ArtScroll® Mesorah Series

Rabbi Nosson Scherman / Rabbi Meir Zlotowitz
General Editors

A PROJECT OF THE

Mesorah Heritage Foundation

דברי רבקה

סליחות

לימים נוראים

מנהג ליטא / ASHKENAZ

Published by

Mesorah Publications, ltd

The Complete
ArtScroll
selichos

Translated by Yaakov Lavon
Edited, with a commentary by Rabbi Avie Gold
Overview by Rabbi Nosson Scherman
Designed by Rabbi Sheah Brander

FIRST EDITION
Fifteen Impressions ... August 1992 — August 2020
Sixteenth Impression ... June 2021

Published and Distributed by
MESORAH PUBLICATIONS, Ltd.
313 Regina Avenue / Rahway, N.J. 07065

Distributed in Europe by
LEHMANNS
Unit E, Viking Industrial Park
Rolling Mill Road
Jarrow, Tyne & Wear NE32 3DP
England

Distributed in Australia & New Zealand by
GOLDS WORLD OF JUDAICA
3-13 William Street
Balaclava, Melbourne 3183
Victoria Australia

Distributed in Israel by
SIFRIATI / A. GITLER — BOOKS
POB 2351
Bnei Brak 51122

Distributed in South Africa by
KOLLEL BOOKSHOP
Northfield Centre, 17 Northfield Avenue
Glenhazel 2192, Johannesburg, South Africa

ARTSCROLL® MESORAH SERIES
"DIVREI RIVKAH / THE COMPLETE SELICHOS SERVICE"
Ashkenaz (Minhag Lita)
© *Copyright 1992, by* MESORAH PUBLICATIONS, Ltd.
313 Regina Avenue / Rahway, N.J. 07065 / (718) 921-9000 / www.artscroll.com

---

ITEM CODE: SLCH
ISBN 10: 0-89906-886-3
ISBN 13: 978-0-89906-886-2

Typography by Compuscribe at ArtScroll Studios, Ltd.

Bound by Sefercraft, Quality Bookbinders, Ltd. Rahway, NJ

*The Complete ArtScroll Selichos
is dedicated to the memory of ...*

Moshe Glaser ז"ל
ר' משה בן ר' אליהו ז"ל
May 7, 2004 — ט"ז אייר תשס"ד

Ruth Glaser ע"ה
רבקה בת ר' ישראל יעקב ע"ה
May 22, 1990 — כ"ז אייר תש"נ

*He was a survivor whose faith in Hashem and dedication to
Torah life survived with him, no matter what the hardship.
He was a famed baal tefillah; the words of the Selichos and tefillos
came from his heart and warmed the souls of all who heard him.*

*She was a woman of valor whose love of children was matched
by her dedication to the promotion of Jewish education and ethics.
Private, selfless, caring, devoted — she was the classic
Jewish wife, mother and grandmother.*

*As husband and wife, they created a home that pulsated
with yearning for Torah chinuch, and throbbed with their tefillos.
These were their legacy, their priceless inheritance.*

... to the memory of

Avigdor Sonnabend ז"ל
אברהם אביגדור בן יוסף דוד ע"ה
December 8, 1956 — ד' טבת תשי"ז

*He was a rescued firebrand who was taken before his time.
A devoted husband and father, he left a wife and three young
daughters. The family he struggled to preserve has grown and brought pride
to his memory and has carried on the Torah life that he held so precious.*

... and to the memory of

Avigdor Glaser ז"ל
יחיאל אברהם אביגדור ז"ל בן אליהו נ"י
September 29, 2005 — כ"ה אלול תשס"ה

*Though he was taken in the prime of life, his noble legacy is kept alive
by להבחל"ח his wife and children; and by Avigdor's Helping Hand,
the worldwide chessed activity that bears his name and perpetuates
his warmth and generosity.*

תנצב"ה

Eli and Yitty Glaser

Avigdor ז"ל and Frumi Glaser
Ari, Tamar, and Elisheva
Sruli and Shandi Glaser   Ruthi, Jackie, Miri, and Rachelli
Shmuly and Mindy Glaser   Moshe, Esti, Shaindy, and Miri
Moshe and Atara Perl   Lily, Ahuva, and Avigdor

৯১ Table of Contents

◆§ Publisher's Preface

The approach of the Days of Awe is a time when the Jew's mind turns to self-examination and improvement. Where have I fallen short? How can I achieve the goals I set for myself a year ago? How can I accomplish more in the coming year than in the last one? How can I better fulfill the will of my Maker and make myself the person He wants me to be?

Such questions flood the mind and heart of the Jew as the season of judgment and repentance draws near. Selichos — the special supplications of this period — are the prayers that express these longings and contemplations. But these moving prayers are so poetic and complex, both in language and construction, that all but scholars of unusual breadth find them extremely difficult. They are so important, yet so distant.

That is why we are especially proud to make this new volume available to the Jewish public. The authors are equal to the challenge. They possess the Torah knowledge and the literary grace to understand the Selichos and present them to the rest of us accurately, beautifully, and movingly. This is a volume that will be the companion of thoughtful, sincere people throughout the Selichos season. It will bring them understanding and inspiration — and, we hope, make the goals of Rosh Hashanah and Yom Kippur much more accessible.

◆§ **Contents** This volume contains the full text of the Selichos according to Nusach Lita [Ashkenaz]. For the convenience of the user, every passage is presented in its entirety every time it appears, so that the reader will not have to turn pages constantly. The Overview presents a hashkafah/philosophical introduction to the concept and historical background of the Selichos.

◆§ **Translation** The translation seeks to balance the lofty beauty of the heavily nuanced text and a readily understood English rendering. Where a choice had to be made, we generally preferred fidelity to the text over inaccurate simplicity, but occasionally, we had to stray from the literal translation in order to capture the essence of a phrase in an accessible English idiom. Often we had to go beyond a strictly literal translation and rely on the commentary to clarify the meaning of the text.

Out of respect for the sanctity and skill of the paytanim, the translators have endeavored to maintain the poetic style and construction of the Hebrew, even though this may occasionally detract from the smooth flow of the English.

◆§ **Layout and Typography** We have followed the pattern of the ArtScroll Siddur and Machzorim, which have been greatly praised for their ease of use and clarity of layout. With its clear instructions, copious subtitles, and precise page headings, this volume was designed to make the Selichos service easy for everyone to follow: The first and last phrases of the translation on each page parallel the first and last phrases of the Hebrew text; paragraphs begin with bold-type words to facilitate the individual tefillos; each paragraph in the translation is introduced with the parallel Hebrew word to ease cross-checking; portions said aloud by the chazzan are indicated by either the symbol ❖ or the word 'chazzan.' An asterisk (*) after a word indicates that that word or phrase is treated in the commentary. Numbered footnotes give the Scriptural and

Talmudic sources of countless passages that have been melded into the prayers, as well as variant readings. A footnote beginning 'Cf.' indicates that the Scriptural source is paraphrased.

❧ **Hebrew Grammar** As a general rule in the Hebrew language, the accent is on the last syllable. Where the accent is on an earlier syllable, it is indicated with a messeg, a vertical line below the accented letter: שִׁירוּ. A נָע שְׁוָא [sh'va na] is indicated by a hyphen mark above the letter: בְּֽרְכוּ; except for a sh'va on the first letter of a word, which is always a sh'va na. In identifying a sh'va na, we have followed the rules of the Vilna Gaon and Rabbi Yaakov Emden.

Acknowledgments

The ArtScroll Series has been privileged to benefit from the advice and support of the venerable Torah leaders of the previous and present generations. MARAN HAGAON HARAV MOSHE FEINSTEIN, MARAN HAGAON HARAV YAAKOV KAMENETSKY, MARAN HAGAON HARAV GEDALIA SCHORR and HARAV HAGAON HARAV SHNEUR KOTLER, זצ"ל. Among today's gedolei Yisrael להבחל"ח MARAN HAGAON HARAV MORDECHAI GIFTER שליט"א has been a father and mentor from the start, and MARAN HAGAON HARAV ZELIK EPSTEIN שליט"א is a treasured counselor.

We are deeply grateful to Maranan HaGeonim HARAV DAVID FEINSTEIN, HARAV DAVID COHEN and HARAV HILLEL DAVID שליט"א for their involvement and for placing their encyclopedic scholarship at our disposal. We are proud that the outstanding Torah scholar, HARAV HERSH GOLDWURM שליט"א, has been associated with the ArtScroll Series virtually since its inception, and is always available for research and guidance.

The authors of this work are RABBI YAAKOV LAVON and RABBI AVIE GOLD. Reb Yaakov, a relative newcomer to the ArtScroll Series, is a gifted translator of difficult material. Reb Avie's earlier works on liturgy are familiar to ArtScroll readers. We are certain that their collaboration in making the often arcane phraseology of the Selichos prayers accessible in readily understood English will enhance the Selichos service and make it more meaningful for thousands of worshipers.

Among those whose guidance was invaluable are such leaders of organizational and rabbinic life as RABBI MOSHE SHERER, RABBI PINCHAS STOLPER, RABBI BORUCH B. BORCHARDT, RABBI JOSHUA FISHMAN, RABBI FABIAN SCHONFELD, RABBI BENJAMIN WALFISH, MR. DAVID H. SCHWARTZ, RABBI YISRAEL H. EIDELMAN, RABBI BURTON JAFFA, and RABBI MICHOEL LEVI.

This work was conceived by our very dear friend, RABBI RAPHAEL BUTLER, whose heroic efforts on behalf of Torah propagation have earned him many admirers — and, more importantly, have brought thousands of people closer to their heritage.

Special recognition and gratitude is due to the trustees of the MESORAH HERITAGE FOUNDATION, which sponsors this and other projects that bring the classics of our heritage to English-speaking Jews. The friendship and selfless efforts of RABBI NETHANIEL STEINBERG on behalf of the projects of the Mesorah Heritage Foundation are gratefully acknowledged.

This volume has been dedicated by MR. AND MRS. ELLIOT GLASER *and their children, in memory of Mr. Glaser's mother, after whom it is named, and Mrs. Glaser's father. The Glasers are people of uncommon kindness and concern for the support of Torah institutions, Jewish children, and the needy wherever they are. Their warmth and generosity have won them friends and admirers wherever they have been, and we are proud to count ourselves among them.*

We are also grateful to the good and loyal friends who dedicated the various editions of the ArtScroll Siddur (in order of their publication): MR. and MRS. ZALMAN MARGULIES; MR. and MRS. JOSEPH BERLINER; MR. and MRS. AARON L. HEIMOWITZ; MRS. MALA WASSNER; MR. and MRS. HIRSCH WOLF; MR. BEREL TENNENBAUM, MR. and MRS. SOLLY KROK; MR. and MRS. DAN SUKENIK, *and* MR. and MRS. MOSHE SUKENIK; *those who have dedicated the Ashkenaz Machzorim (in order of publication):* MRS. EMMA GLICK *and her sons* YITZCHAK (EDWARD) *and* NAFTALI (NORMAN); MRS. TILLIE FEDER *and her children* NORMAN *and* MAUREEN; *the* KUSHNER *and* LAULICHT *families; the sons of* ARNOLD *and* HELEN LEE; MR. *and* MRS. MICHAEL GROSS; *and* MRS. ROCHELLE SORSCHER; *and to* MR. *and* MRS. ELI STERN *and* MR. *and* MRS. JOSEPH STERN, *who dedicated all five Nusach Sefard Machzorim. The* VEGH *and* KISLAK FAMILIES *who dedicated the Ashkenaz edition of the ArtScroll Kinnos/Tishah B'Av Service; and the* EINHORN *and* BRANDER *families who dedicated the Nusach Sefard edition of the ArtScroll Kinnos/Tishah B'Av Service.*

Among the others who have provided the assistance needed to produce such Torah projects, we are grateful to MR. and MRS. LOUIS GLICK, *whose sponsorship of the ArtScroll Mishnah Series with the* YAD AVRAHAM *commentary is a jewel in the crown of Torah dissemination; and* MR. and MRS. IRVING STONE *and* MR. and MRS. MORRY WEISS, *who are sponsoring the forthcoming one-volume* STONE EDITION *of the Chumash.*

We are proud and grateful that MRS. JEROME SCHOTTENSTEIN *and* MR. and MRS. JAY SCHOTTENSTEIN *and their families are continuing to sponsor the monumental* SCHOTTENSTEIN EDITION OF THE TALMUD *in memory of our unforgettable friend* JEROME SCHOTTENSTEIN ע"ה, *and his parents* ע"ה.

The following people have been particularly helpful in making possible the publication of these volumes: MR. JOSEPH A. BERLINER; MR. LAIBEL FRIEDMAN; MR. ABRAHAM FRUCHTHANDLER; RABBI BORUCH GREISMAN; MR. YAAKOV KOVAL; RABBI YEHUDAH LEVI; MR. ALBERT REICHMANN; MR. SHMUEL RIEDER; MR. ELLIS A. SAFDEYE; MR. LAURENCE A. TISCH; MR. WILLY WIESNER; MR. JUDAH SEPTIMUS; and MR. NATHAN SILBERMAN.

Only a fellow craftsman can perceive the excruciating hours that REB SHEAH BRANDER *expended in designing this volume for the mispallel's maximum ease. In this project he has outdone even his own standard of excellence. Moreover, his learned and incisive comments improved every aspect of this work.*

The eminent scholar RABBI AVROHOM YOSEIF ROSENBERG *reviewed the vowelization of the Selichos. We are honored and proud to have a talmid chacham of his stature associated with this work.*

MRS. ESTIE DICKER, MRS. BASSIE GUTMAN, NICHIE FENDRICH, MINDY KOHN, *and* YEHUDA GORDON *typed the manuscript diligently and conscientiously.* RABBI YOSEF GESSER *and* MRS. FAYGIE WEINBAUM *carefully proofread the entire work.*

The entire staff has a share in our service to the community, each in his or her area of responsibility: SHMUEL BLITZ, SHEILA TENNENBAUM, AVROHOM BIDERMAN, *and* EFRAIM PERLOWITZ *of the sales staff;* ELI KROEN, YITZCHOK SAFTLAS, YOSEF TIMINSKY, SAID KOHAN FOLAD, LEA FREIER, MRS. ESTI SCHREIBER *and* RAIZY BRANDER. *We conclude with gratitude to Hashem Yisborach for His infinite blessings and for the opportunity to have been the quill that records His word. May He guide our work in the future for the benefit of His people.*

15 Av 5752 / August 1992
Brooklyn, NY

Rabbis Meir Zlotowitz / Nosson Scherman

An Overview /
Selichos — The Almighty's Own Prayer

אַף עַל פִּי שֶׁהַתְּשׁוּבָה וְהַצְּעָקָה יָפָה לְעוֹלָם, בָּעֲשֶׂרֶת הַיָּמִים שֶׁבֵּין רֹאשׁ
הַשָּׁנָה לְיוֹם הַכִּפּוּרִים הִיא יָפָה בְּיוֹתֵר, וּמִתְקַבֶּלֶת הִיא מִיָּד, שֶׁנֶּאֱמַר דִּרְשׁוּ
ה' בְּהִמָּצְאוֹ

Repentance and outcry [in prayer] *are always proper, but
between Rosh Hashanah and Yom Kippur they are especially
proper and are answered immediately, as it is written (Isaiah
55:6): Seek HASHEM when He is found [call to Him when He is
near] ... (Rambam, Hil. Teshuvah 2:6).*

I. The Father's Hope

The days of awe and judgment, of reflection and repentance, are a time
when Jews use their prayers to seek the Father Who hovers nearby
awaiting their call. The Talmud explains that, of course, God can always be
found and He is always near, but during the ten days from Rosh Hashanah
through Yom Kippur, He is especially available, especially close, especially
hopeful that His children will have the good sense to seek Him out.

Rabbi Bunam of P'shischa used the parable of a king who banished his son
because he failed to live up to his royal responsibilities. The recalcitrant young
man acclimated himself to the rough life of a rural village, and before long
was more a villager than a prince. His father, meanwhile, kept watch over his
beloved, though wayward, son. He accomplished this through agents who
reported back to the palace and unobtrusively shepherded the young man
through frequent difficulties.

Finally, unable to bear the degradation and poverty that his son was
suffering, the king gave him a chance to redeem himself. The king sent an
official with a message: "Your father loves you and is ready to grant you
anything you want. Make a wish."

The prince did not have to think very long. "Tell my father how grateful
I am for his concern. And tell him that it is cold here and my coat is worn.
Please ask him to send me a new, warm, fur-lined coat!"

Can one imagine the heartbreak of the father who wanted his son back in
the palace? The boy could have asked for a chance to visit his family. He could
have asked for a reconciliation. He could have asked for the kingdom. But he
had forgotten where he belonged. He had traded the palace for the corral;
traded his destiny for a coat.

So, too, R' Bunam said, "We come to the Days of Awe when God longs for
us to say, 'Father, we want to come home to You!' And all we think to ask for

in our prayers is a bit more money, a nicer home, a warmer coat. Can we even begin to imagine the extent of our foolishness and the anguish we cause God?"

The Ten Days of Repentance, that begin on Rosh Hashanah and reach their climax with the sunset of Yom Kippur, is our Father's invitation to us to become princes again. One thing should be clear: The call of the season is to return to our roots, to return to the destiny that was mapped out for us in past millennia and is spelled out in our tradition and Torah literature. What should be our goal? Where will we find it? How are we to achieve it? What has the genius of our past told us about the way to remake the future?

II. Origins of Selichos

ORIGINALLY, THE CUSTOM WAS to recite *Selichos* only during the Ten Days of Repentance, from Rosh Hashanah to Yom Kippur (see *Hil. Teshuvah* 3:4).

Early Start But the spiritual genius of the Jewish people decreed that ten days was not enough, that we had to enter the judgment of Rosh Hashanah with the process of prayer and repentance already under way.

Sephardic communities have adopted the practice of reciting *Selichos* from the first day of Elul to Yom Kippur, to commemorate the forty days that Moses spent on Mount Sinai to receive the Second Tablets of the Law. Those forty days were a time of hope and trepidation, because the first time Moses had been away, the people had built the Golden Calf. The people had repented, but what guarantee was there that they would not fall again while Moses was absent? So his forty days on the Mount was a time of intense spiritual striving, when the people had to remember that human aspirations are fragile and require constant encouragement and strengthening.

The climax of the forty days was the tenth of Tishrei, when Moses came back to the camp to find the nation even more elevated than when he had left it, a nation deserving of the Tablets of the Law, which would remain their eternal testimony that God had accepted their repentance and consecrated them once again as His Chosen People [see *Exodus* ch. 32-34].

Just as our ancestors devoted those forty days to self-improvement, so too that period has become a time of striving in all communities — and Sephardic Jews arise every night before dawn to recite *Selichos* as part of the process.

ASHKENAZIC COMMUNITIES began reciting *Selichos* before Rosh Hashanah, and in deciding when to begin the recitation, they based the decision on two

Two Symbols criteria: the twenty-fifth of Elul, and *Motzaei Shabbos* [the night after the Sabbath]. If we can understand the significance of these two considerations, we will go a long way toward understanding the significance of the *Selichos*.

According to Rabbi Eliezer (*Rosh Hashanah* 8a), Adam and Eve were created on Rosh Hashanah, a Friday, which was the sixth day of Creation. This means that Creation began on Sunday, the twenty-fifth of Elul. Therefore, the Jews of Barcelona and its environs adopted the custom of beginning the recitation of *Selichos* on that day (*Ran* to *Rosh Hashanah* 16a). According to this comment, it would seem that the purpose of *Selichos* is nothing less than to remind us that within our minds and hearts we must re-create the pristine state of the beginning of Creation. What is the message of that day?

When God created the world, it was clear that there was only One power in the universe and that everything from the mightiest galaxy to the tiniest gnat owed its existence to Him alone. The Song of the Day of Sunday, which was sung in the Temple by the Levites and which we recite in our Sunday morning prayer, is *Hashem's is the world and its fullness* (*Psalms* 24), because, as the Talmud explains, on that day God created heaven and earth and manifested His sole sovereignty over the universe (*Rosh Hashanah* 31a). When one recognizes that reality, there is no place for sin. Sin is caused by self-deception. As the Talmud puts it, no one sins unless a spirit of foolishness enters him. If someone recognized without a doubt that there is no power or master but the One God, that only He gives the breath of life and the strength to exist, and that no deed goes unrecorded or unrequited by Him, it would be impossible for one to sin — unless one were struck by an attack of lunacy. On the first day of Creation, when God's omnipotence was indisputable, sin was inconceivable. And by beginning to recite *Selichos* on that date, the Jew attempts to re-adopt that primeval conviction.

THE RABBIS ALSO WANTED there to be at least four days of *Selichos* before Rosh Hashanah — to symbolize the four days that an animal must be checked **Motzaei** for flaws before it is used as an offering. This concept brings **Shabbos** home to man that he should analyze himself carefully before he "presents" himself to God on Rosh Hashanah. Consequently, when Rosh Hashanah falls on Monday or Tuesday, *Selichos* must begin sooner — and it is moved up a week, to the previous *Motzaei Shabbos*. Obviously, therefore, the Sabbath, too, is closely related to the beginning of *Selichos*.

The author of *Terumas HaDeshen* explains that the Torah is associated with the Sabbath, the day on which God gave the Ten Commandments. Because the Sabbath is a day when people are free from their weekday activities, they can spend more time studying the Torah, and

> Therefore it is good to begin [reciting *Selichos*] at the beginning of the first day, when people are joyous because of the *mitzvah* of the Torah that they study on the Sabbath, and also because of the pleasure [engendered by] the Sabbath. And as the Talmud teaches (*Shabbos* 30b), the *Shechinah* does not rest amid sadness or laziness, only amid the joy of [the performance of] the commandments. Therefore it is good to begin to pray amid joy of the commandments (*Lekket Yosher*).

As the Torah and the Sages stress, the Sabbath — the culmination of the six days of Creation — bears witness that God is the Creator. So the Sabbath, like the twenty-fifth of Elul, focuses our attention on the beginning of time and it reinforces our responsibility — and, it is to be hoped, our resolve — to do our share in making the world what it was intended to be. For the Jew is called upon to make the world a better place, and the primary way for him to begin is by making himself a better person. After one breaks his mirrors so he will not see his own flaws, it would be vainglorious and futile to think that he can then concentrate on the flaws of everyone else.

JUDAISM TEACHES THAT AN individual human being is a microcosm of the universe. One's primary duty is to perfect *that* universe, his personal one,

Individuals Matter before moving on to change the rest of society. If enough people rise toward perfection, the world will change, not only through the accumulation of many good people, but also because spirituality is indivisible. The very fact that people study the Torah and perform its commandments with sincerity elevates everyone else in the world. Abraham and Sarah were a minority of two in a world awash with idolatry and immorality, yet they saved the entire world from destruction.

Everyone makes a difference. The Sages said that one should imagine that the entire world is balanced between virtue and sin, and that if he performs *one mitzvah*, he will tip the scales of all humanity to the side of merit; but if he commits *one sin*, he will cause the whole world to be condemned. The responsibility is awesome, but so is the privilege. Especially in today's crowded societies, it is easy to think that one lonely individual cannot make a difference and one vote can never matter. That may be true in economics and politics. But Jews are grandchildren of the Patriarchs, the people who proved that majorities are meaningless in determining spiritual accomplishment.

The confluence of the Sabbath and the first day of Creation shed light on what the *Selichos* are meant to, and *can*, accomplish. They are to create a new world, to provide a new resting place for God's Presence, to prepare us for the year that we pray will bring the fulfillment of the prophecies for the coming of Messiah and the End of Days.

III. The Leader of Prayer*

וַיַּעֲבֹר ה׳ עַל פָּנָיו וַיִּקְרָא. אָמַר ר׳ יוֹחָנָן אִלְמָלֵא מִקְרָא כָתוּב אִי אֶפְשָׁר לְאָמְרוּ. מְלַמֵּד שֶׁנִּתְעַטֵּף הַקָּדוֹשׁ בָּרוּךְ הוּא כִּשְׁלִיחַ צִבּוּר וְאָמַר לְמֹשֶׁה, כָּל זְמַן שֶׁיִּשְׂרָאֵל חוֹטְאִים לְפָנַי יַעֲשׂוּ לְפָנַי כְּסֵדֶר הַזֶּה וַאֲנִי מוֹחֵל לָהֶם.
HASHEM passed before him [Moses] *and proclaimed* (Exodus 34:6). R' Yochanan said, "If the Scriptural verse had not been

---

* This section of the Overview is based on *Maharal* in *Be'er HaGolah* and *Chiddushei Aggados, Rosh Hashanah* 17b.

> *written, it would be impossible to say it! This teaches that the*
> *Holy One, Blessed is He, wrapped Himself [in a tallis] like a*
> *leader of prayer, and said to Moses: 'Whenever the Jews sin*
> *before Me, let them perform this procedure and I shall forgive*
> *them' "* (*Rosh Hashanah* 17b).

AFTER THE TRAGIC EPISODE of the Golden Calf, God wrathfully told Moses that Israel was worthy of extermination, and that he, Moses, would become **Moses'** the forerunner of a new and better nation. But Moses could not **Request** bear to see his beloved brethren wiped out, even though they had sinned grievously. He pleaded for them and risked his own survival for their sake, being so bold as to declare that if they were doomed, then he wanted to share their fate (*Exodus* 32:32). God granted his wish and spared the people.

Moses wanted to understand God's ways, to comprehend His justice, and to learn the role of prayer. In response, God told him that no human being, not even Moses, the "master of all prophets," could presume to understand the totality of God's ways, but God showed Moses as much of the Divine glory as he could absorb (ibid. 33: 18-23). After that, God conveyed to Moses the teaching that was not only for him, but for all generations of Jews, the teaching that became the pattern of our order of *Selichos*.

AS CITED ABOVE, GOD APPEARED to Moses in the form of a cantor wrapped in a *tallis*, leading his congregation in prayer. As Moses watched and listened, **God's Tallis** God taught him the prayer that, He assured, would always bring forth God's mercy. Whenever Jews are in distress, let them recite these words, God told Moses, and they will be forgiven. Those words were the Thirteen Attributes of Mercy:

> ה', ה', אֵל, רַחוּם, וְחַנּוּן, אֶרֶךְ אַפַּיִם, וְרַב חֶסֶד, וֶאֱמֶת, נֹצֵר חֶסֶד לָאֲלָפִים,
> נֹשֵׂא עָוֹן, וָפֶשַׁע, וְחַטָּאָה, וְנַקֵּה.
>
> *HASHEM, HASHEM, God, Compassionate and Gracious, Slow to*
> *anger, and Abundant in Kindness and Truth, Preserver of*
> *kindness for thousands of generations, Forgiver of iniquity,*
> *willful sin, and error, and Who cleanses.*

R' Yochanan says, quite understandably, that if the Torah did not allude to this scenario, we would not dare suggest that God gave Moses a personal demonstration, as it were, of how Jews should pray. How did R' Yochanan know that God did so?

Maharal explains that the verses themselves indicate it. The Torah says:

> *HASHEM descended in a cloud and stood with him* [i.e., Moses]
> *there, and He called out with the Name HASHEM. HASHEM passed*
> *before him and proclaimed, HASHEM, HASHEM ...* (*Exodus*
> 34:5-6).

The plain meaning of the verses is that God spoke to Moses and recited the Thirteen Attributes to him, teaching him this new and potent order of prayer.

Because of this, R' Yochanan infers that if God came to teach Moses how to pray, He must have shown him everything he and future generations would need to know — not only the text, but how it should be recited, meaning that God, as it were, "wrapped Himself in a *tallis*." But this merely begs the question, *Maharal* asserts. Why was it so important for God to *demonstrate* the procedure of the prayer?

Moses had begged of God, *"Show me now Your glory"* (ibid. 33:18). He wanted to know how man can attain maximum closeness to God. It was an honest, legitimate request. Moses had seen how even the spiritual height of prophecy can be ephemeral, how the nation that heard God's voice proclaiming, *"I am HASHEM your God"* (ibid. 20:2), had danced around a Golden Calf only forty days later singing, *"This is your god, O Israel"* (ibid. 32:8). If that could happen once, then Moses realized that there had to be a more enduring way to elevate the nation. By appearing in a manner symbolizing someone leading his fellows in prayer, God taught Moses the way to achieve the closeness for which he longed, not only for himself, but for us.

GOD APPEARED AS A LEADER of prayer wrapped in his *tallis*, reciting the Thirteen Attributes of Mercy. The *tallis*, drawn over His head and shielding

Total Concentration His eyes from outside influences and stimuli, was to show how a Jew must react to, and interact with, his prayers. The point is not that all one need do is drape a woolen garment around the shoulders and head of the people's leader; in isolation, such an act is superficial, and superficiality does not lead to spiritual growth. To the contrary, superficiality is harmful, for if a person deceives himself into thinking that he can come closer to God through external deeds, he will only drift further away than he was when he started. God responds to those who seek Him, but only to the extent that they do so sincerely.

In the words of *Maharal*:

> God is just as accessible to a person as the person is accessible to God. If a person concentrates on the content of his prayer and does not turn away from HASHEM, God will be accessible to him completely.

This was the message of the *tallis*. When praying, one must insulate oneself from everything but closeness to God. In the physical sense, the *tallis* shields one's eyes and ears from distraction. But that, too, is not enough — isolation from a corrosive environment enables one to concentrate on the prayers, but it is the *import* of the prayers that matter. What was the prayer to teach?

BY TEACHING MOSES the Attributes of Mercy, God was teaching the Jewish people that in order for their prayers to be efficacious, they must emulate the

Emulating God merciful traits of the One to Whom they pray. As R' Yochanan put it, God told Moses, "Let them *perform* this procedure"; God did not teach Moses words alone; He told him that the message of the words must be carried out. The "procedure" to be performed was the content of the Attributes of Mercy.

God thus showed Moses that in order to merit *God's* mercy, Jews must be merciful to one another — single-mindedly so, for just as the *tallis* draped around them shuts out physical distractions, so it must shut out the thousand reasons why one person does not deserve mercy, another is unworthy of patience, and a third has forfeited his right to forgiveness. By coupling the attitude of prayer with the text that proclaimed the infinite nature of Divine mercy, God was signifying that closeness to God implies emulation of His merciful traits.

How often have Jews wondered why their countless tearful recitations of the Thirteen Attributes have gone unanswered! Did not R' Yochanan teach that they would always be accepted?

Alshich explains that R' Yochanan made it very clear that words are not enough, even if they are recited with feeling. *Perform* this procedure, God pleaded. Do not merely *speak* about *God's* mercy. Show *human* mercy. Only then does God guarantee that He will respond to us in kind (quoted by *Eitz Yosef* to *Ein Yaakov, Rosh Hashanah* 17b).

In the famous homily of *Kedushas Levi,* King David says צִלְּךָ ה', *HASHEM is your protector (Psalms* 121:4). The phrase can also be rendered *HASHEM is your shadow,* for just as a shadow follows and imitates the actions of a person, so God is in a sense, the shadow of a person's deeds. If we are kind, He is kind to us. If we are forgiving, He is forgiving to us. And, unfortunately, vice versa. This is the sort of behavior that God called for, not words but emulation of God's mercy.

IV. Before and After

ה' ה', אֲנִי הוּא קוֹדֶם שֶׁיֶּחֱטָא אָדָם; אֲנִי הוּא לְאַחַר שֶׁיֶּחֱטָא אָדָם וְיַעֲשֶׂה תְשׁוּבָה

[The Talmud explains why the first two Attributes are a repetition of God's Four-letter Name.] *HASHEM, HASHEM . . .* [This means] *I am He before a person sins, and I am He after a person sins and repents (Rosh Hashanah* 17b).

GOD'S FOUR-LETTER NAME SYMBOLIZES His mercy. The repetition of the Name in the Thirteen Attributes, the Talmud teaches, means that He treats **Conditioned** people mercifully both before they sin and after they sin. **to Act** *Rabbeinu Asher* [*Rosh*] asks why it is necessary for God to show mercy *before* the sin; someone who is uncontaminated should not require mercy. He explains that God is merciful even though He knows that someone *will* sin.

It is axiomatic in spiritual matters that nothing happens in a vacuum. When someone sins it is because he has begun to condition himself, emotionally and intellectually, to the idea that it is possible, permissible, even desirable to defy

God's will. Even before he has acted, he has prepared the way for the act. It would be quite logical, therefore, for God to remove His mercy from such a person. But He does not. As long as the *potential* sinner has not become an *actual* sinner, the first Attribute — *HASHEM* — remains in place, and He continues to shower His mercy upon the person who has within himself seeds of defiance that are soon to break through to the surface.

The second Attribute indicated by the Name *HASHEM* is that God is merciful even after one has sinned and repented. Even after repentance, mercy cannot be taken for granted, for it is not at all reasonable to expect that a person should be able to repent from his sins and have them wiped away. By sinning, one has changed himself for the worse. Just as a criminal cannot expect regret to absolve him from all punishment, and a compulsive gambler who has lost a fortune cannot expect his bank account to be replenished because he regrets his foolishness, so too a transgressor cannot logically expect to be made whole again merely because he has repented. But the Attribute of *HASHEM* comes into play in defiance of all logic; even after the sin, God accepts repentance and is merciful to the erstwhile sinner as if the misdeed had never occurred.

Constant Mercy

IN EXPLAINING WHY MERCY IS NEEDED both before and after a sin, *Maharal* disagrees with the basic premise of the *Rosh*. Far from having no need of mercy before he sins, man always requires it; to think otherwise is to ignore his constant needs and deficiencies. Air, water, food, sun, the very breath of life — all these and more are the basic necessities of man's existence. What has he done to earn them, even if he has not sinned? Yet God brings man into a finished world and supplies him with the essentials of life and the ability to enjoy it and find fulfillment. Is this not a display of boundless mercy, even if a sin has never been committed? So it is that man always needs mercy and God always gives it, before the sin and surely after the repentance.

לֹא הָיוּ יִשְׂרָאֵל רְאוּיִּים לְאוֹתוֹ מַעֲשֶׂה אֶלָּא כְּדֵי לְהוֹרוֹת תְּשׁוּבָה לָרַבִּים
Israel would not have been susceptible to that sin [of the Golden Calf] *except to teach repentance to the multitude* (*Avodah Zarah* 4a).

Lesson for the Future*

THAT GOD CHOSE TO BEGIN the Attributes of Mercy with the double use of the Four-letter Name provides an insight into man's mission on earth, especially during the *Selichos* days that call out for our repentance. God uses the same Name for His mercy after the sin as before to show that a sinner can return to the state of purity he enjoyed before he stumbled. The Name is repeated because man has the challenge of coming back after he sins. Thanks to one of God's greatest demonstrations of mercy, repentance can erase sins and bring man back to his pristine state of prior perfection. It can restore him to what he was before he

---

* This section of the Overview is based on *Ohr Gedalyahu*, to *Elul*.

lapsed, so he can once again enjoy the mercy that God extends to those who have not yet fallen short, cognizant though He is that imperfect man is never more than a breath away from stumbling. Sin is cause for chagrin, but never for despair — and certainly not for surrender. HASHEM is always there, before and after, with His support and open arms, awaiting the return of His fallen children.

The lesson of national repentance came in the earliest days of Israel's national history, in the Wilderness, only a few months after the Exodus. As the Sages taught, under normal circumstances, the sin of the Golden Calf would not have happened. The nation that had heard HASHEM announce Himself to them as their God should have been able to withstand the fear and temptation that led them to ask for the Golden Calf. The only reason the sin took place was to demonstrate the power of repentance, and its efficacy in achieving atonement even for a multitude that has sinned (*Avodah Zarah* 4b).

When the Sages tell us that Israel sinned only in order to show the way of repentance, they do not mean to say that God *forced* them to sin. That would have been unjust, and God is never unjust.

What happened in the Wilderness was that God withdrew the mercy that He normally gives before there is a sin. He knew that that august generation could overcome temptation to do evil, because of the combination of their own greatness and God's merciful protection. But He also knew that His people still had flaws that could result in the failure of future generations, which would be neither so lofty nor so worthy of mercy. For such generations, there had to be a well-trodden way back up from the depths of a spiritual fall. If there was any generation that had the capacity to set the example for its offspring, it was the generation that had received the Torah. So God withdrew His mercy, His spiritual shelter, from them so that they could show how Jews can redeem themselves after falling.

They were being tested to see if they could withstand a very powerful temptation, and they would have to do it without Divine assistance. Their downfall was surely not inevitable — for "Israel would not have been susceptible to that sin" (*Avodah Zarah* 4b) — and if God had been giving them the degree of mercy that would normally have been theirs, they would not have sinned. But the mercy was not there and the temptation was — so they danced around the Golden Calf.

That was not the end of it, however. Because of their initial failure, Moses prayed and God appeared to him in the form of a leader of prayer, and taught him the Thirteen Attributes. Only a generation as great as that one could have been worthy of such an exalted teaching, a teaching that has been the mainstay of their offspring for over thirty-three centuries. They taught repentance. They taught that Jews can fall and rise again. They taught that *we* can rise. They became the teachers and the examples of repentance for all generations.

IT IS ILLUSTRATIVE TO SEE what that repentance brought. Prior to the sin of the Golden Calf, Moses had received the Tablets of the Law from Sinai. When **Legacy of the Downfall** he saw the painful spectacle of the nation of God prancing around a false god, he smashed the Tablets — something he had to do because the people no longer deserved them. Then came a long period of prayer, highlighted by the vision of God showing Moses how to pray and what to say, and the promise that if Israel would *perform* this prayer — by making themselves agents of mercy to others — then they could rely on His help in the worst situations. The result was that Moses came back from Mount Sinai on Yom Kippur with the Second Tablets.

This was a lesson for all time. Jews can lose the Torah and get it back. They can lose God's mercy and win it back. God loves us and wants us so much that He shows us how to pray and promises that His ear is always cocked, as it were, waiting for us to call Him, to repent, to evoke His mercy, and to come back to where we were before we fell.

This is the secret of *Selichos*. It is as if God had told Moses and the Children of Israel that He had given them a special service for repentance when they needed it most, when they had lost the greatest gift God had ever given man — the Torah — and longed to get it back. Repentance and Torah went hand in hand, then and now, for the Sages teach that Yom Kippur is a *festival*, because it was the day that God gave the Torah to Israel for a second time (*Taanis* 30b).

Let us take the lesson of *Selichos* to heart. By falling and rising, our ancestors in the Wilderness taught us that hope is never lost, even when the protection of God's mercy is absent. God is merciful when we fall short of His expectations, but only if we emulate Him by being merciful to those who fall short of our expectations of them.

Let us begin, and may this year's *Selichos* be climaxed by a Yom Kippur as climactic as the one when Moses brought back the Second Tablets.

Tammuz 5752   *Rabbi Nosson Scherman*
July 1992

✑ Introduction

W ithin the *Siddur* and synagogue service, the mood of repentance is expressed in the סְלִיחוֹת [*selichos*], *prayers of supplication*. They are of ancient origin; some of them are even mentioned in the Mishnah (*Taanis* ch. 2) where special prayers for rain are discussed, but almost all of them were composed between the eighth and sixteenth centuries. The composers of these *selichos* include some of the outstanding figures of ancient times, among them *Geonim* (7th-10th century Torah authorities) and *Rishonim* (11th-15th century authorities). Consequently, it should be clear that their compositions are not merely inspired poetry.

The central theme of all *selichos*, as well as of the Yom Kippur *Maariv* and *Neilah* services, is שְׁלֹשׁ עֶשְׂרֵה מִדּוֹת הָרַחֲמִים, *the Thirteen Attributes of Mercy*. This passage appears in the Torah (*Exodus* 34:6-7) at the time when God proclaimed His readiness to do away with the Jewish people after the sin of the Golden Calf. According to R' Yochanan's interpretation (*Rosh Hashanah* 17b), Moses felt that Israel's sin was so grievous that there was no possibility of his intercession on their behalf. Thereupon, God appeared to him in the form of a *chazzan* wrapped in a *tallis* and taught him the Thirteen Attributes, saying, 'Whenever Israel sins, let them recite this in its proper order and I will forgive them. Thus, this appeal to God's mercy reassures us both that repentance is always possible and that God always awaits our return to Him. The implication is also plain that if we emulate God's merciful ways, He will treat us mercifully in return.

When it appears in the *Selichos* service, the Thirteen Attributes is introduced by one of two prayers: The first time during each *Selichos* service, it is introduced by אֵל אֶרֶךְ אַפַּיִם, *O God — [You are] slow to anger. . .* All other times, the introduction is אֵל מֶלֶךְ יוֹשֵׁב, *O God, King Who sits. . .* Brief explanations of these introductions, as well as of the Thirteen Attributes, appear in the commentary.* After the Thirteen Attributes there is always a direct prayer for forgiveness, following the example of Moses, who, after being taught the Thirteen Attributes, pleaded that God forgive Israel (*Exodus* 34:8-9).

---

* Among the *Rishonim*, the *Acharonim* and the different schools of philosophical and kabbalistic thought, the Thirteen Attributes have been numbered and explained in many ways. In this volume we have adopted the view of Rabbeinu Tam (*Rosh Hashanah* 17b). The Hebrew reader interested in a deeper understanding and a survey of the various interpretations would do well to study שערי רחמים, by Rabbi Yaakov Y. Hamburger.

Types of Selichos

Each of the *piyutim* (liturgical poems), recited during the *Selichos* service is properly called a סְלִיחָה, *selichah*, literally, *forgiveness*. Certain *selichos*, are further identified by category, according to their poetic form, subject matter or location in the service. Some of these classifications are:

פְּתִיחָה, *pesichah* (opening): A *selichah* recited near the beginning of some *Selichos* services, even before the first recitation of the Thirteen Attributes.

שְׁנִיָּה, *sheniyah* (twofold): A *piyut* composed exclusively of couplets, or two-lined stanzas.

שְׁלִישִׁיָּה, *shelishiyah* (threefold): A *piyut* composed exclusively of triplets, or three-lined stanzas.

שַׁלְמוֹנִית, *shalmonis* (whole): A *piyut* composed exclusively of quatrains, or four-lined stanzas. According to some commentaries, the word *shalmonis* means *of Shlomo*, an allusion to R' Shlomo HaBavli who wrote most of his *piyutim* in this genre.

פִּזְמוֹן, *pizmon* (response; calling out): A *piyut* having a refrain, and usually recited responsively between *chazzan* and congregation. At least one *pizmon* is recited at each *Selichos* service.

שִׁירְשׁוּר, *shirshur* (chain): A *piyut* in which the last word of one stanza (or verse) is repeated as the first word of the next stanza (or verse).

עֲקֵדָה, *akeidah* (binding): A *selichah* that recounts the time Abraham was tested by being asked to sacrifice his son Isaac on the altar. An *akeidah* pleads that the merit of that act should shield the offspring of Abraham and Isaac from harsh judgment when they come before the Heavenly Tribunal.

תּוֹכָחָה, *tochachah* (rebuke): A *piyut* that, unlike the *selichah* which calls upon God to forgive His people, calls on the people to repent and return to God.

חָטָאנוּ, *chatanu* (We have sinned!) A *selichah* with the refrain חָטָאנוּ צוּרֵנוּ, סְלַח לָנוּ יוֹצְרֵנוּ, *We have sinned, our Rock! Forgive us, our Molder!*

שְׁמַע יִשְׂרָאֵל, *Shema Yisrael* (Hear O Israel): A *selichah* with the first verse of the *Shema* as its refrain.

תְּחִנָּה, *techinah* (supplication): A *selichah* juxtaposed with the recital of *tachanun* just before the close of the *Selichos* service.

The Daily Selichos Service

In the various Ashkenazic *Selichos* rites [the best known of which are *Minhag Lita* (Lithuania), *Minhag Polin* (Poland), *Minhag Ungarin* (Hungary), and *Minhag Ashkenaz* (Germany)], different prayers are recited each day of the *Selichos* period. Nevertheless, the basic format is the same every day. The *selichos* compositions are inserted into 'windows' in a 'framework' of Scriptural verses and supplications. In most rites, framework begins with

Ashrei (*Psalm* 145 with added verses) and Half *Kaddish*, followed by some fifty verses, mostly from *Psalms*. It closes with another series of verses, the threefold recitation of the *viduy*/confession (some, however, recite *viduy* only once), more verses, supplications and, finally, *tachanun* and the Full *Kaddish*.

In *Minhag Lita*, the rite used in this volume, the first day's service includes a *pesichah*, two *selichos* and a *pizmon*. On the remaining days before Erev Rosh Hashanah, two *selichos* and a *pizmon* are recited.

The ceremony is much longer on Erev Rosh Hashanah when the recitation includes: a *pesichah*, two *sheniyah*, two *shelishiyah*, five *shalmonis*, four *pizmonim*, an *akeidah*, a *chatanu*, a *Shema Yisrael*, a *techinah* and five other *selichos*. A multipartite supplication is also interpolated at various points during the regular three-fold *viduy* recitation.

In deference to the preparations for Yom Kippur, the *Selichos* service for Erev Yom Kippur comprises only a *sheniyah*, a *shelishiyah*, a *pizmon*, and a greatly abridged framework.

Prayer: Direct to God
or Through Intermediaries

The propriety and permissibility of channeling prayer through angelic intercessors, rather than directly to God, is a point of halachic contention.* The debate revolves around supplications such as, מַבְנִיסֵי רַחֲמִים, *O you who usher in [pleas for] mercy* (p. 46), מַלְאֲבֵי רַחֲמִים, *O angels of mercy* (p. 106), and תְּפִלָּה תִקַּח, *Accept prayer* (p. 436), which request ministering angels to bring our supplications and tears before God, and to beseech Him to accept them favorably.

Some *selichos* do not go quite so far as to request angelic intervention, but nevertheless are not addressed directly to God. Some of these are: שְׁלֹשׁ עֶשְׂרֵה מִדּוֹת, *Thirteen Attributes* (p. 386), which entreats not God but His Attributes; תּוֹרָה הַקְּדוֹשָׁה, *Holy Torah* (p. 528), which pleads with the Torah to act the advocate on Israel's behalf; and שֶׁבֶת הַכִּסֵּא, *May the Throne of Glory* (p. 600), which invokes God's celestial Throne to intercede and pray for us.

Those opposed to the recitation of such prayers cite a passage in the Jerusalem Talmud to support their view:

> When a man supported by a patron finds himself in difficult straits, he does not suddenly enter [his patron's chambers to demand assistance or succor]. Rather, he stands at the door and asks a servant or a family member to announce his presence. [Even then his success

---

* It is not within the scope of this article to even attempt to reconcile the two sides in this centuries-old debate. We have only tried to show that each view is firmly entrenched and based on the tradition of millennia. Those wishing to study the issue further are advised to see the *Mavo* to *Siddur Otzer HaTefillos*, section 3, לְמִי מִתְפַּלְלִין.

is not assured.] Perhaps he will be admitted, perhaps he will not. But with the Holy one, Blessed is He, such is not the case; [for He says.] 'If one is in difficult straits, he should not call to [the angel] Michael or to [the angel] Gabriel. Rather, he should call to me and I will answer him immediately' (*Yerushalmi, Berachos* 9:1).

The *Rishonim* expound on and expand this prohibition. In the fifth of his Thirteen Principles of Faith, Maimonides writes:

It is the Blessed One whom it is proper to worship, to exalt, to propagate His greatness, and to fulfill His commandments. But one must not do so for anything of lower existence [than God Himself], such as the angels, the stars, the spheres, the elements and whatever is composed of them . . . It is likewise improper to pray that they act as intercessors to present [our prayers] to Him. Only to Him shall one's thoughts be directed; and all besides Him should be ignored . . . (*Rambam, Pirush HaMishnayos, Sanhedrin* 10).

Nachmanides writes similarly: 'The third form of idolatry is considering the angels capable of serving as intermediaries between God and His worshipers . . . Realize that even to pray to them for this purpose is forbidden to us . . .' (*Ramban, Toras Hashem Temimah*).

In later generations, the Maharal of Prague wrote strongly against supplications addressed to angelic advocates. In the course of his argument, the Maharal distinguishes between celestial beings on the one hand, and the Patriarchs, Matriarchs and righteous *tzaddikim* of every generation. Why may one seek the intercession of human intermediaries, yet be prohibited from beseeching the angels to advocate his cause? Man is commanded to perform acts of kindness with his fellow man. Thus, by requesting another person to pray for his welfare, one presents his fellow with an opportunity to perform an act of kindness. Angels, on the other hand, are neither commanded nor given the free will to perform such acts. They may only do the specific deed or deeds for which they were created and regarding which they were commanded by God. A request to an angel must therefore be considered not just asking for friendly help, but a prayer; and Heaven forbid that any Jew should utter such a prayer (*Nesivos Olam, nesiv haavodah* 12).

R' Yosef Albo, in a lengthy dissertation, explains that even if there were no halachic problem regarding such prayers, they nevertheless would remain useless for pragmatic reasons. For one to be able to grant the needs of another on an on-going basis; (a) the provider must be eternal and unchanging, then the beneficence will remain unchangingly appropriate and good for the recipient — only God fits this requirement; (b) the provider must be independent and not need the assistance of another party — only God fits this requirement; (c) the provider must be able to supply items of opposite natures, for example, heat and cold, fire and water, because sometimes man needs one, at other times the other — only God fits this requirement; and (d) there must be nothing in the world that can prevent the provider from fulfilling his desire

— only God fits this requirement. Thus, in order for prayer to be effective, it must be received favorably by God, even if it is directed elsewhere. So from a practical sense, prayer should be addressed only to God (*Ikkarim* 4:17).

Elsewhere R' Albo explains that although worshiping an angel is forbidden, showing reverence or honor to the angel as an emissary of God is permitted. For this reason Joshua was able to bow to the angel that appeared to him in Jericho (see *Joshua* 5:13-15). But one who bows to an angel as an act of worship is guilty of idolatry (*Ikkarim* 2:28).

❦ ❦ ❦

Those who permit the recitation of supplications addressed to angelic intercessors cite a passage from *Midrash Shir HaShirim* (not found in extant editions):

> The Congregation of Israel says to the angels standing at the [heavenly] Gates of Prayer and Gates of Tears, 'Usher in my prayer and my tears before the Holy One, Blessed is He; and act as advocates before Him, that He pardon me for both intentional and inadvertent sins.' And so it is stated (*Job* 33:23): *If there be for him but one advocate angel from among a thousand* ... (*Shibbolei HaLeket* 282; *Tanya Rabbasi*, Cremona edition, p. 102a).

Another source for this viewpoint is in the Talmud. 'R' Yochanan says: A person should always seek mercy that all should invigorate and encourage him, and that he not have enemies on high' (*Sanhedrin* 44b). According to *Rashi* this means that one should seek to have the ministering angels plead mercy for him and not become his accusers in heaven.

Another Talmudic passage is cited. 'Rav Yehudah said: A person should never request his needs in the Aramaic tongue. And R' Yochanan said: If anyone requests his needs in the Aramaic tongue, the ministering angels ignore him, for the angels do not understand Aramaic' (*Shabbos* 12b). According to R' Sherira Gaon, Rav Yehudah and R' Yochanan are speaking of a person who directs his request to an angel. One who speaks directly to God, however, may use any language. R' Sherira explains although angels have no independent power to grant bounty or withhold it; some angels are given parameters within which they may function at their own discretion. For example, an angel may be assigned to accompany a traveler and protect him from harm along the road. Nevertheless, the guardian is permitted to remove its protection if the wayfarer acts sinfully. Thus, when God informed Moses that He would send an angel to lead and protect the nation on the way to *Eretz Yisrael*, He warned: *'Be careful before him; follow his words; do not rebel against him, for he will not forgive your rebelliousness, because My Name is within him* (*Exodus* 23:21).

Of course, it is needless to add that the *paytanim* who composed the controversial *selichos* were certainly of the opinion that such prayer is permitted. And their number includes some of the greatest scholars and halachic authorities of all generations.

The Names of God

The Four-Letter Name of *Hashem* [יﭧהﭧוﭧה] indicates that God is timeless and infinite, since the letters of this Name are those of the words הָיָה הֹוֶה וְיִהְיֶה, *He was, He is, and He will be*. This Name is *never* pronounced as it is spelled.

During prayer, or when a blessing is recited, or when Torah verses are read, the Four-Letter Name should be pronounced as if it were spelled אֲדֹנָי, *Adonai,* the Name that identifies God as the Master of All. At other times, it should be pronounced הַשֵּׁם, *Hashem,* literally, ''the Name.''

According to the *Shulchan Aruch,* one should have both meanings — the Master of All and the Timeless, Infinite One — in mind when reciting the Four-Letter Name during prayer (*Orach Chaim* ch. 5). According to *Vilna Gaon,* however, one need have in mind only the meaning of the Name as it is pronounced — the Master of All (ibid.).

When the Name is spelled אֲדֹנָי in the prayer or verse, all agree that one should have in mind that God is the Master of All.

The Name אֱלֹהִים, *God,* refers to Him as the One Who is all-powerful (ibid.).

In this *machzor,* the Four-Letter Name of God is translated ''*Hashem,*'' the pronunciation traditionally used for the Name to avoid pronouncing it unnecessarily. This pronunciation should be used when studying the meanings of the prayers. However, if one prays using the English translation, he should say ''God'' or ''Lord'' or he should pronounce the Name in its proper Hebrew way — *Adonai* — in accord with the ruling of most halachic authorities.

סְלִיחוֹת

דברי רבקה

﴾ יום ראשון ﴿

אַשְׁרֵי יוֹשְׁבֵי בֵיתֶךָ, עוֹד יְהַלְלוּךָ סֶּלָה.[1] אַשְׁרֵי הָעָם שֶׁכָּכָה לוֹ, אַשְׁרֵי הָעָם שֶׁיהוה אֱלֹהָיו.[2]

תהלים קמה

תְּהִלָּה לְדָוִד,

אֲרוֹמִמְךָ* אֱלוֹהַי הַמֶּלֶךְ, וַאֲבָרְכָה שִׁמְךָ לְעוֹלָם וָעֶד.

בְּכָל יוֹם אֲבָרְכֶךָּ,* וַאֲהַלְלָה שִׁמְךָ לְעוֹלָם וָעֶד.

גָּדוֹל יהוה וּמְהֻלָּל מְאֹד, וְלִגְדֻלָּתוֹ אֵין חֵקֶר.*

דּוֹר לְדוֹר יְשַׁבַּח מַעֲשֶׂיךָ, וּגְבוּרֹתֶיךָ יַגִּידוּ.

הֲדַר כְּבוֹד הוֹדֶךָ, וְדִבְרֵי נִפְלְאֹתֶיךָ אָשִׂיחָה.

וֶעֱזוּז נוֹרְאֹתֶיךָ יֹאמֵרוּ, וּגְדֻלָּתְךָ אֲסַפְּרֶנָּה.

זֵכֶר רַב טוּבְךָ יַבִּיעוּ, וְצִדְקָתְךָ יְרַנֵּנוּ.

חַנּוּן וְרַחוּם* יהוה, אֶרֶךְ אַפַּיִם וּגְדָל חָסֶד.

טוֹב יהוה לַכֹּל, וְרַחֲמָיו עַל כָּל מַעֲשָׂיו.

יוֹדוּךָ יהוה כָּל מַעֲשֶׂיךָ, וַחֲסִידֶיךָ יְבָרְכוּכָה.

כְּבוֹד מַלְכוּתְךָ יֹאמֵרוּ, וּגְבוּרָתְךָ יְדַבֵּרוּ.

לְהוֹדִיעַ לִבְנֵי הָאָדָם גְּבוּרֹתָיו, וּכְבוֹד הֲדַר מַלְכוּתוֹ.

מַלְכוּתְךָ מַלְכוּת כָּל עֹלָמִים, וּמֶמְשַׁלְתְּךָ בְּכָל דּוֹר וָדֹר.

סוֹמֵךְ יהוה* לְכָל הַנֹּפְלִים, וְזוֹקֵף לְכָל הַכְּפוּפִים.

אַשְׁרֵי ﴾ / Ashrei

The *Selichos* service is best begun with the recital of the exalted praises of *Kaddish*. However, since *Kaddish* cannot be recited except after Scriptural verses, it is customary to recite psalm 145 [אַשְׁרֵי, *Ashrei*] first (*Levush*). The selection of *Ashrei* is based on the similarity between *Selichos* and the daily *Shacharis* service. Each day's morning prayers begin with *Pesukei D'Zimrah*, of which *Ashrei* is a major component. The *selichah* passages and the Thirteen Attributes recited with them are similar to the *Shemoneh Esrei*. And as with *Shacharis*, the *Selichos* service ends with וִדּוּי, *Confession*, and תַּחֲנוּן, the *Tachanun* supplication. It is noteworthy that the Full *Kaddish*, usually recited after *Shemoneh Esrei*, is also recited after *Selichos*, further adding to the similarity between the regular morning prayers and *Selichos* (*Likkutei Maharich*).

Psalm 145 begins with the verse תְּהִלָּה לְדָוִד; the two preliminary verses, each beginning with the word אַשְׁרֵי, are affixed to תְּהִלָּה לְדָוִד for two reasons: (a) By expressing the idea that those who can dwell in God's house of prayer and

service are praiseworthy, these verses set the stage for the succeeding psalm of praise, for we, the praiseworthy ones, are about to laud the God in Whose house we dwell; and (b) the word אַשְׁרֵי is found three times in these verses. This alludes to the Talmudic dictum that one who recites psalm 145 three times a day is assured of a share in the World to Come (*Berachos* 4b); thus, those who do so are indeed אַשְׁרֵי, *praiseworthy.*

תְּהִלָּה . . . אֲרוֹמִמְךָ — *A psalm . . . I will exalt You.* Beginning with the word אֲרוֹמִמְךָ, the initials of the respective verses follow the order of the *Aleph-Beis*. According to *Abudraham* the *Aleph-Beis* structure symbolizes that we praise God with every sound available to the organs of speech. *Midrash Tadshei* records that the Psalmists and Sages used the *Aleph-Beis* formula in chapters that they wanted people to follow more easily or to memorize.

בְּכָל יוֹם אֲבָרְכֶךָּ — *Every day I will bless You.* True, no mortal can pretend to know God's essence, but each of us is equipped to appreciate life, health, sustenance, sunshine, rainfall, and so on. For them and their daily renewal, we

⚜ **FIRST DAY** ⚜

אַשְׁרֵי *Praiseworthy are those who dwell in Your house; may they always praise You, Selah!*[1] *Praiseworthy is the people for whom this is so, praiseworthy is the people whose God is HASHEM.*[2]

Psalm 145   *A psalm of praise by David:*

א *I will exalt You,* my God the King,*
    and I will bless Your Name forever and ever.

ב *Every day I will bless You,**
    and I will laud Your Name forever and ever.

ג *HASHEM is great and exceedingly lauded,*
    and His greatness is beyond investigation.*

ד *Each generation will praise Your deeds to the next*
    and of Your mighty deeds they will tell;

ה *The splendrous glory of Your power*
    and Your wondrous deeds I shall discuss.

ו *And of Your awesome power they will speak,*
    and Your greatness I shall relate.

ז *A recollection of Your abundant goodness they will utter*
    and of Your righteousness they will sing exultantly.

ח *Gracious and merciful* is HASHEM,*
    slow to anger, and great in [bestowing] kindness.

ט *HASHEM is good to all; His mercies are on all His works.*

י *All Your works shall thank You, HASHEM,*
    and Your devout ones will bless You.

כ *Of the glory of Your kingdom they will speak,*
    and Your power they will tell;

ל *To inform human beings of His mighty deeds,*
    and the glorious splendor of His kingdom.

מ *Your kingdom is a kingdom spanning all eternities,*
    and Your dominion is throughout every generation.

ס *HASHEM supports* all the fallen ones and straightens all the bent.*

---

(1) *Psalms* 84:5. (2) 144:15.

---

give daily blessings (*Siach Yitzchak*).

וְלִגְדֻלָּתוֹ אֵין חֵקֶר — *And His greatness is beyond investigation.* Much though we may try, we can understand neither God's essence nor His ways through human analysis, for He is infinite. We *must* rely on the traditions that have come to us from earlier generations, as the next verse suggests (*Rama*).

חַנּוּן וְרַחוּם — *Gracious and merciful.* Because God is *merciful,* He is אֶרֶךְ אַפַּיִם, *slow to anger,* so that punishment, although deserved, is delayed as long as possible to allow time for repentance. And because He is *gracious,* He is גְּדָל חָסֶד, *great in bestowing kindness* (*Siach Yitzchak*).

סוֹמֵךְ ה' — *HASHEM supports.* No verse in *Ashrei*

begins with a נ, because in the context of this verse that speaks of God supporting the fallen, the letter נ can be taken as an allusion to נְפִילָה, Israel's future *downfall,* ח"ו, and the Psalmist refused to use a letter that could suggest such tragedy. Nevertheless, knowing that downfalls would take place, the Psalmist comforted Israel by saying, *God supports all the fallen ones.* This is an implied guarantee that even when a dreaded downfall happens, the people can look forward to His support (*Berachos* 4b). *Maharsha* comments that by omitting a direct mention of downfall, the Psalmist implies that even when Israel does suffer reverses, those reverses will never be complete. Rather, as the next verse declares, God will support the fallen.

עֵינֵי כֹל אֵלֶיךָ יְשַׂבֵּרוּ,* וְאַתָּה נוֹתֵן לָהֶם אֶת אָכְלָם בְּעִתּוֹ.

פּוֹתֵחַ* אֶת יָדֶךָ, וּמַשְׂבִּיעַ לְכָל חַי רָצוֹן.

❖ צַדִּיק יהוה בְּכָל דְּרָכָיו, וְחָסִיד* בְּכָל מַעֲשָׂיו.

קָרוֹב יהוה לְכָל קֹרְאָיו, לְכֹל אֲשֶׁר יִקְרָאֻהוּ בֶאֱמֶת.

רְצוֹן יְרֵאָיו יַעֲשֶׂה, וְאֶת שַׁוְעָתָם יִשְׁמַע וְיוֹשִׁיעֵם.

שׁוֹמֵר יהוה אֶת כָּל אֹהֲבָיו, וְאֵת כָּל הָרְשָׁעִים יַשְׁמִיד.

תְּהִלַּת יהוה יְדַבֶּר פִּי, וִיבָרֵךְ כָּל בָּשָׂר שֵׁם קָדְשׁוֹ לְעוֹלָם וָעֶד.

וַאֲנַחְנוּ נְבָרֵךְ* יָהּ, מֵעַתָּה וְעַד עוֹלָם, הַלְלוּיָהּ.*[1]

The *chazzan* recites חֲצִי קַדִּישׁ.

יִתְגַּדַּל וְיִתְקַדַּשׁ שְׁמֵהּ רַבָּא.* (.Cong – אָמֵן.*) בְּעָלְמָא דִּי בְרָא כִרְעוּתֵהּ.* וְיַמְלִיךְ מַלְכוּתֵהּ, בְּחַיֵּיכוֹן* וּבְיוֹמֵיכוֹן וּבְחַיֵּי דְכָל בֵּית יִשְׂרָאֵל, בַּעֲגָלָא וּבִזְמַן קָרִיב.* וְאִמְרוּ: אָמֵן.

(.Cong – אָמֵן. יְהֵא שְׁמֵהּ רַבָּא* מְבָרַךְ לְעָלַם וּלְעָלְמֵי עָלְמַיָּא.)

יְהֵא שְׁמֵהּ רַבָּא מְבָרַךְ לְעָלַם וּלְעָלְמֵי עָלְמַיָּא.

יִתְבָּרַךְ* וְיִשְׁתַּבַּח וְיִתְפָּאַר וְיִתְרוֹמַם וְיִתְנַשֵּׂא וְיִתְהַדָּר וְיִתְעַלֶּה וְיִתְהַלָּל שְׁמֵהּ דְּקֻדְשָׁא בְּרִיךְ הוּא. (.Cong – בְּרִיךְ הוּא) לְעֵלָּא מִן כָּל בִּרְכָתָא* וְשִׁירָתָא תֻּשְׁבְּחָתָא וְנֶחֱמָתָא, דַּאֲמִירָן בְּעָלְמָא. וְאִמְרוּ: אָמֵן. (.Cong – אָמֵן.)

עֵינֵי כֹל אֵלֶיךָ יְשַׂבֵּרוּ — *The eyes of all look to You with hope.* Even animals instinctively rely upon God for their sustenance [how much more so should man recognize the beneficence of his Maker!] (*Radak*).

פּוֹתֵחַ — *You open.* When reciting this verse, one should have in mind the translation of the words because this declaration of God's universal goodness is one of the two reasons the Sages required the thrice-daily recitation of this psalm.

צַדִּיק ... וְחָסִיד — *Righteous ... and magnanimous.* That God's ways are just and righteous means that He judges people only according to their deeds. Nevertheless, even when justice calls for grievous punishment, He is *magnanimous* in softening the blow, for He is merciful (*Vilna Gaon*).

וַאֲנַחְנוּ נְבָרֵךְ — *We will bless.* After completing psalm 145 which holds an assurance of the World to Come, we append this verse in which we express the hope that we will bless God *forever* — that is, in both worlds (*Levush*).

הַלְלוּיָהּ — *Halleluyah.* This familiar word is a contraction of two words: הַלְלוּ יָהּ, *praise God.*

The term הַלְלוּ denotes crying out in happy excitement, while the unique meaning implied by the Name יָהּ means 'the One Who is forever.' The Psalmist addresses everyone, saying: Use your energy to be *excited* over God and nothing else (*R' Avigdor Miller*).

קַדִּישׁ / Kaddish

יִתְגַּדַּל וְיִתְקַדַּשׁ שְׁמֵהּ רַבָּא — *May His great Name grow exalted and sanctified.* The ultimate sanctification of God's Name will come when Israel is redeemed; in this sense *Kaddish* is a plea for the final Redemption. It is also an expression of Israel's mission to bring recognition of His sovereignty to all people on earth. This mission is incumbent primarily upon the community as a whole, and *Kaddish* is therefore recited only in the presence of a *minyan* [a quorum of ten males over *bar mitzvah*] (*R' Munk*).

אָמֵן — *Amen.* The word אָמֵן, *Amen,* is the listener's acknowledgment that he believes in what the reader has just said. It is derived from the same root as אֱמוּנָה, *faithfulness* (*Tur, Orach Chaim* 124). Additionally, it stands for אֵל מֶלֶךְ נֶאֱמָן, *God, the trustworthy King* (*Shabbos* 119b).

ע *The eyes of all look to You with hope**
and You give them their food in its proper time;

פ *You open* Your hand,* Concentrate intently while reciting the verse, *'You open. . .*
and satisfy the desire of every living thing.

צ Chazzan— *Righteous is* HASHEM *in all His ways*
and magnanimous* in all His deeds.

ק HASHEM *is close to all who call upon Him —*
to all who call upon Him sincerely.

ר *The will of those who fear Him He will do;*
and their cry He will hear, and save them.

ש HASHEM *protects all who love Him;*
but all the wicked He will destroy.

ת *May my mouth declare the praise of* HASHEM
and may all flesh bless His Holy Name forever and ever.

We will bless* God from this time and forever, Halleluyah!*[1]

The chazzan recites Half-Kaddish:

יִתְגַּדַּל *May His great Name grow exalted and sanctified**
(Cong.— *Amen.**) *in the world that He created as He willed.**
May He give reign to His kingship in your lifetimes* and in your days,
and in the lifetimes of the entire Family of Israel, swiftly and soon.* Now
respond: Amen.

(Cong.— *Amen. May His great Name* be blessed forever and ever.*)
May His great Name be blessed forever and ever.

Blessed,* praised, glorified, exalted, extolled, mighty, upraised, and
lauded be the Name of the Holy One, Blessed is He (Cong.— *Blessed is He*)
— beyond any blessing* and song, praise and consolation that are uttered
in the world. Now respond: Amen. (Cong.— *Amen.*)

---

(1) *Psalms* 115:18.

בְּעָלְמָא דִּי בְרָא כִרְעוּתֵהּ — *In the world that He created as He willed.* God had His concept of a perfect world before He began creation. Then He began to create in accordance with His prior will (*Ran*). Or it refers to the *future*. Only then will mankind function in accordance with God's original intention (*R' Yehudah ben Yakar*).

בְּחַיֵּיכוֹן — *In your lifetimes.* The one reciting the *Kaddish* expresses the hope that his fellow congregants may all live to witness the Redemption of Israel and the sanctification of God's Name (*Abudraham*).

בַּעֲגָלָא וּבִזְמַן קָרִיב — *Swiftly and soon.* May the travail preceding the Messianic epoch be over swiftly and not be drawn out; and may it begin very soon (*Aruch HaShulchan*).

יְהֵא שְׁמֵהּ רַבָּא — *May His great Name.* The Talmud stresses in several places that the response; יְהֵא שְׁמֵהּ רַבָּא, *May His great Name...,* has an enormous cosmic effect. Indeed, the

halachah states that an opportunity to respond to *Kaddish* takes precedence over an opportunity to respond to any other prayer, even *Kedushah* and *Borchu*. Consequently, if *Kaddish* is about to be recited in one room and *Kedushah* in another, one should go to hear *Kaddish* (*Mishnah Berurah* 56:6).

The Talmud (*Shabbos* 19b) teaches that one must respond יְהֵא שְׁמֵהּ רַבָּא 'with all his power,' meaning his total concentration (*Rashi, Tosafos*). Though it is preferable to raise one's voice when saying it, one should not say it so loudly that he will invite ridicule (*R' Yonah*). And it must be enunciated clearly (*Maharal*).

יִתְבָּרַךְ — *Blessed.* This begins a series of praises that continue the central theme of *Kaddish:* namely that in time to come God's greatness will be acknowledged by all of mankind (*Emek Berachah*).

לְעֵלָּא מִן כָּל בִּרְכָתָא — *Beyond any blessing.* No words or ideas can praise God adequately.

All:

לְךָ יהוה הַצְּדָקָה, וְלָנוּ בְּשֶׁת הַפָּנִים.[1] מַה נִּתְאוֹנֵן,[2] מַה נֹּאמַר, מַה נְּדַבֵּר, וּמַה נִּצְטַדָּק.[3] נַחְפְּשָׂה דְרָכֵינוּ וְנַחְקְרָה, וְנָשׁוּבָה אֵלֶיךָ,[4] כִּי יְמִינְךָ פְּשׁוּטָה לְקַבֵּל שָׁבִים. לֹא בְחֶסֶד וְלֹא בְמַעֲשִׂים בָּאנוּ לְפָנֶיךָ, כְּדַלִּים וּכְרָשִׁים דָּפַקְנוּ דְלָתֶיךָ. דְּלָתֶיךָ דָּפַקְנוּ רַחוּם וְחַנּוּן, נָא אַל תְּשִׁיבֵנוּ רֵיקָם מִלְּפָנֶיךָ. מִלְּפָנֶיךָ מַלְכֵּנוּ רֵיקָם אַל תְּשִׁיבֵנוּ, כִּי אַתָּה שׁוֹמֵעַ תְּפִלָּה.

שֹׁמֵעַ תְּפִלָּה,* עָדֶיךָ כָּל בָּשָׂר יָבֹאוּ.[5] יָבוֹא כָּל בָּשָׂר לְהִשְׁתַּחֲוֹת לְפָנֶיךָ יהוה.[6] יָבֹאוּ וְיִשְׁתַּחֲווּ לְפָנֶיךָ אֲדֹנָי, וִיכַבְּדוּ לִשְׁמֶךָ.[7] בֹּאוּ נִשְׁתַּחֲוֶה וְנִכְרָעָה, נִבְרְכָה לִפְנֵי יהוה עֹשֵׂנוּ.[8] נָבוֹאָה לְמִשְׁכְּנוֹתָיו, נִשְׁתַּחֲוֶה לַהֲדֹם רַגְלָיו.*[9] בֹּאוּ שְׁעָרָיו בְּתוֹדָה, חֲצֵרֹתָיו בִּתְהִלָּה, הוֹדוּ לוֹ בָּרְכוּ שְׁמוֹ.[10] רוֹמְמוּ יהוה אֱלֹהֵינוּ, וְהִשְׁתַּחֲווּ לַהֲדֹם רַגְלָיו, קָדוֹשׁ הוּא.[11] רוֹמְמוּ יהוה אֱלֹהֵינוּ, וְהִשְׁתַּחֲווּ לְהַר קָדְשׁוֹ, כִּי קָדוֹשׁ יהוה אֱלֹהֵינוּ.[12] הִשְׁתַּחֲווּ לַיהוה בְּהַדְרַת קֹדֶשׁ,* חִילוּ מִפָּנָיו כָּל הָאָרֶץ.[13] וַאֲנַחְנוּ בְּרֹב חַסְדְּךָ נָבוֹא בֵיתֶךָ, נִשְׁתַּחֲוֶה אֶל הֵיכַל קָדְשְׁךָ בְּיִרְאָתֶךָ.[14] נִשְׁתַּחֲוֶה אֶל הֵיכַל קָדְשְׁךָ וְנוֹדֶה אֶת שְׁמֶךָ, עַל חַסְדְּךָ וְעַל אֲמִתֶּךָ, כִּי הִגְדַּלְתָּ עַל כָּל שִׁמְךָ* אִמְרָתֶךָ.[15] לְכוּ נְרַנְּנָה לַיהוה, נָרִיעָה לְצוּר יִשְׁעֵנוּ.* נְקַדְּמָה פָנָיו בְּתוֹדָה, בִּזְמִרוֹת נָרִיעַ לוֹ.[16] אֲשֶׁר יַחְדָּו נַמְתִּיק סוֹד,* בְּבֵית אֱלֹהִים נְהַלֵּךְ בְּרָגֶשׁ.[17] אֵל נַעֲרָץ בְּסוֹד קְדֹשִׁים רַבָּה, וְנוֹרָא עַל כָּל סְבִיבָיו.[18] שְׂאוּ יְדֵיכֶם קֹדֶשׁ וּבָרְכוּ אֶת יהוה.[19] הִנֵּה בָּרְכוּ אֶת יהוה כָּל עַבְדֵי יהוה, הָעֹמְדִים בְּבֵית יהוה בַּלֵּילוֹת.*[20] אֲשֶׁר מִי

שֹׁמֵעַ תְּפִלָּה ◈ — *You Who hears prayer.* This long selection is the introductory prayer to the daily *Selichos*. It is a collection of verses [some of which have been altered from the singular to the plural], mostly from *Psalms*, but from other parts of Scripture as well. In effect, it speaks simultaneously to God and to Israel. To God, it declares that we acknowledge His complete mastery over everything and His uncontested ability to bring us salvation. To Israel, it urges everyone to join us in worshiping Him and begging forgiveness.

לַהֲדֹם רַגְלָיו ... לְמִשְׁכְּנוֹתָיו — *... to His dwelling places ... at His footstool.* In its Scriptural sense this verse from *Psalms* refers to the Temple. In the context of the *Selichos* service, it refers to our synagogues and study halls, because our places of prayer and Torah study take the place of the Temple, until it is rebuilt (see *Ezekiel* 11:16). The plural form, *dwelling places,* alludes to the fact that the Sanctuary on earth corresponds to the spiritual Sanctuary in heaven. Thus, too, the earthly Sanctuary is like a *footstool* for God, Who hovers above it (*Alshich*).

בְּהַדְרַת קֹדֶשׁ — *In His intensely holy place,* i.e., the Temple. Once again, this alludes, by extension, to our synagogues.

עַל כָּל שִׁמְךָ — *Even beyond Your Name.* Though He is known by Names that suggest strict

All:

לְךָ ה׳ Yours, my Lord, is the righteousness and ours is the shame-facedness.[1] What complaint can we make?[2] What can we say? What can we declare? What justification can we offer?[3] Let us examine our ways and analyze — and return to You,[4] for Your right hand is extended to accept penitents. Neither with kindness nor with [good] deeds do we come before You. As paupers and as beggars do we knock at Your doors. At Your doors we knock, O Compassionate and Gracious One. Please do not turn us away from You empty-handed. Our King, turn us not away from You empty-handed, for You are the One Who hears prayer.

שֹׁמֵעַ תְּפִלָּה You Who hears prayer,* to You all flesh will come.[5] All flesh will come to prostrate itself before You, O HASHEM.[6] They will come and prostrate themselves before You, my Lord, and shall honor Your Name.[7] Come! — let us prostrate ourselves and bow, let us kneel before God, our Maker.[8] Let us come to His dwelling places, let us prostrate ourselves at His footstool.*[9] Enter His gates with thanksgiving, His courts with praise; give thanks to Him, praise His Name.[10] Exalt HASHEM, our God, and bow at His footstool; He is holy![11] Exalt HASHEM, our God, and bow at His holy mountain; for holy is HASHEM, our God.[12] Prostrate yourselves before HASHEM in His intensely holy place,* tremble before Him, everyone on earth.[13] As for us, through Your abundant kindness we will enter Your House; we will prostrate ourselves toward Your Holy Sanctuary in awe of You.[14] We will prostrate ourselves toward Your Holy Sanctuary, and we will give thanks to Your Name for Your kindness and truth for You have exalted Your promise even beyond Your Name.*[15] Come! — let us sing to HASHEM, let us call out to the Rock of our salvation.* Let us greet Him with thanksgiving, with praiseful songs let us call out to Him.[16] For together let us share sweet counsel,* in the house of God let us walk in multitudes.[17] God is dreaded in the hiddenmost counsel of the holy ones, and inspires awe upon all who surround Him.[18] Lift your hands in the Sanctuary and bless HASHEM.[19] Behold, bless HASHEM, all you servants of HASHEM, who stand in the House of HASHEM in the nights.*[20] For what

(1) Daniel 9:7. (2) Cf. Lamentations 3:39. (3) Cf. Genesis 44:16. (4) Cf. Lamentations 3:40. (5) Psalms 65:3. (6) Cf. Isaiah 66:23. (7) Psalms 86:9. (8) 95:6. (9) 132:7. (10) 100:4. (11) 99:5. (12) 99:9. (13) 96:9. (14) Cf. 5:8. (15) Cf. 138:2. (16) 95:1-2. (17) 55:15. (18) 89:8. (19) 134:2. (20) 134:1.

judgment, His promise of mercy overpowers His Attribute of justice (Rashi).

לְצוּר יִשְׁעֵנוּ — To the Rock of our salvation. No matter how imminent Israel's destruction has often seemed, the Rock of our salvation has always prevented the 'inevitable' from happening (Avnei Eliyahu).

נַמְתִּיק סוֹד — Let us share sweet counsel. Let us all gather in the study hall [house of God] to discuss

the pleasant secrets of Torah (Rashi).

הָעֹמְדִים...בַּלֵּילוֹת — Who stand...in the nights. The loyal servants of God bless Him constantly, even at night. 'Night' in this verse can be understood literally: during the nighttime hours, an interpretation that is especially apt regarding the selichos, which are ideally recited during the last third of the night. Or it can have a figurative meaning: They stand in the reverent attitude that

אֵל בַּשָּׁמַיִם וּבָאָרֶץ, אֲשֶׁר יַעֲשֶׂה כְמַעֲשֶׂיךָ וְכִגְבוּרֹתֶךָ.[1] אֲשֶׁר לוֹ
הַיָּם וְהוּא עָשָׂהוּ, וְיַבֶּשֶׁת יָדָיו יָצָרוּ.[2] אֲשֶׁר בְּיָדוֹ מֶחְקְרֵי אָרֶץ,*
וְתוֹעֲפוֹת הָרִים לוֹ.[3] אֲשֶׁר בְּיָדוֹ נֶפֶשׁ כָּל חָי, וְרוּחַ כָּל בְּשַׂר אִישׁ.[4]
וְיוֹדוּ שָׁמַיִם פִּלְאֲךָ יהוה, אַף אֱמוּנָתְךָ בִּקְהַל קְדֹשִׁים.[5] לְךָ זְרוֹעַ
עִם גְּבוּרָה, תָּעֹז יָדְךָ תָּרוּם יְמִינֶךָ.[6]* לְךָ שָׁמַיִם, אַף לְךָ אָרֶץ, תֵּבֵל
וּמְלֹאָהּ אַתָּה יְסַדְתָּם.[7] אַתָּה פוֹרַרְתָּ בְעָזְּךָ יָם, שִׁבַּרְתָּ רָאשֵׁי
תַנִּינִים עַל הַמָּיִם.[8] אַתָּה הִצַּבְתָּ כָּל גְּבוּלוֹת אָרֶץ, קַיִץ וָחֹרֶף
אַתָּה יְצַרְתָּם.[9] אַתָּה רִצַּצְתָּ רָאשֵׁי לִוְיָתָן,* תִּתְּנֶנּוּ מַאֲכָל לְעָם
לְצִיִּים. אַתָּה בָקַעְתָּ מַעְיָן וָנָחַל, אַתָּה הוֹבַשְׁתָּ נַהֲרוֹת אֵיתָן.[10] לְךָ
יוֹם, אַף לְךָ לָיְלָה,* אַתָּה הֲכִינוֹתָ מָאוֹר וָשָׁמֶשׁ.[11] עָשָׂה גְדֹלוֹת עַד
אֵין חֵקֶר, וְנִפְלָאוֹת עַד אֵין מִסְפָּר.[12] כִּי אֵל גָּדוֹל יהוה, וּמֶלֶךְ
גָּדוֹל עַל כָּל אֱלֹהִים.[13] כִּי גָדוֹל אַתָּה וְעֹשֵׂה נִפְלָאוֹת, אַתָּה
אֱלֹהִים לְבַדֶּךָ.[14] כִּי גָדוֹל מֵעַל שָׁמַיִם חַסְדֶּךָ, וְעַד שְׁחָקִים
אֲמִתֶּךָ.[15] גָּדוֹל יהוה וּמְהֻלָּל מְאֹד, וְלִגְדֻלָּתוֹ אֵין חֵקֶר.[16] (כִּי) גָּדוֹל
יהוה וּמְהֻלָּל מְאֹד, נוֹרָא הוּא עַל כָּל אֱלֹהִים.[17] גָּדוֹל יהוה
וּמְהֻלָּל מְאֹד, בְּעִיר אֱלֹהֵינוּ הַר קָדְשׁוֹ.[18] לְךָ יהוה הַגְּדֻלָּה*
וְהַגְּבוּרָה, וְהַתִּפְאֶרֶת וְהַנֵּצַח וְהַהוֹד, כִּי כֹל בַּשָּׁמַיִם וּבָאָרֶץ;
לְךָ יהוה הַמַּמְלָכָה, וְהַמִּתְנַשֵּׂא לְכֹל לְרֹאשׁ.[19] מִי לֹא יִרָאֲךָ
מֶלֶךְ הַגּוֹיִם, כִּי לְךָ יָאָתָה, כִּי בְכָל חַכְמֵי הַגּוֹיִם וּבְכָל מַלְכוּתָם
מֵאֵין כָּמוֹךָ.[20] מֵאַיִן כָּמוֹךָ יהוה, גָּדוֹל אַתָּה וְגָדוֹל שִׁמְךָ בִּגְבוּרָה.[21]
יהוה אֱלֹהֵי צְבָאוֹת, מִי כָמוֹךָ חֲסִין יָהּ, וֶאֱמוּנָתְךָ סְבִיבוֹתֶיךָ.[22]*
יהוה צְבָאוֹת, אֱלֹהֵי יִשְׂרָאֵל, יוֹשֵׁב הַכְּרֻבִים,* אַתָּה הוּא
הָאֱלֹהִים לְבַדֶּךָ.[23] מִי יְמַלֵּל גְּבוּרוֹת יהוה, יַשְׁמִיעַ כָּל תְּהִלָּתוֹ.[24]

---

is proper during praise or prayer, and they remain loyal even during the *night* of suffering and exile.

מֶחְקְרֵי אָרֶץ — *The hidden mysteries of the earth.* God's power is expressed allegorically in earthly terms. He knows the solution to all the earth's mysteries and He reigns over the mightiest peaks.

יָדְךָ . . . יְמִינֶךָ — *Your hand . . . Your right hand.* The verse refers to two hands, as it were. The first is God's 'left hand,' meaning His judgment against the wicked; the second is His 'right hand,' meaning His goodness to the righteous or downtrodden. Whichever mode of conduct God chooses to exercise, no one can resist Him.

רָאשֵׁי לִוְיָתָן — *The heads of Leviathan.* The

Psalmist describes Israel's Exodus from Egypt and God's mercy in the Wilderness. The Egyptian army, which pursued the Jews into the Sea of Reeds, is likened to a sea monster; while Pharaoh and his generals are alluded to as Leviathan heads. God smashed the Egyptians and their leaders and distributed their spoils to Israel, the nation of twelve tribal legions. In the Wilderness, He provided water for Israel and dried the mighty Jordan River so that the people could cross into the Land of Canaan.

יוֹם . . . לָיְלָה — *Day . . . night.* Whether in the *day* of good times or the *night* of exile, the Jewish people maintain their faith in You. To serve as our guide in all seasons, You gave us the Torah,

power is there in heaven or earth that can approximate Your deeds and power?[1] *For His is the sea and He perfected the dry land — His hands fashioned it.*[2] *For in His power are the hidden mysteries of the earth,* and the mountain summits are His.*[3] *For His is the soul of every living thing, and the spirit of all human flesh.*[4] *Heaven will gratefully praise Your wonders,* HASHEM; *also Your faithfulness in the assembly of holy ones.*[5] *Yours is a mighty arm with power, You strengthen Your hand; You exalt Your right hand.**[6] *Yours is the heaven; Yours, too, is the earth; the world and its fullness — You founded them.*[7] *You shattered the sea with Your might, You smashed sea serpents' heads upon the water.*[8] *You established all the boundaries of earth; summer and winter — You fashioned them.*[9] *You crushed the heads of Leviathan,* You served it as food to the nation of legions. You split open fountain and stream, You dried the mighty rivers.*[10] *Yours is the day, Yours as well is the night;* You established luminary and the sun.*[11] *Who performs great deeds that are beyond comprehension, and wonders beyond number.*[12] *For a great God is* HASHEM, *and a great King above all heavenly powers.*[13] *For You are great and work wonders; You alone, O God.*[14] *For great above the very heavens is Your kindness, and until the upper heights is Your truth.*[15] HASHEM *is great and exceedingly lauded, and His greatness is beyond investigation.*[16] *(For)* HASHEM *is great and exceedingly lauded, awesome is He above all heavenly powers.*[17] *Great is* HASHEM *and exceedingly lauded, in the city of our God, Mount of His Holiness.*[18] *Yours,* HASHEM, *is the greatness,* the strength, the splendor, the triumph, and the glory; even everything in heaven and earth; Yours,* HASHEM, *is the kingdom, and sovereignty over every leader.*[19] *Who would not revere You, O King of nations? — for this befits You, for among all the sages of the nations and in all their kingdom there is none like You.*[20] *There is none like You, O* HASHEM, *You are great and Your Name is great with power.*[21] HASHEM, *God of Legions — who is like You, O Strong One, God? — and Your faithfulness surrounds You.**[22] HASHEM, *Master of Legions, God of Israel, enthroned upon the Cherubim,* it is You alone Who is God.*[23] *Who can express the mighty acts of* HASHEM, *who can announce all His praise?*[24]

---

(1) *Deuteronomy* 3:24. (2) *Psalms* 95:5. (3) 95:4. (4) *Job* 12:10. (5) *Psalms* 89:6. (6) 89:14.
(7) 89:12. (8) 74:13. (9) 74:17. (10) 74:14-15. (11) 74:16. (12) *Job* 9:10. (13) *Psalms* 95:3.
(14) 86:10. (15) 108:5. (16) 145:3. (17) 96:4. (18) 48:2. (19) *I Chronicles* 29:11.
(20) *Jeremiah* 10:7. (21) 10:6. (22) *Psalms* 89:9. (23) *Isaiah* 37:16. (24) *Psalms* 106:2.

---

which is our luminary in darkness and our sun in times of joy.

לְךָ ה' הַגְּדֻלָּה — *Yours,* HASHEM, *is the greatness.* David uttered this verse in the presence of the entire congregation at one of the supreme moments of his life, when he had assembled the necessary contributions and materials for his heir, Solomon, to build the Temple. In this moment of public glory, David proclaimed that his every achievement was possible only because God made it so.

וֶאֱמוּנָתְךָ סְבִיבוֹתֶיךָ — *And Your faithfulness surrounds You.* God is surrounded by His angels, who testify to His absolute faithfulness. No word of God goes unfulfilled.

יוֹשֵׁב הַכְּרֻבִים — *Enthroned upon the Cherubim.* God's Presence rested upon the Cherubim in the Holy of Holies. The Cherubim were in the form of angels with the faces of children, carved from the solid gold cover of the Holy Ark in the *Beis HaMikdash.*

כִּי מִי בַשַּׁחַק יַעֲרֹךְ לַיהוה, יִדְמֶה לַיהוה בִּבְנֵי אֵלִים.¹ מַה נֹּאמַר
לְפָנֶיךָ יוֹשֵׁב מָרוֹם, וּמַה נְּסַפֵּר לְפָנֶיךָ שֹׁכֵן שְׁחָקִים. מַה נֹּאמַר
לְפָנֶיךָ יהוה אֱלֹהֵינוּ, מַה נְּדַבֵּר וּמַה נִּצְטַדָּק.² אֵין לָנוּ פֶּה לְהָשִׁיב
וְלֹא מֵצַח לְהָרִים רֹאשׁ, כִּי עֲוֹנוֹתֵינוּ רַבּוּ מִלִּמְנוֹת, וְחַטֹּאתֵינוּ
עָצְמוּ מִסַּפֵּר.³ לְמַעַן שִׁמְךָ יהוה תְּחַיֵּנוּ, וּבְצִדְקָתְךָ תּוֹצִיא מִצָּרָה
נַפְשֵׁנוּ.⁴ דַּרְכְּךָ אֱלֹהֵינוּ* לְהַאֲרִיךְ אַפֶּךָ, לָרָעִים וְלַטּוֹבִים,* וְהִיא
תְהִלָּתֶךָ.* לְמַעַנְךָ אֱלֹהֵינוּ* עֲשֵׂה* וְלֹא לָנוּ, רְאֵה עֲמִידָתֵנוּ, דַּלִים
וְרֵקִים. הַנְּשָׁמָה לָךְ וְהַגּוּף פָּעֳלָךְ, חוּסָה עַל עֲמָלָךְ. הַנְּשָׁמָה לָךְ
וְהַגּוּף שֶׁלָּךְ, יהוה עֲשֵׂה לְמַעַן שְׁמֶךָ.* אָתָאנוּ עַל שִׁמְךָ, יהוה,
עֲשֵׂה לְמַעַן שְׁמֶךָ. בַּעֲבוּר כְּבוֹד שִׁמְךָ, כִּי אֵל חַנּוּן וְרַחוּם שְׁמֶךָ.*
לְמַעַן שִׁמְךָ יהוה, וְסָלַחְתָּ לַעֲוֹנֵנוּ כִּי רַב הוּא.⁵

Congregation, then *chazzan*:

סְלַח לָנוּ אָבִינוּ, כִּי בְרֹב אִוַּלְתֵּנוּ שָׁגִינוּ,
מְחַל לָנוּ מַלְכֵּנוּ, כִּי רַבּוּ עֲוֹנֵינוּ.

סְלִיחָה א (פְּתִיחָה)

All:

(אֱלֹהֵינוּ וֵאלֹהֵי אֲבוֹתֵינוּ:)

אֵיךְ נִפְתַּח פֶּה* לְפָנֶיךָ, דַּר מְתוּחִים,
בְּאֵלוּ פָנִים נִשְׁפֹּךְ שִׂיחִים,
גָּעַלְנוּ נְתִיבוֹתֶיךָ הַיְשָׁרִים וְהַנְּבֹחִים,
דָּבַקְנוּ בְתוֹעֵבוֹת וּבְמַעֲשִׂים זְנוּחִים.
הָלַכְנוּ אַחֲרֵי מַשְׁאוֹת שָׁוְא וּמַדּוּחִים,⁶
וְהִקְשִׁינוּ עֹרֶף וְהֶעֱזַנּוּ מְצָחִים,
זָעַמְתָּ בְּשִׁלֹנוּ, בֵּית מִשְׁכְּנוֹת מִבְטַחִים,*⁷

דַּרְכְּךָ אֱלֹהֵינוּ — *It is Your way, our God.* After the sin of the Golden Calf, Moses pleaded with God, 'Let me know Your way' (*Exodus* 33:13). In response, God taught him the Thirteen Attributes of Mercy, one of which is אֶרֶךְ אַפַּיִם, *Slow to anger.*

לָרָעִים וְלַטּוֹבִים — *Against people both evil and good.* Even good people sin, sometimes seriously. Whether the sinners are good or evil, God waits, giving them a chance to repent.

וְהִיא תְהִלָּתֶךָ — *And this is Your praise.* God Himself says that His patience is praiseworthy (*Isaiah* 48:9). It is easier to lash out at evil than to endure it silently.

לְמַעַנְךָ . . . עֲשֵׂה — *Act for Your sake.* When Israel is downtrodden, non-believers scoff and ask, 'Where is their God?' Therefore, we beg God to help us for the sake of His Own Glory. We do not deserve His mercy for we are spiritually destitute, and totally dependent on Him.

לְמַעַן שְׁמֶךָ — *For Your Name's sake.* Since we are Yours, body and soul, we implore You to spare us for Your sake, though we know we are undeserving.

שְׁמֶךָ — *Is Your Name.* Graciousness and mercy are so intrinsic to You that Your very Name is *Gracious and Merciful God.*

For who in the sky can be compared to HASHEM; be likened to HASHEM
among the angels?[1] What can we say before You Who dwell on high?
And what can we relate to You Who abide in the highest heaven? What
can we say before You, HASHEM, our God? What can we declare? What
justification can we offer?[2] We have neither mouth to respond nor brow
to raise our head, for our iniquities are too numerous to count, and our
sins are too vast to be numbered.[3] For Your Name's sake, HASHEM,
revive us; and with Your righteousness remove our soul from distress.[4]
It is Your way, our God,* to delay Your anger, against people both evil
and good* — and this is Your praise.* Act for Your sake,* our God, and
not for ours, behold our [spiritual] position — destitute and emptyhanded. Chazzan – The soul is Yours and the body is Your handiwork;
take pity on Your labor. The soul is Yours and the body is Yours; O
HASHEM, act for Your Name's sake.* We have come with reliance on
Your Name, O HASHEM, act for Your Name's sake; because of Your
Name's glory — for 'Gracious and Merciful God' is Your Name.* For
Your Name's sake, HASHEM, may You forgive our iniquity, though it is
abundant.[5]

Congregation, then chazzan:
Forgive us, our Father, for in our abundant folly we have erred,
pardon us, our King, for our iniquities are many.

SELICHAH 1

All:
(Our God and the God of our forefathers:)

א How can we open [our] mouth* before You,
O You Who dwell in the stretched-out heavens?

ב In what way can we pour out our prayers?

ג We loathed Your forthright and honest paths;

ד we clung to [idolatrous] abominations and despicable deeds.

ה We went after vain, deceitful prophecies;[6]

ו we made our necks stiff, our brows brazen.

ז You raged at what was ours, the secure Dwelling Place,*[7]

---

(1) *Psalms* 89:7. (2) Cf. *Genesis* 44:16. (3) Cf. *Ezra* 9:6. (4) Cf. *Psalms* 143:11.
(5) Cf. 25:11. (6) *Lamentations* 2:14. (7) Cf. *Isaiah* 32:18.

אֵיךְ נִפְתַּח פֶּה ﭏﭏ — *How can we open [our] mouth.*
This פְּתִיחָה [*pesichah*], introductory *selichah*,
contains an *aleph-beis* acrostic. The *paytan* hid
his name — בִּנְיָמִין — *Binyamin* — in the first two
words of the next-to-last stich: בְּוֹרָאוֹת יְמִינֶךָ. It is
uncertain whether he was R' Binyamin ben
Zerach [see prefatory comment to *selichah* 20] or
another *paytan* with the same first name.

וְצַמְתָּ בְּשֶׁלָּנוּ בֵּית מִשְׁכְּנוֹת מִבְטָחִים — *You raged at
what was ours, the secure Dwelling Place.* The
translation is literal — 'the secure Dwelling Place'
describes 'what was ours' — and is in accord with

both the alphabetical acrostic and the rhyme
scheme. An alternative rendering includes the
word חָרֵב, *was destroyed*, from the next stich as
part of this one. Thus, וְצַמְתָּ בְּשֶׁלָּנוּ, *You raged on
our account*, בֵּית מִשְׁכְּנוֹת מִבְטָחִים חָרֵב, [and] the
secure Dwelling Place was destroyed.

בֵּית מִשְׁכְּנוֹת מִבְטָחִים — *The secure Dwelling
Place.* The juxtaposition of this verse with the
cessation of the Temple offerings indicates that it
refers to the *Beis HaMikdash*. Alternatively, it
may refer to the Land of Israel in general or to
Jerusalem in particular, for that is how the phrase

חָרַב וּפַס רֵיחַ נִיחֹחִים.

טֹרְדוּ וְטֻלְטָלוּ כְּהֶגְנִים מְשׁוּחִים,

יוֹדְעֵי עֶרֶךְ* עוֹלוֹת וּזְבָחִים,

כַּמָּה יִסַּרְתָּנוּ עַל יְדֵי צִירִים וּשְׁלוּחִים,

לֹא הִקְשַׁבְנוּ לִשְׁמֹעַ לְמוֹכִיחִים.

מֵאָז* וְעַד עַתָּה אֲנַחְנוּ נִדָּחִים,

נֶהֱרָגִים וְנִשְׁחָטִים וְנִטְבָּחִים,

שַׂרַדְנוּ מְתֵי מְעַט בֵּין קוֹצִים כְּסוּחִים,*

עֵינֵינוּ כָלוֹת בְּלִי מְצֹא רְוָחִים.

פּוֹרְכֵי עֻמֶּךְ אֲשֶׁר לַבֶּל* שׁוֹחֲחִים,

צֶפֶר וָעֶרֶב לָמָּה מַצְלִיחִים,

קָמִים לְמוּלָךְ נְאָצוֹת שׂוֹחֲחִים,

רְצוּצִים, בַּמָּה אַתֶּם בּוֹטָחִים.

❖ **שׁ**וֹכֵן עַד וְקָדוֹשׁ, צְפֵּה בְּעֶלְבּוֹן אֲנוּחִים,

תְּמוּכִים עָלֶיךָ וּבְךָ מִתְאָחִים,

בְּנוֹרָאוֹת יְמִינְךָ נִוָּשַׁע לִנְצָחִים,

כִּי עַל רַחֲמֶיךָ הָרַבִּים[1] אָנוּ בְטוּחִים.

All:

כִּי עַל רַחֲמֶיךָ הָרַבִּים[1] אָנוּ בְטוּחִים, וְעַל צִדְקוֹתֶיךָ אָנוּ
נִשְׁעָנִים, וְלִסְלִיחוֹתֶיךָ אָנוּ מְקַוִּים, וְלִישׁוּעָתָךְ אָנוּ
מְצַפִּים. אַתָּה הוּא מֶלֶךְ, אוֹהֵב צְדָקוֹת מִקֶּדֶם, מַעֲבִיר עֲווֹנוֹת עַמּוֹ,
וּמֵסִיר חַטֹּאת יְרֵאָיו. כּוֹרֵת בְּרִית לָרִאשׁוֹנִים, וּמְקַיֵּם שְׁבוּעָה
לָאַחֲרוֹנִים. אַתָּה הוּא, שֶׁיָּרַדְתָּ בַּעֲנָן כְּבוֹדֶךָ עַל הַר סִינַי,[2] וְהֶרְאֵיתָ
דַּרְכֵי טוּבְךָ לְמֹשֶׁה עַבְדֶּךָ.[3] וְאָרְחוֹת חֲסָדֶיךָ גִּלִּיתָ לוֹ, וְהוֹדַעְתּוֹ כִּי
אַתָּה אֵל רַחוּם וְחַנּוּן, אֶרֶךְ אַפַּיִם וְרַב חֶסֶד[4] וּמַרְבֶּה לְהֵיטִיב,
וּמַנְהִיג אֶת כָּל הָעוֹלָם כֻּלּוֹ בְּמִדַּת הָרַחֲמִים. ❖ וְכֵן כָּתוּב, וַיֹּאמֶר
אֲנִי אַעֲבִיר כָּל טוּבִי עַל פָּנֶיךָ, וְקָרָאתִי בְשֵׁם יהוה לְפָנֶיךָ, וְחַנֹּתִי
אֶת אֲשֶׁר אָחֹן, וְרִחַמְתִּי אֶת אֲשֶׁר אֲרַחֵם.[5]

---

is used in *Isaiah* (32:18).

יוֹדְעֵי עֶרֶךְ — *Who knew how to arrange.* Alternatively, *who knew the worth of.*

מֵאָז — *From then.* The verses from מ to ר present
the conquering nations in a less-than-favorable
light. Thus, they have been the targets of censor-

ship. In some editions, these verses have been
completely eliminated. In others, they have been
replaced with stanzas that continue the theme of
the כ and ל verses, namely, that Israel did not heed
the reproach of the prophets. The text presented
here is probably the least-altered version and is

ח *[the offerings'] sweet scent was destroyed and ceased.*

ט *Driven out and wandering were the anointed priests,*

י *who knew how to arrange* every form of offering.*

כ *How You chastised us through [the prophets,*
Your] emissaries and messengers!

ל *[But] we were not attentive to listen to those who rebuked [us].*

מ *From then* until now we have been dispersed [in exile],*

נ *slain, slaughtered, and butchered.*

ס *We are left a mere few [scattered] among piercing thorns,**

ע *while our eyes dim without finding relief.*

פ *Those who enslave Your people, they bow to idols* —*

צ *why do they succeed both morning and evening?*

ק *They rise up against You with vexatious talk:*

ר *'You broken-backs! What do you trust in?'*

ש Chazzan — *O He Who dwells eternally, O Holy One,*
behold the shame of those who sigh,

ת *[those] who depend on You, who are like brothers to You.*
By Your right hand's awesome deeds, may we be redeemed forever,
for upon Your abundant mercy[1] do we trust.

All:

כִּי עַל *For upon Your abundant mercy[1] do we trust, and upon Your*
righteousness do we depend, and for Your forgiveness do we
hope, and for Your salvation do we yearn. You are the King Who loves
righteousness since the earliest days, Who overlooks His people's
iniquities and sets aside the sins of those who revere Him. He made
a covenant with the ancestors and keeps [His] vow to the descend-
ants. It is You Who descended in Your cloud of glory on Mount Sinai,[2]
and showed the ways of Your goodness to Your servant Moses.[3]
You revealed Your paths of kindness to him, and let him know that You
are God, Compassionate and Gracious, Slow to anger and Abundant in
Kindness,[4] doing manifold good, and guiding all Your world with the
Attribute of Mercy. Chazzan — *And so it is written: He said, 'I shall pass*
all My good in front of you, and I shall call out the Name of HASHEM
before you; for I will be gracious to whom I will be gracious, and I will
be compassionate with whom I will be compassionate.'[5]

---

(1) *Daniel* 9:18. (2) Cf. *Exodus* 34:5. (3) Cf. 33:13. (4) 34:6. (5) 33:19.

---

the version that appears in virtually all editions of *Selichos* printed during the last century.

בֵּין קוֹצִים כְּסוּחִים — *Among piercing thorns.* The phrase קוֹצִים כְּסוּחִים as used in *Isaiah* (33:12) means *cut thorns.* It refers to the Assyrian hordes who would have eventually be destroyed like thorns that have been cut down and have become dry, easily burned tinder. Perhaps the *paytan* intends both meanings: *Our oppressors presently are like piercing thorns, but, when the proper time ar-*

rives, they will become like cut down thorns that are readily consumed by the fire.

לַבֵּל — *To idols* [lit., *to the Bel*]. The *Bel* or *Baal* was a genre of idolatry common in the days of the prophets. Its use here obviously refers to idolatry in general, since the nations of which this verse speaks do not worship the *Baal* idols. Some early editions of *Selichos* read לַמֵּת, *to the dead*; and that is probably the original uncensored version.

All, while standing:

אֵל אֶֽרֶךְ אַפַּֽיִם אַתָּה, וּבַֽעַל הָרַחֲמִים נִקְרֵֽאתָ,
וְדֶֽרֶךְ תְּשׁוּבָה הוֹרֵֽיתָ.

גְּדֻלַּת רַחֲמֶֽיךָ וַחֲסָדֶֽיךָ,   תִּזְכּוֹר הַיּוֹם וּבְכָל יוֹם לְזֶֽרַע יְדִידֶֽיךָ.

תֵּֽפֶן אֵלֵֽינוּ בְּרַחֲמִים,   כִּי אַתָּה הוּא בַּֽעַל הָרַחֲמִים.

בְּתַחֲנוּן וּבִתְפִלָּה פָּנֶֽיךָ נְקַדֵּם,   כְּהוֹדַֽעְתָּ לֶעָנָיו מִקֶּֽדֶם.

מֵחֲרוֹן אַפְּךָ שׁוּב,[1]   כְּמוֹ בְתוֹרָתְךָ כָּתוּב.[2]

וּבְצֵל כְּנָפֶֽיךָ נֶחֱסֶה[3] וְנִתְלוֹנָן,   כְּיוֹם וַיֵּֽרֶד יהוה בֶּעָנָן.

❖ תַּעֲבוֹר עַל פֶּֽשַׁע וְתִמְחֶה אָשָׁם,   כְּיוֹם וַיִּתְיַצֵּב עִמּוֹ שָׁם.

תַּאֲזִין שַׁוְעָתֵֽנוּ וְתַקְשִׁיב מֶֽנּוּ מַאֲמָר,

כְּיוֹם וַיִּקְרָא בְשֵׁם יהוה,[4] וְשָׁם נֶאֱמַר:

Congregation, then *chazzan*:

וַיַּעֲבֹר יהוה עַל פָּנָיו וַיִּקְרָא:

Congregation and *chazzan* (the words in bold type are recited aloud and in unison):

יהוה, יהוה, * אֵל, **רַחוּם, וְחַנּוּן, אֶֽרֶךְ אַפַּֽיִם, וְרַב חֶֽסֶד,
וֶאֱמֶת, נֹצֵר חֶֽסֶד לָאֲלָפִים, נֹשֵׂא עָוֹן, וָפֶֽשַׁע,
וְחַטָּאָה, וְנַקֵּה.**[5] וְסָלַחְתָּ לַעֲוֹנֵֽנוּ וּלְחַטָּאתֵֽנוּ וּנְחַלְתָּֽנוּ.[6] סְלַח לָֽנוּ
אָבִֽינוּ כִּי חָטָֽאנוּ, מְחַל לָֽנוּ מַלְכֵּֽנוּ כִּי פָשָֽׁעְנוּ. כִּי אַתָּה אֲדֹנָי טוֹב
וְסַלָּח,* וְרַב חֶֽסֶד לְכָל קֹרְאֶֽיךָ.[7]

⊸ּ אֵל אֶֽרֶךְ אַפַּֽיִם ⊱ּ

O God — You Are Slow to Anger

After declaring that God's patience with sinful people and His boundless mercy are our primary hope, we beg Him to be as merciful to us now as He was on the day He taught the Thirteen Attributes to Moses, the epitome of humility, on Mount Sinai. On that day, God assured Moses that He would continue to protect Israel despite the nation's grievous sin. So may He heed and protect us, and be merciful to us now.

⊸ּ **ה' ה' —** *HASHEM, HASHEM.* There are various opinions regarding how to enumerate the Thirteen Attributes. We follow the generally accepted view of *Rabbeinu Tam (Rosh Hashanah* 17b):

(1) **ה' —** *HASHEM.* This Name [containing the letters of הָיָה הֹוֶה וְיִהְיֶה, *He was, He is, He will be*] designates God as the מְהַוֶּה, *Prime Cause*, of everything. It is only natural that He wishes to assure the survival of all that He brought into

---

⊸ּ י"ג מִדּוֹת ⊱ּ

The Thirteen Attributes

The central theme of all the *Selichos* is the שְׁלֹשׁ עֶשְׂרֵה מִדּוֹת הָרַחֲמִים, *Thirteen Attributes of Divine Mercy*, beginning ה' ה', *HASHEM, HASHEM.* This passage appears in the Torah (*Exodus* 34:6-7) at the time when God proclaimed His readiness to do away with Israel after the sin of the Golden Calf. According to R' Yochanan (*Rosh Hashanah* 17b), Moses felt that Israel's sin was so grievous that there was no possibility of his intercession on their behalf. Thereupon, God appeared to him in the guise of a *chazzan* wrapped in a *tallis* and taught him the Thirteen Attributes. God said, 'Whenever Israel sins, let them recite this in its proper order and I will forgive them.' Thus, this appeal for God's mercy reassures us of two things: that repentance is always possible; and that God always awaits our return to Him. The implication is also plain that if we emulate God's merciful ways, He will treat us mercifully in return.

All, while standing:

אֵל אֶרֶךְ אַפַּיִם *O God — You are slow to anger, You are called the Master of Mercy, and You have taught the way of repentance. May You remember this day and every day the greatness of Your mercy and Your kindness to the offspring of Your beloved Ones. Turn to us in mercy for You are the Master of Mercy. With supplication and prayer we approach Your Presence in the manner that You made known to the humble [Moses] in ancient times. Turn back from Your fierce anger;[1] as is written in Your Torah.[2] In the shadow of Your wings may we find shelter[3] and lodging as on the day 'HASHEM descended in a cloud' [to appear to Moses on Sinai].* Chazzan — *Overlook sin and erase guilt as on the day 'He [God] stood there with him [Moses].' Give heed to our cry and be attentive to our declaration as on the day 'He called out with the Name HASHEM,'*[4] *and there it was said:*

Congregation, then chazzan:

And HASHEM passed before him [Moses] and proclaimed:

Congregation and chazzan (the words in bold type are recited aloud and in unison):

ה' ה' HASHEM, HASHEM,* God, Compassionate and Gracious, Slow to anger, and Abundant in Kindness and Truth, Preserver of kindness for thousands [of generations], Forgiver of iniquity, willful sin, and error, and Who cleanses.[5]** *May You forgive our iniquities and our errors and make us Your heritage.[6] Forgive us, our Father, for we have erred; pardon us, our King, for we have willfully sinned; for You, my Lord, are good and forgiving* *and abundantly kind to all who call upon You.[7]*

---

(1) Cf. *Exodus* 32:12. (2) See 32:14. (3) Cf. *Psalms* 36:8.
(4) *Exodus* 34:5. (5) 34:6-7. (6) 34:9. (7) *Psalms* 86:5.

---

being. Consequently, this Name represents the Attribute of Mercy. In addition, the Name's spelling implies God's timelessness. Though man may sin, he can repent and call upon the timeless God to restore him to his original innocent state. As the Talmud states: אֲנִי הוּא קוֹדֶם שֶׁיֶּחֱטָא הָאָדָם, *I am He* [the God of Mercy] *before a person sins, and* וַאֲנִי הוּא לְאַחַר שֶׁיֶּחֱטָא הָאָדָם וְיַעֲשֶׂה תְּשׁוּבָה *I am He after a person sins and repents* (*Rosh Hashanah* 17b). Based on this dictum, *Rabbeinu Tam* counts the twin use of the Name HASHEM as two Attributes. The first is that God is merciful before a person sins, even though He knows that the sin will be committed.

(2) ה' — *HASHEM.* God is merciful after the sin has been committed, by allowing the sinner time to repent, and by accepting his repentance, though it may be imperfect.

(3) אֵל — *God.* This Name denotes the power of God's mercy, which sometimes surpasses even the compassion indicated by the Name HASHEM. He displays this higher degree of mercy to

genuinely righteous people who sin, but repent. In return for their previous behavior, God exerts Himself, as it were, to ensure their survival.

(4) רַחוּם — *Compassionate.* In response to pleas for mercy, God eases the suffering of those being punished for their sins. Another manifestation of compassion is that God does not confront deserving people with overpowering temptation.

(5) וְחַנּוּן — *And Gracious.* God is gracious even to those unworthy of His kindness. Also, if someone finds himself lacking in the will power to avoid sin and he seeks God's help, he will get it.

(6) אֶרֶךְ אַפַּיִם — *Slow to anger.* So that the sinner will have time to repent.

(7) וְרַב חֶסֶד — *And Abundant in Kindness.* God shows great kindness to those who lack personal merits. The Talmud teaches (see below, p. 20), that God exercises this attribute by removing sins from the scale of justice, thus tilting the scales in favor of merit.

(8) וֶאֱמֶת — *And Truth.* God never reneges; His

פסוקי הקדמה לסליחה ב

אָבַד חָסִיד מִן הָאָרֶץ, וְיָשָׁר בָּאָדָם אָיִן.[1] אֵין קוֹרֵא בְשִׁמְךָ
בְּצֶדֶק, מִתְעוֹרֵר לְהַחֲזִיק בָּךְ.[2] הוֹשִׁיעָה יהוה כִּי גָמַר
חָסִיד, כִּי פַסּוּ אֱמוּנִים מִבְּנֵי אָדָם.[3] כִּי עִמְּךָ מְקוֹר חַיִּים, בְּאוֹרְךָ
נִרְאֶה אוֹר.[4] כִּי עִם יהוה הַחֶסֶד, וְהַרְבֵּה עִמּוֹ פְדוּת. וְהוּא יִפְדֶּה
אֶת יִשְׂרָאֵל מִכֹּל עֲוֹנוֹתָיו.[5]

כְּרַחֵם אָב עַל בָּנִים, כֵּן תְּרַחֵם יהוה עָלֵינוּ.[6] לַיהוה הַיְשׁוּעָה,
עַל עַמְּךָ בִרְכָתֶךָ סֶּלָה.[7] יהוה צְבָאוֹת עִמָּנוּ,
מִשְׂגָּב לָנוּ אֱלֹהֵי יַעֲקֹב סֶלָה.[8] יהוה צְבָאוֹת, אַשְׁרֵי אָדָם בֹּטֵחַ
בָּךְ.[9] יהוה הוֹשִׁיעָה, הַמֶּלֶךְ יַעֲנֵנוּ בְיוֹם קָרְאֵנוּ.[10]

In some congregations the following two verses are recited responsively — the chazzan reciting סְלַח,
and the congregation responding וַיֹּאמֶר. In other congregations these verses are recited silently.

סְלַח נָא* לַעֲוֹן הָעָם הַזֶּה כְּגֹדֶל חַסְדֶּךָ, וְכַאֲשֶׁר נָשָׂאתָה לָעָם
הַזֶּה מִמִּצְרַיִם וְעַד הֵנָּה,[11] וְשָׁם נֶאֱמַר:

וַיֹּאמֶר יהוה סָלַחְתִּי כִּדְבָרֶךָ.[12]

All:

הַטֵּה אֱלֹהַי אָזְנְךָ* וּשֲׁמָע, פְּקַח עֵינֶיךָ וּרְאֵה שֹׁמְמֹתֵינוּ, וְהָעִיר
אֲשֶׁר נִקְרָא שִׁמְךָ עָלֶיהָ, כִּי לֹא עַל צִדְקוֹתֵינוּ אֲנַחְנוּ
מַפִּילִים תַּחֲנוּנֵינוּ לְפָנֶיךָ, כִּי עַל רַחֲמֶיךָ הָרַבִּים. אֲדֹנָי שְׁמָעָה,
אֲדֹנָי סְלָחָה, אֲדֹנָי הַקְשִׁיבָה, וַעֲשֵׂה אַל תְּאַחַר, לְמַעַנְךָ אֱלֹהַי, כִּי
שִׁמְךָ נִקְרָא* עַל עִירְךָ וְעַל עַמֶּךָ.[13]

---

promise to reward the deserving will be carried
out unequivocally.

(9) נֹצֵר חֶסֶד לָאֲלָפִים — *Preserver of kindness for
thousands [of generations].* The deeds of the
righteous — especially those who serve Him out
of intense love — bring benefits to their offspring far into the future.

(10) נֹשֵׂא עָוֹן — *Forgiver of iniquity.* God forgives
the intentional sinner, if he repents.

(11) וָפֶשַׁע — *[Forgiver of] willful sin.* Even
those who rebel against God and purposely
seek to anger Him are given an opportunity to
repent.

(12) וְחַטָּאָה — *And [Forgiver of] error.* God
forgives those who repent sins that have been
committed out of carelessness or apathy. Having
already praised God as the forgiver of inten-

tional sin and rebelliousness, why do we revert
to praising Him for this seemingly lesser level
of mercy? Because if someone repents out of
fear rather than love, his intentional sins are
reduced in severity and are treated by God as
if they had been done in error. Thus, even
after having partially forgiven the intentional
sins by reducing their severity, God further
forgives those who continue to repent for these
lesser sins.

(13) וְנַקֵּה — *And Who cleanses.* God wipes away
the sins of those who repent sincerely, as if they
had never existed.

In the Torah the verse continues לֹא יְנַקֶּה, *He
does not cleanse.* The simple interpretation of
the verse is that God does not completely erase
the sin, but He exacts retribution in minute
stages. The Talmud (*Yoma* 86a), however, ex-

PREFATORY VERSES TO SELICHAH 2

אָבַד *The pious are gone from the world, and there is no upright one among men.*[1] *No one calls on Your Name with righteousness, or arouses himself to cling fast to You.*[2] *Save, HASHEM! For the pious have come to an end; for the faithful among men have disappeared.*[3] *For with You is the source of life; by Your light may we see light.*[4] *For with HASHEM is kindness, and with Him abundant redemption. And He shall redeem Israel from all its iniquities.*[5]

כְּרַחֵם אָב *As a father has mercy on his children, so, HASHEM, may You have mercy on us.*[6] *Salvation is HASHEM's, upon Your people is Your blessing, Selah.*[7] *HASHEM, Master of Legions, is with us, a stronghold for us is the God of Jacob, Selah.*[8] *HASHEM, Master of Legions, praiseworthy is the person who trusts in You.*[9] *HASHEM, save! May the King answer us on the day we call.*[10]

In some congregations, the following two verses are recited responsively — the chazzan reciting 'Forgive, please . . . ,' and the congregation responding, 'And HASHEM said . . .' In other congregations these verses are recited silently.

סְלַח נָא *Forgive, please,* the iniquity of this people according to the greatness of Your kindness and as You have forgiven this people from Egypt until now,*[11] *and there it was said:*

And HASHEM said, 'I have forgiven according to your word!'[12]

All:

הַטֵּה *Incline, my God, Your ear,* and listen, open Your eyes and see our desolation and that of the city upon which Your Name is proclaimed; for not because of our righteousness do we cast down our supplications before You, rather because of Your abundant compassion. O my Lord, heed; O my Lord, forgive; O my Lord, be attentive and act, do not delay; for Your sake, my God, for Your Name is proclaimed* upon Your city and upon Your people.*[13]

---

(1) *Micah* 7:2. (2) Cf. *Isaiah* 59:4; 64:6. (3) *Psalms* 12:2. (4) 36:10. (5) 130:7-8. (6) Cf. 103:13. (7) 3:9. (8) 46:8. (9) 84:13. (10) 20:10. (11) *Numbers* 14:19. (12) 14:20. (13) *Daniel* 9:18-19.

---

plains that *He cleanses* the sins of those who truly repent; but *He does not cleanse* the sins of those who do not repent.

טוֹב וְסַלָּח — *Are good and forgiving.* God is *good* to the righteous; even though they may have had difficult lives on earth, their reward will be generous in the World to Come. He is *forgiving* to sinners who try to repent.

סְלַח נָא — *Forgive, please.* This verse was Moses' plea to God that He forgive Israel after the sin of the spies, when the entire nation loudly expressed its lack of faith that God could bring them safely into *Eretz Yisrael.* In

response, God answered, 'סָלַחְתִּי, *I have forgiven.*' In our prayers today, we beg for a similar response.

הַטֵּה אֱלֹהַי אָזְנֶךְ — *Incline, my God, Your ear.* Even if we are not deserving, at least let God help for the sake of His Name that is desecrated by the destruction of His city and the persecution of His people.

כִּי שִׁמְךָ נִקְרָא — *Because Your Name is proclaimed.* Each nation has an angel that is appointed to oversee its fortunes, but God Himself maintains personal dominion over Israel and Jerusalem (*Tikkunei Zohar*).

סליחה ב

All:

אֱלֹהֵינוּ וֵאלֹהֵי אֲבוֹתֵינוּ:

אֵין מִי יִקְרָא בְצֶדֶק,*   אִישׁ טוֹב נִמְשָׁל כְּחֵדֶק,*[2]

בַּקֵּשׁ רַחֲמִים בְּעַד שְׂחוּקֵי הָדָק,   בְּשׁוּם פָּנִים אֵין בֶּדֶק.

גֶּבֶר תָּמִים וְנָבָר אָפֵס,   גָּמַר חָסִיד[3] וְצַדִּיק נִרְפַּס,[4]

דּוֹר עָנִי בַּעֲוֹנוֹ נִתְפַּס,   דְּרָכָיו לְהַגִּיד* מִי יְחָפֵשׂ.

הוֹסַפְנוּ בַחֲטָאֵינוּ חֵמָה לְהַבְעִיר,   הַמִּתְנַדְּבִים כִּבְנֵי בֵית* לְהַפְעִיר,

וּמַה יַּעֲצוֹר כֹּחַ[5] רַב וְצָעִיר,   וִדּוּי וּפֶלֶל לְקַדִּישׁ עָיִיר.[6]

זָחַלְתִּי וְאִירָא בְּעַד מֵחָן,   זַעַק לַחֲווֹת[7] לְחוֹקֵר וּבוֹחֵן,[8]

חָסַר חֶסֶד וְיִתּוּר צָחַן,   חֵן אֵיךְ אֶמְצָא בְּתָחַן.

טוֹב לְקוֹרְאֶיךָ בְּנֶפֶשׁ רַחֵב,   טָרְחָם נְשֹׂא וּלְכַלְכֵּל יַהֲב,

יִקַּר חַסְדְּךָ עָלַי יִרְהַב,   יַעַן קוֹלִי לְהַאֲזִין בְּאַהֲב.

כְּהָגוּן מִדּוֹת וּבִתְפִלָּה שָׁלֵם,   כְּזָקֵן וְרָגִיל* וְלֹא כְגֹלֶם,

לְהַחֲשֵׁב נֶגְדְּךָ דַּכְּאֵי מִלְּהַכְּלֵם,   לְרַוְחָתִי זָכְרָה רַחֲמֶיךָ מֵהִתְעַלֵּם.[9]

מַרְבִּים צְרָכֵינוּ וְאֵין לְהַאֲמֵר,   מִקֻּצֶר דֵּעָה[10] וּמֵרֹב מֶמֶר,

נֶגְדְּךָ הַכֹּל יוֹצֵר חֹמֶר,   נוֹהֵג וְרוֹעֶה צֹאל וְשׁוֹמֵר.[11]

שֵׂרַדְנוּ כְּתָרֵן הַר בְּדוֹדֵנוּ,   סְחִי וּמָאוֹס הוּשַׂם כְּבוֹדֵנוּ,

עֲנֵנוּ וּתְנֵנוּ מִחְיָה בְּשַׁעְבּוּדֵנוּ,   עוֹד לְמִנְיָנְךָ בַּקֵּשׁ אֲבוּדֵינוּ,

פְּקֻדַּת נִגְעֵי תוֹכְחוֹתֶיךָ שְׁבוּטִים,   פְּזוּרִים פְּרוּדִים וּבַגּוֹיִם עֲבוּטִים,

---

§ אֵין מִי יִקְרָא בְצֶדֶק — *There is no one who calls [to You] in righteousness.* This *selichah* follows a double alphabetical scheme. The acrostic of the final quatrain forms the name of the *paytan*, שְׁלֹמֹה, *Shlomo*. Most *selichos* bearing the signature *Shlomo* are ascribed to R' Shlomo bar Yehudah, who was known as R' Shlomo HaBavli. He flourished more than one thousand years ago and passed away about 990. (According to some, he lived a century earlier than that; see commentary to *selichah* 61, s.v., זֶה פַּעֲמַיִם קָצִיר.) R' Shlomo was a contemporary of R' Sherira Gaon and his son R' Hai Gaon. One of Rashi's mentors, R' Yitzchak ben Yehudah, ranks R' Shlomo [together with R' Elazar HaKalir] among the קְדוֹשֵׁי עֶלְיוֹן, *exalted, holy ones*. His *piyutim* are cited by various *Rishonim*.

אִישׁ טוֹב נִמְשָׁל כְּחֵדֶק — *The good man [today] is compared to a thornbush.* The Talmud relates that a non-believer once called the Talmudic sage R' Yehoshua bar Chananiah, 'חֲדָקָאָה, *Thorny one!* For about people like you the prophet (Micah 7:4) states: טוֹבָם כְּחֵדֶק, *The good one among them*

is like a thornbush.'

'Fool,' replied the sage, 'continue the verse: יָשָׁר מִמְּסוּכָה, *the upright is better than a shelter.* Clearly the verse is complimentary, not derogatory! It means that just as thorns guard the breach in a fence, so too, the best of us protects the others' (*Eruvin* 101a).

The *paytan* here, according to most commentaries, follows the derogatory connotation of the phrase, i.e., even the best of men today is merely a vexing thorn. And this interpretation has been used in the translation. An alternative opinion understands the phrase in its Scriptural context. Thus: *There are no longer any of those good people who are compared to protective thorns who can call to You with righteousness.* Both views are cited in the medieval commentary *Arugas HaBosem*.

דְּרָכָיו לְהַגִּיד — *To teach* [lit., *to tell*] *His ways*, i.e., who is capable of teaching God's ways to the iniquitous generation? Or, דְּרָכָיו may be rendered *its ways*, i.e., who can teach this generation the proper way for it to follow? Some

---

SELICHAH 2

All:

Our God and the God of our forefathers:

א *There is no one who calls [to You] in righteousness;*[*1]

א *the good man [today] is compared to a thornbush.*[*2]

ב *To ask mercy for those pounded to dust,*

ב *no one at all can be found.*

ג *Sincere, pure-hearted men have disappeared;*

ג *the pious have come to an end,[3] the righteous are trampled upon.[4]*

ד *A poor generation is caught in its iniquity:*

ד *Who now can be found to teach His ways?*

ה *With our sins we have continued to inflame [God's] rage,*

ה *[while the righteous,] as close [to Him] as family,*
   offered themselves to intercede in prayer.*

ו *How then can strength be mustered[5] by old or young*

ו *to confess and pray to the Holy One, the Ever-Awake?[6]*

ז *I shudder, afraid, on behalf of the Camp [of Israel]*

ז *to voice my cry[7] to the Prober and Searcher of Hearts.[8]*

ח *Lacking deeds of kindness, and reeking greatly [of sin] —*

ח *how then will I find favor with supplication?*

ט *[You Who are] Good to those who call to You with all the soul's strength,*

ט *bearing their trouble and giving them sustenance,*

י *let Your precious kindness flow plentifully upon me,*

י *in order to hearken to my voice with love!*

כ *Like one of good character, skilled in prayer,*

כ *like an experienced elder* and not like a boor —*

ל *so let my broken heart be considered worthy before You, and not be shamed.*

ל *Remember Your mercy and [bring] my relief,*
   not disregarding [my prayer].[9]

מ *Our needs are [so] many, they cannot be expressed,*

מ *because of [our] paucity of knowledge[10] and [our] abundance of bitterness.*

נ *It is all before Your eyes, Molder of Clay,*

נ *[our] Leader and Shepherd, Protector and Guard.[11]*

ס *We are left like a mountain-top beacon in our loneliness,*

ס *our glory made into phlegm and revulsion;*

ע *answer us, give us sustenance in our slavery,*

ע *seek out our lost ones to make up Your [nation's] sum.*

פ *At the behest of those stricken by the blows of Your rebuke,*

פ *scattered, divided, delivered over to the nations,*

---

(1) Cf. *Isaiah* 59:2. (2) Cf. *Micah* 7:4. (3) Cf. *II Samuel* 22:26-27; *Psalms* 18:26-27.
(4) Cf. *Psalms* 12:2. (5) Cf. *II Chronicles* 2:5. (6) Cf. *Daniel* 4:10. (7) Cf. *Job* 32:6.
(8) Some editions read לַחוֹקֵר בְּבוֹחֵן, *to Him Who probes with an examination.*
(9) Cf. *Psalms* 25:6; *Lamentations* 3:56. (10) See tractate *Berachos* 29b. (11) Cf. *Psalms* 80:2; 121:5.

early editions read דְּבָרָיו לְהַגִּיד, which means *to relate its* [i.e., the generation's] *matters* [before God], in other words, to plead its case.

הַמִּתְנַדְּבִים כִּבְנֵי בַיִת — *[While the righteous,] as close [to Him] as family, offered themselves.*

Alternatively, *[even against the righteous] who are as close [to Him] as family and who offered themselves...*

כְּהָגוּן . . . כְּזָקֵן וְרָגִיל — *Like one of good character . . . like an experienced elder.* These are among the

צָפְנֵם בְּסֵכְּךָ מֵרִיב[1] וּשְׁפָטִים,   צָפִית תִּפְאַרְתֵּךְ לָמוֹ מַבָּטִים.

קוֹל כְּחֵךְ לַהַב חוֹצֵב,[2]   קֶצֶב טוֹב וְחִלּוּפוֹ קוֹצֵב,

רֵעֶיךָ דוֹפְקִים בְּקוֹל עֶצֶב,   רְצוֹת נִדְבָתָם וּבְקִרְבָּם הִתְיַצֵּב.

שׁוֹקְדִים בְּצוֹם לִבָּם לְהַכְנִיעַ,   שָׁאוֹנָם מִזַּעַם בַּחֲדָרֶיךָ[3] תַּצְנִיעַ,

תּוֹבְעִים בְּלַחַשׁ שָׂפָה לְהַנִּיעַ,*   תַּאֲנָתָם אַל נָא תַמְנִיעַ.*

❖ שִׁמְךָ אֱלֹהִים חַיִּים מִתְפָּאֵר,   לַחַיִּים טוֹבִים מִמְּךָ נִשְׁאָר,

מְקוֹר חַיִּים עִמְּךָ[4] מִתְבָּאֵר,   הַבִּיטָה וַעֲנֵנוּ וְעֵינֵינוּ הָאֵר.[5]

All, while standing:

אֵל מֶלֶךְ* יוֹשֵׁב עַל כִּסֵּא רַחֲמִים מִתְנַהֵג בַּחֲסִידוּת,* מוֹחֵל עֲוֹנוֹת עַמּוֹ,* מַעֲבִיר רִאשׁוֹן רִאשׁוֹן,*[6] מַרְבֶּה מְחִילָה* לַחַטָּאִים וּסְלִיחָה לַפּוֹשְׁעִים, עֹשֶׂה צְדָקוֹת* עִם כָּל בָּשָׂר וָרוּחַ, לֹא כְרָעָתָם תִּגְמוֹל. ❖ אֵל הוֹרֵיתָ לָּנוּ לוֹמַר* שְׁלֹשׁ עֶשְׂרֵה, וּזְכוֹר לָנוּ הַיּוֹם בְּרִית שְׁלֹשׁ עֶשְׂרֵה,* כְּמוֹ שֶׁהוֹדַעְתָּ לֶעָנָיו* מִקֶּדֶם, כְּמוֹ שֶׁכָּתוּב, וַיֵּרֶד יהוה* בֶּעָנָן וַיִּתְיַצֵּב עִמּוֹ שָׁם, וַיִּקְרָא בְשֵׁם יהוה.*

Congregation, then chazzan:

וַיַּעֲבֹר יהוה עַל פָּנָיו וַיִּקְרָא:

Congregation and chazzan (the words in bold type are recited aloud and in unison):

יהוה, יהוה, אֵל, **רַחוּם,** וְחַנּוּן, אֶרֶךְ **אַפַּיִם,** וְרַב חֶסֶד, וֶאֱמֶת, **נֹצֵר חֶסֶד לָאֲלָפִים, נֹשֵׂא עָוֹן, וָפֶשַׁע, וְחַטָּאָה, וְנַקֵּה.** וְסָלַחְתָּ לַעֲוֹנֵנוּ וּלְחַטָּאתֵנוּ וּנְחַלְתָּנוּ. סְלַח לָנוּ אָבִינוּ כִּי חָטָאנוּ, מְחַל לָנוּ מַלְכֵּנוּ כִּי פָשָׁעְנוּ. כִּי אַתָּה אֲדֹנָי טוֹב וְסַלָּח, וְרַב חֶסֶד לְכָל קֹרְאֶיךָ.

---

qualifications of a *chazzan* enumerated in the Talmud (*Taanis* 16a).

תּוֹבְעִים בְּלַחַשׁ שָׂפָה לְהַנִּיעַ — *They plead in whispered prayer, that the [Accuser's] speech be set aside.* The translation follows *Matteh Levi* who understands שָׂפָה as *speech* or *language*. Others translate שָׂפָה in its literal meaning *lip* and render the verse, *They plead in whispered prayer, [only] their lip moves* (see 1 Samuel 1:13).

אֵל מֶלֶךְ ‎ — *O God, King...* [The commentary to this paragraph is based on *Sh'lah*.] אֵל connotes God as dominating and all-powerful. Despite this awesome strength, He sits on the *throne of mercy,* always anxious to show compassion.

בַּחֲסִידוּת — *With kindness.* A genuinely kind person tends not to avenge himself against those who wrong him. So, too, God finds ways to avoid meting out punishment to sinners.

מוֹחֵל עֲוֹנוֹת עַמּוֹ — *[He] pardons the sins of His people.* This expresses God's kindness in forgiving even those who antagonize Him with their deeds. However, the Talmud (*Rosh Hashanah*

17a-b) notes, this applies to those who subjugate themselves to Him even though they are too weak to avoid sin. [This may be alluded to by the word עַמּוֹ, *His people*; God pardons those who desire to remain *His,* despite their shortcomings.]

מַעֲבִיר רִאשׁוֹן רִאשׁוֹן — *Removes [sins] one by one.* According to the teachings of Beis Hillel, God, Who is רַב חֶסֶד מַטֶּה כְּלַפֵּי חֶסֶד, *Abundant in Kindness,* tips [the scales of justice] toward kindness. The Academy of R' Yishmael explains that God accomplishes this by removing sin one by one. The commentaries explain this in different ways. According to one view, if a person's good deeds are equivalent to his sins, God makes the side of virtue outweigh the side of sin by removing one sin (according to *Rashi*) or two sins (according to *Rambam, Hilchos Teshuvah* 3:5) from the balance. According to another opinion, if a person has committed a particular sin for the first time, God holds it in abeyance and does not include it in the calculation, as long as it has not yet become habitual (*Rif*).

צ *hide them in Your shelter from [gentile] strife*[1] *and [harsh] judgment —*
צ *for they long to gaze on Your glory [revealed].*
ק *The sound of Your might carves out flames,*[2]
ק *apportioning a good portion or its opposite;*
ר *Your loved ones are knocking, with sad voice —*
ר *be pleased with their offered prayer, and stand in their midst.*
ש *They keep their fast so as to subdue their heart;*
ש *hide their multitude from wrath in Your chambers.*[3]
ת *They plead in whispered prayer, that the [Accuser's] speech be set aside;**
ת *please, do not deny them their desire.*
ש Chazzan — *O You Who take glory in Your Name, 'God of life';*
ל *let us remain with a good life [that comes] from You —*
מ *with You wells up the source of life.*[4]
ה *Look down and answer us; give light to our eyes!*[5]

All, while standing:

אֵל מֶלֶךְ *O God, King* Who sits on the throne of mercy; Who acts with kindness,* pardons the iniquities of His people,* removes [sins] one by one,*[6] increasingly grants pardon* to careless sinners and forgiveness to rebels, Who deals righteously* with every living being — You do not repay them in accord with their evil.* Chazzan — *O God, You taught us to recite* the Thirteen [Attributes of Mercy], so remember for us today the covenant of these Thirteen,* as You made known to the humble one* in ancient times, as it is written: And HASHEM descended* in a cloud and stood with him there, and He called out with the Name HASHEM.**

Congregation, then chazzan:

And HASHEM passed before him [Moses] and proclaimed:

Congregation and chazzan (the words in bold type are recited aloud and in unison):

ה' ה' **HASHEM, HASHEM, God, Compassionate and Gracious, Slow to anger, and Abundant in Kindness and Truth, Preserver of kindness for thousands [of generations], Forgiver of iniquity, willful sin, and error, and Who cleanses.** *May You forgive our iniquities and our errors and make us Your heritage. Forgive us, our Father, for we have erred; pardon us, our King, for we have willfully sinned; for You, my Lord, are good and forgiving and abundantly kind to all who call upon You.*

(1) Cf. *Psalms* 31:21. (2) Cf. 29:4,7. (3) Cf. *Isaiah* 26:20. (4) Cf. *Psalms* 36:10.
(5) Cf. 13:4. (6) Tractate *Rosh Hashanah* 17a.

מַרְבֶּה מְחִילָה — *Increasingly grants pardon.* Not only does God forgive those who sin out of carelessness, He even forgives rebels, who sin out of defiance against Him. Furthermore, He pardons *increasingly,* transforming even sins into virtues, provided the sinner's repentance was motivated by love of God (*Yoma* 86b).

עֹשֶׂה צְדָקוֹת — *Who deals righteously.* Although someone may have sinned grievously, God does not withhold reward for any good he may have done. God does not repay them in accord with their evil, i.e., God does not say that they are so evil that even their *mitzvos* deserve to be ignored.

הוֹרֵיתָ לָּנוּ לוֹמַר — *You taught us to recite.* God

instructed Moses that whenever Israel was in a time of crisis, they should pray for mercy by reciting the Thirteen Attributes (see below).

בְּרִית שְׁלֹשׁ עֶשְׂרֵה — *The covenant of these Thirteen.* God sealed a covenant with Moses and Israel that the recitation of the Thirteen Attributes would never be in vain (*Rosh Hashanah* 17b).

לֶעָנָיו — *To the humble one.* Moses was the humblest of men (*Numbers* 12:3).

וַיֵּרֶד ה' — *And HASHEM descended.* God descended, as if to stand with Moses.

וַיִּקְרָא בְשֵׁם ה' — *And He called out with the Name HASHEM.* There, God called out the Name HASHEM,

פסוקי הקדמה לסליחה ג

אַל תָּבֹא בְמִשְׁפָּט עִמָּנוּ, כִּי לֹא יִצְדַּק לְפָנֶיךָ כָל חָי.‏‎1‎‏ תָּבֹא לְפָנֶיךָ תְּפִלָּתֵנוּ,‏‎2‎‏ וְאַל תִּתְעַלַּם מִתְּחִנָּתֵנוּ.‏‎3‎‏ תָּבוֹא לְפָנֶיךָ אֶנְקַת אָסִיר, כְּגֹדֶל זְרוֹעֲךָ הוֹתֵר בְּנֵי תְמוּתָה.‏‎4‎‏ אֲדֹנָי שְׁמָעָה בְקוֹלֵנוּ, תִּהְיֶינָה אָזְנֶיךָ קַשֻּׁבוֹת, לְקוֹל תַּחֲנוּנֵינוּ.‏‎5‎‏ תְּהִי נָא אָזְנְךָ קַשֶּׁבֶת, וְעֵינֶיךָ פְקֻחוֹת עַל עַמְּךָ יִשְׂרָאֵל.‏‎6‎‏

כְּרַחֵם אָב עַל בָּנִים, כֵּן תְּרַחֵם יהוה עָלֵינוּ. לַיהוה הַיְשׁוּעָה, עַל עַמְּךָ בִרְכָתֶךָ סֶּלָה. יהוה צְבָאוֹת עִמָּנוּ, מִשְׂגָּב לָנוּ אֱלֹהֵי יַעֲקֹב סֶלָה. יהוה צְבָאוֹת, אַשְׁרֵי אָדָם בֹּטֵחַ בָּךְ. יהוה הוֹשִׁיעָה, הַמֶּלֶךְ יַעֲנֵנוּ בְיוֹם קָרְאֵנוּ.

In some congregations the following two verses are recited responsively — the *chazzan* reciting סְלַח, and the congregation responding וַיֹּאמֶר. In other congregations these verses are recited silently.

סְלַח נָא לַעֲוֹן הָעָם הַזֶּה כְּגֹדֶל חַסְדֶּךָ, וְכַאֲשֶׁר נָשָׂאתָה לָעָם הַזֶּה מִמִּצְרַיִם וְעַד הֵנָּה, וְשָׁם נֶאֱמַר:

וַיֹּאמֶר יהוה סָלַחְתִּי כִּדְבָרֶךָ.

All:

הַטֵּה אֱלֹהַי אָזְנְךָ וּשְׁמָע, פְּקַח עֵינֶיךָ וּרְאֵה שֹׁמְמֹתֵינוּ, וְהָעִיר אֲשֶׁר נִקְרָא שִׁמְךָ עָלֶיהָ, כִּי לֹא עַל צִדְקוֹתֵינוּ אֲנַחְנוּ מַפִּילִים תַּחֲנוּנֵינוּ לְפָנֶיךָ, כִּי עַל רַחֲמֶיךָ הָרַבִּים. אֲדֹנָי שְׁמָעָה, אֲדֹנָי סְלָחָה, אֲדֹנָי הַקְשִׁיבָה, וַעֲשֵׂה אַל תְּאַחַר, לְמַעַנְךָ אֱלֹהַי, כִּי שִׁמְךָ נִקְרָא עַל עִירְךָ וְעַל עַמֶּךָ.

סליחה ג

אֱלֹהֵינוּ וֵאלֹהֵי אֲבוֹתֵינוּ:

תָּבֹא לְפָנֶיךָ שַׁוְעַת חָנוּן,*   תְּהִי נָא אָזְנְךָ קַשֶּׁבֶת‏‎6‎‏ תַּחֲנוּן,

שִׁמְעָה יהוה צֶדֶק, הַקְשִׁיבָה רִנּוּן,‏‎7‎‏   שָׁר מֵישָׁרִים וּמַעֲלִים מֵרְנּוּן.

רֹאשׁ לְהָרִים נִכְלַמְנוּ בְּשָׁנוּ,‏‎8‎‏   רֵיחַ נִרְדֵּנוּ כִּי הִבְאַשְׁנוּ,

קִלְקַלְנוּ יְשָׁרִים, וְתוֹרוֹת שִׁבַּשְׁנוּ,*   קַרְקַע פָּנֵינוּ בְּכֵן כָּבַשְׁנוּ,

צַר וּמָצוֹק מִכָּל צַד,   צֹאן נִדָּחָה מֵאֵין מִצָּד,

---

as He taught Moses the Thirteen Attributes that begin with that Name.

‏‎⁊‎‏ **תָּבֹא לְפָנֶיךָ שַׁוְעַת חָנוּן** — *Let the cry for mercy come before You.* This *selichah* contains a double תַּשְׁרַ"ק (i.e., reversed *aleph-beis*) acrostic. The author signed his name — שְׁלֹמֹה הַקָּטֹן, *Shlomo, the lesser and the younger,* וְהַצָּעִיר יְחִי

may he live [see prefatory comment to *selichah* 2], as indicated by the bold type. Others read the signature שְׁלֹמֹה הַלֵּוִי, *Shlomo HaLevi*; the letters of הַלֵּוִי, being the initials of the words הַקָּטֹן. . .וְהַצָּעִיר. . .לָאֵלֶף. . .יַחַד.

‏‎⁊‎‏ **וְתוֹרוֹת שִׁבַּשְׁנוּ** — *And [we have] perverted the Torahs.* The plural form alludes to תוֹרה

PREFATORY VERSES TO SELICHAH 3

אַל תָּבֹא *Do not enter into strict judgment with us, for no living creature would be innocent before You.*[1] *Let our prayer come before You;*[2] *do not ignore our supplication.*[3] *Let the prisoner's groan come before You; as befits the greatness of Your power, spare those condemned to die.*[4] *My Lord, hear our voice; may Your ears be attentive to the sound of our supplications.*[5] *Please, let Your ear be attentive, Your eyes open, to Your people Israel.*[6]

כְּרַחֵם אָב *As a father has mercy on his children, so, HASHEM, may You have mercy on us. Salvation is HASHEM's, upon Your people is Your blessing, Selah. HASHEM, Master of Legions, is with us, a stronghold for us is the God of Jacob, Selah. HASHEM, Master of Legions, praiseworthy is the person who trusts in You. HASHEM, save! May the King answer us on the day we call.*

In some congregations, the following two verses are recited responsively — the *chazzan* reciting *'Forgive, please . . . ,'* and the congregation responding, *'And HASHEM said . . . '* In other congregations these verses are recited silently.

סְלַח נָא *Forgive, please, the iniquity of this people according to the greatness of Your kindness and as You have forgiven this people from Egypt until now, and there it was said:*

And HASHEM said, 'I have forgiven according to your word!'

All:

הַטֵּה *Incline, my God, Your ear, and listen, open Your eyes and see our desolation and that of the city upon which Your Name is proclaimed; for not because of our righteousness do we cast down our supplications before You, rather because of Your abundant compassion. O my Lord, heed; O my Lord, forgive; O my Lord, be attentive and act, do not delay; for Your sake, my God, for Your Name is proclaimed upon Your city and upon Your people.*

SELICHAH 3

Our God and the God of our forefathers:

ת *Let the cry for mercy come before You,**

ת *let Your ear be attentive*[6] *to [our] supplication;*

שׁ *hear [our] righteousness, HASHEM, be attentive to [our] song,*[7]

שׁ *You Who look at uprightness and ignore calumny.*

ר *We are embarrassed, ashamed to lift up our head,*[8]

ר *for we have caused our sweet scent to sour;*

ק *we have spoiled straight [paths] and perverted the Torahs,**

ק *and therefore we avert our faces to the ground.*

צ *Trouble and distress on every side,*

צ *[we are] wandering sheep without a fold.*

---

(1) Cf. *Psalms* 143:2. (2) Cf. *Jonah* 2:8. (3) Cf. *Psalms* 55:2. (4) 79:11.
(5) Cf. 130:2. (6) Cf. *Nehemiah* 1:6. (7) Cf. *Psalms* 17:1. (8) Cf. *Ezra* 9:6.

שֶׁבִּכְתָב, *the Written Torah, i.e., Scriptures, and* תּוֹרָה שֶׁבְּעַל פֶּה, *the Oral Torah, i.e., the traditional* interpretation of the Written Torah as taught by Moses and transmitted orally through the gener-

פָּנָה לִימִין וַיָּגְזֹר מַעֲצָד,   פַּחַד מִשְּׂמֹאל וְצַיָּד הַצָּד.

עֵינֶיךָ רוֹאוֹת תִּהְיֶינָה פְּקוּחוֹת,[1]   עָנִי וְעָנָוּ מִצָּרוֹת הַמְּתוּחוֹת,

סֵפֶד לְרִנָּה וּלְרִצּוּי תּוֹכְחוֹת,   סַבּוֹת וַהֲפֹךְ בִּדְרָכֶיךָ הַנְּכֹחוֹת.

נִתַּנּוּ בַּעֲוֹנֵינוּ לַשֶּׁבִי וּלְבִזָּה,   נַחְנוּ מְלָכֵינוּ כֹּהֲנֵינוּ לְבוּזָה;[2]

מָרוֹם נִכְבָּדוֹת וְאַהֲבָה עַזָּה,   מִגְרַתְּ לָאָרֶץ לְשַׁמָּה וּלְעֵזָה.

לֹא חִלִּינוּ פָנֶיךָ לְהַפִּיל תְּחִנָּה,

לְהַשְׂכִּיל בַּאֲמִתָּךְ מֵעֲלוֹת צַחֲנָה,*

כָּלִינוּ כִּסְדוֹם בִּשְׁפַל קוֹל הַטַּחֲנָה,*   כִּמְעַט רֶגַע לוּלֵי תְחִנָּה.[3]

יֶתֶר הַפְּלֵטָה* לְהַשְׁאִיר חָסְתָּ,   יָתֵד וְגָדֵר תַּתָּה וְכִנַּסְתָּ,

טִלְטַלְתָּנוּ כְּנֶגֶד שָׁלֹשׁ* מֵאַסְתָּ,   טִירַת כֶּסֶף* בִּגְלָלֵנוּ רָמַסְתָּ.

חֶבֶל חָבַלְנוּ מַעַל לִמְעַל,   חַבַּלְנוּ מֵעַל אֶל עַל,

זָכֹר צִוִּיתָ בְּלִי לִגְאָל,[4]   זֵרוּיִם לְקַבֵּץ וּבָם לִבְעַל.

וְאַתָּה אַחֲרֵי כָל הַבָּא,[5]   וַדַּאי וְצַדִּיק, וְלָנוּ הַדִּבָּה,

הַיּוֹם כְּמֵאָז בְּלִי סִבָּה,   הִנְּנוּ לְפָנֶיךָ בְּאַשְׁמָה רַבָּה.

דַּלַּת עַם לְקֶלֶס וְחֵרוּף,   דְּחוּפִים סְחוּפִים נְתוּנִים לְטֵרוּף,

גָּלוֹת וְשִׁעְבּוּד בְּנִסָּיוֹן[6] וְצֵרוּף,   גַּלְגֵּל בְּחֶסֶד לִסְלִיחָה וְתֵרוּף,

בְּרַחֲמֶיךָ עוֹד בִּרְבוֹת עִתִּים,*   בְּךָ נִנְשְׁעָה קַיָּם וְהוֹשַׁעְתִּים,[7]

אֵלֶּה מֵרָחוֹק יָבֹאוּ[8] כְתִּים,   וְאֵלֶּה מִצָּפוֹן וְצִיִּים וְכִתִּים.*[9]

שֶׁלְּךָ הֵם עֲבָדֶיךָ וְעַמֶּךָ,   לַבֵּב כִּימֵי קֶדֶם מַנְעִימֶיךָ,*

---

ations until it was formally recorded in the Mishnah and Talmud.

לְהַשְׂכִּיל בַּאֲמִתָּךְ מֵעֲלוֹת צַחֲנָה — *[Nor did we] seek wisdom in Your truth to banish the stench [of sin].* Had we but considered the truth of Your ways, we would have cleansed ourselves of sin. Alternatively, the stich means: *[Nor did we] seek wisdom in Your truth, because we reeked of sin.*

קוֹל הַטַּחֲנָה — *The sound of the millstone,* i.e., the sound of Torah scholars debating and clarifying their subject matter. The Midrash (*Koheles Rabbah* 12:7) explains that Torah study is compared to a flour mill. Just as a mill runs day and night and never ceases to turn, so are we bidden to study Torah day and night, as it is written: וְהָגִיתָ בּוֹ יוֹמָם וָלַיְלָה, *And you shall ponder it day and night* (Joshua 1:8).

יֶתֶר הַפְּלֵטָה — *A surviving remnant.* God allowed a remnant of the nation to survive the destruction of the First Temple, and established them firmly — a stake and a fence — in the Second.

כְּנֶגֶד שָׁלֹשׁ — *[Because of the one sin] equal to the three.* The Talmud compared the underlying causes of the destruction of the two Temples:

Why was the First *Beis HaMikdash* destroyed? Because of three [evil] things — idolatry, adultery and murder... Why then was the Second *Beis HaMikdash* destroyed? Hadn't the nation involved itself in the study of Torah, the performance of *mitzvos*, and acts of kindness? Because of unwarranted hatred [that was prevalent among the people]. This teaches that unwarranted hatred is equal to the three cardinal sins: idolatry, adultery and murder (*Yoma* 9b).

טִירַת כֶּסֶף — *The longed-for Tower.* This is a play on words, for Scriptures alludes to the *Beis HaMikdash* as טִירַת כֶּסֶף, *a Tower of silver* (Song of Songs 8:9). Indeed, many early editions of *Selichos* read כֶּסֶף instead of בֶּסֶף.

בִּרְבוֹת עִתִּים — *In the fullness of time.* The grammatical tense of this verse is ambiguous, and the word רְבוֹת can mean *much* or *many.* Thus, this phrase can have any of three meanings: *In the fullness of time,* i.e., when much time has elapsed; *[which has been exhibited] so many times;* or, *for such a long time.*

וְצִיִּים וְכִתִּים — *On large ships from Rome.* The translation is based on *Rashi's* interpretation of the phrase וְצִים מִיַּד כִּתִּים (*Numbers* 24:24 and

פ *[If we] turn to the right, the axe strikes;*

פ *to the left is fear and the preying hunter.*

ע *Let Your all-seeing eyes be open*[1]

ע *[to view our] poverty and torment from extended troubles.*

ס *Lamenting to song, rebukes to reconciliation —*

ס *turn them and convert them with Your straightforward ways.*

נ *Due to our iniquities we have been delivered to captivity and pillage;*

נ *we, our kings, and our priests to shame.*[2]

מ *From the height of glory and fervent love,*

מ *we are thrown down to earth to [suffer] desolation and defamation.*

ל *We did not beseech You, laying our supplication before You,*

ל *[nor did we] seek wisdom in Your truth to banish the stench [of sin].**

כ *As the sound of the millstone* ebbed,*
we would have been destroyed like Sodom,

כ *in just one fleeting moment, but for Your gracious favor.*[3]

י *You took pity and left a surviving remnant;**

י *You provided a stake and a fence and gathered them in.*

ט *Then You sent us off [again],*
[because of the one sin] equal to the three* that You loathe,

ט *and because of us You trampled the longed-for Tower.**

ח *We have wrought destruction, and committed trespass;*

ח *now we are wounded, from one yoke [of exile] to another.*

ז *Remember! You promised not to despise [us],*[4]

ז *to gather the dispersed, and to rule over them.*

ו *And You, after all that has happened [to us],*[5]

ו *are true and righteous; the fault is ours.*

ה *Today, as of old, without change [of heart],*

ה *we are here before You, full of guilt.*

ד *The poor folk, [exposed] to scorn and reviling,*

ד *pushed, swept away, given over as prey —*

ג *[their] exile and slavery, with trial*[6] *and purification,*

ג *turn now in kindness to pardon and healing.*

ב *In Your mercy yet, in the fullness of time,**

ב *We will be saved by You.*
Fulfill [Your promise], 'I will save them!'[7]

א *Some will come from afar,*[8] *group by group,*

א *some from the north, on large ships from Rome.**[9]

ש *They are Yours: Your servants, Your people.*

ל *Hearten Your sweet ones* as in days of old.*

---

(1) Cf. *Nehemiah* 1:6; *Jeremiah* 32:19. (2) Cf. *Ezra* 9:7; some editions of *Selichos* read לְבִזָּה, *for pillage.*
(3) Cf. 9:8. (4) Cf. *Leviticus* 26:44. (5) Cf. *Ezra* 9:13. (6) Some editions read וְנִסָּיוֹן, but the meaning
is the same. (7) *Hosea* 1:7. (8) *Isaiah* 49:12. (9) Cf. *Numbers* 24:24; *Daniel* 11:30.

Sanhedrin 106a). Elsewhere, *Rashi* renders צִיִּים
כִּתִּים as *Roman legions* (*Daniel* 11:30). R' *Saadiah*
Gaon (ibid.) interprets צִיִּים as *Lombardians* [from
Northern Italy], and כִּתִּים as *Romans* [from
Central Italy]. Accordingly, our text would read
(as it does in some editions) וּמִצִיִּים וְכִתִּים, *and*

from Lombardy and from Rome.

לְבָב. . .מְנָעִימָיךְ — *Hearten Your sweet ones.* The
word לְבָב may also be translated *take to heart* or
cherish. And מְנָעִימָיךְ can mean *those who sing
Your sweet praises.*

מִשְׁכֵנוּ אַחֲרֶיךָ שִׂימֵנוּ בִּרְשׁוּמֶיךָ,

הַכֹּל חֲפֵצִים לְיִרְאָה אֶת שְׁמֶךָ.[1]

❖ הַקָּטֹן לָאֶלֶף גָּדֵל רְחוּמֵנוּ,

וְהַצָּעִיר לְגוֹי לְהָעֲצִים[2] בִּתְחוּמֵנוּ,

יָחַד בְּכָל צִדְקוֹתֶיךָ לְרַחֲמֵנוּ.   יֵשֶׁב נָא אַפֶּךָ וּתְנַחֲמֵנוּ.[3]

All, while standing:

אֵל מֶלֶךְ יוֹשֵׁב עַל כִּסֵּא רַחֲמִים מִתְנַהֵג בַּחֲסִידוּת, מוֹחֵל

עֲוֹנוֹת עַמּוֹ, מַעֲבִיר רִאשׁוֹן רִאשׁוֹן, מַרְבֶּה מְחִילָה

לְחַטָּאִים וּסְלִיחָה לְפוֹשְׁעִים, עֹשֶׂה צְדָקוֹת עִם כָּל בָּשָׂר וָרוּחַ,

לֹא כְרָעָתָם תִּגְמוֹל. ❖ אֵל הוֹרֵיתָ לָּנוּ לוֹמַר שְׁלֹשׁ עֶשְׂרֵה, וּזְכוֹר

לָנוּ הַיּוֹם בְּרִית שְׁלֹשׁ עֶשְׂרֵה, כְּמוֹ שֶׁהוֹדַעְתָּ לֶעָנָיו מִקֶּדֶם, כְּמוֹ

שֶׁכָּתוּב, וַיֵּרֶד יהוה בֶּעָנָן וַיִּתְיַצֵּב עִמּוֹ שָׁם, וַיִּקְרָא בְשֵׁם יהוה.

Congregation, then *chazzan:*

וַיַּעֲבֹר יהוה עַל פָּנָיו וַיִּקְרָא:

Congregation and *chazzan* (the words in bold type are recited aloud and in unison):

יהוה, יהוה, אֵל, רַחוּם, וְחַנּוּן, אֶרֶךְ אַפַּיִם, וְרַב חֶסֶד,

וֶאֱמֶת, נֹצֵר חֶסֶד לָאֲלָפִים, נֹשֵׂא עָוֹן, וָפֶשַׁע,

וְחַטָּאָה, וְנַקֵּה. וְסָלַחְתָּ לַעֲוֹנֵנוּ וּלְחַטָּאתֵנוּ וּנְחַלְתָּנוּ. סְלַח לָנוּ

אָבִינוּ כִּי חָטָאנוּ, מְחַל לָנוּ מַלְכֵּנוּ כִּי פָשָׁעְנוּ. כִּי אַתָּה אֲדֹנָי טוֹב

וְסַלָּח, וְרַב חֶסֶד לְכָל קֹרְאֶיךָ.

סליחה ד (פזמון)

Chazzan, then congregation:

בְּמוֹצָאֵי מְנוּחָה, ∗ קִדַּמְנוּךָ תְּחִלָּה,

הַט אָזְנְךָ מִמָּרוֹם, יוֹשֵׁב תְּהִלָּה,[4]

לִשְׁמֹעַ אֶל הָרִנָּה וְאֶל הַתְּפִלָּה.[5]

Congregation, then *chazzan:*

אֶת יְמִין עֹז עוֹרְרָה, לַעֲשׂוֹת חָיִל,[6]

בְּצֶדֶק נֶעֱקַד, וְנִשְׁחַט תְּמוּרוֹ אָיִל,

גְּנוֹן נָא גִזְעוֹ, בְּזַעֲקָם[7] בְּעוֹד לָיִל,

לִשְׁמֹעַ אֶל הָרִנָּה וְאֶל הַתְּפִלָּה.

בְּמוֹצָאֵי מְנוּחָה ﴾§ — *As [the day of] rest departs.*
This *selichah* is called *pizmon,* which indicates
that it has a refrain. It begins by stating the time
of its recital, on the departure of the Sabbath.
Anonymously written, it follows an *aleph-beis*

acrostic (after the first stanza). It is usually recited
in responsive fashion: the *chazzan* recites the first
stanza which is then repeated by the congregation; each succeeding stanza is recited first by the
congregation, then repeated by the *chazzan.* This

מ Draw us after You, place us among Your inscribed ones,
ה all who desire to revere Your Name.[1]

Chazzan — Make the smallest [people] increase a thousandfold,
   O our Beloved One!

And [let] the younger [son of Isaac] grow into a strong nation[2]
   within our border,

[when we are] united, may You, in all Your righteousness,
   have compassion upon us.

Please turn back Your anger, and console us.[3]

All, while standing:

אֵל מֶלֶךְ O God, King Who sits on the throne of mercy; Who acts with
kindness, pardons the iniquities of His people, removes [sins]
one by one, increasingly grants pardon to careless sinners and forgiveness
to rebels, Who deals righteously with every living being — You do not
repay them in accord with their evil. Chazzan — O God, You taught us to
recite the Thirteen [Attributes of Mercy], so remember for us today the
covenant of these Thirteen, as You made known to the humble one in
ancient times, as it is written: And HASHEM descended in a cloud and
stood with him there, and He called out with the Name HASHEM.

Congregation, then chazzan:

And HASHEM passed before him [Moses] and proclaimed:

Congregation and chazzan (the words in bold type are recited aloud and in unison):

ה' ה' HASHEM, HASHEM, God, Compassionate and Gracious, Slow to
anger, and Abundant in Kindness and Truth, Preserver of
kindness for thousands [of generations], Forgiver of iniquity, willful
sin, and error, and Who cleanses.** May You forgive our iniquities and our
errors and make us Your heritage. Forgive us, our Father, for we have
erred; pardon us, our King, for we have willfully sinned; for You, my Lord,
are good and forgiving and abundantly kind to all who call upon You.

SELICHAH 4

Chazzan, then congregation:

בְּמוֹצָאֵי As [the day of] rest departs,* we come before You first of all;
   bend Your ear from on high,
[O You] Who sits to [hear Israel] praise [Him],[4]
            O [that You] listen to [our] song and to [our] prayer.[5]

Congregation, then chazzan:

א Arouse Your mighty right hand to wage war[6]
   [against the accusing angels],
ב by the merit of [Isaac] who was bound,
   but a ram was slaughtered in his place;
ג please protect his seed when they cry[7] [to You] in the night —
            O [that You] listen to [their] song and to [their] prayer.

---

(1) Cf. *Nehemiah* 1:11. (2) Cf. *Isaiah* 60:22. (3) Cf. 12:1; *Daniel* 9:16; in keeping with the Scriptural verse,
some editions of *Selichos* read בְּכָל, *in accordance with all,* instead of בְּכָל, *in all.* (4) Cf. *Psalms* 22:4.
(5) *I Kings* 8:28. (6) Cf. *Psalms* 118:15. (7) Some editions of *Selichos* read בְּזַעֲקָם, *with their cry.*

Congregation, then *chazzan*:

דְּרוֹשׁ נָא דוֹרְשֶׁיךָ, בְּדׇרְשָׁם פָּנֶיךָ,

הִדָּרֵשׁ לָמוֹ מִשְּׁמֵי מְעוֹנֶךָ,

וּלְשַׁוְעַת חֲנוּנָם אַל תַּעְלֵם אׇזְנֶךָ,[1]

לִשְׁמֹעַ אֶל הָרִנָּה וְאֶל הַתְּפִלָּה.

Congregation, then *chazzan*:

זוֹחֲלִים וְרוֹעֲדִים מִיּוֹם בּוֹאֶךָ,

חָלִים כְּמַבְכִּירָה מֵעֶבְרַת מַשָּׁאֶךָ,

טְנוּפָם מְחֵה נָא וְיוֹדוּ פְלָאֶיךָ,[2]   לִשְׁמֹעַ אֶל הָרִנָּה וְאֶל הַתְּפִלָּה.

Congregation, then *chazzan*:

יוֹצֵר אַתָּה לְכָל יְצִיר נוֹצָר,

כּוֹנַנְתָּ מֵאָז טֶרֶף* לְחַלְּצָם מִמֵּצָר,[3]

לְחוֹנְנָם חִנָּם מֵאוֹצָר הַמְּנְצָר,*   לִשְׁמֹעַ אֶל הָרִנָּה וְאֶל הַתְּפִלָּה.

Congregation, then *chazzan*:

מָרוֹם, אִם עָצְמוּ פִּשְׁעֵי קְהָלֶךָ,

נָא שַׂגְּבֵם מֵאוֹצָר הַמּוּכָן בִּזְבוּלֶךָ,

עָדֶיךָ לָחֹן חִנָּם, בָּאִים אֵלֶיךָ,[4]   לִשְׁמֹעַ אֶל הָרִנָּה וְאֶל הַתְּפִלָּה.

Congregation, then *chazzan*:

פְּנֵה נָא אֶל הַתְּלָאוֹת וְאַל לַחֲטָאוֹת,

צַדֵּק צוֹעֲקֶיךָ מַפְלִיא פְלָאוֹת,

קְשׁוֹב נָא חֲנוּנָם, אֱלֹהִים יהוה צְבָאוֹת,

לִשְׁמֹעַ אֶל הָרִנָּה וְאֶל הַתְּפִלָּה.

Congregation, then *chazzan*:

רְצֵה עֲתִירָתָם בְּעׇמְדָם בַּלֵּילוֹת,

שְׁעֵה נָא בְרָצוֹן כְּקׇרְבַּן כָּלִיל וְעוֹלוֹת,*

תְּרָאֵם נְסֶיךָ עוֹשֵׂה גְדוֹלוֹת,   לִשְׁמֹעַ אֶל הָרִנָּה וְאֶל הַתְּפִלָּה.

---

mode is followed with most of the *selichos* recited
responsively (one or two per day of *selichos*).

כּוֹנַנְתָּ מֵאָז טֶרֶף — *You prepared a cure long ago.*
The Talmud states that seven things were created
before the world itself: Torah, the concept of
teshuvah (repentance), *Gan Eden*, *Gehinnom*, the
Throne of Glory, the *Beis HaMikdash*, and the
name of the Messiah (*Nedarim* 39b). Here the
paytan refers to *teshuvah*, the remedy prepared
long ago to cure the ills of sin.

מֵאוֹצָר הַמְּנְצָר — *From the guarded treasury.*
When God permitted Moses a glimpse of His

glory (see *Exodus* 33:17-23), He displayed before
Moses all of the celestial storehouses in which are
kept the rewards to be meted out to the righteous.
At each, Moses asked its purpose. At one God
said, 'This treasure is for the Torah scholars;' at
another, 'This is for those who honor Torah
scholars;' and at a third, 'Here waits the reward
for those who raise orphans as their own children.' Finally, they reached the largest treasure
house of all. God told Moses, 'Those who perform
mitzvos receive their just compensation from the
appropriate storehouse. But for those who have
not earned their own merits, I provide, by My

Congregation, then chazzan:

ד **Seek, please, those who seek You as they seek Your face;**

ה **come in answer to them from Your Heavenly abode,**

ו **do not turn Your ear away from their supplication's cry[1] —**
            O *[that You] listen to [their] song and to [their] prayer.*

Congregation, then chazzan:

ז **As they shudder and tremble before the day of Your coming,**

ח **shaking before Your burden of wrath, like a woman at her first birth,**

ט **please wipe away their filth [of sin],**
   and they will praise Your wonders[2] —
            O *[that You] listen to [their] song and to [their] prayer.*

Congregation, then chazzan:

י **You are the Creator of every created creature;**

כ **You prepared a cure long ago* to release them from trouble,[3]**

ל **by granting them a free gift from the guarded treasury* —**
            O *[that You] listen to [their] song and to [their] prayer.*

Congregation, then chazzan:

מ **O Most High, if Your congregation's wanton sins have grown great,**

סנ **please, support them from the prepared treasure of Your heavens.**

ע **To You they come to[4] [seek] this free gift —**
            O *[that You] listen to [their] song and to [their] prayer.*

Congregation, then chazzan:

פ **Please turn towards [their] suffering, and not to [their] sins;**

צ **find righteous those who cry to You, O Doer of wonders!**

ק **Please be attentive to their supplication,**
   God, HASHEM, Master of Legions —
            O *[that You] listen to [their] song and to [their] prayer.*

Congregation, then chazzan:

ר **Be pleased with their entreaty as they stand in the night,**

ש **please attend [to it] with favor as [if it were]**
   a completely consumed olah-offering.*

ת **Show them Your miracles, O Doer of great deeds —**
            O *[that You] listen to [their] song and to [their] prayer.*

---

(1) Cf. *Lamentations* 3:56. (2) Cf. *Psalms* 89:6. (3) Some editions read מִמְּעֵצָר, *from the [punishing] constraints [imposed by their sins]*. (4) Cf. *Psalms* 65:3.

---

grace, from this treasury' (*Tanchuma, Ki Sisa* 27; *Shemos Rabbah* 45:6).

כְּקָרְבַּן כָּלִיל וְעוֹלוֹת — *As [if it were] a completely consumed olah-offering* [lit., *as a completely consumed offering and olah-offerings*]. Unlike other personal offerings, the flesh of which is eaten by the owner and/or the *Kohanim,* the *olah*-offering, often referred to as the burnt-offering, is totally consumed by the Altar fire; no part of its flesh is eaten by either the *Kohanim* or the owner. This is usually referred to as כֻּלוֹ כָּלִיל, *entirely consumed.* Thus, the stich 'repeats the same idea

in different words' (*Radak* to *Psalms* 51:21). Alternatively, the word כָּלִיל refers to another Altar-offering completely consumed by the fire, the flour-offering of a *Kohen.* Although a portion of the *minchah,* or flour-offering, of a non-*Kohen* was eaten by the *Kohanim,* the *minchah* of a *Kohen* was completely burnt (ibid.). Additionally, כָּלִיל can mean *completion.* It would then allude to the *tamid,* or continual-offering, which was the final Altar offering each day, and thus 'completed' the day's service. In fact, the reading in some editions is תָּמִיד וְעוֹלוֹת, *the tamid-offering and olah-offerings.*

All, while standing:

אֵל מֶלֶךְ יוֹשֵׁב עַל כִּסֵּא רַחֲמִים מִתְנַהֵג בַּחֲסִידוּת, מוֹחֵל
עֲוֹנוֹת עַמּוֹ, מַעֲבִיר רִאשׁוֹן רִאשׁוֹן, מַרְבֶּה מְחִילָה
לַחַטָּאִים וּסְלִיחָה לַפּוֹשְׁעִים, עֹשֶׂה צְדָקוֹת עִם כָּל בָּשָׂר וָרוּחַ,
לֹא כְרָעָתָם תִּגְמוֹל. אֵל הוֹרֵיתָ לָּנוּ לוֹמַר שְׁלֹשׁ עֶשְׂרֵה, וּזְכוֹר
לָנוּ הַיּוֹם בְּרִית שְׁלֹשׁ עֶשְׂרֵה, כְּמוֹ שֶׁהוֹדַעְתָּ לֶעָנָיו מִקֶּדֶם, כְּמוֹ
שֶׁכָּתוּב, וַיֵּרֶד יהוה בֶּעָנָן וַיִּתְיַצֵּב עִמּוֹ שָׁם, וַיִּקְרָא בְשֵׁם יהוה.

Congregation, then *chazzan*:

וַיַּעֲבֹר יהוה עַל פָּנָיו וַיִּקְרָא:

Congregation and *chazzan* (the words in bold type are recited aloud and in unison):

**יהוה, יהוה, אֵל, רַחוּם, וְחַנּוּן, אֶרֶךְ אַפַּיִם, וְרַב חֶסֶד,
וֶאֱמֶת, נֹצֵר חֶסֶד לָאֲלָפִים, נֹשֵׂא עָוֹן, וָפֶשַׁע,
וְחַטָּאָה, וְנַקֵּה.** וְסָלַחְתָּ לַעֲוֹנֵנוּ וּלְחַטָּאתֵנוּ וּנְחַלְתָּנוּ. סְלַח לָנוּ
אָבִינוּ כִּי חָטָאנוּ, מְחַל לָנוּ מַלְכֵּנוּ כִּי פָשָׁעְנוּ. כִּי אַתָּה אֲדֹנָי טוֹב
וְסַלָּח, וְרַב חֶסֶד לְכָל קֹרְאֶיךָ.

All:

אַל תִּזְכָּר לָנוּ עֲוֹנוֹת רִאשׁוֹנִים, מַהֵר יְקַדְּמוּנוּ רַחֲמֶיךָ, כִּי
דַלּוֹנוּ מְאֹד.[1] חַטֹּאת נְעוּרֵינוּ וּפְשָׁעֵינוּ אַל תִּזְכּוֹר,
כְּחַסְדְּךָ זְכָר לָנוּ אַתָּה, לְמַעַן טוּבְךָ יהוה.[2]

זְכוֹר רַחֲמֶיךָ* יהוה וַחֲסָדֶיךָ, כִּי מֵעוֹלָם הֵמָּה.[3] זָכְרֵנוּ יהוה
בִּרְצוֹן עַמֶּךָ, פָּקְדֵנוּ בִּישׁוּעָתֶךָ.[4] זְכֹר עֲדָתְךָ
קָנִיתָ קֶּדֶם, גָּאַלְתָּ שֵׁבֶט נַחֲלָתֶךָ, הַר צִיּוֹן זֶה שָׁכַנְתָּ בּוֹ.[5] זְכֹר יהוה
חִבַּת יְרוּשָׁלָיִם, אַהֲבַת צִיּוֹן אַל תִּשְׁכַּח לָנֶצַח.[6] אַתָּה תָקוּם
תְּרַחֵם צִיּוֹן, כִּי עֵת לְחֶנְנָהּ כִּי בָא מוֹעֵד.[7] זְכֹר יהוה לִבְנֵי אֱדוֹם
אֵת יוֹם יְרוּשָׁלָיִם,* הָאֹמְרִים עָרוּ עָרוּ עַד הַיְסוֹד בָּהּ.[8] זְכֹר
לְאַבְרָהָם לְיִצְחָק וּלְיִשְׂרָאֵל עֲבָדֶיךָ אֲשֶׁר נִשְׁבַּעְתָּ לָהֶם בָּךְ,
וַתְּדַבֵּר אֲלֵהֶם, אַרְבֶּה אֶת זַרְעֲכֶם כְּכוֹכְבֵי הַשָּׁמָיִם, וְכָל הָאָרֶץ
הַזֹּאת אֲשֶׁר אָמַרְתִּי אֶתֵּן לְזַרְעֲכֶם, וְנָחֲלוּ לְעוֹלָם.[9] ❖ זְכֹר
לַעֲבָדֶיךָ לְאַבְרָהָם לְיִצְחָק וּלְיַעֲקֹב, אַל תֵּפֶן אֶל קְשִׁי הָעָם הַזֶּה
וְאֶל רִשְׁעוֹ וְאֶל חַטָּאתוֹ.[10]

ه‍ **זְכוֹר רַחֲמֶיךָ** — *Remember Your mercies.*
This collection of verses, in a slightly different
order and with some omissions, begins the

conclusion of all *Selichos* services. It has three
themes: (a) a plea that God remember His ancient
promises to the Patriarchs and His covenant to

All, while standing:

אֵל מֶלֶךְ O God, King Who sits on the throne of mercy; Who acts with kindness, pardons the iniquities of His people, removes [sins] one by one, increasingly grants pardon to careless sinners and forgiveness to rebels, Who deals righteously with every living being — You do not repay them in accord with their evil. Chazzan — O God, You taught us to recite the Thirteen [Attributes of Mercy], so remember for us today the covenant of these Thirteen, as You made known to the humble one in ancient times, as it is written: And HASHEM descended in a cloud and stood with him there, and He called out with the Name HASHEM.

Congregation, then *chazzan:*

And HASHEM passed before him [Moses] and proclaimed:

Congregation and *chazzan* (the words in bold type are recited aloud and in unison):

ה' ה' HASHEM, HASHEM, God, Compassionate and Gracious, Slow to anger, and Abundant in Kindness and Truth, Preserver of kindness for thousands [of generations], Forgiver of iniquity, willful sin, and error, and Who cleanses. May You forgive our iniquities and our errors and make us Your heritage. Forgive us, our Father, for we have erred; pardon us, our King, for we have willfully sinned; for You, my Lord, are good and forgiving and abundantly kind to all who call upon You.

All:

אַל תִּזְכָּר Do not recall against us the iniquities of the ancients; speedily — let Your mercy come to meet us for we have fallen very low.[1] Remember not the sins of our youth and our rebellions; may You remember for us [the deeds] worthy of Your kindness, because of Your goodness, HASHEM.[2]

זְכֹר רַחֲמֶיךָ Remember Your mercies,* O HASHEM, and Your kindnesses, for they are from the beginning of the world.[3] Remember us, HASHEM, when You show Your people favor and recall us with Your salvation.[4] Remember Your congregation that You acquired of old, that You redeemed the tribe of Your heritage, and this Mount Zion where You dwelled.[5] Remember, O HASHEM, the affection of Jerusalem, may You never forget the love of Zion.[6] You will arise and show Zion mercy, for it is the time to be gracious to her, for the appointed time will have come.[7] Remember, HASHEM, for the offspring of Edom, the day of Jerusalem* — for those who said: 'Destroy! Destroy to its very foundation!'[8] Remember Abraham, Isaac, and Israel, Your servants, to whom You swore by Your Being, saying to them, 'I shall increase your offspring like the stars of the heavens; and this entire land of which I spoke I will give to your offspring and they will inherit it forever.'[9] Remember for Your servants, for Abraham, for Isaac, and for Jacob; ignore the stubbornness of this people, its wickedness and its sinfulness.[10]

---

(1) *Psalms* 79:8. (2) Cf. 25:7. (3) 25:6. (4) Cf. 106:4. (5) 74:2. (6) This is not a Scriptural verse. (7) *Psalms* 102:14. (8) 137:7. (9) *Exodus* 32:13. (10) *Deuteronomy* 9:27.

---

have mercy on their offspring; (b) a plea that He end our exile and return us to a rebuilt Temple; and (c) a plea for forgiveness.

יוֹם יְרוּשָׁלָיִם — *The day of Jerusalem.* Remember when Rome, the offspring of Edom, destroyed Jerusalem.

Chazzan, then congregation:

אֵל נָא תָשֵׁת עָלֵינוּ חַטָּאת, אֲשֶׁר נוֹאַלְנוּ וַאֲשֶׁר חָטָאנוּ.*[1]

Chazzan, then congregation:

חָטָאנוּ צוּרֵנוּ, סְלַח לָנוּ יוֹצְרֵנוּ.*

All:

זְכוֹר לָנוּ* בְּרִית אָבוֹת, כַּאֲשֶׁר אָמָרְתָּ: וְזָכַרְתִּי אֶת בְּרִיתִי יַעֲקוֹב, וְאַף אֶת בְּרִיתִי יִצְחָק, וְאַף אֶת בְּרִיתִי אַבְרָהָם אֶזְכֹּר, וְהָאָרֶץ אֶזְכֹּר.[2] זְכוֹר לָנוּ בְּרִית רִאשׁוֹנִים, כַּאֲשֶׁר אָמָרְתָּ: וְזָכַרְתִּי לָהֶם בְּרִית רִאשׁוֹנִים, אֲשֶׁר הוֹצֵאתִי אֹתָם מֵאֶרֶץ מִצְרַיִם לְעֵינֵי הַגּוֹיִם, לִהְיוֹת לָהֶם לֵאלֹהִים, אֲנִי יהוה.[3] עֲשֵׂה עִמָּנוּ כְּמָה שֶׁהִבְטַחְתָּנוּ: וְאַף גַּם זֹאת* בִּהְיוֹתָם בְּאֶרֶץ אֹיְבֵיהֶם, לֹא מְאַסְתִּים וְלֹא גְעַלְתִּים לְכַלֹּתָם לְהָפֵר בְּרִיתִי אִתָּם, כִּי אֲנִי יהוה אֱלֹהֵיהֶם.[4] הִמָּצֵא לָנוּ בְּבַקָּשָׁתֵנוּ, כְּמָה שֶׁכָּתוּב: וּבִקַּשְׁתֶּם מִשָּׁם אֶת יהוה אֱלֹהֶיךָ וּמָצָאתָ, כִּי תִדְרְשֶׁנּוּ בְּכָל לְבָבְךָ וּבְכָל נַפְשֶׁךָ.[5] מוֹל אֶת לְבָבֵנוּ* לְאַהֲבָה אֶת שְׁמֶךָ, כְּמָה שֶׁכָּתוּב: וּמָל יהוה אֱלֹהֶיךָ אֶת לְבָבְךָ וְאֶת לְבַב זַרְעֶךָ, לְאַהֲבָה אֶת יהוה אֱלֹהֶיךָ בְּכָל לְבָבְךָ וּבְכָל נַפְשְׁךָ, לְמַעַן חַיֶּיךָ.[6] זְרוֹק עָלֵינוּ מַיִם טְהוֹרִים וְטַהֲרֵנוּ, כְּמָה שֶׁכָּתוּב: וְזָרַקְתִּי עֲלֵיכֶם מַיִם טְהוֹרִים וּטְהַרְתֶּם, מִכֹּל טֻמְאוֹתֵיכֶם וּמִכָּל גִּלּוּלֵיכֶם אֲטַהֵר אֶתְכֶם.[7] מְחֵה פְשָׁעֵינוּ כָּעָב וְכֶעָנָן, כְּמָה שֶׁכָּתוּב: מָחִיתִי כָעָב פְּשָׁעֶיךָ וְכֶעָנָן חַטֹּאתֶיךָ, שׁוּבָה אֵלַי כִּי גְאַלְתִּיךָ.[8] מְחֵה פְשָׁעֵינוּ לְמַעֲנֶךָ, כַּאֲשֶׁר אָמָרְתָּ: אָנֹכִי אָנֹכִי הוּא מֹחֶה פְשָׁעֶיךָ לְמַעֲנִי, וְחַטֹּאתֶיךָ לֹא אֶזְכֹּר.[9] הַלְבֵּן חֲטָאֵינוּ כַּשֶּׁלֶג וְכַצֶּמֶר, כְּמָה שֶׁכָּתוּב: לְכוּ נָא וְנִוָּכְחָה, יֹאמַר יהוה, אִם יִהְיוּ חֲטָאֵיכֶם כַּשָּׁנִים, כַּשֶּׁלֶג יַלְבִּינוּ, אִם יַאְדִּימוּ כַתּוֹלָע, כַּצֶּמֶר יִהְיוּ.[10] רַחֵם עָלֵינוּ וְאַל תַּשְׁחִיתֵנוּ, כְּמָה שֶׁכָּתוּב: כִּי אֵל רַחוּם יהוה אֱלֹהֶיךָ, לֹא יַרְפְּךָ וְלֹא יַשְׁחִיתֶךָ וְלֹא יִשְׁכַּח אֶת בְּרִית אֲבוֹתֶיךָ אֲשֶׁר נִשְׁבַּע לָהֶם.[11] קַבֵּץ נִדָּחֵנוּ כְּמָה שֶׁכָּתוּב: אִם יִהְיֶה נִדַּחֲךָ בִּקְצֵה הַשָּׁמָיִם, מִשָּׁם יְקַבֶּצְךָ יהוה אֱלֹהֶיךָ וּמִשָּׁם יִקָּחֶךָ.[12] הָשֵׁב שְׁבוּתֵנוּ וְרַחֲמֵנוּ,

---

וַאֲשֶׁר חָטָאנוּ — *And what we have sinned.* Though we cannot deny that we have committed sins, we beg God not to reckon them against us, for we have been motivated more by foolishness than by a desire to do evil.

צוּרֵנוּ . . . יוֹצְרֵנוּ — *Our Rock . . . our Molder.* A sin against God is especially serious because we are being ungrateful to *our Rock* and Protector. Nevertheless, He knows our human frailties because He is *our Molder* and Creator. Therefore, we dare beg for forgiveness.

זְכוֹר לָנוּ ⊱ — *Remember for us.* The verses of this supplication appear in a different order in some editions of *Selichos.*

Chazzan, then congregation:
Please, do not reckon for us a sin,
what we have done foolishly and what we have sinned.* 1

Chazzan, then congregation:
We have erred, our Rock! Forgive us, our Molder!*

All:

זְכוֹר לָנוּ *Remember for us** *the covenant of the Patriarchs, as You said:*
'*And I will remember My covenant with Jacob, and also My
covenant with Isaac, and also My covenant with Abraham will I
remember; and the Land will I remember.'* 2 *Remember for us the
covenant of the ancestors, as You said:* '*And I will remember for them the
covenant of the ancestors whom I removed from the land of Egypt in the
very sight of the nations, to be a God to them; I am* HASHEM.' 3 *Do with
us as You promised us:* '*And despite all that,** *when they will be in the
land of their enemies, I will not have despised them nor abhorred them
to destroy them, to annul My covenant with them, for I am* HASHEM *their
God.'* 4 *Be accessible to us in our quest, as it is written: From there you will
seek* HASHEM, *your God, and you will find, when you search for Him with
all your heart and with all your soul.* 5 *Expose our hearts** *to love Your
Name, as it is written:* HASHEM, *your God, will expose your heart and the
heart of your offspring, to love* HASHEM, *your God, with all your heart and
with all your soul, that you may live.* 6 *Pour pure water upon us and purify
us, as it is written: I shall pour pure water upon you and purify you, of
all your contaminations and of all your abominations I will purify you.* 7
*Wipe away our willful sins like a cloud and like a mist, as it is written:
I have wiped away your willful sins like a cloud and your errors like a
mist — repent to Me, for I have redeemed you!** 8 *Wipe away our willful
sins for Your sake, as You said: 'I, only I, am the One Who wipes away
your willful sins for My sake, and I shall not recall your errors.'* 9 *Whiten
our errors like snow and like [pure white] wool, as it is written: 'Come now,
let us reason together,' says* HASHEM, '*though your errors will be like
scarlet, they will become white as snow; though they will be red as
crimson, they will become like [white] wool.'* 10 *Have mercy on us and do
not destroy us, as it is written: For a merciful God is* HASHEM, *your God;
He will not surrender you nor destroy you, and He will not forget the
covenant with your forefathers, which He swore to them.* 11 *Gather in our
dispersed ones, as it is written: If your dispersed were to be at the ends
of heaven, from there* HASHEM, *your God, will gather you in and from there
He will take you.* 12 *Bring back our captivity and have mercy on us,*

(1) *Numbers* 12:11. (2) *Leviticus* 26:42. (3) 26:45. (4) 26:44. (5) *Deuteronomy* 4:29. (6) 30:6.
(7) *Ezekiel* 36:25. (8) *Isaiah* 44:22. (9) 43:25. (10) 1:18. (11) *Deuteronomy* 4:31. (12) 30:4.

וְאַף גַּם זֹאת — *And despite all that.* Even though
Israel may have sinned so gravely that God will
destroy the Temple and exile the people, He will
not permit Israel to be destroyed.

מוֹל אֶת לְבָבֵנוּ — *Expose* [lit., *circumcise*] *our
hearts.* A person's accumulation of sins builds a
barrier of habits, self-justification, and material-

ism over his heart, making it very hard for him to
experience love of God and Torah. When we try
to repent, God helps by cutting away this barrier,
thereby exposing the true inner yearnings of our
heart.

כִּי גְאַלְתִּיךְ — *For I have redeemed you.* Because
God has redeemed Israel from past exiles, we

כְּמָה שֶׁכָּתוּב: וְשָׁב יהוה אֱלֹהֶיךָ אֶת שְׁבוּתְךָ וְרִחֲמֶךָ וְשָׁב וְקִבֶּצְךָ
מִכָּל הָעַמִּים אֲשֶׁר הֱפִיצְךָ יהוה אֱלֹהֶיךָ שָׁמָּה.[1] ❖ תְּבִיאֵנוּ אֶל הַר
קָדְשֶׁךָ, וְשַׂמְּחֵנוּ בְּבֵית תְּפִלָּתֶךָ, כְּמָה שֶׁכָּתוּב: וַהֲבִיאוֹתִים אֶל הַר
קָדְשִׁי, וְשִׂמַּחְתִּים בְּבֵית תְּפִלָּתִי, עוֹלֹתֵיהֶם וְזִבְחֵיהֶם לְרָצוֹן עַל
מִזְבְּחִי, כִּי בֵיתִי בֵּית תְּפִלָּה יִקָּרֵא לְכָל הָעַמִּים.[2]

THE ARK IS OPENED.

The first four verses of the following prayer are recited responsively; *chazzan,* then congregation:

שְׁמַע קוֹלֵנוּ∗ יהוה אֱלֹהֵינוּ, חוּס וְרַחֵם עָלֵינוּ,
וְקַבֵּל בְּרַחֲמִים וּבְרָצוֹן אֶת תְּפִלָּתֵנוּ.[3]
הֲשִׁיבֵנוּ יהוה אֵלֶיךָ וְנָשׁוּבָה, חַדֵּשׁ יָמֵינוּ כְּקֶדֶם.[4]
אַל תַּשְׁלִיכֵנוּ מִלְּפָנֶיךָ, וְרוּחַ קָדְשְׁךָ אַל תִּקַּח מִמֶּנּוּ.[5]
אַל תַּשְׁלִיכֵנוּ לְעֵת זִקְנָה, כִּכְלוֹת כֹּחֵנוּ אַל תַּעַזְבֵנוּ.[6]
אַל תַּעַזְבֵנוּ יהוה, אֱלֹהֵינוּ אַל תִּרְחַק מִמֶּנּוּ.[7]
עֲשֵׂה עִמָּנוּ אוֹת לְטוֹבָה, וְיִרְאוּ שׂוֹנְאֵינוּ וְיֵבֹשׁוּ,
כִּי אַתָּה יהוה עֲזַרְתָּנוּ וְנִחַמְתָּנוּ.[8]
אֲמָרֵינוּ הַאֲזִינָה יהוה, בִּינָה הֲגִיגֵנוּ.[9]
יִהְיוּ לְרָצוֹן אִמְרֵי פִינוּ וְהֶגְיוֹן לִבֵּנוּ לְפָנֶיךָ, יהוה צוּרֵנוּ וְגֹאֲלֵנוּ.[10]
כִּי לְךָ יהוה הוֹחָלְנוּ, אַתָּה תַעֲנֶה אֲדֹנָי אֱלֹהֵינוּ.[11]

THE ARK IS CLOSED.

וידוי

During the recitation of the וִדּוּי, *Confession,*
stand with head and body slightly bowed, in submissive contrition.

אֱלֹהֵינוּ וֵאלֹהֵי אֲבוֹתֵינוּ, תָּבֹא לְפָנֶיךָ תְּפִלָּתֵנוּ,[12] וְאַל תִּתְעַלַּם
מִתְּחִנָּתֵנוּ,[13] שֶׁאֵין אָנוּ עַזֵּי פָנִים וּקְשֵׁי עֹרֶף, לוֹמַר
לְפָנֶיךָ יהוה אֱלֹהֵינוּ וֵאלֹהֵי אֲבוֹתֵינוּ, צַדִּיקִים אֲנַחְנוּ וְלֹא חָטָאנוּ,
אֲבָל אֲנַחְנוּ וַאֲבוֹתֵינוּ חָטָאנוּ.[14]

Strike the left side of the chest with the right fist
while reciting each of the sins in the following confession litany.

אָשַׁמְנוּ, בָּגַדְנוּ, גָּזַלְנוּ, דִּבַּרְנוּ דֹפִי. הֶעֱוִינוּ, וְהִרְשַׁעְנוּ,
זַדְנוּ, חָמַסְנוּ, טָפַלְנוּ שֶׁקֶר. יָעַצְנוּ רָע, כִּזַּבְנוּ,
לַצְנוּ, מָרַדְנוּ, נִאַצְנוּ, סָרַרְנוּ, עָוִינוּ, פָּשַׁעְנוּ, צָרַרְנוּ, קִשִּׁינוּ עֹרֶף.
רָשַׁעְנוּ, שִׁחַתְנוּ, תִּעַבְנוּ, תָּעִינוּ, תִּעְתָּעְנוּ.

---

should repent, for we can be sure He will redeem
us again (*Radak*).

שְׁמַע קוֹלֵנוּ ⧏ — *Hear our voice.* With the Ark
opened and the congregation standing, these

verses are recited aloud and passionately. Their
recitation calls forth strong fervor and emotion in
virtually all congregations. The theme expressed
by this collection of verses is that we must rely

*as it is written: HASHEM, your God, will bring back your captivity and have
mercy on you, and He will again gather you in from all the peoples where
HASHEM, your God, has scattered you.*[1] Chazzan — *Bring us to Your holy
mountain and gladden us in Your house of prayer, as it is written: And I will
bring them to My holy mountain, and I will gladden them in My house of
prayer, their elevation-offerings and their feast offering will find favor on
My Altar, for My House will be called a house of prayer, for all peoples.*[2]

THE ARK IS OPENED.

The first four verses of the following prayer are recited responsively; *chazzan,* then congregation:

שְׁמַע קוֹלֵנוּ *Hear our voice,** HASHEM, *our God,*
   pity and be compassionate to us,
and accept — with compassion and favor — our prayer.[3]
Bring us back to You, HASHEM, and we shall return, renew our days as of old.[4]
Do not cast us away from Yourself,
 and do not remove Your holy spirit from us.[5]
Do not cast us away in old age,
 when our strength gives out do not forsake us.[6]
Do not forsake us, HASHEM, our God, be not distant from us.[7]
Display for us a sign for good, so that our enemies may see it
 and be ashamed, for You, HASHEM, will have helped and consoled us.[8]
To our sayings give ear, HASHEM, perceive our thoughts.[9]
May the expressions of our mouth and the thoughts of our heart
 find favor before You, HASHEM, our Rock and our Redeemer.[10]
Because for You, HASHEM, we waited, You will answer, my Lord, our God.[11]

THE ARK IS CLOSED.

VIDUY/CONFESSION

During the recitation of the וִדּוּי, *Confession,* stand with head and body slightly bowed,
in submissive contrition.

אֱלֹהֵינוּ *Our God and the God of our forefathers, may our prayer come
before You.*[12] *Do not ignore our supplication,*[13] *for we are not so
brazen and obstinate as to say before You,* HASHEM, *our God and the God
of our forefathers, that we are righteous and have not sinned, for in truth,
we and our forefathers have sinned.*[14]

Strike the left side of the chest with the right fist while reciting
each of the sins in the following confession litany.

אָשַׁמְנוּ *We have become guilty;* [ב] *we have betrayed;* [ג] *we have
robbed;* [ד] *we have spoken slander;* [ה] *we have caused perversion;* [ו] *we have caused wickedness;* [ז] *we have sinned willfully;* [ח] *we
have extorted;* [ט] *we have accused falsely;* [י] *we have given evil counsel;*
[כ] *we have been deceitful;* [ל] *we have scorned;* [מ] *we have rebelled;* [נ] *we
have provoked;* [ס] *we have turned away;* [ע] *we have been perverse;*
[פ] *we have acted wantonly;* [צ] *we have persecuted;* [ק] *we have been
obstinate;* [ר] *we have been wicked;* [ש] *we have corrupted;* [ת] *we have
been abominable; we have strayed; You have let us go astray.*

---

(1) *Deuteronomy* 30:3. (2) *Isaiah* 56:7. (3) Weekday *Shemoneh Esrei.* (4) *Lamentations* 5:21.
(5) Cf. *Psalms* 51:13. (6) Cf. 71:9. (7) Cf. 38:22. (8) Cf. 86:17. (9) Cf. 5:2.
(10) Cf. 19:15. (11) Cf. 38:16. (12) Cf. 88:3. (13) Cf. 55:2. (14) Cf. 106:6.

סַרְנוּ מִמִּצְוֹתֶיךָ וּמִמִּשְׁפָּטֶיךָ הַטּוֹבִים וְלֹא שָׁוָה לָּנוּ.[1] וְאַתָּה צַדִּיק עַל כָּל הַבָּא עָלֵינוּ, כִּי אֱמֶת עָשִׂיתָ וַאֲנַחְנוּ הִרְשָׁעְנוּ.[2]

אָשַׁמְנוּ מִכָּל עָם, בֹּשְׁנוּ מִכָּל דּוֹר, גָּלָה מִמֶּנּוּ מָשׂוֹשׂ, דָּוָה לִבֵּנוּ בַּחֲטָאֵינוּ, הֻחַבַּל אִוּוּיֵנוּ, וְנִפְרַע פְּאֵרֵנוּ, זְבוּל בֵּית מִקְדָּשֵׁנוּ חָרַב בַּעֲוֹנֵינוּ, טִירָתֵנוּ הָיְתָה לְשַׁמָּה, יֳפִי אַדְמָתֵנוּ לְזָרִים, כֹּחֵנוּ לְנָכְרִים.

וַעֲדַיִן לֹא שַׁבְנוּ מִטָּעוּתֵנוּ וְהֵיךְ נָעִיז פָּנֵינוּ וְנַקְשֶׁה עָרְפֵּנוּ, לוֹמַר לְפָנֶיךָ יהוה אֱלֹהֵינוּ וֵאלֹהֵי אֲבוֹתֵינוּ, צַדִּיקִים אֲנַחְנוּ וְלֹא חָטָאנוּ, אֲבָל אֲנַחְנוּ וַאֲבוֹתֵינוּ חָטָאנוּ.

Strike the left side of the chest with the right fist while reciting each of the sins in the following confession litany.

אָשַׁמְנוּ, בָּגַדְנוּ, גָּזַלְנוּ, דִּבַּרְנוּ דֹּפִי. הֶעֱוִינוּ, וְהִרְשַׁעְנוּ, זַדְנוּ, חָמַסְנוּ, טָפַלְנוּ שֶׁקֶר. יָעַצְנוּ רָע, כִּזַּבְנוּ, לַצְנוּ, מָרַדְנוּ, נִאַצְנוּ, סָרַרְנוּ, עָוִינוּ, פָּשַׁעְנוּ, צָרַרְנוּ, קִשִּׁינוּ עֹרֶף. רָשַׁעְנוּ, שִׁחַתְנוּ, תִּעַבְנוּ, תָּעִינוּ, תִּעְתָּעְנוּ.

סַרְנוּ מִמִּצְוֹתֶיךָ וּמִמִּשְׁפָּטֶיךָ הַטּוֹבִים וְלֹא שָׁוָה לָּנוּ. וְאַתָּה צַדִּיק עַל כָּל הַבָּא עָלֵינוּ, כִּי אֱמֶת עָשִׂיתָ וַאֲנַחְנוּ הִרְשָׁעְנוּ.

לְעֵינֵנוּ עָשְׁקוּ עֲמָלֵנוּ, מְמֻשָּׁךְ וּמְמוֹרָט מִמֶּנּוּ, נָתְנוּ עֻלָּם עָלֵינוּ, סָבַלְנוּ עַל שִׁכְמֵנוּ, עֲבָדִים מָשְׁלוּ בָנוּ, פֹּרֵק אֵין מִיָּדָם, צָרוֹת רַבּוֹת סְבָבוּנוּ, קְרָאנוּךָ יהוה אֱלֹהֵינוּ, רָחַקְתָּ מִמֶּנּוּ בַּעֲוֹנֵינוּ, שַׁבְנוּ מֵאַחֲרֶיךָ, תָּעִינוּ וְאָבָדְנוּ.

וַעֲדַיִן לֹא שַׁבְנוּ מִטָּעוּתֵנוּ וְהֵיךְ נָעִיז פָּנֵינוּ וְנַקְשֶׁה עָרְפֵּנוּ, לוֹמַר לְפָנֶיךָ יהוה אֱלֹהֵינוּ וֵאלֹהֵי אֲבוֹתֵינוּ, צַדִּיקִים אֲנַחְנוּ וְלֹא חָטָאנוּ, אֲבָל אֲנַחְנוּ וַאֲבוֹתֵינוּ חָטָאנוּ.

Strike the left side of the chest with the right fist while reciting each of the sins in the following confession litany.

אָשַׁמְנוּ, בָּגַדְנוּ, גָּזַלְנוּ, דִּבַּרְנוּ דֹּפִי. הֶעֱוִינוּ, וְהִרְשַׁעְנוּ, זַדְנוּ, חָמַסְנוּ, טָפַלְנוּ שֶׁקֶר. יָעַצְנוּ רָע, כִּזַּבְנוּ, לַצְנוּ, מָרַדְנוּ, נִאַצְנוּ, סָרַרְנוּ, עָוִינוּ, פָּשַׁעְנוּ, צָרַרְנוּ, קִשִּׁינוּ עֹרֶף.

---

(1) Cf. *Job* 33:27. (2) *Nehemiah* 9:33.

upon God to desire our survival and, therefore, to help us come closer to Him through repentance. We acknowledge that we are unworthy, but we also declare that we wish to improve and will do so if God eases the way for us to come back to Him. Therefore, though we are old and 'worn out' in terms of our spiritual freshness, we implore God not to cast us off.

סָרְנוּ *We have turned away from Your commandments and from Your good laws but to no avail.*[1] *Yet You are righteous in all that has come upon us, for You have acted truthfully while we have caused wickedness.*[2]

[א] *We have become the guiltiest of people.* [ב] *We have become the most degraded of all generations.* [ג] *Joy has departed from us.* [ד] *Our heart has been saddened by our sins.* [ה] *Our desirous treasure has been ruined,* [ו] *and our splendor dashed,* [ז] *for our Holy Temple edifice* [ח] *has been destroyed for our iniquities.* [ט] *Our Palace has become desolate.* [י] *[Jerusalem,] the beauty of our Land is given over to aliens,* [כ] *our power to strangers.*

But still we have not returned from our waywardness. So how can we be so brazen and obstinate as to say before You, HASHEM, *our God and the God of our forefathers, that we are righteous and have not sinned, for in truth, both we and our fathers have sinned.*

Strike the left side of the chest with the right fist while reciting
each of the sins in the following confession litany:

אָשַׁמְנוּ *We have become guilty;* [ב] *we have betrayed;* [ג] *we have robbed;* [ד] *we have spoken slander;* [ה] *we have caused perversion;* [ו] *we have caused wickedness;* [ז] *we have sinned willfully;* [ח] *we have extorted;* [ט] *we have accused falsely;* [י] *we have given evil counsel;* [כ] *we have been deceitful;* [ל] *we have scorned;* [מ] *we have rebelled;* [נ] *we have provoked;* [ס] *we have turned away;* [ע] *we have been perverse;* [פ] *we have acted wantonly;* [צ] *we have persecuted;* [ק] *we have been obstinate;* [ר] *we have been wicked;* [ש] *we have corrupted;* [ת] *we have been abominable; we have strayed; You have let us go astray.*

סָרְנוּ *We have turned away from Your commandments and from Your good laws but to no avail. Yet You are righteous in all that has come upon us, for You have acted truthfully while we have caused wickedness.*

[ל] *[The benefit of] our labor has been stolen,* [מ] *pulled away and cut off from us.* [נ] *They have placed their yoke upon us,* [ס] *our burdens upon our shoulders.* [ע] *Slaves have ruled over us,* [פ] *there is no redemption from their hand.* [צ] *Abundant troubles have surrounded us,* [ק] *we called upon You,* HASHEM, *our God,* [ר] *but You have distanced us for our iniquities.* [ש] *We have turned away from following after You;* [ת] *we have strayed; we have become lost.*

But still we have not returned from our waywardness. So how can we be so brazen and obstinate as to say before You, HASHEM, *our God and the God of our forefathers, that we are righteous and have not sinned, for in truth, both we and our fathers have sinned.*

Strike the left side of the chest with the right fist while reciting
each of the sins in the following confession litany:

אָשַׁמְנוּ *We have become guilty;* [ב] *we have betrayed;* [ג] *we have robbed;* [ד] *we have spoken slander;* [ה] *we have caused perversion;* [ו] *we have caused wickedness;* [ז] *we have sinned willfully;* [ח] *we have extorted;* [ט] *we have accused falsely;* [י] *we have given evil counsel;* [כ] *we have been deceitful;* [ל] *we have scorned;* [מ] *we have rebelled;* [נ] *we have provoked;* [ס] *we have turned away;* [ע] *we have been perverse;* [פ] *we have acted wantonly;* [צ] *we have persecuted;* [ק] *we have been obstinate;*

רָשַׁעְנוּ, שִׁחַתְנוּ, תִּעַבְנוּ, תָּעִינוּ, תִּעְתָּעְנוּ.

סַרְנוּ מִמִּצְוֹתֶיךָ וּמִמִּשְׁפָּטֶיךָ הַטּוֹבִים וְלֹא שָׁוָה לָנוּ. וְאַתָּה צַדִּיק עַל כָּל הַבָּא עָלֵינוּ, כִּי אֱמֶת עָשִׂיתָ וַאֲנַחְנוּ הִרְשָׁעְנוּ.

הִרְשַׁעְנוּ* וּפָשַׁעְנוּ, לָכֵן לֹא נוֹשָׁעְנוּ. וְתֵן בְּלִבֵּנוּ לַעֲזוֹב דֶּרֶךְ רֶשַׁע, וְחִישׁ לָנוּ יֶשַׁע, כַּכָּתוּב עַל יַד נְבִיאֶךָ: יַעֲזֹב רָשָׁע דַּרְכּוֹ, וְאִישׁ אָוֶן מַחְשְׁבֹתָיו, וְיָשֹׁב אֶל יהוה וִירַחֲמֵהוּ, וְאֶל אֱלֹהֵינוּ כִּי יַרְבֶּה לִסְלוֹחַ.[1]

מְשִׁיחַ צִדְקֶךָ* אָמַר לְפָנֶיךָ: שְׁגִיאוֹת מִי יָבִין מִנִּסְתָּרוֹת נַקֵּנִי.[2] נַקֵּנוּ יהוה אֱלֹהֵינוּ מִכָּל פְּשָׁעֵינוּ, וְטַהֲרֵנוּ מִכָּל טֻמְאוֹתֵינוּ, וּזְרוֹק עָלֵינוּ מַיִם טְהוֹרִים וְטַהֲרֵנוּ, כַּכָּתוּב עַל יַד נְבִיאֶךָ: וְזָרַקְתִּי עֲלֵיכֶם מַיִם טְהוֹרִים וּטְהַרְתֶּם, מִכֹּל טֻמְאוֹתֵיכֶם וּמִכָּל גִּלּוּלֵיכֶם אֲטַהֵר אֶתְכֶם.*[3]

מִיכָה עַבְדְּךָ אָמַר לְפָנֶיךָ: מִי אֵל כָּמוֹךָ נֹשֵׂא עָוֹן וְעֹבֵר עַל פֶּשַׁע לִשְׁאֵרִית נַחֲלָתוֹ, לֹא הֶחֱזִיק לָעַד אַפּוֹ, כִּי חָפֵץ חֶסֶד הוּא, יָשׁוּב יְרַחֲמֵנוּ, יִכְבֹּשׁ עֲוֹנוֹתֵינוּ, וְתַשְׁלִיךְ בִּמְצֻלוֹת יָם כָּל חַטֹּאתָם.[4] (וְכָל חַטֹּאת עַמְּךָ בֵּית יִשְׂרָאֵל תַּשְׁלִיךְ בִּמְקוֹם אֲשֶׁר לֹא יִזָּכְרוּ, וְלֹא יִפָּקְדוּ, וְלֹא יַעֲלוּ עַל לֵב לְעוֹלָם.) תִּתֵּן אֱמֶת לְיַעֲקֹב חֶסֶד לְאַבְרָהָם אֲשֶׁר נִשְׁבַּעְתָּ לַאֲבוֹתֵינוּ מִימֵי קֶדֶם.[5]

דָּנִיֵּאל אִישׁ חֲמוּדוֹת שִׁוַּע לְפָנֶיךָ: הַטֵּה אֱלֹהַי אָזְנְךָ וּשֲׁמָע, פְּקַח עֵינֶיךָ וּרְאֵה שֹׁמְמֹתֵינוּ וְהָעִיר* אֲשֶׁר נִקְרָא שִׁמְךָ עָלֶיהָ, כִּי לֹא עַל צִדְקֹתֵינוּ אֲנַחְנוּ מַפִּילִים תַּחֲנוּנֵינוּ לְפָנֶיךָ, כִּי עַל רַחֲמֶיךָ הָרַבִּים. אֲדֹנָי שְׁמָעָה, אֲדֹנָי סְלָחָה, אֲדֹנָי הַקְשִׁיבָה, וַעֲשֵׂה אַל תְּאַחַר, לְמַעַנְךָ אֱלֹהַי, כִּי שִׁמְךָ נִקְרָא עַל עִירְךָ וְעַל עַמֶּךָ.[6]

עֶזְרָא הַסּוֹפֵר אָמַר לְפָנֶיךָ: אֱלֹהַי, בֹּשְׁתִּי וְנִכְלַמְתִּי לְהָרִים, אֱלֹהַי, פָּנַי אֵלֶיךָ, כִּי עֲוֹנֹתֵינוּ רָבוּ לְמַעְלָה רֹאשׁ, וְאַשְׁמָתֵנוּ גָדְלָה עַד לַשָּׁמַיִם.[7] וְאַתָּה[8] אֱלוֹהַּ סְלִיחוֹת, חַנּוּן

---

(1) Isaiah 55:7. (2) Psalms 19:13. (3) Ezekiel 36:25. (4) Micah 7:18-19. (5) 7:20. (6) Daniel 9:18-19. (7) Ezra 9:6. (8) Some editions of Selichos insert the word אֱלֹהֵינוּ, our God, at this point.

∴⁍ **הִרְשַׁעְנוּ** — *We have acted wickedly.* Though our deeds have been wicked, God assures us that He does not desire the death of the wicked, but their repentance.

∴⁍ **מְשִׁיחַ צִדְקֶךָ** — *Your righteous anointed*

[David]. These verses deal with the theme of purity — becoming purified from the spiritual contamination of sin, and saying that God will remove from us the contamination that our sins brought upon us.

[ר] *we have been wicked;* [ש] *we have corrupted;* [ת] *we have been abominable; we have strayed; You have let us go astray.*

סַרְנוּ *We have turned away from Your commandments and from Your good laws but to no avail. Yet You are righteous in all that has come upon us, for You have acted truthfully while we have caused wickedness.*

הִרְשַׁעְנוּ *We have acted wickedly* and have sinned willfully, there-fore we have not been saved. Inspire our heart to abandon the path of evil and hasten salvation for us, as it is written by Your prophet: May the wicked one abandon his way and the vicious man his thoughts; may he return to* HASHEM *and He will show him mercy, and to our God, for He is abundantly forgiving.*[1]

מְשִׁיחַ צִדְקֶךָ *Your righteous anointed [David]* said before You: 'Who can discern mistakes? From unperceived faults cleanse me.'*[2] *Cleanse us,* HASHEM, *our God, of all our willful sins and purify us, of all our contaminations. Sprinkle upon us pure water and purify us, as it is written by Your prophet: I shall sprinkle pure water upon you and purify you, of all your contaminations and of all your abominations I will purify you.'*[*3]

מִיכָה עַבְדְּךָ *Micah, Your servant, said before You: 'Who, O God, is like You, Who pardons iniquity and overlooks transgres-sion for the remnant of His heritage? Who has not retained His wrath eternally, for He desires kindness! He will again be merciful to us; He will suppress our iniquities and cast into the depths of the sea all their sins.*[4] *(And all the sins of Your nation the Family of Israel, may You cast away to a place where they will neither be remembered, considered, nor brought to mind — ever.) Grant truth to Jacob, kindness to Abraham, as You swore to our forefathers from ancient times.'*[5]

דָּנִיֵּאל *Daniel, the greatly beloved man, cried out before You: 'Incline, my God, Your ear, and listen, open Your eyes and see our desolation and that of the city* upon which Your Name is proclaimed, for not because of our righteousness do we cast down our supplications before You, rather because of Your abundant compassion. O my Lord, heed; O my Lord, forgive; O my Lord, be attentive and act, do not delay; for Your sake, my God, for Your Name is proclaimed upon Your city and Your people.'*[6]

עֶזְרָא הַסּוֹפֵר *Ezra the Scribe said before You: 'My God, I am embar-rassed and ashamed to lift my face to You, my God — for our iniquities have multiplied above our heads, and our sins extend unto heaven.*[7] *You are*[8] *the God of forgiveness, compassionate*

אַטַהֵר אֶתְכֶם — *I will purify you.* God Himself, as it were, promises to cleanse Israel of its sins. This inspiring pledge makes clear to us that even when we have strayed far from Him, God continues to

love us so much that He personally will remove the filth of our sins.

שִׁמְמוֹתֵינוּ וְהָעִיר — *Our desolation and that of the city.* Both the Jewish people and Jerusalem

וְרַחוּם, אֶרֶךְ אַפַּיִם וְרַב חֶסֶד, וְלֹא עֲזַבְתָּנוּ.[1]

אַל תַּעַזְבֵנוּ אָבִינוּ וְאַל תִּטְּשֵׁנוּ בּוֹרְאֵנוּ, וְאַל תַּזְנִיחֵנוּ יוֹצְרֵנוּ, וְאַל תַּעַשׂ עִמָּנוּ כָּלָה כְּחַטֹּאתֵינוּ. וְקַיֶּם לָנוּ יהוה אֱלֹהֵינוּ, אֶת הַדָּבָר שֶׁהִבְטַחְתָּנוּ בְּקַבָּלָה עַל יְדֵי יִרְמְיָהוּ חוֹזָךְ, כָּאָמוּר: בַּיָּמִים הָהֵם וּבָעֵת הַהִיא, נְאֻם יהוה, יְבֻקַּשׁ אֶת עֲוֹן יִשְׂרָאֵל וְאֵינֶנּוּ וְאֶת חַטֹּאת יְהוּדָה וְלֹא תִמָּצֶאנָה, כִּי אֶסְלַח לַאֲשֶׁר אַשְׁאִיר.[2]

עַמְּךָ וְנַחֲלָתְךָ רְעֵבֵי טוּבְךָ, צְמֵאֵי חַסְדֶּךָ, תְּאֵבֵי יִשְׁעֶךָ, יַכִּירוּ וְיֵדְעוּ כִּי לַיהוה אֱלֹהֵינוּ הָרַחֲמִים וְהַסְּלִיחוֹת.

אֵל רַחוּם* שְׁמֶךָ, אֵל חַנּוּן שְׁמֶךָ, בָּנוּ נִקְרָא שְׁמֶךָ. יהוה עֲשֵׂה לְמַעַן שְׁמֶךָ. עֲשֵׂה לְמַעַן אֲמִתֶּךָ.* עֲשֵׂה לְמַעַן בְּרִיתֶךָ, עֲשֵׂה לְמַעַן גָּדְלְךָ וְתִפְאַרְתֶּךָ, עֲשֵׂה לְמַעַן דָּתֶךָ, עֲשֵׂה לְמַעַן הוֹדֶךָ, עֲשֵׂה לְמַעַן וְעוּדֶךָ, עֲשֵׂה לְמַעַן זִכְרֶךָ, עֲשֵׂה לְמַעַן חַסְדֶּךָ, עֲשֵׂה לְמַעַן טוּבֶךָ, עֲשֵׂה לְמַעַן יְחוּדֶךָ, עֲשֵׂה לְמַעַן כְּבוֹדֶךָ, עֲשֵׂה לְמַעַן לִמּוּדֶךָ, עֲשֵׂה לְמַעַן מַלְכוּתֶךָ, עֲשֵׂה לְמַעַן נִצְחֶךָ, עֲשֵׂה לְמַעַן סוֹדֶךָ, עֲשֵׂה לְמַעַן עֻזֶּךָ, עֲשֵׂה לְמַעַן פְּאֵרֶךָ, עֲשֵׂה לְמַעַן צִדְקָתֶךָ, עֲשֵׂה לְמַעַן קְדֻשָּׁתֶךָ, עֲשֵׂה לְמַעַן רַחֲמֶיךָ הָרַבִּים, עֲשֵׂה לְמַעַן שְׁכִינָתֶךָ, עֲשֵׂה לְמַעַן תְּהִלָּתֶךָ, עֲשֵׂה לְמַעַן אוֹהֲבֶיךָ

---

are desolate.

אֵל רַחוּם — *Merciful God.* The first twenty-two of the verses that begin with עֲשֵׂה לְמַעַן, *act for the sake of,* list attributes of God following the order of the *aleph-beis.* The same list appears in the *Hoshana* service for the first day of *Succos.* These terms are based on Scriptural verses in most cases, and occasionally, on sayings of the Talmudic sages [see ArtScroll *Hoshanos* pp. 38-45 for a full commentary on each of these terms].

Although many editions of *Selichos,* the *Siddur* and the Yom Kippur *Machzor* follow the vowelization that appears above, some vowelize the word endings differently; thus אֲמִתֶּךָ *becomes* אֲמִתָּךְ; and בְּרִיתֶךָ *becomes* בְּרִיתָךְ, etc. The meaning is unchanged.

אֲמִתֶּךָ — *Your truth.* During the long and difficult period of exile, we have seen the fulfillment of the prophecy: וְתַשְׁלֵךְ אֱמֶת אַרְצָה, *It will throw truth to the earth* (Daniel 8:12). Truth has become ridiculed and despised — therefore we pray: *for the sake of Your truth.*

גָּדְלְךָ וְתִפְאַרְתֶּךָ — *Your Greatness and Your Splendor.* This phrase is based on King David's last public declaration of God's praise: *To you* HASHEM *is the greatness* [גְּדֻלָּה] *and the power*

[גְּבוּרָה] *and the splendor* [תִּפְאֶרֶת] (I Chronicles 29:11).

The present stitch deviates from the rest of this stanza by combining two attributes, instead of listing only one. This anomaly is compounded by the exclusion of גְּבוּרָה, *power,* which (a) fits the alphabetical scheme whereas תִּפְאֶרֶת, *splendor,* does not; and (b) follows immediately after *greatness* in King David's formula.

Bnei Yisas'char explains as follows: Kabbalistically, the attributes of גְּדֻלָּה גְּבוּרָה תִּפְאֶרֶת, *greatness, power,* and *splendor,* are equivalent to חֶסֶד דִּין אֱמֶת, *kindness, justice,* and *mercy,* respectively. The latter three are symbolic of the judges on the Heavenly Tribunal through which God passes judgment on His world; each one representing a different response to man's deeds. While Justice tends to strictness, Kindness and Mercy lean toward leniency. Hence, we beseech God, '*Act for the sake of Your Greatness/Kindness and Your Glory/Mercy*' — the attributes of compassion which outweigh the severity of Power/Justice.

דָּתֶךָ ... הוֹדֶךָ — *Your law ... Your glory.* Law refers to the Torah; *glory* to the *Beis HaMikdash.* The *Zohar* relates the destruction of the Holy Temple to the defilement of God's הוֹד, *glory.* Both

and merciful, slow to anger, and abundant in kindness; and You have not forsaken us.'[1]

אַל תַּעַזְבֵנוּ Do not forsake us, our Father; do not cast us off, our Creator; do not abandon us, our Molder; and do not bring about our destruction, as our sins merit. Affirm for us, HASHEM, our God, the promise You made in the tradition through Jeremiah, Your seer, as it is said: 'In those days and at that time' — the words of HASHEM — 'the iniquity of Israel will be sought but there will be none, and the errors of Judah, but they will not be found, for I will have forgiven those whom I leave as a remnant.'[2]

Your people and Your heritage, who hunger for Your goodness, who thirst for Your kindness, who long for Your salvation — may they recognize and know that to HASHEM, our God, belong mercy and forgiveness.

אֵל רַחוּם 'Merciful God'* is Your Name, 'Gracious God' is Your Name, Your Name is called upon us — O HASHEM, act for Your Name's sake. Act for the sake of [א] Your truth;* act for the sake of [ב] Your covenant; act for the sake of [ג] Your greatness and Your splendor;* act for the sake of [ד] Your law; act for the sake of [ה] Your glory;* act for the sake of [ו] Your Meeting House;* act for the sake of [ז] Your remembrance;* act for the sake of [ח] Your kindness; act for the sake of [ט] Your goodness; act for the sake of [י] Your Oneness; act for the sake of [כ] Your honor; act for the sake of [ל] Your teaching;* act for the sake of [מ] Your kingship;* act for the sake of [נ] Your eternality;* act for the sake of [ס] Your counsel; act for the sake of [ע] Your power; act for the sake of [פ] Your beauty; act for the sake of [צ] Your righteousness; act for the sake of [ק] Your sanctity; act for the sake of [ר] Your abundant mercy; act for the sake of [ש] Your Presence, act for the sake of [ת] Your praise; act for the sake of Your beloved ones

---

(1) Cf. *Nehemiah* 9:17. (2) *Jeremiah* 50:20.

---

blows, the destruction and the defilement, can be remedied through the same medium. Only through study of Torah can God's glory be restored; and only through study of Torah can the Holy Temple be rebuilt. Thus the juxtaposition of דָּתֶךָ, *Your law*, i.e., the Torah, with הוֹדֶךָ, *Your Glory*, i.e., the Temple.

וְעוּדְךָ — *Your Meeting House*. This is another allusion to the Holy Temple where the *Shechinah* and Israel came together.

זִכְרְךָ — *Your remembrance*. Moses asked of God: *When I come to the Children of Israel and say to them, 'The God of your ancestors has sent me to you,' and they will respond, 'What is His Name?' What shall I say to them?*

God Replied: 'HASHEM, God of Your ancestors ... זֶה שְׁמִי , *This is My Name eternally*, וְזֶה ... זִכְרִי, *and this is My remembrance in every generation*' (*Exodus* 3:13,15).

לְמוּדְךָ — *Your teaching*. In the World to Come,

Israel shall be taught Torah directly by God, as the prophets declare: *All your children shall be* לִמּוּדֵי ה', *taught by* HASHEM (*Isaiah* 54:33). Just as God is eternal so is His [direct] Teaching eternal. Torah taught in this way can never be forgotten (*Yalkut Shimoni* II 479).

מַלְכוּתֶךָ — *Your kingship*. On *Rosh Hashanah*, just before reciting the *Kaddish* before the *Mussaf*, R' *Levi Yitzchak of Berditchev* would cry out: The czar of Russia claims that the world is his; so it is that every monarch claims possession of the world. But we, Your Jewish nation say, ... יִתְגַּדֵּל וְיִתְקַדֵּשׁ, *May His great Name grow exalted and sanctified in the world* ... וְיַמְלִיךְ מַלְכוּתֵהּ, *and may He give reign to His Kingship*.

Likewise, we pray for salvation which will lead to the day when HASHEM shall be King over the *entire earth* (*Zechariah* 14:9).

נִצְחֶךָ — *Your eternality*. The word also has many other meanings, several of which are accurate in

שׁוֹכְנֵי עָפָר, עֲשֵׂה לְמַעַן אַבְרָהָם יִצְחָק וְיַעֲקֹב, עֲשֵׂה לְמַעַן מֹשֶׁה
וְאַהֲרֹן, עֲשֵׂה לְמַעַן דָּוִד וּשְׁלֹמֹה, עֲשֵׂה לְמַעַן יְרוּשָׁלַיִם עִיר
קָדְשֶׁךָ, עֲשֵׂה לְמַעַן צִיּוֹן מִשְׁכַּן כְּבוֹדֶךָ, עֲשֵׂה לְמַעַן שִׁמְמוֹת
הֵיכָלֶךָ, עֲשֵׂה לְמַעַן הֲרִיסוּת מִזְבְּחֶךָ, עֲשֵׂה לְמַעַן הֲרוּגִים עַל
שֵׁם קָדְשֶׁךָ, עֲשֵׂה לְמַעַן טְבוּחִים עַל יִחוּדֶךָ, עֲשֵׂה לְמַעַן בָּאֵי
בָאֵשׁ וּבַמַּיִם עַל קִדּוּשׁ שְׁמֶךָ, עֲשֵׂה לְמַעַן יוֹנְקֵי שָׁדַיִם שֶׁלֹּא
חָטְאוּ, עֲשֵׂה לְמַעַן גְּמוּלֵי חָלָב שֶׁלֹּא פָשָׁעוּ, עֲשֵׂה לְמַעַן תִּינוֹקוֹת
שֶׁל בֵּית רַבָּן, עֲשֵׂה לְמַעַנְךָ אִם לֹא לְמַעֲנֵנוּ, עֲשֵׂה לְמַעַנְךָ
וְהוֹשִׁיעֵנוּ.

עֲנֵנוּ* יהוה עֲנֵנוּ, עֲנֵנוּ אֱלֹהֵינוּ עֲנֵנוּ, עֲנֵנוּ אָבִינוּ עֲנֵנוּ, עֲנֵנוּ
בּוֹרְאֵנוּ עֲנֵנוּ, עֲנֵנוּ גּוֹאֲלֵנוּ עֲנֵנוּ, עֲנֵנוּ דוֹרְשֵׁנוּ עֲנֵנוּ, עֲנֵנוּ
הָאֵל הַנֶּאֱמָן עֲנֵנוּ, עֲנֵנוּ וָתִיק וְחָסִיד עֲנֵנוּ, עֲנֵנוּ **זַךְ** וְיָשָׁר עֲנֵנוּ,
עֲנֵנוּ **חַי** וְקַיָּם עֲנֵנוּ, עֲנֵנוּ **טוֹב** וּמֵטִיב עֲנֵנוּ, עֲנֵנוּ **יוֹדֵעַ** יֵצֶר עֲנֵנוּ,
עֲנֵנוּ **כּוֹבֵשׁ** כְּעָסִים עֲנֵנוּ, עֲנֵנוּ **לוֹבֵשׁ** צְדָקוֹת עֲנֵנוּ, עֲנֵנוּ **מֶלֶךְ**
מַלְכֵי הַמְּלָכִים עֲנֵנוּ, עֲנֵנוּ **נוֹרָא** וְנִשְׂגָּב עֲנֵנוּ, עֲנֵנוּ **סוֹלֵחַ** וּמוֹחֵל
עֲנֵנוּ, עֲנֵנוּ עוֹנֶה בְּעֵת צָרָה עֲנֵנוּ, עֲנֵנוּ **פּוֹדֶה** וּמַצִּיל עֲנֵנוּ, עֲנֵנוּ
צַדִּיק וְיָשָׁר עֲנֵנוּ, עֲנֵנוּ **קָרוֹב** לְקוֹרְאָיו עֲנֵנוּ, עֲנֵנוּ **רַחוּם** וְחַנּוּן
עֲנֵנוּ, עֲנֵנוּ **שׁוֹמֵעַ** אֶל אֶבְיוֹנִים עֲנֵנוּ, עֲנֵנוּ **תּוֹמֵךְ** תְּמִימִים עֲנֵנוּ,
עֲנֵנוּ אֱלֹהֵי אֲבוֹתֵינוּ עֲנֵנוּ, עֲנֵנוּ אֱלֹהֵי אַבְרָהָם עֲנֵנוּ, עֲנֵנוּ פַּחַד
יִצְחָק עֲנֵנוּ, עֲנֵנוּ אֲבִיר יַעֲקֹב עֲנֵנוּ, עֲנֵנוּ עֶזְרַת הַשְּׁבָטִים עֲנֵנוּ,
עֲנֵנוּ מִשְׂגַּב אִמָּהוֹת עֲנֵנוּ, עֲנֵנוּ קָשֶׁה לִכְעֹס עֲנֵנוּ, עֲנֵנוּ רַךְ
לִרְצוֹת עֲנֵנוּ, עֲנֵנוּ עוֹנֶה בְּעֵת רָצוֹן עֲנֵנוּ, עֲנֵנוּ אֲבִי יְתוֹמִים עֲנֵנוּ,
עֲנֵנוּ דַּיַּן אַלְמָנוֹת עֲנֵנוּ.

מִי שֶׁעָנָה* לְאַבְרָהָם* אָבִינוּ בְּהַר הַמּוֹרִיָּה,   הוּא יַעֲנֵנוּ.
מִי שֶׁעָנָה לְיִצְחָק בְּנוֹ כְּשֶׁנֶּעֱקַד עַל גַּבֵּי הַמִּזְבֵּחַ,   הוּא יַעֲנֵנוּ.

---

the sense of this *piyut: strength, supervision, victory, triumph.*

⁂ **עֲנֵנוּ** — *Answer us.* This *piyut* refers to God in an alphabetical listing of Names and attributes that is based mostly on Scriptural verses, and in some instances, on Talmudic and Midrashic statements.

⁂ **מִי שֶׁעָנָה** — *He Who answered.* Whenever *Eretz Yisrael* is afflicted with a drought, the *beis din* declares a series of public fast days

devoted to prayer and repentance. The special supplications of the day include seven blessings, each of which contains the plea, 'He Who answered . . . may He answer us' (*Taanis* 15a). This litany, in a greatly expanded version, has been appended to the *Selichos* prayers. In this commentary, we will give a very brief description of the particular event to which the verse refers (except for those that are very well known).

אַבְרָהָם — *Abraham* was the first Jew to be saved by God's intervention, when he was rescued

*who rest in the dust; act for the sake of Abraham, Isaac, and Jacob; act
for the sake of Moses and Aaron; act for the sake of David and Solomon;
act for the sake of Jerusalem, Your holy city; act for the sake of Zion, the
abode of Your glory; act for the sake of the desolation of Your Temple;
act for the sake of the ruin of Your Altar; act for the sake of the martyrs
for Your holy Name; act for the sake of those slaughtered for Your
Oneness; act for the sake of those who entered fire and water for the
sanctification of Your Name; act for the nursing infants who did not err;
act for the sake of the weaned babes who did not sin; act for the sake of
children at the schoolroom; act for Your sake if not for ours; act for Your
sake and save us.*

עֲנֵנוּ *Answer us,* HASHEM, answer us; answer us, our God, answer us;
answer us,* [א] *our Father, answer us; answer us,* [ב] *our Creator,
answer us; answer us,* [ג] *our Redeemer, answer us; answer us,* [ד] *You
Who searches us out, answer us; answer us,* [ה] *faithful God, answer us;
answer us,* [ו] *steadfast and kind One, answer us; answer us,* [ז] *pure
and upright One, answer us; answer us,* [ח] *living and enduring
One, answer us; answer us,* [ט] *good and beneficent One, answer us;
answer us,* [י] *You Who knows inclinations, answer us; answer us,* [כ]
You Who suppresses wrath, answer us; answer us, [ל] *You Who dons
righteousness, answer us; answer us,* [מ] *King Who reigns over kings,
answer us; answer us,* [נ] *awesome and powerful One, answer us;
answer us,* [ס] *You Who forgives and pardons, answer us; answer us,*
[ע] *You Who answers in time of distress,*[1] *answer us; answer us,*
[פ] *Redeemer and Rescuer, answer us; answer us,* [צ] *righteous and
upright One, answer us; answer us,* [ק] *He Who is close to those who
call upon Him, answer us; answer us,* [ר] *merciful and gracious One,
answer us; answer us,* [ש] *You Who hears the destitute, answer us;
answer us,* [ת] *You Who supports the wholesome, answer us; answer us,
God of our forefathers, answer us; answer us, God of Abraham, answer
us; answer us, Dread of Isaac, answer us; answer us, Mighty One of
Jacob, answer us; answer us, Helper of the tribes, answer us; answer
us, Stronghold of the Matriarchs, answer us; answer us, You Who are
hard to anger, answer us; answer us, You Who are easy to pacify,
answer us; answer us, You Who answers in a time of favor,*[1] *answer us;
answer us, Father of orphans, answer us; answer us, Judge of widows,
answer us.*

מִי שֶׁעָנָה *He Who answered* our father Abraham* on Mount Moriah,
may He answer us.*

*He Who answered his son Isaac when he was bound atop the altar,
may He answer us.*

---

(1) Some editions of *Selichos* reverse the positions of these two lines.

מִי שֶׁעָנָה לְיַעֲקֹב* בְּבֵית אֵל,   הוּא יַעֲנֵנוּ.

מִי שֶׁעָנָה לְיוֹסֵף בְּבֵית הָאֲסוּרִים,   הוּא יַעֲנֵנוּ.

מִי שֶׁעָנָה לַאֲבוֹתֵינוּ עַל יַם סוּף,   הוּא יַעֲנֵנוּ.

מִי שֶׁעָנָה לְמֹשֶׁה* בְּחוֹרֵב,   הוּא יַעֲנֵנוּ.

מִי שֶׁעָנָה לְאַהֲרֹן* בַּמַּחְתָּה,   הוּא יַעֲנֵנוּ.

מִי שֶׁעָנָה לְפִינְחָס* בְּקוּמוֹ מִתּוֹךְ הָעֵדָה,   הוּא יַעֲנֵנוּ.

מִי שֶׁעָנָה לִיהוֹשֻׁעַ* בַּגִּלְגָּל,   הוּא יַעֲנֵנוּ.

מִי שֶׁעָנָה לִשְׁמוּאֵל* בַּמִּצְפָּה,   הוּא יַעֲנֵנוּ.

מִי שֶׁעָנָה לְדָוִד וּשְׁלֹמֹה בְנוֹ בִּירוּשָׁלַיִם,   הוּא יַעֲנֵנוּ.

מִי שֶׁעָנָה לְאֵלִיָּהוּ בְּהַר הַכַּרְמֶל,   הוּא יַעֲנֵנוּ.

מִי שֶׁעָנָה לֶאֱלִישָׁע* בִּירִיחוֹ,   הוּא יַעֲנֵנוּ.

מִי שֶׁעָנָה לְיוֹנָה בִּמְעֵי הַדָּגָה,   הוּא יַעֲנֵנוּ.

מִי שֶׁעָנָה לְחִזְקִיָּהוּ* מֶלֶךְ יְהוּדָה בְּחָלְיוֹ,   הוּא יַעֲנֵנוּ.

מִי שֶׁעָנָה לַחֲנַנְיָה* מִישָׁאֵל וַעֲזַרְיָה בְּתוֹךְ כִּבְשַׁן הָאֵשׁ,
      הוּא יַעֲנֵנוּ.

מִי שֶׁעָנָה לְדָנִיֵּאל בְּגוֹב הָאֲרָיוֹת,   הוּא יַעֲנֵנוּ.

מִי שֶׁעָנָה לְמָרְדְּכַי וְאֶסְתֵּר בְּשׁוּשַׁן הַבִּירָה,   הוּא יַעֲנֵנוּ.

מִי שֶׁעָנָה לְעֶזְרָא* בַּגּוֹלָה,   הוּא יַעֲנֵנוּ.

מִי שֶׁעָנָה לְכָל הַצַּדִּיקִים וְהַחֲסִידִים וְהַתְּמִימִים וְהַיְשָׁרִים,
      הוּא יַעֲנֵנוּ.

רַחֲמָנָא דְּעָנֵי לַעֲנִיֵּי, עֲנֵינָא. רַחֲמָנָא דְּעָנֵי לִתְבִירֵי לִבָּא,
עֲנֵינָא. רַחֲמָנָא דְּעָנֵי לְמַכִּיכֵי רוּחָא, עֲנֵינָא. רַחֲמָנָא
עֲנֵינָא. רַחֲמָנָא חוּס. רַחֲמָנָא פְּרוֹק. רַחֲמָנָא שְׁזִיב. רַחֲמָנָא
רְחַם עֲלָן. הַשְׁתָּא בַּעֲגָלָא וּבִזְמַן קָרִיב.

---

from Nimrod's attempt to burn him to death. At a later date, on Mount Moriah, when Abraham bound Isaac on the altar, he prayed that God would always come to the defense of the Jewish people in times of future danger (*Yerushalmi, Taanis* 2:4).

יעקב — *Jacob's* vision of the angels on a ladder, and God's promise to protect him, took place at Bethel (*Genesis* 28:19).

משה — *Moses* prayed in Horeb that Israel not be

destroyed for worshiping the Golden Calf (*Deuteronomy* 9:26).

אַהֲרֹן — *Aaron.* When Israel was being struck by a plague, Moses commanded Aaron to take a censer of incense and use it to bring atonement for the people (*Numbers* 17:11).

פִּינְחָס — *Phineas* arose from among the people and single-handedly dealt with the wrongdoers whose lewd acts brought a plague upon Israel (*Numbers* 25:7).

He Who answered Jacob* in Bethel,   *may He answer us.*
He Who answered Joseph in the prison,   *may He answer us.*
He Who answered our forefathers at the Sea of Reeds,

may He answer us.
He Who answered Moses* in Horeb,   *may He answer us.*
He Who answered Aaron* when he offered the censer,

may He answer us.
He Who answered Phineas* when he arose from amid the congregation,

may He answer us.
He Who answered Joshua* in Gilgal,   *may He answer us.*
He Who answered Samuel* in Mitzpah,   *may He answer us.*
He Who answered David and his son Solomon in Jerusalem,

may He answer us.
He Who answered Elijah on Mount Carmel,   *may He answer us.*
He Who answered Elisha* in Jericho,   *may He answer us.*
He Who answered Jonah in the innards of the fish,

may He answer us.
He Who answered Hezekiah,* King of Judah, in his illness,

may He answer us.
He Who answered Chananiah,* Mishael, and Azariah in the fiery oven,

may He answer us.
He Who answered Daniel in the lions' den,   *may He answer us.*
He Who answered Mordechai and Esther in Shushan the capital,

may He answer us.
He Who answered Ezra* in the Exile,   *may He answer us.*
He Who answered all the righteous, the devout, the wholesome,
  and the upright,   *may He answer us.*

רַחֲמָנָא *The Merciful One Who answers the poor, may He answer us.*
The Merciful One Who answers the brokenhearted, may He answer us. The Merciful One Who answers the humble of spirit, may He answer us. O Merciful One, answer us. O Merciful One, pity. O Merciful One, redeem. O Merciful One, deliver. O Merciful One, have mercy on us — now, swiftly and soon.

יְהוֹשֻׁעַ — *Joshua* was encamped in Gilgal when the miraculous conquest of Jericho took place (*Joshua* 6:20).

שְׁמוּאֵל — *Samuel* prayed at Mitzpah for God's help against the Philistines (*I Samuel* 7:9).

אֱלִישָׁע — *Elisha.* At Jericho, Elijah's spirit of prophetic greatness descended upon his disciple Elisha (*II Kings* 2).

חִזְקִיָּהוּ — *Hezekiah* was told by the prophet Isaiah that he would die. Hezekiah prayed to

God, Who responded with a promise that he would live another fifteen years (*II Kings* 20:1-6).

חֲנַנְיָה . . . . — *Chananiah* . . . Nebuchadnezzar ordered that these three Jews (known in Babylonian as Shadrach, Mesach, and Abad Nego) be thrown into a furnace, but God saved them from the flames (*Daniel* 3:22-26).

עֶזְרָא — *Ezra* decided to ascend from Babylonia to *Eretz Yisrael,* and God influenced King Darius to grant all of Ezra's requests (*Ezra* 7:6).

נפילת אפים

In the presence of a Torah Scroll, the following (until יֵבֹשׁוּ רָגַע) is recited with the head resting on the arm, preferably while seated. Elsewhere, it is recited with the head held erect.

(וַיֹּאמֶר דָּוִד אֶל גָּד, צַר לִי מְאֹד נִפְּלָה נָּא בְיַד יהוה,
כִּי רַבִּים רַחֲמָיו, וּבְיַד אָדָם אַל אֶפֹּלָה.[1])

רַחוּם וְחַנּוּן* חָטָאתִי לְפָנֶיךָ. יהוה מָלֵא רַחֲמִים, רַחֵם עָלַי
וְקַבֵּל תַּחֲנוּנָי.

תהלים ו:ב-יא

יהוה אַל בְּאַפְּךָ* תוֹכִיחֵנִי, וְאַל בַּחֲמָתְךָ תְיַסְּרֵנִי. חָנֵּנִי יהוה,
כִּי אֻמְלַל אָנִי, רְפָאֵנִי יהוה, כִּי נִבְהֲלוּ עֲצָמָי. וְנַפְשִׁי
נִבְהֲלָה מְאֹד, וְאַתָּה יהוה, עַד מָתָי.* שׁוּבָה יהוה, חַלְּצָה נַפְשִׁי,
הוֹשִׁיעֵנִי לְמַעַן חַסְדֶּךָ. כִּי אֵין בַּמָּוֶת זִכְרֶךָ, בִּשְׁאוֹל מִי יוֹדֶה לָּךְ.
יָגַעְתִּי בְּאַנְחָתִי, אַשְׂחֶה בְכָל לַיְלָה מִטָּתִי, בְּדִמְעָתִי עַרְשִׂי אַמְסֶה.
עָשְׁשָׁה מִכַּעַס עֵינִי, עָתְקָה בְּכָל צוֹרְרָי. סוּרוּ מִמֶּנִּי כָּל פֹּעֲלֵי אָוֶן,
כִּי שָׁמַע יהוה קוֹל בִּכְיִי. שָׁמַע יהוה תְּחִנָּתִי, יהוה תְּפִלָּתִי יִקָּח.
יֵבֹשׁוּ וְיִבָּהֲלוּ מְאֹד כָּל אֹיְבָי, יָשֻׁבוּ יֵבֹשׁוּ רָגַע.

מַחֵי וּמַסֵּי מְמִית וּמְחַיֶּה, מַסִּיק מִן שְׁאוֹל לְחַיֵּי עָלְמָא, בְּרָא
כַּד חָטֵי אֲבוּהִי לַקְיֵהּ, אֲבוּהִי דְּחָיֵס אַסֵּי לִכְאֵבֵהּ.
עַבְדָּא דְּמָרִיד נָפִיק בְּקוֹלָר, מָרֵהּ תָּאֵיב וְתַבִּיר קוֹלָרֵהּ.

בְּרַךְ בִּכְרָךְ אֲנַן וְחָטֵינַן קַמָּךְ, הָא רָוֵי נַפְשִׁין בְּגִידִין מְרָרִין,
עַבְדָּךְ אֲנַן וּמְרוֹדִינַן קַמָּךְ, הָא בְּבָתָּא, הָא בְּשִׁבְיָא, הָא
בְּמַלְקִיּוּתָא. בְּמָטוּ מִנָּךְ בְּרַחֲמָךְ דִּנְפִישִׁין, אַסֵּי לִכְאֵבִין דִּתְקוֹף
עֲלָן, עַד דְּלָא נֶהֱוֵי גְמִירָא בְּשִׁבְיָא.

מַכְנִיסֵי רַחֲמִים,* הַכְנִיסוּ רַחֲמֵינוּ, לִפְנֵי בַּעַל הָרַחֲמִים.
מַשְׁמִיעֵי תְפִלָּה, הַשְׁמִיעוּ תְפִלָּתֵנוּ,

◆§ נְפִילַת אַפַּיִם / Putting Down the Head

The act of נְפִילַת אַפַּיִם, *putting down the head*, i.e., 'burying' one's face in submissive supplication, is based on the behavior of Moses, Aaron and Joshua. These three cast themselves down before God in times of stress and tragedy (*Numbers* 16:22; *Joshua* 7:6).

This passage is called *Tachanun* and is recited with the head down, resting on the left arm, and preferably in a sitting position. The head should not rest on the bare arm; rather, the arm should be covered with a sleeve, *tallis*, or even a cloth. This posture is an indication of the feelings of despair and guilt that combine with the undying hope that God's mercy will rescue the supplicant no matter how hopeless his plight. Since Scripture states that Joshua cast himself down in the presence of the Holy Ark, the act of putting down the head is done only in the presence of a Torah Scroll, i.e., an Ark containing a Torah Scroll. If a Torah is not present, *Tachanun* is recited with the head held erect.

רַחוּם וְחַנּוּן —*O compassionate and gracious One.* This verse is not of Scriptural origin. It is based on the dictum that God tempers the judgment of someone who confesses that he has sinned (*Etz Yosef*).

PUTTING DOWN THE HEAD

In the presence of a Torah Scroll, the following (until 'instantly shamed') is recited with the head resting on the arm, preferably while seated. Elsewhere, it is recited with the head held erect.

(And David said to Gad, 'I am exceedingly distressed. Let us fall into HASHEM's hand for His mercies are abundant, but let me not fall into human hands.' [1] *)*

רַחוּם וְחַנּוּן *O compassionate and gracious One,* I have sinned before You. HASHEM, Who is full of mercy, have mercy on me and accept my supplications.*

Psalms 6:2-11

'ה *HASHEM, do not rebuke me in Your anger* nor chastise me in Your rage. Favor me, HASHEM, for I am feeble; heal me, HASHEM, for my bones shudder. My soul is utterly confounded, and You, HASHEM, how long?* Desist, HASHEM, release my soul; save me as befits Your kindness. For there is no mention of You in death; in the Lower World who will thank You? I am wearied with my sigh, every night my tears drench my bed, soak my couch. My eye is dimmed because of anger, aged by my tormentors. Depart from me, all evildoers, for HASHEM has heard the sound of my weeping. HASHEM has heard my plea, HASHEM will accept my prayer. Let all my foes be shamed and utterly confounded, they will regret and be instantly shamed.*

מַחֵי וּמַסֵּי *[O God,] He Who smites and heals, causes death and restores life, raises [the dead] from the grave to eternal life: Should a son sin, his father would smack him, but a compassionate father will heal his [son's] pain. When a slave rebels, he is led out in collar-irons, but if his master desires to, he breaks his chains.*

We are Your son, Your firstborn, and we have sinned against You; so our soul has been satiated with bitter wormwood. We are Your servants and we have rebelled against You; so [we have suffered], some with looting, some with captivity, and some with the lash. We beg of You, in Your abundant compassion, heal the pains that have overwhelmed us, before we have been completely wiped out in captivity.

מַכְנִיסֵי רַחֲמִים *O you who usher in [pleas for] mercy,* may you usher in our [plea for] mercy, before the Master of mercy. O you who cause prayer to be heard, may you cause our prayer to be heard,*

---

(1) *II Samuel* 24:14.

אַל בְּאַפְּךָ 'ה — *HASHEM, do not ... in Your anger.* David composed this psalm when he was sick and in pain. He intended his prayer for every person in distress, and particularly for Israel when it suffered oppression and deprivation.

Even if he must be punished for his deeds, David pleaded, let God do so gradually, but not *in anger*, for then it would be beyond human endurance (*Radak*).

עַד מָתָי — *How long?* How long will You watch my suffering and not cure me?

מַכְנִיסֵי רַחֲמִים — *O you who usher in [pleas for] mercy.* The propriety and permissibility of

channeling a prayer through intermediaries — rather than directly to God — is a point of halachic contention. The debate revolves around supplications such as the one before us that request ministering angels to bring our supplications and tears before God, and to beseech Him to accept them favorably.

Shibbolei HaLeket (282) and *Tanya Rabbasi* (Cremona, end of ch. 72, p. 102a) cite a proem from *Midrash Shir HaShirim* (not found in extant editions of the Midrash) upon which this supplication obviously was based:

The Congregation of Israel says to the angels standing at the [heavenly] Gates of Prayer and

לִפְנֵי שׁוֹמֵעַ תְּפִלָּה. מַשְׁמִיעֵי צְעָקָה, הַשְׁמִיעוּ צַעֲקָתֵנוּ, לִפְנֵי שׁוֹמֵעַ צְעָקָה. מַכְנִיסֵי דִמְעָה, הַכְנִיסוּ דִמְעוֹתֵינוּ, לִפְנֵי מֶלֶךְ מִתְרַצֶּה בִּדְמָעוֹת.

הִשְׁתַּדְּלוּ וְהַרְבּוּ תְּחִנָּה וּבַקָּשָׁה, לִפְנֵי מֶלֶךְ אֵל רָם וְנִשָּׂא. הַזְכִּירוּ לְפָנָיו, הַשְׁמִיעוּ לְפָנָיו תּוֹרָה וּמַעֲשִׂים טוֹבִים שֶׁל שׁוֹכְנֵי עָפָר.

יִזְכּוֹר אַהֲבָתָם וִיחַיֶּה זַרְעָם, שֶׁלֹּא תֹאבַד שְׁאֵרִית יַעֲקֹב. כִּי צֹאן רוֹעֶה נֶאֱמָן הָיָה לְחֶרְפָּה, יִשְׂרָאֵל גּוֹי אֶחָד לְמָשָׁל וְלִשְׁנִינָה. מַהֵר עֲנֵנוּ אֱלֹהֵי יִשְׁעֵנוּ, וּפְדֵנוּ מִכָּל גְּזֵרוֹת קָשׁוֹת וְהוֹשִׁיעָה בְּרַחֲמֶיךָ הָרַבִּים, מְשִׁיחַ צִדְקֶךָ וְעַמֶּךָ.

מָרָן דְּבִשְׁמַיָּא לָךְ מִתְחַנְּנַן, כְּבַר שַׁבְיָא דְּמִתְחַנַּן לְשַׁבּוּיֵהּ. כֻּלְּהוֹן בְּנֵי שַׁבְיָא בְּכַסְפָּא מִתְפָּרְקִין, וְעַמָּךְ יִשְׂרָאֵל בְּרַחֲמֵי וּבְתַחֲנוּנֵי, הַב לָן שְׁאֵילָתִין וּבָעוּתִין, דְּלָא נֶהְדַּר רֵיקָם מִן קָדָמָךְ.

מָרָן דְּבִשְׁמַיָּא לָךְ מִתְחַנְּנַן, כְּעַבְדָּא דְּמִתְחַנַּן לְמָרֵיהּ, עֲשִׁיקֵי אֲנַן וּבַחֲשׁוֹכָא שָׁרֵינַן, מְרִירָן נַפְשִׁין מֵעַקְתִין דִּנְפִישִׁין, חֵילָא לֵית בָּן לְרַצּוּיָךְ מָרָן, עֲבִיד בְּדִיל קַיָּמָא דִּגְזַרְתָּ עִם אֲבָהָתָנָא.

שׁוֹמֵר יִשְׂרָאֵל,* שְׁמוֹר שְׁאֵרִית יִשְׂרָאֵל, וְאַל יֹאבַד יִשְׂרָאֵל, הָאֹמְרִים, שְׁמַע יִשְׂרָאֵל.[1]
שׁוֹמֵר גּוֹי אֶחָד, שְׁמוֹר שְׁאֵרִית עַם אֶחָד, וְאַל יֹאבַד גּוֹי אֶחָד, הַמְּיַחֲדִים שְׁמֶךָ, יהוה אֱלֹהֵינוּ יהוה אֶחָד.[1]
שׁוֹמֵר גּוֹי קָדוֹשׁ, שְׁמוֹר שְׁאֵרִית עַם קָדוֹשׁ, וְאַל יֹאבַד גּוֹי קָדוֹשׁ, הַמְּשַׁלְּשִׁים בְּשָׁלֹשׁ קְדֻשּׁוֹת לְקָדוֹשׁ.
מִתְרַצֶּה בְּרַחֲמִים וּמִתְפַּיֵּס בְּתַחֲנוּנִים, הִתְרַצֵּה וְהִתְפַּיֵּס לְדוֹר עָנִי, כִּי אֵין עוֹזֵר. אָבִינוּ מַלְכֵּנוּ, חָנֵּנוּ וַעֲנֵנוּ, כִּי אֵין בָּנוּ מַעֲשִׂים, עֲשֵׂה עִמָּנוּ צְדָקָה וָחֶסֶד וְהוֹשִׁיעֵנוּ.

Gates of Tears, 'Usher in my prayer and my tears before the Holy One, Blessed is He; and act as advocates before Him, that He pardon me for both intentional and inadvertent sins.' And so it is stated: *If there be for him but one advocate angel from among a thousand . . .* (Job 33:23).

שׁוֹמֵר יִשְׂרָאֵל ﴾ — *O Guardian of Israel.* This plea to God as our Guardian enforces the theme that we are helpless and totally dependent on His mercy. However, we do not come to God with nothing in our favor; each of the paragraphs beginning שׁוֹמֵר, *O Guardian,* stresses an aspect of

before the Hearer of prayer. O you who cause outcry to be heard, may you cause our outcry to be heard, before the Hearer of outcry. O you who usher in tears, may you usher in our tears, before the King Who finds favor through tears.

Exert yourselves, and multiply supplication and petition, before the King, God, exalted and most high. Mention before Him, cause to be heard before Him, the Torah and the good deeds of [the Patriarchs and Matriarchs] who dwell in the dust.

May He remember their love and grant life to [their] offspring, that the remnant of Jacob not be lost. For the flock of the faithful shepherd [Moses] has become a disgrace; Israel, the unique nation, a parable and a simile.

Speedily, answer us, O God of our salvation, and redeem us from all harsh decrees; and may You save, in Your abundant mercy, Your righteous anointed and Your people.

מָרָן דִּבִשְׁמַיָּא *Our Master Who is in heaven, to You do we supplicate, as a captive supplicates before his captors; for all captives are redeemed with money, but Your people Israel with compassion and supplication. O grant our requests and our prayers that we not be turned away from You empty handed.*

Our Master Who is in heaven, to You do we supplicate, as a slave supplicates before his master: We are oppressed and we abide in darkness, souls embittered from abundant distress. We have no strength to regain Your favor. Our Master, act for the sake of the covenant that You made with our Patriarchs.

שׁוֹמֵר יִשְׂרָאֵל *O Guardian of Israel,* protect the remnant of Israel; let not Israel be destroyed — those who proclaim, 'Hear O Israel.'*[1]

O Guardian of the unique nation, protect the remnant of the unique people; let not the unique nation be destroyed — those who proclaim the Oneness of Your Name, 'HASHEM is our God, HASHEM, the One and Only!'[1]

O Guardian of the holy nation, protect the remnant of the holy people; let not the holy nation be destroyed — those who proclaim three-fold sanctifications to the Holy One.

Become favorable through compassion and become appeased through supplications. Become favorable and appeased to the poor generation, for there is no helper. Our Father, our King, be gracious with us and answer us, though we have no worthy deeds; treat us with charity and kindness, and save us.

---

(1) *Deuteronomy* 6:4.

Israel's importance to God. Israel deserves God's mercy because: (a) It continues to proclaim its allegiance to God by proclaiming the *Shema*; (b) Israel is unique in that it demonstrates to the world that God is One and Unique; and (c) like the angels, Israel praises and exalts God with the trebled proclamation of His holiness, i.e., *Kedushah*.

וַאֲנַחְנוּ לֹא נֵדַע מַה נַּעֲשֶׂה,* כִּי עָלֶיךָ עֵינֵינוּ.1 זְכֹר רַחֲמֶיךָ
יהוה וַחֲסָדֶיךָ, כִּי מֵעוֹלָם הֵמָּה.2 יְהִי חַסְדְּךָ יהוה
עָלֵינוּ, כַּאֲשֶׁר יִחַלְנוּ לָךְ.3 אַל תִּזְכָּר לָנוּ עֲוֹנֹת רִאשֹׁנִים, מַהֵר
יְקַדְּמוּנוּ רַחֲמֶיךָ, כִּי דַלּוֹנוּ מְאֹד.4 חָנֵּנוּ יהוה חָנֵּנוּ, כִּי רַב שָׂבַעְנוּ
בוּז.5 בְּרֹגֶז רַחֵם תִּזְכּוֹר.6 כִּי הוּא יָדַע יִצְרֵנוּ, זָכוּר כִּי עָפָר אֲנָחְנוּ.7
עָזְרֵנוּ אֱלֹהֵי יִשְׁעֵנוּ עַל דְּבַר כְּבוֹד שְׁמֶךָ, וְהַצִּילֵנוּ וְכַפֵּר עַל
חַטֹּאתֵינוּ לְמַעַן שְׁמֶךָ.8

קדיש שלם
The chazzan recites קַדִּישׁ שָׁלֵם:

יִתְגַּדַּל וְיִתְקַדַּשׁ שְׁמֵהּ רַבָּא. (.Cong – אָמֵן.) בְּעָלְמָא דִּי בְרָא
כִרְעוּתֵהּ, וְיַמְלִיךְ מַלְכוּתֵהּ, בְּחַיֵּיכוֹן וּבְיוֹמֵיכוֹן וּבְחַיֵּי
דְכָל בֵּית יִשְׂרָאֵל, בַּעֲגָלָא וּבִזְמַן קָרִיב. וְאִמְרוּ אָמֵן.
(.Cong – אָמֵן. יְהֵא שְׁמֵהּ רַבָּא מְבָרַךְ לְעָלַם וּלְעָלְמֵי עָלְמַיָּא.)
יְהֵא שְׁמֵהּ רַבָּא מְבָרַךְ לְעָלַם וּלְעָלְמֵי עָלְמַיָּא.
יִתְבָּרַךְ וְיִשְׁתַּבַּח וְיִתְפָּאַר וְיִתְרוֹמַם וְיִתְנַשֵּׂא וְיִתְהַדָּר וְיִתְעַלֶּה
וְיִתְהַלָּל שְׁמֵהּ דְּקוּדְשָׁא בְּרִיךְ הוּא (.Cong – בְּרִיךְ הוּא.) לְעֵלָּא מִן כָּל
בִּרְכָתָא וְשִׁירָתָא תֻּשְׁבְּחָתָא וְנֶחֱמָתָא, דַּאֲמִירָן בְּעָלְמָא. וְאִמְרוּ:
אָמֵן. (.Cong – אָמֵן.)
(.Cong – קַבֵּל בְּרַחֲמִים וּבְרָצוֹן אֶת תְּפִלָּתֵנוּ.)
תִּתְקַבֵּל צְלוֹתְהוֹן וּבָעוּתְהוֹן דְּכָל (בֵּית) יִשְׂרָאֵל קֳדָם אֲבוּהוֹן
דִּי בִשְׁמַיָּא. וְאִמְרוּ אָמֵן. (.Cong – אָמֵן.)
(.Cong – יְהִי שֵׁם יהוה מְבֹרָךְ, מֵעַתָּה וְעַד עוֹלָם.9)
יְהֵא שְׁלָמָא רַבָּא מִן שְׁמַיָּא וְחַיִּים עָלֵינוּ וְעַל כָּל יִשְׂרָאֵל.
וְאִמְרוּ אָמֵן. (.Cong – אָמֵן.)
(.Cong – עֶזְרִי מֵעִם יהוה, עֹשֵׂה שָׁמַיִם וָאָרֶץ.10)

Take three steps back. Bow left and say, עֹשֶׂה . . . ; bow right and say, הוּא יַעֲשֶׂה . . . ;
bow forward and say, וְעַל כָּל . . . אָמֵן.
Remain standing in place for a few moments, then take three steps forward.

עֹשֶׂה שָׁלוֹם בִּמְרוֹמָיו, הוּא יַעֲשֶׂה שָׁלוֹם עָלֵינוּ, וְעַל כָּל
יִשְׂרָאֵל. וְאִמְרוּ אָמֵן. (.Cong – אָמֵן.)

וֹּיֵשׁ וַאֲנַחְנוּ לֹא נֵדַע מַה נַּעֲשֶׂה — *We know not
what to do.* We have prayed in every pos-
sible manner — sitting, standing, and putting
our heads down in supplication. Moses, too,
prayed in these three postures. Now, we beg

of God to help, for 'we know not what else
we can do.' To allude to this thought it is
customary to sit while reciting the first three
words of this prayer and then to stand (*Abudraham*).

וַאֲנַחְנוּ *We know not what to do* — but our eyes are upon You.*[1]
*Remember Your mercies, HASHEM, and Your kindnesses, for
they are from the beginning of the world.*[2] *May Your kindness be upon
us, HASHEM, just as we awaited You.*[3] *Recall not against us the iniquities
of the ancients; may Your mercies meet us swiftly, for we have become
exceedingly impoverished.**[4] *Be gracious to us, HASHEM, be gracious to us,
for we are abundantly sated with scorn.*[5] *Amid rage — remember to be
merciful!*[6] *For He knew our nature, He remembers that we are dust.*[7]
*Chazzan— Assist us, O God of our salvation, for the sake of Your Name's
glory; rescue us and atone for our sins for Your Name's sake.*[8]

FULL KADDISH

The *chazzan* recites the Full Kaddish:

יִתְגַּדַּל *May His great Name grow exalted and sanctified* (Cong. —
Amen.) *in the world that He created as He willed. May He give
reign to His kingship in your lifetimes and in your days, and in the
lifetimes of the entire Family of Israel, swiftly and soon. Now respond:
Amen.*

(Cong. — Amen. May His great Name be blessed forever and ever.)
May His great Name be blessed forever and ever.

*Blessed, praised, glorified, exalted, extolled, mighty, upraised and
lauded be the Name of the Holy One, Blessed is He* (Cong. — *Blessed is He.*)
*beyond any blessing and song, praise, and consolation that are uttered in
the world. Now respond: Amen.* (Cong. — *Amen.*)

(Cong. — Accept our prayers with mercy and favor.)
*May the prayers and supplications of the entire House of Israel be
accepted before their Father Who is in Heaven. Now respond: Amen.*
(Cong. — *Amen.*)

(Cong. — Blessed be the Name of HASHEM from this time and forever.[9]*)*
*May there be abundant peace from Heaven, and life, upon us and upon
all Israel. Now respond: Amen.* (Cong. — *Amen.*)

(Cong. — My help is from HASHEM, Maker of heaven and earth.[10]*)*

Take three steps back. Bow left and say, 'He Who makes peace . . .'; bow right and say,
'may He make peace . . .'; bow forward and say, 'and upon all Israel . . .'
Remain standing in place for a few moments, then take three steps forward.

*He Who makes peace in His heights, may He make peace upon us, and
upon all Israel. Now respond: Amen.* (Cong. — *Amen.*)

---

(1) *II Chronicles* 20:12. (2) *Psalms* 25:6. (3) 33:22. (4) 79:8. (5) 123:3.
(6) *Habakkuk* 3:2. (7) *Psalms* 103:14. (8) 79:9. (9) 113:2. (10) 121:2.

Alternatively: We are like orphaned children
who depend totally on their guardian. Similarly,
we look to God for His help and mercy,
recognizing that only He can rescue us from our
plight (*Etz Yosef*).

כִּי דַלּוֹנוּ מְאֹד — *For we have become exceedingly
impoverished.* The prayer concludes with the
plea that we have already suffered mightily and
that God in His mercy knows that we are
helpless without Him.

❊ יוֹם שֵׁנִי ❊

אַשְׁרֵי יוֹשְׁבֵי בֵיתֶךָ, עוֹד יְהַלְלוּךָ סֶּלָה.[1] אַשְׁרֵי הָעָם שֶׁכָּכָה
לּוֹ, אַשְׁרֵי הָעָם שֶׁיהוה אֱלֹהָיו.[2]

תהלים קמה

תְּהִלָּה לְדָוִד,

אֲרוֹמִמְךָ אֱלוֹהַי הַמֶּלֶךְ, וַאֲבָרְכָה שִׁמְךָ לְעוֹלָם וָעֶד.

בְּכָל יוֹם אֲבָרְכֶךָ, וַאֲהַלְלָה שִׁמְךָ לְעוֹלָם וָעֶד.

גָּדוֹל יהוה וּמְהֻלָּל מְאֹד, וְלִגְדֻלָּתוֹ אֵין חֵקֶר.

דּוֹר לְדוֹר יְשַׁבַּח מַעֲשֶׂיךָ, וּגְבוּרֹתֶיךָ יַגִּידוּ.

הֲדַר כְּבוֹד הוֹדֶךָ, וְדִבְרֵי נִפְלְאֹתֶיךָ אָשִׂיחָה.

וֶעֱזוּז נוֹרְאֹתֶיךָ יֹאמֵרוּ, וּגְדֻלָּתְךָ אֲסַפְּרֶנָּה.

זֵכֶר רַב טוּבְךָ יַבִּיעוּ, וְצִדְקָתְךָ יְרַנֵּנוּ.

חַנּוּן וְרַחוּם יהוה, אֶרֶךְ אַפַּיִם וּגְדָל חָסֶד.

טוֹב יהוה לַכֹּל, וְרַחֲמָיו עַל כָּל מַעֲשָׂיו.

יוֹדוּךָ יהוה כָּל מַעֲשֶׂיךָ, וַחֲסִידֶיךָ יְבָרְכוּכָה.

כְּבוֹד מַלְכוּתְךָ יֹאמֵרוּ, וּגְבוּרָתְךָ יְדַבֵּרוּ.

לְהוֹדִיעַ לִבְנֵי הָאָדָם גְּבוּרֹתָיו, וּכְבוֹד הֲדַר מַלְכוּתוֹ.

מַלְכוּתְךָ מַלְכוּת כָּל עֹלָמִים, וּמֶמְשַׁלְתְּךָ בְּכָל דּוֹר וָדֹר.

סוֹמֵךְ יהוה לְכָל הַנֹּפְלִים, וְזוֹקֵף לְכָל הַכְּפוּפִים.

עֵינֵי כֹל אֵלֶיךָ יְשַׂבֵּרוּ, וְאַתָּה נוֹתֵן לָהֶם אֶת אָכְלָם בְּעִתּוֹ.

Concentrate intently while
reciting the verse, פּוֹתֵחַ.

פּוֹתֵחַ אֶת יָדֶךָ, וּמַשְׂבִּיעַ לְכָל חַי רָצוֹן.

❖ צַדִּיק יהוה בְּכָל דְּרָכָיו, וְחָסִיד בְּכָל מַעֲשָׂיו.

קָרוֹב יהוה לְכָל קֹרְאָיו, לְכֹל אֲשֶׁר יִקְרָאֻהוּ בֶאֱמֶת.

רְצוֹן יְרֵאָיו יַעֲשֶׂה, וְאֶת שַׁוְעָתָם יִשְׁמַע וְיוֹשִׁיעֵם.

שׁוֹמֵר יהוה אֶת כָּל אֹהֲבָיו, וְאֵת כָּל הָרְשָׁעִים יַשְׁמִיד.

תְּהִלַּת יהוה יְדַבֶּר פִּי, וִיבָרֵךְ כָּל בָּשָׂר שֵׁם קָדְשׁוֹ לְעוֹלָם וָעֶד.

וַאֲנַחְנוּ נְבָרֵךְ יָהּ, מֵעַתָּה וְעַד עוֹלָם, הַלְלוּיָהּ.[3]

The chazzan recites חֲצִי קַדִּישׁ.

יִתְגַּדַּל וְיִתְקַדַּשׁ שְׁמֵהּ רַבָּא. (Cong.– אָמֵן.) בְּעָלְמָא דִּי בְרָא כִרְעוּתֵהּ.
וְיַמְלִיךְ מַלְכוּתֵהּ, בְּחַיֵּיכוֹן וּבְיוֹמֵיכוֹן וּבְחַיֵּי דְכָל בֵּית יִשְׂרָאֵל,
בַּעֲגָלָא וּבִזְמַן קָרִיב. וְאִמְרוּ: אָמֵן.

(Cong.– אָמֵן. יְהֵא שְׁמֵהּ רַבָּא מְבָרַךְ לְעָלַם וּלְעָלְמֵי עָלְמַיָּא.)

יְהֵא שְׁמֵהּ רַבָּא מְבָרַךְ לְעָלַם וּלְעָלְמֵי עָלְמַיָּא.

יִתְבָּרַךְ וְיִשְׁתַּבַּח וְיִתְפָּאַר וְיִתְרוֹמַם וְיִתְנַשֵּׂא וְיִתְהַדָּר וְיִתְעַלֶּה וְיִתְהַלָּל
שְׁמֵהּ דְּקֻדְשָׁא בְּרִיךְ הוּא (Cong.– בְּרִיךְ הוּא) לְעֵלָּא מִן כָּל בִּרְכָתָא וְשִׁירָתָא
תֻּשְׁבְּחָתָא וְנֶחֱמָתָא, דַּאֲמִירָן בְּעָלְמָא. וְאִמְרוּ: אָמֵן. (Cong.– אָמֵן.)

⊰ SECOND DAY ⊱

אַשְׁרֵי *Praiseworthy are those who dwell in Your house; may they always praise You, Selah!*[1] *Praiseworthy is the people for whom this is so, praiseworthy is the people whose God is* HASHEM.[2]

Psalm 145   *A psalm of praise by David:*

א *I will exalt You, my God the King, and I will bless Your Name forever and ever.*

ב *Every day I will bless You, and I will laud Your Name forever and ever.*

ג HASHEM *is great and exceedingly lauded,*
and His greatness is beyond investigation.

ד *Each generation will praise Your deeds to the next*
and of Your mighty deeds they will tell;

ה *The splendrous glory of Your power and Your wondrous deeds I shall discuss.*

ו *And of Your awesome power they will speak, and Your greatness I shall relate.*

ז *A recollection of Your abundant goodness they will utter*
and of Your righteousness they will sing exultantly.

ח *Gracious and merciful is* HASHEM,
slow to anger, and great in [bestowing] kindness.

ט HASHEM *is good to all; His mercies are on all His works.*

י *All Your works shall thank You,* HASHEM, *and Your devout ones will bless You.*

כ *Of the glory of Your kingdom they will speak, and of Your power they will tell;*

ל *To inform human beings of His mighty deeds,*
and the glorious splendor of His kingdom.

מ *Your kingdom is a kingdom spanning all eternities,*
and Your dominion is throughout every generation.

ס HASHEM *supports all the fallen ones and straightens all the bent.*

ע *The eyes of all look to You with hope*
and You give them their food in its proper time;

פ *You open Your hand,*   Concentrate intently while reciting the verse, 'You open. . .'
and satisfy the desire of every living thing.

צ Chazzan – *Righteous is* HASHEM *in all His ways*
and magnanimous in all His deeds.

ק HASHEM *is close to all who call upon Him — to all who call upon Him sincerely.*

ר *The will of those who fear Him He will do;*
and their cry He will hear, and save them.

ש HASHEM *protects all who love Him; but all the wicked He will destroy.*

ת *May my mouth declare the praise of* HASHEM
and may all flesh bless His Holy Name forever and ever.

We will bless God from this time and forever, Halleluyah![3]

The *chazzan* recites Half-*Kaddish:*

יִתְגַּדַּל *May His great Name grow exalted and sanctified* (Cong.— *Amen.*) *in the world that He created as He willed. May He give reign to His kingship in your lifetimes and in your days, and in the lifetimes of the entire Family of Israel, swiftly and soon. Now respond: Amen.*

(Cong.— *Amen. May His great Name be blessed forever and ever.*)

May His great Name be blessed forever and ever.

Blessed, praised, glorified, exalted, extolled, mighty, upraised, and lauded be the Name of the Holy One, Blessed is He (Cong.— *Blessed is He*) *— beyond any blessing and song, praise and consolation that are uttered in the world. Now respond: Amen.* (Cong.— *Amen.*)

---

(1) *Psalms* 84:5. (2) 144:15. (3) 115:18.

All:

לְךָ יהוה הַצְּדָקָה, וְלָנוּ בְּשֶׁת הַפָּנִים.[1] מַה נִּתְאוֹנֵן,[2] מַה נֹּאמַר, מַה נְּדַבֵּר, וּמַה נִּצְטַדָּק.[3] נַחְפְּשָׂה דְרָכֵינוּ וְנַחְקֹרָה, וְנָשׁוּבָה אֵלֶיךָ,[4] כִּי יְמִינְךָ פְשׁוּטָה לְקַבֵּל שָׁבִים. לֹא בְחֶסֶד וְלֹא בְמַעֲשִׂים בָּאנוּ לְפָנֶיךָ, כַּדַּלִּים וּכְרָשִׁים דָּפַקְנוּ דְלָתֶיךָ. דְּלָתֶיךָ דָּפַקְנוּ רַחוּם וְחַנּוּן, נָא אַל תְּשִׁיבֵנוּ רֵיקָם מִלְּפָנֶיךָ. מִלְּפָנֶיךָ מַלְכֵּנוּ רֵיקָם אַל תְּשִׁיבֵנוּ, כִּי אַתָּה שׁוֹמֵעַ תְּפִלָּה.

שֹׁמֵעַ תְּפִלָּה, עָדֶיךָ כָּל בָּשָׂר יָבֹאוּ.[5] יָבוֹא כָל בָּשָׂר לְהִשְׁתַּחֲוֹת לְפָנֶיךָ יהוה.[6] יָבֹאוּ וְיִשְׁתַּחֲווּ לְפָנֶיךָ אֲדֹנָי, וִיכַבְּדוּ לִשְׁמֶךָ.[7] בֹּאוּ נִשְׁתַּחֲוֶה וְנִכְרָעָה, נִבְרְכָה לִפְנֵי יהוה עֹשֵׂנוּ.[8] נָבוֹאָה לְמִשְׁכְּנוֹתָיו, נִשְׁתַּחֲוֶה לַהֲדֹם רַגְלָיו.[9] בֹּאוּ שְׁעָרָיו בְּתוֹדָה, חֲצֵרֹתָיו בִּתְהִלָּה, הוֹדוּ לוֹ בָּרְכוּ שְׁמוֹ.[10] רוֹמְמוּ יהוה אֱלֹהֵינוּ, וְהִשְׁתַּחֲווּ לַהֲדֹם רַגְלָיו, קָדוֹשׁ הוּא.[11] רוֹמְמוּ יהוה אֱלֹהֵינוּ, וְהִשְׁתַּחֲווּ לְהַר קָדְשׁוֹ, כִּי קָדוֹשׁ יהוה אֱלֹהֵינוּ.[12] הִשְׁתַּחֲווּ לַיהוה בְּהַדְרַת קֹדֶשׁ, חִילוּ מִפָּנָיו כָּל הָאָרֶץ.[13] וַאֲנַחְנוּ בְּרֹב חַסְדְּךָ נָבוֹא בֵיתֶךָ, נִשְׁתַּחֲוֶה אֶל הֵיכַל קָדְשְׁךָ בְּיִרְאָתֶךָ.[14] נִשְׁתַּחֲוֶה אֶל הֵיכַל קָדְשְׁךָ וְנוֹדֶה אֶת שְׁמֶךָ, עַל חַסְדְּךָ וְעַל אֲמִתֶּךָ, כִּי הִגְדַּלְתָּ עַל כָּל שִׁמְךָ אִמְרָתֶךָ.[15] לְכוּ נְרַנְּנָה לַיהוה, נָרִיעָה לְצוּר יִשְׁעֵנוּ. נְקַדְּמָה פָנָיו בְּתוֹדָה, בִּזְמִרוֹת נָרִיעַ לוֹ.[16] אֲשֶׁר יַחְדָּו נַמְתִּיק סוֹד, בְּבֵית אֱלֹהִים נְהַלֵּךְ בְּרָגֶשׁ.[17] אֵל נַעֲרָץ בְּסוֹד קְדֹשִׁים רַבָּה, וְנוֹרָא עַל כָּל סְבִיבָיו.[18] שְׂאוּ יְדֵיכֶם קֹדֶשׁ וּבָרְכוּ אֶת יהוה.[19] הִנֵּה בָּרְכוּ אֶת יהוה כָּל עַבְדֵי יהוה, הָעֹמְדִים בְּבֵית יהוה בַּלֵּילוֹת.[20] אֲשֶׁר מִי אֵל בַּשָּׁמַיִם וּבָאָרֶץ, אֲשֶׁר יַעֲשֶׂה כְמַעֲשֶׂיךָ וְכִגְבוּרֹתֶיךָ.[21] אֲשֶׁר לוֹ הַיָּם וְהוּא עָשָׂהוּ, וְיַבֶּשֶׁת יָדָיו יָצָרוּ.[22] אֲשֶׁר בְּיָדוֹ מֶחְקְרֵי אָרֶץ, וְתוֹעֲפוֹת הָרִים לוֹ.[23] אֲשֶׁר בְּיָדוֹ נֶפֶשׁ כָּל חָי, וְרוּחַ כָּל בְּשַׂר אִישׁ.[24] וְיוֹדוּ שָׁמַיִם פִּלְאֲךָ יהוה, אַף אֱמוּנָתְךָ בִּקְהַל קְדֹשִׁים.[25] לְךָ זְרוֹעַ עִם גְּבוּרָה, תָּעֹז יָדְךָ תָּרוּם יְמִינֶךָ.[26] לְךָ שָׁמַיִם, אַף לְךָ אָרֶץ, תֵּבֵל וּמְלֹאָהּ אַתָּה יְסַדְתָּם.[27] אַתָּה פוֹרַרְתָּ בְעָזְּךָ יָם, שִׁבַּרְתָּ רָאשֵׁי תַנִּינִים עַל הַמָּיִם.[28] אַתָּה הִצַּבְתָּ כָּל גְּבוּלוֹת אָרֶץ, קַיִץ וָחֹרֶף

(1) *Daniel* 9:7. (2) Cf. *Lamentations* 3:39. (3) Cf. *Genesis* 44:16. (4) Cf. *Lamentations* 3:40.
(5) *Psalms* 65:3. (6) Cf. *Isaiah* 66:23. (7) *Psalms* 86:9. (8) 95:6. (9) 132:7. (10) 100:4.
(11) 99:5. (12) 99:9. (13) 96:9. (14) Cf. 5:8. (15) Cf. 138:2. (16) 95:1-2. (17) 55:15. (18) 89:8.
(19) 134:2. (20) 134:1. (21) *Deuteronomy* 3:24. (22) *Psalms* 95:5. (23) 95:4. (24) *Job* 12:10.
(25) *Psalms* 89:6. (26) 89:14. (27) 89:12. (28) 74:13.

All:

לְךָ ה׳ Yours, my Lord, is the righteousness and ours is the shame-
facedness.[1] What complaint can we make?[2] What can we say?
What can we declare? What justification can we offer?[3] Let us examine
our ways and analyze — and return to You,[4] for Your right hand is
extended to accept penitents. Neither with kindness nor with [good]
deeds do we come before You. As paupers and as beggars do we knock
at Your doors. At Your doors we knock, O Compassionate and Gracious
One. Please do not turn us away from You empty-handed. Our King,
turn us not away from You empty-handed, for You are the One Who
hears prayer.

שֹׁמֵעַ תְּפִלָּה You Who hears prayer, to You all flesh will come.[5] All
flesh will come to prostrate itself before You, O
HASHEM.[6] They will come and prostrate themselves before You, my Lord,
and shall honor Your Name.[7] Come! — let us prostrate ourselves and
bow, let us kneel before God, our Maker.[8] Let us come to His dwelling
places, let us prostrate ourselves at His footstool.[9] Enter His gates with
thanksgiving, His courts with praise; give thanks to Him, praise His
Name.[10] Exalt HASHEM, our God, and bow at His footstool; He is holy![11]
Exalt HASHEM, our God, and bow at His holy mountain; for holy is
HASHEM, our God.[12] Prostrate yourselves before HASHEM in His intensely
holy place, tremble before Him, everyone on earth.[13] As for us, through
Your abundant kindness we will enter Your House; we will prostrate
ourselves toward Your Holy Sanctuary in awe of You.[14] We will
prostrate ourselves toward Your Holy Sanctuary, and we will give
thanks to Your Name for Your kindness and truth for You have exalted
Your promise even beyond Your Name.[15] Come! — let us sing to HASHEM,
let us call out to the Rock of our salvation. Let us greet Him with
thanksgiving, with praiseful songs let us call out to Him.[16] For together
let us share sweet counsel, in the house of God let us walk in
multitudes.[17] God is dreaded in the hiddenmost counsel of the holy ones,
and inspires awe upon all who surround Him.[18] Lift your hands in the
Sanctuary and bless HASHEM.[19] Behold, bless HASHEM, all you servants of
HASHEM, who stand in the House of HASHEM in the nights.[20] For what
power is there in heaven or earth that can approximate Your deeds and
power?[21] For His is the sea and He perfected the dry land — His hands
fashioned it.[22] For in His power are the hidden mysteries of the earth,
and the mountain summits are His.[23] For His is the soul of every living
thing, and the spirit of all human flesh.[24] Heaven will gratefully praise
Your wonders, HASHEM; also Your faithfulness in the assembly of
holy ones.[25] Yours is a mighty arm with power, You strengthen Your
hand; You exalt Your right hand.[26] Yours is the heaven; Yours, too, is the
earth; the world and its fullness — You founded them.[27] You shattered
the sea with Your might, You smashed sea serpents' heads upon the
water.[28] You established all the boundaries of earth; summer and winter

אַתָּה יְצַרְתָּם.[1] אַתָּה רִצַּצְתָּ רָאשֵׁי לִוְיָתָן, תִּתְּנֶנּוּ מַאֲכָל לְעַם לְצִיִּים. אַתָּה בָקַעְתָּ מַעְיָן וָנָחַל, אַתָּה הוֹבַשְׁתָּ נַהֲרוֹת אֵיתָן.[2] לְךָ יוֹם, אַף לְךָ לָיְלָה, אַתָּה הֲכִינוֹתָ מָאוֹר וָשָׁמֶשׁ.[3] עָשָׂה גְדֹלוֹת עַד אֵין חֵקֶר, וְנִפְלָאוֹת עַד אֵין מִסְפָּר.[4] כִּי אֵל גָּדוֹל יְהוָה, וּמֶלֶךְ גָּדוֹל עַל כָּל אֱלֹהִים.[5] כִּי גָדוֹל אַתָּה וְעֹשֵׂה נִפְלָאוֹת, אַתָּה אֱלֹהִים לְבַדֶּךָ.[6] כִּי גָדוֹל מֵעַל שָׁמַיִם חַסְדֶּךָ, וְעַד שְׁחָקִים אֲמִתֶּךָ.[7] גָּדוֹל יְהוָה וּמְהֻלָּל מְאֹד, וְלִגְדֻלָּתוֹ אֵין חֵקֶר.[8] (כִּי) גָּדוֹל יְהוָה וּמְהֻלָּל מְאֹד, נוֹרָא הוּא עַל כָּל אֱלֹהִים.[9] גָּדוֹל יְהוָה וּמְהֻלָּל מְאֹד, בְּעִיר אֱלֹהֵינוּ הַר קָדְשׁוֹ.[10] לְךָ יְהוָה הַגְּדֻלָּה וְהַגְּבוּרָה, וְהַתִּפְאֶרֶת וְהַנֵּצַח וְהַהוֹד, כִּי כֹל בַּשָּׁמַיִם וּבָאָרֶץ; לְךָ יְהוָה הַמַּמְלָכָה, וְהַמִּתְנַשֵּׂא לְכֹל לְרֹאשׁ.[11] מִי לֹא יִרָאֲךָ מֶלֶךְ הַגּוֹיִם, כִּי לְךָ יָאָתָה, כִּי בְכָל חַכְמֵי הַגּוֹיִם וּבְכָל מַלְכוּתָם מֵאֵין כָּמוֹךָ.[12] מֵאֵין כָּמוֹךָ יְהוָה, גָּדוֹל אַתָּה וְגָדוֹל שִׁמְךָ בִּגְבוּרָה.[13] יְהוָה אֱלֹהֵי צְבָאוֹת, מִי כָמוֹךָ חֲסִין יָהּ, וֶאֱמוּנָתְךָ סְבִיבוֹתֶיךָ.[14] יְהוָה צְבָאוֹת, אֱלֹהֵי יִשְׂרָאֵל, יוֹשֵׁב הַכְּרֻבִים, אַתָּה הוּא הָאֱלֹהִים לְבַדֶּךָ.[15] מִי יְמַלֵּל גְּבוּרוֹת יְהוָה, יַשְׁמִיעַ כָּל תְּהִלָּתוֹ.[16] כִּי מִי בַשַּׁחַק יַעֲרֹךְ לַיהוָה, יִדְמֶה לַיהוָה בִּבְנֵי אֵלִים.[17] מַה נֹּאמַר לְפָנֶיךָ יוֹשֵׁב מָרוֹם, וּמַה נְּסַפֵּר לְפָנֶיךָ שֹׁכֵן שְׁחָקִים. מַה נֹּאמַר לְפָנֶיךָ יְהוָה אֱלֹהֵינוּ, מַה נְּדַבֵּר וּמַה נִּצְטַדָּק.[18] אֵין לָנוּ פֶּה לְהָשִׁיב וְלֹא מֵצַח לְהָרִים רֹאשׁ, כִּי עֲווֹנוֹתֵינוּ רַבּוּ מִלִּמְנוֹת, וְחַטֹּאתֵינוּ עָצְמוּ מִסַּפֵּר.[19] לְמַעַן שִׁמְךָ יְהוָה תְּחַיֵּנוּ, וּבְצִדְקָתְךָ תּוֹצִיא מִצָּרָה נַפְשֵׁנוּ.[20] דַּרְכְּךָ אֱלֹהֵינוּ לְהַאֲרִיךְ אַפֶּךָ, לָרָעִים וְלַטּוֹבִים, וְהִיא תְהִלָּתֶךָ. לְמַעַנְךָ אֱלֹהֵינוּ עֲשֵׂה וְלֹא לָנוּ, רְאֵה עֲמִידָתֵנוּ, דַּלִּים וְרֵקִים. ❖ הַנְּשָׁמָה לָךְ וְהַגּוּף פָּעֳלָךְ, חוּסָה עַל עֲמָלָךְ. הַנְּשָׁמָה לָךְ וְהַגּוּף שֶׁלָּךְ, יְהוָה עֲשֵׂה לְמַעַן שְׁמֶךָ. אָתָאנוּ עַל שִׁמְךָ, יְהוָה, עֲשֵׂה לְמַעַן שְׁמֶךָ. בַּעֲבוּר כְּבוֹד שִׁמְךָ, כִּי אֵל חַנּוּן וְרַחוּם שְׁמֶךָ. לְמַעַן שִׁמְךָ יְהוָה, וְסָלַחְתָּ לַעֲוֹנֵנוּ כִּי רַב הוּא.[21]

Congregation, then chazzan:

סְלַח לָנוּ אָבִינוּ, כִּי בְרוֹב אִוַּלְתֵּנוּ שָׁגִינוּ,
מְחַל לָנוּ מַלְכֵּנוּ, כִּי רַבּוּ עֲוֹנֵינוּ.

— *You fashioned them.*[1] *You crushed the heads of Leviathan, You served it as food to the nation of legions. You split open fountain and stream, You dried the mighty rivers.*[2] *Yours is the day, Yours as well is the night; You established luminary and the sun.*[3] *Who performs great deeds that are beyond comprehension, and wonders beyond number.*[4] *For a great God is* HASHEM, *and a great King above all heavenly powers.*[5] *For You are great and work wonders; You alone, O God.*[6] *For great above the very heavens is Your kindness, and until the upper heights is Your truth.*[7] HASHEM *is great and exceedingly lauded, and His greatness is beyond investigation.*[8] *(For)* HASHEM *is great and exceedingly lauded, awesome is He above all heavenly powers.*[9] *Great is* HASHEM *and exceedingly lauded, in the city of our God, Mount of His Holiness.*[10] *Yours,* HASHEM, *is the greatness, the strength, the splendor, the triumph, and the glory; even everything in heaven and earth; Yours,* HASHEM, *is the kingdom, and sovereignty over every leader.*[11] *Who would not revere You, O King of nations?* — *for this befits You, for among all the sages of the nations and in all their kingdom there is none like You.*[12] *There is none like You, O* HASHEM, *You are great and Your Name is great with power.*[13] HASHEM, *God of Legions* — *who is like You, O Strong One, God?* — *and Your faithfulness surrounds You.*[14] HASHEM, *Master of Legions, God of Israel, enthroned upon the Cherubim, it is You alone Who is God.*[15] *Who can express the mighty acts of* HASHEM, *who can announce all His praise?*[16] *For who in the sky can be compared to* HASHEM; *be likened to* HASHEM *among the angels?*[17] *What can we say before You Who dwell on high? And what can we relate to You Who abide in the highest heaven? What can we say before You,* HASHEM, *our God? What can we declare? What justification can we offer?*[18] *We have neither mouth to respond nor brow to raise our head, for our iniquities are too numerous to count, and our sins are too vast to be numbered.*[19] *For Your Name's sake,* HASHEM, *revive us; and with Your righteousness remove our soul from distress.*[20] *It is Your way, our God, to delay Your anger, against people both evil and good* — *and this is Your praise. Act for Your sake, our God, and not for ours, behold our [spiritual] position* — *destitute and emptyhanded.* Chazzan — *The soul is Yours and the body is Your handiwork; take pity on Your labor. The soul is Yours and the body is Yours; O* HASHEM, *act for Your Name's sake. We have come with reliance on Your Name, O* HASHEM, *act for Your Name's sake; because of Your Name's glory* — *for 'Gracious and Merciful God' is Your Name. For Your Name's sake,* HASHEM, *may You forgive our iniquity, though it is abundant.*[21]

Congregation, then chazzan:

Forgive us, our Father, for in our abundant folly we have erred, pardon us, our King, for our iniquities are many.

(1) *Psalms* 74:17. (2) 74:14-15. (3) 74:16. (4) *Job* 9:10. (5) *Psalms* 95:3.
(6) 86:10. (7) 108:5. (8) 145:3. (9) 96:4. (10) 48:2. (11) *I Chronicles* 29:11.
(12) *Jeremiah* 10:7. (13) 10:6. (14) *Psalms* 89:9. (15) *Isaiah* 37:16. (16) *Psalms* 106:2.
(17) 89:7. (18) Cf. *Genesis* 44:16. (19) Cf. *Ezra* 9:6. (20) Cf. *Psalms* 143:11. (21) Cf. 25:11.

All, while standing:

אֵל אֶרֶךְ אַפַּיִם אַתָּה, וּבַעַל הָרַחֲמִים נִקְרֵאתָ,
וְדֶרֶךְ תְּשׁוּבָה הוֹרֵיתָ.

גְּדֻלַּת רַחֲמֶיךָ וַחֲסָדֶיךָ, תִּזְכּוֹר הַיּוֹם וּבְכָל יוֹם לְזֶרַע יְדִידֶיךָ.

תֵּפֶן אֵלֵינוּ בְּרַחֲמִים, כִּי אַתָּה הוּא בַּעַל הָרַחֲמִים.

בְּתַחֲנוּן וּבִתְפִלָּה פָּנֶיךָ נְקַדֵּם, כְּהוֹדַעְתָּ לֶעָנָיו מִקֶּדֶם.

מֵחֲרוֹן אַפְּךָ שׁוּב,[1] כְּמוֹ בְתוֹרָתְךָ כָּתוּב.[2]

וּבְצֵל כְּנָפֶיךָ נֶחֱסֶה[3] וְנִתְלוֹנָן, כְּיוֹם וַיֵּרֶד יהוה בֶּעָנָן.

❖ תַּעֲבוֹר עַל פֶּשַׁע וְתִמְחֶה אָשָׁם, כְּיוֹם וַיִּתְיַצֵּב עִמּוֹ שָׁם.

תַּאֲזִין שַׁוְעָתֵנוּ וְתַקְשִׁיב מֶנּוּ מַאֲמָר,
כְּיוֹם וַיִּקְרָא בְשֵׁם יהוה,[4] וְשָׁם נֶאֱמַר:

Congregation, then *chazzan*:

וַיַּעֲבֹר יהוה עַל פָּנָיו וַיִּקְרָא:

Congregation and *chazzan* (the words in bold type are recited aloud and in unison):

**יהוה, יהוה, אֵל, רַחוּם, וְחַנּוּן, אֶרֶךְ אַפַּיִם, וְרַב חֶסֶד,
וֶאֱמֶת, נֹצֵר חֶסֶד לָאֲלָפִים, נֹשֵׂא עָוֹן, וָפֶשַׁע,
וְחַטָּאָה, וְנַקֵּה.**[5] וְסָלַחְתָּ לַעֲוֹנֵנוּ וּלְחַטָּאתֵנוּ וּנְחַלְתָּנוּ.[6] סְלַח לָנוּ
אָבִינוּ כִּי חָטָאנוּ, מְחַל לָנוּ מַלְכֵּנוּ כִּי פָשָׁעְנוּ. כִּי אַתָּה אֲדֹנָי טוֹב
וְסַלָּח, וְרַב חֶסֶד לְכָל קֹרְאֶיךָ.[7]

פסוקי הקדמה לסליחה ה

אִם עֲוֹנֵינוּ עָנוּ בָנוּ יהוה עֲשֵׂה לְמַעַן שְׁמֶךָ.[8] יהוה אֱלֹהִים
סְלַח נָא לַעֲוֹן יַעֲקֹב כִּי קָטֹן הוּא.[9] כִּי שָׁחָה
לֶעָפָר נַפְשֵׁנוּ, דָּבְקָה לָאָרֶץ בִּטְנֵנוּ.[10] עוּרָה לָמָּה תִישַׁן, אֲדֹנָי,
הָקִיצָה, אַל תִּזְנַח לָנֶצַח.[11] וְעַתָּה יִגְדַּל נָא כֹּחַ אֲדֹנָי, כַּאֲשֶׁר
דִּבַּרְתָּ לֵאמֹר.*[12]

כְּרַחֵם אָב עַל בָּנִים, כֵּן תְּרַחֵם יהוה עָלֵינוּ.[13] לַיהוה הַיְשׁוּעָה,
עַל עַמְּךָ בִרְכָתֶךָ סֶּלָה.[14] יהוה צְבָאוֹת עִמָּנוּ,
מִשְׂגָּב לָנוּ אֱלֹהֵי יַעֲקֹב סֶלָה.[15] יהוה צְבָאוֹת, אַשְׁרֵי אָדָם בֹּטֵחַ
בָּךְ.[16] יהוה הוֹשִׁיעָה, הַמֶּלֶךְ יַעֲנֵנוּ בְיוֹם קָרְאֵנוּ.[17]

וְעַתָּה ... לֵאמֹר — *And now ... [ordaining the
Thirteen Attributes] to be said.* In the Torah, this   verse is part of Moses' prayer for forgiveness after
the nation accepted the spies' slander about *Eretz*

All, while standing:

אֵל אֶרֶךְ אַפַּיִם *O God — You are slow to anger, You are called the Master of Mercy, and You have taught the way of repentance. May You remember this day and every day the greatness of Your mercy and Your kindness to the offspring of Your beloved Ones. Turn to us in mercy for You are the Master of Mercy. With supplication and prayer we approach Your Presence in the manner that You made known to the humble [Moses] in ancient times. Turn back from Your fierce anger;[1] as is written in Your Torah.[2] In the shadow of Your wings may we find shelter[3] and lodging as on the day 'HASHEM descended in a cloud' [to appear to Moses on Sinai].* Chazzan — *Overlook sin and erase guilt as on the day 'He [God] stood there with him [Moses].' Give heed to our cry and be attentive to our declaration as on the day 'He called out with the Name HASHEM,'[4] and there it was said:*

Congregation, then chazzan:

And HASHEM passed before him [Moses] and proclaimed:

Congregation and chazzan (the words in bold type are recited aloud and in unison):

ה' ה' **HASHEM, HASHEM, God, Compassionate and Gracious, Slow to anger, and Abundant in Kindness and Truth, Preserver of kindness for thousands [of generations], Forgiver of iniquity, willful sin, and error, and Who cleanses.**[5] *May You forgive our iniquities and our errors and make us Your heritage.[6] Forgive us, our Father, for we have erred; pardon us, our King, for we have willfully sinned; for You, my Lord, are good and forgiving and abundantly kind to all who call upon You.[7]*

PREFATORY VERSES TO SELICHAH 5

אִם עֲוֹנֵינוּ *Even if our iniquities bear witness against us, HASHEM, act for Your Name's sake.[8] HASHEM, God, please forgive Jacob's sin, for he is [a] small [people].[9] For prostrated to the dust is our soul, stuck to the earth is our belly.[10] Awaken! Why do You [seem to] sleep, O my Lord? Arouse Yourself! Forsake [us] not forever![11] And now, please let [the revelation of] my Lord's strength grow great, as You have spoken, [ordaining the Thirteen Attributes] to be said.*[12]*

כְּרַחֵם אָב *As a father has mercy on his children, so, HASHEM, may You have mercy on us.[13] Salvation is HASHEM's, upon Your people is Your blessing, Selah.[14] HASHEM, Master of Legions, is with us, a stronghold for us is the God of Jacob, Selah.[15] HASHEM, Master of Legions, praiseworthy is the person who trusts in You.[16] HASHEM, save! May the King answer us on the day we call.[17]*

---

(1) Cf. *Exodus* 32:12. (2) See 32:14. (3) Cf. *Psalms* 36:8. (4) *Exodus* 34:5. (5) 34:6-7. (6) 34:9.
(7) *Psalms* 86:5. (8) *Jeremiah* 14:7. (9) Cf. *Amos* 7:2. (10) *Psalms* 44:26. (11) 44:24.
(12) *Numbers* 14:17. (13) Cf. *Psalms* 103:13. (14) 3:9. (15) 46:8. (16) 84:13. (17) 20:10.

Yisrael. There (*Numbers* 14:17), it introduces an abridged version of the Attributes of Mercy.

Here, the reference is to the full version recited after each *selichah* prayer.

In some congregations the following two verses are recited responsively — the *chazzan* reciting סְלַח נָא, and the congregation responding וַיֹּאמֶר. In other congregations these verses are recited silently.

סְלַח נָא לַעֲוֹן הָעָם הַזֶּה כְּגֹדֶל חַסְדֶּךָ, וְכַאֲשֶׁר נָשָׂאתָה לָעָם הַזֶּה מִמִּצְרַיִם וְעַד הֵנָּה,[1] וְשָׁם נֶאֱמַר:

וַיֹּאמֶר יהוה סָלַחְתִּי כִּדְבָרֶךָ.[2]

All:

הַטֵּה אֱלֹהַי אָזְנְךָ וּשֲׁמָע, פְּקַח עֵינֶיךָ וּרְאֵה שֹׁמְמֹתֵינוּ, וְהָעִיר אֲשֶׁר נִקְרָא שִׁמְךָ עָלֶיהָ, כִּי לֹא עַל צִדְקֹתֵינוּ אֲנַחְנוּ מַפִּילִים תַּחֲנוּנֵינוּ לְפָנֶיךָ, כִּי עַל רַחֲמֶיךָ הָרַבִּים. אֲדֹנָי שְׁמָעָה, אֲדֹנָי סְלָחָה, אֲדֹנָי הַקְשִׁיבָה, וַעֲשֵׂה אַל תְּאַחַר, לְמַעַנְךָ אֱלֹהַי, כִּי שִׁמְךָ נִקְרָא עַל עִירְךָ וְעַל עַמֶּךָ.[3]

סליחה ה

All:

אֱלֹהֵינוּ וֵאלֹהֵי אֲבוֹתֵינוּ:

אִם עֲוֹנֵינוּ* רַבּוּ לְהַגְדִּיל,[4]   בָּנוּ עָנוּ[5] עֲבוֹת כְּגָדִיל,*

גָּרְמוּ לָנוּ בֵּינְתַיִם לְהַבְדִּיל,[6]   דַּרְכֵי רַחֲמֶיךָ לֹא תַחְדִּיל.

הִתְנַהֵג בְּמִדַּת חֶסֶד הַתְנִית,   וְאַתָּה הוּא שֶׁמִּקֶּדֶם הָיִיתָ,*

זְכֹר עֲדָתְךָ אֲשֶׁר קָנִיתָ,*[7]   חֵן שִׁירֵי בְכוֹר[8] כָּנִיתָ.

טְעַנְתָּנוּ גַּפֵּי קֶרֶת נְתוּנִים,   יִשַׁבְתָּנוּ שֵׁן סֶלַע אֵיתָנִים,*

כְּאֶחָד דְּכִיתָנוּ בִּמְקוֹם תַּנִּים,[9]   לִרְוָיָה צֵאת כַּמָּה מְתוּנִים.

מֵרֹב פְּקֻדוֹת וּבֶהָלָה מְחַלְחֶלֶת,   נָקְטָה נַפְשִׁי,*[10] לְעָפָר בּוֹחֶלֶת,

סְמֻכָה בֶּטֶן לָאָרֶץ[11] נִשְׁחֶלֶת,   עוֹרָה לָמָּה תִישַׁן[12] תּוֹחֶלֶת.

---

(1) *Numbers* 14:19. (2) 14:20. (3) *Daniel* 9:18-19. (4) Cf. *Ezra* 9:6. (5) Cf. *Jeremiah* 14:7. (6) Cf. *Isaiah* 59:2. (7) Cf. *Psalms* 74:2; some editions read, זְכֹר עֲדָתְךָ קֶדֶם קָנִיתָ, *Remember Your flock that You long ago acquired*. (8) See *Exodus* 4:22. (9) Cf. *Psalms* 44:20. (10) Some editions of *Selichos* read, נָקְטָה שָׁחָה נַפְשִׁי, *My soul is bent, it is in turmoil*; some read, נָקְטָה נַפְשִׁי שָׁחָה, *My soul is in turmoil, it is bent*; but most editions omit the word שָׁחָה. (11) Cf. *Psalms* 44:26. (12) 44:24.

אִם עֲוֹנֵינוּ — *If our iniquities*. The acrostic of this *selichah* forms the *aleph-beis*, followed by the *paytan's* signature, שְׁלֹמֹה הַקָּטָן יְחִי, *Shlomo the lesser, may he live* [see prefatory comment to *selichah* 2].

עֲבוֹת כְּגָדִיל — *Thickly plaited ropes*. The Evil Inclination, or *Yetzer Hara*, at first is as delicate as a spider's strand, but eventually becomes as thick and strong as the rope used to harness a draft animal to its wagon (*Succah* 52a). The *Yetzer Hara* seduces a person to sin in this world, then testifies against him in the future (ibid. 52b).

שֶׁמִּקֶּדֶם הָיִיתָ — *Who was from the beginning*. That is, You have never changed since the beginning of Creation. [Indeed, some editions of

Selichos read: וְאַתָּה הוּא לֹא שָׁנִיתָ, *It is You, You have never changed* (cf. *Malachi* 3:6).] When You created the world, You established it on three pillars: Torah, Divine Worship, and Kindness. Thus it is written: כִּי אָמַרְתִּי עוֹלָם חֶסֶד יִבָּנֶה, *For I have said, 'The world shall be built upon kindness'* (*Psalms* 89:3; *Avos* 1:2 with *Rashi*). So we pray that God fulfill His ancient promise to conduct His affairs with mankind in accordance with His Attribute of Kindness.

אֲשֶׁר קָנִיתָ — *That You have acquired for Yourself*. In the Song at the Sea, Israel is called, עַם זוּ קָנִיתָ, *this people You have acquired for Yourself* (*Exodus* 15:16). The root קנה usually refers to acquisition through a business transaction. In other

In some congregations the following two verses are recited responsively — the chazzan
reciting, 'Forgive, please . . .,' and the congregation responding, 'And HASHEM said . . .'
In other congregations these verses are recited silently.

סְלַח נָא Forgive, please, the iniquity of this people according to the
greatness of Your kindness and as You have forgiven this
people from Egypt until now,[1] and there it was said:

And HASHEM said, 'I have forgiven according to your word!'[2]

All:

הַטֵּה Incline, my God, Your ear, and listen, open Your eyes and see our
desolation and that of the city upon which Your Name is
proclaimed; for not because of our righteousness do we cast down our
supplications before You, rather because of Your abundant compassion.
O my Lord, heed; O my Lord, forgive; O my Lord, be attentive and act,
do not delay; for Your sake, my God, for Your Name is proclaimed upon
Your city and upon Your people.[3]

SELICHAH 5

All:

Our God and the God of our forefathers:

א If our iniquities* have increased greatly,[4]

ב and thickly plaited ropes* bear witness against us,[5]

ג [if our sins] have caused us to create a rift
between the two [of us, God and Israel],[6]

ד You will not withhold Your merciful ways.

ה You have promised to act with the Attribute of Kindness,

ו and it was You Who was from the beginning.*

ז Remember Your flock that You have acquired for Yourself,*[7]

ח and be gracious to the remnants of the ones You called,
'[My] first-born.'[8]

ט You carried us and placed us on the [Holy] City's height,

י You settled us on the Patriarchs' rocky peak.*

כ Suddenly You crushed us in the place of serpents.[9]

ל How long have we waited to go forth [from it] to liberty?

מ Due to the many [evil] occurrences, and the trembling panic,

נ my soul is in turmoil,* [it is bent][10] to the dust it abhors.

ס Prop up the one whose belly sags to the ground![11]

ע Awake! Why do You [pretend to] sleep,[12] [our] Hope?

---

words, the verse implies that God acquired Israel
from someone else! But since everything belongs
to God in the first place, how can He 'acquire'
anything from someone else? Rashi explains that
God did not actually acquire Israel from someone
else. Rather, God's love for Israel is so strong that
it may be compared to a person's love for a
precious possession that he bought for a vast sum
and treasures dearly (ad loc. and Pesachim 87b).

שֶׁן סֶלַע אֵיתָנִים — On the Patriarchs' rocky peak.
The word אֵיתָנִים is a noun and means mighty
ones, a term often used to describe the Patriarchs
Abraham, Isaac and Jacob (see Rosh Hashanah

11a; see also commentary below, s.v., תָּם וְצַבּוּר
(וּבְנֵאי אֵיתָנִי). Since it was in the merit of the
Patriarchs that Israel inherited Eretz Yisrael, a
land that is mountainous and rocky in many
places, the paytan refers to the Land as the
Patriarch's rocky peak.

[Although many commentaries treat אֵיתָנִים as
an adjective and render this phrase on mighty
rocky peaks, the plural form אֵיתָנִים is grammatically inconsistent with the singular noun שֶׁן סֶלַע,
rocky peak.]

נָקְטָה נַפְשִׁי — My soul is in turmoil. The
translation follows Rashi (to Job 10:1). According

פְּקַח קוֹחַ קְרָא אֲסִירֶיךָ[1] חֲפוֹץ,   צוּק הָעִתִּים חֶשְׁבּוֹנָם קְפֹץ,

קַבֵּץ פְּזוּרֶיךָ עֵדֶר הַנָּפֵץ,   רְאוֹת עוֹלָתָה פִּיהָ תִּקְפֹּץ.[2]

שְׁמֹר שְׁבוּעַת חֶסֶד וּתְנַאי,   תָּם וְצִבּוּר וּבְנַאי אֵיתָנַי,*

שְׁלוֹמוֹ יְצַוֶּה לִבְלִי גְנַאי,   הֲפֹךְ וְשַׁוֵּת לְטוֹבָה הַפָּנַאי.

✧ קָטֹן כִּי יַעֲקֹב[3] דַּל,   יָדְוֹעַ חָלִי נִבְזֶה וְחָדַל,[4]

חַיִּים וָחֶסֶד מָעֹז וּמִגְדָּל,   כַּאֲשֶׁר עַתָּה כֹּחֲךָ יִגְדָּל.[5]

All, while standing:

אֵל מֶלֶךְ יוֹשֵׁב עַל כִּסֵּא רַחֲמִים מִתְנַהֵג בַּחֲסִידוּת, מוֹחֵל עֲוֹנוֹת עַמּוֹ, מַעֲבִיר רִאשׁוֹן רִאשׁוֹן,[6] מַרְבֶּה מְחִילָה לַחַטָּאִים וּסְלִיחָה לַפּוֹשְׁעִים, עֹשֶׂה צְדָקוֹת עִם כָּל בָּשָׂר וָרְוּחַ, לֹא כְרָעָתָם תִּגְמוֹל. ✧ אֵל הוֹרֵיתָ לָּנוּ לוֹמַר שְׁלֹשׁ עֶשְׂרֵה, וּזְכוֹר לָנוּ הַיּוֹם בְּרִית שְׁלֹשׁ עֶשְׂרֵה, כְּמוֹ שֶׁהוֹדַעְתָּ לֶעָנָיו מִקֶּדֶם, כְּמוֹ שֶׁכָּתוּב, וַיֵּרֶד יהוה בֶּעָנָן וַיִּתְיַצֵּב עִמּוֹ שָׁם, וַיִּקְרָא בְשֵׁם יהוה.

Congregation, then chazzan:

וַיַּעֲבֹר יהוה עַל פָּנָיו וַיִּקְרָא:

Congregation and chazzan (the words in bold type are recited aloud and in unison):

יהוה, יהוה, אֵל, **רַחוּם,** וְחַנּוּן, אֶרֶךְ אַפַּיִם, וְרַב חֶסֶד, וֶאֱמֶת, **נֹצֵר חֶסֶד לָאֲלָפִים,** נֹשֵׂא עָוֹן, וָפֶשַׁע, וְחַטָּאָה, **וְנַקֵּה.** וְסָלַחְתָּ לַעֲוֹנֵנוּ וּלְחַטָּאתֵנוּ וּנְחַלְתָּנוּ. סְלַח לָנוּ אָבִינוּ כִּי חָטָאנוּ, מְחַל לָנוּ מַלְכֵּנוּ כִּי פָשָׁעְנוּ. כִּי אַתָּה אֲדֹנָי טוֹב וְסַלָּח, וְרַב חֶסֶד לְכָל קֹרְאֶיךָ.

פסוקי הקדמה לסליחה ו

אַף אֹרַח מִשְׁפָּטֶיךָ* יהוה קִוִּינוּךָ, לְשִׁמְךָ וּלְזִכְרְךָ* תַּאֲוַת נָפֶשׁ.[7]

---

to *Targum* and *Ralbag* the meaning is *my soul is doomed.*

תָּם וְצִבּוּר וּבְנַאי אֵיתָנַי — *The wholesome one, the heaped one, and the builder my mighty* [Patriarchs]. The word אֵיתָנַי alludes to the Patriarchs [see above, s.v., שֶׁן סֶלַע אֵיתָנִים]. Jacob is described as אִישׁ תָּם, *a wholesome man* (Genesis 25:27); Isaac is considered as the ashes of an offering צִבּוּר, *heaped*, upon the Altar (*Midrash Tanchuma, Vayeira* 23); and Abraham is called *the builder* because וַיִּבֶן... אֶת הַמִּזְבֵּחַ, *he built the altar*, on which to offer Isaac (*Genesis* 22:9).

אַף אֹרַח מִשְׁפָּטֶיךָ — *Even [in] Your way of judgment.* The commentaries (to *Isaiah* 26:8) vary widely in their understanding of this verse. *Rashi* interprets: Even as we look forward to Your Attributes of Mercy and Beneficence to redeem us from our exile, so do we anticipate Your Attribute

of Strict Justice to mete out retribution to our wicked oppressors.

Rashi interprets: Even though You have until now treated us with Your Attribute of Strict Justice and You have therefore dispersed us among the nations, nevertheless, we hope to You, that You will redeem us from our exile.

לְשִׁמְךָ וּלְזִכְרְךָ — *To Your Name and to Your Remembrance.* Moses asked of God: When I come to the children of Israel and say to them, 'The God of your ancestors has sent me to you,' and they will respond, 'What is His Name?' What shall I say to them? God replied: HASHEM, God of Your ancestors . . . זֶה שְׁמִי, *This is My Name eternally,* וְזֶה זִכְרִי, *and this is My Remembrance in every Generation* (Exodus 3:13, 15).

The Talmud finds this last passage difficult, for although the verse records only one Name — the ineffable Four-Letter Name — repetition of

פ *May it be Your will to cry, 'Undo your fetters!' to Your prisoners,*[1]

צ *[and to] cut short the reckoning for their time of suffering.*

ק *Gather up Your dispersed ones, the scattered flock;*

ר *when wickedness sees [this], it will clamp its mouth shut.*[2]

ש *Keep the vow of kindness and the compact*

ת *of the wholesome one, the heaped one, and the builder, my mighty [Patriarchs].*

May He command His peace [to us], not to [be] shamed, turning and changing the times to good.

Chazzan — *Although Yaakov is small*[3] *and poor, sickly, despised, and [thought] worthless,*[4] *[yet he shall have] life and kindness, a fortress and tower [from God], as now Your strength is [revealed in its] greatness.*[5]

All, while standing:

אֵל מֶלֶךְ O *God, King Who sits on the throne of mercy; Who acts with kindness, pardons the iniquities of His people, removes [sins] one by one,*[6] *increasingly grants pardon to careless sinners and forgiveness to rebels, Who deals righteously with every living being — You do not repay them in accord with their evil.* Chazzan — O *God, You taught us to recite the Thirteen [Attributes of Mercy], so remember for us today the covenant of these Thirteen, as You made known to the humble one in ancient times, as it is written: And* HASHEM *descended in a cloud and stood with him there, and He called out with the Name* HASHEM.

Congregation, then chazzan:

And HASHEM *passed before him [Moses] and proclaimed:*

Congregation and chazzan (the words in bold type are recited aloud and in unison):

ה' ה' HASHEM, HASHEM, **God, Compassionate and Gracious, Slow to anger, and Abundant in Kindness and Truth, Preserver of kindness for thousands [of generations], Forgiver of iniquity, willful sin, and error, and Who cleanses.** *May You forgive our iniquities and our errors and make us Your heritage. Forgive us, our Father, for we have erred; pardon us, our King, for we have willfully sinned; for You, my Lord, are good and forgiving and abundantly kind to all who call upon You.*

PREFATORY VERSES TO SELICHAH 6

אַף *Even [in] Your way of judgment,** HASHEM, *we hope to You; to Your Name and to Your Remembrance,** *[for they are our] soul's desire.*[7]

---

(1) Cf. *Isaiah* 61:1. (2) Cf. *Psalms* 107:42; *Job* 5:16. (3) Cf. *Amos* 7:2. (4) Cf. *Isaiah* 53:3.
(5) Cf. *Numbers* 14:17. (6) Tractate *Rosh Hashanah* 17a. (7) *Isaiah* 26:8.

---

the demonstrative pronoun זֶה, *this*, indicates two names!

Rav Avina explains: God meant, 'Not as My Name is written, is it to be pronounced [or, remembered]. *This is My Name* alludes to the way we spell God's Name, י־ה־ו־ה; *this is My Remembrance* refers to the way we pronounce that Name, as if it were spelled אֲדֹנָי, *Adonai*.

Another verse states: HASHEM *will be the King over all the land; on that day* HASHEM *will be One and His Name will be One* (*Zechariah* 14:9). But does He not have One Name today? R' Nachman bar Yitzchak taught: The world of the future will be unlike the world of today. In the world of today God's Name is spelled one way and pronounced differently, whereas in the world of the future all will be one — the spelling and pronunciation will both be י־ה־ו־ה (*Pesachim* 50a).

קַוֵּה קוֵּינוּ יהוה, וַיֵּט אֵלֵינוּ וַיִּשְׁמַע שַׁוְעָתֵנוּ.[1] וְעַתָּה מַה קּוֵּינוּ
אֲדֹנָי, תּוֹחַלְתֵּנוּ לְךָ הִיא.[2]* אַךְ אֶל אֱלֹהִים דּוּמִיָּה נַפְשֵׁנוּ, מִמֶּנּוּ
יְשׁוּעָתֵנוּ.[3] כְּאַיָּל תַּעֲרֹג עַל אֲפִיקֵי מָיִם, כֵּן נַפְשֵׁנוּ תַעֲרֹג אֵלֶיךָ
אֱלֹהִים.[4] אַךְ טוֹב וָחֶסֶד יִרְדְּפוּנוּ כָּל יְמֵי חַיֵּינוּ, וְשַׁבְנוּ בְּבֵית יהוה
לְאֹרֶךְ יָמִים.[5]

בְּרַחֵם אָב עַל בָּנִים, כֵּן תְּרַחֵם יהוה עָלֵינוּ. לַיהוה הַיְשׁוּעָה,
עַל עַמְּךָ בִרְכָתֶךָ סֶּלָה. יהוה צְבָאוֹת עִמָּנוּ,
מִשְׂגָּב לָנוּ אֱלֹהֵי יַעֲקֹב סֶלָה. יהוה צְבָאוֹת, אַשְׁרֵי אָדָם בֹּטֵחַ בָּךְ.
יהוה הוֹשִׁיעָה, הַמֶּלֶךְ יַעֲנֵנוּ בְיוֹם קָרְאֵנוּ.

In some congregations the following two verses are recited responsively — the *chazzan* reciting סְלַח,
and the congregation responding וַיֹּאמֶר. In other congregations these verses are recited silently.

סְלַח נָא לַעֲוֹן הָעָם הַזֶּה כְּגֹדֶל חַסְדֶּךָ, וְכַאֲשֶׁר נָשָׂאתָה לָעָם
הַזֶּה מִמִּצְרַיִם וְעַד הֵנָּה, וְשָׁם נֶאֱמַר:

וַיֹּאמֶר יהוה סָלַחְתִּי כִּדְבָרֶךָ.

All:

הַטֵּה אֱלֹהַי אָזְנְךָ וּשֲׁמָע, פְּקַח עֵינֶיךָ וּרְאֵה שֹׁמְמֹתֵינוּ, וְהָעִיר
אֲשֶׁר נִקְרָא שִׁמְךָ עָלֶיהָ, כִּי לֹא עַל צִדְקֹתֵינוּ אֲנַחְנוּ
מַפִּילִים תַּחֲנוּנֵינוּ לְפָנֶיךָ, כִּי עַל רַחֲמֶיךָ הָרַבִּים. אֲדֹנָי שְׁמָעָה,
אֲדֹנָי סְלָחָה, אֲדֹנָי הַקְשִׁיבָה, וַעֲשֵׂה אַל תְּאַחַר, לְמַעַנְךָ אֱלֹהַי,
כִּי שִׁמְךָ נִקְרָא עַל עִירְךָ וְעַל עַמֶּךָ.

סליחה ו

All:

אֱלֹהֵינוּ וֵאלֹהֵי אֲבוֹתֵינוּ:

אִוִּיתִיךָ קִוִּיתִיךָ* מֵאֶרֶץ מֶרְחַקִּים.

בְּקִרְבִּי שִׁחַרְתִּיךָ קְרָאתִיךָ מִמַּעֲמַקִּים.

גָּרַסְתִּי לְתַאֲוָתְךָ כְּאַיָּל עַל אֲפִיקִים.

דְּרַשְׁתִּיךָ וּבִקַּשְׁתִּיךָ בָּרְחֹבוֹת וּבַשְּׁוָקִים.

הִנֵּה הָעֵת תְּרַוִּיחַ לִדְחוּקִים.

וְתַעֲשֶׂה דִין וּמִשְׁפָּט לַעֲשׁוּקִים.[6]

תּוֹחַלְתֵּנוּ לְךָ הִיא — *Our longing is to You.* The
translation follows *Radak* (to Psalms 39:8).
According to *Rashi*, this stich is still part of the
previous question: *For what do we hope; what do
we long for from You?*

אִוִּיתִיךָ קִוִּיתִיךָ ‎— *I desire You, I hope for You.*
The verses follow an alphabetical scheme, followed by the composer's signature — אֵלִיָּה בַּר
שְׁמַעְיָהוּ, *Eliyah bar Shemayahu* — as indicated by
the bold type. R' Eliyah lived in Bari, Italy, during

We have greatly hoped for HASHEM — *and He inclined to us and heard our cry.*[1] *And now, for what do we hope, my Lord? Our longing is to You.*[2] *To God alone our souls wait silently; from Him is our salvation.*[3] *As a gazelle longs for brooks of water, so does our soul long for You, O God.*[4] *May only goodness and kindness pursue us all the days of our lives, and we shall dwell in the house of* HASHEM *for long days.*[5]

כְּרַחֵם אָב *As a father has mercy on his children, so,* HASHEM, *may You have mercy on us. Salvation is* HASHEM's, *upon Your people is Your blessing, Selah.* HASHEM, *Master of Legions, is with us, a stronghold for us is the God of Jacob, Selah.* HASHEM, *Master of Legions, praiseworthy is the person who trusts in You.* HASHEM, *save! May the King answer us on the day we call.*

In some congregations the following two verses are recited responsively — the *chazzan* reciting, 'Forgive, please . . .,' and the congregation responding, 'And HASHEM said . . .'
In other congregations these verses are recited silently.

סְלַח נָא *Forgive, please, the iniquity of this people according to the greatness of Your kindness and as You have forgiven this people from Egypt until now, and there it was said:*

And HASHEM said, 'I have forgiven according to your word!'

All:

הַטֵּה *Incline, my God, Your ear, and listen, open Your eyes and see our desolation and that of the city upon which Your Name is proclaimed; for not because of our righteousness do we cast down our supplications before You, rather because of Your abundant compassion. O my Lord, heed; O my Lord, forgive; O my Lord, be attentive and act, do not delay; for Your sake, my God, for Your Name is proclaimed upon Your city and upon Your people.*

SELICHAH 6

All:

Our God and the God of our forefathers:
א *I desire You, I hope for You* *in a far-off land,*
ב *I seek You from within me, I call You from the depths.*
ג *I am broken with desire for You*
  as a gazelle [longs] for brooks of water;
ד *I have sought You and searched for You in the streets*
  and in the market-places.
ה *Behold, it is the time for You to bring relief to the oppressed,*
ו *and make trial and judgment in the cause of the victimized.*[6]

---

(1) Cf. *Psalms* 40:2. (2) Cf. 39:8. (3) Cf. 62:2. (4) Cf. 42:2. (5) Cf. 23:6. (6) Cf. 146:7.

the late-tenth and early-eleventh centuries. About forty of his *selichos* are extant. Character-   istically, they describe the plight of Israel in exile and the nation's hope for a speedy redemption.

זְמוֹרֵיהֶם* שֻׁחֲתוּ וּבְקָקוּם בּוֹקְקִים.[2]
חֲמוּסִים נְגוּשִׁים בְּיַד מַדִּיקִים.
טְפוּלֶיךָ[3] שֶׁעֲשַׁעְתָּ כִּילָדִים רַכִּים.
יָמִים רַבִּים לַחוּצִים וּדְפוּקִים.
כֹּל חָסָרוּ מִטּוּב רֵקִים.
לָבָאִים שְׁנֵיהֶם עֲלֵימוֹ חוֹרְקִים.[4]
מָאַסְתָּ וְזָנַחְתָּ וְנָטַשְׁתָּ דְּבֵקִים.
נֵאַרְתָּ בְּרִית שְׁלֹשֶׁת הַחֲשׁוּקִים.
סֳחִי שַׂמְתָּנוּ מֻכִּים וְלוֹקִים.
עֲצוּמֵי גָזָם וַאֲכוּלֵי יְלָקִים.*
פְּצוּעֵי חַבּוּרוֹת וְאֵבְרִים מִתְפָּרְקִים.
צָרֵי חָדַלְנוּ וְדַלְנוּ מִתַּמְרוּקִים.
קוּמָה עֶזְרָתָה לִנְאֱנָחִים וְנֶאֱנָקִים.
רוֹמֵם מֵאַשְׁפּוֹת וּמֵעָפָר תָּקִים.[5]
שִׁלְטוֹן בְּיָדְךָ יְרוּדֶיךָ לְהָקִים.
תָּקְפֵּךְ בַּשַּׁחַק וּמֶמְשַׁלְתְּךָ בָּאֲרָקִים.
אַךְ לְשִׁמְךָ יוֹדוּ הַצַּדִּיקִים.[6]
בְּנִשְׂאֲךָ רֹאשׁ שִׁבְעָתַיִם מְזֻקָּקִים.
❖ עַתָּה יֹאמְרוּ הַקְּרוֹבִים וְהָרְחוֹקִים.
כְּהוֹשִׁיעֲךָ חוֹכֶיךָ בְּמִצְוֹתֶיךָ מִתְחַזְּקִים.[7]
חֲזַק וְאַמִּיץ דְּבָרוּ הֵקִים.
לַחֲבַצֶּלֶת הַשָּׁרוֹן שׁוֹשַׁנַּת הָעֲמָקִים.[8]

All, while standing:

אֵל מֶלֶךְ יוֹשֵׁב עַל כִּסֵּא רַחֲמִים מִתְנַהֵג בַּחֲסִידוּת, מוֹחֵל
עֲוֹנוֹת עַמּוֹ, מַעֲבִיר רִאשׁוֹן רִאשׁוֹן. מַרְבֶּה מְחִילָה
לְחַטָּאִים וּסְלִיחָה לְפוֹשְׁעִים, עֹשֶׂה צְדָקוֹת עִם כָּל בָּשָׂר וָרוּחַ,
לֹא כְרָעָתָם תִּגְמוֹל. ❖ אֵל הוֹרֵיתָ לָּנוּ לוֹמַר שְׁלֹשׁ עֶשְׂרֵה, וּזְכוֹר
לָנוּ הַיּוֹם בְּרִית שְׁלֹשׁ עֶשְׂרֵה, כְּמוֹ שֶׁהוֹדַעְתָּ לֶעָנָיו מִקֶּדֶם, כְּמוֹ
שֶׁכָּתוּב, וַיֵּרֶד יהוה בֶּעָנָן וַיִּתְיַצֵּב עִמּוֹ שָׁם, וַיִּקְרָא בְשֵׁם יהוה.

Congregation, then chazzan:

וַיַּעֲבֹר יהוה עַל פָּנָיו וַיִּקְרָא:

זְמוֹרֵיהֶם — *Their branches.* Oppressed Israel is compared to a vineyard that has been plun- | dered, its fruits stripped from its vines (see *Hosea* 10:1).

ז Their branches* have been destroyed,
  stripped [of their fruit] by brigands,[1]
ח and they are robbed and coerced by the oppressor's hand.
ט Those who cling to You,[2]
  those whom You [once] dandled like tender children,
י they have been oppressed and battered for many days,
כ deprived of everything, empty of [all the world's] good,
ל [while] lions gnash their teeth at them.[3]
מ You disdained, You rejected,
  You abandoned those who cling [to You];
נ You shook off the covenant of the three dear [Patriarchs].
ס You have made us filthy [in the nations' eyes],
  battered and beaten,
ע overwhelmed by the gazam and eaten by the yelek.*
פ [Covered with] bleeding bruises, [our] limbs disjointed,
צ we have no more balm, and we lack for healing salves.
ק Rise up, O Helper of those who sigh and groan [in suffering]!
ר Lift [us] up from the trash-heaps, raise [us] from the dirt.[4]
ש The power is in Your hand to raise Your fallen [people]:
ת Your might is in the heavens, Your rule in [all] the earth.
  Only the tzaddikim will give thanks to Your Name[5]
  when You raise [Israel's] head, seven times purified.
Chazzan — Now all will say, those near and those far,
  when You redeem those who yearn for You,
    ever-strong in Your commandments,[6]
'The Strong One, the Mighty One, has fulfilled His word
  to the Lily of Sharon, the Rose of the valleys!'[7]

All, while standing:

אֵל מֶלֶךְ O God, King Who sits on the throne of mercy; Who acts with
kindness, pardons the iniquities of His people, removes [sins]
one by one, increasingly grants pardon to careless sinners and forgiveness
to rebels, Who deals righteously with every living being — You do not repay
them in accord with their evil. Chazzan — O God, You taught us to recite the
Thirteen [Attributes of Mercy], so remember for us today the covenant of
these Thirteen, as You made known to the humble one in ancient times, as
it is written: And HASHEM descended in a cloud and stood with him there,
and He called out with the Name HASHEM.

Congregation, then chazzan:
And HASHEM passed before him [Moses] and proclaimed:

---

(1) Cf. *Nahum* 2:3. (2) Some editions read טְלָאֶיךָ, Your flock. (3) Cf. *Psalms* 35:16.
(4) Cf. *I Samuel* 2:8; *Psalms* 113:7. (5) Cf. 140:14. (6) Some editions omit this line and read the next
two lines, חֲזַק וְאִמֵּיץ דִּבְרוֹ הֵקִים, *The Strong One, the Mighty One has fulfilled His word*, קַיֵּם מַאֲמָרוֹ שׁוֹכֵן
שְׁחָקִים, *He Who dwells in the highest heavens has fulfilled His promise.* (7) Cf. *Song of Songs* 2:1.

גַּם ... יְלָקִים — *The gazam ... the yelek.* The
prophet Joel (ch. 1) describes a devastating
visitation of four species of locust coming in four
waves. The species are *gazam, arbeh, yelek* and

chasil. According to *Arugas HaBosem*, these
represent the four kingdoms that would eventually subjugate Israel — Babylon, Persia, Greece
and Rome.

Congregation and *chazzan* (the words in bold type are recited aloud and in unison):

יהוה, יהוה, אֵל, רַחוּם, וְחַנּוּן, אֶרֶךְ אַפַּיִם, וְרַב חֶסֶד, וֶאֱמֶת,
נֹצֵר חֶסֶד לָאֲלָפִים, נֹשֵׂא עָוֹן, וָפֶשַׁע, וְחַטָּאָה,
וְנַקֵּה. וְסָלַחְתָּ לַעֲוֹנֵנוּ וּלְחַטָּאתֵנוּ וּנְחַלְתָּנוּ. סְלַח לָנוּ אָבִינוּ כִּי
חָטָאנוּ, מְחַל לָנוּ מַלְכֵּנוּ כִּי פָשָׁעְנוּ. כִּי אַתָּה אֲדֹנָי טוֹב וְסַלָּח,
וְרַב חֶסֶד לְכָל קֹרְאֶיךָ.

סליחה ז (פזמון)

Chazzan, then congregation:

יִשְׂרָאֵל* נוֹשַׁע בַּיהוה תְּשׁוּעַת עוֹלָמִים,[1]
גַּם הַיּוֹם יִוָּשְׁעוּ מִפִּיךָ, שׁוֹכֵן מְרוֹמִים,
כִּי אַתָּה רַב סְלִיחוֹת וּבַעַל הָרַחֲמִים.

Congregation, then *chazzan*:

שְׁעָרֶיךָ הֵם דּוֹפְקִים כַּעֲנִיִּים וְדַלִּים,
צִקּוּן לַחֲשָׁם קְשָׁב יָהּ שׁוֹכֵן מְעָלִים,
כִּי אַתָּה רַב סְלִיחוֹת וּבַעַל הָרַחֲמִים.

Congregation, then *chazzan*:

פְּחוּדִים הֵם מִכָּל צָרוֹת מִמַּחְרְפֵיהֶם וּמְלוֹחֲצֵיהֶם,[2]
נָא אַל תַּעַזְבֵם, יהוה אֱלֹהֵי אֲבוֹתֵיהֶם,
כִּי אַתָּה רַב סְלִיחוֹת וּבַעַל הָרַחֲמִים.

Congregation, then *chazzan*:

טוֹבוֹתֶיךָ יְקַדְּמוּ לָהֶם בְּיוֹם תּוֹכֵחָה,
וּמִתּוֹךְ צָרָה הַמְצִיאֵם פְּדוּת וּרְוָחָה,
כִּי אַתָּה רַב סְלִיחוֹת וּבַעַל הָרַחֲמִים.

Congregation, then *chazzan*:

יִוָּשְׁעוּ לְעֵין כֹּל, וְאַל יִמְשְׁלוּ בָם רְשָׁעִים,
כַּלֵּה שֵׂעִיר וְחוֹתְנוּ,* וְיַעֲלוּ לְצִיּוֹן מוֹשִׁיעִים,[3]
כִּי אַתָּה רַב סְלִיחוֹת וּבַעַל הָרַחֲמִים.

Congregation, then *chazzan*:

הַקְשִׁיבָה אָדוֹן לְקוֹל שַׁוְעָתָם,
וְלִמְכוֹן שִׁבְתְּךָ הַשָּׁמַיִם תַּעֲלֶה תְפִלָּתָם,
כִּי אַתָּה רַב סְלִיחוֹת וּבַעַל הָרַחֲמִים.

יִשְׂרָאֵל — *Israel*. The acrostic (of the stanzas after the first) spells the author's name — שְׁפַטְיָה, *Shephatiah*. He was a well-known Kabbalist and lived in Oria, Italy. When the Byzantine emperor Basil I issued anti-Jewish decrees (about 873 C.E.), R' Shephatiah traveled to Constantinople in an attempt to convince the emperor to annul his decrees. Although unsuccessful in his overall

Congregation and *chazzan* (the words in bold type are recited aloud and in unison):

ה' ה' **Hashem, Hashem, God, Compassionate and Gracious, Slow to anger, and Abundant in Kindness and Truth, Preserver of kindness for thousands [of generations], Forgiver of iniquity, willful sin, and error, and Who cleanses.** *May You forgive our iniquities and our errors and make us Your heritage. Forgive us, our Father, for we have erred; pardon us, our King, for we have willfully sinned; for You, my Lord, are good and forgiving and abundantly kind to all who call upon You.*

SELICHAH 7

Chazzan, then congregation:

יִשְׂרָאֵל *Israel* is saved by Hashem with an eternal salvation;[1]*
today, too, may they be saved by Your word,
O Dweller in the Heights —
for You are abundantly forgiving, and the Master of mercies.

Congregation, then chazzan:

ש *They knock at Your gates like poor and destitute people;*
hearken to their whispered [heart's] outpouring,
O God Who dwells aloft —
for You are abundantly forgiving, and the Master of mercies.

Congregation, then chazzan:

פ *They are frightened by all the troubles [they undergo],*
of those who disgrace them and those who oppress them;[2]
please do not forsake them, Hashem, God, of their forefathers —
for You are abundantly forgiving, and the Master of mercies.

Congregation, then chazzan:

ט *May Your goodness precede them on the day of admonishment,*
and from amid [their] troubles [may You] bring them
redemption and relief —
for You are abundantly forgiving, and the Master of mercies.

Congregation, then chazzan:

י *May they be saved in everyone's sight,*
and let not the wicked dominate them [any more].
Make an end of Seir and his father-in-law,*
and let saviors go up to Zion[3] —
for You are abundantly forgiving, and the Master of mercies.

Congregation, then chazzan:

ה *Hearken, O Master, to the sound of their outcry;*
and to Your established heavenly dwelling may their prayer ascend —
for You are abundantly forgiving and the Master of all mercies.

---

(1) *Isaiah* 45:17. (2) **Some editions read** וּמִמְּנַדְּפֵיהֶם, *and from those who curse them.* (3) Cf. *Obadiah* 1:1.

mission, while he was in Basil's court, R' Shephatiah cured a daughter of the emperor who had been 'possessed.' As a reward, Basil released the Jews of Oria, as well as four other Jewish communities, from his decrees. Both R' Shephatiah and his son and successor, R' Amittai [see *selichah* 93], often allude to the persecutions and forced con-

versions that Basil inflicted upon the Jews.

שֵׂעִיר וְחוֹתְנוֹ — *Seir and his father-in-law.* Seir refers to Esau [Edom] because he settled on, then took over, Mount Seir (see *Genesis* 32:4 and 36:8). His father-in-law was Ishmael (see ibid. 28:9).

Rashi (to *Zechariah* 5:11) cites a Midrash (*Shocher Tov* 6:1) that states that the four kingdoms

All, while standing:

אֵל מֶלֶךְ יוֹשֵׁב עַל כִּסֵּא רַחֲמִים מִתְנַהֵג בַּחֲסִידוּת, מוֹחֵל עֲוֹנוֹת עַמּוֹ, מַעֲבִיר רִאשׁוֹן רִאשׁוֹן, מַרְבֶּה מְחִילָה לַחַטָּאִים וּסְלִיחָה לַפּוֹשְׁעִים, עֹשֶׂה צְדָקוֹת עִם כָּל בָּשָׂר וָרוּחַ, לֹא כְרָעָתָם תִּגְמוֹל. אֵל הוֹרֵיתָ לָנוּ לוֹמַר שְׁלֹשׁ עֶשְׂרֵה, וּזְכוֹר לָנוּ הַיּוֹם בְּרִית שְׁלֹשׁ עֶשְׂרֵה, כְּמוֹ שֶׁהוֹדַעְתָּ לֶעָנָיו מִקֶּדֶם, כְּמוֹ שֶׁכָּתוּב, וַיֵּרֶד יהוה בֶּעָנָן וַיִּתְיַצֵּב עִמּוֹ שָׁם, וַיִּקְרָא בְשֵׁם יהוה.

Congregation, then chazzan:

וַיַּעֲבֹר יהוה עַל פָּנָיו וַיִּקְרָא:

Congregation and chazzan (the words in bold type are recited aloud and in unison):

יהוה, יהוה, אֵל, רַחוּם, וְחַנּוּן, אֶרֶךְ אַפַּיִם, וְרַב חֶסֶד, וֶאֱמֶת, נֹצֵר חֶסֶד לָאֲלָפִים, נֹשֵׂא עָוֹן, וָפֶשַׁע, וְחַטָּאָה, וְנַקֵּה. וְסָלַחְתָּ לַעֲוֹנֵנוּ וּלְחַטָּאתֵנוּ וּנְחַלְתָּנוּ. סְלַח לָנוּ אָבִינוּ כִּי חָטָאנוּ, מְחַל לָנוּ מַלְכֵּנוּ כִּי פָשָׁעְנוּ. כִּי אַתָּה אֲדֹנָי טוֹב וְסַלָּח, וְרַב חֶסֶד לְכָל קֹרְאֶיךָ.

All:

אַל תִּזְכָּר לָנוּ עֲוֹנוֹת רִאשׁוֹנִים, מַהֵר יְקַדְּמוּנוּ רַחֲמֶיךָ, כִּי דַלּוֹנוּ מְאֹד.[1] חַטַּאת נְעוּרֵינוּ וּפְשָׁעֵינוּ אַל תִּזְכּוֹר, כְּחַסְדְּךָ זְכָר לָנוּ אַתָּה, לְמַעַן טוּבְךָ יהוה.[2]

זְכוֹר רַחֲמֶיךָ יהוה וַחֲסָדֶיךָ, כִּי מֵעוֹלָם הֵמָּה.[3] זָכְרֵנוּ יהוה בִּרְצוֹן עַמֶּךָ, פָּקְדֵנוּ בִּישׁוּעָתֶךָ.[4] זְכֹר עֲדָתְךָ קָנִיתָ קֶּדֶם, גָּאַלְתָּ שֵׁבֶט נַחֲלָתֶךָ, הַר צִיּוֹן זֶה שָׁכַנְתָּ בּוֹ.[5] זְכֹר יהוה חִבַּת יְרוּשָׁלָיִם, אַהֲבַת צִיּוֹן אַל תִּשְׁכַּח לָנֶצַח.[6] אַתָּה תָקוּם תְּרַחֵם צִיּוֹן, כִּי עֵת לְחֶנְנָהּ כִּי בָא מוֹעֵד.[7] זְכֹר יהוה לִבְנֵי אֱדוֹם אֵת יוֹם יְרוּשָׁלָיִם, הָאֹמְרִים עָרוּ עָרוּ עַד הַיְסוֹד בָּהּ.[8] זְכֹר לְאַבְרָהָם לְיִצְחָק וּלְיִשְׂרָאֵל עֲבָדֶיךָ אֲשֶׁר נִשְׁבַּעְתָּ לָהֶם בָּךְ, וַתְּדַבֵּר אֲלֵהֶם, אַרְבֶּה אֶת זַרְעֲכֶם כְּכוֹכְבֵי הַשָּׁמָיִם, וְכָל הָאָרֶץ הַזֹּאת אֲשֶׁר אָמַרְתִּי אֶתֵּן לְזַרְעֲכֶם, וְנָחֲלוּ לְעֹלָם.[9] ❖ זְכֹר לַעֲבָדֶיךָ לְאַבְרָהָם לְיִצְחָק וּלְיַעֲקֹב, אַל תֵּפֶן אֶל קְשִׁי הָעָם הַזֶּה וְאֶל רִשְׁעוֹ וְאֶל חַטָּאתוֹ.[10]

---

that rule over Israel during its four periods of exile were actually eight, for each consisted of two empires: (a) Babylon and Chaldea; (b) Medea and Persia; (c) Greece and Macedonia; and (d) Edom and Ishmael.

Thus, when the fourth kingdom — Seir and his father-in-law — will have ended, then, *the saviors will ascend Mount Zion to judge Esau's mountain, and the kingdom will be HASHEM's* (Obadiah 1:21).

All, while standing:

אֵל מֶלֶךְ O God, King Who sits on the throne of mercy; Who acts with kindness, pardons the iniquities of His people, removes [sins] one by one, increasingly grants pardon to careless sinners and forgiveness to rebels, Who deals righteously with every living being — You do not repay them in accord with their evil. Chazzan – O God, You taught us to recite the Thirteen [Attributes of Mercy], so remember for us today the covenant of these Thirteen, as You made known to the humble one in ancient times, as it is written: And HASHEM descended in a cloud and stood with him there, and He called out with the Name HASHEM.

Congregation, then chazzan:

And HASHEM passed before him [Moses] and proclaimed:

Congregation and chazzan (the words in bold type are recited aloud and in unison):

ה' ה' HASHEM, HASHEM, God, Compassionate and Gracious, Slow to anger, and Abundant in Kindness and Truth, Preserver of kindness for thousands [of generations], Forgiver of iniquity, willful sin, and error, and Who cleanses. May You forgive our iniquities and our errors and make us Your heritage. Forgive us, our Father, for we have erred; pardon us, our King, for we have willfully sinned; for You, my Lord, are good and forgiving and abundantly kind to all who call upon You.

All:

אַל תִּזְכָּר Do not recall against us the iniquities of the ancients; speedily — let Your mercy come to meet us for we have fallen very low.[1] Remember not the sins of our youth and our rebellions; may You remember for us [the deeds] worthy of Your kindness, because of Your goodness, HASHEM.[2]

זְכוֹר רַחֲמֶיךָ Remember Your mercies, O HASHEM, and Your kindnesses, for they are from the beginning of the world.[3] Remember us, HASHEM, when You show Your people favor and recall us with Your salvation.[4] Remember Your congregation that You acquired of old, that You redeemed the tribe of Your heritage, and this Mount Zion where You dwelled.[5] Remember, O HASHEM, the affection of Jerusalem, may You never forget the love of Zion.[6] You will arise and show Zion mercy, for it is the time to be gracious to her, for the appointed time will have come.[7] Remember, HASHEM, for the offspring of Edom, the day of Jerusalem — for those who said: 'Destroy! Destroy to its very foundation!'[8] Remember Abraham, Isaac, and Israel, Your servants, to whom You swore by Your Being, saying to them, 'I shall increase your offspring like the stars of the heavens; and this entire land of which I spoke I will give to your offspring and they will inherit it forever.'[9] Chazzan – Remember for Your servants, for Abraham, for Isaac, and for Jacob; ignore the stubbornness of this people, its wickedness and its sinfulness.[10]

---

(1) Psalms 79:8. (2) Cf. 25:7. (3) 25:6. (4) Cf. 106:4. (5) 74:2. (6) This is not a Scriptural verse. (7) Psalms 102:14. (8) 137:7. (9) Exodus 32:13. (10) Deuteronomy 9:27.

Chazzan, then congregation:

אַל נָא תָשֵׁת עָלֵינוּ חַטָּאת, אֲשֶׁר נוֹאַלְנוּ וַאֲשֶׁר חָטָאנוּ.[1]

Chazzan, then congregation:

חָטָאנוּ צוּרֵנוּ, סְלַח לָנוּ יוֹצְרֵנוּ.

All:

זְכוֹר לָנוּ בְּרִית אָבוֹת, כַּאֲשֶׁר אָמַרְתָּ: וְזָכַרְתִּי אֶת בְּרִיתִי יַעֲקוֹב, וְאַף אֶת בְּרִיתִי יִצְחָק, וְאַף אֶת בְּרִיתִי אַבְרָהָם אֶזְכֹּר, וְהָאָרֶץ אֶזְכֹּר.[2] זְכוֹר לָנוּ בְּרִית רִאשׁוֹנִים, כַּאֲשֶׁר אָמַרְתָּ: וְזָכַרְתִּי לָהֶם בְּרִית רִאשׁוֹנִים, אֲשֶׁר הוֹצֵאתִי אֹתָם מֵאֶרֶץ מִצְרַיִם לְעֵינֵי הַגּוֹיִם, לִהְיוֹת לָהֶם לֵאלֹהִים, אֲנִי יהוה.[3] עֲשֵׂה עִמָּנוּ כְּמָה שֶׁהִבְטַחְתָּנוּ: וְאַף גַּם זֹאת בִּהְיוֹתָם בְּאֶרֶץ אֹיְבֵיהֶם, לֹא מְאַסְתִּים וְלֹא גְעַלְתִּים לְכַלֹּתָם לְהָפֵר בְּרִיתִי אִתָּם, כִּי אֲנִי יהוה אֱלֹהֵיהֶם.[4] הִמָּצֵא לָנוּ בְּבַקָּשָׁתֵנוּ, כְּמָה שֶׁכָּתוּב: וּבִקַּשְׁתֶּם מִשָּׁם אֶת יהוה אֱלֹהֶיךָ וּמָצָאתָ, כִּי תִדְרְשֶׁנּוּ בְּכָל לְבָבְךָ וּבְכָל נַפְשֶׁךָ.[5] מוֹל אֶת לְבָבֵנוּ לְאַהֲבָה וּלְיִרְאָה אֶת שְׁמֶךָ, כְּמָה שֶׁכָּתוּב: וּמָל יהוה אֱלֹהֶיךָ אֶת לְבָבְךָ וְאֶת לְבַב זַרְעֶךָ, לְאַהֲבָה אֶת יהוה אֱלֹהֶיךָ בְּכָל לְבָבְךָ וּבְכָל נַפְשְׁךָ, לְמַעַן חַיֶּיךָ.[6] זְרוֹק עָלֵינוּ מַיִם טְהוֹרִים וְטַהֲרֵנוּ, כְּמָה שֶׁכָּתוּב: וְזָרַקְתִּי עֲלֵיכֶם מַיִם טְהוֹרִים וּטְהַרְתֶּם, מִכֹּל טֻמְאוֹתֵיכֶם וּמִכָּל גִּלּוּלֵיכֶם אֲטַהֵר אֶתְכֶם.[7] מְחֵה פְשָׁעֵינוּ כָּעָב וְכֶעָנָן, כְּמָה שֶׁכָּתוּב: מָחִיתִי כָעָב פְּשָׁעֶיךָ וְכֶעָנָן חַטֹּאתֶיךָ, שׁוּבָה אֵלַי כִּי גְאַלְתִּיךָ.[8] מְחֵה פְשָׁעֵינוּ לְמַעַנְךָ, כַּאֲשֶׁר אָמַרְתָּ: אָנֹכִי אָנֹכִי הוּא מֹחֶה פְשָׁעֶיךָ לְמַעֲנִי, וְחַטֹּאתֶיךָ לֹא אֶזְכֹּר.[9] הַלְבֵּן חֲטָאֵינוּ כַּשֶּׁלֶג וְכַצֶּמֶר, כְּמָה שֶׁכָּתוּב: לְכוּ נָא וְנִוָּכְחָה, יֹאמַר יהוה, אִם יִהְיוּ חֲטָאֵיכֶם כַּשָּׁנִים, כַּשֶּׁלֶג יַלְבִּינוּ, אִם יַאְדִּימוּ כַתּוֹלָע, כַּצֶּמֶר יִהְיוּ.[10] רַחֵם עָלֵינוּ וְאַל תַּשְׁחִיתֵנוּ, כְּמָה שֶׁכָּתוּב: כִּי אֵל רַחוּם יהוה אֱלֹהֶיךָ, לֹא יַרְפְּךָ וְלֹא יַשְׁחִיתֶךָ וְלֹא יִשְׁכַּח אֶת בְּרִית אֲבֹתֶיךָ אֲשֶׁר נִשְׁבַּע לָהֶם.[11] קַבֵּץ נִדָּחֵנוּ כְּמָה שֶׁכָּתוּב: אִם יִהְיֶה נִדַּחֲךָ בִּקְצֵה הַשָּׁמַיִם, מִשָּׁם יְקַבֶּצְךָ יהוה אֱלֹהֶיךָ וּמִשָּׁם יִקָּחֶךָ.[12] הָשֵׁב שְׁבוּתֵנוּ וְרַחֲמֵנוּ, כְּמָה שֶׁכָּתוּב: וְשָׁב יהוה אֱלֹהֶיךָ אֶת שְׁבוּתְךָ וְרִחֲמֶךָ וְשָׁב וְקִבֶּצְךָ מִכָּל הָעַמִּים אֲשֶׁר הֱפִיצְךָ יהוה אֱלֹהֶיךָ שָׁמָּה.[13] ❖ תְּבִיאֵנוּ אֶל הַר קָדְשֶׁךָ, וְשַׂמְּחֵנוּ בְּבֵית תְּפִלָּתֶךָ, כְּמָה שֶׁכָּתוּב: וַהֲבִיאוֹתִים אֶל הַר קָדְשִׁי, וְשִׂמַּחְתִּים בְּבֵית תְּפִלָּתִי, עוֹלֹתֵיהֶם וְזִבְחֵיהֶם לְרָצוֹן עַל מִזְבְּחִי, כִּי בֵיתִי בֵּית תְּפִלָּה יִקָּרֵא לְכָל הָעַמִּים.[14]

THE ARK IS OPENED.

Chazzan, then congregation:
Please, do not reckon for us a sin,
what we have done foolishly and what we have sinned.[1]

Chazzan, then congregation:
We have erred, our Rock! Forgive us, our Molder!

All:

זְכוֹר Remember for us the covenant of the Patriarchs, as You said: 'And I will remember My covenant with Jacob, and also My covenant with Isaac, and also My covenant with Abraham will I remember; and the Land will I remember.'[2] Remember for us the covenant of the ancestors, as You said: 'And I will remember for them the covenant of the ancestors whom I removed from the land of Egypt in the very sight of the nations, to be a God to them; I am HASHEM.'[3] Do with us as You promised us: 'And despite all that, when they will be in the land of their enemies, I will not have despised them nor abhorred them to destroy them, to annul My covenant with them, for I am HASHEM their God.'[4] Be accessible to us in our quest, as it is written: From there you will seek HASHEM, your God, and you will find, when you search for Him with all your heart and with all your soul.[5] Expose our hearts to love Your Name, as it is written: HASHEM, your God, will expose your heart and the heart of your offspring, to love HASHEM, your God, with all your heart and with all your soul, that you may live.[6] Pour pure water upon us and purify us, as it is written: I shall pour pure water upon you and purify you, of all your contaminations and of all your abominations I will purify you.[7] Wipe away our willful sins like a cloud and like a mist, as it is written: I have wiped away your willful sins like a cloud and your errors like a mist — repent to Me, for I have redeemed you![8] Wipe away our willful sins for Your sake, as You said: 'I, only I, am the One Who wipes away your willful sins for My sake, and I shall not recall your errors.'[9] Whiten our errors like snow and like [pure white] wool, as it is written: 'Come now, let us reason together,' says HASHEM, 'though your errors will be like scarlet, they will become white as snow; though they will be red as crimson, they will become like [white] wool.'[10] Have mercy on us and do not destroy us, as it is written: For a merciful God is HASHEM, your God; He will not surrender you nor destroy you, and He will not forget the covenant with your forefathers, which He swore to them.[11] Gather in our dispersed ones, as it is written: If your dispersed were to be at the ends of heaven, from there HASHEM, your God, will gather you in and from there He will take you.[12] Bring back our captivity and have mercy on us, as it is written: HASHEM, your God, will bring back your captivity and have mercy on you, and He will again gather you in from all the peoples where HASHEM, your God, has scattered you.[13] *Chazzan* — Bring us to Your holy mountain and gladden us in Your house of prayer, as it is written: And I will bring them to My holy mountain, and I will gladden them in My house of prayer, their elevation-offerings and their feast offering will find favor on My Altar, for My House will be called a house of prayer, for all peoples.[14]

THE ARK IS OPENED.

---

(1) *Numbers* 12:11. (2) *Leviticus* 26:42. (3) 26:45. (4) 26:44. (5) *Deuteronomy* 4:29.
(6) 30:6. (7) *Ezekiel* 36:25. (8) *Isaiah* 44:22. (9) 43:25. (10) 1:18.
(11) *Deuteronomy* 4:31. (12) 30:4. (13) 30:3. (14) *Isaiah* 56:7.

The first four verses of the following prayer are recited responsively; *chazzan*, then congregation:

שְׁמַע קוֹלֵנוּ יהוה אֱלֹהֵינוּ, חוּס וְרַחֵם עָלֵינוּ,
וְקַבֵּל בְּרַחֲמִים וּבְרָצוֹן אֶת תְּפִלָּתֵנוּ.[1]

הֲשִׁיבֵנוּ יהוה אֵלֶיךָ וְנָשׁוּבָה, חַדֵּשׁ יָמֵינוּ כְּקֶדֶם.[2]

אַל תַּשְׁלִיכֵנוּ מִלְּפָנֶיךָ, וְרוּחַ קָדְשְׁךָ אַל תִּקַּח מִמֶּנּוּ.[3]

אַל תַּשְׁלִיכֵנוּ לְעֵת זִקְנָה, כִּכְלוֹת כֹּחֵנוּ אַל תַּעַזְבֵנוּ.[4]

אַל תַּעַזְבֵנוּ יהוה, אֱלֹהֵינוּ אַל תִּרְחַק מִמֶּנּוּ.[5]

עֲשֵׂה עִמָּנוּ אוֹת לְטוֹבָה, וְיִרְאוּ שׂוֹנְאֵינוּ וְיֵבֹשׁוּ,
כִּי אַתָּה יהוה עֲזַרְתָּנוּ וְנִחַמְתָּנוּ.[6]

אֲמָרֵינוּ הַאֲזִינָה יהוה, בִּינָה הֲגִיגֵנוּ.[7]

יִהְיוּ לְרָצוֹן אִמְרֵי פִינוּ וְהֶגְיוֹן לִבֵּנוּ לְפָנֶיךָ, יהוה צוּרֵנוּ וְגוֹאֲלֵנוּ.[8]

כִּי לְךָ יהוה הוֹחָלְנוּ, אַתָּה תַעֲנֶה אֲדֹנָי אֱלֹהֵינוּ.[9]

THE ARK IS CLOSED.

וידוי

During the recitation of the וִדּוּי stand with head and body slightly bowed,
in submissive contrition.

אֱלֹהֵינוּ וֵאלֹהֵי אֲבוֹתֵינוּ, תָּבֹא לְפָנֶיךָ תְּפִלָּתֵנוּ,[10] וְאַל תִּתְעַלַּם
מִתְּחִנָּתֵנוּ,[11] שֶׁאֵין אָנוּ עַזֵּי פָנִים וּקְשֵׁי עֹרֶף, לוֹמַר
לְפָנֶיךָ יהוה אֱלֹהֵינוּ וֵאלֹהֵי אֲבוֹתֵינוּ, צַדִּיקִים אֲנַחְנוּ וְלֹא חָטָאנוּ,
אֲבָל אֲנַחְנוּ וַאֲבוֹתֵינוּ חָטָאנוּ.[12]

Strike the left side of the chest with the right fist
while reciting each of the sins in the following confession litany.

אָשַׁמְנוּ, בָּגַדְנוּ, גָּזַלְנוּ, דִּבַּרְנוּ דֹפִי. הֶעֱוִינוּ, וְהִרְשַׁעְנוּ, זַדְנוּ,
חָמַסְנוּ, טָפַלְנוּ שֶׁקֶר. יָעַצְנוּ רָע, כִּזַּבְנוּ, לַצְנוּ, מָרַדְנוּ,
נִאַצְנוּ, סָרַרְנוּ, עָוִינוּ, פָּשַׁעְנוּ, צָרַרְנוּ, קִשִּׁינוּ עֹרֶף. רָשַׁעְנוּ, שִׁחַתְנוּ,
תִּעַבְנוּ, תָּעִינוּ, תִּעְתָּעְנוּ.

סַרְנוּ מִמִּצְוֹתֶיךָ וּמִמִּשְׁפָּטֶיךָ הַטּוֹבִים וְלֹא שָׁוָה לָנוּ.[13] וְאַתָּה צַדִּיק
עַל כָּל הַבָּא עָלֵינוּ, כִּי אֱמֶת עָשִׂיתָ וַאֲנַחְנוּ הִרְשָׁעְנוּ.[14]

אָשַׁמְנוּ מִכָּל עָם, בֹּשְׁנוּ מִכָּל דּוֹר, גָּלָה מִמֶּנּוּ מָשׂוֹשׂ, דָּוָה לִבֵּנוּ
בַּחֲטָאֵינוּ, הֻחֲבַּל אֲוִינוּ, וְנִפְרַע פְּאֵרֵנוּ, זְבוּל בֵּית מִקְדָּשֵׁנוּ חָרַב
בַּעֲוֹנֵינוּ, טִירָתֵנוּ הָיְתָה לְשַׁמָּה, יֹפִי אַדְמָתֵנוּ לְזָרִים, כֹּחֵנוּ לְנָכְרִים.
וַעֲדַיִן לֹא שַׁבְנוּ מִטָּעוּתֵנוּ וְהֵיךְ נָעִיז פָּנֵינוּ וְנַקְשֶׁה עָרְפֵּנוּ, לוֹמַר
לְפָנֶיךָ יהוה אֱלֹהֵינוּ וֵאלֹהֵי אֲבוֹתֵינוּ, צַדִּיקִים אֲנַחְנוּ וְלֹא חָטָאנוּ,
אֲבָל אֲנַחְנוּ וַאֲבוֹתֵינוּ חָטָאנוּ.

The first four verses of the following prayer are recited responsively; *chazzan*, then congregation:

שְׁמַע קוֹלֵנוּ *Hear our voice, HASHEM, our God, pity and be compassionate to us, and accept — with compassion and favor — our prayer.*[1]
Bring us back to You, HASHEM, and we shall return, renew our days as of old.[2]
Do not cast us away from Yourself,
    and do not remove Your holy spirit from us.[3]
Do not cast us away in old age,
    when our strength gives out do not forsake us.[4]
Do not forsake us, HASHEM, our God, be not distant from us.[5]
Display for us a sign for good, so that our enemies may see it
    and be ashamed, for You, HASHEM, will have helped and consoled us.[6]
To our sayings give ear, HASHEM, perceive our thoughts.[7]
May the expressions of our mouth and the thoughts of our heart
    find favor before You, HASHEM, our Rock and our Redeemer.[8]
Because for You, HASHEM, we waited, You will answer, my Lord, our God.[9]

THE ARK IS CLOSED.
During the recitation of the וִדּוּי, Confession, stand with head and body slightly bowed,
in submissive contrition.

אֱלֹהֵינוּ *Our God and the God of our forefathers, may our prayer come before You.*[10] *Do not ignore our supplication,*[11] *for we are not so brazen and obstinate as to say before You, HASHEM, our God and the God of our forefathers, that we are righteous and have not sinned, for in truth, we and our forefathers have sinned.*[12]

Strike the left side of the chest with the right fist while reciting
each of the sins in the following confession litany.

אָשַׁמְנוּ *We have become guilty;* [ב] *we have betrayed;* [ג] *we have robbed;* [ד] *we have spoken slander;* [ה] *we have caused perversion;* [ו] *we have caused wickedness;* [ז] *we have sinned willfully;* [ח] *we have extorted;* [ט] *we have accused falsely;* [י] *we have given evil counsel;* [כ] *we have been deceitful;* [ל] *we have scorned;* [מ] *we have rebelled;* [נ] *we have provoked;* [ס] *we have turned away;* [ע] *we have been perverse;* [פ] *we have acted wantonly;* [צ] *we have persecuted;* [ק] *we have been obstinate;* [ר] *we have been wicked;* [ש] *we have corrupted;* [ת] *we have been abominable; we have strayed; You have let us go astray.*

סַרְנוּ *We have turned away from Your commandments and from Your good laws but to no avail.*[13] *Yet You are righteous in all that has come upon us, for You have acted truthfully while we have caused wickedness.*[14]

[א] *We have become the guiltiest of people.* [ב] *We have become the most degraded of all generations.* [ג] *Joy has departed from us.* [ד] *Our heart has been saddened by our sins.* [ה] *Our desirous treasure has been ruined,* [ו] *and our splendor dashed,* [ז] *for our Holy Temple edifice* [ח] *has been destroyed for our iniquities.* [ט] *Our Palace has become desolate.* [י] *[Jerusalem,] the beauty of our Land is given over to aliens,* [כ] *our power to strangers.*

But still we have not returned from our waywardness. So how can we be so brazen and obstinate as to say before You, HASHEM, our God and the God of our forefathers, that we are righteous and have not sinned, for in truth, both we and our fathers have sinned.

(1) Weekday *Shemoneh Esrei.* (2) *Lamentations* 5:21. (3) Cf. *Psalms* 51:13. (4) Cf. 71:9.
(5) Cf. 38:22. (6) Cf. 86:17. (7) Cf. 5:2. (8) Cf. 19:15. (9) Cf. 38:16. (10) Cf. 88:3.
(11) Cf. 55:2. (12) Cf. 106:6. (13) Cf. *Job* 33:27. (14) *Nehemiah* 9:33.

Strike the left side of the chest with the right fist while reciting
each of the sins in the following confession litany.

אָשַׁמְנוּ, בָּגַדְנוּ, גָּזַלְנוּ, דִּבַּרְנוּ דְפִי. הֶעֱוִינוּ, וְהִרְשַׁעְנוּ, זַדְנוּ,
חָמַסְנוּ, טָפַלְנוּ שֶׁקֶר. יָעַצְנוּ רָע, כִּזַּבְנוּ, לַצְנוּ, מָרַדְנוּ,
נִאַצְנוּ, סָרַרְנוּ, עָוִינוּ, פָּשַׁעְנוּ, צָרַרְנוּ, קִשִּׁינוּ עֹרֶף. רָשַׁעְנוּ,
שִׁחַתְנוּ, תִּעַבְנוּ, תָּעִינוּ, תִּעְתָּעְנוּ.

סַרְנוּ מִמִּצְוֹתֶיךָ וּמִמִּשְׁפָּטֶיךָ הַטּוֹבִים וְלֹא שָׁוָה לָנוּ. וְאַתָּה צַדִּיק
עַל כָּל הַבָּא עָלֵינוּ, כִּי אֱמֶת עָשִׂיתָ וַאֲנַחְנוּ הִרְשָׁעְנוּ.

לְעֵינֵנוּ עָשְׁקוּ עֲמָלֵנוּ, מְמֻשָׁךְ וּמְמוֹרָט מִמֶּנּוּ, נָתְנוּ עֻלָּם עָלֵינוּ,
סָבַלְנוּ עַל שִׁכְמֵנוּ, עֲבָדִים מָשְׁלוּ בָנוּ, פֹּרֵק אֵין מִיָּדָם, צָרוֹת רַבּוֹת
סְבָבוּנוּ, קְרָאנוּךָ יהוה אֱלֹהֵינוּ, רָחַקְתָּ מִמֶּנּוּ בַּעֲוֺנֵינוּ, שַׁבְנוּ
מֵאַחֲרֶיךָ, תָּעִינוּ וְאָבָדְנוּ.

וַעֲדַיִן לֹא שַׁבְנוּ מִטָּעוּתֵנוּ וְהֵיךְ נָעִיז פָּנֵינוּ וְנַקְשֶׁה עָרְפֵּנוּ, לוֹמַר
לְפָנֶיךָ יהוה אֱלֹהֵינוּ וֵאלֹהֵי אֲבוֹתֵינוּ, צַדִּיקִים אֲנַחְנוּ וְלֹא חָטָאנוּ,
אֲבָל אֲנַחְנוּ וַאֲבוֹתֵינוּ חָטָאנוּ.

Strike the left side of the chest with the right fist while reciting
each of the sins in the following confession litany.

אָשַׁמְנוּ, בָּגַדְנוּ, גָּזַלְנוּ, דִּבַּרְנוּ דְפִי. הֶעֱוִינוּ, וְהִרְשַׁעְנוּ, זַדְנוּ,
חָמַסְנוּ, טָפַלְנוּ שֶׁקֶר. יָעַצְנוּ רָע, כִּזַּבְנוּ, לַצְנוּ, מָרַדְנוּ,
נִאַצְנוּ, סָרַרְנוּ, עָוִינוּ, פָּשַׁעְנוּ, צָרַרְנוּ, קִשִּׁינוּ עֹרֶף. רָשַׁעְנוּ,
שִׁחַתְנוּ, תִּעַבְנוּ, תָּעִינוּ, תִּעְתָּעְנוּ.

סַרְנוּ מִמִּצְוֹתֶיךָ וּמִמִּשְׁפָּטֶיךָ הַטּוֹבִים וְלֹא שָׁוָה לָנוּ. וְאַתָּה צַדִּיק
עַל כָּל הַבָּא עָלֵינוּ, כִּי אֱמֶת עָשִׂיתָ וַאֲנַחְנוּ הִרְשָׁעְנוּ.

הִרְשַׁעְנוּ וּפָשַׁעְנוּ, לָכֵן לֹא נוֹשָׁעְנוּ. וְתֵן בְּלִבֵּנוּ לַעֲזוֹב דֶּרֶךְ
רֶשַׁע, וְחִישׁ לָנוּ יֶשַׁע, כַּכָּתוּב עַל יַד נְבִיאֶךָ: יַעֲזֹב
רָשָׁע דַּרְכּוֹ, וְאִישׁ אָוֶן מַחְשְׁבֹתָיו, וְיָשֹׁב אֶל יהוה וִירַחֲמֵהוּ, וְאֶל
אֱלֹהֵינוּ כִּי יַרְבֶּה לִסְלוֹחַ.[1]

מְשִׁיחַ צִדְקֶךָ אָמַר לְפָנֶיךָ: שְׁגִיאוֹת מִי יָבִין מִנִּסְתָּרוֹת נַקֵּנִי.[2]
נַקֵּנוּ יהוה אֱלֹהֵינוּ מִכָּל פְּשָׁעֵינוּ, וְטַהֲרֵנוּ מִכָּל

---

(1) Isaiah 55:7. (2) Psalms 19:13.

Strike the left side of the chest with the right fist while reciting
each of the sins in the following confession litany:

אָשַׁמְנוּ *We have become guilty;* [ב] *we have betrayed;* [ג] *we have robbed;*
[ד] *we have spoken slander;* [ה] *we have caused perversion;* [ו] *we*
have caused wickedness; [ז] *we have sinned willfully;* [ח] *we have extorted;*
[ט] *we have accused falsely;* [י] *we have given evil counsel;* [כ] *we have been*
deceitful; [ל] *we have scorned;* [מ] *we have rebelled;* [נ] *we have provoked;*
[ס] *we have turned away;* [ע] *we have been perverse;* [פ] *we have acted*
wantonly; [צ] *we have persecuted;* [ק] *we have been obstinate;* [ר] *we have*
been wicked; [ש] *we have corrupted;* [ת] *we have been abominable; we have*
strayed; You have let us go astray.

סַרְנוּ *We have turned away from Your commandments and from Your*
good laws but to no avail. Yet You are righteous in all that has come
upon us, for You have acted truthfully while we have caused wickedness.

[ל] *[The benefit of] our labor has been stolen,* [מ] *pulled away and cut off*
from us. [נ] *They have placed their yoke upon us,* [ס] *our burdens upon our*
shoulders. [ע] *Slaves have ruled over us,* [פ] *there is no redemption from their*
hand. [צ] *Abundant troubles have surrounded us,* [ק] *we called upon You,*
HASHEM, *our God,* [ר] *but You have distanced us for our iniquities.* [ש] *We*
have turned away from following after You; [ת] *we have strayed; we have*
become lost.

But still we have not returned from our waywardness. So how can we be
so brazen and obstinate as to say before You, HASHEM, *our God and the God*
of our forefathers, that we are righteous and have not sinned, for in truth, both
we and our fathers have sinned.

Strike the left side of the chest with the right fist while reciting
each of the sins in the following confession litany:

אָשַׁמְנוּ *We have become guilty;* [ב] *we have betrayed;* [ג] *we have robbed;*
[ד] *we have spoken slander;* [ה] *we have caused perversion;* [ו] *we*
have caused wickedness; [ז] *we have sinned willfully;* [ח] *we have extorted;*
[ט] *we have accused falsely;* [י] *we have given evil counsel;* [כ] *we have been*
deceitful; [ל] *we have scorned;* [מ] *we have rebelled;* [נ] *we have provoked;*
[ס] *we have turned away;* [ע] *we have been perverse;* [פ] *we have acted*
wantonly; [צ] *we have persecuted;* [ק] *we have been obstinate;* [ר] *we have*
been wicked; [ש] *we have corrupted;* [ת] *we have been abominable; we have*
strayed; You have let us go astray.

סַרְנוּ *We have turned away from Your commandments and from Your*
good laws but to no avail. Yet You are righteous in all that has come
upon us, for You have acted truthfully while we have caused wickedness.

הִרְשַׁעְנוּ *We have acted wickedly and have sinned willfully, therefore we*
have not been saved. Inspire our heart to abandon the path of evil
and hasten salvation for us, as it is written by Your prophet: May the wicked
one abandon his way and the vicious man his thoughts; may he return to
HASHEM *and He will show him mercy, and to our God, for He is abundantly*
forgiving.[1]

מְשִׁיחַ צִדְקֶךָ *Your righteous anointed [David] said before You: 'Who can*
discern mistakes? From unperceived faults cleanse me.'[2]
Cleanse us, HASHEM, *our God, of all our willful sins and purify us, of all our*

טֻמְאוֹתֵינוּ, וּזְרוֹק עָלֵינוּ מַיִם טְהוֹרִים וְטַהֲרֵנוּ, כַּכָּתוּב עַל יַד
נְבִיאֶךָ: וְזָרַקְתִּי עֲלֵיכֶם מַיִם טְהוֹרִים וּטְהַרְתֶּם, מִכֹּל טֻמְאוֹתֵיכֶם
וּמִכָּל גִּלּוּלֵיכֶם אֲטַהֵר אֶתְכֶם.[1]

מִיכָה עַבְדְּךָ אָמַר לְפָנֶיךָ: מִי אֵל כָּמוֹךָ נֹשֵׂא עָוֺן וְעֹבֵר עַל
פֶּשַׁע לִשְׁאֵרִית נַחֲלָתוֹ, לֹא הֶחֱזִיק לָעַד אַפּוֹ, כִּי
חָפֵץ חֶסֶד הוּא, יָשׁוּב יְרַחֲמֵנוּ, יִכְבֹּשׁ עֲוֺנֹתֵינוּ, וְתַשְׁלִיךְ בִּמְצֻלוֹת
יָם כָּל חַטֹּאתָם.[2] (וְכָל חַטֹּאת עַמְּךָ בֵּית יִשְׂרָאֵל תַּשְׁלִיךְ בִּמְקוֹם
אֲשֶׁר לֹא יִזָּכְרוּ, וְלֹא יִפָּקְדוּ, וְלֹא יַעֲלוּ עַל לֵב לְעוֹלָם.) תִּתֵּן אֱמֶת
לְיַעֲקֹב חֶסֶד לְאַבְרָהָם אֲשֶׁר נִשְׁבַּעְתָּ לַאֲבוֹתֵינוּ מִימֵי קֶדֶם.[3]

דָּנִיֵּאל אִישׁ חֲמוּדוֹת שִׁוַּע לְפָנֶיךָ: הַטֵּה אֱלֹהַי אָזְנְךָ וּשְׁמָע,
פְּקַח עֵינֶיךָ וּרְאֵה שֹׁמְמֹתֵינוּ וְהָעִיר אֲשֶׁר נִקְרָא שִׁמְךָ
עָלֶיהָ, כִּי לֹא עַל צִדְקֹתֵינוּ אֲנַחְנוּ מַפִּילִים תַּחֲנוּנֵינוּ לְפָנֶיךָ, כִּי עַל
רַחֲמֶיךָ הָרַבִּים. אֲדֹנָי שְׁמָעָה, אֲדֹנָי סְלָחָה, אֲדֹנָי הַקְשִׁיבָה, וַעֲשֵׂה
אַל תְּאַחַר, לְמַעַנְךָ אֱלֹהַי, כִּי שִׁמְךָ נִקְרָא עַל עִירְךָ וְעַל עַמֶּךָ.[4]

עֶזְרָא הַסּוֹפֵר אָמַר לְפָנֶיךָ: אֱלֹהַי, בֹּשְׁתִּי וְנִכְלַמְתִּי לְהָרִים,
אֱלֹהַי, פָּנַי אֵלֶיךָ, כִּי עֲוֺנֹתֵינוּ רָבוּ לְמַעְלָה
רֹאשׁ, וְאַשְׁמָתֵנוּ גָדְלָה עַד לַשָּׁמָיִם.[5] וְאַתָּה[6] אֱלוֹהַּ סְלִיחוֹת, חַנּוּן
וְרַחוּם, אֶרֶךְ אַפַּיִם וְרַב חֶסֶד, וְלֹא עֲזַבְתָּנוּ.[7]

אַל תַּעַזְבֵנוּ אָבִינוּ וְאַל תִּטְּשֵׁנוּ בּוֹרְאֵנוּ, וְאַל תַּזְנִיחֵנוּ יוֹצְרֵנוּ,
וְאַל תַּעַשׂ עִמָּנוּ כָלָה כְּחַטֹּאתֵינוּ. וְקַיֶּם לָנוּ יהוה
אֱלֹהֵינוּ, אֶת הַדָּבָר שֶׁהִבְטַחְתָּנוּ בְּקַבָּלָה עַל יְדֵי יִרְמְיָהוּ חוֹזָךְ,
כָּאָמוּר: בַּיָּמִים הָהֵם וּבָעֵת הַהִיא, נְאֻם יהוה, יְבֻקַּשׁ אֶת עֲוֺן
יִשְׂרָאֵל וְאֵינֶנּוּ וְאֶת חַטֹּאת יְהוּדָה וְלֹא תִמָּצֶאנָה, כִּי אֶסְלַח
לַאֲשֶׁר אַשְׁאִיר.[8] עַמְּךָ וְנַחֲלָתְךָ רְעֵבֵי טוּבְךָ, צְמֵאֵי חַסְדֶּךָ, תְּאֵבֵי
יִשְׁעֶךָ, יַכִּירוּ וְיֵדְעוּ כִּי לַיהוה אֱלֹהֵינוּ הָרַחֲמִים וְהַסְּלִיחוֹת.

אֵל רַחוּם שְׁמֶךָ, אֵל חַנּוּן שְׁמֶךָ, בָּנוּ נִקְרָא שְׁמֶךָ. יהוה עֲשֵׂה
לְמַעַן שְׁמֶךָ. עֲשֵׂה לְמַעַן אֲמִתֶּךָ, עֲשֵׂה לְמַעַן
בְּרִיתֶךָ, עֲשֵׂה לְמַעַן גָּדְלְךָ וְתִפְאַרְתֶּךָ, עֲשֵׂה לְמַעַן דָּתֶךָ, עֲשֵׂה
לְמַעַן הוֹדֶךָ, עֲשֵׂה לְמַעַן וִעוּדֶךָ, עֲשֵׂה לְמַעַן זִכְרֶךָ, עֲשֵׂה לְמַעַן
חַסְדֶּךָ, עֲשֵׂה לְמַעַן טוּבֶךָ, עֲשֵׂה לְמַעַן יִחוּדֶךָ, עֲשֵׂה לְמַעַן
כְּבוֹדֶךָ, עֲשֵׂה לְמַעַן לִמּוּדֶךָ, עֲשֵׂה לְמַעַן מַלְכוּתֶךָ, עֲשֵׂה לְמַעַן

contaminations. Sprinkle upon us pure water and purify us, as it is written by Your prophet: I shall sprinkle pure water upon you and purify you, of all your contaminations and of all your abominations I will purify you.'[1]

מִיכָה עַבְדְּךָ *Micah, Your servant, said before You: 'Who, O God, is like You, Who pardons iniquity and overlooks transgression for the remnant of His heritage? Who has not retained His wrath eternally, for He desires kindness! He will again be merciful to us; He will suppress our iniquities and cast into the depths of the sea all their sins.[2] (And all the sins of Your nation the Family of Israel, may You cast away to a place where they will neither be remembered, considered, nor brought to mind — ever.) Grant truth to Jacob, kindness to Abraham, as You swore to our forefathers from ancient times.'[3]*

דָּנִיֵּאל *Daniel, the greatly beloved man, cried out before You: 'Incline, my God, Your ear, and listen, open Your eyes and see our desolation and that of the city upon which Your Name is proclaimed, for not because of our righteousness do we cast down our supplications before You, rather because of Your abundant compassion. O my Lord, heed; O my Lord, forgive; O my Lord, be attentive and act, do not delay; for Your sake, my God, for Your Name is proclaimed upon Your city and Your people.'[4]*

עֶזְרָא הַסּוֹפֵר *Ezra the Scribe said before You: 'My God, I am embarrassed and ashamed to lift my face to You, my God — for our iniquities have multiplied above our heads, and our sins extend unto heaven.[5] You are[6] the God of forgiveness, compassionate and merciful, slow to anger, and abundant in kindness; and You have not forsaken us.'[7]*

אַל תַּעַזְבֵנוּ *Do not forsake us, our Father; do not cast us off, our Creator; do not abandon us, our Molder; and do not bring about our destruction, as our sins merit. Affirm for us, HASHEM, our God, the promise You made in the tradition through Jeremiah, Your seer, as it is said: 'In those days and at that time' — the words of HASHEM — 'the iniquity of Israel will be sought but there will be none, and the errors of Judah, but they will not be found, for I will have forgiven those whom I leave as a remnant.'[8]*

Your people and Your heritage, who hunger for Your goodness, who thirst for Your kindness, who long for Your salvation — may they recognize and know that to HASHEM, our God, belong mercy and forgiveness.

אֵל רַחוּם *'Merciful God' is Your Name, 'Gracious God' is Your Name, Your Name is called upon us — O HASHEM, act for Your Name's sake. Act for the sake of [א] Your truth; act for the sake of [ב] Your covenant; act for the sake of [ג] Your greatness and Your splendor; act for the sake of [ד] Your law; act for the sake of [ה] Your glory; act for the sake of [ו] Your Meeting House; act for the sake of [ז] Your remembrance; act for the sake of [ח] Your kindness; act for the sake of [ט] Your goodness; act for the sake of [י] Your Oneness; act for the sake of [כ] Your honor; act for the sake of [ל] Your teaching; act for the sake of [מ] Your kingship; act for the sake of*

---

(1) *Ezekiel* 36:25. (2) *Micah* 7:18-19. (3) 7:20. (4) *Daniel* 9:18-19. (5) *Ezra* 9:6. (6) Some editions of *Selichos* insert the word אֱלֹהֵינוּ, *our God,* at this point. (7) Cf. *Nehemiah* 9:17. (8) *Jeremiah* 50:20.

נִצְחֶךָ, עֲשֵׂה לְמַעַן סוֹדֶךָ, עֲשֵׂה לְמַעַן עֻזֶּךָ, עֲשֵׂה לְמַעַן פְּאֵרֶךָ, עֲשֵׂה לְמַעַן צִדְקָתֶךָ, עֲשֵׂה לְמַעַן קְדֻשָּׁתֶךָ, עֲשֵׂה לְמַעַן רַחֲמֶיךָ הָרַבִּים, עֲשֵׂה לְמַעַן שְׁכִינָתֶךָ, עֲשֵׂה לְמַעַן תְּהִלָּתֶךָ, עֲשֵׂה לְמַעַן אוֹהֲבֶיךָ שׁוֹכְנֵי עָפָר, עֲשֵׂה לְמַעַן אַבְרָהָם יִצְחָק וְיַעֲקֹב, עֲשֵׂה לְמַעַן מֹשֶׁה וְאַהֲרֹן, עֲשֵׂה לְמַעַן דָּוִד וּשְׁלֹמֹה, עֲשֵׂה לְמַעַן יְרוּשָׁלַיִם עִיר קָדְשֶׁךָ, עֲשֵׂה לְמַעַן צִיּוֹן מִשְׁכַּן כְּבוֹדֶךָ, עֲשֵׂה לְמַעַן שִׁמְמוֹת הֵיכָלֶךָ, עֲשֵׂה לְמַעַן הֲרִיסוּת מִזְבְּחֶךָ, עֲשֵׂה לְמַעַן הֲרוּגִים עַל שֵׁם קָדְשֶׁךָ, עֲשֵׂה לְמַעַן טְבוּחִים עַל יִחוּדֶךָ, עֲשֵׂה לְמַעַן בָּאֵי בָאֵשׁ וּבַמַּיִם עַל קִדּוּשׁ שְׁמֶךָ, עֲשֵׂה לְמַעַן יוֹנְקֵי שָׁדַיִם שֶׁלֹּא חָטָאוּ, עֲשֵׂה לְמַעַן גְּמוּלֵי חָלָב שֶׁלֹּא פָשָׁעוּ, עֲשֵׂה לְמַעַן תִּינוֹקוֹת שֶׁל בֵּית רַבָּן, עֲשֵׂה לְמַעַנְךָ אִם לֹא לְמַעֲנֵנוּ, עֲשֵׂה לְמַעַנְךָ וְהוֹשִׁיעֵנוּ.

עֲנֵנוּ יהוה עֲנֵנוּ, עֲנֵנוּ אֱלֹהֵינוּ עֲנֵנוּ, עֲנֵנוּ אָבִינוּ עֲנֵנוּ, עֲנֵנוּ בּוֹרְאֵנוּ עֲנֵנוּ, עֲנֵנוּ גּוֹאֲלֵנוּ עֲנֵנוּ, עֲנֵנוּ דוֹרְשֵׁנוּ עֲנֵנוּ, עֲנֵנוּ הָאֵל הַנֶּאֱמָן עֲנֵנוּ, עֲנֵנוּ וָתִיק וְחָסִיד עֲנֵנוּ, עֲנֵנוּ זַךְ וְיָשָׁר עֲנֵנוּ, עֲנֵנוּ חַי וְקַיָּם עֲנֵנוּ, עֲנֵנוּ טוֹב וּמֵטִיב עֲנֵנוּ, עֲנֵנוּ יוֹדֵעַ יֵצֶר עֲנֵנוּ, עֲנֵנוּ כּוֹבֵשׁ כְּעָסִים עֲנֵנוּ, עֲנֵנוּ לוֹבֵשׁ צְדָקוֹת עֲנֵנוּ, עֲנֵנוּ מֶלֶךְ מַלְכֵי הַמְּלָכִים עֲנֵנוּ, עֲנֵנוּ נוֹרָא וְנִשְׂגָּב עֲנֵנוּ, עֲנֵנוּ סוֹלֵחַ וּמוֹחֵל עֲנֵנוּ, עֲנֵנוּ עוֹנֶה בְּעֵת צָרָה עֲנֵנוּ, עֲנֵנוּ פּוֹדֶה וּמַצִּיל עֲנֵנוּ, עֲנֵנוּ צַדִּיק וְיָשָׁר עֲנֵנוּ, עֲנֵנוּ קָרוֹב לְקוֹרְאָיו עֲנֵנוּ, עֲנֵנוּ רַחוּם וְחַנּוּן עֲנֵנוּ, עֲנֵנוּ שׁוֹמֵעַ אֶל אֶבְיוֹנִים עֲנֵנוּ, עֲנֵנוּ תּוֹמֵךְ תְּמִימִים עֲנֵנוּ, עֲנֵנוּ אֱלֹהֵי אֲבוֹתֵינוּ עֲנֵנוּ, עֲנֵנוּ אֱלֹהֵי אַבְרָהָם עֲנֵנוּ, עֲנֵנוּ פַּחַד יִצְחָק עֲנֵנוּ, עֲנֵנוּ אֲבִיר יַעֲקֹב עֲנֵנוּ, עֲנֵנוּ עֶזְרַת הַשְּׁבָטִים עֲנֵנוּ, עֲנֵנוּ מִשְׂגַּב אִמָּהוֹת עֲנֵנוּ, עֲנֵנוּ קָשֶׁה לִכְעוֹס עֲנֵנוּ, עֲנֵנוּ רַךְ לִרְצוֹת עֲנֵנוּ, עֲנֵנוּ עוֹנֶה בְּעֵת רָצוֹן עֲנֵנוּ, עֲנֵנוּ אֲבִי יְתוֹמִים עֲנֵנוּ, עֲנֵנוּ דַּיַּן אַלְמָנוֹת עֲנֵנוּ.

מִי שֶׁעָנָה לְאַבְרָהָם אָבִינוּ בְּהַר הַמּוֹרִיָּה,	הוּא יַעֲנֵנוּ.
מִי שֶׁעָנָה לְיִצְחָק בְּנוֹ כְּשֶׁנֶּעֱקַד עַל גַּבֵּי הַמִּזְבֵּחַ,	הוּא יַעֲנֵנוּ.
מִי שֶׁעָנָה לְיַעֲקֹב בְּבֵית אֵל,	הוּא יַעֲנֵנוּ.
מִי שֶׁעָנָה לְיוֹסֵף בְּבֵית הָאֲסוּרִים,	הוּא יַעֲנֵנוּ.
מִי שֶׁעָנָה לַאֲבוֹתֵינוּ עַל יַם סוּף,	הוּא יַעֲנֵנוּ.
מִי שֶׁעָנָה לְמֹשֶׁה בְּחוֹרֵב,	הוּא יַעֲנֵנוּ.
מִי שֶׁעָנָה לְאַהֲרֹן בַּמַּחְתָּה,	הוּא יַעֲנֵנוּ.

[נ] Your eternality; act for the sake of [ס] Your counsel; act for the sake of
[ע] Your power; act for the sake of [פ] Your beauty; act for the sake of [צ] Your
righteousness; act for the sake of [ק] Your sanctity; act for the sake of [ר] Your
abundant mercy; act for the sake of [ש] Your Presence, act for the sake of
[ת] Your praise; act for the sake of Your beloved ones who rest in the dust; act
for the sake of Abraham, Isaac, and Jacob; act for the sake of Moses and
Aaron; act for the sake of David and Solomon; act for the sake of Jerusalem,
Your holy city; act for the sake of Zion, the abode of Your glory; act for the
sake of the desolation of Your Temple; act for the sake of the ruin of Your
Altar; act for the sake of the martyrs for Your holy Name; act for the sake of
those slaughtered for Your Oneness; act for the sake of those who entered fire
and water for the sanctification of Your Name; act for the nursing infants
who did not err; act for the sake of the weaned babes who did not sin; act for
the sake of children at the schoolroom; act for Your sake if not for ours; act for
Your sake and save us.

עֲנֵנוּ   Answer us, HASHEM, answer us; answer us, our God, answer us; answer
us, [א] our Father, answer us; answer us, [ב] our Creator, answer us;
answer us, [ג] our Redeemer, answer us; answer us, [ד] You Who searches us
out, answer us; answer us, [ה] faithful God, answer us; answer us, [ו] stead-
fast and kind One, answer us; answer us, [ז] pure and upright One, answer
us; answer us, [ח] living and enduring One, answer us; answer us, [ט] good
and beneficent One, answer us; answer us, [י] You Who knows inclinations,
answer us; answer us, [כ] You Who suppresses wrath, answer us; answer us,
[ל] You Who dons righteousness, answer us; answer us, [מ] King Who reigns
over kings, answer us; answer us, [נ] awesome and powerful One, answer us;
answer us, [ס] You Who forgives and pardons, answer us; answer us, [ע] You
Who answers in time of distress,[1] answer us; answer us, [פ] Redeemer and
Rescuer, answer us; answer us, [צ] righteous and upright One, answer us;
answer us, [ק] He Who is close to those who call upon Him, answer us; answer
us, [ר] merciful and gracious One, answer us; answer us, [ש] You Who hears
the destitute, answer us; answer us, [ת] You Who supports the wholesome,
answer us; answer us, God of our forefathers, answer us; answer us, God of
Abraham, answer us; answer us, Dread of Isaac, answer us; answer us,
Mighty One of Jacob, answer us; answer us, Helper of the tribes, answer us;
answer us, Stronghold of the Matriarchs, answer us; answer us, You Who are
hard to anger, answer us; answer us, You Who are easy to pacify, answer us;
answer us, You Who answers in a time of favor,[1] answer us; answer us,
Father of orphans, answer us; answer us, Judge of widows, answer us.

מִי שֶׁעָנָה   He Who answered our father Abraham on Mount Moriah,
                                                              may He answer us.
He Who answered his son Isaac when he was bound atop the altar,
                                                              may He answer us.
He Who answered Jacob in Bethel,   may He answer us.
He Who answered Joseph in the prison,   may He answer us.
He Who answered our forefathers at the Sea of Reeds,   may He answer us.
He Who answered Moses in Horeb,   may He answer us.
He Who answered Aaron when he offered the censer,   may He answer us.

(1) Some editions of Selichos reverse the positions of these two lines.

מִי שֶׁעָנָה לְפִינְחָס בְּקוּמוֹ מִתּוֹךְ הָעֵדָה,   הוּא יַעֲנֵנוּ.

מִי שֶׁעָנָה לִיהוֹשֻׁעַ בַּגִּלְגָּל,   הוּא יַעֲנֵנוּ.

מִי שֶׁעָנָה לִשְׁמוּאֵל בַּמִּצְפָּה,   הוּא יַעֲנֵנוּ.

מִי שֶׁעָנָה לְדָוִד וּשְׁלֹמֹה בְנוֹ בִּירוּשָׁלָיִם,   הוּא יַעֲנֵנוּ.

מִי שֶׁעָנָה לְאֵלִיָּהוּ בְּהַר הַכַּרְמֶל,   הוּא יַעֲנֵנוּ.

מִי שֶׁעָנָה לֶאֱלִישָׁע בִּירִיחוֹ,   הוּא יַעֲנֵנוּ.

מִי שֶׁעָנָה לְיוֹנָה בִּמְעֵי הַדָּגָה,   הוּא יַעֲנֵנוּ.

מִי שֶׁעָנָה לְחִזְקִיָּהוּ מֶלֶךְ יְהוּדָה בְּחָלְיוֹ,   הוּא יַעֲנֵנוּ.

מִי שֶׁעָנָה לַחֲנַנְיָה מִישָׁאֵל וַעֲזַרְיָה בְּתוֹךְ כִּבְשַׁן הָאֵשׁ,   הוּא יַעֲנֵנוּ.

מִי שֶׁעָנָה לְדָנִיֵּאל בְּגוֹב הָאֲרָיוֹת,   הוּא יַעֲנֵנוּ.

מִי שֶׁעָנָה לְמָרְדְּכַי וְאֶסְתֵּר בְּשׁוּשַׁן הַבִּירָה,   הוּא יַעֲנֵנוּ.

מִי שֶׁעָנָה לְעֶזְרָא בַגּוֹלָה,   הוּא יַעֲנֵנוּ.

מִי שֶׁעָנָה לְכָל הַצַּדִּיקִים וְהַחֲסִידִים וְהַתְּמִימִים וְהַיְשָׁרִים,

הוּא יַעֲנֵנוּ.

רַחֲמָנָא דְּעָנֵי לַעֲנִיֵּי, עֲנֵינָא. רַחֲמָנָא דְּעָנֵי לִתְבִירֵי לִבָּא,
עֲנֵינָא. רַחֲמָנָא דְּעָנֵי לְמַכִּיכֵי רוּחָא, עֲנֵינָא. רַחֲמָנָא
עֲנֵינָא. רַחֲמָנָא חוּס. רַחֲמָנָא פְּרוֹק. רַחֲמָנָא שְׁזֵיב. רַחֲמָנָא
רְחַם עֲלָן. הַשְׁתָּא בַּעֲגָלָא וּבִזְמַן קָרִיב.

נפילת אפים

In the presence of a Torah Scroll, the following (until נַבְשׁוּ רָגַע) is recited with the head resting
on the arm, preferably while seated. Elsewhere, it is recited with the head held erect.

(וַיֹּאמֶר דָּוִד אֶל גָּד, צַר לִי מְאֹד נִפְּלָה נָּא בְיַד יהוה,
כִּי רַבִּים רַחֲמָיו, וּבְיַד אָדָם אַל אֶפֹּלָה.[1])

רַחוּם וְחַנּוּן חָטָאתִי לְפָנֶיךָ. יהוה מָלֵא רַחֲמִים, רַחֵם עָלַי
וְקַבֵּל תַּחֲנוּנָי.

תהלים ו:ב-יא

יהוה אַל בְּאַפְּךָ תוֹכִיחֵנִי, וְאַל בַּחֲמָתְךָ תְיַסְּרֵנִי. חָנֵּנִי יהוה, כִּי
אֻמְלַל אָנִי, רְפָאֵנִי יהוה, כִּי נִבְהֲלוּ עֲצָמָי. וְנַפְשִׁי נִבְהֲלָה
מְאֹד, וְאַתָּה יהוה, עַד מָתָי. שׁוּבָה יהוה, חַלְּצָה נַפְשִׁי, הוֹשִׁיעֵנִי
לְמַעַן חַסְדֶּךָ. כִּי אֵין בַּמָּוֶת זִכְרֶךָ, בִּשְׁאוֹל מִי יוֹדֶה לָּךְ. יָגַעְתִּי
בְּאַנְחָתִי, אַשְׂחֶה בְכָל לַיְלָה מִטָּתִי, בְּדִמְעָתִי עַרְשִׂי אַמְסֶה.
עָשְׁשָׁה מִכַּעַס עֵינִי, עָתְקָה בְּכָל צוֹרְרָי. סוּרוּ מִמֶּנִּי כָּל פֹּעֲלֵי אָוֶן,
כִּי שָׁמַע יהוה קוֹל בִּכְיִי. שָׁמַע יהוה תְּחִנָּתִי, יהוה תְּפִלָּתִי יִקָּח.
יֵבֹשׁוּ וְיִבָּהֲלוּ מְאֹד כָּל אֹיְבָי, יָשֻׁבוּ יֵבֹשׁוּ רָגַע.

He Who answered Phineas when he arose from amid the congregation,
may He answer us.

He Who answered Joshua in Gilgal,   *may He answer us.*
He Who answered Samuel in Mitzpah,   *may He answer us.*
He Who answered David and his son Solomon in Jerusalem,
may He answer us.

He Who answered Elijah on Mount Carmel,   *may He answer us.*
He Who answered Elisha in Jericho,   *may He answer us.*
He Who answered Jonah in the innards of the fish,   *may He answer us.*
He Who answered Hezekiah, King of Judah, in his illness,
may He answer us.

He Who answered Chananiah, Mishael, and Azariah in the fiery oven,
may He answer us.

He Who answered Daniel in the lions' den,   *may He answer us.*
He Who answered Mordechai and Esther in Shushan the capital,
may He answer us.

He Who answered Ezra in the Exile,   *may He answer us.*
He Who answered all the righteous, the devout, the wholesome,
and the upright,   *may He answer us.*

רַחֲמָנָא *The Merciful One Who answers the poor, may He answer us. The Merciful One Who answers the brokenhearted, may He answer us. The Merciful One Who answers the humble of spirit, may He answer us. O Merciful One, answer us. O Merciful One, pity. O Merciful One, redeem. O Merciful One, deliver. O Merciful One, have mercy on us — now, swiftly and soon.*

PUTTING DOWN THE HEAD

In the presence of a Torah Scroll, the following (until *'instantly shamed'*) is recited with the head resting on the arm, preferably while seated. Elsewhere, it is recited with the head held erect.

(*And David said to Gad, 'I am exceedingly distressed. Let us fall into HASHEM's hand for His mercies are abundant, but let me not fall into human hands.'* [1])

רַחוּם וְחַנּוּן *O compassionate and gracious One, I have sinned before You. HASHEM, Who is full of mercy, have mercy on me and accept my supplications.*

Psalms 6:2-11

הׁ *HASHEM, do not rebuke me in Your anger nor chastise me in Your rage. Favor me, HASHEM, for I am feeble; heal me, HASHEM, for my bones shudder. My soul is utterly confounded, and You, HASHEM, how long? Desist, HASHEM, release my soul; save me as befits Your kindness. For there is no mention of You in death; in the Lower World who will thank You? I am wearied with my sigh, every night my tears drench my bed, soak my couch. My eye is dimmed because of anger, aged by my tormentors. Depart from me, all evildoers, for HASHEM has heard the sound of my weeping. HASHEM has heard my plea, HASHEM will accept my prayer. Let all my foes be shamed and utterly confounded, they will regret and be instantly shamed.*

---

(1) *II Samuel* 24:14.

מַחֵי וּמַסֵּי מְמִית וּמְחַיֶּה, מַסִּיק מִן שְׁאוֹל לְחַיֵּי עָלְמָא, בְּרָא
כַּד חָטֵי אֲבוּהִי לַקְיֵהּ, אֲבוּהִי דְחָיֵס אַסֵּי לִכְאֵבָהּ.
עַבְדָּא דְּמָרִיד נָפִיק בְּקוֹלָר, מָרֵהּ תָּאִיב וְתָבִיר קוֹלָרֵהּ.

בְּרָךְ בְּכְרָךְ אֲנַן וְחָטִינַן קַמָּךְ, הָא רָזֵי נַפְשִׁין בְּגִידִין מְרָרִין,
עַבְדָּךְ וּמְרוֹדִינַן קַמָּךְ, הָא בְּבִזְתָּא, הָא בְּשִׁבְיָא, הָא
בְּמַלְקִיּוּתָא. בְּמָטוּ מִנָּךְ בְּרַחֲמָךְ דִּנְפִישִׁין, אַסֵּי לִכְאֵבִין דִּתְקוֹף
עֲלָן, עַד דְּלָא נֶהֱוֵי גְּמִירָא בְּשִׁבְיָא.

מַכְנִיסֵי רַחֲמִים, הַכְנִיסוּ רַחֲמֵינוּ, לִפְנֵי בַּעַל הָרַחֲמִים.
מַשְׁמִיעֵי תְפִלָּה, הַשְׁמִיעוּ תְפִלָּתֵנוּ, לִפְנֵי
שׁוֹמֵעַ תְּפִלָּה. מַשְׁמִיעֵי צְעָקָה, הַשְׁמִיעוּ צַעֲקָתֵנוּ, לִפְנֵי שׁוֹמֵעַ
צְעָקָה. מַכְנִיסֵי דִמְעָה, הַכְנִיסוּ דִמְעוֹתֵינוּ, לִפְנֵי מֶלֶךְ מִתְרַצֶּה
בִּדְמָעוֹת.

הִשְׁתַּדְּלוּ וְהַרְבּוּ תְּחִנָּה וּבַקָּשָׁה, לִפְנֵי מֶלֶךְ אֵל רָם וְנִשָּׂא.
הַזְכִּירוּ לְפָנָיו, הַשְׁמִיעוּ לְפָנָיו תּוֹרָה וּמַעֲשִׂים טוֹבִים שֶׁל שׁוֹכְנֵי
עָפָר.

יִזְכּוֹר אַהֲבָתָם וִיחַיֶּה זַרְעָם, שֶׁלֹּא תֹאבַד שְׁאֵרִית יַעֲקֹב. כִּי צֹאן
רוֹעֶה נֶאֱמָן הָיָה לְחֶרְפָּה, יִשְׂרָאֵל גּוֹי אֶחָד לְמָשָׁל וְלִשְׁנִינָה.
מַהֵר עֲנֵנוּ אֱלֹהֵי יִשְׁעֵנוּ, וּפְדֵנוּ מִכָּל גְּזֵרוֹת קָשׁוֹת וְהוֹשִׁיעָה
בְּרַחֲמֶיךָ הָרַבִּים, מְשִׁיחַ צִדְקֶךָ וְעַמָּךְ.

מָרָן דִּבְשְׁמַיָּא לָךְ מִתְחַנְּנַן, כְּבַר שִׁבְיָא דְּמִתְחַנַּן לְשָׁבוּיֵהּ.
כֻּלְּהוֹן בְּנֵי שִׁבְיָא בְּכַסְפָּא מִתְפָּרְקִין, וְעַמָּךְ
יִשְׂרָאֵל בְּרַחֲמֵי וּבְתַחֲנוּנֵי, הַב לָן שְׁאִילְתִּין וּבָעוּתִין, דְּלָא נֶהֱדַר
רֵיקָם מִן קַדָּמָךְ.

מָרָן דִּבְשְׁמַיָּא לָךְ מִתְחַנְּנַן, כְּעַבְדָּא דְּמִתְחַנַּן לְמָרֵיהּ, עֲשִׁיקֵי
אֲנַן וּבַחֲשׁוֹכָא שָׁרֵינַן, מְרִירָן נַפְשִׁין מֵעַקְתָּן דִּנְפִישִׁין, חֵילָא לֵית
בָּן לְרַצּוּיָךְ מָרָן, עֲבִיד בְּדִיל קְיָמָא דִּגְזַרְתָּ עִם אֲבָהָתָנָא.

שׁוֹמֵר יִשְׂרָאֵל, שְׁמוֹר שְׁאֵרִית יִשְׂרָאֵל, וְאַל יֹאבַד
יִשְׂרָאֵל, הָאוֹמְרִים, שְׁמַע יִשְׂרָאֵל.[1]
שׁוֹמֵר גּוֹי אֶחָד, שְׁמוֹר שְׁאֵרִית עַם אֶחָד, וְאַל יֹאבַד גּוֹי אֶחָד,
הַמְיַחֲדִים שִׁמְךָ, יהוה אֱלֹהֵינוּ יהוה אֶחָד.[1]

מָחִי וּמַסִּי *[O God,] He Who smites and heals, causes death and restores life, raises [the dead] from the grave to eternal life: Should a son sin, his father would smack him, but a compassionate father will heal his [son's] pain. When a slave rebels, he is led out in collar-irons, but if his master desires to, he breaks his chains.*

We are Your son, Your firstborn, and we have sinned against You; so our soul has been satiated with bitter wormwood. We are Your servants and we have rebelled against You; so [we have suffered], some with looting, some with captivity, and some with the lash. We beg of You, in Your abundant compassion, heal the pains that have overwhelmed us, before we have been completely wiped out in captivity.

מַכְנִיסֵי רַחֲמִים *O you who usher in [pleas for] mercy, may you usher in our [plea for] mercy, before the Master of mercy. O you who cause prayer to be heard, may you cause our prayer to be heard, before the Hearer of prayer. O you who cause outcry to be heard, may you cause our outcry to be heard, before the Hearer of outcry. O you who usher in tears, may you usher in our tears, before the King Who finds favor through tears.*

Exert yourselves, and multiply supplication and petition, before the King, God, exalted and most high. Mention before Him, cause to be heard before Him, the Torah and the good deeds of [the Patriarchs and Matriarchs] who dwell in the dust.

May He remember their love and grant life to [their] offspring, that the remnant of Jacob not be lost. For the flock of the faithful shepherd [Moses] has become a disgrace; Israel, the unique nation, a parable and a simile.

Speedily, answer us, O God of our salvation, and redeem us from all harsh decrees; and may You save, in Your abundant mercy, Your righteous anointed and Your people.

מָרָן דִּבְשְׁמַיָּא *Our Master Who is in heaven, to You do we supplicate, as a captive supplicates before his captors; for all captives are redeemed with money, but Your people Israel with compassion and supplication. O grant our requests and our prayers that we not be turned away from You empty-handed.*

Our Master Who is in heaven, to You do we supplicate, as a slave supplicates before his master: We are oppressed and we abide in darkness, souls embittered from abundant distress. We have no strength to regain Your favor. Our Master, act for the sake of the covenant that You made with our Patriarchs.

שׁוֹמֵר יִשְׂרָאֵל *O Guardian of Israel, protect the remnant of Israel; let not Israel be destroyed — those who proclaim, 'Hear O Israel.'[1]*

O Guardian of the unique nation, protect the remnant of the unique people; let not the unique nation be destroyed — those who proclaim the Oneness of Your Name, 'HASHEM is our God, HASHEM, the One and Only!'[1]

---

(1) *Deuteronomy* 6:4.

שׁוֹמֵר גּוֹי קָדוֹשׁ, שְׁמוֹר שְׁאֵרִית עַם קָדוֹשׁ, וְאַל יֹאבַד גּוֹי
קָדוֹשׁ, הַמְשַׁלְּשִׁים בְּשָׁלֹשׁ קְדֻשּׁוֹת לְקָדוֹשׁ.

מִתְרַצֶּה בְרַחֲמִים וּמִתְפַּיֵּס בְּתַחֲנוּנִים, הִתְרַצֵּה וְהִתְפַּיֵּס לְדוֹר
עָנִי, כִּי אֵין עוֹזֵר. אָבִינוּ מַלְכֵּנוּ, חָנֵּנוּ וַעֲנֵנוּ, כִּי אֵין בָּנוּ מַעֲשִׂים,
עֲשֵׂה עִמָּנוּ צְדָקָה וָחֶסֶד וְהוֹשִׁיעֵנוּ.

וַאֲנַחְנוּ לֹא נֵדַע מַה נַּעֲשֶׂה, כִּי עָלֶיךָ עֵינֵינוּ.[1] זְכֹר רַחֲמֶיךָ
יהוה וַחֲסָדֶיךָ, כִּי מֵעוֹלָם הֵמָּה.[2] יְהִי חַסְדְּךָ יהוה
עָלֵינוּ, כַּאֲשֶׁר יִחַלְנוּ לָךְ.[3] אַל תִּזְכָּר לָנוּ עֲוֺנוֹת רִאשׁוֹנִים, מַהֵר
יְקַדְּמוּנוּ רַחֲמֶיךָ, כִּי דַלּוֹנוּ מְאֹד.[4] חָנֵּנוּ יהוה חָנֵּנוּ, כִּי רַב שָׂבַעְנוּ
בוּז.[5] בְּרֹגֶז רַחֵם תִּזְכּוֹר.[6] כִּי הוּא יָדַע יִצְרֵנוּ, זָכוּר כִּי עָפָר אֲנָחְנוּ.[7]
עָזְרֵנוּ אֱלֹהֵי יִשְׁעֵנוּ עַל דְּבַר כְּבוֹד שְׁמֶךָ, וְהַצִּילֵנוּ וְכַפֵּר עַל
חַטֹּאתֵינוּ לְמַעַן שְׁמֶךָ.[8]

קדיש שלם
The *chazzan* recites קַדִּישׁ שָׁלֵם:

יִתְגַּדַּל וְיִתְקַדַּשׁ שְׁמֵהּ רַבָּא. (Cong. – אָמֵן.) בְּעָלְמָא דִּי בְרָא
כִרְעוּתֵהּ, וְיַמְלִיךְ מַלְכוּתֵהּ, בְּחַיֵּיכוֹן וּבְיוֹמֵיכוֹן וּבְחַיֵּי
דְכָל בֵּית יִשְׂרָאֵל, בַּעֲגָלָא וּבִזְמַן קָרִיב. וְאִמְרוּ אָמֵן.
(Cong. – אָמֵן. יְהֵא שְׁמֵהּ רַבָּא מְבָרַךְ לְעָלַם וּלְעָלְמֵי עָלְמַיָּא.)
יְהֵא שְׁמֵהּ רַבָּא מְבָרַךְ לְעָלַם וּלְעָלְמֵי עָלְמַיָּא.
יִתְבָּרַךְ וְיִשְׁתַּבַּח וְיִתְפָּאַר וְיִתְרוֹמַם וְיִתְנַשֵּׂא וְיִתְהַדָּר וְיִתְעַלֶּה
וְיִתְהַלָּל שְׁמֵהּ דְּקֻדְשָׁא בְּרִיךְ הוּא. (Cong. – בְּרִיךְ הוּא.) לְעֵלָּא מִן כָּל
בִּרְכָתָא וְשִׁירָתָא תֻּשְׁבְּחָתָא וְנֶחֱמָתָא, דַּאֲמִירָן בְּעָלְמָא. וְאִמְרוּ:
אָמֵן. (Cong. – אָמֵן.)
(Cong. – קַבֵּל בְּרַחֲמִים וּבְרָצוֹן אֶת תְּפִלָּתֵנוּ.)
תִּתְקַבֵּל צְלוֹתְהוֹן וּבָעוּתְהוֹן דְּכָל (בֵּית) יִשְׂרָאֵל קֳדָם אֲבוּהוֹן
דִּי בִשְׁמַיָּא. וְאִמְרוּ אָמֵן. (Cong. – אָמֵן.)
(Cong. – יְהִי שֵׁם יהוה מְבֹרָךְ, מֵעַתָּה וְעַד עוֹלָם.[9])
יְהֵא שְׁלָמָא רַבָּא מִן שְׁמַיָּא וְחַיִּים עָלֵינוּ וְעַל כָּל יִשְׂרָאֵל.
וְאִמְרוּ אָמֵן. (Cong. – אָמֵן.)
(Cong. – עֶזְרִי מֵעִם יהוה, עֹשֵׂה שָׁמַיִם וָאָרֶץ.[10])

Take three steps back. Bow left and say, . . . עֹשֶׂה; bow right and say, . . . הוּא יַעֲשֶׂה; bow forward and
say, אָמֵן . . . וְעַל כָּל. Remain standing in place for a few moments, then take three steps forward.

עֹשֶׂה שָׁלוֹם בִּמְרוֹמָיו, הוּא יַעֲשֶׂה שָׁלוֹם עָלֵינוּ, וְעַל כָּל יִשְׂרָאֵל.
וְאִמְרוּ אָמֵן. (Cong. – אָמֵן.)

O Guardian of the holy nation, protect the remnant of the holy people; let not the holy nation be destroyed — those who proclaim three-fold sanctifications to the Holy One.

Become favorable through compassion and become appeased through supplications. Become favorable and appeased to the poor generation, for there is no helper. Our Father, our King, be gracious with us and answer us, though we have no worthy deeds; treat us with charity and kindness, and save us.

וַאֲנַחְנוּ We know not what to do — but our eyes are upon You.¹ Remember Your mercies, HASHEM, and Your kindnesses, for they are from the beginning of the world.² May Your kindness be upon us, HASHEM, just as we awaited You.³ Recall not against us the iniquities of the ancients; may Your mercies meet us swiftly, for we have become exceedingly impoverished.⁴ Be gracious to us, HASHEM, be gracious to us, for we are abundantly sated with scorn.⁵ Amid rage — remember to be merciful!⁶ For He knew our nature, He remembers that we are dust.⁷ Chazzan— Assist us, O God of our salvation, for the sake of Your Name's glory; rescue us and atone for our sins for Your Name's sake.⁸

FULL KADDISH
The chazzan recites the Full Kaddish:

יִתְגַּדַּל May His great Name grow exalted and sanctified (Cong. — Amen.) in the world that He created as He willed. May He give reign to His kingship in your lifetimes and in your days, and in the lifetimes of the entire Family of Israel, swiftly and soon. Now respond: Amen.

(Cong. — Amen. May His great Name be blessed forever and ever.)
May His great Name be blessed forever and ever.

Blessed, praised, glorified, exalted, extolled, mighty, upraised and lauded be the Name of the Holy One, Blessed is He (Cong. — Blessed is He.) beyond any blessing and song, praise, and consolation that are uttered in the world. Now respond: Amen. (Cong. — Amen.)

(Cong. — Accept our prayers with mercy and favor.)
May the prayers and supplications of the entire House of Israel be accepted before their Father Who is in Heaven. Now respond: Amen. (Cong. — Amen.)

(Cong. — Blessed be the Name of HASHEM from this time and forever.⁹)
May there be abundant peace from Heaven, and life, upon us and upon all Israel. Now respond: Amen. (Cong. — Amen.)

(Cong. — My help is from HASHEM, Maker of heaven and earth.¹⁰)

Take three steps back. Bow left and say, 'He Who makes peace . . .'; bow right and say, 'may He make peace . . .'; bow forward and say, 'and upon all Israel . . .'
Remain standing in place for a few moments, then take three steps forward.

He Who makes peace in His heights, may He make peace upon us, and upon all Israel. Now respond: Amen. (Cong. — Amen.)

(1) II Chronicles 20:12. (2) Psalms 25:6. (3) 33:22. (4) 79:8. (5) 123:3.
(6) Habakkuk 3:2. (7) Psalms 103:14. (8) 79:9. (9) 113:2. (10) 121:2.

❊ יוֹם שְׁלִישִׁי ❊

אַשְׁרֵי יוֹשְׁבֵי בֵיתֶךָ, עוֹד יְהַלְלוּךָ סֶּלָה.[1] אַשְׁרֵי הָעָם שֶׁכָּכָה לוֹ, אַשְׁרֵי הָעָם שֶׁיהוה אֱלֹהָיו.[2]

תְּהִלָּה לְדָוִד

תהלים קמה

אֲרוֹמִמְךָ אֱלוֹהַי הַמֶּלֶךְ, וַאֲבָרְכָה שִׁמְךָ לְעוֹלָם וָעֶד.

בְּכָל יוֹם אֲבָרְכֶךָּ, וַאֲהַלְלָה שִׁמְךָ לְעוֹלָם וָעֶד.

גָּדוֹל יהוה וּמְהֻלָּל מְאֹד, וְלִגְדֻלָּתוֹ אֵין חֵקֶר.

דּוֹר לְדוֹר יְשַׁבַּח מַעֲשֶׂיךָ, וּגְבוּרֹתֶיךָ יַגִּידוּ.

הֲדַר כְּבוֹד הוֹדֶךָ, וְדִבְרֵי נִפְלְאֹתֶיךָ אָשִׂיחָה.

וֶעֱזוּז נוֹרְאֹתֶיךָ יֹאמֵרוּ, וּגְדֻלָּתְךָ אֲסַפְּרֶנָּה.

זֵכֶר רַב טוּבְךָ יַבִּיעוּ, וְצִדְקָתְךָ יְרַנֵּנוּ.

חַנּוּן וְרַחוּם יהוה, אֶרֶךְ אַפַּיִם וּגְדָל חָסֶד.

טוֹב יהוה לַכֹּל, וְרַחֲמָיו עַל כָּל מַעֲשָׂיו.

יוֹדוּךָ יהוה כָּל מַעֲשֶׂיךָ, וַחֲסִידֶיךָ יְבָרְכוּכָה.

כְּבוֹד מַלְכוּתְךָ יֹאמֵרוּ, וּגְבוּרָתְךָ יְדַבֵּרוּ.

לְהוֹדִיעַ לִבְנֵי הָאָדָם גְּבוּרֹתָיו, וּכְבוֹד הֲדַר מַלְכוּתוֹ.

מַלְכוּתְךָ מַלְכוּת כָּל עֹלָמִים, וּמֶמְשַׁלְתְּךָ בְּכָל דּוֹר וָדֹר.

סוֹמֵךְ יהוה לְכָל הַנֹּפְלִים, וְזוֹקֵף לְכָל הַכְּפוּפִים.

עֵינֵי כֹל אֵלֶיךָ יְשַׂבֵּרוּ, וְאַתָּה נוֹתֵן לָהֶם אֶת אָכְלָם בְּעִתּוֹ.

Concentrate intently while reciting the verse, פּוֹתֵחַ.

פּוֹתֵחַ אֶת יָדֶךָ, וּמַשְׂבִּיעַ לְכָל חַי רָצוֹן.

❖ צַדִּיק יהוה בְּכָל דְּרָכָיו, וְחָסִיד בְּכָל מַעֲשָׂיו.

קָרוֹב יהוה לְכָל קֹרְאָיו, לְכֹל אֲשֶׁר יִקְרָאֻהוּ בֶאֱמֶת.

רְצוֹן יְרֵאָיו יַעֲשֶׂה, וְאֶת שַׁוְעָתָם יִשְׁמַע וְיוֹשִׁיעֵם.

שׁוֹמֵר יהוה אֶת כָּל אֹהֲבָיו, וְאֵת כָּל הָרְשָׁעִים יַשְׁמִיד.

תְּהִלַּת יהוה יְדַבֶּר פִּי, וִיבָרֵךְ כָּל בָּשָׂר שֵׁם קָדְשׁוֹ לְעוֹלָם וָעֶד.

וַאֲנַחְנוּ נְבָרֵךְ יָהּ, מֵעַתָּה וְעַד עוֹלָם, הַלְלוּיָהּ.[3]

The *chazzan* recites חֲצִי קַדִּישׁ.

יִתְגַּדַּל וְיִתְקַדַּשׁ שְׁמֵהּ רַבָּא. (.Cong – אָמֵן.) בְּעָלְמָא דִּי בְרָא כִרְעוּתֵהּ. וְיַמְלִיךְ מַלְכוּתֵהּ, בְּחַיֵּיכוֹן וּבְיוֹמֵיכוֹן וּבְחַיֵּי דְכָל בֵּית יִשְׂרָאֵל, בַּעֲגָלָא וּבִזְמַן קָרִיב. וְאִמְרוּ: אָמֵן.

(.Cong – אָמֵן. יְהֵא שְׁמֵהּ רַבָּא מְבָרַךְ לְעָלַם וּלְעָלְמֵי עָלְמַיָּא.)

יְהֵא שְׁמֵהּ רַבָּא מְבָרַךְ לְעָלַם וּלְעָלְמֵי עָלְמַיָּא.

יִתְבָּרַךְ וְיִשְׁתַּבַּח וְיִתְפָּאַר וְיִתְרוֹמַם וְיִתְנַשֵּׂא וְיִתְהַדָּר וְיִתְעַלֶּה וְיִתְהַלָּל שְׁמֵהּ דְּקֻדְשָׁא בְּרִיךְ הוּא (.Cong – בְּרִיךְ הוּא) לְעֵלָּא מִן כָּל בִּרְכָתָא וְשִׁירָתָא תֻּשְׁבְּחָתָא וְנֶחֱמָתָא, דַּאֲמִירָן בְּעָלְמָא. וְאִמְרוּ: אָמֵן. (.Cong – אָמֵן.)

❊{ **THIRD DAY** }❊

אַשְׁרֵי   *Praiseworthy are those who dwell in Your house; may they always
       praise You, Selah!*[1] *Praiseworthy is the people for whom this is so,
praiseworthy is the people whose God is* HASHEM.[2]

Psalm 145   *A psalm of praise by David:*

א *I will exalt You, my God the King, and I will bless Your Name forever and ever.*

ב *Every day I will bless You, and I will laud Your Name forever and ever.*

ג HASHEM *is great and exceedingly lauded,
       and His greatness is beyond investigation.*

ד *Each generation will praise Your deeds to the next
       and of Your mighty deeds they will tell;*

ה *The splendrous glory of Your power and Your wondrous deeds I shall discuss.*

ו *And of Your awesome power they will speak, and Your greatness I shall relate.*

ז *A recollection of Your abundant goodness they will utter
       and of Your righteousness they will sing exultantly.*

ח *Gracious and merciful is* HASHEM,
       slow to anger, and great in [bestowing] kindness.

ט HASHEM *is good to all; His mercies are on all His works.*

י *All Your works shall thank You,* HASHEM, *and Your devout ones will bless You.*

כ *Of the glory of Your kingdom they will speak, and of Your power they will tell;*

ל *To inform human beings of His mighty deeds,
       and the glorious splendor of His kingdom.*

מ *Your kingdom is a kingdom spanning all eternities,
       and Your dominion is throughout every generation.*

ס HASHEM *supports all the fallen ones and straightens all the bent.*

ע *The eyes of all look to You with hope
       and You give them their food in its proper time;*

פ *You open Your hand,*   Concentrate intently while reciting the verse, 'You open. . .'
       and satisfy the desire of every living thing.

צ Chazzan— *Righteous is* HASHEM *in all His ways
       and magnanimous in all His deeds.*

ק HASHEM *is close to all who call upon Him — to all who call upon Him sincerely.*

ר *The will of those who fear Him He will do;
       and their cry He will hear, and save them.*

ש HASHEM *protects all who love Him; but all the wicked He will destroy.*

ת *May my mouth declare the praise of* HASHEM
       and may all flesh bless His Holy Name forever and ever.

We will bless God from this time and forever, Halleluyah![3]

The *chazzan* recites Half-*Kaddish:*

יִתְגַּדַּל   *May His great Name grow exalted and sanctified* (Cong.— *Amen.*) *in
       the world that He created as He willed. May He give reign to His
kingship in your lifetimes and in your days, and in the lifetimes of the entire
Family of Israel, swiftly and soon. Now respond: Amen.*

(Cong.— *Amen. May His great Name be blessed forever and ever.*)
       May His great Name be blessed forever and ever.

*Blessed, praised, glorified, exalted, extolled, mighty, upraised, and lauded be
the Name of the Holy One, Blessed is He* (Cong.— *Blessed is He*) — *beyond any
blessing and song, praise and consolation that are uttered in the world. Now
respond: Amen.* (Cong.— *Amen.*)

---

(1) *Psalms* 84:5. (2) 144:15. (3) 115:18.

All:

לְךָ יהוה הַצְּדָקָה, וְלָנוּ בְּשֶׁת הַפָּנִים.[1] מַה נִּתְאוֹנֵן,[2] מַה נֹּאמַר, מַה נְּדַבֵּר, וּמַה נִּצְטַדָּק.[3] נַחְפְּשָׂה דְרָכֵינוּ וְנַחְקְרָה, וְנָשׁוּבָה אֵלֶיךָ,[4] כִּי יְמִינְךָ פְּשׁוּטָה לְקַבֵּל שָׁבִים. לֹא בְחֶסֶד וְלֹא בְמַעֲשִׂים בָּאנוּ לְפָנֶיךָ, כְּדַלִּים וּכְרָשִׁים דָּפַקְנוּ דְלָתֶיךָ. דְּלָתֶיךָ דָּפַקְנוּ רַחוּם וְחַנּוּן, נָא אַל תְּשִׁיבֵנוּ רֵיקָם מִלְּפָנֶיךָ. מִלְּפָנֶיךָ מַלְכֵּנוּ רֵיקָם אַל תְּשִׁיבֵנוּ, כִּי אַתָּה שׁוֹמֵעַ תְּפִלָּה.

שׁוֹמֵעַ תְּפִלָּה, עָדֶיךָ כָּל בָּשָׂר יָבֹאוּ.[5] יָבוֹא כָל בָּשָׂר לְהִשְׁתַּחֲוֹת לְפָנֶיךָ יהוה.[6] יָבֹאוּ וְיִשְׁתַּחֲווּ לְפָנֶיךָ אֲדֹנָי, וִיכַבְּדוּ לִשְׁמֶךָ.[7] בְּאוּ נִשְׁתַּחֲוֶה וְנִכְרָעָה, נִבְרְכָה לִפְנֵי יהוה עֹשֵׂנוּ.[8] נָבוֹאָה לְמִשְׁכְּנוֹתָיו, נִשְׁתַּחֲוֶה לַהֲדֹם רַגְלָיו.[9] בְּאוּ שְׁעָרָיו בְּתוֹדָה, חֲצֵרֹתָיו בִּתְהִלָּה, הוֹדוּ לוֹ בָּרְכוּ שְׁמוֹ.[10] רוֹמְמוּ יהוה אֱלֹהֵינוּ, וְהִשְׁתַּחֲווּ לַהֲדֹם רַגְלָיו, קָדוֹשׁ הוּא.[11] רוֹמְמוּ יהוה אֱלֹהֵינוּ, וְהִשְׁתַּחֲווּ לְהַר קָדְשׁוֹ, כִּי קָדוֹשׁ יהוה אֱלֹהֵינוּ.[12] הִשְׁתַּחֲווּ לַיהוה בְּהַדְרַת קֹדֶשׁ, חִילוּ מִפָּנָיו כָּל הָאָרֶץ.[13] וַאֲנַחְנוּ בְּרֹב חַסְדְּךָ נָבוֹא בֵיתֶךָ, נִשְׁתַּחֲוֶה אֶל הֵיכַל קָדְשְׁךָ בְּיִרְאָתֶךָ.[14] נִשְׁתַּחֲוֶה אֶל הֵיכַל קָדְשְׁךָ וְנוֹדֶה אֶת שְׁמֶךָ, עַל חַסְדְּךָ וְעַל אֲמִתֶּךָ, כִּי הִגְדַּלְתָּ עַל כָּל שִׁמְךָ אִמְרָתֶךָ.[15] לְכוּ נְרַנְּנָה לַיהוה, נָרִיעָה לְצוּר יִשְׁעֵנוּ. נְקַדְּמָה פָנָיו בְּתוֹדָה, בִּזְמִרוֹת נָרִיעַ לוֹ.[16] אֲשֶׁר יַחְדָּו נַמְתִּיק סוֹד, בְּבֵית אֱלֹהִים נְהַלֵּךְ בְּרָגֶשׁ.[17] אֵל נַעֲרָץ בְּסוֹד קְדוֹשִׁים רַבָּה, וְנוֹרָא עַל כָּל סְבִיבָיו.[18] שְׂאוּ יְדֵיכֶם קֹדֶשׁ וּבָרְכוּ אֶת יהוה.[19] הִנֵּה בָּרְכוּ אֶת יהוה כָּל עַבְדֵי יהוה, הָעֹמְדִים בְּבֵית יהוה בַּלֵּילוֹת.[20] אֲשֶׁר מִי אֵל בַּשָּׁמַיִם וּבָאָרֶץ, אֲשֶׁר יַעֲשֶׂה כְמַעֲשֶׂיךָ וְכִגְבוּרֹתֶיךָ.[21] אֲשֶׁר לוֹ הַיָּם וְהוּא עָשָׂהוּ, וְיַבֶּשֶׁת יָדָיו יָצָרוּ.[22] אֲשֶׁר בְּיָדוֹ מֶחְקְרֵי אָרֶץ, וְתוֹעֲפוֹת הָרִים לוֹ.[23] אֲשֶׁר בְּיָדוֹ נֶפֶשׁ כָּל חָי, וְרוּחַ כָּל בְּשַׂר אִישׁ.[24] וְיוֹדוּ שָׁמַיִם פִּלְאֲךָ יהוה, אַף אֱמוּנָתְךָ בִּקְהַל קְדֹשִׁים.[25] לְךָ זְרוֹעַ עִם גְּבוּרָה, תָּעֹז יָדְךָ תָּרוּם יְמִינֶךָ.[26] לְךָ שָׁמַיִם, אַף לְךָ אָרֶץ, תֵּבֵל וּמְלֹאָהּ אַתָּה יְסַדְתָּם.[27] אַתָּה פוֹרַרְתָּ בְעָזְּךָ יָם, שִׁבַּרְתָּ רָאשֵׁי תַנִּינִים עַל הַמָּיִם.[28] אַתָּה הִצַּבְתָּ כָּל גְּבוּלוֹת אָרֶץ, קַיִץ וָחֹרֶף

(1) *Daniel* 9:7. (2) Cf. *Lamentations* 3:39. (3) Cf. *Genesis* 44:16. (4) Cf. *Lamentations* 3:40. (5) *Psalms* 65:3. (6) Cf. *Isaiah* 66:23. (7) *Psalms* 86:9. (8) 95:6. (9) 132:7. (10) 100:4. (11) 99:5. (12) 99:9. (13) 96:9. (14) Cf. 5:8. (15) Cf. 138:2. (16) 95:1-2. (17) 55:15. (18) 89:8. (19) 134:2. (20) 134:1. (21) *Deuteronomy* 3:24. (22) *Psalms* 95:5. (23) 95:4. (24) *Job* 12:10. (25) *Psalms* 89:6. (26) 89:14. (27) 89:12. (28) 74:13.

All:

לְךָ הֹ׳ Yours, my Lord, is the righteousness and ours is the shame-
facedness.[1] What complaint can we make?[2] What can we say?
What can we declare? What justification can we offer?[3] Let us examine
our ways and analyze — and return to You,[4] for Your right hand is
extended to accept penitents. Neither with kindness nor with [good]
deeds do we come before You. As paupers and as beggars do we knock
at Your doors. At Your doors we knock, O Compassionate and Gracious
One. Please do not turn us away from You empty-handed. Our King,
turn us not away from You empty-handed, for You are the One Who
hears prayer.

שֹׁמֵעַ תְּפִלָּה You Who hears prayer, to You all flesh will come.[5] All
flesh will come to prostrate itself before You, O
HASHEM.[6] They will come and prostrate themselves before You, my Lord,
and shall honor Your Name.[7] Come! — let us prostrate ourselves and
bow, let us kneel before God, our Maker.[8] Let us come to His dwelling
places, let us prostrate ourselves at His footstool.[9] Enter His gates with
thanksgiving, His courts with praise; give thanks to Him, praise His
Name.[10] Exalt HASHEM, our God, and bow at His footstool; He is holy![11]
Exalt HASHEM, our God, and bow at His holy mountain; for holy is
HASHEM, our God.[12] Prostrate yourselves before HASHEM in His intensely
holy place, tremble before Him, everyone on earth.[13] As for us, through
Your abundant kindness we will enter Your House; we will prostrate
ourselves toward Your Holy Sanctuary in awe of You.[14] We will
prostrate ourselves toward Your Holy Sanctuary, and we will give
thanks to Your Name for Your kindness and truth for You have exalted
Your promise even beyond Your Name.[15] Come! — let us sing to HASHEM,
let us call out to the Rock of our salvation. Let us greet Him with
thanksgiving, with praiseful songs let us call out to Him.[16] For together
let us share sweet counsel, in the house of God let us walk in
multitudes.[17] God is dreaded in the hiddenmost counsel of the holy ones,
and inspires awe upon all who surround Him.[18] Lift your hands in the
Sanctuary and bless HASHEM.[19] Behold, bless HASHEM, all you servants of
HASHEM, who stand in the House of HASHEM in the nights.[20] For what
power is there in heaven or earth that can approximate Your deeds and
power?[21] For His is the sea and He perfected the dry land — His hands
fashioned it.[22] For in His power are the hidden mysteries of the earth,
and the mountain summits are His.[23] For His is the soul of every living
thing, and the spirit of all human flesh.[24] Heaven will gratefully praise
Your wonders, HASHEM; also Your faithfulness in the assembly of
holy ones.[25] Yours is a mighty arm with power, You strengthen Your
hand; You exalt Your right hand.[26] Yours is the heaven; Yours, too, is the
earth; the world and its fullness — You founded them.[27] You shattered
the sea with Your might, You smashed sea serpents' heads upon the
water.[28] You established all the boundaries of earth; summer and winter

אַתָּה יְצַרְתָּם.[1] אַתָּה רִצַּצְתָּ רָאשֵׁי לִוְיָתָן, תִּתְּנֶנּוּ מַאֲכָל לְעָם לְצִיִּים. אַתָּה בָקַעְתָּ מַעְיָן וָנָחַל, אַתָּה הוֹבַשְׁתָּ נַהֲרוֹת אֵיתָן.[2] לְךָ יוֹם, אַף לְךָ לָיְלָה, אַתָּה הֲכִינוֹתָ מָאוֹר וָשָׁמֶשׁ.[3] עֲשֵׂה גְדוֹלוֹת עַד אֵין חֵקֶר, וְנִפְלָאוֹת עַד אֵין מִסְפָּר.[4] כִּי אֵל גָּדוֹל יהוה, וּמֶלֶךְ גָּדוֹל עַל כָּל אֱלֹהִים.[5] כִּי גָדוֹל אַתָּה וְעֹשֵׂה נִפְלָאוֹת, אַתָּה אֱלֹהִים לְבַדֶּךָ.[6] כִּי גָדוֹל מֵעַל שָׁמַיִם חַסְדֶּךָ, וְעַד שְׁחָקִים אֲמִתֶּךָ.[7] גָּדוֹל יהוה וּמְהֻלָּל מְאֹד, וְלִגְדֻלָּתוֹ אֵין חֵקֶר. (כִּי) גָּדוֹל יהוה וּמְהֻלָּל מְאֹד, נוֹרָא הוּא עַל כָּל אֱלֹהִים.[9] גָּדוֹל יהוה וּמְהֻלָּל מְאֹד, בְּעִיר אֱלֹהֵינוּ הַר קָדְשׁוֹ.[10] לְךָ יהוה הַגְּדֻלָּה וְהַגְּבוּרָה, וְהַתִּפְאֶרֶת וְהַנֵּצַח וְהַהוֹד, כִּי כֹל בַּשָּׁמַיִם וּבָאָרֶץ; לְךָ יהוה הַמַּמְלָכָה, וְהַמִּתְנַשֵּׂא לְכֹל לְרֹאשׁ.[11] מִי לֹא יִרָאֲךָ מֶלֶךְ הַגּוֹיִם, כִּי לְךָ יָאָתָה, כִּי בְכָל חַכְמֵי הַגּוֹיִם וּבְכָל מַלְכוּתָם מֵאֵין כָּמוֹךָ.[12] מֵאֵין כָּמוֹךָ יהוה, גָּדוֹל אַתָּה וְגָדוֹל שִׁמְךָ בִּגְבוּרָה.[13] יהוה אֱלֹהֵי צְבָאוֹת, מִי כָמוֹךָ חֲסִין יָהּ, וֶאֱמוּנָתְךָ סְבִיבוֹתֶיךָ.[14] יהוה צְבָאוֹת, אֱלֹהֵי יִשְׂרָאֵל, יוֹשֵׁב הַכְּרֻבִים, אַתָּה הוּא הָאֱלֹהִים לְבַדֶּךָ.[15] מִי יְמַלֵּל גְּבוּרוֹת יהוה, יַשְׁמִיעַ כָּל תְּהִלָּתוֹ.[16] כִּי מִי בַשַּׁחַק יַעֲרֹךְ לַיהוה, יִדְמֶה לַיהוה בִּבְנֵי אֵלִים.[17] מַה נֹּאמַר לְפָנֶיךָ יוֹשֵׁב מָרוֹם, וּמַה נְּסַפֵּר לְפָנֶיךָ שֹׁכֵן שְׁחָקִים. מַה נֹּאמַר לְפָנֶיךָ יהוה אֱלֹהֵינוּ, מַה נְּדַבֵּר וּמַה נִּצְטַדָּק.[18] אֵין לָנוּ פֶּה לְהָשִׁיב וְלֹא מֵצַח לְהָרִים רֹאשׁ, כִּי עֲווֹנוֹתֵינוּ רַבּוּ מִלְמְנוֹת, וְחַטֹּאתֵינוּ עָצְמוּ מִסַּפֵּר.[19] לְמַעַן שִׁמְךָ יהוה תְּחַיֵּנוּ, וּבְצִדְקָתְךָ תוֹצִיא מִצָּרָה נַפְשֵׁנוּ.[20] דַּרְכְּךָ אֱלֹהֵינוּ לְהַאֲרִיךְ אַפֶּךָ, לָרָעִים וְלַטּוֹבִים, וְהִיא תְהִלָּתֶךָ. לְמַעַנְךָ אֱלֹהֵינוּ עֲשֵׂה וְלֹא לָנוּ, רְאֵה עֲמִידָתֵנוּ, דַּלִּים וְרֵקִים. ❖ הַנְּשָׁמָה לָךְ וְהַגּוּף פָּעֳלָךְ, חוּסָה עַל עֲמָלָךְ. הַנְּשָׁמָה לָךְ וְהַגּוּף שֶׁלָּךְ, יהוה עֲשֵׂה לְמַעַן שְׁמֶךָ. אָתָאנוּ עַל שִׁמְךָ, יהוה, עֲשֵׂה לְמַעַן שְׁמֶךָ. בַּעֲבוּר כְּבוֹד שִׁמְךָ, כִּי אֵל חַנּוּן וְרַחוּם שְׁמֶךָ. לְמַעַן שִׁמְךָ יהוה, וְסָלַחְתָּ לַעֲוֹנֵנוּ כִּי רַב הוּא.[21]

Congregation, then *chazzan:*

סְלַח לָנוּ אָבִינוּ, כִּי בְּרֹב אִוַּלְתֵּנוּ שָׁגִינוּ,
מְחַל לָנוּ מַלְכֵּנוּ, כִּי רַבּוּ עֲוֹנֵינוּ.

— You fashioned them.[1] You crushed the heads of Leviathan, You served it as food to the nation of legions. You split open fountain and stream, You dried the mighty rivers.[2] Yours is the day, Yours as well is the night; You established luminary and the sun.[3] Who performs great deeds that are beyond comprehension, and wonders beyond number.[4] For a great God is HASHEM, and a great King above all heavenly powers.[5] For You are great and work wonders; You alone, O God.[6] For great above the very heavens is Your kindness, and until the upper heights is Your truth.[7] HASHEM is great and exceedingly lauded, and His greatness is beyond investigation.[8] (For) HASHEM is great and exceedingly lauded, awesome is He above all heavenly powers.[9] Great is HASHEM and exceedingly lauded, in the city of our God, Mount of His Holiness.[10] Yours, HASHEM, is the greatness, the strength, the splendor, the triumph, and the glory; even everything in heaven and earth; Yours, HASHEM, is the kingdom, and sovereignty over every leader.[11] Who would not revere You, O King of nations? — for this befits You, for among all the sages of the nations and in all their kingdom there is none like You.[12] There is none like You, O HASHEM, You are great and Your Name is great with power.[13] HASHEM, God of Legions — who is like You, O Strong One, God? — and Your faithfulness surrounds You.[14] HASHEM, Master of Legions, God of Israel, enthroned upon the Cherubim, it is You alone Who is God.[15] Who can express the mighty acts of HASHEM, who can announce all His praise?[16] For who in the sky can be compared to HASHEM; be likened to HASHEM among the angels?[17] What can we say before You Who dwell on high? And what can we relate to You Who abide in the highest heaven? What can we say before You, HASHEM, our God? What can we declare? What justification can we offer?[18] We have neither mouth to respond nor brow to raise our head, for our iniquities are too numerous to count, and our sins are too vast to be numbered.[19] For Your Name's sake, HASHEM, revive us; and with Your righteousness remove our soul from distress.[20] It is Your way, our God, to delay Your anger, against people both evil and good — and this is Your praise. Act for Your sake, our God, and not for ours, behold our [spiritual] position — destitute and emptyhanded. Chazzan – The soul is Yours and the body is Your handiwork; take pity on Your labor. The soul is Yours and the body is Yours; O HASHEM, act for Your Name's sake. We have come with reliance on Your Name, O HASHEM, act for Your Name's sake; because of Your Name's glory — for 'Gracious and Merciful God' is Your Name. For Your Name's sake, HASHEM, may You forgive our iniquity, though it is abundant.[21]

Congregation, then chazzan:

Forgive us, our Father, for in our abundant folly we have erred,
pardon us, our King, for our iniquities are many.

(1) *Psalms* 74:17. (2) 74:14-15. (3) 74:16. (4) *Job* 9:10. (5) *Psalms* 95:3.
(6) 86:10. (7) 108:5. (8) 145:3. (9) 96:4. (10) 48:2. (11) *I Chronicles* 29:11.
(12) *Jeremiah* 10:7. (13) 10:6. (14) *Psalms* 89:9. (15) *Isaiah* 37:16. (16) *Psalms* 106:2.
(17) 89:7. (18) Cf. *Genesis* 44:16. (19) Cf. *Ezra* 9:6. (20) Cf. *Psalms* 143:11. (21) Cf. 25:11.

All, while standing:

אֵל אֶרֶךְ אַפַּיִם אַתָּה, וּבַעַל הָרַחֲמִים נִקְרֵאתָ,
וְדֶרֶךְ תְּשׁוּבָה הוֹרֵיתָ.

גְּדֻלַּת רַחֲמֶיךָ וַחֲסָדֶיךָ, תִּזְכֹּר הַיּוֹם וּבְכָל יוֹם לְזֶרַע יְדִידֶיךָ.
תֵּפֶן אֵלֵינוּ בְּרַחֲמִים, כִּי אַתָּה הוּא בַּעַל הָרַחֲמִים.
בְּתַחֲנוּן וּבִתְפִלָּה פָּנֶיךָ נְקַדֵּם, כְּהוֹדַעְתָּ לֶעָנָיו מִקֶּדֶם.
מֵחֲרוֹן אַפְּךָ שׁוּב,¹ כְּמוֹ בְתוֹרָתְךָ כָּתוּב.²
וּבְצֵל כְּנָפֶיךָ נֶחֱסֶה³ וְנִתְלוֹנָן, כְּיוֹם וַיֵּרֶד יהוה בֶּעָנָן.
❖ תַּעֲבוֹר עַל פֶּשַׁע וְתִמְחֶה אָשָׁם, כְּיוֹם וַיִּתְיַצֵּב עִמּוֹ שָׁם.
תַּאֲזִין שַׁוְעָתֵנוּ וְתַקְשִׁיב מֶנּוּ מַאֲמָר,
כְּיוֹם וַיִּקְרָא בְשֵׁם יהוה,⁴ וְשָׁם נֶאֱמַר:

Congregation, then *chazzan:*

וַיַּעֲבֹר יהוה עַל פָּנָיו וַיִּקְרָא:

Congregation and *chazzan* (the words in bold type are recited aloud and in unison):

**יהוה, יהוה, אֵל, רַחוּם, וְחַנּוּן, אֶרֶךְ אַפַּיִם, וְרַב חֶסֶד,
וֶאֱמֶת, נֹצֵר חֶסֶד לָאֲלָפִים, נֹשֵׂא עָוֹן, וָפֶשַׁע,
וְחַטָּאָה, וְנַקֵּה.**⁵ וְסָלַחְתָּ לַעֲוֹנֵנוּ וּלְחַטָּאתֵנוּ וּנְחַלְתָּנוּ.⁶ סְלַח לָנוּ
אָבִינוּ כִּי חָטָאנוּ, מְחַל לָנוּ מַלְכֵּנוּ כִּי פָשָׁעְנוּ. כִּי אַתָּה אֲדֹנָי טוֹב
וְסַלָּח, וְרַב חֶסֶד לְכָל קֹרְאֶיךָ.⁷

פסוקי הקדמה לסליחה ח

אֱלֹהֵינוּ בּוֹשְׁנוּ בְמַעֲשֵׂינוּ וְנִכְלַמְנוּ בַּעֲוֹנֵינוּ. אֱלֹהֵינוּ בּוֹשְׁנוּ
וְנִכְלַמְנוּ לְהָרִים אֱלֹהֵינוּ פָּנֵינוּ אֵלֶיךָ.⁸ לֹא כַחֲטָאֵינוּ
תַּעֲשֶׂה לָּנוּ, וְלֹא כַעֲוֹנוֹתֵינוּ תִּגְמוֹל עָלֵינוּ.⁹ אִם עֲוֹנוֹת תִּשְׁמָר יָהּ,
אֲדֹנָי מִי יַעֲמֹד. כִּי עִמְּךָ הַסְּלִיחָה, לְמַעַן תִּוָּרֵא.*¹⁰ אַל תָּבוֹא
בְמִשְׁפָּט עִמָּנוּ, כִּי לֹא יִצְדַּק לְפָנֶיךָ כָל חָי.¹¹

כְּרַחֵם אָב עַל בָּנִים, כֵּן תְּרַחֵם יהוה עָלֵינוּ.¹² לַיהוה הַיְשׁוּעָה,
עַל עַמְּךָ בִרְכָתֶךָ סֶּלָה.¹³ יהוה צְבָאוֹת עִמָּנוּ,
מִשְׂגָּב לָנוּ אֱלֹהֵי יַעֲקֹב סֶלָה.¹⁴ יהוה צְבָאוֹת, אַשְׁרֵי אָדָם בֹּטֵחַ
בָּךְ.¹⁵ יהוה הוֹשִׁיעָה, הַמֶּלֶךְ יַעֲנֵנוּ בְיוֹם קָרְאֵנוּ.¹⁶

כִּי עִמְּךָ הַסְּלִיחָה לְמַעַן תִּוָּרֵא
— *For with You [alone]
is forgiveness, that You may be feared.* Although
angels may represent God in other areas, He
never delegates them to forgive mankind. As we
read: *Behold I will send an angel before you . . . he
will not forgive your transgression* (Exodus

23:20,21). Otherwise, a sinner might say, I will
transgress at will and then I will appease an angel,
who will give me a dispensation. However, since
forgiveness is in the hands of God alone, people
will truly fear God (*Rashi; Radak*).

• When a person commits a sin he has not merely

All, while standing:

אֵל אֶרֶךְ אַפַּיִם O God — You are slow to anger, You are called the Master of Mercy, and You have taught the way of repentance. May You remember this day and every day the greatness of Your mercy and Your kindness to the offspring of Your beloved Ones. Turn to us in mercy for You are the Master of Mercy. With supplication and prayer we approach Your Presence in the manner that You made known to the humble [Moses] in ancient times. Turn back from Your fierce anger;[1] as is written in Your Torah.[2] In the shadow of Your wings may we find shelter[3] and lodging as on the day 'HASHEM descended in a cloud' [to appear to Moses on Sinai]. Chazzan — Overlook sin and erase guilt as on the day 'He [God] stood there with him [Moses].' Give heed to our cry and be attentive to our declaration as on the day 'He called out with the Name HASHEM,'[4] and there it was said:

Congregation, then chazzan:

And HASHEM passed before him [Moses] and proclaimed:

Congregation and chazzan (the words in bold type are recited aloud and in unison):

ה' ה' HASHEM, HASHEM, God, Compassionate and Gracious, Slow to anger, and Abundant in Kindness and Truth, Preserver of kindness for thousands [of generations], Forgiver of iniquity, willful sin, and error, and Who cleanses.[5]** May You forgive our iniquities and our errors and make us Your heritage.[6] Forgive us, our Father, for we have erred; pardon us, our King, for we have willfully sinned; for You, my Lord, are good and forgiving and abundantly kind to all who call upon You.[7]

PREFATORY VERSES TO SELICHAH 8

אֱלֹהֵינוּ Our God, we are ashamed of our deeds, we are abashed by our iniquities. Our God, we are too ashamed and humiliated to lift, our God, our faces up to You.[8] Do not treat us according to our sins, do not recompense us according to our iniquities.[9] If You preserve iniquities, O God, my Lord, who can survive? For with You [alone] is forgiveness, that You may be feared.*[10] Do not enter into strict judgment with us, for no living creature would be innocent before You.[11]

כְּרַחֵם אָב As a father has mercy on his children, so, HASHEM, may You have mercy on us.[12] Salvation is HASHEM's, upon Your people is Your blessing, Selah.[13] HASHEM, Master of Legions, is with us, a stronghold for us is the God of Jacob, Selah.[14] HASHEM, Master of Legions, praiseworthy is the person who trusts in You.[15] HASHEM, save! May the King answer us on the day we call.[16]

---

(1) Cf. *Exodus* 32:12. (2) See 32:14. (3) Cf. *Psalms* 36:8. (4) *Exodus* 34:5. (5) 34:6-7. (6) 34:9. (7) *Psalms* 86:5. (8) Cf. *Ezra* 9:6. (9) Cf. *Psalms* 103:10. (10) 130:3-4. (11) Cf. 143:2. (12) Cf. *Psalms* 103:13. (13) 3:9. (14) 46:8. (15) 84:13. (16) 20:10.

---

become guilty in a legal sense; rather, he has erected a barrier of dense, profane darkness between himself and God. This obstruction makes the sinner less aware of God's presence and hence diminishes his awe of the Master of the Universe. Thus, when God forgives the sinner,

He does more than wipe away his guilt. Divine pardon means that the barriers which separated the sinner from God are removed. Then the penitent is blessed with new awareness of God, so that he can fear Him with heightened intensity (*Noam Megadim*).

In some congregations the following two verses are recited responsively — the *chazzan* reciting סְלַח, and the congregation responding וַיֹּאמֶר. In other congregations these verses are recited silently.

סְלַח נָא לַעֲוֹן הָעָם הַזֶּה כְּגֹדֶל חַסְדֶּךָ, וְכַאֲשֶׁר נָשָׂאתָה לָעָם הַזֶּה מִמִּצְרַיִם וְעַד הֵנָּה,[1] וְשָׁם נֶאֱמַר:

וַיֹּאמֶר יהוה סָלַחְתִּי כִּדְבָרֶךָ.[2]

All:

הַטֵּה אֱלֹהַי אָזְנְךָ וּשְׁמָע, פְּקַח עֵינֶיךָ וּרְאֵה שֹׁמְמֹתֵינוּ, וְהָעִיר אֲשֶׁר נִקְרָא שִׁמְךָ עָלֶיהָ, כִּי לֹא עַל צִדְקֹתֵינוּ אֲנַחְנוּ מַפִּילִים תַּחֲנוּנֵינוּ לְפָנֶיךָ, כִּי עַל רַחֲמֶיךָ הָרַבִּים. אֲדֹנָי שְׁמָעָה, אֲדֹנָי סְלָחָה, אֲדֹנָי הַקְשִׁיבָה, וַעֲשֵׂה אַל תְּאַחַר, לְמַעַנְךָ אֱלֹהַי, כִּי שִׁמְךָ נִקְרָא עַל עִירְךָ וְעַל עַמֶּךָ.[3]

סליחה ח

All:

אֱלֹהֵינוּ וֵאלֹהֵי אֲבוֹתֵינוּ:

אֵין כְּמִדַּת בָּשָׂר* מִדָּתֶךָ.*   אַיֵּה קְנֵאתָ[4] וַעֲצַת עֲמִידָתֶךָ,[5]
בַּת בֵּרַרְתָּ לְבֵית חֶמְדָּתֶךָ,*   בְּעֻלוֹתָ אֲדוֹנִים[6] וְאֵין לְצִמְיָדָתֶךָ.*
גּוֹעָה, לְדוֹדִי אֲנִי מְאֹרֶסֶת,   גּוֹאֵל רוֹדִי אֵיךְ נִדְרֶסֶת,
דִּין הֶרֶג לְעַצְמָה מְקַנֶּסֶת,*   דְּחוּיָה וְגַם כִּי נֶאֱנֶסֶת.
הָאֵם בְּלִי סֵפֶר שִׁלּוּחַ,[7]   הַבֵּן כִּיתוֹם אוֹבֵד שָׁלוּחַ,
וְגַן נָעוּל[8] הֶפְקֵר כְּמָלוּחַ,*   וּמַעְיָן חָתוּם[8] נִרְפַּס דָּלוּחַ.
זַעַם כְּרֶגַע[9] וְעַתָּה לַהֲפוֹךְ,   זְרֵי קֹדֶשׁ* עַתָּה לִשְׁפּוֹךְ,[10]
חִבַּת רֵעַ כְּקֶרֶן הָפוּךְ,*   חֲשׁוּבָה וַעֲזוּבָה כְּקֹרַעַת בַּפּוּךְ.[11]

(1) *Numbers* 14:19. (2) 14:20. (3) *Daniel* 9:18-19. (4) *Isaiah* 63:15. (5) Cf. *Psalms* 33:11. (6) Cf. *Isaiah* 26:13. (7) Cf. 50:1. (8) *Song of Songs* 4:12. (9) Cf. *Isaiah* 26:20. (10) Cf. *Lamentations* 4:1. (11) Cf. *Jeremiah* 4:30.

אֵין כְּמִדַּת בָּשָׂר 🙰 — *... not like the nature of flesh [and blood].* Ascribed to R' Shlomo HaBavli (whose signature uncharacteristically does not appear in the composition; see prefatory note to *selichah* 2), this *selichah* contains a double *aleph-beis* acrostic.

אֵין כְּמִדַּת בָּשָׂר מִדָּתֶךָ — *Your nature is not like the nature of flesh [and blood].* As Scripture states: *Do You have eyes of flesh? Do You see as man sees?* (*Job* 10:4). Unlike man whose vision is limited, You are able to see everything; nothing is hidden from Your sight (*Arugas HaBosem*).

Alternatively: Unlike man who cannot always fulfill his wishes, You גֹּזֵר וּמְקַיֵּם, *decree and fulfill.* None can prevent You from doing whatever You desire (*Matteh Levi*).

בַּת בֵּרַרְתָּ לְבֵית חֶמְדָּתֶךָ — *The daughter You chose for Your precious House.* The words בַּת, *daugh-*

ter, and בַּיִת, *house,* are often used as a euphemism for *wife.* Thus, when Scripture states that *Mordechai took Esther as a daughter* (*Esther* 2:7), the Sages explain that he married her (*Megillah* 13a). Similarly here, the *paytan* refers to God's chosen mate, Israel (*Arugas HaBosem*).

Other interpret: *The nation You chose to serve in Your Holy Temple.*

וְאֵין לְצִמְיָדָתֶךָ — *And You do not cling to her.* The translation follows *Matteh Levi.* Some commentaries reverse the persons: *And she is unable to cling to You.*

According to *Arugas HaBosem* the phrase modifies אֲדוֹנִים, *[strange] lords,* and means *who cannot compare to You.*

דִּין הֶרֶג לְעַצְמָה מְקַנֶּסֶת — *She accepts a death sentence upon herself.* In every generation, the Jew has proudly surrendered his life to sanctify

In some congregations the following two verses are recited responsively — the *chazzan* reciting, '*Forgive, please . . . ,*' and the congregation responding, '*And HASHEM said . . .*' In other congregations these verses are recited silently.

סְלַח נָא *Forgive, please, the iniquity of this people according to the greatness of Your kindness and as You have forgiven this people from Egypt until now,*[1] *and there it was said:*

And HASHEM said, 'I have forgiven according to your word!'[2]

All:

הַטֵּה *Incline, my God, Your ear, and listen, open Your eyes and see our desolation and that of the city upon which Your Name is proclaimed; for not because of our righteousness do we cast down our supplications before You, rather because of Your abundant compassion. O my Lord, heed; O my Lord, forgive; O my Lord, be attentive and act, do not delay; for Your sake, my God, for Your Name is proclaimed upon Your city and upon Your people.*[3]

SELICHAH 8

All:

Our God and the God of our forefathers:

א *Your nature is not like the nature of flesh [and blood];**

א *where, [then,] is Your jealousy*[4] *[on our behalf],*
　　and Your everlasting counsel?[5]

ב *The daughter You chose for Your precious House**

ב *is ravished by [strange] lords,*[6] *and You do not cling to her.**

ג *She moans, 'I am betrothed to my Beloved!*

ג *How am I, then, trampled by loathsome tyrants?'*

ד *She accepts a death sentence upon herself,**

ד *[why then has she been] pushed out [of her land] and coerced?*

ה *The mother was sent off, without a document [of divorce];*[7]

ה *the son, was sent off like a wandering orphan.*

ו *And the locked garden*[8] *is made ownerless like an inedible weed,**

ו *the sealed-up spring*[8] *is trampled and befouled.*

ז *Your anger [was once] for a [mere] moment,*[9] *but now it has changed.*

ז *The holy tiaras* are now thrown out [like trash]*[10]

ח *The Friend's beloved, [once as lovely] as a brilliant gem,**

ח *is [now] considered and cast-off like a painted harlot.*[11]

God's name. *Meshech Chachmah* (*Genesis* 22:14) explains that martyrdom became ingrained in the Jewish character when the Patriarch Isaac readily encouraged his father, Abraham, to sacrifice him in accordance with God's command.

בְּמַלּוּחַ — *Like an inedible weed.* According to *Rashi* (to *Job* 30:4) and *Arugas HaBosem*, this is the name of a very bitter herb. *Matteh Levi* understands it as an adjective describing herbs grown in אֶרֶץ מְלֵחָה, *salty earth*, and thus lacking in nutritional value.

זֵרֵי קֹדֶשׁ — *The holy tiaras.* In describing the appointments of the *Mishkan* (Tabernacle), the Torah uses the expression זֵר זָהָב סָבִיב, *a gold*

encircling tiara, three times: for the Ark of the Covenant (*Exodus* 25:11); for the Table of the *Panim* Loaves (ibid. v. 24); and for the Incense Altar (ibid. 30:3). According to the Talmud, the tiara of the Ark represents the Crown of Torah scholarship; the tiara of the Table alludes to the Crown of Kingship; and the tiara of the Altar stands for the Crown of Priesthood (*Yoma* 72b with *Rashi*; see also *Avos* 4:17). These Crowns — once borne so proudly by the Sages, the House of David, and the *Kohanim* — have been dashed by our conquerors and discarded like trash.

כְּקֶרֶן הַפּוּךְ — *[Once as lovely] as a brilliant gem.* The reference here is to Job's third daughter Keren Happuch, who with her two older sisters,

טוֹב הַתִּאַר קְדוֹרַנִּית מִפֶּרֶךְ,   טְרִיָּה מַכָּה מִבְּלִי אֶרֶךְ,¹

יוֹם נָקָם² נִסְתַּם דֶּרֶךְ,   יוֹם שָׁלוּם² נֶחְתַּם חֶרֶךְ.

בְּחַ הַסַּבָּל הִכְשִׁיל³ נָטֵל,   כָּסוּל וְשָׁחוּל הַנִּשְׁאָר מְקֻטָּל,

לֹא לְמַרְגּֽעַ נָד וּמְטַלְטָל,   לְעָמֵל וְיָגֵֽעַ וְאַחֵר נוֹטֵל.

מַטַּע קֶֽרֶן* שֶׁמֶן הַמִּדְרָשָׁן,⁴   מִרְמָס מַדּֽוּעַ כַּחַרְלֵי כְבָשָׁן,

נוֹצֵר לְמַעְלָה* לֹא יִישָׁן,   נִטְעוּ לְמִשְׁלֽוֹחַ פָּרוֹת הַבָּשָׁן.*

שׁוֹרֵקָה מַה בֶּצַע וְנִקְטֶפֶת,   סוֹרֵחַת מַה יִתְרוֹן וְנֶחֱטֶפֶת,

עַל יַד חֲקוּקָה וְטוֹטֶפֶת,*   עַל מָה אַהֲבָתָהּ נִשְׁטֶפֶת.⁵

פְּעֻלַּת הָרוֹבִים מְעוּט מְלָאכֶת,*   פְּרִיעַת שָׂכָר רַבָּה וְהוֹלֶכֶת,

צוֹפֶה הַפָּנוֹת וְעַתָּה נִמְשֶׁכֶת,   צָרָה פְּקוּדָה וְאַחֶֽרֶת נִסְמֶכֶת,

קֹֽדֶשׁ רֵאשִׁית* עֲרֵמַת שְׂעָרִים,   קַצְוֵי אֶֽרֶץ זְרוּיִים כִּשְׂעוֹרִים,

רֽוּחַ מְנֻשֶּֽׁבֶת בַּעֲלֵי יְעָרִים,   רָדוּף נִשְׁמֶֽטֶת נָסִים וְנִסְעָרִים,

שְׁמֹנֶה וְתִשְׁעִים הָאָלוֹת הָאֵֽלֶּה.⁶   שָׁלְמוּ אֵֽלֶּה מֵאֵֽלֶּה וְכָאֵֽלֶּה.*

תְּרַחֵם תְּקַבְּצֵֽנוּ מִקְּרָנוֹת אֵֽלֶּה.

אָז יֹאמְרוּ בַגּוֹיִם, הִגְדִּיל יהוה לַעֲשׂוֹת עִם אֵֽלֶּה.⁷

---

(1) Cf. *Isaiah* 1:6. (2) Cf. 34:8; some editions read יוֹם גְּאֻלָּה, a day of redemption, instead of יוֹם שָׁלוּם. (3) Cf. *Nehemiah* 4:4. (4) Cf. *Isaiah* 5:1. (5) Cf. *Song of Songs* 8:7. (6) See *Deuteronomy* 28:15-68. (7) *Psalms* 126:2.

Jemimah and Ketziah, was the fairest in the land (see *Job* 42:14-15). According to the *Targum* and *Metzudos*, קֶרֶן means *shine* and פּוּךְ is the name of a precious stone (see *Isaiah* 54:11). Hence Keren Happuch means *a brilliant gem*. According to Rashi, קֶרֶן means *horn* and refers to a horn-shaped case used to carry פּוּךְ, *mascara* (see *Jeremiah* 4:30).

קֶרֶן — *Corner*. The translation follows *Rashi* (to *Isaiah* 5:1). *Targum*, however, renders *peak*. According to *Ibn Ezra*, the allusion is to a particularly fertile area near Jerusalem. *Radak* understands it as a reference to the Holy Land in general.

נוֹצֵר לְמַעְלָה — *The Watchman on High*. The *Midrash* lists sixteen ways in which Israel is compared to a grapevine. One of these is that just as the vine's watchman stands above it to protect it, so does Israel's Guardian stand over the nation to protect it (*Vayikra Rabbah* 36:2).

פָּרוֹת הַבָּשָׁן — *The cows of Bashan*. The land of Bashan had extremely rich pasturage, and the herds of cattle that grazed there were world renowned for the quality of their meat. The prophet (*Amos* 4:1) uses *cows of Bashan* as an epithet for the wives of wealthy aristocrats who need not work for a living, but fatten themselves on the labor of others (see commentaries to *Avos*

4:1; *Shabbos* 32b). Here, it is a reference to the oppressor nations that plunder the fruits of Israel's labor.

עַל יַד ... וְטוֹטֶפֶת — *On [God's] arm and [His] crown*. The Talmud adduces various verses to show that God wears *tefillin*. Moreover, just as Israel's *tefillin* contain Torah passages that declare God's praises, so do God's *tefillin* contain passages that praise Israel (*Berachos* 6a). Thus, Israel is engraved in the *tefillin* that God wears on His hand and on His head.

פְּעֻלַּת הָרוֹבִים מְעוּט מְלָאכֶת — *[The oppressors, like] youths, do but little work [to serve You]*. The *Midrash* compares Israel's service with that of the other nations with a parable: A king once hired many פּוֹעֲלִים, *laborers*, one of whom toiled long days [thus accomplishing much more than any of the others]. When the workers came to receive their wages, the king took this worker and said, 'To you, my son, will I turn my attention! הָרוֹבִים, *These youths*, who did for me מְלָאכָה הַלָּלוּ, *little work*, I shall give but small wages. But you I shall recompense with great reward in the future!'

So does God say unto Israel, 'To you, My son, will I turn My attention! These nations who did little work on My behalf [i.e., they had only seven *mitzvos* to keep], I shall give but small wages in this world. But you [who fulfilled six hundred

ט The [once-]beautiful one is blackened from hard labor,

ט her wounds raw, with no healing [in sight].[1]

י The way to the day of vengeance[2] is closed off;

י the day of reckoning[2] [is hidden, as if behind] a sealed-up crack.

כ The strength of the bearer [Israel] is broken[3] by the burden [of exile];

כ those left from the slaughter are limping and lame.

ל Without rest they wander from place to place,

ל then toil unto weariness — and others take [the fruits].

מ [Israel, the vine] planted in a fertile, fruitful corner —*[4]

מ why is it trampled like thorns [earmarked] for the furnace?

נ Let the Watchman on High* not sleep.

נ His planting is turned into pasturage for the cows of Bashan.*

ס What gain is [there from] the vine-bough, if [its fruit] has been plucked?

ס What profit is [there from] the spreading vine, if it has been plundered?

ע She who is engraved on [God's] arm and [His] crown —*

ע why is [His] love for her swept away?[5]

פ [The oppressors, like] youths, do but little work [to serve You],*

פ [yet] receive an ever-increasing reward.

צ [We] await Your attention, but its time [of coming] drags on,

צ [while] one trouble strikes and another right after.

ק The holy first-fruits* of piled-up grain

ק is scattered [to] the ends of the earth.

ר Like a wind blows the leaves of the forest,

ר drawn swords chase, as they flee in terror.

ש Chazzan — Those ninety-eight curses [that the Torah decreed];[6]

ש have been fulfilled [upon us], and others and more besides.*

ת Have mercy, gather us in from these corners [of the world];

then they will declare among the nations,

'HASHEM has done great things for these [people]!'[7]

---

and thirteen *mitzvos*] I shall recompense with great reward in the World to Come' (*Sifra, Bechukosai* 2:5:5).

קֹדֶשׁ רֵאשִׁית — *The holy first-fruits.* A reference to Israel, as the prophet proclaims: קֹדֶשׁ יִשְׂרָאֵל לַה', *Israel is holy unto HASHEM,* רֵאשִׁית תְּבוּאָתוֹ, *the first of His grain crop* (Jeremiah 2:3).

שְׁמוֹנָה וְתִשְׁעִים הָאָלוֹת הָאֵלֶּה שְׁלֵמוּ אֵלֶּה מֵאֵלֶּה וְכָאֵלֶּה — *Those ninety-eight curses have been fulfilled, and others and more besides.* The *tochachah* (passage of rebuke) in *Deuteronomy* (28:15-68) contains ninety-eight curses or threats of retribution that will come upon Israel if it will not follow the *mitzvos* of the Torah. The *paytan* here bemoans the fact that many more than ninety-eight punishments, pogroms, exiles, oppressions, and other forms of Divine retribution have come upon us. 'Therefore,' he pleads, 'have mercy and gather us from the four corners of our dispersion.'

Alternatively, the words אֵלֶּה מֵאֵלֶּה וְכָאֵלֶּה, literally, *these, from these, and like these,* allude

to the Altar offerings. *Rashi* (to *Numbers* 29:18) teaches that the fourteen lambs brought as part of the *mussaf*-offering on each of the seven days of Succos served to protect Israel against the ninety-eight (fourteen times seven) curses of *Deuteronomy.* Similarly, the *paytan* here assumes, other Altar offerings must have served the same purpose. Thus, he states: שְׁלֵמוּ, *They have been fulfilled,* i.e., the offerings alluded to by the words אֵלֶּה מֵאֵלֶּה and כָאֵלֶּה. For the last, summarizing verse in the chapter describing the Festival *mussaf*-offerings begins, אֵלֶּה תַּעֲשׂוּ, *These [offerings] shall you make* (*Numbers* 29:39). The laws of the *minchah*-offering state: *You shall bring the minchah-offering that has been made* מֵאֵלֶּה, *from these [aforementioned ingredients]* (*Leviticus* 2:8). And the *mussaf*-offerings of Pesach are summarized; כָּאֵלֶּה תַּעֲשׂוּ, *like these shall you make* (*Numbers* 28:24). Thus, since we are no longer able to bring the offerings described as אֵלֶּה מֵאֵלֶּה and כָאֵלֶּה, we are afflicted with the ninety-eight curses of the *tochachah.*

All, while standing:

אֵל מֶלֶךְ יוֹשֵׁב עַל כִּסֵּא רַחֲמִים מִתְנַהֵג בַּחֲסִידוּת, מוֹחֵל עֲוֹנוֹת עַמּוֹ, מַעֲבִיר רִאשׁוֹן רִאשׁוֹן,[1] מַרְבֶּה מְחִילָה לַחַטָּאִים וּסְלִיחָה לַפּוֹשְׁעִים, עֹשֶׂה צְדָקוֹת עִם כָּל בָּשָׂר וָרוּחַ, לֹא כְרָעָתָם תִּגְמוֹל. ❖ אֵל הוֹרֵיתָ לָּנוּ לוֹמַר שְׁלֹשׁ עֶשְׂרֵה, וּזְכוֹר לָנוּ הַיּוֹם בְּרִית שְׁלֹשׁ עֶשְׂרֵה, כְּמוֹ שֶׁהוֹדַעְתָּ לֶעָנָיו מִקֶּדֶם, כְּמוֹ שֶׁכָּתוּב, וַיֵּרֶד יהוה בֶּעָנָן וַיִּתְיַצֵּב עִמּוֹ שָׁם, וַיִּקְרָא בְשֵׁם יהוה.

Congregation, then *chazzan:*

וַיַּעֲבֹר יהוה עַל פָּנָיו וַיִּקְרָא:

Congregation and *chazzan* (the words in bold type are recited aloud and in unison):

יהוה, יהוה,   אֵל, רַחוּם, וְחַנּוּן, אֶרֶךְ אַפַּיִם, **וְרַב חֶסֶד, וֶאֱמֶת, נֹצֵר חֶסֶד לָאֲלָפִים, נֹשֵׂא עָוֹן, וָפֶשַׁע, וְחַטָּאָה, וְנַקֵּה.** וְסָלַחְתָּ לַעֲוֹנֵנוּ וּלְחַטָּאתֵנוּ וּנְחַלְתָּנוּ. סְלַח לָנוּ אָבִינוּ כִּי חָטָאנוּ, מְחַל לָנוּ מַלְכֵּנוּ כִּי פָשָׁעְנוּ. כִּי אַתָּה אֲדֹנָי טוֹב וְסַלָּח, וְרַב חֶסֶד לְכָל קֹרְאֶיךָ.

פסוקי הקדמה לסליחה ט

נֹשֵׂא לְבָבֵנוּ אֶל כַּפָּיִם, אֶל אֵל בַּשָּׁמָיִם.[2] עֶזְרֵנוּ מֵעִם יהוה, עֹשֵׂה שָׁמַיִם וָאָרֶץ. אַל יִתֵּן לַמּוֹט רַגְלֶךָ, אַל יָנוּם שֹׁמְרֶךָ.[3] הִנֵּה לֹא יָנוּם וְלֹא יִישָׁן שׁוֹמֵר יִשְׂרָאֵל.[4] הוֹשַׁע יהוה אֶת עַמֶּךָ, אֵת שְׁאֵרִית יִשְׂרָאֵל.[5]

כְּרַחֵם אָב עַל בָּנִים, כֵּן תְּרַחֵם יהוה עָלֵינוּ. לַיהוה הַיְשׁוּעָה, עַל עַמְּךָ בִרְכָתֶךָ סֶּלָה. יהוה צְבָאוֹת עִמָּנוּ, מִשְׂגָּב לָנוּ אֱלֹהֵי יַעֲקֹב סֶלָה. יהוה צְבָאוֹת, אַשְׁרֵי אָדָם בֹּטֵחַ בָּךְ. יהוה הוֹשִׁיעָה, הַמֶּלֶךְ יַעֲנֵנוּ בְיוֹם קָרְאֵנוּ.

In some congregations the following two verses are recited responsively — the *chazzan* reciting סְלַח, and the congregation responding וַיֹּאמֶר. In other congregations these verses are recited silently.

סְלַח נָא לַעֲוֹן הָעָם הַזֶּה כְּגֹדֶל חַסְדֶּךָ, וְכַאֲשֶׁר נָשָׂאתָה לָעָם הַזֶּה מִמִּצְרַיִם וְעַד הֵנָּה, וְשָׁם נֶאֱמַר:

וַיֹּאמֶר יהוה סָלַחְתִּי כִּדְבָרֶךָ.

All:

הַטֵּה אֱלֹהַי אָזְנְךָ וּשְׁמָע, פְּקַח עֵינֶיךָ וּרְאֵה שֹׁמְמֹתֵינוּ, וְהָעִיר אֲשֶׁר נִקְרָא שִׁמְךָ עָלֶיהָ, כִּי לֹא עַל צִדְקוֹתֵינוּ אֲנַחְנוּ מַפִּילִים תַּחֲנוּנֵינוּ לְפָנֶיךָ, כִּי עַל רַחֲמֶיךָ הָרַבִּים.

All, while standing:

אֵל מֶלֶךְ O God, King Who sits on the throne of mercy; Who acts with kindness, pardons the iniquities of His people, removes [sins] one by one,[1] increasingly grants pardon to careless sinners and forgiveness to rebels, Who deals righteously with every living being — You do not repay them in accord with their evil. Chazzan — O God, You taught us to recite the Thirteen [Attributes of Mercy], so remember for us today the covenant of these Thirteen, as You made known to the humble one in ancient times, as it is written: And HASHEM descended in a cloud and stood with him there, and He called out with the Name HASHEM.

Congregation, then chazzan:

And HASHEM passed before him [Moses] and proclaimed:

Congregation and chazzan (the words in bold type are recited aloud and in unison):

ה' ה' **HASHEM, HASHEM, God, Compassionate and Gracious, Slow to anger, and Abundant in Kindness and Truth, Preserver of kindness for thousands [of generations], Forgiver of iniquity, willful sin, and error, and Who cleanses.** *May You forgive our iniquities and our errors and make us Your heritage. Forgive us, our Father, for we have erred; pardon us, our King, for we have willfully sinned; for You, my Lord, are good and forgiving and abundantly kind to all who call upon You.*

PREFATORY VERSES TO SELICHAH 9

נִשָּׂא Let us lift our hearts on our hands to God in Heaven.[2] Our help is from HASHEM, Maker of heaven and earth. He will not allow our foot to falter; our Guardian will not slumber.[3] Behold, He neither slumbers nor sleeps — the Guardian of Israel.[4] Save Your people, HASHEM, the remnant of Israel.[5]

כְּרַחֵם אָב As a father has mercy on his children, so, HASHEM, may You have mercy on us. Salvation is HASHEM's, upon Your people is Your blessing, Selah. HASHEM, Master of Legions, is with us, a stronghold for us is the God of Jacob, Selah. HASHEM, Master of Legions, praiseworthy is the person who trusts in You. HASHEM, save! May the King answer us on the day we call.

In some congregations the following two verses are recited responsively — the chazzan reciting, 'Forgive, please . . . ,' and the congregation responding, 'And HASHEM said . . .'
In other congregations these verses are recited silently.

סְלַח נָא Forgive, please, the iniquity of this people according to the greatness of Your kindness and as You have forgiven this people from Egypt until now, and there it was said:

And HASHEM said, 'I have forgiven according to your word!'

All:

הַטֵּה Incline, my God, Your ear, and listen, open Your eyes and see our desolation and that of the city upon which Your Name is proclaimed; for not because of our righteousness do we cast down our supplications before You, rather because of Your abundant compassion.

(1) Tractate *Rosh Hashanah* 17a. (2) *Lamentations* 3:41.
(3) Cf. *Psalms* 121:2-3. (4) 121:4. (5) *Jeremiah* 31:6.

אֲדֹנָי שְׁמָעָה, אֲדֹנָי סְלָחָה, אֲדֹנָי הַקְשִׁיבָה, וַעֲשֵׂה אַל תְּאַחַר, לְמַעַנְךָ אֱלֹהַי, כִּי שִׁמְךָ נִקְרָא עַל עִירְךָ וְעַל עַמֶּךָ.

סליחה ט

All:

אֱלֹהֵינוּ וֵאלֹהֵי אֲבוֹתֵינוּ:

אֲנִי יוֹם אִירָא* אֵלֶיךָ[1] אֶקְרָא,

בַּל יַעַשְׁקוּנִי זֵדִים[2] עוֹזְבֵי יְקָרֶךָ,

גְּמוּל לְהָשִׁיב לָהֶם,[3] שֵׁב לְבַקֵּרָה,

דִּין רָשָׁע וְעָוֶל, מְלוֹאָם[4] יְקָרֵא.*

הַחוֹשְׁבִים לְהַשְׁכִּיחַ שֵׁם קֹדֶשׁ הַנִּכְבָּד,[5]

וּלְהַרְגִּיל שֵׁם טֻמְאָה נִקְלֶה וְנֶעֱבָד,*

זֶה דַרְכָּם, טוֹבֵי עָם אָבָד,

חָשֹׁךְ הַשְׁאֵר מִכָּתְשָׁם בְּבֵית הַבָּד.

טְרֹף טֶרֶף אָדָם, לִמֻּדוּ[6] כִּמְדַבָּר,[7]

יַדּוּ גוֹרָל* כְּעַל הֶפְקֵר בַּמִּדְבָּר,

כִּמְעַט כֻּלּוּ, וְלֹא יַעַדְרוּ דָבָר,

לוּלֵי רַחֲמֶיךָ, אָדוֹן בְּחֶסֶד דַּבֵּר.

מִי יְהַרְהֵר אַחַר מִדּוֹתֶיךָ לְדַיְּנָה,

נָכְחֲךָ לְהָשִׁיב מֵחֲלָצָיו לְזַיְּנָה,

סָרְנוּ וְסָעַרְנוּ,* וְנִשְׁמְטָה חֶרֶב הַיּוֹנָה.*

עִמְּךָ הַדִּין, וְיָדְךָ עַל הָעֶלְיוֹנָה.

פֶּן יֹאמַר יָכָלְתִּי, בַּעַל הַמּוֹט,

צָרֵי יְהוּדָה יָגִילוּ כִּי אֶמּוֹט,[8]

קָרָא לִמְכוּרֵי חִנָּם,* שְׁנַת שָׁמוֹט,

רָשָׁע הַפּוֹשֵׁט יָד, יִסֹּג אָחוֹר וְיִקָּמֵט.

שִׁטְרְךָ קוֹדֵם וְלוֹ נוֹשִׂים מְבַקְשִׁים,

אֲנִי יוֹם אִירָא — *I, on the day I am afraid.* This *selichah* was written by R' Shlomo HaBavli [see prefatory comment to *selichah* 2], whose name appears in the acrostic, after the *aleph-beis*, שְׁלֹמֹה הַקָּטָן יִגְדַּל בְּתוֹרָה, *Shlomo the lesser, may he become great in Torah.* The *selichah* is omitted in some editions, presumably due to Christian censorship. Nevertheless, its omission in those editions is conspicuous because the printers did not renumber the remaining *selichos,* but just skipped over number 9.

דִּין רָשָׁע וְעָוֶל מְלוֹאָם יְקָרֵא — *The wicked and evil*

decrees promulgated at their councils. The translation follows *Arugas HaBosem* and alludes to the anti-Semitic decrees to which the composer was a witness. Others translate this stich as a supplication: *Let the sentence of the wicked and the evildoers be read out in full.* A third opinion repunctuates the verse and synthesizes the first two interpretations: דִּין רָשָׁע, *Let the wicked decree,* וְעָוֶל מְלוֹאָם, *and the evil of their councils,* יְקָרֵא, *be read* [against them].

וּלְהַרְגִּיל שֵׁם טֻמְאָה נִקְלֶה וְנֶעֱבָד — *And to accustom us to an unclean name of vile idolatry.* One of the

*O my Lord, heed; O my Lord, forgive; O my Lord, be attentive and act,
do not delay; for Your sake, my God, for Your Name is proclaimed upon
Your city and upon Your people.*

SELICHAH 9

All:
Our God and the God of our forefathers:

א I, on the day I am afraid,* I call to You,[1]

ב let not the wanton forsakers of the precious [Torah] victimize me.[2]

ג Pay them their due,[3] [when you] sit [in judgment] to examine

ד the wicked and evil decrees promulgated at their councils.*[4]

ה They plot to make [us] oblivious of the holy, revered Name,[5]

ו and to accustom us to an unclean name of vile idolatry.*

ז This method of theirs has ruined the best of our people;

ח save the remnant from being crushed [like olives] in the press.

ט They have learned[6] to rend human prey, as stated [by the prophet].[7]

י [And] they cast lots,* as if for a thing left ownerless in the desert.

כ They almost destroyed [us], and indeed spared no effort,

ל but for Your mercy, Lord Who leads with kindness.

מ Who can criticize Your ways, or debate [about them]?

נ Or arm himself with strength to argue with You?

ס We have turned away [from the Torah's way], and we have been
storm tossed,* and the blood-soaked sword* was loosed.

ע Justice is with You, and You have the upper hand.

פ Lest the master of the yoke say, 'I have won!'

צ Lest the tormenters of Yehudah rejoice when I falter,[8]

ק Proclaim the Sabbatical year for those who were sold for nothing,*

ר while the grasping wicked fall back and wither.

ש Although Your receipt predates [those of all the oppressors,
they, as creditors, demand [payment of their own bill];

---

(1) Cf. *Psalms* 56:4. (2) Cf. 119:122. (3) Cf. *Lamentations* 3:64. (4) Cf. *Job* 36:17. (5) Cf. *Jeremiah* 23:27. (6) Some editions read לֻמְדוּ, they have been taught. (7) Cf. *Ezekiel* 19:3. (8) Cf. *Psalms* 13:5.

---

most heavily censored stiches in all of the *selichos*, this line is omitted entirely in some editions, and altered in many others. One edition went so far as to rewrite the entire verse: וַאֲנַחְנוּ שֵׁם, אֱלֹהֵינוּ נַזְכִּיר לְבָד, *But we mention only the Name of our God.* In most emended versions, however, the words שֵׁם טֻמְאָה, *an unclean name*, are replaced by either שֵׁם אַחֵר, *another's name*, or שֵׁם אֱלִיל, *an idol's name.*

The literal meaning of נִקְלָה is *despised*, while the word וְנֶעֱבָד has been translated as *worshiped* or *manufactured* by man. In some editions the word is spelled וְנֶאֱבָד and means *and ruined*; still other versions read וְנֶעֱכָר, *and murky.*

יַדּוּ גוֹרָל — *They cast lots.* To decide who would get Jerusalem (*Obadiah* 1:11), who would enslave its honored citizens (*Nahum* 3:10), and who would rule over Israel in general (*Joel* 4:3).

וְסֹעֲרְנוּ — *And we have been storm tossed.* The

translation follows *Arugas HaBosem.* According to *Rashi* (to *Isaiah* 54:11), the word may be rendered, *[our hearts] have become turbulent.*

חֶרֶב הַיּוֹנָה — *The blood-soaked sword.* The translation follows *Targum* and *Rashi's* primary interpretation (to *Jeremiah* 46:16), who derive יוֹנָה from יַיִן, *wine*, and paraphrase, *the enemy's sword that is drunk as if with wine.* According to *Radak* and *Rashi's* secondary interpretation, the word is related to אוֹנָאָה and means *oppressive.*

לִמְכוּרֵי חִנָּם — *For those who were sold for nothing*, i.e. they gained nothing from the sinfulness that caused God to give them over into the hands of their captors (*Rashi* to *Isaiah* 52:3). Alternatively, He gave them over to their captors, not for money but as punishment for their sins. Thus, as the verse there continues, they cannot be redeemed with money, but only with repentance (*Radak*)

שֶׁעֲבוּדָךְ לְהַרְחִיק, רַבּוּ צוֹרְרִים קָשִׁים,

תְּחוּמֵי סַמָּנֵי מְצָרֶיךָ, לַעֲקֹר מְבַקְשִׁים

תְּבוּאָה קְדַשְׁתָּ,¹ בְּלוּעָה מְלִילוֹת וְקַשִׁים.*

שֶׁפֶט רָעָה, תָּבֹא עֲלֵיהֶם וְהָאֲשִׁימֵם,¹

לָמוֹ עוֹלֵל, וְהִתְעוֹלֵל בִּכְבֶד יְשִׁימֵם,

מְנָת כּוֹסָם, פֶּחִי מִפַּח הַגְּשָׁמֵם,

הֲשִׁיבֵם שִׁבְעָתַיִם,* נְקַם בְּרִית וְהַשְׁמֵם.

הָעִיר קִרְיַת טִירַת נָנֶךְ, נַהֲלֵנוּ,

יָם גְּאוּלִים דֶּרֶךְ לַעֲבֹר קְהָלֵנוּ,

בְּךָ תוֹחַלְתֵּנוּ, וְאַתָּה רַב (הָאֵל) מְחוֹלֲלֵנוּ,

נַחֲמֵנוּ נָא, יְהִי חַסְדְּךָ עָלֵינוּ.²

All, while standing:

אֵל מֶלֶךְ יוֹשֵׁב עַל כִּסֵּא רַחֲמִים מִתְנַהֵג בַּחֲסִידוּת, מוֹחֵל עֲוֹנוֹת עַמּוֹ, מַעֲבִיר רִאשׁוֹן רִאשׁוֹן, מַרְבֶּה מְחִילָה לַחַטָּאִים וּסְלִיחָה לַפּוֹשְׁעִים, עֹשֶׂה צְדָקוֹת עִם כָּל בָּשָׂר וָרוּחַ, לֹא כְרָעָתָם תִּגְמוֹל. ❖ אֵל הוֹרֵיתָ לָּנוּ לוֹמַר שְׁלֹשׁ עֶשְׂרֵה, וּזְכוֹר לָנוּ הַיּוֹם בְּרִית שְׁלֹשׁ עֶשְׂרֵה, כְּמוֹ שֶׁהוֹדַעְתָּ לֶעָנָיו מִקֶּדֶם, כְּמוֹ שֶׁכָּתוּב, וַיֵּרֶד יהוה בֶּעָנָן וַיִּתְיַצֵּב עִמּוֹ שָׁם, וַיִּקְרָא בְשֵׁם יהוה.

Congregation, then *chazzan:*

וַיַּעֲבֹר יהוה עַל פָּנָיו וַיִּקְרָא:

Congregation and *chazzan* (the words in bold type are recited aloud and in unison):

יהוה, יהוה, אֵל, **רַחוּם, וְחַנּוּן, אֶרֶךְ אַפַּיִם, וְרַב חֶסֶד, וֶאֱמֶת,**

נֹצֵר חֶסֶד לָאֲלָפִים, נֹשֵׂא עָוֹן, וָפֶשַׁע, וְחַטָּאָה,

וְנַקֵּה. וְסָלַחְתָּ לַעֲוֹנֵנוּ וּלְחַטָּאתֵנוּ וּנְחַלְתָּנוּ. סְלַח לָנוּ אָבִינוּ כִּי

מְלִילוֹת וְקַשִׁים — *Grain kernels and straw.* The word מְלִילוֹת refers to the kernels that have been completely separated from the shells and other forms of chaff. Thus, it alludes to the righteous *tzaddikim* who have succeeded in winning their freedom from the *klippos* (spiritual shells) and the *Yetzer Hara* (Evil Inclination) that prevent man from fulfilling his soul's potential. קַשִׁים, straw, has been emptied of its grain and represents those who are devoid of *mitzvos.* The *paytan* intimates that the anti-Semite is not selective in choosing which Jews to oppress; he

will persecute the good along with the bad, the observant along with the irreligious.

מְנָת כּוֹסָם . . . שִׁבְעָתַיִם — *The measure of their cup [of retribution] . . . sevenfold.* The stiches seem to contradict each other. First we pray that they be punished according to *the measure of their cup,* i.e., in equal measure to their acts against us. But then we ask that they be paid back *sevenfold!* Moreover, since it is axiomatic that God always punishes מִדָּה כְּנֶגֶד מִדָּה, *measure for measure,* why do we pray that He pay them back *sevenfold?* Is that not unjust? This very contra-

So many bitter enemies [attempt] to push away Your sovereignty
   [over us]!

ת They seek to uproot the boundary-markers of Your domain,
   and swallow up the wheat that You sanctified,[1]
   both grain kernels and straw.*

שׁ Come upon them and accuse them [with] justice for their evil.[1]

ל Do to them [as they did to us,] and taunt them
   as [You visit] ruin heavily upon them.

מ Rain down on them the measure of their cup [of retribution],
   coals of burning fire;

ה pay them back sevenfold,* the covenant's vengeance,
   and lay them waste.

Lead us to the city of Your dwelling-tower,
[make the] sea a way for the redeemed, our gathered people,
   to pass through.

Our hope is in You, for You are [our] Master, (O God), our Maker;
please comfort us, may Your kindness be upon us.[2]

All, while standing:

אֵל מֶלֶךְ O God, King Who sits on the throne of mercy; Who acts with
   kindness, pardons the iniquities of His people, removes [sins]
one by one, increasingly grants pardon to careless sinners and forgiveness
to rebels, Who deals righteously with every living being — You do not repay
them in accord with their evil. Chazzan — O God, You taught us to recite the
Thirteen [Attributes of Mercy], so remember for us today the covenant of
these Thirteen, as You made known to the humble one in ancient times, as
it is written: And HASHEM descended in a cloud and stood with him there,
and He called out with the Name HASHEM.

Congregation, then chazzan:

And HASHEM passed before him [Moses] and proclaimed:

Congregation and chazzan (the words in bold type are recited aloud and in unison):

ה' ה' HASHEM, HASHEM, God, Compassionate and Gracious, Slow to
   **anger, and Abundant in Kindness and Truth, Preserver of
kindness for thousands [of generations], Forgiver of iniquity, willful
sin, and error, and Who cleanses.** May You forgive our iniquities
and our errors and make us Your heritage. Forgive us, our Father, for

---

(1) Cf. *Jeremiah* 2:3. (2) Cf. *Psalms* 33:22.

diction also appears in Scripture: Jeremiah
prayed, 'Pay them back their due, HASHEM, as
they have done' (*Lamentations* 3:64), i.e., in equal
measure to their sins. But David prayed, 'Pay
back our neighbors sevenfold' (*Psalms* 79:12).
The Midrash (*Yalkut Shimoni* to *Psalms* 79:12
citing *Midrash Eichah*) explains: There is no
contradiction. Jeremiah was referring to the
oppressive nations' acts against Israel, 'Pay them
back their due, as they have done [to us],' while
David spoke of their sins against the Torah

which is described as מְזֻקָּק שִׁבְעָתַיִם, *refined
sevenfold* (ibid. 12:7).

שִׁבְעָתַיִם — *Sevenfold.* Although *Rashi* usually
tries to find a reason for the number seven
whenever it appears in Scriptures (see, e.g.,
Leviticus 26:18; *I Samuel* 2:5), other commentaries understand the number seven as a syn-
onym for *many* (see *Ibn Ezra* and *Radak* ibid.);
or as 'a mystical number whose secret is
known to very few people' (*Ibn Ezra* to *Numbers*
23:1).

חָטָאנוּ, מְחַל לָנוּ מַלְכֵּנוּ כִּי פָשָׁעְנוּ. כִּי אַתָּה אֲדֹנָי טוֹב וְסַלָּח,
וְרַב חֶסֶד לְכָל קֹרְאֶיךָ.

סליחה י (פזמון)

Chazzan, then congregation:

מַלְאֲכֵי רַחֲמִים*   מְשָׁרְתֵי עֶלְיוֹן,
חַלּוּ נָא פְּנֵי אֵל[1] בְּמֵיטַב הַגָּיוֹן,
אוּלַי יָחוֹס עַם עָנִי[2] וְאֶבְיוֹן, אוּלַי יְרַחֵם.

Congregation, then chazzan:

אוּלַי יְרַחֵם שְׁאֵרִית יוֹסֵף,[3]   שְׁפָלִים וְנִבְזִים[4] פְּשׂוּחֵי שֶׁסֶף,
שְׁבוּיֵי חִנָּם מְכוּרֵי בְּלֹא כֶסֶף.[5]
שׁוֹאֲגִים בִּתְפִלָּה וּמְבַקְשִׁים רִשָּׁיוֹן,
אוּלַי יָחוֹס עַם עָנִי וְאֶבְיוֹן, אוּלַי יְרַחֵם.

Congregation, then chazzan:

אוּלַי יְרַחֵם מְעֻנֵּי כֶבֶל,[6]   מְלֻמְּדֵי מַכּוֹת בְּעִנּוּי סֶבֶל,
מְנוֹד רֹאשׁ[7] נְתוּנִים בְּיוֹשְׁבֵי תֵבֵל.
מָשָׁל בָּעַמִּים בְּקֶצֶף וּבְזָיוֹן,
אוּלַי יָחוֹס עַם עָנִי וְאֶבְיוֹן, אוּלַי יְרַחֵם.

Congregation, then chazzan:

אוּלַי יְרַחֵם וְיֵרֶא בָּעֳנִי עַמּוֹ,[8]   וְיַקְשֵׁב וְיִשְׁמַע הַצַּגִים לְעַמּוֹ,
וְעוֹדִים בְּלַחַשׁ מוּסָר לָמוֹ.
וְעֵינֵיהֶם תּוֹלִים לִמְצוֹא רָצוֹן,
אוּלַי יָחוֹס עַם עָנִי וְאֶבְיוֹן, אוּלַי יְרַחֵם.

Congregation, then chazzan:

אוּלַי יְרַחֵם אוֹמְרֵי סְלַח נָא,[9]
אוֹמְצֵי שְׁבָחוֹ בְּכָל עֵת וְעוֹנָה,
אֲגוּדִים בַּצָּרָה לִשְׁפּוֹךְ תְּחִנָּה.
אֶת פְּנֵי אֱלֹהֵיהֶם שׁוֹפְכִים לֵב דִּנְיוֹן,
אוּלַי יָחוֹס עַם עָנִי וְאֶבְיוֹן, אוּלַי יְרַחֵם.

---

§◊ **מַלְאֲכֵי רַחֲמִים** — *O angels of mercy.* The
propriety and permissibility of requesting angelic
intervention in bringing our prayers before God
is a very controversial halachic issue in the area of

prayers. See the introduction for a full discussion.
    The *paytan* signed his name — שְׁמוּאֵל כֹּהֵן יְחִי,
Shmuel the Kohen, may he live — in the acrostic
of the verses, as indicated by the bold type. Some

we have erred; pardon us, our King, for we have willfully sinned; for You, my Lord, are good and forgiving and abundantly kind to all who call upon You.

SELICHAH 10

Chazzan, then congregation:

מַלְאֲכֵי רַחֲמִים *O angels of mercy,* servants of the Supreme,*
please entreat before God[1] with eloquent expression:
'Perhaps He will pity [His] poor and destitute people;[2]
perhaps He will have mercy.'

Congregation, then chazzan:

ש *Perhaps He will have mercy on the remnant of Joseph,[3]*
degraded and disgraced,[4] torn and ripped,
taken captive without reason, sold for no money.[5]
They shout in prayer and plead for permission:
'Perhaps He will pity [His] poor and destitute people;
perhaps He will have mercy.'

Congregation, then chazzan:

מ *Perhaps He will have mercy on those tortured by chains,[6]*
accustomed to blows in the suffering of hard labor,
their heads made to tremble[7] by all inhabitants of the world,
a slogan among the people for wrath and disgrace:
'Perhaps He will pity [His] poor and destitute people;
perhaps He will have mercy.'

Congregation, then chazzan:

ו *Perhaps He will have mercy and see the suffering of His people,[8]*
and hearken and hear those standing before Him,
gathered in silent prayer, chastisement upon them,
with their eyes raised to find favor:
'Perhaps He will pity [His] poor and destitute people;
perhaps He will have mercy.'

Congregation, then chazzan:

א *Perhaps He will have mercy on those who say, 'Please forgive…'[9]*
who intensify His praise at every time and season,
gathered in distress to pour out supplication,
before their God they pour out anguished heart:
'Perhaps He will pity [His] poor and destitute people;
perhaps He will have mercy.'

---

(1) *Malachi* 1:9. (2) Cf. *Zephaniah* 3:12. (3) Cf. *Amos* 5:15; see commentary to *selichah* 68, s.v., בְּכוֹר שׁוֹר. (4) Cf. *Malachi* 2:9. (5) Cf. *Isaiah* 52:3; see commentary to *selichah* 9, s.v., לְמִכּוּרֵי חִנָּם. (6) Cf. *Psalms* 105:18. (7) 44:15. (8) Cf. *Exodus* 3:7. (9) *Numbers* 14:19.

---

speculate that he is R' Shmuel ben R' Yehudah   his wife and children, was martyred during the
HaKohen of Mainz, Germany, who, along with   First Crusade in 1096.

Congregation, then chazzan:

אוּלַי יְרַחֵם לָקְתָה בְכִפְלַיִם,[1] לְעוֹטָה אֲרָיוֹת כְּמוֹ בְּפִי שַׁחֲלַיִם,*
לָקָה וּמִשְׁתַּלֱּמֶת בַּעֲוֹן שׁוּלַיִם.[2]
לֹא שָׁכְחָה בְּכָל זֹאת מִכְתָּב עֹז חֶבְיוֹן,[3]
אוּלַי יָחוֹס עַם עָנִי וְאֶבְיוֹן, אוּלַי יְרַחֵם.

Congregation, then chazzan:

אוּלַי יְרַחֵם **בּ**וֹשֵׁי פָנִים,
הַשּׁוֹמְעִים חֶרְפָּתָם וְלֹא מְשִׁיבִים וְעוֹנִים,
נִצְחוּ מְקֻוִּים וּלִישְׁעוֹ נִשְׁעָנִים.
כִּי לֹא כָלוּ רַחֲמָיו[4] בְּכִלָּיוֹן,
אוּלַי יָחוֹס עַם עָנִי וְאֶבְיוֹן, אוּלַי יְרַחֵם.

Congregation, then chazzan:

אוּלַי יְרַחֵם וְיַחֲלֵץ עָנִי בְעָנְיוֹ,[5]
חֲבוּשׁוֹ יַתִּיר מֵאֶרֶץ שִׁבְיוֹ,
יִגְהֶה מְזוֹרוֹ וְיַחְבּוֹשׁ חָלְיוֹ.
צַעֲקָתוֹ יִשְׁמַע וְיָחִישׁ עֵת פִּדְיוֹן,
אוּלַי יָחוֹס עַם עָנִי וְאֶבְיוֹן, אוּלַי יְרַחֵם.

All, while standing:

אֵל מֶלֶךְ יוֹשֵׁב עַל כִּסֵּא רַחֲמִים מִתְנַהֵג בַּחֲסִידוּת, מוֹחֵל
עֲוֹנוֹת עַמּוֹ, מַעֲבִיר רִאשׁוֹן רִאשׁוֹן, מַרְבֶּה מְחִילָה
לְחַטָּאִים וּסְלִיחָה לְפוֹשְׁעִים, עֹשֶׂה צְדָקוֹת עִם כָּל בָּשָׂר וָרוּחַ,
לֹא כְרָעָתָם תִּגְמוֹל. אֵל הוֹרֵיתָ לָנוּ לוֹמַר שְׁלֹשׁ עֶשְׂרֵה, וּזְכוֹר
לָנוּ הַיּוֹם בְּרִית שְׁלֹשׁ עֶשְׂרֵה, כְּמוֹ שֶׁהוֹדַעְתָּ לֶעָנָיו מִקֶּדֶם, כְּמוֹ
שֶׁכָּתוּב, וַיֵּרֶד יהוה בֶּעָנָן וַיִּתְיַצֵּב עִמּוֹ שָׁם, וַיִּקְרָא בְשֵׁם יהוה.

Congregation, then chazzan:

וַיַּעֲבֹר יהוה עַל פָּנָיו וַיִּקְרָא:

Congregation and chazzan (the words in bold type are recited aloud and in unison):

יהוה, יהוה, אֵל, רַחוּם, וְחַנּוּן, אֶרֶךְ אַפַּיִם, וְרַב חֶסֶד, וֶאֱמֶת,
נֹצֵר חֶסֶד לָאֲלָפִים, נֹשֵׂא עָוֹן, וָפֶשַׁע, וְחַטָּאָה,
וְנַקֵּה. וְסָלַחְתָּ לַעֲוֹנֵנוּ וּלְחַטָּאתֵנוּ וּנְחַלְתָּנוּ. סְלַח לָנוּ אָבִינוּ כִּי
חָטָאנוּ, מְחַל לָנוּ מַלְכֵּנוּ כִּי פָשָׁעְנוּ. כִּי אַתָּה אֲדֹנָי טוֹב וְסַלָּח,
וְרַב חֶסֶד לְכָל קֹרְאֶיךָ.

---

(1) Some editions read לָקְחָה בְּפְלַיִם, *she has received* [lit., *taken*] *double* [*punishment*]; cf. *Isaiah 40:2.*
(2) Cf. *Jeremiah 13:22.* (3) Cf. *Habakkuk 3:4.* (4) *Lamentations 3:22.* (5) *Job 36:15.*

Congregation, then chazzan:

ל Perhaps He will have mercy on the nation
    that was doubly assaulted,[1]
  devoured by lions as by the mouth of vicious lions,*
  beaten and forced to pay for [her] overt sin,[2]
  despite all this, she will not forget the mighty, hidden[3] Written Law:
        'Perhaps He will pity [His] poor and destitute people;
                perhaps He will have mercy.'

Congregation, then chazzan:

כ Perhaps He will have mercy on those who hide their face,
ה who hear their shame and neither respond nor call out;
נ for His triumph they hope and on His salvation they rely,
  for His mercy has not come to a total end — [4]
        'Perhaps He will pity [His] poor and destitute people;
                perhaps He will have mercy.'

Congregation, then chazzan:

י Perhaps He will have mercy
    and deliver the afflicted from his affliction,[5]
ח release His prisoner [Israel] from the land of his [exile] captivity,
י cure his wound and heal his disease.
  O hear his outcry and hasten the time of his redemption:
        'Perhaps He will pity [His] poor and destitute people;
                perhaps He will have mercy.'

All, while standing:

אֵל מֶלֶךְ O God, King Who sits on the throne of mercy; Who acts with
           kindness, pardons the iniquities of His people, removes [sins]
one by one, increasingly grants pardon to careless sinners and forgiveness to rebels, Who deals righteously with every living being — You do
not repay them in accord with their evil. Chazzan – O God, You taught us
to recite the Thirteen [Attributes of Mercy], so remember for us today
the covenant of these Thirteen, as You made known to the humble one in
ancient times, as it is written: And HASHEM descended in a cloud and
stood with him there, and He called out with the Name HASHEM.

Congregation, then chazzan:

And HASHEM passed before him [Moses] and proclaimed:

Congregation and chazzan (the words in bold type are recited aloud and in unison):

ה' ה' HASHEM, HASHEM, God, Compassionate and Gracious, Slow
      to anger, and Abundant in Kindness and Truth, Preserver of
kindness for thousands [of generations], Forgiver of iniquity, willful
sin, and error, and Who cleanses. May You forgive our iniquities
and our errors and make us Your heritage. Forgive us, our Father, for
we have erred; pardon us, our King, for we have willfully sinned; for
You, my Lord, are good and forgiving and abundantly kind to all who
call upon You.

שְׁחָלִים ... אֲרָיוֹת — *Lions ... vicious lions.* The Talmud records six scriptural names for the

lion: אֲרִי, כְּפִיר, לָבִיא, לַיִשׁ, שַׁחַל, שַׁחַץ (*Sanhedrin* 95a).

All:

אַל תִּזְכָּר לָנוּ עֲוֹנוֹת רִאשׁוֹנִים, מַהֵר יְקַדְּמוּנוּ רַחֲמֶיךָ, כִּי דַלּוֹנוּ מְאֹד.[1] חַטַּאת נְעוּרֵינוּ וּפְשָׁעֵינוּ אַל תִּזְכֹּר, כְּחַסְדְּךָ זְכָר לָנוּ אַתָּה, לְמַעַן טוּבְךָ יהוה.[2]

זְכוֹר רַחֲמֶיךָ יהוה וַחֲסָדֶיךָ, כִּי מֵעוֹלָם הֵמָּה.[3] זָכְרֵנוּ יהוה בִּרְצוֹן עַמֶּךָ, פָּקְדֵנוּ בִּישׁוּעָתֶךָ.[4] זְכֹר עֲדָתְךָ קָנִיתָ קֶּדֶם, גָּאַלְתָּ שֵׁבֶט נַחֲלָתֶךָ, הַר צִיּוֹן זֶה שָׁכַנְתָּ בּוֹ.[5] זְכֹר יהוה חִבַּת יְרוּשָׁלָיִם, אַהֲבַת צִיּוֹן אַל תִּשְׁכַּח לָנֶצַח.[6] אַתָּה תָקוּם תְּרַחֵם צִיּוֹן, כִּי עֵת לְחֶנְנָהּ כִּי בָא מוֹעֵד.[7] זְכֹר יהוה לִבְנֵי אֱדוֹם אֵת יוֹם יְרוּשָׁלָיִם, הָאוֹמְרִים עָרוּ עָרוּ עַד הַיְסוֹד בָּהּ.[8] זְכֹר לְאַבְרָהָם לְיִצְחָק וּלְיִשְׂרָאֵל עֲבָדֶיךָ אֲשֶׁר נִשְׁבַּעְתָּ לָהֶם בָּךְ, וַתְּדַבֵּר אֲלֵהֶם, אַרְבֶּה אֶת זַרְעֲכֶם כְּכוֹכְבֵי הַשָּׁמָיִם, וְכָל הָאָרֶץ הַזֹּאת אֲשֶׁר אָמַרְתִּי אֶתֵּן לְזַרְעֲכֶם, וְנָחֲלוּ לְעוֹלָם.[9] ✣ זְכֹר לַעֲבָדֶיךָ לְאַבְרָהָם לְיִצְחָק וּלְיַעֲקֹב, אַל תֵּפֶן אֶל קְשִׁי הָעָם הַזֶּה וְאֶל רִשְׁעוֹ וְאֶל חַטָּאתוֹ.[10]

Chazzan, then congregation:

אַל נָא תָשֵׁת עָלֵינוּ חַטָּאת, אֲשֶׁר נוֹאַלְנוּ וַאֲשֶׁר חָטָאנוּ.[11]

Chazzan, then congregation:

חָטָאנוּ צוּרֵנוּ, סְלַח לָנוּ יוֹצְרֵנוּ.

All:

זְכוֹר לָנוּ בְּרִית אָבוֹת, כַּאֲשֶׁר אָמַרְתָּ: וְזָכַרְתִּי אֶת בְּרִיתִי יַעֲקוֹב, וְאַף אֶת בְּרִיתִי יִצְחָק, וְאַף אֶת בְּרִיתִי אַבְרָהָם אֶזְכֹּר, וְהָאָרֶץ אֶזְכֹּר.[12] זְכוֹר לָנוּ בְּרִית רִאשׁוֹנִים, כַּאֲשֶׁר אָמַרְתָּ: וְזָכַרְתִּי לָהֶם בְּרִית רִאשׁוֹנִים, אֲשֶׁר הוֹצֵאתִי אֹתָם מֵאֶרֶץ מִצְרַיִם לְעֵינֵי הַגּוֹיִם, לִהְיוֹת לָהֶם לֵאלֹהִים, אֲנִי יהוה.[13] עֲשֵׂה עִמָּנוּ כְּמָה שֶׁהִבְטַחְתָּנוּ: וְאַף גַּם זֹאת בִּהְיוֹתָם בְּאֶרֶץ אֹיְבֵיהֶם, לֹא מְאַסְתִּים וְלֹא גְעַלְתִּים לְכַלֹּתָם לְהָפֵר בְּרִיתִי אִתָּם, כִּי אֲנִי יהוה אֱלֹהֵיהֶם.[14] הִמָּצֵא לָנוּ בְּבַקָּשָׁתֵנוּ, כְּמָה שֶׁכָּתוּב: וּבִקַּשְׁתֶּם מִשָּׁם אֶת יהוה אֱלֹהֶיךָ וּמָצָאתָ, כִּי תִדְרְשֶׁנּוּ בְּכָל לְבָבְךָ וּבְכָל נַפְשֶׁךָ.[15] מוֹל אֶת לְבָבֵנוּ לְאַהֲבָה וּלְיִרְאָה אֶת שְׁמֶךָ, כְּמָה שֶׁכָּתוּב: וּמָל יהוה אֱלֹהֶיךָ אֶת לְבָבְךָ וְאֶת לְבַב זַרְעֶךָ, לְאַהֲבָה אֶת יהוה אֱלֹהֶיךָ בְּכָל לְבָבְךָ

All:

אַל תִּזְכׇּר Do not recall against us the iniquities of the ancients; speedily — let Your mercy come to meet us for we have fallen very low.[1] Remember not the sins of our youth and our rebellions; may You remember for us [the deeds] worthy of Your kindness, because of Your goodness, HASHEM.[2]

זְכוֹר רַחֲמֶיךָ Remember Your mercies, O HASHEM, and Your kindnesses, for they are from the beginning of the world.[3] Remember us, HASHEM, when You show Your people favor and recall us with Your salvation.[4] Remember Your congregation that You acquired of old, that You redeemed the tribe of Your heritage, and this Mount Zion where You dwelled.[5] Remember, O HASHEM, the affection of Jerusalem, may You never forget the love of Zion.[6] You will arise and show Zion mercy, for it is the time to be gracious to her, for the appointed time will have come.[7] Remember, HASHEM, for the offspring of Edom, the day of Jerusalem — for those who said: 'Destroy! Destroy to its very foundation!'[8] Remember Abraham, Isaac, and Israel, Your servants, to whom You swore by Your Being, saying to them, 'I shall increase your offspring like the stars of the heavens; and this entire land of which I spoke I will give to your offspring and they will inherit it forever.'[9] Chazzan — Remember for Your servants, for Abraham, for Isaac, and for Jacob; ignore the stubbornness of this people, its wickedness and its sinfulness.[10]

Chazzan, then congregation:
Please, do not reckon for us a sin,
what we have done foolishly and what we have sinned.[11]

Chazzan, then congregation:
We have erred, our Rock! Forgive us, our Molder!

All:

זְכוֹר Remember for us the covenant of the Patriarchs, as You said: 'And I will remember My covenant with Jacob, and also My covenant with Isaac, and also My covenant with Abraham will I remember; and the Land will I remember.'[12] Remember for us the covenant of the ancestors, as You said: 'And I will remember for them the covenant of the ancestors whom I removed from the land of Egypt in the very sight of the nations, to be a God to them; I am HASHEM.'[13] Do with us as You promised us: 'And despite all that, when they will be in the land of their enemies, I will not have despised them nor abhorred them to destroy them, to annul My covenant with them, for I am HASHEM their God.'[14] Be accessible to us in our quest, as it is written: From there you will seek HASHEM, your God, and you will find, when you search for Him with all your heart and with all your soul.[15] Expose our hearts to love Your Name, as it is written: HASHEM, your God, will expose your heart and the heart of your offspring, to love HASHEM, your God, with all your heart

---

(1) *Psalms* 79:8. (2) Cf. 25:7. (3) 25:6. (4) Cf. 106:4. (5) 74:2. (6) This is not a Scriptural verse. (7) *Psalms* 102:14. (8) 137:7. (9) *Exodus* 32:13. (10) *Deuteronomy* 9:27. (11) *Numbers* 12:11. (12) *Leviticus* 26:42. (13) 26:45. (14) 26:44. (15) *Deuteronomy* 4:29.

וּבְכָל נַפְשֶׁךָ, לְמַעַן חַיֶּיךָ.¹ זְרוֹק עָלֵינוּ מַיִם טְהוֹרִים וְטַהֲרֵנוּ, כְּמָה
שֶׁכָּתוּב: וְזָרַקְתִּי עֲלֵיכֶם מַיִם טְהוֹרִים וּטְהַרְתֶּם, מִכֹּל טֻמְאוֹתֵיכֶם
וּמִכָּל גִּלּוּלֵיכֶם אֲטַהֵר אֶתְכֶם.² מְחֵה פְשָׁעֵינוּ כָעָב וְכֶעָנָן, כְּמָה
שֶׁכָּתוּב: מָחִיתִי כָעָב פְּשָׁעֶיךָ וְכֶעָנָן חַטֹּאתֶיךָ, שׁוּבָה אֵלַי כִּי
גְאַלְתִּיךָ.³ מְחֵה פְשָׁעֵינוּ לְמַעַנְךָ, כַּאֲשֶׁר אָמָרְתָּ: אָנֹכִי אָנֹכִי הוּא
מֹחֶה פְשָׁעֶיךָ לְמַעֲנִי, וְחַטֹּאתֶיךָ לֹא אֶזְכֹּר.⁴ הַלְבֵּן חֲטָאֵינוּ כַּשֶּׁלֶג
וְכַצֶּמֶר, כְּמָה שֶׁכָּתוּב: לְכוּ נָא וְנִוָּכְחָה, יֹאמַר יהוה, אִם יִהְיוּ
חֲטָאֵיכֶם כַּשָּׁנִים, כַּשֶּׁלֶג יַלְבִּינוּ, אִם יַאְדִּימוּ כַתּוֹלָע, כַּצֶּמֶר יִהְיוּ.⁵
רַחֵם עָלֵינוּ וְאַל תַּשְׁחִיתֵנוּ, כְּמָה שֶׁכָּתוּב: כִּי אֵל רַחוּם יהוה
אֱלֹהֶיךָ, לֹא יַרְפְּךָ וְלֹא יַשְׁחִיתֶךָ וְלֹא יִשְׁכַּח אֶת בְּרִית אֲבֹתֶיךָ
אֲשֶׁר נִשְׁבַּע לָהֶם.⁶ קַבֵּץ נִדָּחֵינוּ כְּמָה שֶׁכָּתוּב: אִם יִהְיֶה נִדַּחֲךָ בִּקְצֵה
הַשָּׁמָיִם, מִשָּׁם יְקַבֶּצְךָ יהוה אֱלֹהֶיךָ וּמִשָּׁם יִקָּחֶךָ.⁷ הָשֵׁב שְׁבוּתֵנוּ
וְרַחֲמֵנוּ, כְּמָה שֶׁכָּתוּב: וְשָׁב יהוה אֱלֹהֶיךָ אֶת שְׁבוּתְךָ וְרִחֲמֶךָ וְשָׁב
וְקִבֶּצְךָ מִכָּל הָעַמִּים אֲשֶׁר הֱפִיצְךָ יהוה אֱלֹהֶיךָ שָׁמָּה.⁸ ✧ תְּבִיאֵנוּ
אֶל הַר קָדְשֶׁךָ, וְשַׂמְּחֵנוּ בְּבֵית תְּפִלָּתֶךָ, כְּמָה שֶׁכָּתוּב: וַהֲבִיאוֹתִים
אֶל הַר קָדְשִׁי, וְשִׂמַּחְתִּים בְּבֵית תְּפִלָּתִי, עוֹלֹתֵיהֶם וְזִבְחֵיהֶם לְרָצוֹן
עַל מִזְבְּחִי, כִּי בֵיתִי בֵּית תְּפִלָּה יִקָּרֵא לְכָל הָעַמִּים.⁹

THE ARK IS OPENED.

The first four verses of the following prayer are recited responsively; *chazzan*, then congregation:

שְׁמַע קוֹלֵנוּ יהוה אֱלֹהֵינוּ, חוּס וְרַחֵם עָלֵינוּ,
וְקַבֵּל בְּרַחֲמִים וּבְרָצוֹן אֶת תְּפִלָּתֵנוּ.¹⁰

הֲשִׁיבֵנוּ יהוה אֵלֶיךָ וְנָשׁוּבָה, חַדֵּשׁ יָמֵינוּ כְּקֶדֶם.¹¹
אַל תַּשְׁלִיכֵנוּ מִלְּפָנֶיךָ, וְרוּחַ קָדְשְׁךָ אַל תִּקַּח מִמֶּנּוּ.¹²
אַל תַּשְׁלִיכֵנוּ לְעֵת זִקְנָה, כִּכְלוֹת כֹּחֵנוּ אַל תַּעַזְבֵנוּ.¹³
אַל תַּעַזְבֵנוּ יהוה, אֱלֹהֵינוּ אַל תִּרְחַק מִמֶּנּוּ.¹⁴
עֲשֵׂה עִמָּנוּ אוֹת לְטוֹבָה, וְיִרְאוּ שׂוֹנְאֵינוּ וְיֵבֹשׁוּ,
כִּי אַתָּה יהוה עֲזַרְתָּנוּ וְנִחַמְתָּנוּ.¹⁵
אֲמָרֵינוּ הַאֲזִינָה יהוה, בִּינָה הֲגִיגֵנוּ.¹⁶
יִהְיוּ לְרָצוֹן אִמְרֵי פִינוּ וְהֶגְיוֹן לִבֵּנוּ לְפָנֶיךָ, יהוה צוּרֵנוּ וְגֹאֲלֵנוּ.¹⁷
כִּי לְךָ יהוה הוֹחָלְנוּ, אַתָּה תַעֲנֶה אֲדֹנָי אֱלֹהֵינוּ.¹⁸

THE ARK IS CLOSED.

---

(1) *Deuteronomy* 30:6. (2) *Ezekiel* 36:25. (3) *Isaiah* 44:22. (4) 43:25. (5) 1:18.
(6) *Deuteronomy* 4:31. (7) 30:4. (8) 30:3. (9) *Isaiah* 56:7. (10) Weekday *Shemoneh Esrei*.
(11) *Lamentations* 5:21. (12) Cf. *Psalms* 51:13. (13) Cf. 71:9. (14) Cf. 38:22. (15) Cf. 86:17.
(16) Cf. 5:2. (17) Cf. 19:15. (18) Cf. 38:16.

and with all your soul, that you may live.[1] *Pour pure water upon us and purify us, as it is written: I shall pour pure water upon you and purify you, of all your contaminations and of all your abominations I will purify you.*[2] *Wipe away our willful sins like a cloud and like a mist, as it is written: I have wiped away your willful sins like a cloud and your errors like a mist — repent to Me, for I have redeemed you!*[3] *Wipe away our willful sins for Your sake, as You said: 'I, only I, am the One Who wipes away your willful sins for My sake, and I shall not recall your errors.'*[4] *Whiten our errors like snow and like [pure white] wool, as it is written: 'Come now, let us reason together,' says* HASHEM, *'though your errors will be like scarlet, they will become white as snow; though they will be red as crimson, they will become like [white] wool.'*[5] *Have mercy on us and do not destroy us, as it is written: For a merciful God is* HASHEM, *your God; He will not surrender you nor destroy you, and He will not forget the covenant with your forefathers, which He swore to them.*[6] *Gather in our dispersed ones, as it is written: If your dispersed were to be at the ends of heaven, from there* HASHEM, *your God, will gather you in and from there He will take you.*[7] *Bring back our captivity and have mercy on us, as it is written:* HASHEM, *your God, will bring back your captivity and have mercy on you, and He will again gather you in from all the peoples where* HASHEM, *your God, has scattered you.*[8]
Chazzan — *Bring us to Your holy mountain and gladden us in Your house of prayer, as it is written: And I will bring them to My holy mountain, and I will gladden them in My house of prayer, their elevation-offerings and their feast offering will find favor on My Altar, for My House will be called a house of prayer, for all peoples.*[9]

THE ARK IS OPENED.

The first four verses of the following prayer are recited responsively; *chazzan,* then congregation:

שְׁמַע קוֹלֵנוּ *Hear our voice,* HASHEM, *our God, pity and be compassionate to us, and accept — with compassion and favor — our prayer.*[10]

Bring us back to You, HASHEM, *and we shall return,*
    renew our days as of old.[11]
Do not cast us away from Yourself,
    and do not remove Your holy spirit from us.[12]
Do not cast us away in old age,
    when our strength gives out do not forsake us.[13]
Do not forsake us, HASHEM, *our God, be not distant from us.*[14]
Display for us a sign for good, so that our enemies may see it
    and be ashamed, for You, HASHEM, *will have helped and consoled us.*[15]
To our sayings give ear, HASHEM, *perceive our thoughts.*[16]
May the expressions of our mouth and the thoughts of our heart
    find favor before You, HASHEM, *our Rock and our Redeemer.*[17]
Because for You, HASHEM, *we waited,*
    You will answer, my Lord, our God.[18]

THE ARK IS CLOSED.

וִדּוּי

During the recitation of the וִדּוּי stand with head and body slightly bowed,
in submissive contrition.

אֱלֹהֵינוּ וֵאלֹהֵי אֲבוֹתֵינוּ, תָּבֹא לְפָנֶיךָ תְּפִלָּתֵנוּ,[1] וְאַל תִּתְעַלַּם
מִתְּחִנָּתֵנוּ,[2] שֶׁאֵין אָנוּ עַזֵּי פָנִים וּקְשֵׁי עֹרֶף, לוֹמַר
לְפָנֶיךָ יהוה אֱלֹהֵינוּ וֵאלֹהֵי אֲבוֹתֵינוּ, צַדִּיקִים אֲנַחְנוּ וְלֹא חָטָאנוּ,
אֲבָל אֲנַחְנוּ וַאֲבוֹתֵינוּ חָטָאנוּ.[3]

Strike the left side of the chest with the right fist
while reciting each of the sins in the following confession litany.

אָשַׁמְנוּ, בָּגַדְנוּ, גָּזַלְנוּ, דִּבַּרְנוּ דְפִי. הֶעֱוִינוּ, וְהִרְשַׁעְנוּ, זַדְנוּ,
חָמַסְנוּ, טָפַלְנוּ שֶׁקֶר. יָעַצְנוּ רָע, כִּזַּבְנוּ, לַצְנוּ, מָרַדְנוּ,
נִאַצְנוּ, סָרַרְנוּ, עָוִינוּ, פָּשַׁעְנוּ, צָרַרְנוּ, קִשִּׁינוּ עֹרֶף. רָשַׁעְנוּ,
שִׁחַתְנוּ, תִּעַבְנוּ, תָּעִינוּ, תִּעְתָּעְנוּ.

סַרְנוּ מִמִּצְוֹתֶיךָ וּמִמִּשְׁפָּטֶיךָ הַטּוֹבִים וְלֹא שָׁוָה לָנוּ.[4] וְאַתָּה
צַדִּיק עַל כָּל הַבָּא עָלֵינוּ, כִּי אֱמֶת עָשִׂיתָ וַאֲנַחְנוּ
הִרְשָׁעְנוּ.[5]

אָשַׁמְנוּ מִכָּל עָם, בֹּשְׁנוּ מִכָּל דּוֹר, גָּלָה מִמֶּנּוּ מָשׂוֹשׂ, דָּוָה
לִבֵּנוּ בַּחֲטָאֵינוּ, הֻחְבַּל אֲוִוּיֵנוּ, וְנִפְרַע פְּאֵרֵנוּ, זְבוּל בֵּית מִקְדָּשֵׁנוּ
חָרַב בַּעֲוֹנֵינוּ, טִירָתֵנוּ הָיְתָה לְשַׁמָּה, יְפִי אַדְמָתֵנוּ לְזָרִים,
כֹּחֵנוּ לְנָכְרִים.

וַעֲדַיִן לֹא שַׁבְנוּ מִטָּעוּתֵנוּ וְהֵיךְ נָעִיז פָּנֵינוּ וְנַקְשֶׁה עָרְפֵּנוּ, לוֹמַר
לְפָנֶיךָ יהוה אֱלֹהֵינוּ וֵאלֹהֵי אֲבוֹתֵינוּ, צַדִּיקִים אֲנַחְנוּ וְלֹא חָטָאנוּ,
אֲבָל אֲנַחְנוּ וַאֲבוֹתֵינוּ חָטָאנוּ.

Strike the left side of the chest with the right fist
while reciting each of the sins in the following confession litany.

אָשַׁמְנוּ, בָּגַדְנוּ, גָּזַלְנוּ, דִּבַּרְנוּ דְפִי. הֶעֱוִינוּ, וְהִרְשַׁעְנוּ, זַדְנוּ,
חָמַסְנוּ, טָפַלְנוּ שֶׁקֶר. יָעַצְנוּ רָע, כִּזַּבְנוּ, לַצְנוּ, מָרַדְנוּ,
נִאַצְנוּ, סָרַרְנוּ, עָוִינוּ, פָּשַׁעְנוּ, צָרַרְנוּ, קִשִּׁינוּ עֹרֶף. רָשַׁעְנוּ,
שִׁחַתְנוּ, תִּעַבְנוּ, תָּעִינוּ, תִּעְתָּעְנוּ.

סַרְנוּ מִמִּצְוֹתֶיךָ וּמִמִּשְׁפָּטֶיךָ הַטּוֹבִים וְלֹא שָׁוָה לָנוּ.[4] וְאַתָּה
צַדִּיק עַל כָּל הַבָּא עָלֵינוּ, כִּי אֱמֶת עָשִׂיתָ וַאֲנַחְנוּ
הִרְשָׁעְנוּ.[5]

---

(1) Cf. *Psalms* 88:3. (2) Cf. 55:2. (3) Cf. 106:6. (4) Cf. *Job* 33:27. (5) *Nehemiah* 9:33.

VIDUY/CONFESSION

During the recitation of the וִדּוּי, *Confession*, stand with head and body slightly bowed, in submissive contrition.

אֱלֹהֵינוּ *Our God and the God of our forefathers, may our prayer come before You.[1] Do not ignore our supplication,[2] for we are not so brazen and obstinate as to say before You, HASHEM, our God and the God of our forefathers, that we are righteous and have not sinned, for in truth, we and our forefathers have sinned.[3]*

Strike the left side of the chest with the right fist while reciting each of the sins in the following confession litany.

אָשַׁמְנוּ *We have become guilty; [ב] we have betrayed; [ג] we have robbed; [ד] we have spoken slander; [ה] we have caused perversion; [ו] we have caused wickedness; [ז] we have sinned willfully; [ח] we have extorted; [ט] we have accused falsely; [י] we have given evil counsel; [כ] we have been deceitful; [ל] we have scorned; [מ] we have rebelled; [נ] we have provoked; [ס] we have turned away; [ע] we have been perverse; [פ] we have acted wantonly; [צ] we have persecuted; [ק] we have been obstinate; [ר] we have been wicked; [ש] we have corrupted; [ת] we have been abominable; we have strayed; You have let us go astray.*

סַרְנוּ *We have turned away from Your commandments and from Your good laws but to no avail.[4] Yet You are righteous in all that has come upon us, for You have acted truthfully while we have caused wickedness.[5]*

[א] *We have become the guiltiest of people.* [ב] *We have become the most degraded of all generations.* [ג] *Joy has departed from us.* [ד] *Our heart has been saddened by our sins.* [ה] *Our desirous treasure has been ruined,* [ו] *and our splendor dashed,* [ז] *for our Holy Temple edifice* [ח] *has been destroyed for our iniquities.* [ט] *Our Palace has become desolate.* [י] *[Jerusalem,] the beauty of our Land is given over to aliens,* [כ] *our power to strangers.*

But still we have not returned from our waywardness. So how can we be so brazen and obstinate as to say before You, HASHEM, our God and the God of our forefathers, that we are righteous and have not sinned, for in truth, both we and our fathers have sinned.

Strike the left side of the chest with the right fist while reciting each of the sins in the following confession litany.

אָשַׁמְנוּ *We have become guilty; [ב] we have betrayed; [ג] we have robbed; [ד] we have spoken slander; [ה] we have caused perversion; [ו] we have caused wickedness; [ז] we have sinned willfully; [ח] we have extorted; [ט] we have accused falsely; [י] we have given evil counsel; [כ] we have been deceitful; [ל] we have scorned; [מ] we have rebelled; [נ] we have provoked; [ס] we have turned away; [ע] we have been perverse; [פ] we have acted wantonly; [צ] we have persecuted; [ק] we have been obstinate; [ר] we have been wicked; [ש] we have corrupted; [ת] we have been abominable; we have strayed; You have let us go astray.*

סַרְנוּ *We have turned away from Your commandments and from Your good laws but to no avail.[4] Yet You are righteous in all that has come upon us, for You have acted truthfully while we have caused wickedness.[5]*

לְעֵינֵינוּ עָשְׁקוּ עֲמָלֵנוּ, מְמֻשָּׁךְ וּמְמוֹרָט מִמֶּנּוּ, נָתְנוּ עֻלָּם עָלֵינוּ, סָבַלְנוּ עַל שִׁכְמֵנוּ, עֲבָדִים מָשְׁלוּ בָנוּ, פֹּרֵק אֵין מִיָּדָם, צָרוֹת רַבּוֹת סְבָבְוּנוּ, קְרָאנוּךְ יהוה אֱלֹהֵינוּ, רָחַקְתָּ מִמֶּנּוּ בַּעֲוֹנֵינוּ, שַׁבְנוּ מֵאַחֲרֶיךָ, תָּעִינוּ וְאָבָדְנוּ.

וַעֲדַיִן לֹא שַׁבְנוּ מִטָּעוּתֵנוּ וְהֵיךְ נָעִיז פָּנֵינוּ וְנַקְשֶׁה עָרְפֵּנוּ, לוֹמַר לְפָנֶיךָ יהוה אֱלֹהֵינוּ וֵאלֹהֵי אֲבוֹתֵינוּ, צַדִּיקִים אֲנַחְנוּ וְלֹא חָטָאנוּ, אֲבָל אֲנַחְנוּ וַאֲבוֹתֵינוּ חָטָאנוּ.

Strike the left side of the chest with the right fist while reciting
each of the sins in the following confession litany.

אָשַׁמְנוּ, בָּגַדְנוּ, גָּזַלְנוּ, דִּבַּרְנוּ דְפִי. הֶעֱוִינוּ, וְהִרְשַׁעְנוּ, זַדְנוּ, חָמַסְנוּ, טָפַלְנוּ שֶׁקֶר. יָעַצְנוּ רָע, כִּזַּבְנוּ, לַצְנוּ, מָרַדְנוּ, נִאַצְנוּ, סָרַרְנוּ, עָוִינוּ, פָּשַׁעְנוּ, צָרַרְנוּ, קִשִּׁינוּ עֹרֶף. רָשַׁעְנוּ, שִׁחַתְנוּ, תִּעַבְנוּ, תָּעִינוּ, תִּעְתָּעְנוּ.

סַרְנוּ מִמִּצְוֹתֶיךָ וּמִמִּשְׁפָּטֶיךָ הַטּוֹבִים וְלֹא שָׁוָה לָנוּ. וְאַתָּה צַדִּיק עַל כָּל הַבָּא עָלֵינוּ, כִּי אֱמֶת עָשִׂיתָ וַאֲנַחְנוּ הִרְשָׁעְנוּ.

הִרְשַׁעְנוּ וּפָשַׁעְנוּ, לָכֵן לֹא נוֹשָׁעְנוּ. וְתֵן בְּלִבֵּנוּ לַעֲזוֹב דֶּרֶךְ רֶשַׁע, וְחִישׁ לָנוּ יֶשַׁע, כַּכָּתוּב עַל יַד נְבִיאֶךָ: יַעֲזֹב רָשָׁע דַּרְכּוֹ, וְאִישׁ אָוֶן מַחְשְׁבֹתָיו, וְיָשֹׁב אֶל יהוה וִירַחֲמֵהוּ, וְאֶל אֱלֹהֵינוּ כִּי יַרְבֶּה לִסְלוֹחַ.[1]

מְשִׁיחַ צִדְקֶךָ אָמַר לְפָנֶיךָ: שְׁגִיאוֹת מִי יָבִין מִנִּסְתָּרוֹת נַקֵּנִי.[2] נַקֵּנוּ יהוה אֱלֹהֵינוּ מִכָּל פְּשָׁעֵינוּ, וְטַהֲרֵנוּ מִכָּל טֻמְאוֹתֵינוּ, וּזְרוֹק עָלֵינוּ מַיִם טְהוֹרִים וְטַהֲרֵנוּ, כַּכָּתוּב עַל יַד נְבִיאֶךָ: וְזָרַקְתִּי עֲלֵיכֶם מַיִם טְהוֹרִים וּטְהַרְתֶּם, מִכֹּל טֻמְאוֹתֵיכֶם וּמִכָּל גִּלּוּלֵיכֶם אֲטַהֵר אֶתְכֶם.[3]

מִיכָה עַבְדְּךָ אָמַר לְפָנֶיךָ: מִי אֵל כָּמוֹךָ נֹשֵׂא עָוֹן וְעֹבֵר עַל פֶּשַׁע לִשְׁאֵרִית נַחֲלָתוֹ, לֹא הֶחֱזִיק לָעַד אַפּוֹ, כִּי חָפֵץ חֶסֶד הוּא, יָשׁוּב יְרַחֲמֵנוּ, יִכְבֹּשׁ עֲוֺנֹתֵינוּ, וְתַשְׁלִיךְ בִּמְצֻלוֹת יָם כָּל חַטֹּאתָם.[4] (וְכָל חַטֹּאת עַמְּךָ בֵּית

[לְ] *[The benefit of] our labor has been stolen,* [מ] *pulled away and cut off from us.* [נ] *They have placed their yoke upon us,* [ס] *our burdens upon our shoulders.* [ע] *Slaves have ruled over us,* [פ] *there is no redemption from their hand.* [צ] *Abundant troubles have surrounded us,* [ק] *we called upon You, HASHEM, our God,* [ר] *but You have distanced us for our iniquities.* [שׁ] *We have turned away from following after You;* [ת] *we have strayed; we have become lost.*

But still *we have not returned from our waywardness. So how can we be so brazen and obstinate as to say before You, HASHEM, our God and the God of our forefathers, that we are righteous and have not sinned, for in truth, both we and our fathers have sinned.*

Strike the left side of the chest with the right fist while reciting
each of the sins in the following confession litany:

אָשַׁמְנוּ *We have become guilty;* [ב] *we have betrayed;* [ג] *we have robbed;* [ד] *we have spoken slander;* [ה] *we have caused perversion;* [ו] *we have caused wickedness;* [ז] *we have sinned willfully;* [ח] *we have extorted;* [ט] *we have accused falsely;* [י] *we have given evil counsel;* [כ] *we have been deceitful;* [ל] *we have scorned;* [מ] *we have rebelled;* [נ] *we have provoked;* [ס] *we have turned away;* [ע] *we have been perverse;* [פ] *we have acted wantonly;* [צ] *we have persecuted;* [ק] *we have been obstinate;* [ר] *we have been wicked;* [שׁ] *we have corrupted;* [ת] *we have been abominable; we have strayed; You have let us go astray.*

סַרְנוּ *We have turned away from Your commandments and from Your good laws but to no avail. Yet You are righteous in all that has come upon us, for You have acted truthfully while we have caused wickedness.*

הִרְשַׁעְנוּ *We have acted wickedly and have sinned willfully, therefore we have not been saved. Inspire our heart to abandon the path of evil and hasten salvation for us, as it is written by Your prophet: May the wicked one abandon his way and the vicious man his thoughts; may he return to HASHEM and He will show him mercy, and to our God, for He is abundantly forgiving.*[1]

מְשִׁיחַ צִדְקֶךָ *Your righteous anointed [David] said before You: 'Who can discern mistakes? From unperceived faults cleanse me.'*[2] *Cleanse us, HASHEM, our God, of all our willful sins and purify us, of all our contaminations. Sprinkle upon us pure water and purify us, as it is written by Your prophet: I shall sprinkle pure water upon you and purify you, of all your contaminations and of all your abominations I will purify you.'*[3]

מִיכָה עַבְדְּךָ *Micah, Your servant, said before You: 'Who, O God, is like You, Who pardons iniquity and overlooks transgression for the remnant of His heritage? Who has not retained His wrath eternally, for He desires kindness! He will again be merciful to us; He will suppress our iniquities and cast into the depths of the sea all their sins.*[4] (*And all the sins*

(1) *Isaiah* 55:7. (2) *Psalms* 19:13. (3) *Ezekiel* 36:25. (4) *Micah* 7:18-19.

יִשְׂרָאֵל תַּשְׁלִיךְ בִּמְקוֹם אֲשֶׁר לֹא יִזָּכְרוּ, וְלֹא יִפָּקְדוּ, וְלֹא יַעֲלוּ עַל לֵב לְעוֹלָם.) תִּתֵּן אֱמֶת לְיַעֲקֹב חֶסֶד לְאַבְרָהָם אֲשֶׁר נִשְׁבַּעְתָּ לַאֲבוֹתֵינוּ מִימֵי קֶדֶם.[1]

דָּנִיֵּאל אִישׁ חֲמוּדוֹת שִׁוַּע לְפָנֶיךָ: הַטֵּה אֱלֹהַי אָזְנְךָ וּשְׁמָע, פְּקַח עֵינֶיךָ וּרְאֵה שֹׁמְמֹתֵינוּ וְהָעִיר אֲשֶׁר נִקְרָא שִׁמְךָ עָלֶיהָ, כִּי לֹא עַל צִדְקֹתֵינוּ אֲנַחְנוּ מַפִּילִים תַּחֲנוּנֵינוּ לְפָנֶיךָ, כִּי עַל רַחֲמֶיךָ הָרַבִּים. אֲדֹנָי שְׁמָעָה, אֲדֹנָי סְלָחָה, אֲדֹנָי הַקְשִׁיבָה, וַעֲשֵׂה אַל תְּאַחַר, לְמַעַנְךָ אֱלֹהַי, כִּי שִׁמְךָ נִקְרָא עַל עִירְךָ וְעַל עַמֶּךָ.[2]

עֶזְרָא הַסּוֹפֵר אָמַר לְפָנֶיךָ: אֱלֹהַי, בֹּשְׁתִּי וְנִכְלַמְתִּי לְהָרִים, אֱלֹהַי, פָּנַי אֵלֶיךָ, כִּי עֲוֹנֹתֵינוּ רָבוּ לְמַעְלָה רֹאשׁ, וְאַשְׁמָתֵנוּ גָדְלָה עַד לַשָּׁמָיִם.[3] וְאַתָּה[4] אֱלוֹהַּ סְלִיחוֹת, חַנּוּן וְרַחוּם, אֶרֶךְ אַפַּיִם וְרַב חֶסֶד, וְלֹא עֲזַבְתָּנוּ.[5]

אַל תַּעַזְבֵנוּ אָבִינוּ וְאַל תִּטְּשֵׁנוּ בּוֹרְאֵנוּ, וְאַל תַּזְנִיחֵנוּ יוֹצְרֵנוּ, וְאַל תַּעַשׂ עִמָּנוּ כָּלָה כְּחַטֹּאתֵינוּ. וְקַיֵּם לָנוּ יהוה אֱלֹהֵינוּ, אֶת הַדָּבָר שֶׁהִבְטַחְתָּנוּ בְּקַבָּלָה עַל יְדֵי יִרְמְיָהוּ חוֹזָךְ, כָּאָמוּר: בַּיָּמִים הָהֵם וּבָעֵת הַהִיא, נְאֻם יהוה, יְבֻקַּשׁ אֶת עֲוֹן יִשְׂרָאֵל וְאֵינֶנּוּ וְאֶת חַטֹּאת יְהוּדָה וְלֹא תִמָּצֶאנָה, כִּי אֶסְלַח לַאֲשֶׁר אַשְׁאִיר.[6] עַמְּךָ וְנַחֲלָתְךָ רְעֵבֵי טוּבְךָ, צְמֵאֵי חַסְדֶּךָ, תְּאֵבֵי יִשְׁעֶךָ, יַכִּירוּ וְיֵדְעוּ כִּי לַיהוה אֱלֹהֵינוּ הָרַחֲמִים וְהַסְּלִיחוֹת.

אֵל רַחוּם שְׁמֶךָ, אֵל חַנּוּן שְׁמֶךָ, בָּנוּ נִקְרָא שְׁמֶךָ. יהוה עֲשֵׂה לְמַעַן שְׁמֶךָ. עֲשֵׂה לְמַעַן אֲמִתֶּךָ, עֲשֵׂה לְמַעַן בְּרִיתֶךָ, עֲשֵׂה לְמַעַן גָּדְלְךָ וְתִפְאַרְתֶּךָ, עֲשֵׂה לְמַעַן דָּתֶךָ, עֲשֵׂה לְמַעַן הוֹדֶךָ, עֲשֵׂה לְמַעַן וְעוּדֶךָ, עֲשֵׂה לְמַעַן זִכְרֶךָ, עֲשֵׂה לְמַעַן חַסְדֶּךָ, עֲשֵׂה לְמַעַן טוּבֶךָ, עֲשֵׂה לְמַעַן יִחוּדֶךָ, עֲשֵׂה לְמַעַן כְּבוֹדֶךָ, עֲשֵׂה לְמַעַן לִמּוּדֶךָ, עֲשֵׂה לְמַעַן מַלְכוּתֶךָ, עֲשֵׂה לְמַעַן נִצְחֶךָ, עֲשֵׂה לְמַעַן סוֹדֶךָ, עֲשֵׂה לְמַעַן עֻזֶּךָ, עֲשֵׂה לְמַעַן פְּאֵרֶךָ, עֲשֵׂה לְמַעַן צִדְקָתֶךָ, עֲשֵׂה לְמַעַן קְדֻשָּׁתֶךָ, עֲשֵׂה לְמַעַן רַחֲמֶיךָ הָרַבִּים, עֲשֵׂה לְמַעַן שְׁכִינָתֶךָ, עֲשֵׂה לְמַעַן תְּהִלָּתֶךָ, עֲשֵׂה לְמַעַן אוֹהֲבֶיךָ שׁוֹכְנֵי עָפָר, עֲשֵׂה לְמַעַן אַבְרָהָם יִצְחָק וְיַעֲקֹב, עֲשֵׂה

of Your nation the Family of Israel, may You cast away to a place where they will neither be remembered, considered, nor brought to mind — ever.) Grant truth to Jacob, kindness to Abraham, as You swore to our forefathers from ancient times.'[1]

דָּנִיֵּאל *Daniel, the greatly beloved man, cried out before You: 'Incline, my God, Your ear, and listen, open Your eyes and see our desolation and that of the city upon which Your Name is proclaimed, for not because of our righteousness do we cast down our supplications before You, rather because of Your abundant compassion. O my Lord, heed; O my Lord, forgive; O my Lord, be attentive and act, do not delay; for Your sake, my God, for Your Name is proclaimed upon Your city and Your people.'[2]*

עֶזְרָא הַסּוֹפֵר *Ezra the Scribe said before You: 'My God, I am embarrassed and ashamed to lift my face to You, my God — for our iniquities have multiplied above our heads, and our sins extend unto heaven.[3] You are[4] the God of forgiveness, compassionate and merciful, slow to anger, and abundant in kindness; and You have not forsaken us.'[5]*

אַל תַּעַזְבֵנוּ *Do not forsake us, our Father; do not cast us off, our Creator; do not abandon us, our Molder; and do not bring about our destruction, as our sins merit. Affirm for us, HASHEM, our God, the promise You made in the tradition through Jeremiah, Your seer, as it is said: 'In those days and at that time' — the words of HASHEM — 'the iniquity of Israel will be sought but there will be none, and the errors of Judah, but they will not be found, for I will have forgiven those whom I leave as a remnant.'[6] Your people and Your heritage, who hunger for Your goodness, who thirst for Your kindness, who long for Your salvation — may they recognize and know that to HASHEM, our God, belong mercy and forgiveness.*

אֵל רַחוּם *'Merciful God' is Your Name, 'Gracious God' is Your Name, Your Name is called upon us — O HASHEM, act for Your Name's sake. Act for the sake of [א] Your truth; act for the sake of [ב] Your covenant; act for the sake of [ג] Your greatness and Your splendor; act for the sake of [ד] Your law; act for the sake of [ה] Your glory; act for the sake of [ו] Your Meeting House; act for the sake of [ז] Your remembrance; act for the sake of [ח] Your kindness; act for the sake of [ט] Your goodness; act for the sake of [י] Your Oneness; act for the sake of [כ] Your honor; act for the sake of [ל] Your teaching; act for the sake of [מ] Your kingship; act for the sake of [נ] Your eternality; act for the sake of [ס] Your counsel; act for the sake of [ע] Your power; act for the sake of [פ] Your beauty; act for the sake of [צ] Your righteousness; act for the sake of [ק] Your sanctity; act for the sake of [ר] Your abundant mercy; act for the sake of [ש] Your Presence, act for the sake of [ת] Your praise; act for the sake of Your beloved ones who rest in the dust; act for the sake of Abraham, Isaac, and Jacob; act*

---

(1) *Micah* 7:20. (2) *Daniel* 9:18-19. (3) *Ezra* 9:6. (4) Some editions of *Selichos* insert the word אֱלֹהֵינוּ, *our God,* at this point. (5) Cf. *Nehemiah* 9:17. (6) *Jeremiah* 50:20.

לְמַעַן מֹשֶׁה וְאַהֲרֹן, עֲשֵׂה לְמַעַן דָּוִד וּשְׁלֹמֹה, עֲשֵׂה לְמַעַן
יְרוּשָׁלַיִם עִיר קָדְשֶׁךָ, עֲשֵׂה לְמַעַן צִיּוֹן מִשְׁכַּן כְּבוֹדֶךָ, עֲשֵׂה
לְמַעַן שִׁמְמוֹת הֵיכָלֶךָ, עֲשֵׂה לְמַעַן הֲרִיסוֹת מִזְבְּחֶךָ, עֲשֵׂה
לְמַעַן הֲרוּגִים עַל שֵׁם קָדְשֶׁךָ, עֲשֵׂה לְמַעַן טְבוּחִים עַל יִחוּדֶךָ,
עֲשֵׂה לְמַעַן בָּאֵי בָאֵשׁ וּבַמַּיִם עַל קִדּוּשׁ שְׁמֶךָ, עֲשֵׂה לְמַעַן יוֹנְקֵי
שָׁדַיִם שֶׁלֹּא חָטְאוּ, עֲשֵׂה לְמַעַן גְּמוּלֵי חָלָב שֶׁלֹּא פָשְׁעוּ, עֲשֵׂה
לְמַעַן תִּינוֹקוֹת שֶׁל בֵּית רַבָּן, עֲשֵׂה לְמַעַנְךָ אִם לֹא לְמַעֲנֵנוּ, עֲשֵׂה
לְמַעַנְךָ וְהוֹשִׁיעֵנוּ.

עֲנֵנוּ יהוה עֲנֵנוּ, עֲנֵנוּ אֱלֹהֵינוּ עֲנֵנוּ, עֲנֵנוּ אָבִינוּ עֲנֵנוּ, עֲנֵנוּ
בּוֹרְאֵנוּ עֲנֵנוּ, עֲנֵנוּ גּוֹאֲלֵנוּ עֲנֵנוּ, עֲנֵנוּ דוֹרְשֵׁנוּ עֲנֵנוּ, עֲנֵנוּ
הָאֵל הַנֶּאֱמָן עֲנֵנוּ, עֲנֵנוּ וָתִיק וְחָסִיד עֲנֵנוּ, עֲנֵנוּ זַךְ וְיָשָׁר עֲנֵנוּ, עֲנֵנוּ
חַי וְקַיָּם עֲנֵנוּ, עֲנֵנוּ **טוֹב** וּמֵטִיב עֲנֵנוּ, עֲנֵנוּ יוֹדֵעַ יֵצֶר עֲנֵנוּ, עֲנֵנוּ
כּוֹבֵשׁ כְּעָסִים עֲנֵנוּ, עֲנֵנוּ לוֹבֵשׁ צְדָקוֹת עֲנֵנוּ, עֲנֵנוּ מֶלֶךְ מַלְכֵי
הַמְּלָכִים עֲנֵנוּ, עֲנֵנוּ נוֹרָא וְנִשְׂגָּב עֲנֵנוּ, עֲנֵנוּ **סוֹלֵחַ** וּמוֹחֵל עֲנֵנוּ,
עֲנֵנוּ עוֹנֶה בְּעֵת צָרָה עֲנֵנוּ, עֲנֵנוּ **פּוֹדֶה** וּמַצִּיל עֲנֵנוּ, עֲנֵנוּ **צַדִּיק**
וְיָשָׁר עֲנֵנוּ, עֲנֵנוּ **קָרוֹב** לְקוֹרְאָיו עֲנֵנוּ, עֲנֵנוּ **רַחוּם** וְחַנּוּן עֲנֵנוּ, עֲנֵנוּ
שׁוֹמֵעַ אֶל אֶבְיוֹנִים עֲנֵנוּ, עֲנֵנוּ **תּוֹמֵךְ** תְּמִימִים עֲנֵנוּ, עֲנֵנוּ אֱלֹהֵי
אֲבוֹתֵינוּ עֲנֵנוּ, עֲנֵנוּ אֱלֹהֵי אַבְרָהָם עֲנֵנוּ, עֲנֵנוּ פַּחַד יִצְחָק עֲנֵנוּ,
עֲנֵנוּ אֲבִיר יַעֲקֹב עֲנֵנוּ, עֲנֵנוּ עֶזְרַת הַשְּׁבָטִים עֲנֵנוּ, עֲנֵנוּ מִשְׂגָּב
אִמָּהוֹת עֲנֵנוּ, עֲנֵנוּ קָשֶׁה לִכְעוֹס עֲנֵנוּ, עֲנֵנוּ רַךְ לִרְצוֹת עֲנֵנוּ, עֲנֵנוּ
עוֹנֶה בְּעֵת רָצוֹן¹ עֲנֵנוּ, עֲנֵנוּ אֲבִי יְתוֹמִים עֲנֵנוּ, עֲנֵנוּ דַּיַּן אַלְמָנוֹת
עֲנֵנוּ.

מִי שֶׁעָנָה לְאַבְרָהָם אָבִינוּ בְּהַר הַמּוֹרִיָּה,	הוּא יַעֲנֵנוּ.
מִי שֶׁעָנָה לְיִצְחָק בְּנוֹ כְּשֶׁנֶּעֱקַד עַל גַּבֵּי הַמִּזְבֵּחַ,	הוּא יַעֲנֵנוּ.
מִי שֶׁעָנָה לְיַעֲקֹב בְּבֵית אֵל,	הוּא יַעֲנֵנוּ.
מִי שֶׁעָנָה לְיוֹסֵף בְּבֵית הָאֲסוּרִים,	הוּא יַעֲנֵנוּ.
מִי שֶׁעָנָה לַאֲבוֹתֵינוּ עַל יַם סוּף,	הוּא יַעֲנֵנוּ.
מִי שֶׁעָנָה לְמֹשֶׁה בְּחוֹרֵב,	הוּא יַעֲנֵנוּ.
מִי שֶׁעָנָה לְאַהֲרֹן בַּמַּחְתָּה,	הוּא יַעֲנֵנוּ.
מִי שֶׁעָנָה לְפִינְחָס בְּקוּמוֹ מִתּוֹךְ הָעֵדָה,	הוּא יַעֲנֵנוּ.

for the sake of Moses and Aaron; act for the sake of David and Solomon; act for the sake of Jerusalem, Your holy city; act for the sake of Zion, the abode of Your glory; act for the sake of the desolation of Your Temple; act for the sake of the ruin of Your Altar; act for the sake of the martyrs for Your holy Name; act for the sake of those slaughtered for Your Oneness; act for the sake of those who entered fire and water for the sanctification of Your Name; act for the nursing infants who did not err; act for the sake of the weaned babes who did not sin; act for the sake of children at the school-room; act for Your sake if not for ours; act for Your sake and save us.

עֲנֵנוּ *Answer us, HASHEM, answer us; answer us, our God, answer us; answer us, [א] our Father, answer us; answer us, [ב] our Creator, answer us; answer us, [ג] our Redeemer, answer us; answer us, [ד] You Who searches us out, answer us; answer us, [ה] faithful God, answer us; answer us, [ו] stead-fast and kind One, answer us; answer us, [ז] pure and upright One, answer us; answer us, [ח] living and enduring One, answer us; answer us, [ט] good and beneficent One, answer us; answer us, [י] You Who knows inclinations, answer us; answer us, [כ] You Who suppresses wrath, answer us; answer us, [ל] You Who dons righteousness, answer us; answer us, [מ] King Who reigns over kings, answer us; answer us, [נ] awesome and powerful One, answer us; answer us, [ס] You Who forgives and pardons, answer us; answer us, [ע] You Who answers in time of distress,[1] answer us; answer us, [פ] Redeemer and Rescuer, answer us; answer us, [צ] righteous and upright One, answer us; answer us, [ק] He Who is close to those who call upon Him, answer us; answer us, [ר] merciful and gracious One, answer us; answer us, [ש] You Who hears the destitute, answer us; answer us, [ת] You Who supports the wholesome, answer us; answer us, God of our forefathers, answer us; answer us, God of Abraham, answer us; answer us, Dread of Isaac, answer us; answer us, Mighty One of Jacob, answer us; answer us, Helper of the tribes, answer us; answer us, Stronghold of the Matriarchs, answer us; answer us, You Who are hard to anger, answer us; answer us, You Who are easy to pacify, answer us; answer us, You Who answers in a time of favor,[1] answer us; answer us, Father of orphans, answer us; answer us, Judge of widows, answer us.*

מִי שֶׁעָנָה *He Who answered our father Abraham on Mount Moriah,*
may He answer us.
He Who answered his son Isaac when he was bound atop the altar,
may He answer us.
He Who answered Jacob in Bethel,   *may He answer us.*
He Who answered Joseph in the prison,   *may He answer us.*
He Who answered our forefathers at the Sea of Reeds, may He answer us.
He Who answered Moses in Horeb,   *may He answer us.*
He Who answered Aaron when he offered the censer,   may He answer us.
He Who answered Phineas when he arose from amid the congregation,
may He answer us.

(1) Some editions of *Selichos* reverse the positions of these two lines.

מִי שֶׁעָנָה לִיהוֹשֻׁעַ בַּגִּלְגָּל,   הוּא יַעֲנֵנוּ.
מִי שֶׁעָנָה לִשְׁמוּאֵל בַּמִּצְפָּה,   הוּא יַעֲנֵנוּ.
מִי שֶׁעָנָה לְדָוִד וּשְׁלֹמֹה בְנוֹ בִּירוּשָׁלָיִם,   הוּא יַעֲנֵנוּ.
מִי שֶׁעָנָה לְאֵלִיָּהוּ בְּהַר הַכַּרְמֶל,   הוּא יַעֲנֵנוּ.
מִי שֶׁעָנָה לֶאֱלִישָׁע בִּירִיחוֹ,   הוּא יַעֲנֵנוּ.
מִי שֶׁעָנָה לְיוֹנָה בִּמְעֵי הַדָּגָה,   הוּא יַעֲנֵנוּ.
מִי שֶׁעָנָה לְחִזְקִיֵּהוּ מֶלֶךְ יְהוּדָה בְּחָלְיוֹ,   הוּא יַעֲנֵנוּ.
מִי שֶׁעָנָה לַחֲנַנְיָה מִישָׁאֵל וַעֲזַרְיָה בְּתוֹךְ כִּבְשַׁן הָאֵשׁ,   הוּא יַעֲנֵנוּ.
מִי שֶׁעָנָה לְדָנִיֵּאל בְּגוֹב הָאֲרָיוֹת,   הוּא יַעֲנֵנוּ.
מִי שֶׁעָנָה לְמָרְדְּכַי וְאֶסְתֵּר בְּשׁוּשַׁן הַבִּירָה,   הוּא יַעֲנֵנוּ.
מִי שֶׁעָנָה לְעֶזְרָא בַּגּוֹלָה,   הוּא יַעֲנֵנוּ.
מִי שֶׁעָנָה לְכָל הַצַּדִּיקִים וְהַחֲסִידִים וְהַתְּמִימִים וְהַיְשָׁרִים,   הוּא יַעֲנֵנוּ.

רַחֲמָנָא דְּעָנֵי לַעֲנִיֵּי, עֲנֵינָא. רַחֲמָנָא דְּעָנֵי לִתְבִירֵי לִבָּא, עֲנֵינָא. רַחֲמָנָא דְּעָנֵי לְמַכִּיכֵי רוּחָא, עֲנֵינָא. רַחֲמָנָא עֲנֵינָא. רַחֲמָנָא חוּס. רַחֲמָנָא פְּרוֹק. רַחֲמָנָא שְׁזִיב. רַחֲמָנָא רְחַם עֲלָן. הַשְׁתָּא בַּעֲגָלָא וּבִזְמַן קָרִיב.

נְפִילַת אַפַּיִם

In the presence of a Torah Scroll, the following (until וַבֹּשׁוּ רָגַע) is recited with the head resting on the arm, preferably while seated. Elsewhere, it is recited with the head held erect.

(וַיֹּאמֶר דָּוִד אֶל גָּד, צַר לִי מְאֹד נִפְּלָה נָּא בְיַד יהוה,
כִּי רַבִּים רַחֲמָיו, וּבְיַד אָדָם אַל אֶפֹּלָה.[1])

רַחוּם וְחַנּוּן חָטָאתִי לְפָנֶיךָ. יהוה מָלֵא רַחֲמִים, רַחֵם עָלַי וְקַבֵּל תַּחֲנוּנָי.

תְּהִלִּים ו:ב-יא

יהוה אַל בְּאַפְּךָ תוֹכִיחֵנִי, וְאַל בַּחֲמָתְךָ תְיַסְּרֵנִי. חָנֵּנִי יהוה, כִּי אֻמְלַל אָנִי, רְפָאֵנִי יהוה, כִּי נִבְהֲלוּ עֲצָמָי. וְנַפְשִׁי נִבְהֲלָה מְאֹד, וְאַתָּה יהוה, עַד מָתָי. שׁוּבָה יהוה, חַלְּצָה נַפְשִׁי, הוֹשִׁיעֵנִי לְמַעַן חַסְדֶּךָ. כִּי אֵין בַּמָּוֶת זִכְרֶךָ, בִּשְׁאוֹל מִי יוֹדֶה לָּךְ. יָגַעְתִּי בְּאַנְחָתִי, אַשְׂחֶה בְכָל לַיְלָה מִטָּתִי, בְּדִמְעָתִי עַרְשִׂי אַמְסֶה. עָשְׁשָׁה מִכַּעַס עֵינִי, עָתְקָה בְּכָל צוֹרְרָי. סוּרוּ מִמֶּנִּי כָּל פֹּעֲלֵי אָוֶן, כִּי שָׁמַע יהוה קוֹל בִּכְיִי. שָׁמַע יהוה תְּחִנָּתִי, יהוה תְּפִלָּתִי יִקָּח. יֵבֹשׁוּ וְיִבָּהֲלוּ מְאֹד כָּל אֹיְבָי, יָשֻׁבוּ יֵבֹשׁוּ רָגַע.

He Who answered Joshua in Gilgal,   *may He answer us.*
He Who answered Samuel in Mitzpah,   *may He answer us.*
He Who answered David and his son Solomon in Jerusalem,
                                                                              may He answer us.
He Who answered Elijah on Mount Carmel,   *may He answer us.*
He Who answered Elisha in Jericho,   *may He answer us.*
He Who answered Jonah in the innards of the fish,   *may He answer us.*
He Who answered Hezekiah, King of Judah, in his illness,
                                                                              may He answer us.
He Who answered Chananiah, Mishael, and Azariah in the fiery oven,
                                                                              may He answer us.
He Who answered Daniel in the lions' den,   *may He answer us.*
He Who answered Mordechai and Esther in Shushan the capital,
                                                                              may He answer us.
He Who answered Ezra in the Exile,   *may He answer us.*
He Who answered all the righteous, the devout, the wholesome,
   and the upright,   *may He answer us.*

רַחֲמָנָא   The Merciful One Who answers the poor, may He answer us. The
                  Merciful One Who answers the brokenhearted, may He answer
us. The Merciful One Who answers the humble of spirit, may He answer
us. O Merciful One, answer us. O Merciful One, pity. O Merciful One,
redeem. O Merciful One, deliver. O Merciful One, have mercy on us — now,
swiftly and soon.

PUTTING DOWN THE HEAD

In the presence of a Torah Scroll, the following (until *'instantly shamed'*) is recited with the head
resting on the arm, preferably while seated. Elsewhere, it is recited with the head held erect.

(*And David said to Gad, 'I am exceedingly distressed. Let us fall into HASHEM's
hand for His mercies are abundant, but let me not fall into human hands.'* [1])

רַחוּם וְחַנּוּן   O compassionate and gracious One, I have sinned before You.
                    HASHEM, Who is full of mercy, have mercy on me and accept
my supplications.

Psalms 6:2-11

'ה   HASHEM, do not rebuke me in Your anger nor chastise me in Your rage.
        Favor me, HASHEM, for I am feeble; heal me, HASHEM, for my bones
shudder. My soul is utterly confounded, and You, HASHEM, how long?
Desist, HASHEM, release my soul; save me as befits Your kindness. For
there is no mention of You in death; in the Lower World who will thank You?
I am wearied with my sigh, every night my tears drench my bed, soak my
couch. My eye is dimmed because of anger, aged by my tormentors.
Depart from me, all evildoers, for HASHEM has heard the sound of my weeping. HASHEM has heard my plea, HASHEM will accept my prayer. Let all my
foes be shamed and utterly confounded, they will regret and be instantly
shamed.

---

(1) *II Samuel* 24:14.

מְחֵי וּמַסֵּי מֵמִית וּמְחַיֶּה, מַסִּיק מִן שְׁאוֹל לְחַיֵּי עָלְמָא, בְּרָא
כַּד חָטֵי אֲבוּהִי לַקְיֵה, אֲבוּהִי דְחָיֵס אַסִּי לִכְאֵבָהּ.
עַבְדָּא דְמָרִיד נָפִיק בְּקוֹלָר, מָרֵהּ תָּאִיב וְתַבִּיר קוֹלָרֵהּ.

בְּרָךְ בְּכְרָךְ אֲנַן וְחָטֵינַן קַמָּךְ, הָא רָזֵי נַפְשִׁין בְּגִידִין מְרִרִין,
עַבְדָּךְ אֲנַן וּמְרוֹדֵינַן קַמָּךְ, הָא בְּבָזְתָּא, הָא בְּשִׁבְיָא, הָא
בְּמַלְקָיוּתָא. בְּמָטוּ מִנָּךְ בְּרַחֲמָךְ דִּנְפִישִׁין, אַסִּי לִכְאֵבִין דִּתְקוֹף
עֲלָן, עַד דְּלָא נֶהֱוֵי גְמִירָא בְּשִׁבְיָא.

מַכְנִיסֵי רַחֲמִים, הַכְנִיסוּ רַחֲמֵינוּ, לִפְנֵי בַּעַל הָרַחֲמִים.
מַשְׁמִיעֵי תְפִלָּה, הַשְׁמִיעוּ תְפִלָּתֵנוּ, לִפְנֵי
שׁוֹמֵעַ תְּפִלָּה. מַשְׁמִיעֵי צְעָקָה, הַשְׁמִיעוּ צַעֲקָתֵנוּ, לִפְנֵי שׁוֹמֵעַ
צְעָקָה. מַכְנִיסֵי דִמְעָה, הַכְנִיסוּ דִמְעוֹתֵינוּ, לִפְנֵי מֶלֶךְ מִתְרַצֶּה
בִדְמָעוֹת.

הִשְׁתַּדְּלוּ וְהַרְבּוּ תְּחִנָּה וּבַקָּשָׁה, לִפְנֵי מֶלֶךְ אֵל רָם וְנִשָּׂא.
הַזְכִּירוּ לְפָנָיו, הַשְׁמִיעוּ לְפָנָיו תּוֹרָה וּמַעֲשִׂים טוֹבִים שֶׁל שׁוֹכְנֵי
עָפָר.

יִזְכֹּר אַהֲבָתָם וִיחַיֶּה זַרְעָם, שֶׁלֹּא תֹאבַד שְׁאֵרִית יַעֲקֹב. כִּי צֹאן
רֹעֶה נֶאֱמָן הָיָה לְחֶרְפָּה, יִשְׂרָאֵל גּוֹי אֶחָד לְמָשָׁל וְלִשְׁנִינָה.
מַהֵר עֲנֵנוּ אֱלֹהֵי יִשְׁעֵנוּ, וּפְדֵנוּ מִכָּל גְּזֵרוֹת קָשׁוֹת וְהוֹשִׁיעָה
בְּרַחֲמֶיךָ הָרַבִּים, מְשִׁיחַ צִדְקֶךָ וְעַמָּךְ.

מָרָן דְּבִשְׁמַיָּא לָךְ מִתְחַנְּנַן, כְּבַר שַׁבְיָא דְּמִתְחַנַּן לְשָׁבוּיֵהּ.
כֻּלְּהוֹן בְּנֵי שַׁבְיָא בְּכַסְפָּא מִתְפָּרְקִין, וְעַמָּךְ
יִשְׂרָאֵל בְּרַחֲמֵי וּבְתַחֲנוּנֵי, הַב לָן שְׁאֵלְתִּין וּבָעוּתִין, דְּלָא נֶהֱדַר
רֵיקָם מִן קֳדָמָךְ.

מָרָן דְּבִשְׁמַיָּא לָךְ מִתְחַנְּנַן, כְּעַבְדָּא דְּמִתְחַנַּן לְמָרֵיהּ, עֲשִׁיקֵי
אֲנַן וּבַחֲשׁוֹכָא שָׁרֵינַן, מְרִירָן נַפְשִׁין מֵעַקְתִין דִּנְפִישִׁין, חֵילָא לֵית
בָּן לְרַצּוֹיָךְ מָרָן, עֲבִיד בְּדִיל קַיָּמָא דִּגְזַרְתָּ עִם אֲבָהָתָנָא.

שׁוֹמֵר יִשְׂרָאֵל, שְׁמוֹר שְׁאֵרִית יִשְׂרָאֵל, וְאַל יֹאבַד
יִשְׂרָאֵל, הָאוֹמְרִים, שְׁמַע יִשְׂרָאֵל.[1]
שׁוֹמֵר גּוֹי אֶחָד, שְׁמוֹר שְׁאֵרִית עַם אֶחָד, וְאַל יֹאבַד גּוֹי אֶחָד,
הַמְיַחֲדִים שִׁמְךָ, יהוה אֱלֹהֵינוּ יהוה אֶחָד.[1]

מַחֵי וּמַסֵּי *[O God,] He Who smites and heals, causes death and restores
life, raises [the dead] from the grave to eternal life: Should a son
sin, his father would smack him, but a compassionate father will heal his
[son's] pain. When a slave rebels, he is led out in collar-irons, but if his master
desires to, he breaks his chains.*

*We are Your son, Your firstborn, and we have sinned against You; so our
soul has been satiated with bitter wormwood. We are Your servants and we
have rebelled against You; so [we have suffered], some with looting, some
with captivity, and some with the lash. We beg of You, in Your abundant
compassion, heal the pains that have overwhelmed us, before we have been
completely wiped out in captivity.*

מַכְנִיסֵי רַחֲמִים *O you who usher in [pleas for] mercy, may you usher in
our [plea for] mercy, before the Master of mercy. O you
who cause prayer to be heard, may you cause our prayer to be heard,
before the Hearer of prayer. O you who cause outcry to be heard, may you
cause our outcry to be heard, before the Hearer of outcry. O you who usher
in tears, may you usher in our tears, before the King Who finds favor through
tears.*

*Exert yourselves, and multiply supplication and petition, before the King,
God, exalted and most high. Mention before Him, cause to be heard before
Him, the Torah and the good deeds of [the Patriarchs and Matriarchs] who
dwell in the dust.*

*May He remember their love and grant life to [their] offspring, that the
remnant of Jacob not be lost. For the flock of the faithful shepherd [Moses]
has become a disgrace; Israel, the unique nation, a parable and a simile.*

*Speedily, answer us, O God of our salvation, and redeem us from all harsh
decrees; and may You save, in Your abundant mercy, Your righteous
anointed and Your people.*

מָרָן דִּבִשְׁמַיָּא *Our Master Who is in heaven, to You do we supplicate, as
a captive supplicates before his captors; for all captives are
redeemed with money, but Your people Israel with compassion and
supplication. O grant our requests and our prayers that we not be turned
away from You emptyh-anded.*

*Our Master Who is in heaven, to You do we supplicate, as a slave
supplicates before his master: We are oppressed and we abide in darkness,
souls embittered from abundant distress. We have no strength to regain Your
favor. Our Master, act for the sake of the covenant that You made with our
Patriarchs.*

שׁוֹמֵר יִשְׂרָאֵל *O Guardian of Israel, protect the remnant of Israel; let not
Israel be destroyed — those who proclaim, 'Hear O Israel.'* [1]
*O Guardian of the unique nation, protect the remnant of the unique
people; let not the unique nation be destroyed — those who proclaim
the Oneness of Your Name, 'HASHEM is our God, HASHEM, the One and
Only!'* [1]

---

(1) *Deuteronomy* 6:4.

שׁוֹמֵר גּוֹי קָדוֹשׁ, שְׁמוֹר שְׁאֵרִית עַם קָדוֹשׁ, וְאַל יֹאבַד גּוֹי
קָדוֹשׁ, הַמְשַׁלְּשִׁים בְּשָׁלֹשׁ קְדֻשּׁוֹת לְקָדוֹשׁ.

מִתְרַצֶּה בְרַחֲמִים וּמִתְפַּיֵּס בְּתַחֲנוּנִים, הִתְרַצֶּה וְהִתְפַּיֵּס לְדוֹר
עָנִי, כִּי אֵין עוֹזֵר. אָבִינוּ מַלְכֵּנוּ, חָנֵּנוּ וַעֲנֵנוּ, כִּי אֵין בָּנוּ מַעֲשִׂים,
עֲשֵׂה עִמָּנוּ צְדָקָה וָחֶסֶד וְהוֹשִׁיעֵנוּ.

וַאֲנַחְנוּ לֹא נֵדַע מַה נַּעֲשֶׂה, כִּי עָלֶיךָ עֵינֵינוּ.[1] זְכֹר רַחֲמֶיךָ
יהוה וַחֲסָדֶיךָ, כִּי מֵעוֹלָם הֵמָּה.[2] יְהִי חַסְדְּךָ יהוה
עָלֵינוּ, כַּאֲשֶׁר יִחַלְנוּ לָךְ.[3] אַל תִּזְכָּר לָנוּ עֲוֹנוֹת רִאשׁוֹנִים, מַהֵר
יְקַדְּמוּנוּ רַחֲמֶיךָ, כִּי דַלּוֹנוּ מְאֹד.[4] חָנֵּנוּ יהוה חָנֵּנוּ, כִּי רַב שָׂבַעְנוּ
בוּז.[5] בְּרֹגֶז רַחֵם תִּזְכּוֹר.[6] כִּי הוּא יָדַע יִצְרֵנוּ, זָכוּר כִּי עָפָר אֲנָחְנוּ.[7]
עָזְרֵנוּ אֱלֹהֵי יִשְׁעֵנוּ עַל דְּבַר כְּבוֹד שְׁמֶךָ, וְהַצִּילֵנוּ וְכַפֵּר עַל
חַטֹּאתֵינוּ לְמַעַן שְׁמֶךָ.[8]

קדיש שלם

קַדִּישׁ שָׁלֵם The *chazzan* recites:

יִתְגַּדַּל וְיִתְקַדַּשׁ שְׁמֵהּ רַבָּא. (.Cong – אָמֵן.) בְּעָלְמָא דִּי בְרָא
כִרְעוּתֵהּ, וְיַמְלִיךְ מַלְכוּתֵהּ, בְּחַיֵּיכוֹן וּבְיוֹמֵיכוֹן וּבְחַיֵּי
דְכָל בֵּית יִשְׂרָאֵל, בַּעֲגָלָא וּבִזְמַן קָרִיב. וְאִמְרוּ אָמֵן.
(.Cong – אָמֵן. יְהֵא שְׁמֵהּ רַבָּא מְבָרַךְ לְעָלַם וּלְעָלְמֵי עָלְמַיָּא.)
יְהֵא שְׁמֵהּ רַבָּא מְבָרַךְ לְעָלַם וּלְעָלְמֵי עָלְמַיָּא.
יִתְבָּרַךְ וְיִשְׁתַּבַּח וְיִתְפָּאַר וְיִתְרוֹמַם וְיִתְנַשֵּׂא וְיִתְהַדָּר וְיִתְעַלֶּה
וְיִתְהַלָּל שְׁמֵהּ דְּקוּדְשָׁא בְּרִיךְ הוּא (.Cong – בְּרִיךְ הוּא.) לְעֵלָּא מִן כָּל
בִּרְכָתָא וְשִׁירָתָא תֻּשְׁבְּחָתָא וְנֶחֱמָתָא, דַּאֲמִירָן בְּעָלְמָא. וְאִמְרוּ:
אָמֵן. (.Cong – אָמֵן.)
(.Cong – קַבֵּל בְּרַחֲמִים וּבְרָצוֹן אֶת תְּפִלָּתֵנוּ.)
תִּתְקַבֵּל צְלוֹתְהוֹן וּבָעוּתְהוֹן דְּכָל (בֵּית) יִשְׂרָאֵל קֳדָם אֲבוּהוֹן
דִּי בִשְׁמַיָּא. וְאִמְרוּ אָמֵן. (.Cong – אָמֵן.)
(.Cong – יְהִי שֵׁם יהוה מְבֹרָךְ, מֵעַתָּה וְעַד עוֹלָם.[9])
יְהֵא שְׁלָמָא רַבָּא מִן שְׁמַיָּא וְחַיִּים עָלֵינוּ וְעַל כָּל יִשְׂרָאֵל.
וְאִמְרוּ אָמֵן. (.Cong – אָמֵן.)
(.Cong – עֶזְרִי מֵעִם יהוה, עֹשֵׂה שָׁמַיִם וָאָרֶץ.[10])

Take three steps back. Bow left and say, . . . עֹשֶׂה; bow right and say, . . . הוּא יַעֲשֶׂה; bow forward and
say, וְעַל כָּל . . . אָמֵן. Remain standing in place for a few moments, then take three steps forward.

עֹשֶׂה שָׁלוֹם בִּמְרוֹמָיו, הוּא יַעֲשֶׂה שָׁלוֹם עָלֵינוּ, וְעַל כָּל יִשְׂרָאֵל.
וְאִמְרוּ אָמֵן. (.Cong – אָמֵן.)

O Guardian of the holy nation, protect the remnant of the holy people; let not the holy nation be destroyed — those who proclaim three-fold sanctifications to the Holy One.

Become favorable through compassion and become appeased through supplications. Become favorable and appeased to the poor generation, for there is no helper. Our Father, our King, be gracious with us and answer us, though we have no worthy deeds; treat us with charity and kindness, and save us.

וַאֲנַחְנוּ We know not what to do — but our eyes are upon You.[1] Remember Your mercies, HASHEM, and Your kindnesses, for they are from the beginning of the world.[2] May Your kindness be upon us, HASHEM, just as we awaited You.[3] Recall not against us the iniquities of the ancients; may Your mercies meet us swiftly, for we have become exceedingly impoverished.[4] Be gracious to us, HASHEM, be gracious to us, for we are abundantly sated with scorn.[5] Amid rage — remember to be merciful![6] For He knew our nature, He remembers that we are dust.[7] Chazzan— Assist us, O God of our salvation, for the sake of Your Name's glory; rescue us and atone for our sins for Your Name's sake.[8]

FULL KADDISH
The *chazzan* recites the Full Kaddish:

יִתְגַּדַּל May His great Name grow exalted and sanctified (Cong. — Amen.) in the world that He created as He willed. May He give reign to His kingship in your lifetimes and in your days, and in the lifetimes of the entire Family of Israel, swiftly and soon. Now respond: Amen.

(Cong. — Amen. May His great Name be blessed forever and ever.)
May His great Name be blessed forever and ever.

Blessed, praised, glorified, exalted, extolled, mighty, upraised and lauded be the Name of the Holy One, Blessed is He (Cong. — Blessed is He.) beyond any blessing and song, praise, and consolation that are uttered in the world. Now respond: Amen. (Cong. — Amen.)

(Cong. — Accept our prayers with mercy and favor.)
May the prayers and supplications of the entire House of Israel be accepted before their Father Who is in Heaven. Now respond: Amen. (Cong. — Amen.)

(Cong. — Blessed be the Name of HASHEM from this time and forever.[9])
May there be abundant peace from Heaven, and life, upon us and upon all Israel. Now respond: Amen. (Cong. — Amen.)

(Cong. — My help is from HASHEM, Maker of heaven and earth.[10])

Take three steps back. Bow left and say, 'He Who makes peace . . .'; bow right and say,
'may He make peace . . .'; bow forward and say, 'and upon all Israel . . .'
Remain standing in place for a few moments, then take three steps forward.

He Who makes peace in His heights, may He make peace upon us, and upon all Israel. Now respond: Amen. (Cong. — Amen.)

---

(1) *II Chronicles* 20:12. (2) *Psalms* 25:6. (3) 33:22. (4) 79:8. (5) 123:3.
(6) *Habakkuk* 3:2. (7) *Psalms* 103:14. (8) 79:9. (9) 113:2. (10) 121:2.

יום רביעי ﷽

אַשְׁרֵי יוֹשְׁבֵי בֵיתֶךָ, עוֹד יְהַלְלוּךָ סֶּלָה.[1] אַשְׁרֵי הָעָם שֶׁכָּכָה לּוֹ, אַשְׁרֵי הָעָם שֶׁיהוה אֱלֹהָיו.[2]

תְּהִלָּה לְדָוִד,

תהלים קמה

אֲרוֹמִמְךָ אֱלוֹהַי הַמֶּלֶךְ, וַאֲבָרְכָה שִׁמְךָ לְעוֹלָם וָעֶד.

בְּכָל יוֹם אֲבָרְכֶךָּ, וַאֲהַלְלָה שִׁמְךָ לְעוֹלָם וָעֶד.

גָּדוֹל יהוה וּמְהֻלָּל מְאֹד, וְלִגְדֻלָּתוֹ אֵין חֵקֶר.

דּוֹר לְדוֹר יְשַׁבַּח מַעֲשֶׂיךָ, וּגְבוּרֹתֶיךָ יַגִּידוּ.

הֲדַר כְּבוֹד הוֹדֶךָ, וְדִבְרֵי נִפְלְאֹתֶיךָ אָשִׂיחָה.

וֶעֱזוּז נוֹרְאֹתֶיךָ יֹאמֵרוּ, וּגְדֻלָּתְךָ אֲסַפְּרֶנָּה.

זֵכֶר רַב טוּבְךָ יַבִּיעוּ, וְצִדְקָתְךָ יְרַנֵּנוּ.

חַנּוּן וְרַחוּם יהוה, אֶרֶךְ אַפַּיִם וּגְדָל חָסֶד.

טוֹב יהוה לַכֹּל, וְרַחֲמָיו עַל כָּל מַעֲשָׂיו.

יוֹדוּךָ יהוה כָּל מַעֲשֶׂיךָ, וַחֲסִידֶיךָ יְבָרְכוּכָה.

כְּבוֹד מַלְכוּתְךָ יֹאמֵרוּ, וּגְבוּרָתְךָ יְדַבֵּרוּ.

לְהוֹדִיעַ לִבְנֵי הָאָדָם גְּבוּרֹתָיו, וּכְבוֹד הֲדַר מַלְכוּתוֹ.

מַלְכוּתְךָ מַלְכוּת כָּל עֹלָמִים, וּמֶמְשַׁלְתְּךָ בְּכָל דּוֹר וָדֹר.

סוֹמֵךְ יהוה לְכָל הַנֹּפְלִים, וְזוֹקֵף לְכָל הַכְּפוּפִים.

עֵינֵי כֹל אֵלֶיךָ יְשַׂבֵּרוּ, וְאַתָּה נוֹתֵן לָהֶם אֶת אָכְלָם בְּעִתּוֹ.

Concentrate intently while reciting the verse, פּוֹתֵחַ.

פּוֹתֵחַ אֶת יָדֶךָ, וּמַשְׂבִּיעַ לְכָל חַי רָצוֹן.

✧ **צַדִּיק** יהוה בְּכָל דְּרָכָיו, וְחָסִיד בְּכָל מַעֲשָׂיו.

קָרוֹב יהוה לְכָל קֹרְאָיו, לְכֹל אֲשֶׁר יִקְרָאֻהוּ בֶאֱמֶת.

רְצוֹן יְרֵאָיו יַעֲשֶׂה, וְאֶת שַׁוְעָתָם יִשְׁמַע וְיוֹשִׁיעֵם.

שׁוֹמֵר יהוה אֶת כָּל אֹהֲבָיו, וְאֵת כָּל הָרְשָׁעִים יַשְׁמִיד.

תְּהִלַּת יהוה יְדַבֶּר פִּי, וִיבָרֵךְ כָּל בָּשָׂר שֵׁם קָדְשׁוֹ לְעוֹלָם וָעֶד.

וַאֲנַחְנוּ נְבָרֵךְ יָהּ, מֵעַתָּה וְעַד עוֹלָם, הַלְלוּיָהּ.[3]

חֲצִי קַדִּישׁ The chazzan recites.

יִתְגַּדַּל וְיִתְקַדַּשׁ שְׁמֵהּ רַבָּא. (.Cong –אָמֵן) בְּעָלְמָא דִּי בְרָא כִרְעוּתֵהּ. וְיַמְלִיךְ מַלְכוּתֵהּ, בְּחַיֵּיכוֹן וּבְיוֹמֵיכוֹן וּבְחַיֵּי דְכָל בֵּית יִשְׂרָאֵל, בַּעֲגָלָא וּבִזְמַן קָרִיב. וְאִמְרוּ: אָמֵן.

(.Cong –אָמֵן. יְהֵא שְׁמֵהּ רַבָּא מְבָרַךְ לְעָלַם וּלְעָלְמֵי עָלְמַיָּא.)

יְהֵא שְׁמֵהּ רַבָּא מְבָרַךְ לְעָלַם וּלְעָלְמֵי עָלְמַיָּא.

יִתְבָּרַךְ וְיִשְׁתַּבַּח וְיִתְפָּאַר וְיִתְרוֹמַם וְיִתְנַשֵּׂא וְיִתְהַדָּר וְיִתְעַלֶּה וְיִתְהַלָּל שְׁמֵהּ דְּקֻדְשָׁא בְּרִיךְ הוּא (.Cong –בְּרִיךְ הוּא) לְעֵלָּא מִן כָּל בִּרְכָתָא וְשִׁירָתָא תֻּשְׁבְּחָתָא וְנֶחֱמָתָא, דַּאֲמִירָן בְּעָלְמָא. וְאִמְרוּ: אָמֵן. (.Cong –אָמֵן)

⊰ς **FOURTH DAY** ⃫⊱

אַשְׁרֵי *Praiseworthy are those who dwell in Your house; may they always*
praise You, Selah![1] *Praiseworthy is the people for whom this is so,*
praiseworthy is the people whose God is HASHEM.[2]

Psalm 145   *A psalm of praise by David:*

א *I will exalt You, my God the King, and I will bless Your Name forever and ever.*
ב *Every day I will bless You, and I will laud Your Name forever and ever.*
ג *HASHEM is great and exceedingly lauded,*
    and His greatness is beyond investigation.
ד *Each generation will praise Your deeds to the next*
    and of Your mighty deeds they will tell;
ה *The splendrous glory of Your power and Your wondrous deeds I shall discuss.*
ו *And of Your awesome power they will speak, and Your greatness I shall relate.*
ז *A recollection of Your abundant goodness they will utter*
    and of Your righteousness they will sing exultantly.
ח *Gracious and merciful is HASHEM,*
    slow to anger, and great in [bestowing] kindness.
ט *HASHEM is good to all; His mercies are on all His works.*
י *All Your works shall thank You, HASHEM, and Your devout ones will bless You.*
כ *Of the glory of Your kingdom they will speak, and of Your power they will tell;*
ל *To inform human beings of His mighty deeds,*
    and the glorious splendor of His kingdom.
מ *Your kingdom is a kingdom spanning all eternities,*
    and Your dominion is throughout every generation.
ס *HASHEM supports all the fallen ones and straightens all the bent.*
ע *The eyes of all look to You with hope*
    and You give them their food in its proper time;
פ *You open Your hand,*   Concentrate intently while reciting the verse, 'You open. . .'
    and satisfy the desire of every living thing.
צ Chazzan— *Righteous is HASHEM in all His ways*
    and magnanimous in all His deeds.
ק *HASHEM is close to all who call upon Him — to all who call upon Him sincerely.*
ר *The will of those who fear Him He will do;*
    and their cry He will hear, and save them.
ש *HASHEM protects all who love Him; but all the wicked He will destroy.*
ת *May my mouth declare the praise of HASHEM*
    and may all flesh bless His Holy Name forever and ever.
We will bless God from this time and forever, Halleluyah![3]

The chazzan recites Half-Kaddish:

יִתְגַּדַּל *May His great Name grow exalted and sanctified* (Cong.— *Amen.*) *in*
the world that He created as He willed. May He give reign to His
kingship in your lifetimes and in your days, and in the lifetimes of the entire
Family of Israel, swiftly and soon. Now respond: Amen.
          (Cong.— *Amen. May His great Name be blessed forever and ever.*)
          May His great Name be blessed forever and ever.
    Blessed, praised, glorified, exalted, extolled, mighty, upraised, and lauded be
the Name of the Holy One, Blessed is He (Cong.— *Blessed is He*) — *beyond any*
blessing and song, praise and consolation that are uttered in the world. Now
respond: Amen. (Cong.— *Amen.*)

(1) *Psalms* 84:5. (2) 144:15. (3) 115:18.

All:

לְךָ יהוה הַצְּדָקָה, וְלָנוּ בְּשֶׁת הַפָּנִים.¹ מַה נִּתְאוֹנֵן,² מַה נֹּאמַר,
מַה נְּדַבֵּר, וּמַה נִּצְטַדָּק.³ נַחְפְּשָׂה דְרָכֵינוּ וְנַחְקֹרָה,
וְנָשׁוּבָה אֵלֶיךָ,⁴ כִּי יְמִינְךָ פְּשׁוּטָה לְקַבֵּל שָׁבִים. לֹא בְחֶסֶד וְלֹא
בְמַעֲשִׂים בָּאנוּ לְפָנֶיךָ, כְּדַלִּים וּכְרָשִׁים דָּפַקְנוּ דְלָתֶיךָ. דְּלָתֶיךָ
דָּפַקְנוּ רַחוּם וְחַנּוּן, נָא אַל תְּשִׁיבֵנוּ רֵיקָם מִלְּפָנֶיךָ. מִלְּפָנֶיךָ מַלְכֵּנוּ
רֵיקָם אַל תְּשִׁיבֵנוּ, כִּי אַתָּה שׁוֹמֵעַ תְּפִלָּה.

שֹׁמֵעַ תְּפִלָּה, עָדֶיךָ כָּל בָּשָׂר יָבֹאוּ.⁵ יָבוֹא כָל בָּשָׂר לְהִשְׁתַּחֲוֹת
לְפָנֶיךָ יהוה.⁶ יָבֹאוּ וְיִשְׁתַּחֲווּ לְפָנֶיךָ אֲדֹנָי,
וִיכַבְּדוּ לִשְׁמֶךָ.⁷ בָּאוּ נִשְׁתַּחֲוֶה וְנִכְרָעָה, נִבְרְכָה לִפְנֵי יהוה עֹשֵׂנוּ.⁸
נָבוֹאָה לְמִשְׁכְּנוֹתָיו, נִשְׁתַּחֲוֶה לַהֲדֹם רַגְלָיו.⁹ בֹּאוּ שְׁעָרָיו בְּתוֹדָה,
חֲצֵרֹתָיו בִּתְהִלָּה, הוֹדוּ לוֹ בָּרְכוּ שְׁמוֹ.¹⁰ רוֹמְמוּ יהוה אֱלֹהֵינוּ,
וְהִשְׁתַּחֲווּ לַהֲדֹם רַגְלָיו, קָדוֹשׁ הוּא.¹¹ רוֹמְמוּ יהוה אֱלֹהֵינוּ,
וְהִשְׁתַּחֲווּ לְהַר קָדְשׁוֹ, כִּי קָדוֹשׁ יהוה אֱלֹהֵינוּ.¹² הִשְׁתַּחֲווּ לַיהוה
בְּהַדְרַת קֹדֶשׁ, חִילוּ מִפָּנָיו כָּל הָאָרֶץ.¹³ וַאֲנַחְנוּ בְּרֹב חַסְדְּךָ נָבוֹא
בֵיתֶךָ, נִשְׁתַּחֲוֶה אֶל הֵיכַל קָדְשְׁךָ בְּיִרְאָתֶךָ.¹⁴ נִשְׁתַּחֲוֶה אֶל הֵיכַל
קָדְשְׁךָ וְנוֹדֶה אֶת שְׁמֶךָ, עַל חַסְדְּךָ וְעַל אֲמִתֶּךָ, כִּי הִגְדַּלְתָּ עַל כָּל
שִׁמְךָ אִמְרָתֶךָ.¹⁵ לְכוּ נְרַנְּנָה לַיהוה, נָרִיעָה לְצוּר יִשְׁעֵנוּ.¹⁵ נְקַדְּמָה
פָנָיו בְּתוֹדָה, בִּזְמִרוֹת נָרִיעַ לוֹ.¹⁶ אֲשֶׁר יַחְדָּו נַמְתִּיק סוֹד, בְּבֵית
אֱלֹהִים נְהַלֵּךְ בְּרָגֶשׁ.¹⁷ אֵל נַעֲרָץ בְּסוֹד קְדֹשִׁים רַבָּה, וְנוֹרָא עַל
כָּל סְבִיבָיו.¹⁸ שְׂאוּ יְדֵיכֶם קֹדֶשׁ וּבָרְכוּ אֶת יהוה.¹⁹ הִנֵּה בָּרְכוּ אֶת
יהוה כָּל עַבְדֵי יהוה, הָעֹמְדִים בְּבֵית יהוה בַּלֵּילוֹת.²⁰ אֲשֶׁר מִי אֵל
בַּשָּׁמַיִם וּבָאָרֶץ, אֲשֶׁר יַעֲשֶׂה כְמַעֲשֶׂיךָ וְכִגְבוּרֹתֶיךָ.²¹ אֲשֶׁר לוֹ הַיָּם
וְהוּא עָשָׂהוּ, וְיַבֶּשֶׁת יָדָיו יָצָרוּ.²² אֲשֶׁר בְּיָדוֹ מֶחְקְרֵי אָרֶץ,
וְתוֹעֲפֹת הָרִים לוֹ.²³ אֲשֶׁר בְּיָדוֹ נֶפֶשׁ כָּל חָי, וְרוּחַ כָּל בְּשַׂר אִישׁ.²⁴
וְיוֹדוּ שָׁמַיִם פִּלְאֲךָ יהוה, אַף אֱמוּנָתְךָ בִּקְהַל קְדֹשִׁים.²⁵ לְךָ זְרוֹעַ
עִם גְּבוּרָה, תָּעֹז יָדְךָ תָּרוּם יְמִינֶךָ.²⁶ לְךָ שָׁמַיִם, אַף לְךָ אָרֶץ, תֵּבֵל
וּמְלֹאָהּ אַתָּה יְסַדְתָּם.²⁷ אַתָּה פוֹרַרְתָּ בְעָזְּךָ יָם, שִׁבַּרְתָּ רָאשֵׁי
תַנִּינִים עַל הַמָּיִם.²⁸ אַתָּה הִצַּבְתָּ כָּל גְּבוּלוֹת אָרֶץ, קַיִץ וָחֹרֶף

(1) *Daniel* 9:7. (2) Cf. *Lamentations* 3:39. (3) Cf. *Genesis* 44:16. (4) Cf. *Lamentations* 3:40.
(5) *Psalms* 65:3. (6) Cf. *Isaiah* 66:23. (7) *Psalms* 86:9. (8) 95:6. (9) 132:7. (10) 100:4.
(11) 99:5. (12) 99:9. (13) 96:9. (14) Cf. 5:8. (15) Cf. 138:2. (16) 95:1-2. (17) 55:15. (18) 89:8.
(19) 134:2. (20) 134:1. (21) *Deuteronomy* 3:24. (22) *Psalms* 95:5. (23) 95:4. (24) *Job* 12:10.
(25) *Psalms* 89:6. (26) 89:14. (27) 89:12. (28) 74:13.

לְךָ ה׳ *Yours, my Lord, is the righteousness and ours is the shame-facedness.[1] What complaint can we make?[2] What can we say? What can we declare? What justification can we offer?[3] Let us examine our ways and analyze — and return to You,[4] for Your right hand is extended to accept penitents. Neither with kindness nor with [good] deeds do we come before You. As paupers and as beggars do we knock at Your doors. At Your doors we knock, O Compassionate and Gracious One. Please do not turn us away from You empty-handed. Our King, turn us not away from You empty-handed, for You are the One Who hears prayer.*

שֹׁמֵעַ תְּפִלָּה *You Who hears prayer, to You all flesh will come.[5] All flesh will come to prostrate itself before You, O HASHEM.[6] They will come and prostrate themselves before You, my Lord, and shall honor Your Name.[7] Come! — let us prostrate ourselves and bow, let us kneel before God, our Maker.[8] Let us come to His dwelling places, let us prostrate ourselves at His footstool.[9] Enter His gates with thanksgiving, His courts with praise; give thanks to Him, praise His Name.[10] Exalt HASHEM, our God, and bow at His footstool; He is holy![11] Exalt HASHEM, our God, and bow at His holy mountain; for holy is HASHEM, our God.[12] Prostrate yourselves before HASHEM in His intensely holy place, tremble before Him, everyone on earth.[13] As for us, through Your abundant kindness we will enter Your House; we will prostrate ourselves toward Your Holy Sanctuary in awe of You.[14] We will prostrate ourselves toward Your Holy Sanctuary, and we will give thanks to Your Name for Your kindness and truth for You have exalted Your promise even beyond Your Name.[15] Come! — let us sing to HASHEM, let us call out to the Rock of our salvation. Let us greet Him with thanksgiving, with praiseful songs let us call out to Him.[16] For together let us share sweet counsel, in the house of God let us walk in multitudes.[17] God is dreaded in the hiddenmost counsel of the holy ones, and inspires awe upon all who surround Him.[18] Lift your hands in the Sanctuary and bless HASHEM.[19] Behold, bless HASHEM, all you servants of HASHEM, who stand in the House of HASHEM in the nights.[20] For what power is there in heaven or earth that can approximate Your deeds and power?[21] For His is the sea and He perfected the dry land — His hands fashioned it.[22] For in His power are the hidden mysteries of the earth, and the mountain summits are His.[23] For His is the soul of every living thing, and the spirit of all human flesh.[24] Heaven will gratefully praise Your wonders, HASHEM; also Your faithfulness in the assembly of holy ones.[25] Yours is a mighty arm with power, You strengthen Your hand; You exalt Your right hand.[26] Yours is the heaven; Yours, too, is the earth; the world and its fullness — You founded them.[27] You shattered the sea with Your might, You smashed sea serpents' heads upon the water.[28] You established all the boundaries of earth; summer and winter*

אַתָּה יְצַרְתָּם.[1] אַתָּה רִצִּיתָ רָאשֵׁי לְוְיָתָן, תִּתְּנֶנּוּ מַאֲכָל לְעָם לְצִיִּים. אַתָּה בָקַעְתָּ מַעְיָן וָנָחַל, אַתָּה הוֹבַשְׁתָּ נַהֲרוֹת אֵיתָן.[2] לְךָ יוֹם, אַף לְךָ לָיְלָה, אַתָּה הֲכִינוֹתָ מָאוֹר וָשָׁמֶשׁ.[3] עֹשֶׂה גְדֹלוֹת עַד אֵין חֵקֶר, וְנִפְלָאוֹת עַד אֵין מִסְפָּר.[4] כִּי אֵל גָּדוֹל יהוה, וּמֶלֶךְ גָּדוֹל עַל כָּל אֱלֹהִים.[5] כִּי גָדוֹל אַתָּה וְעֹשֵׂה נִפְלָאוֹת, אַתָּה אֱלֹהִים לְבַדֶּךָ.[6] כִּי גָדוֹל מֵעַל שָׁמַיִם חַסְדֶּךָ, וְעַד שְׁחָקִים אֲמִתֶּךָ.[7] גָּדוֹל יהוה וּמְהֻלָּל מְאֹד, וְלִגְדֻלָּתוֹ אֵין חֵקֶר.[8] (כִּי) גָדוֹל יהוה וּמְהֻלָּל מְאֹד, נוֹרָא הוּא עַל כָּל אֱלֹהִים.[9] גָּדוֹל יהוה וּמְהֻלָּל מְאֹד, בְּעִיר אֱלֹהֵינוּ הַר קָדְשׁוֹ.[10] לְךָ יהוה הַגְּדֻלָּה וְהַגְּבוּרָה, וְהַתִּפְאֶרֶת וְהַנֵּצַח וְהַהוֹד, כִּי כֹל בַּשָּׁמַיִם וּבָאָרֶץ; לְךָ יהוה הַמַּמְלָכָה, וְהַמִּתְנַשֵּׂא לְכֹל לְרֹאשׁ.[11] מִי לֹא יִרָאֲךָ מֶלֶךְ הַגּוֹיִם, כִּי לְךָ יָאָתָה, כִּי בְכָל חַכְמֵי הַגּוֹיִם וּבְכָל מַלְכוּתָם מֵאֵין כָּמוֹךָ.[12] מֵאֵין כָּמוֹךָ יהוה, גָּדוֹל אַתָּה וְגָדוֹל שִׁמְךָ בִּגְבוּרָה.[13] יהוה אֱלֹהֵי צְבָאוֹת, מִי כָמוֹךָ חֲסִין יָהּ, וֶאֱמוּנָתְךָ סְבִיבוֹתֶיךָ.[14] יהוה צְבָאוֹת, אֱלֹהֵי יִשְׂרָאֵל, יוֹשֵׁב הַכְּרֻבִים, אַתָּה הוּא הָאֱלֹהִים לְבַדֶּךָ.[15] מִי יְמַלֵּל גְּבוּרוֹת יהוה, יַשְׁמִיעַ כָּל תְּהִלָּתוֹ.[16] כִּי מִי בַשַּׁחַק יַעֲרֹךְ לַיהוה, יִדְמֶה לַיהוה בִּבְנֵי אֵלִים.[17] מַה נֹּאמַר לְפָנֶיךָ יוֹשֵׁב מָרוֹם, וּמַה נְּסַפֵּר לְפָנֶיךָ שֹׁכֵן שְׁחָקִים. מַה נֹּאמַר לְפָנֶיךָ יהוה אֱלֹהֵינוּ, מַה נְּדַבֵּר וּמַה נִּצְטַדָּק.[18] אֵין לָנוּ פֶּה לְהָשִׁיב וְלֹא מֵצַח לְהָרִים רֹאשׁ, כִּי עֲווֹנֹתֵינוּ רַבּוּ מִלִּמְנוֹת, וְחַטֹּאתֵינוּ עָצְמוּ מִסַּפֵּר.[19] לְמַעַן שִׁמְךָ יהוה תְּחַיֵּנוּ, וּבְצִדְקָתְךָ תּוֹצִיא מִצָּרָה נַפְשֵׁנוּ.[20] דַּרְכְּךָ אֱלֹהֵינוּ לְהַאֲרִיךְ אַפֶּךָ, לָרָעִים וְלַטּוֹבִים, וְהִיא תְהִלָּתֶךָ. לְמַעַנְךָ אֱלֹהֵינוּ עֲשֵׂה וְלֹא לָנוּ, רְאֵה עֲמִידָתֵנוּ, דַּלִּים וְרֵקִים. ✧ הַנְּשָׁמָה לָךְ, וְהַגּוּף פָּעֳלֶךְ, חוּסָה עַל עֲמָלֶךְ. הַנְּשָׁמָה לָךְ וְהַגּוּף שֶׁלָּךְ, יהוה עֲשֵׂה לְמַעַן שְׁמֶךָ. אָתָאנוּ עַל שִׁמְךָ, יהוה, עֲשֵׂה לְמַעַן שְׁמֶךָ. בַּעֲבוּר כְּבוֹד שִׁמְךָ, כִּי אֵל חַנּוּן וְרַחוּם שְׁמֶךָ. לְמַעַן שִׁמְךָ יהוה, וְסָלַחְתָּ לַעֲוֺנֵנוּ כִּי רַב הוּא.[21]

Congregation, then chazzan:

סְלַח לָנוּ אָבִינוּ, כִּי בְרֹב אִוַּלְתֵּנוּ שָׁגִינוּ,
מְחַל לָנוּ מַלְכֵּנוּ, כִּי רַבּוּ עֲוֺנֵינוּ.

— *You fashioned them.*[1] *You crushed the heads of Leviathan, You served it as food to the nation of legions. You split open fountain and stream, You dried the mighty rivers.*[2] *Yours is the day, Yours as well is the night; You established luminary and the sun.*[3] *Who performs great deeds that are beyond comprehension, and wonders beyond number.*[4] *For a great God is HASHEM, and a great King above all heavenly powers.*[5] *For You are great and work wonders; You alone, O God.*[6] *For great above the very heavens is Your kindness, and until the upper heights is Your truth.*[7] *HASHEM is great and exceedingly lauded, and His greatness is beyond investigation.*[8] *(For) HASHEM is great and exceedingly lauded, awesome is He above all heavenly powers.*[9] *Great is HASHEM and exceedingly lauded, in the city of our God, Mount of His Holiness.*[10] *Yours, HASHEM, is the greatness, the strength, the splendor, the triumph, and the glory; even everything in heaven and earth; Yours, HASHEM, is the kingdom, and sovereignty over every leader.*[11] *Who would not revere You, O King of nations? — for this befits You, for among all the sages of the nations and in all their kingdom there is none like You.*[12] *There is none like You, O HASHEM, You are great and Your Name is great with power.*[13] *HASHEM, God of Legions — who is like You, O Strong One, God? — and Your faithfulness surrounds You.*[14] *HASHEM, Master of Legions, God of Israel, enthroned upon the Cherubim, it is You alone Who is God.*[15] *Who can express the mighty acts of HASHEM, who can announce all His praise?*[16] *For who in the sky can be compared to HASHEM; be likened to HASHEM among the angels?*[17] *What can we say before You Who dwell on high? And what can we relate to You Who abide in the highest heaven? What can we say before You, HASHEM, our God? What can we declare? What justification can we offer?*[18] *We have neither mouth to respond nor brow to raise our head, for our iniquities are too numerous to count, and our sins are too vast to be numbered.*[19] *For Your Name's sake, HASHEM, revive us; and with Your righteousness remove our soul from distress.*[20] *It is Your way, our God, to delay Your anger, against people both evil and good — and this is Your praise. Act for Your sake, our God, and not for ours, behold our [spiritual] position — destitute and emptyhanded.* Chazzan – *The soul is Yours and the body is Your handiwork; take pity on Your labor. The soul is Yours and the body is Yours; O HASHEM, act for Your Name's sake. We have come with reliance on Your Name, O HASHEM, act for Your Name's sake; because of Your Name's glory — for 'Gracious and Merciful God' is Your Name. For Your Name's sake, HASHEM, may You forgive our iniquity, though it is abundant.*[21]

Congregation, then chazzan:

Forgive us, our Father, for in our abundant folly we have erred,
pardon us, our King, for our iniquities are many.

(1) *Psalms* 74:17. (2) 74:14-15. (3) 74:16. (4) *Job* 9:10. (5) *Psalms* 95:3.
(6) 86:10. (7) 108:5. (8) 145:3. (9) 96:4. (10) 48:2. (11) *I Chronicles* 29:11.
(12) *Jeremiah* 10:7. (13) 10:6. (14) *Psalms* 89:9. (15) *Isaiah* 37:16. (16) *Psalms* 106:2.
(17) 89:7. (18) Cf. *Genesis* 44:16. (19) Cf. *Ezra* 9:6. (20) Cf. *Psalms* 143:11. (21) Cf. 25:11.

All, while standing:

אֵל אֶרֶךְ אַפַּיִם אַתָּה, וּבַעַל הָרַחֲמִים נִקְרֵאתָ, וְדֶרֶךְ תְּשׁוּבָה הוֹרֵיתָ.

גְּדֻלַּת רַחֲמֶיךָ וַחֲסָדֶיךָ, תִּזְכּוֹר הַיּוֹם וּבְכָל יוֹם לְזֶרַע יְדִידֶיךָ. תֵּפֶן אֵלֵינוּ בְּרַחֲמִים, כִּי אַתָּה הוּא בַּעַל הָרַחֲמִים. בְּתַחֲנוּן וּבִתְפִלָּה פָּנֶיךָ נְקַדֵּם, כְּהוֹדַעְתָּ לֶעָנָיו מִקֶּדֶם. מֵחֲרוֹן אַפְּךָ שׁוּב,[1] כְּמוֹ בְתוֹרָתְךָ כָּתוּב.[2] וּבְצֵל כְּנָפֶיךָ[3] נֶחֱסֶה וְנִתְלוֹנָן, כְּיוֹם וַיֵּרֶד יהוה בֶּעָנָן. ❖ תַּעֲבוֹר עַל פֶּשַׁע וְתִמְחֶה אָשָׁם, כְּיוֹם וַיִּתְיַצֵּב עִמּוֹ שָׁם. תַּאֲזִין שַׁוְעָתֵנוּ וְתַקְשִׁיב מֶנּוּ מַאֲמָר, כְּיוֹם וַיִּקְרָא בְשֵׁם יהוה,[4] וְשָׁם נֶאֱמַר:

Congregation, then *chazzan*:

וַיַּעֲבֹר יהוה עַל פָּנָיו וַיִּקְרָא:

Congregation and *chazzan* (the words in bold type are recited aloud and in unison):

יהוה, יהוה, אֵל, רַחוּם, וְחַנּוּן, אֶרֶךְ אַפַּיִם, וְרַב חֶסֶד, וֶאֱמֶת, נֹצֵר חֶסֶד לָאֲלָפִים, נֹשֵׂא עָוֹן, וָפֶשַׁע, וְחַטָּאָה, וְנַקֵּה.[5] וְסָלַחְתָּ לַעֲוֹנֵנוּ וּלְחַטָּאתֵנוּ וּנְחַלְתָּנוּ.[6] סְלַח לָנוּ אָבִינוּ כִּי חָטָאנוּ, מְחַל לָנוּ מַלְכֵּנוּ כִּי פָשָׁעְנוּ. כִּי אַתָּה אֲדֹנָי טוֹב וְסַלָּח, וְרַב חֶסֶד לְכָל קֹרְאֶיךָ.[7]

פסוקי הקדמה לסליחה יא

טוֹב יהוה לְקֹוָו, לְנֶפֶשׁ תִּדְרְשֶׁנּוּ.[8] כָּל הַיּוֹם כִּלְמָתֵנוּ נֶגְדֵּנוּ, וּבֹשֶׁת פָּנֵינוּ כִּסָּתְנוּ.[9] כִּי עָלֶיךָ הֹרַגְנוּ כָל הַיּוֹם, נֶחְשַׁבְנוּ כְּצֹאן טִבְחָה.[10] לֹא נָסוֹג אָחוֹר לִבֵּנוּ, וַתֵּט אֲשֻׁרֵינוּ מִנִּי אָרְחֶךָ.[11] כִּי דֹרֵשׁ דָּמִים אוֹתָם זָכָר, לֹא שָׁכַח צַעֲקַת עֲנָוִים.[12]

בְּרַחֵם אָב עַל בָּנִים, כֵּן תְּרַחֵם יהוה עָלֵינוּ.[13] לַיהוה הַיְשׁוּעָה, עַל עַמְּךָ בִרְכָתֶךָ סֶּלָה.[14] יהוה צְבָאוֹת עִמָּנוּ, מִשְׂגָּב לָנוּ אֱלֹהֵי יַעֲקֹב סֶלָה.[15] יהוה צְבָאוֹת, אַשְׁרֵי אָדָם בֹּטֵחַ בָּךְ.[16] יהוה הוֹשִׁיעָה, הַמֶּלֶךְ יַעֲנֵנוּ בְיוֹם קָרְאֵנוּ.[17]

In some congregations the following two verses are recited responsively — the *chazzan* reciting סְלַח,
and the congregation responding וַיֹּאמֶר. In other congregations these verses are recited silently.

סְלַח נָא לַעֲוֹן הָעָם הַזֶּה כְּגֹדֶל חַסְדֶּךָ, וְכַאֲשֶׁר נָשָׂאתָה לָעָם הַזֶּה מִמִּצְרַיִם וְעַד הֵנָּה,[18] וְשָׁם נֶאֱמַר:

וַיֹּאמֶר יהוה סָלַחְתִּי כִּדְבָרֶךָ.[19]

All, while standing:

אֵל אֶרֶךְ אַפַּיִם O God — You are slow to anger, You are called the Master of Mercy, and You have taught the way of repentance. May You remember this day and every day the greatness of Your mercy and Your kindness to the offspring of Your beloved Ones. Turn to us in mercy for You are the Master of Mercy. With supplication and prayer we approach Your Presence in the manner that You made known to the humble [Moses] in ancient times. Turn back from Your fierce anger;[1] as is written in Your Torah.[2] In the shadow of Your wings may we find shelter[3] and lodging as on the day 'HASHEM descended in a cloud' [to appear to Moses on Sinai]. Chazzan — Overlook sin and erase guilt as on the day 'He [God] stood there with him [Moses].' Give heed to our cry and be attentive to our declaration as on the day 'He called out with the Name HASHEM,'[4] and there it was said:

Congregation, then chazzan:

And HASHEM passed before him [Moses] and proclaimed:

Congregation and chazzan (the words in bold type are recited aloud and in unison):

ה' ה' HASHEM, HASHEM, God, Compassionate and Gracious, Slow to anger, and Abundant in Kindness and Truth, Preserver of kindness for thousands [of generations], Forgiver of iniquity, willful sin, and error, and Who cleanses.[5] May You forgive our iniquities and our errors and make us Your heritage.[6] Forgive us, our Father, for we have erred; pardon us, our King, for we have willfully sinned; for You, my Lord, are good and forgiving and abundantly kind to all who call upon You.[7]

PREFATORY VERSES TO SELICHAH 11

טוֹב HASHEM is good to those who hope for Him, to a soul that seeks Him.[8] All day long our humiliation is before us and our shamefacedness covers us.[9] Because, for Your sake we are killed all the time, we are considered as sheep for the slaughter.[10] Our heart has not turned back, nor have our footsteps strayed from Your path.[11] For the Avenger of blood has remembered them; He has not forgotten the cry of the humble.[12]

כְּרַחֵם אָב As a father has mercy on his children, so, HASHEM, may You have mercy on us.[13] Salvation is HASHEM's, upon Your people is Your blessing, Selah.[14] HASHEM, Master of Legions, is with us, a stronghold for us is the God of Jacob, Selah.[15] HASHEM, Master of Legions, praiseworthy is the person who trusts in You.[16] HASHEM, save! May the King answer us on the day we call.[17]

In some congregations the following two verses are recited responsively — the chazzan reciting, 'Forgive, please . . .,' and the congregation responding, 'And HASHEM said . . .'
In other congregations these verses are recited silently.

סְלַח נָא Forgive, please, the iniquity of this people according to the greatness of Your kindness and as You have forgiven this people from Egypt until now,[18] and there it was said:

And HASHEM said, 'I have forgiven according to your word!'[19]

---

(1) Cf. *Exodus* 32:12. (2) See 32:14. (3) Cf. *Psalms* 36:8. (4) *Exodus* 34:5. (5) 34:6-7. (6) 34:9.
(7) *Psalms* 86:5. (8) *Lamentations* 3:25. (9) Cf. *Psalms* 44:16. (10) 44:23. (11) 44:19. (12) 9:13.
(13) Cf. *Psalms* 103:13. (14) 3:9. (15) 46:8. (16) 84:13. (17) 20:10. (18) *Numbers* 14:19. (19) 14:20.

All:

הַ**טֵּה** אֱלֹהַי אָזְנְךָ וּשֲׁמָע, פְּקַח עֵינֶיךָ וּרְאֵה שֹׁמְמֹתֵינוּ, וְהָעִיר
אֲשֶׁר נִקְרָא שִׁמְךָ עָלֶיהָ, כִּי לֹא עַל צִדְקוֹתֵינוּ אֲנַחְנוּ
מַפִּילִים תַּחֲנוּנֵינוּ לְפָנֶיךָ, כִּי עַל רַחֲמֶיךָ הָרַבִּים. אֲדֹנָי שְׁמָעָה,
אֲדֹנָי סְלָחָה, אֲדֹנָי הַקְשִׁיבָה, וַעֲשֵׂה אַל תְּאַחַר, לְמַעַנְךָ אֱלֹהַי,
כִּי שִׁמְךָ נִקְרָא עַל עִירְךָ וְעַל עַמֶּךָ.[1]

סליחה יא

All:

אֱלֹהֵינוּ וֵאלֹהֵי אֲבוֹתֵינוּ:

אֲ**נִי** קְרָאתִיךָ* כִּי תַעֲנֵנִי אֵל,[2]
בִּקַּשְׁתִּי רַחֲמִים כְּרָשׁ בַּפֶּתַח שׁוֹאֵל,
גִּדֵּל נוֹרְאוֹתֶיךָ בְּצֶדֶק עֲנוֹת הוֹאֵל,[3]
דַּעַת הַכֹּל כִּי יֵשׁ אֱלֹהִים בְּיִשְׂרָאֵל.[4]
הֲלוֹא אַתָּה מִקֶּדֶם אֱלֹהַי קְדֹשִׁי,[5]
וְלָמָּה נָמוּת* בְּלַחַץ וּבְקֶשִׁי,
זְכֹר וְעוֹרֵר חֶסֶד כְּאָז[6] לְחַדְּשִׁי,
חָרְבוֹתַי תָּשִׁיב וְכוֹנֵן מְקוֹם מִקְדָּשִׁי.
טוֹב אַתָּה לְקוֹוֶיךָ* לְנֶפֶשׁ תִּדְרְשֶׁךָ,[7]
יִחַלְנוּ לָךְ בְּעֵת צָרָה לְדָרְשֶׁךָ,
כָּל הַיּוֹם הֹרַגְנוּ עָלֶיךָ[8] עַל שֵׁם קָדְשֶׁךָ,
לֹא נָסוֹג לִבֵּנוּ[9] מִלְּבָרְכֶךָ וּלְהַקְדִּישֶׁךָ.
מִתְגָּרֶת יָדָךְ, כָּלִינוּ[10] בְּאַף וּבְחֵמָה,
נִדְמֵינוּ כִּכְלִי רֵיק וְכִסַּתְנוּ כְלִמָּה,

אֲנִי קְרָאתִיךָ — *I have called to You.* The first
twenty-two lines of this *selichah* form an
aleph-beis acrostic. This is followed by the
paytan's signature, שִׁמְעוֹן בַּר יִצְחָק חֲזַק וֶאֱמָץ,
*Shimon bar Yitzchak, may he be strong and
persevere.* Known as R' Shimon HaGadol, he
lived in Mainz, Germany, about 950-1020, and
he served on that city's *beis din* together with R'
Gershom Meor HaGolah [see prefatory comment
to *selichah* 12].

Because of his great wisdom and impressive
appearance, R' Shimon was often sent by the
community to persuade monarchs and clergymen
to abolish harsh decrees proposed against the
Jews, and in many cases he succeeded. In a
responsum, Rabbeinu Tam describes him as, 'R'
Shimon ben Yitzchak HaGadol, with whom
miracles were common.'

According to a popular story, R' Shimon had
two sons, Yitzchak and Elchanan. Elchanan was
kidnapped by the family's trusted gentile maid,
who handed him over to a monastery where he
was raised in the Christian faith. His keen mind
absorbed so much knowledge that he was
continually raised in rank, until he eventually
became pope. Some time after his son's election,
R' Shimon journeyed to Rome in order to gain an
audience with the new pope and plead with him
to nullify a cruel edict against the Jews. During
this visit the pope invited his guest to play a game
of chess. R' Shimon, a master at chess who had
never before been defeated, was stunned when
the pope checkmated him. R' Shimon, who had
taught chess to his sons, suspected that the pope
might have acquired his chess training from him.
When he questioned the pope concerning his

All:

הַטֵּה *Incline, my God, Your ear, and listen, open Your eyes and see our desolation and that of the city upon which Your Name is proclaimed; for not because of our righteousness do we cast down our supplications before You, rather because of Your abundant compassion. O my Lord, heed; O my Lord, forgive; O my Lord, be attentive and act, do not delay; for Your sake, my God, for Your Name is proclaimed upon Your city and upon Your people.*[1]

SELICHAH 11

All:

Our God and the God of our forefathers:

א *I have called to You,* for [I am certain that] You will answer me, O God;*[2]

ב *I ask for mercy like a pauper begging at the door.*

ג *[With] Your great awesomeness, righteously answer [my] prayers,*[3]

ד *[so] all may know that God is with Israel.*[4]

ה *Have You not been my God, my Holy One, from of old?*[5]

ו *Then why must we perish*, of oppression and hardship?*

ז *Remember [Your] kindness and awaken it,*
to renew [us] as [we were] then;[6]

ח *restore my ruins and re-establish my Holy Temple.*

ט *You are good to those who hope for You*, to the soul that seeks You;*[7]

י *we have looked to You, seeking You in [our] time of trouble.*

כ *Every day we are killed for Your sake,*[8]
for the sake of Your holy Name,

ל *[yet] our heart has not turned away*[9]
from blessing and sanctifying You.

מ *With dread of Your hand, we waste away*[10] *in wrath and rage;*

נ *we are like an empty vessel, and we are covered with humiliation.*

---

(1) *Daniel* 9:18-19. (2) *Psalms* 17:6. (3) Cf. 65:6. (4) Cf. *I Samuel* 17:46. (5) Cf. *Habakkuk* 1:12. (6) Cf. *Jeremiah* 2:2. (7) Cf. *Lamentations* 3:25. (8) Cf. *Psalms* 44:23. (9) Cf. 44:19. (10) Cf. 39:11.

skills, the truth surfaced, and father and son embraced.

After issuing many decrees in favor of the Jews, Elchanan disappeared with his father, and became an outstanding scholar.

וְלָמָּה נָמוּת — *Then why must we perish.* The *paytan* often switches from singular to plural. Sometimes, he speaks as an individual Jew, at other times, he is the voice of the nation collectively. Alternatively, he uses the singular to indicate the nation as a whole, and the plural to show the nation as a group of individuals. [This phenomenon is far from rare in *piyutim*.]

In some cases it is possible to trace the shift of number to the Scriptural source verses upon which the *paytan* bases his words. For example, since the first two stanzas of this *selichah* are written in the first person, we would expect the phrase וְלָמָּה אָמוּת, *then why must I perish*. But

that form does not appear in *Tanach*. However, the plural form וְלָמָּה נָמוּת, appears three times (*Genesis* 47:15,19; *Deuteronomy* 5:22). Thus, the *paytan* used the plural here. Similarly, the later stiches are based on Scriptural verses that appear in the plural and so they are also in the plural here.

טוֹב אַתָּה לְקֹוֶיךָ — *You are good to those who hope for You.* The Talmud resolves two contradictory verses. One verse (*Psalms* 145:9) states: טוֹב ה׳ לַכֹּל, *HASHEM is good to all*; while a second verse (*Lamentations* 3:25) states: טוֹב ה׳ לְקֹוָו, *HASHEM is good to those who hope for Him!* R' Elazar explains this with a parable. When one waters his garden, he waters the entire garden [i.e., once he turns on the hose for the healthy thriving plants, he simultaneously waters every plant in the garden, because little or no extra effort is needed]. However, when he performs chores such as digging and pruning that require additional

סָכַרְנוּ בְּיַד אֲדוֹנִים קָשִׁים[1] לְהוֹמְמָה,

עַד יַשְׁקִיף וְיֵרֶא יהוה מִן הַשָּׁמְיִמָה.[2]

פְּצֵנוּ וְהַצִּילֵנוּ מִיַּד בְּנֵי נֵכָר,[3]

צוּמוֹתִים חַיֵּינוּ בְּשֶׁפֶךְ דָּמֵנוּ לְהַעֲכֶר,

קָרָא שְׁלוּמַת זָרִים גְּמוּל וְשָׁכָר,

רְאוֹת כִּי דֹרֵשׁ דָּמִים אוֹתָם זָכָר.[4]

שׁוּבֵנוּ אֵלֶיךָ וַחֲרוֹן אַפְּךָ הָפֵר,[5]

תְּכַבֵּשׁ עֲוֹנוֹתֵינוּ וְחַטֹּאתֵינוּ תְכַפֵּר,

שֵׁפֶל מְרוּדֵנוּ עֲלֵה וְלֹא נֵחָפֵר,

בְּרֶשֶׁם יְקָרְךָ צוֹפָם חָקְקֵנוּ לְחַיִּים בַּסֵּפֶר.

❖ חֲזַק וְאַמֵּץ יָדַיִם וּבִרְכַּיִם כּוֹשְׁלוֹת,[6]

פַּנֵּה דֶרֶךְ עַמְּךָ וְהָרֵם מִכְשׁוֹלוֹת,[7]

יֶעֱרַב לְפָנֶיךָ תַּחַן כְּשַׁי וְעוֹלוֹת,

וְאַתָּה קָדוֹשׁ יוֹשֵׁב תְּהִלּוֹת.*[8]

All, while standing:

אֵל מֶלֶךְ יוֹשֵׁב עַל כִּסֵּא רַחֲמִים מִתְנַהֵג בַּחֲסִידוּת, מוֹחֵל
עֲוֹנוֹת עַמּוֹ, מַעֲבִיר רִאשׁוֹן רִאשׁוֹן,[9] מַרְבֶּה מְחִילָה
לַחַטָּאִים וּסְלִיחָה לַפּוֹשְׁעִים, עֹשֶׂה צְדָקוֹת עִם כָּל בָּשָׂר וָרוּחַ,
לֹא כְרָעָתָם תִּגְמוֹל. ❖ אֵל הוֹרֵיתָ לָנוּ לוֹמַר שְׁלֹשׁ עֶשְׂרֵה, וּזְכוֹר
לָנוּ הַיּוֹם בְּרִית שְׁלֹשׁ עֶשְׂרֵה, כְּמוֹ שֶׁהוֹדַעְתָּ לֶעָנָיו מִקֶּדֶם, כְּמוֹ
שֶׁכָּתוּב, וַיֵּרֶד יהוה בֶּעָנָן וַיִּתְיַצֵּב עִמּוֹ שָׁם, וַיִּקְרָא בְשֵׁם יהוה.

Congregation, then *chazzan:*

וַיַּעֲבֹר יהוה עַל פָּנָיו וַיִּקְרָא:

Congregation and *chazzan* (the words in bold type are recited aloud and in unison):

יהוה, יהוה, אֵל, **רַחוּם, וְחַנּוּן, אֶרֶךְ אַפַּיִם, וְרַב חֶסֶד, וֶאֱמֶת,
נֹצֵר חֶסֶד לָאֲלָפִים, נֹשֵׂא עָוֹן, וָפֶשַׁע, וְחַטָּאָה,
וְנַקֵּה.** וְסָלַחְתָּ לַעֲוֹנֵנוּ וּלְחַטָּאתֵנוּ וּנְחַלְתָּנוּ. סְלַח לָנוּ אָבִינוּ כִּי
חָטָאנוּ, מְחַל לָנוּ מַלְכֵּנוּ כִּי פָשָׁעְנוּ. כִּי אַתָּה אֲדֹנָי טוֹב וְסַלָּח,
וְרַב חֶסֶד לְכָל קֹרְאֶיךָ.

---

effort for each plant, he attends to the thriving
plants and ignores the others.

Similarly, with regard to sustenance, without
which man cannot survive, HASHEM *is good to all.*
But regarding special Divine protection, HASHEM
*is good to those who hope for Him (Sanhedrin
39b).*

וְאַתָּה קָדוֹשׁ יוֹשֵׁב תְּהִלּוֹת — *For You are the
Holy One, Who sits to hear [Israel's] praises.*
The translation follows *Rashi* (to Psalms 22:4).
Targum renders: *You are the Holy One, Who
established the world upon Israel's praises,*
i.e., the world was created for the sake of Israel's
performance of the Divine service [which, in

ס *We are delivered into the hands of hard masters,*[1] *in constant panic,*
ע *until* HASHEM *looks down from Heaven and takes notice.*[2]
פ *Take us out and rescue us from the aliens' hand.*[3]
צ *They squeeze out our life, spilling our blood*
     [in the attempt] to wipe us out.
ק *Decree retribution for the strangers,*
     [their] recompense and deserts;
ר *[that all may] see that the Avenger of blood*
     remembers their victims.[4]
ש *Bring us back to You, and annul Your burning anger;*[5]
ת *suppress our iniquities, atone our sins.*
     Elevate our wretched lowliness, that we not be ashamed,
     as You inscribe those who look forward to Your glory's [revelation],
        etch us in the Book for life.
     Chazzan — *Strengthen, fortify [our] weakened hands and knees;*[6]
     clear the way for Your people, remove the obstacles.[7]
     May [our] supplication be as pleasing to You
        as presents and olah-offerings,
     for You are the Holy One, Who sits to hear [Israel's] praises.*[8]

All, while standing:

אֵל מֶלֶךְ *O God, King Who sits on the throne of mercy; Who acts with*
     kindness, pardons the iniquities of His people, removes [sins]
one by one,[9] *increasingly grants pardon to careless sinners and forgiveness*
to rebels, Who deals righteously with every living being — You do not repay
them in accord with their evil. Chazzan — *O God, You taught us to recite the*
Thirteen [Attributes of Mercy], so remember for us today the covenant of
these Thirteen, as You made known to the humble one in ancient times, as
it is written: And HASHEM *descended in a cloud and stood with him there,*
and He called out with the Name HASHEM.

Congregation, then chazzan:

And HASHEM *passed before him [Moses] and proclaimed:*

Congregation and chazzan (the words in bold type are recited aloud and in unison):

ה' ה' **HASHEM, HASHEM, God, Compassionate and Gracious, Slow to**
     anger, and Abundant in Kindness and Truth, Preserver of
kindness for thousands [of generations], Forgiver of iniquity, willful
sin, and error, and Who cleanses. *May You forgive our iniquities and*
our errors and make us Your heritage. Forgive us, our Father, for we have
erred; pardon us, our King, for we have willfully sinned; for You, my
Lord, are good and forgiving and abundantly kind to all who call upon
You.

---

(1) Cf. *Isaiah* 19:4; some editions of *Selichos* read צוֹרְרִים קָשִׁים, *hard enemies.*
(2) Cf. *Lamentations* 3:50. (3) Cf. *Psalms* 144:11. (4) 9:13. (5) Cf. 85:5.
(6) Cf. *Isaiah* 35:3. (7) Cf. 57:14. (8) *Psalms* 22:4.(9) Tractate *Rosh Hashanah* 17a.

---

the absence of the *Beis HaMikdash*, is limited
to verbal praise]. This is in accord with the
Mishnah (*Avos* 1:2) that states: 'The world

depends on three things: On Torah study; on the
[Divine] service and on kind deeds.' [See also
Taanis 27b.]

פסוקי הקדמה לסליחה יב

הַבֵּט מִשָּׁמַיִם וּרְאֵה מִזְּבֻל קָדְשְׁךָ וְתִפְאַרְתֶּךָ, אַיֵּה קִנְאָתְךָ וּגְבוּרֹתֶיךָ, הֲמוֹן מֵעֶיךָ וְרַחֲמֶיךָ, אֵלֵינוּ הִתְאַפָּקוּ.[1] אַתָּה פוֹרַרְתָּ בְעָזְּךָ יָם, שִׁבַּרְתָּ רָאשֵׁי תַנִּינִים עַל הַמָּיִם.[2] אִם עֲוֹנֵינוּ עָנוּ בָנוּ, יהוה עֲשֵׂה לְמַעַן שְׁמֶךָ.[3]

בְּרַחֵם אָב עַל בָּנִים, כֵּן תְּרַחֵם יהוה עָלֵינוּ. לַיהוה הַיְשׁוּעָה, עַל עַמְּךָ בִרְכָתֶךָ סֶּלָה. יהוה צְבָאוֹת עִמָּנוּ, מִשְׂגָּב לָנוּ אֱלֹהֵי יַעֲקֹב סֶלָה. יהוה צְבָאוֹת, אַשְׁרֵי אָדָם בֹּטֵחַ בָּךְ. יהוה הוֹשִׁיעָה, הַמֶּלֶךְ יַעֲנֵנוּ בְיוֹם קָרְאֵנוּ.

In some congregations the following two verses are recited responsively — the chazzan reciting סְלַח, and the congregation responding וַיֹּאמֶר. In other congregations these verses are recited silently.

סְלַח נָא לַעֲוֹן הָעָם הַזֶּה כְּגֹדֶל חַסְדֶּךָ, וְכַאֲשֶׁר נָשָׂאתָה לָעָם הַזֶּה מִמִּצְרַיִם וְעַד הֵנָּה, וְשָׁם נֶאֱמַר:

וַיֹּאמֶר יהוה סָלַחְתִּי כִּדְבָרֶךָ.

All:

הַטֵּה אֱלֹהַי אָזְנְךָ וּשֲׁמָע, פְּקַח עֵינֶיךָ וּרְאֵה שֹׁמְמֹתֵינוּ, וְהָעִיר אֲשֶׁר נִקְרָא שִׁמְךָ עָלֶיהָ, כִּי לֹא עַל צִדְקֹתֵינוּ אֲנַחְנוּ מַפִּילִים תַּחֲנוּנֵינוּ לְפָנֶיךָ, כִּי עַל רַחֲמֶיךָ הָרַבִּים. אֲדֹנָי שְׁמָעָה, אֲדֹנָי סְלָחָה, אֲדֹנָי הַקְשִׁיבָה, וַעֲשֵׂה אַל תְּאַחַר, לְמַעַנְךָ אֱלֹהַי, כִּי שִׁמְךָ נִקְרָא עַל עִירְךָ וְעַל עַמֶּךָ.

סליחה יב

All:

אֱלֹהֵינוּ וֵאלֹהֵי אֲבוֹתֵינוּ:

אַיֵּה כָל נִפְלְאוֹתֶיךָ* הַגְּדוֹלוֹת וְהַנּוֹרָאוֹת,

אֲשֶׁר סִפְּרוּ לָנוּ אֲבוֹתֵינוּ,[1] יהוה צְבָאוֹת,

בְּרֶדֶת יִשְׂרָאֵל מִצְרַיְמָה בְּשִׁעְבּוּד וּתְלָאוֹת,

בְּחֶבְלֵי אָדָם מָשְׁכְתָּם[2] וְלֹא בְּשַׁלְשְׁלָאוֹת.*

אַיֵּה כָּל נִפְלְאוֹתֶיךָ § — *Where are all Your … wonders?* This selichah contains an alphabetical acrostic, followed by the paytan's signature, גֵּרְשֹׁם בַּר יְהוּדָה, *Gershom bar Yehudah.* Better known as Rabbeinu Gershom Meor HaGolah [Light of the Diaspora], he lived in Mainz, Germany, in the early part of the eleventh century and maintained a yeshivah there. He was also a member of that city's *beis din* together with R' Shimon HaGadol [see prefatory com-

ment to *selichah* 11].

R' Gershom's best-known contribution are the enactments adopted by rabbinic synods at his behest, and accepted as law throughout Ashkenazic Jewry, and in some instances by the entire Diaspora. Two of these enactments have had a profound effect upon Jewish family life. They are his bans against polygamy, and against divorce without the wife's consent. He also prohibited the shaming of those who renounced

הַבֵּט *Look down from Heaven and see, from Your holy, splendrous abode; where is Your jealousy and Your might? Your inner stirrings and Your mercy is withheld from us.*[1] *You shattered the sea with Your might, You smashed the heads of the serpentine [Egyptians] upon the water.*[2] *Even if our iniquities bear witness against us,* HASHEM, *act for Your Name's sake.*[3]

כְּרַחֵם אָב *As a father has mercy on his children, so,* HASHEM, *may You have mercy on us. Salvation is* HASHEM's, *upon Your people is Your blessing, Selah.* HASHEM, *Master of Legions, is with us, a stronghold for us is the God of Jacob, Selah.* HASHEM, *Master of Legions, praiseworthy is the person who trusts in You.* HASHEM, *save! May the King answer us on the day we call.*

In some congregations the following two verses are recited responsively — the *chazzan* reciting, *'Forgive, please . . .,'* and the congregation responding, *'And* HASHEM *said . . .'* In other congregations these verses are recited silently.

סְלַח נָא *Forgive, please, the iniquity of this people according to the greatness of Your kindness and as You have forgiven this people from Egypt until now, and there it was said:*

And HASHEM said, 'I have forgiven according to your word!'

All:

הַטֵּה *Incline, my God, Your ear, and listen, open Your eyes and see our desolation and that of the city upon which Your Name is proclaimed; for not because of our righteousness do we cast down our supplications before You, rather because of Your abundant compassion. O my Lord, heed; O my Lord, forgive; O my Lord, be attentive and act, do not delay; for Your sake, my God, for Your Name is proclaimed upon Your city and upon Your people.*

SELICHAH 12

All:

Our God and the God of our forefathers:

א *Where are all Your great and awesome wonders,**
א *that our fathers told us of,*[4] *O* HASHEM, *Master of Legions?*
ב *When Israel went down to Egypt in slavery and tribulations,*
ב *with humane ties You drew them [down to Egypt],*[5]
   and not with chains.*

---

(1) Cf. *Isaiah* 63:15. (2) *Psalms* 74:13. (3) *Jeremiah* 14:7. (4) Cf. *Judges* 6:13. (5) Cf. *Hosea* 11:4.

Judaism under duress, once they had returned to the Jewish fold.

This last enactment was necessitated by the common Christian tactic of forcibly converting Jews by threatening them with death or expulsion. Halachah requires Jews to submit to death rather than renounce their faith. Indeed, entire Jewish communities in Germany and France gave up their lives to sanctify God's Name. But some individuals were unable to withstand the test. R' Gershom's only son was compelled to convert to Christianity, and when he died soon after without having had the chance to return to his faith, R' Gershom observed a two-week period of mourning — one week for the loss of his life, and another for the loss of his soul.

The terrible suffering of his people in those times is depicted in R' Gershom's *selichos*.

בְּחַבְלֵי אָדָם מְשַׁכְתָּם וְלֹא בְשַׁלְשְׁלָאוֹת — *With humane ties* [lit., *cords of man*] *You drew them*

גַּם מַעֲבִידֵיהֶם בְּקֶשָׁה עֲבוֹדָה,

גָּזְרוּ בַּיְאוֹר זְכוּרֵיהֶם לְאַבְּדָה,

דָּנְתָּם בְּסַאסְּאָה,[1] מִדָּה בְמִדָּה,

דְּגָלִים הוֹצֵאתָ, בִּרְכוּשׁ כָּל חֶמְדָּה.

הַיָּם וְגַלָּיו בְּעָזְךָ פּוֹרָרוּ,[2]

הַיַּרְדֵּן הוֹבַשְׁתָּ, וּבְרֶגֶל עָבָרוּ,[3]

וּבַמִּדְבָּר כִּלְכַּלְתָּם, וְדָבָר לֹא חָסֵרוּ,[4]

וּמַמְלָכוֹת וַעֲמָמִים בְּיָדָם נִמְסָרוּ.[5]

זָנְחוּ הַטּוֹב,* וּרְדָפוּם[6] מַכְנִיעִים,

זְעָקוּךְ וְשָׁמַעְתָּ, וְהֶעֱמַדְתָּ לָהֶם מוֹשִׁיעִים,

חָנוּ בְאַרְצָם כָּל טוּב שְׂבֵעִים,

חָטְאוּ וְגָלוּ וּפְקַדְתָּם לְשִׁבְעִים.

טָפְלוּ שֶׁקֶר וְנִתְּנוּ לְמִרְמָס,

טְרָדוּם לְמַדְחֵפוֹת אַנְשֵׁי חָמָס,[7]

יָצְאוּ מֵאַרְצָם וְקֵץ חֲזַרְתָּם נִכְמָס,

יָשְׁבוּ בַגּוֹיִם וְהָיוּ לָמַס.[8]

כֹּחַ אַמֵּץ פְּלֵיטָה הַנִּשְׁאֶרֶת,

כָּשַׁל כֹּחָהּ, מִכֹּבֶד רָעָה מְמָאֶרֶת,

לְעֵת רִאשׁוֹנָה פְּקוּדָה מְשֻׁאֶרֶת,[9]

לְבֹא שְׁנִיָּה אָצָה וּמְמַהֶרֶת.[10]

מְעַט לְעֵת צָרָתִי מִרְבָּה,

מִיּוֹם שֶׁעָבַר קָשֶׁה הַבָּא,

נִלְאֵיתִי נְשֹׁא עַל מַדְהֵבָה,

נוֹאֶמֶת מִדֹּד וְהֶבֵא הַבָּאָה רַבָּה.*

סְגֻלָּתְךָ דּוֹחֵק צוֹרֵר הַצָּר,

סִבְרָהּ, לְהָמִיר בֶּאֱמוּנַת נוֹצֵר,*[11]

[down to Egypt], and not with chains. Rabban Yochanan taught that the Patriarch Jacob actually should have descended to Egypt in iron chains [since his descent was the fulfillment of the decree of exile, foretold to Abraham at the Covenant Between the Parts (Genesis 15:13)]. However, his personal merits rescued him from that ignominious fate. Thus, the prophet (Hosea 11:4) states, 'I drew them with cords of man, with bands of love . . .' (Shabbos 89b).

The Midrash explains Jacob's honorable descent to Egypt with a parable. A cow stubbornly

refused to follow its owner to the slaughterhouse. So he led her calf there instead. When the cow saw her calf being led away, she quickly went after it. Thus her owner was able to bring her to the slaughterhouse without having to drag her against her will. Similarly, when God wanted Jacob to leave the HolyLand and go into the Egyptian exile, He first sent Joseph, Jacob's favorite son, down to Egypt. Then Jacob offered no resistance and did not have to go down in chains (Bereishis Rabbah 86:2).

הַטּוֹב — The Good One. The translation follows

ג *Those, too, who enslaved them at hard labor,*
ג *[and] condemned their sons to perish in the Nile —*
ד *You judged them, bushel for bushel,[1] measure for measure,*
ד *[and] brought out the bannered tribes*
    [laden] with all [the Egyptians'] precious possessions.
ה *The sea and its waves were shattered by Your might;[2]*
ה *You dried up the Jordan, and [the tribes] crossed it[3] on foot.*
ו *In the desert You nourished them and they lacked nothing,[4]*
ו *and kingdoms and peoples were delivered into their hand.[5]*
ז *They spurned the Good One,* and subjugating nations pursued them;[6]*
ז *they called to You, and You heard, and established saviors for them.*
ח *They settled in their land, replete with everything good;*
ח *[then] they sinned, and went into exile until You remembered them*
    in seventy-years' time.
ט *They made issues of lies, and were condemned to be trampled;*
ט *violent men chased them away, pushing them out [into exile].[7]*
י *They left their land, their day of return hidden [from them],*
י *they dwelt among nations, and became a tributary.[8]*
כ *Fortify the strength of the surviving remnant,*
כ *[whose] power is exhausted by the burden of evil*
    that causes diminution.
ל *While [the pain of] one calamity still remains,[9]*
ל *the second rushes and hurries its advent.[10]*
מ *From one day to the next my pain increases,*
מ *each day is worse than the one before.*
נ *I am worn out with bearing the yoke of duress,*
נ *[as] the [conquerors] pronounce,*
    'Weigh out [your gold] and bring plenty!'*
ס *The oppressive enemy is pushing Your precious one*
ס *to exchange her Hope for a man-made faith.*[11]*

---

(1) Cf. *Isaiah* 27:8; some editions of *Selichos* read סְאָה בְּסְאָה which has the same meaning. See commentary to *selichah* 94. (2) Cf. *Psalms* 74:13. (3) Cf. *Joshua* 5:1. (4) Cf. *Nehemiah* 9:21. (5) Cf. 9:22. (6) Cf. *Hosea* 8:3. (7) Cf. *Psalms* 140:12. (8) Cf. *Lamentations* 1:3,1. (9) Some editions read מִשְׁמֶרֶת, *guarded*. (10) Cf. *Tractate Sanhedrin* 97a. (11) The two stiches beginning with the letter ס have been the targets of heavy censorship (see commentary); some editions omit one or both of these lines (yet, strangely, include them in the Yiddish translation); some read, סְגֻלָּתְךָ דוֹחֶקֶת פְּקֻדָּתְךָ מִלִּנְצוֹר, *Your precious one is pushed to stop guarding Your laws,* סִבְרָהּ לְהָמִיר כְּבוֹדְךָ בְּעֵת צָר, *[The enemy] hoped [Israel] would exchange Your glory in (times of) stress;* others read, סְגֻלָּתְךָ קוֹרְאִים בַּצַּר, *Your precious ones call out from the straits,* סִבְרָם לְאֵל בּוֹרֵא וְיוֹצֵר, *Their hope is to God, Creator and Maker.*

Ibn Ezra and *Radak* (to *Hosea* 8:3) and is based upon Hezekiah's prayer (*II Chronicles* 30:18), *May* HASHEM, *the Good One, forgive ...* According to *Targum Yonasan* (*Hosea* 8:3), the word הַטּוֹב, *the good,* alludes to the Divine service that is rewarded with God's beneficence and bounty. By rejecting the service, they cut themselves off from the flow of heavenly *goodness* that had sustained them. *Matteh Levi* understands הַטּוֹב as a reference to the Torah, which is described as לֶקַח טוֹב, *a good teaching* (*Proverbs* 4:2).

עַל מַרְהֵבָה ... מְדֹד וְהָבֵא הָבָאָה רַבָּה — *The yoke of duress ... 'Weigh out [your gold] and bring plenty!'* The prophet (*Isaiah* 14:4) refers to Babylon as מַרְהֵבָה, a word most commentaries understand as *abundant with gold,* from the Aramaic דַהֲבָה, *gold.* The Talmud interprets it as a play on words: מַרְהֵבָה is the nation that exclaims, 'מְדֹד וְהָבֵא, *Weigh out and bring!'* Alternatively, 'מְאֹד מְאֹד, *Bring very very much, without measure!'* (*Shabbos* 149b).

סִבְרָהּ לְהָמִיר בֶּאֱמֻנַת נוֹצֵר — *To exchange her Hope for a man-made faith.* See footnote for various

עַד אָנָה יהוה אֶקְרָא מִמֵּצָר,

עֲנֵנִי בַמֶּרְחַב יָהּ[1] כִּי יָדְךָ לֹא תִקְצָר.[2]

פְּשָׁעִים אִם עָצְמוּ בֵּינִי וּבֵינֶךָ לְהַבְדִּילָה,[3]

פַּרְגּוֹד אִם נִגְעַל בִּפְנֵי הַתְּפִלָּה,[4]

צוּר, בְּכִסֵּא כְבוֹדְךָ חֲתָר מְחִלָּה,[5]

צַעֲקָתֵנוּ לְפָנֶיךָ תָבֹא, פְּנֵי כְבוֹדְךָ לְהִתְקַבְּלָה.

קְרָא שְׁנַת רָצוֹן,[6] מֵעֹצֶב לְהַנְפִּישִׁי,

קַבֵּץ נְפוּצוֹתַי וַעֲבֹר בְּרֹאשִׁי,[7]

רִיבָה יהוה רִיבֵי נַפְשִׁי,[8]

רְצֵה לְהַצִּילֵנִי,[9] אֱלֹהַי קָדְשִׁי.

שְׁנֵי רְשָׁעִים בְּחָצָץ תִּגְרֹס,[10]

שָׁכוֹל וְאַלְמוֹן*[11] אוֹתָם תַּהֲרֹס,

תִּשְׁפֹּךְ דָּמָם אַרְצָה לָרוֹס,

תְּמוּתָה* הוֹתֵר[12] וּבֶאֱמוּנָה לְאָרוֹס.[13]

גְּדוֹר פִּרְצַת סֻכַּת דָּוִיד הַנֹּפֶלֶת,*[14]

רוֹמֵם קִרְיָה, עַד עָפָר מֻשְׁפֶּלֶת,[15]

שְׁבוּיֶיהָ נַחֵם, נֶחָמָה מֻכְפֶּלֶת,*

מְאוֹרָהּ הָאֵר, וְתָאִיר מְאַפֶּלֶת.

❖ בְּנֵה עִירְךָ כִּימֵי עוֹלָם,[16]

רַפֵּא מִזְבַּחֲךָ[17] הֵיכָל וְאוּלָם,[18]

יְהוּדָה וְיִשְׂרָאֵל, שָׁם יַעַבְדוּךָ כֻלָּם,

יִגְדַּל שִׁמְךָ מֵעוֹלָם וְעַד עוֹלָם.[19]

All, while standing:

אֵל מֶלֶךְ יוֹשֵׁב עַל כִּסֵּא רַחֲמִים מִתְנַהֵג בַּחֲסִידוּת, מוֹחֵל עֲוֹנוֹת עַמּוֹ, מַעֲבִיר רִאשׁוֹן רִאשׁוֹן, מַרְבֶּה מְחִילָה לַחַטָּאִים וּסְלִיחָה לַפּוֹשְׁעִים, עֹשֶׂה צְדָקוֹת עִם כָּל בָּשָׂר וָרוּחַ,

---

censored versions of this stich. According to *Arugas HaBosem*, the word נוֹצֵר means *the Nazarene* (his text reads בְּתָלוּי נוֹצֵר), and the stich refers to forced baptism and conversions perpetrated throughout the centuries by zealous missionaries. See prefatory comment to this *selichah*.

שָׁכוֹל וְאַלְמוֹן — *[Leaving their mothers] bereaved and [their wives] widowed.* The translation follows the majority of the commentaries to the *Selichos*. According to Rashi (Isaiah 47:9), the

phrase alludes to a land whose citizens have been exiled and whose king has been taken, for the citizens are considered the land's children and the king its husband.

תְּמוּתָה — *Those condemned to die.* The translation follows most commentaries to *Psalms* 79:11, who derive the word from מות, *to die.* According to *Arugas HaBosem*, the word is from תמם, *wholeness* and *perfection*, and means *the wholesome nation.*

ע How long, O HASHEM, must I call out from the straits?

ע Answer me with relief, O God,[1] for Your hand is not short.[2]

פ If [my] sins are so great as to divide between me and You,[3]

פ if the Heavenly Curtain is drawn shut before [my] prayer,[4]

צ O Rock! Delve a tunnel in Your Throne of Glory[5]

צ [so that] our cry may come before You,
  and be accepted before Your glory.

ק Declare a year of good will,[6] to give me rest from misery;

ק gather my dispersed ones, and lead at my head.[7]

ר Fight against those who cause strife to my soul, O HASHEM![8]

ר May it be Your will to rescue me,[9] O my God, my Holy One.

ש Break the teeth of the wicked with gravel;[10]

ש destroy them, [leaving their mothers] bereaved
  [and their wives] widowed.*[11]

ת May their blood be poured upon the earth and mixed [with it],

ת spare those condemned to die*[12] [for Your sake],
  and betroth them with faith.[13]

ג Build up the breaches in David's fallen succah,*[14]

ר uplift the city [of Jerusalem] that is thrown down in the dust.[15]

ש Comfort the captive [nation] with a double consolation:*

ם Kindle her light, and enlighten the darkened one.

  Chazzan — Build Your city as in days of old,[16]
  repair Your Altar[17] [and the] Temple and Antechamber.[18]
  There Judah and Israel, all of them shall serve You there,
  [And] Your Name will be great for all eternity.[19]

All, while standing:

אֵל מֶלֶךְ   O God, King Who sits on the throne of mercy; Who acts with
kindness, pardons the iniquities of His people, removes
[sins] one by one, increasingly grants pardon to careless sinners and
forgiveness to rebels, Who deals righteously with every living being —

---

(1) Cf. *Psalms* 118:5. (2) Cf. *Numbers* 11:23; *Isaiah* 59:1. (3) Cf. *Isaiah* 59:2.
(4) Cf. Tractate *Bava Metzia* 59a. (5) Cf. Tractate *Sanhedrin* 103a. (6) Cf. *Isaiah* 61:2.
(7) Cf. *Micah* 2:12-13. (8) Cf. *Lamentations* 3:58. (9) Cf. *Psalms* 40:14; some editions of *Selichos*
read רְצֵה לְהַצִּילֵנִי, May it be Your will to give me rest. (10) Cf. *Lamentations* 3:16. (11) *Isaiah* 47:9.
(12) Cf. *Psalms* 79:11. (13) Cf. *Hosea* 2:22. (14) *Amos* 9:11. (15) Cf. *Isaiah* 26:5. (16) Cf. *Amos* 9:11.
(17) Cf. *I Kings* 18:30. (18) See 6:3. (19) Cf. *II Samuel* 7:26.

סֻכַּת דָּוִיד הַנֹּפֶלֶת — *David's fallen succah.* This
refers to the Davidic dynasty (*Targum, Rashi,* et
al., to *Amos* 9:11); the *Beis HaMikdash* (*Mahari
Kara,* ibid.); or Jerusalem (*Maglei Tzedek*). This
last interpretation is borne out by the stich below,
בְּנֵה עִירְךָ כִּימֵי עוֹלָם, *Build Your city as in days of
old,* which, without the word עִירְךָ, *Your city,*
appears in the same verse in *Amos* as the phrase
David's fallen succah.

נֶחָמָה מְכֻפֶּלֶת — *A double consolation.* The
Midrash (*Pesikta*) expounds on certain double

expressions found in Scriptures: חָטָא חָטְאָה
יְרוּשָׁלַיִם, *Jerusalem sinned doubly* (*Lamentations*
1:8), and so she was punished, כִּפְלַיִם בְּכָל חַטֹּאתֶיהָ,
double for all her sins (*Isaiah* 40:2). בָּכוֹ תִבְכֶּה, *She
cried doubly* (*Lamentations* 1:2), and so she will
be doubly consoled, as it is written נַחֲמוּ נַחֲמוּ עַמִּי,
Console, console My people (*Isaiah* 40:1).
  Other expressions of double consolation appear in *Isaiah* 51: עוּרִי עוּרִי, *Awaken! Awaken!* (v.
9); אָנֹכִי אָנֹכִי הוּא מְנַחֶמְכֶם, *I, I am He that consoles
you* (v. 12); and הִתְעוֹרְרִי הִתְעוֹרְרִי, *Awaken yourself! Awaken yourself!* (v. 17).

לֹא כְרָעָתָם תִּגְמוֹל. ❖ אֵל הוֹרֵיתָ לָנוּ לוֹמַר שְׁלֹשׁ עֶשְׂרֵה, וּזְכוֹר לָנוּ הַיּוֹם בְּרִית שְׁלֹשׁ עֶשְׂרֵה, כְּמוֹ שֶׁהוֹדַעְתָּ לֶעָנָו מִקֶּדֶם, כְּמוֹ שֶׁכָּתוּב, וַיֵּרֶד יהוה בֶּעָנָן וַיִּתְיַצֵּב עִמּוֹ שָׁם, וַיִּקְרָא בְשֵׁם יהוה.

Congregation, then chazzan:

וַיַּעֲבֹר יהוה עַל פָּנָיו וַיִּקְרָא:

Congregation and chazzan (the words in bold type are recited aloud and in unison):

יהוה, יהוה, אֵל, רַחוּם, וְחַנּוּן, אֶרֶךְ אַפַּיִם, וְרַב חֶסֶד, וֶאֱמֶת, נֹצֵר חֶסֶד לָאֲלָפִים, נֹשֵׂא עָוֹן, וָפֶשַׁע, וְחַטָּאָה, וְנַקֵּה. וְסָלַחְתָּ לַעֲוֹנֵנוּ וּלְחַטָּאתֵנוּ וּנְחַלְתָּנוּ. סְלַח לָנוּ אָבִינוּ כִּי חָטָאנוּ, מְחַל לָנוּ מַלְכֵּנוּ כִּי פָשָׁעְנוּ. כִּי אַתָּה אֲדֹנָי טוֹב וְסַלָּח, וְרַב חֶסֶד לְכָל קֹרְאֶיךָ.

סליחה יג (פזמון)

Chazzan, then congregation:

חוֹקֵר הַכֹּל וְסוֹקֵר,* וּמֵבִין אֵל מִפְעָלַי,
אִם פְּעֻלָּתִי שֶׁקֶר, וּמַהֲתַלּוֹת בַּעֲמָלִי,
אֶת עָוֹנִי לֹא תְבַקֵּר, וְאַל תִּדְרֹשׁ לְמַעֲלָלִי.
יהוה בְּקֶר תִּשְׁמַע קוֹלִי.[1]

Congregation, then chazzan:

יוֹצְרִי אֲשֶׁר בַּזֶּרֶת, תִּכֵּן מְרוֹמֵי קֶרֶת,[2]
לְךָ אֶכְנֶה עֲטֶרֶת,* בַּשְּׁלִישִׁי אַשְׁמֹרֶת,*
אֲשֶׁר תַּאֲזִין הָעֲטֶרֶת, וּלְיִשְׁעֲךָ שׁוֹבֶרֶת,[3]
וְתִשְׁלַח הַמֻּגְאֶרֶת, לְהוֹמִיָּה וְסוֹרֶרֶת,[4]
אֲשֶׁר גָּאֲנָה מְדַבֶּרֶת, וְאֵין בִּלְתָּהּ אוֹמֶרֶת,[5]
וּמְקוֹם מִקְטַר קְטֹרֶת, וְהַדְּבִיר וְהַכַּפֹּרֶת,*
אֲשֶׁר יְשָׁרְתוּ בָם שָׁרֵת, שָׁמוּהוּ מַעֲבֶרֶת,
תִּדְבַּק בָּהּ מַמְאֶרֶת, כְּמוֹ כָּבֵד לְיוֹתֶרֶת,
וַחֲמַת קְרִי יְקַר כָּל מַכָּה וְכָל חֳלִי,[6]   יהוה בְּקֶר תִּשְׁמַע קוֹלִי.

---

§ **חוֹקֵר הַכֹּל וְסוֹקֵר** — *Prober and Searcher of all.* This *selichah* was composed by the otherwise unknown יִצְחָק, *Yitzchak*, whose name appears in the acrostic of the stanzas. This *paytan* lived sometime before 1234, the year in which the commentary *Arugas HaBosem* (which includes this *selichah*) was written.

לְךָ אֶכְנֶה עֲטֶרֶת — *I prepare a diadem for You.* There is an angel ... named Sandalfon ... who stands behind the Divine Chariot weaving

crowns for his Creator (*Chagigah* 13b). These crowns are woven from the prayers of the righteous (*Tosafos*). This is the meaning of the *Kedushah* recited at *Mussaf* [according to *Nusach Sefard*] which begins: כֶּתֶר יִתְּנוּ לְךָ, *A crown will they give You, O Hashem, our God — the angels of the multitude above, together with Your people Israel who are assembled below* (*Rabbeinu Chananel*).

בַּשְּׁלִישִׁי אַשְׁמֹרֶת — *In the third watch [of the*

You do not repay them in accord with their evil. Chazzan — *O God, You taught us to recite the Thirteen [Attributes of Mercy], so remember for us today the covenant of these Thirteen, as You made known to the humble one in ancient times, as it is written: And* HASHEM *descended in a cloud and stood with him there, and He called out with the Name* HASHEM.

Congregation, then *chazzan:*

And HASHEM *passed before him [Moses] and proclaimed:*

Congregation and *chazzan* (the words in bold type are recited aloud and in unison):

ה' ה' HASHEM, HASHEM, God, Compassionate and Gracious, Slow to anger, and Abundant in Kindness and Truth, Preserver of kindness for thousands [of generations], Forgiver of iniquity, willful sin, and error, and Who cleanses. *May You forgive our iniquities and our errors and make us Your heritage. Forgive us, our Father, for we have erred; pardon us, our King, for we have willfully sinned; for You, my Lord, are good and forgiving and abundantly kind to all who call upon You.*

SELICHAH 13

Chazzan, then congregation:

חוֹקֵר הַכֹּל *Prober and Searcher of all,**

Who knows the intent of all my deeds,

if my deeds have been false,

and my toil [on Your behalf] has been a mockery,

examine not my iniquity, inquire not after my wrongdoing:

HASHEM, *at dawn hear my voice!*[1]

Congregation, then *chazzan:*

, *My Maker, Who with His spur laid out the sky's mighty heights,*[2]

I prepare a diadem for You, in the third watch [of the night],**

when You hearken to the prayers

of those who hope for Your salvation.[3]

You will send forth rebuke against the riotous, wayward [oppressor],[4]

who speaks arrogance, saying that there is no [power] besides her.[5]

The place where incense was burnt,

*the Holy of Holies and the Ark Cover,**

where [the Kohanim Gedolim] performed Your service —

[all this] they have turned into a passageway.

May curse adhere to them as the liver to the diaphragm,

and may intense rage come upon them

[with] every kind of wound and sickness[6] —

HASHEM, *at dawn hear my voice!*

---

(1) *Psalms* 5:4. (2) Cf. *Isaiah* 40:12. (3) Cf. *Genesis* 49:18 with *Targum Onkelos*.
(4) Cf. *Proverbs* 7:11. (5) Cf. *Isaiah* 47:8. (6) Cf. *Deuteronomy* 28:61.

night]. The night is divided into watches, the last of which ends at daybreak. The Sages (*Berachos* 3a) dispute whether there are three four-hour watches, or four three-hour watches. If the *paytan* agrees with the view that holds three watches, then he speaks of the final watch which is most propitious for prayer. If, however, he

maintains that there are four watches, then he mentions the third because the *Selichos* service may be recited at any time after midnight when the third watch begins.

וּמְקוֹם מִקְטַר קְטֹרֶת וְהַדְּבִיר וְהַכַּפֹּרֶת — *The place where incense was burnt, the Holy of Holies and the Ark Cover.* This refers to the special incense

Congregation, then *chazzan*:

צוּר שִׁמְךָ אֵל קַנָּא,[1] אַתָּה מַה לְּךָ בַּשֵּׁנָה,[2]

שָׁנָה אַחַר שָׁנָה, יְמִינְךָ נָטְעָה כַנָּה,[3]

מְאֹד נִגַּשׁ וְהוּא נַעֲנָה,[4] זֶה מָכַר וְזֶה קָנָה,

לְאִם בְּשִׁפְלוּת נִתְכַּנָּה, וּשְׁפָלָה אֵינֶנָּה,[5]

מִשְׁפָּטְךָ נְכוֹנָה, אֵין דִּינָא בְּלֹא דַיָּנָא,[6]

אַךְ קַנֵּא לִנְאֶמֶנָה, מִימִינְךָ נִתְּנָה,

וּבָה כָּתוּב מִי מָנָה,[7] וְעַתָּה כַּצֹּאן נִמְנָה,

צוּרִי עוֹרְרָה נָא, (וְהַשְׁחִיתָה מִכַּנָּהּ,

וְאֶת מַלְכוּתָהּ תַּעֲקֵר,) אֱלֹהִים אֲדֹנָי חֵילִי,[8]

יהוה בְּקֶר תִּשְׁמַע קוֹלִי.

Congregation, then *chazzan*:

חָסִין קָרוֹב לְקוֹרְאָיו,[9] וְשׁוֹמֵעַ אֶל אֶבְיוֹנִים,[10]

דָּן דִּין עָנִי וְאֶבְיוֹן,[11] מִשְׁפַּט רְצוּצִים וּמְעָנִים,

וְעֶלְיוֹנִים וְתַחְתּוֹנִים, בְּיָדְךָ אֲדוֹן הָאֲדוֹנִים,

וּמִשְׁפָּטִי מֵאִתְּךָ יֵצֵא,[12] כַּנֹּגַהּ אֵל אֱמוּנִים,

לֹא אִישׁ אֵל וִיכַזֵּב,[13] אֲשֶׁר יַחֲלִיף עִנְיָנִים,

וְגָזַרְתָּ שֵׁשׁ שָׁנִים,* אֲשֶׁר לַעֲבָדִים נְקוֹנִים.[14]

וְכַמָּה שֵׁשׁ חָלְפוּ לִי, וְלֹא אָהַבְתִּי אֲדוֹנִים,[15]

וְאִם נִמְכַּרְתִּי לְעֵקֶר, וְלֹא אֶגָּאֵל בַּשָּׁנִים,

בִּקְרוֹבִים דִּין עֵקֶר, וְאַתָּה קְרוֹבִי וְגוֹאֲלִי,

יהוה בְּקֶר תִּשְׁמַע קוֹלִי.

---

service of Yom Kippur. The *Kohen Gadol* would enter the Holy of Holies bearing a censer filled with burning coals taken from the Altar in one hand and a container of finely ground incense-spices in the other. Once inside, he would place the incense onto the fiery coals and remain there until the Ark's Cover was completely covered with a cloud of smoke (see *Leviticus* 16:12-13).

Some editions of *Selichos* read וְהַמְכַפֶּרֶת, *and the atoner*, in place of הַכַּפֶּרֶת, but the intent may be the same, for both words come from the root כפר, which can mean *to cover, to atone* or *to redeem* (see *Ibn Ezra* to *Exodus* 25:17). However, some translations for וְהַמְכַפֶּרֶת read *the atoning Altar*.

וְגָזַרְתָּ שֵׁשׁ שָׁנִים — *You decreed six years*. From here to the end of the *selichah*, the *paytan* argues that according to Torah law, our exile should have ended many, many years ago. The law of the עֶבֶד עִבְרִי, *Jewish indentured servant*, states that his servitude lasts for six years. In the seventh year, he must be set free. However, if at the end of his six-year term the servant states, 'I love my master, and my slave-wife and children; I do not want to go free!' he remains in the service of his master until *Yoveil*, the Jubilee Year (see *Exodus* 21:2-6). Thus, the *paytan* pleads, 'Our six years have ended many times over, and we have not declared any love for our oppressive foreign masters. So why are we still enslaved?'

Furthermore, the above laws only apply to a

Congregation, then *chazzan:*

צ O Rock, Your name is 'Jealous God'[1]; why do You seem to sleep?[2]
[For] year after year the vine Your right hand planted[3]
is hard-pressed and tormented,[4]
  sold by one [nation] and bought by another.
We are called 'the humbled nation,'
  although we are not humbled.[5]
Your judgments are proper: no
  verdict without [sin as] just cause;[6]
but [at least] avenge for the faithful [Torah],
  given from Your right hand,
and in it is written,
  'Who has counted [the dust of Yaakov]?'[7]
But now he is counted like sheep [to the slaughter].
My Rock, please awake (and raze [Edom's daughter]
  to her foundation;
uproot her kingdom,) O God, my Lord, my Strength[8] —
                    HASHEM, at dawn hear my voice!

Congregation, then *chazzan:*

חק O Mighty One, Who is close to His callers[9]
  and hearkens to the destitute[10] [when they cry to Him],
judge the case of the poor and the destitute,[11]
  the cause of the broken and abused.
For the upper worlds and the lower are in Your hand,
  Lord of lords;
may my sentence issue from You[12] like [the morningstar] Venus,
  O God of faithfulness.
God is not a man, to deceive[13] or change His mind.
You decreed six years* [of servitude]
  for those bought as slaves,[14]
but many times six years have gone by me,
  though I do not love these masters.[15]
And if [You say that] I have been sold to idolatry,
  so that I am not redeemed by [the passing of six] years,
then the law [passes] to my kin [to redeem me] —
  and You are my Kinsman and Redeemer!
                    HASHEM, at dawn hear my voice!

---

(1) Cf. *Exodus* 34:14. (2) Cf. *Psalms* 44:24; 121:4. (3) Cf. 80:16. (4) Cf. *Isaiah* 53:7.
(5) *Leviticus* 13:21,26. (6) Tractate *Berachos* 5b. (7) *Numbers* 23:10. (8) *Habakkuk* 3:19.
(9) Cf. *Psalms* 145:18. (10) Cf. 69:34. (11) *Jeremiah* 22:16. (12) Cf. *Psalms* 17:2.
(13) *Numbers* 23:19. (14) See *Exodus* 21:2. (15) Cf. 21:5.

Jew sold to another Jew. If a Jew is, Heaven forbid, sold to a non-Jew, there is an obligation upon his relatives to redeem him as soon as possible (see *Leviticus* 25:47-49). But You, God, are our closest relative, You are our Redeemer — so, please, redeem us now.

All, while standing:

אֵל מֶלֶךְ יוֹשֵׁב עַל כִּסֵּא רַחֲמִים מִתְנַהֵג בַּחֲסִידוּת, מוֹחֵל עֲוֹנוֹת עַמּוֹ, מַעֲבִיר רִאשׁוֹן רִאשׁוֹן, מַרְבֶּה מְחִילָה לַחַטָּאִים וּסְלִיחָה לַפּוֹשְׁעִים, עֹשֶׂה צְדָקוֹת עִם כָּל בָּשָׂר וָרוּחַ, לֹא כְרָעָתָם תִּגְמוֹל. אֵל הוֹרֵיתָ לָּנוּ לוֹמַר שְׁלֹשׁ עֶשְׂרֵה, וּזְכוֹר לָנוּ הַיּוֹם בְּרִית שְׁלֹשׁ עֶשְׂרֵה, כְּמוֹ שֶׁהוֹדַעְתָּ לֶעָנָיו מִקֶּדֶם, כְּמוֹ שֶׁכָּתוּב, וַיֵּרֶד יהוה בֶּעָנָן וַיִּתְיַצֵּב עִמּוֹ שָׁם, וַיִּקְרָא בְשֵׁם יהוה.

Congregation, then *chazzan*:

וַיַּעֲבֹר יהוה עַל פָּנָיו וַיִּקְרָא:

Congregation and *chazzan* (the words in bold type are recited aloud and in unison):

יהוה, יהוה, אֵל, רַחוּם, וְחַנּוּן, אֶרֶךְ אַפַּיִם, וְרַב חֶסֶד, וֶאֱמֶת, נֹצֵר חֶסֶד לָאֲלָפִים, נֹשֵׂא עָוֹן, וָפֶשַׁע, וְחַטָּאָה, וְנַקֵּה. וְסָלַחְתָּ לַעֲוֹנֵנוּ וּלְחַטָּאתֵנוּ וּנְחַלְתָּנוּ. סְלַח לָנוּ אָבִינוּ כִּי חָטָאנוּ, מְחַל לָנוּ מַלְכֵּנוּ כִּי פָשָׁעְנוּ. כִּי אַתָּה אֲדֹנָי טוֹב וְסַלָּח, וְרַב חֶסֶד לְכָל קֹרְאֶיךָ.

All:

אַל תִּזְכָּר לָנוּ עֲוֹנוֹת רִאשׁוֹנִים, מַהֵר יְקַדְּמוּנוּ רַחֲמֶיךָ, כִּי דַלּוֹנוּ מְאֹד.[1] חַטֹּאת נְעוּרֵינוּ וּפְשָׁעֵינוּ אַל תִּזְכּוֹר, כְּחַסְדְּךָ זְכָר לָנוּ אַתָּה, לְמַעַן טוּבְךָ יהוה.[2]

זְכוֹר רַחֲמֶיךָ יהוה וַחֲסָדֶיךָ, כִּי מֵעוֹלָם הֵמָּה.[3] זָכְרֵנוּ יהוה בִּרְצוֹן עַמֶּךָ, פָּקְדֵנוּ בִּישׁוּעָתֶךָ.[4] זְכֹר עֲדָתְךָ קָנִיתָ קֶּדֶם, גָּאַלְתָּ שֵׁבֶט נַחֲלָתֶךָ, הַר צִיּוֹן זֶה שָׁכַנְתָּ בּוֹ.[5] זְכֹר יהוה חִבַּת יְרוּשָׁלַיִם, אַהֲבַת צִיּוֹן אַל תִּשְׁכַּח לָנֶצַח.[6] אַתָּה תָקוּם תְּרַחֵם צִיּוֹן, כִּי עֵת לְחֶנְנָהּ כִּי בָא מוֹעֵד.[7] זְכֹר יהוה לִבְנֵי אֱדוֹם אֵת יוֹם יְרוּשָׁלָיִם, הָאֹמְרִים עָרוּ עָרוּ עַד הַיְסוֹד בָּהּ.[8] זְכֹר לְאַבְרָהָם לְיִצְחָק וּלְיִשְׂרָאֵל עֲבָדֶיךָ אֲשֶׁר נִשְׁבַּעְתָּ לָהֶם בָּךְ, וַתְּדַבֵּר אֲלֵהֶם, אַרְבֶּה אֶת זַרְעֲכֶם כְּכוֹכְבֵי הַשָּׁמָיִם, וְכָל הָאָרֶץ הַזֹּאת אֲשֶׁר אָמַרְתִּי אֶתֵּן לְזַרְעֲכֶם, וְנָחֲלוּ לְעוֹלָם.[9] ❖ זְכֹר לַעֲבָדֶיךָ לְאַבְרָהָם לְיִצְחָק וּלְיַעֲקֹב, אַל תֵּפֶן אֶל קְשִׁי הָעָם הַזֶּה וְאֶל רִשְׁעוֹ וְאֶל חַטָּאתוֹ.[10]

(1) *Psalms* 79:8. (2) Cf. 25:7. (3) 25:6. (4) Cf. 106:4. (5) 74:2. (6) This is not a Scriptural verse. (7) *Psalms* 102:14. (8) 137:7. (9) *Exodus* 32:13. (10) *Deuteronomy* 9:27.

All, while standing:

אֵל מֶלֶךְ O God, King Who sits on the throne of mercy; Who acts with kindness, pardons the iniquities of His people, removes [sins] one by one, increasingly grants pardon to careless sinners and forgiveness to rebels, Who deals righteously with every living being — You do not repay them in accord with their evil. Chazzan – O God, You taught us to recite the Thirteen [Attributes of Mercy], so remember for us today the covenant of these Thirteen, as You made known to the humble one in ancient times, as it is written: And HASHEM descended in a cloud and stood with him there, and He called out with the Name HASHEM.

Congregation, then chazzan:

And HASHEM passed before him [Moses] and proclaimed:

Congregation and chazzan (the words in bold type are recited aloud and in unison):

ה' ה' HASHEM, HASHEM, God, Compassionate and Gracious, Slow to anger, and Abundant in Kindness and Truth, Preserver of kindness for thousands [of generations], Forgiver of iniquity, willful sin, and error, and Who cleanses. May You forgive our iniquities and our errors and make us Your heritage. Forgive us, our Father, for we have erred; pardon us, our King, for we have willfully sinned; for You, my Lord, are good and forgiving and abundantly kind to all who call upon You.

All:

אַל תִּזְכָּר Do not recall against us the iniquities of the ancients; speedily — let Your mercy come to meet us for we have fallen very low.[1] Remember not the sins of our youth and our rebellions; may You remember for us [the deeds] worthy of Your kindness, because of Your goodness, HASHEM.[2]

זְכוֹר רַחֲמֶיךָ Remember Your mercies, O HASHEM, and Your kindnesses, for they are from the beginning of the world.[3] Remember us, HASHEM, when You show Your people favor and recall us with Your salvation.[4] Remember Your congregation that You acquired of old, that You redeemed the tribe of Your heritage, and this Mount Zion where You dwelled.[5] Remember, O HASHEM, the affection of Jerusalem, may You never forget the love of Zion.[6] You will arise and show Zion mercy, for it is the time to be gracious to her, for the appointed time will have come.[7] Remember, HASHEM, for the offspring of Edom, the day of Jerusalem — for those who said: 'Destroy! Destroy to its very foundation!'[8] Remember Abraham, Isaac, and Israel, Your servants, to whom You swore by Your Being, saying to them, 'I shall increase your offspring like the stars of the heavens; and this entire land of which I spoke I will give to your offspring and they will inherit it forever.'[9] Chazzan – Remember for Your servants, for Abraham, for Isaac, and for Jacob; ignore the stubbornness of this people, its wickedness and its sinfulness.[10]

Chazzan, then congregation:

אֵל נָא תָשֵׁת עָלֵינוּ חַטָּאת, אֲשֶׁר נוֹאַלְנוּ וַאֲשֶׁר חָטָאנוּ.‎¹

Chazzan, then congregation:

חָטָאנוּ צוּרֵנוּ, סְלַח לָנוּ יוֹצְרֵנוּ.

All:

זְכוֹר לָנוּ בְּרִית אָבוֹת, כַּאֲשֶׁר אָמַרְתָּ: וְזָכַרְתִּי אֶת בְּרִיתִי יַעֲקוֹב,
וְאַף אֶת בְּרִיתִי יִצְחָק, וְאַף אֶת בְּרִיתִי אַבְרָהָם אֶזְכֹּר,
וְהָאָרֶץ אֶזְכֹּר.‎² זְכוֹר לָנוּ בְּרִית רִאשׁוֹנִים, כַּאֲשֶׁר אָמַרְתָּ:
לָהֶם בְּרִית רִאשׁוֹנִים, אֲשֶׁר הוֹצֵאתִי אֹתָם מֵאֶרֶץ מִצְרַיִם לְעֵינֵי
הַגּוֹיִם, לִהְיוֹת לָהֶם לֵאלֹהִים, אֲנִי יְהוָה.‎³ עֲשֵׂה עִמָּנוּ כְּמָה
שֶׁהִבְטַחְתָּנוּ: וְאַף גַּם זֹאת בִּהְיוֹתָם בְּאֶרֶץ אֹיְבֵיהֶם, לֹא מְאַסְתִּים
וְלֹא גְעַלְתִּים לְכַלֹּתָם לְהָפֵר בְּרִיתִי אִתָּם, כִּי אֲנִי יְהוָה אֱלֹהֵיהֶם.‎⁴
הִמָּצֵא לָנוּ בְּבַקָּשָׁתֵנוּ, כְּמָה שֶׁכָּתוּב: וּבִקַּשְׁתֶּם מִשָּׁם אֶת יְהוָה
אֱלֹהֶיךָ וּמָצָאתָ, כִּי תִדְרְשֶׁנּוּ בְּכָל לְבָבְךָ וּבְכָל נַפְשֶׁךָ.‎⁵ מוֹל אֶת
לְבָבֵנוּ לְאַהֲבָה וּלְיִרְאָה אֶת שְׁמֶךָ, כְּמָה שֶׁכָּתוּב: וּמָל יְהוָה אֱלֹהֶיךָ
אֶת לְבָבְךָ וְאֶת לְבַב זַרְעֶךָ, לְאַהֲבָה אֶת יְהוָה אֱלֹהֶיךָ בְּכָל לְבָבְךָ
וּבְכָל נַפְשְׁךָ, לְמַעַן חַיֶּיךָ.‎⁶ זְרוֹק עָלֵינוּ מַיִם טְהוֹרִים וְטַהֲרֵנוּ, כְּמָה
שֶׁכָּתוּב: וְזָרַקְתִּי עֲלֵיכֶם מַיִם טְהוֹרִים וּטְהַרְתֶּם, מִכֹּל טֻמְאוֹתֵיכֶם
וּמִכָּל גִּלּוּלֵיכֶם אֲטַהֵר אֶתְכֶם.‎⁷ מְחֵה פְשָׁעֵינוּ כָּעָב וְכֶעָנָן, כְּמָה
שֶׁכָּתוּב: מָחִיתִי כָעָב פְּשָׁעֶיךָ וְכֶעָנָן חַטֹּאתֶיךָ, שׁוּבָה אֵלַי כִּי
גְאַלְתִּיךָ.‎⁸ מְחֵה פְשָׁעֵינוּ לְמַעֲנָךְ, כַּאֲשֶׁר אָמַרְתָּ: אָנֹכִי אָנֹכִי הוּא
מֹחֶה פְשָׁעֶיךָ לְמַעֲנִי, וְחַטֹּאתֶיךָ לֹא אֶזְכֹּר.‎⁹ הַלְבֵּן חֲטָאֵינוּ כַּשֶּׁלֶג
וְכַצֶּמֶר, כְּמָה שֶׁכָּתוּב: לְכוּ נָא וְנִוָּכְחָה, יֹאמַר יְהוָה, אִם יִהְיוּ
חֲטָאֵיכֶם כַּשָּׁנִים, כַּשֶּׁלֶג יַלְבִּינוּ, אִם יַאְדִּימוּ כַתּוֹלָע, כַּצֶּמֶר יִהְיוּ.‎¹⁰
רַחֵם עָלֵינוּ וְאַל תַּשְׁחִיתֵנוּ, כְּמָה שֶׁכָּתוּב: כִּי אֵל רַחוּם יְהוָה
אֱלֹהֶיךָ, לֹא יַרְפְּךָ וְלֹא יַשְׁחִיתֶךָ וְלֹא יִשְׁכַּח אֶת בְּרִית אֲבוֹתֶיךָ
אֲשֶׁר נִשְׁבַּע לָהֶם.‎¹¹ קַבֵּץ נִדָּחֵנוּ כְּמָה שֶׁכָּתוּב: אִם יִהְיֶה נִדַּחֲךָ בִּקְצֵה
הַשָּׁמָיִם, מִשָּׁם יְקַבֶּצְךָ יְהוָה אֱלֹהֶיךָ וּמִשָּׁם יִקָּחֶךָ.‎¹² הָשֵׁב שְׁבוּתֵנוּ
וְרַחֲמֵנוּ, כְּמָה שֶׁכָּתוּב: וְשָׁב יְהוָה אֱלֹהֶיךָ אֶת שְׁבוּתְךָ וְרִחֲמֶךָ וְשָׁב
וְקִבֶּצְךָ מִכָּל הָעַמִּים אֲשֶׁר הֱפִיצְךָ יְהוָה אֱלֹהֶיךָ שָׁמָּה.‎¹³ ❖ תְּבִיאֵנוּ
אֶל הַר קָדְשֶׁךָ, וְשַׂמְּחֵנוּ בְּבֵית תְּפִלָּתֶךָ, כְּמָה שֶׁכָּתוּב: וַהֲבִיאוֹתִים
אֶל הַר קָדְשִׁי, וְשִׂמַּחְתִּים בְּבֵית תְּפִלָּתִי, עוֹלֹתֵיהֶם וְזִבְחֵיהֶם לְרָצוֹן
עַל מִזְבְּחִי, כִּי בֵיתִי בֵּית תְּפִלָּה יִקָּרֵא לְכָל הָעַמִּים.‎¹⁴

THE ARK IS OPENED.

Chazzan, then congregation:
Please, do not reckon for us a sin,
what we have done foolishly and what we have sinned.[1]

Chazzan, then congregation:
We have erred, our Rock! Forgive us, our Molder!

All:

זְכוֹר Remember for us the covenant of the Patriarchs, as You said: 'And
I will remember My covenant with Jacob, and also My covenant with
Isaac, and also My covenant with Abraham will I remember; and the Land
will I remember.'[2] Remember for us the covenant of the ancestors, as You
said: 'And I will remember for them the covenant of the ancestors whom I
removed from the land of Egypt in the very sight of the nations, to be a God
to them; I am HASHEM.'[3] Do with us as You promised us: 'And despite all that,
when they will be in the land of their enemies, I will not have despised them
nor abhorred them to destroy them, to annul My covenant with them, for I
am HASHEM their God.'[4] Be accessible to us in our quest, as it is written: From
there you will seek HASHEM, your God, and you will find, when you search
for Him with all your heart and with all your soul.[5] Expose our hearts to love
Your Name, as it is written: HASHEM, your God, will expose your heart and
the heart of your offspring, to love HASHEM, your God, with all your heart and
with all your soul, that you may live.[6] Pour pure water upon us and purify
us, as it is written: I shall pour pure water upon you and purify you, of all
your contaminations and of all your abominations I will purify you.[7] Wipe
away our willful sins like a cloud and like a mist, as it is written: I have wiped
away your willful sins like a cloud and your errors like a mist — repent to Me,
for I have redeemed you![8] Wipe away our willful sins for Your sake, as You
said: 'I, only I, am the One Who wipes away your willful sins for My sake,
and I shall not recall your errors.'[9] Whiten our errors like snow and like [pure
white]wool, as it is written: 'Come now, let us reason together,' says HASHEM,
'though your errors will be like scarlet, they will become white as snow;
though they will be red as crimson, they will become like [white]wool.'[10] Have
mercy on us and do not destroy us, as it is written: For a merciful God is
HASHEM, your God; He will not surrender you nor destroy you, and He will
not forget the covenant with your forefathers, which He swore to them.[11]
Gather in our dispersed ones, as it is written: If your dispersed were to be at
the ends of heaven, from there HASHEM, your God, will gather you in and from
there He will take you.[12] Bring back our captivity and have mercy on us, as
it is written: HASHEM, your God, will bring back your captivity and have
mercy on you, and He will again gather you in from all the peoples where
HASHEM, your God, has scattered you.[13] Chazzan — Bring us to Your holy
mountain and gladden us in Your house of prayer, as it is written: And I will
bring them to My holy mountain, and I will gladden them in My house of
prayer, their elevation-offerings and their feast offering will find favor on My
Altar, for My House will be called a house of prayer, for all peoples.[14]

THE ARK IS OPENED.

---

(1) *Numbers* 12:11. (2) *Leviticus* 26:42. (3) 26:45. (4) 26:44. (5) *Deuteronomy* 4:29.
(6) 30:6. (7) *Ezekiel* 36:25. (8) *Isaiah* 44:22. (9) 43:25. (10) 1:18.
(11) *Deuteronomy* 4:31. (12) 30:4. (13) 30:3. (14) *Isaiah* 56:7.

The first four verses of the following prayer are recited responsively; chazzan, then congregation:

שְׁמַע קוֹלֵנוּ יהוה אֱלֹהֵינוּ, חוּס וְרַחֵם עָלֵינוּ,
וְקַבֵּל בְּרַחֲמִים וּבְרָצוֹן אֶת תְּפִלָּתֵנוּ.¹

הֲשִׁיבֵנוּ יהוה אֵלֶיךָ וְנָשׁוּבָה, חַדֵּשׁ יָמֵינוּ כְּקֶדֶם.²

אַל תַּשְׁלִיכֵנוּ מִלְּפָנֶיךָ, וְרוּחַ קָדְשְׁךָ אַל תִּקַּח מִמֶּנּוּ.³

אַל תַּשְׁלִיכֵנוּ לְעֵת זִקְנָה, כִּכְלוֹת כֹּחֵנוּ אַל תַּעַזְבֵנוּ.⁴

אַל תַּעַזְבֵנוּ יהוה, אֱלֹהֵינוּ אַל תִּרְחַק מִמֶּנּוּ.⁵

עֲשֵׂה עִמָּנוּ אוֹת לְטוֹבָה, וְיִרְאוּ שׂוֹנְאֵינוּ וְיֵבֹשׁוּ,
כִּי אַתָּה יהוה עֲזַרְתָּנוּ וְנִחַמְתָּנוּ.⁶

אֲמָרֵינוּ הַאֲזִינָה יהוה, בִּינָה הֲגִיגֵנוּ.⁷

יִהְיוּ לְרָצוֹן אִמְרֵי פִינוּ וְהֶגְיוֹן לִבֵּנוּ לְפָנֶיךָ, יהוה צוּרֵנוּ וְגוֹאֲלֵנוּ.⁸

כִּי לְךָ יהוה הוֹחָלְנוּ, אַתָּה תַעֲנֶה אֲדֹנָי אֱלֹהֵינוּ.⁹

THE ARK IS CLOSED.

וידוי

During the recitation of the (וידוי) stand with head and body slightly bowed,
in submissive contrition.

אֱלֹהֵינוּ וֵאלֹהֵי אֲבוֹתֵינוּ, תָּבֹא לְפָנֶיךָ תְּפִלָּתֵנוּ,¹⁰ וְאַל תִּתְעַלַּם
מִתְּחִנָּתֵנוּ,¹¹ שֶׁאֵין אָנוּ עַזֵּי פָנִים וּקְשֵׁי עֹרֶף, לוֹמַר
לְפָנֶיךָ יהוה אֱלֹהֵינוּ וֵאלֹהֵי אֲבוֹתֵינוּ, צַדִּיקִים אֲנַחְנוּ וְלֹא חָטָאנוּ,
אֲבָל אֲנַחְנוּ וַאֲבוֹתֵינוּ חָטָאנוּ.¹²

Strike the left side of the chest with the right fist
while reciting each of the sins in the following confession litany.

אָשַׁמְנוּ, בָּגַדְנוּ, גָּזַלְנוּ, דִּבַּרְנוּ דֹפִי. הֶעֱוִינוּ, וְהִרְשַׁעְנוּ, זַדְנוּ,
חָמַסְנוּ, טָפַלְנוּ שֶׁקֶר. יָעַצְנוּ רָע, כִּזַּבְנוּ, לַצְנוּ, מָרַדְנוּ,
נִאַצְנוּ, סָרַרְנוּ, עָוִינוּ, פָּשַׁעְנוּ, צָרַרְנוּ, קִשִּׁינוּ עֹרֶף. רָשַׁעְנוּ, שִׁחַתְנוּ,
תִּעַבְנוּ, תָּעִינוּ, תִּעְתָּעְנוּ.

סַרְנוּ מִמִּצְוֺתֶיךָ וּמִמִּשְׁפָּטֶיךָ הַטּוֹבִים וְלֹא שָׁוָה לָנוּ.¹³ וְאַתָּה צַדִּיק
עַל כָּל הַבָּא עָלֵינוּ, כִּי אֱמֶת עָשִׂיתָ וַאֲנַחְנוּ הִרְשָׁעְנוּ.¹⁴

אָשַׁמְנוּ מִכָּל עָם, בֹּשְׁנוּ מִכָּל דּוֹר, גָּלָה מִמֶּנּוּ מָשׂוֹשׂ, דָּוָה לִבֵּנוּ
בַּחֲטָאֵינוּ, הֻחְבַּל אִוּוּיֵנוּ, וְנִפְרַע פְּאֵרֵנוּ, זְבוּל בֵּית מִקְדָּשֵׁנוּ חָרַב
בַּעֲוֺנֵינוּ, טִירָתֵנוּ הָיְתָה לְשַׁמָּה, יֹפִי אַדְמָתֵנוּ לְזָרִים, כֹּחֵנוּ לְנָכְרִים.
וַעֲדַיִן לֹא שַׁבְנוּ מִטָּעוּתֵנוּ וְהֵיךְ נָעִיז פָּנֵינוּ וְנַקְשֶׁה עָרְפֵּנוּ, לוֹמַר
לְפָנֶיךָ יהוה אֱלֹהֵינוּ וֵאלֹהֵי אֲבוֹתֵינוּ, צַדִּיקִים אֲנַחְנוּ וְלֹא חָטָאנוּ,
אֲבָל אֲנַחְנוּ וַאֲבוֹתֵינוּ חָטָאנוּ.

The first four verses of the following prayer are recited responsively; chazzan, then congregation:

שְׁמַע קוֹלֵנוּ *Hear our voice, HASHEM, our God, pity and be compassionate to us, and accept — with compassion and favor — our prayer.[1]*
Bring us back to You, HASHEM, and we shall return, renew our days as of old.[2]
Do not cast us away from Yourself,
and do not remove Your holy spirit from us.[3]
Do not cast us away in old age,
when our strength gives out do not forsake us.[4]
Do not forsake us, HASHEM, our God, be not distant from us.[5]
Display for us a sign for good, so that our enemies may see it
and be ashamed, for You, HASHEM, will have helped and consoled us.[6]
To our sayings give ear, HASHEM, perceive our thoughts.[7]
May the expressions of our mouth and the thoughts of our heart
find favor before You, HASHEM, our Rock and our Redeemer.[8]
Because for You, HASHEM, we waited, You will answer, my Lord, our God.[9]

THE ARK IS CLOSED.

During the recitation of the וִדּוּי, Confession, stand with head and body slightly bowed,
in submissive contrition.

אֱלֹהֵינוּ *Our God and the God of our forefathers, may our prayer come before You.[10] Do not ignore our supplication,[11] for we are not so* brazen and obstinate as to say before You, HASHEM, our God and the God of our forefathers, that we are righteous and have not sinned, for in truth, we and our forefathers have sinned.[12]

Strike the left side of the chest with the right fist while reciting
each of the sins in the following confession litany.

אָשַׁמְנוּ *We have become guilty;* [ב] *we have betrayed;* [ג] *we have robbed;* [ד] *we have spoken slander;* [ה] *we have caused perversion;* [ו] *we have caused wickedness;* [ז] *we have sinned willfully;* [ח] *we have extorted;* [ט] *we have accused falsely;* [י] *we have given evil counsel;* [כ] *we have been deceitful;* [ל] *we have scorned;* [מ] *we have rebelled;* [נ] *we have provoked;* [ס] *we have turned away;* [ע] *we have been perverse;* [פ] *we have acted wantonly;* [צ] *we have persecuted;* [ק] *we have been obstinate;* [ר] *we have been wicked;* [ש] *we have corrupted;* [ת] *we have been abominable; we have strayed; You have let us go astray.*

סַרְנוּ *We have turned away from Your commandments and from Your good laws but to no avail.[13] Yet You are righteous in all that has come upon* us, for You have acted truthfully while we have caused wickedness.[14]

[א] *We have become the guiltiest of people.* [ב] *We have become the most degraded of all generations.* [ג] *Joy has departed from us.* [ד] *Our heart has been saddened by our sins.* [ה] *Our desirous treasure has been ruined,* [ו] *and our splendor dashed,* [ז] *for our Holy Temple edifice* [ח] *has been destroyed for our iniquities.* [ט] *Our Palace has become desolate.* [י] *[Jerusalem,] the beauty of our Land is given over to aliens,* [כ] *our power to strangers.*

But still we have not returned from our waywardness. So how can we be so brazen and obstinate as to say before You, HASHEM, our God and the God of our forefathers, that we are righteous and have not sinned, for in truth, both we and our fathers have sinned.

(1) Weekday *Shemoneh Esrei.* (2) *Lamentations* 5:21. (3) Cf. *Psalms* 51:13. (4) Cf. 71:9.
(5) Cf. 38:22. (6) Cf. 86:17. (7) Cf. 5:2. (8) Cf. 19:15. (9) Cf. 38:16. (10) Cf. 88:3.
(11) Cf. 55:2. (12) Cf. 106:6. (13) Cf. *Job* 33:27. (14) *Nehemiah* 9:33.

Strike the left side of the chest with the right fist while reciting
each of the sins in the following confession litany.

אָשַׁמְנוּ, בָּגַדְנוּ, גָּזַלְנוּ, דִּבַּרְנוּ דְפִי. הֶעֱוִינוּ, וְהִרְשַׁעְנוּ, זַדְנוּ,
חָמַסְנוּ, טָפַלְנוּ שֶׁקֶר. יָעַצְנוּ רָע, כִּזַּבְנוּ, לַצְנוּ, מָרַדְנוּ,
נִאַצְנוּ, סָרַרְנוּ, עָוִינוּ, פָּשַׁעְנוּ, צָרַרְנוּ, קִשִּׁינוּ עֹרֶף. רָשַׁעְנוּ,
שִׁחַתְנוּ, תִּעַבְנוּ, תָּעִינוּ, תִּעְתָּעְנוּ.

סַרְנוּ מִמִּצְוֹתֶיךָ וּמִמִּשְׁפָּטֶיךָ הַטּוֹבִים וְלֹא שָׁוָה לָנוּ. וְאַתָּה צַדִּיק
עַל כָּל הַבָּא עָלֵינוּ, כִּי אֱמֶת עָשִׂיתָ וַאֲנַחְנוּ הִרְשָׁעְנוּ.

לְעֵינֵנוּ עָשְׁקוּ עֲמָלֵנוּ, מְמֻשָּׁךְ וּמְמוֹרָט מִמֶּנּוּ, נָתְנוּ עֻלָּם עָלֵינוּ,
סָבַלְנוּ עַל שִׁכְמֵנוּ, עֲבָדִים מָשְׁלוּ בָנוּ, פֹּרֵק אֵין מִיָּדָם, צָרוֹת רַבּוֹת
סְבָבוּנוּ, קְרָאנוּךָ יהוה אֱלֹהֵינוּ, רָחַקְתָּ מִמֶּנּוּ בַּעֲוֹנֵינוּ, שַׁבְנוּ
מֵאַחֲרֶיךָ, תָּעִינוּ וְאָבָדְנוּ.

וַעֲדַיִן לֹא שַׁבְנוּ מִטָּעוּתֵנוּ וְהֵיךְ נָעִיז פָּנֵינוּ וְנַקְשֶׁה עָרְפֵּנוּ, לוֹמַר
לְפָנֶיךָ יהוה אֱלֹהֵינוּ וֵאלֹהֵי אֲבוֹתֵינוּ, צַדִּיקִים אֲנַחְנוּ וְלֹא חָטָאנוּ,
אֲבָל אֲנַחְנוּ וַאֲבוֹתֵינוּ חָטָאנוּ.

Strike the left side of the chest with the right fist while reciting
each of the sins in the following confession litany.

אָשַׁמְנוּ, בָּגַדְנוּ, גָּזַלְנוּ, דִּבַּרְנוּ דְפִי. הֶעֱוִינוּ, וְהִרְשַׁעְנוּ, זַדְנוּ,
חָמַסְנוּ, טָפַלְנוּ שֶׁקֶר. יָעַצְנוּ רָע, כִּזַּבְנוּ, לַצְנוּ, מָרַדְנוּ,
נִאַצְנוּ, סָרַרְנוּ, עָוִינוּ, פָּשַׁעְנוּ, צָרַרְנוּ, קִשִּׁינוּ עֹרֶף. רָשַׁעְנוּ,
שִׁחַתְנוּ, תִּעַבְנוּ, תָּעִינוּ, תִּעְתָּעְנוּ.

סַרְנוּ מִמִּצְוֹתֶיךָ וּמִמִּשְׁפָּטֶיךָ הַטּוֹבִים וְלֹא שָׁוָה לָנוּ. וְאַתָּה צַדִּיק
עַל כָּל הַבָּא עָלֵינוּ, כִּי אֱמֶת עָשִׂיתָ וַאֲנַחְנוּ הִרְשָׁעְנוּ.

הִרְשַׁעְנוּ וּפָשַׁעְנוּ, לָכֵן לֹא נוֹשָׁעְנוּ. וְתֵן בְּלִבֵּנוּ לַעֲזוֹב דֶּרֶךְ
רֶשַׁע, וְחִישׁ לָנוּ יֶשַׁע, כַּכָּתוּב עַל יַד נְבִיאֶךָ: יַעֲזֹב
רָשָׁע דַּרְכּוֹ, וְאִישׁ אָוֶן מַחְשְׁבֹתָיו, וְיָשֹׁב אֶל יהוה וִירַחֲמֵהוּ, וְאֶל
אֱלֹהֵינוּ כִּי יַרְבֶּה לִסְלוֹחַ.[1]

מְשִׁיחַ צִדְקֶךָ אָמַר לְפָנֶיךָ: שְׁגִיאוֹת מִי יָבִין מִנִּסְתָּרוֹת נַקֵּנִי.[2]
נַקֵּנוּ יהוה אֱלֹהֵינוּ מִכָּל פְּשָׁעֵינוּ, וְטַהֲרֵנוּ מִכָּל

---

(1) *Isaiah* 55:7. (2) *Psalms* 19:13.

Strike the left side of the chest with the right fist while reciting
each of the sins in the following confession litany:

אָשַׁמְנוּ *We have become guilty;* [ב] *we have betrayed;* [ג] *we have robbed;*
[ד] *we have spoken slander;* [ה] *we have caused perversion;* [ו] *we*
have caused wickedness; [ז] *we have sinned willfully;* [ח] *we have extorted;*
[ט] *we have accused falsely;* [י] *we have given evil counsel;* [כ] *we have been*
deceitful; [ל] *we have scorned;* [מ] *we have rebelled;* [נ] *we have provoked;*
[ס] *we have turned away;* [ע] *we have been perverse;* [פ] *we have acted*
wantonly; [צ] *we have persecuted;* [ק] *we have been obstinate;* [ר] *we have*
been wicked; [ש] *we have corrupted;* [ת] *we have been abominable; we have*
strayed; You have let us go astray.

סַרְנוּ *We have turned away from Your commandments and from Your*
good laws but to no avail. Yet You are righteous in all that has come
upon us, for You have acted truthfully while we have caused wickedness.

[ל] *[The benefit of] our labor has been stolen,* [מ] *pulled away and cut off*
from us. [נ] *They have placed their yoke upon us,* [ס] *our burdens upon our*
shoulders. [ע] *Slaves have ruled over us,* [פ] *there is no redemption from their*
hand. [צ] *Abundant troubles have surrounded us,* [ק] *we called upon You,*
HASHEM, *our God,* [ר] *but You have distanced us for our iniquities.* [ש] *We*
have turned away from following after You; [ת] *we have strayed; we have*
become lost.

But still we have not returned from our waywardness. So how can we be
so brazen and obstinate as to say before You, HASHEM, *our God and the God*
of our forefathers, that we are righteous and have not sinned, for in truth, both
we and our fathers have sinned.

Strike the left side of the chest with the right fist while reciting
each of the sins in the following confession litany:

אָשַׁמְנוּ *We have become guilty;* [ב] *we have betrayed;* [ג] *we have robbed;*
[ד] *we have spoken slander;* [ה] *we have caused perversion;* [ו] *we*
have caused wickedness; [ז] *we have sinned willfully;* [ח] *we have extorted;*
[ט] *we have accused falsely;* [י] *we have given evil counsel;* [כ] *we have been*
deceitful; [ל] *we have scorned;* [מ] *we have rebelled;* [נ] *we have provoked;*
[ס] *we have turned away;* [ע] *we have been perverse;* [פ] *we have acted*
wantonly; [צ] *we have persecuted;* [ק] *we have been obstinate;* [ר] *we have*
been wicked; [ש] *we have corrupted;* [ת] *we have been abominable; we have*
strayed; You have let us go astray.

סַרְנוּ *We have turned away from Your commandments and from Your*
good laws but to no avail. Yet You are righteous in all that has come
upon us, for You have acted truthfully while we have caused wickedness.

הִרְשַׁעְנוּ *We have acted wickedly and have sinned willfully, therefore we*
have not been saved. Inspire our heart to abandon the path of evil
and hasten salvation for us, as it is written by Your prophet: May the wicked
one abandon his way and the vicious man his thoughts; may he return to
HASHEM *and He will show him mercy, and to our God, for He is abundantly*
forgiving.[1]

מְשִׁיחַ צִדְקֶךָ *Your righteous anointed [David] said before You: 'Who can*
discern mistakes? From unperceived faults cleanse me.'[2]
Cleanse us, HASHEM, *our God, of all our willful sins and purify us, of all our*

טֻמְאוֹתֵינוּ, וּזְרוֹק עָלֵינוּ מַיִם טְהוֹרִים וְטַהֲרֵנוּ, כַּכָּתוּב עַל יַד
נְבִיאֶךָ: וְזָרַקְתִּי עֲלֵיכֶם מַיִם טְהוֹרִים וּטְהַרְתֶּם, מִכֹּל טֻמְאוֹתֵיכֶם
וּמִכָּל גִּלּוּלֵיכֶם אֲטַהֵר אֶתְכֶם.[1]

מִיכָה עַבְדְּךָ אָמַר לְפָנֶיךָ: מִי אֵל כָּמוֹךָ נֹשֵׂא עָוֹן וְעֹבֵר עַל
פֶּשַׁע לִשְׁאֵרִית נַחֲלָתוֹ, לֹא הֶחֱזִיק לָעַד אַפּוֹ, כִּי
חָפֵץ חֶסֶד הוּא, יָשׁוּב יְרַחֲמֵנוּ, יִכְבֹּשׁ עֲוֹנֹתֵינוּ, וְתַשְׁלִיךְ בִּמְצֻלוֹת
יָם כָּל חַטֹּאתָם.[2] (וְכָל חַטֹּאת עַמְּךָ בֵּית יִשְׂרָאֵל תַּשְׁלִיךְ בִּמְקוֹם
אֲשֶׁר לֹא יִזָּכְרוּ, וְלֹא יִפָּקְדוּ, וְלֹא יַעֲלוּ עַל לֵב לְעוֹלָם.) תִּתֵּן אֱמֶת
לְיַעֲקֹב חֶסֶד לְאַבְרָהָם אֲשֶׁר נִשְׁבַּעְתָּ לַאֲבוֹתֵינוּ מִימֵי קֶדֶם.[3]

דָּנִיֵּאל אִישׁ חֲמוּדוֹת שִׁוַּע לְפָנֶיךָ: הַטֵּה אֱלֹהַי אָזְנְךָ וּשְׁמָע,
פְּקַח עֵינֶיךָ וּרְאֵה שֹׁמְמֹתֵינוּ וְהָעִיר אֲשֶׁר נִקְרָא שִׁמְךָ
עָלֶיהָ, כִּי לֹא עַל צִדְקֹתֵינוּ אֲנַחְנוּ מַפִּילִים תַּחֲנוּנֵינוּ לְפָנֶיךָ, כִּי עַל
רַחֲמֶיךָ הָרַבִּים. אֲדֹנָי שְׁמָעָה, אֲדֹנָי סְלָחָה, אֲדֹנָי הַקְשִׁיבָה, וַעֲשֵׂה
אַל תְּאַחַר, לְמַעַנְךָ אֱלֹהַי, כִּי שִׁמְךָ נִקְרָא עַל עִירְךָ וְעַל עַמֶּךָ.[4]

עֶזְרָא הַסּוֹפֵר אָמַר לְפָנֶיךָ: אֱלֹהַי, בֹּשְׁתִּי וְנִכְלַמְתִּי לְהָרִים,
אֱלֹהַי, פָּנַי אֵלֶיךָ, כִּי עֲוֹנֹתֵינוּ רָבוּ לְמַעְלָה
רֹאשׁ, וְאַשְׁמָתֵנוּ גָדְלָה עַד לַשָּׁמָיִם.[5] וְאַתָּה[6] אֱלוֹהַּ סְלִיחוֹת, חַנּוּן
וְרַחוּם, אֶרֶךְ אַפַּיִם וְרַב חֶסֶד, וְלֹא עֲזַבְתָּנוּ.[7]

אַל תַּעַזְבֵנוּ אָבִינוּ וְאַל תִּטְּשֵׁנוּ בּוֹרְאֵנוּ, וְאַל תַּזְנִיחֵנוּ יוֹצְרֵנוּ,
וְאַל תַּעַשׂ עִמָּנוּ כָּלָה כְּחַטֹּאתֵינוּ. וְקַיֶּם לָנוּ יהוה
אֱלֹהֵינוּ, אֶת הַדָּבָר שֶׁהִבְטַחְתָּנוּ בְּקַבָּלָה עַל יְדֵי יִרְמְיָהוּ חוֹזָךְ,
כָּאָמוּר: בַּיָּמִים הָהֵם וּבָעֵת הַהִיא, נְאֻם יהוה, יְבֻקַּשׁ אֶת עֲוֹן
יִשְׂרָאֵל וְאֵינֶנּוּ וְאֶת חַטֹּאת יְהוּדָה וְלֹא תִמָּצֶאנָה, כִּי אֶסְלַח
לַאֲשֶׁר אַשְׁאִיר.[8] עַמְּךָ וְנַחֲלָתְךָ רְעֵבֵי טוּבְךָ, צְמֵאֵי חַסְדֶּךָ, תְּאֵבֵי
יִשְׁעֶךָ, יַכִּירוּ וְיֵדְעוּ כִּי לַיהוה אֱלֹהֵינוּ הָרַחֲמִים וְהַסְּלִיחוֹת.

אֵל רַחוּם שְׁמֶךָ, אֵל חַנּוּן שְׁמֶךָ, בָּנוּ נִקְרָא שְׁמֶךָ. יהוה עֲשֵׂה
לְמַעַן שְׁמֶךָ. עֲשֵׂה לְמַעַן אֲמִתֶּךָ, עֲשֵׂה לְמַעַן
בְּרִיתֶךָ, עֲשֵׂה לְמַעַן גָּדְלְךָ וְתִפְאַרְתֶּךָ, עֲשֵׂה לְמַעַן דָּתֶךָ, עֲשֵׂה
לְמַעַן הוֹדֶךָ, עֲשֵׂה לְמַעַן וִעוּדֶךָ, עֲשֵׂה לְמַעַן זִכְרֶךָ, עֲשֵׂה לְמַעַן
חַסְדֶּךָ, עֲשֵׂה לְמַעַן טוּבֶךָ, עֲשֵׂה לְמַעַן יִחוּדֶךָ, עֲשֵׂה לְמַעַן
כְּבוֹדֶךָ, עֲשֵׂה לְמַעַן לִמּוּדֶךָ, עֲשֵׂה לְמַעַן מַלְכוּתֶךָ, עֲשֵׂה לְמַעַן

contaminations. Sprinkle upon us pure water and purify us, as it is written by Your prophet: I shall sprinkle pure water upon you and purify you, of all your contaminations and of all your abominations I will purify you.'[1]

מִיכָה עַבְדְּךָ *Micah, Your servant, said before You: 'Who, O God, is like You, Who pardons iniquity and overlooks transgression for the remnant of His heritage? Who has not retained His wrath eternally, for He desires kindness! He will again be merciful to us; He will suppress our iniquities and cast into the depths of the sea all their sins.[2] (And all the sins of Your nation the Family of Israel, may You cast away to a place where they will neither be remembered, considered, nor brought to mind — ever.) Grant truth to Jacob, kindness to Abraham, as You swore to our forefathers from ancient times.'[3]*

דָּנִיֵּאל *Daniel, the greatly beloved man, cried out before You: 'Incline, my God, Your ear, and listen, open Your eyes and see our desolation and that of the city upon which Your Name is proclaimed, for not because of our righteousness do we cast down our supplications before You, rather because of Your abundant compassion. O my Lord, heed; O my Lord, forgive; O my Lord, be attentive and act, do not delay; for Your sake, my God, for Your Name is proclaimed upon Your city and Your people.'[4]*

עֶזְרָא הַסּוֹפֵר *Ezra the Scribe said before You: 'My God, I am embarrassed and ashamed to lift my face to You, my God — for our iniquities have multiplied above our heads, and our sins extend unto heaven.[5] You are[6] the God of forgiveness, compassionate and merciful, slow to anger, and abundant in kindness; and You have not forsaken us.'[7]*

אַל תַּעַזְבֵנוּ *Do not forsake us, our Father; do not cast us off, our Creator; do not abandon us, our Molder; and do not bring about our destruction, as our sins merit. Affirm for us, HASHEM, our God, the promise You made in the tradition through Jeremiah, Your seer, as it is said: 'In those days and at that time' — the words of HASHEM — 'the iniquity of Israel will be sought but there will be none, and the errors of Judah, but they will not be found, for I will have forgiven those whom I leave as a remnant.'[8] Your people and Your heritage, who hunger for Your goodness, who thirst for Your kindness, who long for Your salvation — may they recognize and know that to HASHEM, our God, belong mercy and forgiveness.*

אֵל רַחוּם *'Merciful God' is Your Name, 'Gracious God' is Your Name, Your Name is called upon us — O HASHEM, act for Your Name's sake. Act for the sake of [א] Your truth; act for the sake of [ב] Your covenant; act for the sake of [ג] Your greatness and Your splendor; act for the sake of [ד] Your law; act for the sake of [ה] Your glory; act for the sake of [ו] Your Meeting House; act for the sake of [ז] Your remembrance; act for the sake of [ח] Your kindness; act for the sake of [ט] Your goodness; act for the sake of [י] Your Oneness; act for the sake of [כ] Your honor; act for the sake of [ל] Your teaching; act for the sake of [מ] Your kingship; act for the sake of*

---

(1) *Ezekiel* 36:25. (2) *Micah* 7:18-19. (3) 7:20. (4) *Daniel* 9:18-19. (5) *Ezra* 9:6. (6) Some editions of *Selichos* insert the word אֱלֹהֵינוּ, *our God*, at this point. (7) Cf. *Nehemiah* 9:17. (8) *Jeremiah* 50:20.

נִצְחֶךָ, עֲשֵׂה לְמַעַן סוֹדֶךָ, עֲשֵׂה לְמַעַן עֻזֶּךָ, עֲשֵׂה לְמַעַן פְּאֵרֶךָ, עֲשֵׂה לְמַעַן צִדְקָתֶךָ, עֲשֵׂה לְמַעַן קְדֻשָּׁתֶךָ, עֲשֵׂה לְמַעַן רַחֲמֶיךָ הָרַבִּים, עֲשֵׂה לְמַעַן שְׁכִינָתֶךָ, עֲשֵׂה לְמַעַן תְּהִלָּתֶךָ, עֲשֵׂה לְמַעַן אוֹהֲבֶיךָ שׁוֹכְנֵי עָפָר, עֲשֵׂה לְמַעַן אַבְרָהָם יִצְחָק וְיַעֲקֹב, עֲשֵׂה לְמַעַן מֹשֶׁה וְאַהֲרֹן, עֲשֵׂה לְמַעַן דָּוִד וּשְׁלֹמֹה, עֲשֵׂה לְמַעַן יְרוּשָׁלַיִם עִיר קָדְשֶׁךָ, עֲשֵׂה לְמַעַן צִיּוֹן מִשְׁכַּן כְּבוֹדֶךָ, עֲשֵׂה לְמַעַן שִׁמְמוֹת הֵיכָלֶךָ, עֲשֵׂה לְמַעַן הֲרִיסוּת מִזְבְּחֶךָ, עֲשֵׂה לְמַעַן הֲרוּגִים עַל שֵׁם קָדְשֶׁךָ, עֲשֵׂה לְמַעַן טְבוּחִים עַל יִחוּדֶךָ, עֲשֵׂה לְמַעַן בָּאֵי בָאֵשׁ וּבַמַּיִם עַל קִדּוּשׁ שְׁמֶךָ, עֲשֵׂה לְמַעַן יוֹנְקֵי שָׁדַיִם שֶׁלֹּא חָטָאוּ, עֲשֵׂה לְמַעַן גְּמוּלֵי חָלָב שֶׁלֹּא פָשָׁעוּ, עֲשֵׂה לְמַעַן תִּינוֹקוֹת שֶׁל בֵּית רַבָּן, עֲשֵׂה לְמַעַנְךָ אִם לֹא לְמַעֲנֵנוּ, עֲשֵׂה לְמַעַנְךָ וְהוֹשִׁיעֵנוּ.

עֲנֵנוּ יהוה עֲנֵנוּ, עֲנֵנוּ אֱלֹהֵינוּ עֲנֵנוּ, עֲנֵנוּ אָבִינוּ עֲנֵנוּ, עֲנֵנוּ בּוֹרְאֵנוּ עֲנֵנוּ, עֲנֵנוּ גּוֹאֲלֵנוּ עֲנֵנוּ, עֲנֵנוּ דוֹרְשֵׁנוּ עֲנֵנוּ, עֲנֵנוּ הָאֵל הַנֶּאֱמָן עֲנֵנוּ, עֲנֵנוּ וָתִיק וְחָסִיד עֲנֵנוּ, עֲנֵנוּ זַךְ וְיָשָׁר עֲנֵנוּ, עֲנֵנוּ חַי וְקַיָּם עֲנֵנוּ, עֲנֵנוּ טוֹב וּמֵטִיב עֲנֵנוּ, עֲנֵנוּ יוֹדֵעַ יֵצֶר עֲנֵנוּ, עֲנֵנוּ כּוֹבֵשׁ כְּעָסִים עֲנֵנוּ, עֲנֵנוּ לוֹבֵשׁ צְדָקוֹת עֲנֵנוּ, עֲנֵנוּ מֶלֶךְ מַלְכֵי הַמְּלָכִים עֲנֵנוּ, עֲנֵנוּ נוֹרָא וְנִשְׂגָּב עֲנֵנוּ, עֲנֵנוּ סוֹלֵחַ וּמוֹחֵל עֲנֵנוּ, עֲנֵנוּ עוֹנֶה בְּעֵת צָרָה עֲנֵנוּ, עֲנֵנוּ פּוֹדֶה וּמַצִּיל עֲנֵנוּ, עֲנֵנוּ צַדִּיק וְיָשָׁר עֲנֵנוּ, עֲנֵנוּ קָרוֹב לְקוֹרְאָיו עֲנֵנוּ, עֲנֵנוּ רַחוּם וְחַנּוּן עֲנֵנוּ, עֲנֵנוּ שׁוֹמֵעַ אֶל אֶבְיוֹנִים עֲנֵנוּ, עֲנֵנוּ תּוֹמֵךְ תְּמִימִים עֲנֵנוּ, עֲנֵנוּ אֱלֹהֵי אֲבוֹתֵינוּ עֲנֵנוּ, עֲנֵנוּ אֱלֹהֵי אַבְרָהָם עֲנֵנוּ, עֲנֵנוּ פַּחַד יִצְחָק עֲנֵנוּ, עֲנֵנוּ אֲבִיר יַעֲקֹב עֲנֵנוּ, עֲנֵנוּ עֶזְרַת הַשְּׁבָטִים עֲנֵנוּ, עֲנֵנוּ מִשְׂגָּב אִמָּהוֹת עֲנֵנוּ, עֲנֵנוּ קָשֶׁה לִכְעוֹס עֲנֵנוּ, עֲנֵנוּ רַךְ לִרְצוֹת עֲנֵנוּ, עֲנֵנוּ עוֹנֶה בְּעֵת רָצוֹן עֲנֵנוּ, עֲנֵנוּ אֲבִי יְתוֹמִים עֲנֵנוּ, עֲנֵנוּ דַּיַּן אַלְמָנוֹת עֲנֵנוּ.

מִי שֶׁעָנָה לְאַבְרָהָם אָבִינוּ בְּהַר הַמּוֹרִיָּה,	הוּא יַעֲנֵנוּ.
מִי שֶׁעָנָה לְיִצְחָק בְּנוֹ כְּשֶׁנֶּעֱקַד עַל גַּבֵּי הַמִּזְבֵּחַ,	הוּא יַעֲנֵנוּ.
מִי שֶׁעָנָה לְיַעֲקֹב בְּבֵית אֵל,	הוּא יַעֲנֵנוּ.
מִי שֶׁעָנָה לְיוֹסֵף בְּבֵית הָאֲסוּרִים,	הוּא יַעֲנֵנוּ.
מִי שֶׁעָנָה לַאֲבוֹתֵינוּ עַל יַם סוּף,	הוּא יַעֲנֵנוּ.
מִי שֶׁעָנָה לְמֹשֶׁה בְּחוֹרֵב,	הוּא יַעֲנֵנוּ.
מִי שֶׁעָנָה לְאַהֲרֹן בַּמַּחְתָּה,	הוּא יַעֲנֵנוּ.

[**ג**] Your eternality; act for the sake of [**ס**] Your counsel; act for the sake of
[**ע**] Your power; act for the sake of [**פ**] Your beauty; act for the sake of [**צ**] Your
righteousness; act for the sake of [**ק**] Your sanctity; act for the sake of [**ר**] Your
abundant mercy; act for the sake of [**ש**] Your Presence, act for the sake of
[**ת**] Your praise; act for the sake of Your beloved ones who rest in the dust; act
for the sake of Abraham, Isaac, and Jacob; act for the sake of Moses and
Aaron; act for the sake of David and Solomon; act for the sake of Jerusalem,
Your holy city; act for the sake of Zion, the abode of Your glory; act for the
sake of the desolation of Your Temple; act for the sake of the ruin of Your
Altar; act for the sake of the martyrs for Your holy Name; act for the sake of
those slaughtered for Your Oneness; act for the sake of those who entered fire
and water for the sanctification of Your Name; act for the nursing infants
who did not err; act for the sake of the weaned babes who did not sin; act for
the sake of children at the schoolroom; act for Your sake if not for ours; act for
Your sake and save us.

עֲנֵנוּ Answer us, HASHEM, answer us; answer us, our God, answer us; answer
us, [**א**] our Father, answer us; answer us, [**ב**] our Creator, answer us;
answer us, [**ג**] our Redeemer, answer us; answer us, [**ד**] You Who searches us
out, answer us; answer us, [**ה**] faithful God, answer us; answer us, [**ו**] stead-
fast and kind One, answer us; answer us, [**ז**] pure and upright One, answer
us; answer us, [**ח**] living and enduring One, answer us; answer us, [**ט**] good
and beneficent One, answer us; answer us, [**י**] You Who knows inclinations,
answer us; answer us, [**כ**] You Who suppresses wrath, answer us; answer us,
[**ל**] You Who dons righteousness, answer us; answer us, [**מ**] King Who reigns
over kings, answer us; answer us, [**נ**] awesome and powerful One, answer us;
answer us, [**ס**] You Who forgives and pardons, answer us; answer us, [**ע**] You
Who answers in time of distress,[1] answer us; answer us, [**פ**] Redeemer and
Rescuer, answer us; answer us, [**צ**] righteous and upright One, answer us;
answer us, [**ק**] He Who is close to those who call upon Him, answer us; answer
us, [**ר**] merciful and gracious One, answer us; answer us, [**ש**] You Who hears
the destitute, answer us; answer us, [**ת**] You Who supports the wholesome,
answer us; answer us, God of our forefathers, answer us; answer us, God of
Abraham, answer us; answer us, Dread of Isaac, answer us; answer us,
Mighty One of Jacob, answer us; answer us, Helper of the tribes, answer us;
answer us, Stronghold of the Matriarchs, answer us; answer us, You Who are
hard to anger, answer us; answer us, You Who are easy to pacify, answer us;
answer us, You Who answers in a time of favor,[1] answer us; answer us,
Father of orphans, answer us; answer us, Judge of widows, answer us.

מִי שֶׁעָנָה He Who answered our father Abraham on Mount Moriah,
                                                              may He answer us.
He Who answered his son Isaac when he was bound atop the altar,
                                                              may He answer us.
He Who answered Jacob in Bethel,   may He answer us.
He Who answered Joseph in the prison,   may He answer us.
He Who answered our forefathers at the Sea of Reeds,   may He answer us.
He Who answered Moses in Horeb,   may He answer us.
He Who answered Aaron when he offered the censer,   may He answer us.

(1) Some editions of Selichos reverse the positions of these two lines.

מִי שֶׁעָנָה לְפִינְחָס בְּקוּמוֹ מִתּוֹךְ הָעֵדָה,   הוּא יַעֲנֵנוּ.

מִי שֶׁעָנָה לִיהוֹשֻׁעַ בַּגִּלְגָּל,   הוּא יַעֲנֵנוּ.

מִי שֶׁעָנָה לִשְׁמוּאֵל בַּמִּצְפָּה,   הוּא יַעֲנֵנוּ.

מִי שֶׁעָנָה לְדָוִד וּשְׁלֹמֹה בְנוֹ בִּירוּשָׁלָיִם,   הוּא יַעֲנֵנוּ.

מִי שֶׁעָנָה לְאֵלִיֱּהוּ בְּהַר הַכַּרְמֶל,   הוּא יַעֲנֵנוּ.

מִי שֶׁעָנָה לֶאֱלִישָׁע בִּירִיחוֹ,   הוּא יַעֲנֵנוּ.

מִי שֶׁעָנָה לְיוֹנָה בִּמְעֵי הַדָּגָה,   הוּא יַעֲנֵנוּ.

מִי שֶׁעָנָה לְחִזְקִיֱּהוּ מֶלֶךְ יְהוּדָה בְּחָלְיוֹ,   הוּא יַעֲנֵנוּ.

מִי שֶׁעָנָה לַחֲנַנְיָה מִישָׁאֵל וַעֲזַרְיָה בְּתוֹךְ כִּבְשַׁן הָאֵשׁ,   הוּא יַעֲנֵנוּ.

מִי שֶׁעָנָה לְדָנִיֵּאל בְּגוֹב הָאֲרָיוֹת,   הוּא יַעֲנֵנוּ.

מִי שֶׁעָנָה לְמָרְדְּכַי וְאֶסְתֵּר בְּשׁוּשַׁן הַבִּירָה,   הוּא יַעֲנֵנוּ.

מִי שֶׁעָנָה לְעֶזְרָא בַּגּוֹלָה,   הוּא יַעֲנֵנוּ.

מִי שֶׁעָנָה לְכָל הַצַּדִּיקִים וְהַחֲסִידִים וְהַתְּמִימִים וְהַיְשָׁרִים,

הוּא יַעֲנֵנוּ.

רַחֲמָנָא דְּעָנֵי לַעֲנִיֵּי, עֲנֵינָא. רַחֲמָנָא דְּעָנֵי לִתְבִירֵי לִבָּא,
עֲנֵינָא. רַחֲמָנָא דְּעָנֵי לְמַכִּיכֵי רוּחָא, עֲנֵינָא. רַחֲמָנָא
עֲנֵינָא. רַחֲמָנָא חוּס. רַחֲמָנָא פְּרוֹק. רַחֲמָנָא שְׁזֵיב. רַחֲמָנָא
רְחֵם עֲלָן. הַשְׁתָּא בַּעֲגָלָא וּבִזְמַן קָרִיב.

נפילת אפים

In the presence of a Torah Scroll, the following (until יִכְבְּשׁוּ רָגַע) is recited with the head resting
on the arm, preferably while seated. Elsewhere, it is recited with the head held erect.

(וַיֹּאמֶר דָּוִד אֶל גָּד, צַר לִי מְאֹד נִפְּלָה נָּא בְיַד יהוה,
כִּי רַבִּים רַחֲמָיו, וּבְיַד אָדָם אַל אֶפֹּלָה.[1])

רַחוּם וְחַנּוּן חָטָאתִי לְפָנֶיךָ. יהוה מָלֵא רַחֲמִים, רַחֵם עָלַי
וְקַבֵּל תַּחֲנוּנָי.

תהלים ו:ב-יא

יהוה אַל בְּאַפְּךָ תוֹכִיחֵנִי, וְאַל בַּחֲמָתְךָ תְיַסְּרֵנִי. חָנֵּנִי יהוה, כִּי
אֻמְלַל אָנִי, רְפָאֵנִי יהוה, כִּי נִבְהֲלוּ עֲצָמָי. וְנַפְשִׁי נִבְהֲלָה
מְאֹד, וְאַתָּה יהוה, עַד מָתָי. שׁוּבָה יהוה, חַלְּצָה נַפְשִׁי, הוֹשִׁיעֵנִי
לְמַעַן חַסְדֶּךָ. כִּי אֵין בַּמָּוֶת זִכְרֶךָ, בִּשְׁאוֹל מִי יוֹדֶה לָּךְ. יָגַעְתִּי
בְּאַנְחָתִי, אַשְׂחֶה בְכָל לַיְלָה מִטָּתִי, בְּדִמְעָתִי עַרְשִׂי אַמְסֶה.
עָשְׁשָׁה מִכַּעַס עֵינִי, עָתְקָה בְּכָל צוֹרְרָי. סוּרוּ מִמֶּנִּי כָּל פֹּעֲלֵי אָוֶן,
כִּי שָׁמַע יהוה קוֹל בִּכְיִי. שָׁמַע יהוה תְּחִנָּתִי, יהוה תְּפִלָּתִי יִקָּח.
יֵבֹשׁוּ וְיִבָּהֲלוּ מְאֹד כָּל אֹיְבָי, יָשֻׁבוּ יֵבֹשׁוּ רָגַע.

He Who answered Phineas when he arose from amid the congregation,
may He answer us.

He Who answered Joshua in Gilgal, *may He answer us.*
He Who answered Samuel in Mitzpah, *may He answer us.*
He Who answered David and his son Solomon in Jerusalem,
may He answer us.

He Who answered Elijah on Mount Carmel, *may He answer us.*
He Who answered Elisha in Jericho, *may He answer us.*
He Who answered Jonah in the innards of the fish, *may He answer us.*
He Who answered Hezekiah, King of Judah, in his illness,
may He answer us.

He Who answered Chananiah, Mishael, and Azariah in the fiery oven,
may He answer us.

He Who answered Daniel in the lions' den, *may He answer us.*
He Who answered Mordechai and Esther in Shushan the capital,
may He answer us.

He Who answered Ezra in the Exile, *may He answer us.*
He Who answered all the righteous, the devout, the wholesome,
and the upright, *may He answer us.*

רַחֲמָנָא *The Merciful One Who answers the poor, may He answer us. The*
Merciful One Who answers the brokenhearted, may He answer us.
The Merciful One Who answers the humble of spirit, may He answer us. O
Merciful One, answer us. O Merciful One, pity. O Merciful One, redeem. O
Merciful One, deliver. O Merciful One, have mercy on us — now, swiftly and
soon.

PUTTING DOWN THE HEAD

In the presence of a Torah Scroll, the following (until *'instantly shamed'*) is recited with the head
resting on the arm, preferably while seated. Elsewhere, it is recited with the head held erect.

(And David said to Gad, 'I am exceedingly distressed. Let us fall into HASHEM's
hand for His mercies are abundant, but let me not fall into human hands.'[1])

רַחוּם וְחַנּוּן *O compassionate and gracious One, I have sinned before You.*
HASHEM, Who is full of mercy, have mercy on me and accept
my supplications.

Psalms 6:2-11

'ה *HASHEM, do not rebuke me in Your anger nor chastise me in Your rage.*
Favor me, HASHEM, for I am feeble; heal me, HASHEM, for my bones
shudder. My soul is utterly confounded, and You, HASHEM, how long? Desist,
HASHEM, release my soul; save me as befits Your kindness. For there is no
mention of You in death; in the Lower World who will thank You? I am
wearied with my sigh, every night my tears drench my bed, soak my couch.
My eye is dimmed because of anger, aged by my tormentors. Depart from
me, all evildoers, for HASHEM has heard the sound of my weeping. HASHEM
has heard my plea, HASHEM will accept my prayer. Let all my foes be shamed
and utterly confounded, they will regret and be instantly shamed.

(1) *II Samuel* 24:14.

מַחֵי וּמַסֵּי מֵמִית וּמְחַיֶּה, מַסִּיק מִן שְׁאוֹל לְחַיֵּי עָלְמָא, בְּרָא כַּד חָטֵי אֲבוּהִי לַקְיֵהּ, אֲבוּהִי דְחָיֵיס אַסֵּי לִכְאֵבֵהּ. עַבְדָּא דְמָרִיד נָפִיק בְּקוֹלָר, מָרֵהּ תָּאִיב וְתַבִּיר קוֹלָרֵהּ.

בְּרָךְ בִּכְרָךְ אֲנַן וְחָטִינַן קַמָּךְ, הָא רָזֵי נַפְשִׁין בְּגִידִין מְרִירִין, עַבְדָּךְ אֲנַן וּמְרוֹדִינַן קַמָּךְ, הָא בְּבִזְתָא, הָא בְּשִׁבְיָא, הָא בְּמַלְקְיוּתָא. בְּמָטוּ מִנָּךְ בְּרַחֲמָךְ דִּנְפִישִׁין, אַסֵּי לִכְאֵבִין דְּתַקִּיף עֲלָן, עַד דְּלָא נֶהֱוֵי גְּמִירָא בְּשִׁבְיָא.

מַכְנִיסֵי רַחֲמִים, הַכְנִיסוּ רַחֲמֵינוּ, לִפְנֵי בַּעַל הָרַחֲמִים. מַשְׁמִיעֵי תְפִלָּה, הַשְׁמִיעוּ תְפִלָּתֵנוּ, לִפְנֵי שׁוֹמֵעַ תְּפִלָּה. מַשְׁמִיעֵי צְעָקָה, הַשְׁמִיעוּ צַעֲקָתֵנוּ, לִפְנֵי שׁוֹמֵעַ צְעָקָה. מַכְנִיסֵי דִמְעָה, הַכְנִיסוּ דִמְעוֹתֵינוּ, לִפְנֵי מֶלֶךְ מִתְרַצֶּה בִּדְמָעוֹת.

הִשְׁתַּדְּלוּ וְהַרְבּוּ תְּחִנָּה וּבַקָּשָׁה, לִפְנֵי מֶלֶךְ אֵל רָם וְנִשָּׂא. הַזְכִּירוּ לְפָנָיו, הַשְׁמִיעוּ לְפָנָיו תּוֹרָה וּמַעֲשִׂים טוֹבִים שֶׁל שׁוֹכְנֵי עָפָר.

יִזְכֹּר אַהֲבָתָם וִיחַיֶּה זַרְעָם, שֶׁלֹּא תֹאבַד שְׁאֵרִית יַעֲקֹב. כִּי צֹאן רֹעֶה נֶאֱמָן הָיָה לְחֶרְפָּה, יִשְׂרָאֵל גּוֹי אֶחָד לְמָשָׁל וְלִשְׁנִינָה.

מַהֵר עֲנֵנוּ אֱלֹהֵי יִשְׁעֵנוּ, וּפְדֵנוּ מִכָּל גְּזֵרוֹת קָשׁוֹת וְהוֹשִׁיעָה בְּרַחֲמֶיךָ הָרַבִּים, מְשִׁיחַ צִדְקֶךָ וְעַמֶּךָ.

מָרָן דְּבִשְׁמַיָּא לָךְ מִתְחַנְּנָן, כְּבַר שִׁבְיָא דְּמִתְחַנַּן לִשְׁבוּיֵהּ. כֻּלְּהוֹן בְּנֵי שִׁבְיָא בְּכַסְפָּא מִתְפָּרְקִין, וְעַמָּךְ יִשְׂרָאֵל בְּרַחֲמֵי וּבְתַחֲנוּנֵי, הַב לָן שְׁאֵלְתִּין וּבָעוּתִין, דְּלָא נֶהֱדַר רֵיקָם מִן קֳדָמָךְ.

מָרָן דְּבִשְׁמַיָּא לָךְ מִתְחַנְּנָן, כְּעַבְדָּא דְּמִתְחַנַּן לְמָרֵיהּ, עֲשִׁיקֵי אֲנַן וּבַחֲשׁוֹכָא שָׁרֵינַן, מְרִירָן נַפְשִׁין מֵעַקְתִין דִּנְפִישִׁין, חֵילָא לֵית בָּן לְרַצּוּיֵךְ מָרָן, עֲבִיד בְּדִיל קַיָּמָא דִּגְזַרְתְּ עִם אֲבָהָתָנָא.

שׁוֹמֵר יִשְׂרָאֵל, שְׁמוֹר שְׁאֵרִית יִשְׂרָאֵל, וְאַל יֹאבַד יִשְׂרָאֵל, הָאוֹמְרִים, שְׁמַע יִשְׂרָאֵל.[1]

שׁוֹמֵר גּוֹי אֶחָד, שְׁמוֹר שְׁאֵרִית עַם אֶחָד, וְאַל יֹאבַד גּוֹי אֶחָד, הַמְיַחֲדִים שִׁמְךָ, יְהוָה אֱלֹהֵינוּ יְהוָה אֶחָד.[1]

מָחִי וּמַסִּי *[O God,] He Who smites and heals, causes death and restores life, raises [the dead] from the grave to eternal life: Should a son sin, his father would smack him, but a compassionate father will heal his [son's] pain. When a slave rebels, he is led out in collar-irons, but if his master desires to, he breaks his chains.*

We are Your son, Your firstborn, and we have sinned against You; so our soul has been satiated with bitter wormwood. We are Your servants and we have rebelled against You; so [we have suffered], some with looting, some with captivity, and some with the lash. We beg of You, in Your abundant compassion, heal the pains that have overwhelmed us, before we have been completely wiped out in captivity.

מַכְנִיסֵי רַחֲמִים *O you who usher in [pleas for] mercy, may you usher in our [plea for] mercy, before the Master of mercy. O you who cause prayer to be heard, may you cause our prayer to be heard, before the Hearer of prayer. O you who cause outcry to be heard, may you cause our outcry to be heard, before the Hearer of outcry. O you who usher in tears, may you usher in our tears, before the King Who finds favor through tears.*

Exert yourselves, and multiply supplication and petition, before the King, God, exalted and most high. Mention before Him, cause to be heard before Him, the Torah and the good deeds of [the Patriarchs and Matriarchs] who dwell in the dust.

May He remember their love and grant life to [their] offspring, that the remnant of Jacob not be lost. For the flock of the faithful shepherd [Moses] has become a disgrace; Israel, the unique nation, a parable and a simile.

Speedily, answer us, O God of our salvation, and redeem us from all harsh decrees; and may You save, in Your abundant mercy, Your righteous anointed and Your people.

מָרָן דִּבְשְׁמַיָּא *Our Master Who is in heaven, to You do we supplicate, as a captive supplicates before his captors; for all captives are redeemed with money, but Your people Israel with compassion and supplication. O grant our requests and our prayers that we not be turned away from You empty-handed.*

Our Master Who is in heaven, to You do we supplicate as a slave supplicates before his master: We are oppressed and we abide in darkness, souls embittered from abundant distress. We have no strength to regain Your favor. Our Master, act for the sake of the covenant that You made with our Patriarchs.

שׁוֹמֵר יִשְׂרָאֵל *O Guardian of Israel, protect the remnant of Israel; let not Israel be destroyed — those who proclaim, 'Hear O Israel.'[1]*

O Guardian of the unique nation, protect the remnant of the unique people; let not the unique nation be destroyed — those who proclaim the Oneness of Your Name, 'HASHEM is our God, HASHEM, the One and Only!'[1]

---

(1) *Deuteronomy* 6:4.

שׁוֹמֵר גּוֹי קָדוֹשׁ, שְׁמוֹר שְׁאֵרִית עַם קָדוֹשׁ, וְאַל יֹאבַד גּוֹי
קָדוֹשׁ, הַמְשַׁלְּשִׁים בְּשָׁלֹשׁ קְדֻשּׁוֹת לְקָדוֹשׁ.

מִתְרַצֶּה בְרַחֲמִים וּמִתְפַּיֵּס בְּתַחֲנוּנִים, הִתְרַצֵּה וְהִתְפַּיֵּס לְדוֹר
עָנִי, כִּי אֵין עוֹזֵר. אָבִינוּ מַלְכֵּנוּ, חָנֵּנוּ וַעֲנֵנוּ, כִּי אֵין בָּנוּ מַעֲשִׂים,
עֲשֵׂה עִמָּנוּ צְדָקָה וָחֶסֶד וְהוֹשִׁיעֵנוּ.

וַאֲנַחְנוּ לֹא נֵדַע מַה נַּעֲשֶׂה, כִּי עָלֶיךָ עֵינֵינוּ.[1] זְכֹר רַחֲמֶיךָ
יהוה וַחֲסָדֶיךָ, כִּי מֵעוֹלָם הֵמָּה.[2] יְהִי חַסְדְּךָ יהוה
עָלֵינוּ, כַּאֲשֶׁר יִחַלְנוּ לָךְ.[3] אַל תִּזְכָּר לָנוּ עֲוֹנוֹת רִאשׁוֹנִים, מַהֵר
יְקַדְּמוּנוּ רַחֲמֶיךָ, כִּי דַלּוֹנוּ מְאֹד.[4] חָנֵּנוּ יהוה חָנֵּנוּ, כִּי רַב שָׂבַעְנוּ
בוּז.[5] בְּרֹגֶז רַחֵם תִּזְכּוֹר.[6] כִּי הוּא יָדַע יִצְרֵנוּ, זָכוּר כִּי עָפָר אֲנָחְנוּ.[7]
עָזְרֵנוּ אֱלֹהֵי יִשְׁעֵנוּ עַל דְּבַר כְּבוֹד שְׁמֶךָ, וְהַצִּילֵנוּ וְכַפֵּר עַל
חַטֹּאתֵינוּ לְמַעַן שְׁמֶךָ.[8]

קדיש שלם
The chazzan recites קַדִּישׁ שָׁלֵם:

יִתְגַּדַּל וְיִתְקַדַּשׁ שְׁמֵהּ רַבָּא. (Cong. – אָמֵן.) בְּעָלְמָא דִּי בְרָא
כִרְעוּתֵהּ, וְיַמְלִיךְ מַלְכוּתֵהּ, בְּחַיֵּיכוֹן וּבְיוֹמֵיכוֹן וּבְחַיֵּי
דְכָל בֵּית יִשְׂרָאֵל, בַּעֲגָלָא וּבִזְמַן קָרִיב. וְאִמְרוּ אָמֵן.
(Cong. – אָמֵן. יְהֵא שְׁמֵהּ רַבָּא מְבָרַךְ לְעָלַם וּלְעָלְמֵי עָלְמַיָּא.)
יְהֵא שְׁמֵהּ רַבָּא מְבָרַךְ לְעָלַם וּלְעָלְמֵי עָלְמַיָּא.
יִתְבָּרַךְ וְיִשְׁתַּבַּח וְיִתְפָּאַר וְיִתְרוֹמַם וְיִתְנַשֵּׂא וְיִתְהַדָּר וְיִתְעַלֶּה
וְיִתְהַלָּל שְׁמֵהּ דְּקֻדְשָׁא בְּרִיךְ הוּא (Cong. – בְּרִיךְ הוּא.) לְעֵלָּא מִן כָּל
בִּרְכָתָא וְשִׁירָתָא תֻּשְׁבְּחָתָא וְנֶחֱמָתָא, דַּאֲמִירָן בְּעָלְמָא. וְאִמְרוּ:
אָמֵן. (Cong. – אָמֵן.)

(Cong. – קַבֵּל בְּרַחֲמִים וּבְרָצוֹן אֶת תְּפִלָּתֵנוּ.)
תִּתְקַבֵּל צְלוֹתְהוֹן וּבָעוּתְהוֹן דְּכָל (בֵּית) יִשְׂרָאֵל קֳדָם אֲבוּהוֹן
דִּי בִשְׁמַיָּא. וְאִמְרוּ אָמֵן. (Cong. – אָמֵן.)

(Cong. – יְהִי שֵׁם יהוה מְבֹרָךְ, מֵעַתָּה וְעַד עוֹלָם.[9])
יְהֵא שְׁלָמָא רַבָּא מִן שְׁמַיָּא וְחַיִּים עָלֵינוּ וְעַל כָּל יִשְׂרָאֵל.
וְאִמְרוּ אָמֵן. (Cong. – אָמֵן.)

(Cong. – עֶזְרִי מֵעִם יהוה, עֹשֵׂה שָׁמַיִם וָאָרֶץ.[10])

Take three steps back. Bow left and say, . . . עֹשֶׂה; bow right and say, . . . הוּא יַעֲשֶׂה; bow forward and
say, וְעַל כָּל . . . אָמֵן. Remain standing in place for a few moments, then take three steps forward.

עֹשֶׂה שָׁלוֹם בִּמְרוֹמָיו, הוּא יַעֲשֶׂה שָׁלוֹם עָלֵינוּ, וְעַל כָּל יִשְׂרָאֵל.
וְאִמְרוּ אָמֵן. (Cong. – אָמֵן.)

O Guardian of the holy nation, protect the remnant of the holy people; let not the holy nation be destroyed — those who proclaim three-fold sanctifications to the Holy One.

Become favorable through compassion and become appeased through supplications. Become favorable and appeased to the poor generation, for there is no helper. Our Father, our King, be gracious with us and answer us, though we have no worthy deeds; treat us with charity and kindness, and save us.

וַאֲנַחְנוּ We know not what to do — but our eyes are upon You.[1] Remember Your mercies, HASHEM, and Your kindnesses, for they are from the beginning of the world.[2] May Your kindness be upon us, HASHEM, just as we awaited You.[3] Recall not against us the iniquities of the ancients; may Your mercies meet us swiftly, for we have become exceedingly impoverished.[4] Be gracious to us, HASHEM, be gracious to us, for we are abundantly sated with scorn.[5] Amid rage — remember to be merciful![6] For He knew our nature, He remembers that we are dust.[7] Chazzan— Assist us, O God of our salvation, for the sake of Your Name's glory; rescue us and atone for our sins for Your Name's sake.[8]

FULL KADDISH
The chazzan recites the Full Kaddish:

יִתְגַּדַּל May His great Name grow exalted and sanctified (Cong. — Amen.) in the world that He created as He willed. May He give reign to His kingship in your lifetimes and in your days, and in the lifetimes of the entire Family of Israel, swiftly and soon. Now respond: Amen.

(Cong. — Amen. May His great Name be blessed forever and ever.)
May His great Name be blessed forever and ever.

Blessed, praised, glorified, exalted, extolled, mighty, upraised and lauded be the Name of the Holy One, Blessed is He (Cong. — Blessed is He.) beyond any blessing and song, praise, and consolation that are uttered in the world. Now respond: Amen. (Cong. — Amen.)

(Cong. — Accept our prayers with mercy and favor.)
May the prayers and supplications of the entire House of Israel be accepted before their Father Who is in Heaven. Now respond: Amen. (Cong. — Amen.)

(Cong. — Blessed be the Name of HASHEM from this time and forever.[9])
May there be abundant peace from Heaven, and life, upon us and upon all Israel. Now respond: Amen. (Cong. — Amen.)

(Cong. — My help is from HASHEM, Maker of heaven and earth.[10])

Take three steps back. Bow left and say, 'He Who makes peace . . .'; bow right and say,
'may He make peace . . .'; bow forward and say, 'and upon all Israel . . .'
Remain standing in place for a few moments, then take three steps forward.

He Who makes peace in His heights, may He make peace upon us, and upon all Israel. Now respond: Amen. (Cong. — Amen.)

(1) II Chronicles 20:12. (2) Psalms 25:6. (3) 33:22. (4) 79:8. (5) 123:3.
(6) Habakkuk 3:2. (7) Psalms 103:14. (8) 79:9. (9) 113:2. (10) 121:2.

❊ יום חמישי ❊

אַשְׁרֵי יוֹשְׁבֵי בֵיתֶךָ, עוֹד יְהַלְלוּךָ סֶּלָה.[1] אַשְׁרֵי הָעָם שֶׁכָּכָה
לוֹ, אַשְׁרֵי הָעָם שֶׁיהוה אֱלֹהָיו.[2]

תְּהִלָּה לְדָוִד.

תהלים קמה

אֲרוֹמִמְךָ אֱלוֹהַי הַמֶּלֶךְ, וַאֲבָרְכָה שִׁמְךָ לְעוֹלָם וָעֶד.

בְּכָל יוֹם אֲבָרְכֶךָּ, וַאֲהַלְלָה שִׁמְךָ לְעוֹלָם וָעֶד.

גָּדוֹל יהוה וּמְהֻלָּל מְאֹד, וְלִגְדֻלָּתוֹ אֵין חֵקֶר.

דּוֹר לְדוֹר יְשַׁבַּח מַעֲשֶׂיךָ, וּגְבוּרֹתֶיךָ יַגִּידוּ.

הֲדַר כְּבוֹד הוֹדֶךָ, וְדִבְרֵי נִפְלְאֹתֶיךָ אָשִׂיחָה.

וֶעֱזוּז נוֹרְאוֹתֶיךָ יֹאמֵרוּ, וּגְדֻלָּתְךָ אֲסַפְּרֶנָּה.

זֵכֶר רַב טוּבְךָ יַבִּיעוּ, וְצִדְקָתְךָ יְרַנֵּנוּ.

חַנּוּן וְרַחוּם יהוה, אֶרֶךְ אַפַּיִם וּגְדָל חָסֶד.

טוֹב יהוה לַכֹּל, וְרַחֲמָיו עַל כָּל מַעֲשָׂיו.

יוֹדוּךָ יהוה כָּל מַעֲשֶׂיךָ, וַחֲסִידֶיךָ יְבָרְכוּכָה.

כְּבוֹד מַלְכוּתְךָ יֹאמֵרוּ, וּגְבוּרָתְךָ יְדַבֵּרוּ.

לְהוֹדִיעַ לִבְנֵי הָאָדָם גְּבוּרֹתָיו, וּכְבוֹד הֲדַר מַלְכוּתוֹ.

מַלְכוּתְךָ מַלְכוּת כָּל עֹלָמִים, וּמֶמְשַׁלְתְּךָ בְּכָל דּוֹר וָדֹר.

סוֹמֵךְ יהוה לְכָל הַנֹּפְלִים, וְזוֹקֵף לְכָל הַכְּפוּפִים.

עֵינֵי כֹל אֵלֶיךָ יְשַׂבֵּרוּ, וְאַתָּה נוֹתֵן לָהֶם אֶת אָכְלָם בְּעִתּוֹ.

Concentrate intently while
reciting the verse, **פוֹתֵחַ**.   **פּוֹתֵחַ** אֶת יָדֶךָ, וּמַשְׂבִּיעַ לְכָל חַי רָצוֹן.

❖ **צַדִּיק** יהוה בְּכָל דְּרָכָיו, וְחָסִיד בְּכָל מַעֲשָׂיו.

קָרוֹב יהוה לְכָל קֹרְאָיו, לְכֹל אֲשֶׁר יִקְרָאֻהוּ בֶאֱמֶת.

רְצוֹן יְרֵאָיו יַעֲשֶׂה, וְאֶת שַׁוְעָתָם יִשְׁמַע וְיוֹשִׁיעֵם.

שׁוֹמֵר יהוה אֶת כָּל אֹהֲבָיו, וְאֵת כָּל הָרְשָׁעִים יַשְׁמִיד.

תְּהִלַּת יהוה יְדַבֶּר פִּי, וִיבָרֵךְ כָּל בָּשָׂר שֵׁם קָדְשׁוֹ לְעוֹלָם וָעֶד.

וַאֲנַחְנוּ נְבָרֵךְ יָהּ, מֵעַתָּה וְעַד עוֹלָם, הַלְלוּיָהּ.[3]

The chazzan recites חֲצִי קַדִּישׁ.

יִתְגַּדַּל וְיִתְקַדַּשׁ שְׁמֵהּ רַבָּא. (.Cong – אָמֵן) בְּעָלְמָא דִּי בְרָא כִרְעוּתֵהּ,
וְיַמְלִיךְ מַלְכוּתֵהּ, בְּחַיֵּיכוֹן וּבְיוֹמֵיכוֹן וּבְחַיֵּי דְכָל בֵּית יִשְׂרָאֵל,
בַּעֲגָלָא וּבִזְמַן קָרִיב. וְאִמְרוּ: אָמֵן.

(.Cong – אָמֵן. יְהֵא שְׁמֵהּ רַבָּא מְבָרַךְ לְעָלַם וּלְעָלְמֵי עָלְמַיָּא.)

יְהֵא שְׁמֵהּ רַבָּא מְבָרַךְ לְעָלַם וּלְעָלְמֵי עָלְמַיָּא.

יִתְבָּרַךְ וְיִשְׁתַּבַּח וְיִתְפָּאַר וְיִתְרוֹמַם וְיִתְנַשֵּׂא וְיִתְהַדָּר וְיִתְעַלֶּה וְיִתְהַלָּל
שְׁמֵהּ דְּקֻדְשָׁא בְּרִיךְ הוּא (.Cong – בְּרִיךְ הוּא) לְעֵלָּא מִן כָּל בִּרְכָתָא וְשִׁירָתָא
תֻּשְׁבְּחָתָא וְנֶחֱמָתָא, דַּאֲמִירָן בְּעָלְמָא, וְאִמְרוּ: אָמֵן. (.Cong – אָמֵן)

❧ FIFTH DAY ❧

אַשְׁרֵי *Praiseworthy are those who dwell in Your house; may they always praise You, Selah!*[1] *Praiseworthy is the people for whom this is so, praiseworthy is the people whose God is HASHEM.*[2]

Psalm 145   *A psalm of praise by David:*

א *I will exalt You, my God the King, and I will bless Your Name forever and ever.*

ב *Every day I will bless You, and I will laud Your Name forever and ever.*

ג *HASHEM is great and exceedingly lauded,*
   and His greatness is beyond investigation.

ד *Each generation will praise Your deeds to the next*
   and of Your mighty deeds they will tell;

ה *The splendrous glory of Your power and Your wondrous deeds I shall discuss.*

ו *And of Your awesome power they will speak, and Your greatness I shall relate.*

ז *A recollection of Your abundant goodness they will utter*
   and of Your righteousness they will sing exultantly.

ח *Gracious and merciful is HASHEM,*
   slow to anger, and great in [bestowing] kindness.

ט *HASHEM is good to all; His mercies are on all His works.*

י *All Your works shall thank You, HASHEM, and Your devout ones will bless You.*

כ *Of the glory of Your kingdom they will speak, and of Your power they will tell;*

ל *To inform human beings of His mighty deeds,*
   and the glorious splendor of His kingdom.

מ *Your kingdom is a kingdom spanning all eternities,*
   and Your dominion is throughout every generation.

ס *HASHEM supports all the fallen ones and straightens all the bent.*

ע *The eyes of all look to You with hope*
   and You give them their food in its proper time;

פ *You open Your hand,*   Concentrate intently while reciting the verse, 'You open. . .'
   and satisfy the desire of every living thing.

צ Chazzan— *Righteous is HASHEM in all His ways*
   and magnanimous in all His deeds.

ק *HASHEM is close to all who call upon Him — to all who call upon Him sincerely.*

ר *The will of those who fear Him He will do;*
   and their cry He will hear, and save them.

ש *HASHEM protects all who love Him; but all the wicked He will destroy.*

ת *May my mouth declare the praise of HASHEM*
   and may all flesh bless His Holy Name forever and ever.

We will bless God from this time and forever, Halleluyah![3]

The chazzan recites Half-Kaddish:

יִתְגַּדַּל *May His great Name grow exalted and sanctified* (Cong.— *Amen.*) *in the world that He created as He willed. May He give reign to His kingship in your lifetimes and in your days, and in the lifetimes of the entire Family of Israel, swiftly and soon. Now respond: Amen.*

(Cong.— *Amen. May His great Name be blessed forever and ever.*)

May His great Name be blessed forever and ever.

Blessed, praised, glorified, exalted, extolled, mighty, upraised, and lauded be the Name of the Holy One, Blessed is He (Cong.— *Blessed is He*) *— beyond any blessing and song, praise and consolation that are uttered in the world. Now respond: Amen.* (Cong.— *Amen.*)

(1) *Psalms* 84:5. (2) 144:15. (3) 115:18.

All:

לְךָ יהוה הַצְּדָקָה, וְלָנוּ בְּשֶׁת הַפָּנִים.[1] מַה נִּתְאוֹנֵן,[2] מַה נֹּאמַר, מַה נְּדַבֵּר, וּמַה נִּצְטַדָּק.[3] נַחְפְּשָׂה דְרָכֵינוּ וְנַחְקְרָה, וְנָשׁוּבָה אֵלֶיךָ,[4] כִּי יְמִינְךָ פְּשׁוּטָה לְקַבֵּל שָׁבִים. לֹא בְחֶסֶד וְלֹא בְמַעֲשִׂים בָּאנוּ לְפָנֶיךָ, כַּדַּלִּים וּכְרָשִׁים דָּפַקְנוּ דְלָתֶיךָ. דְּלָתֶיךָ דָּפַקְנוּ רַחוּם וְחַנּוּן, נָא אַל תְּשִׁיבֵנוּ רֵיקָם מִלְּפָנֶיךָ. מִלְּפָנֶיךָ מַלְכֵּנוּ רֵיקָם אַל תְּשִׁיבֵנוּ, כִּי אַתָּה שׁוֹמֵעַ תְּפִלָּה.

שְׁמֵעַ תְּפִלָּה, עָדֶיךָ כָּל בָּשָׂר יָבֹאוּ.[5] יָבוֹא כָל בָּשָׂר לְהִשְׁתַּחֲוֹת לְפָנֶיךָ יהוה.[6] יָבֹאוּ וְיִשְׁתַּחֲווּ לְפָנֶיךָ אֲדֹנָי, וִיכַבְּדוּ לִשְׁמֶךָ.[7] בָּאוּ נִשְׁתַּחֲוֶה וְנִכְרָעָה, נִבְרְכָה לִפְנֵי יהוה עֹשֵׂנוּ.[8] נָבוֹאָה לְמִשְׁכְּנוֹתָיו, נִשְׁתַּחֲוֶה לַהֲדֹם רַגְלָיו.[9] בֹּאוּ שְׁעָרָיו בְּתוֹדָה, חֲצֵרֹתָיו בִּתְהִלָּה, הוֹדוּ לוֹ בָּרְכוּ שְׁמוֹ.[10] רוֹמְמוּ יהוה אֱלֹהֵינוּ, וְהִשְׁתַּחֲווּ לַהֲדֹם רַגְלָיו, קָדוֹשׁ הוּא.[11] רוֹמְמוּ יהוה אֱלֹהֵינוּ, וְהִשְׁתַּחֲווּ לְהַר קָדְשׁוֹ, כִּי קָדוֹשׁ יהוה אֱלֹהֵינוּ.[12] הִשְׁתַּחֲווּ לַיהוה בְּהַדְרַת קֹדֶשׁ, חִילוּ מִפָּנָיו כָּל הָאָרֶץ.[13] וַאֲנַחְנוּ בְּרֹב חַסְדְּךָ נָבוֹא בֵיתֶךָ, נִשְׁתַּחֲוֶה אֶל הֵיכַל קָדְשְׁךָ בְּיִרְאָתֶךָ.[14] נִשְׁתַּחֲוֶה אֶל הֵיכַל קָדְשְׁךָ וְנוֹדֶה אֶת שְׁמֶךָ, עַל חַסְדְּךָ וְעַל אֲמִתֶּךָ, כִּי הִגְדַּלְתָּ עַל כָּל שִׁמְךָ אִמְרָתֶךָ.[15] לְכוּ נְרַנְּנָה לַיהוה, נָרִיעָה לְצוּר יִשְׁעֵנוּ. נְקַדְּמָה פָנָיו בְּתוֹדָה, בִּזְמִרוֹת נָרִיעַ לוֹ.[16] אֲשֶׁר יַחְדָּו נַמְתִּיק סוֹד, בְּבֵית אֱלֹהִים נְהַלֵּךְ בְּרָגֶשׁ.[17] אֵל נַעֲרָץ בְּסוֹד קְדוֹשִׁים רַבָּה, וְנוֹרָא עַל כָּל סְבִיבָיו.[18] שְׂאוּ יְדֵיכֶם קֹדֶשׁ וּבָרְכוּ אֶת יהוה.[19] הִנֵּה בָּרְכוּ אֶת יהוה כָּל עַבְדֵי יהוה, הָעֹמְדִים בְּבֵית יהוה בַּלֵּילוֹת.[20] אֲשֶׁר מִי אֵל בַּשָּׁמַיִם וּבָאָרֶץ, אֲשֶׁר יַעֲשֶׂה כְמַעֲשֶׂיךָ וְכִגְבוּרֹתֶיךָ.[21] אֲשֶׁר לוֹ הַיָּם וְהוּא עָשָׂהוּ, וְיַבֶּשֶׁת יָדָיו יָצָרוּ.[22] אֲשֶׁר בְּיָדוֹ מֶחְקְרֵי אָרֶץ, וְתוֹעֲפוֹת הָרִים לוֹ.[23] אֲשֶׁר בְּיָדוֹ נֶפֶשׁ כָּל חָי, וְרוּחַ כָּל בְּשַׂר אִישׁ.[24] וְיוֹדוּ שָׁמַיִם פִּלְאֲךָ יהוה, אַף אֱמוּנָתְךָ בִּקְהַל קְדֹשִׁים.[25] לְךָ זְרוֹעַ עִם גְּבוּרָה, תָּעֹז יָדְךָ תָּרוּם יְמִינֶךָ.[26] לְךָ שָׁמַיִם, אַף לְךָ אָרֶץ, תֵּבֵל וּמְלֹאָהּ אַתָּה יְסַדְתָּם.[27] אַתָּה פוֹרַרְתָּ בְעָזְּךָ יָם, שִׁבַּרְתָּ רָאשֵׁי תַנִּינִים עַל הַמָּיִם.[28] אַתָּה הִצַּבְתָּ כָּל גְּבוּלוֹת אָרֶץ, קַיִץ וָחֹרֶף

(1) *Daniel* 9:7. (2) Cf. *Lamentations* 3:39. (3) Cf. *Genesis* 44:16. (4) Cf. *Lamentations* 3:40. (5) *Psalms* 65:3. (6) Cf. *Isaiah* 66:23. (7) *Psalms* 86:9. (8) 95:6. (9) 132:7. (10) 100:4. (11) 99:5. (12) 99:9. (13) 96:9. (14) Cf. 5:8. (15) Cf. 138:2. (16) 95:1-2. (17) 55:15. (18) 89:8. (19) 134:2. (20) 134:1. (21) *Deuteronomy* 3:24. (22) *Psalms* 95:5. (23) 95:4. (24) *Job* 12:10. (25) *Psalms* 89:6. (26) 89:14. (27) 89:12. (28) 74:13.

All:

לְךָ ה׳ Yours, my Lord, is the righteousness and ours is the shame-facedness.[1] What complaint can we make?[2] What can we say? What can we declare? What justification can we offer?[3] Let us examine our ways and analyze — and return to You,[4] for Your right hand is extended to accept penitents. Neither with kindness nor with [good] deeds do we come before You. As paupers and as beggars do we knock at Your doors. At Your doors we knock, O Compassionate and Gracious One. Please do not turn us away from You empty-handed. Our King, turn us not away from You empty-handed, for You are the One Who hears prayer.

שֹׁמֵעַ תְּפִלָּה You Who hears prayer, to You all flesh will come.[5] All flesh will come to prostrate itself before You, O HASHEM.[6] They will come and prostrate themselves before You, my Lord, and shall honor Your Name.[7] Come! — let us prostrate ourselves and bow, let us kneel before God, our Maker.[8] Let us come to His dwelling places, let us prostrate ourselves at His footstool.[9] Enter His gates with thanksgiving, His courts with praise; give thanks to Him, praise His Name.[10] Exalt HASHEM, our God, and bow at His footstool; He is holy![11] Exalt HASHEM, our God, and bow at His holy mountain; for holy is HASHEM, our God.[12] Prostrate yourselves before HASHEM in His intensely holy place, tremble before Him, everyone on earth.[13] As for us, through Your abundant kindness we will enter Your House; we will prostrate ourselves toward Your Holy Sanctuary in awe of You.[14] We will prostrate ourselves toward Your Holy Sanctuary, and we will give thanks to Your Name for Your kindness and truth for You have exalted Your promise even beyond Your Name.[15] Come! — let us sing to HASHEM, let us call out to the Rock of our salvation. Let us greet Him with thanksgiving, with praiseful songs let us call out to Him.[16] For together let us share sweet counsel, in the house of God let us walk in multitudes.[17] God is dreaded in the hiddenmost counsel of the holy ones, and inspires awe upon all who surround Him.[18] Lift your hands in the Sanctuary and bless HASHEM.[19] Behold, bless HASHEM, all you servants of HASHEM, who stand in the House of HASHEM in the nights.[20] For what power is there in heaven or earth that can approximate Your deeds and power?[21] For His is the sea and He perfected the dry land — His hands fashioned it.[22] For in His power are the hidden mysteries of the earth, and the mountain summits are His.[23] For His is the soul of every living thing, and the spirit of all human flesh.[24] Heaven will gratefully praise Your wonders, HASHEM; also Your faithfulness in the assembly of holy ones.[25] Yours is a mighty arm with power, You strengthen Your hand; You exalt Your right hand.[26] Yours is the heaven; Yours, too, is the earth; the world and its fullness — You founded them.[27] You shattered the sea with Your might, You smashed sea serpents' heads upon the water.[28] You established all the boundaries of earth; summer and winter

אַתָּה יְצַרְתָּם.[1] אַתָּה רָצַצְתָּ רָאשֵׁי לִוְיָתָן, תִּתְּנֶנּוּ מַאֲכָל לְעַם לְצִיִּים. אַתָּה בָקַעְתָּ מַעְיָן וָנָחַל, אַתָּה הוֹבַשְׁתָּ נַהֲרוֹת אֵיתָן.[2] לְךָ יוֹם, אַף לְךָ לָיְלָה, אַתָּה הֲכִינְוֹתָ מָאוֹר וָשָׁמֶשׁ.[3] עֹשֶׂה גְדֹלוֹת עַד אֵין חֵקֶר, וְנִפְלָאוֹת עַד אֵין מִסְפָּר.[4] כִּי אֵל גָּדוֹל יהוה, וּמֶלֶךְ גָּדוֹל עַל כָּל אֱלֹהִים.[5] כִּי גָדוֹל אַתָּה וְעֹשֵׂה נִפְלָאוֹת, אַתָּה אֱלֹהִים לְבַדֶּךָ.[6] כִּי גָדוֹל מֵעַל שָׁמַיִם חַסְדֶּךָ, וְעַד שְׁחָקִים אֲמִתֶּךָ.[7] גָּדוֹל יהוה וּמְהֻלָּל מְאֹד, וְלִגְדֻלָּתוֹ אֵין חֵקֶר.[8] (כִּי) גָּדוֹל יהוה וּמְהֻלָּל מְאֹד, נוֹרָא הוּא עַל כָּל אֱלֹהִים.[9] גָּדוֹל יהוה וּמְהֻלָּל מְאֹד, בְּעִיר אֱלֹהֵינוּ הַר קָדְשׁוֹ.[10] לְךָ יהוה הַגְּדֻלָּה וְהַגְּבוּרָה, וְהַתִּפְאֶרֶת וְהַנֵּצַח וְהַהוֹד, כִּי כֹל בַּשָּׁמַיִם וּבָאָרֶץ; לְךָ יהוה הַמַּמְלָכָה, וְהַמִּתְנַשֵּׂא לְכֹל לְרֹאשׁ.[11] מִי לֹא יִרָאֲךָ מֶלֶךְ הַגּוֹיִם, כִּי לְךָ יָאָתָה, כִּי בְכָל חַכְמֵי הַגּוֹיִם וּבְכָל מַלְכוּתָם מֵאֵין כָּמוֹךָ.[12] מֵאֵין כָּמוֹךָ יהוה, גָּדוֹל אַתָּה וְגָדוֹל שִׁמְךָ בִּגְבוּרָה.[13] יהוה אֱלֹהֵי צְבָאוֹת, מִי כָמוֹךָ חֲסִין יָהּ, וֶאֱמוּנָתְךָ סְבִיבוֹתֶיךָ.[14] יהוה צְבָאוֹת, אֱלֹהֵי יִשְׂרָאֵל, יוֹשֵׁב הַכְּרֻבִים, אַתָּה הוּא הָאֱלֹהִים לְבַדֶּךָ.[15] מִי יְמַלֵּל גְּבוּרוֹת יהוה, יַשְׁמִיעַ כָּל תְּהִלָּתוֹ.[16] כִּי מִי בַשַּׁחַק יַעֲרֹךְ לַיהוה, יִדְמֶה לַיהוה בִּבְנֵי אֵלִים.[17] מַה נֹּאמַר לְפָנֶיךָ יוֹשֵׁב מָרוֹם, וּמַה נְּסַפֵּר לְפָנֶיךָ שֹׁכֵן שְׁחָקִים. מַה נֹּאמַר לְפָנֶיךָ יהוה אֱלֹהֵינוּ, מַה נְּדַבֵּר וּמַה נִּצְטַדָּק.[18] אֵין לָנוּ פֶּה לְהָשִׁיב וְלֹא מֵצַח לְהָרִים רֹאשׁ, כִּי עֲוֹנוֹתֵינוּ רַבּוּ מִלִּמְנוֹת, וְחַטֹּאתֵינוּ עָצְמוּ מִסַּפֵּר.[19] לְמַעַן שִׁמְךָ יהוה תְּחַיֵּנוּ, וּבְצִדְקָתְךָ תוֹצִיא מִצָּרָה נַפְשֵׁנוּ.[20] דַּרְכְּךָ אֱלֹהֵינוּ לְהַאֲרִיךְ אַפֶּךָ, לָרָעִים וְלַטּוֹבִים, וְהִיא תְהִלָּתֶךָ. לְמַעַנְךָ אֱלֹהֵינוּ עֲשֵׂה וְלֹא לָנוּ, רְאֵה עֲמִידָתֵנוּ, דַּלִּים וְרֵקִים. ✧ הַנְּשָׁמָה לָךְ, וְהַגּוּף פָּעֳלָךְ, חוּסָה עַל עֲמָלָךְ. הַנְּשָׁמָה לָךְ וְהַגּוּף שֶׁלָּךְ, יהוה עֲשֵׂה לְמַעַן שְׁמֶךָ. אָתָאנוּ עַל שִׁמְךָ, יהוה, עֲשֵׂה לְמַעַן שְׁמֶךָ. בַּעֲבוּר כְּבוֹד שִׁמְךָ, כִּי אֵל חַנּוּן וְרַחוּם שְׁמֶךָ. לְמַעַן שִׁמְךָ יהוה, וְסָלַחְתָּ לַעֲוֹנֵנוּ כִּי רַב הוּא.[21]

Congregation, then chazzan:

סְלַח לָנוּ אָבִינוּ, כִּי בְרוֹב אִוַּלְתֵּנוּ שָׁגִינוּ,
מְחַל לָנוּ מַלְכֵּנוּ, כִּי רַבּוּ עֲוֹנֵינוּ.

— *You fashioned them.*[1] *You crushed the heads of Leviathan, You served it as food to the nation of legions. You split open fountain and stream, You dried the mighty rivers.*[2] *Yours is the day, Yours as well is the night; You established luminary and the sun.*[3] *Who performs great deeds that are beyond comprehension, and wonders beyond number.*[4] *For a great God is HASHEM, and a great King above all heavenly powers.*[5] *For You are great and work wonders; You alone, O God.*[6] *For great above the very heavens is Your kindness, and until the upper heights is Your truth.*[7] *HASHEM is great and exceedingly lauded, and His greatness is beyond investigation.*[8] *(For) HASHEM is great and exceedingly lauded, awesome is He above all heavenly powers.*[9] *Great is HASHEM and exceedingly lauded, in the city of our God, Mount of His Holiness.*[10] *Yours, HASHEM, is the greatness, the strength, the splendor, the triumph, and the glory; even everything in heaven and earth; Yours, HASHEM, is the kingdom, and sovereignty over every leader.*[11] *Who would not revere You, O King of nations? — for this befits You, for among all the sages of the nations and in all their kingdom there is none like You.*[12] *There is none like You, O HASHEM, You are great and Your Name is great with power.*[13] *HASHEM, God of Legions — who is like You, O Strong One, God? — and Your faithfulness surrounds You.*[14] *HASHEM, Master of Legions, God of Israel, enthroned upon the Cherubim, it is You alone Who is God.*[15] *Who can express the mighty acts of HASHEM, who can announce all His praise?*[16] *For who in the sky can be compared to HASHEM; be likened to HASHEM among the angels?*[17] *What can we say before You Who dwell on high? And what can we relate to You Who abide in the highest heaven? What can we say before You, HASHEM, our God? What can we declare? What justification can we offer?*[18] *We have neither mouth to respond nor brow to raise our head, for our iniquities are too numerous to count, and our sins are too vast to be numbered.*[19] *For Your Name's sake, HASHEM, revive us; and with Your righteousness remove our soul from distress.*[20] *It is Your way, our God, to delay Your anger, against people both evil and good — and this is Your praise. Act for Your sake, our God, and not for ours, behold our [spiritual] position — destitute and emptyhanded.* Chazzan — *The soul is Yours and the body is Your handiwork; take pity on Your labor. The soul is Yours and the body is Yours; O HASHEM, act for Your Name's sake. We have come with reliance on Your Name, O HASHEM, act for Your Name's sake; because of Your Name's glory — for 'Gracious and Merciful God' is Your Name. For Your Name's sake, HASHEM, may You forgive our iniquity, though it is abundant.*[21]

Congregation, then chazzan:
Forgive us, our Father, for in our abundant folly we have erred, pardon us, our King, for our iniquities are many.

(1) *Psalms* 74:17. (2) 74:14-15. (3) 74:16. (4) *Job* 9:10. (5) *Psalms* 95:3.
(6) 86:10. (7) 108:5. (8) 145:3. (9) 96:4. (10) 48:2. (11) *I Chronicles* 29:11.
(12) *Jeremiah* 10:7. (13) 10:6. (14) *Psalms* 89:9. (15) *Isaiah* 37:16. (16) *Psalms* 106:2.
(17) 89:7. (18) Cf. *Genesis* 44:16. (19) Cf. *Ezra* 9:6. (20) Cf. *Psalms* 143:11. (21) Cf. 25:11.

All, while standing:

אֵל אֶרֶךְ אַפַּיִם אַתָּה, וּבַעַל הָרַחֲמִים נִקְרֵאתָ, וְדֶרֶךְ תְּשׁוּבָה הוֹרֵיתָ.

גְּדֻלַּת רַחֲמֶיךָ וַחֲסָדֶיךָ, תִּזְכּוֹר הַיּוֹם וּבְכָל יוֹם לְזֶרַע יְדִידֶיךָ. תֵּפֶן אֵלֵינוּ בְּרַחֲמִים, כִּי אַתָּה הוּא בַּעַל הָרַחֲמִים. בְּתַחֲנוּן וּבִתְפִלָּה פָּנֶיךָ נְקַדֵּם, כְּהוֹדַעְתָּ לֶעָנָיו מִקֶּדֶם. מֵחֲרוֹן אַפְּךָ שׁוּב,[1] כְּמוֹ בְתוֹרָתְךָ כָּתוּב.[2] וּבְצֵל כְּנָפֶיךָ נֶחֱסֶה[3] וְנִתְלוֹנָן, כְּיוֹם וַיֵּרֶד יהוה בֶּעָנָן. ❖ תַּעֲבוֹר עַל פֶּשַׁע וְתִמְחֶה אָשָׁם, כְּיוֹם וַיִּתְיַצֵּב עִמּוֹ שָׁם. תַּאֲזִין שַׁוְעָתֵנוּ וְתַקְשִׁיב מֶנּוּ מַאֲמָר, כְּיוֹם וַיִּקְרָא בְשֵׁם יהוה,[4] וְשָׁם נֶאֱמַר:

Congregation, then chazzan:

וַיַּעֲבֹר יהוה עַל פָּנָיו וַיִּקְרָא:

Congregation and chazzan (the words in bold type are recited aloud and in unison):

יהוה, יהוה, אֵל, רַחוּם, וְחַנּוּן, אֶרֶךְ אַפַּיִם, וְרַב חֶסֶד, וֶאֱמֶת, נֹצֵר חֶסֶד לָאֲלָפִים, נֹשֵׂא עָוֹן, וָפֶשַׁע, וְחַטָּאָה, וְנַקֵּה.[5] וְסָלַחְתָּ לַעֲוֹנֵנוּ וּלְחַטָּאתֵנוּ וּנְחַלְתָּנוּ.[6] סְלַח לָנוּ אָבִינוּ כִּי חָטָאנוּ, מְחַל לָנוּ מַלְכֵּנוּ כִּי פָשָׁעְנוּ. כִּי אַתָּה אֲדֹנָי טוֹב וְסַלָּח, וְרַב חֶסֶד לְכָל קֹרְאֶיךָ.[7]

פסוקי הקדמה לסליחה יד

שׁוּב מֵחֲרוֹן אַפֶּךָ, וְהִנָּחֵם עַל הָרָעָה לְעַמֶּךָ.[8] שׁוּב לְמַעַן עֲבָדֶיךָ, שִׁבְטֵי נַחֲלָתֶךָ.[9] שׁוּבָה יהוה רִבְבוֹת אַלְפֵי יִשְׂרָאֵל.[10] שׁוּבָה יהוה אֶת שְׁבִיתֵנוּ, כַּאֲפִיקִים בַּנֶּגֶב.[11] שׁוּבוּ שׁוּבוּ[12] אָמַרְתָּ לָנוּ, וְעַל הַתְּשׁוּבָה מֵרֹאשׁ הִבְטַחְתָּנוּ. הֲשִׁיבֵנוּ יהוה אֵלֶיךָ וְנָשׁוּבָה, חַדֵּשׁ יָמֵינוּ כְּקֶדֶם.[13]

כְּרַחֵם אָב עַל בָּנִים, כֵּן תְּרַחֵם יהוה עָלֵינוּ.[14] לַיהוה הַיְשׁוּעָה, עַל עַמְּךָ בִרְכָתֶךָ סֶּלָה.[15] יהוה צְבָאוֹת עִמָּנוּ, מִשְׂגָּב לָנוּ אֱלֹהֵי יַעֲקֹב סֶלָה.[16] יהוה צְבָאוֹת, אַשְׁרֵי אָדָם בֹּטֵחַ בָּךְ.[17] יהוה הוֹשִׁיעָה, הַמֶּלֶךְ יַעֲנֵנוּ בְיוֹם קָרְאֵנוּ.[18]

In some congregations the following two verses are recited responsively — the chazzan reciting סְלַח, and the congregation responding וַיֹּאמֶר. In other congregations these verses are recited silently.

סְלַח נָא לַעֲוֹן הָעָם הַזֶּה כְּגֹדֶל חַסְדֶּךָ, וְכַאֲשֶׁר נָשָׂאתָה לָעָם הַזֶּה מִמִּצְרַיִם וְעַד הֵנָּה,[19] וְשָׁם נֶאֱמַר:

All, while standing:

אֵל אֶרֶךְ אַפַּיִם O God — You are slow to anger, You are called the Master of Mercy, and You have taught the way of repentance. May You remember this day and every day the greatness of Your mercy and Your kindness to the offspring of Your beloved Ones. Turn to us in mercy for You are the Master of Mercy. With supplication and prayer we approach Your Presence in the manner that You made known to the humble [Moses] in ancient times. Turn back from Your fierce anger;[1] as is written in Your Torah.[2] In the shadow of Your wings may we find shelter[3] and lodging as on the day 'HASHEM descended in a cloud' [to appear to Moses on Sinai]. Chazzan — Overlook sin and erase guilt as on the day 'He [God] stood there with him [Moses].' Give heed to our cry and be attentive to our declaration as on the day 'He called out with the Name HASHEM,'[4] and there it was said:

Congregation, then chazzan:

And HASHEM passed before him [Moses] and proclaimed:

Congregation and chazzan (the words in bold type are recited aloud and in unison):

ה' ה' **HASHEM, HASHEM, God, Compassionate and Gracious, Slow to anger, and Abundant in Kindness and Truth, Preserver of kindness for thousands [of generations], Forgiver of iniquity, willful sin, and error, and Who cleanses.**[5] May You forgive our iniquities and our errors and make us Your heritage.[6] Forgive us, our Father, for we have erred; pardon us, our King, for we have willfully sinned; for You, my Lord, are good and forgiving and abundantly kind to all who call upon You.[7]

PREFATORY VERSES TO SELICHAH 14

שׁוּב Turn back from Your blasting anger, and reconsider the evil [that You would do] to Your people.[8] Return for the sake of Your servants, the tribes that are Your heritage.[9] Return, HASHEM, to the myriad thousands of Israel.[10] Return, O HASHEM, our captivity, like springs in the desert.[11] 'Return! Return!'[12] You said to us, and promised us of old about repentance. Return us to You, HASHEM, and we shall return; renew our days as of old.[13]

כְּרַחֵם אָב As a father has mercy on his children, so, HASHEM, may You have mercy on us.[14] Salvation is HASHEM's, upon Your people is Your blessing, Selah.[15] HASHEM, Master of Legions, is with us, a stronghold for us is the God of Jacob, Selah.[16] HASHEM, Master of Legions, praiseworthy is the person who trusts in You.[17] HASHEM, save! May the King answer us on the day we call.[18]

In some congregations the following two verses are recited responsively — the chazzan reciting, 'Forgive, please . . . ,' and the congregation responding, 'And HASHEM said . . .'
In other congregations these verses are recited silently.

סְלַח נָא Forgive, please, the iniquity of this people according to the greatness of Your kindness and as You have forgiven this people from Egypt until now,[19] and there it was said:

(1) Cf. Exodus 32:12. (2) See 32:14. (3) Cf. Psalms 36:8. (4) Exodus 34:5. (5) 34:6-7. (6) 34:9. (7) Psalms 86:5. (8) Exodus 32:12. (9) Isaiah 63:17. (10) Numbers 10:36. (11) Psalms 126:4. (12) Ezekiel 33:11. (13) Lamentations 5:21. (14) Cf. Psalms 103:13. (15) 3:9. (16) 46:8. (17) 84:13. (18) 20:10. (19) Numbers 14:19.

וַיֹּאמֶר יהוה סָלַחְתִּי כִּדְבָרֶךָ.[1]

All:

הַטֵּה אֱלֹהַי אָזְנְךָ וּשֲׁמָע, פְּקַח עֵינֶיךָ וּרְאֵה שֹׁמְמֹתֵינוּ, וְהָעִיר
אֲשֶׁר נִקְרָא שִׁמְךָ עָלֶיהָ, כִּי לֹא עַל צִדְקֹתֵינוּ אֲנַחְנוּ
מַפִּילִים תַּחֲנוּנֵינוּ לְפָנֶיךָ, כִּי עַל רַחֲמֶיךָ הָרַבִּים. אֲדֹנָי שְׁמָעָה,
אֲדֹנָי סְלָחָה, אֲדֹנָי הַקְשִׁיבָה, וַעֲשֵׂה אַל תְּאַחַר, לְמַעַנְךָ אֱלֹהַי,
כִּי שִׁמְךָ נִקְרָא עַל עִירְךָ וְעַל עַמֶּךָ.[2]

סליחה יד

All:

אֱלֹהֵינוּ וֵאלֹהֵי אֲבוֹתֵינוּ:

יִשְׂרָאֵל עַמְּךָ* תְּחִנָּה עוֹרְכִים,
שֶׁהֵם מִצְּרִים וּלְהִוָּשַׁע צְרִיכִים,
צָרֵיהֶם עֲלֵיהֶם עַל מַאֲרִיכִים,
כָּל זֹאת הַגַּעְתָּם וְשִׁמְךָ מְבָרְכִים.

חֳלִי וּמַכְאוֹב לְהִכָּתֵב לֹא נִמְסָר,
עֲלוּבִים מִנְּעַר וּמֵהֶם לֹא הוּסָר,
קָדוֹשׁ בְּיָדְךָ לְפַתֵּחַ מוּסָר,
כְּאֶמוּנָתְךָ הַנְּקִיָּה וְלֹא כְּאֶמוּנוֹת בָּשָׂר.

הַלּוֹבֵשׁ צְדָקָה וְלוּ כַּמְּעִיל עֲטוּיָה,[3]
וּמִמַּכָּה עַצְמָה מְתַקֵּן רְטִיָּה,*
קוֹמֵם עֲדָתְךָ מִנְּפִילָתָהּ הַמְּטוּיָה,
בְּכֹחֲךָ הַגָּדוֹל וּבִזְרֹעֲךָ הַנְּטוּיָה.[4]

טְמֵאִים[5] הָאוֹמְרִים נַחֲלָתְךָ לְחַבֵּל,
כְּבוֹדְךָ לְהָמִיר וּבַהֲבֵל לְהִתְהַבֵּל,[6]
נֵצֶר נִתְעָב[7] לֶאֱלוֹהַּ לְקַבֵּל,
וְיִרְאָתְךָ הַקְּדוֹשָׁה לִנְטֹשׁ וּלְנַבֵּל.

בְּאַהֲבָתְךָ וּבְחֶמְלָתְךָ מְנַשֵּׂא וּמְנַטֵּל,[8]
עֲצָתָם תְּסַכֵּל[9] וּמַחְשְׁבוֹתָם תְּבַטֵּל,

‮יִשְׂרָאֵל עַמְּךָ‬ — *Your people, Israel.* This
selichah bewails the tribulations caused by the
First Crusade (1096). It is the work of יִצְחָק הַקָּטָן
בְּרַבִּי מֵאִיר, *Yitzchak the lesser, son of R' Meir*, as
attested to by the acrostic. Best known as רִיבַ"ם,

Rivam, R' Yitzchak was a noted Tosafist, a
grandson to Rashi, and a brother of Rashbam and
Rabbeinu Tam. He lived in Ramerupt, France (c.
1090–c. 1130), and died at a relatively young age,
leaving seven orphans.

And HASHEM said, 'I have forgiven according to your word!'¹

All:

הַטֵּה *Incline, my God, Your ear, and listen, open Your eyes and see our desolation and that of the city upon which Your Name is proclaimed; for not because of our righteousness do we cast down our supplications before You, rather because of Your abundant compassion. O my Lord, heed; O my Lord, forgive; O my Lord, be attentive and act, do not delay; for Your sake, my God, for Your Name is proclaimed upon Your city and upon Your people.²*

SELICHAH 14

All:

Our God and the God of our forefathers:

י *Your people, Israel,* prepares [their] supplication,*
  for they are in travail and need to be helped.

צ *Their oppressors prolong the yoke upon them:*
  All this has befallen them, yet they bless Your name.

ח *[Their] disease and pain cannot be committed to writing;*
  degrading [them] from youth, it has not been removed.

ק *O Holy One, it is in Your power to open [their] bonds,*
  according to Your pure craft, and not like human craft.

ה *He Who dons righteousness, for Whom it is spread like a cloak,³*
  and from the wound itself prepares healing,*

ק *raise Your flock from its abject downfall*
  with Your great strength and Your outstretched arm.⁴

ט *The unclean ones⁵ who say they will destroy Your heritage,*
  to exchange Your glory for emptiness and imbue themselves with it;⁶

נ *To accept the vile offshoot⁷ as a god,*
  and Your holy awesomeness to abandon and revile.

ב *With Your love and Your compassion,*
  O You Who bear [us] and upraise [us],⁸
  confound their counsel⁹ and nullify their intentions.

---

(1) *Numbers* 14:20. (2) *Daniel* 9:18-19. (3) Cf. *Isaiah* 59:17; 61:10. (4) *Deuteronomy* 9:29. (5) This verse and the next have come under the heavy hand of the censors; some editions read, טוֹעִים, *misguided ones*, for טְמֵאִים, *unclean ones*; others omit these two verses altogether. (6) Cf. *Jeremiah* 2:11,5; some editions of *Selichos* read, וּבְהָבֵל לְהִתְבַּלְבֵּל, *and to become confused with emptiness*. (7) Cf. *Isaiah* 14:19; see commentary to selichah 12, s.v., בַּאֲמֶנֶת נוֹצֵר; some editions read, נוֹצֵר אָדָם, *the creation of man*; others read, נְטוֹת מִדְּרָכֶיךָ וְתוֹהוּ לְקַבֵּל, *to leave Your ways and to accept desolate [idols].* (8) Cf. *Isaiah* 63:9. (9) Some editions read, עֲצַת צוֹרְרֶיךָ תְּסַכֵּל, *confound Your enemies' counsel*; others read עֲצַת הָרָעִים תְּמַחֶה, *eradicate the counsel of the evil ones.*

וּמִמַּכָּה עַצְמָהּ מְתַקֵּן רְטִיָּה — *And from the wound itself prepares healing.* God is the Doctor *par excellence*, as the Torah states: כִּי אֲנִי ה' רֹפְאֶךָ, *for I am HASHEM your Healer* (Exodus 15:26). The prophets declared: *Let us go and return to HASHEM, for He has torn and He shall heal us; He has smitten and He shall bandage us* (Hosea 6:1); *Heal me, O HASHEM, and I shall be healed; save me, and I shall be saved* (Jeremiah 17:14); and, *For I shall bring a cure for you, from your very wound*

itself shall I heal you — the word of HASHEM (ibid. 30:17).

The Midrash expounds on the differences between the craft of human physicians and that of HASHEM: The way of the human doctor is that when a person is wounded with a knife, the doctor prepares a bandage for the wound. But that is not My way of healing; rather, *'from your very wound itself shall I heal you.'* God smote Job with a storm wind — *He pushed me with a storm*

רַבָּה מְהוּמָה בֵּינֵיהֶם הַטֵּל,

וּמַלְאָךְ אַכְזָרִי* דּוֹחֶה וּמְטַלְטֵל.

בַּעֲבוּר כְּבוֹד עַצְמְךָ[1] וְשֵׁם קָדְשְׁךָ הַמְהֻלָּל,

נוֹרְאוֹת הַפְלֵא לְכָל בַּגּוֹיִם יִתְחַלָּל,[2]

יוֹעֲצֵיהֶם וְאֵיתָנֵיהֶם תּוֹלִיךְ שׁוֹלָל,[3]

וּבָהֶם תְּעוֹלֵל כַּאֲשֶׁר בִּי הִתְעוֹלָל.[4]

מֵקִים מֵעָפָר דָּל וְאֶבְיוֹן מֵאַשְׁפָּה,[5]

כְּנִסָּתְךָ אַל תִּתֵּן לְכָלָה וּלְחֶרְפָּה,

אִם בְּפִקּוּדֶיךָ מִתְעַצֶּלֶת וּמַרְפָּה,

עַל כָּל פְּשָׁעֶיהָ אַהֲבָתְךָ תְּהֵא מְחַפָּה.[6]

יִתְרָה חִבַּתָם7 לְפָנֶיךָ אֲדֹנֵי הָאֲדוֹנִים,

בֵּין כָּךְ וּבֵין כָּךְ קְרוּאִים לְךָ בָּנִים,*

רַחֲמֶיךָ יְקַדְּמוּנוּ אֱלֹהֵי עֶלְיוֹנִים וְתַחְתּוֹנִים,

טֶרֶם יִשְׁטְפוּנוּ הַמַּיִם הַזֵּידוֹנִים.[8]

❖ חֲפָצֵי קִרְבָתְךָ עַל כָּל הַבָּאוֹת,

הָחִישָׁה לָמוֹ יְשׁוּעוֹת הַנִּבָּאוֹת,

קָדוֹשׁ עֲשֵׂה עִמָּם לְטוֹבָה אוֹת,[9]

חָזָק וְאַמִּיץ גּוֹאֲלָם יהוה צְבָאוֹת.[10]

All, while standing:

אֵל מֶלֶךְ יוֹשֵׁב עַל כִּסֵּא רַחֲמִים מִתְנַהֵג בַּחֲסִידוּת, מוֹחֵל עֲוֹנוֹת עַמּוֹ, מַעֲבִיר רִאשׁוֹן רִאשׁוֹן, מַרְבֶּה מְחִילָה לַחַטָּאִים וּסְלִיחָה לַפּוֹשְׁעִים, עֹשֶׂה צְדָקוֹת עִם כָּל בָּשָׂר וָרוּחַ, לֹא כְרָעָתָם תִּגְמוֹל. ❖ אֵל הוֹרֵיתָ לָּנוּ לוֹמַר שְׁלֹשׁ עֶשְׂרֵה, וּזְכוֹר לָנוּ הַיּוֹם בְּרִית שְׁלֹשׁ עֶשְׂרֵה, כְּמוֹ שֶׁהוֹדַעְתָּ לֶעָנָיו מִקֶּדֶם, כְּמוֹ שֶׁכָּתוּב, וַיֵּרֶד יהוה בֶּעָנָן וַיִּתְיַצֵּב עִמּוֹ שָׁם, וַיִּקְרָא בְשֵׁם יהוה.

---

wind, and caused me multiple wounds (Job 9:17). And He cured him with a storm wind — And HASHEM replied to Job from the storm wind . . . (ibid. 38:1). He caused Israel to be exiled with clouds — Alas, how He has beclouded in His anger . . . (Lamentations 2:1). And He will return Israel from exile with clouds — Who are these that fly like a cloud? (Isaiah 60:8). He dispersed

Israel like doves — And their fugitives will flee and be upon the mountain like doves of the valleys, all of them moaning, each in his sin (Ezekiel 7:16). And will gather them and return them to their land like doves — [Who are these that fly] as doves to their cotes? (Isaiah 60:8). Thus, in God's medical practice, the cure and healing are always derived from the sickness

ר Cast much confusion among them
  and repulse and give no rest to the cruel angel.*

ב For the sake of Your own honor[1] and Your lauded holy Name,
  do awesome wonders, that [Your Name] not be desecrated
      among the nations.[2]

י Lead their advisors and strong men into folly,[3]
  and torment them as they have tormented me.[4]

מ You Who raise the needy from the dust,
      the destitute from the trash heap,[5]
  do not deliver Your congregation to destruction and disgrace.

א Though they be slothful and lax regarding Your commands,
  let Your love cover over all their willful sins.[6]

י Your love for them abounds,[7] O Lord of lords;
  no matter what, they are called Your children.*

ר May Your mercy advance toward us,
      O God of the upper and lower [worlds],
  before the surging waters inundate us.[8]

Chazzan — Those who desire Your nearness, whatever befalls them —
  hasten for them the prophesied salvations.
O Holy One, perform for them a sign of [coming] good,[9]
[for] strong and powerful is their Redeemer,
  HASHEM, Master of Legions.[10]

All, while standing:

אֵל מֶלֶךְ O God, King Who sits on the throne of mercy; Who acts with
          kindness, pardons the iniquities of His people, removes [sins]
one by one, increasingly grants pardon to careless sinners and forgiveness
to rebels, Who deals righteously with every living being — You do not repay
them in accord with their evil. Chazzan — O God, You taught us to recite the
Thirteen [Attributes of Mercy], so remember for us today the covenant of
these Thirteen, as You made known to the humble one in ancient times, as
it is written: And HASHEM descended in a cloud and stood with him there,
and He called out with the Name HASHEM.

---

(1) Some editions read, כְּבוֹד שְׁמֶךָ, Your Name's honor. (2) Cf. Ezekiel 36:23.
(3) Cf. Job 12:17,19. (4) Cf. Lamentations 1:22. (5) Cf. I Samuel 2:8; Psalms 113:7.
(6) Cf. Proverbs 10:12. (7) See Tractate Avos 3:18. (8) Cf. Psalms 124:4-5.
(9) Cf. 86:17. (10) Cf. Isaiah 47:4; Jeremiah 50:34.

---

or wound itself (Mechilta to Shemos 14:24, see
also Pesikta Rabbasi 34:13 for thirty other
examples).

וּמַלְאָךְ אַכְזָרִי — The cruel angel. Repulse and
remove from Your presence the cruel angel who
accuses us before You. Alternatively, send a cruel
angel to repulse and scatter our oppressors
(Arugas HaBosem).

בֵּין כָּךְ וּבֵין כָּךְ קְרוּאִים לְךָ בָּנִים — No matter what
[lit., whether like this or like that], they are called
Your children. The paytan follows the view of R'

Meir in his explanation of the verse, בָּנִים אַתֶּם לַה׳
אֱלֹהֵיכֶם, You are children to HASHEM, your God
(Deuteronomy 14:1). According to R' Yehudah,
this verse applies only when Israel acts like
obedient children. But when they do not act like
obedient children, they are not considered God's
children. R' Meir, however, adduces four verses
(Jeremiah 4:22, Deuteronomy 32:20, Isaiah 1:4,
Hosea 2:1) to prove that בֵּין כָּךְ וּבֵין כָּךְ, whether
like this or like that, i.e., whether or not they are
obedient, they are called [God's] children (Kiddushin 36a).

Congregation, then *chazzan:*

וַיַּעֲבֹר יהוה עַל פָּנָיו וַיִּקְרָא:

Congregation and *chazzan* (the words in bold type are recited aloud and in unison):

יהוה, יהוה, אֵל, רַחוּם, וְחַנּוּן, אֶרֶךְ אַפַּיִם, וְרַב חֶסֶד, וֶאֱמֶת,
נֹצֵר חֶסֶד לָאֲלָפִים, נֹשֵׂא עָוֹן, וָפֶשַׁע, וְחַטָּאָה,
וְנַקֵּה. וְסָלַחְתָּ לַעֲוֹנֵנוּ וּלְחַטָּאתֵנוּ וּנְחַלְתָּנוּ. סְלַח לָנוּ אָבִינוּ כִּי
חָטָאנוּ, מְחַל לָנוּ מַלְכֵּנוּ כִּי פָשָׁעְנוּ. כִּי אַתָּה אֲדֹנָי טוֹב וְסַלָּח, וְרַב
חֶסֶד לְכָל קֹרְאֶיךָ.

פסוקי הקדמה לסליחה טו

אֵלֶיךָ יהוה נַפְשֵׁנוּ נִשָּׂא.[1] נִשָּׂא לְבָבֵנוּ אֶל כַּפָּיִם, אֶל אֵל
בַּשָּׁמָיִם.[2] כִּי עָלֶיךָ הֹרַגְנוּ כָל הַיּוֹם, נֶחְשַׁבְנוּ כְּצֹאן
טִבְחָה. עוּרָה לָמָּה תִישַׁן, אֲדֹנָי, הָקִיצָה, אַל תִּזְנַח לָנֶצַח.
לָמָּה פָנֶיךָ תַסְתִּיר, תִּשְׁכַּח עָנְיֵנוּ וְלַחֲצֵנוּ. כִּי שָׁחָה לֶעָפָר
נַפְשֵׁנוּ, דָּבְקָה לָאָרֶץ בִּטְנֵנוּ. קוּמָה עֶזְרָתָה לָּנוּ, וּפְדֵנוּ לְמַעַן
חַסְדֶּךָ.[3]

כְּרַחֵם אָב עַל בָּנִים, כֵּן תְּרַחֵם יהוה עָלֵינוּ. לַיהוה הַיְשׁוּעָה,
עַל עַמְּךָ בִרְכָתֶךָ סֶּלָה. יהוה צְבָאוֹת עִמָּנוּ, מִשְׂגָּב
לָנוּ אֱלֹהֵי יַעֲקֹב סֶלָה. יהוה צְבָאוֹת, אַשְׁרֵי אָדָם בֹּטֵחַ בָּךְ. יהוה
הוֹשִׁיעָה, הַמֶּלֶךְ יַעֲנֵנוּ בְיוֹם קָרְאֵנוּ.

In some congregations the following two verses are recited responsively — the *chazzan* reciting סְלַח,
and the congregation responding וַיֹּאמֶר. In other congregations these verses are recited silently.

סְלַח נָא לַעֲוֹן הָעָם הַזֶּה כְּגֹדֶל חַסְדֶּךָ, וְכַאֲשֶׁר נָשָׂאתָה לָעָם
הַזֶּה מִמִּצְרַיִם וְעַד הֵנָּה, וְשָׁם נֶאֱמַר:

וַיֹּאמֶר יהוה סָלַחְתִּי כִּדְבָרֶךָ.

All:

הַטֵּה אֱלֹהַי אָזְנְךָ וּשְׁמָע, פְּקַח עֵינֶיךָ וּרְאֵה שֹׁמְמֹתֵינוּ, וְהָעִיר
אֲשֶׁר נִקְרָא שִׁמְךָ עָלֶיהָ, כִּי לֹא עַל צִדְקֹתֵינוּ אֲנַחְנוּ
מַפִּילִים תַּחֲנוּנֵינוּ לְפָנֶיךָ, כִּי עַל רַחֲמֶיךָ הָרַבִּים. אֲדֹנָי שְׁמָעָה,
אֲדֹנָי סְלָחָה, אֲדֹנָי הַקְשִׁיבָה, וַעֲשֵׂה אַל תְּאַחַר, לְמַעַנְךָ אֱלֹהַי,
כִּי שִׁמְךָ נִקְרָא עַל עִירְךָ וְעַל עַמֶּךָ.

Congregation, then *chazzan:*

And HASHEM passed before him [Moses] and proclaimed:

Congregation and *chazzan* (the words in bold type are recited aloud and in unison):

ה' ה' HASHEM, HASHEM, God, Compassionate and Gracious, Slow to anger, and Abundant in Kindness and Truth, Preserver of kindness for thousands [of generations], Forgiver of iniquity, willful sin, and error, and Who cleanses. *May You forgive our iniquities and our errors and make us Your heritage. Forgive us, our Father, for we have erred; pardon us, our King, for we have willfully sinned; for You, my Lord, are good and forgiving and abundantly kind to all who call upon You.*

PREFATORY VERSES TO SELICHAH 15

אֵלֶיךָ *To You, HASHEM, we lift up our souls.[1] Let us lift our hearts with our hands to God in Heaven.[2] Because for Your sake we are killed all the time; we are considered as sheep for the slaughter. Awaken! Why do You [seem to] sleep, O my Lord? Arouse Yourself! Forsake [us] not forever! Why do You conceal Your face; why do you forget our affliction and oppression? For prostrated to the dust is our soul, stuck to the earth is our belly. Arise, assist us, and redeem us for the sake of Your kindness.[3]*

כְּרַחֵם אָב *As a father has mercy on his children, so, HASHEM, may You have mercy on us. Salvation is HASHEM's, upon Your people is Your blessing, Selah. HASHEM, Master of Legions, is with us, a stronghold for us is the God of Jacob, Selah. HASHEM, Master of Legions, praiseworthy is the person who trusts in You. HASHEM, save! May the King answer us on the day we call.*

In some congregations the following two verses are recited responsively — the *chazzan* reciting, 'Forgive, please . . .,' and the congregation responding, 'And HASHEM said . . .' In other congregations these verses are recited silently.

סְלַח נָא *Forgive, please, the iniquity of this people according to the greatness of Your kindness and as You have forgiven this people from Egypt until now, and there it was said:*

And HASHEM said, 'I have forgiven according to your word!'

All:

הַטֵּה *Incline, my God, Your ear, and listen, open Your eyes and see our desolation and that of the city upon which Your Name is proclaimed; for not because of our righteousness do we cast down our supplications before You, rather because of Your abundant compassion. O my Lord, heed; O my Lord, forgive; O my Lord, be attentive and act, do not delay; for Your sake, my God, for Your Name is proclaimed upon Your city and upon Your people.*

---

(1) Cf. *Psalms* 25:1. (2) *Lamentations* 3:41. (3) *Psalms* 44:23-27.

סליחה טו (שניה)

All:

אֱלֹהִים בְּיִשְׂרָאֵל* גָּדוֹל נוֹדָעְתָּ,[1] אַתָּה יהוה אָבִינוּ אָתָּה.[2]

בְּכָל קָרְאֵנוּ אֵלֶיךָ קָרְבֵנוּ,[3] רָם וְנִשָּׂא אַתָּה בְּקִרְבֵּנוּ.[4]*

גְּמַלְתָּנוּ הַטּוֹבוֹת בְּחוֹבֵנוּ, לֹא בְצִדְקוֹתֵינוּ וּבְיֹשֶׁר לְבָבֵנוּ.[5]

דּוֹדֵנוּ גַּם כִּי זְנַחְנוּ,[6] גְּאָלֵנוּ כִּי עֲבָדִים אֲנָחְנוּ.[7]*

הִגַּנּוּ בַּעֲוֹנֵנוּ עַד דַּכָּא,[8] וַתִּקְצַר נֶפֶשׁ לְךָ מֵחַכָּה.

וְאַיֵּה חֲסָדֶיךָ הָרִאשׁוֹנִים[9] עִמָּנוּ, מֵעוֹלָם וְעַד עוֹלָם נֶאֱמָנוּ.

זָעַף נָשָׂא[10] וַתַּשׁ כֹּחֵנוּ, יהוה אַל בְּאַפְּךָ תוֹכִיחֵנוּ.[11]

חַלְחָלוֹת רַבּוֹת בִּלּוּ בְשָׂרֵנוּ, נָא אַל בַּחֲמָתְךָ תְיַסְּרֵנוּ.[11]

טֹרַח הַצָּרוֹת אֵין לְהַסְפֵּר, אַיֵּה שֹׁקֵל וְאַיֵּה סוֹפֵר.[12]

יָדַעְנוּ רִשְׁעֵנוּ כִּי פָשָׁעְנוּ,[13] כִּי אֱמֶת עָשִׂיתָ וַאֲנַחְנוּ הִרְשָׁעְנוּ.[14]

כַּעַס וְחָרוֹן מֶנּוּ יֶחְדָּל,[15] כִּי קָטֹן יַעֲקֹב[16] וָדָל.

לַחַץ יוֹסַר וְעֹל (מֶנּוּ) יֶחְבָּל,[17] כִּי כָשַׁל כֹּחַ הַסַּבָּל.[18]

מְנָת מִדָּתֵנוּ לֹא תַגְבֵּהַּ, כִּי נִשְׁאַרְנוּ מְעַט מֵהַרְבֵּה.[19]

נַחֵם עַל הָרָעָה לְאֻמָּתֶךָ,[20] מַטֵּה כְּלַפֵּי חֶסֶד אֲמָנוּתֶךָ.[21]

סְלָחָה אִם עֲוֹנֵינוּ עָנוּ בָנוּ,[22] עָזְרֵנוּ כִּי עָלֶיךָ נִשְׁעָנּוּ.[23]

עָרְפֵּנוּ כֹף לְךָ לְהִשְׁתַּעְבֵּד, בְּאַהֲבָה וּבְיִרְאָה אוֹתְךָ לַעֲבֹד וּלְכַבֵּד.

פּוֹקְדֶיךָ קִדְּשׁוּ צוֹמוֹת לִקְבֹּעַ, דַּעְתָּם קְצָרָה צָרְכֶם לִתְבֹּעַ.

צַֽקוֹן לַחֲשָׁם[24] אֵלֶיךָ תָבֹא, חַתֵּל לְאִישׁ אִישׁ נִגְעוֹ וּמַכְאוֹבוֹ.[25]

קוֹל יַעֲקֹב נוֹהֵם מִתְּהוֹמוֹתֶיךָ, תִּשְׁמַע הַשָּׁמַיִם מְכוֹן שִׁבְתֶּךָ.[26]

רוֹדֶה רוֹדֵף בְּאַף תְּכַלֶּה, שְׁנַת שִׁלּוּמִים לְרִיב צִיּוֹן[27] תְּגַלֶּה.

---

(1) Cf. *Psalms* 76:2. (2) Cf. *Isaiah* 64:7. (3) Cf. *Deuteronomy* 4:7. (4) Cf. *Isaiah* 57:15.
(5) Cf. *Deuteronomy* 9:5. (6) Some editions read, זְנַחְנוּ, we have forsaken [You].
(7) *Ezra* 9:9. (8) Cf. *Psalms* 90:3. (9) Cf. 89:50. (10) Cf. *Micah* 7:9. (11) Cf. *Psalms* 6:2.
(12) Cf. *Isaiah* 33:18. (13) Cf. *Jeremiah* 14:20. (14) *Nehemiah* 9:33. (15) Some editions read,
כַּעַס יוּפַר וְחָרוֹן יֶחְדָּל, *Let anger be annulled and fury cease*; cf. *Psalms* 85:5.
(16) Cf. *Amos* 7:5. (17) Cf. *Isaiah* 10:27. (18) *Nehemiah* 4:4. (19) *Jeremiah* 42:2.
(20) Cf. *Exodus* 32:12; *Joel* 2:13; *Jonah* 4:2. (21) See commentary p. 20, s.v.,
מַעֲבִיר רִאשׁוֹן רִאשׁוֹן. (22) *Jeremiah* 14:7. (23) Cf. *II Chronicles* 14:10. (24) Cf. *Isaiah* 26:16. (25) Cf. *II Chronicles* 6:29.
(26) *I Kings* 8:39. (27) *Isaiah* 34:8; some editions of *Selichos* omit this line.

אֱלֹהִים בְּיִשְׂרָאֵל — *O God . . . in Israel*. This *selichah*, of unknown authorship, follows an *aleph-beis* acrostic.

רָם וְנִשָּׂא אַתָּה בְּקִרְבֵּנוּ — [Although You are] exalted and uplifted, You are [still] among us. R' Yochanan taught: Wherever you find God's greatness [mentioned in Scripture], there you find His humility. This phenomenon is written in the Torah, repeated in the Prophets, and stated a third time in the Writings . . . It is repeated in the Prophets, as it is written (*Isaiah* 57:15): *For so says* רָם וְנִשָּׂא, *the exalted and uplifted One, Who abides forever and Whose Name is holy,* 'I abide in exaltedness and holiness, but am with the crushed and lowly of spirit, to revive the spirit of the lowly and to revive the heart of the crushed' (*Megillah* 31a).

כִּי עֲבָדִים אֲנָחְנוּ — *For we are slaves.* The phrase

SELICHAH 15

All:

א O God, You are recognized in Israel* as great;[1]
You, are HASHEM, our father are You.[2]

ב Whenever we call upon You, draw us close;[3]
[although You are] exalted and uplifted, You are [still] among us.*[4]

ג You have done [us] favors despite our guilt,
not because of our righteousness and the uprightness of our heart.[5]

ד Our Beloved, though we have been forsaken,[6]
redeem us, for we are slaves.*[7]

ה Because of our iniquities we are now crushed,[8]
vexed is the soul that awaits You;

ו Where, then, are Your earlier kindnesses[9] towards us,
those who have been faithful, forever and ever?

ז We bear [Your] fury[10] and our strength is exhausted;
O HASHEM, do not rebuke us in Your anger.[11]

ח Many convulsions have withered our flesh;
please do not punish us in Your rage.[11]

ט The burden of our distress cannot be measured:
Where is he who can weigh [it]? Where is he who can count [it]?[12]

י We know our wickedness, for we have willfully sinned,[13]
for You have done what is true, while we have been wicked.[14]

כ Let anger and fury cease from us,[15]
for Jacob['s nation] is small[16] and needy;

ל let oppression be removed and [its] yoke be broken,[17]
for the strength of the bearer is spent.[18]

מ Do not exact our full measure [of sins],
for we remain a mere few out of many.[19]

נ Relent from the evil to Your nation,[20]
for Your craft is to tip [the scales] toward kindness.[21]

ס Forgive, though our iniquities testify against us;[22]
help us, for we depend on You.[23]

ע Bend our [stiff] neck to be subservient to You,
with love and reverence to serve and honor You.

פ Those who think of You have sanctified regular fast days;
their awareness is too limited to request their needs.

צ May their whispered prayer[24] come to You,
and may You heal each man's wound and pain.[25]

ק The voice of Jacob moans from Your depths —
may You hear in Heaven, the abode of Your dwelling.[26]

ר May You destroy the pursuing tyrant in Your anger,
and reveal a year of restitution for Zion's grievance.[27]

is taken from *Ezra 9:9*. There it states: *Although we are slaves to Darius, nevertheless, even in our slavery, our God has not abandoned us.* Ac- cordingly, the phrase here should be understood: *Redeem us, for we are slaves* to foreign masters. Some commentaries, however, including the

שָׂרַתָּ וְרָדְתָּ מִנְּעַר קְנוֹתֵנוּ,   וְאַל תַּשְׁלִיכֵנוּ לְעֵת זִקְנָתֵנוּ.[1]

תָּעִינוּ לִשְׂמֹאל וִימִינֶךָ תְּקָרְבֵנוּ,   כִּכְלוֹת כֹּחֵנוּ אַל תַּעַזְבֵנוּ.[1]

❖ תַּבִּיט וְתָצִיץ וְתַשְׁגִּיחַ לְרַחוּמֶיךָ,

תִּתְאַזַּר בַּחֲנִינוּתֶךָ, תִּתְלַבֵּשׁ בְּצִדְקוֹתֶיךָ,

תִּתְכַּסֶּה בְּרַחֲמֶיךָ, וְתִתְעַטֵּף בַּחֲסִידוּתֶךָ,

וְתָבֹא לְפָנֶיךָ מִדַּת טוּבְךָ וְעַנְוְתָנוּתֶךָ.[2]

All, while standing:

אֵל מֶלֶךְ יוֹשֵׁב עַל כִּסֵּא רַחֲמִים מִתְנַהֵג בַּחֲסִידוּת, מוֹחֵל
עֲוֹנוֹת עַמּוֹ, מַעֲבִיר רִאשׁוֹן רִאשׁוֹן, מַרְבֶּה מְחִילָה
לַחַטָּאִים וּסְלִיחָה לַפּוֹשְׁעִים, עֹשֶׂה צְדָקוֹת עִם כָּל בָּשָׂר וָרוּחַ,
לֹא כְרָעָתָם תִּגְמוֹל. ❖ אֵל הוֹרֵיתָ לָּנוּ לוֹמַר שְׁלֹשׁ עֶשְׂרֵה, וּזְכוֹר
לָנוּ הַיּוֹם בְּרִית שְׁלֹשׁ עֶשְׂרֵה, כְּמוֹ שֶׁהוֹדַעְתָּ לֶעָנָיו מִקֶּדֶם, כְּמוֹ
שֶׁכָּתוּב, וַיֵּרֶד יהוה בֶּעָנָן וַיִּתְיַצֵּב עִמּוֹ שָׁם, וַיִּקְרָא בְשֵׁם יהוה.

Congregation, then *chazzan:*

וַיַּעֲבֹר יהוה עַל פָּנָיו וַיִּקְרָא:

Congregation and *chazzan* (the words in bold type are recited aloud and in unison):

יהוה, יהוה, אֵל, **רַחוּם, וְחַנּוּן, אֶרֶךְ אַפַּיִם, וְרַב חֶסֶד, וֶאֱמֶת,
נֹצֵר חֶסֶד לָאֲלָפִים, נֹשֵׂא עָוֹן, וָפֶשַׁע, וְחַטָּאָה,
וְנַקֵּה.** וְסָלַחְתָּ לַעֲוֹנֵנוּ וּלְחַטָּאתֵנוּ וּנְחַלְתָּנוּ. סְלַח לָנוּ אָבִינוּ כִּי
חָטָאנוּ, מְחַל לָנוּ מַלְכֵּנוּ כִּי פָשָׁעְנוּ. כִּי אַתָּה אֲדֹנָי טוֹב וְסַלָּח,
וְרַב חֶסֶד לְכָל קֹרְאֶיךָ.

סְלִיחָה טז (פזמון)

Chazzan, then congregation:

יַשְׁמִיעֵנוּ* סָלַחְתִּי, יֹשֵׁב בְּסֵתֶר עֶלְיוֹן,*[3]

בִּימִין יֵשַׁע לְהוֹשִׁיעַ,[4] עַם עָנִי וְאֶבְיוֹן.

בְּשַׁוְעֵנוּ אֵלֶיךָ, נוֹרָאוֹת בְּצֶדֶק תַּעֲנֵנוּ,[5]   יהוה הֱיֵה עוֹזֵר לָנוּ.[6]

---

(1) Cf. *Psalms* 71:9. (2) See Tractate *Berachos* 16b; these last few lines (beginning תַּבִּיט וְתָצִיץ,
Gaze, peer) do not appear in some early manuscripts and may actually belong to another *selichah.*
(3) *Psalms* 91:1. (4) Cf. 20:7. (5) 65:6. (6) Cf. 30:11.

classic Yiddish translation, insert the word 'Your'
and read: *Redeem us, for we are Your slaves.*

יַשְׁמִיעֵנוּ ❧ — *Let us hear. Matteh Levi*, perhaps
the most popular commentary on *piyutim* in general and *Selichos* in particular, uncharacteristically writes regarding this *pizmon*: 'This *piyut* is
difficult in its entirety, for the composer desired
to tintinnabulate the ears. Thus, he sported with
the phraseology, language and stiches, at almost

every word. Due to the pressure and duress of this
[task], the meaning is so arcane, that the commen-
tator has become wearied trying to interpret his
riddles . . . ' (from *Matteh Levi's* preface to this
selichah).

Beginning with the second stanza the *paytan*
locked himself into the following intricate rhyme
scheme: (a) The first three line endings of each
stanza rhyme with each other; (b) the fourth line

ש *You saw and descended [to Egypt] to acquire us from our youth;*
    do not cast us off in time of old age![1]

ת *We have strayed to the left, but let Your right hand draw us close;*
    when our strength fails, forsake us not.[1]

Chazzan — *Gaze, peer, oversee the objects of Your mercy;*
    gird Yourself in Your graciousness,
        garb Yourself in Your righteousness.
Cover Yourself in Your mercy, wrap Yourself in Your kindness,
    and may Your attribute of goodness and Your humility
        come before You.[2]

All, while standing:

אֵל מֶלֶךְ *O God, King Who sits on the throne of mercy; Who acts with*
    kindness, pardons the iniquities of His people, removes [sins]
one by one, increasingly grants pardon to careless sinners and forgiveness
to rebels, Who deals righteously with every living being — You do not repay
them in accord with their evil. Chazzan — *O God, You taught us to recite the*
Thirteen [Attributes of Mercy], so remember for us today the covenant of
these Thirteen, as You made known to the humble one in ancient times, as
it is written: And HASHEM descended in a cloud and stood with him there,
and He called out with the Name HASHEM.

Congregation, then chazzan:

And HASHEM passed before him [Moses] and proclaimed:

Congregation and chazzan (the words in bold type are recited aloud and in unison):

ה' ה' **HASHEM, HASHEM,** *God,* **Compassionate and Gracious, Slow to**
    anger, and Abundant in Kindness and Truth, Preserver of
kindness for thousands [of generations], Forgiver of iniquity, willful
sin, and error, and Who cleanses. *May You forgive our iniquities and our*
errors and make us Your heritage. Forgive us, our Father, for we have
erred; pardon us, our King, for we have willfully sinned; for You, my Lord,
are good and forgiving and abundantly kind to all who call upon You.

SELICHAH 16

Chazzan, then congregation:

יַשְׁמִיעֵנוּ *Let us hear,* [from] Him Who sits in celestial concealment,**[3]
    'I have forgiven!';
by His right hand's salvation,[4] *may the poor*
    and destitute people be saved.
When we cry out to You,
    in Your righteousness respond to us with awesome deeds[5] —
        O HASHEM, be our Helper![6]

---

ending rhymes with the refrain; (c) the first half
of each line comprises two rhyming words or
phrases. In poetic shorthand the rhyme scheme is:
aab/ccb/ddb/eef/f/ggh/iih/jjh/kkf/f.

As indicated by the acrostic, the *selichah* was
written by שְׁלֹמֹה בְּרַבִּי שְׁמוּאֵל בְּרַבִּי יוֹאֵל, *Shlomo
son of R' Shmuel son of R' Yoel.* However, some
read the grandfather's name as אֵלִיָּה, *Eliyah* (see

commentary, s.v., to וַתֵּק . . . תְּצַלִּיחִי, below). In either case, nothing more is known of the *paytan*,
except that he flourished sometime before 1234,
the year in which the commentary *Arugas Ha-
Bosem* (which includes this *selichah*) was written.

יוֹשֵׁב בְּסֵתֶר עֶלְיוֹן — *[From] Him Who sits in celestial concealment.* In Psalms 91:1, this phrase
refers to those who trust in God's protection, i.e.,

Congregation, then chazzan:

שִׁוִּיתִי עֶזְרָתִי, עַל גִּבּוֹר[1] וְנִשָּׂא,

לִפְנֵי גֹחִי אֶשְׁפֹּךְ שִׂיחִי,[2] אוּלַי פָּנַי יִשָּׂא,[3]

מִדְּתִי כִּוַּנְתִּי, כַּסֵּדֶר אֲשֶׁר עָשָׂה.

הֲלֹא יַקִּיר מְקַרְקַר קִיר,*[4] עוֹד זָכוֹר תִּזְכְּרֶנּוּ,[5]

יהוה הָיָה עוֹזֵר לָנוּ.

Congregation, then chazzan:

בְּבֹא כְּגַל הַגַּלְגַּל,* לְהַחֲלִיף הַשָּׁטָה,

רָעֲיָתָךְ יוֹנָתָךְ,[6] לְךָ פוֹנָה הַבִּיטָה,

בְּאַוַּת נַפְשָׁה הַגִּישָׁה, לִפְתֹּחַ בַּחֲרָטָה.

יָמִין* פְּשׁוּטָה מִלְּמַטָּה, בְּצִפְּיָתֵנוּ צְפִינוּ,[7]

יהוה הָיָה עוֹזֵר לָנוּ.

Congregation, then chazzan:

שׁוֹאֵל חֶסֶד בְּהִנָּסֵד, הִנְנִי תֹאמַר,[8]

מָרוּת יֵצֶר הַבָּצֵר, קָבוּעַ כְּבַמַּסְמָר,

וּלְצַוָּאר כְּמוֹ סַנְאָר, הוּטַל לְמִשְׁמָר.

וּמִי אָזַר[9] זֵר לָזָר, וּמִי אַכְזָר כִּי יְעָרֶנּוּ,[10]

יהוה הָיָה עוֹזֵר לָנוּ.

Congregation, then chazzan:

לַחֲבַצֶּלֶת פְּתַח דֶּלֶת, אֱלוֹהַ מִמַּעַל,

בִּינָה הֲגִיגִי[11] לְהַצִּיגִי, בְּתוֹךְ שַׁעַר הַנִּגְעַל,[12]

רַחֲמֵנוּ קַדְּמֵנוּ, צָרֵי וּמָזוֹר הַתְעַל,

בָּרֵר חִכִּי, לְהַצְדִּיקִי, יְבַקֵּשׁ עָוֹן וְאֵינֶנּוּ,[13]

יהוה הָיָה עוֹזֵר לָנוּ.

Congregation, then chazzan:

יוֹנַת אֵלֶם[14] מְשֻׁלָּם,* חֵלֶק יָפֶה תַּגִּיעַ,

אוֹת צֶדֶק בְּהִצְטַדֵּק, בְּיִרְאָתָךְ לְהוֹשִׁיעָה,

---

he who sits in the refuge of the Most High. Here the *paytan* borrows the phrase to refer to God Who is concealed from us in the celestial heights.

מְקַרְקַר קִיר — *Breaking down the [celestial] barrier*. The phrase is taken from *Isaiah 22:5*, where it refers to the enemies battering down the walls of Jerusalem. The translation here follows *Matteh Levi* who understands it as an allusion to Israel's prayers breaking down the spiritual barrier erected by sins that prevents Israel's prayers from reaching the Throne of Glory. As the Talmud states (*Bava Metzia 59a*): Since the day the *Beis HaMikdash* was destroyed, the gates of prayer have been sealed.

According to *Arugas HaBosem*, קִיר refers to the Assyrian province of Kir (see commentaries to *Isaiah 22:6*) and the stich means: *Kir [read, Assyria] shatters Your precious [Israel]; therefore,*

may You yet remember us.

The Talmud [*Taanis 29a*, according to the reading of *Ain Yaakov*] renders מְקַרְקַר, *crowing*, and קִיר, *wailing*. Thus, *God*, so to speak, *cries like a rooster and wails* about the destruction of Zion and Jerusalem. Following this interpretation, our stich means: *God, as it were, cries and wails over the plight of His precious [Israel], and shall yet remember us.*

הַגַּלְגַּל — *The [evil] wheel*. Just as a storm wave may suddenly roll over a ship and drown it, so does the *Yetzer Hara* (Evil Inclination) attempt to overwhelm a person without warning, in order to turn him from the lane of righteousness and submerge him in the depths of sin. And, measure for measure, this will cause God to turn from His attribute of Mercy to His attribute of Strict Justice.

Alternatively, this alludes to the wheel of mis-

Congregation, then chazzan:

ש I have placed [the burden of] my help on the Mighty,[1] Exalted One.

ל Before Him Who drew me [from the womb], I pour forth my prayer;[2]
perhaps He will turn His countenance toward me.[3]

מ I have arranged my [recitation of the Thirteen] Attributes
in the order He set;

ה Your precious [Israel] is breaking down the [celestial] barrier,*[4]
and You shall yet remember us.[5]   O HASHEM, be our Helper!

Congregation, then chazzan:

ב When the [evil] wheel* comes like a wave to turn over the way,

ר Your mate, Your dove,[6] turns to You — look!

ב At her soul's longing she approaches to begin [her display of] regret:

י [The] right hand* stretching from below, as we await in hope[7]—
O HASHEM, be our Helper!

Congregation, then chazzan:

ש When the gathered [folk] ask for kindness, 'Here I am!' You shall say.[8]

מ The [Evil] Inclination's sovereignty will be denied,
[though it is] fixed in us as with a nail;

ו and it is placed on our shoulders like a beam of wood, to hold us.

א Who has been girded [with strength][9] to throw off the
[satanic] stranger, and who is so truculent as to shove him aside?[10]
O HASHEM, be our Helper!

Congregation, then chazzan:

ל Open the door for the lily, O God on high;

ב perceive my thoughts[11] and put me within the locked gate.[12]

ר Have mercy on us, come to meet us,
bringing the balm and cure [of atonement].

ב Make [the words of] my palate clear, that I may be judged righteous.

י Let sin be searched for, and no longer be.[13]O HASHEM, be our Helper!

Congregation, then chazzan:

יו [Israel] the dove of silence [sent afar[14] into exile] from Jerusalem* —
may she receive a good portion,

א a sign of righteousness, as she achieves righteousness,
through [her] reverence for You to be saved.

---

(1) Cf. *Psalms* 89:20. (2) Cf. 102:1. (3) Cf. *Genesis* 32:21; *Numbers* 6:26.
(4) Cf. *Isaiah* 22:5; most editions of *Selichos* read מְקַרְקֵר, but the source verse reads מְקַרְקַר.
(5) Cf. *Jeremiah* 31:20. (6) Cf. *Songs of Songs* 5:2. (7) *Lamentations* 4:17.
(8) Cf. *Isaiah* 58:9; many editions of *Selichos* read הִנְנִי, but the meaning is the same.
(9) *Arugas HaBosem* reads אָזַר אֵזוֹר, *May He Who has girded Himself . . .* a reading that better fits
the acrostic, but has not been followed in any of the early printed *Selichos*. (10) Cf. *Job* 41:2.
(11) *Psalms* 5:2. (12) See commentary to מְקַרְקֵר קִיר, above. (13) Cf. *Jeremiah* 50:20. (14) *Psalms* 56:1.

---

fortune that may overtake a person and cause him
to lose faith and to abandon his righteous ways
for a life of sin, Heaven forbid.

יָמִין — [The] right hand. According to most commentaries, this refers to the right hand of God, as
it were, which is extended earthward from under
His Throne of Glory to accept penitents. Others,
noting the lack of the possessive suffix (יְמִינְךָ,
Your right hand), understand this as the peni-

tent's right hand stretched upward toward
heaven from earth below.

יוֹנַת אֵלֶם מְשֻׁלָּם — [Israel] the dove of silence [sent
afar into exile] from Jerusalem. The translation
follows the sense of *Psalms* 56:1 which reads, יוֹנַת
אֵלֶם רְחֹקִים, *the distant dove of silence,* a reference
to King David when he was forced to flee from
King Saul and take refuge in Gath, in Philistia.
שָׁלֵם, *Salem,* was an ancient name of Jerusalem.

לְךָ תִּקְרָא עֵת לְשַׁחְרְרָה, אָדוֹן בְּזוֹ הַשָּׁעָה.

נַתֵּק* תִּיק מְנֻרְתָּק, כְּאוֹר תּוֹצִיא דִינֵנוּ,   יהוה הֱיֵה עוֹזֵר לָנוּ.

Congregation, then *chazzan:*

תַּצְלִיחֵי* בְּמִשְׁלָחַי,* אָשִׁיב שׁוֹלְחִי דָבָר,

חֻזַּקְתָּ חֹק חֲקַקְתָּ, עֶשֶׂר וְשָׁלֹשׁ כִּמְדֻבָּר,

מַחֲזִיקָם וְלֹא רֵיקָם,* שָׁלַחְתִּי לְהִתְגַּבֵּר.

וְכֹה תַעֲשֶׂה עָוֹן נִשָּׂא, עַתָּה תָשׁוּב תְּרַחֲמֵנוּ,[1]

יהוה הֱיֵה עוֹזֵר לָנוּ.

All, while standing:

אֵל מֶלֶךְ יוֹשֵׁב עַל כִּסֵּא רַחֲמִים מִתְנַהֵג בַּחֲסִידוּת, מוֹחֵל עֲוֹנוֹת עַמּוֹ, מַעֲבִיר רִאשׁוֹן רִאשׁוֹן, מַרְבֶּה מְחִילָה לְחַטָּאִים וּסְלִיחָה לְפוֹשְׁעִים, עֹשֶׂה צְדָקוֹת עִם כָּל בָּשָׂר וָרוּחַ, לֹא כְרָעָתָם תִּגְמוֹל. אֵל הוֹרֵיתָ לָנוּ לוֹמַר שְׁלֹשׁ עֶשְׂרֵה, וּזְכֹר לָנוּ הַיּוֹם בְּרִית שְׁלֹשׁ עֶשְׂרֵה, כְּמוֹ שֶׁהוֹדַעְתָּ לֶעָנָיו מִקֶּדֶם, כְּמוֹ שֶׁכָּתוּב, וַיֵּרֶד יהוה בֶּעָנָן וַיִּתְיַצֵּב עִמּוֹ שָׁם, וַיִּקְרָא בְשֵׁם יהוה.

Congregation, then *chazzan:*

וַיַּעֲבֹר יהוה עַל פָּנָיו וַיִּקְרָא:

Congregation and *chazzan* (the words in bold type are recited aloud and in unison):

יהוה, יהוה,   אֵל, רַחוּם, וְחַנּוּן, אֶרֶךְ אַפַּיִם, וְרַב חֶסֶד, וֶאֱמֶת, נֹצֵר חֶסֶד לָאֲלָפִים, נֹשֵׂא עָוֹן, וָפֶשַׁע, וְחַטָּאָה, וְנַקֵּה. וְסָלַחְתָּ לַעֲוֹנֵנוּ וּלְחַטָּאתֵנוּ וּנְחַלְתָּנוּ. סְלַח לָנוּ אָבִינוּ כִּי חָטָאנוּ, מְחַל לָנוּ מַלְכֵּנוּ כִּי פָשָׁעְנוּ. כִּי אַתָּה אֲדֹנָי טוֹב וְסַלָּח, וְרַב חֶסֶד לְכָל קֹרְאֶיךָ.

Abraham called the city יִרְאֶה, *Yireh* [Jeru] (see *Genesis* 22:14). Shem, son of Noah [also called Malchi-zedek], called the city שָׁלֵם, *Shalem* [Salem] (see ibid. 14:18). God said, 'If I call it *Yireh* as Abraham did, then the righteous Shem will be distraught. But if I call it *Shalem*, the righteous Abraham will be distraught. Instead I will satisfy both these righteous men by calling it *Yireh-Shalem* [Jeru-Salem]' (*Bereishis Rabbah* 56:10). [Incidentally, this Midrash provides the answer to an often-asked question: Why is the name יְרוּשָׁלַיִם almost always spelled without the second י when it appears in Scriptures? Because the original spelling of שָׁלֵם is thus retained in the new name. (The change from יראה to ירו can be

explained with *gematria,* for both אה and ו have a *gematria* of six. Thus, one may be substituted for the other.)]

Alternatively, שָׁלֵם means *the Perfect One* and refers to God. If so, the stich reads: *Let [Israel] the dove of silence receive a good portion from the Perfect One.*

נַתֵּק . . . תַּצְלִיחֵי — *Loosen . . . Bring me success.* According to *Arugas HaBosem,* these words should be יוּתַּק and תַּצְלִיחֵי. Although the translation remains the same, this reading leads us to a different acrostic for the *paytan's* grandfather's name: The initial letters of בִּינָה, רַחֲמָנוּ, בְּרָר, יוֹנַת, spell יוֹנַת, and the initial letters of אוֹת, לְךָ, יוּתַּק, הַצְלִיחֵי spell בְּרַבִּי אֵלִיָּה, *the son of R' Eliyah.*

ל For Your sake, decree a time to liberate her, O Lord, in this very hour.
Loosen* the cover from the case [of medicine for our souls];
   bring forth our judgment [clear and pure] as light —
                                                    O HASHEM, be our Helper!

Congregation, then chazzan:

Bring me success* in my mission,*
   that I may bring those who sent me an answer.
You have made strong the law You decreed,
   [that the] ten and three [Attributes] as was spoken,
[will] uphold [Israel], and not be for naught;*
   I have been sent to use my strength,
And so may You do, You Who forgives iniquity;
   now, be merciful to us once again[1] —   O HASHEM, be our Helper!

All, while standing:

אֵל מֶלֶךְ O God, King Who sits on the throne of mercy; Who acts with
   kindness, pardons the iniquities of His people, removes
[sins] one by one, increasingly grants pardon to careless sinners and
forgiveness to rebels, Who deals righteously with every living being —
You do not repay them in accord with their evil. Chazzan — O God, You
taught us to recite the Thirteen [Attributes of Mercy], so remember for
us today the covenant of these Thirteen, as You made known to the
humble one in ancient times, as it is written: And HASHEM descended in
a cloud and stood with him there, and He called out with the Name
HASHEM.

Congregation, then chazzan:

And HASHEM passed before him [Moses] and proclaimed:

Congregation and chazzan (the words in bold type are recited aloud and in unison):

ה' ה' HASHEM, HASHEM, God, Compassionate and Gracious, Slow
   **to anger, and Abundant in Kindness and Truth, Preserver of
kindness for thousands [of generations], Forgiver of iniquity, willful
sin, and error, and Who cleanses.** May You forgive our iniquities
and our errors and make us Your heritage. Forgive us, our Father, for
we have erred; pardon us, our King, for we have willfully sinned; for
You, my Lord, are good and forgiving and abundantly kind to all who
call upon You.

---

(1) Cf. Micah 7:19.

תַּצְלִיחִי בְמִשְׁלַחִי — Bring me success in my
mission. This stanza was obviously intended
for the chazzan. Originally, and in some congregations still, only the chazzan would chant
the stanzas of a pizmon (piyut with refrain)
and the congregation would respond with the
refrain.

מְחַזִּיקָם וְלֹא רֵיקָם — [Will] uphold [Israel] and not
be for naught. The Talmud states that a covenant
was sealed with the Thirteen Attributes that
whenever Israel recites them in their fast day
prayers, they will not be returned for naught [but
will accomplish their purpose] (Rosh Hashanah
17b, see Rashi there).

All:

אַל תִּזְכָּר לָנוּ עֲוֹנוֹת רִאשׁוֹנִים, מַהֵר יְקַדְּמוּנוּ רַחֲמֶיךָ, כִּי דַלּוֹנוּ מְאֹד.[1] חַטַּאת נְעוּרֵינוּ וּפְשָׁעֵינוּ אַל תִּזְכּוֹר, כְּחַסְדְּךָ זְכָר לָנוּ אַתָּה, לְמַעַן טוּבְךָ יהוה.[2]

זְכוֹר רַחֲמֶיךָ יהוה וַחֲסָדֶיךָ, כִּי מֵעוֹלָם הֵמָּה.[3] זָכְרֵנוּ יהוה בִּרְצוֹן עַמֶּךָ, פָּקְדֵנוּ בִּישׁוּעָתֶךָ.[4] זְכֹר עֲדָתְךָ קָנִיתָ קֶּדֶם, גָּאַלְתָּ שֵׁבֶט נַחֲלָתֶךָ, הַר צִיּוֹן זֶה שָׁכַנְתָּ בּוֹ.[5] זְכֹר יהוה חִבַּת יְרוּשָׁלַיִם, אַהֲבַת צִיּוֹן אַל תִּשְׁכַּח לָנֶצַח.[6] אַתָּה תָקוּם תְּרַחֵם צִיּוֹן, כִּי עֵת לְחֶנְנָהּ כִּי בָא מוֹעֵד.[7] זְכֹר יהוה לִבְנֵי אֱדוֹם אֵת יוֹם יְרוּשָׁלַיִם, הָאֹמְרִים עָרוּ עָרוּ עַד הַיְסוֹד בָּהּ.[8] זְכֹר לְאַבְרָהָם לְיִצְחָק וּלְיִשְׂרָאֵל עֲבָדֶיךָ אֲשֶׁר נִשְׁבַּעְתָּ לָהֶם בָּךְ, וַתְּדַבֵּר אֲלֵהֶם, אַרְבֶּה אֶת זַרְעֲכֶם כְּכוֹכְבֵי הַשָּׁמָיִם, וְכָל הָאָרֶץ הַזֹּאת אֲשֶׁר אָמַרְתִּי אֶתֵּן לְזַרְעֲכֶם, וְנָחֲלוּ לְעֹלָם.[9] ❖ זְכֹר לַעֲבָדֶיךָ לְאַבְרָהָם לְיִצְחָק וּלְיַעֲקֹב, אַל תֵּפֶן אֶל קְשִׁי הָעָם הַזֶּה וְאֶל רִשְׁעוֹ וְאֶל חַטָּאתוֹ.[10]

Chazzan, then congregation:

אֵל נָא תָשֵׁת עָלֵינוּ חַטָּאת, אֲשֶׁר נוֹאַלְנוּ וַאֲשֶׁר חָטָאנוּ.[11]

Chazzan, then congregation:

חָטָאנוּ צוּרֵנוּ, סְלַח לָנוּ יוֹצְרֵנוּ.

All:

זְכוֹר לָנוּ בְּרִית אָבוֹת, כַּאֲשֶׁר אָמַרְתָּ: וְזָכַרְתִּי אֶת בְּרִיתִי יַעֲקוֹב, וְאַף אֶת בְּרִיתִי יִצְחָק, וְאַף אֶת בְּרִיתִי אַבְרָהָם אֶזְכֹּר, וְהָאָרֶץ אֶזְכֹּר.[12] זְכוֹר לָנוּ בְּרִית רִאשׁוֹנִים, כַּאֲשֶׁר אָמַרְתָּ: וְזָכַרְתִּי לָהֶם בְּרִית רִאשֹׁנִים, אֲשֶׁר הוֹצֵאתִי אֹתָם מֵאֶרֶץ מִצְרַיִם לְעֵינֵי הַגּוֹיִם, לִהְיוֹת לָהֶם לֵאלֹהִים, אֲנִי יהוה.[13] עֲשֵׂה עִמָּנוּ כְּמָה שֶׁהִבְטַחְתָּנוּ: וְאַף גַּם זֹאת בִּהְיוֹתָם בְּאֶרֶץ אֹיְבֵיהֶם, לֹא מְאַסְתִּים וְלֹא גְעַלְתִּים לְכַלֹּתָם לְהָפֵר בְּרִיתִי אִתָּם, כִּי אֲנִי יהוה אֱלֹהֵיהֶם.[14] הִמָּצֵא לָנוּ בְּבַקָּשָׁתֵנוּ, כְּמָה שֶׁכָּתוּב: וּבִקַּשְׁתֶּם מִשָּׁם אֶת יהוה אֱלֹהֶיךָ וּמָצָאתָ, כִּי תִדְרְשֶׁנּוּ בְּכָל לְבָבְךָ וּבְכָל נַפְשֶׁךָ.[15] מוֹל אֶת לְבָבֵנוּ לְאַהֲבָה וּלְיִרְאָה אֶת שְׁמֶךָ, כְּמָה שֶׁכָּתוּב: וּמָל יהוה אֱלֹהֶיךָ אֶת לְבָבְךָ וְאֶת לְבַב זַרְעֶךָ, לְאַהֲבָה אֶת יהוה אֱלֹהֶיךָ בְּכָל לְבָבְךָ

All:

אַל תִּזְכָּר **Do not recall** against us the iniquities of the ancients; speedily — let Your mercy come to meet us for we have fallen very low.[1] Remember not the sins of our youth and our rebellions; may You remember for us [the deeds] worthy of Your kindness, because of Your goodness, HASHEM.[2]

זְכוֹר רַחֲמֶיךָ **Remember** Your mercies, O HASHEM, and Your kindnesses, for they are from the beginning of the world.[3] Remember us, HASHEM, when You show Your people favor and recall us with Your salvation.[4] Remember Your congregation that You acquired of old, that You redeemed the tribe of Your heritage, and this Mount Zion where You dwelled.[5] Remember, O HASHEM, the affection of Jerusalem, may You never forget the love of Zion.[6] You will arise and show Zion mercy, for it is the time to be gracious to her, for the appointed time will have come.[7] Remember, HASHEM, for the offspring of Edom, the day of Jerusalem — for those who said: 'Destroy! Destroy to its very foundation!'[8] Remember Abraham, Isaac, and Israel, Your servants, to whom You swore by Your Being, saying to them, 'I shall increase your offspring like the stars of the heavens; and this entire land of which I spoke I will give to your offspring and they will inherit it forever.'[9] Chazzan — Remember for Your servants, for Abraham, for Isaac, and for Jacob; ignore the stubbornness of this people, its wickedness and its sinfulness.[10]

Chazzan, then congregation:

Please, do not reckon for us a sin,
what we have done foolishly and what we have sinned.[11]

Chazzan, then congregation:

We have erred, our Rock! Forgive us, our Molder!

All:

זְכוֹר **Remember** for us the covenant of the Patriarchs, as You said: 'And I will remember My covenant with Jacob, and also My covenant with Isaac, and also My covenant with Abraham will I remember; and the Land will I remember.'[12] Remember for us the covenant of the ancestors, as You said: 'And I will remember for them the covenant of the ancestors whom I removed from the land of Egypt in the very sight of the nations, to be a God to them; I am HASHEM.'[13] Do with us as You promised us: 'And despite all that, when they will be in the land of their enemies, I will not have despised them nor abhorred them to destroy them, to annul My covenant with them, for I am HASHEM their God.'[14] Be accessible to us in our quest, as it is written: From there you will seek HASHEM, your God, and you will find, when you search for Him with all your heart and with all your soul.[15] Expose our hearts to love Your Name, as it is written: HASHEM, your God, will expose your heart and the heart of your offspring, to love HASHEM, your God, with all your heart

(1) Psalms 79:8. (2) Cf. 25:7. (3) 25:6. (4) Cf. 106:4. (5) 74:2. (6) This is not a Scriptural verse. (7) Psalms 102:14. (8) 137:7. (9) Exodus 32:13. (10) Deuteronomy 9:27. (11) Numbers 12:11. (12) Leviticus 26:42. (13) 26:45. (14) 26:44. (15) Deuteronomy 4:29.

וּבְכָל נַפְשֶׁךָ, לְמַעַן חַיֶּיךָ.[1] זְרוֹק עָלֵינוּ מַיִם טְהוֹרִים וְטַהֲרֵנוּ, כְּמָה
שֶׁכָּתוּב: וְזָרַקְתִּי עֲלֵיכֶם מַיִם טְהוֹרִים וּטְהַרְתֶּם, מִכֹּל טֻמְאוֹתֵיכֶם
וּמִכָּל גִּלּוּלֵיכֶם אֲטַהֵר אֶתְכֶם.[2] מְחֵה פְשָׁעֵינוּ כָּעָב וְכֶעָנָן, כְּמָה
שֶׁכָּתוּב: מָחִיתִי כָעָב פְּשָׁעֶיךָ וְכֶעָנָן חַטֹּאתֶיךָ, שׁוּבָה אֵלַי כִּי
גְאַלְתִּיךָ.[3] מְחֵה פְשָׁעֵינוּ לְמַעֲנָךְ, כַּאֲשֶׁר אָמַרְתָּ: אָנֹכִי אָנֹכִי הוּא
מֹחֶה פְשָׁעֶיךָ לְמַעֲנִי, וְחַטֹּאתֶיךָ לֹא אֶזְכֹּר.[4] הַלְבֵּן חֲטָאֵינוּ כַּשֶּׁלֶג
וְכַצֶּמֶר, כְּמָה שֶׁכָּתוּב: לְכוּ נָא וְנִוָּכְחָה, יֹאמַר יהוה, אִם יִהְיוּ
חֲטָאֵיכֶם כַּשָּׁנִים, כַּשֶּׁלֶג יַלְבִּינוּ, אִם יַאְדִּימוּ כַתּוֹלָע, כַּצֶּמֶר יִהְיוּ.[5]
רַחֵם עָלֵינוּ וְאַל תַּשְׁחִיתֵנוּ, כְּמָה שֶׁכָּתוּב: כִּי אֵל רַחוּם יהוה
אֱלֹהֶיךָ, לֹא יַרְפְּךָ וְלֹא יַשְׁחִיתֶךָ וְלֹא יִשְׁכַּח אֶת בְּרִית אֲבוֹתֶיךָ
אֲשֶׁר נִשְׁבַּע לָהֶם.[6] קַבֵּץ נִדָּחֵינוּ כְּמָה שֶׁכָּתוּב: אִם יִהְיֶה נִדַּחֲךָ בִּקְצֵה
הַשָּׁמָיִם, מִשָּׁם יְקַבֶּצְךָ יהוה אֱלֹהֶיךָ וּמִשָּׁם יִקָּחֶךָ.[7] הָשֵׁב שְׁבוּתֵנוּ
וְרַחֲמֵנוּ, כְּמָה שֶׁכָּתוּב: וְשָׁב יהוה אֱלֹהֶיךָ אֶת שְׁבוּתְךָ וְרִחֲמֶךָ וְשָׁב
וְקִבֶּצְךָ מִכָּל הָעַמִּים אֲשֶׁר הֱפִיצְךָ יהוה אֱלֹהֶיךָ שָׁמָּה.[8] ❖ תְּבִיאֵנוּ
אֶל הַר קָדְשֶׁךָ, וְשַׂמְּחֵנוּ בְּבֵית תְּפִלָּתֶךָ, כְּמָה שֶׁכָּתוּב: וַהֲבִיאוֹתִים
אֶל הַר קָדְשִׁי, וְשִׂמַּחְתִּים בְּבֵית תְּפִלָּתִי, עוֹלֹתֵיהֶם וְזִבְחֵיהֶם
לְרָצוֹן עַל מִזְבְּחִי, כִּי בֵיתִי בֵּית תְּפִלָּה יִקָּרֵא לְכָל הָעַמִּים.[9]

THE ARK IS OPENED.

The first four verses of the following prayer are recited responsively; *chazzan,* then congregation:

שְׁמַע קוֹלֵנוּ יהוה אֱלֹהֵינוּ, חוּס וְרַחֵם עָלֵינוּ,
וְקַבֵּל בְּרַחֲמִים וּבְרָצוֹן אֶת תְּפִלָּתֵנוּ.[10]

הֲשִׁיבֵנוּ יהוה אֵלֶיךָ וְנָשׁוּבָה, חַדֵּשׁ יָמֵינוּ כְּקֶדֶם.[11]
אַל תַּשְׁלִיכֵנוּ מִלְּפָנֶיךָ, וְרוּחַ קָדְשְׁךָ אַל תִּקַּח מִמֶּנּוּ.[12]
אַל תַּשְׁלִיכֵנוּ לְעֵת זִקְנָה, כִּכְלוֹת כֹּחֵנוּ אַל תַּעַזְבֵנוּ.[13]
אַל תַּעַזְבֵנוּ יהוה, אֱלֹהֵינוּ אַל תִּרְחַק מִמֶּנּוּ.[14]
עֲשֵׂה עִמָּנוּ אוֹת לְטוֹבָה, וְיִרְאוּ שׂוֹנְאֵינוּ וְיֵבֹשׁוּ,
כִּי אַתָּה יהוה עֲזַרְתָּנוּ וְנִחַמְתָּנוּ.[15]
אֲמָרֵינוּ הַאֲזִינָה יהוה, בִּינָה הֲגִיגֵנוּ.[16]
יִהְיוּ לְרָצוֹן אִמְרֵי פִינוּ וְהֶגְיוֹן לִבֵּנוּ לְפָנֶיךָ, יהוה צוּרֵנוּ וְגוֹאֲלֵנוּ.[17]
כִּי לְךָ יהוה הוֹחָלְנוּ, אַתָּה תַעֲנֶה אֲדֹנָי אֱלֹהֵינוּ.[18]

THE ARK IS CLOSED.

(1) *Deuteronomy* 30:6. (2) *Ezekiel* 36:25. (3) *Isaiah* 44:22. (4) 43:25. (5) 1:18.
(6) *Deuteronomy* 4:31. (7) 30:4. (8) 30:3. (9) *Isaiah* 56:7. (10) Weekday *Shemoneh Esrei.*
(11) *Lamentations* 5:21. (12) Cf. *Psalms* 51:13. (13) Cf. 71:9. (14) Cf. 38:22. (15) Cf. 86:17.
(16) Cf. 5:2. (17) Cf. 19:15. (18) Cf. 38:16.

and with all your soul, that you may live.[1] Pour pure water upon us and purify us, as it is written: I shall pour pure water upon you and purify you, of all your contaminations and of all your abominations I will purify you.[2] Wipe away our willful sins like a cloud and like a mist, as it is written: I have wiped away your willful sins like a cloud and your errors like a mist — repent to Me, for I have redeemed you![3] Wipe away our willful sins for Your sake, as You said: 'I, only I, am the One Who wipes away your willful sins for My sake, and I shall not recall your errors.'[4] Whiten our errors like snow and like [pure white] wool, as it is written: 'Come now, let us reason together,' says HASHEM, 'though your errors will be like scarlet, they will become white as snow; though they will be red as crimson, they will become like [white] wool.'[5] Have mercy on us and do not destroy us, as it is written: For a merciful God is HASHEM, your God; He will not surrender you nor destroy you, and He will not forget the covenant with your forefathers, which He swore to them.[6] Gather in our dispersed ones, as it is written: If your dispersed were to be at the ends of heaven, from there HASHEM, your God, will gather you in and from there He will take you.[7] Bring back our captivity and have mercy on us, as it is written: HASHEM, your God, will bring back your captivity and have mercy on you, and He will again gather you in from all the peoples where HASHEM, your God, has scattered you.[8]

Chazzan — Bring us to Your holy mountain and gladden us in Your house of prayer, as it is written: And I will bring them to My holy mountain, and I will gladden them in My house of prayer, their elevation-offerings and their feast offering will find favor on My Altar, for My House will be called a house of prayer, for all peoples.[9]

THE ARK IS OPENED.

The first four verses of the following prayer are recited responsively; chazzan, then congregation:

שְׁמַע קוֹלֵנוּ Hear our voice, HASHEM, our God, pity and be compassionate to us, and accept — with compassion and favor — our prayer.[10]

Bring us back to You, HASHEM, and we shall return,
   renew our days as of old.[11]
Do not cast us away from Yourself,
   and do not remove Your holy spirit from us.[12]
Do not cast us away in old age,
   when our strength gives out do not forsake us.[13]
Do not forsake us, HASHEM, our God, be not distant from us.[14]
Display for us a sign for good, so that our enemies may see it
   and be ashamed, for You, HASHEM, will have helped and consoled us.[15]
To our sayings give ear, HASHEM, perceive our thoughts.[16]
May the expressions of our mouth and the thoughts of our heart
   find favor before You, HASHEM, our Rock and our Redeemer.[17]
Because for You, HASHEM, we waited,
   You will answer, my Lord, our God.[18]

THE ARK IS CLOSED.

וִדּוּי

During the recitation of the וִדּוּי stand with head and body slightly bowed,
in submissive contrition.

אֱלֹהֵינוּ וֵאלֹהֵי אֲבוֹתֵינוּ, תָּבֹא לְפָנֶיךָ תְּפִלָּתֵנוּ,[1] וְאַל תִּתְעַלַּם
מִתְּחִנָּתֵנוּ,[2] שֶׁאֵין אָנוּ עַזֵּי פָנִים וּקְשֵׁי עֹרֶף, לוֹמַר
לְפָנֶיךָ יהוה אֱלֹהֵינוּ וֵאלֹהֵי אֲבוֹתֵינוּ, צַדִּיקִים אֲנַחְנוּ וְלֹא חָטָאנוּ,
אֲבָל אֲנַחְנוּ וַאֲבוֹתֵינוּ חָטָאנוּ.[3]

Strike the left side of the chest with the right fist
while reciting each of the sins in the following confession litany.

אָשַׁמְנוּ, בָּגַדְנוּ, גָּזַלְנוּ, דִּבַּרְנוּ דְפִי. הֶעֱוִינוּ, וְהִרְשַׁעְנוּ, זַדְנוּ,
חָמַסְנוּ, טָפַלְנוּ שֶׁקֶר. יָעַצְנוּ רָע, כִּזַּבְנוּ, לַצְנוּ, מָרַדְנוּ,
נִאַצְנוּ, סָרַרְנוּ, עָוִינוּ, פָּשַׁעְנוּ, צָרַרְנוּ, קִשִּׁינוּ עֹרֶף. רָשַׁעְנוּ,
שִׁחַתְנוּ, תִּעַבְנוּ, תָּעִינוּ, תִּעְתָּעְנוּ.

סַרְנוּ מִמִּצְוֹתֶיךָ וּמִמִּשְׁפָּטֶיךָ הַטּוֹבִים וְלֹא שָׁוָה לָנוּ.[4] וְאַתָּה
צַדִּיק עַל כָּל הַבָּא עָלֵינוּ, כִּי אֱמֶת עָשִׂיתָ וַאֲנַחְנוּ
הִרְשָׁעְנוּ.[5]

אָשַׁמְנוּ מִכָּל עָם, בֹּשְׁנוּ מִכָּל דּוֹר, גָּלָה מִמֶּנּוּ מָשׂוֹשׂ, דָּוָה
לִבֵּנוּ בַּחֲטָאֵינוּ, הֻחְבַּל אֲוִיֵּנוּ, וְנִפְרַע פְּאֵרֵנוּ, זְבוּל בֵּית מִקְדָּשֵׁנוּ
חָרַב בַּעֲוֹנֵינוּ, טִירָתֵנוּ הָיְתָה לְשַׁמָּה, יְפִי אַדְמָתֵנוּ לְזָרִים,
כֹּחֵנוּ לְנָכְרִים.

וַעֲדַיִן לֹא שַׁבְנוּ מִטָּעוּתֵנוּ וְהֵיךְ נָעִיז פָּנֵינוּ וְנַקְשֶׁה עָרְפֵּנוּ, לוֹמַר
לְפָנֶיךָ יהוה אֱלֹהֵינוּ וֵאלֹהֵי אֲבוֹתֵינוּ, צַדִּיקִים אֲנַחְנוּ וְלֹא חָטָאנוּ,
אֲבָל אֲנַחְנוּ וַאֲבוֹתֵינוּ חָטָאנוּ.

Strike the left side of the chest with the right fist
while reciting each of the sins in the following confession litany.

אָשַׁמְנוּ, בָּגַדְנוּ, גָּזַלְנוּ, דִּבַּרְנוּ דְפִי. הֶעֱוִינוּ, וְהִרְשַׁעְנוּ, זַדְנוּ,
חָמַסְנוּ, טָפַלְנוּ שֶׁקֶר. יָעַצְנוּ רָע, כִּזַּבְנוּ, לַצְנוּ, מָרַדְנוּ,
נִאַצְנוּ, סָרַרְנוּ, עָוִינוּ, פָּשַׁעְנוּ, צָרַרְנוּ, קִשִּׁינוּ עֹרֶף. רָשַׁעְנוּ,
שִׁחַתְנוּ, תִּעַבְנוּ, תָּעִינוּ, תִּעְתָּעְנוּ.

סַרְנוּ מִמִּצְוֹתֶיךָ וּמִמִּשְׁפָּטֶיךָ הַטּוֹבִים וְלֹא שָׁוָה לָנוּ.[4] וְאַתָּה
צַדִּיק עַל כָּל הַבָּא עָלֵינוּ, כִּי אֱמֶת עָשִׂיתָ וַאֲנַחְנוּ
הִרְשָׁעְנוּ.[5]

---

(1) Cf. *Psalms* 88:3. (2) Cf. 55:2. (3) Cf. 106:6. (4) Cf. *Job* 33:27. (5) *Nehemiah* 9:33.

VIDUY/CONFESSION

During the recitation of the וִדּוּי, *Confession,* stand with head and body slightly bowed,
in submissive contrition.

אֱלֹהֵינוּ *Our God and the God of our forefathers, may our prayer come before You.[1] Do not ignore our supplication,[2] for we are not so brazen and obstinate as to say before You, HASHEM, our God and the God of our forefathers, that we are righteous and have not sinned, for in truth, we and our forefathers have sinned.[3]*

Strike the left side of the chest with the right fist while reciting
each of the sins in the following confession litany.

אָשַׁמְנוּ *We have become guilty; [ב] we have betrayed; [ג] we have robbed; [ד] we have spoken slander; [ה] we have caused perversion; [ו] we have caused wickedness; [ז] we have sinned willfully; [ח] we have extorted; [ט] we have accused falsely; [י] we have given evil counsel; [כ] we have been deceitful; [ל] we have scorned; [מ] we have rebelled; [נ] we have provoked; [ס] we have turned away; [ע] we have been perverse; [פ] we have acted wantonly; [צ] we have persecuted; [ק] we have been obstinate; [ר] we have been wicked; [ש] we have corrupted; [ת] we have been abominable; we have strayed; You have let us go astray.*

סַרְנוּ *We have turned away from Your commandments and from Your good laws but to no avail.[4] Yet You are righteous in all that has come upon us, for You have acted truthfully while we have caused wickedness.[5]*

[א] We have become the guiltiest of people. [ב] We have become the most degraded of all generations. [ג] Joy has departed from us. [ד] Our heart has been saddened by our sins. [ה] Our desirous treasure has been ruined, [ו] and our splendor dashed, [ז] for our Holy Temple edifice [ח] has been destroyed for our iniquities. [ט] Our Palace has become desolate. [י] [Jerusalem,] the beauty of our Land is given over to aliens, [כ] our power to strangers.

But still we have not returned from our waywardness. So how can we be so brazen and obstinate as to say before You, HASHEM, our God and the God of our forefathers, that we are righteous and have not sinned, for in truth, both we and our fathers have sinned.

Strike the left side of the chest with the right fist while reciting
each of the sins in the following confession litany.

אָשַׁמְנוּ *We have become guilty; [ב] we have betrayed; [ג] we have robbed; [ד] we have spoken slander; [ה] we have caused perversion; [ו] we have caused wickedness; [ז] we have sinned willfully; [ח] we have extorted; [ט] we have accused falsely; [י] we have given evil counsel; [כ] we have been deceitful; [ל] we have scorned; [מ] we have rebelled; [נ] we have provoked; [ס] we have turned away; [ע] we have been perverse; [פ] we have acted wantonly; [צ] we have persecuted; [ק] we have been obstinate; [ר] we have been wicked; [ש] we have corrupted; [ת] we have been abominable; we have strayed; You have let us go astray.*

סַרְנוּ *We have turned away from Your commandments and from Your good laws but to no avail.[4] Yet You are righteous in all that has come upon us, for You have acted truthfully while we have caused wickedness.[5]*

לְעֵינֵנוּ עָשְׁקוּ עֲמָלֵנוּ, מְמֻשָּׁךְ וּמְמוֹרָט מִמֶּנּוּ, נָתְנוּ עֻלָּם עָלֵינוּ, סָבַלְנוּ עַל שִׁכְמֵנוּ, עֲבָדִים מָשְׁלוּ בָנוּ, פֹּרֵק אֵין מִיָּדָם, צָרוֹת רַבּוֹת סְבָבְוּנוּ, קְרָאנוּךָ יהוה אֱלֹהֵינוּ, רָחַקְתָּ מִמֶּנּוּ בַּעֲוֹנֵינוּ, שַׁבְנוּ מֵאַחֲרֶיךָ, תָּעִינוּ וְאָבָדְנוּ.

וַעֲדַיִן לֹא שַׁבְנוּ מִטָּעוּתֵנוּ וְהֵיךְ נָעִיז פָּנֵינוּ וְנַקְשֶׁה עָרְפֵּנוּ, לוֹמַר לְפָנֶיךָ יהוה אֱלֹהֵינוּ וֵאלֹהֵי אֲבוֹתֵינוּ, צַדִּיקִים אֲנַחְנוּ וְלֹא חָטָאנוּ, אֲבָל אֲנַחְנוּ וַאֲבוֹתֵינוּ חָטָאנוּ.

Strike the left side of the chest with the right fist while reciting each of the sins in the following confession litany.

אָשַׁמְנוּ, בָּגַדְנוּ, גָּזַלְנוּ, דִּבַּרְנוּ דֹפִי. הֶעֱוִינוּ, וְהִרְשַׁעְנוּ, זַדְנוּ, חָמַסְנוּ, טָפַלְנוּ שֶׁקֶר. יָעַצְנוּ רָע, כִּזַּבְנוּ, לַצְנוּ, מָרַדְנוּ, נִאַצְנוּ, סָרַרְנוּ, עָוִינוּ, פָּשַׁעְנוּ, צָרַרְנוּ, קִשִּׁינוּ עֹרֶף. רָשַׁעְנוּ, שִׁחַתְנוּ, תִּעַבְנוּ, תָּעִינוּ, תִּעְתָּעְנוּ.

סַרְנוּ מִמִּצְוֹתֶיךָ וּמִמִּשְׁפָּטֶיךָ הַטּוֹבִים וְלֹא שָׁוָה לָנוּ. וְאַתָּה צַדִּיק עַל כָּל הַבָּא עָלֵינוּ, כִּי אֱמֶת עָשִׂיתָ וַאֲנַחְנוּ הִרְשָׁעְנוּ.

הִרְשַׁעְנוּ וּפָשַׁעְנוּ, לָכֵן לֹא נוֹשָׁעְנוּ. וְתֵן בְּלִבֵּנוּ לַעֲזוֹב דֶּרֶךְ רֶשַׁע, וְחִישׁ לָנוּ יֶשַׁע, כַּכָּתוּב עַל יַד נְבִיאֶךָ: יַעֲזֹב רָשָׁע דַּרְכּוֹ, וְאִישׁ אָוֶן מַחְשְׁבֹתָיו, וְיָשֹׁב אֶל יהוה וִירַחֲמֵהוּ, וְאֶל אֱלֹהֵינוּ כִּי יַרְבֶּה לִסְלוֹחַ.[1]

מְשִׁיחַ צִדְקֶךָ אָמַר לְפָנֶיךָ: שְׁגִיאוֹת מִי יָבִין מִנִּסְתָּרוֹת נַקֵּנִי.[2] נַקֵּנוּ יהוה אֱלֹהֵינוּ מִכָּל פְּשָׁעֵינוּ, וְטַהֲרֵנוּ מִכָּל טֻמְאוֹתֵינוּ, וּזְרוֹק עָלֵינוּ מַיִם טְהוֹרִים וְטַהֲרֵנוּ, כַּכָּתוּב עַל יַד נְבִיאֶךָ: וְזָרַקְתִּי עֲלֵיכֶם מַיִם טְהוֹרִים וּטְהַרְתֶּם, מִכֹּל טֻמְאוֹתֵיכֶם וּמִכָּל גִּלּוּלֵיכֶם אֲטַהֵר אֶתְכֶם.[3]

מִיכָה עַבְדְּךָ אָמַר לְפָנֶיךָ: מִי אֵל כָּמוֹךָ נֹשֵׂא עָוֹן וְעֹבֵר עַל פֶּשַׁע לִשְׁאֵרִית נַחֲלָתוֹ, לֹא הֶחֱזִיק לָעַד אַפּוֹ, כִּי חָפֵץ חֶסֶד הוּא, יָשׁוּב יְרַחֲמֵנוּ, יִכְבֹּשׁ עֲוֹנוֹתֵינוּ, וְתַשְׁלִיךְ בִּמְצֻלוֹת יָם כָּל חַטֹּאתָם.[4] (וְכָל חַטֹּאת עַמְּךָ בֵּית

[ל] *[The benefit of] our labor has been stolen,* [מ] *pulled away and cut off from us.* [נ] *They have placed their yoke upon us,* [ס] *our burdens upon our shoulders.* [ע] *Slaves have ruled over us,* [פ] *there is no redemption from their hand.* [צ] *Abundant troubles have surrounded us,* [ק] *we called upon You, HASHEM, our God,* [ר] *but You have distanced us for our iniquities.* [ש] *We have turned away from following after You;* [ת] *we have strayed; we have become lost.*

But still we have not returned from our waywardness. So how can we be so brazen and obstinate as to say before You, HASHEM, our God and the God of our forefathers, that we are righteous and have not sinned, for in truth, both we and our fathers have sinned.

Strike the left side of the chest with the right fist while reciting
each of the sins in the following confession litany:

אָשַׁמְנוּ *We have become guilty;* [ב] *we have betrayed;* [ג] *we have robbed;* [ד] *we have spoken slander;* [ה] *we have caused perversion;* [ו] *we have caused wickedness;* [ז] *we have sinned willfully;* [ח] *we have extorted;* [ט] *we have accused falsely;* [י] *we have given evil counsel;* [כ] *we have been deceitful;* [ל] *we have scorned;* [מ] *we have rebelled;* [נ] *we have provoked;* [ס] *we have turned away;* [ע] *we have been perverse;* [פ] *we have acted wantonly;* [צ] *we have persecuted;* [ק] *we have been obstinate;* [ר] *we have been wicked;* [ש] *we have corrupted;* [ת] *we have been abominable; we have strayed; You have let us go astray.*

סַרְנוּ *We have turned away from Your commandments and from Your good laws but to no avail. Yet You are righteous in all that has come upon us, for You have acted truthfully while we have caused wickedness.*

הִרְשַׁעְנוּ *We have acted wickedly and have sinned willfully, therefore we have not been saved. Inspire our heart to abandon the path of evil and hasten salvation for us, as it is written by Your prophet: May the wicked one abandon his way and the vicious man his thoughts; may he return to HASHEM and He will show him mercy, and to our God, for He is abundantly forgiving.*[1]

מְשִׁיחַ צִדְקֶךָ *Your righteous anointed [David] said before You: 'Who can discern mistakes? From unperceived faults cleanse me.'*[2] *Cleanse us, HASHEM, our God, of all our willful sins and purify us, of all our contaminations. Sprinkle upon us pure water and purify us, as it is written by Your prophet: I shall sprinkle pure water upon you and purify you, of all your contaminations and of all your abominations I will purify you.'*[3]

מִיכָה עַבְדְּךָ *Micah, Your servant, said before You: 'Who, O God, is like You, Who pardons iniquity and overlooks transgression for the remnant of His heritage? Who has not retained His wrath eternally, for He desires kindness! He will again be merciful to us; He will suppress our iniquities and cast into the depths of the sea all their sins.*[4] *(And all the sins*

---

(1) *Isaiah* 55:7. (2) *Psalms* 19:13. (3) *Ezekiel* 36:25. (4) *Micah* 7:18-19.

יִשְׂרָאֵל תַּשְׁלִיךְ בִּמְקוֹם אֲשֶׁר לֹא יִזָּבְרוּ, וְלֹא יִפָּקְדוּ, וְלֹא יַעֲלוּ
עַל לֵב לְעוֹלָם.) תִּתֵּן אֱמֶת לְיַעֲקֹב חֶסֶד לְאַבְרָהָם אֲשֶׁר נִשְׁבַּעְתָּ
לַאֲבוֹתֵינוּ מִימֵי קֶדֶם.[1]

דָּנִיֵּאל אִישׁ חֲמוּדוֹת שִׁוַּע לְפָנֶיךָ: הַטֵּה אֱלֹהַי אָזְנְךָ וּשֲׁמָע,
פְּקַח עֵינֶיךָ וּרְאֵה שֹׁמְמֹתֵינוּ וְהָעִיר אֲשֶׁר נִקְרָא שִׁמְךָ
עָלֶיהָ, כִּי לֹא עַל צִדְקֹתֵינוּ אֲנַחְנוּ מַפִּילִים תַּחֲנוּנֵינוּ לְפָנֶיךָ, כִּי
עַל רַחֲמֶיךָ הָרַבִּים. אֲדֹנָי שְׁמָעָה, אֲדֹנָי סְלָחָה, אֲדֹנָי הַקְשִׁיבָה,
וַעֲשֵׂה אַל תְּאַחַר, לְמַעַנְךָ אֱלֹהַי, כִּי שִׁמְךָ נִקְרָא עַל עִירְךָ וְעַל
עַמֶּךָ.[2]

עֶזְרָא הַסּוֹפֵר אָמַר לְפָנֶיךָ: אֱלֹהַי, בֹּשְׁתִּי וְנִכְלַמְתִּי לְהָרִים,
אֱלֹהַי, פָּנַי אֵלֶיךָ, כִּי עֲוֹנֹתֵינוּ רָבוּ לְמַעְלָה
רֹאשׁ, וְאַשְׁמָתֵנוּ גָדְלָה עַד לַשָּׁמָיִם.[3] וְאַתָּה[4] אֱלוֹהַּ סְלִיחוֹת, חַנּוּן
וְרַחוּם, אֶרֶךְ אַפַּיִם וְרַב חֶסֶד, וְלֹא עֲזַבְתָּנוּ.[5]

אַל תַּעַזְבֵנוּ אָבִינוּ וְאַל תִּטְּשֵׁנוּ בּוֹרְאֵנוּ, וְאַל תַּזְנִיחֵנוּ
יוֹצְרֵנוּ, וְאַל תַּעַשׂ עִמָּנוּ כָּלָה כְּחַטֹּאתֵינוּ. וְקַיֶּם
לָנוּ יהוה אֱלֹהֵינוּ, אֶת הַדָּבָר שֶׁהִבְטַחְתָּנוּ בְּקַבָּלָה עַל יְדֵי יִרְמְיָהוּ
חוֹזָךְ, כָּאָמוּר: בַּיָּמִים הָהֵם וּבָעֵת הַהִיא, נְאֻם יהוה, יְבֻקַּשׁ אֶת
עֲוֹן יִשְׂרָאֵל וְאֵינֶנּוּ וְאֶת חַטֹּאת יְהוּדָה וְלֹא תִמָּצֶאנָה, כִּי אֶסְלַח
לַאֲשֶׁר אַשְׁאִיר.[6] עַמְּךָ וְנַחֲלָתְךָ רְעֵבֵי טוּבְךָ, צְמֵאֵי חַסְדֶּךָ, תְּאֵבֵי
יִשְׁעֶךָ, יַכִּירוּ וְיֵדְעוּ כִּי לַיהוה אֱלֹהֵינוּ הָרַחֲמִים וְהַסְּלִיחוֹת.

אֵל רַחוּם שְׁמֶךָ, אֵל חַנּוּן שְׁמֶךָ, בָּנוּ נִקְרָא שְׁמֶךָ. יהוה עֲשֵׂה
לְמַעַן שְׁמֶךָ. עֲשֵׂה לְמַעַן אֲמִתֶּךָ, עֲשֵׂה לְמַעַן
בְּרִיתֶךָ, עֲשֵׂה לְמַעַן **גָּדְלְךָ** וְתִפְאַרְתֶּךָ, עֲשֵׂה לְמַעַן **דָּתֶךָ**, עֲשֵׂה
לְמַעַן **הוֹדֶךָ**, עֲשֵׂה לְמַעַן וְעוּדֶךָ, עֲשֵׂה לְמַעַן **זִכְרֶךָ**, עֲשֵׂה לְמַעַן
חַסְדֶּךָ, עֲשֵׂה לְמַעַן **טוּבֶךָ**, עֲשֵׂה לְמַעַן **יִחוּדֶךָ**, עֲשֵׂה לְמַעַן
כְּבוֹדֶךָ, עֲשֵׂה לְמַעַן **לִמּוּדֶךָ**, עֲשֵׂה לְמַעַן **מַלְכוּתֶךָ**, עֲשֵׂה לְמַעַן
נִצְחֶךָ, עֲשֵׂה לְמַעַן **סוֹדֶךָ**, עֲשֵׂה לְמַעַן עֻזֶּךָ, עֲשֵׂה לְמַעַן **פְּאֵרֶךָ**,
עֲשֵׂה לְמַעַן צִדְקָתֶךָ, עֲשֵׂה לְמַעַן **קְדֻשָּׁתֶךָ**, עֲשֵׂה לְמַעַן **רַחֲמֶיךָ**
הָרַבִּים, עֲשֵׂה לְמַעַן שְׁכִינָתֶךָ, עֲשֵׂה לְמַעַן **תְּהִלָּתֶךָ**, עֲשֵׂה לְמַעַן
אוֹהֲבֶיךָ שׁוֹכְנֵי עָפָר, עֲשֵׂה לְמַעַן אַבְרָהָם יִצְחָק וְיַעֲקֹב, עֲשֵׂה

of Your nation the Family of Israel, may You cast away to a place where they will neither be remembered, considered, nor brought to mind — ever.) Grant truth to Jacob, kindness to Abraham, as You swore to our forefathers from ancient times.'[1]

דָּנִיֵּאל *Daniel, the greatly beloved man, cried out before You: 'Incline, my God, Your ear, and listen, open Your eyes and see our desolation and that of the city upon which Your Name is proclaimed, for not because of our righteousness do we cast down our supplications before You, rather because of Your abundant compassion. O my Lord, heed; O my Lord, forgive; O my Lord, be attentive and act, do not delay; for Your sake, my God, for Your Name is proclaimed upon Your city and Your people.'[2]*

עֶזְרָא הַסּוֹפֵר *Ezra the Scribe said before You: 'My God, I am embarrassed and ashamed to lift my face to You, my God — for our iniquities have multiplied above our heads, and our sins extend unto heaven.[3] You are[4] the God of forgiveness, compassionate and merciful, slow to anger, and abundant in kindness; and You have not forsaken us.'[5]*

אַל תַּעַזְבֵנוּ *Do not forsake us, our Father; do not cast us off, our Creator; do not abandon us, our Molder; and do not bring about our destruction, as our sins merit. Affirm for us, HASHEM, our God, the promise You made in the tradition through Jeremiah, Your seer, as it is said: 'In those days and at that time' — the words of HASHEM — 'the iniquity of Israel will be sought but there will be none, and the errors of Judah, but they will not be found, for I will have forgiven those whom I leave as a remnant.'[6] Your people and Your heritage, who hunger for Your goodness, who thirst for Your kindness, who long for Your salvation — may they recognize and know that to HASHEM, our God, belong mercy and forgiveness.*

אֵל רַחוּם *'Merciful God' is Your Name, 'Gracious God' is Your Name, Your Name is called upon us — O HASHEM, act for Your Name's sake. Act for the sake of [א] Your truth; act for the sake of [ב] Your covenant; act for the sake of [ג] Your greatness and Your splendor; act for the sake of [ד] Your law; act for the sake of [ה] Your glory; act for the sake of [ו] Your Meeting House; act for the sake of [ז] Your remembrance; act for the sake of [ח] Your kindness; act for the sake of [ט] Your goodness; act for the sake of [י] Your Oneness; act for the sake of [כ] Your honor; act for the sake of [ל] Your teaching; act for the sake of [מ] Your kingship; act for the sake of [נ] Your eternity; act for the sake of [ס] Your counsel; act for the sake of [ע] Your power; act for the sake of [פ] Your beauty; act for the sake of [צ] Your righteousness; act for the sake of [ק] Your sanctity; act for the sake of [ר] Your abundant mercy; act for the sake of [ש] Your Presence, act for the sake of [ת] Your praise; act for the sake of Your beloved ones who rest in the dust; act for the sake of Abraham, Isaac, and Jacob; act*

(1) Micah 7:20. (2) Daniel 9:18-19. (3) Ezra 9:6. (4) Some editions of Selichos insert the word אֱלֹהֵינוּ, our God, at this point. (5) Cf. Nehemiah 9:17. (6) Jeremiah 50:20.

לְמַעַן מֹשֶׁה וְאַהֲרֹן, עֲשֵׂה לְמַעַן דָּוִד וּשְׁלֹמֹה, עֲשֵׂה לְמַעַן יְרוּשָׁלַיִם עִיר קָדְשֶׁךָ, עֲשֵׂה לְמַעַן צִיּוֹן מִשְׁכַּן כְּבוֹדֶךָ, עֲשֵׂה לְמַעַן שִׁמְמוֹת הֵיכָלֶךָ, עֲשֵׂה לְמַעַן הֲרִיסוֹת מִזְבְּחֶךָ, עֲשֵׂה לְמַעַן הֲרוּגִים עַל שֵׁם קָדְשֶׁךָ, עֲשֵׂה לְמַעַן טְבוּחִים עַל יִחוּדֶךָ, עֲשֵׂה לְמַעַן בָּאֵי בָאֵשׁ וּבַמַּיִם עַל קִדּוּשׁ שְׁמֶךָ, עֲשֵׂה לְמַעַן יוֹנְקֵי שָׁדַיִם שֶׁלֹּא חָטְאוּ, עֲשֵׂה לְמַעַן גְּמוּלֵי חָלָב שֶׁלֹּא פָשְׁעוּ, עֲשֵׂה לְמַעַן תִּינוֹקוֹת שֶׁל בֵּית רַבָּן, עֲשֵׂה לְמַעַנְךָ אִם לֹא לְמַעֲנֵנוּ, עֲשֵׂה לְמַעַנְךָ וְהוֹשִׁיעֵנוּ.

עֲנֵנוּ יהוה עֲנֵנוּ, עֲנֵנוּ אֱלֹהֵינוּ עֲנֵנוּ, עֲנֵנוּ אָבִינוּ עֲנֵנוּ, עֲנֵנוּ בּוֹרְאֵנוּ עֲנֵנוּ, עֲנֵנוּ גּוֹאֲלֵנוּ עֲנֵנוּ, עֲנֵנוּ דוֹרְשֵׁנוּ עֲנֵנוּ, עֲנֵנוּ הָאֵל הַנֶּאֱמָן עֲנֵנוּ, עֲנֵנוּ וָתִיק וְחָסִיד עֲנֵנוּ, עֲנֵנוּ זַךְ וְיָשָׁר עֲנֵנוּ, עֲנֵנוּ חַי וְקַיָּם עֲנֵנוּ, עֲנֵנוּ טוֹב וּמֵטִיב עֲנֵנוּ, עֲנֵנוּ יוֹדֵעַ יֵצֶר עֲנֵנוּ, עֲנֵנוּ כּוֹבֵשׁ כְּעָסִים עֲנֵנוּ, עֲנֵנוּ לוֹבֵשׁ צְדָקוֹת עֲנֵנוּ, עֲנֵנוּ מֶלֶךְ מַלְכֵי הַמְּלָכִים עֲנֵנוּ, עֲנֵנוּ נוֹרָא וְנִשְׂגָּב עֲנֵנוּ, עֲנֵנוּ סוֹלֵחַ וּמוֹחֵל עֲנֵנוּ, עֲנֵנוּ עוֹנֶה בְּעֵת צָרָה עֲנֵנוּ, עֲנֵנוּ פּוֹדֶה וּמַצִּיל עֲנֵנוּ, עֲנֵנוּ צַדִּיק וְיָשָׁר עֲנֵנוּ, עֲנֵנוּ קָרוֹב לְקוֹרְאָיו עֲנֵנוּ, עֲנֵנוּ רַחוּם וְחַנּוּן עֲנֵנוּ, עֲנֵנוּ שׁוֹמֵעַ אֶל אֶבְיוֹנִים עֲנֵנוּ, עֲנֵנוּ תּוֹמֵךְ תְּמִימִים עֲנֵנוּ, עֲנֵנוּ אֱלֹהֵי אֲבוֹתֵינוּ עֲנֵנוּ, עֲנֵנוּ אֱלֹהֵי אַבְרָהָם עֲנֵנוּ, עֲנֵנוּ פַּחַד יִצְחָק עֲנֵנוּ, עֲנֵנוּ אֲבִיר יַעֲקֹב עֲנֵנוּ, עֲנֵנוּ עֶזְרַת הַשְּׁבָטִים עֲנֵנוּ, עֲנֵנוּ מִשְׂגָּב אִמָּהוֹת עֲנֵנוּ, עֲנֵנוּ קָשֶׁה לִכְעוֹס עֲנֵנוּ, עֲנֵנוּ רַךְ לִרְצוֹת עֲנֵנוּ, עֲנֵנוּ עוֹנֶה בְּעֵת רָצוֹן עֲנֵנוּ, עֲנֵנוּ אֲבִי יְתוֹמִים עֲנֵנוּ, עֲנֵנוּ דַּיַּן אַלְמָנוֹת עֲנֵנוּ.

מִי שֶׁעָנָה לְאַבְרָהָם אָבִינוּ בְּהַר הַמּוֹרִיָּה,	הוּא יַעֲנֵנוּ.
מִי שֶׁעָנָה לְיִצְחָק בְּנוֹ כְּשֶׁנֶּעֱקַד עַל גַּבֵּי הַמִּזְבֵּחַ,	הוּא יַעֲנֵנוּ.
מִי שֶׁעָנָה לְיַעֲקֹב בְּבֵית אֵל,	הוּא יַעֲנֵנוּ.
מִי שֶׁעָנָה לְיוֹסֵף בְּבֵית הָאֲסוּרִים,	הוּא יַעֲנֵנוּ.
מִי שֶׁעָנָה לַאֲבוֹתֵינוּ עַל יַם סוּף,	הוּא יַעֲנֵנוּ.
מִי שֶׁעָנָה לְמֹשֶׁה בְּחוֹרֵב,	הוּא יַעֲנֵנוּ.
מִי שֶׁעָנָה לְאַהֲרֹן בַּמַּחְתָּה,	הוּא יַעֲנֵנוּ.
מִי שֶׁעָנָה לְפִינְחָס בְּקוּמוֹ מִתּוֹךְ הָעֵדָה,	הוּא יַעֲנֵנוּ.

for the sake of Moses and Aaron; act for the sake of David and Solomon; act for the sake of Jerusalem, Your holy city; act for the sake of Zion, the abode of Your glory; act for the sake of the desolation of Your Temple; act for the sake of the ruin of Your Altar; act for the sake of the martyrs for Your holy Name; act for the sake of those slaughtered for Your Oneness; act for the sake of those who entered fire and water for the sanctification of Your Name; act for the nursing infants who did not err; act for the sake of the weaned babes who did not sin; act for the sake of children at the school-room; act for Your sake if not for ours; act for Your sake and save us.

עֲנֵנוּ *Answer us, HASHEM, answer us; answer us, our God, answer us; answer us, [א] our Father, answer us; answer us, [ב] our Creator, answer us; answer us, [ג] our Redeemer, answer us; answer us, [ד] You Who searches us out, answer us; answer us, [ה] faithful God, answer us; answer us, [ו] stead-fast and kind One, answer us; answer us, [ז] pure and upright One, answer us; answer us, [ח] living and enduring One, answer us; answer us, [ט] good and beneficent One, answer us; answer us, [י] You Who knows inclinations, answer us; answer us, [כ] You Who suppresses wrath, answer us; answer us, [ל] You Who dons righteousness, answer us; answer us, [מ] King Who reigns over kings, answer us; answer us, [נ] awesome and powerful One, answer us; answer us, [ס] You Who forgives and pardons, answer us; answer us, [ע] You Who answers in time of distress,[1] answer us; answer us, [פ] Redeemer and Rescuer, answer us; answer us, [צ] righteous and upright One, answer us; answer us, [ק] He Who is close to those who call upon Him, answer us; answer us, [ר] merciful and gracious One, answer us; answer us, [ש] You Who hears the destitute, answer us; answer us, [ת] You Who supports the wholesome, answer us; answer us, God of our forefathers, answer us; answer us, God of Abraham, answer us; answer us, Dread of Isaac, answer us; answer us, Mighty One of Jacob, answer us; answer us, Helper of the tribes, answer us; answer us, Stronghold of the Matriarchs, answer us; answer us, You Who are hard to anger, answer us; answer us, You Who are easy to pacify, answer us; answer us, You Who answers in a time of favor,[1] answer us; answer us, Father of orphans, answer us; answer us, Judge of widows, answer us.*

מִי שֶׁעָנָה *He Who answered our father Abraham on Mount Moriah,*
                                                        may He answer us.
He Who answered his son Isaac when he was bound atop the altar,
                                                        may He answer us.
He Who answered Jacob in Bethel,   *may He answer us.*
He Who answered Joseph in the prison,   *may He answer us.*
He Who answered our forefathers at the Sea of Reeds, *may He answer us.*
He Who answered Moses in Horeb,   *may He answer us.*
He Who answered Aaron when he offered the censer,   *may He answer us.*
He Who answered Phineas when he arose from amid the congregation,
                                                        may He answer us.

_____
(1) Some editions of *Selichos* reverse the positions of these two lines.

מִי שֶׁעָנָה לִיהוֹשֻׁעַ בַּגִּלְגָּל,   הוּא יַעֲנֵנוּ.
מִי שֶׁעָנָה לִשְׁמוּאֵל בַּמִּצְפָּה,   הוּא יַעֲנֵנוּ.
מִי שֶׁעָנָה לְדָוִד וּשְׁלֹמֹה בְנוֹ בִּירוּשָׁלָיִם,   הוּא יַעֲנֵנוּ.
מִי שֶׁעָנָה לְאֵלִיָּהוּ בְּהַר הַכַּרְמֶל,   הוּא יַעֲנֵנוּ.
מִי שֶׁעָנָה לֶאֱלִישָׁע בִּירִיחוֹ,   הוּא יַעֲנֵנוּ.
מִי שֶׁעָנָה לְיוֹנָה בִּמְעֵי הַדָּגָה,   הוּא יַעֲנֵנוּ.
מִי שֶׁעָנָה לְחִזְקִיָּהוּ מֶלֶךְ יְהוּדָה בְּחָלְיוֹ,   הוּא יַעֲנֵנוּ.
מִי שֶׁעָנָה לַחֲנַנְיָה מִישָׁאֵל וַעֲזַרְיָה בְּתוֹךְ כִּבְשַׁן הָאֵשׁ,   הוּא יַעֲנֵנוּ.
מִי שֶׁעָנָה לְדָנִיֵּאל בְּגוֹב הָאֲרָיוֹת,   הוּא יַעֲנֵנוּ.
מִי שֶׁעָנָה לְמָרְדְּכַי וְאֶסְתֵּר בְּשׁוּשַׁן הַבִּירָה,   הוּא יַעֲנֵנוּ.
מִי שֶׁעָנָה לְעֶזְרָא בַּגּוֹלָה,   הוּא יַעֲנֵנוּ.
מִי שֶׁעָנָה לְכָל הַצַּדִּיקִים וְהַחֲסִידִים וְהַתְּמִימִים וְהַיְשָׁרִים,
הוּא יַעֲנֵנוּ.

רַחֲמָנָא דְּעָנֵי לַעֲנִיֵּי, עֲנֵינָא. רַחֲמָנָא דְּעָנֵי לִתְבִירֵי לִבָּא,
עֲנֵינָא. רַחֲמָנָא דְּעָנֵי לְמַכִּיכֵי רוּחָא, עֲנֵינָא. רַחֲמָנָא
עֲנֵינָא. רַחֲמָנָא חוּס. רַחֲמָנָא פְּרוֹק. רַחֲמָנָא שְׁזִיב. רַחֲמָנָא
רְחַם עֲלָן. הַשְׁתָּא בַּעֲגָלָא וּבִזְמַן קָרִיב.

נפילת אפים

In the presence of a Torah Scroll, the following (until וְנַפְשִׁי רָגַע) is recited with the head resting
on the arm, preferably while seated. Elsewhere, it is recited with the head held erect.

(וַיֹּאמֶר דָּוִד אֶל גָּד, צַר לִי מְאֹד נִפְּלָה נָּא בְיַד יהוה,
כִּי רַבִּים רַחֲמָיו, וּבְיַד אָדָם אַל אֶפֹּלָה.[1])

רַחוּם וְחַנּוּן חָטָאתִי לְפָנֶיךָ. יהוה מָלֵא רַחֲמִים, רַחֵם עָלַי
וְקַבֵּל תַּחֲנוּנָי.

תהלים ו:ב-יא

יהוה אַל בְּאַפְּךָ תוֹכִיחֵנִי, וְאַל בַּחֲמָתְךָ תְיַסְּרֵנִי. חָנֵּנִי יהוה, כִּי
אֻמְלַל אָנִי, רְפָאֵנִי יהוה, כִּי נִבְהֲלוּ עֲצָמָי. וְנַפְשִׁי נִבְהֲלָה
מְאֹד, וְאַתָּה יהוה, עַד מָתָי. שׁוּבָה יהוה, חַלְּצָה נַפְשִׁי, הוֹשִׁיעֵנִי
לְמַעַן חַסְדֶּךָ. כִּי אֵין בַּמָּוֶת זִכְרֶךָ, בִּשְׁאוֹל מִי יוֹדֶה לָּךְ. יָגַעְתִּי
בְּאַנְחָתִי, אַשְׂחֶה בְכָל לַיְלָה מִטָּתִי, בְּדִמְעָתִי עַרְשִׂי אַמְסֶה.
עָשְׁשָׁה מִכַּעַס עֵינִי, עָתְקָה בְּכָל צוֹרְרָי. סוּרוּ מִמֶּנִּי כָּל פֹּעֲלֵי אָוֶן,
כִּי שָׁמַע יהוה קוֹל בִּכְיִי. שָׁמַע יהוה תְּחִנָּתִי, יהוה תְּפִלָּתִי יִקָּח.
יֵבֹשׁוּ וְיִבָּהֲלוּ מְאֹד כָּל אֹיְבָי, יָשֻׁבוּ יֵבֹשׁוּ רָגַע.

He Who answered Joshua in Gilgal,   *may He answer us.*
He Who answered Samuel in Mitzpah,   *may He answer us.*
He Who answered David and his son Solomon in Jerusalem,
                                                           may He answer us.
He Who answered Elijah on Mount Carmel,   *may He answer us.*
He Who answered Elisha in Jericho,   *may He answer us.*
He Who answered Jonah in the innards of the fish,   *may He answer us.*
He Who answered Hezekiah, King of Judah, in his illness,
                                                           may He answer us.
He Who answered Chananiah, Mishael, and Azariah in the fiery oven,
                                                           may He answer us.
He Who answered Daniel in the lions' den,   *may He answer us.*
He Who answered Mordechai and Esther in Shushan the capital,
                                                           may He answer us.
He Who answered Ezra in the Exile,   *may He answer us.*
He Who answered all the righteous, the devout, the wholesome,
    and the upright,   *may He answer us.*

רַחֲמָנָא *The Merciful One Who answers the poor, may He answer us. The Merciful One Who answers the brokenhearted, may He answer us. The Merciful One Who answers the humble of spirit, may He answer us. O Merciful One, answer us. O Merciful One, pity. O Merciful One, redeem. O Merciful One, deliver. O Merciful One, have mercy on us — now, swiftly and soon.*

PUTTING DOWN THE HEAD

In the presence of a Torah Scroll, the following (until *'instantly shamed'*) is recited with the head resting on the arm, preferably while seated. Elsewhere, it is recited with the head held erect.

(*And David said to Gad, 'I am exceedingly distressed. Let us fall into HASHEM's hand for His mercies are abundant, but let me not fall into human hands.'*[1])

רַחוּם וְחַנּוּן *O compassionate and gracious One, I have sinned before You. HASHEM, Who is full of mercy, have mercy on me and accept my supplications.*

Psalms 6:2-11

'ה *HASHEM, do not rebuke me in Your anger nor chastise me in Your rage. Favor me, HASHEM, for I am feeble; heal me, HASHEM, for my bones shudder. My soul is utterly confounded, and You, HASHEM, how long? Desist, HASHEM, release my soul; save me as befits Your kindness. For there is no mention of You in death; in the Lower World who will thank You? I am wearied with my sigh, every night my tears drench my bed, soak my couch. My eye is dimmed because of anger, aged by my tormentors. Depart from me, all evildoers, for HASHEM has heard the sound of my weeping. HASHEM has heard my plea, HASHEM will accept my prayer. Let all my foes be shamed and utterly confounded, they will regret and be instantly shamed.*

---

(1) *II Samuel* 24:14.

מָחֵי וּמַסֵּי מֵמִית וּמְחַיֶּה, מַסִּיק מִן שְׁאוֹל לְחַיֵּי עָלְמָא, בְּרָא
כַּד חָטֵי אֲבוּהִי לָקֵיהּ, אֲבוּהִי דְחָיֵס אַסֵּי לִכְאֵבָהּ.
עַבְדָּא דְמָרִיד נָפֵיק בְּקוֹלָר, מָרֵהּ תָּאֵיב וְתַבִּיר קוֹלָרֵהּ.
בְּרָךְ בְּכֵרָךְ אֲנַן וְחָטִינַן קַמָּךְ, הָא רָוֵי נַפְשִׁין בְּגִידִין מְרִירִין,
עַבְדָּךְ אֲנַן וּמְרוֹדִינַן קַמָּךְ, הָא בְּבִזְתָּא, הָא בְּשִׁבְיָא, הָא
בְּמַלְקֻיוּתָא. בְּמָטוּ מִנָּךְ בְּרַחֲמָךְ דִּנְפִישִׁין, אַסֵּי לִכְאֵבִין דִּתְקוֹף
עֲלָן, עַד דְּלָא נֶהֱוֵי גְמִירָא בְּשִׁבְיָא.

מַכְנִיסֵי רַחֲמִים, הַכְנִיסוּ רַחֲמֵינוּ, לִפְנֵי בַּעַל הָרַחֲמִים.
מַשְׁמִיעֵי תְפִלָּה, הַשְׁמִיעוּ תְפִלָּתֵנוּ, לִפְנֵי
שׁוֹמֵעַ תְּפִלָּה. מַשְׁמִיעֵי צְעָקָה, הַשְׁמִיעוּ צַעֲקָתֵנוּ, לִפְנֵי שׁוֹמֵעַ
צְעָקָה. מַכְנִיסֵי דִמְעָה, הַכְנִיסוּ דִמְעוֹתֵינוּ, לִפְנֵי מֶלֶךְ מִתְרַצֶּה
בִדְמָעוֹת.

הִשְׁתַּדְּלוּ וְהַרְבּוּ תְחִנָּה וּבַקָּשָׁה, לִפְנֵי מֶלֶךְ אֵל רָם וְנִשָּׂא.
הַזְכִּירוּ לְפָנָיו, הַשְׁמִיעוּ לְפָנָיו תּוֹרָה וּמַעֲשִׂים טוֹבִים שֶׁל שׁוֹכְנֵי
עָפָר.

יִזְכֹּר אַהֲבָתָם וִיחַיֶּה זַרְעָם, שֶׁלֹּא תֹאבַד שְׁאֵרִית יַעֲקֹב. כִּי צֹאן
רֹעֶה נֶאֱמָן הָיָה לְחֶרְפָּה, יִשְׂרָאֵל גּוֹי אֶחָד לְמָשָׁל וְלִשְׁנִינָה.
מַהֵר עֲנֵנוּ אֱלֹהֵי יִשְׁעֵנוּ, וּפְדֵנוּ מִכָּל גְּזֵרוֹת קָשׁוֹת וְהוֹשִׁיעָה
בְּרַחֲמֶיךָ הָרַבִּים, מְשִׁיחַ צִדְקָךְ וְעַמָּךְ.

מָרָן דִּבִשְׁמַיָּא לָךְ מִתְחַנְּנָן, כְּבַר שִׁבְיָא דְּמִתְחַנַּן לְשָׁבוּיֵהּ.
כֻּלְּהוֹן בְּנֵי שִׁבְיָא בְּכַסְפָּא מִתְפָּרְקִין, וְעַמָּךְ
יִשְׂרָאֵל בְּרַחֲמֵי וּבִתְחַנוּנֵי, הַב לָן שְׁאֵילְתִּין וּבָעוּתִין, דְּלָא נֶהֱדַר
רֵיקָם מִן קַדָּמָךְ.

מָרָן דִּבִשְׁמַיָּא לָךְ מִתְחַנְּנָן, כְּעַבְדָּא דְּמִתְחַנַּן לְמָרֵיהּ, עֲשִׁיקֵי
אֲנַן וּבַחֲשׁוֹכָא שָׁרִינַן, מְרִירָן נַפְשִׁין מֵעָקָתִין דִּנְפִישִׁין, חֵילָא לֵית
בָּן לְרַצוּיָךְ מָרָן, עֲבִיד בְּדִיל קַיָּמָא דִּגְזַרְתָּ עִם אֲבָהָתָנָא.

שׁוֹמֵר יִשְׂרָאֵל, שְׁמֹר שְׁאֵרִית יִשְׂרָאֵל, וְאַל יֹאבַד
יִשְׂרָאֵל, הָאֹמְרִים, שְׁמַע יִשְׂרָאֵל.[1]
שׁוֹמֵר גּוֹי אֶחָד, שְׁמֹר שְׁאֵרִית עַם אֶחָד, וְאַל יֹאבַד גּוֹי אֶחָד,
הַמְיַחֲדִים שִׁמְךָ, יְהוָה אֱלֹהֵינוּ יְהוָה אֶחָד.[1]

מַחֲי וּמַסֵּי [O God,] He Who smites and heals, causes death and restores life, raises [the dead] from the grave to eternal life: Should a son sin, his father would smack him, but a compassionate father will heal his [son's] pain. When a slave rebels, he is led out in collar-irons, but if his master desires to, he breaks his chains.

We are Your son, Your firstborn, and we have sinned against You; so our soul has been satiated with bitter wormwood. We are Your servants and we have rebelled against You; so [we have suffered], some with looting, some with captivity, and some with the lash. We beg of You, in Your abundant compassion, heal the pains that have overwhelmed us, before we have been completely wiped out in captivity.

מַכְנִיסֵי רַחֲמִים O you who usher in [pleas for] mercy, may you usher in our [plea for] mercy, before the Master of mercy. O you who cause prayer to be heard, may you cause our prayer to be heard, before the Hearer of prayer. O you who cause outcry to be heard, may you cause our outcry to be heard, before the Hearer of outcry. O you who usher in tears, may you usher in our tears, before the King Who finds favor through tears.

Exert yourselves, and multiply supplication and petition, before the King, God, exalted and most high. Mention before Him, cause to be heard before Him, the Torah and the good deeds of [the Patriarchs and Matriarchs] who dwell in the dust.

May He remember their love and grant life to [their] offspring, that the remnant of Jacob not be lost. For the flock of the faithful shepherd [Moses] has become a disgrace; Israel, the unique nation, a parable and a simile.

Speedily, answer us, O God of our salvation, and redeem us from all harsh decrees; and may You save, in Your abundant mercy, Your righteous anointed and Your people.

מָרָן דְּבִשְׁמַיָּא Our Master Who is in heaven, to You do we supplicate, as a captive supplicates before his captors; for all captives are redeemed with money, but Your people Israel with compassion and supplication. O grant our requests and our prayers that we not be turned away from You empty-handed.

Our Master Who is in heaven, to You do we supplicate as a slave supplicates before his master: We are oppressed and we abide in darkness, souls embittered from abundant distress. We have no strength to regain Your favor. Our Master, act for the sake of the covenant that You made with our Patriarchs.

שׁוֹמֵר יִשְׂרָאֵל O Guardian of Israel, protect the remnant of Israel; let not Israel be destroyed — those who proclaim, 'Hear O Israel.' [1]

O Guardian of the unique nation, protect the remnant of the unique people; let not the unique nation be destroyed — those who proclaim the Oneness of Your Name, 'HASHEM is our God, HASHEM, the One and Only!' [1]

---

(1) Deuteronomy 6:4.

שׁוֹמֵר גּוֹי קָדוֹשׁ, שְׁמוֹר שְׁאֵרִית עַם קָדוֹשׁ, וְאַל יֹאבַד גּוֹי קָדוֹשׁ, הַמְשַׁלְּשִׁים בְּשָׁלֹשׁ קְדֻשּׁוֹת לְקָדוֹשׁ.

מִתְרַצֶּה בְרַחֲמִים וּמִתְפַּיֵּס בְּתַחֲנוּנִים, הִתְרַצֵּה וְהִתְפַּיֵּס לְדוֹר עָנִי, כִּי אֵין עוֹזֵר. אָבִינוּ מַלְכֵּנוּ, חָנֵּנוּ וַעֲנֵנוּ, כִּי אֵין בָּנוּ מַעֲשִׂים, עֲשֵׂה עִמָּנוּ צְדָקָה וָחֶסֶד וְהוֹשִׁיעֵנוּ.

וַאֲנַחְנוּ לֹא נֵדַע מַה נַּעֲשֶׂה, כִּי עָלֶיךָ עֵינֵינוּ.[1] זְכֹר רַחֲמֶיךָ יהוה וַחֲסָדֶיךָ, כִּי מֵעוֹלָם הֵמָּה.[2] יְהִי חַסְדְּךָ יהוה עָלֵינוּ, כַּאֲשֶׁר יִחַלְנוּ לָךְ.[3] אַל תִּזְכָּר לָנוּ עֲוֹנוֹת רִאשֹׁנִים, מַהֵר יְקַדְּמוּנוּ רַחֲמֶיךָ, כִּי דַלּוֹנוּ מְאֹד.[4] חָנֵּנוּ יהוה חָנֵּנוּ, כִּי רַב שָׂבַעְנוּ בוּז.[5] בְּרֹגֶז רַחֵם תִּזְכּוֹר.[6] כִּי הוּא יָדַע יִצְרֵנוּ, זָכוּר כִּי עָפָר אֲנָחְנוּ.[7] עָזְרֵנוּ אֱלֹהֵי יִשְׁעֵנוּ עַל דְּבַר כְּבוֹד שְׁמֶךָ, וְהַצִּילֵנוּ וְכַפֵּר עַל חַטֹּאתֵינוּ לְמַעַן שְׁמֶךָ.[8]

קַדִּישׁ שָׁלֵם

The *chazzan* recites קַדִּישׁ שָׁלֵם:

יִתְגַּדַּל וְיִתְקַדַּשׁ שְׁמֵהּ רַבָּא. (.Cong – אָמֵן) בְּעָלְמָא דִּי בְרָא כִרְעוּתֵהּ, וְיַמְלִיךְ מַלְכוּתֵהּ, בְּחַיֵּיכוֹן וּבְיוֹמֵיכוֹן וּבְחַיֵּי דְכָל בֵּית יִשְׂרָאֵל, בַּעֲגָלָא וּבִזְמַן קָרִיב. וְאִמְרוּ אָמֵן.

(.Cong – אָמֵן. יְהֵא שְׁמֵהּ רַבָּא מְבָרַךְ לְעָלַם וּלְעָלְמֵי עָלְמַיָּא.)

יְהֵא שְׁמֵהּ רַבָּא מְבָרַךְ לְעָלַם וּלְעָלְמֵי עָלְמַיָּא.

יִתְבָּרַךְ וְיִשְׁתַּבַּח וְיִתְפָּאַר וְיִתְרוֹמַם וְיִתְנַשֵּׂא וְיִתְהַדָּר וְיִתְעַלֶּה וְיִתְהַלָּל שְׁמֵהּ דְּקוּדְשָׁא בְּרִיךְ הוּא (.Cong – בְּרִיךְ הוּא.) לְעֵלָּא מִן כָּל בִּרְכָתָא וְשִׁירָתָא תֻּשְׁבְּחָתָא וְנֶחֱמָתָא, דַּאֲמִירָן בְּעָלְמָא. וְאִמְרוּ: אָמֵן. (.Cong – אָמֵן.)

(.Cong – קַבֵּל בְּרַחֲמִים וּבְרָצוֹן אֶת תְּפִלָּתֵנוּ.)

תִּתְקַבֵּל צְלוֹתְהוֹן וּבָעוּתְהוֹן דְּכָל (בֵּית) יִשְׂרָאֵל קֳדָם אֲבוּהוֹן דִּי בִשְׁמַיָּא. וְאִמְרוּ אָמֵן. (.Cong – אָמֵן.)

(.Cong – יְהִי שֵׁם יהוה מְבֹרָךְ, מֵעַתָּה וְעַד עוֹלָם.[9])

יְהֵא שְׁלָמָא רַבָּא מִן שְׁמַיָּא וְחַיִּים עָלֵינוּ וְעַל כָּל יִשְׂרָאֵל. וְאִמְרוּ אָמֵן. (.Cong – אָמֵן.)

(.Cong – עֶזְרִי מֵעִם יהוה, עֹשֵׂה שָׁמַיִם וָאָרֶץ.[10])

Take three steps back. Bow left and say, . . . עֹשֶׂה; bow right and say, . . . הוּא יַעֲשֶׂה; bow forward and say, וְעַל כָּל . . . אָמֵן. Remain standing in place for a few moments, then take three steps forward.

עֹשֶׂה שָׁלוֹם בִּמְרוֹמָיו, הוּא יַעֲשֶׂה שָׁלוֹם עָלֵינוּ, וְעַל כָּל יִשְׂרָאֵל. וְאִמְרוּ אָמֵן. (.Cong – אָמֵן.)

O *Guardian of the holy nation, protect the remnant of the holy people; let not the holy nation be destroyed — those who proclaim three-fold sanctifications to the Holy One.*

Become favorable through compassion and become appeased through supplications. Become favorable and appeased to the poor generation, for there is no helper. Our Father, our King, be gracious with us and answer us, though we have no worthy deeds; treat us with charity and kindness, and save us.

וַאֲנַחְנוּ *We know not what to do — but our eyes are upon You.[1] Remember Your mercies, HASHEM, and Your kindnesses, for they are from the beginning of the world.[2] May Your kindness be upon us, HASHEM, just as we awaited You.[3] Recall not against us the iniquities of the ancients; may Your mercies meet us swiftly, for we have become exceedingly impoverished.[4] Be gracious to us, HASHEM, be gracious to us, for we are abundantly sated with scorn.[5] Amid rage — remember to be merciful![6] For He knew our nature, He remembers that we are dust.[7]* Chazzan— *Assist us, O God of our salvation, for the sake of Your Name's glory; rescue us and atone for our sins for Your Name's sake.[8]*

FULL KADDISH
The *chazzan* recites the Full Kaddish:

יִתְגַּדַּל *May His great Name grow exalted and sanctified* (Cong. — *Amen.*) *in the world that He created as He willed. May He give reign to His kingship in your lifetimes and in your days, and in the lifetimes of the entire Family of Israel, swiftly and soon. Now respond: Amen.*

(Cong. — *Amen. May His great Name be blessed forever and ever.*)
May His great Name be blessed forever and ever.

Blessed, praised, glorified, exalted, extolled, mighty, upraised and lauded be the Name of the Holy One, Blessed is He (Cong. — *Blessed is He.*) *beyond any blessing and song, praise, and consolation that are uttered in the world. Now respond: Amen.* (Cong. — *Amen.*)

(Cong. — *Accept our prayers with mercy and favor.*)
May the prayers and supplications of the entire House of Israel be accepted before their Father Who is in Heaven. Now respond: Amen. (Cong. — *Amen.*)

(Cong. — *Blessed be the Name of HASHEM from this time and forever.[9]*)
May there be abundant peace from Heaven, and life, upon us and upon all Israel. Now respond: Amen. (Cong. — *Amen.*)

(Cong. — *My help is from HASHEM, Maker of heaven and earth.[10]*)

Take three steps back. Bow left and say, 'He Who makes peace . . .'; bow right and say,
'may He make peace . . .'; bow forward and say, 'and upon all Israel . . .'
Remain standing in place for a few moments, then take three steps forward.

He Who makes peace in His heights, may He make peace upon us, and upon all Israel. Now respond: Amen. (Cong. — *Amen.*)

---

(1) *II Chronicles* 20:12. (2) *Psalms* 25:6. (3) 33:22. (4) 79:8. (5) 123:3.
(6) *Habakkuk* 3:2. (7) *Psalms* 103:14. (8) 79:9. (9) 113:2. (10) 121:2.

יום ששי

אַשְׁרֵי יוֹשְׁבֵי בֵיתֶךָ, עוֹד יְהַלְלוּךָ סֶּלָה.[1] אַשְׁרֵי הָעָם שֶׁכָּכָה
לוֹ, אַשְׁרֵי הָעָם שֶׁיהוה אֱלֹהָיו.[2]

תְּהִלָּה לְדָוִד.

תהלים קמה

אֲרוֹמִמְךָ אֱלוֹהַי הַמֶּלֶךְ, וַאֲבָרְכָה שִׁמְךָ לְעוֹלָם וָעֶד.

בְּכָל יוֹם אֲבָרְכֶךָּ, וַאֲהַלְלָה שִׁמְךָ לְעוֹלָם וָעֶד.

גָּדוֹל יהוה וּמְהֻלָּל מְאֹד, וְלִגְדֻלָּתוֹ אֵין חֵקֶר.

דּוֹר לְדוֹר יְשַׁבַּח מַעֲשֶׂיךָ, וּגְבוּרֹתֶיךָ יַגִּידוּ.

הֲדַר כְּבוֹד הוֹדֶךָ, וְדִבְרֵי נִפְלְאֹתֶיךָ אָשִׂיחָה.

וֶעֱזוּז נוֹרְאֹתֶיךָ יֹאמֵרוּ, וּגְדֻלָּתְךָ אֲסַפְּרֶנָּה.

זֵכֶר רַב טוּבְךָ יַבִּיעוּ, וְצִדְקָתְךָ יְרַנֵּנוּ.

חַנּוּן וְרַחוּם יהוה, אֶרֶךְ אַפַּיִם וּגְדָל חָסֶד.

טוֹב יהוה לַכֹּל, וְרַחֲמָיו עַל כָּל מַעֲשָׂיו.

יוֹדוּךָ יהוה כָּל מַעֲשֶׂיךָ, וַחֲסִידֶיךָ יְבָרְכוּכָה.

כְּבוֹד מַלְכוּתְךָ יֹאמֵרוּ, וּגְבוּרָתְךָ יְדַבֵּרוּ.

לְהוֹדִיעַ לִבְנֵי הָאָדָם גְּבוּרֹתָיו, וּכְבוֹד הֲדַר מַלְכוּתוֹ.

מַלְכוּתְךָ מַלְכוּת כָּל עֹלָמִים, וּמֶמְשַׁלְתְּךָ בְּכָל דּוֹר וָדֹר.

סוֹמֵךְ יהוה לְכָל הַנֹּפְלִים, וְזוֹקֵף לְכָל הַכְּפוּפִים.

עֵינֵי כֹל אֵלֶיךָ יְשַׂבֵּרוּ, וְאַתָּה נוֹתֵן לָהֶם אֶת אָכְלָם בְּעִתּוֹ.

Concentrate intently while reciting the verse, פּוֹתֵחַ.

פּוֹתֵחַ אֶת יָדֶךָ, וּמַשְׂבִּיעַ לְכָל חַי רָצוֹן.

❖ **צַדִּיק** יהוה בְּכָל דְּרָכָיו, וְחָסִיד בְּכָל מַעֲשָׂיו.

קָרוֹב יהוה לְכָל קֹרְאָיו, לְכֹל אֲשֶׁר יִקְרָאֻהוּ בֶאֱמֶת.

רְצוֹן יְרֵאָיו יַעֲשֶׂה, וְאֶת שַׁוְעָתָם יִשְׁמַע וְיוֹשִׁיעֵם.

שׁוֹמֵר יהוה אֶת כָּל אֹהֲבָיו, וְאֵת כָּל הָרְשָׁעִים יַשְׁמִיד.

תְּהִלַּת יהוה יְדַבֶּר פִּי, וִיבָרֵךְ כָּל בָּשָׂר שֵׁם קָדְשׁוֹ לְעוֹלָם וָעֶד.

וַאֲנַחְנוּ נְבָרֵךְ יָהּ, מֵעַתָּה וְעַד עוֹלָם, הַלְלוּיָהּ.[3]

The chazzan recites חֲצִי קַדִּישׁ.

יִתְגַּדַּל וְיִתְקַדַּשׁ שְׁמֵהּ רַבָּא. (.Cong – אָמֵן.) בְּעָלְמָא דִּי בְרָא כִרְעוּתֵהּ,
וְיַמְלִיךְ מַלְכוּתֵהּ, בְּחַיֵּיכוֹן וּבְיוֹמֵיכוֹן וּבְחַיֵּי דְכָל בֵּית יִשְׂרָאֵל,
בַּעֲגָלָא וּבִזְמַן קָרִיב. וְאִמְרוּ: אָמֵן.

(.Cong – אָמֵן. יְהֵא שְׁמֵהּ רַבָּא מְבָרַךְ לְעָלַם וּלְעָלְמֵי עָלְמַיָּא.)

יְהֵא שְׁמֵהּ רַבָּא מְבָרַךְ לְעָלַם וּלְעָלְמֵי עָלְמַיָּא.

יִתְבָּרַךְ וְיִשְׁתַּבַּח וְיִתְפָּאַר וְיִתְרוֹמַם וְיִתְנַשֵּׂא וְיִתְהַדָּר וְיִתְעַלֶּה וְיִתְהַלָּל
שְׁמֵהּ דְּקֻדְשָׁא בְּרִיךְ הוּא (.Cong – בְּרִיךְ הוּא) לְעֵלָּא מִן כָּל בִּרְכָתָא וְשִׁירָתָא
תֻּשְׁבְּחָתָא וְנֶחֱמָתָא, דַּאֲמִירָן בְּעָלְמָא. וְאִמְרוּ: אָמֵן. (.Cong – אָמֵן.)

❧ SIXTH DAY ❧

אַשְׁרֵי *Praiseworthy are those who dwell in Your house; may they always praise You, Selah!*[1] *Praiseworthy is the people for whom this is so, praiseworthy is the people whose God is HASHEM.*[2]

Psalm 145 *A psalm of praise by David:*

א *I will exalt You, my God the King, and I will bless Your Name forever and ever.*

ב *Every day I will bless You, and I will laud Your Name forever and ever.*

ג *HASHEM is great and exceedingly lauded,*
and His greatness is beyond investigation.

ד *Each generation will praise Your deeds to the next*
and of Your mighty deeds they will tell;

ה *The splendrous glory of Your power and Your wondrous deeds I shall discuss.*

ו *And of Your awesome power they will speak, and Your greatness I shall relate.*

ז *A recollection of Your abundant goodness they will utter*
and of Your righteousness they will sing exultantly.

ח *Gracious and merciful is HASHEM,*
slow to anger, and great in [bestowing] kindness.

ט *HASHEM is good to all; His mercies are on all His works.*

י *All Your works shall thank You, HASHEM, and Your devout ones will bless You.*

כ *Of the glory of Your kingdom they will speak, and of Your power they will tell;*

ל *To inform human beings of His mighty deeds,*
and the glorious splendor of His kingdom.

מ *Your kingdom is a kingdom spanning all eternities,*
and Your dominion is throughout every generation.

ס *HASHEM supports all the fallen ones and straightens all the bent.*

ע *The eyes of all look to You with hope*
and You give them their food in its proper time;

פ *You open Your hand,* Concentrate intently while reciting the verse, 'You open...'
and satisfy the desire of every living thing.

צ Chazzan— *Righteous is HASHEM in all His ways*
and magnanimous in all His deeds.

ק *HASHEM is close to all who call upon Him — to all who call upon Him sincerely.*

ר *The will of those who fear Him He will do;*
and their cry He will hear, and save them.

ש *HASHEM protects all who love Him; but all the wicked He will destroy.*

ת *May my mouth declare the praise of HASHEM*
and may all flesh bless His Holy Name forever and ever.

We will bless God from this time and forever, Halleluyah![3]

The chazzan recites Half-Kaddish:

יִתְגַּדַּל *May His great Name grow exalted and sanctified* (Cong.— Amen.) *in the world that He created as He willed. May He give reign to His kingship in your lifetimes and in your days, and in the lifetimes of the entire Family of Israel, swiftly and soon. Now respond: Amen.*

(Cong.— *Amen. May His great Name be blessed forever and ever.*)

May His great Name be blessed forever and ever.

Blessed, praised, glorified, exalted, extolled, mighty, upraised, and lauded be the Name of the Holy One, Blessed is He (Cong.— *Blessed is He*) — *beyond any blessing and song, praise and consolation that are uttered in the world. Now respond: Amen.* (Cong.— *Amen.*)

---

(1) *Psalms* 84:5. (2) 144:15. (3) 115:18.

All:

לְךָ יהוה הַצְּדָקָה, וְלָנוּ בְּשֶׁת הַפָּנִים.[1] מַה נִּתְאוֹנֵן,[2] מַה נֹּאמַר, מַה נְּדַבֵּר, וּמַה נִּצְטַדָּק.[3] נַחְפְּשָׂה דְרָכֵינוּ וְנַחְקֹרָה, וְנָשׁוּבָה אֵלֶיךָ,[4] כִּי יְמִינְךָ פְּשׁוּטָה לְקַבֵּל שָׁבִים. לֹא בְחֶסֶד וְלֹא בְמַעֲשִׂים בָּאנוּ לְפָנֶיךָ, כַּדַּלִּים וּכְרָשִׁים דָּפַקְנוּ דְלָתֶיךָ. דְּלָתֶיךָ דָּפַקְנוּ רַחוּם וְחַנּוּן, נָא אַל תְּשִׁיבֵנוּ רֵיקָם מִלְּפָנֶיךָ. מִלְּפָנֶיךָ מַלְכֵּנוּ רֵיקָם אַל תְּשִׁיבֵנוּ, כִּי אַתָּה שׁוֹמֵעַ תְּפִלָּה.

שֹׁמֵעַ תְּפִלָּה, עָדֶיךָ כָּל בָּשָׂר יָבֹאוּ.[5] יָבוֹא כָל בָּשָׂר לְהִשְׁתַּחֲוֹת לְפָנֶיךָ יהוה.[6] יָבֹאוּ וְיִשְׁתַּחֲווּ לְפָנֶיךָ אֲדֹנָי, וִיכַבְּדוּ לִשְׁמֶךָ.[7] בָּאוּ נִשְׁתַּחֲוֶה וְנִכְרָעָה, נִבְרְכָה לִפְנֵי יהוה עֹשֵׂנוּ.[8] נָבוֹאָה לְמִשְׁכְּנוֹתָיו, נִשְׁתַּחֲוֶה לַהֲדֹם רַגְלָיו.[9] בָּאוּ שְׁעָרָיו בְּתוֹדָה, חֲצֵרֹתָיו בִּתְהִלָּה, הוֹדוּ לוֹ בָּרְכוּ שְׁמוֹ.[10] רוֹמְמוּ יהוה אֱלֹהֵינוּ, וְהִשְׁתַּחֲווּ לַהֲדֹם רַגְלָיו, קָדוֹשׁ הוּא.[11] רוֹמְמוּ יהוה אֱלֹהֵינוּ, וְהִשְׁתַּחֲווּ לְהַר קָדְשׁוֹ, כִּי קָדוֹשׁ יהוה אֱלֹהֵינוּ.[12] הִשְׁתַּחֲווּ לַיהוה בְּהַדְרַת קֹדֶשׁ, חִילוּ מִפָּנָיו כָּל הָאָרֶץ.[13] וַאֲנַחְנוּ בְּרֹב חַסְדְּךָ נָבוֹא בֵיתֶךָ, נִשְׁתַּחֲוֶה אֶל הֵיכַל קָדְשְׁךָ בְּיִרְאָתֶךָ.[14] נִשְׁתַּחֲוֶה אֶל הֵיכַל קָדְשְׁךָ וְנוֹדֶה אֶת שְׁמֶךָ, עַל חַסְדְּךָ וְעַל אֲמִתֶּךָ, כִּי הִגְדַּלְתָּ עַל כָּל שִׁמְךָ אִמְרָתֶךָ.[15] לְכוּ נְרַנְּנָה לַיהוה, נָרִיעָה לְצוּר יִשְׁעֵנוּ. נְקַדְּמָה פָנָיו בְּתוֹדָה, בִּזְמִרוֹת נָרִיעַ לוֹ.[16] אֲשֶׁר יַחְדָּו נַמְתִּיק סוֹד, בְּבֵית אֱלֹהִים נְהַלֵּךְ בְּרָגֶשׁ.[17] אֵל נַעֲרָץ בְּסוֹד קְדוֹשִׁים רַבָּה, וְנוֹרָא עַל כָּל סְבִיבָיו.[18] שְׂאוּ יְדֵיכֶם קֹדֶשׁ וּבָרְכוּ אֶת יהוה.[19] הִנֵּה בָּרְכוּ אֶת יהוה כָּל עַבְדֵי יהוה, הָעֹמְדִים בְּבֵית יהוה בַּלֵּילוֹת.[20] אֲשֶׁר מִי אֵל בַּשָּׁמַיִם וּבָאָרֶץ, אֲשֶׁר יַעֲשֶׂה כְמַעֲשֶׂיךָ וְכִגְבוּרֹתֶיךָ.[21] אֲשֶׁר לוֹ הַיָּם וְהוּא עָשָׂהוּ, וְיַבֶּשֶׁת יָדָיו יָצָרוּ.[22] אֲשֶׁר בְּיָדוֹ מֶחְקְרֵי אָרֶץ, וְתוֹעֲפוֹת הָרִים לוֹ.[23] אֲשֶׁר בְּיָדוֹ נֶפֶשׁ כָּל חָי, וְרוּחַ כָּל בְּשַׂר אִישׁ.[24] וְיוֹדוּ שָׁמַיִם פִּלְאֲךָ יהוה, אַף אֱמוּנָתְךָ בִּקְהַל קְדֹשִׁים.[25] לְךָ זְרוֹעַ עִם גְּבוּרָה, תָּעֹז יָדְךָ תָּרוּם יְמִינֶךָ.[26] לְךָ שָׁמַיִם, אַף לְךָ אָרֶץ, תֵּבֵל וּמְלֹאָהּ אַתָּה יְסַדְתָּם.[27] אַתָּה פוֹרַרְתָּ בְעָזְּךָ יָם, שִׁבַּרְתָּ רָאשֵׁי תַנִּינִים עַל הַמָּיִם.[28] אַתָּה הִצַּבְתָּ כָּל גְּבוּלוֹת אָרֶץ, קַיִץ וָחֹרֶף

(1) *Daniel* 9:7. (2) Cf. *Lamentations* 3:39. (3) Cf. *Genesis* 44:16. (4) Cf. *Lamentations* 3:40. (5) *Psalms* 65:3. (6) Cf. *Isaiah* 66:23. (7) *Psalms* 86:9. (8) 95:6. (9) 132:7. (10) 100:4. (11) 99:5. (12) 99:9. (13) 96:9. (14) Cf. 5:8. (15) Cf. 138:2. (16) 95:1-2. (17) 55:15. (18) 89:8. (19) 134:2. (20) 134:1. (21) *Deuteronomy* 3:24. (22) *Psalms* 95:5. (23) 95:4. (24) *Job* 12:10. (25) *Psalms* 89:6. (26) 89:14. (27) 89:12. (28) 74:13.

All:

לְךָ ה' Yours, my Lord, is the righteousness and ours is the shame-
facedness.[1] What complaint can we make?[2] What can we say?
What can we declare? What justification can we offer?[3] Let us examine
our ways and analyze — and return to You,[4] for Your right hand is
extended to accept penitents. Neither with kindness nor with [good]
deeds do we come before You. As paupers and as beggars do we knock
at Your doors. At Your doors we knock, O Compassionate and Gracious
One. Please do not turn us away from You empty-handed. Our King,
turn us not away from You empty-handed, for You are the One Who
hears prayer.

שְׁמַע תְּפִלָּה You Who hears prayer, to You all flesh will come.[5] All
flesh will come to prostrate itself before You, O
HASHEM.[6] They will come and prostrate themselves before You, my Lord,
and shall honor Your Name.[7] Come! — let us prostrate ourselves and
bow, let us kneel before God, our Maker.[8] Let us come to His dwelling
places, let us prostrate ourselves at His footstool.[9] Enter His gates with
thanksgiving, His courts with praise; give thanks to Him, praise His
Name.[10] Exalt HASHEM, our God, and bow at His footstool; He is holy![11]
Exalt HASHEM, our God, and bow at His holy mountain; for holy is
HASHEM, our God.[12] Prostrate yourselves before HASHEM in His intensely
holy place, tremble before Him, everyone on earth.[13] As for us, through
Your abundant kindness we will enter Your House; we will prostrate
ourselves toward Your Holy Sanctuary in awe of You.[14] We will
prostrate ourselves toward Your Holy Sanctuary, and we will give
thanks to Your Name for Your kindness and truth for You have exalted
Your promise even beyond Your Name.[15] Come! — let us sing to HASHEM,
let us call out to the Rock of our salvation. Let us greet Him with
thanksgiving, with praiseful songs let us call out to Him.[16] For together
let us share sweet counsel, in the house of God let us walk in
multitudes.[17] God is dreaded in the hiddenmost counsel of the holy ones,
and inspires awe upon all who surround Him.[18] Lift your hands in the
Sanctuary and bless HASHEM.[19] Behold, bless HASHEM, all you servants of
HASHEM, who stand in the House of HASHEM in the nights.[20] For what
power is there in heaven or earth that can approximate Your deeds and
power?[21] For His is the sea and He perfected the dry land — His hands
fashioned it.[22] For in His power are the hidden mysteries of the earth,
and the mountain summits are His.[23] For His is the soul of every living
thing, and the spirit of all human flesh.[24] Heaven will gratefully praise
Your wonders, HASHEM; also Your faithfulness in the assembly of
holy ones.[25] Yours is a mighty arm with power, You strengthen Your
hand; You exalt Your right hand.[26] Yours is the heaven; Yours, too, is the
earth; the world and its fullness — You founded them.[27] You shattered
the sea with Your might, You smashed sea serpents' heads upon the
water.[28] You established all the boundaries of earth; summer and winter

אַתָּה יְצַרְתָּם.[1] אַתָּה רִצַּצְתָּ רָאשֵׁי לִוְיָתָן, תִּתְּנֶנּוּ מַאֲכָל לְעַם
לְצִיִּים. אַתָּה בָקַעְתָּ מַעְיָן וָנָחַל, אַתָּה הוֹבַשְׁתָּ נַהֲרוֹת אֵיתָן.[2] לְךָ
יוֹם, אַף לְךָ לָיְלָה, אַתָּה הֲכִינוֹתָ מָאוֹר וָשָׁמֶשׁ.[3] עֹשֶׂה גְדֹלוֹת עַד
אֵין חֵקֶר, וְנִפְלָאוֹת עַד אֵין מִסְפָּר.[4] כִּי אֵל גָּדוֹל יהוה, וּמֶלֶךְ
גָּדוֹל עַל כָּל אֱלֹהִים. כִּי גָדוֹל אַתָּה וְעֹשֵׂה נִפְלָאוֹת, אַתָּה
אֱלֹהִים לְבַדֶּךָ.[6] כִּי גָדוֹל מֵעַל שָׁמַיִם חַסְדֶּךָ, וְעַד שְׁחָקִים
אֲמִתֶּךָ.[7] גָּדוֹל יהוה וּמְהֻלָּל מְאֹד, וְלִגְדֻלָּתוֹ אֵין חֵקֶר.[8] (כִּי) גָדוֹל
יהוה וּמְהֻלָּל מְאֹד, נוֹרָא הוּא עַל כָּל אֱלֹהִים.[9] גָּדוֹל יהוה
וּמְהֻלָּל מְאֹד, בְּעִיר אֱלֹהֵינוּ הַר קָדְשׁוֹ.[10] לְךָ יהוה הַגְּדֻלָּה
וְהַגְּבוּרָה, וְהַתִּפְאֶרֶת וְהַנֵּצַח וְהַהוֹד, כִּי כֹל בַּשָּׁמַיִם וּבָאָרֶץ; לְךָ
יהוה הַמַּמְלָכָה, וְהַמִּתְנַשֵּׂא לְכֹל לְרֹאשׁ.[11] מִי לֹא יִרָאֲךָ מֶלֶךְ
הַגּוֹיִם, כִּי לְךָ יָאָתָה, כִּי בְכָל חַכְמֵי הַגּוֹיִם וּבְכָל מַלְכוּתָם מֵאֵין
כָּמוֹךָ.[12] מֵאֵין כָּמוֹךָ יהוה, גָּדוֹל אַתָּה וְגָדוֹל שִׁמְךָ בִּגְבוּרָה.[13]
יהוה אֱלֹהֵי צְבָאוֹת, מִי כָמוֹךָ חֲסִין יָהּ, וֶאֱמוּנָתְךָ סְבִיבוֹתֶיךָ.[14]
יהוה צְבָאוֹת, אֱלֹהֵי יִשְׂרָאֵל, יוֹשֵׁב הַכְּרֻבִים, אַתָּה הוּא
הָאֱלֹהִים לְבַדֶּךָ.[15] מִי יְמַלֵּל גְּבוּרוֹת יהוה, יַשְׁמִיעַ כָּל תְּהִלָּתוֹ.[16]
כִּי מִי בַשַּׁחַק יַעֲרֹךְ לַיהוה, יִדְמֶה לַיהוה בִּבְנֵי אֵלִים.[17] מַה נֹּאמַר
לְפָנֶיךָ יוֹשֵׁב מָרוֹם, וּמַה נְּסַפֵּר לְפָנֶיךָ שֹׁכֵן שְׁחָקִים. מַה נֹּאמַר
לְפָנֶיךָ יהוה אֱלֹהֵינוּ, מַה נְּדַבֵּר וּמַה נִּצְטַדָּק.[18] אֵין לָנוּ פֶּה
לְהָשִׁיב וְלֹא מֵצַח לְהָרִים רֹאשׁ, כִּי עֲווֹנוֹתֵינוּ רַבּוּ מִלְּמְנוֹת,
וְחַטֹּאתֵינוּ עָצְמוּ מִסַּפֵּר.[19] לְמַעַן שִׁמְךָ יהוה תְּחַיֵּנוּ, וּבְצִדְקָתְךָ
תּוֹצִיא מִצָּרָה נַפְשֵׁנוּ.[20] דַּרְכְּךָ אֱלֹהֵינוּ לְהַאֲרִיךְ אַפֶּךָ, לָרָעִים
וְלַטּוֹבִים, וְהִיא תְהִלָּתֶךָ. לְמַעַנְךָ אֱלֹהֵינוּ עֲשֵׂה וְלֹא לָנוּ, רְאֵה
עֲמִידָתֵנוּ, דַּלִּים וְרֵקִים. ❖ הַנְּשָׁמָה לָךְ וְהַגּוּף פָּעֳלָךְ, חוּסָה עַל
עֲמָלָךְ. הַנְּשָׁמָה לָךְ וְהַגּוּף שֶׁלָּךְ, יהוה עֲשֵׂה לְמַעַן שְׁמֶךָ. אָתָאנוּ
עַל שְׁמֶךָ, יהוה, עֲשֵׂה לְמַעַן שְׁמֶךָ. בַּעֲבוּר כְּבוֹד שִׁמְךָ, כִּי אֵל
חַנּוּן וְרַחוּם שְׁמֶךָ. לְמַעַן שִׁמְךָ יהוה, וְסָלַחְתָּ לַעֲוֹנֵנוּ כִּי רַב
הוּא.[21]

Congregation, then *chazzan:*

סְלַח לָנוּ אָבִינוּ, כִּי בְרוֹב אִוַּלְתֵּנוּ שָׁגִינוּ,
מְחַל לָנוּ מַלְכֵּנוּ, כִּי רַבּוּ עֲוֹנֵינוּ.

— *You fashioned them.*[1] *You crushed the heads of Leviathan, You served it as food to the nation of legions. You split open fountain and stream, You dried the mighty rivers.*[2] *Yours is the day, Yours as well is the night; You established luminary and the sun.*[3] *Who performs great deeds that are beyond comprehension, and wonders beyond number.*[4] *For a great God is* HASHEM, *and a great King above all heavenly powers.*[5] *For You are great and work wonders; You alone, O God.*[6] *For great above the very heavens is Your kindness, and until the upper heights is Your truth.*[7] HASHEM *is great and exceedingly lauded, and His greatness is beyond investigation.*[8] *(For)* HASHEM *is great and exceedingly lauded, awesome is He above all heavenly powers.*[9] *Great is* HASHEM *and exceedingly lauded, in the city of our God, Mount of His Holiness.*[10] *Yours,* HASHEM, *is the greatness, the strength, the splendor, the triumph, and the glory; even everything in heaven and earth; Yours,* HASHEM, *is the kingdom, and sovereignty over every leader.*[11] *Who would not revere You, O King of nations? — for this befits You, for among all the sages of the nations and in all their kingdom there is none like You.*[12] *There is none like You, O* HASHEM, *You are great and Your Name is great with power.*[13] HASHEM, *God of Legions — who is like You, O Strong One, God? — and Your faithfulness surrounds You.*[14] HASHEM, *Master of Legions, God of Israel, enthroned upon the Cherubim, it is You alone Who is God.*[15] *Who can express the mighty acts of* HASHEM, *who can announce all His praise?*[16] *For who in the sky can be compared to* HASHEM; *be likened to* HASHEM *among the angels?*[17] *What can we say before You Who dwell on high? And what can we relate to You Who abide in the highest heaven? What can we say before You,* HASHEM, *our God? What can we declare? What justification can we offer?*[18] *We have neither mouth to respond nor brow to raise our head, for our iniquities are too numerous to count, and our sins are too vast to be numbered.*[19] *For Your Name's sake,* HASHEM, *revive us; and with Your righteousness remove our soul from distress.*[20] *It is Your way, our God, to delay Your anger, against people both evil and good — and this is Your praise. Act for Your sake, our God, and not for ours, behold our [spiritual] position — destitute and emptyhanded.* Chazzan — *The soul is Yours and the body is Your handiwork; take pity on Your labor. The soul is Yours and the body is Yours; O* HASHEM, *act for Your Name's sake. We have come with reliance on Your Name, O* HASHEM, *act for Your Name's sake; because of Your Name's glory — for 'Gracious and Merciful God' is Your Name. For Your Name's sake,* HASHEM, *may You forgive our iniquity, though it is abundant.*[21]

Congregation, then *chazzan:*

Forgive us, our Father, for in our abundant folly we have erred, pardon us, our King, for our iniquities are many.

---

(1) *Psalms* 74:17. (2) 74:14-15. (3) 74:16. (4) *Job* 9:10. (5) *Psalms* 95:3. (6) 86:10. (7) 108:5. (8) 145:3. (9) 96:4. (10) 48:2. (11) *I Chronicles* 29:11. (12) *Jeremiah* 10:7. (13) 10:6. (14) *Psalms* 89:9. (15) *Isaiah* 37:16. (16) *Psalms* 106:2. (17) 89:7. (18) Cf. *Genesis* 44:16. (19) Cf. *Ezra* 9:6. (20) Cf. *Psalms* 143:11. (21) Cf. 25:11.

All, while standing:

אֵל אֶרֶךְ אַפַּיִם אַתָּה, וּבַעַל הָרַחֲמִים נִקְרֵאתָ,
וְדֶרֶךְ תְּשׁוּבָה הוֹרֵיתָ.

גְּדֻלַּת רַחֲמֶיךָ וַחֲסָדֶיךָ,   תִּזְכּוֹר הַיּוֹם וּבְכָל יוֹם לְזֶרַע יְדִידֶיךָ.

תֵּפֶן אֵלֵינוּ בְּרַחֲמִים,   כִּי אַתָּה הוּא בַּעַל הָרַחֲמִים.

בְּתַחֲנוּן וּבִתְפִלָּה פָּנֶיךָ נְקַדֵּם,   כְּהוֹדַעְתָּ לֶעָנָיו מִקֶּדֶם.

מֵחֲרוֹן אַפְּךָ שׁוּב,¹   כְּמוֹ בְתוֹרָתְךָ כָּתוּב.²

וּבְצֵל כְּנָפֶיךָ נֶחֱסֶה³ וְנִתְלוֹנָן,   כְּיוֹם וַיֵּרֶד יהוה בֶּעָנָן.

❖ תַּעֲבוֹר עַל פֶּשַׁע וְתִמְחֶה אָשָׁם,   כְּיוֹם וַיִּתְיַצֵּב עִמּוֹ שָׁם.

תַּאֲזִין שַׁוְעָתֵנוּ וְתַקְשִׁיב מֶנּוּ מַאֲמָר,

כְּיוֹם וַיִּקְרָא בְשֵׁם יהוה,⁴ וְשָׁם נֶאֱמַר:

Congregation, then *chazzan:*

וַיַּעֲבֹר יהוה עַל פָּנָיו וַיִּקְרָא:

Congregation and *chazzan* (the words in bold type are recited aloud and in unison):

יהוה, יהוה, אֵל, **רַחוּם, וְחַנּוּן, אֶרֶךְ אַפַּיִם, וְרַב חֶסֶד, וֶאֱמֶת,**
נֹצֵר חֶסֶד לָאֲלָפִים, נֹשֵׂא עָוֹן, וָפֶשַׁע, וְחַטָּאָה,
וְנַקֵּה.⁵ וְסָלַחְתָּ לַעֲוֹנֵנוּ וּלְחַטָּאתֵנוּ וּנְחַלְתָּנוּ.⁶ סְלַח לָנוּ אָבִינוּ כִּי
חָטָאנוּ, מְחַל לָנוּ מַלְכֵּנוּ כִּי פָשָׁעְנוּ. כִּי אַתָּה אֲדֹנָי טוֹב וְסַלָּח, וְרַב
חֶסֶד לְכָל קֹרְאֶיךָ.⁷

פסוקי הקדמה לסליחה יז

קִדְּמוּ עֵינַי אַשְׁמֻרוֹת, לָשִׂיחַ בְּאִמְרָתֶךָ.⁸ לְאָדָם מַעַרְכֵי לֵב,
וּמֵיהוה מַעֲנֵה לָשׁוֹן.⁹ תְּפִלָּה לְעָנִי כִי יַעֲטֹף, וְלִפְנֵי יהוה
יִשְׁפֹּךְ שִׂיחוֹ.¹⁰ כִּי הִנֵּה יוֹצֵר הָרִים וּבֹרֵא רוּחַ, וּמַגִּיד לְאָדָם
מַה שֵּׂחוֹ, עֹשֵׂה שַׁחַר עֵיפָה, וְדֹרֵךְ עַל בָּמֳתֵי אָרֶץ, יהוה אֱלֹהֵי
צְבָאוֹת שְׁמוֹ.¹¹

כְּרַחֵם אָב עַל בָּנִים, כֵּן תְּרַחֵם יהוה עָלֵינוּ.¹² לַיהוה הַיְשׁוּעָה,
עַל עַמְּךָ בִרְכָתֶךָ סֶּלָה.¹³ יהוה צְבָאוֹת עִמָּנוּ,
מִשְׂגָּב לָנוּ אֱלֹהֵי יַעֲקֹב סֶלָה.¹⁴ יהוה צְבָאוֹת, אַשְׁרֵי אָדָם בֹּטֵחַ
בָּךְ.¹⁵ יהוה הוֹשִׁיעָה, הַמֶּלֶךְ יַעֲנֵנוּ בְיוֹם קָרְאֵנוּ.¹⁶

In some congregations the following two verses are recited responsively — the *chazzan* reciting סְלַח,
and the congregation responding וַיֹּאמֶר. In other congregations these verses are recited silently.

סְלַח נָא לַעֲוֹן הָעָם הַזֶּה כְּגֹדֶל חַסְדֶּךָ, וְכַאֲשֶׁר נָשָׂאתָה לָעָם
הַזֶּה מִמִּצְרַיִם וְעַד הֵנָּה,¹⁷ וְשָׁם נֶאֱמַר:

All, while standing:

אֵל אֶרֶךְ אַפַּיִם **O God** — *You are slow to anger, You are called the Master of Mercy, and You have taught the way of repentance. May You remember this day and every day the greatness of Your mercy and Your kindness to the offspring of Your beloved Ones. Turn to us in mercy for You are the Master of Mercy. With supplication and prayer we approach Your Presence in the manner that You made known to the humble [Moses] in ancient times. Turn back from Your fierce anger;[1] as is written in Your Torah.[2] In the shadow of Your wings may we find shelter[3] and lodging as on the day 'HASHEM descended in a cloud' [to appear to Moses on Sinai]. Chazzan* — Overlook sin and erase guilt as on the day 'He [God] stood there with him [Moses].' Give heed to our cry and be attentive to our declaration as on the day 'He called out with the Name HASHEM,'[4] and there it was said:*

Congregation, then *chazzan:*

And HASHEM passed before him [Moses] and proclaimed:

Congregation and *chazzan* (the words in bold type are recited aloud and in unison):

ה' ה' **HASHEM, HASHEM, God, Compassionate and Gracious, Slow to anger, and Abundant in Kindness and Truth, Preserver of kindness for thousands [of generations], Forgiver of iniquity, willful sin, and error, and Who cleanses.**[5] *May You forgive our iniquities and our errors and make us Your heritage.*[6] *Forgive us, our Father, for we have erred; pardon us, our King, for we have willfully sinned; for You, my Lord, are good and forgiving and abundantly kind to all who call upon You.*[7]

PREFATORY VERSES TO SELICHAH 17

קִדְּמוּ *My eyes preceded the night watches, to discuss Your word.*[8] *The heart's arrangements are man's, but the tongue's answer comes from HASHEM.*[9] *A prayer of the afflicted man when he is bent low, and pours forth his prayer before HASHEM.*[10] *For here is the Former of mountains and Creator of the wind, Who tells man what he has wrought; Who turns dawn to darkness and treads on the heights of the earth; HASHEM, the God of Legions, is His name.*[11]

כְּרַחֵם אָב *As a father has mercy on his children, so, HASHEM, may You have mercy on us.*[12] *Salvation is HASHEM's, upon Your people is Your blessing, Selah.*[13] *HASHEM, Master of Legions, is with us, a stronghold for us is the God of Jacob, Selah.*[14] *HASHEM, Master of Legions, praiseworthy is the person who trusts in You.*[15] *HASHEM, save! May the King answer us on the day we call.*[16]

In some congregations, the following two verses are recited responsively — the *chazzan* reciting 'Forgive, please . . .,' and the congregation responding, 'And HASHEM said . . .' In other congregations these verses are recited silently.

סְלַח נָא *Forgive, please, the iniquity of this people according to the greatness of Your kindness and as You have forgiven this people from Egypt until now,*[17] *and there it was said:*

---

(1) Cf. *Exodus* 32:12. (2) See 32:14. (3) Cf. *Psalms* 36:8. (4) *Exodus* 34:5. (5) 34:6-7. (6) 34:9. (7) *Psalms* 86:5. (8) *Psalms* 119:148. (9) *Proverbs* 16:1. (10) *Psalms* 102:1. (11) *Amos* 4:13. (12) Cf. *Psalms* 103:13. (13) 3:9. (14) 46:8. (15) 84:13. (16) 20:10. (17) *Numbers* 14:19.

וַיֹּאמֶר יהוה סָלַחְתִּי כִּדְבָרֶךָ.¹

All:

הַטֵּה אֱלֹהַי אָזְנְךָ וּשְׁמָע, פְּקַח עֵינֶיךָ וּרְאֵה שֹׁמְמֹתֵינוּ, וְהָעִיר
אֲשֶׁר נִקְרָא שִׁמְךָ עָלֶיהָ, כִּי לֹא עַל צִדְקֹתֵינוּ אֲנַחְנוּ
מַפִּילִים תַּחֲנוּנֵינוּ לְפָנֶיךָ, כִּי עַל רַחֲמֶיךָ הָרַבִּים. אֲדֹנָי שְׁמָעָה,
אֲדֹנָי סְלָחָה, אֲדֹנָי הַקְשִׁיבָה, וַעֲשֵׂה אַל תְּאַחַר, לְמַעַנְךָ אֱלֹהַי,
כִּי שִׁמְךָ נִקְרָא עַל עִירְךָ וְעַל עַמֶּךָ.²

סליחה יז

All:

אֱלֹהֵינוּ וֵאלֹהֵי אֲבוֹתֵינוּ:

אֶקְרָא בְשִׁמְךָ,* לְהַחֲזִיק בְּךָ אֶתְעוֹרֵר,³
בִּתְפִלָּה אֶשְׁמוֹר⁴ אֲקַדֵּם,⁵ שַׁחַר אֲעוֹרֵר,⁶
גַּשְׁתִּי פְנֵי תֵבָה* מֵלֵל לְבָרֵר,
דִּקְדַּקְתִּי מַעַרְכִי, דַּל שְׂפָתַי לְגָרֵר.⁷
הֵן תָּוִי,* יַאֲזִינֵנִי יַעֲנֵנִי* שַׁדַּי,*⁸
וְאֵפוֹא מַפְגִּיעַ⁹ הָגוּן וְאַיֵּה כְּדַי,
זָכִיתִי לִבִּי יֹאמַר,¹⁰ וְקֹשֶׁט מַעֲבָדַי,
חַף אֲנִי¹¹ מִפֶּשַׁע וְזַכּוּ מַעֲשֵׂי יָדַי.
טוֹבָה לְחַיָּבִים גָּמַל,¹² וְלֹא לְכָלוּי,
יֵחָשֵׁב כְּקָרְבָּן מִפֻלָּל, וּכְנִיחֹחַ חָלוּי,
כְּפוּפֶיךָ זְקֹף, הֱיוֹתָם לְרֹאשׁ תָּלוּי,
לֹא תִמָּצֶאנָה חַטֹּאת סֵתֶר וְגָלוּי.
מִשְׂגָּב בַּצָּרָה הֱיֵה,¹³ לְךָ חוֹסֶה,

אֶקְרָא בְשִׁמְךָ ﬄ — *I call in Your Name.* This *selichah* contains an *aleph-beis* acrostic, followed by the author's signature, אֵלִיָּה בַּר שְׁמַעְיָה חֲזָק וֶאֱמָץ, *Eliyah bar Shemayah, may he be strong and persevere* [see prefatory comment to *selichah* 6].

גַּשְׁתִּי פְנֵי תֵבָה — *I have approached before the Ark.* Assumedly, this was written for the *chazzan*.

תָּוִי — *My longing.* This arcane word is from the same root as תַּאֲוָה, *desire*, but with the א elided (see *Targum, Rashi* and *Ibn Ezra* to Job 31:35). Alternatively, תָּוִי may mean *the One for Whom I long*; the stich then reads, *Behold, the One for Whom I long will hearken to me, the Almighty will answer me.* If so, the phrase וְאֵפוֹא מַפְגִּיעַ הָגוּן of the next stich may be interpreted, *but where is*

the *Proper One Who accepts supplication* (see *Rashi* to Isaiah 53:6).

Other interpretations (*Ibn Ezra, Ralbag* ibid.) derive תָּוִי from תָּו, *an inscribed sign* (as in Ezekiel 9:4): *See what I have inscribed [in my heart], O Almighty, hearken to me, answer me.* Or: *See my signs [of repentance] . . .*

The prophet Ezekiel (ibid.) states that God told an angel [Gabriel] to '*pass in the midst of Jerusalem, and mark a sign on the foreheads of the* [righteous] *men who sigh* [in agony over the abominations of the wicked] *and* [of the wicked men] *who groan* [in the death throes about to befall them because of their sinfulness] *for all the abominations that are done within it.*' According to the Talmud (*Shabbos* 55a), the mark was to be the letter ת, and it was to be written in ink on the

And HASHEM said, 'I have forgiven according to your word!'[1]

All:

הַטֵּה *Incline, my God, Your ear, and listen, open Your eyes and see our desolation and that of the city upon which Your Name is proclaimed; for not because of our righteousness do we cast down our supplications before You, rather because of Your abundant compassion. O my Lord, heed; O my Lord, forgive; O my Lord, be attentive and act, do not delay; for Your sake, my God, for Your Name is proclaimed upon Your city and upon Your people.*[2]

SELICHAH 17

All:

Our God and the God of our forefathers:

א *I call in Your Name*; I arouse myself to cling to You.*[3]

ב *I shall be cautious*[4] *to greet [You] with prayer;*[5]
   I awaken the [sleeping] dawn.[6]

ג *I have approached before the Ark* to utter clear speech,*

ד *I have been careful [with] my [prayers'] arrangement,*
   [before] causing my lips to open.[7]

ה *See, my longing* is that the Almighty will hearken to me,*
   He will answer me;*[8]

ו *but where is one who is fit to pray,*[9] *where is there a worthy man*

ז *who can say, 'I have made my heart pure,*[10] *my deeds are true;*

ח *I am clean of willful sin,*[11] *my handiwork is pure'?*

ט *Although [they be] guilty, grant [them] good,*[12]
   and do not eradicate [them];

י *let [their] prayer be deemed sacrifice*
   and [their] supplication pleasing incense.

כ *Straighten Your bent-over people so their heads be held high,*

ל *[and] let no sins be found [among them], neither hidden nor visible.*

מ *Be a fortress-tower in time of trouble*[13]
   to those who take shelter with You;

---

(1) *Numbers* 14:20. (2) *Daniel* 9:18-19. (3) Cf. *Isaiah* 64:6. (4) Some editions read אֶשְׁמוֹר, *the stich then means: With prayer, I greet the [morning] watch*; cf. *Psalms* 119:148. (5) Cf. 88:14. (6) Cf. 57:9. (7) Some editions read מַעֲרְכֵי דַל; *the stich then means: I have been careful to draw my impoverished [heart's] intentions after [the pious words of] my lips.* (8) Cf. *Job* 31:35; some editions read יַאֲזִינֵנוּ יַעֲנֵנ, *hearken to us. . .answer us.* (9) Cf. *Isaiah* 59:16; some editions of *Selichos* read מַפְגִּין, *one who raises an outcry* (10) Cf. *Job* 20:9. (11) Some editions read חֲפוּ, *they are clean, referring to my heart and my deeds* of the previous stich. (12) Cf. Tractate *Berachos* 54b. (13) Cf. *Psalms* 9:10; some editions of *Selichos* read הָיִיתָ, *You have been*; cf. 59:17.

---

foreheads of the righteous, but in blood on the foreheads of the wicked. Various opinions are offered by the Sages regarding the implication of this letter. Among them: Rav says that the inky ת stands for תִּחְיֶה, *you shall live*, while the bloody ת indicates תָּמוּת, *you shall die*. R' Shmuel bar Nachmani says that the inky ת testifies that these people observed the Torah from א to ת (i.e., from A to Z), and the bloody ת alludes to those who desecrated the Torah from א to ת.

Following these interpretations we may translate our stich: *See my* ת [is the ת of תִּחְיֶה, *you shall live*, for I have observed the Torah from א to ת, therefore], *hearken to me, answer me, O Almighty.*

יַעֲנֵנִי — *Answer me.* This can also be translated *testify for me*, i.e., *hearken to me, O Almighty, and testify to my righteousness.* This rendering may be applied with any of the interpretations of תָּוִי given above.

נוֹדֵד אַל תְּגַלֶּה נִדַּח כְּשֶׂה,[1]

שִׂימָה בְּנֹאדְךָ דֶּמַע,[2] עֶרֶשׁ מַמְסֶה,

עֹז לִי בָךְ,[3] מָעֹז וּמַחֲסֶה.[4]

פְּצֵה[5] וְהוֹצֵא לָרְוָיָה,*[6] אֲסִירֶיךָ תַּתִּיר,

צַעֲקוּךְ דְּפָקוּךְ, קְרָאוּךְ בַּצַּר לְהַעְתִּיר,

קִבְּעוּם קוֹבְעִים, וְרָשָׁע צַדִּיק מַכְתִּיר,*

רַב וְשׁוֹפֵט,[7] לָמָה פָנֶיךָ תַסְתִּיר.[8]

שָׁאוֹן* קָמֶיךָ הָעוֹלֶה[9] נֶגְדְּךָ, הָדֵק[10] וְכַלֵּה,

תָּמִיד לְיוֹדְעֵי סוֹדְךָ חֲסָדֶיךָ הַפְלֵה,[11]

אָנָּא, נִדָּח הָשֵׁב, וְקַבֵּץ גּוֹלֶה,

לַמָּרוֹם שָׁפָל[12] הָקֵם, וְיָרוּד הַעֲלֵה.

יֹאמְרוּ בַגּוֹיִם הִגְדִּיל יהוה לַעֲשׂוֹת,[13]

הַנְּשַׁמָּה הָיְתָה לְעֵדֶן, וּלְבִצָּרוֹן הַנֶּהֱרָסוֹת,[14]

בּוֹטְחֶיךָ הַצֵּל, נָסוּ בְּצִלְּךָ לַחֲסוֹת,

רְדִיפָתָם בַּקֵּשׁ, עָלֶיךָ הַדָּבָר לַעֲשׂוֹת.

שִׁמְעָה דַכָּא, בִּיטָה עֶטֶף רוּחוֹ,

❖ **יִהְיוּ** לְרָצוֹן אֲמָרָיו[15] וְשֶׁפֶךְ שִׂיחוֹ,

חַזֵּק רִפְיוֹן וְאַמֵּץ כֹּשֶׁל לְהַרְוִיחוֹ,

כִּי הִנֵּה יוֹצֵר הָרִים וּבֹרֵא רוּחַ,

וּמַגִּיד לְאָדָם מַה שֵּׂחוֹ.*[16]

All, while standing:

אֵל מֶלֶךְ יוֹשֵׁב עַל כִּסֵּא רַחֲמִים מִתְנַהֵג בַּחֲסִידוּת, מוֹחֵל עֲוֹנוֹת עַמּוֹ, מַעֲבִיר רִאשׁוֹן רִאשׁוֹן, מַרְבֶּה מְחִילָה לְחַטָּאִים וּסְלִיחָה לְפוֹשְׁעִים, עֹשֶׂה צְדָקוֹת עִם כָּל בָּשָׂר וָרוּחַ, לֹא כְרָעָתָם תִּגְמוֹל. ❖ אֵל הוֹרֵיתָ לָּנוּ לוֹמַר שְׁלֹשׁ עֶשְׂרֵה, וּזְכֹר

לָרְוָיָה — *Unto [the Land of] satiety.* The translation follows *Radak* (to *Psalms* 66:12). Other interpretations are: *to relief* (*Targum Yonasan*); and *to the fresh air* (*Ibn Ezra*).

Alternatively: R' Yochanan explains why the proselyte רוּת, *Ruth*, was called by that name. It was a prophetic indication that her offspring, King David, רִינְהוּ, *would offer an abundance* of song and praise to God (*Berachos* 7b). Perhaps, then, our stich may be understood as, *Open the way and bring [them] forth, that they may offer You abundant praise.*

מַכְתִּיר — *Surround.* This word is derived from כֶּתֶר, *a crown* that circles the head. Alternatively,

it is not Hebrew but Aramaic and means *await* (see *Ibn Ezra* to *Job* 36:2).

שָׁאוֹן — *The tumult.* The translation follows the commentaries to *Psalms* 74:23. The word can also mean *mob.*

מַה שֵּׂחוֹ — *What he has wrought* [lit., *what is his handiwork*]. The translation follows *Targum Yonasan* to *Amos* 4:13. The Talmud treats the word as if it were spelled שִׂיחוֹ, *his conversation*, and explains that when a person comes before the Heavenly Court for judgments, even his seeming trivial conversations are related to him (*Chagigah* 5b). According to *Ibn Ezra* the word means *intentions.*

נ Do not let the wandering one be exposed; straying like a sheep;[1]

ס Put the tears[2] that drench their bed into Your vessel.

ע My strength is in You,[3] O Fortress and Shelter.[4]

פ Open[5] [the way] and bring [them] forth unto [the Land of] satiety,*[6] [as
You] release Your imprisoned ones;

צ they have cried to You, they have knocked on Your doors,
    they have called to You, to beseech [You when they are] in straits.

ק Robbers have robbed them, and the wicked surround* the righteous —

ר O Master and Judge,[7] why do You hide Your face?[8]

ש The tumult* of Your opponents that rises against You[9] —
    pulverize[10] and annihilate [it].

ת Always set apart[11] Your kindness for those who know
    Your [Torah's] hidden wisdom.

א Please, bring back the lost one and gather the exile,

ל raise the lowly on high[12] and lift the lowly.

י Let them declare among the nations,
    'HASHEM has done greatly [with these]!'[13]

ה The desolate has been made into [a garden of] Eden,
    the ruins into built strength.'[14]

ב Save those who trust in You,
    who have fled to take cover in Your shadow.

ר Demand [judgment] for the persecution [they have suffered]:
    it is Yours to do that.

Hear [the prayer of] the downtrodden, see his failing spirit;

Chazzan — may his expressions and his outpouring of prayer
    find favor [before You].[15]

Strengthen [his] weakness, prop [his] staggering,
    to bring him relief,

for, behold, [You are] the Maker of mountains,
    the Creator of spirit,

Who tells each man [at judgment time] what he has wrought.*[16]

All, while standing:

אֵל מֶלֶךְ O God, King Who sits on the throne of mercy; Who acts
with kindness, pardons the iniquities of His people, removes
[sins] one by one, increasingly grants pardon to careless sinners
and forgiveness to rebels, Who deals righteously with every living being
— You do not repay them in accord with their evil. Chazzan — O God,
You taught us to recite the Thirteen [Attributes of Mercy], so remember

---

(1) Cf. *Isaiah* 16:3. (2) Cf. *Psalms* 56:9. (3) Cf. 46:2; some editions of *Selichos* read לֹי, *his,* in the
selichah as in the Scriptural verse. (4) Cf. *Joel* 4:16. (5) Some editions read צְמָה, *see,* instead of פְּצֵה,
open, but this reading is incongruent with the acrostic. (6) Cf. *Psalms* 66:12. (7) Some editions read
רִיב מִשְׁפָּטָם, *take up their cause.* (8) *Psalms* 44:25; *Job* 13:24. (9) Cf. *Psalms* 74:23. (10) Some editions
read הֲרֹק, which can be translated either, *cause [them] to be spilled out,* or, *draw [a sword against
them].* (11) Some editions read הַפְלֵא, but the meaning is the same; some read לְיוֹדְעֵי סוֹדְךָ גַּלֵּה, *reveal
[Yourself] to those...* (12) Cf. *Job* 5:11. (13) *Psalms* 126:2; some editions of *Selichos* begin this stich
with אָז, *then,* but that is incongruent with the acrostic; some end the stich with עִם אֵלֶּה, but that is
incongruent with the rhyme scheme. (14) Cf. *Ezekiel* 36:35. (15) Cf. *Psalms* 19:15. (16) *Amos* 4:13;
some editions of *Selichos* omit the words כִּי הִנֵּה.

לָנוּ הַיּוֹם בְּרִית שְׁלֹשׁ עֶשְׂרֵה, כְּמוֹ שֶׁהוֹדַעְתָּ לֶעָנָיו מִקֶּדֶם, כְּמוֹ שֶׁכָּתוּב, וַיֵּרֶד יהוה בֶּעָנָן וַיִּתְיַצֵּב עִמּוֹ שָׁם, וַיִּקְרָא בְשֵׁם יהוה.

Congregation, then *chazzan*:

וַיַּעֲבֹר יהוה עַל פָּנָיו וַיִּקְרָא:

Congregation and *chazzan* (the words in bold type are recited aloud and in unison):

יהוה, יהוה, אֵל, רַחוּם, וְחַנּוּן, אֶרֶךְ אַפַּיִם, וְרַב חֶסֶד, **וֶאֱמֶת,** נֹצֵר חֶסֶד לָאֲלָפִים, נֹשֵׂא עָוֹן, וָפֶשַׁע, וְחַטָּאָה, וְנַקֵּה. וְסָלַחְתָּ לַעֲוֹנֵנוּ וּלְחַטָּאתֵנוּ וּנְחַלְתָּנוּ. סְלַח לָנוּ אָבִינוּ כִּי חָטָאנוּ, מְחַל לָנוּ מַלְכֵּנוּ כִּי פָשָׁעְנוּ. כִּי אַתָּה אֲדֹנָי טוֹב וְסַלָּח, וְרַב חֶסֶד לְכָל קֹרְאֶיךָ.

פסוקי הקדמה לסליחה יח

יהוה אֱלֹהֵי צְבָאוֹת, מִי כָמוֹךָ חֲסִין יָהּ, וֶאֱמוּנָתְךָ סְבִיבוֹתֶיךָ.[1] אֲדֹנָי שָׁמַעְתָּ בְקוֹלֵנוּ, תִּהְיֶינָה אָזְנֶיךָ קַשֻּׁבוֹת לְקוֹל תַּחֲנוּנֵינוּ.[2] לַאדֹנָי אֱלֹהֵינוּ הָרַחֲמִים וְהַסְּלִחוֹת, כִּי מָרַדְנוּ בּוֹ.[3] אַל תָּבוֹא בְמִשְׁפָּט עִמָּנוּ, כִּי לֹא יִצְדַּק לְפָנֶיךָ כָל חָי.[4]

כְּרַחֵם אָב עַל בָּנִים, כֵּן תְּרַחֵם יהוה עָלֵינוּ. לַיהוה הַיְשׁוּעָה, עַל עַמְּךָ בִרְכָתֶךָ סֶּלָה. יהוה צְבָאוֹת עִמָּנוּ, מִשְׂגָּב לָנוּ אֱלֹהֵי יַעֲקֹב סֶלָה. יהוה צְבָאוֹת, אַשְׁרֵי אָדָם בֹּטֵחַ בָּךְ. יהוה הוֹשִׁיעָה, הַמֶּלֶךְ יַעֲנֵנוּ בְיוֹם קָרְאֵנוּ.

In some congregations the following two verses are recited responsively — the *chazzan* reciting סְלַח, and the congregation responding וַיֹּאמֶר. In other congregations these verses are recited silently.

סְלַח נָא לַעֲוֹן הָעָם הַזֶּה כְּגֹדֶל חַסְדֶּךָ, וְכַאֲשֶׁר נָשָׂאתָה לָעָם הַזֶּה מִמִּצְרַיִם וְעַד הֵנָּה, וְשָׁם נֶאֱמַר:

וַיֹּאמֶר יהוה סָלַחְתִּי כִּדְבָרֶךָ.

All:

הַטֵּה אֱלֹהַי אָזְנְךָ וּשְׁמָע, פְּקַח עֵינֶיךָ וּרְאֵה שֹׁמְמֹתֵינוּ, וְהָעִיר אֲשֶׁר נִקְרָא שִׁמְךָ עָלֶיהָ, כִּי לֹא עַל צִדְקוֹתֵינוּ אֲנַחְנוּ מַפִּילִים תַּחֲנוּנֵינוּ לְפָנֶיךָ, כִּי עַל רַחֲמֶיךָ הָרַבִּים. אֲדֹנָי שְׁמָעָה, אֲדֹנָי סְלָחָה, אֲדֹנָי הַקְשִׁיבָה, וַעֲשֵׂה אַל תְּאַחַר, לְמַעַנְךָ אֱלֹהַי, כִּי שִׁמְךָ נִקְרָא עַל עִירְךָ וְעַל עַמֶּךָ.

for us today the covenant of these Thirteen, as You made known to the humble one in ancient times, as it is written: And HASHEM descended in a cloud and stood with him there, and He called out with the Name HASHEM.

Congregation, then *chazzan:*

And HASHEM passed before him [Moses] and proclaimed:

Congregation and *chazzan* (the words in bold type are recited aloud and in unison):

ה׳, ה׳ HASHEM, HASHEM, God, Compassionate and Gracious, Slow to anger, and Abundant in Kindness and Truth, Preserver of kindness for thousands [of generations], Forgiver of iniquity, willful sin, and error, and Who cleanses. *May You forgive our iniquities and our errors and make us Your heritage. Forgive us, our Father, for we have erred; pardon us, our King, for we have willfully sinned; for You, my Lord, are good and forgiving and abundantly kind to all who call upon You.*

PREFATORY VERSES TO SELICHAH 18

יהוה HASHEM, God of Legions — who is like You, O Strong One, God, with Your faithfulness [attested to by] Your surrounding [angels]?[1] My Lord, hear our voice; may Your ears be attentive to the sound of our supplications.[2] Mercy and forgiveness belong with my Lord, our God, for we have rebelled against Him.[3] Do not enter into strict judgment with us, for no living creature would be innocent before You.[4]

כְּרַחֵם אָב As a father has mercy on his children, so, HASHEM, may You have mercy on us. Salvation is HASHEM's, upon Your people is Your blessing, Selah. HASHEM, Master of Legions, is with us, a stronghold for us is the God of Jacob, Selah. HASHEM, Master of Legions, praiseworthy is the person who trusts in You. HASHEM, save! May the King answer us on the day we call.

In some congregations the following two verses are recited responsively — the *chazzan* reciting, 'Forgive, please . . .,' and the congregation responding, 'And HASHEM said . . .'
In other congregations these verses are recited silently.

סְלַח נָא Forgive, please, the iniquity of this people according to the greatness of Your kindness and as You have forgiven this people from Egypt until now, and there it was said:

And HASHEM said, 'I have forgiven according to your word!'

All:

הַטֵּה Incline, my God, Your ear, and listen, open Your eyes and see our desolation and that of the city upon which Your Name is proclaimed; for not because of our righteousness do we cast down our supplications before You, rather because of Your abundant compassion. O my Lord, heed; O my Lord, forgive; O my Lord, be attentive and act, do not delay; for Your sake, my God, for Your Name is proclaimed upon Your city and upon Your people.

(1) *Psalms* 89:9. (2) Cf. 130:2. (3) *Daniel* 9:9. (4) Cf. *Psalms* 143:2.

סליחה יח

All:

אֱלֹהֵינוּ וֵאלֹהֵי אֲבוֹתֵינוּ:

אַיֵּה קִנְאָתְךָ* וּגְבוּרֹתֶיךָ,[1]

בַּעֲשׂוֹתְךָ נוֹרָאוֹת[2] לְזֶרַע כֹּרְתֵי בְרִיתֶךָ,[3]

גְּרוּשִׁים נְטוּשִׁים אֲנַחְנוּ מִנַּחֲלָתֶךָ,

יהוה אֱלֹהֵינוּ בְּעָלְוּנוּ אֲדֹנִים זוּלָתֶךָ.[4]

דַּאֲגַת עֲנָיֵיךְ גָּדְלָה עַד לִמְאֹד.

הַסּוֹבְלִים עַל מוֹרָאָךְ בְּלֵב וָנֶפֶשׁ וּמְאֹד,[5]

וְהֵם שָׁחִים וּמֻשְׁפָּלִים עַד מְאֹד,

מַהֵר יְקַדְּמוּנוּ רַחֲמֶיךָ, כִּי דַלּוֹנוּ מְאֹד.[6]

זִיוֵנוּ שׁוּנָּה,[7] מִפְּנֵי מְחָרְפִים יוֹם יוֹם,[8]

חוֹרְקִים שֵׁן וְשׁוֹחֲחִים, אַךְ זֶה הַיּוֹם,[9]

טֶכֶס מֶמְשַׁלְתְּךָ גַּלֵּה, אָיֹם,   כִּי עָלֶיךָ הֹרַגְנוּ כָל הַיּוֹם.[10]

יִחַלְנוּ קֵץ גְּאֻלָּה וְנֶחָמָה,

כִּי כִסַּתְנוּ בוּשָׁה וַעֲטַתְנוּ כְלִמָּה,[11]

לַחוּצִים וַעֲבוּדִים תַּחַת יַד כָּל אֻמָּה,[12]   וְאֵין אִתָּנוּ יוֹדֵעַ עַד מָה.[13]

מֶלֶךְ מְלָכִים, זְכָר רַחֲמֶיךָ הַיְשָׁנִים,

נוֹצְרֵי יְחוּדֶךָ מַלֵּט מֵאוּדִים הָעֲשֵׁנִים,*[14]

סָאַב צַחֲנָתָם לַבֵּן, הַמִּתְלַע כַּשָּׁנִים,[15]

אַל תִּזְכָּר לָנוּ עֲוֹנוֹת רִאשֹׁנִים.[16]

עַל הַר צִיּוֹן שֶׁשָּׁמֵם,[17]

פָּנַי כְּבוּשִׁים וְלִבִּי יִשְׁתּוֹמֵם,[18]

צָרִים אֲשֶׁר שְׁמָמוּהוּ הָאֲשִׁימֵם,

וְהָאֵר פָּנֶיךָ עַל מִקְדָּשְׁךָ הַשָּׁמֵם.[19]

קִנְיָן* הַנִּקְנֶה מֵאָז[20] לְשֵׁם תִּפְאַרְתֶּךָ,

רַחֵם וְאַל תַּשְׁחֵת וְהִיא תְהִלָּתֶךָ,*

אַיֵּה קִנְאָתְךָ — *Where are Your jealousy...*
The author of this *selichah* signed his name,
בִּנְיָמִן, *Binyamin*, after the alphabetic acrostic. He
is probably Binyamin bar Zerach [see prefatory
comment to *selichah* 20].

מֵאוּדִים הָעֲשֵׁנִים — *From the smoking firebrands.*
These are the dying embers that no longer have
the power to burn, yet raise an irritating smoke;
they allude to those nations that rage and
threaten but don't really have the power to wreak

destruction (see *Ibn Ezra* and *Radak* to Isaiah 7:4).
Thus, we pray that God save us, not only from
those capable of destroying us, but even from
those whose bark is worse than their bite.

קִנְיָן — *[Israel,] the possession.* This refers to Israel
the nation. According to the Mishnah (*Avos*
6:10), God singled out five things from the entire
universe that uniquely advance the goals of Creation. One of these is Israel, as it is written: *Until
Your people pass through, HASHEM, until this*

SELICHAH 18

All:

Our God and the God of our forefathers:

א *Where are Your jealousy* and Your mighty deeds[1]*
[that You used to display on our behalf],

ב *when You did awesome deeds[2] for the seed [of the Patriarchs]*
with whom You made Your covenant?[3]

ג *We are chased out and cast off from Your heritage;*
HASHEM, our God, lords other than You have mastered us.[4]

ד *Your poor ones' worries have grown very great,*

ה *they carry the yoke of reverence for You*
with heart and soul and resources,[5]

ו *while they are bowed and abased extremely.*

Speedily let Your mercy come to meet us,
for we have become exceedingly impoverished.[6]

ז *Our [faces'] glow is changed[7] because of the revilers every day,[8]*

ח *[who] gnash their teeth and say, 'Indeed, so this is the day!'[9]*

ט *Reveal the plan of Your sovereignty today, O Awesome One,*
Because for Your sake we are killed all the time.[10]

י *We hope for the time of Redemption and consolation,*

כ *for shame has covered us and humiliation enwrapped us.[11]*

ל *[We are] oppressed and enslaved under every nation's hand,[12]*
and there is none among us who knows how long.[13]

מ *King of kings, remember Your former mercies!*

נ *Rescue those who guard Your Oneness*
from the smoking firebrands.*[14]

ס *Whiten the filth of their [sins'] stench, [though it be] scarlet red;[15]*
Remember not our previous sins.[16]

ע *For Mount Zion that is desolate,[17]*

פ *my face is bent low and my heart is in turmoil.[18]*

צ *Condemn the oppressors who laid [the Temple] waste,*
and let Your countenance shine upon Your desolate Sanctuary.[19]

ק *[Israel,] the possession,* that You acquired long ago[20]*
for the sake of Your splendor,

ר *have mercy [on them] and do not destroy [them],*
for that is Your praise.*

---

(1) *Isaiah* 63:15. (2) 64:2. (3) Cf. *Psalms* 50:5. (4) *Isaiah* 26:13; some editions of *Selichos* read אֱלֹהִים, *God,* instead of אֱלֹהֵינוּ, *our God,* but that reading needlessly alters the Scriptural verse. (5) Cf. *Deuteronomy* 6:5. (6) *Psalms* 79:8. (7) Cf. *Daniel* 5:9. (8) Cf. *Psalms* 102:9. (9) Cf. *Lamentations* 2:16. (10) *Psalms* 44:23. (11) Cf. 71:13. (12) This stich has been a target of the censors and appears in many variant forms; some editions read, תַּחַת יַד רְשָׁעִים [זָרִים] הָעֲצוּמָה, *under the powerful hand of the wicked* [or, *the strangers*]; others read, יַד קֶצֶת אֻמָּה, *the hand of some nation*; some omit the stich altogether; while still others substitute, לֹא עַתָּה קַרְנֵנוּ רָמָה, *Our pride is not raised at present.* (13) Cf. *Psalms* 74:9. (14) Cf. *Isaiah* 7:4. (15) Cf. 1:18. (16) *Psalms* 79:8. (17) *Lamentations* 5:18. (18) Cf. *Psalms* 143:4. (19) *Daniel* 9:17. (20) Cf. *Exodus* 15:16.

---

people You acquired *pass through (Exodus* 15:16). The other four are: Torah; heaven and earth; the Patriarch Abraham; and the Holy Temple.

וְהִיא תְהִלָּתֶךָ — *For that is* Your praise. God Himself declares that His merciful restraint in meting out punishment to sinners is the source of His

שֹׁכֵן הִבְטִיחָנוּ נֶאֱמַן בֵּיתֶךָ,¹

כִּי אֵל רַחוּם יהוה אֱלֹהֶיךָ, לֹא יַרְפְּךָ וְלֹא יַשְׁחִיתֶךָ.²

❖ תִּזְכֹּר תַּבְנִית תָּם בְּכִסְאֲךָ מְחֻקָּה,*

נָאוֹר,* יְלָדָיו מִנַּחַל עֲדָנֶיךָ תַשְׁקֶה,³

יֵשַׁע הַמְצִיאֵם אוֹתָם נַקֵּה,⁴   נֹשֵׂא עָוֹן וָעֹבֵר עַל פֶּשַׁע וְנַקֵּה.⁵

All, while standing:

אֵל מֶלֶךְ יוֹשֵׁב עַל כִּסֵּא רַחֲמִים מִתְנַהֵג בַּחֲסִידוּת, מוֹחֵל עֲוֹנוֹת עַמּוֹ, מַעֲבִיר רִאשׁוֹן רִאשׁוֹן, מַרְבֶּה מְחִילָה לְחַטָּאִים וּסְלִיחָה לְפוֹשְׁעִים, עֹשֶׂה צְדָקוֹת עִם כָּל בָּשָׂר וָרוּחַ, לֹא כְרָעָתָם תִּגְמוֹל. ❖ אֵל הוֹרֵיתָ לָנוּ לוֹמַר שְׁלֹשׁ עֶשְׂרֵה, וּזְכָר לָנוּ הַיּוֹם בְּרִית שְׁלֹשׁ עֶשְׂרֵה, כְּמוֹ שֶׁהוֹדַעְתָּ לֶעָנָיו מִקֶּדֶם, כְּמוֹ שֶׁכָּתוּב, וַיֵּרֶד יהוה בֶּעָנָן וַיִּתְיַצֵּב עִמּוֹ שָׁם, וַיִּקְרָא בְשֵׁם יהוה.

Congregation, then chazzan:

וַיַּעֲבֹר יהוה עַל פָּנָיו וַיִּקְרָא:

Congregation and chazzan (*the words in bold type are recited aloud and in unison*):

יהוה, יהוה, אֵל, רַחוּם, וְחַנּוּן, אֶרֶךְ אַפַּיִם, **וְרַב חֶסֶד, וֶאֱמֶת, נֹצֵר חֶסֶד לָאֲלָפִים, נֹשֵׂא עָוֹן, וָפֶשַׁע, וְחַטָּאָה, וְנַקֵּה.** וְסָלַחְתָּ לַעֲוֹנֵנוּ וּלְחַטָּאתֵנוּ וּנְחַלְתָּנוּ. סְלַח לָנוּ אָבִינוּ כִּי חָטָאנוּ, מְחַל לָנוּ מַלְכֵּנוּ כִּי פָשָׁעְנוּ. כִּי אַתָּה אֲדֹנָי טוֹב וְסַלָּח, וְרַב חֶסֶד לְכָל קֹרְאֶיךָ.

סליחה יט (פזמון)

Chazzan, then congregation:

יֹשֵׁב* בְּסֵתֶר עֶלְיוֹן,*⁶ מָגִנִּי וְצִנָּתִי,*⁷

צַעֲקָתִי הַקְשִׁיבָה, וְהַאֲזִינָה רִנָּתִי,⁸

חֵטְא אֶת חַטָּאתִי, קָדוֹשׁ תֵּן תִּקּוּנָתִי,⁹

נַפְשִׁי בִּשְׁאֵלָתִי, וְעַמִּי בְּבַקָּשָׁתִי.¹⁰

---

praise (see *Isaiah* 48:9). Some translate: *For she [Israel] is [the one that recites] Your praise.* If this is correct, the feminine word הִיא, *she*, does not refer to קִנְיָן, *the possession*, a masculine noun, but to the אֻמָּה, *nation*, which is grammatically feminine.

תַּבְנִית תָּם בְּכִסְאֲךָ מְחֻקָּה — *The image of the whole-hearted [Jacob] graven on Your throne.* According to the Midrash (*Bereishis Rabbah* 68:12), God engraved the image of Jacob [who is called תָּם, *the whole-hearted* or *perfect one* (*Genesis* 25:27)] on His Throne of Glory.

נָאוֹר — *[O You Who are the] Source of light.* The translation follows *Targum*, *Ibn Ezra* and *Radak* (to *Psalms* 76:5). *Rashi* renders, *the One Who destroys those Who oppose Him.*

יֹשֵׁב — *O You Who sit.* The acrostic reads יִצְחָק חֲזַק, *Yitzchak, may he be strong,* but the identity of the composer is otherwise unknown.

יֹשֵׁב בְּסֵתֶר עֶלְיוֹן — *O You Who sit in the hidden heights.* Although in its context in *Psalms* (91:1) this phrase refers to the righteous person *who sits in the refuge of the Exalted One,* the paytan has

שׁ *For so were we promised by [Moses,] the trusted one of Your house:*[1]
                    'For HASHEM, *your God, is a merciful God;*
                    He will neither cast you off nor destroy you.' [2]

ת Chazzan – *Remember the image of the whole-hearted [Jacob]*
         graven on Your throne,*
    [O You Who are the] Source of light,*
    give his children to drink of Your streams of bliss.[3]
Bring forth salvation for them, cleanse them [of sin],[4]
                    O You Who forgives iniquity,
                    and overlooks willful sin and cleanses.[5]

All, while standing:

אֵל מֶלֶךְ *O God, King Who sits on the throne of mercy; Who acts with kindness, pardons the iniquities of His people, removes [sins] one by one, increasingly grants pardon to careless sinners and forgiveness to rebels, Who deals righteously with every living being — You do not repay them in accord with their evil.* Chazzan – *O God, You taught us to recite the Thirteen [Attributes of Mercy], so remember for us today the covenant of these Thirteen, as You made known to the humble one in ancient times, as it is written: And* HASHEM *descended in a cloud and stood with him there, and He called out with the Name* HASHEM.

Congregation, then chazzan:

And HASHEM *passed before him [Moses] and proclaimed:*

Congregation and chazzan (the words in bold type are recited aloud and in unison):

ה' ה' HASHEM, HASHEM, **God, Compassionate and Gracious, Slow to anger, and Abundant in Kindness and Truth, Preserver of kindness for thousands [of generations], Forgiver of iniquity, willful sin, and error, and Who cleanses.** *May You forgive our iniquities and our errors and make us Your heritage. Forgive us, our Father, for we have erred; pardon us, our King, for we have willfully sinned; for You, my Lord, are good and forgiving and abundantly kind to all who call upon You.*

SELICHAH 19

Chazzan, then congregation:

י *O You Who sit** *in the hidden heights,**[6] *my Aegis and my Shield,**[7]
צ *attend to my outcry, and hearken to my prayer's song.*[8]
ח *Cleanse my sin;*   ק *Holy One, realize my hope:*[9]
         '[Spare] my life at my request, and my people at my petition.'[10]

---

(1) Cf. *Numbers* 12:7. (2) *Deuteronomy* 4:31. (3) Cf. *Psalms* 36:9. (4) Cf. *19:14.*
(5) Cf. *Exodus* 34:7; some editions of *Selichos* read, נוֹשֵׂא עָוֹן וָפֶשַׁע וְחַטָּאָה וְנַקֵּה,
Who forgives iniquity, willful sin and error, and Who cleanses, as in the Scriptural verse.
(6) *Psalms* 91:1. (7) Cf. *35:2.* (8) Cf. *17:1.* (9) Cf. *Job* 6:8. (10) *Esther* 7:3.

borrowed the phrase and applied it to God in its entirety.

מָגִנִּי וְצִנָּתִי — *My Aegis and my Shield.* Rashi (to *Jeremiah* 46:3) states that מָגֵן refers to a leather shield coated with oil before a battle; and צִנָּה to a wooden shield. Thus we have translated מָגֵן,

aegis, which in its original usage meant a goatskin shield. *Midrash Shocher Tov* (1:4) describes מָגֵן as a shield that affords protection on three sides of the bearer's body, and צִנָּה as a shield that completely surrounds the carrier (see also *Rashi* to *Psalms* 91:4).

Congregation, then *chazzan:*

צְדָקָה עֲשֵׂה לְעַמֶּךָ, קָדוֹשׁ לְמַעַן שְׁמֶךָ,

כִּי פָסוּ תְמִימֶיךָ, מַעֲבִירֵי זַעֲמֶיךָ, וּמַגִּישֵׁי לַחְמֶךָ,*

לָכֵן עַתָּה בָאתִי,¹   נַפְשִׁי בִּשְׁאֵלָתִי, וְעַמִּי בְּבַקָּשָׁתִי.

Congregation, then *chazzan:*

חַטֹּאת נְעוּרַי תַּצְלִיל, וְיָם יֶהְפְּכוּ כְּצָלִיל,*

וְצֶדֶק זְקֵנִים² תַּסְלִיל, וְשַׁוְעַת נְכָאִים תַּכְלִיל,*

וְעֵת תְּנַקֵּנִי כְּבַעֲלִיל, מַסְטִינִי אָז יֵילִיל, כִּי לִבִּי לְךָ כָּלִיל,

עַתָּה הִנֵּה בָאתִי,³   נַפְשִׁי בִּשְׁאֵלָתִי, וְעַמִּי בְּבַקָּשָׁתִי.

Congregation, then *chazzan:*

חַנּוּן חַי חָגְנִי, לְקוֹל זַעֲקִי בִּגְרוֹנִי,*

בְּשָׁמְעֲךָ תַּעֲנֵנִי, סְלִיחָתְךָ תַּרְבֵּנִי,⁴ חַיִּים תִּכְתְּבֵנִי,

וְעָנִיתָ בִּי צִדְקָתִי,⁵   נַפְשִׁי בִּשְׁאֵלָתִי, וְעַמִּי בְּבַקָּשָׁתִי.

Congregation, then *chazzan:*

זֶה אֵלִי⁶ הוֹשִׁיעָה, וּזְכִיּוֹת הַכְרִיעָה,

וּמִזְּבוּלְךָ הוֹפִיעָה, חֵן סְעָרָה וְסָעָה,

וּמִלָּשְׁנִי הַבְלִיעָה, צֹאנְךָ מִלְהַפְשִׁיעָה, פֶּן אֶרְאֶה בָרָעָה,⁷

בְּאָבְדַן מוֹלַדְתִּי,⁸   נַפְשִׁי בִּשְׁאֵלָתִי, וְעַמִּי בְּבַקָּשָׁתִי.

Congregation, then *chazzan:*

קַדֵּשׁ שֵׁם קָדְשֶׁךָ, חַלְּלוּ בְּמִקְדָּשֶׁךָ,⁹

וְאַחֲרוֹנִים קְדוֹשֶׁיךָ,* מַגִּישֵׁי אִשֶּׁיךָ,¹⁰

לַחְמֶךָ — *Your flour-offering* [lit. *Your bread*]. The translation follows that of the parallel phrase in *Malachi* 3:3. In reality, however, all Altar offerings, whether flour or animal, are called לֶחֶם, *bread* (see, for example, *Leviticus* 3:11, *Numbers* 28:2).

כְּצָלִיל — *Like a [barley] cake.* The *paytan* prays, 'May the sins of my youth be overturned and purified as if they were a barley cake that rolled into the sea.' The strange metaphor of a barley cake turning over alludes to an episode that occurred when Gideon went to attack Midian. God had instructed Gideon to reduce his forces from 32,000 to a mere three hundred men, lest a victorious Israel deny the miraculous nature of its win. As a sign that his skeleton army would prevail over the huge Midianite army, God told Gideon, 'If you are apprehensive about descending [to attack Midian in the valley], then just you and your servant Purah should go down to their camp. Listen to what they say and you will be encouraged.' That night Gideon and Purah went down to spy on the Midianites and their Amalekite allies. There they overheard one soldier tell

another, 'I have dreamt that a cake of barley bread was spinning through the Midianite camp. It came upon a tent, struck it, turned it upside-down, and the tent collapsed.' His friend replied, 'It is naught but the sword of Gideon ben Joash, the Israelite; God has given Midian into his hand!' (See *Judges* ch. 7).

Alternatively, the word צָלִיל means *clear* or *pure*, and the stich reads: *Let the sea turn [the sins of my youth] around [so that they will be] like a pure object.*

וְשַׁוְעַת נְכָאִים תַּכְלִיל — *And make the prayer of the downtrodden a crown [for Yourself].* When all the synagogues have concluded their service, the angel Sandalfon stations himself behind the Divine Chariot where he weaves all the congregational prayers into wreathes with which he crowns God, so to speak (see *Chagigah* 13b with *Tosafos*; *Shemos Rabbah* 21:4).

לְקוֹל זַעֲקִי בִּגְרוֹנִי — *To the sound of my shout that is in my throat.* The prophet proclaimed in the name of God, '*And it will be that before they have called, I shall answer; while they yet speak, I shall hear*' (*Isaiah* 65:24). Thus, we pray that God

Congregation, then *chazzan:*

Deal righteously with Your people,
O Holy One, for Your Name's sake;
for gone are Your whole-hearted ones
   [whose merit] caused Your anger to pass,
and [the Kohanim] who brought Your flour-offering* [to the Altar],
therefore I have come now[1] [to plead],
    '[Spare] my life at my request, and my people at my petition.'

Congregation, then *chazzan:*

Cause the sins of my youth to sink,
and [in the] sea let them be overturned like [a barley] cake.*
Celebrate the righteousness of [our] ancestors,[2]
and make the prayer of the downtrodden a crown [for Yourself].*
Then, when You cleanse me as if in a crucible,
   my Adversary will wail [in despair of overcoming me],
for my heart is utterly Yours; see, now I have come [to plead],[3]
    '[Spare] my life at my request, and my people at my petition.'

Congregation, then *chazzan:*

ח O Gracious, Living One, be gracious to me,
   to the sound of my shout that is in my throat.*
As soon as You hear me, answer me;
   and increase Your forgiveness for me.[4]
Write me down for life,
   and my righteousness shall bear witness for me.[5]
    [Spare] my life at my request, and my people at my petition.

Congregation, then *chazzan:*

ז O [You of Whom we have said,] 'This is my God,'[6]
   save [us], and tilt the scales to [the side of] merit.
Appear from Your dwelling-place [and] show love to the nation
   tossed about by storm and tempest.
And let the Denouncer be swallowed up, no more to accuse Your flock,
lest I see the evil,[7] the destruction of my family.[8]
    [Spare] my life at my request, and my people at my petition.

Congregation, then *chazzan:*

ק Sanctify Your Holy Name that [the conquerors] desecrated
   [when they destroyed] Your Temple,[9]
and the children of Aaron, Your holy ones,*
   who [would] bring Your fire-offerings.[10]

---

(1) Cf. *Joshua* 5:14. (2) Some editions read וְצֶדֶק זְקוּנִים, *the righteousness of [our] old age.*
(3) Cf. *Numbers* 22:38. (4) Cf. *Isaiah* 55:7. (5) *Genesis* 30:33. (6) *Exodus* 15:2.
(7) Cf. *Genesis* 44:34. (8) *Esther* 8:6. (9) Cf. *Ezekiel* 36:23. (10) Cf. *Leviticus* 21:6.

respond to us while our shout is still in our throat.

וְאַהֲרוֹנִים קְדוֹשֶׁיךָ — *And the children of Aaron,
Your holy ones.* It is unclear to which verb this
phrase belongs: Either it is the second subject of
קַדֵּשׁ, *sanctify,* and the stich means, *Sanctify Your*

Name ... *and the children of Aaron [so that they
might once again] bring Your fire-offerings;* or its
antecedent verb is חִלְּלוּ, *that they desecrated,*
and the line means, *Sanctify Your Name and the
children of Aaron, Your holy ones, that [the
gentiles] desecrated ...*

וּמַה יַּעֲשׂוּ קְדוֹשֶׁיךָ, כְּפַסּוּ קָדְשֶׁיךָ, שְׁעֵה נָא מַקְדִּישֶׁיךָ,
כִּפְרַיִם אִם שְׁלַמְתִּי,   נַפְשִׁי בִּשְׁאֵלָתִי, וְעַמִּי בְּבַקָּשָׁתִי.[1]

Congregation, then chazzan:

יֵרָצוּ עֲבָדֶיךָ, לְמַעַן שֵׁם כְּבוֹדֶךָ,
מִיַּחֲרֶיךָ מְעִידֶיךָ, כִּי אֵין בִּלְעָדֶיךָ,[2]
בַּקֵּשׁ נָא אוֹבְדֶיךָ, הֵן בָּאוּ עָדֶיךָ, כִּי טוֹבִים דּוֹדֶיךָ,[3]
פָּנֶיךָ בִּקַּשְׁתִּי,[4]   נַפְשִׁי בִּשְׁאֵלָתִי, וְעַמִּי בְּבַקָּשָׁתִי.

Congregation, then chazzan:

קוֹלִי יֶעֱרַב נָא, כְּמֵחִים תּוֹךְ צִיּוֹנָה,
לְטוֹבָה הִפָּנֶה נָּא, לְהַמְצִיאֵנִי חֲנִינָה,
כִּי אֶל מִי אֶפְנֶה נָּא, בְּאֵין מַשְׁעֵן וּמַשְׁעֵנָה,[5]
לִמְיַחֲלֶיךָ סְלַח נָא,
הַשְׁמִיעֵם סָלַחְתִּי,[6]   נַפְשִׁי בִּשְׁאֵלָתִי, וְעַמִּי בְּבַקָּשָׁתִי.

All, while standing:

אֵל מֶלֶךְ יוֹשֵׁב עַל כִּסֵּא רַחֲמִים מִתְנַהֵג בַּחֲסִידוּת, מוֹחֵל
עֲוֹנוֹת עַמּוֹ, מַעֲבִיר רִאשׁוֹן רִאשׁוֹן, מַרְבֶּה
מְחִילָה לַחַטָּאִים וּסְלִיחָה לַפּוֹשְׁעִים, עֹשֶׂה צְדָקוֹת עִם כָּל
בָּשָׂר וָרוּחַ, לֹא כְרָעָתָם תִּגְמוֹל. אֵל הוֹרֵיתָ לָּנוּ לוֹמַר שְׁלֹשׁ
עֶשְׂרֵה, וּזְכָר לָנוּ הַיּוֹם בְּרִית שְׁלֹשׁ עֶשְׂרֵה, כְּמוֹ שֶׁהוֹדַעְתָּ לֶעָנָיו
מִקֶּדֶם, כְּמוֹ שֶׁכָּתוּב, וַיֵּרֶד יהוה בֶּעָנָן וַיִּתְיַצֵּב עִמּוֹ שָׁם, וַיִּקְרָא
בְשֵׁם יהוה.

Congregation, then chazzan:

וַיַּעֲבֹר יהוה עַל פָּנָיו וַיִּקְרָא:

Congregation and chazzan *(the words in bold type are recited aloud and in unison):*

יהוה, יהוה, אֵל, **רַחוּם,** וְחַנּוּן, **אֶרֶךְ אַפַּיִם,** וְרַב חֶסֶד, **וֶאֱמֶת,**
נֹצֵר חֶסֶד לָאֲלָפִים, נֹשֵׂא עָוֹן, **וָפֶשַׁע,** וְחַטָּאָה,
וְנַקֵּה. וְסָלַחְתָּ לַעֲוֹנֵנוּ וּלְחַטָּאתֵנוּ וּנְחַלְתָּנוּ. סְלַח לָנוּ אָבִינוּ כִּי
חָטָאנוּ, מְחַל לָנוּ מַלְכֵּנוּ כִּי פָשָׁעְנוּ. כִּי אַתָּה אֲדֹנָי טוֹב וְסַלָּח,
וְרַב חֶסֶד לְכָל קֹרְאֶיךָ.

---

(1) Cf. *Hosea* 14:3. (2) Cf. *Isaiah* 44:8. (3) *Song of Songs* 1:2.
(4) Cf. *Psalms* 27:8. (5) Cf. *Isaiah* 3:1. (6) *Numbers* 14:20.

What can Your holy ones do now that Your offerings have stopped?
Pay heed to those who sanctify You,
  as if I had compensated [for my sins] with bulls.[1]
    [Spare] my life at my request, and my people at my petition.

Congregation, then chazzan:

May Your servants find favor [with You],
  for the sake of Your glorious Name,
those who proclaim Your oneness and bear witness
  that there is none besides You.[2]
Please seek Your lost ones; they have come to You,
for Your love is good;[3] *I have sought Your Presence.*[4]
    [Spare] my life at my request, and my people at my petition.

Congregation, then chazzan:

Please let my voice seem as sweet
  as [the odor of] corpulent animal [offerings] in Zion;
please turn to me for good, that I may find graciousness [in Your eyes].
For to whom [else] could I now turn, when every prop is gone?[5]
Please forgive those who hope to You, and let them hear [You say],
  'I have forgiven.'[6]
    [Spare] my life at my request, and my people at my petition.

All, while standing:

אֵל מֶלֶךְ O God, King Who sits on the throne of mercy; Who acts with kindness, pardons the iniquities of His people, removes [sins] one by one, increasingly grants pardon to careless sinners and forgiveness to rebels, Who deals righteously with every living being — You do not repay them in accord with their evil. Chazzan — O God, You taught us to recite the Thirteen [Attributes of Mercy], so remember for us today the covenant of these Thirteen, as You made known to the humble one in ancient times, as it is written: And HASHEM descended in a cloud and stood with him there, and He called out with the Name HASHEM.

Congregation, then chazzan:

And HASHEM passed before him [Moses] and proclaimed:

Congregation and chazzan (the words in bold type are recited aloud and in unison):

ה' ה' HASHEM, HASHEM, God, Compassionate and Gracious, Slow to anger, and Abundant in Kindness and Truth, Preserver of kindness for thousands [of generations], Forgiver of iniquity, willful sin, and error, and Who cleanses.** May You forgive our iniquities and our errors and make us Your heritage. Forgive us, our Father, for we have erred; pardon us, our King, for we have willfully sinned; for You, my Lord, are good and forgiving and abundantly kind to all who call upon You.

All:

אַל תִּזְכָּר לָנוּ עֲוֹנוֹת רִאשׁוֹנִים, מַהֵר יְקַדְּמוּנוּ רַחֲמֶיךָ, כִּי דַלּוֹנוּ מְאֹד.¹ חַטֹּאת נְעוּרֵינוּ וּפְשָׁעֵינוּ אַל תִּזְכֹּר, כְּחַסְדְּךָ זְכָר לָנוּ אַתָּה, לְמַעַן טוּבְךָ יְהוָה.²

זְכוֹר רַחֲמֶיךָ יְהוָה וַחֲסָדֶיךָ, כִּי מֵעוֹלָם הֵמָּה.³ זָכְרֵנוּ יְהוָה בִּרְצוֹן עַמֶּךָ, פָּקְדֵנוּ בִּישׁוּעָתֶךָ.⁴ זְכֹר עֲדָתְךָ קָנִיתָ קֶּדֶם, גָּאַלְתָּ שֵׁבֶט נַחֲלָתֶךָ, הַר צִיּוֹן זֶה שָׁכַנְתָּ בּוֹ.⁵ זְכֹר יְהוָה חִבַּת יְרוּשָׁלָיִם, אַהֲבַת צִיּוֹן אַל תִּשְׁכַּח לָנֶצַח.⁶ אַתָּה תָקוּם תְּרַחֵם צִיּוֹן, כִּי עֵת לְחֶנְנָהּ כִּי בָא מוֹעֵד.⁷ זְכֹר יְהוָה לִבְנֵי אֱדוֹם אֵת יוֹם יְרוּשָׁלָיִם, הָאֹמְרִים עָרוּ עָרוּ עַד הַיְסוֹד בָּהּ.⁸ זְכֹר לְאַבְרָהָם לְיִצְחָק וּלְיִשְׂרָאֵל עֲבָדֶיךָ אֲשֶׁר נִשְׁבַּעְתָּ לָהֶם בָּךְ, וַתְּדַבֵּר אֲלֵהֶם, אַרְבֶּה אֶת זַרְעֲכֶם כְּכוֹכְבֵי הַשָּׁמָיִם, וְכָל הָאָרֶץ הַזֹּאת אֲשֶׁר אָמַרְתִּי אֶתֵּן לְזַרְעֲכֶם, וְנָחֲלוּ לְעֹלָם.⁹ ❖ זְכֹר לַעֲבָדֶיךָ לְאַבְרָהָם לְיִצְחָק וּלְיַעֲקֹב, אַל תֵּפֶן אֶל קְשִׁי הָעָם הַזֶּה וְאֶל רִשְׁעוֹ וְאֶל חַטָּאתוֹ.¹⁰

Chazzan, then congregation:

אַל נָא תָשֵׁת עָלֵינוּ חַטָּאת, אֲשֶׁר נוֹאַלְנוּ וַאֲשֶׁר חָטָאנוּ.¹¹

Chazzan, then congregation:

חָטָאנוּ צוּרֵנוּ, סְלַח לָנוּ יוֹצְרֵנוּ.

All:

זְכוֹר לָנוּ בְּרִית אָבוֹת, כַּאֲשֶׁר אָמַרְתָּ: וְזָכַרְתִּי אֶת בְּרִיתִי יַעֲקוֹב, וְאַף אֶת בְּרִיתִי יִצְחָק, וְאַף אֶת בְּרִיתִי אַבְרָהָם אֶזְכֹּר, וְהָאָרֶץ אֶזְכֹּר.¹² זְכוֹר לָנוּ בְּרִית רִאשׁוֹנִים, כַּאֲשֶׁר אָמַרְתָּ: וְזָכַרְתִּי לָהֶם בְּרִית רִאשׁוֹנִים, אֲשֶׁר הוֹצֵאתִי אֹתָם מֵאֶרֶץ מִצְרַיִם לְעֵינֵי הַגּוֹיִם, לִהְיוֹת לָהֶם לֵאלֹהִים, אֲנִי יְהוָה.¹³ עֲשֵׂה עִמָּנוּ כְּמָה שֶׁהִבְטַחְתָּנוּ: וְאַף גַּם זֹאת בִּהְיוֹתָם בְּאֶרֶץ אֹיְבֵיהֶם, לֹא מְאַסְתִּים וְלֹא גְעַלְתִּים לְכַלֹּתָם לְהָפֵר בְּרִיתִי אִתָּם, כִּי אֲנִי יְהוָה אֱלֹהֵיהֶם.¹⁴ הִמָּצֵא לָנוּ בְּבַקָּשָׁתֵנוּ, כְּמָה שֶׁכָּתוּב: וּבִקַּשְׁתֶּם מִשָּׁם אֶת יְהוָה אֱלֹהֶיךָ וּמָצָאתָ, כִּי תִדְרְשֶׁנּוּ בְּכָל לְבָבְךָ וּבְכָל נַפְשֶׁךָ.¹⁵ מוֹל אֶת לְבָבֵנוּ לְאַהֲבָה וּלְיִרְאָה אֶת שְׁמֶךָ, כְּמָה שֶׁכָּתוּב: וּמָל יְהוָה אֱלֹהֶיךָ אֶת לְבָבְךָ וְאֶת לְבַב זַרְעֶךָ, לְאַהֲבָה אֶת יְהוָה אֱלֹהֶיךָ בְּכָל לְבָבְךָ

All:

אַל תִּזְכָּר *Do not recall against us the iniquities of the ancients; speedily — let Your mercy come to meet us for we have fallen very low.*[1] *Remember not the sins of our youth and our rebellions; may You remember for us [the deeds] worthy of Your kindness, because of Your goodness,* HASHEM.[2]

זְכוֹר רַחֲמֶיךָ *Remember Your mercies, O* HASHEM, *and Your kindnesses, for they are from the beginning of the world.*[3] *Remember us,* HASHEM, *when You show Your people favor and recall us with Your salvation.*[4] *Remember Your congregation that You acquired of old, that You redeemed the tribe of Your heritage, and this Mount Zion where You dwelled.*[5] *Remember, O* HASHEM, *the affection of Jerusalem, may You never forget the love of Zion.*[6] *You will arise and show Zion mercy, for it is the time to be gracious to her, for the appointed time will have come.*[7] *Remember,* HASHEM, *for the offspring of Edom, the day of Jerusalem — for those who said: 'Destroy! Destroy to its very foundation!'*[8] *Remember Abraham, Isaac, and Israel, Your servants, to whom You swore by Your Being, saying to them, 'I shall increase your offspring like the stars of the heavens; and this entire land of which I spoke I will give to your offspring and they will inherit it forever.'*[9] Chazzan — *Remember for Your servants, for Abraham, for Isaac, and for Jacob; ignore the stubbornness of this people, its wickedness and its sinfulness.*[10]

Chazzan, then congregation:
*Please, do not reckon for us a sin,
what we have done foolishly and what we have sinned.*[11]

Chazzan, then congregation:
We have erred, our Rock! Forgive us, our Molder!

All:

זְכוֹר *Remember for us the covenant of the Patriarchs, as You said: 'And I will remember My covenant with Jacob, and also My covenant with Isaac, and also My covenant with Abraham will I remember; and the Land will I remember.'*[12] *Remember for us the covenant of the ancestors, as You said: 'And I will remember for them the covenant of the ancestors whom I removed from the land of Egypt in the very sight of the nations, to be a God to them; I am* HASHEM.'[13] *Do with us as You promised us: 'And despite all that, when they will be in the land of their enemies, I will not have despised them nor abhorred them to destroy them, to annul My covenant with them, for I am* HASHEM *their God.'*[14] *Be accessible to us in our quest, as it is written: From there you will seek* HASHEM, *your God, and you will find, when you search for Him with all your heart and with all your soul.*[15] *Expose our hearts to love Your Name, as it is written:* HASHEM, *your God, will expose your heart and the heart of your offspring, to love* HASHEM, *your God, with all your heart*

(1) *Psalms* 79:8. (2) Cf. 25:7. (3) 25:6. (4) Cf. 106:4. (5) 74:2. (6) This is not a Scriptural verse. (7) *Psalms* 102:14. (8) 137:7. (9) *Exodus* 32:13. (10) *Deuteronomy* 9:27. (11) *Numbers* 12:11. (12) *Leviticus* 26:42. (13) 26:45. (14) 26:44. (15) *Deuteronomy* 4:29.

וּבְכָל נַפְשֶׁךָ, לְמַעַן חַיֶּיךָ.[1] זְרוֹק עָלֵינוּ מַיִם טְהוֹרִים וְטַהֲרֵנוּ, כְּמָה
שֶּׁכָּתוּב: וְזָרַקְתִּי עֲלֵיכֶם מַיִם טְהוֹרִים וּטְהַרְתֶּם, מִכֹּל טֻמְאוֹתֵיכֶם
וּמִכָּל גִּלּוּלֵיכֶם אֲטַהֵר אֶתְכֶם.[2] מְחֵה פְשָׁעֵינוּ כָּעָב וְכֶעָנָן, כְּמָה
שֶּׁכָּתוּב: מָחִיתִי כָעָב פְּשָׁעֶיךָ וְכֶעָנָן חַטֹּאתֶיךָ, שׁוּבָה אֵלַי כִּי
גְאַלְתִּיךָ.[3] מְחֵה פְשָׁעֵינוּ לְמַעַנְךָ, כַּאֲשֶׁר אָמַרְתָּ: אָנֹכִי אָנֹכִי הוּא
מֹחֶה פְשָׁעֶיךָ לְמַעֲנִי, וְחַטֹּאתֶיךָ לֹא אֶזְכֹּר.[4] הַלְבֵּן חֲטָאֵינוּ כַּשֶּׁלֶג
וְכַצֶּמֶר, כְּמָה שֶּׁכָּתוּב: לְכוּ נָא וְנִוָּכְחָה, יֹאמַר יְהוֹה, אִם יִהְיוּ
חֲטָאֵיכֶם כַּשָּׁנִים, כַּשֶּׁלֶג יַלְבִּינוּ, אִם יַאְדִּימוּ כַתּוֹלָע, כַּצֶּמֶר יִהְיוּ.[5]
רַחֵם עָלֵינוּ וְאַל תַּשְׁחִיתֵנוּ, כְּמָה שֶּׁכָּתוּב: כִּי אֵל רַחוּם יְהוֹה
אֱלֹהֶיךָ, לֹא יַרְפְּךָ וְלֹא יַשְׁחִיתֶךָ וְלֹא יִשְׁכַּח אֶת בְּרִית אֲבֹתֶיךָ
אֲשֶׁר נִשְׁבַּע לָהֶם.[6] קַבֵּץ נִדָּחֵינוּ כְּמָה שֶּׁכָּתוּב: אִם יִהְיֶה נִדַּחֲךָ בִּקְצֵה
הַשָּׁמָיִם, מִשָּׁם יְקַבֶּצְךָ יְהוֹה אֱלֹהֶיךָ וּמִשָּׁם יִקָּחֶךָ.[7] הָשֵׁב שְׁבוּתֵנוּ
וְרַחֲמֵנוּ, כְּמָה שֶּׁכָּתוּב: וְשָׁב יְהוֹה אֱלֹהֶיךָ אֶת שְׁבוּתְךָ וְרִחֲמֶךָ וְשָׁב
וְקִבֶּצְךָ מִכָּל הָעַמִּים אֲשֶׁר הֱפִיצְךָ יְהוֹה אֱלֹהֶיךָ שָׁמָּה.[8] ❖ תְּבִיאֵנוּ
אֶל הַר קָדְשֶׁךָ, וְשַׂמְּחֵנוּ בְּבֵית תְּפִלָּתֶךָ, כְּמָה שֶּׁכָּתוּב: וַהֲבִיאוֹתִים
אֶל הַר קָדְשִׁי, וְשִׂמַּחְתִּים בְּבֵית תְּפִלָּתִי, עוֹלֹתֵיהֶם וְזִבְחֵיהֶם
לְרָצוֹן עַל מִזְבְּחִי, כִּי בֵיתִי בֵּית תְּפִלָּה יִקָּרֵא לְכָל הָעַמִּים.[9]

THE ARK IS OPENED.

The first six verses of the following prayer are recited responsively; *chazzan*, then congregation:

שְׁמַע קוֹלֵנוּ יְהוֹה אֱלֹהֵינוּ, חוּס וְרַחֵם עָלֵינוּ,
וְקַבֵּל בְּרַחֲמִים וּבְרָצוֹן אֶת תְּפִלָּתֵנוּ.[10]
הֲשִׁיבֵנוּ יְהוֹה אֵלֶיךָ וְנָשׁוּבָה, חַדֵּשׁ יָמֵינוּ כְּקֶדֶם.[11]
אַל תַּשְׁלִיכֵנוּ מִלְּפָנֶיךָ, וְרוּחַ קָדְשְׁךָ אַל תִּקַּח מִמֶּנּוּ.[12]
אַל תַּשְׁלִיכֵנוּ לְעֵת זִקְנָה, כִּכְלוֹת כֹּחֵנוּ אַל תַּעַזְבֵנוּ.[13]
אַל תַּעַזְבֵנוּ יְהוֹה, אֱלֹהֵינוּ אַל תִּרְחַק מִמֶּנּוּ.[14]
עֲשֵׂה עִמָּנוּ אוֹת לְטוֹבָה, וְיִרְאוּ שׂוֹנְאֵינוּ וְיֵבֹשׁוּ,
כִּי אַתָּה יְהוֹה עֲזַרְתָּנוּ וְנִחַמְתָּנוּ.[15]
אֲמָרֵינוּ הַאֲזִינָה יְהוֹה, בִּינָה הֲגִיגֵנוּ.[16]
יִהְיוּ לְרָצוֹן אִמְרֵי פִינוּ וְהֶגְיוֹן לִבֵּנוּ לְפָנֶיךָ, יְהוֹה צוּרֵנוּ וְגוֹאֲלֵנוּ.[17]
כִּי לְךָ יְהוֹה הוֹחָלְנוּ, אַתָּה תַעֲנֶה אֲדֹנָי אֱלֹהֵינוּ.[18]

THE ARK IS CLOSED.

---

(1) Deuteronomy 30:6. (2) *Ezekiel* 36:25. (3) *Isaiah* 44:22. (4) 43:25. (5) 1:18.
(6) *Deuteronomy* 4:31. (7) 30:4. (8) 30:3. (9) *Isaiah* 56:7. (10) Weekday *Shemoneh Esrei.*
(11) *Lamentations* 5:21. (12) Cf. *Psalms* 51:13. (13) Cf. 71:9. (14) Cf. 38:22. (15) Cf. 86:17.
(16) Cf. 5:2. (17) Cf. 19:15. (18) Cf. 38:16.

and with all your soul, that you may live.[1] Pour pure water upon us and purify us, as it is written: I shall pour pure water upon you and purify you, of all your contaminations and of all your abominations I will purify you.[2] Wipe away our willful sins like a cloud and like a mist, as it is written: I have wiped away your willful sins like a cloud and your errors like a mist — repent to Me, for I have redeemed you![3] Wipe away our willful sins for Your sake, as You said: 'I, only I, am the One Who wipes away your willful sins for My sake, and I shall not recall your errors.'[4] Whiten our errors like snow and like [pure white] wool, as it is written: 'Come now, let us reason together,' says HASHEM, 'though your errors will be like scarlet, they will become white as snow; though they will be red as crimson, they will become like [white] wool.'[5] Have mercy on us and do not destroy us, as it is written: For a merciful God is HASHEM, your God; He will not surrender you nor destroy you, and He will not forget the covenant with your forefathers, which He swore to them.[6] Gather in our dispersed ones, as it is written: If your dispersed were to be at the ends of heaven, from there HASHEM, your God, will gather you in and from there He will take you.[7] Bring back our captivity and have mercy on us, as it is written: HASHEM, your God, will bring back your captivity and have mercy on you, and He will again gather you in from all the peoples where HASHEM, your God, has scattered you.[8] Chazzan — Bring us to Your holy mountain and gladden us in Your house of prayer, as it is written: And I will bring them to My holy mountain, and I will gladden them in My house of prayer, their elevation-offerings and their feast offering will find favor on My Altar, for My House will be called a house of prayer, for all peoples.[9]

THE ARK IS OPENED.

The first four verses of the following prayer are recited responsively; chazzan, then congregation:

שְׁמַע קוֹלֵנוּ Hear our voice, HASHEM, our God, pity and be compassionate to us, and accept — with compassion and favor — our prayer.[10]

Bring us back to You, HASHEM, and we shall return,
    renew our days as of old.[11]

Do not cast us away from Yourself,
    and do not remove Your holy spirit from us.[12]

Do not cast us away in old age,
    when our strength gives out do not forsake us.[13]

Do not forsake us, HASHEM, our God, be not distant from us.[14]

Display for us a sign for good, so that our enemies may see it
    and be ashamed, for You, HASHEM, will have helped and consoled us.[15]

To our sayings give ear, HASHEM, perceive our thoughts.[16]

May the expressions of our mouth and the thoughts of our heart
    find favor before You, HASHEM, our Rock and our Redeemer.[17]

Because for You, HASHEM, we waited,
    You will answer, my Lord, our God.[18]

THE ARK IS CLOSED.

וִדּוּי

During the recitation of the וִדּוּי stand with head and body slightly bowed,
in submissive contrition.

אֱלֹהֵינוּ וֵאלֹהֵי אֲבוֹתֵינוּ, תָּבֹא לְפָנֶיךָ תְּפִלָּתֵנוּ,¹ וְאַל תִּתְעַלַּם מִתְּחִנָּתֵנוּ,² שֶׁאֵין אָנוּ עַזֵּי פָנִים וּקְשֵׁי עֹרֶף, לוֹמַר לְפָנֶיךָ יהוה אֱלֹהֵינוּ וֵאלֹהֵי אֲבוֹתֵינוּ, צַדִּיקִים אֲנַחְנוּ וְלֹא חָטָאנוּ, אֲבָל אֲנַחְנוּ וַאֲבוֹתֵינוּ חָטָאנוּ.³

Strike the left side of the chest with the right fist
while reciting each of the sins in the following confession litany.

אָשַׁמְנוּ, בָּגַדְנוּ, גָּזַלְנוּ, דִּבַּרְנוּ דֹּפִי. הֶעֱוִינוּ, וְהִרְשַׁעְנוּ, זַדְנוּ, חָמַסְנוּ, טָפַלְנוּ שֶׁקֶר. יָעַצְנוּ רָע, כִּזַּבְנוּ, לַצְנוּ, מָרַדְנוּ, נִאַצְנוּ, סָרַרְנוּ, עָוִינוּ, פָּשַׁעְנוּ, צָרַרְנוּ, קִשִּׁינוּ עֹרֶף. רָשַׁעְנוּ, שִׁחַתְנוּ, תִּעַבְנוּ, תָּעִינוּ, תִּעְתָּעְנוּ.

סַרְנוּ מִמִּצְוֹתֶיךָ וּמִמִּשְׁפָּטֶיךָ הַטּוֹבִים וְלֹא שָׁוָה לָנוּ.⁴ וְאַתָּה צַדִּיק עַל כָּל הַבָּא עָלֵינוּ, כִּי אֱמֶת עָשִׂיתָ וַאֲנַחְנוּ הִרְשָׁעְנוּ.⁵

אָשַׁמְנוּ מִכָּל עָם, בֹּשְׁנוּ מִכָּל דּוֹר, גָּלָה מִמֶּנּוּ מָשׂוֹשׂ, דָּוָה לִבֵּנוּ בַּחֲטָאֵינוּ, הֻחְבַּל אֲוֵּינוּ, וְנִפְרַע פְּאֵרֵנוּ, זְבוּל בֵּית מִקְדָּשֵׁנוּ חָרַב בַּעֲוֹנֵינוּ, טִירָתֵנוּ הָיְתָה לְשַׁמָּה, יְפִי אַדְמָתֵנוּ לְזָרִים, כֹּחֵנוּ לְנָכְרִים.

וַעֲדַיִן לֹא שַׁבְנוּ מִטָּעוּתֵנוּ וְהֵיךְ נָעִיז פָּנֵינוּ וְנַקְשֶׁה עָרְפֵּנוּ, לוֹמַר לְפָנֶיךָ יהוה אֱלֹהֵינוּ וֵאלֹהֵי אֲבוֹתֵינוּ, צַדִּיקִים אֲנַחְנוּ וְלֹא חָטָאנוּ, אֲבָל אֲנַחְנוּ וַאֲבוֹתֵינוּ חָטָאנוּ.

Strike the left side of the chest with the right fist
while reciting each of the sins in the following confession litany.

אָשַׁמְנוּ, בָּגַדְנוּ, גָּזַלְנוּ, דִּבַּרְנוּ דֹּפִי. הֶעֱוִינוּ, וְהִרְשַׁעְנוּ, זַדְנוּ, חָמַסְנוּ, טָפַלְנוּ שֶׁקֶר. יָעַצְנוּ רָע, כִּזַּבְנוּ, לַצְנוּ, מָרַדְנוּ, נִאַצְנוּ, סָרַרְנוּ, עָוִינוּ, פָּשַׁעְנוּ, צָרַרְנוּ, קִשִּׁינוּ עֹרֶף. רָשַׁעְנוּ, שִׁחַתְנוּ, תִּעַבְנוּ, תָּעִינוּ, תִּעְתָּעְנוּ.

סַרְנוּ מִמִּצְוֹתֶיךָ וּמִמִּשְׁפָּטֶיךָ הַטּוֹבִים וְלֹא שָׁוָה לָנוּ.⁴ וְאַתָּה צַדִּיק עַל כָּל הַבָּא עָלֵינוּ, כִּי אֱמֶת עָשִׂיתָ וַאֲנַחְנוּ הִרְשָׁעְנוּ.⁵

---

(1) Cf. *Psalms* 88:3. (2) Cf. 55:2. (3) Cf. 106:6. (4) Cf. *Job* 33:27. (5) *Nehemiah* 9:33.

VIDUY/CONFESSION

During the recitation of the וִדּוּי, *Confession*, stand with head and body slightly bowed,
in submissive contrition.

אֱלֹהֵינוּ *Our God and the God of our forefathers, may our prayer come before You.*[1] *Do not ignore our supplication,*[2] *for we are not so brazen and obstinate as to say before You, HASHEM, our God and the God of our forefathers, that we are righteous and have not sinned, for in truth, we and our forefathers have sinned.*[3]

Strike the left side of the chest with the right fist while reciting
each of the sins in the following confession litany.

אָשַׁמְנוּ *We have become guilty;* [ב] *we have betrayed;* [ג] *we have robbed;* [ד] *we have spoken slander;* [ה] *we have caused perversion;* [ו] *we have caused wickedness;* [ז] *we have sinned willfully;* [ח] *we have extorted;* [ט] *we have accused falsely;* [י] *we have given evil counsel;* [כ] *we have been deceitful;* [ל] *we have scorned;* [מ] *we have rebelled;* [נ] *we have provoked;* [ס] *we have turned away;* [ע] *we have been perverse;* [פ] *we have acted wantonly;* [צ] *we have persecuted;* [ק] *we have been obstinate;* [ר] *we have been wicked;* [ש] *we have corrupted;* [ת] *we have been abominable; we have strayed; You have let us go astray.*

סַרְנוּ *We have turned away from Your commandments and from Your good laws but to no avail.*[4] *Yet You are righteous in all that has come upon us, for You have acted truthfully while we have caused wickedness.*[5]

[א] *We have become the guiltiest of people.* [ב] *We have become the most degraded of all generations.* [ג] *Joy has departed from us.* [ד] *Our heart has been saddened by our sins.* [ה] *Our desirous treasure has been ruined,* [ו] *and our splendor dashed,* [ז] *for our Holy Temple edifice* [ח] *has been destroyed for our iniquities.* [ט] *Our Palace has become desolate.* [י] *[Jerusalem,] the beauty of our Land is given over to aliens,* [כ] *our power to strangers.*

But still we have not returned from our waywardness. So how can we be so brazen and obstinate as to say before You, HASHEM, our God and the God of our forefathers, that we are righteous and have not sinned, for in truth, both we and our fathers have sinned.

Strike the left side of the chest with the right fist while reciting
each of the sins in the following confession litany.

אָשַׁמְנוּ *We have become guilty;* [ב] *we have betrayed;* [ג] *we have robbed;* [ד] *we have spoken slander;* [ה] *we have caused perversion;* [ו] *we have caused wickedness;* [ז] *we have sinned willfully;* [ח] *we have extorted;* [ט] *we have accused falsely;* [י] *we have given evil counsel;* [כ] *we have been deceitful;* [ל] *we have scorned;* [מ] *we have rebelled;* [נ] *we have provoked;* [ס] *we have turned away;* [ע] *we have been perverse;* [פ] *we have acted wantonly;* [צ] *we have persecuted;* [ק] *we have been obstinate;* [ר] *we have been wicked;* [ש] *we have corrupted;* [ת] *we have been abominable; we have strayed; You have let us go astray.*

סַרְנוּ *We have turned away from Your commandments and from Your good laws but to no avail.*[4] *Yet You are righteous in all that has come upon us, for You have acted truthfully while we have caused wickedness.*[5]

לְעֵינֵינוּ עָשְׁקוּ עֲמָלֵנוּ, מְמֻשָּׁךְ וּמְמוֹרָט מִמֶּנּוּ, נָתְנוּ עֻלָּם עָלֵינוּ, סָבַלְנוּ עַל שִׁכְמֵנוּ, עֲבָדִים מָשְׁלוּ בָנוּ, פֹּרֵק אֵין מִיָּדָם, צָרוֹת רַבּוֹת סְבָבוּנוּ, קְרָאנוּךְ יהוה אֱלֹהֵינוּ, רָחַקְתָּ מִמֶּנּוּ בַּעֲוֹנֵינוּ, שַׁבְנוּ מֵאַחֲרֶיךָ, תָּעִינוּ וְאָבָדְנוּ.

וַעֲדַיִן לֹא שַׁבְנוּ מִטָּעוּתֵנוּ וְהֵיךְ נָעִיז פָּנֵינוּ וְנַקְשֶׁה עָרְפֵּנוּ, לוֹמַר לְפָנֶיךָ יהוה אֱלֹהֵינוּ וֵאלֹהֵי אֲבוֹתֵינוּ, צַדִּיקִים אֲנַחְנוּ וְלֹא חָטָאנוּ, אֲבָל אֲנַחְנוּ וַאֲבוֹתֵינוּ חָטָאנוּ.

Strike the left side of the chest with the right fist while reciting each of the sins in the following confession litany.

אָשַׁמְנוּ, בָּגַדְנוּ, גָּזַלְנוּ, דִּבַּרְנוּ דֹפִי. הֶעֱוִינוּ, וְהִרְשַׁעְנוּ, זַדְנוּ, חָמַסְנוּ, טָפַלְנוּ שֶׁקֶר. יָעַצְנוּ רָע, כִּזַּבְנוּ, לַצְנוּ, מָרַדְנוּ, נִאַצְנוּ, סָרַרְנוּ, עָוִינוּ, פָּשַׁעְנוּ, צָרַרְנוּ, קִשִּׁינוּ עֹרֶף. רָשַׁעְנוּ, שִׁחַתְנוּ, תִּעַבְנוּ, תָּעִינוּ, תִּעְתָּעְנוּ.

סַרְנוּ מִמִּצְוֹתֶיךָ וּמִמִּשְׁפָּטֶיךָ הַטּוֹבִים וְלֹא שָׁוָה לָנוּ. וְאַתָּה צַדִּיק עַל כָּל הַבָּא עָלֵינוּ, כִּי אֱמֶת עָשִׂיתָ וַאֲנַחְנוּ הִרְשָׁעְנוּ.

הִרְשַׁעְנוּ וּפָשַׁעְנוּ, לָכֵן לֹא נוֹשָׁעְנוּ. וְתֵן בְּלִבֵּנוּ לַעֲזוֹב דֶּרֶךְ רֶשַׁע, וְחִישׁ לָנוּ יֶשַׁע, כַּכָּתוּב עַל יַד נְבִיאֶךָ: יַעֲזֹב רָשָׁע דַּרְכּוֹ, וְאִישׁ אָוֶן מַחְשְׁבֹתָיו, וְיָשֹׁב אֶל יהוה וִירַחֲמֵהוּ, וְאֶל אֱלֹהֵינוּ כִּי יַרְבֶּה לִסְלוֹחַ.[1]

מְשִׁיחַ צִדְקֶךָ אָמַר לְפָנֶיךָ: שְׁגִיאוֹת מִי יָבִין מִנִּסְתָּרוֹת נַקֵּנִי.[2] נַקֵּנוּ יהוה אֱלֹהֵינוּ מִכָּל פְּשָׁעֵינוּ, וְטַהֲרֵנוּ מִכָּל טֻמְאוֹתֵינוּ, וּזְרוֹק עָלֵינוּ מַיִם טְהוֹרִים וְטַהֲרֵנוּ, כַּכָּתוּב עַל יַד נְבִיאֶךָ: וְזָרַקְתִּי עֲלֵיכֶם מַיִם טְהוֹרִים וּטְהַרְתֶּם, מִכֹּל טֻמְאוֹתֵיכֶם וּמִכָּל גִּלּוּלֵיכֶם אֲטַהֵר אֶתְכֶם.[3]

מִיכָה עַבְדְּךָ אָמַר לְפָנֶיךָ: מִי אֵל כָּמוֹךָ נֹשֵׂא עָוֹן וְעֹבֵר עַל פֶּשַׁע לִשְׁאֵרִית נַחֲלָתוֹ, לֹא הֶחֱזִיק לָעַד אַפּוֹ, כִּי חָפֵץ חֶסֶד הוּא, יָשׁוּב יְרַחֲמֵנוּ, יִכְבֹּשׁ עֲוֹנֹתֵינוּ, וְתַשְׁלִיךְ בִּמְצֻלוֹת יָם כָּל חַטֹּאתָם.[4] (וְכָל חַטֹּאת עַמְּךָ בֵּית

[ל] *[The benefit of] our labor has been stolen,* [מ] *pulled away and cut off from us.* [נ] *They have placed their yoke upon us,* [ס] *our burdens upon our shoulders.* [ע] *Slaves have ruled over us,* [פ] *there is no redemption from their hand.* [צ] *Abundant troubles have surrounded us,* [ק] *we called upon You,* HASHEM, *our God,* [ר] *but You have distanced us for our iniquities.* [ש] *We have turned away from following after You;* [ת] *we have strayed; we have become lost.*

But still we have not returned from our waywardness. So how can we be so brazen and obstinate as to say before You, HASHEM, our God and the God of our forefathers, that we are righteous and have not sinned, for in truth, both we and our fathers have sinned.

Strike the left side of the chest with the right fist while reciting each of the sins in the following confession litany:

אָשַׁמְנוּ *We have become guilty;* [ב] *we have betrayed;* [ג] *we have robbed;* [ד] *we have spoken slander;* [ה] *we have caused perversion;* [ו] *we have caused wickedness;* [ז] *we have sinned willfully;* [ח] *we have extorted;* [ט] *we have accused falsely;* [י] *we have given evil counsel;* [כ] *we have been deceitful;* [ל] *we have scorned;* [מ] *we have rebelled;* [נ] *we have provoked;* [ס] *we have turned away;* [ע] *we have been perverse;* [פ] *we have acted wantonly;* [צ] *we have persecuted;* [ק] *we have been obstinate;* [ר] *we have been wicked;* [ש] *we have corrupted;* [ת] *we have been abominable; we have strayed; You have let us go astray.*

סַרְנוּ *We have turned away from Your commandments and from Your good laws but to no avail. Yet You are righteous in all that has come upon us, for You have acted truthfully while we have caused wickedness.*

הִרְשַׁעְנוּ *We have acted wickedly and have sinned willfully, therefore we have not been saved. Inspire our heart to abandon the path of evil and hasten salvation for us, as it is written by Your prophet: May the wicked one abandon his way and the vicious man his thoughts; may he return to* HASHEM *and He will show him mercy, and to our God, for He is abundantly forgiving.*[1]

מְשִׁיחַ צִדְקֶךָ *Your righteous anointed [David] said before You: 'Who can discern mistakes? From unperceived faults cleanse me.'*[2] *Cleanse us,* HASHEM, *our God, of all our willful sins and purify us, of all our contaminations. Sprinkle upon us pure water and purify us, as it is written by Your prophet: I shall sprinkle pure water upon you and purify you, of all your contaminations and of all your abominations I will purify you.'*[3]

מִיכָה עַבְדְּךָ *Micah, Your servant, said before You: 'Who, O God, is like You, Who pardons iniquity and overlooks transgression for the remnant of His heritage? Who has not retained His wrath eternally, for He desires kindness! He will again be merciful to us; He will suppress our iniquities and cast into the depths of the sea all their sins.*[4] *(And all the sins*

(1) *Isaiah* 55:7. (2) *Psalms* 19:13. (3) *Ezekiel* 36:25. (4) *Micah* 7:18-19.

יִשְׂרָאֵל תַּשְׁלִיךְ בְּמָקוֹם אֲשֶׁר לֹא יִזָּכְרוּ, וְלֹא יִפָּקְדוּ, וְלֹא יַעֲלוּ
עַל לֵב לְעוֹלָם.) תִּתֵּן אֱמֶת לְיַעֲקֹב חֶסֶד לְאַבְרָהָם אֲשֶׁר נִשְׁבַּעְתָּ
לַאֲבוֹתֵינוּ מִימֵי קֶדֶם.¹

דָּנִיֵּאל אִישׁ חֲמֻדוֹת שִׁוַּע לְפָנֶיךָ: הַטֵּה אֱלֹהַי אָזְנְךָ וּשְׁמָע,
פְּקַח עֵינֶיךָ וּרְאֵה שֹׁמְמֹתֵינוּ וְהָעִיר אֲשֶׁר נִקְרָא שִׁמְךָ
עָלֶיהָ, כִּי לֹא עַל צִדְקֹתֵינוּ אֲנַחְנוּ מַפִּילִים תַּחֲנוּנֵינוּ לְפָנֶיךָ, כִּי
עַל רַחֲמֶיךָ הָרַבִּים. אֲדֹנָי שְׁמָעָה, אֲדֹנָי סְלָחָה, אֲדֹנָי הַקְשִׁיבָה,
וַעֲשֵׂה אַל תְּאַחַר, לְמַעַנְךָ אֱלֹהַי, כִּי שִׁמְךָ נִקְרָא עַל עִירְךָ וְעַל
עַמֶּךָ.²

עֶזְרָא הַסּוֹפֵר אָמַר לְפָנֶיךָ: אֱלֹהַי, בֹּשְׁתִּי וְנִכְלַמְתִּי לְהָרִים,
אֱלֹהַי, פָּנַי אֵלֶיךָ, כִּי עֲוֹנֹתֵינוּ רָבוּ לְמַעְלָה
רֹאשׁ, וְאַשְׁמָתֵנוּ גָדְלָה עַד לַשָּׁמָיִם.³ וְאַתָּה⁴ אֱלוֹהַּ סְלִיחוֹת, חַנּוּן
וְרַחוּם, אֶרֶךְ אַפַּיִם וְרַב חֶסֶד, וְלֹא עֲזַבְתָּנוּ.⁵

אַל תַּעַזְבֵנוּ אָבִינוּ וְאַל תִּטְּשֵׁנוּ בּוֹרְאֵנוּ, וְאַל תַּזְנִיחֵנוּ
יוֹצְרֵנוּ, וְאַל תַּעַשׂ עִמָּנוּ כָּלָה כְּחַטֹּאתֵינוּ. וְקַיֶּם
לָנוּ יהוה אֱלֹהֵינוּ, אֶת הַדָּבָר שֶׁהִבְטַחְתָּנוּ בְּקַבָּלָה עַל יְדֵי יִרְמְיָהוּ
חוֹזָךְ, כָּאָמוּר: בַּיָּמִים הָהֵם וּבָעֵת הַהִיא, נְאֻם יהוה, יְבֻקַּשׁ אֶת
עֲוֹן יִשְׂרָאֵל וְאֵינֶנּוּ וְאֶת חַטֹּאת יְהוּדָה וְלֹא תִמָּצֶאנָה, כִּי אֶסְלַח
לַאֲשֶׁר אַשְׁאִיר.⁶ עַמְּךָ וְנַחֲלָתְךָ רְעֵבֵי טוּבְךָ, צְמֵאֵי חַסְדֶּךָ, תְּאֵבֵי
יִשְׁעֶךָ, יַכִּירוּ וְיֵדְעוּ כִּי לַיהוה אֱלֹהֵינוּ הָרַחֲמִים וְהַסְּלִיחוֹת.

אֵל רַחוּם שְׁמֶךָ, אֵל חַנּוּן שְׁמֶךָ, בָּנוּ נִקְרָא שְׁמֶךָ. יהוה עֲשֵׂה
לְמַעַן שְׁמֶךָ. עֲשֵׂה לְמַעַן אֲמִתֶּךָ, עֲשֵׂה לְמַעַן
בְּרִיתֶךָ, עֲשֵׂה לְמַעַן גָּדְלְךָ וְתִפְאַרְתֶּךָ, עֲשֵׂה לְמַעַן דָּתֶךָ, עֲשֵׂה
לְמַעַן הוֹדֶךָ, עֲשֵׂה לְמַעַן וְעוּדֶךָ, עֲשֵׂה לְמַעַן זִכְרֶךָ, עֲשֵׂה לְמַעַן
חַסְדֶּךָ, עֲשֵׂה לְמַעַן טוּבֶךָ, עֲשֵׂה לְמַעַן יִחוּדֶךָ, עֲשֵׂה לְמַעַן
כְּבוֹדֶךָ, עֲשֵׂה לְמַעַן לִמּוּדֶךָ, עֲשֵׂה לְמַעַן מַלְכוּתֶךָ, עֲשֵׂה לְמַעַן
נִצְחֶךָ, עֲשֵׂה לְמַעַן סוֹדֶךָ, עֲשֵׂה לְמַעַן עֻזֶּךָ, עֲשֵׂה לְמַעַן פְּאֵרֶךָ,
עֲשֵׂה לְמַעַן צִדְקָתֶךָ, עֲשֵׂה לְמַעַן קְדֻשָּׁתֶךָ, עֲשֵׂה לְמַעַן רַחֲמֶיךָ
הָרַבִּים, עֲשֵׂה לְמַעַן שְׁכִינָתֶךָ, עֲשֵׂה לְמַעַן תְּהִלָּתֶךָ, עֲשֵׂה לְמַעַן
אוֹהֲבֶיךָ שׁוֹכְנֵי עָפָר, עֲשֵׂה לְמַעַן אַבְרָהָם יִצְחָק וְיַעֲקֹב, עֲשֵׂה

of Your nation the Family of Israel, may You cast away to a place where they will neither be remembered, considered, nor brought to mind — ever.) Grant truth to Jacob, kindness to Abraham, as You swore to our forefathers from ancient times.'[1]

דָּנִיֵּאל **Daniel**, the greatly beloved man, cried out before You: 'Incline, my God, Your ear, and listen, open Your eyes and see our desolation and that of the city upon which Your Name is proclaimed, for not because of our righteousness do we cast down our supplications before You, rather because of Your abundant compassion. O my Lord, heed; O my Lord, forgive; O my Lord, be attentive and act, do not delay; for Your sake, my God, for Your Name is proclaimed upon Your city and Your people.'[2]

עֶזְרָא הַסּוֹפֵר **Ezra** the Scribe said before You: 'My God, I am embarrassed and ashamed to lift my face to You, my God — for our iniquities have multiplied above our heads, and our sins extend unto heaven.[3] You are[4] the God of forgiveness, compassionate and merciful, slow to anger, and abundant in kindness; and You have not forsaken us.'[5]

אַל תַּעַזְבֵנוּ **Do not** forsake us, our Father; do not cast us off, our Creator; do not abandon us, our Molder; and do not bring about our destruction, as our sins merit. Affirm for us, HASHEM, our God, the promise You made in the tradition through Jeremiah, Your seer, as it is said: 'In those days and at that time' — the words of HASHEM — 'the iniquity of Israel will be sought but there will be none, and the errors of Judah, but they will not be found, for I will have forgiven those whom I leave as a remnant.'[6] Your people and Your heritage, who hunger for Your goodness, who thirst for Your kindness, who long for Your salvation — may they recognize and know that to HASHEM, our God, belong mercy and forgiveness.

אֵל רַחוּם '**Merciful God**' is Your Name, 'Gracious God' is Your Name, Your Name is called upon us — O HASHEM, act for Your Name's sake. Act for the sake of [א] Your truth; act for the sake of [ב] Your covenant; act for the sake of [ג] Your greatness and Your splendor; act for the sake of [ד] Your law; act for the sake of [ה] Your glory; act for the sake of [ו] Your Meeting House; act for the sake of [ז] Your remembrance; act for the sake of [ח] Your kindness; act for the sake of [ט] Your goodness; act for the sake of [י] Your Oneness; act for the sake of [כ] Your honor; act for the sake of [ל] Your teaching; act for the sake of [מ] Your kingship; act for the sake of [נ] Your eternality; act for the sake of [ס] Your counsel; act for the sake of [ע] Your power; act for the sake of [פ] Your beauty; act for the sake of [צ] Your righteousness; act for the sake of [ק] Your sanctity; act for the sake of [ר] Your abundant mercy; act for the sake of [ש] Your Presence, act for the sake of [ת] Your praise; act for the sake of Your beloved ones who rest in the dust; act for the sake of Abraham, Isaac, and Jacob; act

---

(1) *Micah* 7:20. (2) *Daniel* 9:18-19. (3) *Ezra* 9:6. (4) Some editions of *Selichos* insert the word אֱלֹקֵינוּ, our God, at this point. (5) Cf. *Nehemiah* 9:17. (6) *Jeremiah* 50:20.

לְמַעַן מֹשֶׁה וְאַהֲרֹן, עֲשֵׂה לְמַעַן דָּוִד וּשְׁלֹמֹה, עֲשֵׂה לְמַעַן יְרוּשָׁלַיִם עִיר קָדְשֶׁךָ, עֲשֵׂה לְמַעַן צִיּוֹן מִשְׁכַּן כְּבוֹדֶךָ, עֲשֵׂה לְמַעַן שִׁמְמוֹת הֵיכָלֶךָ, עֲשֵׂה לְמַעַן הֲרִיסוֹת מִזְבְּחֶךָ, עֲשֵׂה לְמַעַן הֲרוּגִים עַל שֵׁם קָדְשֶׁךָ, עֲשֵׂה לְמַעַן טְבוּחִים עַל יִחוּדֶךָ, עֲשֵׂה לְמַעַן בָּאֵי בָאֵשׁ וּבַמַּיִם עַל קִדּוּשׁ שְׁמֶךָ, עֲשֵׂה לְמַעַן יוֹנְקֵי שָׁדַיִם שֶׁלֹּא חָטְאוּ, עֲשֵׂה לְמַעַן גְּמוּלֵי חָלָב שֶׁלֹּא פָשְׁעוּ, עֲשֵׂה לְמַעַן תִּינוֹקוֹת שֶׁל בֵּית רַבָּן, עֲשֵׂה לְמַעַנְךָ אִם לֹא לְמַעֲנֵנוּ, עֲשֵׂה לְמַעַנְךָ וְהוֹשִׁיעֵנוּ.

עֲנֵנוּ יהוה עֲנֵנוּ, עֲנֵנוּ אֱלֹהֵינוּ עֲנֵנוּ, עֲנֵנוּ אָבִינוּ עֲנֵנוּ, עֲנֵנוּ בּוֹרְאֵנוּ עֲנֵנוּ, עֲנֵנוּ גּוֹאֲלֵנוּ עֲנֵנוּ, עֲנֵנוּ דוֹרְשֵׁנוּ עֲנֵנוּ, עֲנֵנוּ הָאֵל הַנֶּאֱמָן עֲנֵנוּ, עֲנֵנוּ וָתִיק וְחָסִיד עֲנֵנוּ, עֲנֵנוּ זַךְ וְיָשָׁר עֲנֵנוּ, עֲנֵנוּ חַי וְקַיָּם עֲנֵנוּ, עֲנֵנוּ טוֹב וּמֵטִיב עֲנֵנוּ, עֲנֵנוּ יוֹדֵעַ יֵצֶר עֲנֵנוּ, עֲנֵנוּ כּוֹבֵשׁ כְּעָסִים עֲנֵנוּ, עֲנֵנוּ לוֹבֵשׁ צְדָקוֹת עֲנֵנוּ, עֲנֵנוּ מֶלֶךְ מַלְכֵי הַמְּלָכִים עֲנֵנוּ, עֲנֵנוּ נוֹרָא וְנִשְׂגָּב עֲנֵנוּ, עֲנֵנוּ סוֹלֵחַ וּמוֹחֵל עֲנֵנוּ, עֲנֵנוּ עוֹנֶה בְּעֵת צָרָה¹ עֲנֵנוּ, עֲנֵנוּ פּוֹדֶה וּמַצִּיל עֲנֵנוּ, עֲנֵנוּ צַדִּיק וְיָשָׁר עֲנֵנוּ, עֲנֵנוּ קָרוֹב לְקוֹרְאָיו עֲנֵנוּ, עֲנֵנוּ רַחוּם וְחַנּוּן עֲנֵנוּ, עֲנֵנוּ שׁוֹמֵעַ אֶל אֶבְיוֹנִים עֲנֵנוּ, עֲנֵנוּ תּוֹמֵךְ תְּמִימִים עֲנֵנוּ, עֲנֵנוּ אֱלֹהֵי אֲבוֹתֵינוּ עֲנֵנוּ, עֲנֵנוּ אֱלֹהֵי אַבְרָהָם עֲנֵנוּ, עֲנֵנוּ פַּחַד יִצְחָק עֲנֵנוּ, עֲנֵנוּ אֲבִיר יַעֲקֹב עֲנֵנוּ, עֲנֵנוּ עֶזְרַת הַשְּׁבָטִים עֲנֵנוּ, עֲנֵנוּ מִשְׂגָּב אִמָּהוֹת עֲנֵנוּ, עֲנֵנוּ קָשֶׁה לִכְעוֹס עֲנֵנוּ, עֲנֵנוּ רַךְ לִרְצוֹת עֲנֵנוּ, עֲנֵנוּ עוֹנֶה בְּעֵת רָצוֹן¹ עֲנֵנוּ, עֲנֵנוּ אֲבִי יְתוֹמִים עֲנֵנוּ, עֲנֵנוּ דַּיַּן אַלְמָנוֹת עֲנֵנוּ.

מִי שֶׁעָנָה לְאַבְרָהָם אָבִינוּ בְּהַר הַמּוֹרִיָּה,	הוּא יַעֲנֵנוּ.
מִי שֶׁעָנָה לְיִצְחָק בְּנוֹ כְּשֶׁנֶּעֱקַד עַל גַּבֵּי הַמִּזְבֵּחַ,	הוּא יַעֲנֵנוּ.
מִי שֶׁעָנָה לְיַעֲקֹב בְּבֵית אֵל,	הוּא יַעֲנֵנוּ.
מִי שֶׁעָנָה לְיוֹסֵף בְּבֵית הָאֲסוּרִים,	הוּא יַעֲנֵנוּ.
מִי שֶׁעָנָה לַאֲבוֹתֵינוּ עַל יַם סוּף,	הוּא יַעֲנֵנוּ.
מִי שֶׁעָנָה לְמֹשֶׁה בְּחוֹרֵב,	הוּא יַעֲנֵנוּ.
מִי שֶׁעָנָה לְאַהֲרֹן בַּמַּחְתָּה,	הוּא יַעֲנֵנוּ.
מִי שֶׁעָנָה לְפִינְחָס בְּקוּמוֹ מִתּוֹךְ הָעֵדָה,	הוּא יַעֲנֵנוּ.

for the sake of Moses and Aaron; act for the sake of David and Solomon; act for the sake of Jerusalem, Your holy city; act for the sake of Zion, the abode of Your glory; act for the sake of the desolation of Your Temple; act for the sake of the ruin of Your Altar; act for the sake of the martyrs for Your holy Name; act for the sake of those slaughtered for Your Oneness; act for the sake of those who entered fire and water for the sanctification of Your Name; act for the nursing infants who did not err; act for the sake of the weaned babes who did not sin; act for the sake of children at the school-room; act for Your sake if not for ours; act for Your sake and save us.

עֲנֵנוּ *Answer us, HASHEM, answer us; answer us, our God, answer us; answer us, [א] our Father, answer us; answer us, [ב] our Creator, answer us; answer us, [ג] our Redeemer, answer us; answer us, [ד] You Who searches us out, answer us; answer us, [ה] faithful God, answer us; answer us, [ו] stead-fast and kind One, answer us; answer us, [ז] pure and upright One, answer us; answer us, [ח] living and enduring One, answer us; answer us, [ט] good and beneficent One, answer us; answer us, [י] You Who knows inclinations, answer us; answer us, [כ] You Who suppresses wrath, answer us; answer us, [ל] You Who dons righteousness, answer us; answer us, [מ] King Who reigns over kings, answer us; answer us, [נ] awesome and powerful One, answer us; answer us, [ס] You Who forgives and pardons, answer us; answer us, [ע] You Who answers in time of distress,[1] answer us; answer us, [פ] Redeemer and Rescuer, answer us; answer us, [צ] righteous and upright One, answer us; answer us, [ק] He Who is close to those who call upon Him, answer us; answer us, [ר] merciful and gracious One, answer us; answer us, [ש] You Who hears the destitute, answer us; answer us, [ת] You Who supports the wholesome, answer us; answer us, God of our forefathers, answer us; answer us, God of Abraham, answer us; answer us, Dread of Isaac, answer us; answer us, Mighty One of Jacob, answer us; answer us, Helper of the tribes, answer us; answer us, Stronghold of the Matriarchs, answer us; answer us, You Who are hard to anger, answer us; answer us, You Who are easy to pacify, answer us; answer us, You Who answers in a time of favor,[1] answer us; answer us, Father of orphans, answer us; answer us, Judge of widows, answer us.*

מִי שֶׁעָנָה *He Who answered our father Abraham on Mount Moriah,*
                                               may He answer us.
He Who answered his son Isaac when he was bound atop the altar,
                                               may He answer us.
He Who answered Jacob in Bethel,   *may He answer us.*
He Who answered Joseph in the prison,   *may He answer us.*
He Who answered our forefathers at the Sea of Reeds,   *may He answer us.*
He Who answered Moses in Horeb,   *may He answer us.*
He Who answered Aaron when he offered the censer,   *may He answer us.*
He Who answered Phineas when he arose from amid the congregation,
                                                 may He answer us.

---

(1) Some editions of *Selichos* reverse the positions of these two lines.

מִי שֶׁעָנָה לִיהוֹשֻׁעַ בַּגִּלְגָּל, הוּא יַעֲנֵנוּ.

מִי שֶׁעָנָה לִשְׁמוּאֵל בַּמִּצְפָּה, הוּא יַעֲנֵנוּ.

מִי שֶׁעָנָה לְדָוִד וּשְׁלֹמֹה בְנוֹ בִּירוּשָׁלַיִם, הוּא יַעֲנֵנוּ.

מִי שֶׁעָנָה לְאֵלִיָּהוּ בְּהַר הַכַּרְמֶל, הוּא יַעֲנֵנוּ.

מִי שֶׁעָנָה לֶאֱלִישָׁע בִּירִיחוֹ, הוּא יַעֲנֵנוּ.

מִי שֶׁעָנָה לְיוֹנָה בִּמְעֵי הַדָּגָה, הוּא יַעֲנֵנוּ.

מִי שֶׁעָנָה לְחִזְקִיָּהוּ מֶלֶךְ יְהוּדָה בְּחָלְיוֹ, הוּא יַעֲנֵנוּ.

מִי שֶׁעָנָה לַחֲנַנְיָה מִישָׁאֵל וַעֲזַרְיָה בְּתוֹךְ כִּבְשַׁן הָאֵשׁ, הוּא יַעֲנֵנוּ.

מִי שֶׁעָנָה לְדָנִיֵּאל בְּגוֹב הָאֲרָיוֹת, הוּא יַעֲנֵנוּ.

מִי שֶׁעָנָה לְמָרְדֳּכַי וְאֶסְתֵּר בְּשׁוּשַׁן הַבִּירָה, הוּא יַעֲנֵנוּ.

מִי שֶׁעָנָה לְעֶזְרָא בַגּוֹלָה, הוּא יַעֲנֵנוּ.

מִי שֶׁעָנָה לְכָל הַצַּדִּיקִים וְהַחֲסִידִים וְהַתְּמִימִים וְהַיְּשָׁרִים,

הוּא יַעֲנֵנוּ.

רַחֲמָנָא דְּעָנֵי לַעֲנִיֵּי, עֲנִינָא. רַחֲמָנָא דְּעָנֵי לִתְבִירֵי לִבָּא,
עֲנִינָא. רַחֲמָנָא דְּעָנֵי לְמַכִּיכֵי רוּחָא, עֲנִינָא. רַחֲמָנָא
עֲנִינָא. רַחֲמָנָא חוּס. רַחֲמָנָא פְּרוֹק. רַחֲמָנָא שְׁזִיב. רַחֲמָנָא
רַחֵם עֲלָן. הַשְׁתָּא בַּעֲגָלָא וּבִזְמַן קָרִיב.

נפילת אפים

In the presence of a Torah Scroll, the following (until יבשו רגע) is recited with the head resting
on the arm, preferably while seated. Elsewhere, it is recited with the head held erect.

(וַיֹּאמֶר דָּוִד אֶל גָּד, צַר לִי מְאֹד נִפְּלָה נָּא בְיַד יהוה,
כִּי רַבִּים רַחֲמָיו, וּבְיַד אָדָם אַל אֶפֹּלָה.[1]

רַחוּם וְחַנּוּן חָטָאתִי לְפָנֶיךָ. יהוה מָלֵא רַחֲמִים, רַחֵם עָלַי
וְקַבֵּל תַּחֲנוּנָי.

תהלים ו:ב-יא

יהוה אַל בְּאַפְּךָ תוֹכִיחֵנִי, וְאַל בַּחֲמָתְךָ תְיַסְּרֵנִי. חָנֵּנִי יהוה, כִּי
אֻמְלַל אָנִי, רְפָאֵנִי יהוה, כִּי נִבְהֲלוּ עֲצָמָי. וְנַפְשִׁי נִבְהֲלָה
מְאֹד, וְאַתָּה יהוה, עַד מָתָי. שׁוּבָה יהוה, חַלְּצָה נַפְשִׁי, הוֹשִׁיעֵנִי
לְמַעַן חַסְדֶּךָ. כִּי אֵין בַּמָּוֶת זִכְרֶךָ, בִּשְׁאוֹל מִי יוֹדֶה לָּךְ. יָגַעְתִּי
בְּאַנְחָתִי, אַשְׂחֶה בְכָל לַיְלָה מִטָּתִי, בְּדִמְעָתִי עַרְשִׂי אַמְסֶה.
עָשְׁשָׁה מִכַּעַס עֵינִי, עָתְקָה בְּכָל צוֹרְרָי. סוּרוּ מִמֶּנִּי כָּל פֹּעֲלֵי אָוֶן,
כִּי שָׁמַע יהוה קוֹל בִּכְיִי. שָׁמַע יהוה תְּחִנָּתִי, יהוה תְּפִלָּתִי יִקָּח.
יֵבֹשׁוּ וְיִבָּהֲלוּ מְאֹד כָּל אֹיְבָי, יָשֻׁבוּ יֵבֹשׁוּ רָגַע.

He Who answered Joshua in Gilgal,   *may He answer us.*
He Who answered Samuel in Mitzpah,   *may He answer us.*
He Who answered David and his son Solomon in Jerusalem,
                                                     may He answer us.

He Who answered Elijah on Mount Carmel,   *may He answer us.*
He Who answered Elisha in Jericho,   *may He answer us.*
He Who answered Jonah in the innards of the fish,   *may He answer us.*
He Who answered Hezekiah, King of Judah, in his illness,
                                                     may He answer us.
He Who answered Chananiah, Mishael, and Azariah in the fiery oven,
                                                     may He answer us.
He Who answered Daniel in the lions' den,   *may He answer us.*
He Who answered Mordechai and Esther in Shushan the capital,
                                                     may He answer us.
He Who answered Ezra in the Exile,   *may He answer us.*
He Who answered all the righteous, the devout, the wholesome,
    and the upright,   *may He answer us.*

רַחֲמָנָא The Merciful One Who answers the poor, may He answer us. The Merciful One Who answers the brokenhearted, may He answer us. The Merciful One Who answers the humble of spirit, may He answer us. O Merciful One, answer us. O Merciful One, pity. O Merciful One, redeem. O Merciful One, deliver. O Merciful One, have mercy on us — now, swiftly and soon.

PUTTING DOWN THE HEAD

In the presence of a Torah Scroll, the following (until 'instantly shamed') is recited with the head resting on the arm, preferably while seated. Elsewhere, it is recited with the head held erect.

(*And David said to Gad, 'I am exceedingly distressed. Let us fall into* HASHEM's *hand for His mercies are abundant, but let me not fall into human hands.'*[1])

רַחוּם וְחַנּוּן O compassionate and gracious One, I have sinned before You. HASHEM, Who is full of mercy, have mercy on me and accept my supplications.

Psalms 6:2-11

'ה HASHEM, do not rebuke me in Your anger nor chastise me in Your rage. Favor me, HASHEM, for I am feeble; heal me, HASHEM, for my bones shudder. My soul is utterly confounded, and You, HASHEM, how long? Desist, HASHEM, release my soul; save me as befits Your kindness. For there is no mention of You in death; in the Lower World who will thank You? I am wearied with my sigh, every night my tears drench my bed, soak my couch. My eye is dimmed because of anger, aged by my tormentors. Depart from me, all evildoers, for HASHEM has heard the sound of my weeping. HASHEM has heard my plea, HASHEM will accept my prayer. Let all my foes be shamed and utterly confounded, they will regret and be instantly shamed.

---

(1) *II Samuel* 24:14.

מַחֵי וּמַסֵּי מֵמִית וּמְחַיֶּה, מַסִּיק מִן שְׁאוֹל לְחַיֵּי עָלְמָא, בְּרָא
כַּד חָטֵי אֲבוּהִי לַקְיֵהּ, אֲבוּהִי דְחָיֵס אַסֵּי לִכְאֵבֵהּ.
עַבְדָּא דְּמָרִיד נָפִיק בְּקוֹלָר, מָרֵהּ תָּאִיב וְתַבִּיר קוֹלָרֵהּ.

בְּרָךְ בְּכְרַךְ אֲנַן וְחָטִינַן קַמָּךְ, הָא רָוֵי נַפְשִׁין בְּגִידִין מְרָרִין,
עַבְדָּךְ אֲנַן וּמְרוֹדִינַן קַמָּךְ, הָא בְּבִזְתָא, הָא בְּשִׁבְיָא, הָא
בְּמַלְקִיוּתָא. בְּמָטוּ מִנָּךְ בְּרַחֲמָךְ דְּנַפִישִׁין, אַסֵּי לִכְאֵבִין דִּתְקוֹף
עֲלָן, עַד דְּלָא נֶהֱוֵי גְּמִירָא בְּשִׁבְיָא.

מַכְנִיסֵי רַחֲמִים, הַכְנִיסוּ רַחֲמֵינוּ, לִפְנֵי בַּעַל הָרַחֲמִים.
מַשְׁמִיעֵי תְפִלָּה, הַשְׁמִיעוּ תְפִלָּתֵנוּ, לִפְנֵי
שׁוֹמֵעַ תְּפִלָּה. מַשְׁמִיעֵי צְעָקָה, הַשְׁמִיעוּ צַעֲקָתֵנוּ, לִפְנֵי שׁוֹמֵעַ
צְעָקָה. מַכְנִיסֵי דִמְעָה, הַכְנִיסוּ דִמְעוֹתֵינוּ, לִפְנֵי מֶלֶךְ מִתְרַצֶּה
בִּדְמָעוֹת.

הִשְׁתַּדְּלוּ וְהַרְבּוּ תְּחִנָּה וּבַקָּשָׁה, לִפְנֵי מֶלֶךְ אֵל רָם וְנִשָּׂא.
הַזְכִּירוּ לְפָנָיו, הַשְׁמִיעוּ לְפָנָיו תּוֹרָה וּמַעֲשִׂים טוֹבִים שֶׁל שׁוֹכְנֵי
עָפָר.

יִזְכֹּר אַהֲבָתָם וִיחַיֶּה זַרְעָם, שֶׁלֹּא תֹאבַד שְׁאֵרִית יַעֲקֹב. כִּי צֹאן
רוֹעֶה נֶאֱמָן הָיָה לְחֶרְפָּה, יִשְׂרָאֵל גּוֹי אֶחָד לְמָשָׁל וְלִשְׁנִינָה.
מַהֵר עֲנֵנוּ אֱלֹהֵי יִשְׁעֵנוּ, וּפְדֵנוּ מִכָּל גְּזֵרוֹת קָשׁוֹת וְהוֹשִׁיעָה
בְּרַחֲמֶיךָ הָרַבִּים, מְשִׁיחַ צִדְקָךְ וְעַמָּךְ.

מָרָן דְּבִשְׁמַיָּא לָךְ מִתְחַנְנַן, כְּבַר שִׁבְיָא דְּמִתְחַנַּן לִשְׁבּוּיֵהּ.
כֻּלְּהוֹן בְּנֵי שִׁבְיָא בְּכַסְפָּא מִתְפָּרְקִין, וְעַמָּךְ
יִשְׂרָאֵל בְּרַחֲמֵי וּבְתַחֲנוּנֵי, הַב לָן שְׁאִילְתִין וּבָעוּתִין, דְּלָא נֶהֱדַר
רֵיקָם מִן קֳדָמָךְ.

מָרָן דְּבִשְׁמַיָּא לָךְ מִתְחַנְנַן, כְּעַבְדָּא דְּמִתְחַנַּן לְמָרֵיהּ, עֲשִׁיקֵי
אֲנַן וּבַחֲשׁוֹכָא שָׁרִינַן, מְרִירָן נַפְשִׁין מֵעַקָתִין דְּנַפִישִׁין, חֵילָא לֵית
בָּן לְרַצּוּיָךְ מָרָן, עֲבִיד בְּדִיל קַיָּמָא דִּגְזַרְתְּ עִם אֲבָהָתָנָא.

שׁוֹמֵר יִשְׂרָאֵל, שְׁמוֹר שְׁאֵרִית יִשְׂרָאֵל, וְאַל יֹאבַד יִשְׂרָאֵל,
הָאוֹמְרִים, שְׁמַע יִשְׂרָאֵל.[1]
שׁוֹמֵר גּוֹי אֶחָד, שְׁמוֹר שְׁאֵרִית עַם אֶחָד, וְאַל יֹאבַד גּוֹי אֶחָד,
הַמְיַחֲדִים שִׁמְךָ, יְהוָה אֱלֹהֵינוּ יְהוָה אֶחָד.[1]

מָחַץ וּמַסֵּי [O God,] He Who smites and heals, causes death and restores life, raises [the dead] from the grave to eternal life: Should a son sin, his father would smack him, but a compassionate father will heal his [son's] pain. When a slave rebels, he is led out in collar-irons, but if his master desires to, he breaks his chains.

We are Your son, Your firstborn, and we have sinned against You; so our soul has been satiated with bitter wormwood. We are Your servants and we have rebelled against You; so [we have suffered], some with looting, some with captivity, and some with the lash. We beg of You, in Your abundant compassion, heal the pains that have overwhelmed us, before we have been completely wiped out in captivity.

מַכְנִיסֵי רַחֲמִים O you who usher in [pleas for] mercy, may you usher in our [plea for] mercy, before the Master of mercy. O you who cause prayer to be heard, may you cause our prayer to be heard, before the Hearer of prayer. O you who cause outcry to be heard, may you cause our outcry to be heard, before the Hearer of outcry. O you who usher in tears, may you usher in our tears, before the King Who finds favor through tears.

Exert yourselves, and multiply supplication and petition, before the King, God, exalted and most high. Mention before Him, cause to be heard before Him, the Torah and the good deeds of [the Patriarchs and Matriarchs] who dwell in the dust.

May He remember their love and grant life to [their] offspring, that the remnant of Jacob not be lost. For the flock of the faithful shepherd [Moses] has become a disgrace; Israel, the unique nation, a parable and a simile.

Speedily, answer us, O God of our salvation, and redeem us from all harsh decrees; and may You save, in Your abundant mercy, Your righteous anointed and Your people.

מָרָן דִּבִשְׁמַיָּא Our Master Who is in heaven, to You do we supplicate, as a captive supplicates before his captors; for all captives are redeemed with money, but Your people Israel with compassion and supplication. O grant our requests and our prayers that we not be turned away from You empty-handed.

Our Master Who is in heaven, to You do we supplicate, as a slave supplicates before his master: We are oppressed and we abide in darkness, souls embittered from abundant distress. We have no strength to regain Your favor. Our Master, act for the sake of the covenant that You made with our Patriarchs.

שׁוֹמֵר יִשְׂרָאֵל O Guardian of Israel, protect the remnant of Israel; let not Israel be destroyed — those who proclaim, 'Hear O Israel.'[1]
O Guardian of the unique nation, protect the remnant of the unique people; let not the unique nation be destroyed — those who proclaim the Oneness of Your Name, 'HASHEM is our God, HASHEM, the One and Only!'[1]

---

(1) Deuteronomy 6:4.

שׁוֹמֵר גּוֹי קָדוֹשׁ, שְׁמוֹר שְׁאֵרִית עַם קָדוֹשׁ, וְאַל יֹאבַד גּוֹי קָדוֹשׁ, הַמְשַׁלְּשִׁים בְּשָׁלֹשׁ קְדֻשּׁוֹת לְקָדוֹשׁ.

מִתְרַצֶּה בְּרַחֲמִים וּמִתְפַּיֵּס בְּתַחֲנוּנִים, הִתְרַצֶּה וְהִתְפַּיֵּס לְדוֹר עָנִי, כִּי אֵין עוֹזֵר. אָבִינוּ מַלְכֵּנוּ, חָנֵּנוּ וַעֲנֵנוּ, כִּי אֵין בָּנוּ מַעֲשִׂים, עֲשֵׂה עִמָּנוּ צְדָקָה וָחֶסֶד וְהוֹשִׁיעֵנוּ.

וַאֲנַחְנוּ לֹא נֵדַע מַה נַּעֲשֶׂה, כִּי עָלֶיךָ עֵינֵינוּ.¹ זְכֹר רַחֲמֶיךָ יהוה וַחֲסָדֶיךָ, כִּי מֵעוֹלָם הֵמָּה.² יְהִי חַסְדְּךָ יהוה עָלֵינוּ, כַּאֲשֶׁר יִחַלְנוּ לָךְ.³ אַל תִּזְכָּר לָנוּ עֲוֹנוֹת רִאשׁוֹנִים, מַהֵר יְקַדְּמוּנוּ רַחֲמֶיךָ, כִּי דַלּוֹנוּ מְאֹד.⁴ חָנֵּנוּ יהוה חָנֵּנוּ, כִּי רַב שָׂבַעְנוּ בוּז.⁵ בְּרֹגֶז רַחֵם תִּזְכּוֹר.⁶ כִּי הוּא יָדַע יִצְרֵנוּ, זָכוּר כִּי עָפָר אֲנָחְנוּ.⁷ עָזְרֵנוּ אֱלֹהֵי יִשְׁעֵנוּ עַל דְּבַר כְּבוֹד שְׁמֶךָ, וְהַצִּילֵנוּ וְכַפֵּר עַל חַטֹּאתֵינוּ לְמַעַן שְׁמֶךָ.⁸

קדיש שלם

קַדִּישׁ שָׁלֵם :The chazzan recites

יִתְגַּדַּל וְיִתְקַדַּשׁ שְׁמֵהּ רַבָּא. (.Cong – אָמֵן) בְּעָלְמָא דִּי בְרָא כִרְעוּתֵהּ, וְיַמְלִיךְ מַלְכוּתֵהּ, בְּחַיֵּיכוֹן וּבְיוֹמֵיכוֹן וּבְחַיֵּי דְכָל בֵּית יִשְׂרָאֵל, בַּעֲגָלָא וּבִזְמַן קָרִיב. וְאִמְרוּ אָמֵן.
(.Cong – אָמֵן. יְהֵא שְׁמֵהּ רַבָּא מְבָרַךְ לְעָלַם וּלְעָלְמֵי עָלְמַיָּא.)

יְהֵא שְׁמֵהּ רַבָּא מְבָרַךְ לְעָלַם וּלְעָלְמֵי עָלְמַיָּא.

יִתְבָּרַךְ וְיִשְׁתַּבַּח וְיִתְפָּאַר וְיִתְרוֹמַם וְיִתְנַשֵּׂא וְיִתְהַדָּר וְיִתְעַלֶּה וְיִתְהַלָּל שְׁמֵהּ דְּקוּדְשָׁא בְּרִיךְ הוּא. (.Cong – בְּרִיךְ הוּא.) לְעֵלָּא מִן כָּל בִּרְכָתָא וְשִׁירָתָא תֻּשְׁבְּחָתָא וְנֶחֱמָתָא, דַּאֲמִירָן בְּעָלְמָא. וְאִמְרוּ: אָמֵן. (.Cong – אָמֵן.)

(.Cong – קַבֵּל בְּרַחֲמִים וּבְרָצוֹן אֶת תְּפִלָּתֵנוּ.)

תִּתְקַבֵּל צְלוֹתְהוֹן וּבָעוּתְהוֹן דְּכָל (בֵּית) יִשְׂרָאֵל קֳדָם אֲבוּהוֹן דִּי בִשְׁמַיָּא. וְאִמְרוּ אָמֵן. (.Cong – אָמֵן.)

(.Cong – יְהִי שֵׁם יהוה מְבֹרָךְ, מֵעַתָּה וְעַד עוֹלָם.⁹)

יְהֵא שְׁלָמָא רַבָּא מִן שְׁמַיָּא וְחַיִּים עָלֵינוּ וְעַל כָּל יִשְׂרָאֵל. וְאִמְרוּ אָמֵן. (.Cong – אָמֵן.)

(.Cong – עֶזְרִי מֵעִם יהוה, עֹשֵׂה שָׁמַיִם וָאָרֶץ.¹⁰)

Take three steps back. Bow left and say, ... עֹשֶׂה; bow right and say, ... הוּא יַעֲשֶׂה; bow forward and say, וְעַל כָּל ... אָמֵן. Remain standing in place for a few moments, then take three steps forward.

עֹשֶׂה שָׁלוֹם בִּמְרוֹמָיו, הוּא יַעֲשֶׂה שָׁלוֹם עָלֵינוּ, וְעַל כָּל יִשְׂרָאֵל. וְאִמְרוּ אָמֵן. (.Cong – אָמֵן.)

O Guardian of the holy nation, protect the remnant of the holy people; let not the holy nation be destroyed — those who proclaim three-fold sanctifications to the Holy One.

Become favorable through compassion and become appeased through supplications. Become favorable and appeased to the poor generation, for there is no helper. Our Father, our King, be gracious with us and answer us, though we have no worthy deeds; treat us with charity and kindness, and save us.

וַאֲנַחְנוּ We know not what to do — but our eyes are upon You.[1] Remember Your mercies, HASHEM, and Your kindnesses, for they are from the beginning of the world.[2] May Your kindness be upon us, HASHEM, just as we awaited You.[3] Recall not against us the iniquities of the ancients; may Your mercies meet us swiftly, for we have become exceedingly impoverished.[4] Be gracious to us, HASHEM, be gracious to us, for we are abundantly sated with scorn.[5] Amid rage — remember to be merciful![6] For He knew our nature, He remembers that we are dust.[7] Chazzan— Assist us, O God of our salvation, for the sake of Your Name's glory; rescue us and atone for our sins for Your Name's sake.[8]

FULL KADDISH
The chazzan recites the Full Kaddish:

יִתְגַּדַּל May His great Name grow exalted and sanctified (Cong. — Amen.) in the world that He created as He willed. May He give reign to His kingship in your lifetimes and in your days, and in the lifetimes of the entire Family of Israel, swiftly and soon. Now respond: Amen.

(Cong. — Amen. May His great Name be blessed forever and ever.)

May His great Name be blessed forever and ever.

Blessed, praised, glorified, exalted, extolled, mighty, upraised and lauded be the Name of the Holy One, Blessed is He (Cong. — Blessed is He.) beyond any blessing and song, praise, and consolation that are uttered in the world. Now respond: Amen. (Cong. — Amen.)

(Cong. — Accept our prayers with mercy and favor.)

May the prayers and supplications of the entire House of Israel be accepted before their Father Who is in Heaven. Now respond: Amen. (Cong. — Amen.)

(Cong. — Blessed be the Name of HASHEM from this time and forever.[9])

May there be abundant peace from Heaven, and life, upon us and upon all Israel. Now respond: Amen. (Cong. — Amen.)

(Cong. — My help is from HASHEM, Maker of heaven and earth.[10])

Take three steps back. Bow left and say, 'He Who makes peace . . .'; bow right and say,
'may He make peace . . .'; bow forward and say, 'and upon all Israel . . .'
Remain standing in place for a few moments, then take three steps forward.

He Who makes peace in His heights, may He make peace upon us, and upon all Israel. Now respond: Amen. (Cong. — Amen.)

(1) II Chronicles 20:12. (2) Psalms 25:6. (3) 33:22. (4) 79:8. (5) 123:3.
(6) Habakkuk 3:2. (7) Psalms 103:14. (8) 79:9. (9) 113:2. (10) 121:2.

יום שביעי ﷼

אַשְׁרֵי יוֹשְׁבֵי בֵיתֶךָ, עוֹד יְהַלְלוּךָ סֶּלָה.[1] אַשְׁרֵי הָעָם שֶׁכָּכָה לוֹ, אַשְׁרֵי הָעָם שֶׁיהוה אֱלֹהָיו.[2]

תהלים קמה

תְּהִלָּה לְדָוִד,

אֲרוֹמִמְךָ אֱלוֹהַי הַמֶּלֶךְ, וַאֲבָרְכָה שִׁמְךָ לְעוֹלָם וָעֶד.

בְּכָל יוֹם אֲבָרְכֶךָּ, וַאֲהַלְלָה שִׁמְךָ לְעוֹלָם וָעֶד.

גָּדוֹל יהוה וּמְהֻלָּל מְאֹד, וְלִגְדֻלָּתוֹ אֵין חֵקֶר.

דּוֹר לְדוֹר יְשַׁבַּח מַעֲשֶׂיךָ, וּגְבוּרֹתֶיךָ יַגִּידוּ.

הֲדַר כְּבוֹד הוֹדֶךָ, וְדִבְרֵי נִפְלְאֹתֶיךָ אָשִׂיחָה.

וֶעֱזוּז נוֹרְאֹתֶיךָ יֹאמֵרוּ, וּגְדֻלָּתְךָ אֲסַפְּרֶנָּה.

זֵכֶר רַב טוּבְךָ יַבִּיעוּ, וְצִדְקָתְךָ יְרַנֵּנוּ.

חַנּוּן וְרַחוּם יהוה, אֶרֶךְ אַפַּיִם וּגְדָל חָסֶד.

טוֹב יהוה לַכֹּל, וְרַחֲמָיו עַל כָּל מַעֲשָׂיו.

יוֹדוּךָ יהוה כָּל מַעֲשֶׂיךָ, וַחֲסִידֶיךָ יְבָרְכוּכָה.

כְּבוֹד מַלְכוּתְךָ יֹאמֵרוּ, וּגְבוּרָתְךָ יְדַבֵּרוּ.

לְהוֹדִיעַ לִבְנֵי הָאָדָם גְּבוּרֹתָיו, וּכְבוֹד הֲדַר מַלְכוּתוֹ.

מַלְכוּתְךָ מַלְכוּת כָּל עֹלָמִים, וּמֶמְשַׁלְתְּךָ בְּכָל דּוֹר וָדֹר.

סוֹמֵךְ יהוה לְכָל הַנֹּפְלִים, וְזוֹקֵף לְכָל הַכְּפוּפִים.

עֵינֵי כֹל אֵלֶיךָ יְשַׂבֵּרוּ, וְאַתָּה נוֹתֵן לָהֶם אֶת אָכְלָם בְּעִתּוֹ.

Concentrate intently while
reciting the verse, פּוֹתֵחַ.

פּוֹתֵחַ אֶת יָדֶךָ, וּמַשְׂבִּיעַ לְכָל חַי רָצוֹן.

✦ **צַדִּיק** יהוה בְּכָל דְּרָכָיו, וְחָסִיד בְּכָל מַעֲשָׂיו.

קָרוֹב יהוה לְכָל קֹרְאָיו, לְכֹל אֲשֶׁר יִקְרָאֻהוּ בֶאֱמֶת.

רְצוֹן יְרֵאָיו יַעֲשֶׂה, וְאֶת שַׁוְעָתָם יִשְׁמַע וְיוֹשִׁיעֵם.

שׁוֹמֵר יהוה אֶת כָּל אֹהֲבָיו, וְאֵת כָּל הָרְשָׁעִים יַשְׁמִיד.

תְּהִלַּת יהוה יְדַבֶּר פִּי, וִיבָרֵךְ כָּל בָּשָׂר שֵׁם קָדְשׁוֹ לְעוֹלָם וָעֶד.

וַאֲנַחְנוּ נְבָרֵךְ יָהּ, מֵעַתָּה וְעַד עוֹלָם, הַלְלוּיָהּ.[3]

חֲצִי קַדִּישׁ The chazzan recites.

יִתְגַּדַּל וְיִתְקַדַּשׁ שְׁמֵהּ רַבָּא. (.Cong –אָמֵן) בְּעָלְמָא דִּי בְרָא כִרְעוּתֵהּ. וְיַמְלִיךְ מַלְכוּתֵהּ, בְּחַיֵּיכוֹן וּבְיוֹמֵיכוֹן וּבְחַיֵּי דְכָל בֵּית יִשְׂרָאֵל, בַּעֲגָלָא וּבִזְמַן קָרִיב. וְאִמְרוּ: אָמֵן.

(.Cong –אָמֵן. יְהֵא שְׁמֵהּ רַבָּא מְבָרַךְ לְעָלַם וּלְעָלְמֵי עָלְמַיָּא.)

יְהֵא שְׁמֵהּ רַבָּא מְבָרַךְ לְעָלַם וּלְעָלְמֵי עָלְמַיָּא.

יִתְבָּרַךְ וְיִשְׁתַּבַּח וְיִתְפָּאַר וְיִתְרוֹמַם וְיִתְנַשֵּׂא וְיִתְהַדָּר וְיִתְעַלֶּה וְיִתְהַלָּל שְׁמֵהּ דְּקֻדְשָׁא בְּרִיךְ הוּא (.Cong –בְּרִיךְ הוּא) לְעֵלָּא מִן כָּל בִּרְכָתָא וְשִׁירָתָא תֻּשְׁבְּחָתָא וְנֶחֱמָתָא, דַּאֲמִירָן בְּעָלְמָא, וְאִמְרוּ: אָמֵן. (.Cong –אָמֵן.)

❧ SEVENTH DAY ❧

אַשְׁרֵי *Praiseworthy are those who dwell in Your house; may they always praise You, Selah![1] Praiseworthy is the people for whom this is so, praiseworthy is the people whose God is HASHEM.[2]*

Psalm 145   *A psalm of praise by David:*

א *I will exalt You, my God the King, and I will bless Your Name forever and ever.*

ב *Every day I will bless You, and I will laud Your Name forever and ever.*

ג *HASHEM is great and exceedingly lauded,*
   and His greatness is beyond investigation.

ד *Each generation will praise Your deeds to the next*
   and of Your mighty deeds they will tell;

ה *The splendrous glory of Your power and Your wondrous deeds I shall discuss.*

ו *And of Your awesome power they will speak, and Your greatness I shall relate.*

ז *A recollection of Your abundant goodness they will utter*
   and of Your righteousness they will sing exultantly.

ח *Gracious and merciful is HASHEM,*
   slow to anger, and great in [bestowing] kindness.

ט *HASHEM is good to all; His mercies are on all His works.*

י *All Your works shall thank You, HASHEM, and Your devout ones will bless You.*

כ *Of the glory of Your kingdom they will speak, and of Your power they will tell;*

ל *To inform human beings of His mighty deeds,*
   and the glorious splendor of His kingdom.

מ *Your kingdom is a kingdom spanning all eternities,*
   and Your dominion is throughout every generation.

ס *HASHEM supports all the fallen ones and straightens all the bent.*

ע *The eyes of all look to You with hope*
   and You give them their food in its proper time;

פ *You open Your hand,*   Concentrate intently while reciting the verse, 'You open. . .'
   and satisfy the desire of every living thing.

צ Chazzan— *Righteous is HASHEM in all His ways*
   and magnanimous in all His deeds.

ק *HASHEM is close to all who call upon Him — to all who call upon Him sincerely.*

ר *The will of those who fear Him He will do;*
   and their cry He will hear, and save them.

ש *HASHEM protects all who love Him; but all the wicked He will destroy.*

ת *May my mouth declare the praise of HASHEM*
   and may all flesh bless His Holy Name forever and ever.

We will bless God from this time and forever, Halleluyah![3]

The chazzan recites Half-Kaddish:

יִתְגַּדַּל *May His great Name grow exalted and sanctified (Cong.— Amen.) in the world that He created as He willed. May He give reign to His kingship in your lifetimes and in your days, and in the lifetimes of the entire Family of Israel, swiftly and soon. Now respond: Amen.*

(Cong.— *Amen. May His great Name be blessed forever and ever.*)
May His great Name be blessed forever and ever.

Blessed, praised, glorified, exalted, extolled, mighty, upraised, and lauded be the Name of the Holy One, Blessed is He (Cong.— Blessed is He) — beyond any blessing and song, praise and consolation that are uttered in the world. Now respond: Amen. (Cong.— Amen.)

---

(1) *Psalms* 84:5. (2) 144:15. (3) 115:18.

All:

לְךָ יהוה הַצְּדָקָה, וְלָנוּ בְּשֶׁת הַפָּנִים.¹ מַה נִּתְאוֹנֵן,² מַה נֹּאמַר, מַה נְּדַבֵּר, וּמַה נִּצְטַדָּק.³ נַחְפְּשָׂה דְרָכֵינוּ וְנַחְקֹרָה, וְנָשׁוּבָה אֵלֶיךָ,⁴ כִּי יְמִינְךָ פְּשׁוּטָה לְקַבֵּל שָׁבִים. לֹא בְחֶסֶד וְלֹא בְמַעֲשִׂים בָּאנוּ לְפָנֶיךָ, כְּדַלִּים וּכְרָשִׁים דָּפַקְנוּ דְלָתֶיךָ. דְּלָתֶיךָ דָּפַקְנוּ רַחוּם וְחַנּוּן, נָא אַל תְּשִׁיבֵנוּ רֵיקָם מִלְּפָנֶיךָ. מִלְּפָנֶיךָ מַלְכֵּנוּ רֵיקָם אַל תְּשִׁיבֵנוּ, כִּי אַתָּה שׁוֹמֵעַ תְּפִלָּה.

שֹׁמֵעַ תְּפִלָּה, עָדֶיךָ כָּל בָּשָׂר יָבֹאוּ.⁵ יָבוֹא כָל בָּשָׂר לְהִשְׁתַּחֲוֺת לְפָנֶיךָ יהוה.⁶ יָבֹאוּ וְיִשְׁתַּחֲווּ לְפָנֶיךָ אֲדֹנָי, וִיכַבְּדוּ לִשְׁמֶךָ.⁷ בָּאוּ נִשְׁתַּחֲוֶה וְנִכְרָעָה, נִבְרְכָה לִפְנֵי יהוה עֹשֵׂנוּ.⁸ נָבוֹאָה לְמִשְׁכְּנוֹתָיו, נִשְׁתַּחֲוֶה לַהֲדֹם רַגְלָיו.⁹ בֹּאוּ שְׁעָרָיו בְּתוֹדָה, חֲצֵרֹתָיו בִּתְהִלָּה, הוֹדוּ לוֹ בָּרְכוּ שְׁמוֹ.¹⁰ רוֹמְמוּ יהוה אֱלֹהֵינוּ, וְהִשְׁתַּחֲווּ לַהֲדֹם רַגְלָיו, קָדוֹשׁ הוּא.¹¹ רוֹמְמוּ יהוה אֱלֹהֵינוּ, וְהִשְׁתַּחֲווּ לְהַר קָדְשׁוֹ, כִּי קָדוֹשׁ יהוה אֱלֹהֵינוּ.¹² הִשְׁתַּחֲווּ לַיהוה בְּהַדְרַת קֹדֶשׁ, חִילוּ מִפָּנָיו כָּל הָאָרֶץ.¹³ וַאֲנַחְנוּ בְּרֹב חַסְדְּךָ נָבוֹא בֵיתֶךָ, נִשְׁתַּחֲוֶה אֶל הֵיכַל קָדְשְׁךָ בְּיִרְאָתֶךָ.¹⁴ נִשְׁתַּחֲוֶה אֶל הֵיכַל קָדְשְׁךָ וְנוֹדֶה אֶת שְׁמֶךָ, עַל חַסְדְּךָ וְעַל אֲמִתֶּךָ, כִּי הִגְדַּלְתָּ עַל כָּל שִׁמְךָ אִמְרָתֶךָ.¹⁵ לְכוּ נְרַנְּנָה לַיהוה, נָרִיעָה לְצוּר יִשְׁעֵנוּ. נְקַדְּמָה פָנָיו בְּתוֹדָה, בִּזְמִרוֹת נָרִיעַ לוֹ.¹⁶ אֲשֶׁר יַחְדָּו נַמְתִּיק סוֹד, בְּבֵית אֱלֹהִים נְהַלֵּךְ בְּרָגֶשׁ.¹⁷ אֵל נַעֲרָץ בְּסוֹד קְדוֹשִׁים רַבָּה, וְנוֹרָא עַל כָּל סְבִיבָיו.¹⁸ שְׂאוּ יְדֵיכֶם קֹדֶשׁ וּבָרְכוּ אֶת יהוה.¹⁹ הִנֵּה בָּרְכוּ אֶת יהוה כָּל עַבְדֵי יהוה, הָעֹמְדִים בְּבֵית יהוה בַּלֵּילוֹת.²⁰ אֲשֶׁר מִי אֵל בַּשָּׁמַיִם וּבָאָרֶץ, אֲשֶׁר יַעֲשֶׂה כְמַעֲשֶׂיךָ וְכִגְבוּרֹתֶיךָ.²¹ אֲשֶׁר לוֹ הַיָּם וְהוּא עָשָׂהוּ, וְיַבֶּשֶׁת יָדָיו יָצָרוּ.²² אֲשֶׁר בְּיָדוֹ מֶחְקְרֵי אָרֶץ, וְתוֹעֲפוֹת הָרִים לוֹ.²³ אֲשֶׁר בְּיָדוֹ נֶפֶשׁ כָּל חָי, וְרוּחַ כָּל בְּשַׂר אִישׁ.²⁴ וְיוֹדוּ שָׁמַיִם פִּלְאֲךָ יהוה, אַף אֱמוּנָתְךָ בִּקְהַל קְדֹשִׁים.²⁵ לְךָ זְרוֹעַ עִם גְּבוּרָה, תָּעֹז יָדְךָ תָּרוּם יְמִינֶךָ.²⁶ לְךָ שָׁמַיִם, אַף לְךָ אָרֶץ, תֵּבֵל וּמְלֹאָהּ אַתָּה יְסַדְתָּם.²⁷ אַתָּה פוֹרַרְתָּ בְעָזְּךָ יָם, שִׁבַּרְתָּ רָאשֵׁי תַנִּינִים עַל הַמָּיִם.²⁸ אַתָּה הִצַּבְתָּ כָּל גְּבוּלוֹת אָרֶץ, קַיִץ וָחֹרֶף

(1) *Daniel* 9:7. (2) Cf. *Lamentations* 3:39. (3) Cf. *Genesis* 44:16. (4) Cf. *Lamentations* 3:40.
(5) *Psalms* 65:3. (6) Cf. *Isaiah* 66:23. (7) *Psalms* 86:9. (8) 95:6. (9) 132:7. (10) 100:4.
(11) 99:5. (12) 99:9. (13) 96:9. (14) Cf. 5:8. (15) Cf. 138:2. (16) 95:1-2. (17) 55:15. (18) 89:8.
(19) 134:2. (20) 134:1. (21) *Deuteronomy* 3:24. (22) *Psalms* 95:5. (23) 95:4. (24) *Job* 12:10.
(25) *Psalms* 89:6. (26) 89:14. (27) 89:12. (28) 74:13.

All:

לְךָ ה׳ Yours, my Lord, is the righteousness and ours is the shame-facedness.[1] What complaint can we make?[2] What can we say? What can we declare? What justification can we offer?[3] Let us examine our ways and analyze — and return to You,[4] for Your right hand is extended to accept penitents. Neither with kindness nor with [good] deeds do we come before You. As paupers and as beggars do we knock at Your doors. At Your doors we knock, O Compassionate and Gracious One. Please do not turn us away from You empty-handed. Our King, turn us not away from You empty-handed, for You are the One Who hears prayer.

שֹׁמֵעַ תְּפִלָּה You Who hears prayer, to You all flesh will come.[5] All flesh will come to prostrate itself before You, O HASHEM.[6] They will come and prostrate themselves before You, my Lord, and shall honor Your Name.[7] Come! — let us prostrate ourselves and bow, let us kneel before God, our Maker.[8] Let us come to His dwelling places, let us prostrate ourselves at His footstool.[9] Enter His gates with thanksgiving, His courts with praise; give thanks to Him, praise His Name.[10] Exalt HASHEM, our God, and bow at His footstool; He is holy![11] Exalt HASHEM, our God, and bow at His holy mountain; for holy is HASHEM, our God.[12] Prostrate yourselves before HASHEM in His intensely holy place, tremble before Him, everyone on earth.[13] As for us, through Your abundant kindness we will enter Your House; we will prostrate ourselves toward Your Holy Sanctuary in awe of You.[14] We will prostrate ourselves toward Your Holy Sanctuary, and we will give thanks to Your Name for Your kindness and truth for You have exalted Your promise even beyond Your Name.[15] Come! — let us sing to HASHEM, let us call out to the Rock of our salvation. Let us greet Him with thanksgiving, with praiseful songs let us call out to Him.[16] For together let us share sweet counsel, in the house of God let us walk in multitudes.[17] God is dreaded in the hiddenmost counsel of the holy ones, and inspires awe upon all who surround Him.[18] Lift your hands in the Sanctuary and bless HASHEM.[19] Behold, bless HASHEM, all you servants of HASHEM, who stand in the House of HASHEM in the nights.[20] For what power is there in heaven or earth that can approximate Your deeds and power?[21] For His is the sea and He perfected the dry land — His hands fashioned it.[22] For in His power are the hidden mysteries of the earth, and the mountain summits are His.[23] For His is the soul of every living thing, and the spirit of all human flesh.[24] Heaven will gratefully praise Your wonders, HASHEM; also Your faithfulness in the assembly of holy ones.[25] Yours is a mighty arm with power, You strengthen Your hand; You exalt Your right hand.[26] Yours is the heaven; Yours, too, is the earth; the world and its fullness — You founded them.[27] You shattered the sea with Your might, You smashed sea serpents' heads upon the water.[28] You established all the boundaries of earth; summer and winter

אַתָּה יְצַרְתָּם.¹ אַתָּה רִצַּצְתָּ רָאשֵׁי לִוְיָתָן, תִּתְּנֶנּוּ מַאֲכָל לְעַם
לְצִיִּים. אַתָּה בָקַעְתָּ מַעְיָן וָנָחַל, אַתָּה הוֹבַשְׁתָּ נַהֲרוֹת אֵיתָן.² לְךָ
יוֹם, אַף לְךָ לָיְלָה, אַתָּה הֲכִינוֹתָ מָאוֹר וָשָׁמֶשׁ.³ עֹשֶׂה גְדֹלוֹת עַד
אֵין חֵקֶר, וְנִפְלָאוֹת עַד אֵין מִסְפָּר.⁴ כִּי אֵל גָּדוֹל יהוה, וּמֶלֶךְ
גָּדוֹל עַל כָּל אֱלֹהִים.⁵ כִּי גָדוֹל אַתָּה וְעֹשֵׂה נִפְלָאוֹת, אַתָּה
אֱלֹהִים לְבַדֶּךָ.⁶ כִּי גָדוֹל מֵעַל שָׁמַיִם חַסְדֶּךָ, וְעַד שְׁחָקִים
אֲמִתֶּךָ.⁷ גָּדוֹל יהוה וּמְהֻלָּל מְאֹד, וְלִגְדֻלָּתוֹ אֵין חֵקֶר. (כִּי) גָּדוֹל⁸
יהוה וּמְהֻלָּל מְאֹד, נוֹרָא הוּא עַל כָּל אֱלֹהִים.⁹ גָּדוֹל יהוה
וּמְהֻלָּל מְאֹד, בְּעִיר אֱלֹהֵינוּ הַר קָדְשׁוֹ.¹⁰ לְךָ יהוה הַגְּדֻלָּה
וְהַגְּבוּרָה, וְהַתִּפְאֶרֶת וְהַנֵּצַח וְהַהוֹד, כִּי כֹל בַּשָּׁמַיִם וּבָאָרֶץ; לְךָ
יהוה הַמַּמְלָכָה, וְהַמִּתְנַשֵּׂא לְכֹל לְרֹאשׁ.¹¹ מִי לֹא יִרָאֲךָ מֶלֶךְ
הַגּוֹיִם, כִּי לְךָ יָאָתָה, כִּי בְכָל חַכְמֵי הַגּוֹיִם וּבְכָל מַלְכוּתָם מֵאֵין
כָּמוֹךָ.¹² מֵאֵין כָּמוֹךָ יהוה, גָּדוֹל אַתָּה וְגָדוֹל שִׁמְךָ בִּגְבוּרָה.¹³
יהוה אֱלֹהֵי צְבָאוֹת, מִי כָמוֹךָ חֲסִין יָהּ, וֶאֱמוּנָתְךָ סְבִיבוֹתֶיךָ.¹⁴
יהוה צְבָאוֹת, אֱלֹהֵי יִשְׂרָאֵל, יוֹשֵׁב הַכְּרֻבִים, אַתָּה הוּא
הָאֱלֹהִים לְבַדֶּךָ.¹⁵ מִי יְמַלֵּל גְּבוּרוֹת יהוה, יַשְׁמִיעַ כָּל תְּהִלָּתוֹ.¹⁶
כִּי מִי בַשַּׁחַק יַעֲרֹךְ לַיהוה, יִדְמֶה לַיהוה בִּבְנֵי אֵלִים.¹⁷ מַה נֹּאמַר
לְפָנֶיךָ יוֹשֵׁב מָרוֹם, וּמַה נְּסַפֵּר לְפָנֶיךָ שֹׁכֵן שְׁחָקִים. מַה נֹּאמַר
לְפָנֶיךָ יהוה אֱלֹהֵינוּ, מַה נְּדַבֵּר וּמַה נִּצְטַדָּק.¹⁸ אֵין לָנוּ פֶּה
לְהָשִׁיב וְלֹא מֵצַח לְהָרִים רֹאשׁ, כִּי עֲווֹנוֹתֵינוּ רַבּוּ מִלִּמְנוֹת,
וְחַטֹּאתֵינוּ עָצְמוּ מִסַּפֵּר.¹⁹ לְמַעַן שִׁמְךָ יהוה תְּחַיֵּנוּ, וּבְצִדְקָתְךָ
תּוֹצִיא מִצָּרָה נַפְשֵׁנוּ.²⁰ דַּרְכְּךָ אֱלֹהֵינוּ לְהַאֲרִיךְ אַפֶּךָ, לָרָעִים
וְלַטּוֹבִים, וְהִיא תְהִלָּתֶךָ. לְמַעַנְךָ אֱלֹהֵינוּ עֲשֵׂה וְלֹא לָנוּ, רְאֵה
עֲמִידָתֵנוּ, דַּלִּים וְרֵקִים. ❖ הַנְּשָׁמָה לָךְ וְהַגּוּף פָּעֳלָךְ, חוּסָה עַל
עֲמָלָךְ. הַנְּשָׁמָה לָךְ וְהַגּוּף שֶׁלָּךְ, יהוה עֲשֵׂה לְמַעַן שְׁמֶךָ. אָתָאנוּ
עַל שִׁמְךָ, יהוה, עֲשֵׂה לְמַעַן שְׁמֶךָ. בַּעֲבוּר כְּבוֹד שִׁמְךָ, כִּי אֵל
חַנּוּן וְרַחוּם שְׁמֶךָ. לְמַעַן שִׁמְךָ יהוה, וְסָלַחְתָּ לַעֲווֹנֵנוּ כִּי רַב
הוּא.²¹

Congregation, then chazzan:

סְלַח לָנוּ אָבִינוּ, כִּי בְרוֹב אִוַּלְתֵּנוּ שָׁגִינוּ,
מְחַל לָנוּ מַלְכֵּנוּ, כִּי רַבּוּ עֲווֹנֵינוּ.

— *You fashioned them.*[1] *You crushed the heads of Leviathan, You served it as food to the nation of legions. You split open fountain and stream, You dried the mighty rivers.*[2] *Yours is the day, Yours as well is the night; You established luminary and the sun.*[3] *Who performs great deeds that are beyond comprehension, and wonders beyond number.*[4] *For a great God is* HASHEM, *and a great King above all heavenly powers.*[5] *For You are great and work wonders; You alone, O God.*[6] *For great above the very heavens is Your kindness, and until the upper heights is Your truth.*[7] HASHEM *is great and exceedingly lauded, and His greatness is beyond investigation.*[8] *(For)* HASHEM *is great and exceedingly lauded, awesome is He above all heavenly powers.*[9] *Great is* HASHEM *and exceedingly lauded, in the city of our God, Mount of His Holiness.*[10] *Yours,* HASHEM, *is the greatness, the strength, the splendor, the triumph, and the glory; even everything in heaven and earth; Yours,* HASHEM, *is the kingdom, and sovereignty over every leader.*[11] *Who would not revere You, O King of nations? — for this befits You, for among all the sages of the nations and in all their kingdom there is none like You.*[12] *There is none like You, O* HASHEM, *You are great and Your Name is great with power.*[13] HASHEM, *God of Legions — who is like You, O Strong One, God? — and Your faithfulness surrounds You.*[14] HASHEM, *Master of Legions, God of Israel, enthroned upon the Cherubim, it is You alone Who is God.*[15] *Who can express the mighty acts of* HASHEM, *who can announce all His praise?*[16] *For who in the sky can be compared to* HASHEM; *be likened to* HASHEM *among the angels?*[17] *What can we say before You Who dwell on high? And what can we relate to You Who abide in the highest heaven? What can we say before You,* HASHEM, *our God? What can we declare? What justification can we offer?*[18] *We have neither mouth to respond nor brow to raise our head, for our iniquities are too numerous to count, and our sins are too vast to be numbered.*[19] *For Your Name's sake,* HASHEM, *revive us; and with Your righteousness remove our soul from distress.*[20] *It is Your way, our God, to delay Your anger, against people both evil and good — and this is Your praise. Act for Your sake, our God, and not for ours, behold our [spiritual] position — destitute and emptyhanded.* Chazzan — *The soul is Yours and the body is Your handiwork; take pity on Your labor. The soul is Yours and the body is Yours; O* HASHEM, *act for Your Name's sake. We have come with reliance on Your Name, O* HASHEM, *act for Your Name's sake; because of Your Name's glory — for 'Gracious and Merciful God' is Your Name. For Your Name's sake,* HASHEM, *may You forgive our iniquity, though it is abundant.*[21]

Congregation, then *chazzan:*

Forgive us, our Father, for in our abundant folly we have erred, pardon us, our King, for our iniquities are many.

---

(1) *Psalms* 74:17. (2) 74:14-15. (3) 74:16. (4) *Job* 9:10. (5) *Psalms* 95:3. (6) 86:10. (7) 108:5. (8) 145:3. (9) 96:4. (10) 48:2. (11) *I Chronicles* 29:11. (12) *Jeremiah* 10:7. (13) 10:6. (14) *Psalms* 89:9. (15) *Isaiah* 37:16. (16) *Psalms* 106:2. (17) 89:7. (18) Cf. *Genesis* 44:16. (19) Cf. *Ezra* 9:6. (20) Cf. *Psalms* 143:11. (21) Cf. 25:11.

All, while standing:

אֵל אֶרֶךְ אַפַּיִם אַתָּה, וּבַעַל הָרַחֲמִים נִקְרֵאתָ,
וְדֶרֶךְ תְּשׁוּבָה הוֹרֵיתָ.

גְּדֻלַּת רַחֲמֶיךָ וַחֲסָדֶיךָ, תִּזְכּוֹר הַיּוֹם וּבְכָל יוֹם לְזֶרַע יְדִידֶיךָ.
תֵּפֶן אֵלֵינוּ בְּרַחֲמִים, כִּי אַתָּה הוּא בַּעַל הָרַחֲמִים.
בְּתַחֲנוּן וּבִתְפִלָּה פָּנֶיךָ נְקַדֵּם, כְּהוֹדַעְתָּ לֶעָנָיו מִקֶּדֶם.
מֵחֲרוֹן אַפְּךָ שׁוּב,[1] כְּמוֹ בְתוֹרָתְךָ כָּתוּב.[2]
וּבְצֵל כְּנָפֶיךָ נֶחֱסֶה[3] וְנִתְלוֹנָן, כְּיוֹם וַיֵּרֶד יהוה בֶּעָנָן.
❖ תַּעֲבוֹר עַל פֶּשַׁע וְתִמְחֶה אָשָׁם, כְּיוֹם וַיִּתְיַצֵּב עִמּוֹ שָׁם.
תַּאֲזִין שַׁוְעָתֵנוּ וְתַקְשִׁיב מֶנּוּ מַאֲמָר,
כְּיוֹם וַיִּקְרָא בְשֵׁם יהוה,[4] וְשָׁם נֶאֱמַר:

Congregation, then *chazzan:*

וַיַּעֲבֹר יהוה עַל פָּנָיו וַיִּקְרָא:

Congregation and *chazzan* (the words in bold type are recited aloud and in unison):

יהוה, יהוה, אֵל, **רַחוּם, וְחַנּוּן, אֶרֶךְ אַפַּיִם, וְרַב חֶסֶד, וֶאֱמֶת,
נֹצֵר חֶסֶד לָאֲלָפִים, נֹשֵׂא עָוֹן, וָפֶשַׁע, וְחַטָּאָה,
וְנַקֵּה.**[5] וְסָלַחְתָּ לַעֲוֹנֵנוּ וּלְחַטָּאתֵנוּ וּנְחַלְתָּנוּ.[6] סְלַח לָנוּ אָבִינוּ כִּי
חָטָאנוּ, מְחַל לָנוּ מַלְכֵּנוּ כִּי פָשָׁעְנוּ. כִּי אַתָּה אֲדֹנָי טוֹב וְסַלָּח, וְרַב
חֶסֶד לְכָל קֹרְאֶיךָ.[7]

פסוקי הקדמה לסליחה כ

עַד מָתַי רְשָׁעִים, יהוה, עַד מָתַי רְשָׁעִים יַעֲלֹזוּ.[8] עַל עַמְּךָ
יַעֲרִימוּ סוֹד, וְיִתְיָעֲצוּ עַל צְפוּנֶיךָ.[9] נָתְנוּ אֶת נִבְלַת
עֲבָדֶיךָ מַאֲכָל לְעוֹף הַשָּׁמַיִם, בְּשַׂר חֲסִידֶיךָ לְחַיְתוֹ אָרֶץ.[10] וּפְרִי
בֶטֶן לֹא יְרַחֵמוּ, עַל בָּנִים לֹא תָחוּס עֵינָם.[11] שְׁפָךְ עֲלֵיהֶם זַעְמֶךָ,
וַחֲרוֹן אַפְּךָ יַשִּׂיגֵם.[12] הֲלֹא אַתָּה תָשׁוּב תְּחַיֵּינוּ, וְעַמְּךָ יִשְׂמְחוּ בָךְ.[13]

בְּרַחֵם אָב עַל בָּנִים, כֵּן תְּרַחֵם יהוה עָלֵינוּ.[14] לַיהוה הַיְשׁוּעָה,
עַל עַמְּךָ בִרְכָתֶךָ סֶּלָה.[15] יהוה צְבָאוֹת עִמָּנוּ,
מִשְׂגָּב לָנוּ אֱלֹהֵי יַעֲקֹב סֶלָה.[16] יהוה צְבָאוֹת, אַשְׁרֵי אָדָם בֹּטֵחַ
בָּךְ.[17] יהוה הוֹשִׁיעָה, הַמֶּלֶךְ יַעֲנֵנוּ בְיוֹם קָרְאֵנוּ.[18]

In some congregations the following two verses are recited responsively — the *chazzan* reciting סְלַח,
and the congregation responding וַיֹּאמֶר. In other congregations these verses are recited silently.

סְלַח נָא לַעֲוֹן הָעָם הַזֶּה כְּגֹדֶל חַסְדֶּךָ, וְכַאֲשֶׁר נָשָׂאתָה לָעָם
הַזֶּה מִמִּצְרַיִם וְעַד הֵנָּה.[19] וְשָׁם נֶאֱמַר:

All, while standing:

אֵל אֶרֶךְ אַפַּיִם *O God — You are slow to anger, You are called the Master of Mercy, and You have taught the way of repentance. May You remember this day and every day the greatness of Your mercy and Your kindness to the offspring of Your beloved Ones. Turn to us in mercy for You are the Master of Mercy. With supplication and prayer we approach Your Presence in the manner that You made known to the humble [Moses] in ancient times. Turn back from Your fierce anger;[1] as is written in Your Torah.[2] In the shadow of Your wings may we find shelter[3] and lodging as on the day 'HASHEM descended in a cloud' [to appear to Moses on Sinai]. Chazzan — Overlook sin and erase guilt as on the day 'He [God] stood there with him [Moses].' Give heed to our cry and be attentive to our declaration as on the day 'He called out with the Name HASHEM,'[4] and there it was said:*

Congregation, then *chazzan:*

And HASHEM passed before him [Moses] and proclaimed:

Congregation and chazzan (the words in bold type are recited aloud and in unison):

ה' ה' **HASHEM, HASHEM, God, Compassionate and Gracious, Slow to anger, and Abundant in Kindness and Truth, Preserver of kindness for thousands [of generations], Forgiver of iniquity, willful sin, and error, and Who cleanses.**[5] *May You forgive our iniquities and our errors and make us Your heritage.[6] Forgive us, our Father, for we have erred; pardon us, our King, for we have willfully sinned; for You, my Lord, are good and forgiving and abundantly kind to all who call upon You.[7]*

PREFATORY VERSES TO SELICHAH 20

עַד מָתַי *How long shall the wicked — O HASHEM — how long shall the wicked exult?[8] Against Your people they take cunning counsel, and consult together against Your sheltered ones.[9] They have given the corpse of Your servants as food for the birds of the sky, the flesh of Your devout ones to the beasts of the earth.[10] Even on infants they have no mercy; their eye does not pity children.[11] Pour Your wrath upon them, let the fury of Your anger overtake them.[12] Shall You not enliven us again that Your people may rejoice in You?[13]*

כְּרַחֵם אָב *As a father has mercy on his children, so, HASHEM, may You have mercy on us.[14] Salvation is HASHEM's, upon Your people is Your blessing, Selah.[15] HASHEM, Master of Legions, is with us, a stronghold for us is the God of Jacob, Selah.[16] HASHEM, Master of Legions, praiseworthy is the person who trusts in You.[17] HASHEM, save! May the King answer us on the day we call.[18]*

In some congregations the following two verses are recited responsively — the chazzan reciting, 'Forgive, please . . .,' and the congregation responding, 'And HASHEM said . . .' In other congregations these verses are recited silently.

סְלַח נָא *Forgive, please, the iniquity of this people according to the greatness of Your kindness and as You have forgiven this people from Egypt until now,[19] and there it was said:*

---

(1) Cf. *Exodus* 32:12. (2) See 32:14. (3) Cf. *Psalms* 36:8. (4) *Exodus* 34:5. (5) 34:6-7. (6) 34:9. (7) *Psalms* 86:5. (8) 94:3. (9) 83:4. (10) 79:2. (11) *Isaiah* 13:18. (12) *Psalms* 69:25. (13) 85:7. (14) Cf. *Psalms* 103:13. (15) 3:9. (16) 46:8. (17) 84:13. (18) 20:10. (19) *Numbers* 14:19.

וַיֹּאמֶר יהוה סָלַחְתִּי כִּדְבָרֶךָ.[1]

All:

הַטֵּה אֱלֹהַי אָזְנְךָ וּשְׁמָע, פְּקַח עֵינֶיךָ וּרְאֵה שֹׁמְמֹתֵינוּ, וְהָעִיר אֲשֶׁר נִקְרָא שִׁמְךָ עָלֶיהָ, כִּי לֹא עַל צִדְקֹתֵינוּ אֲנַחְנוּ מַפִּילִים תַּחֲנוּנֵינוּ לְפָנֶיךָ, כִּי עַל רַחֲמֶיךָ הָרַבִּים. אֲדֹנָי שְׁמָעָה, אֲדֹנָי סְלָחָה, אֲדֹנָי הַקְשִׁיבָה, וַעֲשֵׂה אַל תְּאַחַר, לְמַעַנְךָ אֱלֹהַי, כִּי שִׁמְךָ נִקְרָא עַל עִירְךָ וְעַל עַמֶּךָ.[2]

סליחה כ

All:

אֱלֹהֵינוּ וֵאלֹהֵי אֲבוֹתֵינוּ:

בְּתוּלַת בַּת יְהוּדָה,[3]* רַבַּת תַּאֲנִיָּה וַאֲנִיָּה,[4]
מִתְיַפְּחָה פּוֹרֶשֶׂת כַּף,[5] מֵעָמְקֵי שִׁבְיָהּ,
מִן הַמֵּצַר קְרָאתִיךָ, עֲנֵנִי בַמֶּרְחָב יָהּ,[6]
מֵאֵשׁ וּמִמַּיִם תּוֹצִיאֶנָּה[7] לָרְוָיָה,[8]

נוֹשֵׂאת עַיִן לְעֶזְרָה,[9] וּמַבֶּטֶת הֵנָּה וָהֵנָּה,
מִתְחוֹלֶלֶת כְּמַבְכִּירָה בְּצִירֶיהָ,[10] מִגְּזֵרוֹת עֲדִינָה,[11]*
סוֹפֶקֶת כַּף אֶל כָּף,[12] וְהוֹמָה בְּהֶגְיוֹנָהּ,
אַיֵּה אֵפוֹ תִקְוָתִי, וְתִקְנָתִי מִי יְשׁוּרֶנָּה.[13]

יְדִידוּת נַפְשָׁהּ[14] (וּמִשְׁכְּנוֹתֶיהָ) וּצְבִי גְאוֹנָהּ,[15]*
כְּנִתְּנוּ בְּיַד מְחָרְפֶיהָ וּבְיַד מְעַנָּהּ,
הַשּׁוֹאֲגֶת בְּתוֹךְ מוֹעֲדֶיהָ,[16] וּבְקוֹלָהּ עָלֶיהָ נָתָנָה,
אַיֵּה דְבַר יהוה, יָבוֹא נָא.[17]

מְשֻׁבֵּי לְגָלוּת נְפוּצָה וּשְׁבוּרָה, אִיַּמְתָּךְ,
מִפְּנֵי זַעַם חֲמָתָךְ וּמֵאֵימַת עֶבְרָתֶךָ,
וּבְקֹצֶר רוּחַ בְּקוֹל מַר שׁוֹאֶגֶת לְעַמְתָּךְ,
אַיֵּה קִנְאָתָךְ וּגְבוּרֹתֶיךָ.[18]

נָטַשְׁתָּ עַמְּךָ בֵּית יִשְׂרָאֵל[19] בְּאֶרֶץ שִׁבְיָם,

---

§ **בְּתוּלַת בַּת יְהוּדָה** — *Judah's maiden daughter.* As indicated by the acrostic, this *selichah* was composed by בִּנְיָמִין בַּר זֶרַח, *Binyamin ben Zerach*. According to *Emek HaBacha* (by R' Yosef HaKohen of 16th-century France and Italy), R' Binyamin flourished in late seventh-century Germany and was the first *dayan* (judge of Torah law) in that country. Others find allusions to the First Crusade (1096) in his works

and place him in that era. In either case, he was a prolific *paytan*; seven of his *selichos* appear in the *Selichos of Nusach Lita*, many more in *Nusach Ashkenaz.* The commentary *Arugas HaBosem* refers to him as *R' Binyamin HaGadol* (the Great).

עֲדִינָה — *The pampered nation.* The prophet thus describes the Babylonian conqueror of the First Temple (see *Isaiah 47:8*). Here the *paytan* refers

And HASHEM said, 'I have forgiven according to your word!'[1]

All:

הַטֵּה Incline, my God, Your ear, and listen, open Your eyes and see our desolation and that of the city upon which Your Name is proclaimed; for not because of our righteousness do we cast down our supplications before You, rather because of Your abundant compassion. O my Lord, heed; O my Lord, forgive; O my Lord, be attentive and act, do not delay; for Your sake, my God, for Your Name is proclaimed upon Your city and upon Your people.[2]

SELICHAH 20

All:

Our God and the God of our forefathers:

ב Judah's maiden daughter,*[3] full of moaning and mourning,[4]
sobs, spreading out her hand[5] from the depths of her captivity:
'From the straits I have called upon You;
answer me with relief, O God!'[6]
Bring her out[7] from fire and water to [the Land of] satiety.[8]

ג She raises [her] eye to [seek] help[9] and looks here and there,
she shudders as a woman in first travail[10]
at the pampered nation's* [evil] decrees.[11]
She claps her hands,[12] her thoughts in turmoil:
'Where, then, is my hope?
My hope, who can foresee [its coming]?'[13]

ד Her soul's beloved,[14] [her Tabernacles,]
and the beauty of her grandeur,*[15]
as they were given over into the hand of those who revile her,
into the hand of her tormentor,
those who roar in their assemblies,[16] giving out their voice against her,
'Where is HASHEM's word? Well, then, let it come!'[17]

מ [Jostled] from captivity to exile,
Your [once-]awe-inspiring nation is dispersed and broken
because of Your furious rage and from the dread of Your wrath.
With diminished spirit, she gives forth a bitter shout towards You:
'Where are Your jealousy and Your mighty deeds [on our behalf]?'[18]

נ You abandoned Your people, the House of Israel,[19]
in their land of captivity,

---

(1) *Numbers* 14:20. (2) *Daniel* 9:18-19. (3) Cf. *Lamentations* 1:15. (4) Cf. 2:5. (5) Cf. *Jeremiah* 4:31. (6) Cf. *Psalms* 118:5. (7) Some editions read תּוֹצִיאֵנִי, *bring me out.* (8) Cf. *Psalms* 66:12. See commentary to *selichah* 17. (9) Cf. 121:1. (10) Cf. *Jeremiah* 4:31. (11) Some editions read הַשּׁוֹשַׁנָּה, *the rose,* in place of מִגְּזֵרוֹת עֲדִינָה; the stich then reads, *The rose[-like nation] shudders . . . travail.* (12) Cf. *Ezekiel* 21:19,22. (13) *Job* 17:15. (14) *Jeremiah* 12:7. (15) Cf. *Isaiah* 4:2; 23:9. (16) Cf. *Psalms* 74:4. (17) Cf. *Jeremiah* 17:15. (18) *Isaiah* 63:15. (19) Cf. *Jeremiah* 12:7.

---

to our current oppressors.

יְדִידוּת נַפְשָׁהּ (וּמִשְׁכְּנוֹתֶיהָ) וּצְבִי גְאוֹנָהּ — *Her soul's beloved, (her Tabernacles) and the beauty of her grandeur.* These three expressions refer respec-

tively to the קֹדֶשׁ הַקֳּדָשִׁים, *Holy of Holies,* the Inner Sanctum of the *Beis HaMikdash;* the *Beis HaMikdash* in its entirety; and the Holy Land (*Matteh Levi*).

נָדִים[1] וְנָעִים בְּאֶרֶץ הָאוֹיֵב,[2] כָּאֳנִיָּה בְּלֶב יָם,[3]
לְאָבוֹת שׁוֹאֲלִים עוֹלְלִים, מוֹפְתֵי רוֹעֶה* אִים,
אַיֵּה הַמַּעֲלֵם מִיָּם.[4]

בְּנֵי נָבָל בְּנֵי בְלִי שֵׁם,[5] בּוֹסְסוּ נַחֲלָתֵנוּ,
רְחַקוּנוּ מֵעַל אַדְמָתֵנוּ, וּמִגְּבוּל אַרְצֵנוּ,
אָמְרוּ נִגְזַרְנוּ,[6] אָבְדָה תִקְוָתֵנוּ,[7]
אַיֵּה כָל נִפְלְאוֹתֶיךָ אֲשֶׁר סִפְּרוּ לָנוּ אֲבוֹתֵינוּ.[8]

❖ זְכֹר יהוה לִבְנֵי אֱדוֹם,[9] אֵת חָרְבוֹת הֵיכָלָךְ,
רֶצַח[10] אַבִּירֵי וְנֶפֶץ עוֹלְלֵי קְהָלָךְ,[11]
חֲשֹׂף זְרֹעֲךָ (הַחֲזָקָה) בַּקֵּשׁ מִיָּדָם מַרְעִית חֶבְלָךְ,[12]
אַיֵּה הָעֵדֶר נִתַּן לָךְ.[13]

All, while standing:

אֵל מֶלֶךְ יוֹשֵׁב עַל כִּסֵּא רַחֲמִים מִתְנַהֵג בַּחֲסִידוּת, מוֹחֵל
עֲוֹנוֹת עַמּוֹ, מַעֲבִיר רִאשׁוֹן רִאשׁוֹן, מַרְבֶּה מְחִילָה
לְחַטָּאִים וּסְלִיחָה לְפוֹשְׁעִים, עֹשֶׂה צְדָקוֹת עִם כָּל בָּשָׂר וָרוּחַ,
לֹא כְרָעָתָם תִּגְמוֹל. ❖ אֵל הוֹרֵיתָ לָּנוּ לוֹמַר שְׁלֹשׁ עֶשְׂרֵה, וּזְכוֹר
לָנוּ הַיּוֹם בְּרִית שְׁלֹשׁ עֶשְׂרֵה, כְּמוֹ שֶׁהוֹדַעְתָּ לֶעָנָיו מִקֶּדֶם, כְּמוֹ
שֶׁכָּתוּב, וַיֵּרֶד יהוה בֶּעָנָן וַיִּתְיַצֵּב עִמּוֹ שָׁם, וַיִּקְרָא בְשֵׁם יהוה.

Congregation, then chazzan:

וַיַּעֲבֹר יהוה עַל פָּנָיו וַיִּקְרָא:

Congregation and chazzan (the words in bold type are recited aloud and in unison):

יהוה, יהוה, אֵל **רַחוּם, וְחַנּוּן, אֶרֶךְ אַפַּיִם, וְרַב חֶסֶד, וֶאֱמֶת,
נֹצֵר חֶסֶד לָאֲלָפִים, נֹשֵׂא עָוֹן, וָפֶשַׁע, וְחַטָּאָה,
וְנַקֵּה.** וְסָלַחְתָּ לַעֲוֹנֵנוּ וּלְחַטָּאתֵנוּ וּנְחַלְתָּנוּ. סְלַח לָנוּ אָבִינוּ כִּי
חָטָאנוּ, מְחַל לָנוּ מַלְכֵּנוּ כִּי פָשָׁעְנוּ. כִּי אַתָּה אֲדֹנָי טוֹב וְסַלָּח,
וְרַב חֶסֶד לְכָל קֹרְאֶיךָ.

פסוקי הקדמה לסליחה כא

שׁוּבָה יהוה אֶת שְׁבִיתֵנוּ, כַּאֲפִיקִים בַּנֶּגֶב.[14] שׁוּב מֵחֲרוֹן אַפֶּךָ,
וְהִנָּחֵם עַל הָרָעָה לְעַמֶּךָ.[15] שׁוּבָה יהוה עַד מָתָי, וְהִנָּחֵם
עַל עֲבָדֶיךָ.[16] שׁוּבֵנוּ אֱלֹהֵי יִשְׁעֵנוּ, וְהָפֵר כַּעַסְךָ עִמָּנוּ.[17] אַל תָּבוֹא
בְמִשְׁפָּט עִמָּנוּ, כִּי לֹא יִצְדַּק לְפָנֶיךָ כָל חָי.[18]

---

(1) Some editions read חָגִים, *circling.* (2) Some editions omit the word הָאוֹיֵב and read, בְּאֶרֶץ,
in the land. (3) Cf. *Proverbs* 30:19. (4) *Isaiah* 63:11. (5) Cf. *Job* 30:8. (6) Cf. *Lamentations* 3:54.
(7) Cf. *Ezekiel* 37:11. (8) Cf. *Judges* 6:13. (9) *Psalms* 137:7; some editions of *Selichos* read,
אֲרָם, *Aram,* obviously in deference to the censors. (10) Some editions read, רֶצַח, *the murder.*
(11) Cf. *Psalms* 137:9. (12) Some editions read, זְבֻלָךְ, but the meaning is the same.
(13) *Jeremiah* 13:20. (14) *Psalms* 126:4. (15) *Exodus* 32:12. (16) *Psalms* 90:13. (17) 85:5. (18) Cf. 143:2.

wandering,[1] roaming the enemy's land[2]
like a ship in the heart of the sea.[3]
Babies ask their fathers,
'Where are the wonders of [our] shepherd [Moses]?*
Where is the one who brought [our people] up from the sea?'[4]
ב The children of louts and of nameless folk[5]
have trampled our heritage,
ר have taken us far from our land, the borders of our country.
We said, 'We are cut off,[6] our hope is lost![7]
Where are Your wonders that our fathers told us about?'[8]
ז Chazzan — Remember, HASHEM, for the children of Edom,[9]
Your ruined shrine;
ח the crushing[10] of my strong men
and the dashing of the infants of Your people.[11]
ח Reveal Your (strong) arm,
demand of them [to return] Your heritage-flock,[12] [saying,]
'Where is the flock that was given to you?'[13]

All, while standing:

אֵל מֶלֶךְ O God, King Who sits on the throne of mercy; Who acts with
kindness, pardons the iniquities of His people, removes [sins]
one by one, increasingly grants pardon to careless sinners and forgiveness
to rebels, Who deals righteously with every living being — You do not repay
them in accord with their evil. Chazzan — O God, You taught us to recite the
Thirteen [Attributes of Mercy], so remember for us today the covenant of
these Thirteen, as You made known to the humble one in ancient times, as
it is written: And HASHEM descended in a cloud and stood with him there,
and He called out with the Name HASHEM.

Congregation, then chazzan:

And HASHEM passed before him [Moses] and proclaimed:

Congregation and chazzan (the words in bold type are recited aloud and in unison):

ה' ה' HASHEM, HASHEM, God, **Compassionate and Gracious, Slow to
anger, and Abundant in Kindness and Truth, Preserver of
kindness for thousands [of generations], Forgiver of iniquity, willful
sin, and error, and Who cleanses.** May You forgive our iniquities and our
errors and make us Your heritage. Forgive us, our Father, for we have
erred; pardon us, our King, for we have willfully sinned; for You, my Lord,
are good and forgiving and abundantly kind to all who call upon You.

PREFATORY VERSES TO SELICHAH 21

שׁוּבָה Return, O HASHEM, our captivity, like springs in the desert.[14]
Turn back from Your flaring anger, and relent from the evil
[decreed] against Your people.[15] Return, O HASHEM — how long? and
relent [the evil] against Your servants.[16] Return us, O God of our salvation,
and annul Your anger with us.[17] Do not enter into strict judgment with
us, for no living creature would be innocent before You.[18]

רוֹעֵה — [Our] shepherd [Moses]. This phrase
in Isaiah (63:11) mentions Moses by name.
Nevertheless, Matteh Levi understands the stich

to refer to God. If so, the words Shepherd
(here) and One Who (in the next stich) should be
capitalized.

בְּרַחֵם אָב עַל בָּנִים, כֵּן תְּרַחֵם יהוה עָלֵינוּ. לַיהוה הַיְשׁוּעָה, עַל עַמְּךָ בִרְכָתֶךָ סֶּלָה. יהוה צְבָאוֹת עִמָּנוּ, מִשְׂגָּב לָנוּ אֱלֹהֵי יַעֲקֹב סֶלָה. יהוה צְבָאוֹת, אַשְׁרֵי אָדָם בֹּטֵחַ בָּךְ. יהוה הוֹשִׁיעָה, הַמֶּלֶךְ יַעֲנֵנוּ בְיוֹם קָרְאֵנוּ.

In some congregations the following two verses are recited responsively — the *chazzan* reciting סְלַח, and the congregation responding וַיֹּאמֶר. In other congregations these verses are recited silently.

סְלַח נָא לַעֲוֹן הָעָם הַזֶּה כְּגֹדֶל חַסְדֶּךָ, וְכַאֲשֶׁר נָשָׂאתָה לָעָם הַזֶּה מִמִּצְרַיִם וְעַד הֵנָּה, וְשָׁם נֶאֱמַר:

וַיֹּאמֶר יהוה סָלַחְתִּי כִּדְבָרֶךָ.

All:

הַטֵּה אֱלֹהַי אָזְנְךָ וּשֲׁמָע, פְּקַח עֵינֶיךָ וּרְאֵה שֹׁמְמֹתֵינוּ, וְהָעִיר אֲשֶׁר נִקְרָא שִׁמְךָ עָלֶיהָ, כִּי לֹא עַל צִדְקוֹתֵינוּ אֲנַחְנוּ מַפִּילִים תַּחֲנוּנֵינוּ לְפָנֶיךָ, כִּי עַל רַחֲמֶיךָ הָרַבִּים. אֲדֹנָי שְׁמָעָה, אֲדֹנָי סְלָחָה, אֲדֹנָי הַקְשִׁיבָה, וַעֲשֵׂה אַל תְּאַחַר, לְמַעַנְךָ אֱלֹהַי, כִּי שִׁמְךָ נִקְרָא עַל עִירְךָ וְעַל עַמֶּךָ.

סליחה כא

All:

אֱלֹהֵינוּ וֵאלֹהֵי אֲבוֹתֵינוּ:

אָפֵס הוֹד* כְּבוּדָה נֶאֶלְמָה דַבְּרָנִית,*

בְּשֵׁפֶל יָשְׁבָה הַתָּשָׁה נֶחֱלָשָׁה גְבַרְתָּנִית,

גַּם סוּגָה נוּגָה נְסוּגָה אֲחוֹרַנִית,

דַּלְּלָה אֻמְלְלָה לִוְיָה אַחֲרוֹנִית עֵירָנִית.*

הַהֲלָלָה זַלֲלָה חַלָּלָה וּכְסוּטָה פְרוּעָה,[1]

וְנִזְרִית כְּמוֹ דָוָה וְנִטְמֵאת כְּצָרוּעָה,*

אָפֵס הוֹד ◆ — *Gone is the glory.* The *paytan* signed his name after the *aleph-beis* acrostic — אֵלִיָּה בַּר שְׁמַעְיָה חָזָק, *Eliyah bar Shemayah, may he be strong* [see prefatory comment to *selichah* 6].

נֶאֶלְמָה דַבְּרָנִית — *Silenced is she who spoke [beautiful phrases].* According to most commentaries this stich is based on the phrase וּמִדְבָּרֵךְ נָאוֶה, *and your speech is comely* (Song of Songs 4:3). This refers to either the *Kohen Gadol's* Yom Kippur prayers (*Targum*), or to the songs of the *Leviim* that accompanied the daily *tamid*-offering service (*Metzudas David*). Indeed, the *Kohanim* and *Leviim* are both mentioned below in our stanza. Alternatively, the phrase alludes to the eloquent words of the prophets.

עֵירָנִית — *The lively [one].* Having mentioned the

Kohen (Aaronite) and Levite, the *paytan* speaks of the remainder of the nation, the Israelite, who were alert and lively in the performance of *mitzvos* (*Arugas HaBosem*). Specifically, it refers to the scholars who remain עֵר, *awake,* through the night studying Torah (*Matteh Levi*). An alternative reading is עֵירָנִית which means *villager.* This also alludes to the Israelites who do their work in the villages and farms, as opposed to the *Kohanim* and *Leviim* who serve in the *Beis HaMikdash.*

The two readings are based on two versions (*Rashi* and R' Chananel) of a talmudic dictum. One morning R' Elae did not come to the study hall. His students asked R' Abuhu if he knew where their mentor was 'hiding.' He replied, 'He rejoiced with a young woman, אֲחֲרוֹנִית, *of a*

בְּרַחֵם אָב **As a father has mercy on his children, so, HASHEM, may You have mercy on us. Salvation is HASHEM's, upon Your people is Your blessing, Selah. HASHEM, Master of Legions, is with us, a stronghold for us is the God of Jacob, Selah. HASHEM, Master of Legions, praiseworthy is the person who trusts in You. HASHEM, save! May the King answer us on the day we call.**

In some congregations the following two verses are recited responsively — the *chazzan* reciting, 'Forgive, please . . . ,' and the congregation responding, 'And HASHEM said . . .'
In other congregations these verses are recited silently.

סְלַח נָא **Forgive, please, the iniquity of this people according to the greatness of Your kindness and as You have forgiven this people from Egypt until now, and there it was said:**

And HASHEM said, 'I have forgiven according to your word!'

All:

הַטֵּה **Incline, my God, Your ear, and listen, open Your eyes and see our desolation and that of the city upon which Your Name is proclaimed; for not because of our righteousness do we cast down our supplications before You, rather because of Your abundant compassion. O my Lord, heed; O my Lord, forgive; O my Lord, be attentive and act, do not delay; for Your sake, my God, for Your Name is proclaimed upon Your city and upon Your people.**

SELICHAH 21

All:

Our God and the God of our forefathers:

א *Gone is the glory* of the honored [princess],*
    silenced is she who spoke [beautiful phrases];*

ב *she sits low, exhausted, weakened — she who was the mistress.*

ג *And she, [once] surrounded [with roses]* but [now] woeful,*
    has been turned back.

ד *Wretched, languished are the Levite, the Aaronite, and the lively [one].**

ה *The once-praised is degraded, profaned, as a slatternly wayward wife,[1]*

ו *set aside like a menstruant, unclean like a leper.**

(1) See *Numbers* 5:18; some editions of *Selichos* read, וְכָסוֹטָה פְּרוּעָה, *as slatternly as the wayward wife.*

---

priestly (*Aaronite*) family, אַחֲרוֹנִית, *the latest one*, עִירָנִית, *a lively one*, and she kept him awake all night.' The Talmud understands R' Abuhu's cryptic words in two ways. Either he meant that R' Elae had spent the night with his new wife, who was: the daughter of a *Kohen*; his latest wife (his first wife had passed away); and a vivacious woman whose conversation kept him awake all night. Or, R' Abuhu meant that R' Elae had spent the night studying a new tractate (often referred to allegorically as נַעֲרָה, *a maiden*) which was: of the order *Kodashim* that speaks of the duties of the *Kohanim*; his latest course of study; and so stimulating that he studied through the night (*Eruvin* 53b, according to Rashi).

According to a variant reading of the Talmud, the maiden was עִירָנִית, *a villager*, i.e., his wife was from a family of *Kohanim* who lived in a village, not in Jerusalem. Or, he studied a tractate of order *Kodashim* which was from a far-off village, i.e., not within his usual realm of study; and he began this study late in his life (ibid., according to R' Chananel).

כְּמוֹ דָוָה . . . כְּצָרוּעָה — *Like a menstruant . . . like a leper.* The *niddah* (woman in menses) and the *metzora* (usually translated *leper*, but actually a person afflicted with a leprous disease that is the manifestation of Divine punishment and responds to specific acts of atonement, see *Leviticus* 13-14), as well as the wayward wife mentioned earlier, are set apart from normal marital relations until their status changes. Thus, the exiled nation, alienated from its spouse — God — and unable to carry out its duties to Him in the *Beis HaMikdash*, is compared to these three categories.

זֵרָה נִזְרָה חָלַל וּפְרָזוֹן* גְּדוּעָה,[1]
חָזְרָה נִתְפַּזְּרָה בְּאֶרֶץ לֹא זְרוּעָה.[2]
טְלָאֶיךָ בְּרַעַשׁ וּבְרֹגֶז טָמֵא יְגַמֵּא.[3]
יַחֲרֹק יַעֲרֹק יִשְׁאַף רָעֵב וְצָמֵא.[4]
כֹּחַ גְּבוּרָתֶךָ אֵפוֹא יֻנָּדַע וּבַמֶּה,[5]
לְשׁוּלְחִים זְמוֹרוֹת* אַף[6] (פְּעָמִים) כַּמֶּה וְכַמֶּה.
מִמְשַׁל רַב[7] לְסָרָב לָמֶה הֻחֲלַט.[8]* .
נָבָל בְּנָדִיב, וְכִילַי בְּשׁוֹעַ[9] שָׁלַט,[10]
סָבְרוּ עָלֶיךָ נִקְרָא בְשִׁמְךָ יִמָּלֵט,
עֵזֶר הָיָה תִהְיֶה[11] מִשְׂגָּב וּמִפְלָט.
פְּנֵה אֶל תְּפִלַּת הָעַרְעָר[12] וְלֹא הֶעְתָּר,
צִחַן וַתֵּר כֶּתֶם כַּבֵּס כְּבַנֶּתֶר,[13]
קוֹחַ תִּפְקַח[14] בְּנֵי תְמוּתָה* הוֹתֵר,[15]
רוֹמֵם קוֹמֵם שְׁמָם לְטוֹבָה לְהַנְתֵּר.
שֵׁבֶט[16] מַלֵּבֵּט מְחַבֵּט גֶּדַע וּשְׁבַר,[17]
תָּעִיר קִנְאָה תָּרִיעַ תַּצְרִיחַ כְּגִבּוֹר,[18]
אוֹבְדוֹת נִכְחָדוֹת תִּכְסֹף תֶּאֱסֹף תִּצְבַּר,
לְקַבֵּץ לְרַבֵּץ לְרוֹמֵם (לְדַלּוֹת) לְהַעֲלוֹת מִבּוֹר.
יְשׁוּעָה תִקְרָא תָּשִׁית חֵיל וְחוֹמוֹת,*[19]
הַשְׁפֵּל הַגְּבוֹהוֹת הָמֵךְ רָמֵי הַקּוֹמוֹת,[20]
בּוֹטְחֶיךָ לְנוֹחֲךָ[21] הָשֵׁב בְּפֶקֶד נֶחָמוֹת,
רוֹדִים הַמַּגְדִּילִים יִלְבְּשׁוּ בֹשֶׁת וּכְלִמּוֹת.[22]

וּפְרָזוֹן — *And [her] unwalled villages.* The translation is based on *Judges 5:7,* which speaks of the unwalled cities sitting desolate, abandoned by their inhabitants for the protection afforded by walled cities against the marauding foe. Alternatively, the *paytan* refers to the loss of prophecy, a homiletical interpretation of the verse in *Judges* (see tractate *Pesachim 66b*).

זְמוֹרוֹת — *The putrid odors of [idolatry].* Many interpretations of this word are put forth by the commentators to *Ezekiel 8:17. Targum* renders בֶּהֱתָא, *shame. Radak* explains that *Targum* does not give a literal translation, but a euphemism to avoid explicating the offensiveness of the actual meaning, *a bad smell.* According to *Rashi* the word is derived from זְמַר, *sing,* and refers to the 'singing' that accompanies evacuation. As such, the word refers to vulgar service of the idol Peor, which included uncovering oneself and evacuating before the idol.

Others translate the word זְמוֹרָה, *branch* or *offshoot.* Accordingly, the word alludes to the idol Baal, which the Talmud (*Yerushalmi, Avodah Zarah 3:6*) describes as phallus shaped (*R' Yosef Breuer*). Alternatively, it means those who שׁוּלְחִים, *send forth* (or, *cause to be sent forth*), the punishing *branch* (read *whip*), that will eventually be used against themselves (*Mahari Kara*).

Malbim understands the word זְמוֹרָה to mean *pruning* or *cutting down* and renders, *those who perpetrate slaughter.*

מִמְשַׁל רַב . . . הֻחֲלַט — *Why has such great dominion been established for the rebellious?* At the Exodus, Israel became God's dominions (see *Psalms 114:2*). Why has God's domain, the people of Israel, been given over into the hands of nations that rebel against God's sovereignty? (*Magelei Tzedek*).

Why has the land once ruled by Israel been given over . . . ? (*Arugas HaBosem*).

ז Her crown, her tiara is profaned, [her] unwalled villages* cut off,[1]

ח [and she herself] is again dispersed in an unsown land.[2]

ט Your sheep are swallowed in tumult and rage by the unclean,[3]

י who gnash their teeth, and lust to swallow [their prey,
   to slake] their hunger and thirst.[4]

כ Where and how shall the impact of Your might be made known[5]

ל to those who waft the putrid odors [of idolatry]*[6]
   into their own faces, time and time again?

מ Why has such great dominion[7] been established for the rebellious?*[8]

נ The scoundrel rules the noble, the knave rules the patrician.[9] [10]

ס Let those whose hope is in You, who are called by Your name,
   be spared;

ע surely You will be [their] Aid,[11] Fortress and Haven.

פ Turn to the prayer of the devastated[12] and grant it;

צ overlook the stench [of their sin],
   wash clean the stain as if with scouring sand.[13]

ק Open the prison,[14] spare those condemned to die,*[15]

ר lift up, restore their name, that they be left [alive, to see] good.

ש Whip[16] those who wear [us] out,
   cut down and break those who beat [us];[17]

ת awaken jealousy, trumpet and shout like a warrior![18]

א Long for the lost and perishing ones, gather [them], heap them together,

ל to gather, to cause to rest, to exalt, (to draw forth) and raise from the pit.

י Declare salvation, set up rampart and walls;*[19]

ה humble the haughty, crush those who stand tall.[20]

ב Return those who trust in You to Your repose[21]
   when comfort is ordained,

ר [and] the prodigal tyrants will be clothed with shame and disgrace.[22]

---

(1) Some editions read, גְּרוּעָה, *diminished*. (2) *Jeremiah* 2:2. (3) Cf. *Job* 39:24. (4) Cf. 5:5.
(5) Cf. *Exodus* 33:16. (6) Cf. *Ezekiel* 8:17. (7) Cf. *Daniel* 11:5. (8) In deference to the censors, some
editions read, מוֹשֵׁל אַדִּיר לְךָ הַמֶּמְשָׁלָה הוּכָנָה, *O mighty Ruler, to You is the dominion established*.
(9) *Isaiah* 32:5. (10) This stich has also been censored in some editions which read, נָא כְּבוֹשׁ זַעֲמְךָ בָּנוּ
בַּל יִשְׁלַט, *Please conquer Your wrath, that it not rule over us*. (11) Cf. *Deuteronomy* 33:7.
(12) Cf. *Psalms* 102:18. (13) Cf. *Jeremiah* 2:22. (14) Cf. *Isaiah* 61:1. (15) Cf. *Psalms* 79:11; 102:21.
(16) Some editions read, שֵׁבֶט, *a whip*, the stich then means cut down and break the whip of those who
wear us out by beating us. (17) Some editions read, שְׁעֵה לְעַמְּךָ וְעַל פִּשְׁעָם עֲבוֹר, *Turn to Your people, and
overlook their wanton sins*, a change made to appease the censors. (18) Cf. *Isaiah* 42:13.
(19) Cf. 26:1. (20) Cf. 10:33. (21) Cf. *II Chronicles* 6:41. (22) Cf. *Psalms* 35:26.

Why was any dominion given to the rebellious? (*Matteh Levi*).

An alternative translation for מִמְשַׁל רַב is *a long
period of rule* (*Metzudas David* to *Daniel* 11:5).

בְּנֵי תְמוּתָה — *Those* [lit., *the children*] *condemned
to die*. The translation follows *Targum* to *Psalms*
79:11. *Rashi* (ibid. and 102:21) renders *those who
are fatally ill*. According to *Ibn Ezra* (ibid.), this
phrase refers to those who are prepared to die
[rather than surrender their faith]. *Arugas Ha-
Bosem* derives the word תְמוּתָה from תַּמָּתִי, *My
perfect one* (*Song of Songs* 5:2; 6:9), and interprets,
the children of the nation perfect in its deeds.

חֵיל וְחוֹמוֹת — *Rampart and walls.* חֵיל refers to

the low wall built opposite the tall wall of a fortified city (*Rashi* and *Radak* to *Isaiah* 26:1). Alternatively, חֵיל means *valley* (see *I Kings* 21:23),
and in the sense of fortification refers to the
moat dug around a defensive wall (*Radak* ibid.).

This phrase refers to the city of Jerusalem
which was surrounded by walls until the enemy
breached them when it captured the city. Alternatively, it refers to the *Beis HaMikdash* which was
surrounded by three חוֹמוֹת, *walls* (in the plural)
— the walls of the city, of the Temple Mount, and
of the Temple Courtyard — and the חֵיל (in the
singular), a ten-*amah*-wide strip surrounding the
Courtyard walls and separated from the remainder of the Temple Mount by the סוֹרֵג, *a low fence*

❖ שַׁדַּי מַלֵּט עֲבָדֶיךָ יְדִידֶיךָ הַצְּלַח, חִישׁ זְמַן קָרֵב פְּדוּתָם תִּשְׁלַח. מְחַל לָנוּ אָבִינוּ וְחַטּׂאתֵינוּ סְלַח. כִּי אַתָּה אֲדֹנָי טוֹב וְסַלָּח.¹

All, while standing:

אֵל מֶלֶךְ יוֹשֵׁב עַל כִּסֵּא רַחֲמִים מִתְנַהֵג בַּחֲסִידוּת, מוֹחֵל עֲוֹנוֹת עַמּוֹ, מַעֲבִיר רִאשׁוֹן רִאשׁוֹן, מַרְבֶּה מְחִילָה לְחַטָּאִים וּסְלִיחָה לְפוֹשְׁעִים, עֹשֶׂה צְדָקוֹת עִם כָּל בָּשָׂר וָרוּחַ, לֹא כְרָעָתָם תִּגְמוֹל. ❖ אֵל הוֹרֵיתָ לָנוּ לוֹמַר שְׁלֹשׁ עֶשְׂרֵה, וּזְכוֹר לָנוּ הַיּוֹם בְּרִית שְׁלֹשׁ עֶשְׂרֵה, כְּמוֹ שֶׁהוֹדַעְתָּ לֶעָנָיו מִקֶּדֶם, כְּמוֹ שֶׁכָּתוּב, וַיֵּרֶד יהוה בֶּעָנָן וַיִּתְיַצֵּב עִמּוֹ שָׁם, וַיִּקְרָא בְשֵׁם יהוה.

Congregation, then *chazzan:*

וַיַּעֲבֹר יהוה עַל פָּנָיו וַיִּקְרָא:

Congregation and *chazzan* (the words in bold type are recited aloud and in unison):

יהוה, יהוה, אֵל, רַחוּם, וְחַנּוּן, אֶרֶךְ אַפַּיִם, וְרַב חֶסֶד, וֶאֱמֶת, נֹצֵר חֶסֶד לָאֲלָפִים, נֹשֵׂא עָוֹן, וָפֶשַׁע, וְחַטָּאָה, וְנַקֵּה. וְסָלַחְתָּ לַעֲוֹנֵנוּ וּלְחַטָּאתֵנוּ וּנְחַלְתָּנוּ. סְלַח לָנוּ אָבִינוּ כִּי חָטָאנוּ, מְחַל לָנוּ מַלְכֵּנוּ כִּי פָשָׁעְנוּ. כִּי אַתָּה אֲדֹנָי טוֹב וְסַלָּח, וְרַב חֶסֶד לְכָל קֹרְאֶיךָ.

סְלִיחָה כב (פזמון)

Chazzan, then congregation:

אִם עֲוֹנֵינוּ* עָנוּ בָנוּ,² אָתָנוּ לְךָ³ וּבְשִׁמְךָ בָאנוּ, כְּרַחֵם אָב עַל בָּנִים רַחֲמֵנוּ,⁴ כְּאִישׁ אֲשֶׁר אִמּוֹ תְּנַחֲמֶנּוּ,⁵ אַל בְּאַפְּךָ פֶּן תַּמְעִיטֵנוּ.⁶

Congregation, then *chazzan:*

אַתָּה אֲדֹנָי טוֹב וְסַלָּח אִלֵּחַ,⁷ אוֹתָנוּ רֹעַ יֵצֶר אִלֵּחַ, בָּנֶיךָ בְּיַד פִּשְׁעָם* מְלֻשָּׁלַח,⁸ בְּיַד מַסְרִיּוֹת לִבְּנוּ הַמְּלַח.* אַל בְּאַפְּךָ פֶּן תַּמְעִיטֵנוּ.

(ten handbreadths high). This fence demarcated the point past which neither a non-Jew, nor a Jew who had contracted *tumah*-contamination through contact with a corpse, could enter (see tractate *Middos* 2:3 and *Keilim* 1:8). Thus, our stich is a prayer for the restoration of the *Beis HaMikdash.*

אִם עֲוֹנֵינוּ ❖ — *Even if our iniquities.* This *piz-mon (piyut* with refrain) contains a double alpha-betic acrostic, followed by the composer's signature — שְׁלֹמֹה הַקָּטֹן, *Shlomo the lesser* [see prefatory comment to *selichah* 2].

בְּיַד פִּשְׁעָם — *Into the grip* [lit., *hand*] *of their sin.*

A person who sins creates a destructive angel, the personification of that sin, so to speak. And to that very angel is the sinner delivered for chastisement (see *Rashi* to *Job* 8:4).

לִבְּנוּ הַמְּלַח — *Strengthen our heart.* Although we are in the grip of uncleanness brought about by our errancy in following the whims and wiles of our Evil Inclination, nevertheless, strengthen our hearts that we may return unwavering to Your service.

Arugas HaBosem offers three derivations for the coinage הַמְּלַח: (a) The word is related to מֶלַח, *salt;* its usage here is based on the preservative

Chazzan — *Almighty, rescue Your servants,*
bring success to Your beloved!
Hurry the time, bring it near, send their redemption soon.
Pardon us, our Father, forgive our sins,
for You, my Lord, are good and forgiving.[1]

All, while standing:

אֵל מֶלֶךְ *O God, King Who sits on the throne of mercy; Who acts with*
kindness, pardons the iniquities of His people, removes [sins]
one by one, increasingly grants pardon to careless sinners and forgiveness
to rebels, Who deals righteously with every living being — You do not repay
them in accord with their evil. Chazzan — *O God, You taught us to recite the*
Thirteen [Attributes of Mercy], so remember for us today the covenant of
these Thirteen, as You made known to the humble one in ancient times, as
it is written: And HASHEM *descended in a cloud and stood with him there,*
and He called out with the Name HASHEM.

Congregation, then *chazzan:*

And HASHEM *passed before him [Moses] and proclaimed:*

Congregation and *chazzan* (the words in bold type are recited aloud and in unison):

ה' ה' **HASHEM, HASHEM, God, Compassionate and Gracious, Slow to**
anger, and Abundant in Kindness and Truth, Preserver of
kindness for thousands [of generations], Forgiver of iniquity, willful
sin, and error, and Who cleanses. *May You forgive our iniquities and our*
errors and make us Your heritage. Forgive us, our Father, for we have
erred; pardon us, our King, for we have willfully sinned; for You, my Lord,
are good and forgiving and abundantly kind to all who call upon You.

SELICHAH 22

Chazzan, then congregation:

אִם עֲוֹנֵינוּ *Even if our iniquities* *bear witness against us,*[2]
we come to You [contrite];[3] *we come [trusting] in Your Name.*
As a father is merciful to his children, so have mercy on us,[4]
[comfort us] as a man is comforted by his mother.[5]
[Punish us] not in Your anger, lest You diminish us.[6]

Congregation, then *chazzan:*

א *For You, my Lord, are good and forgiving;*[7]
א *[as for] us, [our] Evil Inclination has caused [our] depravity.*
ב *So that Your children not be delivered into the grip of their sin,**[8]
ב *into the grip of uncleanness, strengthen our heart.**
[Punish us] not in Your anger, lest You diminish us.

---

(1) *Psalms* 86:5. (2) *Jeremiah* 14:7. (3) Cf. 3:22. (4) Cf. *Psalms* 103:13.
(5) *Isaiah* 66:13. (6) Cf. *Jeremiah* 10:24. (7) *Psalms* 86:5. (8) Cf. *Job* 8:4.

---

quality of salt — preserve our hearts that they
not rot as a result of our sins; (b) it is related
to מַלָּח, *an oarsman,* who churns up the salt waters of the sea — our phrase then means
steer our hearts away from the grip of unclean-
ness; (c) it is derived from מְמֻלָּח, a word *Targum*
Onkelos and *Rashi* render *well blended,* and
Ibn Ezra and *Ramban* render *well salted (Exodus*

30:35); according to *Arugas HaBosem,* מְמֻלָּח
there means *fragrant with pure spices* — if so, we
pray that God rescue our hearts from the clutches
of unclean sin, and turn our stagnation into de-
lightfully scented *mitzvah* performance.

It is also possible to understand the first half of
this line as a continuation of the preceding one. *So*
that Your children not be delivered into the grip

Congregation, then chazzan:

גְּדָל חֶסֶד¹ נֹצֵר לָאֲלָפִים,²*   גַּלְגֵּל רַחֲמֶיךָ וַחֲסָדֶיךָ וְלֹא חֲלוּפִים,

דְּבָרְךָ* לֹא רֵיקָם וְסֵלוּפִים,   דְּמֵינוּ חַסְדְּךָ³ כַּעֲיֵפִים וַעֲלוּפִים.

אַל בְּאַפְּךָ פֶּן תַּמְעִיטֵנוּ.

Congregation, then chazzan:

הַסְכֵּת צִית צִיר הִתְבּוֹנֵן,   הָאֵל דְּבָרְךָ אִם לָגוֹנֵן,⁴

וְתִקְתּוֹ דְּרָכֶיךָ חִנּוּן שַׁנֵּן,   וּבָהּ בְּמִדָּה אוֹתָנוּ חַנֵּן.

אַל בְּאַפְּךָ פֶּן תַּמְעִיטֵנוּ.

Congregation, then chazzan:

זוֹכֵר⁵ נִשְׁכָּחוֹת לְךָ הֲלוּל,   זַעַם תַּקְטִין כְּרֶגַע מָלוּל,*

חָתְךָ חַיִּים דִּין פִּלוּל,   חֵן חִנָּם חוֹקְרֶךָ חָלוּל.*

אַל בְּאַפְּךָ פֶּן תַּמְעִיטֵנוּ.

Congregation, then chazzan:

טִיט נִגְרָשׁ תּוֹכוֹ תַצְלִיל,   טוֹעַ⁶ זָדוֹן טָמוּן וַעֲלִיל,

יוֹדֵעַ יֵצֶר מַה מַּעֲלִיל,   יָד לְטוֹבָה עָלֵינוּ תַּגְלִיל.

אַל בְּאַפְּךָ פֶּן תַּמְעִיטֵנוּ.

Congregation, then chazzan:

כְּלָיוֹת בּוֹחֵן וּשְׁבִילֵי לֵב,⁷   כַּשְׁרוּת יְשָׁרוּת וּשְׁרִירוּת הַלֵּב,⁸

לֵב⁹ עָלוּב עִם עוֹלֵב,   לַעַן מָתוֹק שׁוּב וּמַכְלֵב.¹⁰*

אַל בְּאַפְּךָ פֶּן תַּמְעִיטֵנוּ.

Congregation, then chazzan:

מַצִּיל מֻטֵּי דִין הֶרֶג,¹¹   מְקוֹרֶרֶת לְךָ¹² עֶרֶג,

נָקֵל שְׁקֵל עָוֹן¹³ מְהַשְׁתָּרֵג,   נָשׂוּי נָשׂוּי בְּבָא מְקַטְרֵג.

אַל בְּאַפְּךָ פֶּן תַּמְעִיטֵנוּ.

---

(1) Cf. *Psalms* 145:8. (2) Cf. *Exodus* 34:7. (3) Cf. *Psalms* 48:10. (4) Many editions read אִם דְּבָרְךָ לָגוֹנֵן, *whether to shield those who profaned Your word.* (5) Some editions have the imperative, זְכוֹר, *Remember.* (6) Some editions read, תּוֹעַ זָדוֹן, *[Our] wayward wantonness,* but that reading is not in accord with the alphabetic acrostic. (7) Cf. *Jeremiah* 11:20. (8) Cf. 11:8. (9) Some editions read, לְךָ, *to You*; the stich then means, Yours is he who accepts insult silently and the insulter. (10) Cf. *Proverbs* 26:11; some editions of *Selichos* read, שָׁב וּמְלַבְלֵב, *that repents and blossoms.* (11) Cf. *Proverbs* 24:11. (12) Some editions read, מְקוֹר קוֹרוֹת לֵב, but the meaning is essentially the same. (13) Some editions read נָקֵל שְׁקֵל עָוֹן, *lighten the weight of [our] iniquity.*

---

of their sin, into the grip of uncleanness; [rather,] strengthen our hearts.

According to *Pirush HaAruch*, the word הַמֶּלַח has a destructive connotation, e.g., earth sown with salt in which no crops will grow (see *Judges* 9:45), or salt poured on an open wound. Thus, *our hearts have been destroyed by our sin.*

גְּדָל חֶסֶד נֹצֵר לָאֲלָפִים — *[O God,] great in kindness, Who preserves [kindness] for thousands [of generations].* The seventh of the Thirteen Attributes

is רַב חֶסֶד, *Abundant in kindness (Exodus* 34:6), and גְּדָל חֶסֶד assumedly alludes to that Attribute. The ninth Attribute is נֹצֵר חֶסֶד לָאֲלָפִים, *Preserver of kindness for thousands [of generations]* (ibid. 34:7). According to *Rashi* (ibid.), the former Attribute is directed toward those who lack personal merit. God dips into his abundant storehouse of kindness to compensate for their deficiency. The latter Attribute is directed at the thousands of generations that will reap the rewards for the kind deeds of their ancestor, but only if they fol-

Congregation, then *chazzan:*

ג [O God,] great in kindness,[1]
  Who preserves [kindness] for thousands [of generations],*[2]
ג bring around Your mercy and Your kindness [towards us],
  and not their opposite.
ד Your word is neither empty nor twisted;
ד we await Your kindness[3] when we are tired and faint.
                    [Punish us] not in Your anger, lest You diminish us.

Congregation, then *chazzan:*

ה [Moses, Your] messenger, listened attentively and pondered,
ה whether, Your word, O God, would be of protective mercy.[4]
ו You made him practiced in Your ways
  and taught him [about Your] graciousness,
ו in the same way, then, be gracious unto us.
                    [Punish us] not in Your anger, lest You diminish us.

Congregation, then *chazzan:*

ז O Rememberer[5] of forgotten things, praise is Yours,
ז quell Your wrath which lasts only as long as the word 'moment.'*
ח Decree life [for us] as the rendered judgment;
ח grant [us] free grace as You search [our] broken hearts.*
                    [Punish us] not in Your anger, lest You diminish us.

Congregation, then *chazzan:*

ט Throw deep into the midst of the [sea's] unquiet mud
ט [our] mistakes[6] [and our] wanton sins, whether hidden or revealed.
י [O You] Who know what the [Evil] Inclination leads [us] to do,
י stretch forth [Your] hand over us for [our] good.
                    [Punish us] not in Your anger, lest You diminish us.

Congregation, then *chazzan:*

כ [O You] Who probe thoughts and pathways of the heart,[7]
כ [for] propriety, uprightness, and fantasies of the heart;[8]
ל the heart[9] that accepts insult [silently], with the heart that insults,
ל those bitter [with sin], those sweet [with mitzvos], those repentant,
  and those that, doglike, repeat their sin.*[10]
                    [Punish us] not in Your anger, lest You diminish us.

Congregation, then *chazzan:*

מ [O You] Who rescue those who are sentenced to death,[11]
מ from the very source [of our being, we] call longingly to You.[12]
נ Lighten and remove [our] sin,[13] lest it entangle us,
נ [and let it be] forgiven and forgotten when the Accuser comes.
                    [Punish us] not in Your anger, lest You diminish us.

---

low in his righteous ways.

דְּבָרְךָ — *Your word.* A contract was sealed regarding the Thirteen Attributes of Mercy: Whenever they are recited [by Israel, during their fast day prayers (*Rashi*)], they will not be returned empty (*Rosh Hashanah* 17b).

כְּרֶגַע מלּוּל — *Which lasts only as long as the word 'moment.'* The Talmud states that God's anger lasts for a רֶגַע, *moment.* And the length of a mo-

ment is the amount of time it takes to utter the two syllables of its name רֶ-גַע (*Berachos* 7a).

חֲלָל — *[Our] broken hearts.* This usage is based on *Psalms* (109:22), *My heart is* חָלָל *within me.* According to the commentaries there, חָלָל can mean *crushed* (*Targum*); *killed by my troubles* (*Radak*); *hollow* (*Ibn Ezra, Metzudas David*).

שׁוּב וּמַכְלֵב — *Those repentant and those that, doglike, repeat their sins.* King Solomon said: *As*

Congregation, then *chazzan:*

סִרְחוֹן כְּתָב יָד[1] הַנֶּחְתָּם,[2]*   סִפְרוּ זַיִף טַעַן הִסְתַּתָּם,

עוֹז בְּעַיִן עָוֹן הַנִּכְתָּם,[3]   עַל יַד רַחֲמֶיךָ יֻתָּם.

אַל בְּאַפְּךָ פֶּן תַּמְעִיטֵנוּ.

Congregation, then *chazzan:*

פִּנָּה אֶבֶן* מִדַּרְכְּךָ הַתַּקֵּן,   פַּלְגֵי מַיִם פְּנוּי מִלְּהִתְרוֹקֵן,

צוּר, מִכְשׁוֹל* נַעַר וְזָקֵן,   צָמֵת, וּכְרַחֲמָן רַחֵם הַקֵּן.[4]

אַל בְּאַפְּךָ פֶּן תַּמְעִיטֵנוּ.

Congregation, then *chazzan:*

קָרוֹב לְרָצוֹת קְלוּסָךְ אָמוּר,   קוּשִׁי לְגִיוֹנָךְ שָׁנוּי וְתָמוּר,

רִיבָךְ לֹא לָנֶצַח[5] שָׁמוּר,   רַחֵם בְּרָגְזָ[6] דִּין גָּמוּר.

אַל בְּאַפְּךָ פֶּן תַּמְעִיטֵנוּ.

Congregation, then *chazzan:*

שָׁבִים שָׁבִים שֶׁבַח שַׁחֲרוּת,[7]   שְׁתוּלִים יְשַׁר יַלְדוּת בַּחֲרוּת,

תָּגֵן חֵרוּת מִצַּד תַּחֲרוּת,   תָּחֹן תָּו חַיִּים* חָרוּת.

אַל בְּאַפְּךָ פֶּן תַּמְעִיטֵנוּ.

Congregation, then *chazzan:*

שָׁלוֹם שָׁלוֹם בַּשֵּׁר מִתְקָרֵב,[8]   מְעַט סַיַּע קַדֵּשׁ הֶרֶב,*

הַבְּכוֹרוֹת וְחֲלוּפֵיהֶן* כְּאַחַת עָרֵב,   הַקְשֵׁט וְטִינָא[10] יַחַד עָרֵב.

אַל בְּאַפְּךָ פֶּן תַּמְעִיטֵנוּ.

---

(1) Some editions read, עֵד, witness or testimony. (2) Cf. *Job* 37:7. (3) Cf. *Jeremiah* 2:22; some editions of *Selichos* read, עֲוֹן עַיִן הַנִּכְתָּם, iniquity that appears as a stain. (4) Cf. *Deuteronomy* 32:11. (5) Cf. *Psalms* 103:9. (6) Cf. *Habakkuk* 3:2. (7) Some editions read, שֶׁבַח שַׁחֲרוּת, cause [the sins of their] youth to be forgotten. (8) Cf. *Isaiah* 57:19. (9) Cf. *Jeremiah* 24:1-3. (10) Some editions read, הַקֵּשׁ טֶנָא, shake the basket that they be blended as one.

a dog returns to its vomit, so does a fool [read, sinner] repeat his folly (*Proverbs* 26:11).

כְּתָב יָד הַנֶּחְתָּם — [Though] sealed in [the] handwriting [of the accused]. When a person passes on to his eternal home, all of his deeds are detailed before him. They say to him, 'Such and such have you done in such and such place on such and such day!' And he replies, 'It is true!' They then tell him to 'Sign [your confession],' and he signs. As it is said (*Job* 37:7): He seals with the hand of every man (*Taanis* 11a).

אֶבֶן ... מִכְשׁוֹל — The stone ... the stumbling block. The Talmud (*Succah* 52a) records seven names of the Evil Inclination: God called it רָע, Evil (*Genesis* 8:21); Moses called it עָרֵל, Uncircumcised (*Deuteronomy* 10:16); King David called it טָמֵא, Unclean (*Psalms* 51:12); King Solomon called it שׂוֹנֵא, Foe (*Proverbs* 25:21); Isaiah called it מִכְשׁוֹל, Stumbling block (57:14);

Ezekiel called it אֶבֶן, Stone (36:26); and Joel called it צְפוֹנִי, Hidden (2:20). The *paytan* uses two of these seven names in this stanza.

The translation of צוּר מִכְשׁוֹל, O Rock, [see] the stumbling block . . ., follows *Pirush HaAruch*. According to *Arugas HaBosem* and *Matteh Levi*, both words refer to the Evil Inclination. Thus, the rock that is a stumbling block . . .

תָּגֵן חֵרוּת ... תָּו חַיִּים — Protect freedom ... the sign of life. Protect the nation that You brought out of Egyptian slavery to חֵרוּת, freedom, from the rivalry of the Evil Inclination which seeks to lead these away from You. Graciously, inscribe them with the sign of life (*Arugas HaBosem*).

Alternatively, the word תַּחֲרוּת is related to חָרָה, to burn [in anger], and alludes to חֲרוֹן אַף, God's flaming anger. The stich then reads, protect the freed nation from Your flaming anger (*Matteh Levi*).

Congregation, then chazzan:

ס [The Book of] Sin,
    [though] sealed in [the] handwriting[1] [of the accused] — *[2]
ס [the Accuser's] book — declare it false, so that his case be blocked.[3]
ע The sin that stains [us] strongly for all to see,
ע through Your mercy let it come to an end.
       [Punish us] not in Your anger, lest You diminish us.

Congregation, then chazzan:

פ Clear the stone* out of Your way and let it be prepared,
פ turn to [our tears,] streams of water never-empty.
צ O Rock, [see] the stumbling block* of young and old,
צ cut it down; and like the merciful [eagle] have mercy on Your nest.[4]
       [Punish us] not in Your anger, lest You diminish us.

Congregation, then chazzan:

ק Your praise is spoken: '[You are] quick to be appeased.'
ק Let Your legion's difficulty be altered and replaced.
ר Do not hold Your quarrel forever;[5]
ר have mercy [even] in time of anger[6] and strict justice.
       [Punish us] not in Your anger, lest You diminish us.

Congregation, then chazzan:

ש The old can repent, too,
    but praiseworthy are [those contrite in their] youth,[7]
ש well-rooted in uprightness in childhood and adolescence.
ת Protect freedom from every aspect of rivalry;
ת be gracious with those upon whom the sign of life* is inscribed.
       [Punish us] not in Your anger, lest You diminish us.

Congregation, then chazzan:

של Announce 'Peace! Peace!' to the [people]
    approaching [You in repentance];[8]
מ help [those who sanctify themselves] a little to [achieve] great holiness.*
ה Let the first ripe [figs] and their opposites*[9] be sweet all together,
    let the speaker of truth and the fosterer of hatred[10] be blended as one.
       [Punish us] not in Your anger, lest You diminish us.

The *paytan* uses an intricate play on words here. The Talmud (*Shabbos* 55a) explains that the letter ת that God had the angel Gabriel inscribe on the foreheads of the righteous (*Ezekiel* 9:4) was the sign of life. [See our commentary to *selichah* 17, s.v., תָּוִי, *My longing.*] According to one opinion the ת was the initial of תִּחְיֶה, *You shall live.* Another view is that it meant תָּחוֹן זְכוּת אָבוֹת, [God] will be gracious [to us] in the merit of [our] forefathers. The *paytan* writes, תָּגֵּן חֵרוּת מִצַּד תַּחֲרוּת, which may be interpreted: *preserve the letters* חרות *from the word* תחרות, thus granting us חֵרוּת, *freedom*, from our present exile; תָּחוֹן, *be gracious* [with us]; תָּו חַיִּים, and let the remaining ת (of the word תחרות) be the sign of life for us (*Pirush HaAruch*).

מְעַט סַיַּע קַדֵּשׁ הֶרֶב — *Help [those who sanctify themselves] a little to [achieve] great holiness.*

The Talmud homiletically interprets the verse, וְהִתְקַדִּשְׁתֶּם וִהְיִיתֶם קְדֹשִׁים, *and you shall sanctify yourselves and you shall become holy* (*Leviticus* 11:44), not as a command, but as a promise: If a man sanctifies himself a little, they [the Heavenly Tribunal] sanctify him greatly (*Yoma* 39a). It is up to man to raise himself towards the ideal by his own efforts. Heaven will then aid those efforts and help him attain his supreme goal (*Kol HaTorah*).

הַבַּכּוּרוֹת וְחֲלוּפֵיהֶן — *The first ripe [figs] and their opposites.* The Talmud (*Eruvin* 21b) understands the term תְּאֵנֵי הַבַּכּוּרוֹת, *first ripe figs* (*Jeremiah* 24:2), as an allusion to the righteous, and תְּאֵנִים רָעוֹת מְאֹד, *very bad figs*, as an allusion to the wicked. Nevertheless, the sinner can repent, join the righteous, and become sweet again. Thus, the *paytan* prays that they become *sweet all together*.

All, while standing:

אֵל מֶלֶךְ יוֹשֵׁב עַל כִּסֵּא רַחֲמִים מִתְנַהֵג בַּחֲסִידוּת, מוֹחֵל
עֲוֺנוֹת עַמּוֹ, מַעֲבִיר רִאשׁוֹן רִאשׁוֹן, מַרְבֶּה
מְחִילָה לַחַטָּאִים וּסְלִיחָה לַפּוֹשְׁעִים, עֹשֶׂה צְדָקוֹת עִם כָּל
בָּשָׂר וָרוּחַ, לֹא כְרָעָתָם תִּגְמוֹל. ❖ אֵל הוֹרֵיתָ לָּנוּ לוֹמַר שְׁלֹשׁ
עֶשְׂרֵה, וּזְכוֹר לָנוּ הַיּוֹם בְּרִית שְׁלֹשׁ עֶשְׂרֵה, כְּמוֹ שֶׁהוֹדַעְתָּ לֶעָנָיו
מִקֶּדֶם, כְּמוֹ שֶׁכָּתוּב, וַיֵּרֶד יהוה בֶּעָנָן וַיִּתְיַצֵּב עִמּוֹ שָׁם, וַיִּקְרָא
בְשֵׁם יהוה.

Congregation, then *chazzan*:

וַיַּעֲבֹר יהוה עַל פָּנָיו וַיִּקְרָא:

Congregation and *chazzan* (the words in bold type are recited aloud and in unison):

**יהוה, יהוה, אֵל, רַחוּם, וְחַנּוּן, אֶרֶךְ אַפַּיִם, וְרַב חֶסֶד, וֶאֱמֶת,
נֹצֵר חֶסֶד לָאֲלָפִים, נֹשֵׂא עָוֺן, וָפֶשַׁע, וְחַטָּאָה,**
וְנַקֵּה. וְסָלַחְתָּ לַעֲוֺנֵנוּ וּלְחַטָּאתֵנוּ וּנְחַלְתָּנוּ. סְלַח לָנוּ אָבִינוּ כִּי
חָטָאנוּ, מְחַל לָנוּ מַלְכֵּנוּ כִּי פָשָׁעְנוּ. כִּי אַתָּה אֲדֹנָי טוֹב וְסַלָּח,
וְרַב חֶסֶד לְכָל קֹרְאֶיךָ.

All:

אַל תִּזְכָּר לָנוּ עֲוֺנוֹת רִאשׁוֹנִים, מַהֵר יְקַדְּמוּנוּ רַחֲמֶיךָ, כִּי
דַלּוֹנוּ מְאֹד.[1] חַטֹּאת נְעוּרֵינוּ וּפְשָׁעֵינוּ אַל תִּזְכּוֹר,
כְּחַסְדְּךָ זְכָר לָנוּ אַתָּה, לְמַעַן טוּבְךָ יהוה.[2]

זְכוֹר רַחֲמֶיךָ יהוה וַחֲסָדֶיךָ, כִּי מֵעוֹלָם הֵמָּה.[3] זָכְרֵנוּ יהוה
בִּרְצוֹן עַמֶּךָ, פָּקְדֵנוּ בִּישׁוּעָתֶךָ.[4] זְכֹר עֲדָתְךָ
קָנִיתָ קֶּדֶם, גָּאַלְתָּ שֵׁבֶט נַחֲלָתֶךָ, הַר צִיּוֹן זֶה שָׁכַנְתָּ בּוֹ.[5] זְכֹר יהוה
חִבַּת יְרוּשָׁלַיִם, אַהֲבַת צִיּוֹן אַל תִּשְׁכַּח לָנֶצַח.[6] אַתָּה תָקוּם
תְּרַחֵם צִיּוֹן, כִּי עֵת לְחֶנְנָהּ כִּי בָא מוֹעֵד.[7] זְכֹר יהוה לִבְנֵי אֱדוֹם
אֵת יוֹם יְרוּשָׁלָיִם, הָאֹמְרִים עָרוּ עָרוּ עַד הַיְסוֹד בָּהּ.[8] זְכֹר
לְאַבְרָהָם לְיִצְחָק וּלְיִשְׂרָאֵל עֲבָדֶיךָ אֲשֶׁר נִשְׁבַּעְתָּ לָהֶם בָּךְ,
וַתְּדַבֵּר אֲלֵהֶם, אַרְבֶּה אֶת זַרְעֲכֶם כְּכוֹכְבֵי הַשָּׁמָיִם, וְכָל הָאָרֶץ
הַזֹּאת אֲשֶׁר אָמַרְתִּי אֶתֵּן לְזַרְעֲכֶם, וְנָחֲלוּ לְעוֹלָם.[9] ❖ זְכֹר
לַעֲבָדֶיךָ לְאַבְרָהָם לְיִצְחָק וּלְיַעֲקֹב, אַל תֵּפֶן אֶל קְשִׁי הָעָם הַזֶּה
וְאֶל רִשְׁעוֹ וְאֶל חַטָּאתוֹ.[10]

All, while standing:

אֵל מֶלֶךְ O God, King Who sits on the throne of mercy; Who acts with kindness, pardons the iniquities of His people, removes [sins] one by one, increasingly grants pardon to careless sinners and forgiveness to rebels, Who deals righteously with every living being — You do not repay them in accord with their evil. Chazzan – O God, You taught us to recite the Thirteen [Attributes of Mercy], so remember for us today the covenant of these Thirteen, as You made known to the humble one in ancient times, as it is written: And HASHEM descended in a cloud and stood with him there, and He called out with the Name HASHEM.

Congregation, then chazzan:

And HASHEM passed before him [Moses] and proclaimed:

Congregation and chazzan (the words in bold type are recited aloud and in unison):

ה' ה' HASHEM, HASHEM, God, Compassionate and Gracious, Slow to anger, and Abundant in Kindness and Truth, Preserver of kindness for thousands [of generations], Forgiver of iniquity, willful sin, and error, and Who cleanses. May You forgive our iniquities and our errors and make us Your heritage. Forgive us, our Father, for we have erred; pardon us, our King, for we have willfully sinned; for You, my Lord, are good and forgiving and abundantly kind to all who call upon You.

All:

אַל תִּזְכָּר Do not recall against us the iniquities of the ancients; speedily — let Your mercy come to meet us for we have fallen very low.[1] Remember not the sins of our youth and our rebellions; may You remember for us [the deeds] worthy of Your kindness, because of Your goodness, HASHEM.[2]

זְכוֹר רַחֲמֶיךָ Remember Your mercies, O HASHEM, and Your kindnesses, for they are from the beginning of the world.[3] Remember us, HASHEM, when You show Your people favor and recall us with Your salvation.[4] Remember Your congregation that You acquired of old, that You redeemed the tribe of Your heritage, and this Mount Zion where You dwelled.[5] Remember, O HASHEM, the affection of Jerusalem, may You never forget the love of Zion.[6] You will arise and show Zion mercy, for it is the time to be gracious to her, for the appointed time will have come.[7] Remember, HASHEM, for the offspring of Edom, the day of Jerusalem — for those who said: 'Destroy! Destroy to its very foundation!'[8] Remember Abraham, Isaac, and Israel, Your servants, to whom You swore by Your Being, saying to them, 'I shall increase your offspring like the stars of the heavens; and this entire land of which I spoke I will give to your offspring and they will inherit it forever.'[9] Chazzan – Remember for Your servants, for Abraham, for Isaac, and for Jacob; ignore the stubbornness of this people, its wickedness and its sinfulness.[10]

---

(1) Psalms 79:8. (2) Cf. 25:7. (3) 25:6. (4) Cf. 106:4. (5) 74:2. (6) This is not a Scriptural verse. (7) Psalms 102:14. (8) 137:7. (9) Exodus 32:13. (10) Deuteronomy 9:27.

Chazzan, then congregation:

אֵל נָא תָשֵׁת עָלֵינוּ חַטָּאת, אֲשֶׁר נוֹאַלְנוּ וַאֲשֶׁר חָטָאנוּ.¹

Chazzan, then congregation:

חָטָאנוּ צוּרֵנוּ, סְלַח לָנוּ יוֹצְרֵנוּ.

All:

זְכֹר לָנוּ בְּרִית אָבוֹת, כַּאֲשֶׁר אָמַרְתָּ: וְזָכַרְתִּי אֶת בְּרִיתִי יַעֲקוֹב,
וְאַף אֶת בְּרִיתִי יִצְחָק, וְאַף אֶת בְּרִיתִי אַבְרָהָם אֶזְכֹּר,
וְהָאָרֶץ אֶזְכֹּר.² זְכֹר לָנוּ בְּרִית רִאשׁוֹנִים, כַּאֲשֶׁר אָמַרְתָּ: וְזָכַרְתִּי
לָהֶם בְּרִית רִאשׁוֹנִים, אֲשֶׁר הוֹצֵאתִי אֹתָם מֵאֶרֶץ מִצְרַיִם לְעֵינֵי
הַגּוֹיִם, לִהְיוֹת לָהֶם לֵאלֹהִים, אֲנִי יְהוָה.³ עֲשֵׂה עִמָּנוּ כְּמָה
שֶׁהִבְטַחְתָּנוּ: וְאַף גַּם זֹאת בִּהְיוֹתָם בְּאֶרֶץ אֹיְבֵיהֶם, לֹא מְאַסְתִּים
וְלֹא גְעַלְתִּים לְכַלּוֹתָם לְהָפֵר בְּרִיתִי אִתָּם, כִּי אֲנִי יְהוָה אֱלֹהֵיהֶם.⁴
הִמָּצֵא לָנוּ בְּבַקָּשָׁתֵנוּ, כְּמָה שֶׁכָּתוּב: וּבִקַּשְׁתֶּם מִשָּׁם אֶת יְהוָה
אֱלֹהֶיךָ וּמָצָאתָ, כִּי תִדְרְשֶׁנּוּ בְּכָל לְבָבְךָ וּבְכָל נַפְשֶׁךָ.⁵ מוֹל אֶת
לְבָבֵנוּ לְאַהֲבָה וּלְיִרְאָה אֶת שְׁמֶךָ, כְּמָה שֶׁכָּתוּב: וּמָל יְהוָה אֱלֹהֶיךָ
אֶת לְבָבְךָ וְאֶת לְבַב זַרְעֶךָ, לְאַהֲבָה אֶת יְהוָה אֱלֹהֶיךָ בְּכָל לְבָבְךָ
וּבְכָל נַפְשְׁךָ, לְמַעַן חַיֶּיךָ.⁶ זְרוֹק עָלֵינוּ מַיִם טְהוֹרִים וְטַהֲרֵנוּ, כְּמָה
שֶׁכָּתוּב: וְזָרַקְתִּי עֲלֵיכֶם מַיִם טְהוֹרִים וּטְהַרְתֶּם, מִכֹּל טֻמְאוֹתֵיכֶם
וּמִכָּל גִּלּוּלֵיכֶם אֲטַהֵר אֶתְכֶם.⁷ מְחֵה פְשָׁעֵינוּ כָּעָב וְכֶעָנָן, כְּמָה
שֶׁכָּתוּב: מָחִיתִי כָעָב פְּשָׁעֶיךָ וְכֶעָנָן חַטֹּאתֶיךָ, שׁוּבָה אֵלַי כִּי
גְאַלְתִּיךָ.⁸ מְחֵה פְשָׁעֵינוּ לְמַעֲנָךְ, כַּאֲשֶׁר אָמַרְתָּ: אָנֹכִי אָנֹכִי הוּא
מֹחֶה פְשָׁעֶיךָ לְמַעֲנִי, וְחַטֹּאתֶיךָ לֹא אֶזְכֹּר.⁹ הַלְבֵּן חֲטָאֵינוּ כַּשֶּׁלֶג
וְכַצֶּמֶר, כְּמָה שֶׁכָּתוּב: לְכוּ נָא וְנִוָּכְחָה, יֹאמַר יְהוָה, אִם יִהְיוּ
חֲטָאֵיכֶם כַּשָּׁנִים, כַּשֶּׁלֶג יַלְבִּינוּ, אִם יַאְדִּימוּ כַתּוֹלָע, כַּצֶּמֶר יִהְיוּ.¹⁰
רַחֵם עָלֵינוּ וְאַל תַּשְׁחִיתֵנוּ, כְּמָה שֶׁכָּתוּב: כִּי אֵל רַחוּם יְהוָה
אֱלֹהֶיךָ, לֹא יַרְפְּךָ וְלֹא יַשְׁחִיתֶךָ וְלֹא יִשְׁכַּח אֶת בְּרִית אֲבוֹתֶיךָ
אֲשֶׁר נִשְׁבַּע לָהֶם.¹¹ קַבֵּץ נִדָּחֵנוּ כְּמָה שֶׁכָּתוּב: אִם יִהְיֶה נִדַּחֲךָ בִּקְצֵה
הַשָּׁמָיִם, מִשָּׁם יְקַבֶּצְךָ יְהוָה אֱלֹהֶיךָ וּמִשָּׁם יִקָּחֶךָ.¹² הָשֵׁב שְׁבוּתֵנוּ
וְרַחֲמֵנוּ, כְּמָה שֶׁכָּתוּב: וְשָׁב יְהוָה אֱלֹהֶיךָ אֶת שְׁבוּתְךָ וְרִחֲמֶךָ וְשָׁב
וְקִבֶּצְךָ מִכָּל הָעַמִּים אֲשֶׁר הֱפִיצְךָ יְהוָה אֱלֹהֶיךָ שָׁמָּה.¹³ ❖ תְּבִיאֵנוּ
אֶל הַר קָדְשֶׁךָ, וְשַׂמְּחֵנוּ בְּבֵית תְּפִלָּתֶךָ, כְּמָה שֶׁכָּתוּב: וַהֲבִיאוֹתִים
אֶל הַר קָדְשִׁי, וְשִׂמַּחְתִּים בְּבֵית תְּפִלָּתִי, עוֹלֹתֵיהֶם וְזִבְחֵיהֶם לְרָצוֹן
עַל מִזְבְּחִי, כִּי בֵיתִי בֵּית תְּפִלָּה יִקָּרֵא לְכָל הָעַמִּים.¹⁴

THE ARK IS OPENED.

Chazzan, then congregation:
Please, do not reckon for us a sin,
what we have done foolishly and what we have sinned.[1]

Chazzan, then congregation:
We have erred, our Rock! Forgive us, our Molder!

All:

זְכוֹר Remember for us the covenant of the Patriarchs, as You said: 'And
I will remember My covenant with Jacob, and also My covenant with
Isaac, and also My covenant with Abraham will I remember; and the Land
will I remember.'[2] Remember for us the covenant of the ancestors, as You
said: 'And I will remember for them the covenant of the ancestors whom I
removed from the land of Egypt in the very sight of the nations, to be a God
to them; I am HASHEM.'[3] Do with us as You promised us: 'And despite all that,
when they will be in the land of their enemies, I will not have despised them
nor abhorred them to destroy them, to annul My covenant with them, for I
am HASHEM their God.'[4] Be accessible to us in our quest, as it is written: From
there you will seek HASHEM, your God, and you will find, when you search
for Him with all your heart and with all your soul.[5] Expose our hearts to love
Your Name, as it is written: HASHEM, your God, will expose your heart and
the heart of your offspring, to love HASHEM, your God, with all your heart and
with all your soul, that you may live.[6] Pour pure water upon us and purify
us, as it is written: I shall pour pure water upon you and purify you, of all
your contaminations and of all your abominations I will purify you.[7] Wipe
away our willful sins like a cloud and like a mist, as it is written: I have wiped
away your willful sins like a cloud and your errors like a mist — repent to Me,
for I have redeemed you![8] Wipe away our willful sins for Your sake, as You
said: 'I, only I, am the One Who wipes away your willful sins for My sake,
and I shall not recall your errors.'[9] Whiten our errors like snow and like [pure
white] wool, as it is written: 'Come now, let us reason together,' says HASHEM,
'though your errors will be like scarlet, they will become white as snow;
though they will be red as crimson, they will become like [white] wool.'[10] Have
mercy on us and do not destroy us, as it is written: For a merciful God is
HASHEM, your God; He will not surrender you nor destroy you, and He will
not forget the covenant with your forefathers, which He swore to them.[11]
Gather in our dispersed ones, as it is written: If your dispersed were to be at
the ends of heaven, from there HASHEM, your God, will gather you in and from
there He will take you.[12] Bring back our captivity and have mercy on us, as
it is written: HASHEM, your God, will bring back your captivity and have
mercy on you, and He will again gather you in from all the peoples where
HASHEM, your God, has scattered you.[13] Chazzan — Bring us to Your holy
mountain and gladden us in Your house of prayer, as it is written: And I will
bring them to My holy mountain, and I will gladden them in My house of
prayer, their elevation-offerings and their feast offering will find favor on My
Altar, for My House will be called a house of prayer, for all peoples.[14]

THE ARK IS OPENED.

---

(1) *Numbers* 12:11. (2) *Leviticus* 26:42. (3) 26:45. (4) 26:44. (5) *Deuteronomy* 4:29.
(6) 30:6. (7) *Ezekiel* 36:25. (8) *Isaiah* 44:22. (9) 43:25. (10) 1:18.
(11) *Deuteronomy* 4:31. (12) 30:4. (13) 30:3. (14) *Isaiah* 56:7.

The first four verses of the following prayer are recited responsively; *chazzan,* then congregation:

שְׁמַע קוֹלֵנוּ יהוה אֱלֹהֵינוּ, חוּס וְרַחֵם עָלֵינוּ,
וְקַבֵּל בְּרַחֲמִים וּבְרָצוֹן אֶת תְּפִלָּתֵנוּ.¹

הֲשִׁיבֵנוּ יהוה אֵלֶיךָ וְנָשׁוּבָה, חַדֵּשׁ יָמֵינוּ כְּקֶדֶם.²

אַל תַּשְׁלִיכֵנוּ מִלְּפָנֶיךָ, וְרוּחַ קָדְשְׁךָ אַל תִּקַּח מִמֶּנּוּ.³

אַל תַּשְׁלִיכֵנוּ לְעֵת זִקְנָה, כִּכְלוֹת כֹּחֵנוּ אַל תַּעַזְבֵנוּ.⁴

אַל תַּעַזְבֵנוּ יהוה, אֱלֹהֵינוּ אַל תִּרְחַק מִמֶּנּוּ.⁵

עֲשֵׂה עִמָּנוּ אוֹת לְטוֹבָה, וְיִרְאוּ שׂוֹנְאֵינוּ וְיֵבֹשׁוּ,
כִּי אַתָּה יהוה עֲזַרְתָּנוּ וְנִחַמְתָּנוּ.⁶

אֲמָרֵינוּ הַאֲזִינָה יהוה, בִּינָה הֲגִיגֵנוּ.⁷

יִהְיוּ לְרָצוֹן אִמְרֵי פִינוּ וְהֶגְיוֹן לִבֵּנוּ לְפָנֶיךָ, יהוה צוּרֵנוּ וְגוֹאֲלֵנוּ.⁸

כִּי לְךָ יהוה הוֹחָלְנוּ, אַתָּה תַעֲנֶה אֲדֹנָי אֱלֹהֵינוּ.⁹

THE ARK IS CLOSED.

וידוי

During the recitation of the וידוי stand with head and body slightly bowed,
in submissive contrition.

אֱלֹהֵינוּ וֵאלֹהֵי אֲבוֹתֵינוּ, תָּבֹא לְפָנֶיךָ תְּפִלָּתֵנוּ,¹⁰ וְאַל תִּתְעַלַּם
מִתְּחִנָּתֵנוּ,¹¹ שֶׁאֵין אָנוּ עַזֵּי פָנִים וּקְשֵׁי עֹרֶף, לוֹמַר
לְפָנֶיךָ יהוה אֱלֹהֵינוּ וֵאלֹהֵי אֲבוֹתֵינוּ, צַדִּיקִים אֲנַחְנוּ וְלֹא חָטָאנוּ,
אֲבָל אֲנַחְנוּ וַאֲבוֹתֵינוּ חָטָאנוּ.¹²

Strike the left side of the chest with the right fist
while reciting each of the sins in the following confession litany.

אָשַׁמְנוּ, בָּגַדְנוּ, גָּזַלְנוּ, דִּבַּרְנוּ דֹפִי. הֶעֱוִינוּ, וְהִרְשַׁעְנוּ, זַדְנוּ,
חָמַסְנוּ, טָפַלְנוּ שֶׁקֶר. יָעַצְנוּ רָע, כִּזַּבְנוּ, לַצְנוּ, מָרַדְנוּ,
נִאַצְנוּ, סָרַרְנוּ, עָוִינוּ, פָּשַׁעְנוּ, צָרַרְנוּ, קִשִּׁינוּ עֹרֶף, רָשַׁעְנוּ, שִׁחַתְנוּ,
תִּעַבְנוּ, תָּעִינוּ, תִּעְתָּעְנוּ.

סַרְנוּ מִמִּצְוֹתֶיךָ וּמִמִּשְׁפָּטֶיךָ הַטּוֹבִים וְלֹא שָׁוָה לָנוּ.¹³ וְאַתָּה צַדִּיק
עַל כָּל הַבָּא עָלֵינוּ, כִּי אֱמֶת עָשִׂיתָ וַאֲנַחְנוּ הִרְשָׁעְנוּ.¹⁴

אָשַׁמְנוּ מִכָּל עָם, בֹּשְׁנוּ מִכָּל דּוֹר, גָּלָה מִמֶּנּוּ מָשׂוֹשׂ, דָּוָה לִבֵּנוּ
בַּחֲטָאֵינוּ, הֻחְבַּל אִוּוּיֵנוּ, וְנִפְרַע פְּאֵרֵנוּ, זְבוּל בֵּית מִקְדָּשֵׁנוּ חָרַב
בַּעֲוֹנֵינוּ, טִירָתֵנוּ הָיְתָה לְשַׁמָּה, יֹפִי אַדְמָתֵנוּ לְזָרִים, כֹּחֵנוּ לְנָכְרִים.
וַעֲדַיִן לֹא שַׁבְנוּ מִטָּעוּתֵנוּ וְהֵיךְ נָעִיז פָּנֵינוּ וְנַקְשֶׁה עָרְפֵּנוּ, לוֹמַר
לְפָנֶיךָ יהוה אֱלֹהֵינוּ וֵאלֹהֵי אֲבוֹתֵינוּ, צַדִּיקִים אֲנַחְנוּ וְלֹא חָטָאנוּ,
אֲבָל אֲנַחְנוּ וַאֲבוֹתֵינוּ חָטָאנוּ.

The first four verses of the following prayer are recited responsively; *chazzan,* then congregation:

שְׁמַע קוֹלֵנוּ *Hear our voice, HASHEM, our God, pity and be compassionate to us, and accept — with compassion and favor — our prayer.*[1]

Bring us back to You, HASHEM, and we shall return, renew our days as of old.[2]

Do not cast us away from Yourself,
and do not remove Your holy spirit from us.[3]

Do not cast us away in old age,
when our strength gives out do not forsake us.[4]

Do not forsake us, HASHEM, our God, be not distant from us.[5]

Display for us a sign for good, so that our enemies may see it
and be ashamed, for You, HASHEM, will have helped and consoled us.[6]

To our sayings give ear, HASHEM, perceive our thoughts.[7]

May the expressions of our mouth and the thoughts of our heart
find favor before You, HASHEM, our Rock and our Redeemer.[8]

Because for You, HASHEM, we waited, You will answer, my Lord, our God.[9]

THE ARK IS CLOSED.

During the recitation of the וִדּוּי, *Confession,* stand with head and body slightly bowed, in submissive contrition.

אֱלֹהֵינוּ *Our God and the God of our forefathers, may our prayer come before You.*[10] *Do not ignore our supplication,*[11] *for we are not so brazen and obstinate as to say before You, HASHEM, our God and the God of our forefathers, that we are righteous and have not sinned, for in truth, we and our forefathers have sinned.*[12]

Strike the left side of the chest with the right fist while reciting each of the sins in the following confession litany.

אָשַׁמְנוּ *We have become guilty;* [ב] *we have betrayed;* [ג] *we have robbed;* [ד] *we have spoken slander;* [ה] *we have caused perversion;* [ו] *we have caused wickedness;* [ז] *we have sinned willfully;* [ח] *we have extorted;* [ט] *we have accused falsely;* [י] *we have given evil counsel;* [כ] *we have been deceitful;* [ל] *we have scorned;* [מ] *we have rebelled;* [נ] *we have provoked;* [ס] *we have turned away;* [ע] *we have been perverse;* [פ] *we have acted wantonly;* [צ] *we have persecuted;* [ק] *we have been obstinate;* [ר] *we have been wicked;* [ש] *we have corrupted;* [ת] *we have been abominable; we have strayed; You have let us go astray.*

סַרְנוּ *We have turned away from Your commandments and from Your good laws but to no avail.*[13] *Yet You are righteous in all that has come upon us, for You have acted truthfully while we have caused wickedness.*[14]

[א] *We have become the guiltiest of people.* [ב] *We have become the most degraded of all generations.* [ג] *Joy has departed from us.* [ד] *Our heart has been saddened by our sins.* [ה] *Our desirous treasure has been ruined,* [ו] *and our splendor dashed,* [ז] *for our Holy Temple edifice* [ח] *has been destroyed for our iniquities.* [ט] *Our Palace has become desolate.* [י] *[Jerusalem,] the beauty of our Land is given over to aliens,* [כ] *our power to strangers.*

But still we have not returned from our waywardness. So how can we be so brazen and obstinate as to say before You, HASHEM, our God and the God of our forefathers, that we are righteous and have not sinned, for in truth, both we and our fathers have sinned.

---

(1) Weekday *Shemoneh Esrei.* (2) *Lamentations* 5:21. (3) Cf. *Psalms* 51:13. (4) Cf. 71:9. (5) Cf. 38:22. (6) Cf. 86:17. (7) Cf. 5:2. (8) Cf. 19:15. (9) Cf. 38:16. (10) Cf. 88:3. (11) Cf. 55:2. (12) Cf. 106:6. (13) Cf. *Job* 33:27. (14) *Nehemiah* 9:33.

Strike the left side of the chest with the right fist while reciting
each of the sins in the following confession litany.

אָשַׁמְנוּ, בָּגַדְנוּ, גָּזַלְנוּ, דִּבַּרְנוּ דְפִי. הֶעֱוִינוּ, וְהִרְשַׁעְנוּ, זַדְנוּ, חָמַסְנוּ, טָפַלְנוּ שֶׁקֶר. יָעַצְנוּ רָע, כִּזַּבְנוּ, לַצְנוּ, מָרַדְנוּ, נִאַצְנוּ, סָרַרְנוּ, עָוִינוּ, פָּשַׁעְנוּ, צָרַרְנוּ, קִשִּׁינוּ עֹרֶף. רָשַׁעְנוּ, שִׁחַתְנוּ, תִּעַבְנוּ, תָּעִינוּ, תִּעְתָּעְנוּ.

סַרְנוּ מִמִּצְוֹתֶיךָ וּמִמִּשְׁפָּטֶיךָ הַטּוֹבִים וְלֹא שָׁוָה לָנוּ. וְאַתָּה צַדִּיק עַל כָּל הַבָּא עָלֵינוּ, כִּי אֱמֶת עָשִׂיתָ וַאֲנַחְנוּ הִרְשָׁעְנוּ.

לְעֵינֵינוּ עָשְׁקוּ עֲמָלֵנוּ, מְמֻשָּׁךְ וּמְמוֹרָט מִמֶּנּוּ, נָתְנוּ עֻלָּם עָלֵינוּ, סָבַלְנוּ עַל שִׁכְמֵנוּ, עֲבָדִים מָשְׁלוּ בָנוּ, פֹּרֵק אֵין מִיָּדָם, צָרוֹת רַבּוֹת סְבָבוּנוּ, קְרָאנוּךָ יהוה אֱלֹהֵינוּ, רָחַקְתָּ מִמֶּנּוּ בַּעֲוֹנֵינוּ, שַׁבְנוּ מֵאַחֲרֶיךָ, תָּעִינוּ וְאָבָדְנוּ.

וַעֲדַיִן לֹא שַׁבְנוּ מִטָּעוּתֵנוּ וְהֵיךְ נָעִיז פָּנֵינוּ וְנַקְשֶׁה עָרְפֵּנוּ, לוֹמַר לְפָנֶיךָ יהוה אֱלֹהֵינוּ וֵאלֹהֵי אֲבוֹתֵינוּ, צַדִּיקִים אֲנַחְנוּ וְלֹא חָטָאנוּ, אֲבָל אֲנַחְנוּ וַאֲבוֹתֵינוּ חָטָאנוּ.

Strike the left side of the chest with the right fist while reciting
each of the sins in the following confession litany.

אָשַׁמְנוּ, בָּגַדְנוּ, גָּזַלְנוּ, דִּבַּרְנוּ דְפִי. הֶעֱוִינוּ, וְהִרְשַׁעְנוּ, זַדְנוּ, חָמַסְנוּ, טָפַלְנוּ שֶׁקֶר. יָעַצְנוּ רָע, כִּזַּבְנוּ, לַצְנוּ, מָרַדְנוּ, נִאַצְנוּ, סָרַרְנוּ, עָוִינוּ, פָּשַׁעְנוּ, צָרַרְנוּ, קִשִּׁינוּ עֹרֶף. רָשַׁעְנוּ, שִׁחַתְנוּ, תִּעַבְנוּ, תָּעִינוּ, תִּעְתָּעְנוּ.

סַרְנוּ מִמִּצְוֹתֶיךָ וּמִמִּשְׁפָּטֶיךָ הַטּוֹבִים וְלֹא שָׁוָה לָנוּ. וְאַתָּה צַדִּיק עַל כָּל הַבָּא עָלֵינוּ, כִּי אֱמֶת עָשִׂיתָ וַאֲנַחְנוּ הִרְשָׁעְנוּ.

הִרְשַׁעְנוּ וּפָשַׁעְנוּ, לָכֵן לֹא נוֹשָׁעְנוּ. וְתֵן בְּלִבֵּנוּ לַעֲזוֹב דֶּרֶךְ רֶשַׁע, וְחִישׁ לָנוּ יֶשַׁע, כַּכָּתוּב עַל יַד נְבִיאֶךָ: יַעֲזֹב רָשָׁע דַּרְכּוֹ, וְאִישׁ אָוֶן מַחְשְׁבֹתָיו, וְיָשֹׁב אֶל יהוה וִירַחֲמֵהוּ, וְאֶל אֱלֹהֵינוּ כִּי יַרְבֶּה לִסְלוֹחַ.[1]

מְשִׁיחַ צִדְקֵךְ אָמַר לְפָנֶיךָ: שְׁגִיאוֹת מִי יָבִין מִנִּסְתָּרוֹת נַקֵּנִי.[2] נַקֵּנוּ יהוה אֱלֹהֵינוּ מִכָּל פְּשָׁעֵינוּ, וְטַהֲרֵנוּ מִכָּל

---

(1) *Isaiah* 55:7. (2) *Psalms* 19:13.

Strike the left side of the chest with the right fist while reciting
each of the sins in the following confession litany:

אָשַׁמְנוּ *We have become guilty;* [ב] *we have betrayed;* [ג] *we have robbed;* [ד] *we have spoken slander;* [ה] *we have caused perversion;* [ו] *we have caused wickedness;* [ז] *we have sinned willfully;* [ח] *we have extorted;* [ט] *we have accused falsely;* [י] *we have given evil counsel;* [כ] *we have been deceitful;* [ל] *we have scorned;* [מ] *we have rebelled;* [נ] *we have provoked;* [ס] *we have turned away;* [ע] *we have been perverse;* [פ] *we have acted wantonly;* [צ] *we have persecuted;* [ק] *we have been obstinate;* [ר] *we have been wicked;* [ש] *we have corrupted;* [ת] *we have been abominable; we have strayed; You have let us go astray.*

סַרְנוּ *We have turned away from Your commandments and from Your good laws but to no avail. Yet You are righteous in all that has come upon us, for You have acted truthfully while we have caused wickedness.*

[ל] *[The benefit of] our labor has been stolen,* [מ] *pulled away and cut off from us.* [נ] *They have placed their yoke upon us,* [ס] *our burdens upon our shoulders.* [ע] *Slaves have ruled over us,* [פ] *there is no redemption from their hand.* [צ] *Abundant troubles have surrounded us,* [ק] *we called upon You, HASHEM, our God,* [ר] *but You have distanced us for our iniquities.* [ש] *We have turned away from following after You;* [ת] *we have strayed; we have become lost.*

But still we have not returned from our waywardness. So how can we be so brazen and obstinate as to say before You, HASHEM, our God and the God of our forefathers, that we are righteous and have not sinned, for in truth, both we and our fathers have sinned.

Strike the left side of the chest with the right fist while reciting
each of the sins in the following confession litany:

אָשַׁמְנוּ *We have become guilty;* [ב] *we have betrayed;* [ג] *we have robbed;* [ד] *we have spoken slander;* [ה] *we have caused perversion;* [ו] *we have caused wickedness;* [ז] *we have sinned willfully;* [ח] *we have extorted;* [ט] *we have accused falsely;* [י] *we have given evil counsel;* [כ] *we have been deceitful;* [ל] *we have scorned;* [מ] *we have rebelled;* [נ] *we have provoked;* [ס] *we have turned away;* [ע] *we have been perverse;* [פ] *we have acted wantonly;* [צ] *we have persecuted;* [ק] *we have been obstinate;* [ר] *we have been wicked;* [ש] *we have corrupted;* [ת] *we have been abominable; we have strayed; You have let us go astray.*

סַרְנוּ *We have turned away from Your commandments and from Your good laws but to no avail. Yet You are righteous in all that has come upon us, for You have acted truthfully while we have caused wickedness.*

הִרְשַׁעְנוּ *We have acted wickedly and have sinned willfully, therefore we have not been saved. Inspire our heart to abandon the path of evil and hasten salvation for us, as it is written by Your prophet: May the wicked one abandon his way and the vicious man his thoughts; may he return to HASHEM and He will show him mercy, and to our God, for He is abundantly forgiving.*[1]

מְשִׁיחַ צִדְקֶךָ *Your righteous anointed [David] said before You: 'Who can discern mistakes? From unperceived faults cleanse me.'*[2]
Cleanse us, HASHEM, our God, of all our willful sins and purify us, of all our

טֻמְאוֹתֵינוּ, וּזְרוֹק עָלֵינוּ מַיִם טְהוֹרִים וְטַהֲרֵנוּ, כַּכָּתוּב עַל יַד
נְבִיאֶךָ: וְזָרַקְתִּי עֲלֵיכֶם מַיִם טְהוֹרִים וּטְהַרְתֶּם, מִכֹּל טֻמְאוֹתֵיכֶם
וּמִכָּל גִּלּוּלֵיכֶם אֲטַהֵר אֶתְכֶם.[1]

מִיכָה עַבְדְּךָ אָמַר לְפָנֶיךָ: מִי אֵל כָּמוֹךָ נֹשֵׂא עָוֹן וְעֹבֵר עַל
פֶּשַׁע לִשְׁאֵרִית נַחֲלָתוֹ, לֹא הֶחֱזִיק לָעַד אַפּוֹ, כִּי
חָפֵץ חֶסֶד הוּא, יָשׁוּב יְרַחֲמֵנוּ, יִכְבֹּשׁ עֲוֹנוֹתֵינוּ, וְתַשְׁלִיךְ בִּמְצֻלוֹת
יָם כָּל חַטֹּאתָם.[2] (וְכָל חַטֹּאת בֵּית יִשְׂרָאֵל תַּשְׁלִיךְ בִּמְקוֹם
אֲשֶׁר לֹא יִזָּכְרוּ, וְלֹא יִפָּקְדוּ, וְלֹא יַעֲלוּ עַל לֵב לְעוֹלָם.) תִּתֵּן אֱמֶת
לְיַעֲקֹב חֶסֶד לְאַבְרָהָם אֲשֶׁר נִשְׁבַּעְתָּ לַאֲבוֹתֵינוּ מִימֵי קֶדֶם.[3]

דָּנִיֵּאל אִישׁ חֲמֻדוֹת שִׁוַּע לְפָנֶיךָ: הַטֵּה אֱלֹהַי אָזְנְךָ וּשֲׁמָע,
פְּקַח עֵינֶיךָ וּרְאֵה שֹׁמְמֹתֵינוּ וְהָעִיר אֲשֶׁר נִקְרָא שִׁמְךָ
עָלֶיהָ, כִּי לֹא עַל צִדְקֹתֵינוּ אֲנַחְנוּ מַפִּילִים תַּחֲנוּנֵינוּ לְפָנֶיךָ, כִּי עַל
רַחֲמֶיךָ הָרַבִּים. אֲדֹנָי שְׁמָעָה, אֲדֹנָי סְלָחָה, אֲדֹנָי הַקְשִׁיבָה, וַעֲשֵׂה
אַל תְּאַחַר, לְמַעַנְךָ אֱלֹהַי, כִּי שִׁמְךָ נִקְרָא עַל עִירְךָ וְעַל עַמֶּךָ.[4]

עֶזְרָא הַסּוֹפֵר אָמַר לְפָנֶיךָ: אֱלֹהַי, בֹּשְׁתִּי וְנִכְלַמְתִּי לְהָרִים,
אֱלֹהַי, פָּנַי אֵלֶיךָ, כִּי עֲוֹנֹתֵינוּ רָבוּ לְמַעְלָה
רֹאשׁ, וְאַשְׁמָתֵנוּ גָדְלָה עַד לַשָּׁמָיִם.[5] וְאַתָּה[6] אֱלוֹהַּ סְלִיחוֹת, חַנּוּן
וְרַחוּם, אֶרֶךְ אַפַּיִם וְרַב חֶסֶד, וְלֹא עֲזַבְתָּנוּ.[7]

אַל תַּעַזְבֵנוּ אָבִינוּ וְאַל תִּטְּשֵׁנוּ בּוֹרְאֵנוּ, וְאַל תַּזְנִיחֵנוּ יוֹצְרֵנוּ,
וְאַל תַּעַשׂ עִמָּנוּ כָּלָה כְּחַטֹּאתֵינוּ. וְקַיֶּם לָנוּ יהוה
אֱלֹהֵינוּ, אֶת הַדָּבָר שֶׁהִבְטַחְתָּנוּ בְּקַבָּלָה עַל יְדֵי יִרְמְיָהוּ חוֹזָךְ,
כָּאָמוּר: בַּיָּמִים הָהֵם וּבָעֵת הַהִיא, נְאֻם יהוה, יְבֻקַּשׁ אֶת עֲוֹן
יִשְׂרָאֵל וְאֵינֶנּוּ וְאֶת חַטֹּאת יְהוּדָה וְלֹא תִמָּצֶאנָה, כִּי אֶסְלַח
לַאֲשֶׁר אַשְׁאִיר.[8] עַמְּךָ וְנַחֲלָתְךָ רְעֵבֵי טוּבֶךָ, צְמֵאֵי חַסְדֶּךָ, תְּאֵבֵי
יִשְׁעֶךָ, יַכִּירוּ וְיֵדְעוּ כִּי לַיהוה אֱלֹהֵינוּ הָרַחֲמִים וְהַסְּלִיחוֹת.

אֵל רַחוּם שְׁמֶךָ, אֵל חַנּוּן שְׁמֶךָ, בָּנוּ נִקְרָא שְׁמֶךָ. יהוה עֲשֵׂה
לְמַעַן שְׁמֶךָ. עֲשֵׂה לְמַעַן אֲמִתֶּךָ, עֲשֵׂה לְמַעַן
בְּרִיתֶךָ, עֲשֵׂה לְמַעַן גָּדְלְךָ וְתִפְאַרְתֶּךָ, עֲשֵׂה לְמַעַן דָּתֶךָ, עֲשֵׂה
לְמַעַן הוֹדֶךָ, עֲשֵׂה לְמַעַן וִעוּדֶךָ, עֲשֵׂה לְמַעַן זִכְרֶךָ, עֲשֵׂה לְמַעַן
חַסְדֶּךָ, עֲשֵׂה לְמַעַן טוּבֶךָ, עֲשֵׂה לְמַעַן יִחוּדֶךָ, עֲשֵׂה לְמַעַן
כְּבוֹדֶךָ, עֲשֵׂה לְמַעַן לִמּוּדֶךָ, עֲשֵׂה לְמַעַן מַלְכוּתֶךָ, עֲשֵׂה לְמַעַן

contaminations. *Sprinkle upon us pure water and purify us, as it is written by Your prophet: I shall sprinkle pure water upon you and purify you, of all your contaminations and of all your abominations I will purify you.'[1]*

מִיכָה עַבְדְּךָ *Micah, Your servant, said before You: 'Who, O God, is like You, Who pardons iniquity and overlooks transgression for the remnant of His heritage? Who has not retained His wrath eternally, for He desires kindness! He will again be merciful to us; He will suppress our iniquities and cast into the depths of the sea all their sins.[2] (And all the sins of Your nation the Family of Israel, may You cast away to a place where they will neither be remembered, considered, nor brought to mind — ever.) Grant truth to Jacob, kindness to Abraham, as You swore to our forefathers from ancient times.'[3]*

דָּנִיֵּאל *Daniel, the greatly beloved man, cried out before You: 'Incline, my God, Your ear, and listen, open Your eyes and see our desolation and that of the city upon which Your Name is proclaimed, for not because of our righteousness do we cast down our supplications before You, rather because of Your abundant compassion. O my Lord, heed; O my Lord, forgive; O my Lord, be attentive and act, do not delay; for Your sake, my God, for Your Name is proclaimed upon Your city and Your people.'[4]*

עֶזְרָא הַסּוֹפֵר *Ezra the Scribe said before You: 'My God, I am embarrassed and ashamed to lift my face to You, my God — for our iniquities have multiplied above our heads, and our sins extend unto heaven.[5] You are[6] the God of forgiveness, compassionate and merciful, slow to anger, and abundant in kindness; and You have not forsaken us.'[7]*

אַל תַּעַזְבֵנוּ *Do not forsake us, our Father; do not cast us off, our Creator; do not abandon us, our Molder; and do not bring about our destruction, as our sins merit. Affirm for us, HASHEM, our God, the promise You made in the tradition through Jeremiah, Your seer, as it is said: 'In those days and at that time' — the words of HASHEM — 'the iniquity of Israel will be sought but there will be none, and the errors of Judah, but they will not be found, for I will have forgiven those whom I leave as a remnant.'[8]*

Your people and Your heritage, who hunger for Your goodness, who thirst for Your kindness, who long for Your salvation — may they recognize and know that to HASHEM, our God, belong mercy and forgiveness.

אֵל רַחוּם *'Merciful God' is Your Name, 'Gracious God' is Your Name, Your Name is called upon us — O HASHEM, act for Your Name's sake. Act for the sake of [א] Your truth; act for the sake of [ב] Your covenant; act for the sake of [ג] Your greatness and Your splendor; act for the sake of [ד] Your law; act for the sake of [ה] Your glory; act for the sake of [ו] Your Meeting House; act for the sake of [ז] Your remembrance; act for the sake of [ח] Your kindness; act for the sake of [ט] Your goodness; act for the sake of [י] Your Oneness; act for the sake of [כ] Your honor; act for the sake of [ל] Your teaching; act for the sake of [מ] Your kingship; act for the sake of*

---

(1) *Ezekiel* 36:25. (2) *Micah* 7:18-19. (3) 7:20. (4) *Daniel* 9:18-19. (5) *Ezra* 9:6. (6) Some editions of *Selichos* insert the word אֱלֹהֵינוּ, *our God*, at this point. (7) Cf. *Nehemiah* 9:17. (8) *Jeremiah* 50:20.

נִצְחֶךָ, עֲשֵׂה לְמַעַן סוֹדֶךָ, עֲשֵׂה לְמַעַן עֻזֶּךָ, עֲשֵׂה לְמַעַן פְּאֵרֶךָ, עֲשֵׂה לְמַעַן צִדְקָתֶךָ, עֲשֵׂה לְמַעַן קְדֻשָּׁתֶךָ, עֲשֵׂה לְמַעַן רַחֲמֶיךָ הָרַבִּים, עֲשֵׂה לְמַעַן שְׁכִינָתֶךָ, עֲשֵׂה לְמַעַן תְּהִלָּתֶךָ, עֲשֵׂה לְמַעַן אוֹהֲבֶיךָ שׁוֹכְנֵי עָפָר, עֲשֵׂה לְמַעַן אַבְרָהָם יִצְחָק וְיַעֲקֹב, עֲשֵׂה לְמַעַן מֹשֶׁה וְאַהֲרֹן, עֲשֵׂה לְמַעַן דָּוִד וּשְׁלֹמֹה, עֲשֵׂה לְמַעַן יְרוּשָׁלַיִם עִיר קָדְשֶׁךָ, עֲשֵׂה לְמַעַן צִיּוֹן מִשְׁכַּן כְּבוֹדֶךָ, עֲשֵׂה לְמַעַן שִׁמְמוֹת הֵיכָלֶךָ, עֲשֵׂה לְמַעַן הֲרִיסוּת מִזְבְּחֶךָ, עֲשֵׂה לְמַעַן הֲרוּגִים עַל שֵׁם קָדְשֶׁךָ, עֲשֵׂה לְמַעַן טְבוּחִים עַל יִחוּדֶךָ, עֲשֵׂה לְמַעַן בָּאֵי בָאֵשׁ וּבַמַּיִם עַל קִדּוּשׁ שְׁמֶךָ, עֲשֵׂה לְמַעַן יוֹנְקֵי שָׁדַיִם שֶׁלֹּא חָטְאוּ, עֲשֵׂה לְמַעַן גְּמוּלֵי חָלָב שֶׁלֹּא פָשָׁעוּ, עֲשֵׂה לְמַעַן תִּינוֹקוֹת שֶׁל בֵּית רַבָּן, עֲשֵׂה לְמַעַנְךָ אִם לֹא לְמַעֲנֵנוּ, עֲשֵׂה לְמַעַנְךָ וְהוֹשִׁיעֵנוּ.

עֲנֵנוּ יְהוָה עֲנֵנוּ, עֲנֵנוּ אֱלֹהֵינוּ עֲנֵנוּ, עֲנֵנוּ אָבִינוּ עֲנֵנוּ, עֲנֵנוּ בּוֹרְאֵנוּ עֲנֵנוּ, עֲנֵנוּ גוֹאֲלֵנוּ עֲנֵנוּ, עֲנֵנוּ דוֹרְשֵׁנוּ עֲנֵנוּ, עֲנֵנוּ הָאֵל הַנֶּאֱמָן עֲנֵנוּ, עֲנֵנוּ וָתִיק וְחָסִיד עֲנֵנוּ, עֲנֵנוּ זַךְ וְיָשָׁר עֲנֵנוּ, עֲנֵנוּ חַי וְקַיָּם עֲנֵנוּ, עֲנֵנוּ טוֹב וּמֵטִיב עֲנֵנוּ, עֲנֵנוּ יוֹדֵעַ יֵצֶר עֲנֵנוּ, עֲנֵנוּ כּוֹבֵשׁ כְּעָסִים עֲנֵנוּ, עֲנֵנוּ לוֹבֵשׁ צְדָקוֹת עֲנֵנוּ, עֲנֵנוּ מֶלֶךְ מַלְכֵי הַמְּלָכִים עֲנֵנוּ, עֲנֵנוּ נוֹרָא וְנִשְׂגָּב עֲנֵנוּ, עֲנֵנוּ סוֹלֵחַ וּמוֹחֵל עֲנֵנוּ, עֲנֵנוּ עוֹנֶה בְּעֵת צָרָה עֲנֵנוּ, עֲנֵנוּ פּוֹדֶה וּמַצִּיל עֲנֵנוּ, עֲנֵנוּ צַדִּיק וְיָשָׁר עֲנֵנוּ, עֲנֵנוּ קָרוֹב לְקוֹרְאָיו עֲנֵנוּ, עֲנֵנוּ רַחוּם וְחַנּוּן עֲנֵנוּ, עֲנֵנוּ שׁוֹמֵעַ אֶל אֶבְיוֹנִים עֲנֵנוּ, עֲנֵנוּ תּוֹמֵךְ תְּמִימִים עֲנֵנוּ, עֲנֵנוּ אֱלֹהֵי אֲבוֹתֵינוּ עֲנֵנוּ, עֲנֵנוּ אֱלֹהֵי אַבְרָהָם עֲנֵנוּ, עֲנֵנוּ פַּחַד יִצְחָק עֲנֵנוּ, עֲנֵנוּ אֲבִיר יַעֲקֹב עֲנֵנוּ, עֲנֵנוּ עֶזְרַת הַשְּׁבָטִים עֲנֵנוּ, עֲנֵנוּ מִשְׂגָּב אִמָּהוֹת עֲנֵנוּ, עֲנֵנוּ קָשֶׁה לִכְעוֹס עֲנֵנוּ, עֲנֵנוּ רַךְ לִרְצוֹת עֲנֵנוּ, עֲנֵנוּ עוֹנֶה בְּעֵת רָצוֹן[1] עֲנֵנוּ, עֲנֵנוּ אֲבִי יְתוֹמִים עֲנֵנוּ, עֲנֵנוּ דַּיַּן אַלְמָנוֹת עֲנֵנוּ.

מִי שֶׁעָנָה לְאַבְרָהָם אָבִינוּ בְּהַר הַמּוֹרִיָּה,	הוּא יַעֲנֵנוּ.
מִי שֶׁעָנָה לְיִצְחָק בְּנוֹ כְּשֶׁנֶּעֱקַד עַל גַּבֵּי הַמִּזְבֵּחַ,	הוּא יַעֲנֵנוּ.
מִי שֶׁעָנָה לְיַעֲקֹב בְּבֵית אֵל,	הוּא יַעֲנֵנוּ.
מִי שֶׁעָנָה לְיוֹסֵף בְּבֵית הָאֲסוּרִים,	הוּא יַעֲנֵנוּ.
מִי שֶׁעָנָה לַאֲבוֹתֵינוּ עַל יַם סוּף,	הוּא יַעֲנֵנוּ.
מִי שֶׁעָנָה לְמֹשֶׁה בְּחוֹרֵב,	הוּא יַעֲנֵנוּ.
מִי שֶׁעָנָה לְאַהֲרֹן בַּמַּחְתָּה,	הוּא יַעֲנֵנוּ.

[נ] Your eternality; act for the sake of **[ס]** Your counsel; act for the sake of **[ע]** Your power; act for the sake of **[פ]** Your beauty; act for the sake of **[צ]** Your righteousness; act for the sake of **[ק]** Your sanctity; act for the sake of **[ר]** Your abundant mercy; act for the sake of **[ש]** Your Presence, act for the sake of **[ת]** Your praise; act for the sake of Your beloved ones who rest in the dust; act for the sake of Abraham, Isaac, and Jacob; act for the sake of Moses and Aaron; act for the sake of David and Solomon; act for the sake of Jerusalem, Your holy city; act for the sake of Zion, the abode of Your glory; act for the sake of the desolation of Your Temple; act for the sake of the ruin of Your Altar; act for the sake of the martyrs for Your holy Name; act for the sake of those slaughtered for Your Oneness; act for the sake of those who entered fire and water for the sanctification of Your Name; act for the nursing infants who did not err; act for the sake of the weaned babes who did not sin; act for the sake of children at the schoolroom; act for Your sake if not for ours; act for Your sake and save us.

עֲנֵנוּ Answer us, HASHEM, answer us; answer us, our God, answer us; answer us, **[א]** our Father, answer us; answer us, **[ב]** our Creator, answer us; answer us, **[ג]** our Redeemer, answer us; answer us, **[ד]** You Who searches us out, answer us; answer us, **[ה]** faithful God, answer us; answer us, **[ו]** steadfast and kind One, answer us; answer us, **[ז]** pure and upright One, answer us; answer us, **[ח]** living and enduring One, answer us; answer us, **[ט]** good and beneficent One, answer us; answer us, **[י]** You Who knows inclinations, answer us; answer us, **[כ]** You Who suppresses wrath, answer us; answer us, **[ל]** You Who dons righteousness, answer us; answer us, **[מ]** King Who reigns over kings, answer us; answer us, **[נ]** awesome and powerful One, answer us; answer us, **[ס]** You Who forgives and pardons, answer us; answer us, **[ע]** You Who answers in time of distress,[1] answer us; answer us, **[פ]** Redeemer and Rescuer, answer us; answer us, **[צ]** righteous and upright One, answer us; answer us, **[ק]** He Who is close to those who call upon Him, answer us; answer us, **[ר]** merciful and gracious One, answer us; answer us, **[ש]** You Who hears the destitute, answer us; answer us, **[ת]** You Who supports the wholesome, answer us; answer us, God of our forefathers, answer us; answer us, God of Abraham, answer us; answer us, Dread of Isaac, answer us; answer us, Mighty One of Jacob, answer us; answer us, Helper of the tribes, answer us; answer us, Stronghold of the Matriarchs, answer us; answer us, You Who are hard to anger, answer us; answer us, You Who are easy to pacify, answer us; answer us, You Who answers in a time of favor,[1] answer us; answer us, Father of orphans, answer us; answer us, Judge of widows, answer us.

מִי שֶׁעָנָה He Who answered our father Abraham on Mount Moriah,
may He answer us.

He Who answered his son Isaac when he was bound atop the altar,
may He answer us.

He Who answered Jacob in Bethel,   *may He answer us.*
He Who answered Joseph in the prison,   *may He answer us.*
He Who answered our forefathers at the Sea of Reeds,   *may He answer us.*
He Who answered Moses in Horeb,   *may He answer us.*
He Who answered Aaron when he offered the censer,   *may He answer us.*

---

(1) Some editions of *Selichos* reverse the positions of these two lines.

מִי שֶׁעָנָה לְפִינְחָס בְּקוּמוֹ מִתּוֹךְ הָעֵדָה, הוּא יַעֲנֵנוּ.

מִי שֶׁעָנָה לִיהוֹשֻׁעַ בַּגִּלְגָּל, הוּא יַעֲנֵנוּ.

מִי שֶׁעָנָה לִשְׁמוּאֵל בַּמִּצְפָּה, הוּא יַעֲנֵנוּ.

מִי שֶׁעָנָה לְדָוִד וּשְׁלֹמֹה בְנוֹ בִּירוּשָׁלָיִם, הוּא יַעֲנֵנוּ.

מִי שֶׁעָנָה לְאֵלִיָּהוּ בְּהַר הַכַּרְמֶל, הוּא יַעֲנֵנוּ.

מִי שֶׁעָנָה לֶאֱלִישָׁע בִּירִיחוֹ, הוּא יַעֲנֵנוּ.

מִי שֶׁעָנָה לְיוֹנָה בִּמְעֵי הַדָּגָה, הוּא יַעֲנֵנוּ.

מִי שֶׁעָנָה לְחִזְקִיָּהוּ מֶלֶךְ יְהוּדָה בְּחָלְיוֹ, הוּא יַעֲנֵנוּ.

מִי שֶׁעָנָה לַחֲנַנְיָה מִישָׁאֵל וַעֲזַרְיָה בְּתוֹךְ כִּבְשַׁן הָאֵשׁ, הוּא יַעֲנֵנוּ.

מִי שֶׁעָנָה לְדָנִיֵּאל בְּגוֹב הָאֲרָיוֹת, הוּא יַעֲנֵנוּ.

מִי שֶׁעָנָה לְמָרְדְּכַי וְאֶסְתֵּר בְּשׁוּשַׁן הַבִּירָה, הוּא יַעֲנֵנוּ.

מִי שֶׁעָנָה לְעֶזְרָא בַּגּוֹלָה, הוּא יַעֲנֵנוּ.

מִי שֶׁעָנָה לְכָל הַצַּדִּיקִים וְהַחֲסִידִים וְהַתְּמִימִים וְהַיְשָׁרִים, הוּא יַעֲנֵנוּ.

רַחֲמָנָא דְּעָנֵי לַעֲנִיֵּי, עֲנֵינָא. רַחֲמָנָא דְּעָנֵי לִתְבִירֵי לִבָּא, עֲנֵינָא. רַחֲמָנָא דְּעָנֵי לְמַכִּיכֵי רוּחָא, עֲנֵינָא. רַחֲמָנָא עֲנֵינָא. רַחֲמָנָא חוּס. רַחֲמָנָא פְּרוֹק. רַחֲמָנָא שְׁזֵיב. רַחֲמָנָא רְחֵם עֲלָן. הַשְׁתָּא בַּעֲגָלָא וּבִזְמַן קָרִיב.

נפילת אפים

In the presence of a Torah Scroll, the following (until יִבְשׁוּ רָגַע) is recited with the head resting on the arm, preferably while seated. Elsewhere, it is recited with the head held erect.

(וַיֹּאמֶר דָּוִד אֶל גָּד, צַר לִי מְאֹד נִפְּלָה נָּא בְיַד יהוה, כִּי רַבִּים רַחֲמָיו, וּבְיַד אָדָם אַל אֶפֹּלָה.[1])

רַחוּם וְחַנּוּן חָטָאתִי לְפָנֶיךָ. יהוה מָלֵא רַחֲמִים, רַחֵם עָלַי וְקַבֵּל תַּחֲנוּנָי.

תהלים ו:ב-יא

יהוה אַל בְּאַפְּךָ תוֹכִיחֵנִי, וְאַל בַּחֲמָתְךָ תְיַסְּרֵנִי. חָנֵּנִי יהוה, כִּי אֻמְלַל אָנִי, רְפָאֵנִי יהוה, כִּי נִבְהֲלוּ עֲצָמָי. וְנַפְשִׁי נִבְהֲלָה מְאֹד, וְאַתָּה יהוה, עַד מָתָי. שׁוּבָה יהוה, חַלְּצָה נַפְשִׁי, הוֹשִׁיעֵנִי לְמַעַן חַסְדֶּךָ. כִּי אֵין בַּמָּוֶת זִכְרֶךָ, בִּשְׁאוֹל מִי יוֹדֶה לָּךְ. יָגַעְתִּי בְּאַנְחָתִי, אַשְׂחֶה בְכָל לַיְלָה מִטָּתִי, בְּדִמְעָתִי עַרְשִׂי אַמְסֶה. עָשְׁשָׁה מִכַּעַס עֵינִי, עָתְקָה בְּכָל צוֹרְרָי. סוּרוּ מִמֶּנִּי כָּל פֹּעֲלֵי אָוֶן, כִּי שָׁמַע יהוה קוֹל בִּכְיִי. שָׁמַע יהוה תְּחִנָּתִי, יהוה תְּפִלָּתִי יִקָּח. יֵבֹשׁוּ וְיִבָּהֲלוּ מְאֹד כָּל אֹיְבָי, יָשֻׁבוּ יֵבֹשׁוּ רָגַע.

He Who answered Phineas when he arose from amid the congregation,
                                                            may He answer us.

He Who answered Joshua in Gilgal,   *may He answer us.*
He Who answered Samuel in Mitzpah,   *may He answer us.*
He Who answered David and his son Solomon in Jerusalem,
                                                            may He answer us.

He Who answered Elijah on Mount Carmel,   *may He answer us.*
He Who answered Elisha in Jericho,   *may He answer us.*
He Who answered Jonah in the innards of the fish,   *may He answer us.*
He Who answered Hezekiah, King of Judah, in his illness,
                                                            may He answer us.

He Who answered Chananiah, Mishael, and Azariah in the fiery oven,
                                                            may He answer us.

He Who answered Daniel in the lions' den,   *may He answer us.*
He Who answered Mordechai and Esther in Shushan the capital,
                                                            may He answer us.

He Who answered Ezra in the Exile,   *may He answer us.*
He Who answered all the righteous, the devout, the wholesome,
    and the upright,   *may He answer us.*

רַחֲמָנָא *The Merciful One Who answers the poor, may He answer us. The
            Merciful One Who answers the brokenhearted, may He answer us.
The Merciful One Who answers the humble of spirit, may He answer us. O
Merciful One, answer us. O Merciful One, pity. O Merciful One, redeem. O
Merciful One, deliver. O Merciful One, have mercy on us — now, swiftly and
soon.*

PUTTING DOWN THE HEAD

In the presence of a Torah Scroll, the following (until 'instantly shamed') is recited with the head
resting on the arm, preferably while seated. Elsewhere, it is recited with the head held erect.

*(And David said to Gad, 'I am exceedingly distressed. Let us fall into HASHEM's
hand for His mercies are abundant, but let me not fall into human hands.'[1])*

רַחוּם וְחַנּוּן *O compassionate and gracious One, I have sinned before You.
            HASHEM, Who is full of mercy, have mercy on me and accept
my supplications.*

Psalms 6:2-11

'ה *HASHEM, do not rebuke me in Your anger nor chastise me in Your rage.
      Favor me, HASHEM, for I am feeble; heal me, HASHEM, for my bones
shudder. My soul is utterly confounded, and You, HASHEM, how long? Desist,
HASHEM, release my soul; save me as befits Your kindness. For there is no
mention of You in death; in the Lower World who will thank You? I am
wearied with my sigh, every night my tears drench my bed, soak my couch.
My eye is dimmed because of anger, aged by my tormentors. Depart from
me, all evildoers, for HASHEM has heard the sound of my weeping. HASHEM
has heard my plea, HASHEM will accept my prayer. Let all my foes be shamed
and utterly confounded, they will regret and be instantly shamed.*

---

(1) *II Samuel* 24:14.

מָחֵי וּמַסֵּי מֵמִית וּמְחַיֶּה, מַסִּיק מִן שְׁאוֹל לְחַיֵּי עָלְמָא, בְּרָא
כַּד חָטֵי אֲבוּהִי לַקְיֵהּ, אֲבוּהִי דְחָיֵס אַסֵּי לִכְאֵבֵהּ.
עַבְדָּא דְּמָרִיד נָפִיק בְּקוֹלָר, מָרֵהּ תָּאִיב וְתָבִיר קוֹלָרֵהּ.
בְּרָךְ בְּכְרָךְ אֲנַן וְחָטִינָן קַמָּךְ, הָא רָוֵי נַפְשִׁין בְּגִידִין מְרָרִין,
עַבְדָּךְ אֲנַן וּמְרוֹדִינָן קַמָּךְ, הָא בְּבִזְתָּא, הָא בְּשִׁבְיָא, הָא
בְּמַלְקוּתָא. בְּמָטוּ מִנָּךְ בְּרַחֲמָךְ דִּנְפִישִׁין, אַסֵּי לִכְאָבִין דִּתְקוֹף
עֲלָן, עַד דְּלָא נֶהֱוֵי גְמִירָא בְּשִׁבְיָא.

מַכְנִיסֵי רַחֲמִים, הַכְנִיסוּ רַחֲמֵינוּ, לִפְנֵי בַּעַל הָרַחֲמִים.
מַשְׁמִיעֵי תְפִלָּה, הַשְׁמִיעוּ תְפִלָּתֵנוּ, לִפְנֵי
שׁוֹמֵעַ תְּפִלָּה. מַשְׁמִיעֵי צְעָקָה, הַשְׁמִיעוּ צַעֲקָתֵנוּ, לִפְנֵי שׁוֹמֵעַ
צְעָקָה. מַכְנִיסֵי דִמְעָה, הַכְנִיסוּ דִמְעוֹתֵינוּ, לִפְנֵי מֶלֶךְ מִתְרַצֶּה
בִּדְמָעוֹת.

הִשְׁתַּדְּלוּ וְהַרְבּוּ תְחִנָּה וּבַקָּשָׁה, לִפְנֵי מֶלֶךְ אֵל רָם וְנִשָּׂא.
הַזְכִּירוּ לְפָנָיו, הַשְׁמִיעוּ לְפָנָיו תּוֹרָה וּמַעֲשִׂים טוֹבִים שֶׁל שׁוֹכְנֵי
עָפָר.

יִזְכּוֹר אַהֲבָתָם וִיחַיֶּה זַרְעָם, שֶׁלֹּא תֹאבַד שְׁאֵרִית יַעֲקֹב. כִּי צֹאן
רוֹעֶה נֶאֱמָן הָיָה לְחֶרְפָּה, יִשְׂרָאֵל גּוֹי אֶחָד לְמָשָׁל וְלִשְׁנִינָה.
מַהֵר עֲנֵנוּ אֱלֹהֵי יִשְׁעֵנוּ, וּפְדֵנוּ מִכָּל גְּזֵרוֹת קָשׁוֹת וְהוֹשִׁיעָה
בְּרַחֲמֶיךָ הָרַבִּים, מְשִׁיחַ צִדְקֶךָ וְעַמֶּךָ.

מָרָן דִּבִשְׁמַיָּא לָךְ מִתְחַנְּנַן, כְּבַר שַׁבְיָא דְּמִתְחַנַּן לִשְׁבוּיֵהּ.
כֻּלְּהוֹן בְּנֵי שַׁבְיָא בְּכַסְפָּא מִתְפָּרְקִין, וְעַמָּךְ
יִשְׂרָאֵל בְּרַחֲמֵי וּבְתַחֲנוּנֵי, הַב לָן שְׁאֵלְתִּין וּבָעוּתִין, דְּלָא נֶהְדַּר
רֵיקָם מִן קָדָמָךְ.

מָרָן דִּבִשְׁמַיָּא לָךְ מִתְחַנְּנַן, כְּעַבְדָּא דְּמִתְחַנַּן לְמָרֵיהּ, עֲשִׁיקֵי
אֲנַן וּבַחֲשׁוֹכָא שָׁרִינַן, מְרִירָן נַפְשִׁין מֵעַקְתָּין דִּנְפִישִׁין, חֵילָא לֵית
בָּן לְרַצּוּיָךְ מָרָן, עֲבִיד בְּדִיל קַיָּמָא דִּגְזַרְתְּ עִם אֲבָהָתָנָא.

שׁוֹמֵר יִשְׂרָאֵל, שְׁמוֹר שְׁאֵרִית יִשְׂרָאֵל, וְאַל יֹאבַד יִשְׂרָאֵל,
הָאוֹמְרִים, שְׁמַע יִשְׂרָאֵל.[1]
שׁוֹמֵר גּוֹי אֶחָד, שְׁמוֹר שְׁאֵרִית עַם אֶחָד, וְאַל יֹאבַד גּוֹי אֶחָד,
הַמְיַחֲדִים שִׁמְךָ, יְהֹוָה אֱלֹהֵינוּ יְהֹוָה אֶחָד.[1]

מָחַץ וּמַסִּי [O God,] He Who smites and heals, causes death and restores life, raises [the dead] from the grave to eternal life: Should a son sin, his father would smack him, but a compassionate father will heal his [son's] pain. When a slave rebels, he is led out in collar-irons, but if his master desires to, he breaks his chains.

We are Your son, Your firstborn, and we have sinned against You; so our soul has been satiated with bitter wormwood. We are Your servants and we have rebelled against You; so [we have suffered], some with looting, some with captivity, and some with the lash. We beg of You, in Your abundant compassion, heal the pains that have overwhelmed us, before we have been completely wiped out in captivity.

מַכְנִיסֵי רַחֲמִים O you who usher in [pleas for] mercy, may you usher in our [plea for] mercy, before the Master of mercy. O you who cause prayer to be heard, may you cause our prayer to be heard, before the Hearer of prayer. O you who cause outcry to be heard, may you cause our outcry to be heard, before the Hearer of outcry. O you who usher in tears, may you usher in our tears, before the King Who finds favor through tears.

Exert yourselves, and multiply supplication and petition, before the King, God, exalted and most high. Mention before Him, cause to be heard before Him, the Torah and the good deeds of [the Patriarchs and Matriarchs] who dwell in the dust.

May He remember their love and grant life to [their] offspring, that the remnant of Jacob not be lost. For the flock of the faithful shepherd [Moses] has become a disgrace; Israel, the unique nation, a parable and a simile.

Speedily, answer us, O God of our salvation, and redeem us from all harsh decrees; and may You save, in Your abundant mercy, Your righteous anointed and Your people.

מָרָן דְּבִשְׁמַיָּא Our Master Who is in heaven, to You do we supplicate, as a captive supplicates before his captors; for all captives are redeemed with money, but Your people Israel with compassion and supplication. O grant our requests and our prayers that we not be turned away from You empty-handed.

Our Master Who is in heaven, to You do we supplicate, as a slave supplicates before his master: We are oppressed and we abide in darkness, souls embittered from abundant distress. We have no strength to regain Your favor. Our Master, act for the sake of the covenant that You made with our Patriarchs.

שׁוֹמֵר יִשְׂרָאֵל O Guardian of Israel, protect the remnant of Israel; let not Israel be destroyed — those who proclaim, 'Hear O Israel.'[1]

O Guardian of the unique nation, protect the remnant of the unique people; let not the unique nation be destroyed — those who proclaim the Oneness of Your Name, 'HASHEM is our God, HASHEM, the One and Only!'[1]

---

(1) Deuteronomy 6:4.

שׁוֹמֵר גּוֹי קָדוֹשׁ, שְׁמוֹר שְׁאֵרִית עַם קָדוֹשׁ, וְאַל יֹאבַד גּוֹי קָדוֹשׁ, הַמְשַׁלְּשִׁים בְּשָׁלֹשׁ קְדֻשּׁוֹת לְקָדוֹשׁ.

מִתְרַצֶּה בְרַחֲמִים וּמִתְפַּיֵּס בְּתַחֲנוּנִים, הִתְרַצֵּה וְהִתְפַּיֵּס לְדוֹר עָנִי, כִּי אֵין עוֹזֵר. אָבִינוּ מַלְכֵּנוּ, חָנֵּנוּ וַעֲנֵנוּ, כִּי אֵין בָּנוּ מַעֲשִׂים, עֲשֵׂה עִמָּנוּ צְדָקָה וָחֶסֶד וְהוֹשִׁיעֵנוּ.

וַאֲנַחְנוּ לֹא נֵדַע מַה נַּעֲשֶׂה, כִּי עָלֶיךָ עֵינֵינוּ.[1] זְכֹר רַחֲמֶיךָ יהוה וַחֲסָדֶיךָ, כִּי מֵעוֹלָם הֵמָּה.[2] יְהִי חַסְדְּךָ יהוה עָלֵינוּ, כַּאֲשֶׁר יִחַלְנוּ לָךְ.[3] אַל תִּזְכָּר לָנוּ עֲוֹנֹת רִאשׁוֹנִים, מַהֵר יְקַדְּמוּנוּ רַחֲמֶיךָ, כִּי דַלּוֹנוּ מְאֹד.[4] חָנֵּנוּ יהוה חָנֵּנוּ, כִּי רַב שָׂבַעְנוּ בוּז.[5] בְּרֹגֶז רַחֵם תִּזְכּוֹר.[6] כִּי הוּא יָדַע יִצְרֵנוּ, זָכוּר כִּי עָפָר אֲנָחְנוּ.[7] עָזְרֵנוּ אֱלֹהֵי יִשְׁעֵנוּ עַל דְּבַר כְּבוֹד שְׁמֶךָ, וְהַצִּילֵנוּ וְכַפֵּר עַל חַטֹּאתֵינוּ לְמַעַן שְׁמֶךָ.[8]

קדיש שלם

קַדִּישׁ שָׁלֵם: The *chazzan* recites:

יִתְגַּדַּל וְיִתְקַדַּשׁ שְׁמֵהּ רַבָּא. (.Cong – אָמֵן) בְּעָלְמָא דִּי בְרָא כִרְעוּתֵהּ, וְיַמְלִיךְ מַלְכוּתֵהּ, בְּחַיֵּיכוֹן וּבְיוֹמֵיכוֹן וּבְחַיֵּי דְכָל בֵּית יִשְׂרָאֵל, בַּעֲגָלָא וּבִזְמַן קָרִיב. וְאִמְרוּ אָמֵן.

(.Cong – אָמֵן. יְהֵא שְׁמֵהּ רַבָּא מְבָרַךְ לְעָלַם וּלְעָלְמֵי עָלְמַיָּא.)

יְהֵא שְׁמֵהּ רַבָּא מְבָרַךְ לְעָלַם וּלְעָלְמֵי עָלְמַיָּא.

יִתְבָּרַךְ וְיִשְׁתַּבַּח וְיִתְפָּאַר וְיִתְרוֹמַם וְיִתְנַשֵּׂא וְיִתְהַדָּר וְיִתְעַלֶּה וְיִתְהַלָּל שְׁמֵהּ דְּקֻדְשָׁא בְּרִיךְ הוּא (.Cong – בְּרִיךְ הוּא.) לְעֵלָּא מִן כָּל בִּרְכָתָא וְשִׁירָתָא תֻּשְׁבְּחָתָא וְנֶחֱמָתָא, דַּאֲמִירָן בְּעָלְמָא. וְאִמְרוּ: אָמֵן. (.Cong – אָמֵן)

(.Cong – קַבֵּל בְּרַחֲמִים וּבְרָצוֹן אֶת תְּפִלָּתֵנוּ.)

תִּתְקַבֵּל צְלוֹתְהוֹן וּבָעוּתְהוֹן דְּכָל (בֵּית) יִשְׂרָאֵל קֳדָם אֲבוּהוֹן דִּי בִשְׁמַיָּא. וְאִמְרוּ אָמֵן. (.Cong – אָמֵן)

(.Cong – יְהִי שֵׁם יהוה מְבֹרָךְ, מֵעַתָּה וְעַד עוֹלָם.[9])

יְהֵא שְׁלָמָא רַבָּא מִן שְׁמַיָּא וְחַיִּים עָלֵינוּ וְעַל כָּל יִשְׂרָאֵל. וְאִמְרוּ אָמֵן. (.Cong – אָמֵן)

(.Cong – עֶזְרִי מֵעִם יהוה, עֹשֵׂה שָׁמַיִם וָאָרֶץ.[10])

Take three steps back. Bow left and say, . . . עֹשֶׂה; bow right and say, . . . הוּא יַעֲשֶׂה; bow forward and say, וְעַל כָּל . . . אָמֵן. Remain standing in place for a few moments, then take three steps forward.

עֹשֶׂה שָׁלוֹם בִּמְרוֹמָיו, הוּא יַעֲשֶׂה שָׁלוֹם עָלֵינוּ, וְעַל כָּל יִשְׂרָאֵל. וְאִמְרוּ אָמֵן. (.Cong – אָמֵן)

O Guardian of the holy nation, protect the remnant of the holy people; let not the holy nation be destroyed — those who proclaim three-fold sanctifications to the Holy One.

Become favorable through compassion and become appeased through supplications. Become favorable and appeased to the poor generation, for there is no helper. Our Father, our King, be gracious with us and answer us, though we have no worthy deeds; treat us with charity and kindness, and save us.

וַאֲנַחְנוּ We know not what to do — but our eyes are upon You.[1] Remember Your mercies, HASHEM, and Your kindnesses, for they are from the beginning of the world.[2] May Your kindness be upon us, HASHEM, just as we awaited You.[3] Recall not against us the iniquities of the ancients; may Your mercies meet us swiftly, for we have become exceedingly impoverished.[4] Be gracious to us, HASHEM, be gracious to us, for we are abundantly sated with scorn.[5] Amid rage — remember to be merciful![6] For He knew our nature, He remembers that we are dust.[7] Chazzan— Assist us, O God of our salvation, for the sake of Your Name's glory; rescue us and atone for our sins for Your Name's sake.[8]

FULL KADDISH
The chazzan recites the Full Kaddish:

יִתְגַּדַּל May His great Name grow exalted and sanctified (Cong. — Amen.) in the world that He created as He willed. May He give reign to His kingship in your lifetimes and in your days, and in the lifetimes of the entire Family of Israel, swiftly and soon. Now respond: Amen.

(Cong. — Amen. May His great Name be blessed forever and ever.)
May His great Name be blessed forever and ever.

Blessed, praised, glorified, exalted, extolled, mighty, upraised and lauded be the Name of the Holy One, Blessed is He (Cong. — Blessed is He.) beyond any blessing and song, praise, and consolation that are uttered in the world. Now respond: Amen. (Cong. — Amen.)

(Cong. — Accept our prayers with mercy and favor.)
May the prayers and supplications of the entire House of Israel be accepted before their Father Who is in Heaven. Now respond: Amen. (Cong. — Amen.)

(Cong. — Blessed be the Name of HASHEM from this time and forever.[9])
May there be abundant peace from Heaven, and life, upon us and upon all Israel. Now respond: Amen. (Cong. — Amen.)

(Cong. — My help is from HASHEM, Maker of heaven and earth.[10])

Take three steps back. Bow left and say, 'He Who makes peace . . .'; bow right and say, 'may He make peace . . .'; bow forward and say, 'and upon all Israel . . .' Remain standing in place for a few moments, then take three steps forward.

He Who makes peace in His heights, may He make peace upon us, and upon all Israel. Now respond: Amen. (Cong. — Amen.)

---

(1) II Chronicles 20:12. (2) Psalms 25:6. (3) 33:22. (4) 79:8. (5) 123:3. (6) Habakkuk 3:2. (7) Psalms 103:14. (8) 79:9. (9) 113:2. (10) 121:2.

🦋 ערב ראש השנה 🦋

אַשְׁרֵי יוֹשְׁבֵי בֵיתֶךָ, עוֹד יְהַלְלוּךָ סֶּלָה.[1] אַשְׁרֵי הָעָם שֶׁכָּכָה לּוֹ, אַשְׁרֵי הָעָם שֶׁיהוה אֱלֹהָיו.[2]

תהלים קמה

תְּהִלָּה לְדָוִד,

אֲרוֹמִמְךָ אֱלוֹהַי הַמֶּלֶךְ, וַאֲבָרְכָה שִׁמְךָ לְעוֹלָם וָעֶד.

בְּכָל יוֹם אֲבָרְכֶךָּ, וַאֲהַלְלָה שִׁמְךָ לְעוֹלָם וָעֶד.

גָּדוֹל יהוה וּמְהֻלָּל מְאֹד, וְלִגְדֻלָּתוֹ אֵין חֵקֶר.

דּוֹר לְדוֹר יְשַׁבַּח מַעֲשֶׂיךָ, וּגְבוּרֹתֶיךָ יַגִּידוּ.

הֲדַר כְּבוֹד הוֹדֶךָ, וְדִבְרֵי נִפְלְאֹתֶיךָ אָשִׂיחָה.

וֶעֱזוּז נוֹרְאוֹתֶיךָ יֹאמֵרוּ, וּגְדֻלָּתְךָ אֲסַפְּרֶנָּה.

זֵכֶר רַב טוּבְךָ יַבִּיעוּ, וְצִדְקָתְךָ יְרַנֵּנוּ.

חַנּוּן וְרַחוּם יהוה, אֶרֶךְ אַפַּיִם וּגְדָל חָסֶד.

טוֹב יהוה לַכֹּל, וְרַחֲמָיו עַל כָּל מַעֲשָׂיו.

יוֹדוּךָ יהוה כָּל מַעֲשֶׂיךָ, וַחֲסִידֶיךָ יְבָרְכוּכָה.

כְּבוֹד מַלְכוּתְךָ יֹאמֵרוּ, וּגְבוּרָתְךָ יְדַבֵּרוּ.

לְהוֹדִיעַ לִבְנֵי הָאָדָם גְּבוּרֹתָיו, וּכְבוֹד הֲדַר מַלְכוּתוֹ.

מַלְכוּתְךָ מַלְכוּת כָּל עֹלָמִים, וּמֶמְשַׁלְתְּךָ בְּכָל דּוֹר וָדֹר.

סוֹמֵךְ יהוה לְכָל הַנֹּפְלִים, וְזוֹקֵף לְכָל הַכְּפוּפִים.

עֵינֵי כֹל אֵלֶיךָ יְשַׂבֵּרוּ, וְאַתָּה נוֹתֵן לָהֶם אֶת אָכְלָם בְּעִתּוֹ.

פּוֹתֵחַ אֶת יָדֶךָ, וּמַשְׂבִּיעַ לְכָל חַי רָצוֹן.

Concentrate intently while reciting the verse, פּוֹתֵחַ.

❖ **צַדִּיק** יהוה בְּכָל דְּרָכָיו, וְחָסִיד בְּכָל מַעֲשָׂיו.

קָרוֹב יהוה לְכָל קֹרְאָיו, לְכֹל אֲשֶׁר יִקְרָאֻהוּ בֶאֱמֶת.

רְצוֹן יְרֵאָיו יַעֲשֶׂה, וְאֶת שַׁוְעָתָם יִשְׁמַע וְיוֹשִׁיעֵם.

שׁוֹמֵר יהוה אֶת כָּל אֹהֲבָיו, וְאֵת כָּל הָרְשָׁעִים יַשְׁמִיד.

תְּהִלַּת יהוה יְדַבֶּר פִּי, וִיבָרֵךְ כָּל בָּשָׂר שֵׁם קָדְשׁוֹ לְעוֹלָם וָעֶד.

וַאֲנַחְנוּ נְבָרֵךְ יָהּ, מֵעַתָּה וְעַד עוֹלָם, הַלְלוּיָהּ.[3]

חֲצִי קַדִּישׁ The chazzan recites.

יִתְגַּדַּל וְיִתְקַדַּשׁ שְׁמֵהּ רַבָּא. (.Cong – אָמֵן) בְּעָלְמָא דִּי בְרָא כִרְעוּתֵהּ. וְיַמְלִיךְ מַלְכוּתֵהּ, בְּחַיֵּיכוֹן וּבְיוֹמֵיכוֹן וּבְחַיֵּי דְכָל בֵּית יִשְׂרָאֵל, בַּעֲגָלָא וּבִזְמַן קָרִיב. וְאִמְרוּ: אָמֵן.

(.Cong – אָמֵן. יְהֵא שְׁמֵהּ רַבָּא מְבָרַךְ לְעָלַם וּלְעָלְמֵי עָלְמַיָּא.)

יְהֵא שְׁמֵהּ רַבָּא מְבָרַךְ לְעָלַם וּלְעָלְמֵי עָלְמַיָּא.

יִתְבָּרַךְ וְיִשְׁתַּבַּח וְיִתְפָּאַר וְיִתְרוֹמַם וְיִתְנַשֵּׂא וְיִתְהַדָּר וְיִתְעַלֶּה וְיִתְהַלָּל שְׁמֵהּ דְּקֻדְשָׁא בְּרִיךְ הוּא (.Cong – בְּרִיךְ הוּא) לְעֵלָּא מִן כָּל בִּרְכָתָא וְשִׁירָתָא תֻּשְׁבְּחָתָא וְנֶחֱמָתָא, דַּאֲמִירָן בְּעָלְמָא, וְאִמְרוּ: אָמֵן. (.Cong – אָמֵן)

❧ **EREV ROSH HASHANAH** ❧

אַשְׁרֵי *Praiseworthy are those who dwell in Your house; may they always praise You, Selah!*[1] *Praiseworthy is the people for whom this is so, praiseworthy is the people whose God is HASHEM.*[2]

Psalm 145   *A psalm of praise by David:*

א *I will exalt You, my God the King, and I will bless Your Name forever and ever.*

ב *Every day I will bless You, and I will laud Your Name forever and ever.*

ג *HASHEM is great and exceedingly lauded,*
    and His greatness is beyond investigation.

ד *Each generation will praise Your deeds to the next*
    and of Your mighty deeds they will tell;

ה *The splendrous glory of Your power and Your wondrous deeds I shall discuss.*

ו *And of Your awesome power they will speak, and Your greatness I shall relate.*

ז *A recollection of Your abundant goodness they will utter*
    and of Your righteousness they will sing exultantly.

ח *Gracious and merciful is HASHEM,*
    slow to anger, and great in [bestowing] kindness.

ט *HASHEM is good to all; His mercies are on all His works.*

י *All Your works shall thank You, HASHEM, and Your devout ones will bless You.*

כ *Of the glory of Your kingdom they will speak, and of Your power they will tell;*

ל *To inform human beings of His mighty deeds,*
    and the glorious splendor of His kingdom.

מ *Your kingdom is a kingdom spanning all eternities,*
    and Your dominion is throughout every generation.

ס *HASHEM supports all the fallen ones and straightens all the bent.*

ע *The eyes of all look to You with hope*
    and You give them their food in its proper time;

פ *You open Your hand,*   Concentrate intently while reciting the verse, 'You open. . .'
    and satisfy the desire of every living thing.

צ Chazzan— *Righteous is HASHEM in all His ways*
    and magnanimous in all His deeds.

ק *HASHEM is close to all who call upon Him — to all who call upon Him sincerely.*

ר *The will of those who fear Him He will do;*
    and their cry He will hear, and save them.

ש *HASHEM protects all who love Him; but all the wicked He will destroy.*

ת *May my mouth declare the praise of HASHEM*
    and may all flesh bless His Holy Name forever and ever.

We will bless God from this time and forever, Halleluyah![3]

The chazzan recites Half-Kaddish:

יִתְגַּדַּל *May His great Name grow exalted and sanctified* (Cong.— *Amen.*) *in the world that He created as He willed. May He give reign to His kingship in your lifetimes and in your days, and in the lifetimes of the entire Family of Israel, swiftly and soon. Now respond: Amen.*

(Cong.— *Amen. May His great Name be blessed forever and ever.*)

May His great Name be blessed forever and ever.

Blessed, praised, glorified, exalted, extolled, mighty, upraised, and lauded be the Name of the Holy One, Blessed is He (Cong.— *Blessed is He*) *— beyond any blessing and song, praise and consolation that are uttered in the world. Now respond: Amen.* (Cong.— *Amen.*)

---

(1) *Psalms* 84:5. (2) 144:15. (3) 115:18.

All:

לְךָ יהוה הַצְּדָקָה, וְלָנוּ בְּשֶׁת הַפָּנִים.[1] מַה נִּתְאוֹנֵן,[2] מַה נֹּאמַר, מַה נְּדַבֵּר, וּמַה נִּצְטַדָּק.[3] נַחְפְּשָׂה דְרָכֵינוּ וְנַחְקְרָה, וְנָשׁוּבָה אֵלֶיךָ,[4] כִּי יְמִינְךָ פְּשׁוּטָה לְקַבֵּל שָׁבִים. לֹא בְחֶסֶד וְלֹא בְמַעֲשִׂים בָּאנוּ לְפָנֶיךָ, כַּדַּלִּים וּכְרָשִׁים דָּפַקְנוּ דְלָתֶיךָ. דְּלָתֶיךָ דָּפַקְנוּ רַחוּם וְחַנּוּן, נָא אַל תְּשִׁיבֵנוּ רֵיקָם מִלְּפָנֶיךָ. מִלְּפָנֶיךָ מַלְכֵּנוּ רֵיקָם אַל תְּשִׁיבֵנוּ, כִּי אַתָּה שׁוֹמֵעַ תְּפִלָּה.

שֹׁמֵעַ תְּפִלָּה, עָדֶיךָ כָּל בָּשָׂר יָבֹאוּ.[5] יָבוֹא כָל בָּשָׂר לְהִשְׁתַּחֲוֹת לְפָנֶיךָ יהוה.[6] יָבֹאוּ וְיִשְׁתַּחֲווּ לְפָנֶיךָ אֲדֹנָי, וִיכַבְּדוּ לִשְׁמֶךָ.[7] בָּאוּ נִשְׁתַּחֲוֶה וְנִכְרָעָה, נִבְרְכָה לִפְנֵי יהוה עֹשֵׂנוּ.[8] נָבוֹאָה לְמִשְׁכְּנוֹתָיו, נִשְׁתַּחֲוֶה לַהֲדֹם רַגְלָיו.[9] בֹּאוּ שְׁעָרָיו בְּתוֹדָה, חֲצֵרֹתָיו בִּתְהִלָּה, הוֹדוּ לוֹ בָּרְכוּ שְׁמוֹ.[10] רוֹמְמוּ יהוה אֱלֹהֵינוּ, וְהִשְׁתַּחֲווּ לַהֲדֹם רַגְלָיו, קָדוֹשׁ הוּא.[11] רוֹמְמוּ יהוה אֱלֹהֵינוּ, וְהִשְׁתַּחֲווּ לְהַר קָדְשׁוֹ, כִּי קָדוֹשׁ יהוה אֱלֹהֵינוּ.[12] הִשְׁתַּחֲווּ לַיהוה בְּהַדְרַת קֹדֶשׁ, חִילוּ מִפָּנָיו כָּל הָאָרֶץ.[13] וַאֲנַחְנוּ בְּרֹב חַסְדְּךָ נָבוֹא בֵיתֶךָ, נִשְׁתַּחֲוֶה אֶל הֵיכַל קָדְשְׁךָ בְּיִרְאָתֶךָ.[14] נִשְׁתַּחֲוֶה אֶל הֵיכַל קָדְשְׁךָ וְנוֹדֶה אֶת שְׁמֶךָ, עַל חַסְדְּךָ וְעַל אֲמִתֶּךָ, כִּי הִגְדַּלְתָּ עַל כָּל שִׁמְךָ אִמְרָתֶךָ.[15] לְכוּ נְרַנְּנָה לַיהוה, נָרִיעָה לְצוּר יִשְׁעֵנוּ. נְקַדְּמָה פָנָיו בְּתוֹדָה, בִּזְמִרוֹת נָרִיעַ לוֹ.[16] אֲשֶׁר יַחְדָּו נַמְתִּיק סוֹד, בְּבֵית אֱלֹהִים נְהַלֵּךְ בְּרָגֶשׁ.[17] אֵל נַעֲרָץ בְּסוֹד קְדוֹשִׁים רַבָּה, וְנוֹרָא עַל כָּל סְבִיבָיו.[18] שְׂאוּ יְדֵיכֶם קֹדֶשׁ וּבָרְכוּ אֶת יהוה.[19] הִנֵּה בָּרְכוּ אֶת יהוה כָּל עַבְדֵי יהוה, הָעֹמְדִים בְּבֵית יהוה בַּלֵּילוֹת.[20] אֲשֶׁר מִי אֵל בַּשָּׁמַיִם וּבָאָרֶץ, אֲשֶׁר יַעֲשֶׂה כְמַעֲשֶׂיךָ וְכִגְבוּרֹתֶיךָ.[21] אֲשֶׁר לוֹ הַיָּם וְהוּא עָשָׂהוּ, וְיַבֶּשֶׁת יָדָיו יָצָרוּ.[22] אֲשֶׁר בְּיָדוֹ מֶחְקְרֵי אָרֶץ, וְתוֹעֲפוֹת הָרִים לוֹ.[23] אֲשֶׁר בְּיָדוֹ נֶפֶשׁ כָּל חָי, וְרוּחַ כָּל בְּשַׂר אִישׁ.[24] וְיוֹדוּ שָׁמַיִם פִּלְאֲךָ יהוה, אַף אֱמוּנָתְךָ בִּקְהַל קְדֹשִׁים.[25] לְךָ זְרוֹעַ עִם גְּבוּרָה, תָּעֹז יָדְךָ תָּרוּם יְמִינֶךָ.[26] לְךָ שָׁמַיִם, אַף לְךָ אָרֶץ, תֵּבֵל וּמְלֹאָהּ אַתָּה יְסַדְתָּם.[27] אַתָּה פוֹרַרְתָּ בְעָזְּךָ יָם, שִׁבַּרְתָּ רָאשֵׁי תַנִּינִים עַל הַמָּיִם.[28] אַתָּה הִצַּבְתָּ כָּל גְּבוּלוֹת אָרֶץ, קַיִץ וָחֹרֶף אַתָּה יְצַרְתָּם.[29] אַתָּה רִצַּצְתָּ רָאשֵׁי לִוְיָתָן, תִּתְּנֶנּוּ מַאֲכָל לְעָם לְצִיִּים.[29]

(1) Daniel 9:7. (2) Cf. Lamentations 3:39. (3) Cf. Genesis 44:16. (4) Cf. Lamentations 3:40. (5) Psalms 65:3. (6) Cf. Isaiah 66:23. (7) Psalms 86:9. (8) 95:6. (9) 132:7. (10) 100:4. (11) 99:5. (12) 99:9. (13) 96:9. (14) Cf. 5:8. (15) Cf. 138:2. (16) 95:1-2. (17) 55:15. (18) 89:8. (19) 134:2. (20) 134:1. (21) Deuteronomy 3:24. (22) Psalms 95:5. (23) 95:4. (24) Job 12:10. (25) Psalms 89:6. (26) 89:14. (27) 89:12. (28) 74:13. (29) 74:17.

All:

לְךָ ה' Yours, my Lord, is the righteousness and ours is the shame-facedness.[1] What complaint can we make?[2] What can we say? What can we declare? What justification can we offer?[3] Let us examine our ways and analyze — and return to You,[4] for Your right hand is extended to accept penitents. Neither with kindness nor with [good] deeds do we come before You. As paupers and as beggars do we knock at Your doors. At Your doors we knock, O Compassionate and Gracious One. Please do not turn us away from You empty-handed. Our King, turn us not away from You empty-handed, for You are the One Who hears prayer.

שֹׁמֵעַ תְּפִלָּה You Who hears prayer, to You all flesh will come.[5] All flesh will come to prostrate itself before You, O HASHEM.[6] They will come and prostrate themselves before You, my Lord, and shall honor Your Name.[7] Come! — let us prostrate ourselves and bow, let us kneel before God, our Maker.[8] Let us come to His dwelling places, let us prostrate ourselves at His footstool.[9] Enter His gates with thanksgiving, His courts with praise; give thanks to Him, praise His Name.[10] Exalt HASHEM, our God, and bow at His footstool; He is holy![11] Exalt HASHEM, our God, and bow at His holy mountain; for holy is HASHEM, our God.[12] Prostrate yourselves before HASHEM in His intensely holy place, tremble before Him, everyone on earth.[13] As for us, through Your abundant kindness we will enter Your House; we will prostrate ourselves toward Your Holy Sanctuary in awe of You.[14] We will prostrate ourselves toward Your Holy Sanctuary, and we will give thanks to Your Name for Your kindness and truth for You have exalted Your promise even beyond Your Name.[15] Come! — let us sing to HASHEM, let us call out to the Rock of our salvation. Let us greet Him with thanksgiving, with praiseful songs let us call out to Him.[16] For together let us share sweet counsel, in the house of God let us walk in multitudes.[17] God is dreaded in the hiddenmost counsel of the holy ones, and inspires awe upon all who surround Him.[18] Lift your hands in the Sanctuary and bless HASHEM.[19] Behold, bless HASHEM, all you servants of HASHEM, who stand in the House of HASHEM in the nights.[20] For what power is there in heaven or earth that can approximate Your deeds and power?[21] For His is the sea and He perfected the dry land — His hands fashioned it.[22] For in His power are the hidden mysteries of the earth, and the mountain summits are His.[23] For His is the soul of every living thing, and the spirit of all human flesh.[24] Heaven will gratefully praise Your wonders, HASHEM; also Your faithfulness in the assembly of holy ones.[25] Yours is a mighty arm with power, You strengthen Your hand; You exalt Your right hand.[26] Yours is the heaven; Yours, too, is the earth; the world and its fullness — You founded them.[27] You shattered the sea with Your might, You smashed sea serpents' heads upon the water.[28] You established all the boundaries of earth; summer and winter — You fashioned them.[29] You crushed the heads of Leviathan, You served it as food to the nation of legions.

אַתָּה בָקַעְתָּ מַעְיָן וָנָחַל, אַתָּה הוֹבַשְׁתָּ נַהֲרוֹת אֵיתָן.[1] לְךָ יוֹם, אַף
לְךָ לָיְלָה, אַתָּה הֲכִינְוֹתָ מָאוֹר וָשָׁמֶשׁ.[2] עָשָׂה גְדֹלוֹת עַד אֵין חֵקֶר,
וְנִפְלָאוֹת עַד אֵין מִסְפָּר.[3] כִּי אֵל גָּדוֹל יהוה, וּמֶלֶךְ גָּדוֹל עַל כָּל
אֱלֹהִים.[4] כִּי גָדוֹל אַתָּה וְעוֹשֵׂה נִפְלָאוֹת, אַתָּה אֱלֹהִים לְבַדֶּךָ.[5] כִּי
גָדוֹל מֵעַל שָׁמַיִם חַסְדֶּךָ, וְעַד שְׁחָקִים אֲמִתֶּךָ.[6] גָּדוֹל יהוה וּמְהֻלָּל
מְאֹד, וְלִגְדֻלָּתוֹ אֵין חֵקֶר. (כִּי) גָּדוֹל יהוה וּמְהֻלָּל מְאֹד, נוֹרָא הוּא
עַל כָּל אֱלֹהִים.[8] גָּדוֹל יהוה וּמְהֻלָּל מְאֹד, בְּעִיר אֱלֹהֵינוּ הַר
קָדְשׁוֹ.[9] לְךָ יהוה הַגְּדֻלָּה וְהַגְּבוּרָה, וְהַתִּפְאֶרֶת וְהַנֵּצַח וְהַהוֹד, כִּי
כֹל בַּשָּׁמַיִם וּבָאָרֶץ; לְךָ יהוה הַמַּמְלָכָה, וְהַמִּתְנַשֵּׂא לְכֹל לְרֹאשׁ.[10]
מִי לֹא יִרָאֲךָ מֶלֶךְ הַגּוֹיִם, כִּי לְךָ יָאָתָה, כִּי בְכָל חַכְמֵי הַגּוֹיִם וּבְכָל
מַלְכוּתָם מֵאֵין כָּמוֹךָ.[11] מֵאֵין כָּמוֹךָ יהוה, גָּדוֹל אַתָּה וְגָדוֹל שִׁמְךָ
בִּגְבוּרָה.[12] יהוה אֱלֹהֵי צְבָאוֹת, מִי כָמוֹךָ חֲסִין יָהּ, וֶאֱמוּנָתְךָ
סְבִיבוֹתֶיךָ.[13] יהוה צְבָאוֹת, אֱלֹהֵי יִשְׂרָאֵל, יוֹשֵׁב הַכְּרֻבִים, אַתָּה
הוּא הָאֱלֹהִים לְבַדֶּךָ.[14] מִי יְמַלֵּל גְּבוּרוֹת יהוה, יַשְׁמִיעַ כָּל
תְּהִלָּתוֹ.[15] כִּי מִי בַשַּׁחַק יַעֲרֹךְ לַיהוה, יִדְמֶה לַיהוה בִּבְנֵי אֵלִים.[16]

Chazzan, then congregation:

בַּחֲצֹצְרוֹת וְקוֹל שׁוֹפָר, הָרִיעוּ לִפְנֵי הַמֶּלֶךְ יהוה.[17]

Chazzan, then congregation:

אַשְׁרֵי הָעָם יוֹדְעֵי תְרוּעָה, יהוה בְּאוֹר פָּנֶיךָ יְהַלֵּכוּן.[18]

All:

מַה נֹּאמַר לְפָנֶיךָ יוֹשֵׁב מָרוֹם, וּמַה נְּסַפֵּר לְפָנֶיךָ שֹׁכֵן שְׁחָקִים.
מַה נֹּאמַר לְפָנֶיךָ יהוה אֱלֹהֵינוּ, מַה נְּדַבֵּר וּמַה נִּצְטַדָּק.[19] אֵין לָנוּ
פֶּה לְהָשִׁיב וְלֹא מֵצַח לְהָרִים רֹאשׁ, כִּי עֲוֹנוֹתֵינוּ רַבּוּ מִלְמִנּוֹת,
וְחַטֹּאתֵינוּ עָצְמוּ מִסַּפֵּר.[20] לְמַעַן שִׁמְךָ יהוה תְּחַיֵּנוּ, וּבְצִדְקָתְךָ
תּוֹצִיא מִצָּרָה נַפְשֵׁנוּ.[21] דַּרְכְּךָ אֱלֹהֵינוּ לְהַאֲרִיךְ אַפֶּךָ, לָרָעִים
וְלַטּוֹבִים, וְהִיא תְהִלָּתֶךָ. לְמַעַנְךָ אֱלֹהֵינוּ עֲשֵׂה וְלֹא לָנוּ, רְאֵה
עֲמִידָתֵנוּ, דַּלִּים וְרֵקִים. ❖ הַנְּשָׁמָה לָךְ וְהַגּוּף פָּעֳלָךְ, חוּסָה עַל
עֲמָלָךְ. הַנְּשָׁמָה לָךְ וְהַגּוּף שֶׁלָּךְ, יהוה עֲשֵׂה לְמַעַן שְׁמֶךָ. אָתָאנוּ
עַל שִׁמְךָ, יהוה, עֲשֵׂה לְמַעַן שְׁמֶךָ. בַּעֲבוּר כְּבוֹד שִׁמְךָ, כִּי אֵל חַנּוּן
וְרַחוּם שְׁמֶךָ. לְמַעַן שִׁמְךָ יהוה, וְסָלַחְתָּ לַעֲוֹנֵנוּ כִּי רַב הוּא.[22]

---

(1) *Psalms* 74:14-15. (2) 74:16. (3) *Job* 9:10. (4) *Psalms* 95:3. (5) 86:10. (6) 108:5.
(7) 145:3. (8) 96:4. (9) 48:2. (10) *I Chronicles* 29:11. (11) *Jeremiah* 10:7. (12) 10:6.
(13) *Psalms* 89:9. (14) *Isaiah* 37:16. (15) *Psalms* 106:2. (16) 89:7. (17) 98:6. (18) 89:16.
(19) Cf. *Genesis* 44:16. (20) Cf. *Ezra* 9:6. (21) Cf. *Psalms* 143:11. (22) Cf. 25:11.

You split open fountain and stream, You dried the mighty rivers.¹ Yours
is the day, Yours as well is the night; You established luminary and the
sun.² Who performs great deeds that are beyond comprehension, and
wonders beyond number.³ For a great God is HASHEM, and a great King
above all heavenly powers.⁴ For You are great and work wonders; You
alone, O God.⁵ For great above the very heavens is Your kindness, and
until the upper heights is Your truth.⁶ HASHEM is great and exceedingly
lauded, and His greatness is beyond investigation.⁷ (For) HASHEM is
great and exceedingly lauded, awesome is He above all heavenly
powers.⁸ Great is HASHEM and exceedingly lauded, in the city of our
God, Mount of His Holiness.⁹ Yours, HASHEM, is the greatness, the
strength, the splendor, the triumph, and the glory; even everything in
heaven and earth; Yours, HASHEM, is the kingdom, and sovereignty over
every leader.¹⁰ Who would not revere You, O King of nations? — for this
befits You, for among all the sages of the nations and in all their
kingdom there is none like You.¹¹ There is none like You, O HASHEM, You
are great and Your Name is great with power.¹² HASHEM, God of Legions
— who is like You, O Strong One, God? — and Your faithfulness
surrounds You.¹³ HASHEM, Master of Legions, God of Israel, enthroned
upon the Cherubim, it is You alone Who is God.¹⁴ Who can express the
mighty acts of HASHEM, who can announce all His praise?¹⁵ For who in
the sky can be compared to HASHEM; be likened to HASHEM among the
angels?¹⁶

Chazzan, then congregation:

With trumpets and shofar sound, call out before the King, HASHEM.¹⁷

Chazzan, then congregation:

Praises to the people who knew the teruah;
HASHEM, in the light of Your countenance they walk.¹⁸

All:

What can we say before You Who dwell on high? And what can we
relate to You Who abide in the highest heaven? What can we say before
You, HASHEM, our God? What can we declare? What justification can we
offer?¹⁹ We have neither mouth to respond nor brow to raise our head,
for our iniquities are too numerous to count, and our sins are too vast to
be numbered.²⁰ For Your Name's sake, HASHEM, revive us; and with
Your righteousness remove our soul from distress.²¹ It is Your way, our
God, to delay Your anger, against people both evil and good — and this
is Your praise. Act for Your sake, our God, and not for ours, behold our
[spiritual] position — destitute and emptyhanded. Chazzan – The soul is
Yours and the body is Your handiwork; take pity on Your labor. The
soul is Yours and the body is Yours; O HASHEM, act for Your Name's
sake. We have come with reliance on Your Name, O HASHEM, act for
Your Name's sake; because of Your Name's glory — for 'Gracious and
Merciful God' is Your Name. For Your Name's sake, HASHEM, may You
forgive our iniquity, though it is abundant.²²

Congregation, then *chazzan*:

סְלַח לָנוּ אָבִינוּ, כִּי בְרוֹב אִוַּלְתֵּנוּ שָׁגִינוּ,
מְחַל לָנוּ מַלְכֵּנוּ, כִּי רַבּוּ עֲוֹנֵינוּ.

סְלִיחָה כג (פתיחה)

All:

אֲדֹנָי אֱלֹהֵי הַצְּבָאוֹת,¹* נוֹרָא בָּעֶלְיוֹנִים,
אָמַרְתָּ שׁוּבוּ בָּנִים סֵרְבָנִים.²

בָּאוּ עָדֶיךָ בְּתוֹדָה וּבְרָנְנִים,³   בַּקְּשׁוּ פָנֶיךָ⁴ בִּבְכִי וּבְתַחֲנוּנִים.⁵

גַּם כִּי נִסְתְּמָה תְּפִלַּת⁶ הַגְּיוֹנִים,   גַּלֵּי שָׁבִים פְּתוּחִים כֵּיְנִים.⁷

דְּבָרְךָ נִצָּב לְעוֹלְמֵי עֲדָנִים,⁸   דַּרְכֵי טוּבְךָ נֶצַח לֹא שׁוֹנִים.

הִנְנוּ אָתָנוּ לָךְ⁹ כְּדַלִּים וְאֶבְיוֹנִים,   הַצְּדָקוֹת לָךְ, וְלָנוּ הָעֲוֹנִים.

וְעָדֶיךָ שַׁבְנוּ בְּבֹשֶׁת הַפָּנִים,¹⁰   וְעַל דַּלְתוֹתֶיךָ הוֹגִים כַּיוֹנִים.¹¹

זָכְרֵנוּ לְחַיִּים מְתֻקָּנִים,¹²   זַכֵּה כְּתָמֵינוּ צַחִים מְלֻבָּנִים.

חַטֹּאת נְעוּרֵינוּ¹³ מְחֵה כָעֲנָנִים,¹⁴   חַדֵּשׁ יָמֵינוּ כִּימִים קַדְמוֹנִים.¹⁵

טֻמְאָה הַעֲבֵר וְהָתֵם הַזְּדוֹנִים,   טָהֳרָה תִּזְרֹק מַיִם¹⁶ הַנֶּאֱמָנִים.¹⁷

יְדַעְנוּ רִשְׁעֵנוּ¹⁸ סָרְבִים וְסַלּוֹנִים,¹⁹   יַקְשׁוּת עָרְפֵּנוּ חָסֹן כָּאַלּוֹנִים.²⁰

כֶּרֶם נְטַעְנוּ סִגֵּשֵׂג נְצָנִים,²¹   כָּסוּ פָנָיו חֲרֻלִּים קִמְשׁוֹנִים.²²

לִמְּדֵי הָרֵעַ²³ צְמוּדֵי חַמָּנִים,   לוֹקְחֵי שֹׁחַד רוֹדְפֵי שַׁלְמוֹנִים.²⁴*

מַהֵר קִלְקַלְנוּ חֻפַּת חֲתוּנִים,*   מֵאָז הִסַּגְנוּ לְאָחוֹר וְלֹא לְפָנִים.*

נָעוּ זִבְחֵי הַבְּכָרִים קְטֹרֶת סַמָּנִים,*   נִיחֹחֵי רֵיחַ קְטֹרֶת הַמִּשְׁנִים.*

---

(1) Cf. *Amos* 3:13; 9:5. (2) Cf. *Jeremiah* 3:22. (3) Cf. *Psalms* 100:2,4. (4) 27:8. (5) Cf. *Jeremiah* 3:21. (6) Cf. *Lamentations* 3:8. (7) Some editions read כְּחַלּוֹנִים, *windows* (cf. *Daniel* 6:11), i.e., the gates are like open windows. (8) Cf. *Psalms* 119:89. (9) *Jeremiah* 3:22. (10) Cf. *Daniel* 9:7. (11) Cf. *Isaiah* 59:11. (12) Some editions read מְתֻקָּנִים, *proper.* (13) Cf. *Psalms* 25:7. (14) Cf. *Isaiah* 44:22. (15) Cf. *Lamentations* 5:21. (16) Cf. *Ezekiel* 36:25. (17) Cf. *Isaiah* 33:16. (18) Cf. *Jeremiah* 14:20. (19) *Ezekiel* 2:6. (20) Cf. *Amos* 2:9. (21) Cf. *Isaiah* 17:11. (22) Cf. *Proverbs* 24:31; the word קִמְשׁוֹנִים appears only once in Scriptures; some editions read קִמְּשׁוֹנִים, both here and in *Proverbs,* but the meaning is the same. (23) Cf. *Jeremiah* 13:23. (24) Cf. *Isaiah* 1:23.

אֲדֹנָי אֱלֹהֵי הַצְּבָאוֹת — *My Lord, God of Legions.* After a double alphabet, the acrostic of this *pesichah* (introductory *selichah*) reads שְׁלֹמֹה בַּר יִצְחָק, *Shlomo bar Yitzchak.* The composer, better known as *Rashi* (the abbreviation of רַבִּי שְׁלֹמֹה יִצְחָקִי), is considered the greatest of all teacher-commentators on Scriptures and the Talmud. *Rashi* was born in Troyes, France in 1040, and passed away there in 1105 (29 Tammuz 4865). He received his earlier education in his native city, but eventually traveled to Mainz, Germany, and Worms, France, to study under the students of Rabbeinu Gershom [see prefatory comment to *selichah* 12]. *Rashi's* commentary to

the Talmud opened what would have otherwise remained a closed book, inaccessible to the masses. His Torah commentary is the fundamental tool of Biblical interpretation for school child and scholar alike. Literally hundreds of commentaries have been written on *Rashi's* work.

Rashi's later years were marred by the excruciating suffering of the Jews during the First Crusade in 1096, when many important Jewish communities were destroyed. In memorial, *Rashi* composed *selichos* to plead the case of his suffering people before God.

רוֹדְפֵי שַׁלְמוֹנִים — *Pursuers of ill gain.* This phrase describes dishonest judges who pervert justice by

Congregation, then *chazzan*:

*Forgive us, our Father, for in our abundant folly we have erred,
pardon us, our King, for our iniquities are many.*

SELICHAH 23

All:

א My Lord, God of Legions,*[1] revered on high,

א You said, 'Return, stubborn children![2]

ב Come up to Me with thanksgiving-offerings and joyous songs;[3]

ב seek My Presence[4] with weeping and supplication.'[5]

ג Although [our] thoughtful prayer is blocked,[6]

ג the gates for the penitents are open directly[7] before us.

ד Your word stands firm for all eternity,[8]

ד [and] the ways of Your goodness will never change.

ה Here we are; we have come to You[9] as needy and destitute people,

ה [for] Yours is the righteousness, and ours are the iniquities.

ו Now we have returned to You shamefacedly,[10]

ו murmuring like doves[11] around Your doors.

ז Remember us for a sweet[12] life;

ז purify our stains [of sin and make them] clear and clean.

ח Wipe out the sins of our youth[13] like clouds [that pass],[14]

ח [and] renew our days like the days of old.[15]

ט Take away our impurity and make an end of willful sin;

ט throw purity over us,[16] the unfailing water.[17]

י We know our wickedness,[18] [how] stubborn and thorn-like,[19]

י our stiffneckedness as strong as oaks.[20]

כ The vineyard we planted has been overcome by weeds,[21]

כ it is covered over with thorns and brambles.[22]

ל Men accustomed to do evil,[23] devoted to sun worship,

ל takers of bribes, pursuers of ill gain.*[24]

מ We speedily ruined our marriage canopy;*

מ and since then we have moved back instead of forward.

נ Gone are the offerings of fat, healthy sheep;*

נ the satisfying aroma [of the flour-offerings and wine libations];
the spice-compounded incense;*

---

conspiring to protect one another's interest. While being prosecuted before his colleague, a judge would say, 'You champion my cause today. Tomorrow, when you are hailed before my court, I will vindicate you!' (*Rashi* to Isaiah 1:23).

חֻפַּת חֲתוּנִים — *[Our] marriage canopy.* The phrase בְּיוֹם חֲתֻנָּתוֹ, *the day of his wedding* (*Song of Songs* 3:11), alludes to the Giving of the Torah (*Taanis* 26b). While yet at the *chuppah* (Mount Sinai), the bride (Israel) was unfaithful to her betrothed (God) by worshiping the Golden Calf.

הַמִּשְׁנִים — *[The] healthy [ones].* The translation follows *Rashi* (to I Samuel 15:9), who derives the word from שְׁנַיִם, *two*, and interprets it as a

reference to fat, healthy animals that have twice as much meat as others.

נִיחֹחֵי רֵיחַ קְטֹרֶת סַמְמָנִים — *The satisfying aroma [of the flour-offerings and wine libations]; the spice-compounded incense.* The translation follows *Pardes.* Most other commentaries interpret the entire stich as one topic: *The satisfying aroma of the spice-compounded incense.* However, the term רֵיחַ נִיחֹחַ, *satisfying aroma*, as used in Scriptures, refers to either animal and meal-offerings or wine libations. Since the animal offerings are already mentioned in the preceding stich, this one must mean the flour offerings and the wine libations.

שַׂר חֲמִשִּׁים יוֹעֵץ וּנְשׂוּא פָנִים,[1]*   סֶגֶן מָשׂוּחַ לְוִיִּם וְאַחֲרָנִים.

עֲמִידָתֵנוּ רָאָה דַלִּים וְרֵיקָנִים,   עַצְבֵי רְוּחַ מְרוֹרִים[2] כְּלַעֲנִים.

פְּקָדְּנוּךָ בַּצַּר לָחַשׁ צְקוּנִים,   פַּחַד דִּינְךָ דּוֹאֲגִים וּמִתְאוֹנְנִים.[3]

צֶמַח צְדָקָה הַצְמַח לְנֶאֱמָנִים,   צַוֵּה לְהַעֲבִיר עֲוֹנוֹת רִאשׁוֹנִים.

קוֹל הַקּוֹרֵא יַשְׁבִּית מְדָנִים,[4]   קַטֵּגוֹר יַהַס וְיַשְׁתִּיק נִרְגָּנִים.

רְוּחַ נִכְאָה, דִּכְּאוּת לֵב שְׁבָרוֹנִים,[5]   רָצוֹן יַעֲלוּ כְּחֶלְבֵי קָרְבָּנִים.

שְׁבוּעַת אָבוֹת הָקֵם לְבָנִים,   שַׁוְעַת קוֹרְאֶיךָ תִּשְׁמַע מִמְּעוֹנִים.

תָּכִין לִבָּם לְיִרְאָתֶךָ מוּכָנִים,   תַּקְשִׁיב אָזְנְךָ[6] שִׂיחַ חֲנוּנִים.

❖ שׁוּב לְהַעֲלוֹת עַמְּךָ מִשְּׁאוֹנִים,[7]

מַהֵר יְקַדְּמְוּנוּ רַחֲמֶיךָ[8] קַדְמוֹנִים.

בְּרִיבָם יֵצְאוּ חֲנוּנֶיךָ כֵּנִים,   קַיֵּם חֲסָדֶיךָ וְעַל רַחֲמֶיךָ שְׁעוּנִים.

All:

כִּי עַל רַחֲמֶיךָ הָרַבִּים[9] אָנוּ בְטוּחִים, וְעַל צִדְקוֹתֶיךָ אָנוּ נִשְׁעָנִים, וְלִסְלִיחוֹתֶיךָ אָנוּ מְקַוִּים, וְלִישׁוּעָתְךָ אָנוּ מְצַפִּים. אַתָּה הוּא מֶלֶךְ, אוֹהֵב צְדָקוֹת מִקֶּדֶם, מַעֲבִיר עֲוֹנוֹת עַמּוֹ, וּמֵסִיר חַטֹּאת יְרֵאָיו. כּוֹרֵת בְּרִית לָרִאשׁוֹנִים, וּמְקַיֵּם שְׁבוּעָה לָאַחֲרוֹנִים. אַתָּה הוּא, שֶׁיָּרַדְתָּ בַּעֲנַן כְּבוֹדֶךָ עַל הַר סִינַי,[10] וְהֶרְאֵיתָ דַּרְכֵי טוּבְךָ לְמֹשֶׁה עַבְדֶּךָ.[11] וְאָרְחוֹת חֲסָדֶיךָ גִּלִּיתָ לּוֹ, וְהוֹדַעְתּוֹ כִּי אַתָּה אֵל רַחוּם וְחַנּוּן, אֶרֶךְ אַפַּיִם וְרַב חֶסֶד[12] וּמַרְבֶּה לְהֵיטִיב, וּמַנְהִיג אֶת כָּל הָעוֹלָם כֻּלּוֹ בְּמִדַּת הָרַחֲמִים. ❖ וְכֵן כָּתוּב, וַיֹּאמֶר אֲנִי אַעֲבִיר כָּל טוּבִי עַל פָּנֶיךָ, וְקָרָאתִי בְשֵׁם יהוה לְפָנֶיךָ, וְחַנֹּתִי אֶת אֲשֶׁר אָחֹן, וְרִחַמְתִּי אֶת אֲשֶׁר אֲרַחֵם.[13]

All, while standing:

אֵל אֶרֶךְ אַפַּיִם אַתָּה, וּבַעַל הָרַחֲמִים נִקְרֵאתָ, וְדֶרֶךְ תְּשׁוּבָה הוֹרֵיתָ.

גְּדֻלַּת רַחֲמֶיךָ וַחֲסָדֶיךָ,   תִּזְכּוֹר הַיּוֹם וּבְכָל יוֹם לְזֶרַע יְדִידֶיךָ.

תֵּפֶן אֵלֵינוּ בְּרַחֲמִים,   כִּי אַתָּה הוּא בַּעַל הָרַחֲמִים.

---

(1) Cf. *Isaiah* 3:3. (2) Cf. 63:10. (3) Cf. 26:16. (4) Cf. *Proverbs* 18:18; some editions of *Selichos* read מְדָנִים, but the meaning is unchanged. (5) Cf. *Psalms* 51:19. (6) Cf. 10:17. (7) Cf. 40:3. (8) 79:8. (9) *Daniel* 9:18. (10) Cf. *Exodus* 34:5. (11) Cf. 33:13. (12) 34:6. (13) 33:19.

שַׂר חֲמִשִּׁים יוֹעֵץ וּנְשׂוּא פָנִים — *The chief over fifty; the counselor; and the man of dignity*. The Talmud interprets these three terms homiletically. שַׂר חֲמִשִּׁים refers to one who is a master of the Five Books of Moses, for the word חֲמִשִּׁים may be vowelized חֻמָשִׁים), *Chumashim*. A יוֹעֵץ is one

who is familiar with the laws of establishing the New Moon and intercalation of years. And נְשׂוּא פָנִים is the person in whose merit Heaven sustains an entire generation (*Chagigah* 14a). Due to the length and intensity of the present exile, this caliber of people can no longer be found.

ס *the chief over fifty; the counselor; and the man of dignity;*[*1]

ס *the deputy; the anointed [Kohen Gadol]; the Levites;*
       and the children of Aaron.

ע *See our station needy and empty,*

ע *saddened of spirit, bitter[2] as wormwood.*

פ *We have gone to You in distress*
       with an outpouring of whispered prayer,[3]

פ *in fear of Your judgment, worrying and mourning.*

צ *Bring forth a sprout of righteousness for [Your] faithful;*

צ *command that [our] old sins be taken away.*

ק *Let the voice of the chazzan do away with the contentious;[4]*

ק *hush the Accuser, and silence the defamer.*

ר *[May our] submissive spirit [and] humble, broken heart[5]*

ר *ascend with favor like the fats of the offerings.*

ש *[Your] vow to the Patriarchs, make true for their children.*

ש *The outcry of those who call You,*
       may You hear from Your [Heavenly] dwelling-place.

ת *Ready their heart to achieve reverence for You;*

ת *let Your ear listen[6] to [their] pleading prayers.*
       Chazzan — *Lift Your people once again from the clamorous depths;[7]*
       let Your mercy as of old make haste to greet us.[8]
       May Your beloved ones come forth vindicated from their dispute,
       for they hope for Your kindness and depend on Your mercy.

All:

כִּי עַל *For upon Your abundant mercy[9] do we trust, and upon Your*
       righteousness do we depend, and for Your forgiveness do we
hope, and for Your salvation do we yearn. You are the King Who loves
righteousness since the earliest days, Who overlooks His people's
iniquities and sets aside the sins of those who revere Him. He made
a covenant with the ancestors and keeps [His] vow to the descend-
ants. It is You Who descended in Your cloud of glory on Mount Sinai,[10]
and showed the ways of Your goodness to Your servant Moses.[11]
You revealed Your paths of kindness to him, and let him know that You
are God, Compassionate and Gracious, Slow to anger and Abundant in
Kindness,[12] doing manifold good, and guiding all Your world with the
Attribute of Mercy. Chazzan — *And so it is written: He said, 'I shall pass*
all My good in front of you, and I shall call out the Name of HASHEM
before you; for I will be gracious to whom I will be gracious, and I will
be compassionate with whom I will be compassionate.'[13]

All, while standing:

אֵל אֶרֶךְ אַפַּיִם *O God — You are slow to anger, You are called*
       the Master of Mercy, and You have taught the
way of repentance. May You remember this day and every day the
greatness of Your mercy and Your kindness to the offspring of Your
beloved Ones. Turn to us in mercy for You are the Master of Mercy.

בְּתַחֲנוּן וּבִתְפִלָּה פָּנֶיךָ נְקַדֵּם, כְּהוֹדַעְתָּ לֶעָנָיו מִקֶּדֶם.

מֵחֲרוֹן אַפְּךָ שׁוּב,[1] כְּמוֹ בְתוֹרָתְךָ כָּתוּב.[2]

וּבְצֵל כְּנָפֶיךָ נֶחֱסֶה[3] וְנִתְלוֹנָן, כְּיוֹם וַיֵּרֶד יהוה בֶּעָנָן.

❖ תַּעֲבוֹר עַל פֶּשַׁע וְתִמְחֶה אָשָׁם, כְּיוֹם וַיִּתְיַצֵּב עִמּוֹ שָׁם.

תַּאֲזִין שַׁוְעָתֵנוּ וְתַקְשִׁיב מֶנּוּ מַאֲמָר,

כְּיוֹם וַיִּקְרָא בְשֵׁם יהוה,[4] וְשָׁם נֶאֱמַר:

Congregation, then *chazzan*:

וַיַּעֲבֹר יהוה עַל פָּנָיו וַיִּקְרָא:

Congregation and *chazzan* (the words in bold type are recited aloud and in unison):

יהוה, יהוה, אֵל, **רַחוּם, וְחַנּוּן, אֶרֶךְ אַפַּיִם, וְרַב חֶסֶד, וֶאֱמֶת,**

נֹצֵר חֶסֶד לָאֲלָפִים, נֹשֵׂא עָוֹן, וָפֶשַׁע, וְחַטָּאָה,

וְנַקֵּה.[5] וְסָלַחְתָּ לַעֲוֹנֵנוּ וּלְחַטָּאתֵנוּ וּנְחַלְתָּנוּ.[6] סְלַח לָנוּ אָבִינוּ כִּי

חָטָאנוּ, מְחַל לָנוּ מַלְכֵּנוּ כִּי פָשָׁעְנוּ. כִּי אַתָּה אֲדֹנָי טוֹב וְסַלָּח, וְרַב

חֶסֶד לְכָל קֹרְאֶיךָ.[7]

פסוקי הקדמה לסליחה כד

אַל תָּבוֹא בְמִשְׁפָּט עִמָּנוּ, כִּי לֹא יִצְדַּק לְפָנֶיךָ כָל חָי.[8] דִּרְשׁוּ

יהוה בְּהִמָּצְאוֹ, קְרָאֻהוּ בִּהְיוֹתוֹ קָרוֹב.[9] קָרוֹב יהוה

לְכָל קֹרְאָיו, לְכֹל אֲשֶׁר יִקְרָאֻהוּ בֶאֱמֶת.[10] קָרוֹב יהוה לְנִשְׁבְּרֵי לֵב,

וְאֶת דַּכְּאֵי רוּחַ יוֹשִׁיעַ.[11] כִּי מִי גוֹי גָּדוֹל, אֲשֶׁר לוֹ אֱלֹהִים קְרֹבִים

אֵלָיו, כַּיהוה אֱלֹהֵינוּ, בְּכָל קָרְאֵנוּ אֵלָיו.[12] לְמַעַנְךָ אֱלֹהֵינוּ עֲשֵׂה

וְלֹא לָנוּ, רְאֵה עֲמִידָתֵנוּ דַּלִּים וְרֵקִים.[13]

כְּרַחֵם אָב עַל בָּנִים, כֵּן תְּרַחֵם יהוה עָלֵינוּ.[14] לַיהוה הַיְשׁוּעָה,

עַל עַמְּךָ בִרְכָתֶךָ סֶּלָה.[15] יהוה צְבָאוֹת עִמָּנוּ,

מִשְׂגָּב לָנוּ אֱלֹהֵי יַעֲקֹב סֶלָה.[16] יהוה צְבָאוֹת, אַשְׁרֵי אָדָם בֹּטֵחַ

בָּךְ.[17] יהוה הוֹשִׁיעָה, הַמֶּלֶךְ יַעֲנֵנוּ בְיוֹם קָרְאֵנוּ.[18]

In some congregations the following two verses are recited responsively — the *chazzan* reciting סְלַח,
and the congregation responding וַיֹּאמֶר. In other congregations these verses are recited silently.

סְלַח נָא לַעֲוֹן הָעָם הַזֶּה כְּגֹדֶל חַסְדֶּךָ, וְכַאֲשֶׁר נָשָׂאתָה לָעָם

הַזֶּה מִמִּצְרַיִם וְעַד הֵנָּה.[19] וְשָׁם נֶאֱמַר:

וַיֹּאמֶר יהוה סָלַחְתִּי כִּדְבָרֶךָ.[20]

With supplication and prayer we approach Your Presence in the manner that You made known to the humble [Moses] in ancient times. Turn back from Your fierce anger;[1] as is written in Your Torah.[2] In the shadow of Your wings may we find shelter[3] and lodging as on the day 'HASHEM descended in a cloud' [to appear to Moses on Sinai]. Chazzan — *Overlook sin and erase guilt as on the day 'He [God] stood there with him [Moses].' Give heed to our cry and be attentive to our declaration as on the day 'He called out with the Name HASHEM,'[4] and there it was said:*

Congregation, then chazzan:

And HASHEM passed before him [Moses] and proclaimed:

Congregation and chazzan (the words in bold type are recited aloud and in unison):

ה' ה' HASHEM, HASHEM, God, Compassionate and Gracious, Slow to anger, and Abundant in Kindness and Truth, Preserver of kindness for thousands [of generations], Forgiver of iniquity, willful sin, and error, and Who cleanses.[5] *May You forgive our iniquities and our errors and make us Your heritage.[6] Forgive us, our Father, for we have erred; pardon us, our King, for we have willfully sinned; for You, my Lord, are good and forgiving and abundantly kind to all who call upon You.[7]*

PREFATORY VERSES TO SELICHAH 24

אַל תָּבוֹא *Do not enter into strict judgment with us, for no living creature would be innocent before You.[8] Seek HASHEM when He is to be found, call Him when He is near.[9] HASHEM is close to all who call upon Him, to all who call upon Him sincerely.[10] HASHEM is close to the brokenhearted; and those crushed in spirit, He saves.[11] For who is so great a people, that has God as close to it as is HASHEM, our God, whenever we call to Him?[12] Act for Your sake, our God, and not for ours; behold our [spiritual] station, poor and emptyhanded.[13]*

כְּרַחֵם אָב *As a father has mercy on his children, so, HASHEM, may You have mercy on us.[14] Salvation is HASHEM's, upon Your people is Your blessing, Selah.[15] HASHEM, Master of Legions, is with us, a stronghold for us is the God of Jacob, Selah.[16] HASHEM, Master of Legions, praiseworthy is the person who trusts in You.[17] HASHEM, save! May the King answer us on the day we call.[18]*

In some congregations the following two verses are recited responsively — the chazzan reciting, 'Forgive, please ...,' and the congregation responding, 'And HASHEM said ...' In other congregations these verses are recited silently.

סְלַח נָא *Forgive, please, the iniquity of this people according to the greatness of Your kindness and as You have forgiven this people from Egypt until now,[19] and there it was said:*

And HASHEM said, 'I have forgiven according to your word!'[20]

---

(1) Cf. *Exodus* 32:12. (2) See 32:14. (3) Cf. *Psalms* 36:8. (4) *Exodus* 34:5. (5) 34:6-7. (6) 34:9. (7) *Psalms* 86:5. (8) Cf. *Psalms* 143:2. (9) *Isaiah* 55:6. (10) *Psalms* 145:18. (11) 34:19. (12) *Deuteronomy* 4:7. (13) This is not a Scriptural verse; it is taken from the *Selichos* service of Yom Kippur night. (14) Cf. *Psalms* 103:13. (15) 3:9. (16) 46:8. (17) 84:13. (18) 20:10. (19) *Numbers* 14:19. (20) 14:20.

All:

הַטֵּה אֱלֹהַי אָזְנְךָ וּשְׁמָע, פְּקַח עֵינֶיךָ וּרְאֵה שֹׁמְמֹתֵינוּ, וְהָעִיר
אֲשֶׁר נִקְרָא שִׁמְךָ עָלֶיהָ, כִּי לֹא עַל צִדְקֹתֵינוּ אֲנַחְנוּ
מַפִּילִים תַּחֲנוּנֵינוּ לְפָנֶיךָ, כִּי עַל רַחֲמֶיךָ הָרַבִּים. אֲדֹנָי שְׁמָעָה,
אֲדֹנָי סְלָחָה, אֲדֹנָי הַקְשִׁיבָה, וַעֲשֵׂה אַל תְּאַחַר, לְמַעַנְךָ אֱלֹהַי,
כִּי שִׁמְךָ נִקְרָא עַל עִירְךָ וְעַל עַמֶּךָ.[1]

סליחה כד

All:

אֱלֹהֵינוּ וֵאלֹהֵי אֲבוֹתֵינוּ:

אֵיכָכָה אֶפְצֶה פֶּה,* וְאֵיךְ אֶשָּׂא עָיִן,
כִּי אֵין מַעַשׂ, וּבְיָדִי זְכוּת אָיִן,
גָּעִיתִי הָיִיתִי כְּשִׁכּוֹר, וּכְגֶבֶר עֲבָרוֹ יָיִן,[2]
דָּמִיתִי לְגִבּוֹר שֶׁאֵין בְּיָדוֹ כְּלֵי זָיִן.*
הֶחֱרַד לֵב דַּל, וְחָדַל הַהוֹקֵם סַרְסוּר,
וּמַה יִּפְעַר נִבְעָר מִדַּעַת[3] וּבִין חָסוּר,
זְדוֹנוֹ בְּחֻבּוֹ טָמוּן[4] וְאָוֶן[5] בְּקִרְבּוֹ אָסוּר,
חוֹטֵא וְרַב מֶרִי, בְּיַד מְנֻוָּל* מָסוּר.
טֶרֶד לֵב נִבְזֶה הַלָּזֶה הַבָּא לְבַקֵּשׁ,
יָשָׁר הֶעֱוָה,[6] תּוֹכֵחוֹת קָץ,[7] פְּתַלְתּוֹל וְעִקֵּשׁ,[8]
כָּשַׁל בִּרְכָּיו[9] אַשְׁמָתוֹ,* וְצַחֲנָתוֹ לוֹ לְמוֹקֵשׁ,
לִבּוֹ אָוֶן חוֹרֵשׁ,[10] בְּפֹעַל כַּפָּיו נוֹקֵשׁ.[11]
מַעַן טַעַן בְּפִיצָה לְהָשִׁיב מָה אִמְצָא,
נִתְעַבְתִּי וְנֶאֱלַחְתִּי[12] כִּי מָלֵאתִי דֹפִי וְשִׁמְצָה,
סְפֵק מֵימַי לֹא נֶאֱמָנוּ כְּאַכְזָב[13] מוֹצָא,

אֵיכָכָה אֶפְצֶה פֶּה — *How can I open [my]
mouth?* This *selichah* contains an alphabetic
scheme followed by the *paytan's* signature —
אֵלִיָּה בַּר שְׁמַעְיָה, *Eliyah bar Shemayah* [see
prefatory comment to *selichah* 6].

The theme that echoes and re-echoes through
this *selichah* is the anguished words of the
humble and contrite *chazzan*, who pours out his
heart because he feels unqualified and unsuitable
to fulfill the role of intermediary between the
congregation and God.

כְּשִׁכּוֹר . . . כְּלֵי זַיִן — *I am like a
drunk . . . like a warrior with no weapons in his
hand.* Israel's power is in its mouth (see *Bereishis*

Rabbah 65:20; *Bamidbar Rabbah* 20:4). But a
drunk cannot arrange his words properly.
Hence, since I am like a drunk, I have no
weaponry with which to fight (YL).

מְנֻוָּל — *The foul Evil Inclination.* The Talmud
refers to the יֵצֶר הָרָע [*Yetzer Hara*], Evil Inclination, as מְנֻוָּל זֶה, *this foul creature* (*Succah*
52b).

כָּשַׁל בִּרְכָּיו אַשְׁמָתוֹ — *His guilt makes his knees
buckle* [lit., *stumble*]. The prophet often used the
root כשל, *to stumble,* in conjunction with sin:
Israel and Ephraim, וְכָשְׁלוּ בַּעֲוֹנָם, *shall stumble
in their iniquity* (*Hosea* 5:5); *Return, O Israel,*

All:

הַטֵּה *Incline, my God, Your ear, and listen, open Your eyes and see our desolation and that of the city upon which Your Name is proclaimed; for not because of our righteousness do we cast down our supplications before You, rather because of Your abundant compassion. O my Lord, heed; O my Lord, forgive; O my Lord, be attentive and act, do not delay; for Your sake, my God, for Your Name is proclaimed upon Your city and upon Your people.*[1]

SELICHAH 24

All:

Our God and the God of our forefathers:

א *How can I open [my] mouth,* how can I raise an eye?*

ב *I have no deeds [to my credit], no merit is in my hand.*

ג *I moan, [for] I am like a drunk, like one overcome with wine;*[2]

ד *I am like a warrior with no weapons in his hand.**

ה *Impoverished hearts tremble, for the appointed intermediary [between the congregation and God] is gone,*

ו *and how can a witless man open his mouth,*[3] *one who lacks understanding?*

ז *His willful sin is hidden inside him,*[4] *wrongdoing*[5] *locked within him;*

ח *he is a sinner, and full of rebellion, delivered into the power of the foul Evil Inclination.**

ט *The heart of this ignoble one, who comes to ask [mercy], is muddled;*

י *he has made crooked what was straight,*[6] *he has despised rebuke*[7] *— a twisted and perverse [soul].*[8]

כ *His guilt makes his knees buckle,**[9] *the stench [of his sin] is his stumbling block,*

ל *[for] his heart [still] plots wrongdoing,*[10] *he is entrapped by his handiwork.*[11]

מ *What answer or counterclaim can I find, when I open my mouth to refute the charges [against the congregation]?*

נ *I have become loathesome and putrid,*[12] *for I am full of infamy and disgrace.*

ס *My water supply* has not been constant, its source is like a falsifier;*[13]

---

(1) *Daniel* 9:18-19. (2) Cf. *Jeremiah* 23:9; some editions of *Selichos* read כָּאִישׁ שָׁכוֹר for כְּשִׁכּוֹר, thus quoting the Scriptural verse verbatim; the meaning is the same. (3) Cf. 10:14. (4) Cf. *Job* 31:33. (5) Some editions read וַחוּבוֹ, *and his guilt.* (6) Cf. 33:27. (7) Cf. *Proverbs* 3:11. (8) Cf. *Deuteronomy* 32:5. (9) Cf. *Isaiah* 35:3; *Psalms* 109:24. (10) Cf. *Proverbs* 6:18. (11) *Psalms* 9:17. (12) Cf. *Job* 15:16. (13) Cf. *Jeremiah* 15:18.

---

unto HASHEM, *your God,* כִּי כָשַׁלְתָּ, *for you have stumbled in your iniquity* (ibid. 14:2). Thus, the chazzan blames his weak, tottery knees on his own misdeeds (*Masbir*).

Alternatively: This stich is based on the verse, בִּרְכַּי כָּשְׁלוּ מִצּוֹם, *My knees buckle from fasting* (*Psalms* 109:24), and alludes to the custom of fasting on Erev Rosh Hashanah, the day on which this *selichah* is recited. This stich then

means: *Although his knees* [the chazzan speaks of himself in the third person] *buckle from penitential fasting, nevertheless, his guilt and the stench of his sins are his undoing.*

סָפֵק מֵימַי — *My water supply.* Even my tears are unreliable. They should be falling without end, yet have ceased to flow. They are not constant, and thus are false.

עֲצָרוֹתַי אָוֶן[1] וּמִרְמָה וְצוֹמוֹתַי לְרִיב וּמַצָּה.[2]

פֶּשַׁע מְחֵה וְעָוֹן שָׂא וְאָשָׁם כַּפֵּר,

צָעַקְתִּי מִכְּאֵב לֵב,[3] נִכְלָם בּוֹשׁ וְחָפֵר,

קֶצֶף שַׁכֵּךְ וְרֹגֶז הַנַּח וְכַעַס הָפֵר,

רְצֵה מְרַצֶּה וּמְחַבֵּב, וְעָרְבֵב גּוּמָץ חוֹפֵר.[4]*

שִׁבְטֵי פְלִיטֵי יִשְׂרָאֵל הַכִּוּנוּ בְּלֵב נָבָר,

תֹּם הַחֲזִיקוּ, וְתַחַן הָפִיקוּ, נַשְּׁקוּ בַר,[5]*

אֶת יהוה בְּהִמָּצְאוֹ* לְדָרְשׁוֹ[6] חַיִל יַגְבַּר,

לֹא בָזָה וְלֹא שִׁקַּץ עֱנוּת עָנִי[7] וְנִשְׁבָּר.

יוֹם יְשׁוּעָה* וְעֵת רָצוֹן[8] * אִמְצָא לְפָנֶיךָ,

הָגוּן וְרָאוּי וְשָׁלֵם[9] אַחֲשֵׁב בְּעֵינֶיךָ,

בְּעָמְדִי לְהִתְפַּלֵּל וּלְבַקֵּשׁ רַחֲמִים עַל בָּנֶיךָ,

רָצִיתִי אֶתְכֶם[10] הַשְׁמִיעֵנוּ, סָלַחְתִּי[11] נִתְבַּשֵּׂר מִמְּעוֹנֶךָ.

שִׁקְדוּ נָא פְּנֵי עֶלְיוֹן[12] וְהַמְלוּ קָשׁוֹת,

מִכְשׁוֹל הָרִימוּ, פַּנּוּ דֶרֶךְ[13] וְיַשְּׁרוּ מַעֲקַשּׁוֹת,[14]

עָוֹן עִזְבוּ וְהִתְוַדּוּ[15] וְאַל תּוֹסִיפוּ לְהַקְשׁוֹת,[16]

יוֹדֵעַ יָשׁוּב וְנִחָם[17] וְיִקַּח דִּבְרֵי כְבוּשִׁים[18] וּבַקָּשׁוֹת.

❖ הַקְשִׁיבָה אָדוֹן חַנּוּן הַאֲזִינָה אֶרֶךְ שַׁוְעָתִי,[19]

זַעַקְתִּי רְצֵה וְהִתְרַצֵּה וְהִתְפַּיֵּס וְקַבֵּל שַׁוְעָתִי,

קְרָאתִיךָ מִמֵּצַר,[20] קָרַב אֵלַי וּלְכָה לִישׁוּעָתִי,

חוּשָׁה לְעֶזְרָתִי אֲדֹנָי תְּשׁוּעָתִי.[33]

─────

עֲצָרוֹתַי . . . וְצוֹמוֹתַי — *My assemblages . . . and my fasts.* True, we have fulfilled the prophet's words regarding repentance: קַדְּשׁוּ צוֹם, *sanctify a fast*; קִרְאוּ עֲצָרָה, *summon an assemblage* (Joel 2:15), but our good intentions have deteriorated into wrongdoing and deceit; strife and contention.

פֶּשַׁע . . . וְכַעַס — *Rebellious sin . . . anger.* Our sinfulness has been three pronged: rebellious sin, iniquity and guilt. So our remorse is threefold: mortification, shame and abasement. And we beseech God to respond to our repentance in three ways: silencing the fury, laying down the rage and annulling the anger brought about by our sins (*Masbir*).

גּוּמָץ חוֹפֵר — *[The Accuser,] the pit digger.* The Talmud teaches that the Evil Inclination entices man in this world, then testifies against him in the World to Come (*Succah* 52b). Thus, the *Yetzer Hara* digs pits in this world to ensnare man into sinfulness, then points an accusing finger at him before the Heavenly Tribunal. May You, O God, accept favorably the prayers of the *chazzan* [or, the words of the Defender angel] as he attempts to vindicate us and arouse Your love for us, and at the same time confuse the claims of the Accuser angel who caused the iniquities he blames on us.

תֹּם הַחֲזִיקוּ . . . בַר — *Cling whole-heartedly . . . purity [of heart].* The translation follows *Matteh Levi*. According to *Masbir*, the stich is punctuated, תֹּם הַחֲזִיקוּ תַחַן, הָפִיקוּ נַשְּׁקוּ בַר, and is rendered: *Cling whole-heartedly to supplication, bring forth a striving for the purity of Torah.*

בְּהִמָּצְאוֹ — *When He allows Himself to be found.* When does God allow Himself to be found?

ע my assemblages [have turned to] wrongdoing[1] and deceit,
   and my fasts* to strife and contention.[2]

פ 'Wipe away rebellious sin, forbear iniquity, atone for guilt!'

צ I cry from pained heart,[3] mortified, ashamed, abashed.

ק Silence fury, lay down rage, annul anger!*

ר Accept [the prayers of the chazzan,] the peacemaker, arouser of love,
   and confound [the Accuser,] the pit digger.*[4]

ש Tribes of the survivors of Israel,
   prepare yourselves with cleansed hearts!

ת Cling whole-heartedly [to God's mitzvos], bring forth supplication,
   strive for purity [of heart].*[5]

א May strength be increased to seek HASHEM
   when He allows Himself to be found,*[6]

ל [for He] neither despises nor loathes the prayer
   of the poor[7] and broken.

י Let me find before You a day of salvation,* a time of favor;*[8]

ה let me be thought proper, worthy, and whole[9] in Your sight.

ב As I stand in prayer to ask mercy for Your children,

ר let us hear, 'I shall find favor in you';[10] may we hear the news,
   'I have forgiven,'[11] from Your abode.

ש Diligently seek the Presence of the Most High,[12]
   and let [your hearts'] hardness be circumcised;

מ lift away the stumbling block, clear the road[13]
   and straighten the crooked places.[14]

ע Leave off sin, confess[15] and be hard-necked no longer,[16]

י and let he who knows [he has sinned] repent and regret,[17]
   and bring [with him] words of self-reproof[18] and supplication.

ה Chazzan – Be attentive, O gracious Lord; give ear to my prayer service.[19]
   Be pleased with my cry, be favorable and appeased
   and accept my prayer.
   I call to You out of distress;[20]
   draw nigh to me and come to my rescue;
   hasten to my assistance, O my Lord, my Salvation.[21]

---

(1) Cf. *Isaiah* 1:13. (2) Cf. 58:4; see also *Joel* 2:15. (3) Cf. *Isaiah* 65:14; some editions of *Selichos* read
צַעֲקָתִי מִצָּרָה לִי, *I cry from my distress*, cf. *Jonah* 2:3. (4) Cf. *Ecclesiastes* 10:8. (5) *Psalms* 2:12.
(6) Cf. *Isaiah* 55:6. (7) *Psalms* 22:25. (8) Cf. *Isaiah* 49:8. (9) Some editions of *Selichos* add וְזַכֵּן,
and scholarly or, וְרָצוּי, *and favorable*, to this list, see tractate *Taanis* 16a. (10) Cf. *Ezekiel* 43:27.
(11) *Numbers* 14:20. (12) *Lamentations* 3:35; some editions of *Selichos* read, שִׁקְדוּ נָא בְּנֵי עֶלְיוֹן,
Be diligent, O children of the Most High, cf. *Psalms* 82:6. (13) Cf. *Isaiah* 57:14; see commentary to
selichah 22, s.v., אָבֶן... מִכְשׁוֹל. (14) Cf. 42:16. (15) Cf. *Proverbs* 28:13. (16) Cf. *Deuteronomy* 10:16. (17)
Joel 2:14. (18) Cf. *Hosea* 14:3. (19) Cf. *Job* 36:19. (20) Cf. *Psalms* 118:5. (21) 38:23.

During the ten days from Rosh Hashanah [1 Tishrei] until Yom Kippur [10 Tishrei] (*Yevamos* 49b).

יוֹם יְשׁוּעָה — *A day of salvation*. According to all the major commentaries (*Targum*, *Rashi*, *Radak* to *Isaiah* 49:8), the phrase יוֹם יְשׁוּעָה, *a day of salvation*, means a day *that requires salvation*,

i.e., a day of troubles. Here, however, the *paytan* obviously does not plead for such a day. Rather, the phrase must be understood as a day in which God sends us salvation from our present troubles.

עֵת רָצוֹן — *A time of favor*. When is a time of favor? When the congregation prays (*Berachos* 8a).

All, while standing:

אֵל מֶלֶךְ יוֹשֵׁב עַל כִּסֵּא רַחֲמִים מִתְנַהֵג בַּחֲסִידוּת, מוֹחֵל
עֲוֹנוֹת עַמּוֹ, מַעֲבִיר רִאשׁוֹן רִאשׁוֹן,[1] מַרְבֶּה מְחִילָה
לַחַטָּאִים וּסְלִיחָה לַפּוֹשְׁעִים, עֹשֶׂה צְדָקוֹת עִם כָּל בָּשָׂר וָרוּחַ, לֹא
כְרָעָתָם תִּגְמוֹל. ❖ אֵל הוֹרֵיתָ לָּנוּ לוֹמַר שְׁלֹשׁ עֶשְׂרֵה, וּזְכוֹר לָנוּ
הַיּוֹם בְּרִית שְׁלֹשׁ עֶשְׂרֵה, כְּמוֹ שֶׁהוֹדַעְתָּ לֶעָנָיו מִקֶּדֶם, כְּמוֹ
שֶׁכָּתוּב, וַיֵּרֶד יְהוָה בֶּעָנָן וַיִּתְיַצֵּב עִמּוֹ שָׁם, וַיִּקְרָא בְשֵׁם יְהוָה.

Congregation, then *chazzan:*

וַיַּעֲבֹר יְהוָה עַל פָּנָיו וַיִּקְרָא:

Congregation and *chazzan* (the words in bold type are recited aloud and in unison):

יְהוָה, יְהוָה, אֵל, רַחוּם, וְחַנּוּן, אֶרֶךְ אַפַּיִם, וְרַב חֶסֶד, וֶאֱמֶת,
נֹצֵר חֶסֶד לָאֲלָפִים, נֹשֵׂא עָוֹן, וָפֶשַׁע, וְחַטָּאָה,
וְנַקֵּה. וְסָלַחְתָּ לַעֲוֹנֵנוּ וּלְחַטָּאתֵנוּ וּנְחַלְתָּנוּ. סְלַח לָנוּ אָבִינוּ כִּי
חָטָאנוּ, מְחַל לָנוּ מַלְכֵּנוּ כִּי פָשָׁעְנוּ. כִּי אַתָּה אֲדֹנָי טוֹב וְסַלָּח, וְרַב
חֶסֶד לְכָל קֹרְאֶיךָ.

פסוקי הקדמה לסליחה כה

אַל תָּבוֹא בְמִשְׁפָּט עִמָּנוּ, כִּי לֹא יִצְדַּק לְפָנֶיךָ כָל חָי.[2] כִּי
תִקַּח מוֹעֵד, אֱלֹהִים, מֵישָׁרִים תִּשְׁפֹּט.[3] שְׁמַע קוֹל
תַּחֲנוּנֵינוּ בְּשַׁוְּעֵנוּ אֵלֶיךָ, בְּנָשְׂאֵנוּ יָדֵינוּ אֶל דְּבִיר קָדְשֶׁךָ.[4] לְהַצִּיל
מִמָּוֶת נַפְשֵׁנוּ, וּלְחַיּוֹתֵנוּ בָּרָעָב.[5] וְאַתָּה יְהוָה מָגֵן בַּעֲדֵנוּ, כְּבוֹדֵנוּ
וּמֵרִים רֹאשֵׁנוּ.[6]

כְּרַחֵם אָב עַל בָּנִים, כֵּן תְּרַחֵם יְהוָה עָלֵינוּ. לַיהוָה הַיְשׁוּעָה,
עַל עַמְּךָ בִרְכָתֶךָ סֶּלָה. יְהוָה צְבָאוֹת עִמָּנוּ, מִשְׂגָּב
לָנוּ אֱלֹהֵי יַעֲקֹב סֶלָה. יְהוָה צְבָאוֹת, אַשְׁרֵי אָדָם בֹּטֵחַ בָּךְ. יְהוָה
הוֹשִׁיעָה, הַמֶּלֶךְ יַעֲנֵנוּ בְיוֹם קָרְאֵנוּ.

In some congregations the following two verses are recited responsively — the *chazzan* reciting סְלַח,
and the congregation responding וַיֹּאמֶר. In other congregations these verses are recited silently.

סְלַח נָא לַעֲוֹן הָעָם הַזֶּה כְּגֹדֶל חַסְדֶּךָ, וְכַאֲשֶׁר נָשָׂאתָה לָעָם
הַזֶּה מִמִּצְרַיִם וְעַד הֵנָּה, וְשָׁם נֶאֱמַר:

וַיֹּאמֶר יְהוָה סָלַחְתִּי כִּדְבָרֶךָ.

All:

הַטֵּה אֱלֹהַי אָזְנְךָ וּשְׁמָע, פְּקַח עֵינֶיךָ וּרְאֵה שֹׁמְמֹתֵינוּ,
וְהָעִיר אֲשֶׁר נִקְרָא שִׁמְךָ עָלֶיהָ, כִּי לֹא עַל צִדְקוֹתֵינוּ
אֲנַחְנוּ מַפִּילִים תַּחֲנוּנֵינוּ לְפָנֶיךָ, כִּי עַל רַחֲמֶיךָ הָרַבִּים.

All, while standing:

אֵל מֶלֶךְ O God, King Who sits on the throne of mercy; Who acts with kindness, pardons the iniquities of His people, removes [sins] one by one,[1] increasingly grants pardon to careless sinners and forgiveness to rebels, Who deals righteously with every living being — You do not repay them in accord with their evil. Chazzan — O God, You taught us to recite the Thirteen [Attributes of Mercy], so remember for us today the covenant of these Thirteen, as You made known to the humble one in ancient times, as it is written: And HASHEM descended in a cloud and stood with him there, and He called out with the Name HASHEM.

Congregation, then chazzan:

And HASHEM passed before him [Moses] and proclaimed:

Congregation and chazzan (the words in bold type are recited aloud and in unison):

ה' ה' HASHEM, HASHEM, God, Compassionate and Gracious, Slow to anger, and Abundant in Kindness and Truth, Preserver of kindness for thousands [of generations], Forgiver of iniquity, willful sin, and error, and Who cleanses. May You forgive our iniquities and our errors and make us Your heritage. Forgive us, our Father, for we have erred; pardon us, our King, for we have willfully sinned; for You, my Lord, are good and forgiving and abundantly kind to all who call upon You.

PREFATORY VERSES TO SELICHAH 25

אַל תָּבוֹא Do not enter into strict judgment with us, for no living creature would be innocent before You.[2] For You choose the appointed time, O God, and You judge fairly.[3] Hear the sound of our supplications as we cry out to You, as we lift our hands towards Your Holy Sanctuary.[4] To rescue our souls from death, and to sustain us in famine.[5] For You, HASHEM, are a shield for us, for our soul; and the One Who raises our heads.[6]

כְּרַחֵם אָב As a father has mercy on his children, so, HASHEM, may You have mercy on us. Salvation is HASHEM's, upon Your people is Your blessing, Selah. HASHEM, Master of Legions, is with us, a stronghold for us is the God of Jacob, Selah. HASHEM, Master of Legions, praiseworthy is the person who trusts in You. HASHEM, save! May the King answer us on the day we call.

In some congregations the following two verses are recited responsively — the chazzan reciting, 'Forgive, please . . . ,' and the congregation responding, 'And HASHEM said . . .'
In other congregations these verses are recited silently.

סְלַח נָא Forgive, please, the iniquity of this people according to the greatness of Your kindness and as You have forgiven this people from Egypt until now, and there it was said:

And HASHEM said, 'I have forgiven according to your word!'

All:

הַטֵּה Incline, my God, Your ear, and listen, open Your eyes and see our desolation and that of the city upon which Your Name is proclaimed; for not because of our righteousness do we cast down our supplications before You, rather because of Your abundant compassion.

(1) Tractate Rosh Hashanah 17a. (2) Cf. Psalms 143:2. (3) Cf. 75:3. (4) Cf. 28:2. (5) Cf. 33:19. (6) Cf. 3:4.

אֲדֹנָי שְׁמָעָה, אֲדֹנָי סְלָחָה, אֲדֹנָי הַקְשִׁיבָה, וַעֲשֵׂה אַל תְּאַחַר,
לְמַעַנְךָ אֱלֹהַי, כִּי שִׁמְךָ נִקְרָא עַל עִירְךָ וְעַל עַמֶּךָ.

סליחה כה

All:

(אֱלֹהֵינוּ וֵאלֹהֵי אֲבוֹתֵינוּ:)

אָדוֹן מוֹעֵד כְּתִקַּח,* מֵישָׁרִים לִשְׁפּוֹט[1] בְּתַעֲצוּמֶיךָ,

אֶתְיַצְּבָה בְּפֶלֶץ, לְחַלּוֹת פָּנֶיךָ לְרוֹמְמֶךָ,

בְּמַעֲשַׂי לֹא נִשְׁעַנְתִּי, כִּי אִם בְּרַחֲמֶיךָ,[2]   יהוה עֲשֵׂה לְמַעַן שְׁמֶךָ.[3]

גַּזּוּ אֱמוּנִים, גִּבּוֹרֵי כֹחַ בְּמֶרֶץ,

גַּם גּוֹדְרֵי גֶדֶר וְעוֹמְדֵי בַפֶּרֶץ,[4]

דּוֹרְשֵׁי חֶפְצָם בְּכֹחַ, מְשׁוֹכֵן שְׁמֵי עֶרֶץ,   אָבַד חָסִיד מִן הָאָרֶץ.[5]

הֵן קַלּוֹתִי וּמַה אָשִׁיב בְּמוֹ פִי,[6]

הִנְנִי צָעִיר, בְּאֵין מִפְעָלוֹת בְּכַפִּי,[7]

וְאֵיךְ אֲקַוֶּה וַאֲנִי רַב דֹּפִי,   הֱיוֹת לְרָצוֹן אִמְרֵי פִי.[8]

זָחַלְתִּי וָאִירָא מֵחַוּוֹת דֵּעִי,[9]

זְדוֹנִי יָגְרְתִּי וּמֶרֶד רִשְׁעִי,[10]

חַנּוּן, רַחֲמֵנִי בְּהִתְוַדּוֹתִי וְעָזְבִי פְשָׁעִי,[11]   שְׁמַע קוֹל תַּחֲנוּנַי, אֵלֶיךָ בְּשַׁוְּעִי.[12]

טָעִיתִי וְהִנְנִי שָׁב וּמִתְוַדֶּה, עֲשׂוֹת רְצוֹנֶךָ,

טְהוֹר עֵינַיִם,[13] חָשְּׁבֵנִי כְּשָׁלֵם לְפָנֶיךָ,

יָהּ, הַכְנֵס לִי לִפְנִים מִשּׁוּרַת דִּינֶךָ,*   וְאֲדַעֲךָ לְמַעַן אֶמְצָא חֵן בְּעֵינֶיךָ.[14]

❖ כֹּחֲךָ יַגְדִּל נָא[15] וּבִתְפִלָּתִי הִתְנָאֶה,[16]

כְּתִפְלַת זָקֵן וְרָגִיל וּפִרְקוֹ נָאֶה,

לְבָבִי הַנִּשְׁבָּר הַנִּדְכֶּה וְהַנִּכְאֶה,[17]   הַבֵּט מִשָּׁמַיִם וּרְאֵה.[18]

§ אָדוֹן מוֹעֵד כְּתִקַּח — *O Lord, when You choose the appointed time.* This *selichah* and the next are in reality one. In the first half (*selichah* 25), the *chazzan* speaks of his own lack of worth and his inability to achieve the level of perfection attained by the congregational emissaries of earlier generations. The second half (*selichah* 26), continues with the same theme, but in the plural, because this time the *chazzan* speaks of the short-comings of the people who sent him, and of their desire to repent.

In some rites, the *selichah* is not divided, but is

recited without interruption. In some, only the first half is recited on Erev Rosh Hashanah, and the second half is recited at *Neilah* on Yom Kippur.

The complete work contains an *aleph-beis* acrostic [odd-numbered letters — א,ג,... — appear twice; even-numbered letters — ב,ד,... — appear only once], followed by the composer's name — יוֹסֵף בַּר יִצְחָק, *Yosef bar Yitzchak.* R' Yosef was a twelfth-century Tosafist who lived in Orleans, France, and is better known as R' Yosef Bechor Shor.

O my Lord, heed; O my Lord, forgive; O my Lord, be attentive and act, do not delay; for Your sake, my God, for Your Name is proclaimed upon Your city and upon Your people.

SELICHAH 25

All:

(Our God and the God of our forefathers:)

א *O Lord, when You choose the appointed time**
  to judge [the world] fairly[1] in Your might,

א *I stand forth, in trepidation, to entreat [mercy] before You*
  [and] to exalt You.

ב *I rely not on my deeds, but on Your mercy[2] —*
  O HASHEM, act for Your Name's sake![3]

ג *The faithful have vanished, the strong warriors in their vigor;*

ג *those, too, [have vanished] who mend the fence [of Torah]*
  and stand in the breach,[4]

ד *[and] those who [with their great merit] sought their needs*
  forcefully from the Dweller in Awesome Heaven —
  the pious one is gone from the earth.[5]

ה *See, I am [of] light [worth]; what can I answer with my mouth?[6]*

ה *I am but young without [good] deeds in my hand.[7]*

ו *How, then, can I hope, when I am full of infamy,*
  that my mouth's expressions will find favor?[8]

ז *I quail and fear to express my thought;[9]*

ז *I dread [the consequences of] my willful sin*
  and the rebellion of my wickedness.[10]

ח *O Gracious One, have mercy on me,*
  as I confess and abandon my sinfulness.[11]
  Hear the sound of my supplication as I cry out to You.[12]

ט *I have erred, and now I repent and confess, [thus] doing Your will.*

ט *O Pure of Eye,[13] account me as if perfect before You.*

י *O God, for my sake go beyond the line of Your law,**
  that I may know You, that I may find favor in Your eyes.[14]

כ Chazzan — *Please let Your power be increased,[15]*
  and adorn Yourself with my prayer,[16]

כ *as if [it were] the prayer of an elder, experienced [in prayer],*
  whose lifetime has been well spent.

ל *My broken, humbled, and crushed heart[17] —*
  O look down from Heaven and see it![18]

---

(1) Cf. *Psalms* 75:3; some editions of *Selichos* reverse the wording, כְּתִקַּח מוֹעֵד לְשֵׁפֹט מֵישָׁרִים, but the meaning is unchanged. (2) Cf. *Isaiah* 10:20. (3) *Jeremiah* 14:7. (4) Cf. *Ezekiel* 22:30. (5) *Micah* 7:2. (6) Cf. *Job* 40:4. (7) Some editions read וּכְבָנוּ מִפְעֲלוֹת כַּפֵּי, *and the deeds of my hand are as nothing.* (8) Cf. *Psalms* 19:15. (9) *Job* 32:6. (10) Some editions read וּמֶרֶד פַּשְׁעִי, *the rebellion of my sinfulness.* (11) Cf. *Proverbs* 28:13; some editions of *Selichos* read וְעוֹזְבִי רִשְׁעִי, *and I abandon my wickedness.* (12) Cf. *Psalms* 28:2. (13) *Habakkuk* 1:13. (14) *Exodus* 33:13. (15) Cf. *Numbers* 14:17. (16) See *selichah* 13, s.v., לְךָ אֲכַנֶּה עֲטֶרֶת. (17) Cf. *Psalms* 51:19; 109:16. (18) 80:15.

לְפָנִים מִשּׁוּרַת דִּינֶךָ — *Beyond* [lit., *within*] *the line of Your law.* The word לְפָנִים means *within*. Nev- | ertheless, the translation uses *beyond*, because the English expression *within the line of the law* has

All, while standing:

אֵל מֶֽלֶךְ יוֹשֵׁב עַל כִּסֵּא רַחֲמִים מִתְנַהֵג בַּחֲסִידוּת, מוֹחֵל עֲוֹנוֹת עַמּוֹ, מַעֲבִיר רִאשׁוֹן רִאשׁוֹן, מַרְבֶּה מְחִילָה לַחַטָּאִים וּסְלִיחָה לַפּוֹשְׁעִים, עֹשֶׂה צְדָקוֹת עִם כָּל בָּשָׂר וָרֽוּחַ, לֹא כְרָעָתָם תִּגְמוֹל. ✧ אֵל הוֹרֵֽיתָ לָֽנוּ לוֹמַר שְׁלֹשׁ עֶשְׂרֵה, וּזְכוֹר לָֽנוּ הַיּוֹם בְּרִית שְׁלֹשׁ עֶשְׂרֵה, כְּמוֹ שֶׁהוֹדַֽעְתָּ לֶעָנָו מִקֶּֽדֶם, כְּמוֹ שֶׁכָּתוּב, וַיֵּֽרֶד יהוה בֶּעָנָן וַיִּתְיַצֵּב עִמּוֹ שָׁם, וַיִּקְרָא בְשֵׁם יהוה.

Congregation, then *chazzan*:

וַיַּעֲבֹר יהוה עַל פָּנָיו וַיִּקְרָא:

Congregation and *chazzan* (the words in bold type are recited aloud and in unison):

יהוה, יהוה, אֵל, **רַחוּם, וְחַנּוּן, אֶֽרֶךְ אַפַּֽיִם, וְרַב חֶֽסֶד, וֶאֱמֶת,** **נֹצֵר חֶֽסֶד לָאֲלָפִים, נֹשֵׂא עָוֹן, וָפֶֽשַׁע, וְחַטָּאָה,** **וְנַקֵּה.** וְסָלַחְתָּ לַעֲוֹנֵֽנוּ וּלְחַטָּאתֵֽנוּ וּנְחַלְתָּֽנוּ. סְלַח לָֽנוּ אָבִֽינוּ כִּי חָטָֽאנוּ, מְחַל לָֽנוּ מַלְכֵּֽנוּ כִּי פָשָֽׁעְנוּ. כִּי אַתָּה אֲדֹנָי טוֹב וְסַלָּח, וְרַב חֶֽסֶד לְכָל קֹרְאֶֽיךָ.

סליחה כו

All:

(אֱלֹהֵֽינוּ וֵאלֹהֵי אֲבוֹתֵֽינוּ:)

מַרְבִּים צָרְכֵי עַמְּךָ,* וְדַעְתָּם קְצָרָה, מַחְסוֹרָם וּמִשְׁאֲלוֹתָם, בַּל יוּכְלוּ לְסַפְּרָה, נָא בִֽינָה הֲגִיגֵֽנוּ,[1] טֶֽרֶם נִקְרָא,[2]   הָאֵל הַגָּדוֹל הַגִּבּוֹר וְהַנּוֹרָא.[3]

סָפוּ גַם כָּלוּ יוֹדְעֵי פְגִיעָה, סֵֽדֶר תְּפִלּוֹת, בְּמַעֲנֶה לְשׁוֹנָם[4] לְהַבִּיעָה, עֲרָמִים[5] נוֹתַֽרְנוּ וְרָבְתָה (בָֽנוּ) הָרָעָה,   עַל כֵּן לֹא הִשַּׂגְנוּ יְשׁוּעָה.

פָּנִים אֵין לָֽנוּ, פָּנֶֽיךָ לְחַלּוֹת, פְּשָׁעֵֽנוּ וּמָרַֽדְנוּ וְהֶעֱוִֽינוּ[6] מְסִלּוֹת, צְדָקָה לְךָ[7] לְבַד נְבַקֵּשׁ, בְּמַעַרְכֵי תְהִלּוֹת,   הָעוֹמְדִים בְּבֵית יהוה בַּלֵּילוֹת.*[8]

---

the opposite meaning of the Hebrew expression. The phrase לִפְנִים מִשּׁוּרַת הַדִּין implies a merciful lenience that goes far beyond the letter of the law.

מַרְבִּים צָרְכֵי עַמְּךָ — *Your people's needs are many.* This *selichah* is a continuation of *selichah*

25 (see prefatory comment there). The Talmud teaches that one who finds himself in a dangerous place, e.g., where he may be attacked by wild beasts or highwaymen, may recite a very short prayer in place of the regular *Shemoneh Esrei*.

All, while standing:

אֵל מֶלֶךְ *O God, King Who sits on the throne of mercy; Who acts with kindness, pardons the iniquities of His people, removes [sins] one by one, increasingly grants pardon to careless sinners and forgiveness to rebels, Who deals righteously with every living being — You do not repay them in accord with their evil.* Chazzan — *O God, You taught us to recite the Thirteen [Attributes of Mercy], so remember for us today the covenant of these Thirteen, as You made known to the humble one in ancient times, as it is written: And HASHEM descended in a cloud and stood with him there, and He called out with the Name HASHEM.*

Congregation, then *chazzan:*

And HASHEM passed before him [Moses] and proclaimed:

Congregation and *chazzan* (the words in bold type are recited aloud and in unison):

ה' ה' **HASHEM, HASHEM, God, Compassionate and Gracious, Slow to anger, and Abundant in Kindness and Truth, Preserver of kindness for thousands [of generations], Forgiver of iniquity, willful sin, and error, and Who cleanses.** *May You forgive our iniquities and our errors and make us Your heritage. Forgive us, our Father, for we have erred; pardon us, our King, for we have willfully sinned; for You, my Lord, are good and forgiving and abundantly kind to all who call upon You.*

SELICHAH 26

All:

(Our God, and the God of our forefathers:)

מ *Your people's needs are many* and their wit is inadequate, —*

מ *they cannot express their lacks and their wants.*

נ *Please understand our thoughts[1] before we call [to You],[2]*

O great, mighty, and awesome God.[3]

ס *Ended, gone, are those who know [the way of] prayer,*

ס *the order of their prayers, expressed by their eloquent tongue.[4]*

ע *We are left naked [of mitzvos],[5] while evil abounds (in us);*

therefore we have not attained salvation.

פ *We have no approach to beseech before You;*

פ *we have willfully sinned, we have rebelled,*

we have perverted the paths.[6]

צ *Righteousness, which is Yours alone,[7] is what we request,*

through the order of [Your] praises,

[we] who stand in HASHEM's house in the nights.*[8]

---

(1) Cf. *Psalms* 5:2. (2) Cf. *Isaiah* 65:24. (3) *Deuteronomy* 10:17. (4) Cf. *Proverbs* 16:1. (5) See tractates *Shabbos* 14a and *Menachos* 43b. (6) Some editions read וְעִקְּלָנוּ, but the meaning is the same. (7) Cf. *Daniel* 9:7. (8) *Psalms* 134:1.

When he has reached a safe haven he must then recite the *Shemoneh Esrei* he had missed. Various opinions are recorded regarding the text of this blessing. The version that is accepted by the Halachah reads: צָרְכֵי עַמְּךְ יִשְׂרָאֵל מְרֻבִּין וְדַעְתָּם

... קָצְרָה , *The needs of Your people Israel are many, and their wit is inadequate [to express those needs]...* (*Berachos* 29b).

הָעֹמְדִים בְּבֵית ה' בַּלֵּילוֹת — *[We] who stand in HASHEM's house in the nights.* This alludes to our

קָדוֹשׁ, רְאֵה כִּי פָס מֵלִיץ כְּשׁוּרָה,

קַבֵּל נִיבִי כְּמַרְבִּית תְּשׁוּרָה,

רִנְּנָתִי הַיּוֹם תְּהֵא בְּכִתְרְךָ קְשׁוּרָה,[1]   אֵל נֶאְזָר בִּגְבוּרָה.[2]

שַׁוְעָתִי שָׁעֵה, וּתְפִלָּתִי תְהֵא נְעִימָה,

שְׁמַע פְּגִיעָתִי כְּפִגְעָה תַמָּה,

תְּחוֹקְקֵנוּ לַחַיִּים (טוֹבִים), וְתֵיטִיב לָנוּ (הַכְּתִיבָה וְ)הַחֲתִימָה,

תֹּלֶה אֶרֶץ עַל בְּלִימָה.[3]*

יָדְךָ פְּשֹׁט, וְקַבֵּל תְּשׁוּבָתִי בְּמַעֲמָדִי,

סְלַח נָא וּמְחַל רֹעַ מַעֲבָדִי,

פְּנֵה (נָא) וַעֲסֹק בְּטוֹבַת מְשַׁחֲרֶיךָ, דּוֹדִי וּמְעוֹדְדִי,

וְאַתָּה יהוה מָגֵן בַּעֲדִי.[4]

בְּזֶה אַל תִּבְזֶה, הוֹד מְלוּלִי,

רוֹמַמְתִּי הוֹדְךָ כְּפִי מְעוּט שִׂכְלִי,   אֱלֹהִים* אֲדֹנָי חֵילִי.[5]

מַלֵּא לְטוֹבָה תַּאֲוָתִי וּמִשְׁאָלִי,

❖ יֶעֱרַב שִׂיחִי[6] וְתֵעָתֵר בִּתְפִלָּה,

צָרוּף לְחֶשְׁבּוֹן כָּל מִלָּה וּמִלָּה,

חֲשֹׁב קָדוֹשׁ מַעֲמָדִי כְּמִנְחָה בְלוּלָה,[7]

הַאֲזִינָה אֱלֹהֵי יַעֲקֹב סֶלָה.[8]

All, while standing:

אֵל מֶלֶךְ יוֹשֵׁב עַל כִּסֵּא רַחֲמִים מִתְנַהֵג בַּחֲסִידוּת, מוֹחֵל
עֲוֹנוֹת עַמּוֹ, מַעֲבִיר רִאשׁוֹן רִאשׁוֹן, מַרְבֶּה
מְחִילָה לַחַטָּאִים וּסְלִיחָה לַפּוֹשְׁעִים, עֹשֶׂה צְדָקוֹת עִם כָּל
בָּשָׂר וָרוּחַ, לֹא כְרָעָתָם תִּגְמוֹל. ❖ אֵל הוֹרֵיתָ לָּנוּ לוֹמַר שְׁלֹשׁ
עֶשְׂרֵה, וּזְכֹר לָנוּ הַיּוֹם בְּרִית שְׁלֹשׁ עֶשְׂרֵה, כְּמוֹ שֶׁהוֹדַעְתָּ לֶעָנָיו
מִקֶּדֶם, כְּמוֹ שֶׁכָּתוּב וַיֵּרֶד יהוה בֶּעָנָן וַיִּתְיַצֵּב עִמּוֹ שָׁם, וַיִּקְרָא
בְשֵׁם יהוה.

---

recital of *Selichos*, which are ideally said during
the last third of the night.

בְּלִימָה **עַל בְּלִימָה** — *On nothingness.* בְּלִימָה is a composite
of two words בְּלִי, *without*, and מַה, *anything* (Ibn
Ezra and Metzudos to *Job* 26:7).
Midrashically, בְּלִימָה may be interpreted *the
peaceful one*, i.e., one who seeks peace by
remaining silent in the face of argument. The

Talmud cites the teaching of R' Elazar: The world
exists in the merit of the one who seals his lips
(שֶׁבּוֹלֵם עַצְמוֹ) in time of dispute, as Scripture
states: תֹּלֶה אֶרֶץ עַל בְּלִימָה, *He suspends the earth
upon the sealed-lipped one* (Chullin 89a).

אֱלֹהִים — *O HASHEM/God.* Usually, God's Ineffable Four-Letter Name is vowelized ־ּ־ָ־ֳ (in many
siddurim, etc., the vowels are omitted altogether),

ק O Holy One, see how the worthy advocate is gone,

ק so accept my utterance as if an abundant tribute.

ר Let my song today be plaited into Your crown,[1]

O God, Who is girded with strength.[2]

ש Turn to my cry, and let my prayer be pleasant [to You];

ש hear my prayer as if it were a perfect prayer.

ת Inscribe us for (a good) life,

grant us a benevolent, (inscription and) seal,

O You who suspend the world on nothingness.[3*]

יו Extend out Your hand and accept my repentance as I stand [here];

ס please forgive and pardon the evil of my deeds.

פ (Please) turn [towards us] and be involved

with the good of those who seek You,

my Beloved Who encourages me,

for You, HASHEM, are a shield for me.[4]

ב Do not despise the praise of my words;

ר [for] I have exalted Your glory according to my scant understanding.

Fulfill for goodness my desire and my request,

O HASHEM/God, my Lord, my strength.[5]

י May my words be sweet,[6] and may You respond to [my] prayer,

צ adding to the amount [of my merits] each and every word.

חק Consider my standing [here], O Holy One,

as [You would] a flour-offering mixed [with oil];[7]

give ear, O God of Jacob; Selah.[8]

All, while standing:

אֵל מֶלֶךְ O God, King Who sits on the throne of mercy; Who acts with kindness, pardons the iniquities of His people, removes [sins] one by one, increasingly grants pardon to careless sinners and forgiveness to rebels, Who deals righteously with every living being — You do not repay them in accord with their evil. *Chazzan —* O God, You taught us to recite the Thirteen [Attributes of Mercy], so remember for us today the covenant of these Thirteen, as You made known to the humble one in ancient times, as it is written: *And* HASHEM *descended in a cloud and stood with him there, and He called out with the Name* HASHEM.

---

(1) See commentary to selichah 13, s.v., לְךָ אֲכַנֶּה עֲטָרֶת. (2) *Psalms* 65:7.
(3) *Job* 26:7. (4) *Psalms* 3:4. (5) *Habakkuk* 3:19. (6) Cf. *Psalms* 104:34.
(7) Cf. *Leviticus* 2:5. (8) *Psalms* 84:9; see commentary to *selichah* 41.

---

and is pronounced אֲדֹנָי. As such, it refers to God as אָדוֹן, *Lord*, of the entire world, Who הָיָה וְהֹוֶה וְיִהְיֶה, *was, is, and will always be.* This Name, we render HASHEM (lit., *the Name*), which is the way it is expressed when it is used in any context other than prayer, blessing or Torah study. [See the note *The Names of God* at the beginning of this volume.]

However, Scripture occasionally (as in *Habakkuk* 3:19, the source of this stich) uses the vowelization ⸱⸱⸱, in which case the Name is pronounced as if it were spelled אֱלֹהִים, *God.* To indicate this variance, we have translated HASHEM/God. [However, to avoid confusion, we have followed the earlier editions of *Selichos* that spell this Name here as it is pronounced.]

Congregation, then *chazzan:*

וַיַּעֲבֹר יהוה עַל פָּנָיו וַיִּקְרָא:

Congregation and *chazzan* (the words in bold type are recited aloud and in unison):

יהוה, יהוה, אֵל, רַחוּם, וְחַנּוּן, אֶרֶךְ אַפַּיִם, וְרַב חֶסֶד, וֶאֱמֶת,
נֹצֵר חֶסֶד לָאֲלָפִים, נֹשֵׂא עָוֹן, וָפֶשַׁע, וְחַטָּאָה,
וְנַקֵּה. וְסָלַחְתָּ לַעֲוֹנֵנוּ וּלְחַטָּאתֵנוּ וּנְחַלְתָּנוּ. סְלַח לָנוּ אָבִינוּ כִּי
חָטָאנוּ, מְחַל לָנוּ מַלְכֵּנוּ כִּי פָשָׁעְנוּ. כִּי אַתָּה אֲדֹנָי טוֹב וְסַלָּח, וְרַב
חֶסֶד לְכָל קֹרְאֶיךָ.

פסוקי הקדמה לסליחה כז

אַל תָּבוֹא בְמִשְׁפָּט עִמָּנוּ, כִּי לֹא יִצְדַּק לְפָנֶיךָ כָל חָי.[1]
הַאֲזִינָה יהוה תְּפִלָּתֵנוּ, הַקְשִׁיבָה לְקוֹל תַּחֲנוּנֵינוּ.[2]
מַה נֹּאמַר לְפָנֶיךָ יהוה אֱלֹהֵינוּ, מַה נְּדַבֵּר וּמַה נִּצְטַדָּק. חָטָאנוּ עִם
אֲבוֹתֵינוּ הֶעֱוִינוּ וְהִרְשָׁעְנוּ.[3] חַטֹּאת נְעוּרֵינוּ וּפְשָׁעֵינוּ אַל תִּזְכֹּר,
כְּחַסְדְּךָ זְכָר לָנוּ אַתָּה, לְמַעַן טוּבְךָ יהוה.[4]

בְּרַחֵם אָב עַל בָּנִים, כֵּן תְּרַחֵם יהוה עָלֵינוּ. לַיהוה הַיְשׁוּעָה,
עַל עַמְּךָ בִרְכָתֶךָ סֶּלָה. יהוה צְבָאוֹת עִמָּנוּ, מִשְׂגָּב
לָנוּ אֱלֹהֵי יַעֲקֹב סֶלָה. יהוה צְבָאוֹת, אַשְׁרֵי אָדָם בֹּטֵחַ בָּךְ. יהוה
הוֹשִׁיעָה, הַמֶּלֶךְ יַעֲנֵנוּ בְיוֹם קָרְאֵנוּ.

In some congregations the following two verses are recited responsively — the *chazzan* reciting סְלַח,
and the congregation responding וַיֹּאמֶר. In other congregations these verses are recited silently.

סְלַח נָא לַעֲוֹן הָעָם הַזֶּה כְּגֹדֶל חַסְדֶּךָ, וְכַאֲשֶׁר נָשָׂאתָה לָעָם
הַזֶּה מִמִּצְרַיִם וְעַד הֵנָּה, וְשָׁם נֶאֱמַר:

וַיֹּאמֶר יהוה סָלַחְתִּי כִּדְבָרֶךָ.

All:

הַטֵּה אֱלֹהַי אָזְנְךָ וּשְׁמָע, פְּקַח עֵינֶיךָ וּרְאֵה שֹׁמְמֹתֵינוּ,
וְהָעִיר אֲשֶׁר נִקְרָא שִׁמְךָ עָלֶיהָ, כִּי לֹא עַל צִדְקֹתֵינוּ
אֲנַחְנוּ מַפִּילִים תַּחֲנוּנֵינוּ לְפָנֶיךָ, כִּי עַל רַחֲמֶיךָ הָרַבִּים.
אֲדֹנָי שְׁמָעָה, אֲדֹנָי סְלָחָה, אֲדֹנָי הַקְשִׁיבָה, וַעֲשֵׂה אַל תְּאַחַר,
לְמַעַנְךָ אֱלֹהַי, כִּי שִׁמְךָ נִקְרָא עַל עִירְךָ וְעַל עַמֶּךָ.

---

(1) Cf. *Psalms* 143:2. (2) Cf. 86:6. (3) 106:6. (4) Cf. 25:7.

Congregation, then *chazzan:*

And HASHEM *passed before him [Moses] and proclaimed:*

Congregation and chazzan (the words in bold type are recited aloud and in unison):

ה' ה' HASHEM, HASHEM, God, Compassionate and Gracious, Slow to anger, and Abundant in Kindness and Truth, Preserver of kindness for thousands [of generations], Forgiver of iniquity, willful sin, and error, and Who cleanses. *May You forgive our iniquities and our errors and make us Your heritage. Forgive us, our Father, for we have erred; pardon us, our King, for we have willfully sinned; for You, my Lord, are good and forgiving and abundantly kind to all who call upon You.*

PREFATORY VERSES TO SELICHAH 27

אַל תָּבוֹא *Do not enter into strict judgment with us, for no living creature would be innocent before You.*[1] *Give ear,* HASHEM, *to our prayer, heed to the sound of our supplications.*[2] *What can we say before You,* HASHEM, *our God? What can we speak? How can we justify ourselves? We have sinned, like our fathers; we have perpetrated iniquity and wickedness.*[3] *Remember not the sins of our youth and our rebellions; may You remember for us [the deeds] worthy of Your kindness, because of Your goodness,* HASHEM.[4]

כְּרַחֵם אָב *As a father has mercy on his children, so,* HASHEM, *may You have mercy on us. Salvation is* HASHEM's, *upon Your people is Your blessing, Selah.* HASHEM, *Master of Legions, is with us, a stronghold for us is the God of Jacob, Selah.* HASHEM, *Master of Legions, praiseworthy is the person who trusts in You.* HASHEM, *save! May the King answer us on the day we call.*

In some congregations the following two verses are recited responsively — the chazzan reciting, 'Forgive, please . . .,' and the congregation responding, 'And HASHEM said . . .'
In other congregations these verses are recited silently.

סְלַח נָא *Forgive, please, the iniquity of this people according to the greatness of Your kindness and as You have forgiven this people from Egypt until now, and there it was said:*

And HASHEM **said, 'I have forgiven according to your word!'**

All:

הַטֵּה *Incline, my God, Your ear, and listen, open Your eyes and see our desolation and that of the city upon which Your Name is proclaimed; for not because of our righteousness do we cast down our supplications before You, rather because of Your abundant compassion. O my Lord, heed; O my Lord, forgive; O my Lord, be attentive and act, do not delay; for Your sake, my God, for Your Name is proclaimed upon Your city and upon Your people.*

סליחה כז

אֱלֹהֵינוּ וֵאלֹהֵי אֲבוֹתֵינוּ:

אָנָּא עוֹרְרָה אַהֲבָתְךָ הַיְשָׁנָה,*

אֲשֶׁר אָהַבְתָּ לַעֲדַת מִי מָנָה,[1]

בְּכָל כִּנּוּי חִבָּה וְאַחֲוָה* וְרֵעוּת* מְכֻנָּה,

לְמַעַן אַחַי וְרֵעַי אֲדַבְּרָה נָא.[2]

גַּם בְּצַעֲדְךָ עַל הַר גַּבְנוּנִי,*

גִּיל לְשַׁעֲשֵׁעַ חֶמֶד קַדְמוֹנִי,

דְּמִיתָ מַמְלֶכֶת כֹּהֲנִים וְגוֹי קָדוֹשׁ,[3] וּבְנִי,[4]

וְהִיא גַם הִיא אָמְרָה, אָחִי הוּא,[5] מַלְכִּי וַאדוֹנִי.

הוֹרַשְׁתָּ נַחֲלַת צְבִי,[6] חֶבֶל הַנְּעִים,[7]

הִסְתּוֹפֵף לִכְבוֹדְךָ,* בְּלִוְיוֹת צַעֲצֻעִים,

וְהֵן עַתָּה טִלְטָלוּהָ זָרִים, זֵדִים מְרֵעִים,[8]

בְּאֶרֶץ לֹא לָהֶם, הֲלוֹא אַחֶיךָ רוֹעִים.[9]

זְכֹר אַל תִּשְׁכָּח,[10] וְאַל תֶּחֱרַשׁ וְאַל תִּשְׁקֹט אֵל,[11]

זָמְמוּ לְהַכְחִידִי[12] אֱדוֹם וְיִשְׁמָעֵאל,

חַנּוּן, אַתָּה יָדַעְתָּ אֶת כָּל הַתְּלָאוֹת הָאֵל,

כֹּה אָמַר אָחִיךָ יִשְׂרָאֵל.[13]

טָפְלוּ עָלַי וּבְקָקוּנִי בּוֹקְקִים,[14]

טָהֳרָה בְּטֻמְאָה לְהָמִיר,[15] לְחָצוּנִי דּוֹחֲקִים,

יוֹם יוֹם, הִנֵּה עֲבָדֶיךָ מֻכִּים[16] וְלוֹקִים,

קוֹל דְּמֵי אָחִיךָ צוֹעֲקִים.[17]

כָּרוּ לִי שִׁיחוֹת[18] לְמוֹקֵשׁ,

כָּלְתָה וְנִכְסְפָה[19] נַפְשִׁי[20] עֶזְרָתְךָ לְבַקֵּשׁ,

לִישׁוּעָתְךָ לִי עַל פְּתָחַי לְנַקֵּשׁ,

אֶת אַחַי אָנֹכִי מְבַקֵּשׁ.[21]

מִיּוֹם כֶּסֶה,[22] בְּשִׁבְתְּךָ עַל כִּסֵּא כְבוֹדֶךָ,

אָנָּא עוֹרְרָה אַהֲבָתְךָ הַיְשָׁנָה — *Please, awaken Your ancient love.* As in the previous *selichah* (25-26), this work follows an *aleph-beis* acrostic with each odd-numbered letter (א,ג,ה . . .) appearing twice and each even-numbered letter (ב,ד,ו . . .) only once. The remainder of the acrostic spells שלמה חזק, *Shlomo, may he be strong* [see prefatory comment to *selichah* 2]. The last line of each stanza includes some form of the word אָח, *brother* (see next comment).

חִבָּה וְאַחֲוָה וְרֵעוּת — *Love, brotherhood, and friendship.* Each of these terms is used in Scriptures to describe the relationship between God and Israel: חִבָּה, *love,* in the passages חֹבֵב עַמִּים, *He loves the tribes [of Israel]* (Deuteronomy 33:3), and, *You shall be unto Me,* סְגֻלָּה מִכָּל הָעַמִּים (which *Targum Onkelos* renders חֲבִיבִין מִכָּל עַמְמַיָּא), *the most beloved of all peoples* (Exodus 19:5); אַחֲוָה, *brotherhood,* and רֵעוּת, *friendship,* in the verse ([He said,] 'Open [your heart] to Me,

SELICHAH 27

Our God and the God of our forefathers:

א *Please, awaken Your ancient love,**

א *as You [once] loved the uncounted people,[1]*

ב *called by every term of love, brotherhood, and friendship* —*
> *for the sake of my **brothers** and friends*
> *I [the chazzan] beg to speak.[2]*

ג *Then, too, when You stepped forth on Mount Sinai,**

ג *rejoicing to delight [Israel with the Torah, Your] primordial treasure,*

ד *You envisaged [Israel as]*
'a kingdom of priests and a holy nation,'[3] and [as] 'My son';[4]
> *and she [Israel], she too, said,*
> *'He is my **brother**[5] — my King, my Lord!'*

ה *You bequeathed [Israel] a desirable inheritance,[6] the pleasant portion,[7]*

ה *[where] in Your honor they stood* [at the Temple,]*
where the Cherubim stood entwined.

ו *But see, now strangers and malicious evildoers have tossed her about.[8]*
> *In a land not theirs, are not Your **brothers** pasturing?[9]*

ז *'Remember! Do not forget,[10] be not deaf and be not still, O God![11]*

ז *Edom and Ishmael have been plotting to destroy me.[12]*

ח *O Gracious One, You know all these tribulations [of ours],'*
> *thus said Your **brother**, Israel.[13]*

ט *Bandits have surrounded and plundered me,[14]*

ט *oppressors pressure me to exchange [the] pure [Torah]*
for defiled [idolatry].[15]

י *Each day, Your servants are beaten[16] and whipped —*
> *the voice of Your **brother's** blood cries out![17]*

כ *They have dug pits to snare [me];[18]*

כ *my soul pines and yearns[19] to seek help,[20]*

ל *[that You should] knock on my door with salvation for me.*
> *I seek My **brothers**.[21]*

מ *From [Rosh Hashanah,] the day of no moon[22] [onward],*
as You sit on Your Throne of Glory,

---

(1) Cf. *Numbers* 23:10. (2) *Psalms* 122:8. (3) *Exodus* 19:6. (4) 4:22. (5) *Genesis* 20:5. (6) *Jeremiah* 3:19.
(7) Cf. *Psalms* 16:6. (8) In many editions this line omits one or two of the words זָרִים, *strangers*,
זֵדִים, *malicious*, מְרֵעִים, *evildoers*. (9) *Genesis* 15:13; 37:13. (10) *Deuteronomy* 9:7. (11) *Psalms* 83:2.
(12) 83:5. (13) *Numbers* 20:14. (14) Cf. *Nahum* 2:3. (15) Some editions omit this phrase.
(16) Cf. *Exodus* 5:16. (17) *Genesis* 4:10. (18) Cf. *Psalms* 119:85. (19) Cf. 84:3.
(20) Some editions read עֶזְרָתָךְ, *Your help*. (21) *Genesis* 37:16. (22) Cf. *Psalms* 81:4.

אֲחֹתִי, *My sister*, רַעְיָתִי, *My friend!'* (*Song of Songs* 5:2). And it is the theme of brotherly friendship and love between God and Israel that permeates this *piyut*. Thus, the last line of each stanza is a Scriptural fragment that includes some form of the word אָח, *brother*.

הַר גַּבְנֻנִּים — *Mount Sinai*. According to the Midrash (*Tanchuma, Bamidbar* 7). Scripture records six names for Mount Sinai: (a) הַר [הָ]אֱלֹהִים, [*the*]

Mountain of Elokim (*Exodus* 3:1; 18:5; *Psalms* 68:16); (b) הַר בָּשָׁן, *Mount Bashan* (*Psalms* 68:16); (c) הַר גַּבְנֻנִּים, *Mount Gavnunim* (ibid.); (d) הָהָר חָמַד, *the Desired Mountain* (ibid. v. 17); (e) הַר חוֹרֵב, *Mount Horeb* (*Exodus* 3:1, 33:6; *I Kings* 19:8); and (f) הַר סִינַי, *Mount Sinai* (*Exodus* 19:18).

הִסְתּוֹפַף לִכְבוֹדֶךָ — *In Your honor they stood*. Alternatively, *You caused Your honor [the Shechinah] to stand*.

מַבִּיט לִסְקֹר יַחַד, לֵב מוֹרְדֶיךָ וְעוֹבְדֶיךָ,

נִגַּשׁ כָּל בַּעַל מַשָּׁאַת בּוֹגְדֶיךָ,

וַאֲשֶׁר יִהְיֶה לְךָ אֶת אָחִיךָ, תַּשְׁמֵט יָדֶךָ.[1]

סְפָרִים עֵת יִקָּרְאוּ, לִבְרוּאֵי עוֹלָמָךְ,

שְׂאֵת חַיִּים וְחִלּוּף, לְשֶׁעַ נָמָךְ,

עֶלְיוֹן, חֵן נָחֶסֶד בְּאַלְמָךְ,

עֲרֹב עַבְדְּךָ לְטוֹב,[2] וְחִי אָחִיךָ עִמָּךְ.[3]

פְּנֵה אֵלַי וְחָנֵּנִי,[4] וּתְנֵנִי עֶלְיוֹן,

פַּגֵּר מְנַאֲצֶיךָ בְּעֹנִי וְרִשָּׁיוֹן,

צָרְכֵי חֹק טֶרֶף, בְּחֶלְקֵךָ אֶפְסַנְיוֹן,

לֹא תִקְפֹּץ אֶת יָדְךָ, מֵאָחִיךָ הָאֶבְיוֹן.*[5]

קִדַּמְתִּי בַנֶּשֶׁף, וָאֲשַׁוֵּעַ[6] לְךָ מְחוֹלְלִי,

קַדְּמָה חַסְדֶּךָ, וְשָׂא פְּשָׁעִי וּמַעֲלִי,

רַחֲמֶיךָ יִתְגּוֹלְלוּ עָלַי, כְּמַנַחֵם אֲבֵלִי,

מִי יִתֶּנְךָ כְּאָח לִי.[7]

שְׁעֵה שַׁוְעַת עֲנִיֶּיךָ וְצַעֲקָתָם,

שָׂבְעָה בְרָעוֹת נַפְשָׁם[8] וְחַיָּתָם,

תַּשְׁלִיךְ בִּמְצֻלוֹת יָם כָּל חַטֹּאתָם,[9]

אָנָּא, שָׂא נָא פֶשַׁע אַחֶיךָ,[10] וְחַטָּאתָם.

שָׂשׂ אָנֹכִי עַל אִמְרַת מִבְטָחֶיךָ,[11]

לְבַבְתַּנִי, עַל יְדֵי צִירִים שְׁלוּחֶיךָ,

מָתַי תַּחְשֹׂף זְרוֹעֲךָ[12] בְּכֹחֶךָ,

לֵךְ נָא רְאֵה אֶת שְׁלוֹם אַחֶיךָ.[13]

❖ הָיִיתָ מִקֶּדֶם מִקְוֵה יִשְׂרָאֵל, וְחֶרֶב גַּאֲוָתָם,

חַי, זְקֹף גַּם עַתָּה קוֹמָתָם,

וְאַמֵּץ זַרְעָם וְתִשְׁכֹּן בֵּינוֹתָם,

וְאֶת אַחֶיךָ תִּפְקֹד לְשָׁלוֹם, וְאֶת עֲרֻבָּתָם.[14]

All, while standing:

אֵל מֶלֶךְ יוֹשֵׁב עַל כִּסֵּא רַחֲמִים מִתְנַהֵג בַּחֲסִידוּת, מוֹחֵל
עֲוֹנוֹת עַמּוֹ, מַעֲבִיר רִאשׁוֹן רִאשׁוֹן, מַרְבֶּה מְחִילָה
לַחַטָּאִים וּסְלִיחָה לַפּוֹשְׁעִים, עוֹשֶׂה צְדָקוֹת עִם כָּל בָּשָׂר וָרוּחַ,

---

מֵאָחִיךָ הָאֶבְיוֹן — To [lit., from] Your impover-   translated to, in order to accommodate the En-
ished brother. The prefix מ means from. It is here   glish idiom.

מ *peering to search as one, the hearts of those who rebel against You*
    and of those who serve You,
נ *demand debt payment from those who repudiate You,*
                and as for what is due You from Your **brother***,*
                        Your hand must let it drop.[1]

ס *When the Books [of Life and of Death] are read*
    for the creatures of Your world,
ס *bearing [verdicts of] life or the reverse, to rich and to poor,*
ע *Most High! Let love and kindness be in Your hall —*
                insure good for Your servant,[2]
                that Your **brother** *may live with You.*[3]

פ *Turn to me and show me favor,*[4] *and set me supreme;*
פ *devastate those who anger You,*
    [afflicting them] with poverty and destitution.
צ *[As for our] needed measure of nourishment,*
    when You apportion annual provisions,
                You shall not close Your hand to Your impoverished **brother.** *** [5]
ק *I arose before dawn and I cried out*[6] *to You, my Maker,*
ק *'Put forward Your kindness and bear my willful sin and my trespass!'*
ר *Let Your mercy roll over me as if comforting my mourning;*
                would that You were as a **brother** *to me!*[7]
ש *Turn to the outcry of Your poor ones and their shout,*
ש *[for] their souls and lifebloods are satiated with troubles.*[8]
ת *Cast all their sins into the sea's depths;*[9]
                please, bear Your **brothers'** *willful sins*[10] *and their error.*

ש *I rejoice over Your spoken assurance;*[11]
ל *You have drawn my heart [to You]*
    through Your emissaries [the prophets].
מ *When will You unveil Your arm,*[12] *[revealing] Your strength?*
                Please go and see to Your **brothers'** *welfare.*[13]

ה Chazzan — *You have been since antiquity the Hope of Israel,*
    the Sword of their grandeur;
  O Living One, now too straighten their [bent] stature,
  strengthen their arm, and let Yourself dwell among them —
                and visit Your **brothers,** *check on their welfare,*
                and [take] their condition [to heart].[14]

All, while standing:

אֵל מֶלֶךְ *O God, King Who sits on the throne of mercy; Who acts*
  with kindness, pardons the iniquities of His people, removes
[sins] one by one, increasingly grants pardon to careless sinners and
forgiveness to rebels, Who deals righteously with every living being —

---

(1) *Deuteronomy* 15:3. (2) *Psalms* 119:122. (3) *Leviticus* 25:36. (4) *Psalms* 25:16.
(5) Cf. *Deuteronomy* 15:7. (6) *Psalms* 119:147. (7) *Song of Songs* 8:1.
(8) Cf. *Psalms* 88:4. (9) Cf. *Micah* 7:19. (10) Cf. *Genesis* 50:17.
(11) Cf. *Psalms* 119:162. (12) Cf. *Isaiah* 52:10. (13) *Genesis* 37:14. (14) *I Samuel* 17:18.

לֹא כְרָעָתָם תִּגְמוֹל. ❖ אֵל הוֹרֵיתָ לָנוּ לוֹמַר שְׁלֹשׁ עֶשְׂרֵה, וּזְכוֹר לָנוּ הַיּוֹם בְּרִית שְׁלֹשׁ עֶשְׂרֵה, כְּמוֹ שֶׁהוֹדַעְתָּ לֶעָנָיו מִקֶּדֶם, כְּמוֹ שֶׁכָּתוּב, וַיֵּרֶד יהוה בֶּעָנָן וַיִּתְיַצֵּב עִמּוֹ שָׁם, וַיִּקְרָא בְשֵׁם יהוה.

Congregation, then *chazzan:*

וַיַּעֲבֹר יהוה עַל פָּנָיו וַיִּקְרָא:

Congregation and *chazzan* (the words in bold type are recited aloud and in unison):

יהוה, יהוה, אֵל, רַחוּם, וְחַנּוּן, אֶרֶךְ אַפַּיִם, וְרַב חֶסֶד, וֶאֱמֶת, נֹצֵר חֶסֶד לָאֲלָפִים, נֹשֵׂא עָוֹן, וָפֶשַׁע, וְחַטָּאָה, וְנַקֵּה. וְסָלַחְתָּ לַעֲוֹנֵנוּ וּלְחַטָּאתֵנוּ וּנְחַלְתָּנוּ. סְלַח לָנוּ אָבִינוּ כִּי חָטָאנוּ, מְחַל לָנוּ מַלְכֵּנוּ כִּי פָשָׁעְנוּ. כִּי אַתָּה אֲדֹנָי טוֹב וְסַלָּח, וְרַב חֶסֶד לְכָל קֹרְאֶיךָ.

פסוקי הקדמה לסליחה כח

אַל תָּבוֹא בְמִשְׁפָּט עִמָּנוּ, כִּי לֹא יִצְדַּק לְפָנֶיךָ כָל חָי.[1] הַאֲזִינָה יהוה תְּפִלָּתֵנוּ, הַקְשִׁיבָה לְקוֹל תַּחֲנוּנֵינוּ.[2] מַה נֹּאמַר לְפָנֶיךָ יהוה אֱלֹהֵינוּ, מַה נְּדַבֵּר וּמַה נִּצְטַדָּק. אֱלֹהֵינוּ, בֹּשְׁנוּ וְנִכְלַמְנוּ לְהָרִים אֱלֹהֵינוּ פָּנֵינוּ אֵלֶיךָ,[3] כִּי רַבּוּ מְשׁוּבוֹתֵינוּ, לְךָ חָטָאנוּ.[4] חָטָאנוּ עִם אֲבוֹתֵינוּ הֶעֱוִינוּ וְהִרְשָׁעְנוּ.[5] חַטֹּאת נְעוּרֵינוּ וּפְשָׁעֵינוּ אַל תִּזְכֹּר, כְּחַסְדְּךָ זָכָר לָנוּ אַתָּה, לְמַעַן טוּבְךָ יהוה.[6]

בְּרַחֵם אָב עַל בָּנִים, כֵּן תְּרַחֵם יהוה עָלֵינוּ. לַיהוה הַיְשׁוּעָה, עַל עַמְּךָ בִרְכָתֶךָ סֶּלָה. יהוה צְבָאוֹת עִמָּנוּ, מִשְׂגָּב לָנוּ אֱלֹהֵי יַעֲקֹב סֶלָה. יהוה צְבָאוֹת, אַשְׁרֵי אָדָם בֹּטֵחַ בָּךְ. יהוה הוֹשִׁיעָה, הַמֶּלֶךְ יַעֲנֵנוּ בְיוֹם קָרְאֵנוּ.

In some congregations the following two verses are recited responsively — the *chazzan* reciting סְלַח, and the congregation responding וַיֹּאמֶר. In other congregations these verses are recited silently.

סְלַח נָא לַעֲוֹן הָעָם הַזֶּה כְּגֹדֶל חַסְדֶּךָ, וְכַאֲשֶׁר נָשָׂאתָה לָעָם הַזֶּה מִמִּצְרַיִם וְעַד הֵנָּה, וְשָׁם נֶאֱמַר:

וַיֹּאמֶר יהוה סָלַחְתִּי כִּדְבָרֶךָ.

All:

הַטֵּה אֱלֹהַי אָזְנְךָ וּשְׁמָע, פְּקַח עֵינֶיךָ וּרְאֵה שֹׁמְמֹתֵינוּ, וְהָעִיר אֲשֶׁר נִקְרָא שִׁמְךָ עָלֶיהָ, כִּי לֹא עַל צִדְקוֹתֵינוּ אֲנַחְנוּ מַפִּילִים תַּחֲנוּנֵינוּ לְפָנֶיךָ, כִּי עַל רַחֲמֶיךָ הָרַבִּים. אֲדֹנָי שְׁמָעָה, אֲדֹנָי סְלָחָה, אֲדֹנָי הַקְשִׁיבָה, וַעֲשֵׂה אַל תְּאַחַר, לְמַעַנְךָ אֱלֹהַי, כִּי שִׁמְךָ נִקְרָא עַל עִירְךָ וְעַל עַמֶּךָ.

---

(1) Cf. *Psalms* 143:2. (2) Cf. 86:6. (3) Cf. *Ezra* 9:6. (4) *Jeremiah* 14:7. (5) *Psalms* 106:6. (6) Cf. 25:7.

You do not repay them in accord with their evil. Chazzan — O God, You taught
us to recite the Thirteen [Attributes of Mercy], so remember for us today the
covenant of these Thirteen, as You made known to the humble one in ancient
times, as it is written: And HASHEM descended in a cloud and stood with him
there, and He called out with the Name HASHEM.

Congregation, then chazzan:

And HASHEM passed before him [Moses] and proclaimed:

Congregation and chazzan (the words in bold type are recited aloud and in unison):

ה' ה' HASHEM, HASHEM, God, Compassionate and Gracious, Slow
to anger, and Abundant in Kindness and Truth, Preserver of
kindness for thousands [of generations], Forgiver of iniquity, willful
sin, and error, and Who cleanses. May You forgive our iniquities and our
errors and make us Your heritage. Forgive us, our Father, for we have
erred; pardon us, our King, for we have willfully sinned; for You, my Lord,
are good and forgiving and abundantly kind to all who call upon You.

PREFATORY VERSES TO SELICHAH 28

אַל תָּבוֹא Do not enter into strict judgment with us, for no living
creature would be innocent before You.[1] Give ear, HASHEM,
to our prayer, be attentive to the sound of our supplication.[2] What can
we say before You, HASHEM, our God? What can we declare? What
justification can we offer? Our God, we are too ashamed and humiliated
to lift, our God, our faces towards You,[3] for our unruly deeds are so many;
we have sinned unto You.[4] We have sinned, together with our fathers; we
have committed iniquity and wickedness.[5] Remember not the sins of our
youth and our rebellions; may You remember for us [the deeds] worthy
of Your kindness, because of Your goodness, HASHEM.[6]

כְּרַחֵם אָב As a father has mercy on his children, so, HASHEM, may
You have mercy on us. Salvation is HASHEM's, upon Your
people is Your blessing, Selah. HASHEM, Master of Legions, is with us, a
stronghold for us is the God of Jacob, Selah. HASHEM, Master of Legions,
praiseworthy is the person who trusts in You. HASHEM, save! May the
King answer us on the day we call.

In some congregations the following two verses are recited responsively — the chazzan
reciting, 'Forgive, please . . .,' and the congregation responding, 'And HASHEM said . . .'
In other congregations these verses are recited silently.

סְלַח נָא Forgive, please, the iniquity of this people according to the
greatness of Your kindness and as You have forgiven this
people from Egypt until now, and there it was said:
And HASHEM said, 'I have forgiven according to your word!'

All:

הַטֵּה Incline, my God, Your ear, and listen, open Your eyes and see our
desolation and that of the city upon which Your Name is proclaimed; for not because of our righteousness do we cast down our
supplications before You, rather because of Your abundant compassion.
O my Lord, heed; O my Lord, forgive; O my Lord, be attentive and act,
do not delay; for Your sake, my God, for Your Name is proclaimed upon
Your city and upon Your people.

סְלִיחָה כח

אֱלֹהֵינוּ וֵאלֹהֵי אֲבוֹתֵינוּ:

אֶל אֱלוֹהַּ דָּלְפָה עֵינִי,[1]* אֲשַׁוֵּעַ וְיֹאמַר הִנֵּנִי,[2]

אֲמָרַי הַאֲזִינָה בְּהִתְחַנְּנִי,[3] עֲנֵנִי יהוה עֲנֵנִי.[4]

בְּמֹאזְנֵיִם כִּי תְפַלֵּס דַּרְכִּי,[5] בְּמִצְוֹתֶיךָ דַּלּוֹתִי חֶלְקִי וְחִשְׁקִי,*

וְאִם כְּפָעֳלִי תַשְׁלִים חֻקִּי, וָאִירָא כִּי עֵירֹם אָנֹכִי.[6]

גָּרֵשׁ כַּלֵּה חֵטְא וּמֶרִי, גַּלֵּה נַרְתֵּק מַרְפֵּא* וּצְרִי,

וְעָנְתָה בִּי צִדְקָתִי לְיוֹצְרִי, בְּיוֹם מָחָר* כִּי תָבוֹא עַל שְׂכָרִי.[7]

דְּפִי כַּבֵּס וְלַבֵּן אֲדַמְדָּם,[8] דְּרֹשׁ אֶת עֲפַר יְסוֹדָם,[9]

וְאַל תְּשַׁלֵּם כִּגְמוּל יָדָם,[10] כִּי רַבָּה רָעַת הָאָדָם.[11]

הַנֶּפֶשׁ הַחֹטֵאת בַּמֶּה תִתְכַּפֵּר, הוֹן לֹא יוֹעִיל וְרֹב כְּפֶר,[12]

הֶעֱמַדְתָּ עֵד* מְמַהֵר לִסְפֵּר, מִבַּיִת וּמִחוּץ בַּכֹּפֶר.[13]

וּמַה יְּכֻפַּר וּבְיָדוֹ סְדוּרוֹת,* (וְתֵק) עֲוּוֹת מַעֲשָׂיו וְכָל הַקּוֹרוֹת,

וְאֵיךְ יֹאמַר מִי יֹדֵעַ סְפֹרוֹת,[14] וְהִנֵּה הַנֶּגַע בַּקִּירוֹת.[15]

זַכִּים הַמְמֻלָּאִים עִמְּךָ בְּכָל פֶּלֶךְ, זְרִיזִים לְשׁוֹמְרֶךָ בְּכָל אֲשֶׁר תֵּלֵךְ,[16]

אֶל אֱלוֹהַּ דָּלְפָה עֵינִי ⊱ — *My eye drips [tears] to God.* This *selichah* follows a double *aleph-beis* as indicated by the bold type. The fourth line of each quatrain is a Scriptural fragment. The last two stanzas bear the author's signature, יוֹאֵל בַּר יִצְחָק הַלֵּוִי, *Yoel son of Yitzchak the Levite.* R' Yoel studied under R' Ephraim of Regensburg [see prefatory comment to *selichah* 29] and was the son-in-law of the well-known Tosafist and *paytan*, R' Eliezer ben Nassan (*Ravan*). He lived in Bonn, Germany, but in his later years became rabbi of Cologne. His famous son, R' Eliezer (*Ravyah*), took over that position when R' Yoel passed away in the year 1200.

בְּמִצְוֹתֶיךָ דַּלּוֹתִי חֶלְקִי וְחִשְׁקִי — *I am poor [both] in my portion and in my desire for Your mitzvos.* The translation follows virtually all the commentaries. Alternatively, חֶלְקִי, *my Portion* (see Psalms 119:57), and חִשְׁקִי, *my Desire* (see 91:14), refer to God, and the stich reads: *I am poor in Your mitzvos, O my Portion, my Desire* [YL].

גַּלֵּה נַרְתֵּק מַרְפֵּא — *Uncover the vessel of healing.* The primeval light created at the beginning of the world enabled man to see from one end of the world to other. But when God looked into the future and saw the perverse deeds of the generations of the Flood (see Genesis 6:5-12) and of the Dispersal (see ibid. 11:1-9), He concealed that light. In Time to Come, He will unveil that light for the righteous (*Chagigah* 12a).

In Time to Come, God will remove the sun מִנַּרְתִּיקָה, *from its sheath.* The wicked will be punished by it, and the righteous will be healed by it (*Avodah Zarah* 3b). Thus, we pray that God remove the sheath from the sun, that it may become a vessel of healing for us.

בְּיוֹם מָחָר — *On the morrow, [Rosh Hashanah].* The translation reflects most of the commentaries. Alternatively, this stanza is based on three well-known Aggadic passages: (a) the word מָחָר refers to the Day of Reckoning in Time to Come (see preceding comment), for יֵשׁ מָחָר שֶׁהוּא עַכְשָׁיו, *there is an immediate 'tomorrow,'* וְיֵשׁ מָחָר שֶׁהוּא לְאַחַר זְמָן, *and there is a future 'tomorrow'* (*Tanchuma*, *Rashi* to Exodus 13:14); (b) שְׂכַר מִצְוָה בְּהַאי עָלְמָא לֵיכָּא, *a mitzvah's [prime] reward is not given in this world [but in the World to Come]* (*Kiddushin* 39b); and (c) all the mitzvos that Israel does in this world will come forward to testify on their behalf in the World to Come (*Avodah Zarah* 2a).

הֶעֱמַדְתָּ עֵד — *You have appointed a witness.* According to most commentaries this refers to the Evil Inclination which becomes Satan, the Accuser. For, as the Talmud teaches: The Evil Inclination leads a man astray in this world, then testifies against him in the World to Come (*Succah* 52b).

According to *Matteh Levi*, however, the stich is translated, *You have appointed [Yourself] a witness,* and is based on the Mishnah (*Avos* 4:29): He is God; He is the Fashioner; He is the Creator; He is the Discerner; He is the Judge; He is the Witness . . .

SELICHAH 28

Our God and the God of our forefathers:

א My eye drips [tears] to God,*[1]

א I shall cry, and He shall say, 'Here I am'![2]

Hearken to my words as I supplicate,[3]

'Answer me, HASHEM, answer me!'[4]

ב When You weigh out my practices on the scales,[5]

ב I am poor [both] in my portion and in my desire for Your mitzvos;*

if You should mete out my sustenance

according to my accomplishments,

I fear, for I am naked.[6]

ג Chase out, annihilate sin and rebellion;

ג uncover the vessel of healing* salve,

and my righteousness will testify for me to my Creator,

on the morrow, [Rosh Hashanah,]*

when You come to consider my reward.[7]

ד Wash away ignominy, and whiten [sin's bloody] redness;[8]

ד consider the dust that is their base,[9]

and do not recompense them like the deserts of their handiwork,[10]

for man's evil is great.[11]

ה The soul that sins — with what will it atone for itself?

ה Wealth will not avail, nor abundant ransom.[12]

You have appointed a witness* swift to relate

the disbeliever's [thoughts] from within and [deeds] from without.[13]

ו How can man atone, when his own hand has set forth*

ו his twisted deeds (of old) and all his life's events?

How can he say, 'Who knows all their number?'[14]

when, see, the affliction's mark is on the walls?[15]

ז The pure [angels] who accompany You in every place,

ז zealously attending You wherever You go,[16]

---

(1) *Job* 16:20. (2) Cf. *Isaiah* 58:9. (3) Cf. *Psalms* 5:2; 86:6. (4) *I Kings* 18:37.
(5) Cf. *Proverbs* 16:11. (6) *Genesis* 3:10. (7) Cf. 30:33. (8) Cf. *Isaiah* 1:18.
(9) Cf. *Job* 4:19. (10) Cf. *Isaiah* 3:11. (11) *Genesis* 6:5. (12) Cf. *Proverbs* 11:4; *Job* 36:18.
(13) *Genesis* 6:14. (14) Cf. *Psalms* 71:15. (15) *Leviticus* 14:37. (16) Cf. *Genesis* 28:15.

A third interpretation is that a different witness is appointed for each deed. This is based on the Talmud's response to the question: And what if a person will ask, 'Who will testify against me?' Four opinions are cited regarding this point: (a) The stones and beams of a person's house will testify against him; (b) two ministering angels escort a man wherever he goes and will bear witness; (c) a man's own soul will speak against him; and (d) a person's own limbs will testify (*Taanis* 11a). Following this interpretation the next stich, מִבַּיִת וּמִחוּץ בַּכֹּפֶר, would be translated, *whether the disbeliever's acts took place inside* — so that the stones and beams of his house will testify against him — *or outside* — where his angelic escort becomes his witness.

Alternatively, his own soul testifies to his inner thoughts, while his limbs testify against his outward deeds. The *selichah* continues by elaborating on the role of each of these witnesses.

וּבְיָדוֹ סְדָרוֹת — *His own hand has set forth.* At the time of a person's departure to his eternal home, all his wordly deeds take leave of him [variant reading: are delineated before him]. And they say to him, 'Did you do thus and thus at such-and-such place on such-and-such day?' He responds, 'Yes!' They say, 'Sign!' And he signs [to attest to the record's accuracy]. This is all in accord with the verse (*Job* 37:7), בְּיַד כָּל אָדָם יַחְתּוֹם, *He has it signed by the hand of every man* (*Taanis* 11a). Thus, *his own hand has set forth* the litany of his sins.

וְשׁוֹכֶבֶת בְּחֵיק, תָּעִיד בְּעָשִׁיר וָהֵלֶךְ,*   וְעָמְדָה לִפְנֵי הַמֶּלֶךְ.[1]

חַלְתִּי לֹא יִכְחַד כֹּל מֶנְהוּ,[2]   חַוּוֹת לְאָדָם מַה שִּׂיחֵהוּ,[3]

וְאִם עַל הַמִּשְׁכָּב הוּא,*   וְחָשַׁב עִם קוֹנֵהוּ.[4]

טֶרֶם יִתְנַגְּפוּ רַגְלֶיךָ[5] בְּעֶרְבּוֹן,*   טַהֵר עַצְמְךָ מִכָּל עָוֹן,

לֹא יוּכַל לְהִמָּלֵט בְּכָל עִזָּבוֹן,[6]   יֹאמְרוּ הַמּוֹשְׁלִים בָּאוּ חֶשְׁבּוֹן.

יֵעַד אַרְבָּעָה פְרָקִים* וְהָאַחֲרִית,   יָדוּן בֵּמוֹ נַחֲלַת שְׁאֵרִית,

וְאִם מָעֲלוּ בָךְ, הַבֵּט לַבְּרִית,   וְאַל תַּעֲמֹד עַל הַפֶּרֶק לְהַכְרִית.[7]

כִּי בְיוֹם כֶּסֶה* יָבֹא[8]   כָּל מִקְרֵה אִישׁ לִפְנֵי חוֹצְבוֹ,

אִם דַּל אִם עָשִׁיר בְּרִיבוֹ,   עוֹלִים וְיוֹרְדִים בּוֹ.[9]

לְעַמְּךָ מֵלִיץ יְשֶׁר תְּמֻנֶּה,   לְעֵת יָבְאוּ כָּל בְּנֵי

אָדָם בְּשִׁבְטוֹ לְהִמָּנֶה,   תַּעֲבִרְנָה הַצֹּאן עַל יְדֵי מוֹנֶה.[10]

מִשְׁפָּט עַמּוֹ תִּחַלֶּה* בְּקֶרֶב,   מִשְׁחַת תַּעַל חַיָּתָם לְטוֹב תַּעֲרֹב,

וְיָדִין לְאֻמִּים לְבַדָּם מִלַּעֲרֹב,   לְבִלְתִּי הֱיוֹת שָׁם עָרֹב.[11]

נָאוֹר[12] אֵלֶיךָ מִי יֶחְבָּר, נוֹהֵג שֶׁבָּעוֹלָם, אֵין מִשְׁתַּמֵּשׁ בִּכְלִי מְשֻׁבָּר,

---

וָהֵלֶךְ — *And poor* [lit., *traveler or vagrant*]. The Midrash (*Vayikra Rabbah* 34:6; cf. *Midrash Mishlei* 23) lists eight names by which Scripture calls a pauper: עָנִי, *afflicted* (*Exodus* 22:24); אֶבְיוֹן, *unfulfilled* (*ibid.* 23:6); מִסְכֵּן, *endangered* (*Ecclesiastes* 4:13); רָשׁ, *impoverished* (*I Samuel* 18:23); דַּל, *detached* [from his ancestral property] (*Exodus* 23:3); דַּךְ, *oppressed* (*Psalms* 9:10); מָךְ, *trampled upon* (*Leviticus* 27:8); and הֵלֶךְ, *vagrant* (*II Samuel* 12:4).

וְאִם עַל הַמִּשְׁכָּב הוּא — *And even when he is on* [his] *bed*. There is a triple meaning here: (a) Each night while the body lies asleep, the soul leaves the body and ascends to heaven where it must make an accounting for its day; (b) upon his death, all a man's life activities are recounted to him, even his casual words with his wife during their intimacy (*Chagigah* 5b); and (c) 'bed' alludes to man's final resting place, his grave, for each person must give an accounting for his entire life 'before the King Who reigns over kings, the Holy One, Blessed is He' (*Avos* 3:1). According to (a) and (c), this stich is connected to the next one: *And even when he is on his bed, he must make a reckoning with his Master*. According to (b), the stich is a continuation of the previous one: *Man will be told even his casual talk, and even* [that which he speaks] *when he is on his bed*.

טֶרֶם יִתְנַגְּפוּ רַגְלֶיךָ בְּעֶרְבּוֹן — *Before your feet stumble in* [their] *pledge*. This is an allusion to death, as the Talmud (*Succah* 53a) states: A man's feet are his guarantors; [on the day he is to die], they lead him to the place decreed for him [to die].

The Talmud tells a story to illustrate this point. King Solomon had two handsome scribes,

Elicharaf and Achiyah the sons of Shisha. One day, the king saw the Angel of Death looking very sad. He asked, 'Why are you so sad?'

'I am to take the souls of the two handsome men that reside here,' replied the Angel of Death.

Solomon hastily dispatched them to the town of Luz [where the Angel of Death was not permitted entry (see *Nedarim* 46b)]. As they were about to enter the town, they died.

The next day, the king spied the Angel of Death laughing. 'Why are you laughing?' he asked.

'You sent them to the exact spot [the gateway to Luz] where I was to take their souls.' [Yesterday's sadness was not because I had to take their souls; it was because they were not in the right place and I did not know how to get them there.]

Immediately, Solomon said, 'A man's feet are his guarantors; they lead him to the place decreed for him.'

עִזָּבוֹן — *Wares*. In Scriptures, this word is found only in chapter 27 of *Ezekiel* (vs. 12-33), where it is used to describe exported merchandise. Its derivation from the root עזב, *to forsake* or *leave behind*, is discussed by the commentaries. Some of the explanations given are: A dealer *forsakes* his merchandise in the country to which it is exported (*Ibn Janach, Shorashim*); a merchant may sell his wares cheaply, *forsaking* part of its value, in order to attract customers (*R' Eliezer of Beaugency*); any article that is sold is *forsaken* by the seller (*HaKesav VeHaKabbalah* to *Devarim* 32:36); and goods are often *forsaken* in warehouses for long periods of time (*Malbim*). Interestingly, *Targum* (to *Ezekiel*) alternates

and the [soul] that rests in man's breast testifies
  against both rich and poor,*
as it stands before the King.[1]

ח *I tremble — nothing will be hidden from Him;*[2]

ח *Man will be told [even] his casual talk —*[3]
and even when he is on [his] bed —*
he must make reckoning with his Maker.[4]

ט *Before your feet stumble*[5] *in [their] pledge,**

ט *cleanse yourself of every iniquity!*
Man cannot escape, not with all the wares,*
[so] let those who rule [their inclinations] say, 'Come to accounting!' [6]

י *He appointed four junctures [of the year]**
and engraved [their nature in them]:

י *On them He would judge the remnant of His heritage-people.*
If they have betrayed You, look to the covenant,
and do not stand at the juncture [of the year] to destroy.[7]

כ *For on [Rosh Hashanah,] the day of no moon,**[8] *there comes*

כ *man's every event before his Shaper;*
whether rich or poor, [he will come] to his judgment,
ascending and descending by it.[9]

ל *Assign a righteous advocate for Your people,*

ל *[on Rosh Hashanah,] when all the sons of*
Man come to be counted under His rod,
[like] the flock they shall pass before the One Who counts them.[10]

מ *Let Your people's judgment come [before You] first of all,**

מ *raise their souls from ruin and insure their welfare.*
Then judge the peoples separately, unmixed,
That there may be no intermingling there.[11]

נ *O Source of Light,*[12] *who is comparable to You?*

נ *The way of the world is not to use a broken vessel,*

---

(1) *I Kings* 1:2. (2) Cf. *II Samuel* 18:13. (3) Cf. *Amos* 4:13. (4) *Leviticus* 25:50. (5) Cf. *Jeremiah* 13:16. (6) *Numbers* 21:27. (7) *Obadiah* 1:14. (8) Cf. *Proverbs* 7:20; *Psalms* 81:4. (9) *Genesis* 28:12. (10) *Jeremiah* 33:13. (11) *Exodus* 8:18. (12) See commentary to *selichah* 18.

---

between *wares* and *storage houses* for the word עִזָּבוֹן.

In post-Biblical times, the word took on a more specific meaning: the legacy or heritage that one forsakes and passes on to his heirs when he leaves this world. Accordingly, the stich would read, *Man cannot escape, not even with all the wealth he leaves behind.*

אַרְבָּעָה פְרָקִים — *He appointed four junctures [of the year].* The Mishnah teaches: At four junctures [of the year] the world is judged: on Pesach for the grain; on Shavuos for the fruit of the tree; on Rosh Hashanah all who walk the earth pass before Him like young sheep ... and on Succos for the water (*Rosh Hashanah* 16a).

בְּיוֹם כֶּסֶא — *On [Rosh Hashanah,] the day of no moon.* The full Scriptural verse reads: תִּקְעוּ בַחֹדֶשׁ שׁוֹפָר, *Blow the shofar at the moon's renewal,* בַּכֶּסֶה לְיוֹם חַגֵּנוּ, *when it [the moon] is covered for our festive day* (*Psalms* 81:4). All Jewish holidays other than Rosh Hashanah occur in the middle of the month, when the major part of the moon is visible. Only Rosh Hashanah occurs at the very beginning of the month, when the moon is still covered (*Rosh Hashanah* 8a).

Alternatively, the word כֶּסֶא means *appointed time* (Rashi, Radak, Ibn Ezra).

תְּחִלָּה — *First of all.* When a king and his nation are brought before the Heavenly Tribunal for judgment, the king is judged first, lest his fate be sealed by the Divine wrath unleashed by the sins of his people. Similarly, when all the world stands in judgment before the Heavenly Tribunal, Israel is judged first, lest its fate be sealed by the Divine wrath unleashed by the sins of the nations (*Rosh Hashanah* 8b).

הֲיִפָּלֵא מֵיהוה דָּבָר,²   וְלֹא תִבְזֶה, לֵב נִדְכֶּה וְנִשְׁבָּר,¹

סָתְתוּ אֶבֶן נֶגֶף* לְעֵמֶק שָׁוֶה,   סוּרוּ טָמֵא, קָרְאוּ³ כְּסִיל הַמַּחְבֵּא,

כִּי אֵין הַצָּר בְּנֶזֶק שׁוֶה,⁴   הָבָה נִתְחַכְּמָה לוֹ פֶּן יִרְבֶּה.⁵

עוֹבֵד שְׁנֵי אֲדוֹנִים כְּפִי שָׁנָיו,   עֲשׂוֹת לְיוֹצְרוֹ וּלְיִצְרוֹ כִּרְצוֹנָיו,

וְטוֹב הִדָּבֵק לְבוֹרְאוֹ כָּל זְמַנָּיו,   וְעֶבֶד חָפְשִׁי מֵאֲדוֹנָיו.⁶

פְּנוֹת הַיּוֹם* סְעוּדָתוֹ יָכֵן,   פָּעֳלוֹ לָזֶה וְלִבָּא יְהִי נָכוֹן,

וְעוֹשֵׂהוּ בַּשַּׁבָּת מַה יִּסְכֹּן,   מְעֻוָּת לֹא יוּכַל לִתְקֹן.⁷

צְעָקָה לָכֵן קִדַּמְנוּ לְיוֹם הַדִּין, וְתַקְשִׁיב,

צוֹם* וּתְשׁוּבָה שְׁלֵמָה חֲמָתְךָ יָשִׁיב,

וְלֹא כְשָׁב עַל קֵאוֹ⁸ בְּאֶחֱטָא וְאָשִׁיב,⁹

לֹא מָצְאָה יָדוֹ דֵּי הָשִׁיב.¹⁰

קוּמוּ יְשֵׁנֵי מַכְפֵּל* לְסַעֲדִי,   קַלּוֹתִי וּמַעַשׂ אֵין בְּיָדִי,

וְזַעֲקוּ וְהִתְפַּלְּלוּ לְאֵל עִמָּדִי,   וּמכַחֲכָם שִׂחֲדוּ בַעֲדִי.¹¹

רַחֲמִים תְּעוֹרֵר, לָתֵת עָצְמָה לְאֵין אוֹנִים,¹²

רָם, כִּי נִשְׁבְּחוּ זֶה כַּמֶּה שָׁנִים,

שַׁעֲרֵי דְמָעוֹת תִּפְתַּח לְנִטְעֵי נַעֲמָנִים,¹³

בִּבְכִי יָבְאוּ וּבְתַחֲנוּנִים.¹⁴

שַׁדַּי, בְּמֶרְיֵנוּ הֲלוֹא כְּנָכְרִים נֶחְשַׁבְנוּ,¹⁵

שַׁבְנוּ אֵלֶיךָ, וּכְאָב עַל בֵּן תְּרַחֲמֵנוּ,¹⁶

זְכֹר כִּי בָנִים¹⁷ קְרָאתָנוּ, וְאָב אֶחָד לְכֻלָּנוּ,¹⁸

לָמָּה יִגָּרַע שֵׁם אָבִינוּ.¹⁹

תְּשׁוּרָה אֵין בְּיָדִי לְפָנֶיךָ,   תְּמוּרָתָהּ תִּכּוֹן תְּפִלָּתִי וְתַחֲנוּנָי,²⁰

קַח נָא אֶת הַמִּנְחָה הַהוֹלֶכֶת לְפָנָי,²¹

וְיֵדְעוּ (כָל) הָעָם הַזֶּה כִּי אַתָּה יהוה.²²

---

(1) Cf. *Psalms* 51:19. (2) *Genesis* 18:14. (3) Cf. *Lamentations* 4:15. (4) Cf. *Esther* 7:4.
(5) *Exodus* 1:10. (6) *Job* 3:18. (7) *Ecclesiastes* 1:15. (8) Cf. *Proverbs* 26:11.
(9) See tractate *Yoma* 85b. (10) *Leviticus* 25:28. (11) *Job* 6:22. (12) Cf. *Isaiah* 40:29.
(13) Cf. 17:10. (14) *Jeremiah* 31:8. (15) Cf. *Genesis* 31:15. (16) Cf. *Psalms* 103:13.
(17) See *Deuteronomy* 14:1. (18) Cf. *Malachi* 2:10. (19) *Numbers* 27:4.
(20) Cf. *Psalms* 141:2. (21) Cf. *Genesis* 32:20. (22) *I Kings* 18:37.

אֶבֶן נֶגֶף — *The stony obstacle.* This alludes to the Evil Inclination. See commentary to *selichah* 22 (s.v., מכשׁול . . . אֶבֶן) regarding the various names by which the Evil Inclination is known.

פְּנוֹת הַיּוֹם — *Towards [Friday] evening.* The Talmud compares the World to Come to the Sabbath: If one exerts himself on the eve of the Sabbath [i.e., he performs *mitzvos* in this world], he will eat on the Sabbath [i.e., he will reap his reward in the World to Come]; but one who does not exert himself on the eve of the Sabbath, what will he eat on the Sabbath? (*Avodah Zarah* 3a).

yet You do not despise a crushed and broken heart.[1]
Is anything too wonderful for HASHEM?[2]

ס Smooth out the stony obstacle* to a level plain;

ס cry, 'Keep away, Unclean One,'[3] at the hidden fool;
for the oppressor cares nothing for the damage [he causes us].[4]
Come, let us deal wisely with him, lest he increase.[5]

ע [Man,] who serves two masters throughout his years,

ע doing for his Maker or for his [Evil] Inclination,
according to his own will —
better for him to cling to his Creator all his days,
[for then] he is like a [former] slave, free from his [evil] master.[6]

פ If one prepares his meal towards [Friday] evening,*

פ his act stands firm both in this [world] and in the [World] to Come.
But if he makes it on the Sabbath, of what benefit is it?
It is a twisted thing that cannot be made straight.[7]

צ Therefore we cry out before the Day of Judgment,
and You hearken.

צ [Our] fasting* and complete repentance will turn back Your anger.
[We will] not [be] like one who returns to his vomit,[8]
saying, 'I will sin and I will repent,'[9]
but will not find [the time] to fully repent.[10]

ק Arise to my aid, O [you] sleepers in the Machpelah!*

ק I am of light worth, and no [good] deeds are in my hand.
Shout and pray to God along with me,
and from your wealth [of mitzvos] offer a bribe for me.[11]

ר Awaken mercy, to give strength to those who have no might,[12]

ר O Lofty One, for they have been forgotten this many a year.
Open the Gates of Tears to [Israel, Your] delightful plantings;[13]
they will come with crying and with supplications.[14]

ש O Almighty, when we rebelled were we not regarded as strangers
[to You]?[15]

ש [But] we have returned to You; [so now] have mercy on us
as a father on [his] child.[16]
Remember that You called us 'children,'[17] that we all have one Father;[18]
why should our Father's name be diminished?[19]

ת I have no tribute in my hand [to send] before me;

ת in its place, let my prayer and my supplication stand.[20]
Please take this offering that goes before me,[21]
and this (entire) people will know that You are HASHEM.[22]

צום — [Our] fasting. Some editions of Selichos read צְדָקָה, charity. It has been suggested that those people who follow the ancient custom of fasting on Erev Rosh Hashanah should recite the word צום. However, those who are unable to fast should substitute the word צְדָקָה, so their words

do not sound false.

וִישֵׁנֵי מַכְפֵּל — O [you] sleepers in the Machpelah. Four patriarchal couples were buried in the Cave of Machpelah: Adam and Eve; Abraham and Sarah; Isaac and Rebecca; Jacob and Leah (Eruvin 53a; Genesis 49:31).

יָדַע וְהֵכִין[1] מֵרֵאשִׁית תְּשׁוּבָה,*   אֱלֹהִים חָשְׁבָה לְטוֹבָה,[2]

בְּכֵן רְצֹנוּ עָדֶיךָ לָשׁוּבָה,   הֲשִׁיבֵנוּ יהוה אֵלֶיךָ וְנָשׁוּבָה.[3]

❖ יְדִידִים צָעֲקוּ חֵלוּ,[4] קָרוֹת בִּמְהוּמִים,

הַקּוֹל לִמְכוֹן וְעוּדוֹ יִשְׁמַע מִמְּרוֹמִים,

יִכָּמְרוּ רַחֲמָיו, בִּזְכוּת שְׁלֹשֶׁת תְּמִימִים,

אֵל שַׁדַּי, יִתֵּן לָכֶם רַחֲמִים.[5]

All, while standing:

אֵל מֶלֶךְ יוֹשֵׁב עַל כִּסֵּא רַחֲמִים מִתְנַהֵג בַּחֲסִידוּת, מוֹחֵל עֲוֹנוֹת עַמּוֹ, מַעֲבִיר רִאשׁוֹן רִאשׁוֹן,[1] מַרְבֶּה מְחִילָה לְחַטָּאִים וּסְלִיחָה לְפוֹשְׁעִים, עֹשֶׂה צְדָקוֹת עִם כָּל בָּשָׂר וָרוּחַ, לֹא כְרָעָתָם תִּגְמוֹל. ❖ אֵל הוֹרֵיתָ לָּנוּ לוֹמַר שְׁלֹשׁ עֶשְׂרֵה, וּזְכֹר לָנוּ הַיּוֹם בְּרִית שְׁלֹשׁ עֶשְׂרֵה, כְּמוֹ שֶׁהוֹדַעְתָּ לֶעָנָיו מִקֶּדֶם, כְּמוֹ שֶׁכָּתוּב, וַיֵּרֶד יהוה בֶּעָנָן וַיִּתְיַצֵּב עִמּוֹ שָׁם, וַיִּקְרָא בְשֵׁם יהוה.

Congregation, then chazzan:

וַיַּעֲבֹר יהוה עַל פָּנָיו וַיִּקְרָא:

Congregation and chazzan (the words in bold type are recited aloud and in unison):

יהוה, יהוה, אֵל, רַחוּם, וְחַנּוּן, אֶרֶךְ אַפַּיִם, וְרַב חֶסֶד, וֶאֱמֶת, נֹצֵר חֶסֶד לָאֲלָפִים, נֹשֵׂא עָוֹן, וָפֶשַׁע, וְחַטָּאָה, וְנַקֵּה. וְסָלַחְתָּ לַעֲוֹנֵנוּ וּלְחַטָּאתֵנוּ וּנְחַלְתָּנוּ. סְלַח לָנוּ אָבִינוּ כִּי חָטָאנוּ, מְחַל לָנוּ מַלְכֵּנוּ כִּי פָשָׁעְנוּ. כִּי אַתָּה אֲדֹנָי טוֹב וְסַלָּח, וְרַב חֶסֶד לְכָל קֹרְאֶיךָ.

פסוקי הקדמה לסליחה כט

הַצּוּר תָּמִים פָּעֳלוֹ, כִּי כָל דְּרָכָיו מִשְׁפָּט, אֵל אֱמוּנָה וְאֵין עָוֶל, צַדִּיק וְיָשָׁר הוּא.[6] לְמִשְׁפָּטֶיךָ עָמְדוּ הַיּוֹם, כִּי הַכֹּל עֲבָדֶיךָ.[7] תִּקְעוּ בַחֹדֶשׁ שׁוֹפָר, בַּכֶּסֶה לְיוֹם חַגֵּנוּ. כִּי חֹק לְיִשְׂרָאֵל הוּא, מִשְׁפָּט לֵאלֹהֵי יַעֲקֹב.[8] צִדְקָתְךָ כְּהַרְרֵי אֵל, מִשְׁפָּטֶיךָ תְּהוֹם רַבָּה,* אָדָם וּבְהֵמָה תּוֹשִׁיעַ יהוה.[9]

וְהֵכִין מֵרֵאשִׁית תְּשׁוּבָה — *So He prepared repentance from the beginning.* Seven thing were created before the creation of the world [i.e., God laid out their creation in His thoughts (Rabbeinu Nissim)]. They are: Torah, *Teshuvah* (repentance), *Gan Eden, Gehinnom,* the Throne of Glory, the *Beis HaMikdash,* and the name of the Messiah … That *teshuvah* preceded Creation is derived from the passage (*Psalms* 90:2-3): *Before the mountains were born and You had not yet fashioned the earth … You say, 'Repent, O sons*

of man!' (*Nedarim* 39b; see also commentary to *selichah* 46, s.v., אָז טֶרֶם).

צִדְקָתְךָ כְּהַרְרֵי אֵל מִשְׁפָּטֶיךָ תְּהוֹם רַבָּה — *Your righteousness is like the mighty mountains, Your judgments [are like] the vast deep.* Although God's *kindness* and *faithfulness* both encompass the entire world, when the time of judgment arrives, the Almighty differentiates between the righteous and the wicked. Upon the righteous He bestows charities as great as the mighty mountains, while the wicked descend to the lowest

He knew [man would sin],
  so He prepared[1] repentance from the beginning —*
God thought it out for [man's] benefit.[2]
Therefore we run to You in return;
  bring us back to You, HASHEM, and we shall return.[3]
Chazzan — [His] beloved ones cry out, they tremble,[4]
  calling [to Him] in tumultuous assembly;
may the sound [come] to His meeting hall and be heard [there] on high.
May His mercy be aroused by the merit of
  the whole-hearted threesome [the Patriarchs] —
may God Almighty give you mercy.[5]

All, while standing:

אֵל מֶלֶךְ O God, King Who sits on the throne of mercy; Who acts with
  kindness, pardons the iniquities of His people, removes [sins]
one by one,[1] increasingly grants pardon to careless sinners and forgiveness
to rebels, Who deals righteously with every living being — You do not repay
them in accord with their evil. Chazzan — O God, You taught us to recite the
Thirteen [Attributes of Mercy], so remember for us today the covenant of
these Thirteen, as You made known to the humble one in ancient times, as
it is written: And HASHEM descended in a cloud and stood with him there,
and He called out with the Name HASHEM.

Congregation, then chazzan:

And HASHEM passed before him [Moses] and proclaimed:

Congregation and chazzan (the words in bold type are recited aloud and in unison):

ה' ה' HASHEM, HASHEM, God, **Compassionate and Gracious, Slow to
  anger, and Abundant in Kindness and Truth, Preserver of
kindness for thousands [of generations], Forgiver of iniquity, willful
sin, and error, and Who cleanses.** May You forgive our iniquities and our
errors and make us Your heritage. Forgive us, our Father, for we have
erred; pardon us, our King, for we have willfully sinned; for You, my Lord,
are good and forgiving and abundantly kind to all who call upon You.

PREFATORY VERSES TO SELICHAH 29

הַצּוּר The Rock — perfect in His work, for all His paths are justice; a
  faithful God without wrong, righteous and upright is He.[6]
[Heaven and earth] stand to [receive] Your judgment today, for all are
Your servants.[7] Blow the shofar at the moon's renewal, at the time
appointed for our festival day. For it is a decree for Israel, the judgment
of the God of Jacob.[8] Your righteousness is like the mighty mountains,
Your judgments [are like] the vast deep;* You save both man and animal,
HASHEM.[9]

---

(1) Some editions read: יָדַע וְהֵכִין, He made known that He had prepared.
(2) Genesis 50:20. (3) Lamentations 5:21. (4) Some editions read: חִלּוּ, they pray.
(5) Cf. Genesis 43:14. (6) Deuteronomy 32:4. (7) Psalms 119:91. (8) 81:4-5. (9) 36:7.

---

depths of the vast deep.
  The abundance of good is compared to a lofty
mountain peak, because there one is safe from
those evil forces that seek to snatch away the

rewards he has earned in his lifetime. The
punishment of the wicked is likened to the deep,
because there is no escape from its grip (Radak to
Psalms 36:7).

בְּרַחֵם אָב עַל בָּנִים, כֵּן תְּרַחֵם יהוה עָלֵינוּ. לַיהוה הַיְשׁוּעָה, עַל עַמְּךָ בִרְכָתֶךָ סֶּלָה. יהוה צְבָאוֹת עִמָּנוּ, מִשְׂגָּב לָנוּ אֱלֹהֵי יַעֲקֹב סֶלָה. יהוה צְבָאוֹת, אַשְׁרֵי אָדָם בֹּטֵחַ בָּךְ. יהוה הוֹשִׁיעָה, הַמֶּלֶךְ יַעֲנֵנוּ בְיוֹם קָרְאֵנוּ.

In some congregations the following two verses are recited responsively — the *chazzan* reciting סְלַח, and the congregation responding וַיֹּאמֶר. In other congregations these verses are recited silently.

סְלַח נָא לַעֲוֹן הָעָם הַזֶּה כְּגֹדֶל חַסְדֶּךָ, וְכַאֲשֶׁר נָשָׂאתָה לָעָם הַזֶּה מִמִּצְרַיִם וְעַד הֵנָּה, וְשָׁם נֶאֱמַר:

וַיֹּאמֶר יהוה סָלַחְתִּי כִּדְבָרֶךָ.

All:

הַטֵּה אֱלֹהַי אָזְנְךָ וּשֲׁמָע, פְּקַח עֵינֶיךָ וּרְאֵה שֹׁמְמֹתֵינוּ, וְהָעִיר אֲשֶׁר נִקְרָא שִׁמְךָ עָלֶיהָ, כִּי לֹא עַל צִדְקוֹתֵינוּ אֲנַחְנוּ מַפִּילִים תַּחֲנוּנֵינוּ לְפָנֶיךָ, כִּי עַל רַחֲמֶיךָ הָרַבִּים. אֲדֹנָי שְׁמָעָה, אֲדֹנָי סְלָחָה, אֲדֹנָי הַקְשִׁיבָה, וַעֲשֵׂה אַל תְּאַחַר, לְמַעַנְךָ אֱלֹהַי, כִּי שִׁמְךָ נִקְרָא עַל עִירְךָ וְעַל עַמֶּךָ.

סְלִיחָה כט (שלישיה)

All:

אֵל אֱמוּנָה* עֶזְרָה הָבָה,   לְעַמְּךָ כֻּלָּם הֲטִיבָה,

יַחַד **לַמִּשְׁפָּט** נִקְרָבָה.[1]

בּוֹחֵן לִבּוֹת כֻּלָּם,   מוֹשֵׁל בִּגְבוּרָתוֹ עוֹלָם,*[2]

יָבִיא **בְמִשְׁפָּט** עַל כָּל נֶעְלָם.[3]

גְּבוֹהַּ בַּמִּשְׁפָּט הָאֵל,   נִקְדָּשׁ בְּצִדְקוֹתָיו[4] כְּהַרֲרֵי אֵל,

וּמִשְׁפָּטָיו[5] עִם יִשְׂרָאֵל.[6]

דַּלָּה מֵעֹנֶשׁ נְשׂוּאֶיךָ,   בְּחֶסֶד וֶאֱמֶת מְנַשְּׂאֶיךָ,*

צֶדֶק **וּמִשְׁפָּט** מְכוֹן כִּסְאָךְ.[7]

הַיְשַׁר לְפָנֶיךָ לֵב עֲקֹב,   דִּינֶךָ הָדָר יַעֲקֹב,*

מִשְׁפָּט לֵאלֹהֵי יַעֲקֹב.[8]

אֵל אֱמוּנָה — *O faithful God.* This *selichah* comprises twenty-four triplets, and is thus called a שְׁלִישִׁיָה, *threesome*. The first twenty-two follow an alphabetical acrostic, and the twenty-third bears the author's signature, אֶפְרַיִם, *Ephraim*. This *paytan* is usually identified as R' Ephraim of Regensburg [see prefatory comment to *selichah* 52]. The third line of each triplet is a fragment of a Scriptural verse and contains some

form of the word מִשְׁפָּט which can mean *judgment, justice* or *law.*

עוֹלָם — *Forever.* The translation follows *Radak* and *Ibn Ezra* (Psalms 66:7), who understand the word as if it read לְעוֹלָם. *Targum,* however, renders עוֹלָם, *the world,* thus the stich means: *He rules the world with His might.*

... בְּחֶסֶד וֶאֱמֶת מְנַשְּׂאֶיךָ — *Who exalt You with*

כְּרַחֵם אָב As a father has mercy on his children, so, HASHEM, may You have mercy on us. Salvation is HASHEM's, upon Your people is Your blessing, Selah. HASHEM, Master of Legions, is with us, a stronghold for us is the God of Jacob, Selah. HASHEM, Master of Legions, praiseworthy is the person who trusts in You. HASHEM, save! May the King answer us on the day we call.

In some congregations the following two verses are recited responsively — the chazzan reciting, 'Forgive, please . . .,' and the congregation responding, 'And HASHEM said . . .'
In other congregations these verses are recited silently.

סְלַח נָא Forgive, please, the iniquity of this people according to the greatness of Your kindness and as You have forgiven this people from Egypt until now, and there it was said:

And HASHEM said, 'I have forgiven according to your word!'

All:

הַטֵּה Incline, my God, Your ear, and listen, open Your eyes and see our desolation and that of the city upon which YourName is proclaimed; for not because of our righteousness do we cast down our supplications before You, rather because of Your abundant compassion. O my Lord, heed; O my Lord, forgive; O my Lord, be attentive and act, do not delay; for Your sake, my God, for Your Name is proclaimed upon Your city and upon Your people.

SELICHAH 29

All:

א O faithful God,* bring [us] help!
   Do good to all Your people;
   let us approach together for **judgment**.[1]

ב He Who searches all [men's] hearts,
   Who rules with His might forever,*[2]
   brings [us] to **judgment** for every forgotten thing.[3]

ג Lofty in judgment is God,
   hallowed by His righteousness[4] that is like the mighty mountains,
   and [by] His **judgments**[5] of Israel.[6]

ד Raise from punishment those You have borne,
   who exalt You with kindness and truth,*
   [for] righteousness and **justice** are Your Throne's foundation.[7]

ה Straighten before You the crooked heart [of man];
   let Your law pierce the mountain,*
   [for] it is the **judgment** of the God of Jacob.[8]

---

(1) Cf. Isaiah 41:1. (2) Psalms 66:7. (3) Ecclessiastes 12:4. (4) Cf. Isaiah 5:16.
(5) Cf. Psalms 36:7. (6) Deuteronomy 33:21. (7) Cf. Psalms 89:15. (8) 81:5.

---

kindness and truth ... This stich may allude either to God's kindness and truth for which Israel praises him, or to Israel's kindness and truth by which they sanctify and exalt God. Alternatively, this and the next stich form a quotation: They exalt You by [reciting the verse (Psalms 89:15)]: 'Righteousness and justice are Your Throne's foundation; kindness and truth [precede Your countenance].'

דִּינֶךָ הֲרַר יִקַּב — Let Your law pierce the mountain. This Talmudic expression describes the job of the beis din once the litigants stand before the court

וְיֹשֶׁר מְדוֹתֶיךָ נֶחֱמָדוּ,   יוֹשְׁבֵי תֵבֵל צֶדֶק לָמָדוּ,[1]
לְמִשְׁפָּטֶיךָ עָמָדוּ.[2]

זְקוּקָה צְרוּפָה חוֹתֶמֶת,   בִּפְעַל אָדָם נֶחְתֶּמֶת,*
מִשְׁפְּטֵי יהוה אֱמֶת.[3]

חָרַד כָּל מֵדִין בּוֹדֵק,   טוֹחֵן וְשׁוֹחֵק הָדֵק,
מִשְׁפְּטֵי יהוה אֱמֶת וָצֶדֶק.[4]

טוֹב לְמָעוֹז כְּנֶאֱמוֹ,[5]   יוֹם זֶה יִשְׁכַּח זַעֲמוֹ,
לַעֲשׂוֹת מִשְׁפַּט עַמּוֹ.[6]

יַחֵלוּ בְּצִקּוּן דְּבָקֶיךָ,   יְסַלְסְלוּ בְּשָׁלוֹם חֻקֶּיךָ,
עַל מִשְׁפְּטֵי צִדְקֶךָ.[7]

כַּלֵּה פֶּשַׁע נִכְתָּם,   וְאַל יֵבוֹשׁוּ מְיַחֲלֶיךָ בְּמַבָּטָם,
וְעָשִׂיתָ מִשְׁפָּטָם.[8]

לְשִׁמְךָ וּלְזִכְרְךָ הוּקַמְנוּ,   לִבְרִית עוֹלָם הוּשַׂמְנוּ,[9]
וְאַל תָּבוֹא בְמִשְׁפָּט עִמָּנוּ.[10]

מֶלֶךְ בִּקְדוֹשֵׁי אֶרֶץ,[11]   בְּרַחֲמָיו יִגְדֹּר פֶּרֶץ,[12]
בְּמִשְׁפָּט יַעֲמִיד אָרֶץ.[13]

נְגִינוֹתַי כָּל הַיּוֹם[14] יְאַשְּׁרוּהוּ,   שַׂגִּיא כֹחַ לֹא מְצָאנוּהוּ,[15]
כִּי הַמִּשְׁפָּט לֵאלֹהִים הוּא.[16]

שַׂגֵּב חַסְדְּךָ לְעַמֶּךָ,   לְשַׁוְעָתָם פְּתַח שְׁמֶיךָ,
בְּמִשְׁפָּט לְאֹהֲבֵי שְׁמֶךָ.[17]

עָלֶיךָ נַשְׁלִיךְ כָּל יְהָבִים,[18]   כַּף צֶדֶק תַּכְרִיעַ בַּאֲהָבִים,
כִּי מִשְׁפָּטֶיךָ טוֹבִים.[19]

פָּנֶיךָ הָאֵר לִמְחִילָתִי,   בְּבִצְעִי אַל תְּכַבֶּה גַחַלְתִּי,[20]
כִּי לְמִשְׁפָּטֶיךָ יִחָלְתִּי.[21]

צַדְּקֵנוּ כְּאַחַת חֲטִיבָה,   חָשְׁבֵנוּ מִלַּהַט הַיּוֹם הַבָּא,[22]
מִשְׁפָּטֶיךָ תְּהוֹם רַבָּה.[23]

---

(1) Cf. *Isaiah* 26:9. (2) Cf. *Psalms* 119:91. (3) 19:10. (4) Unlike the closing stich of the other stanzas, this one is not a Scriptural verse; some editions read מִשְׁפַּט אֱמֶת וְצֶדֶק, *a true and righteous judgment*, cf. *Zechariah* 7:9; *Psalms* 119:121. (5) *Nahum* 1:7. (6) Cf. *I Kings* 8:59. (7) *Psalms* 119:62. (8) *I Kings* 8:45. (9) Cf. *II Samuel* 23:5. (10) Cf. *Psalms* 143:2. (11) Cf. 89:8. (12) Cf. *Amos* 9:11. (13) *Proverbs* 29:4. (14) Cf. *Lamentations* 3:14. (15) Cf. *Job* 37:23, see Rashi there. (16) *Deuteronomy* 1:17. (17) *Psalms* 119:132. (18) Cf. 55:23. (19) 119:39. (20) Cf. *II Samuel* 14:7. (21) *Psalms* 119:43. (22) Cf. *Malachi* 3:19. (23) *Psalms* 36:7.

---

and the proceedings have started. Until that point, it is proper to attempt mediation that will lead to a settlement agreed upon by both parties. But once the court hearing has begun, 'let the law

ו And the uprightness of Your Attributes which are desirous,
  [to] the inhabitants of earth who have learned righteousness,[1]
  [when] they stand to [receive] Your **judgments**.[2]

ז Clear and pure is the seal [of Your verdict]:
  it is sealed by man's own deed,*
  [for] HASHEM's **judgments** are true.[3]

ח All [men] tremble before the judgment of the Examiner,
  Who grinds and pulverizes [men's deeds and hearts
      to examine them] minutely,
  HASHEM's **judgments** are true and righteous.[4]

ט He Who is a goodly fortress [in time of trouble], as He has said,[5]
  today He will forget His fury
  to pass **judgment** on His people.[6]

י Those who cling to You pray with outpouring,
  they exalt the perfection of Your decrees
  and Your righteous **judgments**.[7]

כ Make an end of staining sin,
  and let those who hope to You not be shamed in their expectation,
  when You pass **judgment** on them.[8]

ל We were established for the sake of Your Name and its revelation;
  we were set as an eternal covenant;[9]
  so do not enter into strict **judgment** with us.[10]

מ He Who is King over awesome, holy [angels],[11]
  in His mercy He will mend the breach [in Israel's wall],[12]
  and with **judgment** He will put the world in order.[13]

נ My songs every day[14] revere Him,
  for never have we found Him [judging us] with His great might
      [but with mercy],[15]
  even though **judgment** belongs to God.[16]

ס Reinforce Your kindness to Your people;
  open Your heavens to their outcry,
  as is **just** for those who love Your Name.[17]

ע We will cast all [our] burdens upon You;[18]
  may You, with love, tilt the scales of vindication,
  for Your **judgments** are good.[19]

פ Let Your countenance shine in forgiveness for me;
  despite my wrongdoing do not extinguish my [soul's] ember,[20]
  for I look expectantly to Your **judgments**.[21]

צ Vindicate us as a single group,
  and save us from the coming Day's flame[22] —
  Your **judgments** are like the vast deep.[23]

---

pierce the mountain,' for nothing in the world, not even the loftiest mountain, can stand in the way of God's justice; the judges must render their decision based on the principles of *halachah* and not continue to attempt a mediated settlement (see *Sanhedrin* 6b).

בְּמִפְעַל אָדָם נֶחְתֶּמֶת — *It is sealed by man's own deed.* See commentary to *selichah* 28 (s.v., וּבְיָדוֹ סְדוּרוֹת). Alternatively, the stich means that it is man's deed that seals his fate, for Divine judgment is based upon man's actions; he is always judged in accordance with his deeds.

קָרֵב יֵשַׁע שְׁבָטֶיךָ,[1]　　אֲחוּזִים בְּחַבְלֵי[2] שְׁפָטֶיךָ,

וְיִוָּשֵׁר **מִשְׁפָּטֶיךָ**.[3]

רֶנֶן מִלֵּב וּבָשָׂר וּנְשָׁמָה,　　יַעֲלֶה לְךָ הַשָּׁמַיְמָה,

מְקוֹם **הַמִּשְׁפָּט** שָׁמָּה.[4]

שׁוֹפְטֵנוּ מְחוֹקְקֵנוּ בְּכַפֶּיךָ,*[5]　　לַמֵּד דְּרָכֶיךָ מְצַפֶּיךָ,

וְכֹל **מִשְׁפְּטֵי** פִיךָ.[6]

תַּשְׁפִּיעַ חַסְדְּךָ דַּיֵּנוּ,　　תַּגְבְּרֵת רַחֲמֶיךָ לְמַאֲוַיֵּינוּ,

כְּמִשְׁפָּטֶיךָ חַיֵּנוּ.[7]

אַפִּרְיוֹן לְעֵי הַשָּׂדֶה,　　מַהֵר לְשַׂכְּלֵל יְסוֹדָהּ,

צִיּוֹן **בְּמִשְׁפָּט** תִּפָּדֶה.[8]

❖ מֵאוֹיְבַי אַנְקְמָה פִּזְּרוּנִי,　　גַּדַּע קַרְנוֹת זֵרוּנִי,

וּמִשְׁפָּטֶיךָ יַעַזְרֻנִי.[9]

All, while standing:

אֵל מֶלֶךְ יוֹשֵׁב עַל כִּסֵּא רַחֲמִים מִתְנַהֵג בַּחֲסִידוּת, מוֹחֵל
עֲוֹנוֹת עַמּוֹ, מַעֲבִיר רִאשׁוֹן רִאשׁוֹן, מַרְבֶּה מְחִילָה
לַחַטָּאִים וּסְלִיחָה לַפּוֹשְׁעִים, עֹשֶׂה צְדָקוֹת עִם כָּל בָּשָׂר וָרוּחַ, לֹא
כְרָעָתָם תִּגְמוֹל. ❖ אֵל הוֹרֵיתָ לָּנוּ לוֹמַר שְׁלֹשׁ עֶשְׂרֵה, וּזְכוֹר לָנוּ
הַיּוֹם בְּרִית שְׁלֹשׁ עֶשְׂרֵה, כְּמוֹ שֶׁהוֹדַעְתָּ לֶעָנָיו מִקֶּדֶם, כְּמוֹ
שֶׁכָּתוּב, וַיֵּרֶד יהוה בֶּעָנָן וַיִּתְיַצֵּב עִמּוֹ שָׁם, וַיִּקְרָא בְשֵׁם יהוה.

Congregation, then chazzan:

וַיַּעֲבֹר יהוה עַל פָּנָיו וַיִּקְרָא:

Congregation and chazzan (the words in bold type are recited aloud and in unison):

יהוה, יהוה,　　אֵל, רַחוּם, וְחַנּוּן, אֶרֶךְ אַפַּיִם, וְרַב חֶסֶד, וֶאֱמֶת,

נֹצֵר חֶסֶד לָאֲלָפִים, נֹשֵׂא עָוֹן, וָפֶשַׁע, וְחַטָּאָה,

וְנַקֵּה. וְסָלַחְתָּ לַעֲוֹנֵנוּ וּלְחַטָּאתֵנוּ וּנְחַלְתָּנוּ. סְלַח לָנוּ אָבִינוּ כִּי
חָטָאנוּ, מְחַל לָנוּ מַלְכֵּנוּ כִּי פָשָׁעְנוּ. כִּי אַתָּה אֲדֹנָי טוֹב וְסַלָּח, וְרַב
חֶסֶד לְכָל קֹרְאֶיךָ.

The Talmud (*Taanis 4a*) relates an exchange
between Israel and God: Israel requested of God,
'Master of the Universe, *place me as a seal on
Your heart, as a seal on Your arm (Song of Songs
8:6).*

God replied, 'My daughter, you request something that at times can be seen and at other times
cannot be seen. [A seal placed on the heart or arm
cannot be seen when a person is clothed.] However, I shall make of you something that can be
seen at all times, הֵן עַל כַּפַּיִם חַקֹּתִיךְ, *behold, on
[My] palms have I engraved you' (Isaiah 49:16).*

ק Bring salvation closer for Your tribes,[1]
   who are caught in the travails[2] of Your admonitions,
   and the righteousness of Your **judgments**.[3]

ר Song — from heart and flesh and soul —
   will arise to You Heavenwards,
   there where Your **judgment** place is.[4]

שׁ Our Judge, You Who have engraved us on Your palm,*[5]
   teach Your ways to those who await You
   and all the **judgments** of Your mouth.[6]

תּ Cause Your kindness to flow in abundance, [until we cry,]
      'It is enough for us!'
   An upsurge of Your mercy to [answer] our longing.
   According to Your **just** way, sustain us in life![7]

[Your] Temple, has become a heap [of rubble] in the field —
   come quickly to re-establish its foundation,
   and let Zion be redeemed through **justice**.[8]

Chazzan — May I have vengeance on my enemies
      who have dispersed me [in Exile];
   lop off the horns of those who scattered me,
   and let Your **judgments** be my aid.[9]

All, while standing:

אֵל מֶלֶךְ O God, King Who sits on the throne of mercy; Who acts with
   kindness, pardons the iniquities of His people, removes [sins]
one by one, increasingly grants pardon to careless sinners and forgiveness
to rebels, Who deals righteously with every living being — You do not
repay them in accord with their evil. Chazzan — O God, You taught us to
recite the Thirteen [Attributes of Mercy], so remember for us today the
covenant of these Thirteen, as You made known to the humble one in
ancient times, as it is written: And HASHEM descended in a cloud and stood
with him there, and He called out with the Name HASHEM.

Congregation, then chazzan:
And HASHEM passed before him [Moses] and proclaimed:

Congregation and chazzan (the words in bold type are recited aloud and in unison):

ה' ה' HASHEM, HASHEM, God, Compassionate and Gracious, Slow
   to anger, and Abundant in Kindness and Truth, Preserver of
kindness for thousands [of generations], Forgiver of iniquity, willful
sin, and error, and Who cleanses. *May You forgive our iniquities and
our errors and make us Your heritage. Forgive us, our Father, for we
have erred; pardon us, our King, for we have willfully sinned; for You,
my Lord, are good and forgiving and abundantly kind to all who call
upon You.*

---

(1) Cf. *Psalms* 85:10. (2) Cf. *Jeremiah* 13:21. (3) Cf. *Psalms* 119:137.
(4) *Ecclesiastes* 3:16. (5) Cf. *Isaiah* 33:22; 49:16. (6) Cf. *Psalms* 119:13.
(7) Cf. 119:156. (8) *Isaiah* 1:27. (9) *Psalms* 119:175.

פסוקי הקדמה לסליחה ל

אַל תָּבוֹא בְמִשְׁפָּט עִמָּנוּ, כִּי לֹא יִצְדַּק לְפָנֶיךָ כָל חָי.[1]
אֱלֹהִים לָנוּ מַחֲסֶה וָעֹז, עֶזְרָה בְצָרוֹת, נִמְצָא
מְאֹד.[2] אֱלֹהִים יְחָנֵּנוּ וִיבָרְכֵנוּ, יָאֵר פָּנָיו אִתָּנוּ סֶלָה.[3] אֱלֹהִים
שׁוֹפֵט, זֶה יַשְׁפִּיל וְזֶה יָרִים.[4] אֱלֹהִים בְּשִׁמְךָ הוֹשִׁיעֵנוּ, וּבִגְבוּרָתְךָ
תְדִינֵנוּ. אֱלֹהִים שִׁמְעָה תְפִלָּתֵנוּ, הַאֲזִינָה לְאִמְרֵי פִינוּ.[5] יהוה
אֱלֹהִים צְבָאוֹת הֲשִׁיבֵנוּ, הָאֵר פָּנֶיךָ וְנִוָּשֵׁעָה.[6]

כְּרַחֵם אָב עַל בָּנִים, כֵּן תְּרַחֵם יהוה עָלֵינוּ. לַיהוה הַיְשׁוּעָה,
עַל עַמְּךָ בִרְכָתֶךָ סֶּלָה. יהוה צְבָאוֹת עִמָּנוּ, מִשְׂגָּב
לָנוּ אֱלֹהֵי יַעֲקֹב סֶלָה. יהוה צְבָאוֹת, אַשְׁרֵי אָדָם בֹּטֵחַ בָּךְ. יהוה
הוֹשִׁיעָה, הַמֶּלֶךְ יַעֲנֵנוּ בְיוֹם קָרְאֵנוּ.

In some congregations the following two verses are recited responsively — the chazzan *reciting* סְלַח,
and the congregation responding וַיֹּאמֶר. *In other congregations these verses are recited silently.*

סְלַח נָא לַעֲוֹן הָעָם הַזֶּה כְּגֹדֶל חַסְדֶּךָ, וְכַאֲשֶׁר נָשָׂאתָה לָעָם
הַזֶּה מִמִּצְרַיִם וְעַד הֵנָּה, וְשָׁם נֶאֱמַר:

וַיֹּאמֶר יהוה סָלַחְתִּי כִּדְבָרֶךָ.

All:

הַטֵּה אֱלֹהַי אָזְנְךָ וּשֲׁמָע, פְּקַח עֵינֶיךָ וּרְאֵה שֹׁמְמֹתֵינוּ, וְהָעִיר
אֲשֶׁר נִקְרָא שִׁמְךָ עָלֶיהָ, כִּי לֹא עַל צִדְקֹתֵינוּ אֲנַחְנוּ
מַפִּילִים תַּחֲנוּנֵינוּ לְפָנֶיךָ, כִּי עַל רַחֲמֶיךָ הָרַבִּים. אֲדֹנָי שְׁמָעָה,
אֲדֹנָי סְלָחָה, אֲדֹנָי הַקְשִׁיבָה, וַעֲשֵׂה אַל תְּאַחַר, לְמַעַנְךָ אֱלֹהַי,
כִּי שִׁמְךָ נִקְרָא עַל עִירְךָ וְעַל עַמֶּךָ.

סְלִיחָה ל (שַׁלְמוֹנִית)

All:

אֱלֹהִים יִרְאֶה לּוֹ* שֶׂה פְזוּרָה[7] וְיוֹשַׁע,
לְקוֹל שַׁוְעָתָה יַקְשִׁיב[8] וְיֵשַׁע,
פֶּן תִּסָּפֶה בַּחֲנִית וּמַסָּע,*[9]

עַל מָה נָאַץ רָשָׁע, אֱלֹהִים.[10]

אֱלֹהִים יִרְאֶה לּוֹ — *God will see for Himself.*
Each stanza of this *selichah* begins with a Scriptural fragment that begins with the word אֱלֹהִים, *God*, and ends with a Scriptural fragment that ends with the same word. It is the word before אֱלֹהִים in the last line that determines the rhyme sound of the stanza. Similarly, in the next three *selichos* the stanzas all begin and end with a theme word: In *selichah* 31 it is אֱמֶת, *truth*; in 32

it is חַיִּים, *life*; and in 33 it is מֶלֶךְ, *King.* Although those three *selichos* are unsigned, the author of *selichah* 30 signed his name — יוֹאֵל בַּר יִצְחָק הַלֵּוִי, *Yoel bar Yitzchak the Levite, may he be strong* [see prefatory comment to *selichah* 28] — in the initial letters of the second word in each stanza. Because of the similarity of style shared by *selichos* 30-33, some editions of *Selichos* ascribe all four to R' Yoel. Although this assump-

PREFATORY VERSES TO SELICHAH 30

אַל תָּבוֹא *Do not enter into strict judgment with us, for no living creature would be innocent before You.*[1] *God is a refuge and strength for us, a help in distress, very accessible.*[2] *May God favor us and bless us; may He shine His countenance upon us, Selah.*[3] *God is Judge: He lowers one and raises another.*[4] *O God, by Your Name, save us, and may Your might vindicate us. O God, hear our prayer; listen to our mouth's utterances.*[5] HASHEM, *God, Master of Legions, return us; let Your countenance shine, and we will be saved.*[6]

כְּרַחֵם אָב *As a father has mercy on his children, so,* HASHEM, *may You have mercy on us. Salvation is* HASHEM's, *upon Your people is Your blessing, Selah.* HASHEM, *Master of Legions, is with us, a stronghold for us is the God of Jacob, Selah.* HASHEM, *Master of Legions, praiseworthy is the person who trusts in You.* HASHEM, *save! May the King answer us on the day we call.*

In some congregations the following two verses are recited responsively — the *chazzan* reciting, 'Forgive, please . . . ,' and the congregation responding, 'And HASHEM said . . .' In other congregations these verses are recited silently.

סְלַח נָא *Forgive, please, the iniquity of this people according to the greatness of Your kindness and as You have forgiven this people from Egypt until now, and there it was said:*

And HASHEM said, 'I have forgiven according to your word!'

All:

הַטֵּה *Incline, my God, Your ear, and listen, open Your eyes and see our desolation and that of the city upon which Your Name is proclaimed; for not because of our righteousness do we cast down our supplications before You, rather because of Your abundant compassion. O my Lord, heed; O my Lord, forgive; O my Lord, be attentive and act, do not delay; for Your sake, my God, for Your Name is proclaimed upon Your city and upon Your people.*

SELICHAH 30

All:

א *God will see for Himself* the scattered sheep,*[7] *[Israel,] and save [them]; to the sound of her outcry He will be attentive*[8] *and turn, lest she be wiped out by spear and sling.**[9]
Why does the wicked man blaspheme **God?**[10]

---

(1) Cf. *Psalms* 143:2. (2) 46:2. (3) 67:2. (4) Cf. 75:8. (5) Cf. 54:3-4. (6) 80:20. (7) Cf. *Genesis* 22:8; *Jeremiah* 50:17. (8) Cf. *Psalms* 5:3. (9) Cf. *Job* 41:18. (10) *Psalms* 10:13.

---

tion may have its merits, it is by no means conclusive.

חֲנִית וּמֶסַע — *Spear and sling.* The term חֲנִית מֶסַע (without the conjunctive prefix ו) appears in *Job* 41:18. Some commentaries understand מֶסַע as an adjective meaning either *very heavy* (Rashi) or *portable* (Ibn Ezra). According to Rashi's first interpretation, Ralbag, and others, מֶסַע is a noun that names an unidentified weapon. *Targum* is

more specific and renders *a sling that hurls stones.* The translation follows this latter opinion.

[It is also possible that the *paytan*, who lived through the Second Crusade (1147-49) and the Third Crusade (1189-92), meant to allude to the atrocities of those periods, for the Hebrew word for Crusade is מַסָּע הַצְּלָב. Moreover, this *selichah* contains a number of other allusions to the

אֱלֹהִים וְאֶהֱמָיָה[1] לְקוֹל שְׁאוֹן שׁוֹאָן,

בְּרַעַשׁ[2] עֲלֵי יְחוּדְךָ לְמָאָן,

וְנַחֲלָתְךָ הַיֵּצֶר לָמָה תְנִיאָן,   אָמַר נָבָל בְּלִבּוֹ אֵין אֱלֹהִים.[3]

אֱלֹהִים אַל דֳּמִי[4] לְדָמֵי שְׁפִיכוֹת,

עֲרִיכַת נְתָחֵינוּ מִלְאוּ לְשָׁכוֹת,

וְלָמָה תַעְלֵם לְבִלְתִּי סְכוֹת,   כִּי חֵרֵף מַעַרְכוֹת אֱלֹהִים.[5]

אֱלֹהִים לָנוּ מַחֲסֶה[6], וְנָרָן בַּאֲבֹד

רְשָׁעִים[7] הָאוֹמְרִים בְּתוֹרָתְךָ מִלְּזֹבֵד,

וּמַה בֶּצַע בְּחָרַתְם בְּאֵל הַכָּבוֹד,   שָׁוְא עָבַד אֱלֹהִים.[8]

אֱלֹהִים בָּאוּ גוֹיִם נַחֲלָתְךָ[9] לְהַלְאוֹת,

בְּפֶסֶל נִסְכָּם שָׂמוּ אוֹתוֹתָם אוֹת,[10]

רָאֵה כִּי גָזְרוּ צֹאן מִמִּכְלָאוֹת,[11]

אָמְרוּ נִירְשָׁה לָנוּ אֵת נְאוֹת אֱלֹהִים.[12]

אֱלֹהִים יַחֲקָר זֹאת[13] כִּי הִכְרִיעוּ לַטֶּבַח,

עוֹלָלִים וְיוֹנְקִים נִתְנַדְּבוּ לָאֶבַח,

וּמִלְאוּ יָדָם לְקָרְבָה אֶת הַזֶּבַח,   אֶל מִזְבַּח אֱלֹהִים.[14]

אֱלֹהִים צְבָאוֹת שׁוּב נָא[15] וְנַקְּמֵנִי,

מִידֵי עֵשָׂו כִּי הִשִּׁיאַנִי,

לֵאמֹר מַה (תְּחַכֶּה) נוֹאָשׁ מִמֶּנִּי,   כִּי נַשַּׁנִי אֱלֹהִים.[16]

אֱלֹהִים חֲדָשִׁים[17] מֵאֲנוּ כִּי שָׁוְא עֲבוֹדָתוֹ,[18]

וְדָבְקוּ בְּיוֹצְרָם וְיָרְקוּ לְעֻמַּת מַחְבַּרְתּוֹ,

וְכָל אֶחָד הִשְׁלִים רוּחוֹ וְגוּיָתוֹ,

וְאֵינֶנּוּ כִּי לָקַח אוֹתוֹ אֱלֹהִים.[19]

אֱלֹהִים קְדוֹשִׁים[20] הֵם פֻּצּוּ, וְהִתְנַדֹּדוּ,

נַפְשׁוֹתָם חַטֹּאתָם לֹא כְחֵדוּ,[21]

לְאֻמּוֹתָם צָרֵחוּ, חוּשָׁה נָא וְעָקְדוּ, אֲשֶׁר בִּי יְכַבְּדוּ אֱלֹהִים.[22]

אֱלֹהִים הוּא יָרֵב לוֹ,[23] כַּאֲשֶׁר מָגֵן

עַמּוֹ לִגְזֹר כְּרֹאשׁ שִׁבֹּלֶת דָּגָן,

תְּצֻרַר (נַפְשָׁם) לְיוֹשְׁבֵי סַהַר אַגָּן,*   (בְּעֵדֶן גָּן)[24] אֱלֹהִים.[25]

---

excesses of Christian zealousness in spreading their faith during that period.]

לְיוֹשְׁבֵי סַהַר אַגָּן — *Together with the sages of the Sanhedrin* [lit., *with those who sit in the round basin*]. The Talmud interprets the phrase אַגָּן הַסַּהַר (Song of Songs 7:3) as an allusion to the Sanhedrin or Highest Court. As the supreme arbiter of Torah law, the Sanhedrin protected (מָגֵן cognate with מָגֵן, *a shield*) the world from disaster. And, in order to allow each of the seventy-one

ר **God!** I am agitated[1] at the sound of the [gentile] horde's tumult,
clamoring[2] [for me] to stop proclaiming Your Oneness.
They press Your heritage-people hard;
   why do You [allow them to] hold us back so?
               [While] the lout says in his heart, 'There is no **God**.'[3]

א **God!** Do not be silent[4] about [our] spilled blood.
Piles of our [severed] limbs, fill [our oppressor's] chambers.
Why, then, do You hide Yourself, not to listen,
               as he blasphemes the troops of **God?**[5]

ל **God** is a refuge for us,[6] and we shall [yet] sing at the demise of
the wicked[7] who tell us not to accept Your Torah [saying]:
'For what gain is there, that you have chosen the God of Glory?
               It is useless to serve **God**.'[8]

ב **God!** Gentiles have come to weary Your heritage-people.[9]
With their poured idol,
   they have made their signs into a [universal] sign.[10]

ר See! They have cut off the flock from its fold;[11]
               they have said,
   'We will take as our inheritance the dwelling place of **God**.'[12]

י **God** will investigate this:[13] that they forced to the slaughter
children, even babies, [who] chose death for themselves,
and who consecrated themselves to be sacrificed,
               to the altar of **God**.[14]

צ **God**, Master of Legions, please return[15] and take vengeance for me
from the hands of Esau, when he urged me [to accept idolatry],
saying, 'What (are you hoping) for?' O has He abandoned me?
               For [it seems as if] I am forgotten by **God**.[16]

ח The new god[17] they [Israel] refused, for his service is meaningless;[18]
they spat at his [New] Book and clung to their Maker.
Each one gave all his soul and body,
               and he is not, for he has been taken by **God**.[19]

ק '**God** is holy!'[20] they said, and they confessed,
their souls did not hide their sins.[21]
[Children] shouted to their mothers,
   'Hurry, please, and bind [me for sacrifice],
               for through me will men glorify **God**.'[22]

ה **God** will take up his [Israel's] cause,[23] just as He [had once] delivered
His people to be cut down like the top of the grain stalks.
Let (the [martyr's] souls)[24] be bound together with the sages
   of the Sanhedrin,*   (in Eden, the garden of)[24] **God**.[25]

---

(1) *Psalms* 77:4. (2) Cf. *Isaiah* 9:4. (3) *Psalms* 53:2. (4) 83:2. (5) *I Samuel* 17:26. (6) *Psalms* 46:2.
(7) Cf. *Proverbs* 11:10. (8) *Malachi* 3:14. (9) Cf. *Psalms* 79:1. (10) Cf. *Psalms* 74:4.
(11) Cf. *Habakkuk* 3:17. (12) *Psalms* 83:13. (13) 44:22. (14) 43:4. (15) 80:15. (16) *Genesis* 41:51.
(17) *Judges* 5:8. (18) Cf. *Malachi* 3:14. (19) *Genesis* 5:24. (20) *Joshua* 24:19. (21) Cf. *Isaiah* 3:9; some
editions of *Selichos* arrange the stiches differently: אֱלֹהִים קְדוֹשִׁים הֵם פְּגוּ, וְהִתְוַדּוּ נַפְשׁוֹתָם, חַטֹּאתָם לֹא
כְחֵדוּ, 'God is Holy!' they said, they confessed what was on their souls, not hiding their sins; but this
arrangement of the words is not in accord with the rhyme scheme of the *selichah*. (22) *Judges* 9:9.
(23) 6:31. (24) These words are not found in all editions. (25) *Ezekiel* 28:13.

אֱלֹהִים, לִבְרִי לְבָבִי[1] עֵינֵי מַיִם נוֹזְלוֹת,

בְּזָכְרִי כִּי בְעָקְבוֹתָם גְּרָרוּם בִּמְסִלּוֹת,

קוֹל מְחָרְפֶיךָ שָׁמַע דּוֹבְרֵי נְבָלוֹת, וְרַב מִהְיוֹת קוֹלוֹת אֱלֹהִים.[2]

אֱלֹהִים וְתִרְצֵנִי[3] הֱיֵה מָעוֹז לַבָּאִים

בְּצֵל כְּנָפֶיךָ לַחֲסוֹת[4] מִפְּנֵי לְבָאִים,

נָסוּ לְעֶזְרָתֶךָ לְהִנָּצֵל מִסּוֹד מְרֵעִים,[5]   כִּי עַם אֱלֹהִים.[6]

אֱלֹהִים, יִפְּלוּ מִמּוֹעֲצוֹתֵיהֶם[7] טוֹפְלֵי טָחִי,

זִכְרָם יָסוּף, זַעַמְךָ עֲלֵיהֶם נְחָה,[8]

קַל מְהֵרָה גְמוּלָם בְּרֹאשָׁם,[9] וּמְחֵה[10]   כָּל גּוֹיִם שְׁכֵחֵי אֱלֹהִים.[11]

אֱלֹהִים חַיִּים,[12] נִפְלָה נָא בְיָדֶךָ,[13]

וּבְיַד רָשָׁע אַל תַּסְגֵּר עֲבָדֶיךָ,

בַּקֵּשׁ אֶת נִרְדָּף[14] בְּנֵי יְדִידֶיךָ,   מַה יָּקָר חַסְדְּךָ אֱלֹהִים.[15]

אֱלֹהִים, זְנַחְתָּנוּ[16] וַאֲנַחְנוּ אֲשֵׁמִים,[17]

בְּכֵן יָחִיל לִבִּי וְאֵשֵׁב מַשְׁמִים,

לְעֶזְרָתִי חוּשָׁה וּמִיַּד קָמִים,   הַצִּילֵנִי מִדָּמִים אֱלֹהִים.[18]

✧ אֱלֹהִים קוֹלִי בְשִׂיחִי[19] וְקוֹל הַצֹּאן,

תָּבֹא לְפָנֶיךָ מִכְּנַף הָאָרֶץ וְקִיצוֹן,

הֲשִׁיבֵנוּ אֵלֶיךָ וְחַלְּצֵנוּ מֵחַצוֹן,

וַאֲנִי תְפִלָּתִי לְךָ יהוה עֵת רָצוֹן, אֱלֹהִים.[20]

All, while standing:

אֵל מֶלֶךְ יוֹשֵׁב עַל כִּסֵּא רַחֲמִים מִתְנַהֵג בַּחֲסִידוּת, מוֹחֵל עֲוֹנוֹת עַמּוֹ, מַעֲבִיר רִאשׁוֹן רִאשׁוֹן, מַרְבֶּה מְחִילָה לַחַטָּאִים וּסְלִיחָה לַפּוֹשְׁעִים, עֹשֶׂה צְדָקוֹת עִם כָּל בָּשָׂר וָרוּחַ, לֹא כְרָעָתָם תִּגְמוֹל. ✧ אֵל הוֹרֵיתָ לָּנוּ לוֹמַר שְׁלֹשׁ עֶשְׂרֵה, וּזְכֹר לָנוּ הַיּוֹם בְּרִית שְׁלֹשׁ עֶשְׂרֵה, כְּמוֹ שֶׁהוֹדַעְתָּ לֶעָנָיו מִקֶּדֶם, כְּמוֹ שֶׁכָּתוּב, וַיֵּרֶד יהוה בֶּעָנָן וַיִּתְיַצֵּב עִמּוֹ שָׁם, וַיִּקְרָא בְשֵׁם יהוה.

Congregation, then chazzan:

וַיַּעֲבֹר יהוה עַל פָּנָיו וַיִּקְרָא:

---

members of this body to see one another, their benches were arranged in a semi-circle, like a   crescent moon (סַהַר). Thus the Sanhedrin was אַגַן הַסַּהַר, a protective crescent (Sanhedrin 37a).

ל *God!* For the pure at heart,[1] *water flows from my eyes,*
  as I remember how [the conquerers] dragged them by their heels
    along the roads.
Hear the voice of those who revile You, those who speak foulness!
        It is enough! [Their] voices should be no more, O **God.**[2]

ו *God!* Favor me,[3] *be a fortress for those who come*
  to take shelter in the shadow of Your wings[4]
    from the lion[-like oppressors].
They have fled to [seek] Your aid,
    to be rescued from the counsel of the wicked[5]
        [by being] with **God.**[6]

י *God!* May they fall from their councils[7] *[in ruin], those plotters of evil;*
  may their memory be gone; may Your rage be upon them.[8]
Fleetly, swiftly, [bring] their just due on their heads,[9] *and blot out*[10]
        all the nations that forget **God.**[11]

ח O living **God!**[12] *Please, let us fall into Your hand,*[13]
  and do not consign Your servants into the hand of the wicked.
Seek out the pursued,[14] *the children of Your beloved [Patriarchs].*
        How precious is Your kindness, O **God!**[15]

ז *God!* You have abandoned us,[16] *but we are the guilty ones;*[17]
  on this account my heart shudders and I sit desolate.
Rush to my aid, and from the foes' clutch
        save me, that my blood not be spilled, O **God!**[18]

ק Chazzan — **God!** *Let my voice in my prayer*[19] *and the voice of [Your] flock*
  come before You, even from the corner and end of the earth.
Return us to You, and release us from oppression.
        As for me, my prayer is to You, Hashem,
        'Let it be a time of favor, O **God.'**[20]

All, while standing:

אֵל מֶלֶךְ O God, King Who sits on the throne of mercy; Who acts with
kindness, pardons the iniquities of His people, removes [sins]
one by one,[1] increasingly grants pardon to careless sinners and forgiveness
to rebels, Who deals righteously with every living being — You do not repay
them in accord with their evil. Chazzan — O God, You taught us to recite the
Thirteen [Attributes of Mercy], so remember for us today the covenant of
these Thirteen, as You made known to the humble one in ancient times, as
it is written: And Hashem descended in a cloud and stood with him there,
and He called out with the Name Hashem.

Congregation, then chazzan:
And Hashem *passed before him [Moses] and proclaimed:*

---

(1) *Psalms* 73:1. (2) *Exodus* 9:28. (3) Cf. *Genesis* 33:10. (4) Cf. *Psalms* 36:8. (5) Cf. 64:3.
(6) *I Samuel* 14:45. (7) *Psalms* 5:11. (8) Some editions read זָכְרָם יָסוּף, וְעַמְּךָ לַךְ נָחֵה, *May their
memory be gone; and may You go to lead Your nation*; cf. *Exodus* 32:34. (9) Cf. *Joel* 4:4.
(10) Some editions read . . . קֵל מְהֵרָה גְּמוּלָם בְּרֹאשָׁם/יְמַחֶה כָּל גּוֹיִם, a reading which does not
change the basic meaning, but also does not fit the rhyme scheme. (11) *Psalms* 9:18.
(12) *Deuteronomy* 5:23. (13) Cf. *II Samuel* 24:14. (14) Cf. *Ecclesiastes* 3:15.
(15) *Psalms* 36:8. (16) 60:3. (17) Cf. *Genesis* 42:21. (18) *Psalms* 51:16. (19) 64:2. (20) 69:14.

Congregation and *chazzan* (the words in bold type are recited aloud and in unison):

יְהוָה, יְהוָה, אֵל, רַחוּם, וְחַנּוּן, אֶרֶךְ אַפַּיִם, וְרַב חֶסֶד, וֶאֱמֶת, **נֹצֵר חֶסֶד לָאֲלָפִים, נֹשֵׂא עָוֹן, וָפֶשַׁע, וְחַטָּאָה, וְנַקֵּה.** וְסָלַחְתָּ לַעֲוֹנֵנוּ וּלְחַטָּאתֵנוּ וּנְחַלְתָּנוּ. סְלַח לָנוּ אָבִינוּ כִּי חָטָאנוּ, מְחַל לָנוּ מַלְכֵּנוּ כִּי פָשָׁעְנוּ. כִּי אַתָּה אֲדֹנָי טוֹב וְסַלָּח, וְרַב חֶסֶד לְכָל קֹרְאֶיךָ.

פסוקי הקדמה לסליחה לא

אַל תָּבוֹא בְמִשְׁפָּט עִמָּנוּ, כִּי לֹא יִצְדַּק לְפָנֶיךָ כָל חָי.[1] יְהוָה יָדַע מַחְשְׁבוֹת אָדָם, כִּי הֵמָּה הָבֶל.[2] תְּהִי נָא אָזְנְךָ קַשֶּׁבֶת וְעֵינֶיךָ פְקֻחוֹת אֶל תְּפִלַּת עַמְּךָ יִשְׂרָאֵל.[3] וְסָלַחְתָּ לְעַמְּךָ אֲשֶׁר חָטְאוּ לָךְ, וּלְכָל פִּשְׁעֵיהֶם אֲשֶׁר פָּשְׁעוּ בָךְ.[4] תִּתֵּן אֱמֶת לְיַעֲקֹב חֶסֶד לְאַבְרָהָם, אֲשֶׁר נִשְׁבַּעְתָּ לַאֲבוֹתֵינוּ מִימֵי קֶדֶם.[5] יְהוָה יְהוָה אֵל רַחוּם וְחַנּוּן אֶרֶךְ אַפַּיִם וְרַב חֶסֶד וֶאֱמֶת.[6]

בְּרַחֵם אָב עַל בָּנִים, כֵּן תְּרַחֵם יְהוָה עָלֵינוּ. לַיהוָה הַיְשׁוּעָה, עַל עַמְּךָ בִרְכָתֶךָ סֶּלָה. יְהוָה צְבָאוֹת עִמָּנוּ, מִשְׂגָּב לָנוּ אֱלֹהֵי יַעֲקֹב סֶלָה. יְהוָה צְבָאוֹת, אַשְׁרֵי אָדָם בֹּטֵחַ בָּךְ. יְהוָה הוֹשִׁיעָה, הַמֶּלֶךְ יַעֲנֵנוּ בְיוֹם קָרְאֵנוּ.

In some congregations the following two verses are recited responsively — the *chazzan* reciting סְלַח, and the congregation responding וַיֹּאמֶר. In other congregations these verses are recited silently.

סְלַח נָא לַעֲוֹן הָעָם הַזֶּה כְּגֹדֶל חַסְדֶּךָ, וְכַאֲשֶׁר נָשָׂאתָה לָעָם הַזֶּה מִמִּצְרַיִם וְעַד הֵנָּה, וְשָׁם נֶאֱמַר:

וַיֹּאמֶר יְהוָה סָלַחְתִּי כִּדְבָרֶךָ.

All:

הַטֵּה אֱלֹהַי אָזְנְךָ וּשֲׁמָע, פְּקַח עֵינֶיךָ וּרְאֵה שֹׁמְמֹתֵינוּ, וְהָעִיר אֲשֶׁר נִקְרָא שִׁמְךָ עָלֶיהָ, כִּי לֹא עַל צִדְקֹתֵינוּ אֲנַחְנוּ מַפִּילִים תַּחֲנוּנֵינוּ לְפָנֶיךָ, כִּי עַל רַחֲמֶיךָ הָרַבִּים. אֲדֹנָי שְׁמָעָה, אֲדֹנָי סְלָחָה, אֲדֹנָי הַקְשִׁיבָה, וַעֲשֵׂה אַל תְּאַחַר, לְמַעַנְךָ אֱלֹהַי, כִּי שִׁמְךָ נִקְרָא עַל עִירְךָ וְעַל עַמֶּךָ.

Congregation and *chazzan* (the words in bold type are recited aloud and in unison):

ה' ה' HASHEM, HASHEM, God, Compassionate and Gracious, Slow to anger, and Abundant in Kindness and Truth, Preserver of kindness for thousands [of generations], Forgiver of iniquity, willful sin, and error, and Who cleanses. *May You forgive our iniquities and our errors and make us Your heritage. Forgive us, our Father, for we have erred; pardon us, our King, for we have willfully sinned; for You, my Lord, are good and forgiving and abundantly kind to all who call upon You.*

PREFATORY VERSES TO SELICHAH 31

אַל תָּבוֹא *Do not enter into strict judgment with us, for no living creature would be innocent before You.*[1] *HASHEM knows man's thoughts, [and knows] that they are futile.*[2] *Please, let Your ear listen and Your eyes be open to the prayer of Your people Israel.*[3] *May You forgive Your people who have sinned against You, and all their willful sins that they have committed willfully against You.*[4] *Grant truth to Jacob, kindness to Abraham, as You swore to our fathers from ancient times.*[5] *HASHEM, HASHEM, God, Merciful and Compassionate, Slow to Anger, and Abundant in Kindness and Truth.*[6]

כְּרַחֵם אָב *As a father has mercy on his children, so, HASHEM, may You have mercy on us. Salvation is HASHEM's, upon Your people is Your blessing, Selah. HASHEM, Master of Legions, is with us, a stronghold for us is the God of Jacob, Selah. HASHEM, Master of Legions, praiseworthy is the person who trusts in You. HASHEM, save! May the King answer us on the day we call.*

In some congregations the following two verses are recited responsively — the *chazzan* reciting, 'Forgive, please . . . ,' and the congregation responding, 'And HASHEM said . . .' In other congregations these verses are recited silently.

סְלַח נָא *Forgive, please, the iniquity of this people according to the greatness of Your kindness and as You have forgiven this people from Egypt until now, and there it was said:*

And HASHEM said, 'I have forgiven according to your word!'

All:

הַטֵּה *Incline, my God, Your ear, and listen, open Your eyes and see our desolation and that of the city upon which Your Name is proclaimed; for not because of our righteousness do we cast down our supplications before You, rather because of Your abundant compassion. O my Lord, heed; O my Lord, forgive; O my Lord, be attentive and act, do not delay; for Your sake, my God, for Your Name is proclaimed upon Your city and upon Your people.*

(1) Cf. *Psalms* 143:2. (2) 94:11. (3) Cf. *I Kings* 8:29, 52.
(4) 8:50. (5) *Micah* 7:20. (6) *Exodus* 34:6.

סליחה לא (שלמונית)

All:

(אֱלֹהֵינוּ וֵאלֹהֵי אֲבוֹתֵינוּ:)

אֱמֶת* אַתָּה הוּא רִאשׁוֹן, וְאֵין רֵאשִׁית לְרֵאשִׁיתֶךָ,

וְאַתָּה הוּא אַחֲרוֹן, וְאֵין סוֹף לְאַחֲרִיתֶךָ,[1]

וַאֲנִי וְדָתָךְ מְעִידִים, כִּי אֵין זוּלָתֶךָ,[2]

צִדְקָתְךָ צֶדֶק לְעוֹלָם, וְתוֹרָתְךָ אֱמֶת.[3]

אֱמֶת בָּרָא אֱלֹהִים אֵת[4] רָמוּז* בְּהוֹדְךָ וַהֲדָרֶךָ,

עַל הַדִּין וְהָאֱמֶת וְהַשָּׁלוֹם הֶעֱמַדְתָּ דְּבִיֶרֶךָ,[5]

עַל כֵּן (אֱלֹהַי) נַאֲמִירְךָ בַּעֲרוֹךְ שִׁירֶיךָ, רֹאשׁ דְּבָרְךָ אֱמֶת.[6]

אֱמֶת גָּמַרְתָּ שִׁשָּׁה פְעָמִים, אֱלֹהִים חַיִּים,

מִבְּרֵאשִׁית וְעַד לַעֲשׂוֹת* חֲתוּמִים תָּוִים,

וְכֻלָּם סוֹפֵי תֵבוֹת הֵמָּה הַגּוֹיִם,

סְמוּכִים לָעַד לְעוֹלָם עֲשׂוּיִם בֶּאֱמֶת.[7]*

אֱמֶת דְּבָרָיו מְרֻחָקִים זֶה מִזֶּה בְּאָרֶךְ,

וְשֶׁקֶר דְּבָרָיו מְקֹרָבִים* וְאֵין לוֹ רֶגֶל דּוֹרֵךְ,*

בָּרוּךְ יהוה מֵצִיץ מֵחֲרָךְ,[8] אֲשֶׁר הִנְחַנִי בְּדֶרֶךְ אֱמֶת.[9]

אֱמֶת הָיְתָה בְּפִיהוּ[10] עוֹלָמוֹ בְּהִתְיַסֵּד,

מִשְׁתַּעֲשַׁעַת עַל בִּרְכּוֹ יַחַד לְהִתְרַפֵּסֵד,

כָּל מַעֲשָׂיו בַּעֲצָתָה לְהִנָּסֵד,* כָּל אָרְחוֹת יהוה חֶסֶד וֶאֱמֶת.[11]

אֱמֶת וַעֲנָוָה וּצְדָקָה[12] עוֹשִׂים זָכוּ לְהִשְׁתַּכֵּר,

אֱמֶת — *True.* Similar to *selichah* 30 in style, this *selichah* revolves around the word and theme אֱמֶת, which may be rendered *truth, truly, true,* or *it is true,* depending on the context. Each stanza begins and ends with the word אֱמֶת as it appears in a Scriptural fragment. The second words of the respective stanzas contain an *aleph-beis* acrostic. [See prefatory comment to *selichah* 30 regarding authorship of this work.]

אֱמֶת בָּרָא אֱלֹהִים אֵת רָמוּז — *'True' is hinted at* [in the phrase] *'God created.'* The first word in the Torah — בְּרֵאשִׁית, *In the beginning* — is followed by the words בָּרָא אֱלֹהִים אֵת, *God created.* These three words end in the letters ת ם א respectively. Thus, the very beginning of the Torah is sealed with the word אֱמֶת. The last line of this stanza teaches that this is the meaning of the verse (Psalms 119:160), רֹאשׁ דְּבָרְךָ אֱמֶת, *the beginning of Your Word is truth.*

אֱמֶת גָּמַרְתָּ שִׁשָּׁה פְעָמִים . . . מִבְּרֵאשִׁית וְעַד לַעֲשׂוֹת — *'True' You completed six times . . . from 'In the beginning . . .' until '. . . to make.'* In addition to the allusion mentioned in the preceding comment, the word אֱמֶת is hinted at five other times in the story of Creation. As the stanza continues, all six allusions are found in the respective final letters of three consecutive words. The six are: בָּרָא אֱלֹהִים אֵת, *God created* (1:1); וַיַּבְרָא אֱלֹהִים אֵת, *And God saw* [the light] (1:4); וַיִּבְרָא, *And God created* [the fish and foul] (1:21); אֱלֹהִים אֵת, *And God created* [man] (1:27); וַיַּרְא, *and God saw* [all that He had made] (1:31); בָּרָא אֱלֹהִים לַעֲשׂוֹת, *God created to make* (2:3). Interestingly, in all six allusions, the middle word is אֱלֹהִים, *God,* which may explain why the *paytan* interjected אֱלֹהִים חַיִּים, *O Living God,* in this stanza.

סְמוּכִים לָעַד לְעוֹלָם עֲשׂוּיִם בֶּאֱמֶת — *They are eter-*

SELICHAH 31

All:

(Our God and the God of our forefathers:)

א **True*** — *You are the first, and nothing precedes Your precedence;*
and You are the last, and there is no end to Your finality.[1]
And I and Your law testify that there is none besides You;[2]
[and that] Your righteousness is an everlasting righteousness,
and Your Torah is **truth.**[3]

ב *'True' is hinted at [in the phrase] 'God created,'*** [4]
in [the Torah,] Your glory and Your splendor.
On justice, truth, and peace You established Your world.[5]
Therefore, (my God,) we will exalt You, in arranging Your songs,
'The beginning of Your Word is **truth.'**[6]

ג *'True' You completed six times, O Living God:*
*From 'In the beginning...' until '...to make'***
[they are] sealed and inscribed,
and all of them spelled out in the words' last letters,
they are eternally juxtaposed, being made of **truth.*** [7]

ד *'True' — its letters are spaced far from one another,*
*but the letters of 'falsehood' are close together,***
*and it has no foot on which to tread.***
Blessed is HASHEM Who peers through the cracks,[8]
Who has guided me in the way of **truth.**[9]

ה **Truth** *was in His mouth*[10] *when His world was established;*
it was dandled on His knee to be his close companion.
*All His actions founded in its counsel;***
all of HASHEM's ways are kindness and truth.[11]

ו **Truth** *and humility and righteousness*[12] —
those who do these merit reward.

---

(1) Cf. *Isaiah* 41:4; 44:6; 48:12. (2) Cf. *II Samuel* 7:22. (3) *Psalms* 119:142. (4) *Genesis* 1:1.
(5) See tractate *Avos* 1:18. (6) *Psalms* 119:160. (7) 111:8. (8) Cf. *Song of Songs* 2:9.
(9) *Genesis* 24:27. (10) *Malachi* 2:6. (11) *Psalms* 25:10. (12) Cf. 45:5.

nally juxtaposed, being made of truth. In its context in *Psalms* (111:8), this verse means, *They [the mitzvos] have steadfast support forever, they are made in truth,* the word סְמוּכִים being similar to סוֹמֵךְ, *he supports* (see *Psalms* 145:14). The *paytan,* however, treats the word in its Talmudic usage סָמוּךְ, *near* (see tractate *Berachos* 10a). Thus, these six allusions are inscribed in the Torah, in words that are immutably juxtaposed to spell the word אֱמֶת.

אֱמֶת דְּבָרָיו מְרֻחָקִים ... שֶׁקֶר דְּבָרָיו מְקֹרבִים — *'Truth' — its letters are spaced far ... but the letters of 'falsehood' are close together.* The Talmud asks why the letters of 'falsehood' (שֶׁקֶר) are near each other [in the alphabet], while the letters of 'truth' (אֱמֶת) are spread out [the א and ת at either end, and the מ at the center of the aleph-

beis]. And answers that falsehood is common and readily found, while truth is uncommon and difficult to find (*Shabbos* 104a).

וְאֵין לוֹ רֶגֶל דּוֹרֵךְ — *And it has no foot on which to tread.* The Talmud continues: Why do the letters of 'falsehood' stand on one foot [i.e., the letters of the word שֶׁקֶר, *falsehood,* all stand on a single point (in the Torah script the three arms of the ש meet at a point)], while the letters of 'truth' have brick-like solidity [i.e., the א and ת each stands on two feet, and the מ has a flat base]? Because truth stands firm while falsehood does not (ibid.).

בַּעֲצָתָהּ לְהִסֵּד — *Founded in its counsel.* According to the Midrash: God took counsel with the Torah, then He created the world (*Tanchuma, Bereishis; Bereishis Rabbah* 1:1). In other words, the Torah is the blueprint of the world.

עוֹשֶׂה מִשְׁפָּט וּצְדָקָה[1] בְּלִי לְהִתְנַכֵּר,

רֶשַׁע עוֹשֶׂה פְּעֻלַּת שֶׁקֶר[3] פִּיהוּ יִסָּכֵר,

וְזֹרֵעַ צְדָקָה שֶׂכֶר אֱמֶת.[2]

אֱמֶת זְכֹר תִּזְכּוֹר לִמְעוּטֵי עַמִּים,

יִשְׂרָאֵל נוֹשַׁע בַּיהוה תְּשׁוּעַת עוֹלָמִים,[4]

עַל כֵּן בָּאוּ לַחֲסוֹת בְּצֵל שׁוֹכֵן מְרוֹמִים,

וְעָבְדוּ אוֹתוֹ בְּתָמִים וּבֶאֱמֶת.[5]

אֱמֶת חָפַצְתָּ בַטָּחוֹת[6] וְאָמַרְתָּ הֵיטִיבוּ דַרְכֵיכֶם,[7]

אֱמֶת וּמִשְׁפַּט שְׁפְטוּ בְּשַׁעֲרֵיכֶם,[8]

עַל כֵּן בְּנֵי יַעֲקֹב הָסִירוּ רַע מַעַלְלֵיכֶם,[9]

וְיִבָּחֲנוּ דִּבְרֵיכֶם הָאֱמֶת.[10]

אֱמֶת טֶכֶס חוֹתָמוֹ, לְהוֹדִיעַ כִּי הוּא*

אֶחָד וְאֵין שֵׁנִי,[11] זֶה אֵלִי וְאַנְוֵהוּ,

אֱלֹהֵי אָבִי וַאֲרֹמְמֶנְהוּ,[12]

קָרוֹב יהוה לְכָל קֹרְאָיו לְכֹל אֲשֶׁר יִקְרָאֻהוּ בֶאֱמֶת.[13]

אֱמֶת יֶהְגֶּה חִכִּי[14] וַאֲדַבְּרָה בְעֵדוֹתֶיךָ,[15]

אֶזְכְּרָה נְגִינָתִי בַּלַּיְלָה[16] דָּבַקְתִּי בְּתוֹרָתֶךָ,

זִכְרָה אֱלֹהִים לְטוֹבָה כָּל בְּנֵי בְרִיתֶךָ,

קָרוֹב אַתָּה יהוה, וְכָל מִצְוֹתֶיךָ אֱמֶת.[17]

אֱמֶת בָּמָה לְךָ בְּשָׂרֵי[18] אֶרֶץ יוֹסֵד,

לְהַצִּיל אֶת עֲבָדֶיךָ מֵעֳנִי וְהֶפְסֵד,

וְרַחֵם כָּל בְּנֵי מוֹצָא מִכֶּשֶׂד,*[19]

צֶדֶק וּמִשְׁפָּט מְכוֹן כִּסְאֶךָ חֶסֶד וֶאֱמֶת.[20]

אֱמֶת לָעַד תִּכּוֹן וְעַד אַרְגִּיעָה[21] זְדוֹנִי,

לַבֹּקֶר* מִשְׁפָּט דִּינוּ[22] עַם נְבוֹנִי,

אַשְׁרֵי חֲמוֹץ[23] כֹּהֲנַי וּזְקֵנַי,

מִשְׁפְּטֵי יהוה אֱמֶת.[24]

אֱמֶת מֵאֶרֶץ תִּצְמָח וְצֶדֶק מִשָּׁמַיִם הַגְבֵּר,[25]

כְּרָחֹק מִזְרָח מִמַּעֲרָב פְּשָׁעִים הַעֲבֵר,[26]

מוֹצָא מִכֶּשֶׂד — [Abraham] whom [You] delivered from Ur Kasdim. Ur Kasdim was the city of Abraham's youth. The name, which means *the inferno of Kasdim*, reflects the flaming kiln into which Abraham (then called Abram) was thrown by Nimrod for destroying his father's idols (see *Rashi* to Genesis 11:28).

אֱמֶת טֶכֶס חוֹתָמוֹ לְהוֹדִיעַ כִּי הוּא — *'Truth' He set as His seal, to let it be known that it is Him.* The Talmud states: חוֹתָמוֹ שֶׁל הקב״ה אֱמֶת, *the seal of the Holy One, Blessed is He, is the word אֱמֶת* (*Sanhedrin* 64a). The *paytan* explains that God chose that word as His signet to teach the world that He is Truth and Truth is He.

He Who does justice and righteousness[1]
   will not act like a stranger [to them].
The wicked, who does false deeds,[2] *will find his mouth stuffed up,*[3]
   but one who sows righteousness will be rewarded with **truth.**[2]

ז *Truly You will remember the smallest of peoples,*
Israel, who are saved by HASHEM with an eternal salvation.[4]
Come, therefore, take shelter in the shadow of the Dweller on High,
   and serve Him whole-heartedly and **truly.**[5]

ח *Truth which You desire is in concealment,*[6]
   yet You said, 'Improve your behavior,[7]
Judge with truth and justice within your gates.'[8]
Therefore, children of Jacob, do away with the evil of your deeds,[9]
   and your words will be examined to see if they are **true.**[10]

ט *'Truth' He set as His seal, to let it be known that it is Him.**
He is One and there is no second;[11] *this is my God and I will glorify Him;*
my father's God and I will exalt Him.[12]

   HASHEM is near to all those who call upon Him,
      to all who call upon Him in **truth.**[13]

י *Truth shall my mouth utter*[14] *and I will speak of Your testimonies;*[15]
I will remember my songs in the night[16] *as I cling to Your Torah.*
Remember, O God, for beneficence, all the people of Your covenant;
      [for] You are near, HASHEM,
         and all Your commandments are **truth.**[17]

כ *Truly my flesh longs for You,*[18] *O Founder of Earth,*
[for You] to rescue Your servants from poverty and decay.
Have mercy on all the children of [Abraham,]
   whom [You] delivered from Ur Kasdim*[19]
      Righteousness and justice are Your throne's foundation,
         kindness and **truth.**[20]

ל *Truth will stand firm forever; my sins for but a moment.*[21]
On the morrow,* sit in judgment[22] *over my discerning people [Israel].*
Hearten the victimized,[23] *my priests and my elders,*
      [with] the laws of HASHEM [for they] are **true.**[24]

מ *Truth may You bring forth from the ground,*
   and strengthen [the flow of] justice from Heaven.[25]
Distance our willful sins [from us] as far as east is from west;[26]

---

(1) Cf. *Jeremiah* 9:23. (2) *Proverbs* 11:18. (3) Cf. *Psalms* 63:12. (4) *Isaiah* 45:17. (5) *Joshua* 24:14.
(6) *Psalms* 51:8. (7) *Jeremiah* 7:3. (8) Cf. *Zechariah* 8:16. (9) *Isaiah* 1:16. (10) *Genesis* 42:16.
(11) *Ecclesiastes* 4:8. (12) *Exodus* 15:2. (13) *Psalms* 145:18. (14) *Proverbs* 8:7. (15) *Psalms* 119:46.
(16) 77:7. (17) 119:151. (18) 63:2. (19) Cf. *Nehemiah* 9:7. (20) *Psalms* 89:15. (21) Cf. *Proverbs* 12:19.
(22) Cf. *Jeremiah* 21:12. (23) *Isaiah* 1:17. (24) *Psalms* 19:10. (25) Cf. 85:12. (26) *Psalms* 103:12.

... לְבֹקֶר — *On the morrow* ..., i.e., tomorrow on Rosh Hashanah. The translation interprets this stanza as the words of Israel, supplicating before the Judge on the eve of the Day of Judgment.

Alternatively: Some commentaries view this as God's admonition to the nation's judges, namely, the priests and elders, that they hear their cases

early in the morning before stuffing themselves with food and drink (see *Radak* to *Jeremiah* 21:12; see also *Exodus* 18:13). Moreover, they should be compassionate to those who have to rely on others for their sustenance, such as the *Kohanim* and the elderly. And, above all, they should always follow the laws of God's Torah for

אַף כִּי אָבַד צַדִּיק עַל מְדֻוֹתָיו עוֹבֵר,

הוֹלֵךְ תָּמִים וּפוֹעֵל צֶדֶק וְדוֹבֵר **אֱמֶת**.[1]

אֱמֶת נֶגְדְּךָ יִכּוֹן לְעוֹלָם וָעֶד,[2]

וְדוֹבֵר שְׁקָרִים לֹא יִכּוֹן[3] בְּיוֹם מוֹעֵד,

מִיּוֹם הַדִּין הֱיוֹת רוֹעֵד, מַצִּיל נְפָשׁוֹת, עַד **אֱמֶת**.[4]

אֱמֶת שָׁשׂ אָנֹכִי כִּי לֹא תִבְזֶה לֵב נִשְׁבָּר,[5]

חֶסֶד חָפַצְתָּ וְלֹא זֶבַח כִּמְדֻבָּר,[6]

זְרוֹעַ תִּשְׁבֵּר לָעוֹבְדִים לָאֵל הַנִּקְבָּר,[7]

וְאַל תַּצֵּל מִפִּי דְבַר **אֱמֶת**.[8]

אֱמֶת עָוֹן צוֹפֶה וְגַם חֶסֶד*,[9]

הַעֲבֵר מֵעָלֵינוּ עָוֹן וְחֶרְפַּת חֶסֶד*.

דְּרָשׁ נָא דוֹרְשֶׁיךָ נֹצֵר חֶסֶד, אֶרֶךְ אַפַּיִם וְרַב חֶסֶד וֶ**אֱמֶת**.[10]

אֱמֶת פְּלִיאִים[11] בַּקְּשׁוּ עָלֵינוּ לַיהוה צְבָאוֹת,

מִיכָאֵל וְגַבְרִיאֵל[12] תֶּשֶׁר הָבִיאוּ לַיהוה לְמוֹרָאוֹת,

וְחַלּוּ נָא פְּנֵי אֵל[13] לְקָרֵב קֵץ הַפְּלָאוֹת,[14]

וּנְתַתֶּם לִי אוֹת **אֱמֶת**.[15]

אֱמֶת צְדָקָה תְּרוֹמֵם גּוֹי הַשְּׁלוּחִים,

וְחֶסֶד לְאֻמִּים חַטָּאת[16] עִם הַתּוֹחִים,

אֲשֶׁר לָעֵץ וְלָאֶבֶן מֵאֱלֵיהֶים,[17] וַיהוה אֱלֹהִים **אֱמֶת**.[18]

אֱמֶת קְנֵה וְאַל תִּמְכֹּר*,[19] לְשָׁרְתוֹ וּלְעָבְדוֹ,

לְרוֹמֵם שֵׁם יהוה כִּי נִשְׂגָּב שְׁמוֹ לְבַדּוֹ,[20]

לְהַשְׂבִּיעַ לְכָל חַי רָצוֹן פּוֹתֵחַ אֶת יָדוֹ,[21]

כִּי גָבַר עָלֵינוּ חַסְדּוֹ וֶ**אֱמֶת**.[22]

אֱמֶת רָאֹה תִרְאֶה בָּעֳנִי יִשְׂרָאֵל,[23]

מִשְׁפָּטֶיךָ תְּהוֹם רַבָּה וְצִדְקָתְךָ כְּהַרְרֵי אֵל.[24]

וְקַבֵּל תְּפִלַּת עַם אֲשֶׁר לְךָ שׁוֹאֵל,

בְּיָדְךָ אַפְקִיד רוּחִי, פָּדִיתָה אוֹתִי, יהוה אֵל **אֱמֶת**.[25]

---

they are the ultimate truth. According to this interpretation, the translation is: *In [early] morning, sit in judgment over My discerning people [Israel], the victimized, My priests and My elders . . .*

חֶסֶד . . . חֶסֶד — *Kindness . . . disgrace.* The word חֶסֶד, which almost always means *kindness,* is also used in the Torah to describe an incestuous relationship between brother and sister (see *Leviticus* 20:17). Some commentaries maintain that this is a

case of a Hebrew word that has two contradictory meanings [such as the root שרש which can mean *to take root* or *to uproot*]. Others explain that חֶסֶד always means *kindness* and offer various reasons for its use in the case of incest (see *Rashi* and *Ramban*). Clearly the *paytan* follows the first view.

אֱמֶת קְנֵה וְאַל תִּמְכֹּר — *Truth — buy it but do not sell it.* This verse (*Proverbs* 23:23) should not be misconstrued as an admonition against sharing one's

even though the righteous man is gone, he who is forbearing,
                        who walks in perfect [innocence],
            who does what is righteous, and who speaks **truth.**[1]

נ The **truthful** person will endure before You forever and ever,[2]
but one who speaks lies will not endure[3] on the appointed Day.
Be in trepidation of the Day of Judgment.
            He saves souls from Gehinnom, the witness who speaks **truth.**[4]

ס **True** it is: I rejoice, for You will not despise a broken heart;[5]
You desire kind deeds, not [unthinking] sacrifices, as it is said.[6]
May You break the might of those who worship the buried god,[7]
            and not deprive my mouth of words of **truth.**[8]

ע **Truly,** You Who look at sin and also kindness,*[9]
remove from us transgression and shameful disgrace.*
Seek, please, those who seek You, O Preserver of Kindness,
            Slow to anger, and Abundant in Kindness and **Truth.**[10]

פ **Truly,** angels of hidden name,[11] ask [forgiveness] for us
    from HASHEM, Master of Legions.
Michael and Gabriel,[12] bring [our prayer
    as] a gift to HASHEM, the Awesome One;
beg before God[13] that He bring near the hidden End [of Days],[14]
            and may you give me a sign of **truth.**[15]

צ **True** it is: righteousness will yet uplift Israel, the weary folk,
but the charity of the nations is a sin,[16] for they are a regretful people,
who make gods out of wood and stone;[17]
            but [only] HASHEM, God, is **true.**[18]

ק **Truth** — buy it but do not sell it;*[19] [use it] to attend Him and serve Him,
to uplift HASHEM's Name, for His Name alone is exalted.[20]
To satisfy the desire of every living thing, He opens His hand,[21]
            for we are overwhelmed with His kindness and **truth.**[22]

ר **Truly** You will see Israel's poverty —[23]
Your judgments are like the vast deep,
    and Your righteousness is like the mighty mountains.[24]
Accept the prayer of the people who petition You [saying]:
                'In Your hand I entrust my spirit;
            may You redeem me, O HASHEM, God of **truth.**'[25]

---

(1) *Psalms* 15:2. (2) Cf. *Proverbs* 12:19. (3) Cf. *Psalms* 101:7. (4) *Proverbs* 14:25. (5) Cf. *Psalms* 51:19.
(6) Cf. *Hosea* 6:6. (7) This stich has been censored out of some editions. (8) *Psalms* 119:43.
(9) Cf. *Proverbs* 15:3. (10) Cf. *Exodus* 34:6-7. (11) See *Judges* 13:18. (12) See introduction to this volume
regarding requests for angelic intervention. (13) *Malachi* 1:9. (14) *Daniel* 12:6. (15) *Joshua* 2:12.
(16) *Proverbs* 14:34. (17) This and the preceding stich have been censored out of some editions.
(18) *Jeremiah* 10:10. (19) *Proverbs* 23:23. (20) *Psalms* 148:13. (21) Cf. *145*:16. (22) 117:2. (23) Cf. *Exodus* 3:7.
(24) Cf. *Psalms* 36:7; see commentary to the introductory verses to *selichah* 29. (25) 31:6.

---

knowledge with others. Quite the opposite. The
Talmud derives that ideally, a Torah teacher
should not accept a salary for teaching Torah.
Just as Moses did not charge a fee for his lessons,
so should you not charge a fee. But what if one
cannot find a teacher who will teach him without
remuneration? Then he should pay someone to

teach him, as it is stated, אֱמֶת קְנֵה, *Buy truth*. Perhaps one may then say, 'Since I have paid for my
knowledge, I will not teach it gratis!' For this reason the verse states, אֱמֶת קְנֵה וְאַל תִּמְכֹּר, *[Even
though you have to] buy truth, [nevertheless,] do
not sell it [but teach it without charge]* (*Berachos*
29a).

אֱמֶת שׁוֹפֵט דַּלִּים וְכִסְאוֹ יִכּוֹן לְדוֹר דּוֹרִים,[1]

מֶלֶךְ בְּמִשְׁפָּט יַעֲמִיד אֶרֶץ[2] וַאֲוִירִים,

יַחֲשֹׁב מַעֲשָׂיו אֶל אַדִּירִים,   אַחֲרֵי הַדְּבָרִים וְהָאֱמֶת.[3]

❖ אֱמֶת תִּתֵּן לְיַעֲקֹב וְחֶסֶד לְאָב הֲמוֹנִי,[4]

כִּי מֵאַהֲבָתָךְ קְרָאתַנִי בְּכוֹרִי וּבְנִי,[5]

הֲלָכֵן חָטָאֵינוּ הָאֲדָמִים כַּשָּׁנִי,[6]

וַאֲנִי תְפִלָּתִי לְךָ יהוה עֵת רָצוֹן,

אֱלֹהִים בְּרָב חַסְדֶּךָ עֲנֵנִי בֶּאֱמֶת.[7]

All, while standing:

אֵל מֶלֶךְ יוֹשֵׁב עַל כִּסֵּא רַחֲמִים מִתְנַהֵג בַּחֲסִידוּת, מוֹחֵל עֲוֹנוֹת עַמּוֹ, מַעֲבִיר רִאשׁוֹן רִאשׁוֹן, מַרְבֶּה מְחִילָה לַחַטָּאִים וּסְלִיחָה לַפּוֹשְׁעִים, עֹשֶׂה צְדָקוֹת עִם כָּל בָּשָׂר וָרוּחַ, לֹא כְרָעָתָם תִּגְמוֹל. ❖ אֵל הוֹרֵיתָ לָּנוּ לוֹמַר שְׁלֹשׁ עֶשְׂרֵה, וּזְכוֹר לָנוּ הַיּוֹם בְּרִית שְׁלֹשׁ עֶשְׂרֵה, כְּמוֹ שֶׁהוֹדַעְתָּ לֶעָנָיו מִקֶּדֶם, כְּמוֹ שֶׁכָּתוּב, וַיֵּרֶד יהוה בֶּעָנָן וַיִּתְיַצֵּב עִמּוֹ שָׁם, וַיִּקְרָא בְשֵׁם יהוה.

Congregation, then chazzan:

וַיַּעֲבֹר יהוה עַל פָּנָיו וַיִּקְרָא:

Congregation and chazzan (the words in bold type are recited aloud and in unison):

יהוה, יהוה, אֵל, **רַחוּם, וְחַנּוּן, אֶרֶךְ אַפַּיִם, וְרַב חֶסֶד, וֶאֱמֶת, נֹצֵר חֶסֶד לָאֲלָפִים, נֹשֵׂא עָוֹן, וָפֶשַׁע, וְחַטָּאָה, וְנַקֵּה.** וְסָלַחְתָּ לַעֲוֹנֵנוּ וּלְחַטָּאתֵנוּ וּנְחַלְתָּנוּ. סְלַח לָנוּ אָבִינוּ כִּי חָטָאנוּ, מְחַל לָנוּ מַלְכֵּנוּ כִּי פָשָׁעְנוּ. כִּי אַתָּה אֲדֹנָי טוֹב וְסַלָּח, וְרַב חֶסֶד לְכָל קֹרְאֶיךָ.

פסוקי הקדמה לסליחה לב

אַל תָּבוֹא בְמִשְׁפָּט עִמָּנוּ, כִּי לֹא יִצְדַּק לְפָנֶיךָ כָל חָי.[8] כִּי עִמְּךָ הַסְּלִיחָה, לְמַעַן תִּוָּרֵא.[9] כִּי עִמְּךָ מְקוֹר חַיִּים, בְּאוֹרְךָ נִרְאֶה אוֹר.[10] חַיִּים וָחֶסֶד תַּעֲשֶׂה עִמָּנוּ, וּפְקֻדָּתְךָ תִּשְׁמוֹר רוּחֵנוּ.[11] חַיִּים נִשְׁאַל מִמְּךָ, תִּתֵּן לָנוּ, אֹרֶךְ יָמִים עוֹלָם וָעֶד.[12]

כְּרַחֵם אָב עַל בָּנִים, כֵּן תְּרַחֵם יהוה עָלֵינוּ. לַיהוה הַיְשׁוּעָה, עַל עַמְּךָ בִרְכָתֶךָ סֶּלָה. יהוה צְבָאוֹת עִמָּנוּ, מִשְׂגָּב לָנוּ אֱלֹהֵי יַעֲקֹב סֶלָה. יהוה צְבָאוֹת, אַשְׁרֵי אָדָם בֹּטֵחַ בָּךְ. יהוה הוֹשִׁיעָה, הַמֶּלֶךְ יַעֲנֵנוּ בְיוֹם קָרְאֵנוּ.

ש **Truly,** the Judge of the poor,
  Whose throne will endure through all generations —[1]
  the King Who with justice establishes the earth[2] and the heavens —
  He, the Mighty of the mighty ones, will reckon [man's] deeds,
                              according to the facts and the **truth.**[3]

ת *Chazzan* — **Truth** — give it to Jacob, and kindness to [Abraham,]
     the Father of my multitude,[4]
  for out of Your love You called me, 'My firstborn, my son.'[5]
  Whiten our sins that are red as scarlet.[6]
     As for me, my prayer is to You, HASHEM: '[May it be] at a time
  of favor; O God, in Your great kindness, answer me with **truth.'**[7]

All, while standing:

אֵל מֶלֶךְ **O God, King Who sits on the throne of mercy; Who acts with**
     kindness, pardons the iniquities of His people, removes [sins]
one by one, increasingly grants pardon to careless sinners and forgiveness
to rebels, Who deals righteously with every living being — You do not repay
them in accord with their evil. *Chazzan* — O God, You taught us to recite the
Thirteen [Attributes of Mercy], so remember for us today the covenant of
these Thirteen, as You made known to the humble one in ancient times, as
it is written: And HASHEM descended in a cloud and stood with him there,
and He called out with the Name HASHEM.

Congregation, then chazzan:

And HASHEM passed before him [Moses] and proclaimed:

Congregation and chazzan (the words in bold type are recited aloud and in unison):

ה' ה' **HASHEM, HASHEM, God, Compassionate and Gracious, Slow**
     to anger, and Abundant in Kindness and Truth, Preserver of
kindness for thousands [of generations], Forgiver of iniquity, willful
sin, and error, and Who cleanses. May You forgive our iniquities and our
errors and make us Your heritage. Forgive us, our Father, for we have
erred; pardon us, our King, for we have willfully sinned; for You, my Lord,
are good and forgiving and abundantly kind to all who call upon You.

PREFATORY VERSES TO SELICHAH 32

אַל תָּבוֹא **Do not enter into strict judgment with us, for no living**
     creature would be innocent before You.[8] For with You [alone]
is forgiveness, that You may be feared.[9] For with You is the source of life;
by Your light may we see light.[10] May You grant life and kindness for us,
and Your law will guard our souls.[11] We ask You for life — may You give
it to us: length of days forever and ever.[12]

כְּרַחֵם אָב **As a father has mercy on his children, so, HASHEM, may**
     You have mercy on us. Salvation is HASHEM's, upon Your
people is Your blessing, Selah. HASHEM, Master of Legions, is with us, a
stronghold for us is the God of Jacob, Selah. HASHEM, Master of Legions,
praiseworthy is the person who trusts in You. HASHEM, save! May the
King answer us on the day we call.

---

(1) Cf. *Proverbs* 29:14. (2) Cf. 29:4. (3) *II Chronicles* 32:1. (4) Cf. *Micah* 7:20.
(5) Cf. *Exodus* 4:22. (6) Cf. *Isaiah* 1:18. (7) *Psalms* 69:14. (8) Cf. 143:2.
(9) 130:4. (10) 36:10. (11) Cf. *Job* 10:12. (12) Cf. *Psalms* 21:5.

In some congregations the following two verses are recited responsively — the *chazzan* reciting סְלַח נָא, and the congregation responding וַיֹּאמֶר. In other congregations these verses are recited silently.

סְלַח נָא לַעֲוֹן הָעָם הַזֶּה כְּגֹדֶל חַסְדֶּךָ, וְכַאֲשֶׁר נָשָׂאתָה לָעָם הַזֶּה מִמִּצְרַיִם וְעַד הֵנָּה, וְשָׁם נֶאֱמַר:

וַיֹּאמֶר יהוה סָלַחְתִּי כִּדְבָרֶךָ.

All:

הַטֵּה אֱלֹהַי אָזְנְךָ וּשְׁמָע, פְּקַח עֵינֶיךָ וּרְאֵה שֹׁמְמֹתֵינוּ, וְהָעִיר אֲשֶׁר נִקְרָא שִׁמְךָ עָלֶיהָ, כִּי לֹא עַל צִדְקוֹתֵינוּ אֲנַחְנוּ מַפִּילִים תַּחֲנוּנֵינוּ לְפָנֶיךָ, כִּי עַל רַחֲמֶיךָ הָרַבִּים. אֲדֹנָי שְׁמָעָה, אֲדֹנָי סְלָחָה, אֲדֹנָי הַקְשִׁיבָה, וַעֲשֵׂה אַל תְּאַחַר, לְמַעַנְךָ אֱלֹהַי, כִּי שִׁמְךָ נִקְרָא עַל עִירְךָ וְעַל עַמֶּךָ.

סליחה לב (שלמונית)

All:

(אֱלֹהֵינוּ וֵאלֹהֵי אֲבוֹתֵינוּ:)

חַיִּים אֲרוּכִים תִּכְתְּבֵנוּ* נָטוּעַ בְּלִי לַעֲקוֹר,
בְּשִׁבְתְּךָ עַל כִּסֵּא מַעֲשִׂים לִסְקוֹר,
כִּי עִמְּךָ מְקוֹר חַיִּים.[1]   הַטּוֹב צְפֵה וְהָרַע אַל תַּחְקוֹר,

חַיִּים בִּרְצוֹנוֹ וְרֶגַע בְּאַפּוֹ[2] נִרְאֵית,
לֹא לָנֶצַח תָּרִיב[3] נַחֲלַת הַנִּלְאֵת,[4]
הַשְׁמִיעֵנִי נָא סָלַחְתִּי[5] עָוֹן לָשֵׂאת,
רְאֵה נָתַתִּי לְפָנֶיךָ הַיּוֹם אֶת הַחַיִּים.[6]

חַיִּים גְּאוֹל מִשַּׁחַת, תְּעַטְּרֵנִי חֶסֶד[7] אֶזְרָח,[8]
וְאֶמֶת יַשְׁרֵשׁ יַעֲקֹב יָצִיץ וּפָרַח,[9]
תַּרְחִיק פְּשָׁעֵינוּ כִּרְחוֹק מַעֲרָב מִמִּזְרָח,[10]
תּוֹדִיעֵנוּ אֹרַח חַיִּים.[11]

חַיִּים דְּבָרְךָ יַדְעֵנוּ*, אֵל גִּבּוֹר וְיוֹעֵץ,[12]
לְהִדָּבֵק בְּתוֹרָתֶךָ, אוֹתָנוּ בְּטוֹבָה לְהַנְעֵץ,
הַגְבֵּר טוֹב עַל צְפוֹנִי[13] לְהָרֵעַ,
לִשְׁמֹר אֶת דֶּרֶךְ עֵץ הַחַיִּים.[14]

↪ **חַיִּים אֲרוּכִים תִּכְתְּבֵנוּ** — *Life of longevity may You inscribe for us.* This is the third in a series of four *selichos*, each of which revolves around a key word that begins and ends each stanza. In the present *selichah*, the theme is חַיִּים, *life, living, live,* or *alive.* [See prefatory com-

In some congregations the following two verses are recited responsively — the *chazzan*
reciting, *'Forgive, please . . .,'* and the congregation responding, *'And HASHEM said . . .'*
In other congregations these verses are recited silently.

סְלַח נָא *Forgive, please, the iniquity of this people according to the
greatness of Your kindness and as You have forgiven this
people from Egypt until now, and there it was said:*

And HASHEM said, 'I have forgiven according to your word!'

All:

הַטֵּה *Incline, my God, Your ear, and listen, open Your eyes and see our
desolation and that of the city upon which Your Name is proclaimed; for not because of our righteousness do we cast down our
supplications before You, rather because of Your abundant compassion.
O my Lord, heed; O my Lord, forgive; O my Lord, be attentive and act,
do not delay; for Your sake, my God, for Your Name is proclaimed upon
Your city and upon Your people.*

SELICHAH 32

All:

(Our God and the God of our forefathers:)

א **Life** *of longevity may You inscribe for us,* planted with none to uproot.
As You sit on [Your] Throne to inspect [men's] deeds,
look at the good and do not investigate the bad,*
                            *for with you is the source of **life.**¹*

ב **Life** *comes from His favor; His anger is apparent for but a moment.²
He will not quarrel forever³ with His wearied heritage-people.⁴
Please let me hear, 'I forgive,⁵ to bear iniquity;*
                            *see, today I have placed before you **life.**'⁶*

ג **Life** *[grant me and] redeem [me] from ruin;
crown me with the kindness⁷ of [Abraham] the Ezrachite.⁸
Let the truth that Jacob implanted [in us] bud and blossom.⁹
Set our willful sins far away, as far as west from east;¹⁰*
                            *inform us of the path of **life.**¹¹*

ד **Live** *is Your word, make it known to us,*
O Mighty God and Counselor,¹²
[to enable us] to cling to Your Torah, to advise [us] well.
Cause the Good [Inclination] to overpower
    my hidden [Evil Inclination],¹³ to break [its power],
                            to guard the way to the Tree of **Life.**¹⁴*

---

(1) *Psalms* 36:10. (2) Cf. 30:6; see commentary to *selichah* 22, s.v., כְּרֶגַע מְלֹוֹל.
(3) Cf. *Isaiah* 57:16. (4) Cf. *Psalms* 68:10. (5) See *Numbers* 14:20. (6) *Deuteronomy* 30:15.
(7) Cf. *Psalms* 103:4. (8) See commentary to *selichah* 83, s.v., אֵיתָן לְמַד דַּעַת.
(9) *Isaiah* 27:6. (10) Cf. *Psalms* 103:12. (11) Cf. 16:11. (12) Cf. *Isaiah* 9:5.
(13) See commentary to *selichah* 22, s.v., אָבֶן. . . מִכְשׁוֹל. (14) *Genesis* 3:24.

---

ments to *selichos* 30 regarding authorship of this
work.]

חַיִּים דְּבָרְךָ יַדְעֵנוּ — *Live is Your word, make it
known to us.* Alternatively: *O Living One, make*

חַיִּים הִיא לַמַּחֲזִיקִים בָּהּ,[1] וּרְפָאוֹת וּמֵרוֹחַ,

תּוֹמְכֶיהָ מְאֻשָּׁרִים[1] בְּאוֹר זָרֻעַ זָרוּחַ,

וְכָל הַדָּבֵק בָּהּ יִהְיֶה שָׂרוּחַ,   כָּל בָּשָׂר אֲשֶׁר בּוֹ רוּחַ חַיִּים.[2]

חַיִּים וְשָׁלוֹם תִּסְמְכֵנוּ, בְּיִרְאָה אוֹתְךָ לַעֲבוֹד,

וְנָגִילָה וְנִשְׂמְחָה בָךְ,[3] רְשָׁעִים בַּאֲבוֹד,

שְׁלֹשׁ מֵאוֹת וַעֲשָׂרָה* אוֹתָנוּ לִזְבּוֹד,

יִרְאַת יהוה עֹשֶׁר וְכָבוֹד וְחַיִּים.[4]

חַיִּים זְכָרֵנִי זֵבֶד טוֹב,[5] גְּדוֹל הָעֵצָה,[6]

מַחֲסֶה לָנוּ עֶזְרָה בַּצָּרוֹת נִמְצָא,[7]

שׁוּבָה אֵלַי וְאָשׁוּבָה,[8] אָמַר בְּפִיצָה,   כִּי מוֹצְאִי מָצָא חַיִּים.[9]

חַיִּים חָנֵּם חָנֵּנִי, אֵל אֱלֹהֵי הָרוּחוֹת,[10]*

עֲוֹן תִּמְחוֹל חָרוּת עַל הַלֻּחוֹת,[11]

וְשׂוֹנְאֶיךָ יִלְבְּשׁוּ בֹשֶׁת[12] בִּיסּוּר תּוֹכָחוֹת,

לֹא יְשׁוּבוּן וְלֹא יַשִּׂיגוּ אָרְחוֹת חַיִּים.[13]

חַיִּים טוֹבִים גְּמוֹל לַעֲבָדֶיךָ,[14] נַפְשָׁם לִגְאוֹל

מֵרְאוֹת שַׁחַת,[15] כְּנָם נִשְׁאָל נִשְׁאָל,[16]*

לֹא כֵן הָרְשָׁעִים[17] שֶׁפֻּרְקוּ עוֹל,

יַשִּׁיא מָוֶת עָלֵימוֹ, יֵרְדוּ שְׁאוֹל חַיִּים.[18]

חַיִּים יוֹדוּךָ כָּמוֹנוּ, וְלֹא קְרוּצֵי קֶרֶץ,*

אָב לַבָּנִים יוֹדִיעַ[19] שִׁבְחֲךָ בְּמֶרֶץ,

וַאֲנַחְנוּ נְבָרֵךְ יָהּ,[20] שִׁבְחֲךָ לְהָאֱרֶץ,

לִרְאוֹת בְּטוּב יהוה בְּאֶרֶץ הַחַיִּים.[21]

חַיִּים כֻּלְּכֶם הַיּוֹם,[22] תַּשְׁמִיעַ טֶרֶף חֻקָּם,[23]

מֵחַטָּאתָם טַהֲרֵם[24] וְאַל תְּשִׁיבֵם רֵיקָם,

מִמְתִים יָדְךָ* יהוה, מַלֵּא סִפְקָם,

מִמְתִים מֵחֶלֶד חֶלְקָם בַּחַיִּים.[25]*

Your word known to us.

שְׁלֹשׁ מֵאוֹת וַעֲשָׂרָה — *Three hundred and ten [worlds].* The very last Mishnah in the Talmud states: In the future, the Holy One, Blessed is He, will grant a heritage of three hundred and ten worlds to each and every righteous person (*Uktzin* 3:12). Thus, we pray that we be found righteous when our judgment is issued, and are among those who receive that portion.

אֱלֹהֵי הָרוּחוֹת — *Lord of the spirits.* According to *Rashi* (Numbers 16:22), this phrase describes God

as the One Who knows the spirits, i.e., the innermost thoughts, of man. It is synonymous with יוֹדֵעַ מַחֲשָׁבוֹת, *Knower of thoughts.* According to *Ibn Ezra* (ibid.), it means that God is Master of all living creatures.

כְּנָם נִשְׁאָל נִשְׁאָל — *As King David stated.* King David, the Psalmist, said: *You will not abandon my soul to the grave; You will not allow Your devout one to see Gehinnom* (Psalms 16:10). He is called נִשְׁאָל נִשְׁאָל [lit., *ask did he ask*, i.e., he asked earnestly] by the *paytan* based on the words of

ה **Life** it is for those who hold fast to it,[1] and healing and salve.
   Those who support it are praiseworthy,[1]
      with shining light sown for them;
      and all who cling to it will have a surplus [of blessing],
                  [over] all flesh that has in it the spirit of **life**.[2]

ו With **life** and peace may You support us,
      [enabling us] to serve You in awe,
   let us rejoice and be happy in You,[3] while the wicked are lost.
   And apportion to us, three hundred and ten [worlds];*
                  for fear of HASHEM [brings] riches, honor, and **life**.[4]

ז **Life** has the Great Counselor[5] apportioned to us, a goodly portion.[6]
   [He is] a shelter for us, a help near at hand in time of trouble.[7]
   'Return to Me and I will return [to you],'[8] He has spoken out clearly,
                  'For He who finds Me has found **life**.'[9]

ח **Life** as a free and undeserved gift, grant me,
      O God, Lord of the spirits;*[10]
   forgive [my] iniquity, [though it be] engraved in stone tablets.[11]
   May Your enemies be clad with shame,[12] with the reproof of suffering.
                  May they neither return nor reach the paths of **life**.[13]

ט **Life** that is good may you grant to Your servants,[14]
      redeeming their souls
   from the sight of Gehinnom,[15] as King David stated.*[16]
   Not so for the wicked[17] who threw off Your yoke;
      incite death against them, may they descend to the grave **alive**.[18]

י **Living** beings will thank You, as we do;
      but not those who have forfeited life.*
   Each father will vigorously teach his children[19] Your praise,
   and we will bless God,[20] exalting Your praise,
      [and so we will] see HASHEM's goodness in the land of the **living**.[21]

כ 'Alive are all of you today'[22] may You announce for them,
      [and] provide their daily needs.[23]
   Purify them from their sin;[24] do not turn them away empty-handed.
   Those destined to die by Your hand,* O HASHEM, — fulfill their need,
      those who die of old age, and their portion is among the **living**.*[25]

---

(1) Cf. *Proverbs* 3:18. (2) Cf. *Genesis* 6:17. (3) Cf. *Psalms* 118:24; *Song of Songs* 1:4. (4) *Proverbs* 22:4.
(5) Cf. *Genesis* 30:20. (6) *Jeremiah* 32:19. (7) Cf. *Psalms* 46:2. (8) *Malachi* 3:7. (9) *Proverbs* 8:35.
(10) *Numbers* 16:22. (11) *Exodus* 32:16. (12) Cf. *Job* 8:22. (13) *Proverbs* 2:19. (14) Cf. *Psalms* 119:17.
(15) Cf. 16:10. (16) Cf. *I Samuel* 20:28. (17) *Psalms* 1:4. (18) 55:16. (19) Cf. *Isaiah* 38:19. (20) *Psalms* 115:18.
(21) Cf. 27:13. (22) *Deuteronomy* 4:4. (23) Cf. *Proverbs* 30:8. (24) Cf. *Psalms* 51:4. (25) Cf. 17:14.

Jonathan when he explained David's absence to King Saul (see *I Samuel* 20:28).

חַיִּים יוֹדוּךָ ... וְלֹא קְרוּצֵי קָרֶץ — *Living beings ... will thank You, but not those who have forfeited life.* The verse states: לֹא הַמֵּתִים יְהַלְלוּ יָהּ, *The dead will not praise God* (*Psalms* 115:17). The people who fail to recognize God's omnipresence and influence over the world resemble *the dead*, who are insensitive to all external stimuli and who are oblivious to reality (R' *Azariah Figo*). However,

the righteous, who are stirred by God's presence, continue to praise God even after their souls depart from their bodies (*Ibn Ezra*).

מְמִתִים יָדֶךָ — *Those destined to die by Your hand.* This alludes to the righteous who will die in their sleep by the hand of God and not suffer violent death (*Rashi* to *Psalms* 17:14).

בַּחַיִּים — *Among the living.* The translation follows *Radak* (to *Psalms* 17:14). *Targum* renders *eternal life*.

חַיִּים לְמַעְלָה לְמַשְׂכִּיל, לְמַעַן סוּר מֵחֶרֶךְ,[1]

אַךְ אֱלֹהִים יִפְדֶּה נַפְשִׁי מִפֶּרֶךְ,[2]

וִיחִי עוֹד לָנֶצַח[3] לְיָמִים אָרֹךְ,

כִּי נֵר מִצְוָה וְתוֹרָה אוֹר וְדֶרֶךְ חַיִּים.[4]

חַיִּים מִסְפָּר יְמַחוּ[5] גְּבָל וּמוֹאָב הַגְּבוֹהִים,

לְבוּל עֵץ סוֹגְדִים[6] וְקֹדִים וּמַאֲלִיהִים,

בַּל יֶחֱזָן רָשָׁע[7] הַמְדֻכֶּה יָדוֹן בִּשְׁלוֹהִים,

כִּי חֶרֶף מַעַרְכוֹת אֱלֹהִים חַיִּים.[8]

חַיִּים נִשְׁבַּעְתָּ בּוֹ לְבִנְךָ יְחִידֶךָ,[9]

שַׁעַר אוֹיְבָיו לְהַנְחִילוֹ[10] תַּתָּה בְיָדֶךָ,

אָנַפְתָּ וְתָשׁוּב עַל כֵּן אוֹדֶךָ,[11]   כִּי טוֹב חַסְדְּךָ מֵחַיִּים.[12]

חַיִּים שֶׂבַע שְׂמָחוֹת אֶת פָּנֶיךָ[13] נוֹרָאוֹת,

חַדֵּשׁ יָמֵינוּ[14] חֵן חֵן תְּשׁוּאוֹת,[15]

תָּשׁוּב תְּרַחֲמֵנוּ[16] יהוה אֱלֹהִים צְבָאוֹת,[17]

כִּי מִמֶּנּוּ תוֹצָאוֹת חַיִּים.[18]

חַיִּים עַל הָאֲדָמָה[19] יְבַשֵּׂר עַמְּךָ מִמְּעוֹנוֹת,

וְתַשְׁלִיךְ בִּמְצוֹלוֹת יָם חֵטְא וַעֲוֹנוֹת,[20]

לֵב טָהוֹר בְּרָא לָנוּ[21] וְהַמְצִיאֵנוּ חֲנִינוֹת,[22]

אֹרֶךְ יָמִים וּשְׁנוֹת חַיִּים.[23]

חַיִּים פִּי צַדִּיק וּפִי רְשָׁעִים מְחַתָּה,[24]

בְּקִרְבְּךָ מִלְחָמוֹת וְשָׁלוֹם וּפַלָּצוּת וּבְעָתָה,

שֹׂבַע וְרָזוֹן וְחִיל[25] הַחַיִּים וְהַמָּוֶת,

הַבְּרָכָה וְהַקְּלָלָה וּבָחַרְתָּ בַּחַיִּים.[26]

חַיִּים צְדָקָה וְכָבוֹד[27] תַּגְדִּיל לְיָפֶה כְּתִרְצָה,[28]

הַזּוֹרַעַת חֶסֶד וְקוֹצֶרֶת[29] בְּלִי שִׂמְצָה,

תְּכוֹנֵן צַדִּיק יהוה וּגְדֹר פִּרְצָה,

רֹדֵף צְדָקָה וָחֶסֶד יִמְצָא חַיִּים.[30]

חַיִּים קַיָּמִים תַּנְחִילֵנוּ, וְחָכְמָה וָדַעַת בְּמוֹעֵצוֹת,[31]

שָׂשׂוֹן וְשִׂמְחָה תַּשְׁמִיעַ מֵעִיר חֻצוֹת,[32]

וְהַעֲבֵר מֵעָלַי עָוֹן, וְהַלְבֵּשׁ מַחֲלָצוֹת,[33]

אֶתְהַלֵּךְ לִפְנֵי יהוה בְּאַרְצוֹת הַחַיִּים.[34]*

בְּאַרְצוֹת הַחַיִּים — *In the lands of the living.* Numerous Midrashim identify *Eretz Yisrael* as the   *land of the living* for it is there that the dead are destined to be resurrected. For this reason, the

ל **Life** [hovers] over the wise man, in order that he keep clear
    of the crevice [of Gehinnom].[1]
May God redeem my soul from backbreaking oppression.[2]
Let it live on for eternity,[3] for length of days,
    for a mitzvah is a lamp, and Torah a light and the road of **life.**[4]

מ **Life** — from its book wipe out[5] haughty Geval and Moab,
those who bow to a piece of wood,[6] kneel and deify it.
Let the wicked oppressor not find grace;[7]
    let him be adjudged to eradication,
        for he has blasphemed the troops of the God of **life.**[8]

נ '**Life**,' You swore [to Abraham] 'for your son, your only son!'[9],
His enemies' gates as his heritage[10] You gave him with Your might.
Though You were angry [with his descendants],
    You will return [to them], and therefore I thank You,[11]
        for Your kindness is better than **life.**[12]

ס **Life** replete with joys before You,[13] O [Worker of] wonders;
renew our days[14] until all acclaim their beauty.[15]
Return [to us] and have mercy on us,[16]
    HASHEM, God, Master of Legions,[17] for from You flows forth **life.**[18]

ע **Life** on earth — [19] may it be announced from Heaven for Your people.
May You throw sin and iniquities into the depths of the sea.[20]
Create a new heart for us[21] and cause us to find grace,[22]
    length of days and years of **life.**[23]

פ **Life** [is in] the mouth of the righteous;
    destruction [in] the mouth of the wicked.[24]
As You apportion wars and peace, fear and panic,
plenty and famine and trembling,[25] life and death,
    blessing and curse — may You chose **life.**[26]

צ **Life**, righteousness and honor[27] may You increase for [Israel]
    who is beautiful when she fulfills Your will,[28]
who sows kindness and reaps[29] [its] untarnished [reward].
Establish the righteous, O HASHEM, and wall up the breach —
    so that he who pursues righteousness and kindness will find **life.**[30]

ק **Life** everlasting cause us to inherit,
    and wisdom and understanding through the [Torah's] counsel;[31]
let us hear [once again] celebration and joy
    from the streets of the [Holy] City.[32]
Remove iniquity from upon me and dress [me] in clean robes;[33]
    that I may walk before HASHEM in the lands of the **living.***[34]

(1) Cf. *Proverbs* 15:24. (2) Cf. *Psalms* 49:16. (3) Cf. 49:10. (4) *Proverbs* 6:23. (5) Cf. *Psalms* 69:29.
(6) Cf. *Isaiah* 44:19; this line (לְבוּל. . .וּמֵאֱלֹהִים) has been censored out of some editions of *Selichos*.
(7) Cf. *Isaiah* 26:10. (8) *I Samuel* 17:36. (9) Cf. *Genesis* 22:16. (10) Cf. 22:17. (11) Cf. *Isaiah* 12:1.
(12) *Psalms* 63:4. (13) 16:11. (14) *Lamentations* 5:21. (15) Cf. *Zechariah* 4:7. (16) Cf. *Micah* 7:19.
(17) *Psalms* 80:5. (18) *Proverbs* 4:23. (19) *Deuteronomy* 4:10. (20) Cf. *Micah* 7:19. (21) Cf. *Psalms* 51:12.
(22) Cf. *Proverbs* 3:4. (23) 3:2. (24) Cf. 10:11. (25) Some editions read וְחָיִל; the translation is then
either, *plenty and famine and [invading] armies*, or, *plenty and famine and wealth*. (26) *Deuteronomy*
30:19. (27) *Proverbs* 21:21. (28) Cf. *Song of Songs* 6:4. (29) Cf. *Hosea* 10:12. (30) *Proverbs* 21:21.
(31) Cf. 22:20. (32) Cf. *Jeremiah* 33:10-11. (33) Cf. *Zechariah* 3:4. (34) *Psalms* 116:9.

חַיִּים רְאֵה עִם סְגֻלָּתְךָ כְּקֶדֶם לְמֵיטוֹב,[1]
לֹא תַחְפּוֹץ בְּמוֹת הַמֵּת, עַד דְּיָתוֹב,[2]
נִשְׁבָּר וְנִדְכֶּה לְפָנֶיךָ חָשׁוּב, הַטּוֹב,
קָדוֹשׁ יֵאָמֶר לוֹ, כָּל הַכָּתוּב **לַחַיִּים**.[3]

חַיִּים שָׁאַל מִמְּךָ נָתַתָּה לּוֹ,* חַיֵּיהוּ מְיוֹמְיִם,[5]
גָּדוֹל כְּבוֹדוֹ בִּישׁוּעָתֶךָ[6] כִּפַּת פַּעֲמָיִם,[7]
הַשְׁקִיפָה מִמְּעוֹן קָדְשְׁךָ מִן הַשָּׁמָיִם,[8]
בַּיּוֹם הַהוּא יֵצְאוּ מַיִם **חַיִּים**.[9]

חַיִּים תַּאֲוָה בָאָה[10] סְלֹחַ אֶל חַטֹּאתֵיכֶם,
תַּשְׁמִיעַ וְאֶת רוּחִי אֶתֵּן בְּקִרְבְּכֶם,[11]
לֵאמֹר מָצָאתִי כֹפֶר,[12] רָצִיתִי אֶתְכֶם,[13]
וְאַתֶּם הַדְּבֵקִים בַּיהוה אֱלֹהֵיכֶם **חַיִּים**.[14]

חַיִּים מִמְּךָ הָאֵל סָמְכָה יוֹנַתְךָ הַמְּשׁוּכָה אַחֲרֶיךָ,[15]
לְהִדָּבֵק בְּךָ כַּדָּת וְכַהֲלָכָה,
תְּבִיאֵנוּ לְהַר צִיּוֹן וְתָשִׁיב הַמְּלוּכָה,
כִּי שָׁם צִוָּה יהוה אֶת הַבְּרָכָה **חַיִּים**.[16]

❖ **חַיִּים** מִמֶּנּוּ נוֹחִיל וְלִישׁוּעָתוֹ קֹנֵינוּ,[17]
עַתָּה יַרְחִיב יהוה לָנוּ וּפָרִינוּ,[18]
יְחַיֵּינוּ מִיּוֹמָיִם בַּיּוֹם הַשְּׁלִישִׁי יְקִימֵנוּ,[19]
אֲנַחְנוּ אֵלֶּה פֹה הַיּוֹם כֻּלָּנוּ **חַיִּים**.[20]

All, while standing:

אֵל מֶלֶךְ יוֹשֵׁב עַל כִּסֵּא רַחֲמִים מִתְנַהֵג בַּחֲסִידוּת, מוֹחֵל
עֲוֹנוֹת עַמּוֹ, מַעֲבִיר רִאשׁוֹן רִאשׁוֹן, מַרְבֶּה מְחִילָה
לְחַטָּאִים וּסְלִיחָה לְפוֹשְׁעִים, עֹשֶׂה צְדָקוֹת עִם כָּל בָּשָׂר וָרוּחַ,
לֹא כְרָעָתָם תִּגְמוֹל. ❖ אֵל הוֹרֵיתָ לָּנוּ לוֹמַר שְׁלֹשׁ עֶשְׂרֵה, וּזְכוֹר
לָנוּ הַיּוֹם בְּרִית שְׁלֹשׁ עֶשְׂרֵה, כְּמוֹ שֶׁהוֹדַעְתָּ לֶעָנָיו מִקֶּדֶם, כְּמוֹ
שֶׁכָּתוּב, וַיֵּרֶד יהוה בֶּעָנָן וַיִּתְיַצֵּב עִמּוֹ שָׁם, וַיִּקְרָא בְשֵׁם יהוה.

Patriarchs and righteous Sages in all generations yearned to be buried in the holy soil. Those who are interred in foreign soil will roll to Israel through subterranean passages prior to their resurrection (*Pesikta Rabbasi* 1; *Yerushalmi, Kesubos* 12:3).

According to *Rashi* (*Psalms* 116:9), *Eretz Yisrael* is called by this name because it is the home of the Living God; in foreign lands, however, idolaters worship lifeless gods.

Moreover, the very air of the Holy Land

makes men healthy and robust and the holy atmosphere grants the mind renewed vitality and alertness. Indeed, the Land of Israel deserves to be called the *land of the living*, for the exiled Jew lives in constant fear of death, but in *Eretz Yisrael* he dwells in safety (*Radak*).

The *Talmud* (*Yoma* 71a) cites the opinion of Rav Yehudah, who identifies the *land of the living* as מְקוֹם שְׁוָוקִים, *the market place*. When Israel wanders in exile, they lack the income to provide the necessities of life. Therefore a market

ר **Living One,** look to Your treasured people
   when they return to You as of old.[1]
You do not wish the wicked to die before repenting;[2]
the broken and crushed are held in esteem before You, O Goodly One,
      'Holy' shall be said of him, of each one inscribed for **life.**[3]

ש **Life** he asked of You and You gave it to him*[4] —
   invigorate him, despite the two Destructions.[5]
Great is his honor in Your salvations,[6]
   as [it was] at the beautiful Pilgrimage [Festivals].[7]
Look down from Your holy abode, from Heaven;[8]
               on that day will go forth the water of **life.**[9]

ת '**Life,** your desire, has come,[10] [with] forgiveness for your sins!' [tell us].
   Let us hear, 'I will put My spirit in your midst.'[11]
Say [to us], 'I have found atonement [for you],[12]
   I have found you favorable.[13]
            And you who cling to HASHEM, your God, have **life.'**[14]

Life is from You, O God, uphold Your dove, [Israel,]
   who is drawn after You,[15]
clinging to You [by doing Your will] according to the Torah and [its] law.
Bring us to Mount Zion and restore the kingdom,
         For there HASHEM commanded the blessing of **life.**[16]
Chazzan — **Life** from Him we await, as we hope for His salvation.[17]
May HASHEM now grant us expansiveness that we may increase.[18]
May He grant us life even after two Destructions —
   may He revive [us] on the day [of] the Third [Temple],[19]
            we who are here today, all of us in **life.**[20]

All, while standing:

אֵל מֶלֶךְ O God, King Who sits on the throne of mercy; Who acts with
         kindness, pardons the iniquities of His people, removes [sins]
one by one, increasingly grants pardon to careless sinners and forgiveness
to rebels, Who deals righteously with every living being — You do not repay
them in accord with their evil. Chazzan — O God, You taught us to recite the
Thirteen [Attributes of Mercy], so remember for us today the covenant of
these Thirteen, as You made known to the humble one in ancient times, as
it is written: And HASHEM descended in a cloud and stood with him there,
and He called out with the Name HASHEM.

---

(1) Cf. *Lamentations* 5:21 with *Targum.* (2) Cf. *Ezekiel* 18:32. (3) *Isaiah* 4:3. (4) *Psalms* 21:5.
(5) Cf. *Hosea* 6:2; see *Rashi.* (6) *Psalms* 21:6. (7) Cf. *Song of Songs* 7:2. (8) *Deuteronomy* 26:15.
(9) *Zechariah* 14:8. (10) *Proverbs* 13:12. (11) *Ezekiel* 36:27. (12) *Job* 33:24. (13) Cf. *Ezekiel* 43:27.
(14) *Deuteronomy* 4:4. (15) The word אַחֲרֶיךָ, *after You,* is absent in some editions; in others
it is the first word of the next line. (16) *Psalms* 133:3. (17) Cf. *Genesis* 49:18. (18) Cf. 26:22.
(19) Cf. *Hosea* 6:2. (20) *Deuteronomy* 5:3.

---

place becomes of vital importance for them
(*Rashi* and *Tosafos Yeshanim,* Yoma 71a).
   Rambam (Hilchos Teshuvah 3:5; 8:7) identifies
'the land of the living' as the World to Come.

חַיִּים שָׁאַל מִמְּךָ נָתַתָּה לּוֹ — *Life he asked of You
and You gave it to him.* The 'he' of this verse al-

ludes to King David's descendant, the Messiah.
The Talmud (*Succah* 52a) relates: God will [in
the future] say to *Mashiach ben David,* may he
be revealed speedily in our days, 'Ask anything
of Me and I shall grant it to you' (*Psalms* 2:8).
Having seen that his precursor *Mashiach ben
Yosef* had been killed, *Mashiach ben David* will

Congregation, then *chazzan*:

וַיַּעֲבֹר יהוה עַל פָּנָיו וַיִּקְרָא:

Congregation and *chazzan* (the words in bold type are recited aloud and in unison):

יהוה, יהוה, אֵל, רַחוּם, וְחַנּוּן, אֶרֶךְ אַפַּיִם, וְרַב חֶסֶד, **וֶאֱמֶת,**
נֹצֵר חֶסֶד לָאֲלָפִים, נֹשֵׂא עָוֹן, וָפֶשַׁע, וְחַטָּאָה,
וְנַקֵּה. וְסָלַחְתָּ לַעֲוֹנֵנוּ וּלְחַטָּאתֵנוּ וּנְחַלְתָּנוּ. סְלַח לָנוּ אָבִינוּ כִּי
חָטָאנוּ, מְחַל לָנוּ מַלְכֵּנוּ כִּי פָשָׁעְנוּ. כִּי אַתָּה אֲדֹנָי טוֹב וְסַלָּח,
וְרַב חֶסֶד לְכָל קֹרְאֶיךָ.

פסוקי הקדמה לסליחה לג

אַל תָּבוֹא בְמִשְׁפָּט עִמָּנוּ, כִּי לֹא יִצְדַּק לְפָנֶיךָ כָל חָי.[1] וְאַתָּה
אֲדוֹנֵינוּ הַמֶּלֶךְ, עֵינֵי כָל יִשְׂרָאֵל עָלֶיךָ.[2] יהוה
מֶלֶךְ,[3] יהוה מָלָךְ,[4] יהוה יִמְלֹךְ לְעֹלָם וָעֶד.[5] אַתָּה הוּא מַלְכֵּנוּ
מִקֶּדֶם, פּוֹעֵל יְשׁוּעוֹת בְּקֶרֶב הָאָרֶץ.[6] אַתָּה הוּא מַלְכֵּנוּ אֱלֹהִים,
צַוֵּה יְשׁוּעוֹת יַעֲקֹב.[7] וְהָיָה יהוה לְמֶלֶךְ עַל כָּל הָאָרֶץ, בַּיּוֹם הַהוּא
יִהְיֶה יהוה אֶחָד וּשְׁמוֹ אֶחָד.[8]

כְּרַחֵם אָב עַל בָּנִים, כֵּן תְּרַחֵם יהוה עָלֵינוּ. לַיהוה הַיְשׁוּעָה,
עַל עַמְּךָ בִרְכָתֶךָ סֶּלָה. יהוה צְבָאוֹת עִמָּנוּ,
מִשְׂגָּב לָנוּ אֱלֹהֵי יַעֲקֹב סֶלָה. יהוה צְבָאוֹת, אַשְׁרֵי אָדָם בֹּטֵחַ בָּךְ.
יהוה הוֹשִׁיעָה, הַמֶּלֶךְ יַעֲנֵנוּ בְיוֹם קָרְאֵנוּ.

In some congregations the following two verses are recited responsively — the *chazzan* reciting סְלַח,
and the congregation responding וַיֹּאמֶר. In other congregations these verses are recited silently.

סְלַח נָא לַעֲוֹן הָעָם הַזֶּה כְּגֹדֶל חַסְדֶּךָ, וְכַאֲשֶׁר נָשָׂאתָה לָעָם
הַזֶּה מִמִּצְרַיִם וְעַד הֵנָּה, וְשָׁם נֶאֱמַר:

וַיֹּאמֶר יהוה סָלַחְתִּי כִּדְבָרֶךָ.

All:

הַטֵּה אֱלֹהַי אָזְנְךָ וּשֲׁמָע, פְּקַח עֵינֶיךָ וּרְאֵה שֹׁמְמֹתֵינוּ, וְהָעִיר
אֲשֶׁר נִקְרָא שִׁמְךָ עָלֶיהָ, כִּי לֹא עַל צִדְקוֹתֵינוּ אֲנַחְנוּ
מַפִּילִים תַּחֲנוּנֵינוּ לְפָנֶיךָ, כִּי עַל רַחֲמֶיךָ הָרַבִּים. אֲדֹנָי שְׁמָעָה,
אֲדֹנָי סְלָחָה, אֲדֹנָי הַקְשִׁיבָה, וַעֲשֵׂה אַל תְּאַחַר, לְמַעַנְךָ אֱלֹהַי,
כִּי שִׁמְךָ נִקְרָא עַל עִירְךָ וְעַל עַמֶּךָ.

reply, 'I ask nothing of You but life!' To this God will respond, 'Long before you asked this of Me, your ancestor David already prophesied, *Life he asked of You and You gave it to him!'* (ibid. 21:5).

Congregation, then *chazzan*:

And HASHEM passed before him [Moses] and proclaimed:

Congregation and *chazzan* (the words in bold type are recited aloud and in unison):

ה' ה' HASHEM, HASHEM, God, Compassionate and Gracious, Slow to anger, and Abundant in Kindness and Truth, Preserver of kindness for thousands [of generations], Forgiver of iniquity, willful sin, and error, and Who cleanses. *May You forgive our iniquities and our errors and make us Your heritage. Forgive us, our Father, for we have erred; pardon us, our King, for we have willfully sinned; for You, my Lord, are good and forgiving and abundantly kind to all who call upon You.*

PREFATORY VERSES TO SELICHAH 33

אַל תָּבוֹא *Do not enter into strict judgment with us, for no living creature would be innocent before You.*[1] *And You, Our Lord the King: the eyes of all Israel are upon You.*[2] *HASHEM reigns,*[3] *HASHEM has reigned,*[4] *HASHEM shall reign forever and ever.*[5] *You are our King from days of old, working salvation in the midst of the earth.*[6] *You are our King, O God; command the salvations of Jacob.*[7] *HASHEM will be King over all the earth; on that day HASHEM will be One and His Name will be One.*[8]

כְּרַחֵם אָב *As a father has mercy on his children, so, HASHEM, may You have mercy on us. Salvation is HASHEM's, upon Your people is Your blessing, Selah. HASHEM, Master of Legions, is with us, a stronghold for us is the God of Jacob, Selah. HASHEM, Master of Legions, praiseworthy is the person who trusts in You. HASHEM, save! May the King answer us on the day we call.*

In some congregations the following two verses are recited responsively — the *chazzan* reciting, 'Forgive, please . . . ,' and the congregation responding, 'And HASHEM said . . .'
In other congregations these verses are recited silently.

סְלַח נָא *Forgive, please, the iniquity of this people according to the greatness of Your kindness and as You have forgiven this people from Egypt until now, and there it was said:*

And HASHEM said, 'I have forgiven according to your word!'

All:

הַטֵּה *Incline, my God, Your ear, and listen, open Your eyes and see our desolation and that of the city upon which Your Name is proclaimed; for not because of our righteousness do we cast down our supplications before You, rather because of Your abundant compassion. O my Lord, heed; O my Lord, forgive; O my Lord, be attentive and act, do not delay; for Your sake, my God, for Your Name is proclaimed upon Your city and upon Your people.*

(1) Cf. *Psalms* 143:2. (2) Cf. *I Kings* 1:20. (3) *Psalms* 10:16. (4) 93:1; etc.
(5) *Exodus* 15:18. (6) Cf. *Psalms* 74:12. (7) Cf. 44:5. (8) *Zechariah* 14:9.

סליחה לג (שלמונית)

All:

(אֱלֹהֵינוּ וֵאלֹהֵי אֲבוֹתֵינוּ:)

מֶלֶךְ אֶחָד יִהְיֶה[1]* אֵל הָעַמִּים מֵרִים נִסִּי,[2]

הַשֵּׁם פָּקַדְתִּי שָׁלוֹם, וְלִצְדָקָה נוֹגְשַׂי,[3]

אֵלָיו אֶתְוַדַּע[4] וְאֹמַר, אַיֵּה אֱלוֹהַּ עֹשָׂי,[5]

אוֹמֵר אֲנִי, מַעֲשַׂי לַמֶּלֶךְ.[6]

מֶלֶךְ בְּמִשְׁפָּט יַעֲמִיד[7] עַמּוֹ יִשְׂרָאֵל,

עַל כֵּן קִדַּמְתִּי לִבְרֹחַ[8] אֶת פְּנֵי הָאֵל,

אֲנִי וּנְעָרַי אָצוּם כֵּן,[9] הֱיוֹת תַּחֲנוּנִים שׁוֹאֵל,

וּבְכֵן אָבוֹא אֶל הַמֶּלֶךְ.

מֶלֶךְ גָּדוֹל עַל כָּל אֱלֹהִים[10]* שָׁמַיִם וָאָרֶץ קוֹנֶה,[11]

סָבִיב לִירֵאָיו מַלְאַךְ יהוה חוֹנֶה,[12]

מַלְאֲכֵי רַחֲמִים חֲלוּ נָא[13] לְשׁוֹכְנִי סְנֶה,

הַסָּרִיסִים הַמְשָׁרְתִים אֶת פְּנֵי הַמֶּלֶךְ.[14]

מֶלֶךְ דָּבָר אַל תַּפֵּל מִכֹּל אֲשֶׁר דִּבַּרְתָּ[15] לְחַזֵּק

אֶת בֶּדֶק הַבַּיִת,[16] וְכַרְמְךָ לְסַקֵּל וּלְעַזֵּק,[17]

אַמֵּץ סַנֵּגוֹר וְהָס קַטֵּגוֹר וְלֹא יִנָּזֵק,

כִּי אֵין הַצָּר שֹׁוֶה בְּנֵזֶק הַמֶּלֶךְ.[18]*

מֶלֶךְ הַטּוֹב בְּעֵינֶיךָ רְאֵה עֲוֹנוֹת לָשֵׂאת,

בְּמַשְׁטִין תִּגְעַר לְהָבִיא הַשֶּׁבֶר וְהַשֵּׁאת,

וְיֵצֵא חָפוּר מֵרֹב פַּחַד וּשְׂאֵת,

כִּי כָלְתָה אֵלָיו הָרָעָה מֵאֵת הַמֶּלֶךְ.[19]

הַמֶּלֶךְ וְדָתוֹ מַגִּיעַ[20] כְּחֹק[21] יוֹם לְהַרְשֵׁם,

לָדִין עַמִּים[22] צַדִּיק וְחוֹטֵא וְאָשֵׁם,

וְעַתָּה יִקָּרְאוּ סוֹפְרֵי הַמֶּלֶךְ[23] הָעוֹצֵר וְהַגּוֹשֵׁם,

כִּתְבוּ עַל הַיְּהוּדִים כַּטּוֹב בְּעֵינֵיכֶם בְּשֵׁם הַמֶּלֶךְ.[24]

מֶלֶךְ אֶחָד יִהְיֶה — *One King shall there be.* This is the final *selichah* in a series of four, each of which revolves around a key word that begins and ends each stanza. In the present *selichah*, the theme is מֶלֶךְ, *King*. [See prefatory comments to *selichos* 30 regarding its authorship.]

כָּל אֱלֹהִים — *All* [heavenly] *powers.* The אֱלֹהִים of this verse refers, of course, to the angels and other forces through whom God exercises His mastery of the universe. Thus, He assigns one force to

provide rainfall, another to heal the sick, a third to regulate the tides, and so on. But no matter how strong and independent these powers seem to be, He is their acknowledged King (*Radak* to Psalms 95:3).

כִּי אֵין הַצָּר שֹׁוֶה בְּנֵזֶק הַמֶּלֶךְ — *For the trouble is not worth the loss to the King.* The prophet declared, 'בְּכָל צָרָתָם לוֹ צָר, *In all their trouble, He is troubled'* (Isaiah 63:9); and the Psalmist said in God's name, 'עִמּוֹ אָנֹכִי בְצָרָה, *I am with him in* [time of]

SELICHAH 33

All:

(Our God and the God of our forefathers:)

א *One **King** shall there be,*[1] *raising my banners to the nations.*[2]
  He will turn the functionaries that rule me to peaceful ways,
      and my oppressors to righteousness.[3]
  I will make myself known to Him[4] [again], as I say,
      'Where is the God Who made me?'[5]
              *And when I say, 'My works are for the **King**.'*[6]

ב *The **King** will cause His people Israel to stand in judgment;*[7]
  therefore I have made haste to flee[8] [from my past,
      and to come] before God.
  I and my attendants will fast, too,[9]
      asking [forgiveness] with supplication,
              *and so I will come to the **King**.*[9]

ג *A **King** great above all [heavenly] powers*[10]
      is the Master of Heaven and earth.[11]
  HASHEM's angel encamps around His reverent ones.[12]
  Angels of mercy, please beseech Him[13] Who dwelt in the thornbush,
              *you courtiers who serve in the presence of the **King**.*[14]

ד *O **King**, let nothing fall short of all that You have said:[15] to strengthen*
  the House [of Israel];[16]
      and to clear the stones from and to fence in Your vineyard.[17]
  Invigorate the Advocate, and hush the Accuser,
      that he may not harm us,
              *for the trouble is not worth the loss to the **King**.*[18]

ה *O **King**, as is good in Your eyes, see how to bear [our] sins.*
  Reprimand the Adversary,
      bringing destruction and ruin [to his arguments against us].
  Let him go forth shamed, full of fear and panic,
              *for calamity had come down on him from the **King**.*[19]

ו *The **King** and His law approach,*[20]
      to inscribe on the day of Rosh Hashanah,[21]
  to judge the nations,[22] the righteous, the sinner,
      and the guilty [all together].
  Now let the scribes of the King Who makes drought and rain
      be summoned[23] [and told]:
          'Write what seems best to you concerning the Jews,
              *in the name of the **King**.'*[24]

(1) Cf. *Ezekiel* 37:22. (2) Cf. *Isaiah* 49:22; some editions of *Selichos* read וּמְרִים with the conjunctive
prefix ו; if so, the translation of the stich would be: *One King shall there be to the nations, and He shall
raise my banners.* (3) Cf. 60:17. (4) *Numbers* 12:6. (5) Cf. *Job* 35:10. (6) *Psalms* 45:2.
(7) *Proverbs* 29:4. (8) *Jonah* 4:2. (9) Cf. *Esther* 4:16. (10) *Psalms* 95:3. (11) Cf. *Genesis* 14:22.
(12) Cf. *Psalms* 34:8. (13) See introduction to this volume regarding the propriety of requesting
angelic intervention. (14) *Esther* 1:10. (15) Cf. 6:10. (16) Cf. *II Kings* 22:5. (17) Cf. *Isaiah* 5:2.
(18) *Esther* 7:4. (19) 7:7. (20) 4:3; some editions of *Selichos* omit this stanza.
(21) See *Psalms* 81:5. (22) *Isaiah* 3:13. (23) Cf. *Esther* 8:9. (24) 8:8.

הַמֶּלֶךְ¹ זָהַר חַמָּה תַּחְפִּיר וְיֵבְשׁוּ² עוֹבְדֵי נְבוֹ,³
וְיִמָּאֲסוּן אִישׁ אֱלִילֵי כַסְפּוֹ וְאִישׁ אֱלִילֵי זְהָבוֹ,⁴
כִּי עַיִן בְּעַיִן יִרְאוּ לְצִיּוֹן בְּשׁוּבוֹ,⁵
וְהִנָּשְׂאוּ פִּתְחֵי עוֹלָם וְיָבוֹא מֶלֶךְ.⁶

הַמֶּלֶךְ חָכָם מִזָּרֶה רָשָׁע⁷ וְגַם בֵּעַר,
וַיֵּשֶׁב עֲלֵיהֶם אוֹפָן⁷ וּבָהֶם יִגְעַר,
גֵּרֵשׁ לֵץ וְיֵצֵא מָדוֹן,⁸ וּפִיהוּ לֹא יִפְעָר,
כִּי אֵין לָבוֹא אֶל שַׁעַר הַמֶּלֶךְ.⁹

הַמֶּלֶךְ טוֹב יֵצֵא דְבַר מַלְכוּת מִלְּפָנָיו¹⁰ מְיֻסָּד,
רַגְלֵי בָנָי אֶשְׁמֹר וְלֹא אָשִׂים אוֹתָם בַּסָּד,¹¹
בַּיּוֹם הַמּוּכָן לָדִין מִי יִצְלַח וּמִי יִפָּסֵד,   כִּי כֵן יִסַּד הַמֶּלֶךְ.¹²

הַמֶּלֶךְ יוֹשֵׁב עַל כִּסֵּא דִין¹³ קָטוֹן וְגָדוֹל מַשְׁלֵב,
וְרוֹאֶה מִי שָׁב בְּכָל לֵב וּמִי שָׁב כְּכֶלֶב,¹⁴
נְקֹם נִקְמַת הַנֶּעֱלָב מִן הָעוֹלֵב,
בַּיּוֹם הַשְּׁבִיעִי כְּטוֹב לֵב הַמֶּלֶךְ.¹⁵

הַמֶּלֶךְ כָּל הָאָרֶץ,¹⁶ הָאֵל הָעוֹנֶה
אוֹתִי בְיוֹם צָרָתִי, וִיהִי עִמָּדִי¹⁷ בְּכָל מַחֲנֶה,
וָעֶד סֶלָה יְסוֹבְבֵנִי פַּלֵּט רָנֵּי,¹⁸ אִם מָצָאתִי חֵן בְּעֵינֵי הַמֶּלֶךְ.¹⁹

הַמֶּלֶךְ לַעֲשׂוֹת יְקָר יוֹתֵר²⁰ לַעֲבָדֶיךָ הוֹאֵל,
תִּיקַר נָא נַפְשָׁם בְּעֵינֶיךָ²¹ לַמְּלָכִים לְמוֹאֵל,²²
לֵרָאוֹת בְּבוֹא כָל יִשְׂרָאֵל,²³
כָּל אִישׁ וְאִשָּׁה אֲשֶׁר יָבוֹא אֶל הַמֶּלֶךְ.²⁴

הַמֶּלֶךְ מְשָׁרְתָיו יְבַקְשׁוּ²⁵ פָּנָיו בְּתַעֲנִית וּטְוָת,
הַמִּתְרִים כָּל הַנּוֹגֵעַ בָּהֶם כְּנוֹגֵעַ בְּבָבַת,²⁶
וְהִנֵּה עָשׂוּ מֵעֻנָּם, אֱמֹר לוֹ, בֶּן נַעֲוַת,
מַדּוּעַ אַתָּה עוֹבֵר אֶת מִצְוַת הַמֶּלֶךְ.²⁷

הַמֶּלֶךְ נוֹרָא עַד מָתַי אָסַפְתָּ בְּמִשְׁמָר,
בְּנֵי זֶרַח וּפֶרֶץ תְּאוֹמֵי תָמָר,²⁸
מַלְכוּתָם הָשֵׁב וַעֲדִינָה²⁹ תֵּעָקֵר כְּנֶאֱמַר,
עַל אֲשֶׁר לֹא עָשְׂתָה אֶת מַאֲמַר הַמֶּלֶךְ.³⁰

trouble' (Psalms 91:15). The Talmud teaches that whenever Israel is exiled because of its sins, the Shechinah (manifestation of the Divine Presence) goes into exile with them; for their trouble is His trouble (Taanis 16a; Megillah 29a). About this, the paytan says: The trouble [inflicted upon the Shechinah when Israel is punished for its misdeeds] is not worth the loss to the King (Pardes).

ז O **King**,[1] put the sun's radiance to shame,
  and idolaters[2] will be disgraced.[3]
Let each man despise his idols of silver, his idols of gold,[4]
for with their own eyes they will see when He returns to Zion.[5]
    Be lifted up, eternal gates, and let enter the **King**.[6]

ח The wise **King** scatters the wicked[7] and the boor;
  He gives them back [their just due like] a turning wheel,[7]
  and reprimands them.
Dismiss the scoffer, let strife take its leave[8] and not open its mouth!
    For [they] may not come to the gate of the **King**.[9]

ט The good **King** — a royal edict will go forth from Him,[10] decreeing:
  'I will guard My children's feet, and not put them in chains,[11]
on the day established for judging who will succeed and who will fail.
    For so has decreed the **King**.'[12]

י The **King** sits on the Throne of Judgment,[13]
  and considers small and great as equal,
He sees who repents wholeheartedly,
  and who returns to his sin like a dog [returns to his vomit].[14]
Wreak vengeance for the abused on the abuser,
    on the [first] day [of the] seventh [month],
    when benevolent is the heart of the **King**.[15]

כ O **King** [over] all the earth,[16] God Who answers me
  in time of my trouble,
Who is with me[17] in every encampment [of my Exile],
evermore may He enwrap me with glad song of rescue,[18]
    if I have found favor in the eyes of the **King**.[19]

ל O **King**, find it favorable to give greater honor to Your servants;[20]
please let their souls be precious in Your eyes,[21] like kings before God,[22]
when all Israel come to appear[23] [for judgment],
    every man and woman who comes to the **King**.[24]

מ The **King's** servants seek[25] His countenance through denial and fasting.
The warning stands:
  'All who touch them are as if touching the pupil of an eye.'[26]
And yet Esau torments them. Tell him, 'Wayward son,
    why do you transgress the command of the **King**?'[27]

נ Awesome **King**, how long will You hold back in [Exile's] prison
the children of Zerach and Peretz, Tamar's twin sons?[28]
Restore their kingdom and uproot the pampered[29] [Edomite] rule,
  as the Torah promises,
    because she has not obeyed the word of the **King**.[30]

---

(1) This entire stanza has been censored out of some editions. (2) Cf. *Isaiah* 24:23. (3) See 46:1. (4) Cf. 31:7. (5) Cf. 52:8. (6) *Psalms* 24:7. (7) Cf. *Proverbs* 20:26. (8) 22:10. (9) *Esther* 4:2. (10) 1:19. (11) 2:12. (12) *Esther* 1:8. (13) Cf. *Proverbs* 20:8. (14) Cf. 26:11. (15) *Esther* 1:10. (16) Cf. *Psalms* 47:8. (17) *Genesis* 35:3. (18) Cf. *Psalms* 32:7. (19) *Esther* 5:8. (20) 6:6. (21) Cf. *I Samuel* 26:21. (22) *Proverbs* 31:4. (23) Cf. *Deuteronomy* 31:11; some editions of *Selichos* read לִרְאוֹת; the translation is then, *and see when all Israel come.* (24) *Esther* 4:11. (25) 2:2. (26) Cf. *Zechariah* 2:12. (27) *Esther* 3:3. (28) See *Genesis* ch. 38. (29) See *Isaiah* 47:8; some editions of *Selichos* read, וְצֹעֵמְלֵק, and . . . *Amalek.* (30) *Esther* 1:15.

הַמֶּלֶךְ שָׂרָיו וַעֲבָדָיו יַקִּיפֻהוּ בְּאַרְמוֹנִי,

יִרְעוּ בָשָׁן וְגִלְעָד לְבָדָד שׁוֹכְנִי,

רְעֵה עַמְּךָ בְּשִׁבְטֶךָ[1] לְרַוְיָה תּוֹצִיאֵנִי,[2]   אַתָּה אֲדֹנִי הַמֶּלֶךְ.[3]

הַמֶּלֶךְ עֵינֵי כָל יִשְׂרָאֵל עָלֶיךָ[4] לְקַבֵּץ הֲמוֹנִי,

עוֹד יֵשְׁבוּ בְשַׁעֲרֵי יְרוּשָׁלַיִם זְקֵנוֹתַי וּזְקֵנַי,[5]

וְאָז יַעַבְדוּךָ יַחַד כֹּהֲנַי וּסְגָנַי,   וְהָיָה יהוה לְמֶלֶךְ.[6]

הַמֶּלֶךְ פְּאֵר בֵּית יהוה[7] עֵינַי יְשַׁבֵּרוּן,

וְכָל הָעָם יַחַד לְשִׁמְךָ יַאַדִּירוּן,

אָז יִמָּלֵא שְׂחוֹק פִּינוּ[8] וְהַכֹּל יְשׁוֹרְרוּן,   וַיְהִי בִישֻׁרוּן מֶלֶךְ.[9]

הַמֶּלֶךְ צָרַי יָגִילוּ,[10] עַד מָתַי הָאֵל,[11]

גָּדְלוּ וְהִצְלֵיחוּ וְהֶחֱרִיבוּ אֲרִיאֵל,[12]

הִנֵּה הֵמָּה אוֹמְרִים יָדֵנוּ לָאֵל,[13]

וַאֲנִי לֹא נִקְרֵאתִי לָבוֹא אֶל הַמֶּלֶךְ.[14]

הַמֶּלֶךְ קָם בַּחֲמָתוֹ[15] לְכַלּוֹת כְּמִדְבָּר,

אוֹכְלֵי בְּשַׂר הַחֲזִיר הַשֶּׁקֶץ וְהָעַכְבָּר,[16]

יָרִיעַ אַף יַצְרִיחַ עַל אוֹיְבָיו יִתְגַּבָּר,[17]   כִּי כֵן דְּבַר הַמֶּלֶךְ.[18]

מֶלֶךְ רַב, הָסֵר מִמֶּנּוּ לֵב הָאָבֶן,[19]

כַּשֶּׁלֶג וְכַצֶּמֶר חֲטָאֵינוּ הַלְבֵּן,[20]

וְדַבְּקֵנוּ בְּךָ כְּמוֹ אָדָם לְלָבֶן.*

מִשְׁפָּטֶיךָ לְמֶלֶךְ תֵּן וְצִדְקָתְךָ לְבֶן מֶלֶךְ.[21]

הַמֶּלֶךְ שׁוֹפֵט בֶּאֱמֶת דַּלִּים,[22] אַתָּה תֶחֱזֶה,

כִּי שְׁבָרֵנוּ גְּאוֹן רוּחֵנוּ כְּהַיּוֹם הַזֶּה,

לֵב נִשְׁבָּר וְנִדְכֶּה אֱלֹהִים לֹא תִבְזֶה.[23]

הַמַּלְאָכָה לְהָבִיא אֶל גִּנְזֵי הַמֶּלֶךְ.[24]

מֶלֶךְ תֵּן צִדְקָתְךָ[25] לְיִשְׂרָאֵל כִּי נַעַר,[26]

לְהִדָּבֶק בּוֹ אִישׁ וְלִוְיָת כְּמֵעַר,[27]

לֹא תִבְזֶה וְתִתְפַּנֶּה אֶל תְּפִלַּת הָעַרְעָר,[28]

וְכָל עַבְדֵי הַמֶּלֶךְ אֲשֶׁר בְּשַׁעַר הַמֶּלֶךְ.[29]

וְדַבְּקֵנוּ בְּךָ כְּמוֹ אָדָם לְלָבֶן — *And cause us to cling to You as red [clings] to white.* There are three partners in a person's formation: God, the father and the mother. The father's contribution is white, and from it comes bones, sinews, nails, the brain and the white of the eye. The mother's contribution is red, and from it comes skin, flesh, [blood,] hair and the black of the eye. God puts into him spirit, soul, facial features, eyesight, hearing, speech . . . (*Niddah* 31a). Thus, we pray that just as our red and white physical components contributed by our parents cling to each other, so may they cling to our spiritual components that are from God (*Pardes*).

ס *The* **King's** *officers and servants will surround Him*
   in our Temple-palace,
[they] will graze [their sheep] in Bashan and Gilead, dwelling securely.
Shepherd Your people with Your staff,[1]
   bring us forth into abundance,[2]   *You, my Lord, the* **King**.[3]

ע O **King**, *the eyes of all Israel are upon You,*[4]
   [waiting for You] to gather my multitudes.
My elderly men and women,
   will yet sit in the gates of Jerusalem,[5]
then my Kohanim [Gedolim] and my deputy Kohanim
   will serve You together,   *and* HASHEM *will be* **King**.[6]

פ O **King**! *My eyes hope to see the glory of* HASHEM'*s house,*[7]
   when all our people together shall exalt Your Name.
Then will our mouths be filled with laughter[8]
   and all will make song,   *for in Jeshurun there is a* **King**.[9]

צ O **King**! *Our oppressors rejoice;*[10] *how long, O God?*[11]
They have grown and succeeded
   and laid waste the leonine Temple.[12]
See, they are saying, 'Our hands are capable!'[13]
              And as for me, I have not been called to come to the **King**.[14]

ק *When the* **King** *will arise in His wrath,*[15]
   as is spoken [in the Torah], to destroy
the eaters of the pig's flesh, the vermin, and the mouse,[16]
He will trumpet and give forth shouts
   as He overcomes His enemies,[17] *for so runs the word of the* **King**.[18]

ר *Great* **King**, *take the heart of stone out of us;*[19]
whiten our sins like snow or wool,[20]
and cause us to cling to You as red [clings] to white.*
              Give Your judgments to the [Messianic] king
              and Your righteousness to the offspring of [David] the **king**.[21]

ש O **King** *Who judges the poor with truth,*[22]
You will see that we have broken our prideful spirit this very day.
God, You will not despise a broken, crushed heart,[23]
              [and You will] bring the work [of repentance]
                 to the treasury of the **King**.[24]

ת O **King**! *Give of Your righteousness*[25] *to Israel,*
   for they [are] Your child;[26]
let it cling to them as a man and his wife are joined.[27]
Do not despise but turn to the prayer of the devastated one,[28]
   and of all the King's servants that are at the gate of the **King**.[29]

---

(1) Cf. *Micah* 7:14; one edition of *Selichos* reads, בְּשָׁבְתְּךָ, *when You sit*, but that is probably a printer's error. (2) Cf. *Psalms* 66:12. (3) *I Kings* 1:13. (4) 1:20. (5) Cf. *Zechariah* 8:4. (6) 14:9.(7) Cf. *Ezra* 7:27. (8) *Psalms* 126:2. (9) *Deuteronomy* 33:5. (10) *Psalms* 13:5. (11) Cf. 74:10. (12) See *Isaiah* 29:1. (13) Cf. *Genesis* 31:29. (14) *Esther* 4:11. (15) 7:7. (16) Cf. *Isaiah* 66:17; some editions of *Selichos* omit the word הַחֲזִיר, *the pig*; some omit the entire line. (17) 42:13. (18) *Esther* 3:9. (19) Cf. *Ezekiel* 11:19. (20) Cf. *Isaiah* 1:18. (21) *Psalms* 72:1. (22) Cf. *Proverbs* 29:14. (23) *Psalms* 51:19. (24) *Esther* 3:9. (25) Cf. *Psalms* 72:1. (26) Cf. *Hosea* 11:1. (27) Cf. *I Kings* 7:36. (28) Cf. *Psalms* 102:18. (29) *Esther* 3:2.

❖ הַמֶּלֶךְ לְהִתְחַנֵּן לוֹ¹ בָּאתִי אוֹתִי לְהִתְוַדּוֹת
לְחַיִּים טוֹבִים, מְדֻשָּׁן בֵּיתוֹ לְהַרְווֹת,²
כָּל הַגּוֹיִם לְשֵׁם יהוה לְהַקְוֹת,³
וְעָלוּ מִדֵּי שָׁנָה בְשָׁנָה לְהִשְׁתַּחֲווֹת לַמֶּלֶךְ.⁴

All, while standing:

אֵל מֶלֶךְ יוֹשֵׁב עַל כִּסֵּא רַחֲמִים מִתְנַהֵג בַּחֲסִידוּת, מוֹחֵל
עֲוֹנוֹת עַמּוֹ, מַעֲבִיר רִאשׁוֹן רִאשׁוֹן, מַרְבֶּה מְחִילָה
לַחַטָּאִים וּסְלִיחָה לַפּוֹשְׁעִים, עֹשֶׂה צְדָקוֹת עִם כָּל בָּשָׂר וָרוּחַ,
לֹא כְרָעָתָם תִּגְמוֹל. ❖ אֵל הוֹרֵיתָ לָּנוּ לוֹמַר שְׁלֹשׁ עֶשְׂרֵה, וּזְכוֹר
לָנוּ הַיּוֹם בְּרִית שְׁלֹשׁ עֶשְׂרֵה, כְּמוֹ שֶׁהוֹדַעְתָּ לֶעָנָיו מִקֶּדֶם, כְּמוֹ
שֶׁכָּתוּב, וַיֵּרֶד יהוה בֶּעָנָן וַיִּתְיַצֵּב עִמּוֹ שָׁם, וַיִּקְרָא בְשֵׁם יהוה.

Congregation, then *chazzan:*

וַיַּעֲבֹר יהוה עַל פָּנָיו וַיִּקְרָא:

Congregation and *chazzan* (the words in bold type are recited aloud and in unison):

יהוה, יהוה, אֵל, רַחוּם, וְחַנּוּן, אֶרֶךְ אַפַּיִם, וְרַב חֶסֶד, וֶאֱמֶת,
נֹצֵר חֶסֶד לָאֲלָפִים, נֹשֵׂא עָוֹן, וָפֶשַׁע, וְחַטָּאָה,
וְנַקֵּה. וְסָלַחְתָּ לַעֲוֹנֵנוּ וּלְחַטָּאתֵנוּ וּנְחַלְתָּנוּ. סְלַח לָנוּ אָבִינוּ כִּי
חָטָאנוּ, מְחַל לָנוּ מַלְכֵּנוּ כִּי פָשָׁעְנוּ. כִּי אַתָּה אֲדֹנָי טוֹב וְסַלָּח,
וְרַב חֶסֶד לְכָל קֹרְאֶיךָ.

פסוקי הקדמה לסליחה לד

אַל תָּבוֹא בְמִשְׁפָּט עִמָּנוּ, כִּי לֹא יִצְדַּק לְפָנֶיךָ כָל חָי.⁵ הֵן
בִּקְדֹשָׁיו לֹא יַאֲמִין, וְשָׁמַיִם לֹא זַכּוּ בְעֵינָיו.⁶ אַף כִּי
אֱנוֹשׁ רִמָּה, וּבֶן אָדָם תּוֹלֵעָה.⁷ הִנֵּנוּ לְפָנֶיךָ בְּאַשְׁמָתֵנוּ, כִּי אֵין
לַעֲמוֹד לְפָנֶיךָ עַל זֹאת.⁸ מִי יֹאמַר זִכִּיתִי לִבִּי, טָהַרְתִּי מֵחַטָּאתִי.⁹

כְּרַחֵם אָב עַל בָּנִים, כֵּן תְּרַחֵם יהוה עָלֵינוּ. לַיהוה הַיְשׁוּעָה,
עַל עַמְּךָ בִרְכָתֶךָ סֶּלָה. יהוה צְבָאוֹת עִמָּנוּ,
מִשְׂגָּב לָנוּ אֱלֹהֵי יַעֲקֹב סֶלָה. יהוה צְבָאוֹת, אַשְׁרֵי אָדָם בֹּטֵחַ בָּךְ.
יהוה הוֹשִׁיעָה, הַמֶּלֶךְ יַעֲנֵנוּ בְיוֹם קָרְאֵנוּ.

In some congregations the following two verses are recited responsively — the *chazzan* reciting סְלַח,
and the congregation responding וַיֹּאמֶר. In other congregations these verses are recited silently.

סְלַח נָא לַעֲוֹן הָעָם הַזֶּה כְּגֹדֶל חַסְדֶּךָ, וְכַאֲשֶׁר נָשָׂאתָה לָעָם
הַזֶּה מִמִּצְרַיִם וְעַד הֵנָּה, וְשָׁם נֶאֱמַר:

וַיֹּאמֶר יהוה סָלַחְתִּי כִּדְבָרֶךָ.

Chazzan — The **King!** I have come to supplicate to Him[1] to mark me down
for a good life, and to fill me with the abundance of His house.[2]
Let all the nations gather in the name of HASHEM,[3]
and ascend each year to bow down to the **King**.[4]

All, while standing:

אֵל מֶלֶךְ O God, King Who sits on the throne of mercy; Who acts with
kindness, pardons the iniquities of His people, removes [sins]
one by one, increasingly grants pardon to careless sinners and forgiveness
to rebels, Who deals righteously with every living being — You do not repay
them in accord with their evil. Chazzan — O God, You taught us to recite the
Thirteen [Attributes of Mercy], so remember for us today the covenant of
these Thirteen, as You made known to the humble one in ancient times, as
it is written: And HASHEM descended in a cloud and stood with him there,
and He called out with the Name HASHEM.

Congregation, then chazzan:

And HASHEM passed before him [Moses] and proclaimed:

Congregation and chazzan (the words in bold type are recited aloud and in unison):

ה' ה' HASHEM, HASHEM, God, Compassionate and Gracious, Slow
to anger, and Abundant in Kindness and Truth, Preserver of
kindness for thousands [of generations], Forgiver of iniquity, willful
sin, and error, and Who cleanses. May You forgive our iniquities and our
errors and make us Your heritage. Forgive us, our Father, for we have
erred; pardon us, our King, for we have willfully sinned; for You, my Lord,
are good and forgiving and abundantly kind to all who call upon You.

PREFATORY VERSES TO SELICHAH 34

אַל תָּבוֹא Do not enter into strict judgment with us, for no living creature would be innocent before You.[5] See, He does not believe
in His holy [angels]; even Heaven is not pure in His sight.[6] Certainly then
man, who is but a worm, the son of man, who is but a maggot.[7] Here we
are before You with our guilt, for on that account we cannot stand up
before You.[8] Who can say, 'I have purified my heart, I am clean of my
sin'?[9]

כְּרַחֵם אָב As a father has mercy on his children, so, HASHEM, may
You have mercy on us. Salvation is HASHEM's, upon Your
people is Your blessing, Selah. HASHEM, Master of Legions, is with us, a
stronghold for us is the God of Jacob, Selah. HASHEM, Master of Legions,
praiseworthy is the person who trusts in You. HASHEM, save! May the
King answer us on the day we call.

In some congregations the following two verses are recited responsively — the chazzan
reciting, 'Forgive, please . . . ,' and the congregation responding, 'And HASHEM said . . .'
In other congregations these verses are recited silently.

סְלַח נָא Forgive, please, the iniquity of this people according to the
greatness of Your kindness and as You have forgiven this
people from Egypt until now, and there it was said:

And HASHEM said, 'I have forgiven according to your word!'

(1) Esther 4:8. (2) Cf. Psalms 36:9. (3) Cf. Jeremiah 3:17. (4) Zechariah 14:16.
(5) Cf. Psalms 143:2. (6) Job 15:15. (7) 25:6. (8) Ezra 9:15. (9) Proverbs 20:9.

All:

הַטֵּה אֱלֹהַי אָזְנְךָ וּשְׁמָע, פְּקַח עֵינֶיךָ וּרְאֵה שֹׁמְמֹתֵינוּ, וְהָעִיר אֲשֶׁר נִקְרָא שִׁמְךָ עָלֶיהָ, כִּי לֹא עַל צִדְקֹתֵינוּ אֲנַחְנוּ מַפִּילִים תַּחֲנוּנֵינוּ לְפָנֶיךָ, כִּי עַל רַחֲמֶיךָ הָרַבִּים. אֲדֹנָי שְׁמָעָה, אֲדֹנָי סְלָחָה, אֲדֹנָי הַקְשִׁיבָה, וַעֲשֵׂה אַל תְּאַחַר, לְמַעַנְךָ אֱלֹהַי, כִּי שִׁמְךָ נִקְרָא עַל עִירְךָ וְעַל עַמֶּךָ.

סְלִיחָה לד (שְׁנִיָּה)

All:

(אֱלֹהֵינוּ וֵאלֹהֵי אֲבוֹתֵינוּ:)

אָדוֹן, בְּפָקְדְךָ אֱנוֹשׁ* לַבְּקָרִים,   בִּמְצוּי הַדִּין אַל תְּמַתַּח.

גּוּף וּנְשָׁמָה אִם תְּרִיבֵם,*   דְּחוּ וְלֹא יוּכְלוּ קוּם.[1]

הֲיוּכַל גֶּבֶר לִזְכּוֹת בַּמִּשְׁפָּט,   וְאִם אֵין בְּיָדוֹ מַעַשׂ לְהִצְטַדָּק.

זֵרוּי יְחוּמוּ מִלְחָה סְרוּחָה,[2]   חֲבוּי אָרְבוּ בְּקִרְבּוֹ מֵעֵת הֻלָּדוֹ.*

טָמוּן בְּחֶבְיוֹן[3] כְּרֶשֶׁת לְרַגְלָיו,   יְסִיתֵהוּ בְכָל יוֹם לְשַׁחַת לְהַפִּילוֹ.

כֹּחַ וּגְבוּרָה בַּגּוּף אֵין   לְפָנָיו לַעֲמֹד וּלְהִתְיַצֵּב.

מִיּוֹם עָמְדוּ עַל דַּעְתּוֹ,   נַפְשׁוֹ יָשִׂים בְּכַפּוֹ לְהָבִיא לַחְמוֹ.[4]

שָׂבַע כָּל יָמָיו כַּעַס וּמַכְאוֹבוֹת,[5]   עַד שׁוּבוֹ לַעֲפָרוֹ[6] לֹא יִשְׁקֹט.

פְּנֵה אָדוֹן בְּעִצְבוֹן רוּחַ,   צְפֵה בְּשִׁבְרוֹן לֵב.

קָרוֹב אַתָּה לָרְחוֹקִים,   רוֹצֶה תְּשׁוּבַת רְשָׁעִים.[7]

שַׁדַּי, הִמָּצֵא לְדוֹרְשֶׁיךָ,   תֹּאמַר הִנְנִי לִמְבַקְשֶׁיךָ.

יְבַשְׂרוּ סָלַחְתִּי[8] קוֹרְאֵי בְשִׁמְךָ,   צַדֵּק בַּמִּשְׁפָּט עַם מְיַחֲדֶךָ.

חֲסֹם מְנַוְּלִי[9] מִלְּהַרְשִׁיעַ,   קְצֹף בְּמַסְטִין מִלְּהַסְטִין.

---

(1) Cf. *Psalms* 36:13. (2) See tractate *Avos* 3:1. (3) Cf. *Job* 31:33. (4) Cf. *Lamentations* 5:9. (5) Cf. *Ecclesiastes* 2:23. (6) Cf. 3:20. (7) Cf. *Ezekiel* 18:23. (8) *Numbers* 14:20. (9) See commentary to *selichah* 24.

אָדוֹן בְּפָקְדְךָ אֱנוֹשׁ — *Lord, when You consider mankind.* This *selichah* contains an *aleph-beis* acrostic, which is followed by the author's signature, יִצְחָק הַכֹּהֵן הֶחָבֵר חֲזַק וֶאֱמָץ, *Yitzchak the Kohen, the chaver* [an ancient title bestowed on certain exceptional people], *may he be strong and persevere.* Nothing is known about R' Yitzchak, except that he lived sometime before 1234, the year in which the commentary *Arugas HaBosem* was written. This *selichah*, as well as the next, is composed entirely of couplets and is therefore classified as a *sheniyah*. Interestingly, both are from among the few *selichos* that are unrhymed.

גּוּף וּנְשָׁמָה אִם תְּרִיבֵם — *If You should adjudicate [the claims of] body and soul [together].* The Talmud relates an insightful discussion between Rabbi [Yehudah HaNassi] and the Roman emperor Antoninus.

The emperor claimed that man's body and soul could exonerate themselves on Judgment Day. The body could argue, 'The soul was the guilty one; for since it left me, I have been lying like a mute rock in the grave;' and the soul could counter, 'The body was the guilty one; for since I left it, I have been flying free as a bird.'

Rabbi responded with a parable: A king ordered two men to guard an orchard of fruit-laden trees. One was lame, the other blind. The lame, sighted one said to his blind companion, 'I see beautiful fruit in the orchard. Let me ride on your shoulders and I will guide you to the trees. We will then be able to eat from them.' And so they

All:

הַטֵּה Incline, my God, Your ear, and listen, open Your eyes and see our
desolation and that of the city upon which Your Name is proclaimed; for not because of our righteousness do we cast down our
supplications before You, rather because of Your abundant compassion.
O my Lord, heed; O my Lord, forgive; O my Lord, be attentive and act,
do not delay; for Your sake, my God, for Your Name is proclaimed upon
Your city and upon Your people.

SELICHAH 34

All:

(Our God and the God of our forefathers:)

א Lord, when You consider mankind* each morning,

ב do not exact rigorous judgment.

ג If You should adjudicate [the claims of] body and soul [together],*

ד they would be thrust down, unable to rise.[1]

ה Can a man win out in judgment,

ו if he has no good deeds to his credit with which to justify himself?

ז The scattered seed of his engendering is but a fetid drop;[2]

ח the lurking enemy is concealed within him from the time of his birth.*

ט Hidden within him,[3] like a net for his feet,

י it incites him every day [to sin], so as to cast him down into Gehinnom.

כ No strength nor might does the body have

ל to stand against it and hold its own.

מ From the day [a man] learns to use his wits,

נ he takes his life in his hands to win bread for himself.[4]

ס [He is] full, his whole life long, with anger and pains;[5]

ע until he returns to the dust,[6] he has no quiet.

פ Consider, Lord, [our] aching spirit;

צ look at [our] broken hearts.

ק You are near to those far off,

ר You desire repentance for the wicked.[7]

ש Almighty, manifest Yourself to those who search for You;

ת say, 'Here I am,' to those who seek You.

י Let those who call out in Your name hear, 'I have forgiven';[8]

צ vindicate in judgment the people who proclaim Your unity.

ח Muzzle the foul [Satan][9] so he cannot prosecute;

ק scold [Satan] the Accuser angrily so he cannot accuse.

---

did for some time, eating the fruit they were set
to protect. When the king returned, he asked
what happened to the ripened figs. The cripple
said, 'Do I have feet to walk over to the trees?' The
blind one said, 'Do I have eyes to see the fruit?' But
the wise king had the lame man hoisted onto the
blind man's shoulders and judged them as one.
So, too, on Judgment Day, God hurls the soul
back into its body and judges them as one (Sanhedrin 91a).

מֵעֵת הִוָּלְדוֹ — From the time of his birth. Another
question posed by Antoninus (ibid.) is: Does the
Evil Inclination enter a person when the embryo
is formed or at birth? Rabbi replied, 'From the formation of the embryo.'

Antoninus retorted, 'If so, it would rebel and
kick its way of out its mother. It cannot enter a
person until he is born.'

Rabbi acceded, saying, 'This matter have I
been taught by Antoninus, and I have found a

הָקֵם לָנוּ מֵלִיץ יְשֶׁר.   כַּפֵּר מָצָאתִי תַּשְׁמִיעַ לַשּׁוֹבָבִים.

הַשְׁלַכְנוּ עָלֶיךָ יְהָבֵנוּ,[1]   נָא אַתָּה תְכַלְכְּלֵנוּ.

הַעְתֵּר לָנוּ בִּתְפִלָּתֵנוּ.   חָפְצֵנוּ וּבַקָּשָׁתֵנוּ מַלֵּא בְּרַחֲמִים.

❖ בְּךָ תָלִינוּ בְטוּחוֹנֵנוּ,   רַחֲמֶיךָ מְהֵרָה יְקַדְּמוּנוּ.

חָזָק וְאַמִּיץ שִׁמְךָ לֹא שָׁכַחְנוּ,   אָנָּא, לָנֶצַח אַל תִּשְׁכָּחֵנוּ.[2]

All, while standing:

אֵל מֶלֶךְ יוֹשֵׁב עַל כִּסֵּא רַחֲמִים מִתְנַהֵג בַּחֲסִידוּת, מוֹחֵל עֲוֹנוֹת עַמּוֹ, מַעֲבִיר רִאשׁוֹן רִאשׁוֹן, מַרְבֶּה מְחִילָה לְחַטָּאִים וּסְלִיחָה לְפוֹשְׁעִים, עֹשֶׂה צְדָקוֹת עִם כָּל בָּשָׂר וָרְוּחַ, לֹא כְרָעָתָם תִּגְמוֹל. ❖ אֵל הוֹרֵיתָ לָנוּ לוֹמַר שְׁלֹשׁ עֶשְׂרֵה, וּזְכוֹר לָנוּ הַיּוֹם בְּרִית שְׁלֹשׁ עֶשְׂרֵה, כְּמוֹ שֶׁהוֹדַעְתָּ לֶעָנָיו מִקֶּדֶם, כְּמוֹ שֶׁכָּתוּב, וַיֵּרֶד יהוה בֶּעָנָן וַיִּתְיַצֵּב עִמּוֹ שָׁם, וַיִּקְרָא בְשֵׁם יהוה.

Congregation, then chazzan:

וַיַּעֲבֹר יהוה עַל פָּנָיו וַיִּקְרָא:

Congregation and chazzan (the words in bold type are recited aloud and in unison):

יהוה, יהוה,   אֵל, רַחוּם, וְחַנּוּן, אֶרֶךְ אַפַּיִם, וְרַב חֶסֶד, וֶאֱמֶת, נֹצֵר חֶסֶד לָאֲלָפִים, נֹשֵׂא עָוֹן, וָפֶשַׁע, וְחַטָּאָה, וְנַקֵּה. וְסָלַחְתָּ לַעֲוֹנֵנוּ וּלְחַטָּאתֵנוּ וּנְחַלְתָּנוּ. סְלַח לָנוּ אָבִינוּ כִּי חָטָאנוּ, מְחַל לָנוּ מַלְכֵּנוּ כִּי פָשָׁעְנוּ. כִּי אַתָּה אֲדֹנָי טוֹב וְסַלָּח, וְרַב חֶסֶד לְכָל קֹרְאֶיךָ.

פסוקי הקדמה לסליחה לה

אַל תָּבוֹא בְמִשְׁפָּט עִמָּנוּ, כִּי לֹא יִצְדַּק לְפָנֶיךָ כָל חָי.[3] כִּי אָכְלוּ אֶת יַעֲקֹב וְאֶת נָוֵהוּ הֵשַׁמּוּ.[4] אָהֳלֵי אֱדוֹם וְיִשְׁמְעֵאלִים מוֹאָב וְהַגְרִים.[5] כִּי שָׁבְעָה בְרָעוֹת נַפְשֵׁנוּ, וְחַיֵּינוּ לִשְׁאוֹל הִגִּיעוּ.[6] וְאַתָּה מַלְכֵּנוּ מִקֶּדֶם, פּוֹעֵל יְשׁוּעוֹת בְּקֶרֶב הָאָרֶץ.[7] וְהוֹצִיא כָאוֹר צִדְקֵנוּ, וּמִשְׁפָּטֵנוּ כַּצָּהֳרָיִם.[8]

בְּרַחֵם אָב עַל בָּנִים, כֵּן תְּרַחֵם יהוה עָלֵינוּ. לַיהוה הַיְשׁוּעָה, עַל עַמְּךָ בִרְכָתֶךָ סֶּלָה. יהוה צְבָאוֹת עִמָּנוּ, מִשְׂגָּב לָנוּ אֱלֹהֵי יַעֲקֹב סֶלָה. יהוה צְבָאוֹת, אַשְׁרֵי אָדָם בֹּטֵחַ בָּךְ. יהוה הוֹשִׁיעָה, הַמֶּלֶךְ יַעֲנֵנוּ בְיוֹם קָרְאֵנוּ.

Scriptural verse to support his view; for it is written, לַפֶּתַח חַטָּאת רֹבֵץ, *Sin crouches at the door (Genesis 4:7).'* [Although the verse speaks in the context of an unrepentant sinner, Rabbi

gave it a novel interpretation: The cause of sin, namely, the Evil Inclination, crouches at the door of the womb, ready to enter the baby as it emerges.]

ה Raise up an advocate [angel] to speak well on our behalf;
כ let Your wayward children hear, 'I have found atonement for you.'
ה We have cast our burden upon You —[1]
נ please, let it be You Who sustain us.
ה Answer us as we pray;
ח fulfill our desire, our request, with mercy.
כ Chazzan – We have put our trust in You;
ר let Your mercy speedily come forth to greet us.
Strong, Mighty One, we have not forgotten Your name;
please do not forget us for all eternity.[2]

All, while standing:

אֵל מֶלֶךְ O God, King Who sits on the throne of mercy; Who acts with
kindness, pardons the iniquities of His people, removes [sins]
one by one, increasingly grants pardon to careless sinners and forgiveness
to rebels, Who deals righteously with every living being — You do not repay
them in accord with their evil. Chazzan — O God, You taught us to recite the
Thirteen [Attributes of Mercy], so remember for us today the covenant of
these Thirteen, as You made known to the humble one in ancient times, as
it is written: And HASHEM descended in a cloud and stood with him there,
and He called out with the Name HASHEM.

Congregation, then chazzan:

And HASHEM passed before him [Moses] and proclaimed:

Congregation and chazzan (the words in bold type are recited aloud and in unison):

ה' ה' HASHEM, HASHEM, God, Compassionate and Gracious, Slow
to anger, and Abundant in Kindness and Truth, Preserver of
kindness for thousands [of generations], Forgiver of iniquity, willful
sin, and error, and Who cleanses. May You forgive our iniquities and our
errors and make us Your heritage. Forgive us, our Father, for we have
erred; pardon us, our King, for we have willfully sinned; for You, my Lord,
are good and forgiving and abundantly kind to all who call upon You.

PREFATORY VERSES TO SELICHAH 35

אַל תָּבוֹא Do not enter into strict judgment with us, for no living creature would be innocent before You.[3] For they have devoured
Jacob, and devastated his habitation[4] — [those who dwell in] the tents of
Edom, the Ishmaelites, Moab and the Egyptians.[5] For our souls are sated
with evils and our life has reached the grave.[6] But You are our King from
of old, Worker of salvations in the midst of the earth.[7] He will bring forth
our righteousness like light, and our judgment like the high noon.[8]

כְּרַחֵם אָב As a father has mercy on his children, so, HASHEM, may
You have mercy on us. Salvation is HASHEM's, upon Your
people is Your blessing, Selah. HASHEM, Master of Legions, is with us, a
stronghold for us is the God of Jacob, Selah. HASHEM, Master of Legions,
praiseworthy is the person who trusts in You. HASHEM, save! May the
King answer us on the day we call.

---

(1) Cf. Psalms 55:23. (2) Cf. Lamentations 5:20. (3) Cf. Psalms 143:2.
(4) Cf. 79:7. (5) 83:7. (6) Cf. 88:4. (7) Cf. 74:12. (8) Cf. 37:6.

In some congregations the following two verses are recited responsively — the *chazzan* reciting סְלַח נָא, and the congregation responding וַיֹאמֶר. In other congregations these verses are recited silently.

סְלַח נָא לַעֲוֹן הָעָם הַזֶּה כְּגֹדֶל חַסְדֶּךָ, וְכַאֲשֶׁר נָשָׂאתָה לָעָם הַזֶּה מִמִּצְרַיִם וְעַד הֵנָּה, וְשָׁם נֶאֱמַר:

וַיֹּאמֶר יהוה סָלַחְתִּי כִּדְבָרֶךָ.[*]

All:

הַטֵּה אֱלֹהַי אָזְנְךָ וּשְׁמָע, פְּקַח עֵינֶיךָ וּרְאֵה שֹׁמְמֹתֵינוּ, וְהָעִיר אֲשֶׁר נִקְרָא שִׁמְךָ עָלֶיהָ, כִּי לֹא עַל צִדְקוֹתֵינוּ אֲנַחְנוּ מַפִּילִים תַּחֲנוּנֵינוּ לְפָנֶיךָ, כִּי עַל רַחֲמֶיךָ הָרַבִּים. אֲדֹנָי שְׁמָעָה, אֲדֹנָי סְלָחָה, אֲדֹנָי הַקְשִׁיבָה, וַעֲשֵׂה אַל תְּאַחַר, לְמַעַנְךָ אֱלֹהַי, כִּי שִׁמְךָ נִקְרָא עַל עִירְךָ וְעַל עַמֶּךָ.

סְלִיחָה לה (שְׁנִיָּה)

All:

(אֱלֹהֵינוּ וֵאלֹהֵי אֲבוֹתֵינוּ:)

תִּזְכֹּר בְּרֹגֶז חַנּוֹת רַחֵם.[1]	אָדוֹן, בְּשָׁפְטְךָ[*] אֱנוֹשׁ רְמָה,
שׁוֹגֵג וָפֶתִי זַכֶּה וְהַצְדֵּק.	בְּעָרְכְּךָ דִין אֲשָׁמִים לְוֹכֵּחַ,
רִיב אֵל תְּמַתַּח לְמָצוּי.	גְּמֹל חֶסֶד וְטוֹבָה לְחַיָּבִים,
קוֹרְאִים אֵלֶיךָ לָמוֹ הִמָּצֵא.	דְּלֵי מַעַשׂ וְרֵיקֵי כְשָׁרוֹן,
צִפְצוּף מַעַן בִּשְׁנוּ לְפוֹצֵץ.	הִנְנוּ לְפָנֶיךָ בְּאַשְׁמָה רַבָּה,
פְּנֵי עֹשֵׂהוּ גֶבֶר הַיִטְהָר.[2]	וְאִם מֵאֱלוֹהַּ אֱנוֹשׁ הַיִצְדָּק,
עָוֹן מָלֵא וָפֶשַׁע רָב.	זָדוֹן בְּחֻבּוֹ[3] אָוֶן בְּקִרְבּוֹ,
סוֹפוֹ לִתֵּן[4] בְּבֹא חֲלִיפָתוֹ.	חֶשְׁבּוֹן נָדִין לְמֶלֶךְ מַלְכֵי הַמְּלָכִים,
נֶגֶד פָּנָיו רִשְׁעוֹ יַעֲנֶה.	טֶבַע חוֹתָם בְּכַפּוֹ נֶחֱרָת,[5]
מַכִּיר אֶבֶן תִּזְעַק וְתִקְרָא.[7]	יוֹרֶה[6] כָּפִיס מֵעֵץ וְיַגִּיד,
לְאֵין חָשׁוּב בְּעָמְדוֹ לְפָנֶיךָ.	כּוֹבֵשׁ פָּנָיו נִדּוֹן וְנִכְלָם,

אָנָּא לְמַעֲשֵׂה יָדֶיךָ הִרָצֵה,   בְּשִׁבְרוֹן רְאֵה שְׁמֹר מִדְּחִי.

❖ עֲבָדֶיךָ יִמָּצְאוּ הַיּוֹם חֲנִינָה,   זַכֵּם קָרֶבְתָּךְ חֲפוֹץ כְּבָרִאשׁוֹנָה.

וְכַשֶּׁלֶג וְכַצֶּמֶר הַלְבֵּן חַטָּאֵי שׁוֹשַׁנָּה,[8] מַלְּטֵם מִכֹּל רָעוֹת בְּזֹאת הַשָּׁנָה.

---

(1) Cf. *Habakkuk* 3:2. (2) Cf. *Job* 4:17. (3) Cf. 31:33. (4) See tractate *Avos* 3:1. (5) See commentary to *selichah* 28, s.v., וּבְיָדוֹ סְדָרוֹת. (6) Some editions read יוֹדֶה, *will testify* (?). (7) Cf. *Habakkuk* 2:11; see commentary to *selichah* 28, s.v., הֶעָמַדְתָּ עַד. (8) Cf. *Isaiah* 1:18.

אָדוֹן בְּשָׁפְטְךָ ❧ — *Lord, when You judge.* This *unrhymed selichah*, by R' Eliyah ben Shemayah [see prefatory comment to *selichah* 6], follows an א״ת ב״ש format. That is, the respective letters from the beginning of the *aleph-beis* are paired with their counterparts from the opposite end. Thus, א, the first letter, is coupled with ת, the last letter; ב, the second, with ש, the second to last; etc. This is followed with a word-by-word acrostic of the *paytan's* name as indicated by the bold type.

In some congregations the following two verses are recited responsively — the *chazzan*
reciting, 'Forgive, please . . .,' and the congregation responding, 'And HASHEM *said* . . .'
In other congregations these verses are recited silently.

סְלַח נָא **Forgive, please, the iniquity of this people according to the**
greatness of Your kindness and as You have forgiven this
people from Egypt until now, and there it was said:

And HASHEM said, 'I have forgiven according to your word!'

All:

הַטֵּה **Incline, my God, Your ear, and listen, open Your eyes and see our**
desolation and that of the city upon which Your Name is proclaimed; for not because of our righteousness do we cast down our
supplications before You, rather because of Your abundant compassion.
O my Lord, heed; O my Lord, forgive; O my Lord, be attentive and act,
do not delay; for Your sake, my God, for Your Name is proclaimed upon
Your city and upon Your people.

SELICHAH 35

All:

(*Our God and the God of our forefathers:*)

א *Lord, when You judge* man, the worm,*
ת *in Your wrath remember [Your] grace and [Your] mercy.*[1]
ב *As You hold trial to adjudge the guilty,*
ש *clear the erring and the foolish, holding them innocent.*
ג *Be kindly and good to the culpable;*
ר *do not draw out the quarrel to its fullest.*
ד *[A people] poor in deeds and empty of ability*
ק *are calling to You to reveal Yourself to them.*
ה *Here we are before You, [confessing our] vast guilt,*
צ *too ashamed to open our mouths and ask mercy.*
ו *For can man come out justified from [before] God?*
פ *Can he be reckoned pure before his Maker?*[2]
ז *Wanton sin in his breast,*[3] *violence within him*
ע *full of iniquity and many rebellious sins.*
ח *An account and reckoning to the King Who is King of kings,*
ס *he must give, in the end, when his time comes to pass on.*[4]
ט *The seal's imprint was set with his own hand;*[5]
נ *his wickedness gives answer before his eyes.*
י *The beam of his house will point*[6] *[to him] and speak out,*
מ *The stones will cry out loud from the wall.*[7]
כ *He covers his face, convicted and shamed,*
ל *reckoned as naught as he stands before You.*
Please find favor with the work of Your hands;
see his brokenness and protect him from pushing.
Chazzan — *May Your servants find grace this day;*
acquit them for they long for Your nearness, as of old.
And make white as snow and wool the Rose-people's sins.[8]
Save them from all evil this year!

All, while standing:

אֵל מֶלֶךְ יוֹשֵׁב עַל כִּסֵּא רַחֲמִים מִתְנַהֵג בַּחֲסִידוּת, מוֹחֵל עֲוֹנוֹת עַמּוֹ, מַעֲבִיר רִאשׁוֹן רִאשׁוֹן, מַרְבֶּה מְחִילָה לַחַטָּאִים וּסְלִיחָה לַפּוֹשְׁעִים, עֹשֶׂה צְדָקוֹת עִם כָּל בָּשָׂר וָרוּחַ, לֹא כְרָעָתָם תִּגְמוֹל. ✧ אֵל הוֹרֵיתָ לָּנוּ לוֹמַר שְׁלֹשׁ עֶשְׂרֵה, וּזְכוֹר לָנוּ הַיּוֹם בְּרִית שְׁלֹשׁ עֶשְׂרֵה, כְּמוֹ שֶׁהוֹדַעְתָּ לֶעָנָיו מִקֶּדֶם, כְּמוֹ שֶׁכָּתוּב, וַיֵּרֶד יהוה בֶּעָנָן וַיִּתְיַצֵּב עִמּוֹ שָׁם, וַיִּקְרָא בְשֵׁם יהוה.

Congregation, then chazzan:

וַיַּעֲבֹר יהוה עַל פָּנָיו וַיִּקְרָא:

Congregation and chazzan (the words in bold type are recited aloud and in unison):

יהוה, יהוה, אֵל, רַחוּם, וְחַנּוּן, אֶרֶךְ אַפַּיִם, וְרַב חֶסֶד, **וֶאֱמֶת, נֹצֵר חֶסֶד לָאֲלָפִים, נֹשֵׂא עָוֹן, וָפֶשַׁע, וְחַטָּאָה, וְנַקֵּה.** וְסָלַחְתָּ לַעֲוֹנֵנוּ וּלְחַטָּאתֵנוּ וּנְחַלְתָּנוּ. סְלַח לָנוּ אָבִינוּ כִּי חָטָאנוּ, מְחַל לָנוּ מַלְכֵּנוּ כִּי פָשָׁעְנוּ. כִּי אַתָּה אֲדֹנָי טוֹב וְסַלָּח, וְרַב חֶסֶד לְכָל קֹרְאֶיךָ.

פסוקי הקדמה לסליחה לו

יהוה, בְּקֶר תִּשְׁמַע קוֹלֵנוּ, בְּקֶר נַעֲרָךְ לְךָ וּנְצַפֶּה.[1] קָרְבָה אֶל נַפְשִׁי גְאָלָהּ, לְמַעַן שְׁמִי פְּדֵנוּ.[2] הַרְאֵנוּ יהוה חַסְדֶּךָ, וְיֶשְׁעֲךָ תִּתֶּן לָנוּ.[3]

כְּרַחֵם אָב עַל בָּנִים, כֵּן תְּרַחֵם יהוה עָלֵינוּ. לַיהוה הַיְשׁוּעָה, עַל עַמְּךָ בִרְכָתֶךָ סֶּלָה. יהוה צְבָאוֹת עִמָּנוּ, מִשְׂגָּב לָנוּ אֱלֹהֵי יַעֲקֹב סֶלָה. יהוה צְבָאוֹת, אַשְׁרֵי אָדָם בֹּטֵחַ בָּךְ. יהוה הוֹשִׁיעָה, הַמֶּלֶךְ יַעֲנֵנוּ בְיוֹם קָרְאֵנוּ.

In some congregations the following two verses are recited responsively — the chazzan reciting סְלַח, and the congregation responding וַיֹּאמֶר. In other congregations these verses are recited silently.

סְלַח נָא לַעֲוֹן הָעָם הַזֶּה כְּגֹדֶל חַסְדֶּךָ, וְכַאֲשֶׁר נָשָׂאתָה לָעָם הַזֶּה מִמִּצְרַיִם וְעַד הֵנָּה, וְשָׁם נֶאֱמַר:

וַיֹּאמֶר יהוה סָלַחְתִּי כִּדְבָרֶךָ.

All:

הַטֵּה אֱלֹהַי אָזְנְךָ וּשְׁמָע, פְּקַח עֵינֶיךָ וּרְאֵה שֹׁמְמֹתֵינוּ, וְהָעִיר אֲשֶׁר נִקְרָא שִׁמְךָ עָלֶיהָ, כִּי לֹא עַל צִדְקֹתֵינוּ אֲנַחְנוּ מַפִּילִים תַּחֲנוּנֵינוּ לְפָנֶיךָ, כִּי עַל רַחֲמֶיךָ הָרַבִּים. אֲדֹנָי שְׁמָעָה, אֲדֹנָי סְלָחָה, אֲדֹנָי הַקְשִׁיבָה, וַעֲשֵׂה אַל תְּאַחַר, לְמַעַנְךָ אֱלֹהַי, כִּי שִׁמְךָ נִקְרָא עַל עִירְךָ וְעַל עַמֶּךָ.

All, while standing:

אֵל מֶלֶךְ O God, King Who sits on the throne of mercy; Who acts with kindness, pardons the iniquities of His people, removes [sins] one by one, increasingly grants pardon to careless sinners and forgiveness to rebels, Who deals righteously with every living being — You do not repay them in accord with their evil. Chazzan — O God, You taught us to recite the Thirteen [Attributes of Mercy], so remember for us today the covenant of these Thirteen, as You made known to the humble one in ancient times, as it is written: And HASHEM descended in a cloud and stood with him there, and He called out with the Name HASHEM.

Congregation, then chazzan:

And HASHEM passed before him [Moses] and proclaimed:

Congregation and chazzan (the words in bold type are recited aloud and in unison):

ה' ה' HASHEM, HASHEM, God, Compassionate and Gracious, Slow to anger, and Abundant in Kindness and Truth, Preserver of kindness for thousands [of generations], Forgiver of iniquity, willful sin, and error, and Who cleanses. May You forgive our iniquities and our errors and make us Your heritage. Forgive us, our Father, for we have erred; pardon us, our King, for we have willfully sinned; for You, my Lord, are good and forgiving and abundantly kind to all who call upon You.

PREFATORY VERSES TO SELICHAH 36

ה' HASHEM, in the morning hear our voice; in the morning as we arrange [our prayer] to You and await [Your answer].[1] Draw near to our soul, redeem it; for Your Name's sake deliver us.[2] Show us Your kindness, HASHEM, and grant us Your salvation.[3]

כְּרַחֵם אָב As a father has mercy on his children, so, HASHEM, may You have mercy on us. Salvation is HASHEM's, upon Your people is Your blessing, Selah. HASHEM, Master of Legions, is with us, a stronghold for us is the God of Jacob, Selah. HASHEM, Master of Legions, praiseworthy is the person who trusts in You. HASHEM, save! May the King answer us on the day we call.

In some congregations the following two verses are recited responsively — the chazzan reciting, 'Forgive, please . . . ,' and the congregation responding, 'And HASHEM said . . .' In other congregations these verses are recited silently.

סְלַח נָא Forgive, please, the iniquity of this people according to the greatness of Your kindness and as You have forgiven this people from Egypt until now, and there it was said:

And HASHEM said, 'I have forgiven according to your word!'

All:

הַטֵּה Incline, my God, Your ear, and listen, open Your eyes and see our desolation and that of the city upon which Your Name is proclaimed; for not because of our righteousness do we cast down our supplications before You, rather because of Your abundant compassion. O my Lord, heed; O my Lord, forgive; O my Lord, be attentive and act, do not delay; for Your sake, my God, for Your Name is proclaimed upon Your city and upon Your people.

(1) Cf. Psalms 5:4. (2) Cf. 69:19. (3) 85:8.

סליחה לו (שלישיה)

All:

אֱלֹהֵינוּ וֵאלֹהֵי אֲבוֹתֵינוּ:

אֶזְעַק אֶל אֱלֹהִים* קוֹלִי,[1] בֹּקֶר אֶעֱרָךְ לְךָ[2] בְּעַד קָהָלִי,
יהוה צוּרִי וְגֹאֲלִי.[3]

גָּשְׁנוּ בְּתַחֲנוּן וּבִתְפִלָּה, דְּלָתֶיךָ שְׁקַדְנוּ רַב עֲלֵילָה,
הָסֵר מֵעָלֵינוּ נֶגַע וּמַחֲלָה.

הַמְצֵא לָנוּ סְלִיחוֹת, וְהַעֲבֵר רָעָה מִנַּפְשׁוּת הָאֲנוּחוֹת,
אֵל אֱלֹהֵי הָרוּחוֹת.[4]

זָעַקְתִּי לְךָ בְּעָנְוִי וּתְלָאָה, חַיָּתִי פְּדֵה נָא מִשַּׁחַת וּשְׁאוֹלָה,
קָרְבָה אֶל נַפְשִׁי גְאָלָהּ.[5]

טוֹב מִבֶּטֶן גֹּחִי,[6] יוֹצְרִי וְשִׂבְרִי וּמִבְטַחִי, בְּיָדְךָ אַפְקִיד רוּחִי.[7]

כְּבֹשׁ כַּעַסְךָ מִידִידֶיךָ, לִרְאוֹת שַׁחַת אַל תִּתֵּן חֲסִידֶיךָ,[8]
עֲנֵנִי יהוה כִּי טוֹב חַסְדֶּךָ.[9]

מַכָּה בְּלִי תְרוּפָה, נֶצַח לְחוֹרְפֶיךָ תִּשְׁלַח בְּהַקְצָפָה,
וּבְעַמְּךָ לֹא לְמַגֵּפָה.[10]

סִגַּפְנוּ בְּיוֹם זֶה,* עִנּוּתָנוּ לֹא תִשְׁקַץ וְלֹא תִבְזֶה,[11]
סְלַח נָא לַעֲוֹן הָעָם הַזֶּה.[12]

פְּשַׁעְנוּ וּמָעַלְנוּ, צוּר לְךָ חֲבוֹל חָבַלְנוּ,[13]
לָכֵן (כִּמְעַט) כָּלִינוּ בְאַפֶּךָ, וּבַחֲמָתְךָ נִבְהָלְנוּ.[14]

קָדוֹשׁ, רִיב אַל תִּמְתַּח, רְאֵה כִּי כַפִּי לְךָ אֶשְׁטַח,[15]
יוֹם אִירָא אֲנִי אֵלֶיךָ אֶבְטָח.[16]

שֶׁפֶךְ שִׂיחַ עַמֶּךָ, תָּחֹן וְתַעַן שְׁלֵמֶיךָ, אַל תִּנְאַץ לְמַעַן שְׁמֶךָ.[17]
שְׁעֵה שַׁוְעַת אֲנוּנִים, לְקוֹרְאֶיךָ מִדְּחַק הַסְכֵּת מִמְּעוֹנִים,
שׁוֹמֵעַ אֶל אֶבְיוֹנִים.[18]

---

§ אֶזְעַק אֶל אֱלֹהִים — *I cry to God.* This *selichah* comprises thirteen triplets and is therefore called a *shelishiyah.* The first and second stiches of the respective stanzas contain an *aleph-beis* acrostic. The *paytan's* signature appears in the final two stanzas and is the subject of controversy. All agree that he signed שְׁלֹמֹה, *Shlomo,* in the twelfth stanza and הַקָּטָן, *the lesser,* in the thirteenth. In some editions of *Selichos,* the order of the stiches in the last stanza is הַחוֹסִיךְ . . . נְדִיבֵי . . . מֶהֵר ; accordingly, the words שְׁלֹמֹה הַקָּטָן form the complete signature. Many editions therefore list the author as *R' Shlomo HaBavli* [see prefatory comment to selichah 2] who often signed his compo-

sitions in this manner. In most editions (as in this one), however, the stiches are arranged נְדִיבֵי . . . מֶהֵר . . . הַחוֹסִיךְ ; accordingly, the name נַעֲמָן, *Naaman,* appears in the acrostic between the words שְׁלֹמֹה and הַקָּטָן. The name Naaman is akin to Naomi and was given to one of Benjamin's sons (see *Genesis* 46:21, and *Rashi* to *Genesis* 43:30) and one of his grandsons (see *Numbers* 26:40). It is unlikely that R' Shlomo HaBavli would use this signature. Moreover, most of R' Shlomo HaBavli's *selichos* are commented upon by *Arugas Ha-Bosem,* while this one is notably absent from that work. Following this view, the *selichah* is by an otherwise unknown *paytan,* R' Shlomo Naaman.

SELICHAH 36

All:

Our God and the God of our forefathers:

א *I cry to God* with my voice;*[1]
ב *in the morning I arrange [my prayer] to You*[2]
   on behalf of my congregation,   HASHEM, my Rock and my Redeemer.[3]
ג *We come forward with supplication and prayer,*
ד *attending at Your doors, O Doer of Great Deeds —*
       remove plague and illness from us!

ה *Bring forth forgiveness for us,*
ו *and dismiss evil from [our] groaning souls,   O God, God of spirits.*[4]
ז *I shout to You out of torment and hardship;*
ח *please deliver my life from ruin and the grave —*
     draw near to my soul, redeem it![5]

ט *O Good One, who drew me forth from the womb,*[6]
י *my Maker, my Hope and my Trust,*
     into Your hand I deliver my spirit.[7]

כ *Suppress Your anger from Your beloved ones;*
ל *allow not Your devout to witness ruin.*[8]
    Answer me, HASHEM, for Your kindness is good.[9]

מ *A wound without any healing,*
נ *everlasting — give in fury to those who revile You,*
    but not to Your people, as a plague.[10]

ס *We are afflicted this day;**
ע *do not loath nor despise our supplication,*[11]
    please forgive this people's iniquity.[12]

פ *We have sinned rebelliously, we have betrayed Your trust.*
צ *O Rock, we have been destructive to You;*[13]
    so we are (almost)consumed by Your anger,
    and confounded by Your wrath.[14]

ק *Holy One, do not draw out the quarrel!*
ר *See how I stretch out my hands to You:*[15]
    on the day that I fear, I trust in You.[16]

ש *The outpouring of Your people's prayer*
ת *accept graciously, and answer Your whole-hearted ones.*
    Do not be enraged, for Your Name's sake.[17]

Pay heed to the grieving people's outcry;
listen from on high to those who call You from out of oppression,
    O You Who hearken to the destitute.[18]

---

(1) Cf. *Psalms* 142:2. (2) 5:4. (3) 19:15. (4) *Numbers* 16:22; see commentary to *selichah* 32.
(5) *Psalms* 69:19. (6) Cf. 22:10. (7) 31:6. (8) Cf. 16:10. (9) 69:17. (10) *I Chronicles* 21:17.
(11) Cf. *Psalms* 22:25. (12) *Numbers* 14:19. (13) Cf. *Nehemiah* 1:7.
(14) *Psalms* 90:7. (15) Cf. 88:10. (16) 56:4. (17) *Jeremiah* 14:21. (18) *Psalms* 69:34.

סַגַּפְנוּ בְּיוֹם זֶה — *We are afflicted this day.* Some commentaries understand this as an allusion to the custom of fasting on Erev Rosh Hashanah and render, 'We are afflicting ourselves today.' However, the verb form סַגַּפְנוּ is not reflexive and so we have translated *we are afflicted.*

❖ נְדִיבֵי עַם מַטַּע נַעֲמָנִים, הַחוֹסִיךְ קֹוֶיךָ טְהוֹרֶיךָ נֶאֱמָנִים, מַהֵר תְּרַחֲמֵם, כְּרַחֵם אָב עַל בָּנִים.[1]

All, while standing:

אֵל מֶלֶךְ יוֹשֵׁב עַל כִּסֵּא רַחֲמִים מִתְנַהֵג בַּחֲסִידוּת, מוֹחֵל עֲוֹנוֹת עַמּוֹ, מַעֲבִיר רִאשׁוֹן רִאשׁוֹן, מַרְבֶּה מְחִילָה לְחַטָּאִים וּסְלִיחָה לְפוֹשְׁעִים, עֹשֶׂה צְדָקוֹת עִם כָּל בָּשָׂר וָרוּחַ, לֹא כְרָעָתָם תִּגְמוֹל. ❖ אֵל הוֹרֵיתָ לָּנוּ לוֹמַר שְׁלֹשׁ עֶשְׂרֵה, וּזְכוֹר לָנוּ הַיּוֹם בְּרִית שְׁלֹשׁ עֶשְׂרֵה, כְּמוֹ שֶׁהוֹדַעְתָּ לֶעָנָיו מִקֶּדֶם, כְּמוֹ שֶׁכָּתוּב, וַיֵּרֶד יהוה בֶּעָנָן וַיִּתְיַצֵּב עִמּוֹ שָׁם, וַיִּקְרָא בְשֵׁם יהוה.

Congregation, then chazzan:

וַיַּעֲבֹר יהוה עַל פָּנָיו וַיִּקְרָא:

Congregation and chazzan (the words in bold type are recited aloud and in unison):

יהוה, יהוה, אֵל, רַחוּם, וְחַנּוּן, אֶרֶךְ אַפַּיִם, וְרַב חֶסֶד, וֶאֱמֶת, **נֹצֵר חֶסֶד לָאֲלָפִים, נֹשֵׂא עָוֹן, וָפֶשַׁע, וְחַטָּאָה, וְנַקֵּה.** וְסָלַחְתָּ לַעֲוֹנֵנוּ וּלְחַטָּאתֵנוּ וּנְחַלְתָּנוּ. סְלַח לָנוּ אָבִינוּ כִּי חָטָאנוּ, מְחַל לָנוּ מַלְכֵּנוּ כִּי פָשָׁעְנוּ. כִּי אַתָּה אֲדֹנָי טוֹב וְסַלָּח, וְרַב חֶסֶד לְכָל קֹרְאֶיךָ.

פסוקי הקדמה לסליחה לז

אַל יָשֹׁב דַּךְ נִכְלָם, עָנִי וְאֶבְיוֹן יְהַלְלוּ שְׁמֶךָ.[2] אַל תִּרְחַק מִמֶּנּוּ כִּי צָרָה קְרוֹבָה, כִּי אֵין עוֹזֵר.[3] כִּי אֶסְלַח לַעֲוֹנָם וּלְחַטָּאתָם לֹא אֶזְכָּר עוֹד.[4] וְסָלַחְתָּ לְעַמְּךָ אֲשֶׁר חָטְאוּ לָךְ, וּלְכָל פִּשְׁעֵיהֶם אֲשֶׁר פָּשְׁעוּ בָךְ, וּנְתַתָּם לְרַחֲמִים לִפְנֵי שׁוֹבֵיהֶם.[5] וְאַתָּה אֱלוֹהַּ סְלִיחוֹת, חַנּוּן וְרַחוּם אֶרֶךְ אַפַּיִם וְרַב חֶסֶד וְלֹא עֲזַבְתָּם.[6]

כְּרַחֵם אָב עַל בָּנִים, כֵּן תְּרַחֵם יהוה עָלֵינוּ. לַיהוה הַיְשׁוּעָה, עַל עַמְּךָ בִרְכָתֶךָ סֶּלָה. יהוה צְבָאוֹת עִמָּנוּ, מִשְׂגָּב לָנוּ אֱלֹהֵי יַעֲקֹב סֶלָה. יהוה צְבָאוֹת, אַשְׁרֵי אָדָם בֹּטֵחַ בָּךְ. יהוה הוֹשִׁיעָה, הַמֶּלֶךְ יַעֲנֵנוּ בְיוֹם קָרְאֵנוּ.

In some congregations the following two verses are recited responsively — the chazzan reciting סְלַח, and the congregation responding וַיֹּאמֶר. In other congregations these verses are recited silently.

סְלַח נָא לַעֲוֹן הָעָם הַזֶּה כְּגֹדֶל חַסְדֶּךָ, וְכַאֲשֶׁר נָשָׂאתָה לָעָם הַזֶּה מִמִּצְרַיִם וְעַד הֵנָּה, וְשָׁם נֶאֱמַר:

וַיֹּאמֶר יהוה סָלַחְתִּי כִּדְבָרֶךָ.

(1) *Psalms* 103:13. (2) 74:21. (3) Cf. 22:12. (4) *Jeremiah* 31:33. (5) *I Kings* 8:50. (6) *Nehemiah* 9:17.

Chazzan — *Your generous-spirited people like a pleasant planting —
who take shelter with You, hope for You,
and are accounted Your pure ones,*
                          *make haste and have mercy on them,
                as a father is merciful towards his children.*[1]

All, while standing:

אֵל מֶלֶךְ *O God, King Who sits on the throne of mercy; Who acts with
kindness, pardons the iniquities of His people, removes [sins]
one by one, increasingly grants pardon to careless sinners and forgiveness
to rebels, Who deals righteously with every living being — You do not repay
them in accord with their evil. Chazzan — O God, You taught us to recite the
Thirteen [Attributes of Mercy], so remember for us today the covenant of
these Thirteen, as You made known to the humble one in ancient times, as
it is written: And HASHEM descended in a cloud and stood with him there,
and He called out with the Name HASHEM.*

Congregation, then *chazzan*:

And HASHEM passed before him [Moses] and proclaimed:

Congregation and *chazzan* (the words in bold type are recited aloud and in unison):

ה' ה' **HASHEM, HASHEM,** God, **Compassionate and Gracious, Slow
to anger,** and **Abundant in Kindness and Truth, Preserver of
kindness for thousands [of generations], Forgiver of iniquity, willful
sin, and error, and Who cleanses.** *May You forgive our iniquities and our
errors and make us Your heritage. Forgive us, our Father, for we have
erred; pardon us, our King, for we have willfully sinned; for You, my Lord,
are good and forgiving and abundantly kind to all who call upon You.*

PREFATORY VERSES TO SELICHAH 37

אַל יָשׁוֹב *Let not the oppressed turn back in shame, let the poor and
destitute praise Your Name.*[2] *Be not far from us, for trouble
is near; for there is none to help.*[3] *For I will forgive their iniquity, and their
sin I will remember no more.*[4] *May You forgive Your people, who have
sinned against You: all their rebellious sins that they have committed
against You; and may You make them the object of mercy for their
captors.*[5] *But You are the God of Forgiveness, Gracious and Merciful, Slow
to anger, Abundant in kindness; and You have not abandoned them.*[6]

בְּרַחֵם אָב *As a father has mercy on his children, so, HASHEM, may
You have mercy on us. Salvation is HASHEM's, upon Your
people is Your blessing, Selah. HASHEM, Master of Legions, is with us, a
stronghold for us is the God of Jacob, Selah. HASHEM, Master of Legions,
praiseworthy is the person who trusts in You. HASHEM, save! May the
King answer us on the day we call.*

In some congregations the following two verses are recited responsively — the *chazzan*
reciting, 'Forgive, please . . . ,' and the congregation responding, 'And HASHEM said . . .'
In other congregations these verses are recited silently.

סְלַח נָא *Forgive, please, the iniquity of this people according to the
greatness of Your kindness and as You have forgiven this
people from Egypt until now, and there it was said:*

And HASHEM said, 'I have forgiven according to your word!'

All:

הַטֵּה אֱלֹהַי אׇזְנְךָ וּשֲׁמָע, פְּקַח עֵינֶיךָ וּרְאֵה שֹׁמְמֹתֵינוּ, וְהָעִיר
אֲשֶׁר נִקְרָא שִׁמְךָ עָלֶיהָ, כִּי לֹא עַל צִדְקוֹתֵינוּ אֲנַחְנוּ
מַפִּילִים תַּחֲנוּנֵינוּ לְפָנֶיךָ, כִּי עַל רַחֲמֶיךָ הָרַבִּים. אֲדֹנָי שְׁמָעָה,
אֲדֹנָי סְלָחָה, אֲדֹנָי הַקְשִׁיבָה, וַעֲשֵׂה אַל תְּאַחַר, לְמַעַנְךָ אֱלֹהַי, כִּי
שִׁמְךָ נִקְרָא עַל עִירְךָ וְעַל עַמֶּךָ.

סליחה לז (שלמונית)

All:

(אֱלֹהֵנוּ וֵאלֹהֵי אֲבוֹתֵינוּ:)

אָב* לְרַחֵם וְרַב סְלָח חוֹלַלְתָּנוּ,
בְּנֵי בְרִית קֹדֶשׁ וְלֹא חִלַּלְתָּנוּ,
גוֹלִים וְאַתָּה בְּקִרְבֵּנוּ* כַּאֲשֶׁר יְחַלְתָּנוּ,
וְסָלַחְתָּ לַעֲוֺנֵנוּ וּלְחַטָּאתֵנוּ וּנְחַלְתָּנוּ.[1]

דָּם וְגָאוּל תָּדִיחַ, דִּין תָּאִיר,
הַחֵטְא יוּעְלַם וּבַל יִמָּצֵא לְהַכְעִיר,
וְעָוֹן יְבֻקַּשׁ וְאֵינֶנּוּ, כְּנֻמְתָּ לְהַבְאִיר, כִּי אֶסְלַח לַאֲשֶׁר אַשְׁאִיר.[2]

זֶהָם מְרֻבֶּה וּפֶסַק נִיחוֹחַ מִמֻּלָּח,
חֲצִיצַת חֲפִיפַת לִכְלוּךְ שֶׁרֶץ הַלָּח,*
טְבִילַת טׇהֳרַת צִנּוֹר מֵימֶיךָ יְקַלָּח, כִּי אַתָּה אֲדֹנָי טוֹב וְסַלָּח.[3]

יַעַן סָרַחְנוּ נִדַּחְנוּ וּמִשַּׁמָּן רָזֶה,
כִּי רַבָּה הַטֻּמְאָה וְאֵין מַזֶּה,
לְמַעַנְךָ יהוה כְּאָז וּלְפָנִים מִזֶּה, סְלַח נָא לַעֲוֺן הָעָם הַזֶּה.[4]
מִסְפַּר עׇצְמוֹ חַסְדֵּי רֹב גְּמוּלֶיךָ,[5]

אָב — O Father. This selichah follows an alphabetical acrostic, three letters to each quatrain. The fourth line of each stanza is a Scriptural fragment that contains some form of the word סְלִיחָה, forgiveness. The author's name, שְׁלֹמֹה, Shlomo, is found in the eighth stanza. Some commentaries read שְׁלֹמֹה בְּיַרְבִּי יְהוּדָה (see footnote 10 below), Shlomo bar R' Yehudah, and ascribe the selichah to R' Shlomo HaBavli [see prefatory comment to selichah 2].

גוֹלִים וְאַתָּה בְּקִרְבֵּנוּ — [We are] exiles, and You are in our midst. As long as Israel is in exile, the שְׁכִינָה [Shechinah] manifestation of the Divine Presence, is in exile with them — as the prophet declares: In all their troubles, He is troubled

(Isaiah 63:9), and as God says: I am with him in [times of] trouble (Psalms 91:15).

The Talmud discusses this at length: Come and observe how beloved Israel is to the Holy One, Blessed is He, for wherever they [Israel] are exiled, the Shechinah is with them. They were exiled to Egypt, the Shechinah was with them, as it is stated: Didn't I appear to your father's household when they were in Egypt? (I Samuel 2:27). They were exiled to Babylon, the Shechinah was with them, as it is stated: For your sake have I been sent to Babylon (Isaiah 43:14). And when they will be redeemed from their present exile, the Shechinah will be with them, as it is stated: HASHEM, Your God, will return [with] your

All:

הַטֵּה *Incline, my God, Your ear, and listen, open Your eyes and see our desolation and that of the city upon which Your Name is proclaimed; for not because of our righteousness do we cast down our supplications before You, rather because of Your abundant compassion. O my Lord, heed; O my Lord, forgive; O my Lord, be attentive and act, do not delay; for Your sake, my God, for Your Name is proclaimed upon Your city and upon Your people.*

SELICHAH 37

All:

א *O Father,* You have formed us
    that You may be compassionate and full of forgiveness [to us];*
ב *[we are] the members of Your holy covenant,
    and You have never profaned us.*
ג *[We are] exiles, and You are in our midst,* as You gave us to hope.
        May You **forgive** our iniquity and our sin,
           and make us Your heritage.*[1]
ד *Wash away the blood and filth [of sin], and brighten our judgment;*
ה *let sin be concealed, no longer there to disfigure us.*
ו *Let transgression be sought and not be there, as You spoke out clearly:
      'For I will **forgive** the remnant that I leave.'*[2]
ז *[Our sinfulness'] stain is great, and the pleasant scent [of sacrifice]
    and well-blended [incense] has ceased.*
ח *This sundering shell of dirt, the taint of fresh sin* —*
ט *[let it become cleansed by] purifying immersion
    in the stream of Your flowing waters,
        for You, my Lord, are good and **forgiving**.*[3]
י *Because of our betrayal we have been exiled,
    and our plenitude has withered away,*
כ *for [our] defilement is great, and there is no one
    to sprinkle [purifying water on us].*
ל *For Your sake, HASHEM, as You used to once long ago,
        Please **forgive** the iniquity of this people.*[4]
מ *Too overwhelming to recount*[5] *are the abundant kindnesses
    You have performed;*

---

(1) *Exodus* 34:9. (2) *Jeremiah* 50:20. (3) *Psalms* 86:5. (4) *Numbers* 14:19. (5) Cf. *Psalms* 40:6.

captivity (Deuteronomy 30:3). The verse does not read וְהֵשִׁיב, He will return [you], but שָׁב, He will return [Himself], this teaches that God returns with them from their exiles (Megillah 29a).

חֲצִיצַת חֲפִיפַת לִבְלוּךְ שֶׁרֶץ הַלַּח — *This sundering shell of dirt, the taint of fresh sin* [lit., moist vermin]. *Eight species of vermin are enumerated in the Torah (Leviticus 11:29-30). Contact with a*

dead member of any of these species imparts a tumah-contamination that can only be removed by immersion in a mikveh (see ibid. 11:29-38). The Talmud teaches that this contamination applies only while the animal's carcass is still moist. If it is already completely dried out, it no longer transmits contamination (Niddah 54b).

In another place (Taanis 16a), the Talmud homiletically compares the would-be penitent

נֵהַגְתָּ לְעַם בֵּית מְרִי לְמוֹלֵךְ,*

סָבְלָם נָא תִשָּׂא כְּמִקֶּדֶם נְטוּלֶיךָ,*

וְסָלַחְתָּ לְעַמְּךָ אֲשֶׁר חָטְאוּ לָךְ. [1]

עָלֵינוּ מִמָּרוֹם רוּחַ קָדְשׁוֹ יְעָרֶה, [2]

פָּרוֹשׁ וְהִתְקַדְּשׁ, וְחָדָשׁ לָנוּ יִבְרָא, [3]

צָרוּף וּמָרוּק בְּלִי יִסּוּרִין תּוֹרָה,

כִּי עִמְּךָ **הַסְּלִיחָה** לְמַעַן תִּוָּרֵא. [4]

קוֹמֵם נְפוּלָה עוֹד מִלְהוֹסִיף דַּאֲבוֹנֵנוּ, [5]

רוּחַ חֵן רַוֵּה שַׂבַּע רְעָבוֹנֵנוּ,

שַׁלְּמוּ תַּמּוּ עֵת רְעוֹעַ בּוֹגְנֵינוּ,

לְמַעַן שִׁמְךָ יהוה, **וְסָלַחְתָּ לַעֲוֹנֵנוּ.** [6]

שִׁירִים הִנֵּנוּ וּמִי כָמוֹךָ נוֹשֵׂא, [7]

לֹא עַל צִדְקוֹתֵינוּ אוֹת נְנַסֶּה,*

מִדַּת הֲמוֹן רַחֲמֶיךָ נַפִּיל[8] מַחֲסֶה,

אֲדֹנָי שְׁמָעָה, אֲדֹנָי **סְלָחָה,** אֲדֹנָי הַקְשִׁיבָה וַעֲשֵׂה. [9]

בְּיִרְאָתֶךָ וּבְתוֹרָתֶךָ הָכֵן פְּעָמֵינוּ לְצָעַד,

בְּיַד עֲוֹנֵינוּ כִּי כָשַׁלְנוּ לִמְעָד,

נָא יֵאָמֶן דְּבָרְךָ הַטּוֹב[10] לִסְעַד,

כִּי **אֶסְלַח** לַעֲוֹנָם, וּלְחַטָּאתָם לֹא אֶזְכָּר עוֹד. [11]

יוֹדֵעַ תַּעֲלוּם כָּל דָּם וּלְחוּם,

חַטָּאתֵינוּ יְדַעְנוּם, וְאִתָּנוּ בְּכָל תְּחוּם,

הִנְנוּ אִתָּנוּ לָךְ, מְצָא כְּפֶר וְתַנְחוּם,

וְאַתָּה אֱלוֹהַּ **סְלִיחוֹת** חַנּוּן וְרַחוּם. [12]

---

who confesses his sin but does not abandon it to one who immerses in the *mikveh* while holding a dead vermin in his hand. All the world's water would be insufficient to cleanse him of his contamination. Yet if he casts the animal from his hand, he can become cleansed in a *mikveh*. Similarly, one who confesses the evils he has perpetrated in the past, yet maintains that same life style, cannot find atonement. However, one who rejects and abandons his former ways may be cleansed by his confession, as it is stated: *One who confesses [his sin] and forsakes [it] will receive mercy* (Proverbs 28:13).

נֵהַגְתָּ לְעַם בֵּית מְרִי לְמוֹלֵךְ — *You have guided a people [though they were] full of rebellion*

towards You. This ambiguous stich may mean either, *You have guided towards You a people full of rebellion,* or, *You have guided a people that is full of rebellion against You.*

סָבְלָם נָא תִשָּׂא כְּמִקֶּדֶם נְטוּלֶיךָ — *Please bear their burden — as of old — the people You carry.* Another ambiguous stich, this may mean either, *Please bear the burden of the people You carry, as [You have] of old;* or, *Please bear the burden of the people You carried of old.*

לֹא עַל צִדְקוֹתֵינוּ אוֹת נְנַסֶּה — *[We can]not [rely] on our righteousness, to test You with a sign.* The righteous King David was able to ask: *Make a good sign for me, that my enemies may see and be abashed* (Psalms 86:17). But we are un-

נ You have guided a people [though they were] full of rebellion
     towards You.*

ס Please bear their burden — as of old — the people You carry;*
          may Your **forgive** Your people who have sinned against You.[1]

ע From on high let His Holy Spirit be poured upon us;[2]

פ [that we may] separate and sanctify [ourselves],
          and that [a] new [heart] may be created in us.[3]

צ Decree that purification and purging [of our sins]
          be without suffering,
                    for **forgiveness** is [only] with You, that You may be feared.[4]

ק Raise up the fallen, that our sorrows may no longer continue;[5]

ר lavish a spirit of graciousness on us; satisfy our hunger.

שת Gone, ended, are those [righteous ones] who built us up
          when we were weakened,
                              [so act] for Your Name's sake, HASHEM,
                                        and **forgive** our iniquity.[6]

ש We are but remnants;
          and who is as forbearing as You?[7]

ל [We can]not [rely] on our righteousness,
          to test You with a sign,*

מה only because of Your Attribute of great mercy
          do we cast [our supplication before You],[8] O Stronghold.
     My Lord, listen! My Lord, forgive! My Lord, hearken and act![9]
Prepare our steps to tread in reverence for You,
          and in Your Torah['s path],
for we have stumbled and fallen,
          in the grip of our iniquities.
Please let Your goodly word, [promising] to prop us up,
     come true:[10]
                    'For I shall **forgive** their transgression,
                         and their sin I shall remember no more.'[11]
You Who Know the secrets of all blood and flesh,
We know our sins, and they are with us in every place.
Here we are!
          We have come to You to find atonement and comfort,
               for You are the God of **Forgiveness**, gracious and merciful.[12]

---

(1) I Kings 8:50. (2) Cf. Isaiah 32:15. (3) Cf. Ezekiel 36:26. (4) Psalms 130:4. (5) Cf. Jeremiah 31:11.
(6) Cf. Psalms 25:11. (7) Cf. Micah 7:18. (8) Cf. Daniel 9:18. (9) 9:19. (10) Cf. I Kings 8:26; according
to the reading of Arugas HaBosem and other manuscripts, this stich reads וִיהִי וְיֵאָמֵן דְּבָרְךָ הַטּוֹב,
Let Your goodly word be and come true; accordingly the paytan's father's name appears in the
stich — יְהִי וְיֵאָמֵן דְּבָרְךָ הַטּוֹב ... בְּיַד ... בְּיִרְאָתֶךָ — for the letters in bold type spell בִּירְבִּי יְהוּדָה,
son of R' Yehudah, and the composer is indeed R' Shlomo bar Yehudah HaBavli. (11) Jeremiah 31:33.
(12) Nehemiah 9:17.

---

able to make a similar request, for we cannot   devotion. Thus, we must rely strictly on Your
even approach David's humility, piety and   great mercy.

All, while standing:

אֵל מֶלֶךְ יוֹשֵׁב עַל כִּסֵּא רַחֲמִים מִתְנַהֵג בַּחֲסִידוּת, מוֹחֵל עֲוֹנוֹת עַמּוֹ, מַעֲבִיר רִאשׁוֹן רִאשׁוֹן, מַרְבֶּה מְחִילָה לַחַטָּאִים וּסְלִיחָה לַפּוֹשְׁעִים, עֹשֶׂה צְדָקוֹת עִם כָּל בָּשָׂר וָרוּחַ, לֹא כְרָעָתָם תִּגְמוֹל. ❖ אֵל הוֹרֵיתָ לָּנוּ לוֹמַר שְׁלֹשׁ עֶשְׂרֵה, וּזְכוֹר לָנוּ הַיּוֹם בְּרִית שְׁלֹשׁ עֶשְׂרֵה, כְּמוֹ שֶׁהוֹדַעְתָּ לֶעָנָיו מִקֶּדֶם, כְּמוֹ שֶׁכָּתוּב, וַיֵּרֶד יהוה בֶּעָנָן וַיִּתְיַצֵּב עִמּוֹ שָׁם, וַיִּקְרָא בְשֵׁם יהוה.

Congregation, then *chazzan:*

וַיַּעֲבֹר יהוה עַל פָּנָיו וַיִּקְרָא:

Congregation and *chazzan* (the words in bold type are recited aloud and in unison):

יהוה, יהוה, אֵל, **רַחוּם, וְחַנּוּן, אֶרֶךְ אַפַּיִם, וְרַב חֶסֶד, וֶאֱמֶת, נֹצֵר חֶסֶד לָאֲלָפִים, נֹשֵׂא עָוֹן, וָפֶשַׁע, וְחַטָּאָה, וְנַקֵּה.** וְסָלַחְתָּ לַעֲוֹנֵנוּ וּלְחַטָּאתֵנוּ וּנְחַלְתָּנוּ. סְלַח לָנוּ אָבִינוּ כִּי חָטָאנוּ, מְחַל לָנוּ מַלְכֵּנוּ כִּי פָשָׁעְנוּ. כִּי אַתָּה אֲדֹנָי טוֹב וְסַלָּח, וְרַב חֶסֶד לְכָל קֹרְאֶיךָ.

פסוקי הקדמה לסליחה לח

לָמָה יהוה תַּעֲמֹד בְּרָחוֹק, תַּעְלִים לְעִתּוֹת בַּצָּרָה.[1] שׁוּב לְמַעַן עֲבָדֶיךָ שִׁבְטֵי נַחֲלָתֶךָ.[2] תִּתֵּן אֱמֶת לְיַעֲקֹב, חֶסֶד לְאַבְרָהָם, אֲשֶׁר נִשְׁבַּעְתָּ לַאֲבוֹתֵינוּ מִימֵי קֶדֶם.[3]

בְּרַחֵם אָב עַל בָּנִים, כֵּן תְּרַחֵם יהוה עָלֵינוּ. לַיהוה הַיְשׁוּעָה, עַל עַמְּךָ בִרְכָתֶךָ סֶּלָה. יהוה צְבָאוֹת עִמָּנוּ, מִשְׂגָּב לָנוּ אֱלֹהֵי יַעֲקֹב סֶלָה. יהוה צְבָאוֹת, אַשְׁרֵי אָדָם בֹּטֵחַ בָּךְ. יהוה הוֹשִׁיעָה, הַמֶּלֶךְ יַעֲנֵנוּ בְיוֹם קָרְאֵנוּ.

In some congregations the following two verses are recited responsively — the *chazzan* reciting סְלַח, and the congregation responding וַיֹּאמֶר. In other congregations these verses are recited silently.

סְלַח נָא לַעֲוֹן הָעָם הַזֶּה כְּגֹדֶל חַסְדֶּךָ, וְכַאֲשֶׁר נָשָׂאתָה לָעָם הַזֶּה מִמִּצְרַיִם וְעַד הֵנָּה, וְשָׁם נֶאֱמַר:
וַיֹּאמֶר יהוה סָלַחְתִּי כִּדְבָרֶךָ.

All:

הַטֵּה אֱלֹהַי אָזְנְךָ וּשֲׁמָע, פְּקַח עֵינֶיךָ וּרְאֵה שֹׁמְמֹתֵינוּ, וְהָעִיר אֲשֶׁר נִקְרָא שִׁמְךָ עָלֶיהָ, כִּי לֹא עַל צִדְקוֹתֵינוּ אֲנַחְנוּ מַפִּילִים תַּחֲנוּנֵינוּ לְפָנֶיךָ, כִּי עַל רַחֲמֶיךָ הָרַבִּים. אֲדֹנָי שְׁמָעָה, אֲדֹנָי סְלָחָה, אֲדֹנָי הַקְשִׁיבָה, וַעֲשֵׂה אַל תְּאַחַר, לְמַעַנְךָ אֱלֹהַי, כִּי שִׁמְךָ נִקְרָא עַל עִירְךָ וְעַל עַמֶּךָ.

All, while standing:

אֵל מֶלֶךְ O God, King Who sits on the throne of mercy; Who acts with kindness, pardons the iniquities of His people, removes [sins] one by one, increasingly grants pardon to careless sinners and forgiveness to rebels, Who deals righteously with every living being — You do not repay them in accord with their evil. Chazzan — O God, You taught us to recite the Thirteen [Attributes of Mercy], so remember for us today the covenant of these Thirteen, as You made known to the humble one in ancient times, as it is written: And HASHEM descended in a cloud and stood with him there, and He called out with the Name HASHEM.

Congregation, then chazzan:

And HASHEM passed before him [Moses] and proclaimed:

Congregation and chazzan (the words in bold type are recited aloud and in unison):

ה' ה' HASHEM, HASHEM, God, Compassionate and Gracious, Slow to anger, and Abundant in Kindness and Truth, Preserver of kindness for thousands [of generations], Forgiver of iniquity, willful sin, and error, and Who cleanses. May You forgive our iniquities and our errors and make us Your heritage. Forgive us, our Father, for we have erred; pardon us, our King, for we have willfully sinned; for You, my Lord, are good and forgiving and abundantly kind to all who call upon You.

PREFATORY VERSES TO SELICHAH 38

לָמָה Why, HASHEM, do You stand far off; do You conceal Yourself in times of trouble?[1] Return for the sake of Your servants, the tribes that are Your heritage.[2] Grant truth to Jacob, kindness to Abraham, as You swore to our forefathers from ancient times.[3]

כְּרַחֵם אָב As a father has mercy on his children, so, HASHEM, may You have mercy on us. Salvation is HASHEM's, upon Your people is Your blessing, Selah. HASHEM, Master of Legions, is with us, a stronghold for us is the God of Jacob, Selah. HASHEM, Master of Legions, praiseworthy is the person who trusts in You. HASHEM, save! May the King answer us on the day we call.

In some congregations the following two verses are recited responsively — the chazzan reciting, 'Forgive, please . . .,' and the congregation responding, 'And HASHEM said . . .' In other congregations these verses are recited silently.

סְלַח נָא Forgive, please, the iniquity of this people according to the greatness of Your kindness and as You have forgiven this people from Egypt until now, and there it was said:

And HASHEM said, 'I have forgiven according to your word!'

All:

הַטֵּה Incline, my God, Your ear, and listen, open Your eyes and see our desolation and that of the city upon which Your Name is proclaimed; for not because of our righteousness do we cast down our supplications before You, rather because of Your abundant compassion. O my Lord, heed; O my Lord, forgive; O my Lord, be attentive and act, do not delay; for Your sake, my God, for Your Name is proclaimed upon Your city and upon Your people.

(1) Psalms 10:1. (2) Isaiah 63:17. (3) Micah 7:20.

סליחה לח (שלמונית)

אֱלֹהֵינוּ וֵאלֹהֵי אֲבוֹתֵינוּ:

Chazzan, then congregation:

שְׁלֹשׁ עֶשְׂרֵה מִדּוֹת* הָאֲמוּרוֹת בַּחֲנִינָה,

נָא כָל מִדָּה נְכוֹנָה, אֲחַלֶּה פְּנֵי מַלְכִּי בִּתְחִנָּה,

לְחַפֵּשׂ זְכוּת כְּנוּיִים, קְרוּאִים שׁוֹשַׁנָּה,[1]

מַלְּטֵם מִכָּל רָעוֹת בְּזֹאת הַשָּׁנָה.

Congregation, then chazzan:

אִם **אַ**שְׁמָתָם גָּדְלָה עַד שְׁמֵי רוֹם וְכוֹכְבֵיהֶם,

נָא כָל מִדָּה נְכוֹנָה, אֲבַקֵּשׁ רַחֲמִים עֲלֵיהֶם,

לְבַ**טֵּל** מֵהֶם כָּתוּב, אָמַרְתִּי אַפְאֵיהֶם,[2]

לָמָּה יֹאמְרוּ הַגּוֹיִם, אַיֵּה נָא אֱלֹהֵיהֶם.[3]

Congregation, then chazzan:

אִם **גָּ**בְרוּ עֲוֹנוֹת וְעָצְמוּ מִלְּסַפְּרָה,

נָא כָל מִדָּה נְכוֹנָה, דְּחֵה אוֹתָם יהוה לְהַסְתִּירָה,

דְּבוּבֵי עֹז בְּתַחַן, לְבַטֵּל מֵהֶם כָּתוּב, אַסְתִּירָה,[4]

לָמָּה יהוה תַּעֲמֹד בְּרָחוֹק, תַּעְלִים לְעִתּוֹת בַּצָּרָה.[5]

Congregation, then chazzan:

אִם **הֶ**עֱווּ פְּנֵי מַלְכָּם בְּעַזּוּת פָּנִים וּמֵצַח,

נָא כָל מִדָּה נְכוֹנָה, אֶתְחַנֵּן לוֹ בְּפֶצַח,

וְנַפְשִׁי שִׁפְכִי כַמַּיִם לִבֵּךְ,[6] נֹכַח אָדָם נָצַח,[7]

לָמָּה אֱלֹהִים זָנַחְתָּ לָנֶצַח.[8]

Congregation, then chazzan:

אִם **זְ**דוֹנוֹת הִשִּׂיאוּ לֵב טִפֵּשׁ[9] וְנִשְׁחָץ,

נָא כָל מִדָּה נְכוֹנָה, חַלֵּץ אוֹתָם יהוה מִמַּחַץ,

חוּשׁ וּבֹא, וְשָׂא קוֹל נַחַץ,

לָמָּה קֵדָר אֶתְהַלֵּךְ בְּלַחַץ.[10]

◀§ **שְׁלֹשׁ עֶשְׂרֵה מִדּוֹת** — *Thirteen Attributes.* This is another of those *selichos* that apparently address some 'higher beings' pleading that they intervene with the Heavenly Tribunal on our behalf. In this case the higher beings are not angels, but God's own Thirteen Attributes of Mercy. The propriety and permissibility of such prayer is discussed in the introduction to this volume. Assumedly to avoid this issue, the

original text of this *selichah* (as it appears in various manuscripts and in the medieval commentary *Arugas HaBosem*) was altered centuries ago. In its present form the supplication addresses God directly, and passages that asked for intercession now are in the first person active voice. For example, in place of the original words, בַּקְּשׁוּ רַחֲמִים, *[you Attributes] seek mercy*, the second stanza now reads, אֲבַקֵּשׁ רַחֲמִים, *I shall seek*

SELICHAH 38

Our God, and the God of our forefathers:

Chazzan, then congregation:

שְׁלֹשׁ עֶשְׂרֵה *[O You Who described Your ways with]*
Thirteen Attributes* pronounced with grace,
O please, *[You Whose]* every Attribute is proper:
I shall pray before [You] my King in supplication,
to seek out merit for the people called a rose,[1]
O save them from all evil during this year.

Congregation, then chazzan:

א If their guilt has grown to the high heavens and their stars,
ב O please, *[You Whose]* every Attribute is proper:
I shall request compassion for them,
to annul that which is written about them:
'[In my heart'] I said that I would cast them away. . .'[2]
Why should the nations say, 'Where now is their God?'[3]

Congregation, then chazzan:

ג If *[Israel's]* iniquities have become overwhelming
and too powerful to recount,
ד O please, *[You Whose]* every Attribute is proper:
push them aside, HASHEM, to concealment.
[I utter] strong words in supplication, to annul for them what is written,
'I shall hide [my face from them].'[4]
Why, HASHEM, do You stand far off,
do You conceal Yourself in times of trouble?'[5]

Congregation, then chazzan:

ה If they have contorted their King's countenance
with their boldness and brazenness,
ו O please, *[You Whose]* every Attribute is proper:
I will supplicate to Him aloud.
And pour out your heart, O my soul, like water[6]
before Him Who is red [with vengeance] and white [with forgiveness].[7]
Why, O God, have You abandoned us forever?[8]

Congregation, then chazzan:

ז If wanton sins have led their suety, conceited heart[9] astray,
ח O please, *[You Whose]* every Attribute is proper:
relieve them, O HASHEM, from the crushing blow.
Hurry, come and bear [their] hasty outcry:
'Why must I go about in gloom and oppression?'[10]

---

(1) See *Song of Songs* 2:1-2. (2) *Deuteronomy* 32:26. (3) *Psalms* 115:2.
(4) *Deuteronomy* 32:20. (5) *Psalms* 10:1. (6) *Lamentations* 2:19.
(7) Cf. *Song of Songs* 5:10. (8) *Psalms* 74:1. (9) Cf. 119:70. (10) Cf. 42:10.

mercy. Other passages were changed by adding God's Name as the object of the supplication. Thus, in the third stanza, דְּחֵי אוֹתָם, *[you Attributes] push them aside*, has been changed to, דְּחֵה

אוֹתָם ה׳, *push them aside, HASHEM.* The present translation conforms to the spirit of these emendations, even in the stiches that have remained unaltered from the original. Thus,

Congregation, then chazzan:

אִם טָפְלוּ שֶׁקֶר בְּהֶגֶה וְהַוּוֹת לְעַמֶּךָ,

נָא כָּל מִדָּה נְכוֹנָה, יְדִידוּת תִּזְכֹּר מִמַּנְעִימֶיךָ,

יִתְגּוֹלְלוּ רַחֲמֶיךָ עַל שְׁאֵרִית עַמֶּךָ,

לָמָה יהוה יֶחֱרֶה אַפְּךָ בְּעַמֶּךָ.[1]

Congregation, then chazzan:

אִם כָּבְדוּ אֹזֶן,[2] לְסַלֵּף מִנִּי הַדֶּרֶךְ,

נָא כָּל מִדָּה נְכוֹנָה, אֲלַחֵשׁ עַל עַמִּי בְּעֶרְךְ,

וְנַפְשִׁי שִׁפְכִי לִבֵּךְ, פְּנֵי קוֹנֵךְ וְצוּרֵךְ,[3]

לָמָה פָּרַצְתָּ גְדֵרֶיהָ, וְאָרוּהָ כָּל עֹבְרֵי דָרֶךְ.[4]

Congregation, then chazzan:

אִם מָרְדוּ בְרֹב פִּשְׁעָם,[5] לְצוּר מַלְכִּי וּקְדוֹשִׁי,

נָא כָּל מִדָּה נְכוֹנָה, נַפְשִׁי נָעַם עֲלֵיהֶם תְּבַקְשִׁי,

לְנוֹרָא מָרוֹם וְקָדוֹשׁ, בְּעֶתֶר אֵלָיו תִּדְרְשִׁי,

לָמָה יהוה תִּזְנַח מִשָּׁלוֹם נַפְשִׁי.[6]

Congregation, then chazzan:

אִם סָרְרוּ כְּפָרָה, מֶרַב עִתִּים וְיָמִים,

נָא כָּל מִדָּה נְכוֹנָה, אֶשָּׂא עַיִן לַמְּרוֹמִים,[7]

עַל עַמִּי אֶפְצֶה פֶה, מְעַטֵּי עַמִּים,

לָמָה לָנֶצַח תִּשְׁכָּחֵנוּ, תַּעַזְבֵנוּ לְאֹרֶךְ יָמִים.[8]

Congregation, then chazzan:

אִם פָּשָׁעֵנוּ עָצְמוּ, וְגָבְרוּ מְאֹד כְּתֵלָא,

נָא כָּל מִדָּה נְכוֹנָה, אֲצַפְצֵף קוֹל לְהַפְלֵא,

צְרוּפָה אִמְרָתְךָ, לַחֲלוֹת עַל עַם אֵלֶּה,

לָמָה תָשִׁיב יָדְךָ וִימִינֶךָ, מִקֶּרֶב חֵיקְךָ כַלֵּה.[9]

Congregation, then chazzan:

אִם קִלְקְלוּ מַעֲשִׂים, לְהָזִיד וּלְהַרְשִׁיעַ,

נָא כָּל מִדָּה נְכוֹנָה, רָחַשׁ לִבִּי לְהוֹשִׁיעַ,

קוּמִי רֹנִּי בַלַּיְלָה[10] לָאֵל הַמּוֹשִׁיעַ,

לָמָה תִהְיֶה כְּאִישׁ נִדְהָם, כְּגִבּוֹר לֹא יוּכַל לְהוֹשִׁיעַ.[11]

כָּל מִדָּה נְכוֹנָה is not translated *every proper Attribute*, but *[You Whose] every Attribute is proper.*

The *selichah* was composed by שְׁלֹמֹה בֶּן מְנַחֵם, *Shlomo ben Menachem*, whose name appears in the acrostic of the first two stanzas. In the original

version, the *paytan's* signature was more obvious, for there the first two lines read שְׁלֹשׁ עֶשְׂרֵה מִדּוֹת הָאֲמוּרוֹת בַּחֲנִינָה/ נָא מִדָּה נְכוֹנָה חַלִּי מַלְכֵּךְ בִּתְחִנָּה. R' Shlomo lived sometime before 1234 when the commentary *Arugas HaBosem* [which includes this *piyut*] was written.

Congregation, then chazzan:

ט If they have falsely made accusation against you
　　in speech or in thought,
י O please, [You Whose] every Attribute is proper:
　　remember the love of those who sing sweetly to You.
　Let Your mercy roll over the remnant of Your people.
　　　　Why, HASHEM, does Your anger flare against Your people?[1]

Congregation, then chazzan:

כ If they have hardened [their] ear [to rebuke],[2]
　causing them to pervert the [Torah's] way,
ל O please, [You Whose] every Attribute is proper:
　　I will whisper [entreaty] for my people in my ordered prayer.
　And pour out your heart, O my soul,
　　before Your Master and Maker [saying]:[3]
　　　　　　　'Why have You breached [Israel's] fences,
　　　　　　　　so that all who pass by strip her bare?'[4]

Congregation, then chazzan:

מ If they have rebelled, with their manifold sins,[5]
　　against the Rock, my King and my Holy One,
נ O please, [You Whose] every Attribute is proper:
　　my soul, ask serenity for them.
　Seek out the Awesome, Lofty and Holy One in powerful prayer:
　　　　'Why, HASHEM, do You abandon my soul without peace?'[6]

Congregation, then chazzan:

ס If they have strayed like a cow
　　because of over-long periods and years [in Exile],
ע O please, [You Whose] every Attribute is proper:
　　I will turn my gaze to the heavens,[7]
　I will open my mouth on behalf of my people,
　　the smallest of nations [saying]:
　　　　'Why should You forget us forever, abandon us for long days?'[8]
פ If their willful sins have grown great, and as overwhelming as a mound,
צ O please, [You Whose] every Attribute is proper:
　　I will twitter [my prayer] in a clear voice.
　Your [Torah's] words are pure enough
　　to beseech [You with them] on this people's behalf:
　　　　　　'Why do You withdraw Your hand, Your right hand
　　　[from punishing our oppressors]? Bring it forth from Your bosom!'[9]
ק If they have corrupted [their] deeds, to be wanton and wicked,
ר O please, [You Whose] every Attribute is proper:
　　my heart stirs [with the desire] to save [them].
　Arise, sing in the night[10] to God Who saves!
　　　　　　　'Why will you act like a man stunned,
　　　　　　　like a warrior who is unable to save?'[11]

_____
(1) Exodus 32:11. (2) Cf. Zechariah 7:11. (3) Cf. Lamentations 2:19. (4) Psalms 80:13.
(5) Cf. Ezekiel 2:3. (6) Cf. Psalms 88:15. (7) Cf. Isaiah 40:26. (8) Lamentations 5:20.
(9) Psalms 74:11. (10) Lamentations 2:19. (11) Jeremiah 14:9.

Congregation, then *chazzan*:

אִם אָמְנָם שָׁבוּ כֻלָּם, בְּלֵב וָנֶפֶשׁ לַחֲלוֹתֶךָ,

נָא כָּל מִדָּה נְכוֹנָה, תַּסְכִּים עִמָּם בִּמְחִילָתֶךָ,

וַעֲשֵׂה אָדוֹן לְמַעַנְךָ, סְלַח וּמְחַל לַעֲדָתֶךָ,

שׁוּב לְמַעַן עֲבָדֶיךָ, שִׁבְטֵי נַחֲלָתֶךָ.[1]

All, while standing:

אֵל מֶלֶךְ יוֹשֵׁב עַל כִּסֵּא רַחֲמִים מִתְנַהֵג בַּחֲסִידוּת, מוֹחֵל עֲוֹנוֹת עַמּוֹ, מַעֲבִיר רִאשׁוֹן רִאשׁוֹן, מַרְבֶּה מְחִילָה לַחַטָּאִים וּסְלִיחָה לַפּוֹשְׁעִים, עֹשֶׂה צְדָקוֹת עִם כָּל בָּשָׂר וָרוּחַ, לֹא כְרָעָתָם תִּגְמוֹל. ❖ אֵל הוֹרֵיתָ לָנוּ לוֹמַר שְׁלֹשׁ עֶשְׂרֵה, וּזְכוֹר לָנוּ הַיּוֹם בְּרִית שְׁלֹשׁ עֶשְׂרֵה, כְּמוֹ שֶׁהוֹדַעְתָּ לֶעָנָיו מִקֶּדֶם, כְּמוֹ שֶׁכָּתוּב, וַיֵּרֶד יהוה בֶּעָנָן וַיִּתְיַצֵּב עִמּוֹ שָׁם, וַיִּקְרָא בְשֵׁם יהוה.

Congregation, then *chazzan*:

וַיַּעֲבֹר יהוה עַל פָּנָיו וַיִּקְרָא:

Congregation and *chazzan* (the words in bold type are recited aloud and in unison):

יהוה, יהוה, אֵל, **רַחוּם, וְחַנּוּן, אֶרֶךְ אַפַּיִם, וְרַב חֶסֶד, וֶאֱמֶת, נֹצֵר חֶסֶד לָאֲלָפִים, נֹשֵׂא עָוֹן, וָפֶשַׁע, וְחַטָּאָה, וְנַקֵּה.** וְסָלַחְתָּ לַעֲוֹנֵנוּ וּלְחַטָּאתֵנוּ וּנְחַלְתָּנוּ. סְלַח לָנוּ אָבִינוּ כִּי חָטָאנוּ, מְחַל לָנוּ מַלְכֵּנוּ כִּי פָשָׁעְנוּ. כִּי אַתָּה אֲדֹנָי טוֹב וְסַלָּח, וְרַב חֶסֶד לְכָל קֹרְאֶיךָ.

פסוקי הקדמה לסליחה לט

אֵלֶיךָ יהוה שִׁוַּעְנוּ, וּבַבֹּקֶר תְּפִלָּתֵנוּ תְקַדְּמֶךָ.[2] יהוה בֹּקֶר תִּשְׁמַע קוֹלֵנוּ, בֹּקֶר נַעֲרָךְ לְךָ וַאֲצַפֶּה.[3] נַפְשֵׁנוּ לַאדֹנָי, מִשֹּׁמְרִים לַבֹּקֶר, שֹׁמְרִים לַבֹּקֶר.[4] זִבְחֵי אֱלֹהִים רוּחַ נִשְׁבָּרָה, לֵב נִשְׁבָּר וְנִדְכֶּה, אֱלֹהִים לֹא תִבְזֶה.[5]

כְּרַחֵם אָב עַל בָּנִים, כֵּן תְּרַחֵם יהוה עָלֵינוּ. לַיהוה הַיְשׁוּעָה, עַל עַמְּךָ בִרְכָתֶךָ סֶּלָה. יהוה צְבָאוֹת עִמָּנוּ, מִשְׂגָּב לָנוּ אֱלֹהֵי יַעֲקֹב סֶלָה. יהוה צְבָאוֹת, אַשְׁרֵי אָדָם בֹּטֵחַ בָּךְ. יהוה הוֹשִׁיעָה, הַמֶּלֶךְ יַעֲנֵנוּ בְיוֹם קָרְאֵנוּ.

In each quatrain (after the first), the first line begins with the word אִם, *if*, followed by a word beginning with the respective letter of the *aleph-beis*; the second line begins with the phrase נָא כָּל מִדָּה נְכוֹנָה, followed by a word beginning with the next letter of the alphabet; the third line repeats the second line's letter; and the fourth line is a Scriptural fragment that begins with the

Congregation, then *chazzan:*

שׁ *And what if they have all repented,*
   with heart and soul beseeching You?
ת *O please, [You Whose] every Attribute is proper:*
   assent to them with Your pardon.
 O Lord, act for Your sake, forgive and pardon Your flock;
 return for the sake of Your servants, your heritage-tribes.[1]

All, while standing:

אֵל מֶלֶךְ *O God, King Who sits on the throne of mercy; Who acts with
         kindness, pardons the iniquities of His people, removes [sins]
one by one, increasingly grants pardon to careless sinners and forgiveness
to rebels, Who deals righteously with every living being — You do not repay
them in accord with their evil.* Chazzan — *O God, You taught us to recite the
Thirteen [Attributes of Mercy], so remember for us today the covenant of
these Thirteen, as You made known to the humble one in ancient times, as
it is written: And* HASHEM *descended in a cloud and stood with him there,
and He called out with the Name* HASHEM.

Congregation, then *chazzan:*

And HASHEM *passed before him [Moses] and proclaimed:*

Congregation and *chazzan* (the words in bold type are recited aloud and in unison):

ה' ה' **HASHEM, HASHEM, God, Compassionate and Gracious, Slow
       to anger, and Abundant in Kindness and Truth, Preserver of
kindness for thousands [of generations], Forgiver of iniquity, willful
sin, and error, and Who cleanses.** *May You forgive our iniquities and
our errors and make us Your heritage. Forgive us, our Father, for we have
erred; pardon us, our King, for we have willfully sinned; for You, my
Lord, are good and forgiving and abundantly kind to all who call upon
You.*

PREFATORY VERSES TO SELICHAH 39

אֵלֶיךָ *To You, HASHEM, we have cried; and in the morning our prayer
        will greet You.*[2] *HASHEM, in the morning hear our voice; in the
morning, as we arrange [our prayer] before You and await [Your
answer].*[3] *Our soul [longs] for my Lord, among those who long for
morning, who long for morning.*[4] *The sacrifices God desires are a broken
spirit; O God, You will not despise a heart broken and humbled.*[5]

כְּרַחֵם אָב *As a father has mercy on his children, so, HASHEM, may
            You have mercy on us. Salvation is HASHEM's, upon Your
people is Your blessing, Selah. HASHEM, Master of Legions, is with us, a
stronghold for us is the God of Jacob, Selah. HASHEM, Master of Legions,
praiseworthy is the person who trusts in You. HASHEM, save! May the
King answer us on the day we call.*

---

(1) *Isaiah* 63:17. (2) Cf. *Psalms* 88:14. (3) Cf. 5:4. (4) Cf. 130:6. (5) 51:19.

word לָמָה, *why.* Some lines deviate from this for-   rated over the years did not take the acrostic into
mula, but that is because the changes incorpo-   account.

In some congregations the following two verses are recited responsively — the *chazzan* reciting סְלַח נָא,
and the congregation responding וַיֹּאמֶר. In other congregations these verses are recited silently.

סְלַח נָא לַעֲוֹן הָעָם הַזֶּה כְּגֹדֶל חַסְדֶּךָ, וְכַאֲשֶׁר נָשָׂאתָה לָעָם
הַזֶּה מִמִּצְרַיִם וְעַד הֵנָּה, וְשָׁם נֶאֱמַר:

וַיֹּאמֶר יהוה סָלַחְתִּי כִּדְבָרֶךָ.

All:

הַטֵּה אֱלֹהַי אָזְנְךָ וּשֲׁמָע, פְּקַח עֵינֶיךָ וּרְאֵה שֹׁמְמֹתֵינוּ, וְהָעִיר
אֲשֶׁר נִקְרָא שִׁמְךָ עָלֶיהָ, כִּי לֹא עַל צִדְקוֹתֵינוּ אֲנַחְנוּ
מַפִּילִים תַּחֲנוּנֵינוּ לְפָנֶיךָ, כִּי עַל רַחֲמֶיךָ הָרַבִּים. אֲדֹנָי שְׁמָעָה,
אֲדֹנָי סְלָחָה, אֲדֹנָי הַקְשִׁיבָה, וַעֲשֵׂה אַל תְּאַחַר, לְמַעַנְךָ אֱלֹהַי, כִּי
שִׁמְךָ נִקְרָא עַל עִירְךָ וְעַל עַמֶּךָ.

סְלִיחָה לט (עֲקֵדָה)

This *piyut* should be recited following the punctuation — not the poetic line endings (see commentary).

All:

אֱלֹהֵינוּ וֵאלֹהֵי אֲבוֹתֵינוּ:

מְפַלְטִי* אֵלִי צוּרִי סִתְרִי וּמָגִנִּי,

וְקֶרֶן יִשְׁעִי מִשְׂגַּבִּי[1] בְּיוֹם צַר לִי וְאוֹנִי,

הִשְׁכַּמְתִּי לַחֲלוֹתְךָ מֶלֶךְ רָב. וַאֲנִי   אֵלֶיךָ יהוה שִׁוַּעְתִּי בַבֹּקֶר.[2]

בֹּקֶר רַחֵם תִּזְכֹּר חֶסֶד אַבְרָהָם אָב אֵיתָנִי,

אֲשֶׁר בְּחַרְתּוֹ וְהֶאֱמִין בְּךָ רֹאשׁ לְמַאֲמִינִי,

זְכֹר בְּרִיתוֹ וְהוֹשִׁיעֵנִי מִטֻּמְאָתִי, יהוה

בֹּקֶר תִּשְׁמַע קוֹלִי **בֹּקֶר**.[3]

בֹּקֶר דִּבַּרְתָּ עִמּוֹ, וְנִסִּיתוֹ לְשַׁלֵּם לוֹ מַשְׂכֹּרֶת,

וְכָרוֹת עִמּוֹ הַבְּרִית לִהְיוֹת עִמּוֹ הַבְּרִית לִהְיוֹת לוֹ לְמִשְׁמֶרֶת,

אֲהַבְתּוֹ וּרְצִיתוֹ וְקִבַּלְתּוֹ כִּקְטֹרֶת   סַמִּים בַּבֹּקֶר **בַּבֹּקֶר**.[4]

בֹּקֶר כּוֹכְבוֹ הֵאִיר, כְּחָפַצְתָּ לְהַרְאוֹת צִדְקָתוֹ הַגְּדוֹלָה,

נִסִּיתוֹ בָּעֲשִׂירִי,* וַתֹּאמֶר לוֹ קַח נָא אֶת בִּנְךָ וְאַל תִּכְלָא,

---

אֶ‎**מְפַלְטִי** — *My Rescuer.* During the period
from Erev Rosh Hashanah until Yom Kippur, an
akeidah is added to the *Selichos* service. As the
name implies, an *akeidah* is a *piyut* that describes
עֲקֵדַת יִצְחָק, *the Binding of Isaac* (Genesis ch. 22),
and pleads that, in its merit, the descendants of
Abraham and Isaac be endowed with Divine
mercy and forgiveness.

In this *piyut*, the word בֹּקֶר, *[in the] morning*,
begins and ends each stanza. The initial letters of
the respective second words of each stanza spell
the composer's name, מָרְדְּכַי הָאָרֹךְ, *Mordechai*

HaAruch [the tall (?)]. Only two things are
known about R' Mordechai: He flourished before
1234 when the commentary *Arugas HaBosem*
[which includes this *akeidah*] was written; and
he wrote another *selichah* for *Minchah* of Yom
Kippur which has become part of the Yom Kippur Kattan *Selichos* service. That latter composition is signed *Mordechai ben Shabsi Aruch.*

The stanzas each comprise four lines, three of
which rhyme; the fourth is a Scriptural fragment
ending with the word בֹּקֶר, *morning.* In an unusual departure, in many stanzas the words of the

In some congregations the following two verses are recited responsively — the *chazzan* reciting, *'Forgive, please . . .,'* and the congregation responding, *'And HASHEM said . . .'*
In other congregations these verses are recited silently.

סְלַח נָא *Forgive, please, the iniquity of this people according to the greatness of Your kindness and as You have forgiven this people from Egypt until now, and there it was said:*

And HASHEM said, 'I have forgiven according to your word!'

All:

הַטֵּה *Incline, my God, Your ear, and listen, open Your eyes and see our desolation and that of the city upon which Your Name is proclaimed; for not because of our righteousness do we cast down our supplications before You, rather because of Your abundant compassion. O my Lord, heed; O my Lord, forgive; O my Lord, be attentive and act, do not delay; for Your sake, my God, for Your Name is proclaimed upon Your city and upon Your people.*

SELICHAH 39

All:

Our God and the God of our forefathers:

מ *My Rescuer,* my God, my Rock, my Refuge and my Shield, my Horn of Salvation, my stronghold[1]*
on the day I am troubled and grieving —
I have risen early to pray to You, O great King,
And I — I cry to You, HASHEM, **in the morning.**[2]

ר **In the morning** *remember mercy,*
[for the sake of] Abraham's kindness, my mighty father,
whom You chose, and who believed in You,
the first of my [people's] believers.
Remember his covenant, and save me from my [sins'] defilement —
HASHEM, in the morning hear my voice, **in the morning!**[3]

ד **In the morning** *You spoke with him,*
testing him so as to pay him reward,
and You made the covenant with him to become a guardian to him.
You loved him, and favored him, accepted him
like the incense spices, each morning, each **morning.**[4]

כ **In the morning** *star's light,*
when You desired to show his great righteousness,
You tested him the tenth time,* and said to him,
'Please take your son — do not hold him back —

---

(1) Cf. *Psalms* 18:3. (2) Cf. 88:14. (3) 5:4. (4) Cf. *Exodus* 30:7.

third and fourth lines flow together, with the third line ending in the middle of a thought. Therefore, it is important that this *piyut* be recited according to the punctuation, not the rhyme scheme; otherwise it will not make sense.

נִסִּיתוֹ בַּעֲשִׂירִי — *You tested him the tenth time.* Abraham's faith was tested ten times by God. The ten trials are enumerated in *Avos deR' Nosson*

(33:2): (a) King Nimrod threw him into the fiery furnace (*Genesis* 11:28, see *Rashi* there; see also commentary to *selichah* 31, s.v., מוֹצָא מִכְּשֶׁד); (b) God commanded him to leave his home to travel to an unknown land (*Genesis* 12:1); (c) when he got to that land, there was a hunger and he had to move again (12:10); (d) in Egypt, his wife Sarah was kidnapped by the king (12:15); (e) in order to

עַל אַחַד הֶהָרִים וְהַעֲלֵהוּ שָׁם לְעֹלָה,[1]

אֶת הַכֶּבֶשׂ אֶחָד תַּעֲשֶׂה בַּבֹּקֶר.[2]

בֹּקֶר יִחַד שִׁמְךָ וְשָׁמַע לְקוֹלֶךָ וְהִרְאָה אַהֲבָתוֹ,

וְשָׂשׂ בְּכָל לֵב עַל אִמְרָתְךָ לַעֲשׂוֹתוֹ,

הָאַהֲבָה קִלְקְלָה הַשּׁוּרָה,* וַיָּקָם בְּשִׂמְחָתוֹ,

וַיַּשְׁכֵּם אַבְרָהָם בַּבֹּקֶר.[3]

בֹּקֶר הֵכִינוּ לִבָּם שְׁנֵיהֶם לַעֲשׂוֹת רְצוֹנָךְ, אָיֹם,

הַבֵּן לָקַח עֵצִים וְהָאָב לָקַח מַאֲכֶלֶת, לִשְׁחֹט בְּלִי פִדְיוֹם,

קְרוּאִים וְהוֹלְכִים לְתֻמָּם,[4] וְרָאוּ כְּבוֹדֶךָ בַּיּוֹם

הַשְּׁלִישִׁי בִּהְיוֹת הַבֹּקֶר.[5]

בֹּקֶר אָזַר כְּגִבּוֹר חֲלָצָיו[6] וְלַעֲקֹד בְּנוֹ קָדַם,

וַיִּקַּח מַאֲכֶלֶת לְשָׁחֲטוֹ וְלֹא חָשַׁב אָדָם,*

וַיֹּאמֶר הַיּוֹם אַקְרִיב עוֹלָתִי וְאֶזְרֹק דָּם

זִבְחִי לֹא יָלִין עַד בֹּקֶר.[7]

בֹּקֶר רַחֲמֶיךָ נִכְמְרוּ עַל בֵּן יָחִיד וְעָלָיו זָרְחוּ,

וַיִּקְרָא אֵלָיו מַלְאַךְ יהוה, אֶל הַנַּעַר יָדַיִם אַל יִשְׁלָחוּ,[8]

כִּי בְיִצְחָק יִקָּרֵא לְךָ זָרַע,[9] וְזִכְרוֹ לְדוֹרוֹת הִנִּיחוּ

לָכֶם לְמִשְׁמֶרֶת עַד הַבֹּקֶר.[10]

בֹּקֶר כָּשְׁרוּ וְיָשְׁרוּ וְצִדְקוֹ יָלִיץ בְּעַד עַם אֵלֶיךָ קָרֵב,

וְאֶפְרוֹ תָּמִיד יֵרָאֶה לְפָנֶיךָ לְכַבֵּסָם הֶרֶב,

תִּנָּתֶן לָהֶם נַפְשָׁם בִּשְׁאֵלָתָם,[11] כִּי לְךָ נִכְסָפָה. וּבְעֶרֶב

הִיא בָאָה וּבַבֹּקֶר.[12]

בֹּקֶר קוֹלָם שְׁמַע,[13] וּתְכַפֵּר עֲוֹנוֹתֵיהֶם,

וְעֶרְךָ תְּפִלָּתָם תֵּחָשֵׁב כְּעֶרֶךְ קָרְבְּנוֹתֵיהֶם,

לָקְחוּ[14] וּבָאוּ בְּזִכְרוֹן צִדְקַת אֲבוֹתֵיהֶם,

וְהֵם הֵבִיאוּ אֵלָיו עוֹד נְדָבָה בַּבֹּקֶר בַּבֹּקֶר.[15]

---

save his nephew Lot, he had to fight the armies of four mighty kings (14:13-16); (f) he was told that his children would be slaves in a foreign land (15:13); (g) he was commanded to have a *bris milah* (17:9-14); (h) his wife Sarah was kidnapped by Abimelech, King of Gerar (20:2); (i) he was commanded to send away Hagar and Ishmael (21:10-12); (j) he was commanded to offer his son Isaac as a sacrifice (22:1-2).

הָאַהֲבָה קִלְקְלָה הַשּׁוּרָה — *Love obliterated the line.* The Torah relates that *Abraham rose early in the*

morning and saddled his donkey (Genesis 22:3) on the morning after he was commanded to sacrifice his son. This teaches that love obliterates the line [that distinguishes between servant and master]. Abraham had many servants to saddle his donkey for him, yet his love of God and his desire to fulfill His command immediately, caused Abraham to act the servant and saddle his donkey on his own. The same lesson is taught by the verse, *Joseph [himself] harnessed his chariot* (ibid. 46:29), when he went to meet his father.

on one of the mountains, and offer him there as an olah-offering.[1]
You shall prepare the one sheep **in the morning.**[2]

In the morning he showed that Your Name is One;
he obeyed Your order and demonstrated his love.
He rejoiced whole-heartedly over Your word, to fulfill it.
Love obliterated the line,* and he rose in his joy;
Abraham arose early **in the morning.**[3]

ה **In the morning** the two prepared themselves to do Your will,
O Awesome One.
The son took wood, and the father took a knife,
[determined] to slaughter without [even thinking of] redemption.
Summoned, they went whole-heartedly,[4] and saw Your glory
on the third day when came **the morning.**[5]

א **In the morning** Abraham girded his loins like a warrior[6]
and went early to bind his son.
He took up the knife to slaughter him, and he did not think a man.*
He said, 'Today I will offer my olah and throw its blood [on the altar];
my sacrifice will not rest until **the morning.**'[7]

ר **In the morning** Your mercy was aroused for the only son's sake,
and it shone upon him,
and the angel of HASHEM called to Abraham,
'Do not put [your] hands out towards the boy,[8]
for through Isaac will offspring be considered yours.[9]
And his remembrance shall you set for [all generations],
that it be unto you a safe-keeping until [Redemption's] **morning.**'[10]

כ **In the morning** let his [Isaac's] worth, his uprightness,
his righteousness, speak for the people that approached You,
and let his ashes always appear before You,
that You may cleanse them thoroughly [of their sins].
Let their soul be given them as their request,[11] since it longs for You,
and in the evening it comes [to You in prayer], and **in the morning.**[12]

In the morning hear their voice[13] and atone for their iniquities;
let their ordered prayers be reckoned as the order of their sacrifices.
They have taken [words of prayer][14] and come,
with the remembrance of their fathers' righteousness,
And they bring another voluntary offering
each morning, each **morning.**[15]

---

(1) *Genesis* 22:2. (2) *Numbers* 28:4. (3) *Genesis* 22:3. (4) *II Samuel* 15:11. (5) Cf. *Exodus* 19:16. (6) Cf. *Job* 38:3. (7) Cf. *Exodus* 23:18; 34:25. (8) Cf. *Genesis* 22:11-12. (9) 21:12. (10) *Exodus* 16:23. (11) Cf. *Esther* 7:3. (12) 2:14. (13) Cf. *Psalms* 5:4. (14) Cf. *Hosea* 14:3. (15) *Exodus* 36:3

Conversely, hatred also obliterates the line, for we find that [Pharaoh] harnessed his own chariot (Exodus 14:6) when he pursued Israel; and Balaam arose early in the morning and saddled his own donkey (Numbers 22:21) when he set out to curse Israel (Bereishis Rabbah 55:8).

וְלֹא חָשַׁב אָדָם — *And he did not think a man.* The translation of this line has purposely been left

ambiguous and arcane. The *paytan* may have meant any of three things with these words. According to many commentaries, Abraham overcame his paternal instinct to spare his son by thinking of Isaac not as a person, but as an animal to be used in God's service. This view is difficult to accept. For one, God commanded Abraham to sacrifice 'your son, your only son, whom

❖ **בְּקֶר** תֵּפֶן אֵלֵינוּ לְרַחֲמֶנוּ, וְרַחֲמֶיךָ עָלֵינוּ יְכָמֶרוּ,
וְתַשְׁלִיךְ בִּמְצֻלוֹת יָם כָּל חַטֹּאתֵינוּ¹ וְלֹא יִזָכְרוּ,
צוּר הַעֲבֵר עֲוֹנֵנוּ מִלְּפָנֶיךָ, וְלֹא יַשְׁאִירוּ   מִמֶּנּוּ עַד **בְּקֶר**.²

All, while standing:

אֵל מֶלֶךְ יוֹשֵׁב עַל כִּסֵּא רַחֲמִים מִתְנַהֵג בַּחֲסִידוּת, מוֹחֵל
עֲוֹנוֹת עַמּוֹ, מַעֲבִיר רִאשׁוֹן רִאשׁוֹן, מַרְבֶּה מְחִילָה
לְחַטָּאִים וּסְלִיחָה לְפוֹשְׁעִים, עֹשֶׂה צְדָקוֹת עִם כָּל בָּשָׂר וָרוּחַ,
לֹא כְרָעָתָם תִּגְמוֹל. ❖ אֵל הוֹרֵיתָ לָנוּ לוֹמַר שְׁלֹשׁ עֶשְׂרֵה, וּזְכוֹר
לָנוּ הַיּוֹם בְּרִית שְׁלֹשׁ עֶשְׂרֵה, כְּמוֹ שֶׁהוֹדַעְתָּ לֶעָנָיו מִקֶּדֶם, כְּמוֹ
שֶׁכָּתוּב, וַיֵּרֶד יהוה בֶּעָנָן וַיִּתְיַצֵּב עִמּוֹ שָׁם, וַיִּקְרָא בְשֵׁם יהוה.

Congregation, then chazzan:

וַיַּעֲבֹר יהוה עַל פָּנָיו וַיִּקְרָא:

Congregation and chazzan (the words in bold type are recited aloud and in unison):

יהוה, יהוה, אֵל, רַחוּם, וְחַנּוּן, אֶרֶךְ אַפַּיִם, **וְרַב חֶסֶד, וֶאֱמֶת,
נֹצֵר חֶסֶד לָאֲלָפִים, נֹשֵׂא עָוֹן, וָפֶשַׁע, וְחַטָּאָה,
וְנַקֵּה.** וְסָלַחְתָּ לַעֲוֹנֵנוּ וּלְחַטָּאתֵנוּ וּנְחַלְתָּנוּ. סְלַח לָנוּ אָבִינוּ כִּי
חָטָאנוּ, מְחַל לָנוּ מַלְכֵּנוּ כִּי פָשָׁעְנוּ. כִּי אַתָּה אֲדֹנָי טוֹב וְסַלָּח,
וְרַב חֶסֶד לְכָל קֹרְאֶיךָ.

פסוקי הקדמה לסליחה מ

THE ARK IS OPENED.

Each of the following verses is recited by the chazzan, then repeated by the congregation.

אַל תָּבוֹא בְּמִשְׁפָּט עִמָּנוּ,* כִּי לֹא יִצְדַּק לְפָנֶיךָ כָל חָי.³
וְהוּא **יִשְׁפֹּט** תֵּבֵל בְּצֶדֶק, וּלְאֻמִּים בְּמֵישָׁרִים.⁴
צֶדֶק **וּמִשְׁפָּט** מְכוֹן כִּסְאֶךָ, חֶסֶד וֶאֱמֶת יְקַדְּמוּ פָנֶיךָ.⁵
מִלְּפָנֶיךָ **מִשְׁפָּטֵנוּ** יֵצֵא, עֵינֶיךָ תֶּחֱזֶינָה מֵישָׁרִים.⁶
וְתוֹצִיא כָאוֹר צִדְקֵנוּ, **וּמִשְׁפָּטֵנוּ** כַּצָּהֳרָיִם.⁷
לְמִשְׁפָּטֶיךָ עָמְדוּ הַיּוֹם, כִּי הַכֹּל עֲבָדֶיךָ.⁸
כִּי יהוה **שֹׁפְטֵנוּ**, יהוה מְחֹקְקֵנוּ, יהוה מַלְכֵּנוּ, הוּא יוֹשִׁיעֵנוּ.⁹
הִנָּשֵׂא **שֹׁפֵט** הָאָרֶץ, הָשֵׁב גְּמוּל עַל גֵּאִים.¹⁰

---

you love, Isaac' (Genesis 22:2). By imagining Isaac to be an animal, or anything less than 'your son, your only son . . . ,' Abraham would, in effect, fail the test placed before him. Another problem is that if this view is correct, the phrase should have read אָדָם חָשַׁב לֹא, he did not think him a man, which would retain the meter while being more explicit.

The two other possible interpretations are: *No man thought* that Abraham would do such a thing; and, *He [Abraham] did not think of what any other man* would say regarding what he was doing.

אַל תָּבוֹא בְּמִשְׁפָּט עִמָּנוּ ﹖— *Do not enter into strict judgment with us.* Although *pizmonim* are not usually preceded by Scriptural verses as are

Chazzan — **In the morning** *turn towards us with mercy —*
let Your mercy be stirred up on our behalf;
and may You throw all our sins into the sea's depths,[1]
that they be not remembered.
O Rock, expel our iniquities from Your presence,
and let none of them remain until **the morning.**[2]

All, while standing:

אֵל מֶלֶךְ O God, King Who sits on the throne of mercy; Who acts with kindness, pardons the iniquities of His people, removes [sins] one by one, increasingly grants pardon to careless sinners and forgiveness to rebels, Who deals righteously with every living being — You do not repay them in accord with their evil. *Chazzan* — O God, You taught us to recite the Thirteen [Attributes of Mercy], so remember for us today the covenant of these Thirteen, as You made known to the humble one in ancient times, as it is written: And HASHEM descended in a cloud and stood with him there, and He called out with the Name HASHEM.

Congregation, then *chazzan*:

And HASHEM passed before him [Moses] and proclaimed:

Congregation and *chazzan* (the words in bold type are recited aloud and in unison):

ה' ה' HASHEM, HASHEM, God, Compassionate and Gracious, Slow to anger, and Abundant in Kindness and Truth, Preserver of kindness for thousands [of generations], Forgiver of iniquity, willful sin, and error, and Who cleanses.** May You forgive our iniquities and our errors and make us Your heritage. Forgive us, our Father, for we have erred; pardon us, our King, for we have willfully sinned; for You, my Lord, are good and forgiving and abundantly kind to all who call upon You.

PREFATORY VERSES TO SELICHAH 40
THE ARK IS OPENED.

Each of the following verses is recited by the *chazzan*, then repeated by the congregation.

אַל תָּבוֹא Do not enter into strict **judgment** with us,* for no living creature would be innocent before You.[3]
He will **judge** the world in righteousness and nations in uprightness.[4]
Righteousness and **justice** form the foundation of Your throne;
kindness and truth precede Your countenance.[5]
May our **judgment** go forth from before You,
and Your eyes behold uprighteousness.[6]
And may You reveal our righteousness like a light,
our **judgment** at high noon.[7]
They stand to [receive] Your **judgment** today, for all are Your servants.[8]
For HASHEM is our **Judge,** HASHEM is our Law-giver,
HASHEM is our King, He will save us.[9]
Be exalted, **Judge** of the earth; render recompense to the haughty.[10]

(1) Cf. *Micah* 7:19. (2) *Numbers* 9:12. (3) Cf. *Psalms* 143:2. (4) Cf. 9:9. (5) 89:15.
(6) Cf. 17:2. (7) Cf. 37:6. (8) 119:91. (9) *Isaiah* 33:22. (10) *Psalms* 94:2.

other *selichos*, an exception is made here and, not only are verses recited, they are recited re-

sponsively, and before the open Ark. Since the theme of the *pizmon* is the judgment that will

חָלִילָה לְּךָ מֵעֲשֹת כַּדָּבָר הַזֶּה, לְהָמִית צַדִּיק עִם רָשָׁע, וְהָיָה
כַצַּדִּיק כָּרָשָׁע, חָלִלָה לָּךְ, הֲשֹפֵט כָּל הָאָרֶץ לֹא יַעֲשֶׂה מִשְׁפָּט.[1]

IN SOME CONGREGATIONS THE ARK IS CLOSED AT THIS POINT.

סליחה מ (פזמון)

Chazzan, then congregation:

שֹפֵט כָּל הָאָרֶץ,[2]* וְאַתָּה בַּמִּשְׁפָּט יַעֲמִיד,[3]
נָא חַיִּים וָחֶסֶד, עַל עַם עָנִי תַּצְמִיד,
אֶת תְּפִלַּת הַשַּׁחַר, בִּמְקוֹם עוֹלָה* תַּעֲמִיד,
כְּעוֹלַת הַבֹּקֶר, אֲשֶׁר לְעוֹלַת הַתָּמִיד.[4]

Congregation, then chazzan:

לוֹבֵשׁ צְדָקָה וּמַעֲטֶה,לְךָ לְבַד הַיִּתְרוֹן,
אִם אֵין בָּנוּ מַעֲשִׂים, זָכְרָה יִשְׁנֵי חֶבְרוֹן,[5]
וְהֵם יַעֲלוּ לְזִכָּרוֹן לִפְנֵי יהוה תָּמִיד,[6]
כְּעוֹלַת הַבֹּקֶר, אֲשֶׁר לְעוֹלַת הַתָּמִיד.

Congregation, then chazzan:

מַטֶּה כְּלַפֵּי חֶסֶד, לְהַטּוֹת אִישׁ לִתְחִיָּה,
עַמְּךָ לְחֶסֶד הַטֶּה, גְּמֹל נָא עָלָיו וְחָיָה,
כְּתֹב תָּו חַיִּים,[7] וְהָיָה עַל מִצְחוֹ תָּמִיד,[8]
כְּעוֹלַת הַבֹּקֶר, אֲשֶׁר לְעוֹלַת הַתָּמִיד.

Congregation, then chazzan:

הֵטִיבָה בִרְצוֹנְךָ אֶת צִיּוֹן,[9] עִיר קָדֹשַׁי,
וְנָתַתָּ יָד וָשֵׁם בְּבֵיתְךָ[10] לְמִקְדָּשַׁי,
וַעֲרִיכַת נֵר לְבֶן יִשַׁי,[11] לְהַעֲלוֹת נֵר תָּמִיד,[12]
כְּעוֹלַת הַבֹּקֶר, אֲשֶׁר לְעוֹלַת הַתָּמִיד.

Congregation, then chazzan:

חִזְקוּ וְאִמְצוּ לְבַבְכֶם,[13] עַמִּי בְּאֵל מָעֻזּוֹ,
עֲדוֹתָיו כִּי תִנְצֹרוּ, גַּם אֵת זוֹ לְעֻמַּת זוֹ,
יְכַפֵּר בַּעַד חַטֹּאתֵיכֶם, וְיִזְכֹּר רַחֵם בְּרָגְזוֹ,[14]
דִּרְשׁוּ יהוה וְעֻזּוֹ, בַּקְּשׁוּ פָנָיו תָּמִיד,[15]
כְּעוֹלַת הַבֹּקֶר, אֲשֶׁר לְעוֹלַת הַתָּמִיד.

THE ARK IS CLOSED.

---

take place on Rosh Hashanah, each of the nine
verses contains some form of the root שפט, *to
judge.*

שֹפֵט כָּל הָאָרֶץ — *Judge of all the earth.*
Opinions vary widely regarding the identity of
the author of this *selichah*, whose name שְׁלֹמֹה,

*It would be sacrilege for You to do such a thing, to slay the righteous along with the wicked, letting the righteous be like the wicked; it would be sacrilege for You; shall the **Judge** of all the earth not do **justice?**[1]*

IN SOME CONGREGATIONS THE ARK IS CLOSED AT THIS POINT.

SELICHAH 40

Chazzan, then congregation:

שׁוֹפֵט *Judge of all the earth,*[2] Who sets it in order through justice,[3]*
    Please conjoin life and kindness upon the afflicted nation.
Set the morning prayer in place of an olah-offering;*
    [let it be] like the morning olah which is a perpetual olah.[4]

ל *You Who garb Yourself in a garment of righteousness,*
    You alone have lofty power.
If we have no good deeds [to our merit],
    then remember those who sleep in Hebron,[5]
and they will ascend as a reminder before HASHEM perpetually,[6]
    like the morning olah which is a perpetual olah.

Congregation, then chazzan:

מ *You Who tip [the scales] towards kindness,*
    tipping man towards [renewed] life,
tip Your people's scales towards kindness;
    please grant them that they may live.
Inscribe the sign of life,[7] let it be on [the people's] forehead perpetually,[8]
    like the morning olah which is a perpetual olah.

Congregation, then chazzan:

ה *In Your favor do good unto Zion,[9] my Holy City,*
    and make a monument and memorial in Your House[10] for my holy ones;
    and a prepared lamp for Jesse's son [the Messiah],[11]
    to kindle a lamp perpetually,[12]
    like the morning olah which is a perpetual olah.

Congregation, then chazzan:

Strengthen and encourage your hearts, my people,[13]
    whose fortress is God,
and when you keep His teachings, then measure for measure
He will atone for your sins and remember mercy amidst His rage.[14]
Seek HASHEM and His might, search for His presence perpetually,[15]
    like the morning olah which is a perpetual olah.

THE ARK IS CLOSED.

---

(1) *Genesis* 18:25. (2) Cf. 18:25. (3) Cf. *Proverbs* 29:4. (4) Cf. *Numbers* 28:23. (5) See commentary to *selichah* 28, s.v., יְשֵׁנֵי מַכְפֵּל. (6) *Exodus* 28:29. (7) See commentary to *selichah* 17, s.v., תָּוֵי, and *selichah* 22, s.v., תָּגֵן חֲרוּת. (8) *Exodus* 28:38. (9) *Psalms* 51:20. (10) Cf. *Isaiah* 56:5. (11) Cf. *Psalms* 132:17. (12) *Exodus* 27:20. (13) Cf. *Psalms* 31:25. (14) Cf. *Habakkuk* 3:2. (15) *Psalms* 105:4.

Shlomo, appears in the acrostic. The opening and closing stanzas each contain four lines, while the three middle stanzas have three lines each. Apparently some lines were lost over the centuries, and, indeed, the Yemenite rite has additional lines in this *selichah*.

תְּפִלַּת הַשַּׁחַר בְּמְקוֹם עוֹלָה — *The morning prayer in place of an olah-offering.* The Talmud records a dispute regarding the origin of the three daily prayers. According to R' Yose bar R' Chanina, the Patriarchs Abraham, Isaac and Jacob, respectively, instituted the morning, afternoon and

All, while standing:

אֵל מֶלֶךְ יוֹשֵׁב עַל כִּסֵּא רַחֲמִים מִתְנַהֵג בַּחֲסִידוּת, מוֹחֵל
עֲוֹנוֹת עַמּוֹ, מַעֲבִיר רִאשׁוֹן רִאשׁוֹן, מַרְבֶּה מְחִילָה
לַחַטָּאִים וּסְלִיחָה לַפּוֹשְׁעִים, עֹשֶׂה צְדָקוֹת עִם כָּל בָּשָׂר וָרוּחַ,
לֹא כְרָעָתָם תִּגְמוֹל. אֵל הוֹרֵיתָ לָנוּ לוֹמַר שְׁלֹשׁ עֶשְׂרֵה, וּזְכוֹר
לָנוּ הַיּוֹם בְּרִית שְׁלֹשׁ עֶשְׂרֵה, כְּמוֹ שֶׁהוֹדַעְתָּ לֶעָנָיו מִקֶּדֶם, כְּמוֹ
שֶׁכָּתוּב, וַיֵּרֶד יהוה בֶּעָנָן וַיִּתְיַצֵּב עִמּוֹ שָׁם, וַיִּקְרָא בְשֵׁם יהוה.

Congregation, then *chazzan:*

וַיַּעֲבֹר יהוה עַל פָּנָיו וַיִּקְרָא:

Congregation and *chazzan* (the words in bold type are recited aloud and in unison):

יהוה, יהוה, אֵל, רַחוּם, וְחַנּוּן, אֶרֶךְ אַפַּיִם, **וְרַב חֶסֶד, וֶאֱמֶת,
נֹצֵר חֶסֶד לָאֲלָפִים, נֹשֵׂא עָוֹן, וָפֶשַׁע, וְחַטָּאָה,**
וְנַקֵּה. וְסָלַחְתָּ לַעֲוֹנֵנוּ וּלְחַטָּאתֵנוּ וּנְחַלְתָּנוּ. סְלַח לָנוּ אָבִינוּ כִּי
חָטָאנוּ, מְחַל לָנוּ מַלְכֵּנוּ כִּי פָשָׁעְנוּ. כִּי אַתָּה אֲדֹנָי טוֹב וְסַלָּח,
וְרַב חֶסֶד לְכָל קֹרְאֶיךָ.

All:

אַל תִּזְכָּר לָנוּ עֲוֹנוֹת רִאשׁוֹנִים, מַהֵר יְקַדְּמוּנוּ רַחֲמֶיךָ, כִּי
דַלּוֹנוּ מְאֹד.[1] חַטֹּאת נְעוּרֵינוּ וּפְשָׁעֵינוּ אַל תִּזְכּוֹר,
כְּחַסְדְּךָ זְכָר לָנוּ אַתָּה, לְמַעַן טוּבְךָ יהוה.[2]

זְכֹר רַחֲמֶיךָ יהוה וַחֲסָדֶיךָ, כִּי מֵעוֹלָם הֵמָּה.[3] זָכְרֵנוּ יהוה
בִּרְצוֹן עַמֶּךָ, פָּקְדֵנוּ בִּישׁוּעָתֶךָ.[4] זְכֹר עֲדָתְךָ
קָנִיתָ קֶּדֶם, גָּאַלְתָּ שֵׁבֶט נַחֲלָתֶךָ, הַר צִיּוֹן זֶה שָׁכַנְתָּ בּוֹ.[5] זְכֹר
יהוה חִבַּת יְרוּשָׁלָיִם, אַהֲבַת צִיּוֹן אַל תִּשְׁכַּח לָנֶצַח.[6] אַתָּה
תָקוּם תְּרַחֵם צִיּוֹן, כִּי עֵת לְחֶנְנָהּ כִּי בָא מוֹעֵד.[7] זְכֹר יהוה
לִבְנֵי אֱדוֹם אֵת יוֹם יְרוּשָׁלָיִם, הָאֹמְרִים עָרוּ עָרוּ עַד הַיְסוֹד
בָּהּ.[8] זְכֹר לְאַבְרָהָם לְיִצְחָק וּלְיִשְׂרָאֵל עֲבָדֶיךָ אֲשֶׁר נִשְׁבַּעְתָּ
לָהֶם בָּךְ, וַתְּדַבֵּר אֲלֵהֶם, אַרְבֶּה אֶת זַרְעֲכֶם כְּכוֹכְבֵי הַשָּׁמָיִם,
וְכָל הָאָרֶץ הַזֹּאת אֲשֶׁר אָמַרְתִּי אֶתֵּן לְזַרְעֲכֶם, וְנָחֲלוּ לְעוֹלָם.[9]

---

nighttime prayers. According to R' Yehoshua ben Levi, the morning prayer was enacted in place of the morning *olah*-offering (see below); the afternoon prayer, in place of the afternoon *olah;* and the nighttime prayer, in place of the organs and fats of the previous day's offerings, which were usually placed on the Altar fire at night (*Berachos* 26b).

The *olah* was an animal offering that was burnt in its entirety on the Altar. No parts of it were eaten either by the bringer or by the *Kohanim.* The Torah ordained that two lambs be offered daily, one each morning, one each afternoon, as the first and last Altar offerings of the day. These are called the תָּמִיד [*tamid*], *continual* or *perpetual* offerings (see *Numbers*

All, while standing:

אֵל מֶלֶךְ O God, King Who sits on the throne of mercy; Who acts with kindness, pardons the iniquities of His people, removes [sins] one by one, increasingly grants pardon to careless sinners and forgiveness to rebels, Who deals righteously with every living being — You do not repay them in accord with their evil. Chazzan — O God, You taught us to recite the Thirteen [Attributes of Mercy], so remember for us today the covenant of these Thirteen, as You made known to the humble one in ancient times, as it is written: And HASHEM descended in a cloud and stood with him there, and He called out with the Name HASHEM.

Congregation, then chazzan:

And HASHEM passed before him [Moses] and proclaimed:

Congregation and chazzan (the words in bold type are recited aloud and in unison):

ה׳ ה׳ HASHEM, HASHEM, God, Compassionate and Gracious, Slow to anger, and Abundant in Kindness and Truth, Preserver of kindness for thousands [of generations], Forgiver of iniquity, willful sin, and error, and Who cleanses. May You forgive our iniquities and our errors and make us Your heritage. Forgive us, our Father, for we have erred; pardon us, our King, for we have willfully sinned; for You, my Lord, are good and forgiving and abundantly kind to all who call upon You.

All:

אַל תִּזְכָּר Do not recall against us the iniquities of the ancients; speedily — let Your mercy come to meet us for we have fallen very low.[1] Remember not the sins of our youth and our rebellions; may You remember for us [the deeds] worthy of Your kindness, because of Your goodness, HASHEM.[2]

זְכוֹר רַחֲמֶיךָ Remember Your mercies, O HASHEM, and Your kindnesses, for they are from the beginning of the world.[3] Remember us, HASHEM, when You show Your people favor and recall us with Your salvation.[4] Remember Your congregation that You acquired of old, that You redeemed the tribe of Your heritage, and this Mount Zion where You dwelled.[5] Remember, O HASHEM, the affection of Jerusalem, may You never forget the love of Zion.[6] You will arise and show Zion mercy, for it is the time to be gracious to her, for the appointed time will have come.[7] Remember, HASHEM, for the offspring of Edom, the day of Jerusalem — for those who said: 'Destroy! Destroy to its very foundation!'[8] Remember Abraham, Isaac, and Israel, Your servants, to whom You swore by Your Being, saying, 'I shall increase your offspring like the stars of the heavens; and this entire land of which I spoke I will give to your offspring and they will inherit it forever.'[9]

---

(1) Psalms 79:8. (2) Cf. 25:7. (3) 25:6. (4) Cf. 106:4. (5) 74:2.
(6) This is not a Scriptural verse. (7) Psalms 102:14. (8) 137:7. (9) Exodus 32:13.

28:1-8). The constantly repeated theme of this selichah is that some aspect of Israel's existence be constantly before God. In the respective verses these aspects are: their prayers; the Patriarchs and Matriarchs; the sign of life; the Messiah; and those who seek God's Presence.

❖ זְכֹר לַעֲבָדֶיךָ לְאַבְרָהָם לְיִצְחָק וּלְיַעֲקֹב, אַל תֵּפֶן אֶל קְשִׁי הָעָם
הַזֶּה וְאֶל רִשְׁעוֹ וְאֶל חַטָּאתוֹ.[1]

Chazzan, then congregation:

אַל נָא תָשֵׁת עָלֵינוּ חַטָּאת, אֲשֶׁר נוֹאַלְנוּ וַאֲשֶׁר חָטָאנוּ.[2]

Chazzan, then congregation:

חָטָאנוּ צוּרֵנוּ, סְלַח לָנוּ יוֹצְרֵנוּ.

סְלִיחָה מא (חטאנו)

All:

אֵלֶיךָ צוּרִי* כַּפֵּי שִׁטַּחְתִּי,[3]   וְגָדֵל וְגָבַהּ לֵב הִנַּחְתִּי,

אָכֵן רוּחַ נִשְׁבָּרָה זָבַחְתִּי,[4]   וַאֲנִי בְּחַסְדְּךָ **בָטַחְתִּי**.[5]

בָטַחְתִּי בָּךְ וְלֹא בְזֵין מִכְּרָזֶל,*   לְהָרֵג כְּנִמְסַרְתִּי רַב וּבַרְזֶל,*

בַּקֵּשׁ יוֹנַת אֵלֶם*[6] וְגוֹזָל,   וְהָשֵׁיב אֶת הַגְּזֵלָה אֲשֶׁר **גָּזָל**.[7]

חָטָאנוּ צוּרֵנוּ, סְלַח לָנוּ יוֹצְרֵנוּ.

גָּזַל וְאִבַּד חֲסִידֵי עֶלְיוֹן וִישִׁישָׁיו,

וְהֶחֱרִיב בֵּיתוֹ וְחִלֵּל מִקְדָּשׁ וְקָדְשָׁיו,

וְגָדֵר הַפָּרְכֶת* וְהָרַג נְבִיאָיו וּקְדוֹשָׁיו,   זֶה דוֹר **דּוֹרְשָׁיו**.[8]

דּוֹרְשָׁיו דָּמָם יְהִי כֻפַּר וּפִדְיוֹם,   לִפְנֵי כִסֵּא כְבוֹדְךָ, אָיֹם,

דְּבוּקִים אַחֲרֶיךָ כִּצְמָדִים וּתְיוֹם,   כִּי עָלֶיךָ הֹרַגְנוּ כָל **הַיּוֹם**.[9]

חָטָאנוּ צוּרֵנוּ, סְלַח לָנוּ יוֹצְרֵנוּ.

הַיּוֹם* הַזֶּה* כַּמָּה רְבָבוֹת נָפְלוּ מֵעַמֶּךָ,

וּמָסְרוּ עַצְמָם עַל יִחוּד שְׁמֶךָ,

אֵלֶיךָ צוּרִי — *To You, my Rock.* Beginning with Erev Rosh Hashanah and continuing until the day before Erev Yom Kippur, a *selichah* with the refrain, חָטָאנוּ צוּרֵנוּ סְלַח לָנוּ יוֹצְרֵנוּ, *We have sinned, our Rock! Forgive us, our Molder!* is recited after the *pizmon*. A *selichah* of this genre is appropriately called a *chatanu*. An intricately designed scheme runs through this *selichah*. Not only do the initial letters of the respective stanzas form the *aleph-beis*, but the first word of each stanza is the same as the last word of the stanza before. Such an arrangement is called a שִׁרְשׁוּר, *shirshur*, or chain. A second *aleph-beis* is formed by the acrostic of the respective third lines. Some editions ascribe this work to an otherwise unknown *paytan* named אֵלִיָּהוּ, *Eliyahu* (see last footnote of this *selichah*).

מִכְּרָזֶל — *Well-made weapons.* One commentary

states that this word is defined in the ancient talmudic dictionary *Aruch* (by R' Nassan ben Yechiel of Rome, 1101) as מְתֻקָּן, *properly made* or *perfected*. However, in the *Aruch* that definition appears under the heading מקרזלות with a ק not a כ. Nevertheless, the letters כ and ק are sometimes interchanged. (See next comment.)

רַב וּבַרְזֶל — *Mentor and disciple* [lit., *teacher and iron*]. The Talmud (*Taanis* 4a) teaches that a *talmid chacham*, literally, *a wise student*, must be hard as iron [in maintaining his principles]. Thus, the *paytan* calls the student בַּרְזֶל, *iron.*

According to some manuscript editions of *Selichos*, the words מִכְּרָזֶל and בַּרְזֶל, discussed in this and the preceding comment, should read מְכֻרְזָל and וְכָרְזָל respectively. If so, the phrase זֵין מְכֻרְזָל means *iron weapon;* and רַב וְכָרְזָל means

Chazzan — Remember for Your servants, for Abraham, for Isaac, and for Jacob; ignore the stubbornness of this people, its wickedness and its sinfulness.[1]

Chazzan, then congregation:
Please, do not reckon for us a sin,
what we have done foolishly and what we have sinned.[2]

Chazzan, then congregation:
We have erred, our Rock! Forgive us, our Molder!

SELICHAH 41

All:

א To You, my Rock,* I stretch out my hands,[3]
conceit and arrogance have I laid aside.

א I have truly offered the sacrifice of a broken spirit,[4]
and as for me — In Your kindness **I have trust.**[5]

ב **I have trust** in You, and not in well-made weapons,*
[even] when I was delivered to death, mentor and disciple* together.

ב Seek out [Israel,] the silent fledgling dove,*[6]
and [Edom] will return the stolen [land] that **he robbed.**[7]

> We have sinned, our Rock! Forgive us, our Molder.

ג **He robbed** and massacred the Exalted's pious ones and His elders,
and laid waste His house, defiling the Sanctuary and its holy things;

ג he slashed the Curtain* and slew His prophets and holy men,
[all] that [in] a generation of **those who sought Him.**[8]

ד **Those who sought Him** — may their blood be atonement
and redemption before Your Throne of Glory, O Awesome One;

ד [For they] cleave after You like inseparable pairs,
and we are killed for Your sake all **the day.**[9]

> We have sinned, our Rock! Forgive us, our Molder.

ה **This day,*** many myriads have fallen from Your people,
they delivered themselves [to death] for the Oneness of Your Name.

---

(1) *Deuteronomy* 9:27. (2) *Numbers* 12:11. (3) Cf. *Psalms* 88:10. (4) Cf. 51:19.
(5) 13:6. (6) Cf. 56:1. (7) *Leviticus* 5:23. (8) *Psalms* 24:6. (9) 44:23.

literally *mentor and disciple,* for the *Aruch* defines כרול as *a shepherd-in-training.*

יוֹנַת אֵלֶם — *[Israel,] the silent . . . dove. Targum* (to *Psalms* 56:1) paraphrases the phrase יוֹנַת אֵלֶם רְחֹקִים [lit., *the distant dove of silence*]: The congregation of Israel which is compared to a silent dove, when they are far from their [Holy] City, yet repent and praise the Master of the Universe.

וְגִדֵּר הַפָּרֶכֶת — *He slashed the Curtain.*
The Talmud (*Gittin* 56b) relates that when Titus captured and entered the Second Temple, he cursed and blasphemed the God of Israel. He dragged a harlot into the Holy of Holies and unrolled a sacred Torah scroll and committed unspeakably lewd acts upon it. He then unsheathed his sword (already bloodied with the

blood of countless Jewish victims) and slashed the פָּרֶכֶת, *Curtain* (that separated the Sanctuary from the Holy of Holies), to shreds. A miracle occurred and blood began to flow from the curtain. Thus Titus imagined that he had actually pieced and slain God Himself!

הַיּוֹם הַזֶּה — *This day.* This phrase seems to refer to Erev Rosh Hashanah. However, the stich continues, *many myriads have fallen from Your people,* yet no major pogrom is known to have taken place on Erev Rosh Hashanah. Thus, the stich should be understood as if it read, עַד הַיּוֹם הַזֶּה, *until this day.*

Alternatively, it means *in this day and age.* If so, the phrase refers to the ever-recurring persecutions and pogroms, and is appropriate to be recited in every generation.

הוֹצֵא לְמַעֲנָם לָאוֹר מִשְׁפָּטָם[1] וְדִינָם מִמְּרוֹמֶיךָ,

וְשָׁמַעְתָּ אֶל תְּחִנַּת עֲבָדֶיךָ וְעַמֶּךָ.[2]

וְעַמְּךָ שׁוֹלְלִים וּבוֹזְזִים וְחֵילָם יָבֹזּוּ,[3]

וּשְׂמֵחִים לְמַחְתָּה וּלְאֵיד יַעֲלֹזוּ,

וּמִי נָתַן לִמְשִׁסָּה יַעֲקֹב, בְּקוֹל יַכְרִיזוּ, הֲלוֹא יהוה זוּ.[4]

חָטָאנוּ צוּרֵנוּ, סְלַח לָנוּ יוֹצְרֵנוּ.

זוּ חֵטְא גָּרַם וְרוֹדֵף חִבַּטְנוּ, סָרַנוּ מִנֵּי דֶרֶךְ[5] וְכַסּוֹרֵרָה[6] בָּעַטְנוּ,

זָעַמְנוּ בְמִדָּה וּכְרֹעַ מַעֲלָלֵינוּ לָעַטְנוּ, לַיהוה אֱלֹהֵינוּ חָטָאנוּ.[7]

חָטָאנוּ וְהִנֵּנוּ בְּאַשְׁמָה גְדוֹלָה,[8] לְלַעַג וָקֶלֶס נְתוּנִים בַּגּוֹלָה,

חֲזוֹן הַמִּקְרָא עָלֵינוּ עָלָה, הִנֵּה יהוה מְטַלְטֶלְךָ טַלְטֵלָה.[9]

חָטָאנוּ צוּרֵנוּ, סְלַח לָנוּ יוֹצְרֵנוּ.

טַלְטֵלָה וְעִצָּבוֹן כִּי גָבְרוּ וְעָצְמוּ, זֹאבֵי עֲרָבוֹת[10] אָבְלוּ הָמָמוּ,

טְרָפוּנוּ וְלַבֹּקֶר לֹא גָרֵמוּ,[11] אַכְזָרִים הֵמָּה וְלֹא יְרַחֵמוּ.[12]

יְרַחֵמוּ מִשָּׁמַיִם עֲשׂוֹת נֵס, וְיַצִּיל עַמּוֹ מִיַּד חָזָק וּמֵאַנֵּס,

יְדִידוּת מִשְׁכְּנוֹתָיו[13] לְאָרֵךְ וְרֹחַב יְפַרְנֵס,

כְּתָרֵן בְּרֹאשׁ הָהָר וְכַנֵּס.[14] חָטָאנוּ צוּרֵנוּ, סְלַח לָנוּ יוֹצְרֵנוּ.

כַּנֵּס נוֹתְרָה שְׁאֵרִית נַחֲלָתוֹ, בְּעָלוּנוּ אֲדוֹנִים זוּלָתוֹ,[15]

בָּעֵת יֵאָמֵר לְיַעֲקֹב[16] בֶּן מְחִילָתוֹ, בָּחַר לוֹ יָהּ יִשְׂרָאֵל לִסְגֻלָּתוֹ.[17]

לִסְגֻלָּתוֹ אַל יְהִי דָוֶה וְשָׁמֵם, כִּימֵי קֶדֶם חָרָבוֹתַי יְקוֹמֵם,[18]

לְמַלְכִּי יִתֶּן עֹז וִירוֹמֵם,[19] מַשְׁפִּיל אַף מְרוֹמֵם.[20]

חָטָאנוּ צוּרֵנוּ, סְלַח לָנוּ יוֹצְרֵנוּ.

מְרוֹמֵם יַרְאֵנִי בְשׁוֹרְרָי,[21] נִקְמָתוֹ וְנִקְמַת בְּחִירָי,

מוּסַר כְּלִמָּתִי[22] לְעָרִי, כִּי נָשָׂאתִי חֶרְפַּת נְעוּרָי.[23]

נְעוּרַי זָכַרְתִּי לוֹ אַהֲבָה כְלוּלָה,[24] לְעֵת זִקְנָה חֶסֶד גּוֹמְלָה,

נָא תִכּוֹן תְּפִלָּתִי כְעוֹלָה, הַאֲזִינָה אֱלֹהֵי יַעֲקֹב סֶלָה.[25]

חָטָאנוּ צוּרֵנוּ, סְלַח לָנוּ יוֹצְרֵנוּ.

(1) Cf. Psalms 37:6. (2) Cf. I Kings 8:30. (3) Cf. Ezekiel 26:12. (4) Cf. Isaiah 42:24. (5) Cf. 30:11.
(6) Cf. Hosea 4:16. (7) Jeremiah 3:25. (8) Cf. Ezra 9:7. (9) Isaiah 22:17. (10) Cf. Jeremiah 5:6.
(11) Cf. Zephaniah 3:3. (12) Jeremiah 50:42. (13) Cf. Psalms 84:2. (14) Cf. Isaiah 30:17.
(15) Cf. 26:13; some editions of Selichos omit this line. (16) Numbers 23:23.
(17) Psalms 135:4. (18) Cf. Isaiah 44:26. (19) Cf. I Samuel 2:10. (20) 2:7.
(21) Cf. Psalms 59:11. (22) Job 20:3. (23) Jeremiah 31:18. (24) Cf. 2:2. (25) Psalms 84:9.

ה Bring forth, for their sake, their [descendants'] judgment[1]
 and sentence, from Your heights into the light,
 and listen to the supplication of Your servants and **Your people.**[2]

ו **Your people** they pillage, and plunder and loot their wealth,[3]
 they rejoice in the terror [they cause], celebrating the disaster.

ו 'And Who has put Jacob to oppression?' they declare in a shout;
 'Did not HASHEM do **this?**'[4]

> We have sinned, our Rock! Forgive us, our Molder.

ז 'This was caused by sin, therefore the pursuer beat us;
 for we turned off the path,[5] and like a balking [cow][6] we kicked.

ז We have been visited by [God's] anger in [just] measure,
 and according to our ill deeds we have swallowed [the bitter cup, for]
 against HASHEM, our God, **we have sinned.**[7]

ח 'We have sinned, and here we are, full of great guilt.[8]
 Given over to mockery and scorn in the Exile.

ח Scripture's vision has loomed up over us:
 Behold, HASHEM will cause you to suffer untold **wandering.**[9]

> We have sinned, our Rock! Forgive us, our Molder.

ט 'Wandering and sorrow have grown greater and stronger.
 Wolves of the night[10] have eaten and confounded [us];

ט they tore us and by morning left not even bones[11] —
 they are cruel, and have no **mercy.**'[12]

י **Mercy,** may it be shown from Heaven; a miracle to work,
 and save His people from the hand of the strong and forceful.

י Let Him provide for His beloved Tabenacle,[13] both length and breadth,
 like a mountaintop signal-post, [held high] **like a banner.**[14]

> We have sinned, our Rock! Forgive us, our Molder.

כ **Like a banner** [abandoned] does the remnant
 of God's heritage-people remain,
 mastered by lords other than Him.[15]

כ Let it be said now to [the House of] Jacob,[16] whom He always forgives,
 'God has chosen for Himself, Israel as **His treasure.**'[17]

ל **His treasure**[-people], may they not suffer faintness and desolation;
 may He re-establish my ruins[18] as in days of old.

ל May He grant might to my king and may He exalt him,[19]
 He Who makes [the exalted] humble and [the humble] **exalted.**[20]

> We have sinned, our Rock! Forgive us, our Molder.

מ **Exalted** One, show me [vengeance] against my watchful foes,[21]
 His vengeance and the vengeance of my Chosen.

מ The punishment of my shame[22] be upon my destroyers,
 For I have borne the disgrace of the sins of **my youth.**[23]

נ **My youth,** I remember it, [our] bridal love.[24]
 In time of old age, treat her [likewise] with kindness!

נ Please let my prayer stand as an olah-offering;
 give ear, O God of Jacob, **eternally.**[25]

> We have sinned, our Rock! Forgive us, our Molder.

סֶלָה* לְקַוֶּיךָ הֱיֵה מִשְׁעֲנָם, לְמַעַנְךָ עֲשֵׂה אִם לֹא לְמַעֲנָם,
שׁוֹטְנֵימוֹ יֵבוֹשׁוּ וְיִכָּלְמוּ[1] בְּמַעֲנָם, אֵל יהוה וְלֹא עָנָם.[2]

עָנָם לְבֵית יִשְׂרָאֵל וְיַחְדּוּךְ, כִּי שַׂמְתָּ מֵעִיר לַגָּל[3] וַחֲמָדוּךְ,
עַל כֵּן בְּאֻרִים כִּבְּדוּךְ,[4] יהוה בַּצַּר פְּקָדוּךְ.[5]
חָטָאנוּ צוּרֵנוּ, סְלַח לָנוּ יוֹצְרֵנוּ.

פְּקָדוּךְ פִּיּוֹת פּוֹנוֹת לְךָ לִקְרָא, חַלְּצֵם מֵעֹנֶשׁ וּמִגְּזֵרָה חֲמוּרָה,
פְּנֵה נָא אֵל הָרֹנָּה וְאֶל הָעֲתִירָה, מֵעָם בְּעֵת צָרָה.[6]

צָרָה וְצוּקָה הָסֵר מֶנִּי מְחוֹלְלִי, וְשַׁעֲרֵי דְמָעוֹת לֹא יִנָּעֲלוּ לִי,
צְבוּרוֹת בְּנֹאדְךָ הֲלֹא בְּסִפְרָתֶךָ[7] גּוֹאֲלִי, שַׁוַּעְתִּי שָׁמַעְתָּ קוֹלִי.[8]
חָטָאנוּ צוּרֵנוּ, סְלַח לָנוּ יוֹצְרֵנוּ.

קוֹלִי אָרִים הֶרֶף בַּקָּשָׁה, מִפְּנֵי עָקַת אוֹיֵב[9] הַמַּרְעִישָׁה,
קְפַחְתַּנִי חֲמַת הַמֵּצִיק[10] הַמִּתְקַשָּׁה, אֵם עַל בָּנִים רֻטָּשָׁה.[11]

רֻטָּשָׁה לְעֵינֶיהָ יַלְדֶיהָ נִשְׁחָטִים, פְּנֵיהָ לִכְלִמּוֹת וּלְחָיֶיהָ לַמּוֹרְטִים,[12]
רוֹזְנִים מִלִּשְׁכַּת הַגָּזִית מִתְמַעֲטִים, שֶׁשָּׁם עָלוּ שְׁבָטִים.[13]

שְׁבָטִים תָּשִׁיב לְנָוַת בֵּית עֲטֶרֶת, לִהְיוֹת שְׁאֵרִית מְכֻתֶּרֶת,
תַּשְׁמִיעַ לִפְלֵיטַת יְהוּדָה הַנִּשְׁאֶרֶת,[14] וְהָיִיתְ עֲטֶרֶת תִּפְאֶרֶת.[15]
חָטָאנוּ צוּרֵנוּ, סְלַח לָנוּ יוֹצְרֵנוּ.

תִּפְאֶרֶת אֱמוּנֶיךָ עַם זוּ קָנִיתָ,[16] לֹא שִׁקַּצְתָּם עַם זוּ קְרָאוּךָ וְעָנִיתָ,
יָחִיד וְעָנִי קוֹרֵא מְשׁוּבָתְךָ הַכְנַתָּ,
וְשָׁמַעְתִּי אֶת תְּפִלָּתָם וְאֶת תְּחִנָּתָם אֲשֶׁר הִתְחַנָּנְתָּ.[17]

הִתְחַנָּנְתָּ עַל בָּנֶיךָ שֶׁכָּלוּ, וּמֵעַל שֻׁלְחָן אֲבִיהֶם גָּלוּ,
אָמַרְתָּ רַחֲמִים עַל מִדּוֹתַי יָגֹלּוּ, בַּיהוה יִצְדְּקוּ וְיִתְהַלֲלוּ.[18]
חָטָאנוּ צוּרֵנוּ, סְלַח לָנוּ יוֹצְרֵנוּ.

---

(1) Cf. *Psalms* 71:13. (2) *II Samuel* 22:42. (3) *Isaiah* 25:2. (4) Cf. 24:15. (5) 26:16.
(6) *Psalms* 37:39. (7) Cf. 56:9. (8) *Jonah* 2:3. (9) Cf. *Psalms* 55:4. (10) *Isaiah* 51:13.
(11) *Hosea* 10:14. (12) Cf. *Isaiah* 50:6. (13) *Psalms* 122:4. (14) Cf. *II Kings* 19:30.
(15) *Isaiah* 62:3. (16) *Exodus* 15:16. (17) Cf. *I Kings* 9:3. (18) Cf. *Isaiah* 45:25.

סֶלָה — *Selah.* Targum and Metzudas Zion (to *Psalms* 3:3) render this word *forever.* This view is supported by the Talmud (*Eruvin* 54a). In the academy of R' Elazar ben Yaakov they taught: Wherever the words נֶצַח סֶלָה וָעֶד are used, they mean *forever, without an end,* as it says, עַד עוֹלָם סֶלָה, *forever, selah!* (*Psalms* 48:9). *Ibn Ezra* disagrees and concludes that the word סֶלָה is always a reaffirmation of a preceding statement, i.e., all of the aforementioned is *true* and *certain. Ibn Ezra* also offers an alternate meaning, endorsed by *Radak* as well, that *selah* is a musical instruction addressed to the singers of the psalm. It indicates special emphasis and a raising of the voice. This theory is supported by the fact that this word *selah* is only to be found in the *Psalms*, a book of songs, and three times in *Habakkuk* who also sings in a style very similar to *Psalms*. These last two views cannot be the meaning the *paytan* had in mind when he began the stanza with the word *selah.*

ס *Eternally,* be a prop for those who hope for You;*
   act for Your sake if not for theirs.

ס *Let their adversaries be disgraced, put to shame[1] in their prayers*
   to HASHEM, *may He leave them without* **answer.**[2]

ע **Answer** *[please] the House of Israel, for they declare Your Oneness;*
   [and] even when You turned the City [of Jerusalem]
       to a heap [of ruins],[3] they still cherished You.

ע *Therefore in the crannies they honored You;[4]*
   HASHEM, *in their distress* **they remembered You [in prayer].**[5]

> *We have sinned, our Rock! Forgive us, our Molder.*

פ **They remembered You [in prayer],** *mouths turning to call to You;*
   therefore save them from punishment and cruel decree.

פ *Please turn to [their] song and ardent prayer,*
   [You Who are] their Stronghold in time of **trouble.**[6]

צ **Trouble** *and anguish turn away from me, O my Creator;*
   let the Gates of Tears not be locked before me.

צ *Are not [my tears] gathered in Your flask,*
   are they not in Your record,[7] my Redeemer?
   I cried out; You heard **my voice.**[8]

> *We have sinned, our Rock! Forgive us, our Molder.*

ק **My voice** *I raise in entreaty,*
   because of the oppression of the tumultuous foe.[9]

ק *The oppressor's ever-wilder rage[10] has suppressed me,*
   the mother over **her children slain.**[11]

ר **[Her] children slain** — *slaughtered before her eyes,*
   her face to humiliation, her cheeks to the plucker's [hands].[12]
   The [Sanhedrin, the Torah's] princes have diminished
       from the Chamber of Hewn Stone,
   whither ascended **the Tribes.**[13]

ש **The Tribes,** *may You bring [them] back to the House*
       that is [Your] diadem,
   that the remnant [once again] be crowned.

ת *Let the fugitive survivors of Judah[14] hear*
   You will be a crown of **glory.**[15]

> *We have sinned, our Rock! Forgive us, our Molder.*

Glory *for Your faithful, this people You acquired[16] —*
You have not abhorred them; they call You, and You answer.
[Even when] a man lone and poor calls,
   You have already prepared Your reply:
'I will hear their prayer and their supplication,
   as you have supplicated for **grace.'**[17]

Grace *have you shown, O* HASHEM, *for Your children*
   who have been devastated,
and have been exiled from their Father's table.
You have said, 'Let My mercy roll over [all] My Attributes;
through HASHEM *will they be justified and* **praised.**[18]

> *We have sinned, our Rock! Forgive us, our Molder.*

❖ **וְיִתְהַלְלוּ**[1] חוֹסֶיךָ תְּפַלָּתָם וּתְפִלָּתִי בַּנְּעִימִים,
וְהִתְנַהֵג עִמָּהֶם בְּמִדַּת צְדָקָה וְרַחֲמִים,
זְכוּתְךָ קַדְּמֵם וּזְכוּת שְׁלֹשֶׁת קְדוּמִים,
אֵל מֶלֶךְ יוֹשֵׁב עַל כִּסֵּא רַחֲמִים.

All:

זְכוֹר לָנוּ בְּרִית אָבוֹת, כַּאֲשֶׁר אָמַרְתָּ: וְזָכַרְתִּי אֶת בְּרִיתִי
יַעֲקוֹב, וְאַף אֶת בְּרִיתִי יִצְחָק, וְאַף אֶת בְּרִיתִי אַבְרָהָם
אֶזְכֹּר, וְהָאָרֶץ אֶזְכֹּר.[2]

סליחה מב (פזמון)

THE ARK IS OPENED.
Chazzan, then congregation:

זְכוֹר בְּרִית אַבְרָהָם* וַעֲקֵדַת יִצְחָק,
וְהָשֵׁב שְׁבוּת אָהֳלֵי יַעֲקֹב,[3] וְהוֹשִׁיעֵנוּ לְמַעַן שְׁמֶךָ.[4]

Congregation, then *chazzan:*

אָבַדְנוּ מֵאֶרֶץ טוֹבָה[5] בְּחִפָּזוֹן,　　אָרְכוּ הַיָּמִים וּדְבַר כָּל חָזוֹן,[6]
בְּיִשְׂרָאֵל חָדְלוּ פְרָזוֹן,[7]　　בְּמִשְׁמַנֵּינוּ שָׁלַח רָזוֹן.[8]
וְשׁוּב בְּרַחֲמִים עַל שְׁאֵרִית יִשְׂרָאֵל, וְהוֹשִׁיעֵנוּ לְמַעַן שְׁמֶךָ.

Congregation, then *chazzan:*

גּוֹלָה אַחַר גּוֹלָה,　　גָּלְתָה יְהוּדָה[9] כֻלָּה,
דָּנָה כָל הַיּוֹם[10] וְכָלָה,　　דּוֹרֵשׁ וּמְבַקֵּשׁ אֵין לָהּ.[11]
וְהָשֵׁב שְׁבוּת אָהֳלֵי יַעֲקֹב, וְהוֹשִׁיעֵנוּ לְמַעַן שְׁמֶךָ.

Congregation, then *chazzan:*

הָעִיר הַקֹּדֶשׁ וְהַמְּחוֹזוֹת,*　　הָיוּ לְחֶרְפָּה וּלְבִזּוֹת,
וְכָל מַחֲמַדֶּיהָ טְבוּעוֹת וּגְנוּזוֹת,*　　וְאֵין שִׁיּוּר רַק הַתּוֹרָה הַזֹּאת.
וְשׁוּב בְּרַחֲמִים עַל שְׁאֵרִית יִשְׂרָאֵל, וְהוֹשִׁיעֵנוּ לְמַעַן שְׁמֶךָ.

---

(1) Some editions find the signature חֲזַק אֵלִיָּהוּ, *Eliyahu, may he be strong,* in the initial letters of the words אֱמוּנֶיךָ לֹא יָחִיד of the stanza beginning וְיִתְהַלְלוּ תִּפְאֶרֶת הַתְחַנֵּן of the second to last stanza; and חוֹסֶיךָ זְכוּתְךָ קַדְּמֵם of the last stanza. (2) *Leviticus* 26:42. (3) Cf. *Jeremiah* 30:18.(4) Cf. *Psalms* 106:8. (5) Cf. *Deuteronomy* 11:17. (6) Cf. *Ezekiel* 12:22-23. (7) Cf. *Judges* 5:7; see commentary to *selichah* 21. (8) Cf. *Isaiah* 10:16. (9) *Lamentations* 1:3. (10) Cf. 1:13. (11) Cf. *Ezekiel* 34:6; *Jeremiah* 30:17.

§⇐ **זְכוֹר בְּרִית אַבְרָהָם** — *Remember the covenant of Abraham.* This *pizmon* differs from others by virtue of its two refrains which alternate after each stanza. Although it originally contained fourteen stanzas, only seven of them have remained in the liturgy. The acrostic of the stiches form a double *aleph-beis* (from ו until ת are omitted today) followed by the *paytan's* signature, גֵּרְשֹׁם בַּר יְהוּדָה חֲזַק, *Gershom bar*

Yehudah, may he be strong [see prefatory comment to *selichah* 12].

הָעִיר הַקֹּדֶשׁ וְהַמְּחוֹזוֹת — *The Holy City and [its outlying] regions.* Some would translate: *The city [of Jerusalem], the Holy [Temple] and the [outlying] regions.* This is based on *Daniel* 9:26, where עִיר and קֹדֶשׁ refer to Jerusalem and the *Beis HaMikdash.* We have not used this translation for two reasons. In *Daniel* the phrase contains

Chazzan – **Praised** will be those who rely on You,[1]
  [may] their prayer and mine [be] pleasant [to You];
  and act towards them with the Attribute of charity and mercy.
Let Your merit and the merit of the three ancestors
  come forward to greet them,
O God, King, Who sits on the Throne of Mercy.

All:

זְכוֹר לָנוּ Remember for us the covenant of the Patriarchs, as You said:
  'And I will remember My covenant with Jacob, and also My
covenant with Isaac, and also My covenant with Abraham will I remember; and the Land will I remember.'[2]

SELICHAH 42

THE ARK IS OPENED.
Chazzan, then congregation:

זְכוֹר Remember the covenant of Abraham* and the binding of Isaac.
  O restore the captivity of Jacob's tents,[3] and save us for Your
Name's sake.[4]

Congregation, then chazzan:

א We have lost our goodly land[5] so quickly;
א long days have passed,
  and every [exile] prophecy's message [has come to pass].[6]
ב Israel can no longer dwell in unfortified cities;[7]
ב a wasting plague is sent on all our prosperity.[8]
  O return with mercy to the remnant of Israel,
    and save us for Your Name's sake.

Congregation, then chazzan:

ג Exile after exile
ג has all of Judah[9] suffered,
ד afflicted all day[10] as they waste away,
ד yet no one seeks or asks about them.[11]
  O restore the captivity of Jacob's tents,
    and save us for Your Name's sake.

Congregation, then chazzan:

ה The Holy City and [its outlying] regions*
ה are turned to shame and to spoils;
ו all its precious things are buried and hidden.*
ו And nothing is left but the Torah [itself].
  O return with mercy to the remnant of Israel,
    and save us for Your Name's sake.

---

only two words הָעִיר וְהַקֹּדֶשׁ, the city and the holy, which are joined by the conjunctive prefix ו, and; in our stich the conjunction is absent and so הַקֹּדֶשׁ is more likely an adjective modifying הָעִיר than an independent noun. Additionally, the order of the stich — city, Temple, outlying regions — would be illogical. The list should be in order of either ascending holiness (outlying, city, Temple)

or descending (Temple, city, outlying), and not haphazard.

וְכָל מַחֲמַדֶּיהָ טְבוּעוֹת וּגְנוּזוֹת — All its precious things are buried and hidden. According to one opinion in the Talmud, before Nebuchadnezzar captured the First Temple, the Holy Ark was hidden beneath the Temple so that it would not be taken by the enemy (see Yoma 53b and Sheka-

Congregation, then *chazzan*:

גּוֹאֵל חָזָק לְמַעַנְךָ פְּדֵנוּ, רְאֵה כִּי אָזְלַת יָדֵנוּ,[1]
שׁוּר כִּי אָבְדוּ חֲסִידֵינוּ,[2] מַפְגִּיעַ אֵין בַּעֲדֵנוּ.[3]
וְהָשֵׁב שְׁבוּת אָהֳלֵי יַעֲקֹב, וְהוֹשִׁיעֵנוּ לְמַעַן שְׁמֶךָ.

Congregation, then *chazzan*:

בְּרִית אָבוֹת וְאִמָּהוֹת וְהַשְּׁבָטִים,
רַחֲמֶיךָ וַחֲסָדֶיךָ בְּרֻבּוֹת עִתִּים,[4]
יָהּ זְכֹר לְמֻכִּים וְנִמְרָטִים,[5] וְעָלֶיךָ כָּל הַיּוֹם נִשְׁחָטִים.[6]
וְשׁוּב בְּרַחֲמִים עַל שְׁאֵרִית יִשְׂרָאֵל, וְהוֹשִׁיעֵנוּ לְמַעַן שְׁמֶךָ.

Congregation, then *chazzan*:

דּוֹרֵשׁ דָּמִים[7] דּוּן דִּינֵנוּ, הָשֵׁב שִׁבְעָתַיִם אֶל חֵיק[8] מְעַנֵּינוּ,
חִנָּם נִמְכַּרְנוּ, וְלֹא בְכֶסֶף פְּדֵנוּ,[9]
זְקֹף בֵּית מִקְדָּשְׁךָ הַשָּׁמֵם[10] לְעֵינֵינוּ.
וְהָשֵׁב שְׁבוּת אָהֳלֵי יַעֲקֹב, וְהוֹשִׁיעֵנוּ לְמַעַן שְׁמֶךָ.

THE ARK IS CLOSED.

All:

זְכוֹר לָנוּ בְּרִית רִאשׁוֹנִים כַּאֲשֶׁר אָמַרְתָּ, וְזָכַרְתִּי לָהֶם בְּרִית
רִאשׁוֹנִים, אֲשֶׁר הוֹצֵאתִי אוֹתָם מֵאֶרֶץ מִצְרַיִם לְעֵינֵי
הַגּוֹיִם, לִהְיוֹת לָהֶם לֵאלֹהִים אֲנִי יהוה.[11]
תִּשְׂגַּב לְבַדְּךָ וְתִמְלוֹךְ עַל כֹּל בְּיִחוּד. כַּכָּתוּב עַל יַד נְבִיאֶךָ, וְהָיָה
יהוה לְמֶלֶךְ עַל כָּל הָאָרֶץ, בַּיּוֹם הַהוּא יִהְיֶה יהוה אֶחָד וּשְׁמוֹ
אֶחָד.[12]

שְׁמַע יִשְׂרָאֵל, יהוה אֱלֹהֵינוּ, יהוה אֶחָד.[13]

מַלְכֵּנוּ בָאנוּ* בְּכֹחַ יִחוּדֶךָ, כִּי אֵין לָנוּ בַּמֶּה לְקַדְּמֶךָ,
כִּי אִם מַלְכוּתְךָ וּמֵעַבְדֶּיךָ, לָכֵן בְּכָל לֵב נְיַחֲדֶךָ.
נְיַחֲדֶךָ יַחַד גְּדוֹלֵינוּ וּקְטַנֵּינוּ, מְחַק נָא שִׁטְרֵי חוֹבוֹתֵינוּ,
וּכְתֹב בְּסֵפֶר הַחַיִּים זִכְרוֹנֵנוּ, וְתִגְזֹר עַתָּה לְהֵיטִיב שְׁנוֹתֵינוּ.
שְׁמַע יִשְׂרָאֵל, יהוה אֱלֹהֵינוּ, יהוה אֶחָד.

(1) Cf. *Deuteronomy* 32:36. (2) Cf. *Micah* 7:2. (3) Cf. *Isaiah* 59:16. (4) Cf. *Nehemiah* 9:28.
(5) Cf. 13:25. (6) Cf. *Psalms* 44:23. (7) 9:13. (8) Cf. 79:12; some editions of *Selichos* omit this stich.
(9) Cf. *Isaiah* 52:3; see commentary to *selichah* 9, s.v., לְמֻכּוֹרֵי חִנָּם. (10) Cf. *Daniel* 9:17.
(11) *Leviticus* 26:45. (12) *Zechariah* 14:9. (13) *Deuteronomy* 6:4.

lim 6:1). The *paytan* follows this view, and refers to the Ark and its contents as 'its precious things.'
מַלְכֵּנוּ בָּאנוּ — *Our King, we have come.* As with the preceding *selichah*, only a small part of this one's original text is recited. The work comprised twenty-two stanzas, and followed an alphabetical theme. Only eight of the stanzas have been retained in the rite. The unknown *paytan* placed the first verse of the *Shema* as the refrain after every second stanza. In the

Congregation, then *chazzan:*

ג O mighty Redeemer, deliver us for Your sake!

ר See how our strength has left [us],[1]

ש look how our pious ones have been lost;[2]

מ so that there is no one to pray for us.[3]

> O restore the captivity of Jacob's tents,
> and save us for Your Name's sake.

Congregation, then *chazzan:*

ב The covenant of the Patriarchs, the Matriarchs, and Tribes;

ר Your mercy and kindness so many times given;[4]

י remember [all this,] O God, on behalf of the beaten and torn,[5]

ו who are slaughtered for Your sake all the time.[6]

> O return with mercy to the remnant of Israel,
> and save us for Your Name's sake.

Congregation, then *chazzan:*

ר Avenger of Blood,[7] judge our cause!

ה Pay back our tormentors sevenfold into their bosom.[8]

ח We were sold [into Exile] for naught; so redeem us,
but not with money,[9]

ז erect Your desolate Holy Temple[10] before our eyes.

> O restore the captivity of Jacob's tents,
> and save us for Your Name's sake.

THE ARK IS CLOSED.

All:

זְכוֹר לָנוּ Remember for us the covenant of the ancestors, as You said:
'And I will remember for them the covenant of the ancestors
whom I brought out of the land of Egypt in the very sight of the nations,
to be a God to them; I am HASHEM.'[11]

May You alone be exalted and reign over all in Oneness, as was written
by Your prophet: HASHEM will become King over all the earth; on that day
HASHEM will be one and His Name will be one.[12]

Hear, O Israel: HASHEM is our God, HASHEM is the One and Only.[13]

מ Our King, we have come* on the strength
of [our proclaiming] Your Oneness,
for we have nothing with which to come to You
except Your Kingship [that we accept]
and Your deeds [that we recognize];
Therefore with all our hearts **we will proclaim Your Oneness.**.

נ We **will proclaim Your Oneness** together,
[our] great and [our] small;
please wipe out the records of our guilt,
and write down a mention of us in the Book of Life;
may you decree now beneficence for our years.
Hear, O Israel: HASHEM is our God, HASHEM is the One and Only.

---

stanzas not separated by the refrain, the last word
of one stanza is identical with the first word of the

next. [For some unknown reason the early
editions do not number this *selichah*.]

סְגֻלָּה אֲשֶׁר פָּדִיתָ בְּמַסּוֹת בְּאוֹתוֹת וּבְנִסִּים,

בְּשִׁמְךָ חוֹסִים, וְעַל שֵׁמַע פּוֹרְסִים,

אֵלֶּה בָרֶכֶב וְאֵלֶּה בַסּוּסִים,

וַאֲנַחְנוּ בְּשֵׁם יהוה אֱלֹהֵינוּ **עוֹמְסִים**.[1]

עוֹמְסִים בְּיִרְאָה וּבְפַחַד וּבְרֶעַד,

לְעוֹדְדָם מֵאֻמּוֹת וּלְהַסְעַד,   כְּמוֹ בְדִבְרֵי קָדְשְׁךָ מוֹעֵד,

הֵמָּה כָּרְעוּ וְנָפָלוּ, וַאֲנַחְנוּ קַמְנוּ וַנִּתְעוֹדָד.[2]

שְׁמַע יִשְׂרָאֵל, יהוה אֱלֹהֵינוּ, יהוה אֶחָד.

פַּסּוּ עֲבוֹדוֹת פְּנִימָה וּשְׂעִירֵי כַפָּרָה,

וְאָפֵס כֹּהֵן לְשַׁבֵּךְ עֶבְרָה,

וְנִשְׁאַרְנוּ כְּלֵב אִשָּׁה מְצֵרָה,

(שְׁעוּנִים בְּאָמְר) יַעַנְךָ יהוה בְּיוֹם **צָרָה**.[3]

צָרָה בִּהְיוֹת לְיַעֲקֹב,   זֶה יֹאמַר לַיהוה אֲנִי בְּלִי לְיַעֲקֹב,

וְזֶה יִקְרָא בְשֵׁם יַעֲקֹב,[4]

וְכֻלָּם שְׁעוּנִים בְּהַבְטָחַת שֵׁם אֱלֹהֵי יַעֲקֹב.[5]

שְׁמַע יִשְׂרָאֵל, יהוה אֱלֹהֵינוּ, יהוה אֶחָד.

שִׁמְךָ בָּנוּ נִקְרָא רַב עֲלִילוֹת,   שְׁעֵה מֶנּוּ שַׁוְעָה וְקַבֵּל תְּפִלּוֹת,

וְהָסֵר מֶנּוּ רֹעַ מַעֲלָלוֹת,   וְאַתָּה קָדוֹשׁ יוֹשֵׁב **תְּהִלּוֹת**.[6]

✧ **תְּהִלּוֹת** דָּר, הָקֵץ רְדוּמִים,   חֲשׁוּכִים בֵּין הָאֵמִים,

פְּדֵם וְנָקָם מִבְּתָמִים,   אֵל מֶלֶךְ יוֹשֵׁב עַל כִּסֵּא רַחֲמִים.

All:

עֲשֵׂה עִמָּנוּ כְּמָה שֶׁהִבְטַחְתָּנוּ: וְאַף גַּם זֹאת בִּהְיוֹתָם בְּאֶרֶץ
אֹיְבֵיהֶם, לֹא מְאַסְתִּים וְלֹא גְעַלְתִּים לְכַלֹּתָם
לְהָפֵר בְּרִיתִי אִתָּם, כִּי אֲנִי יהוה אֱלֹהֵיהֶם.[7] הִמָּצֵא לָנוּ בְּבַקְשָׁתֵנוּ,
כְּמָה שֶׁכָּתוּב: וּבִקַּשְׁתֶּם מִשָּׁם אֶת יהוה אֱלֹהֶיךָ וּמָצָאתָ, כִּי
תִדְרְשֶׁנּוּ בְּכָל לְבָבְךָ וּבְכָל נַפְשֶׁךָ.[8] מוֹל אֶת לְבָבֵנוּ לְאַהֲבָה וּלְיִרְאָה
אֶת שְׁמֶךָ, כְּמָה שֶׁכָּתוּב: וּמָל יהוה אֱלֹהֶיךָ אֶת לְבָבְךָ וְאֶת
לְבַב זַרְעֶךָ, לְאַהֲבָה אֶת יהוה אֱלֹהֶיךָ בְּכָל לְבָבְךָ וּבְכָל נַפְשְׁךָ,
לְמַעַן חַיֶּיךָ.[9] זְרוֹק עָלֵינוּ מַיִם טְהוֹרִים וְטַהֲרֵנוּ, כְּמָה שֶׁכָּתוּב:

---

(1) Cf. *Psalms* 20:8. (2) 20:9. (3) 20:2. (4) Cf. *Isaiah* 44:5 and see *Rashi* there.
(5) *Psalms* 20:2. (6) 22:4. (7) *Leviticus* 26:44. (8) *Deuteronomy* 4:29. (9) 30:6.

ס Your treasured people, whom You redeemed with tests,
　　signs, and miracles —
they take shelter with Your Name, declaring 'Shema Yisrael!'
Some [nations trust] in chariots and some in horses,
but as for us, the name of HASHEM, our God, **we bear.**[1]

ע **We bear** it with reverence, with fear and trembling,
[asking You] to bolster them against the nations,
　　and to support [them].
As is testified in Your Holy Scripture:
'They slump and fall, and we arise and are invigorated.'[2]
　　　Hear, O Israel: HASHEM is our God, HASHEM is the One and Only.

פ The inner Temple service [of Yom Kippur]
　　and the goats that atone are no more,
nor is there any Kohen to calm [Your] fury.
We are left [trembling] like the heart of a woman in travail,
relying on the [Torah's] saying:
　　'HASHEM will answer you in time of **trouble.'**[3]

צ **Trouble** when it comes upon Jacob,
this [righteous] one will say,
　　'I am HASHEM's,' without any deceit.
and this [contrite one] will call in Jacob's name;[4]
and all rely on the promise: the Name of the God of Jacob.[5]
　　　Hear, O Israel: HASHEM is our God, HASHEM is the One and Only.

ר Your Name is called upon us, Doer of Great Deeds;
[therefore] turn to our cry and accept our prayers.
Turn away wicked deeds from us,
the Holy One are **You, Who sits [to hear Israel's] praises.**[6]

ת Chazzan — **[You] Who sits [to hear Israel's] praises,**
　　awaken the slumberers,
those who sit in darkness [exiled] among the nations.
Redeem them and cleanse them of [sin's] stains,
O God, King Who sits on the Throne of Mercy!

All:

עֲשֵׂה עִמָּנוּ Do with us as You promised us: 'And despite all that,
　　　when they will be in the land of their enemies, I will not
have despised them nor abhorred them to destroy them, to annul My
covenant with them, for I am HASHEM their God.'[7] Be accessible to us in
our quest, as it is written: From there you will seek HASHEM, your God,
and you will find, when you search for Him with all your heart and with
all your soul.[8] Expose our hearts to love Your Name, as it is written:
HASHEM, your God, will expose your heart and the heart of your offspring,
to love HASHEM, your God, with all your heart and with all your soul, that
you may live.[9] Pour pure water upon us and purify us, as it is written:

וְזָרַקְתִּי עֲלֵיכֶם מַיִם טְהוֹרִים וּטְהַרְתֶּם, מִכֹּל טֻמְאוֹתֵיכֶם וּמִכָּל
גִּלּוּלֵיכֶם אֲטַהֵר אֶתְכֶם.¹ מָחִה פְשָׁעֵינוּ כָּעָב וְכֶעָנָן, כְּמָה שֶׁכָּתוּב:
מָחִיתִי כָעָב פְּשָׁעֶיךָ וְכֶעָנָן חַטֹּאתֶיךָ, שׁוּבָה אֵלַי כִּי גְאַלְתִּיךָ.²
מְחֵה פְשָׁעֵינוּ לְמַעֲנָךְ, כַּאֲשֶׁר אָמַרְתָּ: אָנֹכִי אָנֹכִי הוּא מֹחֶה פְשָׁעֶיךָ
לְמַעֲנִי, וְחַטֹּאתֶיךָ לֹא אֶזְכֹּר.³ הַלְבֵּן חֲטָאֵינוּ כַּשֶּׁלֶג וְכַצֶּמֶר, כְּמָה
שֶׁכָּתוּב: לְכוּ נָא וְנִוָּכְחָה, יֹאמַר יהוה, אִם יִהְיוּ חֲטָאֵיכֶם כַּשָּׁנִים,
כַּשֶּׁלֶג יַלְבִּינוּ, אִם יַאְדִּימוּ כַתּוֹלָע, כַּצֶּמֶר יִהְיוּ.⁴ רַחֵם עָלֵינוּ וְאַל
תַּשְׁחִיתֵנוּ, כְּמָה שֶׁכָּתוּב: כִּי אֵל רַחוּם יהוה אֱלֹהֶיךָ, לֹא יַרְפְּךָ וְלֹא
יַשְׁחִיתֶךָ וְלֹא יִשְׁכַּח אֶת בְּרִית אֲבֹתֶיךָ אֲשֶׁר נִשְׁבַּע לָהֶם.⁵ קַבֵּץ
נִדָּחֵינוּ כְּמָה שֶׁכָּתוּב: אִם יִהְיֶה נִדַּחֲךָ בִּקְצֵה הַשָּׁמָיִם, מִשָּׁם יְקַבֶּצְךָ
יהוה אֱלֹהֶיךָ וּמִשָּׁם יִקָּחֶךָ.⁶ הָשֵׁב שְׁבוּתֵנוּ וְרַחֲמֵנוּ, כְּמָה שֶׁכָּתוּב:
וְשָׁב יהוה אֱלֹהֶיךָ אֶת שְׁבוּתְךָ וְרִחֲמֶךָ וְשָׁב וְקִבֶּצְךָ מִכָּל הָעַמִּים
אֲשֶׁר הֱפִיצְךָ יהוה אֱלֹהֶיךָ שָׁמָּה.⁷ ❖ תְּבִיאֵנוּ אֶל הַר קָדְשֶׁךָ,
וְשַׂמְּחֵנוּ בְּבֵית תְּפִלָּתֶךָ, כְּמָה שֶׁכָּתוּב: וַהֲבִיאוֹתִים אֶל הַר קָדְשִׁי,
וְשִׂמַּחְתִּים בְּבֵית תְּפִלָּתִי, עוֹלֹתֵיהֶם וְזִבְחֵיהֶם לְרָצוֹן עַל מִזְבְּחִי,
כִּי בֵיתִי בֵּית תְּפִלָּה יִקָּרֵא לְכָל הָעַמִּים.⁸

THE ARK IS OPENED.

The first four verses of the following prayer are recited responsively; *chazzan*, then congregation:

שְׁמַע קוֹלֵנוּ יהוה אֱלֹהֵינוּ, חוּס וְרַחֵם עָלֵינוּ,
וְקַבֵּל בְּרַחֲמִים וּבְרָצוֹן אֶת תְּפִלָּתֵנוּ.⁹

הֲשִׁיבֵנוּ יהוה אֵלֶיךָ וְנָשׁוּבָה, חַדֵּשׁ יָמֵינוּ כְּקֶדֶם.¹⁰

אַל תַּשְׁלִיכֵנוּ מִלְּפָנֶיךָ, וְרוּחַ קָדְשְׁךָ אַל תִּקַּח מִמֶּנּוּ.¹¹

אַל תַּשְׁלִיכֵנוּ לְעֵת זִקְנָה, כִּכְלוֹת כֹּחֵנוּ אַל תַּעַזְבֵנוּ.¹²

אַל תַּעַזְבֵנוּ יהוה, אֱלֹהֵינוּ אַל תִּרְחַק מִמֶּנּוּ.¹³

עֲשֵׂה עִמָּנוּ אוֹת לְטוֹבָה, וְיִרְאוּ שׂוֹנְאֵינוּ וְיֵבֹשׁוּ,
כִּי אַתָּה יהוה עֲזַרְתָּנוּ וְנִחַמְתָּנוּ.¹⁴

אֲמָרֵינוּ הַאֲזִינָה יהוה, בִּינָה הֲגִיגֵנוּ.¹⁵

יִהְיוּ לְרָצוֹן אִמְרֵי פִינוּ וְהֶגְיוֹן לִבֵּנוּ לְפָנֶיךָ, יהוה צוּרֵנוּ וְגֹאֲלֵנוּ.¹⁶

כִּי לְךָ יהוה הוֹחָלְנוּ, אַתָּה תַעֲנֶה אֲדֹנָי אֱלֹהֵינוּ.¹⁷

THE ARK IS CLOSED.

---

(1) *Ezekiel* 36:25. (2) *Isaiah* 44:22. (3) 43:25. (4) 1:18. (5) *Deuteronomy* 4:31. (6) 30:4.
(7) 30:3. (8) *Isaiah* 56:7. (9) Weekday *Shemoneh Esrei*.
(10) *Lamentations* 5:21. (11) Cf. *Psalms* 51:13. (12) Cf. 71:9. (13) Cf. 38:22. (14) Cf. 86:17.
(15) Cf. 5:2. (16) Cf. 19:15. (17) Cf. 38:16.

I shall pour pure water upon you and purify you, of all your contaminations and of all your abominations I will purify you.[1] Wipe away our willful sins like a cloud and like a mist, as it is written: I have wiped away your willful sins like a cloud and your errors like a mist — repent to Me, for I have redeemed you![2] Wipe away our willful sins for Your sake, as You said: 'I, only I, am the One Who wipes away your willful sins for My sake, and I shall not recall your errors.'[3] Whiten our errors like snow and like [pure white] wool, as it is written: 'Come now, let us reason together,' says HASHEM, 'though your errors will be like scarlet, they will become white as snow; though they will be red as crimson, they will become like [white] wool.'[4] Have mercy on us and do not destroy us, as it is written: For a merciful God is HASHEM, your God; He will not surrender you nor destroy you, and He will not forget the covenant with your forefathers, which He swore to them.[5] Gather in our dispersed ones, as it is written: If your dispersed were to be at the ends of heaven, from there HASHEM, your God, will gather you in and from there He will take you.[6] Bring back our captivity and have mercy on us, as it is written: HASHEM, your God, will bring back your captivity and have mercy on you, and He will again gather you in from all the peoples where HASHEM, your God, has scattered you.[7] Chazzan — Bring us to Your holy mountain and gladden us in Your house of prayer, as it is written: And I will bring them to My holy mountain, and I will gladden them in My house of prayer, their elevation-offerings and their feast offering will find favor on My Altar, for My House will be called a house of prayer, for all peoples.[8]

THE ARK IS OPENED.

The first four verses of the following prayer are recited responsively; chazzan, then congregation:

שְׁמַע קוֹלֵנוּ Hear our voice, HASHEM, our God, pity and be compassionate to us, and accept — with compassion and favor —
our prayer.[9]
Bring us back to You, HASHEM, and we shall return,
  renew our days as of old.[10]
Do not cast us away from Yourself,
  and do not remove Your holy spirit from us.[11]
Do not cast us away in old age,
  when our strength gives out do not forsake us.[12]
Do not forsake us, HASHEM, our God, be not distant from us.[13]
Display for us a sign for good, so that our enemies may see it
  and be ashamed, for You, HASHEM, will have helped and consoled us.[14]
To our sayings give ear, HASHEM, perceive our thoughts.[15]
May the expressions of our mouth and the thoughts of our heart
  find favor before You, HASHEM, our Rock and our Redeemer.[16]
Because for You, HASHEM, we waited,
  You will answer, my Lord, our God.[17]

THE ARK IS CLOSED.

בקשות

וּבְכֵן יְהִי רָצוֹן מִלְּפָנֶיךָ, יהוה אֱלֹהֵינוּ וֵאלֹהֵי אֲבוֹתֵינוּ, שֶׁתְּהֵא הַשָּׁנָה הַזֹּאת הַבָּאָה עָלֵינוּ וְעַל כָּל עַמְּךָ בֵּית יִשְׂרָאֵל, קֵץ וְתַכְלִית לְשִׁבְיֵ עַמְּךָ בֵּית יִשְׂרָאֵל, וְעֵת סוֹף לְגָלוּתֵנוּ וּלְאֶבְלֵנוּ, וְאַחֲרִית טוֹב לִימֵי עָנְיֵנוּ וּמְרוּדֵנוּ.[1] כִּי מָשַׁךְ עָלֵינוּ הַשִּׁעְבּוּד, וְאָרַךְ עָלֵינוּ עֹל גָּלִיּוֹת. וְהִנְנוּ בְּכָל יוֹם הוֹלְכִים וְדַלִּים, בְּרֻבּוֹת הַשָּׁנִים אָנוּ נִמְעָטִים, וּבִסְגוֹת הַזְּמַנִּים אָנוּ נִצְעָרִים. וְאֵין לָנוּ לֹא מְנַהֵל וְלֹא מַחֲזִיק בְּיָדֵנוּ, כַּאֲשֶׁר אָמָרְתָּ.[2] כִּי מִי יַחְמֹל עָלַיִךְ יְרוּשָׁלַיִם, וּמִי יָנוּד לָךְ, וּמִי יָסוּר לִשְׁאֹל לְשָׁלוֹם לָךְ.[3] אוֹ מִי יִגְדֹּר גָּדֵר, אוֹ מִי יַעֲמֹד בַּפֶּרֶץ (בַּעֲדֵנוּ).[4] וְאֵין עוֹד נָבִיא וְחוֹזֶה,[5] וְאֵין קוֹרֵא בְשִׁמְךָ בֶּאֱמֶת, מִתְעוֹרֵר לְהַחֲזִיק בָּךְ.[6] כִּי כֻלָּנוּ כַּצֹּאן תָּעִינוּ, אִישׁ אִישׁ לְדַרְכּוֹ הָרָעָה פָנֵינוּ,[7] כָּל גֶּבֶר אַחֲרֵי בִּצְעוֹ, וְכָל אִישׁ אַחֲרֵי שְׁרִירוּת לִבּוֹ הָרָע.[8] וְלֹא דַי לָנוּ בַּעֲוֹנוֹת הָרִאשׁוֹנִים, כִּי אִם הוֹסַפְנוּ עֲלֵיהֶם חֲדָשִׁים. וְלֹא הִזְהַרְנוּ בְּכָל הָאַזְהָרוֹת אֲשֶׁר הִזְהַרְתָּנוּ, וְלֹא הוּכַחְנוּ מִכָּל הַתּוֹכָחוֹת אֲשֶׁר הוֹכַחְתָּנוּ. וּמַה יֵּשׁ לָנוּ עוֹד צְדָקָה, וְלִזְעֹק עוֹד אֶל הַמֶּלֶךְ.[9]

וידוי

During the recitation of the וִדּוּי stand with head and body slightly bowed, in submissive contrition.

אֱלֹהֵינוּ וֵאלֹהֵי אֲבוֹתֵינוּ, תָּבֹא לְפָנֶיךָ תְּפִלָּתֵנוּ,[10] וְאַל תִּתְעַלַּם מִתְּחִנָּתֵנוּ,[11] שֶׁאֵין אָנוּ עַזֵּי פָנִים וּקְשֵׁי עֹרֶף, לוֹמַר לְפָנֶיךָ יהוה אֱלֹהֵינוּ וֵאלֹהֵי אֲבוֹתֵינוּ, צַדִּיקִים אֲנַחְנוּ וְלֹא חָטָאנוּ, אֲבָל אֲנַחְנוּ וַאֲבוֹתֵינוּ חָטָאנוּ.[12]

Strike the left side of the chest with the right fist
while reciting each of the sins in the following confession litany.

אָשַׁמְנוּ, בָּגַדְנוּ, גָּזַלְנוּ, דִּבַּרְנוּ דֹּפִי. הֶעֱוִינוּ, וְהִרְשַׁעְנוּ, זַדְנוּ, חָמַסְנוּ, טָפַלְנוּ שֶׁקֶר. יָעַצְנוּ רָע, כִּזַּבְנוּ, לַצְנוּ, מָרַדְנוּ, נִאַצְנוּ, סָרַרְנוּ, עָוִינוּ, פָּשַׁעְנוּ, צָרַרְנוּ, קִשִּׁינוּ עֹרֶף. רָשַׁעְנוּ, שִׁחַתְנוּ, תִּעַבְנוּ, תָּעִינוּ, תִּעְתָּעְנוּ.

וּבְכֵן יְהִי רָצוֹן ﬤ — *And so, may it be your will.* This lengthy prayer, whose parts are interspersed between the three recitals of the *viduy/confession,* is taken mostly from two supplications written by R' Saadiah Gaon, more than a thousand years ago. Over the centuries, the prayer has been enhanced with additions, but remains basically R' Saadiah's work.

According to his sons' testimony, R' Saadiah was born in 882 in the Al-Fayyum area west of the Nile delta. He was appointed *Gaon* of Sura at the unprecedented young age of only forty-five, in

927. Although he was banished from Sura for a seven-year period beginning two years after he assumed his office, R' Saadiah was subsequently reinstated. Among his many works were an Arabic commentary/translation of Scriptures; *HaEmunos VehaDeos (Faith and Belief)* — the first major work that set forth Jewish philosophy in an organized fashion; many liturgical compositions; and a listing of the 613 *mitzvos* according to his system of counting, written in verse form.

R' Saadiah passed away on 26 Iyar 942, about one month before his sixtieth birthday.

ENTREATIES

וּבְכֵן יְהִי רָצוֹן *And so, may it be Your will, HASHEM, our God and God of our forefathers, that this year now coming toward us, and toward all Your people the House of Israel, be the conclusion and the finish of captivity for Your people the House of Israel; the final end of our Exile and our mourning; and a favorable ending for the days of our afflictions and sorrows.[1] For servitude has drawn out long upon us, and the yoke of exile has extended upon us. And here we are, each day we grow weaker; as the years increase, we decrease; as time piles up, we diminish. We have neither leader, nor one to take our hand, as You said:[2] 'For who will pity you, Jerusalem? Who will lament over you? Who will step aside to seek your welfare?'[3] Or who will rebuild the fence, or who will stand in the breach (for us)?[4] There is no longer a prophet or seer,[5] nor does anyone call truthfully in Your name, being stirred to cling to You.[6] For all of us have strayed like a flock of sheep, each of us turned aside to his evil way:[7] Every man after his pilfer, every person after the evil imaginings of his heart.[8] [Our] earlier iniquities were not enough for us — we have added new ones on top of them. We were not warned by all the warnings with which You warned us; we were not chastened by all the chastisements with which You chastised us. What righteousness do we still have, [that allows us] to continue to cry out to the King?[9]*

VIDUY/CONFESSION

During the recitation of the וִדּוּי, *Confession*, stand with head and body slightly bowed,
in submissive contrition.

אֱלֹהֵינוּ *Our God and the God of our forefathers, may our prayer come before You.[10] Do not ignore our supplication,[11] for we are not so brazen and obstinate as to say before You, HASHEM, our God and the God of our forefathers, that we are righteous and have not sinned, for in truth, we and our forefathers have sinned.[12]*

Strike the left side of the chest with the right fist while reciting
each of the sins in the following confession litany.

אָשַׁמְנוּ *We have become guilty;* [ב] *we have betrayed;* [ג] *we have robbed;* [ד] *we have spoken slander;* [ה] *we have caused perversion;* [ו] *we have caused wickedness;* [ז] *we have sinned willfully;* [ח] *we have extorted;* [ט] *we have accused falsely;* [י] *we have given evil counsel;* [כ] *we have been deceitful;* [ל] *we have scorned;* [מ] *we have rebelled;* [נ] *we have provoked;* [ס] *we have turned away;* [ע] *we have been perverse;* [פ] *we have acted wantonly;* [צ] *we have persecuted;* [ק] *we have been obstinate;* [ר] *we have been wicked;* [ש] *we have corrupted;* [ת] *we have been abominable; we have strayed; You have let us go astray.*

---

(1) Cf. *Lamentations* 1:7. (2) Some editions have the following additional passage here: אֵין מְנַהֵל לָהּ מִכָּל בָּנִים יָלָדָה, וְאֵין מַחֲזִיק בְּיָדָהּ מִכָּל בָּנִים גִּדֵּלָה, *She has no leader from all the children she bore, none to take her hand from all the children she raised* (Isaiah 51:18). וְאֵין מִי יַחֲמוֹל עָלֵינוּ וּמִי, *And we have no one to pity us or comfort us, as You said.* (3) Jeremiah 15:5. וְנַחֲמֵנוּ כַּאֲשֶׁר אָמָרְתָּ, (4) Cf. *Ezekiel* 22:30. (5) Cf. *Psalms* 74:9. (6) *Isaiah* 64:6. (7) Cf. 53:6. (8) Cf. *Jeremiah* 18:12. (9) *II Samuel* 19:29. (10) Cf. *Psalms* 88:3. (11) Cf. 55:2. (12) Cf. 106:6.

סַרְנוּ מִמִּצְוֹתֶיךָ וּמִמִּשְׁפָּטֶיךָ הַטּוֹבִים וְלֹא שָׁוָה לָנוּ.[1] וְאַתָּה צַדִּיק עַל כָּל הַבָּא עָלֵינוּ, כִּי אֱמֶת עָשִׂיתָ וַאֲנַחְנוּ הִרְשָׁעְנוּ.[2]

שִׁבַּחְנוּ אֶת טוֹבוֹתֶיךָ, וְנָשִׁינוּ אֶת רֹב חֲסָדֶיךָ, וּמָרִינוּ אֶת פִּיךָ, וּמִמִּשְׁפָּטֶיךָ סַרְנוּ.[3] וּבְהַבְלֵי הָעוֹלָם הַזֶּה נִהֲבַלְנוּ,[4] אֵל רָהָבִים וְשָׂטֵי כָזָב פָּנִינוּ.[5] וְהִסְכַּלְנוּ הַרְבֵּה מְאֹד.[6] וְאָהַבְנוּ רָע מִטּוֹב, וְשֶׁקֶר מִדַּבֵּר צֶדֶק סֶלָה.[7] וְטֻמְאָה תַּחַת טָהֳרָה, וְשִׁקּוּץ תַּחַת זְכוּת. וְהֶחֱלַפְנוּ עוֹלָם עוֹמֵד בְּעוֹלָם עוֹבֵר, מִדֵּי יוֹם בְּיוֹמוֹ הִשְׁכֵּם וְחָטוֹא עַד אֲשֶׁר עֲווֹנוֹתֵינוּ עָבְרוּ רֹאשֵׁנוּ.[8] וְרַבּוּ מִשַּׂעֲרוֹתֵינוּ, וְעָצְמוּ מִדַּבְּרֵי פִינוּ, וְגָדְלוּ מִצְּעָדֵי רַגְלֵינוּ, וְגָבְהוּ מִנִּשְׁמַת רוּחַ אַפֵּנוּ. טָבַעְנוּ בְּיָוֵן מְצוּלָה וְאֵין מָעֳמָד, בָּאנוּ בְמַעֲמַקֵּי מַיִם וְשִׁבֹּלֶת שְׁטָפָתְנוּ.[9] וְלֹא לְךָ יהוה אֱלֹהֵינוּ הֲרֵעְנוּ כִּי אִם לְנַפְשֵׁנוּ, וְלֹא אוֹתְךָ הִכְעַסְנוּ כִּי אִם אוֹתָנוּ. כִּי אֱנוֹשׁ אִם חָטָא מַה יִּפְעַל לָךְ, וְאִם רַבּוּ פְּשָׁעָיו מַה יַּעֲשֶׂה לָּךְ. אֲבָל אוֹי לִבְנֵי אָדָם אֲשֶׁר חָטְאוּ לָךְ, וְאוֹי לְנַפְשָׁם, כִּי גָמְלוּ לָהֶם רָעָה.[10] אֱלֹהֵינוּ בֹּשְׁנוּ וְנִכְלַמְנוּ לְהָרִים אֱלֹהֵינוּ פָּנֵינוּ אֵלֶיךָ.[11] כִּי אָנוּ כִּכְלִי נִמְאָס. כֵּן נִבְזִינוּ בְּעֵינֵי נַפְשֵׁנוּ, כְּגֶבֶר אֲשֶׁר הֻטְבַּל בְּשַׁחַת, וְתַעֲבוּהוּ שַׂלְמוֹתָיו.[12] וּכְמוֹ בְעָוֹן חוֹלַלְנוּ, כֵּן בְּשֶׁת פָּנֵינוּ כִּסָּתְנוּ.[13]

וְעַתָּה יהוה אֱלֹהֵינוּ, אַחֲרֵי שׁוּבֵנוּ נִחַמְנוּ, וְאַחֲרֵי הִוָּדְעֵנוּ, סָפַקְנוּ עַל יָרֵךְ, בֹּשְׁנוּ וְגַם נִכְלַמְנוּ, כִּי נָשָׂאנוּ חֶרְפַּת נְעוּרֵינוּ.[14] וְעַל זֹאת נִשָּׂא נֶשֶׁר בְּשָׂרֵנוּ בְּשִׁנֵּינוּ, וְנַפְשֵׁנוּ נָשִׂים בְּכַפֵּנוּ.[15] וּבַמֶּה נְקַדְּמָה פָּנֶיךָ יהוה אֱלֹהֵינוּ, וּבַמֶּה נִכַּף לְךָ אֱלֹהֵי מָרוֹם,[16] וּבַמֶּה תִתְרַצֶּה, וּתְכַפֵּר לָנוּ עַל כָּל חַטֹּאתֵנוּ, אֲשֶׁר חָלְפוּ וְעָבְרוּ, כַּמַּיִם הַמֻּגָּרִים אַרְצָה, אֲשֶׁר לֹא יֵאָסֵפוּ.[17]

אִם בִּתְשׁוּבָה וּוִדּוּי תִּתְרַצֶּה, הִנְנוּ שָׁבִים וּמִתְוַדִּים לְפָנֶיךָ יהוה אֱלֹהֵינוּ. חָטָאנוּ וּפָשַׁעְנוּ וְיָשַׁר הֶעֱוִינוּ, וְלֹא שָׁוָה לָנוּ.[18] וְאִם בִּתְפִלָּה וּבְתַחֲנוּנִים תִּמְחָל, הִנְנוּ מַפִּילִים תַּחֲנוּנֵינוּ לְפָנֶיךָ כְּעֵינֵי עֲבָדִים אֶל יַד אֲדוֹנֵיהֶם, וּכְעֵינֵי שִׁפְחָה אֶל יַד גְּבִרְתָּהּ, כֵּן

(1) Cf. Job 33:27. (2) Nehemiah 9:33. (3) Cf. Psalms 119:102. (4) Cf. Job 27:12. (5) Cf. Psalms 40:5. (6) Cf. II Samuel 24:10. (7) Cf. Psalms 52:5. (8) Cf. 38:5. (9) Cf. 69:3. (10) Cf. Isaiah 3:9. (11) Cf. Ezra 9:6. (12) Cf. Job 9:31. (13) Cf. Psalms 44:16. (14) Cf. Jeremiah 31:18. (15) Cf. Job 13:14. (16) Cf. Micah 6:6. (17) Cf. II Samuel 14:14. (18) Cf. Job 33:27.

סַרְנוּ *We have turned away from Your commandments and from Your good laws but to no avail.*[1] *Yet You are righteous in all that has come upon us, for You have acted truthfully while we have caused wickedness.*[2]

שָׁכַחְנוּ *We have forgotten Your beneficence; we have become oblivious to Your manifold kindnesses; we have rebelled against Your word; and we have strayed from Your laws.*[3] *We have flitted after the frivolities of this world;*[4] *we have turned to the arrogant and to strayers after falsehood.*[5] *We have been utterly foolish.*[6] *We have loved evil better than good, lies better than speaking righteously, Selah.*[7] *[We have chosen] defilement instead of purity, foulness instead of merit. We have traded an eternal world for an ephemeral one, every day rising early to sin, until our iniquities have surmounted our heads.*[8] *They are more numerous than our hairs, stronger than the words our mouth [speaks], larger than our legs' stride, taller than the soul that gives us our breath. We have sunk into the deep mud, and there is no foothold; we have entered deep waters and the current sweeps us away.*[9] *We have not done harm to You, HASHEM, our God, but to our own souls; it is not You we have given cause for anger, but ourselves. For if man should sin, what has he accomplished against You? If his sins are many, what has he done to You? Yet woe to people who have sinned against You, and woe to their souls, for they have wrought evil to themselves.*[10] *Our God, we are ashamed and humiliated to lift our faces to You, O our God,*[11] *for we are like a befouled utensil. So are we despised in our own estimation, like a man sunk in a pit, whose very clothes make him odious.*[12] *As we are brought forth in iniquity, so [inevitably] has shame covered our faces over.*[13]

וְעַתָּה *And now, HASHEM, our God, after repenting we regretted [our past misdeeds]; after being made to know [what we had done], we slapped our thighs [in anguish]; we are shamed [on the outside] and humiliated [on the inside], for we must bear the shame of our youthful [sins].*[14] *And for this reason we take our [lips']flesh in our teeth [to silence ourselves from complaining about our deserved lot], and we place our souls in the palm of our hands [offering ourselves to our just deserts].*[15] *For with what [merit] can we come before You, HASHEM, our God? With what shall we humble ourselves to You, God of the Heights?*[16] *With what will You find us favorable and atone for us for all our sins, that have passed and gone by like water running along the ground that cannot be gathered?*[17]

Will You find [us] favorable through repentance and confession? Here we are, repenting and confessing before You, HASHEM, our God: we have sinned erringly, and we have sinned willfully; we have made crooked what was straight, and it is of no use to us.[18] *But if through prayer and supplication You pardon [us], then here we are, we cast down our supplications before You; and as servants' eyes [look] to their masters' hand, as the maidservant's eyes [looks] to her mistress' hand, so are*

עֵינֵינוּ נְשׂוּאוֹת אֵלֶיךָ.[1]

וְאִם בִּבְכִי וּזְעָקָה תִּסְלַח, הִנֵּה בַמִּסְתָּרִים תִּבְכֶּה נַפְשֵׁנוּ מִפְּנֵי חַטֹּאתֵינוּ,[2] וּבַחֲדָרִים תֶּאֱנַח רוּחֵנוּ עַל רֹב פְּשָׁעֵינוּ.

וְאִם בְּשֵׁבֶר רוּחַ תְּכַפֵּר, הִנֵּה נִשְׁבַּר לִבֵּנוּ בְּקִרְבֵּנוּ, וְנִדְכְּאָה רוּחֵנוּ[3] מִן הַצָּרוֹת וּמִן הַתְּלָאוֹת אֲשֶׁר עָבְרוּ עָלֵינוּ, עַד אֲשֶׁר לֹא נוֹתַר מְתוֹם בִּבְשָׂרֵנוּ.[4] לוּלֵי רַחֲמֶיךָ וַחֲסָדֶיךָ, אָז אָבַדְנוּ בַעֲוֹנֵינוּ.[5]

אָשַׁמְנוּ מִכָּל עָם, בֹּשְׁנוּ מִכָּל דּוֹר, גָּלָה מִמֶּנּוּ מָשׂושׂ, דָּוָה לִבֵּנוּ בַּחֲטָאֵינוּ, הֻחְבַּל אִוּוּיֵנוּ, וְנִפְרַע פְּאֵרֵנוּ, זְבוּל בֵּית מִקְדָּשֵׁנוּ חָרַב בַּעֲוֹנֵינוּ, טִירָתֵנוּ הָיְתָה לְשַׁמָּה, יְפִי אַדְמָתֵנוּ לְזָרִים, כֹּחֵנוּ לְנָכְרִים.

וַעֲדַיִן לֹא שַׁבְנוּ מִטָּעוּתֵנוּ וְהֵיךְ נָעִיז פָּנֵינוּ וְנַקְשֶׁה עָרְפֵּנוּ, לוֹמַר לְפָנֶיךָ יהוה אֱלֹהֵינוּ וֵאלֹהֵי אֲבוֹתֵינוּ, צַדִּיקִים אֲנַחְנוּ וְלֹא חָטָאנוּ, אֲבָל אֲנַחְנוּ וַאֲבוֹתֵינוּ חָטָאנוּ.

Strike the left side of the chest with the right fist
while reciting each of the sins in the following confession litany.

אָשַׁמְנוּ, בָּגַדְנוּ, גָּזַלְנוּ, דִּבַּרְנוּ דֹפִי. הֶעֱוִינוּ, וְהִרְשַׁעְנוּ, זַדְנוּ, חָמַסְנוּ, טָפַלְנוּ שֶׁקֶר. יָעַצְנוּ רָע, כִּזַּבְנוּ, לַצְנוּ, מָרַדְנוּ, נִאַצְנוּ, סָרַרְנוּ, עָוִינוּ, פָּשַׁעְנוּ, צָרַרְנוּ, קִשִּׁינוּ עֹרֶף. רָשַׁעְנוּ, שִׁחַתְנוּ, תִּעַבְנוּ, תָּעִינוּ, תִּעְתָּעְנוּ.

סַרְנוּ מִמִּצְוֹתֶיךָ וּמִמִּשְׁפָּטֶיךָ הַטּוֹבִים וְלֹא שָׁוָה לָנוּ. וְאַתָּה צַדִּיק עַל כָּל הַבָּא עָלֵינוּ, כִּי אֱמֶת עָשִׂיתָ וַאֲנַחְנוּ הִרְשָׁעְנוּ.

וְעַתָּה יהוה אֱלֹהֵינוּ אִם עָשִׂינוּ כְּאִוַּלְתֵּנוּ, עֲשֵׂה אַתָּה כֶּאֱמוּנָתֶךָ וּסְלַח, כִּי תְמִים דֵּעִים אָתָּה. אִם שִׁלַּמְנוּ רָעָה תַּחַת טוֹבָה, גְּמָלְנוּ טוֹב וְלֹא רָע. כִּי יֶתֶר מֵרֵעֵהוּ צַדִּיק,[6] וְכָל שֹׁכֵן הַבּוֹרֵא יִתְבָּרַךְ שְׁמוֹ. וְאִם הִרְבִּינוּ לִפְשֹׁעַ, אַתָּה הוּא רַב חֶסֶד וּמַרְבֶּה לִסְלֹחַ, אֲשֶׁר צִדְקוֹתֶיךָ וַחֲסָדֶיךָ רַבּוּ מֵהַרְרֵי אֵל וַעֲמָקוּ מִתְּהוֹם רַבָּה.[7] כִּסָּה שָׁמַיִם הוֹדְךָ וּתְהִלָּתְךָ מָלְאָה

(1) Cf. *Psalms* 123:2. (2) Cf. *Jeremiah* 13:17. (3) Cf. *Psalms* 51:19. (4) Cf. 38:4.
(5) Cf. 119:92. (6) Cf. *Proverbs* 12:26. (7) Cf. *Psalms* 36:7.

our eyes lifted towards You.[1]

Or if through weeping and crying You will forgive [us], see: our soul weeps in [its] hidden places because of our inadvertent sins;[2] our spirit sighs in [its] chambers over our many willful sins.

Or if because of a broken spirit You will atone [for us], see, our hearts are broken within us, and our spirit is crushed[3] by the troubles and hardships that have transpired with us, until no part of our flesh has remained whole.[4] Were it not for Your mercy and Your kindness, we would have been lost in our iniquities.[5]

[א] We have become the guiltiest of people. [ב] We have become the most degraded of all generations. [ג] Joy has departed from us. [ד] Our heart has been saddened by our sins. [ה] Our desirous treasure has been ruined, [ו] and our splendor dashed, [ז] for our Holy Temple edifice [ח] has been destroyed for our iniquities. [ט] Our Palace has become desolate. [י] [Jerusalem,] the beauty of our Land is given over to aliens, [כ] our power to strangers.

But still we have not returned from our waywardness. So how can we be so brazen and obstinate as to say before You, HASHEM, our God and the God of our forefathers, that we are righteous and have not sinned, for in truth, both we and our fathers have sinned.

Strike the left side of the chest with the right fist while reciting
each of the sins in the following confession litany.

אָשַׁמְנוּ *We have become guilty;* [ב] *we have betrayed;* [ג] *we have robbed;* [ד] *we have spoken slander;* [ה] *we have caused perversion;* [ו] *we have caused wickedness;* [ז] *we have sinned willfully;* [ח] *we have extorted;* [ט] *we have accused falsely;* [י] *we have given evil counsel;* [כ] *we have been deceitful;* [ל] *we have scorned;* [מ] *we have rebelled;* [נ] *we have provoked;* [ס] *we have turned away;* [ע] *we have been perverse;* [פ] *we have acted wantonly;* [צ] *we have persecuted;* [ק] *we have been obstinate;* [ר] *we have been wicked;* [ש] *we have corrupted;* [ת] *we have been abominable; we have strayed; You have let us go astray.*

סַרְנוּ *We have turned away from Your commandments and from Your good laws but to no avail. Yet You are righteous in all that has come upon us, for You have acted truthfully while we have caused wickedness.*

וְעַתָּה *And now, HASHEM, our God, though we have done according to our wicked folly, may You do as is Your wont and forgive, for You are the All-Knowing. Though we have paid back evil in place of goodness, nevertheless, grant us good and not bad. For a righteous person is greater souled than his fellow,[6] all the more so the Creator. Though we have willfully sinned many times, You are the Abundant in Kindness and profusely forgiving, for Your righteousness and Your kindnesses are greater than the mighty mountains and deeper than the vast deep waters.[7] Your majesty covers the heavens, and Your praise fills the*

הָאָרֶץ.1 יהוה שְׁמַעֲנוּ שִׁמְעֲךָ,2 כִּי בְּאַחַת הַמִּדּוֹת תִּסְלַח לַאֲשֶׁר
חָטְאוּ לָךְ, וְאַף כִּי בְכֻלָּם. סְלַח נָא לַעֲוֹנֵינוּ וּלְחַטֹּאתֵינוּ,3 וּלְכָל
חַטֹּאת וַעֲוֹנוֹת יִשְׂרָאֵל. וְכַבְּסֵנוּ מֵעֲוֹנֵינוּ וּמֵחַטֹּאתֵינוּ טַהֲרֵנוּ,4 וְאַל
תִּקְצֹף עָלֵינוּ עַד מְאֹד. וְאַל לָעַד תִּזְכֹּר עָוֹן וְאַתָּה רַב לִסְלוֹחַ.

וְאַתָּה יהוה חָשַׁבְתָּ לְצָרֵף סִיגֵנוּ, וּלְהָסִיר בְּדִילֵנוּ,5 וְלִשְׁבֹּר
אֶת לִבֵּנוּ הַזּוֹנָה,6 וּלְהָתֵם טֻמְאָתֵנוּ מִמֶּנּוּ. עַל כֵּן הִגְלִיתָנוּ
וּבַגּוֹיִם זֵרִיתָנוּ.7 הִנֵּה בִּשְׁאוֹן הַמַּלְכֻיּוֹת הִצְלַלְנוּ, וּכְהִתּוּךְ כֶּסֶף
בְּתוֹךְ כּוּר נִתָּכְנוּ.8 וְלֹא מִקְּצֹר יָדְךָ לֹא הוֹשַׁעְתָּנוּ, וְלֹא מִכְּבֹד אָזְנְךָ
לֹא שָׁמַעְתָּ תְּפִלָּתֵנוּ, כִּי הִבְדִּילוּ עֲוֹנוֹתֵינוּ בֵּינֵינוּ וּבֵין יְשׁוּעָתֶךָ.9 לְךָ
אֲדֹנָי הַצְּדָקָה, וְלָנוּ בֹּשֶׁת הַפָּנִים.10 לַאדֹנָי אֱלֹהֵינוּ הָרַחֲמִים
וְהַסְּלִיחוֹת, כִּי מָרַדְנוּ בוֹ.11 וּלְךָ אֲדֹנָי הַחֶסֶד, כִּי אַתָּה תְשַׁלֵּם לְאִישׁ
כְּמַעֲשֵׂהוּ.12 וְאַתָּה יהוה אֱלֹהֵינוּ, גּוֹאֵל יִשְׂרָאֵל וְקִדּוֹשׁוֹ,13 הַלְעוֹלָם
תֶּאֱנַף בָּנוּ, תִּמְשֹׁךְ אַפְּךָ לְדֹר וָדֹר,14 חָלִילָה. הַלְעוֹלָם תִּזְנַח, וְלֹא
תֹסִיף לִרְצוֹת עוֹד, חָלִילָה. כִּי לֹא אָפְסוּ לָנֶצַח חֲסָדֶיךָ,15 וְלֹא כָלוּ
רַחֲמֶיךָ, כִּי הֵמָּה חֲדָשִׁים לַבְּקָרִים,16 יָחִילוּ בְּכָל עֵת וּבְכָל רֶגַע.

וּלְמַעַן שִׁמְךָ יהוה, עֲשֵׂה עִמָּנוּ, כִּי הִיא תְהִלָּתֶךָ. כִּי נִקְרָא שִׁמְךָ
עָלֵינוּ,17 יהוה אֱלֹהֵי יִשְׂרָאֵל. וּלְמַעַן בְּרִית אֲבוֹתֵינוּ, אַבְרָהָם יִצְחָק
וְיַעֲקֹב, אֲשֶׁר כָּרַתָּ לָהֶם, וְאֶת הַשְּׁבוּעָה אֲשֶׁר נִשְׁבַּעְתָּ לָהֶם, זְכוֹר.
וּלְמַעַן תּוֹרָתֶךָ וּלְמַעַן הַקְּדוֹשִׁים וְלוֹמְדֶיהָ, כִּי נִמְעֲטוּ וְשָׁחוּ,18
וְהִבְטַחְתָּנוּ עַל אוֹדוֹתֶיהָ כִּי לֹא תִשָּׁכַח עֵדוּת מִפִּי זַרְעוֹ,19 וּדְבָרַי
אֲשֶׁר שַׂמְתִּי בְּפִיהֶם לֹא יָמוּשׁוּ.20 וּלְמַעַן עַמְּךָ וְנַחֲלָתְךָ אֲשֶׁר
נִשְׁאֲרוּ מְעַט מֵהַרְבֵּה,21 כַּתֹּרֶן בְּרֹאשׁ הָהָר, וְכַנֵּס עַל הַגִּבְעָה.22
וּלְמַעַן יְרוּשָׁלַיִם עִיר קָדְשֶׁךָ, אֲשֶׁר הָיְתָה מִדְבָּר שְׁמָמָה, וְיָצָא
מִמֶּנָּה כָּל הֲדָרָהּ.23 וּלְמַעַן בֵּית חַיֵּינוּ וְתִפְאַרְתֵּנוּ, אֲשֶׁר הִלְלוּךְ
אֲבוֹתֵינוּ אֲשֶׁר הָיָה לִשְׂרֵפַת אֵשׁ, וְכָל מַחֲמַדֵּינוּ הָיוּ לְחָרְבָּה.24
וּלְמַעַן טְבוּחִים עַל יִחוּדֶךָ. וּלְמַעַן הֲרוּגִים עַל שֵׁם קָדְשֶׁךָ. וּלְמַעַן
תּוֹרָתְךָ הַקְּדוֹשָׁה הַשְּׂרוּפָה בָאֵשׁ, וּנְתוּנָה לְמִרְמָס לְכָל עוֹבְרֵי
דָרֶךְ. הַעַל אֵלֶּה תִּתְאַפַּק יהוה, וְתֶחֱשֶׁה וּתְעַנֵּנוּ עַד מְאֹד.25

(1) Cf. *Habakkuk* 3:3. (2) Cf. 3:2. (3) Cf. *Exodus* 34:9. (4) Cf. *Psalms* 51:4. (5) Cf. *Isaiah* 1:25.
(6) Cf. *Ezekiel* 6:9. (7) *Psalms* 44:12. (8) Cf. *Ezekiel* 22:22. (9) Cf. *Isaiah* 59:1-2. (10) *Daniel* 9:7.
(11) 9:9. (12) Cf. *Psalms* 62:13. (13) Cf. *Isaiah* 49:7. (14) *Psalms* 85:6. (15) Cf. 77:8-9.
(16) Cf. *Lamentations* 3:22-23. (17) Cf. *Daniel* 9:19. (18) Cf. *Psalms* 107:39.
(19) Cf. *Deuteronomy* 31:21. (20) Cf. *Isaiah* 59:21. (21) Cf. *Jeremiah* 42:2.
(22) Cf. *Isaiah* 30:17. (23) Cf. *Lamentations* 1:6. (24) Cf. *Isaiah* 64:10. (25) 64:11.

earth.[1] HASHEM, we have heard of Your tidings,[2] how with one of Your Attributes You forgive those who have sinned against You; certainly with all of them. Please forgive our iniquities and our errors,[3] and all the errors and iniquities of Israel. Wash us clean of our iniquities; purify us of our errors.[4] Do not be overly angry with us; do not remember iniquity forever, for You are abundantly forgiving.

וְאַתָּה You, HASHEM, decided to refine us of our dross, to remove our base metal;[5] to break our straying heart;[6] to rid us of our defilement. Therefore You sent us into exile, and scattered us among the nations.[7] See, we have been drowned among the clamorous waves of kingdoms; we have been melted as silver melts in the crucible.[8] It is not because You lack strength that You have not redeemed us; it is not because Your ears are dull that You have not heard our prayer; but because our sins have made a barrier between us and Your salvation.[9] Yours, my Lord, is the righteousness; and ours is the shamefacedness.[10] To my Lord, our God, are mercy and forgiveness, for we have rebelled against Him.[11] And Yours, my Lord, is the kindness, for You reward man according to his deeds[12]. And You, HASHEM, our God, Israel's Redeemer and its Holy One:[13] Will You forever be angry with us, [and] allow Your wrath to endure through the generations?[14] It would be sacrilege! Will You abandon us forever, never to be pleased [with us] again? It would be sacrilege! For Your kindness is not ended forever,[15] Your mercy is not at an end; for they are renewed each morning,[16] brought forth from moment to moment.

So for Your Name's sake, HASHEM, do [kindness] with us, for this is Your praise — for Your Name is called upon us,[17] HASHEM, God of Israel; for the sake of the covenant that You made with our forefathers, Abraham, Isaac, and Jacob, and remember the oath You swore to them; for the sake of Your Torah and the holy one who are its scholars, for they have dwindled and their backs are bent,[18] and You have promised us that the [Torah's] Testimony would never be forgotten from the mouth of [Jacob's] seed:[19] 'And My words, that I have placed in their mouths, shall not stir [from your mouth or from the mouth of your children or your children's children forever];'[20] for the sake of Your people and Your heritage, who are left a few out of many,[21] like a [lonely] signal-post on a mountaintop, like a [forsaken] banner on a hill;[22] for the sake of Jerusalem, Your Holy City that has become a desolate wasteland, all its glory departed;[23] for the sake of [the Temple,] the House of our life and glory, where our fathers praised You, and which was consumed by the fire with all that was most precious to us destroyed;[24] for the sake of those murdered for Your Holy Name; for those slaughtered for Your oneness; for Your holy Torah that is burned in the fire and trampled by all passersby. Will You hold back [Your mercy] from these? Will You keep silent and allow us to be tormented so?[25]

וְהִנֵּה כָּל הַגּוֹיִם יוֹשְׁבִים שְׁלֵוִים וְשֹׁקְטִים, וְאֶבְיוֹנֵי עַמְּךָ דְּוֹוִים סְחוּפִים וּמְדֻלְדָּלִים. וּבְדַלְדּוּלָם הֵם מְבַקְשִׁים פָּנֶיךָ, וּמַפִּילִים תְּחִנָּתָם מוּל אֲרוֹן בְּרִיתֶךָ. יהוה אֱלֹהֵי הַצְּבָאוֹת, עַד מָתַי לֹא תְרַחֵם אֶת יְרוּשָׁלַיִם וְאֵת עָרֵי יְהוּדָה אֲשֶׁר זָעַמְתָּ זֶה כַּמֶּה שָׁנִים.[1] וּרְאֵה אֶת עַמְּךָ מוֹרֵה מְאֹד, וְאֶפֶס עָצוּר וְעָזוּב, וְאֵין עוֹזֵר לְיִשְׂרָאֵל.[2] פָּנִינוּ לְיָמִין וְאֵין עוֹזֵר, לִשְׂמֹאל וְאֵין תּוֹמֵךְ, וַאֲנַחְנוּ אֵין לָנוּ עַל מִי לְהִשָּׁעֵן, כִּי אִם עָלֶיךָ אָבִינוּ שֶׁבַּשָּׁמַיִם.[3] הִנֵּה הָעֵת וְהָעוֹנָה יָאֲתָה לְךָ לְהוֹשִׁיעַ וּלְהִוָּדַע עֹז רַחֲמֶיךָ, אֲשֶׁר מֵעוֹלָם, כִּי רַבּוּ מְאֹד.

וּכְשֶׁחָטְאוּ יִשְׂרָאֵל בַּמִּדְבָּר, עָמַד מֹשֶׁה רַבֵּנוּ בִּתְפִלָּה לְפָנֶיךָ, וּבִקֵּשׁ רַחֲמִים עַל עַמְּךָ בֵּית יִשְׂרָאֵל. וְכַךְ אָמַר בִּתְפִלָּתוֹ, מַלְכִּי וֵאלֹהַי, סְלַח נָא לַעֲוֹן הָעָם הַזֶּה כְּגֹדֶל חַסְדֶּךָ, וְכַאֲשֶׁר נָשָׂאתָה לָעָם הַזֶּה מִמִּצְרַיִם וְעַד הֵנָּה.[4] וְאַתָּה הֲשֵׁבוֹתָ לּוֹ כְּדַרְכֵי טוּבְךָ. וְדִבַּרְתָּ וְאָמַרְתָּ לוֹ, סָלַחְתִּי כִּדְבָרֶךָ.[5] וַאֲנַחְנוּ בֹּשְׁנוּ בְמַעֲשֵׂינוּ, וְנִכְלַמְנוּ בַּעֲוֹנֵינוּ, וְהִשְׁחַרוּ פָנֵינוּ מִפְּנֵי חַטֹּאתֵינוּ. וְנִכְפְּפָה קוֹמָתֵנוּ מִפְּנֵי אַשְׁמָתֵנוּ, וְאֵין לָנוּ פֶּה לְהָשִׁיב, וְלֹא מֵצַח לְהָרִים רֹאשׁ.

לְעֵינֵינוּ עָשְׁקוּ עֲמָלֵנוּ, מְמֻשָּׁךְ וּמְמוֹרָט מִמֶּנּוּ, נָתְנוּ עֻלָּם עָלֵינוּ, סָבַלְנוּ עַל שִׁכְמֵנוּ, עֲבָדִים מָשְׁלוּ בָנוּ, פֹּרֵק אֵין מִיָּדָם, צָרוֹת רַבּוֹת סְבָבוּנוּ, קְרָאֲנוּךָ יהוה אֱלֹהֵינוּ, רָחַקְתָּ מִמֶּנּוּ בַּעֲוֹנֵינוּ, שַׁבְנוּ מֵאַחֲרֶיךָ, תָּעִינוּ וְאָבָדְנוּ.

וַעֲדַיִן לֹא שַׁבְנוּ מִטָּעוּתֵנוּ וְהֵיךְ נָעִיז פָּנֵינוּ וְנַקְשֶׁה עָרְפֵּנוּ, לוֹמַר לְפָנֶיךָ יהוה אֱלֹהֵינוּ וֵאלֹהֵי אֲבוֹתֵינוּ, צַדִּיקִים אֲנַחְנוּ וְלֹא חָטָאנוּ, אֲבָל אֲנַחְנוּ וַאֲבוֹתֵינוּ חָטָאנוּ.

Strike the left side of the chest with the right fist while reciting each of the sins in the following confession litany.

אָשַׁמְנוּ, בָּגַדְנוּ, גָּזַלְנוּ, דִּבַּרְנוּ דֹפִי. הֶעֱוִינוּ, וְהִרְשַׁעְנוּ, זַדְנוּ, חָמַסְנוּ, טָפַלְנוּ שֶׁקֶר. יָעַצְנוּ רָע, כִּזַּבְנוּ, לַצְנוּ, מָרַדְנוּ, נִאַצְנוּ, סָרַרְנוּ, עָוִינוּ, פָּשַׁעְנוּ, צָרַרְנוּ, קִשִּׁינוּ עֹרֶף, רָשַׁעְנוּ, שִׁחַתְנוּ, תִּעַבְנוּ, תָּעִינוּ, תִּעְתָּעְנוּ.

---

(1) Cf. *Zechariah* 1:12. (2) Cf. *II Kings* 14:26. (3) Cf. tractate *Sotah* 49a. (4) *Numbers* 14:19. (5) 14:20.

וְהִנֵּה See, all the nations live serenely and tranquilly, while the impoverished of Your people are full of pain, swept aside and in turmoil. Yet, though in turmoil, they seek Your countenance, and cast down their supplication before the Ark of Your covenant. HASHEM, God of the Legions, until when will You not have mercy on Jerusalem and the cities of Judah, for You have been enraged [against them] for so many years?¹ See Your people, greatly vexed, with nothing preserved and nothing left [to them], and no helper for Israel.² We turn to our right, and there is no helper; to our left, and there is none to support [us]; so as for us, we have not on whom to lean except You, our Father in Heaven.³ See, the time and the season are propitious for You to save [us], and to let be known the fierce strength of Your mercies, which have always been, for they are very great.

וּבְשֶׁחָטְאוּ When Israel sinned in the Wilderness, Moses our Teacher stood up to pray before You, and he asked mercy for Your people the House of Israel. And this is what he said in his prayer: 'My King and my God! Forgive, please, the iniquity of this people according to the greatness of Your kindness, and as You have forgiven this people from Egypt until now.'⁴ And You answered him as befits Your goodly ways, and spoke, and said to him: 'I have forgiven according to your word!'⁵ [Now] we are ashamed of our deeds, humiliated by our iniquities, and our faces have turned black on account of our sins. Our stature is bowed because of our guilt, and we do not have [words in our] mouth to answer, nor the [audaciousness of] brow to lift our heads.

[ל] [The benefit of] our labor has been stolen, [מ] pulled away and cut off from us. [נ] They have placed their yoke upon us, [ס] our burdens upon our shoulders. [ע] Slaves have ruled over us, [פ] there is no redemption from their hand. [צ] Abundant troubles have surrounded us, [ק] we called upon You, HASHEM, our God, [ר] but You have distanced us for our iniquities. [ש] We have turned away from following after You; [ת] we have strayed; we have become lost.

But still we have not returned from our waywardness. So how can we be so brazen and obstinate as to say before You, HASHEM, our God and the God of our forefathers, that we are righteous and have not sinned, for in truth, both we and our fathers have sinned.

Strike the left side of the chest with the right fist while reciting
each of the sins in the following confession litany:

אָשַׁמְנוּ We have become guilty; [ב] we have betrayed; [ג] we have robbed; [ד] we have spoken slander; [ה] we have caused perversion; [ו] we have caused wickedness; [ז] we have sinned willfully; [ח] we have extorted; [ט] we have accused falsely; [י] we have given evil counsel; [כ] we have been deceitful; [ל] we have scorned; [מ] we have rebelled; [נ] we have provoked; [ס] we have turned away; [ע] we have been perverse; [פ] we have acted wantonly; [צ] we have persecuted; [ק] we have been obstinate; [ר] we have been wicked; [ש] we have corrupted; [ת] we have been abominable; we have strayed; You have let us go astray.

סָרְנוּ מִמִּצְוֹתֶיךָ וּמִמִּשְׁפָּטֶיךָ הַטּוֹבִים וְלֹא שָׁוָה לָנוּ. וְאַתָּה צַדִּיק עַל כָּל הַבָּא עָלֵינוּ, כִּי אֱמֶת עָשִׂיתָ וַאֲנַחְנוּ הִרְשָׁעְנוּ.

אָנָּא הַבֵּט בְּצִדְקַת עֲבָדֶיךָ חֲסִידֶיךָ, אֲשֶׁר הֶעֱרוּ נַפְשָׁם לָמוּת עָלֶיךָ,[1] וְלֹא חָסוּ עַל נַפְשָׁם וְעַל זַרְעָם, וְקָצוּ וּמָאֲסוּ בְּחַיֵּי הָעוֹלָם הַזֶּה. וּבִטְּלוּ רְצוֹנָם מִפְּנֵי רְצוֹנֶךָ,[2] וְקִדְּשׁוּ שִׁמְךָ הַגָּדוֹל וְלֹא חִלְּלוּהוּ. וְרָצוּ לַזֶּבַח, וּפָשְׁטוּ צַנָּארָם וְעָמְדוּ בְנִסְיוֹן וְנֶאֱמָנוּ, וְנִבְחֲנוּ בְּצֵרוּף, וְנִמְצְאוּ תְמִימִים. וְנָגְעוּ דְמֵי אָבוֹת וּבָנִים, וּדְמֵי רַחֲמָנִיּוֹת וְיַלְדֵיהֶן, וְנִתְעָרְבוּ דְמֵי אַחִים וַאֲחָיוֹת, וּדְמֵי חֲתָנִים וְכַלּוֹת, וּדְמֵי חֲכָמִים וַחֲכָמוֹת, וּדְמֵי הַגּוּנִים וְהַגּוּנוֹת, וּדְמֵי חֲסִידִים וַחֲסִידוֹת, וּדְמֵי זְקֵנִים וּזְקֵנוֹת, וּדְמֵי בַּחוּרִים וּבְחוּרוֹת, וּדְמֵי פַרְנָסִים וְחַזָּנֵיהֶם, וּדְמֵי דַיָּנִים וְסוֹפְרֵיהֶם, וּדְמֵי מְלַמְּדִים וְתַלְמִידֵיהֶם, וּדְמֵי אֲנָשִׁים וּנְשׁוֹתֵיהֶם, וְנֶהֶרְגוּ כֻלָּם יַחַד, עַל קִדּוּשׁ שִׁמְךָ הַמְּיֻחָד. אֶרֶץ אַל תְּכַסִּי דָמָם, וְאַל יְהִי מָקוֹם לְזַעֲקָתָם.[3] עַד יַשְׁקִיף וְיֵרֶא יהוה מִשָּׁמַיִם.[4] וְיִנְקֹם נִקְמָתוֹ, וְנִקְמַת עַמּוֹ, וְנִקְמַת תּוֹרָתוֹ, וְנִקְמַת דַּם עֲבָדָיו, אֲשֶׁר שָׁפְכוּ דָמָם כַּמַּיִם, כְּהִבְטַחְתָּנוּ בְּיַד אֲבִי חוֹזֶה, הַרְנִינוּ גוֹיִם עַמּוֹ, כִּי דַם עֲבָדָיו יִקּוֹם, וְנָקָם יָשִׁיב לְצָרָיו, וְכִפֶּר אַדְמָתוֹ עַמּוֹ.[5] אֶת אֵלֶּה מִזְבְּחוֹת זְכוֹר, וְאֵלֶּה עֲקֵדוֹת תִּרְאֶה, כִּי עַל אַחַת הִרְעִישׁ הָעוֹלָם, וְהֵן אֶרְאֶלָּם צָעֲקוּ חוּצָה.[6] וְנִשְׁבַּעְתָּ לְבָרֵךְ עוֹקֵד וְנֶעֱקָד.[7] לְהַרְבּוֹת זַרְעָם כְּחוֹל הַיָּם.[7] וְאַף כִּי עַתָּה כַּמָּה וְכַמָּה עָקְדוּ בְנֵיהֶם, עַל יִחוּד שִׁמְךָ הַמְּיֻחָד הַנִּכְבָּד. נָא דוֹרֵשׁ דָּמִים קוֹל דְּמֵי בָנֶיךָ צוֹעֲקִים אֵלֶיךָ מִן הָאֲדָמָה.[8] וְלָאָרֶץ לֹא יְכֻפַּר לַדָּם אֲשֶׁר שֻׁפַּךְ בָּהּ, כִּי אִם בְּדַם שֹׁפְכוֹ.[9] וְהִנָּחֵם, וְשֹׁךְ אַף, וְכַלֵּה חֵמָה, וְתַשְׁבִּית שׁוֹד וָשֶׁבֶר מֵעַמֶּךָ. חוּס וְרַחֵם אֶת יֶתֶר הַפְּלֵיטָה, וְתוֹצִיאֶנָּה מֵאֲפֵלָה לְאוֹרָה. וְחַדֵּשׁ עָלֵינוּ שָׁנָה טוֹבָה, שְׁנַת רָצוֹן וְעֵת גְּאֻלָּה. שַׁדַּי תִּזְכָּר לָנוּ בְּרִית אֶזְרָח, וְתִפְקֹד לָנוּ זְכוּת הַנֶּעֱקָד, וּתְרַחֲמֵנוּ בְּצִדְקַת אִישׁ תָּם. וְאַתָּה צַדִּיק עַל כָּל הַבָּא עָלֵינוּ, כִּי אֱמֶת עָשִׂיתָ וַאֲנַחְנוּ הִרְשָׁעְנוּ.[10]

(1) Cf. Isaiah 53:12. (2) See tractate Avos 2:2. (3) Cf. Job 16:18. (4) Lamentations 3:50. (5) Deuteronomy 32:43. (6) Cf. Isaiah 33:7. (7) See Genesis 22:16-17. (8) Cf. 4:10. (9) Numbers 35:33. (10) Nehemiah 9:33.

סַרְנוּ *We have turned away from Your commandments and from Your good laws but to no avail. Yet You are righteous in all that has come upon us, for You have acted truthfully while we have caused wickedness.*

אָנָּא *Please look to the righteousness of Your servants and Your pious ones, who poured forth their souls [prepared] to die for You.*[1] *They did not pity their souls nor their children; rather, they scorned and disdained the life of this world. They put aside their will before Your will.*[2] *They sanctified Your name and did not profane it. They ran to the sacrifice and stretched forth their necks. They stood firm in the trial and proved faithful. They were tested in the crucible and were found wholehearted. The bloods of fathers and of [their] sons touched; the bloods of compassionate women and their children; the bloods of brothers and sisters mingled; the bloods of grooms and brides; the bloods of wise men and wise women; the bloods of worthy men and worthy women; the bloods of pious men and pious women; the bloods of elderly men and elderly women; the bloods of youths and maidens; the bloods of providers and their deputies; the bloods of judges and their scribes; the bloods of teachers and their students; the bloods of men and their wives. All were slain together so as to sanctify Your Unique Name. Earth, do not cover their blood; and let there be no resting-place for their outcry;*[3] *until* HASHEM *looks down from Heaven and sees,*[4] *and takes His vengeance, His people's vengeance, His Torah's vengeance, and vengeance for the blood of His servants who let their blood be spilled like water. For so You promised us through [Moses] the Father of Prophets: 'O nations, sing the praise of His people, for He will avenge the blood of His servants, and pay back vengeance upon His oppressors, and atone for His Land and His people.'*[5] *Remember these altars, see these bindings for the sacrifice, for over one [such sacrifice, Isaac's,] the whole world was in an uproar, and the angels cried out in the streets.*[6] *You have sworn to bless both [Abraham the] binder and [Isaac the] bound; to increase their offspring as the sand of the sea.*[7] *Certainly now, when many have bound their children [on the altar] to proclaim the Oneness of Your Unique and Glorious Name. Please, Avenger of Blood, the voice of Your children's blood cries out to You from the ground.*[8] *And the earth cannot have atonement for the blood that is spilled into it except with the blood of him that spilled it.*[9] *Reconsider, [then,] quell [Your] anger and dismiss fury, and make an end of pillage and ruin among Your people. Pity and have mercy on our fugitive remnant, and take them out of darkness into light. Renew for us a good year, a year of favor and a time of redemption. O Almighty, remember in our favor [Abraham] the Ezrachite's covenant; for our sake bring to mind the merit of [Isaac] who was bound [on the altar]; and have mercy on us for the sake of the righteousness, whole-hearted [Jacob]. For You are righteous in all that has come upon us, for You have acted truthfully while we have caused wickedness.*[10]

הִרְשַׁעְנוּ וּפָשַׁעְנוּ, לָכֵן לֹא נוֹשַׁעְנוּ. וְתֵן בְּלִבֵּנוּ לַעֲזוֹב דֶּרֶךְ
רֶשַׁע, וְחִישׁ לָנוּ יֶשַׁע, כַּכָּתוּב עַל יַד נְבִיאֶךָ: יַעֲזֹב
רָשָׁע דַּרְכּוֹ, וְאִישׁ אָוֶן מַחְשְׁבֹתָיו, וְיָשֹׁב אֶל יהוה וִירַחֲמֵהוּ, וְאֶל
אֱלֹהֵינוּ כִּי יַרְבֶּה לִסְלוֹחַ.[1]

מְשִׁיחַ צִדְקֶךָ אָמַר לְפָנֶיךָ: שְׁגִיאוֹת מִי יָבִין מִנִּסְתָּרוֹת נַקֵּנִי.[2]
נַקֵּנוּ יהוה אֱלֹהֵינוּ מִכָּל פְּשָׁעֵינוּ, וְטַהֲרֵנוּ מִכָּל
טֻמְאוֹתֵינוּ, וּזְרוֹק עָלֵינוּ מַיִם טְהוֹרִים וְטַהֲרֵנוּ, כַּכָּתוּב עַל יַד
נְבִיאֶךָ: וְזָרַקְתִּי עֲלֵיכֶם מַיִם טְהוֹרִים וּטְהַרְתֶּם, מִכֹּל טֻמְאוֹתֵיכֶם
וּמִכָּל גִּלּוּלֵיכֶם אֲטַהֵר אֶתְכֶם.[3]

מִיכָה עַבְדְּךָ אָמַר לְפָנֶיךָ: מִי אֵל כָּמוֹךָ נֹשֵׂא עָוֹן וְעֹבֵר עַל
פֶּשַׁע לִשְׁאֵרִית נַחֲלָתוֹ, לֹא הֶחֱזִיק לָעַד אַפּוֹ, כִּי
חָפֵץ חֶסֶד הוּא, יָשׁוּב יְרַחֲמֵנוּ, יִכְבֹּשׁ עֲוֹנוֹתֵינוּ, וְתַשְׁלִיךְ בִּמְצֻלוֹת
יָם כָּל חַטֹּאתָם.[4] (וְכָל חַטֹּאת עַמְּךָ בֵּית יִשְׂרָאֵל תַּשְׁלִיךְ בִּמְקוֹם
אֲשֶׁר לֹא יִזָּכְרוּ, וְלֹא יִפָּקְדוּ, וְלֹא יַעֲלוּ עַל לֵב לְעוֹלָם.) תִּתֵּן אֱמֶת
לְיַעֲקֹב חֶסֶד לְאַבְרָהָם אֲשֶׁר נִשְׁבַּעְתָּ לַאֲבוֹתֵינוּ מִימֵי קֶדֶם.[5]

דָּנִיֵּאל אִישׁ חֲמוּדוֹת שִׁוַּע לְפָנֶיךָ: הַטֵּה אֱלֹהַי אָזְנְךָ וּשְׁמָע,
פְּקַח עֵינֶיךָ וּרְאֵה שֹׁמְמֹתֵינוּ וְהָעִיר אֲשֶׁר נִקְרָא שִׁמְךָ
עָלֶיהָ, כִּי לֹא עַל צִדְקוֹתֵינוּ אֲנַחְנוּ מַפִּילִים תַּחֲנוּנֵינוּ לְפָנֶיךָ, כִּי עַל
רַחֲמֶיךָ הָרַבִּים. אֲדֹנָי שְׁמָעָה, אֲדֹנָי סְלָחָה, אֲדֹנָי הַקְשִׁיבָה, וַעֲשֵׂה
אַל תְּאַחַר, לְמַעַנְךָ אֱלֹהַי, כִּי שִׁמְךָ נִקְרָא עַל עִירְךָ וְעַל עַמֶּךָ.[6]

עֶזְרָא הַסּוֹפֵר אָמַר לְפָנֶיךָ: אֱלֹהַי, בֹּשְׁתִּי וְנִכְלַמְתִּי לְהָרִים,
אֱלֹהַי, פָּנַי אֵלֶיךָ, כִּי עֲוֹנוֹתֵינוּ רָבוּ לְמַעְלָה
רֹאשׁ, וְאַשְׁמָתֵנוּ גָדְלָה עַד לַשָּׁמָיִם.[7] וְאַתָּה[8] אֱלוֹהַּ סְלִיחוֹת, חַנּוּן
וְרַחוּם, אֶרֶךְ אַפַּיִם וְרַב חֶסֶד, וְלֹא עֲזַבְתָּנוּ.[9]

אַל תַּעַזְבֵנוּ אָבִינוּ וְאַל תִּטְּשֵׁנוּ בּוֹרְאֵנוּ, וְאַל תַּזְנִיחֵנוּ יוֹצְרֵנוּ,
וְאַל תַּעַשׂ עִמָּנוּ כָּלָה כְּחַטֹּאתֵינוּ. וְקַיֶּם לָנוּ יהוה
אֱלֹהֵינוּ, אֶת הַדָּבָר שֶׁהִבְטַחְתָּנוּ בְּקַבָּלָה עַל יְדֵי יִרְמְיָהוּ חוֹזָךְ,
כָּאָמוּר: בַּיָּמִים הָהֵם וּבָעֵת הַהִיא, נְאֻם יהוה, יְבֻקַּשׁ אֶת עֲוֹן
יִשְׂרָאֵל וְאֵינֶנּוּ וְאֶת חַטֹּאת יְהוּדָה וְלֹא תִמָּצֶאנָה, כִּי אֶסְלַח

---

(1) Isaiah 55:7. (2) Psalms 19:13. (3) Ezekiel 36:25. (4) Micah 7:18-19. (5) 7:20.
(6) Daniel 9:18-19. (7) Ezra 9:6. (8) Some editions of Selichos insert the word אֱלֹהֵינוּ,
our God, at this point. (9) Cf. Nehemiah 9:17.

הִרְשַׁעְנוּ *We have acted wickedly and have sinned willfully, therefore we have not been saved. Inspire our heart to abandon the path of evil and hasten salvation for us, as it is written by Your prophet: May the wicked one abandon his way and the vicious man his thoughts; may he return to* HASHEM *and He will show him mercy, and to our God, for He is abundantly forgiving.*[1]

מְשִׁיחַ צִדְקֶךָ *Your righteous anointed [David] said before You: 'Who can discern mistakes? From unperceived faults cleanse me.'*[2] *Cleanse us,* HASHEM, *our God, of all our willful sins and purify us, of all our contaminations. Sprinkle upon us pure water and purify us, as it is written by Your prophet: I shall sprinkle pure water upon you and purify you, of all your contaminations and of all your abominations I will purify you.'*[3]

מִיכָה עַבְדָּךְ *Micah, Your servant, said before You: 'Who, O God, is like You, Who pardons iniquity and overlooks transgression for the remnant of His heritage? Who has not retained His wrath eternally, for He desires kindness! He will again be merciful to us; He will suppress our iniquities and cast into the depths of the sea all their sins.*[4] *(And all the sins of Your nation the Family of Israel, may You cast away to a place where they will neither be remembered, considered, nor brought to mind — ever.) Grant truth to Jacob, kindness to Abraham, as You swore to our forefathers from ancient times.'*[5]

דָּנִיֵּאל *Daniel, the greatly beloved man, cried out before You: 'Incline, my God, Your ear, and listen, open Your eyes and see our desolation and that of the city upon which Your Name is proclaimed, for not because of our righteousness do we cast down our supplications before You, rather because of Your abundant compassion. O my Lord, heed; O my Lord, forgive; O my Lord, be attentive and act, do not delay; for Your sake, my God, for Your Name is proclaimed upon Your city and Your people.'*[6]

עֶזְרָא הַסּוֹפֵר *Ezra the Scribe said before You: 'My God, I am embarrassed and ashamed to lift my face to You, my God — for our iniquities have multiplied above our heads, and our sins extend unto heaven.*[7] *You are*[8] *the God of forgiveness, compassionate and merciful, slow to anger, and abundant in kindness; and You have not forsaken us.'*[9]

אַל תַּעַזְבֵנוּ *Do not forsake us, our Father; do not cast us off, our Creator; do not abandon us, our Molder; and do not bring about our destruction, as our sins merit. Affirm for us,* HASHEM, *our God, the promise You made in the tradition through Jeremiah, Your seer, as it is said: 'In those days and at that time' — the words of* HASHEM — *'the iniquity of Israel will be sought but there will be none, and the errors of Judah, but they will not be found, for I will have forgiven*

לַאֲשֶׁר אַשְׁאִיר.[1] עַמֶּךָ וְנַחֲלָתֶךָ רְעֵבֵי טוּבֶךָ, צְמֵאֵי חַסְדֶּךָ, תְּאֵבֵי יִשְׁעֶךָ, יַכִּירוּ וְיֵדְעוּ כִּי לַיהוה אֱלֹהֵינוּ הָרַחֲמִים וְהַסְּלִיחוֹת.

אֵל רַחוּם שְׁמֶךָ, אֵל חַנּוּן שְׁמֶךָ, בָּנוּ נִקְרָא שְׁמֶךָ. יהוה עֲשֵׂה לְמַעַן שְׁמֶךָ. עֲשֵׂה לְמַעַן אֲמִתֶּךָ, עֲשֵׂה לְמַעַן בְּרִיתֶךָ, עֲשֵׂה לְמַעַן גָּדְלְךָ וְתִפְאַרְתֶּךָ, עֲשֵׂה לְמַעַן דָּתֶךָ, עֲשֵׂה לְמַעַן הוֹדֶךָ, עֲשֵׂה לְמַעַן וְעוּדֶךָ, עֲשֵׂה לְמַעַן זִכְרֶךָ, עֲשֵׂה לְמַעַן חַסְדֶּךָ, עֲשֵׂה לְמַעַן טוּבֶךָ, עֲשֵׂה לְמַעַן יִחוּדֶךָ, עֲשֵׂה לְמַעַן כְּבוֹדֶךָ, עֲשֵׂה לְמַעַן לִמּוּדֶךָ, עֲשֵׂה לְמַעַן מַלְכוּתֶךָ, עֲשֵׂה לְמַעַן נִצְחֶךָ, עֲשֵׂה לְמַעַן סוֹדֶךָ, עֲשֵׂה לְמַעַן עֻזֶּךָ, עֲשֵׂה לְמַעַן פְּאֵרֶךָ, עֲשֵׂה לְמַעַן צִדְקָתֶךָ, עֲשֵׂה לְמַעַן קְדֻשָּׁתֶךָ, עֲשֵׂה לְמַעַן רַחֲמֶיךָ הָרַבִּים, עֲשֵׂה לְמַעַן שְׁכִינָתֶךָ, עֲשֵׂה לְמַעַן תְּהִלָּתֶךָ, עֲשֵׂה לְמַעַן אוֹהֲבֶיךָ שׁוֹכְנֵי עָפָר, עֲשֵׂה לְמַעַן אַבְרָהָם יִצְחָק וְיַעֲקֹב, עֲשֵׂה לְמַעַן מֹשֶׁה וְאַהֲרֹן, עֲשֵׂה לְמַעַן דָּוִד וּשְׁלֹמֹה, עֲשֵׂה לְמַעַן יְרוּשָׁלַיִם עִיר קָדְשֶׁךָ, עֲשֵׂה לְמַעַן צִיּוֹן מִשְׁכַּן כְּבוֹדֶךָ, עֲשֵׂה לְמַעַן שִׁמְמוֹת הֵיכָלֶךָ, עֲשֵׂה לְמַעַן הֲרִיסוּת מִזְבְּחֶךָ, עֲשֵׂה לְמַעַן הֲרוּגִים עַל שֵׁם קָדְשֶׁךָ, עֲשֵׂה לְמַעַן טְבוּחִים עַל יִחוּדֶךָ, עֲשֵׂה לְמַעַן בָּאֵי בָאֵשׁ וּבַמַּיִם עַל קִדּוּשׁ שְׁמֶךָ, עֲשֵׂה לְמַעַן יוֹנְקֵי שָׁדַיִם שֶׁלֹּא חָטְאוּ, עֲשֵׂה לְמַעַן גְּמוּלֵי חָלָב שֶׁלֹּא פָשְׁעוּ, עֲשֵׂה לְמַעַן תִּינוֹקוֹת שֶׁל בֵּית רַבָּן, עֲשֵׂה לְמַעַנְךָ אִם לֹא לְמַעֲנֵנוּ, עֲשֵׂה לְמַעַנְךָ וְהוֹשִׁיעֵנוּ.

עֲנֵנוּ יהוה עֲנֵנוּ, עֲנֵנוּ אֱלֹהֵינוּ עֲנֵנוּ, עֲנֵנוּ אָבִינוּ עֲנֵנוּ, עֲנֵנוּ בּוֹרְאֵנוּ עֲנֵנוּ, עֲנֵנוּ גּוֹאֲלֵנוּ עֲנֵנוּ, עֲנֵנוּ דוֹרְשֵׁנוּ עֲנֵנוּ, עֲנֵנוּ הָאֵל הַנֶּאֱמָן עֲנֵנוּ, עֲנֵנוּ וָתִיק וְחָסִיד עֲנֵנוּ, עֲנֵנוּ זַךְ וְיָשָׁר עֲנֵנוּ, עֲנֵנוּ חַי וְקַיָּם עֲנֵנוּ, עֲנֵנוּ טוֹב וּמֵטִיב עֲנֵנוּ, עֲנֵנוּ יוֹדֵעַ יֵצֶר עֲנֵנוּ, עֲנֵנוּ כּוֹבֵשׁ כְּעָסִים עֲנֵנוּ, עֲנֵנוּ לוֹבֵשׁ צְדָקוֹת עֲנֵנוּ, עֲנֵנוּ מֶלֶךְ מַלְכֵי הַמְּלָכִים עֲנֵנוּ, עֲנֵנוּ נוֹרָא וְנִשְׂגָּב עֲנֵנוּ, עֲנֵנוּ סוֹלֵחַ וּמוֹחֵל עֲנֵנוּ, עֲנֵנוּ עוֹנֶה בְּעֵת צָרָה[2] עֲנֵנוּ, עֲנֵנוּ פּוֹדֶה וּמַצִּיל עֲנֵנוּ, עֲנֵנוּ צַדִּיק וְיָשָׁר עֲנֵנוּ, עֲנֵנוּ קָרוֹב לְקוֹרְאָיו עֲנֵנוּ, עֲנֵנוּ רַחוּם וְחַנּוּן עֲנֵנוּ, עֲנֵנוּ

---

(1) *Jeremiah* 50:20. (2) Some editions of *Selichos* read בְּעֵת רָצוֹן, *in a time of favor*.

those whom I leave as a remnant.'[1] *Your people and Your heritage, who hunger for Your goodness, who thirst for Your kindness, who long for Your salvation — may they recognize and know that to HASHEM, our God, belong mercy and forgiveness.*

אֵל רַחוּם *'Merciful God' is Your Name, 'Gracious God' is Your Name, Your Name is called upon us — O HASHEM, act for Your Name's sake. Act for the sake of* [א] *Your truth; act for the sake of* [ב] *Your covenant; act for the sake of* [ג] *Your greatness and Your splendor; act for the sake of* [ד] *Your law; act for the sake of* [ה] *Your glory; act for the sake of* [ו] *Your Meeting House; act for the sake of* [ז] *Your remembrance; act for the sake of* [ח] *Your kindness; act for the sake of* [ט] *Your goodness; act for the sake of* [י] *Your Oneness; act for the sake of* [כ] *Your honor; act for the sake of* [ל] *Your teaching; act for the sake of* [מ] *Your kingship; act for the sake of* [נ] *Your eternality; act for the sake of* [ס] *Your counsel; act for the sake of* [ע] *Your power; act for the sake of* [פ] *Your beauty; act for the sake of* [צ] *Your righteousness; act for the sake of* [ק] *Your sanctity; act for the sake of* [ר] *Your abundant mercy; act for the sake of* [ש] *Your Presence, act for the sake of* [ת] *Your praise; act for the sake of Your beloved ones who rest in the dust; act for the sake of Abraham, Isaac, and Jacob; act for the sake of Moses and Aaron; act for the sake of David and Solomon; act for the sake of Jerusalem, Your holy city; act for the sake of Zion, the abode of Your glory; act for the sake of the desolation of Your Temple; act for the sake of the ruin of Your Altar; act for the sake of the martyrs for Your holy Name; act for the sake of those slaughtered for Your Oneness; act for the sake of those who entered fire and water for the sanctification of Your Name; act for the nursing infants who did not err; act for the sake of the weaned babes who did not sin; act for the sake of children at the schoolroom; act for Your sake if not for ours; act for Your sake and save us.*

עֲנֵנוּ *Answer us, HASHEM, answer us; answer us, our God, answer us; answer us,* [א] *our Father, answer us; answer us,* [ב] *our Creator, answer us; answer us,* [ג] *our Redeemer, answer us; answer us,* [ד] *You Who searches us out, answer us; answer us,* [ה] *faithful God, answer us; answer us,* [ו] *stead-fast and kind One, answer us; answer us,* [ז] *pure and upright One, answer us; answer us,* [ח] *living and enduring One, answer us; answer us,* [ט] *good and beneficent One, answer us; answer us,* [י] *You Who knows inclinations, answer us; answer us,* [כ] *You Who suppresses wrath, answer us; answer us,* [ל] *You Who dons righteousness, answer us; answer us,* [מ] *King Who reigns over kings, answer us; answer us,* [נ] *awesome and powerful One, answer us; answer us,* [ס] *You Who forgives and pardons, answer us; answer us,* [ע] *You Who answers in time of distress,*[2] *answer us; answer us,* [פ] *Redeemer and Rescuer, answer us; answer us,* [צ] *righteous and upright One, answer us; answer us,* [ק] *He Who is close to those who call upon Him, answer us; answer us,* [ר] *merciful and gracious One, answer us; answer us,*

שׁוֹמֵעַ אֶל אֶבְיוֹנִים עֲנֵנוּ, עֲנֵנוּ תוֹמֵךְ תְּמִימִים עֲנֵנוּ, עֲנֵנוּ אֱלֹהֵי
אֲבוֹתֵינוּ עֲנֵנוּ, עֲנֵנוּ אֱלֹהֵי אַבְרָהָם עֲנֵנוּ, עֲנֵנוּ פַּחַד יִצְחָק עֲנֵנוּ,
עֲנֵנוּ אֲבִיר יַעֲקֹב עֲנֵנוּ, עֲנֵנוּ עֶזְרַת הַשְּׁבָטִים עֲנֵנוּ, עֲנֵנוּ מִשְׂגָּב
אִמָּהוֹת עֲנֵנוּ, עֲנֵנוּ קָשֶׁה לִכְעוֹס עֲנֵנוּ, עֲנֵנוּ רַךְ לִרְצוֹת עֲנֵנוּ, עֲנֵנוּ
עוֹנֶה בְּעֵת רָצוֹן[1] עֲנֵנוּ, עֲנֵנוּ אֲבִי יְתוֹמִים עֲנֵנוּ, עֲנֵנוּ דַּיַּן אַלְמָנוֹת
עֲנֵנוּ:

הוּא יַעֲנֵנוּ.	**מִי שֶׁעָנָה** לְאַבְרָהָם אָבִינוּ בְּהַר הַמּוֹרִיָּה,
הוּא יַעֲנֵנוּ.	מִי שֶׁעָנָה לְיִצְחָק בְּנוֹ כְּשֶׁנֶּעֱקַד עַל גַּבֵּי הַמִּזְבֵּחַ,
הוּא יַעֲנֵנוּ.	מִי שֶׁעָנָה לְיַעֲקֹב בְּבֵית אֵל,
הוּא יַעֲנֵנוּ.	מִי שֶׁעָנָה לְיוֹסֵף בְּבֵית הָאֲסוּרִים,
הוּא יַעֲנֵנוּ.	מִי שֶׁעָנָה לַאֲבוֹתֵינוּ עַל יַם סוּף,
הוּא יַעֲנֵנוּ.	מִי שֶׁעָנָה לְמֹשֶׁה בְּחוֹרֵב,
הוּא יַעֲנֵנוּ.	מִי שֶׁעָנָה לְאַהֲרֹן בַּמַּחְתָּה,
הוּא יַעֲנֵנוּ.	מִי שֶׁעָנָה לְפִינְחָס בְּקוּמוֹ מִתּוֹךְ הָעֵדָה,
הוּא יַעֲנֵנוּ.	מִי שֶׁעָנָה לִיהוֹשֻׁעַ בַּגִּלְגָּל,
הוּא יַעֲנֵנוּ.	מִי שֶׁעָנָה לִשְׁמוּאֵל בַּמִּצְפָּה,
הוּא יַעֲנֵנוּ.	מִי שֶׁעָנָה לְדָוִד וּשְׁלֹמֹה בְנוֹ בִּירוּשָׁלָיִם,
הוּא יַעֲנֵנוּ.	מִי שֶׁעָנָה לְאֵלִיָּהוּ בְּהַר הַכַּרְמֶל,
הוּא יַעֲנֵנוּ.	מִי שֶׁעָנָה לֶאֱלִישָׁע בִּירִיחוֹ,
הוּא יַעֲנֵנוּ.	מִי שֶׁעָנָה לְיוֹנָה בִּמְעֵי הַדָּגָה,
הוּא יַעֲנֵנוּ.	מִי שֶׁעָנָה לְחִזְקִיָּהוּ מֶלֶךְ יְהוּדָה בְּחָלְיוֹ,
הוּא יַעֲנֵנוּ.	מִי שֶׁעָנָה לַחֲנַנְיָה מִישָׁאֵל וַעֲזַרְיָה בְּתוֹךְ כִּבְשַׁן הָאֵשׁ,
הוּא יַעֲנֵנוּ.	מִי שֶׁעָנָה לְדָנִיֵּאל בְּגוֹב הָאֲרָיוֹת,
הוּא יַעֲנֵנוּ.	מִי שֶׁעָנָה לְמָרְדְּכַי וְאֶסְתֵּר בְּשׁוּשַׁן הַבִּירָה,
הוּא יַעֲנֵנוּ.	מִי שֶׁעָנָה לְעֶזְרָא בַּגּוֹלָה,

מִי שֶׁעָנָה לְכָל הַצַּדִּיקִים וְהַחֲסִידִים וְהַתְּמִימִים וְהַיְשָׁרִים,
הוּא יַעֲנֵנוּ.

רַחֲמָנָא דְּעָנֵי לַעֲנִיֵּי, עֲנֵינָא. רַחֲמָנָא דְּעָנֵי לִתְבִירֵי לִבָּא,
עֲנֵינָא. רַחֲמָנָא דְּעָנֵי לְמַכִּיכֵי רוּחָא, עֲנֵינָא. רַחֲמָנָא
עֲנֵינָא. רַחֲמָנָא חוּס. רַחֲמָנָא פְּרוֹק. רַחֲמָנָא שְׁזִיב. רַחֲמָנָא
רְחַם עֲלָן. הַשְׁתָּא בַּעֲגָלָא וּבִזְמַן קָרִיב.

---

(1) Some editions of *Selichos* read בְּעֵת צָרָה, *in time of distress.*

[ש] You Who hears the destitute, answer us; answer us, [ת] You Who supports the wholesome, answer us; answer us, God of our forefathers, answer us; answer us, God of Abraham, answer us; answer us, Dread of Isaac, answer us; answer us, Mighty One of Jacob, answer us; answer us, Helper of the tribes, answer us; answer us, Stronghold of the Matriarchs, answer us; answer us, You Who are hard to anger, answer us; answer us, You Who are easy to pacify, answer us; answer us, You Who answers in a time of favor,[1] answer us; answer us, Father of orphans, answer us; answer us, Judge of widows, answer us.

מִי שֶׁעָנָה He Who answered our father Abraham on Mount Moriah,
may He answer us.

He Who answered his son Isaac when he was bound atop the altar,
may He answer us.

He Who answered Jacob in Bethel, may He answer us.
He Who answered Joseph in the prison, may He answer us.
He Who answered our forefathers at the Sea of Reeds, may He answer us.

He Who answered Moses in Horeb, may He answer us.
He Who answered Aaron when he offered the censer, may He answer us.

He Who answered Phineas when he arose from amid the congregation,
may He answer us.

He Who answered Joshua in Gilgal, may He answer us.
He Who answered Samuel in Mitzpah, may He answer us.
He Who answered David and his son Solomon in Jerusalem,
may He answer us.

He Who answered Elijah on Mount Carmel, may He answer us.
He Who answered Elisha in Jericho, may He answer us.
He Who answered Jonah in the innards of the fish, may He answer us.
He Who answered Hezekiah, King of Judah, in his illness,
may He answer us.

He Who answered Chananiah, Mishael, and Azariah in the fiery oven,
may He answer us.

He Who answered Daniel in the lions' den, may He answer us.
He Who answered Mordechai and Esther in Shushan the capital,
may He answer us.

He Who answered Ezra in the Exile, may He answer us.
He Who answered all the righteous, the devout, the wholesome, and the upright, may He answer us.

רַחֲמָנָא The Merciful One Who answers the poor, may He answer us. The Merciful One Who answers the brokenhearted, may He answer us. The Merciful One Who answers the humble of spirit, may He answer us. O Merciful One, answer us. O Merciful One, pity. O Merciful One, redeem. O Merciful One, deliver. O Merciful One, have mercy on us — now, swiftly and soon.

נפילת אפים

In the presence of a Torah Scroll, the following (יֵבֹשׁוּ רָגַע until) is recited with the head resting on the arm, preferably while seated. Elsewhere, it is recited with the head held erect.

(וַיֹּאמֶר דָּוִד אֶל גָּד, צַר לִי מְאֹד נִפְּלָה נָּא בְיַד יהוה,
כִּי רַבִּים רַחֲמָיו, וּבְיַד אָדָם אַל אֶפְּלָה.[1]

רַחוּם וְחַנּוּן חָטָאתִי לְפָנֶיךָ. יהוה מָלֵא רַחֲמִים, רַחֵם עָלַי
וְקַבֵּל תַּחֲנוּנָי.

תהלים ו:ב-יא

יהוה אַל בְּאַפְּךָ תוֹכִיחֵנִי, וְאַל בַּחֲמָתְךָ תְיַסְּרֵנִי. חָנֵּנִי יהוה, כִּי
אֻמְלַל אָנִי, רְפָאֵנִי יהוה, כִּי נִבְהֲלוּ עֲצָמָי. וְנַפְשִׁי נִבְהֲלָה
מְאֹד, וְאַתָּה יהוה, עַד מָתָי. שׁוּבָה יהוה, חַלְּצָה נַפְשִׁי, הוֹשִׁיעֵנִי
לְמַעַן חַסְדֶּךָ. כִּי אֵין בַּמָּוֶת זִכְרֶךָ, בִּשְׁאוֹל מִי יוֹדֶה לָּךְ. יָגַעְתִּי
בְּאַנְחָתִי, אַשְׂחֶה בְכָל לַיְלָה מִטָּתִי, בְּדִמְעָתִי עַרְשִׂי אַמְסֶה.
עָשְׁשָׁה מִכַּעַס עֵינִי, עָתְקָה בְּכָל צוֹרְרָי. סוּרוּ מִמֶּנִּי כָּל פֹּעֲלֵי אָוֶן,
כִּי שָׁמַע יהוה קוֹל בִּכְיִי. שָׁמַע יהוה תְּחִנָּתִי, יהוה תְּפִלָּתִי יִקָּח.
יֵבֹשׁוּ וְיִבָּהֲלוּ מְאֹד כָּל אֹיְבָי, יָשֻׁבוּ יֵבֹשׁוּ רָגַע.

סליחה מג (פזמון)

Chazzan, then congregation:

אַנְקַת מְסַלְּדֶיךָ,* תַּעַל לִפְנֵי כִסֵּא כְבוֹדֶךָ,
מַלֵּא מִשְׁאֲלוֹת עַם מְיַחֲדֶיךָ, שׁוֹמֵעַ תְּפִלַּת בָּאֵי עָדֶיךָ.

Congregation, then chazzan:

סְלָחָה מִבּוֹא בַמִּשְׁפָּט, עַל עֲנוּי וְעַל עֲוּוּת מִשְׁפָּט,[2]
כִּי אִם לְפִי מִשְׁפָּט, מִי יִצְדַּק לְפָנֶיךָ אֱלֹהֵי הַמִּשְׁפָּט.[3]
(...אַנְקַת)

Congregation, then chazzan:

יְדֵי עַם הַדְּחוּיִים, תְּחֶזְקְנָה כְּאָז הֱיוֹת לְךָ אֲחוּיִים,
כִּי אִם לְפִי רְאוּיִים, מַה יִּתְרוֹן שֶׁהֵם חַיִּים.
(...אַנְקַת)

Congregation, then chazzan:

לְךָ בְּהִתְחַנְּנִי בְּמוֹ פִי, קַבְּלֵנִי כְּבִמְכַלַל יְפִי,[4]
כִּי אִם לְפִי דְפִי, הֵן אֲנִי יָדִי שַׂמְתִּי לְמוֹ פִי.[5]
(...אַנְקַת)

֎**אַנְקַת מְסַלְּדֶיךָ** — *May the outcry of those who praise You.* Pleading for mercy, compassion and lenience, the theme of this *selichah* is that if God were to judge strictly, none would be found innocent. Thus, the third line of each stanza begins: כִּי אִם לְפִי, *For if [You should judge]*

according to ...

Among the earliest of extant *selichos*, this one was written by R' Silano of ninth-century Venosa, Italy. The *paytan* signed his name — סִילָנוֹ — in the acrostic of the stanzas.

PUTTING DOWN THE HEAD

In the presence of a Torah Scroll, the following (until 'instantly shamed') is recited with the head resting on the arm, preferably while seated. Elsewhere, it is recited with the head held erect.

(*And David said to Gad, 'I am exceedingly distressed. Let us fall into HASHEM's hand for His mercies are abundant, but let me not fall into human hands.'* [1])

רַחוּם וְחַנּוּן O compassionate and gracious One, I have sinned before You. HASHEM, Who is full of mercy, have mercy on me and accept my supplications.

Psalms 6:2-11

'ה HASHEM, do not rebuke me in Your anger nor chastise me in Your rage. Favor me, HASHEM, for I am feeble; heal me, HASHEM, for my bones shudder. My soul is utterly confounded, and You, HASHEM, how long? Desist, HASHEM, release my soul; save me as befits Your kindness. For there is no mention of You in death; in the Lower World who will thank You? I am wearied with my sigh, every night my tears drench my bed, soak my couch. My eye is dimmed because of anger, aged by my tormentors. Depart from me, all evildoers, for HASHEM has heard the sound of my weeping. HASHEM has heard my plea, HASHEM will accept my prayer. Let all my foes be shamed and utterly confounded, they will regret and be instantly shamed.

SELICHAH 43

Chazzan, then congregation:

אֶנְקַת May the outcry of those who praise You*
　　ascend before Your Throne of Glory;
fulfill the requests of the people that declares Your Oneness,
O Hearer of the prayer of those who come to You.

Congregation, then chazzan:

ס Forgive [them], rather than bring [them] to judgment
　　for [their] delay and perversion of justice. [2]
For if [You should judge] according to strict justice,
who can be justified before You, O God of Judgment? [3]
　　　　　　　　　　　　　　　　　　(*May the outcry...*)

Congregation, then chazzan:

י May the hands of the cast-out people
　　be strengthened as of old when they were united with You.
For if [You should judge] according to just deserts,
what benefit is there that they are alive?
　　　　　　　　　　　　　　　　　　(*May the outcry...*)

Congregation, then chazzan:

ל When I supplicate to You in my mouth's prayer,
　　accept me as if I were in the [Temple of] consummate beauty. [4]
For if [You should judge] according to [my] slanderous ways,
behold, I place my hand to [silence] my mouth. [5]
　　　　　　　　　　　　　　　　　　(*May the outcry...*)

---

(1) *II Samuel* 24:14. (2) See *Mishnah Avos* 5:11. (3) Cf. *Psalms* 143:2. (4) Cf. 50:2. (5) *Job* 40:4.

Congregation, then *chazzan:*

נָאוֹר,[1] כְּרֹב חֶסֶד עִמָּנוּ תִפְעַל,　וְלֹא תְשַׁלֵּם לָנוּ כְּמִפְעַל,

כִּי אִם לְפִי פֹעַל,　מִי יֹאמַר זִכִּיתִי לִבִּי מִמַּעַל.[2]　(אֶנְקַת. . .)

Congregation, then *chazzan:*

וְאִם הֶמְרֵנוּ אָמַר,　שָׁעָה וְקַבֵּל זֶמֶר,

כִּי אִם לְפִי מֶמַר,　מַה יַּעֲשׂוּ שׁוֹכְנֵי בָתֵּי חֹמֶר.[3]　(אֶנְקַת. . .)

Congregation, then *chazzan:*

בְּרַחֲמִים וְלֹא בְכַעַס,　הַיּוֹם וּבְכָל יוֹם תַּעַשׂ,

כִּי אִם לְפִי מַעַשׂ,　וַאֲנַחְנוּ לֹא נֵדַע מַה נַּעַשׂ.[4]　(אֶנְקַת. . .)

All:

מַחֵי וּמַסֵּי מֵמִית וּמְחַיֶּה, מַסִּיק מִן שְׁאוֹל לְחַיֵּי עָלְמָא, בְּרָא
כַּד חָטֵי אֲבוּהִי לַקְיֵהּ, אֲבוּהִי דְחָיֵס אַסֵּי לִכְאֵבֵהּ.
עַבְדָא דְמָרִיד נָפִיק בְּקוֹלָר, מָרֵהּ תָּאִיב וְתָבִיר קוֹלָרֵהּ.
בְּרַךְ בְּכְרָךְ אֲנַן וְחָטֵינָן קַמָּךְ, הָא רָוֵי נַפְשִׁין בְּגִידִין מְרִירִין,
עַבְדָּךְ אֲנַן וּמְרוֹדִינַן קַמָּךְ, הָא בְּבִזְתָא, הָא בְּשִׁבְיָא, הָא
בְּמַלְקִיוּתָא. בְּמָטוּ מִנָּךְ בְּרַחֲמָךְ דְּנָפִישִׁין, אַסֵּי לִכְאֵבִין דִּתְקוֹף
עֲלָן, עַד דְּלָא נֶהֱוֵי גְמִירָא בְּשִׁבְיָא.

סליחה מד (תחנה)

All:

תְּפִלָּה תִּקַּח* תְּחִנָּה תִבְחַר,　תְּמוּר נִיחֹחַ תָּמִיד הַשַּׁחַר.

שְׁקֹל לָעוֹמְדִים שִׁמְךָ לְשַׁבֵּחַ,　כְּאִלּוּ זָכוּ תָּרְמוּ מִזְבֵּחַ.[5]

רְצֵה עֲבוֹדָתָם בְּמִקְדַּשׁ שְׁבִיתָם,　כְּבֵית עוֹלָמִים לְעוֹשֵׂי חֲבִיתָם.*[6]

---

(1) See commentary to *selichah* 18. (2) Cf. *Proverbs* 20:9. (3) *Job* 4:19.
(4) Cf. *II Chronicles* 20:12. (5) See tractate *Tamid* 1:2,4. (6) 1:3.

תְּפִלָּה תִּקַּח §— *Accept [our] prayer.* Beginning
on Erev Rosh Hashanah and continuing until the
day before Erev Yom Kippur, a *piyut* is added
just after the recital of *Tachanun.* Because of its
juxtaposition with *Tachanun,* this type of
selichah is called a תְּחִנָּה, *techinah.*

R' Meir bar R' Yitzchak (often called R' Meir
Sheliach Tzibbur) of mid-eleventh-century Germany was a great Torah scholar often quoted by
Rashi and his students. He composed forty-nine
piyutim, forty in Hebrew and nine in Aramaic,
of which about fifteen are extant. His most
celebrated work is *Akdamus,* an awesome exultation of the Torah, God, and Israel, recited on
Shavuos. Tradition records that R' Meir's compositions were so beautiful and inspiring that angels

would sing them before the Throne of Glory, as
if they themselves had written them.

The daily Temple service began with the
preparations and offering of the morning *tamid*
or continual-offering. Likewise, the Altar offering that completed each day's Temple service
was the afternoon *tamid.* One Talmudic tractate,
aptly named *Tamid,* delineates the various
ceremonies, rites and procedures involved in the
bringing of these two daily offerings.

R' Meir Sheliach Tzibbur, in fifty-four pithy
lines, captures the essence of the service. And he
pleads with God to accept our prayers as if we
were performing the Temple and Altar services
being described.

Because of the nature of this *selichah,* a knowl-

Congregation, then *chazzan:*

נ O *Source of Light,*[1] *treat us according to [Your] abundant kindness,*
and do not recompense us according to [our] deeds.
For if [You should judge] according to [our] actions,
who can say, 'I have purified my heart of betrayal'?[2]

(*May the outcry. . .*)

Congregation, then *chazzan:*

ו *Even if we have distorted [Your] word,*
pay heed, and accept our song [of repentance].
For if [You should judge] according to [our] rebelliousness,
what shall those who dwell in houses of mud do?[3]

(*May the outcry. . .*)

Congregation, then *chazzan:*

With mercy and not with anger,
act [for our sake] today and every day.
For if [You should judge] according to [our] deed,
we would not know what we can do.[4] (*May the outcry. . .*)

All:

מָחֵי וּמַסֵּי *[O God,] He Who smites and heals, causes death and*
restores life, raises [the dead] from the grave to eternal life:
Should a son sin, his father would smack him, but a compassionate father
will heal his [son's] pain. When a slave rebels, he is led out in collar-irons,
but if his master desires to, he breaks his chains.

We are Your son, Your firstborn, and we have sinned against You; so
our soul has been satiated with bitter wormwood. We are Your servants
and we have rebelled against You; so [we have suffered], some with
looting, some with captivity, and some with the lash. We beg of You, in
Your abundant compassion, heal the pains that have overwhelmed us,
before we have been completely wiped out in captivity.

SELICHAH 44

All:

ת *Accept [our] prayer,** *and select [our] supplication,*
in place of the sweet scent of morning's tamid-offering.
ש *Account those who stand forth to praise Your Name,*
as if they had won the privilege of removing [the ashes
from upon] the Altar.[5]
ר *Be favorable to their service in their Temple in Exile,*
as [You are] to their chavittin* makers[6] *in the Eternal Temple,*

---

edge of tractate *Tamid* is required, and a full commentary on this *selichah* would require an exhaustive commentary on the *mishnayos* of tractate *Tamid*, an endeavor not within the purview of this work. Therefore, the commentary will be limited to points about which even the erstwhile student of *Tamid* will need clarification. (Unless otherwise indicated, the footnotes refer to the *mishnayos*, not *gemara*, of tractate *Tamid*.)

The acrostic forms a reverse *aleph-beis* (תשר״ק) followed by מֵאִיר בְּרַבִּי יִצְחָק חֲזַק וֶאֱמָץ, *Meir bar R' Yitzchak, may he be strong and persevere.*

חֲבִיתָם — *Their chavittin.* The *chavittin*-offering consisted of one-tenth *ephah* of fine wheat flour that was kneaded with boiling water, shaped into twelve loaves and baked in an oven. Then the loaves were fried in olive oil in a pan called a מַחֲבַת, hence their name חֲבִיתִּין, *chavittin.*

קֶשֶׁב מִקְרָאוֹת וְחִנּוּן סְדָרִים,*   כְּעֵין אֵבָרִים וְעִכּוּל פְּדָרִים.[1]

צֶרֶף שָׁטוּחַ* פְּנֵי טָפוּחַ,   כְּמַעֲלֶה אֵפֶר עַל גַּב תַּפּוּחַ.[1]

פְּאַת קָדִימָה פְּנֵיהֶם יִזְרַח,   כְּסוֹדְרֵי חָזִית כְּלַפֵּי מִזְרָח.[2]

עֶרֶב מַחְבֶּרֶת לְמִדּוֹת עֲרוּכוֹת,*   כְּשָׁרֵת כָּשֵׁר שְׁתֵּי מַעֲרָכוֹת.[3]

סְפֹר לִצְעָדִים לְעָבְדְּךָ גָּשִׁים,*   כְּמוֹ בָעֲזָרָה לְפַיֵּס רוֹגְשִׁים.[4]

נְכוֹן הַשַּׁחַר וְכוֹכָבִים בָּרָן,   בְּרַק הַשַּׁחַר זְכוּת שֶׁבְּחֶבְרוֹן.[5]

מְמֻנֶּה מְזֻרָז* לְהָבִיא טָלֶה,   מִלְּשַׁכַּת טְלָאִים בְּבִקּוּר מוּפְלָא.[6]

לְכוֹס שֶׁל זָהָב יִשְׁלַח לְהַשְׁקוֹת,   בְּבַקְּרוֹ שֵׁנִית לְאוֹר הָאֲבוּקוֹת.[7]

בִּזְכָה בְּתָמִיד וְזִכָּה אֶחָיו,   מָשְׁכוּ וְהוֹלֵךְ לְבֵית מִטְבָּחָיו.[8]

יְדֵי שְׁחִיטָתוֹ זְבַח יַחְדִּ"ל,   עֲדֵי יִפְתַּח הַשַּׁעַר הַגָּדוֹל.[9]

טָרַד עַד שֶׁחִי פָּתוֹחַ כֵּינָן,   שְׁתֵּי מַפְתְּחוֹת לְפָתְחוֹ כִּנָּן.[10]

חֲרָצָיו בְּגַלְגָּלוֹ וְצִירֵי* צְרִיחוֹ,   וְנִשְׁמַע קוֹלוֹ בְּבִקְעַת יְרִיחוֹ.[11]

זְרִיזִים זְהִירִים עֲקֵדָה לִגְמֹר,   בְּיָד וָרֶגֶל[12] כְּיִצְחָק בְּהַר מוֹר.[13]

וְזָכוּ שְׁנִיּוֹת שְׁחִיטָה לַשֶּׁמֶשׁ,   שַׁחַר וָאֶמֶשׁ לְמוּל הַשָּׁמֶשׁ.*[12]

הֵרַמַת שְׁתַּיִם לְאַרְבַּע יִתְּרֵם,*   לְמִזְרָח צָפוֹן לְמַעֲרָב דָּרוֹם.[12]

---

(1) See tractate *Tamid* 1:5. (2) 2:4. (3) 2:5. (4) 3:1. (5) 3:2. (6) 3:3.
(7) 3:4. (8) 3:5. (9) 3:7. (10) 3:6. (11) 3:8. (12) 4:1. (13) *Gemara* 31b.

The Torah ordains that the *Kohen Gadol* bring this offering each day — half of it with the morning *tamid*, half with the afternoon *tamid* (*Leviticus* 6:12-16). The Talmud derives from these verses that the ordinary *Kohen* must also bring a *chavittin*-offering. But, unlike the *Kohen Gadol*, the ordinary *Kohen* brings it only once in his lifetime — the very first day he participates in the Temple service (*Menachos* 51b).

The *chavittin* makers are mentioned because they were the first Temple functionaries to begin their morning preparations (see *Tamid* 1:3).

מִקְרָאוֹת וְחִנּוּן סְדָרִים — [Their] ordered verses and supplication. This refers to the Scriptural verses and *selichah* prayers recited in the *Selichos* service (*Pardes*). Or, 'verses' alludes to the recital of *Shema* and 'supplication' means *Tachanun* (*Masbir*). Alternatively: they refer to *Shema* and *Shemoneh Esrei* (*Matteh Levi*).

צֶרֶף שָׁטוּחַ — Regard what is spread out, i.e., our hands that are spread to the heavens in prayer (*Pardes*). Or, we who are prostrated in prayer (*Masbir*). According to *Arugas HaBosem*, the last word of this stich is תָּפוּחַ, *bloated*. The line then refers to the *chazzan* whose face is contorted in anguish, *spread out and bloated* from torment.

מַחְבֶּרֶת לְמִדּוֹת עֲרוּכוֹת — [Our] union with the order of the [Thirteen] Attributes. The translation

follows *Masbir*. According to *Arugas HaBosem* and *Pardes*, the stich refers to the joining of our blessings, prayers, and supplications with our recital of the Thirteen Attributes. Alternatively: the word מִדּוֹת, lit., *measures*, alludes to footsteps, and by extension, to feet in general. The stich then refers to our feet, joined together while we recite the *Shemoneh Esrei* (*Matteh Levi*).

סְפֹר לִצְעָדִים לְעָבְדְּךָ גָּשִׁים — Count the steps of those who approach to serve You [in prayer]. According to *Matteh Levi* (see above), this would refer to the three steps back and three steps forward taken at the beginning of *Shemoneh Esrei*. According to the others, it alludes to שְׂכַר הֲלִיכָה, *the reward for going* to do a mitzvah (see *Avos* 5:17), which is given over and above the mitzvah's own reward.

מְמֻנֶּה מְזֻרָז — The supervising [Kohen] hurried. From this point until near the end of the *selichah*, the *paytan* no longer compares our synagogue service with the Altar service. Rather, he continues to recount the *tamid* service in all its detail.

חֲרָצָיו ... וְצִירֵי — The hinge ... its socket. The hinges on the Temple doors did not connect the hinges to the doorposts as do the hinges we usually see today. The צִירִים were two *pegs* or *spikes* set into the bottom and top surfaces of the door. They fit into חֲרָצִים, *sockets*, in the doorway, one under

ק *Be attentive to [their] ordered verses and supplication,**
   as [You were to] the limbs and fats consumed on the Altar pyre.[1]

צ *Regard what is spread out* before Heaven,*
   as the heaping of ashes in a mound [on the Altar].[1]

פ *Let their faces shine [as they pray] facing east,*
   as [You did for] those who placed the kindling
      at the east side of the Altar.[2]

ע *May [our] union with the order of the [Thirteen] Attributes**
      be sweet [unto You],
   as the worthy ministrant [Kohen] arranging the two Altar pyres.[3]

ס *Count the steps of those who approach to serve You [in prayer],**
   as [You did] for those running through
      the Temple Court for the lot-casting.[4]

נ *Let those who stand erect at dawn, [joining] the stars*
      [as they] sing [to You],
   recall the merit of [the Patriarchs buried in] Hebron,
      as does the dawn's gleam.[5]

מ *The supervising [Kohen] hurried* to have a lamb brought*
   from the Chamber of Lambs, [where it had been] carefully inspected.[6]

ל *It was sent to drink from a cup of gold,*
   then was inspected again by torchlight.[7]

כ *He who won the privilege for himself and [twelve] colleagues*
      to offer the tamid
   would lead it to the place of slaughtering.[8]

י *He would restrain his hand from slaughtering,*
   until the Great Gate was opened.[9]

ט *He had to reach in up to his armpit to open [the Gate] properly,*
   two keys were needed [one inside, one outside] to open it wide.[10]

ח *As he turned the hinge, creaking in its socket,**
   the sound of it was heard in the valley of Jericho.[11]

ז *The alacritous [Kohanim] carefully completed binding the [animal],*
   foreleg to hind [on each side],[12] *like Isaac on Mount Moriah.*[13]

ו *The second [slaughtering-rings] served for the slaughter,*
   both morning and evening, facing the sun.*[12]

ה *Then [blood] twice thrown was counted as four,**
   on the northeast and the southwest [corners].[12]

---

the door in the threshold, and the other above the door in the lintel.

שְׁנִיּוֹת ... לְמוּל הַשֶּׁמֶשׁ — *The second [slaughtering-rings] .... facing the sun.* The Talmud (*Tamid* 31b) derives from Scriptural verses that the slaughter of the *tamid* had to be done by the light of the sun. Thus, although the usual slaughter of every *olah* could take place anywhere in the northern half of the Temple Courtyard, the *tamid* (which was an *olah*) could only be slaughtered in an area that received direct sunlight. But since the Altar was ten *amos* tall

(15-20 feet), it cast a shadow on its northern side that sometimes reached until the second of six rows of slaughtering-rings (about ten *amos* from the Altar). Consequently, that was the nearest spot to the Altar that the *tamid* could be slaughtered.

הֲרָמַת שְׁתַּיִם לְאַרְבַּע יִתְרֹם — *Then [blood] twice thrown was counted as four.* Immediately after slaughter, the blood of the *tamid* was caught by a *Kohen* in a sacred utensil and dashed on the northeast and southwest corners of the Altar. Blood thrown at one corner would spread

דְּמֵי שִׁירִים יְסוֹד הַדָּרוֹם,¹   וְטָעוּן הֶפְשֵׁט וְכָלִיל לַמָּרוֹם.²

גְּלָל הַנְּתִיחָה מְרֻבָּה בְדִבּוּר,³   שְׁתִיקָה יָפָה וְאֵימַת צִבּוּר.

בְּתִשְׁעָה קָרֵב בְּצֵרוּף זוֹכִים,   חֲבִתִּים וְסֹלֶת וְיַיִן הַנְּסָכִים.⁴

אֲזֵי יַם הַכֶּבֶשׁ מְלֵחוּם וּבָאוּ,   בְּלִשְׁכַּת גָּזִית שְׁמַע יִקְרָאוּ.⁴

מְבָרְכִים בְּמִנּוּי בְּרָכָה אַחַת,   עֲשֶׂרֶת הַדִּבְּרוֹת וּמוֹסִיף בְּנַחַת.⁵

אֱמֶת וַעֲבוֹדָה וּבִרְכַּת כֹּהֲנִים,   יְבָרְכוּ הָעָם⁵ בְּרָכָה נְהֵנִים.

יְבָרְרוּ חֲדָשִׁים לְפַיֵּס קְטֹרֶת,   וְלֹא שָׁנוּ בָהּ וְהִיא מְעַשֶּׂרֶת.⁷

רְבִיעֵי פַּיִס בְּיַחַד נִקְבָּע,   נְתָחִים לְהַעֲלוֹת לְגַב הַמַּרְבֵּעַ.⁶

בְּקוֹל מַגְרֵפָה מַרְבִּים זְמָרִים,⁸   וְקוֹלָהּ נִשְׁמַע בְּעִיר הַתְּמָרִים.⁹

רְגִילִים לְקוֹלָהּ לֵוִים וְכֹהֲנִים,   לְשִׁיר וְהִשְׁתַּחֲוָיָה הָיוּת מְזֻמָּנִים.⁸

בְּמַעֲלוֹת אוּלָם עָלוֹת בִּמְרוּצָה,

מְדַשֵּׁן פְּנִימִי טֶנִי נָטַל וְיָצָא.¹⁰

יְדַשֵּׁן מְנוֹרָה וְכָבָה יַעַרְכוּ,   וְהַכּוֹז נָטַל וְנָחַץ לְדַרְכּוּ.¹⁰

יָרַד זוֹכֶה בְּשׁוּלֵי מַחְתָּה,   לְגַחֲלֵי הָאֵשׁ וְשָׁחָה וְאָתָה.¹¹

צִבּוּר הַקְּטֹרֶת פְּנִימָה חוּץ לוֹ,

מְלַמְּדִין מַקְטִיר בְּלִי כַוּוֹת אֶצִילוֹ.¹²

חֲרֵדִים לְפָרֵשׂ בְּעֵת הַקְטָרָה,¹²   חֲשָׁאֵי כַּפָּרָה לְחֵץ מַטָרָה.¹³

קְבוּעוֹת הָיוּ לְמוּל הַפְּרָצוֹת,   בְּהִשְׁתַּחֲוָיוֹת*¹⁴ לְאֵל חַי לִרְצוֹת.

---

(1) See tractate *Tamid* 4:1. (2) See tractate *Zevachim* 5:4. (3) See tractate *Tamid* 4:2-3.
(4) 4:3. (5) 5:1. (6) 5:2. (7) See tractate *Yoma* 26a. (8) See tractate *Tamid* 5:6. (9) 3:8.
(10) 6:1. (11) 6:2. (12) 6:3. (13) See tractate *Yoma* 44a; *Jeremiah* 9:7.
(14) See tractate *Middos* 2:3; *Yerushalmi, Shekalim* 6:2.

---

out to the two adjacent sides, so there would be some blood on each of the Altar's four sides. Thus, the twice-thrown blood counted as four applications.

קְבוּעוֹת הָיוּ לְמוּל הַפְּרָצוֹת בְּהִשְׁתַּחֲוָיוֹת — *They enacted, opposite the breaches [in the soreig], prostrations.* At a distance of ten cubits outside the walls of the Temple Courtyard stood a low (ten handbreaths, about 30-40 inches) lattice-work fence called the סוֹרֵג, *soreig.* It served to demarcate the point past which neither non-Jews, nor Jews contaminated by contact with a corpse were permitted entry. When the Greeks conquered the Temple compound, they showed their defiance by punching thirteen holes in the *soreig,* symbolically removing the ban. When the Hasmoneans regained control of the Temple, they mended the breaches and enacted that at each breach one must stop and prostrate himself (*Tamid* 2:3; *Yerushalmi Shekalim* 6:2).

[The insertion of these stiches here is strange. Although the Mishnah does mention that the *Kohanim* prostrated themselves before leaving the *Beis HaMikdash* when they concluded their respective duties inside, no mention is made of the prostrations at the *soreig* which was not even within the courtyard! Perhaps, the *paytan* understood the enactment in the following manner: Every time one was required to prostrate himself in the Temple, he had to make thirteen prostrations, corresponding to the breaches.]

Alternatively: The stich is translated, *[the aforementioned services were] necessary to oppose* [i.e., rectify] *the [sinful] breaches [of the people]* (see *Rashi* to Ezekiel 13:5), *[and were accompanied] by prostrations with which to find favor* [i.e., atonement] *before the living God.* Both interpretations of this stich are cited in *Pardes.*

ד The blood remaining [was poured] onto the [Altar's] southern base,[1]
   then the sacrifice had to be skinned and burnt entirely
      for the sake of Heaven.[2]

ג But since cutting up the limbs is so long to tell,[3]
   better it is to be silent out of respect for the congregation.

ב It was brought [to the Altar] by nine [Kohanim],
   among them those privileged [to bear]
   the chavittin, the fine-flour-offering and the wine-libation.[4]

א Then at the west [upper half] of the Altar's ramp
   they salted the limbs, and came
to the Chamber of Hewn Stone to recite the Shema.[4]

מ Following the supervising Kohen,
   they recited one blessing [before Shema],
   then the Ten Commandments and an extra blessing [on the Sabbath].[5]

א [Next the blessings] 'Emes veyatziv,' 'Retzei,' and 'Sim Shalom'
   they blessed with the people,[5] that the blessing be beneficial.

י New [Kohanim] were picked out to draw a lot for the incense,[6]
   one [Kohen] would not do it twice,
      for it brings wealth [to him that offers it].[7]

ד The fourth lot-casting was for all [Kohanim],
   to determine who would bring the limbs up
      onto the four-cornered [Altar].[6]

ב Great song was made at the sound of the magreifah,[8]
   whose sound was heard to [Jericho,] the City of Date-Palms.[9]

ד The Leviim and Kohanim were trained that at its sound
   they must prepare for song and prostration.[8]

ב Then up the Sanctuary steps he ran,
   the [Kohen] who removed the ashes from the inner [Altar]
      took the basket [of ashes] and left.[10]

י The menorah was cleaned, and if its lamps had gone out
      they were rekindled;
   the [Kohen] took the urn [holding ash and wicks]
      and hurried on his way.[10]

י The [Kohen] privileged [to bring the coals] used the bottom
      of the fire-pan to smooth out
   the glowing coals, then prostrated himself, and went out.[11]

צ The [Kohen privileged to offer the incense] heaped the incense
      on the far side [of the Altar],
   he was instructed how to burn [the incense]
      without burning his arm.[12]

ח They hastened to leave the Sanctuary as the incense was burned,[12]
   a secluded atonement for the [tongue's] pointed arrows.[13]

ק They enacted opposite the breaches [in the soreig],
   prostrations*[14] which to find favor before the living God.

חֲגוּרֵי חֶרֶב,* כְּתָב וְלֹא בִכְנוּיִ,   מְבָרְכִין אַחַת וְעַל רֹאשׁ מְנוּיִ.*¹

זְמַן הַגָּדוֹל לְחֶלְקוֹ כּוֹבֵשׁ,   סְגָן מִימִינוֹ עֲלוֹת בַּכֶּבֶשׁ.²

קְרֵבִים אֶצְלוֹ וְלוֹ מַגִּישִׁים,   נְתָחִים לִסְמֹךְ זְרֹק לָאִשִּׁים.²

וְאָז בַּשֵּׁיתִין נְסָכִים סַדֵּר,   וְסְגָן עוֹמֵד וּמֵנִיף בַּסּוּדָר.²

מֵחֲצָרִים בָּאִים עָמַד לוֹ אֵצֶל

(בֶּן אַרְזָא) צְרָדָה מַקִּישׁ לְשֶׁמַע צִלְצֵל.²

לְוִים דִּבְּרוּ בְּשִׁיר הַחֲוָיָה,   לְפֶרֶק תְּקִיעָה וְהִשְׁתַּחֲוָיָה.²

וְזֶה סֵדֶר עֲבוֹדַת תָּמִיד,   בְּבֵית אֱלֹהֵינוּ מְהֵרָה לְהַעֲמִיד.²

תָּמִיד הַבֹּקֶר יְשֻׁלַם בְּסִפּוּר,³   וּלְעוֹלָם זֹאת עַל יְשֻׁרוּן כִּפּוּר.

כְּסִדְרוֹ בַּמִּנְחָה וְנֶסֶךְ קָרֵב,   עֵסֶק בַּשֵּׁנִי לְעִתּוֹת עָרֶב.

בְּאֶחָד עָשָׂר זְכוּת בּוֹ מְחֻזָּרִים,   שָׁנַיִם בְּיָדָם שְׁנֵי גְזִירִים.⁴

כְּבָשִׂים כֹּבְשִׁים עֲוֹנוֹת מְכַבְּסִים,

כְּתִינוֹק בֶּן שְׁנָתוֹ* סְגֻלָּה עוֹשִׂים.

פְּרַקְלִיט סַנֵּגוֹר בְּצֶדֶק לְלוֹנָה,*⁵   בְּעִיר אֱלֹהֵינוּ אֱלֹהִים יְכוֹנְנָה.

דָּמִי אַל תִּתְּנוּ⁶ מְמַנִּים שׁוֹמְרִים,⁷   וְאַתָּה תָקוּם תְּרַחֵם⁸ אוֹמְרִים.

יְרוּשָׁלַיִם בְּנוּיַת עֲרָץ,   יְכוֹנֵן וְיָשִׂים לְשֵׁם בָּאָרֶץ.⁷

---

(1) See tractate *Tamid* 7:2. (2) 7:3. (3) Cf. *Hosea* 14:3. (4) See tractate *Yoma* 2:5. (5) Cf. *Isaiah* 1:21. (6) Cf. 62:7; the propriety and permissibility of addressing prayer to an angel is discussed in the introduction to this volume. (7) Cf. 62:6. (8) Cf. *Psalms* 102:14.

חֲגוּרֵי חֶרֶב — *Girded with [blessing as with] a sword. Behold the couch* [i.e., the Holy Temple] *of the King of peace, sixty warriors round about it ... all gripping the sword ...* (*Song of Songs* 3:7-8). According to the Midrash, this verse alludes to the Priestly Blessing: the 'sixty warriors' are the sixty letters contained in the Blessing; 'the sword' alludes to God's Name within the Blessing, for the Sages proclaimed that any blessing containing God's Name is like a sword that cuts through all obstacles.

The *paytan* therefore refers to the *Kohanim* who pronounced the Priestly Blessing as 'girded with a sword.'

כְּתָב ... וְעַל רֹאשׁ מְנוּיִ — *As it is written ... raised over [their] head.* The bestowal of the Priestly Blessings differed in the Temple from its bestowal in the synagogue in three ways: (a) In the synagogue the Tetragrammaton (Four Letter Divine Name) is pronounced as if it were spelled אֲדֹנָי, but in the *Beis HaMikdash* it was pronounced as it is written; (b) in the synagogue it is recited as three verses, with the congregation responding אָמֵן, *Amen,* after each verse, but in the Temple it was recited as one long sentence;

and (c) in the synagogue the *Kohanim* raise their hands to shoulder level, but in the *Beis HaMikdash* above their heads (*Tamid* 7:2). The *paytan* records all three differences.

כְּבָשִׂים ... כְּתִינוֹק בֶּן שְׁנָתוֹ — *[The tamid] lambs ... [blemish-free] year-old child* [lit., *a baby in its first year*]. God assigned Adam the task of naming the animals He had created, *and whatever Adam called each living being, that is its [proper] name* (*Genesis* 2:19). The Midrash states that this task was so complicated that even the ministering angels were unable to do it, and thus had to concede Adam's superior intelligence (*Bereishis Rabbah* 17:4). It follows from the Midrash that choosing a name is not merely coining a new set of syllables. The name must imply the nature of its object. Thus, every noun in the Holy Tongue, including those assigned by Adam to the various animals, contains within it the essence of the object named.

The *tamid*-offering comprised כְּבָשִׂים בְּנֵי שָׁנָה שְׁנָיִם ... — *two lambs in their first year* (*Numbers* 28:3), and the Sages seek an interpretation of the name כְּבָשִׂים, *lambs,* and its relationship to sacrificial atonement. The Midrash cites three

ח Girded with [blessing as with] a sword,*
    [they pronounced the Name] as it is written and not as we say it,
as they pronounced the [triple] blessing as one,
    [their hands] raised over [their] head.*[1]

ז When the [Kohen] Gadol performed [the daily tasks],
    as was his prerogative,
the Deputy [would accompany him] up the ramp at his right.[2]

ק The priests would come up to him and hand him
    the pieces upon which to lay his hand, then throw into the fire.[2]

וא Then he poured the [wine] libation into the runnels [in the Altar],
    while the Deputy stood and signaled [to the Levite orchestra]
    with a cloth.[2]

מ Two Kohanim with trumpets came and stood by
צ (Ben Arza) who sounded the cymbal, striking it with his thumb.[2]
The Levites sang out praiseful song,
    after each section, trumpeting and prostration.[2]
Now this was the order of the tamid-offering
In the House of our God, may it soon be re-established.[2]
May the morning offering be fulfilled by being retold,[3]
and may this forever be atonement for the people of Jeshurun.
According to the same order,
    accompanied by flour-offering and libation,
was it done for a second time towards evening;
    except that on eleven priests the privilege devolved,
two [more than the morning] to hold two logs of wood.[4]
[The tamid] lambs overpowered [our sins] and washed away iniquity,
and transformed the beloved [people]
    into a [blemish-free] year-old child.*
[They were] advocate and intercessor [for all Israel],
    that they could lie down [each night] in righteousness,*[5]
in the city of our God, may God restore it.
Give yourselves no quiet,[6] you [angels] appointed as watchmen
    [over Jerusalem's walls],[7]
and proclaim always, 'Arise, God, and have mercy on Zion!'[8]
Jerusalem, built in heaven,
    may He re-establish and make famous in the Land.[7]

---

opinions: Beis Shammai, reading the word as if it were spelled כּוֹבֵשׁ, cognate with כּוֹבֵשׁ, *conquerer*, interprets 'they overpower Israel's iniquities' (see *Micah* 7:19); Beis Hillel, reading the word as if it were spelled כְּבָסִים, as in כּוֹבֵס, *launderer*, understands that the lambs 'wash away Israel's iniquities' (see *Isaiah* 1:18); Ben Azzai agrees with Beis Hillel, but adds that כְּבָשִׂים בְּנֵי שָׁנָה means 'they wash away Israel's

iniquities so that the nation remains as sin free as a year-old baby' (*Pesikta Rabbasi* 16). The *paytan* includes all three opinions in this stich.

בְּצֶדֶק לְלוֹנְנָה — [To] lie down [each night] in righteousness. No one in ancient Jerusalem would even retain his sins, for the morning *tamid* would atone for the sins of the night and the afternoon *tamid* would atone for the sins of the day (*Bamidbar Rabbah* 21:21).

וְיַעֲמֹד הַמָּשֵׁל* הַשַּׂר הַגָּדוֹל,

בְּעַד בְּנֵי עַמּוֹ לְחַנֵּן רַע מֵחֲדָל.

תְּחִנַּת שׁוֹעָם לְהַכְתִּיר* תַּעֲרָב,

לְמִזְבֵּחַ מַעֲלָה כְּכָלִיל יְקָרֵב.

וְשַׂר הַפַּחַד* אֲחוֹרֵי הַפַּרְגּוֹד,

בְּיֹשֶׁר תַּמְלִיץ וּבִזְכוּת תֶּאֱגָד.

כְּאָז לַחֲמוּדוֹת בְּלַמֶּדְךָ זְכוּת,

וְזָכִיתָ לַחֲזוֹר לְמֶמְשָׁל וּנְסִיכוּת.*

❖ בְּעַד יִשְׂרָאֵל צֶדֶק לִמְּדוּ,   פְּנֵי הָאָדוֹן יהוה עִמְּדוּ.

צְדָקוֹת לְגַלְגֵּל כְּמֹר נְחוּמִים,*   לְפָנָיו תָּבֹאוּ בְּמִדַּת הָרַחֲמִים.

All:

מַכְנִיסֵי רַחֲמִים, הַכְנִיסוּ רַחֲמֵינוּ, לִפְנֵי בַּעַל הָרַחֲמִים. מַשְׁמִיעֵי תְפִלָּה, הַשְׁמִיעוּ תְפִלָּתֵנוּ, לִפְנֵי שׁוֹמֵעַ תְּפִלָּה. מַשְׁמִיעֵי צְעָקָה, הַשְׁמִיעוּ צַעֲקָתֵנוּ, לִפְנֵי שׁוֹמֵעַ צְעָקָה. מַכְנִיסֵי דִמְעָה, הַכְנִיסוּ דִמְעוֹתֵינוּ, לִפְנֵי מֶלֶךְ מִתְרַצֶּה בִּדְמָעוֹת.

הִשְׁתַּדְּלוּ וְהַרְבּוּ תְּחִנָּה וּבַקָּשָׁה, לִפְנֵי מֶלֶךְ אֵל רָם וְנִשָּׂא. הַזְכִּירוּ לְפָנָיו, הַשְׁמִיעוּ לְפָנָיו תּוֹרָה וּמַעֲשִׂים טוֹבִים שֶׁל שׁוֹכְנֵי עָפָר.

יִזְכֹּר אַהֲבָתָם וִיחַיֶּה זַרְעָם, שֶׁלֹּא תֹאבַד שְׁאֵרִית יַעֲקֹב. כִּי צֹאן רוֹעֶה נֶאֱמָן הָיָה לְחֶרְפָּה, יִשְׂרָאֵל גּוֹי אֶחָד לְמָשָׁל וְלִשְׁנִינָה. מַהֵר עֲנֵנוּ אֱלֹהֵי יִשְׁעֵנוּ, וּפְדֵנוּ מִכָּל גְּזֵרוֹת קָשׁוֹת וְהוֹשִׁיעָה בְּרַחֲמֶיךָ הָרַבִּים, מְשִׁיחַ צִדְקְךָ וְעַמֶּךָ.

מָרָן דְּבִשְׁמַיָּא לָךְ מִתְחַנְּנָן, כְּבַר שַׁבְיָא דְּמִתְחַנֵּן לְשַׁבֻּויֵהּ. כֻּלְּהוֹן בְּנֵי שַׁבְיָא בְּכַסְפָּא מִתְפָּרְקִין, וְעַמָּךְ יִשְׂרָאֵל בְּרַחֲמֵי וּבְתַחֲנוּנֵי, הַב לָן שְׁאֵלְתִּין וּבָעוּתִין, דְּלָא נְהַדַר רֵיקָם מִן קָדָמָךְ.

הַפַּחַד ... הַמָּשֵׁל — [Michael] ... [Gabriel]. Job's friend Bildad said to him: הַמְשֵׁל וָפַחַד, *Dominion and awesomeness are with Him; He brings about peace in His heights* (Job 25:2). *Targum* paraphrases: Michael at His right is composed of fire;

Gabriel at His left is composed of water; in His holy creation, He kneaded fire with water, and with His dominion and awesomeness made peace in His highest heavens.

Thus, the *paytan* refers to Michael and Gabriel

May the great [angelic] prince [Michael]* arise,
to plead for his people, that evil may cease [from among them].
May their pleading outcry be found pleasant,
  to be made into a crown [for God],*
and may it be offered as an olah on the celestial Altar.
The awesome angelic prince [Gabriel],*
  standing behind the [heavenly] partition,
may you advocate justice [for us] and gather [our] merits,
as then, when you pleaded on Daniel's behalf,
and so merited a return to rule and princehood.*
Chazzan — Speak well on behalf of Israel,
standing before the Lord, HASHEM,
and unrolling all our good deeds, igniting conciliation,*
and come before Him with the Attribute of Mercy.

All:

מַכְנִיסֵי רַחֲמִים O you who usher in [pleas for] mercy, may you usher
in our [plea for] mercy, before the Master of mercy. O
you who cause prayer to be heard, may you cause our prayer to be heard,
before the Hearer of prayer. O you who cause outcry to be heard, may
you cause our outcry to be heard, before the Hearer of outcry. O you who
usher in tears, may you usher in our tears, before the King Who finds
favor through tears.

Exert yourselves, and multiply supplication and petition, before the
King, God, exalted and most high. Mention before Him, cause to be heard
before Him, the Torah and the good deeds of [the Patriarchs and
Matriarchs] who dwell in the dust.

May He remember their love and grant life to [their] offspring, that the
remnant of Jacob not be lost. For the flock of the faithful shepherd
[Moses] has become a disgrace; Israel, the unique nation, a parable and
a simile.

Speedily, answer us, O God of our salvation, and redeem us from all
harsh decrees; and may You save, in Your abundant mercy, Your
righteous anointed and Your people.

מָרָן דְּבִשְׁמַיָּא Our Master Who is in heaven, to You do we supplicate,
as a captive supplicates before his captors; for all
captives are redeemed with money, but Your people Israel with
compassion and supplication. O grant our requests and our prayers that
we not be turned away from You emptyhanded.

---

as הַמְשֵׁל and הַפַּחַד, respectively.

אֲחוֹרֵי הַפַּרְגּוֹד ... לְמֶמְשָׁל וּגְסִיכוּת — *Behind the
[heavenly] partition ... for rule and princehood.*
The Talmud relates that Gabriel had been
banished from his exalted position and had been
exiled behind the 'heavenly partition.' He was not
restored to his original status until he had inter-

ceded on behalf of Daniel. We ask Him now to do
the same for us. [The propriety and permissibility
of praying for angelic intercession or of directing
prayer through intermediaries is discussed in the
introduction to this volume.]

כְּמֹר נְחוּמִים — *Igniting conciliation.* Alternatively: *with myrrh-like conciliation.*

מָרָן דְּבִשְׁמַיָּא לָךְ מִתְחַנְּנַן, כְּעַבְדָּא דְּמִתְחַנֵּן לְמָרֵיהּ,
עֲשִׁיקֵי אֲנַן וּבַחֲשׁוֹכָא שָׁרֵינָן, מְרִירָן נַפְשִׁין מֵעַקְתָּין דְּנַפִּישִׁין,
חֵילָא לֵית בָּן לְרַצוּיֵךְ מָרָן, עֲבִיד בְּדִיל קְיָמָא דִּגְזַרְתָּ עִם
אֲבָהָתָנָא.

שׁוֹמֵר יִשְׂרָאֵל, שְׁמוֹר שְׁאֵרִית יִשְׂרָאֵל, וְאַל יֹאבַד יִשְׂרָאֵל,
הָאוֹמְרִים, שְׁמַע יִשְׂרָאֵל.[1]

שׁוֹמֵר גּוֹי אֶחָד, שְׁמוֹר שְׁאֵרִית עַם אֶחָד, וְאַל יֹאבַד גּוֹי אֶחָד,
הַמְּיַחֲדִים שִׁמְךָ, יהוה אֱלֹהֵינוּ יהוה אֶחָד.[1]

שׁוֹמֵר גּוֹי קָדוֹשׁ, שְׁמוֹר שְׁאֵרִית עַם קָדוֹשׁ, וְאַל יֹאבַד גּוֹי
קָדוֹשׁ, הַמְּשַׁלְּשִׁים בְּשָׁלֹשׁ קְדֻשּׁוֹת לְקָדוֹשׁ.

מִתְרַצֶּה בְּרַחֲמִים וּמִתְפַּיֵּס בְּתַחֲנוּנִים, הִתְרַצֶּה וְהִתְפַּיֵּס לְדוֹר
עָנִי, כִּי אֵין עוֹזֵר. אָבִינוּ מַלְכֵּנוּ, חָנֵּנוּ וַעֲנֵנוּ, כִּי אֵין בָּנוּ מַעֲשִׂים,
עֲשֵׂה עִמָּנוּ צְדָקָה וָחֶסֶד וְהוֹשִׁיעֵנוּ.

וַאֲנַחְנוּ לֹא נֵדַע מַה נַּעֲשֶׂה, כִּי עָלֶיךָ עֵינֵינוּ.[2] זְכֹר רַחֲמֶיךָ
יהוה וַחֲסָדֶיךָ, כִּי מֵעוֹלָם הֵמָּה.[3] יְהִי חַסְדְּךָ יהוה
עָלֵינוּ, כַּאֲשֶׁר יִחַלְנוּ לָךְ.[4]

סְלִיחָה מה (פזמון)

All:

אֲדוֹנֵי הָאֲדוֹנִים,* הַשְׁקִיפָה מִמְּעוֹנִים,
וְרַחֵם אֶבְיוֹנִים, כְּרַחֵם אָב עַל בָּנִים,[5]
וּזְכֹר בְּרִית אֱמוּנִים, שִׁבְעָה אֵיתָנִים,
וְאַל תִּזְכָּר לָנוּ עֲוֹנוֹת רִאשׁוֹנִים.[6]

זְכֹר בְּרִית אֶזְרָח,[7] אֲשֶׁר בֵּין חוֹחִים פָּרַח,
וּמִפְּאַת הַמִּזְרָח, כְּצֵאת הַשֶּׁמֶשׁ זָרַח,
וּמֵאַרְצוֹ בָּרַח, וְאַחֲרֶיךָ אֵל אָרַח,
וּלְשִׁמְךָ צָרַח, וְהוּא בֶן שָׁלֹשׁ שָׁנִים.*
וְאַל תִּזְכָּר לָנוּ עֲוֹנוֹת רִאשׁוֹנִים.

אֲדוֹנֵי הָאֲדוֹנִים — *Lord of lords.* The unknown composer of this *pizmon* based his work on the verse: וְזָכַרְתִּי אֶת בְּרִיתִי יַעֲקוֹב, וְאַף אֶת בְּרִיתִי יִצְחָק, וְאַף אֶת בְּרִיתִי אַבְרָהָם אֶזְכֹּר, *and I will remember My covenant with Jacob, and also My covenant* with Isaac, *and also My covenant with Abraham will I remember* (Leviticus 26:42). However, the *paytan* added an additional four patriarchs, giving a total of 'שִׁבְעָה אֵיתָנִים, *seven mighty ones.*' The additional four are Moses, Aaron,

Our Master Who is in heaven, to You do we supplicate, as a slave supplicates before his master: We are oppressed and we abide in darkness, souls embittered from abundant distress. We have no strength to regain Your favor. Our Master, act for the sake of the covenant that You made with our Patriarchs.

שׁוֹמֵר יִשְׂרָאֵל O Guardian of Israel, protect the remnant of Israel; let not Israel be destroyed — those who proclaim, 'Hear O Israel.'[1]

O Guardian of the unique nation, protect the remnant of the unique people; let not the unique nation be destroyed — those who proclaim the Oneness of Your Name, 'HASHEM is our God, HASHEM, the One and Only!'[1]

O Guardian of the holy nation, protect the remnant of the holy people; let not the holy nation be destroyed — those who proclaim three-fold sanctifications to the Holy One.

Become favorable through compassion and become appeased through supplications. Become favorable and appeased to the poor generation, for there is no helper. Our Father, our King, be gracious with us and answer us, though we have no worthy deeds; treat us with charity and kindness, and save us.

וַאֲנַחְנוּ We know not what to do — but our eyes are upon You.[2] Remember Your mercies, HASHEM, and Your kindnesses, for they are from the beginning of the world.[3] May Your kindness be upon us, HASHEM, just as we awaited You.[4]

SELICHAH 45

All:

Lord of lords,* look down from on high
and have mercy on the impoverished
    as a father has mercy on his children.[5]
Remember the covenant with the faithful, the seven mighty ones.
        And do not recall against us former iniquities.[6]
Remember the covenant with Abraham,[7] a blossom among thorns,
and from the eastern corner shone like the rising sun;
how he fled from his land and wandered out after You, O God,
how he called on Your Name when he was only three years old.*
        And do not recall against us former iniquities.

---

(1) *Deuteronomy* 6:4. (2) *II Chronicles* 20:12. (3) *Psalms* 25:6.
(4) 33:22. (5) 103:13. (6) 79:8. (7) See commentary to *selichah* 74.

David and Pinchas/Elijah. [Pinchas and Elijah are counted as one (even though each is accorded his own stanza in the *pizmon*) in accordance with the Midrashic view that Pinchas and Elijah were one and the same (see *Rashi* to *Bava Metzia* 114b).]
וְהוּא בֶּן שָׁלֹשׁ שָׁנִים — *When he was only three*

years old. According to one view cited in the Midrash, Abraham was three years old when he realized that there must be a Higher Power that controls the world, and that that Power was Unique and was the Creator of the universe (*Bereishis Rabbah* 95:3).

זְכֹר בְּרִית אִישׁ חֲמוּדוֹ,   אֲשֶׁר לְפָנֶיךָ עֲקָדוֹ,
וְשָׁלַח אֶת יָדוֹ,   בְּמַאֲכֶלֶת שָׁחַט יְחִידוֹ,[1]
וּפִדְיוֹן שָׂם בַּעֲדוֹ,   אַיִל עוֹלָה בְּמַעֲמָדוֹ,[2]
וְזַרְעוֹ צוּר הוֹדוֹ,   פְּדֵה הַיּוֹם מִזְּדוֹנִים.
וְאַל תִּזְכָּר לָנוּ עֲוֹנוֹת רִאשׁוֹנִים.

זְכֹר בְּרִית אִישׁ תָּמִים,[3]   בָּרַח מֵאִישׁ דָּמִים,
בְּסֻלָּם מִמְּרוֹמִים,   בִּשַּׂרְתּוֹ נִחוּמִים,
וְשָׂרָה אֶת עֲצוּמִים,   וּמָצָא חֶסֶד וְרַחֲמִים,
וְהַעֲבֶר נָא כְתָמִים,   וְהַלְבֵּן כַּשֶּׁלֶג שָׁנִים.[4]
וְאַל תִּזְכָּר לָנוּ עֲוֹנוֹת רִאשׁוֹנִים.

זְכֹר בְּרִית אִישׁ עָנָו,[5]   וְאֶת דַּת הֶגְיוֹנָיו,
וְלִקְהִלּוֹת הֲמוֹנָיו,   וְאֶת דַּת חֶזְיוֹנָיו,
נוֹרָא בְּעֶלְיוֹנָיו,   כְּבוֹדְךָ רָאוּ עֵינָיו,
וּזְכוֹר זֹאת אֲדֹנָיו,   יָדְעוּ פָנִים בְּפָנִים.[6]
וְאַל תִּזְכָּר לָנוּ עֲוֹנוֹת רִאשׁוֹנִים.

זְכֹר בְּרִית שִׁלּוּחֶךָ,[7]   מְכַהֵן בִּמְנוּחֶךָ,
וְשָׁם עוֹלוֹת מֵחֶיךָ,   לְרֵיחַ נִיחוֹחֶךָ,
וְתִמּוֹר רְקוּחֶךָ,   כָּלִיל עַל מִזְבְּחֶךָ,[8]
וְעָלָיו נָחָה רוּחֶךָ,   בְּבוֹאוֹ לִפְנַי וְלִפְנִים.
וְאַל תִּזְכָּר לָנוּ עֲוֹנוֹת רִאשׁוֹנִים.

זְכֹר בְּרִית תָּם בִּלְבָבוֹ,[9]   נָגִיד בָּחַרְתָּ בּוֹ,
אֲשֶׁר מִכָּל סְבִיבוֹ,   הִנַּחְתּוֹ מֵאוֹיְבוֹ,
וְרוּחֲךָ אֶל שִׂגְּבוֹ,   בְּעָמְדוֹ לָצֵאת וְלָבוֹא,[10]
יְקַדְּמוּךָ בְּנִיבוֹ,   כַּמָּה שָׁרִים וְנוֹגְנִים.
וְאַל תִּזְכָּר לָנוּ עֲוֹנוֹת רִאשׁוֹנִים.

זְכֹר הַבְּרִית הַמְּקַנֵּא,[11]   לְדוֹר עִקֵּשׁ מִתְאַנֶּה,
וְהֶעֱלִיתוֹ מִמֶּנָּה,   לִמְבַשֵּׂר וּמְפַנֶּה,[12]
וְעִם עֲלוֹת וּמַעֲנֶה,   אֵלָיו לְטוֹב תִּפְנֶה,
וְשָׁעֵה עַם מְכֻנֶּה,   בְּרַחֲמֶיךָ נִשְׁעָנִים.
וְאַל תִּזְכָּר לָנוּ עֲוֹנוֹת רִאשׁוֹנִים.

Remember the covenant with [Isaac] the son he loved,
  whom he bound before You,
and stretched out his hand to slaughter his only son with the knife;[1]
how he made redemption for him with a ram as an olah in his place.[2]
His seed, whose glory is their Rock, redeem today from wanton sins.
                    And do not recall against us former iniquities.
Remember the covenant with the whole-hearted [Jacob],[3]
  who fled from [Esau], the man of blood.
With a ladder from Heaven, You informed him of solace;
He struggled with angels and received kindness and mercy.
Please clear away [sin's] stain [from his children]
  and whiten its red [blemish] like snow.[4]
                    And do not recall against us former iniquities.
Remember the covenant with [Moses] the humble,[5]
  and the Law of his words,
[that he taught] the congregations of his masses,
  the Law [revealed to him] in his visions.
Awesome One in Your heights, his eyes saw Your glory;
remember that, his Lord, Who knew him face to face.[6]
                    And do not recall against us former iniquities.
Remember the covenant with [Aaron] Your emissary,[7]
  who ministered in Your Tabernacle,
how he made olah-offerings of Your fat animals,
  a pleasing scent for You,
and made a column of smoke of Your compounded incense,
  all burned on Your Altar.[8]
Your spirit rested on him when he came into the Holy of Holies.
                    And do not recall against us former iniquities.
Remember the covenant with whole hearted [King David],[9]
  whom You chose as a prince,
from all that surrounded him You gave him rest from his enemies,
  and Your spirit, O God, encouraged him
when he prepared to go out [to battle] and to return.[10]
They approach You with his words — many singers and musicians.
                    And do not recall against us former iniquities.
Remember the covenant with [Pinchas] the zealous,[11]
  who indicted a rebellious generation,
and You took him up and appointed him
  a herald and preparer [of the Redemption].[12]
Because of his suffering and torment, turn to him for beneficence,
and pay heed to those called [Your] people, who depend on Your mercy.
                    And do not recall against us former iniquities.

---

(1) Cf. *Genesis* 22:10. (2) Some editions read, אַיִל עוֹלָה בְּמַעֲמָדוֹ, *a ram going up in his place.*
(3) See 25:27. (4) Cf. *Isaiah* 1:18. (5) See *Numbers* 12:3. (6) Cf. *Deuteronomy* 5:4.
(7) See *Rashi* to *Malachi* 2:7. (8) Cf. *Deuteronomy* 33:10. (9) See tractate *Sotah* 10b;
Rashi to *Psalms* 16:1. (10) Cf. *Deuteronomy* 31:2. (11) See *Numbers* 25:11. (12) Cf. *Malachi* 3:1.

זְכֹר נְבִיאֵי שָׁוְא הִכְרִית,[1]   הִסְתַּתְּרוּ בְּנַחַל בְּרִית,[2]

וּזְכָר לָנוּ הַבְּרִית,   אֲשֶׁר כָּרַת לְאַחֲרִית,

וְטַהֵר הַשְּׁאֵרִית,   כְּמוֹ נֶתֶר וּכְבוֹרִית,[3]

וּלְשָׁבֵי שַׁעֲרוּרִית,   סְלַח פֶּשַׁע וְזִידוֹנִים.

וְאַל תִּזְכָּר לָנוּ עֲוֹנוֹת רִאשׁוֹנִים.

All:

אַל תִּזְכָּר לָנוּ עֲוֹנוֹת רִאשׁוֹנִים, מַהֵר יְקַדְּמוּנוּ רַחֲמֶיךָ, כִּי דַלּוֹנוּ מְאֹד.[4] חָנֵּנוּ יהוה חָנֵּנוּ, כִּי רַב שָׂבַעְנוּ בוּז.[5] בְּרֹגֶז רַחֵם תִּזְכּוֹר.[6] כִּי הוּא יָדַע יִצְרֵנוּ, זָכוּר כִּי עָפָר אֲנָחְנוּ.[7] עָזְרֵנוּ אֱלֹהֵי יִשְׁעֵנוּ עַל דְּבַר כְּבוֹד שְׁמֶךָ, וְהַצִּילֵנוּ וְכַפֵּר עַל חַטֹּאתֵינוּ לְמַעַן שְׁמֶךָ.[8]

קדיש שלם
The chazzan recites קַדִּישׁ שָׁלֵם:

יִתְגַּדַּל וְיִתְקַדַּשׁ שְׁמֵהּ רַבָּא. (.Cong – אָמֵן.) בְּעָלְמָא דִּי בְרָא כִרְעוּתֵהּ, וְיַמְלִיךְ מַלְכוּתֵהּ, בְּחַיֵּיכוֹן וּבְיוֹמֵיכוֹן וּבְחַיֵּי דְכָל בֵּית יִשְׂרָאֵל, בַּעֲגָלָא וּבִזְמַן קָרִיב. וְאִמְרוּ אָמֵן.

(.Cong – אָמֵן. יְהֵא שְׁמֵהּ רַבָּא מְבָרַךְ לְעָלַם וּלְעָלְמֵי עָלְמַיָּא.)

יְהֵא שְׁמֵהּ רַבָּא מְבָרַךְ לְעָלַם וּלְעָלְמֵי עָלְמַיָּא.

יִתְבָּרַךְ וְיִשְׁתַּבַּח וְיִתְפָּאַר וְיִתְרוֹמַם וְיִתְנַשֵּׂא וְיִתְהַדָּר וְיִתְעַלֶּה וְיִתְהַלָּל שְׁמֵהּ דְּקוּדְשָׁא בְּרִיךְ הוּא (.Cong – בְּרִיךְ הוּא.) לְעֵלָּא מִן כָּל בִּרְכָתָא וְשִׁירָתָא תֻּשְׁבְּחָתָא וְנֶחֱמָתָא, דַּאֲמִירָן בְּעָלְמָא. וְאִמְרוּ: אָמֵן. (.Cong – אָמֵן.)

(.Cong – קַבֵּל בְּרַחֲמִים וּבְרָצוֹן אֶת תְּפִלָּתֵנוּ.)

תִּתְקַבֵּל צְלוֹתְהוֹן וּבָעוּתְהוֹן דְּכָל (בֵּית) יִשְׂרָאֵל קֳדָם אֲבוּהוֹן דִּי בִשְׁמַיָּא. וְאִמְרוּ אָמֵן. (.Cong – אָמֵן.)

(.Cong – יְהִי שֵׁם יהוה מְבֹרָךְ, מֵעַתָּה וְעַד עוֹלָם.[9])

יְהֵא שְׁלָמָא רַבָּא מִן שְׁמַיָּא וְחַיִּים עָלֵינוּ וְעַל כָּל יִשְׂרָאֵל. וְאִמְרוּ אָמֵן. (.Cong – אָמֵן.)

(.Cong – עֶזְרִי מֵעִם יהוה, עֹשֵׂה שָׁמַיִם וָאָרֶץ.[10])

Take three steps back. Bow left and say, ... עֹשֶׂה; bow right and say, . . . הוּא יַעֲשֶׂה; bow forward and say, . . . וְעַל כָּל . . . אָמֵן. Remain standing in place for a few moments, then take three steps forward.

עֹשֶׂה שָׁלוֹם בִּמְרוֹמָיו, הוּא יַעֲשֶׂה שָׁלוֹם עָלֵינוּ, וְעַל כָּל יִשְׂרָאֵל. וְאִמְרוּ אָמֵן. (.Cong – אָמֵן.)

Remember [Elijah], the one who wiped out the false prophets,[1]
   You hid him in the watercourse of Keris;[2]
and recall for us the covenant
   You made [with him] about the End [of Days].
Chazzan — Purify [our] remnant as with scouring sand and soap,[3]
and for those who repent of their waywardness,
   forgive rebellious and wanton sins.
                    And do not recall against us former iniquities.

All:

אַל תִּזְכָּר Recall not against us the iniquities of the ancients; may
         Your mercies meet us swiftly, for we have become
exceedingly impoverished.[4] Be gracious to us, HASHEM, be gracious to us,
for we are abundantly sated with scorn.[5] Amid rage — remember to be
merciful![6] For He knew our nature, He remembers that we are dust.[7]
Chazzan — Assist us, O God of our salvation, for the sake of Your Name's
glory; rescue us and atone for our sins for Your Name's sake.[8]

FULL KADDISH

The chazzan recites the Full Kaddish:

יִתְגַּדַּל May His great Name grow exalted and sanctified (Cong. —
         Amen.) in the world that He created as He willed. May He give
reign to His kingship in your lifetimes and in your days, and in the
lifetimes of the entire Family of Israel, swiftly and soon. Now respond:
Amen.
   (Cong. — Amen. May His great Name be blessed forever and ever.)
         May His great Name be blessed forever and ever.
   Blessed, praised, glorified, exalted, extolled, mighty, upraised and
lauded be the Name of the Holy One, Blessed is He (Cong. — Blessed is He.)
beyond any blessing and song, praise, and consolation that are uttered in
the world. Now respond: Amen. (Cong. — Amen.)
            (Cong. — Accept our prayers with mercy and favor.)
   May the prayers and supplications of the entire House of Israel be
accepted before their Father Who is in Heaven. Now respond: Amen.
(Cong. — Amen.)
      (Cong. — Blessed be the Name of HASHEM from this time and forever.[9])
   May there be abundant peace from Heaven, and life, upon us and upon
all Israel. Now respond: Amen. (Cong. — Amen.)
      (Cong. — My help is from HASHEM, Maker of heaven and earth.[10])
Take three steps back. Bow left and say, 'He Who makes peace . . .'; bow right and say,
      'may He make peace . . .'; bow forward and say, 'and upon all Israel . . .'
   Remain standing in place for a few moments, then take three steps forward.
   He Who makes peace in His heights, may He make peace upon us, and
upon all Israel. Now respond: Amen. (Cong. — Amen.)

(1) See I Kings ch. 18. (2) See 17:3. (3) Cf. Jeremiah 2:22. (4) Psalms 79:8.
(5) 123:3. (6) Habakkuk 3:2. (7) Psalms 103:14. (8) 79:9. (9) 113:2. (10) 121:2.

◈§ סדר התרת נדרים §◈

It is meritorious to annul vows on the day before Rosh Hashanah (see commentary).
The three 'judges' sit while the petitioner seeking annulment stands before them and states:

שִׁמְעוּ נָא רַבּוֹתַי דַּיָּנִים מוּמְחִים. כָּל נֶדֶר אוֹ שְׁבוּעָה אוֹ
אִסָּר אוֹ קוֹנָם אוֹ חֵרֶם שֶׁנָּדַרְתִּי אוֹ נִשְׁבַּעְתִּי בְּהָקִיץ
אוֹ בַּחֲלוֹם, אוֹ נִשְׁבַּעְתִּי בְּשֵׁמוֹת הַקְּדוֹשִׁים שֶׁאֵינָם נִמְחָקִים,
וּבְשֵׁם הֲוָיָ״ה בָּרוּךְ הוּא, וְכָל מִינֵי נְזִירוֹת שֶׁקִּבַּלְתִּי עָלַי, חוּץ
מִנְּזִירוּת שִׁמְשׁוֹן, וְכָל שׁוּם אִסּוּר, וַאֲפִלּוּ אִסּוּר הֲנָאָה
שֶׁאָסַרְתִּי עָלַי אוֹ עַל אֲחֵרִים, בְּכָל לָשׁוֹן שֶׁל אִסּוּר, בֵּין בִּלְשׁוֹן
אִסּוּר אוֹ חֵרֶם אוֹ קוֹנָם, וְכָל שׁוּם קַבָּלָה אֲפִילוּ שֶׁל מִצְוָה
שֶׁקִּבַּלְתִּי עָלַי בֵּין בִּלְשׁוֹן נֶדֶר, בֵּין בִּלְשׁוֹן נְדָבָה, בֵּין בִּלְשׁוֹן
שְׁבוּעָה, בֵּין בִּלְשׁוֹן נְזִירוּת, בֵּין בְּכָל לָשׁוֹן, וְגַם הַנַּעֲשֶׂה
בִּתְקִיעַת כַּף, בֵּין כָּל נֶדֶר, וּבֵין כָּל נְדָבָה, וּבֵין שׁוּם מִנְהַג שֶׁל
מִצְוָה שֶׁנָּהַגְתִּי אֶת עַצְמִי, וְכָל מוֹצָא שְׂפָתַי שֶׁיָּצָא מִפִּי, אוֹ
שֶׁנָּדַרְתִּי וְגָמַרְתִּי בְּלִבִּי לַעֲשׂוֹת שׁוּם מִצְוָה מֵהַמִּצְווֹת, אוֹ אֵיזֶה
הַנְהָגָה טוֹבָה אוֹ אֵיזֶה דָבָר טוֹב, שֶׁנָּהַגְתִּי שָׁלֹשׁ פְּעָמִים, וְלֹא
הִתְנֵיתִי שֶׁיְּהֵא בְּלִי נֶדֶר, הֵן דָּבָר שֶׁעָשִׂיתִי, הֵן עַל עַצְמִי, הֵן עַל
אֲחֵרִים, הֵן אוֹתָן הַיְּדוּעִים לִי, הֵן אוֹתָן שֶׁכְּבָר שָׁכַחְתִּי, בְּכֻלְּהוֹן
אִתְחֲרַטְנָא בְהוֹן מֵעִקָּרָא, וְשׁוֹאֵל וּמְבַקֵּשׁ אֲנִי מִמַּעֲלַתְכֶם
הַתָּרָה עֲלֵיהֶם. כִּי יָרֵאתִי פֶּן אֶכָּשֵׁל וְנִלְכַּדְתִּי, חַס וְשָׁלוֹם, בַּעֲוֹן
נְדָרִים וּשְׁבוּעוֹת וּנְזִירוֹת וַחֲרָמוֹת וְאִסּוּרִין וְקוֹנָמוֹת וְהַסְכָּמוֹת.

◈§ הַתָּרַת נְדָרִים / ANNULMENT OF VOWS §◈

The Torah permits people to accept upon themselves personal obligations and prohibitions, and it gives an owner the right to forbid others to enjoy his property. Such undertakings, known as שְׁבוּעוֹת וּנְדָרִים, *oaths and vows*, must be carried out and have the force of a positive commandment, כְּכָל הַיֹּצֵא מִפִּיו יַעֲשֶׂה, *he shall do whatever he has uttered*, and its violation carries the penalty of a negative commandment, לֹא יַחֵל דְּבָרוֹ, *he shall not desecrate his word* (Numbers 30:3). So serious are these matters that they are the primary subject of three tractates: *Nedarim*, *Nazir*, and *Shevuos*.

That a person's freely chosen wishes can have the force of Torah law is a striking indication of the sanctity that God attaches to a person's word. Consequently, it is considered a fearsome sin for one to violate his vows and oaths and the Sages regard it as an extremely serious matter for one to

approach the Days of Judgment with such violation in hand.

However, the Torah provides a means for one to release himself from such obligations. A 'court' composed of three knowledgeable people has the authority to decide that the oath or vow was undertaken under a mistaken impression and they may annul the obligation retroactively. [This is a very oversimplified explanation of the process of annulment, but the key is that the court has this retroactive power.] One of the pleas that one can make to the court is that he regrets ever having undertaken the obligation as a vow or oath.

In order to free oneself of the sin of such violations before being judged on Rosh Hashanah and Yom Kippur, the halachic authorities urge that one convene a court of at least three people — preferably ten — and seek release from his vows and oaths. However, as the declaration makes clear, this annulment applies

⊰{ ANNULMENT OF VOWS }⊱

It is meritorious to annul vows on the day before Rosh Hashanah (see commentary).
The three 'judges' sit while the petitioner seeking annulment stands before them and states:

שמעו *Listen, please, my masters, expert judges — every vow or oath or prohibition, or restriction that I adopted by use of the term 'konam' or the term 'cherem'; that I vowed or swore while I was awake or in a dream; or that I swore by means of God's Holy Names that it is forbidden to erase or by means of the Name HASHEM, Blessed is He; or any form of nazirism that I accepted upon myself, except the nazirism of Samson [which does not include a prohibition against contact with the dead]; or any prohibition, even a prohibition to derive enjoyment that I imposed upon myself or upon others by means of any expression of prohibition, whether by specifying the term 'prohibition' or by use of the terms 'konam' or 'cherem'; or any commitment — even to perform a mitzvah — that I accepted upon myself, whether the acceptance was in terms of a vow, a voluntary gift, an oath, nazirism, or by means of any other sort of expression, or whether it was made final through a handshake; any form of vow or voluntary gift, or any custom that constitutes a good deed to which I have accustomed myself; and any utterance that escaped my mouth or that I vowed in my heart to perform any of the various optional good deeds, or good practices, or any good thing that I have performed three times but without specifying that the practice does not have the force of a vow; whether the thing I did related to myself or to others; both regarding vows that are known to me and those that I have already forgotten — regarding all of them I regret retroactively and I ask and request of your eminences an annulment of them. [My reason is that] I am fearful that I will stumble and become entrapped, Heaven forbid, in the sin of vows, oaths, nazirism, cherems, prohibitions, konams, and [violation of] agreements.*

---

only to vows for which the *halachah* permits annulments and for which there is a halachically acceptable reason for doing so. Likewise, annulment is valid only if the vows involve only oneself. If, however, the vows were adopted for the sake of, or involve, someone else, they cannot be annulled without the consent of the other party. Also, for an annulment to be effective halachically, the regret must be complete and, preferably, be accompanied by a valid reason for regret (*Yoreh Deah* 228:7). And, as the declaration itself makes clear, the *halachah* requires that the vow be specified [to at least one member of the court (ibid. §14)]. Consequently, the present declaration must be understood not as a halachic annulment, but as a means of repentance from the sin of having abused vows.

A second aspect of the Annulment of Vows is the concluding declaration, in which one states

that his future promises should not have the force of a vow or oath. As the declaration makes clear, this prior nullification is effective only if the person making the vow had forgotten it while making the vow. If he did have the nullification in mind and made the vow anyway, the vow is binding (ibid. 211:2). This nullification does not free him from the obligation to keep his word, it merely removes the severity of sin that attaches to formally proclaimed vows and oaths.

The formula for the Annulment of Vows lists a variety of undertakings. Briefly defined, they are as follows:

• נֶדֶר [*neder*], *vow*. A vow through which one accepts a prohibition upon himself. The standard means to do so is to say, 'This item should be forbidden as if it were a Temple offering.' Thus the prohibition rests on the item.

וְאֵין אֲנִי תוֹהֶא, חַס וְשָׁלוֹם, עַל קִיּוּם הַמַּעֲשִׂים הַטּוֹבִים הָהֵם שֶׁעָשִׂיתִי. רַק אֲנִי מִתְחָרֵט עַל קַבָּלַת הָעִנְיָנִים בִּלְשׁוֹן נֶדֶר אוֹ שְׁבוּעָה אוֹ נְזִירוּת אוֹ אִסּוּר אוֹ חֵרֶם אוֹ קוֹנָם אוֹ הַסְכָּמָה אוֹ קַבָּלָה בְּלֵב, וּמִתְחָרֵט אֲנִי עַל זֶה שֶׁלֹּא אָמַרְתִּי, הִנְנִי עוֹשֶׂה דָבָר זֶה בְּלִי נֶדֶר וּשְׁבוּעָה וּנְזִירוּת וְחֵרֶם וְאִסּוּר וְקוֹנָם וְקַבָּלָה בְּלֵב.

לָכֵן אֲנִי שׁוֹאֵל הַתָּרָה בְּכֻלְּהוֹן. אֲנִי מִתְחָרֵט עַל כָּל הַנִּזְכָּר, בֵּין אִם הָיוּ הַמַּעֲשִׂים מֵהַדְּבָרִים הַנּוֹגְעִים בְּמָמוֹן, בֵּין מֵהַדְּבָרִים הַנּוֹגְעִים בְּגוּף, בֵּין מֵהַדְּבָרִים הַנּוֹגְעִים אֶל הַנְּשָׁמָה. בְּכֻלְּהוֹן אֲנִי מִתְחָרֵט עַל לְשׁוֹן נֶדֶר וּשְׁבוּעָה וּנְזִירוּת וְאִסּוּר וְחֵרֶם וְקוֹנָם וְקַבָּלָה בְּלֵב.

וְהִנֵּה מִצַּד הַדִּין הַמִּתְחָרֵט וְהַמְבַקֵּשׁ הַתָּרָה צָרִיךְ לִפְרוֹט הַנֶּדֶר, אַךְ דְּעוּ נָא רַבּוֹתַי, כִּי אִי אֶפְשָׁר לְפוֹרְטָם כִּי רַבִּים הֵם. וְאֵין אֲנִי מְבַקֵּשׁ הַתָּרָה עַל אוֹתָם הַנְּדָרִים שֶׁאֵין לְהַתִּיר אוֹתָם. עַל כֵּן יִהְיוּ נָא בְעֵינֵיכֶם כְּאִלּוּ הָיִיתִי פוֹרְטָם.

The judges repeat three times:

הַכֹּל יִהְיוּ מֻתָּרִים לָךְ, הַכֹּל מְחוּלִים לָךְ, הַכֹּל שְׁרוּיִם לָךְ, אֵין כָּאן לֹא נֶדֶר וְלֹא שְׁבוּעָה וְלֹא נְזִירוּת וְלֹא חֵרֶם וְלֹא אִסּוּר וְלֹא קוֹנָם וְלֹא נִדּוּי וְלֹא שַׁמְתָּא וְלֹא אָרוּר. אֲבָל יֵשׁ כָּאן מְחִילָה וּסְלִיחָה וְכַפָּרָה. וּכְשֵׁם שֶׁמַּתִּירִים בְּבֵית דִּין שֶׁל מַטָּה, כָּךְ יִהְיוּ מֻתָּרִים בְּבֵית דִּין שֶׁל מַעְלָה.

The petitioner makes the following declaration:

הֲרֵי אֲנִי מוֹסֵר מוֹדָעָה לִפְנֵיכֶם, וַאֲנִי מְבַטֵּל מִכָּאן וּלְהַבָּא כָּל הַנְּדָרִים וְכָל שְׁבוּעוֹת וּנְזִירוֹת וְאִסּוּרִין וְקוֹנָמוֹת וַחֲרָמוֹת וְהַסְכָּמוֹת וְקַבָּלָה בְּלֵב שֶׁאֲקַבֵּל עָלַי בְּעַצְמִי, הֵן בְּהָקִיץ, הֵן בַּחֲלוֹם, חוּץ מִנִּדְרֵי תַעֲנִית בִּשְׁעַת מִנְחָה. וּבְאִם שֶׁאֶשְׁכַּח לִתְנַאי מוֹדָעָה הַזֹּאת, וְאֶדּוֹר מֵהַיּוֹם עוֹד, מֵעַתָּה אֲנִי מִתְחָרֵט עֲלֵיהֶם, וּמַתְנֶה עֲלֵיהֶם, שֶׁיִּהְיוּ כֻלָּן בְּטֵלִין וּמְבֻטָּלִין, לָא שְׁרִירִין וְלָא קַיָּמִין, וְלָא יְהוֹן חָלִין כְּלָל וּכְלָל. בְּכֻלָּן אִתְחֲרַטְנָא בְהוֹן מֵעַתָּה וְעַד עוֹלָם.

I do not regret, Heaven forbid, the performance of the good deeds I have done, rather I regret only having accepted them upon myself with an expression of a vow or oath or nazirism or prohibition or cherem or konam or agreement or acceptance of the heart, and I regret not having said, 'Behold I do this without [adopting it in terms of] a vow, oath, nazirism, cherem, prohibition, konam, or acceptance of the heart.'

Therefore I request annulment for them all. I regret all the aforementioned, whether they were matters relating to money, or whether they are matters relating to the body or whether they were matters relating to the soul. Regarding them all, I regret the terminology of vow, oath, nazirism, prohibition, cherem, konam and acceptance of the heart.

Now behold, according to the law, one who regrets and seeks annulment must specify the vow, but please be informed, my masters, that it is impossible to specify them because they are many. Nor do I seek annulment of those vows that cannot be annulled; therefore may you consider as if I had specified them.

The judges repeat three times:

הַכֹּל *May everything be permitted you, may everything be forgiven you, may everything be allowed you. There does not exist any vow, oath, nazirism, cherem, prohibition, konam, ostracism, excommunication, or curse. But there does exist pardon, forgiveness, and atonement. And just as the earthly court permits them, so may they be permitted in the Heavenly Court.*

The petitioner makes the following declaration:

הֲרֵי *Behold I make formal declaration before you and I cancel from this time onward all vows and all oaths, nazirism, prohibitions, konams, cherems, agreements, and acceptances of the heart that I myself will accept upon myself, whether while I am awake or in a dream, except for vows to fast that I undertake during Minchah. In case I forget the conditions of this declaration and I make a vow from this day onward, from this moment I retroactively regret them and declare of them that they are all totally null and void, without effect and without validity, and they shall not take effect at all. Regarding them all, I regret them from this time and forever.*

• שְׁבוּעָה [shevuah], oath. By means of a shevuah one obligates himself either to do or to refrain from doing something or enjoying something. Thus, in contrast to a neder, a shevuah rests on the person.

• אִסוּר [issur], prohibition. Technically, this falls under one of the above categories. It is mentioned to indicate that the speaker used the word prohibit, rather than the usual formulation

of neder or shevuah as explained by the Talmud.

• קוֹנָם [konam]. In a common form of neder, one says, 'This item should be forbidden as if it were a korban [Temple offering].' Konam is a slang word that came to be used instead of the word korban. Such slang terms are valid.

• חֵרֶם [cherem]. This is a declaration used to dedicate something as the property of the Kohanim or as the property of the Temple.

❈ צום גדליה ❈

אַ֫שְׁרֵי יוֹשְׁבֵי בֵיתֶךָ, עוֹד יְהַלְלוּךָ סֶּלָה.[1] אַשְׁרֵי הָעָם שֶׁכָּכָה לּוֹ, אַשְׁרֵי הָעָם שֶׁיהוה אֱלֹהָיו.[2]

תְּהִלָּה לְדָוִד.

תהלים קמה

אֲרוֹמִמְךָ אֱלוֹהַי הַמֶּלֶךְ, וַאֲבָרְכָה שִׁמְךָ לְעוֹלָם וָעֶד.

בְּכָל יוֹם אֲבָרְכֶךָּ, וַאֲהַלְלָה שִׁמְךָ לְעוֹלָם וָעֶד.

גָּדוֹל יהוה וּמְהֻלָּל מְאֹד, וְלִגְדֻלָּתוֹ אֵין חֵקֶר.

דּוֹר לְדוֹר יְשַׁבַּח מַעֲשֶׂיךָ, וּגְבוּרֹתֶיךָ יַגִּידוּ.

הֲדַר כְּבוֹד הוֹדֶךָ, וְדִבְרֵי נִפְלְאֹתֶיךָ אָשִׂיחָה.

וֶעֱזוּז נוֹרְאֹתֶיךָ יֹאמֵרוּ, וּגְדֻלָּתְךָ אֲסַפְּרֶנָּה.

זֵכֶר רַב טוּבְךָ יַבִּיעוּ, וְצִדְקָתְךָ יְרַנֵּנוּ.

חַנּוּן וְרַחוּם יהוה, אֶרֶךְ אַפַּיִם וּגְדָל חָסֶד.

טוֹב יהוה לַכֹּל, וְרַחֲמָיו עַל כָּל מַעֲשָׂיו.

יוֹדוּךָ יהוה כָּל מַעֲשֶׂיךָ, וַחֲסִידֶיךָ יְבָרְכוּכָה.

כְּבוֹד מַלְכוּתְךָ יֹאמֵרוּ, וּגְבוּרָתְךָ יְדַבֵּרוּ.

לְהוֹדִיעַ לִבְנֵי הָאָדָם גְּבוּרֹתָיו, וּכְבוֹד הֲדַר מַלְכוּתוֹ.

מַלְכוּתְךָ מַלְכוּת כָּל עֹלָמִים, וּמֶמְשַׁלְתְּךָ בְּכָל דּוֹר וָדֹר.

סוֹמֵךְ יהוה לְכָל הַנֹּפְלִים, וְזוֹקֵף לְכָל הַכְּפוּפִים.

עֵינֵי כֹל אֵלֶיךָ יְשַׂבֵּרוּ, וְאַתָּה נוֹתֵן לָהֶם אֶת אָכְלָם בְּעִתּוֹ.

Concentrate intently while reciting the verse, פּוֹתֵחַ.

פּוֹתֵחַ אֶת יָדֶךָ, וּמַשְׂבִּיעַ לְכָל חַי רָצוֹן.

❖ צַדִּיק יהוה בְּכָל דְּרָכָיו, וְחָסִיד בְּכָל מַעֲשָׂיו.

קָרוֹב יהוה לְכָל קֹרְאָיו, לְכֹל אֲשֶׁר יִקְרָאֻהוּ בֶאֱמֶת.

רְצוֹן יְרֵאָיו יַעֲשֶׂה, וְאֶת שַׁוְעָתָם יִשְׁמַע וְיוֹשִׁיעֵם.

שׁוֹמֵר יהוה אֶת כָּל אֹהֲבָיו, וְאֵת כָּל הָרְשָׁעִים יַשְׁמִיד.

תְּהִלַּת יהוה יְדַבֶּר פִּי, וִיבָרֵךְ כָּל בָּשָׂר שֵׁם קָדְשׁוֹ לְעוֹלָם וָעֶד.

וַאֲנַחְנוּ נְבָרֵךְ יָהּ, מֵעַתָּה וְעַד עוֹלָם, הַלְלוּיָהּ.[3]

The chazzan recites חֲצִי קַדִּישׁ.

יִתְגַּדַּל וְיִתְקַדַּשׁ שְׁמֵהּ רַבָּא. (.Cong –אָמֵן.) בְּעָלְמָא דִי בְרָא כִרְעוּתֵהּ, וְיַמְלִיךְ מַלְכוּתֵהּ, בְּחַיֵּיכוֹן וּבְיוֹמֵיכוֹן וּבְחַיֵּי דְכָל בֵּית יִשְׂרָאֵל, בַּעֲגָלָא וּבִזְמַן קָרִיב. וְאִמְרוּ: אָמֵן.

(.Cong –אָמֵן. יְהֵא שְׁמֵהּ רַבָּא מְבָרַךְ לְעָלַם וּלְעָלְמֵי עָלְמַיָּא.)

יְהֵא שְׁמֵהּ רַבָּא מְבָרַךְ לְעָלַם וּלְעָלְמֵי עָלְמַיָּא.

יִתְבָּרַךְ וְיִשְׁתַּבַּח וְיִתְפָּאַר וְיִתְרוֹמַם וְיִתְנַשֵּׂא וְיִתְהַדָּר וְיִתְעַלֶּה וְיִתְהַלָּל שְׁמֵהּ דְּקֻדְשָׁא בְּרִיךְ הוּא (.Cong –בְּרִיךְ הוּא) לְעֵלָּא [וּ]לְעֵלָּא מִכָּל בִּרְכָתָא וְשִׁירָתָא תֻּשְׁבְּחָתָא וְנֶחֱמָתָא, דַּאֲמִירָן בְּעָלְמָא. וְאִמְרוּ: אָמֵן. (.Cong –אָמֵן.)

❖⟨ **FAST OF GEDALIAH** ⟩❖

אַשְׁרֵי *Praiseworthy are those who dwell in Your house; may they always praise You, Selah![1] Praiseworthy is the people for whom this is so, praiseworthy is the people whose God is HASHEM.[2]*

Psalm 145   *A psalm of praise by David:*

א *I will exalt You, my God the King, and I will bless Your Name forever and ever.*

ב *Every day I will bless You, and I will laud Your Name forever and ever.*

ג *HASHEM is great and exceedingly lauded,*
   and His greatness is beyond investigation.

ד *Each generation will praise Your deeds to the next*
   and of Your mighty deeds they will tell;

ה *The splendrous glory of Your power and Your wondrous deeds I shall discuss.*

ו *And of Your awesome power they will speak, and Your greatness I shall relate.*

ז *A recollection of Your abundant goodness they will utter*
   and of Your righteousness they will sing exultantly.

ח *Gracious and merciful is HASHEM,*
   slow to anger, and great in [bestowing] kindness.

ט *HASHEM is good to all; His mercies are on all His works.*

י *All Your works shall thank You, HASHEM, and Your devout ones will bless You.*

כ *Of the glory of Your kingdom they will speak, and of Your power they will tell;*

ל *To inform human beings of His mighty deeds,*
   and the glorious splendor of His kingdom.

מ *Your kingdom is a kingdom spanning all eternities,*
   and Your dominion is throughout every generation.

ס *HASHEM supports all the fallen ones and straightens all the bent.*

ע *The eyes of all look to You with hope*
   and You give them their food in its proper time;

פ *You open Your hand,*   Concentrate intently while reciting the verse, 'You open. . .'
   and satisfy the desire of every living thing.

צ Chazzan— *Righteous is HASHEM in all His ways*
   and magnanimous in all His deeds.

ק *HASHEM is close to all who call upon Him — to all who call upon Him sincerely.*

ר *The will of those who fear Him He will do;*
   and their cry He will hear, and save them.

ש *HASHEM protects all who love Him; but all the wicked He will destroy.*

ת *May my mouth declare the praise of HASHEM*
   and may all flesh bless His Holy Name forever and ever.

We will bless God from this time and forever, Halleluyah![3]

The chazzan recites Half-Kaddish:

יִתְגַּדַּל *May His great Name grow exalted and sanctified (Cong.— Amen.) in the world that He created as He willed. May He give reign to His kingship in your lifetimes and in your days, and in the lifetimes of the entire Family of Israel, swiftly and soon. Now respond: Amen.*

(Cong.— Amen. May His great Name be blessed forever and ever.)

May His great Name be blessed forever and ever.

Blessed, praised, glorified, exalted, extolled, mighty, upraised, and lauded be the Name of the Holy One, Blessed is He (Cong.— Blessed is He) — exceedingly beyond any blessing and song, praise and consolation that are uttered in the world. Now respond: Amen. (Cong.— Amen.)

---

(1) *Psalms* 84:5. (2) 144:15. (3) 115:18.

All:

לְךָ יהוה הַצְּדָקָה, וְלָנוּ בְּשֶׁת הַפָּנִים.[1] מַה נִּתְאוֹנֵן,[2] מַה נֹּאמַר, מַה נְּדַבֵּר, וּמַה נִּצְטַדָּק.[3] נַחְפְּשָׂה דְרָכֵינוּ וְנַחְקֹרָה, וְנָשׁוּבָה אֵלֶיךָ,[4] כִּי יְמִינְךָ פְשׁוּטָה לְקַבֵּל שָׁבִים. לֹא בְחֶסֶד וְלֹא בְמַעֲשִׂים בָּאנוּ לְפָנֶיךָ, כְּדַלִּים וּכְרָשִׁים דָּפַקְנוּ דְלָתֶיךָ. דְּלָתֶיךָ דָּפַקְנוּ רַחוּם וְחַנּוּן, נָא אַל תְּשִׁיבֵנוּ רֵיקָם מִלְּפָנֶיךָ. מִלְּפָנֶיךָ מַלְכֵּנוּ רֵיקָם אַל תְּשִׁיבֵנוּ, כִּי אַתָּה שׁוֹמֵעַ תְּפִלָּה.

שֹׁמֵעַ תְּפִלָּה, עָדֶיךָ כָּל בָּשָׂר יָבֹאוּ.[5] יָבוֹא כָל בָּשָׂר לְהִשְׁתַּחֲוֹת לְפָנֶיךָ יהוה.[6] יָבֹאוּ וְיִשְׁתַּחֲווּ לְפָנֶיךָ אֲדֹנָי, וִיכַבְּדוּ לִשְׁמֶךָ.[7] בֹּאוּ נִשְׁתַּחֲוֶה וְנִכְרָעָה, נִבְרְכָה לִפְנֵי יהוה עֹשֵׂנוּ.[8] נָבוֹאָה לְמִשְׁכְּנוֹתָיו, נִשְׁתַּחֲוֶה לַהֲדֹם רַגְלָיו.[9] בֹּאוּ שְׁעָרָיו בְּתוֹדָה, חֲצֵרֹתָיו בִּתְהִלָּה, הוֹדוּ לוֹ בָּרְכוּ שְׁמוֹ.[10] רוֹמְמוּ יהוה אֱלֹהֵינוּ, וְהִשְׁתַּחֲווּ לַהֲדֹם רַגְלָיו, קָדוֹשׁ הוּא.[11] רוֹמְמוּ יהוה אֱלֹהֵינוּ, וְהִשְׁתַּחֲווּ לְהַר קָדְשׁוֹ, כִּי קָדוֹשׁ יהוה אֱלֹהֵינוּ.[12] הִשְׁתַּחֲווּ לַיהוה בְּהַדְרַת קֹדֶשׁ, חִילוּ מִפָּנָיו כָּל הָאָרֶץ.[13] וַאֲנַחְנוּ בְּרֹב חַסְדְּךָ נָבוֹא בֵיתֶךָ, נִשְׁתַּחֲוֶה אֶל הֵיכַל קָדְשְׁךָ בְּיִרְאָתֶךָ.[14] נִשְׁתַּחֲוֶה אֶל הֵיכַל קָדְשְׁךָ וְנוֹדֶה אֶת שְׁמֶךָ, עַל חַסְדְּךָ וְעַל אֲמִתֶּךָ, כִּי הִגְדַּלְתָּ עַל כָּל שִׁמְךָ אִמְרָתֶךָ.[15] לְכוּ נְרַנְּנָה לַיהוה, נָרִיעָה לְצוּר יִשְׁעֵנוּ. נְקַדְּמָה פָנָיו בְּתוֹדָה, בִּזְמִרוֹת נָרִיעַ לוֹ.[16] אֲשֶׁר יַחְדָּו נַמְתִּיק סוֹד, בְּבֵית אֱלֹהִים נְהַלֵּךְ בְּרָגֶשׁ.[17] אֵל נַעֲרָץ בְּסוֹד קְדֹשִׁים רַבָּה, וְנוֹרָא עַל כָּל סְבִיבָיו.[18] שְׂאוּ יְדֵכֶם קֹדֶשׁ וּבָרְכוּ אֶת יהוה.[19] הִנֵּה בָּרְכוּ אֶת יהוה כָּל עַבְדֵי יהוה, הָעֹמְדִים בְּבֵית יהוה בַּלֵּילוֹת.[20] אֲשֶׁר מִי אֵל בַּשָּׁמַיִם וּבָאָרֶץ, אֲשֶׁר יַעֲשֶׂה כְמַעֲשֶׂיךָ וְכִגְבוּרֹתֶךָ.[21] אֲשֶׁר לוֹ הַיָּם וְהוּא עָשָׂהוּ, וְיַבֶּשֶׁת יָדָיו יָצָרוּ.[22] אֲשֶׁר בְּיָדוֹ מֶחְקְרֵי אָרֶץ, וְתוֹעֲפוֹת הָרִים לוֹ.[23] אֲשֶׁר בְּיָדוֹ נֶפֶשׁ כָּל חָי, וְרוּחַ כָּל בְּשַׂר אִישׁ.[24] וְיוֹדוּ שָׁמַיִם פִּלְאֲךָ יהוה, אַף אֱמוּנָתְךָ בִּקְהַל קְדֹשִׁים.[25] לְךָ זְרוֹעַ עִם גְּבוּרָה, תָּעֹז יָדְךָ תָּרוּם יְמִינֶךָ.[26] לְךָ שָׁמַיִם, אַף לְךָ אָרֶץ, תֵּבֵל וּמְלֹאָהּ אַתָּה יְסַדְתָּם.[27] אַתָּה פוֹרַרְתָּ בְעָזְּךָ יָם, שִׁבַּרְתָּ רָאשֵׁי תַנִּינִים עַל הַמָּיִם.[28] אַתָּה הִצַּבְתָּ כָּל גְּבוּלוֹת אָרֶץ, קַיִץ וָחֹרֶף אַתָּה יְצַרְתָּם.[29] אַתָּה רִצַּצְתָּ רָאשֵׁי לִוְיָתָן, תִּתְּנֶנּוּ מַאֲכָל לְעָם לְצִיִּים.

(1) Daniel 9:7. (2) Cf. Lamentations 3:39. (3) Cf. Genesis 44:16. (4) Cf. Lamentations 3:40. (5) Psalms 65:3. (6) Cf. Isaiah 66:23. (7) Psalms 86:9. (8) 95:6. (9) 132:7. (10) 100:4. (11) 99:5. (12) 99:9. (13) 96:9. (14) Cf. 5:8. (15) 138:2. (16) 95:1-2. (17) 55:15. (18) 89:8. (19) 134:2. (20) 134:1. (21) Deuteronomy 3:24. (22) Psalms 95:5. (23) 95:4. (24) Job 12:10. (25) Psalms 89:6. (26) 89:14. (27) 89:12. (28) 74:13. (29) 74:17.

All:

לְךָ ה׳ *Yours, my Lord, is the righteousness and ours is the shame-facedness.[1] What complaint can we make?[2] What can we say? What can we declare? What justification can we offer?[3] Let us examine our ways and analyze — and return to You,[4] for Your right hand is extended to accept penitents. Neither with kindness nor with [good] deeds do we come before You. As paupers and as beggars do we knock at Your doors. At Your doors we knock, O Compassionate and Gracious One. Please do not turn us away from You empty-handed. Our King, turn us not away from You empty-handed, for You are the One Who hears prayer.*

שׁמֵעַ תְּפִלָּה *You Who hears prayer, to You all flesh will come.[5] All flesh will come to prostrate itself before You, O HASHEM.[6] They will come and prostrate themselves before You, my Lord, and shall honor Your Name.[7] Come! — let us prostrate ourselves and bow, let us kneel before God, our Maker.[8] Let us come to His dwelling places, let us prostrate ourselves at His footstool.[9] Enter His gates with thanksgiving, His courts with praise; give thanks to Him, praise His Name.[10] Exalt HASHEM, our God, and bow at His footstool; He is holy![11] Exalt HASHEM, our God, and bow at His holy mountain; for holy is HASHEM, our God.[12] Prostrate yourselves before HASHEM in His intensely holy place, tremble before Him, everyone on earth.[13] As for us, through Your abundant kindness we will enter Your House; we will prostrate ourselves toward Your Holy Sanctuary in awe of You.[14] We will prostrate ourselves toward Your Holy Sanctuary, and we will give thanks to Your Name for Your kindness and truth for You have exalted Your promise even beyond Your Name.[15] Come! — let us sing to HASHEM, let us call out to the Rock of our salvation. Let us greet Him with thanksgiving, with praiseful songs let us call out to Him.[16] For together let us share sweet counsel, in the house of God let us walk in multitudes.[17] God is dreaded in the hiddenmost counsel of the holy ones, and inspires awe upon all who surround Him.[18] Lift your hands in the Sanctuary and bless HASHEM.[19] Behold, bless HASHEM, all you servants of HASHEM, who stand in the House of HASHEM in the nights.[20] For what power is there in heaven or earth that can approximate Your deeds and power?[21] For His is the sea and He perfected the dry land — His hands fashioned it.[22] For in His power are the hidden mysteries of the earth, and the mountain summits are His.[23] For His is the soul of every living thing, and the spirit of all human flesh.[24] Heaven will gratefully praise Your wonders, HASHEM; also Your faithfulness in the assembly of holy ones.[25] Yours is a mighty arm with power, You strengthen Your hand; You exalt Your right hand.[26] Yours is the heaven; Yours, too, is the earth; the world and its fullness — You founded them.[27] You shattered the sea with Your might, You smashed sea serpents' heads upon the water.[28] You established all the boundaries of earth; summer and winter — You fashioned them.[29] You crushed the heads of Leviathan, You served it as food to the nation of legions.*

אַתָּה בָקַעְתָּ מַעְיָן וָנָחַל, אַתָּה הוֹבַשְׁתָּ נַהֲרוֹת אֵיתָן.‎[1] לְךָ יוֹם, אַף
לְךָ לָיְלָה, אַתָּה הֲכִינוֹתָ מָאוֹר וָשָׁמֶשׁ.‎[2] עֹשֶׂה גְדֹלוֹת עַד אֵין חֵקֶר,
וְנִפְלָאוֹת עַד אֵין מִסְפָּר.‎[3] כִּי אֵל גָּדוֹל יהוה, וּמֶלֶךְ גָּדוֹל עַל כָּל
אֱלֹהִים.‎[4] כִּי גָדוֹל אַתָּה וְעֹשֵׂה נִפְלָאוֹת, אַתָּה אֱלֹהִים לְבַדֶּךָ.‎[5] כִּי
גָדוֹל מֵעַל שָׁמַיִם חַסְדֶּךָ, וְעַד שְׁחָקִים אֲמִתֶּךָ.‎[6] גָּדוֹל יהוה וּמְהֻלָּל
מְאֹד, וְלִגְדֻלָּתוֹ אֵין חֵקֶר; (כִּי) גָּדוֹל יהוה וּמְהֻלָּל מְאֹד, נוֹרָא
הוּא עַל כָּל אֱלֹהִים.‎[7] גָּדוֹל יהוה וּמְהֻלָּל מְאֹד, בְּעִיר אֱלֹהֵינוּ הַר
קָדְשׁוֹ.‎[8] לְךָ יהוה הַגְּדֻלָּה וְהַגְּבוּרָה, וְהַתִּפְאֶרֶת וְהַנֵּצַח וְהַהוֹד, כִּי
כֹל בַּשָּׁמַיִם וּבָאָרֶץ; לְךָ יהוה הַמַּמְלָכָה, וְהַמִּתְנַשֵּׂא לְכֹל
לְרֹאשׁ.‎[9] מִי לֹא יִרָאֲךָ מֶלֶךְ הַגּוֹיִם, כִּי לְךָ יָאָתָה, כִּי בְכָל חַכְמֵי
הַגּוֹיִם וּבְכָל מַלְכוּתָם מֵאֵין כָּמוֹךָ.‎[10] מֵאֵין כָּמוֹךָ יהוה, גָּדוֹל אַתָּה
וְגָדוֹל שִׁמְךָ בִּגְבוּרָה.‎[11] יהוה אֱלֹהֵי צְבָאוֹת, מִי כָמוֹךָ חֲסִין יָהּ,
וֶאֱמוּנָתְךָ סְבִיבוֹתֶיךָ.‎[12] יהוה צְבָאוֹת, אֱלֹהֵי יִשְׂרָאֵל, יוֹשֵׁב
הַכְּרֻבִים, אַתָּה הוּא הָאֱלֹהִים לְבַדֶּךָ.‎[13] מִי יְמַלֵּל גְּבוּרוֹת יהוה,
יַשְׁמִיעַ כָּל תְּהִלָּתוֹ.‎[14] כִּי מִי בַשַּׁחַק יַעֲרֹךְ לַיהוה, יִדְמֶה לַיהוה
בִּבְנֵי אֵלִים.‎[15] מַה נֹּאמַר לְפָנֶיךָ יוֹשֵׁב מָרוֹם, וּמַה נְּסַפֵּר לְפָנֶיךָ
שֹׁכֵן שְׁחָקִים. מַה נֹּאמַר לְפָנֶיךָ יהוה אֱלֹהֵינוּ, מַה נְּדַבֵּר וּמַה
נִּצְטַדָּק.‎[16] אֵין לָנוּ פֶּה לְהָשִׁיב וְלֹא מֵצַח לְהָרִים רֹאשׁ, כִּי
עֲוֹנוֹתֵינוּ רַבּוּ מִלִּמְנוֹת, וְחַטֹּאתֵינוּ עָצְמוּ מִסַּפֵּר.‎[17] לְמַעַן שִׁמְךָ
יהוה תְּחַיֵּנוּ, וּבְצִדְקָתְךָ תּוֹצִיא מִצָּרָה נַפְשֵׁנוּ.‎[18] דַּרְכְּךָ אֱלֹהֵינוּ
לְהַאֲרִיךְ אַפֶּךָ, לָרָעִים וְלַטּוֹבִים, וְהִיא תְהִלָּתֶךָ. לְמַעַנְךָ אֱלֹהֵינוּ
עֲשֵׂה וְלֹא לָנוּ, רְאֵה עֲמִידָתֵנוּ, דַּלִּים וְרֵקִים. ✧ הַנְּשָׁמָה לָךְ וְהַגּוּף
פָּעֳלָךְ, חוּסָה עַל עֲמָלָךְ. הַנְּשָׁמָה לָךְ וְהַגּוּף שֶׁלָּךְ, יהוה עֲשֵׂה
לְמַעַן שְׁמֶךָ. אָתָאנוּ עַל שִׁמְךָ, יהוה, עֲשֵׂה לְמַעַן שְׁמֶךָ. בַּעֲבוּר
כְּבוֹד שִׁמְךָ, כִּי אֵל חַנּוּן וְרַחוּם שְׁמֶךָ. לְמַעַן שִׁמְךָ יהוה, וְסָלַחְתָּ
לַעֲוֹנֵנוּ כִּי רַב הוּא.‎[20]

Congregation, then *chazzan:*

סְלַח לָנוּ אָבִינוּ, כִּי בְרֹב אִוַּלְתֵּנוּ שָׁגִינוּ,
מְחַל לָנוּ מַלְכֵּנוּ, כִּי רַבּוּ עֲוֹנֵינוּ.

(1) *Psalms* 74:14-15. (2) 74:16. (3) *Job* 9:10. (4) *Psalms* 95:3. (5) 86:10. (6) 108:5.
(7) 145:3. (8) 96:4. (9) 48:2. (10) *I Chronicles* 29:11. (11) *Jeremiah* 10:7. (12) 10:6.
(13) *Psalms* 89:9. (14) *Isaiah* 37:16. (15) *Psalms* 106:2. (16) 89:7.
(17) Cf. *Genesis* 44:16. (18) Cf. *Ezra* 9:6. (19) Cf. *Psalms* 143:11. (20) Cf. 25:11.

You split open fountain and stream, You dried the mighty rivers.[1] Yours is the day, Yours as well is the night; You established luminary and the sun.[2] Who performs great deeds that are beyond comprehension, and wonders beyond number.[3] For a great God is HASHEM, and a great King above all heavenly powers.[4] For You are great and work wonders; You alone, O God.[5] For great above the very heavens is Your kindness, and until the upper heights is Your truth.[6] HASHEM is great and exceedingly lauded, and His greatness is beyond investigation.[7] (For) HASHEM is great and exceedingly lauded, awesome is He above all heavenly powers.[8] Great is HASHEM and exceedingly lauded, in the city of our God, Mount of His Holiness.[9] Yours, HASHEM, is the greatness, the strength, the splendor, the triumph, and the glory; even everything in heaven and earth; Yours, HASHEM, is the kingdom, and sovereignty over every leader.[10] Who would not revere You, O King of nations? — for this befits You, for among all the sages of the nations and in all their kingdom there is none like You.[11] There is none like You, O HASHEM, You are great and Your Name is great with power.[12] HASHEM, God of Legions — who is like You, O Strong One, God? — and Your faithfulness surrounds You.[13] HASHEM, Master of Legions, God of Israel, enthroned upon the Cherubim, it is You alone Who is God.[14] Who can express the mighty acts of HASHEM, who can announce all His praise?[15] For who in the sky can be compared to HASHEM; be likened to HASHEM among the angels?[16] What can we say before You Who dwell on high? And what can we relate to You Who abide in the highest heaven? What can we say before You, HASHEM, our God? What can we declare? What justification can we offer?[17] We have neither mouth to respond nor brow to raise our head, for our iniquities are too numerous to count, and our sins are too vast to be numbered.[18] For Your Name's sake, HASHEM, revive us; and with Your righteousness remove our soul from distress.[19] It is Your way, our God, to delay Your anger, against people both evil and good — and this is Your praise. Act for Your sake, our God, and not for ours, behold our [spiritual] position — destitute and emptyhanded. Chazzan – The soul is Yours and the body is Your handiwork; take pity on Your labor. The soul is Yours and the body is Yours; O HASHEM, act for Your Name's sake. We have come with reliance on Your Name, O HASHEM, act for Your Name's sake; because of Your Name's glory — for 'Gracious and Merciful God' is Your Name. For Your Name's sake, HASHEM, may You forgive our iniquity, though it is abundant.[20]

Congregation, then chazzan:

Forgive us, our Father, for in our abundant folly we have erred, pardon us, our King, for our iniquities are many.

סליחה מו (פתיחה)

All:

אָז טֶרֶם* נִמְתְּחוּ נִבְלֵי שְׁכָבִים.[1]

בָּאָרֶץ עַד לֹא דָּבְקוּ רְגָבִים.[2]

גַּבָּךְ שִׁבְעָה דְּבָרִים הָיוּ מְגֻבָּבִים.

דָּת[3] נָכֵס[4] וּרְטִיַּת בָּנִים שׁוֹבָבִים.[5]

הוֹד גַּן עֵדֶן וְעֶלֶק הַכְּהָבִים.[6]

וּמָקוֹם כַּפָּרָה עַל יְדֵי מַקְרִיבִים.

זְהַר שֵׁם יִנּוֹן*[7] מְחוֹלָל מֵחוֹבִים.

חִבְּרוּ אֲלָפַיִם קֹדֶם בְּרִיאַת יְשׁוּבִים.

טְכוּסִים עַל רָקִיעַ בּוֹטִים כְּשָׁבִיבִים.

יְעוּרִים וּמְשָׁרְשִׁים פְּנֵי יוֹשֵׁב הַכְּרוּבִים.

כִּסֵּא הָיָה מֻנָּח בָּרָקִיעַ בִּיצוּבִים.

לְמוֹשַׁב מֶלֶךְ וְנוֹרָא עַל סְבִיבִים.[8]

מִימִינוֹ אֵשׁ דָּת[9] חֲקוּקָה בִּכְתָבִים.

נְתוּנָה עַל בִּרְכּוֹ בְּשַׁעֲשׁוּעַ[10] אֲהָבִים.

סָדוּר עַל הַדָּרוֹם גַּן רְטוּבִים.

עָרוּךְ עַל הַצָּפוֹן*[11] תִּפְתֶּה שַׁלְהֲבִים.

פְּנֵי הַמִּזְרָח יְרוּשָׁלַיִם הַבְּנוּיָה בְּמַחֲצָבִים.

צָפוֹן בְּתוֹכָהּ מִקְדָּשׁ אֵל בִּישׁוּבִים.

קָבוּעַ בָּאֶמְצַע מִזְבֵּחַ כִּפּוּר חַיָּבִים.[12]

רְבוּצָה עָלָיו אֶבֶן שְׁתִיַּת חֲטוּבִים.*

שֵׁם יִנּוֹן עָלֶיהָ חָקוּק בְּמִכְתָּבִים.

תֹּאַר שֵׁם הַמְפֹרָשׁ* בְּתָוֵי גְלוּבִים.

⁊§ אָז טֶרֶם — *Then, before.* This *pesichah* (introductory *selichah*) was composed by *Rashi*, the best known and greatest of all commentaries on Scriptures and the Talmud [see prefatory comment to *selichah* 23]. The acrostic of the stiches comprises the *aleph-beis* followed by *Rashi's* signature, שְׁלֹמֹה בְּרַבִּי יִצְחָק, *Shlomo son of R' Yitzchak*.

The *selichah* is based on the Talmud's teaching that seven things were created before the world itself: Torah, the concept of *teshuvah* (repentance), *Gan Eden, Gehinnom*, the Throne of Glory, the [heavenly] *Beis HaMikdash*, and the name of the Messiah (*Nedarim* 39b; *Pesachim* 54a).

The Midrash describes the scene: Seven things preceded the world by two thousand years . . .

The Torah, written with black fire [as the ink] on white fire [as the parchment], is lying on God's knees [so to speak]. God is sitting on the Throne of Glory . . . with *Gan Eden* at His right [south], *Gehinnom* at His left [north]. The *Beis HaMikdash* is before Him, with the Messiah's name engraved on a precious stone upon the Altar. A heavenly voice calls out, 'Repent! O sons of man . . .' (*Shocheir Tov* 90:12).

שֵׁם יִנּוֹן — *The [Messiah's] . . . name, 'Yinon.'* According to one opinion in the Talmud, the Messiah's name is יִנּוֹן, *Yinon*, as it is stated (*Psalms* 72:17): *May his name endure forever; before the sun [was created]*, יִנּוֹן שְׁמוֹ, *his name was Yinon* (*Sanhedrin* 98b).

סָדוּר עַל הַדָּרוֹם . . . עָרוּךְ עַל הַצָּפוֹן — *Set to the south*

SELICHAH 46

All:

א Then, before* the water-skin clouds were spread out to bring rainfall,[1]

ב before earth-clumps were bound together to form the earth,[2]

ג seven things were gathered before You:

ד The Torah,[3] the Throne [of Glory],[4]
  and the healing [of repentance] for wayward children,[5]

ה the glory of the Garden of Eden, and the thirsty leech [Gehinnom],[6]

ו the place of atonement through [Altar] offerings,

ז the [Messiah's] shining name 'Yinon'*[7] that [our] sins have profaned—

ח these were conjoined two thousand [years] before the world's creation,

ט arrayed over the firmament, looking like sparks of fire,

י burgeoning well-rooted before Him Who sits on the Cherubim.

כ The Throne was set firmly upon the Heavenly expanse,

ל a seat for the King whose awe is all around Him;[8]

מ at His right the fiery Law[9] was engraved in writing,

נ placed on His knee to be dandled[10] lovingly;

ס set to the south was the flourishing Garden;

ע arranged to the north* was flaming Tofes [Gehinnom].[11]

פ Before Him, to the east was Jerusalem, built of hewn stones,

צ and hidden within it God's [Celestial] Sanctuary,
  [corresponding to the Temple] on inhabited earth,

ק set in its center, the Altar of atonement for sinners,[12]

ר and upon it lying the stone from which [the conduit to]
  the foundation was hewn.*

ש The [Messiah's] name 'Yinon' is engraved upon it in letters,

ת and also the Ineffable Name of God* in lapidary letters.

---

(1) Cf. *Job* 38:37. (2) Cf. 38:38. (3) See *Deuteronomy* 33:2. (4) See *Exodus* 17:16.
(5) See *Jeremiah* 3:14. (6) See *Proverbs* 30:15. (7) Cf. *Psalms* 72:17. (8) Cf. 89:8.
(9) *Deuteronomy* 33:2. (10) Cf. *Proverbs* 8:30-31; *Isaiah* 66:12. (11) See *Jeremiah* 7:32.
(12) Some editions read, מִזְבַּח כַּפּוּר חַיָּבִים, *the Altar, to atone for sinners.*

... *arranged to the north.* The *paytan* has changed right and left (of the Midrash's description) to south and north respectively. From the viewpoint of the *Shechinah* (Divine Presence) resting upon the top of the Ark in the Holy of Holies, facing the entranceway to the Sanctuary, east is before Him, west behind Him, south to His right and north to His left. Thus, east is called קֶדֶם, *before*, and west is called אָחוֹר, *behind* (see *Psalms* 139:5; *Chagigah* 12a with *Rashi*); south is called יָמִין, *right*, and north is called שְׂמֹאל, *left* (see *Targum Onkelos* to *Genesis* 13:9).

אֶבֶן שְׁתִיָּה חֲטוּבִים — *The stone from which [the conduit to] the foundation was hewn.* The Talmud states that there was a rock that protruded three handbreadths above the floor of the Holy of Holies. That stone was called אֶבֶן שְׁתִיָּה, *Foundation Stone*, for it was the basis, or central point, from which the world was created (*Yoma* 54b). The *paytan* borrows the term אֶבֶן שְׁתִיָּה and uses

it to describe another stone in the *Beis HaMikdash*, namely, the אֶבֶן יְקָרָה, *precious stone*, that the Midrash cited above states was on the Altar and had the Messiah's name engraved upon it. Moreover, he identifies that stone with another upon which King David had engraved the Ineffable Name of God. The Talmud relates that when King David prepared the foundations for the future Temple that his son Solomon would build, he excavated deep pits beneath the site of the Altar, into which the wine and water libations would flow. David dug so deep that he penetrated the subterranean reservoirs of water that had been stored beneath the earth's crust since Creation. The waters erupted from the reservoir and threatened to inundate the world. David then inscribed a Divine Name on a shard and cast it into the waters, which receded ... (*Succah* 53).

תֹּאַר שֵׁם הַמְפֹרָשׁ — *And also the Ineffable Name of God*, [lit., *the form of the Ineffable Name*]. See

שָׁמָּה בַּתְּוֶךְ לִפְנֵי מַאֲזִין מֵאֶשְׁנַבִּים.*¹

לַוִּי תְּשׁוּבָה אֶרֶךְ לְנִדְוִים וְכֹאֲבִים.

מְעֻתֶּרֶת לְכַבֵּס צוֹאִים, וּלְהַלְבִּישׁ מוּטָבִים.*²

הָרֵק שֶׁמֶן הַטּוֹב עַל רֹאשׁ שָׁבִים.

בְּכֵן אָתְנוּ לְךָ עֲלָמִים וְשָׁבִים.

רַחֵץ מִצַּחַן וְהַשְׁלֵךְ טְמוּס סְאָבִים.

בִּתְפִלָּה יְקַדְּמוּךָ בָּנִים שׁוֹבָבִים.

יוֹם יוֹם לְדָרְשֶׁךָ בְּפִיץ נִיבִים.

❖ יֵחָשֵׁב אֲמָרֵינוּ כְּהֶקְטֵר דָּמִים וַחֲלָבִים.*

צִפְצוּפֵנוּ יְקַבֵּל כְּפִסּוּגֵי פָרִים וּכְשָׂבִים.

חֲטָאֵינוּ הַצְלֵל בְּקַרְקַע נִטְפֵי מַרְזֵבִים.

קָרְבֵנוּ אֵלֶיךָ בִּרְחִיפַת רַחֲמֶיךָ הָרַבִּים.

All:

כִּי עַל רַחֲמֶיךָ הָרַבִּים³ אָנוּ בְטוּחִים, וְעַל צִדְקוֹתֶיךָ אָנוּ נִשְׁעָנִים, וְלִסְלִיחוֹתֶיךָ אָנוּ מְקַוִּים, וְלִישׁוּעָתְךָ אָנוּ מְצַפִּים. אַתָּה הוּא מֶלֶךְ, אוֹהֵב צְדָקוֹת מִקֶּדֶם, מַעֲבִיר עֲוֹנוֹת עַמּוֹ, וּמֵסִיר חַטֹּאת יְרֵאָיו. כּוֹרֵת בְּרִית לָרִאשׁוֹנִים, וּמְקַיֵּם שְׁבוּעָה לָאַחֲרוֹנִים. אַתָּה הוּא, שֶׁיָּרַדְתָּ בַּעֲנַן כְּבוֹדְךָ עַל הַר סִינַי,⁴ וְהֶרְאֵיתָ דַּרְכֵי טוּבְךָ לְמֹשֶׁה עַבְדֶּךָ.⁵ וְאָרְחוֹת חֲסָדֶיךָ גִּלִּיתָ לּוֹ, וְהוֹדַעְתּוֹ כִּי אַתָּה אֵל רַחוּם וְחַנּוּן, אֶרֶךְ אַפַּיִם וְרַב חֶסֶד⁶ וּמַרְבֶּה לְהֵיטִיב, וּמַנְהִיג אֶת כָּל הָעוֹלָם כֻּלּוֹ בְּמִדַּת הָרַחֲמִים. ❖ וְכֵן כָּתוּב, וַיֹּאמֶר אֲנִי אַעֲבִיר כָּל טוּבִי עַל פָּנֶיךָ, וְקָרָאתִי בְשֵׁם יהוה לְפָנֶיךָ, וְחַנֹּתִי אֶת אֲשֶׁר אָחֹן, וְרִחַמְתִּי אֶת אֲשֶׁר אֲרַחֵם.⁷

All, while standing:

אֵל אֶרֶךְ אַפַּיִם אַתָּה, וּבַעַל הָרַחֲמִים נִקְרֵאתָ, וְדֶרֶךְ תְּשׁוּבָה הוֹרֵיתָ.

גְּדֻלַּת רַחֲמֶיךָ וַחֲסָדֶיךָ, תִּזְכּוֹר הַיּוֹם וּבְכָל יוֹם לְזֶרַע יְדִידֶיךָ.

---

the preceding comment for the interpretation of this phrase. Alternatively, the stich should be understood in its literal sense, and connected to the one before it. Thus, the Messiah's name that is carved into the stone takes the same form as God's Name. Just as in God's Name the first and third letters are י and ו, so in the Messiah's name Yinon the first and third letters are י and ו. And just as in God's Name the second and fourth letters are the same (ה), so in the name Yinon are the second

and fourth letters the same (נ). Moreover, in one of the kabbalistic permutations of the *aleph-beis* (known as א"ט ב"ח), the letters ה and נ form a pair in which one may be substituted for the other. Accordingly, the two stiches read: *The [Messiah's] name Yinon is engraved upon it in letters that form the Ineffable ...*

מַאֲזִין מֵאֶשְׁנַבִּים — *Who gives ear ... from the windows ...* Some editions of *Selichos* read מְטוֹב

שׁ *There in the middle of the firmament, before Him*
   Who gives ear [to prayer] from the windows [of Heaven],[1]
ל *was the juncture of repentance — healing for the pained and sorrowful,*
מ *primed to launder [their] befouled [garments]*
   and enrobe [them with] proper ones,[2]
ה *to pour beneficial oil on the heads of the repentant.*
ב *Therefore we have come to You, young and old,*
ר *to wash us of the stench [of sin]*
   and cast away the tome of our defiling deeds.
כ *Your wayward children approach You with prayer,*
י *seeking You each day, speaking words [of prayers].*
י Chazzan — *Let our words be accounted as bloods and fats*
   burning [on the Altar];
צ *accept our twittering [prayer] as*
   [You would the prescribed] parts of bulls and sheep [on the Altar].
ח *Sink our sins in the depths of the earth where water flows;*
ק *bring us near to You as Your great mercy hovers over us.*

All:

בִּי עַל For upon Your abundant mercy[3] do we trust, and upon Your
righteousness do we depend, and for Your forgiveness do we
hope, and for Your salvation do we yearn. You are the King Who loves
righteousness since the earliest days, Who overlooks His people's
iniquities and sets aside the sins of those who revere Him. He made
a covenant with the ancestors and keeps [His] vow to the descendants. It is You Who descended in Your cloud of glory on Mount Sinai,[4]
and showed the ways of Your goodness to Your servant Moses.[5]
You revealed Your paths of kindness to him, and let him know that You
are God, Compassionate and Gracious, Slow to anger and Abundant in
Kindness,[6] doing manifold good, and guiding all Your world with the
Attribute of Mercy. Chazzan — And so it is written: He said, 'I shall pass
all My good in front of you, and I shall call out the Name of HASHEM before
you; for I will be gracious to whom I will be gracious, and I will be
compassionate with whom I will be compassionate.'[7]

All, while standing:

אֵל אֶרֶךְ אַפַּיִם O God — You are slow to anger, You are called the
Master of Mercy, and You have taught the way of
repentance. May You remember this day and every day the greatness of
Your mercy and Your kindness to the offspring of Your beloved Ones.

---

(1) Some editions read מַזִּיב מַשְׁאַבִּים, see commentary. (2) Cf. Zechariah 3:4.
(3) Daniel 9:18. (4) Cf. Exodus 34:5. (5) Cf. 33:13. (6) 34:6. (7) 33:19.

מַשְׁאַבִּים, *from which the waters flow.* The phrase
then refers to the אֶבֶן שְׁתִיָּה, *Foundation Stone,*
mentioned earlier, from which flow all the waters
of the world.

מוּטָבִים ... צוֹאִים — *Befouled [garments] ...*
proper ones. The prophet (Zechariah 3:2) describes the effects of sin as befouled garments and

repentance as the donning of fresh clothing.

בְּהַקְטֵר דָּמִים וַחֲלָבִים — *As bloods and fats burning*
[on the Altar]. The expression הַקְטֵר דָּמִים, *burning*
bloods, is difficult. Nowhere in Scriptures or Talmud do we find blood placed upon the Altar fire.
The blood of sacrificial animals was placed on the
sides or corners of the Altar, not on the fire. In-

תִּפֶּן אֵלֵינוּ בְּרַחֲמִים, כִּי אַתָּה הוּא בַּעַל הָרַחֲמִים. בְּתַחֲנוּן וּבִתְפִלָּה פָּנֶיךָ נְקַדֵּם, כְּהוֹדַעְתָּ לֶעָנָיו מִקֶּדֶם. מֵחֲרוֹן אַפְּךָ שׁוּב,[1] כְּמוֹ בְתוֹרָתְךָ כָּתוּב.[2] וּבְצֵל כְּנָפֶיךָ נֶחֱסֶה[3] וְנִתְלוֹנָן, כְּיוֹם וַיֵּרֶד יהוה בֶּעָנָן. ❖ תַּעֲבוֹר עַל פֶּשַׁע וְתִמְחֶה אָשָׁם, כְּיוֹם וַיִּתְיַצֵּב עִמּוֹ שָׁם. תַּאֲזִין שַׁוְעָתֵנוּ וְתַקְשִׁיב מֶנּוּ מַאֲמָר, כְּיוֹם וַיִּקְרָא בְשֵׁם יהוה,[4] וְשָׁם נֶאֱמַר:

Congregation, then chazzan:

וַיַּעֲבֹר יהוה עַל פָּנָיו וַיִּקְרָא:

Congregation and chazzan (the words in bold type are recited aloud and in unison):

יהוה, יהוה, אֵל, רַחוּם, וְחַנּוּן, אֶרֶךְ אַפַּיִם, וְרַב חֶסֶד, וֶאֱמֶת, **נֹצֵר חֶסֶד לָאֲלָפִים, נֹשֵׂא עָוֹן, וָפֶשַׁע, וְחַטָּאָה, וְנַקֵּה.**[5] וְסָלַחְתָּ לַעֲוֹנֵנוּ וּלְחַטָּאתֵנוּ וּנְחַלְתָּנוּ.[6] סְלַח לָנוּ אָבִינוּ כִּי חָטָאנוּ, מְחַל לָנוּ מַלְכֵּנוּ כִּי פָשָׁעְנוּ. כִּי אַתָּה אֲדֹנָי טוֹב וְסַלָּח, וְרַב חֶסֶד לְכָל קֹרְאֶיךָ.[7]

פסוקי הקדמה לסליחה מז

דִּרְשׁוּ יהוה בְּהִמָּצְאוֹ, קְרָאֻהוּ בִּהְיוֹתוֹ קָרוֹב.[8] שׁוּבוּ אֵלַי וְאָשׁוּבָה אֲלֵיכֶם אָמַר יהוה צְבָאוֹת.[9] מִי יוֹדֵעַ יָשׁוּב, וְנִחַם הָאֱלֹהִים,* וְשָׁב מֵחֲרוֹן אַפּוֹ וְלֹא נֹאבֵד.[10] מִי יוֹדֵעַ יָשׁוּב וְנִחָם, וְהִשְׁאִיר אַחֲרָיו בְּרָכָה.[11] וְקִרְעוּ לְבַבְכֶם וְאַל בִּגְדֵיכֶם, וְשׁוּבוּ אֶל יהוה אֱלֹהֵיכֶם, כִּי חַנּוּן וְרַחוּם הוּא, אֶרֶךְ אַפַּיִם וְרַב חֶסֶד, וְנִחָם עַל הָרָעָה.[12]

בְּרַחֵם אָב עַל בָּנִים, כֵּן תְּרַחֵם יהוה עָלֵינוּ.[13] לַיהוה הַיְשׁוּעָה, עַל עַמְּךָ בִרְכָתֶךָ סֶּלָה.[14] יהוה צְבָאוֹת עִמָּנוּ, מִשְׂגָּב לָנוּ אֱלֹהֵי יַעֲקֹב סֶּלָה.[15] יהוה צְבָאוֹת, אַשְׁרֵי אָדָם בֹּטֵחַ בָּךְ.[16] יהוה הוֹשִׁיעָה, הַמֶּלֶךְ יַעֲנֵנוּ בְיוֹם קָרְאֵנוּ.[17]

In some congregations the following two verses are recited responsively — the chazzan reciting סְלַח, and the congregation responding וַיֹּאמֶר. In other congregations these verses are recited silently.

סְלַח נָא לַעֲוֹן הָעָם הַזֶּה כְּגֹדֶל חַסְדֶּךָ, וְכַאֲשֶׁר נָשָׂאתָה לָעָם הַזֶּה מִמִּצְרַיִם וְעַד הֵנָּה,[18] וְשָׁם נֶאֱמַר:

---

teresting, none of the commentaries raise this question. There is however at least one ancient manuscript that reads בְּשָׂמִים, spices, instead of דָּמִים, blood. If so, the word refers to the Incense offered twice daily on the Golden (Inner) Altar.

מִי יוֹדֵעַ יָשׁוּב וְנִחַם הָאֱלֹהִים — Let the one who knows [that he has sinned] repent, then God will reconsider. The translation follows Targum, Rashi, et al. (to Jonah 3:9). Alternatively: the object of the verb 'knows' is God's disposition, i.e.,

Turn to us in mercy for You are the Master of Mercy. With supplication and prayer we approach Your Presence in the manner that You made known to the humble [Moses] in ancient times. Turn back from Your fierce anger;[1] as is written in Your Torah.[2] In the shadow of Your wings may we find shelter[3] and lodging as on the day 'HASHEM descended in a cloud' [to appear to Moses on Sinai]. Chazzan — *Overlook sin and erase guilt as on the day 'He [God] stood there with him [Moses].' Give heed to our cry and be attentive to our declaration as on the day 'He called out with the Name HASHEM,'[4] and there it was said:*

Congregation, then chazzan:

And HASHEM passed before him [Moses] and proclaimed:

Congregation and chazzan (the words in bold type are recited aloud and in unison):

ה' ה' HASHEM, HASHEM, God, Compassionate and Gracious, Slow **to anger, and Abundant in Kindness and Truth, Preserver of kindness for thousands [of generations], Forgiver of iniquity, willful sin, and error, and Who cleanses.**[5] *May You forgive our iniquities and our errors and make us Your heritage.[6] Forgive us, our Father, for we have erred; pardon us, our King, for we have willfully sinned; for You, my Lord, are good and forgiving and abundantly kind to all who call upon You.[7]*

PREFATORY VERSES TO SELICHAH 47

דִּרְשׁוּ *Seek HASHEM when He is to be found, call Him when He is near.[8] 'Return to Me and I will return to you,' says HASHEM, Master of Legions.[9] Let the one who knows [that he has sinned] repent, then God will reconsider* and turn back from His blasting anger, so we will not be lost.[10] Let the one who knows [that he has sinned] repent, then [God will] reconsider and leave blessing in his wake.[11] So rend your hearts, not your garments, and return to HASHEM your God. For He is endlessly loving and merciful, slow to anger, and reconsiders the evil [decree].[12]*

כְּרַחֵם אָב *As a father has mercy on his children, so, HASHEM, may You have mercy on us.[13] Salvation is HASHEM's, upon Your people is Your blessing, Selah.[14] HASHEM, Master of Legions, is with us, a stronghold for us is the God of Jacob, Selah.[15] HASHEM, Master of Legions, praiseworthy is the person who trusts in You.[16] HASHEM, save! May the King answer us on the day we call.[17]*

In some congregations the following two verses are recited responsively — the chazzan reciting, 'Forgive, please . . .,' and the congregation responding, 'And HASHEM said . . .'
In other congregations these verses are recited silently.

סְלַח נָא *Forgive, please, the iniquity of this people according to the greatness of Your kindness and as You have forgiven this people from Egypt until now,[18] and there it was said:*

---

(1) Cf. *Exodus* 32:12. (2) See 32:14. (3) Cf. *Psalms* 36:8. (4) *Exodus* 34:5. (5) 34:6-7. (6) 34:9. (7) *Psalms* 86:5. (8) *Isaiah* 55:6. (9) *Malachi* 3:7. (10) *Jonah* 3:9. (11) *Joel* 2:14. (12) 2:13. (13) Cf. *Psalms* 103:13. (14) 3:9. (15) 46:8. (16) 84:13. (17) 20:10. (18) *Numbers* 14:19.

Who knows whether God will turn back and reconsider? (Radak). This same phrase appears in the next verse recited during *Selichos (Joel* 2:14), but without the mentioning הָאֱלֹהִים, *God. Nevertheless, God is the implied subject of* וְנִחַם, *He will reconsider (Targum, Ibn Ezra).*

וַיֹּאמֶר יהוה סָלַחְתִּי כִּדְבָרֶךָ.[1]

All:

הַטֵּה אֱלֹהַי אָזְנְךָ וּשֲׁמָע, פְּקַח עֵינֶיךָ וּרְאֵה שֹׁמְמֹתֵינוּ, וְהָעִיר אֲשֶׁר נִקְרָא שִׁמְךָ עָלֶיהָ, כִּי לֹא עַל צִדְקוֹתֵינוּ אֲנַחְנוּ מַפִּילִים תַּחֲנוּנֵינוּ לְפָנֶיךָ, כִּי עַל רַחֲמֶיךָ הָרַבִּים. אֲדֹנָי שְׁמָעָה, אֲדֹנָי סְלָחָה, אֲדֹנָי הַקְשִׁיבָה, וַעֲשֵׂה אַל תְּאַחַר, לְמַעַנְךָ אֱלֹהַי, כִּי שִׁמְךָ נִקְרָא עַל עִירְךָ וְעַל עַמֶּךָ.[2]

סליחה מז

All:

אֶת יהוה בְּהִמָּצְאוֹ* לְדָרְשׁוֹ[3] קִדַּמְתִּי,*

בְּעַד עֲוֹנוֹת לְכַפֵּר, כִּי כַתּוֹלָע נֶאֱדַמְתִּי,[4]

גִּלְגַּל הַלֵּב וְטִמְטֵם, וּכְיָשֵׁן נִרְדַּמְתִּי,

כִּמְעַט כִּסְדֹם הָיְיתִי וְלַעֲמוֹרָה דָמֶיתִי.[5]

דָּמֶיתִי לְסוֹטָה פְרוּעָה[6] מְנָאֶפֶת וַחֲלָלָה,[7]

הָיְיתִי כְבֶגֶד עִדִּים,[8] וְהוֹשַׁעְתִּי כְּשִׂמְלָה מְגוֹלָלָה,[9]

וְחָסַרְתִּי מַפְגִּיעַ, וְיוֹדֵעַ אֵין לְפַלְלָה,

רְאֵה יהוה וְהַבִּיטָה, כִּי הָיְיתִי זוֹלֵלָה.[10]

זוֹלֵלָה כְּבוֹדָה נֶהְפְּכָה בְּיַד מְגֹאָל,

חִנָּם נִמְכְּרָה לִצְמִיתוּת, וְאֵין גּוֹאֵל,[11]

טֶבַע נָכוֹן וְנִשָּׂא וְחָרֵב אֲרִיאֵל,*

הִשְׁלִיךְ מִשָּׁמַיִם אֶרֶץ תִּפְאֶרֶת יִשְׂרָאֵל.[12]

יִשְׂרָאֵל לְבוֹזְזִים וְלִמְשִׁסָּה,[13] עַד מָתַי,

כְּאָרְבֶּה רַבּוּ עוֹרְקַי, וְעָצְמוּ מַצְמִיתַי,

לַלֵּב בְּשׁוּמִי, הֲרִיסוֹתַי חָרְבוֹתַי וְשׁוֹמְמוֹתַי,[14]

וַתִּבְחַר מַחֲנָק נַפְשִׁי, מָוֶת מֵעַצְמוֹתָי.[15]

מֵעַצְמוֹתַי הַמֻּפְצָצוֹת וְהַמֻּפְלָחוֹת, מִמַּכְעִיסֶיךָ וּמִמַּזְעִיעֶיךָ,

נֶאֱמָתִי, נִלְאֵיתִי נְשֹׂא חֲרוֹנְךָ וְזַעֲמֶךָ,

שִׂים לֵב לִגְאֹל חַיַּת נְעִימֶיךָ,

כִּי שִׁמְךָ נִקְרָא, עַל עִירְךָ וְעַל עַמֶּךָ.[16]

אֶת ה׳ בְּהִמָּצְאוֹ — ...HASHEM when He is to be *found.* In the intricate tapestry of this *selichah,* the first three lines of the respective quatrains form an *aleph-beis* acrostic followed by the composer's name חֲזָק שְׁמַעְיָה בַּר אֵלִיָּה, *Eliyah bar She-* *mayah, may he be strong* [see prefatory comment

to *selichah* 6]. The last line of each stanza is a Scriptural fragment, the last word of which is repeated as the first word of the next stanza.

אֶת ה׳ בְּהִמָּצְאוֹ לְדָרְשׁוֹ קִדַּמְתִּי — *I have come early* *to seek* HASHEM *when He is to be found.* This

And HASHEM said, 'I have forgiven according to your word!'[1]

All:

הַטֵּה *Incline, my God, Your ear, and listen, open Your eyes and see our desolation and that of the city upon which Your Name is proclaimed; for not because of our righteousness do we cast down our supplications before You, rather because of Your abundant compassion. O my Lord, heed; O my Lord, forgive; O my Lord, be attentive and act, do not delay; for Your sake, my God, for Your Name is proclaimed upon Your city and upon Your people.*[2]

SELICHAH 47

All:

א *I have come early to seek HASHEM when He is to be found,*[3]

ב *[asking Him] to atone for my iniquities,*
    for I am reddened [with sin] like a scarlet thread.[4]

ג *My heart is overturned and obstructed; I drowse like a sleeper.*
    *I have almost become like Sodom; and to Amorah, **I am likened**.*[5]

ד ***I am likened** to a suspected wife, her tresses disarrayed,*[6]
    to an adulteress, to a dishonored daughter.[7]

ה *I have been like a soiled garment,*[8]
    I am made like a cloak befouled with blood.[9]

ו *Now I lack one to pray for me,*
    for there is none who knows how to pray.
        *See, HASHEM, and observe how I have become **degraded**.*[10]

ז ***Degraded** is the august lady, turned about by the defiler.*

ח *She has been sold for naught, eternally, with no redeemer.*[11]

ט *The well-founded, lofty Temple, is sunk; Ariel* is destroyed;*
        *flung down from Heaven to earth is the glory of **Israel**.*[12]

י ***Israel** given over to pillagers and oppressors*[13] *— until when?*

כ *Many pursuers are abundant as locusts; my despoilers are powerful.*

ל *When I take to heart my wreckage, my ruins, and my desolation,*[14]
    *my soul chooses suffocation, death rather than [life in] **my bones**.*[15]

מ ***My bones** that are broken and split*
    by those who anger and enrage You,

נ *I declare, 'I am wearied of bearing Your fury and Your rage.*

ס *Take to heart to redeem the lifeblood*
    of those who sing of Your pleasantness,
        *for Your Name is proclaimed on Your city and on **Your people**.'*[16]

---

(1) *Numbers* 14:20. (2) *Daniel* 9:18-19. (3) Cf. *Isaiah* 55:6. (4) Cf. 1:18. (5) Cf. 1:9.
(6) See *Numbers* ch. 5. (7) See *Leviticus* 21:9. (8) Cf. *Isaiah* 64:5. (9) Cf. 9:4.
(10) *Lamentations* 1:11. (11) Cf. *Isaiah* 52:3; *Leviticus* 25:30. (12) *Lamentations* 2:1.
(13) Cf. *Isaiah* 42:24. (14) Cf. 49:19. (15) *Job* 7:15. (16) *Daniel* 9:19.

opening stich has a double significance for the Fast of Gedaliah: (a) It is based on *Isaiah* 55:6, the first verse of the *haftarah* read at Minchah on fast days; and (b) the Talmud (*Rosh Hashanah* 18a) states that 'when He is to be found' refers to the ten-day period from Rosh Hashanah to Yom Kip-

pur, and today is the first day during that period on which *Selichos* is recited.

אֲרִיאֵל — *Ariel*. This compound word literally means *lion of God*. In the book of *Ezekiel* (43:15-16), it refers to the Altar fire, for the fire that originally descended from heaven when King

עַמְּךָ זְרוּיִים פְּזוּרִים בְּכָל מוֹשָׁבוֹת,

פְּקָדוּךָ בַּצָּר, פְּחָדוּךָ בְּמַעַשׂ וּבְמַחֲשָׁבוֹת,

צְלַל זָדוֹן, וְהַעֲבֵר וְרַפֵּא מְשׁוּבוֹת,

אֲדֹנָי, שִׁמְעָה בְקוֹלֵנוּ, תִּהְיֶינָה אָזְנֶיךָ קַשֻׁבוֹת.[1]

קַשֻׁבוֹת תִּהְיֶינָה אָזְנֶיךָ, לְשֶׁפֶךְ שִׂיחֵנוּ,

רֹן שְׂפָתֵינוּ קַבֵּל כְּרֵיחַ נִיחֹחֵינוּ,[2]

שַׂחֲרְנוּךָ מָגִנֵּנוּ וּבְךָ יַהֵב מִבְטָחֵנוּ,

וְשִׁמְךָ עָלֵינוּ נִקְרָא אַל תַּנִּיחֵנוּ.[3]

תַּנִּיחֵנוּ אָדוֹן זֶה כַּמֶּה שָׁנִים לָמָּה,

לְשַׁמָּה לְמָשָׁל וְלִשְׁנִינָה[4] לַלַעַג לְבֹשֶׁת וְלִכְלִמָּה,

יֵאָמֵן וְיוּחַשׁ הַמֻּבְטָח, שֶׁהִבְטַחְתָּ לַשׁוֹמֵמָה,

אֲנִי יְהוָה בָּנִיתִי הַנֶּהֱרָסוֹת, נָטַעְתִּי הַנְּשַׁמָּה.[5]

❖ הַנְּשַׁמָּה בְּרַחֲמִים גְּדוֹלִים תִּבָּנֶה וּתְכוֹנָנָה,

שְׁמַע יָהּ חֲנוּנָה, כִּי בָא עֵת לְחֶנְנָה,[6]

חַזֵּק מַאֲמִירֶיךָ, בְּצֵל יָדְךָ לְגוֹנְנָה,

וּפְדוּיֵי יְהוָה יְשֻׁבוּן וּבָאוּ צִיּוֹן בְּרִנָּה.[7]

All, while standing:

אֵל מֶלֶךְ יוֹשֵׁב עַל כִּסֵּא רַחֲמִים מִתְנַהֵג בַּחֲסִידוּת, מוֹחֵל
עֲוֹנוֹת עַמּוֹ, מַעֲבִיר רִאשׁוֹן רִאשׁוֹן,[8] מַרְבֶּה מְחִילָה
לְחַטָּאִים וּסְלִיחָה לְפוֹשְׁעִים, עֹשֶׂה צְדָקוֹת עִם כָּל בָּשָׂר וָרוּחַ,
לֹא כְרָעָתָם תִּגְמוֹל. ❖ אֵל הוֹרֵיתָ לָּנוּ לוֹמַר שְׁלֹשׁ עֶשְׂרֵה, וּזְכוֹר
לָנוּ הַיּוֹם בְּרִית שְׁלֹשׁ עֶשְׂרֵה, כְּמוֹ שֶׁהוֹדַעְתָּ לֶעָנָיו מִקֶּדֶם, כְּמוֹ
שֶׁכָּתוּב, וַיֵּרֶד יְהוָה בֶּעָנָן וַיִּתְיַצֵּב עִמּוֹ שָׁם, וַיִּקְרָא בְשֵׁם יְהוָה.

Congregation, then *chazzan*:

וַיַּעֲבֹר יְהוָה עַל פָּנָיו וַיִּקְרָא:

Congregation and *chazzan* (the words in bold type are recited aloud and in unison):

יְהוָה, יְהוָה, אֵל רַחוּם, וְחַנּוּן, אֶרֶךְ אַפַּיִם, וְרַב חֶסֶד, וֶאֱמֶת,
נֹצֵר חֶסֶד לָאֲלָפִים, נֹשֵׂא עָוֹן, וָפֶשַׁע, וְחַטָּאָה,
וְנַקֵּה. וְסָלַחְתָּ לַעֲוֹנֵנוּ וּלְחַטָּאתֵנוּ וּנְחַלְתָּנוּ. סְלַח לָנוּ אָבִינוּ כִּי
חָטָאנוּ, מְחַל לָנוּ מַלְכֵּנוּ כִּי פָשָׁעְנוּ. כִּי אַתָּה אֲדֹנָי טוֹב וְסַלָּח,
וְרַב חֶסֶד לְכָל קֹרְאֶיךָ.

Solomon inaugurated the Temple (*II Chronicles*
7:1) was in the shape of a crouching lion (*Yoma*
21b). In *Isaiah* (29:1-2) it refers either to the Altar
(*Targum* to v. 1; *Rashi*); the Temple itself which,
like a crouching lion, was wider in front and nar-
rower in back (*Rashi* based on *Berachos* 18a); or
the City of Jerusalem in which the Temple and
the Altar stood (*Targum* to v. 2; *Ibn Ezra*).

ע **Your people** are strewn and scattered in all settled places,

פ remembering You in their distress,

        expressing fear of You in thought and deed.

צ Sink wantonness deep; push aside and heal misdeeds.

                  My Lord, hear our voice, may Your ears be **attentive.**[1]

ק **Attentive** let Your ears be to the outpouring of our prayer;

ר accept our lips' song like our [Temple] offerings pleasing aroma.[2]

ש We seek You, our Shield, and in You is our trust placed.

            Your Name is called upon us; do not **abandon us.**[3]

ת **Abandoned us** have You, O Lord, for so many years — why?

    To be a wonderment, a metaphor, an example,[4]

      a mockery, a shame and a disgrace?

    Let the promise You made about the desolate [Land]

      be speedily made true:

      'I, HASHEM, have rebuilt the razed, I have planted **the desolate.**'[5]

Chazzan — **The desolate** land — may You rebuild and re-establish it

    with great mercy.

Hear, O God, her supplication,

    for the time has come to show her favor.[6]

Strengthen those who exalt You,

    shielding them in the shadow of Your hand,

and may those redeemed by HASHEM return,

    and come to Zion with glad song.[7]

All, while standing:

אֵל מֶלֶךְ O God, King Who sits on the throne of mercy; Who acts with kindness, pardons the iniquities of His people, removes [sins] one by one,[8] increasingly grants pardon to careless sinners and forgiveness to rebels, Who deals righteously with every living being — You do not repay them in accord with their evil. Chazzan — O God, You taught us to recite the Thirteen [Attributes of Mercy], so remember for us today the covenant of these Thirteen, as You made known to the humble one in ancient times, as it is written: And HASHEM descended in a cloud and stood with him there, and He called out with the Name HASHEM.

Congregation, then chazzan:

And HASHEM passed before him [Moses] and proclaimed:

Congregation and chazzan (the words in bold type are recited aloud and in unison):

ה' ה' HASHEM, HASHEM, God, Compassionate and Gracious, Slow to anger, and Abundant in Kindness and Truth, Preserver of kindness for thousands [of generations], Forgiver of iniquity, willful sin, and error, and Who cleanses. May You forgive our iniquities and our errors and make us Your heritage. Forgive us, our Father, for we have erred; pardon us, our King, for we have willfully sinned; for You, my Lord, are good and forgiving and abundantly kind to all who call upon You.

(1) Cf. *Psalms* 130:2. (2) See *Hosea* 14:3. (3) *Jeremiah* 14:9. (4) *Deuteronomy* 28:37. (5) *Ezekiel* 36:36. (6) *Psalms* 102:14. (7) *Isaiah* 35:10; 51:11. (8) Tractate *Rosh Hashanah* 17a.

פסוקי הקדמה לסליחה מח

דִּרְשׁוּ יהוה וְעֻזּוֹ בַּקְּשׁוּ פָנָיו תָּמִיד.[1] דִּרְשׁוּ יהוה בְּהִמָּצְאוֹ,
קְרָאֻהוּ בִּהְיוֹתוֹ קָרוֹב. יַעֲזֹב רָשָׁע דַּרְכּוֹ וְאִישׁ אָוֶן
מַחְשְׁבֹתָיו, וְיָשֹׁב אֶל יהוה וִירַחֲמֵהוּ, וְאֶל אֱלֹהֵינוּ כִּי יַרְבֶּה
לִסְלוֹחַ.[2] שׁוּבָה יִשְׂרָאֵל עַד יהוה אֱלֹהֶיךָ, כִּי כָשַׁלְתָּ בַּעֲוֹנֶךָ.[3]

בְּרַחֵם אָב עַל בָּנִים, כֵּן תְּרַחֵם יהוה עָלֵינוּ. לַיהוה הַיְשׁוּעָה,
עַל עַמְּךָ בִרְכָתֶךָ סֶּלָה. יהוה צְבָאוֹת עִמָּנוּ, מִשְׂגָּב
לָנוּ אֱלֹהֵי יַעֲקֹב סֶלָה. יהוה צְבָאוֹת, אַשְׁרֵי אָדָם בֹּטֵחַ בָּךְ. יהוה
הוֹשִׁיעָה, הַמֶּלֶךְ יַעֲנֵנוּ בְיוֹם קָרְאֵנוּ.

In some congregations the following two verses are recited responsively — the *chazzan* reciting סְלַח,
and the congregation responding וַיֹּאמֶר. In other congregations these verses are recited silently.

סְלַח נָא לַעֲוֹן הָעָם הַזֶּה כְּגֹדֶל חַסְדֶּךָ, וְכַאֲשֶׁר נָשָׂאתָה לָעָם
הַזֶּה מִמִּצְרַיִם וְעַד הֵנָּה, וְשָׁם נֶאֱמַר:

וַיֹּאמֶר יהוה סָלַחְתִּי כִּדְבָרֶךָ.

All:

הַטֵּה אֱלֹהַי אָזְנְךָ וּשֲׁמָע, פְּקַח עֵינֶיךָ וּרְאֵה שֹׁמְמֹתֵינוּ,
וְהָעִיר אֲשֶׁר נִקְרָא שִׁמְךָ עָלֶיהָ, כִּי לֹא עַל צִדְקֹתֵינוּ
אֲנַחְנוּ מַפִּילִים תַּחֲנוּנֵינוּ לְפָנֶיךָ, כִּי עַל רַחֲמֶיךָ הָרַבִּים.
אֲדֹנָי שְׁמָעָה, אֲדֹנָי סְלָחָה, אֲדֹנָי הַקְשִׁיבָה, וַעֲשֵׂה אַל תְּאַחַר,
לְמַעַנְךָ אֱלֹהַי, כִּי שִׁמְךָ נִקְרָא עַל עִירְךָ וְעַל עַמֶּךָ.

סליחה מח

אֱלֹהֵינוּ וֵאלֹהֵי אֲבוֹתֵינוּ:

אָבְלָה נַפְשִׁי* וְחָשַׁךְ תָּאֳרִי,
בֵּית תִּפְאַרְתִּי כְּנָשַׁף* בּוֹ הָאֲרִי,[4]
גַּם פְּלֵיטָתִי אֲשֶׁר עָזְבוּ וּשְׁאָרִי,
דְּעָכוּ כְּהַיּוֹם בִּשְׁלֹשָׁה בְתִשְׁרִי.
הָאֵשׁ וְהַמַּיִם הַזֵּידוֹנִים שְׁטָפוּנִי[5] בְּדָלְקָם,
וּבָסְסוּ מִקְדָּשׁ וּבָזְזוּ חֶלְקָם,
זִקְנֵי שְׁאֵרִית אֲשֶׁר פָּלְטוּ מִיּוֹם נָקָם,

---

§ אָבְלָה נַפְשִׁי — *My soul mourned.* This
selichah contains an *aleph-beis* acrostic. It is
written by R' Saadiah Gaon [see commentary
page 416].

כְּנָשַׁף — *When ... breathed out* [*destruction*].
The translation follows the commentaries to

Isaiah 40:24. With a mere puff of breath, that is,
in a comparatively easy manner, was Nebuchadnezzar able to capture the *Beis HaMikdash*
(*Masbir*).

According to others, the word is cognate to
נֶשֶׁף, *evening*, and means *when he lodged*

PREFATORY VERSES TO SELICHAH 48

דִּרְשׁוּ Seek HASHEM and His might, search for His presence always.[1]
Seek HASHEM when He is to be found, call Him when He is near.
Let the wicked man abandon his way, the wrongdoer his designs; let him return to HASHEM, and He will have mercy on him, to our God, for He forgives abundantly.[2] Return, Israel, to HASHEM, your God, for you have stumbled in your iniquity.[3]

כְּרַחֵם אָב As a father has mercy on his children, so, HASHEM, may You have mercy on us. Salvation is HASHEM's, upon Your people is Your blessing, Selah. HASHEM, Master of Legions, is with us, a stronghold for us is the God of Jacob, Selah. HASHEM, Master of Legions, praiseworthy is the person who trusts in You. HASHEM, save! May the King answer us on the day we call.

In some congregations the following two verses are recited responsively — the chazzan reciting, 'Forgive, please . . .,' and the congregation responding, 'And HASHEM said . . .'
In other congregations these verses are recited silently.

סְלַח נָא Forgive, please, the iniquity of this people according to the greatness of Your kindness and as You have forgiven this people from Egypt until now, and there it was said:

And HASHEM said, 'I have forgiven according to your word!'

All:

הַטֵּה Incline, my God, Your ear, and listen, open Your eyes and see our desolation and that of the city upon which Your Name is proclaimed; for not because of our righteousness do we cast down our supplications before You, rather because of Your abundant compassion. O my Lord, heed; O my Lord, forgive; O my Lord, be attentive and act, do not delay; for Your sake, my God, for Your Name is proclaimed upon Your city and upon Your people.

SELICHAH 48

Our God and the God of our forefathers:

א My soul mourned,* my face was darkened,
ב when the lion [Nebuchadnezzar]*[4] breathed out [destruction]*
against my glorious Temple.
ג Even my refugees whom they left [in the Land], and my remnant,
ד were smashed on this day, on the Third of Tishrei.
ה The fire and the treacherous waters have inundated us[5]
in their pursuit;
ו they smashed the Temple and looted their share.
ז The elders of our remnant, that escaped the day of vengeance,

---

(1) Psalms 105:4. (2) Isaiah 55:6-7. (3) Hosea 14:2. (4) See Jeremiah 50:17. (5) Cf. Psalms 124:4-5.

there. Thus did Nebuchadnezzar fulfill the verse (Isaiah 1:21), Righteousness had once lodged there [in Jerusalem], but now murderers (Beis Levi).

Others relate the word to וִישׁוּפְךָ and תְּשׁוּפֶנּוּ (Genesis 3:15), which Ibn Ezra renders he will smite you and you will smite him, respectively.

יֶתֶר הַגָּזָם אָכַל הָאַרְבֶּה — What the gazam left over, the arbeh devoured. During the days of the prophet Joel, four species of locust — gazam, arbeh, yelek and chasil — plagued the land in rapid succession: What the gazam left over, the arbeh devoured; what the arbeh left over, the yelek devoured; and what the yelek left over, the

חָבְלוּ עַתָּה בְּיוֹם צוֹם גְּדַלְיָה בֶּן אֲחִיקָם.

טָרְפוּ דַלַּת עַם הָאָרֶץ,

יֶתֶר הַגָּזָם אָכַל הָאַרְבֶּה*[1] בְּמֶרֶץ,

כּוֹרְמִים וְיוֹגְבִים[2] פְּקֻדַּת מַרְגִּיז הָאָרֶץ,[3]

לָהֲטוּ וְלֹא הָיָה בָם גֶּדֶר גָּדֵר וְעוֹמֵד בַּפֶּרֶץ.[4]

מָה אֲסַפֵּר, וְאַנְחוֹתַי עֲצוּמוֹת,

נָקְטָה נַפְשִׁי,*[5] וּמַקְהֵלוֹתַי עֲגוּמוֹת.

שְׂרִיגֵינוּ אֲשֶׁר נִשְׁאֲרוּ מִיקוֹד אֵשׁ לְתַעֲצוּמוֹת.

עוֹד הֵם לֹא נִתְקַיְּמוּ וְנִתְּשׁוּ בְּחֵמוֹת.

פָּנֶיךָ עַד מָתַי מִמֶּנּוּ תַסְתִּיר,[6]

צַעֲקָתֵנוּ שְׁמַע וַאֲסִירֵינוּ תַּתִּיר,

קָדוֹשׁ בְּיָטָה כִּי אֵין בַּעֲדֵנוּ מַעְתִּיר,

רְאֵה בְדַלּוּתֵנוּ וְשַׁבְחֲךָ בְּפֶה נַכְתִּיר.

❖ שַׁדַּדְנוּ מָדוֹר לְדוֹר וּמִקֵּץ לְקֵץ,

שָׁרֵשׁ צֶפַע מְעוֹפֵף אוֹתָנוּ עוֹקֵץ,

תַּקִּיף, לְמִשְׁפָּטֵנוּ הָעֵר וְהָקֵץ,[7]

תְּכַפֵּר לַעֲוֹנוֹתֵינוּ וְתֹאמַר קֵץ.

All, while standing:

אֵל מֶלֶךְ יוֹשֵׁב עַל כִּסֵּא רַחֲמִים מִתְנַהֵג בַּחֲסִידוּת, מוֹחֵל עֲוֹנוֹת עַמּוֹ, מַעֲבִיר רִאשׁוֹן רִאשׁוֹן, מַרְבֶּה מְחִילָה לַחַטָּאִים וּסְלִיחָה לַפּוֹשְׁעִים, עֹשֶׂה צְדָקוֹת עִם כָּל בָּשָׂר וָרוּחַ, לֹא כְרָעָתָם תִּגְמוֹל. ❖ אֵל הוֹרֵיתָ לָנוּ לוֹמַר שְׁלֹשׁ עֶשְׂרֵה, וּזְכוֹר לָנוּ הַיּוֹם בְּרִית שְׁלֹשׁ עֶשְׂרֵה, כְּמוֹ שֶׁהוֹדַעְתָּ לֶעָנָיו מִקֶּדֶם, כְּמוֹ שֶׁכָּתוּב, וַיֵּרֶד יהוה בֶּעָנָן וַיִּתְיַצֵּב עִמּוֹ שָׁם, וַיִּקְרָא בְשֵׁם יהוה.

Congregation, then chazzan:

וַיַּעֲבֹר יהוה עַל פָּנָיו וַיִּקְרָא:

Congregation and chazzan (the words in bold type are recited aloud and in unison):

יהוה, יהוה, אֵל, רַחוּם, וְחַנּוּן, אֶרֶךְ אַפַּיִם, וְרַב חֶסֶד, וֶאֱמֶת, **נֹצֵר חֶסֶד לָאֲלָפִים, נֹשֵׂא עָוֹן, וָפֶשַׁע, וְחַטָּאָה, וְנַקֵּה.** וְסָלַחְתָּ לַעֲוֹנֵנוּ וּלְחַטָּאתֵנוּ וּנְחַלְתָּנוּ. סְלַח לָנוּ אָבִינוּ כִּי חָטָאנוּ, מְחַל לָנוּ מַלְכֵּנוּ כִּי פָשָׁעְנוּ. כִּי אַתָּה אֲדֹנָי טוֹב וְסַלָּח, וְרַב חֶסֶד לְכָל קֹרְאֶיךָ.

---

chasil devoured (Joel 1:4). Similarly, after the
Destruction, Nebuchadnezzar had allowed a
remnant of Israel to remain in the Land. But when
Ishmael ben Nesaniah slew Gedaliahu ben

ח were stricken now, on the day of the Fast of Gedaliah ben Achikam.

ט The poor people of the country were torn asunder;

י what the gazam left over, the arbeh devoured.*[1]

כ Vineyardists and farmers[2] commanded [to remain] by the
One Who made the earth tremble,[3]

ל were burnt up, with none to erect a fence or to stand in the breach.[4]

מ What can I tell over? My sighs are so deep;

נ my soul contends [against life],*[5] my communities grieve.

ס The branches of our vine that were left from the blazing fire

ע they had not yet been re-established, and they were driven out with fury.

פ How long will You hide Your countenance from us?[6]

צ Hear our cry and release our prisoners!

ק O Holy One, observe that there is no one to pray for us;

ר see our poverty [and redeem us,]
and with Your praise in [our] mouth we will crown You.

ש Chazzan — We have been pillaged from generation to generation,
from one [expected] end [of exile] to another;
the darting viper born of a snake bites us.

ת O Forceful One, awaken and rise to our judgment![7]
May You atone for our sins and declare an end [to our exile].

All, while standing:

אֵל מֶלֶךְ O God, King Who sits on the throne of mercy; Who acts with
kindness, pardons the iniquities of His people, removes [sins]
one by one, increasingly grants pardon to careless sinners and forgiveness
to rebels, Who deals righteously with every living being — You do not repay
them in accord with their evil. Chazzan — O God, You taught us to recite the
Thirteen [Attributes of Mercy], so remember for us today the covenant of
these Thirteen, as You made known to the humble one in ancient times, as
it is written: And HASHEM descended in a cloud and stood with him there,
and He called out with the Name HASHEM.

Congregation, then chazzan:

And HASHEM passed before him [Moses] and proclaimed:

Congregation and chazzan (the words in bold type are recited aloud and in unison):

ה' ה' HASHEM, HASHEM, God, Compassionate and Gracious, Slow to
anger, and Abundant in Kindness and Truth, Preserver of
kindness for thousands [of generations], Forgiver of iniquity, willful
sin, and error, and Who cleanses. May You forgive our iniquities and our
errors and make us Your heritage. Forgive us, our Father, for we have
erred; pardon us, our King, for we have willfully sinned; for You, my Lord,
are good and forgiving and abundantly kind to all who call upon You.

(1) Joel 1:4. (2) See Jeremiah 52:16. (3) See Isaiah 14:16.
(4) Ezekiel 22:30. (5) Job 10:1. (6) Cf. Psalms 13:2. (7) Cf. Psalms 35:23.

Achikam, even that remnant was banished. Thus, what Nebuchadnezzar left over, Ishmael ben Nesaniah devoured.

נָקְטָה נַפְשִׁי — My soul contends [against life]. The translation follows Rashi to Job 10:1, which also contains the interpolated phrase. According to Targum, the word נקטה means cut off. Thus, my soul is cut off even while I am yet alive (Metzudas David). Others translate my soul is melancholy (Masbir).

פסוקי הקדמה לסליחה מט

דִּרְשׁוּ יהוה בְּהִמָּצְאוֹ, קְרָאֻהוּ בִּהְיוֹתוֹ קָרוֹב.¹ שׁוּבוּ בָּנִים
שׁוֹבָבִים, אֶרְפָּא מְשׁוּבֹתֵיכֶם, הִנְנוּ אָתָנוּ לָךְ, כִּי אַתָּה
יהוה אֱלֹהֵינוּ.² שׁוּבָה יִשְׂרָאֵל עַד יהוה אֱלֹהֶיךָ, כִּי כָשַׁלְתָּ בַּעֲוֺנֶךָ.³

כְּרַחֵם אָב עַל בָּנִים, כֵּן תְּרַחֵם יהוה עָלֵינוּ. לַיהוה הַיְשׁוּעָה,
עַל עַמְּךָ בִרְכָתֶךָ סֶּלָה. יהוה צְבָאוֹת עִמָּנוּ, מִשְׂגָּב
לָנוּ אֱלֹהֵי יַעֲקֹב סֶלָה. יהוה צְבָאוֹת, אַשְׁרֵי אָדָם בֹּטֵחַ בָּךְ. יהוה
הוֹשִׁיעָה, הַמֶּלֶךְ יַעֲנֵנוּ בְיוֹם קָרְאֵנוּ.

In some congregations the following two verses are recited responsively — the chazzan reciting סְלַח,
and the congregation responding וַיֹּאמֶר. In other congregations these verses are recited silently.

סְלַח נָא לַעֲוֺן הָעָם הַזֶּה כְּגֹדֶל חַסְדֶּךָ, וְכַאֲשֶׁר נָשָׂאתָה לָעָם
הַזֶּה מִמִּצְרַיִם וְעַד הֵנָּה, וְשָׁם נֶאֱמַר:

וַיֹּאמֶר יהוה סָלַחְתִּי כִּדְבָרֶךָ.

All:

הַטֵּה אֱלֹהַי אָזְנְךָ וּשְׁמָע, פְּקַח עֵינֶיךָ וּרְאֵה שֹׁמְמֹתֵינוּ, וְהָעִיר
אֲשֶׁר נִקְרָא שִׁמְךָ עָלֶיהָ, כִּי לֹא עַל צִדְקֹתֵינוּ אֲנַחְנוּ
מַפִּילִים תַּחֲנוּנֵינוּ לְפָנֶיךָ, כִּי עַל רַחֲמֶיךָ הָרַבִּים. אֲדֹנָי שְׁמָעָה,
אֲדֹנָי סְלָחָה, אֲדֹנָי הַקְשִׁיבָה, וַעֲשֵׂה אַל תְּאַחַר, לְמַעַנְךָ אֱלֹהַי, כִּי
שִׁמְךָ נִקְרָא עַל עִירְךָ וְעַל עַמֶּךָ.

סליחה מט

אֱלֹהֵינוּ וֵאלֹהֵי אֲבוֹתֵינוּ:

אִמַּנְתָּ מֵאָז* אֲרֶשֶׁת נִיב שְׂפָתַיִם,
בִּתְפִלָּה וּבְתַחֲנוּן דְּפַק שַׁעֲרֵי דְלָתַיִם,
גְּשָׁתֵנוּ עָדֶיךָ בְּזָרִיזוּת וְלֹא בַעֲצַלְתַּיִם,
דְּחוֹת רַע פֻּרְעָנִיּוֹת הַמִּתְרַגְּשׁוֹת לְעִתּוֹתָיִם.
הִנְנוּ אָתָנוּ לָךְ⁴ בְּשִׁבְרוֹן רוּחַ וְדַכְּאוּת לֵב,⁵
וַדּוּת לְפָנֶיךָ כָּל פָּתוּל וְעִקְשׁוּת לֵב,
זֶה⁶ חוֹקֵר לְבָבוֹת, הָרוֹפֵא לִשְׁבוּרֵי לֵב,⁷
חַדֵּשׁ רוּחַ נָכוֹן בְּקִרְבֵּנוּ, וּבְרָא לָנוּ טְהוֹר לֵב.⁸
טִכַּסְתָּ מִקֶּדֶם אֵלּוּ יָמִים עֲשָׂרָה,
יָחִיד בָּם לָשׁוּב וְלִמְצֹא כַפָּרָה,
כָּל הַשָּׁנָה כֻּלָּהּ לָרַבִּים מְסוּרָה,

PREFATORY VERSES TO SELICHAH 49

דְּרְשׁוּ Seek HASHEM when He is to be found; call Him when He is near.[1] Return, wayward children; I will heal your waywardness. Here we are, we have come to You, for You are HASHEM, our God.[2] Return, Israel, to HASHEM, your God, for you have stumbled in your iniquity.[3]

כְּרַחֵם אָב As a father has mercy on his children, so, HASHEM, may You have mercy on us. Salvation is HASHEM's, upon Your people is Your blessing, Selah. HASHEM, Master of Legions, is with us, a stronghold for us is the God of Jacob, Selah. HASHEM, Master of Legions, praiseworthy is the person who trusts in You. HASHEM, save! May the King answer us on the day we call.

In some congregations the following two verses are recited responsively — the chazzan reciting, 'Forgive, please . . .,' and the congregation responding, 'And HASHEM said . . .'
In other congregations these verses are recited silently.

סְלַח נָא Forgive, please, the iniquity of this people according to the greatness of Your kindness and as You have forgiven this people from Egypt until now, and there it was said:

And HASHEM said, 'I have forgiven according to your word!'

All:

הַטֵּה Incline, my God, Your ear, and listen, open Your eyes and see our desolation and that of the city upon which Your Name is proclaimed; for not because of our righteousness do we cast down our supplications before You, rather because of Your abundant compassion. O my Lord, heed; O my Lord, forgive; O my Lord, be attentive and act, do not delay; for Your sake, my God, for Your Name is proclaimed upon Your city and upon Your people.

SELICHAH 49

Our God and the God of our forefathers:

א You taught [us] from of old* how [our] lips should speak out,
ב with prayer and supplication to knock on [Your] gates.
ג So we have approached You, with alacrity and not with indolence,
ד to ward off the catastrophes that amass themselves time after time.
ה Here we are, we have come to You[4]
with broken spirit and crushed heart,[5]
ו confessing before You all [our] foolishness and perversion of heart.
ז This is [my God,][6] the Searcher of Hearts,
Healer of the broken-hearted.[7]
ח Renew within us a steadfast spirit, and create a pure heart for us.[8]
ט You planned out these Ten Days [of Repentance] from of old,
י when [even] an individual can repent and find atonement —
כ all the rest of the year is given over [only] to the community,

---

(1) Isaiah 55:6. (2) Jeremiah 3:22. (3) Hosea 14:2. (4) Jeremiah 3:22.
(5) Cf. Psalms 51:19. (6) Exodus 15:2; Isaiah 25:9. (7) Psalms 147:3. (8) Cf. 51:12.

⊷§ אָמְנָתָ מֵאָז — *You taught [us] from of old.* The *selichah* contains an alphabetical acrostic, fol- lowed by the author's name בִּנְיָמִין, *Binyamin* [see introductory comment to *selichah* 20].

לְשַׁוֵּעַ וְלַעֲנוֹת בְּכָל עֵת צוּקָה וְצָרָה.

מְהֵר הַיָּחִיד וְשָׁב בֵּינָתַיִם, מוֹחֲלִין לוֹ,

נוֹאַשׁ וְלֹא שָׁב, אֵין תַּקָּנָה לְעַוְלוֹ,

סִדֵּר וְעָרַךְ כָּל אֵילֵי נְבָיוֹת לְהוֹעִילוֹ,

עוֹתֵר וְצוֹעֵק וְאֵין שׁוֹמֵעַ לוֹ.

פְּגִיעַת הָרַבִּים וְהַיָּחִיד לְךָ לְבַד עוֹלָה,

צוּר, כִּי אַתָּה שׁוֹמֵעַ תְּפִלָּה.

קַבְּלֵנוּ בְרָצוֹן וְהַמְצִיאֵנוּ מְחִילָה,

רְצֵנוּ כְּקָרְבַּן כָּלִיל וְעוֹלָה.[1]

❖ שָׁפוֹט תִּשְׁפֹּט אוֹתָנוּ בְּרַחֲמִים וְחֶמְלָה,

בָּנֶיךָ יְחוּסֶיךָ לְקוּחִים לְךָ לִסְגֻלָּה,

יֶקֶשׁ מִרְיָם יֻצְלַל בִּמְצוּלָה,

נֶצַח לְהַלֶּלְךָ בְּכָל מִינֵי תְהִלָּה.

All, while standing:

אֵל מֶלֶךְ יוֹשֵׁב עַל כִּסֵּא רַחֲמִים מִתְנַהֵג בַּחֲסִידוּת, מוֹחֵל עֲוֹנוֹת עַמּוֹ, מַעֲבִיר רִאשׁוֹן רִאשׁוֹן, מַרְבֶּה מְחִילָה לְחַטָּאִים וּסְלִיחָה לְפוֹשְׁעִים, עֹשֶׂה צְדָקוֹת עִם כָּל בָּשָׂר וָרוּחַ, לֹא כְרָעָתָם תִּגְמוֹל. ❖ אֵל הוֹרֵיתָ לָנוּ לוֹמַר שְׁלֹשׁ עֶשְׂרֵה, וּזְכוֹר לָנוּ הַיּוֹם בְּרִית שְׁלֹשׁ עֶשְׂרֵה, כְּמוֹ שֶׁהוֹדַעְתָּ לֶעָנָיו מִקֶּדֶם, כְּמוֹ שֶׁכָּתוּב, וַיֵּרֶד יהוה בֶּעָנָן וַיִּתְיַצֵּב עִמּוֹ שָׁם, וַיִּקְרָא בְשֵׁם יהוה.

Congregation, then chazzan:

וַיַּעֲבֹר יהוה עַל פָּנָיו וַיִּקְרָא:

Congregation and chazzan (the words in bold type are recited aloud and in unison):

יהוה, יהוה, אֵל, **רַחוּם, וְחַנּוּן, אֶרֶךְ אַפַּיִם, וְרַב חֶסֶד, וֶאֱמֶת, נֹצֵר חֶסֶד לָאֲלָפִים, נֹשֵׂא עָוֹן, וָפֶשַׁע, וְחַטָּאָה, וְנַקֵּה.** וְסָלַחְתָּ לַעֲוֹנֵנוּ וּלְחַטָּאתֵנוּ וּנְחַלְתָּנוּ. סְלַח לָנוּ אָבִינוּ כִּי חָטָאנוּ, מְחַל לָנוּ מַלְכֵּנוּ כִּי פָשָׁעְנוּ. כִּי אַתָּה אֲדֹנָי טוֹב וְסַלָּח, וְרַב חֶסֶד לְכָל קֹרְאֶיךָ.

פסוקי הקדמה לסליחה נ

אַל תִּזְכָּר לָנוּ עֲוֹנוֹת רִאשׁוֹנִים, מַהֵר יְקַדְּמוּנוּ רַחֲמֶיךָ, כִּי דַלּוֹנוּ מְאֹד.[2] כִּי שׁוֹמֵעַ אֶל אֶבְיוֹנִים יהוה, וְאֶת אֲסִירָיו לֹא בָזָה.[3] כִּי כָלוּ בְיָגוֹן חַיֵּינוּ, וּשְׁנוֹתֵינוּ בַּאֲנָחָה.[4] כִּי עָלֶיךָ הֹרַגְנוּ כָל הַיּוֹם, נֶחְשַׁבְנוּ כְּצֹאן טִבְחָה.[5] כִּי לֹא יִזְנַח לְעוֹלָם אֲדֹנָי.[6]

ל to cry out in prayer in every time of distress and trouble.
מ If the individual hurries and repents between them,
    they [the Heavenly Tribunal] pardon him;
נ if he despairs and does not repent, there is no remedy for his sinfulness;
ס though he were to prepare and arrange all the choicest rams
    [for sacrifice] on his behalf,
ע [though] he will pray and shout, there is none who will listen to him.
פ The prayer of the many and of the individual to You alone ascend,
צ O Rock, for You are the Hearer of Prayer.
ק Accept us favorably and make pardon accessible;
ר be pleased with us as You are
    with a completely consumed olah-offering.[1]
ש Chazzan – May You ever judge us with mercy and compassion,
ב [for we are] Your children in whom You take pride,
    who are taken to You as [Your] beloved [people].
י May the snare of their rebelliousness be sunk in the deep sea,
נ that they may eternally praise You with every kind of praise.

All, while standing:

אֵל מֶלֶךְ O God, King Who sits on the throne of mercy; Who acts with kindness, pardons the iniquities of His people, removes [sins] one by one, increasingly grants pardon to careless sinners and forgiveness to rebels, Who deals righteously with every living being — You do not repay them in accord with their evil. Chazzan – O God, You taught us to recite the Thirteen [Attributes of Mercy], so remember for us today the covenant of these Thirteen, as You made known to the humble one in ancient times, as it is written: And HASHEM descended in a cloud and stood with him there, and He called out with the Name HASHEM.

Congregation, then chazzan:

And HASHEM passed before him [Moses] and proclaimed:

Congregation and chazzan (the words in bold type are recited aloud and in unison):

ה' ה' **HASHEM, HASHEM, God, Compassionate and Gracious, Slow to anger, and Abundant in Kindness and Truth, Preserver of kindness for thousands [of generations], Forgiver of iniquity, willful sin, and error, and Who cleanses.** May You forgive our iniquities and our errors and make us Your heritage. Forgive us, our Father, for we have erred; pardon us, our King, for we have willfully sinned; for You, my Lord, are good and forgiving and abundantly kind to all who call upon You.

PREFATORY VERSES TO SELICHAH 50

אַל Do not recall former iniquities against us; let Your mercy come quickly towards us, for we are greatly impoverished.[2] For HASHEM hears [the cry of] the destitute, and He does not despise His prisoners.[3] For our life wastes away in sorrow, our years in sighing.[4] Because for Your sake we are killed all the time; we are considered as sheep for the slaughter.[5] For my Lord will not reject [us] forever.[6]

(1) See last comment to selichah 4. (2) Psalms 79:8.
(3) 69:34. (4) Cf. 31:11. (5) 44:23. (6) Lamentations 3:31.

בְּרַחֵם אָב עַל בָּנִים, כֵּן תְּרַחֵם יהוה עָלֵינוּ. לַיהוה הַיְשׁוּעָה,
עַל עַמְּךָ בִרְכָתֶךָ סֶּלָה. יהוה צְבָאוֹת עִמָּנוּ, מִשְׂגָּב
לָנוּ אֱלֹהֵי יַעֲקֹב סֶלָה. יהוה צְבָאוֹת, אַשְׁרֵי אָדָם בֹּטֵחַ בָּךְ. יהוה
הוֹשִׁיעָה, הַמֶּלֶךְ יַעֲנֵנוּ בְיוֹם קָרְאֵנוּ.

In some congregations the following two verses are recited responsively — the chazzan reciting סְלַח,
and the congregation responding וַיֹּאמֶר. In other congregations these verses are recited silently.

סְלַח נָא לַעֲוֹן הָעָם הַזֶּה כְּגֹדֶל חַסְדֶּךָ, וְכַאֲשֶׁר נָשָׂאתָה לָעָם
הַזֶּה מִמִּצְרַיִם וְעַד הֵנָּה, וְשָׁם נֶאֱמַר:
וַיֹּאמֶר יהוה סָלַחְתִּי כִּדְבָרֶךָ.

All:

הַטֵּה אֱלֹהַי אָזְנְךָ וּשֲׁמָע, פְּקַח עֵינֶיךָ וּרְאֵה שֹׁמְמֹתֵינוּ, וְהָעִיר
אֲשֶׁר נִקְרָא שִׁמְךָ עָלֶיהָ, כִּי לֹא עַל צִדְקֹתֵינוּ אֲנַחְנוּ
מַפִּילִים תַּחֲנוּנֵינוּ לְפָנֶיךָ, כִּי עַל רַחֲמֶיךָ הָרַבִּים. אֲדֹנָי שְׁמָעָה,
אֲדֹנָי סְלָחָה, אֲדֹנָי הַקְשִׁיבָה, וַעֲשֵׂה אַל תְּאַחַר, לְמַעַנְךָ אֱלֹהַי, כִּי
שִׁמְךָ נִקְרָא עַל עִירְךָ וְעַל עַמֶּךָ.

סליחה נ (שלישית)

אֱלֹהֵינוּ וֵאלֹהֵי אֲבוֹתֵינוּ:

אוֹרְךָ וַאֲמִתְּךָ שְׁלַח,[1]*   אֱמוּנֶיךָ בְּטוּב הַצְלַח,
כִּי אַתָּה אֲדֹנָי טוֹב וְסַלָּח.[2]

בִּיטָה בְעִנּוּי נֶפֶשׁ,   בְּטוּבְךָ הוֹצִיאֵנוּ לַחֹפֶשׁ,
כִּי בָאוּ מַיִם עַד נָפֶשׁ.[3]

גַּעֲיוֹתֵינוּ יְהוּ נִקְשָׁבִים,   גָּלוּתֵנוּ הָשֵׁב לְיִשּׁוּבִים,
כִּי גֵרִים אֲנַחְנוּ וְתוֹשָׁבִים.[4]

דָּפַקְנוּ דְלָתֶיךָ לִתְמֹד,   דָּבַקְנוּ אֵלֶיךָ לִצְמֹד,   כִּי דַלּוֹנוּ מְאֹד.[5]

הֱלִיצוּנוּ זֵדִים[6] בְּמִצְרֵינוּ,   הַצִּילֵנוּ וְנוֹדְךָ צוּרֵנוּ,
כִּי הוֹשַׁעְתָּנוּ מִצָּרֵינוּ.[7]

זְרוּיֶיךָ מְיַחֲלִים לְעוֹדְדָם,   זַכֵּם[8] בְּיִרְאָתְךָ לְסַעֲדָם,
כִּי זֶה כָּל הָאָדָם.[9]*

אוֹרְךָ וַאֲמִתְּךָ שְׁלַח — Send [us] Your light and
Your truth. The acrostic of this selichah spells the
aleph-beis. The last line bears the signature
שִׁמְעוֹן, Shimon [see prefatory comment to
selichah 11].

בְּיִרְאָתְךָ . . . כִּי זֶה כָּל הָאָדָם — In [their] fear of You,
for that is the entire [purpose of] man. After two

hundred and twenty verses of mussar, ethical
teachings, admonishment, and deep insights into
man, his duties and the purpose of his existence,
the wise King Solomon writes in the penultimate
verse of Ecclesiastes (12:13): The end of the matter
is, after all has been heard, that You should fear
God and keep His mitzvos, for that is the entire

כְּרַחֵם אָב As a father has mercy on his children, so, HASHEM, may You have mercy on us. Salvation is HASHEM's, upon Your people is Your blessing, Selah. HASHEM, Master of Legions, is with us, a stronghold for us is the God of Jacob, Selah. HASHEM, Master of Legions, praiseworthy is the person who trusts in You. HASHEM, save! May the King answer us on the day we call.

In some congregations the following two verses are recited responsively — the chazzan reciting, 'Forgive, please . . .,' and the congregation responding, 'And HASHEM said . . .'
In other congregations these verses are recited silently.

סְלַח נָא Forgive, please, the iniquity of this people according to the greatness of Your kindness and as You have forgiven this people from Egypt until now, and there it was said:

And HASHEM said, 'I have forgiven according to your word!'

All:

הַטֵּה Incline, my God, Your ear, and listen, open Your eyes and see our desolation and that of the city upon which Your Name is proclaimed; for not because of our righteousness do we cast down our supplications before You, rather because of Your abundant compassion. O my Lord, heed; O my Lord, forgive; O my Lord, be attentive and act, do not delay; for Your sake, my God, for Your Name is proclaimed upon Your city and upon Your people.

SELICHAH 50

Our God and the God of our forefathers:

א *Send [us] Your light and Your truth;*[1]
א *give goodly success to Your faithful ones,*
          for You, my Lord, are good and forgiving.[2]

ב *Look at the affliction of soul,*
ב *[and] in Your goodness bring us out to freedom,*
          for the waters have reached until the soul.[3]

ג *Let our lowing in prayer be heard:*
ג *Return our Exile to [our] settlements,*
          for we are sojourners and tenants.[4]

ד *We knock on Your doors continually,*
ד *we cling to You to become united,*
          for we are greatly impoverished.[5]

ה *Wanton men taunted us*[6] *in our straits;*
ה *save us and we will thank You, our Rock,*
          for You have saved us from our oppressors.[7]

ז *Your scattered children hope for You to enhearten them;*
ז *cleanse them*[8] *to support them in [their] fear of You,*
          for that is the entire [purpose of] man.[9]*

---

(1) Cf. *Psalms* 43:3. (2) 86:5. (3) 69:2. (4) Cf. *I Chronicles* 29:15; *Genesis* 23:4.
(5) *Psalms* 79:8. (6) Cf. 119:51. (7) 44:8. (8) See *Job* 9:30; some editions of *Selichos* read, זַכִּים, *the pure ones*, i.e., the righteous. (9) *Ecclesiastes* 12:13.

man [i.e., that is why man was created (*Rashi*)].
In the same vein, the Talmud teaches: הַכּל בִּידֵי

שָׁמַיִם חוּץ מִיִּרְאַת שָׁמַיִם, *Everything is in the hands of Heaven, except fear of Hashem* (*Berachos* 33b).

חֻקּוֹת הָעַמִּים תֹּהוּ,[1] חֲשׁוּקֶיךָ אַחֲרֶיךָ יִנָּהוּ,[2]
כִּי חַנּוּן וְרַחוּם הוּא.[3]

טִירָתְךָ הֲשַׁמָּה לְעִיִּים,[4] טַיְבָה בְּחוֹמוֹת בְּנוּיִים,[4]
כִּי טוֹב חַסְדְּךָ מֵחַיִּים.[6]

יָגַעְתִּי וְאָשִׁיחָה בְּמַעֲנִי,[7] יֵבוֹשׁ וְיִכָּלֵם מְעַנִּי,
כִּי יַעֲשֶׂה יהוה דִּין עָנִי.[8]

כָּבְדוּ שְׂפָתַי קָמַי, כָּל הַיּוֹם[9] מַזְעִימַי, כִּי כָלוּ בְעָשָׁן יָמַי.[10]
לָהֶם יָשִׁיב כְּפָעֳלָם,*[11] לְעַמּוֹ יְלַמֵּד לְהוֹעִילָם,[12]
כִּי לֹא יִזְנַח לְעוֹלָם.[13]

מֵרַחֲמוֹ יִתֵּן מַאֲנָיו, מִמֶּנּוּ יָסִיר דָּפְיוֹ, כִּי מַה טּוּבוֹ וּמַה יָפְיוֹ.[14]
נְשַׁמּוֹת הוֹשַׁתּוּ עָרַי,[15] וְנָכְרִים בָּאוּ שְׁעָרַי,[16]
כִּי נָשָׂאתִי חֶרְפַּת נְעוּרָי.[17]

שׂוֹשׂ אָשִׂישׂ עָלֶיךָ,[18] שִׂיחַ לַעֲנוֹת גְּאוּלֶיךָ,
כִּי שִׂמַּחְתַּנִי יהוה בְּפָעֳלֶךָ.[19]

עֻזּוּז נוֹרָא וְאָיֹם, עַתָּה הַמְצִיאֵנוּ פִדְיוֹם,
כִּי עָלֶיךָ הֹרַגְנוּ כָל הַיּוֹם.[20]

פְּנֵה דֶרֶךְ עֲקֹב,[21] פָּאֵר הַלּוֹלֵךְ לְנַקֵּב,
כִּי גָאַל יהוה אֶת יַעֲקֹב.[22]

צָרִים לְכַלּוֹת בְּחָרֶץ,* צָפָה מִשְּׁמֵי עָרֶץ,
כִּי צֵל יָמֵינוּ עֲלֵי אָרֶץ.[23]

קָרֵב קֵץ עֶדְנָי,[24] קוֹל לְהַשְׁמִיעַ לְעוֹנָי,[25] כִּי קָרוֹב יוֹם יהוה.[26]
רָם זְרֹעֲךָ תֵּרָאֶה,[25] רְעִיתְךָ פָּנִים הִתְרָאֶה,
כִּי רָם יהוה וְשָׁפָל יִרְאֶה.[27]

שְׁמַע קוֹל תַּחֲנוּנַי,[28] שַׁוְעָתִי תַּעֲלֶה לִמְעוֹנָי,[29]
כִּי שׁוֹמֵעַ אֶל אֶבְיוֹנִים, יהוה.[30]

תַּחַן כְּתוֹדָה תִּרְצֶה, תֹּאמַר לְעַמְּךָ אֶתְרַצֶּה,
כִּי תוֹרָה מֵאִתִּי תֵצֵא.[31]

(1) Cf. Jeremiah 10:3; in some editions of Selichos this stanza has been censored to read חֶלְקֵנוּ אַתָּה, It is You Who are our portion, חֲשׁוּקָיו אַחֲרָיו יִנָּהוּ, those who desire Him follow after Him. . .; in some editions the first two stiches of the stanza have been omitted. (2) Cf. I Samuel 7:2. (3) Joel 2:13. (4) Cf. Psalms 79:1. (5) Cf. 51:20. (6) 63:4. (7) Some editions read, יָדַעְתִּי, I am aware. (8) Psalms 140:13. (9) Cf. Lamentations 3:62. (10) Psalms 102:4. (11) Cf. Jeremiah 25:14. (12) Cf. Isaiah 48:17. (13) Lamentations 3:31. (14) Zechariah 9:17. (15) Cf. Isaiah 54:3. (16) Cf. Obadiah 1:11. (17) Jeremiah 31:18. (18) Isaiah 61:10. (19) Psalms 92:5. (20) 44:23. (21) Cf. Isaiah 40:3-4. (22) Jeremiah 31:10. (23) Job 8:9. (24) Cf. Lamentations 4:18. (25) Cf. Isaiah 30:30. (26) Joel 1:15. (27) Psalms 138:6. (28) 28:2. (29) See 90:1. (30) 69:34. (31) Isaiah 51:4.

ח [Knowing that] the nations' customs are void,[1]

ח those who desire You follow after You,[2] [saying:]
'For He is gracious and merciful.'[3]

ט Your Temple-tower has been turned to heaps of rubble![4]

ט Repair it with built-up walls,[5]
for Your kindness is better than life itself.[6]

י I am exhausted,[7] yet I speak out in my prayer:

י 'Let my tormentor be shamed and humiliated!'
for HASHEM will champion the cause of the poor.[8]

כ My adversaries' lips weigh heavily [upon me],

כ they vex me all the time,[9]   for my days disappear in smoke.[10]

ל He shall pay them back according to their deeds,*[11]

ל and teach His people to their benefit,[12]
for He will not reject [them] forever.[13]

מ He Who has mercy on him [Israel] will grant his desire,

מ and remove his ignominy from him,
for how good and how beautiful he will then be.[14]

נ Our cities have been made desolate;[15]

נ gentiles have entered our gates;[16]
for I have borne the shame of my youth[ful sins].[17]

ס Yet I will rejoice over You,[18]

ס when You answer the prayer of Your redeemed ones,
for You have gladdened me, HASHEM, with Your deeds.[19]

ע O Mighty, Awesome and Fearsome One,

ע bring forth redemption for us now,
because for Your sake we are killed all the time.[20]

פ Clear the crooked road,[21]

פ that [we may] pronounce the glory of Your praise:
'For HASHEM has redeemed Jacob.'[22]

צ As the oppressors press to destroy [us],*

צ look down from the mighty heavens,
[and see] that our days on the earth are like a shadow.[23]

ק Bring near the End, my time [of Redemption],[24]

ק let my tormentors hear the sound,[25]   as the Day of HASHEM nears.[26]

ר Lofty One, show Your strong arm![25]

ר Let Your countenance appear to Your beloved [Israel],
for though HASHEM is lofty, he sees the lowly.[27]

ש Hear the sound of my supplication,[28]

ש let my outcry rise to You, my eternal abode,[29]
for HASHEM hears [the cry of] the destitute.[30]

ת Favor our supplication as [if it were] a thanksgiving-offering;

ת say to Your people, 'I am appeased,
for Torah shall go forth from Me.'[31]

כְּפָעֳלָם — *According to their deeds.* This stich is ambiguous and could mean either He shall reward the righteous for their deeds, or He shall punish the oppressors for theirs.

צָרִים לְכַלּוֹת בְּחָרָץ — *As the oppressors press to destroy [us].* The stich is ambiguous and may also be rendered: *The oppressors* — *[may You] press to destroy [them].*

שֶׁקֶל מֹאזְנַיִם יִכְבָּשׁ,   עֹז (נֶצַח) יַעֲטֶה וְיִלְבָּשׁ,[1]
כִּי הוּא יַכְאִיב וְיֶחְבָּשׁ.[2]

All, while standing:

אֵל מֶלֶךְ יוֹשֵׁב עַל כִּסֵּא רַחֲמִים מִתְנַהֵג בַּחֲסִידוּת, מוֹחֵל
עֲוֹנוֹת עַמּוֹ, מַעֲבִיר רִאשׁוֹן רִאשׁוֹן, מַרְבֶּה
מְחִילָה לְחַטָּאִים וּסְלִיחָה לְפוֹשְׁעִים, עֹשֶׂה צְדָקוֹת עִם כָּל
בָּשָׂר וָרוּחַ, לֹא כְרָעָתָם תִּגְמוֹל. ❖ אֵל הוֹרֵיתָ לָּנוּ לוֹמַר שְׁלֹשׁ
עֶשְׂרֵה, וּזְכוֹר לָנוּ הַיּוֹם בְּרִית שְׁלֹשׁ עֶשְׂרֵה, כְּמוֹ שֶׁהוֹדַעְתָּ
לֶעָנָיו מִקֶּדֶם, כְּמוֹ שֶׁכָּתוּב, וַיֵּרֶד יהוה בֶּעָנָן וַיִּתְיַצֵּב עִמּוֹ שָׁם,
וַיִּקְרָא בְשֵׁם יהוה.

Congregation, then *chazzan:*

וַיַּעֲבֹר יהוה עַל פָּנָיו וַיִּקְרָא:

Congregation and *chazzan* (the words in bold type are recited aloud and in unison):

יהוה, יהוה, אֵל, רַחוּם, וְחַנּוּן, אֶרֶךְ אַפַּיִם, וְרַב חֶסֶד, וֶאֱמֶת,
נֹצֵר חֶסֶד לָאֲלָפִים, נֹשֵׂא עָוֹן, וָפֶשַׁע, וְחַטָּאָה,
וְנַקֵּה. וְסָלַחְתָּ לַעֲוֹנֵנוּ וּלְחַטָּאתֵנוּ וּנְחַלְתָּנוּ. סְלַח לָנוּ אָבִינוּ כִּי
חָטָאנוּ, מְחַל לָנוּ מַלְכֵּנוּ כִּי פָשָׁעְנוּ. כִּי אַתָּה אֲדֹנָי טוֹב וְסַלָּח, וְרַב
חֶסֶד לְכָל קֹרְאֶיךָ.

פסוקי הקדמה לסליחה נא

תָּשׁוּב תְּרַחֲמֵנוּ, תִּכְבֹּשׁ עֲוֹנֹתֵינוּ, וְתַשְׁלִיךְ בִּמְצֻלוֹת יָם
כָּל חַטֹּאותָם.[3] שׁוּב מֵחֲרוֹן אַפֶּךָ, וְהִנָּחֵם
עַל הָרָעָה לְעַמֶּךָ.[4] שׁוּבָה יהוה אֶת שְׁבִיתֵנוּ כַּאֲפִיקִים בַּנֶּגֶב.[5]
הֲשִׁיבֵנוּ יהוה אֵלֶיךָ וְנָשׁוּבָה, חַדֵּשׁ יָמֵינוּ כְּקֶדֶם.[6]

כְּרַחֵם אָב עַל בָּנִים, כֵּן תְּרַחֵם יהוה עָלֵינוּ. לַיהוה הַיְשׁוּעָה,
עַל עַמְּךָ בִרְכָתֶךָ סֶּלָה. יהוה צְבָאוֹת עִמָּנוּ, מִשְׂגָּב
לָנוּ אֱלֹהֵי יַעֲקֹב סֶלָה. יהוה צְבָאוֹת, אַשְׁרֵי אָדָם בֹּטֵחַ בָּךְ. יהוה
הוֹשִׁיעָה, הַמֶּלֶךְ יַעֲנֵנוּ בְיוֹם קָרְאֵנוּ.

In some congregations the following two verses are recited responsively — the *chazzan* reciting סְלַח,
and the congregation responding וַיֹּאמֶר. In other congregations these verses are recited silently.

סְלַח נָא לַעֲוֹן הָעָם הַזֶּה כְּגֹדֶל חַסְדֶּךָ, וְכַאֲשֶׁר נָשָׂאתָה לָעָם
הַזֶּה מִמִּצְרַיִם וְעַד הֵנָּה, וְשָׁם נֶאֱמַר:

וַיֹּאמֶר יהוה סָלַחְתִּי כִּדְבָרֶךָ.

Chazzan — *May He tip the scales [towards mercy],*
donning and wearing (eternal) might,[1]
for He causes pain and He heals [the wound].[2]

All, while standing:

אֵל מֶלֶךְ *O God, King Who sits on the throne of mercy; Who acts with*
kindness, pardons the iniquities of His people, removes [sins]
one by one, increasingly grants pardon to careless sinners and forgiveness
to rebels, Who deals righteously with every living being — You do not repay
them in accord with their evil. Chazzan — *O God, You taught us to recite the*
Thirteen [Attributes of Mercy], so remember for us today the covenant of
these Thirteen, as You made known to the humble one in ancient times, as
it is written: And HASHEM descended in a cloud and stood with him there,
and He called out with the Name HASHEM.

Congregation, then chazzan:

And HASHEM passed before him [Moses] and proclaimed:

Congregation and chazzan (the words in bold type are recited aloud and in unison):

ה' ה' **HASHEM, HASHEM,** God, **Compassionate and Gracious, Slow to**
anger, and **Abundant in Kindness and Truth, Preserver of**
kindness for thousands [of generations], Forgiver of iniquity, willful
sin, and error, and Who cleanses. *May You forgive our iniquities and our*
errors and make us Your heritage. Forgive us, our Father, for we have
erred; pardon us, our King, for we have willfully sinned; for You, my Lord,
are good and forgiving and abundantly kind to all who call upon You.

PREFATORY VERSES TO SELICHAH 51

תָּשׁוּב תְּרַחֲמֵנוּ *May You once again have mercy on us; may You quell*
our transgressions, and cast all our sins into the sea's
depths.[3] Turn back from Your blasting anger, and reconsider the evil [that
You would do] to Your people.[4] Return, O HASHEM, our captivity like
springs in the desert.[5] Return us, HASHEM, to You, and we will return;
renew our days as of old.[6]

כְּרַחֵם אָב *As a father has mercy on his children, so, HASHEM, may*
You have mercy on us. Salvation is HASHEM's, upon Your
people is Your blessing, Selah. HASHEM, Master of Legions, is with us, a
stronghold for us is the God of Jacob, Selah. HASHEM, Master of Legions,
praiseworthy is the person who trusts in You. HASHEM, save! May the
King answer us on the day we call.

In some congregations the following two verses are recited responsively — the chazzan
reciting, 'Forgive, please . . .,' and the congregation responding, 'And HASHEM said . . .'
In other congregations these verses are recited silently.

סְלַח נָא *Forgive, please, the iniquity of this people according to the*
greatness of Your kindness and as You have forgiven this
people from Egypt until now, and there it was said:

And HASHEM said, 'I have forgiven according to your word!'

---

(1) Cf. *Psalms* 93:1. (2) *Job* 5:18. (3) Cf. *Micah* 7:19.
(4) *Exodus* 32:12. (5) *Psalms* 126:4. (6) *Lamentations* 5:21.

All:

הַטֵּה אֱלֹהַי אָזְנְךָ וּשֲׁמָע, פְּקַח עֵינֶיךָ וּרְאֵה שֹׁמְמֹתֵינוּ, וְהָעִיר
אֲשֶׁר נִקְרָא שִׁמְךָ עָלֶיהָ, כִּי לֹא עַל צִדְקֹתֵינוּ אֲנַחְנוּ
מַפִּילִים תַּחֲנוּנֵינוּ לְפָנֶיךָ, כִּי עַל רַחֲמֶיךָ הָרַבִּים. אֲדֹנָי שְׁמָעָה,
אֲדֹנָי סְלָחָה, אֲדֹנָי הַקְשִׁיבָה, וַעֲשֵׂה אַל תְּאַחַר, לְמַעַנְךָ אֱלֹהַי, כִּי
שִׁמְךָ נִקְרָא עַל עִירְךָ וְעַל עַמֶּךָ.

סְלִיחָה נא (שְׁלמוֹנִית)

אֱלֹהֵינוּ וֵאלֹהֵי אֲבוֹתֵינוּ:

תָּשׁוּב תְּרַחֲמֵנוּ;[1] שׁוּב שְׁבִיתֵנוּ[2] כְּנֶאֱמָךְ,
שׁוּב כְּקֶדֶם חַדֵּשׁ חִבַּת לְאֻמֶּךָ,
רַחֵק רֹגֶז וְקָרֵב שֹׂךְ זַעֲמֶךָ,
שׁוּב מֵחֲרוֹן אַפֶּךָ, וְהִנָּחֵם עַל הָרָעָה לְעַמֶּךָ.[3]

קַבֵּץ וּבַקֵּשׁ אֲבֵדוֹת וְחַזֵּק נַחֲלָתֶךָ,[4]
צֹאן הַהֲרֵגָה וְהַגְּזוּזָה בִּדְחִילָתֶךָ,[5]
פֶּשַׁע אִם רַב בִּבְנֵי מְחִילָתֶךָ,*
שׁוּב לְמַעַן עֲבָדֶיךָ שִׁבְטֵי נַחֲלָתֶךָ.[6]

עֲוֹן אֲבוֹתֵינוּ הַטְעֵינוּ, וּבְסֵר הַטְעִימָנוּ;[7]
סַף רַעַל הַשְׁקֵנוּ[8] הִלְעֵינֶנּוּ וְהִזְעִימָנוּ,
נָא כְּאָז בְּשֵׁכֶן יַחַד הִנְעִימָנוּ,[9]
שׁוּבֵנוּ* אֱלֹהֵי יִשְׁעֵנוּ, וְהָפֵר כַּעַסְךָ עִמָּנוּ.[10]

מָאוֹס לֹא מְאַסְתָּ[11] חוֹסֶיךָ מְעִידֶיךָ,
לְקַיֵּם כְּסוֹרֵחַ, וּלְהִתְמָרֵחַ סְבָרָם עָדֶיךָ,
בַּעַס לִרְצוֹת כְּמִדַּת יֹשֶׁר מַעֲבָדֶיךָ,
שׁוּבָה יהוה עַד מָתַי, וְהִנָּחֵם עַל עֲבָדֶיךָ.[12]

יוֹם יוֹם נְצַפֶּה גִּלּוּי סוֹדֶךָ,
טָמוּם וְעָמוּם וּבָלָה בְּשַׂר[13] חֲסִידֶיךָ,

◆§ **תָּשׁוּב תְּרַחֲמֵנוּ** — *May You once again have mercy on us.* The respective first three lines of each quatrain form a reverse alphabetical acrostic (תשר"ק) followed by the author's signature, שלמה, *Shlomo* [see prefatory comment to *selichah 2*]. The fourth line of each stanza is a Scriptural fragment that begins with some form of the word שוב, *return* or *turn back*.

בִּבְנֵי מְחִילָתֶךָ — *Among those You are wont to forgive.* The translation follows *Arugas Ha-*

Bosem. According to *Masbir*, the phrase means *those who seek Your forgiveness.*

...כְּאָז בְּשֵׁכֶן יַחַד הִנְעִימָנוּ שׁוּבֵנוּ — *As of old when [we] dwelt in unity and our life was pleasant, return us ...* The translation follows *Arugas HaBosem*. However, *Matteh Levi* (based on *Targum* and *Rashi* to Psalms 85:5) renders, *As of old when Your Presence dwelt among us and made our life pleasant, so return to us ...*

All:

הַטֵּה *Incline, my God, Your ear, and listen, open Your eyes and see our desolation and that of the city upon which Your Name is proclaimed; for not because of our righteousness do we cast down our supplications before You, rather because of Your abundant compassion. O my Lord, heed; O my Lord, forgive; O my Lord, be attentive and act, do not delay; for Your sake, my God, for Your Name is proclaimed upon Your city and upon Your people.*

SELICHAH 51

Our God and the God of our forefathers:

ת *May You once again have mercy on us:*[*1]
   return our captivity[2] *as You have said.*

ש *Once again, as of old, renew Your love for Your nation.*

ר *Set rage at a distance, and draw Your fury's quiescence near;*
         turn back *from Your blasting anger, and reconsider
            the evil [that You would do] to Your people.*[3]

ק *Gather together and seek out the lost ones,*
   and strengthen Your heritage-people,[4]

צ *the flock of the slaughter, shorn [by the gentiles]*
   because they fear You.[5]

פ *Even if sin is rife among those You are wont to forgive,*
         turn back *[Your anger] for the sake of Your servants,
            Your heritage tribes.*[6]

ע *Our fathers' iniquity lies heavy upon us,*
   causing us to taste sour grapes.[7]

ס *They gave us a bowl of poison to drink,*[8]
   filling us with wormwood and with rage.

נ *Please, as of old when [we] dwelt in unity and our life was pleasant,*[9]
      return *us,* *God of our salvation, and annul Your anger with us.*[10]

מ *You have not utterly despised*[11] *those who take shelter with You,*
   who bear witness to You;

ל *though they are punished when they sin,*
   for the balm [of atonement] they hope to You,

כ *to placate [Your] anger, according to Your upright ways.*
   Return, HASHEM; *how long? and relent concerning Your servants.*[12]

י *Every day we look forward to Your secret revealed,*

ט *yet it is sealed up and cloaked,*
   and [by now] Your pious ones' flesh is worn out.[13]

---

(1) Cf. *Micah* 7:19. (2) Cf. *Psalms* 126:4. (3) *Exodus* 32:12. (4) Cf. *Ezekiel* 34:16.
(5) Many editions of *Selichos* [and almost all manuscript versions] read וְהַגְּזוּזָה בְּרְחֵלוֹתָיִךְ,
and the shorn of Your ewes, or כְּרְחֵלוֹתָיִךְ, like Your ewes. (6) *Isaiah* 63:17. (7) Cf. *Jeremiah* 31:29.
(8) Cf. *Zechariah* 12:2; some editions of *Selichos* read סַף רַעַל רִשְׁעֵנוּ, *Our wickedness is a bowl of poison* [for us]. (9) Cf. *Psalms* 133:1. (10) 85:5. (11) Cf. *Jeremiah* 14:19; *Lamentations* 5:22; *Leviticus* 26:44. (12) *Psalms* 90:13. (13) Cf. *Lamentations* 3:4; some editions of *Selichos* read וְכָלָה, cf. *Proverbs* 5:10, but the meaning is unchanged.

חֶרְפָּה שָׁבְרָה לִבֵּנוּ[1] מְקַוִּים חֲסָדֶיךָ,

שׁוּבָה יהוה חַלְצָה נַפְשֵׁנוּ, וְהוֹשִׁיעֵנוּ לְמַעַן חַסְדֶּךָ.[2]

זַנַחְנוּ וְנֶחְשַׁבְנוּ עִם יוֹרְדֵי רֶגֶב,

וַיְהִי לְאֵבֶל כִּנּוֹר וְשִׁיר וְעֻגָב,[3]

הַקּוֹדְרִים בְּרִנָּה וְתוֹדָה הִתְהַלֵּךְ בְּשֶׂגֶב,[4]

שׁוּבָה יהוה אֶת שְׁבִיתֵנוּ כַּאֲפִיקִים בַּנֶּגֶב.[5]

דִּמְעָה לֶחֶם[6] חוֹסֵיךְ צוּרֵי אֵל,

גּוֹאֵל אַיֵּה בְּחֶרֶף צָרֵי אֵל,[7]

בְּחִזָּיוֹן אָז כְּדַבֶּרְתָּ[8] לְיִשְׁרֵי אֵל,

שׁוּבָה יהוה רִבְבוֹת אַלְפֵי יִשְׂרָאֵל.[9]

שִׁמְעָה יהוה הַטֵּה אָזְנְךָ[10] וְהַקְשִׁיבָה,

לְמְחַלֵּי סְלַח נָא סָלַחְתִּי הָשִׁיבָה,[11]

מְשׁוּבוֹתֵינוּ רַבּוּ וּפָתַחְתָּ יִשְׂרָאֵל שׁוּבָה,[12]

הֲשִׁיבֵנוּ יהוה אֵלֶיךָ וְנָשׁוּבָה.[13]

All, while standing:

אֵל מֶלֶךְ יוֹשֵׁב עַל כִּסֵּא רַחֲמִים מִתְנַהֵג בַּחֲסִידוּת, מוֹחֵל עֲוֹנוֹת עַמּוֹ, מַעֲבִיר רִאשׁוֹן רִאשׁוֹן, מַרְבֶּה מְחִילָה לְחַטָּאִים וּסְלִיחָה לְפוֹשְׁעִים, עֹשֶׂה צְדָקוֹת עִם כָּל בָּשָׂר וָרוּחַ, לֹא כְרָעָתָם תִּגְמוֹל. ✣ אֵל הוֹרֵיתָ לָנוּ לוֹמַר שְׁלֹשׁ עֶשְׂרֵה, וּזְכוֹר לָנוּ הַיּוֹם בְּרִית שְׁלֹשׁ עֶשְׂרֵה, כְּמוֹ שֶׁהוֹדַעְתָּ לֶעָנָיו מִקֶּדֶם, כְּמוֹ שֶׁכָּתוּב, וַיֵּרֶד יהוה בֶּעָנָן וַיִּתְיַצֵּב עִמּוֹ שָׁם, וַיִּקְרָא בְשֵׁם יהוה.

Congregation, then chazzan:

וַיַּעֲבֹר יהוה עַל פָּנָיו וַיִּקְרָא:

Congregation and chazzan (the words in bold type are recited aloud and in unison):

יהוה, יהוה, אֵל, רַחוּם, וְחַנּוּן, אֶרֶךְ אַפַּיִם, **וְרַב חֶסֶד, וֶאֱמֶת, נֹצֵר חֶסֶד לָאֲלָפִים, נֹשֵׂא עָוֹן, וָפֶשַׁע, וְחַטָּאָה, וְנַקֵּה.** וְסָלַחְתָּ לַעֲוֹנֵנוּ וּלְחַטָּאתֵנוּ וּנְחַלְתָּנוּ. סְלַח לָנוּ אָבִינוּ כִּי חָטָאנוּ, מְחַל לָנוּ מַלְכֵּנוּ כִּי פָשָׁעְנוּ. כִּי אַתָּה אֲדֹנָי טוֹב וְסַלָּח, וְרַב חֶסֶד לְכָל קֹרְאֶיךָ.

ח Humiliation has broken our hearts[1] that hope for Your kindness.
Return, HASHEM, release our soul,
and save us for the sake of Your kindness.[2]

ז We are abandoned, reckoned with those gone down to the grave,
ו and harp and song and flute have turned to mourning.[3]

ה The downcast people will stride with vigor,[4] with song and thanks —
[when You,] HASHEM, **return** our captivity
like springs in the desert.[5]

ד Tears are the bread[6] of those who take shelter with You,
my Rock, God,

ג while God's enemies blaspheme:[7] 'Where is the redeemer?'

ב As You once spoke in visions[8] to God's upright [prophets],
'**Return**, HASHEM, to the myriad thousands of Israel.'[9]

ש Hear, HASHEM; bend Your ear[10] and be attentive,

ל to those who beg, 'Please forgive!'
give the answer, 'I have forgiven.'[11]

מ Our waywardness has been great,
yet You have proclaimed, 'Israel, return!'[12]

ה **Return** us to You, HASHEM, and we will return.[13]

All, while standing:

אֵל מֶלֶךְ O God, King Who sits on the throne of mercy; Who acts with
kindness, pardons the iniquities of His people, removes [sins]
one by one, increasingly grants pardon to careless sinners and forgiveness
to rebels, Who deals righteously with every living being — You do not
repay them in accord with their evil. *Chazzan* — O God, You taught us to
recite the Thirteen [Attributes of Mercy], so remember for us today the
covenant of these Thirteen, as You made known to the humble one in
ancient times, as it is written: And HASHEM descended in a cloud and stood
with him there, and He called out with the Name HASHEM.

Congregation, then chazzan:

And HASHEM passed before him [Moses] and proclaimed:

Congregation and chazzan (the words in bold type are recited aloud and in unison):

ה' ה' HASHEM, HASHEM, God, Compassionate and Gracious, Slow
to anger, and Abundant in Kindness and Truth, Preserver of
kindness for thousands [of generations], Forgiver of iniquity, willful
sin, and error, and Who cleanses. *May You forgive our iniquities and
our errors and make us Your heritage. Forgive us, our Father, for we
have erred; pardon us, our King, for we have willfully sinned; for You,
my Lord, are good and forgiving and abundantly kind to all who call
upon You.*

---

(1) Cf. *Psalms* 69:21. (2) Cf. 6:5. (3) Cf. *Job* 30:31. (4) Cf. 5:11; *Psalms* 43:2. (5) 126:4.
(6) Cf. 80:6. (7) Cf. 74:10. (8) Cf. 89:20. (9) *Numbers* 10:36. (10) Cf. *Daniel* 9:18.
(11) See *Numbers* 14:19-20. (12) Cf. *Hosea* 14:2. (13) *Lamentations* 5:21.

פסוקי הקדמה לסליחה נב

שׁוּבָה יהוה חַלְּצָה נַפְשֵׁנוּ, וְהוֹשִׁיעֵנוּ לְמַעַן חַסְדֶּךָ.[1] שׁוּבוּ
שׁוּבוּ[2] אָמַרְתָּ לָנוּ, וְעַל הַתְּשׁוּבָה מֵרֹאשׁ הִבְטַחְתָּנוּ.
זִבְחֵי אֱלֹהִים רוּחַ נִשְׁבָּרָה, לֵב נִשְׁבָּר וְנִדְכֶּה, אֱלֹהִים לֹא תִבְזֶה.[3]
תָּבוֹא לְפָנֶיךָ אֶנְקַת אָסִיר, כְּגֹדֶל זְרוֹעֲךָ הוֹתֵר בְּנֵי תְמוּתָה.[4] תִּתֵּן
אֱמֶת לְיַעֲקֹב חֶסֶד לְאַבְרָהָם, אֲשֶׁר נִשְׁבַּעְתָּ לַאֲבֹתֵינוּ מִימֵי קֶדֶם.[5]

כְּרַחֵם אָב עַל בָּנִים, כֵּן תְּרַחֵם יהוה עָלֵינוּ. לַיהוה הַיְשׁוּעָה,
עַל עַמְּךָ בִרְכָתֶךָ סֶּלָה. יהוה צְבָאוֹת עִמָּנוּ, מִשְׂגָּב
לָנוּ אֱלֹהֵי יַעֲקֹב סֶלָה. יהוה צְבָאוֹת, אַשְׁרֵי אָדָם בֹּטֵחַ בָּךְ. יהוה
הוֹשִׁיעָה, הַמֶּלֶךְ יַעֲנֵנוּ בְיוֹם קָרְאֵנוּ.

In some congregations the following two verses are recited responsively — the *chazzan* reciting סְלַח,
and the congregation responding וַיֹּאמֶר. In other congregations these verses are recited silently.

סְלַח נָא לַעֲוֹן הָעָם הַזֶּה כְּגֹדֶל חַסְדֶּךָ, וְכַאֲשֶׁר נָשָׂאתָה לָעָם
הַזֶּה מִמִּצְרַיִם וְעַד הֵנָּה, וְשָׁם נֶאֱמַר:

וַיֹּאמֶר יהוה סָלַחְתִּי כִּדְבָרֶךָ.

All:

הַטֵּה אֱלֹהַי אָזְנְךָ וּשְׁמָע, פְּקַח עֵינֶיךָ וּרְאֵה שֹׁמְמֹתֵינוּ, וְהָעִיר
אֲשֶׁר נִקְרָא שִׁמְךָ עָלֶיהָ, כִּי לֹא עַל צִדְקוֹתֵינוּ אֲנַחְנוּ
מַפִּילִים תַּחֲנוּנֵינוּ לְפָנֶיךָ, כִּי עַל רַחֲמֶיךָ הָרַבִּים. אֲדֹנָי שְׁמָעָה,
אֲדֹנָי סְלָחָה, אֲדֹנָי הַקְשִׁיבָה, וַעֲשֵׂה אַל תְּאַחַר, לְמַעַנְךָ אֱלֹהַי, כִּי
שִׁמְךָ נִקְרָא עַל עִירְךָ וְעַל עַמֶּךָ.

סליחה נב (עקדה)

אֱלֹהֵינוּ וֵאלֹהֵי אֲבוֹתֵינוּ:

אִם אָפֵס רֹבַע הַקֵּן,*   אֹהֶל שֹׁכֵן אִם רִקֵּן,
אַל נֹאבְדָה[6] עַל כֵּן,   יֵשׁ לָנוּ אָב זָקֵן.[7]
פָּנִים לוֹ תַכִּיר,[8]   וְצִדְקוֹ לְפָנֶיךָ נַזְכִּיר,
צִוִּיתוֹ, קַח נָא אֶת בִּנְךָ[9] יַקִּיר,   וְנִמְצָה דָמוֹ עַל קִיר.*[10]

אִם אָפֵס רֹבַע הַקֵּן — *Even if the bird offering
has ceased.* The binding of Isaac on the altar on
Mount Moriah (see *Genesis* ch. 22) is described
and its merit is invoked in this *piyut* that is
appropriately called an עֲקֵידָה, *akeidah*. The
composer signed his name — אֶפְרַיִם בַּר רַבִּי יִצְחָק,
Ephraim bar R' Yitzchak, may he be strong
— in the acrostic of the stanzas. R' Ephraim

flourished in twelfth-century Regensburg, Germany. He was a disciple of Rabbeinu Tam and
author of *Arbaah Panim,* a Talmud commentary
that, unfortunately, is no longer extant.

רֹבַע הַקֵּן — *The bird offering.* The word רֹבַע
means *a quarter* and here refers to a quarter of a
dinar, the price assigned to a קֵן, *nesting pair of*

PREFATORY VERSES TO SELICHAH 52

שׁוּבָה *Return, HASHEM! Release our soul, and save us for the sake of Your kindness.¹ 'Return! Return!'² You have said to us, and promised us from the start about repentance. The sacrifices of God are a broken spirit, a heart broken and humbled, O God, You will not despise.³ Let the prisoner's groan come before You; as befits Your great power, spare those condemned to death.⁴ Grant truth to Jacob, kindness to Abraham, as You swore to our forefathers from ancient times.⁵*

כְּרַחֵם אָב *As a father has mercy on his children, so, HASHEM, may You have mercy on us. Salvation is HASHEM's, upon Your people is Your blessing, Selah. HASHEM, Master of Legions, is with us, a stronghold for us is the God of Jacob, Selah. HASHEM, Master of Legions, praiseworthy is the person who trusts in You. HASHEM, save! May the King answer us on the day we call.*

In some congregations the following two verses are recited responsively — the chazzan reciting, 'Forgive, please . . .,' and the congregation responding, 'And HASHEM said . . .'
In other congregations these verses are recited silently.

סְלַח נָא *Forgive, please, the iniquity of this people according to the greatness of Your kindness and as You have forgiven this people from Egypt until now, and there it was said:*

And HASHEM said, 'I have forgiven according to your word!'

All:

הַטֵּה *Incline, my God, Your ear, and listen, open Your eyes and see our desolation and that of the city upon which Your Name is proclaimed; for not because of our righteousness do we cast down our supplications before You, rather because of Your abundant compassion. O my Lord, heed; O my Lord, forgive; O my Lord, be attentive and act, do not delay; for Your sake, my God, for Your Name is proclaimed upon Your city and upon Your people.*

SELICHAH 52

Our God and the God of our forefathers:

א *Even if the bird offering* has ceased,**
  even if the Tabernacle in which He dwelt is empty,
  we need not be lost⁶ on that account,
  for we have [the merits of] an ancient Patriarch [Abraham].⁷
ב *Show him favor,⁸*
  as we mention his righteousness before You.
  You commanded him, 'Take now your dear son,⁹
  and let his blood be squeezed out on the [altar's] wall.'*¹⁰

---

(1) Cf. *Psalms* 6:5. (2) *Ezekiel* 33:11. (3) *Psalms* 51:19. (4) 79:11. (5) *Micah* 7:20. (6) Cf. *Jonah* 1:14. (7) *Genesis* 44:20. (8) Cf. *Deuteronomy* 16:19. (9) *Genesis* 22:2. (10) *Leviticus* 1:15.

doves, to be brought as a bird offering (see *Rosh Hashanah* 11b). The intent of the stich is that even the least of the Altar offerings is no longer available to atone for our sins.

וְנִמְצָה דָמוֹ עַל קִיר — *And let his blood be squeezed out on the [altar's] wall.* Since the *piyut* began by mentioning the bird offering, the metaphor of Isaac as a bird offering is continued here.

רָץ אֶל הַנַּעַר וְהִקְדִּישׁוֹ,   וְנַפְשׁוֹ קְשׁוּרָה בְנַפְשׁוֹ,[1]

עִטְּרוֹ בָעֵצִים וְאִשּׁוֹ,*   וְנֵזֶר אֱלֹהָיו עַל רֹאשׁוֹ.*[2]

יָחִיד רַךְ הוּקַל כַּצְּבִי,   עָנָה וְאָמַר אָבִי,

הִנֵּה הָאֵשׁ וְהָעֵצִים[3] נָבִיא,   וּתְשׁוּרָה אֵין לְהָבִיא.[4]

מִלִּין הֵשִׁיבוּ מִלְּהַבְהִילוּ,   עָנָה אָבִיו וְאָמַר לוֹ,

אֱלֹהִים יִרְאֶה לּוֹ,[5]   וְיָדַע יהוה אֶת אֲשֶׁר לוֹ.[6]

בְּמִצְוֹתֶיךָ שְׁנֵיהֶם נִזְהָרִים,   וְאַחֲרֶיךָ לֹא מְהַרְהֲרִים,

חָשׁוּ מְאֹד נִמְהָרִים,   עַל אַחַד הֶהָרִים.[7]

רָאוּ אֵשׁ תְּלוּלָה,   מִהֲרוּ עֲצֵי עוֹלָה,

יַחַד בְּאַהֲבָה כְלוּלָה,   יָשְׁרוּ בָּעֲרָבָה מְסִלָּה.[8]

רָאָה יָחִיד כִּי הוּא הַשֶּׂה,   נָאַם לְהוֹרוֹ הַמְנֻסֶּה,

אָתִי כְּכֶבֶשׂ תַּעֲשֶׂה,   לֹא תַחְמֹל וְלֹא תְכַסֶּה.[9]

כִּי חָפֵץ וְנִכְסָף,   לְבָבִי לוֹ אֶחְשֹׂף,

הַאִם תִּמְנָעֵנִי סוֹף,   רוּחִי וְנִשְׁמָתִי אֵלָיו יֵאָסֵף.[10]

יָדָיו וְרַגְלָיו עָקַד,   וְחַרְבוֹ עָלָיו פָּקַד,

לְשׂוּמוֹ עַל עֵצִים שָׁקַד,   וְהָאֵשׁ עַל הַמִּזְבֵּחַ תּוּקַד.[11]

צַוָּאר פָּשַׁט מֵאֵלָיו,   וְאָבִיו נִגַּשׁ אֵלָיו,

לְשָׁחֲטוֹ לְשֵׁם בְּעָלָיו,[12]   וְהִנֵּה יהוה נִצָּב עָלָיו.[13]

חָקַר אֶת אֲשֶׁר נַעֲשָׂה,   הָאָב עַל בְּנוֹ לֹא חָסָה,

לִבּוֹ אֶל כַּפָּיו נָשָׂא,[14]   וַיַּרְא אֱלֹהִים אֵת כָּל אֲשֶׁר עָשָׂה.[15]

קָרָא לְמֵרֵחֵם מְשַׂחָר,[16]   תְּמוּר בִּנְךָ תִּבְחָר,

הִנֵּה אַיִל אַחַר,[17]   וַעֲשֵׂה וְאַל תְּאַחַר.[18]

חֲלִיפֵי אַזְכָּרָתוֹ,   תְּכַן הַקְטָרָתוֹ,

וְתַעֲלֶה תְמֻרָתוֹ,   וְהָיָה הוּא וּתְמוּרָתוֹ.[19]

עִטְּרוֹ בָעֵצִים וְאִשּׁוֹ — *He garlanded him with wood and his fire.* A simple rendering of *Genesis 22:6* yields the following: *Abraham took the wood for the offering and placed it on Isaac his son; he took in his hand the fire and the knife, and the two of them went together.* The logical antecedent of the pronoun 'he' in the phrase 'he took . . . the fire . . .' is Abraham. Yet the *paytan* implies that Isaac carried both the wood and the fire! If so, Isaac, not Abraham, is the subject of the clause 'he took . . .' Perhaps the *paytan* understands the Scriptural passage in the following manner. Isaac would never allow his father to carry a burden in his presence, as long as Isaac was able to handle it himself. However, the bundle of wood was too

heavy for Isaac to swing unto his shoulders unassisted. Therefore, *Abraham took the wood . . . and placed it on Isaac.* But the fire and knife were light, so he [Isaac] took [them] in his hand without waiting for his father to hand them to him.

וְנֵזֶר אֱלֹהָיו עַל רֹאשׁוֹ — *The diadem of his God on his head.* Although the Scriptural passage from which this phrase is taken (*Numbers 6:7*) speaks of a *nazir*, the *paytan* borrows the expression to describe Abraham as a *Kohen Gadol* (see *Yalkut Shimoni, Shir HaShirim 987*), for one of the eight vestments of the *Kohen Gadol*, the golden צִיץ, *forehead plate*, is also referred to as נֵזֶר הַקֹּדֶשׁ, *the holy diadem* (see *Exodus 29:6*).

ר He ran to the boy and consecrated him [as a sacrifice],
   although his soul was bound up with his [son's] soul.[1]
   He garlanded him with wood and his fire,*
   the diadem of his God on his head.*[2]

י The tender only [son] went lightly as a deer;
   he spoke up and said, 'My father...
   here is the fire and the wood[3] that we are bringing,
   but there is no offering to bring.'[4]

ם He answered him words that would not alarm him.
   His father answered and said to him, 'God will see for Himself,[5]
   for HASHEM will make known the one that is His.'[6]

כ Both were careful to do Your commandments,
   and did not question Your will.
   They went quickly, as fast as fast can be, on one of the mountains.[7]

ר They saw fire suspended [between heaven and earth]
   and hurried along with the wood for the offering.
   Together, with perfect love,
   they made a straight path through the wilderness.[8]

ר The only [son] realized that he was the [sacrificial] lamb,
   and said to his father, who was being tested [by God],
   'Offer me like a sheep; do not have mercy, do not shelter me.[9]

בי 'It is in me that He desires and in whom He delights;
   I will bare my heart to Him.
   Even were you to withhold me to the end?
   He will [nevertheless] gather my spirit and soul to Him.'[10]

י He bound his [son's] hands and feet,
   and set his blade towards him, he hied to place him on the wood,
   and the fire was burning on the altar.[11]

צ He stretched out his throat on his own,
   and his father drew up to him,
   to slaughter him in his Master's name —[12]
   when see, HASHEM was standing over him.[13]

ח [God] investigated what was being done;
   the father had not pitied his son,
   and raised his heart with his hands [in prayer].[14]
   And God saw all that he had done.[15]

ק He called [to Abraham], who knew Him [almost] from birth,[16]
   'Choose something in your son's place;
   behold a ram behind [you],[17] so offer it, do not delay.'[18]

ח May the exchange of his offering
   stand in his stead through its burning; and may its smoke ascend,
   so that he and his replacement shall be [considered as offered].[19]

(1) Genesis 44:30. (2) Cf. Numbers 6:7. (3) Genesis 22:7. (4) I Samuel 9:7.
(5) Genesis 22:8. (6) Numbers 16:5. (7) Genesis 22:2. (8) Isaiah 40:3. (9) Deuteronomy 13:9.
(10) Cf. Job 34:14. (11) Leviticus 6:5. (12) See tractate Zevachim 2a. (13) Genesis 28:13.
(14) Cf. Lamentations 3:41, see Rashi there. (15) Genesis 1:31. (16) Cf. Psalms 110:3.
(17) Cf. Genesis 22:13. (18) Daniel 9:19. (19) Leviticus 27:33.

זִכָּרוֹן לְפָנֶיךָ בַּשַּׁחַק,‏[1] לָעַד בְּסֵפֶר יוּחָק,
בְּרִית עוֹלָם לֹא נִמְחַק,‏[2] אֶת אַבְרָהָם וְאֶת יִצְחָק.
❖ קוֹרְאֶיךָ בָּאִים לִקוֹד, בְּצֶדֶק עֲקֵדָה תִשְׁקֹד,
צֹאנְךָ בְּרַחֲמִים תִּפְקֹד, פְּנֵי הַצֹּאן אֶל עָקֹד.‏[3]

All, while standing:

אֵל מֶלֶךְ יוֹשֵׁב עַל כִּסֵּא רַחֲמִים מִתְנַהֵג בַּחֲסִידוּת, מוֹחֵל
עֲוֹנוֹת עַמּוֹ, מַעֲבִיר רִאשׁוֹן רִאשׁוֹן, מַרְבֶּה מְחִילָה
לְחַטָּאִים וּסְלִיחָה לְפוֹשְׁעִים, עֹשֶׂה צְדָקוֹת עִם כָּל בָּשָׂר וָרוּחַ,
לֹא כְרָעָתָם תִּגְמוֹל. ❖ אֵל הוֹרֵיתָ לָּנוּ לוֹמַר שְׁלֹשׁ עֶשְׂרֵה, וּזְכוֹר
לָנוּ הַיּוֹם בְּרִית שְׁלֹשׁ עֶשְׂרֵה, כְּמוֹ שֶׁהוֹדַעְתָּ לֶעָנָיו מִקֶּדֶם, כְּמוֹ
שֶׁכָּתוּב, וַיֵּרֶד יְהוֹה בֶּעָנָן וַיִּתְיַצֵּב עִמּוֹ שָׁם, וַיִּקְרָא בְשֵׁם יְהוֹה.

Congregation, then chazzan:

וַיַּעֲבֹר יְהוֹה עַל פָּנָיו וַיִּקְרָא:

Congregation and chazzan *(the words in bold type are recited aloud and in unison):*

**יְהוֹה, יְהוֹה, אֵל, רַחוּם, וְחַנּוּן, אֶרֶךְ אַפַּיִם, וְרַב חֶסֶד, וֶאֱמֶת,
נֹצֵר חֶסֶד לָאֲלָפִים, נֹשֵׂא עָוֹן, וָפֶשַׁע, וְחַטָּאָה,
וְנַקֵּה.** וְסָלַחְתָּ לַעֲוֹנֵנוּ וּלְחַטָּאתֵנוּ וּנְחַלְתָּנוּ. סְלַח לָנוּ אָבִינוּ כִּי
חָטָאנוּ, מְחַל לָנוּ מַלְכֵּנוּ כִּי פָשָׁעְנוּ. כִּי אַתָּה אֲדֹנָי טוֹב וְסַלָּח,
וְרַב חֶסֶד לְכָל קֹרְאֶיךָ.

סְלִיחָה נג (פזמון)

Chazzan, then congregation:

הוֹרֵיתָ דֶּרֶךְ תְּשׁוּבָה,* לְבַת הַשּׁוֹבֵבָה,‏[4]
בֵּין כֶּסֶה לֶעָשׂוֹר,* עָדֶיךָ לָשׁוּבָה,
הֲשִׁיבֵנוּ יְהוֹה אֵלֶיךָ, וְנָשׁוּבָה.‏[5]

Congregation, then chazzan:

אָז מֵאָז מִקֶּדֶם, הִקְדַּמְתָּ תְּשׁוּבָה,‏[6]
בְּטֶרֶם הִמְתַּחְתָּ אֶרֶץ וִיסוֹדֵי רְגוּבָה,

הוֹרֵיתָ דֶּרֶךְ תְּשׁוּבָה §— *You have taught the
way of repentance.* Various Scriptural personali-
ties sinned and were given the opportunity to
repent. Some even become paradigms for the
penitent to emulate, others were contrite, but in
their own way. Their stories are related in *Tanach*
to teach the lesson of *teshuvah*, repentance, on
different levels — individual, communal, royal
... Six of them are mentioned in this *selichah*:
Adam, Cain, Reuben, Judah, Ahab and the

citizens of Nineveh in Jonah's time.

The *paytan's* signature — בִּנְיָמִן, *Binyamin* [see
prefatory note to *selichah* 1] — appears after the
alphabetical acrostic.

Although the refrain of this *pizmon* comprises
the entire introductory stanza, many congregations repeat only the third line.

בֵּין כֶּסֶה לֶעָשׂוֹר — *Between Rosh Hashanah and
Yom Kippur.* The word כֶּסֶה means covered, and

ז *[Let it be] a memorial before You in Heaven,*
inscribed in the Book forever,[1]
an eternal covenant, never to be erased:
with Abraham and with Isaac.[2]
ק Chazzan — *Those who call You are coming to bow [in prayer];*
keep in mind the righteous deed of the Akeidah.
Remember Your flock with mercy,
for the face of the flock looks to [the merits of] the bound one.[3]

All, while standing:

אֵל מֶלֶךְ *O God, King Who sits on the throne of mercy; Who acts with*
kindness, pardons the iniquities of His people, removes [sins]
one by one, increasingly grants pardon to careless sinners and forgiveness
to rebels, Who deals righteously with every living being — *You do not repay*
them in accord with their evil. Chazzan — *O God, You taught us to recite the*
Thirteen [Attributes of Mercy], so remember for us today the covenant of
these Thirteen, as You made known to the humble one in ancient times, as
it is written: And HASHEM descended in a cloud and stood with him there,
and He called out with the Name HASHEM.

Congregation, then chazzan:

And HASHEM passed before him [Moses] and proclaimed:

Congregation and chazzan (the words in bold type are recited aloud and in unison):

ה' ה' **HASHEM, HASHEM, God, Compassionate and Gracious, Slow to**
anger, and Abundant in Kindness and Truth, Preserver of
kindness for thousands [of generations], Forgiver of iniquity, willful
sin, and error, and Who cleanses. *May You forgive our iniquities and our*
errors and make us Your heritage. Forgive us, our Father, for we have
erred; pardon us, our King, for we have willfully sinned; for You, my Lord,
are good and forgiving and abundantly kind to all who call upon You.

SELICHAH 53

Chazzan, then congregation:

הוֹרֵיתָ *You have taught the way of repentance**
to the wayward daughter,[4]
between Rosh Hashanah and Yom Kippur* to return to You.
Return us to You, HASHEM, and we will return![5]

Congregation, then chazzan:

א *Then, back then, from of old You made repentance first,*[6]
ב *before You stretched out the heavens and the foundations of earth.*

---

(1) Cf. *Job* 19:23. (2) Cf. *Exodus* 2:24. (3) *Genesis* 30:40. (4) Cf. *Jeremiah* 31:21.
(5) *Lamentations* 5:21. (6) See commentary to *selichah* 4, s.v., כּוֹנַנְתָּ מֵאָז תָּרֶף.

the phrase from which it is taken, בְּכֶסֶה לְיוֹם חַגֵּנוּ (*Psalms* 81:4), means *on the festive day when the moon is covered*. But that can only refer to Rosh Hashanah which coincides with the New Moon, for all other Scripturally ordained festivals fall between the First Quarter and Third Quarter of their respective months (*Rosh Hashanah* 8a). Alternatively, the word כֶּסֶה is cognate to כסא

and means either *appointed time* (Rashi) or *throne* (Sforno), and alludes to Rosh Hashanah as the day appointed for judgment, or the day on which God sits in the Throne of Judgment.

The term עָשׂוֹר, *tenth*, refers to Yom Kippur, the tenth of Tishrei. Taken together, the Ten Days of Penitence — from Rosh Hashanah to Yom Kippur — are thus called בֵּין כֶּסֶה לֶעָשׂוֹר.

גַּם לְכָל הַשָּׁבִים,* צָרֵי וּמַרְפֵּא חֲשׁוּבָה,
דּוֹפְקֵי דְלָתֶיךָ רֵיקָם מִלְּהָשִׁיבָה.
(הוֹרֵיתָ דֶּרֶךְ תְּשׁוּבָה, לְבַת הַשּׁוֹבֵבָה, בֵּין כֶּסֶה לֶעָשׂוֹר, עָדֶיךָ לָשׁוּבָה,)
הֲשִׁיבֵנוּ יהוה אֵלֶיךָ, וְנָשׁוּבָה.

Congregation, then chazzan:

הֵן רֹאשׁ עַפְרוֹת תֵּבֵל,¹ אֲשֶׁר רִאשׁוֹן נוֹצָר,
וְנִסִּיתוֹ בְּמִצְוָה קַלָּה,* וְאוֹתָהּ לֹא נָצָר,
זָעַמְתָּ וְאָנַפְתָּ עָלָיו, שְׁנוֹתָיו לְקַצֵּר,
חָזַר בִּתְשׁוּבָה² וְכָאִישׁוֹן הַנְצָר.
(הוֹרֵיתָ דֶּרֶךְ תְּשׁוּבָה, לְבַת הַשּׁוֹבֵבָה, בֵּין כֶּסֶה לֶעָשׂוֹר, עָדֶיךָ לָשׁוּבָה,)
הֲשִׁיבֵנוּ יהוה אֵלֶיךָ, וְנָשׁוּבָה.

Congregation, then chazzan:

טָעָה גִזְעוֹ דְּמֵי אָחִיו בְּשָׁפְכוֹ,³
יִסַּרְתּוֹ בְּנָע וָנָד,⁴ לֶכֶת כֹּה וָכֹה,
בָּעֵת שָׁב אֵלֶיךָ, וְעָזַב רַע דַּרְכּוֹ,⁵
לְשִׁבְעָתַיִם הָאֱרַכְתּוֹ, כָּל מוֹצְאוֹ בְּלִי לְהַכּוֹ.⁶
(הוֹרֵיתָ דֶּרֶךְ תְּשׁוּבָה, לְבַת הַשּׁוֹבֵבָה, בֵּין כֶּסֶה לֶעָשׂוֹר, עָדֶיךָ לָשׁוּבָה,)
הֲשִׁיבֵנוּ יהוה אֵלֶיךָ, וְנָשׁוּבָה.

Congregation, then chazzan:

מְחַלֵּל⁷ יְצוּעֵי יוֹלְדוֹ, אֲשֶׁר פֵּחַז כַּמַּיִם,⁸
נָטָיוּ רַגְלָיו כִּמְעַט,⁹ לוּלֵי שָׁפַךְ לֵב כַּמַּיִם,¹⁰
סָרַח גּוּר אַרְיֵה, בִּקְדֻשָּׁה הִיא בָעֵינַיִם,¹¹
עָוֹנוֹ הוֹדָה,¹² וְהִכְרַעְתּוֹ לְצֶדֶק בְּמֹאזְנַיִם.
(הוֹרֵיתָ דֶּרֶךְ תְּשׁוּבָה, לְבַת הַשּׁוֹבֵבָה, בֵּין כֶּסֶה לֶעָשׂוֹר, עָדֶיךָ לָשׁוּבָה,)
הֲשִׁיבֵנוּ יהוה אֵלֶיךָ, וְנָשׁוּבָה.

Congregation, then chazzan:

פָּרַץ גְּדֵרוֹת עוֹלָם, בֶּן עָמְרִי בְּרֶשַׁע,
צַלְמֵי אֲשֵׁרִים חָשַׁק, וְהוֹסִיף עַל חַטָּאתוֹ פֶּשַׁע,¹³
קָרַעְתָּ גְזַר דִּינוֹ בְּשׁוּבוֹ מִלְּפְשַׁע,¹⁴
רַחֵם כְּמוֹדֶה וְעוֹזֵב,¹⁵ וּבְךָ נוֹשַׁע.
(הוֹרֵיתָ דֶּרֶךְ תְּשׁוּבָה, לְבַת הַשּׁוֹבֵבָה, בֵּין כֶּסֶה לֶעָשׂוֹר, עָדֶיךָ לָשׁוּבָה,)
הֲשִׁיבֵנוּ יהוה אֵלֶיךָ, וְנָשׁוּבָה.

גַּם לְכָל הַשָּׁבִים — *Also for all penitents,* i.e., not only those mentioned in this *piyut,* but also all others who are contrite and remorseful about their sinful past may find balm and healing in *teshuvah.*

בְּמִצְוָה קַלָּה — *With a slight commandment.* While yet in the Garden of Eden, Adam had

ג Also for all penitents,* it is balm and healing,
ד that those who knock on Your doors
   may not be sent back empty-handed.
> (You have taught ... to return to You.)
> Return us to You, HASHEM, and we will return!

Congregation, then chazzan:

ה [Adam,] the first [created] of earth's dust,[1]
   who was formed first of all,
ו whom You tried with a slight commandment,*
   but he did not keep it —
ז You raged and were furious at him,
   [so You decreed] to cut his years short,
ח [yet] when he repented,[2] You guarded him like the pupil of the eye.
> (You have taught ... to return to You.)
> Return us to You, HASHEM, and we will return!

Congregation, then chazzan:

ט His child [Cain] went astray and spilled his brother's blood;[3]
י You punished him with endless wandering,[4] moving here and there.
כ [Yet] when he returned to You and abandoned the evil of his way,[5]
ל You gave him seven generations' stay,
   that any who found him might not smite him.[6]
> (You have taught ... to return to You.)
> Return us to You, HASHEM, and we will return!

Congregation, then chazzan:

מ [Reuben] debased[7] his father's couch, he was impetuous as water,[8]
נ his feet almost led him astray[9]
   — but then he poured out his heart in prayer.[10]
ס The lion's cub [Judah] sinned with a harlot at the crossroads;[11]
ע he confessed his transgression,[12]
   and You tipped the scales for him to the side of righteousness.
> (You have taught ... to return to You.)
> Return us to You, HASHEM, and we will return!

Congregation, then chazzan:

פ [Ahab] the son of Omri breached all the world's fences
   in [his] wickedness,
צ lusting after Asheirah-idols, adding rebellion to his sin.[13]
ק Yet You tore up his decree of retribution when he repented his sins,[14]
ר and he received mercy, as befits one who confesses and leaves off sin,[15]
   and found salvation with You.
> (You have taught ... to return to You.)
> Return us to You, HASHEM, and we will return!

---

(1) Cf. *Proverbs* 8:26. (2) See tractate *Eruvin* 18b. (3) See *Genesis* 4:8. (4) 4:12. (5) See 4:13.
(6) Cf. 4:15. (7) See commentaries to 35:22. (8) Cf. 49:4. (9) Cf. *Psalms* 73:2. (10) Cf. *Lamentations*
2:19; see tractate *Sotah* 7b. (11) See *Genesis* ch. 38. (12) See 38:26; see tractate *Sotah* 7b.
(13) See *I Kings* 16:29ff; see tractate *Sanhedrin* 102b. (14) See *I Kings* 21:27-29. (15) Cf. *Proverbs* 28:13.

---

been given but one *mitzvah*: From all the trees of
the Garden you may eat. But from the Tree-of-
Knowledge-between-Good-and-Bad — you shall
not eat from it (Genesis 2:16-17).

Congregation, then *chazzan:*

שָׁנֵנוּ לְשׁוֹנָם כְּחֵץ, אַנְשֵׁי עִיר הַגְּדוֹלָה,
שִׁגְיוֹנָם וּזְדוֹנָם רַבּוּ עַד לְמַעְלָה,[1]
תִּתֶּךְ חֲזוֹן הַפִּיכָתָם,[2] אֲחָזוּם רֶתֶת וְחַלְחָלָה,
תְּשׁוּבָה עָשׂוּ כְּהָגֵן,[3] וְלִפְנֵי כִסֵּא כְבוֹדְךָ נִתְקַבְּלָה.[4]
(הוֹרֵיתָ דֶּרֶךְ תְּשׁוּבָה, לְבַת הַשּׁוֹבֵבָה, בֵּין כֶּסֶה לֶעָשׂוֹר, עָדֶיךָ לָשׁוּבָה,)
הֲשִׁיבֵנוּ יהוה אֵלֶיךָ, וְנָשׁוּבָה.

Congregation, then *chazzan:*

בּוֹחֵן כְּלָיוֹת וָלֵב, נֶאְזָר בִּגְבוּרָה,
יַדְּעֵנוּ מַדַּע לֶכֶת בְּאֹרַח יְשָׁרָה,
מְשׁוּבוֹתֵינוּ אִם רַבּוּ[5] בְּפֶשַׁע וּסְרָרָה,
נָא לְמַעַנְךָ הֲשִׁיבֵנוּ, עֲשׂוֹת תְּשׁוּבָה כְּשׁוּרָה.
(הוֹרֵיתָ דֶּרֶךְ תְּשׁוּבָה, לְבַת הַשּׁוֹבֵבָה, בֵּין כֶּסֶה לֶעָשׂוֹר, עָדֶיךָ לָשׁוּבָה,)
הֲשִׁיבֵנוּ יהוה אֵלֶיךָ, וְנָשׁוּבָה.

All, while standing:

אֵל מֶלֶךְ יוֹשֵׁב עַל כִּסֵּא רַחֲמִים מִתְנַהֵג בַּחֲסִידוּת, מוֹחֵל
עֲוֹנוֹת עַמּוֹ, מַעֲבִיר רִאשׁוֹן רִאשׁוֹן, מַרְבֶּה מְחִילָה
לַחַטָּאִים וּסְלִיחָה לַפּוֹשְׁעִים, עֹשֶׂה צְדָקוֹת עִם כָּל בָּשָׂר וָרוּחַ, לֹא
כְרָעָתָם תִּגְמוֹל. ❖ אֵל הוֹרֵיתָ לָנוּ לוֹמַר שְׁלֹשׁ עֶשְׂרֵה, וּזְכוֹר לָנוּ
הַיּוֹם בְּרִית שְׁלֹשׁ עֶשְׂרֵה, כְּמוֹ שֶׁהוֹדַעְתָּ לֶעָנָיו מִקֶּדֶם, כְּמוֹ
שֶׁכָּתוּב, וַיֵּרֶד יהוה בֶּעָנָן וַיִּתְיַצֵּב עִמּוֹ שָׁם, וַיִּקְרָא בְשֵׁם יהוה.

Congregation, then *chazzan:*

וַיַּעֲבֹר יהוה עַל פָּנָיו וַיִּקְרָא:

Congregation and *chazzan* (the words in bold type are recited aloud and in unison):

יהוה, יהוה, אֵל, **רַחוּם,** וְחַנּוּן, **אֶרֶךְ אַפַּיִם,** וְרַב **חֶסֶד,**
וֶאֱמֶת, **נֹצֵר חֶסֶד לָאֲלָפִים,** נֹשֵׂא עָוֹן **וָפֶשַׁע,**
וְחַטָּאָה, **וְנַקֵּה.** וְסָלַחְתָּ לַעֲוֹנֵנוּ וּלְחַטָּאתֵנוּ וּנְחַלְתָּנוּ. סְלַח לָנוּ
אָבִינוּ כִּי חָטָאנוּ, מְחַל לָנוּ מַלְכֵּנוּ כִּי פָשָׁעְנוּ. כִּי אַתָּה אֲדֹנָי טוֹב
וְסַלָּח, וְרַב חֶסֶד לְכָל קֹרְאֶיךָ.

All:

אַל תִּזְכָּר לָנוּ עֲוֹנוֹת רִאשׁוֹנִים; מַהֵר יְקַדְּמוּנוּ רַחֲמֶיךָ, כִּי
דַלּוֹנוּ מְאֹד.[6] חַטֹּאת נְעוּרֵינוּ וּפְשָׁעֵינוּ אַל תִּזְכּוֹר,
כְּחַסְדְּךָ זְכָר לָנוּ אַתָּה, לְמַעַן טוּבְךָ, יהוה.[7]

Congregation, then *chazzan:*

ש *The people of [Nineveh] the great city*
spoke with sharp tongues against You;
their sins, both inadvertent and intentional,
increased until the heavens.[1]

ת *When You revealed the vision of their overthrow,*[2]
shuddering and quaking seized them;
they repented properly[3] —
and were accepted before Your Throne of Glory.[4]

(*You have taught . . . to return to You.*)
Return us to You, HASHEM, and we will return!

Congregation, then *chazzan:*

ב *O Searcher of thoughts and hearts, [You Who are] girded with might,*
י *teach us the knowledge of walking in the straight path.*
מ *If our waywardness has been great,*[5] *with rebellious sin and straying,*
נ *please, for Your own sake, return us, that we may properly repent.*

(*You have taught . . . to return to You.*)
Return us to You, HASHEM, and we will return!

All, while standing:

אֵל מֶלֶךְ O *God, King Who sits on the throne of mercy; Who acts with*
kindness, pardons the iniquities of His people, removes [sins]
one by one, increasingly grants pardon to careless sinners and forgiveness
to rebels, Who deals righteously with every living being — *You do not repay*
them in accord with their evil. Chazzan — O *God, You taught us to recite the*
Thirteen [Attributes of Mercy], so remember for us today the covenant of
these Thirteen, as You made known to the humble one in ancient times, as
it is written: And HASHEM descended in a cloud and stood with him there,
and He called out with the Name HASHEM.

Congregation, then *chazzan:*

And HASHEM passed before him [Moses] and proclaimed:

Congregation and *chazzan* (the words in bold type are recited aloud and in unison):

ה' ה' **HASHEM, HASHEM, God, Compassionate and Gracious, Slow to**
anger, and Abundant in Kindness and Truth, Preserver of
kindness for thousands [of generations], Forgiver of iniquity, willful
sin, and error, and Who cleanses. *May You forgive our iniquities and our*
errors and make us Your heritage. Forgive us, our Father, for we have
erred; pardon us, our King, for we have willfully sinned; for You, my Lord,
are good and forgiving and abundantly kind to all who call upon You.

All:

אַל תִּזְכָּר Do *not recall against us the iniquities of the ancients;*
speedily — *let Your mercy come to meet us for we have fallen*
very low.[6] *Remember not the sins of our youth and our rebellions; may*
You remember for us [the deeds] worthy of Your kindness, because of
Your goodness, HASHEM.[7]

---

(1) See *Jonah* 1:2. (2) See 3:4. (3) See 3:5-8. (4) See 3:10.
(5) Cf. *Jeremiah* 14:7. (6) *Psalms* 79:8. (7) Cf. 25:7.

זְכוֹר רַחֲמֶיךָ יהוה וַחֲסָדֶיךָ, כִּי מֵעוֹלָם הֵמָּה.[1] זָכְרֵנוּ יהוה
בִּרְצוֹן עַמֶּךָ, פָּקְדֵנוּ בִּישׁוּעָתֶךָ.[2] זְכֹר עֲדָתְךָ
קָנִיתָ קֶּדֶם, גָּאַלְתָּ שֵׁבֶט נַחֲלָתֶךָ, הַר צִיּוֹן זֶה שָׁכַנְתָּ בּוֹ.[3] זְכֹר
יהוה חִבַּת יְרוּשָׁלַיִם, אַהֲבַת צִיּוֹן אַל תִּשְׁכַּח לָנֶצַח.[4] אַתָּה
תָקוּם תְּרַחֵם צִיּוֹן, כִּי עֵת לְחֶנְנָהּ כִּי בָא מוֹעֵד.[5] זְכֹר יהוה
לִבְנֵי אֱדוֹם אֵת יוֹם יְרוּשָׁלָיִם, הָאֹמְרִים עָרוּ עָרוּ עַד הַיְסוֹד
בָּהּ.[6] זְכֹר לְאַבְרָהָם לְיִצְחָק וּלְיִשְׂרָאֵל עֲבָדֶיךָ אֲשֶׁר נִשְׁבַּעְתָּ
לָהֶם בָּךְ, וַתְּדַבֵּר אֲלֵהֶם, אַרְבֶּה אֶת זַרְעֲכֶם כְּכוֹכְבֵי הַשָּׁמַיִם,
וְכָל הָאָרֶץ הַזֹּאת אֲשֶׁר אָמַרְתִּי אֶתֵּן לְזַרְעֲכֶם, וְנָחֲלוּ לְעוֹלָם.[7]
❖ זְכֹר לַעֲבָדֶיךָ לְאַבְרָהָם לְיִצְחָק וּלְיַעֲקֹב, אַל תֵּפֶן אֶל קְשִׁי הָעָם
הַזֶּה וְאֶל רִשְׁעוֹ וְאֶל חַטָּאתוֹ.[8]

Chazzan, then congregation:

אַל נָא תָשֵׁת עָלֵינוּ חַטָּאת, אֲשֶׁר נוֹאַלְנוּ וַאֲשֶׁר חָטָאנוּ.[9]

Chazzan, then congregation:

חָטָאנוּ צוּרֵנוּ, סְלַח לָנוּ יוֹצְרֵנוּ.

סְלִיחָה נד (חטאנו)

IN SOME EDITIONS OF SELICHOS, THE ORDER OF THIS SELICHAH AND THE NEXT IS REVERSED.

All:

יָקְרוּ רֵעֶיךָ*[10] רַב מְחוֹלֵל,   אֱדוֹם לַיהוה וְאֶתְחוֹלֵל,[11]
בְּאוֹיֵב אֲשֶׁר בְּעַמִּי מִסְתּוֹלֵל,   וְעַל זֹאת **יִתְפַּלֵּל.**[12]

יִתְפַּלֵּל כָּל חָסִיד[12] וְיִלְבַּשׁ שַׂקִּים,   לִפְתֹּחַ רַגְלֵי אֲסוּרֵי בְזִקִּים,
וְעַתָּה הִנֵּה עֲבָדֶיךָ לוֹקִים,[13]   וְאֵלּוּ הֵן **הַלּוֹקִין.**[14]

חָטָאנוּ צוּרֵנוּ, סְלַח לָנוּ יוֹצְרֵנוּ.

לוֹקִין וְחוֹבְטִין בְּשׁוֹטִים יְחִידָתִי,   שֻׁקַּי בְּבִכְי מָסַכְתִּי,[15]
מִבּוֹר תַּחְתִּיּוֹת שִׁמְךָ קָרָאתִי,[16]   אַיֵּה אֵפוֹא **תִּקְוָתִי.**[17]

☙ **יָקְרוּ רֵעֶיךָ** — *[How] precious are Your friends.*
This *selichah* is by R' Yoel ben Yitzchak HaLevi
[see prefatory comment to *selichah* 28]. Each
stanza ends with a fragment of either a Scriptural
verse or a Mishnaic passage, the last word of
which is repeated as the first word of the next
stanza. This poetic form, called שִׁרְשׁוּר, *shirshur,*
is found in many of the *chatanu selichos* (see, e.g.,
selichos 41, 85 and 94).

The opening phrase is from *Psalms* 139:17, and
is interpreted by the Talmud (*Sanhedrin* 38b;
Avodah Zarah 5b) as an allusion to R' Akiva and
his colleagues, the עֲשָׂרָה הֲרוּגֵי מַלְכוּת, *Ten*

Martyrs. Numerous *piyutim, kinnos* and *selichos*
have been written about the Ten Martyrs, all of
which seemingly place them as contemporane-
ous. It should be noted, however, that while all ten
of these righteous men were murdered by the
Romans during the Mishnaic period, their execu-
tions did not take place at the same time, nor
could they have, since two of the ten did not even
live in the same generation as the other eight.
Namely, Rabban Shimon ben Gamliel (the only
one mentioned by name in this *piyut*) and Rabbi
Yishmael the *Kohen Gadol* lived before the
Destruction of the Second Temple, and were

זְכוֹר רַחֲמֶיךָ Remember Your mercies, O HASHEM, and Your kindnesses, for they are from the beginning of the world.[1]
Remember us, HASHEM, when You show Your people favor and recall us
with Your salvation.[2] Remember Your congregation that You acquired of
old, that You redeemed the tribe of Your heritage, and this Mount Zion
where You dwelled.[3] Remember, O HASHEM, the affection of Jerusalem,
may You never forget the love of Zion.[4] You will arise and show Zion
mercy, for it is the time to be gracious to her, for the appointed time will
have come.[5] Remember, HASHEM, for the offspring of Edom, the day of
Jerusalem — for those who said: 'Destroy! Destroy to its very foundation!'[6] Remember Abraham, Isaac, and Israel, Your servants, to whom
You swore by Your Being, saying to them, 'I shall increase your offspring
like the stars of the heavens; and this entire land of which I spoke I will
give to your offspring and they will inherit it forever.'[7] Chazzan – Remember for Your servants, for Abraham, for Isaac, and for Jacob; ignore the
stubbornness of this people, its wickedness and its sinfulness.[8]

Chazzan, then congregation:

Please, do not reckon for us a sin,
what we have done foolishly and what we have sinned.[9]

Chazzan, then congregation:

We have erred, our Rock! Forgive us, our Molder!

SELICHAH 54

IN SOME EDITIONS OF SELICHOS, THE ORDER OF THIS SELICHAH AND THE NEXT IS REVERSED.

All:

יָקְרוּ [How] precious are Your friends,*[10] O Master, O Creator!
I remain silent before HASHEM and hope for Him[11]
[to take vengeance] on the enemy that oppresses my people;
About this [let every pious man] pray.[12]
Let every man pious man pray[12] and put on sackcloth
to free the feet of those bound with chains.
As for now, see, Your servants are beaten —[13]
And these are the flogged.[14]

We have sinned, our Rock! Forgive us, our Molder!

Flogged and cudgeled with whips is my one and only.
I mixed my drink with tears.[15]
Out of the nethermost pit I called Your name:[16]
'Where, then, is my hope?'[17]

(1) Psalms 25:6. (2) Cf. 106:4. (3) 74:2. (4) This is not a Scriptural verse. (5) Psalms 102:14.
(6) 137:7. (7) Exodus 32:13. (8) Deuteronomy 9:27. (9) Numbers 12:11. (10) Psalms 139:17.
(11) Cf. 37:7. (12) 32:6. (13) Cf. Exodus 5:16. (14) Mishnah, Makkos 3:1. (15) Cf. Psalms 102:10.
(16) Cf. Lamentations 3:55. (17) Cf. Job 17:15.

---

murdered shortly thereafter, while the others were all killed after the Bar Kochba revolt, more than sixty years later. The liturgical accounts of the martyrdom were not meant as historical records, but as dramatic accounts of the story, in order to evoke feelings of loss and repentance on the part of the congregation.

Their story is included in the Selichos service and in the Mussaf of Yom Kippur (in the piyut titled אֵלֶּה אֶזְכְּרָה, These shall I recall) because the Talmud (Moed Katan 28a) states: 'The death of the righteous atones for the sins of Israel,' and so

תִּקְוָתִי לְשָׁלוֹם וּמֵחֲדָרִים אֵימוֹת,[1] וּפָנַי לֹא הִסְתַּרְתִּי מִכְּלִמּוֹת,[2]
הַצְּבִי יִשְׂרָאֵל עַל בָּמוֹתֶיךָ חָלָל,[3] אֵלּוּ הֵן הָאֲשֵׁמוֹת.[4]
חָטָאנוּ צוּרֵנוּ, סְלַח לָנוּ יוֹצְרֵנוּ.

אֲשֵׁמוֹת עָצְמוּ וְנַחֲלָתְךָ יְעַנּוּ,[5] וְכַצֹּאן לַטֶּבַח נֶחְשַׁבְנוּ,[6]
וְטוּבֵינוּ נִתְפְּשׂוּ בַּעֲוֹנֵינוּ, אֲבָל אֲשֵׁמִים אֲנַחְנוּ עַל אַחֵינוּ.[7]
אַחֵינוּ הַיְּהוּדִים הָאֻמְלָלִים, כֹּל שֻׁפַּךְ דָּמָם כַּגִּלּוּלִים,[8]
וְנִדָּשׁ בְּשָׂרָם אֶת הַקּוֹצִים וְהַחֲרוּלִים,[9] אֵלּוּ הֵן הַנִּסְקָלִין.[10]
חָטָאנוּ צוּרֵנוּ, סְלַח לָנוּ יוֹצְרֵנוּ.

נִסְקָלִין לְעֵינֶיךָ עֲלֻמוֹת עֲלֵי מָוֶת, וְהֵכִין לוֹ אוֹיֵב כְּלֵי מָוֶת,[11]
וַיֹּאמֶר אָכֵן סָר מַר הַמָּוֶת,[12] וְקִוִּינוּ לָאוֹר וְשָׁמָּה לְצַלְמָוֶת.[13]
לְצַלְמָוֶת בִּמְקוֹם חֹשֶׁךְ קוֹלָם מְצַפְצְפִים,*
וּמִקּוֹל הַקּוֹרֵא נָעוּ אֵבָרֵי וּמִתְרוֹפְפִים,
עָמְדוּ בְנִסָּיוֹן וְנִמְצְאוּ צְרוּפִים, אֵלּוּ הֵן הַנִּשְׂרָפִין.[14]
חָטָאנוּ צוּרֵנוּ, סְלַח לָנוּ יוֹצְרֵנוּ.

נִשְׂרָפִין בְּסִפְרֵיהֶן כְּרָכוּם עַל מוֹקְדָם יַחַד,
וְהִקְדִּישׁוּ אֶת קְדוֹשׁ יַעֲקֹב[15] הַמְיֻחָד,
וַיַּעֲנוּ כָל הָעָם קוֹל אֶחָד,[16] וְהוּא בְאֶחָד.*[17]
בְּאֶחָד יָצְאוּ נִשְׁמָתָם רַכִּים וַעֲנֻגִים, וְלָזֶה הַיּוֹם נַפְשׁוֹתָם עוֹרְגִים,
מָסְרוּ עַצְמָם לַחֲרָמִין וּלַהֲרוּגִים, אֵלּוּ הֵן הַנֶּהֱרָגִין.*[18]
חָטָאנוּ צוּרֵנוּ, סְלַח לָנוּ יוֹצְרֵנוּ.

נֶהֱרָגִין רַבּוּ, תַּלְמִיד עִם רַב, נְשָׁכָם נָחָשׁ שָׂרָף וְעַקְרָב,[19]

---

(1) Cf. *Deuteronomy* 32:25. (2) Cf. *Isaiah* 50:6. (3) Cf. *II Samuel* 1:19. (4) A play on the *Mishnah*, *Zevachim* 5:5. (5) *Psalms* 94:5. (6) Cf. 44:23. (7) Cf. *Genesis* 42:21. (8) Cf. *Zephaniah* 1:17. (9) Cf. *Judges* 8:7. (10) *Mishnah, Sanhedrin* 7:4. (11) Cf. *Psalms* 7:14. (12) *I Samuel* 15:32. (13) Cf. *Jeremiah* 13:16. (14) *Mishnah, Sanhedrin* 9:1; *Temurah* 7:5. (15) *Isaiah* 29:23. (16) Cf. *Exodus* 24:3. (17) Cf. *Job* 23:13. (18) Cf. *Mishnah, Sanhedrin* 7:3. (19) *Deuteronomy* 8:15.

on these days we invoke the merit of the martyrs. The Yom Kippur version of this story explains that the death of the Ten Martyrs was an atonement for the sin of the ten sons of Jacob in the sale of Joseph into slavery (see *Genesis* ch. 37). That act sowed the seeds of future dissension and senseless hatred in Israel. But it was not until the Second Temple was destroyed due to שִׂנְאַת חִנָּם, *baseless hatred*, that Israel reaped the bitter fruits of that deed (*Yoma* 9b). Then, after the Temple's destruction, God brought about the death of ten holy martyrs who sanctified His Name in atonement for the sin of the ten brothers, for it was the still-present

influence of their act that continued to prevent their offspring from living in brotherhood and harmony.

The *selichah* does not speak only of the Ten Martyrs, but bewails all those, throughout the generations, who sacrificed their lives עַל קִדּוּשׁ הַשֵּׁם, *in sanctification of God's Name.*

לְצַלְמָוֶת בִּמְקוֹם חֹשֶׁךְ קוֹלָם מְצַפְצְפִים — *'To a death-shadow in the place of darkness!'* the [enemies'] voice twitters [on]. Alternatively: The voice refers to Israel — *Even in the shadow of death, in the place of darkness, their voice twitters [in prayer].*

My hope is for peace, but terror is [even] in my rooms.[1]
I have not hidden my face from humiliation.[2]
Desirous Israel lies dead on the high places[3] —
and these are the result of **our sins**.[4]

                 We have sinned, our Rock! Forgive us, our Molder!

Our sins have grown powerful;
  and they afflict Your heritage-people,[5]
who are reckoned like a flock for slaughtering.[6]
Our best have been seized for our iniquities;
but we are guilty about **our brothers**.[7]
Our brothers, the unfortunate Jews,
 all their blood poured out like dung,[8]
and their flesh is threshed with thorns and thistles[9] —
and these are the **stoned**.[10]

                 We have sinned, our Rock! Forgive us, our Molder!

Stoned before Your eyes are the youthful maidens
  who love You unto [a martyr's] death,
for the enemy has readied his instruments of death.[11]
He said [to us], 'Indeed, the bitterness of death has come!'[12]
We hoped for light, but he turned it **to a death-shadow**.[13]
To a death-shadow in the place of darkness!'
  the [enemies'] voice twitters [on],*
and at the sound of the outcry, my limbs shudder and turn limp.
They withstood the trial and were found pure —
these are the **burnt**.[14]

                 We have sinned, our Rock! Forgive us, our Molder!

Burnt, wrapped in their scrolls, together on their pyre,
they sanctified the Holy One of Jacob,[15] the One and Only.
And all the people answered with one voice,[16]
'He is **One**!'*[17]
At '**One**!' their souls left them, tender and delicate,
and it was for this day that their souls had pined.
They gave themselves over to spoliaters and murderers —
these are the **slain**.[18]

                 We have sinned, our Rock! Forgive us, our Molder!

Slain are so many — disciple with master.
Serpent, viper, and scorpion[19] bit them,

וְהוּא בְּאֶחָד — 'He is One!' That is, as they prepared for their martyrdom, they recited the verse of Shema which ends with the words 'ה אֱחָד, HASHEM is One. And, as the next stanza relates, and as the Talmud (Berachos 61b) states regarding the death of R' Akiva, their souls expired as they pronounced the word אֶחָד. Moreover, when R' Akiva's disciples saw his body being mutilated with iron rakes, and saw him calmly preparing to recite the Shema, they asked him, 'Even this far!' He replied, 'All my life I have longed to fulfill the verse, You shall love HASHEM, your God, with all your heart (Deuteronomy 6:5), which means that one must love God even at the cost of his life. Now that its fulfillment has come into my grasp, shall I not fulfill it?' He then extended his recital of the Shema until his soul departed at the word אֶחָד.

וְדָמָם עַל צְחִיחַ סֶלַע נִתְעָרֵב,[1]   וְנָפַל מִמֶּנּוּ רָב.[2]*

רָב* וְצָעִיר וַאֲנָשִׁים צַדִּיקִים,

הַנְּעִימִים בְּחַיֵּיהֶם וּבְמוֹתָם לֹא פוֹרָקִים,[3]

עָלָךְ מְקַבְּלִים מוּמָתִים תַּשְׁנוּקִים,   אֵלּוּ הֵן הַנֶּחֱנָקִין.[4]

חָטָאנוּ צוּרֵנוּ, סְלַח לָנוּ יוֹצְרֵנוּ.

נֶחֱנָקִין יָצְאוּ לְפָעֳלָם וְלִמְעוֹנָתָם יִרְבָּצוּן,[5]

הָאוֹיֵב מְחָרֵף וּלְשִׁמְךָ יְנַאֲצוּן,

וּמְבַשְּׂרֵי לֹא יִשְׁבָּעוּן[6] וְיִמְחָצוּן,   וְגַם אֶת הַמֵּת יֶחֱצוּן.[7]

יֶחֱצוּן נְתָחִים נְתָחִים אֲמוּלִים,

וּשְׁטָחוּם עֲרֵמִים בְּדָמִים מְגֻלָלִים,

וַיִּלְעֲגוּ לָמוֹ וְאֵין מַכְלִים,[8]   אֵלּוּ הֵן הַגּוֹלִים.[9]

חָטָאנוּ צוּרֵנוּ, סְלַח לָנוּ יוֹצְרֵנוּ.

גּוֹלִים, יִתְנַבְּלוּ לָמוֹ מִדְוָי,   דְּרֹשׁ אֶל הַמֵּתִים* הַנִּקְלָה בְּעֵינָי,

וְנָמוּ הוֹצֵא אֶת הַמְּקַלֵּל[10] שַׁלַּח מֵעַל פָּנָי,

מִי יִתֵּן מוּתֵנוּ בְּיַד יהוה.[11]

יהוה בְּיָדְךָ מִמֵּתִים חֹמֶר וָצֶבוּר,

וְסִדְּרוּ מַעֲרָכוֹת אֵשׁ לְחוֹבַת צִבּוּר,

וְדָמָם לְפָנֶיךָ יְהִי צָבוּר,   אֵלּוּ הֵן חַטֹּאת הַצִּבּוּר.[12]

חָטָאנוּ צוּרֵנוּ, סְלַח לָנוּ יוֹצְרֵנוּ.

צִבּוּר אֵשׁ שָׁלְחוּ בְיָדוֹ לְהַבְדֵּק,

וְלֹא אֵחֲרוּ הַבָּנִים לַקֹּדֶשׁ מִלְּדַקְדֵּק,

וְהוֹצִיאָם מִלִּשְׁכַּת הַטְּלָאִים* בְּלִי בֶדֶק, כִּי שָׁם יִזְבְּחוּ זִבְחֵי צֶדֶק.[13]

צֶדֶק וּמִשְׁפָּט תַּעֲטֶה לִנְקֹם נִקְמָתִי,

כִּי הִשְׁמִידוּ הַיּוֹרֵשׁ וְכִבּוּ גַחַלְתִּי,[14]

לָמָה כְאֹיְבִי נֵצַח אֲנוּשָׁה מַכָּתִי,[15]

וְאֵלּוּ לַעֲבָדִים וְלִשְׁפָחוֹת נִמְכַּרְנוּ הֶחֱרַשְׁתִּי.[16]

חָטָאנוּ צוּרֵנוּ, סְלַח לָנוּ יוֹצְרֵנוּ.

הֶחֱרַשְׁתִּי חֵרֵשׁ וְאוֹיֵב מְנָאֵץ וּמְנַבֵּל,

לִנְטֹשׁ יִרְאָתְךָ וְלֶכֶת אַחֲרֵי הַהֶבֶל,[17]

רָב . . . — *Many, Elder.* The word רָב or רַב can mean *much, many; chief, rabbi, elder,* etc. In the Hebrew, the last word of one stanza is רָב, *many;* the next stanza begins, רָב, *elder.*

דְּרֹשׁ אֶל הַמֵּתִים — *Seek the dead.* An allusion to the heathen practice of consulting the spirits of the dead through black magic, a practice forbidden by the Torah (see *Deuteronomy* 18:11). Some

and their blood mixed as it ran over the dry stones —[1]
and there fell from them **many.***[2]
Elder* and youth and righteous men,
pleasant in their lifetimes and in their death not removing
Your yoke,[3] but accepting it, while being choked to death —
these are the **strangled.**[4]

>   We have sinned, our Rock! Forgive us, our Molder!

Strangled, they went to their deeds' reward
   and reposed in their eternal abode,[5]
while the enemy reviled and blasphemed Your Name.
Still they were not sated with my flesh,[6] and they lashed out again,
and the dead also **they hack to pieces.**[7]
They hack to pieces the unfortunate ones,
and strew them naked, befouled with blood,
mocking them with none to rebuke[8] — these are the **exiled.**[9]

>   We have sinned, our Rock! Forgive us, our Molder!

Exiled, their foes plot against them,
[to make them] seek the dead,* which is worthless in my eyes.
They said, 'Take out the reviler[10] [of our God],
   send him from my presence [to his death]!'
Would only that we could die by the hand of **HASHEM.**[11]
HASHEM, those who died holding Your hand are piled in heaps,
and the perpetrators arranged bonfires to the detriment of the masses.
Then let their blood be gathered before You!
These are [due to] the sins of **the masses.**[12]

>   We have sinned, our Rock! Forgive us, our Molder!

The masses themselves set the fire, to be tested by it,
and the children were not slow to sanctify the Name without question.
The parents brought them out from the Sheep Chamber*
   without reservation,
for there they would offer sacrifices of **righteousness.**[13]
Righteousness and justice may You don, to take vengeance for me,
for they have destroyed the heir and extinguished my ember [of hope].[14]
Why must my pain go on endlessly, my wound be mortal?[15]
If we were sold as servants and handmaidens I would be **silent.**[16]

>   We have sinned, our Rock! Forgive us, our Molder!

Silent and mute have I been while the enemy blasphemed and cursed,
to abandon Your reverence and go after the vanity [of idolatry].[17]

(1) Cf. Ezekiel 24:7. (2) Exodus 19:21. (3) Cf. II Samuel 1:23. (4) Mishnah, Sanhedrin 11:1.
(5) Cf. Psalms 104:22-23. (6) Cf. Job 19:22. (7) Exodus 21:35. (8) Cf. Job 11:3. (9) Mishnah, Makkos
2:1. (10) Leviticus 24:14. (11) Exodus 16:3. (12) Mishnah, Zevachim 5:3. (13) Deuteronomy 33:19.
(14) Cf. II Samuel 14:7. (15) Cf. Jeremiah 15:18. (16) Esther 7:4. (17) Cf. Jeremiah 2:5.

editions of Selichos read אֶל הַמֵּת, the dead [in the singular], and the verse then alludes to the dead god whom the oppressors worship.

מִלִּשְׁכַּת הַטְּלָאִים — From the Sheep Chamber. This was a Temple chamber in which sheep were inspected and sequestered prior to their being brought as the daily tamid-offerings (Arachin 13a). Here the term indicates the parents' lack of hesitation in fulfilling the mitzvah of קִידּוּשׁ הַשֵּׁם, Sanctification of God's Holy Name.

וַיְמָאֵן בְּבֶצַע וְכֹפֶר לְקַבֵּל,   כִּי נֶפֶשׁ הוּא **חוֹבֵל**.[1]

חוֹבֵל בִּקַּע הָרִיּוֹתֵיהֶן בְּטַנְמוֹ,   וְהִכְרִעָנָה יַלְדֵיהֶן תְּפַלֵּחְמוֹ,

וַיֹּאמֶר אַיֵּה אֱלֹהֵימוֹ[2] וּמִיָּדִי יוֹשִׁיעֵמוֹ,[3]

וְאִילּוּ הָאֶחָד שִׁיפּוֹל וְאֵין לַהֲקִימוֹ.[4]

חָטָאנוּ צוּרֵנוּ, סְלַח לָנוּ יוֹצְרֵנוּ.

לַהֲקִימָה קוּמָה עַד מָתַי יְנַאֲצוּנִי,[5]

וְהָיָה כָל מוֹצְאַי יַהַרְגֵנִי,[6]

לָכֵן אֲמָרֵר בִּבְכִי אַל תָּאִיצוּ לְנַחֲמֵנִי,[7]

וְעוֹלַלְתִּי בֶעָפָר קַרְנִי.[8]

קַרְנִי נִגְדְּעָה בְּגוּמִּין אֲשֶׁר כָּרוּ זָרִים,

וּקְבָרוּם חַיִּים בְּנִקְרַת הַצּוּרִים,

וַתְּכַס עֲלֵיהֶם הָאָרֶץ[9] וּמֵתוּ בֵּין הַגְּזָרִים,

אֵלּוּ הֵן **הַנִּקְבָּרִים.**[10]   חָטָאנוּ צוּרֵנוּ, סְלַח לָנוּ יוֹצְרֵנוּ.

נִקְבָּרִין הֲרוּגָה יַעֲלוּ כִּקְטֹרֶת מְתֻקָּן,

לָתֵת לָנוּ מִחְיָה[11] שְׁאֵרִית וּפִרְקָן,

וְיָגֶל אֶבֶן מִבְּאֵרוֹת בְּנֵי יַעֲקָן,[12]

יִשְׂמַח צַדִּיק כִּי חָזָה יוֹם **נָקָם.**[13]

❖ **נָקָם** יָשִׁיב לְצָרָיו[14] אֱדוֹם[15] וְיִשְׁמָעֵאל,

כִּי חִלְּלוּ מִקְדָּשִׁי וְחָבְרוּ רַבָּן שִׁמְעוֹן בֶּן גַּמְלִיאֵל,

אַל תֶּחֱרַשׁ לְדָמָם וְאַל תִּשְׁקֹט אֵל,[16]

נְקֹם נִקְמַת בְּנֵי יִשְׂרָאֵל.[17]   חָטָאנוּ צוּרֵנוּ, סְלַח לָנוּ יוֹצְרֵנוּ.

All:

זְכוֹר לָנוּ בְּרִית אָבוֹת, כַּאֲשֶׁר אָמַרְתָּ: וְזָכַרְתִּי אֶת בְּרִיתִי

יַעֲקוֹב, וְאַף אֶת בְּרִיתִי יִצְחָק, וְאַף אֶת בְּרִיתִי אַבְרָהָם

אֶזְכֹּר, וְהָאָרֶץ אֶזְכֹּר.[18]

סליחה נה (פזמון)

IN SOME EDITIONS OF SELICHOS, THE ORDER OF
THIS AND THE PRECEDING SELICHAH IS REVERSED.
THE ARK IS OPENED.

Chazzan, then congregation:

זְכוֹר בְּרִית אַבְרָהָם* וַעֲקֵדַת יִצְחָק,

וְהָשֵׁב שְׁבוּת אָהֳלֵי יַעֲקֹב,[19] וְהוֹשִׁיעֵנוּ לְמַעַן שְׁמֶךָ.[20]

He refused to take ransom or any payment,
for it is the soul he seeks **to destroy.**[1]
To destroy, *he sundered her gravid women to get at the fetal progeny;*
as they sank to their knees, their babies fell.
Then he said, 'Where is their God?[2]
Let Him save them from my power![3]
But if the One People should fall, then there is none **to raise them.'**[4]
We have sinned, our Rock! Forgive us, our Molder!

To raise them, *arise! How long must they vex me?*[5]
It will be that all who find me will kill me.[6]
Therefore I weep bitterly; do not be quick to comfort me,[7]
for in the dust have I soiled **my strength.**[8]
My strength *was lopped off in the pits that the strangers dug,*
as they buried [our people] alive in the clefts of the rocks.
The earth covered them over,[9] *they died among the corpses —*
these are **the buried.**[10]
We have sinned, our Rock; forgive us, our Molder.

The buried *slain — may they ascend like compounded incense,*
to give us sustenance,[11] *a remnant, and redemption.*
Let the stone be rolled off the well of the suffering people;[12]
let the righteous one rejoice, when he sees the day of **vengeance.**[13]
Chazzan — **Vengeance** *may He repay to His enemies,*[14] *Edom*[15] *and Ishmael,*
for they desecrated my holy [R' Yishmael Kohen Gadol],
and his companion, Rabban Shimon ben Gamliel.
Be not deaf to their blood, be not still, O God![16]
Wreak vengeance for the Children of Israel.[17]
We have sinned, our Rock! Forgive us, our Molder!

All:

זְכוֹר לָנוּ *Remember for us the covenant of the Patriarchs, as You said:*
'And I will remember My covenant with Jacob, and also My
covenant with Isaac, and also My covenant with Abraham will I remem-
ber; and the Land will I remember.'[18]

SELICHAH 55

IN SOME EDITIONS OF SELICHOS, THE ORDER OF
THIS AND THE PRECEDING SELICHAH IS REVERSED.

THE ARK IS OPENED.

Chazzan, then congregation:

זְכוֹר *Remember the covenant of Abraham* and the binding of Isaac.*
O restore the captivity of Jacob's tents,[19] *and save us for Your*
Name's sake.[20]

---

(1) *Deuteronomy* 24:6. (2) Cf. 32:37. (3) Cf. *Isaiah* 37:20. (4) Cf. *Ecclesiastes* 4:10.
(5) Cf. *Numbers* 14:11. (6) *Genesis* 4:14. (7) *Isaiah* 22:4. (8) *Job* 16:15. (9) *Numbers* 16:33.
(10) *Mishnah, Temurah* 7:4. (11) Cf. *Ezra* 9:9. (12) Cf. *Genesis* 29:10; *Deuteronomy* 10:6.
(13) Cf. *Psalms* 58:11. (14) Cf. *Deuteronomy* 32:41. (15) Some editions read אֲרָם, *Aram,*
a commonly used substitute for Edom, to appease the censors. (16) Cf. *Psalms* 83:2.
(17) *Numbers* 31:2. (18) *Leviticus* 26:42. (19) Cf. *Jeremiah* 30:18. (20) Cf. *Psalms* 106:8.

Congregation, then *chazzan:*

אֲשַׁמְתָּנוּ כִּי רַבָּה,*[1]   בֵּית מִקְדָּשֵׁנוּ[2] לְחוֹבָה,

בָּגַדְנוּ בְּיִתְרָה חִבָּה,   וַתְּהִי לְהֶפֶךְ סִבָּה.

וְשׁוּב בְּרַחֲמִים עַל שְׁאֵרִית יִשְׂרָאֵל, וְהוֹשִׁיעֵנוּ לְמַעַן שְׁמֶךָ.

Congregation, then *chazzan:*

פְּעֻלַּת רִאשׁוֹנִים חֲסִידֶיךָ,   זְכוֹר עֹז יְדִידֶיךָ,

צַוֵּה יְשׁוּעַת עֲבָדֶיךָ,   גַּלֵּה כָּמוּס סוֹדֶיךָ.

וְהָשֵׁב שְׁבוּת אָהֳלֵי יַעֲקֹב, וְהוֹשִׁיעֵנוּ לְמַעַן שְׁמֶךָ.

Congregation, then *chazzan:*

קָשַׁרְנוּ בְּאַחֲוָה וְתוֹפֶל,   וְלִמְאֹד שִׂיחֵנוּ שָׁפֵל,

רָם, הֲקִימֵנוּ מִנֹּפֶל,   וְתוֹצִיא לָאוֹר מֵאֹפֶל.

וְשׁוּב בְּרַחֲמִים עַל שְׁאֵרִית יִשְׂרָאֵל, וְהוֹשִׁיעֵנוּ לְמַעַן שְׁמֶךָ.

Congregation then *chazzan:*

שֶׁטֶף אֵשׁ וְלֶהָבָה,   לְהַשְׁבִּית נוֹגֵשׂ וּמַדְהֵבָה,[3]

מִצַּר עֲזַרְתֵּנוּ הָבָה,[4]   הָקִיצָה לְעוֹרֵר אַהֲבָה.

וְהָשֵׁב שְׁבוּת אָהֳלֵי יַעֲקֹב, וְהוֹשִׁיעֵנוּ לְמַעַן שְׁמֶךָ.

Congregation, then *chazzan:*

חַי לֹא יִישָׁן,   זְכֹר עֲדַת שׁוֹשָׁן,

קוּמָה כְּחִק הַיָּשָׁן,   וְיָפוּצוּ אוֹיְבֶיךָ[5] כְּעָשָׁן.

וְשׁוּב בְּרַחֲמִים עַל שְׁאֵרִית יִשְׂרָאֵל, וְהוֹשִׁיעֵנוּ לְמַעַן שְׁמֶךָ.

Congregation, then *chazzan:*

גּוֹאֵל חָזָק לְמַעַנְךָ פְּדֵנוּ,   רְאֵה כִּי אָזְלַת יָדֵנוּ,[6]

שׁוּר כִּי אָבְדוּ חֲסִידֵינוּ,[7]   מַפְגִּיעַ אֵין בַּעֲדֵנוּ.[8]

וְהָשֵׁב שְׁבוּת אָהֳלֵי יַעֲקֹב, וְהוֹשִׁיעֵנוּ לְמַעַן שְׁמֶךָ.

Congregation, then *chazzan:*

בְּרִית אָבוֹת וְאִמָּהוֹת וְהַשְּׁבָטִים,

רַחֲמֶיךָ וַחֲסָדֶיךָ בְּרֻבּוֹת עִתִּים,[9]

אֲשַׁמְתָּנוּ כִּי רַבָּה ❧ — *Because of our great guilt.* This *selichah* is condensed from a much longer one that contained the complete alphabet in the acrostic, followed by the composer's signature — שְׁלֹמֹה חֲזָק, *Shlomo, may he be strong.* Of the original work, only the verses beginning with א,ב,פ,צ,ק,ר and the author's name have been retained. Because of its similarity to *selichah* 42 (from where it borrows its double refrain), three stanzas of that *piyut* have been appended here. Ironically, they are the stanzas which bear the signature of that *selichah's* composer in their acrostic. For this reason, some editions mistakenly ascribe this work to R' Gershom bar Yehudah.

Congregation, then *chazzan:*

א *Because of our great guilt,*[*1]
   our Holy Temple[2] *was taken away in payment.*

ב *We betrayed God's great love for us,*
   and so it was turned into its opposite.

> O *return with mercy to the remnant of Israel,*
>   *and save us for Your Name's sake.*

Congregation, then *chazzan:*

ס *The accomplishments of Your ancient pious ones,*
   remember Your powerful beloved ones.

צ *Command the salvation of Your servants,*
   reveal the hidden secret [about when redemption will come].

> O *restore the captivity of Jacob's tents,*
>   *and save us for Your Name's sake.*

Congregation, then *chazzan:*

ק *We bound ourselves in a brotherhood of falsehood,*
   and our prayers are utterly debased.

ר *Lofty One, stand us up erect from our lowliness,*
   and bring us out into the light from the darkness.

> O *return with mercy to the remnant of Israel,*
>   *and save us for Your Name's sake.*

Congregation, then *chazzan:*

ש *[Pour] a stream of fire and flame,*

ל *to destroy oppressor and tormentor.*[3]

מ *Bring us help from distress;*[4]

ה *Awake, to arouse love!*   O *restore the captivity of Jacob's tents,*
                            and save us for Your Name's sake.

Congregation, then *chazzan:*

ח O *Living One, who sleeps not,*

ז *Remember the rose-like congregation.*

ק *Arise as You once used to,*
   and let Your enemies disperse[5] *like smoke.*

> O *return with mercy to the remnant of Israel,*
>   *and save us for Your Name's sake.*

Congregation, then *chazzan:*

ג O *mighty Redeemer, deliver us for Your sake!*

ר *See how our strength has left [us],*[6]

ש *look how our pious ones have been lost;*[7]

מ *so that there is no one to pray for us.*[8]

> O *restore the captivity of Jacob's tents,*
>   *and save us for Your Name's sake.*

ב *The covenant of the Patriarchs, the Matriarchs, and Tribes;*

ר *your mercy and kindness so many times given;*[9] —

---

(1) *II Chronicles* 28:13. (2) Some editions read בֵּית תִּפְאַרְתֵּנוּ, *the House of our splendor,*
a reference to the Holy Temple. (3) Cf. *Isaiah* 14:4; see commentary to *selichah* 12.
(4) Cf. *Psalms* 60:13. (5) Cf. *Numbers* 10:35. (6) Cf. *Deuteronomy* 32:36. (7) Cf. *Micah* 7:2.
(8) Cf. *Isaiah* 59:16. (9) Cf. *Nehemiah* 9:28.

יָהּ זְכֹר לְמֻכִּים וְנִמְרָטִים,¹ וְעָלֶיךָ כָּל הַיּוֹם נֶחְשָׁטִים.² וְשׁוּב בְּרַחֲמִים עַל שְׁאֵרִית יִשְׂרָאֵל, וְהוֹשִׁיעֵנוּ לְמַעַן שְׁמֶךָ.

Congregation, then *chazzan:*

דּוֹרֵשׁ דָּמִים³ דּוֹן דִּינֵנוּ, הָשֵׁב שִׁבְעָתַיִם אֶל חֵיק מְעַנֵּינוּ,⁴ חִנָּם נִמְכַּרְנוּ, וְלֹא בְכֶסֶף פְּדֵנוּ,⁵ זְקֹף בֵּית מִקְדָּשְׁךָ⁶ הַשָּׁמֵם לְעֵינֵינוּ. וְהָשֵׁב שְׁבוּת אָהֳלֵי יַעֲקֹב, וְהוֹשִׁיעֵנוּ לְמַעַן שְׁמֶךָ.

THE ARK IS CLOSED.

All:

זְכֹר לָנוּ בְּרִית רִאשׁוֹנִים כַּאֲשֶׁר אָמַרְתָּ, וְזָכַרְתִּי לָהֶם בְּרִית רִאשׁוֹנִים, אֲשֶׁר הוֹצֵאתִי אוֹתָם מֵאֶרֶץ מִצְרַיִם לְעֵינֵי הַגּוֹיִם, לִהְיוֹת לָהֶם לֵאלֹהִים אֲנִי יהוה.⁷

סליחה נו (שמע ישראל)

שְׁמַע יִשְׂרָאֵל, יהוה אֱלֹהֵינוּ, יהוה אֶחָד.⁸

אֶחָד צוּרִי* בְּרוֹב הוֹדָאוֹת, בִּלְתּוֹ אֶפֶס מַפְלִיא פְּלָאוֹת, גְּבוּרָתוֹ אֲשַׁגֵּן בְּעֹז נוֹרָאוֹת, (לְהִשְׁתַּחֲוֹת) לְמֶלֶךְ יהוה צְבָאוֹת.⁹ דַּרְכּוֹ סוּפָה וּבִסְעָרָה הֲלִיכָתוֹ,¹⁰ הַמֵּאִיר לָעוֹלָם וְחֹשֶׁךְ סִבְּתוֹ,¹¹ וְכָל מְשָׁרְתָיו זְרִיזִים בִּמְלַאכְתּוֹ, בָּרוּךְ שֵׁם כְּבוֹד מַלְכוּתוֹ.

שְׁמַע יִשְׂרָאֵל, יהוה אֱלֹהֵינוּ, יהוה אֶחָד.

זְוָעוֹת וּזְקִים וּרְעָמִים, חָשִׁים וְרָצִים לְהַלְּלוֹ בַּנְּעִימִים, טָהוֹר מַרְעִישׁ עוֹלָם בִּזְעָמִים, יהוה מָלָךְ יִרְגְּזוּ עַמִּים.¹² יְרוֹפְפוּ עַמּוּדֵי שָׁמַיִם וְתָמוּהִים,¹³ כּוֹכָבִים וּמַזָּלוֹת וּצְבָאוֹת נְגוֹהִים, לְפָנָיו בּוֹרְכִים רַבִּים וּגְבוֹהִים, כִּי מֶלֶךְ כָּל הָאָרֶץ אֱלֹהִים.¹⁴

שְׁמַע יִשְׂרָאֵל, יהוה אֱלֹהֵינוּ, יהוה אֶחָד.

אֶחָד צוּרִי — *I shall affirm my Rock's Oneness.* The acrostic of the first three lines of the respective stanzas in this *piyut* form the *aleph-beis,* followed by the composer's signature — יוֹסֵף בַּר שְׁמוּאֵל חָזָק, *Yosef bar Shmuel, may he be strong.* However, most editions omit two of the stanzas that contain part of the signature — סברשמ — leading some to identify the composer as יוֹאֵל, *Yoel.* In this edition those stanzas have been inserted in parentheses. The fourth line of each stanza is a Scriptural fragment that contains some

form of the root מלך, such as *king, kingdom, reign.*

Also known as R' Yosef Tuv Elem, the composer was an excellent and punctilious scribe, author and editor of various works on *halachah,* a prolific *paytan* (more than seventy of his *piyutim* are extant), and leader of the Jewish communities of Limoges and Anjou, France, early in the eleventh century. Of special importance is his *yotzer* for *Shabbos HaGadol* (the Sabbath before Pesach), a halachic-liturgical work quoted extensively by *Tosafos.*

י remember [all this,] O God, on behalf of the beaten and torn,[1]

ו who are slaughtered for Your sake all the time.[2]

O return with mercy to the remnant of Israel,
and save us for Your Name's sake.

Congregation, then *chazzan*:

ר Avenger of Blood,[3] judge our cause!

ה Pay back our tormentors sevenfold into their bosom.[4]

ח We were sold [into Exile] for naught; so redeem us, but not with money,[5]

ז erect Your desolate Holy Temple[6] before our eyes.

O restore the captivity of Jacob's tents,
and save us for Your Name's sake.

THE ARK IS CLOSED.

All:

זְכוֹר לָנוּ Remember for us the covenant of the ancestors, as You said:
'And I will remember for them the covenant of the ancestors
whom I brought out of the land of Egypt in the very sight of the nations,
to be a God to them; I am HASHEM.'[7]

SELICHAH 56

Hear, O Israel, HASHEM is our God, HASHEM is the One and Only![8]

א I shall affirm my Rock's Oneness* with abundant thanks.

ב Other than Him there is none who works wonders.

ג I shall speak clearly of His might, powerfully of [His] awesome deeds.
[and bow] to the **King**, HASHEM, Master of Legions.[9]

ד His path is the tempest and His going is in storm,[10]

ה He gives light to the world,
but His dwelling is [hidden, as if] in darkness.[11]

ו And all His ministering angels are alacritous in His mission.
Blessed is the Name of His glorious **kingdom**.
Hear, O Israel, HASHEM is our God, HASHEM is the One and Only!

ז Earthquakes, shooting stars and thunderbolts

ח hurry and run to praise Him in pleasant song,

ט [for He is] the Pure One Who shakes the world in times of fury,
when all [mankind] will acknowledge HASHEM as **King**,
the peoples shall tremble.[12]

י The pillars of Heaven quake in bewilderment,[13]

כ stars, constellations and radiant hosts,

ל before Him the many and the exalted bend their knee,
for God is **King** of all the earth.[14]
Hear, O Israel, HASHEM is our God, HASHEM is the One and Only!

---

(1) Cf. *Nehemiah* 13:25. (2) Cf. *Psalms* 44:23. (3) 9:13. (4). Cf. 79:12; in some editions of *Selichos* this line is omitted. (5) Cf. *Isaiah* 52:3; see commentary to *selichah* 9, s.v., לְמְכוּרֵי חִנָּם. (6) Cf. *Daniel* 9:17. (7) *Leviticus* 26:45. (8) *Deuteronomy* 6:4. (9) *Zechariah* 14:16; the interpolated word appears both in the Scriptural verse and in manuscript editions of *Selichos*. (10) Cf. *Nahum* 1:3. (11) Cf. *II Samuel* 22:12. (12) *Psalms* 99:1. (13) Cf. *Job* 26:11. (14) *Psalms* 47:8.

מוֹשֵׁל עוֹלָם מוֹחֵץ וְחוֹבֵשׁ,   **נוֹצֵר חֶסֶד**[1] עֲוֹנוֹת כּוֹבֵשׁ,[2]

סוֹפֵר צְעָדִים[3] יַמִּים מְיַבֵּשׁ,[4]   יהוה **מֶלֶךְ** גֵּאוּת לָבֵשׁ.[5]

עוֹלָם חֲמֵשׁ מֵאוֹת מַהֲלָךְ,*   **פּוֹחֲדִים** וְרוֹתְתִים מִפְּנֵי נָפֶלֶךְ,

צָעַד בְּרַעַד מִשְׁתַּחֲוִים לַמֶּלֶךְ,   וְיֹאמְרוּ בָעַמִּים יהוה **מֶלֶךְ**.[6]

שְׁמַע יִשְׂרָאֵל, יהוה אֱלֹהֵינוּ, יהוה אֶחָד.

קוֹלִי אֶתֵּן בְּכָל עֶדְנִי,   **רוֹמְמוֹת** אֵל לְצַלְצֵל בְּעָדוֹנִי,

שׁוֹמְרֵי עֵדוּת וְיוֹדְעֵי דִינִי,   הָרִיעוּ לִפְנֵי **הַמֶּלֶךְ** יהוה.[7]

תַּקִּיף מִפַּעֲנֵחַ נֶעְלָמִים,   **יָחִיד** וּמְיֻחָד נֶחֱלָמִים,

וּמַעֲרִיצִים תְּקֶף יְשִׁישִׁים וְעוֹלָמִים,

מַלְכוּתְךָ **מַלְכוּת** כָּל עוֹלָמִים.[8]

שְׁמַע יִשְׂרָאֵל, יהוה אֱלֹהֵינוּ, יהוה אֶחָד.

(סִירִים סְבוּכִים כּוֹרְעִים לַמֶּלֶךְ,   **פִּימוֹ** יִסָּכֵר כַּסּוּחָה לְהַשְׁלֵךְ,

בִּקְדוֹשָׁיו יְהָדַר חוּג מִתְהַלֵּךְ,[9]   **הֵן** לְצֶדֶק יִמְלָךְ **מֶלֶךְ**.[10]

רַבּוּ פְּלָאֶיךָ וְעָצְמוּ בַּסְּגוּיִים,   **שִׁבְחֲךָ** הוֹפַעְתָּ בִּקְהַל דְּגוּיִים,[11]

מְעִידִים יִחוּדְךָ בְּדָתְךָ הַגּוּיִים,   מִי לֹא יִרָאֲךָ **מֶלֶךְ** הַגּוֹיִם.[12]

שְׁמַע יִשְׂרָאֵל, יהוה אֱלֹהֵינוּ, יהוה אֶחָד.)

וָתִיק מְרוֹמִים מְהֻדָּר בִּזְבוּלָךְ,   **אָתָנוּ** לְפָנֶיךָ לְהַזְכִּיר גָּדְלָךְ,

לְמַעַנְךָ רַחֵם וּגְאוֹל קְהָלָךְ,   יהוה מֶלֶךְ, יהוה **מָלָךְ**.

❖ **חֵי** עוֹלָמִים תּוֹמֵךְ וְסוֹעֵד,   **זְרוֹעֵנוּ** תְּאַמֵּץ בְּלִי לְהַמְעֵד,

קַבֵּץ קוֹרֶיךָ עֲדָתְךָ וּבָם תִּנָּעֵד,   יהוה **יִמְלֹךְ** לְעֹלָם וָעֶד.[13]

שְׁמַע יִשְׂרָאֵל, יהוה אֱלֹהֵינוּ, יהוה אֶחָד.

All:

עֲשֵׂה עִמָּנוּ כְּמָה שֶׁהִבְטַחְתָּנוּ: וְאַף גַּם זֹאת בִּהְיוֹתָם בְּאֶרֶץ
אֹיְבֵיהֶם, לֹא מְאַסְתִּים וְלֹא גְעַלְתִּים לְכַלֹּתָם
לְהָפֵר בְּרִיתִי אִתָּם, כִּי אֲנִי יהוה אֱלֹהֵיהֶם.[14] הִמָּצֵא לָנוּ בְּבַקָּשָׁתֵנוּ,
כְּמָה שֶׁכָּתוּב: וּבִקַּשְׁתֶּם מִשָּׁם אֶת יהוה אֱלֹהֶיךָ וּמָצָאתָ, כִּי
תִדְרְשֶׁנּוּ בְּכָל לְבָבְךָ וּבְכָל נַפְשֶׁךָ.[15] מוֹל אֶת לְבָבֵנוּ לְאַהֲבָה וּלְיִרְאָה
אֶת שְׁמֶךָ, כְּמָה שֶׁכָּתוּב: וּמָל יהוה אֱלֹהֶיךָ אֶת לְבָבְךָ וְאֶת לְבַב

---

(1) *Exodus* 34:7. (2) *Cf. Micah* 7:19. (3) *Cf. Job* 14:16. (4) *Cf. Nahum* 1:4. (5) *Psalms* 93:1.
(6) *Cf. I Chronicles* 16:31. (7) *Psalms* 98:6. (8) 145:13. (9) *Cf. Job* 22:14. (10) *Isaiah* 32:1. (11) See
Genesis 48:16. (12) *Jeremiah* 10:7. (13) *Exodus* 15:18. (14) *Leviticus* 26:44. (15) *Deuteronomy* 4:29.

חֲמֵשׁ מֵאוֹת מַהֲלָךְ — *A five-hundred[-year] jour-*
ney. The Talmud teaches that a five-hundred-

year journey separates heaven from earth
(*Chagigah* 13a).

מ Ruler of the world, Smiter and Healer,

נ Preserver of kindness[1] and Queller of iniquities,[2]

ס Counter of footsteps,[3] all our steps, Who dries up the seas —[4]
when all [mankind] will acknowledge HASHEM as **King**,
> He will have donned grandeur.[5]

ע In the universe, a five-hundred[-year] journey,*

פ [the inhabitants] fear and quiver in every sector.

צ Stepping forward atremble, they bow to the King,
and it is said among the nations, 'HASHEM is **King!**[6]
> Hear, O Israel, HASHEM is our God, HASHEM is the One and Only!

ק I shall give forth my voice through all of my days,

ר to ring out God's exaltedness, in my delight.

ש Keepers of the Testimony, knowers of my laws,
blow [the shofar] before the **King**, HASHEM![7]

ת O Forceful One Who unravels mysteries,

י 'the One,' 'the Only' are fitting [titles for You alone.]

ו Old and young revere You with [all their] strength [saying],
'Your **kingdom** is a **kingdom** spanning all eternities.'[8]
> Hear, O Israel, HASHEM is our God, HASHEM is the One and Only!

ס The tangled thorns kneel to the Molech,

פ stop up their mouths, cast them away like dung.

ב He is glorified by His holy angels that move in [their] circuit,[9]
behold, the **King** shall reign in righteousness.[10]

ר Numerous are Your marvels and powerfully eminent.

ש You have shone Your praise on the fish-like[11] congregation [of Israel],

מ they testify to Your Oneness, they pore over Your Law.
Who would not fear You, O **King** of the nations?[12]
> Hear, O Israel, HASHEM is our God, HASHEM is the One and Only!)

ו All-worthy One in the heights, glorified in Your dwelling,

א we have come before You to declare Your greatness.

ל For Your own sake have mercy and redeem Your congregation —
HASHEM Who **reigns**, HASHEM Who has **reigned.**

ח Chazzan — Eternally Living, Supporter and Helper,

ו strengthen our arms that we may not falter.

ק Gather those who hope for You, Your flock, and meet with them —
[for You] HASHEM shall **reign** forever and ever.[13]
> Hear, O Israel, HASHEM is our God, HASHEM is the One And Only!

All:

עֲשֵׂה עִמָּנוּ Do with us as You promised us: 'And despite all that,
when they will be in the land of their enemies, I will not
have despised them nor abhorred them to destroy them, to annul My
covenant with them, for I am HASHEM their God.'[14] Be accessible to us
in our quest, as it is written: From there you will seek HASHEM, your
God, and you will find, when you search for Him with all your heart
and with all your soul.[15] Expose our hearts to love Your Name, as it
is written: HASHEM, your God, will expose your heart and the heart of

זַרְעֶךָ, לְאַהֲבָה אֶת יהוה אֱלֹהֶיךָ בְּכָל לְבָבְךָ וּבְכָל נַפְשְׁךָ, לְמַעַן חַיֶּיךָ.[1] וְזָרַקְתִּי עֲלֵיכֶם מַיִם טְהוֹרִים וּטְהַרְתֶּם, מִכֹּל טֻמְאוֹתֵיכֶם וּמִכָּל גִּלּוּלֵיכֶם אֲטַהֵר אֶתְכֶם.[2] מָחִיתִי כָעָב פְּשָׁעֶיךָ וְכֶעָנָן חַטֹּאותֶיךָ, שׁוּבָה אֵלַי כִּי גְאַלְתִּיךָ.[3] מֹחֶה פְשָׁעֶיךָ וְכֶעָנָן חַטֹּאתֶיךָ, כַּאֲשֶׁר אָמָרְתָּ: אָנֹכִי אָנֹכִי הוּא מֹחֶה פְשָׁעֶיךָ לְמַעֲנִי, וְחַטֹּאתֶיךָ לֹא אֶזְכֹּר.[4] הֲלָבֵן חֲטָאֵינוּ כַּשֶּׁלֶג וְכַצֶּמֶר, כְּמָה שֶׁכָּתוּב: לְכוּ נָא וְנִוָּכְחָה, יֹאמַר יהוה, אִם יִהְיוּ חֲטָאֵיכֶם כַּשָּׁנִים, כַּשֶּׁלֶג יַלְבִּינוּ, אִם יַאְדִּימוּ כַתּוֹלָע, כַּצֶּמֶר יִהְיוּ.[5] רַחֵם עָלֵינוּ וְאַל תַּשְׁחִיתֵנוּ, כְּמָה שֶׁכָּתוּב: כִּי אֵל רַחוּם יהוה אֱלֹהֶיךָ, לֹא יַרְפְּךָ וְלֹא יַשְׁחִיתֶךָ וְלֹא יִשְׁכַּח אֶת בְּרִית אֲבֹתֶיךָ אֲשֶׁר נִשְׁבַּע לָהֶם.[6] קַבֵּץ נִדָּחֵינוּ כְּמָה שֶׁכָּתוּב: אִם יִהְיֶה נִדַּחֲךָ בִּקְצֵה הַשָּׁמָיִם, מִשָּׁם יְקַבֶּצְךָ יהוה אֱלֹהֶיךָ וּמִשָּׁם יִקָּחֶךָ.[7] הָשֵׁב שְׁבוּתֵנוּ וְרַחֲמֵנוּ, כְּמָה שֶׁכָּתוּב: וְשָׁב יהוה אֱלֹהֶיךָ אֶת שְׁבוּתְךָ וְרִחֲמֶךָ וְשָׁב וְקִבֶּצְךָ מִכָּל הָעַמִּים אֲשֶׁר הֱפִיצְךָ יהוה אֱלֹהֶיךָ שָׁמָּה.[8] ❖ תְּבִיאֵנוּ אֶל הַר קָדְשֶׁךָ, וְשַׂמְּחֵנוּ בְּבֵית תְּפִלָּתֶךָ, כְּמָה שֶׁכָּתוּב: וַהֲבִיאוֹתִים אֶל הַר קָדְשִׁי, וְשִׂמַּחְתִּים בְּבֵית תְּפִלָּתִי, עוֹלֹתֵיהֶם וְזִבְחֵיהֶם לְרָצוֹן עַל מִזְבְּחִי, כִּי בֵיתִי בֵּית תְּפִלָּה יִקָּרֵא לְכָל הָעַמִּים.[9]

THE ARK IS OPENED.

The first four verses of the following prayer are recited responsively; *chazzan*, then congregation:

שְׁמַע קוֹלֵנוּ יהוה אֱלֹהֵינוּ, חוּס וְרַחֵם עָלֵינוּ, וְקַבֵּל בְּרַחֲמִים וּבְרָצוֹן אֶת תְּפִלָּתֵנוּ.[10]

הֲשִׁיבֵנוּ יהוה אֵלֶיךָ וְנָשׁוּבָה, חַדֵּשׁ יָמֵינוּ כְּקֶדֶם.[11]

אַל תַּשְׁלִיכֵנוּ מִלְּפָנֶיךָ, וְרוּחַ קָדְשְׁךָ אַל תִּקַּח מִמֶּנּוּ.[12]

אַל תַּשְׁלִיכֵנוּ לְעֵת זִקְנָה, כִּכְלוֹת כֹּחֵנוּ אַל תַּעַזְבֵנוּ.[13]

אַל תַּעַזְבֵנוּ יהוה, אֱלֹהֵינוּ אַל תִּרְחַק מִמֶּנּוּ.[14]

עֲשֵׂה עִמָּנוּ אוֹת לְטוֹבָה, וְיִרְאוּ שׂוֹנְאֵינוּ וְיֵבֹשׁוּ, כִּי אַתָּה יהוה עֲזַרְתָּנוּ וְנִחַמְתָּנוּ.[15]

אֲמָרֵינוּ הַאֲזִינָה יהוה, בִּינָה הֲגִיגֵנוּ.[16]

יִהְיוּ לְרָצוֹן אִמְרֵי פִינוּ וְהֶגְיוֹן לִבֵּנוּ לְפָנֶיךָ, יהוה צוּרֵנוּ וְגוֹאֲלֵנוּ.[17]

כִּי לְךָ יהוה הוֹחָלְנוּ, אַתָּה תַעֲנֶה אֲדֹנָי אֱלֹהֵינוּ.[18]

THE ARK IS CLOSED.

your offspring, to love HASHEM, your God, with all your heart and with all your soul, that you may live.[1] *Pour pure water upon us and purify us, as it is written: I shall pour pure water upon you and purify you, of all your contaminations and of all your abominations I will purify you.*[2] *Wipe away our willful sins like a cloud and like a mist, as it is written: I have wiped away your willful sins like a cloud and your errors like a mist — repent to Me, for I have redeemed you!*[3] *Wipe away our willful sins for Your sake, as You said: 'I, only I, am the One Who wipes away your willful sins for My sake, and I shall not recall your errors.'*[4] *Whiten our errors like snow and like [pure white] wool, as it is written: 'Come now, let us reason together,' says HASHEM, 'though your errors will be like scarlet, they will become white as snow; though they will be red as crimson, they will become like [white] wool.'*[5] *Have mercy on us and do not destroy us, as it is written: For a merciful God is HASHEM, your God; He will not surrender you nor destroy you, and He will not forget the covenant with your forefathers, which He swore to them.*[6] *Gather in our dispersed ones, as it is written: If your dispersed were to be at the ends of heaven, from there HASHEM, your God, will gather you in and from there He will take you.*[7] *Bring back our captivity and have mercy on us, as it is written: HASHEM, your God, will bring back your captivity and have mercy on you, and He will again gather you in from all the peoples where HASHEM, your God, has scattered you.*[8]

Chazzan — *Bring us to Your holy mountain and gladden us in Your house of prayer, as it is written: And I will bring them to My holy mountain, and I will gladden them in My house of prayer, their elevation-offerings and their feast offering will find favor on My Altar, for My House will be called a house of prayer, for all peoples.*[9]

THE ARK IS OPENED.

The first four verses of the following prayer are recited responsively; *chazzan*, then congregation:

שְׁמַע *Hear our voice, HASHEM, our God, pity and be compassionate to us, and accept — with compassion and favor — our prayer.*[10]

Bring us back to You, HASHEM, and we shall return, renew our days as of old.[11]

Do not cast us away from Yourself, and do not remove Your holy spirit from us.[12]

Do not cast us away in old age, when our strength gives out do not forsake us.[13]

Do not forsake us, HASHEM, our God, be not distant from us.[14]

Display for us a sign for good, so that our enemies may see it and be ashamed, for You, HASHEM, will have helped and consoled us.[15]

To our sayings give ear, HASHEM, perceive our thoughts.[16]

May the expressions of our mouth and the thoughts of our heart find favor before You, HASHEM, our Rock and our Redeemer.[17]

Because for You, HASHEM, we waited, You will answer, my Lord, our God.[18]

THE ARK IS CLOSED.

---

(1) *Deuteronomy* 30:6. (2) *Ezekiel* 36:25. (3) *Isaiah* 44:22. (4) 43:25. (5) 1:18. (6) *Deuteronomy* 4:31. (7) 30:4. (8) 30:3. (9) *Isaiah* 56:7. (10) Weekday *Shemoneh Esrei*. (11) *Lamentations* 5:21. (12) Cf. *Psalms* 51:13. (13) Cf. 71:9. (14) Cf. 38:22. (15) Cf. 86:17. (16) Cf. 5:2. (17) Cf. 19:15. (18) Cf. 38:16.

סליחה נז (תוכחה)

All:

יַעֲזֹב רָשָׁע נְתִיבוֹ,* וְיַכְנִיעַ רוּם לְבָבוֹ,

וְיָשֹׁב אֶל יהוה וִירַחֲמֵהוּ בְּשׁוּבוֹ,[1]

בְּטֶרֶם יִסָּפֶה אוֹ יוֹמוֹ יָבוֹא.[2]

עֲזָב נָא בֶן אָדָם עֲזָב נָא –

עֲזֹב שֶׁמֶץ וְדִבָּה,   בְּטֶרֶם תִּתְעוֹפֵף, כַּיּוֹנִים אֶל אֲרֻבָּה,[3]

וְהַנּוֹשֶׁה בָּא לָקַחַת הָעֲרֵבָה,   לָכֵן שׁוּב וּזְכֹר אֶת הַיּוֹם הַבָּא,

כִּי הַיּוֹם קָצֵר וְהַמְּלָאכָה מְרֻבָּה.[4]   מִי יִתֵּן אֶל לִבּוֹ,

בְּטֶרֶם יִסָּפֶה אוֹ יוֹמוֹ יָבוֹא.

עֲזָב נָא בֶן אָדָם עֲזָב נָא –

עֲזֹב הַבְלֵי הָעוֹלָם הַזֶּה וְהַרְחֵק,

כִּי מָחָר תִּבְכֶּה, מֵאֲשֶׁר בּוֹ הַיּוֹם תִּשְׂחָק,

וּבִכְתָב אִישׁ יְרִיבֶךָ, כְּתָבְךָ[5] לֹא יִמָּחֵק,

וְלֹא יוֹעִיל מַתָּן, וְלֹא שְׁחַד בַּחֵק,[6]

וְהַפּוֹעֲלִים עֲצֵלִים, וּבַעַל הַבַּיִת דּוֹחֵק,[7]

אִישׁ הָרִיב נִגָּשׁ, וְגַם נִצָּב לָרִיבוֹ,   **בְּטֶרֶם יִסָּפֶה אוֹ יוֹמוֹ יָבוֹא.**

עֲזָב נָא בֶן אָדָם עֲזָב נָא –

עֲזֹב יְקָר עוֹלָם נוֹדֵד נָדוֹד,   כִּי עָרוּךְ תָּפְתֶּה,[8] בְּכָל לַהַב וְכִידוֹד,*[9]

זְכָר נָא אַחֲרִיתְךָ, בְּעֵת תּוּשַׁד שָׁדוֹד,[10]

כִּי כָל אָח יֹאמַר הֶאָח, וְכָל דּוֹד יָדוֹד,[11]

לָכֵן שׁוּב, וְהַתְקֵן עַצְמְךָ בַּפְּרוֹזְדוֹד[12]

כְּדֵי שֶׁתִּכָּנֵס לַטְּרַקְלִין   וְטוּבוֹ,   **בְּטֶרֶם יִסָּפֶה אוֹ יוֹמוֹ יָבוֹא.**

עֲזָב נָא בֶן אָדָם עֲזָב נָא –

עֲזֹב יֵצֶר אֶת אֲשֶׁר נַפְשְׁךָ אוֹהֶבֶת,

וְתֹאמַר נַפְשִׁי מוּטָב שֶׁתִּהְיִי כּוֹאֶבֶת,

מִשֶּׁתִּחְפְּצִי מִבּוֹר אַחֵר שׁוֹאֶבֶת,*

---

§ **יַעֲזֹב רָשָׁע נְתִיבוֹ** — *Let the wicked one forsake his path.* Based on the verse, *Let the wicked one forsake his way, the man of evil his thoughts; let him return to* HASHEM *Who will have mercy on him . . .* (Isaiah 55:7), which is read during the *haftarah* of *Minchah* on fast days, this anonymous *piyut* is of the genre known as תוֹכָחָה

[*tochachah*], *reproach* or *rebuke.* Unlike the *selichah* which places the burden of forgiveness on God's mercy, compassion and grace, the *tochahah* puts the burden on man. If you want to be forgiven, repent. If you want to be pardoned, return to the proper path. If you seek atonement, forsake your evils.

SELICHAH 57

All:

יַעֲזֹב *Let the wicked one forsake his path**
and humble his arrogant heart,
Let him return to HASHEM,
Who will have mercy on him in his repentance.[1]
> *While he is not yet cut off, nor his [last] day come.[2]*

Forsake, O son of man, forsake!
Forsake the grime [of sin] and evil talk,
before you go flying [from this world] like doves to [their] cote,[3]
and the Collector comes to retrieve the pledge.
Therefore, repent! And remember the day that must come,
for the day is short and the work is great.[4]
O who will take this to his heart —
> *while he is not yet cut off, nor his [last] day come?*

Forsake, O son of man, forsake!
Forsake the vain indulgences of this world, distance yourself [from them],
for tomorrow you shall weep over what you laugh at today.
And in your Adversary's book your writing[5] will not be erased;
no payment will avail nor a bribe secretly passed.[6]
The workers are lazy, the Employer urgent,[7]
for the Adversary is coming, he stands ready with his case —
> *while he is not yet cut off, nor his [last] day come.*

Forsake, O son of man, forsake!
Forsake the world's ephemeral values,
for Gehinnom is arranged[8] with every flame and torch.*[9]
Please remember your end when you will robbed of all,[10]
for every 'brother' will say, 'Hoo-hah!' and every 'friend' wander off.[11]
Therefore repent! And prepare yourself in the vestibule [of this world],[12]
in order to enter the banquet hall [of the World to Come]
and its goodness.
> *While he is not yet cut off, nor his [last] day come.*

Forsake, O son of man, forsake!
Forsake the Evil Inclination that your soul loves,
and say, 'My soul, better that you should be in pain,
than be gratified by drawing from another well.'*

---

(1) Cf. *Isaiah* 55:7. (2) *I Samuel* 26:10. (3) Cf. *Isaiah* 60:8. (4) *Mishnah, Avos* 2:20.
(5) See commentary to *selichah* 28, s.v., וּבְיָדוֹ סְדוּרוֹת. (6) Cf. *Proverbs* 21:14. (7) *Mishnah, Avos* 2:20.
(8) Cf. *Isaiah* 30:33. (9) Cf. *Job* 41:11. (10) Cf. *Isaiah* 33:1. (11) Cf. *Jeremiah* 9:3ff.
(12) *Mishnah, Avos* 4:21; the *Mishnah's* פְּרוֹזְדוֹר and the *paytan's* פְּרוֹזְדוֹד have the same meaning.

לַהַב וְכִידוֹד — *Flame and torch.* The word כִּידוֹד
appears only once in Scriptures: כִּידוֹדֵי אֵשׁ (*Job*
4:11). It is translated by the commentaries
according to its context, and can mean *torch*
(Rashi), *cauldron* (Ibn Ezra), or *spark* (Ralbag).

מִבּוֹר אַחֵר שׁוֹאָבֶת — *Drawing from another well*

[lit., *pit*]. The Torah is a בְּאֵר מַיִם חַיִּים, *a well of
living water.* Any other source is בְּאֵר אַחֶרֶת, an expression with various connotations: *another well;*
*another's well; an unfaithful well; the well of
idolatry* (from אֱלֹהִים אֲחֵרִים, *gods of others*); *the
well of the Evil Inclination* (from סִטְרָא אַחֲרָא, *the
other side*, an Aramaic term for the *Yetzer Hara*).

וְאִם תֹּאמַר מִי יְעִידֵנִי שֶׁאֲנִי שׁוֹכֶבֶת,

הַפִּנְקָס פָּתוּחַ, וְהַיָּד כּוֹתֶבֶת.[1]   שׁוּבִי וְתִזְכִּי לֶעָתִיד לָבֹא.

בְּטֶרֶם יִסָּפֶה אוֹ יוֹמוֹ יָבוֹא.

עֲזֹב נָא בֶּן אָדָם עֲזֹב נָא –

עֲזֹב נַחַת הָעוֹלָם הַזֶּה וְשִׂמְחָה,

בְּטֶרֶם נוֹד רוּחֲךָ, בְּכָל פִּנָּה וּרְוָחָה,

וְעֵינֶיךָ תִרְאֶינָה גֵּיהִנֹּם פְּתוּחָה,

וְשָׁם תִּהְיֶה נַפְשְׁךָ שְׂרוּפָה וְגַם כְּסוּחָה,

וּמֵאַיִן בָּאתָ, מְלֵחָה סְרוּחָה,

וְאַתָּה הוֹלֵךְ לִמְקוֹם שַׁחַת וְשׁוּחָה.

וְחֶשְׁבּוֹן תִּתֵּן לְשָׁם עָבִים רְכוּבוֹ,[2]   **בְּטֶרֶם יִסָּפֶה אוֹ יוֹמוֹ יָבוֹא.**

וידוי

During the recitation of the (וידוי) stand with head and body slightly bowed,
in submissive contrition.

אֱלֹהֵינוּ וֵאלֹהֵי אֲבוֹתֵינוּ, תָּבֹא לְפָנֶיךָ תְּפִלָּתֵנוּ,[3] וְאַל תִּתְעַלַּם
מִתְּחִנָּתֵנוּ,[4] שֶׁאֵין אָנוּ עַזֵּי פָנִים וּקְשֵׁי עֹרֶף, לוֹמַר
לְפָנֶיךָ יהוה אֱלֹהֵינוּ וֵאלֹהֵי אֲבוֹתֵינוּ, צַדִּיקִים אֲנַחְנוּ וְלֹא חָטָאנוּ,
אֲבָל אֲנַחְנוּ וַאֲבוֹתֵינוּ חָטָאנוּ.[5]

Strike the left side of the chest with the right fist
while reciting each of the sins in the following confession litany.

אָשַׁמְנוּ, בָּגַדְנוּ, גָּזַלְנוּ, דִּבַּרְנוּ דֹפִי. הֶעֱוִינוּ, וְהִרְשַׁעְנוּ, זַדְנוּ,
חָמַסְנוּ, טָפַלְנוּ שֶׁקֶר. יָעַצְנוּ רָע, כִּזַּבְנוּ, לַצְנוּ, מָרַדְנוּ,
נִאַצְנוּ, סָרַרְנוּ, עָוִינוּ, פָּשַׁעְנוּ, צָרַרְנוּ, קִשִּׁינוּ עֹרֶף. רָשַׁעְנוּ,
שִׁחַתְנוּ, תִּעַבְנוּ, תָּעִינוּ, תִּעְתָּעְנוּ.

סַרְנוּ מִמִּצְוֹתֶיךָ וּמִמִּשְׁפָּטֶיךָ הַטּוֹבִים וְלֹא שָׁוָה לָנוּ.[6] וְאַתָּה
צַדִּיק עַל כָּל הַבָּא עָלֵינוּ, כִּי אֱמֶת עָשִׂיתָ וַאֲנַחְנוּ
הִרְשָׁעְנוּ.[7]

אָשַׁמְנוּ מִכָּל עָם, בַּשְׁנוּ מִכָּל דּוֹר, גָּלָה מִמֶּנּוּ מָשׂוֹשׂ, דָּוָה
לִבֵּנוּ בַּחֲטָאֵינוּ, הֻחְבַּל אֻוּיֵּנוּ, וְנִפְרַע פְּאָרֵנוּ, זְבוּל בֵּית מִקְדָּשֵׁנוּ
חָרַב בַּעֲוֹנֵינוּ, טִירָתֵנוּ הָיְתָה לְשַׁמָּה, יְפִי אַדְמָתֵנוּ לְזָרִים,
כֹּחֵנוּ לְנָכְרִים.

And if your soul should say, 'Who will testify what I do lying [in bed]?'
[Tell it,] 'The book is open and the Hand is writing;[1]
so repent, and be worthy in the time to come.'
While he is not yet cut off, nor his [last] day come.

Forsake, O son of man, forsake!
Forsake this world's pleasure and joy,
before your spirit wanders in every corner and direction.
And your eyes see an open Gehinnom,
where your soul will be burned and cut off.
For where did you come from but a fetid ooze?
And you go to a place of ruin and the grave,
and you will render account to Him who makes the clouds His chariot.[2]
While he is not yet cut off, nor his [last] day come.

VIDUY/CONFESSION

During the recitation of the וִדּוּי stand with head and body slightly bowed,
in submissive contrition.

אֱלֹהֵינוּ *Our God and the God of our forefathers, may our prayer come*
before You.[3] *Do not ignore our supplication,*[4] *for we are not so*
brazen and obstinate as to say before You, HASHEM, our God and the God
of our forefathers, that we are righteous and have not sinned, for in truth,
we and our forefathers have sinned.[5]

Strike the left side of the chest with the right fist while reciting
each of the sins in the following confession litany.

אָשַׁמְנוּ *We have become guilty; [ב] we have betrayed; [ג] we have*
robbed; [ד] we have spoken slander; [ה] we have caused
perversion; [ו] we have caused wickedness; [ז] we have sinned willfully;
[ח] we have extorted; [ט] we have accused falsely; [י] we have given evil
counsel; [כ] we have been deceitful; [ל] we have scorned; [מ] we have
rebelled; [נ] we have provoked; [ס] we have turned away; [ע] we have
been perverse; [פ] we have acted wantonly; [צ] we have persecuted;
[ק] we have been obstinate; [ר] we have been wicked; [ש] we have
corrupted; [ת] we have been abominable; we have strayed; You have let
us go astray.

סַרְנוּ *We have turned away from Your commandments and from Your*
good laws but to no avail.[6] *Yet You are righteous in all that has*
come upon us, for You have acted truthfully while we have caused
wickedness.[7]

[א] We have become the guiltiest of people. [ב] We have become the
most degraded of all generations. [ג] Joy has departed from us. [ד] Our
heart has been saddened by our sins. [ה] Our desirous treasure has been
ruined, [ו] and our splendor dashed, [ז] for our Holy Temple edifice
[ח] has been destroyed for our iniquities. [ט] Our Palace has become
desolate. [י] [Jerusalem,] the beauty of our Land is given over to aliens,
[כ] our power to strangers.

---

(1) *Mishnah, Avos* 3:20. (2) Cf. 3:1. (3) Cf. *Psalms* 88:3.
(4) Cf. 55:2. (5) Cf. 106:6. (6) Cf. *Job* 33:27. (7) *Nehemiah* 9:33.

וַעֲדַיִן לֹא שַׁבְנוּ מִטָּעוּתֵנוּ וְהֵיךְ נָעִיז פָּנֵינוּ וְנַקְשֶׁה עָרְפֵּנוּ, לוֹמַר לְפָנֶיךָ יְהוָה אֱלֹהֵינוּ וֵאלֹהֵי אֲבוֹתֵינוּ, צַדִּיקִים אֲנַחְנוּ וְלֹא חָטָאנוּ, אֲבָל אֲנַחְנוּ וַאֲבוֹתֵינוּ חָטָאנוּ.

Strike the left side of the chest with the right fist
while reciting each of the sins in the following confession litany.

אָשַׁמְנוּ, בָּגַדְנוּ, גָּזַלְנוּ, דִּבַּרְנוּ דֹפִי. הֶעֱוִינוּ, וְהִרְשַׁעְנוּ, זַדְנוּ, חָמַסְנוּ, טָפַלְנוּ שֶׁקֶר. יָעַצְנוּ רָע, כִּזַּבְנוּ, לַצְנוּ, מָרַדְנוּ, נִאַצְנוּ, סָרַרְנוּ, עָוִינוּ, פָּשַׁעְנוּ, צָרַרְנוּ, קִשִּׁינוּ עֹרֶף. רָשַׁעְנוּ, שִׁחַתְנוּ, תִּעַבְנוּ, תָּעִינוּ, תִּעְתָּעְנוּ.

סַרְנוּ מִמִּצְוֹתֶיךָ וּמִמִּשְׁפָּטֶיךָ הַטּוֹבִים וְלֹא שָׁוָה לָנוּ. וְאַתָּה צַדִּיק עַל כָּל הַבָּא עָלֵינוּ, כִּי אֱמֶת עָשִׂיתָ וַאֲנַחְנוּ הִרְשָׁעְנוּ.

לְעֵינֵינוּ עָשְׁקוּ עֲמָלֵנוּ, מְמֻשָּׁךְ וּמְמוֹרָט מִמֶּנּוּ, נָתְנוּ עֻלָּם עָלֵינוּ, סָבַלְנוּ עַל שִׁכְמֵנוּ, עֲבָדִים מָשְׁלוּ בָנוּ, פֹּרֵק אֵין מִיָּדָם, צָרוֹת רַבּוֹת סְבָבוּנוּ, קְרָאנוּךָ יְהוָה אֱלֹהֵינוּ, רָחַקְתָּ מִמֶּנּוּ בַּעֲוֹנֵינוּ, שַׁבְנוּ מֵאַחֲרֶיךָ, תָּעִינוּ וְאָבָדְנוּ.

וַעֲדַיִן לֹא שַׁבְנוּ מִטָּעוּתֵנוּ וְהֵיךְ נָעִיז פָּנֵינוּ וְנַקְשֶׁה עָרְפֵּנוּ, לוֹמַר לְפָנֶיךָ יְהוָה אֱלֹהֵינוּ וֵאלֹהֵי אֲבוֹתֵינוּ, צַדִּיקִים אֲנַחְנוּ וְלֹא חָטָאנוּ, אֲבָל אֲנַחְנוּ וַאֲבוֹתֵינוּ חָטָאנוּ.

Strike the left side of the chest with the right fist while reciting
each of the sins in the following confession litany.

אָשַׁמְנוּ, בָּגַדְנוּ, גָּזַלְנוּ, דִּבַּרְנוּ דֹפִי. הֶעֱוִינוּ, וְהִרְשַׁעְנוּ, זַדְנוּ, חָמַסְנוּ, טָפַלְנוּ שֶׁקֶר. יָעַצְנוּ רָע, כִּזַּבְנוּ, לַצְנוּ, מָרַדְנוּ, נִאַצְנוּ, סָרַרְנוּ, עָוִינוּ, פָּשַׁעְנוּ, צָרַרְנוּ, קִשִּׁינוּ עֹרֶף. רָשַׁעְנוּ, שִׁחַתְנוּ, תִּעַבְנוּ, תָּעִינוּ, תִּעְתָּעְנוּ.

סַרְנוּ מִמִּצְוֹתֶיךָ וּמִמִּשְׁפָּטֶיךָ הַטּוֹבִים וְלֹא שָׁוָה לָנוּ. וְאַתָּה צַדִּיק עַל כָּל הַבָּא עָלֵינוּ, כִּי אֱמֶת עָשִׂיתָ וַאֲנַחְנוּ הִרְשָׁעְנוּ.

But still we have not returned from our waywardness. So how can we be so brazen and obstinate as to say before You, HASHEM, our God and the God of our forefathers, that we are righteous and have not sinned, for in truth, both we and our fathers have sinned.

Strike the left side of the chest with the right fist while reciting each of the sins in the following confession litany.

אָשַׁמְנוּ We have become guilty; [ב] we have betrayed; [ג] we have robbed; [ד] we have spoken slander; [ה] we have caused perversion; [ו] we have caused wickedness; [ז] we have sinned willfully; [ח] we have extorted; [ט] we have accused falsely; [י] we have given evil counsel; [כ] we have been deceitful; [ל] we have scorned; [מ] we have rebelled; [נ] we have provoked; [ס] we have turned away; [ע] we have been perverse; [פ] we have acted wantonly; [צ] we have persecuted; [ק] we have been obstinate; [ר] we have been wicked; [ש] we have corrupted; [ת] we have been abominable; we have strayed; You have let us go astray.

סַרְנוּ We have turned away from Your commandments and from Your good laws but to no avail. Yet You are righteous in all that has come upon us, for You have acted truthfully while we have caused wickedness.

[ל] [The benefit of] our labor has been stolen, [מ] pulled away and cut off from us. [נ] They have placed their yoke upon us, [ס] our burdens upon our shoulders. [ע] Slaves have ruled over us, [פ] there is no redemption from their hand. [צ] Abundant troubles have surrounded us, [ק] we called upon You, HASHEM, our God, [ר] but You have distanced us for our iniquities. [ש] We have turned away from following after You; [ת] we have strayed; we have become lost.

But still we have not returned from our waywardness. So how can we be so brazen and obstinate as to say before You, HASHEM, our God and the God of our forefathers, that we are righteous and have not sinned, for in truth, both we and our fathers have sinned.

Strike the left side of the chest with the right fist while reciting each of the sins in the following confession litany:

אָשַׁמְנוּ We have become guilty; [ב] we have betrayed; [ג] we have robbed; [ד] we have spoken slander; [ה] we have caused perversion; [ו] we have caused wickedness; [ז] we have sinned willfully; [ח] we have extorted; [ט] we have accused falsely; [י] we have given evil counsel; [כ] we have been deceitful; [ל] we have scorned; [מ] we have rebelled; [נ] we have provoked; [ס] we have turned away; [ע] we have been perverse; [פ] we have acted wantonly; [צ] we have persecuted; [ק] we have been obstinate; [ר] we have been wicked; [ש] we have corrupted; [ת] we have been abominable; we have strayed; You have let us go astray.

סַרְנוּ We have turned away from Your commandments and from Your good laws but to no avail. Yet You are righteous in all that has come upon us, for You have acted truthfully while we have caused wickedness.

הִרְשַׁעְנוּ וּפָשַׁעְנוּ, לָכֵן לֹא נוֹשָׁעְנוּ. וְתֵן בְּלִבֵּנוּ לַעֲזוֹב דֶּרֶךְ רֶשַׁע, וְחִישׁ לָנוּ יֶשַׁע, כַּכָּתוּב עַל יַד נְבִיאֶךָ: יַעֲזֹב רָשָׁע דַּרְכּוֹ, וְאִישׁ אָוֶן מַחְשְׁבֹתָיו, וְיָשֹׁב אֶל יהוה וִירַחֲמֵהוּ, וְאֶל אֱלֹהֵינוּ כִּי יַרְבֶּה לִסְלוֹחַ.[1]

מְשִׁיחַ צִדְקֶךָ אָמַר לְפָנֶיךָ: שְׁגִיאוֹת מִי יָבִין מִנִּסְתָּרוֹת נַקֵּנִי.[2] נַקֵּנוּ יהוה אֱלֹהֵינוּ מִכָּל פְּשָׁעֵינוּ, וְטַהֲרֵנוּ מִכָּל טֻמְאוֹתֵינוּ, וּזְרוֹק עָלֵינוּ מַיִם טְהוֹרִים וְטַהֲרֵנוּ, כַּכָּתוּב עַל יַד נְבִיאֶךָ: וְזָרַקְתִּי עֲלֵיכֶם מַיִם טְהוֹרִים וּטְהַרְתֶּם, מִכֹּל טֻמְאוֹתֵיכֶם וּמִכָּל גִּלּוּלֵיכֶם אֲטַהֵר אֶתְכֶם.[3]

מִיכָה עַבְדְּךָ אָמַר לְפָנֶיךָ: מִי אֵל כָּמוֹךָ נֹשֵׂא עָוֹן וְעֹבֵר עַל פֶּשַׁע לִשְׁאֵרִית נַחֲלָתוֹ, לֹא הֶחֱזִיק לָעַד אַפּוֹ, כִּי חָפֵץ חֶסֶד הוּא, יָשׁוּב יְרַחֲמֵנוּ, יִכְבֹּשׁ עֲוֹנֹתֵינוּ, וְתַשְׁלִיךְ בִּמְצֻלוֹת יָם כָּל חַטֹּאתָם.[4] (וְכָל חַטֹּאת עַמְּךָ בֵּית יִשְׂרָאֵל תַּשְׁלִיךְ בִּמְקוֹם אֲשֶׁר לֹא יִזָּכְרוּ, וְלֹא יִפָּקְדוּ, וְלֹא יַעֲלוּ עַל לֵב לְעוֹלָם.) תִּתֵּן אֱמֶת לְיַעֲקֹב חֶסֶד לְאַבְרָהָם אֲשֶׁר נִשְׁבַּעְתָּ לַאֲבוֹתֵינוּ מִימֵי קֶדֶם.[5]

דָּנִיֵּאל אִישׁ חֲמוּדוֹת שִׁוַּע לְפָנֶיךָ: הַטֵּה אֱלֹהַי אָזְנְךָ וּשְׁמָע, פְּקַח עֵינֶיךָ וּרְאֵה שֹׁמְמֹתֵינוּ וְהָעִיר אֲשֶׁר נִקְרָא שִׁמְךָ עָלֶיהָ, כִּי לֹא עַל צִדְקֹתֵינוּ אֲנַחְנוּ מַפִּילִים תַּחֲנוּנֵינוּ לְפָנֶיךָ, כִּי עַל רַחֲמֶיךָ הָרַבִּים. אֲדֹנָי שְׁמָעָה, אֲדֹנָי סְלָחָה, אֲדֹנָי הַקְשִׁיבָה, וַעֲשֵׂה אַל תְּאַחַר, לְמַעַנְךָ אֱלֹהַי, כִּי שִׁמְךָ נִקְרָא עַל עִירְךָ וְעַל עַמֶּךָ.[6]

עֶזְרָא הַסּוֹפֵר אָמַר לְפָנֶיךָ: אֱלֹהַי, בֹּשְׁתִּי וְנִכְלַמְתִּי לְהָרִים, אֱלֹהַי, פָּנַי אֵלֶיךָ, כִּי עֲוֹנֹתֵינוּ רָבוּ לְמַעְלָה רֹּאשׁ, וְאַשְׁמָתֵנוּ גָדְלָה עַד לַשָּׁמָיִם.[7] וְאַתָּה[8] אֱלוֹהַּ סְלִיחוֹת, חַנּוּן וְרַחוּם, אֶרֶךְ אַפַּיִם וְרַב חֶסֶד, וְלֹא עֲזַבְתָּנוּ.[9]

אַל תַּעַזְבֵנוּ אָבִינוּ וְאַל תִּטְּשֵׁנוּ בּוֹרְאֵנוּ, וְאַל תַּזְנִיחֵנוּ יוֹצְרֵנוּ, וְאַל תַּעַשׂ עִמָּנוּ כָּלָה כְּחַטֹּאתֵינוּ. וְקַיֶּם לָנוּ יהוה אֱלֹהֵינוּ, אֶת הַדָּבָר שֶׁהִבְטַחְתָּנוּ בְּקַבָּלָה עַל יְדֵי יִרְמְיָהוּ חוֹזָךְ, כָּאָמוּר: בַּיָּמִים הָהֵם וּבָעֵת הַהִיא, נְאֻם יהוה, יְבֻקַּשׁ אֶת עֲוֹן יִשְׂרָאֵל וְאֵינֶנּוּ וְאֶת חַטֹּאת יְהוּדָה וְלֹא תִמָּצֶאנָה, כִּי אֶסְלַח

---

(1) *Isaiah* 55:7. (2) *Psalms* 19:13. (3) *Ezekiel* 36:25. (4) *Micah* 7:18-19. (5) 7:20.
(6) *Daniel* 9:18-19. (7) *Ezra* 9:6. (8) Some editions of *Selichos* insert the word אֱלֹהֵינוּ,
our God, at this point. (9) Cf. *Nehemiah* 9:17.

הִרְשַׁעְנוּ We have acted wickedly and have sinned willfully, therefore we have not been saved. Inspire our heart to abandon the
path of evil and hasten salvation for us, as it is written by Your prophet:
May the wicked one abandon his way and the vicious man his thoughts;
may he return to HASHEM and He will show him mercy, and to our God,
for He is abundantly forgiving.[1]

מְשִׁיחַ צִדְקֶךָ Your righteous anointed [David] said before You: 'Who
can discern mistakes? From unperceived faults cleanse
me.'[2] Cleanse us, HASHEM, our God, of all our willful sins and purify us,
of all our contaminations. Sprinkle upon us pure water and purify us, as
it is written by Your prophet: I shall sprinkle pure water upon you and
purify you, of all your contaminations and of all your abominations I will
purify you.'[3]

מִיכָה עַבְדְּךָ Micah, Your servant, said before You: 'Who, O God, is
like You, Who pardons iniquity and overlooks transgression for the remnant of His heritage? Who has not retained His wrath
eternally, for He desires kindness! He will again be merciful to us; He will
suppress our iniquities and cast into the depths of the sea all their sins.[4]
(And all the sins of Your nation the Family of Israel, may You cast away
to a place where they will neither be remembered, considered, nor brought
to mind — ever.) Grant truth to Jacob, kindness to Abraham, as You
swore to our forefathers from ancient times.'[5]

דָּנִיֵּאל Daniel, the greatly beloved man, cried out before You: 'Incline,
my God, Your ear, and listen, open Your eyes and see our
desolation and that of the city upon which Your Name is proclaimed, for
not because of our righteousness do we cast down our supplications
before You, rather because of Your abundant compassion. O my Lord,
heed; O my Lord, forgive; O my Lord, be attentive and act, do not delay;
for Your sake, my God, for Your Name is proclaimed upon Your city and
Your people.'[6]

עֶזְרָא הַסּוֹפֵר Ezra the Scribe said before You: 'My God, I am embarrassed and ashamed to lift my face to You, my God —
for our iniquities have multiplied above our heads, and our sins extend
unto heaven.[7] You are[8] the God of forgiveness, compassionate and
merciful, slow to anger, and abundant in kindness; and You have not
forsaken us.'[9]

אַל תַּעַזְבֵנוּ Do not forsake us, our Father; do not cast us off, our
Creator; do not abandon us, our Molder; and do not
bring about our destruction, as our sins merit. Affirm for us, HASHEM,
our God, the promise You made in the tradition through Jeremiah,
Your seer, as it is said: 'In those days and at that time' — the words of
HASHEM — 'the iniquity of Israel will be sought but there will be none, and
the errors of Judah, but they will not be found, for I will have forgiven

לַאֲשֶׁר אַשְׁאִיר.[1] עַמְּךָ וְנַחֲלָתְךָ רְעֵבֵי טוּבְךָ, צְמֵאֵי חַסְדֶּךָ, תְּאֵבֵי יִשְׁעֶךָ, יַכִּירוּ וְיֵדְעוּ כִּי לַיהוה אֱלֹהֵינוּ הָרַחֲמִים וְהַסְּלִיחוֹת.

אֵל רַחוּם שְׁמֶךָ, אֵל חַנּוּן שְׁמֶךָ, בָּנוּ נִקְרָא שְׁמֶךָ. יהוה עֲשֵׂה לְמַעַן שְׁמֶךָ. עֲשֵׂה לְמַעַן אֲמִתֶּךָ, עֲשֵׂה לְמַעַן בְּרִיתֶךָ, עֲשֵׂה לְמַעַן **גָּדְלְךָ** וְתִפְאַרְתֶּךָ, עֲשֵׂה לְמַעַן **דָּתֶךָ**, עֲשֵׂה לְמַעַן **הוֹדֶךָ**, עֲשֵׂה לְמַעַן וְעוּדֶךָ, עֲשֵׂה לְמַעַן **זִכְרֶךָ**, עֲשֵׂה לְמַעַן חַסְדֶּךָ, עֲשֵׂה לְמַעַן **טוּבֶךָ**, עֲשֵׂה לְמַעַן **יִחוּדֶךָ**, עֲשֵׂה לְמַעַן כְּבוֹדֶךָ, עֲשֵׂה לְמַעַן **לִמּוּדֶךָ**, עֲשֵׂה לְמַעַן **מַלְכוּתֶךָ**, עֲשֵׂה לְמַעַן **נִצְחֶךָ**, עֲשֵׂה לְמַעַן **סוֹדֶךָ**, עֲשֵׂה לְמַעַן עֻזֶּךָ, עֲשֵׂה לְמַעַן **פְּאֵרֶךָ**, עֲשֵׂה לְמַעַן **צִדְקָתֶךָ**, עֲשֵׂה לְמַעַן **קְדֻשָּׁתֶךָ**, עֲשֵׂה לְמַעַן **רַחֲמֶיךָ** הָרַבִּים, עֲשֵׂה לְמַעַן **שְׁכִינָתֶךָ**, עֲשֵׂה לְמַעַן **תְּהִלָּתֶךָ**, עֲשֵׂה לְמַעַן אוֹהֲבֶיךָ שׁוֹכְנֵי עָפָר, עֲשֵׂה לְמַעַן אַבְרָהָם יִצְחָק וְיַעֲקֹב, עֲשֵׂה לְמַעַן מֹשֶׁה וְאַהֲרֹן, עֲשֵׂה לְמַעַן דָּוִד וּשְׁלֹמֹה, עֲשֵׂה לְמַעַן יְרוּשָׁלַיִם עִיר קָדְשֶׁךָ, עֲשֵׂה לְמַעַן צִיּוֹן מִשְׁכַּן כְּבוֹדֶךָ, עֲשֵׂה לְמַעַן שִׁמְמוֹת הֵיכָלֶךָ, עֲשֵׂה לְמַעַן הֲרִיסוֹת מִזְבְּחֶךָ, עֲשֵׂה לְמַעַן הֲרוּגִים עַל שֵׁם קָדְשֶׁךָ, עֲשֵׂה לְמַעַן טְבוּחִים עַל יִחוּדֶךָ, עֲשֵׂה לְמַעַן בָּאֵי בָאֵשׁ וּבַמַּיִם עַל קִדּוּשׁ שְׁמֶךָ, עֲשֵׂה לְמַעַן יוֹנְקֵי שָׁדַיִם שֶׁלֹּא חָטְאוּ, עֲשֵׂה לְמַעַן גְּמוּלֵי חָלָב שֶׁלֹּא פָשָׁעוּ, עֲשֵׂה לְמַעַן תִּינוֹקוֹת שֶׁל בֵּית רַבָּן, עֲשֵׂה לְמַעַנְךָ אִם לֹא לְמַעֲנֵנוּ, עֲשֵׂה לְמַעַנְךָ וְהוֹשִׁיעֵנוּ.

עֲנֵנוּ יהוה עֲנֵנוּ, עֲנֵנוּ אֱלֹהֵינוּ עֲנֵנוּ, עֲנֵנוּ אָבִינוּ עֲנֵנוּ, עֲנֵנוּ בּוֹרְאֵנוּ עֲנֵנוּ, עֲנֵנוּ גּוֹאֲלֵנוּ עֲנֵנוּ, עֲנֵנוּ דּוֹרְשֵׁנוּ עֲנֵנוּ, עֲנֵנוּ הָאֵל הַנֶּאֱמָן עֲנֵנוּ, עֲנֵנוּ וָתִיק וְחָסִיד עֲנֵנוּ, עֲנֵנוּ זַךְ וְיָשָׁר עֲנֵנוּ, עֲנֵנוּ חַי וְקַיָּם עֲנֵנוּ, עֲנֵנוּ טוֹב וּמֵטִיב עֲנֵנוּ, עֲנֵנוּ יוֹדֵעַ יֵצֶר עֲנֵנוּ, עֲנֵנוּ כּוֹבֵשׁ כְּעָסִים עֲנֵנוּ, עֲנֵנוּ לוֹבֵשׁ צְדָקוֹת עֲנֵנוּ, עֲנֵנוּ מֶלֶךְ מַלְכֵי הַמְּלָכִים עֲנֵנוּ, עֲנֵנוּ נוֹרָא וְנִשְׂגָּב עֲנֵנוּ, עֲנֵנוּ סוֹלֵחַ וּמוֹחֵל עֲנֵנוּ, עֲנֵנוּ עוֹנֶה בְּעֵת צָרָה[2] עֲנֵנוּ, עֲנֵנוּ פּוֹדֶה וּמַצִּיל עֲנֵנוּ, עֲנֵנוּ צַדִּיק וְיָשָׁר עֲנֵנוּ, עֲנֵנוּ קָרוֹב לְקוֹרְאָיו עֲנֵנוּ, עֲנֵנוּ רַחוּם וְחַנּוּן עֲנֵנוּ, עֲנֵנוּ

---

(1) *Jeremiah* 50:20. (2) Some editions of *Selichos* read בְּעֵת רָצוֹן, *in a time of favor.*

those whom I leave as a remnant.'[1] Your people and Your heritage, who
hunger for Your goodness, who thirst for Your kindness, who long for
Your salvation — may they recognize and know that to HASHEM, our God,
belong mercy and forgiveness.

אֵל רַחוּם 'Merciful God' is Your Name, 'Gracious God' is Your Name,
Your Name is called upon us — O HASHEM, act for Your
Name's sake. Act for the sake of [א] Your truth; act for the sake of
[ב] Your covenant; act for the sake of [ג] Your greatness and Your
splendor; act for the sake of [ד] Your law; act for the sake of [ה] Your
glory; act for the sake of [ו] Your Meeting House; act for the sake of
[ז] Your remembrance; act for the sake of [ח] Your kindness; act for the
sake of [ט] Your goodness; act for the sake of [י] Your Oneness; act for
the sake of [כ] Your honor; act for the sake of [ל] Your teaching; act for
the sake of [מ] Your kingship; act for the sake of [נ] Your eternality; act
for the sake of [ס] Your counsel; act for the sake of [ע] Your power; act
for the sake of [פ] Your beauty; act for the sake of [צ] Your righteousness;
act for the sake of [ק] Your sanctity; act for the sake of [ר] Your abundant
mercy; act for the sake of [ש] Your Presence, act for the sake of [ת] Your
praise; act for the sake of Your beloved ones who rest in the dust; act for
the sake of Abraham, Isaac, and Jacob; act for the sake of Moses and
Aaron; act for the sake of David and Solomon; act for the sake of Jerusalem, Your holy city; act for the sake of Zion, the abode of Your glory;
act for the sake of the desolation of Your Temple; act for the sake of the
ruin of Your Altar; act for the sake of the martyrs for Your holy Name;
act for the sake of those slaughtered for Your Oneness; act for the sake
of those who entered fire and water for the sanctification of Your Name;
act for the nursing infants who did not err; act for the sake of the weaned
babes who did not sin; act for the sake of children at the schoolroom; act
for Your sake if not for ours; act for Your sake and save us.

עֲנֵנוּ Answer us, HASHEM, answer us; answer us, our God, answer us;
answer us, [א] our Father, answer us; answer us, [ב] our Creator,
answer us; answer us, [ג] our Redeemer, answer us; answer us, [ד] You
Who searches us out, answer us; answer us, [ה] faithful God, answer us;
answer us, [ו] stead-fast and kind One, answer us; answer us, [ז] pure
and upright One, answer us; answer us, [ח] living and enduring One,
answer us; answer us, [ט] good and beneficent One, answer us; answer
us, [י] You Who knows inclinations, answer us; answer us, [כ] You Who
suppresses wrath, answer us; answer us, [ל] You Who dons righteousness, answer us; answer us, [מ] King Who reigns over kings, answer us;
answer us, [נ] awesome and powerful One, answer us; answer us, [ס] You
Who forgives and pardons, answer us; answer us, [ע] You Who answers
in time of distress,[2] answer us; answer us, [פ] Redeemer and Rescuer,
answer us; answer us, [צ] righteous and upright One, answer us;
answer us, [ק] He Who is close to those who call upon Him, answer
us; answer us, [ר] merciful and gracious One, answer us; answer us,

שׁוֹמֵעַ אֶל אֶבְיוֹנִים עֲנֵנוּ, עֲנֵנוּ תּוֹמֵךְ תְּמִימִים עֲנֵנוּ, עֲנֵנוּ אֱלֹהֵי
אֲבוֹתֵינוּ עֲנֵנוּ, עֲנֵנוּ אֱלֹהֵי אַבְרָהָם עֲנֵנוּ, עֲנֵנוּ פַּחַד יִצְחָק עֲנֵנוּ, עֲנֵנוּ
אֲבִיר יַעֲקֹב עֲנֵנוּ, עֲנֵנוּ עֶזְרַת הַשְּׁבָטִים עֲנֵנוּ, עֲנֵנוּ מִשְׂגָּב אִמָּהוֹת
עֲנֵנוּ, עֲנֵנוּ קָשֶׁה לִכְעוֹס עֲנֵנוּ, עֲנֵנוּ רַךְ לִרְצוֹת עֲנֵנוּ, עֲנֵנוּ עוֹנֶה בְּעֵת
רָצוֹן¹ עֲנֵנוּ, עֲנֵנוּ אֲבִי יְתוֹמִים עֲנֵנוּ, עֲנֵנוּ דַּיַּן אַלְמָנוֹת עֲנֵנוּ.

מִי שֶׁעָנָה לְאַבְרָהָם אָבִינוּ בְּהַר הַמּוֹרִיָּה,   הוּא יַעֲנֵנוּ.

מִי שֶׁעָנָה לְיִצְחָק בְּנוֹ כְּשֶׁנֶּעֱקַד עַל גַּבֵּי הַמִּזְבֵּחַ,   הוּא יַעֲנֵנוּ.

מִי שֶׁעָנָה לְיַעֲקֹב בְּבֵית אֵל,   הוּא יַעֲנֵנוּ.

מִי שֶׁעָנָה לְיוֹסֵף בְּבֵית הָאֲסוּרִים,   הוּא יַעֲנֵנוּ.

מִי שֶׁעָנָה לַאֲבוֹתֵינוּ עַל יַם סוּף,   הוּא יַעֲנֵנוּ.

מִי שֶׁעָנָה לְמֹשֶׁה בְּחוֹרֵב,   הוּא יַעֲנֵנוּ.

מִי שֶׁעָנָה לְאַהֲרֹן בַּמַּחְתָּה,   הוּא יַעֲנֵנוּ.

מִי שֶׁעָנָה לְפִינְחָס בְּקוּמוֹ מִתּוֹךְ הָעֵדָה,   הוּא יַעֲנֵנוּ.

מִי שֶׁעָנָה לִיהוֹשֻׁעַ בַּגִּלְגָּל,   הוּא יַעֲנֵנוּ.

מִי שֶׁעָנָה לִשְׁמוּאֵל בַּמִּצְפָּה,   הוּא יַעֲנֵנוּ.

מִי שֶׁעָנָה לְדָוִד וּשְׁלֹמֹה בְּנוֹ בִּירוּשָׁלָיִם,   הוּא יַעֲנֵנוּ.

מִי שֶׁעָנָה לְאֵלִיָּהוּ בְּהַר הַכַּרְמֶל,   הוּא יַעֲנֵנוּ.

מִי שֶׁעָנָה לֶאֱלִישָׁע בִּירִיחוֹ,   הוּא יַעֲנֵנוּ.

מִי שֶׁעָנָה לְיוֹנָה בִּמְעֵי הַדָּגָה,   הוּא יַעֲנֵנוּ.

מִי שֶׁעָנָה לְחִזְקִיָּהוּ מֶלֶךְ יְהוּדָה בְּחָלְיוֹ,   הוּא יַעֲנֵנוּ.

מִי שֶׁעָנָה לַחֲנַנְיָה מִישָׁאֵל וַעֲזַרְיָה בְּתוֹךְ כִּבְשַׁן הָאֵשׁ,   הוּא יַעֲנֵנוּ.

מִי שֶׁעָנָה לְדָנִיֵּאל בְּגוֹב הָאֲרָיוֹת,   הוּא יַעֲנֵנוּ.

מִי שֶׁעָנָה לְמָרְדְּכַי וְאֶסְתֵּר בְּשׁוּשַׁן הַבִּירָה,   הוּא יַעֲנֵנוּ.

מִי שֶׁעָנָה לְעֶזְרָא בַּגּוֹלָה,   הוּא יַעֲנֵנוּ.

מִי שֶׁעָנָה לְכָל הַצַּדִּיקִים וְהַחֲסִידִים וְהַתְּמִימִים וְהַיְשָׁרִים,

הוּא יַעֲנֵנוּ.

רַחֲמָנָא דְּעָנֵי לַעֲנִיֵּי, עֲנִינָא. רַחֲמָנָא דְּעָנֵי לִתְבִירֵי לִבָּא,
עֲנִינָא. רַחֲמָנָא דְּעָנֵי לְמַכִּיכֵי רוּחָא, עֲנִינָא. רַחֲמָנָא
עֲנִינָא. רַחֲמָנָא חוּס. רַחֲמָנָא פְּרוֹק. רַחֲמָנָא שֵׁזִיב. רַחֲמָנָא
רְחֵם עֲלָן. הַשְׁתָּא בַּעֲגָלָא וּבִזְמַן קָרִיב.

---

(1) Some editions of *Selichos* read בְּעֵת צָרָה, *in time of distress.*

[ש] You Who hears the destitute, answer us; answer us, [ת] You Who
supports the wholesome, answer us; answer us, God of our forefathers,
answer us; answer us, God of Abraham, answer us; answer us, Dread of
Isaac, answer us; answer us, Mighty One of Jacob, answer us; answer us,
Helper of the tribes, answer us; answer us, Stronghold of the Matriarchs,
answer us; answer us, You Who are hard to anger, answer us; answer us,
You Who are easy to pacify, answer us; answer us, You Who answers in
a time of favor,¹ answer us; answer us, Father of orphans, answer us;
answer us, Judge of widows, answer us.

מִי שֶׁעָנָה He Who answered our father Abraham on Mount Moriah,
may He answer us.

He Who answered his son Isaac when he was bound atop the altar,
may He answer us.

He Who answered Jacob in Bethel,   may He answer us.
He Who answered Joseph in the prison,   may He answer us.
He Who answered our forefathers at the Sea of Reeds,   may He
answer us.

He Who answered Moses in Horeb,   may He answer us.
He Who answered Aaron when he offered the censer, may He answer
us.

He Who answered Phineas when he arose from amid the congregation,
may He answer us.

He Who answered Joshua in Gilgal,   may He answer us.
He Who answered Samuel in Mitzpah,   may He answer us.
He Who answered David and his son Solomon in Jerusalem,
may He answer us.

He Who answered Elijah on Mount Carmel,   may He answer us.
He Who answered Elisha in Jericho,   may He answer us.
He Who answered Jonah in the innards of the fish,   may He answer
us.

He Who answered Hezekiah, King of Judah, in his illness,
may He answer us.

He Who answered Chananiah, Mishael, and Azariah in the fiery oven,
may He answer us.

He Who answered Daniel in the lions' den,   may He answer us.
He Who answered Mordechai and Esther in Shushan the capital,
may He answer us.

He Who answered Ezra in the Exile,   may He answer us.
He Who answered all the righteous, the devout, the wholesome,
and the upright,   may He answer us.

רַחֲמָנָא The Merciful One Who answers the poor, may He answer us.
The Merciful One Who answers the brokenhearted, may He
answer us. The Merciful One Who answers the humble of spirit, may He
answer us. O Merciful One, answer us. O Merciful One, pity. O Merciful
One, redeem. O Merciful One, deliver. O Merciful One, have mercy on
us — now, swiftly and soon.

נפילת אפים

In the presence of a Torah Scroll, the following (until יַבֹּשׁוּ רָגַע) is recited with the head resting on the arm, preferably while seated. Elsewhere, it is recited with the head held erect.

(וַיֹּאמֶר דָּוִד אֶל גָּד, צַר לִי מְאֹד נִפְּלָה נָּא בְיַד יהוה,
כִּי רַבִּים רַחֲמָיו, וּבְיַד אָדָם אַל אֶפֹּלָה.[1])

רַחוּם וְחַנּוּן חָטָאתִי לְפָנֶיךָ. יהוה מָלֵא רַחֲמִים, רַחֵם עָלַי
וְקַבֵּל תַּחֲנוּנָי.

תהלים ו:ב-יא

יהוה אַל בְּאַפְּךָ תוֹכִיחֵנִי, וְאַל בַּחֲמָתְךָ תְיַסְּרֵנִי. חָנֵּנִי יהוה, כִּי
אֻמְלַל אָנִי, רְפָאֵנִי יהוה, כִּי נִבְהֲלוּ עֲצָמָי. וְנַפְשִׁי נִבְהֲלָה
מְאֹד, וְאַתָּה יהוה, עַד מָתָי. שׁוּבָה יהוה, חַלְּצָה נַפְשִׁי, הוֹשִׁיעֵנִי
לְמַעַן חַסְדֶּךָ. כִּי אֵין בַּמָּוֶת זִכְרֶךָ, בִּשְׁאוֹל מִי יוֹדֶה לָּךְ. יָגַעְתִּי
בְּאַנְחָתִי, אַשְׂחֶה בְכָל לַיְלָה מִטָּתִי, בְּדִמְעָתִי עַרְשִׂי אַמְסֶה.
עָשְׁשָׁה מִכַּעַס עֵינִי, עָתְקָה בְּכָל צוֹרְרָי. סוּרוּ מִמֶּנִּי כָּל פֹּעֲלֵי אָוֶן,
כִּי שָׁמַע יהוה קוֹל בִּכְיִי. שָׁמַע יהוה תְּחִנָּתִי, יהוה תְּפִלָּתִי יִקָּח.
יֵבֹשׁוּ וְיִבָּהֲלוּ מְאֹד כָּל אֹיְבָי, יָשֻׁבוּ יֵבֹשׁוּ רָגַע.

All:

מָחֵי וּמַסֵּי מְמִית וּמְחַיֶּה, מַסִּיק מִן שְׁאוֹל לְחַיֵּי עָלְמָא, בְּרָא
כַּד חָטֵי אֲבוּהִי לַקְיֵהּ, אֲבוּהִי דְּחַיֵּס אַסֵּי לִכְאֵבֵהּ.
עַבְדָּא דְּמָרִיד נָפִיק בְּקוֹלָר, מָרֵהּ תָּאִיב וְתַבִּיר קוֹלָרֵהּ.
בְּרַךְ בְּכְרַךְ אֲנָן וְחָטֵינָן קַמָּךְ, הָא רְוֵי נַפְשִׁין בְּגִידִין מְרָרִין,
עַבְדָּךְ אֲנָן וּמְרוֹדִינָן קַמָּךְ, הָא בְּבִזְתָּא, הָא בְּשִׁבְיָא, הָא
בְּמַלְקְיוּתָא. בְּמָטוּ מִנָּךְ בְּרַחֲמָךְ דְּנַפִישִׁין, אַסֵּי לִכְאֵבִין דִּתְקוֹף
עֲלָן, עַד דְּלָא נֶהֱוֵי גְּמִירָא בְּשִׁבְיָא.

סליחה נח (תחנה)

All:

תּוֹרָה הַקְּדוֹשָׁה,* הִתְחַנְּנִי בְּבַקָּשָׁה,*[2]
פְּנֵי הַצּוּר נַעֲרֹץ בִּקְדֻשָׁה.
שִׁפְכִי שִׂיחַ עָרֵב, וְזִכְרִי מַעֲשֵׂה חֹרֵב,[3]
בְּנַעֲשֶׂה וְנִשְׁמַע[4] נֻמּוּ לְהִתְקָרֵב.

◄§ **תּוֹרָה הַקְּדוֹשָׁה** — *Holy Torah.* The *paytan* recalls Israel's acceptance of the Torah in the face of the gentiles' rejection of it; describes their devotion to its study and its mitzvos; and beseeches the Torah to pray for Israel's redemption. [See the introduction to this volume regard-

ing the propriety and permissibility of request-ing outside intervention in our prayers.]

This תְּחִנָּה, *supplication,* consists of a series of triplets the acrostic of which forms a reverse *aleph-beis* (תשר"ק), followed by the composer's signature — שִׁמְעוֹן בַּר יִצְחָק חֲזַק, *Shimon bar*

PUTTING DOWN THE HEAD

In the presence of a Torah Scroll, the following (until 'instantly shamed') is recited with the head resting on the arm, preferably while seated. Elsewhere, it is recited with the head held erect.

(*And David said to Gad, 'I am exceedingly distressed. Let us fall into HASHEM's hand for His mercies are abundant, but let me not fall into human hands.'*[1])

רַחוּם וְחַנּוּן *O compassionate and gracious One, I have sinned before You. HASHEM, Who is full of mercy, have mercy on me and accept my supplications.*

Psalms 6:2-11

ה' *HASHEM, do not rebuke me in Your anger nor chastise me in Your rage. Favor me, HASHEM, for I am feeble; heal me, HASHEM, for my bones shudder. My soul is utterly confounded, and You, HASHEM, how long? Desist, HASHEM, release my soul; save me as befits Your kindness. For there is no mention of You in death; in the Lower World who will thank You? I am wearied with my sigh, every night my tears drench my bed, soak my couch. My eye is dimmed because of anger, aged by my tormentors. Depart from me, all evildoers, for HASHEM has heard the sound of my weeping. HASHEM has heard my plea, HASHEM will accept my prayer. Let all my foes be shamed and utterly confounded, they will regret and be instantly shamed.*

All:

מָחֵי וּמַסֵּי *[O God,] He Who smites and heals, causes death and re- stores life, raises [the dead] from the grave to eternal life: Should a son sin, his father would smack him, but a compassionate fa- ther will heal his [son's] pain. When a slave rebels, he is led out in collar- irons, but if his master desires to, he breaks his chains.*

We are Your son, Your firstborn, and we have sinned against You; so our soul has been satiated with bitter wormwood. We are Your servants and we have rebelled against You; so [we have suffered], some with looting, some with captivity, and some with the lash. We beg of You, in Your abundant compassion, heal the pains that have overwhelmed us, before we have been completely wiped out in captivity.

SELICHAH 58

All:

ת *Holy Torah,* supplicate in petition,**[2]
   before the Rock revered in [His] holiness.

ש *Pour out a mellifluous prayer, and mention the event at Mount Sinai,*[3]
   [where] they said, 'We will do and we will listen!'[4]
      to be able to approach.

---

(1) *II Samuel* 24:14. (2) See the introduction to this volume regarding the propriety of requesting intervention from another source in bringing our prayers before God. (3) See commentary to *selichah* 27, s.v., הַר גַּבְנוּנִּי. (4) See *Exodus* 24:7.

Yitzchak, *may he be strong* [see prefatory comment to *selichah* 11]. In an unusual depar- ture, R' Shimon combined the word חֲזַק with his father's name. Instead of writing יִצְחָק חֲזַק, he inserted the ו of חֲזַק between the ח and ק of יִצְחָק,

so that the signature ends יִצְחָק.

הִתְחַנְּנִי בְּבַקָּשָׁה — *Supplicate in petition.* The Torah itself prayed for Israel on a previous occasion. As the Midrash relates: Israel asked two

רָגְנוּ שֵׂעִיר וּפָארָן,   דָּתוֹתֶיךָ לִשְׁמָרָן,*

עָמַד וּמְדָדָן רָאָה וְהִתִּירָן.[1]

קָדוֹשׁ הִתֵּיקָם,   לְלֹא שָׁמְרוּ חֻקָם,

בְּאַף וּבְחֵמָה עֲשׂוֹת בָּהֶם נָקָם.[2]

צָעַד מֵרְבָבוֹת,   וְנִקְדַּשׁ בָּעֲרָבוֹת,*

מִימִינוֹ אֵשׁ דָּת,[3] וְלַהַב שַׁלְהֶבוֹת.

פָּנִים מַסְבִּירוֹת,   אֵלָיו מִתְחַבְּרוֹת,

הַנְשִׁקוּ מִפִּיו עֲשֶׂרֶת הַדִּבְּרוֹת.*

עוֹלָם נִתְבַּסָּס,   אֲשֶׁר מִתְּנָאוֹ נִמְסָס,

וּכְמוֹצֵא שָׁלָל רָב עַל אִמְרָתְךָ שָׂשׂ.[4]

סוֹדֵי פִקּוּדֶיךָ,   נִמְסְרוּ לְדוֹדֶיךָ,

מֵאָז וְעַד עַתָּה הֵמָּה מְכַבְּדֶיךָ.

נָדִים וְגַם נָעִים,   וּבְרָגֶז שְׁבֵעִים,

בִּנְפֶת צוּפֶיךָ[5] תָּמִיד מִשְׁתַּעְשְׁעִים.

מַסֹּרֶת לַיָּפֶה,   בִּכְתָב וּבְעַל פֶּה,

יְקָרוּ אֲמָרֶיךָ מִשַּׁחַם וְיָשְׁפֶה.*

לִבִּי לְחוֹקְקֶיךָ,   בַּעֲלִיל מְזוּקָקֶיךָ,[6]

קוֹבְעֵי עִתּוֹתָם לְפַלֵּשׁ פְּקוּדֶיךָ.

---

things of God, that they might see His glory and hear His voice. At Mount Sinai, this request was granted. But the nation did not have the strength to endure that great revelation, and so their souls flew out of the bodies. Then the Torah pleaded mercy on their behalf, 'Does a King [God] marry off his daughter [the Torah], then slay his household [Israel]? Shall the whole world celebrate [the Giving of the Torah], while Your children are dead?' With that their souls returned (Shemos Rabbah 29:4).

דָּתוֹתֶיךָ לִשְׁמָרָן — *About keeping Your laws* [lit., *to keep Your laws*]. The wording is ambiguous. The other nations complaints about the Torah and its mitzvos are twofold: First, they refused to accept the Torah when it was offered to them, before the Jews accepted it at Sinai, 'We cannot live up to its laws, our lifestyle is based on killing [or, stealing, or adultery]!' Each nation had a different reason for rejecting it. Second, in the future, when the nations will witness Israel's reward for its loyalty to the Torah, they will complain that they never had the chance to fulfill as many mitzvos as Israel had. 'Had the Torah been given to us, we would have been just as loyal' (*Avodah Zarah* 2b).

It is not clear to which of these complaints the *paytan* refers: *Seir [Edom] and Paran [Ishmael] complained that they could not keep the Torah and so rejected it;* or, *Seir and Paran complained that they were not given a chance to observe all 613 mitzvos.*

The Talmud continues that because of their complaints, God reviewed their observance of the seven Noahide *mitzvos* and found them lacking in their fulfillment. Seeing this, He released them from their obligations. But, the Talmud asks, isn't that rewarding the sinner? The Talmud concludes, He didn't release them completely, He lessened their reward; even if they would fulfill their *mitzvos*, their reward would be only that of one who is not commanded but does the *mitzvah* on his own, a level of performance that the Sages find less exalted than a *mitzvah* performed by one who is commanded in its fulfillment (ibid.). Thus, the *paytan* continues: *So He went and measured [their fulfillment of their own seven mitzvos], and saw [their performance as inadequate], and excused them.*

וְנִקְדַּשׁ בָּעֲרָבוֹת — *And was hallowed in Aravos.* This stich alludes to God Who is sanctified in

ר Seir and Paran complained about keeping your laws;*
    so He went and measured, and saw, and excused them.[1]

ק The Holy One cut them off,
    for not keeping even their own law,
    with anger and fury exacting.[2]

צ He strode out from the myriads [of angels],
    and was hallowed in Aravos,*
    at His right the fire of Law,[3] a blazing conflagration.

פ Faces beaming with favor, they [Israel] cleaved to Him,
    and were kissed from His mouth with the Ten Commandments.*

ע The world then became founded,
    though its proviso would have it melt,
    and like the finder of abundant spoils,
      it rejoiced over your word [O Torah].[4]

ס The secrets of your commandments
    were given to your beloved ones,
    and from then until now they are the ones who honor you.

נ Roving and roaming, replete with torment,
    they ever delight in your [words, sweeter than] honeycombs.[5]

מ They enhance the tradition, both Written and Oral;
    they value your words, more than shoham and yashpeh.*

ל My heart is to those who decide your Law,
    who refine you[r words] with lucidity,[6]
    who devote their time to opening your sealed [teachings].

---

(1) Cf. *Habakkuk* 3:6. (2) Cf. *Micah* 5:14. (3) Cf. *Deuteronomy* 33:2.
(4) Cf. *Psalms* 119:162. (5) See 19:11. (6) Cf. *Psalms* 12:7.

---

the seven heavens. The Talmud names and describes the seven heavens. In ascending order, they are:

(1) וִילוֹן, *Vilon* [lit., *curtain*]; although nothing happens within this heaven, in the morning it withdraws [like a curtain, allowing the daylight to shine through (*Rashi*)], and in the evening it goes forth [preventing the light of the sun from reaching Earth (*Rashi*)], thus it renews the work of Creation each day . . .

(2) רָקִיעַ, *Rakia* [lit., *firmament*]; in which the sun, moon, stars and constellations are suspended . . .

(3) שְׁחָקִים, *Shechakim* [lit., *powders* or *pulverizers*]; in which stand millstones that grind manna for the righteous . . .

(4) זְבוּל, *Zevul* [lit., *Temple*]; in which are built the heavenly Jerusalem, Temple and the Altar upon which the great angelic prince Michael sacrifices offerings . . .

(5) מָעוֹן, *Maon* [lit., *dwelling*]; in which groups of ministering angels recite songs [of praise to God] through the night, but remain silent by day in deference to Israel . . .

(6) מָכוֹן, *Machon* [lit., *foundation* or *establishment*]; in which are storehouses of snow, storehouses of hail, the attics in which harmful dew and heavy rainfall are stored, and

the chamber of the whirlwind and the tempest, the grotto of smoke with its doors of fire [all of them used for retribution against the wicked (*Rashi*)] . . .

and (7) עֲרָבוֹת, *Aravos* [lit., *willows* or *darkenings* or *mixtures*]; in which are Righteousness, Justice and Charity; caches of Life, Peace, and Blessing; the souls of the righteous, the spirits and souls that are destined to be born; and the life-giving dew with which God will resurrect the dead . . . (*Chagigah* 12b).

הָנְקָשׁוּ מִפִּיו עֲשֶׂרֶת הַדִּבְּרוֹת — *And were kissed from His mouth with the Ten Commandments.* The Midrash relates that the personification of each of the Ten Commandments approached each Jew at Mount Sinai and said, 'Accept me upon yourself! I entail so-and-so many *mitzvos*; so-and-so many laws; so-and-so many punishments; so-and-so many decrees; so-and-so many leniencies and stringencies; so-and-so many rewards.' Each Jew replied, 'Yes! Yes!' And the Commandment kissed him on his mouth (*Shir HaShirim Rabbah* to 1:2).

מִשֹּׁהַם וְיָשְׁפֵה — *Than shoham and yashpeh.* These are two of the twelve precious stones worn by the *Kohen Gadol* on his חֹשֶׁן, breastplate (*Exodus* 28:20).

בְּלָלוֹת וּפְרָטוֹת,   לִרְאוֹת וּלְהַטּוֹת,*
שְׁנָתָם נוֹדֶדֶת בַּחֲדַר הַמִּטּוֹת.

יוֹם יוֹם יִדְרְשׁוּן,[1]   בְּלִבָּם יַחֲרְשׁוּן,
לֶאֱסֹר וּלְהַתִּיר בְּפִיהֶם יִפְרְשׁוּן.

טֻמְאוֹת וּטְהוֹרוֹת,   לְהַבְדִּיל וּלְהוֹרוֹת,[2]
מְלַחֵץ וְדָחַק עֵינֵיהֶם מַנְהִירוֹת.[3]

חֻקִּים וּמִשְׁפָּטִים,   עַל פִּימוֹ שְׁפוּטִים,
וְאוֹיְבֵיהֶם פְּלִילִים וּבָהֶם נִשְׁפָּטִים.

זִכְרִי זֹאת תְּעוּדָה,   הוֹגַיִךְ לְהִתְעוֹדָדָה,
וּמְלִיצֵי הֶגְיוֹנַיִךְ לַעֲזֹר וּלְסַעֲדָה.

וְחָנְנִי פְּנֵי קוֹנֵךְ,   בְּמַעַן חֲנוּנֵךְ,
כִּי הוּא אֱלֹהַיִךְ יוֹצְרֵךְ וַאֲדוֹנֵךְ.

הֲלֹא אִם אֵין תַּמָּה,   הוֹגֶה בִּתְמִימָה,
הֵן בְּקֶרֶן זָוִית נְתוּנָה וּמִשְׁתּוֹמְמָה.[4]

דִּק נֶחֱלַד עֲבוּרָה,   עוֹמְדִים בִּגְבֵרָה,
בְּיִרְאָה הַטְּהוֹרָה, וּבְמִצְוָה בָרָה.[5]

גַּבְּרִי רְנוּנִים,[6]   וְשִׁפְכִי תַחֲנוּנִים,
עֲבֹר תְּפַלְּטֵנוּ בְּאֵין סְכוּךְ עֲנָנִים.[7]

בָּאֵי עָדָיו[8] בְּתַחַן,   לְנַקּוֹתָם מִצַּחַן,
מַאֲנָיִם יִתֵּן יִכְמֹר וְגַם יָחֹן.

אֱסֹף עֲדַת מִי מָנָה,[9]   לְקִרְיָה נֶאֱמָנָה,[10]
וּכְאֶדֶר בְּתוֹךְ הַדַּבְּרוֹ, מֵאָדָם תִּהִימֶנָּה.[11]

שְׁבוּיִם יְמַלֵּט,   מֵאַשְׁמַנֵּי עֵלֶט,
עֲדֵי עַד יְסוֹבְבָם עֹז, רָנֵּי פַלֵּט.[12]

וּבְשׁוּבָה* וָנַחַת,   נוֹשָׁעִים מְשַׁחַת,[13]
בַּקֵּשׁ צֹאן אוֹבְדוֹת וְגַם הַנִּדַּחַת.[14]

רְפָאוֹת הַנַּחֲלָה,   יָסִיר כָּל מַחֲלָה,
צִיּוֹן לְמַלֹּאות עִיר הַמְּהֻלָּלָה.

❖ חֲבֹשׁ הַנִּשְׁבֶּרֶת,[14]   זַלְזַל הַגָּבֶרֶת,
קַנֵּא קִנְאָה גְדוֹלָה, לְעִיר הַמֻּחְבֶּרֶת.[15]

לִרְאוֹת וּלְהַטּוֹת — *To see and to incline towards.*
An opinion may be accepted by the *Halachah*
in one of three ways: הֲלָכָה, *halachah*, מֵטִין,
inclining towards, or נִרְאִין, *appearing indicated*
(*Eruvin* 46b). According to *Rashi,* statements
regarded as הֲלָכָה may be publicized at popular
lectures and may be relied upon as practical
halachic guidelines; those considered מֵטִין
may be followed in individual cases, under
certain circumstances, but are not to be publi-

כ [Studying] generalities and particulars, to see and to incline towards,*
   sleep eludes them, even in their bedroom.

י Each day they investigate [the Law],[1] they meditate in their hearts,
   [whether] to forbid or to permit, and they explain [their decision] orally.

ט [Between] impurities and purities,
   to distinguish and determine;[2] according to the Law —
   despite [Exile's] oppression and affliction, their eyes shine bright.[3]

ח Laws and statutes are judged by their word,
   yet their enemies have become arbiters, who judge over them.

ז Remember this, O Torah, to invigorate your students,
   and to aid and support those who expound your ideas.

ו Plead before your Maker, with your well-spoken supplication,
   for He is your God, your Maker, and your Lord.

ה If not for [Israel] the wholesome [nation]
   pondering the perfect [Torah],
   it would be left in the corner, and [all would be] confounded.[4]

ד Because of her, heaven and earth stand strong,
   with pure reverence and clear commandments.[5]

ג [O Torah,] sing loud [your] prayer,[6] [for us] pour forth supplication,
   that our prayers may pass through [to God]
   with no obstruction of clouds.[7]

ב Those who come to Him[8] with supplications,
   that they be cleansed of [sin's] stench —
   may He grant their wish, may He be compassionate and gracious.

א Gather the uncountable people[9] to [Jerusalem,] the faithful city;[10]
   and as a flock in its fold, let it resound with the noise of man.[11]

ש May He let captives escape   מ from [Exile's] dark shadows;

ע eternally, may [Torah's] might surround them [with] songs of rescue.[12]

ו With calm spirit* and severity   נ they will be saved from ruin —[13]

ב O seek out the lost and straying sheep![14]

ר May he heal the sick,   י remove all illness,

צ and repopulate Zion, the lauded city.

ח Chazzan — Bind up the broken people,[14]

ז and scorn the [gentile] mistress;

ק and take great vengeance for [Jerusalem,]
   the city united [with its celestial counterpart].[15]

---

(1) *Isaiah* 58:2. (2) Cf. *Leviticus* 10:10-11. (3) Some editions read נוֹהֲרוֹת, the stich then reads, *even though their eyes are dimmed by [Exile's] oppression and affliction.* (4) See tractate *Kiddushin* 66a.
(5) Cf. *Psalms* 19:9-10; some editions of *Selichos* read, בְּיִרְאָה הַקָּדוֹשָׁה, *with holy reverence.*
(6) Some editions read, גְּבְּרֵי תַּחֲנוּנִים, *give forth strong supplication.* (7) Cf. *Lamentations* 3:44.
(8) Some editions read, עָדֶיךָ, *to You.* (9) See *Numbers* 23:10. (10) *Isaiah* 1:21. (11) Cf. *Micah* 2:12.
(12) Cf. *Psalms* 32:7. (13) Cf. *Isaiah* 30:15. (14) Cf. *Ezekiel* 34:16. (15) Cf. *Psalms* 122:3.

---

cized to the masses at public lectures; and those opinions classified as נְרָאִין are not to be relied upon in rendering decisions, but if one in fact did rely on such a view, the decision is not reversed.

וּבְשׁוּבָה — *With calm spirit.* The translation is

literal and follows the commentaries to *Isaiah* 30:15. The Talmud understands the word homiletically as an allusion to תְּשׁוּבָה, *repentance.* Thus, it is through repentance that Israel will attain serenity on their own land (*Sanhedrin* 97b).

All:

מַכְנִיסֵי רַחֲמִים, הַכְנִיסוּ רַחֲמֵינוּ, לִפְנֵי בַּעַל הָרַחֲמִים.
מַשְׁמִיעֵי תְפִלָּה, הַשְׁמִיעוּ תְפִלָּתֵנוּ, לִפְנֵי
שׁוֹמֵעַ תְּפִלָּה. מַשְׁמִיעֵי צְעָקָה, הַשְׁמִיעוּ צַעֲקָתֵנוּ, לִפְנֵי שׁוֹמֵעַ
צְעָקָה. מַכְנִיסֵי דִמְעָה, הַכְנִיסוּ דִמְעוֹתֵינוּ, לִפְנֵי מֶלֶךְ מִתְרַצֶּה
בִּדְמָעוֹת.

הִשְׁתַּדְּלוּ וְהַרְבּוּ תְּחִנָּה וּבַקָּשָׁה, לִפְנֵי מֶלֶךְ אֵל רָם וְנִשָּׂא.
הַזְכִּירוּ לְפָנָיו, הַשְׁמִיעוּ לְפָנָיו תּוֹרָה וּמַעֲשִׂים טוֹבִים שֶׁל שׁוֹכְנֵי
עָפָר.

יִזְכֹּר אַהֲבָתָם וִיחַיֶּה זַרְעָם, שֶׁלֹּא תֹאבַד שְׁאֵרִית יַעֲקֹב. כִּי צֹאן
רוֹעֶה נֶאֱמָן הָיָה לְחֶרְפָּה, יִשְׂרָאֵל גּוֹי אֶחָד לְמָשָׁל וְלִשְׁנִינָה.
מַהֵר עֲנֵנוּ אֱלֹהֵי יִשְׁעֵנוּ, וּפְדֵנוּ מִכָּל גְּזֵרוֹת קָשׁוֹת וְהוֹשִׁיעָה
בְּרַחֲמֶיךָ הָרַבִּים, מְשִׁיחַ צִדְקֶךָ וְעַמֶּךָ.

מָרָן דִּבִשְׁמַיָּא לָךְ מִתְחַנְּנַן, כְּבַר שַׁבְיָא דְּמִתְחַנַּן לְשִׁבוּיֵהּ.
כֻּלְּהוֹן בְּנֵי שַׁבְיָא בְּכַסְפָּא מִתְפָּרְקִין, וְעַמָּךְ
יִשְׂרָאֵל בְּרַחֲמֵי וּבְתַחֲנוּנֵי, הַב לָן שְׁאִילָתִין וּבָעוּתִין, דְּלָא נֶהְדַּר
רֵיקָם מִן קֳדָמָךְ.

מָרָן דִּבִשְׁמַיָּא לָךְ מִתְחַנְּנַן, כְּעַבְדָּא דְּמִתְחַנַּן לְמָרֵיהּ,
עֲשִׁיקֵי אֲנַן וּבַחֲשׁוֹכָא שַׁרְיַנָן, מְרִירָן נַפְשִׁין מֵעַקְתִין דִּנְפִישִׁין,
חֵילָא לֵית בָּן לְרַצּוּיָךְ מָרָן, עֲבִיד בְּדִיל קְיָמָא דִּגְזַרְתָּ עִם
אֲבָהָתָנָא.

שׁוֹמֵר יִשְׂרָאֵל, שְׁמוֹר שְׁאֵרִית יִשְׂרָאֵל, וְאַל יֹאבַד יִשְׂרָאֵל,
הָאוֹמְרִים, שְׁמַע יִשְׂרָאֵל.[1]
שׁוֹמֵר גּוֹי אֶחָד, שְׁמוֹר שְׁאֵרִית עַם אֶחָד, וְאַל יֹאבַד גּוֹי אֶחָד,
הַמְיַחֲדִים שִׁמְךָ, יְהוָה אֱלֹהֵינוּ יְהוָה אֶחָד.[1]
שׁוֹמֵר גּוֹי קָדוֹשׁ, שְׁמוֹר שְׁאֵרִית עַם קָדוֹשׁ, וְאַל יֹאבַד גּוֹי
קָדוֹשׁ, הַמְשַׁלְּשִׁים בְּשָׁלֹשׁ קְדֻשּׁוֹת לְקָדוֹשׁ.
מִתְרַצֶּה בְּרַחֲמִים וּמִתְפַּיֵּס בְּתַחֲנוּנִים, הִתְרַצֵּה וְהִתְפַּיֵּס לְדוֹר
עָנִי, כִּי אֵין עוֹזֵר. אָבִינוּ מַלְכֵּנוּ, חָנֵּנוּ וַעֲנֵנוּ, כִּי אֵין בָּנוּ מַעֲשִׂים,
עֲשֵׂה עִמָּנוּ צְדָקָה וָחֶסֶד וְהוֹשִׁיעֵנוּ.

---

(1) Deuteronomy 6:4.

All:

מַכְנִיסֵי רַחֲמִים O you who usher in [pleas for] mercy, may you usher in our [plea for] mercy, before the Master of mercy. O you who cause prayer to be heard, may you cause our prayer to be heard, before the Hearer of prayer. O you who cause outcry to be heard, may you cause our outcry to be heard, before the Hearer of outcry. O you who usher in tears, may you usher in our tears, before the King Who finds favor through tears.

Exert yourselves, and multiply supplication and petition, before the King, God, exalted and most high. Mention before Him, cause to be heard before Him, the Torah and the good deeds of [the Patriarchs and Matriarchs] who dwell in the dust.

May He remember their love and grant life to [their] offspring, that the remnant of Jacob not be lost. For the flock of the faithful shepherd [Moses] has become a disgrace; Israel, the unique nation, a parable and a simile.

Speedily, answer us, O God of our salvation, and redeem us from all harsh decrees; and may You save, in Your abundant mercy, Your righteous anointed and Your people.

מָרָן דְּבִשְׁמַיָּא Our Master Who is in heaven, to You do we supplicate, as a captive supplicates before his captors; for all captives are redeemed with money, but Your people Israel with compassion and supplication. O grant our requests and our prayers that we not be turned away from You empty-handed.

Our Master Who is in heaven, to You do we supplicate, as a slave supplicates before his master: We are oppressed and we abide in darkness, souls embittered from abundant distress. We have no strength to regain Your favor. Our Master, act for the sake of the covenant that You made with our Patriarchs.

שׁוֹמֵר יִשְׂרָאֵל O Guardian of Israel, protect the remnant of Israel; let not Israel be destroyed — those who proclaim, 'Hear O Israel.'[1]

O Guardian of the unique nation, protect the remnant of the unique people; let not the unique nation be destroyed — those who proclaim the Oneness of Your Name, 'HASHEM is our God, HASHEM, the One and Only!'[1]

O Guardian of the holy nation, protect the remnant of the holy people; let not the holy nation be destroyed — those who proclaim three-fold sanctifications to the Holy One.

Become favorable through compassion and become appeased through supplications. Become favorable and appeased to the poor generation, for there is no helper. Our Father, our King, be gracious with us and answer us, though we have no worthy deeds; treat us with charity and kindness, and save us.

סליחה נט

גְּרוֹנִי נִחַר*[1] זוֹעֵק חָמָס,[2]
רְאוֹתִי רָשָׁע נוֹתֵן קֹדֶשׁ לְמִרְמָס,[3]
שׁוַּעְתִּי הוֹשִׁיעָה לְיוֹם נָקָם נִכְמָס,
מֵעַי עַל כֵּן אוֹחִילָה[4] וְלִבִּי נָמָס.[5]

אָדוֹן אֶרֶץ קִדַּשְׁתָּ בְּעֶשֶׂר קְדֻשּׁוֹת,[6]
בְּתוֹכָהּ שָׁכַנְתָּ לְכַפָּרַת נְפָשׁוֹת,
גְּאוֹן עֻזְּךָ[7] כּוֹנְנוּ יָדֶיךָ הַקְּדוֹשׁוֹת,
דָּשׁוּ בּוֹ שׁוּעָלִים וְנֶחְרַשׁ בְּמַחֲרֵשׁוֹת.
מֵעַי עַל כֵּן אוֹחִילָה וְלִבִּי נָמָס.

הָעִיר כְּלִילַת יֹפִי[8] קִרְיָה נֶאֱמָנָה,[9]
וּמָקוֹם בּוֹ מִתְכַּפְּרִים אַחַת בַּשָּׁנָה,
זָעַמְתָּ וְאָנַפְתָּ עָלָיו זֶה כַּמֶּה שָׁנָה,*
חֲרוֹן אַפְּךָ שָׁפַכְתָּ[10] וְלֹא רִחַמְתָּ לַחֲנֻנָּה.
מֵעַי עַל כֵּן אוֹחִילָה וְלִבִּי נָמָס.

טַבּוּר הָאָרֶץ בִּקִקְתָּ בַּלַּקְתָּ,[11]
יַעַר הַלְּבָנוֹן* הִסַּקְתָּ הִדְלַקְתָּ,
כַּבִּיר, יוֹשְׁבִים הוֹרַדְתָּ סִלַּקְתָּ,
לְקוּחֶיךָ בְּיוֹם אַף טָבַחְתָּ מָלַקְתָּ.[12]
מֵעַי עַל כֵּן אוֹחִילָה וְלִבִּי נָמָס.

מֵאֶרֶץ חֶמְדָּה יָצְאוּ רְחוּמֶיךָ,
נוֹדְדִים בַּגּוֹלָה וּמְהַלְלִים שְׁמֶךָ,
שׂוֹנְאִים בְּלַחַץ לְהוֹנוֹת עַמֶּךָ,
עִם יהוה אַתָּה וְגוֹלֶה מִמְּקוֹמֶךָ.[13]
מֵעַי עַל כֵּן אוֹחִילָה וְלִבִּי נָמָס.

פָּתוֹחַ נִפְתַּח פִּינוּ וּלְךָ נַצְדִּיק,
צוּר עַל כָּל הַבָּא אַתָּה צַדִּיק,[14]

גְּרוֹנִי נִחַר — *My throat is dried out.* A
description of the Destruction of the *Beis HaMikdash* is followed by the acceptance of blame, for
it was the national sinfulness that caused it to
happen. That acknowledged, this *selichah* pleads
that our *teshuvah* put an end to our suffering in
exile. With the change of theme, from confession

to supplication, comes a new refrain of roseate
optimism to replace the bleak picture painted by
the earlier refrain.

Rabbeinu Gershom [see prefatory comment to
selichah 12] signed his name in the acrostic of the
first stanza. The acrostic continues with the
aleph-beis, then concludes גֵּרְשׁוֹם בַּר יְהוּדָה חֲזַק

SELICHAH 59

ג My throat is dried out*[1] from crying, 'Corruption!'[2]

ר When I see the wicked make the holy for trampling.[3]

ש I shout, 'Save us!', longing for the day of vengeance.

מ And so my innards shudder[4] and my heart melts.[5]

א Lord, You hallowed [our] land with ten levels of holiness;[6]

ב You dwelt in its midst to give atonement for [our] souls.

ג Your holy hands established [the Temple,] the pride of Your strength[7]

ד and now foxes run through it, and it is furrowed by plows.

And so my innards shudder and my heart melts.

ה The city [that was] perfect in its beauty,[8] the faithful town,[9]

ו and in it, the place of the once-a-year [Yom Kippur] atonement service.

ז So many years now* You have raged and stormed against it;

ח You poured out Your anger,[10] You have had no mercy to favor it.

And so my innards shudder and my heart melts.

ט You emptied and laid waste the [Holy] Land,[11] the navel of the world,

י You kindled and burned Lebanon's forest.*

כ O powerful One, You dragged down the land's

inhabitants and placed them afar;

ל those You had taken as Your own

You slaughtered and strangled in the day of anger.[12]

And so my innards shudder and my heart melts.

מ Your beloved ones went forth from the desirable land,

נ wandering through Exile, yet praising Your name.

ס The enemies use pressure to taunt Your people:

ע 'You are God's people, yet you have been exiled from your land?'[13]

And so my innards shudder and my heart melts.

פ We shall open our mouths and justify You:

צ Creator, for all that may happen, You are righteous.[14]

---

(1) Cf. *Psalms* 69:4. (2) Cf. *Habakkuk* 1:2. (3) Cf. *Daniel* 8:13. (4) Cf. *Jeremiah* 4:19.
(5) Cf. *Psalms* 22:15. (6) See Mishnah, *Keilim* 1:6-9. (7) Cf. *Ezekiel* 24:21.
(8) Cf. *Lamentations* 2:15. (9) *Isaiah* 1:26. (10) Cf. *Lamentations* 4:11. (11) Cf. *Isaiah* 24:1.
(12) Cf. *Lamentations* 2:22. (13) Cf. *Ezekiel* 36:20. (14) Cf. *Nehemiah* 9:33.

וֶאֱמָץ, *Gershom bar Yehudah, may he be strong and persevere.*

זֶה כַּמָּה שָׁנָה — *So many years now.* In its original version this read תֵּשַׁע מֵאוֹת וַחֲמִשִּׁים וְעוֹד שָׁנָה, *some nine hundred and fifty-plus years.* Over the years, however, various editions updated the stich to יוֹתֵר מֵאֶלֶף שָׁנָה, *more than a thousand years.* One manuscript read זֶה אֶלֶף שָׁנָה וְשִׁבְעִים שָׁנָה, *this 1070 years.* The present version has been used for many centuries, for the Destruction took place almost two millennia ago.

יַעַר הַלְּבָנוֹן — *Lebanon's forest.* Moses beseeched

God to permit him entry into the Holy Land, that he might see הָהָר הַטּוֹב הַזֶּה וְהַלְּבָנוֹן, *this good mountain and the Lebanon* (*Deuteronomy* 3:25). Although the name Lebanon refers to a forest in which grew towering cedars, the Sages understand Moses' request as more than just the desire to visit nature's wonderland. Lebanon alludes to the *Beis HaMikdash* ... And why is it called לְבָנוֹן, *Lebanon,* a word related to לָבָן, *white?* Because it cleanses the sins of Israel; as it is stated: *If your sins are as scarlet, as snow will He whiten them* (*Isaiah* 1:18; *Sifri* 3:25).

קָדוֹשׁ הַדִּין עִמָּךְ לְמָסְרֵנוּ בְּיַד מַדִּיק,
רוֹפֵשׁ בְּרֶגֶל וְחֹרֵק שֵׁן וּמַדִּיק.*[1]
מֵעַי עַל כֵּן אוֹחִילָה וְלִבִּי נָמָס.

שָׁחֲתוּ דֶרֶךְ אָבוֹת, עוֹנָם סֵבֶל נִתְפַּסְנוּ,
תַּחַת כִּי מַעֲשֵׂימוֹ סֵבֶל תָּפַסְנוּ,
גָּעַר מְלָאוּנוּ נִגְעַלְנוּ נִמְאַסְנוּ,
רָעוֹת רַבּוֹת וְצָרוֹת לְהַמְצִיא[2] נִקְנַסְנוּ.
מֵעַי עַל כֵּן אוֹחִילָה וְלִבִּי נָמָס.

שׁוּב עָדֶיךָ אָדוֹן נִמְלַכְנוּ נִסְכַּכְמְנוּ,
מְאֹד אַחֲרֵי שׁוּבֵנוּ נֶחֱרַטְנוּ נִחַמְנוּ,[3]
בְּרַחֲמֶיךָ חָנֵנוּ כִּי כָלִינוּ תַמְנוּ,
יְרִיבֵינוּ אַל יִשְׂמְחוּ כִּי נָפַלְנוּ קָמְנוּ.[4]
מֵעַי עַל כֵּן אוֹחִילָה וְלִבִּי נָמָס.

הָשֵׁב שְׁבוּת זְרוּיִים בְּאַשְׁמָה רַבָּה,
וְקַבְּצֵם מִן הַגּוֹיִם בְּיִתְרָה חִבָּה,
דְּבָרְךָ יֵאָמֵן שְׁלוּחֲךָ הַחוֹזֶה נָבָא,
הָקֵם סֻכַּת דָּוִד הַנּוֹפֶלֶת וַחֲרֵבָה.[5]
וְאָז מֵעַי יָגִילוּ וְלִבִּי יִשְׂמַח.

חֶסֶד נְעוּרִים זְכָרָה[6] וּבְרִית רִאשׁוֹנִים,
זְכוּת אָבוֹת תִּזְכֹּר וְאַל יֹאבְדוּ בָנִים,
קוֹמְמִיּוּת יֵלְכוּ בִּבְכִי וּבְתַחֲנוּנִים,*[7]
מִצָּפוֹן וּמִיָּם וּמֵאֶרֶץ צְפוֹנִים.
וְאָז מֵעַי יָגִילוּ וְלִבִּי יִשְׂמַח.

❖ וְעַתָּה בַּצַּר פְּקַדְנוּךְ בּוֹשִׁים וְנִכְלָמִים,
אוֹמְרִים חָטָאנוּ סְלַח נָא נוֹאֲמִים,
מִדַּת הַדִּין הֲפָךְ נָא לְמִדַּת רַחֲמִים,
צִדְקָתֵנוּ הָאֵר כְּאוֹר שִׁבְעַת יָמִים.[8]
וְאָז מֵעַי יָגִילוּ וְלִבִּי יִשְׂמַח.

Another reason why the Temple is called Lebanon is that timber for the Temple was brought from the forest of Lebanon (see *I Kings* 5:20-28; *Song of Songs* 3:9).

רוֹפֵשׁ בְּרֶגֶל וְחֹרֵק שֵׁן וּמַדִּיק — *Who tramples [us] underfoot, gnashes [his] teeth and crushes [us].* In Daniel's version of the four ferocious beasts that represented the four kingdoms

ק Holy One, the right is with You to deliver us
   into the grinder's hand,
ר who tramples [us] underfoot,
   gnashes [his] teeth and crushes [us].*[1]
                    And so my innards shudder and my heart melts.

ש Our fathers perverted [their] way,
   and we are compelled to suffer for their iniquity.
ת since we have grasped their deeds in our hands.
ג We are replete with [God's] rebuke,
   we have become despicable and detestable,
ר many evils and troubles have been brought forth[2] to punish us.
                    And so my innards shudder and my heart melts.

ש We have considered and agreed to return to You, O Lord;
מ after our repentance, we still sorely regret, we rue our deeds.[3]
בר Favor for us in Your mercy, for we are exhausted, we are ended!
י Let not our foes rejoice when we fall, for we rise again.[4]
                    And so my innards shudder and my heart melts.

ה Bring back the captives, dispersed for [their] great guilt,
ו and gather them from among the nations with exceeding love.
ר Fulfill Your words that Your emissary the seer prophesied;
ה raise up David's fallen and destroyed Tabernacle.[5]
                    And then my innards will rejoice, and my heart will be glad.

ח Remember the youthful kindness[6] and the ancestors' covenant;
ו remember the Patriarchs' merit, and let not the children perish.
ק Let them go with upright stature,
   with weeping and with supplications,*[7]
   from north and from west and from the land of the concealed.
                    And then my innards will rejoice, and my heart will be glad.

ו Chazzan — And now, in distress we come to You,
   shamed and humiliated;
א saying, 'We have sinned', declaring, 'Please forgive!'
מ Please turn the Attribute of Judgment to the Attribute of Mercy,
צ and shine forth Your kindly justice
   like the light of [Creation's] seven days.[8]
                    And then my innards will rejoice, and my heart will be glad.

---

(1) Cf. *Daniel* 7:7. (2) Cf. *Deuteronomy* 31:17. (3) Cf. *Jeremiah* 31:18.
(4) Cf. *Micah* 7:8. (5) Cf. *Amos* 9:11. (6) Cf. *Jeremiah* 2:2. (7) Cf. 31:8. (8) Cf. *Isaiah* 30:26.

---

into whose power Israel would be exiled, the
fourth and fiercest of them is described as
*excessively terrifying, awesome and strong;
with immense iron teeth, it was eating and
crushing and trampling the rest underfoot …*
(*Daniel* 7:7). That beast represents the present
Edomite exile.

בִּבְכִי וּבְתַחֲנוּנִים — *With weeping and with
supplications.* The translation follows *Rashi* (to
Jeremiah 31:8). Weeping and prayer will bring
the Redemption. Alternatively, at the time of the
Redemption, we will cry tears of joy, and find
favor [תַּחֲנוּנִים, from חֵן, *favor*, and חֲנִינָה,
graciousness] (*Radak*).

All:

וַאֲנַחְנוּ לֹא נֵדַע מַה נַּעֲשֶׂה, כִּי עָלֶיךָ עֵינֵינוּ.[1] זְכֹר רַחֲמֶיךָ יהוה וַחֲסָדֶיךָ, כִּי מֵעוֹלָם הֵמָּה.[2] יְהִי חַסְדְּךָ יהוה עָלֵינוּ, כַּאֲשֶׁר יִחַלְנוּ לָךְ.[3]

אַל תִּזְכָּר לָנוּ עֲוֹנוֹת רִאשׁוֹנִים, מַהֵר יְקַדְּמוּנוּ רַחֲמֶיךָ, כִּי דַלּוֹנוּ מְאֹד.[4] חָנֵּנוּ יהוה חָנֵּנוּ, כִּי רַב שָׂבַעְנוּ בוּז.[5] בְּרֹגֶז רַחֵם תִּזְכּוֹר.[6] כִּי הוּא יָדַע יִצְרֵנוּ, זָכוּר כִּי עָפָר אֲנָחְנוּ.[7] עָזְרֵנוּ אֱלֹהֵי יִשְׁעֵנוּ עַל דְּבַר כְּבוֹד שְׁמֶךָ, וְהַצִּילֵנוּ וְכַפֵּר עַל חַטֹּאתֵינוּ לְמַעַן שְׁמֶךָ.[8]

קדיש שלם

קַדִּישׁ שָׁלֵם: The chazzan recites

יִתְגַּדַּל וְיִתְקַדַּשׁ שְׁמֵהּ רַבָּא. (.Cong – אָמֵן.) בְּעָלְמָא דִּי בְרָא כִרְעוּתֵהּ, וְיַמְלִיךְ מַלְכוּתֵהּ, בְּחַיֵּיכוֹן וּבְיוֹמֵיכוֹן וּבְחַיֵּי דְכָל בֵּית יִשְׂרָאֵל, בַּעֲגָלָא וּבִזְמַן קָרִיב. וְאִמְרוּ אָמֵן.

(.Cong – אָמֵן. יְהֵא שְׁמֵהּ רַבָּא מְבָרַךְ לְעָלַם וּלְעָלְמֵי עָלְמַיָּא.)

יְהֵא שְׁמֵהּ רַבָּא מְבָרַךְ לְעָלַם וּלְעָלְמֵי עָלְמַיָּא.

יִתְבָּרַךְ וְיִשְׁתַּבַּח וְיִתְפָּאַר וְיִתְרוֹמַם וְיִתְנַשֵּׂא וְיִתְהַדָּר וְיִתְעַלֶּה וְיִתְהַלָּל שְׁמֵהּ דְּקוּדְשָׁא בְּרִיךְ הוּא (.Cong – בְּרִיךְ הוּא.) לְעֵלָּא [וּ]לְעֵלָּא מִכָּל בִּרְכָתָא וְשִׁירָתָא תֻּשְׁבְּחָתָא וְנֶחֱמָתָא, דַּאֲמִירָן בְּעָלְמָא. וְאִמְרוּ: אָמֵן. (.Cong – אָמֵן.)

(.Cong – קַבֵּל בְּרַחֲמִים וּבְרָצוֹן אֶת תְּפִלָּתֵנוּ.)

תִּתְקַבֵּל צְלוֹתְהוֹן וּבָעוּתְהוֹן דְּכָל (בֵּית) יִשְׂרָאֵל קֳדָם אֲבוּהוֹן דִּי בִשְׁמַיָּא. וְאִמְרוּ אָמֵן. (.Cong – אָמֵן.)

(.Cong – יְהִי שֵׁם יהוה מְבֹרָךְ, מֵעַתָּה וְעַד עוֹלָם.[9])

יְהֵא שְׁלָמָא רַבָּא מִן שְׁמַיָּא וְחַיִּים עָלֵינוּ וְעַל כָּל יִשְׂרָאֵל. וְאִמְרוּ אָמֵן. (.Cong – אָמֵן.)

(.Cong – עֶזְרִי מֵעִם יהוה, עֹשֵׂה שָׁמַיִם וָאָרֶץ.[10])

Take three steps back. Bow left and say, . . . עֹשֶׂה; bow right and say, . . . הוּא יַעֲשֶׂה; bow forward and say, וְעַל כָּל . . . אָמֵן. Remain standing in place for a few moments, then take three steps forward.

עֹשֶׂה [הַ]שָּׁלוֹם בִּמְרוֹמָיו, הוּא יַעֲשֶׂה שָׁלוֹם עָלֵינוּ, וְעַל כָּל יִשְׂרָאֵל. וְאִמְרוּ אָמֵן. (.Cong – אָמֵן.)

All:

וַאֲנַחְנוּ *We know not what to do — but our eyes are upon You.*[1] *Remember Your mercies,* HASHEM, *and Your kindnesses, for they are from the beginning of the world.*[2] *May Your kindness be upon us,* HASHEM, *just as we awaited You.*[3]

אַל תִּזְכָּר *Recall not against us the iniquities of the ancients; may Your mercies meet us swiftly, for we have become exceedingly impoverished.*[4] *Be gracious to us,* HASHEM, *be gracious to us, for we are abundantly sated with scorn.*[5] *Amid rage — remember to be merciful!*[6] *For He knew our nature, He remembers that we are dust.*[7] Chazzan— *Assist us, O God of our salvation, for the sake of Your Name's glory; rescue us and atone for our sins for Your Name's sake.*[8]

FULL KADDISH

The chazzan recites the Full Kaddish:

יִתְגַּדַּל *May His great Name grow exalted and sanctified* (Cong. — *Amen.*) *in the world that He created as He willed. May He give reign to His kingship in your lifetimes and in your days, and in the lifetimes of the entire Family of Israel, swiftly and soon. Now respond: Amen.*

(Cong. — *Amen. May His great Name be blessed forever and ever.*)
May His great Name be blessed forever and ever.

Blessed, praised, glorified, exalted, extolled, mighty, upraised and lauded be the Name of the Holy One, Blessed is He (Cong. — *Blessed is He.*) *exceedingly beyond any blessing and song, praise, and consolation that are uttered in the world. Now respond: Amen.* (Cong. — *Amen.*)

(Cong. — *Accept our prayers with mercy and favor.*)
May the prayers and supplications of the entire House of Israel be accepted before their Father Who is in Heaven. Now respond: Amen. (Cong. — *Amen.*)

(Cong. — *Blessed be the Name of* HASHEM *from this time and forever.*[9])
May there be abundant peace from Heaven, and life, upon us and upon all Israel. Now respond: Amen. (Cong. — *Amen.*)

(Cong. — *My help is from* HASHEM, *Maker of heaven and earth.*[10])

Take three steps back. Bow left and say, 'He Who makes peace . . .'; bow right and say,
'may He make peace . . .'; bow forward and say, 'and upon all Israel . . .'
Remain standing in place for a few moments, then take three steps forward.

He Who makes [the] peace in His heights, may He make peace upon us, and upon all Israel. Now respond: Amen. (Cong. — *Amen.*)

---

(1) *II Chronicles* 20:12. (2) *Psalms* 25:6. (3) 33:22. (4) 78:8. (5) 123:3.
(6) *Habakkuk* 3:2. (7) *Psalms* 103:14. (8) 79:9. (9) 113:2. (10) 121:2.

❀ יוֹם שֵׁנִי שֶׁל עֲשֶׂרֶת יְמֵי תְשׁוּבָה ❀

אַשְׁרֵי יוֹשְׁבֵי בֵיתֶךָ, עוֹד יְהַלְלְוּךָ סֶּלָה.[1] אַשְׁרֵי הָעָם שֶׁכָּכָה
לוֹ, אַשְׁרֵי הָעָם שֶׁיהוה אֱלֹהָיו.[2]

תְּהִלָּה לְדָוִד.

_{תהלים קמה}

אֲרוֹמִמְךָ אֱלוֹהַי הַמֶּלֶךְ, וַאֲבָרְכָה שִׁמְךָ לְעוֹלָם וָעֶד.

בְּכָל יוֹם אֲבָרְכֶךָּ, וַאֲהַלְלָה שִׁמְךָ לְעוֹלָם וָעֶד.

גָּדוֹל יהוה וּמְהֻלָּל מְאֹד, וְלִגְדֻלָּתוֹ אֵין חֵקֶר.

דּוֹר לְדוֹר יְשַׁבַּח מַעֲשֶׂיךָ, וּגְבוּרֹתֶיךָ יַגִּידוּ.

הֲדַר כְּבוֹד הוֹדֶךָ, וְדִבְרֵי נִפְלְאֹתֶיךָ אָשִׂיחָה.

וֶעֱזוּז נוֹרְאוֹתֶיךָ יֹאמֵרוּ, וּגְדֻלָּתְךָ אֲסַפְּרֶנָּה.

זֵכֶר רַב טוּבְךָ יַבִּיעוּ, וְצִדְקָתְךָ יְרַנֵּנוּ.

חַנּוּן וְרַחוּם יהוה, אֶרֶךְ אַפַּיִם וּגְדָל חָסֶד.

טוֹב יהוה לַכֹּל, וְרַחֲמָיו עַל כָּל מַעֲשָׂיו.

יוֹדוּךָ יהוה כָּל מַעֲשֶׂיךָ, וַחֲסִידֶיךָ יְבָרְכוּכָה.

כְּבוֹד מַלְכוּתְךָ יֹאמֵרוּ, וּגְבוּרָתְךָ יְדַבֵּרוּ.

לְהוֹדִיעַ לִבְנֵי הָאָדָם גְּבוּרֹתָיו, וּכְבוֹד הֲדַר מַלְכוּתוֹ.

מַלְכוּתְךָ מַלְכוּת כָּל עֹלָמִים, וּמֶמְשַׁלְתְּךָ בְּכָל דּוֹר וָדֹר.

סוֹמֵךְ יהוה לְכָל הַנֹּפְלִים, וְזוֹקֵף לְכָל הַכְּפוּפִים.

עֵינֵי כֹל אֵלֶיךָ יְשַׂבֵּרוּ, וְאַתָּה נוֹתֵן לָהֶם אֶת אָכְלָם בְּעִתּוֹ.

<sub>Concentrate intently while
reciting the verse, פּוֹתֵחַ.</sub>

פּוֹתֵחַ אֶת יָדֶךָ, וּמַשְׂבִּיעַ לְכָל חַי רָצוֹן.

❖ **צַדִּיק** יהוה בְּכָל דְּרָכָיו, וְחָסִיד בְּכָל מַעֲשָׂיו.

קָרוֹב יהוה לְכָל קֹרְאָיו, לְכֹל אֲשֶׁר יִקְרָאֻהוּ בֶאֱמֶת.

רְצוֹן יְרֵאָיו יַעֲשֶׂה, וְאֶת שַׁוְעָתָם יִשְׁמַע וְיוֹשִׁיעֵם.

שׁוֹמֵר יהוה אֶת כָּל אֹהֲבָיו, וְאֵת כָּל הָרְשָׁעִים יַשְׁמִיד.

תְּהִלַּת יהוה יְדַבֶּר פִּי, וִיבָרֵךְ כָּל בָּשָׂר שֵׁם קָדְשׁוֹ לְעוֹלָם וָעֶד.

וַאֲנַחְנוּ נְבָרֵךְ יָהּ, מֵעַתָּה וְעַד עוֹלָם, הַלְלוּיָהּ.[3]

_{חֲצִי קַדִּישׁ. The chazzan recites}

יִתְגַּדַּל וְיִתְקַדַּשׁ שְׁמֵהּ רַבָּא. (.Cong – אָמֵן.) בְּעָלְמָא דִּי בְרָא כִרְעוּתֵהּ.
וְיַמְלִיךְ מַלְכוּתֵהּ, בְּחַיֵּיכוֹן וּבְיוֹמֵיכוֹן וּבְחַיֵּי דְכָל בֵּית יִשְׂרָאֵל,
בַּעֲגָלָא וּבִזְמַן קָרִיב. וְאִמְרוּ: אָמֵן.

(.Cong – אָמֵן. יְהֵא שְׁמֵהּ רַבָּא מְבָרַךְ לְעָלַם וּלְעָלְמֵי עָלְמַיָּא.)

יְהֵא שְׁמֵהּ רַבָּא מְבָרַךְ לְעָלַם וּלְעָלְמֵי עָלְמַיָּא.

יִתְבָּרַךְ וְיִשְׁתַּבַּח וְיִתְפָּאַר וְיִתְרוֹמַם וְיִתְנַשֵּׂא וְיִתְהַדָּר וְיִתְעַלֶּה וְיִתְהַלָּל
שְׁמֵהּ דְּקֻדְשָׁא בְּרִיךְ הוּא (.Cong – בְּרִיךְ הוּא) לְעֵלָּא [וּ]לְעֵלָּא מִכָּל בִּרְכָתָא
וְשִׁירָתָא תֻּשְׁבְּחָתָא וְנֶחֱמָתָא, דַּאֲמִירָן בְּעָלְמָא. וְאִמְרוּ: אָמֵן. (.Cong – אָמֵן.)

❧ SECOND DAY OF REPENTANCE ❧

אַשְׁרֵי *Praiseworthy are those who dwell in Your house; may they always praise You, Selah!*[1] *Praiseworthy is the people for whom this is so, praiseworthy is the people whose God is HASHEM.*[2]

Psalm 145   *A psalm of praise by David:*

א *I will exalt You, my God the King, and I will bless Your Name forever and ever.*

ב *Every day I will bless You, and I will laud Your Name forever and ever.*

ג *HASHEM is great and exceedingly lauded,*
      and His greatness is beyond investigation.

ד *Each generation will praise Your deeds to the next*
      and of Your mighty deeds they will tell;

ה *The splendrous glory of Your power and Your wondrous deeds I shall discuss.*

ו *And of Your awesome power they will speak, and Your greatness I shall relate.*

ז *A recollection of Your abundant goodness they will utter*
      and of Your righteousness they will sing exultantly.

ח *Gracious and merciful is HASHEM,*
      slow to anger, and great in [bestowing] kindness.

ט *HASHEM is good to all; His mercies are on all His works.*

י *All Your works shall thank You, HASHEM, and Your devout ones will bless You.*

כ *Of the glory of Your kingdom they will speak, and of Your power they will tell;*

ל *To inform human beings of His mighty deeds,*
      and the glorious splendor of His kingdom.

מ *Your kingdom is a kingdom spanning all eternities,*
      and Your dominion is throughout every generation.

ס *HASHEM supports all the fallen ones and straightens all the bent.*

ע *The eyes of all look to You with hope*
      and You give them their food in its proper time;

פ *You open Your hand,*   *Concentrate intently while reciting the verse, 'You open...'*
      and satisfy the desire of every living thing.

צ *Chazzan—* *Righteous is HASHEM in all His ways*
      and magnanimous in all His deeds.

ק *HASHEM is close to all who call upon Him — to all who call upon Him sincerely.*

ר *The will of those who fear Him He will do;*
      and their cry He will hear, and save them.

ש *HASHEM protects all who love Him; but all the wicked He will destroy.*

ת *May my mouth declare the praise of HASHEM*
      and may all flesh bless His Holy Name forever and ever.

We will bless God from this time and forever, Halleluyah![3]

The chazzan recites Half-Kaddish:

יִתְגַּדַּל *May His great Name grow exalted and sanctified* (Cong.— *Amen.*) *in the world that He created as He willed. May He give reign to His kingship in your lifetimes and in your days, and in the lifetimes of the entire Family of Israel, swiftly and soon. Now respond: Amen.*

(Cong.— *Amen. May His great Name be blessed forever and ever.*)

May His great Name be blessed forever and ever.

Blessed, praised, glorified, exalted, extolled, mighty, upraised, and lauded be the Name of the Holy One, Blessed is He (Cong.— *Blessed is He*) *— exceedingly beyond any blessing and song, praise and consolation that are uttered in the world. Now respond: Amen.* (Cong.— *Amen.*)

---

(1) *Psalms* 84:5. (2) 144:15. (3) 115:18.

All:

לְךָ יהוה הַצְּדָקָה, וְלָנוּ בְּשֶׁת הַפָּנִים.[1] מַה נִּתְאוֹנֵן,[2] מַה נֹּאמַר, מַה נְּדַבֵּר, וּמַה נִּצְטַדָּק.[3] נַחְפְּשָׂה דְרָכֵינוּ וְנַחְקֹרָה, וְנָשׁוּבָה אֵלֶיךָ,[4] כִּי יְמִינְךָ פְּשׁוּטָה לְקַבֵּל שָׁבִים. לֹא בְחֶסֶד וְלֹא בְמַעֲשִׂים בָּאנוּ לְפָנֶיךָ, כְּדַלִּים וּכְרָשִׁים דָּפַקְנוּ דְלָתֶיךָ. דְּלָתֶיךָ דָּפַקְנוּ רַחוּם וְחַנּוּן, נָא אַל תְּשִׁיבֵנוּ רֵיקָם מִלְּפָנֶיךָ. מִלְּפָנֶיךָ מַלְכֵּנוּ רֵיקָם אַל תְּשִׁיבֵנוּ, כִּי אַתָּה שׁוֹמֵעַ תְּפִלָּה.

שְׁמַע תְּפִלָּה, עָדֶיךָ כָּל בָּשָׂר יָבֹאוּ.[5] יָבוֹא כָל בָּשָׂר לְהִשְׁתַּחֲוֹת לְפָנֶיךָ יהוה.[6] יָבֹאוּ וְיִשְׁתַּחֲווּ לְפָנֶיךָ אֲדֹנָי, וִיכַבְּדוּ לִשְׁמֶךָ.[7] בֹּאוּ נִשְׁתַּחֲוֶה וְנִכְרָעָה, נִבְרְכָה לִפְנֵי יהוה עֹשֵׂנוּ.[8] נָבוֹאָה לְמִשְׁכְּנוֹתָיו, נִשְׁתַּחֲוֶה לַהֲדֹם רַגְלָיו.[9] בֹּאוּ שְׁעָרָיו בְּתוֹדָה, חֲצֵרֹתָיו בִּתְהִלָּה, הוֹדוּ לוֹ בָּרְכוּ שְׁמוֹ.[10] רוֹמְמוּ יהוה אֱלֹהֵינוּ, וְהִשְׁתַּחֲווּ לַהֲדֹם רַגְלָיו, קָדוֹשׁ הוּא.[11] רוֹמְמוּ יהוה אֱלֹהֵינוּ, וְהִשְׁתַּחֲווּ לְהַר קָדְשׁוֹ, כִּי קָדוֹשׁ יהוה אֱלֹהֵינוּ.[12] הִשְׁתַּחֲווּ לַיהוה בְּהַדְרַת קֹדֶשׁ, חִילוּ מִפָּנָיו כָּל הָאָרֶץ.[13] וַאֲנַחְנוּ בְּרֹב חַסְדְּךָ נָבוֹא בֵיתֶךָ, נִשְׁתַּחֲוֶה אֶל הֵיכַל קָדְשְׁךָ בְּיִרְאָתֶךָ.[14] נִשְׁתַּחֲוֶה אֶל הֵיכַל קָדְשְׁךָ וְנוֹדֶה אֶת שְׁמֶךָ, עַל חַסְדְּךָ וְעַל אֲמִתֶּךָ, כִּי הִגְדַּלְתָּ עַל כָּל שִׁמְךָ אִמְרָתֶךָ.[15] לְכוּ נְרַנְּנָה לַיהוה, נָרִיעָה לְצוּר יִשְׁעֵנוּ. נְקַדְּמָה פָנָיו בְּתוֹדָה, בִּזְמִרוֹת נָרִיעַ לוֹ.[16] אֲשֶׁר יַחְדָּו נַמְתִּיק סוֹד, בְּבֵית אֱלֹהִים נְהַלֵּךְ בְּרָגֶשׁ.[17] אֵל נַעֲרָץ בְּסוֹד קְדֹשִׁים רַבָּה, וְנוֹרָא עַל כָּל סְבִיבָיו.[18] שְׂאוּ יְדֵכֶם קֹדֶשׁ וּבָרְכוּ אֶת יהוה.[19] הִנֵּה בָּרְכוּ אֶת יהוה כָּל עַבְדֵי יהוה, הָעֹמְדִים בְּבֵית יהוה בַּלֵּילוֹת.[20] אֲשֶׁר מִי אֵל בַּשָּׁמַיִם וּבָאָרֶץ, אֲשֶׁר יַעֲשֶׂה כְמַעֲשֶׂיךָ וְכִגְבוּרֹתֶיךָ.[21] אֲשֶׁר לוֹ הַיָּם וְהוּא עָשָׂהוּ, וְיַבֶּשֶׁת יָדָיו יָצָרוּ.[22] אֲשֶׁר בְּיָדוֹ מֶחְקְרֵי אָרֶץ, וְתוֹעֲפוֹת הָרִים לוֹ.[23] אֲשֶׁר בְּיָדוֹ נֶפֶשׁ כָּל חָי, וְרוּחַ כָּל בְּשַׂר אִישׁ.[24] וְיוֹדוּ שָׁמַיִם פִּלְאֲךָ יהוה, אַף אֱמוּנָתְךָ בִּקְהַל קְדֹשִׁים.[25] לְךָ זְרוֹעַ עִם גְּבוּרָה, תָּעֹז יָדְךָ תָּרוּם יְמִינֶךָ.[26] לְךָ שָׁמַיִם, אַף לְךָ אָרֶץ, תֵּבֵל וּמְלֹאָהּ אַתָּה יְסַדְתָּם.[27] אַתָּה פוֹרַרְתָּ בְעָזְּךָ יָם, שִׁבַּרְתָּ רָאשֵׁי תַנִּינִים עַל הַמָּיִם.[28] אַתָּה הִצַּבְתָּ כָּל גְּבוּלוֹת אָרֶץ, קַיִץ וָחֹרֶף אַתָּה יְצַרְתָּם.[29] אַתָּה רִצַּצְתָּ רָאשֵׁי לִוְיָתָן, תִּתְּנֶנּוּ מַאֲכָל לְעָם לְצִיִּים.

(1) *Daniel* 9:7. (2) Cf. *Lamentations* 3:39. (3) Cf. *Genesis* 44:16. (4) Cf. *Lamentations* 3:40. (5) *Psalms* 65:3. (6) Cf. *Isaiah* 66:23. (7) *Psalms* 86:9. (8) 95:6. (9) 132:7. (10) 100:4. (11) 99:5. (12) 99:9. (13) 96:9. (14) Cf. 5:8. (15) Cf. 138:2. (16) 95:1-2. (17) 55:15. (18) 89:8. (19) 134:2. (20) 134:1. (21) *Deuteronomy* 3:24. (22) *Psalms* 95:5. (23) 95:4. (24) *Job* 12:10. (25) *Psalms* 89:6. (26) 89:14. (27) 89:12. (28) 74:13. (29) 74:17.

All:

לְךָ ה׳ *Yours, my Lord, is the righteousness and ours is the shame-*
facedness.[1] *What complaint can we make?*[2] *What can we say?*
What can we declare? What justification can we offer?[3] *Let us examine*
our ways and analyze — and return to You,[4] *for Your right hand is*
extended to accept penitents. Neither with kindness nor with [good]
deeds do we come before You. As paupers and as beggars do we knock
at Your doors. At Your doors we knock, O Compassionate and Gracious
One. Please do not turn us away from You empty-handed. Our King, turn
us not away from You empty-handed, for You are the One Who hears
prayer.

שֹׁמֵעַ תְּפִלָּה *You Who hears prayer, to You all flesh will come.*[5] *All*
flesh will come to prostrate itself before You, O HASHEM.[6]
They will come and prostrate themselves before You, my Lord, and shall
honor Your Name.[7] *Come! — let us prostrate ourselves and bow, let us*
kneel before God, our Maker.[8] *Let us come to His dwelling places, let us*
prostrate ourselves at His footstool.[9] *Enter His gates with thanksgiving,*
His courts with praise; give thanks to Him, praise His Name.[10] *Exalt*
HASHEM, our God, and bow at His footstool; He is holy![11] *Exalt HASHEM,*
our God, and bow at His holy mountain; for holy is HASHEM, our God.[12]
Prostrate yourselves before HASHEM in His intensely holy place, tremble
before Him, everyone on earth.[13] *As for us, through Your abundant*
kindness we will enter Your House; we will prostrate ourselves toward
Your Holy Sanctuary in awe of You.[14] *We will prostrate ourselves toward*
Your Holy Sanctuary, and we will give thanks to Your Name for Your
kindness and truth for You have exalted Your promise even beyond Your
Name.[15] *Come! — let us sing to HASHEM, let us call out to the Rock of our*
salvation. Let us greet Him with thanksgiving, with praiseful songs let us
call out to Him.[16] *For together let us share sweet counsel, in the house of*
God let us walk in multitudes.[17] *God is dreaded in the hiddenmost*
counsel of the holy ones, and inspires awe upon all who surround Him.[18]
Lift your hands in the Sanctuary and bless HASHEM.[19] *Behold, bless*
HASHEM, all you servants of HASHEM, who stand in the House of HASHEM
in the nights.[20] *For what power is there in heaven or earth that can*
approximate Your deeds and power?[21] *For His is the sea and He*
perfected the dry land — His hands fashioned it.[22] *For in His power are*
the hidden mysteries of the earth, and the mountain summits are His.[23]
For His is the soul of every living thing, and the spirit of all human flesh.[24]
Heaven will gratefully praise Your wonders, HASHEM; also Your
faithfulness in the assembly of holy ones.[25] *Yours is a mighty arm with*
power, You strengthen Your hand; You exalt Your right hand.[26] *Yours is*
the heaven; Yours, too, is the earth; the world and its fullness — You
founded them.[27] *You shattered the sea with Your might, You smashed sea*
serpents' heads upon the water.[28] *You established all the boundaries*
of earth; summer and winter — You fashioned them.[29] *You crushed*
the heads of Leviathan, You served it as food to the nation of legions.

אַתָּה בָקַעְתָּ מַעְיָן וָנָחַל, אַתָּה הוֹבַשְׁתָּ נַהֲרוֹת אֵיתָן.‏[1] לְךָ יוֹם, אַף
לְךָ לָיְלָה, אַתָּה הֲכִינוֹתָ מָאוֹר וָשָׁמֶשׁ.‏[2] עֹשֶׂה גְדֹלוֹת עַד אֵין חֵקֶר,
וְנִפְלָאוֹת עַד אֵין מִסְפָּר.‏[3] כִּי אֵל גָּדוֹל יהוה, וּמֶלֶךְ גָּדוֹל עַל כָּל
אֱלֹהִים.‏[4] כִּי גָדוֹל אַתָּה וְעֹשֵׂה נִפְלָאוֹת, אַתָּה אֱלֹהִים לְבַדֶּךָ.‏[5] כִּי
גָדוֹל מֵעַל שָׁמַיִם חַסְדֶּךָ, וְעַד שְׁחָקִים אֲמִתֶּךָ.‏[6] גָּדוֹל יהוה וּמְהֻלָּל
מְאֹד, וְלִגְדֻלָּתוֹ אֵין חֵקֶר.‏[7] (כִּי) גָּדוֹל יהוה וּמְהֻלָּל מְאֹד, נוֹרָא
הוּא עַל כָּל אֱלֹהִים.‏[8] גָּדוֹל יהוה וּמְהֻלָּל מְאֹד, בְּעִיר אֱלֹהֵינוּ הַר
קָדְשׁוֹ.‏[9] לְךָ יהוה הַגְּדֻלָּה וְהַגְּבוּרָה, וְהַתִּפְאֶרֶת וְהַנֵּצַח וְהַהוֹד, כִּי
כֹל בַּשָּׁמַיִם וּבָאָרֶץ; לְךָ יהוה הַמַּמְלָכָה, וְהַמִּתְנַשֵּׂא לְכֹל
לְרֹאשׁ.‏[10] מִי לֹא יִרָאֲךָ מֶלֶךְ הַגּוֹיִם, כִּי לְךָ יָאָתָה, כִּי בְכָל חַכְמֵי
הַגּוֹיִם וּבְכָל מַלְכוּתָם מֵאֵין כָּמוֹךָ.‏[11] מֵאֵין כָּמוֹךָ יהוה, גָּדוֹל אַתָּה
וְגָדוֹל שִׁמְךָ בִּגְבוּרָה.‏[12] יהוה אֱלֹהֵי צְבָאוֹת, מִי כָמוֹךָ חֲסִין יָהּ,
וֶאֱמוּנָתְךָ סְבִיבוֹתֶיךָ.‏[13] יהוה צְבָאוֹת, אֱלֹהֵי יִשְׂרָאֵל, יוֹשֵׁב
הַכְּרֻבִים, אַתָּה הוּא הָאֱלֹהִים לְבַדֶּךָ.‏[14] מִי יְמַלֵּל גְּבוּרוֹת יהוה,
יַשְׁמִיעַ כָּל תְּהִלָּתוֹ.‏[15] כִּי מִי בַשַּׁחַק יַעֲרֹךְ לַיהוה, יִדְמֶה לַיהוה
בִּבְנֵי אֵלִים.‏[16] מַה נֹּאמַר לְפָנֶיךָ יוֹשֵׁב מָרוֹם, וּמַה נְּסַפֵּר לְפָנֶיךָ
שֹׁכֵן שְׁחָקִים. מַה נֹּאמַר לְפָנֶיךָ יהוה אֱלֹהֵינוּ, מַה נְּדַבֵּר וּמַה
נִּצְטַדָּק.‏[17] אֵין לָנוּ פֶּה לְהָשִׁיב וְלֹא מֵצַח לְהָרִים רֹאשׁ, כִּי
עֲוֹנוֹתֵינוּ רַבּוּ מִלְמְנוֹת, וְחַטֹּאתֵינוּ עָצְמוּ מִסַּפֵּר.‏[18] לְמַעַן שִׁמְךָ
יהוה תְּחַיֵּנוּ, וּבְצִדְקָתְךָ תּוֹצִיא מִצָּרָה נַפְשֵׁנוּ.‏[19] דַּרְכְּךָ אֱלֹהֵינוּ
לְהַאֲרִיךְ אַפֶּךָ, לָרָעִים וְלַטּוֹבִים, וְהִיא תְהִלָּתֶךָ. לְמַעַנְךָ אֱלֹהֵינוּ
עֲשֵׂה וְלֹא לָנוּ, רְאֵה עֲמִידָתֵנוּ, דַּלִּים וְרֵקִים. ❖ הַנְּשָׁמָה לָךְ וְהַגּוּף
פָּעֳלָךְ, חוּסָה עַל עֲמָלָךְ. הַנְּשָׁמָה לָךְ וְהַגּוּף שֶׁלָּךְ, יהוה עֲשֵׂה
לְמַעַן שְׁמֶךָ. אָתָאנוּ עַל שְׁמֶךָ, יהוה, עֲשֵׂה לְמַעַן שְׁמֶךָ. בַּעֲבוּר
כְּבוֹד שִׁמְךָ, כִּי אֵל חַנּוּן וְרַחוּם שְׁמֶךָ. לְמַעַן שִׁמְךָ יהוה, וְסָלַחְתָּ
לַעֲוֹנֵנוּ כִּי רַב הוּא.‏[20]

Congregation, then *chazzan:*

סְלַח לָנוּ אָבִינוּ, כִּי בְרֹב אִוַּלְתֵּנוּ שָׁגִינוּ,
מְחַל לָנוּ מַלְכֵּנוּ, כִּי רַבּוּ עֲוֹנֵינוּ.

(1) Psalms 74:14-15. (2) 74:16. (3) Job 9:10. (4) Psalms 95:3. (5) 86:10. (6) 108:5.
(7) 145:3. (8) 96:4. (9) 48:2. (10) I Chronicles 29:11. (11) Jeremiah 10:7. (12) 10:6.
(13) Psalms 89:9. (14) Isaiah 37:16. (15) Psalms 106:2. (16) 89:7.
(17) Cf. Genesis 44:16. (18) Cf. Ezra 9:6. (19) Cf. Psalms 143:11. (20) Cf. 25:11.

You split open fountain and stream, You dried the mighty rivers.[1] Yours is the day, Yours as well is the night; You established luminary and the sun.[2] Who performs great deeds that are beyond comprehension, and wonders beyond number.[3] For a great God is HASHEM, and a great King above all heavenly powers.[4] For You are great and work wonders; You alone, O God.[5] For great above the very heavens is Your kindness, and until the upper heights is Your truth.[6] HASHEM is great and exceedingly lauded, and His greatness is beyond investigation.[7] (For) HASHEM is great and exceedingly lauded, awesome is He above all heavenly powers.[8] Great is HASHEM and exceedingly lauded, in the city of our God, Mount of His Holiness.[9] Yours, HASHEM, is the greatness, the strength, the splendor, the triumph, and the glory; even everything in heaven and earth; Yours, HASHEM, is the kingdom, and sovereignty over every leader.[10] Who would not revere You, O King of nations? — for this befits You, for among all the sages of the nations and in all their kingdom there is none like You.[11] There is none like You, O HASHEM, You are great and Your Name is great with power.[12] HASHEM, God of Legions — who is like You, O Strong One, God? — and Your faithfulness surrounds You.[13] HASHEM, Master of Legions, God of Israel, enthroned upon the Cherubim, it is You alone Who is God.[14] Who can express the mighty acts of HASHEM, who can announce all His praise?[15] For who in the sky can be compared to HASHEM; be likened to HASHEM among the angels?[16] What can we say before You Who dwell on high? And what can we relate to You Who abide in the highest heaven? What can we say before You, HASHEM, our God? What can we declare? What justification can we offer?[17] We have neither mouth to respond nor brow to raise our head, for our iniquities are too numerous to count, and our sins are too vast to be numbered.[18] For Your Name's sake, HASHEM, revive us; and with Your righteousness remove our soul from distress.[19] It is Your way, our God, to delay Your anger, against people both evil and good — and this is Your praise. Act for Your sake, our God, and not for ours, behold our [spiritual] position — destitute and emptyhanded. Chazzan — The soul is Yours and the body is Your handiwork; take pity on Your labor. The soul is Yours and the body is Yours; O HASHEM, act for Your Name's sake. We have come with reliance on Your Name, O HASHEM, act for Your Name's sake; because of Your Name's glory — for 'Gracious and Merciful God' is Your Name. For Your Name's sake, HASHEM, may You forgive our iniquity, though it is abundant.[20]

Congregation, then chazzan:

Forgive us, our Father, for in our abundant folly we have erred, pardon us, our King, for our iniquities are many.

סליחה ס (פתיחה)

All:

אֵלֶיךָ לֵב וָנֶפֶשׁ נִשְׁפֹּךְ* כַּמַּיִם,[1]
כֻּלָּנוּ אֶל אֵל בַּשָּׁמָיִם.[2]

אָתִיו זְקֵנִים עִם עוֹלְלֵיכֶם, הַזַּכּוּ וְהָסִירוּ רֹעַ מַעַלְלֵיכֶם,[3]
לְפָנָיו נַרְבֶּה תְחִנָּה וּבַקָּשָׁה, עַל זֹאת מֵאֱלֹהֵינוּ נְבַקְשָׁה.[4]

יִרְגַּז הַטּוֹב עַל מִנְעָל,[5] דַּרְכּוֹ יַעֲזֹב פּוֹשֵׁעַ וְעָוָל.[6]
הָכִינוּ לֵב וְהֵטִיבוּ מַחֲשָׁבָה, כִּי גָדוֹל כֹּחַ הַתְּשׁוּבָה.[7]

בְּקָהָל עָם מִלִּין נַכְבִּיר,[8] וְלֹא יִמְאַס אֵל כַּבִּיר.[9]
רוֹצֶה תְשׁוּבַת בּוֹגֵד וְנִשְׁחָת,[10] לְהָשִׁיב נַפְשׁוֹ מִנִּי שָׁחַת.[11]

שְׁמַע תַּחֲנוּן הַעֲתֵר לִמְבַקְשֶׁיךָ, בְּנָשְׂאֵנוּ יָדֵינוּ אֶל דְּבִיר קָדְשֶׁךָ.[12]
יִהְיוּ נָא אִמְרֵי פִינוּ לְרָצוֹן,[13] וְכַפֵּר עַל חַטֹּאתֵינוּ[14] אֹנֶס וְרָצוֹן,

❖ חֲשֹׁב זֵכֶר קְרִיאַת נְעִימֶיךָ, וְהִנָּחֵם עַל הָרָעָה לְעַמֶּךָ.[15]
וַעֲשֵׂה חֵפֶץ עֲבָדֶיךָ וִישַׁעְשְׁעוּן תַּנְחוּמֶיךָ,[16]
סְמוּכִים בְּחַסְדֶּךָ וּבְטוּחִים עַל רַחֲמֶיךָ.

All:

כִּי עַל רַחֲמֶיךָ הָרַבִּים[17] אָנוּ בְטוּחִים, וְעַל צִדְקוֹתֶיךָ אָנוּ
נִשְׁעָנִים, וְלִסְלִיחוֹתֶיךָ אָנוּ מְקַוִּים, וְלִישׁוּעָתְךָ אָנוּ
מְצַפִּים. אַתָּה הוּא מֶלֶךְ, אוֹהֵב צְדָקוֹת מִקֶּדֶם, מַעֲבִיר עֲוֹנוֹת עַמּוֹ,
וּמֵסִיר חַטֹּאת יְרֵאָיו. כּוֹרֵת בְּרִית לָרִאשׁוֹנִים, וּמְקַיֵּם שְׁבוּעָה
לָאַחֲרוֹנִים. אַתָּה הוּא, שֶׁיָּרַדְתָּ בַּעֲנַן כְּבוֹדְךָ עַל הַר סִינַי,[18]
וְהֶרְאֵיתָ דַּרְכֵי טוּבְךָ לְמֹשֶׁה עַבְדֶּךָ.[19] וְאָרְחוֹת חֲסָדֶיךָ גִּלִּיתָ לּוֹ,
וְהוֹדַעְתּוֹ כִּי אַתָּה אֵל רַחוּם וְחַנּוּן, אֶרֶךְ אַפַּיִם וְרַב חֶסֶד[20] וּמַרְבֶּה
לְהֵטִיב, וּמַנְהִיג אֶת כָּל הָעוֹלָם כֻּלּוֹ בְּמִדַּת הָרַחֲמִים. ❖ וְכֵן כָּתוּב,
וַיֹּאמֶר אֲנִי אַעֲבִיר כָּל טוּבִי עַל פָּנֶיךָ, וְקָרָאתִי בְשֵׁם יהוה לְפָנֶיךָ,
וְחַנֹּתִי אֶת אֲשֶׁר אָחֹן, וְרִחַמְתִּי אֶת אֲשֶׁר אֲרַחֵם.[21]

---

(1) Cf. *Lamentations* 2:19. (2) 3:41. (3) Cf. *Isaiah* 1:16. (4) Cf. *Ezra* 8:23.
(5) See tractate *Berachos* 5a; see also commentary to *selichah* 24. (6) Cf. *Isaiah* 55:7.
(7) See tractate *Yoma* 86a. (8) *Job* 35:16. (9) Cf. 36:5. (10) See *Ezekiel* 18:23. (11) *Job* 33:30.
(12) Cf. *Psalms* 28:2. (13) 19:15. (14) 79:9. (15) *Exodus* 32:12. (16) Cf. *Psalms* 94:19.
(17) *Daniel* 9:18. (18) Cf. *Exodus* 34:5. (19) Cf. 33:13. (20) 34:6. (21) 33:19.

אֵלֶיךָ לֵב וָנֶפֶשׁ נִשְׁפֹּךְ ﴾ — *To You we pour out
heart and soul.* This פְּתִיחָה, *introductory
selichah,* contains the signature אֵלִיָּה בַּר שְׁמַעְיָה

חֲזַק, *Eliyah bar Shemayah, may he be strong* [see
prefatory comment to *selichah* 6].

SELICHAH 60

All:

אֵלֶיךָ *To You we pour out heart and soul* like water,*[1]
all of us, to God in Heaven.[2]

א *Come, O elders, with your children;*
purify yourselves and cast off the evil of your deeds.[3]

ל *Let us increase supplication and entreaty before Him,*
and let us request this of our God:[4]

י *'Let the Good Inclination be angered against the reprobate;*[5]
let the willful sinner and wrongdoer abandon his way.[6]

ה *Prepare [our] heart, turn our thought to good,*
for great is the power of repentance.'[7]

ב *Among the congregated people, let us increase words*[8] *[of prayer],*
for the Almighty God will not show contempt.[9]

ר *He desires the repentance of the rebellious and corrupt,*[10]
to retrieve his soul from ruin.[11]

ש *O Hear [our] supplication;*
accede to the prayer of those who appeal to You,
as we raise our hands towards Your Holy Sanctuary.[12]

י *Please let the expressions of our mouths find favor,*[13]
and atone for our sins,[14] *both accidental and deliberate.*

ח Chazzan — *Consider, remember the call*
of Your pleasing ones [our Patriarchs],
and reconsider the evil [You would do] to Your people.[15]
Grant Your servants' desire, and let Your solace delight them,[16]
[for] they rely on Your kindness, and trust in Your mercy.

All:

כִּי עַל *For upon Your abundant mercy*[17] *do we trust, and upon Your*
righteousness do we depend, and for Your forgiveness do we
hope, *and for Your salvation do we yearn. You are the King Who loves*
righteousness since the earliest days, Who overlooks His people's
iniquities and sets aside the sins of those who revere Him. He made
a covenant with the ancestors and keeps [His] vow to the descend-
ants. It is You Who descended in Your cloud of glory on Mount Sinai,[18]
and showed the ways of Your goodness to Your servant Moses.[19] *You*
revealed Your paths of kindness to him, and let him know that You
are God, Compassionate and Gracious, Slow to anger and Abundant
in Kindness,[20] *doing manifold good, and guiding all Your world with*
the Attribute of Mercy. Chazzan — *And so it is written: He said, 'I*
shall pass all My good in front of you, and I shall call out the Name
of HASHEM *before you; for I will be gracious to whom I will be*
gracious, and I will be compassionate with whom I will be compassion-
ate.'[21]

All, while standing:

אֵל אֶרֶךְ אַפַּיִם אַתָּה, וּבַעַל הָרַחֲמִים נִקְרֵאתָ,
וְדֶרֶךְ תְּשׁוּבָה הוֹרֵיתָ.

גְּדֻלַּת רַחֲמֶיךָ וַחֲסָדֶיךָ, תִּזְכּוֹר הַיּוֹם וּבְכָל יוֹם לְזֶרַע יְדִידֶיךָ.

תֵּפֶן אֵלֵינוּ בְּרַחֲמִים, כִּי אַתָּה הוּא בַּעַל הָרַחֲמִים.

בְּתַחֲנוּן וּבִתְפִלָּה פָּנֶיךָ נְקַדֵּם, כְּהוֹדַעְתָּ לֶעָנָיו מִקֶּדֶם.

מֵחֲרוֹן אַפְּךָ שׁוּב,[1] כְּמוֹ בְתוֹרָתְךָ כָּתוּב.[2]

וּבְצֵל כְּנָפֶיךָ נֶחֱסֶה[3] וְנִתְלוֹנָן, כְּיוֹם וַיֵּרֶד יהוה בֶּעָנָן.

❖ תַּעֲבוֹר עַל פֶּשַׁע וְתִמְחֶה אָשָׁם, כְּיוֹם וַיִּתְיַצֵּב עִמּוֹ שָׁם.

תַּאֲזִין שַׁוְעָתֵנוּ וְתַקְשִׁיב מֶנּוּ מַאֲמָר, כְּיוֹם וַיִּקְרָא בְשֵׁם יהוה,[4] וְשָׁם נֶאֱמַר:

Congregation, then *chazzan*:

וַיַּעֲבֹר יהוה עַל פָּנָיו וַיִּקְרָא:

Congregation and *chazzan* (the words in bold type are recited aloud and in unison):

יהוה, יהוה, אֵל, **רַחוּם, וְחַנּוּן, אֶרֶךְ אַפַּיִם, וְרַב חֶסֶד, וֶאֱמֶת,**
נֹצֵר חֶסֶד לָאֲלָפִים, נֹשֵׂא עָו‍ֹן, וָפֶשַׁע, וְחַטָּאָה,
וְנַקֵּה.[5] וְסָלַחְתָּ לַעֲו‍ֹנֵנוּ וּלְחַטָּאתֵנוּ וּנְחַלְתָּנוּ.[6] סְלַח לָנוּ אָבִינוּ כִּי
חָטָאנוּ, מְחַל לָנוּ מַלְכֵּנוּ כִּי פָשָׁעְנוּ. כִּי אַתָּה אֲדֹנָי טוֹב וְסַלָּח, וְרַב
חֶסֶד לְכָל קֹרְאֶיךָ.[7]

פסוקי הקדמה לסליחה סא

יִשְׂרָאֵל נוֹשַׁע בַּיהוה תְּשׁוּעַת עוֹלָמִים, לֹא תֵבֹשׁוּ וְלֹא
תִכָּלְמוּ עַד עוֹלְמֵי עַד.[8] מִקְוֵה יִשְׂרָאֵל יהוה, מוֹשִׁיעוֹ
בְּעֵת צָרָה.[9] מִקְוֵה יִשְׂרָאֵל יהוה, כָּל עֹזְבֶיךָ יֵבֹשׁוּ.[10] וְיֵשׁ
תִּקְוָה לְאַחֲרִיתֵךְ, נְאֻם יהוה, וְשָׁבוּ בָנִים לִגְבוּלָם.[11] קַוֵּה קִוִּיתִי
יהוה, וַיֵּט אֵלַי וַיִּשְׁמַע שַׁוְעָתִי.[12] לְךָ אֲדֹנָי הַצְּדָקָה, וְלָנוּ בֹּשֶׁת
הַפָּנִים, כַּיּוֹם הַזֶּה.[13] הֵיטִיבָה בִרְצוֹנְךָ אֶת צִיּוֹן, תִּבְנֶה חוֹמוֹת
יְרוּשָׁלָיִם.[14]

כְּרַחֵם אָב עַל בָּנִים, כֵּן תְּרַחֵם יהוה עָלֵינוּ.[15] לַיהוה הַיְשׁוּעָה,
עַל עַמְּךָ בִרְכָתֶךָ סֶּלָה.[16] יהוה צְבָאוֹת עִמָּנוּ,
מִשְׂגָּב לָנוּ אֱלֹהֵי יַעֲקֹב סֶלָה.[17] יהוה צְבָאוֹת, אַשְׁרֵי אָדָם בֹּטֵחַ
בָּךְ.[18] יהוה הוֹשִׁיעָה, הַמֶּלֶךְ יַעֲנֵנוּ בְיוֹם קָרְאֵנוּ.[19]

All, while standing:

אֵל אֶרֶךְ אַפַּיִם *O God — You are slow to anger, You are called the Master of Mercy, and You have taught the way of repentance. May You remember this day and every day the greatness of Your mercy and Your kindness to the offspring of Your beloved Ones. Turn to us in mercy for You are the Master of Mercy. With supplication and prayer we approach Your Presence in the manner that You made known to the humble [Moses] in ancient times. Turn back from Your fierce anger;[1] as is written in Your Torah.[2] In the shadow of Your wings may we find shelter[3] and lodging as on the day 'HASHEM descended in a cloud' [to appear to Moses on Sinai]. Chazzan — Overlook sin and erase guilt as on the day 'He [God] stood there with him [Moses].' Give heed to our cry and be attentive to our declaration as on the day 'He called out with the Name HASHEM,'[4] and there it was said:*

Congregation, then *chazzan:*

And HASHEM passed before him [Moses] and proclaimed:

Congregation and *chazzan* (the words in bold type are recited aloud and in unison):

ה' ה' **HASHEM, HASHEM, God, Compassionate and Gracious, Slow to anger, and Abundant in Kindness and Truth, Preserver of kindness for thousands [of generations], Forgiver of iniquity, willful sin, and error, and Who cleanses.**[5] *May You forgive our iniquities and our errors and make us Your heritage.[6] Forgive us, our Father, for we have erred; pardon us, our King, for we have willfully sinned; for You, my Lord, are good and forgiving and abundantly kind to all who call upon You.[7]*

PREFATORY VERSES TO SELICHAH 61

יִשְׂרָאֵל *Israel is saved by HASHEM, an eternal salvation; you shall not be ashamed nor humiliated forever and ever.[8] HASHEM is Israel's hope, their savior in time of trouble.[9] HASHEM is Israel's hope: all who abandon You will be shamed.[10] There is hope for you at the end, says HASHEM, and your children shall return to their borders.[11] I have hoped greatly for HASHEM; He inclined toward me and heard my outcry.[12] Yours, my Lord, is the righteousness, and ours is the shamefacedness, this day.[13] Do good in Your favor unto Zion; build the walls of Jerusalem.[14]*

כְּרַחֵם אָב *As a father has mercy on his children, so, HASHEM, may You have mercy on us.[15] Salvation is HASHEM's, upon Your people is Your blessing, Selah.[16] HASHEM, Master of Legions, is with us, a stronghold for us is the God of Jacob, Selah.[17] HASHEM, Master of Legions, praiseworthy is the person who trusts in You.[18] HASHEM, save! May the King answer us on the day we call.[19]*

---

(1) Cf. *Exodus* 32:12. (2) See 32:14. (3) Cf. *Psalms* 36:8. (4) *Exodus* 34:5. (5) 34:6-7. (6) 34:9. (7) *Psalms* 86:5. (8) *Isaiah* 45:17. (9) Cf. *Jeremiah* 14:8. (10) 17:13. (11) 31:16. (12) *Psalms* 40:2. (13) *Daniel* 9:7. (14) *Psalms* 51:20. (15) Cf. 103:13. (16) 3:9. (17) 46:8. (18) 84:13. (19) 20:10.

In some congregations the following two verses are recited responsively — the *chazzan* reciting סְלַח, and the congregation responding וַיֹּאמֶר. In other congregations these verses are recited silently.

סְלַח נָא לַעֲוֹן הָעָם הַזֶּה כְּגֹדֶל חַסְדֶּךָ, וְכַאֲשֶׁר נָשָׂאתָה לָעָם הַזֶּה מִמִּצְרַיִם וְעַד הֵנָּה,[1] וְשָׁם נֶאֱמַר:

וַיֹּאמֶר יהוה סָלַחְתִּי כִּדְבָרֶךָ.[2]

All:

הַטֵּה אֱלֹהַי אָזְנְךָ וּשֲׁמָע, פְּקַח עֵינֶיךָ וּרְאֵה שֹׁמְמֹתֵינוּ, וְהָעִיר אֲשֶׁר נִקְרָא שִׁמְךָ עָלֶיהָ, כִּי לֹא עַל צִדְקֹתֵינוּ אֲנַחְנוּ מַפִּילִים תַּחֲנוּנֵינוּ לְפָנֶיךָ, כִּי עַל רַחֲמֶיךָ הָרַבִּים. אֲדֹנָי שְׁמָעָה, אֲדֹנָי סְלָחָה, אֲדֹנָי הַקְשִׁיבָה, וַעֲשֵׂה אַל תְּאַחַר, לְמַעַנְךָ אֱלֹהַי, כִּי שִׁמְךָ נִקְרָא עַל עִירְךָ וְעַל עַמֶּךָ.[3]

סליחה סא

All:

(אֱלֹהֵינוּ וֵאלֹהֵי אֲבוֹתֵינוּ:)

אַךְ בְּךָ מִקְוֵה יִשְׂרָאֵל יהוה,[4]*

אָחוֹר וָקֶדֶם עַם נוֹשַׁע בַּיהוה,[5]

וּמַדּוּעַ **בּ**וֹשֵׁשׁ יוֹם זֶה כַּמָּה עֶדְנַי,   לִישׁוּעָתְךָ קִוִּיתִי יהוה.[6]

גֵּרְתִּי וְאַחֵר[7] מֶשֶׁךְ יְמֵי עֲגוּנִי,

גֵּיא גּוֹי נָבָל וְעַם גְּנַאי,

וּמַדּוּעַ **דַּל** כָּכָה[8] כָּבוֹד וְלִי דִינַי,

קַוֵּה אֶל יהוה, חֲזַק וְיַאֲמֵץ לִבֶּךָ, וְקַוֵּה אֶל יהוה.[9]

הֲלֹא אַתָּה מִקֶּדֶם חֶרֶב גְּאַנְתָּנוּ,

הִקְוִינוּךָ אַף אֹרַח מִשְׁפָּטֶיךָ תְּאַוְּתָנוּ,[10]

וּמַדּוּעַ וְאֵין אִישׁ מְכַפֵּר[11] עַל חוֹבוֹתֵינוּ,

וּמִ**דַּ**אֲבוֹנֵינוּ אוֹמְרִים יָבְשׁוּ עַצְמוֹתֵינוּ אָבְדָה תִקְוָתֵנוּ.[12]

זָכַרְנוּ חֶשְׁבּוֹנוֹת מִקֶּדֶם וּמִדָּתָם קָצָרָה,

זֶה פַּעֲמַיִם קָצִיר* וְעוֹד עֲצָרָה,[13]

אַךְ בְּךָ מִקְוֵה יִשְׂרָאֵל ה׳ — *Only in You, HASHEM, is Israel's hope.* The acrostic forms the *aleph-beis* with odd-numbered letters (. . . ה,ג,א) appearing twice, and even-numbered letters (. . . ו,ד,ב) appearing only once and that after the word וּמַדּוּעַ, *Why, then?* The fourth line of each alphabetical stanza is a Scriptural fragment that contains some form of the root קוה, *hope.* The *paytan* signed his name שְׁלֹמֹה הַקָּטָן יִגְדַּל בִּתְשׁוּבָה, *Shlomo the lesser, may he grow in repentance* [see

prefatory comment to *selichah* 2], in the last three stanzas.

זֶה פַּעֲמַיִם קָצִיר — *This [exile] has been a double harvest.* The present exile is more difficult than the previous ones because of both its severity and its duration. The *paytan* speaks of its intensity as *a double harvest,* i.e., so many more have been slaughtered during our present exile than during earlier exiles.

In some congregations the following two verses are recited responsively — the *chazzan* reciting, 'Forgive, please . . .,' and the congregation responding, 'And HASHEM said . . .' In other congregations these verses are recited silently.

סְלַח נָא *Forgive, please, the iniquity of this people according to the greatness of Your kindness and as You have forgiven this people from Egypt until now,*[1] *and there it was said:*

And HASHEM said, 'I have forgiven according to your word!'[2]

All:

הַטֵּה *Incline, my God, Your ear, and listen, open Your eyes and see our desolation and that of the city upon which Your Name is proclaimed; for not because of our righteousness do we cast down our supplications before You, rather because of Your abundant compassion. O my Lord, heed; O my Lord, forgive; O my Lord, be attentive and act, do not delay; for Your sake, my God, for Your Name is proclaimed upon Your city and upon Your people.*[3]

SELICHAH 61

All:

(*Our God and the God of our forefathers:*)

א Only in You, HASHEM, is Israel's hope,*[4]

א to the last, from the first, a people saved by HASHEM.[5]

ב Why, then, does the day of Redemption lag back for so very long?

I **hope** *for Your salvation, HASHEM.*[6]

ג I sojourned and tarried[7] for the length of my period of desolation,

ג in the valley of the sordid nation, the ignoble people.

ד Why, then, has [my] esteem sunk so low?[8] Why am I so condemned?

Hope *to HASHEM; strengthen yourself, and He will let your heart persevere, and* **hope** *to HASHEM.*[9]

ה Were You not from of old the sword of our grandeur?[10]

ה We have placed our hope in You;

our desire is even for Your way of judgment.

ו Why, then, is there no one to atone[11] for our sins?

And due to our anguish we are wont to say, 'Our bones are dried up! Our **hope** *is lost!'*[12]

ז We remember earlier reckonings and their term was short;

ז this [exile] has been a double harvest,* yet still reigns strong.[13]

---

(1) *Numbers* 14:19. (2) 14:20. (3) *Daniel* 9:18-19. (4) *Jeremiah* 17:13. (5) *Deuteronomy* 33:29; cf. *Isaiah* 45:17. (6) *Genesis* 49:18. (7) 32:5. (8) Cf. *II Samuel* 13:4. (9) *Psalms* 27:14. (10) Cf. *Isaiah* 26:8. (11) Cf. 50:2, *Proverbs* 16:14. (12) Cf. *Ezekiel* 37:11. (13) Many editions read זֶה פַּעֲמַיִם קְצָרָה וְעוֹד פָּצְרָה, *But this one has been twice the short term, yet still presses hard.*

Additionally, according to *Arugas HaBosem*, the *paytan* had another meaning in mind with the expression פַּעֲמַיִם קְצָרָה. The word קָצִיר has a *gematria* (numerical value) of 400 [ק=100; צ=90, י=10; ר=200]; double קָצִיר is then 800. Thus, the stich means, *this exile is already eight hundred years long, yet still reigns strong.* Based on this interpretation, some commentaries claim that this selichah must have been written soon after the year 870, eight hundred years after the Destruc-

tion of the Second Temple. Nevertheless, most feel that the composer, R' Shlomo HaBavli, lived about a century later. [Perhaps the mathematical calculation should include the word וְעוֹד, *and still,* which can also mean *and more.* How much more? The *gematria* of וְעוֹד, which is 86. This would then date the work from about 956, and the stich would mean: *Even though this exile is already 886 years long, it still reigns strong.*]

וּמַדּוּעַ חֶשְׁבֵּנוּ כַּבְּהֵמָה כִּנְטַמֵּינוּ[1] מִשְׁטַת הַשּׁוּרָה,

מִקְוֵה יִשְׂרָאֵל יהוה מוֹשִׁיעוֹ בְּעֵת צָרָה.[2]

טוֹעֲנִים וּפוֹרְקִים בָּנִים הַכָּתוּב סְבָלָם,*

טְרוּדֵי חֶבְלָם וְחָרֵב בֵּית זְבוּלָם,

וּמַדּוּעַ יַסְתִּיר הָאָב[3] שְׁבִילָם הָאָמוּר בְּגִלְלָם,

וְיֵשׁ תִּקְוָה לְאַחֲרִיתֵךְ נְאֻם יהוה, וְשָׁבוּ בָנִים לִגְבוּלָם.[4]

כִּמְעַט נָטָיו רַגְלַי וְשֻׁפְּכוּ אֲשׁוּרִים,

כִּי קִנֵּאתִי בַהוֹלְלִים[5] מְעַרְבְּבֵי מֵישָׁרִים,

וּמַדּוּעַ לֹא תִקְצַר וְתִשְׁבֵּר רָמַת הַקּוֹשְׁרִים,

וְקוֹיֵ* יהוה יַחֲלִיפוּ כֹחַ, יַעֲלוּ אֵבֶר כַּנְּשָׁרִים.[6]

מָלֵא רְדַפְתִּי וְחָסְרָה שְׁנַת גְּאוּלִי,*

מְסוּרִים לַמַּכִּים וּמוֹרְטִים[7] וּלְתִקְנָה אוּלַי,[8]

וּמַדּוּעַ נִסְחֲפוּ אֲבִירַי[9] וּמְתֵי שִׁיר אַיָּלַי,*

קַוֵּה קִוִּיתִי (אֶל) יהוה וַיֵּט אֵלַי.[10]

סוּגֵיךְ שְׁרִיגֵיךְ בְּקֶקוּם בּוֹלְקִים[11] וְהִבְאִישׁוּ,

סִירִים סוּרֶיךְ גָּבְשׁוּ וְלֹא עָבְשׁוּ,

וּמַדּוּעַ עָתְקוּ גָּבְרוּ כְּמִדְבָּר לֹא יֵבוֹשׁוּ,

מִקְוֵה יִשְׂרָאֵל יהוה כָּל עֹזְבֶיךָ יֵבֹשׁוּ.[12]

פּוֹעֲלֵי שֶׁקֶר יִתְאַמְּרוּ[13] אוֹיְנוּ רָאֵינוּ,

פָּשְׁטוּ אֶמֶת אוֹתוֹתֵינוּ שַׂמְנוּ[14] הִתְוֵינוּ,

וּמַדּוּעַ צָלְחָה דַרְכָּם,[15] וְחַסְדְּךָ דִּמְּינוּ[16] נִדְוֵינוּ,

יהוה חָנֵּנוּ לְךָ קִוִּינוּ.[17]

קִימַת סֻכַּת שָׁלֹשׁ עֶשְׂרֵה פֶּרֶץ,[18]

טוֹעֲנִים וּפוֹרְקִים בָּנִים הַכָּתוּב סְבָלָם — [Whether]
they bear or cast off their burden [of mitzvos], the
Torah calls them [God's] children. The Jewish
people are God's children even when they do not
uphold His commands. Various Scriptural verses
describe them as foolish (Jeremiah 4:22), disloyal
(Deuteronomy 32:20), or corrupt (Isaiah 1:4), yet
call them His children (Arugas HaBosem, based
on Kiddushin 36a).

Others understand the stich as a description of
Israel's fate to constantly load (טוֹעֲנִים) and unload
(פּוֹרְקִים) the burdens of the evil taskmasters in
whose lands they have been exiled (Masbir).

וְקוֹיֵ — While those who hope. The vowelization
follows virtually all editions. However, according
to Radak (Isaiah 40:31), the word is pronounced
as if it were spelled וְקוֹוֵי.

מָלֵא רְדַפְתִּי וְחָסְרָה שְׁנַת גְּאוּלִי — I have been chased
to the full, but the year of my redemption is lacking. The Midrash states that whenever the word
רוֹדֵף, pursuer, appears in Scriptures, it is spelled
deficiently (רֹדֵף), without the letter (ו), except once:
וַיֵּלְכוּ בְלֹא כֹחַ לִפְנֵי רוֹדֵף, they went without any
strength before the pursuer (Lamentations 1:6).
This indicates that the enemy after the Destruction of Jerusalem set out after the remaining Jews
in full pursuit. Similarly, the word גּוֹאֵל, Redeemer, is always spelled deficiently (גֹּאֵל), except
once: וּבָא לְצִיּוֹן גּוֹאֵל, A Redeemer shall come to
Zion (Isaiah 59:20). This indicates that just as their
pursuit was a full pursuit, so will their Redemption be a full Redemption (Eichah Rabbasi 1:33).
Rashi (to Lamentations 1:6), however, seems to
have had a different reading in the Midrash (or

ח Why, then, are we reckoned as animals,
  and blocked off[1] from [fulfillment of] the Scriptural verse,
      'HASHEM is Israel's **hope**, their savior in time of trouble.'[2]

ט [Whether] they bear or cast off their burden [of mitzvos],
  the Torah calls them [God's] children;*

ט [yet] they are evicted from their heritage,
  and their Temple is destroyed.

י Why, then, should the Father hide[3] their path
  of which it is said for their sake,
      'There is **hope** for you in the end, says HASHEM,
        and your children shall return to their borders'?[4]

כ My feet were almost turned astray, my steps washed aside,

כ for we envied the scoffers,[5] the perverters of the straight.

ל Why, then, should the plotters' arrogance not be cut short and broken;
    while those who **hope*** for HASHEM gain new strength,
      growing wings like the eagles?[6]

מ I have been chased to the full, but the year of my redemption is lacking,*

מ given over to beaters and pluckers,[7] uncertain of hope.[8]

נ Why, then, have my men of valor been thrown down,[9]
    along with the men of my ram-offerings' song?*
  I have **hoped** greatly (for) HASHEM, and He has inclined toward me.[10]

ס Bandits have ravaged [Israel,] Your fenced-off branching vine,[11]
  which now lies rotting;

ס while the thorns who turn away from You climb high, free of blight.

ע Why, then, do they gather strength, overpower,
  yet not come to shame, as was said:
    'HASHEM is Israel's **hope**: all that leave You will be shamed'?[12]

פ The perpetrators of falsehood glorify themselves,[13]
  'What we longed for, we have seen!'

פ They expound, 'True are our signs that we set[14] and inscribed!'

צ Why, then, is this way of theirs successful,[15]
  whereas we grieve while we hope for Your kindness?[16]
      HASHEM, be gracious towards us; we **hope** to You![17]

ק The re-erection of Your Temple-succah
  [in which were made] thirteen breaches,[18]

---

(1) Cf. *Job* 18:3; many editions read נֶחְשַׁבְנוּ instead of חֲשַׁבְנוּ, a reading that does not change the meaning and is a more direct quote from the Scriptural source; however, the expected initial letter after the word וּמַדּוּעַ is ח not נ. (2) Cf. *Jeremiah* 14:8. (3) Cf. *I Samuel* 20:2. (4) *Jeremiah* 31:16. (5) Cf. *Psalms* 73:2-3. (6) *Isaiah* 40:31. (7) Cf. 50:6. (8) Cf. *Lamentations* 3:29. (9) Cf. *Jeremiah* 46:15. (10) *Psalms* 40:2. (11) Cf. *Nahum* 2:3; *Hosea* 10:1. (12) *Jeremiah* 17:13. (13) Cf. *Psalms* 94:4. (14) Cf. 74:4. (15) Cf. *Jeremiah* 12:1. (16) Cf. *Psalms* 48:10. (17) *Isaiah* 33:2. (18) Cf. *Amos* 9:11; see commentary to *selichah* 44, s.v., לְמוּל הַפְּרָצוֹת.

---

based his commentary on another Midrash that is no longer extant). He explains that the word גְּאוּלַי, *my redemption*, is spelled deficiently [without the ו] in the verse: שְׁנַת גְּאוּלַי בָּאָה, *The year of my redemption has come* (Isaiah 63:4). This, says *Rashi*, is what the *paytan* means by the stich מָלֵא רַדְפַתִּי, *I have been chased to the full* [as

indicated by the full spelling of וְחָסְרָה שְׁנַת [רוֹדֵף, גְּאוּלַי, *but the year of my redemption is lacking* [as indicated by the missing ו of גְּאוּלַי].

וּמְחֵי שִׁיר אֵילַי — *The men of my ram-offerings song.* Each day in the Temple, the Levite choir would sing the Song of the Day during the service

קָצֶה רָחַק, וְלַמִּקְרָא עָלָה הַפּוֹרֵץ,[1]

וּמַדּוּעַ רְשָׁעִים יִחְיוּ[2] וְלֹא יִדְּמוּ קֶרֶץ,*

וְקֹוֵי יהוה הֵמָּה יִירְשׁוּ אָרֶץ.[3]

שׁוֹסֵי נַחֲלָתִי[4] חֶבֶל מֶחְלְקָךְ לְגָרְשֵׁנוּ,

שׁוּבִי שׁוּבִי הַשּׁוּלַמִּית[5] בְּפִיהֶם לְהַפְרִישֵׁנוּ,

וּמַדּוּעַ תִּתְנַשָּׂאוּ[6] וְזֶה לָזֶה תִּנְאָמוּ נַפְרִישֵׁנוּ,

טוֹב יהוה **לְקֹוָיו** לְנֶפֶשׁ תִּדְרְשֶׁנוּ.[7]

שַׁדַּי תְּשׁוּבַת מַדּוּעֵינוּ פִּינוּ נְמַלֵּא,

לַיהוה אֱלֹהֵינוּ חָטָאנוּ[8] וַתִּקְרֶאנָה אוֹתָנוּ כָּאֵלֶּה,[9]

מִשְׁפָּטֶיךָ אֱמֶת וְאַתָּה מָרוֹם מִתְעַלֶּה,

הַצְּדָקָה לְךָ וְלָנוּ הַבּשֶׁת[10] נִגְלֶה.

הֶעָרְתָּ רַבּוֹת וְנֹאמַר לֹא נַקְשִׁיב,[11]

קוֹל טִיף נְבִיאֶיךָ בָּזִינוּ לְהַקְשִׁיב,

יִגְדַּל כֹּחַ[12] סֶלָה יְחִידִים מוֹשִׁיב,[13]

בִּתְשׁוּבָה שְׁלֵמָה אוֹתָנוּ לְהָשִׁיב.

✧ מַדּוּעַ אָדָם לְלְבוּשֶׁךְ[14] תְּקָרֵב עוֹנָתוֹ,

וְיֵז נִצְחָם עַל בִּגְדֵי עֲטִיָּתוֹ,

נוֹדֶה סֶלָה יוֹם הַבָּא בְּשַׁעְתוֹ,

זֶה יהוה **קִוִּינוּ** לוֹ, נָגִילָה וְנִשְׂמְחָה בִּישׁוּעָתוֹ.[15]

All, while standing:

אֵל מֶלֶךְ יוֹשֵׁב עַל כִּסֵּא רַחֲמִים מִתְנַהֵג בַּחֲסִידוּת, מוֹחֵל
עֲונות עַמּוֹ, מַעֲבִיר רִאשׁוֹן רִאשׁוֹן,[16] מַרְבֶּה מְחִילָה
לְחַטָּאִים וּסְלִיחָה לְפוֹשְׁעִים, עֹשֶׂה צְדָקוֹת עִם כָּל בָּשָׂר וָרוּחַ,
לֹא כְרָעָתָם תִּגְמוֹל. ✧ אֵל הוֹרֵיתָ לָּנוּ לוֹמַר שְׁלֹשׁ עֶשְׂרֵה, וּזְכוֹר
לָנוּ הַיּוֹם בְּרִית שְׁלֹשׁ עֶשְׂרֵה, כְּמוֹ שֶׁהוֹדַעְתָּ לֶעָנָיו מִקֶּדֶם, כְּמוֹ
שֶׁכָּתוּב, וַיֵּרֶד יהוה בֶּעָנָן וַיִּתְיַצֵּב עִמּוֹ שָׁם, וַיִּקְרָא בְשֵׁם יהוה.

Congregation, then chazzan:

וַיַּעֲבֹר יהוה עַל פָּנָיו וַיִּקְרָא:

---

of the *tamid* [perpetual] offering. That offering was a male sheep in its first year. Although such a sheep is usually called a כֶּבֶשׂ, the *paytan* here calls it an אַיִל, a name that specifies a male sheep from thirteen to twenty-four months old, possibly to fit the rhyme scheme. [See prefatory commentary to *selichah* 44.]

וְלֹא יִדְּמוּ קֶרֶץ — *And not be stilled with slaughter.* The translation follows *Radak* and *Metzudos* (to *Jeremiah* 46:20). *Targum*, however, renders *murderous nations*; accordingly, the translation would read either *and not be stilled by murderous nations*, or, *and the murderous nation not be stilled.*

ק its time is far off, as is [the promise of] the verse,
  'The King [Messiah] has ascended!'[1]
ר Why, then, should the wicked go on living,[2]
  and not be stilled, with slaughter?*
      But those who **hope** to HASHEM, they shall inherit the earth.[3]
ש Those who despoil [Your] heritage[4] [seek] to evict us from Your portion,
ש [the call,] 'Turn away! Turn away, O Shulamite!'[5]
  is in their mouths, to separate us [from You].
ת But [we reply:] "Why should you be so pompous,[6]
  urging each other on: 'Let us separate them [from their God]!'?
          [Do you not know that] HASHEM is good to those
          who **hope** for Him, to the soul that seeks Him."[7]
ש Almighty, the answer to our 'Why, then's' fills our mouths:
ל We have sinned against HASHEM, our God,[8]
  and so this has happened to us.[9]
מ Your judgments are true and You are lofty and exalted —
ה Yours is the righteousness, and ours is the shamefacedness[10]
  for all to see.
  You cautioned us many times, yet we said,
  'We will not pay attention!'[11]
  We despised Your prophets' admonitions, [refusing] to pay heed.
  Now let the greatness of Your power be shown,[12]
  [You] Who settle the solitary [into a family];[13]
  and return us [to You] in whole-hearted repentance.
  Chazzan — O bring near that time [of vengeance
  when the oppressors will say:] 'Why are your clothes stained red?'[14]
  When their life blood will spatter over Your enwrapping robes!
  We will praise You forever, when that day comes in its due time:
          'This is HASHEM to whom we **hoped**,
          let us rejoice and be glad in His salvation.'[15]

All, while standing:

אֵל מֶלֶךְ O God, King Who sits on the throne of mercy; Who acts with
  kindness, pardons the iniquities of His people, removes [sins]
one by one,[16] increasingly grants pardon to careless sinners and forgiveness
to rebels, Who deals righteously with every living being — You do not repay
them in accord with their evil. Chazzan — O God, You taught us to recite the
Thirteen [Attributes of Mercy], so remember for us today the covenant of
these Thirteen, as You made known to the humble one in ancient times, as
it is written: And HASHEM descended in a cloud and stood with him there,
and He called out with the Name HASHEM.

Congregation, then chazzan:
And HASHEM passed before him [Moses] and proclaimed:

---

(1) Cf. *Micah* 2:13. (2) *Job* 21:7. (3) *Psalms* 37:9. (4) Cf. *Jeremiah* 50:11. (5) *Song of Songs* 7:1.
(6) *Numbers* 16:3. (7) *Lamentations* 3:25. (8) *Jeremiah* 3:25. (9) Cf. *Leviticus* 10:19.
(10) Cf. *Daniel* 9:7. (11) Cf. *Jeremiah* 6:17. (12) Cf. *Numbers* 14:17. (13) Cf. *Psalms* 68:7.
(14) *Isaiah* 63:2. (15) 25:9. (16) Tractate *Rosh Hashanah* 17a.

Congregation and *chazzan* (the words in bold type are recited aloud and in unison):

יְהוָה, יְהוָה, אֵל, רַחוּם, וְחַנּוּן, אֶרֶךְ אַפַּיִם, וְרַב חֶסֶד, **וֶאֱמֶת,**
נֹצֵר חֶסֶד לָאֲלָפִים, נֹשֵׂא עָוֹן, וָפֶשַׁע, **וְחַטָּאָה,**
וְנַקֵּה. וְסָלַחְתָּ לַעֲוֹנֵנוּ וּלְחַטָּאתֵנוּ וּנְחַלְתָּנוּ. סְלַח לָנוּ אָבִינוּ כִּי
חָטָאנוּ, מְחַל לָנוּ מַלְכֵּנוּ כִּי פָשָׁעְנוּ. כִּי אַתָּה אֲדֹנָי טוֹב וְסַלָּח, וְרַב
חֶסֶד לְכָל קֹרְאֶיךָ.

פסוקי הקדמה לסליחה סב

הוֹשִׁיעָה יְהוָה כִּי גָמַר חָסִיד, כִּי פַסּוּ אֱמוּנִים מִבְּנֵי אָדָם.[1]
אָבַד חָסִיד מִן הָאָרֶץ, וְיָשָׁר בָּאָדָם אָיִן.[2] רְאֵה כִּי אֵין
אִישׁ, וְהִשְׁתּוֹמֵם כִּי אֵין מַפְגִּיעַ.[3] אַתָּה הוּא מַלְכֵּנוּ אֱלֹהִים, צַוֵּה
יְשׁוּעוֹת יַעֲקֹב.[4] יַחֵל יִשְׂרָאֵל אֶל יְהוָה מֵעַתָּה וְעַד עוֹלָם.[5]

כְּרַחֵם אָב עַל בָּנִים, כֵּן תְּרַחֵם יְהוָה עָלֵינוּ. לַיהוָה הַיְשׁוּעָה,
עַל עַמְּךָ בִרְכָתֶךָ סֶּלָה. יְהוָה צְבָאוֹת עִמָּנוּ, מִשְׂגָּב
לָנוּ אֱלֹהֵי יַעֲקֹב סֶלָה. יְהוָה צְבָאוֹת, אַשְׁרֵי אָדָם בֹּטֵחַ בָּךְ. יְהוָה
הוֹשִׁיעָה, הַמֶּלֶךְ יַעֲנֵנוּ בְיוֹם קָרְאֵנוּ.

In some congregations the following two verses are recited responsively — the *chazzan* reciting סְלַח נָא, and the congregation responding וַיֹּאמֶר. In other congregations these verses are recited silently.

סְלַח נָא לַעֲוֹן הָעָם הַזֶּה כְּגֹדֶל חַסְדֶּךָ, וְכַאֲשֶׁר נָשָׂאתָה לָעָם
הַזֶּה מִמִּצְרַיִם וְעַד הֵנָּה, וְשָׁם נֶאֱמַר:
וַיֹּאמֶר יְהוָה סָלַחְתִּי כִּדְבָרֶךָ.

All:

הַטֵּה אֱלֹהַי אָזְנְךָ וּשְׁמָע, פְּקַח עֵינֶיךָ וּרְאֵה שֹׁמְמֹתֵינוּ, וְהָעִיר
אֲשֶׁר נִקְרָא שִׁמְךָ עָלֶיהָ, כִּי לֹא עַל צִדְקֹתֵינוּ אֲנַחְנוּ
מַפִּילִים תַּחֲנוּנֵינוּ לְפָנֶיךָ, כִּי עַל רַחֲמֶיךָ הָרַבִּים. אֲדֹנָי שְׁמָעָה,
אֲדֹנָי סְלָחָה, אֲדֹנָי הַקְשִׁיבָה, וַעֲשֵׂה אַל תְּאַחַר, לְמַעַנְךָ אֱלֹהַי,
כִּי שִׁמְךָ נִקְרָא עַל עִירְךָ וְעַל עַמֶּךָ.

סליחה סב

אֱלֹהֵינוּ וֵאלֹהֵי אֲבוֹתֵינוּ:

אַרְיֵה בַיַּעַר* דָּמִיתִי** וְנִמְשַׁלְתִּי בְּחוֹבַי,
בְּטוּיֵי נוֹאָל, מִלָּתִי לְשׁוֹן הֲבִי,

אַרְיֵה בַּיַּעַר — *... a lion in the forest.* The first three verses of the respective stanzas form an *aleph-beis* acrostic, followed by the composer's signature, אֵלִיָּה בַּר שְׁמַעְיָה חֲזַק, *Eliyah bar Shemaya, may he be strong* [see prefatory comment to *selichah* 6]. The last word of each stanza is also the first word of the following one.

Congregation and chazzan (the words in bold type are recited aloud and in unison):

ה' ה' HASHEM, HASHEM, God, Compassionate and Gracious, Slow to anger, and Abundant in Kindness and Truth, Preserver of kindness for thousands [of generations], Forgiver of iniquity, willful sin, and error, and Who cleanses. *May You forgive our iniquities and our errors and make us Your heritage. Forgive us, our Father, for we have erred; pardon us, our King, for we have willfully sinned; for You, my Lord, are good and forgiving and abundantly kind to all who call upon You.*

PREFATORY VERSES TO SELICHAH 62

הוֹשִׁיעָה *Save [us], HASHEM, for the devout one is no more, for truthful men have vanished from mankind.[1] The devout one is lost from the land; there is none honest among men.[2] See how there is no worthy man; consider how there is no intercessor.[3] Only You are our King, O God; command the salvations of Jacob.[4] Let Israel hope to HASHEM, from now and forever.[5]*

כְּרַחֵם אָב *As a father has mercy on his children, so, HASHEM, may You have mercy on us. Salvation is HASHEM's, upon Your people is Your blessing, Selah. HASHEM, Master of Legions, is with us, a stronghold for us is the God of Jacob, Selah. HASHEM, Master of Legions, praiseworthy is the person who trusts in You. HASHEM, save! May the King answer us on the day we call.*

In some congregations the following two verses are recited responsively — the chazzan reciting, 'Forgive, please . . .,' and the congregation responding, 'And HASHEM said . . .'
In other congregations these verses are recited silently.

סְלַח נָא *Forgive, please, the iniquity of this people according to the greatness of Your kindness and as You have forgiven this people from Egypt until now, and there it was said:*

And HASHEM said, 'I have forgiven according to your word!'

All:

הַטֵּה *Incline, my God, Your ear, and listen, open Your eyes and see our desolation and that of the city upon which Your Name is proclaimed; for not because of our righteousness do we cast down our supplications before You, rather because of Your abundant compassion. O my Lord, heed; O my Lord, forgive; O my Lord, be attentive and act, do not delay; for Your sake, my God, for Your Name is proclaimed upon Your city and upon Your people.*

SELICHAH 62

Our God and God of our forefathers:

א *I am likened unto a lion in the forest,**[6]
I am considered so because of my sins;
ב *my speech is folly, my word an idle one;*

---

(1) *Psalms* 12:2. (2) *Micah* 7:2. (3) Cf. *Isaiah* 59:16. (4) Cf. *Psalms* 44:5. (5) 131:3. (6) Cf. *Jeremiah* 12:8.

אַרְיֵה בְיַעַר דָּמִיתִי — *I am likened to a lion in the forest.* The prophet Jeremiah, speaking in God's voice, admonished: *My heritage-people was to me like a lion in the forest; she gave her voice against Me, therefore have I hated her* (Jeremiah 12:8). The Talmud interprets the phrase *she gave her voice against Me* as an allusion to a person who, because of character flaws and sinful ways,

גָּרַעְתִּי מַקִּישׁ כְּבֶן קִישׁ וּמִסְפַּר בִּגְוַי,[*][1]

כָּל רֹאשׁ לָחֳלִי וְכָל לֵבָב דַּוָּי.[2]

דַּוָּי גוֹלֶה וְנִקְלֶה הִכְאַבְתִּי וְנֶעֱכַּרְתִּי,

הוּנַעְתִּי חָגַגְתִּי וְרָוִיתִי רוֹשׁ וְנִשְׁבַּרְתִּי,

וּמִדְּחַק אֲדוֹנִים חִנָּם לָהֶם נִמְכַּרְתִּי,[3]

בְּהִתְעַטֵּף עָלַי נַפְשִׁי, אֶת יהוה זָכָרְתִּי.[4]

זָכַרְתִּי חַסְדֶּךָ[5] וְאַהֲבָתָךְ עָלַי כְּהַדְרִגִילוּ,[6]

חוֹבוֹת הֶעֱבִירוּ וְאוֹתִי לְךָ הִסְגִּילוּ,

טְלָאֶיךָ עַתָּה בְּתַחַן וָפֶלֶל יַרְגִּילוּ,

אֶבְיוֹנֵי אָדָם בִּקְדוֹשׁ יִשְׂרָאֵל יָגִילוּ.[7]

יָגִילוּ יָרֹנּוּ עֲבָדֶיךָ בְּפֶקֶד חוֹמוֹתַי,

כְּדַרְכֹּד וְאַבְנֵי חֵפֶץ תַּגְבִּילֵם[8] אֵימָתַי,

לְתֵל עוֹלָם עִירִי[9] וְלַשֵּׁפֶל רָמוֹתַי,

וְאַתָּה יהוה עַד מָתַי.[10]

מָתַי תְּחַיֵּנוּ וּמִתְּהוֹמוֹת תַּעֲלֵנוּ,[11]

נָאוֹר,[12] הָסֵר וְהָקֵל סִמְלוֹן עָלֵנוּ,

שְׂבַע מַלֵּא אֲסָמֵינוּ,[13] וְהַצְלִיחָה מִפְעָלֵנוּ,

יְהִי חַסְדְּךָ יהוה עָלֵינוּ.[14]

עָלֵינוּ הַמָּלֵא רַחֲמִים בְּצָרָה דְּרַשְׁתִּיךָ,

פֵּרַשְׂתִּי יָדַי אֵלֶיךָ[15] בְּקִרְבִּי שִׁחַרְתִּיךָ,[16]

צָמְאָה לְךָ נַפְשִׁי[17] בַּלַּיְלָה כִּי אִוִּיתִיךָ,[18]

יהוה אַל אֵבוֹשָׁה כִּי קְרָאתִיךָ.[19]

קְרָאתִיךָ[20] מֵעָמְקֵי דָּלוּ עֵינַי,

רוּם יָדַי נָשָׂאתִי[21] הֲפִיצוֹתִי מַעְיָנַי,

שׁוּר כִּשְׁרוֹן מְחֵה וְהַעֲבֵר זְדוֹנַי,

יהוה שָׁמְעָה תְפִלָּתִי הַאֲזִינָה אֶל תַּחֲנוּנָי.[22]

---

is unfit to serve as *chazzan*, yet fills the role solely because of his fine voice (*Taanis* 16b, see *Maharsha*). Sending a wicked person, one despised by God, to represent the congregation in its prayers, is a travesty. About such a congregation does God add, *therefore have I hated her.* The *paytan*, in the voice of the *chazzan*, humbly stands before the Ark, and pleads that his prayers be answered. Although he knows that he is really unworthy, his speech is foolish, and he cannot set the words of the prayer properly, nevertheless, since truly righteous intercessors

are no longer available to us, he has no choice but to lead the service, despite his shortcomings.

כְּבֶן קִישׁ וּמִסְפַּר בִּגְוַי — *Like [Mordechai] the son of Kish and Mispar Bigvai.* In the Book of Esther, Kish is listed as one of Mordechai's forebears. Although the genealogy there (2:5) is incomplete, three of Mordechai's progenitors are mentioned: *Mordechai son of Yair son of Shimi son of Kish.* The Talmud explains that these names were chosen to be listed because they describe Mordechai's prowess in prayer: יָאִיר, *Yair,* from

ג I am cut off from those who could knock [on the gates of Heaven],
 like [Mordechai] the son of Kish and Mispar Bigvai.*[1]
 Every head is filled with illness, every heart is **ill**.[2]

ד **Ill**, exiled and demeaned, I have become achy and troubled,

ה I have been driven about, reeling, satiated with gall,
 I have become drunk.

ו Yet from the oppression of lords to whom I was sold for naught,[3]
 as my soul fainted in me, HASHEM **I remembered**.[4]

ז **I remembered** Your kindness and Your love for me[5]
 when [You led my] bannered [tribes in the Wilderness],[6]

ח they pushed aside my sins and made me Your beloved [nation].

ט Your flock now is wont [to approach You] in supplication and prayer:
 'In the Holy One of Israel may the poorest of men **rejoice!**'[7]

י **Rejoice** and sing shall Your servants
 when my [Holy City's] walls are restored!

כ O when will You surround them with kadkod and precious stones?[8]

ל My city [has been made] into a mound of eternal ruin,[9]
 my lofty places into lowliness,
 and You, O HASHEM — until **when?**[10]

מ **When** will You enliven us and raise us from the depths?[11]

נ O Source of light,[12] remove [our burden]
 and loosen the harness of our yoke.

ס Fill our granaries with satiation,[13] and bring success to our endeavors;
 please let Your kindness, HASHEM, be **upon us**.[14]

ע **Upon us** may [Your] mercy be full, for I seek You in distress.

פ I spread forth my hands to You,[15] within myself I pray to You.[16]

צ My soul thirsts for You[17] in the [galus-]night, for I desire You;[18]
 HASHEM, let me not be shamed, when **I call You**.[19]

ק **I call You** from the depths,[20] my eyes are turned upwards,

ר I lift my hands heavenwards,[21]
 I cause my wellsprings [of tears] to flow forth.

ש Consider [my] proper deeds; wipe away,
 dismiss [even] my deliberate sins.
 HASHEM, hear my prayer; lend an ear **to my supplications**.[22]

---

(1) See *Ezra* 2:2. (2) *Isaiah* 1:5. (3) Cf. 52:3; see commentary to *selichah* 9, s.v., לְמָכוּרֵי חִנָּם.
(4) *Jonah* 2:8. (5) Cf. *Jeremiah* 2:2. (6) Cf. *Song of Songs* 2:4. (7) Cf. *Isaiah* 29:19. (8) Cf. 54:12.
(9) Cf. *Deuteronomy* 13:17. (10) *Psalms* 6:4. (11) Cf. 71:20. (12) See commentary to *selichah* 18.
(13) Cf. *Proverbs* 3:10. (14) *Psalms* 33:22. (15) 143:6. (16) Cf. *Isaiah* 26:9. (17) *Psalms* 63:2.
(18) *Isaiah* 26:9. (19) *Psalms* 31:18. (20) Cf. 130:1. (21) Cf. *Habakkuk* 3:10. (22) Cf. *Psalms* 143:1.

---

the root אוֹר, *light*, indicates that he lit up Israel's
eyes with his prayers; שִׁמְעִי, *Shimi*, from שָׁמַע,
hear, because his prayers were heard by God;
and קִישׁ, *Kish*, a word related to מַקִּישׁ, *to bang*,
for he banged on the Gates of Mercy until they
were opened for him. Furthermore, Scriptures
call Mordechai בִּלְשָׁן, *Bilshan* (*Ezra* 2:2; Nehemiah 7:7), a word derived from בִּיל לָשׁוֹן, *he
mixed language*, because of his mastery with
words (*Menachos* 65a).

Mispar Bigvai is listed in *Ezra* (2:2) among the
colleagues of Mordechai who returned with
Zerubavel to Jerusalem at the end of the seventy-
year exile following the Destruction of the First
Temple. Some commentaries read the two words
as the name of one person (since there is no
conjunctive prefix ו); others read them as the
names of two people (since these names appear
in the middle of the list, there is no need for the
conjunctive prefix).

תַּחֲנוּנַי אֱזֹן אוֹמְנִי מְחוֹלְלִי וּפַדְגוּגִי,

לְךָ גָלוּי וְצָפוּי תַּאַב רְגוּגִי,

יִצָּלַל זָדוֹן וִיכֻפַּר חֵטְא שְׁגָגִי,

אֲמָרַי הַאֲזִינָה יהוה, בִּינָה הֲגִיגִי.¹

הֲגִיגִי בַּר יֵחָשֵׁב וְיִכּוֹן פְּלוּלִי,

שְׁמַע יָהּ סְלָחָה דְּפִי עֲקוּלִי,

חַזֵּק מַאֲמִירֶךְ וּלְרָצוֹן יְהִי מִלּוּלִי,

הֶגְיוֹן לִבִּי לְפָנֶיךָ יהוה צוּרִי וְגוֹאֲלִי.²

All, while standing:

אֵל מֶלֶךְ יוֹשֵׁב עַל כִּסֵּא רַחֲמִים מִתְנַהֵג בַּחֲסִידוּת, מוֹחֵל עֲוֹנוֹת עַמּוֹ, מַעֲבִיר רִאשׁוֹן רִאשׁוֹן, מַרְבֶּה מְחִילָה לְחַטָּאִים וּסְלִיחָה לְפוֹשְׁעִים, עֹשֶׂה צְדָקוֹת עִם כָּל בָּשָׂר וָרוּחַ, לֹא כְרָעָתָם תִּגְמוֹל. ❖ אֵל הוֹרֵיתָ לָּנוּ לוֹמַר שְׁלֹשׁ עֶשְׂרֵה, וּזְכוֹר לָנוּ הַיּוֹם בְּרִית שְׁלֹשׁ עֶשְׂרֵה, כְּמוֹ שֶׁהוֹדַעְתָּ לֶעָנָיו מִקֶּדֶם, כְּמוֹ שֶׁכָּתוּב, וַיֵּרֶד יהוה בֶּעָנָן וַיִּתְיַצֵּב עִמּוֹ שָׁם, וַיִּקְרָא בְשֵׁם יהוה.

Congregation, then *chazzan:*

וַיַּעֲבֹר יהוה עַל פָּנָיו וַיִּקְרָא:

Congregation and *chazzan* (the words in bold type are recited aloud and in unison):

יהוה, יהוה, אֵל, **רַחוּם, וְחַנּוּן, אֶרֶךְ אַפַּיִם, וְרַב חֶסֶד, וֶאֱמֶת, נֹצֵר חֶסֶד לָאֲלָפִים, נֹשֵׂא עָוֹן, וָפֶשַׁע, וְחַטָּאָה, וְנַקֵּה.** וְסָלַחְתָּ לַעֲוֹנֵנוּ וּלְחַטָּאתֵנוּ וּנְחַלְתָּנוּ. סְלַח לָנוּ אָבִינוּ כִּי חָטָאנוּ, מְחַל לָנוּ מַלְכֵּנוּ כִּי פָשָׁעְנוּ. כִּי אַתָּה אֲדֹנָי טוֹב וְסַלָּח, וְרַב חֶסֶד לְכָל קֹרְאֶיךָ.

פסוקי הקדמה לסליחה סג

שׁוּבָה יִשְׂרָאֵל עַד יהוה אֱלֹהֶיךָ, כִּי כָשַׁלְתָּ בַּעֲוֹנֶךָ.³ יהוה אַל בְּאַפְּךָ תוֹכִיחֵנוּ, וְאַל בַּחֲמָתְךָ תְיַסְּרֵנוּ.⁴ טָבַעְנוּ בְיָוֵן מְצוּלָה וְאֵין מָעֳמָד, בָּאנוּ בְמַעֲמַקֵּי מַיִם וְשִׁבֹּלֶת שְׁטָפָתְנוּ.⁵ הֲשִׁיבֵנוּ יהוה אֵלֶיךָ וְנָשׁוּבָה, חַדֵּשׁ יָמֵינוּ כְּקֶדֶם.⁶

כְּרַחֵם אָב עַל בָּנִים, כֵּן תְּרַחֵם יהוה עָלֵינוּ. לַיהוה הַיְשׁוּעָה, עַל עַמְּךָ בִרְכָתֶךָ סֶּלָה. יהוה צְבָאוֹת עִמָּנוּ, מִשְׂגָּב לָנוּ אֱלֹהֵי יַעֲקֹב סֶלָה. יהוה צְבָאוֹת, אַשְׁרֵי אָדָם בֹּטֵחַ בָּךְ. יהוה הוֹשִׁיעָה, הַמֶּלֶךְ יַעֲנֵנוּ בְיוֹם קָרְאֵנוּ.

ת **To my supplications,** *lend an ear,*
    my Nurturer, my Maker, my Teacher!
ל To You is open and revealed my innermost desire.
י Let my intentional sin be sunk deep,
    and my inadvertent error be atoned;
            lend an ear to my words, HASHEM; perceive **my thought.**[1]
ה **My thought,** *may it be adjudged pure, and may my prayer stand firm.*
Hear, O God, and forgive my perverse slander.
Strengthen those who exalt You; let my words find favor,
                        and my heart's thought, before You,
                        HASHEM, my Rock and my Redeemer.[2]

All, while standing:

אֵל מֶלֶךְ O God, King Who sits on the throne of mercy; Who acts with
        kindness, pardons the iniquities of His people, removes [sins]
one by one, increasingly grants pardon to careless sinners and forgiveness
to rebels, Who deals righteously with every living being — You do not repay
them in accord with their evil. Chazzan — O God, You taught us to recite the
Thirteen [Attributes of Mercy], so remember for us today the covenant of
these Thirteen, as You made known to the humble one in ancient times, as
it is written: And HASHEM descended in a cloud and stood with him there,
and He called out with the Name HASHEM.

Congregation, then chazzan:

And HASHEM passed before him [Moses] and proclaimed:

Congregation and chazzan (the words in bold type are recited aloud and in unison):

ה' ה' HASHEM, HASHEM, God, Compassionate and Gracious, Slow to
        anger, and Abundant in Kindness and Truth, Preserver of
kindness for thousands [of generations], Forgiver of iniquity, willful
sin, and error, and Who cleanses. May You forgive our iniquities and our
errors and make us Your heritage. Forgive us, our Father, for we have
erred; pardon us, our King, for we have willfully sinned; for You, my Lord,
are good and forgiving and abundantly kind to all who call upon You.

PREFATORY VERSES TO SELICHAH 63

שׁוּבָה יִשְׂרָאֵל Return, O Israel, to HASHEM, your God, for you have
        stumbled in your iniquity.[3] HASHEM, do not rebuke us
in Your anger, do not chastise us in Your rage.[4] We have sunk into the
mire of the shadowy depths, and there is no foothold; we have entered
deep waters and a rushing current has swept us away.[5] Return us to You,
HASHEM, and we will return; renew our days as of old.[6]

כְּרַחֵם אָב As a father has mercy on his children, so, HASHEM, may
        You have mercy on us. Salvation is HASHEM's, upon Your
people is Your blessing, Selah. HASHEM, Master of Legions, is with us, a
stronghold for us is the God of Jacob, Selah. HASHEM, Master of Legions,
praiseworthy is the person who trusts in You. HASHEM, save! May the
King answer us on the day we call.

(1) *Psalms* 5:2. (2) *19:15.* (3) *Hosea* 14:2. (4) Cf. *Psalms* 6:2. (5) Cf. *69:3.* (6) *Lamentations* 5:21.

In some congregations the following two verses are recited responsively — the *chazzan* reciting סְלַח,
and the congregation responding וַיֹּאמֶר. In other congregations these verses are recited silently.

סְלַח נָא לַעֲוֹן הָעָם הַזֶּה כְּגֹדֶל חַסְדֶּךָ, וְכַאֲשֶׁר נָשָׂאתָה לָעָם
הַזֶּה מִמִּצְרַיִם וְעַד הֵנָּה, וְשָׁם נֶאֱמַר:

וַיֹּאמֶר יהוה סָלַחְתִּי כִּדְבָרֶךָ.

All:

הַטֵּה אֱלֹהַי אָזְנְךָ וּשְׁמָע, פְּקַח עֵינֶיךָ וּרְאֵה שֹׁמְמֹתֵינוּ, וְהָעִיר
אֲשֶׁר נִקְרָא שִׁמְךָ עָלֶיהָ, כִּי לֹא עַל צִדְקוֹתֵינוּ אֲנַחְנוּ
מַפִּילִים תַּחֲנוּנֵינוּ לְפָנֶיךָ, כִּי עַל רַחֲמֶיךָ הָרַבִּים. אֲדֹנָי שְׁמָעָה,
אֲדֹנָי סְלָחָה, אֲדֹנָי הַקְשִׁיבָה, וַעֲשֵׂה אַל תְּאַחַר, לְמַעַנְךָ אֱלֹהַי, כִּי
שִׁמְךָ נִקְרָא עַל עִירְךָ וְעַל עַמֶּךָ.

סְלִיחָה סג (שְׁלִישִׁיָּה)

אֱלֹהִים אֵין בִּלְתֶּךָ,[1]*   לְדוֹר דּוֹרִים מֶמְשַׁלְתֶּךָ,[2]
וְלָעַד קִיּוּם בְּרִיתֶךָ.

בִּימִינְךָ אֵין מַעֲצָר,[3]   יָדְךָ לֹא תִקְצָר,[4]
אֵל עוֹנֶה בַּצָּר.[5]

גָּבְרוּ מְאֹד נִפְלְאוֹתֶיךָ,   וְלָעַד שִׁלְטוֹן מַלְכוּתֶךָ,
וְלֹא יִתַּמּוּ שְׁנוֹתֶיךָ.[6]

דּוֹרֵשׁ דָּמִים,[7]   הִצַּלְתָּנוּ כַּמָּה פְעָמִים,
וְהִשְׁפַּלְתָּ מְלָכִים רָמִים.[8]

הֵן אַתָּה לֹא שָׁנִיתָ,[9]   וְאַתָּה הוּא שֶׁהָיִיתָ,
בְּנֵי יַעֲקֹב לֹא כִלִּיתָ.[9]

וּמִבְּנֵי בְנֵיהֶם אֲנַחְנוּ,[10]   לָמָּה לָנֶצַח זְנַחְתָּנוּ,
וְכַמֶּה מִלֵּב נִשְׁכַּחְנוּ.[11]

זְרוּיִים בְּכָל פִּנָּה,   עֲבוּדִים בְּכָל מְדִינָה,
וְאֵין לָנוּ חֲנִינָה.[12]

חֲשׁוּכִים[13] בֵּין כָּל אֻמָּה,   נְתוּנִים לְבֹשֶׁת וְלִכְלִמָּה,[14]
לְגוֹיֵי אֲדָמָה.

טָבַעְנוּ בְּצוּל מַעֲמַקִּים,[15]   יָרַדְנוּ וְאֵין מָקִים,[16]
לְךָ לְבַד נוֹאֲקִים.

---

§ **אֱלֹהִים אֵין בִּלְתֶּךָ** — *God, there is none besides
You.* The acrostic follows the *aleph-beis*, then
spells the *paytan's* name זְבַדְיָה, *Zevadiah.* Not
much is known about him, except that he wrote

many *piyutim* that appear in various liturgies. He
is thought to have lived in ninth or tenth-century
Southern Italy.

    The translation regards the opening word,

In some congregations the following two verses are recited responsively — the chazzan
reciting, 'Forgive, please . . .,' and the congregation responding, 'And HASHEM said . . .'
In other congregations these verses are recited silently.

סְלַח נָא *Forgive, please, the iniquity of this people according to the greatness of Your kindness and as You have forgiven this people from Egypt until now, and there it was said:*

And HASHEM said, 'I have forgiven according to your word!'

All:

הַטֵּה *Incline, my God, Your ear, and listen, open Your eyes and see our desolation and that of the city upon which Your Name is proclaimed; for not because of our righteousness do we cast down our supplications before You, rather because of Your abundant compassion. O my Lord, heed; O my Lord, forgive; O my Lord, be attentive and act, do not delay; for Your sake, my God, for Your Name is proclaimed upon Your city and upon Your people.*

SELICHAH 63

א *God, there is none besides You;*[1]*
Your rule extends to generation after generation,[2]
and Your covenant stands forever.

ב *There is no restraint in Your right hand;[3] Your hand does not fall short,[4]*
O God Who answers [us] in distress.[5]

ג *Your wonders are very powerful; Your kingship's dominion is forever,*
and Your years never end.[6]

ד *Avenger of blood,[7] You have saved us so many times,*
You have humbled haughty kings![8]

ה *See, You have not changed,[9] for it is You Who always were,*
the Children of Jacob You have not annihilated.[9]

ו *But we are their children's children!*
Why are we abandoned eternally?[10]
And why are we forgotten, as the dead [is forgotten] from the heart?[11]

ז *Scattered to every corner [of the world], enslaved in every province,*
there is no grace granted us.[12]

ח *[Sitting] in the dark[13] among each nation,*
given over to shame and humiliation[14]
among the folks of the earth.

ט *We have sunk in the shadowy depths;[15]*
we have descended, and there is none to set [us] erect;[16]
to You alone do we cry.

---

(1) I Samuel 2:2. (2) Cf. Psalms 145:13. (3) Cf. I Samuel 14:6. (4) Cf. Numbers 11:23; Isaiah 59:1.
(5) Cf. Genesis 35:3. (6) Cf. Psalms 102:28. (7) 9:13. (8) Cf. II Samuel 22:28; some editions of Selichos
read, (וְהִשְׁפַּלְתָּ גֵּאִים וְרָמִים), You have humbled the proud and the haughty. (9) Cf. Malachi 3:6.
(10) Cf. Psalms 74:1. (11) Cf. 31:13. (12) Cf. Jeremiah 16:13. (13) Some editions read חֲשׂוּכִים,
imprisoned. (14) Cf. Psalms 35:26. (15) Cf. 69:3. (16) Cf. Jeremiah 50:32.

אֱלֹהִים, God, as sacred. Thus, as in every selichah that begins with a Divine Name, the introductory phrase אֱלֹהֵינוּ וֵאלֹהֵי אֲבוֹתֵינוּ, Our God and the God of our forefathers, is omitted. Alternatively: the word is not sacred but refers to idols: and the stich is rendered: There is no other god besides You. If so, the introductory phrase should be recited.

יוֹשְׁבִים כְּעֵדֵי שְׁקָרִים,   בְּלִי רֹאשׁ לְהָרִים,
לַעֲנָה וָרֹאשׁ שְׁכוּרִים.

בְּשַׁלְנוּ בַּצָּהֳרִים כְּבַלַּיְלָה,   כְּעִוְרִים נְגַשֵׁשׁ בָּאֲפֵלָה,[1]
וְאֵין לֵידַע קֵץ הַגְּאֻלָּה.

לְקוּחֵי כֶסֶף* לְחֵרוּת יוֹצְאִים,   וַאֲנַחְנוּ יוֹם וָלֵיל נִלְאִים,
וּמָנוֹחַ לֹא מוֹצְאִים.[2]

מַה כֹּחִי לִסְבֹּל טִיט רְפָשִׁי,   וּמַה קִּצִּי כִּי אַאֲרִיךְ נַפְשִׁי,[3]
עַד זְמַן תּוֹצִיאֵנִי לַחָפְשִׁי.

נֹאמַר בְּקֶר מִי יִתֵּן עֶרֶב,   וּבָעֶרֶב מִי יִתֵּן בֹּקֶר יִקְרַב,
מִפַּחַד לֵב נֶקְרַב.[4]

שֶׂה פְזוּרָה אָנוּ מְשׁוּלִים,   כָּל מוֹצְאֵינוּ אוֹתָנוּ אוֹכְלִים,[5]
וְעַל נַפְשׁוֹתֵינוּ לֹא חוֹמְלִים.

עֵינַי סָבִיב הֲרִימְוֹתִי,   שְׂמֹאל וְיָמִין צִפִּיתִי,
וּמַכִּיר לִי לֹא רָאִיתִי.[6]

פָּנִיתִי לְכָל צַד וְאֵין עֶזְרָה,   צָעַקְתִּי לְךָ נָאֶקְרָא,
אֵל עֲוֹנָה בְּעֵת צָרָה.[7]

צוּר יָדְךָ לֹא קָצְרָה,[8]   לְךָ הַכֹּחַ וְהַגְּבוּרָה,
לָמָּה תִישָׁן עוּרָה.[9]

קְשֹׁב תַּחַן שִׂיחֵנוּ,   רְאֵה בְּתַשׁוּת כֹּחֵנוּ,
וְאַל בְּאַפְּךָ תוֹכִיחֵנוּ.[10]

שׁוּר בְּשִׁפְלוּת דּוֹרֵנוּ,   תַּבִּיט בְּכֹבֶד צַעֲרֵנוּ,
וְאַל בַּחֲמָתְךָ תְיַסְּרֵנוּ.[10]

זַעֲקָתֵנוּ שְׁעֵה מִמְּעוֹנֶךָ,   בִּיטָה בְּאַנְקַת בָּנֶיךָ,
וְאַל תְּשִׁיבֵנוּ רֵיקָם מִלְּפָנֶיךָ.

❖דִּרְשָׁנוּךָ בְּחִין וְשַׁוְעָה,   יָהּ הַרְצֵה לָנוּ בְּזוּ הַשָּׁעָה,
וְתַחֲנוּנֵינוּ[11] יהוה שְׁמָעָה.

All, while standing:

אֵל מֶלֶךְ יוֹשֵׁב עַל כִּסֵּא רַחֲמִים מִתְנַהֵג בַּחֲסִידוּת, מוֹחֵל
עֲווֹנוֹת עַמּוֹ, מַעֲבִיר רִאשׁוֹן רִאשׁוֹן, מַרְבֶּה
מְחִילָה לַחַטָּאִים וּסְלִיחָה לַפּוֹשְׁעִים, עֹשֶׂה צְדָקוֹת עִם כָּל
בָּשָׂר וָרוּחַ, לֹא כְרָעָתָם תִּגְמוֹל. ❖ אֵל הוֹרֵיתָ לָנוּ לוֹמַר

לְקוּחֵי כֶסֶף — *Those bought for money,* i.e., even slaves for whom the master has paid a tidy sum are often able to have themselves set free (see *Kid-* *dushin* 22b). Yet we, who were given over to our oppressors without any cost to them (see *Isaiah* 52:3,5), cannot acquire our freedom (*Masbir*).

י We sit in shame like false witnesses exposed,
   unable to lift our heads, drunk with wormwood and gall.

כ We stumble at noon as if at night;
   like blind men we grope through the gloom,[1]
   with no way to know when the Redemption will come.

ל Those bought for money* go out to freedom,
   yet we are wearied day and night, rest [we] cannot find.[2]

מ What is my strength to bear this clinging mud?
   And what is my [exile's] end, that I should extend [hope in] my soul,[3]
   until the time You bring me forth to freedom?

נ In the morning we say, 'Would it were evening!'
   and in the evening, 'Would that morning draw nigh!'
   filled with fear of heart and innard.[4]

ס We are compared to scattered sheep: all who find us devour us,[5]
   upon our souls they have no compassion.

ע I raised my eyes all around [me], I looked left and right,
   but I saw none that recognizes me.[6]

פ I have turned to each side, and there was no aid;
   I have shouted to You and called out,
   'O God, Who answers in time of trouble!'[7]

צ O Rock, Your hand does not fall short;[8]
   Yours is the power and the might.
   Why do You [seem to] sleep? Awake![9]

ק Be attentive to our prayer of supplication;

ר see how our strength is failing,
   and do not rebuke us in Your wrath.[10]

ש See the degradation of our generation;

ת look at the heaviness of our pain,
   and do not chastise us in Your rage.[10]

ז Heed our outcry from Your heavenly abode;

כ look at Your children's groan,
   and do not send us away empty-handed from before You.

ד Chazzan – We have sought You with supplication and cry;

יה O God, find favor with us at this time,
   and hear our supplications,[11] HASHEM!

All, while standing:

אֵל מֶלֶךְ O God, King Who sits on the throne of mercy; Who acts with
kindness, pardons the iniquities of His people, removes [sins]
one by one, increasingly grants pardon to careless sinners and forgiveness
to rebels, Who deals righteously with every living being — You do not
repay them in accord with their evil. Chazzan – O God, You taught us to recite

---

(1) Cf. *Isaiah* 59:9-10. (2) Cf. *Lamentations* 1:3. (3) Cf. *Job* 6:11. (4) Cf. *Deuteronomy* 28:67.
(5) Cf. *Jeremiah* 50:17. (6) Cf. *Psalms* 142:5. (7) Cf. 20:2; *Genesis* 35:3. (8) Cf. *Isaiah* 59:1.
(9) Cf. *Psalms* 44:24. (10) Cf. 6:2. (11) Some editions read אֲמָרֵינוּ, our words.

Alternatively: לְקוּחֵי כֶסֶף is to be understood as
לוֹקְחֵי כֶסֶף, *those who took the silver*, i.e., those

who looted the Temple treasury (see *Joel* 4:5),
לְחֵרוּת יוֹצְאִים, *go about freely* (*Pardes*).

שָׁלֹשׁ עֶשְׂרֵה, וּזְכוֹר לָנוּ הַיּוֹם בְּרִית שְׁלֹשׁ עֶשְׂרֵה, כְּמוֹ שֶׁהוֹדַעְתָּ
לֶעָנָיו מִקֶּדֶם, כְּמוֹ שֶׁכָּתוּב, וַיֵּרֶד יהוה בֶּעָנָן וַיִּתְיַצֵּב עִמּוֹ שָׁם,
וַיִּקְרָא בְשֵׁם יהוה.

Congregation, then *chazzan:*

וַיַּעֲבֹר יהוה עַל פָּנָיו וַיִּקְרָא:

Congregation and *chazzan* (the words in bold type are recited aloud and in unison):

יהוה, יהוה, אֵל, רַחוּם, וְחַנּוּן, אֶרֶךְ אַפַּיִם, וְרַב חֶסֶד, וֶאֱמֶת,
נֹצֵר חֶסֶד לָאֲלָפִים, נֹשֵׂא עָוֹן, וָפֶשַׁע, וְחַטָּאָה,
וְנַקֵּה. וְסָלַחְתָּ לַעֲוֹנֵנוּ וּלְחַטָּאתֵנוּ וּנְחַלְתָּנוּ. סְלַח לָנוּ אָבִינוּ כִּי
חָטָאנוּ, מְחַל לָנוּ מַלְכֵּנוּ כִּי פָשָׁעְנוּ. כִּי אַתָּה אֲדֹנָי טוֹב וְסַלָּח, וְרַב
חֶסֶד לְכָל קֹרְאֶיךָ.

פסוקי הקדמה לסליחה סד

כִּי כָל הָעַמִּים יֵלְכוּ אִישׁ בְּשֵׁם אֱלֹהָיו, וַאֲנַחְנוּ נֵלֵךְ בְּשֵׁם
יהוה אֱלֹהֵינוּ לְעוֹלָם וָעֶד.[1] וַאֲנַחְנוּ בְּחַסְדְּךָ בָטָחְנוּ,
יָגֵל לִבֵּנוּ בִּישׁוּעָתֶךָ.[2] וַאֲנַחְנוּ נָשִׁיר עֻזֶּךָ, נְרַנֵּן לַבֹּקֶר חַסְדֶּךָ.[3]
וַאֲנַחְנוּ בְּרֹב חַסְדְּךָ נָבוֹא בֵיתֶךָ, נִשְׁתַּחֲוֶה אֶל הֵיכַל קָדְשְׁךָ
בְּיִרְאָתֶךָ.[4]

בְּרַחֵם אָב עַל בָּנִים, כֵּן תְּרַחֵם יהוה עָלֵינוּ. לַיהוה הַיְשׁוּעָה,
עַל עַמְּךָ בִרְכָתֶךָ סֶּלָה. יהוה צְבָאוֹת עִמָּנוּ, מִשְׂגָּב
לָנוּ אֱלֹהֵי יַעֲקֹב סֶלָה. יהוה צְבָאוֹת, אַשְׁרֵי אָדָם בֹּטֵחַ בָּךְ. יהוה
הוֹשִׁיעָה, הַמֶּלֶךְ יַעֲנֵנוּ בְיוֹם קָרְאֵנוּ.

In some congregations the following two verses are recited responsively — the *chazzan* reciting סְלַח,
and the congregation responding וַיֹּאמֶר. In other congregations these verses are recited silently.

סְלַח נָא לַעֲוֹן הָעָם הַזֶּה כְּגֹדֶל חַסְדֶּךָ, וְכַאֲשֶׁר נָשָׂאתָה לָעָם
הַזֶּה מִמִּצְרַיִם וְעַד הֵנָּה, וְשָׁם נֶאֱמַר:

וַיֹּאמֶר יהוה סָלַחְתִּי כִּדְבָרֶךָ.

All:

הַטֵּה אֱלֹהַי אָזְנְךָ וּשֲׁמָע, פְּקַח עֵינֶיךָ וּרְאֵה שֹׁמְמֹתֵינוּ, וְהָעִיר
אֲשֶׁר נִקְרָא שִׁמְךָ עָלֶיהָ, כִּי לֹא עַל צִדְקוֹתֵינוּ אֲנַחְנוּ
מַפִּילִים תַּחֲנוּנֵינוּ לְפָנֶיךָ, כִּי עַל רַחֲמֶיךָ הָרַבִּים. אֲדֹנָי שְׁמָעָה,
אֲדֹנָי סְלָחָה, אֲדֹנָי הַקְשִׁיבָה, וַעֲשֵׂה אַל תְּאַחַר, לְמַעַנְךָ אֱלֹהַי, כִּי
שִׁמְךָ נִקְרָא עַל עִירְךָ וְעַל עַמֶּךָ.

the Thirteen [Attributes of Mercy], so remember for us today the covenant of these Thirteen, as You made known to the humble one in ancient times, as it is written: And HASHEM descended in a cloud and stood with him there, and He called out with the Name HASHEM.

Congregation, then chazzan:

And HASHEM passed before him [Moses] and proclaimed:

Congregation and chazzan (the words in bold type are recited aloud and in unison):

ה' ה' **HASHEM, HASHEM, God, Compassionate and Gracious, Slow to anger, and Abundant in Kindness and Truth, Preserver of kindness for thousands [of generations], Forgiver of iniquity, willful sin, and error, and Who cleanses.** *May You forgive our iniquities and our errors and make us Your heritage. Forgive us, our Father, for we have erred; pardon us, our King, for we have willfully sinned; for You, my Lord, are good and forgiving and abundantly kind to all who call upon You.*

PREFATORY VERSES TO SELICHAH 64

כִּי כָל *For all the nations proceed, each in the name of its god, but we will go in the name of HASHEM, our God, for ever and ever.[1] But as for us, we trust in Your kindness; our heart will exult in Your salvation.[2] But as for us, we shall sing of Your might; we will rejoice toward morning in Your kindness.[3] But as for us, through Your abundant kindness, we will enter Your House; we will prostrate ourselves towards Your Holy Sanctuary in awe of You.[4]*

כְּרַחֵם אָב *As a father has mercy on his children, so, HASHEM, may You have mercy on us. Salvation is HASHEM's, upon Your people is Your blessing, Selah. HASHEM, Master of Legions, is with us, a stronghold for us is the God of Jacob, Selah. HASHEM, Master of Legions, praiseworthy is the person who trusts in You. HASHEM, save! May the King answer us on the day we call.*

In some congregations the following two verses are recited responsively — the chazzan reciting, 'Forgive, please . . .,' and the congregation responding, 'And HASHEM said . . .'
In other congregations these verses are recited silently.

סְלַח נָא *Forgive, please, the iniquity of this people according to the greatness of Your kindness and as You have forgiven this people from Egypt until now, and there it was said:*

And HASHEM said, 'I have forgiven according to your word!'

All:

הַטֵּה *Incline, my God, Your ear, and listen, open Your eyes and see our desolation and that of the city upon which Your Name is proclaimed; for not because of our righteousness do we cast down our supplications before You, rather because of Your abundant compassion. O my Lord, heed; O my Lord, forgive; O my Lord, be attentive and act, do not delay; for Your sake, my God, for Your Name is proclaimed upon Your city and upon Your people.*

---

(1) *Micah* 4:5. (2) Cf. *Psalms* 13:6. (3) Cf. 59:17. (4) Cf. 5:8.

סליחה סד (שלמונית)

All:

אֱלֹהֵינוּ וֵאלֹהֵי אֲבוֹתֵינוּ:

אֵיךְ אוּכַל לָבֹא* עָדֶיךָ,[1]

וְעוֹבְדֵי זוּלָתֶךָ לֹא עֲזָבוּנִי לְעָבְדֶךָ,[2]

וְהֵמָּה בִקְשׁוּ לְהַפְרִידִי מִמָּךְ,

וַאֲנִי לֹא עָזַבְתִּי פִּקֻּדֶיךָ.[3]

אֵיךְ גָּלִיתִי וָאֵלֵךְ בְּכָל הֵלֶךְ וָפֶלֶךְ,

וּמָלְכוּ עָלַי מַמְלִיכִים לְמֶלֶךְ,[2]

וְהֵמָּה דִינָם עוֹמֵד וּמַלְכָּם מוֹלֵךְ,[2]

וַאֲנִי לֹא נִקְרֵאתִי לָבוֹא אֶל הַמֶּלֶךְ.[4]

אֵיךְ הָלְכוּ נְחָלִים מִדֶּלֶף דִּמְעִי הַדָּלוּף,

וְנִמְסַרְתִּי לְפוֹעֲלֵי אָוֶן וְסִלּוּף,

וְהֵמָּה וּבְנֵיהֶם יוֹרוּנִי חֵץ שָׁלוּף,

וַאֲנִי כְּכֶבֶשׂ אַלּוּף.[5]

אֵיךְ זְמַן קִצִּי נֶחְתָּם וְלֹא נוֹדָע,

וְקַרְנִי גֻדַּע אוֹיְבִי[6] מַשְׁחַת פֻּדָּע,[7]

וְהֵמָּה חוֹשְׁבִים חָכְמָתָם כְּהֵימָן וְדַרְדַּע,*[8]

וַאֲנִי בַעַר וְלֹא אֵדָע.[9]

אֵיךְ טֹרְפָה מַלְכוּת, מַמְלֶכֶת עַם סְגֻלָּה,

וְאָרְכָה מְלוּכָה לְמַלְכֵי בְּנֵי עַוְלָה,[2]

וְהֵמָּה יוֹשְׁבִים לָבֶטַח בְּשִׂמְחָה וְגִילָה,

וַאֲנִי בְתוֹךְ הַגּוֹלָה.[10]

אֵיךְ כּוֹס הַתַּרְעֵלָה שָׁתִיתִי[11] וָאֶגְמְעָה,

בָּכִיתִי וְאַדְמְעָה מֵעַל מַשָּׂא וּמִשְׁמְעָה,*[12]

וְהֵמָּה לוֹעֲגִים עָלַי הַקְשִׁיבָה וּשְׁמַע,

וַאֲנִי כְּחֵרֵשׁ לֹא אֶשְׁמָע.[13]

────────

§ אֵיךְ אוּכַל לָבֹא — *How can I come?* In the intricate pattern of this *selichah*, the first line of each stanza begins with the word אֵיךְ, *How*; the third line begins הֵמָּה, *And as for them*; and the fourth line is a Scriptural fragment that begins וַאֲנִי, *But as for me.* An *aleph-beis* acrostic is formed by the initial letters of the words following אֵיךְ and וְהֵמָּה respectively. After the

alphabet, the acrostic continues with the *paytan's* signature — יִצְחָק בַּר סַעַדְיָה חֲזַק, *Yitzchak bar Saadiah, may he be strong.* Nothing is known about this *paytan* except that he was highly praised by R' Shimon Duran in his responsa (*Tashbeitz*), and that he lived sometime before 1234 when the commentary *Arugas HaBosem* [which contains this *selichah*] was written.

SELICHAH 64

All:

Our God and the God of our forefathers:

א **How** can I come* unto You,[1]
when those who serve other-than-You have not let me serve You?[2]

ב **And as for them** — they attempt to separate me from You;
but as for me — I have not forsaken Your orders.[3]

ג **How** have I been exiled? I go along every road, through every area,
while those who make Molech their ruler have ruled over me.[2]

ד **And as for them** — their laws endure, their king rules;[2]
but as for me — I have not been called to come to the King.[4]

ה **How** rivers have flowed from the drops of my dripping tears!
For I have been delivered over to workers of evil and distortion.

ו **And as for them** and their children — they shoot drawn arrows at me;
but as for me — and I am like a choice lamb
[prepared for the slaughter].[5]

ז **How** is it that the time of my [exile's] end is sealed up, not to be known,
while my enemy, who has cut down my dignity,[6]
are saved from ruin?[7]

ח **And as for them** — they think their wisdom
equals that of Moses and his generation;*[8]
but as for me — [they think] I am a boor and know nothing.[9]

ט **How** sundered is the kingdom, the kingdom of [Your] treasured people,
whereas kingship is extended for the kings of iniquitous folk![2]

י **And as for them** — they dwell securely, in gladness and exultation;
but as for me — I am in the midst of the Exile.[10]

כ **How** have I drunk and swallowed the poisoned cup?[11]
I have wept and shed tears from the yoke of Ishmael's children.*[12]

ל **And as for them** they mock at me,
[demanding that I] be attentive and listen [to their preaching];
but as for me — I am like a deaf man and I do not listen.[13]

---

(1) Cf. *Psalms* 65:3. (2) This line has been censored out of some editions. (3) *Psalms* 119:87. (4) *Esther* 4:11; cf. *Hosea* 8:4. (5) *Jeremiah* 11:19. (6) Cf. *Lamentations* 2:3. (7) Cf. *Job* 33:24. (8) See *I Kings* 5:11. (9) *Psalms* 73:22. (10) *Ezekiel* 1:1. (11) Cf. *Isaiah* 51:17. (12) Cf. *Genesis* 15:14. (13) *Psalms* 38:14.

כְּהֵימָן וְדַרְדַּע — *Equals that of Moses and his generation.* The prophet describes Solomon as wiser מִכָּל אָדָם, *than any man;* מֵאֵיתָן הָאֶזְרָחִי, *than Eisan the Ezrachite,* וְכַלְכֹּל וְדַרְדַּע, *and Heiman, Chalcal and Darda,* בְּנֵי מָחוֹל, *the sons of Machol* (*I Kings* 5:11). *Rashi* and *Radak* cite a Midrash (*Pesikta*) that interprets these names homiletically: מִכָּל אָדָם alludes to Adam, who, in his wisdom, named all the animals in the world; אֵיתָן is Abraham (see prefatory comment to selichah 83); הֵימָן is Moses, of whom it is stated: *Of all My household,* נֶאֱמָן, *he is the faithful one* (*Numbers* 12:7); וְכַלְכֹּל refers to Joseph who supplied food (כִּלְכֵּל) during the famine; וְדַרְדַּע

alludes to that generation of the Wilderness that received the Torah at Mount Sinai and therefore was called דּוֹר דֵעָה, *the generation of knowledge;* and בְּנֵי מָחוֹל also means that same generation, for they were granted forgiveness (מְחִילָה) from the sin of the Golden Calf.

Thus, the *paytan* speaks of the idolaters who place their writings on the same level as the Torah given through Moses to the Generation of Knowledge.

מַשָּׂא וּמִשְׁמָע — *Ishmael's children.* These are two of the children of Ishmael (listed in *Genesis* 25:13-15). The *paytan* plays on the name מַשָּׂא which means *a burden;* thus, מֵעֹל מַשָּׂא, *from the*

אֵיךְ מְחָצַנִי אֱלֹהַי, וּמַכְאוֹבִי לֹא חָבָשׁ,
וּמְעִיל תִּפְאַרְתִּי לִבְנֵי אֱדוֹם הִלְבָּשׁ,
וְהֵמָּה נְפָת אוֹכְלִים חָלָב וּדְבַשׁ,
וַאֲנִי כָּעֶשֶׂב אִיבָשׁ.[1]

אֵיךְ סְבָבוּנִי קֵדָר* כִּתְּרוּנִי דְדָן וּשְׁבָא,*
הַקּוֹרְאִים נָבִיא לְאִישׁ מֵעוֹלָם לֹא נִבָּא,
וְהֵמָּה עוֹשִׂים חַיִל גְּדוּד וּצְבָא,
וַאֲנִי אָנָה אֲנִי בָא.[2]

אֵיךְ פָּקַדְתָּ עָלַי כַּאֲשֶׁר הֲרֵעוֹתִי וְהִסְכַּלְתִּי,
בְּשִׁנֵּי אֲרָיוֹת וּלְבָאִים נֶאֱכַלְתִּי,
וְהֵמָּה צָעִיר וָרַב אוֹמְרִים מְצָאתִי וְגַם יָכָלְתִּי,
וַאֲנִי כַּאֲשֶׁר שָׁכְלְתִּי שָׁכָלְתִּי.[3]

אֵיךְ קָדְרוּ כּוֹכְבַי וְחָזְרוּ גַלְגַּלִּי,
וְעוֹבְדֵי גִלּוּלִים גֻּלְלוּ גְלִילִי,*
וְהֵמָּה רָחֲקוּ רַגְלַי מֵעֲלוֹת רַגְלַי,
וַאֲנִי כִּמְעַט נָטָיוּ רַגְלָי.[4]

אֵיךְ שָׁמַרְתָּ מַעֲנָיַי וּנְטַרְתַּנִי חוֹבִי,
וּמְרִיבֵי נַפְשִׁי לֹא רַבְתָּ רִיבִי,[5]
וְהֵמָּה תַקְפָּם וְכֹחָם לְהַכְאִיבִי וּלְהַדְאִיבִי,
וַאֲנִי בְחַסְדְּךָ בָטַחְתִּי יָגֵל לִבִּי.[6]

אֵיךְ יָשַׁבְתִּי בָדָד[7] וָאֱהִי לְנִידָה,[8]
מִכָּבוֹד יְרוּדָה בַּגּוֹיִם נְדוּדָה,[9]
וְהֵמָּה צָלְחוּ וּמָלְכוּ וּמֶמְשַׁלְתָּם עָמְדָה,
וַאֲנִי שְׁכוּלָה וְגַלְמוּדָה.[10]

אֵיךְ חֵרְפוּנִי מְעוֹלְלַי וּמְהוֹלֲלַי[11] כֻּלְּהֶם,
צֶלֶם אֶצְלָם לֹא סָר מֵעֲלֵיהֶם,[12]
וְהֵמָּה קָרְאוּ הֶאָח הֶאָח[13] בְּמִלֵּיהֶם,
וַאֲנִי הָיִיתִי חֶרְפָּה לָהֶם.[14]

אֵיךְ בֵּינֵיהֶם נִשְׁאַרְתִּי דּוֹאֵג וְדוֹאֵב,
מִפַּלְגֵי יְגוֹנָם* וּמִמְּקוֹרָם שׁוֹאֵב,

---

(1) Psalms 102:12. (2) Genesis 37:30. (3) 43:14. (4) Psalms 73:2. (5) Cf. 35:1. (6) 13:6.
(7) Cf. Lamentations 1:1. (8) Cf. 1:8; many editions of Selichos read, וָאֱהִי לְנִדָּה,
and I became [like] a menstruant, cf. Lamentations 1:17. (9) Cf. Hosea 9:17. (10) Isaiah 49:21.
(11) Cf. Psalms 102:9. (12) Cf. Numbers 14:9. (13) Cf. Psalms 40:16. (14) 109:25.

מ **How** my God has crushed me, and my wounds are not bound up!
My cloak of splendor is draped around Edom's children.

נ **And as for them** — they feast on nectar, milk and honey;
but as for me — I wither away like grass.[1]

ס **How** the people of Araby* have surrounded us
and the Hamites* cut us off!
They call a man who had never prophesied 'the Prophet.'

ע **And as for them** — they build army, troop and legion;
but as for me — where will I go?[2]

פ **How** have You visited punishment upon me,
according to how evil and foolish I have been?
I have been devoured by the teeth of lions and lionesses.

צ **And as for them** — both young and old, they declare,
'I have found and I have also conquered!'
But as for me — as I was bereaved, so was I [again] bereaved.[3]

ק **How** have my stars gone dark,
and the spheres of Heaven turned back?
Idol worshipers have turned my territories into heaps of rubble.*

ר **And as for them** — they have distanced my feet
from ascending for my pilgrimage festivals;
but as for me — my legs almost foundered.[4]

ש **How** have You kept my sins in mind, and been attentive to my guilt;
but have not taken up my cause against those
who contend with my soul?[5]

ת **And as for them** — they use all their strength and power
to pain me and grieve me;
but as for me — I trust in Your kindness, and my heart will rejoice.[6]

י **How** have I sat alone[7] and become a wanderer,[8]
descended from glory, wandering among the nations?[9]

צ **And as for them** — they have succeeded and reigned
and their dominion has endured;
but as for me — I am bereaved of my children and forsaken.[10]

ח **How** is it that my tormentors, my mockers, all vilify me?[11]
Their protective shadow is with them,
it has not turned away from them.[12]

ק **And as for them** — they call out with [taunting] word, 'Aha! Aha!'[13]
But as for me — I have become an object of disgrace to them.[14]

כ **How** am I left worried and aching among them,
I draw [troubles] from their wellsprings of sorrow*
and their source [of ill].

---

yoke of the burden.

קֵדָר — *The people of Araby* [lit., *Kedar*]. This son of Ishmael (*Genesis* 25:13) is identified by *Targum Yonasan* as עֲרָב, *Araby.*

דְּדָן וּשְׁבָא — *The Hamites.* Dedan and Sheba were great-grandsons of Ham (see *Genesis* 10:7).

גָּלְלוּ גְלִילַי — *Have turned my territories into*

heaps of rubble. The word גְּלָלִים is cognate with גַּל, *heap* (*Arugas HaBosem*). Others derive גָּלְלוּ from גָּלָל, *filth*, and translate, *have befouled my territories* (*Masbir*).

מִפִּלְגֵי יְגוֹנָם — *From their wellsprings of sorrow*, i.e., the flood of troubles the oppressors bring upon Israel (*Arugas HaBosem*). Alternatively: *from [my] flowing [tears] brought on by the*

וְהֵמָּה רוֹבְצִים וְשׁוֹכְבִים כְּעוֹרֵב וְכִזְאָב,[1*]

וַאֲנִי עָנִי וְכוֹאֵב.[2]

אֵיךְ שׂוֹנְאַי כָּל טָהֲרָה שָׁכְנוּ בְצִיּוֹן,

מִי הֶאֱמִין כֶּזֶה מִי עָלָה לוֹ בְּרַצְיוֹן,[3*]

וְהֵמָּה עֲשִׁירִים נְשִׂיאִים נְתוּנִים עֶלְיוֹן,

וַאֲנִי עָנִי וְאֶבְיוֹן.[4]

אֵיךְ דָרוּ בְהֵיכָלוֹתַי וְשָׁכְנוּ בָם שָׁכוֹן,

מֵעֶלְיוֹן לְתַחְתּוֹן וּמִתַּחְתּוֹן לְתִיכוֹן,[5*]

וְהֵמָּה יָרְשׁוּ הוֹן זָהָב וַאֲדַרְכוֹן,

וַאֲנִי לְצֶלַע נָכוֹן.[6]

❖ אֵיךְ חֶשְׁבּוֹנוֹתַי נָפוֹצוּ וְהֵמָּה עָלוּ בְּמַחְשְׁבוֹתֶיךָ,

זָכְרֵנוּ נָא וּפָקְדֵנוּ בִּישׁוּעָתֶךָ,[7] מֵעוֹבְדֵי בִלְתֶּךָ,

וְהֵמָּה קַלְּעֵם וּבַלְּעֵם מִמְּכוֹן שִׁבְתֶּךָ,

וַאֲנִי בְּרֹב חַסְדְּךָ אָבוֹא בֵיתֶךָ.[8]

All, while standing:

אֵל מֶלֶךְ יוֹשֵׁב עַל כִּסֵּא רַחֲמִים מִתְנַהֵג בַּחֲסִידוּת, מוֹחֵל עֲוֹנוֹת עַמּוֹ, מַעֲבִיר רִאשׁוֹן רִאשׁוֹן, מַרְבֶּה מְחִילָה לְחַטָּאִים וּסְלִיחָה לְפוֹשְׁעִים, עֹשֶׂה צְדָקוֹת עִם כָּל בָּשָׂר וָרוּחַ, לֹא כְרָעָתָם תִּגְמוֹל. ❖ אֵל הוֹרֵיתָ לָּנוּ לוֹמַר שְׁלֹשׁ עֶשְׂרֵה, וּזְכוֹר לָנוּ הַיּוֹם בְּרִית שְׁלֹשׁ עֶשְׂרֵה, כְּמוֹ שֶׁהוֹדַעְתָּ לֶעָנָיו מִקֶּדֶם, כְּמוֹ שֶׁכָּתוּב, וַיֵּרֶד יהוה בֶּעָנָן וַיִּתְיַצֵּב עִמּוֹ שָׁם, וַיִּקְרָא בְשֵׁם יהוה.

Congregation, then *chazzan:*

וַיַּעֲבֹר יהוה עַל פָּנָיו וַיִּקְרָא:

Congregation and *chazzan* (the words in bold type are recited aloud and in unison):

יהוה, יהוה, אֵל, **רַחוּם,** וְחַנּוּן, **אֶרֶךְ אַפַּיִם,** וְרַב חֶסֶד, **וֶאֱמֶת,** נֹצֵר חֶסֶד לָאֲלָפִים, נֹשֵׂא עָוֹן, **וָפֶשַׁע,** וְחַטָּאָה, **וְנַקֵּה.** וְסָלַחְתָּ לַעֲוֹנֵנוּ וּלְחַטָּאתֵנוּ וּנְחַלְתָּנוּ. סְלַח לָנוּ אָבִינוּ כִּי

---

sorrows they placed upon me (Masbir).

כְּעוֹרֵב וְכִזְאָב — *Like raven and wolf.* Having robbed us of our all, the oppressor nations lie comfortably and satiated, just as the predatory raven and wolf do after devouring their prey. Alternatively: The phrase alludes to עוֹרֵב, *Oreb,* and זְאֵב, *Zeeb,* two Midianite generals who tormented Israel freely, yet rested securely, until they were defeated by Gideon's men (see *Judges* 7:25). Both in-

terpretations appear in *Arugas HaBosem.*

בְּרַצְיוֹן — *As [his] desire,* i.e., 'Who could possibly desire such a thing?' Alternatively: *As [His] desire,* i.e., 'Who could imagine that God would desire such a thing?'

מֵעֶלְיוֹן לְתַחְתּוֹן וּמִתַּחְתּוֹן לְתִיכוֹן — *From the upper section to the lower, and from the lower to the middle.* The enemy took over the entire Temple

ר *And as for them* — *they sprawl and lie back like raven and wolf;*[*1]
but as for me — *I am afflicted and in pain.*[2]

ס *How is it that haters of all that is pure now dwell in Zion?*
Who would have believed anything like this?
Who would have conjured this up as [his] desire?[*3]

ע *And as for them* — *they are rich men, princes, placed on high;*
but as for me — *and I am poor and destitute.*[4]

ר *How have they come to live in my Temples*
and establish a dwelling therein,
from the upper section to the lower,
and from the lower to the middle?[*5]

יה *And as for them* — *they have inherited a horde of gold and of coin;*
but as for me — *I am prone to crippling pain.*[6]

ח Chazzan — *How has my reckoning been disarrayed,*
while they occupy Your thoughts?

ז *Please remember us and recall us with Your salvation*[7]
from those who worship other-than-You.

ק *And as for them* — *hurl them out from Your dwelling place*
and swallow them up,
but as for me — *through Your abundant kindness,*
I will enter Your house.[8]

All, while standing:

אֵל מֶלֶךְ O God, King Who sits on the throne of mercy; Who acts with
kindness, pardons the iniquities of His people, removes [sins]
one by one, increasingly grants pardon to careless sinners and forgiveness
to rebels, Who deals righteously with every living being — You do not repay
them in accord with their evil. Chazzan — O God, You taught us to recite the
Thirteen [Attributes of Mercy], so remember for us today the covenant of
these Thirteen, as You made known to the humble one in ancient times, as
it is written: And HASHEM descended in a cloud and stood with him there,
and He called out with the Name HASHEM.

Congregation, then chazzan:

And HASHEM passed before him [Moses] and proclaimed:

Congregation and chazzan (the words in bold type are recited aloud and in unison):

ה' ה' HASHEM, HASHEM, God, Compassionate and Gracious, Slow
**to anger, and Abundant in Kindness and Truth, Preserver of
kindness for thousands [of generations], Forgiver of iniquity,
willful sin, and error, and Who cleanses.** *May You forgive our iniquities
and our errors and make us Your heritage. Forgive us, our Father, for*

---

(1) Cf. *Judges* 7:25; *Psalms* 83:12. (2) 69:30. (3) Some editions read בְּרַעֲיוֹן, *in [his] thought.*
(4) *Psalms* 40:18. (5) Cf. *Ezekiel* 41:7. (6) Cf. *Psalms* 38:18. (7) Cf. 106:4. (8) 5:8.

---

complex, from the Temple Mount [עֶלְיוֹן, *heights*]
to the Courtyard [which was six cubits *lower*
than the Sanctuary itself] to the Temple [which
stood in the *center* of the complex] (*Arugas Ha-
Bosem*).
    Alternatively: The entire stich alludes to the

Temple edifice, which was surrounded on three
sides by a U-shaped structure of three stories, *the
lowest ascending to the highest by way of the
middle* (*Ezekiel* 41:7). Thus, the *paytan* means
that the enemy made itself at home in every section of the Temple.

חָטָאנוּ, מְחַל לָנוּ מַלְכֵּנוּ כִּי פָשָׁעְנוּ. כִּי אַתָּה אֲדֹנָי טוֹב וְסַלָּח, וְרַב חֶסֶד לְכָל קֹרְאֶיךָ.

פסוקי הקדמה לסליחה סה

יִזְכֹּר אֱלֹהִים אֶת בְּרִיתוֹ אֶת אַבְרָהָם אֶת יִצְחָק וְאֶת יַעֲקֹב.[1] (וַיֹּאמֶר) כִּי נִשְׁבַּעְתִּי נְאֻם יְהוָה, כִּי יַעַן אֲשֶׁר עָשִׂיתָ אֶת הַדָּבָר הַזֶּה, וְלֹא חָשַׂכְתָּ אֶת בִּנְךָ אֶת יְחִידֶךָ. כִּי בָרֵךְ אֲבָרֶכְךָ, וְהַרְבָּה אַרְבֶּה אֶת זַרְעֲךָ כְּכוֹכְבֵי הַשָּׁמַיִם, וְכַחוֹל אֲשֶׁר עַל שְׂפַת הַיָּם, וְיִרַשׁ זַרְעֲךָ אֵת שַׁעַר אֹיְבָיו. וְהִתְבָּרְכוּ בְזַרְעֲךָ כֹּל גּוֹיֵי הָאָרֶץ, עֵקֶב אֲשֶׁר שָׁמַעְתָּ בְּקֹלִי.[2]

כְּרַחֵם אָב עַל בָּנִים, כֵּן תְּרַחֵם יְהוָה עָלֵינוּ. לַיהוָה הַיְשׁוּעָה, עַל עַמְּךָ בִרְכָתֶךָ סֶּלָה. יְהוָה צְבָאוֹת עִמָּנוּ, מִשְׂגָּב לָנוּ אֱלֹהֵי יַעֲקֹב סֶלָה. יְהוָה צְבָאוֹת, אַשְׁרֵי אָדָם בֹּטֵחַ בָּךְ. יְהוָה הוֹשִׁיעָה, הַמֶּלֶךְ יַעֲנֵנוּ בְיוֹם קָרְאֵנוּ.

In some congregations the following two verses are recited responsively — the *chazzan* reciting סְלַח נָא, and the congregation responding וַיֹּאמֶר. In other congregations these verses are recited silently.

סְלַח נָא לַעֲוֹן הָעָם הַזֶּה כְּגֹדֶל חַסְדֶּךָ, וְכַאֲשֶׁר נָשָׂאתָה לָעָם הַזֶּה מִמִּצְרַיִם וְעַד הֵנָּה, וְשָׁם נֶאֱמַר:

וַיֹּאמֶר יְהוָה סָלַחְתִּי כִּדְבָרֶךָ.

All:

הַטֵּה אֱלֹהַי אָזְנְךָ וּשֲׁמָע, פְּקַח עֵינֶיךָ וּרְאֵה שֹׁמְמֹתֵינוּ, וְהָעִיר אֲשֶׁר נִקְרָא שִׁמְךָ עָלֶיהָ, כִּי לֹא עַל צִדְקוֹתֵינוּ אֲנַחְנוּ מַפִּילִים תַּחֲנוּנֵינוּ לְפָנֶיךָ, כִּי עַל רַחֲמֶיךָ הָרַבִּים. אֲדֹנָי שְׁמָעָה, אֲדֹנָי סְלָחָה, אֲדֹנָי הַקְשִׁיבָה, וַעֲשֵׂה אַל תְּאַחַר, לְמַעַנְךָ אֱלֹהַי, כִּי שִׁמְךָ נִקְרָא עַל עִירְךָ וְעַל עַמֶּךָ.

סליחה סה (עקדה)

אֱלֹהֵינוּ וֵאלֹהֵי אֲבוֹתֵינוּ:

אֶזְרָחִי[3] מֵעֵבֶר הַנָּהָר,*[4] אֵלֶיךָ רָץ וְלֹא אָחַר.
בְּחָנְתּוֹ בְּנִסְיוֹנוֹת עֶשֶׂר,[5] וְנִמְצָא שָׁלֵם בְּלִי חָסֵר.
גֵּרַשׁ מֵאֶרֶץ מוֹלַדְתּוֹ, גּוֹי בָּעוֹלָם שְׁמָתוֹ.
דְּבָרְךָ הֵקִים וְלֹא הֵפֵר, וְנָם אָנֹכִי עָפָר וָאֵפֶר.[6]

אֶזְרָחִי מֵעֵבֶר הַנָּהָר — *[Abraham,] the Ezra-chite from across the River [Euphrates].* The Tal-mud teaches that Eisan the Ezrachite (*Psalms* 89:1) was Abraham. He was called Ezrachite be-cause he came from a country that was to the east [מִזְרָח, *mizrach*] of *Eretz Yisrael* (*Bava Basra* 15a).

*we have erred; pardon us, our King, for we have willfully sinned; for You,
my Lord, are good and forgiving and abundantly kind to all who call upon
You.*

יִזְכּוֹר *May God remember His covenant with Abraham, with Isaac,
and with Jacob.*[1] *(And [the angel] said:) 'By Myself I swear,' says*
H*ASHEM,* '*that since you have done this thing, and have not withheld your
son, your only one, I shall surely bless you, and greatly increase your seed
as the stars of the heavens and the sand on the seashore; and your seed
shall inherit the gate of its enemy. All the nations of the earth shall bless
themselves by your seed, because you have listened to My voice.*[2]

כְּרַחֵם אָב *As a father has mercy on his children, so,* H*ASHEM, may
You have mercy on us. Salvation is* H*ASHEM's, upon Your
people is Your blessing, Selah.* H*ASHEM, Master of Legions, is with us, a
stronghold for us is the God of Jacob, Selah.* H*ASHEM, Master of Legions,
praiseworthy is the person who trusts in You.* H*ASHEM, save! May the
King answer us on the day we call.*

In some congregations the following two verses are recited responsively — the *chazzan*
reciting, 'Forgive, please . . .,' and the congregation responding, 'And H*ASHEM* said . . .'
In other congregations these verses are recited silently.

סְלַח נָא *Forgive, please, the iniquity of this people according to the
greatness of Your kindness and as You have forgiven this
people from Egypt until now, and there it was said:*

And H*ASHEM* said, 'I have forgiven according to your word!'

All:

הַטֵּה *Incline, my God, Your ear, and listen, open Your eyes and see our
desolation and that of the city upon which Your Name is proclaimed; for not because of our righteousness do we cast down our
supplications before You, rather because of Your abundant compassion.
O my Lord, heed; O my Lord, forgive; O my Lord, be attentive and act,
do not delay; for Your sake, my God, for Your Name is proclaimed upon
Your city and upon Your people.*

SELICHAH 65

Our God and the God of our forefathers:

א *[Abraham,] the Ezrachite,*[3] *from across the River [Euphrates],*[*4]
  ran to You without delay.

ב *You tested him with ten tests,*[5]
  and he was found whole, without a lack.

ג *[Though] he was driven from his homeland,
  You made him into the major nation of the world.*

ד *He upheld Your word and did not oppose [it],
  and he said, 'I am dust and ashes.'*[6]

(1) Cf. *Exodus* 2:24. (2) *Genesis* 22:16-18. (3) See commentary to *selichah* 83, s.v., אֵיתָן לְמַד דֵּעַת.
(4) Cf. *Joshua* 24:2. (5) See *Mishnah, Avos* 5:4. (6) Cf. *Genesis* 18:27.

This unsigned *selichah* follows an *aleph-beis*
acrostic. It is one of the genre called *akeidah*, for

it first describes Abraham's binding of Isaac (see
Genesis ch. 22), and then pleads for mercy in the

הִקְרִיב חָלָב וְחֶמְאָה,¹ וְנַחַט פְּרִי לְמֵאָה.²

וְנָאֱמַת לוֹ הַעֲלֵהוּ לְעוֹלָה, בְּקַע עֵצִים וְעָרֹךְ וְהַעֲלָה.

זְכָר לָנוּ הַיּוֹם עֲקֵדָתוֹ, וְהַשְׁלָמַת יְחִידָתוֹ.*

חָן הַיּוֹם שִׁבְטֵי תָם,³ וְתִשְׁכֹּן בְּמִקְהֲלוֹתָם.

טִיעַת מַטּוֹת שְׁנֵים עָשָׂר, מֶזֶג מֵהֶם אַל יֶחְסָר.⁴

יְדִידוּת מִשְׁבְּנוֹתֶיךָ תְּבִיאֵם, בְּהַר נַחֲלָתְךָ תִּטָּעֵם.⁵

כַּנֵּס כָּל פְּזוּרֵי נִדָּחֵיהֶם, נַהֲגֵם לְבֵית מַאֲוַיֵּיהֶם.

לְקוּחִים⁶ מִמָּוֶת תַּחְשֹׂךְ, פֶּה מַשְׁטִין סְתֹם וַחֲשֹׁךְ.

נַשְּׂאֵנוּ וְנַטְּלֵנוּ כִּימֵי עוֹלָם,⁷ וְכַפֵּר לָנוּ כָּל זָדוֹן וְעֶלֶם.

סְלַח וַעֲבֹר עַל פֶּשַׁע,⁸ וּמְחַל אַשְׁמָה וָרֶשַׁע.

עֲנֵה הַיּוֹם כָּל מְיַחֲלֶיךָ, כִּי עֵינֵינוּ נְשׂוּאוֹת אֵלֶיךָ.⁹

פְּדֵנוּ מִצָּרָה וְצוּקָה, וְתַעֲלֵנוּ מְשׁוּחָה עֲמֻקָּה.

צַעֲקָתֵנוּ הַיּוֹם תְּקַבֵּל, וְתַצִּילֵנוּ מִידֵי מְחַבֵּל.

קוֹמֵם בֵּית שְׁכִינַת הוֹדֶךָ, וְאַל תְּנַבֵּל כִּסֵּא כְבוֹדֶךָ.¹⁰

רְפָא עַמְּךָ מִכָּל שֶׁבֶר, כִּי בָאוּ בָנִים עַד מַשְׁבֵּר.¹¹

שָׁבָץ אֲחָזַתְנוּ¹² כַּיּוֹלֵדָה, וְכֹחַ אַיִן לְלֵדָה.¹¹

❖ תִּגְאַל עַמְּךָ מֵהַבְדֵּהַב, כִּי עָלֶיךָ מַשְׁלִיכִים יְהָב.¹³

תַּנְחֵם לְעִיר הַבְּנוּיָה, תְּמַהֵר תִּשְׁבִּי מְנַחֵם* וּנְחֶמְיָה.*

---

(1) See *Genesis* 18:8. (2) See 21:5. (3) See 25:27. (4) Cf. *Song of Songs* 7:3.
(5) Cf. *Exodus* 15:17. (6) See 6:7. (7) Cf. *Isaiah* 63:9. (8) Cf. *Micah* 7:18. (9) Cf. *Psalms* 123:1.
(10) Cf. *Jeremiah* 14:21. (11) *II Kings* 19:3. (12) Cf. *II Samuel* 1:9. (13) Cf. *Psalms* 55:23.

---

merit of that deed.

וְהַשְׁלָמַת יְחִידָתוֹ — *How he gave over his soul.* The soul is called by five names in Hebrew, but not all of them are translatable into English. The Midrash lists the five names and their implications, as follows: (a) נֶפֶשׁ, the *lifeblood*, so to speak, since Scripture describes the power of life as residing in the blood (*Deuteronomy* 12:23); (b) רוּחַ, the *spirit*, is man's spiritual capability to rise up, but also to fall back down (see *Ecclesiastes* 3:21); (c) חַיָּה, *life* — man's body dies eventually, but the soul lives on forever; (d) נְשָׁמָה, man's higher *soul*; his intelligence and personality; and (c) יְחִידָה, the soul's *uniqueness* among the many components of man, because virtually all of man's limbs and organs come in pairs — even the heart and brain have pairs of chambers or hemispheres — but there is only one soul (*Bereishis Rabbah* 14:9).

Various Midrashim refer to נֶפֶשׁ מְסִירַת, *self-sacrifice*, as הַשְׁלָמַת הַנֶּפֶשׁ. Thus, our stich alludes to Isaac's act of self-sacrifice in allowing himself to be slaughtered.

According to *Masbir* (based on *Psalms* 78:50), the terms חַיָּה and יְחִידָה may also refer to the body of man. Thus, the translation would be: *how he gave over his body.* Nevertheless, the stich still alludes to Isaac's self-sacrifice.

Alternatively: הַשְׁלָמָה refers to *whole-heartedness*, and יְחִידָתוֹ to his *one and only [son]*. Thus, the stich alludes to Abraham's act of wholeheartedly offering his one and only son (*Matteh Levi*). [The expected grammatical form in this case would be in the masculine, יְחִידוֹ (= שֶׁלּוֹ יָחִיד), rather than the feminine יְחִידָתוֹ (= שֶׁלּוֹ יְחִידָה). Presumably, according to *Matteh Levi*, the *paytan* used the feminine form יְחִידָתוֹ to fit the rhyme scheme.]

מְנַחֵם — *The Messiah.* The Talmud states four opinions regarding the Messiah's given name: מְנַחֵם, *Menachem*; שִׁילֹה, *Shiloh*; יִנּוֹן, *Yinon* (see commentary to *selichah* 60); and חֲנִינָה, *Chaninah* (*Sanhedrin* 98b). It is noteworthy that the initial letters of these four names spell מָשִׁיחַ, *Messiah.*

ה He offered [the angels] milk and butter,[1]
and bore fruit, [Isaac,] at age one hundred.[2]

ו Then You said to him,
'Bring him up[on the altar] as an olah-offering,'
so he cut and arranged the wood and brought him up.

ז Remember his binding [of Isaac] today in our favor,
how he gave over his soul.*

ח Show graciousness today for the tribes of [Jacob]
the whole-hearted,[3]
and dwell among their assemblies.

ט The plant [that flourished from the root] of twelve tribes —
let them not be deprived of the wine prepared[4]
[for the righteous].

י bring them to Your beloved Sanctuary,
and plant them on the mount of Your heritage.[5]

כ Gather in all their scattered exiles
and bring them to the Temple of their longing.

למ Save from death the people taken [to be Yours];[6]
seal and thwart the Adversary's mouth.

נ Carry us and bear us as in days of old,[7]
and atone for us, every deliberate or inadvertent [sin].

ס Forgive, and pass over [our] rebelliousness,[8]
and pardon [us our] guilt and wickedness.

ע Today may You answer all those who hope to You,
for our eyes are lifted to You.[9]

פ Redeem us from trouble and hardship
and raise us from the deep pit.

צ Today may You accept our cry,
and save us from the hands of the spoliater.

ק Stand erect the House of Your glorious Presence,
and demean not Your Throne of Glory.[10]

ר Heal Your people of every fracture,
for [Your] children have reached the birthing stool.[11]

ש Spasms have seized us,[12] like a woman in travail,
but there is no strength [left in us] to deliver.[11]

ת Chazzan — Redeem Your people from Gehinnom,
for they cast their burden upon You.[13]
Lead them to the rebuilt city of [Jerusalem];
hasten [Elijah] the Tishbite, the Messiah,* and Nehemiah.*

וּנְחֶמְיָה — *And Nehemiah.* The inclusion of the name Nehemiah here is puzzling. Some interpret it as another form of מְנַחֵם [*Menachem*, lit., *Comforter*], since both are derived from נֶחָמָה, *comfort*. Thus, it is another name for the Messiah (*Masbir*; *Matteh Levi*).

According to *Pardes*, the name refers to Nehemiah ben Hachaliah, the leader of those who returned to Jerusalem after the seventy-year exile that followed the Destruction of the First Temple, and the architect and builder of the Second Temple. Thus, the stich prays for the advent of Elijah, the Messiah, and the builder of the Third Temple.

All, while standing:

אֵל מֶלֶךְ יוֹשֵׁב עַל כִּסֵּא רַחֲמִים מִתְנַהֵג בַּחֲסִידוּת, מוֹחֵל
עֲוֹנוֹת עַמּוֹ, מַעֲבִיר רִאשׁוֹן רִאשׁוֹן, מַרְבֶּה מְחִילָה
לְחַטָּאִים וּסְלִיחָה לְפוֹשְׁעִים, עֹשֶׂה צְדָקוֹת עִם כָּל בָּשָׂר וָרוּחַ,
לֹא כְרָעָתָם תִּגְמוֹל. ּ אֵל הוֹרֵיתָ לָּנוּ לוֹמַר שְׁלֹשׁ עֶשְׂרֵה, וּזְכוֹר
לָנוּ הַיּוֹם בְּרִית שְׁלֹשׁ עֶשְׂרֵה, כְּמוֹ שֶׁהוֹדַעְתָּ לֶעָנָיו מִקֶּדֶם, כְּמוֹ
שֶׁכָּתוּב, וַיֵּרֶד יהוה בֶּעָנָן וַיִּתְיַצֵּב עִמּוֹ שָׁם, וַיִּקְרָא בְשֵׁם יהוה.

Congregation, then *chazzan:*

וַיַּעֲבֹר יהוה עַל פָּנָיו וַיִּקְרָא:

Congregation and *chazzan* (the words in bold type are recited aloud and in unison):

יהוה, יהוה, אֵל, **רַחוּם, וְחַנּוּן, אֶרֶךְ אַפַּיִם, וְרַב חֶסֶד, וֶאֱמֶת,**
נֹצֵר חֶסֶד לָאֲלָפִים, נֹשֵׂא עָוֹן, וָפֶשַׁע, וְחַטָּאָה,
וְנַקֵּה. וְסָלַחְתָּ לַעֲוֹנֵנוּ וּלְחַטָּאתֵנוּ וּנְחַלְתָּנוּ. סְלַח לָנוּ אָבִינוּ כִּי
חָטָאנוּ, מְחַל לָנוּ מַלְכֵּנוּ כִּי פָשָׁעְנוּ. כִּי אַתָּה אֲדֹנָי טוֹב וְסַלָּח,
וְרַב חֶסֶד לְכָל קֹרְאֶיךָ.

סְלִיחָה סו (פזמון)

Chazzan, then congregation:

בְּאַשְׁמֶרֶת הַבֹּקֶר* קְרָאתִיךָ אֵל מְהֻלָּל,¹
יֶעֱרַב לְךָ חִין עֶרְכִּי, יוֹם לִבִּי לְךָ סוֹלֵל,
וְתַגִּיהַּ אֶת חָשְׁכִּי²⁰ וּכְאוֹר בֹּקֶר יְהֻלָּל,
מַלְכִּי וֵאלֹהַי כִּי אֵלֶיךָ אֶתְפַּלָּל.³

Congregation, then *chazzan:*

צָרֵי מַזְעִימֶיךָ בְּאַף חֵרְפוּ עַמֶּךָ,
וְנָשָׂאתִי אֵימֶךָ⁴ בְּרֶגֶשׁ שְׁאוֹן קָמֶיךָ,⁵
שְׁפֹךְ עֲלֵיהֶם זַעְמֶךָ וַחֲרוֹן אַף⁶ מִמְּרוֹמֶיךָ,
וְקַנֵּא אֶל לִשְׁמֶךָ⁷ אֲשֶׁר בַּגּוֹיִם מְחֻלָּל,⁸
מַלְכִּי וֵאלֹהַי כִּי אֵלֶיךָ אֶתְפַּלָּל.

Congregation, then *chazzan:*

חַי רוֹכֵב עַל עָב קַל,⁹ אִם תַּעֲלֵנִי בְמִשְׁקָל,
צִדְקִי כְּחוֹל יָם יִתְקַל,¹⁰ וּרְשָׁעַי כְּנוֹצָה יֵקַל,

בְּאַשְׁמֶרֶת הַבֹּקֶר ❧ — *At the morning's watch.*
The night is divided into three (or four) periods,
called מִשְׁמָרוֹת, *watches*, during which different
legions of angels sing praises before the Throne
of Glory (see *Berachos* 3a). The last of these peri-

ods is called אַשְׁמֶרֶת הַבֹּקֶר (see *Exodus* 14:24 with
Rashi), and is the ideal time for reciting the *selichos* prayers.

The *paytan* signed his name — יִצְחָק, *Yitzchak*
— in the initial letters of the second line of the

All, while standing:

אֵל מֶלֶךְ *O God, King Who sits on the throne of mercy; Who acts with kindness, pardons the iniquities of His people, removes [sins] one by one, increasingly grants pardon to careless sinners and forgiveness to rebels, Who deals righteously with every living being — You do not repay them in accord with their evil.* Chazzan — *O God, You taught us to recite the Thirteen [Attributes of Mercy], so remember for us today the covenant of these Thirteen, as You made known to the humble one in ancient times, as it is written: And* HASHEM *descended in a cloud and stood with him there, and He called out with the Name* HASHEM.

Congregation, then chazzan:

And HASHEM *passed before him [Moses] and proclaimed:*

Congregation and chazzan (the words in bold type are recited aloud and in unison):

ה' ה' HASHEM, HASHEM, **God, Compassionate and Gracious, Slow to anger, and Abundant in Kindness and Truth, Preserver of kindness for thousands** [of generations], **Forgiver of iniquity, willful sin, and error, and Who cleanses.** *May You forgive our iniquities and our errors and make us Your heritage. Forgive us, our Father, for we have erred; pardon us, our King, for we have willfully sinned; for You, my Lord, are good and forgiving and abundantly kind to all who call upon You.*

SELICHAH 66

Chazzan, then congregation:

בְּאַשְׁמֹרֶת *At the morning's watch,* *
I call You, O praised God; [1]

י *let my ordered prayer be sweet to You on the day my heart extols You, and brighten my darkness* [2] *until it shines like morning's light,*
> *O my King and my God, for to You alone do I pray.* [3]

Congregation, then chazzan:

צ *My oppressors, who infuriate You, with anger abuse Your people, but I have borne [my] awe of You,* [4]
despite the massing of Your opponents. [5]
Pour out Your wrath upon them, and fierce anger [6] *from Your heights, and take vengeance, God, for Your Name,* [7]
that is desecrated among the nations, [8]
> *O my King and my God, for to You alone do I pray.*

Congregation, then chazzan:

ח *O Living One, who rides upon a light cloud,* [9]
if You should lift me onto a scale,
let my righteousness weigh [as heavy] as the sea's sand [10]
and my wickedness as light as a feather;

---

(1) Cf. *Psalms* 18:4. (2) Cf. 18:29. (3) 5:3. (4) Cf. 88:16. (5) 74:23. (6) Cf. 69:25.
(7) Cf. *Ezekiel* 39:25. (8) Cf. 36:23. (9) *Isaiah* 19:1. (10) Cf. *Job* 6:2-3.

first stanza and the first words of the others. All we know of R' Yitzchak is that he flourished some time before 1234, because his *selichah* is commented upon in *Arugas HaBosem*, which was written in that year. Although some identify the composer as R' Yitzchak ben Yehudah ibn Gias of eleventh-century Lucena, Spain, there is no solid basis for this assertion.

וְאִם נָתִיב אָרְחִי מֵעֲקֹל וְדִינִי כְּשׁוֹר הַנִּסְקָל,*
שְׁקֵלָה בְּפֶלֶס מַהֲלָל, אִישׁ מִפְּשָׁעִים מְחוֹלָל,*[1]
מַלְכִּי וֵאלֹהַי כִּי אֵלֶיךָ אֶתְפַּלָל.

Congregation, then chazzan:

קוֹמֵם אָרוֹן וּבַדָּיו, וְהַלְבֵּשׁ אַהֲרֹן מַדָּיו,
וְרוֹבֶה וְצוֹדֶה* בְּצֵידָיו יֹאכַל פְּרִי מַעֲבָדָיו,
וְאִישׁ נוֹחֵם עַל מְרָדָיו[2] לְשׁוֹן אֵשׁ תֹּאכַל בַּדָּיו,[3]
וּבָעֲרוּ שְׁנֵיהֶם יַחְדָּו[4] כַּאֲשֶׁר יְבַעֵר הַגָּלָל,[5]
מַלְכִּי וֵאלֹהַי כִּי אֵלֶיךָ אֶתְפַּלָל.

Congregation, then chazzan:

קָדוֹשׁ עַל כָּל אָדוֹן, עִם כָּל יְצוּרָיו נָדוֹן,
חֲזֵה יְרִיבֵי אִישׁ מָדוֹן מְדַבֵּר עָלַי בְּזָדוֹן,
וְנוֹכְחִי יְעוֹרֵר כִּידוֹן וְתוֹתָח בִּי יָדוֹן,
תְּנָה אֶת נַפְשִׁי לְשָׁלָל, מוֹלִיךְ יוֹעֲצִים שׁוֹלָל,
מַלְכִּי וֵאלֹהַי כִּי אֵלֶיךָ אֶתְפַּלָל.

All, while standing:

אֵל מֶלֶךְ יוֹשֵׁב עַל כִּסֵּא רַחֲמִים מִתְנַהֵג בַּחֲסִידוּת, מוֹחֵל
עֲוֹנוֹת עַמּוֹ, מַעֲבִיר רִאשׁוֹן רִאשׁוֹן, מַרְבֶּה מְחִילָה
לַחַטָּאִים וּסְלִיחָה לַפּוֹשְׁעִים, עֹשֶׂה צְדָקוֹת עִם כָּל בָּשָׂר וָרוּחַ,
לֹא כְרָעָתָם תִּגְמוֹל. ❖ אֵל הוֹרֵיתָ לָנוּ לוֹמַר שְׁלֹשׁ עֶשְׂרֵה, וּזְכוֹר
לָנוּ הַיּוֹם בְּרִית שְׁלֹשׁ עֶשְׂרֵה, כְּמוֹ שֶׁהוֹדַעְתָּ לֶעָנָיו מִקֶּדֶם, כְּמוֹ
שֶׁכָּתוּב, וַיֵּרֶד יהוה בֶּעָנָן וַיִּתְיַצֵּב עִמּוֹ שָׁם, וַיִּקְרָא בְשֵׁם יהוה.

Congregation, then chazzan:

וַיַּעֲבֹר יהוה עַל פָּנָיו וַיִּקְרָא:

Congregation and chazzan (the words in bold type are recited aloud and in unison):

יהוה, יהוה, אֵל, רַחוּם, וְחַנּוּן, אֶרֶךְ אַפַּיִם, וְרַב חֶסֶד, וֶאֱמֶת,
נֹצֵר חֶסֶד לָאֲלָפִים, נֹשֵׂא עָוֹן, וָפֶשַׁע, וְחַטָּאָה,
וְנַקֵּה. וְסָלַחְתָּ לַעֲוֹנֵנוּ וּלְחַטָּאתֵנוּ וּנְחַלְתָּנוּ. סְלַח לָנוּ אָבִינוּ כִּי
חָטָאנוּ, מְחַל לָנוּ מַלְכֵּנוּ כִּי פָשָׁעְנוּ. כִּי אַתָּה אֲדֹנָי טוֹב וְסַלָּח,
וְרַב חֶסֶד לְכָל קֹרְאֶיךָ.

כְּשׁוֹר הַנִּסְקָל — *That of the stoned ox.* The Torah
decrees death by stoning as the punishment of
an ox that kills a person (see *Exodus* 21:28).

אִישׁ מִפְּשָׁעִים מְחוֹלָל — *A man desecrated by
wanton sins.* The translation is based on the
commentaries to *Isaiah* 53:5. Other renderings

are: *man who is created sinful* (*Arugas Ha-
Bosem*, based on *Genesis* 8:21 and *Deuteronomy*
32:18); *man who is conceived in sin* (*Masbir*; see
Rashi to *Psalms* 51:7).

וְרוֹבֶה וְצוֹדֶה — *The archer and the trapper.*
Ishmael is described as an archer (*Genesis*

and if my path is crooked, and my sentence is that of the stoned ox,*
take a better scale [to weigh] a man desecrated by wanton sins,*[1]
O my King and my God, for to You alone do I pray.

Congregation, then *chazzan*:

ק *Stand erect the Holy Ark and its golden rods,*
and dress Aaron['s descendant] in his [priestly] vestments;
and let the archer and the trapper* with his traps,
each have his just deserts for his deeds.
And he that roars out his rebellion[2] —
let a tongue of fire consume his descendants;[3]
let both of them together be swept away[4]
as one sweeps away dung,[5]
O my King and my God, for to You alone do I pray.

Congregation, then *chazzan*:

O Holy One, Who is higher than every lord,
Who passes judgment upon all His creatures,
see how my contentious Adversary speaks cruelly about me,
arouses his spear toward me and fires his weapon at me,
Grant my soul escape,
[O God] Who leads counselors [of evil] into folly,
O my King and my God, for to You alone do I pray.

All, while standing:

אֵל מֶלֶךְ O God, King Who sits on the throne of mercy; Who acts with
kindness, pardons the iniquities of His people, removes [sins]
one by one, increasingly grants pardon to careless sinners and forgiveness
to rebels, Who deals righteously with every living being — You do not repay
them in accord with their evil. *Chazzan —* O God, You taught us to recite the
Thirteen [Attributes of Mercy], so remember for us today the covenant of
these Thirteen, as You made known to the humble one in ancient times, as
it is written: And HASHEM descended in a cloud and stood with him there,
and He called out with the Name HASHEM.

Congregation, then *chazzan*:

And HASHEM *passed before him [Moses] and proclaimed:*

Congregation and *chazzan* (the words in bold type are recited aloud and in unison):

ה' ה' HASHEM, HASHEM, **God, Compassionate and Gracious, Slow to
anger, and Abundant in Kindness and Truth, Preserver of
kindness for thousands [of generations], Forgiver of iniquity, willful
sin, and error, and Who cleanses.** May You forgive our iniquities and our
errors and make us Your heritage. Forgive us, our Father, for we have
erred; pardon us, our King, for we have willfully sinned; for You, my Lord,
are good and forgiving and abundantly kind to all who call upon You.

---

(1) Cf. *Isaiah* 53:5. (2) Cf. 5:29. (3) Cf. 5:24; *Job* 18:13. (4) *Isaiah* 1:31. (5) *I Kings* 14:10.

21:20), Esau as a hunter (ibid. 25:27; 27:3).
Thus, the phrase refers to their descendants who
have oppressed Israel throughout the centuries
(*Masbir*). Alternatively: Both terms refer to

Ishmael; while the stich about the one who
roars out his rebellion alludes to Esau (*Arugas
HaBosem*) or Assyria (*Pardes* based on *Isaiah*
5:29).

All:

אַל תִּזְכָּר לָנוּ עֲוֹנוֹת רִאשׁוֹנִים, מַהֵר יְקַדְּמוּנוּ רַחֲמֶיךָ, כִּי דַלּוֹנוּ מְאֹד.[1] חַטֹּאת נְעוּרֵינוּ וּפְשָׁעֵינוּ אַל תִּזְכּוֹר, כְּחַסְדְּךָ זְכָר לָנוּ אַתָּה, לְמַעַן טוּבְךָ יהוה.[2]

זְכֹר רַחֲמֶיךָ יהוה וַחֲסָדֶיךָ, כִּי מֵעוֹלָם הֵמָּה.[3] זָכְרֵנוּ יהוה בִּרְצוֹן עַמֶּךָ, פָּקְדֵנוּ בִּישׁוּעָתֶךָ.[4] זְכֹר עֲדָתְךָ קָנִיתָ קֶּדֶם, גָּאַלְתָּ שֵׁבֶט נַחֲלָתֶךָ, הַר צִיּוֹן זֶה שָׁכַנְתָּ בּוֹ.[5] זְכֹר יהוה חִבַּת יְרוּשָׁלָיִם, אַהֲבַת צִיּוֹן אַל תִּשְׁכַּח לָנֶצַח.[6] אַתָּה תָקוּם תְּרַחֵם צִיּוֹן, כִּי עֵת לְחֶנְנָהּ כִּי בָא מוֹעֵד.[7] זְכֹר יהוה לִבְנֵי אֱדוֹם אֵת יוֹם יְרוּשָׁלָיִם, הָאֹמְרִים עָרוּ עָרוּ עַד הַיְסוֹד בָּהּ.[8] זְכֹר לְאַבְרָהָם לְיִצְחָק וּלְיִשְׂרָאֵל עֲבָדֶיךָ אֲשֶׁר נִשְׁבַּעְתָּ לָהֶם בָּךְ, וַתְּדַבֵּר אֲלֵהֶם, אַרְבֶּה אֶת זַרְעֲכֶם כְּכוֹכְבֵי הַשָּׁמָיִם, וְכָל הָאָרֶץ הַזֹּאת אֲשֶׁר אָמַרְתִּי אֶתֵּן לְזַרְעֲכֶם, וְנָחֲלוּ לְעוֹלָם.[9] ❖ זְכֹר לַעֲבָדֶיךָ לְאַבְרָהָם לְיִצְחָק וּלְיַעֲקֹב, אַל תֵּפֶן אֶל קְשִׁי הָעָם הַזֶּה וְאֶל רִשְׁעוֹ וְאֶל חַטָּאתוֹ.[10]

Chazzan, then congregation:

אֵל נָא תָשֵׁת עָלֵינוּ חַטָּאת, אֲשֶׁר נוֹאַלְנוּ וַאֲשֶׁר חָטָאנוּ.[11]

Chazzan, then congregation:

חָטָאנוּ צוּרֵנוּ, סְלַח לָנוּ יוֹצְרֵנוּ.

סְלִיחָה סז (חטאנו)

All:

אָדוֹן בִּינָה הֲגִיגֵנוּ,* אֱזֹן שִׁיחֵנוּ בְּשַׁאֲגֵנוּ,
בַּעֲוֹנֵינוּ אַל תְּמוֹגְגֵנוּ, בְּרִשְׁעֵנוּ אַל תַּכְלִימֵנוּ.
גָּבְרוּ דִבְרֵי עֲוֹנוֹת, גָּדְלוּ עַד לִמְעוֹנוֹת,
דַּוֻּי נְפָשׁוֹת נַעֲנוֹת, דּוֹד שְׁעֵה לַעֲנוֹת.

חָטָאנוּ צוּרֵנוּ, סְלַח לָנוּ יוֹצְרֵנוּ.

הַרְגִּזְנוּךָ אֱלֹהֵי תְהִלָּתֵנוּ, הַכְעַסְנוּךָ בְּרֹב אֻוַּלְתֵּנוּ,
וְלָכֵן נִמְשְׁכָה תוֹחַלְתֵּנוּ, וּלְזָרִים נֶהְפְּכָה נַחֲלָתֵנוּ.
זֹרֵנוּ מִבֵּית חַיֵּינוּ, זְלַלְנוּ בֵּית מַאֲוַיֵּינוּ,

---

(1) *Psalms* 79:8. (2) Cf. 25:7. (3) 25:6. (4) Cf. 106:4. (5) 74:2. (6) This is not a Scriptural verse. (7) *Psalms* 102:14. (8) 137:7. (9) *Exodus* 32:13. (10) *Deuteronomy* 9:27. (11) *Numbers* 12:11.

⊱ אָדוֹן בִּינָה הֲגִיגֵנוּ ⊰ — *O Lord, understand our thoughts.* This *selichah* contains a double alpha-betical acrostic. The identity of the author has not been established.

All:

אַל תִּזְכָּר **Do not recall** against us the iniquities of the ancients; speedily — let Your mercy come to meet us for we have fallen very low.[1] Remember not the sins of our youth and our rebellions; may You remember for us [the deeds] worthy of Your kindness, because of Your goodness, HASHEM.[2]

זְכוֹר רַחֲמֶיךָ **Remember** Your mercies, O HASHEM, and Your kindnesses, for they are from the beginning of the world.[3] Remember us, HASHEM, when You show Your people favor and recall us with Your salvation.[4] Remember Your congregation that You acquired of old, that You redeemed the tribe of Your heritage, and this Mount Zion where You dwelled.[5] Remember, O HASHEM, the affection of Jerusalem, may You never forget the love of Zion.[6] You will arise and show Zion mercy, for it is the time to be gracious to her, for the appointed time will have come.[7] Remember, HASHEM, for the offspring of Edom, the day of Jerusalem — for those who said: 'Destroy! Destroy to its very foundation!'[8] Remember Abraham, Isaac, and Israel, Your servants, to whom You swore by Your Being, saying to them, 'I shall increase your offspring like the stars of the heavens; and this entire land of which I spoke I will give to your offspring and they will inherit it forever.'[9] Chazzan — Remember for Your servants, for Abraham, for Isaac, and for Jacob; ignore the stubbornness of this people, its wickedness and its sinfulness.[10]

Chazzan, then congregation:

Please, do not reckon for us a sin,
what we have done foolishly and what we have sinned.[11]

Chazzan, then congregation:

We have erred, our Rock! Forgive us, our Molder!

SELICHAH 67

All:

א O Lord, understand our thoughts;*
  give ear to our prayers as we cry out [to You].

ב Do not let us waste away for our sins,
  do not put us to shame for our wickedness.

ג [Our] iniquitous words have waxed strong,
  they have grown until the very Heavens.

ד The wandering of [our] afflicted souls,
  O Beloved, pay heed to answer.
        We have sinned, our Rock! Forgive us, our Molder!

ה We have enraged You, God of our praise;
  we have angered You with our abundant foolishness.

ו Therefore our hope of Redemption has been drawn out,
  and our heritage has been turned over to strangers.

ז They have scattered us far from the House of our life,
  and we have degraded the Temple of our longings.

חָרֵב מְקוֹם אַוֵּינוּ,   חָדְלוּ נִיחוֹחֵי רְצוֹנֵנוּ,
חָטָאנוּ צוּרֵנוּ, סְלַח לָנוּ יוֹצְרֵנוּ.

טָעִינוּ מִנְּתִיב יְשָׁר,   טִפַּשְׁנוּ צַעַד מִלְּיֹשֶׁר,
יַעַן כִּי מְאַסְנוּ כְּשֵׁר,¹   יְרִיבֵנוּ הִדְאִיתָ כַּנֶּשֶׁר.²

כֶּבֶשׁ פּוּל קְהָלִי,   בִּלָּה כֹּחִי וְהִבְהִילִי,
לַחֲלַח וְחָבוֹר הוֹבִילִי,³   לְהַרְחִיקִי מֵעַל גְּבוּלִי,
חָטָאנוּ צוּרֵנוּ, סְלַח לָנוּ יוֹצְרֵנוּ.

מַצֶּבֶת קֹדֶשׁ נִשְׁאָרָה,*   מֵעִיר קֹדֶשׁ הַמְעֻטָּרָה,
נָמָה לְנֶגְדָּךְ סָרָה,   נַעֲלֵיתָ וְרוּחֲךָ סָרָה.
סָחַף נְבוֹ* כָּל גִּבּוֹרַי,   סִלָּה כָל אַבִּירַי,⁴
עֶצֶם כָּל אֵבָרַי,   עֻלְּפְתִּי בִּידֵי שׁוֹבְרַי.
חָטָאנוּ צוּרֵנוּ, סְלַח לָנוּ יוֹצְרֵנוּ.

פְּלָצְנוּ מֵרֹב תְּלָאוֹת,   פְּצָמְנוּ מִכֹּבֶד תַּחֲלוּאוֹת,
צִפִּינוּ יֶשַׁע לְהַרְאוֹת,   צָרוֹת אוֹתָנוּ קוֹרְאוֹת.
קְדוֹשׁ יִשְׂרָאֵל הַבִּיטָה,   קָלוֹן רְעִיָּתָךְ הַמְלַבְּטָה,
רָדָה מִכְּבוֹדָהּ וְנִתְמוֹטָטָה,   רָפָה שְׁבָרֶיהָ כִּי מָטָה.⁵
חָטָאנוּ צוּרֵנוּ, סְלַח לָנוּ יוֹצְרֵנוּ.

שְׁמַע פֵּלֶל פִּיּוֹת,   שַׂכְלֵל בָּנוּי לְתַלְפִּיּוֹת,*⁶
שׁוּבָה אֱלֹהֵי בְרִיּוֹת,   שׁוֹבֵב נִדְחֵי אֲרָיוֹת.⁷
❖ תַּחֲבֹשׁ נָא מַכּוֹתֵינוּ,   תַּעֲלֶה נָא אֲרוּכָתֵנוּ,⁸
תַּקְשִׁיב קוֹל רִנָּתֵנוּ,   תְּקַבֵּל בְּרַחֲמִים וּבְרָצוֹן אֶת תְּפִלָּתֵנוּ.
חָטָאנוּ צוּרֵנוּ, סְלַח לָנוּ יוֹצְרֵנוּ.

All:

זְכוֹר לָנוּ בְּרִית אָבוֹת, כַּאֲשֶׁר אָמַרְתָּ: וְזָכַרְתִּי אֶת בְּרִיתִי
יַעֲקוֹב, וְאַף אֶת בְּרִיתִי יִצְחָק, וְאַף אֶת בְּרִיתִי אַבְרָהָם
אֶזְכֹּר, וְהָאָרֶץ אֶזְכֹּר.⁹

(1) Cf. Leviticus 26:15. (2) Cf. Deuteronomy 28:49. (3) Cf. I Chronicles 5:26. (4) Lamentations 1:15. (5) Psalms 60:4. (6) Song of Songs 4:4. (7) Cf. Jeremiah 50:17. (8) Cf. 30:17. (9) Leviticus 26:42.

מַצֶּבֶת קֹדֶשׁ נִשְׁאָרָה — A holy outpost was left to remain. Although the Assyrian king had exiled the ten tribes of the Kingdom of Israel, the tribes of Benjamin and Judah remained in their land, until they were ousted by Nebuchanezzar (see Jeremiah 50:17).

נְבוֹ — Nebo. One of the Babylonian gods, used here in poetic fashion as an allusion to Nebuchadnezzar who worshiped Nebo (see Isaiah 46:1).

שַׂכְלֵל בָּנוּי לְתַלְפִּיּוֹת — Complete the Temple, built for all to turn in prayer. The translation follows the Talmud's interpretation which considers תַּלְפִּיּוֹת a composite word — תֵּל, a hill, to which פִּיּוֹת, mouths, turn in prayer [as King Solomon declared when he dedicated the Beis HaMikdash

ח Destroyed is the place we long for,
  gone are the satisfying aromas of our [offerings of] favor.
                    We have sinned, our Rock! Forgive us, our Molder!

ט We have wandered from the straight path;
  we have been too foolish to straighten our steps.

י Because we despised proper [ways],[1]
  You made our foe fly at us like an eagle.[2]

כ The king of Assyria conquered my people;
  he wore down my strength and threw me into panic;

ל He shipped me off to exile in Halach and Havor,[3]
  to set me far away from my borders.
                    We have sinned, our Rock! Forgive us, our Molder!

מ A holy outpost was left to remain*
  from [the people of] the crowned Holy City.

נ But she spoke against You with wayward word,
  so You rose up and Your Spirit departed.

ס Nebo* swept away all my valiant men, trampled all my heroes,[4]

ע crushed all my limbs —
  [until] I fainted in the grip of those who would break me.
                    We have sinned, our Rock! Forgive us, our Molder!

פ We have shuddered from abundant travail;
  we have been broken by the weight of [our] afflictions.

צ We have looked to see salvation — but troubles came upon us.

ק O Holy One of Israel, look
  at the shame of Your beloved one who has stumbled.

ר She is descended from her glory and been toppled;
  heal her fractures, for she totters.[5]
                    We have sinned, our Rock! Forgive us, our Molder!

ש Hear [our] mouths' prayer;
  complete the Temple, built for all to turn to in prayer.*[6]
  Return, O God of [all] creatures!
  Bring back those far flung by the leonine [conquerors].[7]

ת Chazzan — Bind up our wounds, please;[8] bring our healing, please;
  be attentive to the sound of our [prayerful] song;
  accept our prayer with mercy and favor.
                    We have sinned, our Rock! Forgive us, our Molder!

All:

זְכוֹר לָנוּ Remember for us the covenant of the Patriarchs, as You said:
  'And I will remember My covenant with Jacob, and also My
covenant with Isaac, and also My covenant with Abraham will I remember; and the Land will I remember.'[9]

(I Kings 8:35-36): 'When they will pray towards
this place and will praise Your Name ... then
may You hearken from the heavens ...'] (Berachos 30a).
    Other interpretations offered for this rare word
תַּלְפִּיּוֹת include: adornment, the Temple was so

called because all gazed upon it to study its
beautiful forms and the masterwork of its design
(Rashi); a landmark (Ibn Yanach); a place to hang
swords (לִתְלוֹת פִּיּוֹת) [i.e., a fortress] (Ibn Ezra);
and teaching, training, to guide the traveler, for
its height made it visible from afar (Metzudos).

זְכוֹר לָנוּ בְּרִית רִאשׁוֹנִים כַּאֲשֶׁר אָמַרְתָּ, וְזָכַרְתִּי לָהֶם בְּרִית רִאשׁוֹנִים, אֲשֶׁר הוֹצֵאתִי אוֹתָם מֵאֶרֶץ מִצְרַיִם לְעֵינֵי הַגּוֹיִם, לִהְיוֹת לָהֶם לֵאלֹהִים אֲנִי יהוה.[1] עֲשֵׂה עִמָּנוּ כְּמָה שֶׁהִבְטַחְתָּנוּ: וְאַף גַּם זֹאת בִּהְיוֹתָם בְּאֶרֶץ אֹיְבֵיהֶם, לֹא מְאַסְתִּים וְלֹא גְעַלְתִּים לְכַלֹּתָם לְהָפֵר בְּרִיתִי אִתָּם, כִּי אֲנִי יהוה אֱלֹהֵיהֶם.[2] הִמָּצֵא לָנוּ בְּבַקָּשָׁתֵנוּ, כְּמָה שֶׁכָּתוּב: וּבִקַּשְׁתֶּם מִשָּׁם אֶת יהוה אֱלֹהֶיךָ וּמָצָאתָ, כִּי תִדְרְשֶׁנּוּ בְּכָל לְבָבְךָ וּבְכָל נַפְשֶׁךָ.[3] מוֹל אֶת לְבָבֵנוּ לְאַהֲבָה וּלְיִרְאָה אֶת שְׁמֶךָ, כְּמָה שֶׁכָּתוּב: וּמָל יהוה אֱלֹהֶיךָ אֶת לְבָבְךָ וְאֶת לְבַב זַרְעֶךָ, לְאַהֲבָה אֶת יהוה אֱלֹהֶיךָ בְּכָל לְבָבְךָ וּבְכָל נַפְשְׁךָ, לְמַעַן חַיֶּיךָ.[4] זְרוֹק עָלֵינוּ מַיִם טְהוֹרִים וְטַהֲרֵנוּ, כְּמָה שֶׁכָּתוּב: וְזָרַקְתִּי עֲלֵיכֶם מַיִם טְהוֹרִים וּטְהַרְתֶּם, מִכֹּל טֻמְאוֹתֵיכֶם וּמִכָּל גִּלּוּלֵיכֶם אֲטַהֵר אֶתְכֶם.[5] מְחֵה פְשָׁעֵינוּ כָּעָב וְכֶעָנָן, כְּמָה שֶׁכָּתוּב: מָחִיתִי כָעָב פְּשָׁעֶיךָ וְכֶעָנָן חַטֹּאתֶיךָ, שׁוּבָה אֵלַי כִּי גְאַלְתִּיךָ.[6] מְחֵה פְשָׁעֵינוּ לְמַעַנְךָ, כַּאֲשֶׁר אָמַרְתָּ: אָנֹכִי אָנֹכִי הוּא מֹחֶה פְשָׁעֶיךָ לְמַעֲנִי, וְחַטֹּאתֶיךָ לֹא אֶזְכֹּר.[7] הַלְבֵּן חֲטָאֵינוּ כַּשֶּׁלֶג וְכַצֶּמֶר, כְּמָה שֶׁכָּתוּב: לְכוּ נָא וְנִוָּכְחָה, יֹאמַר יהוה, אִם יִהְיוּ חֲטָאֵיכֶם כַּשָּׁנִים, כַּשֶּׁלֶג יַלְבִּינוּ, אִם יַאְדִּימוּ כַתּוֹלָע, כַּצֶּמֶר יִהְיוּ.[8] רַחֵם עָלֵינוּ וְאַל תַּשְׁחִיתֵנוּ, כְּמָה שֶׁכָּתוּב: כִּי אֵל רַחוּם יהוה אֱלֹהֶיךָ, לֹא יַרְפְּךָ וְלֹא יַשְׁחִיתֶךָ וְלֹא יִשְׁכַּח אֶת בְּרִית אֲבֹתֶיךָ אֲשֶׁר נִשְׁבַּע לָהֶם.[9] קַבֵּץ נִדָּחֵנוּ כְּמָה שֶׁכָּתוּב: אִם יִהְיֶה נִדַּחֲךָ בִּקְצֵה הַשָּׁמַיִם, מִשָּׁם יְקַבֶּצְךָ יהוה אֱלֹהֶיךָ וּמִשָּׁם יִקָּחֶךָ.[10] הָשֵׁב שְׁבוּתֵנוּ וְרַחֲמֵנוּ, כְּמָה שֶׁכָּתוּב: וְשָׁב יהוה אֱלֹהֶיךָ אֶת שְׁבוּתְךָ וְרִחֲמֶךָ וְשָׁב וְקִבֶּצְךָ מִכָּל הָעַמִּים אֲשֶׁר הֱפִיצְךָ יהוה אֱלֹהֶיךָ שָׁמָּה.[11] ❖ תְּבִיאֵנוּ אֶל הַר קָדְשֶׁךָ, וְשַׂמְּחֵנוּ בְּבֵית תְּפִלָּתֶךָ, כְּמָה שֶׁכָּתוּב: וַהֲבִיאוֹתִים אֶל הַר קָדְשִׁי, וְשִׂמַּחְתִּים בְּבֵית תְּפִלָּתִי, עוֹלֹתֵיהֶם וְזִבְחֵיהֶם לְרָצוֹן עַל מִזְבְּחִי, כִּי בֵיתִי בֵּית תְּפִלָּה יִקָּרֵא לְכָל הָעַמִּים.[12]

THE ARK IS OPENED.

The first four verses of the following prayer are recited responsively; *chazzan*, then congregation:

שְׁמַע קוֹלֵנוּ יהוה אֱלֹהֵינוּ, חוּס וְרַחֵם עָלֵינוּ, וְקַבֵּל בְּרַחֲמִים וּבְרָצוֹן אֶת תְּפִלָּתֵנוּ.[13]
הֲשִׁיבֵנוּ יהוה אֵלֶיךָ וְנָשׁוּבָה, חַדֵּשׁ יָמֵינוּ כְּקֶדֶם.[14]
אַל תַּשְׁלִיכֵנוּ מִלְּפָנֶיךָ, וְרוּחַ קָדְשְׁךָ אַל תִּקַּח מִמֶּנּוּ.[15]

זְכוֹר לָנוּ *Remember for us the covenant of the ancestors, as You said: 'And I will remember for them the covenant of the ancestors whom I brought out of the land of Egypt in the very sight of the nations, to be a God to them; I am HASHEM.'* [1] *Do with us as You promised us: 'And despite all that, when they will be in the land of their enemies, I will not have despised them nor abhorred them to destroy them, to annul My covenant with them, for I am HASHEM their God.'* [2] *Be accessible to us in our quest, as it is written: From there you will seek HASHEM, your God, and you will find, when you search for Him with all your heart and with all your soul.* [3] *Expose our hearts to love Your Name, as it is written: HASHEM, your God, will expose your heart and the heart of your offspring, to love HASHEM, your God, with all your heart and with all your soul, that you may live.* [4] *Pour pure water upon us and purify us, as it is written: I shall pour pure water upon you and purify you, of all your contaminations and of all your abominations I will purify you.* [5] *Wipe away our willful sins like a cloud and like a mist, as it is written: I have wiped away your willful sins like a cloud and your errors like a mist — repent to Me, for I have redeemed you!* [6] *Wipe away our willful sins for Your sake, as You said: 'I, only I, am the One Who wipes away your willful sins for My sake, and I shall not recall your errors.'* [7] *Whiten our errors like snow and like [pure white] wool, as it is written: 'Come now, let us reason together,' says HASHEM, 'though your errors will be like scarlet, they will become white as snow; though they will be red as crimson, they will become like [white] wool.'* [8] *Have mercy on us and do not destroy us, as it is written: For a merciful God is HASHEM, your God; He will not surrender you nor destroy you, and He will not forget the covenant with your forefathers, which He swore to them.* [9] *Gather in our dispersed ones, as it is written: If your dispersed were to be at the ends of heaven, from there HASHEM, your God, will gather you in and from there He will take you.* [10] *Bring back our captivity and have mercy on us, as it is written: HASHEM, your God, will bring back your captivity and have mercy on you, and He will again gather you in from all the peoples where HASHEM, your God, has scattered you.* [11] Chazzan — *Bring us to Your holy mountain and gladden us in Your house of prayer, as it is written: And I will bring them to My holy mountain, and I will gladden them in My house of prayer, their elevation-offerings and their feast offering will find favor on My Altar, for My House will be called a house of prayer, for all peoples.* [12]

THE ARK IS OPENED.

The first four verses of the following prayer are recited responsively; chazzan, then congregation:

שְׁמַע *Hear our voice, HASHEM, our God, pity and be compassionate to us, and accept — with compassion and favor — our prayer.* [13]
Bring us back to You, HASHEM, and we shall return, renew our days as of old. [14]
Do not cast us away from Yourself, and do not remove Your holy spirit from us. [15]

(1) *Leviticus* 26:45. (2) 26:44. (3) *Deuteronomy* 4:29. (4) 30:6. (5) *Ezekiel* 36:25.
(6) *Isaiah* 44:22. (7) 43:25. (8) 1:18. (9) *Deuteronomy* 4:31. (10) 30:4. (11) 30:3.
(12) *Isaiah* 56:7. (13) Weekday *Shemoneh Esrei*. (14) *Lamentations* 5:21. (15) Cf. *Psalms* 51:13.

אַל תַּשְׁלִיכֵנוּ לְעֵת זִקְנָה, כִּכְלוֹת כֹּחֵנוּ אַל תַּעַזְבֵנוּ.¹

אַל תַּעַזְבֵנוּ יהוה, אֱלֹהֵינוּ אַל תִּרְחַק מִמֶּנּוּ.²

עֲשֵׂה עִמָּנוּ אוֹת לְטוֹבָה, וְיִרְאוּ שׂוֹנְאֵינוּ וְיֵבֹשׁוּ,

כִּי אַתָּה יהוה עֲזַרְתָּנוּ וְנִחַמְתָּנוּ.³

אֲמָרֵינוּ הַאֲזִינָה יהוה, בִּינָה הֲגִיגֵנוּ.⁴

יִהְיוּ לְרָצוֹן אִמְרֵי פִינוּ וְהֶגְיוֹן לִבֵּנוּ לְפָנֶיךָ, יהוה צוּרֵנוּ וְגוֹאֲלֵנוּ.⁵

כִּי לְךָ יהוה הוֹחָלְנוּ, אַתָּה תַעֲנֶה אֲדֹנָי אֱלֹהֵינוּ.⁶

THE ARK IS CLOSED.

וידוי

During the recitation of the וידוי stand with head and body slightly bowed, in submissive contrition.

אֱלֹהֵינוּ וֵאלֹהֵי אֲבוֹתֵינוּ, תָּבֹא לְפָנֶיךָ תְּפִלָּתֵנוּ,⁷ וְאַל תִּתְעַלַּם מִתְּחִנָּתֵנוּ,⁸ שֶׁאֵין אָנוּ עַזֵּי פָנִים וּקְשֵׁי עֹרֶף, לוֹמַר לְפָנֶיךָ יהוה אֱלֹהֵינוּ וֵאלֹהֵי אֲבוֹתֵינוּ, צַדִּיקִים אֲנַחְנוּ וְלֹא חָטָאנוּ, אֲבָל אֲנַחְנוּ וַאֲבוֹתֵינוּ חָטָאנוּ.⁹

Strike the left side of the chest with the right fist
while reciting each of the sins in the following confession litany.

אָשַׁמְנוּ, בָּגַדְנוּ, גָּזַלְנוּ, דִּבַּרְנוּ דֹפִי. הֶעֱוִינוּ, וְהִרְשַׁעְנוּ, זַדְנוּ, חָמַסְנוּ, טָפַלְנוּ שֶׁקֶר. יָעַצְנוּ רָע, כִּזַּבְנוּ, לַצְנוּ, מָרַדְנוּ, נִאַצְנוּ, סָרַרְנוּ, עָוִינוּ, פָּשַׁעְנוּ, צָרַרְנוּ, קִשִּׁינוּ עֹרֶף. רָשַׁעְנוּ, שִׁחַתְנוּ, תִּעַבְנוּ, תָּעִינוּ, תִּעְתָּעְנוּ.

סַרְנוּ מִמִּצְוֹתֶיךָ וּמִמִּשְׁפָּטֶיךָ הַטּוֹבִים וְלֹא שָׁוָה לָנוּ.¹⁰ וְאַתָּה צַדִּיק עַל כָּל הַבָּא עָלֵינוּ, כִּי אֱמֶת עָשִׂיתָ וַאֲנַחְנוּ הִרְשָׁעְנוּ.¹¹

אָשַׁמְנוּ מִכָּל עָם, בֹּשְׁנוּ מִכָּל דּוֹר, גָּלָה מִמֶּנּוּ מָשׂוֹשׂ, דָּוָה לִבֵּנוּ בַּחֲטָאֵינוּ, הֻחַבַּל אִוּוּיֵנוּ, וְנִפְרַע פְּאֵרֵנוּ, זְבוּל בֵּית מִקְדָּשֵׁנוּ חָרַב בַּעֲוֹנֵינוּ, טִירָתֵנוּ הָיְתָה לְשַׁמָּה, יְפִי אַדְמָתֵנוּ לְזָרִים, כֹּחֵנוּ לְנָכְרִים. וַעֲדַיִן לֹא שַׁבְנוּ מִטָּעוּתֵנוּ וְהֵיךְ נָעִיז פָּנֵינוּ וְנַקְשֶׁה עָרְפֵּנוּ, לוֹמַר לְפָנֶיךָ יהוה אֱלֹהֵינוּ וֵאלֹהֵי אֲבוֹתֵינוּ, צַדִּיקִים אֲנַחְנוּ וְלֹא חָטָאנוּ, אֲבָל אֲנַחְנוּ וַאֲבוֹתֵינוּ חָטָאנוּ.

Strike the left side of the chest with the right fist while reciting
each of the sins in the following confession litany.

אָשַׁמְנוּ, בָּגַדְנוּ, גָּזַלְנוּ, דִּבַּרְנוּ דֹפִי. הֶעֱוִינוּ, וְהִרְשַׁעְנוּ, זַדְנוּ,

(1) Cf. Psalms 71:9. (2) Cf. 38:22. (3) Cf. 86:17. (4) Cf. 5:2. (5) Cf. 19:15. (6) Cf. 38:16.
(7) Cf. 88:3. (8) Cf. 55:2. (9) Cf. 106:6. (10) Cf. Job 33:27. (11) Nehemiah 9:33.

Do not cast us away in old age,
    when our strength gives out do not forsake us.[1]
Do not forsake us, HASHEM, our God, be not distant from us.[2]
Display for us a sign for good, so that our enemies may see it
    and be ashamed, for You, HASHEM, will have helped and consoled us.[3]
To our sayings give ear, HASHEM, perceive our thoughts.[4]
May the expressions of our mouth and the thoughts of our heart
    find favor before You, HASHEM, our Rock and our Redeemer.[5]
Because for You, HASHEM, we waited, You will answer, my Lord, our God.[6]

THE ARK IS CLOSED.

VIDUY/CONFESSION

During the recitation of the וִדּוּי stand with head and body slightly bowed, in submissive contrition.

אֱלֹהֵינוּ *Our God and the God of our forefathers, may our prayer come* *before You.[7] Do not ignore our supplication,[8] for we are not so brazen and obstinate as to say before You, HASHEM, our God and the God of our forefathers, that we are righteous and have not sinned, for in truth, we and our forefathers have sinned.[9]*

Strike the left side of the chest with the right fist while reciting
each of the sins in the following confession litany.

אָשַׁמְנוּ *We have become guilty;* [ב] *we have betrayed;* [ג] *we have robbed;* [ד] *we have spoken slander;* [ה] *we have caused perversion;* [ו] *we have caused wickedness;* [ז] *we have sinned willfully;* [ח] *we have extorted;* [ט] *we have accused falsely;* [י] *we have given evil counsel;* [כ] *we have been deceitful;* [ל] *we have scorned;* [מ] *we have rebelled;* [נ] *we have provoked;* [ס] *we have turned away;* [ע] *we have been perverse;* [פ] *we have acted wantonly;* [צ] *we have persecuted;* [ק] *we have been obstinate;* [ר] *we have been wicked;* [ש] *we have corrupted;* [ת] *we have been abominable; we have strayed; You have let us go astray.*

סַרְנוּ *We have turned away from Your commandments and from Your good laws but to no avail.[10] Yet You are righteous in all that has come upon us, for You have acted truthfully while we have caused wickedness.[11]*

[א] *We have become the guiltiest of people.* [ב] *We have become the most degraded of all generations.* [ג] *Joy has departed from us.* [ד] *Our heart has been saddened by our sins.* [ה] *Our desirous treasure has been ruined,* [ו] *and our splendor dashed,* [ז] *for our Holy Temple edifice* [ח] *has been destroyed for our iniquities.* [ט] *Our Palace has become desolate.* [י] *[Jerusalem,] the beauty of our Land is given over to aliens,* [כ] *our power to strangers.*

But still we have not returned from our waywardness. So how can we be so brazen and obstinate as to say before You, HASHEM, our God and the God of our forefathers, that we are righteous and have not sinned, for in truth, both we and our fathers have sinned.

Strike the left side of the chest with the right fist while reciting
each of the sins in the following confession litany.

אָשַׁמְנוּ *We have become guilty;* [ב] *we have betrayed;* [ג] *we have robbed;* [ד] *we have spoken slander;* [ה] *we have caused perversion;* [ו] *we have caused wickedness;* [ז] *we have sinned willfully;*

חָמַסְנוּ, טָפַלְנוּ שֶׁקֶר. יָעַצְנוּ רָע, כִּזַּבְנוּ, לַצְנוּ, מָרַדְנוּ, נִאַצְנוּ, סָרַרְנוּ, עָוְינוּ, פָּשַׁעְנוּ, צָרַרְנוּ, קִשִּׁינוּ עֹרֶף. רָשַׁעְנוּ, שִׁחַתְנוּ, תִּעַבְנוּ, תָּעְינוּ, תִּעְתָּעְנוּ.

סַרְנוּ מִמִּצְוֹתֶיךָ וּמִמִּשְׁפָּטֶיךָ הַטּוֹבִים וְלֹא שָׁוָה לָנוּ. וְאַתָּה צַדִּיק עַל כָּל הַבָּא עָלֵינוּ, כִּי אֱמֶת עָשִׂיתָ וַאֲנַחְנוּ הִרְשָׁעְנוּ.

לְעֵינֵינוּ עָשְׁקוּ עֲמָלֵנוּ, מְמֻשָּׁךְ וּמְמוֹרָט מִמֶּנּוּ, נָתְנוּ עֻלָּם עָלֵינוּ, סָבַלְנוּ עַל שִׁכְמֵנוּ, עֲבָדִים מָשְׁלוּ בָנוּ, פֹּרֵק אֵין מִיָּדָם, צָרוֹת רַבּוֹת סְבָבוּנוּ, קְרָאנוּךְ יהוה אֱלֹהֵינוּ, רָחַקְתָּ מִמֶּנּוּ בַּעֲוֹנֵינוּ, שַׁבְנוּ מֵאַחֲרֶיךָ, תָּעִינוּ וְאָבַדְנוּ.

וַעֲדַיִן לֹא שַׁבְנוּ מִטָּעוּתֵנוּ וְהֵיךְ נָעִיז פָּנֵינוּ וְנַקְשֶׁה עָרְפֵּנוּ, לוֹמַר לְפָנֶיךָ יהוה אֱלֹהֵינוּ וֵאלֹהֵי אֲבוֹתֵינוּ, צַדִּיקִים אֲנַחְנוּ וְלֹא חָטָאנוּ, אֲבָל אֲנַחְנוּ וַאֲבוֹתֵינוּ חָטָאנוּ.

Strike the left side of the chest with the right fist while reciting
each of the sins in the following confession litany.

אָשַׁמְנוּ, בָּגַדְנוּ, גָּזַלְנוּ, דִּבַּרְנוּ דֹפִי. הֶעֱוִינוּ, וְהִרְשַׁעְנוּ, זַדְנוּ, חָמַסְנוּ, טָפַלְנוּ שֶׁקֶר. יָעַצְנוּ רָע, כִּזַּבְנוּ, לַצְנוּ, מָרַדְנוּ, נִאַצְנוּ, סָרַרְנוּ, עָוְינוּ, פָּשַׁעְנוּ, צָרַרְנוּ, קִשִּׁינוּ עֹרֶף. רָשַׁעְנוּ, שִׁחַתְנוּ, תִּעַבְנוּ, תָּעִינוּ, תִּעְתָּעְנוּ.

סַרְנוּ מִמִּצְוֹתֶיךָ וּמִמִּשְׁפָּטֶיךָ הַטּוֹבִים וְלֹא שָׁוָה לָנוּ. וְאַתָּה צַדִּיק עַל כָּל הַבָּא עָלֵינוּ, כִּי אֱמֶת עָשִׂיתָ וַאֲנַחְנוּ הִרְשָׁעְנוּ.

הִרְשַׁעְנוּ וּפָשַׁעְנוּ, לָכֵן לֹא נוֹשָׁעְנוּ. וְתֵן בְּלִבֵּנוּ לַעֲזוֹב דֶּרֶךְ רֶשַׁע, וְחִישׁ לָנוּ יֶשַׁע, כַּכָּתוּב עַל יַד נְבִיאֶךָ: יַעֲזֹב רָשָׁע דַּרְכּוֹ, וְאִישׁ אָוֶן מַחְשְׁבֹתָיו, וְיָשֹׁב אֶל יהוה וִירַחֲמֵהוּ, וְאֶל אֱלֹהֵינוּ כִּי יַרְבֶּה לִסְלוֹחַ.[1]

מָשִׁיחַ צִדְקֶךָ אָמַר לְפָנֶיךָ: שְׁגִיאוֹת מִי יָבִין מִנִּסְתָּרוֹת נַקֵּנִי.[2] נַקֵּנוּ יהוה אֱלֹהֵינוּ מִכָּל פְּשָׁעֵינוּ, וְטַהֲרֵנוּ מִכָּל טֻמְאוֹתֵינוּ, וּזְרוֹק עָלֵינוּ מַיִם טְהוֹרִים וְטַהֲרֵנוּ, כַּכָּתוּב עַל יַד נְבִיאֶךָ: וְזָרַקְתִּי עֲלֵיכֶם מַיִם טְהוֹרִים וּטְהַרְתֶּם, מִכֹּל טֻמְאוֹתֵיכֶם וּמִכָּל גִּלּוּלֵיכֶם אֲטַהֵר אֶתְכֶם.[3]

---
(1) *Isaiah* 55:7. (2) *Psalms* 19:13. (3) *Ezekiel* 36:25.

[ח] we have extorted; [ט] we have accused falsely; [י] we have given evil counsel; [כ] we have been deceitful; [ל] we have scorned; [מ] we have rebelled; [נ] we have provoked; [ס] we have turned away; [ע] we have been perverse; [פ] we have acted wantonly; [צ] we have persecuted; [ק] we have been obstinate; [ר] we have been wicked; [ש] we have corrupted; [ת] we have been abominable; we have strayed; You have let us go astray.

סַרְנוּ We have turned away from Your commandments and from Your good laws but to no avail. Yet You are righteous in all that has come upon us, for You have acted truthfully while we have caused wickedness.

[ל] [The benefit of] our labor has been stolen, [מ] pulled away and cut off from us. [נ] They have placed their yoke upon us, [ס] our burdens upon our shoulders. [ע] Slaves have ruled over us, [פ] there is no redemption from their hand. [צ] Abundant troubles have surrounded us, [ק] we called upon You, HASHEM, our God, [ר] but You have distanced us for our iniquities. [ש] We have turned away from following after You; [ת] we have strayed; we have become lost.

But still we have not returned from our waywardness. So how can we be so brazen and obstinate as to say before You, HASHEM, our God and the God of our forefathers, that we are righteous and have not sinned, for in truth, both we and our fathers have sinned.

Strike the left side of the chest with the right fist while reciting
each of the sins in the following confession litany:

אָשַׁמְנוּ We have become guilty; [ב] we have betrayed; [ג] we have robbed; [ד] we have spoken slander; [ה] we have caused perversion; [ו] we have caused wickedness; [ז] we have sinned willfully; [ח] we have extorted; [ט] we have accused falsely; [י] we have given evil counsel; [כ] we have been deceitful; [ל] we have scorned; [מ] we have rebelled; [נ] we have provoked; [ס] we have turned away; [ע] we have been perverse; [פ] we have acted wantonly; [צ] we have persecuted; [ק] we have been obstinate; [ר] we have been wicked; [ש] we have corrupted; [ת] we have been abominable; we have strayed; You have let us go astray.

סַרְנוּ We have turned away from Your commandments and from Your good laws but to no avail. Yet You are righteous in all that has come upon us, for You have acted truthfully while we have caused wickedness.

הִרְשַׁעְנוּ We have acted wickedly and have sinned willfully, there-fore we have not been saved. Inspire our heart to abandon the path of evil and hasten salvation for us, as it is written by Your prophet: May the wicked one abandon his way and the vicious man his thoughts; may he return to HASHEM and He will show him mercy, and to our God, for He is abundantly forgiving.[1]

מָשִׁיחַ Your righteous anointed [David] said before You: 'Who can discern mistakes? From unperceived faults cleanse me.'[2] Cleanse us, HASHEM, our God, of all our willful sins and purify us, of all our contam-inations. Sprinkle upon us pure water and purify us, as it is written by Your prophet: I shall sprinkle pure water upon you and purify you, of all your contaminations and of all your abominations I will purify you.'[3]

מִיכָה עַבְדְּךָ אָמַר לְפָנֶיךָ: מִי אֵל כָּמוֹךָ נֹשֵׂא עָוֹן וְעֹבֵר עַל
פֶּשַׁע לִשְׁאֵרִית נַחֲלָתוֹ, לֹא הֶחֱזִיק לָעַד אַפּוֹ, כִּי
חָפֵץ חֶסֶד הוּא, יָשׁוּב יְרַחֲמֵנוּ, יִכְבֹּשׁ עֲוֹנֹתֵינוּ, וְתַשְׁלִיךְ בִּמְצֻלוֹת
יָם כָּל חַטֹּאתָם.¹ (וְכָל חַטֹּאת עַמְּךָ בֵּית יִשְׂרָאֵל תַּשְׁלִיךְ בִּמְקוֹם
אֲשֶׁר לֹא יִזָּכְרוּ, וְלֹא יִפָּקְדוּ, וְלֹא יַעֲלוּ עַל לֵב לְעוֹלָם.) תִּתֵּן אֱמֶת
לְיַעֲקֹב חֶסֶד לְאַבְרָהָם אֲשֶׁר נִשְׁבַּעְתָּ לַאֲבוֹתֵינוּ מִימֵי קֶדֶם.²

דָּנִיֵּאל אִישׁ חֲמוּדוֹת שִׁוַּע לְפָנֶיךָ: הַטֵּה אֱלֹהַי אָזְנְךָ וּשְׁמָע,
פְּקַח עֵינֶיךָ וּרְאֵה שֹׁמְמֹתֵינוּ וְהָעִיר אֲשֶׁר נִקְרָא שִׁמְךָ
עָלֶיהָ, כִּי לֹא עַל צִדְקֹתֵינוּ אֲנַחְנוּ מַפִּילִים תַּחֲנוּנֵינוּ לְפָנֶיךָ, כִּי עַל
רַחֲמֶיךָ הָרַבִּים. אֲדֹנָי שְׁמָעָה, אֲדֹנָי סְלָחָה, אֲדֹנָי הַקְשִׁיבָה, וַעֲשֵׂה
אַל תְּאַחַר, לְמַעַנְךָ אֱלֹהַי, כִּי שִׁמְךָ נִקְרָא עַל עִירְךָ וְעַל עַמֶּךָ.³

עֶזְרָא הַסּוֹפֵר אָמַר לְפָנֶיךָ: אֱלֹהַי, בֹּשְׁתִּי וְנִכְלַמְתִּי לְהָרִים,
אֱלֹהַי, פָּנַי אֵלֶיךָ, כִּי עֲוֹנֹתֵינוּ רָבוּ לְמַעְלָה
רֹאשׁ, וְאַשְׁמָתֵנוּ גָדְלָה עַד לַשָּׁמָיִם.⁴ וְאַתָּה⁵ אֱלוֹהַּ סְלִיחוֹת, חַנּוּן
וְרַחוּם, אֶרֶךְ אַפַּיִם וְרַב חֶסֶד, וְלֹא עֲזַבְתָּנוּ.⁶

אַל תַּעַזְבֵנוּ אָבִינוּ וְאַל תִּטְּשֵׁנוּ בּוֹרְאֵנוּ, וְאַל תַּזְנִיחֵנוּ
יוֹצְרֵנוּ, וְאַל תַּעַשׂ עִמָּנוּ כָּלָה כְּחַטֹּאתֵינוּ. וְקַיֵּם
לָנוּ יהוה אֱלֹהֵינוּ, אֶת הַדָּבָר שֶׁהִבְטַחְתָּנוּ בְּקַבָּלָה עַל יְדֵי יִרְמְיָהוּ
חוֹזָךְ, כָּאָמוּר: בַּיָּמִים הָהֵם וּבָעֵת הַהִיא, נְאֻם יהוה, יְבֻקַּשׁ אֶת עֲוֹן
יִשְׂרָאֵל וְאֵינֶנּוּ וְאֶת חַטֹּאת יְהוּדָה וְלֹא תִמָּצֶאנָה, כִּי אֶסְלַח
לַאֲשֶׁר אַשְׁאִיר.⁷ עַמְּךָ וְנַחֲלָתְךָ רְעֵבֵי טוּבְךָ, צְמֵאֵי חַסְדֶּךָ, תְּאֵבֵי
יִשְׁעֶךָ, יַכִּירוּ וְיֵדְעוּ כִּי לַיהוה אֱלֹהֵינוּ הָרַחֲמִים וְהַסְּלִיחוֹת.

אֵל רַחוּם שְׁמֶךָ. אֵל חַנּוּן שְׁמֶךָ, בָּנוּ נִקְרָא שְׁמֶךָ. יהוה עֲשֵׂה
לְמַעַן שְׁמֶךָ. עֲשֵׂה לְמַעַן אֲמִתֶּךָ, עֲשֵׂה לְמַעַן
בְּרִיתֶךָ, עֲשֵׂה לְמַעַן גָּדְלְךָ וְתִפְאַרְתֶּךָ, עֲשֵׂה לְמַעַן דָּתֶךָ, עֲשֵׂה
לְמַעַן הוֹדֶךָ, עֲשֵׂה לְמַעַן וִעוּדֶךָ, עֲשֵׂה לְמַעַן זִכְרֶךָ, עֲשֵׂה לְמַעַן
חַסְדֶּךָ, עֲשֵׂה לְמַעַן טוּבֶךָ, עֲשֵׂה לְמַעַן יִחוּדֶךָ, עֲשֵׂה לְמַעַן כְּבוֹדֶךָ,
עֲשֵׂה לְמַעַן לִמּוּדֶךָ, עֲשֵׂה לְמַעַן מַלְכוּתֶךָ, עֲשֵׂה לְמַעַן נִצְחֶךָ,
עֲשֵׂה לְמַעַן סוֹדֶךָ, עֲשֵׂה לְמַעַן עֻזֶּךָ, עֲשֵׂה לְמַעַן פְּאֵרֶךָ, עֲשֵׂה
לְמַעַן צִדְקָתֶךָ, עֲשֵׂה לְמַעַן קְדֻשָּׁתֶךָ, עֲשֵׂה לְמַעַן רַחֲמֶיךָ הָרַבִּים,

---

(1) *Micah* 7:18-19. (2) *Micah* 7:20. (3) *Daniel* 9:18-19. (4) *Ezra* 9:6. (5) Some editions of *Selichos* insert the word אֱלֹהֵינוּ, *our God*, at this point. (6) Cf. *Nehemiah* 9:17. (7) *Jeremiah* 50:20.

מִיכָה עַבְדְּךָ Micah, Your servant, said before You: 'Who, O God, is like You, Who pardons iniquity and overlooks transgression for the remnant of His heritage? Who has not retained His wrath eternally, for He desires kindness! He will again be merciful to us; He will suppress our iniquities and cast into the depths of the sea all their sins.[1] (And all the sins of Your nation the Family of Israel, may You cast away to a place where they will neither be remembered, considered, nor brought to mind — ever.) Grant truth to Jacob, kindness to Abraham, as You swore to our forefathers from ancient times.'[2]

דָּנִיֵּאל Daniel, the greatly beloved man, cried out before You: 'Incline, my God, Your ear, and listen, open Your eyes and see our desolation and that of the city upon which Your Name is proclaimed, for not because of our righteousness do we cast down our supplications before You, rather because of Your abundant compassion. O my Lord, heed; O my Lord, forgive; O my Lord, be attentive and act, do not delay; for Your sake, my God, for Your Name is proclaimed upon Your city and Your people.'[3]

עֶזְרָא הַסּוֹפֵר Ezra the Scribe said before You: 'My God, I am embarrassed and ashamed to lift my face to You, my God — for our iniquities have multiplied above our heads, and our sins extend unto heaven.[4] You are[5] the God of forgiveness, compassionate and merciful, slow to anger, and abundant in kindness; and You have not forsaken us.'[6]

אַל תַּעַזְבֵנוּ Do not forsake us, our Father; do not cast us off, our Creator; do not abandon us, our Molder; and do not bring about our destruction, as our sins merit. Affirm for us, HASHEM, our God, the promise You made in the tradition through Jeremiah, Your seer, as it is said: 'In those days and at that time' — the words of HASHEM — 'the iniquity of Israel will be sought but there will be none, and the errors of Judah, but they will not be found, for I will have forgiven those whom I leave as a remnant.'[7] Your people and Your heritage, who hunger for Your goodness, who thirst for Your kindness, who long for Your salvation — may they recognize and know that to HASHEM, our God, belong mercy and forgiveness.

אֵל רַחוּם 'Merciful God' is Your Name, 'Gracious God' is Your Name, Your Name is called upon us — O HASHEM, act for Your Name's sake. Act for the sake of [א] Your truth; act for the sake of [ב] Your covenant; act for the sake of [ג] Your greatness and Your splendor; act for the sake of [ד] Your law; act for the sake of [ה] Your glory; act for the sake of [ו] Your Meeting House; act for the sake of [ז] Your remembrance; act for the sake of [ח] Your kindness; act for the sake of [ט] Your goodness; act for the sake of [י] Your Oneness; act for the sake of [כ] Your honor; act for the sake of [ל] Your teaching; act for the sake of [מ] Your kingship; act for the sake of [נ] Your eternality; act for the sake of [ס] Your counsel; act for the sake of [ע] Your power; act for the sake of [פ] Your beauty; act for the sake of [צ] Your righteousness; act for the sake of [ק] Your sanctity; act for the sake of [ר] Your abundant mercy;

עֲשֵׂה לְמַעַן שְׁכִינָתֶךָ, עֲשֵׂה לְמַעַן תְּהִלָּתֶךָ, עֲשֵׂה לְמַעַן אֹהֲבֶיךָ
שׁוֹכְנֵי עָפָר, עֲשֵׂה לְמַעַן אַבְרָהָם יִצְחָק וְיַעֲקֹב, עֲשֵׂה לְמַעַן מֹשֶׁה
וְאַהֲרֹן, עֲשֵׂה לְמַעַן דָּוִד וּשְׁלֹמֹה, עֲשֵׂה לְמַעַן יְרוּשָׁלַיִם עִיר
קָדְשֶׁךָ, עֲשֵׂה לְמַעַן צִיּוֹן מִשְׁכַּן כְּבוֹדֶךָ, עֲשֵׂה לְמַעַן שִׁמְמוֹת
הֵיכָלֶךָ, עֲשֵׂה לְמַעַן הֲרִיסוּת מִזְבְּחֶךָ, עֲשֵׂה לְמַעַן הַהֲרוּגִים עַל שֵׁם
קָדְשֶׁךָ, עֲשֵׂה לְמַעַן טְבוּחִים עַל יִחוּדֶךָ, עֲשֵׂה לְמַעַן בָּאֵי בָאֵשׁ
וּבַמַּיִם עַל קִדּוּשׁ שְׁמֶךָ, עֲשֵׂה לְמַעַן יוֹנְקֵי שָׁדַיִם שֶׁלֹּא חָטְאוּ, עֲשֵׂה
לְמַעַן גְּמוּלֵי חָלָב שֶׁלֹּא פָשָׁעוּ, עֲשֵׂה לְמַעַן תִּינוֹקוֹת שֶׁל בֵּית רַבָּן,
עֲשֵׂה לְמַעַנְךָ אִם לֹא לְמַעֲנֵנוּ, עֲשֵׂה לְמַעַנְךָ וְהוֹשִׁיעֵנוּ.

עֲנֵנוּ יהוה עֲנֵנוּ, עֲנֵנוּ אֱלֹהֵינוּ עֲנֵנוּ, עֲנֵנוּ אָבִינוּ עֲנֵנוּ, עֲנֵנוּ
בּוֹרְאֵנוּ עֲנֵנוּ, עֲנֵנוּ גּוֹאֲלֵנוּ עֲנֵנוּ, עֲנֵנוּ דוֹרְשֵׁנוּ עֲנֵנוּ, עֲנֵנוּ
הָאֵל הַנֶּאֱמָן עֲנֵנוּ, עֲנֵנוּ וָתִיק וְחָסִיד עֲנֵנוּ, עֲנֵנוּ זַךְ וְיָשָׁר עֲנֵנוּ, עֲנֵנוּ
חַי וְקַיָּם עֲנֵנוּ, עֲנֵנוּ טוֹב וּמֵטִיב עֲנֵנוּ, עֲנֵנוּ יוֹדֵעַ יֵצֶר עֲנֵנוּ, עֲנֵנוּ
כּוֹבֵשׁ כְּעָסִים עֲנֵנוּ, עֲנֵנוּ לוֹבֵשׁ צְדָקוֹת עֲנֵנוּ, עֲנֵנוּ מֶלֶךְ מַלְכֵי
הַמְּלָכִים עֲנֵנוּ, עֲנֵנוּ נוֹרָא וְנִשְׂגָּב עֲנֵנוּ, עֲנֵנוּ סוֹלֵחַ וּמוֹחֵל עֲנֵנוּ,
עֲנֵנוּ עוֹנֶה בְּעֵת צָרָה עֲנֵנוּ, עֲנֵנוּ פּוֹדֶה וּמַצִּיל עֲנֵנוּ, עֲנֵנוּ צַדִּיק
וְיָשָׁר עֲנֵנוּ, עֲנֵנוּ קָרוֹב לְקוֹרְאָיו עֲנֵנוּ, עֲנֵנוּ רַחוּם וְחַנּוּן עֲנֵנוּ, עֲנֵנוּ
שׁוֹמֵעַ אֶל אֶבְיוֹנִים עֲנֵנוּ, עֲנֵנוּ תּוֹמֵךְ תְּמִימִים עֲנֵנוּ, עֲנֵנוּ אֱלֹהֵי
אֲבוֹתֵינוּ עֲנֵנוּ, עֲנֵנוּ אֱלֹהֵי אַבְרָהָם עֲנֵנוּ, עֲנֵנוּ פַּחַד יִצְחָק עֲנֵנוּ,
עֲנֵנוּ אֲבִיר יַעֲקֹב עֲנֵנוּ, עֲנֵנוּ עֶזְרַת הַשְּׁבָטִים עֲנֵנוּ, עֲנֵנוּ
מִשְׂגָּב אִמָּהוֹת עֲנֵנוּ, עֲנֵנוּ קָשֶׁה לִכְעוֹס עֲנֵנוּ, עֲנֵנוּ רַךְ לִרְצוֹת
עֲנֵנוּ, עֲנֵנוּ עוֹנֶה בְּעֵת רָצוֹן¹ עֲנֵנוּ, עֲנֵנוּ אֲבִי יְתוֹמִים עֲנֵנוּ, עֲנֵנוּ דַּיַּן
אַלְמָנוֹת עֲנֵנוּ.

מִי שֶׁעָנָה לְאַבְרָהָם אָבִינוּ בְּהַר הַמּוֹרִיָּה,	הוּא יַעֲנֵנוּ.
מִי שֶׁעָנָה לְיִצְחָק בְּנוֹ כְּשֶׁנֶּעֱקַד עַל גַּבֵּי הַמִּזְבֵּחַ,	הוּא יַעֲנֵנוּ.
מִי שֶׁעָנָה לְיַעֲקֹב בְּבֵית אֵל,	הוּא יַעֲנֵנוּ.
מִי שֶׁעָנָה לְיוֹסֵף בְּבֵית הָאֲסוּרִים,	הוּא יַעֲנֵנוּ.
מִי שֶׁעָנָה לַאֲבוֹתֵינוּ עַל יַם סוּף,	הוּא יַעֲנֵנוּ.
מִי שֶׁעָנָה לְמֹשֶׁה בְּחוֹרֵב,	הוּא יַעֲנֵנוּ.
מִי שֶׁעָנָה לְאַהֲרֹן בַּמַּחְתָּה,	הוּא יַעֲנֵנוּ.

---

(1) Some editions of *Selichos* reverse the positions of these two lines.

act for the sake of [שׁ] *Your Presence, act for the sake of* [ת] *Your praise; act for the sake of Your beloved ones who rest in the dust; act for the sake of Abraham, Isaac, and Jacob; act for the sake of Moses and Aaron; act for the sake of David and Solomon; act for the sake of Jerusalem, Your holy city; act for the sake of Zion, the abode of Your glory; act for the sake of the desolation of Your Temple; act for the sake of the ruin of Your Altar; act for the sake of the martyrs for Your holy Name; act for the sake of those slaughtered for Your Oneness; act for the sake of those who entered fire and water for the sanctification of Your Name; act for the nursing infants who did not err; act for the sake of the weaned babes who did not sin; act for the sake of children at the schoolroom; act for Your sake if not for ours; act for Your sake and save us.*

עֲנֵנוּ *Answer us, HASHEM, answer us; answer us, our God, answer us; answer us,* [א] *our Father, answer us; answer us,* [ב] *our Creator, answer us; answer us,* [ג] *our Redeemer, answer us; answer us,* [ד] *You Who searches us out, answer us; answer us,* [ה] *faithful God, answer us; answer us,* [ו] *stead-fast and kind One, answer us; answer us,* [ז] *pure and upright One, answer us; answer us,* [ח] *living and enduring One, answer us; answer us,* [ט] *good and beneficent One, answer us; answer us,* [י] *You Who knows inclinations, answer us; answer us,* [כ] *You Who suppresses wrath, answer us; answer us,* [ל] *You Who dons righteousness, answer us; answer us,* [מ] *King Who reigns over kings, answer us; answer us,* [נ] *awesome and powerful One, answer us; answer us,* [ס] *You Who forgives and pardons, answer us; answer us,* [ע] *You Who answers in time of distress,*[1] *answer us; answer us,* [פ] *Redeemer and Rescuer, answer us; answer us,* [צ] *righteous and upright One, answer us; answer us,* [ק] *He Who is close to those who call upon Him, answer us; answer us,* [ר] *merciful and gracious One, answer us; answer us,* [שׁ] *You Who hears the destitute, answer us; answer us,* [ת] *You Who supports the wholesome, answer us; answer us, God of our forefathers, answer us; answer us, God of Abraham, answer us; answer us, Dread of Isaac, answer us; answer us, Mighty One of Jacob, answer us; answer us, Helper of the tribes, answer us; answer us, Stronghold of the Matriarchs, answer us; answer us, You Who are hard to anger, answer us; answer us, You Who are easy to pacify, answer us; answer us, You Who answers in a time of favor,*[1] *answer us; answer us, Father of orphans, answer us; answer us, Judge of widows, answer us.*

מִי שֶׁעָנָה *He Who answered our father Abraham on Mount Moriah,*
may He answer us.
He Who answered his son Isaac when he was bound atop the altar,
may He answer us.
He Who answered Jacob in Bethel, *may He answer us.*
He Who answered Joseph in the prison, *may He answer us.*
He Who answered our forefathers at the Sea of Reeds, *may He answer us.*
He Who answered Moses in Horeb, *may He answer us.*
He Who answered Aaron when he offered the censer, *may He answer us.*

מִי שֶׁעָנָה לְפִינְחָס בְּקוּמוֹ מִתּוֹךְ הָעֵדָה,   הוּא יַעֲנֵנוּ.

מִי שֶׁעָנָה לִיהוֹשֻׁעַ בַּגִּלְגָּל,   הוּא יַעֲנֵנוּ.

מִי שֶׁעָנָה לִשְׁמוּאֵל בַּמִּצְפָּה,   הוּא יַעֲנֵנוּ.

מִי שֶׁעָנָה לְדָוִד וּשְׁלֹמֹה בְנוֹ בִּירוּשָׁלָיִם,   הוּא יַעֲנֵנוּ.

מִי שֶׁעָנָה לְאֵלִיָּהוּ בְּהַר הַכַּרְמֶל,   הוּא יַעֲנֵנוּ.

מִי שֶׁעָנָה לֶאֱלִישָׁע בִּירִיחוֹ,   הוּא יַעֲנֵנוּ.

מִי שֶׁעָנָה לְיוֹנָה בִּמְעֵי הַדָּגָה,   הוּא יַעֲנֵנוּ.

מִי שֶׁעָנָה לְחִזְקִיָּהוּ מֶלֶךְ יְהוּדָה בְּחָלְיוֹ,   הוּא יַעֲנֵנוּ.

מִי שֶׁעָנָה לַחֲנַנְיָה מִישָׁאֵל וַעֲזַרְיָה בְּתוֹךְ כִּבְשַׁן הָאֵשׁ,   הוּא יַעֲנֵנוּ.

מִי שֶׁעָנָה לְדָנִיֵּאל בְּגוֹב הָאֲרָיוֹת,   הוּא יַעֲנֵנוּ.

מִי שֶׁעָנָה לְמָרְדְּכַי וְאֶסְתֵּר בְּשׁוּשַׁן הַבִּירָה,   הוּא יַעֲנֵנוּ.

מִי שֶׁעָנָה לְעֶזְרָא בַּגּוֹלָה,   הוּא יַעֲנֵנוּ.

מִי שֶׁעָנָה לְכָל הַצַּדִּיקִים וְהַחֲסִידִים וְהַתְּמִימִים וְהַיְשָׁרִים,   הוּא יַעֲנֵנוּ.

רַחֲמָנָא דְּעָנֵי לַעֲנִיֵּי, עֲנֵינָא. רַחֲמָנָא דְּעָנֵי לִתְבִירֵי לִבָּא, עֲנֵינָא. רַחֲמָנָא דְּעָנֵי לְמַכִּיכֵי רוּחָא, עֲנֵינָא. רַחֲמָנָא עֲנֵינָא. רַחֲמָנָא חוּס. רַחֲמָנָא פְּרוֹק. רַחֲמָנָא שְׁזִיב. רַחֲמָנָא רְחֵם עֲלָן. הַשְׁתָּא בַּעֲגָלָא וּבִזְמַן קָרִיב.

נפילת אפים

In the presence of a Torah Scroll, the following (until יַכְסוּ רָגַע) is recited with the head resting on the arm, preferably while seated. Elsewhere, it is recited with the head held erect.

(וַיֹּאמֶר דָּוִד אֶל גָּד, צַר לִי מְאֹד נִפְּלָה נָּא בְיַד יהוה, כִּי רַבִּים רַחֲמָיו, וּבְיַד אָדָם אַל אֶפֹּלָה.[1])

רַחוּם וְחַנּוּן חָטָאתִי לְפָנֶיךָ. יהוה מָלֵא רַחֲמִים, רַחֵם עָלַי וְקַבֵּל תַּחֲנוּנָי.

תהלים ו:ב-יא

יהוה אַל בְּאַפְּךָ תוֹכִיחֵנִי, וְאַל בַּחֲמָתְךָ תְיַסְּרֵנִי. חָנֵּנִי יהוה, כִּי אֻמְלַל אָנִי, רְפָאֵנִי יהוה, כִּי נִבְהֲלוּ עֲצָמָי. וְנַפְשִׁי נִבְהֲלָה מְאֹד, וְאַתָּה יהוה, עַד מָתָי. שׁוּבָה יהוה, חַלְּצָה נַפְשִׁי, הוֹשִׁיעֵנִי לְמַעַן חַסְדֶּךָ. כִּי אֵין בַּמָּוֶת זִכְרֶךָ, בִּשְׁאוֹל מִי יוֹדֶה לָּךְ. יָגַעְתִּי בְּאַנְחָתִי, אַשְׂחֶה בְכָל לַיְלָה מִטָּתִי, בְּדִמְעָתִי עַרְשִׂי אַמְסֶה. עָשְׁשָׁה מִכַּעַס עֵינִי, עָתְקָה בְּכָל צוֹרְרָי. סוּרוּ מִמֶּנִּי כָּל פֹּעֲלֵי אָוֶן, כִּי שָׁמַע יהוה קוֹל בִּכְיִי. שָׁמַע יהוה תְּחִנָּתִי, יהוה תְּפִלָּתִי יִקָּח. יֵבֹשׁוּ וְיִבָּהֲלוּ מְאֹד כָּל אֹיְבָי, יָשֻׁבוּ יֵבֹשׁוּ רָגַע.

He Who answered Phineas when he arose from amid the congregation,
may He answer us.
He Who answered Joshua in Gilgal,   *may He answer us.*
He Who answered Samuel in Mitzpah,   *may He answer us.*
He Who answered David and his son Solomon in Jerusalem,
may He answer us.
He Who answered Elijah on Mount Carmel,   *may He answer us.*
He Who answered Elisha in Jericho,   *may He answer us.*
He Who answered Jonah in the innards of the fish,   *may He answer us.*
He Who answered Hezekiah, King of Judah, in his illness,
may He answer us.
He Who answered Chananiah, Mishael, and Azariah in the fiery oven,
may He answer us.
He Who answered Daniel in the lions' den,   *may He answer us.*
He Who answered Mordechai and Esther in Shushan the capital,
may He answer us.
He Who answered Ezra in the Exile,   *may He answer us.*
He Who answered all the righteous, the devout, the wholesome,
and the upright,   *may He answer us.*

רַחֲמָנָא *The Merciful One Who answers the poor, may He answer us.*
The Merciful One Who answers the brokenhearted, may He answer us. The Merciful One Who answers the humble of spirit, may He answer us. O Merciful One, answer us. O Merciful One, pity. O Merciful One, redeem. O Merciful One, deliver. O Merciful One, have mercy on us — now, swiftly and soon.

PUTTING DOWN THE HEAD

In the presence of a Torah Scroll, the following (until *'instantly shamed'*) is recited with the head resting on the arm, preferably while seated. Elsewhere, it is recited with the head held erect.

(And David said to Gad, 'I am exceedingly distressed. Let us fall into HASHEM's hand for His mercies are abundant, but let me not fall into human hands.' [1]*)*

רַחוּם וְחַנּוּן *O compassionate and gracious One, I have sinned before You. HASHEM, Who is full of mercy, have mercy on me and accept my supplications.*

Psalms 6:2-11

ה' *HASHEM, do not rebuke me in Your anger nor chastise me in Your rage. Favor me, HASHEM, for I am feeble; heal me, HASHEM, for my bones shudder. My soul is utterly confounded, and You, HASHEM, how long? Desist, HASHEM, release my soul; save me as befits Your kindness. For there is no mention of You in death; in the Lower World who will thank You? I am wearied with my sigh, every night my tears drench my bed, soak my couch. My eye is dimmed because of anger, aged by my tormentors. Depart from me, all evildoers, for HASHEM has heard the sound of my weeping. HASHEM has heard my plea, HASHEM will accept my prayer. Let all my foes be shamed and utterly confounded, they will regret and be instantly shamed.*

---

(1) *II Samuel* 24:14.

מְחֵי וּמַסֵּי מֵמִית וּמְחַיֶּה, מַסִּיק מִן שְׁאוֹל לְחַיֵּי עָלְמָא, בְּרָא
כַּד חָטֵי אֲבְוּהִי לַקְיֵהּ, אֲבְוּהִי דְּחָיֵס אַסֵּי לִכְאֵבֵהּ.
עַבְדָּא דְּמָרִיד נָפִיק בְּקוֹלָר, מָרֵהּ תָּאִיב וְתַבִּיר קוֹלָרֵהּ.
בְּרָךְ בְּכָרֵךְ אֲנָן וְחָטֵינַן קַמָּךְ, הָא רְזֵי נַפְשִׁין בְּגִידִין מְרִירִין,
עַבְדָּךְ אֲנָן וּמְרוֹדִינַן קַמָּךְ, הָא בְּבִזְּתָא, הָא בְּשִׁבְיָא, הָא
בְּמַלְקְיוּתָא. בְּמָטוּ מִנָּךְ בְּרַחֲמָךְ דִּנְפִישִׁין, אַסֵּי לִכְאֵבִין דִּתְקוֹף
עֲלָן, עַד דְּלָא נֶהֱוֵי גְּמִירָא בְּשִׁבְיָא.

סְלִיחָה סח (תחנה)

אֱלֹהֵינוּ וֵאלֹהֵי אֲבוֹתֵינוּ

שֶׁבֶת הַכִּסֵּא,* אֲשֶׁר לְמַעְלָה מְנֻשָּׂא,
יְחַלֶּה בַּעֲדֵנוּ לְצוּר הַמִּתְנַשֵּׂא.
מֶלֶךְ עַל כִּסֵּא לְעַמּוֹ יְהִי מַחְסֶה,
וְיַבִּיט בְּצוּרַת תָּם חֲקוּקָה בַּכִּסֵּא.*
עַל הַיָּמִין אַרְיֵה, יְחַלֶּה פְּנֵי אֶהְיֶה,[1]
יָחֹן וְיָחוֹס לְזֶרַע כֹּה יִהְיֶה.[2]
וְיִשְׁעֵנוּ יִהְיֶה, וְאוֹתָנוּ יְחַיֶּה,
וְיָשִׁיב הַמְּלוּכָה לְזֶרַע גּוּר אַרְיֵה.[3]
נָא מֵהַשְּׂמֹאל שׁוֹר, פְּגִיעָתֵנוּ יִתְשַׁר,
לְלַמְּדֵנוּ הֵיטִיב חֲמוּצֵנוּ לְאַשֵּׁר.
בִּרְכוֹת יַחֲשָׁר, וּמְרוֹדֵינוּ יַעֲשֹׁר,
וְיָשִׁיב לְבִצָּרוֹן הַדְרַת הַהוֹד בְּכוֹר שׁוֹר.*[4]
רְאִיַּת פְּנֵי אָדָם, תְּחִנָּתֵנוּ יְקַדֵּם,
לִפְנֵי צוּר מָעוֹז יוֹצֵר הָאָדָם.
יַלְבִּין הַמְּאָדָם,[5] וִיעוֹרֵר הַנִּרְדָּם,
וְיַרְבֶּה הַמִּשְׂרָה לִקְרוּאֵי צֹאן אָדָם.[6]
צְפִצוּף הַנֶּשֶׁר, בִּכְנָפָיו יְחַשֵּׁר,
וְיָלִיץ צִדְקֵנוּ פְּנֵי אוֹהֵב יֹשֶׁר.

שֶׁבֶת הַכִּסֵּא — *May the Throne of Glory* [lit., *may the seat of the Throne*]. R' Shimon HaGadol signed this supplication in the acrostic of the stanzas — שמעון בר יצחק, *Shimon bar Yitzchak* [see prefatory comment to *selichah* 11].

The first chapter of *Ezekiel* is a deep, mystical record of the angelic forms that the prophet saw in his Vision of the Chariot, that is, the Throne of Glory and the angels that bear it. Four *Chayos*,

each with four faces — *The semblance of their faces: the face of a man, with the face of a lion to the right of the four of them, the face of an ox to the left of the four of them, and the face of an eagle to the four of them (Ezekiel 1:10)* — were the bearers of the Chariot.

The *paytan* beseeches the Throne and its angelic bearers to pray before God for Israel's welfare. [The propriety and halachic significance

מָחִי וּמַסֵּי *[O God,] He Who smites and heals, causes death and re-*
stores life, raises [the dead] from the grave to eternal life:
Should a son sin, his father would smack him, but a compassionate father
will heal his [son's] pain. When a slave rebels, he is led out in collar-irons,
but if his master desires to, he breaks his chains.

We are Your son, Your firstborn, and we have sinned against You; so
our soul has been satiated with bitter wormwood. We are Your servants
and we have rebelled against You; so [we have suffered], some with loot-
ing, some with captivity, and some with the lash. We beg of You, in Your
abundant compassion, heal the pains that have overwhelmed us, before
we have been completely wiped out in captivity.

SELICHAH 68

Our God and God of our forefathers —

ש *May the Throne of Glory,* that is exalted Above,*
pray for our sake, before the Exalted Creator.

מ *May the King on His Throne be a shelter for His people,*
gazing at [Jacob] the perfect one's likeness carved in the Throne.*

ע *May the lion on the right*
pray before [God Who calls Himself] I-shall-be[1]
that He grant grace and pity to [Abraham's] offspring
that would be [numerous as the stars].[2]

ו *May He be our salvation and grant us life,*
and restore the kingdom to the offspring of the lion cub [Judah].[3]

נ *Please, may the ox on the left offer our prayer as tribute;*
that He may teach us well to rectify our haughtiness.

ב *May He rain down blessings and make wealthy our poor,*
and bring back to the walled city [Jerusalem] the glory
of [Joseph's] ox-like greatness.*[4]

ר *May the semblance of a man's face proffer our supplication*
before the Rock, the Stronghold, the Maker of Man.

י *May He whiten [sin's] redness,[5]*
and awaken the slumbering [sinners]
and give power and rule to [Israel] called Sheep, Man.[6]

צ *May the twittering of the eagle*
with its wings cause a flow [of prayer to God],
and recommend our righteousness before Him Who loves uprightness.

---

(1) See *Exodus* 3:14. (2) Cf. *Genesis* 15:5. (3) 49:9. (4) Cf. *Deuteronomy* 33:17.
(5) Cf. *Isaiah* 1:18. (6) Cf. *Ezekiel* 36:37-38.

of prayer through intercessors are discussed in
the introduction to this volume.]

חֲקוּקָה בַּכִּסֵּא — *Carved in the Throne.* The face of
a man that was the face of each of the *Chayos*
mentioned above, was the face of the Patriarch
Jacob (*Rashi* to *Ezekiel* 1:5, based on *Bereishis
Rabbah* 68:12).

בְּכוֹר שׁוֹר — *[Joseph's] ox-like greatness.* This
description of Joseph is found in Moses' blessings

to the tribes before his death (see *Deuteronomy*
33:17). But the reference here is not limited to the
offspring of Joseph, for why would the *paytan*
single out one tribe over the others? All Israel is
called by Joseph's name (*Amos* 5:15) for a variety
of reasons: Joseph supported and sustained the
fledgling tribes when they first came down to
Egypt (*Rashi*); most of the kings of the Northern
Kingdom were descended from Joseph's sons

חֶלְקֵנוּ יְבַשֵּׂר, וְעַפְעַפֵּינוּ יְיַשֵּׁר,
וִידַבֵּר בִּצְדָקָה לְעַם נְשׂוּאֵי נֶשֶׁר.[1]

❖ קְדִישֵׁי עֶלְיוֹנִים, שְׂרָפִים וְאוֹפַנִּים,
הַפִּילוּ תְחִנַּתֵנוּ[2] פְּנֵי אֲדוֹנֵי הָאֲדוֹנִים.
וְיִזְכֹּר רִאשׁוֹנִים, וְאַהֲבַת אֵיתָנִים,
וִיקַיֵּם שְׁבוּעָה לְדוֹרוֹת אַחֲרוֹנִים.

All:

מַכְנִיסֵי רַחֲמִים, הַכְנִיסוּ רַחֲמֵינוּ, לִפְנֵי בַּעַל הָרַחֲמִים.
מַשְׁמִיעֵי תְפִלָּה, הַשְׁמִיעוּ תְפִלָּתֵנוּ, לִפְנֵי
שׁוֹמֵעַ תְּפִלָּה. מַשְׁמִיעֵי צְעָקָה, הַשְׁמִיעוּ צַעֲקָתֵנוּ, לִפְנֵי שׁוֹמֵעַ
צְעָקָה. מַכְנִיסֵי דִמְעָה, הַכְנִיסוּ דִמְעוֹתֵינוּ, לִפְנֵי מֶלֶךְ מִתְרַצֶּה
בִּדְמָעוֹת.

הִשְׁתַּדְּלוּ וְהַרְבּוּ תְּחִנָּה וּבַקָּשָׁה, לִפְנֵי מֶלֶךְ אֵל רָם וְנִשָּׂא.
הַזְכִּירוּ לְפָנָיו, הַשְׁמִיעוּ לְפָנָיו תּוֹרָה וּמַעֲשִׂים טוֹבִים שֶׁל שׁוֹכְנֵי
עָפָר.

יִזְכֹּר אַהֲבָתָם וִיחַיֶּה זַרְעָם, שֶׁלֹּא תֹאבַד שְׁאֵרִית יַעֲקֹב. כִּי צֹאן
רוֹעֶה נֶאֱמָן הָיָה לְחֶרְפָּה, יִשְׂרָאֵל גּוֹי אֶחָד לְמָשָׁל וְלִשְׁנִינָה.
מַהֵר עֲנֵנוּ אֱלֹהֵי יִשְׁעֵנוּ, וּפְדֵנוּ מִכָּל גְּזֵרוֹת קָשׁוֹת וְהוֹשִׁיעָה
בְּרַחֲמֶיךָ הָרַבִּים, מְשִׁיחַ צִדְקָךְ וְעַמָּךְ.

מָרָן דְּבִשְׁמַיָּא לָךְ מִתְחַנְּנַן, כְּבַר שַׁבְיָא דְּמִתְחַנֵּן לְשָׁבוּיֵהּ.
כֻּלְּהוֹן בְּנֵי שַׁבְיָא בְּכַסְפָּא מִתְפָּרְקִין, וְעַמָּךְ
יִשְׂרָאֵל בְּרַחֲמֵי וּבְתַחֲנוּנֵי, הַב לָן שְׁאֵלְתִין וּבָעוּתִין, דְּלָא נֶהְדַּר
רֵיקָם מִן קָדָמָךְ.

מָרָן דְּבִשְׁמַיָּא לָךְ מִתְחַנְּנַן, כְּעַבְדָּא דְּמִתְחַנֵּן לְמָרֵיהּ,
עֲשִׁיקֵי אֲנַן וּבַחֲשׁוֹכָא שָׁרֵינַן, מְרִירָן נַפְשִׁין מֵעַקְתִין דִּנְפִישִׁין,
חֵילָא לֵית בָּן לְרַצּוּיָךְ מָרָן, עֲבִיד בְּדִיל קְיָמָא דִּגְזַרְתָּ עִם אֲבָהָתָנָא.

שׁוֹמֵר יִשְׂרָאֵל, שְׁמוֹר שְׁאֵרִית יִשְׂרָאֵל, וְאַל יֹאבַד יִשְׂרָאֵל,
הָאֹמְרִים, שְׁמַע יִשְׂרָאֵל.[3]
שׁוֹמֵר גּוֹי אֶחָד, שְׁמוֹר שְׁאֵרִית עַם אֶחָד, וְאַל יֹאבַד גּוֹי אֶחָד,
הַמְיַחֲדִים שִׁמְךָ, יהוה אֱלֹהֵינוּ יהוה אֶחָד.[3]

Ephraim and Menasseh (Ibn Ezra); and the
Northern Kingdom was called Ephraim

[and also Joseph] for the tribe of its first king
(Radak).

ה May He herald our portion, and set our flitting eyes straight,
  and speak charitably about the people borne by the eagle.[1]

ק Chazzan – Holy ones on high, Seraphim and Ofanim
   [of the Heavenly Chariot],
  cast our supplications[2] before the Lord of lords!
  May He remember our ancestors' merit
  and the Patriarchs who loved Him,
  and fulfill the oath [he swore to them], in these latter generations.

All:

מַכְנִיסֵי רַחֲמִים O you who usher in [pleas for] mercy, may you usher
                    in our [plea for] mercy, before the Master of mercy. O
you who cause prayer to be heard, may you cause our prayer to be heard,
before the Hearer of prayer. O you who cause outcry to be heard, may you
cause our outcry to be heard, before the Hearer of outcry. O you who
usher in tears, may you usher in our tears, before the King Who finds
favor through tears.

Exert yourselves, and multiply supplication and petition, before the
King, God, exalted and most high. Mention before Him, cause to be heard
before Him, the Torah and the good deeds of [the Patriarchs and Matri-
archs] who dwell in the dust.

May He remember their love and grant life to [their] offspring, that the
remnant of Jacob not be lost. For the flock of the faithful shepherd [Moses]
has become a disgrace; Israel, the unique nation, a parable and a simile.

Speedily, answer us, O God of our salvation, and redeem us from all
harsh decrees; and may You save, in Your abundant mercy, Your righteous anointed and Your people.

מָרָן דְּבִשְׁמַיָּא Our Master Who is in heaven, to You do we supplicate,
                  as a captive supplicates before his captors; for all cap-
tives are redeemed with money, but Your people Israel with compassion
and supplication. O grant our requests and our prayers that we not be
turned away from You empty-handed.

Our Master Who is in heaven, to You do we supplicate, as a slave
supplicates before his master: We are oppressed and we abide in darkness, souls embittered from abundant distress. We have no strength to
regain Your favor. Our Master, act for the sake of the covenant that You
made with our Patriarchs.

שׁוֹמֵר יִשְׂרָאֵל O Guardian of Israel, protect the remnant of Israel; let
                  not Israel be destroyed — those who proclaim, 'Hear O
                  Israel.'[3]

O Guardian of the unique nation, protect the remnant of the unique
people; let not the unique nation be destroyed — those who proclaim
the Oneness of Your Name, 'HASHEM is our God, HASHEM, the One and
Only!'[3]

---

(1) Cf. *Exodus* 19:4. (2) Some editions read הַשְׁמִיעֵנוּ תְּפִלּוֹתֵנוּ,
cause our prayers to be heard. (3) *Deuteronomy* 6:4.

שׁוֹמֵר גּוֹי קָדוֹשׁ, שְׁמוֹר שְׁאֵרִית עַם קָדוֹשׁ, וְאַל יֹאבַד גּוֹי קָדוֹשׁ,
הַמְשַׁלְּשִׁים בְּשָׁלֹשׁ קְדֻשּׁוֹת לְקָדוֹשׁ.

מִתְרַצֶּה בְּרַחֲמִים וּמִתְפַּיֵּס בְּתַחֲנוּנִים, הִתְרַצֵּה וְהִתְפַּיֵּס לְדוֹר
עָנִי, כִּי אֵין עוֹזֵר. אָבִינוּ מַלְכֵּנוּ, חָנֵּנוּ וַעֲנֵנוּ, כִּי אֵין בָּנוּ מַעֲשִׂים,
עֲשֵׂה עִמָּנוּ צְדָקָה וָחֶסֶד וְהוֹשִׁיעֵנוּ.

וַאֲנַחְנוּ לֹא נֵדַע מַה נַּעֲשֶׂה, כִּי עָלֶיךָ עֵינֵינוּ.[1] זְכֹר רַחֲמֶיךָ
יהוה וַחֲסָדֶיךָ, כִּי מֵעוֹלָם הֵמָּה.[2] יְהִי חַסְדְּךָ יהוה עָלֵינוּ,
כַּאֲשֶׁר יִחַלְנוּ לָךְ.[3]

אַל תִּזְכָּר לָנוּ עֲוֹנוֹת רִאשׁוֹנִים, מַהֵר יְקַדְּמוּנוּ רַחֲמֶיךָ, כִּי
דַלּוֹנוּ מְאֹד.[4] חָנֵּנוּ יהוה חָנֵּנוּ, כִּי רַב שָׂבַעְנוּ בוּז.[5]
בְּרֹגֶז רַחֵם תִּזְכּוֹר.[6] כִּי הוּא יָדַע יִצְרֵנוּ, זָכוּר כִּי עָפָר אֲנָחְנוּ.[7] עָזְרֵנוּ
אֱלֹהֵי יִשְׁעֵנוּ עַל דְּבַר כְּבוֹד שְׁמֶךָ, וְהַצִּילֵנוּ וְכַפֵּר עַל חַטֹּאתֵינוּ
לְמַעַן שְׁמֶךָ.[8]

קַדִּישׁ שָׁלֵם
The chazzan recites קַדִּישׁ שָׁלֵם:

יִתְגַּדַּל וְיִתְקַדַּשׁ שְׁמֵהּ רַבָּא. (.Cong – אָמֵן.) בְּעָלְמָא דִּי בְרָא
כִרְעוּתֵהּ, וְיַמְלִיךְ מַלְכוּתֵהּ, בְּחַיֵּיכוֹן וּבְיוֹמֵיכוֹן וּבְחַיֵּי דְכָל
בֵּית יִשְׂרָאֵל, בַּעֲגָלָא וּבִזְמַן קָרִיב. וְאִמְרוּ אָמֵן.
(.Cong – אָמֵן. יְהֵא שְׁמֵהּ רַבָּא מְבָרַךְ לְעָלַם וּלְעָלְמֵי עָלְמַיָּא.)
יְהֵא שְׁמֵהּ רַבָּא מְבָרַךְ לְעָלַם וּלְעָלְמֵי עָלְמַיָּא.
יִתְבָּרַךְ וְיִשְׁתַּבַּח וְיִתְפָּאַר וְיִתְרוֹמַם וְיִתְנַשֵּׂא וְיִתְהַדָּר וְיִתְעַלֶּה וְיִתְהַלָּל
שְׁמֵהּ דְּקוּדְשָׁא בְּרִיךְ הוּא (.Cong – בְּרִיךְ הוּא.) לְעֵלָּא [וּ]לְעֵלָּא מִכָּל
בִּרְכָתָא וְשִׁירָתָא תֻּשְׁבְּחָתָא וְנֶחֱמָתָא, דַּאֲמִירָן בְּעָלְמָא. וְאִמְרוּ: אָמֵן.
(.Cong – אָמֵן.)
(.Cong – קַבֵּל בְּרַחֲמִים וּבְרָצוֹן אֶת תְּפִלָּתֵנוּ.)
תִּתְקַבֵּל צְלוֹתְהוֹן וּבָעוּתְהוֹן דְּכָל (בֵּית) יִשְׂרָאֵל קֳדָם אֲבוּהוֹן דִּי
בִשְׁמַיָּא. וְאִמְרוּ אָמֵן. (.Cong – אָמֵן.)
(.Cong – יְהִי שֵׁם יהוה מְבֹרָךְ, מֵעַתָּה וְעַד עוֹלָם.[9])
יְהֵא שְׁלָמָא רַבָּא מִן שְׁמַיָּא וְחַיִּים עָלֵינוּ וְעַל כָּל יִשְׂרָאֵל. וְאִמְרוּ אָמֵן
(.Cong – אָמֵן.)
(.Cong – עֶזְרִי מֵעִם יהוה, עֹשֵׂה שָׁמַיִם וָאָרֶץ.[10])

Take three steps back. Bow left and say, . . . עֹשֶׂה; bow right and say, . . . הוּא יַעֲשֶׂה; bow forward and say,
וְעַל כָּל . . . אָמֵן. Remain standing in place for a few moments, then take three steps forward.

עֹשֶׂה [הַ]שָׁלוֹם בִּמְרוֹמָיו, הוּא יַעֲשֶׂה שָׁלוֹם עָלֵינוּ, וְעַל כָּל יִשְׂרָאֵל.
וְאִמְרוּ אָמֵן. (.Cong – אָמֵן.)

O Guardian of the holy nation, protect the remnant of the holy people; let not the holy nation be destroyed — those who proclaim three-fold sanctifications to the Holy One.

Become favorable through compassion and become appeased through supplications. Become favorable and appeased to the poor generation, for there is no helper. Our Father, our King, be gracious with us and answer us, though we have no worthy deeds; treat us with charity and kindness, and save us.

וַאֲנַחְנוּ We know not what to do — but our eyes are upon You.[1] Remember Your mercies, HASHEM, and Your kindnesses, for they are from the beginning of the world.[2] May Your kindness be upon us, HASHEM, just as we awaited You.[3]

אַל תִּזְכָּר Recall not against us the iniquities of the ancients; may Your mercies meet us swiftly, for we have become exceedingly impoverished.[4] Be gracious to us, HASHEM, be gracious to us, for we are abundantly sated with scorn.[5] Amid rage — remember to be merciful![6] For He knew our nature, He remembers that we are dust.[7] Chazzan— Assist us, O God of our salvation, for the sake of Your Name's glory; rescue us and atone for our sins for Your Name's sake.[8]

FULL KADDISH

The chazzan recites the Full Kaddish:

יִתְגַּדַּל May His great Name grow exalted and sanctified (Cong. — Amen.) in the world that He created as He willed. May He give reign to His kingship in your lifetimes and in your days, and in the lifetimes of the entire Family of Israel, swiftly and soon. Now respond: Amen.

(Cong. — Amen. May His great Name be blessed forever and ever.)
May His great Name be blessed forever and ever.

Blessed, praised, glorified, exalted, extolled, mighty, upraised and lauded be the Name of the Holy One, Blessed is He (Cong. — Blessed is He.) exceedingly beyond any blessing and song, praise, and consolation that are uttered in the world. Now respond: Amen. (Cong. — Amen.)

(Cong. — Accept our prayers with mercy and favor.)
May the prayers and supplications of the entire House of Israel be accepted before their Father Who is in Heaven. Now respond: Amen. (Cong. — Amen.)

(Cong. — Blessed be the Name of HASHEM from this time and forever.[9])
May there be abundant peace from Heaven, and life, upon us and upon all Israel. Now respond: Amen. (Cong. — Amen.)

(Cong. — My help is from HASHEM, Maker of heaven and earth.[10])

Take three steps back. Bow left and say, 'He Who makes peace . . .'; bow right and say, 'may He make peace . . .'; bow forward and say, 'and upon all Israel . . .'
Remain standing in place for a few moments, then take three steps forward.

He Who makes peace in His heights, may He make peace upon us, and upon all Israel. Now respond: Amen. (Cong. — Amen.)

---

(1) II Chronicles 20:12. (2) Psalms 25:6. (3) 33:22. (4) 79:8. (5) 123:3.
(6) Habakkuk 3:2. (7) Psalms 103:14. (8) 79:9. (9) 113:2. (10) 121:2.

﷽ יום שלישי של עשרת ימי תשובה ﷽

אַשְׁרֵי יוֹשְׁבֵי בֵיתֶךָ, עוֹד יְהַלְלוּךָ סֶּלָה.[1] אַשְׁרֵי הָעָם שֶׁכָּכָה לּוֹ, אַשְׁרֵי הָעָם שֶׁיהוה אֱלֹהָיו.[2]

תְּהִלָּה לְדָוִד,

תהלים קמה

אֲרוֹמִמְךָ אֱלוֹהַי הַמֶּלֶךְ, וַאֲבָרְכָה שִׁמְךָ לְעוֹלָם וָעֶד.

בְּכָל יוֹם אֲבָרְכֶךָּ, וַאֲהַלְלָה שִׁמְךָ לְעוֹלָם וָעֶד.

גָּדוֹל יהוה וּמְהֻלָּל מְאֹד, וְלִגְדֻלָּתוֹ אֵין חֵקֶר.

דּוֹר לְדוֹר יְשַׁבַּח מַעֲשֶׂיךָ, וּגְבוּרֹתֶיךָ יַגִּידוּ.

הֲדַר כְּבוֹד הוֹדֶךָ, וְדִבְרֵי נִפְלְאֹתֶיךָ אָשִׂיחָה.

וֶעֱזוּז נוֹרְאֹתֶיךָ יֹאמֵרוּ, וּגְדֻלָּתְךָ אֲסַפְּרֶנָּה.

זֵכֶר רַב טוּבְךָ יַבִּיעוּ, וְצִדְקָתְךָ יְרַנֵּנוּ.

חַנּוּן וְרַחוּם יהוה, אֶרֶךְ אַפַּיִם וּגְדָל חָסֶד.

טוֹב יהוה לַכֹּל, וְרַחֲמָיו עַל כָּל מַעֲשָׂיו.

יוֹדוּךָ יהוה כָּל מַעֲשֶׂיךָ, וַחֲסִידֶיךָ יְבָרְכוּכָה.

כְּבוֹד מַלְכוּתְךָ יֹאמֵרוּ, וּגְבוּרָתְךָ יְדַבֵּרוּ.

לְהוֹדִיעַ לִבְנֵי הָאָדָם גְּבוּרֹתָיו, וּכְבוֹד הֲדַר מַלְכוּתוֹ.

מַלְכוּתְךָ מַלְכוּת כָּל עֹלָמִים, וּמֶמְשַׁלְתְּךָ בְּכָל דּוֹר וָדֹר.

סוֹמֵךְ יהוה לְכָל הַנֹּפְלִים, וְזוֹקֵף לְכָל הַכְּפוּפִים.

עֵינֵי כֹל אֵלֶיךָ יְשַׂבֵּרוּ, וְאַתָּה נוֹתֵן לָהֶם אֶת אָכְלָם בְּעִתּוֹ.

פּוֹתֵחַ אֶת יָדֶךָ, וּמַשְׂבִּיעַ לְכָל חַי רָצוֹן.

Concentrate intently while
reciting the verse, פּוֹתֵחַ.

❖ **צַדִּיק** יהוה בְּכָל דְּרָכָיו, וְחָסִיד בְּכָל מַעֲשָׂיו.

קָרוֹב יהוה לְכָל קֹרְאָיו, לְכֹל אֲשֶׁר יִקְרָאֻהוּ בֶאֱמֶת.

רְצוֹן יְרֵאָיו יַעֲשֶׂה, וְאֶת שַׁוְעָתָם יִשְׁמַע וְיוֹשִׁיעֵם.

שׁוֹמֵר יהוה אֶת כָּל אֹהֲבָיו, וְאֵת כָּל הָרְשָׁעִים יַשְׁמִיד.

תְּהִלַּת יהוה יְדַבֶּר פִּי, וִיבָרֵךְ כָּל בָּשָׂר שֵׁם קָדְשׁוֹ לְעוֹלָם וָעֶד.

וַאֲנַחְנוּ נְבָרֵךְ יָהּ, מֵעַתָּה וְעַד עוֹלָם, הַלְלוּיָהּ.[3]

The chazzan recites חֲצִי קַדִּישׁ.

יִתְגַּדַּל וְיִתְקַדַּשׁ שְׁמֵהּ רַבָּא. (.Cong — אָמֵן.) בְּעָלְמָא דִּי בְרָא כִרְעוּתֵהּ,
וְיַמְלִיךְ מַלְכוּתֵהּ, בְּחַיֵּיכוֹן וּבְיוֹמֵיכוֹן וּבְחַיֵּי דְכָל בֵּית יִשְׂרָאֵל,
בַּעֲגָלָא וּבִזְמַן קָרִיב. וְאִמְרוּ: אָמֵן.

(.Cong — אָמֵן. יְהֵא שְׁמֵהּ רַבָּא מְבָרַךְ לְעָלַם וּלְעָלְמֵי עָלְמַיָּא.)

יְהֵא שְׁמֵהּ רַבָּא מְבָרַךְ לְעָלַם וּלְעָלְמֵי עָלְמַיָּא.

יִתְבָּרַךְ וְיִשְׁתַּבַּח וְיִתְפָּאַר וְיִתְרוֹמַם וְיִתְנַשֵּׂא וְיִתְהַדָּר וְיִתְעַלֶּה וְיִתְהַלָּל
שְׁמֵהּ דְּקֻדְשָׁא בְּרִיךְ הוּא (.Cong — בְּרִיךְ הוּא.) לְעֵלָּא [וּ]לְעֵלָּא מִכָּל בִּרְכָתָא
וְשִׁירָתָא תֻּשְׁבְּחָתָא וְנֶחֱמָתָא, דַּאֲמִירָן בְּעָלְמָא. וְאִמְרוּ: אָמֵן. (.Cong — אָמֵן.)

ᵛᴸ THIRD DAY OF REPENTANCE ᴵᵉ

אַשְׁרֵי *Praiseworthy are those who dwell in Your house; may they always praise You, Selah!*[1] *Praiseworthy is the people for whom this is so, praiseworthy is the people whose God is HASHEM.*[2]

Psalm 145   *A psalm of praise by David:*

א *I will exalt You, my God the King, and I will bless Your Name forever and ever.*

ב *Every day I will bless You, and I will laud Your Name forever and ever.*

ג *HASHEM is great and exceedingly lauded,*
    and His greatness is beyond investigation.

ד *Each generation will praise Your deeds to the next*
    and of Your mighty deeds they will tell;

ה *The splendrous glory of Your power and Your wondrous deeds I shall discuss.*

ו *And of Your awesome power they will speak, and Your greatness I shall relate.*

ז *A recollection of Your abundant goodness they will utter*
    and of Your righteousness they will sing exultantly.

ח *Gracious and merciful is HASHEM,*
    slow to anger, and great in [bestowing] kindness.

ט *HASHEM is good to all; His mercies are on all His works.*

י *All Your works shall thank You, HASHEM, and Your devout ones will bless You.*

כ *Of the glory of Your kingdom they will speak, and of Your power they will tell;*

ל *To inform human beings of His mighty deeds,*
    and the glorious splendor of His kingdom.

מ *Your kingdom is a kingdom spanning all eternities,*
    and Your dominion is throughout every generation.

ס *HASHEM supports all the fallen ones and straightens all the bent.*

ע *The eyes of all look to You with hope*
    and You give them their food in its proper time;

פ *You open Your hand,*   Concentrate intently while reciting the verse, 'You open. . .'
    and satisfy the desire of every living thing.

צ Chazzan— *Righteous is HASHEM in all His ways*
    and magnanimous in all His deeds.

ק *HASHEM is close to all who call upon Him — to all who call upon Him sincerely.*

ר *The will of those who fear Him He will do;*
    and their cry He will hear, and save them.

ש *HASHEM protects all who love Him; but all the wicked He will destroy.*

ת *May my mouth declare the praise of HASHEM*
    and may all flesh bless His Holy Name forever and ever.

We will bless God from this time and forever, Halleluyah![3]

The *chazzan* recites *Half-Kaddish:*

יִתְגַּדַּל *May His great Name grow exalted and sanctified* (Cong.— *Amen.*) *in the world that He created as He willed. May He give reign to His kingship in your lifetimes and in your days, and in the lifetimes of the entire Family of Israel, swiftly and soon. Now respond: Amen.*

(Cong.— *Amen. May His great Name be blessed forever and ever.*)
May His great Name be blessed forever and ever.

Blessed, praised, glorified, exalted, extolled, mighty, upraised, and lauded be the Name of the Holy One, Blessed is He (Cong.— *Blessed is He*) — *exceedingly beyond any blessing and song, praise and consolation that are uttered in the world. Now respond: Amen.* (Cong.— *Amen.*)

---

(1) *Psalms* 84:5. (2) 144:15. (3) 115:18.

All:

לְךָ יהוה הַצְּדָקָה, וְלָנוּ בְּשֶׁת הַפָּנִים.[1] מַה נִּתְאוֹנֵן,[2] מַה נֹּאמַר, מַה נְּדַבֵּר, וּמַה נִּצְטַדָּק.[3] נַחְפְּשָׂה דְרָכֵינוּ וְנַחְקְרָה, וְנָשׁוּבָה אֵלֶיךָ,[4] כִּי יְמִינְךָ פְּשׁוּטָה לְקַבֵּל שָׁבִים. לֹא בְחֶסֶד וְלֹא בְמַעֲשִׂים בָּאנוּ לְפָנֶיךָ, כְּדַלִּים וּכְרָשִׁים דָּפַקְנוּ דְלָתֶיךָ. דְּלָתֶיךָ דָּפַקְנוּ רַחוּם וְחַנּוּן, נָא אַל תְּשִׁיבֵנוּ רֵיקָם מִלְּפָנֶיךָ. מִלְּפָנֶיךָ מַלְכֵּנוּ רֵיקָם אַל תְּשִׁיבֵנוּ, כִּי אַתָּה שׁוֹמֵעַ תְּפִלָּה.

שֹׁמֵעַ תְּפִלָּה, עָדֶיךָ כָּל בָּשָׂר יָבֹאוּ.[5] יָבוֹא כָל בָּשָׂר לְהִשְׁתַּחֲוֹת לְפָנֶיךָ יהוה.[6] יָבֹאוּ וְיִשְׁתַּחֲווּ לְפָנֶיךָ אֲדֹנָי, וִיכַבְּדוּ לִשְׁמֶךָ.[7] בֹּאוּ נִשְׁתַּחֲוֶה וְנִכְרָעָה, נִבְרְכָה לִפְנֵי יהוה עֹשֵׂנוּ.[8] נָבוֹאָה לְמִשְׁכְּנוֹתָיו, נִשְׁתַּחֲוֶה לַהֲדֹם רַגְלָיו.[9] בֹּאוּ שְׁעָרָיו בְּתוֹדָה, חֲצֵרֹתָיו בִּתְהִלָּה, הוֹדוּ לוֹ בָּרְכוּ שְׁמוֹ.[10] רוֹמְמוּ יהוה אֱלֹהֵינוּ, וְהִשְׁתַּחֲווּ לַהֲדֹם רַגְלָיו, קָדוֹשׁ הוּא.[11] רוֹמְמוּ יהוה אֱלֹהֵינוּ, וְהִשְׁתַּחֲווּ לְהַר קָדְשׁוֹ, כִּי קָדוֹשׁ יהוה אֱלֹהֵינוּ.[12] הִשְׁתַּחֲווּ לַיהוה בְּהַדְרַת קֹדֶשׁ, חִילוּ מִפָּנָיו כָּל הָאָרֶץ.[13] וַאֲנַחְנוּ בְּרֹב חַסְדְּךָ נָבוֹא בֵיתֶךָ, נִשְׁתַּחֲוֶה אֶל הֵיכַל קָדְשְׁךָ בְּיִרְאָתֶךָ.[14] נִשְׁתַּחֲוֶה אֶל הֵיכַל קָדְשְׁךָ וְנוֹדֶה אֶת שְׁמֶךָ, עַל חַסְדְּךָ וְעַל אֲמִתֶּךָ, כִּי הִגְדַּלְתָּ עַל כָּל שִׁמְךָ אִמְרָתֶךָ.[15] לְכוּ נְרַנְּנָה לַיהוה, נָרִיעָה לְצוּר יִשְׁעֵנוּ. נְקַדְּמָה פָנָיו בְּתוֹדָה, בִּזְמִרוֹת נָרִיעַ לוֹ.[16] אֲשֶׁר יַחְדָּו נַמְתִּיק סוֹד, בְּבֵית אֱלֹהִים נְהַלֵּךְ בְּרָגֶשׁ.[17] אֵל נַעֲרָץ בְּסוֹד קְדֹשִׁים רַבָּה, וְנוֹרָא עַל כָּל סְבִיבָיו.[18] שְׂאוּ יְדֵיכֶם קֹדֶשׁ וּבָרְכוּ אֶת יהוה.[19] הִנֵּה בָּרְכוּ אֶת יהוה כָּל עַבְדֵי יהוה, הָעֹמְדִים בְּבֵית יהוה בַּלֵּילוֹת.[20] אֲשֶׁר מִי אֵל בַּשָּׁמַיִם וּבָאָרֶץ, אֲשֶׁר יַעֲשֶׂה כְמַעֲשֶׂיךָ וְכִגְבוּרֹתֶיךָ.[21] אֲשֶׁר לוֹ הַיָּם וְהוּא עָשָׂהוּ, וְיַבֶּשֶׁת יָדָיו יָצָרוּ.[22] אֲשֶׁר בְּיָדוֹ מֶחְקְרֵי אָרֶץ, וְתוֹעֲפוֹת הָרִים לוֹ.[23] אֲשֶׁר בְּיָדוֹ נֶפֶשׁ כָּל חָי, וְרוּחַ כָּל בְּשַׂר אִישׁ.[24] וְיוֹדוּ שָׁמַיִם פִּלְאֲךָ יהוה, אַף אֱמוּנָתְךָ בִּקְהַל קְדֹשִׁים.[25] לְךָ זְרוֹעַ עִם גְּבוּרָה, תָּעֹז יָדְךָ תָּרוּם יְמִינֶךָ.[26] לְךָ שָׁמַיִם, אַף לְךָ אָרֶץ, תֵּבֵל וּמְלֹאָהּ אַתָּה יְסַדְתָּם.[27] אַתָּה פוֹרַרְתָּ בְעָזְּךָ יָם, שִׁבַּרְתָּ רָאשֵׁי תַנִּינִים עַל הַמָּיִם.[28] אַתָּה הִצַּבְתָּ כָּל גְּבוּלוֹת אָרֶץ, קַיִץ וָחֹרֶף אַתָּה יְצַרְתָּם.[29] אַתָּה רִצַּצְתָּ רָאשֵׁי לִוְיָתָן, תִּתְּנֶנּוּ מַאֲכָל לְעָם לְצִיִּים.

---

(1) Daniel 9:7. (2) Cf. Lamentations 3:39. (3) Cf. Genesis 44:16. (4) Cf. Lamentations 3:40.
(5) Psalms 65:3. (6) Cf. Isaiah 66:23. (7) Psalms 86:9. (8) 95:6. (9) 132:7. (10) 100:4.
(11) 99:5. (12) 99:9. (13) 96:9. (14) Cf. 138:2. (15) 55:15. (18) 89:8.
(19) 134:2. (20) 134:1. (21) Deuteronomy 3:24. (22) Psalms 95:5. (23) 95:4. (24) Job 12:10.
(25) Psalms 89:6. (26) 89:14. (27) 89:12. (28) 74:13. (29) 74:17.

All:

לְךָ ה' Yours, my Lord, is the righteousness and ours is the shame-facedness.[1] What complaint can we make?[2] What can we say? What can we declare? What justification can we offer?[3] Let us examine our ways and analyze — and return to You,[4] for Your right hand is extended to accept penitents. Neither with kindness nor with [good] deeds do we come before You. As paupers and as beggars do we knock at Your doors. At Your doors we knock, O Compassionate and Gracious One. Please do not turn us away from You empty-handed. Our King, turn us not away from You empty-handed, for You are the One Who hears prayer.

שֹׁמֵעַ תְּפִלָּה You Who hears prayer, to You all flesh will come.[5] All flesh will come to prostrate itself before You, O HASHEM.[6] They will come and prostrate themselves before You, my Lord, and shall honor Your Name.[7] Come! — let us prostrate ourselves and bow, let us kneel before God, our Maker.[8] Let us come to His dwelling places, let us prostrate ourselves at His footstool.[9] Enter His gates with thanksgiving, His courts with praise; give thanks to Him, praise His Name.[10] Exalt HASHEM, our God, and bow at His footstool; He is holy![11] Exalt HASHEM, our God, and bow at His holy mountain; for holy is HASHEM, our God.[12] Prostrate yourselves before HASHEM in His intensely holy place, tremble before Him, everyone on earth.[13] As for us, through Your abundant kindness we will enter Your House; we will prostrate ourselves toward Your Holy Sanctuary in awe of You.[14] We will prostrate ourselves toward Your Holy Sanctuary, and we will give thanks to Your Name for Your kindness and truth for You have exalted Your promise even beyond Your Name.[15] Come! — let us sing to HASHEM, let us call out to the Rock of our salvation. Let us greet Him with thanksgiving, with praiseful songs let us call out to Him.[16] For together let us share sweet counsel, in the house of God let us walk in multitudes.[17] God is dreaded in the hiddenmost counsel of the holy ones, and inspires awe upon all who surround Him.[18] Lift your hands in the Sanctuary and bless HASHEM.[19] Behold, bless HASHEM, all you servants of HASHEM, who stand in the House of HASHEM in the nights.[20] For what power is there in heaven or earth that can approximate Your deeds and power?[21] For His is the sea and He perfected the dry land — His hands fashioned it.[22] For in His power are the hidden mysteries of the earth, and the mountain summits are His.[23] For His is the soul of every living thing, and the spirit of all human flesh.[24] Heaven will gratefully praise Your wonders, HASHEM; also Your faithfulness in the assembly of holy ones.[25] Yours is a mighty arm with power, You strengthen Your hand; You exalt Your right hand.[26] Yours is the heaven; Yours, too, is the earth; the world and its fullness — You founded them.[27] You shattered the sea with Your might, You smashed sea serpents' heads upon the water.[28] You established all the boundaries of earth; summer and winter — You fashioned them.[29] You crushed the heads of Leviathan, You served it as food to the nation of legions.

אַתָּה בָקַעְתָּ מַעְיָן וָנָחַל, אַתָּה הוֹבַשְׁתָּ נַהֲרוֹת אֵיתָן.[1] לְךָ יוֹם, אַף
לְךָ לָיְלָה, אַתָּה הֲכִינוֹתָ מָאוֹר וָשָׁמֶשׁ.[2] עָשָׂה גְדֹלוֹת עַד אֵין חֵקֶר,
וְנִפְלָאוֹת עַד אֵין מִסְפָּר.[3] כִּי אֵל גָּדוֹל יהוה, וּמֶלֶךְ גָּדוֹל עַל כָּל
אֱלֹהִים.[4] כִּי גָדוֹל אַתָּה וְעֹשֵׂה נִפְלָאוֹת, אַתָּה אֱלֹהִים לְבַדֶּךָ.[5] כִּי
גָדוֹל מֵעַל שָׁמַיִם חַסְדֶּךָ, וְעַד שְׁחָקִים אֲמִתֶּךָ.[6] גָּדוֹל יהוה וּמְהֻלָּל
מְאֹד, וְלִגְדֻלָּתוֹ אֵין חֵקֶר.[7] (כִּי) גָדוֹל יהוה וּמְהֻלָּל מְאֹד, נוֹרָא
הוּא עַל כָּל אֱלֹהִים.[8] גָּדוֹל יהוה וּמְהֻלָּל מְאֹד, בְּעִיר אֱלֹהֵינוּ הַר
קָדְשׁוֹ.[9] לְךָ יהוה הַגְּדֻלָּה וְהַגְּבוּרָה, וְהַתִּפְאֶרֶת וְהַנֵּצַח וְהַהוֹד, כִּי
כֹל בַּשָּׁמַיִם וּבָאָרֶץ; לְךָ יהוה הַמַּמְלָכָה, וְהַמִּתְנַשֵּׂא לְכֹל
לְרֹאשׁ.[10] מִי לֹא יִרָאֲךָ מֶלֶךְ הַגּוֹיִם, כִּי לְךָ יָאָתָה, כִּי בְכָל חַכְמֵי
הַגּוֹיִם וּבְכָל מַלְכוּתָם מֵאֵין כָּמוֹךָ.[11] מֵאֵין כָּמוֹךָ יהוה, גָּדוֹל אַתָּה
וְגָדוֹל שִׁמְךָ בִּגְבוּרָה.[12] יהוה אֱלֹהֵי צְבָאוֹת, מִי כָמוֹךָ חֲסִין יָהּ,
וֶאֱמוּנָתְךָ סְבִיבוֹתֶיךָ.[13] יהוה צְבָאוֹת, אֱלֹהֵי יִשְׂרָאֵל, יוֹשֵׁב
הַכְּרֻבִים, אַתָּה הוּא הָאֱלֹהִים לְבַדֶּךָ.[14] מִי יְמַלֵּל גְּבוּרוֹת יהוה,
יַשְׁמִיעַ כָּל תְּהִלָּתוֹ.[15] כִּי מִי בַשַּׁחַק יַעֲרֹךְ לַיהוה, יִדְמֶה לַיהוה
בִּבְנֵי אֵלִים.[16] מַה נֹּאמַר לְפָנֶיךָ לֹא מֶצַח לְהָרִים רֹאשׁ, כִּי
שָׁכֵן שְׁחָקִים. מַה נֹּאמַר לְפָנֶיךָ יהוה אֱלֹהֵינוּ, מַה נְּדַבֵּר וּמַה
נִּצְטַדָּק.[17] אֵין לָנוּ פֶּה לְהָשִׁיב וְלֹא מֶצַח לְהָרִים רֹאשׁ, כִּי
עֲוֹנוֹתֵינוּ רַבּוּ מִלִּמְנוֹת, וְחַטֹּאתֵינוּ עָצְמוּ מִסַּפֵּר.[18] לְמַעַן שִׁמְךָ
יהוה תְּחַיֵּנוּ, וּבְצִדְקָתְךָ תּוֹצִיא מִצָּרָה נַפְשֵׁנוּ.[19] דַּרְכְּךָ אֱלֹהֵינוּ
לְהַאֲרִיךְ אַפֶּךָ, לָרָעִים וְלַטּוֹבִים, וְהִיא תְהִלָּתֶךָ. לְמַעַנְךָ אֱלֹהֵינוּ
עֲשֵׂה וְלֹא לָנוּ, רְאֵה עֲמִידָתֵנוּ, דַּלִּים וְרֵקִים. ❖ הַנְּשָׁמָה לְךָ וְהַגּוּף
פָּעֳלָךְ, חוּסָה עַל עֲמָלָךְ. הַנְּשָׁמָה לָךְ וְהַגּוּף שֶׁלָּךְ, יהוה עֲשֵׂה
לְמַעַן שְׁמֶךָ. אָתָאנוּ עַל שִׁמְךָ, יהוה, עֲשֵׂה לְמַעַן שְׁמֶךָ. בַּעֲבוּר
כְּבוֹד שִׁמְךָ, כִּי אֵל חַנּוּן וְרַחוּם שְׁמֶךָ. לְמַעַן שִׁמְךָ יהוה, וְסָלַחְתָּ
לַעֲוֹנֵנוּ כִּי רַב הוּא.[20]

Congregation, then *chazzan:*

סְלַח לָנוּ אָבִינוּ, כִּי בְרוֹב אִוַּלְתֵּנוּ שָׁגִינוּ,
מְחַל לָנוּ מַלְכֵּנוּ, כִּי רַבּוּ עֲוֹנֵינוּ.

(1) *Psalms* 74:14-15. (2) 74:16. (3) *Job* 9:10. (4) *Psalms* 95:3. (5) 86:10. (6) 108:5.
(7) 145:3. (8) 96:4. (9) 48:2. (10) *I Chronicles* 29:11. (11) *Jeremiah* 10:7. (12) 10:6.
(13) *Psalms* 89:9. (14) *Isaiah* 37:16. (15) *Psalms* 106:2. (16) 89:7.
(17) Cf. *Genesis* 44:16. (18) Cf. *Ezra* 9:6. (19) Cf. *Psalms* 143:11. (20) Cf. 25:11.

You split open fountain and stream, You dried the mighty rivers.[1] Yours is the day, Yours as well is the night; You established luminary and the sun.[2] Who performs great deeds that are beyond comprehension, and wonders beyond number.[3] For a great God is HASHEM, and a great King above all heavenly powers.[4] For You are great and work wonders; You alone, O God.[5] For great above the very heavens is Your kindness, and until the upper heights is Your truth.[6] HASHEM is great and exceedingly lauded, and His greatness is beyond investigation.[7] (For) HASHEM is great and exceedingly lauded, awesome is He above all heavenly powers.[8] Great is HASHEM and exceedingly lauded, in the city of our God, Mount of His Holiness.[9] Yours, HASHEM, is the greatness, the strength, the splendor, the triumph, and the glory; even everything in heaven and earth; Yours, HASHEM, is the kingdom, and sovereignty over every leader.[10] Who would not revere You, O King of nations? — for this befits You, for among all the sages of the nations and in all their kingdom there is none like You.[11] There is none like You, O HASHEM, You are great and Your Name is great with power.[12] HASHEM, God of Legions — who is like You, O Strong One, God? — and Your faithfulness surrounds You.[13] HASHEM, Master of Legions, God of Israel, enthroned upon the Cherubim, it is You alone Who is God.[14] Who can express the mighty acts of HASHEM, who can announce all His praise?[15] For who in the sky can be compared to HASHEM; be likened to HASHEM among the angels?[16] What can we say before You Who dwell on high? And what can we relate to You Who abide in the highest heaven? What can we say before You, HASHEM, our God? What can we declare? What justification can we offer?[17] We have neither mouth to respond nor brow to raise our head, for our iniquities are too numerous to count, and our sins are too vast to be numbered.[18] For Your Name's sake, HASHEM, revive us; and with Your righteousness remove our soul from distress.[19] It is Your way, our God, to delay Your anger, against people both evil and good — and this is Your praise. Act for Your sake, our God, and not for ours, behold our [spiritual] position — destitute and empty-handed. Chazzan — The soul is Yours and the body is Your handiwork; take pity on Your labor. The soul is Yours and the body is Yours; O HASHEM, act for Your Name's sake. We have come with reliance on Your Name, O HASHEM, act for Your Name's sake; because of Your Name's glory — for 'Gracious and Merciful God' is Your Name. For Your Name's sake, HASHEM, may You forgive our iniquity, though it is abundant.[20]

Congregation, then chazzan:

Forgive us, our Father, for in our abundant folly we have erred, pardon us, our King, for our iniquities are many.

סליחה סט (פתיחה)

All:

(אֱלֹהֵינוּ וֵאלֹהֵי אֲבוֹתֵינוּ:)

שַׁחַרְנוּךְ בְּקַשְׁנוּךְ* יוֹצֵר הָרִים, **מַגִּיד לְאָדָם שִׂיחַ**¹ וּדְבָרִים,

וְחִלִּינוּךְ וּדְרַשְׁנוּךְ בּוֹשִׁים וַחֲפוּרִים,

אֶת חַטֹּאתֵינוּ הַיּוֹם² אָנוּ מְסַפְּרִים.

לְהָקְנוּ וַעֲדֵנוּ זְקֵנִים וּנְעָרִים, **בְּבֵית הַתְּפִלָּה מִקְדַּשׁ מְזֹעָרִים,**³

רְפוּיֵי יָדַיִם מְעוּדֵי אֲבָרִים, **בְּהוֹלִים וְסֹעֲרִים מִכָּל עֲבָרִים.**

יְגוֹרְנוּ וְדָאַגְנוּ מִשְּׁנֵי גוֹלְיָרִים, **אַף וְחֵמָה*⁴ שְׁנֵיהֶם קַטֵּגוֹרִים,**

בְּפִשְׁפְּשֵׁנוּ מַעֲשִׂים וְהִנָּם מְכֹעָרִים,

רֶתֶת אֲחָזַתְנוּ חֲבָלִים וְצִירִים.⁵

הֻשְׁחֲרוּ פָנֵינוּ וְהָלַכְנוּ קֹדְרִים,

מוֹט הִתְמוֹטַטְנוּ וְנַעֲשִׂינוּ פְרוּרִים,⁶

❖ חָלְחָלוּ מָתְנֵינוּ וְכַיּוֹלֵדָה מְצִירִים,⁷

זָחַלְנוּ וַנִּירָא מֵעֲוֹנוֹתֵינוּ הַיְתֵרִים,

קַחֵנוּ דְבָרִים בְּשָׁלוֹם פָּרִים,⁸

תְּמוּכִים בְּטוּחִים וּלְרַחֲמֶיךָ מְסַבְּרִים.

All:

כִּי עַל רַחֲמֶיךָ הָרַבִּים⁹ אָנוּ בְּטוּחִים, וְעַל צִדְקוֹתֶיךָ אָנוּ נִשְׁעָנִים, וְלִסְלִיחוֹתֶיךָ אָנוּ מְקַוִּים, וְלִישׁוּעָתְךָ אָנוּ מְצַפִּים. אַתָּה הוּא מֶלֶךְ, אוֹהֵב צְדָקוֹת מִקֶּדֶם, מַעֲבִיר עֲוֹנוֹת עַמּוֹ וּמֵסִיר חַטֹּאת יְרֵאָיו. כּוֹרֵת בְּרִית לָרִאשׁוֹנִים, וּמְקַיֵּם שְׁבוּעָה לָאַחֲרוֹנִים. אַתָּה הוּא, שֶׁיָּרַדְתָּ בֶּעָנָן כְּבוֹדֶךָ עַל הַר סִינַי,¹⁰ וְהֶרְאֵיתָ דַרְכֵי טוּבְךָ לְמֹשֶׁה עַבְדֶּךָ.¹¹ וְאָרְחוֹת חֲסָדֶיךָ גִּלִּיתָ לוֹ, וְהוֹדַעְתּוֹ כִּי אַתָּה אֵל רַחוּם וְחַנּוּן, אֶרֶךְ אַפַּיִם וְרַב חֶסֶד¹² וּמַרְבֶּה לְהֵטִיב, וּמַנְהִיג אֶת כָּל הָעוֹלָם כֻּלּוֹ בְּמִדַּת הָרַחֲמִים. ❖ וְכֵן כָּתוּב, וַיֹּאמֶר אֲנִי אַעֲבִיר כָּל טוּבִי עַל פָּנֶיךָ, וְקָרָאתִי בְשֵׁם יהוה לְפָנֶיךָ, וְחַנֹּתִי אֶת אֲשֶׁר אָחֹן, וְרִחַמְתִּי אֶת אֲשֶׁר אֲרַחֵם.¹³

שַׁחַרְנוּךְ בְּקַשְׁנוּךְ ❧ — *We have beseeched You, we have petitioned You.* The composer of this selichah signed his name — שְׁמוּאֵל בְּרַבִּי אַבְרָהָם חֲזַק, *Shmuel bar R' Avraham, may he be strong* — in the initial letters of the respective stiches. He is identified as R' Shmuel bar R' Avraham HaLevi Bonfant, a disciple of R' Simchah of Speyer of late-12th-early-13th-century Germany.

מַגִּיד לְאָדָם שִׂיחַ — *Who tells man what were [his] conversation* . . . When a person is brought before the Heavenly Tribunal for his final judgment, his entire life is paraded before him, even his casual conversations with his wife. Can one hope to save himself from retribution when his every

SELICHAH 69

All:

(*Our God and the God of our forefathers:*)

ש *We have beseeched You, we have petitioned You,**
     Maker of the mountains,
מ *Who tells man what were [his] conversation** [1] *and words;*
ו *we beseech You, we seek for You, shamed and abashed,*
א *for our sins that we relate today.* [2]
ל *We have assembled, gathered ourselves old and young*
ב *in the synagogue, the Miniature Temple,* [3]
ר *with weakened hands, faltering limbs,*
ב *panicked and agitated by [events on] all sides.*
י *We anxiously dread Your two minor angels*
א *Af and Cheimah** [4] *who are both accusers.*
ב *As we probe [our] deeds, we see they are reprehensible.*
ר *Wwe are seized with trembling, travail and pangs.* [5]
ה *Our faces are darkened, we walk in gloom,*
ם *We are utterly tottery and broken into fragments.* [6]
ח Chazzan — *Our loins shudder like a woman in birth pangs,* [7]
ז *we are scared and we fear because of our many sins.*
ק *We bring these words instead of bull-offerings,* [8]
     confident, trusting, and awaiting Your mercy.

All:

כִּי עַל *For upon Your abundant mercy* [9] *do we trust, and upon Your
righteousness do we depend, and for Your forgiveness do we
hope, and for Your salvation do we yearn. You are the King Who loves
righteousness since the earliest days, Who overlooks His people's
iniquities and sets aside the sins of those who revere Him. He made a
covenant with the ancestors and keeps [His] vow to the descendants. It
is You Who descended in Your cloud of glory on Mount Sinai,* [10] *and
showed the ways of Your goodness to Your servant Moses.* [11] *You revealed
Your paths of kindness to him, and let him know that You are God,
Compassionate and Gracious, Slow to anger and Abundant in Kindness,* [12] *doing manifold good, and guiding all Your world with the
Attribute of Mercy.* Chazzan — *And so it is written: He said, 'I shall pass
all My good in front of you, and I shall call out the Name of H*ASHEM *before
you; for I will be gracious to whom I will be gracious, and I will be
compassionate with whom I will be compassionate.'* [13]

---

(1) Cf. *Amos* 4:13. (2) Cf. *Genesis* 41:9. (3) See *Ezekiel* 11:16 with *Targum.*
(4) Cf. *Deuteronomy* 9:19. (5) Cf. *Isaiah* 13:8. (6) Cf. 24:19. (7) Cf. 21:3. (8) Cf. *Hosea* 14:3.
(9) *Daniel* 9:18. (10) Cf. *Exodus* 34:5. (11) Cf. 33:13. (12) 34:6. (13) 33:19.

word has been recorded and the testimony
against him is irrefutable? (*Chagigah* 5b, based on
Amos 4:13).

גּוּלְיָרִים אַף וְחֵמָה — *Minor angels Af and Cheimah.* The Midrash shows how Moses' relationship with the celestial beings changed after the

sin of the Golden Calf. At first even the arch-
angels Michael and Gabriel were unable to look
Moses in the face. But after Israel sinned, Moses
was unable to look directly at even the minor angels אַף וְחֵמָה, *Af and Cheimah* [lit., *Anger and
Fury*] (*Pesikta Rabbasi* 15:3).

All, while standing:

אֵל אֶרֶךְ אַפַּיִם אַתָּה, וּבַעַל הָרַחֲמִים נִקְרֵאתָ,
וְדֶרֶךְ תְּשׁוּבָה הוֹרֵיתָ.

גְּדֻלַּת רַחֲמֶיךָ וַחֲסָדֶיךָ, תִּזְכּוֹר הַיּוֹם וּבְכָל יוֹם לְזֶרַע יְדִידֶיךָ.
תֵּפֶן אֵלֵינוּ בְּרַחֲמִים, כִּי אַתָּה הוּא בַּעַל הָרַחֲמִים.
בְּתַחֲנוּן וּבִתְפִלָּה פָּנֶיךָ נְקַדֵּם, כְּהוֹדַעְתָּ לֶעָנָיו מִקֶּדֶם.
מֵחֲרוֹן אַפְּךָ שׁוּב,¹ כְּמוֹ בְתוֹרָתְךָ כָּתוּב.²
וּבְצֵל כְּנָפֶיךָ נֶחֱסֶה³ וְנִתְלוֹנָן, כְּיוֹם וַיֵּרֶד יהוה בֶּעָנָן.
❖ תַּעֲבוֹר עַל פֶּשַׁע וְתִמְחֶה אָשָׁם, כְּיוֹם וַיִּתְיַצֵּב עִמּוֹ שָׁם.
תַּאֲזִין שַׁוְעָתֵנוּ וְתַקְשִׁיב מֶנּוּ מַאֲמָר,
כְּיוֹם וַיִּקְרָא בְשֵׁם יהוה,⁴ וְשָׁם נֶאֱמַר:

Congregation, then *chazzan:*

וַיַּעֲבֹר יהוה עַל פָּנָיו וַיִּקְרָא:

Congregation and *chazzan* (the words in bold type are recited aloud and in unison):

יהוה, יהוה, **אֵל, רַחוּם, וְחַנּוּן, אֶרֶךְ אַפַּיִם, וְרַב חֶסֶד, וֶאֱמֶת,**
נֹצֵר חֶסֶד לָאֲלָפִים, נֹשֵׂא עָוֹן, וָפֶשַׁע, וְחַטָּאָה,
וְנַקֵּה.⁵ וְסָלַחְתָּ לַעֲוֹנֵנוּ וּלְחַטָּאתֵנוּ וּנְחַלְתָּנוּ.⁶ סְלַח לָנוּ אָבִינוּ כִּי
חָטָאנוּ, מְחַל לָנוּ מַלְכֵּנוּ כִּי פָשָׁעְנוּ. כִּי אַתָּה אֲדֹנָי טוֹב וְסַלָּח, וְרַב
חֶסֶד לְכָל קֹרְאֶיךָ.⁷

פְּסוּקֵי הַקְדָּמָה לִסְלִיחָה ע

אֵלֶיךָ יהוה שִׁוַּעְנוּ וּבַבֹּקֶר תְּפִלָּתֵנוּ תְקַדְּמֶךָּ.⁸ אֵלֶיךָ נָשָׂאנוּ אֶת
עֵינֵינוּ.⁹ נִשָּׂא לְבָבֵנוּ אֶל כַּפָּיִם, אֶל
אֵל בַּשָּׁמָיִם.¹⁰ אֱלֹהִים מַלְכֵּנוּ מִקֶּדֶם, פֹּעֵל יְשׁוּעוֹת בְּקֶרֶב
הָאָרֶץ.¹¹ אַתָּה הוּא מַלְכֵּנוּ אֱלֹהִים, צַוֵּה יְשׁוּעוֹת יַעֲקֹב.¹² הוֹשַׁע
יהוה אֶת עַמֶּךָ, אֵת שְׁאֵרִית יִשְׂרָאֵל.¹³ הוֹשִׁיעֵנוּ אֱלֹהֵי יִשְׁעֵנוּ,
וְקַבְּצֵנוּ וְהַצִּילֵנוּ מִן הַגּוֹיִם, לְהוֹדוֹת לְשֵׁם קָדְשֶׁךָ לְהִשְׁתַּבֵּחַ
בִּתְהִלָּתֶךָ.¹⁴

כְּרַחֵם אָב עַל בָּנִים, כֵּן תְּרַחֵם יהוה עָלֵינוּ.¹⁵ לַיהוה הַיְשׁוּעָה,
עַל עַמְּךָ בִרְכָתֶךָ סֶּלָה.¹⁶ יהוה צְבָאוֹת עִמָּנוּ,
מִשְׂגָּב לָנוּ אֱלֹהֵי יַעֲקֹב סֶלָה.¹⁷ יהוה צְבָאוֹת, אַשְׁרֵי אָדָם בֹּטֵחַ
בָּךְ.¹⁸ יהוה הוֹשִׁיעָה, הַמֶּלֶךְ יַעֲנֵנוּ בְיוֹם קָרְאֵנוּ.¹⁹

All, while standing:

אֵל אֶרֶךְ אַפַּיִם *O God — You are slow to anger, You are called the Master of Mercy, and You have taught the way of repentance. May You remember this day and every day the greatness of Your mercy and Your kindness to the offspring of Your beloved Ones. Turn to us in mercy for You are the Master of Mercy. With supplication and prayer we approach Your Presence in the manner that You made known to the humble [Moses] in ancient times. Turn back from Your fierce anger;[1] as is written in Your Torah.[2] In the shadow of Your wings may we find shelter[3] and lodging as on the day 'HASHEM descended in a cloud' [to appear to Moses on Sinai]. Chazzan — Overlook sin and erase guilt as on the day 'He [God] stood there with him [Moses].' Give heed to our cry and be attentive to our declaration as on the day 'He called out with the Name HASHEM,'[4] and there it was said:*

Congregation, then chazzan:

And HASHEM passed before him [Moses] and proclaimed:

Congregation and chazzan (the words in bold type are recited aloud and in unison):

ה' ה' **HASHEM, HASHEM, God, Compassionate and Gracious, Slow to anger, and Abundant in Kindness and Truth, Preserver of kindness for thousands [of generations], Forgiver of iniquity, willful sin, and error, and Who cleanses.**[5] *May You forgive our iniquities and our errors and make us Your heritage.*[6] *Forgive us, our Father, for we have erred; pardon us, our King, for we have willfully sinned; for You, my Lord, are good and forgiving and abundantly kind to all who call upon You.*[7]

PREFATORY VERSES TO SELICHAH 70

אֵלֶיךָ *To You, HASHEM, have we cried, and in the morning our prayer will greet You.*[8] *To You we raised our eyes, [O You] Who dwell in the heavens.*[9] *Let us lift our hearts with our hands, to God in Heaven.*[10] *God is our King from [days] of old, working salvations in the midst of the earth.*[11] *Only You are our King, O God; command the salvations of Jacob.*[12] *O HASHEM, save Your people, the remnant of Israel.*[13] *Save us, O God of our salvation, gather us and rescue us from the nations, to thank Your holy Name and to glory in Your praise.*[14]

כְּרַחֵם אָב *As a father has mercy on his children, so, HASHEM, may You have mercy on us.*[15] *Salvation is HASHEM's, upon Your people is Your blessing, Selah.*[16] *HASHEM, Master of Legions, is with us, a stronghold for us is the God of Jacob, Selah.*[17] *HASHEM, Master of Legions, praiseworthy is the person who trusts in You.*[18] *HASHEM, save! May the King answer us on the day we call.*[19]

---

(1) Cf. Exodus 32:12. (2) See 32:14. (3) Cf. Psalms 36:8. (4) Exodus 34:5. (5) 34:6-7. (6) 34:9. (7) Psalms 86:5. (8) Cf. 88:14. (9) Cf. 123:1. (10) Lamentations 3:41. (11) Cf. Psalms 74:12. (12) Cf. 44:5. (13) Jeremiah 31:6. (14) I Chronicles 16:35. (15) Cf. Psalms 103:13. (16) 3:9. (17) 46:8. (18) 84:13. (19) 20:10.

In some congregations the following two verses are recited responsively — the *chazzan* reciting סְלַח, and the congregation responding וַיֹאמֶר. In other congregations these verses are recited silently.

סְלַח נָא לַעֲוֹן הָעָם הַזֶּה כְּגֹדֶל חַסְדֶּךָ, וְכַאֲשֶׁר נָשָׂאתָה לָעָם הַזֶּה מִמִּצְרַיִם וְעַד הֵנָּה,[1] וְשָׁם נֶאֱמָר:

וַיֹּאמֶר יהוה סָלַחְתִּי כִּדְבָרֶךָ.[2]

All:

הַטֵּה אֱלֹהַי אָזְנְךָ וּשְׁמָע, פְּקַח עֵינֶיךָ וּרְאֵה שֹׁמְמֹתֵינוּ, וְהָעִיר אֲשֶׁר נִקְרָא שִׁמְךָ עָלֶיהָ, כִּי לֹא עַל צִדְקֹתֵינוּ אֲנַחְנוּ מַפִּילִים תַּחֲנוּנֵינוּ לְפָנֶיךָ, כִּי עַל רַחֲמֶיךָ הָרַבִּים. אֲדֹנָי שְׁמָעָה, אֲדֹנָי סְלָחָה, אֲדֹנָי הַקְשִׁיבָה, וַעֲשֵׂה אַל תְּאַחַר, לְמַעַנְךָ אֱלֹהַי, כִּי שִׁמְךָ נִקְרָא עַל עִירְךָ וְעַל עַמֶּךָ.[3]

סליחה ע

All:

אֱלֹהֵינוּ וֵאלֹהֵי אֲבוֹתֵינוּ:

אֵלֶיךָ הָאֵל עֵינֵי כָל יְצִיר תְּלוּיוֹת,*

בַּעַד כִּי לְפָנֶיךָ מְכֻסּוֹת גְּלוּיוֹת,

גְּדוֹל הָעֵצָה וְרַב הָעֲלִילִיּוֹת,[4]

דַּיָּן אֱמֶת וּמוֹכִיחַ, עֵד וּבַעַל דִּין לַבְּרִיּוֹת.[5]

הֵן אֵין לְפָנֶיךָ מַשּׂוֹא פָנִים,[5]

וְשֽׁוֹעַ וָדַל[6] בְּשָׁוֶה נִדּוֹנִים,

זַכִּיּוֹת תְּחַפֵּשׂ לְזֶרַע אֱמוּנִים,*

חֲמֹל עֲלֵיהֶם כְּרַחֵם אָב עַל בָּנִים.[7]

טְכַסְתָּ וְהִקְדַּמְתָּ תְּשׁוּבָה לִיצוּרִים,[8]

יַדְּוֹת רֹעַ מַעַשׂ וְלִבְרֹר מַעֲשִׂים הַבְּרוּרִים,

כְֹּחַ יֵצֶר רַע הַמֵּסִית וְהַמַּדִּיחַ מִנְּעוּרִים,[9]

לְמַעַנְךָ תַּדְּרִיכֵנוּ בְּלִי לְהַכְשִׁיל לֵב הָעֲצוּרִים.

מִלְּפָנֶיךָ כּוֹנֵן לָנוּ תְּשׁוּבָה שְׁלֵמָה,

נָאוֹר[10] בְּיָדְךָ חַדְרֵי רֽוּחַ וּנְשָׁמָה,

סַרְעַפֵּינוּ תְטַהֵר מֵחֵטְא וְאַשְׁמָה,

עָדֶיךָ לָשׁוּב בְּלִי עָוֶל וּמִרְמָה.

אֵלֶיךָ הָאֵל עֵינֵי כָל יְצִיר תְּלוּיוֹת — To You, O God, every creature's eyes are turned. The acrostic of the verses of this *selichah* forms the *aleph-beis*. The *paytan* signed his name — בִּנְיָמִן, Binyamin — in the penultimate stich [see prefatory comment to *selichah* 20].

In some congregations the following two verses are recited responsively — the *chazzan*
reciting, '*Forgive, please . . . ,*' and the congregation responding, '*And HASHEM said . . .*'
In other congregations these verses are recited silently.

סְלַח נָא *Forgive, please, the iniquity of this people according to the*
greatness of Your kindness and as You have forgiven this
people from Egypt until now,[1] *and there it was said:*

And HASHEM said, 'I have forgiven according to your word!'[2]

All:

הַטֵּה *Incline, my God, Your ear, and listen, open Your eyes and see our*
desolation and that of the city upon which Your Name is
proclaimed; for not because of our righteousness do we cast down our
supplications before You, rather because of Your abundant compassion.
O my Lord, heed; O my Lord, forgive; O my Lord, be attentive and act,
do not delay; for Your sake, my God, for Your Name is proclaimed upon
Your city and upon Your people.[3]

SELICHAH 70

All:

Our God and the God of our forefathers:

א *To You, O God, every creature's eyes are turned,**

ב *for before You secrets are revealed —*

ג *great in counsel, mighty in deeds,*[4]

ד *True Judge, Rebuker, Witness and Plaintiff of all creatures.*[5]

ה *For before You there are no favorites;*[5]

ו *rich and poor*[6] *are alike adjudged.*

ז *Search for merits for the offspring of [Your] faithful ones;**

ח *have mercy on them as a father has mercy on his children.*[7]

ט *Before there were creatures, You arranged and set repentance,*[8]

י *by which to discard bad deeds and choose flawless ones.*

כ *The Evil Inclination's power,*
that tempts and leads astray from youth,[9]

ל *for Your own sake, cast it out,*
that it no longer corrupt the hearts of the ensnared.

מ *Prepare before You whole-hearted repentance for us.*

נ *O Source of Light,*[10]
the chambers of [our] spirit and soul are in Your hand.

ס *Purify our thoughts from sin and fault,*

ע *[that we be able] to return to You without perversity or falsehood.*

---

(1) *Numbers* 14:19. (2) 14:20. (3) *Daniel* 9:18-19. (4) Cf. *Jeremiah* 32:19.
(5) Cf. *Mishnah Avos* 4:29. (6) Cf. *Job* 34:19. (7) *Psalms* 103:13. (8) See commentary to *selichah* 4,
s.v., כּוֹנַנְתָּ מֵאָז תֶּרֶף. (9) Cf. *Genesis* 8:21. (10) See commentary to *selichah* 18.

לְזֶרַע אֲמוּנִים — *For the offspring of [Your] faith-*
ful ones. We are the children of Abraham of
whom Scripture (*Nehemiah* 9:7-8) states: *You se-*
lected Abram, brought him out of Ur Kasdim and
made his name Abraham. And You found his
heart faithful before You (*Matteh Levi*). Alternatively: זֶרַע אֲמוּנִים means *the faithful offspring,*
i.e., Israel.

פְּלָאֶיךָ רַבִּים פְּלָאוֹת,   צִדְקוֹתֶיךָ צֶדֶק נוֹרָאוֹת,

קוֹרְאֶיךָ בְּחַיִל וּמוֹרָאוֹת,

רַחֵשׁם שְׁעֵה נָא וַעֲשֵׂה עִמָּהֶם לְטוֹבָה אוֹת.[1]

❖ שִׁחַרְנוּךָ קֹדֶם עַמּוּד הַשַּׁחַר,*

תָּאִיר לָנוּ פָנֶיךָ[2] כְּעַפְעַפֵּי שָׁחַר,[3]

בְּנוֹגְהֶךָ יָהִיל מָאוֹר נִשְׁקְפָה כְּמוֹ שָׁחַר,[4]

אֲדֹנָי שְׁמָעָה, אֲדֹנָי סְלָחָה, אֲדֹנָי הַקְשִׁיבָה וַעֲשֵׂה, אַל תְּאַחַר.[5]

All, while standing:

אֵל מֶלֶךְ יוֹשֵׁב עַל כִּסֵּא רַחֲמִים מִתְנַהֵג בַּחֲסִידוּת, מוֹחֵל
עֲוֹנוֹת עַמּוֹ, מַעֲבִיר רִאשׁוֹן רִאשׁוֹן, מַרְבֶּה מְחִילָה
לַחַטָּאִים וּסְלִיחָה לַפּוֹשְׁעִים, עֹשֶׂה צְדָקוֹת עִם כָּל בָּשָׂר וָרוּחַ,
לֹא כְרָעָתָם תִּגְמוֹל. ❖ אֵל הוֹרֵיתָ לָנוּ לוֹמַר שְׁלֹשׁ עֶשְׂרֵה, וּזְכוֹר
לָנוּ הַיּוֹם בְּרִית שְׁלֹשׁ עֶשְׂרֵה, כְּמוֹ שֶׁהוֹדַעְתָּ לֶעָנָיו מִקֶּדֶם, כְּמוֹ
שֶׁכָּתוּב, וַיֵּרֶד יהוה בֶּעָנָן וַיִּתְיַצֵּב עִמּוֹ שָׁם, וַיִּקְרָא בְשֵׁם יהוה.

Congregation, then chazzan:

וַיַּעֲבֹר יהוה עַל פָּנָיו וַיִּקְרָא:

Congregation and chazzan (the words in bold type are recited aloud and in unison):

יהוה, יהוה,   אֵל, רַחוּם, וְחַנּוּן, אֶרֶךְ אַפַּיִם, וְרַב חֶסֶד, וֶאֱמֶת,
נֹצֵר חֶסֶד לָאֲלָפִים, נֹשֵׂא עָוֹן, וָפֶשַׁע, וְחַטָּאָה,
וְנַקֵּה. וְסָלַחְתָּ לַעֲוֹנֵנוּ וּלְחַטָּאתֵנוּ וּנְחַלְתָּנוּ. סְלַח לָנוּ אָבִינוּ כִּי
חָטָאנוּ, מְחַל לָנוּ מַלְכֵּנוּ כִּי פָשָׁעְנוּ. כִּי אַתָּה אֲדֹנָי טוֹב וְסַלָּח,
וְרַב חֶסֶד לְכָל קֹרְאֶיךָ.

פסוקי הקדמה לסליחה עא

כְּאַיָּל תַּעֲרֹג עַל אֲפִיקֵי מָיִם, כֵּן נַפְשִׁי תַעֲרֹג אֵלֶיךָ אֱלֹהִים.[6]
אֱלֹהִים, זֵדִים קָמוּ עָלֵינוּ, וַעֲדַת עָרִיצִים בִּקְשׁוּ נַפְשֵׁנוּ,
וְלֹא שָׂמוּךָ לְנֶגְדָּם, סֶלָה.[7] אֲשֶׁר אָמְרוּ נִירָשָׁה לָּנוּ, אֵת נְאוֹת
אֱלֹהִים.[8] הַעַל אֵלֶּה תִתְאַפַּק יהוה, תֶּחֱשֶׁה וּתְעַנֵּנוּ עַד מְאֹד.[9]

כְּרַחֵם אָב עַל בָּנִים, כֵּן תְּרַחֵם יהוה עָלֵינוּ. לַיהוה הַיְשׁוּעָה,
עַל עַמְּךָ בִרְכָתֶךָ סֶּלָה. יהוה צְבָאוֹת עִמָּנוּ,
מִשְׂגָּב לָנוּ אֱלֹהֵי יַעֲקֹב סֶלָה. יהוה צְבָאוֹת, אַשְׁרֵי אָדָם בֹּטֵחַ בָּךְ.
יהוה הוֹשִׁיעָה, הַמֶּלֶךְ יַעֲנֵנוּ בְיוֹם קָרְאֵנוּ.

קֹדֶם עַמּוּד הַשַּׁחַר — *Before the first ray of dawn.* The ideal time for reciting the *Selichos* service is before dawn during the latter part of the night.

פ *Your wonders are abundantly wondrous;*
צ *Your righteous justice is awesomely just;*
ק *they call on You with trembling and fear —*
ר *please turn to their prayer and show them a sign for the good.*[1]
ש Chazzan — *We have beseeched You before the first ray of dawn.**
ת *Shine Your countenance upon us*[2] *like the twinkling of dawn.*[3]
In Your glow will shine [Redemption's] lamp,
  gleaming forth like the dawn[4] —
O my Lord, heed! O my Lord, forgive!
O my Lord, be attentive and act, do not delay![5]

All, while standing:

אֵל מֶלֶךְ O God, King Who sits on the throne of mercy; Who acts with
kindness, pardons the iniquities of His people, removes [sins]
one by one, increasingly grants pardon to careless sinners and forgiveness
to rebels, Who deals righteously with every living being — You do not repay
them in accord with their evil. Chazzan — O God, You taught us to recite the
Thirteen [Attributes of Mercy], so remember for us today the covenant of
these Thirteen, as You made known to the humble one in ancient times, as
it is written: And HASHEM descended in a cloud and stood with him there,
and He called out with the Name HASHEM.

Congregation, then *chazzan:*

And HASHEM passed before him [Moses] and proclaimed:

Congregation and *chazzan* (the words in bold type are recited aloud and in unison):

ה' ה' HASHEM, HASHEM, God, Compassionate and Gracious, Slow to
anger, and Abundant in Kindness and Truth, Preserver of
kindness for thousands [of generations], Forgiver of iniquity, willful
sin, and error, and Who cleanses. *May You forgive our iniquities and our
errors and make us Your heritage. Forgive us, our Father, for we have
erred; pardon us, our King, for we have willfully sinned; for You, my Lord,
are good and forgiving and abundantly kind to all who call upon You.*

PREFATORY VERSES TO SELICHAH 71

כְּאַיָּל *As a gazelle longs for springs of water, so does our soul long for
You, O God.*[6] *O God, wicked men have arisen against us, and a
company of ruthless men has sought our souls, and they have not set You
before them, Selah.*[7] *For they have said, 'We will take possession for
ourselves of God's pleasant habitations.'*[8] *Will You hold Yourself back
from these, HASHEM? Will You be silent and allow us to be tormented so?*[9]

כְּרַחֵם אָב *As a father has mercy on his children, so, HASHEM, may
You have mercy on us. Salvation is HASHEM's, upon Your
people is Your blessing, Selah. HASHEM, Master of Legions, is with us, a
stronghold for us is the God of Jacob, Selah. HASHEM, Master of Legions,
praiseworthy is the person who trusts in You. HASHEM, save! May the
King answer us on the day we call.*

---

(1) Cf. *Psalms* 86:17. (2) Cf. *Numbers* 6:25. (3) Cf. *Job* 3:9 [8]. (4) Cf. *Song of Songs* 6:10.
(5) *Daniel* 9:19. (6) Cf. *Psalms* 42:2. (7) Cf. 86:14. (8) 83:13. (9) *Isaiah* 64:11.

In some congregations the following two verses are recited responsively — the *chazzan* reciting סְלַח,
and the congregation responding וַיֹּאמֶר. In other congregations these verses are recited silently.

סְלַח נָא לַעֲוֹן הָעָם הַזֶּה כְּגֹדֶל חַסְדֶּךָ, וְכַאֲשֶׁר נָשָׂאתָה לָעָם
הַזֶּה מִמִּצְרַיִם וְעַד הֵנָּה, וְשָׁם נֶאֱמַר:

וַיֹּאמֶר יהוה סָלַחְתִּי כִּדְבָרֶךָ.

All:

הַטֵּה אֱלֹהַי אָזְנְךָ וּשְׁמָע, פְּקַח עֵינֶיךָ וּרְאֵה שֹׁמְמֹתֵינוּ, וְהָעִיר
אֲשֶׁר נִקְרָא שִׁמְךָ עָלֶיהָ, כִּי לֹא עַל צִדְקוֹתֵינוּ אֲנַחְנוּ
מַפִּילִים תַּחֲנוּנֵינוּ לְפָנֶיךָ, כִּי עַל רַחֲמֶיךָ הָרַבִּים. אֲדֹנָי שְׁמָעָה,
אֲדֹנָי סְלָחָה, אֲדֹנָי הַקְשִׁיבָה, וַעֲשֵׂה אַל תְּאַחַר, לְמַעַנְךָ אֱלֹהַי,
כִּי שִׁמְךָ נִקְרָא עַל עִירְךָ וְעַל עַמֶּךָ.

סליחה עא

אֱלֹהֵינוּ וֵאלֹהֵי אֲבוֹתֵינוּ:

תַּעֲרֹג אֵלֶיךָ* כְּאַיָּל עַל אֲפִיקִים,[1]

שָׁחָה* לְקֵץ רְוָיָה וְאֵין מְפִיקִים,

רָחוֹק וְעָמֹק וְלַדַּלּוּת לֹא מַסְפִּיקִים,

קוֹיִם וְחוֹכִים, וַאֲמָנָה לֹא מַפְסִיקִים.

צְמֵאֶיךָ צוּק לָהֶם יָחוּל לְבָבָם,

פָּנֶיךָ לְרָאוֹת בֵּית מְעוֹן חֲבִיבָם,*

עָבַר בַּסָּךְ[2] וְעַמּוּד אֵשׁ* סְבִיבָם,

סוּר עָרֵל וְטָמֵא[3] בַּעֲלֵי דְבָבָם.

נִכְחִידֵם נִירָשָׁה[4] לָמוֹ נָמוּ חָרְשׁוּ,

מִירֻשָּׁתְךָ אֲשֶׁר הוֹרַשְׁתָּ עַמְּךָ גֵּרֵשׁוּ,[5]

לְהַשְׁמִיד יוֹם יוֹם עוֹד יִדְרְשׁוּ,[6]

כְּנֹס מַס וְחָמָס וַעֲנָיֶיךָ יְרוֹשֵׁשׁוּ.

יָבוֹזוּ יִבְזוּ יְדִידֶךָ יְכַנּוּם כְּלָבִים,

טִפֵּשׁ וְנָבָל כְּמֶר תַּעַר הַגַּלָּבִים.*[7]

‎‫תַּעֲרֹג אֵלֶיךָ‬ — *She [Israel] longs for You.* This *selichah* bears an alphabetical scheme, followed by the *paytan's* signature — ‎שְׁלֹמֹה הַקָּטָן, *Shlomo the lesser* [see prefatory comment to *selichah* 2].

‎תַּעֲרֹג ... שָׁחָה — *She [Israel] longs ... leaning forward [in anticipation].* The translation follows *Masbir* and *Matteh Levi* who understand the feminine verb forms as an allusion to ‎כְּנֶסֶת יִשְׂרָאֵל, the Assembly of Israel. According to *Arugas Ha-*

Bosem, the reference is to the speaker's soul which has been bent to the ground in unfulfilled anticipation (see Psalms 44:26).

‎מְעוֹן חֲבִיבָם — *Their beloved Dwelling.* The translation follows *Arugas HaBosem* and *Matteh Levi.* Alternatively: *the Dwelling of [You,] their Beloved,* or, *the Dwelling that is [in the portion of Benjamin who is called God's] beloved (Pardes).*

‎וְעַמּוּד אֵשׁ — *With a pillar of fire.* The angels are

In some congregations the following two verses are recited responsively — the chazzan
reciting, 'Forgive, please . . .,' and the congregation responding, 'And HASHEM said . . .'
In other congregations these verses are recited silently.

סְלַח נָא *Forgive, please, the iniquity of this people according to the
greatness of Your kindness and as You have forgiven this
people from Egypt until now, and there it was said:*

And HASHEM said, 'I have forgiven according to your word!'

All:

הַטֵּה *Incline, my God, Your ear, and listen, open Your eyes and see our
desolation and that of the city upon which YourName is proclaimed; for not because of our righteousness do we cast down our
supplications before You, rather because of Your abundant compassion.
O my Lord, heed; O my Lord, forgive; O my Lord, be attentive and act,
do not delay; for Your sake, my God, for Your Name is proclaimed upon
Your city and upon Your people.*

SELICHAH 71

Our God and God of our forefathers:

ת *She [Israel] longs for You* like a gazelle for springs,[1]*

ש *leaning forward [in anticipation]* of the relief
of the [Redemption's] end, but not reaching it;*

ר *it is far away, deep down, they are unable to draw it up.*

ק *They wait, they hope, they do not pause in [their] faith.*

צ *Pour forth their heart's hope, [for] those who thirst for You,*

פ *to appear before You in the Temple, their beloved Dwelling,**

ע *to pass among their multitude[2] with a pillar of fire* around them,*

ס *turn away their enemies, the uncircumcised and unclean.*[3]*

נ *'Let us cut them off! Let us take possession of their heritage!'[4]
they said, they intimated.*

מ *They have banished [Your people] from Your inheritance
that You bequeathed Your people.[5]*

ל *They still seek[6] to destroy [Israel], day by day,*

כ *gathering taxes and booty,
making Your poor people yet more destitute.*

י *They despoil, they revile Your beloved people, they call them 'dogs.'*

ט *[So speaks] the fool, the wretch, the razor-shorn priest.*[7]*

---

(1) Cf. *Psalms* 42:2. (2) Cf. 42:5. (3) *Isaiah* 52:1. (4) Cf. *Psalms* 83:5,13. (5) Cf. *II Chronicles* 20:11.
(6) Cf. *Isaiah* 58:2. (7) Cf. *Ezekiel* 5:1; in some editions of *Selichos* this stich has been censored to read,
טִפְּשִׁים יִשְׁמָעֵאל, the *Ishmaelite fools* [or טִפַּשׁ גּוֹי, the *foolish nation*], נָבָל תַּעַר הַגַּלָּבִים, wretched,
razor-shorn; in others it has been changed to, טְהוֹרֵי לֵב עָלֶיךָ מַשְׁלִיכִים יְהָבִים, [while] *the pure of heart
cast their burden upon You* (based on *Psalms* 55:23).

called pillars of fire (*Arugas HaBosem*). Just as we
merited to be led through the Wilderness by a
pillar of fire when we left Egypt, so may we merit
to be led out of our present exile by a pillar of fire
(*Pardes*).

סוּר עָרֵל וְטָמֵא — *Turn away . . . the uncircumcised
and unclean.* This term includes all the nations
that are hostile to Israel (see *Jeremiah* 9:25). Alternatively: עָרֵל, *Uncircumcised*, and טָמֵא, *Unclean*,
are two of the seven names of the Evil Inclination
(*Succos* 52a; see commentary to *selichah* 22, s.v.,
אָכֵן . . . מִכְשׁוֹל).

כְּמַר תַּעַר הַגַּלָּבִים — *The razor-shorn priest.* The
priests, friars, and other church functionaries of
medieval times were [as are certain of their
present-day counterparts] virulent anti-Semites.

חֶרְפָּתָם שׁוֹמְעִים עֲלוּבִים וְלֹא עוֹלְבִים,[1]

זָר לֹא נִשְׁלָבִים וְעָלֶיךָ נִצְלָבִים.

וַאֲנַחְנוּ נֶגְדְּךָ זֶה עִנְוַיְנוּ,

הַעַל אֵלֶּה תִּתְאַפַּק תֶּחֱשֶׁה וּתְעַנֵּנוּ,[2]

דְּכִיתָנוּ בִּמְקוֹם תַּנִּים[3] וְאֵלֶיךָ עֵינֵינוּ,[4]

גַּם גֵּיא צַלְמָוֶת,[3] שָׂמוּ מְעוֹנֵנוּ.

בָּנוּ נִקְרָא שִׁמְךָ אַל יִתְחַלָּל,

בְּךָ כָּל זֶרַע יִשְׂרָאֵל יִתְהַלָּל,

אִם עֲוֹנֵינוּ רַבּוּ וּמָלְאוּ חָלָל,

אָנֹכִי מוֹחֶה פְשָׁעֶיךָ,[5] פִּיךָ מִלָּל.

שְׁגִיאוֹת שִׂים זֵדִים וְלֹא קוֹנֵס,

לִפְנִים מִשּׁוּרַת הַדִּין לָנוּ הַכָּנֵס,

מִפְּנֵי קֹשֶׁט סֶלָה, יֵבוֹשׁ הָאוֹנֵס,

הַנֵּס יִתְנוֹסֵס[6] וְנִדְחֵי יִשְׂרָאֵל יְכַנֵּס.[7]

✣ הָרֵץ בַּת פּוּצִי וְקָרְבָּן תֶּשַׁע,

קַבֵּץ יַחַד עֲשִׂירִית עִם תֵּשַׁע,*

טַבַּע חֵטְא וְלֹא יִזָּכֵר רֶשַׁע,

נֹשֵׂא עָוֹן וְעֹבֵר עַל פֶּשַׁע.[8]

All, while standing:

אֵל מֶלֶךְ יוֹשֵׁב עַל כִּסֵּא רַחֲמִים מִתְנַהֵג בַּחֲסִידוּת, מוֹחֵל
עֲוֹנוֹת עַמּוֹ, מַעֲבִיר רִאשׁוֹן רִאשׁוֹן, מַרְבֶּה מְחִילָה
לְחַטָּאִים וּסְלִיחָה לְפוֹשְׁעִים, עֹשֶׂה צְדָקוֹת עִם כָּל בָּשָׂר וָרוּחַ, לֹא
כְרָעָתָם תִּגְמוֹל. ✣ אֵל הוֹרֵיתָ לָנוּ לוֹמַר שְׁלֹשׁ עֶשְׂרֵה, וּזְכוֹר לָנוּ
הַיּוֹם בְּרִית שְׁלֹשׁ עֶשְׂרֵה, כְּמוֹ שֶׁהוֹדַעְתָּ לֶעָנָיו מִקֶּדֶם, כְּמוֹ
שֶׁכָּתוּב, וַיֵּרֶד יהוה בֶּעָנָן וַיִּתְיַצֵּב עִמּוֹ שָׁם, וַיִּקְרָא בְשֵׁם יהוה.

Congregation, then *chazzan:*

וַיַּעֲבֹר יהוה עַל פָּנָיו וַיִּקְרָא:

Congregation and *chazzan* **(the words in bold type are recited aloud and in unison):**

יהוה, יהוה, אֵל **רַחוּם, וְחַנּוּן,** אֶרֶךְ **אַפַּיִם, וְרַב חֶסֶד, וֶאֱמֶת,**
נֹצֵר חֶסֶד לָאֲלָפִים, נֹשֵׂא עָוֹן, וָפֶשַׁע, וְחַטָּאָה,
וְנַקֵּה. וְסָלַחְתָּ לַעֲוֹנֵנוּ וּלְחַטָּאתֵנוּ וּנְחַלְתָּנוּ. סְלַח לָנוּ אָבִינוּ כִּי

עֲשִׂירִית עִם תֵּשַׁע — *The Tenth [Exile], together*
with the nine [preceding it]. The commentary

Arugas HaBosem cites various Midrashim that
discuss the stages by which Israel was exiled from

ח They [Your people] hear their abuse,
  and remain insulted but do not insult;[1]

ו they embrace no strange [god], and are gibbeted for Your sake.

נ As for us — let this torment of ours be considered before You.

ה Will You hold Yourself back from these?
  Will You stay silent and allow us to be tormented?[2]

ר You have crushed us in the place of serpents,[3] yet our eyes are to You,

ג even though they have turned our dwellings
  into the valley of the shadow of death.[3]

ב We are called by Your Name — let it not be desecrated!
  Through You all the seed of Israel are praised.

א Though our sins are many, enough to fill the world's expanse,
  'I wipe away your sins,'[5] Your mouth has said.

ש Consider deliberate sin as error, and do not punish;

ל do more for us than the strict line of the law.

מ For the sake of truth eternal, let the oppressor be put to shame;

ה let the [Messiah's] banner be raised on high,[6]
  and let Him gather in the outcast of Israel.[7]

ה Chazzan — Find favor with the daughter of my scattered nation,
  and turn to [her prayer in lieu of] offering;

ק gather in the Tenth [Exile], together with the nine [preceding it].*

ט Drown sin, and let wickedness not be remembered,

נ O God Who bears iniquity and passes over sin.[8]

All, while standing:

אֵל מֶלֶךְ O God, King Who sits on the throne of mercy; Who acts with
kindness, pardons the iniquities of His people, removes [sins]
one by one, increasingly grants pardon to careless sinners and forgiveness
to rebels, Who deals righteously with every living being — You do not repay
them in accord with their evil. Chazzan — O God, You taught us to recite the
Thirteen [Attributes of Mercy], so remember for us today the covenant of
these Thirteen, as You made known to the humble one in ancient times, as
it is written: And HASHEM descended in a cloud and stood with him there,
and He called out with the Name HASHEM.

Congregation, then chazzan:

And HASHEM passed before him [Moses] and proclaimed:

Congregation and chazzan (the words in bold type are recited aloud and in unison):

ה' ה' HASHEM, HASHEM, God, Compassionate and Gracious, Slow to
anger, and Abundant in Kindness and Truth, Preserver of
kindness for thousands [of generations], Forgiver of iniquity,
willful sin, and error, and Who cleanses. May You forgive our iniquities
and our errors and make us Your heritage. Forgive us, our Father, for

---

(1) Cf. tractate *Shabbos* 88b. (2) Cf. *Isaiah* 64:11. (3) Cf. *Psalms* 44:20. (4) Cf. *II Chronicles* 20:12;
Psalms 123:2. (5) Cf. *Isaiah* 43:25. (6) Cf. *Psalms* 60:6. (7) Cf. 147:2. (8) *Micah* 7:18.

the Land, during and after the First Destruction   Nebuchadnezzar (*Tanchuma, Masei* 13), and four
and after the Second. He counts six for the First   for the Second (*Seder Olam*), culminating in the
Temple — three by Sennacherib and three by   almost two-thousand-year *galus* of today.

חָטָאנוּ, מְחַל לָנוּ מַלְכֵּנוּ כִּי פָשָׁעְנוּ. כִּי אַתָּה אֲדֹנָי טוֹב וְסַלָּח, וְרַב חֶסֶד לְכָל קֹרְאֶיךָ.

פסוקי הקדמה לסליחה עב

אֵין לָנוּ פֶּה לְהָשִׁיב, וְלֹא מֵצַח לְהָרִים רֹאשׁ.[1] אָח לֹא פָדֹה יִפְדֶּה אִישׁ, לֹא יִתֵּן לֵאלֹהִים כָּפְרוֹ.[2] פְּדֵה אֱלֹהִים אֶת יִשְׂרָאֵל מִכֹּל צָרוֹתָיו.[3] חָנֵּנוּ יהוה כְּחַסְדֶּךָ, בְּרוֹב רַחֲמֶיךָ פְּנֵה אֵלֵינוּ.[4] פּוֹדֶה יהוה נֶפֶשׁ עֲבָדָיו, וְלֹא יֶאְשְׁמוּ כָּל הַחוֹסִים בּוֹ.[5]

כְּרַחֵם אָב עַל בָּנִים, כֵּן תְּרַחֵם יהוה עָלֵינוּ. לַיהוה הַיְשׁוּעָה, עַל עַמְּךָ בִרְכָתֶךָ סֶּלָה. יהוה צְבָאוֹת עִמָּנוּ, מִשְׂגָּב לָנוּ אֱלֹהֵי יַעֲקֹב סֶלָה. יהוה צְבָאוֹת, אַשְׁרֵי אָדָם בֹּטֵחַ בָּךְ. יהוה הוֹשִׁיעָה, הַמֶּלֶךְ יַעֲנֵנוּ בְיוֹם קָרְאֵנוּ.

In some congregations the following two verses are recited responsively — the chazzan reciting סְלַח,
and the congregation responding וַיֹּאמֶר. In other congregations these verses are recited silently.

סְלַח נָא לַעֲוֹן הָעָם הַזֶּה כְּגֹדֶל חַסְדֶּךָ, וְכַאֲשֶׁר נָשָׂאתָה לָעָם הַזֶּה מִמִּצְרַיִם וְעַד הֵנָּה, וְשָׁם נֶאֱמַר:

וַיֹּאמֶר יהוה סָלַחְתִּי כִּדְבָרֶךָ.

All:

הַטֵּה אֱלֹהַי אָזְנְךָ וּשֲׁמָע, פְּקַח עֵינֶיךָ וּרְאֵה שֹׁמְמֹתֵינוּ, וְהָעִיר אֲשֶׁר נִקְרָא שִׁמְךָ עָלֶיהָ, כִּי לֹא עַל צִדְקֹתֵינוּ אֲנַחְנוּ מַפִּילִים תַּחֲנוּנֵינוּ לְפָנֶיךָ, כִּי עַל רַחֲמֶיךָ הָרַבִּים. אֲדֹנָי שְׁמָעָה, אֲדֹנָי סְלָחָה, אֲדֹנָי הַקְשִׁיבָה, וַעֲשֵׂה אַל תְּאַחַר, לְמַעַנְךָ אֱלֹהַי, כִּי שִׁמְךָ נִקְרָא עַל עִירְךָ וְעַל עַמֶּךָ.

━━━━━━ סליחה עב (שלישיה) ━━━━━━

אֱלֹהֵינוּ וֵאלֹהֵי אֲבוֹתֵינוּ:

שׁוֹמֵמְתִּי* בְּרֹב יְגוֹנִי, לְיוֹם יִפָּקֵד זְדוֹנִי, **מָה** אֹמַר לַאדֹנָי.[6] אֻמְלַלְתִּי וְנֶאֱלַמְתִּי, בְּזָכְרִי אֲשֶׁר אָשַׁמְתִּי, בְּשַׁתִּי וְגַם נִכְלַמְתִּי.[7] בְּהֶבֶל כָּלוּ יָמַי,[8] מִפְּנֵי בֹשֶׁת עֲלוּמַי,[9] אֵין שָׁלוֹם בַּעֲצָמַי.[10]

⦁§ **שׁוֹמֵמְתִּי** — *I am desolate.* R' Shlomo ben Yehudah ibn Gabirol (Spain, c. 1021-1058) was a prolific *paytan* and philosopher about whom R' Moshe ibn Ezra (Spain, c. 1070-1140) writes, 'By subduing his natural instincts and inclinations in order to purify his body and soul, he achieved sublime holiness and ascended to heights unpar-

alleled by his contemporaries.' From this purity of soul welled poems and hymns which have been incorporated into the festival liturgy. (However, many, if not most, of the *Selichos* signed Shlomo ben Yehudah are not by Ibn Gabriol, but by his namesake, R' Shlomo ben Yehudah HaBavli; see prefatory comment to *selichah* 2.)

we have erred; pardon us, our King, for we have willfully sinned; for You, my Lord, are good and forgiving and abundantly kind to all who call upon You.

PREFATORY VERSES TO SELICHAH 72

אֵין לָנוּ *We have no mouth to reply, nor the brazenness to lift up our heads.[1] A man cannot redeem [his] brother; he cannot give God his ransom.[2] Redeem Israel, O God, from all its troubles![3] Show us favor, O God, as befits Your kindness; in Your abundant mercy turn to us.[4] HASHEM redeems the souls of His servants, and all who take shelter with Him will not be condemned.[5]*

כְּרַחֵם אָב *As a father has mercy on his children, so, HASHEM, may You have mercy on us. Salvation is HASHEM's, upon Your people is Your blessing, Selah. HASHEM, Master of Legions, is with us, a stronghold for us is the God of Jacob, Selah. HASHEM, Master of Legions, praiseworthy is the person who trusts in You. HASHEM, save! May the King answer us on the day we call.*

In some congregations the following two verses are recited responsively — the *chazzan* reciting, '*Forgive, please . . .*' and the congregation responding, '*And HASHEM said . . .*'
In other congregations these verses are recited silently.

סְלַח נָא *Forgive, please, the iniquity of this people according to the greatness of Your kindness and as You have forgiven this people from Egypt until now, and there it was said:*

And HASHEM said, 'I have forgiven according to your word!'

All:

הַטֵּה *Incline, my God, Your ear, and listen, open Your eyes and see our desolation and that of the city upon which Your Name is proclaimed; for not because of our righteousness do we cast down our supplications before You, rather because of Your abundant compassion. O my Lord, heed; O my Lord, forgive; O my Lord, be attentive and act, do not delay; for Your sake, my God, for Your Name is proclaimed upon Your city and upon Your people.*

SELICHAH 72

Our God and the God of our forefathers:

שׁ *I am desolate* in my abundant anguish.*
ל *On the day that my sins are considered,*
מה *what will I say to my Lord?[6]*
א *I am wretched and fall silent*
    when I remember what guilty deeds I have done;
    I am ashamed and disgraced.[7]
ב *My days are consumed in frivolity;[8]*
    because of the shame of my youth[9] my bones have no peace.[10]

---

(1) This is not a Scriptural verse. (2) *Psalms* 49:8. (3) 25:22. (4) Cf. 51:3; 69:17. (5) 34:23.
(6) Cf. *Genesis* 44:16. (7) *Jeremiah* 31:18. (8) Cf. *Psalms* 102:4. (9) Cf. *Isaiah* 54:4. (10) *Psalms* 38:4.

R' Shlomo signed his name in the acrostic of the first stanza. The remaining stanzas follow an *aleph-beis* acrostic, and the last stich of each is a fragment of a Scriptural verse.

גָּחַלְתִּי[1] בִּי קוֹדַחַת, כִּי מְגֻלָּה נִמְתַּחַת, וְהַנּוּשָׁה בָּא לָקַחַת.[2]

דָּבַקְתִּי בְּמַחְשַׁכֵּי, וְנַפְשִׁי לֹא יָדְעָה, כִּי גֵר וְתוֹשָׁב אָנֹכִי.[3]

הוֹי כִּי יָבֹא יוֹמִי,[4] אֲזַי אֵיקַץ מֵחֲלוֹמִי, וְאָשׁוּבָה אֶל מְקוֹמִי.[5]

וְעַל חֲטָאַי אֲשֶׁר עָבַר, וְעַל פְּשָׁעַי אֲשֶׁר גָּבַר,

מָה אָשִׁיב שֹׁלְחִי דָבָר.[6]

זָדוֹן לִבִּי הִשִּׁיאַנִי,[7] עַל עָוֹן אֲשֶׁר הֶלְאַנִי, מִבֶּטֶן קְרָאַנִי.[8]

חוֹשֵׁב בְּנַפְשׁוֹ נָבָל, כְּעֵץ שָׁתוּל עַל יוּבָל,[9]

וְהוּא לִקְבָרוֹת יוּבָל.[10]

טָפַל שֶׁקֶר בְּתוֹכוֹ, וְנָמֵס מִמַּהֲלָכוֹ, וַיִּפֶן כֹּה וָכֹה.*[11]

יֵשַׁלַּךְ כְּאֶבֶן דּוּמָה, וְלֹא יִשָּׂא לְבֵית מְהוּמָה,

מִכָּל אֲשֶׁר לוֹ מְאוּמָה.[12]

כֹּחוֹ לֹא סְמָכַתְהוּ, עֵת נַפְשׁוֹ נְשָׁאַתְהוּ, אַף כִּי אֵשׁ אֲכָלָתְהוּ.[13]

לְכָדַתְנִי אַשְׁמָתִי, הֲלֹא זֶה דְבַר נִשְׁמָתִי, עַד הֱיוֹתִי עַל אַדְמָתִי.[14]

לְזֹאת נַפְשִׁי נְשָׁמָה, כְּאִישׁ שׁוֹכֵב בְּכִלְמָה, עָרֹם אָשׁוּב שָׁמָּה.[15]

מְשׁוּגָתִי נָשָׂאתִי, וּבִלְבָבִי קְרָאתִי, אָנֹכִי חָטָאתִי.[16]

נְכוֹחָה לֹא חָשַׁקְתִּי, וּבִשְׁרִירוּת לִבִּי דָבַקְתִּי, מַה לְּךָ כִּי נִזְעַקְתִּי.[17]

שְׂאִי נַפְשִׁי אַשְׁמָתֶךָ, רְאִי חַטָּאתֵךְ לְעֻמָּתֵךְ,

גַּם אַתְּ שְׂאִי כְלִמָּתֵךְ.[18]

עֵת אֶדְאַג לַעֲוֹנִי, הֱשִׁיבוּנִי רַעְיוֹנִי, נִפְלָה נָא בְיַד יהוה.[19]

פְּנֵה מִמְּכוֹן שִׁבְתֶּךָ, וּפְתַח לִי דְלָתֶיךָ, כִּי אֵין בִּלְתֶּךָ.[20]

צוּר הָגֵן בַּעֲדֵנִי, וּמְעוֹנִי פְּדֵנִי, וְתוֹרָתְךָ לַמְּדֵנִי.

קוֹלִי שִׁמְעָה כְחַסְדֶּךָ,[21] בְּיוֹם אֶעֱמֹד נֶגְדֶּךָ, אַל תַּט בְּאַף עַבְדֶּךָ.[22]

רְאֵה עָנְיִי וַעֲנֵנִי, אֲנִי בְיָדְךָ הִנֵּנִי, וְאַתָּה יהוה חָנֵּנִי.[23]

✧ שְׁלַח אֲמִתְּךָ וַחֲסָדֶיךָ, לְעַם צוֹעֲקִים נֶגְדֶּךָ, וְלִי אֲנִי עַבְדֶּךָ.[24]

תִּסְלַח אַשְׁמָתֵנוּ, וְאַל תִּפְקֹד עֲלוּמֵנוּ, כִּי כְצֵל יָמֵינוּ,[25]

---

(1) See II Samuel 14:7. (2) II Kings 4:1. (3) Genesis 23:4. (4) Cf. Psalms 37:13.
(5) Cf. Hosea 5:15. (6) II Samuel 24:13. (7) Cf. Obadiah 1:3. (8) Isaiah 49:1. (9) Cf. Jeremiah 17:8.
(10) Job 21:32. (11) Exodus 2:12. (12) I Samuel 25:21. (13) Cf. Ezekiel 15:5. (14) Cf. Jonah 4:2.
(15) Cf. Job 1:21. (16) Joshua 7:20. (17) Cf. Judges 18:23. (18) Ezekiel 16:52. (19) II Samuel 24:14.
(20) I Samuel 2:2. (21) Psalms 119:149. (22) 27:9. (23) 41:11. (24) I Kings 1:26. (25) Cf. Job 8:9.

טָפַל שֶׁקֶר... כֹּה וָכֹה —*He has heaped falsehood ...
this way and that [trying to escape].* The translation follows *Pardes* (based on Ezekiel 21:12), who
understands the subject of the verbs 'melts' and
'turns' as the sinner's heart בְּתוֹכוֹ, *within him.*

According to *Masbir* the subject is the sinner
himself whose strength melts as he ages. God
causes this to happen as a warning that one
should begin re-examining — this way and that
— the falsehood with which he has been living.

ג *My coal[1] burns within me, for the scroll [of misdeeds] is unrolled*
   and the Collector comes to take [payment].[2]

ד *I have clung to my [ways of] darkness;*
   even my soul did not know that
   I am but a sojourner and a foreign-resident [in this world].[3]

ה *Woe! when my day comes,[4] then shall I awake from this dream*
   and return to my place.[5]

ו *As for my sins of the past, and my overwhelming rebelliousness,*
   what answer can I make to Him that sent me?[6]

ז *My wanton heart led me astray[7] to the iniquity that wearied me,*
   it has called me from the womb.[8]

ח *A villain thinks of himself as a tree planted by a stream,[9]*
   even as he is borne to his grave.[10]

ט *He has heaped falsehood within himself,*
   but it melts as he goes [to his grave]
   and he turns this way and that [trying to escape].[11]

י *He is thrown like a stone into [the grave's] silence,*
   and carries not to his sudden home anything of all that was his.[12]

כ *His strength did not support him when his soul bore him [in life],*
   certainly [it will not support him] now that the fire devours him.[13]

ל *'My guilt has entrapped me!' Has this not been my soul's phrase,*
   since I have been in my [place on] earth?[14]

ל *And therefore my soul is desolate, like one lying in shame;*
   for I shall return there naked.[15]

מ *I bear my misdeeds, and in my heart I call out, 'I have sinned!'[16]*

נ *I did not desire what was upright,*
   but I clung to my heart's haughtiness;
   so what is it to You if I cry out?[17]

ס *Bear your guilt, O my soul! See how your sin is before you;*
   so you also must bear your shame.[18]

ע *When I worry about my sins, my thought answers me back,*
   'Please, let us fall into HASHEM's hands.'[19]

פ *Turn to me from Your Heavenly Dwelling,*
   and open Your doors for me! For there is none besides You.[20]

צ *O Rock, be a shield for me, redeem me from my iniquity,*
   and teach me Your Torah.

ק *Hear my voice in accordance with Your kindness;[21]*
   on the day that I stand before You, repel not Your servant in anger.[22]

ר *See my destitute state, and answer me.*
   As for me, here I am in Your hand;
   but as for You, HASHEM, may You be gracious towards me.[23]

ש Chazzan — *Send Your truth and Your kindnesses*
   to Your people, who cry out before You;
   and to me, for I am Your servant.[24]

ת *Forgive our guilt, and reckon not our immaturities,*
   for our days are like a shadow.[25]

All, while standing:

אֵל מֶלֶךְ יוֹשֵׁב עַל כִּסֵּא רַחֲמִים מִתְנַהֵג בַּחֲסִידוּת, מוֹחֵל עֲוֹנוֹת עַמּוֹ, מַעֲבִיר רִאשׁוֹן רִאשׁוֹן, מַרְבֶּה מְחִילָה לַחַטָּאִים וּסְלִיחָה לַפּוֹשְׁעִים, עֹשֶׂה צְדָקוֹת עִם כָּל בָּשָׂר וָרוּחַ, לֹא כְרָעָתָם תִּגְמוֹל. ❖ אֵל הוֹרֵיתָ לָנוּ לוֹמַר שְׁלֹשׁ עֶשְׂרֵה, וּזְכֹר לָנוּ הַיּוֹם בְּרִית שְׁלֹשׁ עֶשְׂרֵה, כְּמוֹ שֶׁהוֹדַעְתָּ לֶעָנָיו מִקֶּדֶם, כְּמוֹ שֶׁכָּתוּב, וַיֵּרֶד יהוה בֶּעָנָן וַיִּתְיַצֵּב עִמּוֹ שָׁם, וַיִּקְרָא בְשֵׁם יהוה.

Congregation, then *chazzan*:

וַיַּעֲבֹר יהוה עַל פָּנָיו וַיִּקְרָא:

Congregation and *chazzan* (the words in bold type are recited aloud and in unison):

יהוה, יהוה, אֵל, רַחוּם, וְחַנּוּן, אֶרֶךְ אַפַּיִם, וְרַב חֶסֶד, וֶאֱמֶת, נֹצֵר חֶסֶד לָאֲלָפִים, נֹשֵׂא עָוֹן, וָפֶשַׁע, וְחַטָּאָה, וְנַקֵּה. וְסָלַחְתָּ לַעֲוֹנֵנוּ וּלְחַטָּאתֵנוּ וּנְחַלְתָּנוּ. סְלַח לָנוּ אָבִינוּ כִּי חָטָאנוּ, מְחַל לָנוּ מַלְכֵּנוּ כִּי פָשָׁעְנוּ. כִּי אַתָּה אֲדֹנָי טוֹב וְסַלָּח, וְרַב חֶסֶד לְכָל קֹרְאֶיךָ.

פסוקי הקדמה לסליחה עג

גָּדוֹל יהוה וּמְהֻלָּל מְאֹד, בְּעִיר אֱלֹהֵינוּ הַר קָדְשׁוֹ. יְפֵה נוֹף, מְשׂוֹשׂ כָּל הָאָרֶץ, הַר צִיּוֹן יַרְכְּתֵי צָפוֹן, קִרְיַת מֶלֶךְ רָב.[1] הֵיטִיבָה בִרְצוֹנְךָ אֶת צִיּוֹן, תִּבְנֶה חוֹמוֹת יְרוּשָׁלָיִם.[2] יָשֵׁב נָא אַפְּךָ וַחֲמָתְךָ מֵעִירְךָ יְרוּשָׁלַיִם הַר קָדְשֶׁךָ.[3] לְסַפֵּר בְּצִיּוֹן שֵׁם יהוה, וּתְהִלָּתוֹ בִּירוּשָׁלָיִם.[4] וְעָרְבָה לַיהוה מִנְחַת יְהוּדָה וִירוּשָׁלָיִם, כִּימֵי עוֹלָם וּכְשָׁנִים קַדְמֹנִיּוֹת.[5] בּוֹנֵה יְרוּשָׁלַיִם יהוה, נִדְחֵי יִשְׂרָאֵל יְכַנֵּס.[6] כִּי לֹא יִטֹּשׁ יהוה עַמּוֹ וְנַחֲלָתוֹ לֹא יַעֲזֹב.[7]

כְּרַחֵם אָב עַל בָּנִים, כֵּן תְּרַחֵם יהוה עָלֵינוּ. לַיהוה הַיְשׁוּעָה, עַל עַמְּךָ בִרְכָתֶךָ סֶּלָה. יהוה צְבָאוֹת עִמָּנוּ, מִשְׂגָּב לָנוּ אֱלֹהֵי יַעֲקֹב סֶלָה. יהוה צְבָאוֹת, אַשְׁרֵי אָדָם בֹּטֵחַ בָּךְ. יהוה הוֹשִׁיעָה, הַמֶּלֶךְ יַעֲנֵנוּ בְיוֹם קָרְאֵנוּ.

In some congregations the following two verses are recited responsively — the *chazzan* reciting סְלַח, and the congregation responding וַיֹּאמֶר. In other congregations these verses are recited silently.

סְלַח נָא לַעֲוֹן הָעָם הַזֶּה כְּגֹדֶל חַסְדֶּךָ, וְכַאֲשֶׁר נָשָׂאתָה לָעָם הַזֶּה מִמִּצְרַיִם וְעַד הֵנָּה, וְשָׁם נֶאֱמַר:

וַיֹּאמֶר יהוה סָלַחְתִּי כִּדְבָרֶךָ.

All, while standing:

אֵל מֶלֶךְ *O God, King Who sits on the throne of mercy; Who acts with kindness, pardons the iniquities of His people, removes [sins] one by one, increasingly grants pardon to careless sinners and forgiveness to rebels, Who deals righteously with every living being — You do not repay them in accord with their evil.* Chazzan — *O God, You taught us to recite the Thirteen [Attributes of Mercy], so remember for us today the covenant of these Thirteen, as You made known to the humble one in ancient times, as it is written: And HASHEM descended in a cloud and stood with him there, and He called out with the Name HASHEM.*

Congregation, then *chazzan:*

And HASHEM passed before him [Moses] and proclaimed:

Congregation and *chazzan* (the words in bold type are recited aloud and in unison):

ה' ה' **HASHEM, HASHEM, God, Compassionate and Gracious, Slow to anger, and Abundant in Kindness and Truth, Preserver of kindness for thousands [of generations], Forgiver of iniquity, willful sin, and error, and Who cleanses.** *May You forgive our iniquities and our errors and make us Your heritage. Forgive us, our Father, for we have erred; pardon us, our King, for we have willfully sinned; for You, my Lord, are good and forgiving and abundantly kind to all who call upon You.*

PREFATORY VERSES TO SELICHAH 73

גָּדוֹל *Great is HASHEM and much praised, in the city of our God, mount of His holiness: Fairest of sites, joy of all the earth, Mount Zion, at the northern side of the great King's city.[1] Do good in Your favor unto Zion; build the walls of Jerusalem.[2] Please let Your anger and fury turn away from Your city Jerusalem, Your holy mountain.[3] To declare in Zion the Name of HASHEM, and His praise in Jerusalem.[4] Then the offering of Judah and Jerusalem will be pleasing to HASHEM, as in days of old and in former years.[5] The Builder of Jerusalem is HASHEM; the outcast of Israel He will gather in.[6] For HASHEM will not forsake His people, nor will He abandon His heritage.[7]*

כְּרַחֵם אָב *As a father has mercy on his children, so, HASHEM, may You have mercy on us. Salvation is HASHEM's, upon Your people is Your blessing, Selah. HASHEM, Master of Legions, is with us, a stronghold for us is the God of Jacob, Selah. HASHEM, Master of Legions, praiseworthy is the person who trusts in You. HASHEM, save! May the King answer us on the day we call.*

In some congregations the following two verses are recited responsively — the *chazzan* reciting, 'Forgive, please . . . ,' and the congregation responding, 'And HASHEM said . . .' In other congregations these verses are recited silently.

סְלַח נָא *Forgive, please, the iniquity of this people according to the greatness of Your kindness and as You have forgiven this people from Egypt until now, and there it was said:*

And HASHEM said, 'I have forgiven according to your word!'

(1) *Psalms* 48:2-3. (2) 51:20. (3) *Daniel* 9:16. (4) *Psalms* 102:22.
(5) *Malachi* 3:4. (6) *Psalms* 147:2. (7) 94:14.

All:

הַטֵּה אֱלֹהַי אָזְנְךָ וּשְׁמָע, פְּקַח עֵינֶיךָ וּרְאֵה שֹׁמְמֹתֵינוּ, וְהָעִיר
אֲשֶׁר נִקְרָא שִׁמְךָ עָלֶיהָ, כִּי לֹא עַל צִדְקֹתֵינוּ אֲנַחְנוּ
מַפִּילִים תַּחֲנוּנֵינוּ לְפָנֶיךָ, כִּי עַל רַחֲמֶיךָ הָרַבִּים. אֲדֹנָי שְׁמָעָה,
אֲדֹנָי סְלָחָה, אֲדֹנָי הַקְשִׁיבָה, וַעֲשֵׂה אַל תְּאַחַר, לְמַעַנְךָ אֱלֹהַי, כִּי
שִׁמְךָ נִקְרָא עַל עִירְךָ וְעַל עַמֶּךָ.

סליחה עג (שלמונית)

אֱלֹהֵינוּ וֵאלֹהֵי אֲבוֹתֵינוּ:

יְרוּשָׁלַיִם* אֶת יהוה הַלְלִי[1] דָּגוּל מֵרְבָבוֹת,

הַדּוֹרֵשׁ מֵרֵאשִׁית אַחֲרִית בְּגֶשֶׁם נְדָבוֹת,[2]

בְּנוֹתַיִךְ כְּזָוִיוֹת תַּבְנִית הֵיכָל מְחֻטָּבוֹת,[3]

פִּצְחוּ רַנְּנוּ יַחְדָּו חָרְבוֹת **יְרוּשָׁלָיִם.**[4]

יְרוּשָׁלַיִם בְּנוּיָה כְּעִיר שֶׁחֻבְּרָה לָּהּ בִּתְיוֹם,[5]

אִישׁ וְאִישׁ יֻלַּד בָּהּ, וְהוּא יְכוֹנְנֶהָ עֶלְיוֹן,[6]

יִסְפֹּר בִּכְתוֹב עַמִּים,*[7] אִים,

זָכֹר יהוה לִבְנֵי אֱדוֹם אֵת יוֹם **יְרוּשָׁלָיִם.**[8]

יְרוּשָׁלַיִם גָּנוֹן וְהִצִּיל[9] לְצָרַי וְתָעַל,

לְחֶפַת כָּבוֹד הֶיֵה לָהּ,[10] מוֹדֵד בַּשְׁעַל,[11]

לְגוֹנְנָהּ כְּצִפֳּרִים עָפוֹת מִמַּעַל,

כֵּן יָגֵן יהוה צְבָאוֹת עַל **יְרוּשָׁלָיִם.**[12]

יְרוּשָׁלַיִם דּוֹרֵשׁ אֵין לָךְ[13] שְׁכֵחוּךְ אוֹהֲבַיִךְ,

אוֹתָךְ לֹא יִדְרְשׁוּ,[14] וּבָטְלוּ יוֹעֲצַיִךְ,

יֵאָמֵן נָא דְבָרֶךְ,[15] וְאָשִׁיבָה שׁוֹפְטַיִךְ,[16]

כִּי מִי יַחְמֹל עָלָיִךְ **יְרוּשָׁלָיִם.**[17]

יְרוּשָׁלַיִם הָרִים סָבִיב לָהּ[18] עוֹמְדִים כַּחוֹמוֹת,

וַיהוה סָבִיב לְעַמּוֹ[18] יוֹסֵד הַדּוֹמוֹת,

עֲדִינָה תַּפִּיל לְאֵין תְּקוּמוֹת,

וְתִבָּנֶה חוֹמוֹת **יְרוּשָׁלָיִם.**[19]

יְרוּשָׁלַיִם — *Jerusalem.* Jerusalem, once the fairest of cities, lies in ruin. It was destroyed because of its inhabitant's iniquities. But it shall one day return to its former glory. Our sins caused its destruction; our repentance will re-establish its splendor. In what seems more like a *kinnah* for Tishah B'Av than a *selichah* for the Ten Days of Repentance, the anonymous *paytan* bewails what once was, and prays for the time it will be again.

Each stanza begins with the word Jerusalem, followed by the respective letters of the *aleph-*

All:

הַטֵּה Incline, my God, Your ear, and listen, open Your eyes and see our
        desolation and that of the city upon which Your Name is pro-
claimed; for not because of our righteousness do we cast down our
supplications before You, rather because of Your abundant compassion.
O my Lord, heed; O my Lord, forgive; O my Lord, be attentive and act,
do not delay; for Your sake, my God, for Your Name is proclaimed upon
Your city and upon Your people.

SELICHAH 73

Our God and the God of our forefathers:

א **Jerusalem,** * praise HASHEM,[1] bannered by myriad [angels],
   Who visits from [the year's] beginning until [its] end
      with generous rain.[2]
   Your daughters are like cornerstones, crafted in palatial form.[3]
   Burst out in song all together, O ruins of   **Jerusalem!**[4]

ב **Jerusalem** built up, like a city united to its [Heavenly] twin;[5]
   [of her exiles it will be said,] 'This man, as well as that man,
      was born in her,' and He will establish her supreme.[6]
   The Awesome One will count when He records the nations.*[7]
   Remember, HASHEM, for the children of Edom,
      the day of [the Destruction of]   **Jerusalem!**[8]

ג **Jerusalem** — protect and save it![9] Be balm and healing for it.
   Be a canopy of honor for it.[10] [Please come] with measured footsteps [11]
   to protect it as high-flying birds [are protected];
      for so shall HASHEM, Master of Legions, protect   **Jerusalem.**[12]

ד **Jerusalem,** there is none who seeks you;[13]
      all your paramours have forgotten you,
   they seek you not,[14] and your counselors are no more.
   [O God,] let Your word be shown true:[15]
      'I shall bring back your judges.'[16]
   For who will have pity on you,   **Jerusalem?**[17]

ה **Jerusalem** — mountains surround it,[18] standing like walls,
   and HASHEM, Who founded the terrestrial footstool,
      surrounds His people.
   May You cast down the pampered [oppressors],
      that they never rise [again],
   and rebuild the walls of   **Jerusalem.**[19]

---

(1) Cf. *Psalms* 147:12. (2) Cf. *Deuteronomy* 11:11-12. (3) Cf. *Psalms* 144:12. (4) *Isaiah* 52:9.
(5) Cf. *Psalms* 122:3; see *Rashi* there. (6) 87:5. (7) 87:6. (8) 137:7. (9) *Isaiah* 31:5.
(10) Cf. 4:5. (11) Cf. 40:12. (12) Cf. 31:5. (13) Cf. *Jeremiah* 30:17. (14) Cf. 30:14.
(15) *I Kings* 8:26. (16) *Isaiah* 1:26. (17) *Jeremiah* 15:5. (18) *Psalms* 125:2. (19) Cf. 51:20.

---

beis. The last verse of each stanza is a Scriptural
fragment ending in the word Jerusalem.

אִישׁ וְאִישׁ . . . וְסָפַר בִּכְתוֹב עַמִּים — *This man, as
well as that man . . . [He] will count when He
records the nations.* During the millennia of

Exile, many thousands of Jews have become mingled among the nations. Innocent babes who
never knew their exalted lineage were raised
as gentiles. Through no fault of theirs, they
lived the life-style of their host country. But
when the Day of Reckoning comes for the gen-

יְרוּשָׁלַיִם וְעַמֵּךְ לְחֶרְפָּה[1] לְפַלָּצוּת וּבְעָתָה,
חוֹמַת בַּת צִיּוֹן הוֹרִידִי כַּנַּחַל דִּמְעָתָה,[2]
עָרֵי קׇדְשְׁךָ הָיוּ מִדְבָּר וּבְעָתָה,
צִיּוֹן מִדְבָּר הָיְתָה
וִירוּשָׁלָיִם.[3]

יְרוּשָׁלַיִם זָכְרָה יְמֵי עׇנְיָהּ[4] כִּי נִטְמָאֵת,
בְּסָךְ לֹא תוּכַל עוֹד לָבֹא וְלָצֵאת,
וּמַדּוּעַ לֹא תֵרָאֶה נַחֲלָתְךָ הַנִּלְאֵית,
עַד מָתַי אַתָּה לֹא תְרַחֵם אֶת
יְרוּשָׁלָיִם.[5]

יְרוּשָׁלַיִם חֵטְא חָטְאָה עַל כֵּן הָיְתָה לְנִידָה,[6]
הוֹצֵא לָרְוָיָה הַיּוֹשֶׁבֶת בְּדוֹדָה,
אֵיכָכָה תוּכַל וְרָאִיתָ בְּאׇבְדָהּ,[7]
וְעׇרְבָה לַיהוה מִנְחַת יְהוּדָה
וִירוּשָׁלָיִם.[8]

יְרוּשָׁלַיִם טֻמְאָתֵךְ עַד מָתַי תָּלִין בְּקִרְבֵּךְ,[9]
כִּטְמֵא נֶחְשָׁבִים סָבֵךְ וְרַבֵּךְ,
רֶשַׁע וְעָוֺן טָמוּן בְּחֻבֵּךְ,[10]
כַּבְּסִי מֵרָעָה לִבֵּךְ
יְרוּשָׁלָיִם.[9]

יְרוּשָׁלַיִם יִשְׁלָיוּ אוֹהֲבָיִךְ[11] וְנִבְנוּ הֶחֳרָבוֹת,[12]
תַּחַת כִּי נִתְקַלְּסוּ בָּךְ הָרְחוֹקוֹת וְהַקְּרוֹבוֹת,
לְקַיֵּם חֲזוֹן יְשׁוּעוֹת טוֹבוֹת,
עוֹד יֵשְׁבוּ זְקֵנִים וּזְקֵנוֹת בִּרְחוֹבוֹת
יְרוּשָׁלָיִם.[13]

יְרוּשָׁלַיִם כִּסֵּא יהוה תִּקָּרֵא לְעִתּוֹת הַבָּאוֹת,[14]
אֶת הָאֶבֶן הָרֹאשָׁה חֵן חֵן תְּשֻׁאוֹת,[15]
בְּבוֹא כָּל יִשְׂרָאֵל לֵרָאוֹת,[16]
לְבַקֵּשׁ אֶת יהוה צְבָאוֹת
בִּירוּשָׁלָיִם.[17]

יְרוּשָׁלַיִם לָבֶטַח תּוֹשִׁיב אֶרֶץ צְבִי,
אֲשֶׁר בָּנֶיהָ עֻלְּפוּ וְהָלְכוּ בַּשֶּׁבִי,
כַּנֵּהּ תְּבִיאֶנָּה לְעִירָהּ כַּאֲשֶׁר נָם נָבִיא,
הִתְנַעֲרִי מֵעָפָר קוּמִי שְׁבִי
יְרוּשָׁלָיִם.[18]

יְרוּשָׁלַיִם מֵרֹב אָדָם, פְּרָזוֹת תֵּשֵׁב יְשִׁיבָתֵךְ,[19]
בַּיּוֹם הַהוּא תִּנָּשְׂעִי עַל אַדְמָתֵךְ,
עֲזוּבָה וּשְׂנוּאָה תַּחַת הֱיוֹתֵךְ,[20]
לִבְשִׁי בִּגְדֵי תִפְאַרְתֵּךְ
יְרוּשָׁלָיִם.[21]

ו **Jerusalem** and Your people are put to shame,[1]
to trembling and to terror.
O wall of [Jerusalem,] daughter of Zion, shed tears like a river![2]
Your holy cities have become wilderness and desolation.
Zion has become a wilderness, and [so has] **Jerusalem.**[3]

ז **Jerusalem** remembers her days of ruin,[4] when she became impure.
Her people can no longer come and go [to the Temple], in multitudes.
Why do You not look upon Your wearied heritage?
How long will You refuse to have mercy on **Jerusalem?**[5]

ח **Jerusalem** committed sin; therefore she has become a wanderer.[6]
Bring her who sits alone out into contentment!
How are You able to oberve [silently] her annihilation?[7]
[O for the days when] sweet unto HASHEM
will be the offering of Judah and **Jerusalem.**[8]

ט **Jerusalem!** How long will your impurity linger on within you?[9]
Your elders and your youth are considered impure [because of sin].
Wickedness and iniquity are hidden within you;[10]
wash your heart clean of evil, O **Jerusalem!**[9]

י **Jerusalem,** may those who love you be serene;[11]
and may [your] ruins be rebuilt —[12]
for near [cities] and far once made you the paradigm of praise —
to uphold the vision of goodly salvations:
'Elderly men and women
will once again inhabit the streets of **Jerusalem.'**[13]

כ **Jerusalem,** in times to come you will be called the Throne of God,[14]
its plumb line will be accorded accolades of grace,[15]
when all Israel come to appear,[16]
to seek HASHEM, Master of Legions, in **Jerusalem.**[17]

ל **Jerusalem,** the land of [our] desire, may You return it to security,
she whose children fainted from weakness
when they went into captivity.
Bring Your vine to her city, as the prophet spoke:
'Shake the dust off of you; rise, return to **Jerusalem.'**[18]

מ **Jerusalem!** So many will be your people that your inhabitants
will dwell in open villages [outside your walls].[19]
On that day you will find salvation upon your land,
in place of having been abandoned and hated.[20]
Don your splendid raiment, O **Jerusalem!**[21]

---

(1) *Daniel* 9:16. (2) Cf. *Lamentations* 2:18. (3) Cf. *Isaiah* 64:9. (4) Cf. *Lamentations* 1:7.
(5) *Zechariah* 1:12. (6) Cf. *Lamentations* 1:8; many editions of *Selichos* read הָיְתָה לְנִדָּה, *she has become a menstruant*, a reading that seems patently wrong, and which probably stems from confusion between verses 1:8 and 1:17 of *Lamentations*. (7) Cf. *Esther* 8:6. (8) *Malachi* 3:4. (9) *Jeremiah* 4:14. (10) Cf. *Job* 31:33. (11) Cf. *Psalms* 122:6. (12) *Ezekiel* 36:33. (13) *Zechariah* 8:4. (14) Cf. *Jeremiah* 3:17. (15) Cf. *Zechariah* 4:7. (16) *Deuteronomy* 31:11. (17) *Zechariah* 8:22. (18) *Isaiah* 52:2. (19) Cf. *Zechariah* 2:8. (20) Cf. *Isaiah* 60:15. (21) 52:1.

---

tile nations, God will identify each and every one of these lost souls and proclaim, 'This one was born a Jew! That one was born a Jew!' He will then separate them from the nations and return them to Zion (based on *Rashi* to *Psalms* 87:5-6).

יְרוּשָׁלַיִם נוֹצְרִים בָּאוּ לָךְ[1] לְהָרִיב וּלְחַרְחֵר,

הַצְּפוֹנִי[2] גָּרַם לָךְ בְּהִשְׁתַּחֲוֺת לְאֵל אַחֵר,

יִגְעַר יהוה בְּךָ הַשָּׂטָן, הַבּוֹחֵר,

וְיִגְעַר יהוה בְּךָ, הַבּוֹחֵר **בִּירוּשָׁלָיִם.**[3]

יְרוּשָׁלַיִם שִׂמְחוּ אַתָּה כָּל אוֹהֲבֶיהָ[4] מִי נָמִי,

בְּנֵי יַעֲקֹב וְיוֹסֵף,[5] וְאַל תִּתְּנוּ דֳמִי,

עַד יָשִׂים בֵּית אוּלָמִי,[6]

הִתְעוֹרְרִי הִתְעוֹרְרִי קוּמִי **יְרוּשָׁלָיִם.**[7]

יְרוּשָׁלַיִם עִיר הַקֹּדֶשׁ רָוִית לַעַד,

מַדּוּעַ כִּי בָזִית מִצְוֺתָיו יַעַן וּבְיַעַן,[8]

עוֹד מַלְכֵּךְ יִהְיֶה לָךְ לְמִשְׁעָן,[9]

לְמַעַן צִיּוֹן לֹא אֶחֱשֶׁה וּלְמַעַן **יְרוּשָׁלָיִם.**[10]

יְרוּשָׁלַיִם פֶּן תֵּקַע נַפְשִׁי מִמֵּךְ,[11] אָמַר עֶלְיוֹן,

עוֹד יָבֹא וְיִמְלֹךְ וְיוֹאֵל בְּצִבְיוֹן,

וְחָפְרָה הַלְּבָנָה וּבוֹשָׁה הַחַמָּה בִּכְהוֹי רָאִיוֹן,

כִּי מָלַךְ יהוה צְבָאוֹת בְּהַר צִיּוֹן **וּבִירוּשָׁלָיִם.**[12]

יְרוּשָׁלַיִם צַהֲלִי וָרֹנִּי[13] לִצְבִי וּלְתִפְאָרֶת,

לִבְשִׁי עֻזֵּךְ וְלִבְשִׁי אַדֶּרֶת,[14]

פִּצְחִי רִנָּה וְצַהֲלִי[15] כִּמְּסֹרֶת,

הָרִימִי בַכֹּחַ קוֹלֵךְ מְבַשֶּׂרֶת **יְרוּשָׁלָיִם.**[16]

יְרוּשָׁלַיִם קֹדֶשׁ, זָרִים לֹא יַעַבְרוּ עוֹד,[17]

כּוֹס הַתַּרְעֵלָה לֹא תוֹסִיפִי לִשְׁתּוֹתָהּ עוֹד,[18]

יְכוֹנֵן דְּרָכֵיךְ וְקַרְסֻלֵּךְ לֹא יִמְעַד,

וְנִחַם יהוה אֶת צִיּוֹן וּבָחַר עוֹד **בִּירוּשָׁלָיִם.**[19]

יְרוּשָׁלַיִם רָנִּי וְשִׂמְחִי שִׁיר לְחַדֵּשׁ,

וְהַר הַלְּבָנוֹן יִתְרוֹמֵם בְּגֹדֶשׁ,

וְיָבֹא כָל בָּשָׂר מִדֵּי חֹדֶשׁ בְּחָדְשׁוֹ,

וְהִשְׁתַּחֲווּ לַיהוה[20] בְּהַר הַקֹּדֶשׁ **בִּירוּשָׁלָיִם.**[21]

יְרוּשָׁלַיִם שְׁמָמָה וְעָרֶיהָ נִצְּתוּ בְּזָדוֹנִי,

הַשְׁלֵךְ חַטֹּאתֶיהָ בִּמְצוֹלוֹת זְדוֹנִי,

וְהַעֲלֵה לְרֹאשׁ בִּזְכוּת אֵיתָנִי,

נ *Jerusalem! Besiegers have come to you[1] to fight and quarrel;*
   the [Evil Inclination] hidden[2] [in man] caused this,
      when he enticed you to bow to the god of others.
   HASHEM shall denounce you, O Satan;
      [HASHEM] Who chooses [Jerusalem];
   HASHEM shall repeatedly denounce you,
      [HASHEM] Who chooses   *Jerusalem.[3]*

ס *Jerusalem, may all who love her rejoice with her,[4] whoever they may be.*
   O children of Jacob and Joseph,[5] let there be no silence [before God]
      until He restores my Holy Temple.[6]
   Wake up! Wake up! Arise, O   *Jerusalem![7]*

ע *Jerusalem, Holy City, satiated with wormwood,*
   why did you so despise His commandments, for this reason or that?[8]
   Nevertheless, your King will again be [your] support.[9]
   For Zion's sake I will not be silent, and for the sake of   *Jerusalem.[10]*

פ *Jerusalem! 'Lest My soul be estranged from you,'[11]*
      warned the Most High.
   But He will yet come and rule, and show you good will.
   Then the moon will be abashed and the sun shamed,
      when [their] light will be dimmed,
      for HASHEM, Master of Legions, reigns on Mount Zion and in Jerusalem.[12]

צ *Jerusalem, exult and sing for joy[13] over your beauty and grandeur;*
   don your power, don [your] cloak [of majesty].[14]
   Burst with joyous song, exult[15] as was prophesied:
   'Lift up your voice in strength, O herald of   *Jerusalem.'[16]*

ק *Jerusalem [shall be] sanctified,*
      and strangers shall not come through it again;[17]
   no more will you drink the cup of poison.[18]
   He shall set your ways well, and your feet shall not falter.
   HASHEM will comfort Zion, and once again will choose   *Jerusalem.[19]*

ר *Jerusalem, sing and rejoice, compose a new song,*
      as the mount of the whitening Temple rises every higher.
   All flesh will come from month to month
   and prostrate themselves to HASHEM[20]
      at the holy mountain, in   *Jerusalem.[21]*

ש *Jerusalem is desolate; her cities were burned for my willful sins.*
   Throw her sins into the raging sea's depths!
   Through my Patriarchs' merit, raise her premier;

---

(1) Cf. *Jeremiah* 4:16; because the word נוֹצְרִים can also mean *Christians*, this stich was censored in many editions of *Selichos*; some read אוֹיְבִים, *enemies*, or נוֹקְמִים, *avengers*, instead of נוֹצְרִים, *besiegers*; others omit the first three stiches of the stanzas altogether. (2) See commentary to *selichah* 22, s.v., אָבֶן... מִכְשׁוֹל. (3) Cf. *Zechariah* 3:2; some editions of *Selichos* read הַשָּׂטָן הַצּוֹרֵר, *O murderous Satan*, in place of הַצּוֹרֵר, the first time it appears in this stanza. (4) Cf. *Isaiah* 66:10. (5) *Psalms* 77:16; see commentary to *selichah* 68, s.v., בְּכוֹר שׁוֹר. (6) Cf. *Isaiah* 62:7. (7) 51:17. (8) Cf. *Leviticus* 26:43. (9) Cf. *Psalms* 18:19. (10) *Isaiah* 62:1. (11) *Jeremiah* 6:8. (12) *Isaiah* 24:23. (13) Cf. *Isaiah* 12:6. (14) Cf. 52:1. (15) 54:1. (16) 40:9. (17) Cf. *Joel* 4:17. (18) Cf. *Isaiah* 51:22. (19) Cf. *Zechariah* 1:17. (20) Cf. *Isaiah* 66:23. (21) 27:13.

וְנִקְּווּ אֵלֶיהָ כָל הַגּוֹיִם לְשֵׁם יהוה **לִירוּשָׁלֵָיִם.**[1]

יְרוּשָׁלֵַיִם תְּהִלָּה בָּאָרֶץ תָּשִׂים[2] בָּאִים,

אֶשְׁכָּר וָשַׁי יָבִיאוּ שְׁבָא וּסְבָא[3] וְכוּשִׁיִים,

לְךָ לִישׁוּעָתָה לָנוּ[4] לְפִדְיוֹן שְׁבוּיִים,

בַּיּוֹם הַהוּא יֵצְאוּ מַיִם חַיִּים **מִירוּשָׁלֵָיִם.**[5]

יְרוּשָׁלֵַיִם עַל רֹאשׁ שִׂמְחָה תַּעֲלֶה[6] בְּאוֹרֵךְ,

לְהָשִׁיב[7] מֵשִׁיר צִיּוֹן בְּשִׁיר[8] דְּבִירֵךְ,

נְקֵבָה תְּסוֹבֵב גֶּבֶר[9]* בְּפִי בְּנֵךְ בְּכוֹרֵךְ,

יֵשֶׁב נָא אַפֵּךְ וַחֲמָתֵךְ מֵעִירֵךְ **יְרוּשָׁלֵָיִם.**[10]

All, while standing:

אֵל מֶלֶךְ יוֹשֵׁב עַל כִּסֵּא רַחֲמִים מִתְנַהֵג בַּחֲסִידוּת, מוֹחֵל עֲוֹנוֹת עַמּוֹ, מַעֲבִיר רִאשׁוֹן רִאשׁוֹן, מַרְבֶּה מְחִילָה לַחַטָּאִים וּסְלִיחָה לַפּוֹשְׁעִים, עֹשֶׂה צְדָקוֹת עִם כָּל בָּשָׂר וָרוּחַ, לֹא כְרָעָתָם תִּגְמוֹל. ✧ אֵל הוֹרֵיתָ לָנוּ לוֹמַר שְׁלֹשׁ עֶשְׂרֵה, וּזְכוֹר לָנוּ הַיּוֹם בְּרִית שְׁלֹשׁ עֶשְׂרֵה, כְּמוֹ שֶׁהוֹדַעְתָּ לֶעָנָיו מִקֶּדֶם, כְּמוֹ שֶׁכָּתוּב, וַיֵּרֶד יהוה בֶּעָנָן וַיִּתְיַצֵּב עִמּוֹ שָׁם, וַיִּקְרָא בְשֵׁם יהוה.

Congregation, then *chazzan*:

וַיַּעֲבֹר יהוה עַל פָּנָיו וַיִּקְרָא:

Congregation and *chazzan* (the words in bold type are recited aloud and in unison):

יהוה, יהוה, אֵל, רַחוּם, וְחַנּוּן, אֶרֶךְ אַפַּיִם, וְרַב חֶסֶד, **וֶאֱמֶת, נֹצֵר חֶסֶד לָאֲלָפִים, נֹשֵׂא עָוֹן, וָפֶשַׁע, וְחַטָּאָה, וְנַקֵּה.** וְסָלַחְתָּ לַעֲוֹנֵנוּ וּלְחַטָּאתֵנוּ וּנְחַלְתָּנוּ. סְלַח לָנוּ אָבִינוּ כִּי חָטָאנוּ, מְחַל לָנוּ מַלְכֵּנוּ כִּי פָשָׁעְנוּ. כִּי אַתָּה אֲדֹנָי טוֹב וְסַלָּח, וְרַב חֶסֶד לְכָל קֹרְאֶיךָ.

פסוקי הקדמה לסליחה עד

זִבְחֵי אֱלֹהִים רוּחַ נִשְׁבָּרָה, לֵב נִשְׁבָּר וְנִדְכֶּה אֱלֹהִים לֹא תִבְזֶה.[11] אָז תַּחְפֹּץ זִבְחֵי צֶדֶק עוֹלָה וְכָלִיל, אָז יַעֲלוּ עַל מִזְבַּחֲךָ פָרִים.[12] וְחֶסֶד יהוה מֵעוֹלָם וְעַד עוֹלָם עַל יְרֵאָיו, וְצִדְקָתוֹ לִבְנֵי בָנִים.[13] וַיֹּאמֶר, בִּי נִשְׁבַּעְתִּי נְאֻם יהוה, כִּי יַעַן אֲשֶׁר עָשִׂיתָ אֶת הַדָּבָר הַזֶּה, וְלֹא חָשַׂכְתָּ אֶת בִּנְךָ אֶת יְחִידֶךָ.[14]

---

(1) *Jeremiah* 3:17. (2) Cf. *Isaiah* 62:7. (3) Cf. *Psalms* 72:10. (4) 80:3. (5) *Zechariah* 14:8. (6) Cf. *Psalms* 137:6. (7) Some editions read לָשִׁיר, *to sing*. (8) *Psalms* 137:3. (9) *Jeremiah* 31:21. (10) *Daniel* 9:16. (11) *Psalms* 51:19. (12) 51:21. (13) 103:17. (14) *Genesis* 22:16.

then all the nations will gather to her,
     for HASHEM's sake, to   **Jerusalem.**¹

ת **Jerusalem** — make it be made the praise of the land² and the isles;
Sheba, Seba, and Cushites will bring tribute and gifts.³
Go forth to be salvation for us,⁴ to ransom captives,
[and] on that day living water will go forth from   **Jerusalem.**⁵

Jerusalem — elevate it above the foremost of joys⁶
     with Your [salvation's] light,
to bring back⁷ the songs of Zion with melody⁸
     to Your Sanctuary.
feminine [song] will turn to masculine*⁹ in the mouth of [Israel,]
     Your firstborn —
please turn back Your furious anger from Your city   **Jerusalem.**¹⁰

All, while standing:

אֵל מֶלֶךְ O God, King Who sits on the throne of mercy; Who acts with
     kindness, pardons the iniquities of His people, removes [sins]
one by one, increasingly grants pardon to careless sinners and forgiveness
to rebels, Who deals righteously with every living being — You do not repay
them in accord with their evil. Chazzan — O God, You taught us to recite the
Thirteen [Attributes of Mercy], so remember for us today the covenant of
these Thirteen, as You made known to the humble one in ancient times, as
it is written: And HASHEM descended in a cloud and stood with him there,
and He called out with the Name HASHEM.

Congregation, then chazzan:

And HASHEM passed before him [Moses] and proclaimed:

Congregation and chazzan (the words in bold type are recited aloud and in unison):

ה' ה' **HASHEM, HASHEM, God, Compassionate and Gracious, Slow
     to anger, and Abundant in Kindness and Truth, Preserver of
kindness for thousands [of generations], Forgiver of iniquity, willful
sin, and error, and Who cleanses.** May You forgive our iniquities and our
errors and make us Your heritage. Forgive us, our Father, for we have
erred; pardon us, our King, for we have willfully sinned; for You, my Lord,
are good and forgiving and abundantly kind to all who call upon You.

PREFATORY VERSES TO SELICHAH 74

זִבְחֵי The offerings of God are a broken spirit; a heart broken and
     crushed, O God, You will not despise.¹¹ Then You will desire the
sacrifices of righteousness, the olah-offering and the whole-offering; then
bulls will go up on Your Altar.¹² HASHEM's kindness is forever and ever
on those who fear Him, and His righteousness is upon children's
children.¹³ He said: 'By Myself I swear,' declared HASHEM, 'that since you
have done this thing, and not withheld your son, your only one . . .'¹⁴

נְקֵבָה תְּסוֹבֵב גֶּבֶר — Feminine [song] will turn to
masculine. The word for song appears in Scripture in the masculine gender — שִׁיר — and in the
feminine — שִׁירָה. In the feminine form, it refers
to songs of joy in the world of the present. After

every song of joy, a new tragedy is born, just as
a female gives birth to one child after another. But
the song of the World to Come is in the masculine
form, because it is the song which will beget no
further misfortunes (Rashi to Arachin 13b).

כְּרַחֵם אָב עַל בָּנִים, כֵּן תְּרַחֵם יהוה עָלֵינוּ. לַיהוה הַיְשׁוּעָה,
עַל עַמְּךָ בִרְכָתֶךָ סֶּלָה. יהוה צְבָאוֹת עִמָּנוּ, מִשְׂגָּב
לָנוּ אֱלֹהֵי יַעֲקֹב סֶלָה. יהוה צְבָאוֹת, אַשְׁרֵי אָדָם בֹּטֵחַ בָּךְ. יהוה
הוֹשִׁיעָה, הַמֶּלֶךְ יַעֲנֵנוּ בְיוֹם קָרְאֵנוּ.

In some congregations the following two verses are recited responsively — the *chazzan* reciting סְלַח,
and the congregation responding וַיֹּאמֶר. In other congregations these verses are recited silently.

סְלַח נָא לַעֲוֹן הָעָם הַזֶּה כְּגֹדֶל חַסְדֶּךָ, וְכַאֲשֶׁר נָשָׂאתָה לָעָם
הַזֶּה מִמִּצְרַיִם וְעַד הֵנָּה, וְשָׁם נֶאֱמַר:

וַיֹּאמֶר יהוה סָלַחְתִּי כִּדְבָרֶךָ.

All:

הַטֵּה אֱלֹהַי אָזְנְךָ וּשֲׁמָע, פְּקַח עֵינֶיךָ וּרְאֵה שֹׁמְמֹתֵינוּ, וְהָעִיר
אֲשֶׁר נִקְרָא שִׁמְךָ עָלֶיהָ, כִּי לֹא עַל צִדְקוֹתֵינוּ אֲנַחְנוּ
מַפִּילִים תַּחֲנוּנֵינוּ לְפָנֶיךָ, כִּי עַל רַחֲמֶיךָ הָרַבִּים. אֲדֹנָי שְׁמָעָה,
אֲדֹנָי סְלָחָה, אֲדֹנָי הַקְשִׁיבָה, וַעֲשֵׂה אַל תְּאַחַר, לְמַעַנְךָ אֱלֹהַי, כִּי
שִׁמְךָ נִקְרָא עַל עִירְךָ וְעַל עַמֶּךָ.

סְלִיחָה עד (עקדה)

אֱלֹהֵינוּ וֵאלֹהֵי אֲבוֹתֵינוּ:

אֶזְרָחִי[1] הֵעִיר מִמִּזְרָח,*   בְּרַגְלוֹ צֶדֶק זָרַח,[2]

גִּבּוֹר לָרוּץ אֹרַח,[3]   דָּגוּל כְּשׁוֹשַׁן פָּרַח.

הוּא אַבְרָהָם הוּעַד,*   וְצִדְקָתוֹ עוֹמֶדֶת לָעַד,[4]

זֶרַע לְמֵאָה נִסְעָד,   חוֹנֵן צַדִּיק וְסָעַד.*

טַכְסִיסֵי מַלְכוּת לָמַד,   יָעַץ נְדִיבוֹת וְלִמַּד,

כַּזָּהָב מְזֻקָּק וְנֶחְמָד,   לַאֲשֶׁר נִסָּה[5] וְעָמָד.

מוֹרִיָּה יְחִידוֹ הֶעֱלָה,   נְצַטַּנָּה מִנְּשִׂאִים לְמָעְלָה,*

סִנְסִינוֹ כִּגְדִישׁ עוֹלָה,   עָקוּד כְּכֶבֶשׂ וְטָלֶה.

פָּקוּד כְּשׁוֹרָה שָׁמַר,   צְפָצֵף וּבְלֵב גָּמַר,

---

§ אֶזְרָחִי הֵעִיר מִמִּזְרָח — *Abraham awoke from
the east.* This anonymously written *akeidah*
follows an *aleph-beis* acrostic.

הוּא אַבְרָהָם הוּעַד — *He was appointed to be
Abraham.* His original name, אַבְרָם, *Abram*,
implies אַב אֲרָם, *patriarch of Aram*, his homeland. But the name given him by God, אַבְרָהָם,
Abraham, implies אַב הֲמוֹן גּוֹיִם, *patriarch of
multitude of nations* (Genesis 17:5; Berachos 13a).

חוֹנֵן צַדִּיק וְסָעַד — *[Because] he was gracious,*

righteous and supplied [wayfarers their] needs.
Alternatively, this stich refers not to Abraham,
but to God. The translation then is: *[by God] the
Gracious One, the Righteous One, the Supplier [of
all needs]*; or, *the One Who is gracious to the
righteous person and supplies [his needs].*

מוֹרִיָּה . . . מִנְּשִׂאִים לְמָעְלָה — *On [Mount] Moriah
. . . Him Who is above the clouds.* The word
נְשִׂאִים here means *the bearers*, specifically, the
clouds that bear the rain (see, e.g., Psalms 135:7).

כְּרַחֵם אָב *As a father has mercy on his children, so, HASHEM, may You have mercy on us. Salvation is HASHEM's, upon Your people is Your blessing, Selah. HASHEM, Master of Legions, is with us, a stronghold for us is the God of Jacob, Selah. HASHEM, Master of Legions, praiseworthy is the person who trusts in You. HASHEM, save! May the King answer us on the day we call.*

In some congregations the following two verses are recited responsively — the chazzan reciting, 'Forgive, please . . .,' and the congregation responding, 'And HASHEM said . . .' In other congregations these verses are recited silently.

סְלַח נָא *Forgive, please, the iniquity of this people according to the greatness of Your kindness and as You have forgiven this people from Egypt until now, and there it was said:*

And HASHEM said, 'I have forgiven according to your word!'

All:

הַטֵּה *Incline, my God, Your ear, and listen, open Your eyes and see our desolation and that of the city upon which YourName is proclaimed; for not because of our righteousness do we cast down our supplications before You, rather because of Your abundant compassion. O my Lord, heed; O my Lord, forgive; O my Lord, be attentive and act, do not delay; for Your sake, my God, for Your Name is proclaimed upon Your city and upon Your people.*

SELICHAH 74

Our God and the God of our forefathers:

א *Abraham[1] awoke from the east;**
ב *at his foot righteousness shone,[2]*
ג *a powerful warrior to run the course,[3]*
ד *outstanding as a blooming rose.*
ה *He was appointed to be Abraham,**
ו *His righteousness endures forever.[4]*
ז *At one hundred years of age he was supplied with offspring,*
ח *[because] he was gracious,*
      righteous and supplied [wayfarers their] needs.*
ט *He learned the ways of [God's] kingship,*
י *he counseled and taught generosity.*
כ *Like precious refined gold,*
ל *he faced ten trials[5] and stood them all.*
מ *On [Mount] Moriah he offered up his only [son],*
נ *commanded by Him Who is above the clouds.**
ס *His offspring considered like the heaped up [incense offering]*
ע *was bound like a sheep or lamb.*
פ *He kept the commandment exactly,*
צ *speech and heart united,*

---

(1) See commentary to selichah 83, s.v., אֵיתָן לְמַד דַּעַת. (2) Cf. Isaiah 41:2.
(3) Cf. Psalms 19:6. (4) 111:3. (5) See commentary to selichah 39, s.v., נִסִּיתוֹ בַּעֲשִׂירִי.

Alternatively: this word is the plural of נָשִׂיא, prince, a title by which the Hittites called Abraham (Genesis 23:6). Accordingly, these two lines read: On [Mount] Moriah he who is

קַחַת בְּלֶב תָּמָר,*   רְצוּיוֹ כְּנִיחוֹחַ לְתָמָר.

שֵׁבוּ יַחְדָּו שְׁנֵיהֶם,   עֲשׂוֹת רְצוֹן קוֹנֵיהֶם,

תִּזְכֹּר מִנְחַת דִּשְׁנֵיהֶם,   אַחֲרֵיהֶם לִבְנֵי בְנֵיהֶם.

❖ תָּרִיחַ קְטֹרֶת מַתְכָּנְתָּם,   תְּעָרֵב תְּכוּנַת עֲמִידָתָם,

תִּסְתַּכֵּל חֲקִיקַת תָּם,[1]   תְּרַחֵם עַל שְׁאֵרִיתָם.

All, while standing:

אֵל מֶֽלֶךְ יוֹשֵׁב עַל כִּסֵּא רַחֲמִים מִתְנַהֵג בַּחֲסִידוּת, מוֹחֵל
עֲוֹנוֹת עַמּוֹ, מַעֲבִיר רִאשׁוֹן רִאשׁוֹן, מַרְבֶּה מְחִילָה
לַחַטָּאִים וּסְלִיחָה לַפּוֹשְׁעִים, עֹשֶׂה צְדָקוֹת עִם כָּל בָּשָׂר וָרֽוּחַ,
לֹא כְרָעָתָם תִּגְמוֹל. ❖ אֵל הוֹרֵיתָ לָּנוּ לוֹמַר שְׁלֹשׁ עֶשְׂרֵה, וּזְכוֹר
לָֽנוּ הַיּוֹם בְּרִית שְׁלֹשׁ עֶשְׂרֵה, כְּמוֹ שֶׁהוֹדַעְתָּ לֶעָנָו מִקֶּֽדֶם, כְּמוֹ
שֶׁכָּתוּב, וַיֵּֽרֶד יהוה בֶּעָנָן וַיִּתְיַצֵּב עִמּוֹ שָׁם, וַיִּקְרָא בְשֵׁם יהוה.

Congregation, then *chazzan:*

וַיַּעֲבֹר יהוה עַל פָּנָיו וַיִּקְרָא:

Congregation and *chazzan* (the words in bold type are recited aloud and in unison):

יהוה, יהוה, אֵל, רַחוּם, וְחַנּוּן, אֶֽרֶךְ אַפַּֽיִם, וְרַב חֶֽסֶד, וֶאֱמֶת,
נֹצֵר חֶֽסֶד לָאֲלָפִים, נֹשֵׂא עָוֹן, וָפֶֽשַׁע, וְחַטָּאָה,
וְנַקֵּה. וְסָלַחְתָּ לַעֲוֹנֵֽנוּ וּלְחַטָּאתֵֽנוּ וּנְחַלְתָּֽנוּ. סְלַח לָֽנוּ אָבִֽינוּ כִּי
חָטָֽאנוּ, מְחַל לָֽנוּ מַלְכֵּֽנוּ כִּי פָשָֽׁעְנוּ. כִּי אַתָּה אֲדֹנָי טוֹב וְסַלָּח, וְרַב
חֶֽסֶד לְכָל קֹרְאֶֽיךָ.

סְלִיחָה עה (פזמון)

Chazzan, then congregation:

שַֽׁחַר קַמְתִּי* לְהוֹדוֹת לָךְ[2] אֱלֹהֵי תְהִלָּתִי,[3]

וָאֲרַנֵּן לְךָ בְּקֶר[4] וְאוֹדִיעֲךָ חַטָּאתִי,[5]

תִּנָּֽתֶן לִי[6] בָּזֶה שָׂכָר לִפְעֻלָּתִי,[7]

נַפְשִׁי בִּשְׁאֵלָתִי, וְעַמִּי בְּבַקָּשָׁתִי.[6]

---

pre-eminent among princes was commanded to offer up his only [son].

בְּלֶב תָּמָר — *With undivided heart* [lit., *with date-palm heart*]. Just as the date-palm has but one heart [its sap travels but one route, without sidetracking into branches (Rashi)], so has Israel but one heart, dedicated to its Father in heaven (*Succah* 45b).

שַֽׁחַר קַמְתִּי — *I have risen at dawn.* Although most of the *selichos* bearing the signature שְׁלֹמֹה

הַקָּטָן חֲזָק, *Shlomo the lesser, may he be strong,* are attributed to R' Shlomo HaBavli [see prefatory comment to *selichah* 2], this one is ascribed to R' Shlomo Ibn Gabriol [see prefatory comment to *selichah* 72]. Like *selichah* 19, this *selichah* uses the words of Queen Esther, נֶפְשִׁי בִּשְׁאֵלָתִי, *[Spare] my life at my request,* וְעַמִּי בְּבַקָּשָׁתִי, *and my people at my petition* (*Esther* 7:3), as its refrain. But the similarity does not end there, for the meters and rhyme schemes of the two *selichos* are

ק to take his son with undivided heart*
ר and let his smoke rise as a pleasing, favorable offering.
ש The two of them returned together
　　[from] the fulfillment of their Creator's will.
ת Remember their lavish sacrifice
　　for [the sake of] their children after them.
Chazzan — Smell the [fragrance of those children's prayer,
　　like] compounded incense;
let the order of their standing [prayer] be sweet.
Gaze upon the [likeness of] whole-hearted Jacob,
　　graven on Your Throne,[1]
and have mercy on their remnant.

All, while standing:

אֵל מֶלֶךְ O God, King Who sits on the throne of mercy; Who acts with kindness, pardons the iniquities of His people, removes [sins] one by one, increasingly grants pardon to careless sinners and forgiveness to rebels, Who deals righteously with every living being — You do not repay them in accord with their evil. Chazzan — O God, You taught us to recite the Thirteen [Attributes of Mercy], so remember for us today the covenant of these Thirteen, as You made known to the humble one in ancient times, as it is written: And HASHEM descended in a cloud and stood with him there, and He called out with the Name HASHEM.

Congregation, then chazzan:

And HASHEM passed before him [Moses] and proclaimed:

Congregation and chazzan (the words in bold type are recited aloud and in unison):

ה' ה' HASHEM, HASHEM, God, Compassionate and Gracious, Slow to anger, and Abundant in Kindness and Truth, Preserver of kindness for thousands [of generations], Forgiver of iniquity, willful sin, and error, and Who cleanses.** May You forgive our iniquities and our errors and make us Your heritage. Forgive us, our Father, for we have erred; pardon us, our King, for we have willfully sinned; for You, my Lord, are good and forgiving and abundantly kind to all who call upon You.

SELICHAH 75

Chazzan, then congregation:

ש I have risen at dawn* to offer thanks to You,[2] O God of my praise;[3]
　　I will sing to You in the morning[4] and let You know my [every] sin.[5]
For this may I be granted[6] reward for my labor:[7]
　　[Spare] my life at my request, and my people at my petition.[6]

---

(1) See commentary to selichah 68, s.v., חֲקוּקָה בַּכִּסֵּא. (2) Cf. Psalms 119:62.
(3) 109:1. (4) Cf. 59:17. (5) Cf. 32:5. (6) Esther 7:3. (7) Cf. Jeremiah 31:15.

also very close to each other. If indeed this one is the work of Ibn Gabriol and selichah 19 is by Ibn Gias, the similarity may be more than coincidence. The two paytanim lived in Southern Spain at the same time, and were about the same age. Moreover, for a time, they were both supported by (and may have been students of) R' Shmuel HaNaggid.

Congregation, then *chazzan:*

לְפָנִים זֹאת בְּיִשְׂרָאֵל[1] מַקְרִיבֵי הַקָּרְבָּן,
אִם חָטָאתִי כַּשֵּׁנִי כֻּלּוֹ הָפַךְ לָבָן,[2]
וְאֶדַּדֶּה כָל שְׁנוֹתַי[3]* וַאֲאַנִּין עַל הַחֻרְבָּן,
וְאֵין לִי לְבַד מִלָּתִי, וְעוֹלָתִי תְפִלָּתִי,
נַפְשִׁי בִּשְׁאֵלָתִי, וְעַמִּי בְּבַקָּשָׁתִי.

Congregation, then *chazzan:*

מִזְבֵּחַ בִּהְיוֹתוֹ וְקָדָשִׁים לְזָבְחָה,
וְהֵבִיא אִישׁ אֶת זִבְחוֹ וְחַטָּאתוֹ נִמְחָה,[4]
אָפֵס מֶנִּי מִכַּהֵן, וְאֵין זֶבַח וְאֵין מִנְחָה,
תּוֹדָתִי וְזִבְחָתִי, שִׂיחָתִי מִנְחָתִי,
נַפְשִׁי בִּשְׁאֵלָתִי, וְעַמִּי בְּבַקָּשָׁתִי.

Congregation, then *chazzan:*

הֵן בִּהְיוֹת הָעֲבוֹדָה וְכֹהֲנִים עַל מִשְׁמֶרֶת,
הֲלֹא חַטָּאת מְכַפֶּרֶת וְהָעוֹלָה מַכְשֶׁרֶת,
וְאֵין חַטָּאת וְאֵין עוֹלָה וְלֹא חֵלֶב וְיוֹתֶרֶת,
וְאֶשְׁפֹּךְ אֶת רִנָּתִי וְאָפִיל תְּחִנָּתִי,
נַפְשִׁי בִּשְׁאֵלָתִי, וְעַמִּי בְּבַקָּשָׁתִי.

Congregation, then *chazzan:*

הֵן קֶדֶם בַּמִּקְדָּשׁ בְּקוּם זְרִיזִים בְּאַשְׁמֹרֶת,
טְהוֹרִים נִצְּבוּ לְהָפִיס, חֲדָשִׁים לִקְטֹרֶת,*
וְאֵין לְבוֹנָה וְאֵין קְטֹרֶת, וְנִשְׁאַרְתִּי שְׁחַרְחֹרֶת,
בְּהִתְוַדּוּת חַטָּאתִי תְּהִי כְקָרְבָּן תּוֹדָתִי,
נַפְשִׁי בִּשְׁאֵלָתִי, וְעַמִּי בְּבַקָּשָׁתִי.

Congregation, then *chazzan:*

חֹזֶה קָדוֹשׁ כִּי יָדַי כָּבְדָה עַל אֲנָחָתִי,[5]
וְאֵין מִי יַעֲמֹד בַּעֲדִי, וְאֵין לִי בֵית מְנוּחָתִי,[6]
לְבַד בְּךָ אַזְכִּיר שְׁמֶךָ,[7] מָעוֹז צוּר יְשׁוּעָתִי,[8]
הַעֲבֵר אֶת אַשְׁמָתִי, וְעַתָּה בִּי צִדְקָתִי,[9]
נַפְשִׁי בִּשְׁאֵלָתִי, וְעַמִּי בְּבַקָּשָׁתִי.

וְאֶדַּדֶּה כָּל שְׁנוֹתַי — *[Therefore] I will leave my sleep behind* [lit., *I will wander all my sleep*]. The translation follows *Rashi* (to Isaiah 38:15) who considers שְׁנוֹתַי a derivative of שֵׁנָה, *sleep.* According to *Targum*, the word is derived from

שָׁנָה, *year,* and the phrase means, *I shall wander all my years.*

חֲדָשִׁים לִקְטֹרֶת — *[Which] new ones [among them would offer] the incense.* Whenever possible, the Incense service was limited to *Kohanim* who had

Congregation, then *chazzan*:

ל Formerly among Israel,¹ those who offered sacrifice,
   were my sin as scarlet it would all turn white.²
   [Therefore] I will leave my sleep behind*³
     and mourn the [Temple's] destruction,
   for now I have naught but my word; my prayer is my olah-offering:
      '[Spare] my life at my request, and my people at my petition.'

Congregation, then *chazzan*:

מ When there was the Altar,
   as well as sanctified offerings for slaughter,
   a man would bring his sacrifice and his sin was wiped away.⁴
   But the Kohen is gone from me,
     and there is neither animal offering nor meal offering.
   My confession is my animal offering, my prayer is my meal offering.
     '[Spare] my life at my request, and my people at my petition.'

Congregation, then *chazzan*:

ה Lo, when there was the Temple service,
   and the priests [served] at their watches,
   a sin-offering atoned, an olah-offering set matters right.
   [But today] there is neither sin- nor olah-offering,
     neither fat nor organs [to place on the Altar],
   so I pour out my song and offer my supplication:
      '[Spare] my life at my request, and my people at my petition.'

Congregation, then *chazzan*:

הק Lo, [in] earlier [times] in the Holy Temple,
   when the alacritous [Kohanim] rose before dawn,
טנ the purified ones would stand to cast lots:
   [which] new ones [among them would offer] the incense.*
   [But today] there is neither frankincense nor incense,
     so I remain blackened [by sin];
   [thus] as I confess my sins,
     let my confession be [considered] as an offering.
      [Spare] my life at my request, and my people at my petition.

Congregation, then *chazzan*:

See, O Holy One, how my smite is heavier than my sigh,⁵
and there is none to stand up for me;
   nor do I have [my Temple,] my House of Rest.⁶
[I call] only upon You, I mention [only] Your Name,⁷
   O Rock of my Salvation;⁸
clear away my guilt, and let my righteousness answer for me:⁹
     '[Spare] my life at my request, and my people at my petition.'

---

(1) Cf. *Ruth* 4:7. (2) Cf. *Isaiah* 1:18; *Leviticus* 13:13. (3) Cf. *Isaiah* 38:15. (4) Some editions read, וְנִתְכַּפֵּר בִּסְלִיחָה, *and he was atoned with forgiveness.* (5) *Job* 23:2; see *Targum* and *Rashi* there. (6) Cf. *I Chronicles* 28:2. (7) Cf. *Isaiah* 26:13. (8) Cf. *Psalms* 31:3; 28:8. (9) Genesis 30:33.

never yet burned the incense. Tradition, based on *Deuteronomy* 33:10-11, teaches that this service increased the wealth of the *Kohen* who performed it. Therefore, care was taken to give every *Kohen* at least one opportunity to burn the incense (*Yoma* 26a).

All, while standing:

אֵל מֶ֫לֶךְ יוֹשֵׁב עַל כִּסֵּא רַחֲמִים מִתְנַהֵג בַּחֲסִידוּת, מוֹחֵל עֲוֹנוֹת עַמּוֹ, מַעֲבִיר רִאשׁוֹן רִאשׁוֹן, מַרְבֶּה מְחִילָה לְחַטָּאִים וּסְלִיחָה לְפוֹשְׁעִים, עֹשֶׂה צְדָקוֹת עִם כָּל בָּשָׂר וָר֫וּחַ, לֹא כְרָעָתָם תִּגְמוֹל. ❖ אֵל הוֹרֵ֫יתָ לָ֫נוּ לוֹמַר שְׁלֹשׁ עֶשְׂרֵה, וּזְכוֹר לָ֫נוּ הַיּוֹם בְּרִית שְׁלֹשׁ עֶשְׂרֵה, כְּמוֹ שֶׁהוֹדַ֫עְתָּ לֶעָנָו מִקֶּ֫דֶם, כְּמוֹ שֶׁכָּתוּב, וַיֵּ֫רֶד יהוה בֶּעָנָן וַיִּתְיַצֵּב עִמּוֹ שָׁם, וַיִּקְרָא בְשֵׁם יהוה.

Congregation, then *chazzan:*

וַיַּעֲבֹר יהוה עַל פָּנָיו וַיִּקְרָא:

Congregation and *chazzan* (the words in bold type are recited aloud and in unison):

יהוה, יהוה, אֵל, רַחוּם, וְחַנּוּן, אֶ֫רֶךְ אַפַּ֫יִם, וְרַב חֶ֫סֶד, וֶאֱמֶת, נֹצֵר חֶ֫סֶד לָאֲלָפִים, נֹשֵׂא עָוֹן, וָפֶ֫שַׁע, וְחַטָּאָה, וְנַקֵּה. וְסָלַחְתָּ לַעֲוֹנֵ֫נוּ וּלְחַטָּאתֵ֫נוּ וּנְחַלְתָּ֫נוּ. סְלַח לָ֫נוּ אָבִ֫ינוּ כִּי חָטָ֫אנוּ, מְחַל לָ֫נוּ מַלְכֵּ֫נוּ כִּי פָשָׁ֫עְנוּ. כִּי אַתָּה אֲדֹנָי טוֹב וְסַלָּח, וְרַב חֶ֫סֶד לְכָל קֹרְאֶ֫יךָ.

All:

אַל תִּזְכָּר לָ֫נוּ עֲוֹנוֹת רִאשׁוֹנִים, מַהֵר יְקַדְּמ֫וּנוּ רַחֲמֶ֫יךָ, כִּי דַלּ֫וֹנוּ מְאֹד.[1] חַטַּאת נְעוּרֵ֫ינוּ וּפְשָׁעֵ֫ינוּ אַל תִּזְכּוֹר, כְּחַסְדְּךָ זְכָר לָ֫נוּ אַתָּה, לְמַ֫עַן טוּבְךָ יהוה.[2]

זְכוֹר רַחֲמֶ֫יךָ יהוה וַחֲסָדֶ֫יךָ, כִּי מֵעוֹלָם הֵ֫מָּה.[3] זָכְרֵ֫נוּ יהוה בִּרְצוֹן עַמֶּ֫ךָ, פָּקְדֵ֫נוּ בִּישׁוּעָתֶ֫ךָ.[4] זְכֹר עֲדָתְךָ קָנִ֫יתָ קֶּ֫דֶם, גָּאַ֫לְתָּ שֵׁ֫בֶט נַחֲלָתֶ֫ךָ, הַר צִיּוֹן זֶה שָׁכַ֫נְתָּ בּוֹ.[5] זְכֹר יהוה חִבַּת יְרוּשָׁלָ֫יִם, אַהֲבַת צִיּוֹן אַל תִּשְׁכַּח לָנֶ֫צַח.[6] אַתָּה תָקוּם תְּרַחֵם צִיּוֹן, כִּי עֵת לְחֶֽנְנָהּ כִּי בָא מוֹעֵד.[7] זְכֹר יהוה לִבְנֵי אֱדוֹם אֵת יוֹם יְרוּשָׁלָ֫יִם, הָאֹמְרִים עָ֫רוּ עָ֫רוּ עַד הַיְסוֹד בָּהּ.[8] זְכֹר לְאַבְרָהָם לְיִצְחָק וּלְיִשְׂרָאֵל עֲבָדֶ֫יךָ אֲשֶׁר נִשְׁבַּ֫עְתָּ לָהֶם בָּךְ, וַתְּדַבֵּר אֲלֵהֶם, אַרְבֶּה אֶת זַרְעֲכֶם כְּכוֹכְבֵי הַשָּׁמָ֫יִם, וְכָל הָאָ֫רֶץ הַזֹּאת אֲשֶׁר אָמַ֫רְתִּי אֶתֵּן לְזַרְעֲכֶם, וְנָחֲלוּ לְעוֹלָם.[9] ❖ זְכֹר לַעֲבָדֶ֫יךָ לְאַבְרָהָם לְיִצְחָק וּלְיַעֲקֹב, אַל תֵּ֫פֶן אֶל קְשִׁי הָעָם הַזֶּה וְאֶל רִשְׁעוֹ וְאֶל חַטָּאתוֹ.[10]

All, while standing:

אֵל מֶלֶךְ O God, King Who sits on the throne of mercy; Who acts with kindness, pardons the iniquities of His people, removes [sins] one by one, increasingly grants pardon to careless sinners and forgiveness to rebels, Who deals righteously with every living being — You do not repay them in accord with their evil. Chazzan — O God, You taught us to recite the Thirteen [Attributes of Mercy], so remember for us today the covenant of these Thirteen, as You made known to the humble one in ancient times, as it is written: And HASHEM descended in a cloud and stood with him there, and He called out with the Name HASHEM.

Congregation, then chazzan:

And HASHEM passed before him [Moses] and proclaimed:

Congregation and chazzan (the words in bold type are recited aloud and in unison):

ה' ה' HASHEM, HASHEM, God, Compassionate and Gracious, Slow to anger, and Abundant in Kindness and Truth, Preserver of kindness for thousands [of generations], Forgiver of iniquity, willful sin, and error, and Who cleanses. May You forgive our iniquities and our errors and make us Your heritage. Forgive us, our Father, for we have erred; pardon us, our King, for we have willfully sinned; for You, my Lord, are good and forgiving and abundantly kind to all who call upon You.

All:

אַל תִּזְכָּר Do not recall against us the iniquities of the ancients; speedily — let Your mercy come to meet us for we have fallen very low.[1] Remember not the sins of our youth and our rebellions; may You remember for us [the deeds] worthy of Your kindness, because of Your goodness, HASHEM.[2]

זְכוֹר רַחֲמֶיךָ Remember Your mercies, O HASHEM, and Your kindnesses, for they are from the beginning of the world.[3] Remember us, HASHEM, when You show Your people favor and recall us with Your salvation.[4] Remember Your congregation that You acquired of old, that You redeemed the tribe of Your heritage, and this Mount Zion where You dwelled.[5] Remember, O HASHEM, the affection of Jerusalem, may You never forget the love of Zion.[6] You will arise and show Zion mercy, for it is the time to be gracious to her, for the appointed time will have come.[7] Remember, HASHEM, for the offspring of Edom, the day of Jerusalem — for those who said: 'Destroy! Destroy to its very foundation!'[8] Remember Abraham, Isaac, and Israel, Your servants, to whom You swore by Your Being, saying to them, 'I shall increase your offspring like the stars of the heavens; and this entire land of which I spoke I will give to your offspring and they will inherit it forever.'[9] Chazzan — Remember for Your servants, for Abraham, for Isaac, and for Jacob; ignore the stubbornness of this people, its wickedness and its sinfulness.[10]

---

(1) *Psalms* 79:8. (2) Cf. 25:7. (3) 25:6. (4) Cf. 106:4. (5) 74:2. (6) This is not a Scriptural verse. (7) *Psalms* 102:14. (8) 137:7. (9) *Exodus* 32:13. (10) *Deuteronomy* 9:27.

Chazzan, then congregation:

אֵל נָא תָשֵׁת עָלֵינוּ חַטָּאת, אֲשֶׁר נוֹאַלְנוּ וַאֲשֶׁר חָטָאנוּ.[1]

Chazzan, then congregation:

חָטָאנוּ צוּרֵנוּ, סְלַח לָנוּ יוֹצְרֵנוּ.

סליחה עו (חטאנו)

All:

יוֹשֵׁב בְּגָבְהֵי מְרוֹמִים*   וּמַבִּיט בְּעָמְקֵי הֲדוֹמִים,

וְיוֹדֵעַ כָּל תַּעֲלוּמִים,   וּמֵבִין כָּל סְתוּמִים,

אִם עֲווֹנוֹת[2] נֶעֱצָמִים,   וּפְשָׁעִים[2] נִכְתָּמִים,

נָא יְכֻבְּשׁוּ רַחֲמִים,   כַּעַס וּזְעָמִים,[3]

אֵל מֶלֶךְ יוֹשֵׁב עַל כִּסֵּא רַחֲמִים.

חָטָאנוּ צוּרֵנוּ, סְלַח לָנוּ יוֹצְרֵנוּ.

וְאִם הִרְבֵּית אַשְׁמָה,   עֲנִיָּה וַעֲגוּמָה,

דַּיָּהּ כִּי נִזְעָמָה   בְּאַף וּבְחֵמָה,

וְנִתְּנָה לְשַׁמָּה,   וַאֲבֵלָה וְשׁוֹמֵמָה,

וּמֵעַת נִכְלָמָה   עוֹד לֹא רֻחָמָה.[4]

חָטָאנוּ צוּרֵנוּ, סְלַח לָנוּ יוֹצְרֵנוּ.

שְׂרִידֵי אֲשׁוּרִי   כְּנָפְלוּ בְּיַד הָאֲרִי,

וַיְמַלֵּא טֶרֶף חוֹרִי,   וּמְעוֹנוֹתָיו עֵגֶל וּמְרִיא,[5]

סָמוּךְ דֹּב אַחֲרִי,   וְנָמֵר בְּצֵרוּף חָמְרִי,

וְצֶפַע* נוֹשֵׁךְ בַּחֲרִי   בְּאֵין חוֹבֵשׁ וְצָרִי.

חָטָאנוּ צוּרֵנוּ, סְלַח לָנוּ יוֹצְרֵנוּ.

פָּנַי[6] כְּבָבַת נְצוּרָה,   נֶהֶפְכוּ כְּשׁוּלֵי קְדֵרָה,

כִּי עֲנִיָּה נִשְׁאָרָה,   בְּאֵין גְּבוּרָה,

פָּנֶיהָ לֹא הִסְתִּירָה,   מִכְּלִמָּה וְעֶבְרָה,

כָּתוּב וְלֹא כָתוּב בַּתּוֹרָה[7]   אוֹתָהּ הִקְרָה.

חָטָאנוּ צוּרֵנוּ, סְלַח לָנוּ יוֹצְרֵנוּ.

יוֹשֵׁב בְּגָבְהֵי מְרוֹמִים — [O God] Who dwells in lofty heights. The acrostic reads יוֹסֵף חֲזַק, Yosef, may he be strong, but nothing else is known about the author's identity.

הָאֲרִי . . . דֹּב . . . נָמֵר . . . וְצֶפַע — The [Babylonian] lion . . . the [Persian] bear . . . the [Greek] leopard . . . the [Roman] Monster. Throughout the Talmud and Midrash, and based on the Book of Daniel (ch. 8), Israel's long series of exiles and

persecutions are always treated as four main periods of subjugation to foreign oppressors — either in Eretz Yisrael or in the Diaspora. These periods are known collectively as אַרְבַּע מַלְכֻיּוֹת, the Four Kingdoms (Daniel 8:22), and each is called by the name of the empire dominant in the world at that particular time.

The first, called גָּלוּת בָּבֶל, the Babylonian Exile, began when Nebuchadnezzar king of Babylon

Chazzan, then congregation:

Please, do not reckon for us a sin,
what we have done foolishly and what we have sinned.[1]

Chazzan, then congregation:

We have erred, our Rock! Forgive us, our Molder!

SELICHAH 76

All:

י [O God] Who dwells in lofty heights,*
Who looks into the depths of the earth,
Who knows of all hidden things, Who understands every enigma:
If [Israel's] iniquities[2] are overpowering,
and they are stained with rebellion,[2]
please let [Your] mercy overcome,
[Your] anger and fury [at her],[3]
O God, King Who sits on the Throne of Mercy!
        We have sinned, our Rock! Forgive us, our Molder!

י If she has increased guilt, [she,] the poor and grieving [nation],
it is enough that she has suffered from wrath and fury;
she has been given over to desolation, mourning and devastation.
And from when she was shamed she has as yet found no mercy.[4]
        We have sinned, our Rock! Forgive us, our Molder!

ס Those who escaped Assyria
fell into the hand of the [Babylonian] lion,
who filled his den with prey, his lairs with calf and fattened ox.[5]
Close after him came the [Persian] bear,
and the [Greek] leopard bringing trials and upheaval.
Then the [Roman] monster,* biting viciously,
[a bite] without bandage or balm.
        We have sinned, our Rock! Forgive us, our Molder!

פ The face of the one[6] [You] would guard like the pupil [of the eye]
has become [black] like the bottom of a pot,
for she was left destitute without any strength.
She has not hidden her face,
[for she is used] to humiliation and enmity.
[All the curses, both those] written in the Torah
        and [those] unwritten,[7] have come upon her.
        We have sinned, our Rock! Forgive us, our Molder!

---

(1) *Numbers* 12:11. (2) In some editions of *Selichos* the word עֲוֹנוֹת, *iniquities,* and פְּשָׁעִים, *rebellions,* are reversed. (3) This stich does not appear in all editions. (4) Cf. *Hosea* 1:6. (5) Cf. *Nahum* 2:13. (6) Some editions read, פָּנַי, *my face*; if so, the *paytan* changes from third person to first person for this stich. (7) Cf. *Deuteronomy* 28:61.

conquered the land of Israel and destroyed the First Temple. The second, called גָּלוּת מָדַי וּפָרַס, *the Median-Persian Exile* (ibid. 8:20), began when that empire captured the Babylonians and became the leading world power. Although the Medes permitted the Jewish return to *Eretz* *Yisrael* and the building of the Second Temple, the early years of that *Beis HaMikdash* were still considered a part of the exile, because Israel was not sovereign in its Land. During the entire third period, גָּלוּת יָוָן, *the Greek Exile* (ibid. 8:21), paradoxically, Israel lived on its Land and the

חַיֶּיהָ תְּלוּאִים,   מִפְּחָדִים הַבָּאִים,[1]

כִּי כְגִדְיֵי טְלָאִים,   בֵּין כְּפִירֵי לְבָאִים,

חֲשׁוּכִים וְנִדְכָּאִים,   פְּצוּעִים וְחֶלְכָּאִים,

כָּל מְצֹרָעִים וּטְמֵאִים,   בְּאֶצְבַּע אוֹתָם מַרְאִים.

חָטָאנוּ צוּרֵנוּ, סְלַח לָנוּ יוֹצְרֵנוּ.

זְרִיּוֹת הֲדוֹמָךְ,[2]   וּשְׂרֵפַת אוּלָמָךְ,

הַבֵּט מִמְּרוֹמָךְ,   וְעַל הַגּוֹיִם שְׁפֹךְ זַעֲמָךְ,[3]

זְכוֹר נְאוּמָךְ,   אֲשֶׁר פֵּצְתָּ לְעַמָּךְ,

אִם בִּקְצֵה הָאָרֶץ אֲשִׁימֵךְ,   מִשָּׁם אֲקַבֶּצֵךְ וַאֲנַחֲמֵךְ.[4]

חָטָאנוּ צוּרֵנוּ, סְלַח לָנוּ יוֹצְרֵנוּ.

קָצַבְתָּ לִנְמְכָּרִים,[5]   מִשְׁנֶה שְׂכַר שְׂכִירִים[6]

הֵם בִּקְצָווֹת פְּזוּרִים,   וְכַמָּה שָׁנִים לֹא זְכוּרִים,

קַיֶּם נָא מַאֲמָרִים,   בְּיַד בֶּן אָמוֹץ אֲמוּרִים,

אִם יָמוֹשׁוּ גְבָעוֹת וְצוּרִים,   חַסְדִּי וּבְרִיתִי מֵאִתֵּךְ לֹא סָרִים.[7]

חָטָאנוּ צוּרֵנוּ, סְלַח לָנוּ יוֹצְרֵנוּ.

All:

זְכוֹר לָנוּ בְּרִית אָבוֹת, כַּאֲשֶׁר אָמַרְתָּ: וְזָכַרְתִּי אֶת בְּרִיתִי יַעֲקוֹב, וְאַף אֶת בְּרִיתִי יִצְחָק, וְאַף אֶת בְּרִיתִי אַבְרָהָם אֶזְכֹּר, וְהָאָרֶץ אֶזְכֹּר.[8]

זְכוֹר לָנוּ בְּרִית רִאשׁוֹנִים כַּאֲשֶׁר אָמַרְתָּ, וְזָכַרְתִּי לָהֶם בְּרִית רִאשׁוֹנִים, אֲשֶׁר הוֹצֵאתִי אוֹתָם מֵאֶרֶץ מִצְרַיִם לְעֵינֵי הַגּוֹיִם, לִהְיוֹת לָהֶם לֵאלֹהִים אֲנִי יְהוָה.[9] עֲשֵׂה עִמָּנוּ כְּמָה שֶׁהִבְטַחְתָּנוּ: וְאַף גַּם זֹאת בִּהְיוֹתָם בְּאֶרֶץ אֹיְבֵיהֶם, לֹא מְאַסְתִּים וְלֹא גְעַלְתִּים לְכַלֹּתָם לְהָפֵר בְּרִיתִי אִתָּם, כִּי אֲנִי יְהוָה אֱלֹהֵיהֶם.[10] הִמָּצֵא לָנוּ בְּבַקָּשָׁתֵנוּ, כְּמָה שֶׁכָּתוּב: וּבִקַּשְׁתֶּם מִשָּׁם אֶת יְהוָה אֱלֹהֶיךָ וּמָצָאתָ, כִּי תִדְרְשֶׁנּוּ בְּכָל לְבָבְךָ וּבְכָל נַפְשֶׁךָ.[11] מוֹל אֶת לְבָבֵנוּ לְאַהֲבָה וּלְיִרְאָה אֶת שְׁמֶךָ, כְּמָה שֶׁכָּתוּב:

Temple stood. Nevertheless, it was a very turbulent era marked with civil strife, foreign domination, vicious anti-religious campaigns, and the rejection of Torah values by a large number of Jews who adopted Greek culture with all its abominations. The downfall of the Greek Empire and the rise of Rome marked the beginning of גָּלוּת אֱדוֹם, *the Edomite or Roman*

Exile. It is this millennia-long exile that we are still in today.

In his Vision of the Four Beasts, Daniel was shown allegorically the four nations in whose domains Israel would be exiled. The first exile, the Babylonian, was represented by a lion with eagle's wings; the second, the Median-Persian, by a bear; the third, the Greek, by a

ח Her [people's] lives are suspended by a thread
for fearful events that are coming,[1]
for they are like young sheep among the youthful lions.
Plunged into darkness and crushed, wounded and weak,
all the lepers and the unclean point a finger at them [in disdain].
We have sinned, our Rock! Forgive us, our Molder!

ז [At your people] scattered across [the earth,] Your footstool,[2]
and [at] the burning of Your Temple,
look down from Your heights,
and pour out Your wrath on the nations [responsible].[3]
Remember Your words, that You spoke to Your people:
'Even if I put You at the end of the earth,
from there I will gather you in and comfort you.'[4]
We have sinned, our Rock! Forgive us, our Molder!

ק You fixed a term [of six years] for those sold [as servants],[5]
twice the years of a hired man;[6]
but they are scattered to the ends [of the earth],
and not remembered for so many years!
Please uphold all the words spoken by [Isaiah] the son of Amoz:
'Though the hills and boulders may move,
My kindness and My covenant will not depart from you,'[7]
We have sinned, our Rock! Forgive us, our Molder!

All:

זְכוֹר לָנוּ Remember for us the covenant of the Patriarchs, as You said:
'And I will remember My covenant with Jacob, and also My
covenant with Isaac, and also My covenant with Abraham will I remember; and the Land will I remember.'[8]

זְכוֹר לָנוּ Remember for us the covenant of the ancestors, as You said:
'And I will remember for them the covenant of the ancestors
whom I brought out of the land of Egypt in the very sight of the nations,
to be a God to them; I am HASHEM.'[9] Do with us as You promised us: 'And
despite all that, when they will be in the land of their enemies, I will not
have despised them nor abhorred them to destroy them, to annul My
covenant with them, for I am HASHEM their God.'[10] Be accessible to us in
our quest, as it is written: From there you will seek HASHEM, your God,
and you will find, when you search for Him with all your heart and with
all your soul.[11] Expose our hearts to love Your Name, as it is written:

---

(1) Cf. *Deuteronomy* 28:66. (2) See *Isaiah* 66:1; some editions of *Selichos* read זְרִיבַת הֲדוֹמֶךָ, *the burning
of [the Temple,] Your footstool*; see *Lamentations* 2:1. (3) Cf. *Psalms* 69:25; in some editions of
Selichos this stich has been omitted or altered to suit the censors; some read וְעַל הַמַּיִם, *on the waters*;
some read וְעַל הָעוֹבְדֵי אֱלִילִים, *on the [pagan] idol worshipers*. (4) Cf. *Deuteronomy* 30:4. (5) See
Exodus 21:2. (6) See *Deuteronomy* 15:18 and *Isaiah* 16:14; see also *Tosafos* to *Kiddushin* 17a, s.v., חלה.
(7) Cf. *Isaiah* 54:10. (8) Cf. *Jeremiah* 30:18. (9) *Leviticus* 26:45. (10) 26:44. (11) *Deuteronomy* 4:29.

---

four-headed, four-winged leopard; and the last, the Roman, by an unnamed ten-horned, iron-toothed ferocious beast (see *Daniel* 7:4-7). Although the *paytan* refers to the fourth beast as צֶפַע, *a poisonous serpent*, the translation reads *monster*, in keeping with the Scriptural passage that does not identify the animal.

וּמָל יהוה אֱלֹהֶיךָ אֶת לְבָבְךָ וְאֶת לְבַב זַרְעֶךָ, לְאַהֲבָה אֶת יהוה
אֱלֹהֶיךָ בְּכָל לְבָבְךָ וּבְכָל נַפְשְׁךָ, לְמַעַן חַיֶּיךָ.[1] זְרוֹק עָלֵינוּ מַיִם
טְהוֹרִים וְטַהֲרֵנוּ, כְּמָה שֶׁכָּתוּב: וְזָרַקְתִּי עֲלֵיכֶם מַיִם טְהוֹרִים
וּטְהַרְתֶּם, מִכֹּל טֻמְאוֹתֵיכֶם וּמִכָּל גִּלּוּלֵיכֶם אֲטַהֵר אֶתְכֶם.[2] מְחֵה
פְשָׁעֵינוּ כָּעָב וְכֶעָנָן, כְּמָה שֶׁכָּתוּב: מָחִיתִי כָעָב פְּשָׁעֶיךָ וְכֶעָנָן
חַטֹּאתֶיךָ, שׁוּבָה אֵלַי כִּי גְאַלְתִּיךָ.[3] מְחֵה פְשָׁעֵינוּ לְמַעֲנָךְ, כַּאֲשֶׁר
אָמַרְתָּ: אָנֹכִי אָנֹכִי הוּא מֹחֶה פְשָׁעֶיךָ לְמַעֲנִי, וְחַטֹּאתֶיךָ לֹא אֶזְכֹּר.[4]
הַלְבֵּן חֲטָאֵינוּ כַּשֶּׁלֶג וְכַצֶּמֶר, כְּמָה שֶׁכָּתוּב: לְכוּ נָא וְנִוָּכְחָה, יֹאמַר
יהוה, אִם יִהְיוּ חֲטָאֵיכֶם כַּשָּׁנִים, כַּשֶּׁלֶג יַלְבִּינוּ, אִם יַאְדִּימוּ כַתּוֹלָע,
כַּצֶּמֶר יִהְיוּ.[5] רַחֵם עָלֵינוּ וְאַל תַּשְׁחִיתֵנוּ, כְּמָה שֶׁכָּתוּב: כִּי אֵל רַחוּם
יהוה אֱלֹהֶיךָ, לֹא יַרְפְּךָ וְלֹא יַשְׁחִיתֶךָ וְלֹא יִשְׁכַּח אֶת בְּרִית
אֲבוֹתֶיךָ אֲשֶׁר נִשְׁבַּע לָהֶם.[6] קַבֵּץ נִדָּחֵינוּ כְּמָה שֶׁכָּתוּב: אִם יִהְיֶה
נִדַּחֲךָ בִּקְצֵה הַשָּׁמָיִם, מִשָּׁם יְקַבֶּצְךָ יהוה אֱלֹהֶיךָ וּמִשָּׁם יִקָּחֶךָ.[7]
הָשֵׁב שְׁבוּתֵנוּ וְרַחֲמֵנוּ, כְּמָה שֶׁכָּתוּב: וְשָׁב יהוה אֱלֹהֶיךָ אֶת שְׁבוּתְךָ
וְרִחֲמֶךָ וְשָׁב וְקִבֶּצְךָ מִכָּל הָעַמִּים אֲשֶׁר הֱפִיצְךָ יהוה אֱלֹהֶיךָ
שָׁמָּה.[8] ❖ תְּבִיאֵנוּ אֶל הַר קָדְשֶׁךָ, וְשַׂמְּחֵנוּ בְּבֵית תְּפִלָּתֶךָ, כְּמָה
שֶׁכָּתוּב: וַהֲבִיאוֹתִים אֶל הַר קָדְשִׁי, וְשִׂמַּחְתִּים בְּבֵית תְּפִלָּתִי,
עוֹלֹתֵיהֶם וְזִבְחֵיהֶם לְרָצוֹן עַל מִזְבְּחִי, כִּי בֵיתִי בֵּית תְּפִלָּה יִקָּרֵא
לְכָל הָעַמִּים.[9]

THE ARK IS OPENED.

The first four verses of the following prayer are recited responsively; *chazzan*, then congregation:

שְׁמַע קוֹלֵנוּ יהוה אֱלֹהֵינוּ, חוּס וְרַחֵם עָלֵינוּ,
וְקַבֵּל בְּרַחֲמִים וּבְרָצוֹן אֶת תְּפִלָּתֵנוּ.[10]

הֲשִׁיבֵנוּ יהוה אֵלֶיךָ וְנָשׁוּבָה, חַדֵּשׁ יָמֵינוּ כְּקֶדֶם.[11]

אַל תַּשְׁלִיכֵנוּ מִלְּפָנֶיךָ, וְרוּחַ קָדְשְׁךָ אַל תִּקַּח מִמֶּנּוּ.[12]

אַל תַּשְׁלִיכֵנוּ לְעֵת זִקְנָה, כִּכְלוֹת כֹּחֵנוּ אַל תַּעַזְבֵנוּ.[13]

אַל תַּעַזְבֵנוּ יהוה, אֱלֹהֵינוּ אַל תִּרְחַק מִמֶּנּוּ.[14]

עֲשֵׂה עִמָּנוּ אוֹת לְטוֹבָה, וְיִרְאוּ שׂוֹנְאֵינוּ וְיֵבֹשׁוּ,
כִּי אַתָּה יהוה עֲזַרְתָּנוּ וְנִחַמְתָּנוּ.[15]

אֲמָרֵינוּ הַאֲזִינָה יהוה, בִּינָה הֲגִיגֵנוּ.[16]

יִהְיוּ לְרָצוֹן אִמְרֵי פִינוּ וְהֶגְיוֹן לִבֵּנוּ לְפָנֶיךָ, יהוה צוּרֵנוּ וְגֹאֲלֵנוּ.[17]

כִּי לְךָ יהוה הוֹחָלְנוּ, אַתָּה תַעֲנֶה אֲדֹנָי אֱלֹהֵינוּ.[18]

THE ARK IS CLOSED.

HASHEM, your God, will expose your heart and the heart of your offspring,
to love HASHEM, your God, with all your heart and with all your soul, that
you may live.[1] Pour pure water upon us and purify us, as it is written: I shall
pour pure water upon you and purify you, of all your contaminations and
of all your abominations I will purify you.[2] Wipe away our willful sins like
a cloud and like a mist, as it is written: I have wiped away your willful sins
like a cloud and your errors like a mist — repent to Me, for I have redeemed
you![3] Wipe away our willful sins for Your sake, as You said: 'I, only I, am
the One Who wipes away your willful sins for My sake, and I shall not recall
your errors.'[4] Whiten our errors like snow and like [pure white] wool, as it
is written: 'Come now, let us reason together,' says HASHEM, 'though your
errors will be like scarlet, they will become white as snow; though they will
be red as crimson, they will become like [white] wool.'[5] Have mercy on us
and do not destroy us, as it is written: For a merciful God is HASHEM, your
God; He will not surrender you nor destroy you, and He will not forget the
covenant with your forefathers, which He swore to them.[6] Gather in our
dispersed ones, as it is written: If your dispersed were to be at the ends of
heaven, from there HASHEM, your God, will gather you in and from there He
will take you.[7] Bring back our captivity and have mercy on us, as it is
written: HASHEM, your God, will bringback your captivity and have mercy
on you, and He will again gather you in from all the peoples where HASHEM,
your God, has scattered you.[8] Chazzan — Bring us to Your holy mountain and
gladden us in Your house of prayer, as it is written: And I will bring them
to My holy mountain, and I will gladden them in My house of prayer, their
elevation-offerings and their feast offering will find favor on My Altar, for
My House will be called a house of prayer, for all peoples.[9]

THE ARK IS OPENED.

The first four verses of the following prayer are recited responsively; chazzan, then congregation:

שְׁמַע Hear our voice, HASHEM, our God, pity and be compassionate to us,
  and accept — with compassion and favor — our prayer.[10]
Bring us back to You, HASHEM, and we shall return,
  renew our days as of old.[11]
Do not cast us away from Yourself,
  and do not remove Your holy spirit from us.[12]
Do not cast us away in old age,
  when our strength gives out do not forsake us.[13]
Do not forsake us, HASHEM, our God, be not distant from us.[14]
Display for us a sign for good, so that our enemies may see it
  and be ashamed, for You, HASHEM, will have helped and consoled us.[15]
To our sayings give ear, HASHEM, perceive our thoughts.[16]
May the expressions of our mouth and the thoughts of our heart
  find favor before You, HASHEM, our Rock and our Redeemer.[17]
Because for You, HASHEM, we waited, You will answer, my Lord, our God.[18]

THE ARK IS CLOSED.

(1) Deuteronomy 30:6. (2) Ezekiel 36:25. (3) Isaiah 44:22. (4) 43:25. (5) 1:18. (6) Deuteronomy 4:31.
(7) 30:4. (8) 30:3. (9) Isaiah 56:7. (10) Weekday Shemoneh Esrei. (11) Lamentations 5:21.
(12) Cf. Psalms 51:13. (13) Cf. 71:9. (14) Cf. 38:22. (15) Cf. 86:17. (16) Cf. 5:2. (17) Cf. 19:15. (18) Cf. 38:16.

וִדּוּי

During the recitation of the וִדּוּי stand with head and body slightly bowed, in submissive contrition.

אֱלֹהֵינוּ וֵאלֹהֵי אֲבוֹתֵינוּ, תָּבֹא לְפָנֶיךָ תְּפִלָּתֵנוּ,[1] וְאַל תִּתְעַלַּם מִתְּחִנָּתֵנוּ,[2] שֶׁאֵין אֲנוּ עַזֵּי פָנִים וּקְשֵׁי עֹרֶף, לוֹמַר לְפָנֶיךָ יהוה אֱלֹהֵינוּ וֵאלֹהֵי אֲבוֹתֵינוּ, צַדִּיקִים אֲנַחְנוּ וְלֹא חָטָאנוּ, אֲבָל אֲנַחְנוּ וַאֲבוֹתֵינוּ חָטָאנוּ.[3]

Strike the left side of the chest with the right fist
while reciting each of the sins in the following confession litany.

אָשַׁמְנוּ, בָּגַדְנוּ, גָּזַלְנוּ, דִּבַּרְנוּ דֹפִי. הֶעֱוִינוּ, וְהִרְשַׁעְנוּ, זַדְנוּ, חָמַסְנוּ, טָפַלְנוּ שֶׁקֶר. יָעַצְנוּ רָע, כִּזַּבְנוּ, לַצְנוּ, מָרַדְנוּ, נִאַצְנוּ, סָרַרְנוּ, עָוִינוּ, פָּשַׁעְנוּ, צָרַרְנוּ, קִשִּׁינוּ עֹרֶף. רָשַׁעְנוּ, שִׁחַתְנוּ, תִּעַבְנוּ, תָּעִינוּ, תִּעְתָּעְנוּ.

סַרְנוּ מִמִּצְוֹתֶיךָ וּמִמִּשְׁפָּטֶיךָ הַטּוֹבִים וְלֹא שָׁוָה לָנוּ.[4] וְאַתָּה צַדִּיק עַל כָּל הַבָּא עָלֵינוּ, כִּי אֱמֶת עָשִׂיתָ וַאֲנַחְנוּ הִרְשָׁעְנוּ.[5]

אָשַׁמְנוּ מִכָּל עָם, בֹּשְׁנוּ מִכָּל דּוֹר, גָּלָה מִמֶּנּוּ מָשׂוֹשׂ, דָּוָה לִבֵּנוּ בַּחֲטָאֵינוּ, הֻחַבַּל אֲוֵּינוּ, וְנִפְרַע פְּאֵרֵנוּ, זְבוּל בֵּית מִקְדָּשֵׁנוּ חָרַב בַּעֲוֹנֵינוּ, טִירָתֵנוּ הָיְתָה לְשַׁמָּה, יְפִי אַדְמָתֵנוּ לְזָרִים, כֹּחֵנוּ לְנָכְרִים.

וַעֲדַיִן לֹא שַׁבְנוּ מִטָּעוּתֵנוּ וְהֵיךְ נָעִיז פָּנֵינוּ וְנַקְשֶׁה עָרְפֵּנוּ, לוֹמַר לְפָנֶיךָ יהוה אֱלֹהֵינוּ וֵאלֹהֵי אֲבוֹתֵינוּ, צַדִּיקִים אֲנַחְנוּ וְלֹא חָטָאנוּ, אֲבָל אֲנַחְנוּ וַאֲבוֹתֵינוּ חָטָאנוּ.

Strike the left side of the chest with the right fist while reciting
each of the sins in the following confession litany.

אָשַׁמְנוּ, בָּגַדְנוּ, גָּזַלְנוּ, דִּבַּרְנוּ דֹפִי. הֶעֱוִינוּ, וְהִרְשַׁעְנוּ, זַדְנוּ, חָמַסְנוּ, טָפַלְנוּ שֶׁקֶר. יָעַצְנוּ רָע, כִּזַּבְנוּ, לַצְנוּ, מָרַדְנוּ, נִאַצְנוּ, סָרַרְנוּ, עָוִינוּ, פָּשַׁעְנוּ, צָרַרְנוּ, קִשִּׁינוּ עֹרֶף. רָשַׁעְנוּ, שִׁחַתְנוּ, תִּעַבְנוּ, תָּעִינוּ, תִּעְתָּעְנוּ.

סַרְנוּ מִמִּצְוֹתֶיךָ וּמִמִּשְׁפָּטֶיךָ הַטּוֹבִים וְלֹא שָׁוָה לָנוּ. וְאַתָּה צַדִּיק עַל כָּל הַבָּא עָלֵינוּ, כִּי אֱמֶת עָשִׂיתָ וַאֲנַחְנוּ הִרְשָׁעְנוּ.

---

(1) Cf. *Psalms* 88:3. (2) Cf. 55:2. (3) Cf. 106:6. (4) Cf. *Job* 33:27. (5) *Nehemiah* 9:33.

VIDUY/CONFESSION

During the recitation of the וִדּוּי stand with head and body slightly bowed, in submissive contrition.

אֱלֹהֵינוּ *Our God and the God of our forefathers, may our prayer come before You.[1] Do not ignore our supplication,[2] for we are not so brazen and obstinate as to say before You, HASHEM, our God and the God of our forefathers, that we are righteous and have not sinned, for in truth, we and our forefathers have sinned.[3]*

Strike the left side of the chest with the right fist while reciting
each of the sins in the following confession litany.

אָשַׁמְנוּ *We have become guilty; [ב] we have betrayed; [ג] we have robbed; [ד] we have spoken slander; [ה] we have caused perversion; [ו] we have caused wickedness; [ז] we have sinned willfully; [ח] we have extorted; [ט] we have accused falsely; [י] we have given evil counsel; [כ] we have been deceitful; [ל] we have scorned; [מ] we have rebelled; [נ] we have provoked; [ס] we have turned away; [ע] we have been perverse; [פ] we have acted wantonly; [צ] we have persecuted; [ק] we have been obstinate; [ר] we have been wicked; [ש] we have corrupted; [ת] we have been abominable; we have strayed; You have let us go astray.*

סַרְנוּ *We have turned away from Your commandments and from Your good laws but to no avail.[4] Yet You are righteous in all that has come upon us, for You have acted truthfully while we have caused wickedness.[5]*

[א] We have become the guiltiest of people. [ב] We have become the most degraded of all generations. [ג] Joy has departed from us. [ד] Our heart has been saddened by our sins. [ה] Our desirous treasure has been ruined, [ו] and our splendor dashed, [ז] for our Holy Temple edifice [ח] has been destroyed for our iniquities. [ט] Our Palace has become desolate. [י] [Jerusalem,] the beauty of our Land is given over to aliens, [כ] our power to strangers.

But still we have not returned from our waywardness. So how can we be so brazen and obstinate as to say before You, HASHEM, our God and the God of our forefathers, that we are righteous and have not sinned, for in truth, both we and our fathers have sinned.

Strike the left side of the chest with the right fist while reciting
each of the sins in the following confession litany.

אָשַׁמְנוּ *We have become guilty; [ב] we have betrayed; [ג] we have robbed; [ד] we have spoken slander; [ה] we have caused perversion; [ו] we have caused wickedness; [ז] we have sinned willfully; [ח] we have extorted; [ט] we have accused falsely; [י] we have given evil counsel; [כ] we have been deceitful; [ל] we have scorned; [מ] we have rebelled; [נ] we have provoked; [ס] we have turned away; [ע] we have been perverse; [פ] we have acted wantonly; [צ] we have persecuted; [ק] we have been obstinate; [ר] we have been wicked; [ש] we have corrupted; [ת] we have been abominable; we have strayed; You have let us go astray.*

סַרְנוּ *We have turned away from Your commandments and from Your good laws but to no avail. Yet You are righteous in all that has come upon us, for You have acted truthfully while we have caused wickedness.*

לְעֵינֵנוּ עָשְׁקוּ עֲמָלֵנוּ, מְמֻשָּׁךְ וּמְמוֹרָט מִמֶּנּוּ, נָתְנוּ עֻלָּם עָלֵינוּ,
סָבַלְנוּ עַל שִׁכְמֵנוּ, עֲבָדִים מָשְׁלוּ בָנוּ, פֹּרֵק אֵין מִיָּדָם, צָרוֹת רַבּוֹת
סְבָבוּנוּ, קְרָאנוּךְ יהוה אֱלֹהֵינוּ, רָחַקְתָּ מִמֶּנּוּ בַּעֲוֹנֵינוּ, שַׁבְנוּ
מֵאַחֲרֶיךָ, תָּעִינוּ וְאָבָדְנוּ.

וַעֲדַיִן לֹא שַׁבְנוּ מִטָּעוּתֵנוּ וְהֵיךְ נָעִיז פָּנֵינוּ וְנַקְשֶׁה עָרְפֵּנוּ,
לוֹמַר לְפָנֶיךָ יהוה אֱלֹהֵינוּ וֵאלֹהֵי אֲבוֹתֵינוּ, צַדִּיקִים אֲנַחְנוּ וְלֹא
חָטָאנוּ, אֲבָל אֲנַחְנוּ וַאֲבוֹתֵינוּ חָטָאנוּ.

*Strike the left side of the chest with the right fist while reciting
each of the sins in the following confession litany.*

אָשַׁמְנוּ, בָּגַדְנוּ, גָּזַלְנוּ, דִּבַּרְנוּ דֹּפִי. הֶעֱוִינוּ, וְהִרְשַׁעְנוּ, זַדְנוּ,
חָמַסְנוּ, טָפַלְנוּ שֶׁקֶר. יָעַצְנוּ רָע, כִּזַּבְנוּ, לַצְנוּ, מָרַדְנוּ,
נִאַצְנוּ, סָרַרְנוּ, עָוִינוּ, פָּשַׁעְנוּ, צָרַרְנוּ, קִשִּׁינוּ עֹרֶף. רָשַׁעְנוּ,
שִׁחַתְנוּ, תִּעַבְנוּ, תָּעִינוּ, תִּעְתָּעְנוּ.

סַרְנוּ מִמִּצְוֹתֶיךָ וּמִמִּשְׁפָּטֶיךָ הַטּוֹבִים וְלֹא שָׁוָה לָנוּ. וְאַתָּה
צַדִּיק עַל כָּל הַבָּא עָלֵינוּ, כִּי אֱמֶת עָשִׂיתָ וַאֲנַחְנוּ
הִרְשָׁעְנוּ.

הִרְשַׁעְנוּ וּפָשַׁעְנוּ, לָכֵן לֹא נוֹשָׁעְנוּ. וְתֵן בְּלִבֵּנוּ לַעֲזוֹב דֶּרֶךְ
רֶשַׁע, וְחִישׁ לָנוּ יֶשַׁע, כַּכָּתוּב עַל יַד נְבִיאֶךָ: יַעֲזֹב רָשָׁע
דַּרְכּוֹ, וְאִישׁ אָוֶן מַחְשְׁבֹתָיו, וְיָשֹׁב אֶל יהוה וִירַחֲמֵהוּ, וְאֶל אֱלֹהֵינוּ
כִּי יַרְבֶּה לִסְלוֹחַ.[1]

מָשִׁיחַ צִדְקֶךָ אָמַר לְפָנֶיךָ: שְׁגִיאוֹת מִי יָבִין מִנִּסְתָּרוֹת נַקֵּנִי.[2]
נַקֵּנוּ יהוה אֱלֹהֵינוּ מִכָּל פְּשָׁעֵינוּ, וְטַהֲרֵנוּ מִכָּל
טֻמְאוֹתֵינוּ, וּזְרוֹק עָלֵינוּ מַיִם טְהוֹרִים וְטַהֲרֵנוּ, כַּכָּתוּב עַל יַד
נְבִיאֶךָ: וְזָרַקְתִּי עֲלֵיכֶם מַיִם טְהוֹרִים וּטְהַרְתֶּם, מִכֹּל טֻמְאוֹתֵיכֶם
וּמִכָּל גִּלּוּלֵיכֶם אֲטַהֵר אֶתְכֶם.[3]

מִיכָה עַבְדְּךָ אָמַר לְפָנֶיךָ: מִי אֵל כָּמוֹךָ נֹשֵׂא עָוֹן וְעֹבֵר עַל
פֶּשַׁע לִשְׁאֵרִית נַחֲלָתוֹ, לֹא הֶחֱזִיק לָעַד אַפּוֹ, כִּי
חָפֵץ חֶסֶד הוּא, יָשׁוּב יְרַחֲמֵנוּ, יִכְבֹּשׁ עֲוֹנֹתֵינוּ, וְתַשְׁלִיךְ בִּמְצֻלוֹת
יָם כָּל חַטֹּאתָם.[4] (וְכָל חַטֹּאת עַמְּךָ בֵּית יִשְׂרָאֵל תַּשְׁלִיךְ בִּמְקוֹם
אֲשֶׁר לֹא יִזָּכְרוּ, וְלֹא יִפָּקְדוּ, וְלֹא יַעֲלוּ עַל לֵב לְעוֹלָם.) תִּתֵּן אֱמֶת
לְיַעֲקֹב חֶסֶד לְאַבְרָהָם אֲשֶׁר נִשְׁבַּעְתָּ לַאֲבוֹתֵינוּ מִימֵי קֶדֶם.[5]

---

(1) *Isaiah* 55:7. (2) *Psalms* 19:13. (3) *Ezekiel* 36:25. (4) *Micah* 7:18-19. (5) 7:20.

[ל] *[The benefit of] our labor has been stolen,* [מ] *pulled away and cut off from us.* [נ] *They have placed their yoke upon us,* [ס] *our burdens upon our shoulders.* [ע] *Slaves have ruled over us,* [פ] *there is no redemption from their hand.* [צ] *Abundant troubles have surrounded us,* [ק] *we called upon You,* HASHEM, *our God,* [ר] *but You have distanced us for our iniquities.* [ש] *We have turned away from following after You;* [ת] *we have strayed; we have become lost.*

But still we have not returned from our waywardness. So how can we be so brazen and obstinate as to say before You, HASHEM, our God and the God of our forefathers, that we are righteous and have not sinned, for in truth, both we and our fathers have sinned.

Strike the left side of the chest with the right fist while reciting
each of the sins in the following confession litany:

אָשַׁמְנוּ *We have become guilty;* [ב] *we have betrayed;* [ג] *we have robbed;* [ד] *we have spoken slander;* [ה] *we have caused perversion;* [ו] *we have caused wickedness;* [ז] *we have sinned willfully;* [ח] *we have extorted;* [ט] *we have accused falsely;* [י] *we have given evil counsel;* [כ] *we have been deceitful;* [ל] *we have scorned;* [מ] *we have rebelled;* [נ] *we have provoked;* [ס] *we have turned away;* [ע] *we have been perverse;* [פ] *we have acted wantonly;* [צ] *we have persecuted;* [ק] *we have been obstinate;* [ר] *we have been wicked;* [ש] *we have corrupted;* [ת] *we have been abominable; we have strayed; You have let us go astray.*

סַרְנוּ *We have turned away from Your commandments and from Your good laws but to no avail. Yet You are righteous in all that has come upon us, for You have acted truthfully while we have caused wickedness.*

הִרְשַׁעְנוּ *We have acted wickedly and have sinned willfully, therefore we have not been saved. Inspire our heart to abandon the path of evil and hasten salvation for us, as it is written by Your prophet: May the wicked one abandon his way and the vicious man his thoughts; may he return to* HASHEM *and He will show him mercy, and to our God, for He is abundantly forgiving.*[1]

מָשִׁיחַ *Your righteous anointed [David] said before You: 'Who can discern mistakes? From unperceived faults cleanse me.'*[2] *Cleanse us,* HASHEM, *our God, of all our willful sins and purify us, of all our contaminations. Sprinkle upon us pure water and purify us, as it is written by Your prophet: I shall sprinkle pure water upon you and purify you, of all your contaminations and of all your abominations I will purify you.'*[3]

מִיכָה עַבְדְּךָ *Micah, Your servant, said before You: 'Who, O God, is like You, Who pardons iniquity and overlooks transgression for the remnant of His heritage? Who has not retained His wrath eternally, for He desires kindness! He will again be merciful to us; He will suppress our iniquities and cast into the depths of the sea all their sins.*[4] *(And all the sins of Your nation the Family of Israel, may You cast away to a place where they will neither be remembered, considered, nor brought to mind — ever.) Grant truth to Jacob, kindness to Abraham, as You swore to our forefathers from ancient times.'*[5]

דָּנִיֵּאל אִישׁ חֲמוּדוֹת שִׁוַּע לְפָנֶיךָ: הַטֵּה אֱלֹהַי אָזְנְךָ וּשְׁמָע,
פְּקַח עֵינֶיךָ וּרְאֵה שֹׁמְמֹתֵינוּ וְהָעִיר אֲשֶׁר נִקְרָא שִׁמְךָ
עָלֶיהָ, כִּי לֹא עַל צִדְקֹתֵינוּ אֲנַחְנוּ מַפִּילִים תַּחֲנוּנֵינוּ לְפָנֶיךָ, כִּי עַל
רַחֲמֶיךָ הָרַבִּים. אֲדֹנָי שְׁמָעָה, אֲדֹנָי סְלָחָה, אֲדֹנָי הַקְשִׁיבָה, וַעֲשֵׂה
אַל תְּאַחַר, לְמַעַנְךָ אֱלֹהַי, כִּי שִׁמְךָ נִקְרָא עַל עִירְךָ וְעַל עַמֶּךָ.[1]

עֶזְרָא הַסּוֹפֵר אָמַר לְפָנֶיךָ: אֱלֹהַי, בֹּשְׁתִּי וְנִכְלַמְתִּי לְהָרִים,
אֱלֹהַי, פָּנַי אֵלֶיךָ, כִּי עֲוֹנֹתֵינוּ רָבוּ לְמַעְלָה
רֹאשׁ, וְאַשְׁמָתֵנוּ גָדְלָה עַד לַשָּׁמָיִם.[2] וְאַתָּה[3] אֱלֽוֹהַּ סְלִיחוֹת, חַנּוּן
וְרַחוּם, אֶרֶךְ אַפַּיִם וְרַב חֶסֶד, וְלֹא עֲזַבְתָּנוּ.[4]

אַל תַּעַזְבֵנוּ אָבִינוּ וְאַל תִּטְּשֵׁנוּ בּוֹרְאֵנוּ, וְאַל תַּזְנִיחֵנוּ
יוֹצְרֵנוּ, וְאַל תַּעַשׂ עִמָּנוּ כָּלָה כְּחַטֹּאתֵינוּ. וְקַיֵּם
לָנוּ יהוה אֱלֹהֵינוּ, אֶת הַדָּבָר שֶׁהִבְטַחְתָּנוּ בְּקַבָּלָה עַל יְדֵי יִרְמְיָהוּ
חוֹזָךְ, כָּאָמוּר: בַּיָּמִים הָהֵם וּבָעֵת הַהִיא, נְאֻם יהוה, יְבֻקַּשׁ אֶת עֲוֹן
יִשְׂרָאֵל וְאֵינֶנּוּ וְאֶת חַטֹּאת יְהוּדָה וְלֹא תִמָּצֶאנָה, כִּי אֶסְלַח
לַאֲשֶׁר אַשְׁאִיר.[5] עַמְּךָ וְנַחֲלָתְךָ רְעֵבֵי טוּבְךָ, צְמֵאֵי חַסְדֶּךָ, תְּאֵבֵי
יִשְׁעֶךָ, יַכִּירוּ וְיֵדְעוּ כִּי לַיהוה אֱלֹהֵינוּ הָרַחֲמִים וְהַסְּלִיחוֹת.

אֵל רַחוּם שְׁמֶךָ. אֵל חַנּוּן שְׁמֶךָ. בָּנוּ נִקְרָא שְׁמֶךָ. יהוה עֲשֵׂה
לְמַעַן שְׁמֶךָ. עֲשֵׂה לְמַעַן אֲמִתֶּךָ, עֲשֵׂה לְמַעַן
בְּרִיתֶךָ, עֲשֵׂה לְמַעַן גָּדְלְךָ וְתִפְאַרְתֶּךָ, עֲשֵׂה לְמַעַן דָּתֶךָ, עֲשֵׂה
לְמַעַן הוֹדֶךָ, עֲשֵׂה לְמַעַן וִעוּדֶךָ, עֲשֵׂה לְמַעַן זִכְרֶךָ, עֲשֵׂה לְמַעַן
חַסְדֶּךָ, עֲשֵׂה לְמַעַן טוּבֶךָ, עֲשֵׂה לְמַעַן יִחוּדֶךָ, עֲשֵׂה לְמַעַן כְּבוֹדֶךָ,
עֲשֵׂה לְמַעַן לִמּוּדֶךָ, עֲשֵׂה לְמַעַן מַלְכוּתֶךָ, עֲשֵׂה לְמַעַן נִצְחֶךָ,
עֲשֵׂה לְמַעַן סוֹדֶךָ, עֲשֵׂה לְמַעַן עֻזֶּךָ, עֲשֵׂה לְמַעַן פְּאֵרֶךָ, עֲשֵׂה
לְמַעַן צִדְקָתֶךָ, עֲשֵׂה לְמַעַן קְדֻשָּׁתֶךָ, עֲשֵׂה לְמַעַן רַחֲמֶיךָ הָרַבִּים,
עֲשֵׂה לְמַעַן שְׁכִינָתֶךָ, עֲשֵׂה לְמַעַן תְּהִלָּתֶךָ, עֲשֵׂה לְמַעַן אוֹהֲבֶיךָ
שׁוֹכְנֵי עָפָר, עֲשֵׂה לְמַעַן אַבְרָהָם יִצְחָק וְיַעֲקֹב, עֲשֵׂה לְמַעַן מֹשֶׁה
וְאַהֲרֹן, עֲשֵׂה לְמַעַן דָּוִד וּשְׁלֹמֹה, עֲשֵׂה לְמַעַן יְרוּשָׁלַיִם עִיר
קָדְשֶׁךָ, עֲשֵׂה לְמַעַן צִיּוֹן מִשְׁכַּן כְּבוֹדֶךָ, עֲשֵׂה לְמַעַן שִׁמְמוֹת
הֵיכָלֶיךָ, עֲשֵׂה לְמַעַן הֲרִיסוּת מִזְבְּחֶךָ, עֲשֵׂה לְמַעַן הֲרוּגִים עַל שֵׁם
קָדְשֶׁךָ, עֲשֵׂה לְמַעַן טְבוּחִים עַל יִחוּדֶךָ, עֲשֵׂה לְמַעַן בָּאֵי בָאֵשׁ

דָּנִיֵּאל Daniel, the greatly beloved man, cried out before You: 'Incline, my God, Your ear, and listen, open Your eyes and see our desolation and that of the city upon which Your Name is proclaimed, for not because of our righteousness do we cast down our supplications before You, rather because of Your abundant compassion. O my Lord, heed; O my Lord, forgive; O my Lord, be attentive and act, do not delay; for Your sake, my God, for Your Name is proclaimed upon Your city and Your people.'[1]

עֶזְרָא הַסּוֹפֵר Ezra the Scribe said before You: 'My God, I am embarrassed and ashamed to lift my face to You, my God — for our iniquities have multiplied above our heads, and our sins extend unto heaven.[2] You are[3] the God of forgiveness, compassionate and merciful, slow to anger, and abundant in kindness; and You have not forsaken us.'[4]

אַל תַּעַזְבֵנוּ Do not forsake us, our Father; do not cast us off, our Creator; do not abandon us, our Molder; and do not bring about our destruction, as our sins merit. Affirm for us, HASHEM, our God, the promise You made in the tradition through Jeremiah, Your seer, as it is said: 'In those days and at that time' — the words of HASHEM — 'the iniquity of Israel will be sought but there will be none, and the errors of Judah, but they will not be found, for I will have forgiven those whom I leave as a remnant.'[5] Your people and Your heritage, who hunger for Your goodness, who thirst for Your kindness, who long for Your salvation — may they recognize and know that to HASHEM, our God, belong mercy and forgiveness.

אֵל רַחוּם 'Merciful God' is Your Name, 'Gracious God' is Your Name, Your Name is called upon us — O HASHEM, act for Your Name's sake. Act for the sake of [א] Your truth; act for the sake of [ב] Your covenant; act for the sake of [ג] Your greatness and Your splendor; act for the sake of [ד] Your law; act for the sake of [ה] Your glory; act for the sake of [ו] Your Meeting House; act for the sake of [ז] Your remembrance; act for the sake of [ח] Your kindness; act for the sake of [ט] Your goodness; act for the sake of [י] Your Oneness; act for the sake of [כ] Your honor; act for the sake of [ל] Your teaching; act for the sake of [מ] Your kingship; act for the sake of [נ] Your eternality; act for the sake of [ס] Your counsel; act for the sake of [ע] Your power; act for the sake of [פ] Your beauty; act for the sake of [צ] Your righteousness; act for the sake of [ק] Your sanctity; act for the sake of [ר] Your abundant mercy; act for the sake of [ש] Your Presence, act for the sake of [ת] Your praise; act for the sake of Your beloved ones who rest in the dust; act for the sake of Abraham, Isaac, and Jacob; act for the sake of Moses and Aaron; act for the sake of David and Solomon; act for the sake of Jerusalem, Your holy city; act for the sake of Zion, the abode of Your glory; act for the sake of the desolation of Your Temple; act for the sake of the ruin of Your Altar; act for the sake of the martyrs for Your holy Name; act for the sake of those slaughtered for Your Oneness; act for the sake of those who entered fire

(1) *Daniel* 9:18-19. (2) *Ezra* 9:6. (3) Some editions of *Selichos* insert the word אֱלֹהֵינוּ, our God, at this point. (4) Cf. *Nehemiah* 9:17. (5) *Jeremiah* 50:20.

וּבְמַיִם עַל קְדוּשׁ שְׁמֶךָ, עֲשֵׂה לְמַעַן יוֹנְקֵי שָׁדַיִם שֶׁלֹּא חָטָאוּ, עֲשֵׂה לְמַעַן גְּמוּלֵי חָלָב שֶׁלֹּא פָשֳׁעוּ, עֲשֵׂה לְמַעַן תִּינוֹקוֹת שֶׁל בֵּית רַבָּן, עֲשֵׂה לְמַעַנְךָ אִם לֹא לְמַעֲנֵנוּ, עֲשֵׂה לְמַעַנְךָ וְהוֹשִׁיעֵנוּ.

עֲנֵנוּ יהוה עֲנֵנוּ, עֲנֵנוּ אֱלֹהֵינוּ עֲנֵנוּ, עֲנֵנוּ אָבִינוּ עֲנֵנוּ, עֲנֵנוּ בּוֹרְאֵנוּ עֲנֵנוּ, עֲנֵנוּ גּוֹאֲלֵנוּ עֲנֵנוּ, עֲנֵנוּ דוֹרְשֵׁנוּ עֲנֵנוּ, עֲנֵנוּ הָאֵל הַנֶּאֱמָן עֲנֵנוּ, עֲנֵנוּ וָתִיק וְחָסִיד עֲנֵנוּ, עֲנֵנוּ זַךְ וְיָשָׁר עֲנֵנוּ, עֲנֵנוּ חַי וְקַיָּם עֲנֵנוּ, עֲנֵנוּ טוֹב וּמֵטִיב עֲנֵנוּ, עֲנֵנוּ יוֹדֵעַ יֵצֶר עֲנֵנוּ, עֲנֵנוּ כּוֹבֵשׁ כְּעָסִים עֲנֵנוּ, עֲנֵנוּ לוֹבֵשׁ צְדָקוֹת עֲנֵנוּ, עֲנֵנוּ מֶלֶךְ מַלְכֵי הַמְּלָכִים עֲנֵנוּ, עֲנֵנוּ נוֹרָא וְנִשְׂגָּב עֲנֵנוּ, עֲנֵנוּ סוֹלֵחַ וּמוֹחֵל עֲנֵנוּ, עֲנֵנוּ עוֹנֶה בְּעֵת צָרָה¹ עֲנֵנוּ, עֲנֵנוּ פּוֹדֶה וּמַצִּיל עֲנֵנוּ, עֲנֵנוּ צַדִּיק וְיָשָׁר עֲנֵנוּ, עֲנֵנוּ קָרוֹב לְקוֹרְאָיו עֲנֵנוּ, עֲנֵנוּ רַחוּם וְחַנּוּן עֲנֵנוּ, עֲנֵנוּ שׁוֹמֵעַ אֶל אֶבְיוֹנִים עֲנֵנוּ, עֲנֵנוּ תּוֹמֵךְ תְּמִימִים עֲנֵנוּ, עֲנֵנוּ אֱלֹהֵי אֲבוֹתֵינוּ עֲנֵנוּ, עֲנֵנוּ אֱלֹהֵי אַבְרָהָם עֲנֵנוּ, עֲנֵנוּ פַּחַד יִצְחָק עֲנֵנוּ, עֲנֵנוּ אֲבִיר יַעֲקֹב עֲנֵנוּ, עֲנֵנוּ עֶזְרַת הַשְּׁבָטִים עֲנֵנוּ, עֲנֵנוּ מִשְׂגַּב אִמָּהוֹת עֲנֵנוּ, עֲנֵנוּ קָשֶׁה לִכְעוֹס עֲנֵנוּ, עֲנֵנוּ רַךְ לִרְצוֹת עֲנֵנוּ, עֲנֵנוּ עוֹנֶה בְּעֵת רָצוֹן¹ עֲנֵנוּ, עֲנֵנוּ אֲבִי יְתוֹמִים עֲנֵנוּ, עֲנֵנוּ דַּיַּן אַלְמָנוֹת עֲנֵנוּ.

מִי שֶׁעָנָה לְאַבְרָהָם אָבִינוּ בְּהַר הַמּוֹרִיָּה,	הוּא יַעֲנֵנוּ.
מִי שֶׁעָנָה לְיִצְחָק בְּנוֹ כְּשֶׁנֶּעֱקַד עַל גַּבֵּי הַמִּזְבֵּחַ,	הוּא יַעֲנֵנוּ.
מִי שֶׁעָנָה לְיַעֲקֹב בְּבֵית אֵל,	הוּא יַעֲנֵנוּ.
מִי שֶׁעָנָה לְיוֹסֵף בְּבֵית הָאֲסוּרִים,	הוּא יַעֲנֵנוּ.
מִי שֶׁעָנָה לַאֲבוֹתֵינוּ עַל יַם סוּף,	הוּא יַעֲנֵנוּ.
מִי שֶׁעָנָה לְמֹשֶׁה בְּחוֹרֵב,	הוּא יַעֲנֵנוּ.
מִי שֶׁעָנָה לְאַהֲרֹן בַּמַּחְתָּה,	הוּא יַעֲנֵנוּ.
מִי שֶׁעָנָה לְפִינְחָס בְּקוּמוֹ מִתּוֹךְ הָעֵדָה,	הוּא יַעֲנֵנוּ.
מִי שֶׁעָנָה לִיהוֹשֻׁעַ בַּגִּלְגָּל,	הוּא יַעֲנֵנוּ.
מִי שֶׁעָנָה לִשְׁמוּאֵל בַּמִּצְפָּה,	הוּא יַעֲנֵנוּ.
מִי שֶׁעָנָה לְדָוִד וּשְׁלֹמֹה בְנוֹ בִּירוּשָׁלָיִם,	הוּא יַעֲנֵנוּ.
מִי שֶׁעָנָה לְאֵלִיָּהוּ בְּהַר הַכַּרְמֶל,	הוּא יַעֲנֵנוּ.
מִי שֶׁעָנָה לֶאֱלִישָׁע בִּירִיחוֹ,	הוּא יַעֲנֵנוּ.
מִי שֶׁעָנָה לְיוֹנָה בִּמְעֵי הַדָּגָה,	הוּא יַעֲנֵנוּ.

(1) Some editions of *Selichos* reverse the positions of these two lines.

and water for the sanctification of Your Name; act for the nursing infants who did not err; act for the sake of the weaned babes who did not sin; act for the sake of children at the schoolroom; act for Your sake if not for ours; act for Your sake and save us.

עֲנֵנוּ *Answer us, HASHEM, answer us; answer us, our God, answer us; answer us, [א] our Father, answer us; answer us, [ב] our Creator, answer us; answer us, [ג] our Redeemer, answer us; answer us, [ד] You Who searches us out, answer us; answer us, [ה] faithful God, answer us; answer us, [ו] stead-fast and kind One, answer us; answer us, [ז] pure and upright One, answer us; answer us, [ח] living and enduring One, answer us; answer us, [ט] good and beneficent One, answer us; answer us, [י] You Who knows inclinations, answer us; answer us, [כ] You Who suppresses wrath, answer us; answer us, [ל] You Who dons righteousness, answer us; answer us, [מ] King Who reigns over kings, answer us; answer us, [נ] awesome and powerful One, answer us; answer us, [ס] You Who forgives and pardons, answer us; answer us, [ע] You Who answers in time of distress,[1] answer us; answer us, [פ] Redeemer and Rescuer, answer us; answer us, [צ] righteous and upright One, answer us; answer us, [ק] He Who is close to those who call upon Him, answer us; answer us, [ר] merciful and gracious One, answer us; answer us, [ש] You Who hears the destitute, answer us; answer us, [ת] You Who supports the wholesome, answer us; answer us, God of our forefathers, answer us; answer us, God of Abraham, answer us; answer us, Dread of Isaac, answer us; answer us, Mighty One of Jacob, answer us; answer us, Helper of the tribes, answer us; answer us, Stronghold of the Matriarchs, answer us; answer us, You Who are hard to anger, answer us; answer us, You Who are easy to pacify, answer us; answer us, You Who answers in a time of favor,[1] answer us; answer us, Father of orphans, answer us; answer us, Judge of widows, answer us.*

מִי שֶׁעָנָה *He Who answered our father Abraham on Mount Moriah,*
                                                                      may He answer us.
He Who answered his son Isaac when he was bound atop the altar,
                                                                      may He answer us.

He Who answered Jacob in Bethel,   *may He answer us.*
He Who answered Joseph in the prison,   *may He answer us.*
He Who answered our forefathers at the Sea of Reeds,   *may He answer us.*
He Who answered Moses in Horeb,   *may He answer us.*
He Who answered Aaron when he offered the censer,   *may He answer us.*
He Who answered Phineas when he arose from amid the congregation,
                                                                      may He answer us.

He Who answered Joshua in Gilgal,   *may He answer us.*
He Who answered Samuel in Mitzpah,   *may He answer us.*
He Who answered David and his son Solomon in Jerusalem,
                                                                      may He answer us.

He Who answered Elijah on Mount Carmel,   *may He answer us.*
He Who answered Elisha in Jericho,   *may He answer us.*
He Who answered Jonah in the innards of the fish,   *may He answer us.*

מִי שֶׁעָנָה לְחִזְקִיָּהוּ מֶלֶךְ יְהוּדָה בְּחָלְיוֹ,　　הוּא יַעֲנֵנוּ.

מִי שֶׁעָנָה לַחֲנַנְיָה מִישָׁאֵל וַעֲזַרְיָה בְּתוֹךְ כִּבְשַׁן הָאֵשׁ,　הוּא יַעֲנֵנוּ.

מִי שֶׁעָנָה לְדָנִיֵּאל בְּגוֹב הָאֲרָיוֹת,　　הוּא יַעֲנֵנוּ.

מִי שֶׁעָנָה לְמָרְדֳּכַי וְאֶסְתֵּר בְּשׁוּשַׁן הַבִּירָה,　　הוּא יַעֲנֵנוּ.

מִי שֶׁעָנָה לְעֶזְרָא בַּגּוֹלָה,　　הוּא יַעֲנֵנוּ.

מִי שֶׁעָנָה לְכָל הַצַּדִּיקִים וְהַחֲסִידִים וְהַתְּמִימִים וְהַיְשָׁרִים,
הוּא יַעֲנֵנוּ.

רַחֲמָנָא דְּעָנֵי לַעֲנִיֵּי, עֲנִינָא. רַחֲמָנָא דְּעָנֵי לִתְבִירֵי לִבָּא,
עֲנִינָא. רַחֲמָנָא דְּעָנֵי לְמַכִּיכֵי רוּחָא, עֲנִינָא. רַחֲמָנָא
עֲנִינָא. רַחֲמָנָא חוּס. רַחֲמָנָא פְּרוֹק. רַחֲמָנָא שְׁזִיב. רַחֲמָנָא
רְחַם עֲלָן. הַשְׁתָּא בַּעֲגָלָא וּבִזְמַן קָרִיב.

נפילת אפים

In the presence of a Torah Scroll, the following (until יַבְשׁוּ רָגַע) is recited with the head resting
on the arm, preferably while seated. Elsewhere, it is recited with the head held erect.

(וַיֹּאמֶר דָּוִד אֶל גָּד, צַר לִי מְאֹד נִפְּלָה נָּא בְיַד יְהוָה,
כִּי רַבִּים רַחֲמָיו, וּבְיַד אָדָם אַל אֶפֹּלָה.[1]

רַחוּם וְחַנּוּן חָטָאתִי לְפָנֶיךָ. יְהוָה מָלֵא רַחֲמִים, רַחֵם עָלַי
וְקַבֵּל תַּחֲנוּנָי.

תהלים ו:ב-יא

יְהוָה אַל בְּאַפְּךָ תוֹכִיחֵנִי, וְאַל בַּחֲמָתְךָ תְיַסְּרֵנִי. חָנֵּנִי יְהוָה, כִּי
אֻמְלַל אָנִי, רְפָאֵנִי יְהוָה, כִּי נִבְהֲלוּ עֲצָמָי. וְנַפְשִׁי נִבְהֲלָה
מְאֹד, וְאַתָּה יְהוָה, עַד מָתָי. שׁוּבָה יְהוָה, חַלְּצָה נַפְשִׁי, הוֹשִׁיעֵנִי
לְמַעַן חַסְדֶּךָ. כִּי אֵין בַּמָּוֶת זִכְרֶךָ, בִּשְׁאוֹל מִי יוֹדֶה לָּךְ. יָגַעְתִּי
בְּאַנְחָתִי, אַשְׂחֶה בְכָל לַיְלָה מִטָּתִי, בְּדִמְעָתִי עַרְשִׂי אַמְסֶה.
עָשְׁשָׁה מִכַּעַס עֵינִי, עָתְקָה בְּכָל צוֹרְרָי. סוּרוּ מִמֶּנִּי כָּל פֹּעֲלֵי אָוֶן,
כִּי שָׁמַע יְהוָה קוֹל בִּכְיִי. שָׁמַע יְהוָה תְּחִנָּתִי, יְהוָה תְּפִלָּתִי יִקָּח.
יֵבֹשׁוּ וְיִבָּהֲלוּ מְאֹד כָּל אֹיְבָי, יָשֻׁבוּ יֵבֹשׁוּ רָגַע.

מַחֵי וּמַסֵּי מֵמִית וּמְחַיֶּה, מַסִּיק מִן שְׁאוֹל לְחַיֵּי עָלְמָא, בְּרָא
כַּד חָטֵי אֲבוּהִי לַקְיֵהּ, אֲבוּהִי דְּחָיֵס אַסֵּי לִכְאֵבֵהּ.

עַבְדָּא דְּמָרִיד נָפִיק בְּקוֹלָר, מָרֵהּ תָּאִיב וְתַבִּיר קוֹלָרֵהּ.

בְּרַךְ בְּכַרְךְ אֲנַן וְחָטֵינַן קַמָּךְ, הָא רָזֵי נַפְשִׁין בְּגִידִין מְרִירִין,
עַבְדָּךְ אֲנַן וּמְרוֹדִינַן קַמָּךְ, הָא בְּבִזְתָּא, הָא בְּשִׁבְיָא, הָא
בְּמַלְקְיוּתָא. בְּמָטוּ מִנָּךְ בְּרַחֲמָךְ הַנְפִישִׁין, אַסֵּי לִכְאֵבִין דִּתְקוֹף
עֲלָן, עַד דְּלָא נֶהֱוֵי גְּמִירָא בְּשִׁבְיָא.

He Who answered Hezekiah, King of Judah, in his illness, may He answer us.
He Who answered Chananiah, Mishael, and Azariah in the fiery oven,
                                                        may He answer us.
He Who answered Daniel in the lions' den,   may He answer us.
He Who answered Mordechai and Esther in Shushan the capital,
                                                        may He answer us.
He Who answered Ezra in the Exile,   may He answer us.
He Who answered all the righteous, the devout, the wholesome,
    and the upright,   may He answer us.

רַחֲמָנָא The Merciful One Who answers the poor, may He answer us.
            The Merciful One Who answers the brokenhearted, may He
answer us. The Merciful One Who answers the humble of spirit, may He
answer us. O Merciful One, answer us. O Merciful One, pity. O Merciful
One, redeem. O Merciful One, deliver. O Merciful One, have mercy on us —
now, swiftly and soon.

PUTTING DOWN THE HEAD

In the presence of a Torah Scroll, the following (until 'instantly shamed') is recited with the head
resting on the arm, preferably while seated. Elsewhere, it is recited with the head held erect.
(And David said to Gad, 'I am exceedingly distressed. Let us fall into HASHEM's
hand for His mercies are abundant, but let me not fall into human hands.'[1])

רַחוּם וְחַנּוּן O compassionate and gracious One, I have sinned before
                You. HASHEM, Who is full of mercy, have mercy on me and
accept my supplications.

Psalms 6:2-11

'ה HASHEM, do not rebuke me in Your anger nor chastise me in Your rage.
     Favor me, HASHEM, for I am feeble; heal me, HASHEM, for my bones
shudder. My soul is utterly confounded, and You, HASHEM, how long? Desist, HASHEM, release my soul; save me as befits Your kindness. For there is
no mention of You in death; in the Lower World who will thank You? I am
wearied with my sigh, every night my tears drench my bed, soak my couch.
My eye is dimmed because of anger, aged by my tormentors. Depart from
me, all evildoers, for HASHEM has heard the sound of my weeping. HASHEM
has heard my plea, HASHEM will accept my prayer. Let all my foes be
shamed and utterly confounded, they will regret and be instantly shamed.

מַחֲי וּמַסֵּי [O God,] He Who smites and heals, causes death and re-
                stores life, raises [the dead] from the grave to eternal life:
Should a son sin, his father would smack him, but a compassionate father
will heal his [son's] pain. When a slave rebels, he is led out in collar-irons,
but if his master desires to, he breaks his chains.
    We are Your son, Your firstborn, and we have sinned against You; so
our soul has been satiated with bitter wormwood. We are Your servants
and we have rebelled against You; so [we have suffered], some with looting, some with captivity, and some with the lash. We beg of You, in Your
abundant compassion, heal the pains that have overwhelmed us, before
we have been completely wiped out in captivity.

---

(1) *II Samuel* 24:14.

סליחה עז (תחנה)

שַׁעֲרֵי שָׁמַיִם,* בְּלוּלֵי אֵשׁ וּמַיִם,*

שְׁלֹשׁ מֵאוֹת וְתִשְׁעִים כְּמִנְיַן שָׁמַיִם,*

הִפָּתְחוּ לְחַנּוּן יְפַת פַּעֲמַיִם,   **וְתַעַל** תְּפִלָּתָם לְאֵל הַשָּׁמַיִם.[1]

שַׁעֲרֵי רָקִיעַ,   בּוֹ מְאוֹרוֹת הִתְקִיעַ,

וּמִמֶּנּוּ זוֹרְחִים בִּמְקוֹמָם לְהַשְׁקִיעַ,

הִפָּתְחוּ לְחַנּוּן יָם לָמוֹ הַבְּקִיעַ, **וְתַעַל** תְּפִלָּתָם פְּנֵי מַעֲבִיב רָקִיעַ.

שַׁעֲרֵי זְבוּל,   שֶׁבּוֹ מִזְבֵּחַ סָבוּל,

וְהַשַּׂר מַקְטִיר עָלָיו כְּמִכְּבֶן בְּכַרְבּוּל,

הִפָּתְחוּ לְחַנּוּן נִדְחָקִים בְּחִבּוּל, **וְתַעַל** תְּפִלָּתָם פְּנֵי יָשַׁב לַמַּבּוּל.[2]

שַׁעֲרֵי וִילוֹן,   נִכְנָס וְיוֹצֵא בְּגִלְגָּלוֹן,*

וּמְחַדֵּשׁ בְּכָל יוֹם מִפִּתְחֵי חַלּוֹן,

הִפָּתְחוּ לְחַנּוּן מַצַּבְתָּהּ כָּאֵלּוֹן,   **וְתַעַל** תְּפִלָּתָם פְּנֵי רוּם וִילוֹן.

שַׁעֲרֵי שְׁחָקִים,   שֶׁבּוֹ רֵחַיִם שׁוֹחֲקִים,

עוֹמְדוֹת וְטוֹחֲנוֹת מָן לַצַּדִּיקִים,

הִפָּתְחוּ לְחַנּוּן זְרוּיִים בְּמֶרְחַקִּים,

וְתַעַל תְּפִלָּתָם פְּנֵי שׁוֹכֵן שְׁחָקִים.

שַׁעֲרֵי מָכוֹן,   שֶׁבּוֹ שְׁלָגִים יִתְכּוֹן,

וּמְעָרַת קִיטוֹר וְסַעַר בּוֹ יִשְׁכּוֹן,

הִפָּתְחוּ לְחַנּוּן עַם לִבּוֹ יִכּוֹן,   **וְתַעַל** תְּפִלָּתָם פְּנֵי דָר רוּם מָכוֹן.

---

§ **שַׁעֲרֵי שָׁמַיִם** — *O Gates of Heaven*. The Talmud names and describes seven heavens, each a higher level than the preceding one. They are:

(1) וִילוֹן, *Vilon* [lit., *curtain*], although nothing happens within this heaven, in the morning it withdraws [like a curtain, allowing the daylight to shine through (*Rashi*)] and in the evening it goes forth [preventing the light of the sun from reaching Earth (*Rashi*)], thus it renews the work of Creation each day;

(2) רָקִיעַ, *Rakia* [lit., *firmament*], in which the sun, moon, stars and constellations are suspended;

(3) שְׁחָקִים, *Shechakim* [lit., *powders* or *pulverizers*], in which stand millstones that grind manna for the righteous;

(4) זְבוּל, *Zevul* [lit., *Temple*], in which stands the heavenly Jerusalem, Temple and Altar upon which the great angelic prince Michael sacrifices offerings;

(5) מָעוֹן, *Maon* [lit., *dwelling*], in which groups of ministering angels recite songs [of praise to God] through the night, but remain silent by day

in deference to Israel;

(6) מָכוֹן, *Machon* [lit., *foundation* or *establishment*], in which are storehouses of snow and of hail, the attics in which harmful dew and heavy rainfall are stored, and the chamber of the whirlwind and the tempest, the grotto of smoke with its doors of fire [all of them used for retribution against the wicked (*Rashi*)];

and (7) עֲרָבוֹת, *Aravos* [lit., *willows* or *darkenings* or *mixtures*], in which are Righteousness, Justice and Charity; caches of Life, Peace, and Blessing; the souls of the righteous, the spirits and souls that are destined to be born; and the life-giving dew with which God will resurrect the dead (*Chagigah* 12b).

The *paytan* petitions all the heavens to open so that Israel's prayers may pour through them to the Throne of Glory. The first stanza speaks to all seven heavens at once, while each of the remaining stanzas addresses a particular heaven. The order of the heavens as enumerated in the *selichah* does not follow that of the Talmud (although in some editions the stanzas have been re-arranged

SELICHAH 77

שַׁעֲרֵי שָׁמַיִם   O *Gates* of Heaven,*
   which is made of fire mixed with water,
three hundred and ninety [in all], like the sum of שָׁמַיִם,*
   open *before the supplication of [Israel]*
   whose pilgrimage footsteps are so beautiful,
   and let their prayer ascend *to God of the Heavens.* [1]
O *Gates* of Rakia — *in which the stars are fixed,*
   whence they shine forth and in their places to set —
   open *before the supplication of [Israel] for whom He split the sea,*
   and let their prayer ascend *before Him Who enclouds the sky.*
O *Gates* of Zevul — *in which the Altar is borne,*
   and the angel raises smoke on it like the turbaned Kohen —
   open *before the supplication of [Israel] oppressed in chains,*
   and let their prayer ascend *before Him Who sat alone at the Deluge.* [2]
O *Gates* of Vilon, *that spreads open and folds back*
   so renewing each day the [celestial] window's opening,
   open *before the supplication of [Israel]*
   who stands sturdy like an oak,
   and let their prayer ascend *before Him Who dwells above Vilon.*
O *Gates* of Shechakim — *in which the millstones turn,*
   that stand and grind manna for the righteous —
   open *before the supplication of [Israel] scattered in far-off places,*
   and let their prayer ascend *before Him Who dwells in Shechakim.*
O *Gates* of Machon — *in which snows are stored up,*
   and the cavern where vapors and winds dwell —
   open *before the supplication of [Israel] whose heart is upright,*
   and let their prayer ascend *before Him Who dwells above Machon.*

---

(1) Some editions read אֶל הַשָּׁמַיִם, *to the heavens.* (2) Cf. *Psalms* 29:10; see *Rashi* there; some editions of *Selichos* read, יוֹשֵׁב בִּזְבוּל, *Who is enthroned in Zevul.*

to conform to the talmudic listing). The propriety and permissibility of directing prayer to any entity other than God is discussed in the introduction to this volume.

Although this *selichah* is apparently unsigned, some attribute it to R' Shimon ben Yitzchak [see prefatory comment to *selichah* 11].

בְּלוּלֵי אֵשׁ וּמַיִם — *Made of fire mixed with water.* This phrase describes not the Gates of Heaven, but Heaven itself. According to one view in the Talmud (*Chagigah* 12a; see also *Rashi* to *Genesis* 1:8) the word שָׁמַיִם, *heavens,* is a composite of אֵשׁ וּמַיִם, *fire and water,* because God combined these two elements and formed the heavens.

שְׁלֹשׁ מֵאוֹת וְתִשְׁעִים כְּמִנְיַן שָׁמַיִם — *Three hundred and ninety [in all], like the sum of* שָׁמַיִם. The

gematria of the word שָׁמַיִם is 390 [שׁ=300; מ=40; י=10; ם=40]. The stich refers to the Aggadah (*Derech Eretz Rabbah* 2) that states: God is One, His Name is One, and He sits among three hundred and ninety firmaments each with its name upon it.

The *paytan* cites this teaching here to answer a question regarding the previously cited talmudic proem (see preceding comment): If the heavens are compounded of אֵשׁ and מַיִם, they should be called אַשְׁמַיִם; why was the א dropped from their name? The answer is that the name שָׁמַיִם alludes to the number of firmaments the heavens comprise (*Masbir*).

נִכְנָס וְיוֹצֵא בְּגִלְלוֹן — *That spreads open and folds back.* This describes the function of Vilon, not its gates (see the talmudic passage cited in the prefatory comment).

שַׁעֲרֵי מָעוֹן, בּוֹ מְשׁוֹרְרִים יִשְׁעוֹן,
וּבַיּוֹם הֵם חָשִׁים לְסֶגֶל יִשְׁמְעוֹן.

הִפָּתְחוּ לְחַנּוּן נִמְרָרִים לְלָעוֹן, **וְתַעַל** תְּפִלָּתָם פְּנֵי דָר רוֹם מָעוֹן.

❖ **שַׁעֲרֵי עֲרָבוֹת,** שֶׁבּוֹ בִּרְכוֹת רַבּוֹת,
וְגִנְזֵי צְדָקָה וָחֶסֶד וְכָל טוֹבוֹת,

הִפָּתְחוּ לְחַנּוּן בְּנֵי שְׁלֹשֶׁת אָבוֹת,

וְתַעַל תְּפִלָּתָם פְּנֵי רוֹכֵב עֲרָבוֹת.[1]

All:

מַכְנִיסֵי רַחֲמִים, הַכְנִיסוּ רַחֲמֵינוּ, לִפְנֵי בַּעַל הָרַחֲמִים.
מַשְׁמִיעֵי תְפִלָּה, הַשְׁמִיעוּ תְפִלָּתֵנוּ, לִפְנֵי
שׁוֹמֵעַ תְּפִלָּה. מַשְׁמִיעֵי צְעָקָה, הַשְׁמִיעוּ צַעֲקָתֵנוּ, לִפְנֵי שׁוֹמֵעַ
צְעָקָה. מַכְנִיסֵי דִמְעָה, הַכְנִיסוּ דִמְעוֹתֵינוּ, לִפְנֵי מֶלֶךְ מִתְרַצֶּה
בִּדְמָעוֹת.

הִשְׁתַּדְּלוּ וְהַרְבּוּ תְּחִנָּה וּבַקָּשָׁה, לִפְנֵי מֶלֶךְ אֵל רָם וְנִשָּׂא.
הַזְכִּירוּ לְפָנָיו, הַשְׁמִיעוּ לְפָנָיו תּוֹרָה וּמַעֲשִׂים טוֹבִים שֶׁל שׁוֹכְנֵי
עָפָר.

יִזְכֹּר אַהֲבָתָם וְיַחֲיֶה זַרְעָם, שֶׁלֹּא תֹאבַד שְׁאֵרִית יַעֲקֹב. כִּי צֹאן
רוֹעֶה נֶאֱמָן הָיָה לְחֶרְפָּה, יִשְׂרָאֵל גּוֹי אֶחָד לְמָשָׁל וְלִשְׁנִינָה.
מַהֵר עֲנֵנוּ אֱלֹהֵי יִשְׁעֵנוּ, וּפְדֵנוּ מִכָּל גְּזֵרוֹת קָשׁוֹת וְהוֹשִׁיעָה
בְּרַחֲמֶיךָ הָרַבִּים, מְשִׁיחַ צִדְקָךְ וְעַמָּךְ.

מָרָן דְּבִשְׁמַיָּא לָךְ מִתְחַנְּנָן, כְּבָר שַׁבְיָא דְּמִתְחַנַּן לְשַׁבוּיֵהּ.
כֻּלְּהוֹן בְּנֵי שַׁבְיָא בְּכַסְפָּא מִתְפָּרְקִין, וְעַמָּךְ
יִשְׂרָאֵל בְּרַחֲמֵי וּבְתַחֲנוּנֵי, הַב לָן שְׁאִילְתִין וּבָעוּתִין, דְּלָא נֶהֱדַר
רֵיקָם מִן קֳדָמָךְ.

מָרָן דְּבִשְׁמַיָּא לָךְ מִתְחַנְּנָן, כְּעַבְדָּא דְּמִתְחַנַּן לְמָרֵיהּ,
עֲשִׁיקֵי אֲנָן וּבַחֲשׁוֹכָא שָׁרֵינָן, מְרִירָן נַפְשִׁין מֵעַקְתִין דִּנְפִישִׁין,
חֵילָא לֵית בָּן לְרַצּוּיָךְ מָרָן, עֲבִיד בְּדִיל קַיָּמָא דִּגְזַרְתָּ עִם אַבָהָתָנָא.

שׁוֹמֵר יִשְׂרָאֵל, שְׁמוֹר שְׁאֵרִית יִשְׂרָאֵל, וְאַל יֹאבַד יִשְׂרָאֵל,
הָאוֹמְרִים, שְׁמַע יִשְׂרָאֵל.[2]

שׁוֹמֵר גּוֹי אֶחָד, שְׁמוֹר שְׁאֵרִית עַם אֶחָד, וְאַל יֹאבַד גּוֹי אֶחָד,
הַמְּיַחֲדִים שִׁמְךָ, יהוה אֱלֹהֵינוּ יהוה אֶחָד.[2]

O Gates of Maon — in which [angelic] choristers sing out [at night]
   and by day are silent to hear the treasured [people's prayers] —
   open before the supplication of [Israel] embittered by wormwood,
   and let their prayer ascend before Him Who dwells above Maon.

Chazzan — *O Gates* of Aravos — where is manifold blessing
   and the storehouses of righteousness, kindness, and all good —
   open before the supplication of [Israel] the three Patriarchs' children,
   and let their prayer ascend to Him Who rides upon Aravos.[1]

All:

מַכְנִיסֵי רַחֲמִים   *O you who usher in [pleas for] mercy, may you usher
                       in our [plea for] mercy, before the Master of mercy. O*
you who cause prayer to be heard, may you cause our prayer to be heard,
before the Hearer of prayer. O you who cause outcry to be heard, may
you cause our outcry to be heard, before the Hearer of outcry. O you who
usher in tears, may you usher in our tears, before the King Who finds
favor through tears.

   Exert yourselves, and multiply supplication and petition, before the
King, God, exalted and most high. Mention before Him, cause to be heard
before Him, the Torah and the good deeds of [the Patriarchs and
Matriarchs] who dwell in the dust.

   May He remember their love and grant life to [their] offspring, that the
remnant of Jacob not be lost. For the flock of the faithful shepherd
[Moses] has become a disgrace; Israel, the unique nation, a parable and a
simile.

   Speedily, answer us, O God of our salvation, and redeem us from all
harsh decrees; and may You save, in Your abundant mercy, Your
righteous anointed and Your people.

מָרָן דְּבִשְׁמַיָּא   *Our Master Who is in heaven, to You do we supplicate,
                       as a captive supplicates before his captors; for all*
captives are redeemed with money, but Your people Israel with
compassion and supplication. O grant our requests and our prayers that
we not be turned away from You empty-handed.

   Our Master Who is in heaven, to You do we supplicate, as a slave
supplicates before his master: We are oppressed and we abide in
darkness, souls embittered from abundant distress. We have no strength
to regain Your favor. Our Master, act for the sake of the covenant that
You made with our Patriarchs.

שׁוֹמֵר יִשְׂרָאֵל   *O Guardian of Israel, protect the remnant of Israel; let
                     not Israel be destroyed — those who proclaim, 'Hear O
                     Israel.'*[2]

   O Guardian of the unique nation, protect the remnant of the unique
people; let not the unique nation be destroyed — those who proclaim
the Oneness of Your Name, 'HASHEM is our God, HASHEM, the One and
Only!'[2]

---

(1) Cf. *Psalms* 68:5. (2) *Deuteronomy* 6:4.

שׁוֹמֵר גּוֹי קָדוֹשׁ, שְׁמוֹר שְׁאֵרִית עַם קָדוֹשׁ, וְאַל יֹאבַד גּוֹי קָדוֹשׁ,
הַמְשַׁלְּשִׁים בְּשָׁלֹשׁ קְדֻשּׁוֹת לְקָדוֹשׁ.

מִתְרַצֶּה בְּרַחֲמִים וּמִתְפַּיֵּס בְּתַחֲנוּנִים, הִתְרַצֵּה וְהִתְפַּיֵּס לְדוֹר
עָנִי, כִּי אֵין עוֹזֵר. אָבִינוּ מַלְכֵּנוּ, חָנֵּנוּ וַעֲנֵנוּ, כִּי אֵין בָּנוּ מַעֲשִׂים,
עֲשֵׂה עִמָּנוּ צְדָקָה וָחֶסֶד וְהוֹשִׁיעֵנוּ.

וַאֲנַחְנוּ לֹא נֵדַע מַה נַּעֲשֶׂה, כִּי עָלֶיךָ עֵינֵינוּ.¹ זְכֹר רַחֲמֶיךָ
יהוה וַחֲסָדֶיךָ, כִּי מֵעוֹלָם הֵמָּה.² יְהִי חַסְדְּךָ יהוה עָלֵינוּ,
כַּאֲשֶׁר יִחַלְנוּ לָךְ.³

אַל תִּזְכָּר לָנוּ עֲוֹנוֹת רִאשׁוֹנִים, מַהֵר יְקַדְּמוּנוּ רַחֲמֶיךָ, כִּי
דַלּוֹנוּ מְאֹד.⁴ חָנֵּנוּ יהוה חָנֵּנוּ, כִּי רַב שָׂבַעְנוּ בוּז.⁵
בְּרֹגֶז רַחֵם תִּזְכּוֹר.⁶ כִּי הוּא יָדַע יִצְרֵנוּ, זָכוּר כִּי עָפָר אֲנָחְנוּ.⁷ עָזְרֵנוּ
אֱלֹהֵי יִשְׁעֵנוּ עַל דְּבַר כְּבוֹד שְׁמֶךָ, וְהַצִּילֵנוּ וְכַפֵּר עַל חַטֹּאתֵינוּ
לְמַעַן שְׁמֶךָ.⁸

קדיש שלם

The *chazzan* recites קַדִּישׁ שָׁלֵם:

יִתְגַּדַּל וְיִתְקַדַּשׁ שְׁמֵהּ רַבָּא. (.Cong – אָמֵן.) בְּעָלְמָא דִּי בְרָא
כִרְעוּתֵהּ, וְיַמְלִיךְ מַלְכוּתֵהּ, בְּחַיֵּיכוֹן וּבְיוֹמֵיכוֹן וּבְחַיֵּי דְכָל
בֵּית יִשְׂרָאֵל, בַּעֲגָלָא וּבִזְמַן קָרִיב. וְאִמְרוּ אָמֵן.
(.Cong – אָמֵן. יְהֵא שְׁמֵהּ רַבָּא מְבָרַךְ לְעָלַם וּלְעָלְמֵי עָלְמַיָּא.)
יְהֵא שְׁמֵהּ רַבָּא מְבָרַךְ לְעָלַם וּלְעָלְמֵי עָלְמַיָּא.
יִתְבָּרַךְ וְיִשְׁתַּבַּח וְיִתְפָּאַר וְיִתְרוֹמַם וְיִתְנַשֵּׂא וְיִתְהַדָּר וְיִתְעַלֶּה וְיִתְהַלָּל
שְׁמֵהּ דְּקוּדְשָׁא בְּרִיךְ הוּא (.Cong – בְּרִיךְ הוּא.) לְעֵלָּא [וּ]לְעֵלָּא מִכָּל
בִּרְכָתָא וְשִׁירָתָא תֻּשְׁבְּחָתָא וְנֶחֱמָתָא, דַּאֲמִירָן בְּעָלְמָא. וְאִמְרוּ: אָמֵן.
(.Cong – אָמֵן.)
(.Cong – קַבֵּל בְּרַחֲמִים וּבְרָצוֹן אֶת תְּפִלָּתֵנוּ.)
תִּתְקַבֵּל צְלוֹתְהוֹן וּבָעוּתְהוֹן דְּכָל (בֵּית) יִשְׂרָאֵל קֳדָם אֲבוּהוֹן דִּי
בִשְׁמַיָּא. וְאִמְרוּ אָמֵן. (.Cong – אָמֵן.)
(.Cong – יְהִי שֵׁם יהוה מְבֹרָךְ, מֵעַתָּה וְעַד עוֹלָם.⁹)
יְהֵא שְׁלָמָא רַבָּא מִן שְׁמַיָּא וְחַיִּים עָלֵינוּ וְעַל כָּל יִשְׂרָאֵל. וְאִמְרוּ אָמֵן
(.Cong – אָמֵן.)
(.Cong – עֶזְרִי מֵעִם יהוה, עֹשֵׂה שָׁמַיִם וָאָרֶץ.¹⁰)

Take three steps back. Bow left and say, . . . עֹשֶׂה; bow right and say, . . . הוּא יַעֲשֶׂה; bow forward and say,
וְעַל כָּל . . . אָמֵן. Remain standing in place for a few moments, then take three steps forward.

עֹשֶׂה [הַ]שָּׁלוֹם בִּמְרוֹמָיו, הוּא יַעֲשֶׂה שָׁלוֹם עָלֵינוּ, וְעַל כָּל יִשְׂרָאֵל.
וְאִמְרוּ אָמֵן. (.Cong – אָמֵן.)

O Guardian of the holy nation, protect the remnant of the holy people; let not the holy nation be destroyed — those who proclaim three-fold sanctifications to the Holy One.

Become favorable through compassion and become appeased through supplications. Become favorable and appeased to the poor generation, for there is no helper. Our Father, our King, be gracious with us and answer us, though we have no worthy deeds; treat us with charity and kindness, and save us.

וַאֲנַחְנוּ We know not what to do — but our eyes are upon You.[1] Remember Your mercies, HASHEM, and Your kindnesses, for they are from the beginning of the world.[2] May Your kindness be upon us, HASHEM, just as we awaited You.[3]

אַל תִּזְכָּר Recall not against us the iniquities of the ancients; may Your mercies meet us swiftly, for we have become exceedingly impoverished.[4] Be gracious to us, HASHEM, be gracious to us, for we are abundantly sated with scorn.[5] Amid rage — remember to be merciful![6] For He knew our nature, He remembers that we are dust.[7] Chazzan— Assist us, O God of our salvation, for the sake of Your Name's glory; rescue us and atone for our sins for Your Name's sake.[8]

FULL KADDISH

The chazzan recites the Full Kaddish:

יִתְגַּדַּל May His great Name grow exalted and sanctified (Cong. – Amen.) in the world that He created as He willed. May He give reign to His kingship in your lifetimes and in your days, and in the lifetimes of the entire Family of Israel, swiftly and soon. Now respond: Amen.

(Cong. – Amen. May His great Name be blessed forever and ever.)

May His great Name be blessed forever and ever.

Blessed, praised, glorified, exalted, extolled, mighty, upraised and lauded be the Name of the Holy One, Blessed is He (Cong. – Blessed is He.) exceedingly beyond any blessing and song, praise, and consolation that are uttered in the world. Now respond: Amen. (Cong. – Amen.)

(Cong. – Accept our prayers with mercy and favor.)

May the prayers and supplications of the entire House of Israel be accepted before their Father Who is in Heaven. Now respond: Amen. (Cong. – Amen.)

(Cong. – Blessed be the Name of HASHEM from this time and forever.[9])

May there be abundant peace from Heaven, and life, upon us and upon all Israel. Now respond: Amen. (Cong. – Amen.)

(Cong. – My help is from HASHEM, Maker of heaven and earth.[10])

Take three steps back. Bow left and say, 'He Who makes peace . . .'; bow right and say, 'may He make peace . . .'; bow forward and say, 'and upon all Israel . . .'
Remain standing in place for a few moments, then take three steps forward.

He Who makes [the] peace in His heights, may He make peace upon us, and upon all Israel. Now respond: Amen. (Cong. – Amen.)

---

(1) II Chronicles 20:12. (2) Psalms 25:6. (3) 33:22. (4) 79:8. (5) 123:3.
(6) Habakkuk 3:2. (7) Psalms 103:14. (8) 79:9. (9) 113:2. (10) 121:2.

WHEN YOM KIPPUR FALLS ON MONDAY OR THURSDAY SOME CONGREGATIONS
REVERSE THE ORDER OF THE FOURTH AND FIFTH DAYS OF REPENTANCE

יום רביעי של עשרת ימי תשובה

אַשְׁרֵי יוֹשְׁבֵי בֵיתֶךָ, עוֹד יְהַלְלוּךָ סֶּלָה. אַשְׁרֵי הָעָם שֶׁכָּכָה לּוֹ, אַשְׁרֵי הָעָם שֶׁיהוה אֱלֹהָיו. תְּהִלָּה לְדָוִד,

אֲרוֹמִמְךָ אֱלוֹהַי הַמֶּלֶךְ, וַאֲבָרְכָה שִׁמְךָ לְעוֹלָם וָעֶד.

בְּכָל יוֹם אֲבָרְכֶךָּ, וַאֲהַלְלָה שִׁמְךָ לְעוֹלָם וָעֶד.

גָּדוֹל יהוה וּמְהֻלָּל מְאֹד, וְלִגְדֻלָּתוֹ אֵין חֵקֶר.

דּוֹר לְדוֹר יְשַׁבַּח מַעֲשֶׂיךָ, וּגְבוּרֹתֶיךָ יַגִּידוּ.

הֲדַר כְּבוֹד הוֹדֶךָ, וְדִבְרֵי נִפְלְאֹתֶיךָ אָשִׂיחָה.

וֶעֱזוּז נוֹרְאוֹתֶיךָ יֹאמֵרוּ, וּגְדֻלָּתְךָ אֲסַפְּרֶנָּה.

זֵכֶר רַב טוּבְךָ יַבִּיעוּ, וְצִדְקָתְךָ יְרַנֵּנוּ.

חַנּוּן וְרַחוּם יהוה, אֶרֶךְ אַפַּיִם וּגְדָל חָסֶד.

טוֹב יהוה לַכֹּל, וְרַחֲמָיו עַל כָּל מַעֲשָׂיו.

יוֹדוּךָ יהוה כָּל מַעֲשֶׂיךָ, וַחֲסִידֶיךָ יְבָרְכוּכָה.

כְּבוֹד מַלְכוּתְךָ יֹאמֵרוּ, וּגְבוּרָתְךָ יְדַבֵּרוּ.

לְהוֹדִיעַ לִבְנֵי הָאָדָם גְּבוּרֹתָיו, וּכְבוֹד הֲדַר מַלְכוּתוֹ.

מַלְכוּתְךָ מַלְכוּת כָּל עֹלָמִים, וּמֶמְשַׁלְתְּךָ בְּכָל דּוֹר וָדֹר.

סוֹמֵךְ יהוה לְכָל הַנֹּפְלִים, וְזוֹקֵף לְכָל הַכְּפוּפִים.

עֵינֵי כֹל אֵלֶיךָ יְשַׂבֵּרוּ, וְאַתָּה נוֹתֵן לָהֶם אֶת אָכְלָם בְּעִתּוֹ.

Concentrate intently while reciting the verse, פּוֹתֵחַ.

פּוֹתֵחַ אֶת יָדֶךָ, וּמַשְׂבִּיעַ לְכָל חַי רָצוֹן.

❖ צַדִּיק יהוה בְּכָל דְּרָכָיו, וְחָסִיד בְּכָל מַעֲשָׂיו.

קָרוֹב יהוה לְכָל קֹרְאָיו, לְכֹל אֲשֶׁר יִקְרָאֻהוּ בֶאֱמֶת.

רְצוֹן יְרֵאָיו יַעֲשֶׂה, וְאֶת שַׁוְעָתָם יִשְׁמַע וְיוֹשִׁיעֵם.

שׁוֹמֵר יהוה אֶת כָּל אֹהֲבָיו, וְאֵת כָּל הָרְשָׁעִים יַשְׁמִיד.

תְּהִלַּת יהוה יְדַבֶּר פִּי, וִיבָרֵךְ כָּל בָּשָׂר שֵׁם קָדְשׁוֹ לְעוֹלָם וָעֶד.

וַאֲנַחְנוּ נְבָרֵךְ יָהּ, מֵעַתָּה וְעַד עוֹלָם, הַלְלוּיָהּ.[3]

The chazzan recites חֲצִי קַדִּישׁ.

יִתְגַּדַּל וְיִתְקַדַּשׁ שְׁמֵהּ רַבָּא. (.Cong – אָמֵן) בְּעָלְמָא דִּי בְרָא כִרְעוּתֵהּ. וְיַמְלִיךְ מַלְכוּתֵהּ, בְּחַיֵּיכוֹן וּבְיוֹמֵיכוֹן וּבְחַיֵּי דְכָל בֵּית יִשְׂרָאֵל, 1.31,

בַּעֲגָלָא וּבִזְמַן קָרִיב. וְאִמְרוּ: אָמֵן.

(.Cong – אָמֵן. יְהֵא שְׁמֵהּ רַבָּא מְבָרַךְ לְעָלַם וּלְעָלְמֵי עָלְמַיָּא.)

יְהֵא שְׁמֵהּ רַבָּא מְבָרַךְ לְעָלַם וּלְעָלְמֵי עָלְמַיָּא.

יִתְבָּרַךְ וְיִשְׁתַּבַּח וְיִתְפָּאַר וְיִתְרוֹמַם וְיִתְנַשֵּׂא וְיִתְהַדָּר וְיִתְעַלֶּה וְיִתְהַלָּל שְׁמֵהּ דְּקֻדְשָׁא בְּרִיךְ הוּא (.Cong – בְּרִיךְ הוּא) לְעֵלָּא [וּ]לְעֵלָּא מִכָּל בִּרְכָתָא וְשִׁירָתָא תֻּשְׁבְּחָתָא וְנֶחֱמָתָא, דַּאֲמִירָן בְּעָלְמָא, וְאִמְרוּ: אָמֵן. (.Cong – אָמֵן)

WHEN YOM KIPPUR FALLS ON MONDAY OR THURSDAY SOME CONGREGATIONS
REVERSE THE ORDER OF THE FOURTH AND FIFTH DAYS OF REPENTANCE

☙ FOURTH DAY OF REPENTANCE ❧

אַשְׁרֵי *Praiseworthy are those who dwell in Your house; may they always praise You, Selah! Praiseworthy is the people for whom this is so, praiseworthy is the people whose God is HASHEM.*

Psalm 145   *A psalm of praise by David:*

א *I will exalt You, my God the King, and I will bless Your Name forever and ever.*
ב *Every day I will bless You, and I will laud Your Name forever and ever.*
ג *HASHEM is great and exceedingly lauded,*
       and His greatness is beyond investigation.
ד *Each generation will praise Your deeds to the next*
       and of Your mighty deeds they will tell;
ה *The splendrous glory of Your power and Your wondrous deeds I shall discuss.*
ו *And of Your awesome power they will speak, and Your greatness I shall relate.*
ז *A recollection of Your abundant goodness they will utter*
       and of Your righteousness they will sing exultantly.
ח *Gracious and merciful is HASHEM, slow to anger, and great in [bestowing] kindness.*
ט *HASHEM is good to all; His mercies are on all His works.*
י *All Your works shall thank You, HASHEM, and Your devout ones will bless You.*
כ *Of the glory of Your kingdom they will speak, and of Your power they will tell;*
ל *To inform human beings of His mighty deeds,*
       and the glorious splendor of His kingdom.
מ *Your kingdom is a kingdom spanning all eternities,*
       and Your dominion is throughout every generation.
ס *HASHEM supports all the fallen ones and straightens all the bent.*
ע *The eyes of all look to You with hope*
       and You give them their food in its proper time;
פ *You open Your hand,*   Concentrate intently while reciting the verse, 'You open...'
       and satisfy the desire of every living thing.
צ Chazzan— *Righteous is HASHEM in all His ways*
       and magnanimous in all His deeds.
ק *HASHEM is close to all who call upon Him — to all who call upon Him sincerely.*
ר *The will of those who fear Him He will do;*
       and their cry He will hear, and save them.
ש *HASHEM protects all who love Him; but all the wicked He will destroy.*
ת *May my mouth declare the praise of HASHEM*
       and may all flesh bless His Holy Name forever and ever.
We will bless God from this time and forever, Halleluyah!

The chazzan recites Half-*Kaddish:*

יִתְגַּדַּל *May His great Name grow exalted and sanctified* (Cong.— *Amen.*) *in the world that He created as He willed. May He give reign to His kingship in your lifetimes and in your days, and in the lifetimes of the entire Family of Israel, swiftly and soon. Now respond: Amen.*

(Cong.— *Amen. May His great Name be blessed forever and ever.*)
       May His great Name be blessed forever and ever.
Blessed, praised, glorified, exalted, extolled, mighty, upraised, and lauded be the Name of the Holy One, Blessed is He (Cong.— *Blessed is He*) *— exceedingly beyond any blessing and song, praise and consolation that are uttered in the world. Now respond: Amen.* (Cong.— *Amen.*)

All:

לְךָ יהוה הַצְּדָקָה, וְלָנוּ בֹּשֶׁת הַפָּנִים.[1] מַה נִּתְאוֹנֵן,[2] מַה נֹּאמַר, מַה נְּדַבֵּר, וּמַה נִּצְטַדָּק.[3] נַחְפְּשָׂה דְרָכֵינוּ וְנַחְקְרָה, וְנָשׁוּבָה אֵלֶיךָ,[4] כִּי יְמִינְךָ פְּשׁוּטָה לְקַבֵּל שָׁבִים. לֹא בְחֶסֶד וְלֹא בְמַעֲשִׂים בָּאנוּ לְפָנֶיךָ, כְּדַלִּים וּכְרָשִׁים דָּפַקְנוּ דְלָתֶיךָ. דְּלָתֶיךָ דָּפַקְנוּ רַחוּם וְחַנּוּן, נָא אַל תְּשִׁיבֵנוּ רֵיקָם מִלְּפָנֶיךָ. מִלְּפָנֶיךָ מַלְכֵּנוּ רֵיקָם אַל תְּשִׁיבֵנוּ, כִּי אַתָּה שׁוֹמֵעַ תְּפִלָּה.

שֹׁמֵעַ תְּפִלָּה, עָדֶיךָ כָּל בָּשָׂר יָבֹאוּ.[5] יָבוֹא כָל בָּשָׂר לְהִשְׁתַּחֲוֹת לְפָנֶיךָ יהוה.[6] יָבֹאוּ וְיִשְׁתַּחֲווּ לְפָנֶיךָ אֲדֹנָי, וִיכַבְּדוּ לִשְׁמֶךָ.[7] בֹּאוּ נִשְׁתַּחֲוֶה וְנִכְרָעָה, נִבְרְכָה לִפְנֵי יהוה עֹשֵׂנוּ.[8] נָבוֹאָה לְמִשְׁכְּנוֹתָיו, נִשְׁתַּחֲוֶה לַהֲדֹם רַגְלָיו.[9] בֹּאוּ שְׁעָרָיו בְּתוֹדָה, חֲצֵרֹתָיו בִּתְהִלָּה, הוֹדוּ לוֹ בָּרְכוּ שְׁמוֹ.[10] רוֹמְמוּ יהוה אֱלֹהֵינוּ, וְהִשְׁתַּחֲווּ לַהֲדֹם רַגְלָיו, קָדוֹשׁ הוּא.[11] רוֹמְמוּ יהוה אֱלֹהֵינוּ, וְהִשְׁתַּחֲווּ לְהַר קָדְשׁוֹ, כִּי קָדוֹשׁ יהוה אֱלֹהֵינוּ.[12] הִשְׁתַּחֲווּ לַיהוה בְּהַדְרַת קֹדֶשׁ, חִילוּ מִפָּנָיו כָּל הָאָרֶץ.[13] וַאֲנַחְנוּ בְּרֹב חַסְדְּךָ נָבוֹא בֵיתֶךָ, נִשְׁתַּחֲוֶה אֶל הֵיכַל קָדְשְׁךָ בְּיִרְאָתֶךָ.[14] נִשְׁתַּחֲוֶה אֶל הֵיכַל קָדְשְׁךָ וְנוֹדֶה אֶת שְׁמֶךָ, עַל חַסְדְּךָ וְעַל אֲמִתֶּךָ, כִּי הִגְדַּלְתָּ עַל כָּל שִׁמְךָ אִמְרָתֶךָ.[15] לְכוּ נְרַנְּנָה לַיהוה, נָרִיעָה לְצוּר יִשְׁעֵנוּ. נְקַדְּמָה פָנָיו בְּתוֹדָה, בִּזְמִרוֹת נָרִיעַ לוֹ.[16] אֲשֶׁר יַחְדָּו נַמְתִּיק סוֹד, בְּבֵית אֱלֹהִים נְהַלֵּךְ בְּרָגֶשׁ.[17] אֵל נַעֲרָץ בְּסוֹד קְדֹשִׁים רַבָּה, וְנוֹרָא עַל כָּל סְבִיבָיו.[18] שְׂאוּ יְדֵיכֶם קֹדֶשׁ וּבָרְכוּ אֶת יהוה.[19] הִנֵּה בָּרְכוּ אֶת יהוה כָּל עַבְדֵי יהוה, הָעֹמְדִים בְּבֵית יהוה בַּלֵּילוֹת.[20] אֲשֶׁר מִי אֵל בַּשָּׁמַיִם וּבָאָרֶץ, אֲשֶׁר יַעֲשֶׂה כְמַעֲשֶׂיךָ וְכִגְבוּרֹתֶיךָ.[21] אֲשֶׁר לוֹ הַיָּם וְהוּא עָשָׂהוּ, וְיַבֶּשֶׁת יָדָיו יָצָרוּ.[22] אֲשֶׁר בְּיָדוֹ מֶחְקְרֵי אָרֶץ, וְתוֹעֲפוֹת הָרִים לוֹ.[23] אֲשֶׁר בְּיָדוֹ נֶפֶשׁ כָּל חָי, וְרוּחַ כָּל בְּשַׂר אִישׁ.[24] וְיוֹדוּ שָׁמַיִם פִּלְאֲךָ יהוה, אַף אֱמוּנָתְךָ בִּקְהַל קְדֹשִׁים.[25] לְךָ זְרוֹעַ עִם גְּבוּרָה, תָּעֹז יָדְךָ תָּרוּם יְמִינֶךָ.[26] לְךָ שָׁמַיִם, אַף לְךָ אָרֶץ, תֵּבֵל וּמְלֹאָהּ אַתָּה יְסַדְתָּם.[27] אַתָּה פוֹרַרְתָּ בְעָזְּךָ יָם, שִׁבַּרְתָּ רָאשֵׁי תַנִּינִים עַל הַמָּיִם.[28] אַתָּה הִצַּבְתָּ כָּל גְּבוּלוֹת אָרֶץ, קַיִץ וָחֹרֶף אַתָּה יְצַרְתָּם.[29] אַתָּה רִצַּצְתָּ רָאשֵׁי לִוְיָתָן, תִּתְּנֶנּוּ מַאֲכָל לְעַם לְצִיִּים.

(1) *Daniel* 9:7. (2) Cf. *Lamentations* 3:39. (3) Cf. *Genesis* 44:16. (4) Cf. *Lamentations* 3:40.
(5) *Psalms* 65:3. (6) Cf. *Isaiah* 66:23. (7) *Psalms* 86:9. (8) 95:6. (9) 132:7. (10) 100:4.
(11) 99:5. (12) 99:9. (13) 96:9. (14) Cf. 5:8. (15) Cf. 138:2. (16) 95:1-2. (17) 55:15. (18) 89:8.
(19) 134:2. (20) 134:1. (21) *Deuteronomy* 3:24. (22) *Psalms* 95:5. (23) 95:4. (24) *Job* 12:10.
(25) *Psalms* 89:6. (26) 89:14. (27) 89:12. (28) 74:13. (29) 74:17.

All:

לְךָ ה׳ *Yours, my Lord, is the righteousness and ours is the shame-facedness.¹ What complaint can we make?² What can we say? What can we declare? What justification can we offer?³ Let us examine our ways and analyze — and return to You,⁴ for Your right hand is extended to accept penitents. Neither with kindness nor with [good] deeds do we come before You. As paupers and as beggars do we knock at Your doors. At Your doors we knock, O Compassionate and Gracious One. Please do not turn us away from You empty-handed. Our King, turn us not away from You empty-handed, for You are the One Who hears prayer.*

שֹׁמֵעַ תְּפִלָּה *You Who hears prayer, to You all flesh will come.⁵ All flesh will come to prostrate itself before You, O HASHEM.⁶ They will come and prostrate themselves before You, my Lord, and shall honor Your Name.⁷ Come! — let us prostrate ourselves and bow, let us kneel before God, our Maker.⁸ Let us come to His dwelling places, let us prostrate ourselves at His footstool.⁹ Enter His gates with thanksgiving, His courts with praise; give thanks to Him, praise His Name.¹⁰ Exalt HASHEM, our God, and bow at His footstool; He is holy!¹¹ Exalt HASHEM, our God, and bow at His holy mountain; for holy is HASHEM, our God.¹² Prostrate yourselves before HASHEM in His intensely holy place, tremble before Him, everyone on earth.¹³ As for us, through Your abundant kindness we will enter Your House; we will prostrate ourselves toward Your Holy Sanctuary in awe of You.¹⁴ We will prostrate ourselves toward Your Holy Sanctuary, and we will give thanks to Your Name for Your kindness and truth for You have exalted Your promise even beyond Your Name.¹⁵ Come! — let us sing to HASHEM, let us call out to the Rock of our salvation. Let us greet Him with thanksgiving, with praiseful songs let us call out to Him.¹⁶ For together let us share sweet counsel, in the house of God let us walk in multitudes.¹⁷ God is dreaded in the hiddenmost counsel of the holy ones, and inspires awe upon all who surround Him.¹⁸ Lift your hands in the Sanctuary and bless HASHEM.¹⁹ Behold, bless HASHEM, all you servants of HASHEM, who stand in the House of HASHEM in the nights.²⁰ For what power is there in heaven or earth that can approximate Your deeds and power?²¹ For His is the sea and He perfected the dry land — His hands fashioned it.²² For in His power are the hidden mysteries of the earth, and the mountain summits are His.²³ For His is the soul of every living thing, and the spirit of all human flesh.²⁴ Heaven will gratefully praise Your wonders, HASHEM; also Your faithfulness in the assembly of holy ones.²⁵ Yours is a mighty arm with power, You strengthen Your hand; You exalt Your right hand.²⁶ Yours is the heaven; Yours, too, is the earth; the world and its fullness — You founded them.²⁷ You shattered the sea with Your might, You smashed sea serpents' heads upon the water.²⁸ You established all the boundaries of earth; summer and winter — You fashioned them.²⁹ You crushed the heads of Leviathan, You served it as food to the nation of legions.*

אַתָּה בָקַעְתָּ מַעְיָן וָנָחַל, אַתָּה הוֹבַשְׁתָּ נַהֲרוֹת אֵיתָן.[1] לְךָ יוֹם, אַף
לְךָ לָיְלָה, אַתָּה הֲכִינוֹתָ מָאוֹר וָשָׁמֶשׁ.[2] עָשָׂה גְדֹלוֹת עַד אֵין חֵקֶר,
וְנִפְלָאוֹת עַד אֵין מִסְפָּר.[3] כִּי אֵל גָּדוֹל יהוה, וּמֶלֶךְ גָּדוֹל עַל כָּל
אֱלֹהִים.[4] כִּי גָדוֹל אַתָּה וְעֹשֵׂה נִפְלָאוֹת, אַתָּה אֱלֹהִים לְבַדֶּךָ.[5] כִּי
גָדוֹל מֵעַל שָׁמַיִם חַסְדֶּךָ, וְעַד שְׁחָקִים אֲמִתֶּךָ.[6] גָּדוֹל יהוה וּמְהֻלָּל
מְאֹד, וְלִגְדֻלָּתוֹ אֵין חֵקֶר.[7] (כִּי) גָדוֹל יהוה וּמְהֻלָּל מְאֹד, נוֹרָא
הוּא עַל כָּל אֱלֹהִים.[8] גָּדוֹל יהוה וּמְהֻלָּל מְאֹד, בְּעִיר אֱלֹהֵינוּ הַר
קָדְשׁוֹ.[9] לְךָ יהוה הַגְּדֻלָּה וְהַגְּבוּרָה, וְהַתִּפְאֶרֶת וְהַנֵּצַח וְהַהוֹד, כִּי
כֹל בַּשָּׁמַיִם וּבָאָרֶץ; לְךָ יהוה הַמַּמְלָכָה, וְהַמִּתְנַשֵּׂא לְכֹל
לְרֹאשׁ.[10] מִי לֹא יִרָאֲךָ מֶלֶךְ הַגּוֹיִם, כִּי לְךָ יָאֶתָה, כִּי בְכָל חַכְמֵי
הַגּוֹיִם וּבְכָל מַלְכוּתָם מֵאֵין כָּמוֹךָ.[11] מֵאֵין כָּמוֹךָ יהוה, גָּדוֹל אַתָּה
וְגָדוֹל שִׁמְךָ בִּגְבוּרָה.[12] יהוה אֱלֹהֵי צְבָאוֹת, מִי כָמוֹךָ חֲסִין יָהּ,
וֶאֱמוּנָתְךָ סְבִיבוֹתֶיךָ.[13] יהוה צְבָאוֹת, אֱלֹהֵי יִשְׂרָאֵל, יוֹשֵׁב
הַכְּרֻבִים, אַתָּה הוּא הָאֱלֹהִים לְבַדֶּךָ.[14] מִי יְמַלֵּל גְּבוּרוֹת יהוה,
יַשְׁמִיעַ כָּל תְּהִלָּתוֹ.[15] כִּי מִי בַשַּׁחַק יַעֲרֹךְ לַיהוה, יִדְמֶה לַיהוה
בִּבְנֵי אֵלִים.[16] מַה נֹּאמַר לְפָנֶיךָ יוֹשֵׁב מָרוֹם, וּמַה נְּסַפֵּר לְפָנֶיךָ
שֹׁכֵן שְׁחָקִים. מַה נֹּאמַר לְפָנֶיךָ יהוה אֱלֹהֵינוּ, מַה נְּדַבֵּר וּמַה
נִּצְטַדָּק.[17] אֵין לָנוּ פֶּה לְהָשִׁיב וְלֹא מֵצַח לְהָרִים רֹאשׁ, כִּי
עֲוֹנוֹתֵינוּ רַבּוּ מִלְמְנוֹת, וְחַטֹּאתֵינוּ עָצְמוּ מִסַּפֵּר.[18] לְמַעַן שִׁמְךָ
יהוה תְּחַיֵּנוּ, וּבְצִדְקָתְךָ תּוֹצִיא מִצָּרָה נַפְשֵׁנוּ.[19] דַּרְכְּךָ אֱלֹהֵינוּ
לְהַאֲרִיךְ אַפֶּךָ, לָרָעִים וְלַטּוֹבִים, וְהִיא תְהִלָּתֶךָ. לְמַעַנְךָ אֱלֹהֵינוּ
עֲשֵׂה וְלֹא לָנוּ, רְאֵה עֲמִידָתֵנוּ, דַּלִּים וְרֵקִים. ❖ הַנְּשָׁמָה לָךְ וְהַגּוּף
פָּעֳלָךְ, חוּסָה עַל עֲמָלָךְ. הַנְּשָׁמָה לָךְ וְהַגּוּף שֶׁלָּךְ, יהוה עֲשֵׂה
לְמַעַן שְׁמֶךָ. אָתָאנוּ עַל שִׁמְךָ, יהוה, עֲשֵׂה לְמַעַן שְׁמֶךָ. בַּעֲבוּר
כְּבוֹד שִׁמְךָ, כִּי אֵל חַנּוּן וְרַחוּם שְׁמֶךָ. לְמַעַן שִׁמְךָ יהוה, וְסָלַחְתָּ
לַעֲוֹנֵנוּ כִּי רַב הוּא.[20]

Congregation, then chazzan:

סְלַח לָנוּ אָבִינוּ, כִּי בְרֹב אִוַּלְתֵּנוּ שָׁגִינוּ,
מְחַל לָנוּ מַלְכֵּנוּ, כִּי רַבּוּ עֲוֹנֵינוּ.

(1) *Psalms* 74:14-15. (2) 74:16. (3) *Job* 9:10. (4) *Psalms* 95:3. (5) 86:10. (6) 108:5.
(7) 145:3. (8) 96:4. (9) 48:2. (10) *I Chronicles* 29:11. (11) *Jeremiah* 10:7. (12) 10:6.
(13) *Psalms* 89:9. (14) *Isaiah* 37:16. (15) *Psalms* 106:2. (16) 89:7.
(17) Cf. *Genesis* 44:16. (18) Cf. *Ezra* 9:6. (19) Cf. *Psalms* 143:11. (20) Cf. 25:11.

You split open fountain and stream, You dried the mighty rivers.[1] Yours is the day, Yours as well is the night; You established luminary and the sun.[2] Who performs great deeds that are beyond comprehension, and wonders beyond number.[3] For a great God is HASHEM, and a great King above all heavenly powers.[4] For You are great and work wonders; You alone, O God.[5] For great above the very heavens is Your kindness, and until the upper heights is Your truth.[6] HASHEM is great and exceedingly lauded, and His greatness is beyond investigation.[7] (For) HASHEM is great and exceedingly lauded, awesome is He above all heavenly powers.[8] Great is HASHEM and exceedingly lauded, in the city of our God, Mount of His Holiness.[9] Yours, HASHEM, is the greatness, the strength, the splendor, the triumph, and the glory; even everything in heaven and earth; Yours, HASHEM, is the kingdom, and sovereignty over every leader.[10] Who would not revere You, O King of nations? — for this befits You, for among all the sages of the nations and in all their kingdom there is none like You.[11] There is none like You, O HASHEM, You are great and Your Name is great with power.[12] HASHEM, God of Legions — who is like You, O Strong One, God? — and Your faithfulness surrounds You.[13] HASHEM, Master of Legions, God of Israel, enthroned upon the Cherubim, it is You alone Who is God.[14] Who can express the mighty acts of HASHEM, who can announce all His praise?[15] For who in the sky can be compared to HASHEM; be likened to HASHEM among the angels?[16] What can we say before You Who dwell on high? And what can we relate to You Who abide in the highest heaven? What can we say before You, HASHEM, our God? What can we declare? What justification can we offer?[17] We have neither mouth to respond nor brow to raise our head, for our iniquities are too numerous to count, and our sins are too vast to be numbered.[18] For Your Name's sake, HASHEM, revive us; and with Your righteousness remove our soul from distress.[19] It is Your way, our God, to delay Your anger, against people both evil and good — and this is Your praise. Act for Your sake, our God, and not for ours, behold our [spiritual] position — destitute and emptyhanded. Chazzan – The soul is Yours and the body is Your handiwork; take pity on Your labor. The soul is Yours and the body is Yours; O HASHEM, act for Your Name's sake. We have come with reliance on Your Name, O HASHEM, act for Your Name's sake; because of Your Name's glory — for 'Gracious and Merciful God' is Your Name. For Your Name's sake, HASHEM, may You forgive our iniquity, though it is abundant.[20]

Congregation, then chazzan:

Forgive us, our Father, for in our abundant folly we have erred, pardon us, our King, for our iniquities are many.

סליחה עח (פתיחה)

All:

אֵשֶׁת נְעוּרִים הָאֲהוּבָה,*¹   אֲשֶׁר אֵרַשְׂתָּ² בְּרֹב מֹהַר וְרֹב טוֹבָה,

וְאֵיךְ עַתָּה יוֹשֶׁבֶת עֲלוּבָה,   גְּעוּלָה וּמְאוּסָה וַעֲזוּבָה.

לְבוּשָׁה בַּעֲדִי עֲדָיִים,*³   אֲשֶׁר הִתְנֵיתָ בִּבְרִית וּבִתְנָאִים,

וְאֵיךְ עַתָּה סוֹבֶבֶת דְּלָתַיִם,   וְשׁוֹכֶבֶת בֵּין שְׁפַתָּיִם.*⁴

חֲשׁוּבָה בְּשֵׁשׁ וּמֶשִׁי כְּלוּלָה,⁵   הִיא הָיְתָה בְּכָל הָאָרֶץ מְהֻלָּלָה,⁶

וְאֵיךְ עַתָּה נֶחְשֶׁבֶת מְחֻלָּלָה,   לְלַעַג וּלְבֹשֶׁת וְלִקְלָלָה.

נְוַת פַּעֲמַיִם בִּנְעָלֶיהָ,⁷   אֲשֶׁר כְּנָפֶיךָ פְּרוּשִׂים עָלֶיהָ,⁸

וְאֵיךְ עַתָּה נִגְּפוּ רַגְלֶיהָ,   עַל הֶהָרִים⁹ אַחַר עוֹלָלֶיהָ.

❖ נָא יוֹשֵׁב הַכְּרוּבִים,¹⁰   תֵּרֶא בְּכָל זֹאת לֹא אַתָּה פָנִיתָ אֶל רְהָבִים,¹¹

לֹא עַל פָּרָשִׁים וְלֹא עַל רוֹכְבִים,¹²   כִּי עַל רַחֲמֶיךָ הָרַבִּים.¹³

All:

כִּי עַל רַחֲמֶיךָ הָרַבִּים¹³ אָנוּ בְטוּחִים, וְעַל צִדְקוֹתֶיךָ אָנוּ נִשְׁעָנִים, וְלִסְלִיחוֹתֶיךָ אָנוּ מְקַוִּים, וְלִישׁוּעָתְךָ אָנוּ מְצַפִּים. אַתָּה הוּא מֶלֶךְ, אוֹהֵב צְדָקוֹת מִקֶּדֶם, מַעֲבִיר עֲוֹנוֹת עַמּוֹ, וּמֵסִיר חַטַּאת יְרֵאָיו. כּוֹרֵת בְּרִית לָרִאשׁוֹנִים, וּמְקַיֵּם שְׁבוּעָה לָאַחֲרוֹנִים. אַתָּה הוּא, שֶׁיָּרַדְתָּ בַּעֲנַן כְּבוֹדֶךָ עַל הַר סִינַי,¹⁴ וְהֶרְאֵיתָ דַּרְכֵי טוּבְךָ לְמֹשֶׁה עַבְדֶּךָ.¹⁵ וְאָרְחוֹת חֲסָדֶיךָ גִּלִּיתָ לּוֹ, וְהוֹדַעְתּוֹ כִּי אַתָּה אֵל רַחוּם וְחַנּוּן, אֶרֶךְ אַפַּיִם וְרַב חֶסֶד¹⁶ וּמַרְבֶּה לְהֵטִיב, וּמַנְהִיג אֶת כָּל הָעוֹלָם כֻּלּוֹ בְּמִדַּת הָרַחֲמִים. ❖ וְכֵן כָּתוּב, וַיֹּאמֶר אֲנִי אַעֲבִיר כָּל טוּבִי עַל פָּנֶיךָ, וְקָרָאתִי בְשֵׁם יהוה לְפָנֶיךָ, וְחַנֹּתִי אֶת אֲשֶׁר אָחֹן, וְרִחַמְתִּי אֶת אֲשֶׁר אֲרַחֵם.¹⁷

⳨⳾ אֵשֶׁת נְעוּרִים הָאֲהוּבָה — *[Israel,] the beloved wife of earliest* [lit., *youthful*] *days.* The acrostic of this *selichah* spells the *paytan's* name אֶלְחָנָן, *Elchanan.* R' Elchanan of Dampierre, France, was a Tosafist of the academy of his father, R' Yitzchak, best known as the Ri. He met a martyr's death in 1184 and his son Shmuel was raised by his father.

Each of the first four stanzas compares Israel of the glorious past with the embittered nation of the millennia-long exile. First, two lines exult about ancient days, then the transitional phrase *'how is it that now . . .'* introduces two lines that bewail her present situation. The final stanza is a plea that she be redeemed, for despite her condition, despite the pressure of her captors, she nevertheless staunchly refuses to place her faith in anything or anyone but God's mercy.

עֲדִי עֲדָיִים — *Twin Torah crowns.* When Israel was asked to accept the Torah, the nation cried out, נַעֲשֶׂה וְנִשְׁמָע, *We will do and we will hear'* (*Exodus* 24:7), placing נַעֲשֶׂה, *we will do*, before נִשְׁמָע, *we will hear.* Thus, they undertook to fulfill all of God's commandments, even before they knew what was expected of them. This devotion was rewarded when 600,000 ministering angels approached Israel and placed two crowns upon each Jew's head — one for נַעֲשֶׂה, and one for נִשְׁמָע (*Shabbos* 88a).

בֵּין שְׁפַתָּיִם — *On the open roadsides* [lit., *between the borders*]. The translation and interpretation follow *Rashi* (*Genesis* 49:14 and *Psalms* 68:14). When the Jews were exiled from Jerusalem in chains, captive women were not permitted to sleep in the cities they passed on their way to

SELICHAH 78

All:

א [Israel,] the beloved wife of earliest days,*[1]
whom You betrothed[2] with abundant dowry and abundant goodness —
how is it that now she sits in disgrace, loathed, despised, and neglected?

ל She was once clothed with twin Torah crowns,*[3]
that You had stipulated with a covenant and [nuptial] agreements.
How is it that now she goes begging from door to door
and sleeps on the open roadside?*[4]

ה Once enwrapped in the finest linen and silk,[5]
she was the praise of all the earth.[6]
How is it that now she is reckoned profaned,
[put] to mockery, to shame, and to curse?

ג She whose footsteps were so lovely in pilgrim's sandals,[7]
over whom Your wings were spread —[8]
how is it that now her feet are bruised
on the mountains[9] [of the Diaspora as she stumbles] after her children?

ג Chazzan – Please, O You Who sit upon the Cherubim,[10]
see how despite all this she has not turned to the arrogant [for help],[11]
nor to charioteers, nor to horsemen,[12]
but only to Your abundant mercy.[13]

All:

כִּי עַל For upon Your abundant mercy[13] do we trust, and upon Your
righteousness do we depend, and for Your forgiveness do we
hope, and for Your salvation do we yearn. You are the King Who loves
righteousness since the earliest days, Who overlooks His people's
iniquities and sets aside the sins of those who revere Him. He made a
covenant with the ancestors and keeps [His] vow to the descendants. It
is You Who descended in Your cloud of glory on Mount Sinai,[14] and
showed the ways of Your goodness to Your servant Moses.[15] You revealed
Your paths of kindness to him, and let him know that You are God,
Compassionate and Gracious, Slow to anger and Abundant in Kindness,[16] doing manifold good, and guiding all Your world with the
Attribute of Mercy. Chazzan – And so it is written: He said, 'I shall pass
all My good in front of you, and I shall call out the Name of HASHEM before
you; for I will be gracious to whom I will be gracious, and I will be
compassionate with whom I will be compassionate.'[17]

---

(1) Cf. *Isaiah* 54:6. (2) Some editions read אֵרַשְׂתָּה, but the meaning is virtually unchanged.
(3) Cf. *Ezekiel* 16:7. (4) Cf. *Psalms* 68:14. (5) Cf. *Ezekiel* 16:10. (6) Cf. 16:14. (7) *Song of Songs* 7:2.
(8) Cf. *Ezekiel* 16:8. (9) Cf. *Jeremiah* 13:16. (10) *I Samuel* 4:4. (11) Cf. *Psalms* 40:5. (12) Cf. 20:8.
(13) *Daniel* 9:18. (14) Cf. *Exodus* 34:5. (15) Cf. 33:13. (16) 34:6. (17) 33:19.

Babylon, but had to sleep out in the open, exposed
to the elements. Some interpret that these women
were publicly violated when they were made to
lie on the roadsides.

Other interpretations of this phrase are: The
noble daughters were forced to work as kitchen
slaves and had to sleep among the rows of pots

(*Ibn Ezra* to *Psalms* 68:14); they were forced to till
the soil and sleep between the furrows (*Rashbam*
to *Genesis* 49:14); they were forced to carry heavy
double burdens and collapsed under their weight
(*Sforno* ibid.). None of these views are mutually
exclusive, for all of these atrocities may have been
perpetrated against the captives.

All, while standing:

אֵל אֶרֶךְ אַפַּיִם אַתָּה, וּבַעַל הָרַחֲמִים נִקְרֵאתָ,
וְדֶרֶךְ תְּשׁוּבָה הוֹרֵיתָ.

גְּדֻלַּת רַחֲמֶיךָ וַחֲסָדֶיךָ, תִּזְכּוֹר הַיּוֹם וּבְכָל יוֹם לְזֶרַע יְדִידֶיךָ.
תֵּפֶן אֵלֵינוּ בְּרַחֲמִים, כִּי אַתָּה הוּא בַּעַל הָרַחֲמִים.
בְּתַחֲנוּן וּבִתְפִלָּה פָּנֶיךָ נְקַדֵּם, כְּהוֹדַעְתָּ לֶעָנָיו מִקֶּדֶם.
מֵחֲרוֹן אַפְּךָ שׁוּב,[1] כְּמוֹ בְתוֹרָתְךָ כָּתוּב.[2]
וּבְצֵל כְּנָפֶיךָ נֶחֱסֶה[3] וְנִתְלוֹנָן, כְּיוֹם וַיֵּרֶד יהוה בֶּעָנָן.
❖ תַּעֲבוֹר עַל פֶּשַׁע וְתִמְחֶה אָשָׁם, כְּיוֹם וַיִּתְיַצֵּב עִמּוֹ שָׁם.
תַּאֲזִין שַׁוְעָתֵנוּ וְתַקְשִׁיב מֶנּוּ מַאֲמָר, כְּיוֹם וַיִּקְרָא בְשֵׁם יהוה,[4] וְשָׁם נֶאֱמַר:

Congregation, then *chazzan:*

וַיַּעֲבֹר יהוה עַל פָּנָיו וַיִּקְרָא:

Congregation and *chazzan* (the words in bold type are recited aloud and in unison):

יהוה, יהוה, אֵל, רַחוּם, וְחַנּוּן, אֶרֶךְ אַפַּיִם, וְרַב חֶסֶד, וֶאֱמֶת,
נֹצֵר חֶסֶד לָאֲלָפִים, נֹשֵׂא עָוֹן, וָפֶשַׁע, וְחַטָּאָה,
וְנַקֵּה.[5] וְסָלַחְתָּ לַעֲוֹנֵנוּ וּלְחַטָּאתֵנוּ וּנְחַלְתָּנוּ.[6] סְלַח לָנוּ אָבִינוּ כִּי
חָטָאנוּ, מְחַל לָנוּ מַלְכֵּנוּ כִּי פָשָׁעְנוּ. כִּי אַתָּה אֲדֹנָי טוֹב וְסַלָּח, וְרַב
חֶסֶד לְכָל קֹרְאֶיךָ.[7]

פסוקי הקדמה לסליחה עט

מֵאֵין כָּמוֹךָ יהוה, גָּדוֹל אַתָּה וְגָדוֹל שִׁמְךָ בִּגְבוּרָה.[8] נוֹדָע
בִּיהוּדָה אֱלֹהִים, בְּיִשְׂרָאֵל גָּדוֹל שְׁמוֹ.[9] עֶזְרֵנוּ יהוה
אֱלֹהֵינוּ, כִּי עָלֶיךָ נִשְׁעַנּוּ, וּבְשִׁמְךָ בָאנוּ.[10] כְּשִׁמְךָ אֱלֹהִים כֵּן
תְּהִלָּתְךָ, עַל קַצְוֵי אֶרֶץ, צֶדֶק מָלְאָה יְמִינֶךָ.[11] מִגְדַּל עֹז שֵׁם יהוה,
בּוֹ יָרוּץ צַדִּיק וְנִשְׂגָּב.[12]

כְּרַחֵם אָב עַל בָּנִים, כֵּן תְּרַחֵם יהוה עָלֵינוּ.[13] לַיהוה הַיְשׁוּעָה,
עַל עַמְּךָ בִרְכָתֶךָ סֶּלָה.[14] יהוה צְבָאוֹת עִמָּנוּ,
מִשְׂגָּב לָנוּ אֱלֹהֵי יַעֲקֹב סֶלָה.[15] יהוה צְבָאוֹת, אַשְׁרֵי אָדָם בֹּטֵחַ
בָּךְ.[16] יהוה הוֹשִׁיעָה, הַמֶּלֶךְ יַעֲנֵנוּ בְיוֹם קָרְאֵנוּ.[17]

In some congregations the following two verses are recited responsively — the *chazzan* reciting סְלַח,
and the congregation responding וַיֹּאמֶר. In other congregations these verses are recited silently.

סְלַח נָא לַעֲוֹן הָעָם הַזֶּה כְּגֹדֶל חַסְדֶּךָ, וְכַאֲשֶׁר נָשָׂאתָה לָעָם
הַזֶּה מִמִּצְרַיִם וְעַד הֵנָּה.[18] וְשָׁם נֶאֱמַר:

All, while standing:

אֵל אֶרֶךְ אַפַּיִם O God — You are slow to anger, You are called the Master of Mercy, and You have taught the way of repentance. May You remember this day and every day the greatness of Your mercy and Your kindness to the offspring of Your beloved Ones. Turn to us in mercy for You are the Master of Mercy. With supplication and prayer we approach Your Presence in the manner that You made known to the humble [Moses] in ancient times. Turn back from Your fierce anger;[1] as is written in Your Torah.[2] In the shadow of Your wings may we find shelter[3] and lodging as on the day 'HASHEM descended in a cloud' [to appear to Moses on Sinai]. Chazzan — Overlook sin and erase guilt as on the day 'He [God] stood there with him [Moses].' Give heed to our cry and be attentive to our declaration as on the day 'He called out with the Name HASHEM,'[4] and there it was said:

Congregation, then chazzan:

And HASHEM passed before him [Moses] and proclaimed:

Congregation and chazzan (the words in bold type are recited aloud and in unison):

ה' ה' HASHEM, HASHEM, God, Compassionate and Gracious, Slow to anger, and Abundant in Kindness and Truth, Preserver of kindness for thousands [of generations], Forgiver of iniquity, willful sin, and error, and Who cleanses.[5] May You forgive our iniquities and our errors and make us Your heritage.[6] Forgive us, our Father, for we have erred; pardon us, our King, for we have willfully sinned; for You, my Lord, are good and forgiving and abundantly kind to all who call upon You.[7]

PREFATORY VERSES TO SELICHAH 79

מֵאֵין There is none like You, O HASHEM, You are great and Your Name is great in power.[8] God is recognized in Judah; in Israel His Name is great.[9] Help us, O HASHEM, our God, for we depend upon You, and we have come in Your name.[10] Like Your Name, O God, so is Your praise — to the ends of the earth; righteousness fills Your right hand.[11] HASHEM's Name is a tower of strength, with which the righteous may run and be uplifted.[12]

כְּרַחֵם אָב As a father has mercy on his children, so, HASHEM, may You have mercy on us.[13] Salvation is HASHEM's, upon Your people is Your blessing, Selah.[14] HASHEM, Master of Legions, is with us, a stronghold for us is the God of Jacob, Selah.[15] HASHEM, Master of Legions, praiseworthy is the person who trusts in You.[16] HASHEM, save! May the King answer us on the day we call.[17]

In some congregations the following two verses are recited responsively — the chazzan reciting, 'Forgive, please . . .,' and the congregation responding, 'And HASHEM said . . .'
In other congregations these verses are recited silently.

סְלַח נָא Forgive, please, the iniquity of this people according to the greatness of Your kindness and as You have forgiven this people from Egypt until now,[18] and there it was said:

---

(1) Cf. Exodus 32:12. (2) See 32:14. (3) Cf. Psalms 36:8. (4) Exodus 34:5. (5) 34:6-7. (6) 34:9.
(7) Psalms 86:5. (8) Jeremiah 10:6. (9) Psalms 76:2. (10) II Chronicles 14:10. (11) Psalms 48:11.
(12) Proverbs 18:10. (13) Cf. Psalms 103:13. (14) 3:9. (15) 46:8. (16) 84:13. (17) 20:10. (18) Numbers 14:19.

וַיֹּאמֶר יהוה סָלַחְתִּי כִּדְבָרֶךָ.[1]

All:

הַטֵּה אֱלֹהַי אָזְנְךָ וּשֲׁמָע, פְּקַח עֵינֶיךָ וּרְאֵה שֹׁמְמֹתֵינוּ, וְהָעִיר אֲשֶׁר נִקְרָא שִׁמְךָ עָלֶיהָ, כִּי לֹא עַל צִדְקוֹתֵינוּ אֲנַחְנוּ מַפִּילִים תַּחֲנוּנֵינוּ לְפָנֶיךָ, כִּי עַל רַחֲמֶיךָ הָרַבִּים. אֲדֹנָי שְׁמָעָה, אֲדֹנָי סְלָחָה, אֲדֹנָי הַקְשִׁיבָה, וַעֲשֵׂה אַל תְּאַחַר, לְמַעַנְךָ אֱלֹהַי, כִּי שִׁמְךָ נִקְרָא עַל עִירְךָ וְעַל עַמֶּךָ.[2]

סליחה עט

All:

אֱלֹהֵינוּ וֵאלֹהֵי אֲבוֹתֵינוּ:

אָמְנָם אֲנַחְנוּ חָטָאנוּ*[3] וְהֶעֱוִינוּ,   **בָּ**גוֹד בָּגַדְנוּ בְּךָ אָבִינוּ,

גָּלִינוּ מִבְּלִי דַעַת[4] וְנִדְוֵינוּ,   **דְּ**חוּיִים דְּחוּפִים לִישׁוּעָתְךָ קִוִּינוּ.[5]

הַעֲבֵר אָדוֹן עֲוֹן עֲבָדֶיךָ,[6]   **וְ**אַל תַּט בְּאַף[7] זֶרַע יְדִידֶיךָ,

זְכֹר רַחֲמֶיךָ יהוה וַחֲסָדֶיךָ,[8]   **חֶ**סֶד וֶאֱמֶת נִשְׁבַּעְתָּ לִידִידֶיךָ.[9]

טָרוּד וְעָנוּי מִדֶּרֶךְ פְּשָׁעָם,[10]   **יִ**סּוּרֵי תוֹכָחוֹת שְׁמוֹנָה וְתִשְׁעִים,[11]

כָּרַתָּ וְהִכְתַּבְתָּ לְאִים פּוֹשְׁעִים,   **לֹ**א תַאֲשִׁים אוֹם בְּךָ נוֹשְׁעִים.[12]

מִפְשַׁע רַב נַקֵּה בָנֶיךָ,[13]   **נִ**כְנָעִים שָׁבִים וּמִתְחַנְּנִים לְפָנֶיךָ,

סִרְחוֹן כִּתְמָם לַבֵּן בְּהַעֲבָרַת סַמְמָנֶיךָ,*

עֲוֹנָם תִּכְבֹּשׁ וְתַשְׁלִיךְ בְּצוּל שְׁאוֹנֶךָ.[14]

פְּקַח קוֹחַ אֲסוּרֶיךָ לְהַתִּר,[15]   **צַ**חַן שִׁמְצָתֵנוּ תַּעֲבִיר כְּבַנֶּתֶר,

קָרַע שְׁטָרֵינוּ וְחוֹבוֹתֵינוּ וַתֵּר,   **רַ**חֵם תִּזְכֹּר[16] פָּנִים בְּהַסְתֵּר.

שְׁבוּעָה זְכֹר וּבְרִית קַדְמוֹנִית,

תָּחֹן בִּזְכוּת אָבוֹת מְנוּיֵי אֲחוֹרַנִּית,*

גְּדֵרַת הַגִּינָה[17] מְלֶאכֶת הַתַּבְנִית,   **רְ**צֵה לְהַחֲזִיר חִבָּה רִאשׁוֹנִית.[18]

---

§ **אָמְנָם אֲנַחְנוּ חָטָאנוּ** — *Truly, we have sinned.* The acrostic of this *selichah* follows the *aleph-beis,* then spells the *paytan's* signature — גֵּרְשֹׁם בֶּן יְהוּדָה חֲזָק, *Gershom ben Yehudah, may he be strong* [see prefatory comment to *selichah* 12].

בְּהַעֲבָרַת סַמְמָנֶיךָ — *Treating it with Your herbs* [lit., *by passing Your spices*]. Metaphorically, this refers to cleansing the stain of sin as one would launder a garment with soap and other cleansers (see *Isaiah* 1:18 and *Jeremiah* 2:22). On another plane, the stich refers to the קְטֹרֶת הַסַּמִּים, *incense spices.* For we find that when a plague struck the nation after Korach's rebellion (*Numbers* 17:6-15), Moses told Aaron to place coals from the Al-

tar into a pan, place incense spices upon them, stand among the people, וְכַפֵּר עֲלֵיהֶם, *and atone for them* (ibid. 17:11). Aaron did so, וַיְכַפֵּר עַל הָעָם, *and he brought atonement for the people* (ibid. 17:12). Thus, the *paytan* pleads for the return of the Temple and its service, so that our sins can once again be atoned for by the incense offering.

אָבוֹת מְנוּיֵי אֲחוֹרַנִּית — *The Patriarchs, recorded in reverse order.* The Torah (*Leviticus* 26:42) states: *And I shall remember My covenant with Jacob, and also My covenant with Isaac, and also My covenant with Abraham shall I remember …* listing the three Patriarchs in reverse order of their ages.

And HASHEM said, 'I have forgiven according to your word!'[1]

All:

הַטֵּה *Incline, my God, Your ear, and listen, open Your eyes and see our desolation and that of the city upon which Your Name is proclaimed; for not because of our righteousness do we cast down our supplications before You, rather because of Your abundant compassion. O my Lord, heed; O my Lord, forgive; O my Lord, be attentive and act, do not delay; for Your sake, my God, for Your Name is proclaimed upon Your city and upon Your people.*[2]

SELICHAH 79

All:

Our God and the God of our forefathers:

א *Truly, we have sinned,*[*3] *and we have caused perversion;*

ב *we have utterly betrayed You, our Father.*

ג *We have been exiled for our lack of wit,*[4] *and we have been pained,*

ד *We have been thrown aside and hard pressed,*
      [yet] we hope for Your salvation.[5]

ה *Dismiss, O Lord, Your servants' iniquity,*[6]

ו *and do not repel Your beloved's seed in anger.*[7]

ז *Remember Your mercies, O HASHEM, and Your kindnesses,*[8]

ח *the kindness and truth that You swore to Your beloved [Patriarchs].*[9]

ט *Expulsion and torment for [our] sinful way,*[10]

י *and the sufferings promised in the ninety-eight Rebukes*[11]

כ *that You decreed and wrote [in the Torah] to put fear into sinners;*

ל *[after all this,] do not hold guilty the nation*
      whose salvation is from You.[12]

מ *Cleanse Your children of [their] great rebelliousness,*[13]

נ *for they humbly repent and supplicate before You [for forgiveness].*

ס *Whiten their sin's stain, treating it with Your herbs;*[*]

ע *quell their iniquity and throw it into the depths*
      of Your tumultuous sea.[14]

פ *Cry freedom to release [Israel,] Your imprisoned ones;*[15]

צ *remove our sin's stench, as if with soap;*

ק *rip up our records and waive our culpability —*

ר *remember [Your] mercy,*[16] *even when [Your] countenance is hidden.*

ש *Remember Your oath and covenant of old.*

ת *Show us grace in the merit of the Patriarchs, recorded in reverse order.*[*]

ג *The perfect stonemasonry*[17]
      and [carefully] measure work [of the Holy Temple][18]

ר *Your ancient love — find favor to restore.*

---

(1) *Numbers* 14:20. (2) *Daniel* 9:18-19. (3) Cf. *Joshua* 7:20. (4) Cf. *Isaiah* 5:13. (5) Cf. *Genesis* 49:18. (6) Cf. *II Samuel* 24:10. (7) Cf. *Psalms* 27:9. (8) 25:6. (9) Cf. *Micah* 7:20; *Genesis* 22:16; some editions of *Selichos* read, לַעֲבָדֶיךָ, to Your servants. (10) Cf. *Psalms* 107:17. (11) See *Deuteronomy* 28:15-68. (12) Cf. *Deuteronomy* 33:29. (13) Cf. *Psalms* 19:14. (14) Cf. *Micah* 7:19. (15) Cf. *Isaiah* 61:1. (16) *Habakkuk* 3:2. (17) Cf. *Ezekiel* 42:12. (18) Cf. 43:10.

שָׁפְטָה מִשְׁפָּטֵי מְזִדִים עוֹשְׁקִים,   מֵאֲנוּ לְשַׁלְּחֵנוּ וּבְנוּ מַחֲזִיקִים,

בְּנֵי יְהוּדָה וְיִשְׂרָאֵל הָעֲשׁוּקִים,[1]   יָהּ שׁוּב שְׁבִיתָם כְּבַנֶּגֶב אֲפִיקִים.*[2]

הַבֵּט מִשָּׁמַיִם מִזְּבוּל מְרוֹמֶיךָ,   וְגַל יִתְגַּלּוּ הֲמוֹן מֵעֶיךָ וְרַחֲמֶיךָ,[3]

דִּי תֹאמַר לְיִסּוּרֵי נְעִימֶיךָ,   הֵיטִיבָה בִרְצוֹנְךָ עִירְךָ וְעַמֶּךָ.[4]

❖ חַטָּאתֵינוּ בִּמְצֹלוֹת יָם תַּצְלִיל,[5]

זְבוּל קָדְשְׁךָ בִּמְרוֹם הָרִים תַּתְלִיל,[6]

קְנוּיֶיךָ יֵלְכוּ בְּשִׂמְחַת לֵבָב וְחָלִיל,[7]

אָז תַּחְפֹּץ זִבְחֵי צֶדֶק עוֹלָה וְכָלִיל.[8]

All, while standing:

אֵל מֶלֶךְ יוֹשֵׁב עַל כִּסֵּא רַחֲמִים מִתְנַהֵג בַּחֲסִידוּת, מוֹחֵל עֲוֹנוֹת עַמּוֹ, מַעֲבִיר רִאשׁוֹן רִאשׁוֹן,[9] מַרְבֶּה מְחִילָה לְחַטָּאִים וּסְלִיחָה לְפוֹשְׁעִים, עֹשֶׂה צְדָקוֹת עִם כָּל בָּשָׂר וָרוּחַ, לֹא כְרָעָתָם תִּגְמוֹל. ❖ אֵל הוֹרֵיתָ לָּנוּ לוֹמַר שְׁלֹשׁ עֶשְׂרֵה, וּזְכֹר לָנוּ הַיּוֹם בְּרִית שְׁלֹשׁ עֶשְׂרֵה, כְּמוֹ שֶׁהוֹדַעְתָּ לֶעָנָיו מִקֶּדֶם, כְּמוֹ שֶׁכָּתוּב, וַיֵּרֶד יהוה בֶּעָנָן וַיִּתְיַצֵּב עִמּוֹ שָׁם, וַיִּקְרָא בְשֵׁם יהוה.

Congregation, then chazzan:

וַיַּעֲבֹר יהוה עַל פָּנָיו וַיִּקְרָא:

Congregation and chazzan (the words in bold type are recited aloud and in unison):

יהוה, יהוה, אֵל, **רַחוּם, וְחַנּוּן, אֶרֶךְ אַפַּיִם, וְרַב חֶסֶד, וֶאֱמֶת, נֹצֵר חֶסֶד לָאֲלָפִים, נֹשֵׂא עָוֹן, וָפֶשַׁע, וְחַטָּאָה, וְנַקֵּה.** וְסָלַחְתָּ לַעֲוֹנֵנוּ וּלְחַטָּאתֵנוּ וּנְחַלְתָּנוּ. סְלַח לָנוּ אָבִינוּ כִּי חָטָאנוּ, מְחַל לָנוּ מַלְכֵּנוּ כִּי פָשָׁעְנוּ. כִּי אַתָּה אֲדֹנָי טוֹב וְסַלָּח, וְרַב חֶסֶד לְכָל קֹרְאֶיךָ.

פסוקי הקדמה לסליחה פ

אֱלֹהִים, בָּאוּ גוֹיִם בְּנַחֲלָתֶךָ, טִמְּאוּ אֶת הֵיכַל קָדְשֶׁךָ, שָׂמוּ אֶת יְרוּשָׁלַיִם לְעִיִּים.[10] שְׁפֹךְ עֲלֵיהֶם זַעְמֶךָ, וַחֲרוֹן אַפְּךָ יַשִּׂיגֵם.[11] הִנָּשֵׂא שֹׁפֵט הָאָרֶץ, הָשֵׁב גְּמוּל עַל גֵּאִים.[12] תֵּן לָהֶם כְּפָעֳלָם וּכְרֹעַ מַעַלְלֵיהֶם, כְּמַעֲשֵׂה יְדֵיהֶם תֵּן לָהֶם, הָשֵׁב גְּמוּלָם לָהֶם.[13] הֵיטִיבָה בִרְצוֹנְךָ אֶת צִיּוֹן, תִּבְנֶה חוֹמוֹת יְרוּשָׁלָיִם.[14]

---

(1) Cf. *Jeremiah* 50:33. (2) Cf. *Psalms* 126:4. (3) Cf. *Isaiah* 63:15. (4) Cf. *Psalms* 51:20. (5) Cf. *Micah* 7:19. (6) Cf. *Isaiah* 63:15; 37:24. (7) Cf. 30:29. (8) *Psalms* 51:21; see commentary to *selichah* 4. (9) Tractate *Rosh Hashanah* 17a. (10) *Psalms* 79:1. (11) 69:25. (12) 94:2. (13) 28:4. (14) 51:20.

כְּבַנֶּגֶב אֲפִיקִים — *Like springs in the desert.* The commentaries (to *Psalms* 126:4) explains this simile in various ways: Just as water turns a seemingly barren desert into a flourishing garden, so

will we be transformed and gladdened when God delivers us from our exile (*Rashi*).

One who plants in dry soil always wonders how his crop will fare. If a hidden stream unex-

שׁ Render justice for me against the wanton oppressors,
מ who refuse to set us free, but hold us tight [in their grasp].
בנ The oppressed children of Judah and Israel,[1]
י O God, bring back their captivity like springs in the desert.*[2]
ה Look down from Heaven, from Your celestial Temple,
ו and let Your inner feelings and mercy[3] be overwhelming.
ד Say, 'Enough!' to the sufferings of Your pleasant ones;
ה Do good in Your favor unto Your city and Your people.[4]
ח Chazzan — Sink our sins into the depths of the sea,[5]
ז and raise high Your Holy Temple on the highest of mountains.[6]
ק May the people You acquired for Yourself
        go there with joyful heart and flute,[7]
    for then You will desire the sacrifices of righteousness,
        the olah-offering and whole-offering.[8]

All, while standing:

אֵל מֶלֶךְ O God, King Who sits on the throne of mercy; Who acts with
        kindness, pardons the iniquities of His people, removes [sins]
one by one,[9] increasingly grants pardon to careless sinners and forgiveness
to rebels, Who deals righteously with every living being — You do not repay
them in accord with their evil. Chazzan — O God, You taught us to recite the
Thirteen [Attributes of Mercy], so remember for us today the covenant of
these Thirteen, as You made known to the humble one in ancient times, as
it is written: And HASHEM descended in a cloud and stood with him there,
and He called out with the Name HASHEM.

Congregation, then chazzan:

And HASHEM passed before him [Moses] and proclaimed:

Congregation and chazzan (the words in bold type are recited aloud and in unison):

ה' ה' HASHEM, HASHEM, God, Compassionate and Gracious, Slow to
        anger, and Abundant in Kindness and Truth, Preserver of
kindness for thousands [of generations], Forgiver of iniquity, willful
sin, and error, and Who cleanses. May You forgive our iniquities and our
errors and make us Your heritage. Forgive us, our Father, for we have
erred; pardon us, our King, for we have willfully sinned; for You, my Lord,
are good and forgiving and abundantly kind to all who call upon You.

PREFATORY VERSES TO SELICHAH 80

אֱלֹהִים O God, nations have entered into Your heritage; they have
        defiled the Sanctuary of Your holiness, they have turned
Jerusalem into heaps of rubble.[10] Pour Your wrath upon them; and let the
fierceness of Your anger overtake them.[11] Arise, O Judge of the earth,
render recompense to the haughty.[12] Give them according to their deeds
and according to the evil of their endeavors; according to their handiwork
give them, render their recompense to them.[13] Do good in Your favor unto
Zion; build the walls of Jerusalem.[14]

---

pectedly springs forth to water them, the farmer
is beside himself with joy. Such will be our joy at
the redemption, which will follow so much despair (Radak).

When occasional rains fill the dry river beds
and crevices in the desert, water gushes through
them in a mighty torrent. So will our joy be a
powerful surge of happiness (Meiri).

בְּרַחֵם אָב עַל בָּנִים, כֵּן תְּרַחֵם יהוה עָלֵינוּ. לַיהוה הַיְשׁוּעָה,
עַל עַמְּךָ בִרְכָתֶךָ סֶּלָה. יהוה צְבָאוֹת עִמָּנוּ, מִשְׂגָּב
לָנוּ אֱלֹהֵי יַעֲקֹב סֶלָה. יהוה צְבָאוֹת, אַשְׁרֵי אָדָם בֹּטֵחַ בָּךְ. יהוה
הוֹשִׁיעָה, הַמֶּלֶךְ יַעֲנֵנוּ בְיוֹם קָרְאֵנוּ.

In some congregations the following two verses are recited responsively — the *chazzan* reciting סְלַח,
and the congregation responding וַיֹּאמֶר. In other congregations these verses are recited silently.

סְלַח נָא לַעֲוֹן הָעָם הַזֶּה כְּגֹדֶל חַסְדֶּךָ, וְכַאֲשֶׁר נָשָׂאתָה לָעָם
הַזֶּה מִמִּצְרַיִם וְעַד הֵנָּה, וְשָׁם נֶאֱמַר:
וַיֹּאמֶר יהוה סָלַחְתִּי כִּדְבָרֶךָ.

All:

הַטֵּה אֱלֹהַי אָזְנְךָ וּשְׁמָע, פְּקַח עֵינֶיךָ וּרְאֵה שֹׁמְמֹתֵינוּ, וְהָעִיר
אֲשֶׁר נִקְרָא שִׁמְךָ עָלֶיהָ, כִּי לֹא עַל צִדְקוֹתֵינוּ אֲנַחְנוּ
מַפִּילִים תַּחֲנוּנֵינוּ לְפָנֶיךָ, כִּי עַל רַחֲמֶיךָ הָרַבִּים. אֲדֹנָי שְׁמָעָה,
אֲדֹנָי סְלָחָה, אֲדֹנָי הַקְשִׁיבָה, וַעֲשֵׂה אַל תְּאַחַר, לְמַעַנְךָ אֱלֹהַי, כִּי
שִׁמְךָ נִקְרָא עַל עִירְךָ וְעַל עַמֶּךָ.

סליחה פ

אֱלֹהֵינוּ וֵאלֹהֵי אֲבוֹתֵינוּ:

אַרְבָּעָה אֲבוֹת נְזִיקִין הֵן,[1]*
הַזְּאֵב וְהָאֲרִי וְהַדֹּב וְגוּרֵיהֶן,
נָמֵר[2] שׁוֹקֵד עַל עָרֵיהֶם וַחֲזִיר עִמָּהֶם,
תֵּן לָהֶם כְּפָעֳלָם וּכְרֹעַ מַעַלְלֵיהֶם.[3]
נוֹגֵחַ הוּא מֵאֶתְמוֹל שִׁלְשֹׁם[4] אֲשֶׁר בּוֹר כָּרָה,[5]*
יֵאָחֲזוּמוֹ צִיר וְצָרָה כְּמַבְכִּירָה,[6]
בְּקֶרֶב מַחֲנֶךָ הִכְנִיסוּ זָרָה,   וַיַּשְׁלִיכוּ אוֹתִי הַבּוֹרָה.[7]

There are two possible forms which the redemption may take. If we are especially meritorious, God promises to bring it about swiftly
[אֲחִישֶׁנָּה; see *Sanhedrin* 98a based on *Isaiah*
60:22]. In that case, it will burst about us suddenly, like a newly revealed spring which spurts
from the arid desert (*Malbim*).

אַרְבָּעָה אֲבוֹת נְזִיקִין הֵן ✍ — *There are four primary damagers.* In a veiled allusion to the nations
that have subjugated Israel during its four Exiles,
the *paytan* [whose signature in the acrostic — אֲנִי
מֹשֶׁה בְּרַבִּי יוֹסֵף הַכֹּהֵן, *I am Moshe son of R' Yosef
the Kohen* — is all that is known about him] cites
two *mishnayos* from the first chapter of tractate
Bava Kamma. The opening *mishnah* of that tractate lists four primary categories of damagers. But

after citing the introductory phrase of that *mishnah*, the *paytan* skips to the last *mishnah* of the
chapter and lists four of the six wild beasts that
are considered extremely dangerous — wolf, lion,
bear and leopard. To this roster, he adds the pig.

In his vision, Daniel (ch. 7) saw four beasts,
each of which represented one of the exiles to
which Israel had been or would be subjected to
[see commentary to *selichah* 76, s.v., דֹּב . . . הָאֲרִי
. . . וְנָמֵר . . . וָצֶפַע]. The first, a lion, alluded to
Babylon. The second is described as דְּמָה לְדֹב, *like
a dov*, but the word דֹּב can be translated in two
ways. The Hebrew word דּוֹב means *bear*, but in
Aramaic (the language of this chapter of *Daniel*)
דֻּבָּא means *wolf*. Various Midrashim (e.g., *Bereishis Rabbah* 99:2) identify the wolf (in *Jeremiah*

כְּרַחֵם אָב *As a father has mercy on his children, so, HASHEM, may You have mercy on us. Salvation is HASHEM's, upon Your people is Your blessing, Selah. HASHEM, Master of Legions, is with us, a stronghold for us is the God of Jacob, Selah. HASHEM, Master of Legions, praiseworthy is the person who trusts in You. HASHEM, save! May the King answer us on the day we call.*

> In some congregations the following two verses are recited responsively — the *chazzan* reciting, 'Forgive, please . . .,' and the congregation responding, 'And HASHEM said . . .'
> In other congregations these verses are recited silently.

סְלַח נָא *Forgive, please, the iniquity of this people according to the greatness of Your kindness and as You have forgiven this people from Egypt until now, and there it was said:*

And HASHEM said, 'I have forgiven according to your word!'

> All:

הַטֵּה *Incline, my God, Your ear, and listen, open Your eyes and see our desolation and that of the city upon which YourName is proclaimed; for not because of our righteousness do we cast down our supplications before You, rather because of Your abundant compassion. O my Lord, heed; O my Lord, forgive; O my Lord, be attentive and act, do not delay; for Your sake, my God, for Your Name is proclaimed upon Your city and upon Your people.*

SELICHAH 80

Our God and the God of our forefathers:

א *There are four primary damagers;*[1]
   the [Median] wolf, the [Babylonian] lion, the [Persian] bear,
      and their young;
   the [Greek] leopard[2] swift over their cities,
      and the [Roman] boar after them —
   give them according to their deeds and the evil of their endeavors![3]
ב *He who gores [us] from yesterday and before,[4]*
   who dug a pit [for us] —[5]
let pangs and pain seize him, like a woman's in her first birth.[6]
For he brought a false god into the midst of Your camp,
   and threw me into the pit.[7]

---

(1) *Mishnah, Bava Kamma* 1:1. (2) 1:4. (3) *Psalms* 28:4. (4) Cf. *Exodus* 21:29. (5) Cf. 21:33. (6) Cf. *Isaiah* 21:3; *Jeremiah* 4:31. (7) Cf. *Genesis* 37:24.

5:6) with Media, while the Talmud (*Megillah* 11a) compared the Persians to bears. In wishing to retain the wording of the Mishnah, the *paytan* cites both wolf and bear, thus counting Media and Persia separately. Nevertheless, his count remains at four because these two empires represent only one exile. The third, a leopard, represented Greece. The fourth beast not identified by species referred to the fourth *galus*, that of the Roman Empire (in all its metamorphoses) from which we still seek redemption. However, the Talmud (*Pesachim* 118b, based on *Psalms* 80:14) identifies this beast as a type of wild boar.

נוֹגֵחַ . . . בּוֹר כָּרָה — *He who gores . . . who dug a pit.* The four primary damagers mentioned in the Mishnah are: הַשּׁוֹר הַבּוֹר הַמַּבְעֶה וְהַהֶבְעֵר, *the bull, the pit, the maveh, and the fire.* Specifically, according to the Talmudic sage Shmuel, 'bull' includes damages perpetrated by the animal while walking (this class is also called רֶגֶל, *foot*); and 'maveh' includes damages that occur while the animal is eating (also called שֵׁן, *tooth*). According to the Talmudic sage Rav, 'bull' comprises three sub-divisions: קֶרֶן, *horn* (i.e., goring), שֵׁן, *tooth*, and רֶגֶל, *foot*, while 'maveh' is אָדָם, *man*.
   In continuing the metaphor of the four dam-

יָבֹא דְבָרְךָ וְלֹא יְאַחֵר,[1]   תַּכְרִית נִין וּשְׁאָר וְטוּבוֹ סוֹחֵר,[2]

וּטְבֹחַ טֶבַח וְהָכֵן[3] תְּהִי עוֹקֵר וְנוֹחֵר,

כִּי שָׁלַח אֶת הַבְּעֵרָה וּבָעֵר בִּשְׂדֵה אַחֵר.[4]

מַה כֹּחִי לִסָּבֵל עַל רוֹדִים,   לְהַכְחִידִי מִגּוֹי יַחַד מִתְוַעֲדִים,

שׁוֹדֵד בְּשָׁמְעִי בְּאָזְנַי קוֹל פְּחָדִים,

וְכָל הָעָם רוֹאִים אֶת הַקּוֹלוֹת וְאֶת הַלַּפִּידִים.[6]

שֶׁבְּעָתַיִם הָשֵׁב, חֲלָלִים הַפִּילֵם,

בָּאֶבֶן יִרְגְּמוּ אוֹתָם,[7] וְחֶרֶב יהוה תֹּאכְלֵם,

בָּנֶיךָ מֵעֹמֶק בּוֹר הַעֲלֵם,   וּבַעַל הַבּוֹר יְשַׁלֵּם.[8]

הַעַל אֵלֶּה לֹא תִפְקֹד[9] בְּאַף וְעֶבְרָה,

לְהָשִׁיב תַּשְׁלוּם לְנַחֲלָה לְךָ שְׁפֵרָה,[10]

הָשֵׁב תָּשִׁיב לִבְעָלֶיהָ הָעֲטָרָה,

שַׁלֵּם יְשַׁלֵּם הַמַּבְעִיר אֶת הַבְּעֵרָה.[11]

בַּת עַמִּי צוּר יִגְאָלֶנָּה בְּכֶסֶף,

וְיִטְעָנֶנָּה בְּהַר קָדְשׁוֹ יַחַד בְּהִתְאַסֵּף,

לִקְנוֹת שֵׁנִית יָדוֹ יוֹסֵף,[12] וְיָצְאָה חִנָּם אֵין כָּסֶף.[13]

רְאֵה תִרְאֶה בָּעֳנִי עַם נִבְזֶה,[14] יָהּ, הַצִּילֵם מִצַּר בּוֹזֶה,

זְכֹר רַחֲמֶיךָ וַחֲסָדֶיךָ נֶחֱזֶה,   וְהָסֵר מֵעָלַי רַק אֶת הַמָּוֶת הַזֶּה.[15]

בְּכָל פֶּה אֲכָלוּם כַּזְּאֵבִים,   וְעִתֵּי יְשׁוּעוֹת אָרְכוּ, וְהִנָּם כּוֹאֲבִים,

הֲלֹא הֵם עַל סֵפֶר כְּתוּבִים,[16] וְהֵמָּה בִקְשׁוּ חִשְּׁבוֹנוֹת רַבִּים.[17]

יֵבוֹשׁוּ זֵדִים כִּי אָכְלוּ מְנַת גּוֹרָלֶךָ,

הַחוֹסִים בְּצִלְּךָ, נַחֲלָתְךָ וְחֶבְלֶךָ,

רַחוּם וְחַנּוּן עֵינֵינוּ תְלוּיוֹת אֵלֶיךָ,

וְעַתָּה אֲדֹנָי הַמֶּלֶךְ עֵינֵי כָל יִשְׂרָאֵל עָלֶיךָ.[18]

יְהִי חַסְדְּךָ לְרַחֵם עַם בָּחַרְתָּ,   וְקַיֵּם עָלֵימוֹ הַדָּבָר אֲשֶׁר הִבְטַחְתָּ,

זְרוּיֶיךָ קַבֵּץ מִקְצֵה אֶרֶץ אָמַרְתָּ,[19]

וְאַל תַּפֵּל דָּבָר מִכֹּל אֲשֶׁר דִּבַּרְתָּ.[20]

וְאַתָּה תָקוּם תְּרַחֵם כִּי בָא עֵת לְחֶנְנָהּ,[21]

---

(1) Cf. *Habakkuk* 2:3. (2) Cf. *Proverbs* 11:27. (3) *Genesis* 43:16. (4) Cf. *Exodus* 22:4.
(5) Cf. *Psalms* 83:5. (6) *Exodus* 20:15. (7) *Leviticus* 20:27. (8) Cf. *Exodus* 21:34.
(9) Cf. *Jeremiah* 5:9. (10) Cf. *Psalms* 16:6. (11) *Exodus* 22:5. (12) Cf. *Isaiah* 11:11.
(13) *Exodus* 21:11. (14) Cf. 3:7. (15) Cf. 10:17. (16) Cf. *Esther* 10:2. (17) *Ecclesiastes* 7:29.
(18) *I Kings* 1:20. (19) See *Deuteronomy* 30:4. (20) *Esther* 6:10. (21) Cf. *Psalms* 102:14.

ᵍ Let Your word come true without delay.[1]
Cut down [his] scion and relative who seeks only his own good.[2]
Prepare a slaughter for him,[3] that he be torn and stabbed,
for he has sent out the beast, that devoured in another's field.[4]

מ What strength have I to bear the tyrants' yoke?
Together they plot my destruction as a nation.[5]
When I hear the marauder, it is a fearsome sound in my ears,
and all the people can see the sounds and the flares.[6]

שׁ Pay them back sevenfold! Strike them down corpses!
Let them be bombarded with stones,[7]
   and let HASHEM's sword devour them.
Raise Your children from the depths of the pit,
and let the pit's owner pay.[8]

ה Will You not take account of such things,[9] with wrath and fury,
and make reparation to Your heritage[-people, Israel],
   so beautiful for You?[10]
Surely You will return the tiara to its owner [the Davidic dynasty];
and the one who lit the fire shall certainly pay.[11]

ב The daughter of my people [Israel],
   may the Rock redeem her with desire,
and may He plant her upon the holy mountain, all gathered together.
Let His hand once again acquire [her as His own],[12]
and let her go free for naught, without price.[13]

ר Look well at the affliction of the despised nation;[14]
O God, save them from the degrading enemy.
Remember Your mercy! Let us see Your kindness,
and remove this death from me.[15]

ב With full mouth they gobble them up like wolves,
and the times of salvation are so long, while they are yet in pain!
Are they not written in the book[16] [of Daniel]?
But men have demanded many calculations.[17]

ᵍ Let the wanton be put to shame,
   for they have devoured [Israel,] Your destined lot,
who shelter in Your shadow, Your heritage-people, Your portion,
O Merciful One, O Gracious One, our eyes depend upon You;
and now, my Lord the King, the eyes of all Israel are upon You.[18]

ᵍ Let Your kindness serve to be compassionate
   to the people You have chosen,
and fulfill for them what You have promised.
Gather Your dispersed from the end of the earth, [as] You have said,[19]
and do not leave out anything of all that You have spoken![20]

ו And You will arise and have mercy,
   for the time to favor her will have come;[21]

---

agers, the *paytan* mentions these various classifications in this and the subsequent stanzas. He also
cites the Scriptural verses in Exodus from which
these categories are derived.

תְּרַחֵם צִיּוֹן וַעֲדַת מִי מָנָה,‎ הָשֵׁב שְׁבוּתָם אֱלֹהֵי קֶדֶם מְעוֹנָה,¹
אֶל מְקוֹם הַמִּזְבֵּחַ אֲשֶׁר עָשָׂה שָׁם בָּרִאשׁוֹנָה.²

סְחַרְחַר לִבִּי כִּי רַב זַעֲמֶךָ,‎ שׁוּב מֵחֲרוֹנְךָ וְקַיֵּם נְאֻמֶךָ,
רִיבָה רִיבִי מֵעַם חֶרְמֶךָ,³ הִנֵּה עֲבָדֶיךָ מֻכִּים וְחַטַּאת עַמֶּךָ.⁴

פָּנֶיךָ הָאֵר, בְּעֵינֶיךָ חֵן נִמְצָא, וְהוֹצִיאֵנוּ מִמַּסְגֵּר וְאַחֲרֶיךָ נָרוּצָה,
כְּקֶדֶם כְּאָז עַמְּךָ יֵצֵא, וַיָּנָס וַיֵּצֵא הַחוּצָה.⁵

הַט אָזְנְךָ כִּי לְךָ הוֹחַלְתִּי, חָנֵּנִי כְּאִמְרָתְךָ וְלִישׁוּעָתְךָ קִוִּיתִי,
בְּכָל לֵב פָּנֶיךָ חִלִּיתִי,⁶ נַפְשִׁי בִּשְׁאֵלָתִי וְעַמִּי בְּבַקָּשָׁתִי.⁷

כָּלוּ עֵינַי וְאֵין בְּפִי מִלָּה, רְאֵה וְהַבִּיטָה כִּי הָיִיתִי זוֹלֵלָה,⁸
הָיִיתִי בַיּוֹם בְּבִכְיִי וּבִילָלָה, אֲכָלַנִי חֹרֶב וְקֶרַח בַּלָּיְלָה.⁹

הָיִיתִי שְׂחוֹק וְכָל הַיּוֹם נִכְלַמְנוּ,
בְּרִית אֶזְרָח¹⁰ זְכֹר קוּמָה וְהוֹשִׁיעֵנוּ,
הֶן הַבֶּט נָא עַמְּךָ כֻלָּנוּ,¹¹ בְּנֵי אִישׁ אֶחָד נָחְנוּ.¹²

❖ נִדְבוֹת פִּינוּ רְצֵה¹³ וְהַסְכֵּת תְּפִלָּה,
שְׂפָתֵינוּ לְשַׁלֵּם מִנְחָה וְעוֹלָה,¹⁴
נַהֵל עַמְּךָ אֶל הַמְּנוּחָה וְאֶל הַנַּחֲלָה,¹⁵
מָקוֹם אֲשֶׁר הָיָה שָׁם אָהֳלֹה בַּתְּחִלָּה.¹⁶

All, while standing:

אֵל מֶלֶךְ יוֹשֵׁב עַל כִּסֵּא רַחֲמִים מִתְנַהֵג בַּחֲסִידוּת, מוֹחֵל
עֲוֹנוֹת עַמּוֹ, מַעֲבִיר רִאשׁוֹן רִאשׁוֹן, מַרְבֶּה מְחִילָה
לְחַטָּאִים וּסְלִיחָה לְפוֹשְׁעִים, עֹשֶׂה צְדָקוֹת עִם כָּל בָּשָׂר וָרוּחַ, לֹא
כְרָעָתָם תִּגְמוֹל. ❖ אֵל הוֹרֵיתָ לָּנוּ לוֹמַר שְׁלֹשׁ עֶשְׂרֵה, וּזְכוֹר לָנוּ
הַיּוֹם בְּרִית שְׁלֹשׁ עֶשְׂרֵה, כְּמוֹ שֶׁהוֹדַעְתָּ לֶעָנָיו מִקֶּדֶם, כְּמוֹ
שֶׁכָּתוּב, וַיֵּרֶד יְהוָה בֶּעָנָן וַיִּתְיַצֵּב עִמּוֹ שָׁם, וַיִּקְרָא בְשֵׁם יְהוָה.

Congregation, then *chazzan:*

וַיַּעֲבֹר יְהוָה עַל פָּנָיו וַיִּקְרָא:

Congregation and *chazzan* (the words in bold type are recited aloud and in unison):

יְהוָה, יְהוָה, אֵל, **רַחוּם, וְחַנּוּן, אֶרֶךְ אַפַּיִם, וְרַב חֶסֶד, וֶאֱמֶת,
נֹצֵר חֶסֶד לָאֲלָפִים, נֹשֵׂא עָוֹן, וָפֶשַׁע, וְחַטָּאָה,
וְנַקֵּה.** וְסָלַחְתָּ לַעֲוֹנֵנוּ וּלְחַטָּאתֵנוּ וּנְחַלְתָּנוּ. סְלַח לָנוּ אָבִינוּ כִּי

(1) Cf. *Deuteronomy* 33:27. (2) *Genesis* 13:4. (3) Cf. *Isaiah* 34:5. (4) Cf. *Exodus* 5:16.
(5) *Genesis* 39:12. (6) Cf. *Psalms* 119:58. (7) *Esther* 7:3. (8) Cf. *Lamentations* 1:11. (9) *Genesis* 31:40.
(10) See commentary to *selichah* 83, s.v., אִיתָן לִמֵּד דָּעַת. (11) *Isaiah* 64:8. (12) *Genesis* 42:11.
(13) Cf. *Psalms* 119:108. (14) Cf. *Hosea* 14:3. (15) Cf. *Deuteronomy* 12:9. (16) Cf. *Genesis* 13:3.

have mercy on Zion and the uncountable congregation of [Israel].
Bring back their captivity,
    God Who was in Heaven from the earliest time,[1]
to the site of the Altar that was made there at the beginning.[2]

ס *My heart spins round, for great is Your wrath;*
turn back from Your anger and fulfill Your word.
Take up my cause against the people with whom You do battle —[3]
behold, Your servants are beaten, because Your people has sinned.[4]

פ *Shine Your countenance [on us]; let us find favor in Your eyes,*
and take us out of prison, that we may run after You.
Your people shall go forth as of old, as then [at the Exodus],
when he fled, and went forth, out[5] [of Egypt's land].

ה *Bend Your ear, for to You I hope;*
be gracious to me as You said, for I hope for Your salvation.
With full heart I beseech You:[6]
'[Spare] my soul at my request, and my people at my petition.'[7]

כ *My eyes are worn out, and I have no word in my mouth;*
see, observe that I have been degraded![8]
All day I have been sobbing and wailing;
the dry sun ate me, and the ice at night.[9]

ה *I have become a laughing stock, we are humiliated all day long.*
Remember Abraham's covenant;[10] arise and save us!
Please look now, we are all Your people,[11]
the sons of one man are we.[12]

נ Chazzan — *Be pleased with our mouth's appeal;[13] listen to our prayer,*
let our lips stand in place of minchah and olah-offering.[14]
Lead Your people to the place of rest and the heritage,[15]
the place where His Tabernacle was at the beginning.[16]

All, while standing:

אֵל מֶלֶךְ *O God, King Who sits on the throne of mercy; Who acts with*
    kindness, pardons the iniquities of His people, removes [sins]
one by one, increasingly grants pardon to careless sinners and forgiveness
to rebels, Who deals righteously with every living being — You do not repay
them in accord with their evil. Chazzan — *O God, You taught us to recite the*
Thirteen [Attributes of Mercy], so remember for us today the covenant of
these Thirteen, as You made known to the humble one in ancient times, as
it is written: And HASHEM descended in a cloud and stood with him there,
and He called out with the Name HASHEM.

Congregation, then chazzan:

And HASHEM passed before him [Moses] and proclaimed:

Congregation and chazzan (the words in bold type are recited aloud and in unison):

ה' ה' **HASHEM, HASHEM, God, Compassionate and Gracious, Slow to**
    anger, and Abundant in Kindness and Truth, Preserver of
kindness for thousands [of generations], Forgiver of iniquity, willful
sin, and error, and Who cleanses. *May You forgive our iniquities*
and our errors and make us Your heritage. Forgive us, our Father, for

חָטָאנוּ, מְחַל לָנוּ מַלְכֵּנוּ כִּי פָשָׁעְנוּ. כִּי אַתָּה אֲדֹנָי טוֹב וְסַלָּח, וְרַב
חֶסֶד לְכָל קֹרְאֶיךָ.

פסוקי הקדמה לסליחה פא

תָּבוֹא לְפָנֶיךָ תְּפִלָּתֵנוּ,[1] וְאַל תִּתְעַלַּם מִתְּחִנָּתֵנוּ.[2] תָּבוֹא לְפָנֶיךָ
אֶנְקַת אָסִיר, כְּגֹדֶל זְרוֹעֲךָ הוֹתֵר בְּנֵי תְמוּתָה.[3] אַתָּה
תָקוּם תְּרַחֵם צִיּוֹן, כִּי עֵת לְחֶנְנָהּ כִּי בָא מוֹעֵד.[4]

כְּרַחֵם אָב עַל בָּנִים, כֵּן תְּרַחֵם יהוה עָלֵינוּ. לַיהוה הַיְשׁוּעָה,
עַל עַמְּךָ בִרְכָתֶךָ סֶּלָה. יהוה צְבָאוֹת עִמָּנוּ, מִשְׂגָּב
לָנוּ אֱלֹהֵי יַעֲקֹב סֶלָה. יהוה צְבָאוֹת, אַשְׁרֵי אָדָם בֹּטֵחַ בָּךְ. יהוה
הוֹשִׁיעָה, הַמֶּלֶךְ יַעֲנֵנוּ בְיוֹם קָרְאֵנוּ.

In some congregations the following two verses are recited responsively — the *chazzan* reciting סְלַח,
and the congregation responding וַיֹּאמֶר. In other congregations these verses are recited silently.

סְלַח נָא לַעֲוֹן הָעָם הַזֶּה כְּגֹדֶל חַסְדֶּךָ, וְכַאֲשֶׁר נָשָׂאתָה לָעָם
הַזֶּה מִמִּצְרַיִם וְעַד הֵנָּה, וְשָׁם נֶאֱמַר:
וַיֹּאמֶר יהוה סָלַחְתִּי כִּדְבָרֶךָ.

All:

הַטֵּה אֱלֹהַי אָזְנְךָ וּשֲׁמָע, פְּקַח עֵינֶיךָ וּרְאֵה שֹׁמְמֹתֵינוּ, וְהָעִיר
אֲשֶׁר נִקְרָא שִׁמְךָ עָלֶיהָ, כִּי לֹא עַל צִדְקוֹתֵינוּ אֲנַחְנוּ
מַפִּילִים תַּחֲנוּנֵינוּ לְפָנֶיךָ, כִּי עַל רַחֲמֶיךָ הָרַבִּים. אֲדֹנָי שְׁמָעָה,
אֲדֹנָי סְלָחָה, אֲדֹנָי הַקְשִׁיבָה, וַעֲשֵׂה אַל תְּאַחַר, לְמַעַנְךָ אֱלֹהַי, כִּי
שִׁמְךָ נִקְרָא עַל עִירְךָ וְעַל עַמֶּךָ.

סליחה פא (שלישיה)

אֱלֹהֵינוּ וֵאלֹהֵי אֲבוֹתֵינוּ:

אַתָּה חֶלְקִי* וְצוּר לְבָבִי,[5]   אִוִּיתִיךָ בַּלַּיְלָה[6] עַל מִשְׁכָּבִי,[7]
אֵלֶיךָ יהוה אֶקְרָא בַּעֲטֹף לִבִּי.[8]

בָּגַדְנוּ וְהִרְבִּינוּ חֵמוֹת וּכְעָסִים,   לְמִרְמָס אָנוּ מְעָשִׂים,
כִּי אֵין בָּנוּ מַעֲשִׂים.

גָּבְרוּ מְאֹד מְצוּקוֹתֵינוּ,   בְּרוֹאֶה שַׁגִּינוּ פְּלִילוֹת פּוּקוֹתֵינוּ,[9]
וּכְבֶגֶד עֵדִים כָּל צִדְקוֹתֵינוּ.[10]

⊰§ **אַתָּה חֶלְקִי** — *You are my portion.* Comprising
twenty-four triplets, this *selichah* follows an alphabetical acrostic. The last two stanzas bear the

author's signature — אֵלִיָּה בַּר שְׁמַעְיָה חֲזַק וֶאֱמָץ,
*Eliyah bar Shemayah, may he be strong and per-
severe* [see prefatory comment to *selichah* 6].

we have erred; pardon us, our King, for we have willfully sinned; for You, my Lord, are good and forgiving and abundantly kind to all who call upon You.

PREFATORY VERSES TO SELICHAH 81

תָּבוֹא Let our prayer come before You;[1] do not disregard our supplication.[2] Let the prisoner's groan come before You; as befits the greatness of Your power; spare those condemned to die.[3] You will arise and show Zion mercy, for [there will come] the time to favor her, for the appointed time will have come.[4]

כְּרַחֵם אָב As a father has mercy on his children, so, HASHEM, may You have mercy on us. Salvation is HASHEM's, upon Your people is Your blessing, Selah. HASHEM, Master of Legions, is with us, a stronghold for us is the God of Jacob, Selah. HASHEM, Master of Legions, praiseworthy is the person who trusts in You. HASHEM, save! May the King answer us on the day we call.

In some congregations the following two verses are recited responsively — the chazzan reciting, 'Forgive, please . . .,' and the congregation responding, 'And HASHEM said . . .'
In other congregations these verses are recited silently.

סְלַח נָא Forgive, please, the iniquity of this people according to the greatness of Your kindness and as You have forgiven this people from Egypt until now, and there it was said:

And HASHEM said, 'I have forgiven according to your word!'

All:

הַטֵּה Incline, my God, Your ear, and listen, open Your eyes and see our desolation and that of the city upon which Your Name is proclaimed; for not because of our righteousness do we cast down our supplications before You, rather because of Your abundant compassion. O my Lord, heed; O my Lord, forgive; O my Lord, be attentive and act, do not delay; for Your sake, my God, for Your Name is proclaimed upon Your city and upon Your people.

SELICHAH 81

Our God and the God of our forefathers:

א You are my portion,* the Rock of my heart;[5]
  I long for You in the night[6] on my bed.[7]
  To You, HASHEM, I call when my heart grows faint.[8]

ב We have betrayed [You], we have built up furies and angers;
  now we have become for trampling,
  for we have no [worthy] deeds.

ג Our hardships have become very overwhelming,
  [for] we scorned the prophets and made justice a lie,[9]
  and all our merits are like a dirty rag.[10]

---

(1) Cf. *Psalms* 88:3. (2) Cf. 55:2. (3) 79:11. (4) 102:14. (5) Cf. 73:26. (6) *Isaiah* 26:9.
(7) Cf. *Song of Songs* 3:1. (8) Cf. *Psalms* 61:3; to conform to the Scriptural verse, some editions of *Selichos* omit the Divine Name from this stich. (9) Cf. *Isaiah* 28:7, see *Rashi* there. (10) 64:5.

דַּעַת חָסַרְנוּ פְּתָאִים מֵעָרְמָה,[1]   תְּהִלָּה תָּשִׂים בְּמַלְאֲכֵי רוּמָה,[2]
אַף כִּי אֱנוֹשׁ רִמָּה.[3]

הֵן אִיִּם תִּטֹּל כַּדָּק,[4]   וְאִם עַוְלָתָה תְּחַפֵּשׂ וְתִבְדָּק,
מַה נְּדַבֵּר וּמַה נִּצְטַדָּק.[5]

וָאֲבַקֵּשׁ גּוֹדֵר גָּדֵר וְעוֹמֵד בַּפֶּרֶץ,[6]   וְיָשָׁר אַיִן פָּנִים לְהָרֶץ,
אָבַד חָסִיד מִן הָאָרֶץ.[7]

זְמַן קִצִּי סָתוּם מִלֵּדַע,   עֲוֺנוֹתַי הִטּוּ קַרְנַי לְהַגְדֵּעַ,
כִּי פְשָׁעַי אֲנִי אֵדָע.[8]

חָמָס אֶזְעַק וְאֵין מוֹשִׁיעַ,[9]   לָמָּה צַדִּיק מַכְתִּיר מַרְשִׁיעַ,[10]
וְלֹא קָצְרָה יָדְךָ מֵהוֹשִׁיעַ.[11]

טְלָאֶיךָ דוֹפְקִים כַּיָּם הוֹמִים,   אֲנוּסִים חֲמוּסִים בְּיַד אֵמִים,
לָמָּה לָנֶצַח תִּשְׁכָּחֵנוּ, תַּעַזְבֵנוּ לְאֹרֶךְ יָמִים.[12]

יַעֲקֹב לִמְשִׁסָּה וְיִשְׂרָאֵל לְבוֹזְזִים,[13]
כְּבוֹדָהּ שִׁבְעַת חֻפּוֹת חֲזִיזִים,*   כְּרָחֵל נֶאֱלָמָה לִפְנֵי גוֹזְזִים.[14]

בֵּילַי[15] וְנָבָל כְּמֶלֶךְ בִּמְסִבּוֹ,   נָדִיב וְשׁוֹעַ[15] נִטְרָד בְּחוֹבוֹ,
כִּכְלִי אֵין חֵפֶץ בּוֹ.[16]

לֹא לְעוֹלָם תִּטֹּר[17] לְהַחֲרִיבֵנִי,
שְׂמֹאלָךְ דְּחִיתַנִי יְמִינָךְ תְּקָרְבֵנִי,*   אֲדֹנָי עָשְׁקָה לִּי עָרְבֵנִי.[18]

מֵאָז תָּמִיד לָנוּ הַדִּבָּה,   הַקֻּוֵּיתָ* שָׁבִים בְּרוּחַ נְדִיבָה,
אֶרְפָּא מְשׁוּבָתָם אֹהֲבֵם נְדָבָה.[19]

נוֹבְעוֹת (עֵינַי) כְּנַחַל אֲגָלַי,   הוֹלֵל שׁוֹקֵט וְשָׁבְתוּ גִילַי,
וַאֲנִי כִּמְעַט נָטָיוּ רַגְלָי.[20]

שֶׂה אֹבֵד בַּקֵּשׁ עִם נוֹשֵׁעַ,   אָוֶן מָצָא מִבֶּטֶן פֶּשַׁע.*
צַדִּיק מָט לִפְנֵי רָשָׁע.[21]

שִׁבְעַת חֻפּוֹת חֲזִיזִים — **Seven canopies of clouds.**
During its forty-year sojourn in the Wilderness,
the nation was accompanied by the protective
עַנְנֵי הַכָּבוֹד, *Clouds of Glory.* According to one
view in the Midrash (*Bamidbar Rabbah* 1:2), there
were seven clouds. Not just ordinary clouds, the
four situated to the east, west, north and south
protected Israel from any arrows or missiles that
may be aimed at them; a fifth cloud was overhead
to protect them from the heat of the desert sun; a
sixth cloud formed a mat beneath their feet, pro-
tecting them from serpents and scorpions and
leveling the ground to ease their travel; and a seventh, the עַמּוּד הֶעָנָן, *column of cloud,* stayed some
distance ahead of the encampment, leading them
through the Wilderness.

שְׂמֹאלָךְ דְּחִיתַנִי יְמִינָךְ תְּקָרְבֵנִי — *Your left hand
pushed me away, may Your right hand bring me
close.* The Talmud teaches a lesson in pedagogy:
Always push away [a wayward student] with the
left hand, yet draw him close with the right (*Sanhedrin* 107b). *Maharsha* explains that מִדַּת הַדִּין,
the Attribute of Strict Justice, is represented by
the left hand; מִדַּת הָרַחֲמִים, *the Attribute of
Mercy,* by the right. Thus, even when Justice requires a master to push away his disciple, Mercy
demands that he draw him close. According to
Iyun Yaakov (to *Sotah* 47a), it is only with the
weaker left hand that one may punish, but with
the stronger right hand one should reward.

In either case, the *paytan* pleads that we have
already been pushed away; it is now time for God

ד We lacked knowledge, fools without cunning,[1]
You regard even the angels on high as foolish,[2]
certainly man, who is but a worm.[3]

ה Behold, You will cast away the islands like dust;[4]
and if You should examine and seek out sin,
what can we say? How can we be justified?[5]

ו I have sought a righteous man to mend fences
and stand [in prayer] in the breach,[6]
but there is no upright man to restore Your good will;
the pious man is gone from the earth.[7]

ז The time of my [salvation's] end is sealed beyond knowing;
my sins have pulled down my pride, to be lopped off,
for I recognize my rebellious sins.[8]

ח I shout, 'Violence!' but there is no savior.[9]
Why is the righteous man encircled by the wicked?[10]
Yet Your hand is not too short to save [me].[11]

ט Your sheep are knocking, tumultuous as the sea,
plundered and robbed by the nations' hand.
Why have You forgotten us eternally, abandoned us for so long?[12]

י Jacob['s seed are given] to oppression; Israel to the looters.[13]
Once dignified by seven canopies of cloud;*
she has become silent as a sheep before the shearers.[14]

כ The scheming, vile man[15] is like a king on his couch,
while the generous and lordly[15] is exiled for his guilt,
like a vessel in which there is no interest.[16]

ל You will not hold resentment forever,[17] to destroy me;
Your left hand pushed me away,
may Your right hand bring me close.*
O my Lord, kidnap me [from the oppressors] and grant me surety.[18]

מ Always, from the start, the blame has been on us,
yet You have encouraged* penitents with a generous spirit:
[by saying:] 'I will heal their rebelliousness; I will love them freely.'[19]

נ (My eyes) flow with tears like a stream,
for the scoffer is serene, while my joys are ended;
and as for me — my feet almost foundered.[20]

ס Seek [Your] lost sheep, the people saved [by You],
that has found wrongdoing, sinfulness from birth.*
The righteous man is abased before the wicked.[21]

---

(1) Cf. *Proverbs* 1:4. (2) Cf. *Job* 4:18. (3) 25:6. (4) Cf. *Isaiah* 40:15. (5) *Genesis* 44:16.
(6) Cf. *Ezekiel* 22:30. (7) *Micah* 7:2. (8) *Psalms* 51:5. (9) Cf. *Habakkuk* 1:2. (10) Cf. 1:4.
(11) Cf. *Isaiah* 59:1. (12) *Lamentations* 5:20; some editions of *Selichos* read אַל תִּשְׁכָּחֵנוּ לָנֶצַח,
do not forget us eternally. (13) Cf. *Isaiah* 42:24. (14) Cf. 53:7. (15) Cf. 32:5. (16) *Hosea* 8:8.
(17) Cf. *Jeremiah* 3:12. (18) *Isaiah* 38:14; some editions of *Selichos* read this entire stanza in the plural,
using the suffix נו, *us*, in place of יִ, *me*. (19) *Hosea* 14:5. (20) *Psalms* 73:2. (21) *Proverbs* 25:6.

---

to draw us to Him.

הַקְוִית — *You have encouraged*. The translation
follows *Pardes* and *Matteh Levi* who derive the
word from תִּקְוָה, *hope*, i.e., You have given hope,

You have encouraged. According to *Masbir*, the
word is cognate to מִקְוֶה, *a gathering of water*, and
means *You have gathered in*.

מִבֶּטֶן פֶּשַׁע — *Sinfulness from birth* [lit., *from the*

עֵדוּת בְּיַעֲקֹב בִּתְעוּדָה נֶחְתָּם,   בְּאֶרֶץ אוֹיֵב הִבְטַחְתָּ לְהַחֲיוֹתָם,
וְאַף גַּם זֹאת בִּהְיוֹתָם.[1]

פְּשָׁעִים תַּעֲבִיר וְחוֹבוֹת תִּמְחֹק,   הַרְחִיבָה שְׁאוֹל נַפְשָׁהּ לִדְחֹק,
וּפָעֲרָה פִּיהָ לִבְלִי חֹק.[2]

צָפָה נַחְשׁוֹל קָרֵב לְחַפְּשֵׁנוּ,[3]   דְּלֵנוּ וְהַעֲלֵנוּ מִטִּיט רְפָשֵׁנוּ,
שׁוּבָה יהוה חַלְּצָה נַפְשֵׁנוּ.[4]

קַדְּשֵׁנוּ צוֹם בִּתְפִלָּה לְקַדֵּם,   חֲבֹשׁ וְצָרֵי לְמַכָּתֵנוּ הַקְדֵּם,
זְכֹר עֲדָתְךָ קָנִיתָ קֶּדֶם.[5]

רֹגֶז הַנַּח, כַּעַס יֶחְשָׁךְ,   אֲסוּרִים בַּעֲבוֹתוֹת, אֱהָב וְהַמְשֵׁךְ,*[6]
מִבֵּית כֶּלֶא יוֹשְׁבֵי חֹשֶׁךְ.[7]

שְׁלוּחַ קְרָא לִשְׁבוּרָה וְלִשְׁמוּטָה,   בָּרִיחַ גְּדַע שֶׁבֶר מוֹטָה,
רְפָּה שְׁבָרֶיהָ כִּי מָטָה.[8]

תְּשׁוּבָה הֲשֵׁבְתִּי לְתַנִּין וְזוֹחֵל,[9]   תִּקְנָתִי הוּא סוֹלֵחַ וּמוֹחֵל,
הֵן (אִם) יִקְטְלֵנִי לוֹ אֲיַחֵל.[10]

אֵלֶיךָ הַטֵּה בּוֹרֵא אָזְנֶךָ,

שְׁמַע יָהּ דוֹרְשֶׁיךָ הַקְשִׁיבָה מְחַנְּנֶיךָ,[11]
תִּכּוֹן תְּפִלָּתִי קְטֹרֶת לְפָנֶיךָ.[12]

❖ חַזֵּק כּוֹשֵׁל וְאַמֵּץ רִפְיוֹן,   מִקְדָּשׁ יַסֵּד, יַשֵׁב אַפִּרְיוֹן,
הֵיטִיבָה בִרְצוֹנְךָ אֶת צִיּוֹן.[13]

All, while standing:

אֵל מֶלֶךְ יוֹשֵׁב עַל כִּסֵּא רַחֲמִים מִתְנַהֵג בַּחֲסִידוּת, מוֹחֵל
עֲוֹנוֹת עַמּוֹ, מַעֲבִיר רִאשׁוֹן רִאשׁוֹן, מַרְבֶּה
מְחִילָה לַחֲטָאִים וּסְלִיחָה לַפּוֹשְׁעִים, עֹשֶׂה צְדָקוֹת עִם כָּל
בָּשָׂר וָרוּחַ, לֹא כְרָעָתָם תִּגְמוֹל. ❖ אֵל הוֹרֵיתָ לָנוּ לוֹמַר שְׁלֹשׁ
עֶשְׂרֵה, וּזְכוֹר לָנוּ הַיּוֹם בְּרִית שְׁלֹשׁ עֶשְׂרֵה, כְּמוֹ שֶׁהוֹדַעְתָּ
לֶעָנָיו מִקֶּדֶם, כְּמוֹ שֶׁכָּתוּב, וַיֵּרֶד יהוה בֶּעָנָן וַיִּתְיַצֵּב עִמּוֹ שָׁם,
וַיִּקְרָא בְשֵׁם יהוה.

---

womb, rebelliousness]. The period of Egyptian
enslavement is considered as the womb from
which the nation of Israel emerged. From their
very birth as a nation, the people were rebellious,
as Moses said (*Deuteronomy 9:7*), 'From the day

*you went forth from Egypt, until you have
reached this place, you have been rebellious
against HASHEM*' (based on *Rashi* and *Radak* to
Isaiah 48:8.)

ע *Witness of Jacob's future is set forth in the Torah.*
   In the enemy's land You have promised to nurture them,
   'And this, too, even when they are in their enemies' land.'[1]

פ *Dismiss rebellious deeds, and erase guilt;*
   Gehinnom broadens itself to push [in more souls],
   and has stretched its mouth unrestrictedly.[2]

צ *See the storm [upon us]; come to set us free,*[3]
   pull us out, lift us up out of the mud we have made;
   return, O HASHEM, release our soul![4]

ק *We have sanctified a fast*
      on which we shall come to You with prayer;
   bring forward bandage and balm for our wound;
   remember Your congregation, that You acquired long ago.[5]

ר *Put aside rage, let anger be annulled;*
   those bound in chains, show love and draw forth*[6]
   from the prison-house, those who dwell in darkness.[7]

ש *Declare liberation for those broken and abandoned;*
   cut through the bolt, break the yoke!
   Heal her fragments, for she totters.[8]

ת *I have answered back the serpent, the reptilian,*[9]
   'My hope is in Him Who forgives and pardons;
   though He slay me, I will look hopefully to Him.'[10]
   Lean Your ear to us, O Creator!
   Hear, O God, those who seek You,
      be attentive to those who supplicate before You.[11]
   Let my prayer stand as incense before You.[12]
   Chazzan — *Strengthen the stumbler, give vigor to the weak.*
   Re-found the Sanctuary; restore the Temple;
   do good in Your favor unto Zion.[13]

All, while standing:

אֵל מֶלֶךְ *O God, King Who sits on the throne of mercy; Who acts with
kindness, pardons the iniquities of His people, removes [sins]
one by one, increasingly grants pardon to careless sinners and forgiveness
to rebels, Who deals righteously with every living being — You do not repay
them in accord with their evil.* Chazzan — *O God, You taught us to recite the
Thirteen [Attributes of Mercy], so remember for us today the covenant of
these Thirteen, as You made known to the humble one in ancient times, as
it is written: And HASHEM descended in a cloud and stood with him there,
and He called out with the Name HASHEM.*

---

(1) *Leviticus* 26:44. (2) *Isaiah* 5:14. (3) Some editions read לְחַפְּשֵׂנוּ, *to search for us.* (4) Cf. *Psalms* 6:5.
(5) 74:2. (6) Some editions read, אֲסוּרִים בַּעֲבוֹתוֹת אַהַב הַמְשֵׁךְ, *draw forth with chains of love those who
are bound,* see *Hosea* 11:4; others read, אֲסוּרֵי אַהַב בַּעֲבוֹתוֹת הַמְשֵׁךְ, *draw forth with chains the prisoners
of love.* (7) *Isaiah* 42:7. (8) *Psalms* 60:4. (9) Cf. *Deuteronomy* 32:24, 33. (10) *Job* 13:15; the word אִם,
included in some editions of *Selichos,* does not appear in the Scriptural verse, and does not change
the meaning of the stich. (11) Cf. *Daniel* 9:17-18. (12) *Psalms* 141:2. (13) 51:20.

Congregation, then *chazzan:*

וַיַּעֲבֹר יהוה עַל פָּנָיו וַיִּקְרָא:

Congregation and *chazzan* (the words in bold type are recited aloud and in unison):

יהוה, יהוה, אֵל, רַחוּם, וְחַנּוּן, אֶרֶךְ אַפַּיִם, וְרַב חֶסֶד, וֶאֱמֶת,
נֹצֵר חֶסֶד לָאֲלָפִים, נֹשֵׂא עָוֹן, וָפֶשַׁע, וְחַטָּאָה,
וְנַקֵּה. וְסָלַחְתָּ לַעֲוֹנֵנוּ וּלְחַטָּאתֵנוּ וּנְחַלְתָּנוּ. סְלַח לָנוּ אָבִינוּ כִּי
חָטָאנוּ, מְחַל לָנוּ מַלְכֵּנוּ כִּי פָשָׁעְנוּ. כִּי אַתָּה אֲדֹנָי טוֹב וְסַלָּח, וְרַב
חֶסֶד לְכָל קֹרְאֶיךָ.

פסוקי הקדמה לסליחה פב

רַבַּת שָׂבְעָה לָּהּ נַפְשֵׁנוּ, עִם שׂוֹנֵא שָׁלוֹם.[1] אֲנִי שָׁלוֹם, וְכִי
אֲדַבֵּר, הֵמָּה לַמִּלְחָמָה.[2] יְהִי שָׁלוֹם בְּחֵילֵךְ, שַׁלְוָה
בְּאַרְמְנוֹתָיִךְ.[3] שָׁלוֹם שָׁלוֹם לָרָחוֹק וְלַקָּרוֹב, אָמַר יהוה
וּרְפָאתִיו.[4] יהוה תִּשְׁפֹּת שָׁלוֹם לָנוּ, כִּי גַּם כָּל מַעֲשֵׂינוּ פָּעַלְתָּ
לָּנוּ.[5] יהוה עֹז לְעַמּוֹ יִתֵּן, יהוה יְבָרֵךְ אֶת עַמּוֹ בַשָּׁלוֹם.[6] הַמְשֵׁל
וָפַחַד עִמּוֹ, עֹשֶׂה שָׁלוֹם בִּמְרוֹמָיו.[7] כִּי בְשִׂמְחָה תֵצֵאוּ וּבְשָׁלוֹם
תּוּבָלוּן.[8]

כְּרַחֵם אָב עַל בָּנִים, כֵּן תְּרַחֵם יהוה עָלֵינוּ. לַיהוה הַיְשׁוּעָה,
עַל עַמְּךָ בִרְכָתֶךָ סֶּלָה. יהוה צְבָאוֹת עִמָּנוּ, מִשְׂגָּב
לָנוּ אֱלֹהֵי יַעֲקֹב סֶלָה. יהוה צְבָאוֹת, אַשְׁרֵי אָדָם בֹּטֵחַ בָּךְ. יהוה
הוֹשִׁיעָה, הַמֶּלֶךְ יַעֲנֵנוּ בְיוֹם קָרְאֵנוּ.

In some congregations the following two verses are recited responsively — the *chazzan* reciting סְלַח נָא,
and the congregation responding וַיֹּאמֶר. In other congregations these verses are recited silently.

סְלַח נָא לַעֲוֹן הָעָם הַזֶּה כְּגֹדֶל חַסְדֶּךָ, וְכַאֲשֶׁר נָשָׂאתָה לָעָם
הַזֶּה מִמִּצְרַיִם וְעַד הֵנָּה, וְשָׁם נֶאֱמַר:

וַיֹּאמֶר יהוה סָלַחְתִּי כִּדְבָרֶךָ.

All:

הַטֵּה אֱלֹהַי אָזְנְךָ וּשֲׁמָע, פְּקַח עֵינֶיךָ וּרְאֵה שֹׁמְמֹתֵינוּ, וְהָעִיר
אֲשֶׁר נִקְרָא שִׁמְךָ עָלֶיהָ, כִּי לֹא עַל צִדְקֹתֵינוּ אֲנַחְנוּ
מַפִּילִים תַּחֲנוּנֵינוּ לְפָנֶיךָ, כִּי עַל רַחֲמֶיךָ הָרַבִּים. אֲדֹנָי שְׁמָעָה,
אֲדֹנָי סְלָחָה, אֲדֹנָי הַקְשִׁיבָה, וַעֲשֵׂה אַל תְּאַחַר, לְמַעַנְךָ אֱלֹהַי, כִּי
שִׁמְךָ נִקְרָא עַל עִירְךָ וְעַל עַמֶּךָ.

Congregation, then chazzan:

And HASHEM passed before him [Moses] and proclaimed:

Congregation and chazzan (the words in bold type are recited aloud and in unison):

'ה 'ה HASHEM, HASHEM, God, Compassionate and Gracious, Slow to
anger, and Abundant in Kindness and Truth, Preserver of
kindness for thousands [of generations], Forgiver of iniquity, willful
sin, and error, and Who cleanses. *May You forgive our iniquities and
our errors and make us Your heritage. Forgive us, our Father, for we have
erred; pardon us, our King, for we have willfully sinned; for You, my
Lord, are good and forgiving and abundantly kind to all who call upon
You.*

PREFATORY VERSES TO SELICHAH 82

רַבַּת *Long has our soul dwelt with those who hate peace!*[1] *I am peace;
but when I speak, they are for war.*[2] *May there be peace within
your wall, serenity within your palaces.*[3] *'Peace, peace, for far and near,'
says HASHEM, 'and I shall heal him.'*[4] *HASHEM, may You settle peace upon
us, for indeed all that we do, You have done for us.*[5] *HASHEM will give
might to His people; HASHEM will bless His people with peace.*[6] *Rule and
fear are with Him; He makes peace in His heights.*[7] *For in gladness shall
you go out and in peace shall you arrive.*[8]

כְּרַחֵם אָב *As a father has mercy on his children, so, HASHEM, may
You have mercy on us. Salvation is HASHEM's, upon Your
people is Your blessing, Selah. HASHEM, Master of Legions, is with us, a
stronghold for us is the God of Jacob, Selah. HASHEM, Master of Legions,
praiseworthy is the person who trusts in You. HASHEM, save! May the
King answer us on the day we call.*

In some congregations the following two verses are recited responsively — the chazzan
reciting, 'Forgive, please . . .,' and the congregation responding, 'And HASHEM said . . .'
In other congregations these verses are recited silently.

סְלַח נָא *Forgive, please, the iniquity of this people according to the
greatness of Your kindness and as You have forgiven this
people from Egypt until now, and there it was said:*

And HASHEM said, 'I have forgiven according to your word!'

All:

הַטֵּה *Incline, my God, Your ear, and listen, open Your eyes and see our
desolation and that of the city upon which Your Name is proclaimed; for not because of our righteousness do we cast down our
supplications before You, rather because of Your abundant compassion.
O my Lord, heed; O my Lord, forgive; O my Lord, be attentive and act,
do not delay; for Your sake, my God, for Your Name is proclaimed upon
Your city and upon Your people.*

---

(1) Cf. *Psalms* 120:6. (2) 120:7. (3) 122:7. (4) *Isaiah* 57:19.
(5) 26:12. (6) *Psalms* 29:11. (7) *Job* 25:2. (8) *Isaiah* 55:12.

סליחה פב

אֱלֹהֵינוּ וֵאלֹהֵי אֲבוֹתֵינוּ:

שָׁלוֹם תִּשְׁפֹּת לָנוּ,[1]* אוֹתָנוּ לְחַיִּים לְחוֹקְקָה,
שׁוּעַ נַעֲרֹךְ לְפָנֶיךָ, תְּשׁוּבָה תְּפִלָּה וּצְדָקָה,*
נֶחֱזֶה פָנֶיךָ, בַּיהוה אֱלֹהִים לְהִדָּבְקָה,
וְהָיָה מַעֲשֵׂה הַצְּדָקָה שָׁלוֹם.[2]

שָׁלוֹם* לָרָחוֹק וְלַקָּרוֹב*[3] אֶל עִיר מָצוֹר,*
עִיר קְטַנָּה וּמֶלֶךְ גָּדוֹל סוֹבְבָה לִנְצוֹר,
מִסְכֵּן וְחָכָם יְמַלֵּט עִיר[4] בְּלִי לִבְצֹר,
יֵצֶר סָמוּךְ תִּצֹּר שָׁלוֹם.[5]

שָׁלוֹם רָב לְאוֹהֲבֵי תוֹרָתֶךָ, וְאֵין לָמוֹ מַדְוֶה,[6]
מוֹשִׁיעַ אֶת עַמֶּךָ, מָעוֹז וּמָנוֹס וּמִקְוֶה,
תִּשְׁפֹּט בְּרַחֲמִים עַמֶּךָ, יְשׁוּעוֹת יַעֲקֹב צַוֵּה,[7]
וְיָשַׁב עַמֶּךָ בִּנְוֵה שָׁלוֹם.[8]

שָׁלוֹם, קִוִּינוּ טוֹב,[9] וְהָיָה לָנוּ הַשֶּׁבֶר וְהַשֵּׁאת,[10]
לַיּוֹצֵא וְלַבָּא אֵין לָבֹא וְלָצֵאת,[11]
וְאִם יִשָּׂא לַחֲטֹאתֵינוּ כְּיַד הַמֶּלֶךְ מַשְׂאֵת,[12]
אָז הָיִיתִי בְעֵינָיו כְּמוֹצְאֵת שָׁלוֹם.

שָׁלוֹם צְדָקָה וָחֶסֶד לְהַלְבִּין לָשׁוֹן שֶׁל זְהוֹרִית,*

---

§ שָׁלוֹם תִּשְׁפֹּת לָנוּ — *Peace may You settle upon us.* Each stanza of this *selichah* begins and ends with the word שָׁלוֹם, *peace*. The translation of some of these sentences may seem to have a convoluted syntax; this was done to maintain 'peace'. The initial letters of the second words of the respective stanzas form a reverse *aleph-beis* (תשר״ק). In the last line of each stanza, the next-to-the-last word rhymes with the last words of the first three lines. Some read the name בִּנְיָמִן, *Binyamin*, in the final stanza [see prefatory comment to *selichah* 1].

Besides meaning *peace*, the word שָׁלוֹם is a Divine Name. It is used to describe God as מֶלֶךְ שֶׁהַשָּׁלוֹם שֶׁלּוֹ, *the King to Whom peace belongs*, or as the Source of all Peace. Such usage is indicated in the translation by the word PEACE appearing in capital letters.

תְּשׁוּבָה תְּפִלָּה וּצְדָקָה — *Repentance, prayer and charity.* This phrase is taken from the Rosh Hashanah and Yom Kippur prayers. It describes the formula with which man can cause the severity of his judgment to be mitigated or annulled. The combination of repentance, prayer and charity can influence God to cast aside the harshness of the decree (*Midrash Rabbah Bereishis* 44:15).

In almost all editions of the Rosh Hashanah and Yom Kippur *machzor*, the words וּתְשׁוּבָה וּתְפִלָּה וּצְדָקָה, *repentance, prayer, and charity*, are crowned in smaller type with the words צוֹם קוֹל מָמוֹן, *fast, voice, money*. These superscripts are meant to indicate that sincere repentance includes fasting, prayer is to be recited in a loud voice, and charity means monetary donations.

Interestingly, the *gematrios* (numeric equivalents) of each of the three words קוֹל צוֹם מָמוֹן are the same, 136 [ק=100 ו=6 ל=30; צ=90 ו=6 ם=40; מ=40 מ=40 ו=6 ן=50]. This alludes to the fact that the three are equally important in attaining atonement.

שָׁלוֹם שָׁלוֹם — *Peace, Peace.* Although many editions do not repeat the word שָׁלוֹם in this stanza, it does appear in some editions and seems to belong for two reasons: (a) So reads the Scriptural verse (*Isaiah* 57:19); and (b) according to the תשר״ק arrangement of the initial letters of the second words in the respective stanzas, the letter שׁ should follow the word שָׁלוֹם in this stanza.

לָרָחוֹק וְלַקָּרוֹב — *To the far and to the near.* The Talmud (*Berachos* 34b; *Sanhedrin* 99a) records a

SELICHAH 82

Our God and God of our forefathers:

ת **Peace** may You settle upon us,*[1] to inscribe us for life.
We arrange prayer before You: repentance, prayer, and charity.*
May we see Your countenance, to be able to cling to HASHEM, God,
and the effect of charity will be **peace**.[2]

ש **Peace**, peace,* to the far and to the near,*[3] to the beleaguered city,*
a tiny city, that the great King walks around to guard.
The poor wise man can save the city[4] without need to fortify.
The Good Inclination depends [on You]; guard it for **peace**.[5]

ר **Peace** in abundance for those who love Your Torah,
and they shall know no illness.[6]
Savior of Your people, Fortress, Refuge, and Hope,
judge Your people mercifully and command salvation for Jacob,[7]
and let Your people dwell in the habitation of **peace**.[8]

ק **PEACE**, we have hoped for goodness,[9]
but instead we had ruin and destruction.[10]
Those who would go or come [have no peace and so]
cannot come or go.[11]
But if He should bear with our sins, as His kingly gift,[12]
then I would be in His eyes like one who finds **peace**.

צ **Peace**, charity, and kindness with which to whiten
the strip of red wool —*

---

(1) Cf. *Isaiah* 26:12. (2) 32:17. (3) 57:19. (4) Cf. *Ecclesiastes* 9:14-15.
(5) *Isaiah* 26:3. (6) Cf. *Psalms* 119:165. (7) Cf. 44:5. (8) Cf. *Isaiah* 32:18.
(9) Cf. *Job* 30:26; early editions of *Selichos* printed in Vilna omit the word טוב, *goodness*;
the stich then means, we have hoped for peace, and is not based on the verse from *Job*.
(10) Cf. *Lamentations* 3:47. (11) Cf. *Zechariah* 8:10; *II Chronicles* 15:5. (12) Cf. *Esther* 2:18.

---

dispute regarding the relative stations of the person who was righteous from birth, having never sunk into sinful ways, and the true penitent who, despite his years of waywardness, has returned wholeheartedly to the path of life. The interpretation of *the far* and *the near* is dependent on one's point of view regarding the always righteous and the penitent. If the always righteous is on a higher plane, then he would be mentioned first in the Scriptural verse. Thus, רָחוֹק, *the far one*, refers to a person who has always remained far from sin, while קָרוֹב, *the near one*, refers to one who had been near to sin, but is presently far removed from it. [According to *Rashi* and *Targum* to *Isaiah* 57:19, *far* and *near* speak of time, i.e., distant times and recent times. The רָחוֹק has been righteous from long ago, but the קָרוֹב has recently turned righteous.]

If, however, the penitent is on a loftier level than one who has not tasted of sin, then a רָחוֹק is one who had been far but is now near, while a קָרוֹב is one who has always been near.

אֶל עִיר מָצוֹר — *To the beleaguered city.* King Solomon tells a story: *There was a small city with only a few inhabitants; and a mighty king came*

upon it and surrounded it, and build great seige works over it. Present in the city was a poor wise man, who, by his wisdom, saved the city. Yet no one remembered that poor man (*Ecclesiastes* 9:14-15).

The Talmud explains the allegory: The small city is the human body; the inhabitants, the body's limbs and organs; the mighty king with his siege works is the *Yetzer Hara* [Evil Inclination] with his machinations and temptations; the poor wise man with his plan to save the city is the *Yetzer Tov* [Good Inclination] urging repentance and good deeds. And even though the *Yetzer Tov* saved the man/city, the penitent may not let down his guard for a moment. For should the *Yetzer Hara* gain ascendancy again, all the accomplishment of the *Yetzer Tov* will be washed away and forgotten (*Nedarim* 32b).

לָשׁוֹן שֶׁל זְהוֹרִית — *Strip of red wool.* Part of the Yom Kippur Temple service included the Kohen Gadol's drawing of lots to determine which of two identical billy goats would become an Altar sacrifice [לַה׳, *to* HASHEM], and which would be pushed off a cliff in the Wilderness [לַעֲזָאזֵל, *to Azazel*] (see *Leviticus* 16:7-10). To identify the

הוֹשִׁיעָה יהוה אֶת עַמְּךָ אֶת שְׁאֵרִית,[1]
תִּכְרֹת לָהֶם בְּרִית כְּנָם נָבִיא וְהַחֲרִית,
וְכָרַתִּי לָהֶם בְּרִית שָׁלוֹם.[2]

שָׁלוֹם פָּתַח לְיוֹנָתָךְ תַּמָּתָךְ הַשְׁמִיעִינִי אֶת קוֹלֵךְ,
כִּי קוֹלֵךְ עָרֵב וּמַרְאֵךְ נָאוֶה[3] בְּהִתְפַּלְלֵךְ,
הַרְחִיבִי מְקוֹם אָהֳלֵךְ,[4] אֲבִיר יַעֲקֹב גּוֹאֲלֵךְ,[5]
הַשָׁם גְּבוּלֵךְ שָׁלוֹם.[6]

שָׁלוֹם עוֹשֶׂה בִּמְרוֹמָיו[7] יַעֲשֶׂה שָׁלוֹם לְעַם נִבְזֶה,
גּוֹי קַו קַו וּמְבוּסָה מִצַּר בּוֹזֶה,[8]
מִמְשָׁךְ וּמוֹרָט יוּבַל שַׁי[9] כְּמַאֲמַר חוֹזֶה,
וְהָיָה זֶה שָׁלוֹם.[10]

שָׁלוֹם סָבִיב לְעַמּוֹ יַחֲנֶה[11] הֱיוֹת לָמוֹ לְמִסְעַד,
אַלּוּפֵי אֱדוֹם יֹאחֲזֵמוֹ רָעַד.[12]
וּלְבָנֶיךָ שָׁלַח אֵלָיְךָ מִתּוֹשְׁבֵי גִלְעָד,[13]
יוֹעֵץ אֵל גִּבּוֹר אֲבִי עַד שַׂר שָׁלוֹם.[14]*

שָׁלוֹם נִקְרָא שְׁמוֹ וְאָדוֹן לְכָל רֹאשׁ מִתְנַשֵּׂא.[15]
מוֹחֵל עֲוֹנוֹת עַמּוֹ וּפְשָׁעִים מְכַסֶּה,
מְקַבֵּל שָׁבִים וּפוֹשֵׁט יָד, וְלִירֵאָיו מַחְסֶה,
הַמְשֵׁל וָפַחַד עִמּוֹ עֹשֶׂה שָׁלוֹם.[16]

שָׁלוֹם, מְבַשֵּׂר טוֹב וּמַשְׁמִיעַ יְשׁוּעָה[17] מִמְּרוֹמוֹ,
מֶלֶךְ עַל כֹּל, יהוה צְבָאוֹת שְׁמוֹ,
בִּדְבָרוֹ תִּרְגַּז כָּל הָאָרֶץ לְמִשְׁפָּט בְּקוּמוֹ,[18]
יהוה עֹז לְעַמּוֹ יִתֵּן, יהוה יְבָרֵךְ אֶת עַמּוֹ בַשָּׁלוֹם.[19]

שָׁלוֹם לָכֶם אַל תִּירָאוּ,[20] לִרְאוֹת[21] כִּי תָבֹאוּ,
עַל בִּרְכַּיִם תְּשָׁעֳשָׁעוּ, וְעַל צַד תִּנָּשֵׂאוּ,[22]
בְּשׁוּב יהוה צִיּוֹן עַיִן בְּעַיִן תִּרְאוּ,[23]
כִּי בְשִׂמְחָה תֵצֵאוּ וּבְשָׁלוֹם.[24]

---

goats after their selection, a strip of red wool was
tied to the head of the Azazel goat and another
strip was tied around the neck of the Altar goat
(Mishnah, *Yoma* 4:2). But, the strip on the Azazel
goat's head served a second purpose. If God had
chosen to forgive the nation's sins that year, the
red wool, a symbol of sin (see *Isaiah* 1:18), would
miraculously turn white, a symbol of innocence
(ibid.; Mishnah, *Yoma* 6:9).

Since today we do not have the Temple Service

by which to attain atonement, the *paytan* tells us
that peace, charity and kindness will serve the
same purpose as the Azazel goat.

יוֹעֵץ אֵל גִּבּוֹר אֲבִי עַד שַׂר שָׁלוֹם — *O Advisor,
Mighty God, Eternal Father, [send the Messiah,]
the Prince of Peace.* This list of descriptive names
is taken from *Isaiah* 9:5. There the prophet speaks
of the impending birth of the righteous king
Hezekiah (*Chizkiyahu*). The passage begins,

O HASHEM, save Your people, the remnant![1]
Make a covenant with them, as the prophet said and inscribed,
'I will make with them a covenant of **peace**.'[2]

פ **PEACE**, call to Your dove, Your whole-hearted one,
   'Let Me hear your voice,
   for your voice is sweet and your countenance graceful[3] as you pray.
   Widen the area of your tent,[4]
      for the Mighty One of Jacob is your Savior,[5]
   He Who puts your border at **peace**.'[6]

ע **Peace** — may He Who makes it in His heights[7]
   make peace for the despised nation,
   the people who pay measure for measure [for their sins],
      trampled by the ravening foe.[8]
   The abused, torn folk will be brought as a gift to Him,[9]
      as the prophet said,
   'And this will be **peace**.'[10]

ס **PEACE** will encamp around His people[11] being a support unto them.
   Let trembling seize the chieftains of Edom,[12]
   and send Elijah the Giladite to Your children,[13]
   O Advisor, Mighty God, Eternal Father,
   [send the Messiah,] the Prince of **Peace**!*[14]

נ **PEACE** is His name, and He is the Lord, exalted over every leader;[15]
   He pardons His people's iniquities
      and covers over their rebellious sins;
   He accepts the repentant, stretching out His hand to them,
      and is a shelter for those who revere Him.
   Rule and fear are with Him; He makes **peace**.[16]

מ **PEACE**, Herald of good, announcing salvation[17] from His heights;
   King over everything, HASHEM, Master of Legions, is His name!
   At His word all the earth will shudder as He rises to judge.[18]
   HASHEM will give might to His people;
      HASHEM will bless His people with **peace**.[19]

ל **Peace** unto you; do not fear[20] when you come [to Jerusalem]
   to see [the glory of HASHEM].[21]
   You will be dandled on [His] knees and carried at [His] side;[22]
   when HASHEM returns to Zion you will see it eye to eye,[23]
   for you will go forth in joy, and in **peace**.[24]

---

(1) Cf. *Jeremiah* 31:6. (2) *Ezekiel* 34:25. (3) *Song of Songs* 2:14. (4) *Isaiah* 54:2. (5) Cf. 49:26.
(6) *Psalms* 147:14. (7) Cf. *Job* 25:2. (8) Cf. *Isaiah* 18:2. (9) Cf. 18:7. (10) *Micah* 5:4. (11) Cf. *Psalms* 125:2.
(12) Cf. *Exodus* 15:15. (13) Cf. *I Kings* 17:1. (14) *Isaiah* 9:5. (15) Cf. *I Chronicles* 29:11. (16) *Job* 25:2.
(17) Cf. *Isaiah* 52:7. (18) Cf. *Psalms* 76:10. (19) 29:11. (20) *Genesis* 43:23. (21) Some editions read
לֵרָאוֹת, *to be seen* [*by* HASHEM]; cf. *Isaiah* 1:12. (22) Cf. 66:12. (23) Cf. 52:8. (24) 55:12.

... וַיִּקְרָא שְׁמוֹ פֶּלֶא יוֹעֵץ, literally, *And he will call his name Wonder, Advisor* ... The Sages are split regarding the interpretation of this list of appellations. According to the Talmud, the eight names all refer to Hezekiah who was to be: פֶּלֶא, *a wonder*; יוֹעֵץ, *an advisor*; אֵל, *mighty* [in this

sense, this word is not a Divine Name — see *Psalms* 36:7 and 80:11 for other examples of this usage]; גִּבּוֹר, *a warrior*; אֲבִי, *a father* [to his nation]; עַד, [whose deeds would be] *eternal*; שַׂר, *a prince*; and שָׁלוֹם, *peace* [would reign in his time] (*Sanhedrin* 94a; see Ibn Ezra to *Isaiah* 9:5). If so,

שָׁלוֹם כַּנָּהָר נְטֵה[1] וְשִׂים לְאַבְנֵי חֵפֶץ גְּבוּלֶיהָ,[2]
כַּנָּה אֲשֶׁר נָטְעָה יְמִינֶךְ[3] וְקַבֵּץ עוֹלֶלֶיהָ,
וְזָרַק מַיִם טְהוֹרִים[4] וְטַהֵר טֻמְאַת שׁוּלֶיהָ,[5]
וְקָרָאתָ אֵלֶיהָ **לְשָׁלוֹם**.[6]

שָׁלוֹם יַחְדָּו אֶשְׁכְּבָה וְאִישָׁן,[7] וַיהוה נַפְשִׁי שָׁמְרָה,[8]
אַל תִּזְנַח לָנֶצַח, לָמָה תִישַׁן, עוּרָה,[9]
וְתוֹצִיא כָאוֹר צִדְקֵנוּ,[10] וְהָכֵן נָבִיא מְהֵרָה,
לְמַרְבֵּה הַמִּשְׂרָה **וּלְשָׁלוֹם**.[11]

שָׁלוֹם טוֹב מֵאָדוֹן טוֹב, לַבָּאִים אֵלֶיךָ לְהִבָּדֵק,
אַל תָּשִׂים פָּנֶיךָ עִמָּנוּ בַּדִּין לְדַקְדֵּק,
תִּתֵּן אֱמֶת לְיַעֲקֹב וְחֶסֶד לְאַבְרָהָם[12] לְהִצְטַדֵּק,
חֶסֶד וֶאֱמֶת נִפְגָּשׁוּ צֶדֶק **וְשָׁלוֹם**.[13]

שָׁלוֹם חֵלֶב חִטִּים תַּשְׂבִּיעַ[14] לְכָל בְּנֵי עֵבֶר,
קֹנֵי יהוה יַחֲלִיפוּ כֹחַ,[15] יַעֲלוּ אֵבֶר,
וְיַעֲבֹר מַלְכָּם לִפְנֵיהֶם,[16] עַל פֶּשַׁע עוֹבֵר,[17]
דּוֹרֵשׁ טוֹב לְעַמּוֹ וְדֹבֵר **שָׁלוֹם**.[18]

שָׁלוֹם זֶרַע בֵּרַךְ יהוה,[19] אִם נָאֲוָה שְׁחַרְחֹרֶת,[20]
שִׂימֶנָּה לִתְהִלָּה לְכָבוֹד וּלְתִפְאָרֶת,
וְקַיֵּם לָהּ חָזוֹן אֲשֶׁר הִתְוֵיתָ בְּחֶרֶת,
וְגִלֵּיתִי לָהֶם עֲתֶרֶת **שָׁלוֹם**.[21]

שָׁלוֹם וּבְרִית עוֹלָם יִהְיֶה[22] אֵל עַם קְרוֹבוֹ,
אֲשֶׁר צָפוּן לִירֵאָיו מָה רַב טוּבוֹ,[23]
כִּי עַיִן בְּעַיִן יִרְאוּ לְצִיּוֹן בְּשׁוּבוֹ,[24]
וְכָל הָעָם הַזֶּה עַל מְקוֹמוֹ יָבֹא **בְשָׁלוֹם**.[25]

שָׁלוֹם הִנֵּה מַר לִי מָר[26] כִּי בָזְאוּ
אַרְצִי, [27] שְׁלָלוּ שָׂסוּ גָּבְרוּ וְגָאוּ,
עַמִּים שָׁמְמוּ עָרִים עַד אֲשֶׁר שָׁאוּ,[28]
הַנּוֹשְׁכִים בְּשִׁנֵּיהֶם וְקָרְאוּ **שָׁלוֹם**.[29]

---

in our *selichah*, all these names refer to the Messiah, and the translation should be adjusted accordingly.

However, *Targum*, followed by *Rashi*, translates the verse: ... אָבִי עַד ... שְׁמוֹ פֶּלֶא וַיִּקְרָא, *The Wondrous Advisor, Mighty God, Eternal Father will call his [Hezekiah's] name 'Prince of Peace.'*

These particular attributes are used to describe God in this verse that heralds Hezekiah's birth, because they are all apropos for Hezekiah and his reign (*Radak*). Our translation follows this interpretation, applying the appellation 'Prince of Peace' to the Messiah, and all the preceding ones to God.

כ **Peace** make flow [in Jerusalem] like a river,[1]
   and turn her boundaries to precious stones;[2]
and [Israel,] the vine Your right hand planted,[3]
   gather in her youngsters.
Cast purifying water[4] and cleanse her skirt's contamination,[5]
and call to it to make **peace.**[6]

י **Peace** and unity [reign], [therefore] I can lie down and sleep,[7]
   for HASHEM watches my soul.[8]
Forsake not forever; why do You [seem to] sleep? Awake![9]
And reveal our righteousness like a light.[10]
   Raise up [Elijah the] prophet for us quickly,
to enhance [God's] rulership and to make **peace.**[11]

ט **Peace** that is good, from the Lord Who is good,
   to those who come to cling to You;
do not set Your countenance towards us in strict judgment.
.Give truth to Jacob['s children] and kindness
   to Abraham['s descendants],[12] that they may be justified;
kindness and truth have met righteousness and **peace.**[13]

ח **Peace** , may You satisfy all the Hebrew children
   with the cream of the wheat.[14]
Let those who hope for HASHEM renew strength continually,
   and sprout new wings.[15]
Let their King go before them,[16] Who bears with sin,[17]
Who seeks the good of His people, and speaks **peace.**[18]

ז **Peace** [upon] the seed blessed by HASHEM,[19] the comely nation
   [cleansed by] having been blackened [by their sins].[20]
Bring upon them praise, honor, and splendor,
   and make true for them the vision inscribed in Scriptures:
'I will reveal to them an abundance of **peace.'**[21]

ו **Peace** and an eternal covenant shall there be[22]
   for the people near to Him,
Who has concealed [the reward] for those who revere Him,
   how abundant is His goodness![23]
For eye to eye they will see when He returns to Zion,[24]
   and all this people will reach its place in **peace.**[25]

ה **Peace** is become bitter, bitter to me;[26] for they have plundered,
   my land[27] have they looted, pillaged, conquered;
   and they have become haughty.
These peoples laid cities waste unto desolation;[28]
   they gnaw with their teeth, and call for **peace.**[29]

---

(1) Cf. *Isaiah* 66:12. (2) Cf. 54:12. (3) Cf. *Psalms* 80:16. (4) Cf. *Ezekiel* 36:25. (5) Cf. *Lamentations* 1:9.
(6) *Deuteronomy* 20:10. (7) Cf. *Psalms* 4:9. (8) Cf. 86:2. (9) Cf. 44:24. (10) Cf. 37:6.
(11) *Isaiah* 9:6. (12) *Micah* 7:20. (13) *Psalms* 85:11. (14) Cf. 147:14. (15) Cf. *Isaiah* 40:31; see
commentary to *selichah* 61, s.v., קוֹי. (16) *Micah* 2:13. (17) Cf. 7:18. (18) *Esther* 10:3. (19) *Isaiah* 61:9.
(20) See *Song of Songs* 1:5-6 with *Rashi*. (21) *Jeremiah* 33:6. (22) Cf. *Ezekiel* 37:26.
(23) Cf. *Psalms* 31:20. (24) Cf. *Isaiah* 52:8. (25) Cf. *Exodus* 18:23.
(26) Cf. *Isaiah* 38:17. (27) Cf. 18:7. (28) Cf. 6:11. (29) *Micah* 3:5.

שָׁלוֹם דַּבֵּר אֶל בְּנֵי יִשְׂרָאֵל וּבַקֵּשׁ לְהַעֲלוֹתָם מִבּוֹר,

מִמִּזְרָח וּמִמַּעֲרָב[1] שְׁאֵרִיתָם לְצַבֵּר,

מֵאֱדוֹם וּמִמּוֹאָב עָלָם הַכָּבֵד תִּשְׁבֹּר,

יִרְדְּפֵם יַעֲבוֹר שָׁלוֹם.[2]

שָׁלוֹם גְּמֹל לַעֲבָדֶיךָ שָׁמַיִם וָאָרֶץ קוֹנֶה,[3]

בְּעֵת צָרָה לְעַמּוֹ בַּמֶּרְחָב יָהּ עוֹנֶה,[4]

אֵיכָה יוּעַם זָהָב וְהֻכֵּתֶם הַטּוֹב יִשְׂנֵא,[5]

רַבַּת שָׁכְנָה לָהּ נַפְשֵׁנוּ, עִם שׂוֹנֵא שָׁלוֹם.[6]

שָׁלוֹם בָּאָרֶץ תִּתֵּן[7] וְעַמִּים תַּחְתֵּנוּ יַדְבֵּר,

לְאֻמִּים תַּחַת נַפְשֵׁנוּ[8] מִשְׁנֶה שִׁבָּרוֹן יְשַׁבֵּר,

כִּי בָאֵשׁ יהוה נִשְׁפָּט[9] וַחֲיָלִים יְגַבֵּר,[10]

אֶשְׁמְעָה מַה יְדַבֵּר הָאֵל יהוה, כִּי יְדַבֵּר שָׁלוֹם.[11]

❖ **שָׁלוֹם** אֵין קֵץ עַל כִּסֵּא גֶזַע גּוּר אַרְיֵה,[12]

בְּהִלּוֹ נֵרוֹ לְעוֹלָם וָעֶד בְּלִי לְאַטְפוּיֵי,

יְחַיֵּנוּ מִיּוֹמָיִם, בַּיּוֹם הַשְּׁלִישִׁי יְקִימֵנוּ וְנִחְיֶה,[13]

לְדָוִד וּלְזַרְעוֹ וּלְכִסְאוֹ יִהְיֶה שָׁלוֹם.[14]

All, while standing:

אֵל מֶלֶךְ יוֹשֵׁב עַל כִּסֵּא רַחֲמִים מִתְנַהֵג בַּחֲסִידוּת, מוֹחֵל עֲוֹנוֹת עַמּוֹ, מַעֲבִיר רִאשׁוֹן רִאשׁוֹן, מַרְבֶּה מְחִילָה לַחַטָּאִים וּסְלִיחָה לַפּוֹשְׁעִים, עֹשֶׂה צְדָקוֹת עִם כָּל בָּשָׂר וָרוּחַ, לֹא כְרָעָתָם תִּגְמוֹל. ❖ אֵל הוֹרֵיתָ לָּנוּ לוֹמַר שְׁלֹשׁ עֶשְׂרֵה, וּזְכָר לָנוּ הַיּוֹם בְּרִית שְׁלֹשׁ עֶשְׂרֵה, כְּמוֹ שֶׁהוֹדַעְתָּ לֶעָנָיו מִקֶּדֶם, כְּמוֹ שֶׁכָּתוּב, וַיֵּרֶד יהוה בֶּעָנָן וַיִּתְיַצֵּב עִמּוֹ שָׁם, וַיִּקְרָא בְשֵׁם יהוה.

Congregation, then chazzan:

וַיַּעֲבֹר יהוה עַל פָּנָיו וַיִּקְרָא:

Congregation and chazzan (the words in bold type are recited aloud and in unison):

יהוה, יהוה, אֵל, **רַחוּם, וְחַנּוּן, אֶרֶךְ אַפַּיִם, וְרַב חֶסֶד, וֶאֱמֶת, נֹצֵר חֶסֶד לָאֲלָפִים, נֹשֵׂא עָוֹן, וָפֶשַׁע, וְחַטָּאָה,** וְנַקֵּה. וְסָלַחְתָּ לַעֲוֹנֵנוּ וּלְחַטָּאתֵנוּ וּנְחַלְתָּנוּ. סְלַח לָנוּ אָבִינוּ כִּי חָטָאנוּ, מְחַל לָנוּ מַלְכֵּנוּ כִּי פָשָׁעְנוּ. כִּי אַתָּה אֲדֹנָי טוֹב וְסַלָּח, וְרַב חֶסֶד לְכָל קֹרְאֶיךָ.

ר **Peace** , *speak unto the Children of Israel,*
    and seek [just cause] to raise them from the pit,
to gather their remnant together from east and from west.[1]
Break off their heavy yoke set by Edom and Moab;
[the Messiah] will have pursued them and returned in **peace.**[2]

ג **Peace** *grant unto Your servants, O Creator of heaven and earth!*[3]
In time of trouble for His people, God answers them with relief.[4]
How has their gold become dimmed, their goodly metal debased?[5]
So long has our soul dwelt with the hater of **peace!**[6]

ב **Peace** *grant in [our] land,*[7] *and subdue peoples under us;*
may the nations, instead of us, be broken twice over.[8]
For HASHEM *punishes with fire,*[9]
    and yet encourages His warriors.[10]
I will hear what the Almighty God, HASHEM, *will say,*
    for He speaks of **peace.**[11]

א Chazzan – **Peace** *without end upon the throne of the [Judean] lion cub,*[12]
as his light shines forever, without being extinguished.
He will revive us after our two exiles,
    and raise us up the third time, that we may live.[13]
Unto David, his seed, and his throne may there be **peace.**[14]

All, while standing:

אֵל מֶלֶךְ O God, King Who sits on the throne of mercy; Who acts with
    kindness, pardons the iniquities of His people, removes [sins]
one by one, increasingly grants pardon to careless sinners and forgiveness
to rebels, Who deals righteously with every living being — You do not repay
them in accord with their evil. Chazzan – O God, You taught us to recite the
Thirteen [Attributes of Mercy], so remember for us today the covenant of
these Thirteen, as You made known to the humble one in ancient times, as
it is written: And HASHEM descended in a cloud and stood with him there,
and He called out with the Name HASHEM.

Congregation, then chazzan:

And HASHEM passed before him [Moses] and proclaimed:

Congregation and chazzan (the words in bold type are recited aloud and in unison):

**ה' ה' ** HASHEM, HASHEM, God, Compassionate and Gracious, Slow
    to anger, and Abundant in Kindness and Truth, Preserver of
kindness for thousands [of generations], Forgiver of iniquity, willful
sin, and error, and Who cleanses. May You forgive our iniquities and
our errors and make us Your heritage. Forgive us, our Father, for we have
erred; pardon us, our King, for we have willfully sinned; for You, my
Lord, are good and forgiving and abundantly kind to all who call upon
You.

---

(1) *Psalms* 107:3. (2) *Isaiah* 41:3. (3) Cf. *Genesis* 14:19. (4) Cf. *Psalms* 118:5. (5) Cf. *Lamentations* 4:1.
(6) Cf. *Psalms* 120:6. (7) Cf. *Leviticus* 26:6. (8) Cf. *Psalms* 47:4; this line has been censored out of some
editions of *Selichos*. (9) *Isaiah* 66:16. (10) *Ecclesiastes* 10:10. (11) *Psalms* 85:9. (12) Cf. *Isaiah* 9:6.
(13) *Hosea* 6:2. (14) Cf. *I Kings* 2:33.

פסוקי הקדמה לסליחה פג

זִבְחֵי אֱלֹהִים רוּחַ נִשְׁבָּרָה, לֵב נִשְׁבָּר וְנִדְכֶּה, אֱלֹהִים לֹא
תִבְזֶה.¹ תִּתֵּן אֱמֶת לְיַעֲקֹב חֶסֶד לְאַבְרָהָם, אֲשֶׁר נִשְׁבַּעְתָּ
לַאֲבֹתֵינוּ מִימֵי קֶדֶם.² וְחֶסֶד יהוה מֵעוֹלָם וְעַד עוֹלָם עַל יְרֵאָיו,
וְצִדְקָתוֹ לִבְנֵי בָנִים.³ קָרוֹב יהוה לְנִשְׁבְּרֵי לֵב, וְאֶת דַּכְּאֵי רוּחַ
יוֹשִׁיעַ.⁴

כְּרַחֵם אָב עַל בָּנִים, כֵּן תְּרַחֵם יהוה עָלֵינוּ. לַיהוה הַיְשׁוּעָה,
עַל עַמְּךָ בִרְכָתֶךָ סֶּלָה. יהוה צְבָאוֹת עִמָּנוּ, מִשְׂגָּב
לָנוּ אֱלֹהֵי יַעֲקֹב סֶלָה. יהוה צְבָאוֹת, אַשְׁרֵי אָדָם בֹּטֵחַ בָּךְ. יהוה
הוֹשִׁיעָה, הַמֶּלֶךְ יַעֲנֵנוּ בְיוֹם קָרְאֵנוּ.

In some congregations the following two verses are recited responsively — the *chazzan* reciting סְלַח,
and the congregation responding וַיֹּאמֶר. In other congregations these verses are recited silently.

סְלַח נָא לַעֲוֹן הָעָם הַזֶּה כְּגֹדֶל חַסְדֶּךָ, וְכַאֲשֶׁר נָשָׂאתָה לָעָם
הַזֶּה מִמִּצְרַיִם וְעַד הֵנָּה, וְשָׁם נֶאֱמַר:

וַיֹּאמֶר יהוה סָלַחְתִּי כִּדְבָרֶךָ.

All:

הַטֵּה אֱלֹהַי אָזְנְךָ וּשֲׁמָע, פְּקַח עֵינֶיךָ וּרְאֵה שֹׁמְמֹתֵינוּ, וְהָעִיר
אֲשֶׁר נִקְרָא שִׁמְךָ עָלֶיהָ, כִּי לֹא עַל צִדְקוֹתֵינוּ אֲנַחְנוּ
מַפִּילִים תַּחֲנוּנֵינוּ לְפָנֶיךָ, כִּי עַל רַחֲמֶיךָ הָרַבִּים. אֲדֹנָי שְׁמָעָה,
אֲדֹנָי סְלָחָה, אֲדֹנָי הַקְשִׁיבָה, וַעֲשֵׂה אַל תְּאַחַר, לְמַעַנְךָ אֱלֹהַי, כִּי
שִׁמְךָ נִקְרָא עַל עִירְךָ וְעַל עַמֶּךָ.

סְלִיחָה פג (עֲקֵדָה)

אֱלֹהֵינוּ וֵאלֹהֵי אֲבוֹתֵינוּ:

אֵיתָן לִמֵּד דַּעַת,*   טֶרֶם לַכֹּל מוּדַעַת.

בֵּאֵר שִׁמְךָ לְכָל בָּאֵי עוֹלָם,   גִּלָּה כָּל סָתוּם וְנֶעְלָם.

גְּלוּלִים מָאַס וְשִׁבֵּר,*   תּוֹעִים לְשִׁמְךָ חִבֵּר.

דֶּרֶךְ מִישׁוֹר בָּחַר,   תּוֹרָה וּמִצְוֹת שָׁמַר וְלֹא אַחַר.

אֵיתָן לִמֵּד דַּעַת ⇐ — *Abraham taught knowledge [of God].* The Psalmist records a psalm by אֵיתָן הָאֶזְרָחִי, *Ethan the Ezrachite,* whom the Talmud identifies as the Patriarch Abraham (*Bava Basra* 15a; see also *Rashi* to *I Kings* 5:11). He is called אֵיתָן, literally, *the mighty one,* for the Patriarchs are the pillars of the world (see *Rosh Hashanah* 11a); and הָאֶזְרָחִי, literally, *the East-*

erner, because he hailed from Aram which is to the east of *Eretz Yisrael* (see *Sanhedrin* 108b).

All *akeidah piyutim* extol the virtues and merits of Abraham and Isaac when they went forth to fulfill God's command to sacrifice Isaac. This *akeidah,* however, goes a few steps further than most, for it also involves the merit of Jacob, the Matriarchs, and the twelve sons of Jacob. The

PREFATORY VERSES TO SELICHAH 83

זִבְחֵי *The sacrifices God desires are a broken spirit, a broken, crushed heart; [these]God will not despise.[1] Grant truth to Jacob, kindness to Abraham, as You swore to our forefathers from ancient times.[2] For HASHEM's kindness is forever and ever upon those who fear Him, and His righteousness is upon children's children.[3] HASHEM is close to the broken-hearted, and those crushed in spirit He saves.[4]*

כְּרַחֵם אָב *As a father has mercy on his children, so, HASHEM, may You have mercy on us. Salvation is HASHEM's, upon Your people is Your blessing, Selah. HASHEM, Master of Legions, is with us, a stronghold for us is the God of Jacob, Selah. HASHEM, Master of Legions, praiseworthy is the person who trusts in You. HASHEM, save! May the King answer us on the day we call.*

In some congregations the following two verses are recited responsively — the *chazzan* reciting, *'Forgive, please . . . ,'* and the congregation responding, *'And HASHEM said . . .'*
In other congregations these verses are recited silently.

סְלַח נָא *Forgive, please, the iniquity of this people according to the greatness of Your kindness and as You have forgiven this people from Egypt until now, and there it was said:*

And HASHEM said, 'I have forgiven according to your word!'

All:

הַטֵּה *Incline, my God, Your ear, and listen, open Your eyes and see our desolation and that of the city upon which Your Name is proclaimed; for not because of our righteousness do we cast down our supplications before You, rather because of Your abundant compassion. O my Lord, heed; O my Lord, forgive; O my Lord, be attentive and act, do not delay; for Your sake, my God, for Your Name is proclaimed upon Your city and upon Your people.*

SELICHAH 83

Our God and the God of our forefathers:
א *Abraham taught knowledge [of God],**
   when it was not yet known to all.
ב *He interpreted Your Name to all dwellers in the world,*
   he revealed every hidden, obscure thing.
ג *He despised and shattered [his father's] idols;**
   he taught the errant to hold fast to Your Name.
ד *He chose the straight path,*
   he kept Torah and mitzvos without delay.

(1) *Psalms* 51:19. (2) *Micah* 7:20. (3) *Psalms* 103:17. (4) 34:19.

initial letters of the twenty-two couplets form the *aleph-beis*.

גִּלּוּלִים מָאַס וְשִׁבֵּר — *He despised and shattered [his father's]idols.* Terach, an idol manufacturer, asked his young son Abram to mind the business. When his father had left, Abram took a club and smashed all the idols except the largest one. Then

he placed the club into that idol's hands.
   Upon returning, Terach demanded, 'Who did this to my idols?'
   Abram explained, 'When I placed food before them, the idols began arguing, each claiming the right to the first portion. Finally, the largest of them settled the argument by smashing the others with his club.'

הַצַּלְתּוֹ מֵאוּר כַּשְׂדִּים,   גִּנַּנְתּוֹ בְּעֵמֶק הַשִּׂדִּים.*

וְעֶדְתּוֹ שְׂכָרְךָ הַרְבֵּה מְאֹד,[1]   וַתְּתַקְּנֵהוּ רֹב עֹשֶׁר וְכָבוֹד.

זָעַק וְהֵשִׁיב מַה תִּתֶּן לִי,[2]   שֹׁרֶשׁ וְעָנָף אֵין לִי.

חִיַּלְתּוֹ בִּרְאִיַּת מַחֲזֶה,   בְּשַׂרְתּוֹ לֹא יִירָשְׁךָ זֶה.[3]

טֶנֶא בִּכּוּרִים לְמֵאָה חֲנַנְתּוֹ,   לְקׇרְבָּן נִיחוֹחַ חֲשַׁקְתּוֹ.

יַחְדָּו בְּכָל לִבָּם דָּצוּ,   לַעֲשׂוֹת רְצוֹנְךָ רָצוּ.

כָּבַשׁ רַחֲמָיו לַעֲשׂוֹת רְצוֹנֶךָ,*

כֵּן יִכְבְּשׁוּ רַחֲמֶיךָ אֶת כַּעַסְךָ מֵעַל צֹאנֶךָ.

לִבָּם וְנַפְשָׁם הָיָה נָכוֹן,[4]   לָכֵן תִּפְלָטֵנוּ לְפָנֶיךָ כִּקְטֹרֶת תִּכּוֹן.[5]

מִהֵר וְלָקַח מַאֲכֶלֶת,[6]   לָכֵן זַרְעָם תַּצִּיל מִמִּיתָה מְשֻׁכֶּלֶת.

נֶעֱקַד יָחִיד כְּשֶׂה לָטֶבַח,   לָכֵן תִּפְלָטֵנוּ תִּרְצֶה כְּעוֹלָה וָזֶבַח.

סִדֵּר עֵצִים וְהִצִּית עֲלֵיהֶם אֵשׁ,   לָכֵן בַּעֲמִידָתֵנוּ הַיּוֹם לֹא נִתְבַּיֵּשׁ.

עֲנִיתוֹ מִשְּׁמֵי שָׁמַיִם,   לָכֵן נִשְׁבַּעְתָּ לּוֹ בְּשִׁמְךָ פַּעֲמָיִם.[7]

פָּדִיתָ אוֹתוֹ בְּאַיִל בַּסְּבַךְ אָחוּז,[8]   לָכֵן עֲמִידָתֵנוּ וְעִנּוּיֵנוּ לֹא תָבוּז.

צַעֲקָתֵנוּ שְׁמַע וְשַׁוְעָתֵנוּ סְכֹת,   בִּזְכוּת אָב נָסַע סֻכֹּת,[9]

קוֹל מְבַשֵּׂר יִשָּׁמַע בָּעוֹלָם,   לִגְאֹל עַם גֶּזַע גִּבְעוֹת עוֹלָם.[10]

רַחֵם קְהַל עֲדַת מְקֻשָּׁטִים,   טִיעַת שְׁנַיִם עָשָׂר שְׁבָטִים.

❖ שְׁכִינָתְךָ תִּשְׁכֹּן בְּתוֹכֵנוּ,   תְּנַהֲגֵנוּ לִגְבוּל אַדְמָתֵנוּ.

תָּפֶן אֵלֵינוּ בְּרַחֲמִים,   כִּי כֵן נִקְרֵאתָ מָלֵא רַחֲמִים.

All:

אֵל מֶלֶךְ יוֹשֵׁב עַל כִּסֵּא רַחֲמִים מִתְנַהֵג בַּחֲסִידוּת, מוֹחֵל עֲוֹנוֹת עַמּוֹ, מַעֲבִיר רִאשׁוֹן רִאשׁוֹן, מַרְבֶּה מְחִילָה לַחַטָּאִים וּסְלִיחָה לַפּוֹשְׁעִים, עֹשֶׂה צְדָקוֹת עִם כָּל בָּשָׂר וָרוּחַ,

'What are you saying?' cried the incredulous Terach. 'Do they know what's happening?'

To which Abram replied, 'Would that your ears would hear what your mouth just said [i.e., Why do you worship them if they do not know what is happening?]!'

Not knowing how to handle his son's 'blasphemy,' Terach hauled Abram before King Nimrod. The king ordered the lad to bow to the fire. Abram replied, 'But water extinguishes fire; perhaps we should bow to the water?' The king agreed. Then Abram said, 'But the clouds are stronger for they carry the water; perhaps we should bow to the clouds?' Nimrod agreed. Once again Abram argued, 'But the wind blows the clouds wherever it pleases; perhaps we should bow to the wind?'

Finally, Nimrod got the point. 'You are trying

to sidetrack me with your words. I bow only to the fire. And I shall throw you into it. Let us see whether the God to Whom you bow can save you from it.' Thereupon, he had Abram cast into a fiery furnace; but the fire miraculously had no power over the young Patriarch, and he emerged unscathed. For this reason the place became known as אוּר כַּשְׂדִּים, *Ur* [lit., *fire*]*of the Chaldees* (*Bereishis Rabbah* 38:13).

בְּעֵמֶק הַשִּׂדִּים — *In the Valley of Siddim*, where he battled and defeated the four kings who had taken his nephew Lot captive (see *Genesis* ch. 14).

כָּבַשׁ רַחֲמָיו לַעֲשׂוֹת רְצוֹנֶךָ — *He [Abraham] quelled his mercy to do Your will.* According to the Midrash, after God told Abraham to sacrifice the ram in place of Isaac, Abraham prayed, ' . . . just as I quelled my mercy to do Your will, so may it be Your will . . .' (*Bereishis Rabbah* 56:10).

ה You saved him from Ur of the Chaldees,
   and watched over him in the Valley of Siddim.*

ו You told him, 'Your reward is very great!'[1]
   and fortified him with abundant wealth and honor.

ז He answered back with a cry, 'What can You give me,[2]
   when root and branch have I not?'

ח You strengthened him with a vision before his eyes,
   You informed him, 'This [Eliezer] would not inherit you.'[3]

ט At a hundred years of age you granted him a basket of first fruits,
   then desired [that son] for a pleasant-scented sacrifice.

י Together they rejoiced with all their hearts; they ran to do Your will.

כ He [Abraham] quelled his mercy to do Your will;*
   therefore may Your mercy quell Your anger against Your flock.

ל Their heart and soul stood firm;[4]
   therefore may our prayer stand as incense before You.[5]

מ Swiftly [Abraham] took a knife;[6]
   therefore may You rescue their seed from untimely death.

נ The only son was bound like a sheep for slaughter;
   therefore may You be pleased with our prayer
      as with olah- and peace-offering.

ס He arranged the logs and lit the fire upon them;
   therefore in our standing prayer today let us not be put to shame.

ע You had answered him from the highest heavens;
   for You had sworn to him twice in Your Name
      [that his seed would be many].[7]

פ You redeemed him [Isaac] with a ram caught in the thicket;[8]
   therefore You will not despise our standing prayer and our fast.

צ Hear our cry, listen to our shout,
   by the merit of the Patriarch [Jacob], who traveled to Succos.[9]

ק Let the voice of the herald be heard in the world,
   to redeem the people, descendants of [the Matriarchs,
      whose merit is]eternal [as the]hills.[10]

ר Have mercy on the assembled flock, adorned with truth,
   the plant [sown] by the twelve tribes.

ש Chazzan – May Your Presence dwell in our midst,
   and may You lead us to the borders of our land.

ת Turn to us with mercy,
   for so You are called: '[God] full of mercy.'

All, while standing:

אֵל מֶלֶךְ O God, King Who sits on the throne of mercy; Who acts with kindness, pardons the iniquities of His people, removes [sins] one by one, increasingly grants pardon to careless sinners and forgiveness to rebels, Who deals righteously with every living being —

(1) Genesis 15:1. (2) 15:2. (3) 15:4. (4) Cf. Psalms 78:37. (5) Cf. 141:2.
(6) Cf. Genesis 22:10. (7) See Genesis 13:16 and 15:5. (8) Cf. 22:13.
(9) See 33:17. (10) See Targum Yerushalmi to Genesis 49:26 and Deuteronomy 33:15.

לֹא כִרְעָתָם תִּגְמוֹל. ❖ אֵל הוֹרֵיתָ לָנוּ לוֹמַר שְׁלֹשׁ עֶשְׂרֵה, וּזְכוֹר
לָנוּ הַיּוֹם בְּרִית שְׁלֹשׁ עֶשְׂרֵה, כְּמוֹ שֶׁהוֹדַעְתָּ לֶעָנָיו מִקֶּדֶם, כְּמוֹ
שֶׁכָּתוּב, וַיֵּרֶד יהוה בֶּעָנָן וַיִּתְיַצֵּב עִמּוֹ שָׁם, וַיִּקְרָא בְשֵׁם יהוה.

Congregation, then chazzan:

וַיַּעֲבֹר יהוה עַל פָּנָיו וַיִּקְרָא:

Congregation and chazzan (the words in bold type are recited aloud and in unison):

יהוה, יהוה, אֵל, רַחוּם, וְחַנּוּן, אֶרֶךְ אַפַּיִם, וְרַב חֶסֶד, וֶאֱמֶת,
נֹצֵר חֶסֶד לָאֲלָפִים, נֹשֵׂא עָוֹן, וָפֶשַׁע, וְחַטָּאָה,
וְנַקֵּה. וְסָלַחְתָּ לַעֲוֹנֵנוּ וּלְחַטָּאתֵנוּ וּנְחַלְתָּנוּ. סְלַח לָנוּ אָבִינוּ כִּי
חָטָאנוּ, מְחַל לָנוּ מַלְכֵּנוּ כִּי פָשָׁעְנוּ. כִּי אַתָּה אֲדֹנָי טוֹב וְסַלָּח,
וְרַב חֶסֶד לְכָל קֹרְאֶיךָ.

סְלִיחָה פד (פזמון)

Chazzan, then congregation:

בֵּין כֶּסֶה לֶעָשׂוֹר* הַשְׁלַכְנוּ רַע שְׂאוֹר,*
צַדְּקֵנוּ בַּמִּשְׁפָּט בְּאוֹר הַחַיִּים לָאוֹר,[1]
הִנְנוּ אָתָנוּ לְךָ[2] אַדִּיר וְנָאוֹר,
כִּי עִמְּךָ מְקוֹר חַיִּים, בְּאוֹרְךָ נִרְאֶה אוֹר.[3]

Congregation, then chazzan:

אָדוֹן עִמְּךָ סְלִיחָה,[4] סְלַח וּמְחַל לְשָׁבֶיךָ,
לְעֵת חָתוּם גְּזַר דִּינֶךָ, לְטוֹבָה זָכְרָה אֲהוּבֶיךָ,
יִוָּדַע כִּי אֱלֹהִים[5] בִּישֻׁרוּן קְרוֹבֶיךָ,
וְשִׂימֵנִי כַחוֹתָם עַל לִבֶּךָ.[6]   בֵּין כֶּסֶה לֶעָשׂוֹר...

Congregation, then chazzan:

עֲבָדֶיךָ לְטוֹב תַּעֲרֹב,[7] צַו כִּתְמָם לְמָחֳקָה,
זָכְרָה מְצוּקֵי תֵבֵל,[8] פְּעֻלָּתָם אִם פָּסְקָה,
רַחֵם בְּרָגֶז תִּזְכּוֹר,[9] בָּנֶיךָ עֵת חֲקוּקָה,
כָּתְבָה עַל לוּחַ אִתָּם וְעַל סֵפֶר חֻקָּה.[10]   בֵּין כֶּסֶה לֶעָשׂוֹר...

☙ בֵּין כֶּסֶה לֶעָשׂוֹר — *Between Rosh Hashanah and Yom Kippur.* [See *selichah* 53 for the derivation of this expression.] The acrostic of this *pizmon* reads, אֱלִיעֶזֶר בְּרַבִּי שְׁלֹמֹה הָאֵל יִגְמְלֵהוּ חֶסֶד, *Eliezer son of R' Shlomo, may God grant him kindness.* He is thought to be the former disciple of Rabbeinu Tam [France, 1100-1171] whose correspondence with R' Tam appears in *Sefer HaYashar* (§58-59).

In this *pizmon*, the *paytan* refers repeatedly to a well-known Talmudic teaching: Three books

are opened [before the Heavenly Tribunal] on Rosh Hashanah — one for the unquestionably wicked; one for the unquestionably righteous; and one for those between [these extremes]. The unquestionably righteous are immediately inscribed and sealed for life; the unquestionably wicked are immediately inscribed and sealed for death. [But the judgment of] those between stands in abeyance from Rosh Hashanah until Yom Kippur. If they are found worthy, they are inscribed for life; if they are not found

You do not repay them in accord with their evil. Chazzan — *O God, You taught us to recite the Thirteen [Attributes of Mercy], so remember for us today the covenant of these Thirteen, as You made known to the humble one in ancient times, as it is written: And HASHEM descended in a cloud and stood with him there, and He called out with the Name HASHEM.*

Congregation, then *chazzan:*

And HASHEM passed before him [Moses] and proclaimed:

Congregation and *chazzan* (the words in bold type are recited aloud and in unison):

'ה 'ה HASHEM, HASHEM, God, Compassionate and Gracious, Slow to anger, and Abundant in Kindness and Truth, Preserver of kindness for thousands [of generations], Forgiver of iniquity, willful sin, and error, and Who cleanses. *May You forgive our iniquities and our errors and make us Your heritage. Forgive us, our Father, for we have erred; pardon us, our King, for we have willfully sinned; for You, my Lord, are good and forgiving and abundantly kind to all who call upon You.*

SELICHAH 84

Chazzan, then congregation:

בֵּין *Between Rosh Hashanah and Yom Kippur**
we cast off the Evil Inclination;*
bring us out victorious from the judgment, to bask in the light of life.[1]
Here we are! We have come to You,[2] Grand and Illuminating One,
for with You is the source of life; by Your light may we see light.[3]

Congregation, then *chazzan:*

א *O Lord, with You is forgiveness,[4] forgive,*
pardon those who return to You.

ל *When the seal is put on Your decree,*
remember Your beloved [people] for beneficence.

י *Let it be known that God[5] is among Jeshurun, the people close to You,*
and put me as a seal upon Your heart[6] —
between Rosh Hashanah and Yom Kippur...

Congregation, then *chazzan:*

ע *Be Your servants' guarantor for good;[7]*
command that their [sin's] stain be erased.

ז *Remember the [patriarchal] pillars of the world;[8]*
even if their merit has ended.

ר *Remember mercy amidst anger.[9]*
When the time comes to inscribe Your children['s judgment],
write it down on a tablet amongst them;
inscribe it in the Book [of Life][10] —
between Rosh Hashanah and Yom Kippur...

---

(1) Cf. *Job* 33:30. (2) *Jeremiah* 3:22. (3) *Psalms* 36:10. (4) Cf. *130:4*. (5) Cf. *I Kings* 18:36. (6) Cf. *Song of Songs* 8:6. (7) Cf. *Psalms* 119:122. (8) Cf. *I Samuel* 2:8. (9) Cf. *Habakkuk* 3:2. (10) *Isaiah* 30:8; many editions of Selichos paraphrase this verse, ... כָּתְבָהּ עַל לוּחַ אוֹתָם, *write them [Your children(?)] on a tablet...; some editions read, ...*כְּתוֹב עַל לוּחַ חוֹתָם, *write on the tablet seal...*

---

worthy, they are inscribed for death (*Rosh Hashanah* 6b).   הַשְׁלַכְנוּ רַע שְׂאוֹר — *We cast off the Evil Inclination* [lit., *the evil yeast*]. The Talmud refers to

Congregation, then *chazzan:*

בְּתַחֲנוּנִים כְּרָשׁ וְדַל, לְפָנֶיךָ קָרֵבוּ,

רְאֵה עָנְיָם מֹרֶה מְאֹד,¹ בְּלַחַץ בַּשֵּׁפֶל יֵשֵׁבוּ,

בְּיוֹם חִפּוּשׂ תַּעֲלוּמוֹת, עֶלְיוֹן בְּךָ עֵינֵיךָ יֵיטִיבוּ,

וְעַל סִפְרְךָ כֻּלָּם יִכָּתֵבוּ.²   בֵּין כֶּסֶה לֶעָשׂוֹר...

Congregation, then *chazzan:*

שׁוֹחֲרֶיךָ הַמָּצֵא לְחַנְּנָךְ עוֹמְדִים הַשְׁכֵּם,

לְבַל יָעֹז קַטֵּגוֹר בְּעֵינֶיךָ בַּל יִתְחַכֵּם,

מְלִיצִים וּפְרַקְלִיטִים בְּחַסְדְּךָ עִמָּם הַסְכֵּם,

כִּתְבוּ עַל הַיְּהוּדִים כַּטּוֹב בְּעֵינֵיכֶם.³   בֵּין כֶּסֶה לֶעָשׂוֹר...

Congregation, then *chazzan:*

הֵן רוּחַ וְלֵב עַמְּךָ שָׁבוּר וְחוֹלֶה,

הֵן חַטָּאת וְאָשָׁם וְנֶדֶר אֲשֶׁר יַפְלֶא,

אֱמוּנִים וּבֵינוּנִים חָתֹם חוֹתָם מָלֵא,

אֵלֶּה לְחַיֵּי עוֹלָם וְאֵלֶּה.⁴   בֵּין כֶּסֶה לֶעָשׂוֹר...

Congregation, then *chazzan:*

לֹא לְפִי רְאוּיִם תִּשְׁפֹּט הֲמוֹנַי,

יְשֻׁרוּן מְיַחֲדֶיךָ אַף בְּלַחַץ מוֹנַי,

גְּלִיפַת כְּתָב צַוֵּה לְשֶׁבַח וְלֹא לִגְנַאי,

מִפְתַּח פִּתּוּחֵי חוֹתָם קֹדֶשׁ לַיהוה.⁵   בֵּין כֶּסֶה לֶעָשׂוֹר...

Congregation, then *chazzan:*

לְפַתּוֹתָךְ בְּתַחַן, עֲבָדֶיךָ מַסְכִּימִים,

הַפָּתַח לָמוֹ וּזְכָר נְחוּמִים,

חַסְדְּךָ הַפְלֵא, וְהַעֲבֵר כְּתָמִים,

אֵל מֶלֶךְ יוֹשֵׁב עַל כִּסֵּא רַחֲמִים.   בֵּין כֶּסֶה לֶעָשׂוֹר...

All, while standing:

אֵל מֶלֶךְ יוֹשֵׁב עַל כִּסֵּא רַחֲמִים מִתְנַהֵג בַּחֲסִידוּת, מוֹחֵל עֲוֹנוֹת עַמּוֹ, מַעֲבִיר רִאשׁוֹן רִאשׁוֹן, מַרְבֶּה מְחִילָה לְחַטָּאִים וּסְלִיחָה לְפוֹשְׁעִים, עֹשֶׂה צְדָקוֹת עִם כָּל בָּשָׂר וָרוּחַ, לֹא כְרָעָתָם תִּגְמוֹל. ❖ אֵל הוֹרֵיתָ לָּנוּ לוֹמַר שְׁלֹשׁ עֶשְׂרֵה, וּזְכֹר לָנוּ הַיּוֹם בְּרִית שְׁלֹשׁ עֶשְׂרֵה, כְּמוֹ שֶׁהוֹדַעְתָּ לֶעָנָו מִקֶּדֶם, כְּמוֹ שֶׁכָּתוּב, וַיֵּרֶד יהוה בֶּעָנָן וַיִּתְיַצֵּב עִמּוֹ שָׁם, וַיִּקְרָא בְשֵׁם יהוה.

---

the Evil Inclination as שְׂאוֹר שֶׁבְּעִיסָה, *the yeast in the batter (Berachos* 17a), because it leavens the   heart, causing it to ferment (*Rashi*), and leading man to sin.

Congregation, then *chazzan:*

ב With supplications, like a poor man and beggar,
   they have drawn near to You;
ר see their pain, how very troubled;[1]
   how they dwell in oppression, in lowliness,
בי On the day when hidden things are searched out, O Exalted One,
   may they be found good in Your eyes,
   and may all of them be written in the Book [of Life][2] —
                    between Rosh Hashanah and Yom Kippur...

Congregation, then *chazzan:*

ש Be manifest to those who seek You, who rise at dawn to beseech You,
ל that the Adversary not become bold and not seem cogent in Your eyes.
מ In Your kindness, concur with [our angelic] advocates and defenders;
   write whatever is good in Your eyes about the Jews[3] —
                    between Rosh Hashanah and Yom Kippur...

Congregation, then *chazzan:*

ה See, Your people's spirit and heart are broken and infirm;
ה they are [their] sin- and guilt- and declared vow-offerings.
א Seal with a full seal both the steadfast and the mediocre among them
   — these are for eternal life, and these [too][4] —
                    between Rosh Hashanah and Yom Kippur...

Congregation, then *chazzan:*

ל Not according to their deserts must You judge my multitudes,
י for Jeshurun declares Your Oneness
   even when coerced by my oppressors.
ג Command that their inscription be written for praise and not shame,
מ an engraving carved like a signet rign, holy to HASHEM[5] —
                    between Rosh Hashanah and Yom Kippur...

Congregation, then *chazzan:*

ל Your servants have agreed to persuade You with supplication;
הו let [Your gates] be opened to them,
   and remember the comfort [You promised them].
   Show forth Your kindness and remove [their sins'] stains,
   O God, King Who sits on the Throne of Mercy,
                    between Rosh Hashanah and Yom Kippur...

All, while standing:

אֵל מֶלֶךְ O God, King Who sits on the throne of mercy; Who acts with
   kindness, pardons the iniquities of His people, removes [sins]
one by one, increasingly grants pardon to careless sinners and forgiveness
to rebels,Who deals righteously with every living being — You do not repay
them in accord with their evil. Chazzan – O God, You taught us to recite the
Thirteen [Attributes of Mercy], so remember for us today the covenant of
these Thirteen, as You made known to the humble one in ancient times, as
it is written: And HASHEM descended in a cloud and stood with him there,
and He called out with the Name HASHEM.

---

(1) Cf. *II Kings* 14:26. (2) *Psalms* 139:16. (3) *Esther* 8:8. (4) *Daniel* 12:2. (5) Cf. *Exodus* 39:30.

Congregation, then *chazzan*:

וַיַּעֲבֹר יהוה עַל פָּנָיו וַיִּקְרָא:

Congregation and *chazzan* (the words in bold type are recited aloud and in unison):

יהוה, יהוה, אֵל, רַחוּם, וְחַנּוּן, אֶרֶךְ אַפַּיִם, וְרַב חֶסֶד, וֶאֱמֶת, נֹצֵר חֶסֶד לָאֲלָפִים, נֹשֵׂא עָוֹן, וָפֶשַׁע, וְחַטָּאָה, **וְנַקֵּה.** וְסָלַחְתָּ לַעֲוֹנֵנוּ וּלְחַטָּאתֵנוּ וּנְחַלְתָּנוּ. סְלַח לָנוּ אָבִינוּ כִּי חָטָאנוּ, מְחַל לָנוּ מַלְכֵּנוּ כִּי פָשָׁעְנוּ. כִּי אַתָּה אֲדֹנָי טוֹב וְסַלָּח, וְרַב חֶסֶד לְכָל קֹרְאֶיךָ.

All:

אַל תִּזְכָּר לָנוּ עֲוֹנוֹת רִאשׁוֹנִים, מַהֵר יְקַדְּמוּנוּ רַחֲמֶיךָ, כִּי דַלּוֹנוּ מְאֹד.[1] חַטֹּאת נְעוּרֵינוּ וּפְשָׁעֵינוּ אַל תִּזְכּוֹר, כְּחַסְדְּךָ זְכָר לָנוּ אַתָּה, לְמַעַן טוּבְךָ יהוה.[2]

זְכוֹר רַחֲמֶיךָ יהוה וַחֲסָדֶיךָ, כִּי מֵעוֹלָם הֵמָּה.[3] זָכְרֵנוּ יהוה בִּרְצוֹן עַמֶּךָ, פָּקְדֵנוּ בִּישׁוּעָתֶךָ.[4] זְכֹר עֲדָתְךָ קָנִיתָ קֶּדֶם, גָּאַלְתָּ שֵׁבֶט נַחֲלָתֶךָ, הַר צִיּוֹן זֶה שָׁכַנְתָּ בּוֹ.[5] זְכֹר יהוה חִבַּת יְרוּשָׁלָיִם, אַהֲבַת צִיּוֹן אַל תִּשְׁכַּח לָנֶצַח.[6] אַתָּה תָקוּם תְּרַחֵם צִיּוֹן, כִּי עֵת לְחֶנְנָהּ כִּי בָא מוֹעֵד.[7] זְכֹר יהוה לִבְנֵי אֱדוֹם אֵת יוֹם יְרוּשָׁלָיִם, הָאֹמְרִים עָרוּ עָרוּ עַד הַיְסוֹד בָּהּ.[8] זְכֹר לְאַבְרָהָם לְיִצְחָק וּלְיִשְׂרָאֵל עֲבָדֶיךָ אֲשֶׁר נִשְׁבַּעְתָּ לָהֶם בָּךְ, וַתְּדַבֵּר אֲלֵהֶם, אַרְבֶּה אֶת זַרְעֲכֶם כְּכוֹכְבֵי הַשָּׁמָיִם, וְכָל הָאָרֶץ הַזֹּאת אֲשֶׁר אָמַרְתִּי אֶתֵּן לְזַרְעֲכֶם, וְנָחֲלוּ לְעוֹלָם.[9] ❖ זְכֹר לַעֲבָדֶיךָ לְאַבְרָהָם לְיִצְחָק וּלְיַעֲקֹב, אַל תֵּפֶן אֶל קְשִׁי הָעָם הַזֶּה וְאֶל רִשְׁעוֹ וְאֶל חַטָּאתוֹ.[10]

Chazzan, then congregation:

אַל נָא תָשֵׁת עָלֵינוּ חַטָּאת, אֲשֶׁר נוֹאַלְנוּ וַאֲשֶׁר חָטָאנוּ.[11]

Chazzan, then congregation:

חָטָאנוּ צוּרֵנוּ, סְלַח לָנוּ יוֹצְרֵנוּ.

סליחה פה (חטאנו)

All:

אָרִיד בְּשִׂיחִי,*[12] בְּשִׂיחִי לְגוֹחִי, לְגוֹחִי בַּהֲשִׂיחִי,[13] כִּי אִם בְּרוּחִי.[14] **בְּרוּחִי** בִּלְשׁוֹנִי, בִּלְשׁוֹנִי עֶלְבּוֹנִי, עֶלְבּוֹנִי לְקוֹנִי, נֶחַר גְּרוֹנִי.[15]

---

§ **אָרִיד בְּשִׂיחִי** — *I delve deep in my prayer.* The first twenty-two stanzas of this intricately woven *selichah* contain an alphabetical acrostic. But here the similarity to other *piyutim* ends. Each stanza   contains four two-word stiches. The initial letters of the respective stanzas form the *aleph-beis*; and the last word of each stanza is the same as the first word of the following stanza. The second word of

Congregation, then chazzan:

And HASHEM passed before him [Moses] and proclaimed:

Congregation and chazzan (the words in bold type are recited aloud and in unison):

ה' ה' HASHEM, HASHEM, God, Compassionate and Gracious, Slow to anger, and Abundant in Kindness and Truth, Preserver of kindness for thousands [of generations], Forgiver of iniquity, willful sin, and error, and Who cleanses. *May You forgive our iniquities and our errors and make us Your heritage. Forgive us, our Father, for we have erred; pardon us, our King, for we have willfully sinned; for You, my Lord, are good and forgiving and abundantly kind to all who call upon You.*

All:

אַל תִּזְכָּר *Do not recall against us the iniquities of the ancients; speedily — let Your mercy come to meet us for we have fallen very low.*[1] *Remember not the sins of our youth and our rebellions; may You remember for us [the deeds] worthy of Your kindness, because of Your goodness, HASHEM.*[2]

זְכוֹר רַחֲמֶיךָ *Remember Your mercies, O HASHEM, and Your kindnesses, for they are from the beginning of the world.*[3] *Remember us, HASHEM, when You show Your people favor and recall us with Your salvation.*[4] *Remember Your congregation that You acquired of old, that You redeemed the tribe of Your heritage, and this Mount Zion where You dwelled.*[5] *Remember, O HASHEM, the affection of Jerusalem, may You never forget the love of Zion.*[6] *You will arise and show Zion mercy, for it is the time to be gracious to her, for the appointed time will have come.*[7] *Remember, HASHEM, for the offspring of Edom, the day of Jerusalem — for those who said: 'Destroy! Destroy to its very foundation!'*[8] *Remember Abraham, Isaac, and Israel, Your servants, to whom You swore by Your Being, saying to them, 'I shall increase your offspring like the stars of the heavens; and this entire land of which I spoke I will give to your offspring and they will inherit it forever.'*[9] *Chazzan — Remember for Your servants, for Abraham, for Isaac, and for Jacob; ignore the stubbornness of this people, its wickedness and its sinfulness.*[10]

Chazzan, then congregation:

Please, do not reckon for us a sin,
what we have done foolishly and what we have sinned.[11]

Chazzan, then congregation:

We have erred, our Rock! Forgive us, our Molder!

SELICHAH 85

All:

א *I delve deep in my prayer,**[12] *in my prayer to my Creator;*
  to my Creator I bow[13] *but with my spirit!*[14]

ב *With my spirit, with my tongue, with my tongue is my shame,*
  my shame before my Master — raw is my throat.[15]

---

(1) *Psalms* 79:8. (2) Cf. 25:7. (3) 25:6. (4) Cf. 106:4. (5) 74:2. (6) This is not a Scriptural verse. (7) *Psalms* 102:14. (8) 137:7. (9) *Exodus* 32:13. (10) *Deuteronomy* 9:27. (11) *Numbers* 12:11. (12) *Psalms* 55:3. (13) Some editions read, בְּחַשִׂיחִי, *as I say* [or, *pray*]. (14) *Zechariah* 4:6. (15) *Psalms* 69:4.

גְּרוֹנִי וּשְׂפָתַיִם, וּשְׂפָתַיִם בִּשְׁתַּיִם,

בִּשְׁתַּיִם נְתִיבוֹתַיִם, נְתִיבוֹתַיִם דְּלָתַיִם.[1]

דְּלָתַיִם לִתְשׁוּבָה, לִתְשׁוּבָה מְשׁוּבָה,

מְשׁוּבָה וּמְשׁוּבָבָה, הֲבַת הַשּׁוֹבֵבָה.[2]

חָטָאנוּ צוּרֵנוּ, סְלַח לָנוּ יוֹצְרֵנוּ.

הַשּׁוֹבֵבָה נַעֲוֵית, נַעֲוֵית וְנִדְוֵית,

נִדְוֵית (וְנִכְוֵית, וְנִכְוֵית) וְנִתְוֵית, לַאֲבַדּוֹן וָמָוֶת.[3]

וָמָוֶת וְצוּקָה, וְצוּקָה מְצִיקָה, מְצִיקָה הֶחֱזִיקָה, וַתֵּלֶךְ הָלוֹךְ וְזָעֲקָה.[4]

זָעֲקָה מִגַּעֲרָתֶךָ, מִגַּעֲרָתֶךָ וְקִנְאָתֶךָ,

וְקִנְאָתֶךָ וּגְבוּרָתֶךָ, סָמְכָה חֲמָתֶךָ.[5]

חֲמָתֶךָ מָלְאָה, מָלְאָה וְנִלְאָה, נִלְאָה נִכְאָה, אַף הִיא טְמֵאָה.[6]

חָטָאנוּ צוּרֵנוּ, סְלַח לָנוּ יוֹצְרֵנוּ.

טְמֵאָה כִּצְרוּעָה, כִּצְרוּעָה פְּרוּעָה,

פְּרוּעָה מֵרֵעָה, וְהִיא לֹא יָדֵעָה.[7]

יָדֵעָה וְנֶאֱלָמָה, נֶאֱלָמָה נֶעֱלָמָה, נֶעֱלָמָה חָכְמָה, כִּסַּתָּה כְלִמָּה.[8]

כְּלִמָּה וְחֶרְפָּה, וְחֶרְפָּה פְּרוּפָה, פְּרוּפָה צְרוּפָה, הָיְתָה לִשְׂרֵפָה.[9]

לִשְׂרֵפָה חֲבוּשָׁה, חֲבוּשָׁה רְטוּשָׁה,

רְטוּשָׁה נְטוּשָׁה, גְּרוּשָׁה מֵאִישָׁה.[10]

חָטָאנוּ צוּרֵנוּ, סְלַח לָנוּ יוֹצְרֵנוּ.

מֵאִישָׁה לְבִזָּיוֹן, לְבִזָּיוֹן וְכִלָּיוֹן, וְכִלָּיוֹן בְּצִיּוֹן, לֹא תוּכַל נִקָּיוֹן.[11]

נִקָּיוֹן וְכַפָּרָה, כַּפָּרָה מַחְסָרָה, מַחְסָרָה מִגְרָה, כִּפָּרָה סוֹרֲרָה.[12]

סוֹרֲרָה בְּבַעֲלָה, בְּבַעֲלָה מַעֲלָה, מַעֲלָה מְעִילָה, וְאֵין דֵּי עוֹלָה.[13]

עוֹלָה וּמִנְחָה, מִנְחָה זְנוּחָה, זְנוּחָה נֶאֱנָחָה, בְּמִכְנֶה פָּרְחָה.[14]

חָטָאנוּ צוּרֵנוּ, סְלַח לָנוּ יוֹצְרֵנוּ.

פָּרְחָה טְמֵאָה, טְמֵאָה וְקִנְאָה, וְקִנְאָה תַּקְנִיאָה, לְךָ צָמְאָה.[15]

צָמְאָה נַפְשִׁי, נַפְשִׁי לְהַנְפִּישִׁי, לְהַנְפִּישִׁי מַרְפְּשִׁי, אֱלֹהֵי קְדוֹשִׁי.[16]

קְדוֹשִׁי וּמוֹשִׁיעִי, מוֹשִׁיעִי מְמַרְשִׁיעִי,

מִמַּרְשִׁיעִי תְּשַׁעְשְׁעִי, יְהוֹה רוֹעִי.[17]

the first stich and the first word of the second are identical. Likewise, the second word of the second stich is the same as the first word of the third stich. The fourth stich is a Scriptural fragment.

This pattern changes slightly in the penulti-mate stanza, which contain the *paytan's* signature — יִצְחָק בַּר יָקָר, *Yitzchak bar Yakar* — and about whom nothing certain is known. He is thought to have lived in Germany sometime before 1300.

ג My throat and lips, lips going two ways;
   two ways [good and bad,] two paths, two paths with two doors.[1]

ד Doors to repentance, to repentance for rebellion,
   for rebellion and for the rebellious, the wayward daughter.[2]

   We have sinned, our Rock! Forgive us, our Molder!

ה The wayward daughter has become perverted,
   perverted and anguished, anguished (and burning,
   burning) and marked for destruction and death.[3]

ו Death and torment, torment [and] agony,
   agony seized her, and she went her way in crying.[4]

ז Crying from Your rebuke; from Your rebuke and Your jealousy;
   and Your jealously and Your might weighed down Your wrath.[5]

ח Your wrath is full, full and exhausting,
   exhausting and crushing, and even contaminated.[6]

   We have sinned, our Rock! Forgive us, our Molder!

ט Contaminated like a leper, like a leper unkempt,
   unkempt from her evil, [of sin] she was not aware.[7]

י Aware [perhaps,] but silent, silent and forgetting,
   forgetting wisdom, covered with shame.[8]

כ Shame and humiliation; humiliation surrounding [her],
   surrounding her and attached, to be put to the burning.[9]

ל To the burning, imprisoned, imprisoned and forsaken;
   forsaken and abandoned, separated from her Husband.[10]

   We have sinned, our Rock! Forgive us, our Molder!

מ From her Husband to degradation, from degradation to devastation;
   devastation in the dry land [of Exile],
   where she cannot attain cleansing.[11]

נ Cleansing and atonement; atonement that is lacking,
   lacking, estranged, like a cow that is stubborn.[12]

ס Stubborn to her husband, her husband she betrayed,
   she betrayed a betrayal,
   for which there is no sufficient olah-offering.[13]

ע Olah-offering and flour-offering — flour-offering abandoned,
   abandoned, sighing, leperous sores spreading.[14]

   We have sinned, our Rock! Forgive us, our Molder!

פ Spreading contamination, contamination and jealousy;
   jealousy air on her behalf, because for You she thirsts![15]

צ She thirsts, my soul, my soul longs for respite,
   respite from the muck [of my sins], O my God, my Holy One![16]

ק My Holy One, my Savior, my Savior from those who harm me;
   from those who harm me give me pleasure, HASHEM, my Shepherd![17]

---

(1) Some editions read לְפָנָיו דְּלָתַיִם, before him two doors; Isaiah 45:1. (2) Jeremiah 31:21.
(3) Job 28:22. (4) II Samuel 13:19. (5) Psalms 88:5. (6) This line has been censored in all the
Lithuanian editions; therefore it is not a Scriptural fragment as expected; the original reads,
עַל אֲדָמָה טְמֵאָה, upon contaminated soil; Amos 7:17. (7) Hosea 2:10. (8) Jeremiah 51:51.
(9) Cf. Isaiah 9:4. (10) Leviticus 21:7. (11) Cf. Hosea 8:5. (12) 4:16. (13) Cf. Isaiah 40:16.
(14) Leviticus 13:25. (15) Cf. Psalms 63:2. (16) Habakkuk 1:12. (17) Psalms 23:1.

רוֹעִי וְאֵלִי, וְאֵלִי וּמַצִּילִי, וּמַצִּילִי תַנְחִילִי, כַּרְמִי שֶׁלִּי.[1] חֲטָאנוּ צוּרֵנוּ, סְלַח לָנוּ יוֹצְרֵנוּ.

שֶׁלִּי וְשֶׁלָּךְ, וְשֶׁלָּךְ לְמוּלָךְ, לְמוּלָךְ נָאֲצוּ לָךְ, וּלְשׁוֹנָם תְּהַלָּךְ.[2] תְּהַלָּךְ גָּזַרְתָּ, גָּזַרְתָּ הֶעֱבַרְתָּ, הֶעֱבַרְתָּ וְיִתַּרְתָּ, עַם זוּ יָצַרְתָּ.[3] ❖ יָצַרְתָּ **חֹק** לִי, בָּרֵר יְשַׁר מִלּוּלִי, מִלּוּלִי לְאֵלִי. אֱלֹהִים אֲדֹנָי חֵילִי.[4] חֵילִי חַזְּקֵנוּ, חַזְּקֵנוּ **וְאַמְּצֵנוּ**, וְאַמְּצֵנוּ מַלְכֵּנוּ, יהוה מְחוֹקְקֵנוּ.[5] חֲטָאנוּ צוּרֵנוּ, סְלַח לָנוּ יוֹצְרֵנוּ.

All:

זְכוֹר לָנוּ בְּרִית אָבוֹת, כַּאֲשֶׁר אָמַרְתָּ: וְזָכַרְתִּי אֶת בְּרִיתִי יַעֲקוֹב, וְאַף אֶת בְּרִיתִי יִצְחָק, וְאַף אֶת בְּרִיתִי אַבְרָהָם אֶזְכֹּר, וְהָאָרֶץ אֶזְכֹּר.[6]

זְכוֹר לָנוּ בְּרִית רִאשׁוֹנִים כַּאֲשֶׁר אָמַרְתָּ, וְזָכַרְתִּי לָהֶם בְּרִית רִאשׁוֹנִים, אֲשֶׁר הוֹצֵאתִי אוֹתָם מֵאֶרֶץ מִצְרַיִם לְעֵינֵי הַגּוֹיִם, לִהְיוֹת לָהֶם לֵאלֹהִים אֲנִי יהוה.[7] עָשֶׂה עִמָּנוּ כְּמָה שֶׁהִבְטַחְתָּנוּ: וְאַף גַּם זֹאת בִּהְיוֹתָם בְּאֶרֶץ אֹיְבֵיהֶם, לֹא מְאַסְתִּים וְלֹא גְעַלְתִּים לְכַלֹּתָם לְהָפֵר בְּרִיתִי אִתָּם, כִּי אֲנִי יהוה אֱלֹהֵיהֶם.[8] הִמָּצֵא לָנוּ בְּבַקָּשָׁתֵנוּ, כְּמָה שֶׁכָּתוּב: וּבִקַּשְׁתֶּם מִשָּׁם אֶת יהוה אֱלֹהֶיךָ וּמָצָאתָ, כִּי תִדְרְשֶׁנּוּ בְּכָל לְבָבְךָ וּבְכָל נַפְשֶׁךָ.[9] מוֹל אֶת לְבָבֵנוּ לְאַהֲבָה וּלְיִרְאָה אֶת שְׁמֶךָ, כְּמָה שֶׁכָּתוּב: וּמָל יהוה אֱלֹהֶיךָ אֶת לְבָבְךָ וְאֶת לְבַב זַרְעֶךָ, לְאַהֲבָה אֶת יהוה אֱלֹהֶיךָ בְּכָל לְבָבְךָ וּבְכָל נַפְשְׁךָ, לְמַעַן חַיֶּיךָ.[10] זְרוֹק עָלֵינוּ מַיִם טְהוֹרִים וְטַהֲרֵנוּ, כְּמָה שֶׁכָּתוּב: וְזָרַקְתִּי עֲלֵיכֶם מַיִם טְהוֹרִים וּטְהַרְתֶּם, מִכֹּל טֻמְאוֹתֵיכֶם וּמִכֹּל גִּלּוּלֵיכֶם אֲטַהֵר אֶתְכֶם.[11] מְחֵה פְשָׁעֵינוּ כָּעָב וְכֶעָנָן, כְּמָה שֶׁכָּתוּב: מָחִיתִי כָעָב פְּשָׁעֶיךָ וְכֶעָנָן חַטֹּאתֶיךָ, שׁוּבָה אֵלַי כִּי גְאַלְתִּיךָ.[12] מְחֵה פְשָׁעֵינוּ לְמַעַנְךָ, כַּאֲשֶׁר אָמַרְתָּ: אָנֹכִי אָנֹכִי הוּא מֹחֶה פְשָׁעֶיךָ לְמַעֲנִי, וְחַטֹּאתֶיךָ לֹא אֶזְכֹּר.[13] הַלְבֵּן חֲטָאֵינוּ כַּשֶּׁלֶג וְכַצֶּמֶר, כְּמָה שֶׁכָּתוּב: לְכוּ נָא וְנִוָּכְחָה, יֹאמַר יהוה, אִם יִהְיוּ חֲטָאֵיכֶם כַּשָּׁנִים, כַּשֶּׁלֶג יַלְבִּינוּ, אִם יַאְדִּימוּ כַתּוֹלָע, כַּצֶּמֶר יִהְיוּ.[14] רַחֵם עָלֵינוּ וְאַל תַּשְׁחִיתֵנוּ, כְּמָה שֶׁכָּתוּב: כִּי אֵל רַחוּם יהוה

---

(1) *Song of Songs* 1:6; 8:12. (2) *Psalms* 73:9. (3) Cf. *Isaiah* 43:21. (4) *Habakkuk* 3:19.
(5) *Isaiah* 33:22. (6) *Leviticus* 26:42. (7) 26:45. (8) 26:44.
(9) *Deuteronomy* 4:29. (10) 30:6. (11) *Ezekiel* 36:25. (12) *Isaiah* 44:22. (13) 43:25. (14) 1:18.

ר My Shepherd and my God, My God and my Rescuer,
   My Rescuer grant me my inheritance, the vineyard that is mine.¹
                    We have sinned, our Rock! Forgive us, our Molder!
ש Mine and Yours, Yours is before You;
   before You have they blasphemed You, their tongues on the move.²
ת On the move, You split [the Sea];
   You split [the Sea] and You passed [them] across;
   You passed them across and elevated them,
   this people You have created.³
   You have fashioned a decree for me,
   to choose the precious words in my prayer, my prayer to my God,
   God, my Lord, my Strength.⁴
   My Strength, strengthen us!
   Strengthen us and give us courage; give us courage, our King,
   HASHEM, our Lawgiver.⁵
                    We have sinned, our Rock! Forgive us, our Molder!

                                    All:

זְכוֹר לָנוּ Remember for us the covenant of the Patriarchs, as You
            said: 'And I will remember My covenant with Jacob, and
also My covenant with Isaac, and also My covenant with Abraham will
I remember; and the Land will I remember.'⁶

זְכוֹר לָנוּ Remember for us the covenant of the ancestors, as You said:
            'And I will remember for them the covenant of the ancestors
whom I brought out of the land of Egypt in the very sight of the nations,
to be a God to them; I am HASHEM.'⁷ Do with us as You promised us:
'And despite all that, when they will be in the land of their enemies, I
will not have despised them nor abhorred them to destroy them, to
annul My covenant with them, for I am HASHEM their God.'⁸ Be
accessible to us in our quest, as it is written: From there you will seek
HASHEM, your God, and you will find, when you search for Him with
all your heart and with all your soul.⁹ Expose our hearts to love
Your Name, as it is written: HASHEM, your God, will expose your heart
and the heart of your offspring, to love HASHEM, your God, with all your
heart and with all your soul, that you may live.¹⁰ Pour pure water upon us
and purify us, as it is written: I shall pour pure water upon you and purify
you, of all your contaminations and of all your abominations I will purify
you.¹¹ Wipe away our willful sins like a cloud and like a mist, as it is
written: I have wiped away your willful sins like a cloud and your errors
like a mist — repent to Me, for I have redeemed you!¹² Wipe away our
willful sins for Your sake, as You said: 'I, only I, am the One Who wipes
away your willful sins for My sake, and I shall not recall your errors.'¹³
Whiten our errors like snow and like [pure white] wool, as it is written:
'Come now, let us reason together,' says HASHEM, 'though your errors
will be like scarlet, they will become white as snow; though they will
be red as crimson, they will become like [white] wool.'¹⁴ Have mercy on
us and do not destroy us, as it is written: For a merciful God is HASHEM,

אֱלֹהֶיךָ, לֹא יַרְפְּךָ וְלֹא יַשְׁחִיתֶךָ וְלֹא יִשְׁכַּח אֶת בְּרִית אֲבוֹתֶיךָ
אֲשֶׁר נִשְׁבַּע לָהֶם.¹ קַבֵּץ נִדָּחֵינוּ כְּמָה שֶׁכָּתוּב: אִם יִהְיֶה נִדַּחֲךָ בִּקְצֵה
הַשָּׁמָיִם, מִשָּׁם יְקַבֶּצְךָ יהוה אֱלֹהֶיךָ וּמִשָּׁם יִקָּחֶךָ.² הָשֵׁב שְׁבוּתֵנוּ
וְרַחֲמֵנוּ, כְּמָה שֶׁכָּתוּב: וְשָׁב יהוה אֱלֹהֶיךָ אֶת שְׁבוּתְךָ וְרִחֲמֶךָ וְשָׁב
וְקִבֶּצְךָ מִכָּל הָעַמִּים אֲשֶׁר הֱפִיצְךָ יהוה אֱלֹהֶיךָ שָׁמָּה.³ ❖ תְּבִיאֵנוּ
אֶל הַר קָדְשֶׁךָ, וְשַׂמְּחֵנוּ בְּבֵית תְּפִלָּתֶךָ, כְּמָה שֶׁכָּתוּב: וַהֲבִיאוֹתִים
אֶל הַר קָדְשִׁי, וְשִׂמַּחְתִּים בְּבֵית תְּפִלָּתִי, עוֹלֹתֵיהֶם וְזִבְחֵיהֶם לְרָצוֹן
עַל מִזְבְּחִי, כִּי בֵיתִי בֵּית תְּפִלָּה יִקָּרֵא לְכָל הָעַמִּים.⁴

THE ARK IS OPENED.

The first four verses of the following prayer are recited responsively; *chazzan,* then congregation:

שְׁמַע קוֹלֵנוּ יהוה אֱלֹהֵינוּ, חוּס וְרַחֵם עָלֵינוּ,
וְקַבֵּל בְּרַחֲמִים וּבְרָצוֹן אֶת תְּפִלָּתֵנוּ.⁵
הֲשִׁיבֵנוּ יהוה אֵלֶיךָ וְנָשׁוּבָה, חַדֵּשׁ יָמֵינוּ כְּקֶדֶם.⁶
אַל תַּשְׁלִיכֵנוּ מִלְּפָנֶיךָ, וְרוּחַ קָדְשְׁךָ אַל תִּקַּח מִמֶּנּוּ.⁷
אַל תַּשְׁלִיכֵנוּ לְעֵת זִקְנָה, כִּכְלוֹת כֹּחֵנוּ אַל תַּעַזְבֵנוּ.⁸
אַל תַּעַזְבֵנוּ יהוה, אֱלֹהֵינוּ אַל תִּרְחַק מִמֶּנּוּ.⁹
עֲשֵׂה עִמָּנוּ אוֹת לְטוֹבָה, וְיִרְאוּ שׂוֹנְאֵינוּ וְיֵבֹשׁוּ,
כִּי אַתָּה יהוה עֲזַרְתָּנוּ וְנִחַמְתָּנוּ.¹⁰
אֲמָרֵינוּ הַאֲזִינָה יהוה, בִּינָה הֲגִיגֵנוּ.¹¹
יִהְיוּ לְרָצוֹן אִמְרֵי פִינוּ וְהֶגְיוֹן לִבֵּנוּ לְפָנֶיךָ, יהוה צוּרֵנוּ וְגוֹאֲלֵנוּ.¹²
כִּי לְךָ יהוה הוֹחָלְנוּ, אַתָּה תַעֲנֶה אֲדֹנָי אֱלֹהֵינוּ.¹³

THE ARK IS CLOSED.

וידוי

During the recitation of the וידוי stand with head and body slightly bowed, in submissive contrition.

אֱלֹהֵינוּ וֵאלֹהֵי אֲבוֹתֵינוּ, תָּבֹא לְפָנֶיךָ תְּפִלָּתֵנוּ,¹⁴ וְאַל תִּתְעַלַּם
מִתְּחִנָּתֵנוּ,¹⁵ שֶׁאֵין אָנוּ עַזֵּי פָנִים וּקְשֵׁי עֹרֶף, לוֹמַר
לְפָנֶיךָ יהוה אֱלֹהֵינוּ וֵאלֹהֵי אֲבוֹתֵינוּ, צַדִּיקִים אֲנַחְנוּ וְלֹא חָטָאנוּ,
אֲבָל אֲנַחְנוּ וַאֲבוֹתֵינוּ חָטָאנוּ.¹⁶

Strike the left side of the chest with the right fist
while reciting each of the sins in the following confession litany.

אָשַׁמְנוּ, בָּגַדְנוּ, גָּזַלְנוּ, דִּבַּרְנוּ דֹפִי. הֶעֱוִינוּ, וְהִרְשַׁעְנוּ, זַדְנוּ,
חָמַסְנוּ, טָפַלְנוּ שֶׁקֶר. יָעַצְנוּ רָע, כִּזַּבְנוּ, לַצְנוּ, מָרַדְנוּ,

---

(1) *Deuteronomy* 4:31. (2) 30:4. (3) 30:3. (4) *Isaiah* 56:7. (5) Weekday *Shemoneh Esrei.*
(6) *Lamentations* 5:21. (7) Cf. *Psalms* 51:13. (8) Cf. 71:9. (9) Cf. 38:22. (10) Cf. 86:17.
(11) Cf. 5:2. (12) Cf. 19:15. (13) Cf. 38:16. (14) Cf. 88:3. (15) Cf. 55:2. (16) Cf. 106:6.

your God; He will not surrender you nor destroy you, and He will not forget the covenant with your forefathers, which He swore to them.[1] Gather in our dispersed ones, as it is written: If your dispersed were to be at the ends of heaven, from there HASHEM, your God, will gather you in and from there He will take you.[2] Bring back our captivity and have mercy on us, as it is written: HASHEM, your God, will bringback your captivity and have mercy on you, and He will again gather you in from all the peoples where HASHEM, your God, has scattered you.[3] Chazzan — Bring us to Your holy mountain and gladden us in Your house of prayer, as it is written: And I will bring them to My holy mountain, and I will gladden them in My house of prayer, their elevation-offerings and their feast offering will find favor on My Altar, for My House will be called a house of prayer, for all peoples.[4]

THE ARK IS OPENED.

The first four verses of the following prayer are recited responsively; chazzan, then congregation:

שְׁמַע Hear our voice, HASHEM, our God, pity and be compassionate to us, and accept — with compassion and favor — our prayer.[5]

Bring us back to You, HASHEM, and we shall return, renew our days as of old.[6]

Do not cast us away from Yourself, and do not remove Your holy spirit from us.[7]

Do not cast us away in old age, when our strength gives out do not forsake us.[8]

Do not forsake us, HASHEM, our God, be not distant from us.[9]

Display for us a sign for good, so that our enemies may see it and be ashamed, for You, HASHEM, will have helped and consoled us.[10]

To our sayings give ear, HASHEM, perceive our thoughts.[11]

May the expressions of our mouth and the thoughts of our heart find favor before You, HASHEM, our Rock and our Redeemer.[12]

Because for You, HASHEM, we waited, You will answer, my Lord, our God.[13]

THE ARK IS CLOSED.

VIDUY/CONFESSION

During the recitation of the וִדּוּי stand with head and body slightly bowed, in submissive contrition.

אֱלֹהֵינוּ Our God and the God of our forefathers, may our prayer come before You.[14] Do not ignore our supplication,[15] for we are not so brazen and obstinate as to say before You, HASHEM, our God and the God of our forefathers, that we are righteous and have not sinned, for in truth, we and our forefathers have sinned.[16]

Strike the left side of the chest with the right fist while reciting
each of the sins in the following confession litany.

אָשַׁמְנוּ We have become guilty; [ב] we have betrayed; [ג] we have robbed; [ד] we have spoken slander; [ה] we have caused perversion; [ו] we have caused wickedness; [ז] we have sinned willfully; [ח] we have extorted; [ט] we have accused falsely; [י] we have given evil counsel; [כ] we have been deceitful; [ל] we have scorned; [מ] we have

נִאַצְנוּ, סָרַרְנוּ, עָוִינוּ, פָּשַׁעְנוּ, צָרַרְנוּ, קִשִּׁינוּ עֹרֶף. רָשַׁעְנוּ, שִׁחַתְנוּ, תִּעַבְנוּ, תָּעִינוּ, תִּעְתָּעְנוּ.

סַרְנוּ מִמִּצְוֹתֶיךָ וּמִמִּשְׁפָּטֶיךָ הַטּוֹבִים וְלֹא שָׁוָה לָנוּ.[1] וְאַתָּה צַדִּיק עַל כָּל הַבָּא עָלֵינוּ, כִּי אֱמֶת עָשִׂיתָ וַאֲנַחְנוּ הִרְשָׁעְנוּ.[2]

אָשַׁמְנוּ מִכָּל עָם, בּשְׁנוּ מִכָּל דּוֹר, גָּלָה מִמֶּנּוּ מָשׂוֹשׂ, דָּוָה לִבֵּנוּ בַּחֲטָאֵינוּ, הֻחַבַּל אֲוֵּינוּ, וְנִפְרַע פְּאֵרֵנוּ, זְבוּל בֵּית מִקְדָּשֵׁנוּ חָרֵב בַּעֲוֹנֵינוּ, טִירָתֵנוּ הָיְתָה לְשַׁמָּה, יְפִי אַדְמָתֵנוּ לְזָרִים, כֹּחֵנוּ לְנָכְרִים.

וַעֲדַיִן לֹא שַׁבְנוּ מִטָּעוּתֵנוּ וְהֵיךְ נָעִיז פָּנֵינוּ וְנַקְשֶׁה עָרְפֵּנוּ, לוֹמַר לְפָנֶיךָ יהוה אֱלֹהֵינוּ וֵאלֹהֵי אֲבוֹתֵינוּ, צַדִּיקִים אֲנַחְנוּ וְלֹא חָטָאנוּ, אֲבָל אֲנַחְנוּ וַאֲבוֹתֵינוּ חָטָאנוּ.

Strike the left side of the chest with the right fist while reciting
each of the sins in the following confession litany.

אָשַׁמְנוּ, בָּגַדְנוּ, גָּזַלְנוּ, דִּבַּרְנוּ דֹפִי. הֶעֱוִינוּ, וְהִרְשַׁעְנוּ, זַדְנוּ, חָמַסְנוּ, טָפַלְנוּ שֶׁקֶר. יָעַצְנוּ רָע, כִּזַּבְנוּ, לַצְנוּ, מָרַדְנוּ, נִאַצְנוּ, סָרַרְנוּ, עָוִינוּ, פָּשַׁעְנוּ, צָרַרְנוּ, קִשִּׁינוּ עֹרֶף. רָשַׁעְנוּ, שִׁחַתְנוּ, תִּעַבְנוּ, תָּעִינוּ, תִּעְתָּעְנוּ.

סַרְנוּ מִמִּצְוֹתֶיךָ וּמִמִּשְׁפָּטֶיךָ הַטּוֹבִים וְלֹא שָׁוָה לָנוּ. וְאַתָּה צַדִּיק עַל כָּל הַבָּא עָלֵינוּ, כִּי אֱמֶת עָשִׂיתָ וַאֲנַחְנוּ הִרְשָׁעְנוּ.

לְעֵינֵינוּ עָשְׁקוּ עֲמָלֵנוּ, מְמֻשָּׁךְ וּמְמוֹרָט מִמֶּנּוּ, נָתְנוּ עֻלָּם עָלֵינוּ, סָבַלְנוּ עַל שִׁכְמֵנוּ, עֲבָדִים מָשְׁלוּ בָנוּ, פֹּרֵק אֵין מִיָּדָם, צָרוֹת רַבּוֹת סְבָבוּנוּ, קְרָאנוּךָ יהוה אֱלֹהֵינוּ, רָחַקְתָּ מִמֶּנּוּ בַּעֲוֹנֵינוּ, שַׁבְנוּ מֵאַחֲרֶיךָ, תָּעִינוּ וְאָבָדְנוּ.

וַעֲדַיִן לֹא שַׁבְנוּ מִטָּעוּתֵנוּ וְהֵיךְ נָעִיז פָּנֵינוּ וְנַקְשֶׁה עָרְפֵּנוּ, לוֹמַר לְפָנֶיךָ יהוה אֱלֹהֵינוּ וֵאלֹהֵי אֲבוֹתֵינוּ, צַדִּיקִים אֲנַחְנוּ וְלֹא חָטָאנוּ, אֲבָל אֲנַחְנוּ וַאֲבוֹתֵינוּ חָטָאנוּ.

---

(1) Cf. *Job* 33:27. (2) *Nehemiah* 9:33.

rebelled; [נ] we have provoked; [ס] we have turned away; [ע] we have been perverse; [פ] we have acted wantonly; [צ] we have persecuted; [ק] we have been obstinate; [ר] we have been wicked; [ש] we have corrupted; [ת] we have been abominable; we have strayed; You have let us go astray.

סַרְנוּ We have turned away from Your commandments and from Your good laws but to no avail.¹ Yet You are righteous in all that has come upon us, for You have acted truthfully while we have caused wickedness.²

[א] We have become the guiltiest of people. [ב] We have become the most degraded of all generations. [ג] Joy has departed from us. [ד] Our heart has been saddened by our sins. [ה] Our desirous treasure has been ruined, [ו] and our splendor dashed, [ז] for our Holy Temple edifice [ח] has been destroyed for our iniquities. [ט] Our Palace has become desolate. [י] [Jerusalem,] the beauty of our Land is given over to aliens, [כ] our power to strangers.

But still we have not returned from our waywardness. So how can we be so brazen and obstinate as to say before You, HASHEM, our God and the God of our forefathers, that we are righteous and have not sinned, for in truth, both we and our fathers have sinned.

Strike the left side of the chest with the right fist while reciting
each of the sins in the following confession litany.

אָשַׁמְנוּ We have become guilty; [ב] we have betrayed; [ג] we have robbed; [ד] we have spoken slander; [ה] we have caused perversion; [ו] we have caused wickedness; [ז] we have sinned willfully; [ח] we have extorted; [ט] we have accused falsely; [י] we have given evil counsel; [כ] we have been deceitful; [ל] we have scorned; [מ] we have rebelled; [נ] we have provoked; [ס] we have turned away; [ע] we have been perverse; [פ] we have acted wantonly; [צ] we have persecuted; [ק] we have been obstinate; [ר] we have been wicked; [ש] we have corrupted; [ת] we have been abominable; we have strayed; You have let us go astray.

סַרְנוּ We have turned away from Your commandments and from Your good laws but to no avail. Yet You are righteous in all that has come upon us, for You have acted truthfully while we have caused wickedness.

[ל] [The benefit of] our labor has been stolen, [מ] pulled away and cut off from us. [נ] They have placed their yoke upon us, [ס] our burdens upon our shoulders. [ע] Slaves have ruled over us, [פ] there is no redemption from their hand. [צ] Abundant troubles have surrounded us, [ק] we called upon You, HASHEM, our God, [ר] but You have distanced us for our iniquities. [ש] We have turned away from following after You; [ת] we have strayed; we have become lost.

But still we have not returned from our waywardness. So how can we be so brazen and obstinate as to say before You, HASHEM, our God and the God of our forefathers, that we are righteous and have not sinned, for in truth, both we and our fathers have sinned.

Strike the left side of the chest with the right fist while reciting
each of the sins in the following confession litany.

אָשַׁמְנוּ, בָּגַדְנוּ, גָּזַלְנוּ, דִּבַּרְנוּ דְפִי. הֶעֱוִינוּ, וְהִרְשַׁעְנוּ, זַדְנוּ, חָמַסְנוּ, טָפַלְנוּ שֶׁקֶר. יָעַצְנוּ רָע, כִּזַּבְנוּ, לַצְנוּ, מָרַדְנוּ, נִאַצְנוּ, סָרַרְנוּ, עָוִינוּ, פָּשַׁעְנוּ, צָרַרְנוּ, קִשִּׁינוּ עֹרֶף. רָשַׁעְנוּ, שִׁחַתְנוּ, תִּעַבְנוּ, תָּעִינוּ, תִּעְתָּעְנוּ.

סַרְנוּ מִמִּצְוֹתֶיךָ וּמִמִּשְׁפָּטֶיךָ הַטּוֹבִים וְלֹא שָׁוָה לָנוּ. וְאַתָּה צַדִּיק עַל כָּל הַבָּא עָלֵינוּ, כִּי אֱמֶת עָשִׂיתָ וַאֲנַחְנוּ הִרְשָׁעְנוּ.

הִרְשַׁעְנוּ וּפָשַׁעְנוּ, לָכֵן לֹא נוֹשָׁעְנוּ. וְתֵן בְּלִבֵּנוּ לַעֲזוֹב דֶּרֶךְ רֶשַׁע, וְחִישׁ לָנוּ יֶשַׁע, כַּכָּתוּב עַל יַד נְבִיאֶךָ: יַעֲזֹב רָשָׁע דַּרְכּוֹ, וְאִישׁ אָוֶן מַחְשְׁבֹתָיו, וְיָשֹׁב אֶל יהוה וִירַחֲמֵהוּ, וְאֶל אֱלֹהֵינוּ כִּי יַרְבֶּה לִסְלוֹחַ.[1]

מָשִׁיחַ צִדְקֶךָ אָמַר לְפָנֶיךָ: שְׁגִיאוֹת מִי יָבִין מִנִּסְתָּרוֹת נַקֵּנִי.[2] נַקֵּנוּ יהוה אֱלֹהֵינוּ מִכָּל פְּשָׁעֵינוּ, וְטַהֲרֵנוּ מִכָּל טֻמְאוֹתֵינוּ, וּזְרוֹק עָלֵינוּ מַיִם טְהוֹרִים וְטַהֲרֵנוּ, כַּכָּתוּב עַל יַד נְבִיאֶךָ: וְזָרַקְתִּי עֲלֵיכֶם מַיִם טְהוֹרִים וּטְהַרְתֶּם, מִכֹּל טֻמְאוֹתֵיכֶם וּמִכָּל גִּלּוּלֵיכֶם אֲטַהֵר אֶתְכֶם.[3]

מִיכָה עַבְדְּךָ אָמַר לְפָנֶיךָ: מִי אֵל כָּמוֹךָ נֹשֵׂא עָוֹן וְעֹבֵר עַל פֶּשַׁע לִשְׁאֵרִית נַחֲלָתוֹ, לֹא הֶחֱזִיק לָעַד אַפּוֹ, כִּי חָפֵץ חֶסֶד הוּא, יָשׁוּב יְרַחֲמֵנוּ, יִכְבֹּשׁ עֲוֹנוֹתֵינוּ, וְתַשְׁלִיךְ בִּמְצֻלוֹת יָם כָּל חַטֹּאתָם.[4] (וְכָל חַטֹּאת עַמְּךָ בֵּית יִשְׂרָאֵל תַּשְׁלִיךְ בִּמְקוֹם אֲשֶׁר לֹא יִזָּכְרוּ, וְלֹא יִפָּקְדוּ, וְלֹא יַעֲלוּ עַל לֵב לְעוֹלָם.) תִּתֵּן אֱמֶת לְיַעֲקֹב חֶסֶד לְאַבְרָהָם אֲשֶׁר נִשְׁבַּעְתָּ לַאֲבוֹתֵינוּ מִימֵי קֶדֶם.[5]

דָּנִיֵּאל אִישׁ חֲמוּדוֹת שִׁוַּע לְפָנֶיךָ: הַטֵּה אֱלֹהַי אָזְנְךָ וּשְׁמָע, פְּקַח עֵינֶיךָ וּרְאֵה שֹׁמְמֹתֵינוּ וְהָעִיר אֲשֶׁר נִקְרָא שִׁמְךָ עָלֶיהָ, כִּי לֹא עַל צִדְקֹתֵינוּ אֲנַחְנוּ מַפִּילִים תַּחֲנוּנֵינוּ לְפָנֶיךָ, כִּי עַל רַחֲמֶיךָ הָרַבִּים. אֲדֹנָי שְׁמָעָה, אֲדֹנָי סְלָחָה, אֲדֹנָי הַקְשִׁיבָה, וַעֲשֵׂה אַל תְּאַחַר, לְמַעַנְךָ אֱלֹהַי, כִּי שִׁמְךָ נִקְרָא עַל עִירְךָ וְעַל עַמֶּךָ.[6]

---

(1) Isaiah 55:7. (2) Psalms 19:13. (3) Ezekiel 36:25. (4) Micah 7:18-19. (5) 7:20. (6) Daniel 9:18-19.

Strike the left side of the chest with the right fist while reciting
each of the sins in the following confession litany:

אָשַׁמְנוּ We have become guilty; [ב] we have betrayed; [ג] we have
robbed; [ד] we have spoken slander; [ה] we have caused
perversion; [ו] we have caused wickedness; [ז] we have sinned willfully;
[ח] we have extorted; [ט] we have accused falsely; [י] we have given evil
counsel; [כ] we have been deceitful; [ל] we have scorned; [מ] we have
rebelled; [נ] we have provoked; [ס] we have turned away; [ע] we have been
perverse; [פ] we have acted wantonly; [צ] we have persecuted; [ק] we have
been obstinate; [ר] we have been wicked; [ש] we have corrupted; [ת] we
have been abominable; we have strayed; You have let us go astray.

סַרְנוּ We have turned away from Your commandments and from Your
good laws but to no avail. Yet You are righteous in all that has
come upon us, for You have acted truthfully while we have caused
wickedness.

הִרְשַׁעְנוּ We have acted wickedly and have sinned willfully, therefore we have not been saved. Inspire our heart to abandon the
path of evil and hasten salvation for us, as it is written by Your prophet:
May the wicked one abandon his way and the vicious man his thoughts;
may he return to HASHEM and He will show him mercy, and to our God, for
He is abundantly forgiving.[1]

מָשִׁיחַ Your righteous anointed [David] said before You: 'Who can discern
mistakes? From unperceived faults cleanse me.'[2] Cleanse us,
HASHEM, our God, of all our willful sins and purify us, of all our contaminations. Sprinkle upon us pure water and purify us, as it is written by Your
prophet: I shall sprinkle pure water upon you and purify you, of all your
contaminations and of all your abominations I will purify you.'[3]

מִיכָה עַבְדְּךָ Micah, Your servant, said before You: 'Who, O God, is like
You, Who pardons iniquity and overlooks transgression for
the remnant of His heritage? Who has not retained His wrath eternally, for
He desires kindness! He will again be merciful to us; He will suppress our
iniquities and cast into the depths of the sea all their sins.[4] (And all the sins
of Your nation the Family of Israel, may You cast away to a place where
they will neither be remembered, considered, nor brought to mind — ever.)
Grant truth to Jacob, kindness to Abraham, as You swore to our forefathers
from ancient times.'[5]

דָּנִיֵּאל Daniel, the greatly beloved man, cried out before You: 'Incline,
my God, Your ear, and listen, open Your eyes and see our
desolation and that of the city upon which Your Name is proclaimed, for
not because of our righteousness do we cast down our supplications before
You, rather because of Your abundant compassion. O my Lord, heed; O my
Lord, forgive; O my Lord, be attentive and act, do not delay; for Your sake,
my God, for Your Name is proclaimed upon Your city and Your people.'[6]

עֶזְרָא הַסּוֹפֵר אָמַר לְפָנֶיךָ: אֱלֹהַי, בְּשְׁתִּי וְנִכְלַמְתִּי לְהָרִים,
אֱלֹהַי, פָּנַי אֵלֶיךָ, כִּי עֲוֹנֹתֵינוּ רָבוּ לְמַעְלָה
רֹאשׁ, וְאַשְׁמָתֵנוּ גָדְלָה עַד לַשָּׁמָיִם.¹ וְאַתָּה² אֱלוֹהַּ סְלִיחוֹת, חַנּוּן
וְרַחוּם, אֶרֶךְ אַפַּיִם וְרַב חֶסֶד, וְלֹא עֲזַבְתָּנוּ.³

אַל תַּעַזְבֵנוּ אָבִינוּ וְאַל תִּטְּשֵׁנוּ בּוֹרְאֵנוּ, וְאַל תַּזְנִיחֵנוּ
יוֹצְרֵנוּ, וְאַל תַּעַשׂ עִמָּנוּ כָּלָה כְּחַטֹּאתֵינוּ. וְקַיֵּם
לָנוּ יהוה אֱלֹהֵינוּ, אֶת הַדָּבָר שֶׁהִבְטַחְתָּנוּ בְּקַבָּלָה עַל יְדֵי יִרְמְיָהוּ
חוֹזָךְ, כָּאָמוּר: בַּיָּמִים הָהֵם וּבָעֵת הַהִיא, נְאֻם יהוה, יְבֻקַּשׁ אֶת עֲוֹן
יִשְׂרָאֵל וְאֵינֶנּוּ וְאֶת חַטֹּאת יְהוּדָה וְלֹא תִמָּצֶאנָה, כִּי אֶסְלַח
לַאֲשֶׁר אַשְׁאִיר.⁴ עַמְּךָ וְנַחֲלָתְךָ רְעֵבֵי טוּבְךָ, צְמֵאֵי חַסְדֶּךָ, תְּאֵבֵי
יִשְׁעֶךָ, יַכִּירוּ וְיֵדְעוּ כִּי לַיהוה אֱלֹהֵינוּ הָרַחֲמִים וְהַסְּלִיחוֹת.

אֵל רַחוּם שְׁמֶךָ. אֵל חַנּוּן שְׁמֶךָ. בָּנוּ נִקְרָא שְׁמֶךָ. יהוה עֲשֵׂה
לְמַעַן שְׁמֶךָ. עֲשֵׂה לְמַעַן אֲמִתֶּךָ, עֲשֵׂה לְמַעַן
בְּרִיתֶךָ, עֲשֵׂה לְמַעַן גָּדְלְךָ וְתִפְאַרְתֶּךָ, עֲשֵׂה לְמַעַן דָּתֶךָ, עֲשֵׂה
לְמַעַן הוֹדֶךָ, עֲשֵׂה לְמַעַן וְעוּדֶךָ, עֲשֵׂה לְמַעַן זִכְרֶךָ, עֲשֵׂה לְמַעַן
חַסְדֶּךָ, עֲשֵׂה לְמַעַן טוּבֶךָ, עֲשֵׂה לְמַעַן יִחוּדֶךָ, עֲשֵׂה לְמַעַן כְּבוֹדֶךָ,
עֲשֵׂה לְמַעַן לִמּוּדֶךָ, עֲשֵׂה לְמַעַן מַלְכוּתֶךָ, עֲשֵׂה לְמַעַן נִצְחֶךָ,
עֲשֵׂה לְמַעַן סוֹדֶךָ, עֲשֵׂה לְמַעַן עֻזֶּךָ, עֲשֵׂה לְמַעַן פְּאֵרֶךָ, עֲשֵׂה לְמַעַן
צִדְקָתֶךָ, עֲשֵׂה לְמַעַן קְדֻשָּׁתֶךָ, עֲשֵׂה לְמַעַן רַחֲמֶיךָ הָרַבִּים, עֲשֵׂה
לְמַעַן שְׁכִינָתֶךָ, עֲשֵׂה לְמַעַן תְּהִלָּתֶךָ, עֲשֵׂה לְמַעַן אוֹהֲבֶיךָ שׁוֹכְנֵי
עָפָר, עֲשֵׂה לְמַעַן אַבְרָהָם יִצְחָק וְיַעֲקֹב, עֲשֵׂה לְמַעַן מֹשֶׁה וְאַהֲרֹן,
עֲשֵׂה לְמַעַן דָּוִד וּשְׁלֹמֹה, עֲשֵׂה לְמַעַן יְרוּשָׁלַיִם עִיר קָדְשֶׁךָ, עֲשֵׂה
לְמַעַן צִיּוֹן מִשְׁכַּן כְּבוֹדֶךָ, עֲשֵׂה לְמַעַן שִׁמְמוֹת הֵיכָלֶךָ, עֲשֵׂה לְמַעַן
הֲרִיסוּת מִזְבְּחֶךָ, עֲשֵׂה לְמַעַן הֲרוּגִים עַל שֵׁם קָדְשֶׁךָ, עֲשֵׂה לְמַעַן
טְבוּחִים עַל יִחוּדֶךָ, עֲשֵׂה לְמַעַן בָּאֵי בָאֵשׁ וּבַמַּיִם עַל קִדּוּשׁ שְׁמֶךָ,
עֲשֵׂה לְמַעַן יוֹנְקֵי שָׁדַיִם שֶׁלֹּא חָטְאוּ, עֲשֵׂה לְמַעַן גְּמוּלֵי חָלָב שֶׁלֹּא
פָשְׁעוּ, עֲשֵׂה לְמַעַן תִּינוֹקוֹת שֶׁל בֵּית רַבָּן, עֲשֵׂה לְמַעַנְךָ אִם לֹא
לְמַעֲנֵנוּ, עֲשֵׂה לְמַעַנְךָ וְהוֹשִׁיעֵנוּ.

עֲנֵנוּ יהוה עֲנֵנוּ, עֲנֵנוּ אֱלֹהֵינוּ עֲנֵנוּ, עֲנֵנוּ אָבִינוּ עֲנֵנוּ, עֲנֵנוּ
בּוֹרְאֵנוּ עֲנֵנוּ, עֲנֵנוּ גּוֹאֲלֵנוּ עֲנֵנוּ, עֲנֵנוּ דוֹרְשֵׁנוּ עֲנֵנוּ, עֲנֵנוּ

---

(1) *Ezra* 9:6. (2) Some editions of *Selichos* insert the word אֱלֹהֵינוּ,
our God, at this point. (3) Cf. *Nehemiah* 9:17. (4) *Jeremiah* 50:20.

עֶזְרָא הַסּוֹפֵר Ezra the Scribe said before You: 'My God, I am embarrassed and ashamed to lift my face to You, my God — for our iniquities have multiplied above our heads, and our sins extend unto heaven.[1] You are[2] the God of forgiveness, compassionate and merciful, slow to anger, and abundant in kindness; and You have not forsaken us.'[3]

אַל תַּעַזְבֵנוּ Do not forsake us, our Father; do not cast us off, our Creator; do not abandon us, our Molder; and do not bring about our destruction, as our sins merit. Affirm for us, HASHEM, our God, the promise You made in the tradition through Jeremiah, Your seer, as it is said: 'In those days and at that time' — the words of HASHEM — 'the iniquity of Israel will be sought but there will be none, and the errors of Judah, but they will not be found, for I will have forgiven those whom I leave as a remnant.'[4] Your people and Your heritage, who hunger for Your goodness, who thirst for Your kindness, who long for Your salvation — may they recognize and know that to HASHEM, our God, belong mercy and forgiveness.

אֵל רַחוּם 'Merciful God' is Your Name, 'Gracious God' is Your Name, Your Name is called upon us — O HASHEM, act for Your Name's sake. Act for the sake of [א] Your truth; act for the sake of [ב] Your covenant; act for the sake of [ג] Your greatness and Your splendor; act for the sake of [ד] Your law; act for the sake of [ה] Your glory; act for the sake of [ו] Your Meeting House; act for the sake of [ז] Your remembrance; act for the sake of [ח] Your kindness; act for the sake of [ט] Your goodness; act for the sake of [י] Your Oneness; act for the sake of [כ] Your honor; act for the sake of [ל] Your teaching; act for the sake of [מ] Your kingship; act for the sake of [נ] Your eternality; act for the sake of [ס] Your counsel; act for the sake of [ע] Your power; act for the sake of [פ] Your beauty; act for the sake of [צ] Your righteousness; act for the sake of [ק] Your sanctity; act for the sake of [ר] Your abundant mercy; act for the sake of [ש] Your Presence, act for the sake of [ת] Your praise; act for the sake of Your beloved ones who rest in the dust; act for the sake of Abraham, Isaac, and Jacob; act for the sake of Moses and Aaron; act for the sake of David and Solomon; act for the sake of Jerusalem, Your holy city; act for the sake of Zion, the abode of Your glory; act for the sake of the desolation of Your Temple; act for the sake of the ruin of Your Altar; act for the sake of the martyrs for Your holy Name; act for the sake of those slaughtered for Your Oneness; act for the sake of those who entered fire and water for the sanctification of Your Name; act for the nursing infants who did not err; act for the sake of the weaned babes who did not sin; act for the sake of children at the schoolroom; act for Your sake if not for ours; act for Your sake and save us.

עֲנֵנוּ Answer us, HASHEM, answer us; answer us, our God, answer us; answer us, [א] our Father, answer us; answer us, [ב] our Creator, answer us; answer us, [ג] our Redeemer, answer us; answer us, [ד] You Who

הָאֵל הַנֶּאֱמָן עֲנֵנוּ, עֲנֵנוּ וָתִיק וְחָסִיד עֲנֵנוּ, עֲנֵנוּ זַךְ וְיָשָׁר עֲנֵנוּ, עֲנֵנוּ חַי וְקַיָּם עֲנֵנוּ, עֲנֵנוּ טוֹב וּמֵטִיב עֲנֵנוּ, עֲנֵנוּ יוֹדֵעַ יֵצֶר עֲנֵנוּ, עֲנֵנוּ כּוֹבֵשׁ כְּעָסִים עֲנֵנוּ, עֲנֵנוּ לוֹבֵשׁ צְדָקוֹת עֲנֵנוּ, עֲנֵנוּ מֶלֶךְ מַלְכֵי הַמְּלָכִים עֲנֵנוּ, עֲנֵנוּ נוֹרָא וְנִשְׂגָּב עֲנֵנוּ, עֲנֵנוּ סוֹלֵחַ וּמוֹחֵל עֲנֵנוּ, עֲנֵנוּ עוֹנֶה בְּעֵת צָרָה[1] עֲנֵנוּ, עֲנֵנוּ פּוֹדֶה וּמַצִּיל עֲנֵנוּ, עֲנֵנוּ צַדִּיק וְיָשָׁר עֲנֵנוּ, עֲנֵנוּ קָרוֹב לְקוֹרְאָיו עֲנֵנוּ, עֲנֵנוּ רַחוּם וְחַנּוּן עֲנֵנוּ, עֲנֵנוּ שׁוֹמֵעַ אֶל אֶבְיוֹנִים עֲנֵנוּ, עֲנֵנוּ תּוֹמֵךְ תְּמִימִים עֲנֵנוּ, עֲנֵנוּ אֱלֹהֵי אֲבוֹתֵינוּ עֲנֵנוּ, עֲנֵנוּ אֱלֹהֵי אַבְרָהָם עֲנֵנוּ, עֲנֵנוּ פַּחַד יִצְחָק עֲנֵנוּ, עֲנֵנוּ אֲבִיר יַעֲקֹב עֲנֵנוּ, עֲנֵנוּ עֶזְרַת הַשְּׁבָטִים עֲנֵנוּ, עֲנֵנוּ מִשְׂגַּב אִמָּהוֹת עֲנֵנוּ, עֲנֵנוּ קָשֶׁה לִכְעוֹס עֲנֵנוּ, עֲנֵנוּ רַךְ לִרְצוֹת עֲנֵנוּ, עֲנֵנוּ עוֹנֶה בְּעֵת רָצוֹן[1] עֲנֵנוּ, עֲנֵנוּ אֲבִי יְתוֹמִים עֲנֵנוּ, עֲנֵנוּ דַּיַּן אַלְמָנוֹת עֲנֵנוּ.

מִי שֶׁעָנָה לְאַבְרָהָם אָבִינוּ בְּהַר הַמּוֹרִיָּה,	הוּא יַעֲנֵנוּ.
מִי שֶׁעָנָה לְיִצְחָק בְּנוֹ כְּשֶׁנֶּעֱקַד עַל גַּבֵּי הַמִּזְבֵּחַ,	הוּא יַעֲנֵנוּ.
מִי שֶׁעָנָה לְיַעֲקֹב בְּבֵית אֵל,	הוּא יַעֲנֵנוּ.
מִי שֶׁעָנָה לְיוֹסֵף בְּבֵית הָאֲסוּרִים,	הוּא יַעֲנֵנוּ.
מִי שֶׁעָנָה לַאֲבוֹתֵינוּ עַל יַם סוּף,	הוּא יַעֲנֵנוּ.
מִי שֶׁעָנָה לְמֹשֶׁה בְּחוֹרֵב,	הוּא יַעֲנֵנוּ.
מִי שֶׁעָנָה לְאַהֲרֹן בַּמַּחְתָּה,	הוּא יַעֲנֵנוּ.
מִי שֶׁעָנָה לְפִינְחָס בְּקוּמוֹ מִתּוֹךְ הָעֵדָה,	הוּא יַעֲנֵנוּ.
מִי שֶׁעָנָה לִיהוֹשֻׁעַ בַּגִּלְגָּל,	הוּא יַעֲנֵנוּ.
מִי שֶׁעָנָה לִשְׁמוּאֵל בַּמִּצְפָּה,	הוּא יַעֲנֵנוּ.
מִי שֶׁעָנָה לְדָוִד וּשְׁלֹמֹה בְנוֹ בִּירוּשָׁלָיִם,	הוּא יַעֲנֵנוּ.
מִי שֶׁעָנָה לְאֵלִיָּהוּ בְּהַר הַכַּרְמֶל,	הוּא יַעֲנֵנוּ.
מִי שֶׁעָנָה לֶאֱלִישָׁע בִּירִיחוֹ,	הוּא יַעֲנֵנוּ.
מִי שֶׁעָנָה לְיוֹנָה בִּמְעֵי הַדָּגָה,	הוּא יַעֲנֵנוּ.
מִי שֶׁעָנָה לְחִזְקִיָּהוּ מֶלֶךְ יְהוּדָה בְּחָלְיוֹ,	הוּא יַעֲנֵנוּ.
מִי שֶׁעָנָה לַחֲנַנְיָה מִישָׁאֵל וַעֲזַרְיָה בְּתוֹךְ כִּבְשַׁן הָאֵשׁ,	הוּא יַעֲנֵנוּ.
מִי שֶׁעָנָה לְדָנִיֵּאל בְּגוֹב הָאֲרָיוֹת,	הוּא יַעֲנֵנוּ.

---

(1) Some editions of *Selichos* reverse the positions of these two lines.

searches us out, answer us; answer us, [ה] *faithful God, answer us; answer us,* [ו] *stead-fast and kind One, answer us; answer us,* [ז] *pure and upright One, answer us; answer us,* [ח] *living and enduring One, answer us; answer us,* [ט] *good and beneficent One, answer us; answer us,* [י] *You Who knows inclinations, answer us; answer us,* [כ] *You Who suppresses wrath, answer us; answer us,* [ל] *You Who dons righteousness, answer us; answer us,* [מ] *King Who reigns over kings, answer us; answer us,* [נ] *awesome and powerful One, answer us; answer us,* [ס] *You Who forgives and pardons, answer us; answer us,* [ע] *You Who answers in time of distress,*[1] *answer us; answer us,* [פ] *Redeemer and Rescuer, answer us; answer us,* [צ] *righteous and upright One, answer us; answer us,* [ק] *He Who is close to those who call upon Him, answer us; answer us,* [ר] *merciful and gracious One, answer us; answer us,* [ש] *You Who hears the destitute, answer us; answer us,* [ת] *You Who supports the wholesome, answer us; answer us, God of our forefathers, answer us; answer us, God of Abraham, answer us; answer us, Dread of Isaac, answer us; answer us, Mighty One of Jacob, answer us; answer us, Helper of the tribes, answer us; answer us, Stronghold of the Matriarchs, answer us; answer us, You Who are hard to anger, answer us; answer us, You Who are easy to pacify, answer us; answer us, You Who answers in a time of favor,*[1] *answer us; answer us, Father of orphans, answer us; answer us, Judge of widows, answer us.*

מִי שֶׁעָנָה   *He Who answered our father Abraham on Mount Moriah,*
                                    may He answer us.
He Who answered his son Isaac when he was bound atop the altar,
                                    may He answer us.
He Who answered Jacob in Bethel,   *may He answer us.*
He Who answered Joseph in the prison,   *may He answer us.*
He Who answered our forefathers at the Sea of Reeds, *may He answer us.*
He Who answered Moses in Horeb,   *may He answer us.*
He Who answered Aaron when he offered the censer,   *may He answer us.*
He Who answered Phineas when he arose from amid the congregation,
                                    may He answer us.
He Who answered Joshua in Gilgal,   *may He answer us.*
He Who answered Samuel in Mitzpah,   *may He answer us.*
He Who answered David and his son Solomon in Jerusalem,
                                    may He answer us.
He Who answered Elijah on Mount Carmel,   *may He answer us.*
He Who answered Elisha in Jericho,   *may He answer us.*
He Who answered Jonah in the innards of the fish,   *may He answer us.*
He Who answered Hezekiah, King of Judah, in his illness,
                                    may He answer us.
He Who answered Chananiah, Mishael, and Azariah in the fiery oven,
                                    may He answer us.
He Who answered Daniel in the lions' den,   *may He answer us.*

מִי שֶׁעָנָה לְמָרְדְּכַי וְאֶסְתֵּר בְּשׁוּשַׁן הַבִּירָה,   הוּא יַעֲנֵנוּ.

מִי שֶׁעָנָה לְעֶזְרָא בַּגּוֹלָה,   הוּא יַעֲנֵנוּ.

מִי שֶׁעָנָה לְכָל הַצַּדִּיקִים וְהַחֲסִידִים וְהַתְּמִימִים וְהַיְּשָׁרִים,

הוּא יַעֲנֵנוּ.

רַחֲמָנָא דְּעָנֵי לַעֲנִיֵּי, עֲנֵינָא. רַחֲמָנָא דְּעָנֵי לִתְבִירֵי לִבָּא,

עֲנֵינָא. רַחֲמָנָא דְּעָנֵי לְמַכִּיכֵי רוּחָא, עֲנֵינָא. רַחֲמָנָא

עֲנֵינָא. רַחֲמָנָא חוּס. רַחֲמָנָא פְּרוֹק. רַחֲמָנָא שֵׁזִיב. רַחֲמָנָא

רְחֵם עֲלָן. הַשְׁתָּא בַּעֲגָלָא וּבִזְמַן קָרִיב.

נפילת אפים

In the presence of a Torah Scroll, the following (until יִבְֽשׁוּ רֶגַע) is recited with the head resting on the arm, preferably while seated. Elsewhere, it is recited with the head held erect.

(וַיֹּאמֶר דָּוִד אֶל גָּד, צַר לִי מְאֹד נִפְּלָה נָּא בְיַד יהוה,

כִּי רַבִּים רַחֲמָיו, וּבְיַד אָדָם אַל אֶפֹּלָה.[1])

רַחוּם וְחַנּוּן חָטָאתִי לְפָנֶיךָ. יהוה מָלֵא רַחֲמִים, רַחֵם עָלַי

וְקַבֵּל תַּחֲנוּנָי.

תהלים ו:ב-יא

יהוה אַל בְּאַפְּךָ תוֹכִיחֵנִי, וְאַל בַּחֲמָתְךָ תְיַסְּרֵנִי. חָנֵּנִי יהוה, כִּי

אֻמְלַל אָנִי, רְפָאֵנִי יהוה, כִּי נִבְהֲלוּ עֲצָמָי. וְנַפְשִׁי נִבְהֲלָה

מְאֹד, וְאַתָּה יהוה, עַד מָתָי. שׁוּבָה יהוה, חַלְּצָה נַפְשִׁי, הוֹשִׁיעֵנִי

לְמַעַן חַסְדֶּךָ. כִּי אֵין בַּמָּוֶת זִכְרֶךָ, בִּשְׁאוֹל מִי יוֹדֶה לָּךְ. יָגַעְתִּי

בְּאַנְחָתִי, אַשְׂחֶה בְכָל לַיְלָה מִטָּתִי, בְּדִמְעָתִי עַרְשִׂי אַמְסֶה.

עָשְׁשָׁה מִכַּעַס עֵינִי, עָתְקָה בְּכָל צוֹרְרָי. סוּרוּ מִמֶּנִּי כָּל פֹּעֲלֵי אָוֶן,

כִּי שָׁמַע יהוה קוֹל בִּכְיִי. שָׁמַע יהוה תְּחִנָּתִי, יהוה תְּפִלָּתִי יִקָּח.

יֵבֹשׁוּ וְיִבָּהֲלוּ מְאֹד כָּל אֹיְבָי, יָשֻׁבוּ יֵבֹשׁוּ רָגַע.

מַחֵי וּמַסֵּי מֵמִית וּמְחַיֶּה, מַסִּיק מִן שְׁאוֹל לְחַיֵּי עָלְמָא, בְּרָא

כַּד חָטֵי אֲבוּהִי לַקְיֵהּ, אֲבוּהִי דְחָיֵס אַסֵּי לִכְאֵבֵהּ.

עַבְדָּא דְּמָרִיד נָפִיק בְּקוֹלָר, מָרֵהּ תָּאִיב וְתַבִּיר קוֹלָרֵהּ.

בְּרַךְ בְּכָרַךְ אֲנַן וְחָטִינַן קַמָּךְ, הָא רָזֵי נַפְשִׁין בְּגִידִין מְרִירִין,

עַבְדָּךְ אֲנַן וּמְרוֹדִינַן קַמָּךְ, הָא בְּבִזְתָּא, הָא בְּשִׁבְיָא, הָא

בְּמַלְקְיוּתָא. בְּמָטוּ מִנָּךְ בְּרַחֲמָךְ דִּנְפִישִׁין, אַסֵּי לִכְאֵבִין דִּתְקוֹף

עֲלָן, עַד דְּלָא נֶהֱוֵי גְמִירָא בְּשִׁבְיָא.

He Who answered Mordechai and Esther in Shushan the capital,
may He answer us.

He Who answered Ezra in the Exile,   may He answer us.

He Who answered all the righteous, the devout, the wholesome,
  and the upright,   may He answer us.

רַחֲמָנָא The Merciful One Who answers the poor, may He answer us.
The Merciful One Who answers the brokenhearted, may He
answer us. The Merciful One Who answers the humble of spirit, may He
answer us. O Merciful One, answer us. O Merciful One, pity. O Merciful
One, redeem. O Merciful One, deliver. O Merciful One, have mercy on us —
now, swiftly and soon.

PUTTING DOWN THE HEAD

In the presence of a Torah Scroll, the following (until 'instantly shamed') is recited with the head
resting on the arm, preferably while seated. Elsewhere, it is recited with the head held erect.

(And David said to Gad, 'I am exceedingly distressed. Let us fall into HASHEM's
hand for His mercies are abundant, but let me not fall into human hands.'[1])

רַחוּם וְחַנּוּן O compassionate and gracious One, I have sinned before
You. HASHEM, Who is full of mercy, have mercy on me and
accept my supplications.

Psalms 6:2-11

ה' HASHEM, do not rebuke me in Your anger nor chastise me in Your rage.
Favor me, HASHEM, for I am feeble; heal me, HASHEM, for my bones
shudder. My soul is utterly confounded, and You, HASHEM, how long?
Desist, HASHEM, release my soul; save me as befits Your kindness. For
there is no mention of You in death; in the Lower World who will thank
You? I am wearied with my sigh, every night my tears drench my bed, soak
my couch. My eye is dimmed because of anger, aged by my tormentors.
Depart from me, all evildoers, for HASHEM has heard the sound of my
weeping. HASHEM has heard my plea, HASHEM will accept my prayer. Let
all my foes be shamed and utterly confounded, they will regret and be
instantly shamed.

מַחֲי וּמַסִּי [O God,] He Who smites and heals, causes death and
restores life, raises [the dead] from the grave to eternal life:
Should a son sin, his father would smack him, but a compassionate father
will heal his [son's] pain. When a slave rebels, he is led out in collar-irons,
but if his master desires to, he breaks his chains.

We are Your son, Your firstborn, and we have sinned against You; so
our soul has been satiated with bitter wormwood. We are Your servants
and we have rebelled against You; so [we have suffered], some with
looting, some with captivity, and some with the lash. We beg of You, in
Your abundant compassion, heal the pains that have overwhelmed us,
before we have been completely wiped out in captivity.

(1) II Samuel 24:14.

סליחה פו (תחנה)

All:

מֶלֶךְ מַלְכִים* רָם עַל רָמִים.

שׁוֹכֵן שְׁחָקִים וְיוֹשֵׁב בַּמְּרוֹמִים.

הַמְּהֻלָּל וְהַמְּשֻׁבָּח לְעוֹלְמֵי עוֹלָמִים.

בָּרוּךְ וּמְבֹרָךְ בְּפִי כָל יְקוּמִים.

רְאֵה בְּעָנְוִּי אֲנוּנִים וַעֲגוּמִים.

שׁוּר נָא בְּשִׁפְלוּת מְעוּטֵי עַמִּים.¹

מְפֻזָּרִים וּמְפֹרָדִים בֵּין כָּל הָאֻמִּים.²

וּבְבָשְׁת וּכְלִמָּה נֶחְפָּרִים וְנִכְלָמִים.

אֲבֵלִים וּבְדוּדִים נְזוּפִים וְנִזְעָמִים.

לַמַּכִּים נְתוּנִים גֵּוֶם לְמַהֲלֻמִים.³

בַּבֹּקֶר מִי יִתֵּן עֶרֶב נוֹאֲמִים.

רֶמֶשׂ אוֹמְרִים מִי יְקָרֵב אוֹר יָמִים.⁴

אֵין לָהֶם מְנוּחָה וְשֶׁקֶט וּשְׁלוֹמִים.

בַּמֶּה לְהִתְנַחֵם וְלִמְצֹא תַנְחוּמִים.

שָׁלוֹם מְצַפִּים וְהִנֵּה נִלְחָמִים.

לְטוֹבָה מְקַוִּים⁵ וְהִנֵּה רֹעַ תַּשְׁלוּמִים.

וַתִּבְחַר נַפְשָׁם מִיתַת רְדוּמִים.⁶

מַה נִּתְאוֹנֵן וּמַה נֹּאמַר וַעֲוֹנוֹתֵינוּ גּוֹרְמִים.

חָטָאנוּ רָשַׁעְנוּ סַרְנוּ מֵחֻקֶּיךָ הַנְּעִימִים.

זְכֹר רַחֲמֶיךָ יהוה וַחֲסָדֶיךָ הָעֲצוּמִים.⁷

קוּמָה וְהִמָּלֵא עָלֵינוּ רַחֲמִים.

וְקַבֵּץ פְּזוּרֵינוּ מֵאַרְצוֹת וְיַמִּים.

אֲשֶׁר מָכַרְתָּ חִנָּם לֶאֱדוֹמִים.

❖ מַהֵר לְגָאֳלָם בְּלֹא כֶסֶף וְדָמִים.⁸

צַוֵּה יְשׁוּעוֹת יַעֲקֹב,⁹ הַצּוּר תָּמִים.

כִּי לְךָ אֲדֹנָי הַסְּלִיחוֹת וְהָרַחֲמִים.¹⁰

---

§§ מֶלֶךְ מַלְכִים — *King of kings.* The acrostic
spells the *paytan's* name — מֹשֶׁה בַּר שְׁמוּאֵל בַּר
אַבְשָׁלוֹם חֲזַק וְאֱמָץ, *Moshe bar Shmuel bar*

Avshalom, may he be strong and persevere.
Nothing more is known about him.

SELICHAH 86

All:

מ *King of kings,* high above the high,*

שׁ *Who dwells in heaven and sits in the heights,*

ה *Who is praised and lauded until all eternity,*

ב *blessed and extolled*
    by the mouth of all living creatures:

ר *See the torment of the mourning and gloomy;*

שׁ *please look at how lowly is*
    that smallest among peoples,[1]

מ *scattered and dispersed among all the nations,*[2]

ו *with shame and humiliation*
    they are disgraced and humiliated.

א *Mourning, alone, upbraided, angrily spurned,*

ל *given over to beaters, their bodies to blows;*[3]

ב *in the morning they say,*
    'Would that it were evening!'

ר *and at dusk they say,*
    'Would that morning light could come sooner!'[4]

א *They do not have rest, or quiet, or peace*

ב *in which to take comfort and find consolation.*

שׁ *They look forward to peace, but are warred upon,*

ל *they hope for good [times],*[5] *and are paid with bad.*

ו *Their souls choose the sleep of death;*[6]

מ *How can we complain? What can we say?*
    Our own sins are the cause!

ח *We have sinned, we have been wicked,*
    we have turned away from Your pleasant decrees.

ז *Remember Your mercies, HASHEM,*
    and Your powerful kindnesses.[7]

ק *Arise, and fill Yourself with mercy for us,*

ו *and gather Your scattered people*
    from the lands and seas.

א *Those whom You sold for naught to the Edomites,*

מ *Chazzan — make haste to redeem them*
    for no money or price.[8]

צ *Command the salvations for Jacob,*[9]
    O Perfect Rock,

for Yours, my Lord, are forgiveness and mercy.[10]

---

(1) Cf. *Deuteronomy* 7:7. (2) Cf. *Esther* 3:8. (3) Cf. *Isaiah* 50:6.
(4) Cf. *Deuteronomy* 28:67. (5) Cf. *Jeremiah* 8:15. (6) Cf. *Job* 7:15.
(7) Cf. *Psalms* 25:6. (8) Cf. *Isaiah* 52:3; see commentary to *selichah* 9, s.v., לִמְכוּרֵי חִנָּם.
(9) *Psalms* 44:5. (10) Cf. *Daniel* 9:9.

All:

מַכְנִיסֵי רַחֲמִים, הַכְנִיסוּ רַחֲמֵינוּ, לִפְנֵי בַּעַל הָרַחֲמִים. מַשְׁמִיעֵי תְפִלָּה, הַשְׁמִיעוּ תְפִלָּתֵנוּ, לִפְנֵי שׁוֹמֵעַ תְּפִלָּה. מַשְׁמִיעֵי צְעָקָה, הַשְׁמִיעוּ צַעֲקָתֵנוּ, לִפְנֵי שׁוֹמֵעַ צְעָקָה. מַכְנִיסֵי דִמְעָה, הַכְנִיסוּ דִמְעוֹתֵינוּ, לִפְנֵי מֶלֶךְ מִתְרַצֶּה בִּדְמָעוֹת.

הִשְׁתַּדְּלוּ וְהַרְבּוּ תְּחִנָּה וּבַקָּשָׁה, לִפְנֵי מֶלֶךְ אֵל רָם וְנִשָּׂא. הַזְכִּירוּ לְפָנָיו, הַשְׁמִיעוּ לְפָנָיו תּוֹרָה וּמַעֲשִׂים טוֹבִים שֶׁל שׁוֹכְנֵי עָפָר.

יִזְכֹּר אַהֲבָתָם וִיחַיֶּה זַרְעָם, שֶׁלֹּא תֹאבַד שְׁאֵרִית יַעֲקֹב. כִּי צֹאן רוֹעֶה נֶאֱמָן הָיָה לְחֶרְפָּה, יִשְׂרָאֵל גּוֹי אֶחָד לְמָשָׁל וְלִשְׁנִינָה.

מַהֵר עֲנֵנוּ אֱלֹהֵי יִשְׁעֵנוּ, וּפְדֵנוּ מִכָּל גְּזֵרוֹת קָשׁוֹת וְהוֹשִׁיעָה בְּרַחֲמֶיךָ הָרַבִּים, מְשִׁיחַ צִדְקֶךָ וְעַמֶּךָ.

מָרָן דְּבִשְׁמַיָּא לָךְ מִתְחַנְּנַן, כְּבַר שַׁבְיָא דְּמִתְחַנֵּן לִשְׁבוֹיֵהּ. כֻּלְּהוֹן בְּנֵי שַׁבְיָא בְּכַסְפָּא מִתְפָּרְקִין, וְעַמָּךְ יִשְׂרָאֵל בְּרַחֲמֵי וּבְתַחֲנוּנֵי, הַב לָן שְׁאֵלְתִּין וּבָעוּתִין, דְּלָא נֶהֱדַר רֵיקָם מִן קָדָמָךְ.

מָרָן דְּבִשְׁמַיָּא לָךְ מִתְחַנְּנַן, כְּעַבְדָּא דְּמִתְחַנֵּן לְמָרֵיהּ, עֲשִׁיקֵי אֲנַן וּבַחֲשׁוֹכָא שָׁרִינַן, מְרִירָן נַפְשִׁין מֵעַקְתִין דִּנְפִישִׁין, חֵילָא לֵית בָּן לְרַצּוּיָךְ מָרָן, עֲבִיד בְּדִיל קַיָּמָא דִּגְזַרְתָּ עִם אֲבָהָתָנָא.

שׁוֹמֵר יִשְׂרָאֵל, שְׁמוֹר שְׁאֵרִית יִשְׂרָאֵל, וְאַל יֹאבַד יִשְׂרָאֵל, הָאֹמְרִים, שְׁמַע יִשְׂרָאֵל.[1]

שׁוֹמֵר גּוֹי אֶחָד, שְׁמוֹר שְׁאֵרִית עַם אֶחָד, וְאַל יֹאבַד גּוֹי אֶחָד, הַמְיַחֲדִים שִׁמְךָ, יהוה אֱלֹהֵינוּ יהוה אֶחָד.[1]

שׁוֹמֵר גּוֹי קָדוֹשׁ, שְׁמוֹר שְׁאֵרִית עַם קָדוֹשׁ, וְאַל יֹאבַד גּוֹי קָדוֹשׁ, הַמְשַׁלְּשִׁים בְּשָׁלֹשׁ קְדֻשּׁוֹת לְקָדוֹשׁ.

מִתְרַצֶּה בְּרַחֲמִים וּמִתְפַּיֵּס בְּתַחֲנוּנִים, הִתְרַצֵּה וְהִתְפַּיֵּס לְדוֹר עָנִי, כִּי אֵין עוֹזֵר. אָבִינוּ מַלְכֵּנוּ, חָנֵּנוּ וַעֲנֵנוּ, כִּי אֵין בָּנוּ מַעֲשִׂים, עֲשֵׂה עִמָּנוּ צְדָקָה וָחֶסֶד וְהוֹשִׁיעֵנוּ.

All:

מַכְנִיסֵי רַחֲמִים O you who usher in [pleas for] mercy, may you usher in our [plea for] mercy, before the Master of mercy. O you who cause prayer to be heard, may you cause our prayer to be heard, before the Hearer of prayer. O you who cause outcry to be heard, may you cause our outcry to be heard, before the Hearer of outcry. O you who usher in tears, may you usher in our tears, before the King Who finds favor through tears.

Exert yourselves, and multiply supplication and petition, before the King, God, exalted and most high. Mention before Him, cause to be heard before Him, the Torah and the good deeds of [the Patriarchs and Matriarchs] who dwell in the dust.

May He remember their love and grant life to [their] offspring, that the remnant of Jacob not be lost. For the flock of the faithful shepherd [Moses] has become a disgrace; Israel, the unique nation, a parable and a simile.

Speedily, answer us, O God of our salvation, and redeem us from all harsh decrees; and may You save, in Your abundant mercy, Your righteous anointed and Your people.

מָרָן דְּבִשְׁמַיָּא Our Master Who is in heaven, to You do we supplicate, as a captive supplicates before his captors; for all captives are redeemed with money, but Your people Israel with compassion and supplication. O grant our requests and our prayers that we not be turned away from You empty-handed.

Our Master Who is in heaven, to You do we supplicate as a slave supplicates before his master: We are oppressed and we abide in darkness, souls embittered from abundant distress. We have no strength to regain Your favor. Our Master, act for the sake of the covenant that You made with our Patriarchs.

שׁוֹמֵר יִשְׂרָאֵל O Guardian of Israel, protect the remnant of Israel; let not Israel be destroyed — those who proclaim, 'Hear O Israel.'[1]

O Guardian of the unique nation, protect the remnant of the unique people; let not the unique nation be destroyed — those who proclaim the Oneness of Your Name, 'HASHEM is our God, HASHEM, the One and Only!'[1]

O Guardian of the holy nation, protect the remnant of the holy people; let not the holy nation be destroyed — those who proclaim three-fold sanctifications to the Holy One.

Become favorable through compassion and become appeased through supplications. Become favorable and appeased to the poor generation, for there is no helper. Our Father, our King, be gracious with us and answer us, though we have no worthy deeds; treat us with charity and kindness, and save us.

---

(1) Deuteronomy 6:4.

וַאֲנַחְנוּ לֹא נֵדַע מַה נַּעֲשֶׂה, כִּי עָלֶיךָ עֵינֵינוּ.[1] זְכֹר רַחֲמֶיךָ
יהוה וַחֲסָדֶיךָ, כִּי מֵעוֹלָם הֵמָּה.[2] יְהִי חַסְדְּךָ יהוה עָלֵינוּ,
כַּאֲשֶׁר יִחַלְנוּ לָךְ.[3]

אַל תִּזְכָּר לָנוּ עֲוֹנוֹת רִאשׁוֹנִים, מַהֵר יְקַדְּמוּנוּ רַחֲמֶיךָ, כִּי
דַלּוֹנוּ מְאֹד.[4] חָנֵּנוּ יהוה חָנֵּנוּ, כִּי רַב שָׂבַעְנוּ בוּז.[5]
בְּרֹגֶז רַחֵם תִּזְכּוֹר.[6] כִּי הוּא יָדַע יִצְרֵנוּ, זָכוּר כִּי עָפָר אֲנָחְנוּ.[7] עָזְרֵנוּ
אֱלֹהֵי יִשְׁעֵנוּ עַל דְּבַר כְּבוֹד שְׁמֶךָ, וְהַצִּילֵנוּ וְכַפֵּר עַל חַטֹּאתֵינוּ
לְמַעַן שְׁמֶךָ.[8]

קדיש שלם

The *chazzan* recites קַדִּישׁ שָׁלֵם:

יִתְגַּדַּל וְיִתְקַדַּשׁ שְׁמֵהּ רַבָּא. (.Cong – אָמֵן.) בְּעָלְמָא דִּי בְרָא
כִרְעוּתֵהּ, וְיַמְלִיךְ מַלְכוּתֵהּ, בְּחַיֵּיכוֹן וּבְיוֹמֵיכוֹן וּבְחַיֵּי
דְכָל בֵּית יִשְׂרָאֵל, בַּעֲגָלָא וּבִזְמַן קָרִיב. וְאִמְרוּ אָמֵן.
(.Cong – אָמֵן. יְהֵא שְׁמֵהּ רַבָּא מְבָרַךְ לְעָלַם וּלְעָלְמֵי עָלְמַיָּא.)
יְהֵא שְׁמֵהּ רַבָּא מְבָרַךְ לְעָלַם וּלְעָלְמֵי עָלְמַיָּא.
יִתְבָּרַךְ וְיִשְׁתַּבַּח וְיִתְפָּאַר וְיִתְרוֹמַם וְיִתְנַשֵּׂא וְיִתְהַדָּר וְיִתְעַלֶּה
וְיִתְהַלָּל שְׁמֵהּ דְּקוּדְשָׁא בְּרִיךְ הוּא (.Cong – בְּרִיךְ הוּא.) לְעֵלָּא
[וּ]לְעֵלָּא מִכָּל בִּרְכָתָא וְשִׁירָתָא תֻּשְׁבְּחָתָא וְנֶחֱמָתָא, דַּאֲמִירָן
בְּעָלְמָא. וְאִמְרוּ: אָמֵן. (.Cong – אָמֵן.)
(.Cong – קַבֵּל בְּרַחֲמִים וּבְרָצוֹן אֶת תְּפִלָּתֵנוּ.)
תִּתְקַבֵּל צְלוֹתְהוֹן וּבָעוּתְהוֹן דְּכָל (בֵּית) יִשְׂרָאֵל קֳדָם אֲבוּהוֹן דִּי
בִשְׁמַיָּא. וְאִמְרוּ אָמֵן. (.Cong – אָמֵן.)
(.Cong – יְהִי שֵׁם יהוה מְבֹרָךְ, מֵעַתָּה וְעַד עוֹלָם.[9])
יְהֵא שְׁלָמָא רַבָּא מִן שְׁמַיָּא וְחַיִּים עָלֵינוּ וְעַל כָּל יִשְׂרָאֵל. וְאִמְרוּ
אָמֵן. (.Cong – אָמֵן.)
(.Cong – עֶזְרִי מֵעִם יהוה, עֹשֵׂה שָׁמַיִם וָאָרֶץ.[10])

Take three steps back. Bow left and say, . . . עֹשֶׂה; bow right and say, . . . הוּא יַעֲשֶׂה; bow forward and say,
אָמֵן . . . וְעַל כָּל. Remain standing in place for a few moments, then take three steps forward.

עֹשֶׂה [הַ]שָּׁלוֹם בִּמְרוֹמָיו, הוּא יַעֲשֶׂה שָׁלוֹם עָלֵינוּ, וְעַל כָּל
יִשְׂרָאֵל. וְאִמְרוּ אָמֵן. (.Cong – אָמֵן.)

וַאֲנַחְנוּ We know not what to do — but our eyes are upon You.[1] Remember Your mercies, HASHEM, and Your kindnesses, for they are from the beginning of the world.[2] May Your kindness be upon us, HASHEM, just as we awaited You.[3]

אַל תִּזְכָּר Recall not against us the iniquities of the ancients; may Your mercies meet us swiftly, for we have become exceedingly impoverished.[4] Be gracious to us, HASHEM, be gracious to us, for we are abundantly sated with scorn.[5] Amid rage — remember to be merciful![6] For He knew our nature, He remembers that we are dust.[7] Chazzan— Assist us, O God of our salvation, for the sake of Your Name's glory; rescue us and atone for our sins for Your Name's sake.[8]

FULL KADDISH
The chazzan recites the Full Kaddish:

יִתְגַּדַּל May His great Name grow exalted and sanctified (Cong. – Amen.) in the world that He created as He willed. May He give reign to His kingship in your lifetimes and in your days, and in the lifetimes of the entire Family of Israel, swiftly and soon. Now respond: Amen.

(Cong. – Amen. May His great Name be blessed forever and ever.)
May His great Name be blessed forever and ever.

Blessed, praised, glorified, exalted, extolled, mighty, upraised and lauded be the Name of the Holy One, Blessed is He (Cong. – Blessed is He.) exceedingly beyond any blessing and song, praise, and consolation that are uttered in the world. Now respond: Amen. (Cong. – Amen.)

(Cong. – Accept our prayers with mercy and favor.)
May the prayers and supplications of the entire House of Israel be accepted before their Father Who is in Heaven. Now respond: Amen. (Cong. – Amen.)

(Cong. – Blessed be the Name of HASHEM from this time and forever.[9])
May there be abundant peace from Heaven, and life, upon us and upon all Israel. Now respond: Amen. (Cong. – Amen.)

(Cong. – My help is from HASHEM, Maker of heaven and earth.[10])
Take three steps back. Bow left and say, 'He Who makes peace . . .'; bow right and say,
'may He make peace . . .'; bow forward and say, 'and upon all Israel . . .'
Remain standing in place for a few moments, then take three steps forward.

He Who makes [the] peace in His heights, may He make peace upon us, and upon all Israel. Now respond: Amen. (Cong. – Amen.)

---

(1) II Chronicles 20:12. (2) Psalms 25:6. (3) 33:22. (4) 79:8. (5) 123:3.
(6) Habakkuk 3:2. (7) Psalms 103:14. (8) 79:9. (9) 113:2. (10) 121:2.

WHEN YOM KIPPUR FALLS ON MONDAY OR THURSDAY SOME CONGREGATIONS
REVERSE THE ORDER OF THE FOURTH AND FIFTH DAYS OF REPENTANCE

יום חמישי של עשרת ימי תשובה

אַשְׁרֵי יוֹשְׁבֵי בֵיתֶךָ, עוֹד יְהַלְלוּךָ סֶּלָה. אַשְׁרֵי הָעָם שֶׁכָּכָה
לּוֹ, אַשְׁרֵי הָעָם שֶׁיהוה אֱלֹהָיו. תְּהִלָּה לְדָוִד,
אֲרוֹמִמְךָ אֱלוֹהַי הַמֶּלֶךְ, וַאֲבָרְכָה שִׁמְךָ לְעוֹלָם וָעֶד.
בְּכָל יוֹם אֲבָרְכֶךָּ, וַאֲהַלְלָה שִׁמְךָ לְעוֹלָם וָעֶד.
גָּדוֹל יהוה וּמְהֻלָּל מְאֹד, וְלִגְדֻלָּתוֹ אֵין חֵקֶר.
דּוֹר לְדוֹר יְשַׁבַּח מַעֲשֶׂיךָ, וּגְבוּרֹתֶיךָ יַגִּידוּ.
הֲדַר כְּבוֹד הוֹדֶךָ, וְדִבְרֵי נִפְלְאֹתֶיךָ אָשִׂיחָה.
וֶעֱזוּז נוֹרְאוֹתֶיךָ יֹאמֵרוּ, וּגְדֻלָּתְךָ אֲסַפְּרֶנָּה.
זֵכֶר רַב טוּבְךָ יַבִּיעוּ, וְצִדְקָתְךָ יְרַנֵּנוּ.
חַנּוּן וְרַחוּם יהוה, אֶרֶךְ אַפַּיִם וּגְדָל חָסֶד.
טוֹב יהוה לַכֹּל, וְרַחֲמָיו עַל כָּל מַעֲשָׂיו.
יוֹדוּךָ יהוה כָּל מַעֲשֶׂיךָ, וַחֲסִידֶיךָ יְבָרְכוּכָה.
כְּבוֹד מַלְכוּתְךָ יֹאמֵרוּ, וּגְבוּרָתְךָ יְדַבֵּרוּ.
לְהוֹדִיעַ לִבְנֵי הָאָדָם גְּבוּרֹתָיו, וּכְבוֹד הֲדַר מַלְכוּתוֹ.
מַלְכוּתְךָ מַלְכוּת כָּל עֹלָמִים, וּמֶמְשַׁלְתְּךָ בְּכָל דּוֹר וָדֹר.
סוֹמֵךְ יהוה לְכָל הַנֹּפְלִים, וְזוֹקֵף לְכָל הַכְּפוּפִים.
עֵינֵי כֹל אֵלֶיךָ יְשַׂבֵּרוּ, וְאַתָּה נוֹתֵן לָהֶם אֶת אָכְלָם בְּעִתּוֹ.

Concentrate intently while reciting the verse, פּוֹתֵחַ.

פּוֹתֵחַ אֶת יָדֶךָ, וּמַשְׂבִּיעַ לְכָל חַי רָצוֹן.
✣ צַדִּיק יהוה בְּכָל דְּרָכָיו, וְחָסִיד בְּכָל מַעֲשָׂיו.
קָרוֹב יהוה לְכָל קֹרְאָיו, לְכֹל אֲשֶׁר יִקְרָאֻהוּ בֶאֱמֶת.
רְצוֹן יְרֵאָיו יַעֲשֶׂה, וְאֶת שַׁוְעָתָם יִשְׁמַע וְיוֹשִׁיעֵם.
שׁוֹמֵר יהוה אֶת כָּל אֹהֲבָיו, וְאֵת כָּל הָרְשָׁעִים יַשְׁמִיד.
תְּהִלַּת יהוה יְדַבֶּר פִּי, וִיבָרֵךְ כָּל בָּשָׂר שֵׁם קָדְשׁוֹ לְעוֹלָם וָעֶד.
וַאֲנַחְנוּ נְבָרֵךְ יָהּ, מֵעַתָּה וְעַד עוֹלָם, הַלְלוּיָהּ.³

The chazzan recites חֲצִי קַדִּישׁ.

יִתְגַּדַּל וְיִתְקַדַּשׁ שְׁמֵהּ רַבָּא. (.Cong – אָמֵן.) בְּעָלְמָא דִּי בְרָא כִרְעוּתֵהּ.
וְיַמְלִיךְ מַלְכוּתֵהּ, בְּחַיֵּיכוֹן וּבְיוֹמֵיכוֹן וּבְחַיֵּי דְכָל בֵּית יִשְׂרָאֵל, 1.31
בַּעֲגָלָא וּבִזְמַן קָרִיב. וְאִמְרוּ: אָמֵן.

(.Cong – אָמֵן. יְהֵא שְׁמֵהּ רַבָּא מְבָרַךְ לְעָלַם וּלְעָלְמֵי עָלְמַיָּא.)
יְהֵא שְׁמֵהּ רַבָּא מְבָרַךְ לְעָלַם וּלְעָלְמֵי עָלְמַיָּא.
יִתְבָּרַךְ וְיִשְׁתַּבַּח וְיִתְפָּאַר וְיִתְרוֹמַם וְיִתְנַשֵּׂא וְיִתְהַדָּר וְיִתְעַלֶּה וְיִתְהַלָּל שְׁמֵהּ
דְּקֻדְשָׁא בְּרִיךְ הוּא (.Cong – בְּרִיךְ הוּא) לְעֵלָּא [וּ]לְעֵלָּא מִכָּל בִּרְכָתָא
וְשִׁירָתָא תֻּשְׁבְּחָתָא וְנֶחֱמָתָא, דַּאֲמִירָן בְּעָלְמָא. וְאִמְרוּ: אָמֵן. (.Cong – אָמֵן.)

WHEN YOM KIPPUR FALLS ON MONDAY OR THURSDAY SOME CONGREGATIONS
REVERSE THE ORDER OF THE FOURTH AND FIFTH DAYS OF REPENTANCE

❧ FIFTH DAY OF REPENTANCE ❧

אַשְׁרֵי *Praiseworthy are those who dwell in Your house; may they always praise You, Selah! Praiseworthy is the people for whom this is so, praiseworthy is the people whose God is HASHEM.*

Psalm 145   *A psalm of praise by David:*

א *I will exalt You, my God the King, and I will bless Your Name forever and ever.*

ב *Every day I will bless You, and I will laud Your Name forever and ever.*

ג *HASHEM is great and exceedingly lauded,*
and His greatness is beyond investigation.

ד *Each generation will praise Your deeds to the next*
and of Your mighty deeds they will tell;

ה *The splendrous glory of Your power and Your wondrous deeds I shall discuss.*

ו *And of Your awesome power they will speak, and Your greatness I shall relate.*

ז *A recollection of Your abundant goodness they will utter*
and of Your righteousness they will sing exultantly.

ח *Gracious and merciful is HASHEM, slow to anger, and great in [bestowing]kindness.*

ט *HASHEM is good to all; His mercies are on all His works.*

י *All Your works shall thank You, HASHEM, and Your devout ones will bless You.*

כ *Of the glory of Your kingdom they will speak, and of Your power they will tell;*

ל *To inform human beings of His mighty deeds,*
and the glorious splendor of His kingdom.

מ *Your kingdom is a kingdom spanning all eternities,*
and Your dominion is throughout every generation.

ס *HASHEM supports all the fallen ones and straightens all the bent.*

ע *The eyes of all look to You with hope*
and You give them their food in its proper time;

פ *You open Your hand,*   Concentrate intently while reciting the verse, 'You open. . .'
and satisfy the desire of every living thing.

צ Chazzan— *Righteous is HASHEM in all His ways*
and magnanimous in all His deeds.

ק *HASHEM is close to all who call upon Him — to all who call upon Him sincerely.*

ר *The will of those who fear Him He will do;*
and their cry He will hear, and save them.

ש*HASHEM protects all who love Him; but all the wicked He will destroy.*

ת *May my mouth declare the praise of HASHEM*
and may all flesh bless His Holy Name forever and ever.

We will bless God from this time and forever, Halleluyah!

The chazzan recites Half-Kaddish:

יִתְגַּדַּל *May His great Name grow exalted and sanctified* (Cong.— *Amen.*) *in the world that He created as He willed. May He give reign to His kingship in your lifetimes and in your days, and in the lifetimes of the entire Family of Israel, swiftly and soon. Now respond: Amen.*

(Cong.— *Amen. May His great Name be blessed forever and ever.*)
May His great Name be blessed forever and ever.

Blessed, praised, glorified, exalted, extolled, mighty, upraised, and lauded be the Name of the Holy One, Blessed is He (Cong.— *Blessed is He*) — *exceedingly beyond any blessing and song, praise and consolation that are uttered in the world. Now respond: Amen.* (Cong.— *Amen.*)

All:

לְךָ יהוה הַצְּדָקָה, וְלָנוּ בֹּשֶׁת הַפָּנִים.[1] מַה נִּתְאוֹנֵן,[2] מַה נֹּאמַר, מַה נְּדַבֵּר, וּמַה נִּצְטַדָּק.[3] נַחְפְּשָׂה דְרָכֵינוּ וְנַחְקֹרָה, וְנָשׁוּבָה אֵלֶיךָ,[4] כִּי יְמִינְךָ פְשׁוּטָה לְקַבֵּל שָׁבִים. לֹא בְחֶסֶד וְלֹא בְמַעֲשִׂים בָּאנוּ לְפָנֶיךָ, כְּדַלִּים וּכְרָשִׁים דָּפַקְנוּ דְלָתֶיךָ. דְּלָתֶיךָ דָּפַקְנוּ רַחוּם וְחַנּוּן, נָא אַל תְּשִׁיבֵנוּ רֵיקָם מִלְּפָנֶיךָ. מִלְּפָנֶיךָ מַלְכֵּנוּ רֵיקָם אַל תְּשִׁיבֵנוּ, כִּי אַתָּה שׁוֹמֵעַ תְּפִלָּה.

שֹׁמֵעַ תְּפִלָּה, עָדֶיךָ כָּל בָּשָׂר יָבֹאוּ.[5] יָבוֹא כָל בָּשָׂר לְהִשְׁתַּחֲוֹת לְפָנֶיךָ יהוה.[6] יָבֹאוּ וְיִשְׁתַּחֲווּ לְפָנֶיךָ אֲדֹנָי, וִיכַבְּדוּ לִשְׁמֶךָ.[7] בֹּאוּ נִשְׁתַּחֲוֶה וְנִכְרָעָה, נִבְרְכָה לִפְנֵי יהוה עֹשֵׂנוּ.[8] נָבוֹאָה לְמִשְׁכְּנוֹתָיו, נִשְׁתַּחֲוֶה לַהֲדֹם רַגְלָיו.[9] בֹּאוּ שְׁעָרָיו בְּתוֹדָה, חֲצֵרֹתָיו בִּתְהִלָּה, הוֹדוּ לוֹ בָּרְכוּ שְׁמוֹ.[10] רוֹמְמוּ יהוה אֱלֹהֵינוּ, וְהִשְׁתַּחֲווּ לַהֲדֹם רַגְלָיו, קָדוֹשׁ הוּא.[11] רוֹמְמוּ יהוה אֱלֹהֵינוּ, וְהִשְׁתַּחֲווּ לְהַר קָדְשׁוֹ, כִּי קָדוֹשׁ יהוה אֱלֹהֵינוּ.[12] הִשְׁתַּחֲווּ לַיהוה בְּהַדְרַת קֹדֶשׁ, חִילוּ מִפָּנָיו כָּל הָאָרֶץ.[13] וַאֲנַחְנוּ בְּרֹב חַסְדְּךָ נָבוֹא בֵיתֶךָ, נִשְׁתַּחֲוֶה אֶל הֵיכַל קָדְשְׁךָ בְּיִרְאָתֶךָ.[14] נִשְׁתַּחֲוֶה אֶל הֵיכַל קָדְשְׁךָ וְנוֹדֶה אֶת שְׁמֶךָ, עַל חַסְדְּךָ וְעַל אֲמִתֶּךָ, כִּי הִגְדַּלְתָּ עַל כָּל שִׁמְךָ אִמְרָתֶךָ.[15] לְכוּ נְרַנְּנָה לַיהוה, נָרִיעָה לְצוּר יִשְׁעֵנוּ. נְקַדְּמָה פָנָיו בְּתוֹדָה, בִּזְמִרוֹת נָרִיעַ לוֹ.[16] אֲשֶׁר יַחְדָּו נַמְתִּיק סוֹד, בְּבֵית אֱלֹהִים נְהַלֵּךְ בְּרָגֶשׁ.[17] אֵל נַעֲרָץ בְּסוֹד קְדוֹשִׁים רַבָּה, וְנוֹרָא עַל כָּל סְבִיבָיו.[18] שְׂאוּ יְדֵיכֶם קֹדֶשׁ וּבָרְכוּ אֶת יהוה.[19] הִנֵּה בָּרְכוּ אֶת יהוה כָּל עַבְדֵי יהוה, הָעֹמְדִים בְּבֵית יהוה בַּלֵּילוֹת.[20] אֲשֶׁר מִי אֵל בַּשָּׁמַיִם וּבָאָרֶץ, אֲשֶׁר יַעֲשֶׂה כְמַעֲשֶׂיךָ וְכִגְבוּרֹתֶיךָ.[21] אֲשֶׁר לוֹ הַיָּם וְהוּא עָשָׂהוּ, וְיַבֶּשֶׁת יָדָיו יָצָרוּ.[22] אֲשֶׁר בְּיָדוֹ מֶחְקְרֵי אָרֶץ, וְתוֹעֲפוֹת הָרִים לוֹ.[23] אֲשֶׁר בְּיָדוֹ נֶפֶשׁ כָּל חָי, וְרוּחַ כָּל בְּשַׂר אִישׁ.[24] וְיוֹדוּ שָׁמַיִם פִּלְאֲךָ יהוה, אַף אֱמוּנָתְךָ בִּקְהַל קְדֹשִׁים.[25] לְךָ זְרוֹעַ עִם גְּבוּרָה, תָּעֹז יָדְךָ תָּרוּם יְמִינֶךָ.[26] לְךָ שָׁמַיִם, אַף לְךָ אָרֶץ, תֵּבֵל וּמְלֹאָהּ אַתָּה יְסַדְתָּם.[27] אַתָּה פוֹרַרְתָּ בְעָזְּךָ יָם, שִׁבַּרְתָּ רָאשֵׁי תַנִּינִים עַל הַמָּיִם.[28] אַתָּה הִצַּבְתָּ כָּל גְּבוּלוֹת אָרֶץ, קַיִץ וָחֹרֶף אַתָּה יְצַרְתָּם.[29] אַתָּה רִצַּצְתָּ רָאשֵׁי לִוְיָתָן, תִּתְּנֶנּוּ מַאֲכָל לְעַם לְצִיִּים.

---

(1) *Daniel* 9:7. (2) Cf. *Lamentations* 3:39. (3) Cf. *Genesis* 44:16. (4) Cf. *Lamentations* 3:40.
(5) *Psalms* 65:3. (6) Cf. *Isaiah* 66:23. (7) *Psalms* 86:9. (8) 95:6. (9) 132:7. (10) 100:4.
(11) 99:5. (12) 99:9. (13) 96:9. (14) Cf. 5:8. (15) Cf. 138:2. (16) 95:1-2. (17) 55:15. (18) 89:8.
(19) 134:2. (20) 134:1. (21) *Deuteronomy* 3:24. (22) *Psalms* 95:5. (23) 95:4. (24) *Job* 12:10.
(25) *Psalms* 89:6. (26) 89:14. (27) 89:12. (28) 74:13. (29) 74:17.

לְךָ ה׳ *Yours, my Lord, is the righteousness and ours is the shame-*
facedness.[1] *What complaint can we make?*[2] *What can we say?*
What can we declare? What justification can we offer?[3] *Let us examine*
our ways and analyze — and return to You,[4] *for Your right hand is*
extended to accept penitents. Neither with kindness nor with [good]
deeds do we come before You. As paupers and as beggars do we knock
at Your doors. At Your doors we knock, O Compassionate and Gracious
One. Please do not turn us away from You empty-handed. Our King, turn
us not away from You empty-handed, for You are the One Who hears
prayer.

שֹׁמֵעַ תְּפִלָּה *You Who hears prayer, to You all flesh will come.*[5] *All*
flesh will come to prostrate itself before You, O HASHEM.[6]
They will come and prostrate themselves before You, my Lord, and shall
honor Your Name.[7] *Come! — let us prostrate ourselves and bow, let us*
kneel before God, our Maker.[8] *Let us come to His dwelling places, let us*
prostrate ourselves at His footstool.[9] *Enter His gates with thanksgiving,*
His courts with praise; give thanks to Him, praise His Name.[10] *Exalt*
HASHEM, our God, and bow at His footstool; He is holy![11] *Exalt HASHEM,*
our God, and bow at His holy mountain; for holy is HASHEM, our God.[12]
Prostrate yourselves before HASHEM in His intensely holy place, tremble
before Him, everyone on earth.[13] *As for us, through Your abundant*
kindness we will enter Your House; we will prostrate ourselves toward
Your Holy Sanctuary in awe of You.[14] *We will prostrate ourselves toward*
Your Holy Sanctuary, and we will give thanks to Your Name for Your
kindness and truth for You have exalted Your promise even beyond Your
Name.[15] *Come! — let us sing to HASHEM, let us call out to the Rock of our*
salvation. Let us greet Him with thanksgiving, with praiseful songs let us
call out to Him.[16] *For together let us share sweet counsel, in the house of*
God let us walk in multitudes.[17] *God is dreaded in the hiddenmost*
counsel of the holy ones, and inspires awe upon all who surround Him.[18]
Lift your hands in the Sanctuary and bless HASHEM.[19] *Behold, bless*
HASHEM, all you servants of HASHEM, who stand in the House of HASHEM
in the nights.[20] *For what power is there in heaven or earth that can*
approximate Your deeds and power?[21] *For His is the sea and He*
perfected the dry land — His hands fashioned it.[22] *For in His power are*
the hidden mysteries of the earth, and the mountain summits are His.[23]
For His is the soul of every living thing, and the spirit of all human flesh.[24]
Heaven will gratefully praise Your wonders, HASHEM; also Your
faithfulness in the assembly of holy ones.[25] *Yours is a mighty arm with*
power, You strengthen Your hand; You exalt Your right hand.[26] *Yours is*
the heaven; Yours, too, is the earth; the world and its fullness — You
founded them.[27] *You shattered the sea with Your might, You smashed sea*
serpents' heads upon the water.[28] *You established all the boundaries*
of earth; summer and winter — You fashioned them.[29] *You crushed*
the heads of Leviathan, You served it as food to the nation of legions.

אַתָּה בָקַעְתָּ מַעְיָן וָנָחַל, אַתָּה הוֹבַשְׁתָּ נַהֲרוֹת אֵיתָן.[1] לְךָ יוֹם, אַף
לְךָ לָיְלָה, אַתָּה הֲכִינְוֹתָ מָאוֹר וָשָׁמֶשׁ.[2] עָשָׂה גְדֹלוֹת עַד אֵין חֵקֶר,
וְנִפְלָאוֹת עַד אֵין מִסְפָּר.[3] כִּי אֵל גָּדוֹל יהוה, וּמֶלֶךְ גָּדוֹל עַל כָּל
אֱלֹהִים.[4] כִּי גָדוֹל אַתָּה וְעוֹשֵׂה נִפְלָאוֹת, אַתָּה אֱלֹהִים לְבַדֶּךָ.[5] כִּי
גָדוֹל מֵעַל שָׁמַיִם חַסְדֶּךָ, וְעַד שְׁחָקִים אֲמִתֶּךָ.[6] גָּדוֹל יהוה וּמְהֻלָּל
מְאֹד, וְלִגְדֻלָּתוֹ אֵין חֵקֶר.[7] (כִּי) גָּדוֹל יהוה וּמְהֻלָּל מְאֹד, נוֹרָא
הוּא עַל כָּל אֱלֹהִים.[8] גָּדוֹל יהוה וּמְהֻלָּל מְאֹד, בְּעִיר אֱלֹהֵינוּ הַר
קָדְשׁוֹ.[9] לְךָ יהוה הַגְּדֻלָּה וְהַגְּבוּרָה, וְהַתִּפְאֶרֶת וְהַנֵּצַח וְהַהוֹד, כִּי
כֹל בַּשָּׁמַיִם וּבָאָרֶץ; לְךָ יהוה הַמַּמְלָכָה, וְהַמִּתְנַשֵּׂא לְכֹל
לְרֹאשׁ.[10] מִי לֹא יִרָאֲךָ מֶלֶךְ הַגּוֹיִם, כִּי לְךָ יָאָתָה, כִּי בְכָל חַכְמֵי
הַגּוֹיִם וּבְכָל מַלְכוּתָם מֵאֵין כָּמוֹךָ.[11] מֵאֵין כָּמוֹךָ יהוה, גָּדוֹל אַתָּה
וְגָדוֹל שִׁמְךָ בִּגְבוּרָה.[12] יהוה אֱלֹהֵי צְבָאוֹת, מִי כָמוֹךָ חֲסִין יָהּ,
וֶאֱמוּנָתְךָ סְבִיבוֹתֶיךָ.[13] יהוה צְבָאוֹת, אֱלֹהֵי יִשְׂרָאֵל, יוֹשֵׁב
הַכְּרֻבִים, אַתָּה הוּא הָאֱלֹהִים לְבַדֶּךָ.[14] מִי יְמַלֵּל גְּבוּרוֹת יהוה,
יַשְׁמִיעַ כָּל תְּהִלָּתוֹ.[15] כִּי מִי בַשַּׁחַק יַעֲרֹךְ לַיהוה, יִדְמֶה לַיהוה
בִּבְנֵי אֵלִים.[16] מַה נֹּאמַר לְפָנֶיךָ יוֹשֵׁב מָרוֹם, וּמַה נְּסַפֵּר לְפָנֶיךָ
שֹׁכֵן שְׁחָקִים. מַה נֹּאמַר לְפָנֶיךָ יהוה אֱלֹהֵינוּ, מַה נְּדַבֵּר וּמַה
נִּצְטַדָּק.[17] אֵין לָנוּ פֶּה לְהָשִׁיב וְלֹא מֵצַח לְהָרִים רֹאשׁ, כִּי
עֲוֺנוֹתֵינוּ רַבּוּ מִלְמְנוֹת, וְחַטֹּאתֵינוּ עָצְמוּ מִסַּפֵּר.[18] לְמַעַן שִׁמְךָ
יהוה תְּחַיֵּנוּ, וּבְצִדְקָתְךָ תּוֹצִיא מִצָּרָה נַפְשֵׁנוּ.[19] דַּרְכְּךָ אֱלֹהֵינוּ
לְהַאֲרִיךְ אַפֶּךָ, לָרָעִים וְלַטּוֹבִים, וְהִיא תְהִלָּתֶךָ. לְמַעַנְךָ אֱלֹהֵינוּ
עֲשֵׂה וְלֹא לָנוּ, רְאֵה עֲמִידָתֵנוּ, דַּלִּים וְרֵקִים. ❖ הַנְּשָׁמָה לָךְ וְהַגּוּף
פָּעֳלָךְ, חוּסָה עַל עֲמָלָךְ. הַנְּשָׁמָה לָךְ וְהַגּוּף שֶׁלָּךְ, יהוה עֲשֵׂה
לְמַעַן שְׁמֶךָ. אָתָאנוּ עַל שִׁמְךָ, יהוה, עֲשֵׂה לְמַעַן שְׁמֶךָ. בַּעֲבוּר
כְּבוֹד שִׁמְךָ, כִּי אֵל חַנּוּן וְרַחוּם שְׁמֶךָ. לְמַעַן שִׁמְךָ יהוה, וְסָלַחְתָּ
לַעֲוֺנֵנוּ כִּי רַב הוּא.[20]

Congregation, then *chazzan:*

סְלַח לָנוּ אָבִינוּ, כִּי בְרֹב אִוַּלְתֵּנוּ שָׁגִינוּ,
מְחַל לָנוּ מַלְכֵּנוּ, כִּי רַבּוּ עֲוֺנֵינוּ.

(1) *Psalms* 74:14-15. (2) 74:16. (3) *Job* 9:10. (4) *Psalms* 95:3. (5) 86:10. (6) 108:5.
(7) 145:3. (8) 96:4. (9) 48:2. (10) *I Chronicles* 29:11. (11) *Jeremiah* 10:7. (12) 10:6.
(13) *Psalms* 89:9. (14) *Isaiah* 37:16. (15) *Psalms* 106:2. (16) 89:7.
(17) Cf. *Genesis* 44:16. (18) Cf. *Ezra* 9:6. (19) Cf. *Psalms* 143:11. (20) Cf. 25:11.

You split open fountain and stream, You dried the mighty rivers.[1] *Yours is the day, Yours as well is the night; You established luminary and the sun.*[2] *Who performs great deeds that are beyond comprehension, and wonders beyond number.*[3] *For a great God is HASHEM, and a great King above all heavenly powers.*[4] *For You are great and work wonders; You alone, O God.*[5] *For great above the very heavens is Your kindness, and until the upper heights is Your truth.*[6] *HASHEM is great and exceedingly lauded, and His greatness is beyond investigation.*[7] *(For) HASHEM is great and exceedingly lauded, awesome is He above all heavenly powers.*[8] *Great is HASHEM and exceedingly lauded, in the city of our God, Mount of His Holiness.*[9] *Yours, HASHEM, is the greatness, the strength, the splendor, the triumph, and the glory; even everything in heaven and earth; Yours, HASHEM, is the kingdom, and sovereignty over every leader.*[10] *Who would not revere You, O King of nations? — for this befits You, for among all the sages of the nations and in all their kingdom there is none like You.*[11] *There is none like You, O HASHEM, You are great and Your Name is great with power.*[12] *HASHEM, God of Legions — who is like You, O Strong One, God? — and Your faithfulness surrounds You.*[13] *HASHEM, Master of Legions, God of Israel, enthroned upon the Cherubim, it is You alone Who is God.*[14] *Who can express the mighty acts of HASHEM, who can announce all His praise?*[15] *For who in the sky can be compared to HASHEM; be likened to HASHEM among the angels?*[16] *What can we say before You Who dwell on high? And what can we relate to You Who abide in the highest heaven? What can we say before You, HASHEM, our God? What can we declare? What justification can we offer?*[17] *We have neither mouth to respond nor brow to raise our head, for our iniquities are too numerous to count, and our sins are too vast to be numbered.*[18] *For Your Name's sake, HASHEM, revive us; and with Your righteousness remove our soul from distress.*[19] *It is Your way, our God, to delay Your anger, against people both evil and good — and this is Your praise. Act for Your sake, our God, and not for ours, behold our [spiritual] position — destitute and emptyhanded.* Chazzan – *The soul is Yours and the body is Your handiwork; take pity on Your labor. The soul is Yours and the body is Yours; O HASHEM, act for Your Name's sake. We have come with reliance on Your Name, O HASHEM, act for Your Name's sake; because of Your Name's glory — for 'Gracious and Merciful God' is Your Name. For Your Name's sake, HASHEM, may You forgive our iniquity, though it is abundant.*[20]

Congregation, then chazzan:

Forgive us, our Father, for in our abundant folly we have erred, pardon us, our King, for our iniquities are many.

סליחה פז (פתיחה)

All:

עַם יהוה חִזְקוּ* וְנִתְחַזְקָה,¹   וְקִרְאוּ אֶל אֱלֹהִים בְּחָזְקָה.²

אִישׁ אָוֶן יִתְוַדֶּה אַשְׁמֵהוּ,   וְיָשֹׁב אֶל יהוה וִירַחֲמֵהוּ.³

לִקְרֹא לְלֹא יָנוּם וְלֹא יִישָׁן,   שׁוֹמֵר יִשְׂרָאֵל⁴ עוּרָה לָמָּה תִישָׁן.⁵

יַשֵּׁר זֵכֶר וְכִשְׁרוֹן מַעֲשֶׂה,   וַיהוה הַטּוֹב בְּעֵינָיו יַעֲשֶׂה.⁶

הַבְטִיחָנוּ אֱלֹהִים אֱמֶת,*   כִּי לֹא אֶחְפֹּץ בְּמוֹת הַמֵּת.⁷

בְּהִמָּצְאוֹ דִּרְשׁוּהוּ בְּתַחַן לְקָרֹב,   קְרָאֻהוּ בִּהְיוֹתוֹ קָרוֹב.⁸

רַצּוּהוּ חַלּוּהוּ בְּאֵימָה עִבְדוּהוּ,   כָּל זֶרַע יַעֲקֹב כַּבְּדוּהוּ.⁹

שָׁקֹד דַּלְתוֹת אֶרֶךְ אַפַּיִם,   נִשָּׂא לְבָבֵנוּ אֶל כַּפָּיִם.¹⁰

מִי יוֹדֵעַ רַצוֹת וְיוֹאֵל,   הִכּוֹן לִקְרַאת אֱלֹהֶיךָ יִשְׂרָאֵל.¹¹

עִרְכוּ שֶׁוַע וּתְפִלָּה לְצָרָה,   קַדְּשׁוּ צוֹם קִרְאוּ עֲצָרָה.¹²

יְבַקֵּשׁ יְפַלֵּל אֱלֹהִים עוֹבֵד,   וְשָׁב מֵחֲרוֹן אַפּוֹ וְלֹא נֹאבֵד.¹³

הֲיִרְצֶה שַׁי וָתֶשֶׁר מֵהַשָּׁמֵן,*   בְּרִבְבוֹת נַחֲלֵי שָׁמֶן.¹⁴

חָפֵץ שְׁמֹעַ מִתְקָרֶבֶת עוֹלִים,   לְהַקְשִׁיב מֵחֵלֶב אֵילִים.¹⁵

❖ זְכוּת לַמֵּד וְיַשֵּׁר עָקֹב,¹⁶   זְכֹר אֵלֶּה לְיַעֲקֹב.¹⁷

קְחוּ עִמָּכֶם דְּבָרִים   וְשַׂפָּה בְשָׁלוֹם פָּרִים.

All:

כִּי עַל רַחֲמֶיךָ הָרַבִּים¹⁸ אָנוּ בְטוּחִים, וְעַל צִדְקוֹתֶיךָ אָנוּ נִשְׁעָנִים, וְלִסְלִיחוֹתֶיךָ אָנוּ מְקַוִּים, וְלִישׁוּעָתְךָ אָנוּ מְצַפִּים. אַתָּה הוּא מֶלֶךְ, אוֹהֵב צְדָקוֹת מִקֶּדֶם, מַעֲבִיר עֲוֹנוֹת עַמּוֹ, וּמֵסִיר חַטַּאת יְרֵאָיו. כּוֹרֵת בְּרִית לָרִאשׁוֹנִים, וּמְקַיֵּם שְׁבוּעָה לָאַחֲרוֹנִים. אַתָּה הוּא, שֶׁיָּרַדְתָּ בַּעֲנַן כְּבוֹדֶךָ עַל הַר סִינַי,¹⁹ וְהֶרְאֵיתָ דַּרְכֵי טוּבְךָ לְמֹשֶׁה עַבְדֶּךָ.²⁰ וְאָרְחוֹת חֲסָדֶיךָ גִּלִּיתָ לּוֹ, וְהוֹדַעְתּוֹ כִּי אַתָּה אֵל רַחוּם וְחַנּוּן, אֶרֶךְ אַפַּיִם וְרַב חֶסֶד²¹ וּמַרְבֶּה לְהֵיטִיב, וּמַנְהִיג אֶת כָּל הָעוֹלָם כֻּלּוֹ

---

(1) Cf. *I Chronicles* 19:13. (2) Cf. *Jonah* 3:8. (3) *Isaiah* 55:7. (4) Cf. *Psalms* 121:4; some editions of *Selichos* omit these two words. (5) 44:24. (6) *I Chronicles* 19:13. (7) *Ezekiel* 18:32. (8) *Isaiah* 55:6. (9) *Psalms* 22:24. (10) *Lamentations* 3:41. (11) *Amos* 4:12. (12) *Joel* 2:15. (13) *Jonah* 3:9. (14) *Micah* 6:7. (15) *I Samuel* 15:22. (16) Some editions read, כְּוֹת וְיֵשֶׁר עָקֹב, [*turn into*] *merit and uprightness that which has been made crooked* [*by our sins*]. (17) Cf. *Isaiah* 44:21; some editions read, זְכֹר אֱלֹהֵי יַעֲקֹב, *remember, O God of Jacob.* (18) Cf. *Hosea* 14:3. (19) *Daniel* 9:18. (20) Cf. *Exodus* 34:5. (21) Cf. 33:13.

עַם ה' חִזְקוּ ﴾— *People of HASHEM, be strong.* This *selichah* calls upon Israel to arouse itself to repentance. The acrostic reads, אֵלִיָּה בַּר שְׁמַעְיָה חֲזַק, *Eliyah bar Shemayah, may he be strong* [see prefatory comment to *selichah* 6].

הַבְטִיחָנוּ אֱלֹהִים אֱמֶת — *The God of Truth*

promised us. The translation follows the classic Yiddish version of *Selichos*. Alternatively, the stich means, *God promised us truly.*

מֵהַשָּׁמֵן — *From the [person] fattened.* This describes either: the wicked man whose heart is so saturated with spiritual fat, that it prevents him

---

SELICHAH 87

All:

People of HASHEM, be strong* and let us strengthen each other,[1]
and call out loudly to God![2]

א *Let the sinner confess his guilt,*
and return to HASHEM, who will have mercy on him.[3]

ל *To cry to the One who neither slumbers nor sleeps:*
'O Guardian of Israel,[4] *awake! Why do You [seem to] sleep?*[5]

י *'Remember uprightness and proper deeds.'*
And HASHEM will do what is good in His judgment.[6]

ה *The God of Truth promised us,**
'I do not desire that the condemned should die.'[7]

ב *Seek Him when He is to be found, to draw near [to Him] in supplication;*
call to Him when He is near.[8]

ר *Reconcile Him, beseech Him, serve Him with reverence;*
all the seed of Jacob, honor Him![9]

ש *Wait upon the doors of Him Who is slow to anger;*
let us lift up our hearts with our hands.[10]

מ *Whoever knows how to find favor, that He will be appeased,*
prepare to approach your God, O Israel![11]

ע *Arrange an outcry and a prayer in time of trouble;*
declare a fast, summon an assembly![12]

י *Let him that serves God beseech and pray [on our behalf],*
that He may turn back from His flaring anger, that we not be lost.[13]

ה *Will He be pleased with gift and offering from the [person] fattened**
or with myriad rivers of oil?[14]

ח *He desires obedience more than the bringing of olah-offerings;*
to be heeded, more than the offering of rams' fat.[15]

ז *Chazzan — [O God] advocate merit and rectify the perverse —* [16]
remember these for the sake of Jacob.[17]

ק *Take words [of prayer] with you, and lips instead of sacrificial bulls.*

All:

כִּי עַל *For upon Your abundant mercy*[18] *do we trust, and upon Your*
righteousness do we depend, and for Your forgiveness do we
hope, and for Your salvation do we yearn. You are the King Who
loves righteousness since the earliest days, Who overlooks His people's
iniquities and sets aside the sins of those who revere Him. He made
a covenant with the ancestors and keeps [His] vow to the descendants.
It is You Who descended in Your cloud of glory on Mount Sinai,[19]
and showed the ways of Your goodness to Your servant Moses.[20]
You revealed Your paths of kindness to him, and let him know that
You are God, Compassionate and Gracious, Slow to anger and Abund-
ant in Kindness,[21] *doing manifold good, and guiding all Your world*

---

from repenting (*Arugas HaBosem*); the wealthy man who brings many fat animals as offerings, yet does not repent in his heart (*Masbir*); or the penitent whose heart was once stuffed with spiritual fat, but who has repented and brought many Altar offerings (*Matteh Levi*).

בְּמִדַּת הָרַחֲמִים. ❖ וְכֵן כָּתוּב, וַיֹּאמֶר אֲנִי אַעֲבִיר כָּל טוּבִי עַל
פָּנֶיךָ, וְקָרָאתִי בְשֵׁם יהוה לְפָנֶיךָ, וְחַנֹּתִי אֶת אֲשֶׁר אָחֹן, וְרִחַמְתִּי
אֶת אֲשֶׁר אֲרַחֵם.¹

All, while standing:

אֵל אֶרֶךְ אַפַּיִם אַתָּה, וּבַעַל הָרַחֲמִים נִקְרֵאתָ,
וְדֶרֶךְ תְּשׁוּבָה הוֹרֵיתָ.

גְּדֻלַּת רַחֲמֶיךָ וַחֲסָדֶיךָ,   תִּזְכּוֹר הַיּוֹם וּבְכָל יוֹם לְזֶרַע יְדִידֶיךָ.
תֵּפֶן אֵלֵינוּ בְּרַחֲמִים,   כִּי אַתָּה הוּא בַּעַל הָרַחֲמִים.
בְּתַחֲנוּן וּבִתְפִלָּה פָּנֶיךָ נְקַדֵּם,   כְּהוֹדַעְתָּ לֶעָנָיו מִקֶּדֶם.
מֵחֲרוֹן אַפְּךָ שׁוּב,²   כְּמוֹ בְּתוֹרָתְךָ כָּתוּב.³
וּבְצֵל כְּנָפֶיךָ נֶחֱסֶה⁴ וְנִתְלוֹנָן,   כְּיוֹם וַיֵּרֶד יהוה בֶּעָנָן.
❖ תַּעֲבוֹר עַל פֶּשַׁע וְתִמְחֶה אָשָׁם,   כְּיוֹם וַיִּתְיַצֵּב עִמּוֹ שָׁם.
תַּאֲזִין שַׁוְעָתֵנוּ וְתַקְשִׁיב מֶנּוּ מַאֲמַר,
כְּיוֹם וַיִּקְרָא בְשֵׁם יהוה,⁵ וְשָׁם נֶאֱמַר:

Congregation, then chazzan:

וַיַּעֲבֹר יהוה עַל פָּנָיו וַיִּקְרָא:

Congregation and chazzan (the words in bold type are recited aloud and in unison):

יהוה, יהוה, אֵל, **רַחוּם, וְחַנּוּן, אֶרֶךְ אַפַּיִם, וְרַב חֶסֶד, וֶאֱמֶת,
נֹצֵר חֶסֶד לָאֲלָפִים, נֹשֵׂא עָוֹן, וָפֶשַׁע, וְחַטָּאָה,
וְנַקֵּה.**⁶ וְסָלַחְתָּ לַעֲוֹנֵנוּ וּלְחַטָּאתֵנוּ וּנְחַלְתָּנוּ.⁷ סְלַח לָנוּ אָבִינוּ כִּי
חָטָאנוּ, מְחַל לָנוּ מַלְכֵּנוּ כִּי פָשָׁעְנוּ. כִּי אַתָּה אֲדֹנָי טוֹב וְסַלָּח, וְרַב
חֶסֶד לְכָל קֹרְאֶיךָ.⁸

פסוקי הקדמה לסליחה פח

הַאֲזִינָה אֱלֹהִים תְּפִלָּתִי, וְאַל תִּתְעַלַּם מִתְּחִנָּתִי.⁹ תִּכּוֹן
תְּפִלָּתֵנוּ קְטֹרֶת לְפָנֶיךָ, מַשְׂאַת כַּפֵּינוּ מִנְחַת עָרֶב.¹⁰
הַאֲזִינָה יהוה תְּפִלָּתֵנוּ, הַקְשִׁיבָה לְקוֹל תַּחֲנוּנֵינוּ.¹¹ הַקְשִׁיבָה לְקוֹל
שַׁוְעָתֵנוּ, מַלְכֵּנוּ וֵאלֹהֵינוּ, כִּי אֵלֶיךָ נִתְפַּלָּל.¹² יהוה אֱלֹהֵי יִשְׂרָאֵל
צַדִּיק אַתָּה, כִּי נִשְׁאַרְנוּ פְּלֵיטָה כְּהַיּוֹם הַזֶּה.¹³

בְּרַחֵם אָב עַל בָּנִים, כֵּן תְּרַחֵם יהוה עָלֵינוּ.¹⁴ לַיהוה הַיְשׁוּעָה,
עַל עַמְּךָ בִרְכָתֶךָ סֶּלָה.¹⁵ יהוה צְבָאוֹת עִמָּנוּ,
מִשְׂגָּב לָנוּ אֱלֹהֵי יַעֲקֹב סֶלָה.¹⁶ יהוה צְבָאוֹת, אַשְׁרֵי אָדָם בֹּטֵחַ
בָּךְ.¹⁷ יהוה הוֹשִׁיעָה, הַמֶּלֶךְ יַעֲנֵנוּ בְיוֹם קָרְאֵנוּ.¹⁸

with the Attribute of Mercy. Chazzan — *And so it is written: He said, 'I shall pass all My good in front of you, and I shall call out the Name of HASHEM before you; for I will be gracious to whom I will be gracious, and I will be compassionate with whom I will be compassionate.'* [1]

All, while standing:

אֵל אֶרֶךְ אַפַּיִם *O God — You are slow to anger, You are called the Master of Mercy, and You have taught the way of repentance. May You remember this day and every day the greatness of Your mercy and Your kindness to the offspring of Your beloved Ones. Turn to us in mercy for You are the Master of Mercy. With supplication and prayer we approach Your Presence in the manner that You made known to the humble [Moses] in ancient times. Turn back from Your fierce anger;* [2] *as is written in Your Torah.* [3] *In the shadow of Your wings may we find shelter* [4] *and lodging as on the day 'HASHEM descended in a cloud' [to appear to Moses on Sinai].* Chazzan — *Overlook sin and erase guilt as on the day 'He [God] stood there with him [Moses].' Give heed to our cry and be attentive to our declaration as on the day 'He called out with the Name HASHEM,'* [5] *and there it was said:*

Congregation, then *chazzan:*

And HASHEM passed before him [Moses] and proclaimed:

Congregation and *chazzan* (the words in bold type are recited aloud and in unison):

ה' ה' HASHEM, HASHEM, God, Compassionate and Gracious, Slow to anger, and Abundant in Kindness and Truth, Preserver of kindness for thousands [of generations], Forgiver of iniquity, willful sin, and error, and Who cleanses. [6] *May You forgive our iniquities and our errors and make us Your heritage.* [7] *Forgive us, our Father, for we have erred; pardon us, our King, for we have willfully sinned; for You, my Lord, are good and forgiving and abundantly kind to all who call upon You.* [8]

PREFATORY VERSES TO SELICHAH 88

הַאֲזִינָה *Listen, O God, to my prayer, and do not conceal Yourself from my supplication.* [9] *May our prayer stand as incense before You: the lifting of our hands as an evening offering.* [10] *Give ear, HASHEM, to our prayer; be attentive to the sound of our supplication.* [11] *Be attentive to the sound of our outcry, our King and our God, for to You alone do we pray.* [12] *HASHEM, God of Israel, You are righteous, in that we are left a remnant as today.* [13]

כְּרַחֵם אָב *As a father has mercy on his children, so, HASHEM, may You have mercy on us.* [14] *Salvation is HASHEM's, upon Your people is Your blessing, Selah.* [15] *HASHEM, Master of Legions, is with us, a stronghold for us is the God of Jacob, Selah.* [16] *HASHEM, Master of Legions, praiseworthy is the person who trusts in You.* [17] *HASHEM, save! May the King answer us on the day we call.* [18]

---

(1) *Exodus* 33:19. (2) Cf. 32:12. (3) See 32:14. (4) Cf. *Psalms* 36:8. (5) *Exodus* 34:5. (6) 34:6-7. (7) 34:9. (8) *Psalms* 86:5. (9) 55:2; some editions of *Selichos* pluralize the pronouns of this verse: תְּפִלָּתֵנוּ, our prayer and מִתְּחִנָּתֵנוּ, *from our supplication.* (10) Cf. 141:2. (11) Cf. 86:6. (12) Cf. 5:3. (13) *Ezra* 9:15. (14) Cf. *Psalms* 103:13. (15) 3:9. (16) 46:8. (17) 84:13. (18) 20:10.

In some congregations the following two verses are recited responsively — the *chazzan* reciting סְלַח,
and the congregation responding וַיֹּאמֶר. In other congregations these verses are recited silently.

סְלַח נָא לַעֲוֹן הָעָם הַזֶּה כְּגֹדֶל חַסְדֶּךָ, וְכַאֲשֶׁר נָשָׂאתָה לָעָם
הַזֶּה מִמִּצְרַיִם וְעַד הֵנָּה,[1] וְשָׁם נֶאֱמַר:

וַיֹּאמֶר יהוה סָלַחְתִּי כִּדְבָרֶךָ.[2]

All:

הַטֵּה אֱלֹהַי אָזְנְךָ וּשֲׁמָע, פְּקַח עֵינֶיךָ וּרְאֵה שֹׁמְמֹתֵינוּ, וְהָעִיר
אֲשֶׁר נִקְרָא שִׁמְךָ עָלֶיהָ, כִּי לֹא עַל צִדְקֹתֵינוּ אֲנַחְנוּ
מַפִּילִים תַּחֲנוּנֵינוּ לְפָנֶיךָ, כִּי עַל רַחֲמֶיךָ הָרַבִּים. אֲדֹנָי שְׁמָעָה,
אֲדֹנָי סְלָחָה, אֲדֹנָי הַקְשִׁיבָה, וַעֲשֵׂה אַל תְּאַחַר, לְמַעַנְךָ אֱלֹהַי, כִּי
שִׁמְךָ נִקְרָא עַל עִירְךָ וְעַל עַמֶּךָ.[3]

סליחה פח

All:

יהוה **אֱלֹהֵי יִשְׂרָאֵל*** אַתָּה צַדִּיק[4] אֱלוֹהַּ סְלִיחוֹת,[5]
בְּלֵב נִדְכֶּה (וְנִשְׁבָּר) בָּאנוּ לְחַלּוֹתָךְ וּבְשִׁבְרוֹן רוּחוֹת,[6]
גַּם עֶשְׁתּוֹנוֹת קָשַׁטְנוּ וְהֵבַנּוּ סִתְרֵי טוּחוֹת,
דָּגוּל תְּהִי נָא אָזְנְךָ[7] קַשֶּׁבֶת וְעֵינֶיךָ פְּקוּחוֹת.[8]
הַשְׁקְדָה הִשְׂרְגָה עָלַי[9] עֲלִיַּת חֶרֶף מַכָּה,
(**וְרוֹפֵא**) אוּמָן וּבָקִי אַיִן לְהַעֲלוֹת אֲרוּכָה,
זֵד שׁוּחַ כּוֹרֶה,[10] וְעֵינָיו תִּצְפֵּינָה לְחֶלְכָּה,[11]
חֲלַקְלַק רֶשֶׁת בְּרַגְלָיו, וְיִתְהַלֵּךְ עַל שְׁבָכָה.[12]
טֹרְדוּ חַתּוּ יְדִידֶיךָ הָעַתִּיקוּ מִלִּים וְטַעֲנָה,[13]
יְהוּדָה וְיִשְׂרָאֵל הוּסַר מֵהֶם מַשְׁעֵן וּמִשְׁעֵנָה,[14]
כְּרֹאשׁ שִׁבֹּלֶת נִמְלוּ[15] וְנַפְשָׁם דָּאֲבָה וְנַעֲנָה,
לְרֹעָבָם מְרוֹרִים שָׂבֵעוּ וְלִצְמָאָם רָווּ לַעֲנָה.[16]
מַעַרְכֵי לֵב מַשֹּׁוֶה כָּל נָבוֹן וְרַבָּן,
נֶעֱלָם מֶשֶׁךְ הָעֵדָן וְנִסְתַּם בֶּשֶׁשׁ הַחֻרְבָּן,
סָפוּ תַמּוּ תְמִידֵי כַפָּרָה וּבָטֵל הַקָּרְבָּן,

פ⦿ **ה' אֱלֹהֵי יִשְׂרָאֵל** — *HASHEM, God of Israel.*
Throughout our long, seemingly interminable,
galus, we have remained loyal to our God. Despite blows and murder, torment and torture,
Israel has not succumbed to the pressure of its oppressors to forsake the God of Israel and worship
strange gods. Therefore, O God, as long as we
must remain in exile, hear our pleas and accept
our prayers as if they were Temple offerings.

The acrostic of this *selichah* follows the *aleph-
beis*, then spells the author's name — אֵלִיָּה בַּר
שְׁמַעְיָה חֲזַק, *Eliyah bar Shemayah, may he live* [see
prefatory comment to *selichah* 6].

פ⦿ **וּפְרָזוֹן חָדֵל** — *For prophecy has ceased.* The translation follows *Arugas HaBosem* and is based on
the Talmud's interpretation of חָדְלוּ פְרָזוֹן (*Judges*
5:7; *Pesachim* 66b). Others understand פְּרָזוֹן as

In some congregations the following two verses are recited responsively — the *chazzan*
reciting, 'Forgive, please . . .,' and the congregation responding, 'And HASHEM said . . .'
In other congregations these verses are recited silently.

סְלַח נָא *Forgive, please, the iniquity of this people according to the
greatness of Your kindness and as You have forgiven this
people from Egypt until now,*[1] *and there it was said:*
And HASHEM said, 'I have forgiven according to your word!'[2]

All:

הַטֵּה *Incline, my God, Your ear, and listen, open Your eyes and see our
desolation and that of the city upon which Your Name is
proclaimed; for not because of our righteousness do we cast down our
supplications before You, rather because of Your abundant compassion.
O my Lord, heed; O my Lord, forgive; O my Lord, be attentive and act,
do not delay; for Your sake, my God, for Your Name is proclaimed upon
Your city and upon Your people.*[3]

SELICHAH 88

All:

א *HASHEM, God of Israel!* You are righteous,*[4] *the God of forgiveness.*[5]

ב *With crushed (and broken) heart and with broken spirits*[6]
we have come to beseech You.

ג *[Our] thoughts, too, we have corrected, and we have prepared
[the lists of] our inner secrets;*

ד *Resplendent One, please let Your ear be attentive*[7]
and Your eyes wide open.[8]

ה *The mounting string of blows*[9] *has come repeatedly upon us,*

ו *and there is no (doctor,) nurse or specialist to bring healing.*

ז *The wanton one digs a pit,*[10] *his eyes looking for the weak;*[11]

ח *the net is smooth at his feet, and he walks onto the web.*[12]

ט *Your beloved ones are dismayed, cowed,
words and argument have left them.*[13]

י *Judah and Israel, every support or prop
has been removed from them;*[14]

כ *they are tumbled about like the tip of a wheatstalk,*[15]
their souls aching and afflicted;

ל *their hunger is sated with bitters,
their thirst quenched with wormwood.*[16]

מ *[Although] every man of understanding and rabbi
lays out the plan of [his] heart*

נ *concealed [from them all] is the length of the [Exile's] term;
hidden is the duration of the Destruction period.*

ס *The atoning continual-offering is gone, at an end; sacrifice has ceased —*

---

(1) *Numbers* 14:19. (2) 14:20. (3) *Daniel* 9:18-19. (4) *Ezra* 9:15. (5) *Nehemiah* 9:17. (6) Cf. *Psalms* 51:19.
(7) Cf. 130:2. (8) Cf. *Daniel* 9:18. (9) Cf. *Lamentations* 1:14. (10) Cf. *Psalms* 119:85. (11) Cf. 10:8.
(12) Cf. *Job* 18:8. (13) Cf. 32:15. (14) Cf. *Isaiah* 3:1. (15) Cf. *Job* 24:24. (16) Cf. *Lamentations* 3:15.

---

open, unwalled cities. No longer is Israel safe in
unwalled cities (*Targum* and *Rashi* to *Judges* 5:17;

Masbir, Pardes; see also commentary to *selichah*
21, s.v., וּפְרָזוֹן).

עֲבָדֶיךָ בְּקֹצֶר רְוּחַ, וּבְשַׁלְוָה יָהִיר וְסָרְבָן.

פּוֹדָם וּמַצִּילָם, הֲנָשִׁיתָ חֲמֹל, וְשָׁכַחְתָּ חֲנוֹת,[1]

צָפִיתָ הַבַּטְתָּ מֵעַל, וְלָעַד זָכַרְתָּ צַחֲנוֹת,[2]

קָצַפְתָּ עַד מְאֹד,[3] וְסָתַמְתָּ זַעַק וּתְחִנּוֹת,

רִבְבוֹת אֵלֶיךָ שׁוּבָה,[4] וּשְׁכֹן בְּקֶרֶב הַמַּחֲנוֹת.

שָׁח גַּבְהוּת יִשְׂרָאֵל וְרוּם יְהוּדָה שָׁפֵל,[5]

תַּלְפִּיּוֹת[6] חָרֵב, לֹא נִגַּהּ לוֹ וְאָפֵל,[7]

אוֹר לְצַלְמָוֶת הוּשַׁם, וְגִיהַּ הוּשַׁת לַעֲרָפֶל,[8]

לְאָן שַׁעַן הוֹרִים וּזְכוּת יְשֵׁנֵי מַכְפֵּל.[9]

יוֹצְרֵנוּ בְּדִינְךָ אִישׁ לֹא נִשָּׂא וְנִגְדָּל,

הֲשָׁוָה שׁוֹעַ וְלֹא נִכַּר לִפְנֵי דָל,[10]

בָּזוּי לָמָה נִכְבַּד, וְקָטוֹן[11] גָּבַהּ וְגָדַל,

רָצוּי יֶלֶד שַׁעֲשׁוּעַ[12] עָצוּר וּפִרְזוֹן חָדַל.*[13]

שְׁלֵמֶיךָ לֹא בָטְחוּ בַחֶרֶב וְסָבְרוּ בַחֲנִית,

מַשְׁעֵנָם צוֹם וָשַׂק, וּמִבְטְחָם תְּפִלָּה וְתַעֲנִית,

עוֹד תּוֹסִיף יָדְךָ עֲלוּבֶיךָ לִקְנוֹת שֵׁנִית,[14]

יְדֻמּוּ וְיָחִלוּ לְךָ[15] מִתַּחַת עַל רַגְזָנִית.

❖ הַאֲזִינָה עַם בָּזוּי וְשָׂסוּי מְדֻכָּא וּמְחֻלָּל,

חַנּוּן זַעַק קָשֵׁב וְקַבֵּל בְּרָצוֹן מִפְלָל,

קְטֹרֶת תְּפִלָּה תִּכּוֹן[16] וּכְקָרְבָּן תְּכַלָּל,

הַקְשִׁיבָה לְקוֹל שַׁוְעִי מַלְכִּי וֵאלֹהָי כִּי אֵלֶיךָ אֶתְפַּלָּל.[17]

All, while standing:

אֵל מֶלֶךְ יוֹשֵׁב עַל כִּסֵּא רַחֲמִים מִתְנַהֵג בַּחֲסִידוּת, מוֹחֵל עֲוֹנוֹת עַמּוֹ, מַעֲבִיר רִאשׁוֹן רִאשׁוֹן,[18] מַרְבֶּה מְחִילָה לַחַטָּאִים וּסְלִיחָה לַפּוֹשְׁעִים, עֹשֶׂה צְדָקוֹת עִם כָּל בָּשָׂר וָרְוּחַ, לֹא כְרָעָתָם תִּגְמוֹל. ❖ אֵל הוֹרֵיתָ לָּנוּ לוֹמַר שְׁלֹשׁ עֶשְׂרֵה, וּזְכוֹר לָנוּ הַיּוֹם בְּרִית שְׁלֹשׁ עֶשְׂרֵה, כְּמוֹ שֶׁהוֹדַעְתָּ לֶעָנָיו מִקֶּדֶם, כְּמוֹ שֶׁכָּתוּב, וַיֵּרֶד יהוה בֶּעָנָן וַיִּתְיַצֵּב עִמּוֹ שָׁם, וַיִּקְרָא בְשֵׁם יהוה.

(1) Cf. *Psalms* 77:10. (2) Cf. *Isaiah* 64:8. (3) Cf. *Lamentations* 5:22. (4) Cf. *Numbers* 10:36.
(5) Cf. *Isaiah* 2:11. (6) See commentary to *selichah* 67, s.v., שֶׁכָּלֵל בְּנוּי לְתַלְפִּיּוֹת. (7) Cf. *Amos* 5:20.
(8) Cf. *Jeremiah* 13:16. (9) See commentary to *selichah* 28. (10) Cf. *Job* 34:19. (11) See *Jeremiah* 49:15.
(12) Cf. 31:19. (13) Cf. *Judges* 5:7. (14) Cf. *Isaiah* 11:11. (15) Cf. *Psalms* 37:7. (16) Cf. 141:2.
(17) 5:3. (18) Tractate *Rosh Hashanah* 17a.

ע Your servants are short of spirit, while the arrogant,
   rebellious one has serenity.

פ O their Redeemer! O their Savior! Have You lost thoughts of mercy?
   Have you forgotten graciousness?[1]

צ Do You look at, do You observe misdeed?
   Do You remember [sins'] stench forever?[2]

ק You have been extremely wrathful;[3]
   You have blocked out cry and supplications.

ר Return to Your myriad thousands [of Israel],[4]
   and dwell amidst the [tribal] camps!

ש Israel's eminence is bent, Judah's stature is low;[5]

ת the Temple that all turned to in prayer[6] is destroyed;
   it has no light, but darkness.[7]

א Light has been turned to death-shadow, radiance to murky gloom.[8]

ל Where is the support of the Patriarchs?
   The merit of those who sleep in Machpelah?[9]

י Our Molder, in Your justice no man is exalted or great.

ה The rich are set even, not shown recognition before the poor.[10]

ב Why, then, is the despised [Edom][11] now eminent,
   the lowly one tall and great?

ר And Your child of delight,[12] who so pleased You, is restricted,
   for prophecy has ceased.*[13]

ש Your wholehearted people do not trust in the sword,
   nor put hope in the spear;

מ their reliance is on fast and sackcloth,
   and their trust is in prayer and affliction.

ע You will once again stretch out Your hand
   to take Your humbled people [as Your own] anew.[14]

י So they keep silent and hope for You[15]
   under the yoke of a furious mistress.

ה Chazzan – Give ear to the degraded, oppressed,
   crushed and profaned people;

חו be attentive to cried out supplication and accept prayer with favor.

ק Let prayer stand in lieu of incense[16] and burnt offering;
   be attentive to the sound of my outcry, my King and my God,
   for to You alone do I pray.[17]

All, while standing:

אֵל מֶלֶךְ O God, King Who sits on the throne of mercy; Who acts with
kindness, pardons the iniquities of His people, removes [sins]
one by one,[18] increasingly grants pardon to careless sinners and forgiveness
to rebels, Who deals righteously with every living being — You do not repay
them in accord with their evil. Chazzan — O God, You taught us to recite the
Thirteen [Attributes of Mercy], so remember for us today the covenant of
these Thirteen, as You made known to the humble one in ancient times, as
it is written: And HASHEM descended in a cloud and stood with him there,
and He called out with the Name HASHEM.

Congregation, then *chazzan:*

וַיַּעֲבֹר יהוה עַל פָּנָיו וַיִּקְרָא:

Congregation and *chazzan* (the words in bold type are recited aloud and in unison):

יהוה, יהוה, אֵל, רַחוּם, וְחַנּוּן, אֶרֶךְ אַפַּיִם, וְרַב חֶסֶד, וֶאֱמֶת,
נֹצֵר חֶסֶד לָאֲלָפִים, נֹשֵׂא עָוֹן, וָפֶשַׁע, וְחַטָּאָה,
וְנַקֵּה. וְסָלַחְתָּ לַעֲוֹנֵנוּ וּלְחַטָּאתֵנוּ וּנְחַלְתָּנוּ. סְלַח לָנוּ אָבִינוּ כִּי
חָטָאנוּ, מְחַל לָנוּ מַלְכֵּנוּ כִּי פָשָׁעְנוּ. כִּי אַתָּה אֲדֹנָי טוֹב וְסַלָּח, וְרַב
חֶסֶד לְכָל קֹרְאֶיךָ.

פסוקי הקדמה לסליחה פט

לָמָה יהוה תַּעֲמֹד בְּרָחוֹק, תַּעְלִים לְעִתּוֹת בַּצָּרָה.[1] לָמָה יהוה
יֶחֱרֶה אַפְּךָ בְּעַמֶּךָ, אֲשֶׁר הוֹצֵאתָ מֵאֶרֶץ מִצְרָיִם.[2] וְעַתָּה
יִגְדַּל נָא כֹּחַ אֲדֹנָי, כַּאֲשֶׁר דִּבַּרְתָּ לֵאמֹר.[3] שְׁמַע קוֹלֵנוּ יהוה
אֱלֹהֵינוּ, וְקַבֵּל בְּרַחֲמִים וּבְרָצוֹן אֶת תְּפִלָּתֵנוּ.[4] לָמָה לָנֶצַח
תִּשְׁכָּחֵנוּ, תַּעַזְבֵנוּ לְאֹרֶךְ יָמִים.[5]

בְּרַחֵם אָב עַל בָּנִים, כֵּן תְּרַחֵם יהוה עָלֵינוּ. לַיהוה הַיְשׁוּעָה,
עַל עַמְּךָ בִרְכָתֶךָ סֶּלָה. יהוה צְבָאוֹת עִמָּנוּ, מִשְׂגָּב
לָנוּ אֱלֹהֵי יַעֲקֹב סֶלָה. יהוה צְבָאוֹת, אַשְׁרֵי אָדָם בֹּטֵחַ בָּךְ. יהוה
הוֹשִׁיעָה, הַמֶּלֶךְ יַעֲנֵנוּ בְיוֹם קָרְאֵנוּ.

In some congregations the following two verses are recited responsively — the *chazzan* reciting סְלַח,
and the congregation responding וַיֹּאמֶר. In other congregations these verses are recited silently.

סְלַח נָא לַעֲוֹן הָעָם הַזֶּה כְּגֹדֶל חַסְדֶּךָ, וְכַאֲשֶׁר נָשָׂאתָה לָעָם
הַזֶּה מִמִּצְרַיִם וְעַד הֵנָּה, וְשָׁם נֶאֱמַר:

וַיֹּאמֶר יהוה סָלַחְתִּי כִּדְבָרֶךָ.

All:

הַטֵּה אֱלֹהַי אָזְנְךָ וּשְׁמָע, פְּקַח עֵינֶיךָ וּרְאֵה שֹׁמְמֹתֵינוּ, וְהָעִיר
אֲשֶׁר נִקְרָא שִׁמְךָ עָלֶיהָ, כִּי לֹא עַל צִדְקוֹתֵינוּ אֲנַחְנוּ
מַפִּילִים תַּחֲנוּנֵינוּ לְפָנֶיךָ, כִּי עַל רַחֲמֶיךָ הָרַבִּים. אֲדֹנָי שְׁמָעָה,
אֲדֹנָי סְלָחָה, אֲדֹנָי הַקְשִׁיבָה, וַעֲשֵׂה אַל תְּאַחַר, לְמַעַנְךָ אֱלֹהַי, כִּי
שִׁמְךָ נִקְרָא עַל עִירְךָ וְעַל עַמֶּךָ.

---

(1) *Psalms* 10:1. (2) *Exodus* 32:11. (3) *Numbers* 14:17; see commentary to prefatory
verses to *selichah* 5. (4) From the weekday *Shemoneh Esrei.* (5) *Lamentations* 5:20.

Congregation, then *chazzan:*

And HASHEM passed before him [Moses] and proclaimed:

Congregation and *chazzan* (the words in bold type are recited aloud and in unison):

ה' ה' **HASHEM, HASHEM, God, Compassionate and Gracious, Slow to anger, and Abundant in Kindness and Truth, Preserver of kindness for thousands [of generations], Forgiver of iniquity, willful sin, and error, and Who cleanses.** *May You forgive our iniquities and our errors and make us Your heritage. Forgive us, our Father, for we have erred; pardon us, our King, for we have willfully sinned; for You, my Lord, are good and forgiving and abundantly kind to all who call upon You.*

PREFATORY VERSES TO SELICHAH 89

לָמָה *Why, HASHEM, do You stand far off, do You conceal Yourself in times of trouble?[1] Why, HASHEM, does Your fury rage against Your people, whom You brought out of the land of Egypt?[2] And now, please let [the revelation of] my Lord's strength grow great, as You have spoken, [ordaining the Thirteen Attributes] to be said.[3] Hear our voice, HASHEM our God, and accept — with compassion and favor — our prayer.[4] Why do You forget us for eternity, forsake us for so long?[5]*

כְּרַחֵם אָב *As a father has mercy on his children, so, HASHEM, may You have mercy on us. Salvation is HASHEM's, upon Your people is Your blessing, Selah. HASHEM, Master of Legions, is with us, a stronghold for us is the God of Jacob, Selah. HASHEM, Master of Legions, praiseworthy is the person who trusts in You. HASHEM, save! May the King answer us on the day we call.*

In some congregations the following two verses are recited responsively — the *chazzan* reciting, *'Forgive, please . . . ,'* and the congregation responding, *'And HASHEM said . . .'* In other congregations these verses are recited silently.

סְלַח נָא *Forgive, please, the iniquity of this people according to the greatness of Your kindness and as You have forgiven this people from Egypt until now, and there it was said:*

And HASHEM said, 'I have forgiven according to your word!'

All:

הַטֵּה *Incline, my God, Your ear, and listen, open Your eyes and see our desolation and that of the city upon which YourName is proclaimed; for not because of our righteousness do we cast down our supplications before You, rather because of Your abundant compassion. O my Lord, heed; O my Lord, forgive; O my Lord, be attentive and act, do not delay; for Your sake, my God, for Your Name is proclaimed upon Your city and upon Your people.*

סליחה פט

אֱלֹהֵינוּ וֵאלֹהֵי אֲבוֹתֵינוּ:

אֱזֹן תַּחַן* וְהַסְכֵּת עֲתִירָה,   אַף הָפֵר וְשַׂכֵּךְ עֶבְרָה,

בָּאֵי לְחַלּוֹתְךָ בְּנֶפֶשׁ מָרָה,   בְּשִׁמְךָ הַגָּדוֹל יִמְצְאוּ עֶזְרָה.[1*]

גָּעִית נֶאֱנָחִים עֲנֹתָם חֲזֵה,   גְּחִינַת קוֹמָתָם נָא אַל תִּבְזֶה,

דְּרֹשׁ עֶלְבּוֹנָם (מִצַּר בּוֹזֶה,   דְּרֹךְ פּוּרָה וְנִצְחָם יַזֶּה).[2]

הֲלֹא אַתָּה הָיִיתָ וְהִנֶּךָּ,   הָיוּ תִהְיֶה בַּהֲדַר גְּאוֹנֶךָ,

וְנֶאֱמְתָּ יִכּוֹן זֶרַע אֱמוּנֶיךָ,[3]   וְהֵנָם כָּלִים מִתִּגְרַת חֲרוֹנֶךָ.[4]

זָעֲמוּ בְעֵוּוּיִם וּמִמַּאֲוַיִּם נִסָּחוּ,   זֹרוּ בָּאֲפָסִים וְלֹא נָחוּ,

חֻבְּלָה רוּחָם[5] וְלֶעָפָר שָׁחוּ,   חָרְשׁוּ חוֹרְשִׁים וּמַעֲנִית הִמְתִּיחוּ.[7]

טָבְעוּ בַבֹּץ וְאֵין פּוֹצֶה,   טוֹרְפֵיהֶם שָׁלוּ מִקָּצֶה אֶל קָצֶה,

יוֹם יוֹם לוֹחֲמָם מְנַצֶּה,   יַד פּוֹרְשִׂים מַלְחָץ לֵיצֵא.

כָּלוּ חַיֵּיהֶם בְּיָגוֹן וַאֲנָחָה,   כְּשֵׁל[8] רַבָּה וְעָרְבָה שִׂמְחָה,

לְיֵשַׁע חוֹכִים וְהִנֵּה צְוָחָה,   לַבְּטוּם קָמִים וְכָרוּ שׁוּחָה.[9]

מַעֲרִימִים סוֹד מִמְּךָ לְהַדִּיחָם,   מַכְבִּידִים עֹל לְהַכְשִׁיל כֹּחָם,

נָאֳקִים אֵלֶיךָ בְּהִתְעַטֵּף רוּחָם,   נַחַת לִמְצֹא מְכֻבָּד טָרְחָם.

שִׂיחַ צָקִים בְּמַעֲמָד צָפוּף,   סְלִיחָה מְבַקְּשִׁים בְּקָדְקֹד כָּפוּף,

עוֹשְׁקֵיהֶם יַקְנִיאוּם, וּנְתָנוּם לִשְׁסוּף,[10]

עֵוִים יְמַסְּכוּ[11] וְיִהְיוּ לִסְפוּף.

פְּדֵה דְבֵקֶיךָ מֵחֶרֶץ וְכִלּוּי,   פַּלְּטֵם מְצוֹרֵר וּתְנֵם לְעִלּוּי,

צַוֵּה יְשׁוּעוֹת מְשַׁחֲרֶיךָ בְּחִלּוּי,   צַדְּקֵם בְּדִינֶךָ מִסְתָּר וְגָלוּי.[12]

קַנֹּא וְנוֹקֵם קַנֵּא לִשְׁמֶךָ,   קַצֵּץ סַמְלוֹנִים מִצַּוַּאר עַמֶּךָ,

רְאֵה עֲמָלֵנוּ וְשׁוּב מִזַּעְמֶךָ,   רִיבָה רִיבֵנוּ מֵעַם חֶרְמֶךָ.[13]

---

(1) Cf. *Psalms* 124:8. (2) Cf. *Isaiah* 63:3; some editions of *Selichos* omit the passage in parentheses. (3) Cf. *Psalms* 102:29. (4) Cf. 39:11. (5) Cf. *Job* 17:1. (6) Cf. *Psalms* 44:26. (7) Cf. 129:3. (8) Cf. 31:11. (9) Cf. *Jeremiah* 18:20. (10) This stich is another instance of censorship; some editions omit all or part of the stich; the original text reads, *The persecutors who provoke them,* בְּנֶצֶר נָאָפוּף, *with the branch grown from adultery.* (11) Cf. *Isaiah* 19:4. (12) Another censored line; this one originally read: צַמֵּת בְּקִצְפְּךָ שׁוֹחֲחֵי לְתָלוּי, *utterly destroy in Your anger those who bow to one hanging*; some editions read, צוּר עוֹלָמִים הוֹשִׁיעֵנוּ בְּגָלוּי, *May the Rock of the Universe openly save us.* (13) Cf. *Isaiah* 34:5.

אֱזֹן תַּחַן ⧉ — *Give ear to supplication.* This anonymous *selichah* contains a double *aleph-beis* acrostic, although in some editions a few lines are omitted, presumably to appease the censor.

בְּשִׁמְךָ הַגָּדוֹל יִמְצְאוּ עֶזְרָה — *May they find help by*

[invoking] *Your great Name.* The translation is based on *Metzudos David* to *Psalms* 124:8. According to *Pardes* the stich means: *For the sake of Your Name* [i.e., that it not be profaned when their prayer is ignored], *let them find help.*

SELICHAH 89

Our God and the God of our forefathers:

א *Give ear to supplication;* hearken to prayer;*

א *dismiss anger and quell wrath.*

ב *Those who come with bitter soul to beseech You,*

ב *may they find help by [invoking] Your great Name.*1*

ג *[Hear] the sigh of the groaners, see their affliction;*

ג *please do not despise their bent low spines.*

ד *Seek justice for their humiliation (from the rapacious enemies.*

ד *Trample [them like grapes in] the vat and let their lifeblood spatter)!2*

ה *Have You not [always] been, and are now?*

ה *You will always be, in Your glorious majesty.*

ו *And You said that the seed of Your faithful would stand fast;3*

ו *yet here they are, withering away under the attack of Your fury.4*

ז *For their iniquity they suffered [Your] anger,*
and were expelled from [the Land of] their longing,

ז *dispersed to the ends [of the earth] without resting.*

ח *Their spirit wounded,5 they are bowed to the dust,6*

ח *while the [oppressive] plowers plow [over them as if a field],*
lengthening the furrow.7

ט *They drown in the [Exile's] mud with none to release [them].*

ט *From one end of the world to the other,*
those who prey on them are at ease.

י *Each day those who wage war against them attack.*

י *So they stretch out their hands [to Heaven,*
asking] to be released from suffering.

כ *Their lives wither away in grief and groan;*

כ *amid much stumbling,8 and diminution of joy.*

ל *They hope for salvation, but there is screaming.*

ל *Opponents weaken them, and dig a pit.9*

מ *The [gentiles] plot deviously to turn [Israel] away [from You];*

מ *[the oppressors] make heavier the yoke to weaken their strength.*

נ *[But] they cry out to You as their spirit grows faint,*

נ *to find solace from the heaviness of their burden.*

ס *They pour out prayer, standing crowded together,*

ס *they seek forgiveness with bowed heads.*

ע *The persecutors who provoke [Israel] and deliver them to the sword —10*

ע *may madness be poured upon the [oppressors],11 that they be put to an end!*

פ *Redeem those who cling to You from destruction and annihilation;*

פ *rescue them from the foe and set them on high.*

צ *Command salvations for those who seek You in prayer;*

צ *justify them in Your judgment, from both concealed and revealed [sins].12*

ק *Jealous, avenging [God], be jealous on behalf of Your Name!*

ק *Cut off the harness-ropes from Your people's neck.*

ר *See our toil, and turn back from Your wrath;*

ר *take up our cause against the people You have condemned.13*

❖ (שֶׁבְעָתַיִם הָשֵׁב לְחֵיק¹ מַאֲנִינָי,

שַׂכֵּר חֵצֶיךָ מִדַּם מְעָנָי)²

תַּטֶּה אָזְנְךָ לְקוֹל תַּחֲנוּנָי,³

תִּרְצֵנִי בְּקָרְאֵי יהוה יהוה.

All, while standing:

אֵל מֶלֶךְ יוֹשֵׁב עַל כִּסֵּא רַחֲמִים מִתְנַהֵג בַּחֲסִידוּת, מוֹחֵל
עֲוֹנוֹת עַמּוֹ, מַעֲבִיר רִאשׁוֹן רִאשׁוֹן, מַרְבֶּה
מְחִילָה לְחַטָּאִים וּסְלִיחָה לְפוֹשְׁעִים, עֹשֶׂה צְדָקוֹת עִם כָּל
בָּשָׂר וָרוּחַ, לֹא כְרָעָתָם תִּגְמוֹל. ❖ אֵל הוֹרֵיתָ לָּנוּ לוֹמַר שְׁלֹשׁ
עֶשְׂרֵה, וּזְכוֹר לָנוּ הַיּוֹם בְּרִית שְׁלֹשׁ עֶשְׂרֵה, כְּמוֹ שֶׁהוֹדַעְתָּ
לֶעָנָיו מִקֶּדֶם, כְּמוֹ שֶׁכָּתוּב, וַיֵּרֶד יהוה בֶּעָנָן וַיִּתְיַצֵּב עִמּוֹ שָׁם,
וַיִּקְרָא בְשֵׁם יהוה.

Congregation, then chazzan:

וַיַּעֲבֹר יהוה עַל פָּנָיו וַיִּקְרָא:

Congregation and chazzan *(the words in bold type are recited aloud and in unison):*

יהוה, יהוה, אֵל, **רַחוּם, וְחַנּוּן, אֶרֶךְ אַפַּיִם, וְרַב חֶסֶד, וֶאֱמֶת,**
נֹצֵר חֶסֶד לָאֲלָפִים, נֹשֵׂא עָוֹן, וָפֶשַׁע, וְחַטָּאָה,
וְנַקֵּה. וְסָלַחְתָּ לַעֲוֹנֵנוּ וּלְחַטָּאתֵנוּ וּנְחַלְתָּנוּ. סְלַח לָנוּ אָבִינוּ כִּי
חָטָאנוּ, מְחַל לָנוּ מַלְכֵּנוּ כִּי פָשָׁעְנוּ. כִּי אַתָּה אֲדֹנָי טוֹב וְסַלָּח,
וְרַב חֶסֶד לְכָל קֹרְאֶיךָ.

פְּסוּקֵי הַקְדָּמָה לִסְלִיחָה צ

כִּי אָדָם אֵין צַדִּיק בָּאָרֶץ, אֲשֶׁר יַעֲשֶׂה טּוֹב וְלֹא יֶחֱטָא.⁴ כִּי
יֵצֶר לֵב הָאָדָם רַע מִנְּעֻרָיו.⁵ כִּי תְבַקֵּשׁ לַעֲוֹנֵנוּ
וּלְחַטֹּאתֵנוּ תִדְרוֹשׁ.⁶ שַׁתָּ עֲוֹנֹתֵינוּ לְנֶגְדֶּךָ, עֲלֻמֵנוּ לִמְאוֹר פָּנֶיךָ.⁷
אֱנוֹשׁ כֶּחָצִיר יָמָיו, כְּצִיץ הַשָּׂדֶה כֵּן יָצִיץ.⁸ וְאַתָּה אֲדֹנָי חַנּוּן
וְרַחוּם אֶרֶךְ אַפַּיִם וְרַב חֶסֶד וֶאֱמֶת.⁹

בְּרַחֵם אָב עַל בָּנִים, כֵּן תְּרַחֵם יהוה עָלֵינוּ. לַיהוה הַיְשׁוּעָה,
עַל עַמְּךָ בִרְכָתֶךָ סֶּלָה. יהוה צְבָאוֹת עִמָּנוּ,
מִשְׂגָּב לָנוּ אֱלֹהֵי יַעֲקֹב סֶלָה. יהוה צְבָאוֹת, אַשְׁרֵי אָדָם בֹּטֵחַ בָּךְ.
יהוה הוֹשִׁיעָה, הַמֶּלֶךְ יַעֲנֵנוּ בְיוֹם קָרְאֵנוּ.

שׁ Chazzan – *(Pay back sevenfold[1] those who torment me;*
שׁ *let Your arrows be drunk on my oppressor's blood.)* [2]
ת *Turn Your ear towards the sound of my supplication,*[3]
ת *and favor me as I cry, 'HASHEM, HASHEM. . .'*

All, while standing:

אֵל מֶלֶךְ O God, King Who sits on the throne of mercy; Who acts with
kindness, pardons the iniquities of His people, removes [sins]
one by one, increasingly grants pardon to careless sinners and forgiveness
to rebels, Who deals righteously with every living being — You do not repay
them in accord with their evil. Chazzan – O God, You taught us to recite the
Thirteen [Attributes of Mercy], so remember for us today the covenant of
these Thirteen, as You made known to the humble one in ancient times, as
it is written: And HASHEM descended in a cloud and stood with him there,
and He called out with the Name HASHEM.

Congregation, then chazzan:

And HASHEM passed before him [Moses] and proclaimed:

Congregation and chazzan (the words in bold type are recited aloud and in unison):

ה' ה' **HASHEM, HASHEM, God, Compassionate and Gracious, Slow to
anger, and Abundant in Kindness and Truth, Preserver of
kindness for thousands [of generations], Forgiver of iniquity, willful
sin, and error, and Who cleanses.** May You forgive our iniquities and
our errors and make us Your heritage. Forgive us, our Father, for we have
erred; pardon us, our King, for we have willfully sinned; for You, my
Lord, are good and forgiving and abundantly kind to all who call upon
You.

PREFATORY VERSES TO SELICHAH 90

כִּי אָדָם For there is no man so wholly righteous on earth that he
[always] does good and never sins.[4] For the inclination of
man's heart is evil from his youth.[5] For You search for our iniquity, and
seek out our sin.[6] You have set our iniquities before You, our youth[ful
deeds] in the light of Your countenance.[7] Frail man's days are like grass;
like a sprout in the field, so he sprouts.[8] But You, my Lord, are gracious
and merciful, slow to anger, and abundant in kindness and truth.[9]

כְּרַחֵם אָב As a father has mercy on his children, so, HASHEM, may
You have mercy on us. Salvation is HASHEM's, upon Your
people is Your blessing, Selah. HASHEM, Master of Legions, is with us, a
stronghold for us is the God of Jacob, Selah. HASHEM, Master of Legions,
praiseworthy is the person who trusts in You. HASHEM, save! May the
King answer us on the day we call.

---

(1) Cf. *Psalms* 79:12. (2) Cf. *Deuteronomy* 32:42; some editions of *Selichos* omit the passage in
parentheses (some also omit the stanza before it); still others have altered versions: שְׁכִינָתְךָ הָשֵׁב
לִמְקוֹם מַאֲוַיִי, *Return Your Presence to the place of my longing* [or, לְחֵיק אַרְמוֹנִי, *to the bosom of my
Palace*], שָׁבָה בְּצִיּוֹן לְוַיֵי וְכֹהֲנַי, *returned (?) to Zion, my Leviim and Kohanim* [or, שֶׁאֲנָן הוּשַׁב לְוַיֵי וְכֹהֲנַי, *let
my Leviim and Kohanim be returned with serenity*]. (3) Cf. *Psalms* 86:1,6. (4) *Ecclesiastes* 7:20.
(5) *Genesis* 8:21. (6) Cf. *Job* 10:6. (7) *Psalms* 90:8; see commentary below, s.v., עֲלוּמֵי, *My youth* [ful
deeds.*] (8) 103:15. (9) Cf. 86:15.

In some congregations the following two verses are recited responsively — the chazzan reciting סְלַח,
and the congregation responding וַיֹּאמֶר. In other congregations these verses are recited silently.

סְלַח נָא לַעֲוֹן הָעָם הַזֶּה כְּגֹדֶל חַסְדֶּךָ, וְכַאֲשֶׁר נָשָׂאתָה לָעָם
הַזֶּה מִמִּצְרַיִם וְעַד הֵנָּה, וְשָׁם נֶאֱמַר:

וַיֹּאמֶר יהוה סָלַחְתִּי כִּדְבָרֶךָ.

All:

הַטֵּה אֱלֹהַי אָזְנְךָ וּשֲׁמָע, פְּקַח עֵינֶיךָ וּרְאֵה שֹׁמְמֹתֵינוּ, וְהָעִיר
אֲשֶׁר נִקְרָא שִׁמְךָ עָלֶיהָ, כִּי לֹא עַל צִדְקוֹתֵינוּ אֲנַחְנוּ
מַפִּילִים תַּחֲנוּנֵינוּ לְפָנֶיךָ, כִּי עַל רַחֲמֶיךָ הָרַבִּים. אֲדֹנָי שְׁמָעָה,
אֲדֹנָי סְלָחָה, אֲדֹנָי הַקְשִׁיבָה, וַעֲשֵׂה אַל תְּאַחַר, לְמַעַנְךָ אֱלֹהַי, כִּי
שִׁמְךָ נִקְרָא עַל עִירְךָ וְעַל עַמֶּךָ.

סְלִיחָה צ (שלישיה)

אֱלֹהִים אֲדֹנָי חֵילִי,*[1] יוֹצְרִי וּמְחוֹלְלִי, לְךָ אֲנִי וְכָל אֲשֶׁר לִי.[2]

בְּסַאסְּאָה אַל תָּרִיב,[3] פֶּן תַּשְׁחִית וְתַחֲרִיב, נֶפֶשׁ כִּי תַקְרִיב.[4]

גֵּרְדֹּם לַדּוֹן, רֵאשִׁית מָדוֹן,[5] אֵשׁ הִיא עַד אֲבַדּוֹן.[6]

דְּרָכַי הַסְכַּנְתָּ,[7] עֲלוּמַי* לְאוֹר שַׁתָּה,[8] אַל תִּהְיֶה לִי לִמְחִתָּה.[9]

הֲלִיכוֹת לוֹ עוֹלָם,*[10] הֵן עַל כָּל נֶעְלָם,[11] אַל יָשׁוֹב דַּךְ נִכְלָם.[12]

וְכִי רַבּוּ מְשׁוּבוֹתַי,[13] לֵב הוּתַל בְּמַחְשְׁבוֹתַי, כִּי לֹא מַחְשְׁבוֹתַי.*[14]

זַמּוֹתִי הַכֹּל הֶבֶל,[15] בְּכָל מַעֲשֵׂה תֵבֶל, נֶפֶשׁ הוּא חוֹבֵל.[16]

חוֹשֵׁב מַאֲוִיו לְסַפֵּק, קוֹל דּוֹדִי דוֹפֵק,[17] זָמְמוֹ אַל תָּפֵק.*[18]

טָהוֹר יְצִירְךָ עֲשִׂיתוֹ, וְרַע לֵב מְסִיתוֹ, כִּי תִרְאֶה עָוֹן וְכִסִּיתוֹ.[19]

יְשׁוּעָתְךָ לְנַפְשִׁי אֱמֹר,[20] הַאִם תַּמֵּנוּ לִגְמֹר,[21] אִם עֲוֹנוֹת תִּשְׁמָר.[22]

---

(1) Habakkuk 3:19. (2) I Kings 20:4. (3) Cf. Isaiah 27:8; see commentary to selichah 94.
(4) Cf. Leviticus 2:1. (5) Cf. Proverbs 17:14. (6) Cf. Job 31:12. (7) Psalms 139:3. (8) Cf. 90:8.
(9) Cf. Jeremiah 17:17. (10) Cf. Habakkuk 3:6. (11) Cf. Ecclesiastes 12:14. (12) Psalms 74:21.
(13) Cf. Jeremiah 14:7. (14) Isaiah 58:8. (15) Ecclesiastes 1:2. (16) Deuteronomy 24:6.
(17) Song of Songs 5:2. (18) Psalms 140:9. (19) Cf. Isaiah 58:7. (20) Cf. Psalms 35:3.
(21) Cf. Numbers 17:28. (22) Cf. Psalms 130:3.

אֱלֹהִים אֲדֹנָי חֵילִי — *God, my Lord, my
Strength.* After an alphabetic acrostic, the paytan
signed his name — אֶפְרַיִם בַּר יִצְחָק, *Ephraim bar
Yitzchak* [see prefatory comment to *selichah* 52].

עֲלוּמַי — *My youth[ful deeds].* The translation
follows *Targum* and *Rashi* to Psalms 90:8. According to *Radak* and *Ibn Ezra* the word means
my hidden [deeds], i.e., my inadvertent sins that
I am unaware of.

הֲלִיכוֹת לוֹ עוֹלָם — *The ways [known only] to him
are eternal.* Although this stich is borrowed from
the Scriptural verse: הֲלִיכוֹת עוֹלָם לוֹ, *the ways of
the world are His* (Habakkuk 3:6), the phrase can-

not be so translated here. By interjecting the word
לוֹ between הֲלִיכוֹת and עוֹלָם, the paytan indicates
that he is not alluding to the ways of the world.
Rather, he wishes to state that God's ways are in-
comprehensible to finite man for they are infinite
and inscrutable. Thus, He may render a favorable
decision for someone who seems to deserve the
harshest punishment, for His judgment is based
on much more than meets the eye. Moreover,
since He knows even the thoughts concealed in
one's heart, He will not reject the petition of the
oppressed person who cannot choose the appropriate phrases for his prayer.

וְכִי רַבּוּ מְשׁוּבוֹתַי . . . כִּי לֹא מַחְשְׁבוֹתַי — *And though*

In some congregations the following two verses are recited responsively — the *chazzan* reciting, *'Forgive, please . . .,'* and the congregation responding, *'And* HASHEM *said . . .'* In other congregations these verses are recited silently.

סְלַח נָא *Forgive, please, the iniquity of this people according to the greatness of Your kindness and as You have forgiven this people from Egypt until now, and there it was said:*

And HASHEM said, 'I have forgiven according to your word!'

All:

הַטֵּה *Incline, my God, Your ear, and listen, open Your eyes and see our desolation and that of the city upon which Your Name is proclaimed; for not because of our righteousness do we cast down our supplications before You, rather because of Your abundant compassion. O my Lord, heed; O my Lord, forgive; O my Lord, be attentive and act, do not delay; for Your sake, my God, for Your Name is proclaimed upon Your city and upon Your people.*

SELICHAH 90

א *God, my Lord, my Strength,*[1] *my Molder and my Creator,*
to You am I, and all that is mine.[2]

ב *Do not demand measure for measure,*[3] *lest You destroy and lay in ruin,*
the soul that would draw near [to You].[4]

ג *In the courtroom for judgment, the initial accusation*[5]
would consign one to the fire that reaches to Gehinnom.[6]

ד *You know well my ways;*[7]
*my youth[ful deeds] *You have set in the light —*[8]
do not be unto me as a destroyer.[9]

ה *The ways [known only] to Him are eternal;*[10]
[He knows] even all that is concealed,[11]
so the broken in spirit will not suffer shame.[12]

ו *And though my rebellions have been many,*[13]
[my] foolish heart [seemingly misled] by my thoughts —
*yet [these are] not my intentions.**[14]

ז *I have thought futile*[15] *each deed done in the world,*
[for] it causes Him to punish the soul.[16]

ח *Man thinks to satisfy his desire,*
[but hark] the sound of my Beloved knocking [to warn him],[17]
*'Do not carry out [the Evil Inclination's] scheme!'**[18]

ט *You made Your creature pure, but the heart's evil seduces him,*
*'When you see sin, cover it over.'**[19]

י *Tell my soul about Your salvation;*[20]
for would we not be utterly ruined,[21] *if You should preserve iniquities?*[22]

---

my rebellions have been many . . . yet these are not my intention. I have been misled my *Yetzer Hara* [Evil Inclination] and have rebelled against You in ways that I would never have done and never really intended to do (*Matteh Levi*).

קוֹל דּוֹדִי דוֹפֵק דְּמָמוֹ אַל תָּפֵק — *[But hark] the sound of my Beloved knocking [to warn him], 'Do not*

carry out [the Evil Inclination's] scheme!' The translation follows *Matteh Levi*. According to *Pardes* the passage means: *[But when he hears] the sound of my Beloved knocking, his desires will not have been fulfilled.*

כִּי תִרְאֶה עָוֹן וְכִסִּיתוֹ — *'When you see sin, cover it over.'* The translation follows *Pardes* who under-

כָּלוּ בַהֶבֶל יָמַי,[1] וּמִכְּבֶד אַשְׁמַי, נִבְהֲלוּ עֲצָמַי.[2]

לַבֶּן אֲדַמְדָּם,[3] הַמְאַחֵר וְהַמַּקְדִּים, יֵצֶר לֵב הָאָדָם.[4]

מְשַׁשְׁתָּ אֶת כֹּל,[5] חַדְרֵי לֵב עָקֹל, מַה מָּצָאתָ מִכֹּל.

נְעַם חֶפְצְךָ בִּי, טָמוּן עָוֹן בְּחֻבִּי,[6] חַם לִבִּי בְּקִרְבִּי.[7]

סְמֹךְ נַפְשִׁי מִפֶּחַת, וּמַה בֶּצַע לָקַחַת, בְּרִדְתִּי אֶל שַׁחַת.[8]

עָלַי בְּרַחֲמִים שׁוּב, כִּי בַמֶּה חָשׁוּב, רוּחַ הוֹלֵךְ וְלֹא יָשׁוּב.[9]

פִּצְעֵי לְפִי פְשָׁעַי, וְשַׂק וָאֵפֶר מַצָּעַי,[10] עַל כֵּן הָמוּ מֵעָי.[11]

צוּקוֹת עִם צָרוֹת, אֲשֶׁר הֵנָּה חוֹבְרוֹת, לֹא יָדַעְתִּי סְפוֹרוֹת.[12]

קְשֵׁה רְוּחַ אָנִי,[13] הֲלֹא תִרְאֶה בְעָנְיִי,[14] כִּי תְבַקֵּשׁ לַעֲוֹנִי.[15]

רַחֲשִׁי לְךָ יֶעֱרַב, וּלְפָנֶיךָ תִקְרַב, וְנִקֵּיתִי מִפֶּשַׁע רָב.[16]

שִׁבְרֵי פֶשַׁע תְּנַקֶּה, בְּלֵב נִשְׁבָּר וְנִדְכֶּה,[17] וְאִם יִתְמַהְמָהּ חַכֵּה.[18]

תְּשׁוּבָתוֹ תְּצַפֶּה,[19] וְעַל חֲטָאָיו תְּחַפֶּה, לְשָׂטָן בַּסֵּתֶר יִכְפֶּה.[20]

אֵל עָוֹן וְחֵטְא נוֹשֵׂא,[21] אִם פֶּשַׁע יִפְשָׂה,[22] וְעָשִׂיתָ לּוֹ מִכְסֶה.[23]

פְּדֵנוּ מֵעֲבֹר בַּשֶּׁלַח,[24] לְפָנֶיךָ תְּפִלָּתִי תִצְלַח, אֵל טוֹב וְסַלָּח.[25]

רֹן תְּפִלָּתִי תִּשַּׁע, וּמְחֵה כָעָב פֶּשַׁע,[26]

כִּי לֹא אֵל חָפֵץ רֶשַׁע.[27]

יִגְמְלֵנִי יהוה כְּצִדְקוֹ,[28] תָּמִיד יִצְפְּנֵנִי בְּסֻכּוֹ,[29]

הָאֵל תָּמִים דַּרְכּוֹ.[30]

מֵעֹמֶק בּוֹר קְרָאתִיךָ, מִכְּאֵב לֵב שְׁחַרְתִּיךָ, כִּי זָכוֹר זְכַרְתִּיךָ.

בְּרַחֲמֶיךָ תִּלְבַּשׁ, וְאֶת חַטָּאַי תְּכַבֵּשׁ,[31] וְאֵדַע כִּי לֹא אֵבוֹשׁ.[32]

רַבִּים אוֹמְרִים לְנַפְשִׁי,[33] בָּאֵפֶר הִתְפַּלְּשִׁי,[34]

וְלֹא תֵצֵא חָפְשִׁי.[35]

יֶהֱמוּ הֲמוֹן מֵעֶיךָ, זְכֹר חֶסֶד יוֹדְעֶיךָ, וְלִי מַה יָּקְרוּ רֵעֶיךָ.[36]*

צֵא עַל אוֹיְבֶיךָ כְּגִבּוֹר,[37] זְרוֹעַ רוֹדְפַי תִּשְׁבֹּר,

כִּי שָׂמוּ אוֹתִי בַּבּוֹר.[38]

---

(1) Cf. *Psalms* 78:33. (2) 6:3. (3) Cf. *Isaiah* 1:18. (4) *Genesis* 8:21. (5) Cf. 31:37. (6) *Job* 31:33. (7) *Psalms* 39:4. (8) Cf. 30:10. (9) 78:39. (10) Cf. *Isaiah* 58:5. (11) *Jeremiah* 31:19. (12) *Psalms* 71:15. (13) Cf. *I Samuel* 1:15. (14) Cf. 1:11. (15) *Job* 10:6. (16) *Psalms* 19:14. (17) Cf. 51:19. (18) Cf. *Habakkuk* 3:2. (19) Cf. 2:1. (20) Cf. *Proverbs* 21:14. (21) Cf. *Exodus* 34:6-7. (22) Cf. *Leviticus* 13:35. (23) Cf. *Exodus* 26:14. (24) Cf. *Job* 33:18. (25) Cf. *Psalms* 86:5. (26) Cf. *Isaiah* 44:22. (27) *Psalms* 5:5. (28) Cf. 18:21. (29) Cf. 27:5. (30) 18:31. (31) Cf. *Micah* 7:19. (32) *Isaiah* 50:7. (33) *Psalms* 3:3. (34) Cf. *Jeremiah* 6:26. (35) Cf. *Exodus* 21:5. (36) *Psalms* 139:17. (37) Cf. *Isaiah* 42:13. (38) *Genesis* 40:15.

---

stands this phrase as the seductive chant of the Evil Inclination. According to *Matteh Levi*, this is a plea to God to overlook man's sin caused by the Evil Inclination. Thus, the translation is: *So when You see [a man's] sin, cover it over.*

רֵעֶיךָ — *Your dear ones.* The translation follows *Targum* and *Rashi* (to *Psalms* 139:17) and alludes to the righteous *tzaddikim* of every generation. Others render: *Your thoughts,* from רַעְיוֹן (*Ibn Ezra*, *Radak*).

כ My days wither away in emptiness;[1]
and from the weight of my guilt, my bones shudder with terror.[2]

ל Make white the red stain [of sins],[3]
the later ones as well as the early ones —
the Evil Inclination of man's heart.[4]

מ You have probed every[5] chamber of the twisted heart;
what did You find of all[5]

נ the gracious things that gave You delight in me?
Iniquity lurks in my innards;[6] my heart is hot within me.[7]

ס Prop up my soul against decay!
What good will it do You to take it [from me],
so that I descend to the grave?[8]

ע Return to me, with mercy; for what worth is
a spirit that goes and does not return?[9]

פ My wounds are according to my rebellious sins;
sackcloth and ashes are my couch; [10]
therefore my innards are in tumult.[11]

צ Torments and troubles that are connected to each other
so that I know not [their] numbers.[12]

ק I am heavy of spirit;[13] will You not look at my affliction,[14]
when You inquire after my iniquity?[15]

ר May my prayer be sweet to You, and approach close to You,
that I may be cleansed of great transgression.[16]

ש May You cleanse those who repent of their rebellious sin
with broken, crushed heart;[17] and if he is hesitant, wait![18]

ת Look forward to his repentance,[19] and cover over his inadvertent sins,
while secret [charity] beats down the Adversary.[20]

א O God who bears iniquity and inadvertent sin![21]
If [sins' blemish] is spreading,[22] make a covering for it.[23]

פ Redeem us from the [Angel of Death and his] sword; [24]
let my prayer succeed before You, O God, Who is good and forgiving.[25]

ר Turn to the song of my prayer, and wipe away sin like a cloud,[26]
for God does not desire wickedness.[27]

י May HASHEM recompense me according to His righteousness,[28]
and conceal me ever in His Tabernacle —[29]
O God, Whose way is perfect.[30]

מ I call You from the depths of the pit,
I beseech with an aching heart, for I constantly remember You.

כ Don Your [robes of] mercy and quell my sins,[31]
and then I will know that I will not be put to shame.[32]

ר Many say to my soul,[33] 'Writhe in the dust,[34] for you will not go free!'[35]

י May Your innards be moved deeply;
remember the kindness of those intimate with You;
to me — how precious are Your dear ones.*[36]

צ Stride forth against Your enemies like a warrior, [37]
and break the arm of my pursuers,
for they have placed me into the pit.[38]

❖ חָצַי, בָּהֶם תְּכַלֶּה,¹ אַסִּירֶיךָ מֵהֶם תַּעֲלֶה, וְיִהְיוּ דְבָרַי אֵלֶּה. קְרוֹבִים² וַעֲרֵבִים, אֲהוּבִים וַחֲבִיבִים, יהוה צְבָאוֹת יוֹשֵׁב הַכְּרוּבִים.³

All, while standing:

אֵל מֶלֶךְ יוֹשֵׁב עַל כִּסֵּא רַחֲמִים מִתְנַהֵג בַּחֲסִידוּת, מוֹחֵל עֲוֹנוֹת עַמּוֹ, מַעֲבִיר רִאשׁוֹן רִאשׁוֹן, מַרְבֶּה מְחִילָה לְחַטָּאִים וּסְלִיחָה לְפוֹשְׁעִים, עֹשֶׂה צְדָקוֹת עִם כָּל בָּשָׂר וָרוּחַ, לֹא כְרָעָתָם תִּגְמוֹל. ❖ אֵל הוֹרֵיתָ לָּנוּ לוֹמַר שְׁלֹשׁ עֶשְׂרֵה, וּזְכוֹר לָנוּ הַיּוֹם בְּרִית שְׁלֹשׁ עֶשְׂרֵה, כְּמוֹ שֶׁהוֹדַעְתָּ לֶעָנָו מִקֶּדֶם, כְּמוֹ שֶׁכָּתוּב, וַיֵּרֶד יהוה בֶּעָנָן וַיִּתְיַצֵּב עִמּוֹ שָׁם, וַיִּקְרָא בְשֵׁם יהוה.

Congregation, then chazzan:

וַיַּעֲבֹר יהוה עַל פָּנָיו וַיִּקְרָא:

Congregation and chazzan (the words in bold type are recited aloud and in unison):

יהוה, יהוה, אֵל **רַחוּם, וְחַנּוּן, אֶרֶךְ אַפַּיִם, וְרַב חֶסֶד, וֶאֱמֶת, נֹצֵר חֶסֶד לָאֲלָפִים, נֹשֵׂא עָוֹן, וָפֶשַׁע, וְחַטָּאָה, וְנַקֵּה.** וְסָלַחְתָּ לַעֲוֹנֵנוּ וּלְחַטָּאתֵנוּ וּנְחַלְתָּנוּ. סְלַח לָנוּ אָבִינוּ כִּי חָטָאנוּ, מְחַל לָנוּ מַלְכֵּנוּ כִּי פָשָׁעְנוּ. כִּי אַתָּה אֲדֹנָי טוֹב וְסַלָּח, וְרַב חֶסֶד לְכָל קֹרְאֶיךָ.

פסוקי הקדמה לסליחה צא

יֹאחֵז צַדִּיק דַּרְכּוֹ, וּטְהָר יָדַיִם יוֹסִיף אֹמֶץ.⁴ חִזְקוּ וְיַאֲמֵץ לְבַבְכֶם, כָּל הַמְיַחֲלִים לַיהוה.⁵ בַּצַּר לָנוּ נִקְרָא יהוה, וְאֶל אֱלֹהֵינוּ נְשַׁוֵּעַ, וַיִּשְׁמַע מֵהֵיכָלוֹ קוֹלֵנוּ, וְשַׁוְעָתֵנוּ לְפָנָיו תָּבֹא.⁶ עֲנֵנוּ יהוה כִּי טוֹב חַסְדֶּךָ, כְּרֹב רַחֲמֶיךָ פְּנֵה אֵלֵינוּ.⁷

כְּרַחֵם אָב עַל בָּנִים, כֵּן תְּרַחֵם יהוה עָלֵינוּ. לַיהוה הַיְשׁוּעָה, עַל עַמְּךָ בִרְכָתֶךָ סֶּלָה. יהוה צְבָאוֹת עִמָּנוּ, מִשְׂגָּב לָנוּ אֱלֹהֵי יַעֲקֹב סֶלָה. יהוה צְבָאוֹת, אַשְׁרֵי אָדָם בֹּטֵחַ בָּךְ. יהוה הוֹשִׁיעָה, הַמֶּלֶךְ יַעֲנֵנוּ בְיוֹם קָרְאֵנוּ.

In some congregations the following two verses are recited responsively — the chazzan reciting סְלַח, and the congregation responding וַיֹּאמֶר. In other congregations these verses are recited silently.

סְלַח נָא לַעֲוֹן הָעָם הַזֶּה כְּגֹדֶל חַסְדֶּךָ, וְכַאֲשֶׁר נָשָׂאתָה לָעָם הַזֶּה מִמִּצְרַיִם וְעַד הֵנָּה, וְשָׁם נֶאֱמַר:

---

(1) Cf. *Deuteronomy* 32:23. (2) Cf. *I Kings* 8:59. (3) *I Samuel* 4:4.
(4) Cf. *Job* 17:9. (5) *Psalms* 31:25. (6) Cf. 18:7. (7) Cf. 69:17.

ח Exhaust Your arrows against them,[1]
and raise up Your prisoner-people from among them,
and let these words of mine be
ק close [to You][2] and sweet, beloved and dear,
O HASHEM, Master of legions, Who sits upon the Cherubim![3]

All, while standing:

אֵל מֶלֶךְ O God, King Who sits on the throne of mercy; Who acts with
kindness, pardons the iniquities of His people, removes [sins]
one by one, increasingly grants pardon to careless sinners and forgiveness
to rebels, Who deals righteously with every living being — You do not repay
them in accord with their evil. Chazzan — O God, You taught us to recite the
Thirteen [Attributes of Mercy], so remember for us today the covenant of
these Thirteen, as You made known to the humble one in ancient times, as
it is written: And HASHEM descended in a cloud and stood with him there,
and He called out with the Name HASHEM.

Congregation, then chazzan:

And HASHEM passed before him [Moses] and proclaimed:

Congregation and chazzan (the words in bold type are recited aloud and in unison):

ה' ה' **HASHEM, HASHEM, God, Compassionate and Gracious, Slow to
anger, and Abundant in Kindness and Truth, Preserver of
kindness for thousands [of generations], Forgiver of iniquity, willful
sin, and error, and Who cleanses.** May You forgive our iniquities and our
errors and make us Your heritage. Forgive us, our Father, for we have
erred; pardon us, our King, for we have willfully sinned; for You, my Lord,
are good and forgiving and abundantly kind to all who call upon You.

PREFATORY VERSES TO SELICHAH 91

יֹאחֵז Let the righteous man hold fast in his way, and the pure-handed
increase courage.[4] Be strong, and let your hearts take courage, all
who long for HASHEM.[5] In our distress, we would call upon HASHEM, and
to our God we would cry for salvation; from His Palace He would hear
our voice, and our outcry would come before Him.[6] Answer us, HASHEM,
for Your kindness is good; according to the abundance of Your mercy,
turn to us.[7]

כְּרַחֵם אָב As a father has mercy on his children, so, HASHEM, may
You have mercy on us. Salvation is HASHEM's, upon Your
people is Your blessing, Selah. HASHEM, Master of Legions, is with us, a
stronghold for us is the God of Jacob, Selah. HASHEM, Master of Legions,
praiseworthy is the person who trusts in You. HASHEM, save! May the
King answer us on the day we call.

In some congregations the following two verses are recited responsively — the chazzan
reciting, 'Forgive, please . . .,' and the congregation responding, 'And HASHEM said . . .'
In other congregations these verses are recited silently.

סְלַח נָא Forgive, please, the iniquity of this people according to the
greatness of Your kindness and as You have forgiven this
people from Egypt until now, and there it was said:

וַיֹּאמֶר יהוה סָלַחְתִּי כִּדְבָרֶךָ.

All:

הַטֵּה אֱלֹהַי אָזְנְךָ וּשֲׁמָע, פְּקַח עֵינֶיךָ וּרְאֵה שֹׁמְמֹתֵינוּ, וְהָעִיר
אֲשֶׁר נִקְרָא שִׁמְךָ עָלֶיהָ, כִּי לֹא עַל צִדְקוֹתֵינוּ אֲנַחְנוּ
מַפִּילִים תַּחֲנוּנֵינוּ לְפָנֶיךָ, כִּי עַל רַחֲמֶיךָ הָרַבִּים. אֲדֹנָי שְׁמָעָה,
אֲדֹנָי סְלָחָה, אֲדֹנָי הַקְשִׁיבָה, וַעֲשֵׂה אַל תְּאַחַר, לְמַעַנְךָ אֱלֹהַי, כִּי
שִׁמְךָ נִקְרָא עַל עִירְךָ וְעַל עַמֶּךָ.

סליחה צא

אֱלֹהֵינוּ וֵאלֹהֵי אֲבוֹתֵינוּ:

אֹמֶץ יוֹסִיף טְהָר יָדַיִם,[1]* וְכֹחוֹ יִגְדַּל[2] וְיִישָׁר,

בְּמִקְרָא אַלְמָלֵא כָּתוּב לְאָמְרוֹ אִי אֶפְשָׁר,

גֵּאֶה נִתְעַטֵּף כִּשְׁלִיחַ צִבּוּר וּשְׁלֹשׁ עֶשְׂרֵה מִדּוֹת הִכְשִׁיר,[3]

דִּבְּרַת יְקָרוֹ הֶעֱבִיר וְהֶרְאָה לְמֹשֶׁה קֶשֶׁר הַמְקֻשָּׁר,[4]

הִזְהִירוֹ וְאָמַר לוֹ, כָּל זְמַן שֶׁחוֹטְאִין בָּנַי,

וְכַסֵּדֶר הַזֶּה יִהְיוּ עוֹשִׂין לְפָנַי,

זוֹ הִיא הַמִּדָּה לִסְלֹחַ, אֲנִי יהוה יהוה,[5]

חַנּוּן קֹדֶם שֶׁיֶּחֱטָא, וְאַחַר שֶׁיֶּחֱטָא וְיָשׁוּב,[3] אֵלּוּ דְרָכַי וְעִנְיָנַי.

טוֹב וְסַלָּח וְרַב חֶסֶד[6] כְּלַפֵּי חֶסֶד מַגְבִּיר,[7]

יָשׁוּב יְרַחֵם כּוֹבֵשׁ וְנוֹשֵׂא[8] וּפָנִים מַסְבִּיר,

כַּךְ הִיא הַמִּדָּה, רִאשׁוֹן רִאשׁוֹן מַעֲבִיר,[7]

לִמְחֹל וְלִסְלֹחַ, רַחֲמָיו וַחֲסָדָיו לְהַגְבִּיר.

כָּמוֹךְ מִי מוֹרֶה[9] תַחְבֹּשֶׁת חָסִיד וְרוֹפֵא אָמָן,

לְפִי הַמַּכָּה גְדוֹלָה מְלוּגְמָתְךָ תְּזַמָּן,

מוּעֲטִים דָּמִים חוֹלֶה הַבָּא אֶצְלְךָ לְיָדוֹ זְמָן,[10]

נִשְׁתַּיֵּר מְשֶׁלָּךְ חִנָּם חָנֵנוּ רַחֲמָן וְנֶאֱמָן.

סַמֵּךְ סַם חַיִּים (רְטִיָּה) מִפְלָאָה לְמַלָּנִית,

עִקָּרֵי כּוֹסְךָ יָפִים וְקִלּוּרֵי מַטְלָנִית,

⯈ **אֹמֶץ יוֹסִיף טְהָר יָדָיִם** — *May the Pure-
Handed increase courage*, i.e., may God encourage the righteous (*Arugas HaBosem, Pardes*)
thereby making manifest a greater portion of
His infinite strength.

This *selichah* follows an alphabetical ac-

rostic. Although it contains no signature, R'
Elazar of Worms (best known as the *Rokeach*)
of twelfth-century Germany testified that it
is one of the compositions of R' Meir bar
R' Yitzchak [see prefatory comment to *selichah*
44].

And HASHEM said, 'I have forgiven according to your word!'

All:

הַטֵּה *Incline, my God, Your ear, and listen, open Your eyes and see our desolation and that of the city upon which Your Name is proclaimed; for not because of our righteousness do we cast down our supplications before You, rather because of Your abundant compassion. O my Lord, heed; O my Lord, forgive; O my Lord, be attentive and act, do not delay; for Your sake, my God, for Your Name is proclaimed upon Your city and upon Your people.*

SELICHAH 91

Our God and the God of our forefathers:

א *May the Pure-Handed increase courage,*[1]*
  and His [revealed] strength will be increased[2] and aligned.*

ב *Were it not written in the Torah, one could never say it:*

ג *The Grand One wrapped Himself [in a tallis] like a chazzan,
  and arranged the Thirteen Attributes [of Mercy].[3]*

ד *He caused the procession of His glory to pass by,
  then showed Moses the binding [tefillin-]knot.[4]*

ה *Then He instructed [Moses], and said to him,
  'Every time My children will have sinned,*

ו *and they will [ruefully] set forth this order before Me,*

ז *this will be the way to [achieve] forgiveness,
  for I am [the One Whose Attributes are]: HASHEM, HASHEM. . .[5]*

ח *Gracious before man sins, and after he sins and repents;[3]
  these are My ways and My practices.'*

ט *O Beneficent One, O Forgiving One Who is full of kindness,[6]
  Who tips [the scales] towards kindness,[7]*

י *return, be merciful, O Queller and Bearer [of iniquity][8]
  Who shows favorable countenance.*

כ *That is the way [You work], removing [sins] one by one,[7]*

ל *to pardon and to forgive, to overwhelm with His mercy
  and His kindness.*

כ *Who can teach healing like You,[9] O Kind One and expert Healer?*

ל *According to the greatness of the wound, You prepare Your salve.*

מ *Little is the payment that the sick who comes to You has prepared;[10]*

נ *the remainder must come from Your grace — so be gracious to us,
  O Merciful One, O Faithful One!*

ס *Your elixir is the elixir of life, wondrous (salve) for [Israel,]
  the one blackened [with sin];*

ע *the herbal roots in Your cup are just right,
  likewise the medicaments on [Your] bandage.*

---

(1) Cf. *Job* 17:9. (2) Cf. *Numbers* 14:17. (3) Tractate *Rosh Hashanah* 17b; see commentary p. 14.
(4) Tractate *Berachos* 7a. (5) *Exodus* 34:6. (6) *Psalms* 86:5. (7) See commentary, p. 20.
(8) Cf. *Micah* 7:19,18. (9) Cf. *Job* 36:22. (10) Some editions read יְמַן, some read אְמַן, some read יְמַז, but all mean the same.

פָּתוֹחַ בְּיָדְךָ כֵּיוָן נִרְתַּק הָאַסְפְּלָנִית,

צָרִי לְהַתְעִיל מַחַץ חַבַּת חוֹלָנִית.

פּוֹעֵל עִם בַּעַל הַבַּיִת וּבֶאֱמוּנָה נוֹהֵג בּוֹ,

צוֹפֶה לִתֵּן שְׂכָרוֹ מַה שְׁבָחוֹ וּמַה טוּבוֹ,

קִלְקֵל וְנִתְעַצֵּל בִּמְלַאכְתּוֹ שֶׁבַח רַבּוֹ אִם קֵרְבוֹ,

לַאדֹנָי אֱלֹהֵינוּ הָרַחֲמִים וְהַסְּלִיחוֹת, כִּי מָרַדְנוּ בּוֹ.[1]

:קֹשֶׁט מִדּוֹתֶיךָ תְּרוּמוֹת וַהֲגוּנוֹת,

רָאִית דְּגִמָתְךָ לְמַסְפִּיק לְמוֹרְדָיו מְזוֹנוֹת,

שְׁאֵרִית יוֹסֵף[2] מְקַוֶּה מָצָא סְלִיחָה לַעֲוֹנוֹת,

תִּגְמֹל הַטּוֹב כְּיוֹסֵף לְאֶחָיו צִדְקוֹתֶיךָ נֶצַח לְתַנּוֹת.[3]

All, while standing:

אֵל מֶלֶךְ יוֹשֵׁב עַל כִּסֵּא רַחֲמִים מִתְנַהֵג בַּחֲסִידוּת, מוֹחֵל עֲוֹנוֹת עַמּוֹ, מַעֲבִיר רִאשׁוֹן רִאשׁוֹן, מַרְבֶּה מְחִילָה לַחַטָּאִים וּסְלִיחָה לַפּוֹשְׁעִים, עֹשֶׂה צְדָקוֹת עִם כָּל בָּשָׂר וָרוּחַ, לֹא כְרָעָתָם תִּגְמוֹל. אֵל הוֹרֵיתָ לָנוּ לוֹמַר שְׁלֹשׁ עֶשְׂרֵה, וּזְכוֹר לָנוּ הַיּוֹם בְּרִית שְׁלֹשׁ עֶשְׂרֵה, כְּמוֹ שֶׁהוֹדַעְתָּ לֶעָנָיו מִקֶּדֶם, כְּמוֹ שֶׁכָּתוּב, וַיֵּרֶד יהוה בֶּעָנָן וַיִּתְיַצֵּב עִמּוֹ שָׁם, וַיִּקְרָא בְשֵׁם יהוה.

Congregation, then chazzan:

וַיַּעֲבֹר יהוה עַל פָּנָיו וַיִּקְרָא:

Congregation and chazzan (the words in bold type are recited aloud and in unison):

יהוה, יהוה, אֵל, **רַחוּם, וְחַנּוּן, אֶרֶךְ אַפַּיִם, וְרַב חֶסֶד, וֶאֱמֶת, נֹצֵר חֶסֶד לָאֲלָפִים, נֹשֵׂא עָוֹן, וָפֶשַׁע, וְחַטָּאָה, וְנַקֵּה.** וְסָלַחְתָּ לַעֲוֹנֵנוּ וּלְחַטָּאתֵנוּ וּנְחַלְתָּנוּ. סְלַח לָנוּ אָבִינוּ כִּי חָטָאנוּ, מְחַל לָנוּ מַלְכֵּנוּ כִּי פָשָׁעְנוּ. כִּי אַתָּה אֲדֹנָי טוֹב וְסַלָּח, וְרַב חֶסֶד לְכָל קֹרְאֶיךָ.

פסוקי הקדמה לסליחה צב

אָז תַּחְפֹּץ זִבְחֵי צֶדֶק עוֹלָה וְכָלִיל, אָז יַעֲלוּ עַל מִזְבַּחֲךָ פָרִים.[4] תִּתֵּן אֱמֶת לְיַעֲקֹב, חֶסֶד לְאַבְרָהָם, אֲשֶׁר נִשְׁבַּעְתָּ לַאֲבֹתֵינוּ מִימֵי קֶדֶם.[5] וְחֶסֶד יהוה מֵעוֹלָם וְעַד עוֹלָם עַל יְרֵאָיו, וְצִדְקָתוֹ לִבְנֵי בָנִים.[6]

---

(1) *Daniel* 9:9. (2) See commentary to *selichah* 68, s.v., בְּכוֹר שׁוֹר.
(3) Cf. *Judges* 5:11. (4) *Psalms* 51:21. (5) *Micah* 7:20. (6) *Psalms* 103:17.

פ *Open directly with Your hand the case of cure,*
צ *bringing balm to heal the wounds of [Israel,]*
   she who is sick with love [for You].
פ *If one works for an employer dealing with him in good faith,*
צ *[and the employer] seeks to pay his wages, what is his*
   [the employer's] praise and what is his beneficence?
ק *But if [the worker is] destructive and lazy in his work,*
   how praiseworthy is his Master if He draws him near.
   To HASHEM, *our God, are mercy and forgiveness,*
   although we have rebelled against Him.[1]
ק Chazzan – *The epitome of Truth —*
   Your lofty and praiseworthy Attributes —
ר *can be seen through Your example of supplying sustenance*
   to those who rebel against Him?
ש *The remnant of Joseph['s people][2] hope to find forgiveness*
   for [their] iniquities.
ת *Be beneficent [to them], as Joseph to his brothers;*
   that Your righteousness forever be retold. [3]

All, while standing:

אֵל מֶלֶךְ *O God, King Who sits on the throne of mercy; Who acts with*
   kindness, pardons the iniquities of His people, removes [sins]
one by one, increasingly grants pardon to careless sinners and forgiveness
to rebels, Who deals righteously with every living being — You do not repay
them in accord with their evil. Chazzan – *O God, You taught us to recite the*
Thirteen [Attributes of Mercy], so remember for us today the covenant of
these Thirteen, as You made known to the humble one in ancient times, as
it is written: And HASHEM *descended in a cloud and stood with him there,*
and He called out with the Name HASHEM.

Congregation, then chazzan:

And HASHEM *passed before him [Moses] and proclaimed:*

Congregation and chazzan (the words in bold type are recited aloud and in unison):

ה' ה' **HASHEM, HASHEM, God, Compassionate and Gracious, Slow**
   to anger, and Abundant in Kindness and Truth, Preserver of
kindness for thousands [of generations], Forgiver of iniquity, willful
sin, and error, and Who cleanses. *May You forgive our iniquities and our*
errors and make us Your heritage. Forgive us, our Father, for we have
erred; pardon us, our King, for we have willfully sinned; for You, my Lord,
are good and forgiving and abundantly kind to all who call upon You.

PREFATORY VERSES TO SELICHAH 92

אָז תַּחְפֹּץ *Then You will desire sacrifices of righteousness, the*
   olah-offering and completely consumed [flour-]offering;
then bulls will go up on Your altar.[4] *Grant truth to Jacob, kindness to*
Abraham, as You swore to our forefathers from ancient times.[5] *For*
HASHEM's *kindness is forever and ever upon those who fear Him, and His*
righteousness is upon children's children.[6]

כְּרַחֵם אָב עַל בָּנִים, כֵּן תְּרַחֵם יהוה עָלֵינוּ. לַיהוה הַיְשׁוּעָה, עַל עַמְּךָ בִרְכָתֶךָ פֶּלָה. יהוה צְבָאוֹת עִמָּנוּ, מִשְׂגָּב לָנוּ אֱלֹהֵי יַעֲקֹב סֶלָה. יהוה צְבָאוֹת, אַשְׁרֵי אָדָם בֹּטֵחַ בָּךְ. יהוה הוֹשִׁיעָה, הַמֶּלֶךְ יַעֲנֵנוּ בְיוֹם קָרְאֵנוּ.

In some congregations the following two verses are recited responsively — the chazzan reciting סְלַח,
and the congregation responding וַיֹּאמֶר. In other congregations these verses are recited silently.

סְלַח נָא לַעֲוֺן הָעָם הַזֶּה כְּגֹדֶל חַסְדֶּךָ, וְכַאֲשֶׁר נָשָׂאתָה לָעָם הַזֶּה מִמִּצְרַיִם וְעַד הֵנָּה, וְשָׁם נֶאֱמַר:

וַיֹּאמֶר יהוה סָלַחְתִּי כִּדְבָרֶךָ.

All:

הַטֵּה אֱלֹהַי אָזְנְךָ וּשְׁמָע, פְּקַח עֵינֶיךָ וּרְאֵה שֹׁמְמֹתֵינוּ, וְהָעִיר אֲשֶׁר נִקְרָא שִׁמְךָ עָלֶיהָ, כִּי לֹא עַל צִדְקוֹתֵינוּ אֲנַחְנוּ מַפִּילִים תַּחֲנוּנֵינוּ לְפָנֶיךָ, כִּי עַל רַחֲמֶיךָ הָרַבִּים. אֲדֹנָי שְׁמָעָה, אֲדֹנָי סְלָחָה, אֲדֹנָי הַקְשִׁיבָה, וַעֲשֵׂה אַל תְּאַחַר, לְמַעַנְךָ אֱלֹהַי, כִּי שִׁמְךָ נִקְרָא עַל עִירְךָ וְעַל עַמֶּךָ.

סליחה צב (עקדה)

אֱלֹהֵינוּ וֵאלֹהֵי אֲבוֹתֵינוּ

אָז בְּהַר מֹר* דָּץ יוֹנַת אִלֵּם,[1]

בְּקַחְתּוֹ אֵיתָן[2] לְעוֹלָה וְשָׁלֵם,

גֵּאֶה בְּחָנוּ קַח נָא זֶה הָעֶלֶם,   תְּרוּמָה לַיהוה קֹדֶשׁ.[3]

דָּת הַטֶּנֶא לְפָנֵי לְהַנִּיחֵהוּ,[4]

הֵן קַח נָא אֶת בִּנְךָ[5] לְאַשְׁכָּר סְפָחֵהוּ,

וַאֲנִי בְּחַרְתִּיו קוּם מְשָׁחֵהוּ,[6]   שֶׁמֶן מִשְׁחַת קֹדֶשׁ.[7]

זַךְ בְּשָׁמְעוֹ לִבּוֹ לֹא דָאַב,

חֵפֶץ צוּרוֹ חָשַׁק וְתָאַב,

טָפְלוּ שְׁנֵיהֶם הַבֵּן וְהָאָב,   וְהִשְׁתַּחֲווּ[9] לַיהוה בְּהַדְרַת קֹדֶשׁ.[10]

יָעַד עֵצִים וְלִשְׁפֹת עָרַךְ,

כָּמַהּ וְתָמַהּ יָחִיד וָרַךְ,

לַהַג אַיֵּה הַשֶּׂה[11] הַנֶּעֱרָךְ,   לְהַקְדִּישׁוֹ בְּמִקְדָּשׁ קֹדֶשׁ.[12]

אָז בְּהַר מֹר — *Then, on Mount Moriah.* This *selichah*, of the *akeidah* genre, contains an *aleph-beis* acrostic, followed by the *paytan's* signature שְׁלֹמֹה בַּר יְהוּדָה גַּבִּירוֹל, *Shlomo bar Ye-*

hudah [ibn] Gabirol [see prefatory comment to *selichah* 72]. The fourth line of each stanza is a Scriptural fragment that ends in the word קֹדֶשׁ, *holy, holiness,* or *Sanctuary.*

כְּרַחֵם אָב As a father has mercy on his children, so, HASHEM, may You have mercy on us. Salvation is HASHEM's, upon Your people is Your blessing, Selah. HASHEM, Master of Legions, is with us, a stronghold for us is the God of Jacob, Selah. HASHEM, Master of Legions, praiseworthy is the person who trusts in You. HASHEM, save! May the King answer us on the day we call.

In some congregations the following two verses are recited responsively — the chazzan reciting, 'Forgive, please . . .,' and the congregation responding, 'And HASHEM said . . .' In other congregations these verses are recited silently.

סְלַח נָא Forgive, please, the iniquity of this people according to the greatness of Your kindness and as You have forgiven this people from Egypt until now, and there it was said:

And HASHEM said, 'I have forgiven according to your word!'

All:

הַטֵּה Incline, my God, Your ear, and listen, open Your eyes and see our desolation and that of the city upon which Your Name is proclaimed; for not because of our righteousness do we cast down our supplications before You, rather because of Your abundant compassion. O my Lord, heed; O my Lord, forgive; O my Lord, be attentive and act, do not delay; for Your sake, my God, for Your Name is proclaimed upon Your city and upon Your people.

SELICHAH 92

Our God and the God of our forefathers:

א Then, on Mount Moriah,* [Isaac,] the dove of silence rejoiced,[1]

ב when Abraham[2] took him for an olah-offering and a peace-offering.

ג The Grand One tested [Abraham], 'Please take this youth,
to be uplifted unto HASHEM **holy'.**[3]

ד 'Such is the law of the [first fruits] basket, it is to be placed before Me.[4]

ה So, take now your son[5] as part of your offering,

ו for I have chosen him; rise, anoint him[6]
with anointing oil that is **holy.'**[7]

ז When the pure[-hearted Abraham] heard this,
his heart was not pained;

ח he wished, desired to do his Molder's will.

ט The two stayed united, the son and the father,[8]
and prostrated themselves[9] to HASHEM in splendrous **holiness.**[10]

י He prepared wood and arranged it for the pyre.

כ While the delicate only [son] longed and wondered,

ל he asked, 'Where is the lamb[11] to be set out,
to be consecrated with the sanctity of **holiness?**[12]

---

(1) *Psalms* 56:1. (2) See commentary to *selichah* 83, s.v., אֵיתָן לְמַד דֵּעַת.
(3) *Ezekiel* 45:1. (4) See *Deuteronomy* 26:4. (5) *Genesis* 22:2. (6) *I samuel* 16:12.
(7) *Exodus* 30:25. (8) Cf. *Genesis* 22:6,8. (9) Cf. 22:5. (10) Cf. *Psalms* 29:2.
(11) Cf. *Genesis* 22:7. (12) Cf. *I Chronicles* 23:13.

מָרוֹם יִרְאֶה לּוֹ הַשֶּׂה[1] וְהוּא יָשִׁיב,

נֶפֶשׁ אִם עֲקֶרֶת שִׂמְחָה לְהָשִׁיב,[2]

יִשְׁלַח עֶזְרְךָ מִקֹּדֶשׁ.[3]   סוֹכֵר סְפוּנוֹת בְּנֵי שַׁוְעָךְ יַקְשִׁיב,

עָמַד נָא אָבִי וּקְשֹׁר הַטֶּבַח,

פֶּן אָגוּר מִפְּנֵי הָאָבַח,

וּלְהַבְדִּיל בֵּין הַקֹּדֶשׁ.[4]*   צַמְּדֵנִי פֶּן אֲחַלֵּל הַזֶּבַח,

קָפַץ לִבְכּוֹת כְּפֶר אֶשְׁכּוֹל,

רָאוֹתוֹ אָבִיו נִשְׁכַּל שָׁכוֹל,

מְלֶאכֶת עֲבוֹדַת הַקֹּדֶשׁ.[5]   שָׁלַח יָדוֹ לַעֲשׂוֹת אֶת כָּל

תַּרְשִׁישִׁים* צָעֲקוּ בִּשְׁמֵי מְרוֹמִי,

שָׁחֹט יוֹנַת אֵלֶם הֲיוּכַל יֶחֱזֶה מִי,

שְׂאוּ יְדֵיכֶם קֹדֶשׁ.[7]   לָז לְלָז יֶהְגּוּ אַל תִּתְּנוּ דָמִי,[6]

מָרוֹם הִבִּיט עוֹקֵד וְנֶעֱקָד,

הַשֶּׂה עָקוּד וְהָאֵשׁ תּוּקַד,

וְנִשְׁמַע קוֹלוֹ בְּבֹאוֹ אֶל הַקֹּדֶשׁ.[8]   בּוֹחֵן טָהָר לֵב זָכָר וּפָקַד,

רָחַשׁ מֵלִיץ בְּקַחְתּוֹ מִשְׁלַחַת,

יְחִידְךָ פְּדָעֵהוּ מֵרֶדֶת שַׁחַת,[9]

פְּתוּחֵי חוֹתָם קֹדֶשׁ.[11]   הִנֵּה כְתוּבָה לְפָנַי[10] פֶּתַח מִפְתַּחַת,

וַאֲנִי יָדַעְתִּי דַרְכְּךָ בְּשֶׁפֶר,

דּוּץ וְרוּץ וְקַח אַיִל תַּחַת עֹפֶר,

הֲכִינוֹתִי כְפֶר לְאֶשְׁכֹּל הַכֹּפֶר, וְהָיָה הוּא וּתְמוּרָתוֹ יִהְיֶה קֹדֶשׁ.[12]   גָּמוּל נִמְלַט מֵאֶבַח הַנִּשְׁחָז,

בְּפָשְׁטוֹ צַוָּארוֹ דָמוֹ לֹא נִפְחַז,

לְהַקְדִּישׁוֹ לַיהוה קֹדֶשׁ.[13]   יְמִינוּ אָחַז בְּיוֹבֵל הַנֶּאֱחָז,

❖ רַחוּם תִּתֵּן שָׁלוֹם לְאַחֲרִיתוֹ,

וּזְכוֹר הַיּוֹם לְגִזְעוֹ בְּרִיתוֹ,

תִּהְיֶה פְּלֵיטָה וְהָיָה קֹדֶשׁ.[14]   לְיַתֵּר הַפְּלֵיטָה וּשְׁאָר שְׁאֵרִיתוֹ,

---

וּלְהַבְדִּיל בֵּין הַקֹּדֶשׁ — *And to distinguish what is holy.* Isaac asked that he be bound tightly for two reasons: (a) lest he shudder and cause the knife to make an invalid incision; and (b) to distinguish between the slaughter of a well-tied altar offering and a hastily bound animal to be slaughtered for food (*Pardes*).

According to *Arugas HaBosem* the conjunctive ו, *and*, is omitted from the text. Thus, Isaac gave only one reason: that he not invalidate the offering, but that it remain holy.

Alternatively: Isaac said, 'Bind me tight lest I desecrate the sacrifice and thus separate myself from God's Holiness!' (*Masbir*).

מ *'The Most High will pick the lamb for Himself,*[1] *and He will revive*
נ *the barren mother's soul, restoring her joy.*[2]
ס *The Examiner of hidden things, my son,*
    will be attentive to your prayer,
                and He will send His aid from the **Sanctuary.**' [3]

ע *'Please rise up, my father, and bind [me for] the slaughter,*
פ *lest I shudder in fear before the blade.*
צ *Bind me tight lest I desecrate the sacrifice,*
                and to distinguish what is **holy.**'*[4]

ק *Suddenly, [Isaac] the cluster of henna began to weep,*
ר *seeing his father bereaved, left childless.*
ש *But he [Abraham] stretched forth his hand to do all*
                the service of the **Holy.**' [5]

ת *The angels* *cried out in the Heavenly heights,*
ש *'Who can bear to see the dove of silence slaughtered?'*
ל *They said one to another, 'Give Him no silence!*[6]
           Lift up your hands [to pray] in **holiness.**' [7]

מ *When the Most High observed the binder and the bound,*
ה *the lamb bound and the fire kindled,*
ב *the Tester of pure hearts remembered and recalled,*
         and His voice was heard as He entered the **Sanctuary.**[8]

ר *The advocate [angel] called out, as he [Abraham] took the knife,*
י *'Redeem your only son from descending to the grave!*[9]
ה *See, it is all written before Me,*[10] *deeply engraved,*
            an engraved seal, made in **holiness.**[11]

ו *'And as for Me, I know how lovely is your way;*
ר *rejoice, run and take a ram instead of [Isaac,] the gazelle.*
ה *I have prepared ransom for the cluster of henna,*
         and both he and his substitute shall be **holy.**' [12]

ג *Reprieved, rescued from the sharp blade;*
ב *though he had stretched out his neck, his blood was not shed.*
י *His right hand grasped the ram tangled [in the thicket],*
         to consecrate it, to HASHEM **holy.**[13]

ר *O Merciful One, grant peace to his posterity,*
ו *and remember his covenant today in his descendants' favor.*
ל *For the surviving remnant and his remaining folk,*
         may there be rescue, and may they be **holy.**[14]

---

(1) *Genesis* 22:8. (2) Cf. *Psalms* 113:9. (3) 20:3. (4) *Leviticus* 10:10. (5) Cf. *Exodus* 36:1.
(6) Cf. *Isaiah* 62:7. (7) *Psalms* 134:2. (8) *Exodus* 28:35. (9) *Job* 33:24. (10) *Isaiah* 65:6.
(11) *Exodus* 28:36 (12) *Leviticus* 27:10. (13) Cf. *I chronicles* 23:13. (14) *Obadiah* 1:17.)

תַּרְשִׁישִׁים — *Angels.* Rambam (*Yesodei HaTorah* 2:7) notes that there are ten levels of angels. Their names are *Chayos, Ofanim, Erelim, Chashmalim, Seraphim, Malachim, Elohim, Bnei Elohim, Cherubim,* and *Ishim.* [We do not have the vocabulary to translate these names.] The prophet (*Ezekiel* 1:16) describes the appearance of the *Ofanim,* as similar to that of תַּרְשִׁישׁ, *tarshish,* a beautiful, clear gem which *Rashi* identifies as crystal. the *paytanim* have borrowed the term *Tarshishim* for the *Ofanim* in particular, and all angels in general.

All, while standing:

אֵל מֶלֶךְ יוֹשֵׁב עַל כִּסֵּא רַחֲמִים מִתְנַהֵג בַּחֲסִידוּת, מוֹחֵל
עֲוֹנוֹת עַמּוֹ, מַעֲבִיר רִאשׁוֹן רִאשׁוֹן, מַרְבֶּה מְחִילָה
לַחַטָּאִים וּסְלִיחָה לַפּוֹשְׁעִים, עֹשֶׂה צְדָקוֹת עִם כָּל בָּשָׂר וָרוּחַ, לֹא
כְרָעָתָם תִּגְמוֹל. ❖ אֵל הוֹרֵיתָ לָּנוּ לוֹמַר שְׁלֹשׁ עֶשְׂרֵה, וּזְכוֹר לָנוּ
הַיּוֹם בְּרִית שְׁלֹשׁ עֶשְׂרֵה, כְּמוֹ שֶׁהוֹדַעְתָּ לֶעָנָיו מִקֶּדֶם, כְּמוֹ
שֶׁכָּתוּב, וַיֵּרֶד יהוה בֶּעָנָן וַיִּתְיַצֵּב עִמּוֹ שָׁם, וַיִּקְרָא בְשֵׁם יהוה.

Congregation, then *chazzan:*

וַיַּעֲבֹר יהוה עַל פָּנָיו וַיִּקְרָא:

Congregation and *chazzan* (the words in bold type are recited aloud and in unison):

יהוה, יהוה, אֵל, רַחוּם, וְחַנּוּן, אֶרֶךְ אַפַּיִם, וְרַב חֶסֶד, וֶאֱמֶת,
נֹצֵר חֶסֶד לָאֲלָפִים, נֹשֵׂא עָוֹן, וָפֶשַׁע, וְחַטָּאָה,
וְנַקֵּה. וְסָלַחְתָּ לַעֲוֹנֵנוּ וּלְחַטָּאתֵנוּ וּנְחַלְתָּנוּ. סְלַח לָנוּ אָבִינוּ כִּי
חָטָאנוּ, מְחַל לָנוּ מַלְכֵּנוּ כִּי פָשָׁעְנוּ. כִּי אַתָּה אֲדֹנָי טוֹב וְסַלָּח, וְרַב
חֶסֶד לְכָל קֹרְאֶיךָ.

סליחה צג (פזמון)

[In some congregations, the paragraph beginning ה' ה'
is repeated by the congregation after each stanza.]

Chazzan, then congregation:

יהוה, יהוה, * אֵל רַחוּם, וְחַנּוּן, אֶרֶךְ אַפַּיִם, וְרַב חֶסֶד, וֶאֱמֶת,
נֹצֵר חֶסֶד לָאֲלָפִים, נֹשֵׂא עָוֹן, וָפֶשַׁע, וְחַטָּאָה,
וְנַקֵּה.[1] וְסָלַחְתָּ לַעֲוֹנֵנוּ וּלְחַטָּאתֵנוּ וּנְחַלְתָּנוּ.[2]

Congregation, then *chazzan:*

אֶזְכְּרָה אֱלֹהִים וְאֶהֱמָיָה,[3]
בִּרְאוֹתִי כָל עִיר עַל תִּלָּהּ בְּנוּיָה,*[4]
וְעִיר הָאֱלֹהִים מֻשְׁפֶּלֶת עַד שְׁאוֹל תַּחְתִּיָה,
וּבְכָל זֹאת אָנוּ לְיָהּ וְעֵינֵינוּ לְיָהּ.[5]

Congregation, then *chazzan:*

מִדַּת הָרַחֲמִים עָלֵינוּ הִתְגַּלְגָּלִי,*
וְלִפְנֵי קוֹנֵךְ תְּחִנָּתֵנוּ הַפִּילִי,

ה' ה' — *Hashem, Hashem.* The theme of this *selichah* is, appropriately, the Thirteen Attributes of Mercy, because God promised Moses that those who beseech Him with these sacred words will not be turned away empty-handed

(*Rosh Hashanah* 17b).

The acrostic spells the author's name, אֲמִתַּי, *Amittai*, son and successor to R' Shephatiah in ninth-century Oria, Italy [see prefatory comment in *selichah* 7].

All, while standing:

אֵל מֶלֶךְ   *O God, King Who sits on the throne of mercy; Who acts with kindness, pardons the iniquities of His people, removes [sins] one by one, increasingly grants pardon to careless sinners and forgiveness to rebels, Who deals righteously with every living being — You do not repay them in accord with their evil.* Chazzan — *O God, You taught us to recite the Thirteen [Attributes of Mercy], so remember for us today the covenant of these Thirteen, as You made known to the humble one in ancient times, as it is written: And H*ASHEM *descended in a cloud and stood with him there, and He called out with the Name H*ASHEM.

Congregation, then *chazzan:*

*And H*ASHEM *passed before him [Moses] and proclaimed:*

Congregation and *chazzan* (the words in bold type are recited aloud and in unison):

ה' ה'   **H**ASHEM, **H**ASHEM, **God, Compassionate and Gracious, Slow to anger, and Abundant in Kindness and Truth, Preserver of kindness for thousands [of generations], Forgiver of iniquity, willful sin, and error, and Who cleanses.** *May You forgive our iniquities and our errors and make us Your heritage. Forgive us, our Father, for we have erred; pardon us, our King, for we have willfully sinned; for You, my Lord, are good and forgiving and abundantly kind to all who call upon You.*

SELICHAH 93

[In some congregations, the paragraph beginning H*ASHEM, H*ASHEM, is repeated by the congregation after each stanza.]

Chazzan, then congregation:

ה' ה'   *H*ASHEM, *H*ASHEM,* *God, Compassionate and Gracious, Slow to anger, and Abundant in Kindness and Truth. Preserver of kindness for thousands of generations, Forgiver of iniquity, willful sin, and error, and Who cleanses.[1] May You forgive our iniquities and our errors and make us Your heritage.[2]*

Congregation, then *chazzan:*

א *I shall remember, O God, and I shall moan,[3]*
when I see every city built on its hilltop,[4]
while the City of God is degraded to the nethermost depth.
But despite all this, we are God's and our eyes look to God.[5]

Congregation, then *chazzan:*

מ *O Attribute of Mercy, overflow upon us,**
and before Your Creator cast our supplication;

---

(1) *Exodus* 34:6-7. (2) 34:9. (3) *Psalms* 77:4. (4) Cf. *Jeremiah* 30:18. (5) See tractate *Succah* 51b.

עַל תִּלָּהּ בְּנוּיָה — *Built on its hilltop.* The prophet (Jeremiah 30:18) promises that Israel will be redeemed and Jerusalem rebuilt. Now, in exile, we contrast Jerusalem, which still has mosques on its holiest place, with the proud, arrogant cities of our oppressors and those who have historically been indifferent to our suffering.

עָלֵינוּ הִתְגַּלְגְּלִי — *Overflow upon us.* In this stanza, we plead 'to' God's Attribute of Mercy as if it were a tangible being that has the power to determine the fate of people's prayers. The propriety and permissibility of such prayer is discussed in the introduction to this volume.

וּבְעַד עַמְּךָ רַחֲמִים שַׁאֲלִי, כִּי כָל לֵבָב דַּוָּי וְכָל רֹאשׁ לָחֳלִי.[1]

Congregation, then *chazzan:*

תָּמַכְתִּי יְתֵדוֹתִי* בִּשְׁלֹשׁ עֶשְׂרֵה תֵבוֹת,
וּבְשַׁעֲרֵי דְמָעוֹת כִּי לֹא נִשְׁלָבוֹת,*
לָכֵן שָׁפַכְתִּי שִׂיחַ פְּנֵי בוֹחֵן לְבוֹת,
בָּטוּחַ אֲנִי בְּאֵלֶּה* וּבִזְכוּת שְׁלֹשֶׁת אָבוֹת.

Congregation, then *chazzan:*

יְהִי רָצוֹן מִלְּפָנֶיךָ שׁוֹמֵעַ קוֹל בְּכִיּוֹת,[2]
שֶׁתָּשִׂים דִּמְעוֹתֵינוּ בְּנֹאדְךָ לִהְיוֹת,[3]
וְתַצִּילֵנוּ מִכָּל גְּזֵרוֹת אַכְזָרִיּוֹת, כִּי לְךָ לְבַד עֵינֵינוּ תְלוּיוֹת.

All, while standing:

אֵל מֶלֶךְ יוֹשֵׁב עַל כִּסֵּא רַחֲמִים מִתְנַהֵג בַּחֲסִידוּת, מוֹחֵל
עֲוֹנוֹת עַמּוֹ, מַעֲבִיר רִאשׁוֹן רִאשׁוֹן, מַרְבֶּה מְחִילָה
לְחַטָּאִים וּסְלִיחָה לְפוֹשְׁעִים, עֹשֶׂה צְדָקוֹת עִם כָּל בָּשָׂר וָרוּחַ, לֹא
כְרָעָתָם תִּגְמוֹל. ❖ אֵל הוֹרֵיתָ לָנוּ לוֹמַר שְׁלֹשׁ עֶשְׂרֵה, וּזְכוֹר לָנוּ
הַיּוֹם בְּרִית שְׁלֹשׁ עֶשְׂרֵה, כְּמוֹ שֶׁהוֹדַעְתָּ לֶעָנָיו מִקֶּדֶם, כְּמוֹ
שֶׁכָּתוּב, וַיֵּרֶד יהוה בֶּעָנָן וַיִּתְיַצֵּב עִמּוֹ שָׁם, וַיִּקְרָא בְשֵׁם יהוה.

Congregation, then *chazzan:*

וַיַּעֲבֹר יהוה עַל פָּנָיו וַיִּקְרָא:

Congregation and *chazzan* (the words in bold type are recited aloud and in unison):

יהוה, יהוה, אֵל, רַחוּם, וְחַנּוּן, אֶרֶךְ אַפַּיִם, וְרַב חֶסֶד, וֶאֱמֶת,
נֹצֵר חֶסֶד לָאֲלָפִים, נֹשֵׂא עָוֹן, וָפֶשַׁע, וְחַטָּאָה,
וְנַקֵּה. וְסָלַחְתָּ לַעֲוֹנֵנוּ וּלְחַטָּאתֵנוּ וּנְחַלְתָּנוּ. סְלַח לָנוּ אָבִינוּ כִּי
חָטָאנוּ, מְחַל לָנוּ מַלְכֵּנוּ כִּי פָשָׁעְנוּ. כִּי אַתָּה אֲדֹנָי טוֹב וְסַלָּח, וְרַב
חֶסֶד לְכָל קֹרְאֶיךָ.

All:

אַל תִּזְכָּר לָנוּ עֲוֹנוֹת רִאשׁוֹנִים, מַהֵר יְקַדְּמוּנוּ רַחֲמֶיךָ, כִּי
דַלּוֹנוּ מְאֹד.[4] חַטֹּאת נְעוּרֵינוּ וּפְשָׁעֵינוּ אַל תִּזְכּוֹר,
כְּחַסְדְּךָ זְכָר לָנוּ אַתָּה, לְמַעַן טוּבְךָ יהוה.[5]

זְכוֹר רַחֲמֶיךָ יהוה וַחֲסָדֶיךָ, כִּי מֵעוֹלָם הֵמָּה.[6] זָכְרֵנוּ יהוה
בִּרְצוֹן עַמֶּךָ, פָּקְדֵנוּ בִּישׁוּעָתֶךָ.[7] זְכֹר עֲדָתְךָ קָנִיתָ

תָּמַכְתִּי יְתֵדוֹתִי — *I have place my reliance.* Since God has promised to take note of prayers containing the Thirteen Attributes of Mercy, we express our confidence that our *Selichos* prayers will help save us from a harsh decree.

כִּי לֹא נִשְׁלָבוֹת — *For they are never closed.* Even when the Gates of Prayer are sealed, the Gates of Tears are always open (*Berachos* 32b).

for the sake of Your people request mercy,
for every heart is pained and every head is ill.[1]

Congregation, then *chazzan:*

ת *I have placed my reliance* on the Thirteen Attributes,*
and on the gates of tears for they are never closed,*
therefore I have poured out my prayer to Him Who tests hearts.
I trust in these* and in the merit of the three Patriarchs.

Congregation, then *chazzan:*

י *May it be Your will, You Who hear the sound of weeping,* [2]
that You place our tears in Your flask permanently,[3]
and that You rescue us from all cruel decrees,
for on You alone are our eyes fixed.

All, while standing:

אֵל מֶלֶךְ *O God, King Who sits on the throne of mercy; Who acts with*
kindness, pardons the iniquities of His people, removes [sins]
one by one, increasingly grants pardon to careless sinners and forgiveness
to rebels, Who deals righteously with every living being — You do not repay
them in accord with their evil. Chazzan – *O God, You taught us to recite the*
Thirteen [Attributes of Mercy], so remember for us today the covenant of
these Thirteen, as You made known to the humble one in ancient times, as
it is written: And HASHEM descended in a cloud and stood with him there,
and He called out with the Name HASHEM.

Congregation, then *chazzan:*

And HASHEM passed before him [Moses] and proclaimed:

Congregation and *chazzan* (the words in bold type are recited aloud and in unison):

ה' ה' **HASHEM, HASHEM, God, Compassionate and Gracious, Slow to**
anger, and Abundant in Kindness and Truth, Preserver of
kindness for thousands [of generations], Forgiver of iniquity, willful
sin, and error, and Who cleanses. *May You forgive our iniquities and our*
errors and make us Your heritage. Forgive us, our Father, for we have
erred; pardon us, our King, for we have willfully sinned; for You, my Lord,
are good and forgiving and abundantly kind to all who call upon You.

All:

אַל תִּזְכָּר *Do not recall against us the iniquities of the ancients;*
speedily — let Your mercy come to meet us for we have fallen
very low.[4] *Remember not the sins of our youth and our rebellions; may*
You remember for us [the deeds] worthy of Your kindness, because of
Your goodness, HASHEM.[5]

זְכוֹר רַחֲמֶיךָ *Remember Your mercies, O HASHEM, and Your kind-*
nesses, for they are from the beginning of the world.[6]
Remember us, HASHEM, when You show Your people favor and recall us
with Your salvation.[7] *Remember Your congregation that You acquired*

---

(1) Cf. *Isaiah* 1:5. (2) Cf. *Psalms* 6:9. (3) Cf. 56:9. (4) 79:8. (5) Cf. 25:7. (6) *Psalms* 25:6. (7) Cf. 106:5.

בָּטוּחַ אֲנִי בְּאֵלֶּה — *I trust in these,* i.e., in the
efficacy of the Thirteen Attributes and in the
power of tearful prayer. Some editions have the
singular pronoun בְּזֹאת, *in this,* i.e., in the efficacy of the tearful recitation of the Thirteen
Attributes.

קֶדֶם, גָּאַלְתָּ שֵׁבֶט נַחֲלָתֶךָ, הַר צִיּוֹן זֶה שָׁכַנְתָּ בּוֹ.[1] זְכֹר יהוה חִבַּת
יְרוּשָׁלַיִם, אַהֲבַת צִיּוֹן אַל תִּשְׁכַּח לָנֶצַח.[2] אַתָּה תָקוּם תְּרַחֵם צִיּוֹן,
כִּי עֵת לְחֶנְנָהּ כִּי בָא מוֹעֵד.[3] זְכֹר יהוה לִבְנֵי אֱדוֹם אֵת יוֹם
יְרוּשָׁלַיִם, הָאֹמְרִים עָרוּ עָרוּ עַד הַיְסוֹד בָּהּ.[4] זְכֹר לְאַבְרָהָם
לְיִצְחָק וּלְיִשְׂרָאֵל עֲבָדֶיךָ אֲשֶׁר נִשְׁבַּעְתָּ לָהֶם בָּךְ, וַתְּדַבֵּר אֲלֵהֶם,
אַרְבֶּה אֶת זַרְעֲכֶם כְּכוֹכְבֵי הַשָּׁמָיִם, וְכָל הָאָרֶץ הַזֹּאת אֲשֶׁר
אָמַרְתִּי אֶתֵּן לְזַרְעֲכֶם, וְנָחֲלוּ לְעֹלָם.[5] ❖ זְכֹר לַעֲבָדֶיךָ לְאַבְרָהָם
לְיִצְחָק וּלְיַעֲקֹב, אַל תֵּפֶן אֶל קְשִׁי הָעָם הַזֶּה וְאֶל רִשְׁעוֹ וְאֶל
חַטָּאתוֹ.[6]

Chazzan, then congregation:

אַל נָא תָשֵׁת עָלֵינוּ חַטָּאת, אֲשֶׁר נוֹאַלְנוּ וַאֲשֶׁר חָטָאנוּ.[7]

Chazzan, then congregation:

חָטָאנוּ צוּרֵנוּ, סְלַח לָנוּ יוֹצְרֵנוּ.

סליחה צד (חטאנו)

All:

אֵיךְ נֶאֶנְחָה בְּמִשְׁבָּר,*[8]   אֲדוּקָה מִקֶּדֶם כְּבָר,
אֲרוּכָה בְּכָל מַעֲבָר,[9]   וַתֵּלֶךְ וַתֵּתַע בַּמִּדְבָּר.[10]
בַּמִּדְבָּר בֵּין פְּרָאִים,[11]   בְּעָלוּהָ גוּרֵי לְבָאִים,
בִּגְדֵי נָקָם הַנָּאִים,   הָשֵׁב גָּמוּל עַל גֵּאִים.[12]

חָטָאנוּ צוּרֵנוּ, סְלַח לָנוּ יוֹצְרֵנוּ.

גֵּאִים חֶחֱזַקְתָּ בְּיָדָם,   גְּבוּלֵי הֶחֱרִיבוּ בְּסוֹדָם,
גָּבְרוּ עָלַי בְּמַעֲמָדָם,   וַיְמַהֲרוּ לִשְׁפָּךְ דָּם.[13]
דָּם שָׁפְכוּ כַמַּיִם,   דָּרְכוּ כְּגַת יְפַת פַּעֲמַיִם,
דִּמְעָה הִזִּילוּ כַמַּיִם,   וְאַתָּה תִשְׁמַע הַשָּׁמָיִם.[14]

חָטָאנוּ צוּרֵנוּ, סְלַח לָנוּ יוֹצְרֵנוּ.

הַשָּׁמַיִם יָד הֵרִימוּ,   הֶחֱלִיף קְדָשָׁתְךָ דְּמוּ,
הֵן אוֹתִי הֶחֱרִימוּ,   מְלָכִים יִרְאוּ וָקָמוּ.[15]
וָקָמוּ עַל נַחֲלָתִי,   וַיְשַׁסּוּ אֶת בֵּיתִי,
וּמֵאָז בְּיָדָם סְגַרְתִּי,   עַל כֵּן זָחַלְתִּי.[16]

חָטָאנוּ צוּרֵנוּ, סְלַח לָנוּ יוֹצְרֵנוּ.

אֵיךְ נֶאֶנְחָה בְּמִשְׁבָּר — *How she sighs bro-kenly.* In this intricately woven tapestry, the first three lines of the respective stanzas for a triple *aleph-beis* acrostic. The penultimate stanza con-

tains the *paytan's* signature — יִצְחָק בַּר יַקִּיר, *Yitzchak bar Yakir* (or *Yakar*) [see prefatory comment to *selichah* 85]. The last line of each stanza is a Scriptural fragment, the last word of

*of old, that You redeemed the tribe of Your heritage, and this Mount Zion
where You dwelled.*[1] *Remember, O* HASHEM, *the affection of Jerusalem,
may You never forget the love of Zion.*[2] *You will arise and show Zion
mercy, for it is the time to be gracious to her, for the appointed time will
have come.*[3] *Remember,* HASHEM, *for the offspring of Edom, the day of
Jerusalem — for those who said: 'Destroy! Destroy to its very foundation!'*[4] *Remember Abraham, Isaac, and Israel, Your servants, to whom
You swore by Your Being, saying to them, 'I shall increase your offspring
like the stars of the heavens; and this entire land of which I spoke I will
give to your offspring and they will inherit it forever.'*[5] Chazzan – *Remember for Your servants, for Abraham, for Isaac, and for Jacob; ignore the
stubbornness of this people, its wickedness and its sinfulness.*[6]

Chazzan, then congregation:

*Please, do not reckon for us a sin,
what we have done foolishly and what we have sinned.*[7]

Chazzan, then congregation:

We have erred, our Rock! Forgive us, our Molder!

SELICHAH 94

All:

א *How she sighs brokenly,*[*8] *she who of old cleaved [to God].
Plucked by every passer-by,*[9]
*and she goes wandering **in the Exile's desert.***[10]
ב ***In the [Exile's] desert** among the wanton,*[11]
*she is ravaged by young lions.
[O God, don Your] fine robes of vengeance,
render recompense to **the haughty!***[12]

We have sinned, our Rock! Forgive us, our Molder!

ג ***The haughty** when You encouraged their hand,
they destroyed my boundary in their counsel.
They overpowered me from their battle stations,
then they hastened to spill **blood.***[13]
ד ***Blood** they spilled like water,
they trampled like grapes, the people of the beautiful pilgrimage.
They shed tears like water — and You, may You hear us in **Heaven!***[14]

We have sinned, our Rock! Forgive, us our Molder!

ה ***Heaven** — they have raised hand against it,
thinking to [force us] to exchange Your holiness [for their idols].
See, they have decreed doom for me,
when those [very] kings saw [me at an early time], **they rose.***[15]
ו ***They rose** against my heritage-land and demolished my Temple.
And since then I have been given over into their hand;
therefore **I am afraid.***[16]

We have sinned, our Rock! Forgive us, our Molder!

---

(1) *Ps*alms 74:2. (2) This is not a Scriptural verse. (3) *Psalms* 102:14. (4) 137:7. (5) *Exodus* 32:13. (6) *Deut.*
9:27. (7) *Numbers* 12:11. (8) Cf. *Ezekiel* 21:11. (9) Cf. *Psalms* 80:13. (10) Cf. *Genesis* 21:14. (11) Cf. *Job* 24:5.
(12) *Psalms* 94:2. (13) Cf. *Isaiah* 59:7; *Proverbs* 1:16. (14) *I Kings* 8:32, 34, etc. (15) *Isaiah* 49:7. (16) *Job* 32:6.

זָחַלְתִּי מִזְּעַם לְשׁוֹנָם,   זוּ לַעֲגָם[1] בְּרִנּוּנָם,

זָרִים לְהַעֲלוֹת עֲשָׁנָם,   כִּי לָקַח עַמִּי חִנָּם.[2]

חִנָּם חָנֵּנוּ כְּמַעֲלָלֶךָ,   חוֹן זֶרַע חֲבָלֶךָ,

חַיֵּינוּ כְּמִלּוּלֶיךָ,   טַל אוֹרוֹת טַלֶּךָ.[3]

חָטָאנוּ צוּרֵנוּ, סְלַח לָנוּ יוֹצְרֵנוּ.

טַלֶּךָ הַגְשִׁימֵנוּ מִקָּב,   טַהֲרֵנוּ עֻזְּךָ מִלַּעֲקֹב,

טֶנֶף מַרְשִׁיעֵי יְרָקָב,   כִּי אָכְלוּ אֶת יַעֲקֹב.[4]

יַעֲקֹב בָּחַרְתָּ לְעַלֵּה,   יִחוּד אֱלֹהוּתָךְ עָלָיו לְהַגְלֵה,

יַחַד צֶאֱצָאָיו הַעֲלֵה,   אֲסִירִים מִבֵּית כֶּלֶא.[5]

חָטָאנוּ צוּרֵנוּ, סְלַח לָנוּ יוֹצְרֵנוּ.

כֶּלֶא בְּזִקִּים אֲסַרְתָּנוּ,   כְּהִזְהַרְתָּנוּ וְלֹא שָׁמָעֵנוּ,

כַּעַסְךָ הָפֵר עִמָּנוּ,[6]   תִּשְׁפֹּת שָׁלוֹם לָנוּ.[7]

לָנוּ שְׁכִינָתָךְ לְהוֹעֵד,   לְמַעֲנֶךָ תּוֹמֵךְ וְסוֹעֵד,

לָנֶצַח סֶלָה וָעֵד,   אֵשֵׁב בְּהַר מוֹעֵד.[8]

חָטָאנוּ צוּרֵנוּ, סְלַח לָנוּ יוֹצְרֵנוּ.

מוֹעֵד קֵץ מִלְחַמְתֶּךָ,   מֵעַלי שַׁכֵּךְ חֲמָתֶךָ,

מִמִּתְקוֹמְמִים בְּהַר נַחֲלָתֶךָ,   אֶרְאֶה נִקְמָתֶךָ.[9]

נִקְמָתָךְ תַּרְאֵנוּ וְנָגִילָה,   נֵחֵנוּ בִּישֶׁר מְסִלָּה,

נְעַם זְמִירָתָךְ נְמַלְּלָה,   אֱלֹהֵי יַעֲקֹב סֶלָה.[10]

חָטָאנוּ צוּרֵנוּ, סְלַח לָנוּ יוֹצְרֵנוּ.

סֶלָה נִצְחָךְ יֹאמֵרוּ,   סִלּוּדֶיךָ הַכֹּל יֹאמֵרוּ,

סָאסְּאָה* תָּמוּר כְּפָאֲרוּ,   הָאוֹמְרִים עָרוּ עָרוּ.[11]

עָרוּ יְסוֹדוֹת[11] וּמִגְדָּלִים,   עוֹד שָׁדְּדוּ אֹהָלִים,

עָרִים שָׂמוּ לְגַלִּים,   וְאוֹיְבֵינוּ פְּלִילִים.[12]

חָטָאנוּ צוּרֵנוּ, סְלַח לָנוּ יוֹצְרֵנוּ.

פְּלִילִים שְׁפָטְוּנוּ בִּמְצוּקָה,   פָּנִים נִצְרְבוּ לִירוּקָה,

פְּנֵה אֵלֵינוּ וְנִצְטַדָּקָה,   וּלְךָ תִּהְיֶה צְדָקָה.[13]

---

(1) Hosea 7:16. (2) Isaiah 52:5. (3) 26:19. (4) Jeremiah 10:25. (5) Cf. Isaiah 42:7. (6) Cf. Psalms 85:5. (7) Isaiah 26:12. (8) Cf. Isaiah 14:13. (9) Jeremiah 11:20. (10) Psalms 84:9; see commentary to selichah 41, s.v., סֶלָה. (11) Cf. 137:7. (12) Deuteronomy 32:31. (13) 24:13.

---

which is the same as the first word of the following stanza. The refrain is repeated after every second stanza.

סָאסְּאָה — *Measure for Measure.* The Talmud

adduces a Scriptural verse (Isaiah 27:8) as proof that God recompenses man's deeds in the same measure as they are performed: בְּסַאסְּאָה בְּשַׁלְחָהּ תְּרִיבֶנָּה, *When You banish her, You demand from*

ז *I am afraid of their tongue's fury,*
  this is their mockery[1] in their ridiculing chant,
  [urging us] to burn incense to foreign gods,
  *for my people is taken by them **for naught**.[2]*

ח **For naught** *be gracious to us, as is Your way;*
  be gracious to the seed of Your heritage[-people].
  Enliven us today, as Your word:
  *'[Resuscitating] dew of lights is **Your dew**.[3]*
                    We have sinned, our Rock! Forgive us, our Molder!

ט **Your dew** *let rain down on us [to protect us] from curse;*
  purify us, that we may not corrupt Your mighty [Torah].
  *Let the squalid who do me evil rot, for they have devoured **Jacob**.[4]*

י **Jacob** *have You chosen to elevate,*
  the Oneness of Your Divinity to be revealed upon him.
  Now bring up his descendants all as one,
  *the prisoners from the house of **[our] confinement**.[5]*
                    We have sinned, our Rock! Forgive us, our Molder!

כ **[Our] confinement!** *You have bound us [there] in chains,*
  as You had warned us; but we did not listen.
  *Now annul Your anger against us,[6] and set peace **unto us!**[7]*

ל **Unto us** *may Your Presence come,*
  for Your sake, O Supporter and Sustainer.
  Then forever and ever and ever,
  *I shall dwell [in the Temple] on the Mount of **the Appointed Time**.[8]*
We have sinned our Rock! Forgive us, our Molder!

מ **The appointed time** *for the end of Your battle,*
  put down Your anger against me.
  And from those who rise up against the mount of Your heritage,
  *may I witness **Your vengeance**.[9]*

נ **Your vengeance** *show us, that we may rejoice.*
  Lead us on the straight path. We shall sing out Your pleasant song,
  *for You are the God of Jacob **forever**.[10]*
                    We have sinned our Rock! Forgive us, our Molder!

ס **Forever** *shall mankind speak of Your eternality,*
  and all will speak of Your praises,
  When You pay back measure for measure* for their vainglory,
            *those who said, 'Destroy [Jerusalem]! **Destroy!**[11]*

ע **Destroy** *they did, foundations[11] and towers,*
  and went on to plunder homes. They turned cities into heaps of rubble,
  *when our enemies became **the judges**.[12]*
                    We have sinned, our Rock! Forgive us, our Molder!

פ **The judges** *have judged us harshly, so our faces are scorched and green.*
  Turn to us and let us be vindicated,
  *and it will be for You a deed of **charity**.[13]*

---

her measure (Sotah 8b). The word בְּסָאסְאָה is
thus to be understood as if it were written סְאָה

בְּסָאה, bushel for bushel, i.e., measure for measure.

צְדָקָה בְּקַשְׁתֶּיךָ לְהוֹעִילִי, צַוֵּה יְשׁוּעוֹת אֵלִי,
צָרוֹת לְבָבִי לְהַחְדִּילִי, שְׁמַע אֱלֹהִים קוֹלִי.¹
חָטָאנוּ צוּרֵנוּ, סְלַח לָנוּ יוֹצְרֵנוּ.

קוֹלִי תִשְׁמַע הַשָּׁמַיְמָה,² קַנֵּא וּנְקַם נְקָמָה,
קָרֵב קֵץ נֶחָמָה, יַד יהוה רָמָה.³
רָמָה יָדְךָ כִּנְאוּמֶךָ, רִיבָה רִיב עַמֶּךָ,
רַחוּם שַׁכֵּךְ זַעֲמֶךָ, גּוֹאֲלֵנוּ מֵעוֹלָם שְׁמֶךָ.⁴
חָטָאנוּ צוּרֵנוּ, סְלַח לָנוּ יוֹצְרֵנוּ.

שִׁמְךָ עָלֵינוּ נִקְרָא,⁵ שַׁדַּי דָּר בִּנְהוֹרָא,
שׁוּב לְגָאֳלֵנוּ מְהֵרָה, מִצִּיּוֹן תֵּצֵא תּוֹרָה.⁶
תּוֹרָה וְסֵפֶר נִחוּמִים, תַּמְצִיאֵנוּ מָלֵא רַחֲמִים,
תְּנַהֲלֵנוּ לְעוֹלָמִים, יהוה לְאֹרֶךְ יָמִים.⁷
חָטָאנוּ צוּרֵנוּ, סְלַח לָנוּ יוֹצְרֵנוּ.

❖ יָמִים צֵאת לְיֶשַׁע, חַי וְקַיָּם וְנוֹשַׁע,
בְּרַחֲמִים יִפְקֹד וְיוֹשַׁע, יַקִּיר יֶלֶד מִשְׁעֲשֵׁעַ.⁸
מִשְׁעֲשֵׁעַ כִּנְאוּמוֹ, לָעַד לְיוֹם קוּמוֹ,⁹
וְנִשְׂגָּב לְבַדּוֹ שְׁמוֹ,⁹ כִּי נִחַם יהוה עַמּוֹ.¹⁰
חָטָאנוּ צוּרֵנוּ, סְלַח לָנוּ יוֹצְרֵנוּ.

All:

זְכוֹר לָנוּ בְּרִית אָבוֹת, כַּאֲשֶׁר אָמַרְתָּ: וְזָכַרְתִּי אֶת בְּרִיתִי
יַעֲקוֹב, וְאַף אֶת בְּרִיתִי יִצְחָק, וְאַף אֶת בְּרִיתִי אַבְרָהָם
אֶזְכֹּר, וְהָאָרֶץ אֶזְכֹּר.¹¹

סליחה צה (פזמון)

THE ARK IS OPENED.

Chazzan, then congregation:

זְכוֹר בְּרִית אַבְרָהָם* וַעֲקֵדַת יִצְחָק,
וְהָשֵׁב שְׁבוּת אָהֳלֵי יַעֲקֹב,¹² וְהוֹשִׁיעֵנוּ לְמַעַן שְׁמֶךָ.¹³

זְכוֹר בְּרִית אַבְרָהָם — **זְכוֹר בְּרִית אַבְרָהָם** — *Remember the covenant of Abraham.* This *pizmon* differs from others by virtue of its two refrains which alternate after each stanza. Although it originally contained fourteen stanzas, only seven of them have re- mained in the liturgy. The acrostic of the stiches form a double *aleph-beis* (from ו until ת are omit- ted today) followed by the *paytan's* signature, גֵּרְשֹׁם בַּר יְהוּדָה חֲזַק, *Gershom bar Yehudah, may he be strong* [see prefatory comment to *selichah* 12].

צ **Charity** have I asked of You, to benefit me;
command salvation for me, O my God,
that my heart's afflictions may come to an end.
O God, **hear my voice!**[1]

           We have sinned, our Rock! Forgive us, our Molder!

ק **Hear my voice** in Heaven,[2]
be jealous and take vengeance [for us].
Bring nearer the time of consolation,
when HASHEM's hand will be **manifest.**[3]

ר **Manifest** is Your hand, as You have said;
fight, then, Your people's fight.
O Merciful One, quell Your fury, [since]
'Our Redeemer' has always been **Your Name.**[4]

           We have sinned, our Rock! Forgive us, our Molder!

ש **Your Name** is called upon us,[5]
Almighty Who dwells in light.
Return and redeem us swiftly,
so that from Zion shall go forth **Torah.**[6]

ת **Torah** and the book of the prophet's consolation,
bring them about for us, O [God] full of mercy!
Lead us in Your way for all eternity,
O HASHEM, unto length of **days.**[7]

           We have sinned, our Rock! Forgive us, our Molder!

יצ *Chazzan* – **Days** bringing forth to salvation,

חק [Israel will be] alive, enduring, and saved.

בר In mercy may He consider [us] and save

יקיר His dear child in whom **He delights.**[8]

     He delights, as He said, forever, on the day that He arises;
and His name alone will be exalted,[9]
when HASHEM has comforted His people.[10]

           We have sinned, our Rock! Forgive us, our Molder!

All:

זְכוֹר לָנוּ Remember for us the covenant of the Patriarchs, as You said:
     'And I will remember My covenant with Jacob, and also My
covenant with Isaac, and also My covenant with Abraham will I remember; and the Land will I remember.'[11]

SELICHAH 95

THE ARK IS OPENED.
Chazzan, then congregation:

זְכוֹר Remember the covenant of Abraham* and the binding of Isaac.
     O restore the captivity of Jacob's tents,[12] and save us for Your
Name's sake.[13]

---

(1) *Psalms* 64:2. (2) Cf. *I Kings* 8:32, 34, etc. (3) Cf. *Psalms* 118:16; *Isaiah* 26:11. (4) *Isaiah* 63:16. (5) Cf. *Jeremiah* 14:9. (6) *Isaiah* 2:3. (7) *Psalms* 23:6. (8) Cf. *Jeremiah* 31:19. (9) Cf. *Psalms* 138:13. (10) *Isaiah* 49:13. (11) *Leviticus* 26:42. (12) Cf. *Jeremiah* 30:18. (13) Cf. *Psalms* 106:8.

Congregation, then *chazzan:*

אָבַדְנוּ מֵאֶרֶץ טוֹבָה[1] בְּחִפָּזוֹן,   אָרְכוּ הַיָּמִים וּדְבַר כָּל חָזוֹן,[2]

בְּיִשְׂרָאֵל חָדְלוּ פְרָזוֹן,[3]   בְּמִשְׁמַנֵּינוּ שָׁלַח רָזוֹן.[4]

וְשׁוּב בְּרַחֲמִים עַל שְׁאֵרִית יִשְׂרָאֵל, וְהוֹשִׁיעֵנוּ לְמַעַן שְׁמֶךָ.

Congregation, then *chazzan:*

גּוֹלָה אַחַר גּוֹלָה,   גָּלְתָה יְהוּדָה[5] כֻלָּה,

דָּוָה כָל הַיּוֹם[7] וְכָלָה,   דּוֹרֵשׁ וּמְבַקֵּשׁ אֵין לָהּ.[7]

וְהָשֵׁב שְׁבוּת אָהֳלֵי יַעֲקֹב, וְהוֹשִׁיעֵנוּ לְמַעַן שְׁמֶךָ.

Congregation, then *chazzan:*

הָעִיר הַקֹּדֶשׁ וְהַמְּחוֹזוֹת,*   הָיוּ לְחֶרְפָּה וּלְבִזּוֹת,

וְכָל מַחֲמַדֶּיהָ טְבוּעוֹת וּגְנוּזוֹת,*   וְאֵין שִׁיּוּר רַק הַתּוֹרָה הַזֹּאת.

וְשׁוּב בְּרַחֲמִים עַל שְׁאֵרִית יִשְׂרָאֵל, וְהוֹשִׁיעֵנוּ לְמַעַן שְׁמֶךָ.

Congregation, then *chazzan:*

גּוֹאֵל חָזָק לְמַעַנְךָ פְּדֵנוּ,   רְאֵה כִּי אָזְלַת יָדֵנוּ,[8]

שׁוּר כִּי אָבְדוּ חֲסִידֵינוּ,[9]   מַפְגִּיעַ אֵין בַּעֲדֵנוּ.[10]

וְהָשֵׁב שְׁבוּת אָהֳלֵי יַעֲקֹב, וְהוֹשִׁיעֵנוּ לְמַעַן שְׁמֶךָ.

Congregation, then *chazzan:*

בְּרִית אָבוֹת וְאִמָּהוֹת וְהַשְּׁבָטִים,

רַחֲמֶיךָ וַחֲסָדֶיךָ בְּרֻבּוֹת עִתִּים,[11]

יָהּ זְכֹר לְמֻכִּים וְנִמְרָטִים,[12]   וְעָלֶיךָ כָּל הַיּוֹם נִשְׁחָטִים.[13]

וְשׁוּב בְּרַחֲמִים עַל שְׁאֵרִית יִשְׂרָאֵל, וְהוֹשִׁיעֵנוּ לְמַעַן שְׁמֶךָ.

Congregation, then *chazzan:*

דּוֹרֵשׁ דָּמִים[14] דּוֹן דִּינֵנוּ,   הָשֵׁב שִׁבְעָתַיִם אֶל חֵיק[15] מְעַנֵּינוּ,

חִנָּם נִמְכַּרְנוּ, וְלֹא בְכֶסֶף פְּדֵנוּ,[16]

זְקֹף בֵּית מִקְדָּשְׁךָ הַשָּׁמֵם[17] לְעֵינֵינוּ.

וְהָשֵׁב שְׁבוּת אָהֳלֵי יַעֲקֹב, וְהוֹשִׁיעֵנוּ לְמַעַן שְׁמֶךָ.

THE ARK IS CLOSED.

---

(1) Cf. *Deuteronomy* 11:17. (2) Cf. *Ezekiel* 12:22-23. (3) Cf. *Judges* 5:7; see commentary to *selichah* 21. (4) Cf. *Isaiah* 10:16. (5) *Lamentations* 1:3. (6) Cf. 1:13. (7) Cf. *Ezekiel* 34:6; *Jeremiah* 30:17. (8) Cf. *Deuteronomy* 32:36. (9) Cf. *Micah* 7:2. (10) Cf. *Isaiah* 59:16. (11) Cf. *Nehemiah* 9:28. (12) Cf. 13:25. (13) Cf. *Psalms* 44:23. (14) 9:13. (15) Cf. 79:12; some editions of *Selichos* omit this stich. (16) Cf. *Isaiah* 52:3; see commentary to *selichah* 9, s.v., לְמֹכְרֵי חִנָּם. (17) Cf. *Daniel* 9:17.

הָעִיר הַקֹּדֶשׁ וְהַמְּחוֹזוֹת — *The Holy City and [its outlying] regions.* Some would translate: *The city [of Jerusalem], the Holy [Temple] and the [outlying] regions.* This is based on *Daniel* 9:26, where עִיר and קֹדֶשׁ refer to Jerusalem and the *Beis HaMikdash.* We have not used this translation for two reasons. In *Daniel* the phrase contains only two words הַקֹּדֶשׁ וְהָעִיר, *the city and the holy,* which are joined by the conjunctive prefix וְ, *and;* in our stich the conjunction is absent and so הַקֹּדֶשׁ is more likely an adjective modifying הָעִיר than an independent noun. Additionally, the order of the stich — city, Temple, outlying regions — would be illogical. The list should be in order of

Congregation, then chazzan:

א *We have lost our goodly land¹ so quickly;*
long days have passed,
and every [exile] prophecy's message [has come to pass].²

ב *Israel can no longer dwell in unfortified cities;³*
a wasting plague is sent on all our prosperity.⁴

> *O return with mercy to the remnant of Israel,*
> *and save us for Your Name's sake.*

Congregation, then chazzan:

ג *Exile after exile has all of Judah⁵ suffered,*

ד *afflicted all day⁶ as they waste away,*
yet no one seeks or asks about them.⁷

> *O restore the captivity of Jacob's tents,*
> *and save us for Your Name's sake.*

Congregation, then chazzan:

ה *The Holy City and [its outlying] regions**
are turned to shame and to spoils;

ו *all its precious things are buried and hidden.**
And nothing is left but the Torah [itself].

> *O return with mercy to the remnant of Israel,*
> *and save us for Your Name's sake.*

Congregation, then chazzan:

ג *O mighty Redeemer, deliver us for Your sake!*

ר *See how our strength has left [us],⁸*

ש *look how our pious ones have been lost;⁹*

מ *so that there is no one to pray for us.¹⁰*

> *O restore the captivity of Jacob's tents,*
> *and save us for Your Name's sake.*

Congregation, then chazzan:

ב *The covenant of the Patriarchs, the Matriarchs, and Tribes;*

ר *Your mercy and kindness so many times given;¹¹*

י *remember [all this,] O God, on behalf of the beaten and torn,¹²*

ו *who are slaughtered for Your sake all the time.¹³*

> *O return with mercy to the remnant of Israel,*
> *and save us for Your Name's sake.*

Congregation, then chazzan:

ר *Avenger of Blood,¹⁴ judge our cause!*

ה *Pay back our tormentors sevenfold into their bosom.¹⁵*

ח *We were sold [into Exile] for naught; so redeem us,*
but not with money,¹⁶

ז *erect Your desolate Holy Temple¹⁷ before our eyes.*

> *O restore the captivity of Jacob's tents,*
> *and save us for Your Name's sake.*

THE ARK IS CLOSED.

---

either ascending holiness (outlying, city, Temple) or descending (Temple, city, outlying), and not haphazard.

וְכָל מַחֲמַדֶּיהָ טְבוּעוֹת וּגְנוּזוֹת — *All its precious things are buried and hidden.* According to one opinion in the Talmud, before Nebuchadnezzar

All:

זְכוֹר לָנוּ בְּרִית רִאשׁוֹנִים כַּאֲשֶׁר אָמַרְתָּ, וְזָכַרְתִּי לָהֶם בְּרִית
רִאשׁוֹנִים, אֲשֶׁר הוֹצֵאתִי אוֹתָם מֵאֶרֶץ מִצְרַיִם לְעֵינֵי
הַגּוֹיִם, לִהְיוֹת לָהֶם לֵאלֹהִים אֲנִי יהוה.¹

סליחה צו (שמע ישראל)

All:

שְׁמַע יִשְׂרָאֵל, יהוה אֱלֹהֵינוּ, יהוה אֶחָד.²

אָמוֹן פִּתְחֵי תְשׁוּבָה,*   בְּכָל הַתּוֹרָה נֶחְשָׁבָה,*
תָּמִיד עֵינַי בָּהּ.²

בָּהּ לְפָרֵשׁ יָאוּת,   בְּשִׁבְרוֹן לֵב וְדִכְּאוּת,
בְּנַחַת וְלֹא בְלֵאוּת,   לוֹבֵשׁ גֵּאוּת.³*

שְׁמַע יִשְׂרָאֵל, יהוה אֱלֹהֵינוּ, יהוה אֶחָד.

גֵּאוּת וּנְקָמָה מְלֻבָּשׁ,   לְהוֹשִׁיעַ עַם מְכֻבָּשׁ,
לְךָ עֶצֶב יֵחָבַשׁ,   בְּהַנְחִילוֹ מְתוּקִים מִדְּבָשׁ.⁴

דְּבַשׁ וְחָלָב בִּלְשׁוֹנֶךָ,⁵   שְׁמַע יִשְׂרָאֵל בְּשַׁנֶּנֶךָ,
וּבְקוֹלֵנוּ* עֲרֵב בְּהִתְחַנְּנֶךָ,   כַּבֵּד אֶת יהוה מֵהוֹנֶךָ.⁶*

שְׁמַע יִשְׂרָאֵל, יהוה אֱלֹהֵינוּ, יהוה אֶחָד.

---

captured the First Temple, the Holy Ark was hidden beneath the Temple so that it would not be taken by the enemy (see *Yoma* 53b and *Shekalim* 6:1). The *paytan* follows this view, and refers to the Ark and its contents as 'its precious things.'

אָמוֹן פִּתְחֵי תְשׁוּבָה — *O Mentor [Who makes] openings for repentance.* No manuscripts of this anonymous *selichah* are known to exist, and less than half of the original has been preserved in the printed editions. The acrostic of the extant portion follows the alphabet from א to ח, then skips to ש and ת. Each stanza comprises four stiches, and ends with a Scriptural fragment, the last word of which is repeated as the first word of the next stanza.

The opening stanza is particularly difficult because it has only three stiches and they do not seem to fit together. It is not known whether the *paytan*, for some arcane reason, did this intentionally or whether he wrote four lines, one of which has been lost. And if wrote four lines, which one is missing? The fourth, which according to the poetic pattern must be a Scriptural fragment ending with בָּהּ, is present. And since the first extant stich begins with an א, we may assume it is the opening phrase of the composition. However, we do not know whether the middle stich before us is the second or third line of the stanza.

The word אָמוֹן has a variety of meanings.

According to most commentaries, the phrase וָאֶהְיֶה אֶצְלוֹ אָמוֹן (*Proverbs* 8:30) means, *I [the Torah] was a nursling to Him.* Thus אָמוֹן describes someone nurtured by an אוֹמֵן, *nurse* or *nurturer.* Nevertheless, the Midrash renders this same phrase four different ways: I was a *pedagogue* unto Him; I was *clothed royally* by Him; I was *concealed* by Him; and, I was a *prince* unto him (*Bereishis Rabbah* 1:1, see *Rashi* there). The meaning 'pedagogue' seems to fit best in our stich.

God, the Mentor and Nurturer of Israel, says: 'My children, make for Me one [tiny] opening of repentance [even if it be only] like the point of a needle, then I shall make for you openings [so large] that wagons and coaches could pass through them!' (*Shir HaShirim Rabbah* 5:2:2).

בְּכָל הַתּוֹרָה נֶחְשָׁבָה — *Which is considered like the entire Torah.* Although the word בְּכָל means *in the entire,* most commentaries understand it here as if it read כְּכָל, *like the entire.* [In fact, some editions read כְּכָל.]

The *paytan*'s intention here is unclear. Although various *mitzvos* are considered by the Talmud as equal to all the *mitzvos* of the Torah combined [e.g., circumcision (*Nedarim* 32a); tzitzis (*Menachos* 43b); charity (*Bava Basra* 9a); Shabbos (*Yerushalmi Berachos* 1:5)], no such statement appears regarding repentance!

All:

זְכוֹר לָנוּ *Remember for us the covenant of the ancestors, as You said:*
'And I will remember for them the covenant of the ancestors
whom I brought out of the land of Egypt in the very sight of the nations,
to be a God to them; I am HASHEM.'[1]

SELICHAH 96

All:

Hear, O Israel: HASHEM *is our God,* HASHEM *is the One and Only.*[2]

א *O Mentor, [make] openings for repentance**
*which is considered like the entire Torah**
my eyes are ever upon **it**.[2]

ב *It requires man to spell out [his sins] properly,*
with broken heart and crushed [spirit], deliberately, not feebly,
[before Him] Who is **dressed in grandeur.***[3]

Hear, O Israel, HASHEM *is our God;* HASHEM, *the One and Only.*

ג **Dressed in grandeur** *and vengeance to save the conquered people.*
He will heal your pain
by granting [the Torah,] a heritage sweeter than **honey**.[4]

ד **Honey** *and milk is on your tongue*[5] *when you recite 'Shema Yisrael;'*
*and you beseech Him with your sweet voice,**
honoring HASHEM *with* **your possessions.***[6]

Hear, O Israel, HASHEM *is our God;* HASHEM, *the One and Only.*

---

(1) *Leviticus* 26:45. (2) *Deuteronomy* 6:4. (3) Cf. 11:12. (4) Cf. *Psalms* 93:1.
(5) Cf. 19:11. (6) Cf. *Song of Songs* 4:11. (7) *Proverbs* 3:9.

Perhaps the *paytan* alludes to either of two midrashic statements (*Eliyahu Zuta* 22). The first reads: 'Repentance is equal to all the Altar offerings in the Torah.' It is possible that the missing stich in this stanza fills in the words 'Altar offerings.'

A second passage in the Midrash states: 'Repentance is greater than charity.' If so, the *paytan* may have reasoned: Since charity is equal to all the other *mitzvos* (*Bava Basra* 9a) and repentance is greater than charity, therefore repentance must be greater than (or, at least, equal to) all the *mitzvos* of the Torah.

לוֹבֵשׁ גַּאוּת — *[Before Him] Who is dressed in grandeur.* Unlike the previous stiches that describes the penitents posture, this one refers to God. Alternatively: This stich is continuation of the preceding one, with the word לֹא, *not*, serving double duty, i.e., the penitent's soul should not be robed in pride and grandeur.

וּבְקוֹלֵנוּ — *And with your [lit., our] . . . voice* For some unexplained reason, the *paytan* switched from second person singular [your] to first person plural [our] for this one word. Some editions, however, maintain the person and read וּבְקוֹלְךָ, *and with your voice.*

שְׁמַע יִשְׂרָאֵל . . . וּבְקוֹלֵנוּ עָרֵב . . . כַּבֵּד אֶת ה' מֵהוֹנֶךָ — *'Shema Yisrael' . . . with your sweet voice . . .*

honoring HASHEM *with your possessions.* According to the Midrash (*Tanchuma, Re'eh* 12), 'your possessions' refers to more than just fiscal and material assets.

Scripture states, *honor* HASHEM *with your possessions* (*Proverbs* 3:9). One way of understanding 'possessions' is talents. Thus, one who has a sweet voice should use it to serve as *chazzan* and lead the recital of the *Shema*. He will thereby honor God with the talent he possesses. This is the meaning of the present stanza.

The same Midrash further states that one who is scrupulous regarding tithing his possessions, will be granted ever-increasing wealth and well-being. But one who is careless about the tithes will lose both his property and his health. This is the theme of the next stanza: Proper use of Your possessions — tithing properly, giving charity — will free you from the worries of supporting and sustaining your family, leaving you plenty of time to rest from your labors and display your love of God.

A third interpretation in the Midrash is: A person who, though endowed with physical attractiveness, nevertheless resists the seductive overtures of illicit and forbidden suitors, honors God by using wisely the possessions He granted. This is the intent of the stich (below) *and your body is removed from evil.*

הוֹנְךָ בְּמַתְּנוֹת יַחְפִּישֶׁךָ,   וְלִפְנֵי גְדוֹלִים יַנְפִּישֶׁךָ,
אֱהֹב פּוֹדְךָ מֵרַפְּשֶׁךָ,   בְּכָל לְבָבְךָ וּבְכָל **נַפְשֶׁךָ.**[1]

וְנַפְשְׁךָ שְׁמוֹרָה מֵרַע,[2]   וּבְעוֹבְדָךְ לְצוּרְךָ תִּכְרַע,
וְגוּפָךְ הוֹסַר מֵרַע,   וְתַשִּׂיג אֶת **זֶרַע.**[3]

שְׁמַע יִשְׂרָאֵל, יהוה אֱלֹהֵינוּ, יהוה אֶחָד.

זֶרַע קֹדֶשׁ דְּגוֹיִים,[4]   תָּמִיד זְבוּחִים כִּגְדָיִים,
וּבִכְנַף מֶלֶךְ חֲסוּיִים,[5]   הַדְּבֵקִים בֵּאלֹהִים **חַיִּים.**[6]

חַיִּים וָסַיִף נִשְׁלָבִים,   יַעֲסֹק בְּגִרְסָא וּבִכְתוּבִים,
יֻצַּל מִשֶּׁסֶף לְהָבִים,   הֵיטִיבָה יהוה לַטּוֹבִים.[7]

שְׁמַע יִשְׂרָאֵל, יהוה אֱלֹהֵינוּ, יהוה אֶחָד.

שׁוֹמֵר כְּנִיסָה וּקְהָלָה,   צַמְצֵם שְׁכִינָתוֹ לְהַנְחִילָה,
לְהָאִירָהּ מֵאֲפֵלָה לְהָלָּה,   לַיְשָׁרִים נָאוָה **תְהִלָּה.**[8]

❖ **תְהִלָּה** וָעֹז לְגוֹאֲלֵנוּ,   מַחֲסֵנוּ וְסִתְרֵנוּ,
הָאֵר פָּנֶיךָ אֵלֵינוּ,   יְהִי חַסְדְּךָ יהוה עָלֵינוּ.[9]

שְׁמַע יִשְׂרָאֵל, יהוה אֱלֹהֵינוּ, יהוה אֶחָד.

All:

עֲשֵׂה עִמָּנוּ כְּמָה שֶׁהִבְטַחְתָּנוּ: וְאַף גַּם זֹאת בִּהְיוֹתָם בְּאֶרֶץ
אֹיְבֵיהֶם, לֹא מְאַסְתִּים וְלֹא גְעַלְתִּים לְכַלֹּתָם
לְהָפֵר בְּרִיתִי אִתָּם, כִּי אֲנִי יהוה אֱלֹהֵיהֶם.[10] הִמָּצֵא לָנוּ
בְּבַקָּשָׁתֵנוּ, כְּמָה שֶׁכָּתוּב: וּבִקַּשְׁתֶּם מִשָּׁם אֶת יהוה אֱלֹהֶיךָ
וּמָצָאתָ, כִּי תִדְרְשֶׁנּוּ בְּכָל לְבָבְךָ וּבְכָל נַפְשֶׁךָ.[11] מוֹל אֶת לְבָבֵנוּ
לְאַהֲבָה וּלְיִרְאָה אֶת שְׁמֶךָ, כְּמָה שֶׁכָּתוּב: וּמָל יהוה אֱלֹהֶיךָ אֶת
לְבָבְךָ וְאֶת לְבַב זַרְעֶךָ, לְאַהֲבָה אֶת יהוה אֱלֹהֶיךָ בְּכָל לְבָבְךָ וּבְכָל
נַפְשְׁךָ, לְמַעַן חַיֶּיךָ.[12] זְרוֹק עָלֵינוּ מַיִם טְהוֹרִים וְטַהֲרֵנוּ, כְּמָה
שֶׁכָּתוּב: וְזָרַקְתִּי עֲלֵיכֶם מַיִם טְהוֹרִים וּטְהַרְתֶּם, מִכֹּל טֻמְאוֹתֵיכֶם
וּמִכָּל גִּלּוּלֵיכֶם אֲטַהֵר אֶתְכֶם.[13] מְחֵה פְשָׁעֵינוּ כָּעָב וְכֶעָנָן, כְּמָה
שֶׁכָּתוּב: מָחִיתִי כָעָב פְּשָׁעֶיךָ וְכֶעָנָן חַטֹּאותֶיךָ, שׁוּבָה אֵלַי כִּי
גְאַלְתִּיךָ.[14] מְחֵה פְשָׁעֵינוּ לְמַעַנְךָ, כַּאֲשֶׁר אָמַרְתָּ: אָנֹכִי אָנֹכִי הוּא
מֹחֶה פְשָׁעֶיךָ לְמַעֲנִי, וְחַטֹּאתֶיךָ לֹא אֶזְכֹּר.[15] הַלְבֵּן חֲטָאֵינוּ כַּשֶּׁלֶג
וְכַצֶּמֶר, כְּמָה שֶׁכָּתוּב: לְכוּ נָא וְנִוָּכְחָה, יֹאמַר יהוה, אִם יִהְיוּ

---

(1) Cf. *Deuteronomy* 6:5. (2) Cf. *Psalms* 121:7. (3) Cf. *Leviticus* 26:5. (4) Cf. *Genesis* 48:16.
(5) Cf. *Psalms* 91:4. (6) Cf. *Deuteronomy* 4:4. (7) *Psalms* 125:4. (8) 33:1. (9) 33:22.
(10) *Leviticus* 26:44. (11) *Deuteronomy* 4:29. (12) 30:6. (13) *Ezekiel* 36:25. (14) *Isaiah* 44:22. (15) 43:25.

ה **Your possessions** used for giving will set you free,
and give you rest among the great.
Love Him Who redeems you from your mud[dy troubles],
with all your heart and with all **your soul!**[1]

ו **Your soul** will be guarded from evil;[2]
as you serve your Molder, bend your knee,
with your body removed from evil,
then you will be granted **[holy] offspring.**[3]

    Hear, O Israel, HASHEM is our God; HASHEM, the One and Only.

ז **Holy offspring,** [burgeoning] like the fish [in the sea],[4]
ever and again slaughtered like kids —
they find shelter under the King's wing,[5]
they are cleaved to God, so they have **life.**[6]

ח **Life** and sword are intertwined;
therefore one who involves himself with Talmud and Scriptures
will be saved from death by the fiery blade.
Do good, O HASHEM, to those who are good.[7]

    Hear, O Israel, HASHEM is our God; HASHEM, the One and Only.

ש The Guardian of assembly and congregation
constricted His Presence to bequeath to her [Israel],
to enlighten her, from gloom to radiance.
How fitting for the upright is **praise!**[8]

ת Chazzan – **Praise** and might to our Redeemer, our Shelter and our Refuge!
Let Your countenance shine towards us;
let Your kindness, HASHEM, be upon us.[9]

    Hear, O Israel, HASHEM is our God; HASHEM, the One and Only.

All:

עֲשֵׂה עִמָּנוּ Do with us as You promised us: 'And despite all that, when
they will be in the land of their enemies, I will not have
despised them nor abhorred them to destroy them, to annul My covenant
with them, for I am HASHEM their God.'[10] Be accessible to us in our quest,
as it is written: From there you will seek HASHEM, your God, and you will
find, when you search for Him with all your heart and with all your
soul.[11] Expose our hearts to love Your Name, as it is written: HASHEM, your
God, will expose your heart and the heart of your offspring, to love HASHEM,
your God, with all your heart and with all your soul, that you may live.[12]
Pour pure water upon us and purify us, as it is written: I shall pour pure
water upon you and purify you, of all your contaminations and of all your
abominations I will purify you.[13] Wipe away our willful sins like a cloud
and like a mist, as it is written: I have wiped away your willful sins like a
cloud and your errors like a mist — repent to Me, for I have redeemed you![14]
Wipe away our willful sins for Your sake, as You said: 'I, only I, am the One
Who wipes away your willful sins for My sake, and I shall not recall
your errors.'[15] Whiten our errors like snow and like [pure white] wool,
as it is written: 'Come now, let us reason together,' says HASHEM, 'though

חֲטָאֵיכֶם כַּשָּׁנִים, כַּשֶּׁלֶג יַלְבִּינוּ, אִם יַאְדִּימוּ כַתּוֹלָע, כַּצֶּמֶר יִהְיוּ.[1]
רַחֵם עָלֵינוּ וְאַל תַּשְׁחִיתֵנוּ, כְּמָה שֶׁכָּתוּב: כִּי אֵל רַחוּם יהוה
אֱלֹהֶיךָ, לֹא יַרְפְּךָ וְלֹא יַשְׁחִיתֶךָ וְלֹא יִשְׁכַּח אֶת בְּרִית אֲבוֹתֶיךָ
אֲשֶׁר נִשְׁבַּע לָהֶם.[2] קַבֵּץ נִדָּחֵינוּ כְּמָה שֶׁכָּתוּב: אִם יִהְיֶה נִדַּחֲךָ בִּקְצֵה
הַשָּׁמָיִם, מִשָּׁם יְקַבֶּצְךָ יהוה אֱלֹהֶיךָ וּמִשָּׁם יִקָּחֶךָ.[3] הָשֵׁב שְׁבוּתֵנוּ
וְרַחֲמֵנוּ, כְּמָה שֶׁכָּתוּב: וְשָׁב יהוה אֱלֹהֶיךָ אֶת שְׁבוּתְךָ וְרִחֲמֶךָ וְשָׁב
וְקִבֶּצְךָ מִכָּל הָעַמִּים אֲשֶׁר הֱפִיצְךָ יהוה אֱלֹהֶיךָ שָׁמָּה.[4] ❖ תְּבִיאֵנוּ
אֶל הַר קָדְשֶׁךָ, וְשַׂמְּחֵנוּ בְּבֵית תְּפִלָּתֶךָ, כְּמָה שֶׁכָּתוּב: וַהֲבִיאוֹתִים
אֶל הַר קָדְשִׁי, וְשִׂמַּחְתִּים בְּבֵית תְּפִלָּתִי, עוֹלֹתֵיהֶם וְזִבְחֵיהֶם לְרָצוֹן
עַל מִזְבְּחִי, כִּי בֵיתִי בֵּית תְּפִלָּה יִקָּרֵא לְכָל הָעַמִּים.[5]

THE ARK IS OPENED.

The first four verses of the following prayer are recited responsively; *chazzan,* then congregation:

שְׁמַע קוֹלֵנוּ יהוה אֱלֹהֵינוּ, חוּס וְרַחֵם עָלֵינוּ,
וְקַבֵּל בְּרַחֲמִים וּבְרָצוֹן אֶת תְּפִלָּתֵנוּ.[6]
הֲשִׁיבֵנוּ יהוה אֵלֶיךָ וְנָשׁוּבָה, חַדֵּשׁ יָמֵינוּ כְּקֶדֶם.[7]
אַל תַּשְׁלִיכֵנוּ מִלְּפָנֶיךָ, וְרוּחַ קָדְשְׁךָ אַל תִּקַּח מִמֶּנּוּ.[8]
אַל תַּשְׁלִיכֵנוּ לְעֵת זִקְנָה, כִּכְלוֹת כֹּחֵנוּ אַל תַּעַזְבֵנוּ.[9]
אַל תַּעַזְבֵנוּ יהוה, אֱלֹהֵינוּ אַל תִּרְחַק מִמֶּנּוּ.[10]
עֲשֵׂה עִמָּנוּ אוֹת לְטוֹבָה, וְיִרְאוּ שׂוֹנְאֵינוּ וְיֵבֹשׁוּ,
כִּי אַתָּה יהוה עֲזַרְתָּנוּ וְנִחַמְתָּנוּ.[11]
אֲמָרֵינוּ הַאֲזִינָה יהוה, בִּינָה הֲגִיגֵנוּ.[12]
יִהְיוּ לְרָצוֹן אִמְרֵי פִינוּ וְהֶגְיוֹן לִבֵּנוּ לְפָנֶיךָ, יהוה צוּרֵנוּ וְגוֹאֲלֵנוּ.[13]
כִּי לְךָ יהוה הוֹחָלְנוּ, אַתָּה תַעֲנֶה אֲדֹנָי אֱלֹהֵינוּ.[14]

THE ARK IS CLOSED.

וידוי

During the recitation of the וידוי stand with head and body slightly bowed, in submissive contrition.

אֱלֹהֵינוּ וֵאלֹהֵי אֲבוֹתֵינוּ, תָּבֹא לְפָנֶיךָ תְּפִלָּתֵנוּ,[15] וְאַל תִּתְעַלַּם
מִתְּחִנָּתֵנוּ,[16] שֶׁאֵין אָנוּ עַזֵּי פָנִים וּקְשֵׁי עֹרֶף, לוֹמַר
לְפָנֶיךָ יהוה אֱלֹהֵינוּ וֵאלֹהֵי אֲבוֹתֵינוּ, צַדִּיקִים אֲנַחְנוּ וְלֹא חָטָאנוּ,
אֲבָל אֲנַחְנוּ וַאֲבוֹתֵינוּ חָטָאנוּ.[17]

Strike the left side of the chest with the right fist
while reciting each of the sins in the following confession litany.

אָשַׁמְנוּ, בָּגַדְנוּ, גָּזַלְנוּ, דִּבַּרְנוּ דֹפִי. הֶעֱוִינוּ, וְהִרְשַׁעְנוּ, זַדְנוּ,

your errors will be like scarlet, they will become white as snow; though they will be red as crimson, they will become like [white] wool.'¹ Have mercy on us and do not destroy us, as it is written: For a merciful God is HASHEM, your God; He will not surrender you nor destroy you, and He will not forget the covenant with your forefathers, which He swore to them.² Gather in our dispersed ones, as it is written: If your dispersed were to be at the ends of heaven, from there HASHEM, your God, will gather you in and from there He will take you.³ Bring back our captivity and have mercy on us, as it is written: HASHEM, your God, will bringback your captivity and have mercy on you, and He will again gather you in from all the peoples where HASHEM, your God, has scattered you.⁴ Chazzan — Bring us to Your holy mountain and gladden us in Your house of prayer, as it is written: And I will bring them to My holy mountain, and I will gladden them in My house of prayer, their elevation-offerings and their feast offering will find favor on My Altar, for My House will be called a house of prayer, for all peoples.⁵

THE ARK IS OPENED.

The first four verses of the following prayer are recited responsively; chazzan, then congregation:

שְׁמַע Hear our voice, HASHEM, our God, pity and be compassionate to us, and accept — with compassion and favor — our prayer.⁶

Bring us back to You, HASHEM, and we shall return, renew our days as of old.⁷

Do not cast us away from Yourself,
  and do not remove Your holy spirit from us.⁸

Do not cast us away in old age,
  when our strength gives out do not forsake us.⁹

Do not forsake us, HASHEM, our God, be not distant from us.¹⁰

Display for us a sign for good, so that our enemies may see it
  and be ashamed, for You, HASHEM, will have helped and consoled us.¹¹

To our sayings give ear, HASHEM, perceive our thoughts.¹²

May the expressions of our mouth and the thoughts of our heart
  find favor before You, HASHEM, our Rock and our Redeemer.¹³

Because for You, HASHEM, we waited, You will answer, my Lord, our God.¹⁴

THE ARK IS CLOSED.

VIDUY/CONFESSION

During the recitation of the וִדּוּי stand with head and body slightly bowed, in submissive contrition.

אֱלֹהֵינוּ Our God and the God of our forefathers, may our prayer come before You.¹⁵ Do not ignore our supplication,¹⁶ for we are not so brazen and obstinate as to say before You, HASHEM, our God and the God of our forefathers, that we are righteous and have not sinned, for in truth, we and our forefathers have sinned.¹⁷

Strike the left side of the chest with the right fist while reciting
each of the sins in the following confession litany.

אָשַׁמְנוּ We have become guilty; [ב] we have betrayed; [ג] we have robbed; [ד] we have spoken slander; [ה] we have caused per-version; [ו] we have caused wickedness; [ז] we have sinned willfully;

---

(1) Isaiah 1:18. (2) Deuteronomy 4:31. (3) 30:4. (4) 30:3. (5) Isaiah 56:7. (6) Weekday Shemoneh Esrei.
(7) Lamentations 5:21. (8) Cf. Psalms 51:13. (9) Cf. 71:9. (10) Cf. 38:22. (11) Cf. 86:17.
(12) Cf. 5:2. (13) Cf. 19:15. (14) Cf. 38:16. (15) Cf. 88:3. (16) Cf. 55:2. (17) Cf. 106:6.

חָמַסְנוּ, **טָפַלְנוּ** שֶׁקֶר. יָעַצְנוּ רָע, כִּזַּבְנוּ, לַצְנוּ, מָרַדְנוּ, נִאַצְנוּ, סָרַרְנוּ, עָוִינוּ, פָּשַׁעְנוּ, צָרַרְנוּ, קִשִּׁינוּ עֹרֶף. רָשַׁעְנוּ, שִׁחַתְנוּ, תִּעַבְנוּ, תָּעִינוּ, תִּעְתָּעְנוּ.

סַרְנוּ מִמִּצְוֹתֶיךָ וּמִמִּשְׁפָּטֶיךָ הַטּוֹבִים וְלֹא שָׁוָה לָנוּ.[1] וְאַתָּה צַדִּיק עַל כָּל הַבָּא עָלֵינוּ, כִּי אֱמֶת עָשִׂיתָ וַאֲנַחְנוּ הִרְשָׁעְנוּ.[2]

אָשַׁמְנוּ מִכָּל עָם, בֹּשְׁנוּ מִכָּל דּוֹר, גָּלָה מִמֶּנּוּ מָשׂוֹשׂ, דָּוָה לִבֵּנוּ בַּחֲטָאֵינוּ, הֻחַבַּל אַוּוּיֵנוּ, וְנִפְרַע פְּאֵרֵנוּ, זְבוּל בֵּית מִקְדָּשֵׁנוּ חָרַב בַּעֲוֺנֵינוּ, טִירָתֵנוּ הָיְתָה לְשַׁמָּה, יֳפִי אַדְמָתֵנוּ לְזָרִים, כֹּחֵנוּ לְנָכְרִים.

וַעֲדַיִן לֹא שַׁבְנוּ מִטָּעוּתֵנוּ וְהֵיךְ נָעִיז פָּנֵינוּ וְנַקְשֶׁה עָרְפֵּנוּ, לוֹמַר לְפָנֶיךָ יהוה אֱלֹהֵינוּ וֵאלֹהֵי אֲבוֹתֵינוּ, צַדִּיקִים אֲנַחְנוּ וְלֹא חָטָאנוּ, אֲבָל אֲנַחְנוּ וַאֲבוֹתֵינוּ חָטָאנוּ.

Strike the left side of the chest with the right fist while reciting each of the sins in the following confession litany.

אָשַׁמְנוּ, בָּגַדְנוּ, גָּזַלְנוּ, דִּבַּרְנוּ דֹפִי. הֶעֱוִינוּ, וְהִרְשַׁעְנוּ, זַדְנוּ, חָמַסְנוּ, **טָפַלְנוּ** שֶׁקֶר. יָעַצְנוּ רָע, כִּזַּבְנוּ, לַצְנוּ, מָרַדְנוּ, נִאַצְנוּ, סָרַרְנוּ, עָוִינוּ, פָּשַׁעְנוּ, צָרַרְנוּ, קִשִּׁינוּ עֹרֶף. רָשַׁעְנוּ, שִׁחַתְנוּ, תִּעַבְנוּ, תָּעִינוּ, תִּעְתָּעְנוּ.

סַרְנוּ מִמִּצְוֹתֶיךָ וּמִמִּשְׁפָּטֶיךָ הַטּוֹבִים וְלֹא שָׁוָה לָנוּ. וְאַתָּה צַדִּיק עַל כָּל הַבָּא עָלֵינוּ, כִּי אֱמֶת עָשִׂיתָ וַאֲנַחְנוּ הִרְשָׁעְנוּ.

לְעֵינֵנוּ עָשְׁקוּ עֲמָלֵנוּ, מְמֻשָּׁךְ וּמְמוֹרָט מִמֶּנּוּ, נָתְנוּ עֻלָּם עָלֵינוּ, סָבַלְנוּ עַל שִׁכְמֵנוּ, עֲבָדִים מָשְׁלוּ בָנוּ, פֹּרֵק אֵין מִיָּדָם, צָרוֹת רַבּוֹת סְבָבוּנוּ, קְרָאנוּךָ יהוה אֱלֹהֵינוּ, רָחַקְתָּ מִמֶּנּוּ בַּעֲוֺנֵינוּ, שַׁבְנוּ מֵאַחֲרֶיךָ, תָּעִינוּ וְאָבָדְנוּ.

וַעֲדַיִן לֹא שַׁבְנוּ מִטָּעוּתֵנוּ וְהֵיךְ נָעִיז פָּנֵינוּ וְנַקְשֶׁה עָרְפֵּנוּ, לוֹמַר לְפָנֶיךָ יהוה אֱלֹהֵינוּ וֵאלֹהֵי אֲבוֹתֵינוּ, צַדִּיקִים אֲנַחְנוּ וְלֹא חָטָאנוּ, אֲבָל אֲנַחְנוּ וַאֲבוֹתֵינוּ חָטָאנוּ.

(1) Cf. *Job* 33:27. (2) *Nehemiah* 9:33.

[ח] *we have extorted;* [ט] *we have accused falsely;* [י] *we have given evil counsel;* [כ] *we have been deceitful;* [ל] *we have scorned;* [מ] *we have rebelled;* [נ] *we have provoked;* [ס] *we have turned away;* [ע] *we have been perverse;* [פ] *we have acted wantonly;* [צ] *we have persecuted;* [ק] *we have been obstinate;* [ר] *we have been wicked;* [ש] *we have corrupted;* [ת] *we have been abominable; we have strayed; You have let us go astray.*

סַרְנוּ *We have turned away from Your commandments and from Your good laws but to no avail.*[1] *Yet You are righteous in all that has come upon us, for You have acted truthfully while we have caused wickedness.*[2]

[א] *We have become the guiltiest of people.* [ב] *We have become the most degraded of all generations.* [ג] *Joy has departed from us.* [ד] *Our heart has been saddened by our sins.* [ה] *Our desirous treasure has been ruined,* [ו] *and our splendor dashed,* [ז] *for our Holy Temple edifice* [ח] *has been destroyed for our iniquities.* [ט] *Our Palace has become desolate.* [י] *[Jerusalem,] the beauty of our Land is given over to aliens,* [כ] *our power to strangers.*

But still we have not returned from our waywardness. So how can we be so brazen and obstinate as to say before You, HASHEM, our God and the God of our forefathers, that we are righteous and have not sinned, for in truth, both we and our fathers have sinned.

Strike the left side of the chest with the right fist while reciting
each of the sins in the following confession litany.

אָשַׁמְנוּ *We have become guilty;* [ב] *we have betrayed;* [ג] *we have robbed;* [ד] *we have spoken slander;* [ה] *we have caused perversion;* [ו] *we have caused wickedness;* [ז] *we have sinned willfully;* [ח] *we have extorted;* [ט] *we have accused falsely;* [י] *we have given evil counsel;* [כ] *we have been deceitful;* [ל] *we have scorned;* [מ] *we have rebelled;* [נ] *we have provoked;* [ס] *we have turned away;* [ע] *we have been perverse;* [פ] *we have acted wantonly;* [צ] *we have persecuted;* [ק] *we have been obstinate;* [ר] *we have been wicked;* [ש] *we have corrupted;* [ת] *we have been abominable; we have strayed; You have let us go astray.*

סַרְנוּ *We have turned away from Your commandments and from Your good laws but to no avail. Yet You are righteous in all that has come upon us, for You have acted truthfully while we have caused wickedness.*

[ל] *[The benefit of] our labor has been stolen,* [מ] *pulled away and cut off from us.* [נ] *They have placed their yoke upon us,* [ס] *our burdens upon our shoulders.* [ע] *Slaves have ruled over us,* [פ] *there is no redemption from their hand.* [צ] *Abundant troubles have surrounded us,* [ק] *we called upon You, HASHEM, our God,* [ר] *but You have distanced us for our iniquities.* [ש] *We have turned away from following after You;* [ת] *we have strayed; we have become lost.*

But still we have not returned from our waywardness. So how can we be so brazen and obstinate as to say before You, HASHEM, our God and the God of our forefathers, that we are righteous and have not sinned, for in truth, both we and our fathers have sinned.

Strike the left side of the chest with the right fist while reciting
each of the sins in the following confession litany.

אָשַׁמְנוּ, בָּגַדְנוּ, גָּזַלְנוּ, דִּבַּרְנוּ דְֹפִי. הֶעֱוִינוּ, וְהִרְשַׁעְנוּ, זַדְנוּ,
חָמַסְנוּ, טָפַלְנוּ שֶׁקֶר. יָעַצְנוּ רָע, כִּזַּבְנוּ, לַצְנוּ, מָרַדְנוּ,
נִאַצְנוּ, סָרַרְנוּ, עָוִינוּ, פָּשַׁעְנוּ, צָרַרְנוּ, קִשִּׁינוּ עֹרֶף. רָשַׁעְנוּ,
שִׁחַתְנוּ, תִּעַבְנוּ, תָּעִינוּ, תִּעְתָּעְנוּ.

סַרְנוּ מִמִּצְוֹתֶיךָ וּמִמִּשְׁפָּטֶיךָ הַטּוֹבִים וְלֹא שָׁוָה לָנוּ. וְאַתָּה
צַדִּיק עַל כָּל הַבָּא עָלֵינוּ, כִּי אֱמֶת עָשִׂיתָ וַאֲנַחְנוּ
הִרְשָׁעְנוּ.

הִרְשַׁעְנוּ וּפָשַׁעְנוּ, לָכֵן לֹא נוֹשָׁעְנוּ. וְתֵן בְּלִבֵּנוּ לַעֲזוֹב דֶּרֶךְ
רֶשַׁע, וְחִישׁ לָנוּ יֶשַׁע, כַּכָּתוּב עַל יַד נְבִיאֶךָ: יַעֲזֹב רָשָׁע
דַּרְכּוֹ, וְאִישׁ אָוֶן מַחְשְׁבֹתָיו, וְיָשֹׁב אֶל יהוה וִירַחֲמֵהוּ, וְאֶל אֱלֹהֵינוּ
כִּי יַרְבֶּה לִסְלוֹחַ.¹

מָשִׁיחַ צִדְקֶךָ אָמַר לְפָנֶיךָ: שְׁגִיאוֹת מִי יָבִין מִנִּסְתָּרוֹת נַקֵּנִי.²
נַקֵּנוּ יהוה אֱלֹהֵינוּ מִכָּל פְּשָׁעֵינוּ, וְטַהֲרֵנוּ מִכָּל
טֻמְאוֹתֵינוּ, וּזְרוֹק עָלֵינוּ מַיִם טְהוֹרִים וְטַהֲרֵנוּ, כַּכָּתוּב עַל יַד
נְבִיאֶךָ: וְזָרַקְתִּי עֲלֵיכֶם מַיִם טְהוֹרִים וּטְהַרְתֶּם, מִכֹּל טֻמְאוֹתֵיכֶם
וּמִכָּל גִּלּוּלֵיכֶם אֲטַהֵר אֶתְכֶם.³

מִיכָה עַבְדְּךָ אָמַר לְפָנֶיךָ: מִי אֵל כָּמוֹךָ נֹשֵׂא עָוֹן וְעֹבֵר עַל
פֶּשַׁע לִשְׁאֵרִית נַחֲלָתוֹ, לֹא הֶחֱזִיק לָעַד אַפּוֹ, כִּי
חָפֵץ חֶסֶד הוּא, יָשׁוּב יְרַחֲמֵנוּ, יִכְבֹּשׁ עֲוֹנֹתֵינוּ, וְתַשְׁלִיךְ בִּמְצֻלוֹת
יָם כָּל חַטֹּאתָם.⁴ (וְכָל חַטֹּאת עַמְּךָ בֵּית יִשְׂרָאֵל תַּשְׁלִיךְ בִּמְקוֹם
אֲשֶׁר לֹא יִזָּכְרוּ, וְלֹא יִפָּקְדוּ, וְלֹא יַעֲלוּ עַל לֵב לְעוֹלָם.) תִּתֵּן אֱמֶת
לְיַעֲקֹב חֶסֶד לְאַבְרָהָם אֲשֶׁר נִשְׁבַּעְתָּ לַאֲבוֹתֵינוּ מִימֵי קֶדֶם.⁵

דָּנִיֵּאל אִישׁ חֲמוּדוֹת שִׁוַּע לְפָנֶיךָ: הַטֵּה אֱלֹהַי אָזְנְךָ וּשְׁמָע,
פְּקַח עֵינֶיךָ וּרְאֵה שֹׁמְמֹתֵינוּ וְהָעִיר אֲשֶׁר נִקְרָא שִׁמְךָ
עָלֶיהָ, כִּי לֹא עַל צִדְקֹתֵינוּ אֲנַחְנוּ מַפִּילִים תַּחֲנוּנֵינוּ לְפָנֶיךָ, כִּי עַל
רַחֲמֶיךָ הָרַבִּים. אֲדֹנָי שְׁמָעָה, אֲדֹנָי סְלָחָה, אֲדֹנָי הַקְשִׁיבָה, וַעֲשֵׂה
אַל תְּאַחַר, לְמַעַנְךָ אֱלֹהַי, כִּי שִׁמְךָ נִקְרָא עַל עִירְךָ וְעַל עַמֶּךָ.⁶

(1) *Isaiah* 55:7. (2) *Psalms* 19:13. (3) *Ezekiel* 36:25. (4) *Micah* 7:18-19. (5) 7:20. (6) *Daniel* 9:18-19.

Strike the left side of the chest with the right fist while reciting
each of the sins in the following confession litany:

אָשַׁמְנוּ We have become guilty; [ב] we have betrayed; [ג] we have robbed; [ד] we have spoken slander; [ה] we have caused perversion; [ו] we have caused wickedness; [ז] we have sinned willfully; [ח] we have extorted; [ט] we have accused falsely; [י] we have given evil counsel; [כ] we have been deceitful; [ל] we have scorned; [מ] we have rebelled; [נ] we have provoked; [ס] we have turned away; [ע] we have been perverse; [פ] we have acted wantonly; [צ] we have persecuted; [ק] we have been obstinate; [ר] we have been wicked; [ש] we have corrupted; [ת] we have been abominable; we have strayed; You have let us go astray.

סַרְנוּ We have turned away from Your commandments and from Your good laws but to no avail. Yet You are righteous in all that has come upon us, for You have acted truthfully while we have caused wickedness.

הִרְשַׁעְנוּ We have acted wickedly and have sinned willfully, therefore we have not been saved. Inspire our heart to abandon the path of evil and hasten salvation for us, as it is written by Your prophet: May the wicked one abandon his way and the vicious man his thoughts; may he return to Hashem and He will show him mercy, and to our God, for He is abundantly forgiving.[1]

מָשִׁיחַ Your righteous anointed [David] said before You: 'Who can discern mistakes? From unperceived faults cleanse me.'[2] Cleanse us, Hashem, our God, of all our willful sins and purify us, of all our contaminations. Sprinkle upon us pure water and purify us, as it is written by Your prophet: I shall sprinkle pure water upon you and purify you, of all your contaminations and of all your abominations I will purify you.'[3]

מִיכָה עַבְדְּךָ Micah, Your servant, said before You: 'Who, O God, is like You, Who pardons iniquity and overlooks transgression for the remnant of His heritage? Who has not retained His wrath eternally, for He desires kindness! He will again be merciful to us; He will suppress our iniquities and cast into the depths of the sea all their sins.[4] (And all the sins of Your nation the Family of Israel, may You cast away to a place where they will neither be remembered, considered, nor brought to mind — ever.) Grant truth to Jacob, kindness to Abraham, as You swore to our forefathers from ancient times.'[5]

דָּנִיֵּאל Daniel, the greatly beloved man, cried out before You: 'Incline, my God, Your ear, and listen, open Your eyes and see our desolation and that of the city upon which Your Name is proclaimed, for not because of our righteousness do we cast down our supplications before You, rather because of Your abundant compassion. O my Lord, heed; O my Lord, forgive; O my Lord, be attentive and act, do not delay; for Your sake, my God, for Your Name is proclaimed upon Your city and Your people.'[6]

עֶזְרָא הַסּוֹפֵר אָמַר לְפָנֶיךָ: אֱלֹהַי, בְּשְׁתִּי וְנִכְלַמְתִּי לְהָרִים,
אֱלֹהַי, פָּנַי אֵלֶיךָ, כִּי עֲוֹנֹתֵינוּ רָבוּ לְמַעְלָה
רֹאשׁ, וְאַשְׁמָתֵנוּ גָדְלָה עַד לַשָּׁמָיִם.[1] וְאַתָּה[2] אֱלוֹהַּ סְלִיחוֹת, חַנּוּן
וְרַחוּם, אֶרֶךְ אַפַּיִם וְרַב חֶסֶד, וְלֹא עֲזַבְתָּנוּ.[3]

אַל תַּעַזְבֵנוּ אָבִינוּ וְאַל תִּטְּשֵׁנוּ בּוֹרְאֵנוּ, וְאַל תַּזְנִיחֵנוּ
יוֹצְרֵנוּ, וְאַל תַּעַשׂ עִמָּנוּ כָּלָה כְּחַטֹּאתֵינוּ. וְקַיֵּם
לָנוּ יהוה אֱלֹהֵינוּ, אֶת הַדָּבָר שֶׁהִבְטַחְתָּנוּ בְּקַבָּלָה עַל יְדֵי יִרְמְיָהוּ
חוֹזָךְ, כָּאָמוּר: בַּיָּמִים הָהֵם וּבָעֵת הַהִיא, נְאֻם יהוה, יְבֻקַּשׁ אֶת עֲוֹן
יִשְׂרָאֵל וְאֵינֶנּוּ וְאֶת חַטֹּאת יְהוּדָה וְלֹא תִמָּצֶאנָה, כִּי אֶסְלַח
לַאֲשֶׁר אַשְׁאִיר.[4] עַמְּךָ וְנַחֲלָתְךָ רְעֵבֵי טוּבְךָ, צְמֵאֵי חַסְדֶּךָ, תְּאֵבֵי
יִשְׁעֶךָ, יַכִּירוּ וְיֵדְעוּ כִּי לַיהוה אֱלֹהֵינוּ הָרַחֲמִים וְהַסְּלִיחוֹת.

אֵל רַחוּם שְׁמֶךָ. אֵל חַנּוּן שְׁמֶךָ, בָּנוּ נִקְרָא שְׁמֶךָ. יהוה עֲשֵׂה
לְמַעַן שְׁמֶךָ. עֲשֵׂה לְמַעַן אֲמִתֶּךָ, עֲשֵׂה לְמַעַן
בְּרִיתֶךָ, עֲשֵׂה לְמַעַן גָּדְלְךָ וְתִפְאַרְתֶּךָ, עֲשֵׂה לְמַעַן דָּתֶךָ, עֲשֵׂה
לְמַעַן הוֹדֶךָ, עֲשֵׂה לְמַעַן וְעוּדֶךָ, עֲשֵׂה לְמַעַן זִכְרֶךָ, עֲשֵׂה לְמַעַן
חַסְדֶּךָ, עֲשֵׂה לְמַעַן טוּבֶךָ, עֲשֵׂה לְמַעַן יִחוּדֶךָ, עֲשֵׂה לְמַעַן כְּבוֹדֶךָ,
עֲשֵׂה לְמַעַן לִמּוּדֶךָ, עֲשֵׂה לְמַעַן מַלְכוּתֶךָ, עֲשֵׂה לְמַעַן נִצְחֶךָ,
עֲשֵׂה לְמַעַן סוֹדֶךָ, עֲשֵׂה לְמַעַן עֻזֶּךָ, עֲשֵׂה לְמַעַן פְּאֵרֶךָ, עֲשֵׂה לְמַעַן
צִדְקָתֶךָ, עֲשֵׂה לְמַעַן קְדֻשָּׁתֶךָ, עֲשֵׂה לְמַעַן רַחֲמֶיךָ הָרַבִּים, עֲשֵׂה
לְמַעַן שְׁכִינָתֶךָ, עֲשֵׂה לְמַעַן תְּהִלָּתֶךָ, עֲשֵׂה לְמַעַן אוֹהֲבֶיךָ שׁוֹכְנֵי
עָפָר, עֲשֵׂה לְמַעַן אַבְרָהָם יִצְחָק וְיַעֲקֹב, עֲשֵׂה לְמַעַן מֹשֶׁה וְאַהֲרֹן,
עֲשֵׂה לְמַעַן דָּוִד וּשְׁלֹמֹה, עֲשֵׂה לְמַעַן יְרוּשָׁלַיִם עִיר קָדְשֶׁךָ, עֲשֵׂה
לְמַעַן צִיּוֹן מִשְׁכַּן כְּבוֹדֶךָ, עֲשֵׂה לְמַעַן שִׁמְמוֹת הֵיכָלֶךָ, עֲשֵׂה לְמַעַן
הֲרִיסוּת מִזְבְּחֶךָ, עֲשֵׂה לְמַעַן הֲרוּגִים עַל שֵׁם קָדְשֶׁךָ, עֲשֵׂה לְמַעַן
טְבוּחִים עַל יִחוּדֶךָ, עֲשֵׂה לְמַעַן בָּאֵי בָאֵשׁ וּבַמַּיִם עַל קִדּוּשׁ שְׁמֶךָ,
עֲשֵׂה לְמַעַן יוֹנְקֵי שָׁדַיִם שֶׁלֹּא חָטְאוּ, עֲשֵׂה לְמַעַן גְּמוּלֵי חָלָב שֶׁלֹּא
פָשְׁעוּ, עֲשֵׂה לְמַעַן תִּינוֹקוֹת שֶׁל בֵּית רַבָּן, עֲשֵׂה לְמַעַנְךָ אִם לֹא
לְמַעֲנֵנוּ, עֲשֵׂה לְמַעַנְךָ וְהוֹשִׁיעֵנוּ.

עֲנֵנוּ יהוה עֲנֵנוּ, עֲנֵנוּ אֱלֹהֵינוּ עֲנֵנוּ, עֲנֵנוּ אָבִינוּ עֲנֵנוּ, עֲנֵנוּ
בּוֹרְאֵנוּ עֲנֵנוּ, עֲנֵנוּ גּוֹאֲלֵנוּ עֲנֵנוּ, עֲנֵנוּ דוֹרְשֵׁנוּ עֲנֵנוּ, עֲנֵנוּ

(1) *Ezra* 9:6. (2) Some editions of *Selichos* insert the word אֱלֹהֵינוּ, *our God,* at this point. (3) Cf. *Nehemiah* 9:17. (4) *Jeremiah* 50:20.

עֶזְרָא הַסוֹפֵר Ezra the Scribe said before You: 'My God, I am embarrassed and ashamed to lift my face to You, my God — for our iniquities have multiplied above our heads, and our sins extend unto heaven.[1] You are[2] the God of forgiveness, compassionate and merciful, slow to anger, and abundant in kindness; and You have not forsaken us.'[3]

אַל תַּעַזְבֵנוּ Do not forsake us, our Father; do not cast us off, our Creator; do not abandon us, our Molder; and do not bring about our destruction, as our sins merit. Affirm for us, HASHEM, our God, the promise You made in the tradition through Jeremiah, Your seer, as it is said: 'In those days and at that time' — the words of HASHEM — 'the iniquity of Israel will be sought but there will be none, and the errors of Judah, but they will not be found, for I will have forgiven those whom I leave as a remnant.'[4] Your people and Your heritage, who hunger for Your goodness, who thirst for Your kindness, who long for Your salvation — may they recognize and know that to HASHEM, our God, belong mercy and forgiveness.

אֵל רַחוּם 'Merciful God' is Your Name, 'Gracious God' is Your Name, Your Name is called upon us — O HASHEM, act for Your Name's sake. Act for the sake of [א] Your truth; act for the sake of [ב] Your covenant; act for the sake of [ג] Your greatness and Your splendor; act for the sake of [ד] Your law; act for the sake of [ה] Your glory; act for the sake of [ו] Your Meeting House; act for the sake of [ז] Your remembrance; act for the sake of [ח] Your kindness; act for the sake of [ט] Your goodness; act for the sake of [י] Your Oneness; act for the sake of [כ] Your honor; act for the sake of [ל] Your teaching; act for the sake of [מ] Your kingship; act for the sake of [נ] Your eternality; act for the sake of [ס] Your counsel; act for the sake of [ע] Your power; act for the sake of [פ] Your beauty; act for the sake of [צ] Your righteousness; act for the sake of [ק] Your sanctity; act for the sake of [ר] Your abundant mercy; act for the sake of [ש] Your Presence, act for the sake of [ת] Your praise; act for the sake of Your beloved ones who rest in the dust; act for the sake of Abraham, Isaac, and Jacob; act for the sake of Moses and Aaron; act for the sake of David and Solomon; act for the sake of Jerusalem, Your holy city; act for the sake of Zion, the abode of Your glory; act for the sake of the desolation of Your Temple; act for the sake of the ruin of Your Altar; act for the sake of the martyrs for Your holy Name; act for the sake of those slaughtered for Your Oneness; act for the sake of those who entered fire and water for the sanctification of Your Name; act for the nursing infants who did not err; act for the sake of the weaned babes who did not sin; act for the sake of children at the schoolroom; act for Your sake if not for ours; act for Your sake and save us.

עֲנֵנוּ Answer us, HASHEM, answer us; answer us, our God, answer us; answer us, [א] our Father, answer us; answer us, [ב] our Creator, answer us; answer us, [ג] our Redeemer, answer us; answer us, [ד] You Who

הָאֵל הַנֶּאֱמָן עֲנֵנוּ, עֲנֵנוּ וָתִיק וְחָסִיד עֲנֵנוּ, עֲנֵנוּ זַךְ וְיָשָׁר עֲנֵנוּ, עֲנֵנוּ חַי וְקַיָּם עֲנֵנוּ, עֲנֵנוּ טוֹב וּמֵטִיב עֲנֵנוּ, עֲנֵנוּ יוֹדֵעַ יֵצֶר עֲנֵנוּ, עֲנֵנוּ כּוֹבֵשׁ כְּעָסִים עֲנֵנוּ, עֲנֵנוּ לוֹבֵשׁ צְדָקוֹת עֲנֵנוּ, עֲנֵנוּ מֶלֶךְ מַלְכֵי הַמְּלָכִים עֲנֵנוּ, עֲנֵנוּ נוֹרָא וְנִשְׂגָּב עֲנֵנוּ, עֲנֵנוּ סוֹלֵחַ וּמוֹחֵל עֲנֵנוּ, עֲנֵנוּ עוֹנֶה בְּעֵת צָרָה¹ עֲנֵנוּ, עֲנֵנוּ פּוֹדֶה וּמַצִּיל עֲנֵנוּ, עֲנֵנוּ צַדִּיק וְיָשָׁר עֲנֵנוּ, עֲנֵנוּ קָרוֹב לְקוֹרְאָיו עֲנֵנוּ, עֲנֵנוּ רַחוּם וְחַנּוּן עֲנֵנוּ, עֲנֵנוּ שׁוֹמֵעַ אֶל אֶבְיוֹנִים עֲנֵנוּ, עֲנֵנוּ תּוֹמֵךְ תְּמִימִים עֲנֵנוּ, עֲנֵנוּ אֱלֹהֵי אֲבוֹתֵינוּ עֲנֵנוּ, עֲנֵנוּ אֱלֹהֵי אַבְרָהָם עֲנֵנוּ, עֲנֵנוּ פַּחַד יִצְחָק עֲנֵנוּ, עֲנֵנוּ אֲבִיר יַעֲקֹב עֲנֵנוּ, עֲנֵנוּ עֶזְרַת הַשְּׁבָטִים עֲנֵנוּ, עֲנֵנוּ מִשְׂגָּב אִמָּהוֹת עֲנֵנוּ, עֲנֵנוּ קָשֶׁה לִכְעוֹס עֲנֵנוּ, עֲנֵנוּ רַךְ לִרְצוֹת עֲנֵנוּ, עֲנֵנוּ עוֹנֶה בְּעֵת רָצוֹן¹ עֲנֵנוּ, עֲנֵנוּ אֲבִי יְתוֹמִים עֲנֵנוּ, עֲנֵנוּ דַּיַּן אַלְמָנוֹת עֲנֵנוּ.

מִי שֶׁעָנָה לְאַבְרָהָם אָבִינוּ בְּהַר הַמּוֹרִיָּה,	הוּא יַעֲנֵנוּ.
מִי שֶׁעָנָה לְיִצְחָק בְּנוֹ כְּשֶׁנֶּעֱקַד עַל גַּבֵּי הַמִּזְבֵּחַ,	הוּא יַעֲנֵנוּ.
מִי שֶׁעָנָה לְיַעֲקֹב בְּבֵית אֵל,	הוּא יַעֲנֵנוּ.
מִי שֶׁעָנָה לְיוֹסֵף בְּבֵית הָאֲסוּרִים,	הוּא יַעֲנֵנוּ.
מִי שֶׁעָנָה לַאֲבוֹתֵינוּ עַל יַם סוּף,	הוּא יַעֲנֵנוּ.
מִי שֶׁעָנָה לְמֹשֶׁה בְּחוֹרֵב,	הוּא יַעֲנֵנוּ.
מִי שֶׁעָנָה לְאַהֲרֹן בַּמַּחְתָּה,	הוּא יַעֲנֵנוּ.
מִי שֶׁעָנָה לְפִינְחָס בְּקוּמוֹ מִתּוֹךְ הָעֵדָה,	הוּא יַעֲנֵנוּ.
מִי שֶׁעָנָה לִיהוֹשֻׁעַ בַּגִּלְגָּל,	הוּא יַעֲנֵנוּ.
מִי שֶׁעָנָה לִשְׁמוּאֵל בַּמִּצְפָּה,	הוּא יַעֲנֵנוּ.
מִי שֶׁעָנָה לְדָוִד וּשְׁלֹמֹה בְנוֹ בִּירוּשָׁלָיִם,	הוּא יַעֲנֵנוּ.
מִי שֶׁעָנָה לְאֵלִיָּהוּ בְּהַר הַכַּרְמֶל,	הוּא יַעֲנֵנוּ.
מִי שֶׁעָנָה לֶאֱלִישָׁע בִּירִיחוֹ,	הוּא יַעֲנֵנוּ.
מִי שֶׁעָנָה לְיוֹנָה בִּמְעֵי הַדָּגָה,	הוּא יַעֲנֵנוּ.
מִי שֶׁעָנָה לְחִזְקִיָּהוּ מֶלֶךְ יְהוּדָה בְּחָלְיוֹ,	הוּא יַעֲנֵנוּ.
מִי שֶׁעָנָה לַחֲנַנְיָה מִישָׁאֵל וַעֲזַרְיָה בְּתוֹךְ כִּבְשַׁן הָאֵשׁ,	
	הוּא יַעֲנֵנוּ.
מִי שֶׁעָנָה לְדָנִיֵּאל בְּגוֹב הָאֲרָיוֹת,	הוּא יַעֲנֵנוּ.

---

(1) Some editions of *Selichos* reverse the positions of these two lines.

searches us out, answer us; answer us, [ה] *faithful God, answer us; answer us,* [ו] *stead-fast and kind One, answer us; answer us,* [ז] *pure and upright One, answer us; answer us,* [ח] *living and enduring One, answer us; answer us,* [ט] *good and beneficent One, answer us; answer us,* [י] *You Who knows inclinations, answer us; answer us,* [כ] *You Who suppresses wrath, answer us; answer us,* [ל] *You Who dons righteousness, answer us; answer us,* [מ] *King Who reigns over kings, answer us; answer us,* [נ] *awesome and powerful One, answer us; answer us,* [ס] *You Who forgives and pardons, answer us; answer us,* [ע] *You Who answers in time of distress,*[1] *answer us; answer us,* [פ] *Redeemer and Rescuer, answer us; answer us,* [צ] *righteous and upright One, answer us; answer us,* [ק] *He Who is close to those who call upon Him, answer us; answer us,* [ר] *merciful and gracious One, answer us; answer us,* [ש] *You Who hears the destitute, answer us; answer us,* [ת] *You Who supports the wholesome, answer us; answer us, God of our forefathers, answer us; answer us, God of Abraham, answer us; answer us, Dread of Isaac, answer us; answer us, Mighty One of Jacob, answer us; answer us, Helper of the tribes, answer us; answer us, Stronghold of the Matriarchs, answer us; answer us, You Who are hard to anger, answer us; answer us, You Who are easy to pacify, answer us; answer us, You Who answers in a time of favor,*[1] *answer us; answer us, Father of orphans, answer us; answer us, Judge of widows, answer us.*

מִי שֶׁעָנָה *He Who answered our father Abraham on Mount Moriah,*
may He answer us.
He Who answered his son Isaac when he was bound atop the altar,
may He answer us.
He Who answered Jacob in Bethel,   *may He answer us.*
He Who answered Joseph in the prison,   *may He answer us.*
He Who answered our forefathers at the Sea of Reeds, may He answer us.
He Who answered Moses in Horeb,   *may He answer us.*
He Who answered Aaron when he offered the censer,   may He answer us.
He Who answered Phineas when he arose from amid the congregation,
may He answer us.
He Who answered Joshua in Gilgal,   *may He answer us.*
He Who answered Samuel in Mitzpah,   *may He answer us.*
He Who answered David and his son Solomon in Jerusalem,
may He answer us.
He Who answered Elijah on Mount Carmel,   *may He answer us.*
He Who answered Elisha in Jericho,   *may He answer us.*
He Who answered Jonah in the innards of the fish,   *may He answer us.*
He Who answered Hezekiah, King of Judah, in his illness,
may He answer us.
He Who answered Chananiah, Mishael, and Azariah in the fiery oven,
may He answer us.
He Who answered Daniel in the lions' den,   *may He answer us.*

מִי שֶׁעָנָה לְמָרְדְּכַי וְאֶסְתֵּר בְּשׁוּשַׁן הַבִּירָה, ‎ הוּא יַעֲנֵנוּ.

מִי שֶׁעָנָה לְעֶזְרָא בַּגּוֹלָה, ‎ הוּא יַעֲנֵנוּ.

מִי שֶׁעָנָה לְכָל הַצַּדִּיקִים וְהַחֲסִידִים וְהַתְּמִימִים וְהַיְשָׁרִים,

הוּא יַעֲנֵנוּ.

רַחֲמָנָא דְּעָנֵי לַעֲנִיֵּי, עֲנֵינָא. רַחֲמָנָא דְּעָנֵי לִתְבִירֵי לִבָּא,

עֲנֵינָא. רַחֲמָנָא דְּעָנֵי לְמַכִּיכֵי רוּחָא, עֲנֵינָא. רַחֲמָנָא

עֲנֵינָא. רַחֲמָנָא חוּס. רַחֲמָנָא פְּרוֹק. רַחֲמָנָא שֵׁזִיב. רַחֲמָנָא

רְחֵם עֲלָן. הַשְׁתָּא בַּעֲגָלָא וּבִזְמַן קָרִיב.

נפילת אפים

In the presence of a Torah Scroll, the following (until וַיִּבֹּשׁוּ רֶגַע) is recited with the head resting on the arm, preferably while seated. Elsewhere, it is recited with the head held erect.

(וַיֹּאמֶר דָּוִד אֶל גָּד, צַר לִי מְאֹד נִפְּלָה נָּא בְיַד יהוה,

כִּי רַבִּים רַחֲמָיו, וּבְיַד אָדָם אַל אֶפֹּלָה.[1]

רַחוּם וְחַנּוּן חָטָאתִי לְפָנֶיךָ. יהוה מָלֵא רַחֲמִים, רַחֵם עָלַי

וְקַבֵּל תַּחֲנוּנָי.

תהלים ו:ב-יא

יהוה אַל בְּאַפְּךָ תוֹכִיחֵנִי, וְאַל בַּחֲמָתְךָ תְיַסְּרֵנִי. חָנֵּנִי יהוה, כִּי

אֻמְלַל אָנִי, רְפָאֵנִי יהוה, כִּי נִבְהֲלוּ עֲצָמָי. וְנַפְשִׁי נִבְהֲלָה

מְאֹד, וְאַתָּה יהוה, עַד מָתָי. שׁוּבָה יהוה, חַלְּצָה נַפְשִׁי, הוֹשִׁיעֵנִי

לְמַעַן חַסְדֶּךָ. כִּי אֵין בַּמָּוֶת זִכְרֶךָ, בִּשְׁאוֹל מִי יוֹדֶה לָּךְ. יָגַעְתִּי

בְּאַנְחָתִי, אַשְׂחֶה בְכָל לַיְלָה מִטָּתִי, בְּדִמְעָתִי עַרְשִׂי אַמְסֶה.

עָשְׁשָׁה מִכַּעַס עֵינִי, עָתְקָה בְּכָל צוֹרְרָי. סוּרוּ מִמֶּנִּי כָּל פֹּעֲלֵי אָוֶן,

כִּי שָׁמַע יהוה קוֹל בִּכְיִי. שָׁמַע יהוה תְּחִנָּתִי, יהוה תְּפִלָּתִי יִקָּח.

יֵבֹשׁוּ וְיִבָּהֲלוּ מְאֹד כָּל אֹיְבָי, יָשֻׁבוּ יֵבֹשׁוּ רָגַע.

מַחֵי וּמַסֵּי מֵמִית וּמַחֲיֶה, מַסִּיק מִן שְׁאוֹל לְחַיֵּי עָלְמָא, בְּרָא

כַד חָטֵי אֲבוּהִי לַקְיֵהּ, אֲבוּהִי דְחָיֵס אַסֵּי לִכְאֵבֵהּ.

עַבְדָּא דְמָרִיד נָפִיק בְּקוֹלָר, מָרֵהּ תָּאִיב וְתַבִּיר קוֹלָרֵהּ.

בְּרַךְ בְּכְרַךְ אֲנָן וְחָטֵינָן קַמָּךְ, הָא רָוֵי נַפְשִׁין בְּגִידִין מְרִירִין,

עַבְדָּךְ אֲנָן וּמְרוֹדִינַן קַמָּךְ, הָא בְּבֹדְתָא, הָא בְּשִׁבְיָא, הָא

בְּמַלְקִיוּתָא. בְּמָטוּ מִנָּךְ בְּרַחֲמָךְ דִּנְפִישִׁין, אַסֵּי לִכְאֵבִין דִּתְקוֹף

עֲלָן, עַד דְּלָא נֶהֱוֵי גְמִירָא בְּשִׁבְיָא.

He Who answered Mordechai and Esther in Shushan the capital,
*   may He answer us.*
He Who answered Ezra in the Exile,   may He answer us.
He Who answered all the righteous, the devout, the wholesome,
*   and the upright,   may He answer us.*

רַחֲמָנָא *The Merciful One Who answers the poor, may He answer us.*
*   The Merciful One Who answers the brokenhearted, may He*
answer us. The Merciful One Who answers the humble of spirit, may He
answer us. O Merciful One, answer us. O Merciful One, pity. O Merciful
One, redeem. O Merciful One, deliver. O Merciful One, have mercy on us —
now, swiftly and soon.

PUTTING DOWN THE HEAD

In the presence of a Torah Scroll, the following (until *'instantly shamed'*) is recited with the head
resting on the arm, preferably while seated. Elsewhere, it is recited with the head held erect.
(And David said to Gad, 'I am exceedingly distressed. Let us fall into HASHEM's
hand for His mercies are abundant, but let me not fall into human hands.' [1])

רַחוּם וְחַנּוּן *O compassionate and gracious One, I have sinned before*
*   You. HASHEM, Who is full of mercy, have mercy on me and*
accept my supplications.

Psalms 6:2-11

'ה *HASHEM, do not rebuke me in Your anger nor chastise me in Your rage.*
*   Favor me, HASHEM, for I am feeble; heal me, HASHEM, for my bones*
shudder. My soul is utterly confounded, and You, HASHEM, how long?
Desist, HASHEM, release my soul; save me as befits Your kindness. For
there is no mention of You in death; in the Lower World who will thank
You? I am wearied with my sigh, every night my tears drench my bed, soak
my couch. My eye is dimmed because of anger, aged by my tormentors.
Depart from me, all evildoers, for HASHEM has heard the sound of my
weeping. HASHEM has heard my plea, HASHEM will accept my prayer. Let
all my foes be shamed and utterly confounded, they will regret and be
instantly shamed.

מָחִי וּמַסִּי *[O God,] He Who smites and heals, causes death and*
*   restores life, raises [the dead] from the grave to eternal life:*
Should a son sin, his father would smack him, but a compassionate father
will heal his [son's] pain. When a slave rebels, he is led out in collar-irons,
but if his master desires to, he breaks his chains.

*   We are Your son, Your firstborn, and we have sinned against You; so*
our soul has been satiated with bitter wormwood. We are Your servants
and we have rebelled against You; so [we have suffered], some with
looting, some with captivity, and some with the lash. We beg of You, in
Your abundant compassion, heal the pains that have overwhelmed us,
before we have been completely wiped out in captivity.

(1) *II Samuel* 24:14.

סליחה צז (תחנה)

All:

מִקְוֵה יִשְׂרָאֵל* מוֹשִׁיעוֹ בְּעֵת צָרָה.[1]

שׁוֹמְרוּ וְצַלּוּ[2] וּמַצִּילוֹ בְּיוֹם עֶבְרָה.

הַמָּלֵא רַחֲמִים עַל עֲנִיָּה סֹעֲרָה.[3]

בְּדוּדָה וּשְׁדוּדָה כְּאוּבָה וְצְעוּרָה.

רְמוּסָה בְּיַד צָר וּבֶעָפָר מְעֻפָּרָה.

שְׁכוּלָה וְגַלְמוּדָה גוֹלָה וְסוּרָה.

מֵאֲרָיוֹת וְדֻבִּים דְּרוּסָה וּשְׁבוּרָה.

וּכְצֹאן בְּלִי רוֹעֶה תּוֹעָה וּפְזוּרָה.

אָדוֹן עַד מָתַי לֹא תַבִּיט בַּצָּרָה.

לָמָּה לָנֶצַח תַּעַזְבֶנָּה בְּיַד עוֹכְרָה.

בְּרַחֲמֶיךָ הוֹצִיאֶהָ מֵאֲפֵלָה לְאוֹרָה.

אַל תִּנְאַץ לְמַעַן שִׁמְךָ[4] כַּחַמָּה בָּרָה.[5]

בָּחַרְתָּ מִכָּל עָם בְּשָׂפָה בְרוּרָה.*[6]

שׁוּר נָא בְּעָנְיָהּ וְנַעֲרָהּ מֵעַפְרָהּ.[7]

לְחַם לוֹחֲמָהּ[8] וּצְרֹר צוֹרְרָהּ,[9]

וּנְקֹם נִקְמָתָהּ[10] וְנִקְמַת בֵּית הַבְּחִירָה.

מִגָּרוּ וּפִגְּרוּ וְהִסִּיקוּ בוֹ הַבְעָרָה.

חִלְּלוּ וְנִאֲצוּ שֵׁם הַנִּכְבָּד וְהַנּוֹרָא.[11]

זְכֹר חֶרְפַּת נָבָל[12] חֵרֵף בַּאֲמִירָה.

קוּמָה יהוה בְּאַפֶּךָ וְהִנָּשֵׂא לְהִתְגַּבְּרָה,[13]

וְאַל תִּשְׁכַּח קוֹל צוֹרְרֶיךָ עוֹלֶה בִּתְדִירָה.[14]

❖ **אַ**בֵּד וְגַדַּע מַלְכוּת אֲרוּרָה.

מְבַשֵּׂר שָׁלוֹם לְעַמְּךָ תִּשְׁלַח מְהֵרָה.

צִיּוֹן לְנַחֵם וּפְרָצוֹתֶיהָ לְגָדְרָה.[15]

כִּי לְךָ יהוה הַגְּדֻלָּה וְהַגְּבוּרָה.[16]

◆§ **מִקְוֵה יִשְׂרָאֵל** — *Hope of Israel.* The acrostic of this *selichah* reads מֹשֶׁה בַּר שְׁמוּאֵל בַּר אַבְשָׁלוֹם חֲזַק וֶאֱמָץ, *Moshe bar Shmuel bar Avshalom, may he be strong and persevere* [see prefatory comment to *selichah* 86].

בָּחַרְתָּ מִכָּל עָם בְּשָׂפָה בְרוּרָה — *You chose her from all people with a clear language.* Human language is capable of capturing sublime and complex ideas, but God chose Israel and granted it the language of the Torah, the language that en-

SELICHAH 87

All:

מ Hope of Israel,* its Savior in time of trouble,[1]

ש its Guardian, its Sheltering Shadow, and its Rescuer[2]
    in the day of wrath,

ה be filled with mercy for the poor, storm-tossed [nation],[3]

ב lonely, plundered, aching and troubled.

ר She is trampled by the enemy, covered with dust,

ש bereaved, left alone, exiled and wandering,

מ torn and broken by lions and bears,

ו straying and scattered like sheep without shepherd.

א O Lord, how long will You not look at [her] trouble?

ל Why will You leave her forever
    in the grip of her assailants?

בר In Your mercy bring her out of gloom into light;

א for Your Name's sake, do not reject [her],[4]
    she who shines like the sun.[5]

ב You chose her from all peoples,
    with a clear language;*[6]

ש please look at her poverty
    and shake her free of her dust.[7]

ל Fight her attacker,[8] persecute her persecutor,[9]

ו and take vengeance for her[10] and for the Chosen Temple.

מ They razed it, destroyed it, set it on fire,

ח profaning and contemning
    [Your] honored and awesome Name.[11]

ז Remember the lout's insolence[12]
    when he spoke shameful blasphemy.

ק Stand erect, HASHEM, in Your wrath,
    arise to overcome [him].[13]

ו Do not forget the sound of Your enemies
    that arises continually;[14]

א destroy and chop down the accursed kingdom.[15]

מ Send the herald of peace swiftly to Your people,

צ to comfort Zion and to mend her breaches,
    for Yours, HASHEM, is the greatness and the might.[16]

---

(1) *Jeremiah* 14:8. (2) Cf. *Psalms* 121:5. (3) *Isaiah* 54:11. (4) *Jeremiah* 14:21.
(5) Cf. *Song of Songs* 6:10. (6) Cf. *Zephaniah* 3:9. (7) Cf. *Isaiah* 52:2.
(8) Cf. *Psalms* 35:1. (9) Cf. *Exodus* 23:22. (10) Cf. *Numbers* 31:2.
(11) Cf. *Deuteronomy* 28:58. (12) *Psalms* 39:9. (13) Cf. 7:7. (14) Cf. 74:23.
(15) This stich has been censored out of some editions. (16) *I Chronicles* 29:11.

---

compasses God's own wisdom and that is uniquely suited to expressing concepts of holiness.

According to *Ibn Ezra* (*Zephaniah* 3:9), the Holy Tongue is called שָׂפָה בְרוּרָה, *a clear language*, because it is the only language in which God is called by His Holy Name, the Tetragrammaton.

All:

מַכְנִיסֵי רַחֲמִים, הַכְנִיסוּ רַחֲמֵינוּ, לִפְנֵי בַּעַל הָרַחֲמִים.
מַשְׁמִיעֵי תְפִלָּה, הַשְׁמִיעוּ תְפִלָּתֵנוּ, לִפְנֵי
שׁוֹמֵעַ תְּפִלָּה. מַשְׁמִיעֵי צְעָקָה, הַשְׁמִיעוּ צַעֲקָתֵנוּ, לִפְנֵי שׁוֹמֵעַ
צְעָקָה. מַכְנִיסֵי דִמְעָה, הַכְנִיסוּ דִמְעוֹתֵינוּ, לִפְנֵי מֶלֶךְ מִתְרַצֶּה
בִּדְמָעוֹת.

הִשְׁתַּדְּלוּ וְהַרְבּוּ תְחִנָּה וּבַקָּשָׁה, לִפְנֵי מֶלֶךְ אֵל רָם וְנִשָּׂא.
הַזְכִּירוּ לְפָנָיו, הַשְׁמִיעוּ לְפָנָיו תּוֹרָה וּמַעֲשִׂים טוֹבִים שֶׁל שׁוֹכְנֵי
עָפָר.

יִזְכֹּר אַהֲבָתָם וִיחַיֶּה זַרְעָם, שֶׁלֹּא תֹאבַד שְׁאֵרִית יַעֲקֹב. כִּי צֹאן
רוֹעֶה נֶאֱמָן הָיָה לְחֶרְפָּה, יִשְׂרָאֵל גּוֹי אֶחָד לְמָשָׁל וְלִשְׁנִינָה.
מַהֵר עֲנֵנוּ אֱלֹהֵי יִשְׁעֵנוּ, וּפְדֵנוּ מִכָּל גְּזֵרוֹת קָשׁוֹת וְהוֹשִׁיעָה
בְּרַחֲמֶיךָ הָרַבִּים, מְשִׁיחַ צִדְקֶךָ וְעַמָּךְ.

מָרָן דְּבִשְׁמַיָּא לָךְ מִתְחַנְּנַן, כְּבַר שַׁבְיָא דְּמִתְחַנַּן לְשָׁבוּיֵהּ.
כֻּלְּהוֹן בְּנֵי שִׁבְיָא בְּכַסְפָּא מִתְפָּרְקִין, וְעַמָּךְ
יִשְׂרָאֵל בְּרַחֲמֵי וּבְתַחֲנוּנֵי, הַב לָן שְׁאֵלְתִין וּבָעוּתִין, דְּלָא נֶהְדַּר
רֵיקָם מִן קֳדָמָךְ.

מָרָן דְּבִשְׁמַיָּא לָךְ מִתְחַנְּנַן, כְּעַבְדָּא דְּמִתְחַנַּן לְמָרֵיהּ,
עֲשִׁיקֵי אֲנָן וּבַחֲשׁוֹכָא שָׁרִינַן, מְרִירָן נַפְשִׁין מֵעַקְתִּין דִּנְפִישִׁין,
חֵילָא לֵית בָּן לְרַצּוּיָךְ מָרָן, עֲבִיד בְּדִיל קַיָּמָא דִּגְזַרְתְּ עִם אֲבָהָתָנָא.

שׁוֹמֵר יִשְׂרָאֵל, שְׁמֹר שְׁאֵרִית יִשְׂרָאֵל, וְאַל יֹאבַד יִשְׂרָאֵל,
הָאוֹמְרִים, שְׁמַע יִשְׂרָאֵל.[1]
שׁוֹמֵר גּוֹי אֶחָד, שְׁמֹר שְׁאֵרִית עַם אֶחָד, וְאַל יֹאבַד גּוֹי אֶחָד,
הַמְיַחֲדִים שִׁמְךָ, יהוה אֱלֹהֵינוּ יהוה אֶחָד.[1]
שׁוֹמֵר גּוֹי קָדוֹשׁ, שְׁמֹר שְׁאֵרִית עַם קָדוֹשׁ, וְאַל יֹאבַד גּוֹי קָדוֹשׁ,
הַמְשַׁלְּשִׁים בְּשָׁלֹשׁ קְדֻשּׁוֹת לְקָדוֹשׁ.
מִתְרַצֶּה בְּרַחֲמִים וּמִתְפַּיֵּס בְּתַחֲנוּנִים, הִתְרַצֵּה וְהִתְפַּיֵּס לְדוֹר
עָנִי, כִּי אֵין עוֹזֵר. אָבִינוּ מַלְכֵּנוּ, חָנֵּנוּ וַעֲנֵנוּ, כִּי אֵין בָּנוּ מַעֲשִׂים,
עֲשֵׂה עִמָּנוּ צְדָקָה וָחֶסֶד וְהוֹשִׁיעֵנוּ.

All:

מַכְנִיסֵי רַחֲמִים O you who usher in [pleas for] mercy, may you usher in our [plea for] mercy, before the Master of mercy. O you who cause prayer to be heard, may you cause our prayer to be heard, before the Hearer of prayer. O you who cause outcry to be heard, may you cause our outcry to be heard, before the Hearer of outcry. O you who usher in tears, may you usher in our tears, before the King Who finds favor through tears.

Exert yourselves, and multiply supplication and petition, before the King, God, exalted and most high. Mention before Him, cause to be heard before Him, the Torah and the good deeds of [the Patriarchs and Matriarchs] who dwell in the dust.

May He remember their love and grant life to [their] offspring, that the remnant of Jacob not be lost. For the flock of the faithful shepherd [Moses] has become a disgrace; Israel, the unique nation, a parable and a simile.

Speedily, answer us, O God of our salvation, and redeem us from all harsh decrees; and may You save, in Your abundant mercy, Your righteous anointed and Your people.

מָרָן דְּבִשְׁמַיָּא Our Master Who is in heaven, to You do we supplicate, as a captive supplicates before his captors; for all captives are redeemed with money, but Your people Israel with compassion and supplication. O grant our requests and our prayers that we not be turned away from You empty-handed.

Our Master Who is in heaven, to You do we supplicate as a slave supplicates before his master: We are oppressed and we abide in darkness, souls embittered from abundant distress. We have no strength to regain Your favor. Our Master, act for the sake of the covenant that You made with our Patriarchs.

שׁוֹמֵר יִשְׂרָאֵל O Guardian of Israel, protect the remnant of Israel; let not Israel be destroyed — those who proclaim, 'Hear O Israel.'[1]

O Guardian of the unique nation, protect the remnant of the unique people; let not the unique nation be destroyed — those who proclaim the Oneness of Your Name, 'HASHEM is our God, HASHEM, the One and Only!'[1]

O Guardian of the holy nation, protect the remnant of the holy people; let not the holy nation be destroyed — those who proclaim three-fold sanctifications to the Holy One.

Become favorable through compassion and become appeased through supplications. Become favorable and appeased to the poor generation, for there is no helper. Our Father, our King, be gracious with us and answer us, though we have no worthy deeds; treat us with charity and kindness, and save us.

---

(1) Deuteronomy 6:4.

וַאֲנַחְנוּ לֹא נֵדַע מַה נַּעֲשֶׂה, כִּי עָלֶיךָ עֵינֵינוּ.[1] זְכֹר רַחֲמֶיךָ יהוה וַחֲסָדֶיךָ, כִּי מֵעוֹלָם הֵמָּה.[2] יְהִי חַסְדְּךָ יהוה עָלֵינוּ, כַּאֲשֶׁר יִחַלְנוּ לָךְ.[3]

אַל תִּזְכָּר לָנוּ עֲוֹנוֹת רִאשׁוֹנִים, מַהֵר יְקַדְּמוּנוּ רַחֲמֶיךָ, כִּי דַלּוֹנוּ מְאֹד.[4] חָנֵּנוּ יהוה חָנֵּנוּ, כִּי רַב שָׂבַעְנוּ בוּז.[5] בְּרֹגֶז רַחֵם תִּזְכּוֹר.[6] כִּי הוּא יָדַע יִצְרֵנוּ, זָכוּר כִּי עָפָר אֲנָחְנוּ.[7] עָזְרֵנוּ אֱלֹהֵי יִשְׁעֵנוּ עַל דְּבַר כְּבוֹד שְׁמֶךָ, וְהַצִּילֵנוּ וְכַפֵּר עַל חַטֹּאתֵינוּ לְמַעַן שְׁמֶךָ.[8]

קדיש שלם

The *chazzan* recites קַדִּישׁ שָׁלֵם:

יִתְגַּדַּל וְיִתְקַדַּשׁ שְׁמֵהּ רַבָּא. (.Cong – אָמֵן) בְּעָלְמָא דִּי בְרָא כִרְעוּתֵהּ, וְיַמְלִיךְ מַלְכוּתֵהּ, בְּחַיֵּיכוֹן וּבְיוֹמֵיכוֹן וּבְחַיֵּי דְכָל בֵּית יִשְׂרָאֵל, בַּעֲגָלָא וּבִזְמַן קָרִיב. וְאִמְרוּ אָמֵן.

(.Cong – אָמֵן. יְהֵא שְׁמֵהּ רַבָּא מְבָרַךְ לְעָלַם וּלְעָלְמֵי עָלְמַיָּא.)

יְהֵא שְׁמֵהּ רַבָּא מְבָרַךְ לְעָלַם וּלְעָלְמֵי עָלְמַיָּא.

יִתְבָּרַךְ וְיִשְׁתַּבַּח וְיִתְפָּאַר וְיִתְרוֹמַם וְיִתְנַשֵּׂא וְיִתְהַדָּר וְיִתְעַלֶּה וְיִתְהַלָּל שְׁמֵהּ דְּקוּדְשָׁא בְּרִיךְ הוּא (.Cong – בְּרִיךְ הוּא.) לְעֵלָּא [וּ]לְעֵלָּא מִכָּל בִּרְכָתָא וְשִׁירָתָא תֻּשְׁבְּחָתָא וְנֶחֱמָתָא, דַּאֲמִירָן בְּעָלְמָא. וְאִמְרוּ: אָמֵן. (.Cong – אָמֵן)

(.Cong – קַבֵּל בְּרַחֲמִים וּבְרָצוֹן אֶת תְּפִלָּתֵנוּ.)

תִּתְקַבֵּל צְלוֹתְהוֹן וּבָעוּתְהוֹן דְּכָל (בֵּית) יִשְׂרָאֵל קֳדָם אֲבוּהוֹן דִּי בִשְׁמַיָּא. וְאִמְרוּ אָמֵן. (.Cong – אָמֵן)

(.Cong – יְהִי שֵׁם יהוה מְבֹרָךְ, מֵעַתָּה וְעַד עוֹלָם.[9])

יְהֵא שְׁלָמָא רַבָּא מִן שְׁמַיָּא וְחַיִּים עָלֵינוּ וְעַל כָּל יִשְׂרָאֵל. וְאִמְרוּ אָמֵן. (.Cong – אָמֵן)

(.Cong – עֶזְרִי מֵעִם יהוה, עֹשֵׂה שָׁמַיִם וָאָרֶץ.[10])

Take three steps back. Bow left and say, . . . עֹשֶׂה; bow right and say, . . . הוּא יַעֲשֶׂה; bow forward and say, וְעַל כָּל . . . אָמֵן. Remain standing in place for a few moments, then take three steps forward.

עֹשֶׂה [הַ]שָּׁלוֹם בִּמְרוֹמָיו, הוּא יַעֲשֶׂה שָׁלוֹם עָלֵינוּ, וְעַל כָּל יִשְׂרָאֵל. וְאִמְרוּ אָמֵן. (.Cong – אָמֵן)

וַאֲנַחְנוּ *We know not what to do — but our eyes are upon You.*[1] *Remember Your mercies, HASHEM, and Your kindnesses, for they are from the beginning of the world.*[2] *May Your kindness be upon us, HASHEM, just as we awaited You.*[3]

אַל תִּזְכָּר *Recall not against us the iniquities of the ancients; may Your mercies meet us swiftly, for we have become exceedingly impoverished.*[4] *Be gracious to us, HASHEM, be gracious to us, for we are abundantly sated with scorn.*[5] *Amid rage — remember to be merciful!*[6] *For He knew our nature, He remembers that we are dust.*[7] Chazzan— *Assist us, O God of our salvation, for the sake of Your Name's glory; rescue us and atone for our sins for Your Name's sake.*[8]

FULL KADDISH
The *chazzan* recites the Full Kaddish:

יִתְגַּדַּל *May His great Name grow exalted and sanctified* (Cong. — *Amen.*) *in the world that He created as He willed. May He give reign to His kingship in your lifetimes and in your days, and in the lifetimes of the entire Family of Israel, swiftly and soon. Now respond: Amen.*

(Cong. — Amen. May His great Name be blessed forever and ever.)
May His great Name be blessed forever and ever.

Blessed, praised, glorified, exalted, extolled, mighty, upraised and lauded be the Name of the Holy One, Blessed is He (Cong. — *Blessed is He.*) *exceedingly beyond any blessing and song, praise, and consolation that are uttered in the world. Now respond: Amen.* (Cong. — *Amen.*)

(Cong. — Accept our prayers with mercy and favor.)

May the prayers and supplications of the entire House of Israel be accepted before their Father Who is in Heaven. Now respond: Amen. (Cong. — *Amen.*)

(Cong. — Blessed be the Name of HASHEM from this time and forever.[9]*)*

May there be abundant peace from Heaven, and life, upon us and upon all Israel. Now respond: Amen. (Cong. — *Amen.*)

*(*Cong. — *My help is from HASHEM, Maker of heaven and earth.*[10]*)*

Take three steps back. Bow left and say, 'He Who makes peace . . .'; bow right and say,
'may He make peace . . .'; bow forward and say, 'and upon all Israel . . .'
Remain standing in place for a few moments, then take three steps forward.

He Who makes [the] peace in His heights, may He make peace upon us, and upon all Israel. Now respond: Amen. (Cong. — *Amen.*)

---

(1) *II Chronicles* 20:12. (2) *Psalms* 25:6. (3) 33:22. (4) *Psalms* 79:8.
(5) 123:3. (6) *Habakkuk* 3:2. (7) *Psalms* 103:14. (8) 79:9. (9) 113:2. (10) 121:2.

❧ ערב יום כפור ❧

אַשְׁרֵי יוֹשְׁבֵי בֵיתֶךָ, עוֹד יְהַלְלוּךָ סֶּלָה.[1] אַשְׁרֵי הָעָם שֶׁכָּכָה
לוֹ, אַשְׁרֵי הָעָם שֶׁיהוה אֱלֹהָיו.[2]

תְּהִלָּה לְדָוִד,

תהלים קמה

אֲרוֹמִמְךָ אֱלוֹהַי הַמֶּלֶךְ, וַאֲבָרְכָה שִׁמְךָ לְעוֹלָם וָעֶד.

בְּכָל יוֹם אֲבָרְכֶךָּ, וַאֲהַלְלָה שִׁמְךָ לְעוֹלָם וָעֶד.

גָּדוֹל יהוה וּמְהֻלָּל מְאֹד, וְלִגְדֻלָּתוֹ אֵין חֵקֶר.

דּוֹר לְדוֹר יְשַׁבַּח מַעֲשֶׂיךָ, וּגְבוּרֹתֶיךָ יַגִּידוּ.

הֲדַר כְּבוֹד הוֹדֶךָ, וְדִבְרֵי נִפְלְאֹתֶיךָ אָשִׂיחָה.

וֶעֱזוּז נוֹרְאוֹתֶיךָ יֹאמֵרוּ, וּגְדֻלָּתְךָ אֲסַפְּרֶנָּה.

זֵכֶר רַב טוּבְךָ יַבִּיעוּ, וְצִדְקָתְךָ יְרַנֵּנוּ.

חַנּוּן וְרַחוּם יהוה, אֶרֶךְ אַפַּיִם וּגְדָל חָסֶד.

טוֹב יהוה לַכֹּל, וְרַחֲמָיו עַל כָּל מַעֲשָׂיו.

יוֹדוּךָ יהוה כָּל מַעֲשֶׂיךָ, וַחֲסִידֶיךָ יְבָרְכוּכָה.

כְּבוֹד מַלְכוּתְךָ יֹאמֵרוּ, וּגְבוּרָתְךָ יְדַבֵּרוּ.

לְהוֹדִיעַ לִבְנֵי הָאָדָם גְּבוּרֹתָיו, וּכְבוֹד הֲדַר מַלְכוּתוֹ.

מַלְכוּתְךָ מַלְכוּת כָּל עֹלָמִים, וּמֶמְשַׁלְתְּךָ בְּכָל דּוֹר וָדֹר.

סוֹמֵךְ יהוה לְכָל הַנֹּפְלִים, וְזוֹקֵף לְכָל הַכְּפוּפִים.

עֵינֵי כֹל אֵלֶיךָ יְשַׂבֵּרוּ, וְאַתָּה נוֹתֵן לָהֶם אֶת אָכְלָם בְּעִתּוֹ.

Concentrate intently while reciting the verse, פּוֹתֵחַ. **פּוֹתֵחַ** אֶת יָדֶךָ, וּמַשְׂבִּיעַ לְכָל חַי רָצוֹן.

❖ צַדִּיק יהוה בְּכָל דְּרָכָיו, וְחָסִיד בְּכָל מַעֲשָׂיו.

קָרוֹב יהוה לְכָל קֹרְאָיו, לְכֹל אֲשֶׁר יִקְרָאֻהוּ בֶאֱמֶת.

רְצוֹן יְרֵאָיו יַעֲשֶׂה, וְאֶת שַׁוְעָתָם יִשְׁמַע וְיוֹשִׁיעֵם.

שׁוֹמֵר יהוה אֶת כָּל אֹהֲבָיו, וְאֵת כָּל הָרְשָׁעִים יַשְׁמִיד.

תְּהִלַּת יהוה יְדַבֶּר פִּי, וִיבָרֵךְ כָּל בָּשָׂר שֵׁם קָדְשׁוֹ לְעוֹלָם וָעֶד.

וַאֲנַחְנוּ נְבָרֵךְ יָהּ, מֵעַתָּה וְעַד עוֹלָם, הַלְלוּיָהּ.[3]

The *chazzan* recites חֲצִי קַדִּישׁ.

יִתְגַּדַּל וְיִתְקַדַּשׁ שְׁמֵהּ רַבָּא. (.Cong – אָמֵן.) בְּעָלְמָא דִּי בְרָא כִרְעוּתֵהּ.
וְיַמְלִיךְ מַלְכוּתֵהּ, בְּחַיֵּיכוֹן וּבְיוֹמֵיכוֹן וּבְחַיֵּי דְכָל בֵּית יִשְׂרָאֵל,
בַּעֲגָלָא וּבִזְמַן קָרִיב. וְאִמְרוּ: אָמֵן.

(.Cong –) אָמֵן. יְהֵא שְׁמֵהּ רַבָּא מְבָרַךְ לְעָלַם וּלְעָלְמֵי עָלְמַיָּא.)

יְהֵא שְׁמֵהּ רַבָּא מְבָרַךְ לְעָלַם וּלְעָלְמֵי עָלְמַיָּא.

יִתְבָּרַךְ וְיִשְׁתַּבַּח וְיִתְפָּאַר וְיִתְרוֹמַם וְיִתְנַשֵּׂא וְיִתְהַדָּר וְיִתְעַלֶּה וְיִתְהַלָּל
שְׁמֵהּ דְּקֻדְשָׁא בְּרִיךְ הוּא (.Cong – בְּרִיךְ הוּא) לְעֵלָּא [וּ]לְעֵלָּא מִכָּל בִּרְכָתָא
וְשִׁירָתָא תֻּשְׁבְּחָתָא וְנֶחֱמָתָא, דַּאֲמִירָן בְּעָלְמָא. וְאִמְרוּ: אָמֵן. (.Cong – אָמֵן.)

❖❈ EREV YOM KIPPUR ❈❖

אַשְׁרֵי *Praiseworthy are those who dwell in Your house; may they always praise You, Selah!*[1] *Praiseworthy is the people for whom this is so, praiseworthy is the people whose God is HASHEM.*[2]

Psalm 145   *A psalm of praise by David:*

א *I will exalt You, my God the King, and I will bless Your Name forever and ever.*

ב *Every day I will bless You, and I will laud Your Name forever and ever.*

ג *HASHEM is great and exceedingly lauded,*
   and His greatness is beyond investigation.

ד *Each generation will praise Your deeds to the next*
   and of Your mighty deeds they will tell;

ה *The splendrous glory of Your power and Your wondrous deeds I shall discuss.*

ו *And of Your awesome power they will speak, and Your greatness I shall relate.*

ז *A recollection of Your abundant goodness they will utter*
   and of Your righteousness they will sing exultantly.

ח *Gracious and merciful is HASHEM,*
   slow to anger, and great in [bestowing] kindness.

ט *HASHEM is good to all; His mercies are on all His works.*

י *All Your works shall thank You, HASHEM, and Your devout ones will bless You.*

כ *Of the glory of Your kingdom they will speak, and of Your power they will tell;*

ל *To inform human beings of His mighty deeds,*
   and the glorious splendor of His kingdom.

מ *Your kingdom is a kingdom spanning all eternities,*
   and Your dominion is throughout every generation.

ס *HASHEM supports all the fallen ones and straightens all the bent.*

ע *The eyes of all look to You with hope*
   and You give them their food in its proper time;

פ *You open Your hand,*   Concentrate intently while reciting the verse, 'You open...'
   and satisfy the desire of every living thing.

צ Chazzan— *Righteous is HASHEM in all His ways*
   and magnanimous in all His deeds.

ק *HASHEM is close to all who call upon Him — to all who call upon Him sincerely.*

ר *The will of those who fear Him He will do;*
   and their cry He will hear, and save them.

ש *HASHEM protects all who love Him; but all the wicked He will destroy.*

ת *May my mouth declare the praise of HASHEM*
   and may all flesh bless His Holy Name forever and ever.

We will bless God from this time and forever, Halleluyah![3]

The chazzan recites Half-*Kaddish:*

יִתְגַּדַּל *May His great Name grow exalted and sanctified* (Cong.— *Amen.*) *in the world that He created as He willed. May He give reign to His kingship in your lifetimes and in your days, and in the lifetimes of the entire Family of Israel, swiftly and soon. Now respond: Amen.*

(Cong.— *Amen. May His great Name be blessed forever and ever.*)
May His great Name be blessed forever and ever.

Blessed, praised, glorified, exalted, extolled, mighty, upraised, and lauded be the Name of the Holy One, Blessed is He (Cong.— *Blessed is He*) *— exceedingly beyond any blessing and song, praise and consolation that are uttered in the world. Now respond: Amen.* (Cong.— *Amen.*)

---

(1) *Psalms* 84:5. (2) 144:15. (3) 115:18.

All:

לְךָ יהוה הַצְּדָקָה, וְלָנוּ בֹּשֶׁת הַפָּנִים.¹ מַה נִּתְאוֹנֵן,² מַה נֹּאמַר,
מַה נְּדַבֵּר, וּמַה נִּצְטַדָּק.³ נַחְפְּשָׂה דְרָכֵינוּ וְנַחְקְרָה,
וְנָשׁוּבָה אֵלֶיךָ,⁴ כִּי יְמִינְךָ פְּשׁוּטָה לְקַבֵּל שָׁבִים. לֹא בְחֶסֶד וְלֹא
בְמַעֲשִׂים בָּאנוּ לְפָנֶיךָ, כְּדַלִּים וּכְרָשִׁים דָּפַקְנוּ דְלָתֶיךָ. ❖ דְּלָתֶיךָ
דָּפַקְנוּ רַחוּם וְחַנּוּן, נָא אַל תְּשִׁיבֵנוּ רֵיקָם מִלְּפָנֶיךָ. מִלְּפָנֶיךָ מַלְכֵּנוּ
רֵיקָם אַל תְּשִׁיבֵנוּ, כִּי אַתָּה שׁוֹמֵעַ תְּפִלָּה.

All, while standing:

אֵל אֶרֶךְ אַפַּיִם אַתָּה, וּבַעַל הָרַחֲמִים נִקְרֵאתָ,
וְדֶרֶךְ תְּשׁוּבָה הוֹרֵיתָ.

גְּדֻלַּת רַחֲמֶיךָ וַחֲסָדֶיךָ,   תִּזְכּוֹר הַיּוֹם וּבְכָל יוֹם לְזֶרַע יְדִידֶיךָ.
תֵּפֶן אֵלֵינוּ בְּרַחֲמִים,   כִּי אַתָּה הוּא בַּעַל הָרַחֲמִים.
בְּתַחֲנוּן וּבִתְפִלָּה פָּנֶיךָ נְקַדֵּם,   כְּהוֹדַעְתָּ לֶעָנָיו מִקֶּדֶם.
מֵחֲרוֹן אַפְּךָ שׁוּב,⁵   כְּמוֹ בְתוֹרָתְךָ כָּתוּב.⁶
וּבְצֵל כְּנָפֶיךָ נֶחֱסֶה⁷ וְנִתְלוֹנָן,   כְּיוֹם וַיֵּרֶד יהוה בֶּעָנָן.
❖ תַּעֲבוֹר עַל פֶּשַׁע וְתִמְחֶה אָשָׁם,   כְּיוֹם וַיִּתְיַצֵּב עִמּוֹ שָׁם.
תַּאֲזִין שַׁוְעָתֵנוּ וְתַקְשִׁיב מֶנּוּ מַאֲמַר,
כְּיוֹם וַיִּקְרָא בְשֵׁם יהוה,⁸ וְשָׁם נֶאֱמַר:

Congregation, then *chazzan:*

וַיַּעֲבֹר יהוה עַל פָּנָיו וַיִּקְרָא:

Congregation and *chazzan* (the words in bold type are recited aloud and in unison):

יהוה, יהוה, אֵל, **רַחוּם, וְחַנּוּן,** אֶרֶךְ **אַפַּיִם, וְרַב חֶסֶד, וֶאֱמֶת,
נֹצֵר חֶסֶד לָאֲלָפִים,** נֹשֵׂא **עָוֹן, וָפֶשַׁע, וְחַטָּאָה,
וְנַקֵּה.**⁹ וְסָלַחְתָּ לַעֲוֹנֵנוּ וּלְחַטָּאתֵנוּ וּנְחַלְתָּנוּ.¹⁰ סְלַח לָנוּ אָבִינוּ כִּי
חָטָאנוּ, מְחַל לָנוּ מַלְכֵּנוּ כִּי פָשָׁעְנוּ. כִּי אַתָּה אֲדֹנָי טוֹב וְסַלָּח, וְרַב
חֶסֶד לְכָל קֹרְאֶיךָ.¹¹

פסוקי הקדמה לסליחה צח

אַל תָּבוֹא בְמִשְׁפָּט עִמָּנוּ, כִּי לֹא יִצְדַּק לְפָנֶיךָ כָל חָי.¹² הֵן
בִּקְדֹשָׁו לֹא יַאֲמִין, וְשָׁמַיִם לֹא זַכּוּ בְעֵינָיו.¹³ אַף
כִּי אֱנוֹשׁ רִמָּה, וּבֶן אָדָם תּוֹלֵעָה.¹⁴ הִנְּנוּ לְפָנֶיךָ בְּאַשְׁמָתֵינוּ, כִּי
אֵין לַעֲמוֹד לְפָנֶיךָ עַל זֹאת.¹⁵ מִי יֹאמַר זִכִּיתִי לִבִּי, טָהַרְתִּי
מֵחַטָּאתִי.¹⁶

All:

לְךָ ה' Yours, my Lord, is the righteousness and ours is the shame-facedness.[1] What complaint can we make?[2] What can we say? What can we declare? What justification can we offer?[3] Let us examine our ways and analyze — and return to You,[4] for Your right hand is extended to accept penitents. Neither with kindness nor with [good] deeds do we come before You. As paupers and as beggars do we knock at Your doors. Chazzan – At Your doors we knock, O Compassionate and Gracious One. Please do not turn us away from You empty-handed. Our King, turn us not away from You empty-handed, for You are the One Who hears prayer.

All, while standing:

אֵל אֶרֶךְ אַפַּיִם O God — You are slow to anger, You are called the Master of Mercy, and You have taught the way of repentance. May You remember this day and every day the greatness of Your mercy and Your kindness to the offspring of Your beloved Ones. Turn to us in mercy for You are the Master of Mercy. With supplication and prayer we approach Your Presence in the manner that You made known to the humble [Moses] in ancient times. Turn back from Your fierce anger;[5] as is written in Your Torah.[6] In the shadow of Your wings may we find shelter[7] and lodging as on the day 'HASHEM descended in a cloud' [to appear to Moses on Sinai]. Chazzan – Overlook sin and erase guilt as on the day 'He [God] stood there with him [Moses].' Give heed to our cry and be attentive to our declaration as on the day 'He called out with the Name HASHEM,'[8] and there it was said:

Congregation, then chazzan:

And HASHEM passed before him [Moses] and proclaimed:

Congregation and chazzan (the words in bold type are recited aloud and in unison):

ה' ה' HASHEM, HASHEM, God, Compassionate and Gracious, Slow to anger, and Abundant in Kindness and Truth, Preserver of kindness for thousands [of generations], Forgiver of iniquity, willful sin, and error, and Who cleanses.[9] May You forgive our iniquities and our errors and make us Your heritage.[10] Forgive us, our Father, for we have erred; pardon us, our King, for we have willfully sinned; for You, my Lord, are good and forgiving and abundantly kind to all who call upon You.[11]

PREFATORY VERSES TO SELICHAH 98

אַל תָּבוֹא Do not enter into strict judgment with us, for no living crea-ture would be innocent before You.[12] See, He does not believe in His holy [angels]; even Heaven is not pure in His sight.[13] Certainly then man, who is but a worm, the son of man, who is but a maggot.[14] Here we are before You with our guilt, for on that account we cannot stand up before You.[15] Who can say, 'I have purified my heart, I am clean of my sin'?[16]

---

(1) Daniel 9:7. (2) Cf. Lamentations 3:39. (3) Cf. Genesis 44:16. (4) Cf. Lamentations 3:40. (5) Cf. Exodus 32:12. (6) See 32:14. (7) Cf. Psalms 36:8. (8) Exodus 34:5. (9) 34:6-7. (10) 34:9. (11) Psalms 86:5. (12) Cf. Psalms 143:2. (13) Job 15:15. (14) 25:6. (15) Ezra 9:15. (16) Proverbs 20:9.

בְּרַחֵם אָב עַל בָּנִים, כֵּן תְּרַחֵם יהוה עָלֵינוּ. לַיהוה הַיְשׁוּעָה, עַל עַמְּךָ בִרְכָתֶךָ סֶּלָה. יהוה צְבָאוֹת עִמָּנוּ, מִשְׂגָּב לָנוּ אֱלֹהֵי יַעֲקֹב סֶלָה. יהוה צְבָאוֹת, אַשְׁרֵי אָדָם בֹּטֵחַ בָּךְ. יהוה הוֹשִׁיעָה, הַמֶּלֶךְ יַעֲנֵנוּ בְיוֹם קָרְאֵנוּ.

In some congregations the following two verses are recited responsively — the *chazzan* reciting סְלַח, and the congregation responding וַיְֹּאמֶר. In other congregations these verses are recited silently.

סְלַח נָא לַעֲוֹן הָעָם הַזֶּה כְּגֹדֶל חַסְדֶּךָ, וְכַאֲשֶׁר נָשָׂאתָה לָעָם הַזֶּה מִמִּצְרַיִם וְעַד הֵנָּה, וְשָׁם נֶאֱמַר:

וַיְֹּאמֶר יהוה סָלַחְתִּי כִּדְבָרֶךָ.

All:

הַטֵּה אֱלֹהַי אָזְנְךָ וּשְׁמָע, פְּקַח עֵינֶיךָ וּרְאֵה שֹׁמְמֹתֵינוּ, וְהָעִיר אֲשֶׁר נִקְרָא שִׁמְךָ עָלֶיהָ, כִּי לֹא עַל צִדְקוֹתֵינוּ אֲנַחְנוּ מַפִּילִים תַּחֲנוּנֵינוּ לְפָנֶיךָ, כִּי עַל רַחֲמֶיךָ הָרַבִּים. אֲדֹנָי שְׁמָעָה, אֲדֹנָי סְלָחָה, אֲדֹנָי הַקְשִׁיבָה, וַעֲשֵׂה אַל תְּאַחַר, לְמַעַנְךָ אֱלֹהַי, כִּי שִׁמְךָ נִקְרָא עַל עִירְךָ וְעַל עַמֶּךָ.

סְלִיחָה צח (שְׁנִיָּה)

All:

(אֱלֹהֵינוּ וֵאלֹהֵי אֲבוֹתֵינוּ:)

אָדוֹן, בְּפָקְדְּךָ אֱנוֹשׁ* לַבְּקָרִים,   בִּמְצוּי הַדִּין אַל תְּמַתַּח.
גּוּף וּנְשָׁמָה אִם תְּרִיבֵם,*   דְּחוּ וְלֹא יוּכְלוּ קוּם.[1]
הֲיוּכַל גֶּבֶר לִזְכּוֹת בַּמִּשְׁפָּט,   וְאִם אֵין בְּיָדוֹ מַעַשׂ לְהִצְטַדָּק.
זֵרוּי יֵחוֹמוּ מְלֵחָה סְרוּחָה,*   חָבוּי אָרְבוּ בְּקִרְבּוֹ מֵעֵת הִוָּלְדוֹ.*
טָמוּן בְּחֶבְאוֹ[3] כְּרֶשֶׁת לְרַגְלָיו,   יְסִיתֵהוּ בְכָל יוֹם לְשַׁחַת לְהַפִּילוֹ.
כֹּחַ וּגְבוּרָה בַּגּוּף אָיִן   לְפָנָיו לַעֲמֹד וּלְהִתְיַצֵּב.

⧆ אָדוֹן בְּפָקְדְּךָ אֱנוֹשׁ — *Lord, when You consider mankind.* This *selichah* contains an *aleph-beis* acrostic, which is followed by the author's signature, יִצְחָק הַכֹּהֵן הֶחָבֵר חֲזַק וֶאֱמָץ, *Yitzchak the Kohen, the chaver* [an ancient title bestowed on certain exceptional people], *may he be strong and persevere.* Nothing is known about R' Yitzchak, except that he lived sometime before 1234, the year in which the commentary *Arugas HaBosem* was written. This *selichah* is composed entirely of couplets and is therefore classified as a *sheniyah.* It is from among the few *selichos* that are unrhymed.

גּוּף וּנְשָׁמָה אִם תְּרִיבֵם — *If You should adjudicate [the claims of] body and soul [together].* The Talmud relates an insightful discussion between

Rabbi [Yehudah HaNassi] and the Roman emperor Antoninus.

The emperor claimed that man's body and soul could exonerate themselves on Judgment Day. The body could argue, 'The soul was the guilty one; for since it left me, I have been lying like a mute rock in the grave;' and the soul could counter, 'The body was the guilty one; for since I left it, I have been flying free as a bird.'

Rabbi responded with a parable: A king ordered two men to guard an orchard of fruit-laden trees. One was lame, the other blind. The lame, sighted one said to his blind companion, 'I see beautiful fruit in the orchard. Let me ride on your shoulders and I will guide you to the trees. We will then be able to eat from them.' And so they

כְּרַחֵם אָב *As a father has mercy on his children, so, HASHEM, may You have mercy on us. Salvation is HASHEM's, upon Your people is Your blessing, Selah. HASHEM, Master of Legions, is with us, a stronghold for us is the God of Jacob, Selah. HASHEM, Master of Legions, praiseworthy is the person who trusts in You. HASHEM, save! May the King answer us on the day we call.*

In some congregations the following two verses are recited responsively — the *chazzan* reciting, '*Forgive, please . . .,*' and the congregation responding, '*And HASHEM said . . .*' In other congregations these verses are recited silently.

סְלַח נָא *Forgive, please, the iniquity of this people according to the greatness of Your kindness and as You have forgiven this people from Egypt until now, and there it was said:*

And HASHEM said, 'I have forgiven according to your word!'

All:

הַטֵּה *Incline, my God, Your ear, and listen, open Your eyes and see our desolation and that of the city upon which Your Name is proclaimed; for not because of our righteousness do we cast down our supplications before You, rather because of Your abundant compassion. O my Lord, heed; O my Lord, forgive; O my Lord, be attentive and act, do not delay; for Your sake, my God, for Your Name is proclaimed upon Your city and upon Your people.*

SELICHAH 98

All:

(Our God and the God of our forefathers:)

א *Lord, when You consider mankind* each morning,*

ב *do not exact rigorous judgment.*

ג *If You should adjudicate [the claims of] body and soul [together],**

ד *they would be thrust down, unable to rise.*[1]

ה *Can a man win out in judgment,*

ו *if he has no good deeds to his credit with which to justify himself?*

ז *The scattered seed of his engendering is but a fetid drop;*[2]

ח *the lurking enemy is concealed within him from the time of his birth.**

ט *Hidden within him,*[3] *like a net for his feet,*

י *it incites him every day [to sin], so as to cast him down into Gehinnom.*

כ *No strength nor might does the body have*

ל *to stand against it and hold its own.*

---

(1) Cf. *Psalms* 36:13. (2) See tractate *Avos* 3:1. (3) Cf. *Job* 31:33.

---

did for some time, eating the fruit they were set to protect. When the king returned, he asked what happened to the ripened figs. The cripple said, 'Do I have feet to walk over to the trees?' The blind one said, 'Do I have eyes to see the fruit?' But the wise king had the lame man hoisted onto the blind man's shoulders and judged them as one. So, too, on Judgment Day, God hurls the soul back into its body and judges them as one (*Sanhedrin* 91a).

מֵעֵת הִוָּלְדוֹ — *From the time of his birth.* Another question posed by Antoninus (ibid.) is: Does the Evil Inclination enter a person when the embryo is formed or at birth? Rabbi replied, 'From the formation of the embryo.'

Antoninus retorted, 'If so, it would rebel and kick its way out of its mother. It cannot enter a person until he is born.'

Rabbi acceded, saying, 'This matter have I been taught by Antoninus, and I have found a

מִיּוֹם עָמְדוּ עַל דַּעְתּוֹ,   נַפְשׁוֹ יָשִׂים בְּכַפּוֹ לְהָבִיא לַחֲמוֹ.[1]

שֶׁבַע כָּל יָמָיו כַּעַס וּמַכְאוֹבוֹת,[2]   עַד שׁוּבוֹ לַעֲפָרוֹ[3] לֹא יִשְׁקֹט.

פְּנֵה אָדוֹן בְּעִצְּבוֹן רוּחַ,   צְפֵה בְּשִׁבְרוֹן לֵב.

קָרוֹב אַתָּה לָרְחוֹקִים,   רוֹצֶה תְּשׁוּבַת רְשָׁעִים.[4]

שַׁדַּי, הַמֹּצֵא לְדוֹרְשֶׁיךָ,   תֹּאמַר הִנְנִי לִמְבַקְשֶׁיךָ.

יְבֻשְּׁרוּ סָלַחְתִּי[5] קוֹרְאֵי בִשְׁמֶךָ,   צַדֵּק בַּמִּשְׁפָּט עַם מְיַחֲדֶךָ.

חֲסֹם מְגֻנֶּ[6] מִלְּהַרְשִׁיעַ,   קְצֹף בְּמַסְטִין מִלְּהַסְטִין.

הָקֵם לָנוּ מֵלִיץ יֹשֶׁר.   כְּפֹר מָצָאתִי תַּשְׁמִיעַ לַשּׁוֹבָבִים.

הַשְּׁלַכְנוּ עָלֶיךָ יְהָבֵנוּ,[7]   נָא אַתָּה תְכַלְכְּלֵנוּ.

הֵעָתֵר לָנוּ בִּתְפִלָּתֵנוּ.   חָפְצֵנוּ וּבַקָּשָׁתֵנוּ מַלֵּא בְרַחֲמִים.

❖ בְּךָ תָלִינוּ בִטְחוֹנֵנוּ,   רַחֲמֶיךָ מְהֵרָה יְקַדְּמוּנוּ.

חֲזַק וְאַמֵּיץ שְׁמָךְ לֹא שָׁכֵחְנוּ,   אָנָּא, לָנֶצַח אַל תִּשְׁכָּחֵנוּ.[8]

All, while standing:

אֵל מֶלֶךְ יוֹשֵׁב עַל כִּסֵּא רַחֲמִים מִתְנַהֵג בַּחֲסִידוּת, מוֹחֵל עֲוֹנוֹת עַמּוֹ, מַעֲבִיר רִאשׁוֹן רִאשׁוֹן, מַרְבֶּה מְחִילָה לְחַטָּאִים וּסְלִיחָה לְפוֹשְׁעִים, עֹשֶׂה צְדָקוֹת עִם כָּל בָּשָׂר וָרוּחַ, לֹא כְרָעָתָם תִּגְמוֹל. ❖ אֵל הוֹרֵיתָ לָנוּ לוֹמַר שְׁלֹשׁ עֶשְׂרֵה, וּזְכוֹר לָנוּ הַיּוֹם בְּרִית שְׁלֹשׁ עֶשְׂרֵה, כְּמוֹ שֶׁהוֹדַעְתָּ לֶעָנָיו מִקֶּדֶם, כְּמוֹ שֶׁכָּתוּב, וַיֵּרֶד יהוה בֶּעָנָן וַיִּתְיַצֵּב עִמּוֹ שָׁם, וַיִּקְרָא בְשֵׁם יהוה.

Congregation, then chazzan:

וַיַּעֲבֹר יהוה עַל פָּנָיו וַיִּקְרָא:

Congregation and chazzan (the words in bold type are recited aloud and in unison):

יהוה, יהוה, אֵל, רַחוּם, וְחַנּוּן, אֶרֶךְ אַפַּיִם, וְרַב חֶסֶד, וֶאֱמֶת, נֹצֵר חֶסֶד לָאֲלָפִים, נֹשֵׂא עָוֹן, וָפֶשַׁע, וְחַטָּאָה, וְנַקֵּה. וְסָלַחְתָּ לַעֲוֹנֵנוּ וּלְחַטָּאתֵנוּ וּנְחַלְתָּנוּ. סְלַח לָנוּ אָבִינוּ כִּי חָטָאנוּ, מְחַל לָנוּ מַלְכֵּנוּ כִּי פָשָׁעְנוּ. כִּי אַתָּה אֲדֹנָי טוֹב וְסַלָּח, וְרַב חֶסֶד לְכָל קֹרְאֶיךָ.

Scriptural verse to support his view; for it is written, לַפֶּתַח חַטָּאת רֹבֵץ, *Sin crouches at the door (Genesis 4:7).'* [Although the verse speaks in the context of an unrepentant sinner, Rabbi gave it a novel interpretation: The cause of sin, namely, the Evil Inclination, crouches at the door of the womb, ready to enter the baby as it emerges.]

מ *From the day [a man] learns to use his wits,*
נ *he takes his life in his hands to win bread for himself.*[1]
ס *[He is] full, his whole life long, with anger and pains;*[2]
ע *until he returns to the dust,*[3] *he has no quiet.*
פ *Consider, Lord, [our] aching spirit;*
צ *look at [our] broken hearts.*
ק *You are near to those far off,*
ר *You desire repentance for the wicked.*[4]
ש *Almighty, manifest Yourself to those who search for You;*
ת *say, 'Here I am,' to those who seek You.*
י *Let those who call out in Your name hear, 'I have forgiven';*[5]
צ *vindicate in judgment the people who proclaim Your unity.*
ח *Muzzle the foul [Satan]*[6] *so he cannot prosecute;*
ק *scold [Satan] the Accuser angrily so he cannot accuse.*
ה *Raise up an advocate [angel] to speak well on our behalf;*
כ *let Your wayward children hear, 'I have found atonement for you.'*
ה *We have cast our burden upon You —*[7]
נ *please, let it be You Who sustain us.*
ה *Answer us as we pray;*
ח *fulfill our desire, our request, with mercy.*
ב Chazzan — *We have put our trust in You;*
ר *let Your mercy speedily come forth to greet us.*
Strong, Mighty One, we have not forgotten Your name;
please do not forget us for all eternity.[8]

All, while standing:

אֵל מֶלֶךְ *O God, King Who sits on the throne of mercy; Who acts with
kindness, pardons the iniquities of His people, removes [sins]
one by one, increasingly grants pardon to careless sinners and forgiveness
to rebels, Who deals righteously with every living being — You do not repay
them in accord with their evil.* Chazzan — *O God, You taught us to recite the
Thirteen [Attributes of Mercy], so remember for us today the covenant of
these Thirteen, as You made known to the humble one in ancient times, as
it is written: And Hashem descended in a cloud and stood with him there,
and He called out with the Name Hashem.*

Congregation, then chazzan:

And Hashem passed before him [Moses] and proclaimed:

Congregation and chazzan (the words in bold type are recited aloud and in unison):

ה' ה' **Hashem, Hashem, God, Compassionate and Gracious, Slow
to anger, and Abundant in Kindness and Truth, Preserver of
kindness for thousands [of generations], Forgiver of iniquity, willful
sin, and error, and Who cleanses.** *May You forgive our iniquities and our
errors and make us Your heritage. Forgive us, our Father, for we have
erred; pardon us, our King, for we have willfully sinned; for You, my Lord,
are good and forgiving and abundantly kind to all who call upon You.*

---

(1) Cf. *Lamentations* 5:9. (2) Cf. *Ecclesiastes* 2:23. (3) Cf. 3:20. (4) Cf. *Ezekiel* 18:23. (5) *Numbers* 14:20.
(6) See commentary to *selichah* 24. (7) Cf. *Psalms* 55:23. (8) Cf. *Lamentations* 5:20.

פסוקי הקדמה לסליחה צט

אַל תַּעַזְבֵנוּ יהוה, אֱלֹהֵינוּ אַל תִּרְחַק מִמֶּנּוּ.[1] אַל תִּרְחַק
מִמֶּנּוּ, כִּי צָרָה קְרוֹבָה, כִּי אֵין עוֹזֵר.[2] עֶזְרֵנוּ מֵעִם
יהוה, עֹשֵׂה שָׁמַיִם וָאָרֶץ. אַל יִתֵּן לַמּוֹט רַגְלֶנוּ, וְאַל יָנוּם שׁוֹמְרֵנוּ.[3]
יהוה הוֹשִׁיעָה, הַמֶּלֶךְ יַעֲנֵנוּ בְיוֹם קָרְאֵנוּ.[4]

כְּרַחֵם אָב עַל בָּנִים, כֵּן תְּרַחֵם יהוה עָלֵינוּ. לַיהוה הַיְשׁוּעָה,
עַל עַמְּךָ בִרְכָתֶךָ סֶּלָה. יהוה צְבָאוֹת עִמָּנוּ, מִשְׂגָּב
לָנוּ אֱלֹהֵי יַעֲקֹב סֶלָה. יהוה צְבָאוֹת, אַשְׁרֵי אָדָם בֹּטֵחַ בָּךְ. יהוה
הוֹשִׁיעָה, הַמֶּלֶךְ יַעֲנֵנוּ בְיוֹם קָרְאֵנוּ.

In some congregations the following two verses are recited responsively — the *chazzan* reciting סְלַח,
and the congregation responding וַיֹּאמֶר. In other congregations these verses are recited silently.

סְלַח נָא לַעֲוֹן הָעָם הַזֶּה כְּגֹדֶל חַסְדֶּךָ, וְכַאֲשֶׁר נָשָׂאתָה לָעָם
הַזֶּה מִמִּצְרַיִם וְעַד הֵנָּה, וְשָׁם נֶאֱמַר:

וַיֹּאמֶר יהוה סָלַחְתִּי כִּדְבָרֶךָ.

All:

הַטֵּה אֱלֹהַי אָזְנְךָ וּשְׁמָע, פְּקַח עֵינֶיךָ וּרְאֵה שֹׁמְמֹתֵינוּ, וְהָעִיר
אֲשֶׁר נִקְרָא שִׁמְךָ עָלֶיהָ, כִּי לֹא עַל צִדְקוֹתֵינוּ אֲנַחְנוּ
מַפִּילִים תַּחֲנוּנֵינוּ לְפָנֶיךָ, כִּי עַל רַחֲמֶיךָ הָרַבִּים. אֲדֹנָי שְׁמָעָה,
אֲדֹנָי סְלָחָה, אֲדֹנָי הַקְשִׁיבָה, וַעֲשֵׂה אַל תְּאַחַר, לְמַעַנְךָ אֱלֹהַי, כִּי
שִׁמְךָ נִקְרָא עַל עִירְךָ וְעַל עַמֶּךָ.

סליחה צט (שלישיה)

(אֱלֹהֵינוּ וֵאלֹהֵי אֲבוֹתֵינוּ:)

אָדוֹן דִּין אִם יְדַקְדַּק,∗ בְּחֵקֶר פֹּעַל אִם יְבְדַּק,
גֶּבֶר לְפָנֶיךָ לֹא יִצְדַּק.[5]
דְּפִי תִתֶּן[6] בִּצְבָא מַעְלָה, הֵן בְּמַלְאָכֶיךָ תָּשִׂים תָּהֳלָה,[7]
וְאַף שׁוֹתֶה כַמַּיִם עַוְלָה.[8]
זְכוּת וּצְדָקָה אֵין בָּנוּ, חֵטְא וְרֶשַׁע כֻּלָּנוּ,
טוֹב, אַל תָּבֹא בְמִשְׁפָּט עִמָּנוּ.[9]

∗ **אָדוֹן דִּין אִם יְדַקְדַּק** — *O Lord, if judgment were to be rigorously precise.* The acrostic of this *selichah* forms the *aleph-beis* followed by

the *paytan's* name — חֲזַק זְבַדְיָה, *Zevadiah, may he be strong* [see prefatory comment to *selichah* 63].

PREFATORY VERSES TO SELICHAH 99

אַל תַּעַזְבֵנוּ *Do not forsake us, HASHEM; our God, do not distance Yourself from us.*[1] *Do not distance Yourself from us, lest trouble be near, for there is none to help [besides You].*[2] *Our help is from HASHEM, Maker of heaven and earth. He will not allow our foot to falter; our Guardian will not slumber.*[3] *HASHEM, save! May the King answer us on the day we call.*[4]

כְּרַחֵם אָב *As a father has mercy on his children, so, HASHEM, may You have mercy on us. Salvation is HASHEM's, upon Your people is Your blessing, Selah. HASHEM, Master of Legions, is with us, a stronghold for us is the God of Jacob, Selah. HASHEM, Master of Legions, praiseworthy is the person who trusts in You. HASHEM, save! May the King answer us on the day we call.*

In some congregations the following two verses are recited responsively — the *chazzan* reciting, '*Forgive, please . . .,*' and the congregation responding, '*And HASHEM said . . .*' In other congregations these verses are recited silently.

סְלַח נָא *Forgive, please, the iniquity of this people according to the greatness of Your kindness and as You have forgiven this people from Egypt until now, and there it was said:*

And HASHEM said, 'I have forgiven according to your word!'

All:

הַטֵּה *Incline, my God, Your ear, and listen, open Your eyes and see our desolation and that of the city upon which Your Name is proclaimed; for not because of our righteousness do we cast down our supplications before You, rather because of Your abundant compassion. O my Lord, heed; O my Lord, forgive; O my Lord, be attentive and act, do not delay; for Your sake, my God, for Your Name is proclaimed upon Your city and upon Your people.*

SELICHAH 99

(Our God and the God of our forefathers:)
א *Our Lord, if judgment were to be rigorously precise,*＊
ב *if each action were examined through an investigation,*
ג *man will never be found innocent before You.*[5]
ד *You have reason to rebuff*[6] *the celestial host,*
ה *You find folly even among Your angels*[7] —
ו *how much more so [man], who drinks sin like water.*[8]
ז *Merit and righteousness are not within us,*
ח *our entire being is sin and wickedness,*
ט *O Good One, enter not into strict judgment with us.*[9]

---

(1) Cf. *Psalms* 38:22. (2) Cf. 22:12. (3) Cf. 121:2-3. (4) 20:10. (5) Cf. 143:2.
(6) See 50:20 with *Rashi*. (7) Cf. *Job* 4:18. (8) Cf. 15:16. (9) Cf. *Psalms* 143:2.

יֶהֱמוּ מֵעֶיךָ עָלֵינוּ,[1]   בְּרוֹב רַחֲמֶיךָ פְּנֵה אֵלֵינוּ,[2]
לְבִלְתִּי כְּרֹעַ מַעֲלָלֵינוּ.

מְשׁוּבָתֵינוּ רַבּוּ מִלְמְנוֹת,[3]   נִיחוֹחִים אַיִן וְקָרְבָּנוֹת,
סְלִיחָה מְצָא לַעֲוֹנוֹת.

עַל צִדְקוֹתֵינוּ אֵין אָנוּ סְמוּכִים,[4]   פֶּשַׁע וְעָוֹן מְכַלְכְּלִים,
צְדָקָה מְצָא תַּחַן עוֹרְכִים.

קַו אַל תִּמְתַּח בְּאוֹרְחוֹתֵינוּ,   רִמָּה וְתוֹלֵעָה אַחֲרִיתֵנוּ,[5]
שָׁוְא וְהֶבֶל שְׁנוֹתֵינוּ.

תָּשׁוּב עַל הָרָעָה תִּנָּחֵם,[6]   זֶה דַרְכְּךָ חִנָּם מְרַחֵם,
בְּרַחֲמֶיךָ הָרַבִּים עָלֵינוּ רַחֵם.

דְּרָכֶיךָ הוֹדַעְתָּ[7] לֶעָנָו לְהוֹרוֹת,   יְדַעְתּוֹ שְׁלֹשׁ עֶשְׂרֵה סְדוּרוֹת,
הִבְטַחְתּוֹ שֶׁאֵין רֵיקָם חוֹזְרוֹת.[8]

❖ חַנּוּן,[9] בָּם סִדַּרְנוּ לְפָנֶיךָ,   זְעַק קֶשֶׁב מִמִּתְחַנְּנֶיךָ,
וְאַל תְּשִׁיבֵנוּ רֵיקָם מִלְּפָנֶיךָ.

All, while standing:

אֵל מֶלֶךְ יוֹשֵׁב עַל כִּסֵּא רַחֲמִים מִתְנַהֵג בַּחֲסִידוּת, מוֹחֵל
עֲוֹנוֹת עַמּוֹ, מַעֲבִיר רִאשׁוֹן רִאשׁוֹן, מַרְבֶּה מְחִילָה
לְחַטָּאִים וּסְלִיחָה לְפוֹשְׁעִים, עֹשֶׂה צְדָקוֹת עִם כָּל בָּשָׂר וָרוּחַ, לֹא
כְרָעָתָם תִּגְמוֹל. ❖ אֵל הוֹרֵיתָ לָּנוּ לוֹמַר שְׁלֹשׁ עֶשְׂרֵה, וּזְכוֹר לָנוּ
הַיּוֹם בְּרִית שְׁלֹשׁ עֶשְׂרֵה, כְּמוֹ שֶׁהוֹדַעְתָּ לֶעָנָיו מִקֶּדֶם, כְּמוֹ
שֶׁכָּתוּב, וַיֵּרֶד יהוה בֶּעָנָן וַיִּתְיַצֵּב עִמּוֹ שָׁם, וַיִּקְרָא בְשֵׁם יהוה.

Congregation, then chazzan:

וַיַּעֲבֹר יהוה עַל פָּנָיו וַיִּקְרָא:

Congregation and chazzan (the words in bold type are recited aloud and in unison):

יהוה, יהוה, אֵל, **רַחוּם, וְחַנּוּן, אֶרֶךְ אַפַּיִם, וְרַב חֶסֶד, וֶאֱמֶת,
נֹצֵר חֶסֶד לָאֲלָפִים, נֹשֵׂא עָוֹן, וָפֶשַׁע, וְחַטָּאָה,
וְנַקֵּה.** וְסָלַחְתָּ לַעֲוֹנֵנוּ וּלְחַטָּאתֵנוּ וּנְחַלְתָּנוּ. סְלַח לָנוּ אָבִינוּ כִּי
חָטָאנוּ, מְחַל לָנוּ מַלְכֵּנוּ כִּי פָשָׁעְנוּ. כִּי אַתָּה אֲדֹנָי טוֹב וְסַלָּח, וְרַב
חֶסֶד לְכָל קֹרְאֶיךָ.

---

(1) Cf. *Jeremiah* 31:19. (2) Cf. *Psalms* 69:17. (3) Cf. *Jeremiah* 14:7. (4) Cf. *Daniel* 9:18.
(5) Cf. *Job* 25:6; Mishnah, *Avos* 3:1. (6) Cf. *Exodus* 32:12. (7) Cf. 33:13.
(8) See tractate *Rosh HaShanah* 17b. (9) Some editions read חַנּוּן, [our] supplication.

י Let Your innards arouse [compassion] for us;[1]

ב turn to us in accord with Your abundant mercies,[2]

ל but not in accord with the evil of our deeds.

מ Our wayward deeds are too numerous to count.[3]

נ There are no offerings with [their] satisfying aroma

ס to evoke forgiveness for [our] iniquities.

ע Upon our righteousness we do not rely,[4]

פ [for we are] filthy with willful sin and iniquity;

צ [rather,] we arrange [our] supplication to evoke charity.

ק [Therefore,] do not extend a tape measure over our ways;

ר worm and maggot are our end,[5]

ש worthlessness and emptiness are our years.

ת Reverse the evil judgment, relent,[6]

ז [for] this is Your way, being graciously compassionate;

ב O, with Your great mercies, may You have mercy on us.

ד You made Your ways known[7] to the humble [Moses]
that he may teach;

י You let him know how the Thirteen [Attributes] are arranged;

ה You promised him they would never be turned back empty.[8]

ח O Gracious One,[9] we have arranged them before You.

זק Attend to the cries of those who supplicate before You,
and do not turn us away from You empty-handed.

All, while standing:

אֵל מֶלֶךְ O God, King Who sits on the throne of mercy; Who acts with
kindness, pardons the iniquities of His people, removes [sins]
one by one, increasingly grants pardon to careless sinners and forgiveness
to rebels, Who deals righteously with every living being — You do not repay
them in accord with their evil. Chazzan — O God, You taught us to recite the
Thirteen [Attributes of Mercy], so remember for us today the covenant of
these Thirteen, as You made known to the humble one in ancient times, as
it is written: And HASHEM descended in a cloud and stood with him there,
and He called out with the Name HASHEM.

Congregation, then chazzan:

And HASHEM passed before him [Moses] and proclaimed:

Congregation and chazzan (the words in bold type are recited aloud and in unison):

ה' ה' HASHEM, HASHEM, God, Compassionate and Gracious, Slow
to anger, and Abundant in Kindness and Truth, Preserver of
kindness for thousands [of generations], Forgiver of iniquity, willful
sin, and error, and Who cleanses. May You forgive our iniquities and
our errors and make us Your heritage. Forgive us, our Father, for we have
erred; pardon us, our King, for we have willfully sinned; for You, my
Lord, are good and forgiving and abundantly kind to all who call upon
You.

סליחה ק (פזמון)

Chazzan, then congregation:

יֵרָצֶה צוֹם עַמְּךָ* אֲשֶׁר דָּמוֹ לְךָ מַזֶּה,
חָשַׁב חֶלְבּוֹ כְּעַל זֶבַח* וְקָרְבָּנוֹ אַל תִּבְזֶה,
חֲתֹם עָלָיו אוֹת חַיִּים,[1] וּתְפִלָּתוֹ תֶּחֱזֶה —

מָחָר יִהְיֶה הָאוֹת הַזֶּה.[2]

Congregation, then chazzan:

צִדְקָתְךָ הִתְאַזָּר, שׁוֹכֵן עַד וּמְרוֹמָם,[3]
סְמֹךְ נָא הַנִּכְשָׁלִים, שְׁלַח יָדְךָ לַהֲקִימָם,
אֲשֶׁר דִּמְעָם שְׁקוּיָם וְאַנְחָתָם הִיא לַחְמָם,[4]
וְתִנְקֹם דַּם עֲבָדֶיךָ מֵאוֹיְבֶיךָ עַד תֻּמָּם.
וְתִדְרֹשׁ לְשֶׁפֶךְ דָּמָם,
לָדַעַת מַה זֶּה וְעַל מַה זֶּה*[5] —   מָחָר יִהְיֶה הָאוֹת הַזֶּה.

Congregation, then chazzan:

חַנּוּן חֹן עַמְּךָ אֲשֶׁר לְשִׁמְךָ הוּא מַאֲמִין,
סַנֵּגוֹר עָלַי תְּמַנֶּה אֲשֶׁר חֲטָאתִי יַטְמִין,
וְחוֹבִי בִּשְׂמֹאל יַכְמִין, זְכוּתִי יַעֲלֶה בְיָמִין,
וְאֵפֶר יִצְחָק* יַזְמִין,
אֲשֶׁר יֹאמַר כִּי הוּא זֶה[6] —   מָחָר יִהְיֶה הָאוֹת הַזֶּה.

Congregation, then chazzan:

קָרֵב וּשְׁמַע רִנָּתִי, לְזַעֲקָתִי תִּפְתַּח שַׁעַר,
לְזַכּוֹת אֶת חַטָּאתִי כְּמוֹ בֶן שָׁנָה נַעַר,*

---

§ יֵרָצֶה צוֹם עַמְּךָ — *May the fast of Your nation ... be acceptable.* This *pizmon* is signed יִצְחָק, *Yitzchak*, in the acrostic of the first four stanzas. Some read בַּר אֲבִיגְדוֹר, *bar Avigdor*, in the acrostic of stanzas five and six. Nothing more is known about this *paytan* except that he wrote before 1234 when the commentary *Arugas HaBosem* [which includes this work] was written.

חָשַׁב חֶלְבּוֹ כְּעַל זֶבַח — *Consider its fat as if it were a sacrifice.* The concept that one's fasting is reckoned as if he had sanctified himself on the Altar is the subject of a prayer, originally recited by the talmudic Sage R' Shaishes (*Berachos* 17a), generally recited at the end of the *Minchah Amidah* on fast days:

'Master of all worlds, it is revealed and known before You that, when the Holy Temple stood, one who sinned would offer an animal — its fat and its blood — upon the Altar, and it would

atone for him. Now I have engaged in a fast and my own fat and blood have been diminished. May it be Your will that the diminution of my fat and blood be considered as if I had offered them upon the Altar, and may You show me favor.'

לָדַעַת מַה זֶּה וְעַל מַה זֶּה — *To know what this is and why this is.* The commentaries vary widely on the meaning of this stich:

Investigate to learn why their tears have become their drinks, and why have their sighs have become their bread (*Masbir*).

Investigate to determine whether the spilled blood of Your people falls into the category of קִדּוּשׁ הַשֵּׁם, *martyrdom* (*Matteh Levi*).

Seek [and refute] the excuses the gentiles used for spilling Jewish blood, so that they will know why Your vengeance is upon them (*Selichos HaMeforash*).

וְאֵפֶר יִצְחָק — *Isaac's ashes.* Many sources in the Talmud and Midrash speak of God's mercy

---

SELICHAH 100

Chazzan, then congregation:

י May the fast of Your nation that sprinkles its blood to You
    be acceptable;*
consider its fat as if it were a sacrifice,* and disparage not its offering.
Seal it[s verdict] with a sign of life,¹ and accept its prayer.
                 On the morrow, may this sign be [ours].²

Congregation, then chazzan:

צ Gird Yourself in righteousness,
    O You Who live eternally and are exalted;³
please support those who stumble,
    send forth Your hand to raise them,
those whose tear is their drink and whose sigh is their bread.⁴
Avenge your servants' blood
    until You have made an end to Your enemies,
and seek an understanding of their spilled blood
to know what this is and why this is.⁵*
               On the morrow, may this sign be [ours].

Congregation, then chazzan:

ח O Gracious One, favor Your people who believe in Your Name,
assign for me an advocate [angel]
    who will conceal my inadvertent sin;
who will suppress my guilt with his left hand,
and elevate my merit with his right;
who will exhibit Isaac's ashes,*
about which he will say, 'This is it!'⁶
              On the morrow, may this sign be [ours].

Congregation, then chazzan:

ק Draw near and listen to my prayerful song,
    open the [heavenly] Gate [of Prayer] before my cry,
to cleanse me of my sin, as if [I were] a year-old child.*

---

(1) See commentary to *selichah* 17, s.v., תֵּן. (2) Cf. *Exodus* 8:19. (3) Cf. *Isaiah* 57:15.
(4) Cf. *Psalms* 80:6; also 102:10; *Job* 3:24. (5) *Esther* 4:5. (6) *Exodus* 22:8.

being evoked by the merit of Isaac's willingness to be offered as a sacrifice. Those merits are referred to as Isaac's ashes (see for example *Taanis* 16a where, according to one view, the fast day custom of placing ashes on the Ark in which the Torah Scrolls are kept is based on recalling the merit of Isaac's ashes.) But our *paytan* asks for more than just a verbal allusion to the *Akeidah*; he asks for an advocate who will *display* Isaac's ashes, as if Isaac were actually burned and his ashes are real!?

The Talmud relates that when King David bought the land upon which his son Solomon would eventually build the *Beis HaMikdash*, he was able to determine the exact spot on which the Altar would stand. But how did David know the exact location? According to one view, he saw the

ashes of Isaac heaped up on that spot (*Zevachim* 62a). Similarly, when God sent a destroying angel to visit a death plague on Israel during the days of King David, when the angel began his destruction of Jerusalem, HASHEM *saw and relented about the evil decrees* (I *Chronicles* 21:15). But, asks the Talmud, what did God see that caused him to relent? One opinion answers that He saw Isaac's ashes (*Berachos* 62b). Thus, according to at least two Sages of the Talmud, Isaac's ashes are not just a concept, but are a visible entity. It is to these views that the *paytan* subscribes when he asks that the ashes be displayed.

כְּמוֹ בֶן שָׁנָה נָעַר — *As if [I were] a year-old child.* The simile of a one-year-old as a symbol of innocence is taken from Scriptures' description of

וְתַחְסֹם לְשׁוֹן מַשְׂטִינִי וְאֶת פִּיהוּ לֹא יִפְעָר,

יהוה בַּשָּׂטָן יִגְעַר,[1]

קוּם רֵד מַהֵר מִזֶּה —[2]   מָחָר יִהְיֶה הָאוֹת הַזֶּה.

Congregation, then chazzan:

בַּמֶּה אֲקַדֵּם וְאֶכַּף[3] פְּנֵי לֹא יִקַּח שֹׁחַד,[4]

וּבְיָדִי אֵין מַעַשׂ וְעַל זֹאת לִבִּי יִפְחַד,

אֲבָל עַתָּה בְּזָכְרִי מַלְכוּת שֵׁם הַמְּיֻחָד,

וְעַל זֹאת אֲנִי בוֹטֵחַ[5] בְּאוֹמְרִים יהוה אֶחָד,

וּמוֹשְׁכִים כֻּלָּם יַחַד,

מִזֶּה אֶחָד וּמִזֶּה —[6]   מָחָר יִהְיֶה הָאוֹת הַזֶּה.

Congregation, then chazzan:

רְאֵה אֵין מְכַפֵּר בַּעֲדִי, וְאֵין סוֹדֵר לִי סֵדֶר,

וּבְגָדַי לָבָן אַיִן, וְאֵין לוֹבֵשׁ הָאֵדֶר,

וְגַם אֵין קָרְבָּן חוֹבָה וְלֹא נְדָבָה וָנֶדֶר,

וְאַתָּה תְּכַפֵּר עָלַי, בּוֹחֵן כְּלָיוֹת וָחֵדֶר,

גָּדֵר פִּרְצַת צֹאנֶךְ וְשִׂים רֶוַח לָעֵדֶר,

וְתִבְנֶה לָמוֹ גָדֵר,

מִזֶּה וְגָדֵר מִזֶּה —[7]   מָחָר יִהְיֶה הָאוֹת הַזֶּה.

Congregation, then chazzan:

צֵל קוֹרָתְךָ בָּאוּ בָנִים אֲשֶׁר נִגְרֵשׁוּ,

בֵּיתְךָ כְּנִתְוַעֲדוּ רָעֲשׁוּ וְגַם נִתְגָּעֲשׁוּ,

חֶסֶד אֲבוֹתָם תִּזְכֹּר עֵת לָרִיב יִגְּשׁוּ,

אֱמֶת וְשָׁלוֹם נִפְגָּשׁוּ,[8]

גַּם אֶת זֶה לְעֻמַּת זֶה —[9]   מָחָר יִהְיֶה הָאוֹת הַזֶּה.

All, while standing:

אֵל מֶלֶךְ יוֹשֵׁב עַל כִּסֵּא רַחֲמִים מִתְנַהֵג בַּחֲסִידוּת, מוֹחֵל
עֲוֹנוֹת עַמּוֹ, מַעֲבִיר רִאשׁוֹן רִאשׁוֹן, מַרְבֶּה מְחִילָה
לְחַטָּאִים וּסְלִיחָה לְפוֹשְׁעִים, עֹשֶׂה צְדָקוֹת עִם כָּל בָּשָׂר וָרוּחַ, לֹא
כְרָעָתָם תִּגְמוֹל. ✦ אֵל הוֹרֵיתָ לָנוּ לוֹמַר שְׁלֹשׁ עֶשְׂרֵה, וּזְכֹר לָנוּ
הַיּוֹם בְּרִית שְׁלֹשׁ עֶשְׂרֵה, כְּמוֹ שֶׁהוֹדַעְתָּ לֶעָנָיו מִקֶּדֶם, כְּמוֹ

(1) Cf. *Zechariah* 3:2. (2) *Deuteronomy* 9:12. (3) Cf. *Micah* 6:6. (4) Cf. *Deuteronomy* 10:17.
(5) Cf. *Psalms* 27:3. (6) *Exodus* 17:12. (7) *Numbers* 22:24. (8) Cf. *Psalms* 85:11. (9) Cf. *Ecclesiastes* 7:14.

King Saul: *Saul was a year old when he became*   was as innocent] as a one-year-old child who has
king (*I Samuel* 13:1). The Talmud interprets: [He   not tasted of sin (*Yoma* 22b).

Muzzle the speech of my satanic Accuser, that he not open his mouth.
O HASHEM, denounce the Satan,[1]
'Stand up! Descend quickly from here!'[2]
                              On the morrow, may this sign be [ours].

Congregation, then *chazzan:*

With what shall I [the chazzan] approach and humble myself[3]
    before Him Who takes no bribe?[4]
In my hand is no [worthy] deed, and for this my heart is fearful.
Yet when I recall [how Israel accepts the yoke of] the sovereignty
    of the Oneness of [Your] Name,
on this do I place my trust[5] *[for their future],*
    when they recite, 'HASHEM is One,'
and all together as one they draw out the word 'One',
from this side [of the congregation] and from that.[6]
                              On the morrow, may this sign be [ours].

Congregation, then *chazzan:*

See, there is no [Kohen Gadol] to atone for me, no one to perform
    the order of the [Yom Kippur Temple] service for me;
the [Kohen Gadol's] white [linen vestments] are not here,
    and there is no one to wear the [priestly] mantle,
and there is no obligatory offering,
    nor voluntary, nor promissory offering.
But You will atone for me,
    O Prober of man's internal organs and chamber.
So fence up Your flock's breaches, and give the herd room,
build for them a fence on this side and a fence on that side.[7]
                              On the morrow, may this sign be [ours].

Congregation, then *chazzan:*

Your children who had been banished
    have come under the protective shadow of Your beam,
as they assemble themselves in Your synagogue,
    they are tremulous and apprehensive [about their verdict].
Recall the kindness of their Patriarchs,
    when they approach to plead [their cases].
Truth and peace will meet among them,[8]
as they ask forgiveness one from the other.[9]
                              On the morrow, may this sign be [ours].

All, while standing:

אֵל מֶלֶךְ *O God, King Who sits on the throne of mercy; Who acts with*
            kindness, pardons the iniquities of His people, removes [sins]
one by one, increasingly grants pardon to careless sinners and forgiveness
to rebels, Who deals righteously with every living being — You do not repay
them in accord with their evil. Chazzan — *O God, You taught us to recite the*
Thirteen [Attributes of Mercy], so remember for us today the covenant of
these Thirteen, as You made known to the humble one in ancient times, as

שֶׁכָּתוּב, וַיֵּרֶד יהוה בֶּעָנָן וַיִּתְיַצֵּב עִמּוֹ שָׁם, וַיִּקְרָא בְשֵׁם יהוה.

Congregation, then chazzan:

וַיַּעֲבֹר יהוה עַל פָּנָיו וַיִּקְרָא:

Congregation and chazzan (the words in bold type are recited aloud and in unison):

יהוה, יהוה, אֵל, רַחוּם, וְחַנּוּן, אֶרֶךְ אַפַּיִם, וְרַב חֶסֶד, וֶאֱמֶת, נֹצֵר חֶסֶד לָאֲלָפִים, נֹשֵׂא עָוֹן, וָפֶשַׁע, וְחַטָּאָה, **וְנַקֵּה.** וְסָלַחְתָּ לַעֲוֹנֵנוּ וּלְחַטָּאתֵנוּ וּנְחַלְתָּנוּ. סְלַח לָנוּ אָבִינוּ כִּי חָטָאנוּ, מְחַל לָנוּ מַלְכֵּנוּ כִּי פָשָׁעְנוּ. כִּי אַתָּה אֲדֹנָי טוֹב וְסַלָּח, וְרַב חֶסֶד לְכָל קֹרְאֶיךָ.

All:

אַל תִּזְכָּר לָנוּ עֲוֹנוֹת רִאשׁוֹנִים, מַהֵר יְקַדְּמוּנוּ רַחֲמֶיךָ, כִּי דַלּוֹנוּ מְאֹד.[1] חַטֹּאת נְעוּרֵינוּ וּפְשָׁעֵינוּ אַל תִּזְכּוֹר, כְּחַסְדְּךָ זְכָר לָנוּ אַתָּה, לְמַעַן טוּבְךָ יהוה.[2]

זְכוֹר רַחֲמֶיךָ יהוה וַחֲסָדֶיךָ, כִּי מֵעוֹלָם הֵמָּה.[3] זָכְרֵנוּ יהוה בִּרְצוֹן עַמֶּךָ, פָּקְדֵנוּ בִּישׁוּעָתֶךָ.[4] זְכֹר עֲדָתְךָ קָנִיתָ קֶּדֶם, גָּאַלְתָּ שֵׁבֶט נַחֲלָתֶךָ, הַר צִיּוֹן זֶה שָׁכַנְתָּ בּוֹ.[5] זְכֹר יהוה חִבַּת יְרוּשָׁלַיִם, אַהֲבַת צִיּוֹן אַל תִּשְׁכַּח לָנֶצַח.[6] אַתָּה תָקוּם תְּרַחֵם צִיּוֹן, כִּי עֵת לְחֶנְנָהּ כִּי בָא מוֹעֵד.[7] זְכֹר יהוה לִבְנֵי אֱדוֹם אֵת יוֹם יְרוּשָׁלַיִם, הָאֹמְרִים עָרוּ עָרוּ עַד הַיְסוֹד בָּהּ.[8] זְכֹר לְאַבְרָהָם לְיִצְחָק וּלְיִשְׂרָאֵל עֲבָדֶיךָ אֲשֶׁר נִשְׁבַּעְתָּ לָהֶם בָּךְ, וַתְּדַבֵּר אֲלֵהֶם, אַרְבֶּה אֶת זַרְעֲכֶם כְּכוֹכְבֵי הַשָּׁמַיִם, וְכָל הָאָרֶץ הַזֹּאת אֲשֶׁר אָמַרְתִּי אֶתֵּן לְזַרְעֲכֶם, וְנָחֲלוּ לְעוֹלָם.[9] ❖ זְכֹר לַעֲבָדֶיךָ לְאַבְרָהָם לְיִצְחָק וּלְיַעֲקֹב, אַל תֵּפֶן אֶל קְשִׁי הָעָם הַזֶּה וְאֶל רִשְׁעוֹ וְאֶל חַטָּאתוֹ.[10]

Chazzan, then congregation:

אַל נָא תָשֵׁת עָלֵינוּ חַטָּאת, אֲשֶׁר נוֹאַלְנוּ וַאֲשֶׁר חָטָאנוּ.[11]

Chazzan, then congregation:

חָטָאנוּ צוּרֵנוּ, סְלַח לָנוּ יוֹצְרֵנוּ.

All:

זְכוֹר לָנוּ בְּרִית אָבוֹת, כַּאֲשֶׁר אָמַרְתָּ: וְזָכַרְתִּי אֶת בְּרִיתִי יַעֲקוֹב, וְאַף אֶת בְּרִיתִי יִצְחָק, וְאַף אֶת בְּרִיתִי אַבְרָהָם אֶזְכֹּר, וְהָאָרֶץ אֶזְכֹּר.[12]

it is written: And HASHEM descended in a cloud and stood with him there, and He called out with the Name HASHEM.

Congregation, then *chazzan:*

And HASHEM passed before him [Moses] and proclaimed:

Congregation and *chazzan* (the words in bold type are recited aloud and in unison):

ה׳ ה׳ **HASHEM, HASHEM, God, Compassionate and Gracious, Slow to anger, and Abundant in Kindness and Truth, Preserver of kindness for thousands [of generations], Forgiver of iniquity, willful sin, and error, and Who cleanses.** *May You forgive our iniquities and our errors and make us Your heritage. Forgive us, our Father, for we have erred; pardon us, our King, for we have willfully sinned; for You, my Lord, are good and forgiving and abundantly kind to all who call upon You.*

All:

אַל תִּזְכָּר *Do not recall against us the iniquities of the ancients; speedily — let Your mercy come to meet us for we have fallen very low.*[1] *Remember not the sins of our youth and our rebellions; may You remember for us [the deeds] worthy of Your kindness, because of Your goodness, HASHEM.*[2]

זְכוֹר רַחֲמֶיךָ *Remember Your mercies, O HASHEM, and Your kindnesses, for they are from the beginning of the world.*[3] *Remember us, HASHEM, when You show Your people favor and recall us with Your salvation.*[4] *Remember Your congregation that You acquired of old, that You redeemed the tribe of Your heritage, and this Mount Zion where You dwelled.*[5] *Remember, O HASHEM, the affection of Jerusalem, may You never forget the love of Zion.*[6] *You will arise and show Zion mercy, for it is the time to be gracious to her, for the appointed time will have come.*[7] *Remember, HASHEM, for the offspring of Edom, the day of Jerusalem — for those who said: 'Destroy! Destroy to its very foundation!'*[8] *Remember Abraham, Isaac, and Israel, Your servants, to whom You swore by Your Being, saying to them, 'I shall increase your offspring like the stars of the heavens; and this entire land of which I spoke I will give to your offspring and they will inherit it forever.'*[9] Chazzan — *Remember for Your servants, for Abraham, for Isaac, and for Jacob; ignore the stubbornness of this people, its wickedness and its sinfulness.*[10]

Chazzan, then congregation:

Please, do not reckon for us a sin,
what we have done foolishly and what we have sinned.[11]

Chazzan, then congregation:

We have erred, our Rock! Forgive us, our Molder!

All:

זְכוֹר לָנוּ *Remember for us the covenant of the Patriarchs, as You said: 'And I will remember My covenant with Jacob, and also My covenant with Isaac, and also My covenant with Abraham will I remember; and the Land will I remember.'*[12]

---

(1) *Psalms* 79:8. (2) Cf. 25:7. (3) 25:6. (4) Cf. 106:4. (5) 74:2. (6) This is not a Scriptural verse. (7) *Psalms* 102:14. (8)137:7. (9) *Exodus* 32:13. (10) *Deuteronomy* 9:27. (11) *Numbers* 12:11. (12) *Leviticus* 26:42.

THE ARK IS OPENED.

The first four verses of the following prayer are recited responsively; *chazzan,* then congregation:

שְׁמַע קוֹלֵנוּ יהוה אֱלֹהֵינוּ, חוּס וְרַחֵם עָלֵינוּ,
וְקַבֵּל בְּרַחֲמִים וּבְרָצוֹן אֶת תְּפִלָּתֵנוּ.¹

הֲשִׁיבֵנוּ יהוה אֵלֶיךָ וְנָשׁוּבָה, חַדֵּשׁ יָמֵינוּ כְּקֶדֶם.²

אַל תַּשְׁלִיכֵנוּ מִלְּפָנֶיךָ, וְרוּחַ קָדְשְׁךָ אַל תִּקַּח מִמֶּנּוּ.³

אַל תַּשְׁלִיכֵנוּ לְעֵת זִקְנָה, כִּכְלוֹת כֹּחֵנוּ אַל תַּעַזְבֵנוּ.⁴

אַל תַּעַזְבֵנוּ יהוה, אֱלֹהֵינוּ אַל תִּרְחַק מִמֶּנּוּ.⁵

עֲשֵׂה עִמָּנוּ אוֹת לְטוֹבָה, וְיִרְאוּ שׂוֹנְאֵינוּ וְיֵבֹשׁוּ,
כִּי אַתָּה יהוה עֲזַרְתָּנוּ וְנִחַמְתָּנוּ.⁶

אֲמָרֵינוּ הַאֲזִינָה יהוה, בִּינָה הֲגִיגֵנוּ.⁷

יִהְיוּ לְרָצוֹן אִמְרֵי פִינוּ וְהֶגְיוֹן לִבֵּנוּ לְפָנֶיךָ, יהוה צוּרֵנוּ וְגוֹאֲלֵנוּ.⁸

כִּי לְךָ יהוה הוֹחָלְנוּ, אַתָּה תַעֲנֶה אֲדֹנָי אֱלֹהֵינוּ.⁹

THE ARK IS CLOSED.

וידוי

During the recitation of the וידוי) stand with head and body slightly bowed,
in submissive contrition.

אֱלֹהֵינוּ וֵאלֹהֵי אֲבוֹתֵינוּ, תָּבֹא לְפָנֶיךָ תְּפִלָּתֵנוּ,¹⁰ וְאַל
תִּתְעַלַּם מִתְּחִנָּתֵנוּ,¹¹ שֶׁאֵין אָנוּ עַזֵּי פָנִים וּקְשֵׁי עֹרֶף,
לוֹמַר לְפָנֶיךָ יהוה אֱלֹהֵינוּ וֵאלֹהֵי אֲבוֹתֵינוּ, צַדִּיקִים אֲנַחְנוּ וְלֹא
חָטָאנוּ, אֲבָל אֲנַחְנוּ וַאֲבוֹתֵינוּ חָטָאנוּ.¹²

Strike the left side of the chest with the right fist
while reciting each of the sins in the following confession litany.

אָשַׁמְנוּ, בָּגַדְנוּ, גָּזַלְנוּ, דִּבַּרְנוּ דֹפִי. הֶעֱוִינוּ, וְהִרְשַׁעְנוּ, זַדְנוּ,
חָמַסְנוּ, טָפַלְנוּ שֶׁקֶר. יָעַצְנוּ רָע, כִּזַּבְנוּ, לַצְנוּ, מָרַדְנוּ,
נִאַצְנוּ, סָרַרְנוּ, עָוִינוּ, פָּשַׁעְנוּ, צָרַרְנוּ, קִשִּׁינוּ עֹרֶף. רָשַׁעְנוּ,
שִׁחַתְנוּ, תִּעַבְנוּ, תָּעִינוּ, תִּעְתָּעְנוּ.

הִרְשַׁעְנוּ וּפָשַׁעְנוּ, לָכֵן לֹא נוֹשָׁעְנוּ. וְתֵן בְּלִבֵּנוּ לַעֲזוֹב דֶּרֶךְ
רֶשַׁע, וְחִישׁ לָנוּ יֶשַׁע, כַּכָּתוּב עַל יַד נְבִיאֶךָ: יַעֲזֹב
רָשָׁע דַּרְכּוֹ, וְאִישׁ אָוֶן מַחְשְׁבֹתָיו, וְיָשֹׁב אֶל יהוה וִירַחֲמֵהוּ, וְאֶל
אֱלֹהֵינוּ כִּי יַרְבֶּה לִסְלוֹחַ.¹³

THE ARK IS OPENED.

The first four verses of the following prayer are recited responsively; *chazzan,* then congregation:

שְׁמַע Hear our voice, HASHEM, our God, pity and be compassionate to us,
and accept — with compassion and favor — our prayer.[1]

Bring us back to You, HASHEM, and we shall return, renew our days as of old.[2]
Do not cast us away from Yourself,
and do not remove Your holy spirit from us.[3]
Do not cast us away in old age,
when our strength gives out do not forsake us.[4]
Do not forsake us, HASHEM, our God, be not distant from us.[5]
Display for us a sign for good, so that our enemies may see it
and be ashamed, for You, HASHEM, will have helped and consoled us.[6]
To our sayings give ear, HASHEM, perceive our thoughts.[7]
May the expressions of our mouth and the thoughts of our heart
find favor before You, HASHEM, our Rock and our Redeemer.[8]
Because for You, HASHEM, we waited, You will answer, my Lord, our God.[9]

THE ARK IS CLOSED.

VIDUY/CONFESSION

During the recitation of the וִדּוּי stand with head and body slightly bowed,
in submissive contrition.

אֱלֹהֵינוּ Our God and the God of our forefathers, may our prayer come
before You.[10] Do not ignore our supplication,[11] for we are not so
brazen and obstinate as to say before You, HASHEM, our God and the God
of our forefathers, that we are righteous and have not sinned, for in truth,
we and our forefathers have sinned.[12]

Strike the left side of the chest with the right fist while reciting
each of the sins in the following confession litany.

אָשַׁמְנוּ We have become guilty; [ב] we have betrayed; [ג] we have
robbed; [ד] we have spoken slander; [ה] we have caused perversion; [ו] we have caused wickedness; [ז] we have sinned willfully; [ח] we
have extorted; [ט] we have accused falsely; [י] we have given evil counsel;
[כ] we have been deceitful; [ל] we have scorned; [מ] we have rebelled; [נ] we
have provoked; [ס] we have turned away; [ע] we have been perverse;
[פ] we have acted wantonly; [צ] we have persecuted; [ק] we have been
obstinate; [ר] we have been wicked; [ש] we have corrupted; [ת] we have
been abominable; we have strayed; You have let us go astray.

הִרְשַׁעְנוּ We have acted wickedly and have sinned willfully, therefore we have not been saved. Inspire our heart to abandon the
path of evil and hasten salvation for us, as it is written by Your prophet:
May the wicked one abandon his way and the vicious man his thoughts;
may he return to HASHEM and He will show him mercy, and to our God, for
He is abundantly forgiving.[13]

---

(1) Weekday *Shemoneh Esrei.* (2) *Lamentations* 5:21. (3) Cf. *Psalms* 51:13. (4) Cf. 71:9.
(5) Cf. 38:22. (6) Cf. 86:17. (7) Cf. 5:2. (8) Cf. 19:15. (9) Cf. 38:16. (10) Cf. 88:3.
(11) Cf. 55:2. (12) Cf. 106:6. (13) *Isaiah* 55:7.

מָשִׁיחַ צִדְקֶךָ אָמַר לְפָנֶיךָ: שְׁגִיאוֹת מִי יָבִין מִנִּסְתָּרוֹת נַקֵּנִי.[1] נַקֵּנוּ יהוה אֱלֹהֵינוּ מִכָּל פְּשָׁעֵינוּ, וְטַהֲרֵנוּ מִכָּל טֻמְאוֹתֵינוּ, וּזְרוֹק עָלֵינוּ מַיִם טְהוֹרִים וְטַהֲרֵנוּ, כַּכָּתוּב עַל יַד נְבִיאֶךָ: וְזָרַקְתִּי עֲלֵיכֶם מַיִם טְהוֹרִים וּטְהַרְתֶּם, מִכֹּל טֻמְאוֹתֵיכֶם וּמִכָּל גִּלּוּלֵיכֶם אֲטַהֵר אֶתְכֶם.[2]

עַמְּךָ וְנַחֲלָתְךָ רְעֵבֵי טוּבְךָ, צְמֵאֵי חַסְדֶּךָ, תְּאֵבֵי יִשְׁעֶךָ, יַכִּירוּ וְיֵדְעוּ כִּי לַיהוה אֱלֹהֵינוּ הָרַחֲמִים וְהַסְּלִיחוֹת.

קדיש שלם

The *chazzan* recites קַדִּישׁ שָׁלֵם:

יִתְגַּדַּל וְיִתְקַדַּשׁ שְׁמֵהּ רַבָּא. (.Cong – אָמֵן) בְּעָלְמָא דִּי בְרָא כִרְעוּתֵהּ, וְיַמְלִיךְ מַלְכוּתֵהּ, בְּחַיֵּיכוֹן וּבְיוֹמֵיכוֹן וּבְחַיֵּי דְכָל בֵּית יִשְׂרָאֵל, בַּעֲגָלָא וּבִזְמַן קָרִיב. וְאִמְרוּ אָמֵן.

(.Cong – אָמֵן. יְהֵא שְׁמֵהּ רַבָּא מְבָרַךְ לְעָלַם וּלְעָלְמֵי עָלְמַיָּא.)

יְהֵא שְׁמֵהּ רַבָּא מְבָרַךְ לְעָלַם וּלְעָלְמֵי עָלְמַיָּא.

יִתְבָּרַךְ וְיִשְׁתַּבַּח וְיִתְפָּאַר וְיִתְרוֹמַם וְיִתְנַשֵּׂא וְיִתְהַדָּר וְיִתְעַלֶּה וְיִתְהַלָּל שְׁמֵהּ דְּקוּדְשָׁא בְּרִיךְ הוּא (.Cong – בְּרִיךְ הוּא) לְעֵלָּא [וּ]לְעֵלָּא מִכָּל בִּרְכָתָא וְשִׁירָתָא תֻּשְׁבְּחָתָא וְנֶחֱמָתָא, דַּאֲמִירָן בְּעָלְמָא. וְאִמְרוּ: אָמֵן. (.Cong – אָמֵן)

(.Cong – קַבֵּל בְּרַחֲמִים וּבְרָצוֹן אֶת תְּפִלָּתֵנוּ.)

תִּתְקַבֵּל צְלוֹתְהוֹן וּבָעוּתְהוֹן דְּכָל (בֵּית) יִשְׂרָאֵל קֳדָם אֲבוּהוֹן דִּי בִשְׁמַיָּא. וְאִמְרוּ אָמֵן. (.Cong – אָמֵן)

(.Cong – יְהִי שֵׁם יהוה מְבֹרָךְ, מֵעַתָּה וְעַד עוֹלָם.[3])

יְהֵא שְׁלָמָא רַבָּא מִן שְׁמַיָּא וְחַיִּים עָלֵינוּ וְעַל כָּל יִשְׂרָאֵל. וְאִמְרוּ אָמֵן. (.Cong – אָמֵן)

(.Cong – עֶזְרִי מֵעִם יהוה, עֹשֵׂה שָׁמַיִם וָאָרֶץ.[4])

Take three steps back. Bow left and say, ...עֹשֶׂה; bow right and say, ...הוּא יַעֲשֶׂה; bow forward and say, וְעַל כָּל . . . . אָמֵן. Remain standing in place for a few moments, then take three steps forward.

עֹשֶׂה [הַ]שָּׁלוֹם בִּמְרוֹמָיו, הוּא יַעֲשֶׂה שָׁלוֹם עָלֵינוּ, וְעַל כָּל יִשְׂרָאֵל. וְאִמְרוּ אָמֵן. (.Cong – אָמֵן)

מָשִׁיחַ **Your** righteous anointed [David] said before You: 'Who can discern mistakes? From unperceived faults cleanse me.'[1] Cleanse us, HASHEM, our God, of all our willful sins and purify us, of all our contaminations. Sprinkle upon us pure water and purify us, as it is written by Your prophet: I shall sprinkle pure water upon you and purify you, of all your contaminations and of all your abominations I will purify you.'[2]

עַמְּךָ **Your** people and Your heritage, who hunger for Your goodness, who thirst for Your kindness, who long for Your salvation — may they recognize and know that to HASHEM, our God, belong mercy and forgiveness.

FULL KADDISH
The chazzan recites the Full Kaddish:

יִתְגַּדַּל **May** His great Name grow exalted and sanctified (Cong. — Amen.) in the world that He created as He willed. May He give reign to His kingship in your lifetimes and in your days, and in the lifetimes of the entire Family of Israel, swiftly and soon. Now respond: Amen.

(Cong. — Amen. May His great Name be blessed forever and ever.)
May His great Name be blessed forever and ever.

Blessed, praised, glorified, exalted, extolled, mighty, upraised and lauded be the Name of the Holy One, Blessed is He (Cong. — Blessed is He.) exceedingly beyond any blessing and song, praise, and consolation that are uttered in the world. Now respond: Amen. (Cong. — Amen.)

(Cong. — Accept our prayers with mercy and favor.)

May the prayers and supplications of the entire House of Israel be accepted before their Father Who is in Heaven. Now respond: Amen. (Cong. — Amen.)

(Cong. — Blessed be the Name of HASHEM from this time and forever.[3])

May there be abundant peace from Heaven, and life, upon us and upon all Israel. Now respond: Amen. (Cong. — Amen.)

(Cong. — My help is from HASHEM, Maker of heaven and earth.[4])

Take three steps back. Bow left and say, 'He Who makes peace . . .'; bow right and say,
'may He make peace . . .'; bow forward and say, 'and upon all Israel . . .'
Remain standing in place for a few moments, then take three steps forward.

He Who makes [the] peace in His heights, may He make peace upon us, and upon all Israel. Now respond: Amen. (Cong. — Amen.)

---

(1) *Psalms* 19:13. (2) *Ezekiel* 36:25. (3) *Psalms* 79:9. (4) 113:2. (10) 121:2.

﴾ סדר כפרות ﴿

The *Kaparos* ritual may be performed between Rosh Hashanah and Yom Kippur.
However, the preferred time is just after dawn of Erev Yom Kippur.

Take the chicken (or money) in the right hand (some say נֶפֶשׁ תַּחַת נָפֶשׁ, *A life for a life*, as they do so), and recite the following paragraph. Then — while reciting the appropriate paragraph on the next page — revolve the chicken or money around the head (some do this three times). Follow this procedure three times. (Alternatively, recite the following paragraph three times. Then — while revolving the chicken or the money around the head — recite the appropriate paragraph on page 702 three times.)

בְּנֵי אָדָם,* יֹשְׁבֵי חֹשֶׁךְ וְצַלְמָוֶת, אֲסִירֵי עֳנִי וּבַרְזֶל.¹ יוֹצִיאֵם* מֵחֹשֶׁךְ וְצַלְמָוֶת, וּמוֹסְרוֹתֵיהֶם יְנַתֵּק.² אֱוִלִים מִדֶּרֶךְ פִּשְׁעָם, וּמֵעֲוֹנֹתֵיהֶם יִתְעַנּוּ. כָּל אֹכֶל תְּתַעֵב נַפְשָׁם,* וַיַּגִּיעוּ עַד שַׁעֲרֵי מָוֶת. וַיִּזְעֲקוּ אֶל יהוה בַּצַּר לָהֶם, מִמְּצֻקוֹתֵיהֶם יוֹשִׁיעֵם.* יִשְׁלַח דְּבָרוֹ וְיִרְפָּאֵם,* וִימַלֵּט מִשְּׁחִיתוֹתָם. יוֹדוּ לַיהוה חַסְדּוֹ, וְנִפְלְאוֹתָיו לִבְנֵי אָדָם.*³ אִם יֵשׁ עָלָיו מַלְאָךְ מֵלִיץ אֶחָד* מִנִּי אָלֶף, לְהַגִּיד לְאָדָם יָשְׁרוֹ. וַיְחֻנֶּנּוּ וַיֹּאמֶר, פְּדָעֵהוּ מֵרֶדֶת שַׁחַת, מָצָאתִי כֹפֶר.⁴

﴿ כַּפָּרוֹת / ATONEMENT ﴾

The ancient ritual of *Kaparos*/Atonement is cited by the early *Geonim* (see *Rosh, Yoma* 8:23; *Tur Orach Chaim* 605). *Rashi* (*Shabbos* 81b) describes a vastly different form of this custom. But that form is no longer practiced.

The ritual is designed to imbue people with the awareness that their lives are at stake as Yom Kippur approaches, and that they must repent and seek atonement. The ceremony symbolizes that our sins cry out for atonement, that our good deeds and repentance can save us from the punishment we deserve. The form of the ritual calls for a chicken to be moved in a circular motion around the penitent's head (see instructions accompanying the text). The chicken is later slaughtered [symbolizing the concept that a sinner deserves to forfeit his soul for not having used it to do God's will] and either the chicken or its cash value is given to the poor, for charity is an indispensable part of repentance — and the combination of the two can achieve atonement. [In giving the *Kaparos* chicken to the poor, one must be extremely careful not to embarrass the recipient or to cause him to feel that the donor is ridding himself of his sins and placing them on this poor man's head (*Matteh Ephraim*).] The entrails are left for birds and animals, because this exemplifies the same kind of compassion that we pray God will show us.

Technically, any animal should be acceptable for the *Kaparos* ritual. However, in order that the ritual not be misconstrued as a sacrificial offering — an act prohibited in the absence of the *Beis HaMikdash* — the animal used for *Kaparos* may not be one that is suitable for such sacrifice, e.g., a dove. A chicken was chosen because the Hebrew word גֶּבֶר means both *man* and *rooster*. Thus, use of this particular bird alludes to the person performing the ritual.

In the original and preferable form, a white rooster was taken for a male and a white hen for a female, because the color white symbolizes atonement (see *Isaiah* 1:18). Nevertheless, it is forbidden to make strenuous efforts to find birds of such color, lest it appear that one is following the idolaters' practice of using only white birds in their ceremonies (see *Avodah Zarah* 13b-14a).

Some use a separate chicken for each person while others perform the ritual for all the males simultaneously using one rooster, and for all the females simultaneously with one hen. A pregnant woman uses two hens — one for herself and one in case she is carrying a female child — and one rooster, in case she is carrying a male.

Many people use money for this ritual instead of a rooster. The money is then given to the poor (see *Orach Chaim* 605).

בְּנֵי אָדָם — *Children of Man.* The nine verses of this paragraph are all taken directly from Scripture, but this opening phrase was added only for the purpose of this ritual. The term בֶּן אָדָם, literally, *son of Adam,* is used throughout the Book of *Ezekiel*, where it indicates one who remains loyal to the great mission for the sake of which God created Adam, the first human being (see *Overview* to ArtScroll *Yechezkel*). It is

⊰{ KAPAROS / ATONEMENT }⊱

The *Kaparos* ritual may be performed between Rosh Hashanah and Yom Kippur.
However, the preferred time is just after dawn of Erev Yom Kippur.

Take the chicken (or money) in the right hand (some say נֶפֶשׁ תַּחַת נֶפֶשׁ, *A life for a life*, as they do so), and recite the following paragraph. Then — while reciting the appropriate paragraph on the next page — revolve the chicken or money around the head (some do this three times). Follow this procedure three times. (Alternatively, recite the following paragraph three times. Then — while revolving the chicken or the money around the head — recite the appropriate paragraph on the next page three times.)

בְּנֵי אָדָם *Children of Man,* who sat in darkness* and the shadow of death, shackled in affliction and iron.[1] He removed them* from darkness and the shadow of death, and broke open their shackles.[2] The fools — because of their sinful path and their iniquities they were afflicted. Their soul abhorred all food,* and they reached the portals of death. Then they cried out to HASHEM in their distress; from their woes He spared them.* He dispatched His word and cured them,* and let them escape their destruction. Let them thank HASHEM for His kindness and for His wonders to mankind.*[3] If there will be for someone but a single defending angel* out of a thousand to declare a man's uprightness on his behalf, then He will be gracious to him and say, "Redeem him from descending to the Pit; I have found atonement."[4]*

(1) *Psalms* 107:10. (2) 107:14. (3) 107:17-21. (4) *Job* 33:23-24.

used here to stress that we seek atonement for our sins because we want to become worthy of God's purpose.

יֹשְׁבֵי חֹשֶׁךְ — *Who sat in darkness.* Psalm 107 tells of people who must express their gratitude to God for saving them from mortal danger. The verses from this psalm that are used here refer to a person who was imprisoned and shackled in a dark dungeon and to someone who lay gravely ill. Both afflictions are the fruit of sin. In the first case, imprisonment, one is suddenly cast into darkness by a major transgression that causes a sudden change in his outlook, performance, or life. The second, illness, is the gradual process of a person whose persistent sinning causes a steady change in his character until he becomes gravely ill in a spiritual sense. In either case we pray that God will help us repent so that we can escape the danger (*Radak*).

יוֹצִיאֵם — *He removed them.* God has many ways of liberating innocent captives from their dark dungeons and their heavy chains. He may even implant a spark of compassion in the hearts of the captors, who will be moved to free their prisoners (*Radak*).

כָּל אֹכֶל תְּתַעֵב נַפְשָׁם — *Their soul abhorred all food.* There are many symptoms of illness — fever, nausea, pain — yet the Psalmist chose abhorrence of food because it indicates the loss of desire to enjoy or even to sustain life. This proves that one has reached the portals of death

and has no hope of survival (*Rabbi A. C. Feuer*).

וַיִּזְעֲקוּ אֶל ה' בַּצַּר לָהֶם מִמְּצֻקוֹתֵיהֶם יוֹשִׁיעֵם — *Then they cried out to HASHEM in their distress; from their woes He spared them.* The sick man finally realizes that his distresses are his own sins which plague him, and that he can be saved only by sincere prayer and repentance (*Alshich*).

יִשְׁלַח דְּבָרוֹ וְיִרְפָּאֵם — *He dispatched His word and cured them.* No cure is effective on its own. God Himself must speak and decree, "This herb will cure that disease! This doctor will heal that malady!" (*Ibn Ezra; Alshich*).

וְנִפְלְאוֹתָיו לִבְנֵי אָדָם — *And for His wonders to mankind* [lit., *children of man*]. When a king does favors for his subjects it is not necessarily genuine kindness, because every leader tries to ingratiate himself with his followers to inspire their loyalty. Not so is the kindness of God, Who has no need for the assistance of any person. Thus, His wonderful works are truly for the benefit of mankind — not for Himself (*Alshich*).

מַלְאָךְ מֵלִיץ אֶחָד — *But a single defending angel.* Commenting on this verse and the next, the Talmud (*Shabbos* 32a) teaches that when someone is in danger and is surrounded by angry accusers on all sides, he can be saved by the pleas of even one defending angel. What is this defending angel? Repentance and good deeds. Sometimes, even a single sincere good deed can save one from destruction.

Recite the applicable paragraph.
(When money is used, substitute the bracketed phrase for the phrase preceding it.)
Each time the paragraph is recited, the bird or money is circled around the head.

— A man performing the ritual for himself

זֶה חֲלִיפָתִי, זֶה תְּמוּרָתִי,* זֶה כַּפָּרָתִי. זֶה הַתַּרְנְגוֹל יֵלֵךְ לְמִיתָה [זֶה הַכֶּסֶף יֵלֵךְ לִצְדָקָה], וַאֲנִי אֶכָּנֵס וְאֵלֵךְ לְחַיִּים טוֹבִים אֲרוּכִים וּלְשָׁלוֹם.

— Two or more men performing the ritual for themselves

זֶה חֲלִיפָתֵנוּ, זֶה תְּמוּרָתֵנוּ, זֶה כַּפָּרָתֵנוּ. זֶה הַתַּרְנְגוֹל יֵלֵךְ לְמִיתָה [זֶה הַכֶּסֶף יֵלֵךְ לִצְדָקָה], וַאֲנַחְנוּ נִכָּנֵס וְנֵלֵךְ לְחַיִּים טוֹבִים אֲרוּכִים וּלְשָׁלוֹם.

— One performing the ritual for a man

זֶה חֲלִיפָתָךְ, זֶה תְּמוּרָתָךְ, זֶה כַּפָּרָתָךְ. זֶה הַתַּרְנְגוֹל יֵלֵךְ לְמִיתָה [זֶה הַכֶּסֶף יֵלֵךְ לִצְדָקָה], וְאַתָּה תִּכָּנֵס וְתֵלֵךְ לְחַיִּים טוֹבִים אֲרוּכִים וּלְשָׁלוֹם.

— One performing the ritual for two or more men

זֶה חֲלִיפַתְכֶם, זֶה תְּמוּרַתְכֶם, זֶה כַּפָּרַתְכֶם. זֶה הַתַּרְנְגוֹל יֵלֵךְ לְמִיתָה [זֶה הַכֶּסֶף יֵלֵךְ לִצְדָקָה], וְאַתֶּם תִּכָּנְסוּ וְתֵלְכוּ לְחַיִּים טוֹבִים אֲרוּכִים וּלְשָׁלוֹם.

— A woman performing the ritual for herself

זֹאת חֲלִיפָתִי, זֹאת תְּמוּרָתִי, זֹאת כַּפָּרָתִי. זֹאת הַתַּרְנְגֹלֶת תֵּלֵךְ לְמִיתָה [זֶה הַכֶּסֶף יֵלֵךְ לִצְדָקָה], וַאֲנִי אֶכָּנֵס וְאֵלֵךְ לְחַיִּים טוֹבִים אֲרוּכִים וּלְשָׁלוֹם.

— Two or more women performing the ritual for themselves

זֹאת חֲלִיפָתֵנוּ, זֹאת תְּמוּרָתֵנוּ, זֹאת כַּפָּרָתֵנוּ. זֹאת הַתַּרְנְגֹלֶת תֵּלֵךְ לְמִיתָה [זֶה הַכֶּסֶף יֵלֵךְ לִצְדָקָה], וַאֲנַחְנוּ נִכָּנֵס וְנֵלֵךְ לְחַיִּים טוֹבִים אֲרוּכִים וּלְשָׁלוֹם.

— One performing the ritual for a woman

זֹאת חֲלִיפָתֵךְ, זֹאת תְּמוּרָתֵךְ, זֹאת כַּפָּרָתֵךְ. זֹאת הַתַּרְנְגֹלֶת תֵּלֵךְ לְמִיתָה [זֶה הַכֶּסֶף יֵלֵךְ לִצְדָקָה], וְאַתְּ תִּכָּנְסִי וְתֵלְכִי לְחַיִּים טוֹבִים אֲרוּכִים וּלְשָׁלוֹם.

— One performing the ritual for two or more women

זֹאת חֲלִיפַתְכֶן, זֹאת תְּמוּרַתְכֶן, זֹאת כַּפָּרַתְכֶן. זֹאת הַתַּרְנְגֹלֶת תֵּלֵךְ לְמִיתָה [זֶה הַכֶּסֶף יֵלֵךְ לִצְדָקָה], וְאַתֶּן תִּכָּנֵסְנָה וְתֵלַכְנָה לְחַיִּים טוֹבִים אֲרוּכִים וּלְשָׁלוֹם.

— A pregnant woman performing the ritual for herself

אֵלּוּ חֲלִיפוֹתֵינוּ, אֵלּוּ תְּמוּרוֹתֵינוּ, אֵלּוּ כַּפָּרוֹתֵינוּ. אֵלּוּ הַתַּרְנְגוֹלִים יֵלְכוּ לְמִיתָה [זֶה הַכֶּסֶף יֵלֵךְ לִצְדָקָה], וַאֲנַחְנוּ נִכָּנֵס וְנֵלֵךְ לְחַיִּים טוֹבִים אֲרוּכִים וּלְשָׁלוֹם.

— One performing the ritual for a pregnant woman

אֵלּוּ חֲלִיפוֹתֵיכֶם, אֵלּוּ תְּמוּרוֹתֵיכֶם, אֵלּוּ כַּפָּרוֹתֵיכֶם. אֵלּוּ הַתַּרְנְגוֹלִים יֵלְכוּ לְמִיתָה [זֶה הַכֶּסֶף יֵלֵךְ לִצְדָקָה], וְאַתֶּם תִּכָּנְסוּ וְתֵלְכוּ לְחַיִּים טוֹבִים אֲרוּכִים וּלְשָׁלוֹם.

חֲלִיפָתִי ... תְּמוּרָתִי — *My exchange ... my substitute.* In the Hebrew idiom, חִלּוּף, *exchange,* refers to putting a superior thing in place of an inferior one. As long as a person is a sinner, even

Recite the applicable paragraph.
(When money is used, substitute the bracketed phrase for the phrase preceding it.)
Each time the paragraph is recited, the bird or money is circled around the head.

A man performing— *This is my exchange, this is my substitute,* this is my*
the ritual   *atonement. This rooster will go to its death [this money will*
for himself   *go to charity] while I will enter and proceed to a good long*
              life, and to peace.

Two or more men— *This is our exchange, this is our substitute, this is our*
performing the ritual *atonement. This rooster will go to its death [this money*
for themselves *will go to charity] while we will enter and proceed to a*
              good long life, and to peace.

One performing— *This is your exchange, this is your substitute, this is your*
the ritual for a man *atonement. This rooster will go to its death [this money will*
              go to charity] while you will enter and proceed to a good
              long life, and to peace.

One performing— *This is your exchange, this is your substitute, this is your*
the ritual for *atonement. This rooster will go to its death [this money will*
two or more men *go to charity] while you will enter and proceed to a good*
              long life, and to peace.

A woman— *This is my exchange, this is my substitute, this is my*
performing the ritual *atonement. This hen will go to its death [this money will*
for herself   *go to charity] while I will enter and proceed to a good long*
              life, and to peace.

Two or more women— *This is our exchange, this is our substitute, this is our*
performing the ritual *atonement. This hen will go to its death [this money will go*
for themselves *to charity] while we will enter and proceed to a good long*
              life, and to peace.

One performing— *This is your exchange, this is your substitute, this is your*
the ritual for a *atonement. This hen will go to its death [this money will go*
woman   *to charity] while you will enter and proceed to a good long*
              life, and to peace.

One performing— *This is your exchange, this is your substitute, this is your*
the ritual for two or *atonement. This hen will go to its death [this money will go*
more women   *to charity] while you will enter and proceed to a good long*
              life, and to peace.

A pregnant woman— *This is our exchange, this is our substitute, this is our*
performing the *atonement. These chickens will go to their deaths [this*
ritual for herself *money will go to charity] while we will enter and proceed*
              to a good long life, and to peace.

One performing— *This is your exchange, this is your substitute, this is your*
the ritual for *atonement. These chickens will go to their deaths [this*
a pregnant woman *money will go to charity] while you will enter and proceed*
              to a good long life, and to peace.

---

a rooster is considered superior to him. On the other hand תְּמוּרָה, *substitute*, refers to the use of an inferior thing to take the place of a superior one. In the context of *Kaparos*, once someone has repented, he is infinitely better than the rooster that takes his place.